Tolley's Orange Tax
Post-Brexit Suppleme

While every care has been taken to ensure the accuracy of this work, no responsibility for loss or damage occasioned to any person acting or refraining from action as a result of any statement in it can be accepted by the authors, editors or publishers.

Tolley's Orange Tax Handbook

Post-Brexit Supplement

LexisNexis® UK & Worldwide

United Kingdom	RELX (UK) Limited trading as LexisNexis®, 1–3 Strand, London WC2N 5JR and 9–10 St Andrew Square, Edinburgh EH2 2AF
LNUK Global Partners	LexisNexis® encompasses authoritative legal publishing brands dating back to the 19th century including: Butterworths® in the United Kingdom, Canada and the Asia-Pacific region; Les Editions du Juris Classeur in France; and Matthew Bender® worldwide. Details of LexisNexis® locations worldwide can be found at www.lexisnexis.com

© 2021 RELX (UK) Ltd.

Published by LexisNexis®

All rights reserved. No part of this publication may be reproduced in any material form (including photocopying or storing it in any medium by electronic means and whether or not transiently or incidentally to some other use of this publication) without the written permission of the copyright owner except in accordance with the provisions of the Copyright, Designs and Patents Act 1988 or under the terms of a licence issued by the Copyright Licensing Agency Ltd, Saffron House, 6–10 Kirby Street, London EC1N 8TS. Applications for the copyright owner's written permission to reproduce any part of this publication should be addressed to the publisher.

Warning: The doing of an unauthorised act in relation to a copyright work may result in both a civil claim for damages and criminal prosecution.

Crown copyright material is reproduced with the permission of the Controller of HMSO and the Queen's Printer for Scotland. Parliamentary copyright material is reproduced with the permission of the Controller of Her Majesty's Stationery Office on behalf of Parliament. Any European material in this work which has been reproduced from EUR-lex, the official European Communities legislation website, is European Communities copyright.

LexisNexis® and the Knowledge Burst logo are registered trademarks of RELX Group plc, used under license. Butterworths® and Tolley® are registered trademarks of RELX (UK) Ltd. Matthew Bender® is a registered trademark of Matthew Bender & Company Inc. Other products and services may be trademarks or registered trademarks of their respective companies.

ISBN: 9781474320351

A CIP Catalogue record for this book is available from the British Library.

Printed and bound by CPI Group (UK) Limited, Croydon, CR0 4YY

Visit Tolley at www.tolley.co.uk or email the editorial department on: yellowandorange@lexisnexis.co.uk

Publishers' Note

Tolley's Orange Tax Handbook Post-Brexit Supplement brings together the key VAT legislation, fully updated to reflect the position following the end of the Brexit transition period.

The Brexit-related changes to UK VAT legislation had originally been drafted on the basis of no agreement being reached on the UK's future relationship with the EU. Having struck a deal at the end of 2020 on a framework for the future, significant changes have been made to the legislation, including amendments to reflect the operation of the Ireland/Northern Ireland Protocol.

This special edition of the Orange Book includes the up to date, consolidated key UK VAT legislation, along with a "snapshot" of the EU VAT Directives as they stood at 11pm on 31 December 2020 (Implementation Period Completion Day).

This edition contains texts as they applied at 1 March 2021.

Previous versions of the legislation are included in the Orange Tax Handbook archives on TolleyLibrary: bit.ly/TolleyOrangeArchive (subscription sensitive).

March 2021

Contents

Part 1: Value Added Tax Statutes
(including VATA 1994)
Part 2: Value Added Tax Statutory Instruments
(including VAT Regulations 1995)
Part 3: EU material
EU VAT Directives as at 31 December 2020
Retained EU VAT Implementing Regulation
Trade and Cooperation Agreement – Protocol on administrative cooperation, combating VAT fraud and mutual assistance etc
Index and Words & Phrases

Part 1

VAT Statutes

Value Added Tax Statutes

Contents

Interpretation Act 1978
Customs and Excise Management Act 1979
Customs and Excise Duties (General Reliefs) Act 1979
Value Added Tax Act 1994
Finance Act 2003
Finance Act 2007
Finance Act 2008
Finance Act 2009
Finance Act 2011
Finance Act 2016
Finance (No 2) Act 2017
Taxation (Cross-border Trade) Act 2018
Taxation (Post-transition Period) Act 2020
European Union (Future Relationship) Act 2020

VAT Statutes

INTERPRETATION ACT 1978
(1978 Chapter 30)
ARRANGEMENT OF SECTIONS

General provisions as to enactment and operation

1	Words of enactment.
3	Judicial notice.
4	Time of commencement.

Interpretation and construction

5	Definitions.
6	Gender and number.
7	References to service by post.
10	References to the Sovereign.
11	Construction of subordinate legislation.

Statutory powers and duties

12	Continuity of powers and duties.
13	Anticipatory exercise of powers.
14	Implied power to amend.
14A	Power to include sunset and review provisions in subordinate legislation.

Repealing enactments

15	Repeal of repeal.
16	General savings.
17	Repeal and re-enactment.

Miscellaneous

18	Duplicated offences.
19	Citation of other Acts.
20	References to other enactments.
20A	References to Community instruments

Supplementary

21	Interpretation etc.
22	Application to Acts and Measures
23	Application to other instruments
23ZA	Retained direct EU legislation
23A	Acts of the Scottish Parliament etc
23B	Measures and Acts of the National Assembly for Wales etc]
24	Application to Northern Ireland
25	Repeals and savings
26	Commencement.
27	Short title.
	Schedules:
	Schedule 1—Words and expressions defined.
	Schedule 2—Application of Act to existing enactments.
Part I	—Acts.
Part II	—Subordinate legislation.

General provisions as to enactment and operation

1 Words of enactment
Every section of an Act takes effect as a substantive enactment without introductory words.

3 Judicial notice
Every Act is a public Act to be judicially noticed as such, unless the contrary is expressly provided by the Act.

4 Time of commencement
An Act or provision of an Act comes into force—
- (a) where provision is made for it to come into force on a particular day, at the beginning of that day;
- (b) where no provision is made for its coming into force, at the beginning of the day on which the Act receives the Royal Assent.

Interpretation and construction

5 Definitions
In any Act, unless the contrary intention appears, words and expressions listed in Schedule 1 to this Act are to be construed according to that Schedule.

6 Gender and number
In any Act, unless the contrary intention appears,—
- (a) words importing the masculine gender include the feminine;
- (b) words importing the feminine gender include the masculine;
- (c) words in the singular include the plural and words in the plural include the singular.

7 References to service by post
Where an Act authorises or requires any document to be served by post (whether the expression "serve" or the expression "give" or "send" or any other expression is used) then, unless the contrary intention appears, the service is deemed to be effected by properly addressing, pre-paying and posting a letter containing the document and, unless the contrary is proved, to have been effected at the time at which the letter would be delivered in the ordinary course of post.

10 References to the Sovereign
In any Act a reference to the Sovereign reigning at the time of the passing of the Act is to be construed, unless the contrary intention appears, as a reference to the Sovereign for the time being.

11 Construction of subordinate legislation
Where an Act confers power to make subordinate legislation, expressions used in that legislation have, unless the contrary intention appears, the meaning which they bear in the Act.

Statutory powers and duties

12 Continuity of powers and duties
(1) Where an Act confers a power or imposes a duty it is implied, unless the contrary intention appears, that the power may be exercised, or the duty is to be performed, from time to time as occasion requires.
(2) Where an Act confers a power or imposes a duty on the holder of an office as such, it is implied, unless the contrary intention appears, that the power may be exercised, or the duty is to be performed, by the holder for the time being of the office.

13 Anticipatory exercise of powers
Where an Act which (or any provision of which) does not come into force immediately on its passing confers power to make subordinate legislation, or to make appointments, give notices, prescribe forms or do any other thing for the purposes of the Act, then, unless the contrary intention appears, the power may be exercised, and any instrument made thereunder may be made so as to come into force, at any time after the passing of the Act so far as may be necessary or expedient for the purpose—
- (a) of bringing the Act or any provision of the Act into force; or
- (b) of giving full effect to the Act or any such provision at or after the time when it comes into force.

14 Implied power to amend
Where an Act confers power to make—
- (a) rules, regulations or byelaws; or
- (b) Orders in Council, orders or other subordinate legislation to be made by statutory instrument,

it implies, unless the contrary intention appears, a power, exercisable in the same manner and subject to the same conditions or limitations, to revoke, amend or re-enact any instrument made under the power.

[14A Power to include sunset and review provisions in subordinate legislation
(1) This section applies where an Act confers a power or a duty on a person to make subordinate legislation except to the extent that—
- (a) the power or duty is exercisable by the Scottish Ministers, or
- (b) the power or duty is exercisable by any other person within devolved competence (within the meaning of the Scotland Act 1998).

(2) The subordinate legislation may include—

(a) provision requiring the person to review the effectiveness of the legislation within a specified period or at the end of a specified period;
(b) provision for the legislation to cease to have effect at the end of a specified day or a specified period;
(c) if the power or duty is being exercised to amend other subordinate legislation, provision of the kind mentioned in paragraph (a) or (b) in relation to that other legislation.
(3) The provision that may be made by virtue of subsection (2)(a) includes provision requiring the person to consider whether the objectives which it was the purpose of the legislation to achieve remain appropriate and, if so, whether they could be achieved in another way.
(4) Subordinate legislation including provision of a kind mentioned in subsection (2) may make such provision generally or only in relation to specified provisions of the legislation or specified cases or circumstances.
(5) Subordinate legislation including provision of a kind mentioned in subsection (2) may make transitional, consequential, incidental or supplementary provision or savings in connection with such provision.
(6) In this section, "specified" means specified in the subordinate legislation.][1]

Amendments—[1] Section 14A inserted by the Enterprise and Regulatory Reform Act 2013 s 59(1), (2) with effect from 25 April 2013.

Repealing enactments

15 Repeal of repeal

Where an Act repeals a repealing enactment, the repeal does not revive any enactment previously repealed unless words are added reviving it.

16 General savings

(1) Without prejudice to section 15, where an Act repeals an enactment, the repeal does not, unless the contrary intention appears,—
   (a) revive anything not in force or existing at the time at which the repeal takes effect;
   (b) affect the previous operation of the enactment repealed or anything duly done or suffered under that enactment;
   (c) affect any right, privilege, obligation or liability acquired, accrued or incurred under that enactment;
   (d) affect any penalty, forfeiture or punishment incurred in respect of any offence committed against that enactment;
   (e) affect any investigation, legal proceeding or remedy in respect of any such right, privilege, obligation, liability, penalty, forfeiture or punishment;
and any such investigation, legal proceeding or remedy may be instituted, continued or enforced, and any such penalty, forfeiture or punishment may be imposed, as if the repealing Act had not been passed.
(2) This section applies to the expiry of a temporary enactment as if it were repealed by an Act.

17 Repeal and re-enactment

(1) Where an Act repeals a previous enactment and substitutes provisions for the enactment repealed, the repealed enactment remains in force until the substituted provisions come into force.
(2) Where an Act repeals and re-enacts, with or without modification, a previous enactment then, unless the contrary intention appears,—
   (a) any reference in any other enactment to the enactment so repealed shall be construed as a reference to the provision re-enacted;
   (b) in so far as any subordinate legislation made or other thing done under the enactment so repealed, or having effect as if so made or done, could have been made or done under the provision re-enacted, it shall have effect as if made or done under that provision.

Miscellaneous

18 Duplicated offences

Where an act or omission constitutes an offence under two or more Acts, or both under an Act and at common law, the offender shall, unless the contrary intention appears, be liable to be prosecuted and punished under either or any of those Acts or at common law, but shall not be liable to be punished more than once for the same offence.

19 Citation of other Acts

(1) Where an Act cites another Act by year, statute, session or chapter, or a section or other portion of another Act by number or letter, the reference shall, unless the contrary intention appears, be read as referring—
   (a) in the case of Acts included in any revised edition of the statutes printed by authority, to that edition;
   (b) in the case of Acts not so included but included in the edition prepared under the direction of the Record Commission, to that edition;

(c) in any other case, to the Acts printed by the Queen's Printer, or under the superintendence or authority of Her Majesty's Stationery Office.

(2) An Act may continue to be cited by the short title authorised by any enactment notwithstanding the repeal of that enactment.

20 References to other enactments [etc]

(1) Where an Act describes or cites a portion of an enactment by referring to words, sections or other parts from or to which (or from and to which) the portion extends, the portion described or cited includes the words, sections or other parts referred to unless the contrary intention appears.

(2) Where an Act refers to an enactment, the reference, unless the contrary intention appears, is a reference to that enactment as amended, and includes a reference thereto as extended or applied, by or under any other enactment, including any other provision of that Act.

[(2A) Where—
  (a) an Act passed on or after IP completion day refers to any treaty relating to the EU or any instrument or other document of an EU entity, and
  (b) the treaty, instrument of document has effect by virtue of section 7A or 7B of the European Union (Withdrawal) Act 2018 (general implementation of remainder of EU withdrawal agreement etc),
the reference, unless the contrary intention appears and so far as required for the purposes of relevant separation agreement law, is a reference to the treaty, instrument or document as it so has effect (including, so far as so required, as it has effect from time to time).][3]

[(3) [Subject to subsection (2A), where][3] an Act passed on or after [IP completion day][2] refers to any EU regulation, EU decision, EU tertiary legislation or provision of the EEA agreement, the reference, unless the contrary intention appears, is a reference to the EU regulation, EU decision, EU tertiary legislation or provision of the EEA agreement as it forms part of domestic law by virtue of section 3 of the European Union (Withdrawal) Act 2018.

(4) Subsection (3) does not determine any question as to whether the reference is to be read as a reference to the EU regulation, EU decision, EU tertiary legislation or provision of the EEA agreement as modified by domestic law (and, accordingly, is without prejudice to subsection (2)).

(5) Any expression in [subsections (2A) to][3] (4) which is defined in the European Union (Withdrawal) Act 2018 has the same meaning in [the subsection concerned][3] as in that Act.][1]

[(6) In this section, "treaty" includes any international agreement (and any protocol or annex to a treaty or international agreement).][3]

Amendments—[1] Sub-ss (3)–(5) inserted by the European Union (Withdrawal) Act 2018 (Consequential Modifications and Repeals and Revocations) (EU Exit) Regulations, SI 2019/628 reg 3(1), (2) with effect from IP completion day (11pm UK time on 31 December 2020) (see EU(WA)A 2020 Sch 5 para 1(1)).

[2] In sub-s (3) above, words substituted for words "exit day" by the European Union (Withdrawal Agreement) Act 2020 s 41, Sch 5 paras 8, 9 with effect from IP completion day (11pm UK time on 31 December 2020) (see EU(WA)A 2020 Sch 5 para 1(1)).

[3] Word in heading inserted, sub-ss (2A) and (6) inserted, and words in sub-ss (3) and (5) substituted, by the European Union Withdrawal (Consequential Modifications) (EU Exit) Regulations, SI 2020/1447 reg 2(1), (2) with effect from IP completion day (11pm UK time on 31 December 2020) (see EU(WA)A 2020 Sch 5 para 1(1)).

[20A References to [certain][3] [EU instruments][2]

Where an Act passed after the commencement of this section refers to an [EU instrument][2] that has been amended, extended or applied by another such instrument, the reference, unless the contrary intention appears, is a reference to that instrument as so amended, extended or applied.][1]

Amendments—[1] This section inserted by the Legislative and Regulatory Reform Act 2006, s 25(1) with effect from 8 January 2007.

[2] In section heading and in main text, words substituted by the European Union (Amendment) Act 2008, s 3(3), Schedule, Pt 2 with effect from 1 December 2009 (by virtue of SI 2009/3143 art 2). Note that the European Union (Withdrawal) Act 2018 Sch 9 repeals the European Union (Amendment) Act 2008 with effect from IP completion day (11pm on 31 December 2020) by virtue of SI 2020/1622 reg 3(o). See also transitional and savings provisions in SI 2020/1622 regs 8, 9.

[3] Word in section heading inserted by the European Union Withdrawal (Consequential Modifications) (EU Exit) Regulations, SI 2020/1447 reg 2(1), (3) with effect from IP completion day (11pm on 31 December 2020) (see EU(WA)A 2020 Sch 5 para 1(1)).

Supplementary

21 Interpretation etc

(1) In this Act "Act" includes a local and personal or private Act; and "subordinate legislation" means Orders in Council, orders, rules, regulations, schemes, warrants, byelaws and other instruments made or to be made under any Act [or made or to be made on or after exit day under retained direct EU CAP legislation as defined in section 2 of the Direct Payments to Farmers (Legislative Continuity) Act 2020][1] [or made or to be made on or after IP completion day under any retained direct EU legislation other than retained direct EU CAP legislation as so defined][2].

(2) This Act binds the Crown.

Amendments—[1] In sub-s (1) words inserted by the Direct Payments to Farmers (Legislative Continuity) Act 2020 (Consequential Amendments) Regulations, SI 2020/463 reg 2(1), (2) with effect from 30 April 2020.

[2] In sub-s (1), words inserted by the European Union (Withdrawal) Act 2018 s 23(5), Sch 8 paras 18, 19 (as amended by SI 2020/463 reg 8) with effect from IP completion day (11pm on 31 December 2020) by virtue of SI 2020/1622 reg 3(i), (n).

22 Application to Acts and Measures

(1) This Act applies to itself, to any Act passed after the commencement of this Act [(subject[, in the case of section [20(2A) to (6)]³, to the provision made in [in section 20(2A) or (3)]³ and]², in the case of section 20A, to the provision made in that section)]¹ and, to the extent specified in Part I of Schedule 2, to Acts passed before the commencement of this Act.

(2) In any of the foregoing provisions of this Act a reference to an Act is a reference to an Act to which that provision applies; but this does not affect the generality of references to enactments or of the references in section 19(1) to other Acts.

(3) This Act applies to Measures of the General Synod of the Church of England (and, so far as it relates to Acts passed before the commencement of this Act, to Measures of the Church Assembly passed after 28th May 1925) as it applies to Acts.

Amendments—[1] In sub-s (1), words inserted by the Legislative and Regulatory Reform Act 2006 s 25(2) with effect from 8 January 2007.
[2] In sub-s (1), words inserted by the European Union (Withdrawal) Act 2018 (Consequential Modifications and Repeals and Revocations) (EU Exit) Regulations, SI 2019/628 reg 3(1), (3) with effect from IP completion day (11pm UK time on 31 December 2020) (see EU(WA)A 2020 Sch 5 para 1(1)).
[3] In sub-s (1), words substituted by the European Union Withdrawal (Consequential Modifications) (EU Exit) Regulations, SI 2020/1447 reg 2(1), (4) with effect from IP completion day (11pm UK time on 31 December 2020) (see EU(WA)A 2020 Sch 5 para 1(1)).

23 Application to other instruments

(1) The provisions of this Act, except sections 1 to 3 and 4(b), apply, so far as applicable and unless the contrary intention appears, to subordinate legislation made after the commencement of this Act and, to the extent specified in Part II of Schedule 2, to subordinate legislation made before the commencement of this Act, as they apply to Acts.

(2) In the application of this Act to Acts passed or subordinate legislation made after the commencement of this Act, all references to an enactment include an enactment comprised in subordinate legislation whenever made, and references to the passing or repeal of an enactment are to be construed accordingly.

(3) Sections 9 and 19(1) also apply to deeds and other instruments and documents as they apply to Acts and subordinate legislation; and in the application of section 17(2)(a) to Acts passed or subordinate legislation made after the commencement of this Act, the reference to any other enactment includes any deed or other instrument or document.

(4) Subsections (1) and (2) of this section do not apply to Orders in Council made under section 5 of the Statutory Instruments Act 1946, section 1(3) of the Northern Ireland (Temporary Provisions) Act 1972 or Schedule 1 to the Northern Ireland Act 1974.

[23ZA Retained direct EU legislation

(1) The provisions of this Act (except sections 1 to 4, 13 and 19(2)) apply, so far as applicable and unless the contrary intention appears, to any retained direct EU legislation so far as it—
  (a) is amended by an Act, subordinate legislation or devolution legislation, and
  (b) is not subordinate legislation,
as they apply to an Act passed at the corresponding time.

(2) In their application by virtue of subsection (1)—
  (a) section 10 has effect as if the reference to the passing of the Act were a reference to the corresponding time,
  (b) section 11 has effect as if the second reference to an Act included a reference to the retained direct EU legislation so far as unamended (as well as a reference to that legislation so far as amended), and
  (c) section 16(1) has effect as if the reference to the repealing Act not being passed were a reference to the repeal not having been made.

(3) References in this Act to the repeal of an enactment are to be read, in the case of an enactment which is retained direct EU legislation, as references to the revocation of the enactment.

(4) In Schedule 1—
  (a) in the definition of "Commencement", the references to an enactment do not include any retained direct EU legislation other than—
    (i) any such legislation to which subsection (1) applies, . . .²
    [(iia) any instrument made on or after exit day under retained direct EU CAP legislation as defined in section 2 of the Direct Payments to Farmers (Legislative Continuity) Act 2020, or]²
    (ii) any instrument[, not falling within sub-paragraph (ia),]² made on or after [IP completion day]³ under any retained direct EU legislation, and
  (b) in the definitions of "The Corporation Tax Acts" and "The Income Tax Acts", the references to an enactment do not include any retained direct EU legislation.

(5) For the application of this Act to retained direct EU legislation which is subordinate legislation, see section 23(1) and (2).
(6) In this section—
"corresponding time" means the time when the amending Act, subordinate legislation or devolution legislation was passed or (as the case may be) made, and
"devolution legislation" means—
- (a) an Act of the Scottish Parliament,
- (b) a Measure or Act of the National Assembly for Wales,
- (c) Northern Ireland legislation (for the meaning of which see section 24(5)), or
- (d) an instrument made under anything falling within paragraph (a), (b) or (c).][1]

AMENDMENTS—
[1] Section 23ZA inserted by the European Union (Withdrawal) Act 2018 s 23(5), Sch 8 paras 18, 20 with effect from 4 July 2018 (by virtue of SI 2018/808 reg 3(g)(i), (ii)).
[2] In sub-s (4)(a), in sub-para (i) word "or" repealed, sub-para (ia) inserted, and sub-para (ii) words inserted, by the Direct Payments to Farmers (Legislative Continuity) Act 2020 (Consequential Amendments) Regulations, SI 2020/463 reg 2(1), (3) with effect from 30 April 2020.
[3] In sub-s (4)(a)(ii), words substituted for word "exit day" by the European Union (Withdrawal Agreement) Act 2020 s 41(4), Sch 5 paras 8, 11 with effect from 11pm on 31 January 2020.

[23A Acts of the Scottish Parliament etc
(1) This Act applies in relation to an Act of the Scottish Parliament and an instrument made under such an Act only to the extent provided in this section.
(2) Except as provided in subsection (3) below, sections 15 to 18 apply to—
- (a) an Act of the Scottish Parliament as they apply to an Act,
- (b) an instrument made under an Act of the Scottish Parliament as they apply to subordinate legislation.

(3) In the application of those sections to an Act and to subordinate legislation—
- (a) references to an enactment include an enactment comprised in, or in an instrument made under, an Act of the Scottish Parliament, and
- (b) the reference in section 17(2)(b) to subordinate legislation includes an instrument made under an Act of the Scottish Parliament.

(4) In the application of section 20 to an Act and to subordinate legislation, references to an enactment include an enactment comprised in, or in an instrument made under, an Act of the Scottish Parliament.][1]

Amendments—[1] Section 23A inserted by the Scotland Act 1998 s 125, Sch 8 para 16(2) with effect from 1 July 1999 (by virtue of SI 1998/3178 art 2(1)).

[23B Application of this Act to Welsh legislation
(1) The provisions of this Act, except sections 1 to 3, apply to the following as they apply to an Act—
- (a) a Measure of the National Assembly for Wales, and
- (b) an Act of the National Assembly for Wales, other than the Legislation (Wales) Act 2019, which receives Royal Assent before [1 January 2020 (the day on which Part 2 of that Act comes fully into force)][2].

(2) The provisions of this Act apply to an instrument—
- (a) made under a Measure or Act of the National Assembly for Wales, and
- (b) made before [1 January 2020][2],

as they apply to other subordinate legislation.
(3) The provisions of this Act apply to an instrument made under an Act of Parliament or retained direct EU legislation, and made by the Welsh Ministers or any other devolved Welsh authority, only if—
- (a) the instrument is made before [1 January 2020][2],
- (b) the instrument is made (at any time) with any other person who is not a devolved Welsh authority, or
- (c) the instrument contains any provision that applies otherwise than in relation to Wales.

(4) Nothing in subsection (2) or (3) limits the operation of sections 12 to 14A in relation to a power or duty to make an instrument to which Part 2 of the Legislation (Wales) Act 2019 applies, but section 11 does not apply in relation to such an instrument.
(5) In the application of this Act to a Measure or Act of the National Assembly for Wales, references to the passing of an Act or an enactment are to be read as references to the enactment of the Measure or Act.
(6) In this section, "devolved Welsh authority" and "Wales" have the same meanings as in the Government of Wales Act 2006 (see sections 157A and 158 of that Act).][1]

Amendments—[1] Section 23B substituted by the Legislation (Wales) Act 2019 s 41, Sch 2 para 1 with effect from 11 September 2019.

[2] In sub-s (1)(b), words substituted for words "the day on which Part 2 of that Act (interpretation and operation of Welsh legislation) comes fully into force", and in sub-ss (2)(b) and (3)(a), words substituted for words "the day on which Part 2 of the Legislation (Wales) Act 2019 comes fully into force", by SI 2019/1333 reg 4 with effect from 11 October 2019.

[23C Interpretation of this Act in relation to Welsh legislation
(1) In this Act, references to an enactment include an enactment comprised in—
    (a) a Measure of the National Assembly for Wales
    (b) an Act of the National Assembly for Wales (whenever the Act receives Royal Assent),
    (c) an instrument made under such an Act or Measure (whenever the instrument is made), or
    (d) an instrument made under an Act of Parliament or retained direct EU legislation, and made by the Welsh Ministers or any other devolved Welsh authority (whenever the instrument is made, and whether or not it is made with any other person),
but the reference in section 16(2) to a temporary enactment does not include an enactment comprised in legislation to which Part 2 of the Legislation (Wales) Act 2019 applies (see section 3(1) of that Act).
(2) In section 17(2)(b), the reference to subordinate legislation includes an instrument to which Part 2 of the Legislation (Wales) Act 2019 applies.
(3) In section 18, the reference to an act or omission which constitutes an offence under two or more Acts includes an act or omission which constitutes an offence under—
    (a) any legislation to which that section applies, and
    (b) any legislation to which Part 2 of the Legislation (Wales) Act 2019 applies,
and the reference to "those Acts" is to be read accordingly.
(4) In section 19(1), references to "another Act" include—
    (a) a Measure of the National Assembly for Wales, and
    (b) an Act of the National Assembly for Wales (whenever the Act receives Royal Assent),
and the reference in paragraph (c) to "Acts" is to be read accordingly.][1]

AMENDMENTS—
[1] Section 23C inserted by the Legislation (Wales) Act 2019 s 41, Sch 2 para 1 with effect from 11 September 2019.

24 Application to Northern Ireland
(1) This Act extends to Northern Ireland so far as it applies to Acts or subordinate legislation which so extend.
(2) In the application of this Act to Acts passed or subordinate legislation made after the commencement of this Act, all references to an enactment include an enactment comprised in Northern Ireland legislation whenever passed or made; and in relation to such legislation references to the passing or repeal of an enactment include the making or revocation of an Order in Council.
(3) In the application of section 14 to Acts passed after the commencement of this Act which extend to Northern Ireland, "statutory instrument" includes statutory rule for the purposes of the [Statutory Rules Northern Ireland Order 1979][1].
[(3A) Section 20A applies to Northern Ireland legislation as it applies to Acts.][4]
(4) The following definitions contained in Schedule 1, namely those of—
. . .[2]
    The Communities . . .[5];
    The Corporation Tax Acts;
    [ECSC Treaty;][5]
    [EEC Treaty;][5]
    [EEA agreement and EEA state;][4]
    [Entry date;][5]
    [The EU or the European Union;][5]
    [EU institution;][5]
    [EU instrument;][5]
    [Euratom, Economic Community and Coal and Steel Community;][5]
    [Euratom Treaty;][5]
    [European Court;][5]
    The Income Tax Acts;
    [Member (in the expression "member State");][5]
    The Tax Acts;
    [The Treaties or the EU Treaties][5],
apply unless the contrary intention appears, to Northern Ireland legislation as they apply to Acts.
(5) In this section "Northern Ireland legislation" means—
    (a) Acts of the Parliament of Ireland;
    (b) Acts of the Parliament of Northern Ireland;
    (c) Orders in Council under section 1(3) of the Northern Ireland (Temporary Provisions) Act 1972;
    [(d) Measures of the Northern Ireland Assembly established under section 1 of the Northern Ireland Assembly Act 1973;

(e) orders in Council under Schedule 1 to the Northern Ireland Act 1974;
(f) Acts of the Northern Ireland Assembly; and
(g) Orders in Council under section 85 of the Northern Ireland Act 1998.][3]

Amendments—[1] Sub-s (3) amended by the Statutory Rules (Northern Ireland) Order, SI 1979/1573, art 11(1), Sch 4, para 25.
[2] In sub-s (4), definition "British subject and Commonwealth citizen;" repealed by the British Nationality Act 1981 s 52(8), Sch 9.
[3] Sub-s (5)(d)–(g) substituted by the Northern Ireland Act 1998 s 99, Sch 13 para 3 with effect from 2 December 1999 (by virtue of SI 1999/3209 art 2, Schedule).
[4] Sub-s (3A) inserted, and in sub-s (4), definition "EEA agreement and EEA state;" inserted, by the Legislative and Regulatory Reform Act 2006 ss 25(3), 26(2) with effect from 8 January 2007.
[5] In sub-s (4), the following amendments made by the European Union (Withdrawal) Act 2018 s 23(5), Sch 8 paras 18, 21 with effect from IP completion day (11pm on 31 December 2020) by virtue of SI 2020/1622 reg 3(*i*), (*n*)—
- in definition "The Communities and related expressions" words "and related expressions" repealed; and
- definitions "ECSC Treaty;", "EEC Treaty;", "Entry date;", "The EU or the European Union;", "EU institution;", "EU instrument;", "Euratom, Economic Community and Coal and Steel Community;", "Euratom Treaty;", "European Court;", "Member (in the expression "member State");", "The Treaties or the EU Treaties", inserted.

25 Repeals and savings

(1) The enactments described in Schedule 3 are repealed to the extent specified in the third column of that Schedule.
(2) Without prejudice to section 17(2)(*a*), a reference to the Interpretation Act 1889, to any provision of that Act or to any other enactment repealed by this Act, whether occurring in another Act, in subordinate legislation, in Northern Ireland legislation or in any deed or other instrument or document, shall be construed as referring to this Act, or to the corresponding provision of this Act, as it applies to Acts passed at the time of the reference.
(3) The provisions of this Act relating to Acts passed after any particular time do not affect the construction of Acts passed before that time, though continued or amended by Acts passed thereafter.

26 Commencement

This Act shall come into force on 1st January 1979.

27 Short title

This Act may be cited as the Interpretation Act 1978.

SCHEDULES

SCHEDULE 1

WORDS AND EXPRESSIONS DEFINED

Section 5

Note: The years or dates which follow certain entries in the Schedule are relevant for the purposes of paragraph 4 of Schedule 2 (application to existing enactments).

Definitions

"Associated state" means a territory maintaining a status of association with the United Kingdom in accordance with the West Indies Act 1967. [16th February 1967]

"Bank of England" means, as the context requires, the Governor and Company of the Bank of England or the bank of the Governor and Company of the Bank of England.

"Bank of Ireland" means, as the context requires, the Governor and Company of the Bank of Ireland or the bank of the Governor and Company of the Bank of Ireland.

"British Islands" means the United Kingdom, the Channel Islands and the Isle of Man. [1889]

["British overseas territory" has the same meaning as in the British Nationality Act 1981.]

"British possession" means any part of Her Majesty's dominions outside the United Kingdom; and where parts of such dominions are under both a central and a local legislature, all parts under the central legislature are deemed, for the purposes of this definition, to be one British possession. [1889]

. . .

"Building regulations", in relation to England and Wales, [has the meaning given by section 122 of the Building Act 1984].

"Central funds", in an enactment providing in relation to England and Wales for the payment of costs out of central funds, means money provided by Parliament.

["Charity Commission" means the Charity Commission for England and Wales (see section 13 of the Charities Act 2011).]

"Church Commissioners" means the Commissioners constituted by the Church Commissioners Measure 1947.

["Civil partnership" means a civil partnership which exists under or by virtue of the Civil Partnership Act 2004 (and any reference to a civil partner is to be read accordingly).]

"Colonial legislature", and "legislature" in relation to a British possession, mean the authority, other than the Parliament of the United Kingdom or Her Majesty in Council, competent to make laws for the possession. [1889]

"Colony" means any part of Her Majesty's dominions outside the British Islands except—
  (a) countries having fully responsible status within the Commonwealth;
  (b) territories for whose external relations a country other than the United Kingdom is responsible;
  (c) associated states;

and where parts of such dominions are under both a central and a local legislature, all parts under the central legislature are deemed for the purposes of this definition to be one colony. [1889]

"Commencement", in relation to an Act or enactment, means the time when the Act or enactment comes into force.

"Committed for trial" means—
  (a) in relation to England and Wales, committed in custody or on bail by a magistrates' court pursuant to [section 6 of the Magistrates' Courts Act 1980], or by any judge or other authority having power to do so, with a view to trial before a judge and jury; [1889]
  (b) in relation to Northern Ireland, committed in custody or on bail by a magistrates' court pursuant to [Article 37 of the Magistrates' Courts (Northern Ireland) Order 1981], or by a court, judge, resident magistrate, . . . or other authority having power to do so, with a view to trial on indictment. [1st January 1979]

["The EU" or "the EU Treaties"] and other expressions defined by section 1 of and Schedule 1 to the European Communities Act 1972 have the meanings prescribed by that Act.

"Comptroller and Auditor General" means the Comptroller-General of the receipt and issue of Her Majesty's Exchequer and Auditor-General of Public Accounts . . . .

"Consular officer" has the meaning assigned by Article 1 of the Vienna Convention set out in Schedule 1 to the Consular Relations Act 1968.

["The Corporation Tax Acts" means the enactments relating to the taxation of the income and chargeable gains of companies and of company distributions (including provisions relating to income tax).]

"County court" means—
  (a) in relation to England and Wales, [the county court established under section A1 of] [the County Courts Act 1984]; [1846]
  (b) in relation to Northern Ireland, a court held . . . under the County Courts [(Northern Ireland) Order 1980]. [1889]

"Court of Appeal" means—
  (a) in relation to England and Wales, Her Majesty's Court of Appeal in England;
  (b) in relation to Northern Ireland, Her Majesty's Court of Appeal in Northern Ireland.

["Court of Judicature"' means the Court of Judicature of Northern Ireland.]

"Court of summary jurisdiction", "summary conviction" and "Summary Jurisdiction Acts", in relation to Northern Ireland, have the same meanings as in Measures of the Northern Ireland Assembly and Acts of the Parliament of Northern Ireland.

"Crown Court" means—
  (a) in relation to England and Wales, the Crown Court constituted by section 4 of the Courts Act 1971;
  (b) in relation to Northern Ireland, the Crown Court constituted by section 4 of the Judicature (Northern Ireland) Act 1978.

"Crown Estate Commissioners" means the Commissioners referred to in section 1 of the Crown Estate Act 1961.

. . .

["Enactment" [includes any retained direct EU legislation but] does not include an enactment comprised in, or in an instrument made under, an Act of the Scottish Parliament.]

"England" means, subject to any alteration of boundaries under Part IV of the Local Government Act 1972 the area consisting of the countries established by section 1 of that Act, Greater London and the Isles of Scilly. [1st April 1974]

"Financial year" means, in relation to matters relating to the Consolidated Fund, the National Loans Fund, or moneys provided by Parliament, or to the Exchequer or to central taxes or finance, the twelve months ending with 31st March. [1889]

"Governor-General" includes any person who for the time being has the powers of the Governor-General, and "Governor", in relation to any British possession, includes the officer for the time being administering the government of that possession. [1889]

["Her Majesty's Revenue and Customs" has the meaning given by section 4 of the Commissioners for Revenue and Customs Act 2005.]

"High Court" means—
　(a) in relation to England and Wales, Her Majesty's High Court of Justice in England;
　(b) in relation to Northern Ireland, Her Majesty's High Court of Justice in Northern Ireland.

"The Income Tax Acts" means all enactments relating to income tax, including any provisions of the Corporation Tax Acts which relate to income tax.

"Land" includes buildings and other structures, land covered with water, and any estate, interest, easement, servitude or right in or over land. [1st January 1979]

"Land Clauses Acts" means—
　(a) in relation to England and Wales, the Land Clauses Consolidation Act 1845 and the Lands Clauses Consolidation Acts Amendment Act 1860, and any Acts for the time being in force amending those Acts; [1889]
　(b) in relation to Scotland, the Lands Clauses Consolidation (Scotland) Act 1845 and the Lands Clauses Consolidation Acts Amendment Act 1860, and any Acts for the time being in force amending those Acts; [1889]
　(c) in relation to Northern Ireland, the enactments defined as such by section 46(1) of the Interpretation Act (Northern Ireland) 1954. [1889]

"Local land charges register", in relation to England and Wales, means [the register] kept pursuant to section 3 of the Local Land Charges Act 1975 . . . .

["Local policing body" has the meaning given by section 101(1) of the Police Act 1996.]

"London borough" means a borough described in Schedule 1 to the London Government Act 1963 "inner London borough" means one of the boroughs so described and numbered from 1 to 12 and "outer London borough" means one of the boroughs so described and numbered from 13 to 32, subject (in each case) to any alterations made under Part IV of the Local Government Act 1972[, Part 2 of the Local Government Act 1992 or Part 1 of the Local Government and Public Involvement in Health Act 2007].

"Lord Chancellor" means the Lord High Chancellor of Great Britain.

"Magistrates' court" has the meaning assigned to it—
　(a) in relation to England and Wales, by [section 148 of the Magistrates' Courts Act 1980];
　(b) in relation to Northern Ireland, by [Article 2(2) of the Magistrates' Courts (Northern Ireland) Order 1981].

"Month" means calendar month. [1850]

"National Debt Commissioners" means the Commissioners for the Reduction of the National Debt.

"Northern Ireland legislation" has the meaning assigned by section 24(5) of this Act. [1st January 1979]

"Oath" and "affidavit" include affirmation and declaration, and "swear" includes affirm and declare.

["Officer of a provider of probation services" in relation to England and Wales, has the meaning given by section 9(1) of the Offender Management Act 2007;]

["Officer of Revenue and Customs" has the meaning given by section 2(1) of the Commissioners for Revenue and Customs Act 2005.]

"Ordnance Map" means a map made under powers conferred by the Ordnance Survey Act 1841 or the Boundary Survey (Ireland) Act 1854.

"Parliamentary Election" means the election of a Member to serve in Parliament for a constituency. [1889]

["PAYE income" has the meaning given by section 683 of the Income Tax (Earnings and Pensions) Act 2003.]

["PAYE regulations" means regulations under section 684 of that Act.]

"Person" includes a body of persons corporate or unincorporate. [1889]

["Police and crime commissioner" means a police and crime commissioner established under section 1 of the Police Reform and Social Responsibility Act 2011]

"Police area" . . . and other expressions relating to the police have the meaning or effect described—
　(a) in relation to England and Wales, by [section 101(1) of the Police Act 1996];
　(b) in relation to Scotland, by sections 50 and 51(4) of the Police (Scotland) Act 1967.

["Police authority", in relation to Scotland, has the meaning or effect described by sections 50 and 51(4) of the Police (Scotland) Act 1967.]

["Police Service of Northern Ireland" and "Police Service of Northern Ireland Reserve" have the same meaning as in the Police (Northern Ireland) Act 2000.]

"The Privy Council" means the Lords and others of Her Majesty's Most Honourable Privy Council.

["Provider of probation services", in relation to England and Wales, has the meaning given by section 3(6) of the Offender Management Act 2007;]

["Registered" in relation to nurses, to midwives or to nursing associates, means registered in the register maintained under article 5 of the Nursing and Midwifery Order 2001 by virtue of a qualification which is an approved qualification for the purposes of registration in the relevant part of that register.]

"Registered medical practitioner" means a fully registered person within the meaning of the Medical Act 1983 who holds a licence to practise under that Act.".

["Registered provider of social housing'"has the meaning given by section 80(2) of the Housing and Regeneration Act 2008 (and "non-profit" and "profit-making" in connection with a provider have the meanings given by section 115 of that Act).]

"Rules of Court" in relation to any court means rules made by the authority having power to make rules or orders regulating the practice and procedure of that court, and in Scotland includes Acts of Adjournal and Acts of Sederunt; and the power of the authority to make rules of court (as above defined) includes power to make such rules for the purpose of any Act which directs or authorises anything to be done by rules of court. [1889]

"Secretary of State" means one of Her Majesty's Principal Secretaries of State.

["Senior Courts'"means the Senior Courts of England and Wales.]

["Sent for trial" means, in relation to England and Wales, sent by a magistrates' court to the Crown Court for trial pursuant to section 51 or 51A of the Crime and Disorder Act 1998.]

["The Sentencing Code" means the code contained in the Sentencing Act 2020 (see section 1 of that Act).]

["Sewerage undertaker, in relation to England and Wales, shall be construed in accordance with [section 6 of the Water Industry Act 1991].]

["Sheriff" is to be construed in accordance with section 134(2) and (3) of the Courts Reform (Scotland) Act 2014.]

["The standard scale", with reference to a fine or penalty for an offence triable only summarily,—
- (a) in relation to England and Wales, [has the meaning given by section 122 of the Sentencing Code (or, in the case of an offence of which the offender was convicted before that Act came into force, section 37 of the Criminal Justice Act 1982)];
- (b) in relation to Scotland, has the meaning given by section 289G of the Criminal Procedure (Scotland) Act 1975;
- (c) in relation to Northern Ireland, has the meaning given by Article 5 of the Fines and Penalties (Northern Ireland) Order 1984.]

"Statutory declaration" means a declaration made by virtue of the Statutory Declarations Act 1835.

["Statutory maximum", with reference to a fine or penalty on summary conviction for an offence,—
- (a) in relation to England and Wales, means the prescribed sum within the meaning of section 32 of the Magistrates' Courts Act 1980;
- (b) in relation to Scotland, means the prescribed sum within the meaning of section 289B(6) of the Criminal Procedure (Scotland) Act 1975; and
- (c) in relation to Northern Ireland, means the prescribed sum within the meaning of Article 4 of the Fines and Penalties (Northern Ireland) Order 1984.]

["Supreme Court" means the Supreme Court of the United Kingdom.]

["The Tax Acts" means the Income Tax Acts and the Corporation Tax Acts.]

["Transfer for trial" means the transfer of proceedings against an accused to the Crown Court for trial under section 7 of the Magistrates' Courts Act 1980.]

"The Treasury" means the Commissioners of Her Majesty's Treasury.

["Trust of land" and "trustees of land", in relation to England and Wales, have the same meanings as in the Trusts of Land and Appointment of Trustees Act 1996.]

"United Kingdom" means Great Britain and Northern Ireland. [12th April 1927]

["Wales" means the combined area of counties which were created by section 20 of the Local Government Act 1972, as originally enacted, but subject to any alteration made under section 73 of that Act (consequential alteration of boundary following alteration of watercourse).]

["Water undertaker", in relation to England and Wales, shall be construed in accordance with [section 6 of the Water Industry Act 1991].]

"Writing" includes typing, printing, lithography, photography and other modes of representing or reproducing words in a visible form, and expressions referring to writing are construed accordingly.

. . .

Construction of certain expressions relating to offences

In relation to England and Wales—
- (a) "indictable offence" means an offence which, if committed by an adult, is triable on indictment, whether it is exclusively so triable or triable either way;
- (b) "summary offence" means an offence which, if committed by an adult, is triable only summarily;
- (c) "offence triable either way" means an offence [, other than an offence triable on indictment only by virtue of Part V of the Criminal Justice Act 1988] which, if committed by an adult, is triable either on indictment or summarily;

and the terms "indictable", "summary" and "triable either way", in their application to offences, are to be construed accordingly.

In the above definitions references to the way or ways in which an offence is triable are to be construed without regard to the effect, if any, of [section 22 of the Magistrates' Courts Act 1980] on the mode of trial in a particular case.

[Construction of certain references to relationships

In relation to England and Wales—
- (a) references (however expressed) to any relationship between two persons;
- (b) references to a person whose father and mother were or were not married to[, or civil partners of,] each other at the time of his birth; and
- (c) references cognate with references falling within paragraph (b) above,

shall be construed in accordance with section 1 of the Family Law Reform Act 1987. [4th April 1988]]

[Definitions relating to the EU and the United Kingdom's withdrawal

"The Communities" means Euratom, the Economic Community and the Coal and Steel Community, but a reference to any or all of those Communities is to be treated as being or including (as the context requires) a reference to the EU.

"ECSC Treaty" means the Treaty establishing the European Coal and Steel Community, signed at Paris on 18 April 1951.

"EEA agreement" means the agreement on the European Economic Area signed at Oporto on 2 May 1992, together with the Protocol adjusting that Agreement signed at Brussels on 17 March 1993, as modified or supplemented from time to time, but does not include any retained direct EU legislation. [8 January 2007]

"EEA state", in relation to a time, means—
- (a) a state which at that time is a member State, or
- (b) any other state which at that time is a party to the EEA agreement. [8 January 2007]

"EEC Treaty" means the Treaty establishing the European Economic Community, signed at Rome on 25 March 1957.

"Entry date" means the date on which the United Kingdom became a member of the Communities (which neither includes nor is a reference to the EU).

"The EU" or "the European Union" means the European Union, being the Union established by the Treaty on European Union signed at Maastricht on 7 February 1992 (as amended by any later Treaty); and includes, so far as the context permits or requires, Euratom.

"EU institution" means any institution of the EU.

"EU instrument" means any instrument issued by an EU institution other than any retained direct EU legislation.

"Euratom", "Economic Community" and "Coal and Steel Community" mean respectively the European Atomic Energy Community, the European Economic Community and the European Coal and Steel Community (but see the definition of "the Communities" for provision as to the construction of references to those Communities).

"Euratom Treaty" means the Treaty establishing the European Atomic Energy Community, signed at Rome on 25 March 1957.

"European Court" means the Court of Justice of the European Union.

"Exit day" (and related expressions) have the same meaning as in the European Union (Withdrawal) Act 2018 (see section 20(1) to (5) of that Act).

"Member", in the expression "member State", refers to membership of the EU.

"Retained EU law", "retained direct minor EU legislation", "retained direct principal EU legislation" and "retained direct EU legislation" have the same meaning as in the European Union (Withdrawal) Act 2018 (see sections 6(7), 7(6) and 20(1) of that Act) [(see also paragraph 7 of Schedule 1 to the Direct Payments to Farmers (Legislative Continuity) Act 2020)]].

"Retained EU obligation" means an obligation that—
  (a) was created or arose by or under the EU Treaties before exit day, and
  (b) forms part of retained EU law,
    as modified from time to time.

"The Treaties" or "the EU Treaties" means the Treaties or EU Treaties, within the meaning given by section 1(2) of the European Communities Act 1972 as that Act had effect immediately before its repeal by section 1 of the European Union (Withdrawal) Act 2018, as at immediately before exit day.]

Note—Omitted provisions are outside the scope of this publication.

Cross references—See TA 1988 s 834(1) (meaning of "financial year" for the purposes of Corporation Tax Acts).

See the European Union (Withdrawal) Act 2018 and European Union (Withdrawal Agreement) Act 2020 (Commencement, Transitional and Savings Provisions) Regulations, SI 2020/1622 reg 7 (repeal of definitions of "the Treaties" and "the EU Treaties" and replacement of those definitions by EUWA 2018 Sch 8 para 22(e) does not affect the interpretation of those provisions in pre-IP completion day legislation on and after IP completion day in relation to a time before IP completion day).

Modifications—See the Police and Fire Reform (Scotland) Act 2012 (Consequential Provisions and Modifications) Order, SI 2013/602 art 26, Sch 2 para 15 (modification of this Schedule in its application to Scotland).

Amendments—

The definition of "British overseas territory" inserted by the British Overseas Territories Act 2002 s 1(3) with effect from 26 February 2002.

The definitions of "British subject" and "Commonwealth citizen" repealed by the British Nationality Act 1981 Sch 9.

Words in the definition of "Building regulations" substituted by the Building Act 1984 Sch 6 para 19.

Definition "Charity Commission" substituted by the Charities Act 2011 s 354, Sch 7, para 34 with effect from 16 January 2012.

Definition "Civil partnership" inserted by the Civil Partnership Act 2004 s 261(1), Sch 27 para 59 with effect from 5 December 2005 (by virtue of SI 2005/3175).

Words in the definition of "Committed for trial" substituted by the Magistrates' Courts Act 1980 Sch 7 para 169 and the Magistrates' Courts (Northern Ireland) Order, SI 1981/1675 Sch 6 para 56. The whole of para (a) of this definition is repealed by the Criminal Justice and Public Order Act 1994 Sch 4 para 28(a), Sch 11 with effect for certain purposes from 8 June 2012 (see SI 2012/1320 art 4(1)(a), (b), (c)(iii)–(v), (d), for certain other purposes from 5 November 2012 (see SI 2012/2574 art 2(1)(a)–(d), (2), (3), Schedule, and for remaining purposes from a date to be appointed.

Words in the definition of "Committed for trial" repealed by the Justice (Northern Ireland) Act 2002 s 86, Sch 13 with effect from 1 April 2005 (by virtue of SR 2005/109).

In definition of "Committed for trial", para (a) repealed by the Criminal Justice Act 2003 ss 41, 332, Sch 3 para 49(a), Sch 37 Pt 4. This amendment has effect from 28 May 2013 in relation to certain local justice areas (see SI 2013/1103).

Words in definition of "Comptroller and Auditor General" repealed by the Budget Responsibility and National Audit Act 2011 s 26, Sch 5 para 12 with effect from 1 April 2012 (SI 2011/2576 art 5).

The definition of "The Corporation Tax Acts" substituted by FA 1987 s 71 Sch 15 para 12.

Words in the definition of "County court" substituted by the County Courts Act 1984 Sch 2 para 68 and the County Courts (Northern Ireland) Order, SI 1980/397 Sch 1 Pt II.

In definition of "county court", in para (a), words substituted by the Crime and Courts Act 2013 s 17, Sch 9 para 94 with effect from 22 April 2014 (by virtue of SI 2014/954 art 2(c)).

In definition of "county court", para (b), words "for a division" repealed by the Justice Act (Northern Ireland) 2015 s 6, Sch 1 para 75, s 106, Sch 9 Pt 1 with effect from 31 October 2016 (by virtue of SR 2016/387 art 2(k), (m)).

The definition of "Court of Judicature" inserted by the Constitutional Reform Act 2005 s 59, Sch 11 para 24(b) with effect from 1 October 2009 (by virtue of SI 2009/1604 art 2(d)).

Definition "Enactment" inserted by the Scotland Act 1998 s 125, Sch 8 para 16(3) with effect from 1 July 1999 (SI 1998/3178, art 2(1)).

In definition "Enactment", words inserted by the European Union (Withdrawal) Act 2018 s 23(5), Sch 8 paras 18, 22(d) for the purposes of the use of the term "enactment" in ss 15, 16, 17, with effect from 4 July 2018 (by virtue of SI 2018/808 regs 2, 3(g)(iii), (iv)).

Under the heading "Definitions relating to the EU and the United Kingdom's withdrawal", definitions " 'exit day' (and related expressions)", "retained EU law", "retained direct minor EU legislation", "retained direct principal EU legislation", "retained direct EU legislation", and "retained EU obligation", inserted by the European Union (Withdrawal) Act 2018 s 23(5), Sch 8 paras 18, 22(e) with effect from 4 July 2018 (by virtue of SI 2018/808 regs 2, 3(g)(iii), (iv)). Remaining definitions inserted with effect from IP completion day (11pm on 31 December 2020) by virtue of SI 2020/1622 reg 3(n). Note that, in its application to an Act passed, or subordinate legislation made, before 19 June 2008, the definition of "the Communities" as inserted by EUWA 2018 Sch 8 para 22(e) has effect on and after IP completion day, in its application in relation to a time before 19 June 2008, as if the words from "but" to the end were omitted.

In the entry for "retained EU law", "retained direct minor EU legislation", "retained direct principal EU legislation" and "retained direct EU legislation", words in squared brackets inserted by the Direct Payments to Farmers (Legislative Continuity) Act 2020) s 6, Sch 1 para 3.

Definitions "'The EU' or 'the EU Treaties'", "EEA agreement" and "EEA state" repealed by the European Union (Withdrawal) Act 2018 s 23(5), Sch 8 paras 18, 22(a)–(c) with effect from IP completion day (11pm on 31 December 2020) by virtue of SI 2020/1622 reg 3(n). Note that the replacement of definitions of "the Treaties" and "the EU Treaties" does not affect the interpretation of those expressions in pre-IP completion day legislation on and after IP completion day in relation to a time before IP completion day (see SI 2020/1622 reg 7).

Definition of "Her Majesty's Revenue and Customs" inserted by CRCA 2005 s 4(3) with effect from 7 April 2005 (by virtue of SI 2005/1126).

Words in the definition "local land charges register" substituted for words "a register", and words "and "the appropriate local land charges register" has the meaning assigned by section 4 of that Act" repealed by the Infrastructure Act 2015 s 34(1), (2)(c), Sch 5 para 34 with effect from 12 April 2015.

Definitions "Local Policing Body and "Police Authority" inserted by Police Reform and Social Responsibility Act 2011 s 97(1), (2), (5) with effect from 16 January 2012 (by virtue of SI 2011/3019 art 2, Sch 1(aaa)).

Words in the definition of "London borough" substituted by the Local Government and Public Involvement in Health Act 2007 s 22, Sch 1 para 14 with effect from 1 November 2007 (by virtue of SI 2007/3136, art 2(b)).

Words in para (a) of the definition of "Magistrates' court" substituted by the Magistrates' Courts Act 1980 s 154 Sch 7 para 169 and, in para (b), by the Magistrates' Court (Northern Ireland) Order, SI 1981/1675 art 170(2) Sch 6 Pt I para 56.

Definition of "Officer of a provider of probation services" inserted by the Offender Management Act 2007 s 39, Sch 3 para 2 with effect from 1 April 2008 (by virtue of SI 2008/504 art 3(1)).

Definition of "Officer of Revenue and Customs" inserted by CRCA 2005 s 2(7) with effect from 7 April 2005 (by virtue of SI 2005/1126).

Definitions of "PAYE income" and "PAYE regulations" inserted by ITEPA 2003 s 722, Sch 6 para 148 with effect, for income tax purposes, from 2003–04; and for corporation tax purposes, for accounting periods ending after 5 April 2003. For transitional provisions and savings see ITEPA 2003 s 723, Sch 7.

Definition of "police and crime commissioner" inserted by Police Reform and Social Responsibility Act 2001, s 97(3) with effect from 22 November 2012 (by virtue of SI 2012/2892 art 2(a)).

Words in the definition of "police area" substituted by the Police Act 1996 Sch 7 para 32.

Words in the definition of "Police area" repealed by Police Reform and Social Responsibility Act 2011 s 97(1), (4), with effect from 16 January 2012 (by virtue of SI 2011/3019 art 2, Sch 1(*aaa*)).

Definition of "Police authority" inserted by the Police Reform and Social Responsibility Act 2011 s 97(1), (5) with effect from 16 January 2012 (by virtue of SI 2011/3019 art 3, Sch 1 para (*aaa*)).

Definition of "Police Service of Northern Ireland" and "Police Service of Northern Ireland Reserve" inserted by the Police (Northern Ireland) Act 2000 s 78(1), Sch 6 para 5 with effect from 4 December 2001 (by virtue of SR 2001/396).

Definition of "Provider of probation services" inserted by the Offender Management Act 2007 s 39, Sch 3 para 2 with effect from 1 April 2008 (by virtue of SI 2008/504 art 3(l)).

Definition of "Registered" substituted by the Nursing and Midwifery (Amendment) Order, SI 2018/838 art 2(3), Sch 3 para 1 with effect from 28 January 2019.

"Registered" in relation to nurses and midwives, means registered in the register maintained under article 5 of the Nurses and Midwives Order 2001 by virtue of qualifications in nursing or midwifery, as the case may be.".

Definition of "Registered medical practitioner" substituted by the Medical Act 1983 (Amendment) Order, SI 2002/3135 art 16(1), Sch 1 para 10 with effect from 16 November 2009.

The definition of "Registered provider of social housing" inserted by the Housing and Regeneration Act 2008 s 277, Sch 9 para 5 with effect from 1 April 2010 (by virtue of SI 2010/844, art 1(2)

The definition of "Senior Courts" inserted by the Constitutional Reform Act 2005 s 59, Sch 11 para 24(*b*) with effect from 1 October 2009 (by virtue of SI 2009/1604 art 2(d)).

The definition of "Sent for trial" inserted by the Criminal Justice Act 2003 s 41, Sch 3, Pt 2, para 49(*b*) with effect from 9 May 2005 (by virtue of SI 2005/1267).

The definition of "The Sentencing Code" inserted by the Sentencing Act 2020 s 410, Sch 24 para 39(1), (2) with effect from 1 December 2020 (by virtue of SI 2020/1236).

The definition of "Sewerage undertaker" inserted by the Water Act 1989 s 190(1), Sch 25 para 55(1), (2), as amended by the Water Consolidation (Consequential Provisions) Act 1991 s 2(1) Sch 1 para 32.

Definition of "Sheriff" substituted by the Courts Reform (Scotland) Act 2014 (Consequential Provisions and Modifications) Order, SI 2015/700 art 10, Schedule para 10, with effect for certain purposes from 11 November 2014 and for remaining purposes from a date to be appointed (see SI 2015/700 art 1(11)(*h*) and the Court Reform Act ss 134, 138). Definition previously read as follows—

""'Sheriff', in relation to Scotland, includes sheriff principal."

The definition of "The standard scale" inserted by the Criminal Justice Act 1988 s 170(1) Sch 15 para 58(*a*).

In definition of "The standard scale" in para (*a*) words substituted for words "has the meaning given by section 37 of the Criminal Justice Act 1982" by the Sentencing Act 2020 s 410, Sch 24 para 39(1), (3) with effect from 1 December 2020 (by virtue of SI 2020/1236).

The definition of "Statutory maximum" inserted by the Criminal Justice Act 1988 s 170(1) Sch 15 para 58(*b*).

The definition of "Supreme Court" substituted by the Constitutional Reform Act 2005 s 59, Sch 11 para 24(*a*) with effect from 1 October 2009 (by virtue of SI 2009/1604 art 2(d)).

The definition of "The Tax Acts" substituted by FA 1987 s 71 Sch 15 para 12.

The definition "Transfer for trial" inserted by the Criminal Justice and Public Order Act 1994 Sch 4 para 28(*b*), as from a day to be appointed.

The definitions of "Trust of land" and trustees of land" inserted by the Trusts of Land and Appointment of Trustees Act 1996 s 25(1), Sch 3 para 16, as from a day to be appointed.

The definition of "Wales" substituted by the Local Government (Wales) Act 1994 Sch 2 para 9.

The definition of "Water undertaker" substituted for the definitions "Water authority" and "Water authority area" by the Water Act 1989 s 190(1) Sch 25 para 55(1), (3), as amended by the Water Consolidation (Consequential Provisions) Act 1991 s 2(1) Sch 1 para 32.

The entry relating to the construction of certain expressions relating to children is repealed by the Children Act 1989 s 108(7) Sch 15.

In the entry relating to the construction of certain expressions relating to offences (i) the words in the definition "offence triable either way" inserted by the Criminal Justice Act 1988 s 170(1) Sch 15 para 59; (ii) the words "section 22 of the Magistrates' Courts Act 1980" substituted by the Magistrates' Courts Act 1980 s 154 Sch 7 para 169.

The entry relating to the construction of references to relationships added at the end by the Family Law Reform Act 1987 s 33(1), Sch 2 para 73.

In entry relating to the construction of certain references to relationships, in para (*b*) words inserted by the Civil Partnership (Opposite-sex Couples) Regulations, SI 2019/1458 reg 41(a), Sch 3 para 6 with effect from 2 December 2019.

The following definitions inserted by the European Union (Withdrawal) Act 2018 s 23(5), Sch 8 paras 18, 22(e) with effect from 4 July 2018 (by virtue of SI 2018/808 regs 2, 3(g)(iii), (iv))—

- " 'exit day' (and related expressions)",
- "Retained EU law",
- "retained direct minor EU legislation",
- "retained direct principal EU legislation",
- "retained direct EU legislation", and
- "retained EU obligation".

SCHEDULE 2
APPLICATION OF ACT TO EXISTING ENACTMENTS
PART I
ACTS

1 The following provisions of this Act apply to Acts whenever passed—
Section 6(*a*) and (*c*) so far as applicable to enactments relating to offences punishable on indictment or on summary conviction
    Section 9
    Section 10
    Section 11 so far as it relates to subordinate legislation made after the year 1889
    [Section 14A][1]
    Section 18
    Section 19(2).

Amendments—[1] Entry for "Section 14A" inserted by the Enterprise and Regulatory Reform Act 2013 s 59(1), (3) with effect from 25 April 2013.

2 The following apply to Acts passed after the year 1850—
    Section 1
    Section 3
    Section 6(*a*) and (*c*) so far as not applicable to such Acts by virtue of paragraph 1
    Section 15
    Section 17(1)

3 The following apply to Acts passed after the year 1889—
    Section 4
    Section 7
    Section 12
    Section 13
    Section 14 so far as it relates to rules, regulations or byelaws
    Section 16(1)
    Section 17(2)(*a*)
    Section 19(1)
    Section 20(1)

4—(1) Subject to the following provisions of this paragraph—
    (*a*) paragraphs of Schedule 1 at the end of which a year or date . . . [1] is specified [or described][2] apply, so far as applicable, to Acts passed on or after the date, or after the year, so specified [or described][2]; and

(*b*) paragraphs of the Schedule at the end of which no year or date is specified [or described][2] apply, so far as applicable, to Acts passed at any time.

(4) The definition of "Lord Chancellor" does not apply to Acts passed before 1st October 1921 in which that expression was used in relation to Ireland only.

(5) The definition of "person", so far as it includes bodies corporate, applies to any provision of an Act whenever passed relating to an offence punishable on indictment or on summary conviction.

Amendments—[1] Words in sub-para (1)(*a*) repealed by the Family Law Reform Act 1987 s 33(1) Sch 2 para 74, Sch 4, with effect from 4 April 1988, by virtue of the Family Law Reform Act 1987 (Commencement No 1) Order, SI 1988/425.

[2] Words in sub-para (1)(*a*), (*b*) inserted by the Family Law Reform Act 1987 s 33(1) Sch 2 para 74, Sch 4, with effect from 4 April 1988, by virtue of the Family Law Reform Act 1987 (Commencement No 1) Order, SI 1988/425.

5 The following definitions shall be treated as included in Schedule 1 for the purposes specified in this paragraph—

(*a*) in any Act passed before 1st April 1974, a reference to England includes Berwick upon Tweed and Monmouthshire and, in the case of an Act passed before the Welsh Language Act 1967 Wales;

(*b*) in any Act passed before the commencement of this Act and after the year 1850, "land", includes messuages, tenements and hereditaments, houses and buildings of any tenure;

(*c*) in any Act passed before the commencement of the Criminal Procedure (Scotland) Act 1975 "the Summary Jurisdiction (Scotland) Acts" means Part II of that Act.

PART II
SUBORDINATE LEGISLATION

7 The definition in Schedule 1 of "county court", in relation to England and Wales, applies to Orders in Council made after the year 1846.

[**8** The definition in Schedule 1 of "enactment", in so far as it relates to retained direct EU legislation, applies to subordinate legislation made at any time before the commencement of this Act as it applies to Acts passed at that time.][1]

Amendments—[1] Para 8 inserted by the European Union Withdrawal (Consequential Modifications) (EU Exit) Regulations, SI 2020/1447 reg 2(1), (5) with effect from IP completion day (11pm UK time on 31 December 2020) (see EU(WA)A 2020 Sch 5 para 1(1)).

CUSTOMS AND EXCISE MANAGEMENT ACT 1979

(1979 Chapter 2)

ARRANGEMENT OF SECTIONS

PART I
PRELIMINARY

1	Interpretation.
5	Time of importation, exportation, etc.

PART II
ADMINISTRATION

Appointment and duties of Commissioners, officers, etc

6	Appointment and general duties of Commissioners, etc. (repealed)

Offences in connection with Commissioners, officers, etc

15	Bribery and collusion. (repealed)
16	Obstruction of officers, etc. (repealed)

Commissioners' receipts and expenses

17	Disposal of duties, etc. (repealed)

PART III
CUSTOMS AND EXCISE CONTROL AREAS

19	Appointment of ports, etc.
21	Control of movement of aircraft, etc into and out of the United Kingdom.

PART IV
CONTROL OF IMPORTATION
Inward entry and clearance

37	Entry of goods on importation. (repealed)
37A	*Initial and supplementary entries.* (repealed)
37B	*Postponed entry.* (repealed)
37C	*Provisions supplementary to ss 37A and 37B.* (repealed)
38	Acceptance of incomplete entry. (repealed)
38A	Examination of goods for purpose of making entry. (repealed)
38B	*Correction and cancellation of entry.* (repealed)
41	Failure to comply with provisions as to entry.
42	Power to regulate unloading, removal, etc of imported goods.

Provisions as to duty on imported goods

43	Duty on imported goods.
44	Exclusion of s 43(1) for importers etc keeping standing deposits.
45	*Deferred payment of customs duty.* (repealed)
46	*Goods to be warehoused without payment of duty.* (repealed)
47	*Relief from payment of duty of goods entered for transit or transhipment.* (repealed)
48	*Relief from payment of duty of goods temporarily imported.* (repealed)

Forfeiture, offences, etc in connection with importation

49	Forfeiture of goods improperly imported.
50	Penalty for improper importation of goods.

PART VII
CUSTOMS AND EXCISE CONTROL: SUPPLEMENTARY PROVISIONS
Additional provisions as to information

77	Information in relation to goods imported or exported.
77A	Information powers.
78	Customs and excise control of persons entering or leaving the United Kingdom.
79	Power to require evidence in support of information.

PART VIII
WAREHOUSES AND QUEEN'S WAREHOUSES AND RELATED PROVISIONS ABOUT PIPE-LINES

92	Approval of warehouses.

PART VIIIA
FREE ZONES

100A	Designation of free zones.
100B	Free zone regulations. (repealed)
100C	Free zone goods: customs duties, etc. (repealed)
100D	Free zone regulations: supplemental. (repealed)
100E	Control of trading in free zones. (repealed)
100F	Powers of search.

PART X
DUTIES AND DRAWBACKS—GENERAL PROVISIONS
General provisions relating to imported goods

125	*Valuation of goods for purposes of ad valorem duties.* (repealed)
127	Determination of disputes as to duties on imported goods. (repealed)

PART XI
DETENTION OF PERSONS, FORFEITURE AND LEGAL PROCEEDINGS
Detention of persons

138	Provisions as to detention of persons.

Forfeiture

139	Provisions as to detention, seizure and condemnation of goods, etc.

General provisions as to legal proceedings

145	Institution of proceedings.
146	Service of process.

146A	Time limits for proceedings
147	Proceedings for offences.
148	Place of trial for offences.
149	Non-payment of penalties, etc: maximum terms of imprisonment.
150	Incidental provisions as to legal proceedings.
151	Application of penalties.
152	Power of Commissioners to mitigate penalties, etc.
153	*Proof of certain documents.* (repealed)
154	Proof of certain other matters.
155	Persons who may conduct proceedings.
156	Saving for outlying enactments of certain general provisions as to offences.

PART XII
GENERAL AND MISCELLANEOUS
General powers, etc

157	Bonds and security.
157A	General information powers in relation to persons entering or leaving the United Kingdom.
158	Power to require provision of facilities.
159	Power to examine and take account of goods.
164	Power to search persons.
164A	Powers to search for cash

General offences

167	Untrue declarations, etc.
168	Counterfeiting documents, etc.
171	General provisions as to offences and penalties.
	Schedules
	Schedule 2A—Supplementary provisions relating to the detention of things as liable to forfeiture
	Schedule 3—Provisions relating to forfeiture.

PART I
PRELIMINARY

1 Interpretation

(1) In this Act, unless the context otherwise requires—

"aerodrome" means any area of land or water designed, equipped, set apart or commonly used for affording facilities for the landing and departure of aircraft;
. . .[15]

"approved wharf" has the meaning given by [section 20A][8] below;

"armed forces" means the Royal Navy, the Royal Marines, the regular army and the regular air force, and any reserve or auxiliary force of any of those services which has been called out on permanent service, [. . .][24] or embodied;

["assigned matter" means any matter in relation to which the Commissioners, or officers of Revenue and Customs, have a power or duty[, except that it does not include any matter relating to a devolved tax within the meaning of the Scotland Act 1998][31] [or the Government of Wales Act 2006][36];][27]

"boarding station" means a boarding station for the time being appointed under section 19 below;

"boundary" means the land boundary of Northern Ireland;

"British ship" means a British ship within the meaning of the [Merchant Shipping Act 1995][21];

"claimant", in relation to proceedings for the condemnation of any thing as being forfeited, means a person claiming that the thing is not liable to forfeiture;
. . .[38]

"commander", in relation to an aircraft, includes any person having or taking the charge or command of the aircraft;

["the Commissioners" means the Commissioners for Her Majesty's Revenue and Customs;][27]
. . .[38]

"container" includes any bundle or package and any [baggage,][28] box, cask or other receptacle whatsoever;

"the customs and excise Acts" means the Customs and Excise Acts 1979 and any other enactment for the time being in force relating to customs or excise;

"the Customs and Excise Acts 1979" means—

this Act,

the Customs and Excise Duties (General Reliefs) Act 1979

the Alcoholic Liquor Duties Act 1979
the Hydrocarbon Oil Duties Act 1979
. . . [13] and
the Tobacco Products Duty Act 1979;
"customs warehouse" means a place of security approved by the Commissioners under subsection (2) (whether or not it is also approved under subsection (1)) of section 92 below;[9]
"customs and excise airport" has the meaning given by section 21(7) below;
"customs and excise station" has the meaning given by section 26 below;
["customs formalities", in relation to any goods, means the requirements made by or under this Act, or by or under Part 1 of the Taxation (Cross-border Trade) Act 2018, that apply in relation to the importation or exportation of the goods;
"customs warehouse" means premises approved under regulations under Schedule 2 to the Taxation (Cross-border Trade) Act 2018 for the purposes of a storage procedure;][38]
["designation order" has the meaning given by section 100A(5);][4]
"drawback goods" means goods in the case of which a claim for drawback has been or is to be made;
"dutiable goods", except in the expression "dutiable or restricted goods", means goods of a class or description subject to any duty of customs or excise, whether or not those goods are in fact chargeable with that duty, and whether or not that duty has been paid thereon;
"dutiable or restricted goods" has the meaning given by section 52 below;
"examination station" has the meaning given by [section 22A][8] below;
["excise duty point" has the meaning given by section 1 of the Finance (No 2) Act 1992;][11]
"excise licence trade" means, subject to subsection (5) below, a trade or business for the carrying on of which an excise licence is required;
"excise warehouse" means a place of security approved by the Commissioners under subsection (1) . . . [38] of section 92 below, and, except in that section, also includes a distiller's warehouse;
"exporter", in relation to goods for exportation or for use as stores, includes the shipper of the goods and any person performing in relation to an aircraft functions corresponding with those of a shipper;
["free zone" has the meaning given by section 100A(2);][4]
["free zone goods" are goods which are within a free zone][18]
. . . [10]
"goods" includes stores and [containers][33];
"holiday", in relation to any part of the United Kingdom, means any day that is a bank holiday in that part of the United Kingdom under the Banking and Financial Dealings Act 1971 Christmas Day, Good Friday and the day appointed for the purposes of customs and excise for the celebration of Her Majesty's birthday;
"hovercraft" means a hovercraft within the meaning of the Hovercraft Act 1968;
"importer", in relation to any goods at any time between their importation and the time when [all customs formalities have been complied with in respect of the goods][38], includes any owner or other person for the time being possessed of or beneficially interested in the goods and, in relation to goods imported by means of a pipe-line, includes the owner of the pipe-line;
"justice" and "justice of the peace" in Scotland includes a sheriff and in Northern Ireland, in relation to any powers and duties which can under any enactment for the time being in force be exercised and performed only by a resident magistrate, means a resident magistrate;
"land" and "landing", in relation to aircraft, include alighting on water;
"law officer of the Crown" means the Attorney General or [for the purpose of criminal proceedings in Scotland, the Lord Advocate or, for the purpose of civil proceedings in Scotland, the appropriate Law Officer within the meaning of section 4A of the Crown Suits (Scotland) Act 1857][25] or in Northern Ireland the Attorney General for Northern Ireland;
"licence year", in relation to an excise licence issuable annually, means the period of 12 months ending on the date on which that licence expires in any year;
"master", in relation to a ship, includes any person having or taking the charge or command of the ship;
. . . [6]
"night" means the period between 11 pm and 5 am;
["nuclear material" has the same meaning as in the Nuclear Material (Offences) Act 1983 (see section 6 of that Act);][30]
"occupier", in relation to any bonded premises, [includes any][12] person who has given security to the Crown in respect of those premises;
"officer" means, subject to section 8(2) below, a person commissioned by the Commissioners;
"owner", in relation to an aircraft, includes the operator of the aircraft;

"owner", in relation to a pipe-line, means (except in the case of a pipe-line vested in the Crown which in pursuance of arrangements in that behalf is operated by another) the person in whom the line is vested and, in the said excepted case, means the person operating the line;
"perfect entry" means an entry made in accordance with [regulation 5 of the Customs Controls on Importation of Goods Regulations 1991][14] or warehousing regulations, as the case may require;[20]
"pipe-line" has the meaning given by section 65 of the Pipe-lines Act 1962 (that Act being taken, for the purposes of this definition, to extend to Northern Ireland);
"port" means a port appointed by the Commissioners under section 19 below;
"prescribed area" means such an area in Northern Ireland adjoining the boundary as the Commissioners may by regulations prescribe;
"prescribed sum", in relation to the penalty provided for an offence, has the meaning given by section 171(2) below;
"prohibited or restricted goods" means goods of a class or description of which the importation, exportation or carriage coastwise is for the time being prohibited or restricted under or by virtue of any enactment;
"proper", in relation to the person by, with or to whom, the place at which, anything is to be done, means the person or place appointed or authorised in that behalf by the Commissioners;
"proprietor", in relation to any goods, includes any owner, importer, exporter, shipping or other person for the time being possessed of or beneficially interested in those goods;
"Queen's warehouse" means any place provided by the Crown or appointed by the Commissioners for the deposit of goods for security thereof and of the duties chargeable thereon;
["railway customs area" has the meaning given by section 26(1ZA)(c);][38]
["registered excise dealer and shipper" means a revenue trader approved and registered by the Commissioners under section 100G below;
"registered excise dealers and shippers regulations" means regulations under section 100G below;][19]
"representative", in relation to any person from whom the Commissioners assess an amount as being excise duty due, means his personal representative, trustee in bankruptcy[, trustee or interim trustee in a sequestration][37], any receiver or liquidator appointed in relation to him or any of his property or any other person acting in a representative capacity in relation to him;
"the revenue trade provisions of the customs and excise Acts" means—

(a) the provisions of the customs and excise Acts relating to the protection, security, collection or management of the revenues derived from the duties of excise on goods produced or manufactured in the United Kingdom;

(b) the provisions of the customs and excise Acts relating to any activity or facility for the carrying on or provision of which an excise licence is required; . . . [16]

(c) the provisions of [the Betting and Gaming Duties Act 1981][3] (so far as not included in paragraph (b) above); . . . [22]

[(d) the provisions of Chapter II of Part I of the Finance Act 1993;][16]

[(e) the provisions of section 10 to 15 of, and Schedule 1 to, the Finance Act 1997;][22]

[(f) the provisions of Part 1 of Schedule 24 to the Finance Act 2012;][32]

[(g) the provisions of Part 3 of the Finance Act 2014;][34]

"revenue trader" means—

[(a)] [2]any person carrying on a trade or business subject to any of the revenue trade provisions of the customs and excise Acts, [or which consists of or includes—

(i) the buying, selling, importation, exportation, dealing in or handling of any goods of a class or description which is subject to a duty of excise (whether or not duty is chargeable on the goods);][7] . . . [17]

[(ia) the buying, selling, importation, exportation, dealing in or handling of tickets or chances on the taking of which lottery duty is or will be chargeable;] . . . [23]

[(ib) being (within the meaning of sections 10 to 15 of the Finance Act 1997) the provider of any premises for gaming;][23]

[(ic) the organisation, management or promotion of [any activity that constitutes betting or gaming for the purposes of Part 3 of the Finance Act 2014 (see sections 150, 183 and 188)][34]; . . . [3]][23]

[(id) being responsible for premises where relevant machines are located (within the meaning of Part 1 of Schedule 24 to the Finance Act 2012); or][3]

[(ie) the management or administration of any Chapter 1 stake fund, Chapter 2 stake fund or gaming prize fund within the meaning of Part 3 of the Finance Act 2014 (see sections 134, 143 and 154);][34]

[(ii) the financing or facilitation of any such transactions or activities][7] [as are mentioned in sub-paragraph (i)[, (ia), (ib) [(ic)[, (id) or (ie)][34]][32]][23] above][17]

whether or not that trade or business is an excise licence trade[; and[2]

[(b) any person who is a wholesaler or an occupier of an excise warehouse (so far as not included in paragraph (a) above),

and includes a registered club;][2]

"ship", and "vessel" include any boat or other vessel whatsoever (and, to the extent provided in section 2 below, any hovercraft);

"shipment" includes loading into an aircraft, and "shipped" and cognate expressions shall be construed accordingly;

"stores" means, subject to subsection (4) below, goods for use in a [ship, aircraft or railway vehicle][38] and includes fuel and spare parts and other articles of equipment, whether or not for immediate fitting;

["temporary storage facility" has the meaning given by section 25A;][38]

"tons register" means the tons of a ship's net tonnage as ascertained and registered according to the tonnage regulations of the [Merchant Shipping Act 1995][21] or, in the case of a ship which is not registered under that Act, ascertained in like manner as if it were to be so registered;

"transit goods" [means chargeable goods declared for a transit procedure;][38]

. . .[38]

. . .[38]

["tribunal" means the First-tier Tribunal or, where determined by or under Tribunal Procedure Rules, the Upper Tribunal;][29]

["United Kingdom waters" means any waters (including inland waters) within the seaward limits of the Territorial sea of the United Kingdom.][6]

["vehicle" includes—

(a) a ship,

(b) an aircraft, and

(c) a railway vehicle;

and any reference to goods being in or on board a vehicle include their being conveyed by the vehicle (for example, by being on or otherwise attached to it);][38]

["vehicle operator" means—

(a) in the case a ship, the master of the ship,

(b) in the case of an aircraft, the commander of the aircraft,

(c) in the case of a railway vehicle, the person designated as train manager by the person operating the international service on which the railway vehicle is engaged, and

(d) in the case of any other vehicle, the person in charge of the vehicle;][38]

. . .[38]

"warehouse", except in the expressions "Queen's warehouse" and "distiller's warehouse", means a place of security approved by the Commissioners under subsection (1) . . . [38] of section 92 below and, except in that section, also includes a distiller's warehouse; and "warehoused" and cognate expressions shall, subject to . . . [38] [and any regulations made by virtue of section 93(2)(da)(i) or (ee) or (4) below][11], be construed accordingly;

"warehousing regulations" means regulations under section 93 below.

(2) This Act and the other Acts included in the Customs and Excise Acts 1979 shall be construed as one Act but where a provision of this Act refers to this Act that reference is not to be construed as including a reference to any of the others.

(3) Any expression used in this Act or in any instrument made under this Act to which a meaning is given by any other Act included in the Customs and Excise Acts 1979 has, except where the context otherwise requires, the same meaning in this Act or any such instrument as in that Act; . . .

[(3A) Any expression used in this Act or in any instrument made under this Act to which a meaning is given by Part 1 of the Taxation (Crossborder Trade) Act 2018 has, except where the context otherwise requires, the same meaning in this Act or any such instrument as in that Part; and for ease of reference the following is a list of the expressions concerned—

"the applicable export provisions"

"authorised use procedure"

"chargeable goods"

"Customs declaration" (including any expression relating to a Customs declaration such as the documents accompanying it or its acceptance)

"Customs procedure" (including expressions relating to a Customs procedure such as goods being released to or discharged from the procedure)

"inward processing procedure"

"storage procedure"

"territory outside the United Kingdom"

"temporary admission procedure"

"transit procedure".][38]

[(4) Goods for use in a ship or aircraft as merchandise for sale to persons carried in the ship or aircraft shall be treated for the purposes of the customs and excise Acts as stores if, and only if—
   (a) the goods are to be sold by retail either—
      (i) in the course of a [journey made by the ship or aircraft][36], or
      (ii) for consumption on board;
   and
   (b) the goods are not treated as exported by virtue of regulations under section 12 of the Customs and Excise Duties (General Reliefs) Act 1979 (goods for use in naval ships or establishments).
(4A) . . .[35]
(4B) In relation to goods treated as stores by virtue of subsection (4) above, any reference in the customs and excise Acts to the consumption of stores shall be construed as referring to the sale of the goods as mentioned in paragraph (a) of that subsection.][26]
(5) A person who deals in or sells tobacco products in the course of a trade or business carried on by him shall be deemed for the purposes of this Act to be carrying on an excise licence trade (and to be a revenue trader) notwithstanding that no excise licence is required for carrying on that trade or business.
(6) In computing for the purposes of this Act any period expressed therein as a period of clear days no account shall be taken of the day of the event from which the period is computed or of any Sunday or holiday.
(7) . . .[38]

Amendments—[2] "(a)", para (b) and the word "and" preceding it in the definition of "revenue trader" in sub-s (1) inserted by FA 1981 Sch 8 para 1(1).
[3] Words in para (c) of the definition of "the revenue trade provisions of the customs and excise Acts" in sub-s (1) substituted by Betting and Gaming Duties Act 1981 Sch 5 para 5(a).
[4] Definitions inserted by FA 1984 Sch 4 Pt II, para 1.
[6] Definition of "United Kingdom waters" inserted, and definition of "nautical mile" repealed, by Territorial Sea Act 1987 s 3(1), (4), Sch 1 para 4(1), Sch 2 with effect from 1 October 1987; see SI 1987/1270.
[7] Words in the definition of "revenue trader" inserted by FA 1991 s 11(2).
[8] Words in the definitions of "approved wharf", "examination station" in sub-s (1) substituted by Customs Controls on Importation of Goods Regulations, SI 1991/2724 reg 6(1), (2).
[9] Definition of "customs warehouse" repealed by Customs Warehousing Regulations, SI 1991/2725 regs 3(1), (2), 4, except in relation to its application to VAT by virtue of VATA 1994 s 16.
[10] Definition of "free zone regulations" repealed by Free Zone Regulations, SI 1991/2727 reg 4, with effect from 1 January 1992.
[11] Definition of "excise duty point" and words in the definition of "warehouse" in sub-s (1) inserted by F(No 2)A 1992 ss 1(8), 3 and Sch 1 para 1 and Sch 2 para 1 with effect from 9 December 1992 by virtue of F(No 2)A 1992 (Commencement No 3) Order, SI 1992/3104.
[12] Words in the definition of "occupier" in sub-s (1) substituted for the words "means the" by F(No 2)A 1992 s 3 and Sch 2 para 1 with effect from 9 December 1992 by virtue of F(No 2)A 1992 (Commencement No 3) Order, SI 1992/3104.
[13] Words omitted from the definition of "the Customs and Excise Acts 1979" in sub-s (1) repealed by F(No 2)A 1992 Sch 18 Pt II with effect from 1 January 1993.
[14] Words in the definition of "perfect entry" in sub-s (1) substituted by the Customs and Excise (Single Market etc) Regulations, SI 1992/3095 Sch 1 para 2 with effect from 1 January 1993.
[15] Definition of "approved route" in sub-s (1) repealed by the Customs and Excise (Single Market etc) Regulations, SI 1992/3095 regs 2, 3(1) and Sch 2 with effect from 1 January 1993.
[16] Word "and" in the definition of "revenue trade provisions of the customs and excise Acts" repealed and para (d) added to that definition by FA 1993 ss 30(1), (2), 41, 213, Sch 23 Pt I.
[17] Word "or" in the definition of "revenue trader" repealed and sub-para (ia) and the words in sub-para (ii) inserted in that definition by FA 1993 ss 30(1), (2)(a), (b), 41, 213, Sch 23 Pt I.
[18] Definition "free zone goods" substituted by VATA 1994 s 100, Sch 14 para 6.
[19] Definitions "registered excise dealer and shipper" and "registered excise dealers and shippers regulations" inserted by FA 1991 s 11(1).
[20] Definition "perfect entry" in sub-s (1) is repealed with effect from a day to be appointed by C & E Commissioners by FA 1981 Sch 19 Pt I.
[21] Words in the definitions of "British ship" and "tons register" substituted by Merchant Shipping Act 1995 Sch 13 para 53(1), (2) with effect from 1 January 1996.
[22] Word "and" in the definition of "revenue trade provisions of the customs and excise Acts" repealed and para (e) added to that definition by FA 1997 s 13, Sch 2 para 2, Sch 18 Pt II with effect from 19 March 1997.
[23] Word "or" in the definition of "revenue trader" repealed, sub-paras (a)(ib) and (a)(ic) inserted and words in sub-para (a)(ii) substituted by FA 1997 s 13, Sch 2 para 2, Sch 18 Part II with effect from 19 March 1997.
[24] Words "or called into actual service" in the definition of "armed forces" repealed by The Reserved Forces Act 1996 (Consequential Provisions etc.) Regulations 1998 reg 10(3), with effect from 1 January 1999.
[25] Words in the definition "law officer of the Crown" substituted by Scotland Act 1998 (Consequential Modifications) (No 1) Order, SI 1999/1042 Article 4 Sch 2 Part 1 para 6 with effect from 20 May 1999.
[26] Sub-ss (4), (4A), (4B) substituted by FA 1999 s 10 with effect from 1 July 1999.
[27] Definitions of "assigned matter" and "the Commissioners" substituted by Commissioners for Revenue and Customs Act 2005 s 50, Sch 4 para 22 with effect from 18 April 2005 by virtue of the Commissioners for Revenue and Customs Act 2005 (Commencement) Order, SI 2005/1126, art 2(2).

[28] Word in definition of "container" inserted by FA 2008 s 117(1), (2) with effect from 21 July 2008.
[29] Definition of "tribunal" inserted by the Transfer of Tribunal Functions and Revenue and Customs Appeals Order, SI 2009/56 art 3, Sch 1 paras 88, 89 with effect from 1 April 2009.
[30] In sub-s (1), definition of "nuclear material" inserted by the Criminal Justice and Immigration Act 2008 s 75, Sch 17 para 8(1), (2) with effect from 30 November 2009 (by virtue of SI 2009/3074 art 2(i), (q)).
[31] In sub-s (1), in definition of "assigned matter", words inserted by the Scotland Act 2012 s 24(7) with effect from 1 July 2012.
[32] In sub-s (1), in definition of "the revenue trade provisions of the customs and excise Acts", para (f) inserted; in definition of "revenue trader", word at end of para (a)(ic) repealed, para (a)(id) inserted, and in sub-para (ii), words substituted by FA 2012 s 191, Sch 24 para 41 with effect in relation to the playing of machine games on or after 1 February 2013.
[33] In sub-s (1) in definition of "goods", word substituted for word "baggage" by FA 2013 s 225 with effect from 17 July 2013.
[34] In sub-s (1) in definition of "the revenue trade provisions of the customs and excise Acts", para (g) inserted, in definition of "revenue trader", in para (a)(ic) words substituted for words "gaming within the meaning of the Betting and Gaming Duties Act 1981 (see section 33(1))", para (a)(ie) inserted, and in para (ii) words substituted for words "or (id)", by FA 2014 s 196, Sch 28 paras 10, 11 with effect from 1 December 2014 (FA 2014 s 198(2)), subject to transitional provisions and savings in FA 2014 Sch 29.
[35] In sub-s (4)(a)(i), words substituted, and subs (4A) repealed, by FA 2014 s 101, Sch 21 para 1 with effect from 1 April 2015 (by virtue of SI 2015/812 art 2).
[36] In definition of "assigned matter", words inserted by the Wales Act 2014 s 7(1) with effect from 17 February 2015 (Wales Act 2014 s 29(2)(b)).
[37] In definition of "representative", words substituted by the Bankruptcy (Scotland) Act 2016 (Consequential Provisions and Modifications) Order, SI 2016/1034, art 7(1), Sch 1 para 3 with effect from 30 November 2016.
[38] The following amendments made by the Taxation (Cross-border Trade) Act 2018 s 29, Sch 7 paras 3, 4 with effect from IP completion day (11pm on 31 December 2020), by virtue of SI 2020/1642 reg 4(a)—
- definitions of "coasting ship", "Community transit goods", "transit or transhipment", "transit shed", and "victualling warehouse" repealed; definitions of "customs formalities", "customs warehouse", "railway customs area", "temporary storage facility", and "vehicle operator" inserted;
- in definition of "excise warehouse" words "(whether or not it is also approved under subsection (2))" repealed;
- in definition of "importer", words substituted for words "they are delivered out of charge";
- in definition of "stores", words substituted for words "ship or aircraft";
- in definition of "transit goods", words substituted for words "except in the expression "Community transit goods", means imported goods entered on importation for transit or transhipment";
- definition of "vehicle" substituted;
- in definition of "warehouse", words "or (2) or subsections (1) and (2)" and "subsection (4) of that section and" repealed;
- sub-s (3A) inserted; and
- sub-s (7) repealed.

These amendments are subject to savings and modifications in relation to Northern Ireland. TCBTA 2018 Sch 7 para 158 preserves the continued application of this Act for various purposes as if these amendments (except for the repeal of sub-s (7)) had not been made and with certain modifications. These savings and modifications relate to the application of this Act for any purposes in connection with duty under the following provisions of TCBTA 2018—
- s 30A(3) (non-EU goods imported into the UK as a result of entry into Northern Ireland are subject to duty charged in accordance with Union customs legislation);
- s 30C (goods removed from Northern Ireland to Great Britain which are not Qualifying Northern Ireland Goods are chargeable to customs duty)
- s 40A (goods moving to Northern Ireland from Great Britain, that are not domestic goods or are 'at risk' of subsequently being moved into the EU are chargeable to customs duty in accordance with Union customs legislation).

Definitions previously read as follows—
"coasting ship" has the meaning given by section 69 below;
"Community transit goods"—
  (a) in relation to imported goods, means—
    (i) goods which have been imported under the internal or external Community transit procedure for transit through the United Kingdom with a view to exportation where the importation was and the transit and exportation are to be part of one Community transit operation; or
    (ii) goods which have, at the port or airport at which they were imported, been placed under the internal or external Community transit procedure for transit through the United Kingdom with a view to exportation where the transit and exportation are to be part of one Community transit operation;
  (b) in relation to goods for exportation, means—
    (i) goods which have been imported as mentioned in paragraph (a)(i) of this definition and are to be exported as part of the Community transit operation in the course of which they were imported; or
    (ii) goods which have, under the internal or external Community transit procedure, transited the United Kingdom from the port or airport at which they were imported and are to be exported as part of the Community transit operation which commenced at that port or airport;
    and for the purposes of para (a)(i) above the Isle of Man shall be treated as if it were part of the United Kingdom;

"transit or transhipment", in relation to the entry of goods, means transit through the United Kingdom or transhipment with a view to the re-exportation of the goods in question or transhipment of those goods for use as stores;
"transit shed" has the meaning given by section 25A below;
"vehicle" includes a railway vehicle;
"victualling warehouse" means a place of security approved by the Commissioners under subsection (2) (whether or not it is also a place approved under subsection (1) of section 92 below).
Sub-s (7) previously read as follows—
"(7) The provisions of this Act in so far as they relate to customs duties apply, notwithstanding that any duties are imposed for the benefit of the Communities, as if the revenue from duties so imposed remained part of the revenues of the Crown.".

5 Time of importation, exportation, etc

(1) The provisions of this section shall have effect for the purposes of the customs and excise Acts.
(2) Subject to [subsections (2A)]² and (6) below, the time of importation of any goods shall be deemed to be—
   (a) where the goods are brought by sea, the time when the ship carrying them comes within the limits of a port;
   (b) where the goods are brought by air, the time when the aircraft carrying them lands in the United Kingdom or the time when the goods are unloaded in the United Kingdom, whichever is the earlier;
   (c) where the goods are brought by land, the time when the goods [enter the United Kingdom]².
[(2A) If there is a relevant international arrangement with a country or territory outside the United Kingdom, the Commissioners may by regulations provide for the time of importation of any goods to be a time—
   (a) which is earlier than the times set out in paragraph (a), (b) or (c) of subsection (2), and
   (b) which is specified by reference to movement in or out of an area in the country or territory.
(2B) "Relevant international arrangement" means an arrangement between Her Majesty's government in the United Kingdom and the government of the country or territory which includes provision in relation to the time at which goods are to be regarded as imported into the United Kingdom.]²
(3) . . .²
(4) Subject to subsections (5)[, (5A)]² and (7) below, the time of exportation of any goods from the United Kingdom shall be deemed to be—
   (a) where the goods are exported by sea or air, the time when the goods are shipped for exportation;
   (b) where the goods are exported by land, the time when they are cleared by the proper officer at the last customs and excise station on their way to the boundary.
(5) In the case of goods of a class or description with respect to the exportation of which any prohibition or restriction is for the time being in force under or by virtue of any enactment which are exported by sea or air, the time of exportation shall be deemed to be the time when the exporting ship or aircraft departs from the last port or customs and excise airport at which it is cleared before departing for a destination outside the United Kingdom.
[(5A) If there is a relevant international arrangement with a country or territory outside the United Kingdom, the Commissioners may by regulations provide for the time of exportation of any goods to be a time—
   (a) which is earlier than the times set out in paragraph (a) or (b) of subsection (4), and
   (b) which is specified by reference to movement in or out of an area in the country or territory.
(5B) "Relevant international arrangement" means an arrangement between Her Majesty's government in the United Kingdom and the government of the country or territory which includes provision in relation to the time at which goods are to be regarded as exported from the United Kingdom.]²
(6) Goods imported by means of a pipe-line shall be treated as imported at the time when they are brought within the limits of a port [or otherwise when they enter the United Kingdom]².
(7) Goods exported by means of a pipe-line shall be treated as exported at the time when they are charged into that pipe-line for exportation.
(8) A ship shall be deemed to have arrived at or departed from a port at the time when the ship comes within or, as the case may be, leaves the limits of that port.

Commentary—*De Voil Indirect Tax Service* **V3.307, V4.307**.
Amendments—[1] Words in sub-s (3) substituted by Customs and Excise (Single Market etc) Regulations, SI 1992/3095 Sch 1 para 3 with effect from 1 January 1993.
[2] In sub-s (2) words substituted for words "subsections (3)", and in sub-s (2)(c) words substituted for words "are brought across the boundary into Northern Ireland", sub-ss (2A), (2B), (5A), (5B) inserted, sub-s (3) repealed, in sub-s (4), words inserted, and in sub-s (6) words substituted for words "or brought across the boundary into Northern Ireland", by the Taxation (Cross-border Trade) Act 2018 s 29, Sch 7 paras 3, 6 with effect from IP completion day (11pm on 31 December 2020), by virtue of SI 2020/1642 reg 4(a).

[2] These amendments are subject to savings and modifications in relation to Northern Ireland. TCBTA 2018 Sch 7 para 158 preserves the continued application of this Act for various purposes as if these amendments had not been made and with certain modifications. These savings and modifications relate to the application of this Act for any purposes in connection with duty under the following provisions of TCBTA 2018—
- s 30A(3) (non-EU goods imported into the UK as a result of entry into Northern Ireland are subject to duty charged in accordance with Union customs legislation);
- s 30C (goods removed from Northern Ireland to Great Britain which are not Qualifying Northern Ireland Goods are chargeable to customs duty)
- s 40A (goods moving to Northern Ireland from Great Britain, that are not domestic goods or are 'at risk' of subsequently being moved into the EU are chargeable to customs duty in accordance with Union customs legislation).

Sub-s (3) previously read as follows—
"(3) In the case of goods brought by sea of which entry is not required under regulation 5 of the Customs Controls on Importation of Goods Regulations 1991, the time of importation shall be deemed to be the time when the ship carrying them came within the limits of the port at which the goods are discharged.".

PART III
CUSTOMS AND EXCISE CONTROL AREAS

19 Appointment of ports, etc

(1) The Commissioners may by order made by statutory instrument appoint and name as a port for the purposes of customs and excise any area in the United Kingdom specified in the order.
(2) The appointment of any port for those purposes made before 1st August 1952 may be revoked, and the name or limits of any such port may be altered, by an order under subsection (1) above as if the appointment had been made by an order under that subsection.
(3) The Commissioners may in any port from time to time appoint boarding stations for the purpose of the boarding of or disembarkation from ships by officers.

Commentary—*De Voil Indirect Tax Service* **V3.307, V4.251**

21 Control of movement of aircraft, etc into and out of the United Kingdom
(1)–(6) . . .
(7) In this Act "customs and excise airport" means an aerodrome for the time being designated as a place for the landing or departure of aircraft for the purposes of the customs and excise Acts by an order made by the Secretary of State with the concurrence of the Commissioners which is in force under an Order in Council made in pursuance of [section 60 of the Civil Aviation Act 1982][1].
(8) . . .

Commentary—*De Voil Indirect Tax Service* **V3.307**.
Amendments—[1] Words substituted by Civil Aviation Act 1982 Sch 15 para 23.

PART IV
CONTROL OF IMPORTATION

Inward entry and clearance

[37A Initial and supplementary entries
[(1) The Commissioners may—
  (a) give such directions as they think fit for enabling an entry under regulation 5 of the Customs Controls on Importation of Goods Regulations 1991 to consist of an initial entry and a supplementary entry where the importer is authorised for the purposes of this section in accordance with the directions; and
  (b) include in the directions such supplementary provision in connection with entries consisting of initial and supplementary entries as they think fit.][5]
[(1A) Without prejudice to section 37 above, a direction under that section may—
  (a) provide that where the importer is not authorised for the purposes of this section but a person who is so authorised is appointed as his agent for the purpose of entering the goods, the entry may consist of an initial entry made by the person so appointed and a supplementary entry so made; and
  (b) make such supplementary provision in connection with entries consisting of initial and supplementary entries made as mentioned in paragraph (a) above as the Commissioners think fit.][2]
[(2) Where—
  (a) an initial entry made under subsection (1) above has been accepted and the importer has given security by deposit of money or otherwise to the satisfaction of the Commissioners for payment of the unpaid duty, or
  (b) an initial entry made under subsection (1A) above has been accepted and the person making the entry on the importer's behalf has given such security as is mentioned in paragraph (a) above,
the goods may][3] be delivered without payment of any duty chargeable in respect of the goods, but any such duty shall be paid within such time as the Commissioners may direct.
(3) An importer who makes an initial entry [under subsection (1) above][2] shall complete the entry by delivering the supplementary entry within such time as the Commissioners may direct.

[(3A) A person who makes an initial entry under subsection (1A) above on behalf of an importer shall complete the entry by delivering the supplementary entry within such time as the Commissioners may direct.]²
(4) For the purposes of the customs and excise Acts an entry of goods shall be taken to have been delivered when an initial entry of the goods has been delivered, and accepted when an initial entry has been accepted.]¹, ⁴

Commentary—*De Voil Indirect Tax Service* **V3.308**
Amendments—¹   This section inserted by FA 1984 Sch 5 para 2.
²   Sub-ss (1A), (3A) and words in sub-s (3) inserted by FA 1990 s 7 and Sch 3 paras 1, 2(1), (3), (6), in relation to goods imported after 25 July 1990.
³   Words in sub-s (2) substituted by FA 1990 s 7 and Sch 3 paras 1, 2(1), (4) in relation to goods imported after 25 July 1990.
⁴   Section 37A repealed by the Taxation (Cross-border Trade) Act 2018 s 29, Sch 7 paras 3, 29 with effect from IP completion day (11pm on 31 December 2020), by virtue of SI 2020/1642 reg 4(*a*).
These amendments are subject to savings and modifications in relation to Northern Ireland. TCBTA 2018 Sch 7 para 158 preserves the continued application of this Act for various purposes as if these amendments had not been made and with certain modifications. These savings and modifications relate to the application of this Act for any purposes in connection with duty under the following provisions of TCBTA 2018—
-    s 30A(3) (non-EU goods imported into the UK as a result of entry into Northern Ireland are subject to duty charged in accordance with Union customs legislation);
-    s 30C (goods removed from Northern Ireland to Great Britain which are not Qualifying Northern Ireland Goods are chargeable to customs duty)
-    s 40A (goods moving to Northern Ireland from Great Britain, that are not domestic goods or are 'at risk' of subsequently being moved into the EU are chargeable to customs duty in accordance with Union customs legislation).

[37B Postponed entry

(1) The Commissioners may, if they think fit, direct that where—
   (a) such goods as may be specified in the direction are imported by an importer authorised for the purposes of this subsection;
   (b) the importer has delivered a document relating to the goods to the proper officer, in such form and manner, containing such particulars and accompanied by such documents as the Commissioners may direct; and
   (c) the document has been accepted by the proper officer,
the goods may be delivered before an entry of them has been delivered or any duty chargeable in respect of them has been paid.
[(1A) The Commissioners may, if they think fit, direct that where—
   (a) such goods as may be specified in the direction are imported by an importer who is not authorised for the purposes of this subsection;
   (b) a person who is authorised for the purposes of this subsection is appointed as his agent for the purpose of entering the goods;
   (c) the person so appointed has delivered a document relating to the goods to the proper officer, in such form and manner, containing such particulars and accompanied by such documents as the Commissioners may direct; and
   (d) the document has been accepted by the proper officer,
the goods may be delivered before an entry of them has been delivered or any duty chargeable in respect of them has been paid.]²
(2) The Commissioners may, if they think fit, direct that where—
   (a) such goods as may be specified in the direction are imported by an importer authorised for the purposes of this subsection;
   (b) the goods have been removed from the place of importation to a place approved by the Commissioners for the clearance out of charge of such goods; and
   (c) the conditions mentioned in subsection (3) below have been satisfied,
the goods may be delivered before an entry of them has been delivered or any duty chargeable in respect of them has been paid.
(3) The conditions are that—
   (a) on the arrival of the goods at the approved place the importer delivers to the proper officer a notice of the arrival of the goods in such form and containing such particulars as may be required by the directions;
   (b) within such time as may be so required the importer enters such particulars of the goods and such other information as may be so required in a record maintained by him at such place as the proper officer may require; and
   (c) the goods are kept secure in the approved place for such period as may be required by the directions.
[(3A) The Commissioners may, if they think fit, direct that where—
   (a) such goods as may be specified in the direction are imported by an importer who is not authorised for the purposes of this subsection;

(b) a person who is authorised for the purposes of this subsection is appointed as his agent for the purpose of entering the goods;
   (c) the goods have been removed from the place of importation to a place approved by the Commissioners for the clearance out of charge of such goods; and
   (d) the conditions mentioned in subsection (3B) below have been satisfied,
the goods may be delivered before an entry of them has been delivered or any duty chargeable in respect of them has been paid.]^2
[(3B) the conditions are that—
   (a) on the arrival of the goods at the approved place the person appointed as the agent of the importer for the purpose of entering the goods delivers to the proper officer a notice of the arrival of the goods in such form and containing such particulars as may be required by the directions;
   (b) within such time as may be so required the person appointed as the agent of the importer for the purpose of entering the goods enters such particulars of the goods and such other information as may be so required in a record maintained by him at such place as the proper officer may require; and
   (c) the goods are kept secure in the approved place for such period as may be required by the directions.]^3
(4) The Commissioners may direct that the condition mentioned in subsection (3)(a) [or (3B) (a)]^3 above shall not apply in relation to any goods specified in the direction and such a direction may substitute another condition.
(5) No goods shall be delivered under [subsection (1) or (2) above]^4 unless the importer gives security by deposit of money or otherwise to the satisfaction of the Commissioners for the payment of any duty chargeable in respect of the goods which is unpaid.
[(5A) No goods shall be delivered under subsection (1A) or (3A) above unless the person appointed as the agent of the importer for the purpose of entering the goods gives security by deposit of money or otherwise to the satisfaction of the Commissioners for the payment of any duty chargeable in respect of the goods which is unpaid.]^2
(6) Where goods of which no entry has been made have been delivered under [sub-section (1) or (2) above]^4, the importer shall deliver an entry of the goods under [regulation 5 of the Customs Controls on Importation of Goods Regulations 1991]^5 within such time as the Commissioners may direct.
[(6A) Where goods of which no entry has been made have been delivered under sub-section (1A) or (3A) above, the person appointed as the agent of the importer for the purpose of entering the goods shall deliver an entry of the goods under section 37(1) above within such time as the Commissioners may direct.]^2
(7) For the purposes of section 43(2)(a) below such an entry shall be taken to have been accepted—
   (a) in the case of goods delivered by virtue of a direction under subsection (1) [or (1A)]^3 above, on the date on which the document mentioned in that subsection was accepted; and
   (b) in the case of goods delivered by virtue of a direction under subsection (2) above, on the date on which particulars of the goods were entered as mentioned in subsection (3)(b) above;]^1 [and]^2
   [(c) in the case of goods delivered by virtue of a direction under subsection (3A) above, on the date on which particulars of the goods were entered as mentioned in subsection (3B)(b) above.]^2, ^{6}

Commentary—*De Voil Indirect Tax Service* **V3.308, V3.313**.
Amendments—[1] This section inserted by FA 1984 Sch 5 para 2.
[2] Sub-ss (1A), (3A), (3B), (5A), (6A), (7)(c) inserted by FA 1990 s 7 and Sch 3 paras 1, 3(1), (2), (3), (6), (8), (9)(b) in relation to goods imported after 25 July 1990.
[3] Words in sub-ss (4), (7)(a) inserted by FA 1990 s 7 and Sch 3 paras 1, 3(1), (4), (9)(a).
[4] Words in sub-ss (5), (6) substituted by FA 1990 s 7 and Sch 3 paras 1, 3(1), (5), (7).
[5] Words in sub-s (6) substituted by Customs and Excise (Single Market etc) Regulations, SI 1992/3095 Sch 1 para 6 with effect from 1 January 1993.
[6] Section 37B repealed by the Taxation (Cross-border Trade) Act 2018 s 29, Sch 7 paras 3, 30 with effect from IP completion day (11pm on 31 December 2020), by virtue of SI 2020/1642 reg 4(a).
These amendments are subject to savings and modifications in relation to Northern Ireland. TCBTA 2018 Sch 7 para 158 preserves the continued application of this Act for various purposes as if these amendments had not been made and with certain modifications. These savings and modifications relate to the application of this Act for any purposes in connection with duty under the following provisions of TCBTA 2018—
   – s 30A(3) (non-EU goods imported into the UK as a result of entry into Northern Ireland are subject to duty charged in accordance with Union customs legislation);
   – s 30C (goods removed from Northern Ireland to Great Britain which are not Qualifying Northern Ireland Goods are chargeable to customs duty)
   – s 40A (goods moving to Northern Ireland from Great Britain, that are not domestic goods or are 'at risk' of subsequently being moved into the EU are chargeable to customs duty in accordance with Union customs legislation).

[37C Provisions supplementary to ss 37A and 37B
(1) The Commissioners may, if they think fit—

(a) authorise any [person]² for the purposes of section 37A, or 37B(1) [, (1A), (2) or (3A)]³ above; and
(b) suspend or cancel the authorisation of any [person]² where it appears to them that he has failed to comply with any requirement imposed on him by or under this Part of this Act or that there is other reasonable cause for suspension or cancellation.
(2) The Commissioners may give directions—
(a) imposing such requirements as they think fit on any [person]² authorised under this section; or
(b) varying any such requirements previously imposed.
(3) If any person without reasonable excuse contravenes any requirement imposed by or under section 37A, 37B or this section he shall be liable on summary conviction to a penalty of level 4 on the standard scale.]¹, ⁴

Commentary—*De Voil Indirect Tax Service* **V3.308**.
Amendments—¹ This section inserted by FA 1984 Sch 5 para 2.
² Word in sub-ss (1)(a), (b), (2)(a) substituted by FA 1990 s 7 and Sch 3 paras 1, 4 in relation to goods imported after 25 July 1990.
³ Words in sub-s (1)(a) substituted by FA 1990 s 7 and Sch 3 paras 1, 4 in relation to goods imported after 25 July 1990.
⁴ Section 37C repealed by the Taxation (Cross-border Trade) Act 2018 s 29, Sch 7 paras 3, 31 with effect from IP completion day (11pm on 31 December 2020), by virtue of SI 2020/1642 reg 4(a).
These amendments are subject to savings and modifications in relation to Northern Ireland. TCBTA 2018 Sch 7 para 158 preserves the continued application of this Act for various purposes as if these amendments had not been made and with certain modifications. These savings and modifications relate to the application of this Act for any purposes in connection with duty under the following provisions of TCBTA 2018—
– s 30A(3) (non-EU goods imported into the UK as a result of entry into Northern Ireland are subject to duty charged in accordance with Union customs legislation);
– s 30C (goods removed from Northern Ireland to Great Britain which are not Qualifying Northern Ireland Goods are chargeable to customs duty)
– s 40A (goods moving to Northern Ireland from Great Britain, that are not domestic goods or are 'at risk' of subsequently being moved into the EU are chargeable to customs duty in accordance with Union customs legislation).

[38B Correction and cancellation of entry
(1) Where goods have been entered for home use or for free circulation the importer may correct any of the particulars contained in an entry of the goods after it has been accepted if—
(a) the goods have not been cleared from customs and excise charge;
(b) he has not been notified by an officer that the goods are to be examined; and
(c) the entry has not been found by an officer to be incorrect.
(2) The proper officer may permit or require any correction allowed by subsection (1) above to be made by the delivery of a substituted entry.
(3) An entry of goods may at the request of the importer be cancelled at any time before the goods are cleared from customs and excise charge if the importer proves to the satisfaction of the Commissioners that the entry was delivered by mistake or that the goods cannot be cleared for free circulation.]¹, ²

Commentary—*De Voil Indirect Tax Service* **V3.308**.
Amendments—¹ This section inserted by FA 1981 s 10(1), Sch 6 para 4 with effect from 1 April 1982; see FA 1981 (Import Procedures) (Commencement) Order, SI 1982/205.
² Section 38B repealed by the Taxation (Cross-border Trade) Act 2018 s 29, Sch 7 paras 3, 32 with effect from IP completion day (11pm on 31 December 2020), by virtue of SI 2020/1642 reg 4(a).
These amendments are subject to savings and modifications in relation to Northern Ireland. TCBTA 2018 Sch 7 para 158 preserves the continued application of this Act for various purposes as if these amendments had not been made and with certain modifications. These savings and modifications relate to the application of this Act for any purposes in connection with duty under the following provisions of TCBTA 2018—
– s 30A(3) (non-EU goods imported into the UK as a result of entry into Northern Ireland are subject to duty charged in accordance with Union customs legislation);
– s 30C (goods removed from Northern Ireland to Great Britain which are not Qualifying Northern Ireland Goods are chargeable to customs duty)
– s 40A (goods moving to Northern Ireland from Great Britain, that are not domestic goods or are 'at risk' of subsequently being moved into the EU are chargeable to customs duty in accordance with Union customs legislation).

41 Failure to comply with [customs formalities]

Without prejudice to any liability under any other provision of the Customs and Excise Acts 1979[—
(a) any person importing goods who contravenes or fails to comply with any of the requirements made by or under this Part of this Act, or
(b) any person who contravenes or fails to comply with any of the requirements made by or under Part 1 of the Taxation (Cross-border Trade) Act 2018 in connection with the presentation of goods to Customs on import, the making of a declaration relating to the storage of goods or the making of a Customs declaration,
shall]² be liable on summary conviction to a penalty of [level 2 on the standard scale]¹ and the goods in question shall be liable to forfeiture . . . ²

Amendments—[1] Words substituted by virtue of Criminal Justice Act 1982 ss 37, 46.
[2] In the heading, words inserted for words "provisions as to entry", and words substituted and repealed, by the Taxation (Cross-border Trade) Act 2018 s 29, Sch 7 paras 3, 35 with effect from IP completion day (11pm on 31 December 2020), by virtue of SI 2020/1642 reg 4(*a*).

These amendments are subject to savings and modifications in relation to Northern Ireland. TCBTA 2018 Sch 7 para 158 preserves the continued application of this Act for various purposes as if these amendments had not been made and with certain modifications. These savings and modifications relate to the application of this Act for any purposes in connection with duty under the following provisions of TCBTA 2018—
- s 30A(3) (non-EU goods imported into the UK as a result of entry into Northern Ireland are subject to duty charged in accordance with Union customs legislation);
- s 30C (goods removed from Northern Ireland to Great Britain which are not Qualifying Northern Ireland Goods are chargeable to customs duty)
- s 40A (goods moving to Northern Ireland from Great Britain, that are not domestic goods or are 'at risk' of subsequently being moved into the EU are chargeable to customs duty in accordance with Union customs legislation).

Before these amendments, section 41 read as follows—

"Without prejudice to any liability under any other provision of the Customs and Excise Acts 1979, any person making entry of goods on their importation who fails to comply with any of the requirements of this Part of this Act in connection with that entry shall be liable on summary conviction to a penalty of level 2 on the standard scale and the goods in question shall be liable to forfeiture but this section shall not apply to—
  (*a*) any failure which has been or may be remedied by virtue of section 38B(1); or
  (*b*) any failure in respect of an entry which by virtue of section 38B(3) has been or may be cancelled at his request.".

42 Power to regulate unloading, removal, etc of imported goods

(1) The Commissioners may make regulations—
  (*a*) prescribing the procedure to be followed by a ship arriving at a port, an aircraft arriving at a customs and excise airport, [any other vehicle entering the United Kingdom][2] or a person conveying goods into [the United Kingdom][2] by land;
  (*b*) regulating the unloading, landing, movement and removal of goods on their importation;
and different regulations may be made with respect to importation by sea, air or land respectively.

(2) If any person contravenes or fails to comply with any regulation made under this section or with any direction given by the Commissioners or the proper officer in pursuance of any such regulation, he shall be liable on summary conviction to a penalty of [level 3 on the standard scale][1] and any goods in respect of which the offence was committed shall be liable to forfeiture.

(3) . . .[2]

Amendments—[1] Words in sub-s (2) substituted by virtue of Criminal Justice Act 1982 ss 37, 38, 46.
[2] In sub-s (1)(*a*) words inserted and words substituted for words "Northern Ireland", and sub-s (3) repealed, by the Taxation (Cross-border Trade) Act 2018 s 29, Sch 7 paras 3, 36 with effect from IP completion day (11pm on 31 December 2020), by virtue of SI 2020/1642 reg 4(*a*).

These amendments are subject to savings and modifications in relation to Northern Ireland. TCBTA 2018 Sch 7 para 158 preserves the continued application of this Act for various purposes as if these amendments had not been made and with certain modifications. These savings and modifications relate to the application of this Act for any purposes in connection with duty under the following provisions of TCBTA 2018—
- s 30A(3) (non-EU goods imported into the UK as a result of entry into Northern Ireland are subject to duty charged in accordance with Union customs legislation);
- s 30C (goods removed from Northern Ireland to Great Britain which are not Qualifying Northern Ireland Goods are chargeable to customs duty)
- s 40A (goods moving to Northern Ireland from Great Britain, that are not domestic goods or are 'at risk' of subsequently being moved into the EU are chargeable to customs duty in accordance with Union customs legislation).

Sub-s (3) previously read as follows—

"(3) Subsection (1)(*b*) above shall not apply in relation to goods imported on or after 1st January 1992 from a place outside the customs territory of the Community or to any goods which are moving under the procedure specified in Article 165 of Council Regulation (EEC) No 2913/92 and Article 311 of Commission Regulation (EEC) No 2454/93 (transit procedures).".

Provisions as to duty on imported goods

43 [Excise duty] on imported goods

(1) Save as permitted by or under the customs and excise Acts . . .[8], no imported goods shall be delivered or removed on importation until the importer has paid to the proper officer any [excise][8] duty chargeable thereon, and that duty shall, in the case of goods of which entry is made, be paid on making the entry.

(2) [Subject to subsections (2A), (2B) [(2C) and (2D)][7] below,][3] the duties of . . .[8] excise and the rates thereof chargeable on imported goods—
  [(*a*) if entry is made thereof, except where the entry is for warehousing, or if they are declared under section 78 below, shall be those in force with respect to such goods at the time when the entry is accepted or the declaration is made;][1]
  (*b*) if entry *or, in the case of goods entered by bill of sight, perfect entry* is made thereof for warehousing, shall be ascertained in accordance with warehousing regulations;
  [(*c*) if no entry is made thereof and the goods are not declared under section 78 below shall be—

(i) . . . [8]
(ii) . . . [8] those in force with respect to such goods at the time of their importation.][4]
(2A)–(2C) . . . [8]
[(2D) Nothing in the provisions of subsections (1) and (2) above or of subsection (6) below or in any exception to any of those provisions made by or under [section 44][8] below shall have effect for the purposes of any duty of excise chargeable on any goods for which—
  (a) the excise duty point is fixed by regulations under section 1 of the Finance (No 2) Act 1992; and
  (b) the applicable rate of duty is determined in accordance with subsection (2) of that section.][6]
(3) Any goods brought or coming into the United Kingdom by sea otherwise than as cargo, stores or baggage carried in a ship shall be chargeable with the like [excise][8] duty, if any, as would be applicable to those goods if they had been imported as merchandise . . . [8].
(4) Where, in accordance with approval given by the Commissioners, entry of goods is made by any method involving the use of a computer, subsection (2) above shall have effect as if the reference in paragraph (a) to the time of the delivery of the entry were a reference to the time when particulars contained in the entry are accepted by the computer.
(5) Subject to sections 10 and 11 of the Customs and Excise Duties (General Reliefs) Act 1979 (reliefs for re-imported goods) and save as provided by or under any such enactments or instruments as are mentioned in subsection (1) above, any goods which are re-imported into the United Kingdom after exportation from the United Kingdom or the Isle of Man, whether they were manufactured or produced in or outside the United Kingdom and whether or not any [excise][8] duty was paid thereon at a previous importation, shall be treated for the purpose of charging [excise][8] duty—
  (a) as if they were being imported for the first time; and
  (b) in the case of goods manufactured or produced in the United Kingdom, as if they had not been so manufactured or produced.
[(6) Where entry of goods is made otherwise than for warehousing and there is a reduction in the rate of duty of . . . [8] excise chargeable on the goods between—
  (a) the time mentioned in subsection (2)(a) above; and
  (b) the time when the goods are cleared from . . . [8] excise charge,
the rate of the [excise][8] duty chargeable on the goods shall, if the importer so requests, be that in force at the time mentioned in paragraph (b) above unless clearance of the goods has been delayed by reason of any act or omission for which the importer is responsible.][2]
[(7) Notwithstanding section 6(5) of the European Communities Act 1972 "duty of customs" in subsection (6) above does not include any agricultural levy.][2]
(8), (9) . . . [8]

Commentary—*De Voil Indirect Tax Service* V3.312.
Amendments—[1] Sub-s (2)(a) substituted by FA 1981 s 10(3) and Sch 6 para 7(2) with effect from 1 April 1982; see FA 1981 (Import Procedures) (Commencement) Order, SI 1982/205.
[2] Sub-ss (6), (7) inserted by FA 1981 s 10(3) and Sch 6 para 7(2) with effect from 1 April 1982; see FA 1981 (Import Procedures) (Commencement) Order, SI 1982/205.
[3] Words at the beginning of sub-s (2) substituted by Customs Duty Regulations, SI 1982/1324 reg 2(2).
[4] Sub-s (2)(c) substituted by Customs Duty Regulations, SI 1982/1324 reg 2(3) with effect from 15 October 1982.
[6] Sub-s (2D) inserted by F(No 2)A 1992 s 1(8) and Sch 1 para 2 with effect from 1 December 1992 by virtue of F(No 2)A 1992 (Commencement No 2 and Transitional Provisions) Order, SI 1992/2979 art 4 and Schedule, Pt II.
[7] Words in sub-s (2) substituted by F(No 2)A 1992 s 1(8) and Sch 1 para 2 with effect from 1 December 1992 by virtue of F(No 2)A 1992 (Commencement No 2 and Transitional Provisions) Order, SI 1992/2979 art 4 and Schedule, Pt II.
[8] The following amendments made by the Taxation (Cross-border Trade) Act 2018 s 29, Sch 7 paras 3, 37 with effect from IP completion day (11pm on 31 December 2020), by virtue of SI 2020/1642 reg 4(a)—
  – in heading, words substituted for word "Duty";
  – in sub-s (1) words "or section 2(2) of the European Communities Act 1972 or any Community regulation or other instrument having the force of law" repealed, and words inserted;
  – in sub-s (2) words "customs or" repealed;
  – sub-s (2)(c)(i) repealed;
  – in sub-s (2)(c)(ii), words "as respects other duties," repealed;
  – sub-ss (2A)–(2C), (8), (9) repealed;
  – in sub-s (2D) words substituted for words "any of sections 44 to 48";
  – in sub-s (3) word inserted, and words "; and if any question arises as to the origin of the goods they shall, unless that question is determined under section 120 below, section 14 of the Customs and Excise Duties (General Reliefs) Act 1979 (produce of the sea or continental shelf) or under a Community regulation or other instrument having the force of law, be deemed to be the produce of such country as the Commissioners may on investigation determine" repealed;
  – in sub-s (5) after word "excise" inserted (in both places);
  – in sub-s (6) words "customs or" repealed; and
  – in sub-s (6)(b), words "customs and" repealed, and in the words after that paragraph word inserted.
These amendments are subject to savings and modifications in relation to Northern Ireland. TCBTA 2018 Sch 7 para 158 preserves the continued application of this Act for various purposes as if these amendments had not been made and with certain modifications. These savings and modifications relate to the application of this Act for any purposes in connection with duty under the following provisions of TCBTA 2018—

- s 30A(3) (non-EU goods imported into the UK as a result of entry into Northern Ireland are subject to duty charged in accordance with Union customs legislation);
- s 30C (goods removed from Northern Ireland to Great Britain which are not Qualifying Northern Ireland Goods are chargeable to customs duty)
- s 40A (goods moving to Northern Ireland from Great Britain, that are not domestic goods or are 'at risk' of subsequently being moved into the EU are chargeable to customs duty in accordance with Union customs legislation).

Before these amendments, section 43 read as follows—

"(1) Save as permitted by or under the customs and excise Acts or section 2(2) of the European Communities Act 1972 or any Community regulation or other instrument having the force of law, no imported goods shall be delivered or removed on importation until the importer has paid to the proper officer any duty chargeable thereon, and that duty shall, in the case of goods of which entry is made, be paid on making the entry.

(2) Subject to subsections (2A), (2B), (2C) and (2D) below, the duties of customs or excise and the rates thereof chargeable on imported goods—

   (a)   if entry is made thereof, except where the entry is for warehousing, or if they are declared under section 78 below, shall be those in force with respect to such goods at the time when the entry is accepted or the declaration is made;

   (b)   if entry is made thereof for warehousing, shall be ascertained in accordance with warehousing regulations;

   (c)   if no entry is made thereof and the goods are not declared under section 78 below shall be—

      (i)   as respects Community customs duties, those in force with respect to such goods at the time of their entry into the customs territory of the Community; and

      (ii)   as respects other duties, those in force with respect to such goods at the time of their importation.

(2A) Where the Commissioners require a duty of customs to be paid because of a failure to comply with a condition or other obligation imposed under section 47 or 48 below (not being a condition or obligation required to be complied with before the goods were allowed to be removed or delivered) the duty shall be charged as if entry of the goods had been accepted at the time when the non-compliance occurred.

(2B) Where any duties of customs are chargeable in respect of waste or debris resulting from the destruction of imported goods in free circulation, those duties and their rates shall be those in force at the time when the goods were destroyed.

(2C) As respects goods which have been unlawfully removed from customs charge, subsection (2)(c) above shall have effect with respect to any duties of customs as if they had entered the customs territory of the Community, or, as the case may be, had been imported at the time of their removal.

(2D) Nothing in the provisions of subsections (1) and (2) above or of subsection (6) below or in any exception to any of those provisions made by or under any of sections 44 to 48 below shall have effect for the purposes of any duty of excise chargeable on any goods for which—

   (a)   the excise duty point is fixed by regulations under section 1 of the Finance (No 2) Act 1992; and

   (b)   the applicable rate of duty is determined in accordance with subsection (2) of that section.

(3) Any goods brought or coming into the United Kingdom by sea otherwise than as cargo, stores or baggage carried in a ship shall be chargeable with the like duty, if any, as would be applicable to those goods if they had been imported as merchandise; and if any question arises as to the origin of the goods they shall, unless that question is determined under section 120 below, section 14 of the Customs and Excise Duties (General Reliefs) Act 1979 (produce of the sea or continental shelf) or under a Community regulation or other instrument having the force of law, be deemed to be the produce of such country as the Commissioners may on investigation determine.

(4) . . .

(5) Subject to sections 10 and 11 of the Customs and Excise Duties (General Reliefs) Act 1979 (reliefs for re-imported goods) and save as provided by or under any such enactments or instruments as are mentioned in subsection (1) above, any goods which are re-imported into the United Kingdom after exportation from the United Kingdom or the Isle of Man, whether they were manufactured or produced in or outside the United Kingdom and whether or not any excise duty was paid thereon at a previous importation, shall be treated for the purpose of charging excise duty—

   (a)   as if they were being imported for the first time; and

   (b)   in the case of goods manufactured or produced in the United Kingdom, as if they had not been so manufactured or produced.

(6) Where entry of goods is made otherwise than for warehousing and there is a reduction in the rate of duty of customs or excise chargeable on the goods between—

   (a)   the time mentioned in subsection (2)(a) above; and

   (b)   the time when the goods are cleared from customs and excise charge,

the rate of the duty chargeable on the goods shall, if the importer so requests, be that in force at the time mentioned in paragraph (b) above unless clearance of the goods has been delayed by reason of any act or omission for which the importer is responsible.

(7) Notwithstanding section 6(5) of the European Communities Act 1972 "duty of customs" in subsection (6) above does not include any agricultural levy.

(8) Where samples are taken of goods under section 38A above and the quantity of the goods covered by the entry which is subsequently delivered does not include the samples the duties of customs and the rates of those duties chargeable on the samples shall be those in force at the time when the application under subsection (1) of that section was made and shall be determined by reference to the particulars contained in the application.

(9) Where a substituted entry is delivered under section 38(2) or 38B(2) above the entry referred to in subsection (2)(a) above is the original entry.".

Prospective amendments—Words in italics in sub-s (2)(b) and whole of sub-s (4) to be repealed by FA 1981 Sch 19 Pt I, with effect from a date to be appointed.

44 Exclusion of section 43(1) for importers etc keeping standing deposits

Where the Commissioners so direct, section 43(1) above shall not apply if and so long as the importer or his agent pays to, and keeps deposited with, the Commissioners a sum by way of standing deposit sufficient in their opinion to cover any [excise][1] duty which may become payable in respect of goods entered by that importer or agent, and if the importer or agent complies with such other conditions as the Commissioners may impose.

Commentary—*De Voil Indirect Tax Service* **V5.117, V5.118**.
Amendments—[1]　Word inserted after words "to cover any" by the Taxation (Cross-border Trade) Act 2018 s 29, Sch 7 paras 3, 38 with effect from IP completion day (11pm on 31 December 2020), by virtue of SI 2020/1642 reg 4(*a*).
These amendments are subject to savings and modifications in relation to Northern Ireland. TCBTA 2018 Sch 7 para 158 preserves the continued application of this Act for various purposes as if these amendments had not been made and with certain modifications. These savings and modifications relate to the application of this Act for any purposes in connection with duty under the following provisions of TCBTA 2018—
– s 30A(3) (non-EU goods imported into the UK as a result of entry into Northern Ireland are subject to duty charged in accordance with Union customs legislation);
– s 30C (goods removed from Northern Ireland to Great Britain which are not Qualifying Northern Ireland Goods are chargeable to customs duty)
– s 40A (goods moving to Northern Ireland from Great Britain, that are not domestic goods or are 'at risk' of subsequently being moved into the EU are chargeable to customs duty in accordance with Union customs legislation).

45 Deferred payment of customs duty

(1) The Commissioners may by regulations provide for the payment of customs duty to be deferred in such cases as may be specified by the regulations and subject to such conditions as may be imposed by or under the regulations; and duty of which payment is deferred under the regulations shall be treated, for such purposes as may be specified thereby, as if it had been paid.

(2) Regulations under this section may make different provision for goods of different descriptions or for goods of the same description in different circumstances.[1]

Commentary—*De Voil Indirect Tax Service* **V5.117**.
Regulations—See Customs Duties (Deferred Payment) Regulations, SI 1976/1223.
Customs and Excise (Deferred Payment) (RAF Airfields and Offshore Installations) (No 2) Regulations, SI 1988/1898.
Excise Duties (Deferred Payment) Regulations, SI 1992/3152.
Amendments—[1]　Section 45 repealed by the Taxation (Cross-border Trade) Act 2018 s 29, Sch 7 paras 3, 39 with effect from IP completion day (11pm on 31 December 2020), by virtue of SI 2020/1642 reg 4(*a*).
These amendments are subject to savings and modifications in relation to Northern Ireland. TCBTA 2018 Sch 7 para 158 preserves the continued application of this Act for various purposes as if these amendments had not been made and with certain modifications. These savings and modifications relate to the application of this Act for any purposes in connection with duty under the following provisions of TCBTA 2018—
– s 30A(3) (non-EU goods imported into the UK as a result of entry into Northern Ireland are subject to duty charged in accordance with Union customs legislation);
– s 30C (goods removed from Northern Ireland to Great Britain which are not Qualifying Northern Ireland Goods are chargeable to customs duty)
– s 40A (goods moving to Northern Ireland from Great Britain, that are not domestic goods or are 'at risk' of subsequently being moved into the EU are chargeable to customs duty in accordance with Union customs legislation).

46 Goods to be warehoused without payment of duty

Any goods which are on their importation permitted to be entered for warehousing shall be allowed, subject to such conditions or restrictions as may be imposed by or under warehousing regulations, to be warehoused without payment of duty.[1]

Commentary—*De Voil Indirect Tax Service* **V3.332**.
Amendments—[1]　Section 46 repealed by the Taxation (Cross-border Trade) Act 2018 s 29, Sch 7 paras 3, 40 with effect from IP completion day (11pm on 31 December 2020), by virtue of SI 2020/1642 reg 4(*a*).
These amendments are subject to savings and modifications in relation to Northern Ireland. TCBTA 2018 Sch 7 para 158 preserves the continued application of this Act for various purposes as if these amendments had not been made and with certain modifications. These savings and modifications relate to the application of this Act for any purposes in connection with duty under the following provisions of TCBTA 2018—
– s 30A(3) (non-EU goods imported into the UK as a result of entry into Northern Ireland are subject to duty charged in accordance with Union customs legislation);
– s 30C (goods removed from Northern Ireland to Great Britain which are not Qualifying Northern Ireland Goods are chargeable to customs duty)
– s 40A (goods moving to Northern Ireland from Great Britain, that are not domestic goods or are 'at risk' of subsequently being moved into the EU are chargeable to customs duty in accordance with Union customs legislation).

47 Relief from payment of duty of goods entered for transit or transhipment

Where any goods are entered for transit or transhipment, the Commissioners may allow the goods to be removed for that purpose, subject to such conditions and restrictions as they see fit, without payment of duty.[1]

Commentary—*De Voil Indirect Tax Service* **V3.333**.
Amendments—[1]　Section 47 repealed by the Taxation (Cross-border Trade) Act 2018 s 29, Sch 7 paras 3, 41 with effect from IP completion day (11pm on 31 December 2020), by virtue of SI 2020/1642 reg 4(*a*).
These amendments are subject to savings and modifications in relation to Northern Ireland. TCBTA 2018 Sch 7 para 158 preserves the continued application of this Act for various purposes as if these amendments had not been made and with certain modifications. These savings and modifications relate to the application of this Act for any purposes in connection with duty under the following provisions of TCBTA 2018—

- s 30A(3) (non-EU goods imported into the UK as a result of entry into Northern Ireland are subject to duty charged in accordance with Union customs legislation);
- s 30C (goods removed from Northern Ireland to Great Britain which are not Qualifying Northern Ireland Goods are chargeable to customs duty)
- s 40A (goods moving to Northern Ireland from Great Britain, that are not domestic goods or are 'at risk' of subsequently being moved into the EU are chargeable to customs duty in accordance with Union customs legislation).

48 Relief from payment of duty of goods temporarily imported

In such cases as the Commissioners may by regulations prescribe, where the Commissioners are satisfied that goods are imported only temporarily with a view to subsequent re-exportation, they may permit the goods to be delivered on importation, subject to such conditions as they see fit to impose, without payment of duty.[1]

Commentary—*De Voil Indirect Tax Service* V3.338.

Amendments—[1] Section 48 repealed by the Taxation (Cross-border Trade) Act 2018 s 29, Sch 7 paras 3, 42 with effect from IP completion day (11pm on 31 December 2020), by virtue of SI 2020/1642 reg 4(a).

These amendments are subject to savings and modifications in relation to Northern Ireland. TCBTA 2018 Sch 7 para 158 preserves the continued application of this Act for various purposes as if these amendments had not been made and with certain modifications. These savings and modifications relate to the application of this Act for any purposes in connection with duty under the following provisions of TCBTA 2018—
- s 30A(3) (non-EU goods imported into the UK as a result of entry into Northern Ireland are subject to duty charged in accordance with Union customs legislation);
- s 30C (goods removed from Northern Ireland to Great Britain which are not Qualifying Northern Ireland Goods are chargeable to customs duty)
- s 40A (goods moving to Northern Ireland from Great Britain, that are not domestic goods or are 'at risk' of subsequently being moved into the EU are chargeable to customs duty in accordance with Union customs legislation).

Forfeiture, offences, etc in connection with importation

49 Forfeiture of goods improperly imported

(1) Where—
   (a) except as provided by or under the Customs and Excise [Acts 1979 or by or under the Taxation (Cross-border Trade) Act 2018, any imported goods, being goods chargeable by reference to][1] their importation with customs or excise duty, are, without payment of that duty—
      (i) unshipped in any port,
      (ii) unloaded from any aircraft in the United Kingdom,
      [(iii) unloaded from any other vehicle which has entered the United Kingdom, or][1]
      (iv) removed from their place of importation or from any approved wharf, examination station or [temporary storage facility or any place specified by an officer of Revenue and Customs under Part 1 of the Taxation (Cross-border Trade) Act 2018 as a place where the goods are required to be kept][1]; or
   (b) any goods are imported, landed or unloaded contrary to any prohibition or restriction for the time being in force with respect thereto under or by virtue of any enactment; or
   (c) any goods, being goods chargeable with any duty or goods the importation of which is for the time being prohibited or restricted by or under any enactment, are found, whether before or after the unloading thereof, to have been concealed in any manner on board any ship or aircraft or, while in Northern Ireland, in [any other vehicle][1]; or
   (d) any goods are imported concealed in a container holding goods of a different description; or
   [(e) any goods are found, whether before or after being released to or discharged from a Customs procedure, not to correspond with any information provided under Part 1 of the Taxation (Cross-border Trade) Act 2018;][1]
   (f) any imported goods concealed or packed in any manner appearing to be intended to deceive an officer,

those goods shall, subject to subsection (2) below, be liable to forfeiture.

(2) Where any goods, the importation of which is for the time being prohibited or restricted by or under any enactment, are on their importation either—
   [(a) declared as intended for exportation in the same vehicle,
   (b) declared for a transit procedure or a storage procedure, or
   (c) are otherwise to be warehoused for exportation or for use as stores,][1]

the Commissioners may, if they see fit, permit the goods to be dealt with accordingly.

Amendments—[1] The following amendments made by the Taxation (Cross-border Trade) Act 2018 s 29, Sch 7 paras 3, 43 with effect from IP completion day (11pm on 31 December 2020), by virtue of SI 2020/1642 reg 4(a)—
- in sub-s (1)(a) words substituted for words "Acts 1979, any imported goods, being goods chargeable on";
- sub-s (1)(a)(iii) substituted;
- in sub-s (1)(a)(iv), words substituted for words "transit shed";
- in sub-s (1)(c) words substituted for words "any vehicle"; and
- sub-ss (1)(e), (2)(a)–(c) substituted.

These amendments are subject to savings and modifications in relation to Northern Ireland. TCBTA 2018 Sch 7 para 158 preserves the continued application of this Act for various purposes as if these amendments had not been made and with certain modifications. These savings and modifications relate to the application of this Act for any purposes in connection with duty under the following provisions of TCBTA 2018—
- s 30A(3) (non-EU goods imported into the UK as a result of entry into Northern Ireland are subject to duty charged in accordance with Union customs legislation);
- s 30C (goods removed from Northern Ireland to Great Britain which are not Qualifying Northern Ireland Goods are chargeable to customs duty)
- s 40A (goods moving to Northern Ireland from Great Britain, that are not domestic goods or are 'at risk' of subsequently being moved into the EU are chargeable to customs duty in accordance with Union customs legislation).

Before these amendments, section 49 read as follows—

"(1) Where—
 (a) except as provided by or under the Customs and Excise Acts 1979, any imported goods, being goods chargeable on their importation with customs or excise duty, are, without payment of that duty—
  (i) unshipped in any port,
  (ii) unloaded from any aircraft in the United Kingdom,
  (iii) unloaded from any vehicle in, or otherwise brought across the boundary into, Northern Ireland, or
  (iv) removed from their place of importation or from any approved wharf, examination station or transit shed; or
 (b) any goods are imported, landed or unloaded contrary to any prohibition or restriction for the time being in force with respect thereto under or by virtue of any enactment; or
 (c) any goods, being goods chargeable with any duty or goods the importation of which is for the time being prohibited or restricted by or under any enactment, are found, whether before or after the unloading thereof, to have been concealed in any manner on board any ship or aircraft or, while in Northern Ireland, in any vehicle; or
 (d) any goods are imported concealed in a container holding goods of a different description; or
 (e) any imported goods are found, whether before or after delivery, not to correspond with the entry made thereof; or
 (f) any imported goods concealed or packed in any manner appearing to be intended to deceive an officer,
those goods shall, subject to subsection (2) below, be liable to forfeiture.
 (2) Where any goods, the importation of which is for the time being prohibited or restricted by or under any enactment, are on their importation either—
  (a) reported as intended for exportation in the same ship, aircraft or vehicle; or
  (b) entered for transit or transhipment; or
  (c) entered to be warehoused for exportation or for use as stores,
the Commissioners may, if they see fit, permit the goods to be dealt with accordingly.".

50 Penalty for improper importation of goods

(1) Subsection (2) below applies to goods of the following descriptions, that is to say—
 (a) goods chargeable with a duty which has not been paid; and
 (b) goods the importation, landing or unloading of which is for the time being prohibited or restricted by or under any enactment.

(2) If any person with intent to defraud Her Majesty of any such duty or to evade any such prohibition or restriction as is mentioned in subsection (1) above—
 (a) unships or lands in any port or unloads from any aircraft in the United Kingdom or from [any other vehicle which has entered the United Kingdom][9] any goods to which this subsection applies, or assists or is otherwise concerned in such unshipping, landing or unloading; or
 (b) removes from their place of importation or from any approved wharf, examination station, [temporary storage facility, any place specified by an officer of Revenue and Customs under Part 1 of the Taxation (Cross-border Trade) Act 2018 as a place where the goods are required to be kept][9] or customs and excise station any goods to which this subsection applies or assists or is otherwise concerned in such removal,
he shall be guilty of an offence under this subsection and may be [arrested.][3]

(3) If any person imports or is concerned in importing any goods contrary to any prohibition or restriction for the time being in force under or by virtue of any enactment with respect to those goods, whether or not the goods are unloaded, and does so with intent to evade the prohibition or restriction, he shall be guilty of an offence under this subsection and may be [arrested.][3]

(4) Subject to subsection [(5), (5A)[, (5B) or (5C)][7]][1] below, a person guilty of an offence under subsection (2) or (3) above shall be liable—
 (a) on summary conviction, to a penalty of [£20,000][8] or of three times the value of the goods, whichever is the greater, or to imprisonment for a term not exceeding 6 months, or to both; or
 (b) on conviction on indictment, to a penalty of any amount, or to imprisonment for a term not exceeding [7 years][4], or to both.

(5) In the case of an offence under subsection (2) or (3) above in connection with a prohibition or restriction on importation having effect by virtue of section 3 of the Misuse of Drugs Act 1971 subsection (4) above shall have effect subject to the modifications specified in Schedule 1 to this Act.

[(5A) In the case of—

(a) an offence under subsection (2) or (3) above committed in Great Britain in connection with a prohibition or restriction on the importation of any weapon or ammunition that is of a kind mentioned in section 5(1)(a), (ab), (aba), (ac), (ad), (ae), (af) or (c) or (1A)(a) of the Firearms Act 1968,

(b) any such offence committed in Northern Ireland in connection with a prohibition or restriction on the importation of any weapon or ammunition that is of a kind mentioned in [Article 45(1)(a), (b), (c), (d), (e) or (g) or (2)(a)][6] of the Firearms (Northern Ireland) Order [2004][6], or

(c) any such offence committed in connection with the prohibition contained in section 20 of the Forgery and Counterfeiting Act 1981,

subsection (4)(b) above shall have effect as if for the words "7 years" there were substituted the words "10 years".][5]

[(5B) In the case of an offence under subsection (2) or (3) above in connection with the prohibition contained in regulation 2 of the Import of Seal Skins Regulations 1996, subsection (4) above shall have effect as if—

(a) for paragraph (a) there were substituted the following—

"(a) on summary conviction, to a fine not exceeding [£20,000][8] or to imprisonment for a term not exceeding three months, or both"; and

(b) in paragraph (b) for the words "7 years" there were substituted the words "2 years".".][1]

[(5C) In the case of an offence under subsection (2) or (3) above in connection with a prohibition or restriction relating to the importation of nuclear material, subsection (4)(b) above shall have effect as if for the words "7 years" there were substituted the words "14 years".][7]

(6) If any person—

(a) imports or causes to be imported any goods concealed in a container holding goods of a different description; or

[(b) directly or indirectly imports, or causes to be imported, any chargeable goods found, whether before or after being released to a Customs procedure, not to correspond with any information provided under Part 1 of the Taxation (Cross-border Trade) Act 2018,][9]

he shall be liable on summary conviction to a penalty of three times the value of the goods or [level 3 on the standard scale][2], whichever is the greater.

(7) In any case where a person would, apart from this subsection, be guilty of—

(a) an offence under this section in connection with the importation of goods contrary to a prohibition or restriction; and

(b) a corresponding offence under the enactment or other instrument imposing the prohibition or restriction, being an offence for which a fine or other penalty is expressly provided by that enactment or other instrument,

he shall not be guilty of the offence mentioned in paragraph (a) of this subsection.

Modification—Controlled Drugs (Drug Precursors) (Community External Trade) Regulations, SI 2008/296 reg 7 (modification of sub-s (4)(a), (b) in relation to breaches of Articles 20 and 12 of Council Regulation (EC) No 111/2005).

Forest Law Enforcement, Governance and Trade Regulations, SI 2012/178 reg 12 (modification of sub-s (4)(b) in relation to breaches of Article 4(1) of the FLEGT Regulation (EC) No 2173/2005).

Export Control (North Korea and Ivory Coast Sanctions and Syria Amendment) Order, SI 2013/3182 reg 12 (modification of sub-s (4)(b) in relation to the prohibitions of importation in Articles 2(3) or 4a(1)(b) of the North Korea Regulation (Council Regulation (EC) No 329/2007)).

Export Control (Syria Sanctions) Order, SI 2013/2012 reg 17 (modification of sub-s (4)(b) in relation to the prohibitions of importation in Articles 6(a) or 11(a)(1)(b) of the Syria Regulation (Council Regulation (EU) No 36/2012)).

Amendments—[1] Words in sub-s (4) substituted, and sub-s (5B) inserted, by the Import of Seal Skins Regulations, SI 1996/2686 reg 4(1), with effect from 15 November 1996.

[2] Words in sub-s (6) substituted by virtue of Criminal Justice Act 1982 ss 37, 38, 46.

[3] Words in sub-ss (2), (3) substituted by Police and Criminal Evidence Act 1984 s 114(1) with effect from 1 January 1986; see Police and Criminal Evidence Act 1984 (Commencement No 3) Order, SI 1985/1934.

[4] Words in sub-s (4)(b) substituted by FA 1988 s 12(1)(a).

[5] Sub-s (5A) substituted by the Criminal Justice Act 2003 s 293(1), (2) with effect from 22 January 2004 (by virtue of SI 2004/81), except in relation to any offences committed before that date.

[6] Words and figure in sub-s (5A) substituted by the Firearms (Northern Ireland) Order, SI 2004/702 art 82(1), Sch 7 para 3 with effect from 1 February 2005 (by virtue of SR 2005/4).

[7] In sub-s (4) words substituted for words "or (5B)", and sub-s (5C) inserted, by the Criminal Justice and Immigration Act 2008 s 75, Sch 17 para 8(1), (3) with effect from 30 November 2009 (by virtue of SI 2009/3074 art 2(i), (q)).

[8] In sub-ss (4)(a) and para (a) of inserted text in (5B)(a), figure substituted by the Legal Aid, Sentencing and Punishment of Offenders Act 2012 (Fines on Summary Conviction) Regulations, SI 2015/664 reg 2(2), Sch 2 paras 1, 3 with effect from 12 March 2015 in relation to England and Wales only.

[9] In sub-s (2)(a) words substituted for words "any vehicle in Northern Ireland", in sub-s (2)(b) words substituted for words "transit shed", and sub-s (6)(b) substituted, by the Taxation (Cross-border Trade) Act 2018 s 29, Sch 7 paras 3, 44 with effect from IP completion day (11pm on 31 December 2020), by virtue of SI 2020/1642 reg 4(a).

[9] These amendments are subject to savings and modifications in relation to Northern Ireland. TCBTA 2018 Sch 7 para 158 preserves the continued application of this Act for various purposes as if these amendments had not been made and with certain modifications. These savings and modifications relate to the application of this Act for any purposes in connection with duty under the following provisions of TCBTA 2018—
- s 30A(3) (non-EU goods imported into the UK as a result of entry into Northern Ireland are subject to duty charged in accordance with Union customs legislation);
- s 30C (goods removed from Northern Ireland to Great Britain which are not Qualifying Northern Ireland Goods are chargeable to customs duty)
- s 40A (goods moving to Northern Ireland from Great Britain, that are not domestic goods or are 'at risk' of subsequently being moved into the EU are chargeable to customs duty in accordance with Union customs legislation).

Sub-s (6)(*b*) previously read as follows—

"(*b*) directly or indirectly imports or causes to be imported or entered any goods found, whether before or after delivery, not to correspond with the entry made thereof,".

Prospective amendments—In sub-s (5A)(a), after "(af)" words ", (ag), (ba)" to be inserted, and in sub-s (5A)(a), after "(e)", words ", (ea), (fa)" to be inserted, by the Offensive Weapons Act 2019 s 56, Sch 2, paras 1, 2 with effect from a date to be appointed (see the Offensive Weapons Act 2019, ss 31, 70(1)).

PART VII
CUSTOMS AND EXCISE CONTROL: SUPPLEMENTARY PROVISIONS

Additional provisions as to information

77 Information in relation to goods imported or exported

(1) An officer may require any person—
   (a) concerned with the . . . [2] shipment for carriage coastwise of goods of which [for that purpose [a declaration is required as a result of Part 1 of the Taxation (Cross-border Trade) Act 2018][4]][3]; or
   (b) concerned in the carriage, unloading, landing or loading of goods which are being or have been imported or exported,

to furnish in such form as the officer may require any information relating to the goods and to produce and allow the officer to inspect and take extracts from or make copies of any invoice, bill of lading or other book or document whatsoever relating to the goods.

(2) If any person without reasonable cause fails to comply with a requirement imposed on him under subsection (1) above he shall be liable on summary conviction to a penalty of [level 3 on the standard scale.][1]

(3) Where any prohibition or restriction to which this subsection applies, that is to say, any prohibition or restriction under or by virtue of any enactment with respect to—
   (a) the exportation of goods to any particular destination; or
   (b) the exportation of goods of any particular class or description to any particular destination,

is for the time being in force, then, if any person about to ship for exportation or to export any goods or, as the case may be, any goods of that class or description, in the course of making [a declaration in respect of the goods][4] before shipment or exportation makes a [statement][4] as to the ultimate destination thereof, and the Commissioners have reason to suspect that the [statement][4] is untrue in any material particular, the goods may be detained until the Commissioners are satisfied as to the truth of the [statement][4], and if they are not so satisfied the goods shall be liable to forfeiture.

(4) Any person concerned in the exportation of any goods which are subject to any prohibition or restriction to which subsection (3) above applies shall, if so required by the Commissioners, satisfy the Commissioners that those goods have not reached any destination other than that mentioned in the [declaration made][4] in respect of the goods.

(5) If any person required under subsection (4) above to satisfy the Commissioners as mentioned in that subsection fails to do so, then, unless he proves—
   (a) that he did not consent to or connive at the goods reaching any destination other than that mentioned in the [declaration made][4] in respect of the goods; and
   (b) that he took all reasonable steps to secure that the ultimate destination of the goods was not other than that so mentioned,

he shall be liable on summary conviction to a penalty of three times the value of the goods or [level 3 on the standard scale][2], whichever is the greater.

Amendments—[1] Words in sub-ss (2) and (5) substituted by virtue of Criminal Justice Act 1982 ss 37, 38, 46.
[2] Words in sub-s (1)(a) repealed by FA 1987 ss 10, 72(7) and Sch 16 Pt III.
[3] Words in sub-s (1) substituted by Customs and Excise (Single Market etc) Regulations, SI 1992/3095 reg 10(1), Sch 1 para 7.
[4] In sub-s (1)(*a*) words substituted for words "an entry is required by regulation 5 of the Customs Controls on Importation of Goods Regulations 1991 or an entry or specification is required by or under this Act", in sub-s (3) words substituted for words "entry thereof", and word substituted for word "declaration" in each place, in sub-s (4), words substituted for words "entry delivered", and in sub-s (5)(*a*) words substituted for words "entry delivered", by the Taxation (Cross-border Trade) Act 2018 s 29, Sch 7 paras 3, 76 with effect from IP completion day (11pm on 31 December 2020), by virtue of SI 2020/1642 reg 4(*a*).

These amendments are subject to savings and modifications in relation to Northern Ireland. TCBTA 2018 Sch 7 para 158 preserves the continued application of this Act for various purposes as if these amendments had not been made and with certain modifications. These savings and modifications relate to the application of this Act for any purposes in connection with duty under the following provisions of TCBTA 2018—
- s 30A(3) (non-EU goods imported into the UK as a result of entry into Northern Ireland are subject to duty charged in accordance with Union customs legislation);
- s 30C (goods removed from Northern Ireland to Great Britain which are not Qualifying Northern Ireland Goods are chargeable to customs duty)
- s 40A (goods moving to Northern Ireland from Great Britain, that are not domestic goods or are 'at risk' of subsequently being moved into the EU are chargeable to customs duty in accordance with Union customs legislation).

[77A Information powers

(1) Every person who is concerned (in whatever capacity) in the importation or exportation of goods for which [for that purpose an entry is required by regulation 5 of the Customs Controls on Importation of Goods Regulations 1991 or an entry or specification is required by or under this Act][2] shall—
   (a) furnish to the Commissioners, within such time and in such form as they may reasonably require, such information relating to the goods or to the importation or exportation as the Commissioners may reasonably specify; and
   (b) if so required by an officer, produce or cause to be produced for inspection by the officer—
      (i) at the principal place of business of the person upon whom the demand is made or at such other place as the officer may reasonably require, and
      (ii) at such time as the officer may reasonably require,
   any documents relating to the goods or to the importation or exportation.
(2) Where, by virtue of subsection (1) above, an officer has power to require the production of any documents from any such person as is referred to in that subsection, he shall have the like power to require production of the documents concerned from any other person who appears to the officer to be in possession of them; but where any such other person claims a lien on any document produced by him, the production shall be without prejudice to the lien.
(3) An officer may take copies of, or make extracts from, any document produced under subsection (1) or subsection (2) above.
(4) If it appears to him to be necessary to do so, an officer may, at a reasonable time and for a reasonable period, remove any document produced under subsection (1) or subsection (2) above and shall, on request, provide a receipt for any document so removed; and where a lien is claimed on a document produced under subsection (2) above, the removal of the document under this subsection shall not be regarded as breaking the lien.
(5) Where a document removed by an officer under subsection (4) above is reasonably required for the proper conduct of a business, the officer shall, as soon as practicable, provide a copy of the document, free of charge, to the person by whom it was produced or caused to be produced.
(6) Where any documents removed under the powers conferred by this section are lost or damaged, the Commissioners shall be liable to compensate their owner for any expenses reasonably incurred by him in replacing or repairing the documents.
(7) If any person fails to comply with a requirement under this section, he shall be liable on summary conviction to a penalty of level 3 on the standard scale.][1]

Amendments—[1]   This section inserted by FA 1987 s 10.
[2]   Words in sub-s (1) substituted by virtue of Customs and Excise (Single Market etc) Regulations, SI 1992/3095 reg 10(1) and Sch 1 para 7.

78 Customs and Excise control of persons entering or leaving the United Kingdom

(1) Any person entering the United Kingdom shall, at such place and in such manner as the Commissioners may direct, declare any thing contained in his baggage or carried with him which—
   (a) he has obtained outside the United Kingdom; or
   (b) being dutiable goods or [taxable][4] goods, he has obtained in the United Kingdom without payment of duty or tax,
and in respect of which he is not entitled to exemption from duty and tax by virtue of [provision made by regulations under section 19 of the Taxation (Cross-border Trade) Act 2018 relating to any relief conferred on persons entering the United Kingdom or][4] any order under section 13 of the Customs and Excise Duties (General Reliefs) Act 1979 (personal reliefs).
In this [subsection "taxable goods" means][4] goods on the importation of which value added tax is chargeable or goods obtained in the United Kingdom before 1st April 1973 which are chargeable goods within the meaning of the Purchase Tax Act 1963; and "tax" means value added tax or purchase tax.
[(1A) Subsection (1) above does not apply to a person entering the United Kingdom from the Isle of Man as respects anything obtained by him in the Island unless it is chargeable there with duty or value added tax and he has obtained it without payment of the duty or tax.][1]

(1B) . . . [4]

(2) Any person entering or leaving the United Kingdom shall answer such questions as the proper officer may put to him with respect to his baggage and any thing contained therein or carried with him, and shall, if required by the proper officer, produce that baggage and any such thing for examination at such place as the Commissioners may direct.

[(2A) Subject to subsection (1A) above, where the journey of a person arriving by air in the United Kingdom is continued or resumed by air to a destination in the United Kingdom which is not the place where he is regarded for the purposes of this section as entering the United Kingdom, subsections (1) and (2) above shall apply in relation to that person on his arrival at that destination as they apply in relation to a person entering the United Kingdom.][3]

(3) Any person failing to declare any thing or to produce any baggage or thing as required by this section shall be liable on summary conviction to a penalty of three times the value of the thing not declared or of the baggage or thing not produced, as the case may be, or [level 3 on the standard scale][2], whichever is the greater.

(4) Any thing chargeable with any duty or tax which is found concealed, or is not declared, and any thing which is being taken into or out of the United Kingdom contrary to any prohibition or restriction for the time being in force with respect thereto under or by virtue of any enactment, shall be liable to forfeiture.

Commentary—*De Voil Indirect Tax Service* **V3.345, V3.346**.
Amendments—[1] Sub-s (1A) inserted by Isle of Man Act 1979 s 13, Sch 1.
[2] Words in sub-s (3) substituted by virtue of Criminal Justice Act 1982 ss 37, 38, 46.
[3] Sub-s (2A) inserted by F(No 2)A 1992 s 5 with effect from 1 January 1993.
[4] In sub-s (1)(*b*) word substituted for word "chargeable", in the words after sub-s (1)(*b*), words inserted, and in the second sentence, words substituted for words "subsection "chargeable goods" means", and sub-s (1B) repealed, by the Taxation (Cross-border Trade) Act 2018 s 29, Sch 7 paras 3, 78 with effect from IP completion day (11pm on 31 December 2020), by virtue of SI 2020/1642 reg 4(*a*). Note that savings apply preserving the effect of sub-s (1B) with modifications in connection with duty under TCBTA 2018 s 30A(3) (see TCBTA 2018 Sch 7 para 158).

Sub-s (1B) previously read as follows—
"(1B) Subsection (1) above does not apply to a person entering the United Kingdom from another member State, except—
 (*a*) where he arrives at a customs and excise airport in an aircraft in which he began his journey in a place outside the member States; or
 (*b*) as respects such of his baggage as—
  (i) is carried in the hold of the aircraft in which he arrives at a customs and excise airport, and
  (ii) notwithstanding that it was transferred on one or more occasions from aircraft to aircraft at an airport in a member State, began its journey by air from a place outside the member States.".

79 Power to require evidence in support of information

(1) The Commissioners may, if they consider it necessary, require evidence to be produced to their satisfaction in support of any information required by or under Parts III to VII of this Act to be provided in respect of goods imported or exported.

(2) Without prejudice to subsection (1) above, where any question as to the duties chargeable on any imported goods, or the operation of any prohibition or restriction on importation depends on any question as to the place from which the goods were consigned, or any question where they or other goods are to be treated as grown, manufactured or produced, or any question as to payments made or relief from duty allowed in any country or territory, then—
 (*a*) the Commissioners may require the importer of the goods to furnish to them, in such form as they may prescribe, proof of—
  (i) any statement made to them as to any fact necessary to determine that question, or
  (ii) the accuracy of any certificate or other document furnished in connection with the importation of the goods and relating to the matter in issue,
 and if such proof is not furnished to their satisfaction, the question may be determined without regard to that statement or to that certificate or document; and
 (*b*) if in any proceedings relating to the goods or to the duty chargeable thereon the accuracy of any such certificate or document comes in question, it shall be for the person relying on it to furnish proof of its accuracy.

PART VIII
WAREHOUSES AND QUEEN'S WAREHOUSES AND RELATED PROVISIONS ABOUT PIPE-LINES

92 Approval of warehouses

(1) The Commissioners may approve, for such periods and subject to such conditions as they think fit, places of security for the deposit, keeping and securing—
 (*a*) of imported goods chargeable as such with excise duty (whether or not also chargeable with customs duty) without payment of the excise duty;
 (*b*) of goods for exportation or for use as stores, being goods not eligible for home use;

(c) of goods manufactured or produced in the United Kingdom [or the Isle of Man][1] and permitted by or under the customs and excise Acts to be warehoused without payment of any duty of excise chargeable thereon;

(d) of goods imported into or manufactured or produced in the United Kingdom [or the Isle of Man][1] and permitted by or under the customs and excise Acts to be warehoused on drawback,

subject to and in accordance with warehousing regulations; and any place of security so approved is referred to in this Act as an "excise warehouse".

(2)–(4) . . .[3]

(5) The Commissioners may from time to time give directions—
   (a) as to the goods which may or may not be deposited in any particular warehouse or class of warehouse;
   (b) as to the part of any warehouse in which any class or description of goods may be kept or secured.

(6) If, after the approval of a warehouse as an excise warehouse, the occupier thereof makes without the previous consent of the Commissioners any alteration therein or addition thereto, [the making of the alteration or addition shall attract a penalty under section 9 of the Finance Act 1994 (civil penalties).][2]

(7) The Commissioners may at any time for reasonable cause revoke or vary the terms of their approval of any warehouse under this section.

[(8) Where any person contravenes or fails to comply with any condition imposed or direction given by the Commissioners under this section, his contravention or failure to comply shall attract a penalty under section 9 of the Finance Act 1994 (civil penalties).][2]

Commentary—*De Voil Indirect Tax Service* **V3.138, V3.332, V5.141**.

Amendments—[1] Words in sub-s (1)(c), (d) inserted by Isle of Man Act 1979 s 13, Sch 1 para 21.
[2] Sub-s (8) and words in sub-s (6) substituted by FA 1994 Sch 4 paras 1, 2.
[3] Sub-ss (2)–(4) repealed by the Taxation (Cross-border Trade) Act 2018 s 29, Sch 7 paras 3, 84 with effect from IP completion day (11pm on 31 December 2020), by virtue of SI 2020/1642 reg 4(*a*).

These amendments are subject to savings and modifications in relation to Northern Ireland. TCBTA 2018 Sch 7 para 158 preserves the continued application of this Act for various purposes as if these amendments had not been made and with certain modifications. These savings and modifications relate to the application of this Act for any purposes in connection with duty under the following provisions of TCBTA 2018—
- s 30A(3) (non-EU goods imported into the UK as a result of entry into Northern Ireland are subject to duty charged in accordance with Union customs legislation);
- s 30C (goods removed from Northern Ireland to Great Britain which are not Qualifying Northern Ireland Goods are chargeable to customs duty)
- s 40A (goods moving to Northern Ireland from Great Britain, that are not domestic goods or are 'at risk' of subsequently being moved into the EU are chargeable to customs duty in accordance with Union customs legislation).

Those subsections previously read as follows—

"(2) The Commissioners may approve, for such periods and subject to such conditions as they think fit, places of security for the deposit, keeping and securing—
   (a) of imported goods chargeable with customs duty or otherwise not for the time being in free circulation in member States (whether or not also chargeable with excise duty) without payment of the customs duty;
   (b) of such other goods as the Commissioners may allow to be warehoused—
      (i) for exportation or for use as stores in cases where relief from or repayment of any customs duty or other payment is conditional on their exportation or use as stores; or
      (ii) for exportation or for use for a purpose referred to in a Community regulation in cases where payment of an export refund under such a regulation is conditional on their exportation or use for such a purpose,

subject to and in accordance with warehousing regulations; and any place of security so approved is referred to in this Act as a "customs warehouse".

(3) The same place may be approved under this section both as a customs and as an excise warehouse.

(4) Notwithstanding subsection (2) above and the terms of the approval of the warehouse but subject to directions under subsection (5) below, goods of the following descriptions, not being goods chargeable with excise duty which has not been paid, that is to say—
   (a) goods originating in member States;
   (b) goods which are in free circulation in member States; and
   (c) goods placed on importation under a customs procedure (other than warehousing) involving the suspension of, or the giving of relief from, customs duties,

may be kept, without being warehoused, in a customs warehouse.".

PART VIIIA
FREE ZONES

Amendments—This Part (ie ss 100A–100F) inserted by FA 1984 Sch 4 Pt I.

[100A Designation of free zones

(1) The Treasury may by order designate any area in the United Kingdom as a special area for customs purposes.

(2) An area so designated shall be known as a "free zone".

(3) An order under subsection (1) above—

(a) shall have effect for such period as shall be specified in the order;
(b) may be made so as to take effect, in relation to the area or any part of the area designated by a previous order under this section, on the expiry of the period specified in the previous order;
(c) shall appoint one or more persons as the responsible authority or authorities for the free zone;
(d) may impose on any responsible authority such conditions or restrictions as may be specified; and
(e) may be revoked if the Commissioners are satisfied that there has been a failure to comply with any condition or restriction.
(4) The Treasury may by order—
    (a) from time to time vary—
        (i) the conditions or restrictions imposed by a designation order; or
        (ii) with the agreement of the responsible authority, the area designated; or
    (b) appoint one or more persons as the responsible authority or authorities for a free zone either in addition to or in substitution for any person appointed as such by a designation order.
(5) In this Act "designation order" means an order made under subsection (1) above.
(6) Any order under this section shall be made by statutory instrument.][1]

Commentary—*De Voil Indirect Tax Service* **V3.331**.
Orders—See Free Zone (Birmingham Airport) Designation Order, SI 1991/1737; Free Zone (Humberside) Designation Order, SI 1994/144; Free Zone (Port of Sheerness) Designation Order, SI 1994/2898; Free Zone (Southampton) Designation Order, SI 2001/2880; Free Zone (Liverpool) Designation Order, SI 2001/2881; Free Zone (Prestwick Airport) Designation Order, SI 2001/2882; Free Zone (Port of Tilbury) Order, SI 2002/1418.
Amendments—[1] This section inserted by FA 1984 Sch 4 Pt I.

[100F Powers of search
(1) Any person entering or leaving a free zone shall answer such questions as any officer may put to him with respect to any goods and shall, if required by the officer, produce those goods for examination at such place as the Commissioners may direct.
(2) At a time while a vehicle is entering or leaving a free zone, any officer may board the vehicle and search any part of it.
(3) Any officer may at any time enter upon and inspect a free zone and all buildings and goods within the zone.][1]

Commentary—*De Voil Indirect Tax Service* **V3.331**.
Amendments—[1] This section inserted by FA 1984 Sch 4 Pt I.

PART X
DUTIES AND DRAWBACKS—GENERAL PROVISIONS

General provisions relating to imported goods

125 Valuation of goods for purposes of ad valorem duties
(1), (2) . . .
(3) The Commissioners may make regulations for the purpose of giving effect to the foregoing provisions of this section, and in particular for requiring any importer or other person concerned with the importation of goods—
    (a) to furnish to the Commissioners in such form as they may require, such information as is in their opinion necessary for a proper valuation of the goods; and
    (b) to produce any books of account or other documents of whatever nature relating to the purchase, importation or sale of the goods by that person.
(4) If any person contravenes or fails to comply with any regulation made under sub-section (3) above he shall be liable on summary conviction to a penalty of [level 3 on the standard scale].[1], [2]

Commentary—*De Voil Indirect Tax Service* **V3.314**.
Amendments—[1] Words in sub-s (4) substituted by virtue of Criminal Justice Act 1982 ss 37, 38, 46.
[2] Section 125 repealed by the Taxation (Cross-border Trade) Act 2018 s 29, Sch 7 paras 3, 96 with effect from IP completion day (11pm on 31 December 2020), by virtue of SI 2020/1642 reg 4(a).
These amendments are subject to savings and modifications in relation to Northern Ireland. TCBTA 2018 Sch 7 para 158 preserves the continued application of this Act for various purposes as if these amendments had not been made and with certain modifications. These savings and modifications relate to the application of this Act for any purposes in connection with duty under the following provisions of TCBTA 2018—
    – s 30A(3) (non-EU goods imported into the UK as a result of entry into Northern Ireland are subject to duty charged in accordance with Union customs legislation);
    – s 30C (goods removed from Northern Ireland to Great Britain which are not Qualifying Northern Ireland Goods are chargeable to customs duty)
    – s 40A (goods moving to Northern Ireland from Great Britain, that are not domestic goods or are 'at risk' of subsequently being moved into the EU are chargeable to customs duty in accordance with Union customs legislation).

PART XI
[ARREST] OF PERSONS, FORFEITURE AND LEGAL PROCEEDINGS
[Arrest] of persons

Amendments—Words in square brackets substituted by Police and Criminal Evidence Act 1984 s 114(1) with effect from 1 January 1986; see Police and Criminal Evidence Act 1984 (Commencement No 3) Order, SI 1985/1934.

138 Provisions as to [arrest][1] of persons

(1) Any person who has committed, or whom there are reasonable grounds to suspect of having committed, any offence for which he is liable to be [arrested][1] under the customs and excise Acts may be [arrested][1] by any officer . . . [2] or any member of Her Majesty's armed forces or coastguard at any time within [20 years][4] from the date of the commission of the offence.

(2) Where it was not practicable to [arrest][1] any person so liable at the time of the commission of the offence, or where any such person having been then or subsequently [arrested][1] for that offence has escaped, he may be [arrested][1] by any officer . . . [2] or any member of Her Majesty's armed forces or coastguard at any time and may be proceeded against in like manner as if the offence had been committed at the date when he was finally [arrested][1].

(3) Where any person who is a member of the crew of any ship in Her Majesty's employment or service is [arrested][1] by an officer for an offence under the customs and excise Acts, the commanding officer of the ship shall, if so required by the [arresting][1] officer, keep that person secured on board that ship until he can be brought before a court and shall then deliver him up to the proper officer.

[(4) Where any person has been arrested by a person who is not an officer—
  (a) by virtue of this section; or
  (b) by virtue of section 24 [or 24A][6] of the Police and Criminal Evidence Act 1984 in its application to offences under the customs and excise Acts, [or][5]
  [(c) by virtue of Article 26 of the Police and Criminal Evidence (Northern Ireland) Order 1989 in its application to such offences][5]
the person arresting him shall give notice of the arrest to an officer at the nearest convenient office of customs and excise.][3]

Amendments—
[1] Words in sub-ss (1)–(3) substituted by Police and Criminal Evidence Act 1984 s 114(1) with effect from 1 January 1986; see Police and Criminal Evidence Act 1984 (Commencement No 3) Order, SI 1985/1934.
[2] Words in sub-ss (1), (2) repealed by Police and Criminal Evidence Act 1984 ss 26(1), 119(2), 120, Sch 7 with effect from 1 January 1986; see Police and Criminal Evidence Act 1984 (Commencement No 3) Order, SI 1985/1934.
[3] Sub-s (4) substituted by Police and Criminal Evidence Act 1984 s 119(1), Sch 6 Pt II, para 37 with effect from 1 January 1986; see Police and Criminal Evidence Act 1984 (Commencement No 3) Order, SI 1985/1934.
[4] Words in sub-s (1) substituted by FA 1988 s 11(1), (2).
[5] Words in sub-s (4) inserted by Police and Criminal Evidence (Northern Ireland) Order, SI 1989/1341 art 90(1), Sch 6 para 9.
[6] In sub-s (4)(b), words inserted by the Serious Organised Crime and Police Act 2005 s 111, Sch 7 para 54 with effect from 1 January 2006, see Serious Organised Crime and Police Act 2005 (Commencement No 4 and Transitory Provision), SI 2005/3495, art 2(1)(m).

Forfeiture

139 Provisions as to detention, seizure and condemnation of goods, etc

(1) Any thing liable to forfeiture under the customs and excise Acts may be seized or detained by any officer or constable or any member of Her Majesty's armed forces or coastguard.

[(1A) A person mentioned in subsection (1) who reasonably suspects that any thing may be liable to forfeiture under the customs and excise Acts may detain that thing.

(1B) References in this section and Schedule 2A to a thing detained as liable to forfeiture under the customs and excise Acts include a thing detained under subsection (1A).][2]

(2) Where any thing is seized or detained as liable to forfeiture under the customs and excise Acts by a person other than an officer, that person shall, subject to subsection (3) below, [deliver that thing to an officer][2]

(3) Where the person seizing or detaining any thing as liable to forfeiture under the customs and excise Acts is a constable and that thing is or may be required for use in connection with any proceedings to be brought otherwise than under those Acts it may, subject to subsection (4) below, be retained in the custody of the police until either those proceedings are completed or it is decided that no such proceedings shall be brought.

(4) The following provisions apply in relation to things retained in the custody of the police by virtue of subsection (3) above, that is to say—
  (a) notice in writing of the seizure or detention and of the intention to retain the thing in question in the custody of the police, together with full particulars as to that thing, shall be given to [an officer][2];
  (b) any officer shall be permitted to examine that thing and take account thereof at any time while it remains in the custody of the police;
  (c) nothing in the Police (Property) Act 1897 shall apply in relation to that thing.

(2) Where any such offence was committed at some place outside the area of any commission of the peace, the place of the commission of the offence shall, for the purposes of the jurisdiction of any court, be deemed to be any place in the United Kingdom where the offender is found or to which he is first brought after the commission of the offence.
(3) The jurisdiction under subsection (2) above shall be in addition to and not in derogation of any jurisdiction or power of any court under any other enactment.
Commentary—*De Voil Indirect Tax Service* **V5.304**.

149 Non-payment of penalties, etc: maximum terms of imprisonment

(1) Where, in any proceedings for an offence under the customs and excise Acts, a magistrates' court in England or Wales or a court of summary jurisdiction in Scotland, in addition to ordering the person convicted to pay a penalty for the offence—
   (*a*) orders him to be imprisoned for a term in respect of the same offence; and
   (*b*) further (whether at the same time or subsequently) orders him to be imprisoned for a term in respect of non-payment of that penalty or default of a sufficient distress to satisfy the amount of that penalty,
the aggregate of the terms for which he is so ordered to be imprisoned shall not exceed 15 months.
[(1A) [2]
(2) . . . [1]
(3) Where, under any enactment for the time being in force in Northern Ireland, a court of summary jurisdiction has power to order a person to be imprisoned in respect of the non-payment of a penalty, or of the default of a sufficient distress to satisfy the amount of that penalty, for a term in addition and succession to a term of imprisonment imposed for the same offence as the penalty, then in relation to a sentence for an offence under the customs and excise Acts the aggregate of those terms of imprisonment may, notwithstanding anything in any such enactment, by any period not exceeding 15 months.
Commentary—*De Voil Indirect Tax Service* **V5.308**.
Amendments—[1] Sub-s (2) repealed by Criminal Justice (Scotland) Act 1980 Sch 8.
[2] Sub-s (1A) inserted by the Tribunals, Courts and Enforcement Act 2007 s 50, Sch 10 paras 44 with effect from 6 April 2014 (by virtue of SI 2014/768).

150 Incidental provisions as to legal proceedings

(1) Where liability for any offence under the customs and excise Acts is incurred by two or more persons jointly, those persons shall each be liable for the full amount of any pecuniary penalty and may be proceeded against jointly or severally as [prosecuting authority (within the meaning of section 146A)][1] may see fit.
(2) In any proceedings for an offence under the customs and excise Acts instituted in England, Wales or Northern Ireland, any court by whom the matter is considered may mitigate any pecuniary penalty as they see fit.
(3) In any proceedings for an offence or for the condemnation of any thing as being forfeited under the customs and excise Acts, the fact that security has been given by bond or otherwise for the payment of any duty or for compliance with any condition in respect of the non-payment of which or non-compliance with which the proceedings are instituted shall not be a defence.
Commentary—*De Voil Indirect Tax Service* **V5.304, V5.307**.
Amendment—[1] Words in sub-s (1) substituted for words "the Director of Public Prosecutions (in relation to proceedings instituted in England and Wales) or the Commissioners (in relation to proceedings instituted in Scotland or Northern Ireland)" by FA 2016 s 174(1),(3) with effect in relation to proceedings commenced on or after 15 September 2016.

151 Application of penalties

The balance of any sum paid or recovered on account of any penalty imposed under the customs and excise Acts, after paying any such compensation or costs as are mentioned in [section 139 of the Magistrates' Courts Act 1980][1] to persons other than the Commissioners shall, notwithstanding any local or other special right or privilege of whatever origin, be accounted for and paid to the Commissioners or as they direct.
Amendments—[1] Words substituted by Magistrates' Courts Act 1980 Sch 7 para 177.

152 Power of Commissioners to mitigate penalties, etc

The Commissioners may, as they see fit—
   (*a*) stay, sist or [compound an offence (whether or not proceedings have been instituted in respect of it) and compound proceedings][1] or for the condemnation of any thing as being forfeited under the customs and excise Acts; or
   (*b*) restore, subject to such conditions (if any) as they think proper, any thing forfeited or seized under those Acts; or
      (*c*), (*d*) . . . [2]
but paragraph (*a*) above shall not apply to proceedings on indictment in Scotland.
Commentary—*De Voil Indirect Tax Service* **V5.308**.

Amendments—[1] Words substituted by Commissioners for Revenue and Customs Act 2005 s 50, Sch 4 para 26 with effect from 18 April 2005 by virtue of the Commissioners for Revenue and Customs Act 2005 (Commencement) Order, SI 2005/1126, art 2(2).
[2] Paras (c), (d) repealed by the Commissioners for Revenue and Customs Act 2005 s 52, Sch 5 with effect from 18 April 2005 by virtue of SI 2005/1126, art 2(2)(i).

154 Proof of certain other matters

(1) An averment in any process in proceedings under the customs and excise Acts—
 (a) that those proceedings were instituted by the order of the Commissioners; or
 (b) that any person is or was a Commissioner, officer or constable, or a member of Her Majesty's armed forces or coastguard; or
 (c) that any person is or was appointed or authorised by the Commissioners to discharge, or was engaged by the orders or with the concurrence of the Commissioners in the discharge of, any duty; or
 (d) that the Commissioners have or have not been satisfied as to any matter as to which they are required by any provision of those Acts to be satisfied; or
 (e) that any ship is a British ship; or
 (f) that any goods thrown overboard, staved or destroyed were so dealt with in order to prevent or avoid the seizure of those goods,
shall, until the contrary is proved, be sufficient evidence of the matter in question.

(2) Where in any proceedings relating to customs or excise any question arises as to the place from which any goods have been brought or as to whether or not—
 (a) any duty has been paid or secured in respect of any goods; or
 (b) any goods or other things whatsoever are of the description or nature alleged in the information, writ or other process; or
 (c) any goods have been lawfully imported or lawfully unloaded from any [ship, aircraft or railway vehicle][1]; or
 (d) any goods have been lawfully loaded into any [ship, aircraft or railway vehicle][1] or lawfully exported or were lawfully waterborne; or
 (e) any goods were lawfully brought to any place for the purpose of being loaded into any [ship, aircraft or railway vehicle][1] or exported; or
 (f) any goods are or were subject to any prohibition of or restriction on their importation or exportation,
then, where those proceedings are brought by or against the Commissioners, a law officer of the Crown or an officer, or against any other person in respect of anything purporting to have been done in pursuance of any power or duty conferred or imposed on him by or under the customs and excise Acts, the burden of proof shall lie upon the other party to the proceedings.

Commentary—*De Voil Indirect Tax Service* **V5.305**.
Amendments—[1] In sub-s (2)(c), (d), (e), words substituted for words "ship or aircraft" by the Taxation (Cross-border Trade) Act 2018 s 29, Sch 7 paras 3, 106 with effect from IP completion day (11pm on 31 December 2020), by virtue of SI 2020/1642 reg 4(a).

155 Persons who may conduct proceedings

[(1) An officer of Revenue and Customs or other person authorised by the Commissioners may conduct criminal proceedings relating to an assigned matter before a court of summary jurisdiction in Scotland or Northern Ireland.][1]

[(2) Any person who has been admitted as a solicitor and is employed by the Commissioners may act as a solicitor in any proceedings in England, Wales or Northern Ireland relating to any assigned matter notwithstanding that he does not hold a current practising certificate.][2]

Commentary—*De Voil Indirect Tax Service* **V5.305**.
Amendments—[1] Sub-s (1) substituted by Commissioners for Revenue and Customs Act 2005 s 50, Sch 4 para 27 with effect from 18 April 2005 by virtue of the Commissioners for Revenue and Customs Act 2005 (Commencement) Order, SI 2005/1126, art 2(2).
[2] Sub-s (2) repealed by Commissioners for Revenue and Customs Act 2005 ss 50, 52, Sch 4 para 21 and Sch 5 with effect from 18 April 2005 by virtue of the Commissioners for Revenue and Customs Act 2005 (Commencement) Order, SI 2005/1126, art 2(2).

Saving for outlying enactments of certain general provisions as to offences

156 Saving for outlying enactments of certain general provisions as to offences

(1) In subsections (2), (3) and (4) below (which reproduce certain enactments not required as general provisions for the purposes of the enactments re-enacted in the Customs and Excise Acts 1979) "the outlying provisions of the customs and excise Acts" [means the provisions][1] of the customs and excise Acts, as for the time being amended, which were passed before the commencement of this Act and are not re-enacted in the Customs and Excise Acts 1979 [or the Betting and Gaming Duties Act 1981][1].

(2) It is hereby declared that any act or omission in respect of which a pecuniary penalty (however described) is imposed by any of the outlying provisions of the customs and excise Acts is an offence under that provision; and accordingly in this Part of this Act any reference to an offence under the customs and excise Acts includes a reference to such an act or omission.

(3) Subject to any express provision made by the enactment in question, an offence under any of the outlying provisions of the customs and excise Acts—
(a) where it is punishable with imprisonment for a term of 2 years, with or without a pecuniary penalty, shall be punishable either on summary conviction or on conviction on indictment;
(b) in any other case, shall be punishable on summary conviction.

. . .²

[(4) The maximum term of imprisonment which may be imposed on summary conviction in the sheriff court of an offence under any of the outlying provisions of the customs and excise Acts shall be 6 months.

(5) Where, in Scotland, an offence under any of the outlying provisions of the customs and excise Acts is triable only summarily by virtue of subsection (3)(b) above, the penalty for the offence shall be that to which a person was liable on summary conviction of the offence immediately before 29th July 1977 (the date of the passing of the Criminal Law Act 1977) subject to any increase by virtue of section 289C(5) of the Criminal Procedure (Scotland) Act 1975 or Part IV of the Criminal Justice Act 1982.]³

Amendments—[1] Words sub-s (1) substituted by the Betting and Gaming Duties Act 1981, s 34(1), Sch 5, para 5.
[2] Words omitted repealed by the Criminal Justice Act 1982, ss 77, 78, Sch 14, para 43, Sch 16.
[3] Sub-ss (4), (5) substituted for original sub-s (4) by the Criminal Justice Act 1982, s 77, Sch 14, para 43.

PART XII
GENERAL AND MISCELLANEOUS

General powers, etc

157 Bonds and security

(1) Without prejudice to any express requirement as to security contained in the customs and excise Acts, the Commissioners may, if they see fit, require any person to give security [(or further security) by bond, guarantee]¹ or otherwise for the observance of any condition in connection with customs or excise.

(1A) . . .³

(2) Any bond[, guarantee or other security]² taken for the purposes of any assigned matter—
(a) shall be taken [on behalf of Her Majesty]³; and
(b) shall be valid notwithstanding that it is entered into by a person under full age; and
(c) may be cancelled at any time by or by order of the Commissioners.

. . .³

Amendments—[1] Words in sub-s (1) substituted by the Finance Act 2000, s 27(1), (2) with effect from 28 July 2000.
[2] Words in sub-s (2) inserted by the Finance Act 2000, s 27(1), (4) with effect from 28 July 2000.
[3] Sub-s (1A) repealed, and in sub-s (2), in para (a), words substituted for words "either on behalf of Her Majesty or on behalf of Her Majesty and the tax authorities of each member State other than the United Kingdom", and sentence after para (c) repealed, by the Taxation (Cross-border Trade) Act 2018 s 50, Sch 9 paras 1, 3 with effect from IP completion day (11pm on 31 December 2020), by virtue of SI 2020/1642 reg 4(c). Note that this section continues to have effect for any purpose in connection with duty charged as a result of the Taxation (Post-transition Period) Act 2020 s 4(1), and in relation to goods in Northern Ireland, as if these amendments had not been made (see TCBTA 2018 Sch 9 para 10).

Sub-s (1A) previously read as follows—
"(1A) For the purposes of this section "condition in connection with excise" includes a condition in connection with excise duty charged, under the law of a member State other than the United Kingdom, on—
(a) manufactured tobacco,
(b) alcohol or alcoholic beverages, or
(c) energy products.
The expressions used in paragraphs (a) to (c) above have the same meaning as in Council Directive 2008/118/EC.".

Sentence after sub-s (2)(c) previously read as follows—
"In this subsection "assigned matter" includes any excise duty charged as mentioned in subsection (1A) above.".

[157A General information powers in relation to persons entering or leaving the United Kingdom

(1) The proper officer of Revenue and Customs may require any person entering or leaving the United Kingdom—
(a) to produce the person's passport or travel documents for examination, or
(b) to answer any questions put by the proper officer of Revenue and Customs about the person's journey.

(2) In subsection (1) "passport" means—
(a) a United Kingdom passport (within the meaning of the Immigration Act 1971),

(b) a passport issued by or on behalf of the authorities of a country or territory outside the United Kingdom, or by or on behalf of an international organisation, or (c) a document that can be used (in some or all circumstances) instead of a passport.

(3) Subsections (1) and (2) apply in relation to a transit air passenger arriving at the passenger's final destination in the United Kingdom as they apply in relation to a person entering the United Kingdom.

(4) For the purposes of subsection (3) a transit air passenger is a person—
- (a) who has arrived by air in the United Kingdom; and
- (b) whose journey is continued or resumed by air to a destination in the United Kingdom which is not the place where the person is regarded for the purposes of this section as entering the United Kingdom; and the passenger's final destination is the destination of the continued or resumed journey.][1]

Amendments—[1] This section inserted by the Policing and Crime Act 2009 s 98(1) with effect from 25 January 2010 (by virtue of SI 2010/52 art 2).

158 Power to require provision of facilities

(1) A person to whom this section applies, that is to say, a revenue trader and any person required by the Commissioners under the Customs and Excise Acts 1979 to give security in respect of any premises or place to be used for the examination of goods by an officer, shall—
- (a) provide and maintain such appliances and afford such other facilities reasonably necessary to enable an officer to take any account or make any examination or search or to perform any other of his duties on the premises of that trader or at the bonded premises or place as the Commissioners may direct;
- (b) keep any appliances so provided in a convenient place approved by the proper officer for that purpose; and
- (c) allow the proper officer at any time to use anything so provided and give him any assistance necessary for the performance of his duties.

(2) Any person who contravenes or fails to comply with any provision of subsection (1) above shall be liable on summary conviction to a penalty of [level 3 on the standard scale][1].

(3) A person to whom this section applies shall provide and maintain any fitting required for the purpose of affixing any lock which the proper officer may require to affix to the premises of that person or any part thereof or to any vessel, utensil or other apparatus whatsoever kept thereon, and in default—
- (a) the fitting may be provided or any work necessary for its maintenance may be carried out by the proper officer, and any expenses so incurred shall be paid on demand by that person; and
- (b) if that person fails to pay those expenses on demand, he shall in addition be liable on summary conviction to a penalty of [level 3 on the standard scale][1].

(4) If any person to whom this section applies or any servant of his—
- (a) wilfully destroys or damages any such fitting as is mentioned in subsection (3) above or any lock or key provided for use therewith, or any label or seal placed on any such lock; or
- (b) improperly obtains access to any place or article secured by any such lock; or
- (c) has any such fitting or any article intended to be secured by means thereof so constructed that that intention is defeated,

he shall be liable on summary conviction to a penalty of [£20,000][3] and may be [arrested][2].

Amendments—[1] References in sub-ss (2), (3) to level 3 on the standard scale substituted by virtue of the Criminal Justice Act 1982, ss 37, 38, 46.

[2] In sub-s (4), word substituted by the Police and Criminal Evidence Act 1984, s 114(1).

[3] In sub-s (4), figure substituted by the Legal Aid, Sentencing and Punishment of Offenders Act 2012 (Fines on Summary Conviction) Regulations, SI 2015/664 reg 2(2), Sch 2 paras 1, 17 with effect from 12 March 2015 in relation to England and Wales only.

159 Power to examine and take account of goods

(1) Without prejudice to any other power conferred by the Customs and Excise Acts 1979, an officer may examine and take account of any goods—
- (a) which are imported; or
- [(aa) which are subject to the control of any officer of Revenue and Customs as a result of Part 1 of the Taxation (Cross-border Trade) Act 2018; or
- (ab) which have been discharged from a Customs procedure under Part 1 of the Taxation (Cross-border Trade) Act 2018 so far as necessary for the purpose of verifying any Customs declaration or any document required to accompany it; or][7]
- (b) which are in a warehouse or Queen's warehouse; or
- [(bb) which are in a free zone; or][2]
- (c) which have been loaded into any ship or aircraft at any place in the United Kingdom [or the Isle of Man][1]; or
- (d) which are [declared][7] for exportation or for use as stores; or
- (e) which are brought to any place in the United Kingdom for exportation or for shipment for exportation or as stores; or

(f) in the case of which any claim for drawback, allowance, rebate, remission or repayment of duty is made;
and may for that purpose [open or unpack any container or]⁵ require any container to be opened or unpacked [and search it or anything in it.]⁵

(2) Any examination of goods by an officer under the Customs and Excise Acts 1979 shall be made at such place as the Commissioners appoint for the purpose.

(3) In the case of such goods as the Commissioners may direct, and subject to such conditions as they see fit to impose, an officer may permit goods to be skipped on the quay or bulked, sorted, lotted, packed or repacked before account is taken thereof.

(4) Any opening, unpacking, weighing, measuring, repacking, bulking, sorting, lotting, marking, numbering, loading, unloading, carrying or landing of goods or their containers for the purposes of, or incidental to, the examination by an officer, removal or warehousing thereof shall be done, and any facilities or assistance required for any such examination shall be provided, by or at the expense of the proprietor of the goods[; but if an officer opens or unpacks any container, or searches it or anything in it, the Commissioners are to bear the expense of doing so.]⁵

[(4A) But, in the case of anything done for the purpose of verifying any Customs declaration or any document required to accompany it—
   (a) the reference in subsection (4) to the proprietor of the goods is a reference to the declarant, and
   (b) if, while the goods are being moved to a place for examination, an act which was not authorised by the Commissioners is, without reasonable excuse, done by any person in relation to the goods, the declarant is liable on summary conviction to a penalty of level 3 on the standard scale.

(4B) In subsection (4A) "the declarant", in relation to a Customs declaration in respect of any goods, means—
   (a) the person who has made the declaration, or
   (b) the person on whose behalf it was made.]⁷

(5) If any imported goods which an officer has power under the Customs and Excise Acts 1979 to examine are without the authority of the proper officer removed from customs and excise charge before they have been examined, those goods shall be liable to forfeiture.

(6) If any goods falling within subsection (5) above are removed by a person with intent to defraud Her Majesty of any duty chargeable thereon or to evade any prohibition or restriction for the time being in force with respect thereto under or by virtue of any enactment, that person shall be guilty of an offence under this subsection and may be [arrested]³.

(7) A person guilty of an offence under subsection (6) above shall be liable—
   (a) on summary conviction, to a penalty of [£20,000]⁶ or of three times the value of the goods, whichever is the greater, or to imprisonment for a term not exceeding 6 months, or to both; or
   (b) on conviction on indictment, to a penalty of any amount, or to imprisonment for a term not exceeding [7 years]⁴, or to both.

(8) Without prejudice to the foregoing provisions of this section, where by this section or by or under any other provision of the Customs and Excise Acts 1979 an account is authorised or required to be taken of any goods for any purpose by an officer, the Commissioners may, with the consent of the proprietor of the goods, accept as the account of those goods for that purpose an account taken by such other person as may be approved in that behalf by both the Commissioners and the proprietor of the goods.

Amendments— ¹ Words in sub-s (1)(c) inserted by Isle of Man Act 1979 s 13, Sch 1, para 22.
² Sub-s (1)(bb) inserted by FA 1984 Sch 4 Pt II, para 5.
³ Word in sub-s (6) substituted by Police and Criminal Evidence Act 1984 s 114(1) with effect from 1 January 1986; see Police and Criminal Evidence Act 1984 (Commencement No 3) Order, SI 1985/1934.
⁴ Words in sub-s (7)(b) substituted by FA 1988 s 12(1)(a).
⁵ Words in sub-ss (1), (4) inserted by FA 2008 s 117(3)–(5) with effect from 21 July 2008.
⁶ In sub-s (7)(a), figure substituted by the Legal Aid, Sentencing and Punishment of Offenders Act 2012 (Fines on Summary Conviction) Regulations, SI 2015/664 reg 2(2), Sch 2 paras 1, 18 with effect from 12 March 2015 in relation to England and Wales only.
⁷ Sub-ss (1)(aa), (ab), (4A), (4B) inserted, and in sub-s (1)(d) word substituted for word "entered", by the Taxation (Cross-border Trade) Act 2018 s 29, Sch 7 paras 3, 107 with effect from IP completion day (11pm on 31 December 2020), by virtue of SI 2020/1642 reg 4(a).

164 Power to search persons

(1) Where there are reasonable grounds to suspect that any person to whom this section applies [(referred to in this section as "the suspect")]² is carrying any article—
   (a) which is chargeable with any duty which has not been paid or secured or
   (b) with respect to the importation or exportation of which any prohibition or restriction is for the time being in force under or by virtue of any enactment,

[an officer may exercise the powers conferred by subsection (2) below and, if the suspect is not under arrest, may detain him for so long as may be necessary for the exercise of those powers and (where applicable) the exercise of the rights conferred by subsection (3) below.]³
[(2) The officer may require the suspect—
   (a) to permit such a search of any article which he has with him; and
   (b) subject to subsection (3) below, to submit to such searches of his person, whether rub-down, strip or intimate,
as the officer may consider necessary or expedient; but no such requirement may be imposed under paragraph (b) above without the officer informing the suspect of the effect of subsection (3) below.]⁴
[(3) If the suspect is required to submit to a search of his person, he may require to be taken—
   (a) except in the case of a rub-down search, before a justice of the peace or a superior of the officer concerned; and
   (b) in the excepted case, before such a superior;
and the justice or superior shall consider the grounds for suspicion and direct accordingly whether the suspect is to submit to the search.]⁴
[(3A) A rub-down or strip search shall not be carried out except by a person of the same sex as the suspect; and an intimate search shall not be carried out except by a suitably qualified person.]⁴
(4) This section applies to the following persons, namely—
   (a) any person who is on board or has landed from any ship or aircraft;
   (b) any person entering or about to leave the United Kingdom;
   (c) any person within the dock area of a port;
   (d) any person at a customs and excise airport;
   [(da) any person in, entering or leaving a railway customs area;
   (db) any person who is on board a railway vehicle which—
      (i) is in a railway customs area,
      (ii) has entered the United Kingdom but has not yet arrived at a railway customs area in the course of its journey, or
      (iii) has left a railway customs area and has not yet left the United Kingdom in the course of its journey;]⁶
   (e) any person in, entering or leaving any approved wharf or [temporary storage facility]⁶ which is not in a port;
   [(ee) any person in, entering or leaving a free zone;]¹
   (f) in Northern Ireland, any person travelling from or to any place which is on or beyond the boundary.
[(5) In this section—
   "intimate search" means any search which involves a physical examination (that is, an examination which is more than simply a visual examination) of a person's body orifices;
   "rub-down search" means any search which is neither an intimate search nor a strip search;
   "strip search" means any search which is not an intimate search but which involves the removal of an article of clothing which—
      (a) is being worn (wholly or partly) on the trunk; and
      (b) is being so worn either next to the skin or next to an article of underwear;
   "suitably qualified person" means a registered medical practitioner or a registered nurse.]⁵
[(6) Notwithstanding anything in subsection (4) of section 48 of the Criminal Justice (Scotland) Act 1987 (detention and questioning by customs officers), detention of the suspect under subsection (1) above shall not prevent his subsequent detention under subsection (1) of that section.]⁵

Amendments—¹ Sub-s (4)(ee) inserted by FA 1984 Sch 4 Pt II, para 6.
² Words in sub-s (1) inserted by FA 1988 s 10(1)(a).
³ Words in sub-s (1) substituted by FA 1988 s 10(1)(b).
⁴ Sub-ss (2), (3), (3A) substituted for sub-ss (2), (3) by FA 1988 s 10(2).
⁵ Sub-ss (5), (6) inserted by FA 1988 s 10(3).
⁶ Sub-s (4)(da), (db) inserted, and in sub-s (4)(e) words substituted for words "transit shed", by the Taxation (Cross-border Trade) Act 2018 s 29, Sch 7 paras 3, 112 with effect from IP completion day (11pm on 31 December 2020), by virtue of SI 2020/1642 reg 4(a).

[164A Powers to search for cash
(1) The provisions of this Act which fall within subsection (2) (search powers for officers of Revenue and Customs etc) apply in accordance with subsection (3)—
   (a) for the purposes of searching for cash—
      (i) which is recoverable property or is intended by any person for use in unlawful conduct; and
      (ii) the amount of which is not less than the minimum amount;
   (b) for the purposes of searching for cash to ensure compliance with the Cash Control Regulation; or
   (c) for purposes connected to any such purposes.
(2) The provisions of this Act which fall within this subsection are—

(a) section 28(1) (powers of access etc);
(b) section 77(1) and (2) (information powers);
(c) section 159(1) to (4) (powers to examine and take account of goods); and
(d) section 164 (power to search persons including intimate searches).
(3) Those provisions apply for the purposes mentioned in subsection (1) as if—
    (a) any reference in them to goods included a reference to cash; and
    (b) in section 164(1)—
        (i) the reference to an article were a reference to cash; and
        (ii) paragraphs (a) and (b) were omitted.
(4) The Treasury may by regulations provide for—
    (a) any provision of this Act to apply with modifications for the purposes of the provisions applied by subsections (1) to (3), or
    (b) any other enactment to apply, with or without modifications, for the purposes of the provisions so applied.
(5) This section does not limit the scope of any powers that exist apart from this section (whether under this Act or otherwise).
(6) In this section—
    "the 2002 Act" means the Proceeds of Crime Act 2002;
    "cash"—
        (a) so far as relating to purposes falling within subsection (1)(a) above, has the meaning given by section 289(6) and (7) of the 2002 Act; and
        (b) so far as relating to purposes falling within subsection (1)(b) above, has the same meaning as in the Cash Control Regulation;
    "the Cash Control Regulation" means Regulation (EC) No 1889/2005 of the European Parliament and of the Council of 26 October 2005 on controls of cash entering or leaving the Community;
    "minimum amount" has the meaning given by section 303 of the 2002 Act;
    "modifications" includes omissions;
    "recoverable property" has the meaning given by section 316(1) of the 2002 Act;
    "unlawful conduct" has the meaning given by section 241 of the 2002 Act.][1]

Amendments—[1] This section inserted by the Policing and Crime Act 2009 s 99(1) with effect from 25 January 2010 (by virtue of SI 2010/52 art 2).

General offences

167 Untrue declarations, etc

(1) If any person either knowingly or recklessly—
    (a) makes or signs, or causes to be made or signed, or delivers or causes to be delivered to the Commissioners or any officer, any declaration, notice, certificate or other document whatsoever; or
    (b) makes any statement in answer to any question put to him by an officer which he is required by or under any enactment to answer,
being a document or statement produced or made for any purpose of any assigned matter, which is untrue in any material particular, he shall be guilty of an offence under this subsection and may be [arrested][2]; and any goods in relation to which the document or statement was made shall be liable to forfeiture.
(2) Without prejudice to subsection (4) below, a person who commits an offence under subsection (1) above shall be liable—
    (a) on summary conviction, to a penalty of [£20,000][4], or to imprisonment for a term not exceeding 6 months, or to both; or
    (b) on conviction on indictment, to a penalty of any amount, or to imprisonment for a term not exceeding 2 years, or to both.
(3) If any person—
    (a) makes or signs, or causes to be made or signed, or delivers or causes to be delivered to the Commissioners or an officer, any declaration, notice, certificate or other document whatsoever; or
    (b) makes any statement in answer to any question put to him by an officer which he is required by or under any enactment to answer,
being a document or statement produced or made for any purpose of any assigned matter, which is untrue in any material particular, then, without prejudice to subsection (4) below, he shall be liable on summary conviction to a penalty of [level 4 on the standard scale.][1]
(4) Where by reason of any such document or statement as is mentioned in subsection (1) or (3) above the full amount of any duty payable is not paid or any overpayment is made in respect of any drawback, allowance, rebate of repayment of duty, the amount of the duty unpaid or of the overpayment shall be recoverable as a debt to the Crown or may be summarily recovered as a civil debt.

[(5) An amount of excise duty, or the amount of an overpayment in respect of any drawback, allowance, rebate or repayment of any excise duty, shall not be recoverable as mentioned in subsection (4) above unless the Commissioners have assessed the amount of the duty or of the overpayment as being excise duty due from the person mentioned in subsection (1) or (3) above and notified him or his representative accordingly.][3]

Commentary—*De Voil Indirect Tax Service* **V5.304**.
Amendments—[1] Words in sub-s (3) substituted by virtue of Criminal Justice Act 1982 ss 37, 38, 46.
[2] Word in sub-s (1) substituted by Police and Criminal Evidence Act 1984 s 114(1) with effect from 1 January 1986; see Police and Criminal Evidence Act 1984 (Commencement No 3) Order, SI 1985/1934.
[3] Sub-s (5) inserted by FA 1997 s 50(2), Sch 6 para 5 with effect from 1 June 1997 (by virtue of SI 1997/1305 art 2).
[4] In sub-s (2)(*a*), figure substituted by the Legal Aid, Sentencing and Punishment of Offenders Act 2012 (Fines on Summary Conviction) Regulations, SI 2015/664 reg 2(2), Sch 2 paras 1, 19 with effect from 12 March 2015 in relation to England and Wales only.

168 Counterfeiting documents, etc

(1) If any person—
  (*a*) counterfeits or falsifies any document which is required by or under any enactment relating to an assigned matter or which is used in the transaction of any business relating to an assigned matter; or
  (*b*) knowingly accepts, receives or uses any such document so counterfeited or falsified; or
  (*c*) alters any such document after it is officially issued; or
  (*d*) counterfeits any seal, signature, initials or other mark of, or used by, any officer for the verification of such a document or for the security of goods or for any other purpose relating to an assigned matter,
he shall be guilty of an offence under this section and may be [arrested.][1]
(2) A person guilty of an offence under this section shall be liable—
  (*a*) on summary conviction, to a penalty of [£20,000][2], or to imprisonment for a term not exceeding 6 months, or to both; or
  (*b*) on conviction on indictment, to a penalty of any amount, or to imprisonment for a term not exceeding 2 years, or to both.

Commentary—*De Voil Indirect Tax Service* **V5.304**.
Amendments—[1] Word in sub-s (1) substituted by Police and Criminal Evidence Act 1984 s 114(1) with effect from 1 January 1986; see Police and Criminal Evidence Act 1984 (Commencement No 3) Order, SI 1985/1934.
[2] In sub-s (2)(*a*), figure substituted by the Legal Aid, Sentencing and Punishment of Offenders Act 2012 (Fines on Summary Conviction) Regulations, SI 2015/664 reg 2(2), Sch 2 paras 1, 20 with effect from 12 March 2015 in relation to England and Wales only.

171 General provisions as to offences and penalties

(1) Where—
  (*a*) by any provision of any enactment relating to an assigned matter a punishment is prescribed for any offence thereunder or for any contravention of or failure to comply with any regulation, direction, condition or requirement made, given or imposed thereunder; and
  (*b*) any person is convicted in the same proceedings of more than one such offence, contravention or failure,
that person shall be liable to that punishment for each such offence, contravention or failure of which he is so convicted.
(2) In this Act the "prescribed sum", in relation to the penalty provided for an offence, means—
  (*a*) if the offence was committed in England [or Wales][2], the prescribed sum within the meaning of [section 32 of the Magistrates' Courts Act 1980 (£1,000 or other sum substituted by order under section 143(1) of that Act)][1];
  (*b*) if the offence was committed in Scotland, the prescribed sum within the meaning of section 289B of the Criminal Procedure (Scotland) Act 1975 (£1,000 or other sum substituted by order under section 289D(1) of that Act);
  [(*c*) if the offence was committed in Northern Ireland, the prescribed sum within the meaning of Article 4 of the Fines and Penalties (Northern Ireland) Order 1984 ([£5,000][3] or other sum substituted by order under Article 17 of that Order);][2]
and in subsection (1)(a) above, the reference to a provision by which a punishment is prescribed includes a reference to a provision which makes a person liable to a penalty of the prescribed sum within the meaning of this subsection.
[(2A) . . .][5]
(3) Where a penalty for an offence under any enactment relating to an assigned matter is required to be fixed by reference to the value of any goods, that value shall be taken as the price which those goods might reasonably be expected to have fetched, after payment of any duty or tax chargeable thereon, if they had been sold in the open market at or about the date of the commission of the offence for which the penalty is imposed.

(4) Where an offence under any enactment relating to an assigned matter which has been committed by a body corporate is proved to have been committed with the consent or connivance of, or to be attributable to any neglect on the part of, any director, manager, secretary or other similar officer of the body corporate or any person purporting to act in any such capacity, he as well as the body corporate shall be guilty of that offence and shall be liable to be proceeded against and punished accordingly.

In this subsection "director", in relation to any body corporate established by or under any enactment for the purpose of carrying on under national ownership any industry or part of an industry or undertaking, being a body corporate whose affairs are managed by the members thereof, means a member of that body corporate.

[(4A) Subsection (4) shall not apply to an offence which relates to a matter listed in Schedule 1 to the Commissioners for Revenue and Customs Act 2005 (former Inland Revenue matters).][6]

(5) Where in any proceedings for an offence under the customs and excise Acts any question arises as to the duty or the rate thereof chargeable on any imported goods, and it is not possible to ascertain [the time at which a liability to import duty is incurred][7] [or the relevant excise duty point][4], that duty or rate shall be determined [as if the time when the proceedings were commenced was the time at which the liability to import duty was incurred][7] [or, as the case may be, as if the time when the proceedings were commenced was the relevant excise duty point][4].

Commentary—*De Voil Indirect Tax Service* **V5.306, V5.307**.
Amendments—[1] Words in sub-s (2)(*a*) substituted by Magistrates' Courts Act 1980 Sch 7 para 178.
[2] Words in sub-s (2)(*a*) substituted and sub-s (2)(*c*) inserted by Fines and Penalties (Northern Ireland) Order, SI 1984/703 art 19(1), Sch 6 para 7 with effect from 19 July 1984.
[3] Figure in square brackets in sub-s (2)(*c*) substituted for the figure "£2,000" by virtue of Criminal Justice (Northern Ireland) Order, SI 1994/2795 art 3(1) with effect from a day to be appointed.
[4] Words in sub-s (5) inserted by F(No 2)A 1992 s 3 and Sch 2 para 9 with effect from 9 December 1992 by virtue of F(No 2)A 1992 (Commencement No 3) Order, SI 1992/3104.
[5] Sub-s (2A) repealed by Statute Law (Repeals) Act 1993 s 1(1), Sch 1 Pt XIV.
[6] Sub-s (4A) inserted by Commissioners for Revenue and Customs Act 2005 s 50, Sch 4 para 28 with effect from 18 April 2005 by virtue of the Commissioners for Revenue and Customs Act 2005 (Commencement) Order, SI 2005/1126, art 2(2).
[7] In sub-s (5) words substituted for words "the relevant time specified in section 43 above", and words substituted for words "as if the goods had been imported without entry at the time when the proceedings were commenced", by the Taxation (Cross-border Trade) Act 2018 s 29, Sch 7 paras 3, 115 with effect from IP completion day (11pm on 31 December 2020), by virtue of SI 2020/1642 reg 4(*a*).

SCHEDULES

[SCHEDULE 2A

SUPPLEMENTARY PROVISIONS RELATING TO THE DETENTION OF THINGS AS LIABLE TO FORFEITURE]

Section 139(5A)

Amendments—Schedule 2A inserted by FA 2013 s 226(7) with effect in relation to things detained on or after 17 July 2013.

[Interpretation

1 In this Schedule, references (however expressed) to a thing being detained are references to a thing being detained as liable to forfeiture under the customs and excise Acts.][1]

Amendments—[1] Schedule 2A inserted by FA 2013 s 226(7) with effect in relation to things detained on or after 17 July 2013.

[Period of detention

2—(1) This paragraph applies where a thing is detained.
(2) The thing may be detained for 30 days beginning with the day on which the thing is first detained.
(3) The thing is deemed to be seized as liable to forfeiture under the customs and excise Acts if its detention ceases to be authorised under this paragraph.][1]

Amendments—[1] Schedule 2A inserted by FA 2013 s 226(7) with effect in relation to things detained on or after 17 July 2013.

[Notice of detention

3—(1) The Commissioners must take reasonable steps to give written notice of the detention of any thing, and of the grounds for the detention, to any person who to their knowledge was, at the time of the detention, the owner or one of the owners of the thing.
(2) But notice need not be given under sub-paragraph (1) if the detention occurred in the presence of—
    (*a*) the person whose offence or suspected offence occasioned the detention,
    (*b*) the owner or any of the owners of the thing detained or any servant or agent of such an owner, . . . [2]

[(*ba*) a person who has (or appears to have) possession or control of the thing being detained,][2]
(*c*) in the case of any thing detained on [or from][2] a ship or aircraft, the master or commander[,or
(*d*) in the case of any thing detained on or from [any other vehicle, the vehicle operator][3].][2]][1]

Amendments—[1] Schedule 2A inserted by FA 2013 s 226(7) with effect in relation to things detained on or after 17 July 2013.
[2] In sub-para (2)(*b*), word "or" repealed, sub-para (2)(*ba*), (*d*) and preceding word inserted, and words in sub-para (2)(*c*) inserted, by FA 2016 s 175(1)–(3) with effect in relation to things detained or seized on or after 15 September 2016.
[3] In sub-para (2)(*d*), words substituted for words "a vehicle, the driver of the vehicle" by the Taxation (Cross-border Trade) Act 2018 s 29, Sch 7 paras 3, 117(1), (2) with effect from IP completion day (11pm on 31 December 2020), by virtue of SI 2020/1642 reg 4(*a*).

[Unauthorised removal or disposal: penalties etc

4—(1) This paragraph applies where a thing is detained and, with the agreement of a person within sub-paragraph (2) ("the responsible person"), the thing remains at the place where it is first detained (rather than being removed and detained elsewhere).
(2) A person is within this sub-paragraph if the person is—
[(*a*) the person whose offence or suspected offence occasioned the detention,
(*b*) the owner or any of the owners of the thing detained or any servant or agent of such an owner,
(*c*) a person who has (or appears to have) possession or control of the thing being detained,
(*d*) in the case of any thing detained on a ship or aircraft, the master or commander,
(*e*) in the case of any thing detained on [any other vehicle, the vehicle operator][3], or
(*f*) a person whom the person who detains the thing reasonably believes to be a person within any of paragraphs (*a*) to (*e*).][2]
(3) If the responsible person fails to prevent the unauthorised removal or disposal of the thing from the place where it is detained, that failure attracts a penalty under section 9 of the Finance Act 1994 (civil penalties).
(4) The removal or disposal of the thing is unauthorised unless it is done with the permission of a proper officer of Revenue and Customs.
(5) Where any duty of excise is payable in respect of the thing—
(*a*) the penalty is to be calculated by reference to the amount of that duty (whether it has been paid or not), and
(*b*) section 9 of the Finance Act 1994 has effect as if in subsection (2)(*a*) the words "5 per cent of" were omitted.
(6) If no duty of excise is payable in respect of the thing, that section has effect as if the penalty provided for by subsection (2)(*b*) of that section were whichever is the greater of—
(*a*) the value of the thing at the time it was first detained, or
(*b*) £250.][1]

Amendments—[1] Schedule 2A inserted by FA 2013 s 226(7) with effect in relation to things detained on or after 17 July 2013.
[2] Sub-para (2)(*a*)–(*f*) substituted for previous sub-para (2)(*a*), (*b*) by FA 2016 s 175(1), (4) with effect in relation to things detained or seized on or after 15 September 2016.
[3] In sub-para (2)(*e*), words substituted for words "a vehicle, the driver of the vehicle" by the Taxation (Cross-border Trade) Act 2018 s 29, Sch 7 paras 3, 117(1), (3) with effect from IP completion day (11pm on 31 December 2020), by virtue of SI 2020/1642 reg 4(*a*).

[**5**—(1) This paragraph applies where—
(*a*) a thing is detained at a revenue trader's premises,
(*b*) the thing is liable to forfeiture under the customs and excise Acts, and
(*c*) without the permission of a proper officer of Revenue and Customs, the thing is removed from the trader's premises, or otherwise disposed of, by any person.
(2) The Commissioners may seize, as liable to forfeiture under the customs and excise Acts, goods of equivalent value to the thing, from the revenue trader's stock.
(3) For the purposes of this paragraph, a revenue trader's premises include any premises used to hold or store anything for the purposes of the revenue trader's trade, regardless of who owns or occupies the premises.][1]

Amendments—[1] Schedule 2A inserted by FA 2013 s 226(7) with effect in relation to things detained on or after 17 July 2013.

SCHEDULE 3
PROVISIONS RELATING TO FORFEITURE
Sections 139, 143, 145

Notice of seizure

1—(1) The Commissioners shall, except as provided in sub-paragraph (2) below, give notice of the seizure of any thing as liable to forfeiture and of the grounds therefor to any person who to their knowledge was at the time of the seizure the owner or one of the owners thereof.

(2) Notice need not be given under this paragraph if the seizure was made in the presence of—
- (a) the person whose offence or suspected offence occasioned the seizure; or
- (b) the owner or any of the owners of the thing seized or any servant or agent of his; or
- [(ba) a person who has (or appears to have) possession or control of the thing being seized; or]²
- (c) in the case of any thing seized [on or from]² any ship or aircraft, the master or commander[; or
- (d) in the case of any thing seized on or from a vehicle, the driver of the vehicle.]²

2 Notice under paragraph 1 above shall be given in writing and shall be deemed to have been duly served on the person concerned—
- (a) if delivered to him personally; or
- (b) if addressed to him and left or forwarded by post to him at his usual or last known place of abode or business or, in the case of a body corporate, at their registered or principal office; or
- (c) where he has no address within the United Kingdom [or the Isle of Man]¹, or his address is unknown, by publication of notice of the seizure in the London, Edinburgh or Belfast Gazette.

Amendments—¹ Words in para 2(c) inserted by Isle of Man Act 1979 s 13 and Sch 1, para 23.
² Sub-para (2)(ba), (d) inserted, and in sub-para (2)(c), words substituted for word "in" by FA 2016 s 175(1), (5) with effect in relation to things detained or seized on or after 15 September 2016.

Notice of claim

3 Any person claiming that any thing seized as liable to forfeiture is not so liable shall, within one month of the date of the notice of seizure or, where no such notice has been served on him, within one month of the date of the seizure, give notice of his claim in writing to the Commissioners at any office of customs and excise.

4—(1) Any notice under paragraph 3 above shall specify the name and address of the claimant and, in the case of a claimant who is outside the United Kingdom [and the Isle of Man]¹, shall specify the name and address of a solicitor in the United Kingdom who is authorised to accept service of process and to act on behalf of the claimant.

(2) Service of process upon a solicitor so specified shall be deemed to be proper service upon the claimant.

Amendments—¹ Words in para 4(1) inserted by Isle of Man Act 1979 s 13 and Sch 1. para 24.

Condemnation

5 If on the expiration of the relevant period under paragraph 3 above for the giving of notice of claim in respect of any thing no such notice has been given to the Commissioners, or if, in the case of any such notice given, any requirement of paragraph 4 above is not complied with, the thing in question shall be deemed to have been duly condemned as forfeited.

6 Where notice of claim in respect of any thing is duly given in accordance with paragraphs 3 and 4 above, the Commissioners shall take proceedings for the condemnation of that thing by the court, and if the court finds that the thing was at the time of seizure liable to forfeiture the court shall condemn it as forfeited.

7 Where any thing is in accordance with either of paragraphs 5 or 6 above condemned or deemed to have been condemned as forfeited, then, without prejudice to any delivery up or sale of the thing by the Commissioners under paragraph 16 below, the forfeiture shall have effect as from the date when the liability to forfeiture arose.

Proceedings for condemnation by court

8 Proceedings for condemnation shall be civil proceedings and may be instituted—
- (a) in England or Wales either in the High Court or in a magistrates' court;
- (b) in Scotland either in the Court of Session or in the sheriff court;
- (c) in Northern Ireland either in the High Court or in a court of summary jurisdiction.

9 Proceedings for the condemnation of any thing instituted in a magistrates' court in England or Wales, in the sheriff court in Scotland or in a court of summary jurisdiction in Northern Ireland may be so instituted—
   (*a*) in any such court having jurisdiction in the place where any offence in connection with that thing was committed or where any proceedings for such an offence are instituted; or
   (*b*) in any such court having jurisdiction in the place where the claimant resides or, if the claimant has specified a solicitor under paragraph 4 above, in the place where that solicitor has his office; or
   (*c*) in any such court having jurisdiction in the place where that thing was found, detained or seized or to which it is first brought after being found, detained or seized.

10—(1) In any proceedings for condemnation instituted in England, Wales or Northern Ireland, the claimant or his solicitor shall make oath that the thing seized was, or was to the best of his knowledge and belief, the property of the claimant at the time of the seizure.
(2) In any such proceedings instituted in the High Court, the claimant shall give such security for the costs of the proceedings as may be determined by the Court.
(3) If any requirement of this paragraph is not complied with, the court shall give judgment for the Commissioners.

11—(1) In the case of any proceedings for condemnation instituted in a magistrates' court in England or Wales, without prejudice to any right to require the statement of a case for the opinion of the High Court, either party may appeal against the decision of that court to the Crown Court.
(2) In the case of any proceedings for condemnation instituted in a court of summary jurisdiction in Northern Ireland, without prejudice to any right to require the statement of a case for the opinion of the High Court, either party may appeal against the decision of that court to the county court.

12 Where an appeal, including an appeal by way of case stated, has been made against the decision of the court in any proceedings for the condemnation of any thing, that thing shall, pending the final determination of the matter, be left with the Commissioners or at any convenient office of customs and excise.

Provisions as to proof

13 In any proceedings arising out of the seizure of any thing, the fact, form and manner of the seizure shall be taken to have been as set forth in the process without any further evidence thereof, unless the contrary is proved.

14 In any proceedings, the condemnation by a court of any thing as forfeited may be proved by the production either of the order or certificate of condemnation or of a certified copy thereof purporting to be signed by an officer of the court by which the order or certificate was made or granted.

Special provisions as to certain claimants

15 For the purposes of any claim to, or proceedings for the condemnation of, any thing, where that thing is at the time of seizure the property of a body corporate, of two or more partners or of any number of persons exceeding five, the oath required by paragraph 10 above to be taken and any other thing required by this Schedule or by any rules of the court to be done by, or by any person authorised by, the claimant or owner may be taken or done by, or by any other person authorised by, the following persons respectively, that is to say—
   (*a*) where the owner is a body corporate, the secretary or some duly authorised officer of that body;
   (*b*) where the owners are in partnership, any one of those owners;
   (*c*) where the owners are any number of persons exceeding five not being in partnership, any two of those persons on behalf of themselves and their co-owners.

Power to deal with seizures before condemnation, etc

16 Where any thing has been seized as liable to forfeiture the Commissioners may at any time if they see fit and notwithstanding that the thing has not yet been condemned, or is not yet deemed to have been condemned, as forfeited—
   (*a*) deliver it up to any claimant upon his paying to the Commissioners such sum as they think proper, being a sum not exceeding that which in their opinion represents the value of the thing, including any duty or tax chargeable thereon which has not been paid;
   (*b*) if the thing seized is a living creature or is in the opinion of the Commissioners of a perishable nature, sell or destroy it.

17—(1) If, where any thing is delivered up, sold or destroyed under paragraph 16 above, it is held in proceedings taken under this Schedule that the thing was not liable to forfeiture at the time of its seizure, the Commissioners shall, subject to any deduction allowed under sub-paragraph (2) below, on demand by the claimant tender to him—
   (a) an amount equal to any sum paid by him under sub-paragraph (a) of that paragraph; or
   (b) where they have sold the thing, an amount equal to the proceeds of sale; or
   (c) where they have destroyed the thing, an amount equal to the market value of the thing at the time of its seizure.
(2) Where the amount to be tendered under sub-paragraph (1)(a), (b) or (c) above includes any sum on account of any duty or tax chargeable on the thing which had not been paid before its seizure the Commissioners may deduct so much of that amount as represents that duty or tax.
(3) If the claimant accepts any amount tendered to him under sub-paragraph (1) above, he shall not be entitled to maintain any action on account of the seizure, detention, sale or destruction of the thing.
(4) For the purposes of sub-paragraph (1)(c) above, the market value of any thing at the time of its seizure shall be taken to be such amount as the Commissioners and the claimant may agree or, in default of agreement, as may be determined by a referee appointed by the Lord Chancellor (not being an official of any government department [or an office-holder in, or a member of the staff of, the Scottish Administration][1]), whose decision shall be final and conclusive; and the procedure on any reference to a referee shall be such as may be determined by the referee.
[(5) The Lord Chancellor may make an appointment under sub-paragraph (4) only with the concurrence—
   (a) where the proceedings referred to in sub-paragraph (1) were taken in England and Wales, of the Lord Chief Justice of England and Wales;
   (b) where those proceedings were taken in Scotland, of the Lord President of the Court of Session;
(c) where those proceedings were taken in Northern Ireland, of the Lord Chief Justice of Northern Ireland.
(6) The Lord Chief Justice of England and Wales may nominate a judicial office holder (as defined in section 109(4) of the Constitutional Reform Act 2005) to exercise his functions under this paragraph.
(7) The Lord President of the Court of Session may nominate a judge of the Court of Session who is a member of the First or Second Division of the Inner House of that Court to exercise his functions under this paragraph.
(8) The Lord Chief Justice of Northern Ireland may nominate any of the following to exercise his functions under this paragraph—
   (a) the holder of one of the offices listed in Schedule 1 to the Justice (Northern Ireland) Act 2002;
   (b) a Lord Justice of Appeal (as defined in section 88 of that Act).][2]

Amendments—[1] Words in para (4) inserted by The Scotland Act 1998 (Consequential Modifications) (No 2) Order, SI 1999/1820 s 59, which comes into force on the "principle appointed day", currently 1 July 1999, by virtue of the Scotland Act 1998 (Commencement) Order 1998/3178.
[2] Sub-paras (5)–(8) inserted by the Constitutional Reform Act 2005 s 15, Sch 4 para 97 with effect from 3 April 2006 (by virtue of SI 2006/1014, art 2(a), Sch 1, para 11).

CUSTOMS AND EXCISE DUTIES (GENERAL RELIEFS) ACT 1979

(1979 Chapter 3)

. . . Reliefs from . . . excise duties

[7 Power to provide for reliefs from [excise] duty and value added tax in respect of imported legacies
(1) The Commissioners may by order make provision for conferring reliefs from [excise][2] duty and value added tax in respect of goods imported into the United Kingdom by or for any person who has become entitled to them as legatee.
(2) Any such relief may take the form either of an exemption from payment of [excise][2] duty and tax or of a provision whereby the sum payable by way of [excise][2] duty or tax is less than it would otherwise be.
(3) . . . [2]
(4) An order under this section—
   (a) may make any relief for which it provides . . . [2] subject to conditions, including conditions which are to be complied with after the importation of the goods to which the relief applies;
   (b) may, in relation to any relief conferred by order made under this section, contain such incidental and supplementary provisions as the Commissioners think necessary or expedient; and
   (c) may make different provision for different cases.

(5) In this section—

. . .[2]

[''excise duty'' means any duty of excise chargeable on goods and includes any addition to the duty by virtue of section 1 of the Excise Duties (Surcharges or Rebates) Act 1979;][2]

''legatee'' means any person taking under a testamentary disposition or donatio mortis causa or on an intestacy; and

''value added tax'' means value added tax chargeable on the importation of goods.][1]

Commentary—*De Voil Indirect Tax Service* **V3.341**.

Orders—See Customs and Excise Duties (Personal Reliefs for Goods Permanently Imported) Order, SI 1992/3193.

Amendments—[1] This section substituted by FA 1984 s 14(1), (3) with effect from 1 July 1984.

[2] In heading before s 7, words "miscellaneous" and "customs and" repealed, in heading to s 7 and in sub-ss (1), (2) words inserted , sub-s (3) repealed, in sub-s (4)(a) words "or any Community relief" repealed, and in sub-s (5) definition of "Community relief" repealed and definition of "excise duty" substituted for previous definition of "duty", by the Taxation (Cross-border Trade) Act 2018 s 29, Sch 7 paras 118, 124, 125 with effect from IP completion day (11pm on 31 December 2020), by virtue of SI 2020/1642 reg 4(a).

These amendments are subject to savings and modifications in relation to Northern Ireland. TCBTA 2018 Sch 7 para 158(4) preserves the continued application of this Act for various purposes as if these amendments had not been made and with certain modifications. These savings and modifications relate to the application of this Act for any purposes in connection with duty under the following provisions of TCBTA 2018—

– s 30A(3) (non-EU goods imported into the UK as a result of entry into Northern Ireland are subject to duty charged in accordance with Union customs legislation);
– s 40A (goods moving to Northern Ireland from Great Britain, that are not domestic goods or are 'at risk' of subsequently being moved into the EU are chargeable to customs duty in accordance with Union customs legislation).

Sub-s (3) previously read as follows—

"(3) The Commissioners may by order make provision supplementing any Community relief, in such manner as they think necessary or expedient.".

Definitions previously read as follows—

" "Community relief " means any relief which is conferred by a Community instrument and is of a kind, or of a kind similar to that, which could otherwise be conferred by order made under this section;

"duty" means customs or excise duty chargeable on goods imported into the United Kingdom and, in the case of excise duty, includes any addition to the duty by virtue of section 1 of the Excise Duties (Surcharges or Rebates) Act 1979;".

8 Relief from . . . excise duty on trade samples, labels, etc

The Commissioners may allow the delivery without payment of . . . [2] excise duty on importation, subject to such conditions and restrictions as they see fit—

(a) of trade samples of such goods as they see fit, whether imported as samples or drawn from the goods on their importation;

(b) of labels or other articles supplied without charge for the purpose of being re-exported with goods manufactured or produced in, and to be exported from, the United Kingdom [or the Isle of Man.][1]

Commentary—*De Voil Indirect Tax Service* **V3.342, 3.343**.

Amendments—[1] Words in para (b) inserted by Isle of Man Act 1979 s 13, Sch 1 para 26.

[2] In heading and in opening words, words "customs or" repealed, by the Taxation (Cross-border Trade) Act 2018 s 29, Sch 7 paras 118, 126 with effect from IP completion day (11pm on 31 December 2020), by virtue of SI 2020/1642 reg 4(a).

These amendments are subject to savings and modifications in relation to Northern Ireland. TCBTA 2018 Sch 7 para 158(4) preserves the continued application of this Act for various purposes as if these amendments had not been made and with certain modifications. These savings and modifications relate to the application of this Act for any purposes in connection with duty under the following provisions of TCBTA 2018—

– s 30A(3) (non-EU goods imported into the UK as a result of entry into Northern Ireland are subject to duty charged in accordance with Union customs legislation);
– s 40A (goods moving to Northern Ireland from Great Britain, that are not domestic goods or are 'at risk' of subsequently being moved into the EU are chargeable to customs duty in accordance with Union customs legislation).

9 Relief from . . . excise duty on antiques, prizes, etc

The Commissioners may allow the delivery without payment of . . . [1] excise duty on importation—

(a) of any goods (other than spirits or wine) which are proved to the satisfaction of the Commissioners to have been manufactured or produced more than 100 years before the date of importation;

(b) of articles which are shown to the satisfaction of the Commissioners to have been awarded abroad to any person for distinction in art, literature, science or sport, or for public service, or otherwise as a record of meritorious achievement or conduct, and to be imported by or on behalf of that person.

Commentary—*De Voil Indirect Tax Service* **V3.344**.

Amendments—[1] In heading and in opening words, words "customs or" repealed by the Taxation (Cross-border Trade) Act 2018 s 29, Sch 7 paras 118, 127 with effect from IP completion day (11pm on 31 December 2020), by virtue of SI 2020/1642 reg 4(a).

These amendments are subject to savings and modifications in relation to Northern Ireland. TCBTA 2018 Sch 7 para 158(4) preserves the continued application of this Act for various purposes as if these amendments had not been made and with certain modifications. These savings and modifications relate to the application of this Act for any purposes in connection with duty under the following provisions of TCBTA 2018—
- s 30A(3) (non-EU goods imported into the UK as a result of entry into Northern Ireland are subject to duty charged in accordance with Union customs legislation);
- s 40A (goods moving to Northern Ireland from Great Britain, that are not domestic goods or are 'at risk' of subsequently being moved into the EU are chargeable to customs duty in accordance with Union customs legislation).

Personal reliefs

13 Power to provide, in relation to persons entering the United Kingdom, for reliefs from [excise] duty and value added tax and for simplified computation of [excise] duty and tax

(1) The Commissioners may by order make provision for conferring on persons entering the United Kingdom reliefs from [excise]^7 duty and value added tax; and any such relief may take the form either of an exemption from payment of [excise]^7 duty and tax or of a provision whereby the sum payable by way of [excise]^7 duty or tax is less than it would otherwise be.

[(1A) The Commissioners may by order make provision supplementing any Community relief, in such manner as they think necessary or expedient.]^1

(2) Without prejudice to subsection (1) above, the Commissioners may by order make provision whereby, in such cases and to such extent as may be specified in the order, a sum calculated at a rate specified in the order is treated as the aggregate amount payable by way of [excise]^7 duty and tax in respect of goods imported by a person entering the United Kingdom; but any order making such provision shall enable the person concerned to elect that [excise]^7 duty and tax shall be charged on the goods in question at the rate which would be applicable apart from that provision.

(3) An order under this section—
   (a) may make any relief for which it provides, . . .^{7} subject to conditions, including conditions which are to be complied with after the importation of the goods to which the relief applies [and conditions with respect to the conduct in relation to the goods of persons other than the person on whom the relief is conferred and of persons whose identity cannot be ascertained at the time of importation]^2;
   (b) may [, in relation to any relief conferred by order made under this section,]^1 contain such incidental and supplementary provisions as the Commissioners think necessary or expedient, including [provisions requiring any person to whom a condition of the relief at any time relates to notify the Commissioners of any non-compliance with the condition and]^2 provisions for the forfeiture of goods in the event of non-compliance with any condition subject to which they have been relieved from [excise]^7 duty or tax; and
   (c) may make a different provision for different cases,

[(3A) An order under this section may provide, in relation to any relief which under such an order is made subject to a condition, for there to be a presumption that, in such cases as may be described in the order by reference—
   (a) to the quantity of goods in question; or
   (b) to any other factor which the Commissioners consider appropriate,
the condition is to be treated, unless the Commissioners are satisfied to the contrary, as not being complied with.]^3

[(3B) An order under this section may provide, in relation to any requirement of such an order for the Commissioners to be notified of non-compliance with a condition to which any relief from payment of any duty of excise is made subject, for goods to be exempt from forfeiture under section 124 of the Customs and Excise Management Act 1979 (forfeiture for breach of certain conditions) in respect of non-compliance with that condition if—
   (a) the non-compliance is notified to the Commissioners in accordance with that requirement;
   (b) any [excise]^7 duty which becomes payable on those goods by virtue of the non-compliance is paid; and
   (c) the circumstances are otherwise such as may be described in the order.]^3

[(3C) If any person fails to comply with any requirement of an order under this section to notify the Commissioners of any non-compliance with a condition to which any relief is made subject—
   (a) he shall be liable, on summary conviction, to a penalty of an amount not exceeding [£20,000]^5; and
   (b) the goods in respect of which the offence was committed shall be liable to forfeiture.]^3

(4) In this section—
   . . .^{7}
   ["conduct", in relation to any person who has or may acquire possession or control of any goods, includes that person's intentions at any time in relation to those goods;]^4
   ["excise duty" means any duty of excise chargeable on goods and includes any addition to excise duty by virtue of section 1 of the Excise Duties (Surcharges or Rebates) Act 1979;]^7
   "value added tax" or "tax" means value added tax chargeable on the importation of goods
   . . .^{6}

(5) Nothing in any order under this section shall be construed as authorising any person to import any thing in contravention of any prohibition or restriction for the time being in force with respect thereto under or by virtue of any enactment.
Commentary—*De Voil Indirect Tax Service* **V3.345, 3.346**.
Northern Ireland—See Sch 9ZA para 76 (Northern Ireland: this section has effect in relation to NI acquisition VAT as if, in sub-s (4), in definition of "value added tax" after "goods" there were inserted "or on the acquisition of goods from a member State").
Orders—See Customs and Excise Duties (Personal Reliefs for Goods Permanently Imported) Order, SI 1992/3193; Travellers' Allowances Order, SI 1994/955; Travellers' Reliefs (Fuel and Lubricants) Order, SI 1995/1777.
Cross reference—See the Travellers' Allowances and Miscellaneous Provisions (EU Exit) Regulations, SI 2020/1412 reg 9 (any reference in any provision made by or under any enactment to orders made under sub-s (1) is to be read as including a reference to any regulations made under TCBTA 2018 s 51 that grant relief from VAT or excise duty to persons entering the UK).
Amendments—
[1] Words in sub-s (3)(*a*), (*b*) inserted by FA 1984 s 15(1)–(5), (8) with effect from 31 March 1984.
[2] Words in sub-s (3)(*a*), (*b*) inserted by F(No 2)A 1992 s 1(8), Sch 1 para 8 with effect from 1 December 1992 by virtue of F(No 2)A 1992 (Commencement No 2 and Transitional Provisions) Order, SI 1992/2979 art 4 and Schedule, Pt II.
[3] Sub-ss (3A)–(3C) inserted by F(No 2)A 1992 s 1(8), Sch 1 para 8 with effect from 1 December 1992 by virtue of F(No 2)A 1992 (Commencement No 2 and Transitional Provisions) Order, SI 1992/2979 art 4 and Schedule, Pt II.
[4] Definition of "conduct" in sub-s (4) inserted by F(No 2)A 1992 s 1(8), Sch 1 para 8 with effect from 1 December 1992 by virtue of F(No 2)A 1992 (Commencement No 2 and Transitional Provisions) Order, SI 1992/2979 art 4 and Schedule, Pt II.
[5] In sub-s (3C)(*a*), figure substituted by the Legal Aid, Sentencing and Punishment of Offenders Act 2012 (Fines on Summary Conviction) Regulations, SI 2015/664 reg 2(2), Sch 2 para 2(1), (2) with effect from 12 March 2015 in relation to England and Wales only.
[6] In sub-s (4), in definition of "value added tax", words "from places outside the member States or on the acquisition of goods from member States other than the United Kingdom" repealed by the Taxation (Cross-border Trade) Act 2018 s 43, Sch 8 para 105 with effect from IP completion day (11pm on 31 December 2020), by virtue of SI 2020/1642 reg 4(*b*).
[7] The following amendments made by the Taxation (Cross-border Trade) Act 2018 s 29, Sch 7 paras 118, 131 with effect from IP completion day (11pm on 31 December 2020), by virtue of SI 2020/1642 reg 4(*a*)—
  – in heading, and in sub-ss (1), (2), (3), (3B)(*b*), words inserted;
  – sub-s (1A) repealed;
  – in sub-s (3)(*a*) words ", or any Community relief" repealed; and
  – in sub-s (4) definition of "Community relief" repealed, and definition of "excise duty" substituted for previous definition of "duty".
These amendments are subject to savings and modifications in relation to Northern Ireland. TCBTA 2018 Sch 7 para 158(4) preserves the continued application of this Act for various purposes as if these amendments had not been made and with certain modifications. These savings and modifications relate to the application of this Act for any purposes in connection with duty under the following provisions of TCBTA 2018—
  – s 30A(3) (non-EU goods imported into the UK as a result of entry into Northern Ireland are subject to duty charged in accordance with Union customs legislation);
  – s 40A (goods moving to Northern Ireland from Great Britain, that are not domestic goods or are 'at risk' of subsequently being moved into the EU are chargeable to customs duty in accordance with Union customs legislation).
Sub-s (1A) previously read as follows—
  "(1A) The Commissioners may by order make provision supplementing any Community relief, in such manner as they think necessary or expedient.".
Definitions previously read as follows—
  " "Community relief" means any relief which is conferred by a Community instrument and is of a kind, or of a kind similar to that, which could otherwise be conferred by order made under this section;".
  " "duty" means customs or excise duty chargeable on goods imported into the United Kingdom and, in the case of excise duty, includes any addition thereto by virtue of section 1 of the Excise Duties (Surcharges or Rebates) Act 1979;".

[13A Reliefs from duties and taxes for persons enjoying certain immunities and privileges

(1) The Commissioners may by order make provision for conferring in respect of any persons to whom this section applies reliefs, by way of remission or repayment, from payment by them or others of [any relevant levy, any duty of excise,][2] value added tax or car tax.
(2) An order under this section may make any relief for which it provides subject to such conditions binding the person in respect of whom the relief is conferred and, if different, the person liable apart from the relief for payment of the tax or duty (including conditions which are to be complied with after the time when, apart from the relief, the duty or tax would become payable) as may be imposed by or under the order.
(3) An order under this section may include any of the provisions mentioned in subsection (4) below for cases where—
  (*a*) relief from payment of [any relevant levy, any duty of excise,][2] value added tax or car tax chargeable on any goods, or on the supply of any goods or services or the importation of any goods has been conferred (whether by virtue of an order under this section or otherwise) in respect of any person to whom this section applies, and
  (*b*) any condition required to be complied with in connection with the relief is not complied with.
(4) The provisions referred to in subsection (3) above are—
  (*a*) provision for payment to the Commissioners of the tax or duty by—
    (i) the person liable, apart from the relief, for its payment, or
    (ii) any person bound by the condition, or

(iii) any person who is or has been in possession of the goods or has received the benefit of the services,

or for two or more of those persons to be jointly and severally liable for such payment, and
(b) in the case of goods, provision for forfeiture of the goods.
(5) An order under this section—
(a) may contain such incidental and supplementary provisions as the Commissioners think necessary or expedient, and
(b) may make different provision for different cases.
(6) In this section and section 13C of this Act—
["relevant levy" means][2] any agricultural levy within the meaning of section 6 of the European Communities Act 1972 chargeable on goods imported into the United Kingdom, and "duty of excise" means any duty of excise chargeable on goods and includes any addition to excise duty by virtue of section 1 of the Excise Duties (Surcharges or Rebates) Act 1979.
(7) For the purposes of this section and section 13C of this Act, where in respect of any person to whom this section applies relief is conferred (whether by virtue of an order under this section or otherwise) in relation to the use of goods by any persons or for any purposes, the relief is to be treated as conferred subject to a condition binding on him that the goods will be used only by those persons or for those purposes.
(8) Nothing in any order under this section shall be construed as authorising a person to import any thing in contravention of any prohibition or restriction for the time being in force with respect to it under or by virtue of any enactment.][1]

Commentary—*De Voil Indirect Tax Service* **V3.347**.
Orders—See Customs and Excise (Personal Reliefs for Special Visitors) Order, SI 1992/3156.
Amendments—[1] This section inserted by FA 1989 s 28(1).
[2] In sub-s (1) words substituted for words "duties of customs or excise," in sub-s (3)(a) words substituted for words "any duty of customs or excise," and in sub-s (6) words substituted for words ""duty of customs" includes", by the Taxation (Cross-border Trade) Act 2018 s 29, Sch 7 paras 118, 132 with effect from IP completion day (11pm on 31 December 2020), by virtue of SI 2020/1642 reg 4(a).
These amendments are subject to savings and modifications in relation to Northern Ireland. TCBTA 2018 Sch 7 para 158(4) preserves the continued application of this Act for various purposes as if these amendments had not been made and with certain modifications. These savings and modifications relate to the application of this Act for any purposes in connection with duty under the following provisions of TCBTA 2018—
- s 30A(3) (non-EU goods imported into the UK as a result of entry into Northern Ireland are subject to duty charged in accordance with Union customs legislation);
- s 40A (goods moving to Northern Ireland from Great Britain, that are not domestic goods or are 'at risk' of subsequently being moved into the EU are chargeable to customs duty in accordance with Union customs legislation).

[13B Persons to whom section 13A applies

(1) The persons to whom section 13A of this Act applies are—
(a) any person who, for the purposes of any provision of the Visiting Forces Act 1952 or the International Headquarters and Defence Organisations Act 1964 is—
(i) a member of a visiting force or of a civilian component of such a force or a dependant of such a member, or
(ii) a headquarters, a member of a headquarters or a dependant of such a member,
(b) any person enjoying any privileges or immunities under or by virtue of—
(i) the Diplomatic Privileges Act 1964
(ii) the Commonwealth Secretariat Act 1966
(iii) the Consular Relations Act 1968
(iv) the International Organisations Act 1968 or
[(v) the International Development Act 2002.][2]
(c) . . .[3]
(2) The Secretary of State may by order amend subsection (1) above to include any persons enjoying any privileges or immunities similar to those enjoyed under or by virtue of the enactments referred to in paragraph (b) of that subsection.
(3) No order shall be made under this section unless a draft of the order has been laid before and approved by resolution of each House of Parliament.][1]

Commentary—*De Voil Indirect Tax Service* **V3.347**.
Amendments—[1] This section inserted by FA 1989 s 28(1).
[2] In sub-s (1), para (b)(v) substituted by the International Development Act 2002 s 19, Sch 3 para 7 with effect from 17 June 2002 (by virtue of SI 2002/1408).
[3] Sub-s (1)(c) repealed by the Taxation (Cross-border Trade) Act 2018 s 29, Sch 7 paras 118, 133 with effect from IP completion day (11pm on 31 December 2020), by virtue of SI 2020/1642 reg 4(a).
These amendments are subject to savings and modifications in relation to Northern Ireland. TCBTA 2018 Sch 7 para 158(4) preserves the continued application of this Act for various purposes as if these amendments had not been made and with certain modifications. These savings and modifications relate to the application of this Act for any purposes in connection with duty under the following provisions of TCBTA 2018—

- s 30A(3) (non-EU goods imported into the UK as a result of entry into Northern Ireland are subject to duty charged in accordance with Union customs legislation);
- s 40A (goods moving to Northern Ireland from Great Britain, that are not domestic goods or are 'at risk' of subsequently being moved into the EU are chargeable to customs duty in accordance with Union customs legislation).

Sub-s (1)(c) previously read as follows—

"(c) any person enjoying, under or by virtue of section 2 of the European Communities Act 1972 any privileges or immunities similar to those enjoyed under or by virtue of the enactments referred to in paragraph (b) above.".

[13C Offence where relieved goods used, etc, in breach of condition

(1) Subsection (2) below applies where—
  (a) any relief from payment of [any relevant levy, any duty of excise,][4] value added tax or car tax chargeable on, or on the supply or importation of, any goods has been conferred (whether by virtue of an order under section 13A of this Act or otherwise) in respect of any person to whom that section applies subject to any condition as to the persons by whom or the purposes for which the goods may be used, and
  (b) if the tax or duty has subsequently become payable, it has not been paid.
(2) If any person—
  (a) acquires the goods for his own use, where he is not permitted by the condition to use them, or for use for a purpose that is not permitted by the condition or uses them for such a purpose, or
  (b) acquires the goods for use, or causes or permits them to be used, by a person not permitted by the condition to use them or by a person for a purpose that is not permitted by the condition or disposes of them to a person not permitted by the condition to use them,

with intent to evade payment or any tax or duty that has become payable or that, by reason of the disposal, acquisition or use, becomes or will become payable, he is guilty of an offence.

(3) For the purposes of this section—
  (a) in the case of a condition as to the persons by whom goods may be used, a person is not permitted by the condition to use them unless he is a person referred to in the condition as permitted to use them, and
  (b) in relation to a condition as to the purposes for which goods may be used, a purpose is not permitted by the condition unless it is a purpose referred to in the condition as a permitted purpose,

and in this section "dispose" includes "lend" and "let on hire", and "acquire" shall be interpreted accordingly.

(4) A person guilty of an offence under this section may be detained and shall be liable—
  (a) on summary conviction, to a penalty of [£20,000][3] or of three times the value of the goods (whichever is the greater), or to imprisonment for a term not exceeding six months, or to both, or
  (b) on conviction on indictment, to a penalty of any amount, or to imprisonment for a term not exceeding seven years, or to both.][1]

[(5) Where any person is guilty of an offence under this section, the goods in respect of which the offence was committed shall be liable to forfeiture.][2]

Commentary—*De Voil Indirect Tax Service* **V5.303**.

Amendments—[1] This section inserted by FA 1989 s 28(1), (2) and has effect where relief is conferred after 26 July 1989.

[2] Sub-s (5) added by F(No 2)A 1992 s 3, Sch 2 para 10 with effect from 9 December 1992 by virtue of F(No 2)A 1992 (Commencement No 3) Order, SI 1992/3104.

[3] In sub-s (4)(a), figure substituted by the Legal Aid, Sentencing and Punishment of Offenders Act 2012 (Fines on Summary Conviction) Regulations, SI 2015/664 reg 2(2), Sch 2 para 2(1), (3) with effect from 12 March 2015 in relation to England and Wales only.

[4] In sub-s (1)(a) words substituted for words "any duty of customs or excise," by the Taxation (Cross-border Trade) Act 2018 s 29, Sch 7 paras 118, 134 with effect from IP completion day (11pm on 31 December 2020), by virtue of SI 2020/1642 reg 4(a).

These amendments are subject to savings and modifications in relation to Northern Ireland. TCBTA 2018 Sch 7 para 158(4) preserves the continued application of this Act for various purposes as if these amendments had not been made and with certain modifications. These savings and modifications relate to the application of this Act for any purposes in connection with duty under the following provisions of TCBTA 2018—

- s 30A(3) (non-EU goods imported into the UK as a result of entry into Northern Ireland are subject to duty charged in accordance with Union customs legislation);
- s 40A (goods moving to Northern Ireland from Great Britain, that are not domestic goods or are 'at risk' of subsequently being moved into the EU are chargeable to customs duty in accordance with Union customs legislation).

VALUE ADDED TAX ACT 1994

(1994 Chapter 23)

ARRANGEMENT OF SECTIONS

PART I THE CHARGE TO TAX

Imposition and rate of VAT

1	Value added tax.
2	Rate of VAT.
3	Taxable persons and registration.
3A	Supplies of electronic, telecommunication and broadcasting services: special accounting schemes.

Supply of goods or services in the United Kingdom

4	Scope of VAT on taxable supplies.
5	Meaning of supply: alteration by Treasury order.
5A	Supplies of goods facilitated by online marketplaces: deemed supply.
6	Time of supply.
7	Place of supply of goods.
7AA	Reverse charge on goods supplied from abroad.
7A	Place of supply of services.
8	Reverse charge on supplies received from abroad.
9	Place where supplier or recipient of services belongs.
9A	Reverse charge on gas, electricity, heat or cooling supplied by persons outside the United Kingdom.

Acquisition of goods from member States

10	*Scope of VAT on acquisitions from member States.* (repealed)
11	*Meaning of acquisition of goods from another member State.*(repealed)
12	*Time of acquisition.* (repealed)
13	*Place of acquisition.*(repealed)
14	*Acquisitions from persons belonging in other member States.*(repealed)

Goods supplied between the UK and member States under call-off stock arrangements

14A	*Call-off stock arrangements.* (repealed)

Importation of goods...

15	Meaning of "importation of goods" into the United Kingdom
16	Application of customs enactments.
16A	Postal packets
17	Free zone regulations.

Goods subject to a warehousing regime

18	Place and time of... supply.
18A	Fiscal warehousing.
18B	Fiscally warehoused goods: relief.
18C	Warehouses and fiscal warehouses: services.
18D	Removal from warehousing: accountability.
18E	Deficiency in fiscally warehoused goods.
18F	Sections 18A to 18E: supplementary.

Determination of value

19	Value of supply of goods or services.
20	*Valuation of acquisitions from other member States.* (repealed)
21	Value of imported goods.
22	*Value of certain goods.* (repealed)
23	Value of supplies involving relevant machine games.
23A	Meaning of "relevant machine game"

Payment of VAT by taxable persons

24	Input tax and output tax.
25	Payment by reference to accounting periods and credit for input tax against output tax.
26	Input tax allowable under section 25.
26A	Disallowance of input tax where consideration not paid.
26AA	Disapplication of disallowance under section 26A in insolvency.
26AB	Adjustment of output tax in respect of supplies under section 55A.
26B	Flat-rate scheme.

27	Goods imported for private purposes.
28	Payments on account of VAT.
29	Invoices provided by recipients of goods or services.

PART II RELIEFS, EXEMPTIONS AND REPAYMENTS
Reliefs etc generally available

29A	Reduced rate.
30	Zero-rating.
31	Exempt supplies.
32	*Relief on supply of certain second-hand goods.* (repealed)
33	Refunds of VAT in certain cases.
33A	Refunds of VAT to museums and galleries.
33B	Refunds of VAT to academies.
33C	Refunds of VAT to charities within section 33D.
33D	Charities to which section 33C applies.
33E	Power to extend refunds of VAT to other persons.
34	Capital goods.
35	Refund of VAT to persons constructing certain buildings.
36	Bad debts.

Acquisitions

36A	*Relief from VAT on acquisition if importation would attract relief.*(repealed)

Imports, overseas businesses etc

37	Relief from VAT on importation of goods.
38	Importation of goods by taxable persons.
39	Repayment of VAT to those in business overseas.
39A	Applications for forwarding of VAT repayment claims to other member States.
40	*Refunds in relation to new means of transport supplied to other member States.* (repealed)

PART III APPLICATION OF ACT IN PARTICULAR CASES

40A	Northern Ireland Protocol.
41	Application to the Crown.
41A	Supply of goods or services by public bodies.
42	Local authorities.
43	Groups of companies.
43A	Groups: eligibility.
43AZA	Section 43A: control test.
43AA	Power to alter eligibility for grouping.
43B	Groups: applications.
43C	Groups: termination of membership.
43D	Groups: duplication.
44	Supplies to groups.
45	Partnerships.
46	Business carried on in divisions or by unincorporated bodies, personal representatives etc.
47	Agents etc.
48	VAT representatives and security.
49	Transfers of going concerns.
50	Terminal markets.
50A	Margin schemes.
51	Buildings and land.
51A	*Co-owners etc of buildings and land.* (repealed)
51B	Face-value vouchers issued before 1 January 2019.
51C	Vouchers issued on or after 1 January 2019.
51D	Postage stamps issued on or after 1 January 2019.
52	Trading stamp schemes.
53	Tour operators.
54	Farmers etc.
55	Customers to account for tax on supplies of gold etc.
55A	Customers to account for tax on supplies of goods or services of a kind used in missing trader... fraud.
56	*Fuel for private use.* (repealed)
57	*Determination of consideration for fuel supplied for private use.* (repealed)

PART IV ADMINISTRATION, COLLECTION AND ENFORCEMENT

General administrative provisions

58	General provisions relating to the administration and collection of VAT.

Disclosure of avoidance schemes

58ZA	International VAT arrangements.
58A	*Disclosure of avoidance schemes.* (repealed)
58B	Payment by cheque.

Default surcharges and other penalties and criminal offences

59	The default surcharge.
59A	Default surcharge: payments on account.
59B	Relationship between sections 59 and 59A.
60	VAT evasion: conduct involving dishonesty.
61	VAT evasion: liability of directors etc.
62	Incorrect certificates as to zero-rating etc.
63	*Penalty for misdeclaration or neglect resulting in VAT loss for one accounting period equalling or exceeding certain amounts.* (repealed)
64	*Repeated misdeclarations.* (repealed)
65	Inaccuracies in section 55A statements.
66	Failure to submit section 55A statement.
67	Failure to notify and unauthorised issue of invoices. (repealed)
68	Breaches of walking possession agreements.
69	Breaches of regulatory provisions.
69A	Breach of record-keeping requirements etc in relation to transactions in gold.
69B	Breach of record-keeping requirements imposed by directions.
69C	Penalty for transactions connected with VAT fraud etc.
69D	Penalties under section 69C: officers' liability.
69E	Publication of details of persons liable to penalties under section 69C.
70	Mitigation of penalties under sections 60, 63, 64, 67, 69A and 69C.
71	Construction of sections 59 to 70.
72	Offences.

Assessments of VAT and other payments due

73	Failure to make returns etc.
74	Interest on VAT recovered or recoverable by assessment.
75	*Assessments in cases of acquisitions of certain goods by non-taxable persons.* (repealed)
76	Assessment of amounts due by way of penalty, interest or surcharge.
76A	*Section 76: cases involving special accounting schemes.* (repealed)
77	*Assessments: time limits and supplementary assessments.* (repealed)

Liability for unpaid VAT of another

77A	Joint and several liability of traders in supply chain where tax unpaid.

Online marketplaces

77B	Joint and several liability: sellers identified as non-compliant by the Commissioners.
77BA	Joint and several liability: non-UK sellers in breach of Schedule 1A registration requirement.
77C	Joint and several liability under section 77B or 77BA: assessments.
77D	Joint and several liability under section 77B or 77BA: interest.
77E	Display of VAT registration numbers.
77F	Exception from liability under section 5A.

Interest, repayment supplements etc payable by Commissioners

78	Interest in certain cases of official error.
78A	Assessment for interest overpayments.
79	Repayment supplement in respect of certain delayed payments or refunds.
80	Credit for, or repayment of, overstated or overpaid VAT.
80A	Arrangements for reimbursing customers.
80B	Assessments of amounts due under section 80A arrangements.
81	Interest given by way of credit and set-off of credits.

PART V REVIEWS AND APPEALS

82	Meaning of "tribunal".
83	Appeals.
83A	Offer of review.

83B	Right to require review.
83C	Review by HMRC.
83D	Extensions of time.
83E	Review out of time.
83F	Nature of review.
83G	Bringing of appeals.
84	Further provisions relating to appeals.
85	Settling appeals by agreement.
85A	Payment of tax on determination of appeal
85B	Payment of tax where there is a further appeal
86	*Appeals to Court of Appeal.* (repealed)
87	*Enforcement of registered or recorded tribunal decisions etc.* (repealed)

PART VI SUPPLEMENTARY PROVISIONS

Change in rate of VAT etc and disclosure of information

88	Supplies spanning change of rate etc.
89	Adjustments of contracts on changes in VAT.
90	Failure of resolution under Provisional Collection of Taxes Act 1968.
91	Disclosure of information for statistical purposes.

Interpretative provisions

92	*Taxation under the laws of other member States etc.* (repealed)
93	*Territories included in references to other member States etc.* (repealed)
94	Meaning of "business" etc.
95	*Meaning of "new means of transport".* (repealed)
95A	Meaning of "online marketplace" and "operator" etc.
96	Other interpretative provisions.

Supplementary provisions

97	Orders, rules and regulations.
97A	Place of supply orders: transitional provision.
98	Service of notices.
99	Refund of VAT to Government of Northern Ireland.
100	Savings and transitional provisions, consequential amendments and repeals.
101	Commencement and extent.
102	Short title.

Schedules:
Schedule A1— *Charge at reduced rate.* (repealed)
Schedule 1— Registration in respect of taxable supplies: UK establishment.
Schedule 1A— Registration in respect of taxable supplies: non-UK establishment.
Schedule 2— *Registration in respect of supplies from other member States.* (repealed)
Schedule 3— *Registration in respect of acquisitions from other member States.* (repealed)
Schedule 3A— Registration in respect of disposals of assets for which a VAT repayment is claimed
Schedule 3B— *Electronic, telecommunication and broadcasting services: non-Union scheme.* (repealed)
Schedule 3BA— *Electronic, telecommunication and broadcasting services: Union scheme.* (repealed)
Schedule 4— Matters to be treated as supply of goods or services.
Schedule 4A— Place of Supply of Services: Special Rules.
Schedule 4B— Call-off stock arrangements
Schedule 5— Services supplied where received.
Schedule 5A— Goods eligible to be fiscally warehoused.
Schedule 6— Valuation: special cases.
Part I— Valuation of supplies of fuel for private use.
Part 2— Other provisions.
Schedule 7— *Valuation of acquisitions from other member States: special cases.* (repealed)
Schedule 7A— Charge at reduced rate
Schedule 8— Zero-rating.
Part I— Index to zero-rated supplies of goods and services.
Part II— The Groups.
Schedule 9— Exemptions.
Part I— Index to exempt supplies of goods and services.
Part II— The Groups.
Schedule 9ZA— VAT on acquisitions in Northern Ireland from member States.
Schedule 9ZB— Goods removed to or from Northern Ireland and supply rules.

Schedule 9ZC— Online sales by overseas persons and low value importations: modifications relating to the Northern Ireland Protocol
Schedule 9A— Anti-avoidance provisions: groups.
Schedule 10— Buildings and land.
Schedule 10A— Face-value vouchers issued before 1 January 2019.
Schedule 10B— VAT treatment of vouchers issued on or after 1 January 2019.
Schedule 11— Administration, collection and enforcement.
Schedule 11A— Disclosure of avoidance schemes. (repealed)
Schedule 12— Constitution and procedure of tribunals. (repealed)
Schedule 13— Transitional provisions and savings.
Schedule 14— Consequential amendments.
Schedule 15— Repeals. (not printed)

PART I
THE CHARGE TO TAX

Imposition and rate of VAT

1 Value added tax
(1) Value added tax shall be charged, in accordance with the provisions of this Act—
  (*a*) on the supply of goods or services in the United Kingdom (including anything treated as such a supply),
  (*b*) . . . [1] and
  [(*c*) on the importation of goods into the United Kingdom,][2]
and references in this Act to VAT are references to value added tax.
(2) VAT on any supply of goods or services is a liability of the person making the supply and (subject to provisions about accounting and payment) becomes due at the time of supply.
(3) . . . [3]
(4) VAT on the importation of goods [into the United Kingdom][3] shall be charged and payable as if it were [import duty][3].

Commentary—*De Voil Indirect Tax Service* **V3.101, V3.301**.
HMRC Manuals—VAT Single Market VATSM3315 (main UK primary law provisions).
Northern Ireland—See Sch 9ZA below (VAT on acquisitions in Northern Ireland from member States).
Amendments—[1] In sub-s (1)(*b*) repealed by the Taxation (Cross-border Trade) Act 2018 s 41(1), (2) with effect from IP completion day (11pm on 31 December 2020), by virtue of SI 2020/1642 reg 4(*b*). Sub-s (1)(*b*) previously read as follows—
  "(*b*) on the acquisition in the United Kingdom from other member States of any goods, and".
[2] Sub-s (1)(*c*) substituted by the Taxation (Cross-border Trade) Act 2018 s 41(1), (2)(*b*) with effect from IP completion day (11pm on 31 December 2020), by virtue of SI 2020/1642 reg 4(*b*). This amendment had effect from 28 January 2018 (by virtue of SI 2019/104 reg 2) to the extent that it related to, and for the purpose of, the interpretation of the definition of "import VAT" in the Value Added Tax (Postal Packets and Amendment) (EU Exit) Regulations 2018/1376 reg 2. SI 2018/1376 was revoked by SI 2020/1495 reg 26(*a*) with effect from 11pm on 31 December 2020.
  Sub-s (1)(*c*) previously read as follows—
  "(*c*) on the importation of goods from places outside the member States,".
[3] Sub-s (3) repealed, and in sub-s (4) words substituted for words "from places outside the member States", and words "a duty of customs", by the Taxation (Cross-border Trade) Act 2018 s 43, Sch 8 paras 1, 2 with effect from IP completion day (11pm on 31 December 2020), by virtue of SI 2020/1642 reg 4(*b*). Sub-s (3) previously read as follows—
  "(3) VAT on any acquisition of goods from another member State is a liability of the person who acquires the goods and (subject to provisions about accounting and payment) becomes due at the time of acquisition.".

2 Rate of VAT
(1) Subject to the following provisions of this section [and to the provisions of section 29A[2]] . . . [1], VAT shall be charged at the rate of [20 per cent][5] and shall be charged—
  (*a*) on the supply of goods or services, by reference to the value of the supply as determined under this Act; and
  (*b*) . . . [6]
  (*c*) on the importation of goods . . . [6], by reference to the value of the goods as determined under this Act.
(1A)–(1C) . . . [2],
(2) The Treasury may by order increase or decrease the rate of VAT for the time being in force [under this section][3] by such percentage thereof not exceeding 25 per cent as may be specified in the order, but any such order [that has not previously expired or been revoked][4] shall cease to be in force at the expiration of a period of one year from the date on which it takes effect, unless continued in force by a further order under this subsection.
(3) In relation to an order made under subsection (2) above to continue, vary or replace a previous order, the reference in that subsection to the rate for the time being in force [under this section][3] is a reference to the rate which would be in force if no order under that subsection had been made.

Commentary—*De Voil Indirect Tax Service* **V1.121, V131, V3.151**.
Northern Ireland—See Sch 9ZA para 35 (Northern Ireland: supplies spanning change of rate).
Amendments—[1] Words omitted from sub-s (1) repealed by FA 1995 s 21(2), (6), with effect in relation to any supply made after 31 March 1995 and any acquisition or importation taking place after that date.

² Words in sub-s (1) inserted, and sub-s (1A), (1B) repealed by FA 2001 s 99(2), (3) with effect for supplies made, and acquisitions and importations taking place, after 31 October 2001. Sub-s (1C) repealed by FA 2001 s 99(2), (3) with effect from 1 November 2001.
³ Words in sub-ss (2), (3) inserted by FA 2001 s 99(6), Sch 31 para 2 with effect for orders under sub-s (2) that make changes only in the rate of VAT that is in force at times after 31 October 2001.
⁴ Words in sub-s (2) inserted by FA 2009 Sch 3 para 25(2) with effect from 21 July 2009.
⁵ In sub-s (1), words substituted for words "17.5 per cent" by F(No 2)A 2010 s 3(1) with effect in relation to any supply made on or after 4 January 2011 and any acquisition or importation taking place on or after that date.
⁶ In sub-s (1), para (b), and in para (c) words "from a place outside the member States", repealed, by the Taxation (Cross-border Trade) Act 2018 s 43, Sch 8 paras 1, 3 with effect from IP completion day (11pm on 31 December 2020), by virtue of SI 2020/1642 reg 4(b).

Those paras previously read as follows—
"(b) on the acquisition of goods from another member State, by reference to the value of the acquisition as determined under this Act; and
(c) on the importation of goods from a place outside the member States, by reference to the value of the goods as determined under this Act.".

3 Taxable persons and registration

(1) A person is a taxable person for the purposes of this Act while he is, or is required to be, registered under this Act.
(2) [Schedules 1 to 3A]¹ shall have effect with respect to registration [(and see also Parts 8 and 9 of Schedule 9ZA which contain further provisions about registration)]².
(3) Persons registered under any of those Schedules [and Part 8 and 9 of Schedule 9ZA]² shall be registered in a single register kept by the Commissioners for the purposes of this Act; and, accordingly, references in this Act to being registered under this Act are references to being registered under any of those Schedules [or those Parts]².
(4) The Commissioners may by regulations make provision as to the inclusion and correction of information in that register with respect to the Schedule under which any person is registered.

Commentary—*De Voil Indirect Tax Service* **V2.101**.
HMRC VAT Manuals—VAT Taxable Person Manual VTAXPER22000 (scope and legal basis of VAT: defining and identifying the taxable person).
VAT Registration Manual VATREG02150 (meaning of taxable person).
Regulations—See VAT Regulations, SI 1995/2518 regs 5–7.
VAT (Amendment) (No 2) Regulations, SI 2012/1899.
Cross-references—See the Value Added Tax (Disclosure of Information Relating to VAT Registration) (EU Exit) Regulations, SI 2018/1228 (HMRC may, in response to an enquiry about a VAT registration number, disclose whether or not the number is a VAT registration number allocated to a person registered in the UK's VAT register and, if it is, disclose that person's name and address). Those Regulations came into force on 1 December 2020 (by virtue of SI 2020/1333 reg 2).
Amendments—¹ Words in sub-s (2) substituted by FA 2000 s 136(1), with effect for supplies made after 20 March 2000.
² In sub-ss (2), (3) words inserted by the Taxation (Post-transition Period) Act 2020 s 3, Sch 2 para 3 with effect from IP completion day (11pm on 31 December 2020), by virtue of SI 2020/1642 reg 9.

[3A [Supplies of electronic, telecommunication and broadcasting services: special accounting schemes]

(1) Schedule 3B (scheme enabling persons who supply electronically supplied services[, telecommunication services or broadcasting services]³ in any member State, but who are not established in a member State, to account for and pay VAT in the United Kingdom on those supplies) has effect.
[(1A) Schedule 3BA—
  (a) establishes a special accounting scheme for use by persons established in the UK and supplying electronically supplied services, telecommunication services or broadcasting services in other member States, and
  (b) makes provision about corresponding schemes in other member States.]³
(2) The Treasury may by order amend Schedule 3B [or 3BA]².
(3) The power of the Treasury by order to amend [Schedules 3B and 3BA]² includes power to make such incidental, supplemental, consequential and transitional provision in connection with any amendment of that Schedule as they think fit.]¹, ⁴

Amendments—¹ This section inserted by FA 2003 s 23, Sch 2 paras 1, 2 in relation to qualifying supplies made after 30 June 2003, see FA 2003 s 23(2).
² In sub-s (2), words inserted, and in sub-s (3), words substituted for words "Schedule 3B", by FA 2014 s 103, Sch 22 para 2 with effect in relation to supplies made on or after 1 January 2015.
³ In sub-s (1), words inserted, sub-s (1A) inserted, and in section heading words substituted for words "Supply of electronic services in member States: special accounting scheme" by FA 2014 s 103, Sch 22 paras 11, 12 with effect in relation to supplies made on or after 1 January 2015.
⁴ Section 3A repealed by the Taxation (Cross-border Trade) Act 2018 s 43, Sch 8 paras 1, 4 with effect from IP completion day (11pm on 31 December 2020), by virtue of SI 2020/1642 reg 4(b).

Supply of goods or services in the United Kingdom

4 Scope of VAT on taxable supplies
(1) VAT shall be charged on any supply of goods or services made in the United Kingdom, where it is a taxable supply made by a taxable person in the course or furtherance of any business carried on by him.
(2) A taxable supply is a supply of goods or services made in the United Kingdom other than an exempt supply.
Commentary—*De Voil Indirect Tax Service* **V3.122, V3.131, V3.421**.
HMRC Manuals—VAT Business/Non-Business Manual VBNB14000 (scope of VAT on taxable supplies).
VAT Place of Supply Of Service VATPOSS01200 (introduction: background to the rules).

5 Meaning of supply: alteration by Treasury order
(1) Schedule 4 shall apply for determining what is, or is to be treated as, a supply of goods or a supply of services.
(2) Subject to any provision made by that Schedule and to Treasury orders under subsections (3) to (6) below—
   (*a*) "supply" in this Act includes all forms of supply, but not anything done otherwise than for a consideration;
   (*b*) anything which is not a supply of goods but is done for a consideration (including, if so done, the granting, assignment or surrender of any right) is a supply of services.
(3) The Treasury may by order provide with respect to any description of transaction—
   (*a*) that it is to be treated as a supply of goods and not as a supply of services; or
   (*b*) that it is to be treated as a supply of services and not as a supply of goods; or
   (*c*) that it is to be treated as neither a supply of goods nor a supply of services;
and without prejudice to the foregoing, such an order may further provide that paragraph 5(4) of Schedule 4 is not to apply, in relation to goods of any prescribed description used or made available for use in prescribed circumstances, so as to make that a supply of services under that paragraph . . . [1]
[(3A) An order under subsection (3) may provide that paragraph 30 of Schedule 9ZB does not apply, in such circumstances as may be described in the order, so as to make a removal of assets a supply of goods under that paragraph.][2]
(4) Without prejudice to subsection (3) above, the Treasury may by order make provision for securing, with respect to services of any description specified in the order, that where—
   (*a*) a person carrying on a business does anything which is not a supply of services but would, if done for a consideration, be a supply of services of a description specified in the order; and
   (*b*) such other conditions as may be specified in the order are satisfied,
such services are treated for the purposes of this Act as being supplied by him in the course or furtherance of that business.
(5) The Treasury may by order make provision for securing, subject to any exceptions provided for by or under the order, that where in such circumstances as may be specified in the order goods of a description so specified are taken possession of or produced by a person in the course or furtherance of a business carried on by him and—
   (*a*) are neither supplied to another person nor incorporated in other goods produced in the course or furtherance of that business; but
   (*b*) are used by him for the purpose of a business carried on by him,
the goods are treated for the purposes of this Act as being both supplied to him for the purpose of that business and supplied by him in the course or furtherance of it.
(6) The Treasury may by order make provision for securing, with respect to services of any description specified in the order, that where—
   (*a*) a person, in the course or furtherance of a business carried on by him, does anything for the purpose of that business which is not a supply of services but would, if done for a consideration, be a supply of services of a description specified in the order; and
   (*b*) such other conditions as may be specified in the order are satisfied,
such services are treated for the purposes of this Act as being both supplied to him for the purpose of that business and supplied by him in the course or furtherance of it.
(7) For the purposes of this section, where goods are manufactured or produced from any other goods, those other goods shall be treated as incorporated in the first-mentioned goods.
(8) An order under subsection (4) or (6) above may provide for the method by which the value of any supply of services which is treated as taking place by virtue of the order is to be calculated.
Commentary—*De Voil Indirect Tax Service* **V3.102, V3.111, V3.114**.
HMRC Manuals—VAT Supply And Consideration VATSC03510 (supply of services).
Orders—See VAT (Treatment of Transactions) (No 1) Order, SI 1973/325; VAT (Treatment of Transactions) Order, SI 1986/896; VAT (Tour Operators) Order, SI 1987/1806; VAT (Self-supply of Construction Services) Order, SI 1989/472; VAT (Water) Order, SI 1989/1114; VAT (Treatment of Transactions) Order, SI 1992/630; VAT (Removal of Goods) Order, SI 1992/3111; VAT (Cars) Order, SI 1992/3122; VAT (Supply of Temporarily Imported Goods) Order, SI 1992/3130; VAT (Supply of Services) Order, SI 1993/1507; VAT (Treatment of Transactions) Order, SI 1995/958; VAT (Special Provisions) Order, SI 1995/1268; VAT

(Fiscal Warehousing) (Treatment of Transactions) Order, SI 1996/1255; VAT (Removal of Gas, Electricity, Heat and Cooling) Order, SI 2010/2925; VAT (Removal of Goods) (Amendment) Order, SI 2012/2953.

Amendments—[1] In sub-s (3), words "and may provide that paragraph 6 of that Schedule shall not apply, in such circumstances as may be described in the order, so as to make a removal of assets a supply of goods under that paragraph." revoked by the Taxation (Cross-border Trade) Act 2018 s 43, Sch 8 paras 1, 5 with effect from IP completion day (11pm on 31 December 2020), by virtue of SI 2020/1642 reg 4(*b*).

[2] Sub-s (3A) inserted by the Taxation (Post-transition Period) Act 2020 s 3, Sch 2 para 4. The Act came into force generally on IP completion day (11pm UK time on 31 December 2020, by virtue of SI 2020/1642 reg 9), but from 17 December 2020 in relation to making provision for anything to be done by regulations or order (see s 11(1)).

[5A Supplies of goods facilitated by online marketplaces: deemed supply

(1) This section applies where—
- (*a*) a person ("P") makes a taxable supply of goods in the course or furtherance of a business to another person ("R"),
- (*b*) that supply is facilitated by an online marketplace, and
- [(*c*) one of the following applies—
    - (i) the imported consignment condition is met, or
    - (ii) the supply of goods to R does not involve those goods being imported, but P is established outside the United Kingdom.][2]

[(1A) But this section does not apply in a case where P is established outside the United Kingdom and the imported consignment condition is not met if—
- (*a*) R is registered under this Act,
- (*b*) R has provided the operator of the online marketplace with R's VAT registration number, and
- (*c*) the operator of the online marketplace has provided P with that number and details of the supply before the end of the relevant period.][2]

(2) For the purposes of this Act—
- (*a*) P is to be treated as having supplied the goods to the operator of the online marketplace, and
- (*b*) the operator is to be treated as having supplied the goods to R in the course or furtherance of a business carried on by the operator.

(3) The imported consignment condition is met where—
- (*a*) the supply of the goods to R involves those goods being imported,
- (*b*) the intrinsic value of the consignment of which the goods are part is not more than £135, and
- (*c*) the consignment of which the goods are part—
    - (i) does not contain excepted goods, and
    - (ii) is not a consignment in relation to which a postal operator established outside the United Kingdom has an obligation under an agreement with the Commissioners to pay any import VAT that is chargeable on the importation of that consignment into the United Kingdom.

(4) For the purposes of subsection (3)(*c*)(i), "excepted goods" means goods of a class or description subject to any duty of excise whether or not those goods are in fact chargeable with that duty, and whether or not that duty has been paid on the goods.

(5) The Commissioners may by regulations[—
- (*a*) specify the details that must be provided for the purposes of subsection (1A)(*c*);
- (*b*)] [2] substitute a different figure for a figure that is at any time specified in subsection (3)(*b*).

[(6) In this section—
"relevant period" means the period of 7 days beginning with the day on which the supply is treated as taking place under section 6 or such longer period as the Commissioners may allow in general or specific directions;
"VAT registration number" means the number allocated by the Commissioners to a person registered under this Act.][2]][1]

Commentary—*De Voil Indirect Tax Service* **V1.308**.
HMRC Manuals—VAT Supplies In Warehouse And Fiscal Warehousing VWRHS5400 (goods eligible to be fiscally warehoused).
Northern Ireland—See VATA 1994 Sch 9ZC para 1(*a*) (online sales by overseas persons and low value importations: modifications relating to the Northern Ireland Protocol): references in sub-s (3) to goods being imported do not include goods imported into the UK as a result of their entry into Northern Ireland or goods treated as having been imported into the UK as a result of their being removed from Northern Ireland to Great Britain.
See also VATA 1994 Sch 9ZC para 1A (this section is modified to cover cases where the goods are located in Great Britain at the point of sale but where the seller is established outside the UK, as follows:
as if in sub-s (1)(*c*)(ii) after "outside the United Kingdom" there were inserted "and prior to the supply the goods were located in Great Britain".''
Cross-references—See s 77F below (liability of operators of online marketplaces for VAT in cases of deemed supply: exception from liability under s 5A).
Amendments—[1] Section 5A inserted by the Taxation (Post-transition Period) Act 2020 s 7, Sch 3 paras 1, 2 with effect from IP completion day (11pm on 31 December 2020), by virtue of SI 2020/1642 reg 9.
[2] Sub-s (1)(*c*) substituted, sub-ss (1A), (6) inserted, and in sub-s (5) words inserted, by the Taxation (Post-transition Period) Act 2020 s 7, Sch 3 paras 1, 3 with effect from IP completion day (11pm on 31 December 2020), by virtue of SI 2020/1642 reg 9.

6 Time of supply

(1) The provisions of this section shall apply, subject to [sections 18, 18B and 18C][1], for determining the time when a supply of goods or services is to be treated as taking place for the purposes of the charge to VAT.

(2) Subject to subsections (4) to (14) below, a supply of goods shall be treated as taking place—
 (a) if the goods are to be removed, at the time of the removal;
 (b) if the goods are not to be removed, at the time when they are made available to the person to whom they are supplied;
 (c) if the goods (being sent or taken on approval or sale or return or similar terms) are removed before it is known whether a supply will take place, at the time when it becomes certain that the supply has taken place or, if sooner, 12 months after the removal.

(3) Subject to subsections (4) to (14) below, a supply of services shall be treated as taking place at the time when the services are performed.

(4) If, before the time applicable under subsection (2) or (3) above, the person making the supply issues a VAT invoice in respect of it or if, before the time applicable under subsection (2)(a) or (b) or (3) above, he receives a payment in respect of it, the supply shall, to the extent covered by the invoice or payment, be treated as taking place at the time the invoice is issued or the payment is received.

(5) If, within 14 days after the time applicable under subsection (2) or (3) above, the person making the supply issues a VAT invoice in respect of it, then, unless he has notified the Commissioners in writing that he elects not to avail himself of this subsection, the supply shall (to the extent that it is not treated as taking place at the time mentioned in subsection (4) above) be treated as taking place at the time the invoice is issued.

(6) The Commissioners may, at the request of a taxable person, direct that subsection (5) above shall apply in relation to supplies made by him (or such supplies made by him as may be specified in the direction) as if for the period of 14 days there were substituted such longer period as may be specified in the direction.

(7), (8) . . .[5]

(9) . . .[3]

(10) The Commissioners may, at the request of a taxable person, by direction alter the time at which supplies made by him (or such supplies made by him as may be specified in the direction) are to be treated as taking place, either—
 (a) by directing those supplies to be treated as taking place—
  (i) at times or on dates determined by or by reference to the occurrence of some event described in the direction; or
  (ii) at times or on dates determined by or by reference to the time when some event so described would in the ordinary course of events occur,
  the resulting times or dates being in every case earlier than would otherwise apply; or
 (b) by directing that, notwithstanding subsections (5) and (6) above, those supplies shall (to the extent that they are not treated as taking place at the time mentioned in subsection (4) above) be treated as taking place—
  (i) at the beginning of the relevant working period (as defined in his case in and for the purposes of the direction); or
  (ii) at the end of the relevant working period (as so defined).

(11) Where goods are treated as supplied by an order under section 5(5), the supply is treated as taking place when they are appropriated to the use mentioned in that section.

(12) Where there is a supply of goods by virtue only of paragraph 5(1) of Schedule 4, the supply is treated as taking place when the goods are transferred or disposed of as mentioned in that paragraph.

(13) Where there is a supply of services by virtue only of paragraph 5(4) of Schedule 4, the supply is treated as taking place when the goods are appropriated to the use mentioned in that paragraph.

(14) The Commissioners may by regulations make provision with respect to the time at which (notwithstanding [subsections (2) to (6)][5] and (11) to (13) above or section 55(4)) a supply is to be treated as taking place in cases where—
 (a) it is a supply of goods or services for a consideration the whole or part of which is determined or payable periodically, or from time to time, or at the end of any period, or
 (b) it is a supply of goods for a consideration the whole or part of which is determined at the time when the goods are appropriated for any purpose, or
 (c) there is a supply to which section 55 applies, or
 (d) there is a supply of services by virtue of paragraph 5(4) of Schedule 4 or an order under section 5(4);

and for any such case as is mentioned in this subsection the regulations may provide for goods or services to be treated as separately and successively supplied at prescribed times or intervals.

[(14A) . . . ,[4] This section and any regulations under this section or section 8(4) shall have effect subject to section 97A.][2]

(15) In this Act "VAT invoice" means such an invoice as is required under [paragraph 2A]³ of Schedule 11, or would be so required if the person to whom the supply is made were a person to whom such an invoice should be issued.

Commentary—*De Voil Indirect Tax Service* **V3.131, V3.134, V3.135**.
HMRC Manuals—VAT Time Of Supply VATTOS2200 (UK primary law (VAT Act 1994)).
Northern Ireland—See VATA 1994 Sch 9ZB para 28: time of supply rules: where any supply of goods involves both the removal of the goods from Northern Ireland and their acquisition in a member State by a person who is liable for VAT on the acquisition in accordance with provisions of the law of that member State corresponding, in relation to that member State, to the provisions of Sch 9ZB para 2 (valuation of goods imported into UK as a result of their entry into NI), sub-ss (2), (4)–(6) and (10)–(12) of this section do not apply and the supply is treated for the purposes of this Act as taking place on whichever is the earlier of the following days—
- the 15th day of the month following that in which the removal in question takes place; and
- the day of the issue, in respect of the supply, of a VAT invoice or of an invoice of such other description as the Commissioners may by regulations prescribe.

Sub-s (14) is accordingly modified to have effect as if after "section 55(4)" there were inserted "or paragraph 28 of Schedule 9ZB" (Sch 9ZB para 28(3)).
Regulations—See VAT Regulations, SI 1995/2518 regs 81, 84–86, 88–95.
VAT (Amendment) (No 3) Regulations, SI 2012/2951.
Amendments—¹ Words in sub-s (1) substituted by FA 1996 Sch 3 para 1 with effect in relation to any supply taking place on or after 1 June 1996; see Finance Act 1996, Section 26, (Appointed Day) Order, SI 1996/1249.
² Sub-s (14A) inserted by FA 1998 s 22 with effect from 17 March 1998.
³ Sub-s (9) repealed, and in sub-s (15), words substituted by FA 2002 ss 24(1)(a), (4)(a), (5), 139, Sch 40 Pt 2(2) with effect from 1 December 2003 (by virtue of SI 2003/3043).
⁴ In sub-s (14A) words "In relation to any services of a description specified in an order under section 7(11)" repealed by FA 2009 s 76, Sch 36 para 2 with effect from 1 January 2010.
⁵ Sub-ss (7), (8) repealed, and in sub-s (14) words substituted for words "subsections (2) to (8)", by the Taxation (Cross-border Trade) Act 2018 s 43, Sch 8 paras 1, 6 with effect from IP completion day (11pm on 31 December 2020), by virtue of SI 2020/1642 reg 4(*b*).
Sub-ss (7), (8) previously read as follows—
"(7) Where any supply of goods involves both—
  (*a*) the removal of the goods from the United Kingdom; and
  (*b*) their acquisition in another member State by a person who is liable for VAT on the acquisition in accordance with provisions of the law of that member State corresponding, in relation to that member State, to the provisions of section 10,
subsections (2), (4) to (6) and (10) to (12) of this section shall not apply and the supply shall be treated for the purposes of this Act as taking place on whichever is the earlier of the days specified in subsection (8) below.
(8) The days mentioned in subsection (7) above are—
  (*a*) the 15th day of the month following that in which the removal in question takes place; and
  (*b*) the day of the issue, in respect of the supply, of a VAT invoice or of an invoice of such other description as the Commissioners may by regulations prescribe.".

7 Place of supply [of goods]

(1) This section shall apply (subject to [sections . . . ³ 18 and 18B]¹) for determining, for the purposes of this Act, whether goods . . . ² are supplied in the United Kingdom.
(2) Subject to the following provisions of this section, if the supply of any goods does not involve their removal from or to the United Kingdom they shall be treated as supplied in the United Kingdom if they are in the United Kingdom and otherwise shall be treated as supplied outside the United Kingdom.
(3) Goods shall be treated—
  (*a*) as supplied in the United Kingdom where their supply involves their installation or assembly at a place in the United Kingdom to which they are removed; and
  (*b*) as supplied outside the United Kingdom where their supply involves their installation or assembly at a place outside the United Kingdom to which they are removed.
(4), (5) . . . ³
[(5A) Goods whose place of supply is not determined under any of the preceding provisions of this section shall be treated as supplied outside the United Kingdom where the supply—
  (*a*) meets the imported consignment condition in section 5A; and
  (*b*) is deemed to be to the operator of an online marketplace.
(5B) Goods whose place of supply is not determined under any of the preceding provisions of this section shall be treated as supplied in the United Kingdom where—
  (*a*) they are supplied by a person in the course or furtherance of a business carried on by that person;
  (*b*) the supply involves the goods being imported;
  (*c*) the intrinsic value of the consignment of which the goods are part is not more than £135; and
  (*d*) the consignment of which the goods are part—
    (i) does not contain goods of a class or description subject to any duty of excise whether or not those goods are in fact chargeable with that duty, and whether or not that duty has been paid on the goods; and

(ii) is not a consignment in relation to which a postal operator established outside the United Kingdom has an obligation under an agreement with the Commissioners to pay any import VAT that is chargeable on the importation of that consignment into the United Kingdom.]⁴

(6) Goods whose place of supply is not determined under any of the preceding provisions of this section shall be treated as supplied in the United Kingdom where—
  (a) their supply involves their being imported . . . ³; and
  (b) the person who supplies them is the person by whom, or under whose directions, they are so imported.

(7) Goods whose place of supply is not determined under any of the preceding provisions of this section but whose supply involves their removal to or from the United Kingdom shall be treated—
  (a) as supplied in the United Kingdom where their supply involves their removal from the United Kingdom without also involving their previous removal to the United Kingdom; and
  (b) as supplied outside the United Kingdom in any other case.

(8) For the purposes of the preceding provisions of this section, where goods, in the course of their removal from a place in the United Kingdom to another place in the United Kingdom, leave and re-enter the United Kingdom the removal shall not be treated as a removal from or to the United Kingdom.

(9) . . . ³

[(9A) The Commissioners may by regulations substitute a different figure for a figure that is at any time specified in subsection (5B)(c).]⁴

(10) . . . ²

(11) The Treasury may by order provide, in relation to goods . . . ² generally or to particular goods . . . ² specified in the order, for varying the rules for determining where a supply of goods . . . ² is made.

[(12) The Commissioners may by regulations provide that any rule for determining where a supply of goods is made is subject to such conditions relating to the notification of matters to the Commissioners, or such other conditions, as may be specified in the regulations.]³

Commentary—*De Voil Indirect Tax Service* **V3.172, V3.173, V3.186**.
HMRC Manuals—VAT Place of Supply (Goods) VATPOSG3200 (scope of VATA 1994 s 7).
VATPOSG3600–VATPOSG3700 (imported and exported goods).
Northern Ireland—See VATA 1994 Sch 9ZB para 29: place of supply of goods: reinstatement of EU-wide distance-selling rules in respect of goods sold by businesses based in Northern Ireland to non-business customers in member States, and by businesses in the EU to non-business customers in Northern Ireland.
Section 7 has effect accordingly as if the references in subsections (5A) to (7) to "the preceding provisions of this section" included Sch 9ZB para 29(1), (2), as follows—
  "(1) Goods whose place of supply is not determined under subsection (2) or (3) of section 7 (place of supply of goods) are treated as supplied in the United Kingdom where—
    (a) the supply involves the removal of the goods to Northern Ireland by or under the directions of the person who supplies them,
    (b) the supply is a transaction in pursuance of which the goods are acquired in Northern Ireland from a member State by a person who is not a taxable person,
    (c) the supplier—
      (i) is liable to be registered under Part 9 of Schedule 9ZA, or
      (ii) would be so liable if the supplier were not already registered under this Act or liable to be registered under Schedule 1 or 1A, and
    (d) the supply is neither a supply of goods consisting in a new means of transport nor anything which is treated as a supply for the purposes of this Act by virtue only of paragraph 5(1) of Schedule 4 or paragraph 30 of Schedule 9ZB.
  (2) Goods whose place of supply is not determined under sub-paragraph (1) or subsection (2) or (3) of section 7 and which do not consist in a new means of transport are treated as supplied outside the United Kingdom where—
    (a) the supply involves the removal of the goods from Northern Ireland, by or under the directions of the person who supplies them, to a member State,
    (b) the person who makes the supply is taxable in a member State, and
    (c) provisions of the law of that member State corresponding, in relation to that member State, to the provisions made by sub-paragraph (1) make that person liable to VAT on the supply.".
See VATA 1994 Sch 9ZC para 1(b) (online sales by overseas persons and low value importations: modifications relating to the Northern Ireland Protocol): reference in sub-s (5B)(b) to goods being imported does not include goods imported into the UK as a result of their entry into Northern Ireland or goods treated as having been imported into the UK as a result of their being removed from Northern Ireland to Great Britain.
Regulations—See VAT Regulations, SI 1995/2518 reg 98.
Orders—See VAT (Tour Operators) Order, SI 1987/1806; VAT (Place of Supply of Services) Order, SI 1992/3121; VAT (Place of Supply of Goods) (Amendment) Order, SI 2010/2923.
Value Added Tax (Place of Supply of Goods) (Amendment) Order, SI 2019/1507.
Amendments—¹ Words in sub-s (1) substituted by FA 1996 Sch 3 para 2, with effect in relation to any supply taking place on or after 1 June 1996; see Finance Act 1996, Section 26, (Appointed Day) Order, SI 1996/1249.
² Words inserted in heading, and words "or services" in sub-ss (1), (11) and whole of sub-s (10) repealed, by FA 2009 s 76, Sch 36 paras 1, 3 with effect in relation to supplies made on or after 1 January 2010.

[3] In sub-s (1) reference "14" repealed, sub-ss (4), (5), (9) repealed, in sub-s (6)(*a*) words "from a place outside the member States" repealed, and sub-s (12) inserted, by the Taxation (Cross-border Trade) Act 2018 s 43, Sch 8 paras 1, 7 with effect from IP completion day (11pm on 31 December 2020), by virtue of SI 2020/1642 reg 4(*b*).

Sub-ss (4), (5), (9) previously read as follows—

"(4) Goods whose place of supply is not determined under any of the preceding provisions of this section shall be treated as supplied in the United Kingdom where—

(*a*) the supply involves the removal of the goods to the United Kingdom by or under the directions of the person who supplies them;

(*b*) the supply is a transaction in pursuance of which the goods are acquired in the United Kingdom from another member State by a person who is not a taxable person;

(*c*) the supplier—
  (i) is liable to be registered under Schedule 2; or
  (ii) would be so liable if he were not already registered under this Act or liable to be registered under Schedule 1 or 1A; and

(*d*) the supply is neither a supply of goods consisting in a new means of transport nor anything which is treated as a supply for the purposes of this Act by virtue only of paragraph 5(1) or 6 of Schedule 4.

(5) Goods whose place of supply is not determined under any of the preceding provisions of this section and which do not consist in a new means of transport shall be treated as supplied outside the United Kingdom where—

(*a*) the supply involves the removal of the goods, by or under the directions of the person who supplies them, to another member State;

(*b*) the person who makes the supply is taxable in another member State; and

(*c*) provisions of the law of that member State corresponding, in relation to that member State, to the provisions made by subsection (4) above make that person liable to VAT on the supply;

but this subsection shall not apply in relation to any supply in a case where the liability mentioned in paragraph (c) above depends on the exercise by any person of an option in the United Kingdom corresponding to such an option as is mentioned in paragraph 1(2) of Schedule 2 unless that person has given, and has not withdrawn, a notification to the Commissioners that he wishes his supplies to be treated as taking place outside the United Kingdom where they are supplies in relation to which the other requirements of this subsection are satisfied.".

"(9) The Commissioners may by regulations provide that a notification for the purposes of subsection (5) above is not to be given or withdrawn except in such circumstances, and in such form and manner, as may be prescribed.".

[4] Sub-ss (5A), (5B), (9A) inserted by the Taxation (Post-transition Period) Act 2020 s 7, Sch 3 paras 1, 4 with effect from IP completion day (11pm on 31 December 2020), by virtue of SI 2020/1642 reg 9.

[7AA Reverse charge on goods supplied from abroad

(1) This section applies where—
  (*a*) goods are supplied by a person ("A") to another person ("B"),
  (*b*) B is registered under this Act,
  (*c*) the supply involves the goods being imported,
  (*d*) the intrinsic value of the consignment of which the goods are part is not more than £135, and
  (*e*) the consignment of which the goods are part—
    (i) does not contain goods of a class or description subject to any duty of excise whether or not those goods are in fact chargeable with that duty, and whether or not that duty has been paid on the goods, and
    (ii) is not a consignment in relation to which a postal operator established outside the United Kingdom has an obligation under an agreement with the Commissioners to pay any import VAT that is chargeable on the importation of that consignment into the United Kingdom.

(2) This Act has effect as if, instead of there being a supply of the goods by A to B—
  (*a*) there were a supply of the goods by B in the course of furtherance of a business carried on by B, and
  (*b*) that supply were a taxable supply.

(3) The Commissioners may by regulations substitute a different figure for a figure that is at any time specified in subsection (1)(*d*).][1]

Commentary—*De Voil Indirect Tax Service* V1.308.

Northern Ireland—See VATA 1994 Sch 9ZC para 1(*c*) (online sales by overseas persons and low value importations: modifications relating to the Northern Ireland Protocol): reference in sub-s (1)(*c*) to goods being imported does not include goods imported into the UK as a result of their entry into Northern Ireland or goods treated as having been imported into the UK as a result of their being removed from Northern Ireland to Great Britain.

Amendments—[1] Section 7AA inserted by the Taxation (Post-transition Period) Act 2020 s 7, Sch 3 paras 1, 5 with effect from IP completion day (11pm on 31 December 2020), by virtue of SI 2020/1642 reg 9.

[7A Place of supply of services

(1) This section applies for determining, for the purposes of this Act, the country in which services are supplied.

(2) A supply of services is to be treated as made—
  (*a*) in a case in which the person to whom the services are supplied is a relevant business person, in the country in which the recipient belongs, and
  (*b*) otherwise, in the country in which the supplier belongs.

(3) The place of supply of a right to services is the same as that in which the supply of the services would be treated as made if made by the supplier of the right to the recipient of the right (whether or not the right is exercised); and for this purpose a right to services includes any right, option or priority with respect to the supply of services and an interest deriving from a right to services.
[(4) For the purposes of this Act a person is a relevant business person in relation to a supply of services if—
 (a) the person carries on a business, and
 (b) the services are not received by the person wholly for private purposes,
whether or not the services are received in the course of business.]²
(5) Subsection (2) has effect subject to Schedule 4A.
(6) The Treasury may by order—
 (a) amend subsection (4),
 (b) amend Schedule 4A, or
 (c) otherwise make provision for exceptions from either or both of the paragraphs of subsection (2).
(7) An order under subsection (6) may include incidental, supplemental, consequential and transitional provision.]¹

Commentary—*De Voil Indirect Tax Service* **V3.182, V3.186**.
HMRC Manuals—VAT Place Of Supply Of Service VATPOSS01000 (place of supply of services: introduction).
Orders—VAT (Exceptions Relating to Supplies not Made to Relevant Business Person) Order, SI 2010/3017.
VAT (Place of Supply of Services) (Transport of Goods) Order, SI 2012/2787.
VAT (Place of Supply of Services) (Exceptions Relating to Supplies Not Made to Relevant Business Person) Order, SI 2014/2726.
Value Added Tax (Place of Supply of Services: Exceptions Relating to Supplies Made to Relevant Business Person) Order, SI 2016/726.
Value Added Tax (Place of Supply of Services) (Telecommunication Services) Order, SI 2017/778.
Value Added Tax (Place of Supply of Services) (Supplies of Electronic, Telecommunication and Broadcasting Services) Order, SI 2018/1194.
Value Added Tax (Place of Supply of Services) (Supplies of Electronic, Telecommunication and Broadcasting Services) (Amendment and Revocation) (EU Exit) Order, SI 2019/404.
Amendments—¹ Section 7A inserted by FA 2009 s 76, Sch 3 paras 1, 4 with effect in relation to supplies made on or after 1 January 2010, except the powers contained in sub-s (6) which may be exercised at any time from 21 July 2009.
² Sub-s (4) substituted by the Taxation (Cross-border Trade) Act 2018 s 43, Sch 8 paras 1, 8 with effect from IP completion day (11pm on 31 December 2020), by virtue of SI 2020/1642 reg 4(b). Note that, where these amendments remove a reference to the principal VAT Directive (2006/112/EC) or the Implementing VAT Regulation ((EU) No 282/2011), the removal is not to be taken as implying that the Directive or Regulation is no longer relevant for determining the meaning and effect of this section (Taxation (Cross-border Trade) Act 2018 Sch 8 para 99).
Sub-s (4) previously read as follows—
 "(4) For the purposes of this Act a person is a relevant business person in relation to a supply of services if the person—
 (a) is a taxable person within the meaning of Article 9 of Council Directive 2006/112/EC,
 (b) is registered under this Act,
 (c) is identified for the purposes of VAT in accordance with the law of a member State other than the United Kingdom, or
 (d) is registered under an Act of Tynwald for the purposes of any tax imposed by or under an Act of Tynwald which corresponds to value added tax,
and the services are received by the person otherwise than wholly for private purposes.".

8 Reverse charge on supplies received from abroad

[(1) Where services are supplied by a person who belongs in a country other than the United Kingdom in circumstances in which this subsection applies, this Act has effect as if (instead of there being a supply of the services by that person)—
 (a) there were a supply of the services by the recipient in the United Kingdom in the course or furtherance of a business carried on by the recipient, and
 (b) that supply were a taxable supply.
(2) Subsection (1) above applies if—
 (a) the recipient is a relevant business person who belongs in the United Kingdom, and
 (b) the place of supply of the services is inside the United Kingdom,
and, where the supply of the services is one to which any paragraph of Part 1 or 2 of Schedule 4A applies, the recipient is registered under this Act.]²
(3) Supplies which are treated as made by the recipient under subsection (1) above are not to be taken into account as supplies made by him when determining any allowance of input tax in his case under section 26(1).
(4) In applying subsection (1) above, the supply of services treated as made by the recipient shall be assumed to have been made at a time to be determined in accordance with regulations prescribing rules for attributing a time of supply in cases within that subsection.
[(4A) Subsection (1) does not apply to services of any of the descriptions specified in Schedule 9.]²
(5) The Treasury may by order [amend subsection (4A) by altering the descriptions of services specified in that subsection]².
(6) . . . ²

[(7) The power of the Treasury by order to [amend subsection (4A)]² shall include power to make such incidental, supplemental, consequential and transitional provision in connection with any [amendment of that subsection]² as they think fit.]¹

[(8) Without prejudice to the generality of subsection (7) above, the provision that may be made under that subsection includes—
  (a) provision making such modifications of section 43(2A) to (2E) as the Treasury may think fit in connection with any [amendment of subsection (4A)]²; and
  (b) provision modifying the effect of any regulations under subsection (4) above in relation to any services added to [that subsection]².]¹

Commentary—*De Voil Indirect Tax Service* **V3.231**.
HMRC Manuals—VAT Place Of Supply Of Service VATPOSS14200 (reverse charge). VATPOSS14300 (examples).
Regulations—See VAT Regulations, SI 1995/2518 reg 82.
VAT (Reverse Charge) (Anti-avoidance) Order, SI 1997/1523.
Amendments—¹ Sub-s (7) and (8) inserted by FA 1997 s 42 with effect from 19 March 1997.
² Sub-ss (1), (2), words "add to or vary Schedule 5" in sub-ss (5), (7), "addition to or variation of that Schedule" in sub-ss (7), (8)(a), "the Schedule" in sub-s (8)(b) substituted, sub-s (4A) inserted and sub-s (6) repealed, by FA 2009 s 76, Sch 36 paras 1, 5 with effect in relation to supplies made on or after 1 January 2010.

[9 Place where supplier or recipient of services belongs
(1) This section has effect for determining for the purposes of section 7A (or Schedule 4A) or section 8, in relation to any supply of services, whether a person who is the supplier or recipient belongs in one country or another.
(2) A person who is a relevant business person is to be treated as belonging in the relevant country.
(3) In subsection (2) "the relevant country" means—
  (a) if the person has a business establishment, or some other fixed establishment, in a country (and none in any other country), that country,
  (b) if the person has a business establishment, or some other fixed establishment or establishments, in more than one country, the country in which the relevant establishment is, and
  (c) otherwise, the country in which the person's usual place of residence [or permanent address]² is.
(4) In subsection (3)(b) "relevant establishment" means whichever of the person's business establishment, or other fixed establishments, is most directly concerned with the supply.
(5) A person who is not a relevant business person is to be treated as [belonging—
  (a) in the country in which the person's usual place of residence or permanent address is (except in the case of a body corporate or other legal person);
  (b) in the case of a body corporate or other legal person, in the country in which the place where it is established is.]²
[(6) . . . ³]¹

Commentary—*De Voil Indirect Tax Service* **V3.182**.
HMRC Manuals—VAT Place Of Supply Of Service VATPOSS04000 (place of supply of services: belonging).
Amendments—¹ Section substituted by FA 2009 s 76, Sch 36 paras 1, 6 with effect in relation to supplies made on or after 1 January 2010.
² In sub-s (3)(c), words inserted, and in sub-s (5), words substituted, by FA 2014 s 104 with effect in relation to supplies made on or after 1 January 2015.
³ Sub-s (6) repealed by the Taxation (Cross-border Trade) Act 2018 s 43, Sch 8 paras 1, 9 with effect from IP completion day (11pm on 31 December 2020), by virtue of SI 2020/1642 reg 4(b).
  Sub-s (6) previously read as follows—
    "(6) The reference in subsection (5)(b) to the place where a body corporate or other legal person "is established" is to be read in accordance with Article 13a of Implementing Regulation (EU) No 282/2011 (which is inserted by Council Implementing Regulation (EU) No 1042/2013).".

[9A Reverse charge on gas[, electricity, heat or cooling] . . .
(1) This section applies if relevant goods are supplied—
  (a) by a person who is outside the United Kingdom,
  (b) to a person who is registered under this Act,
for the purposes of any business carried on by the recipient.
[(1A) This section also applies if relevant goods are supplied by a person ("A") to another person ("B") for the purposes of any business carried on by B and—
  (a) A is in Great Britain and B is registered under this Act and is identified for the purposes of VAT in Northern Ireland, or
  (b) A is in Northern Ireland and B is so registered but is not so identified.]⁴
(2) The same consequences follow under this Act (and particularly so much as charges VAT on a supply and entitles a taxable person to credit for input tax) as if—
  (a) the recipient had himself supplied the relevant goods in the course or furtherance of his business, and
  (b) that supply were a taxable supply.

(3) But supplies which are treated as made by the recipient under subsection (2) are not to be taken into account as supplies made by him when determining any allowance of input tax in his case under section 26(1).
(4) In applying subsection (2) the supply of relevant goods treated as made by the recipient shall be assumed to have been made at a time to be determined in accordance with regulations prescribing rules for attributing a time of supply in cases to which this section applies.
[(5) "Relevant goods" means—
 (a) gas supplied through a natural gas system [in [Great Britain]⁴]³ or any network connected to [a natural gas system in [Great Britain]²]³,
 [(aa) gas supplied through a natural gas system situated within Northern Ireland or the territory of a member State or any network connected to such a system,]⁴
 (b) electricity, and
 (c) heat or cooling supplied through a network.]²
(6) Whether a person is outside the United Kingdom[, in Great Britain or in Northern Ireland]⁴ is to be determined in accordance with an order made by the Treasury.]¹

Commentary—*De Voil Indirect Tax Service* **V3.232**.
HMRC Manuals—VAT Place of Supply (Goods) VATPOSG5700 (gas and electricity: reverse charge).
Northern Ireland—The reference in sub-s (1A) to a person identified for the purposes of VAT in Northern Ireland includes a registered person who is not so identified but who undertakes a business activity from a place in Northern Ireland (see SI 2020/1546 reg 31).
Amendments—¹ This section inserted by FA 2004 s 21 with effect for supplies made after 31 December 2004.
² Sub-s (5) substituted, and words in heading substituted for words "and electricity", by F(No 3)A 2010 s 20(1) with effect in relation to supplies made on or after 1 January 2011.
³ In sub-s (5)(a), words substituted for words "situated within the territory of a member State" and "such a system" by the Taxation (Cross-border Trade) Act 2018 s 43, Sch 8 paras 1, 10 with effect from IP completion day (11pm on 31 December 2020), by virtue of SI 2020/1642 reg 4(b).
⁴ In the heading, words "supplied by persons outside the United Kingdom" repealed, sub-s (1A) inserted, in sub-para (5)(a) words substituted for words "the United Kingdom" in both places, sub-para (5)(aa) inserted, and in sub-s (6) words inserted, by the Taxation (Post-transition Period) Act 2020 s 3, Sch 2 para 5 with effect from IP completion day (11pm on 31 December 2020), by virtue of SI 2020/1642 reg 9.

Acquisition of goods from member States

Northern Ireland—See Sch 9ZA below (VAT on acquisitions in Northern Ireland from member States).

10 Scope of VAT on acquisitions from member States
(1) VAT shall be charged on any acquisition from another member State of any goods where—
 (a) the acquisition is a taxable acquisition and takes place in the United Kingdom;
 (b) the acquisition is otherwise than in pursuance of a taxable supply; and
 (c) the person who makes the acquisition is a taxable person or the goods are subject to a duty of excise or consist in a new means of transport.
(2) An acquisition of goods from another member State is a taxable acquisition if—
 (a) it falls within subsection (3) below or the goods consist in a new means of transport; and
 (b) it is not an exempt acquisition.
(3) An acquisition of goods from another member State falls within this subsection if—
 (a) the goods are acquired in the course or furtherance of—
  (i) any business carried on by any person; or
  (ii) any activities carried on otherwise than by way of business by any body corporate or by any club, association, organisation or other unincorporated body;
 (b) it is the person who carries on that business or, as the case may be, those activities who acquires the goods; and
 (c) the supplier—
  (i) is taxable in another member State at the time of the transaction in pursuance of which the goods are acquired; and
  *(ii) in participating in that transaction, acts in the course or furtherance of a business carried on by him.*¹

Northern Ireland—See Sch 9ZA para 2 below (scope of NI acquisition VAT).
Amendments—¹ Sections 10–14 and preceding heading repealed by the Taxation (Cross-border Trade) Act 2018 s 43, Sch 8 paras 1, 11 with effect from IP completion day (11pm on 31 December 2020), by virtue of SI 2020/1642 reg 4(b).

11 Meaning of acquisition of goods from another member State
(1) Subject to the following provisions of this section, references in this Act to the acquisition of goods from another member State shall be construed as references to any acquisition of goods in pursuance of a transaction in relation to which the following conditions are satisfied, that is to say—
 (a) the transaction is a supply of goods (including anything treated for the purposes of this Act as a supply of goods); and
 (b) the transaction involves the removal of the goods from another member State;
and references in this Act, in relation to such an acquisition, to the supplier shall be construed accordingly.

(2) It shall be immaterial for the purposes of subsection (1) above whether the removal of the goods from the other member State is by or under the directions of the supplier or by or under the directions of the person who acquires them or any other person.
(3) Where the person with the property in any goods does not change in consequence of anything which is treated for the purposes of this Act as a supply of goods, that supply shall be treated for the purposes of this Act as a transaction in pursuance of which there is an acquisition of goods by the person making it.
(4) The Treasury may by order provide with respect to any description of transaction that the acquisition of goods in pursuance of a transaction of that description is not to be treated for the purposes of this Act as the acquisition of goods from another member State.[1]

Commentary—*De Voil Indirect Tax Service* **V2.181**.
Northern Ireland—See Sch 9ZA para 3 below (Northern Ireland: meaning of acquisition of goods from a member State).
Orders—See VAT (Treatment of Transactions) (No 2) Order, SI 1992/3132; VAT (Special Provisions) Order, SI 1995/1268.
Amendments—[1] Sections 10–14 and preceding heading repealed by the Taxation (Cross-border Trade) Act 2018 s 43, Sch 8 paras 1, 11 with effect from IP completion day (11pm on 31 December 2020), by virtue of SI 2020/1642 reg 4(*b*).

12 Time of acquisition

(1) Subject to [sections 18 and 18B][1] and any regulations under subsection (3) below, where goods are acquired from another member State, the acquisition shall be treated for the purposes of this Act as taking place on whichever is the earlier of—
   (a) the 15th day of the month following that in which the event occurs which, in relation to that acquisition, is the first relevant event for the purposes of taxing the acquisition; and
   (b) the day of the issue, in respect of the transaction in pursuance of which the goods are acquired, of an invoice of such a description as the Commissioners may by regulations prescribe.
(2) For the purposes of this Act the event which, in relation to any acquisition of goods from another member State, is the first relevant event for the purposes of taxing the acquisition is the first removal of the goods which is involved in the transaction in pursuance of which they are acquired.
(3) The Commissioners may by regulations make provision with respect to the time at which an acquisition is to be treated as taking place in prescribed cases where the whole or part of any consideration comprised in the transaction in pursuance of which the goods are acquired is determined or payable periodically, or from time to time, or at the end of a period; and any such regulations may provide, in relation to any case to which they apply, for goods to be treated as separately and successively acquired at prescribed times or intervals.[2]

Commentary—*De Voil Indirect Tax Service* **V3.388**.
Northern Ireland—See Sch 9ZA para 4 below (Northern Ireland: time of acquisition).
Regulations—See VAT Regulations, SI 1995/2518 regs 83, 87.
VAT (Amendment) (No 3) Regulations, SI 2012/2951.
Amendments—[1] Words in sub-s (1) substituted by FA 1996 Sch 3 para 3, with effect in relation to any acquisition of goods from another member State taking place on or after 1 June 1996; see Finance Act 1996, Section 26, (Appointed Day) Order, SI 1996/1249.
[2] Sections 10–14 and preceding heading repealed by the Taxation (Cross-border Trade) Act 2018 s 43, Sch 8 paras 1, 11 with effect from IP completion day (11pm on 31 December 2020), by virtue of SI 2020/1642 reg 4(*b*).

13 Place of acquisition

(1) This section shall apply (subject to [sections 18 and 18B][1]) for determining for the purposes of this Act whether goods acquired from another member State are acquired in the United Kingdom.
(2) The goods shall be treated as acquired in the United Kingdom if they are acquired in pursuance of a transaction which involves their removal to the United Kingdom and does not involve their removal from the United Kingdom, and (subject to the following provisions of this section) shall otherwise be treated as acquired outside the United Kingdom.
(3) Subject to subsection (4) below, the goods shall be treated as acquired in the United Kingdom if they are acquired by a person who, for the purposes of their acquisition, makes use of a number assigned to him for the purposes of VAT in the United Kingdom.
(4) Subsection (3) above shall not require any goods to be treated as acquired in the United Kingdom where it is established, in accordance with regulations made by the Commissioners for the purposes of this section that VAT—
   (a) has been paid in another member State on the acquisition of those goods; and
   (b) fell to be paid by virtue of provisions of the law of that member State corresponding, in relation to that member State, to the provision made by subsection (2) above.
(5) The Commissioners may by regulations make provision for the purposes of this section—
   (a) for the circumstances in which a person is to be treated as having been assigned a number for the purposes of VAT in the United Kingdom;
   (b) for the circumstances in which a person is to be treated as having made use of such a number for the purposes of the acquisition of any goods; and
   (c) for the refund, in prescribed circumstances, of VAT paid in the United Kingdom on acquisitions of goods in relation to which the conditions specified in subsection (4)(a) and (b) above are satisfied.[2]

Northern Ireland—See Sch 9ZA para 5 below (Northern Ireland: place of acquisition).
Amendments—[1] Words in sub-s (1) substituted by FA 1996 Sch 3 para 4, with effect in relation to any acquisition of goods from another member State taking place on or after 1 June 1996; see Finance Act 1996, Section 26, (Appointed Day) Order, SI 1996/1249.
[2] Sections 10–14 and preceding heading repealed by the Taxation (Cross-border Trade) Act 2018 s 43, Sch 8 paras 1, 11 with effect from IP completion day (11pm on 31 December 2020), by virtue of SI 2020/1642 reg 4(b).

14 Acquisitions from persons belonging in other member States
(1) Subject to subsection (3) below, where—
 (a) a person ("the original supplier") makes a supply of goods to a person who belongs in another member State ("the intermediate supplier");
 (b) that supply involves the removal of the goods from another member State and their removal to the United Kingdom but does not involve the removal of the goods from the United Kingdom;
 (c) both that supply and the removal of the goods to the United Kingdom are for the purposes of the making of a supply by the intermediate supplier to another person ("the customer") who is registered under this Act;
 (d) neither of those supplies involves the removal of the goods from a member State in which the intermediate supplier is taxable at the time of the removal without also involving the previous removal of the goods to that member State; and
 (e) there would be a taxable acquisition by the customer if the supply to him involved the removal of goods from another member State to the United Kingdom,
the supply by the original supplier to the intermediate supplier shall be disregarded for the purposes of this Act and the supply by the intermediate supplier to the customer shall be treated for the purposes of this Act, other than Schedule 3, as if it did involve the removal of the goods from another member State to the United Kingdom.
(2) Subject to subsection (3) below, where—
 (a) a person belonging in another member State makes such a supply of goods to a person who is registered under this Act as involves their installation or assembly at a place in the United Kingdom to which they are removed; and
 (b) there would be a taxable acquisition by the registered person if that supply were treated as not being a taxable supply but as involving the removal of the goods from another member State to the United Kingdom,
that supply shall be so treated except for the purposes of Schedule 3.
(3) Neither subsection (1) nor subsection (2) above shall apply in relation to any supply unless the intermediate supplier or, as the case may be, the person making the supply complies with such requirements as to the furnishing (whether before or after the supply is made) of invoices and other documents, and of information, to—
 (a) the Commissioners, and
 (b) the person supplied,
as the Commissioners may by regulations prescribe; and regulations under this subsection may provide for the times at which, and the form and manner in which, any document or information is to be furnished and for the particulars which it is to contain.
(4) Where this section has the effect of treating a taxable acquisition as having been made, section 12(1) shall apply in relation to that acquisition with the omission of the words from "whichever" to "acquisition; and" at the end of paragraph (a).
(5) For the purposes of this section a person belongs in another member State if—
 (a) he does not have any business establishment or other fixed establishment in the United Kingdom and does not have his usual place of residence in the United Kingdom;
 (b) he is neither registered under this Act nor required to be so registered;
 (c) he does not have a VAT representative and is not for the time being required to appoint one; and
 (d) he is taxable in another member State;
but, in determining for the purposes of paragraph (b) above whether a person is required to be registered under this Act, there shall be disregarded any supplies which, if he did belong in another member State and complied with the requirements prescribed under subsection (3) above, would fall to be disregarded by virtue of this section.
(6) Without prejudice to section 13(4), where—
 (a) any goods are acquired from another member State in a case which corresponds, in relation to another member State, to the case specified in relation to the United Kingdom in subsection (1) above; and
 (b) the person who acquires the goods is registered under this Act and would be the intermediate supplier in relation to that corresponding case,
the supply to him of those goods and the supply by him of those goods to the person who would be the customer in that corresponding case shall both be disregarded for the purposes of this Act, other than the purposes of the information provisions referred to in section 92(7).

(7) References in this section to a person being taxable in another member State shall not include references to a person who is so taxable by virtue only of provisions of the law of another member State corresponding to the provisions of this Act by virtue of which a person who is not registered under this Act is a taxable person if he is required to be so registered.
(8) This section does not apply in relation to any supply of goods by an intermediate supplier to whom the goods were supplied before 1st August 1993.[1]

Northern Ireland—See Sch 9ZA para 6 below (Northern Ireland: acquisitions from persons belonging in member States).
Regulations—See VAT Regulations, SI 1995/2518 regs 11, 12, 17–19.
Amendments—[1] Sections 10–14 and preceding heading repealed by the Taxation (Cross-border Trade) Act 2018 s 43, Sch 8 paras 1, 11 with effect from IP completion day (11pm on 31 December 2020), by virtue of SI 2020/1642 reg 4(b).

[Goods supplied between the UK and member States under call-off stock arrangements

14A Call-off stock arrangements

Schedule 4B (call-off stock arrangements) has effect.][1], [2]

Northern Ireland—See Sch 9ZA Part 10 (paras 57–65): businesses moving own goods from Northern Ireland to EU member State or vice versa under call-off stock provisions.
Amendments—[1] Section 14A inserted by FA 2020 s 80(1), (2) with effect from 22 July 2020.
[2] Section 14A and Schedule 4B repealed by the Taxation (Post-transition Period) Act 2020 s 3, Sch 2 para 7(1) with effect from IP completion day (11pm on 31 December 2020), by virtue of SI 2020/1642 reg 9.

Importation of goods . . .

[15 Meaning of "importation of goods" into the United Kingdom

(1) This section determines for the purposes of this Act when, and by whom, goods are imported into the United Kingdom.
(2) Goods are imported when they are declared for a Customs procedure under Part 1 of TCTA 2018.
(3) But—
   (a) in the case of goods declared under TCTA 2018 for a storage procedure, a transit procedure or an inward processing procedure, the goods are imported when a liability to import duty is, or on the relevant assumptions would be, incurred in respect of them under section 4 of that Act, and
   (b) in the case of goods which are liable to forfeiture as a result of section 5(1) of, or paragraph 1(5) or 3(4) of Schedule 1 to, that Act (goods not presented to Customs or Customs declaration not made), the goods are imported when they become liable to forfeiture as a result of those provisions.
(4) Each person who is, or on the relevant assumptions would be, liable to import duty in respect of goods imported into the United Kingdom is a person who has imported the goods.
(5) For the purposes of this section "the relevant assumptions" are—
   (a) an assumption that a liability to import duty at a nil rate is replaced by a liability to import duty at a higher rate, and
   (b) an assumption that no relief from import duty is available.
(6) If two or more persons are regarded as importing goods, those persons are jointly and severally liable to any VAT that is payable on the importation.
(7) The preceding provisions of this section are to be ignored in reading any reference to importation or to an importer in anything applied for the purposes of this Act by section 16(1) or (2).
(8) But subsection (7) does not apply so far as the context otherwise requires or provision to the contrary is contained in regulations under section 16(3).][1]

Commentary—*De Voil Indirect Tax Service* V3.302, V1.308.
Northern Ireland—See Sch 9ZA para 1(5): section 15 is modified as follows, so that VAT on the importation of non-EU goods imported into the UK as a result of their entry into Northern Ireland is charged and payable as if it were "relevant NI import duty" (broadly, duty charged under TCBTA 2018 s 30A(3))—
   – as if any reference to import duty were to relevant NI import duty;
   – as if the references in sub-ss (2), (3) to a Customs, storage, transit or inward processing procedure were to a procedure corresponding to such a procedure under Union customs legislation; and
   – as if the reference in sub-s (3)(b) to TCBTA 2018 s 5(1) or Sch 1 para 1(5) or 3(4) included any provision (including any provision of Union customs legislation) corresponding to those provisions that may apply to those goods.
See also VATA 1994 Sch 9ZC para 4 (online sales by overseas persons and low value importations: modifications relating to the Northern Ireland Protocol): in the circumstances set out in Sch 9ZC para 4(1), where certain goods are imported into the UK as a result of their entry into Northern Ireland in the course or furtherance of a business by a person (P), the person who is treated as having imported the goods is—
   (a) in a case where the supply is facilitated by an online marketplace, the operator of the online marketplace, or
   (b) in any other case, P.
Amendments—[1] In heading before s 15, words "from outside the member States" repealed, and s 15 substituted, by the Taxation (Cross-border Trade) Act 2018 ss 41(1), (3), 43, Sch 8 paras 1, 12 with effect from IP completion day (11pm on 31 December 2020), by virtue of SI 2020/1642 reg 4(b).
Section 15 previously read as follows—

   "**15 General provisions relating to imported goods**
   (1) For the purposes of this Act goods are imported from a place outside the member States where—
      (a) having been removed from a place outside the member States, they enter the territory of the European Union;

(b) they enter that territory by being removed to the United Kingdom or are removed to the United Kingdom after entering that territory; and
(c) the circumstances are such that it is on their removal to the United Kingdom or subsequently while they are in the United Kingdom that any EU customs debt in respect of duty on their entry into the territory of the European Union would be incurred.
(2) Accordingly—
  (a) goods shall not be treated for the purposes of this Act as imported at any time before a EU customs debt in respect of duty on their entry into the territory of the European Union would be incurred, and
  (b) the person who is to be treated for the purposes of this Act as importing any goods from a place outside the member States is the person who would be liable to discharge any such EU customs debt.
(3) Subsections (1) and (2) above shall not apply, except in so far as the context otherwise requires or provision to the contrary is contained in regulations under section 16(1), for construing any references to importation or to an importer in any enactment or subordinate legislation applied for the purposes of this Act by section 16(1)."

[16 Application of customs enactments

(1) The provision made by or under—
  (a) the Customs and Excise Acts 1979 (as defined in the Management Act), and
  (b) the other enactments for the time being having effect generally in relation to duties of customs and excise charged by reference to the importation of goods into the United Kingdom,
apply (so far as relevant) in relation to any VAT chargeable on the importation of goods into the United Kingdom as they apply in relation to any duty of customs or excise.
(2) The provision made by section 1(4) for VAT on the importation of goods to be charged and payable as if it were import duty is to be taken as applying, in relation to any VAT chargeable on the importation of the goods, the provision made by or under Part 1 of TCTA 2018.
(3) The Commissioners may by regulations—
  (a) provide for exceptions from the effect of subsection (1) or (2), or
  (b) provide for the provision mentioned in subsection (1) or (2) to have effect with modifications specified in the regulations.
(4) Subsections (1) and (2) do not apply so far as the context otherwise requires.
(5) Regulations under section 105 of the Postal Services Act 2000 (which provides for the application of customs enactments to postal packets) may make special provision in relation to VAT.][1]

Commentary—*De Voil Indirect Tax Service* **V1.225, V1.227, V3.301**.
HMRC Manuals—Imports Manual IMPS01200 (introduction: law and regulations).
Northern Ireland—See Sch 9ZA para 1(6): section 16 is modified as follows, so that VAT on the importation of non-EU goods imported into the UK as a result of their entry into Northern Ireland is charged and payable as if it were "relevant NI import duty" (broadly, duty charged under TCBTA 2018 s 30A(3))—
– sub-s (1) applies to the importation of such goods as if the reference to "other enactments for the time being having effect generally in relation to duties of customs and excise charged by reference to the importation of goods into the United Kingdom" included any provision of Union customs legislation that applies in relation to relevant NI import duty; and
Modifications—Value Added Tax (Accounting Procedures for Import VAT for VAT Registered Persons and Amendment) (EU Exit) Regulations, SI 2019/60: the effect of sub-s (2) is modified to the extent that SI 2019/60 makes different provision for accounting for import VAT on relevant goods. See regs 4–6 (accounting for import VAT).
VAT (Miscellaneous and Transitional Provisions, Amendment and Revocation) (EU Exit) Regulations, SI 2020/1495 reg 5: the effect of sub-s (2) is modified to the extent that SI 2020/1495 Part 2 Chapter 2 makes different provision for accounting for import VAT, including the timing of such accounting, on a relevant importation.
Amendments—[1] Section 16 substituted by the Taxation (Cross-border Trade) Act 2018 s 43, Sch 8 paras 1, 13 with effect from IP completion day (11pm on 31 December 2020), by virtue of SI 2020/1642 reg 4(b).
Section 16 previously read as follows—

"**16 Application of customs enactments**

(1) Subject to such exceptions and adaptations as the Commissioners may by regulations prescribe and except where the contrary intention appears—
  (a) the provision made by or under the Customs and Excise Acts 1979 and the other enactments and subordinate legislation for the time being having effect generally in relation to duties of customs and excise charged on the importation of goods into the United Kingdom; and
  (b) the EU legislation for the time being having effect in relation to EU customs duties charged on goods entering the territory of the European Union,
shall apply (so far as relevant) in relation to any VAT chargeable on the importation of goods from places outside the member States as they apply in relation to any such duty of customs or excise or, as the case may be, EU customs duties.
(2) Regulations under section 105 of the Postal Services Act 2000 (which provides for the application of customs enactments to postal packets) may make special provision in relation to VAT."

[16A Postal packets

(1) The Commissioners may by regulations impose a liability to VAT on a person outside the United Kingdom in respect of the entry of goods into the United Kingdom if the person sent, or arranged for the sending of, the goods to their recipient in a postal packet . . .[2]

(2) The regulations may—
  (a) provide that a liability to VAT arises only in relation to goods of a value described in the regulations,
  (b) provide that in cases specified in the regulations, other persons are jointly and severally liable for the VAT, and
  (c) provide that the entry of the goods into the United Kingdom is not an importation for the purposes of this Act.
(3) Among other provision that may be made by the regulations, the regulations may make provision—
  (a) requiring persons to register under the regulations for the purpose of accounting for VAT imposed under the regulations,
  (b) modifying the application of this Act in relation to cases dealt with by the regulations, and
  (c) requiring persons to provide information to the Commissioners about the goods or the person who sent, or arranged for the sending of, the goods.
(4) Regulations under this section may make different provision for different purposes.][1]
Commentary—*De Voil Indirect Tax Service* **V1.308**.
Regulations—Value Added Tax (Miscellaneous Amendments, Revocation and Transitional Provisions) (EU Exit) Regulations, SI 2019/513.
Value Added Tax (Miscellaneous and Transitional Provisions, Amendment and Revocation) (EU Exit) Regulation, SI 2020/1495.
Amendments—[1] Section 16A inserted by the Taxation (Cross-border Trade) Act 2018 s 43, Sch 8 paras 1, 14 with effect from 16 December 2018 (by virtue of SI 2018/1362 reg 2).
[2] In Sub-s (1) words "(within the meaning of the Postal Services Act 2000)" repealed by the Taxation (Post-transition Period) Act 2020 s 7, Sch 3 paras 1, 6 with effect from IP completion day (11pm on 31 December 2020), by virtue of SI 2020/1642 reg 9.

17 Free zone regulations

(1) This section applies in relation to VAT chargeable on the importation of goods . . . [1]; and in this section "free zone" has the meaning given by section 100A(2) of the Management Act.
(2) . . . [1] Goods which are chargeable with VAT may be moved into a free zone and may remain as free zone goods without payment of VAT.
(3) The Commissioners may by regulations ("free zone regulations") make provision with respect to the movement of goods into, and the removal of goods from, any free zone and the keeping, securing and treatment of goods which are within a free zone, and subject to any provision of the regulations, "free zone goods" means goods which are within a free zone.
(4) Without prejudice to the generality of subsection (3), free zone regulations may make provision—
  (a) for enabling the Commissioners to allow goods to be removed from a free zone without payment of VAT in such circumstances and subject to such conditions as they may determine;
  (b) for determining where any VAT becomes payable in respect of goods which cease to be free zone goods—
    (i) the rates of any VAT applicable; and
    (ii) the time at which those goods cease to be free zone goods;
  (c) for determining for the purpose of enabling VAT to be charged in respect of free zone goods in a case where a person wishes to pay that VAT notwithstanding that the goods will continue to be free zone goods, the rate of VAT to be applied; and
  (d) permitting free zone goods to be destroyed without payment of VAT in such circumstances and subject to such conditions as the Commissioners may determine.
(5) The Commissioners, with respect to free zone goods or the movement of goods into any free zone, may by regulations make provision—
  (a) for relief from the whole or part of any VAT chargeable on the importation of goods . . . [1] in such circumstances as they may determine;
  (b) in place of, or in addition to, any provision made by section 6 or any other enactment, for determining the time when a supply of goods which are or have been free zone goods is to be treated as taking place for the purposes of the charge to VAT; and
  (c) as to the treatment, for the purposes of VAT, of goods which are manufactured or produced within a free zone from other goods or which have other goods incorporated in them while they are free zone goods.
Amendments—[1] The following words repealed by the Taxation (Cross-border Trade) Act 2018 s 43, Sch 8 paras 1, 15 with effect from IP completion day (11pm on 31 December 2020), by virtue of SI 2020/1642 reg 4(b)—
  – in sub-s (1): "from places outside the member States";
  – in sub-s (2): "Subject to any contrary provision made by any directly applicable Community provision,"; and
  – in sub-s (5)(a): "into the United Kingdom".

Goods subject to a warehousing regime

18 Place and time of . . . supply

[(1) A supply of goods which are subject to a warehousing regime is to be treated, for the purposes of this Act, as taking place outside the United Kingdom where—
  (a) those goods have been brought into the United Kingdom,

(b) the material time of that supply is while those goods are subject to that regime and before the duty point, and
(c) those goods are not mixed with any dutiable goods which were produced or manufactured in the United Kingdom.]³
[(1A) The Commissioners may by regulations prescribe circumstances in which subsection (1) above shall not apply.]²
(2) Subsection (3) below applies where—
   (a) . . . ³
   (b) any person makes a supply of—
      (i) any dutiable goods which were produced or manufactured in the United Kingdom . . . ³; or
      (ii) any goods comprising a mixture of goods falling within sub-paragraph (i) above and other goods.
(3) Where this subsection applies and the material time for the . . . ³ supply mentioned in subsection (2) above is while the goods in question are subject to a warehousing regime and before the duty point, that . . . ³ supply shall be treated for the purposes of this Act as taking place outside the United Kingdom if the material time for any subsequent supply of those goods is also while the goods are subject to the warehousing regime and before the duty point.
(4) Where the material time for any . . . ³ supply of any goods in relation to which subsection (3) above applies is while the goods are subject to a warehousing regime and before the duty point but the . . . ³ supply nevertheless falls, for the purposes of this Act, to be treated as taking place in the United Kingdom—
   (a) that . . . ³ supply shall be treated for the purposes of this Act as taking place at the earlier of the following times, that is to say, the time when the goods are removed from the warehousing regime and the duty point; and
   (b) . . . ³ any VAT payable on the supply shall be paid (subject to any regulations under subsection (5) below)—
      (i) at the time when the supply is treated as taking place under paragraph (a) above; and
      (ii) by the person by whom the goods are so removed or, as the case may be, together with the duty or agricultural levy, by the person who is required to pay the duty or levy.
[(5) The Commissioners may by regulations make provision for enabling a taxable person to pay the VAT he is required to pay by virtue of paragraph (b) of subsection (4) above at a time later than that provided for by that paragraph.]¹
[(5A) Regulations under subsection (5) above may in particular make provision for either or both of the following—
   (a) for the taxable person to pay the VAT together with the VAT chargeable on other supplies by him of goods and services;
   (b) for the taxable person to pay the VAT together with any duty of excise deferment of which has been granted to him under section 127A of the Customs and Excise Management Act 1979;
and they may make different provision for different descriptions of taxable person and for different descriptions of goods.]¹
(6) In this section—
   "dutiable goods" means any goods which are subject—
      (a) to a duty of excise; or
      (b) in accordance with any provision for the time being having effect for transitional purposes in connection with the accession of any State to the European Union, to any . . . ³ agricultural levy of the Economic Union;
   "the duty point", in relation to any goods, means—
      (a) in the case of goods which are subject to a duty of excise, the time when the requirement to pay the duty on those goods takes effect; and
      (b) in the case of goods which are not so subject, the time when [import duty is incurred in respect of the goods]³ or, as the case may be, [the time a debt in respect of any]³ levy as is mentioned in paragraph (b) of the definition of dutiable goods [is incurred in respect of the goods]³;
   "material time"—
      (a) in relation to any . . . ³ supply the time of which is determined in accordance with regulations under section 6(14) . . . ³, means such time as may be prescribed for the purpose of this section by those regulations;
      (b) . . . ³ and
      (c) in relation to any other supply, means the time when the supply would be treated as taking place in accordance with subsection (2) of section 6 if paragraph (c) of that subsection were omitted;

"warehouse" means any warehouse where goods may be stored in [the United Kingdom][3] without payment of any one or more of the following, that is to say—

[(a) import duty;][3]

(b) any agricultural levy of the European Union;

(c) VAT on the importation of the goods . . . [3];

(d) any duty of excise . . . [3].

(7) References in this section to goods being subject to a warehousing regime is a reference to goods being kept in a warehouse or being transported between warehouses . . . [3] without the payment . . . [3] of any duty, levy or VAT; and references to the removal of goods from a warehousing regime shall be construed accordingly.

Commentary—*De Voil Indirect Tax Service* **V5.141, V3.173, V3.138.**

HMRC Manuals—VAT Supplies In Warehouse And Fiscal Warehousing VWRHS2020 – 2040 (supplies of imported goods within a warehousing regime).

VWRHS2100 (joint and several liability).

Northern Ireland—See Sch 9ZB para 15(1): warehouses and fiscal warehouses in Northern Ireland: section 18 has effect as if—
- every reference to the United Kingdom were to Great Britain, other than the references in the phrases "taking place outside the United Kingdom" and "taking place in the United Kingdom" and in the definition of "warehouse" in sub-s (6);
- in sub-s (6), in the definition of "the duty point", in para (b), after "import duty" there were inserted "or duty under section 30C of TCTA 2018", and in the definition of "warehouse", in para (a), after "import duty" there were inserted "or duty under section 30C of TCTA 2018".

See also VATA 1994 Sch 9ZB para 16 for place and time of supply rules in relation to Northern Ireland warehouses.

Regulations—VAT Regulations, SI 1995/2518 reg 43.

Amendments—[1] Sub-ss (5), (5A) substituted for original sub-s (5) by FA 1995 s 29.

[2] Sub-s (1A) inserted by F(No 2)A 2005 s 1 with effect from 20 July 2005.

[3] The following amendments made by the Taxation (Cross-border Trade) Act 2018 s 43, Sch 8 paras 1, 15 with effect from IP completion day (11pm on 31 December 2020), by virtue of SI 2020/1642 reg 4(b)—
- sub-s (1) substituted;
- in sub-s (2), para (a) and word "and" at the end repealed;
- in sub-s (2)(b)(i), words "or acquired from another member State" repealed;
- in sub-s (3), words "acquisition or" repealed in both places;
- in sub-s (4), in opening words and in para (a), words "acquisition or" repealed in both places, and in para (b) words "in the case of a supply," repealed;
- in sub-s (6), in definition of "dutiable goods", in para (b), words "EU customs duty or" repealed;
- in sub-s (6), in definition of "the duty point", in para (b)—
    (a) words substituted for words "any Community customs debt in respect of duty on the entry of the goods into the territory of the Community would be incurred";
    (b) words substituted for words "the corresponding time in relation to any such duty or"; and
    (c) words inserted;
- in sub-s (6), in definition of "material time", in para (a), words "acquisition or" and "or 12(3)" repealed, and para (b) (but not the word "and" at the end) repealed;
- in sub-s (6), in definition of "warehouse"—
    (a) in the opening words, words substituted for words "any member State";
    (b) para (a) substituted;
    (c) in para (c), words "into any member State" repealed; and
    (d) in para (d), words from repealed;
- in sub-s (7), words "(whether in the same or different member States)" and "in a member State" repealed; and
- in the heading, words "acquisition or" repealed.

Before the above amendments, this section previously read as follows—

"18 Place and time of acquisition or supply

(1A) The Commissioners may by regulations prescribe circumstances in which subsection (1) above shall not apply.

(2) Subsection (3) below applies where—

(a) any dutiable goods are acquired from another member State; or

(b) any person makes a supply of—

(i) any dutiable goods which were produced or manufactured in the United Kingdom or acquired from another member State; or

(ii) any goods comprising a mixture of goods falling within sub-paragraph (i) above and other goods.

(3) Where this subsection applies and the material time for the acquisition or supply mentioned in subsection (2) above is while the goods in question are subject to a warehousing regime and before the duty point, that acquisition or supply shall be treated for the purposes of this Act as taking place outside the United Kingdom if the material time for any subsequent supply of those goods is also while the goods are subject to the warehousing regime and before the duty point.

(4) Where the material time for any acquisition or supply of any goods in relation to which subsection (3) above applies is while the goods are subject to a warehousing regime and before the duty point but the acquisition or supply nevertheless falls, for the purposes of this Act, to be treated as taking place in the United Kingdom—

(a) that acquisition or supply shall be treated for the purposes of this Act as taking place at the earlier of the following times, that is to say, the time when the goods are removed from the warehousing regime and the duty point; and

(b) in the case of a supply, any VAT payable on the supply shall be paid (subject to any regulations under subsection (5) below)—

(i) at the time when the supply is treated as taking place under paragraph (a) above; and

(ii) by the person by whom the goods are so removed or, as the case may be, together with the duty or agricultural levy, by the person who is required to pay the duty or levy.

(5) The Commissioners may by regulations make provision for enabling a taxable person to pay the VAT he is required to pay by virtue of paragraph (b) of subsection (4) above at a time later than that provided for by that paragraph.

(5A) Regulations under subsection (5) above may in particular make provision for either or both of the following—
 (a) for the taxable person to pay the VAT together with the VAT chargeable on other supplies by him of goods and services;
 (b) for the taxable person to pay the VAT together with any duty of excise deferment of which has been granted to him under section 127A of the Customs and Excise Management Act 1979;
and they may make different provision for different descriptions of taxable person and for different descriptions of goods.

(6) In this section—
 "dutiable goods" means any goods which are subject—
  (a) to a duty of excise; or
  (b) in accordance with any provision for the time being having effect for transitional purposes in connection with the accession of any State to the European Union, to any EU customs duty or agricultural levy of the European Union;
 "the duty point", in relation to any goods, means—
  (a) in the case of goods which are subject to a duty of excise, the time when the requirement to pay the duty on those goods takes effect; and
  (b) in the case of goods which are not so subject, the time when any EU customs debt in respect of duty on the entry of the goods into the territory of the European Union would be incurred or, as the case may be, the corresponding time in relation to any such duty or levy as is mentioned in paragraph (b) of the definition of dutiable goods;
 "material time"—
  (a) in relation to any acquisition or supply the time of which is determined in accordance with regulations under section 6(14) or 12(3), means such time as may be prescribed for the purpose of this section by those regulations;
  (b) in relation to any other acquisition, means the time of the event which, in relation to the acquisition, is the first relevant event for the purposes of taxing it; and
  (c) in relation to any other supply, means the time when the supply would be treated as taking place in accordance with subsection (2) of section 6 if paragraph (c) of that subsection were omitted;
 "warehouse" means any warehouse where goods may be stored in any member State without payment of any one or more of the following, that is to say—
  (a) EU customs duty;
  (b) any agricultural levy of the European Union;
  (c) VAT on the importation of the goods into any member State;
  (d) any duty of excise or any duty which is equivalent in another member State to a duty of excise.

(7) References in this section to goods being subject to a warehousing regime is a reference to goods being kept in a warehouse or being transported between warehouses (whether in the same or different member States) without the payment in a member State of any duty, levy or VAT; and references to the removal of goods from a warehousing regime shall be construed accordingly.".

[18A Fiscal warehousing

(1) The Commissioners may, if it appears to them proper, upon application approve any registered person as a fiscal warehouse keeper; and such approval shall be subject to such conditions as they shall impose.

(2) Subject to those conditions and to regulations made under section 18F such a person shall be entitled to keep a fiscal warehouse.

(3) "Fiscal warehouse" means such place in the United Kingdom in the occupation or under the control of the fiscal warehouse keeper, not being retail premises, as he shall notify to the Commissioners in writing; and such a place shall become a fiscal warehouse on receipt by the Commissioners of that notification or on the date stated in it as the date from which it is to have effect, whichever is the later, and, subject to subsection (6) below, shall remain a fiscal warehouse so long as it is in the occupation or under the control of the fiscal warehouse keeper or until he shall notify the Commissioners in writing that it is to cease to be a fiscal warehouse.

(4) The Commissioners may in considering an application by a person to be a fiscal warehousekeeper take into account any matter which they consider relevant, and may without prejudice to the generality of that provision take into account all or any one or more of the following—
 (a) his record of compliance and ability to comply with the requirements of this Act and regulations made hereunder;
 (b) his record of compliance and ability to comply with the requirements of the customs and excise Acts . . . [4] and regulations made thereunder;
 (c), (d) . . . [4]
 (e) if the applicant is a company the records of compliance and ability to comply with the matters set out at [(a) and (b)][4] above of its directors, persons connected with its directors, its managing officers, any shadow directors or any of those persons, and, if it is a close company, the records of compliance and ability to comply with the matters set out at [(a) and (b)][4] above of the beneficial owners of the shares of the company or any of them; and

(f) if the applicant is an individual the records of compliance and ability to comply with the matters set out at [(a) and (b)]⁴ above of any company of which he is or has been a director, managing officer or shadow director or, in the case of a close company, a shareholder or the beneficial owner of shares.

. . . ⁵

[(4A) For the purposes of paragraphs (e) and (f) of subsection (4)—
   (a) a person is "connected" with a director if that person is the director's spouse or civil partner, or is a relative, or the spouse or civil partner of a relative, of the director or of the director's spouse or civil partner;
   (b) "managing officer" in relation to a body corporate, means any manager, secretary or other similar officer of the body corporate or any person purporting to act in any such capacity or as a director;
   (c) "shadow director" has the meaning given by section 251 of the Companies Act 2006;
   (d) "close company" has the meaning it has in the Corporation Tax Acts (see Chapter 2 of Part 10 of the Corporation Tax Act 2010).]⁵

(5) Subject to subsection (6) below, a person approved under subsection (1) shall remain a fiscal warehouse keeper until he ceases to be a registered person or until he shall notify the Commissioners in writing that he is to cease to be a fiscal warehouse keeper.

(6) The Commissioners may if they consider it appropriate from time to time—
   (a) impose conditions on a fiscal warehouse keeper in addition to those conditions, if any, which they imposed under subsection (1), and vary or revoke any conditions previously imposed;
   (b) withdraw approval of any person as a fiscal warehouse keeper, and
   (c) withdraw fiscal warehouse status from any premises.

(7) Any application by or on behalf of a person to be a fiscal warehousekeeper shall be in writing in such form as the Commissioners may direct and shall be accompanied by such information as they shall require.

(8) Any approval by the Commissioners under subsection (1) above, and any withdrawal of approval or other act by them under subsection (6) above, shall be notified by them to the fiscal warehousekeeper in writing and shall take effect on such notification being made or on any later date specified for the purpose in the notification.

(9) Without prejudice to the provisions of section 43 concerning liability for VAT, in subsections (1) and (2) above "registered person" includes any [person who]³ under that section is for the time being treated as a member of a group.]¹

Commentary—*De Voil Indirect Tax Service* **V3.388B**.

HMRC Manuals—VAT Supplies In Warehouse And Fiscal Warehousing VWRHS4010-4020 (fiscal warehouses: aim and definition).

Northern Ireland—See Sch 9ZB para 15(2): warehouses and fiscal warehouses in Northern Ireland: section 18A has effect as if the reference to "such place in the United Kingdom" in sub-s (3) were to "such place in Great Britain".

See also VATA Sch 9ZB para 17 for provision in relation to Northern Ireland fiscal warehouses, and para 18 for conversion of relevant fiscal warehouses.

Amendments—¹   This section, and ss 18B–18F, inserted by FA 1996 Sch 3 para 5, with effect from 1 June 1996; see Finance Act 1996, Section 26, (Appointed Day) Order, SI 1996/1249, and applying to any acquisition of goods from another member State and any supply taking place on or after that day, except in so far as these sections confer power to make regulations, when they come into force on 29 April 1996.

³   In sub-s (9), words substituted for words "body corporate which" by FA 2019 s 53, Sch 18 paras 3, 4 with effect from 1 November 2019 (see SI 2019/1348).

⁴   In sub-s (4), the following amendments made by the Taxation (Cross-border Trade) Act 2018 s 43, Sch 8 paras 1, 17 with effect from IP completion day (11pm on 31 December 2020), by virtue of SI 2020/1642 reg 4(b)—
   –   in para (b), words "(as defined in the Management Act)" repealed;
   –   paras (c), (d) repealed;
   –   in para (e), words substituted for words "(a) to (d)" in both places; and
   –   in para (f), words substituted for words "(a) to (d)".

Sub-s (4)(c), (d) previously read as follows—
   "(c)   his record of compliance and ability to comply with EU customs provisions;
   (d)   his record of compliance and ability to comply with the requirements of other member States relating to VAT and duties equivalent to duties of excise;".

⁵   In sub-s (4) the words after para (f) repealed, and sub-s (4A) inserted, by the Taxation (Post-transition Period) Act 2020 s 3, Sch 2 para 6 with effect from IP completion day (11pm on 31 December 2020), by virtue of SI 2020/1642 reg 9.

Repealed words previously read as follows—
"and for the purposes of paragraphs (e) and (f) "connected" shall have the meaning given by section 24(7), "managing officer" the meaning given by section 61(6), "shadow director" the meaning given by section 251 of the Companies Act 2006 and "close company" the meaning given by the Taxes Act.".

[18B Fiscally warehoused goods: relief

(1) . . . ¹

(2) Subsections (3) and (4) below . . . ¹ apply where—
   (a) there is a supply of goods;

(b) those goods are eligible goods;
(c) either—
  (i) that supply takes place while the goods are subject to a fiscal warehousing regime; or
  (ii) after that supply but before the supply, if any, of those goods which next occurs, the person to whom the former supply is made causes the goods to be placed in a fiscal warehousing regime;
(d) in a case falling within paragraph (c)(ii) above, the person to whom the supply is made gives the supplier, not later than the time of the supply, a certificate . . . [2] that he will cause paragraph (c)(ii) to be satisfied; and
(e) the supply is not a retail transaction.
[(2A) A certificate under subsection . . . [1] (2)(d) must be in such form as may be specified by regulations or by the Commissioners in accordance with regulations.][2]
(3) The . . . [1] supply in question shall be treated for the purposes of this Act as taking place outside the United Kingdom if any subsequent supply of those goods is while they are subject to the fiscal warehousing regime.
(4) Where subsection (3) does not apply and the . . . [1] supply in question falls, for the purposes of this Act, to be treated as taking place in the United Kingdom, that . . . [1] supply shall be treated for the purposes of this Act as taking place when the goods are removed from the fiscal warehousing regime.
[(5) VAT is chargeable on a supply made by a person who is not a taxable person, but who would be were it not for paragraph 1(9) of Schedule 1, where—
  (a) subsection (4) applies to that supply, and
  (b) that supply is taxable and not zero-rated.][3]
[(6) In this section "eligible goods" means goods—
  (a) of a description falling within Schedule 5A,
  (b) in the case of imported goods—
    (i) upon which any import duty has been paid or deferred (by virtue of the customs and excise Acts or any subordinate legislation made under those Acts), and
    (ii) upon which any VAT chargeable under section 1(1)(c) has been paid, or deferred (by virtue of the customs and excise Acts or any subordinate legislation made under those Acts), and
  (c) in the case of goods subject to a duty of excise, upon which any excise duty has been paid or deferred under section 127A of the Management Act.][3]
(7) For the purposes of this section, apart from subsection (4), [a supply][3] shall be treated as taking place at the material time for [the supply][3].
(8) The Treasury may by order vary Schedule 5A by adding to or deleting from it any goods or varying any description of any goods.][1]

Commentary—*De Voil Indirect Tax Service* **V5.141A, V3.176, V3.388B.**
HMRC Manuals—VAT Supplies In Warehouse And Fiscal Warehousing VWRHS3070 (certificate required to secure zero-rating of services).
VAT Civil Penalties VCP11311 (penalty for incorrect issue of a certificate).

NORTHERN IRELAND—
See VATA Sch 9ZB para 19 for provision in relation to Northern Ireland fiscal warehouses.
See also Sch 9ZB para 20: modification of this section so that sub-s (5) has effect as if after "Schedule 1" there were inserted "and paragraphs 38(6) and 48(7) of Schedule 9ZA, or any of those provisions".
Regulations—VAT (Amendment) (No 2) Regulations, SI 2012/1899.
Amendments—[1] This section inserted by FA 1996 Sch 3 para 5, with effect from 1 June 1996; (see Finance Act 1996, Section 26, (Appointed Day) Order, SI 1996/1249), and applying to any acquisition of goods from another member State and any supply taking place on or after that day, except in so far as it confers power to make regulations, when it comes into force on 29 April 1996.
[2] In sub-s (2)(d), words "in such form as the Commissioners may by regulations specify" repealed, and sub-s (2A) inserted, by FA 2012 s 204, Sch 29 paras 1, 2 with effect from 17 July 2012.
[3] The following amendments made by the Taxation (Cross-border Trade) Act 2018 s 43, Sch 8 paras 1, 18 with effect from IP completion day (11pm on 31 December 2020), by virtue of SI 2020/1642 reg 4(b)—
  – sub-s (1) repealed;
  – in sub-s (2), word "also" repealed;
  – in sub-s (2A) words "(1)(d) or" repealed;
  – in sub-s (3), and in sub-s (4) in both places, words "acquisition or" repealed;
  – sub-ss (5), (6) substituted; and
  – in sub-s (7), words substituted for words "an acquisition or supply", and words "the supply" substituted for words "the acquisition or supply".

Before these amendments, section 18B previously read as follows—

"**18B Fiscally warehoused goods: relief**
(1) Subsections (3) and (4) below apply where—
  (a) there is an acquisition of goods from another member State;
  (b) those goods are eligible goods;
  (c) either—

(i) the acquisition takes place while the goods are subject to a fiscal warehousing regime; or
(ii) after the acquisition but before the supply, if any, of those goods which next occurs, the acquirer causes the goods to be placed in a fiscal warehousing regime; and
(d) the acquirer, not later than the time of the acquisition, prepares and keeps a certificate that the goods are subject to a fiscal warehousing regime, or (as the case may be) that he will cause paragraph (c)(ii) above to be satisfied; and the certificate shall be kept for such period as the Commissioners may by regulations specify.

(2) Subsections (3) and (4) below also apply where—
(a) there is a supply of goods;
(b) those goods are eligible goods;
(c) either—
(i) that supply takes place while the goods are subject to a fiscal warehousing regime; or
(ii) after that supply but before the supply, if any, of those goods which next occurs, the person to whom the former supply is made causes the goods to be placed in a fiscal warehousing regime;
(d) in a case falling within paragraph (c)(ii) above, the person to whom the supply is made gives the supplier, not later than the time of the supply, a certificate that he will cause paragraph (c)(ii) to be satisfied; and
(e) the supply is not a retail transaction.

(2A) A certificate under subsection (1)(d) or (2)(d) must be in such form as may be specified by regulations or by the Commissioners in accordance with regulations.

(3) The acquisition or supply in question shall be treated for the purposes of this Act as taking place outside the United Kingdom if any subsequent supply of those goods is while they are subject to the fiscal warehousing regime.

(4) Where subsection (3) does not apply and the acquisition or supply in question falls, for the purposes of this Act, to be treated as taking place in the United Kingdom, that acquisition or supply shall be treated for the purposes of this Act as taking place when the goods are removed from the fiscal warehousing regime.

(5) Where—
(a) subsection (4) above applies to an acquisition or a supply,
(b) the acquisition or supply is taxable and not zero-rated, and
(c) the acquirer or supplier is not a taxable person but would be were it not for paragraph 1(9) of Schedule 1, paragraph 1(7) of Schedule 2 and paragraph 1(6) of Schedule 3, or any of those provisions,

VAT shall be chargeable on that acquisition or supply notwithstanding that the acquirer or the supplier is not a taxable person.

(6) In this section "eligible goods" means goods—
(a) of a description falling within Schedule 5A;
(b) upon which any import duties, as defined in article 4(10) of the Community Customs Code of 12th October 1992 (Council Regulation (EEC) No 2913/92), either have been paid or have been deferred under article 224 of that Code or regulations made under section 45 of the Management Act;
(c) (in the case of goods imported from a place outside the member States) upon which any VAT chargeable under section 1(1)(c) has been either paid or deferred in accordance with EU customs provisions, and
(d) (in the case of goods subject to a duty of excise) upon which that duty has been either paid or deferred under section 127A of the Management Act.

(7) For the purposes of this section, apart from subsection (4), an acquisition or supply shall be treated as taking place at the material time for the acquisition or supply.

(8) The Treasury may by order vary Schedule 5A by adding to or deleting from it any goods or varying any description of any goods.".

[18C Warehouses and fiscal warehouses: services

(1) Where—
(a) a taxable person makes a supply of specified services;
(b) those services are wholly performed on or in relation to goods while those goods are subject to a warehousing or fiscal warehousing regime;
(c) (except where the services are the supply by an occupier of a warehouse or a fiscal warehousekeeper of warehousing or fiscally warehousing the goods) the person to whom the supply is made gives the supplier a certificate . . . [2] that the services are so performed;
(d) the supply of services would (apart from this section) be taxable and not zero-rated; and
(e) the supplier issues to the person to whom the supply is made an invoice of such a description as the Commissioners may by regulations prescribe,

his supply shall be zero-rated.

[(1A) A certificate under subsection (1)(c) must be in such form as may be specified by regulations or by the Commissioners in accordance with regulations.][2]

(2) If a supply of services is zero-rated under subsection (1) above ("the zero-rated supply of services") then, unless there is a supply of the goods in question the material time for which is—
(a) while the goods are subject to a warehousing or fiscal warehousing regime, and
(b) after the material time for the zero-rated supply of services,

subsection (3) below shall apply.

(3) Where this subsection applies—
(a) a supply of services identical to the zero-rated supply of services shall be treated for the purposes of this Act as being, at the time the goods are removed from the warehousing or

fiscal warehousing regime or (if earlier) at the duty point, both made (for the purposes of his business) to the person to whom the zero-rated supply of services was actually made and made by him in the course or furtherance of his business,
- (b) that supply shall have the same value as the zero-rated supply of services,
- (c) that supply shall be a taxable (and not a zero-rated) supply, and
- (d) VAT shall be charged on that supply even if the person treated as making it is not a taxable person.

(4) In this section "specified services" means—
- (a) services of an occupier of a warehouse or a fiscal warehousekeeper of keeping the goods in question in a warehousing or fiscal warehousing regime;
- (b) in relation to goods subject to a warehousing regime, services of carrying out on the goods operations which are permitted to be carried out under [the customs and excise Acts or any subordinate legislation made under those Acts][3] as the case may be; and
- (c) in relation to goods subject to a fiscal warehousing regime, services of carrying out on the goods any physical operations (other than any prohibited by regulations made under section 18F), for example, and without prejudice to the generality of the foregoing words, preservation and repacking operations.][1]

Commentary—*De Voil Indirect Tax Service* **V4.209, V5.141A**.
HMRC Manuals—VAT Supplies In Warehouse And Fiscal Warehousing VWRHS3030 (how supplies of services may be relieved).
VWRHS3035 (subsequent taxation of previously zero-rated services).
Northern Ireland—See VATA 1994 Sch 9ZB para 21: section 18C is modified in relation to Northern Ireland warehouses and fiscal warehouses, as if and reference to—
- "a warehousing or fiscal warehousing regime" were to "a warehousing, Northern Ireland warehousing, fiscal warehousing, or Northern Ireland fiscal warehousing regime";
- "a warehouse or a fiscal warehousekeeper" were to "a warehouse, Northern Ireland warehouse, fiscal or Northern Ireland fiscal warehousekeeper";
- "a warehousing regime" were to "a warehousing or Northern Ireland warehousing regime";
- "a fiscal warehousing regime" were to "a fiscal or Northern Ireland fiscal warehousing regime".

Subsection (2) has effect in relation to goods subject to a Northern Ireland warehousing or Northern Ireland fiscal warehousing regime as if the term "material time" had the meaning defined in VATA 1994 Sch 9ZB para 25(1).
Subsection (3) has effect in relation to goods subject to a Northern Ireland warehousing or Northern Ireland fiscal warehousing regime as if the term "duty point" had the meaning it has in VATA 1994 Sch 9ZB para 16.
Subsection (4)(b) has effect in relation to goods subject to a Northern Ireland fiscal warehousing regime as if after "carried out under" there were inserted "Union customs legislation (within the meaning of Schedule 9ZB) or under".
Regulations—VAT (Amendment) (No 2) Regulations, SI 2012/1899.
Amendments—[1] This section inserted by FA 1996 Sch 3 para 5, with effect from 1 June 1996; (see Finance Act 1996, Section 26, (Appointed Day) Order, SI 1996/1249), and applying to any acquisition of goods from another member State and any supply taking place on or after that day, except in so far as it confers power to make regulations, when it comes into force on 29 April 1996.
[2] In sub-s (1)(c), words ", in such a form as the Commissioners may by regulations specify," repealed, and sub-s (1A) inserted, by FA 2012 s 204, Sch 29 paras 1, 3 with effect from 17 July 2012.
[3] In sub-s (4)(b), words substituted for words "EU customs provisions or warehousing regulations", by the Taxation (Cross-border Trade) Act 2018 s 43, Sch 8 paras 1, 19 with effect from IP completion day (11pm on 31 December 2020), by virtue of SI 2020/1642 reg 4(b).

[18D Removal from warehousing: accountability

(1) This section applies to any supply to which section 18B(4) or section 18C(3) applies (supply treated as taking place on removal or duty point) and . . . [2]
(2) Any VAT payable on the supply . . . [2] shall (subject to any regulations under subsection (3) below) be paid—
- (a) at the time when the supply . . . [2] is treated as taking place under the section in question; and
- (b) by the person by whom the goods are removed or, as the case may be, together with the excise duty, by the person who is required to pay that duty.

(3) The Commissioners may by regulations make provision for enabling a taxable person to pay the VAT he is required to pay by virtue of subsection (2) above at a time later than that provided by that subsection; and they may make different provisions for different descriptions of taxable persons and for different descriptions of goods and services.][1]

Amendments—[1] This section inserted by FA 1996 Sch 3 para 5, with effect from 1 June 1996 (see Finance Act 1996, Section 26, (Appointed Day) Order, SI 1996/1249), and applies to any acquisition of goods from another member State and any supply taking place on or after that day, except in so far as it confers power to make regulations, when it comes into force on 29 April 1996.
[2] In sub-s (1), words "any acquisition to which section 18B(5) applies (acquisition treated as taking place on removal where acquirer not a taxable person)." repealed, and in sub-s (2), words "or acquisition" repealed in both places, by the Taxation (Cross-border Trade) Act 2018 s 43, Sch 8 paras 1, 20 with effect from IP completion day (11pm on 31 December 2020), by virtue of SI 2020/1642 reg 4(b).

[18E Deficiency in fiscally warehoused goods

(1) This section applies where goods have been subject to a fiscal warehousing regime and, before being lawfully removed from the fiscal warehouse, they are found to be missing or deficient.

(2) In any case where this section applies, unless it is shown to the satisfaction of the Commissioners that the absence of or deficiency in the goods can be accounted for by natural waste or other legitimate cause, the Commissioners may require the fiscal warehousekeeper to pay immediately in respect of the missing goods or of the whole or any part of the deficiency, as they see fit, the VAT that would have been chargeable.

(3) In subsection (2) "VAT that would have been chargeable" means VAT that would have been chargeable on a supply of the missing goods, or the amount of goods by which the goods are deficient, taking place at the time immediately before the absence arose or the deficiency occurred, if the value of that supply were the open market value; but where that time cannot be ascertained to the Commissioners' satisfaction, that VAT shall be the greater of the amounts of VAT which would have been chargeable on a supply of those goods—

   (a) if the value of that supply were the highest open market value during the period (the relevant period) commencing when the goods were placed in the fiscal warehousing regime and ending when the absence or deficiency came to the notice of the Commissioners, or
   (b) if the rate of VAT chargeable on that supply were the highest rate chargeable on a supply of such goods during the relevant period and the value of that supply were the highest open market value while that rate prevailed.

(4) This section has effect without prejudice to any penalty incurred under any other provision of this Act or regulations made under it.]

Commentary—*De Voil Indirect Tax Service* **V3.396, V5.141A**.
HMRC Manuals—VAT Supplies In Warehouse And Fiscal Warehousing VWRHS4160 (deficiencies of warehoused goods).
Northern Ireland—See VATA 1994 Sch 9ZB para 23: section 18E applies to goods which have been subject to a Northern Ireland fiscal warehousing regime as it applies to goods which have been subject to a fiscal warehousing regime, and to a Northern Ireland fiscal warehousekeeper as it applies to a fiscal warehousekeeper.
Amendments—This section inserted by FA 1996 Sch 3 para 5, with effect from 1 June 1996 (see Finance Act 1996, Section 26, (Appointed Day) Order, SI 1996/1249).

[18F Sections 18A to 18E: supplementary

(1) In sections 18A to 18E and this section—
   ["the customs and excise Acts" has the same meaning as in the Management Act;][2]
   "duty point" has the meaning given by section 18(6);
   "eligible goods" has the meaning given by section 18B(6);
   "fiscal warehouse" means a place notified to the Commissioners under section 18A(3) and from which such status has not been withdrawn;
   "fiscal warehousekeeper" means a person approved under section 18A(1);
   "material time"—

   (a) in relation to any . . . [2] supply the time of which is determined in accordance with regulations under section 6(14) . . . [2], means such time as may be prescribed for the purpose of this section by those regulations;
   (b) . . . [2]
   (c) in relation to any other supply of goods, means the time when the supply would be treated as taking place in accordance with subsection (2) of section 6 if paragraph (c) of that subsection were omitted; and
   (d) in relation to any other supply of services, means the time when the services are performed;
   "warehouse", except in the expression "fiscal warehouse", has the meaning given by section 18(6);
   . . . [2]

(2) Any reference in sections 18A to 18E or this section to goods being subject to a fiscal warehousing regime is, subject to any regulations made under subsection (8)(e) below, a reference to eligible goods being kept in a fiscal warehouse or being transferred between fiscal warehouses in accordance with such regulations; and any reference to the removal of goods from a fiscal warehousing regime shall be construed accordingly.

(3) Subject to subsection (2) above, any reference in sections 18C and 18D to goods being subject to a warehousing regime or to the removal of goods from a warehousing regime shall have the same meaning as in section 18(7).

(4) Where as a result of an operation on eligible goods subject to a fiscal warehousing regime they change their nature but the resulting goods are also eligible goods, the provisions of sections 18B to 18E and this section shall apply as if the resulting goods were the original goods.

(5) Where as a result of an operation on eligible goods subject to a fiscal warehousing regime they cease to be eligible goods, on their ceasing to be so sections 18B to 18E shall apply as if they had at that time been removed from the fiscal warehousing regime; and for that purpose the proprietor of the goods shall be treated as if he were the person removing them.

(6) Where—
   (a) any person ceases to be a fiscal warehouse keeper; or
   (b) any premises cease to have fiscal warehouse status,
sections 18B to 18E and this section shall apply as if the goods of which he is the fiscal warehousekeeper, or the goods in the fiscal warehouse, as the case may be, had at that time been removed from the fiscal warehousing regime; and for that purpose the proprietor of the goods shall be treated as if he were the person removing them.
(7) The Commissioners may make regulations governing the deposit, keeping, securing and treatment of goods in a fiscal warehouse, and the removal of goods from a fiscal warehouse.
(8) Regulations may, without prejudice to the generality of subsection (7) above, include provisions—
   (a) in relation to—
      (i) goods which are, have been or are to be subject to a fiscal warehousing regime,
      (ii) other goods which are, have been or are to be kept in fiscal warehouses,
      (iii) fiscal warehouse premises, and
      (iv) fiscal warehousekeepers and their businesses,
   as to the keeping, preservation and production of records and the furnishing of returns and information by fiscal warehousekeepers and any other persons;
   (b) requiring goods deposited in a fiscal warehouse to be produced to or made available for inspection by an authorised person on request by him;
   (c) prohibiting the carrying out on fiscally warehoused goods of such operations as they may prescribe;
   (d) regulating the transfer of goods from one fiscal warehouse to another;
   (e) concerning goods which, though kept in a fiscal warehouse, are not eligible goods or are not intended by a relevant person to be goods in respect of which reliefs are to be enjoyed under sections 18A to 18E and this section;
   (f) prohibiting the fiscal warehouse keeper from allowing goods to be removed from the fiscal warehousing regime without payment of any VAT payable under section 18D on or by reference to that removal and, if in breach of that prohibition he allows goods to be so removed, making him liable for the VAT jointly and severally with the remover,
and may contain such incidental or supplementary provisions as the Commissioners think necessary or expedient.
(9) Regulations may make different provision for different cases, including different provision for different fiscal warehousekeepers or descriptions of fiscal warehousekeeper, for fiscal warehouses of different descriptions or for goods of different classes or descriptions or of the same class or description in different circumstances.][1]

Commentary—*De Voil Indirect Tax Service* **V3.388B, V3.388**.
HMRC Manuals—VAT Supplies In Warehouse And Fiscal Warehousing VWRHS4020 (definition and approval of a fiscal warehouse).
Amendments—[1] This section inserted by FA 1996 Sch 3 para 5, with effect from 1 June 1996; (see Finance Act 1996, Section 26, (Appointed Day) Order, SI 1996/1249)., and applying to any acquisition of goods from another member State and any supply taking place on or after that day, except in so far as it confers power to make regulations, when it comes into force on 29 April 1996.
[2]   In sub-s (1), the following amendments made by the Taxation (Cross-border Trade) Act 2018 s 43, Sch 8 paras 1, 21 with effect from IP completion day (11pm on 31 December 2020), by virtue of SI 2020/1642 reg 4(b)—
   –   definition of "the customs and excise Acts" inserted;
   –   in definition of "material time, in para (a) words "acquisition or" and words "or 12(3)" repealed, and para (b) repealed; and
   –   definition of "warehousing regulations" repealed.
   In definition of "material time", para (b) previously read as follows—
      "(b)   in relation to any other acquisition, means the time when the goods reach the destination to which they are despatched from the member State in question;".
   Definition of "warehousing regulations" previously read as follows—
      " "warehousing regulations" has the same meaning as in the Management Act.".

Determination of value

19 Value of supply of goods or services

(1) For the purposes of this Act the value of any supply of goods or services shall, except as otherwise provided by or under this Act, be determined in accordance with this section and Schedule 6, and for those purposes subsections (2) to (4) below have effect subject to that Schedule.
(2) If the supply is for a consideration in money its value shall be taken to be such amount as, with the addition of the VAT chargeable, is equal to the consideration.
(3) If the supply is for a consideration not consisting or not wholly consisting of money, its value shall be taken to be such amount in money as, with the addition of the VAT chargeable, is equivalent to the consideration.

(4) Where a supply of any goods or services is not the only matter to which a consideration in money relates, the supply shall be deemed to be for such part of the consideration as is properly attributable to it.
(5) For the purposes of this Act the open market value of a supply of goods or services shall be taken to be the amount that would fall to be taken as its value under subsection (2) above if the supply were for such consideration in money as would be payable by a person standing in no such relationship with any person as would affect that consideration.

Commentary—*De Voil Indirect Tax Service* **V3.152, V3.161, V3.103**.
HMRC Manuals—VAT Registration VATREG02300 (meaning of taxable turnover).
VAT Business/Non-Business Manual VBNB60420 (subscription or other consideration?).
VAT Valuation Manual VATVAL07200 (relationship between s 19 and Sch 6).
Northern Ireland—Sch 9ZB para 5: where goods are moved from Northern Ireland to Great Britain in the course of a supply they must be valued under s 19 (which covers supplies) and not s 21 (which covers imports).

20 Valuation of acquisitions from other member States

(1) [Subject to section 18C,][1] For the purposes of this Act the value of any acquisition of goods from another member State shall be taken to be the value of the transaction in pursuance of which they are acquired.
(2) Where goods are acquired from another member State otherwise than in pursuance of a taxable supply, the value of the transaction in pursuance of which they are acquired shall be determined for the purposes of subsection (1) above in accordance with this section and Schedule 7, and for those purposes—
    (a) subsections (3) to (5) below have effect subject to that Schedule; and
    (b) section 19 and Schedule 6 shall not apply in relation to the transaction.
(3) If the transaction is for a consideration in money, its value shall be taken to be such amount as is equal to the consideration.
(4) If the transaction is for a consideration not consisting or not wholly consisting of money, its value shall be taken to be such amount in money as is equivalent to the consideration.
(5) Where a transaction in pursuance of which goods are acquired from another member State is not the only matter to which a consideration in money relates, the transaction shall be deemed to be for such part of the consideration as is properly attributable to it.[2]

Commentary—*De Voil Indirect Tax Service* **V3.388**.
Northern Ireland—Sch 9ZB paras 3 and 4 apply to a removal of goods from Northern Ireland to Great Britain or vice versa, instead of s 15. However, para 5 provides that, where goods are moved from NI to GB in the course of a supply, they must be valued under s 19 above (which covers supplies as opposed to imports under s 21).
Amendments—[1] Words in sub-s (1) inserted by FA 1996 Sch 3 para 6, with effect to any acquisition of goods from another member State taking place on or after 1 June 1996; (see Finance Act 1996, Section 26, (Appointed Day) Order, SI 1996/1249).
[2] Section 20 repealed by the Taxation (Cross-border Trade) Act 2018 s 43, Sch 8 paras 1, 22 with effect from IP completion day (11pm on 31 December 2020), by virtue of SI 2020/1642 reg 4(b).

21 Value of imported goods

[(1) For the purposes of this Act, the value of imported goods is (subject to subsections (2) to (4)) their value as if determined under TCTA 2018 for the purposes of import duty (whether or not the goods are subject to import duty).][8]
(2) For the purposes of this Act the value of any goods imported . . . [8] shall [(subject to subsection (2A) below)][5] be taken to include the following so far as they are not already included in that value in accordance with the rules mentioned in subsection (1) above, that is to say—
    (a) all taxes, duties and other charges levied either outside or, by reason of importation, within the United Kingdom (except VAT); . . . [2]
    [(b) all incidental expenses, such as commission, packing, transport and insurance costs, up to the goods' first destination in the United Kingdom; and
    (c) if at the time of the importation of the goods . . . [8] a further destination for the goods is known, and that destination is within the United Kingdom . . . [8], all such incidental expenses in so far as they result from the transport of the goods to that other destination;
and in this subsection "the goods' first destination" means the place mentioned on the consignment note or any other document by means of which the goods are imported into the United Kingdom, or in the absence of such documentation it means the place of the first transfer of cargo in the United Kingdom.][2]
[(2A) Where—
    (a) any goods falling within subsection (5) below are sold by auction at a time when they are subject to [the temporary admission procedure under Part 1 of TCTA 2018][8], and
    (b) arrangements made by or on behalf of the purchaser of the goods following the sale by auction result in the importation of the goods . . . [8],
the value of the goods shall not be taken for the purposes of this Act to include, in relation to that importation, any commission or premium payable to the auctioneer in connection with the sale of the goods.
(2B) . . . [8]

(3) Subject to subsection (2) above, where—
- (a) goods are imported . . . [8] for a consideration which is or includes a price in money payable as on the transfer of property;
- (b) the terms on which those goods are so imported allow a discount for prompt payment of that price;
- (c) those terms do not include provision for payment of that price by instalments; and
- (d) payment of that price is made in accordance with those terms so that the discount falls to be allowed,

the value of the goods shall be taken for the purposes of this Act to be reduced by the amount of the discount.

[(4) [Subject to subsection (6D) below,][3] for the purposes of this Act, the value of any goods falling within subsection (5) below which are imported . . . [8] shall be taken to be an amount equal to [25 per cent][7] of the amount which, apart from this subsection, would be their value for those purposes.][1]

[(5) The goods that fall within this subsection are—
- (a) any work of art;
- (b) any antique, not falling within paragraph (a) above or (c) below, that is more than one hundred years old;
- (c) any collection or collector's piece that is of zoological, botanical, mineralogical, anatomical, historical, archaeological, palaeontological, ethnographic, numismatic or philatelic interest.

(6) In this section "work of art" means, subject to subsections (6A) and (6B) below—
- (a) any mounted or unmounted painting, drawing, collage, decorative plaque or similar picture that was executed by hand;
- (b) any original engraving, lithograph or other print which—
  - (i) was produced from one or more plates executed by hand by an individual who executed them without using any mechanical or photomechanical process; and
  - (ii) either is the only one produced from the plate or plates or is comprised in a limited edition;
- (c) any original sculpture or statuary, in any material;
- (d) any sculpture cast which—
  - (i) was produced by or under the supervision of the individual who made the mould or became entitled to it by succession on the death of that individual; and
  - (ii) either is the only cast produced from the mould or is comprised in a limited edition;
- (e) any tapestry or other hanging which—
  - (i) was made by hand from an original design; and
  - (ii) either is the only one made from the design or is comprised in a limited edition;
- (f) any ceramic executed by an individual and signed by him;
- (g) any enamel on copper which—
  - (i) was executed by hand;
  - (ii) is signed either by the person who executed it or by someone on behalf of the studio where it was executed;
  - (iii) either is the only one made from the design in question or is comprised in a limited edition; and
  - (iv) is not comprised in an article of jewellery or an article of a kind produced by goldsmiths or silversmiths;
- (h) any mounted or unmounted photograph which—
  - (i) was printed by or under the supervision of the photographer;
  - (ii) is signed by him; and
  - (iii) either is the only print made from the exposure in question or is comprised in a limited edition;

(6A) The following do not fall within subsection (5) above by virtue of subsection (6)(a) above, that is to say—
- (a) any technical drawing, map or plan;
- (b) any picture comprised in a manufactured article that has been hand-decorated; or
- (c) anything in the nature of scenery, including a backcloth.

(6B) An item comprised in a limited edition shall be taken to be so comprised for the purposes of subsection (6)(d) to (h) above only if—
- (a) in the case of sculpture casts—
  - (i) the edition is limited so that the number produced from the same mould does not exceed eight; or
  - (ii) the edition comprises a limited edition of nine or more casts made before 1st January 1989 which the Commissioners have directed should be treated, in the exceptional circumstances of the case, as a limited edition for the purposes of subsection (6)(d) above;

(b) in the case of tapestries and hangings, the edition is limited so that the number produced from the same design does not exceed eight;

(c) in the case of enamels on copper—
  (i) the edition is limited so that the number produced from the same design does not exceed eight; and
  (ii) each of the enamels in the edition is numbered and is signed as mentioned in subsection (6)(g)(ii) above;

(d) in the case of photographs—
  (i) the edition is limited so that the number produced from the same exposure does not exceed thirty; and
  (ii) each of the prints in the edition is numbered and is signed as mentioned in subsection (6)(h)(ii) above.

(6C) For the purposes of this section a collector's piece is of philatelic interest if—
  (a) it is a postage or revenue stamp, a postmark, a first-day cover or an item of pre-stamped stationery; and
  (b) it is franked or (if unfranked) it is not legal tender and is not intended for use as such.

(6D) Subsection (4) above does not apply in the case of [imported goods][8] if—
  (a) the whole of the VAT chargeable on their importation falls to be relieved by virtue of an order under section 37(1); or
  (b) they were exported from the United Kingdom during the period of twelve months ending with the date of their importation [in circumstances where the exportation and subsequent importation were effected to obtain the benefit of that subsection][6].][4]

(7) An order under section 2(2) may contain provision making such alteration of the percentage for the time being specified in subsection (4) above as the Treasury consider appropriate in consequence of any increase or decrease by that order of the rate of VAT.][1]

Commentary—*De Voil Indirect Tax Service* **V1.298, V3.306**.

HMRC Manuals—Imports Manual IMPS04100 (UK law).
IMPS05200 (permanent imports: works of art, antiques and collectors' items).
VAT Margin Scheme VATMARG02100 (works of art, collectors items and antiques : meaning).

Northern Ireland—See Sch 9ZA para 2: sub-para (1) provides that, for the purposes of this Act, the value of goods imported into the UK as a result of their entry into Northern Ireland is their value as if determined for the purposes of relevant NI import duty, whether or not the goods are subject to that duty. Accordingly, sub-s (1) of this section does not apply in relation to such goods. Subsections (2)–(7) apply in relation to such goods as if—
- the reference in sub-s (2) to the rules mentioned in sub-s (1) were to the adapted import valuation rules mentioned above in Sch 9ZB para 2(1);
- in sub-s (2)(c), after "United Kingdom" there were inserted "or a member State"; and
- the reference in sub-s (2A) to the temporary admission procedure under TCBTA 2018 Part 1 were to the procedure that corresponds to that procedure under Union customs legislation.

Amendments—[1] Sub-ss (4)–(7) inserted by FA 1995 s 22 with effect in relation to goods imported at any time on or after 1 May 1995.

[2] In sub-s (2)(a) word repealed, and sub-s (2)(b), (c) and words following substituted for previous sub-s (2)(b), by FA 1996 s 27, Sch 41 Pt IV(3) with effect in relation to goods imported after 31 December 1995.

[3] Words in sub-s (4) inserted by FA 1999 s 12 in relation to goods imported at any time from 27 July 1999.

[4] Sub-ss (5)–(6D) substituted for previous sub-ss (5), (6) by FA 1999 s 12 in relation to goods imported at any time from 27 July 1999.

[5] In sub-s (2) words inserted, and sub-ss (2A), (2B) inserted, by FA 2006 s 18 with effect from 1 September 2006 (by virtue of SI 2006/2149).

[6] In sub-s (6D)(b), words inserted by the Enactment of Extra-Statutory Concessions Order, SI 2009/730 art 17 with effect in relation to importations on or after 6 April 2009.

[7] In sub-s (4), words substituted for words "28.58 per cent" by F(No 2)A 2010 s 3(2) with effect in relation to goods imported on or after 4 January 2011.

[8] The following amendments made by the Taxation (Cross-border Trade) Act 2018 s 43, Sch 8 paras 1, 23 with effect from IP completion day (11pm on 31 December 2020), by virtue of SI 2020/1642 reg 4(b)—
- sub-s (1) substituted;
- in sub-s (2), words "from a place outside the member States" repealed in both places;
- in sub-s (2A), in para (a), words substituted for words "the procedure specified in subsection (2B) below", and in para (b), words "from a place outside the member States" repealed;
- sub-s (2B) repealed;
- in sub-ss (3)(a), (4), words "from a place outside the member States" repealed; and
- in sub-s (6D), words substituted for words "any goods imported from outside the member States".

Before these amendments, section 21 read as follows—

"(1) For the purposes of this Act, the value of goods imported from a place outside the member States shall (subject to subsections (2) to (4) below) be determined according to the rules applicable in the case of EU customs duties, whether or not the goods' in question are subject to any such duties.

(2) For the purposes of this Act the value of any goods imported from a place outside the member States shall (subject to subsection (2A) below) be taken to include the following so far as they are not already included in that value in accordance with the rules mentioned in subsection (1) above, that is to say—

  (a) all taxes, duties and other charges levied either outside or, by reason of importation, within the United Kingdom (except VAT);

(b) all incidental expenses, such as commission, packing, transport and insurance costs, up to the goods' first destination in the United Kingdom; and

(c) if at the time of the importation of the goods from a place outside the member States a further destination for the goods is known, and that destination is within the United Kingdom or another member State, all such incidental expenses in so far as they result from the transport of the goods to that other destination;

and in this subsection "the goods' first destination" means the place mentioned on the consignment note or any other document by means of which the goods are imported into the United Kingdom, or in the absence of such documentation it means the place of the first transfer of cargo in the United Kingdom.

(2A) Where—

(a) any goods falling within subsection (5) below are sold by auction at a time when they are subject to the procedure specified in subsection (2B) below, and

(b) arrangements made by or on behalf of the purchaser of the goods following the sale by auction result in the importation of the goods from a place outside the member States,

the value of the goods shall not be taken for the purposes of this Act to include, in relation to that importation, any commission or premium payable to the auctioneer in connection with the sale of the goods.

(2B) That procedure is the customs procedure for temporary importation with total relief from import duties provided for in Articles 137 to 141 of Council Regulation 2913/92/EEC establishing the Community Customs Code.

(3) Subject to subsection (2) above, where—

(a) goods are imported from a place outside the member States for a consideration which is or includes a price in money payable as on the transfer of property;

(b) the terms on which those goods are so imported allow a discount for prompt payment of that price;

(c) those terms do not include provision for payment of that price by instalments; and

(d) payment of that price is made in accordance with those terms so that the discount falls to be allowed,

the value of the goods shall be taken for the purposes of this Act to be reduced by the amount of the discount.

(4) Subject to subsection (6D) below, for the purposes of this Act, the value of any goods falling within subsection (5) below which are imported from a place outside the member States shall be taken to be an amount equal to 25 per cent of the amount which, apart from this subsection, would be their value for those purposes.

(5) The goods that fall within this subsection are—

(a) any work of art;

(b) any antique, not falling within paragraph (a) above or (c) below, that is more than one hundred years old;

(c) any collection or collector's piece that is of zoological, botanical, mineralogical, anatomical, historical, archaeological, palaeontological, ethnographic, numismatic or philatelic interest.

(6) In this section "work of art" means, subject to subsections (6A) and (6B) below—

(a) any mounted or unmounted painting, drawing, collage, decorative plaque or similar picture that was executed by hand;

(b) any original engraving, lithograph or other print which—

(i) was produced from one or more plates executed by hand by an individual who executed them without using any mechanical or photomechanical process; and

(ii) either is the only one produced from the plate or plates or is comprised in a limited edition;

(c) any original sculpture or statuary, in any material;

(d) any sculpture cast which—

(i) was produced by or under the supervision of the individual who made the mould or became entitled to it by succession on the death of that individual; and

(ii) either is the only cast produced from the mould or is comprised in a limited edition;

(e) any tapestry or other hanging which—

(i) was made by hand from an original design; and

(ii) either is the only one made from the design or is comprised in a limited edition;

(f) any ceramic executed by an individual and signed by him;

(g) any enamel on copper which—

(i) was executed by hand;

(ii) is signed either by the person who executed it or by someone on behalf of the studio where it was executed;

(iii) either is the only one made from the design in question or is comprised in a limited edition; and

(iv) is not comprised in an article of jewellery or an article of a kind produced by goldsmiths or silversmiths;

(h) any mounted or unmounted photograph which—

(i) was printed by or under the supervision of the photographer;

(ii) is signed by him; and

(iii) either is the only print made from the exposure in question or is comprised in a limited edition;

(6A) The following do not fall within subsection (5) above by virtue of subsection (6)(a) above, that is to say—

(a) any technical drawing, map or plan;

(b) any picture comprised in a manufactured article that has been hand-decorated; or

(c) anything in the nature of scenery, including a backcloth.

(6B) An item comprised in a limited edition shall be taken to be so comprised for the purposes of subsection (6)(d) to (h) above only if—

(a) in the case of sculpture casts—

(i) the edition is limited so that the number produced from the same mould does not exceed eight; or

(ii) the edition comprises a limited edition of nine or more casts made before 1st January 1989 which the Commissioners have directed should be treated, in the exceptional circumstances of the case, as a limited edition for the purposes of subsection (6)(d) above;

(b) in the case of tapestries and hangings, the edition is limited so that the number produced from the same design does not exceed eight;
(c) in the case of enamels on copper—
   (i) the edition is limited so that the number produced from the same design does not exceed eight; and
   (ii) each of the enamels in the edition is numbered and is signed as mentioned in subsection (6)(g)(ii) above;
(d) in the case of photographs—
   (i) the edition is limited so that the number produced from the same exposure does not exceed thirty; and
   (ii) each of the prints in the edition is numbered and is signed as mentioned in subsection (6)(h)(ii) above.
(6C) For the purposes of this section a collector's piece is of philatelic interest if—
(a) it is a postage or revenue stamp, a postmark, a first-day cover or an item of pre-stamped stationery; and
(b) it is franked or (if unfranked) it is not legal tender and is not intended for use as such.
(6D) Subsection (4) above does not apply in the case of any goods imported from outside the member States if—
(a) the whole of the VAT chargeable on their importation falls to be relieved by virtue of an order under section 37(1); or
(b) they were exported from the United Kingdom during the period of twelve months ending with the date of their importation in circumstances where the exportation and subsequent importation were effected to obtain the benefit of that subsection.
(7) An order under section 2(2) may contain provision making such alteration of the percentage for the time being specified in subsection (4) above as the Treasury consider appropriate in consequence of any increase or decrease by that order of the rate of VAT.".

[23 Value of supplies involving relevant machine games

(1) If a person plays a relevant machine game, then for the purposes of VAT the amount paid by the person is to be treated as consideration for a supply of services to that person.
(2) "Relevant machine game" is defined in section 23A.
(3) The value to be taken as the value of supplies made by a person ("the supplier") in the circumstances mentioned in subsection (1) in any period is to be determined as if the consideration for the supplies were reduced by an amount equal to X.
(4) X is the amount (if any) paid out in that period by way of winnings in respect of relevant machine games made available by the supplier (whether the games were played in the same period or an earlier one).
(5) X does not include any winnings paid out to the supplier or a person acting on the supplier's behalf.
(6) Inserting a token into a machine on which a relevant machine game is played is to be treated for the purposes of subsection (1) as the payment of an amount equal to that for which the token can be obtained.
(7) Providing a specified kind of token by way of winnings is to be treated for the purposes of subsection (4) as the payment out of an amount by way of winnings equal to the value of the token.
(8) A specified kind of token is—
   (a) a token that can be inserted into the same machine to enable games to be played on the machine, or
   (b) a token that is not of such a kind but can be exchanged for money.
(9) The value of a specified kind of token is—
   (a) for a token within subsection (8)(a), an amount equal to that for which the token can be obtained, and
   (b) for a token within subsection (8)(b), an amount equal to that for which the token can be exchanged.
(10) If it is not reasonably practicable to attribute payments and winnings to relevant machine games or to apportion them between relevant machine games and other games or other activities, any attribution or apportionment is to be done on a just and reasonable basis.
(11) For the purposes of this section, a person plays a game if the person participates in the game—
   (a) whether or not there are other participants in the game, and
   (b) whether or not a computer generates images or data taken to represent the actions of other participants in the game.][1]

Amendments—[1] Sections 23, 23A substituted for former s 23 by FA 2012 s 191, Sch 24 para 63 with effect in relation to supplies made on or after 1 February 2013.

[23A Meaning of "relevant machine game"

(1) A "relevant machine game" is a game (whether of skill or chance or both) that—
   (a)
   (b)
(a) is played on a machine for a prize, and
(b) is not excluded by subsection (2).
(2) A game is excluded by this subsection if—
   (a) takings and payouts in respect of it are taken into account in determining any charge to machine games duty,
   (b) it involves betting on future real events,

(c) bingo duty is charged on the playing of it or would be so charged but for paragraphs 1 to 5 of Schedule 3 to the Betting and Gaming Duties Act 1981 (exemptions from bingo duty),
(d) lottery duty is charged on the taking of a ticket or chance in it or would be so charged but for an express exception,
(e) lottery duty is charged on the taking of a ticket or chance in it or would be so charged but for an express exception,
(f) playing it amounts to remote gaming within the meaning of [section 154(1) of the Finance Act 2014 (meaning of remote gaming)]².
(3) In this section—
"game" does not include a sport;
"machine" means any apparatus that uses or applies mechanical power, electrical power or both;
"prize", in relation to a game, does not include the opportunity to play the game again;
"real game of chance" means a game of chance (within the meaning of [Part 3 of the Finance Act 2014 (see section 188(1)(b))]²) that is non-virtual.
(4) The Treasury may by order amend this section.]¹

Commentary—*De Voil Indirect Tax Service* **V3.264**.
HMRC Manuals—VAT Betting And Gaming Guidance VBANDG08210 (definition of a relevant machine game).
Amendments—¹ Sections 23, 23A substituted for former s 23 by FA 2012 s 191, Sch 24 para 63 with effect in relation to supplies made on or after 1 February 2013.
² In sub-s (2)(f), words substituted for words "section 26A of the Betting and Gaming Duties Act 1981 (remote gaming duty: interpretation)", and in sub-s (3), words substituted for words "the Betting and Gaming Duties Act 1981", by FA 2014 s 196, Sch 28 para 19 with effect from 1 December 2014 (FA 2014 s 198(2)), subject to transitional provisions and savings in FA 2014 Sch 29.

Payment of VAT by taxable persons

24 Input tax and output tax

(1) Subject to the following provisions of this section, "input tax", in relation to a taxable person, means the following tax, that is to say—
(a) VAT on the supply to him of any goods or services;
(b) . . . ⁴ and
(c) VAT paid or payable by him on the importation of any goods . . . ⁴,
being (in each case) goods or services used or to be used for the purpose of any business carried on or to be carried on by him.
(2) Subject to the following provisions of this section, "output tax", in relation to a taxable person, means VAT on supplies which he makes . . . ⁴.
(3) . . . ³
(4) The Treasury may by order provide with respect to any description of goods or services that, where goods or services of that description are supplied to a person who is not a taxable person, they shall, in such circumstances as may be specified in the order, be treated for the purposes of subsections (1) and (2) above as supplied to such other person as may be determined in accordance with the order.
(5) Where goods or services supplied to a taxable person . . . ⁴ or goods imported by a taxable person . . . ⁴ are used or to be used partly for the purposes of a business carried on or to be carried on by him and partly for other purposes[—
(a) VAT on supplies . . . ⁴ and importations shall be apportioned so that so much as is referable to the taxable person's business purposes is counted as that person's input tax, and
(b) the remainder of that VAT ("the non-business VAT") shall count as that person's input tax only to the extent (if any) provided for by regulations under subsection (6)(e).]²
[(5A) For the purposes of subsections (1) and (5), a relevant asset held for the purposes of a business carried on or to be carried on by a taxable person is not, in any circumstances, to be regarded as used or to be used for the purposes of the business if, and to the extent that, it is used or to be used for that person's private use or the private use of that person's staff.
(5B) In subsection (5A) "relevant asset" means—
(a) any interest in land,
(b) any building or part of a building,
(c) any civil engineering work or part of such a work,
(d) any goods incorporated or to be incorporated in a building or civil engineering work (whether by being installed as fixtures or fittings or otherwise),
(e) any ship, boat or other vessel, or
(f) any aircraft.]³
(6) Regulations may provide—
(a) for VAT on the supply of goods or services to a taxable person . . . ⁴ and VAT paid or payable by a taxable person on the importation of goods . . . ⁴ to be treated as his input tax only if and to the extent that the charge to VAT is evidenced and quantified by reference to such documents [or other information]¹ as may be specified in the regulations or the Commissioners may direct either generally or in particular cases or classes of cases;

(b) for a taxable person to count as his input tax, in such circumstances, to such extent and subject to such conditions as may be prescribed, VAT on the supply to him of goods or services . . . [4] or paid by him on the importation of goods . . . [4] notwithstanding that he was not a taxable person at the time of the supply . . . [4] or payment;

(c) for a taxable person that is a body corporate to count as its input tax, in such circumstances, to such extent and subject to such conditions as may be prescribed, VAT on the supply . . . [4] or importation of goods before the company's incorporation for appropriation to the company or its business or on the supply of services before that time for its benefit or in connection with its incorporation;

(d) in the case of a person who has been, but is no longer, a taxable person, for him to be paid by the Commissioners the amount of any VAT on a supply of services made to him for the purposes of the business carried on by him when he was a taxable person;

[(e) in cases where an apportionment is made under subsection (5), for the non-business VAT to be counted as the taxable person's input tax for the purposes of any provision made by or under section 26 in such circumstances, to such extent and subject to such conditions as may be prescribed.][2]

[(6A) Regulations under subsection (6) may contain such supplementary, incidental, consequential and transitional provisions as appear to the Commissioners to be necessary or expedient.][2]

(7) . . . [3]

Commentary—*De Voil Indirect Tax Service* **V3.421, V3.501**.
HMRC Manuals—VAT Input Tax VIT25400 - 5450 (Input tax : method of apportionment).
VAT Fraud VATF34600 (business and taxable person).
Northern Ireland—See Sch 9ZA para 14 (sub-ss (5)–(6A) apply to NI acquisition VAT as they apply to VAT on the supply or importation of goods).
Orders—See VAT Regulations, SI 1995/2518.
VAT (Input Tax) (Reimbursement by Employers of Employees' Business Use of Road Fuel) Regulations, SI 2005/3290.
VAT (Input Tax) (Person Supplied) Order, SI 2005/3291.
Amendments—[1] Words in sub-s (6)(a) inserted by FA 2003, s 17(2) with effect from 10 April 2003.

[2] In sub-s (5), words substituted for words ", VAT on supplies, acquisitions and importations shall be apportioned so that only so much as is referable to his business purposes is counted as his input tax.", and sub-ss (6)(e), (6A) inserted, by F(No 3)A 2010 s 19, Sch 8 para 1(1), (3), (5), (6) with effect from 16 December 2010.

[3] Sub-ss (3), (7) repealed and sub-ss (5A), (5B) inserted, by F(No 3)A 2010 s 19, Sch 8 para 1(1), (2), (4), (7) with effect in relation to VAT incurred by a taxable person on or after 1 January 2011. The VAT "incurred" by a person in respect of an asset is VAT on the supply to the person of the asset, VAT on the supply to the person of any goods or services the expenditure on which constitutes expenditure related to the asset, VAT on the acquisition by the person from another member State of the asset or anything comprised in it, and VAT paid or payable by the person on the importation of the asset or anything comprised in it from a place outside the member States, and such VAT is incurred at the time of the supply, acquisition or importation in question (F(No 3)A 2010 Sch 8 para 1(9)).

[4] The following amendments made by the Taxation (Cross-border Trade) Act 2018 s 43, Sch 8 paras 1, 24 with effect from IP completion day (11pm on 31 December 2020), by virtue of SI 2020/1642 reg 4(b)—
- in sub-s (1), para (b) repealed, and in para (c), words "from a place outside the member States" repealed;
- in sub-s (2), words "or on the acquisition by him from another member State of goods (including VAT which is also to be counted as input tax by virtue of subsection (1)(b) above)" repealed;
- in sub-s (5), the following words repealed—
    (a) in the opening words, words ", goods acquired by a taxable person from another member State" and "from a place outside the member States"; and
    (b) in para (a), word ", acquisitions";
- in sub-s (6), the following words repealed—
    (a) in para (a), words ", VAT on the acquisition of goods by a taxable person from other member States" and "from places outside the member States";
    (b) in para (b), words "or on the acquisition of goods by him from another member State", "from places outside the member States" and ", acquisition"; and
    (c) in para (c), word ", acquisition".

Before these amendments, section 24 read as follows—

"(1) Subject to the following provisions of this section, "input tax", in relation to a taxable person, means the following tax, that is to say—
  (a) VAT on the supply to him of any goods or services;
  (b) VAT on the acquisition by him from another member State of any goods; and
  (c) VAT paid or payable by him on the importation of any goods from a place outside the member States,
being (in each case) goods or services used or to be used for the purpose of any business carried on or to be carried on by him.

(2) Subject to the following provisions of this section, "output tax", in relation to a taxable person, means VAT on supplies which he makes . . . .

(3) . . .

(4) The Treasury may by order provide with respect to any description of goods or services that, where goods or services of that description are supplied to a person who is not a taxable person, they shall, in such circumstances as may be specified in the order, be treated for the purposes of subsections (1) and (2) above as supplied to such other person as may be determined in accordance with the order.

(5) Where goods or services supplied to a taxable person, goods acquired by a taxable person from another member State or goods imported by a taxable person from a place outside the member States are used or to be used partly for the purposes of a business carried on or to be carried on by him and partly for other purposes—

(a) VAT on supplies, acquisitions and importations shall be apportioned so that so much as is referable to the taxable person's business purposes is counted as that person's input tax, and

(b) the remainder of that VAT ("the non-business VAT") shall count as that person's input tax only to the extent (if any) provided for by regulations under subsection (6)(e).

(5A) For the purposes of subsections (1) and (5), a relevant asset held for the purposes of a business carried on or to be carried on by a taxable person is not, in any circumstances, to be regarded as used or to be used for the purposes of the business if, and to the extent that, it is used or to be used for that person's private use or the private use of that person's staff.

(5B) In subsection (5A) "relevant asset" means—

(a) any interest in land,

(b) any building or part of a building,

(c) any civil engineering work or part of such a work,

(d) any goods incorporated or to be incorporated in a building or civil engineering work (whether by being installed as fixtures or fittings or otherwise),

(e) any ship, boat or other vessel, or

(f) any aircraft.

(6) Regulations may provide—

(a) for VAT on the supply of goods or services to a taxable person, VAT on the acquisition of goods by a taxable person from other member States and VAT paid or payable by a taxable person on the importation of goods from places outside the member States to be treated as his input tax only if and to the extent that the charge to VAT is evidenced and quantified by reference to such documents or other information as may be specified in the regulations or the Commissioners may direct either generally or in particular cases or classes of cases;

(b) for a taxable person to count as his input tax, in such circumstances, to such extent and subject to such conditions as may be prescribed, VAT on the supply to him of goods or services or on the acquisition of goods by him from another member State or paid by him on the importation of goods from places outside the member States notwithstanding that he was not a taxable person at the time of the supply, acquisition or payment;

(c) for a taxable person that is a body corporate to count as its input tax, in such circumstances, to such extent and subject to such conditions as may be prescribed, VAT on the supply, acquisition or importation of goods before the company's incorporation for appropriation to the company or its business or on the supply of services before that time for its benefit or in connection with its incorporation;

(d) in the case of a person who has been, but is no longer, a taxable person, for him to be paid by the Commissioners the amount of any VAT on a supply of services made to him for the purposes of the business carried on by him when he was a taxable person;

(e) in cases where an apportionment is made under subsection (5), for the non-business VAT to be counted as the taxable person's input tax for the purposes of any provision made by or under section 26 in such circumstances, to such extent and subject to such conditions as may be prescribed.

(6A) Regulations under subsection (6) may contain such supplementary, incidental, consequential and transitional provisions as appear to the Commissioners to be necessary or expedient.

(7) . . . ".

25 Payment by reference to accounting periods and credit for input tax against output tax

(1) A taxable person shall—

(a) in respect of supplies made by him, . . . [1]

(b) . . . [1]

account for and pay VAT by reference to such periods (in this Act referred to as "prescribed accounting periods") at such time and in such manner as may be determined by or under regulations and regulations may make different provision for different circumstances.

(2) Subject to the provisions of this section, he is entitled at the end of each prescribed accounting period to credit for so much of his input tax as is allowable under section 26, and then to deduct that amount from any output tax that is due from him.

(3) If either no output tax is due at the end of the period, or the amount of the credit exceeds that of the output tax then, subject to subsections (4) and (5) below, the amount of the credit or, as the case may be, the amount of the excess shall be paid to the taxable person by the Commissioners; and an amount which is due under this subsection is referred to in this Act as a "VAT credit".

(4) The whole or any part of the credit may, subject to and in accordance with regulations, be held over to be credited in and for a subsequent period; and the regulations may allow for it to be so held over either on the taxable person's own application or in accordance with general or special directions given by the Commissioners from time to time.

(5) Where at the end of any period a VAT credit is due to a taxable person who has failed to submit returns for any earlier period as required by this Act, the Commissioners may withhold payment of the credit until he has complied with that requirement.

(6) A deduction under subsection (2) above and payment of a VAT credit shall not be made or paid except on a claim made in such manner and at such time as may be determined by or under regulations; and, in the case of a person who has made no taxable supplies in the period concerned or any previous period, payment of a VAT credit shall be made subject to such conditions (if any) as the Commissioners think fit to impose, including conditions as to repayment in specified circumstances.

(7) The Treasury may by order provide, in relation to such supplies . . . [1] and importations as the order may specify, that VAT charged on them is to be excluded from any credit under this section; and—
  (a) any such provision may be framed by reference to the description of goods or services supplied or goods . . . [1] imported, the person by whom they are supplied . . . [1] or imported or to whom they are supplied, the purposes for which they are supplied . . . [1] or imported, or any circumstances whatsoever; and
  (b) such an order may contain provision for consequential relief from output tax.

Commentary—*De Voil Indirect Tax Service* **V3.418, V3.401**.
HMRC Manuals—VAT Annual Manual VATAC1530 (legal framework for VAT payments).
VAT Assessments And Error Correction VAEC8320 (error correction for VAT).
Security Guidance Manual SG29200 (meaning of VAT credit)
Northern Ireland—See Sch 9ZA para 15 (payment of Northern Ireland acquisition VAT).
Note—The reference in sub-s (2) to output tax due from the taxable person does not include any VAT that the taxable person is liable to pay to another member State under a non-UK special scheme (VATA 1994 Sch 3BA para 19(5)).
Regulations—See VAT Regulations, SI 1995/2518.
VAT (Annual Accounting) Regulations, SI 1996/542.
VAT (Amendment) Regulations, SI 2012/33.
VAT (Amendment) (No 2) Regulations, SI 2012/1899.
VAT (Amendment) (No 2) Regulations, SI 2014/1497.
VAT (Amendment) Regulations, SI 2015/1978.
VAT (Amendment) Regulations, SI 2018/261.
Amendments—[1] In sub-s (1), para (b) and preceding word "and" repealed; and in sub-s (7), in opening words, word ", acquisitions" and in para (a), words "acquired or" and ", acquired" (in both places), repealed, by the Taxation (Cross-border Trade) Act 2018 s 43, Sch 8 paras 1, 25 with effect from IP completion day (11pm on 31 December 2020), by virtue of SI 2020/1642 reg 4(b).
  Sub-s (1)(b) previously read as follows—
    "(b) in respect of the acquisition by him from other member States of any goods,".

26 Input tax allowable under section 25

(1) The amount of input tax for which a taxable person is entitled to credit at the end of any period shall be so much of the input tax for the period (that is input tax on supplies . . . [2] and importations in the period) as is allowable by or under regulations as being attributable to supplies within subsection (2) below.
(2) The supplies within this subsection are the following supplies made or to be made by the taxable person in the course or furtherance of his business—
  (a) taxable supplies;
  (b) supplies outside the United Kingdom which would be taxable supplies if made in the United Kingdom;
  (c) such other supplies outside the United Kingdom and such exempt supplies as the Treasury may by order specify for the purposes of this subsection.
(3) The Commissioners shall make regulations for securing a fair and reasonable attribution of input tax to supplies within subsection (2) above, and any such regulations may provide for—
  (a) determining a proportion by reference to which input tax for any prescribed accounting period is to be provisionally attributed to those supplies;
  (b) adjusting, in accordance with a proportion determined in like manner for any longer period comprising two or more prescribed accounting periods or parts thereof, the provisional attribution for any of those periods;
  (c) the making of payments in respect of input tax, by the Commissioners to a taxable person (or a person who has been a taxable person) or by a taxable person (or a person who has been a taxable person) to the Commissioners, in cases where events prove inaccurate an estimate on the basis of which an attribution was made; and
  (d) preventing input tax on a supply which, under or by virtue of any provision of this Act, a person makes to himself from being allowable as attributable to that supply.
(4) Regulations under subsection (3) above may make different provision for different circumstances and, in particular (but without prejudice to the generality of that subsection) for different descriptions of goods or services; and may contain such incidental[, supplementary, consequential and transitional][1] provisions as appear to the Commissioners necessary or expedient.

Commentary—*De Voil Indirect Tax Service* **V3.460, V3.465**.
HMRC Manuals—VAT Place Of Supply Of Services VATPOSS03200 (recovery of input tax).
VAT Finance Manual VATFIN1550 (input tax recovery).
VAT Supply and consideration VATSC10223 (whether supplies are goods or services).
Northern Ireland—Sub-s (1) has effect as if the reference to "input tax on supplies and importations" included input tax on acquisitions in Northern Ireland from a member State (see Sch 9ZA para 15(4)).
Orders—VAT (Input Tax) (Specified Supplies) Order, SI 1999/3121.
Value Added Tax (Input Tax) (Specified Supplies) (Amendment) Order, SI 2018/1328.
Regulations—See VAT Regulations, SI 1995/2518 regs 99–111.
VAT (Amendment) (No 2) Regulations, SI 2012/1899.
VAT (Amendment) Regulations, SI 2015/1978.

Amendments—[1] In sub-s (4), words substituted for words "and supplementary" by F(No 3)A 2010 s 19, Sch 8 para 2 with effect from 16 December 2010.
[2] In sub-s (1), word ", acquisitions" repealed by the Taxation (Cross-border Trade) Act 2018 s 43, Sch 8 paras 1, 26 with effect from IP completion day (11pm on 31 December 2020), by virtue of SI 2020/1642 reg 4(b).

[26A Disallowance of input tax where consideration not paid
(1) Where—
  (a) a person has become entitled to credit for any input tax, and
  (b) the consideration for the supply to which that input tax relates, or any part of it, is unpaid at the end of the period of six months following the relevant date,
he shall be taken, as from the end of that period, not to have been entitled to credit for input tax in respect of the VAT that is referable to the unpaid consideration or part.
[(1A) Subsection (1) is subject to section 26AA (disapplication of disallowance under section 26A in insolvency).][2]
(2) For the purposes of subsection (1) above "the relevant date", in relation to any sum representing consideration for a supply, is—
  (a) the date of the supply; or
  (b) if later, the date on which the sum became payable.
(3) Regulations may make such supplementary, incidental, consequential or transitional provisions as appear to the Commissioners to be necessary or expedient for the purposes of this section.
(4) Regulations under this section may in particular—
  (a) make provision for restoring the whole or any part of an entitlement to credit for input tax where there is a payment after the end of the period mentioned in subsection (1) above;
  (b) make rules for ascertaining whether anything paid is to be taken as paid by way of consideration for a particular supply;
  (c) make rules dealing with particular cases, such as those involving payment of part of the consideration or mutual debts.
(5) Regulations under this section may make different provision for different circumstances.
(6) Section 6 shall apply for determining the time when a supply is to be treated as taking place for the purposes of construing this section.]¹
Commentary—*De Voil Indirect Tax Service* **V3.450.**
HMRC Manuals—VAT Finance Manual VATF42500 (the supplies have not been paid for).
Amendments—[1] This section inserted by FA 2002 s 22(1), (3) with effect for supplies made after 31 December 2002 (by virtue of SI 2002/3028).
[2] Sub-s (1A) inserted by the Enactment of Extra-Statutory Concessions Order, SI 2017/495 art 7(1), (2) with effect in relation to supplies made on or after 6 April 2017.

[26AA Disapplication of disallowance under section 26A in insolvency
(1) Section 26A(1) does not apply to a person in relation to credit for input tax which relates to a supply where—
  (a) at the time of the supply, no insolvency procedure had effect in relation to the person,
  (b) at any time during the relevant period, an insolvency procedure had effect in relation to that person ("the insolvent person"), and
  (c) the Commissioners have been notified in writing of the matter mentioned in paragraph (b) by or on behalf of a person authorised to deal with the insolvent person's affairs.
(2) But where the insolvency procedure mentioned in subsection (1)(b) is a bankruptcy order, award of sequestration, protected trust deed or voluntary arrangement and that bankruptcy order is annulled, that award of sequestration is recalled or that protected trust deed or voluntary arrangement has come to an end prematurely—
  (a) the disapplication of section 26A(1) by subsection (1) above ceases to have effect, and
  (b) the person to which the bankruptcy order, award of sequestration, protected trust deed or voluntary arrangement relates is to be taken for the purposes of section 26A(1) as not being entitled to the credit for the input tax concerned as from whichever is the later of—
    (i) the end of the relevant period, and
    (ii) the date on which the bankruptcy order was annulled, the award of sequestration recalled or the protected trust deed or voluntary arrangement has come to an end prematurely.
(3) Where the person mentioned in section 26A(1) is entitled as a member of a partnership to credit for input tax this section has effect as if—
  (a) the references in subsections (1)(a) and (b) to "the person" and "that person" were references to the partnership,
  (b) the reference in subsection (1)(c) to "the insolvent person's affairs" were a reference to the insolvent partnership's affairs, and
  (c) the reference in subsection (2)(b) to "the person", in connection with a bankruptcy order or a voluntary arrangement, were a reference to the person who is a member of the partnership to which the bankruptcy order or voluntary arrangement relates.

(4) Subsection (1) does not apply where the insolvency procedure referred to in subsection (1)(*b*) has effect as part of, or as a consequence of, arrangements where the main purpose, or one of the main purposes, of those arrangements is to obtain a tax advantage by the operation of this section.

(5) Regulations may make such supplementary, incidental, consequential or transitional provisions as appear to the Commissioners to be necessary or expedient for the purposes of this section.

(6) For the purposes of this section "the relevant period", in relation to a supply, is the period beginning immediately after the supply took place and ending six months after—
- (*a*) the date of that supply, or
- (*b*) if later, the date on which the relevant part of the consideration for the supply is payable.

(7) For the purposes of subsection (6) the relevant part of the consideration is the part of the consideration referable to the credit for input tax which would (ignoring the effect of this section) be disallowed under section 26A(1).

(8) For the purposes of this section an insolvency procedure has effect in relation to a person at a time when any of the following apply—
- (*a*) a bankruptcy order has been made under Chapter 1 of Part 9 of the Insolvency Act 1986 in relation to that person and has not been annulled,
- (*b*) a warrant has been granted for a petition for sequestration to be served on that person which has resulted in the sequestration of that person's estate or an award of sequestration has been made on an application by that person, in both cases under section 22 of the Bankruptcy (Scotland) Act 2016, and in either case the award of sequestration has not been recalled,
- (*c*) a bankruptcy order has been made under Chapter 1 of Part 9 of the Insolvency (Northern Ireland) Order 1989 in relation to that person and has not been annulled,
- (*d*) where that person is a company registered under the Companies Act 2006 in England and Wales or Scotland or an unregistered company as defined in section 220 of the Insolvency Act 1986 which is deemed to be registered in England and Wales or Scotland under section 221 of that Act, a petition has been presented to the court which has resulted in a winding-up order being made under Chapter 6 of Part 4 or Part 5 of the Insolvency Act 1986 in relation to that person and that person has not been dissolved or that winding-up order has not been stayed or sisted,
- (*e*) where that person is a company registered under the Companies Act 2006 in Northern Ireland, or an unregistered company as defined in article 184 of the Insolvency (Northern Ireland) Order 1989 which is deemed to be registered in Northern Ireland under article 185 of that Order, a petition has been presented to the court which has resulted in a winding-up order being made under Part 5 or Part 6 of the Insolvency (Northern Ireland) Order 1989 and that person has not been dissolved or that winding-up order has not been stayed,
- (*f*) that person is in administration for the purposes of Schedule B1 to the Insolvency Act 1986 or Schedule B1 to the Insolvency (Northern Ireland) Order 1989,
- (*g*) an appointment of an administrative receiver is in force in relation to that person disregarding any temporary vacancy in the office of receiver,
- (*h*) an appointment of a liquidator is in force as a consequence of a creditors' voluntary winding up under Chapter 4 of Part 4 of the Insolvency Act 1986 or Chapter 4 of Part 5 of the Insolvency (Northern Ireland) Order 1989 in relation to that person disregarding any temporary vacancy in the office of liquidator,
- (*i*) a voluntary arrangement has been approved in accordance with Part 1 or Part 8 of the Insolvency Act 1986 or Part 2 or Chapter 2 of Part 8 of the Insolvency (Northern Ireland) Order 1989 in relation to that person and that voluntary arrangement has not come to an end prematurely,
- (*j*) a county court administration order has been made under Part 6 of the County Courts Act 1984 or Part 6 of the Judgments Enforcement (Northern Ireland) Order 1981 in relation to that person and has not ceased to take effect,
- (*k*) a compromise or arrangement sanctioned by the court and delivered to the registrar in accordance with section 899 of the Companies Act 2006 is in place in relation to that person,
- [(*ka*) a compromise or arrangement sanctioned by the court and delivered to the registrar or (as the case may be) published in the Gazette in accordance with section 901F of the Companies Act 2006 is in place in relation to that person,][2]
- (*l*) that person's estate is vested in any other person as that person's trustee under a trust deed and that trust deed has become a protected trust deed,
- (*m*) that person has died and an insolvency administration order has been made which has not been discharged in respect of that person's estate in accordance with an order under section 421 of the Insolvency Act 1986 or article 365 of the Insolvency (Northern Ireland) Order 1989 or that person's estate has been sequestrated under section 22 of the Bankruptcy (Scotland) Act 2016 and the award of sequestration has not been recalled,
- (*n*) a voluntary arrangement has been approved in accordance with Part 1 of the Insolvency Act 1986 as applied by Part 2 of the Insolvent Partnerships Order 1994 or Part 2 of the Insolvency

(Northern Ireland) Order 1989 as applied by Part 2 of the Insolvent Partnerships Order (Northern Ireland) 1995 in relation to that person and that voluntary arrangement has not come to an end prematurely,
  (o) an appointment of a liquidator is in force as a consequence of a creditors' voluntary winding up under Chapter 4 of Part 4 of the Insolvency Act 1986 as applied by Parts 4 and 5 of the Insolvent Partnerships Order 1994, or Chapter 4 of Part 5 of the Insolvency (Northern Ireland) Order 1989 as applied by Part 4 of the Insolvent Partnerships Order (Northern Ireland) 1995 in relation to that person disregarding any temporary vacancy in the office of liquidator,
  (p) that person is in administration for the purposes of Schedule B1 to the Insolvency Act 1986 as applied by Part 3 of the Insolvent Partnerships Order 1994 or Schedule B1 to the Insolvency (Northern Ireland) Order 1989 as applied by Part 3 of the Insolvent Partnerships Order (Northern Ireland) 1995,
  (q) a voluntary arrangement has been approved in accordance with Part 1 of the Insolvency Act 1986 as applied by Part 4 of the Limited Liability Partnerships Regulations 2001 or Part 2 of the Insolvency (Northern Ireland) Order 1989 as applied by Part 4 of the Limited Liability Partnerships Regulations (Northern Ireland) 2004 in relation to that person and that voluntary arrangement has not come to an end prematurely,
  (r) an appointment of a liquidator is in force as a consequence of a creditors' voluntary winding up under Chapter 4 of Part 4 of the Insolvency Act 1986 as applied by Part 4 of the Limited Liability Partnerships Regulations 2001 or Chapter 4 of Part 5 of the Insolvency (Northern Ireland) Order 1989 as applied by Part 4 of the Limited Liability Partnerships Regulations (Northern Ireland) 2004 in relation to that person disregarding any temporary vacancy in the office of liquidator,
  (s) that person is in administration for the purposes of Schedule B1 to the Insolvency Act 1986 as applied by Part 4 of the Limited Liability Partnerships Regulations 2001 or Schedule B1 to the Insolvency (Northern Ireland) Order 1989 as applied by Part 4 of the Limited Liability Partnerships Regulations (Northern Ireland) 2004.
(9) In this section—
  "administrative receiver" means an administrative receiver within the meaning of section 251 of the Insolvency Act 1986 or article 5(1) of the Insolvency (Northern Ireland) Order 1989;
  "protected trust deed" has the same meaning as in the Bankruptcy (Scotland) Act 2016;
  "tax advantage" has the same meaning as in Schedule 11A; and
  "trust deed" has the same meaning as in the Bankruptcy (Scotland) Act 2016.
(10) In this section a voluntary arrangement comes to an end prematurely if it would be regarded as having come to an end prematurely under—
  (a) section 7B or section 262C of the Insolvency Act 1986; or
  (b) article 20B or article 236C of the Insolvency (Northern Ireland) Order 1989.
(11) Section 6 applies for determining the time when a supply is to be treated as taking place for the purposes of construing this section.][1]

Commentary—*De Voil Indirect Tax Service* **V3.450**.
Modifications—Sub-s (8)(*t*) treated as having been inserted by the Further Education Bodies (Insolvency) Regulations, SI 2019/138 reg 35 with effect from 31 January 2019 and in relation to certain statutory corporations and companies conducting designated further education institutions in England and Wales. Sub-s (8)(*t*) reads as follows—
"(*t*) an education administration order under Chapter 4 of Part 2 of the Technical and Further Education Act 2017 has been made in respect of that person and had not been set aside.".
Amendments—[1] Section 26AA inserted by the Enactment of Extra-Statutory Concessions Order, SI 2017/495 art 7(1), (3) with effect in relation to supplies made on or after 6 April 2017.
[2] Sub-s (8)(*ka*) inserted by the Corporate Insolvency and Governance Act 2020 s 7, Sch 9 para 15 with effect from 26 June 2020.

[26AB Adjustment of output tax in respect of supplies under section 55A

(1) This section applies if—
  (a) a person is, as a result of section 26A, taken not to have been entitled to any credit for input tax in respect of any supply, and
  (b) the supply is one in respect of which the person is required under section 55A(6) to account for and pay VAT.
(2) The person is entitled to make an adjustment to the amount of VAT which he is so required to account for and pay.
(3) The amount of the adjustment is to be equal to the amount of the credit for the input tax to which the person is taken not to be entitled.
(4) Regulations may make such supplementary, incidental, consequential or transitional provisions as appear to the Commissioners to be necessary or expedient for the purposes of this section.
(5) Regulations under this section may in particular—
  (a) make provision for the manner in which, and the period for which, the adjustment is to be given effect,
  (b) require the adjustment to be evidenced and quantified by reference to such records and other documents as may be specified by or under the regulations,

(c) require the person entitled to the adjustment to keep, for such period and in such form and manner as may be so specified, those records and documents,
(d) make provision for readjustments if any credit for input tax is restored under section 26A.
(6) Regulations under this section may make different provision for different circumstances.][1]

Commentary—*De Voil Indirect Tax Service* **V3.450, V3.233**.
HMRC Manuals—VAT Traders' Records Manual VATREC13080 (when do regulation 38 adjustments need to be made to the VAT account?).
Regulations—VAT (Amendment) (No 2) Regulations, SI 2012/1899.
Amendments—[1] Section inserted by FA 2006 s 19(2), (8) in relation to supplies made on or after 1 June 2007 (by virtue of the Finance Act 2006, section 19, (Appointed Day) Order, SI 2007/1419).

[26B Flat-rate scheme

(1) The Commissioners may by regulations make provision under which, where a taxable person so elects, the amount of his liability to VAT in respect of his relevant supplies in any prescribed accounting period shall be the appropriate percentage of his relevant turnover for that period.
A person whose liability to VAT is to any extent determined as mentioned above is referred to in this section as participating in the flat-rate scheme.
(2) For the purposes of this section—
   (a) a person's "relevant supplies" are all supplies made by him except supplies made at such times or of such descriptions as may be specified in the regulations;
   (b) the "appropriate percentage" is the percentage so specified for the category of business carried on by the person in question;
   (c) a person's "relevant turnover" is the total of—
      (i) the value of those of his relevant supplies that are taxable supplies, together with the VAT chargeable on them, and
      (ii) the value of those of his relevant supplies that are exempt supplies.
(3) The regulations may designate certain categories of business as categories in relation to which the references in subsection (1) above to liability to VAT are to be read as references to entitlement to credit for VAT.
(4) The regulations may provide for persons to be eligible to participate in the flat-rate scheme only in such cases and subject to such conditions and exceptions as may be specified in, or determined by or under, the regulations.
(5) Subject to such exceptions as the regulations may provide for, a participant in the flat-rate scheme shall not be entitled to credit for input tax.
This is without prejudice to subsection (3) above.
(6) The regulations may—
   (a) provide for the appropriate percentage to be determined by reference to the category of business that a person is expected, on reasonable grounds, to carry on in a particular period;
   (b) provide, in such circumstances as may be prescribed, for different percentages to apply in relation to different parts of the same prescribed accounting period;
   (c) make provision for determining the category of business to be regarded as carried on by a person carrying on businesses in more than one category.
(7) The regulations may provide for the following matters to be determined in accordance with notices published by the Commissioners—
   (a) when supplies are to be treated as taking place for the purposes of ascertaining a person's relevant turnover for a particular period;
   (b) the method of calculating any adjustments that fall to be made in accordance with the regulations in a case where a person begins or ceases to participate in the flat-rate scheme.
(8) The regulations may make provision enabling the Commissioners—
   (a) to authorise a person to participate in the flat-rate scheme with effect from—
      (i) a day before the date of his election to participate, or
      (ii) a day that is not earlier than that date but is before the date of the authorisation;
   (b) to direct that a person shall cease to be a participant in the scheme with effect from a day before the date of the direction.
The day mentioned in paragraph (a)(i) above may be a day before the date on which the regulations come into force.
(9) Regulations under this section—
   (a) may make different provision for different circumstances;
   (b) may make such incidental, supplemental, consequential or transitional provision as the Commissioners think fit, including provision disapplying or applying with modifications any provision contained in or made under this Act.][1]

Regulations—Value Added Tax (Amendment) (No 2) Regulations, SI 2010/2240.
Value Added Tax (Amendment) Regulations, SI 2017/295.
Amendments—[1] This section inserted by FA 2002 s 23(1), (4) and deemed to have come into force on 24 April 2002

27 Goods imported for private purposes

(1) Where goods are imported by a taxable person . . . [1] and—

(*a*) at the time of importation they belong wholly or partly to another person; and
(*b*) the purposes for which they are to be used include private purposes either of himself or of the other,
VAT paid or payable by the taxable person on the importation of the goods shall not be regarded as input tax to be deducted or credited under section 25; but he may make a separate claim to the Commissioners for it to be repaid.
(2) The Commissioners shall allow the claim if they are satisfied that to disallow it would result, in effect, in a double charge to VAT; and where they allow it they shall do so only to the extent necessary to avoid the double charge.
(3) In considering a claim under this section, the Commissioners shall have regard to the circumstances of the importation and, so far as appearing to them to be relevant, things done with, or occurring in relation to, the goods at any subsequent time.
(4) Any amount allowed by the Commissioners on the claim shall be paid by them to the taxable person.
(5) The reference above to a person's private purposes is to purposes which are not those of any business carried on by him.
Commentary—*De Voil Indirect Tax Service* **V5.153**.
Amendments—[1] In sub-s (1), words "from a place outside the member States" repealed by the Taxation (Cross-border Trade) Act 2018 s 43, Sch 8 paras 1, 27 with effect from IP completion day (11pm on 31 December 2020), by virtue of SI 2020/1642 reg 4(*b*).

28 Payments on account of VAT
(1) The Treasury may make an order under this section if they consider it desirable to do so in the interests of the national economy.
(2) An order under this section may provide that a taxable person of a description specified in the order shall be under a duty—
(*a*) to pay, on account of any VAT he may become liable to pay in respect of a prescribed accounting period, amounts determined in accordance with the order, and
(*b*) to do so at such times as are so determined.
[(2AA) An order under this section may provide for the matters with respect to which an appeal under section 83 lies to a tribunal to include such decisions of the Commissioners under that or any other order under this section as may be specified in the order.][2]
[(2A) The Commissioners may give directions, to persons who are or may become liable by virtue of any order under this section to make payments on account of VAT, about the manner in which they are to make such payments; and where such a direction has been given to any person and has not subsequently been withdrawn, any duty of that person by virtue of such an order to make such a payment shall have effect as if it included a requirement for the payment to be made in the manner directed.][1]
(3) Where an order is made under this section, the Commissioners may make regulations containing such supplementary, incidental or consequential provisions as appear to the Commissioners to be necessary or expedient.
(4) A provision of an order or regulations under this section may be made in such way as the Treasury or, as the case may be, the Commissioners think fit (whether by amending provisions of or made under the enactments relating to VAT or otherwise).
(5) An order or regulations under this section may make different provision for different circumstances.
Commentary—*De Voil Indirect Tax Service* **V5.110**.
HMRC Manuals—VAT Payments On Account Regime VPOA7000 (commissioners' directions).
Regulations—See VAT Regulations, SI 1995/2518 regs 44–48.
Orders—See VAT (Payments on Account) Order, SI 1993/2001.
Amendments—[1] Sub-s (2A) inserted by FA 1996 s 34.
[2] Sub-s (2AA) inserted by FA 1997 s 43 with effect from 19 March 1997.

29 Invoices provided by recipients of goods or services
Where—
(*a*) a taxable person ("the recipient") provides a document to himself which purports to be an invoice in respect of a taxable supply of goods or services to him by another taxable person; and
(*b*) that document understates the VAT chargeable on the supply,
the Commissioners may, by notice served on the recipient and on the supplier, elect that the amount of VAT understated by the document shall be regarded for all purposes as VAT due from the recipient and not from the supplier.

PART II
RELIEFS, EXEMPTIONS AND REPAYMENTS

Reliefs etc generally available

[29A Reduced rate
(1) VAT charged on—
   (*a*) any supply that is of a description for the time being specified in Schedule 7A, or
   (*b*) any equivalent . . . [2] importation,
shall be charged at the rate of 5 per cent.
[(2) The reference in subsection (1) to an equivalent importation, in relation to any supply that is of a description for the time being specified in Schedule 7A, is a reference to any importation of any goods the supply of which would be such a supply.][2]
(3) The Treasury may by order vary Schedule 7A by adding to or deleting from it any description of supply or by varying any description of supply for the time being specified in it.
(4) The power to vary Schedule 7A conferred by subsection (3) above may be exercised so as to describe a supply of goods or services by reference to matters unrelated to the characteristics of the goods or services themselves.
In the case of a supply of goods, those matters include, in particular, the use that has been made of the goods.][1]

Commentary—*De Voil Indirect Tax Service* **V4.401**.
HMRC Manuals—VAT Construction VCONST01200 (introduction: laws and regulations).
Northern Ireland—See Sch 9ZA para 16 (reduced rate: application in relation to Northern Ireland acquisition VAT).
Orders—VAT (Reduced Rate) (Cable-Suspended Passenger Transport Systems) Order, SI 2013/430.
VAT (Independence Payment) Order, SI 2013/601.
VAT (Reduced Rate) (Hospitality and Tourism) (Coronavirus) Order, SI 2020/728.
VAT (Reduced Rate) (Hospitality and Tourism) (Extension of Time Period) (Coronavirus) Order, SI 2020/1413.
Amendments—[1] This section inserted by FA 2001 s 99(4), (7)(*c*) with effect for sub-ss (1), (2) in relation to supplies made and acquisitions and importations taking place, after 31 October 2001.
[2] In sub-s (1)(*b*), words "acquisition or" repealed, and sub-s (2) substituted, by the Taxation (Cross-border Trade) Act 2018 s 43, Sch 8 paras 1, 28 with effect from IP completion day (11pm on 31 December 2020), by virtue of SI 2020/1642 reg 4(*b*). Sub-s (2) previously read as follows—
"(2) The reference in subsection (1) above to an equivalent acquisition or importation, in relation to any supply that is of a description for the time being specified in Schedule 7A, is a reference (as the case may be) to—
   (*a*) any acquisition from another member State of goods the supply of which would be such a supply; or
   (*b*) any importation from a place outside the member States of any such goods.".

30 Zero-rating
(1) Where a taxable person supplies goods or services and the supply is zero-rated, then, whether or not VAT would be chargeable on the supply apart from this section—
   (*a*) no VAT shall be charged on the supply; but
   (*b*) it shall in all other respects be treated as a taxable supply;
and accordingly the rate at which VAT is treated as charged on the supply shall be nil.
(2) A supply of goods or services is zero-rated by virtue of this subsection if the goods or services are of a description for the time being specified in Schedule 8 or the supply is of a description for the time being so specified.
[(2A) A supply by a person of services which consist of applying a treatment or process to another person's goods is zero-rated by virtue of this subsection if by doing so he produces goods, and either—
   (*a*) those goods are of a description for the time being specified in Schedule 8; or
   (*b*) a supply by him of those goods to the person to whom he supplies the services would be of a description so specified.][2]
(3) Where goods of a description for the time being specified in that Schedule, or of a description forming part of a description of supply for the time being so specified, are [imported, no VAT shall be chargeable on their importation][3] except as otherwise provided in that Schedule.
(4) The Treasury may by order vary Schedule 8 by adding to or deleting from it any description or by varying any description for the time being specified in it.
[(5) The export of any goods by a charity . . . [3] shall for the purposes of this Act be treated as a supply made by the charity—
   (*a*) in the United Kingdom, and
   (*b*) in the course or furtherance of a business carried on by the charity.][1]
(6) A supply of goods is zero-rated by virtue of this subsection if the Commissioners are satisfied that the person supplying the goods—
   (*a*) has exported them . . . [3]; or
   (*b*) has shipped them for use as stores on a voyage or flight to an eventual destination outside the United Kingdom, or as merchandise for sale by retail to persons carried on such a voyage or flight in a ship or aircraft,

and in either case if such other conditions, if any, as may be specified in regulations or the Commissioners may impose are fulfilled.

(7) Subsection (6)(*b*) above shall not apply in the case of goods shipped for use as stores on a voyage or flight to be made by the person to whom the goods were supplied and to be made for a purpose which is private.

(8) Regulations may provide for the zero-rating of supplies of goods, or of such goods as may be specified in the regulations, in cases where—

[(*a*) the Commissioners are satisfied that the goods have been or are to be exported to such places as may be specified in the regulations, and][3]

(*b*) such other conditions, if any, as may be specified in the regulations or the Commissioners may impose are fulfilled.

[(8A) . . .[3]

(9) Regulations may provide for the zero-rating of a supply of services which is made where goods are let on hire and the Commissioners are satisfied that the goods have been or are to be [exported][3] during the period of the letting, and such other conditions, if any, as may be specified in the regulations or the Commissioners may impose are fulfilled.

(10) Where the supply of any goods has been zero-rated by virtue of subsection (6) above or in pursuance of regulations made under [subsection (8) or (9)][3] above and—

(*a*) the goods are found in the United Kingdom after the date on which they were alleged to have been or were to be exported or shipped . . .[3]; or

(*b*) any condition specified in the relevant regulations under [subsection (6), (8) or (9)][3] above or imposed by the Commissioners is not complied with,

and the presence of the goods in the United Kingdom after that date or the non-observance of the condition has not been authorised for the purposes of this subsection by the Commissioners, the goods shall be liable to forfeiture under the Management Act and the VAT that would have been chargeable on the supply but for the zero-rating shall become payable forthwith by the person to whom the goods were supplied or by any person in whose possession the goods are found in the United Kingdom; but the Commissioners may, if they think fit, waive payment of the whole or part of that VAT.

Commentary—*De Voil Indirect Tax Service* **V4.201, V4.210.**

HMRC Manuals—VAT Export And Removal Of Goods From The UK VEXP90900 (use of the power in VAT act 1994 section 30(10)).

VEXP20300 (direct and indirect exports).

VEXP80310 (direct export to a non-EU branch).

Northern Ireland—See Sch 9ZA para 17 (sub-s (3) applies to an acquisition of goods in Northern Ireland from a member State as it would apply to an importation of those goods, and sub-s (10) applies to a supply of goods that has been zero-rated in pursuance of regulations made under Sch 9ZA para 17(3) as it applies to a supply of goods that has been zero-rated in pursuance of regulations made under sub-s (8) or (9)).

See Sch 9ZB Part 3 (paras 8–14): a number of modifications apply in relation to movements of goods by charities—

- Sub-s (5) has effect as if the reference to the export of goods included the removal of goods from Great Britain to Northern Ireland, and did not include the export of goods from Northern Ireland to a place in the member States.
- Sub-s (6) has effect as if reference to the export of goods did not include the export of goods from Northern Ireland to a place in the member States.
- Sub-s (8) has effect as if reference to the export of goods included the removal of goods from Northern Ireland to Great Britain, or vice versa, and did not include the export of goods from Northern Ireland to a place in the member States.
- Sub-s (9) has effect as if the reference to the export of goods did not include the export of goods from Northern Ireland to a place in the member States.
- Where a supply of goods has been zero-rated under VATA 1994 Sch 9ZB para 3(1), or as a result of regulations under sub-s (8), on the basis that the goods have been or are to be removed from Northern Ireland to Great Britain, sub-s (10) applies in relation to that supply as if any reference to the United Kingdom were to Northern Ireland.
- Where a supply of goods has been zero-rated under VATA 1994 Sch 9ZB para 3(1), or as a result of regulations under sub-s (8), on the basis that the goods have been or are to be removed from Great Britain to Northern Ireland, sub-s (10) applies in relation to that supply as if any reference to the United Kingdom were to Great Britain.

See Sch 9ZB para 33 (modifications in relation to exports – goods removed to Isle of Man): sub-s (8) has effect as if reference to the export of goods included the removal of goods from Northern Ireland to the Isle of Man; where a supply of goods has been zero-rated as a result of Sch 9ZB para 3(1) or regulations under sub-s (8), on the basis that the goods have been or are to be removed from Northern Ireland to the Isle of Man, sub-s (10) applies in relation to that supply as if any reference to the United Kingdom were to Northern Ireland.

Regulations—See VAT Regulations, SI 1995/2518 regs 127–135.

Value Added Tax (Amendment) (No 2) Regulations, SI 2019/1509.

Orders—See VAT (Tour Operators) Order, SI 1987/1806.

VAT (Drugs and Medicines) Order, SI 2009/2972.

VAT (Relief for European Research Infrastructure Consortia) Order, SI 2012/2907.

VAT (Independence Payment) Order, SI 2013/601.

Value Added Tax (Amendment) (No 2) Regulations, SI 2013/2241.

Value Added Tax (Drugs and Medicines) Order, SI 2014/1111.

Value Added Tax (Caravans) Order, SI 2015/1949.

Value Added Tax (Drugs, Medicines, Aids and Charities, etc.) Order, SI 2016/620.

Value Added Tax (Drugs and Medicines) Order, SI 2020/250.

Value Added Tax (Zero Rate for Personal Protective Equipment) (Coronavirus) Order, SI 2020/458.
Value Added Tax (Extension of Zero-Rating to Electronically Supplied Books etc) (Coronavirus) Order, SI 2020/459.
Amendments—[1] Sub-s (5) substituted by FA 1995 s 28 with effect in relation to transactions occurring on or after 1 May 1995.
[2] Sub-s (2A) inserted by FA 1996 s 29(2), with effect in relation to supplies made after 31 December 1995.
[3] The following amendments made by the Taxation (Cross-border Trade) Act 2018 s 43, Sch 8 paras 1, 29 with effect from IP completion day (11pm on 31 December 2020), by virtue of SI 2020/1642 reg 4(b)—
- in sub-s (3), words substituted for words "acquired in the United Kingdom from another member State or imported from a place outside the member States, no VAT shall be chargeable on their acquisition or importation,";
- in sub-ss (5), (6)(a), words "to a place outside the member States" repealed;
- in sub-s (8), para (a) substituted;
- sub-s (8A) repealed;
- in sub-s (9), word substituted for words "removed from the United Kingdom";
- in sub-s (10)—
    (a) in the opening words, words substituted for words "subsection (8), (8A) or (9)";
    (b) in para (a), words "or otherwise removed from the United Kingdom" repealed; and
    (c) in para (b), words "subsection (6), (8) or (9)" substituted for words "subsection (6), (8), (8A) or (9)".

Before these amendments, section 30 read as follows—

"(1) Where a taxable person supplies goods or services and the supply is zero-rated, then, whether or not VAT would be chargeable on the supply apart from this section—
  (a) no VAT shall be charged on the supply; but
  (b) it shall in all other respects be treated as a taxable supply;
and accordingly the rate at which VAT is treated as charged on the supply shall be nil.

(2) A supply of goods or services is zero-rated by virtue of this subsection if the goods or services are of a description for the time being specified in Schedule 8 or the supply is of a description for the time being so specified.

(2A) A supply by a person of services which consist of applying a treatment or process to another person's goods is zero-rated by virtue of this subsection if by doing so he produces goods, and either—
  (a) those goods are of a description for the time being specified in Schedule 8; or
  (b) a supply by him of those goods to the person to whom he supplies the services would be of a description so specified.

(3) Where goods of a description for the time being specified in that Schedule, or of a description forming part of a description of supply for the time being so specified, are acquired in the United Kingdom from another member State or imported from a place outside the member States, no VAT shall be chargeable on their acquisition or importation, except as otherwise provided in that Schedule.

(4) The Treasury may by order vary Schedule 8 by adding to or deleting from it any description or by varying any description for the time being specified in it.

(5) The export of any goods by a charity to a place outside the member States shall for the purposes of this Act be treated as a supply made by the charity—
  (a) in the United Kingdom, and
  (b) in the course or furtherance of a business carried on by the charity.

(6) A supply of goods is zero-rated by virtue of this subsection if the Commissioners are satisfied that the person supplying the goods—
  (a) has exported them to a place outside the member States; or
  (b) has shipped them for use as stores on a voyage or flight to an eventual destination outside the United Kingdom, or as merchandise for sale by retail to persons carried on such a voyage or flight in a ship or aircraft,
and in either case if such other conditions, if any, as may be specified in regulations or the Commissioners may impose are fulfilled.

(7) Subsection (6)(b) above shall not apply in the case of goods shipped for use as stores on a voyage or flight to be made by the person to whom the goods were supplied and to be made for a purpose which is private.

(8) Regulations may provide for the zero-rating of supplies of goods, or of such goods as may be specified in the regulations, in cases where—
  (a) the Commissioners are satisfied that the goods have been or are to be exported to a place outside the member States or that the supply in question involves both—
    (i) the removal of the goods from the United Kingdom; and
    (ii) their acquisition in another member State by a person who is liable for VAT on the acquisition in accordance with provisions of the law of that member State corresponding, in relation to that member State, to the provisions of section 10; and
  (b) such other conditions, if any, as may be specified in the regulations or the Commissioners may impose are fulfilled.

(8A) Regulations may provide for the zero-rating of supplies of goods, or of such goods as may be specified in regulations, in cases where—
  (a) the Commissioners are satisfied that the supply in question involves both—
    (i) the removal of the goods from a fiscal warehousing regime within the meaning of section 18F(2); and
    (ii) their being placed in a warehousing regime in another member State, or in such member State or States as may be prescribed, where that regime is established by provisions of the law of that member State corresponding, in relation to that member State, to the provisions of sections 18A and 18B; and
  (b) such other conditions, if any, as may be specified in the regulations or the Commissioners may impose are fulfilled.

(9) Regulations may provide for the zero-rating of a supply of services which is made where goods are let on hire and the Commissioners are satisfied that the goods have been or are to be removed from the United Kingdom during the period of the letting, and such other conditions, if any, as may be specified in the regulations or the Commissioners may impose are fulfilled.

(10) Where the supply of any goods has been zero-rated by virtue of subsection (6) above or in pursuance of regulations made under subsection (8), (8A) or (9) above and—

(a) the goods are found in the United Kingdom after the date on which they were alleged to have been or were to be exported or shipped or otherwise removed from the United Kingdom; or
(b) any condition specified in the relevant regulations under subsection (6), (8), (8A) or (9) above or imposed by the Commissioners is not complied with,

and the presence of the goods in the United Kingdom after that date or the non-observance of the condition has not been authorised for the purposes of this subsection by the Commissioners, the goods shall be liable to forfeiture under the Management Act and the VAT that would have been chargeable on the supply but for the zero-rating shall become payable forthwith by the person to whom the goods were supplied or by any person in whose possession the goods are found in the United Kingdom; but the Commissioners may, if they think fit, waive payment of the whole or part of that VAT.".

31 Exempt supplies . . .

(1) A supply of goods or services is an exempt supply if it is of a description for the time being specified in Schedule 9 . . . [2].
(2) The Treasury may by order vary that Schedule by adding to or deleting from it any description of supply or by varying any description of supply for the time being specified in it, and the Schedule may be varied so as to describe a supply of goods by reference to the use which has been made of them or to other matters unrelated to the characteristics of the goods themselves.
[(3) The Treasury may by regulations make an exemption of a group 16 supply of a description specified in the regulations subject to conditions.
(4) Regulations under subsection (3) may—
    (a) make different provision for different cases, and
    (b) make consequential or transitional provision (including provision amending this Act).
(5) In subsection (3) "group 16 supply" means a supply falling within Group 16 of Schedule 9.][1]

Commentary—*De Voil Indirect Tax Service* **V3.121, V4.101**.
Orders—Value Added Tax (Land Exemption) Order, SI 2012/58.
Value Added Tax (Education) Order, SI 2013/1897.
Value Added Tax (Sport) Order, SI 2014/3185.
Value Added Tax (Finance) (EU Exit) Order, SI 2019/43.
Value Added Tax (Finance) (EU Exit) (Revocation) Order, SI 2019/1014.
Value Added Tax (Finance) Order, SI 2020/209.
Regulations—Value Added Tax (Miscellaneous Amendments and Transitional Provisions) (EU Exit) Regulations, SI 2019/1214.
Amendments—[1] Sub-ss (3)–(5) inserted by FA 2012 s 197(3) with effect from 17 July 2012.
[2] In sub-s (1), words "and an acquisition of goods from another member State is an exempt acquisition if the goods are acquired in pursuance of an exempt supply" repealed, and in heading, words "and acquisitions" repealed, by the Taxation (Cross-border Trade) Act 2018 s 43, Sch 8 paras 1, 30 with effect from IP completion day (11pm on 31 December 2020), by virtue of SI 2020/1642 reg 4(b).

33 Refunds of VAT in certain cases

(1) Subject to the following provisions of this section, where—
    [(a) VAT is chargeable on the supply of goods or services to, or on the importation of goods by, a body to which this section applies, and][7]
    (b) the supply . . . [7] or importation is not for the purpose of any business carried on by the body,
the Commissioners shall, on a claim made by the body at such time and in such form and manner as the Commissioners may determine, refund to it the amount of the VAT so chargeable.
(2) Where goods or services so supplied to . . . [7] or imported by the body cannot be conveniently distinguished from goods or services supplied to . . . [7] or imported by it for the purpose of a business carried on by it, the amount to be refunded under this section shall be such amount as remains after deducting from the whole of the VAT chargeable on any supply to . . . [7] or importation by the body such proportion thereof as appears to the Commissioners to be attributable to the carrying on of the business; but where—
    (a) the VAT so attributable is or includes VAT attributable, in accordance with regulations under section 26, to exempt supplies by the body, and
    (b) the VAT attributable to the exempt supplies is in the opinion of the Commissioners an insignificant proportion of the VAT so chargeable,
they may include it in the VAT refunded under this section.
(3) The bodies to which this section applies are—
    (a) a local authority [and a combined authority established by an order made under section 103(1) of the Local Democracy, Economic Development and Construction Act 2009][6];
    [(aa) a fire and rescue authority under the Fire and Rescue Services Act 2004, if the authority does not fall within paragraph (a);
    (ab) the Scottish Fire and Rescue Service;][6]
    (b) a river purification board established under section 135 of the Local Government (Scotland) Act 1973 and a water development board within the meaning of section 109 of the Water (Scotland) Act 1980;

(c) an internal drainage board;
[(d) an Integrated Transport Authority, Passenger Transport Authority or Passenger Transport Executive for the purposes of Part 2 of the Transport Act 1968;][3]
(e) a port health authority within the meaning of the Public Health (Control of Disease) Act 1984 . . .[4];
(f) [a police and crime commissioner, the Mayor's Office for Policing and Crime and][5] . . .[6] the Receiver for the Metropolitan Police District;
[(fa) the Scottish Police Authority;
(fb) the Police Service of Northern Ireland and the Northern Ireland Policing Board;][6]
(g) a development corporation within the meaning of the New Towns Act 1981 or the New Towns (Scotland) Act 1968 a new town commission within the meaning of the New Towns Act (Northern Ireland) 1965 and the Commission for the New Towns;
(h) a general lighthouse authority within the meaning of [Part VIII of the Merchant Shipping Act 1995][1];
(i) the British Broadcasting Corporation;
[(j) the appointed news provider referred to in section 280 of the Communications Act 2003; and][2]
(k) any body specified for the purposes of this section by an order made by the Treasury.
(4) No VAT shall be refunded under this section to a general lighthouse authority which in the opinion of the Commissioners is attributable to activities other than those concerned with the provision, maintenance or management of lights or other navigational aids.
(5) No VAT shall be refunded under this section to [an appointed][2] news provider which in the opinion of the Commissioners is attributable to activities other than the provision of news programmes for broadcasting by holders of regional Channel 3 licences (within the meaning of Part I of the Broadcasting Act 1990).
(6) References in this section to VAT chargeable do not include any VAT which, by virtue of any order under section 25(7), is excluded from credit under that section.

Commentary—*De Voil Indirect Tax Service* **V5.162**.
HMRC Manuals—VAT Isle of Man VIOM02600 (refunds under section 33 of VATA 1994).
VAT Repayment Supplement VATRS10210 (who do we pay repayment supplement to?).
Northern Ireland—See Sch 9ZA para 18 (sections 33–33C, 33E, 34 apply to an acquisition of goods from a member State as they apply to a supply of those goods).
Orders—See VAT (Refund of Tax) Orders, SI 1973/2121, SI 1976/2028, SI 1985/1101, SI 1986/336, SI 1986/532, SI 1989/1217, SI 1995/1978, SI 1995/2999, SI 1997/2558, SI 1999/2076, SI 2000/1046, SI 2001/3453, 2006/1793.
VAT (Refund of Tax to Charter Trustees and Conservators) Order, SI 2009/1177.
VAT (Refund of VAT to Chief Constables and the Commissioner of Police of the Metropolis) Order, SI 2012/2393.
VAT (Refund of Tax to the Natural Resources Body for Wales) Order, SI 2013/412.
Value Added Tax (Refund of Tax) Order, SI 2014/1112.
Value Added Tax (Refund of Tax to the London Legacy Development Corporation) Order, SI 2015/449.
Value Added Tax (Refund of Tax to the Tees Valley and West Midlands Combined Authorities) Order, SI 2016/993.
Value Added Tax (Refund of Tax to Museums and Galleries) (Amendment) Order, SI 2017/905.
Value Added Tax (Refund of Tax to the Cambridgeshire and Peterborough Combined Authority) Order, SI 2017/1203.
Value Added Tax (Refund of Tax to the Essex Police, Fire and Crime Commissioner Fire and Rescue Authority) Order, SI 2018/16.
Value Added Tax (Refund of Tax to the Charter Trustees for Bournemouth and the Charter Trustees for Poole) Order, SI 2020/1113.
Amendments—[1] Words in sub-s (3)(h) substituted by the Merchant Shipping Act 1995 Sch 13 para 95 with effect from 1 January 1996.
[2] Sub-s (3)(j) substituted, and words in sub-s (5) substituted, by the Communications Act 2003 s 406, Sch 17 para 129(1), (2) with effect from 29 December 2003 (by virtue of SI 2003/3142).
[3] Sub-s (3)(d) substituted, in relation to England and Wales, by the Local Transport Act 2008 s 77(5), Sch 4 para 59 with effect from 9 February 2009 (by virtue of SI 2009/107 art 2(1), Sch 1 Pt 1).
[4] In sub-s (3)(e), words "and a port local authority and joint port local authority constituted under Part X of the Public Health (Scotland) Act 1897" repealed by the Public Health etc (Scotland) Act 2008 s 126(1), Sch 3 Pt 1 with effect from 1 October 2009 (by virtue of SSI 2009/319 art 2(a), Sch 1).
[5] In sub-s (3)(f) words inserted by the Police Reform and Social Responsibility Act 2011, s 99, Sch 16, Pt 3, para 217 with effect from 16 January 2012 (by virtue of SI 2011/3019 art 3, Sch 1 para nnn (iii)).
[6] In sub-s (3)(a), words inserted, sub-s (3)(aa), (ab), (fa), (fb) inserted, and in sub-s (3)(f), words "a police authority and" repealed, by FA 2018 s 39 with effect in relation to supplies made, and acquisitions and importations taking place, on or after 15 March 2018.
[7] In sub-s (1), para (a) substituted, and in para (b), word ", acquisition" repealed; and in sub-s (2), words "or acquired" (in both places) and "or acquisition" repealed, by the Taxation (Cross-border Trade) Act 2018 s 43, Sch 8 paras 1, 31 with effect from IP completion day (11pm on 31 December 2020), by virtue of SI 2020/1642 reg 4(b).
Sub-s (1)(a) previously read as follows—
"(a) VAT is chargeable on the supply of goods or services to a body to which this section applies, on the acquisition of any goods by such a body from another member State or on the importation of any goods by such a body from a place outside the member States, and".
Prospective amendments—In sub-s (3)(f), words "and the Receiver for the Metropolitan Police District" to be repealed by the Greater London Authority Act 1999, s 325, Sch 27 para 68 with effect from a day to be appointed.

[33A Refunds of VAT to museums and galleries
(1) Subsections (2) to (5) below apply where—
  [(a) VAT is chargeable on the supply of goods or services to, or on the importation of goods by, a body to which this section applies,]³
  (b) the supply . . . ³ or importation is attributable to the provision by the body of free rights of admission to a relevant museum or gallery, and
  (c) the supply is made, or the . . . ³ importation takes place, on or after 1st April 2001.
(2) The Commissioners shall, on a claim made by the body in such form and manner as the Commissioners may determine, refund to the body the amount of VAT so chargeable.
(3) The claim must be made before the end of the claim period.
(4) Subject to subsection (5) below, "the claim period" is the period of [4 years]² beginning with the day on which the supply is made or the . . . ³ importation takes place.
(5) If the Commissioners so determine, the claim period is such shorter period beginning with that day as the Commissioners may determine.
(6) Subsection (7) below applies where goods or services supplied to, . . . ³ or imported by, a body to which this section applies that are attributable to free admissions cannot conveniently be distinguished from goods or services supplied to, . . . ³ or imported by, the body that are not attributable to free admissions.
(7) The amount to be refunded on a claim by the body under this section shall be such amount as remains after deducting from the VAT related to the claim such proportion of that VAT as appears to the Commissioners to be attributable otherwise than to free admissions.
(8) For the purposes of subsections (6) and (7) above—
  (a) goods or services are, and VAT is, attributable to free admissions if they are, or it is, attributable to the provision by the body of free rights of admission to a relevant museum or gallery;
  (b) the VAT related to a claim is the whole of the VAT chargeable on—
    (i) the supplies to the body, and
    (ii) the . . . ³ importations by the body,
  to which the claim relates.
(9) The Treasury may by order—
  (a) specify a body as being a body to which this section applies;
  (b) when specifying a body under paragraph (a), specify any museum or gallery that, for the purposes of this section, is a "relevant" museum or gallery in relation to the body;
  (c) specify an additional museum or gallery as being, for the purposes of this section, a "relevant" museum or gallery in relation to a body to which this section applies;
  (d) when specifying a museum or gallery under paragraph (b) or (c), provide that this section shall have effect in the case of the museum or gallery as if in subsection (1)(c) there were substituted for 1st April 2001 a later date specified in the order.
(10) References in this section to VAT do not include any VAT which, by virtue of any order under section 25(7), is excluded from credit under that section.]¹

Commentary—*De Voil Indirect Tax Service* **V5.162A**.
HMRC Manuals—VAT Business and Non- business Manual VBNB44400 (VAT treatment of museums and galleries).
VAT Repayment Supplement VATRS10210 (who do we pay repayment supplement to?).
Northern Ireland—See Sch 9ZA para 18 (sections 33–33C, 33E, 34 apply to an acquisition of goods from a member State as they apply to a supply of those goods).
Orders—See VAT (Refund of Tax to Museums and Galleries) Order, SI 2001/2879.
VAT (Refund of Tax to Museums and Galleries) (Amendment), SI 2016/235.
VAT (Refund of Tax to Museums and Galleries) (Amendment) Order, SI 2020/1167.
Amendments—¹ This section inserted by FA 2001 s 98(2), (10), (11) with effect from 11 May 2001 for the purpose only of the exercise of the power to make orders under sub-s (9). Subject to that, this section comes into force on 1 September 2001.
² In sub-s (4) words substituted for words "3 years" by FA 2008 s 118, Sch 39 paras 32, 33 with effect from 1 April 2009 (by virtue of SI 2009/403). FA 2008 Sch 39 para 33 is disregarded where, for the purposes of VATA 1994 s 33A, the day on which the supply was made or the acquisition or importation took place was on or before 31 March 2006 (SI 2009/403 art 3).
³ The following amendments made by the Taxation (Cross-border Trade) Act 2018 s 43, Sch 8 paras 1, 32 with effect from IP completion day (11pm on 31 December 2020), by virtue of SI 2020/1642 reg 4(b)—
  – in sub-s (1)—
    (a) para (a) substituted;
    (b) in para (b), word ", acquisition" repealed; and
    (c) in para (c), words "acquisition or" repealed;
  – in sub-s (4), words "acquisition or" repealed;
  – in sub-s (6), words "or acquired" repealed (in both places); and
  – in sub-s (8)(b)(ii), words "acquisitions and" repealed.
Sub-s (1)(a) previously read as follows—
  "(a) VAT is chargeable on—
    (i) the supply of goods or services to a body to which this section applies,
    (ii) the acquisition of any goods by such a body from another member State, or
    (iii) the importation of any goods by such a body from a place outside the member States,".

[33B Refunds of VAT to Academies

(1) This section applies where—
   [(a) VAT is chargeable on the supply of goods or services to, or on the importation of goods by, the proprietor of an Academy, and][2]
   (b) the supply . . . [2] or importation is not for the purposes of any business carried on by the proprietor of the Academy.

(2) The Commissioners shall, on a claim made by the proprietor of the Academy at such time and in such form and manner as the Commissioners may determine, refund to that proprietor the amount of VAT so chargeable.

(3) Subject to subsection (4), the claim must be made before the end of the period of 4 years beginning with the day on which the supply is made or the . . . [2] importation takes place.

(4) If the Commissioners so determine, the claim period is such shorter period beginning with that day as the Commissioners may determine.

(5) Subsection (6) applies where goods or services supplied to, . . . [2] or imported by, the proprietor of the Academy cannot be conveniently distinguished from goods or services supplied to, . . . [2] or imported by, it for the purpose of a business carried on by that proprietor.

(6) The amount to be refunded under this section is such amount as remains after deducting from the whole of the VAT chargeable on any supply to, . . . [2] or importation by, the proprietor of the Academy such proportion of that VAT as appears to the Commissioners to be attributable to the carrying on of the business.

(7) References in this section to VAT do not include any VAT which, by virtue of an order under section 25(7), is excluded from credit under section 25.

(8) In this section—
   (a) references to the proprietor of an Academy are to the proprietor of the Academy acting in that capacity, and
   (b) "Academy" and "proprietor" have the same meaning as in the Education Act 1996 (see section 579 of that Act).][1]

Commentary—*De Voil Indirect Tax Service* V5.162C.
HMRC Manuals—VAT Repayment Supplement VATRS10210 (who do we pay repayment supplement to?).
Northern Ireland—See Sch 9ZA para 18 (sections 33–33C, 33E, 34 apply to an acquisition of goods from a member State as they apply to a supply of those goods).
Amendments—[1] Section 33B inserted by FA 2011 s 76(1) with effect in relation to supplies made, and acquisitions and importations taking place, on or after 1 April 2011.

[2] The following amendments made by the Taxation (Cross-border Trade) Act 2018 s 43, Sch 8 paras 1, 33 with effect from IP completion day (11pm on 31 December 2020), by virtue of SI 2020/1642 reg 4(b)—
   – in sub-s (1)—
       (a) para (a) substituted;
       (b) in para (b), word ", acquisition" repealed;
   – in sub-s (3), words "acquisition or" repealed;
   – in sub-s (5), words "or acquired" repealed (in both places); and
   – in sub-s (6), words "or acquisition" repealed.
   Sub-s (1)(a) previously read as follows—
       "(a) VAT is chargeable on—
           (i) the supply of goods or services to the proprietor of an Academy,
           (ii) the acquisition of any goods from another member State by the proprietor of an Academy, or
           (iii) the importation of any goods from a place outside the member States by the proprietor of an Academy, and".

[33C Refunds of VAT to charities within section 33D

(1) This section applies to a charity that falls within any of the descriptions in section 33D. A charity to which this section applies is referred to in this section as a "qualifying charity".

(2) This section applies where—
   [(a) VAT is chargeable on the supply of goods or services to, or on the importation of goods by, a qualifying charity, and][2]
   (b) the supply . . . [2] or importation is not for the purpose of any business carried on by the qualifying charity.

(3) The Commissioners shall, on a claim made by the qualifying charity at such time and in such form and manner as the Commissioners may determine, refund to the qualifying charity the amount of the VAT so chargeable.

(4) A claim under subsection (3) above in respect of a [supply or][2] importation must be made before the end of the period of 4 years beginning with the day on which the supply is made or [the importation][2] takes place.

(5) Subsection (6) applies where goods or services supplied to, . . . [2] or imported by, a qualifying charity otherwise than for the purpose of any business carried on by the qualifying charity cannot be conveniently distinguished from goods or services supplied to, . . . [2] or imported by, the qualifying charity for the purpose of such a business.

(6) The amount to be refunded under this section is such amount as remains after deducting from the whole of the VAT chargeable on any supply to, . . . [2] or importation by, the qualifying charity such proportion of that VAT as appears to the Commissioners to be attributable to the carrying on of the business.
(7) References in this section to VAT do not include any VAT which, by virtue of an order under section 25(7), is excluded from credit under section 25.][1]
Commentary—*De Voil Indirect Tax Service* **V5.162D**.
HMRC Manuals—VAT Repayment Supplement VATRS10210 (who do we pay repayment supplement to?).
Northern Ireland—See Sch 9ZA para 18 (sections 33–33C, 33E, 34 apply to an acquisition of goods from a member State as they apply to a supply of those goods).
Amendments—[1] Sections 33C, 33D inserted by FA 2015 s 66(1) with effect in relation to supplies made, and acquisitions and importations taking place, on or after 1 April 2015.
[2] The following amendments made by the Taxation (Cross-border Trade) Act 2018 s 43, Sch 8 paras 1, 34 with effect from IP completion day (11pm on 31 December 2020), by virtue of SI 2020/1642 reg 4(*b*)—
- in sub-s (2)—
  - (a) para (*a*) substituted;
  - (b) in para (*b*), word ", acquisition" repealed;
- in sub-s (4), words substituted for words "supply, acquisition or", and "the acquisition or importation";
- in sub-s (5), words "or acquired" repealed (in both places); and
- in sub-s (6), words "or acquisition" repealed.

Sub-s (2)(*a*) previously read as follows—
"(*a*) VAT is chargeable on—
  (i) the supply of goods or services to a qualifying charity,
  (ii) the acquisition of any goods from another member State by a qualifying charity, or
  (iii) the importation of any goods from a place outside the member States by a qualifying charity, and".

[33D Charities to which section 33C applies
Palliative care charities
(1) "Palliative care charity" means a charity the main purpose of which is the provision of palliative care at the direction of, or under the supervision of, a medical professional to persons who are in need of such care as a result of having a terminal illness.
(2) In subsection (1) "medical professional" means—
(*a*) a registered medical practitioner, or
(*b*) a registered nurse.
Air ambulance charities
(3) "Air ambulance charity" means a charity the main purpose of which is to provide an air ambulance service in pursuance of arrangements made by, or at the request of, a relevant NHS body.
(4) In subsection (3) "relevant NHS body" means a body the main purpose of which is to provide ambulance services and which is—
(*a*) an NHS foundation trust in England,
(*b*) an NHS trust in Wales,
(*c*) a Special Health Board constituted under section 2 of the National Health Service (Scotland) Act 1978, or
(*d*) a Health and Social Care trust established under the Health and Personal Social Services (Northern Ireland) Order 1991.
Search and rescue charities
(5) "Search and rescue charity" means a charity that meets condition A or B.
(6) Condition A is that—
(*a*) the main purpose of the charity is to carry out search and rescue activities in the United Kingdom or the UK marine area, and
(*b*) the search and rescue activities carried out by the charity are co-ordinated by a relevant authority.
(7) Condition B is that the main purpose of the charity is to support, develop and promote the activities of a charity which meets condition A.
(8) For the purposes of subsection (6)—
"search and rescue activities" means searching for, and rescuing, persons who are, or may be, at risk of death or serious injury;
"relevant authority" means—
(*a*) the Secretary of State;
(*b*) a police force;
(*c*) the Scottish Fire and Rescue Service;
(*d*) any other person or body specified for the purposes of subsection (6) by an order made by the Treasury;
"police force" means—
(*a*) a police force within the meaning of the Police Act 1996;
(*b*) the Police Service of Scotland;
(*c*) the Police Service of Northern Ireland;

    (d) the Police Service of Northern Ireland Reserve;
    (e) the British Transport Police Force;
    (f) the Civil Nuclear Constabulary;
    (g) the Ministry of Defence Police;
"UK marine area" has the meaning given by section 42(1) of the Marine and Coastal Access Act 2009.

Medical courier charities
(9) "Medical courier charity" means a charity that meets condition A or B.
(10) Condition A is that the main purpose of the charity is to provide services for the transportation of items intended for use for medical purposes, including in particular—
    (a) blood;
    (b) medicines and other medical supplies;
    (c) items relating to people who are undergoing medical treatment.
(11) Condition B is that the main purpose of the charity is to support, develop and promote the activities of a charity which meets condition A.
(12) In subsection (10) "item" includes any substance.][1]

Amendments—[1] Sections 33C, 33D inserted by FA 2015 s 66(1) with effect in relation to supplies made, and acquisitions and importations taking place, on or after 1 April 2015.

[33E Power to extend refunds of VAT to other persons
(1) This section applies where—
    [a] VAT is chargeable on the supply of goods or services to, or on the importation of goods by, a specified person, and][2]
    (b) the supply . . . [2] or importation is not for the purpose of—
        (i) any business carried on by the person, or
        (ii) a supply by the person which, by virtue of section 41A, is treated as a supply in the course or furtherance of a business.
(2) If and to the extent that the Treasury so direct, the Commissioners shall, on a claim made by the specified person at such time and in such form and manner as the Commissioners may determine, refund to the person the amount of the VAT so chargeable. This is subject to subsection (3) below.
(3) A specified person may not make a claim under subsection (2) above unless it has been agreed with the Treasury that, in the circumstances specified in the agreement, the amount of the person's funding is to be reduced by all or part of the amount of the VAT so chargeable.
(4) A claim under subsection (2) above in respect of a supply . . . [2] or importation must be made on or before the relevant day.
(5) The "relevant day" is—
    (a) in the case of a person who is registered, the last day on which the person may make a return under this Act for the prescribed accounting period containing the last day of the financial year in which the supply is made or the . . . [2] importation takes place;
    (b) in the case of a person who is not registered, the last day of the period of 3 months beginning immediately after the end of the financial year in which the supply is made or the . . . [2] importation takes place.
(6) Subsection (7) applies where goods or services supplied to, . . . [2] or imported by, a specified person otherwise than for the purpose of—
    (a) any business carried on by the person, or
    (b) a supply falling within subsection (1)(b)(ii) above,
cannot be conveniently distinguished from goods or services supplied to, . . . [2] or imported by, the person for such a purpose.
(7) The amount to be refunded under this section is such amount as remains after deducting from the whole of the VAT chargeable on any supply to, . . . [2] or importation by, the specified person such proportion of that VAT as appears to the Commissioners to be attributable to the carrying on of the business or (as the case may be) the making of the supply.
(8) In this section, "specified person" means a person specified in an order made by the Treasury.
(9) An order under subsection (8) may make transitional provision or savings.
(10) References in this section to VAT do not include any VAT which, by virtue of an order under section 25(7), is excluded from credit under section 25.][1]

Commentary—*De Voil Indirect Tax Service* **V5.162E.**
HMRC Manuals—VAT Government and Public Bodies VATGPB9640 (section 33E bodies).
Northern Ireland—See Sch 9ZA para 18 (sections 33–33C, 33E, 34 apply to an acquisition of goods from a member State as they apply to a supply of those goods).
Orders—Value Added Tax (Refund of Tax) Order, SI 2020/185: the following persons are specified for the purpose of this section—
    – High Speed Two (HS2) Limited, an executive non departmental public body registered at Companies House under company number 06791686;
    – the East West Railway Company Limited, a non-departmental public body registered at Companies House under company number 11072935;

- Transport for Wales, a not-for-profit company limited by guarantee registered at Companies House under company number 09476013; and
- the Single Financial Guidance Body, a body corporate with functions relating to financial guidance established by section 1(1) of the Financial Guidance and Claims Act 2018.

Amendments—[1] Section 33E inserted by FA 2016 s 122 with effect from 15 September 2016.
[2] The following amendments made by the Taxation (Cross-border Trade) Act 2018 s 43, Sch 8 paras 1, 35 with effect from IP completion day (11pm on 31 December 2020), by virtue of SI 2020/1642 reg 4(*b*).
- in sub-s (1)—
    - (a) para (*a*) substituted;
    - (b) in para (*b*), word ", acquisition" repealed;
- in sub-s (4), word ", acquisition" repealed;
- in sub-s (5), words "acquisition or" repealed (in both places);
- in sub-s (6), words "or acquired" repealed (in both places); and
- in sub-s (7), words "or acquisition" repealed.

Sub-s (1)(*a*) previously read as follows—
"(*a*) VAT is chargeable on—
   (i) the supply of goods or services to a specified person,
   (ii) the acquisition of any goods from another member State by a specified person, or
   (iii) the importation of any goods from a place outside the member States by a specified person, and".

34 Capital goods
(1) The Treasury may by order make provision for the giving of relief, in such cases, to such extent and subject to such exceptions as may be specified in the order, from VAT paid on the supply . . . [1] or importation for the purpose of a business carried on by any person of machinery or plant or any specified description of machinery or plant in cases where that VAT or part of that VAT cannot be credited under section 25 and such other conditions are satisfied as may be specified in the order.
(2) Without prejudice to the generality of subsection (1) above, an order under this section may provide for relief to be given by deduction or refunding of VAT and for aggregating or excluding the aggregation of value where goods of the same description are supplied . . . [1] or imported together.

Commentary—*De Voil Indirect Tax Service* **V5.166**.

Northern Ireland—See Sch 9ZA para 18 (sections 33–33C, 33E, 34 apply to an acquisition of goods from a member State as they apply to a supply of those goods).

Amendments—[1] In sub-s (1) word ", acquisition", and in sub-s (2) word ", acquired", repealed, by the Taxation (Cross-border Trade) Act 2018 s 43, Sch 8 paras 1, 36 with effect from IP completion day (11pm on 31 December 2020), by virtue of SI 2020/1642 reg 4(*b*).

35 Refund of VAT to persons constructing certain buildings
[(1) Where—
   (*a*) a person carries out works to which this section applies,
   (*b*) his carrying out of the works is lawful and otherwise than in the course or furtherance of any business, and
   (*c*) VAT is chargeable on the supply . . . [4] or importation of any goods used by him for the purposes of the works,
the Commissioners shall, on a claim made in that behalf, refund to that person the amount of VAT so chargeable.
(1A) The works to which this section applies are—
   (*a*) the construction of a building designed as a dwelling or number of dwellings;
   (*b*) the construction of a building for use solely for a relevant residential purpose or relevant charitable purpose; and
   (*c*) a residential conversion.
(1B) For the purposes of this section goods shall be treated as used for the purposes of works to which this section applies by the person carrying out the works in so far only as they are building materials which, in the course of the works, are incorporated in the building in question or its site.
(1C) Where—
   (*a*) a person ("the relevant person") carries out a residential conversion by arranging for any of the work of the conversion to be done by another ("a contractor"),
   (*b*) the relevant person's carrying out of the conversion is lawful and otherwise than in the course or furtherance of any business,
   (*c*) the contractor is not acting as an architect, surveyor or consultant or in a supervisory capacity, and
   (*d*) VAT is chargeable on services consisting in the work done by the contractor,
the Commissioners shall, on a claim made in that behalf, refund to the relevant person the amount of VAT so chargeable.
(1D) For the purposes of this section works constitute a residential conversion to the extent that they consist in the conversion of a non-residential building, or a non-residential part of a building, into—
   (*a*) a building designed as a dwelling or a number of dwellings;
   (*b*) a building intended for use solely for a relevant residential purpose; or

(c) anything which would fall within paragraph (a) or (b) above if different parts of a building were treated as separate buildings.]¹

(2) The Commissioners shall not be required to entertain a claim for a refund of VAT under this section unless the claim—

(a) is made within such time and in such form and manner, and
(b) contains such information, and
(c) is accompanied by such documents, whether by way of evidence or otherwise,

[as may be specified by regulations or by the Commissioners in accordance with regulations.]³.

(3) . . .⁴

[(4) The notes to Group 5 of Schedule 8 shall apply for construing this section as they apply for construing that Group [but this is subject to subsection (4A) below.]²

[(4A) The meaning of "non-residential" given by Note (7A) of Group 5 of Schedule 8 (and not that given by Note (7) of that Group) applies for the purposes of this section but as if—

(a) references in that Note to item 3 of that Group were references to this section, and
(b) paragraph (b)(iii) of that Note were omitted.]²

(5) The power of the Treasury by order under section 30 to vary Schedule 8 shall include—

(a) power to apply any variation made by the order for the purposes of this section; and
(b) power to make such consequential modifications of this section as they may think fit.]¹

Commentary—*De Voil Indirect Tax Service* **V5.164**.
HMRC Manuals—VAT Construction VCONST24100 (entitlement to refund).
Regulations—See VAT Regulations, SI 1995/2518 regs 200, 201.
VAT (Amendment) (No 2) Regulations, SI 2012/1899.
Amendments—¹ Sub-ss (1), (1A)–(1D) substituted for sub-s (1), and sub-ss (4), (5) added by FA 1996 s 30, with effect in relation to any case in which a claim for repayment under this section is made at any time on or after 29 April 1996.
² Sub-s (4) amended, and sub-s (4A) inserted, by the VAT (Conversion of Buildings) Order, SI 2001/2305 arts 1, 4 with effect for supplies made after 31 July 2001.
³ In sub-s (2), words substituted for words "as the Commissioners may by regulations prescribe or, in the case of documents, as the Commissioners may determine in accordance with the regulations.", by FA 2012 s 204, Sch 29 paras 1, 4 with effect from 17 July 2012.
⁴ In sub-s (1)(c) word ", acquisition", and whole of sub-s (3), repealed, by the Taxation (Cross-border Trade) Act 2018 s 43, Sch 8 paras 1, 37 with effect from IP completion day (11pm on 31 December 2020), by virtue of SI 2020/1642 reg 4(b). Sub-s (3) previously read as follows—

"(3) This section shall have effect—
(a) as if the reference in subsection (1) above to the VAT chargeable on the supply of any goods included a reference to VAT chargeable on the supply in accordance with the law of another member State; and
(b) in relation to VAT chargeable in accordance with the law of another member State, as if references to refunding VAT to any person were references to paying that person an amount equal to the VAT chargeable in accordance with the law of that member State;

and the provisions of this Act and of any other enactment or subordinate legislation (whenever passed or made) so far as they relate to a refund under this section shall be construed accordingly.".

36 Bad debts

(1) Subsection (2) below applies where—

(a) a person has supplied goods or services [. . .]² and has accounted for and paid VAT on the supply,
(b) the whole or any part of the consideration for the supply has been written off in his accounts as a bad debt, and
(c) a period of 6 months (beginning with the date of the supply) has elapsed.

(2) Subject to the following provisions of this section and to regulations under it the person shall be entitled, on making a claim to the Commissioners, to a refund of the amount of VAT chargeable by reference to the outstanding amount.

[(3) In subsection (2) above "the outstanding amount" means—

(a) if at the time of the claim no part of the consideration written off in the claimant's accounts as a bad debt has been received, an amount equal to the amount of the consideration so written off;
(b) if at that time any part of the consideration so written off has been received, an amount by which that part is exceeded by the amount of the consideration written off;

and in this subsection "received" means received either by the claimant or by a person to whom has been assigned a right to receive the whole or any part of the consideration written off.]⁵

[(3A) For the purposes of this section, where the whole or any part of the consideration for the supply does not consist of money, the amount in money that shall be taken to represent any non-monetary part of the consideration shall be so much of the amount made up of—

(a) the value of the supply, and
(b) the VAT charged on the supply,

as is attributable to the non-monetary consideration in question.]⁴

(4) A person shall not be entitled to a refund under subsection (2) above unless—

(a) the value of the supply is equal to or less than its open market value, . . . ¹

(b) . . .¹
(4A) . . . ⁷
(5) Regulations under this section may—
- (a) require a claim to be made at such time and in such form and manner as may be specified by or under the regulations;
- (b) require a claim to be evidenced and quantified by reference to such records and other documents as may be so specified;
- (c) require the claimant to keep, for such period and in such form and manner as may be so specified, those records and documents and a record of such information relating to the claim and to [anything subsequently received]³ by way of consideration as may be so specified;
- (d) require the repayment of a refund allowed under this section where any requirement of the regulations is not complied with;
- (e) require the repayment of the whole or, as the case may be, an appropriate part of a refund allowed under this section [where any part (or further part) of the consideration written off in the claimant's accounts as a bad debt is subsequently received either by the claimant or, except in such circumstances as may be prescribed, by a person to whom has been assigned a right to receive the whole or any part of that consideration;]⁶
- (ea) . . . ⁷
- (f) include such supplementary, incidental, consequential or transitional provisions as appear to the Commissioners to be necessary or expedient for the purposes of this section;
- (g) make different provision for different circumstances.

(6) The provisions which may be included in regulations by virtue of subsection (5)(f) above may include rules for ascertaining—
- (a) whether, when and to what extent consideration is to be taken to have been written off in accounts as a bad debt;
- (b) whether [anything received]³ is to be taken as received by way of consideration for a particular supply;
- (c) whether, and to what extent, [anything received]³ is to be taken as received by way of consideration written off in accounts as a bad debt.

(7) The provisions which may be included in regulations by virtue of subsection (5)(f) above may include rules dealing with particular cases, such as those involving [receipt of part of the consideration]³ or mutual debts; and in particular such rules may vary the way in which the following amounts are to be calculated—
- (a) the outstanding amount mentioned in subsection (2) above, and
- (b) the amount of any repayment where a refund has been allowed under this section.

(8) Section 6 shall apply for determining the time when a supply is to be treated as taking place for the purposes of construing this section.

Commentary—*De Voil Indirect Tax Service* **V5.156**.
HMRC Manuals—VAT Cash Accounting Scheme VCAS6300 (claiming bad debt relief).
Regulations—VAT Regulations, SI 1995/2518 regs 156–172.
VAT (Amendment) (No 3) Regulations, SI 2014/2430.
Amendments—¹ Sub-s (4)(b), and the word "and" immediately preceding it, repealed by FA 1997 s 39(1), Sch 18 Pt IV(3) in respect of any claim made under this section in relation to a supply of goods made after 19 March 1997.
² In sub-s (1)(a) the words "for a consideration in money" repealed by FA 1998 s 23(1), Sch 27 Part II with effect from 31 July 1998.
³ Words in sub-ss (3)(a), (b), (5)(c), (6)(b), (c) and (7) substituted by FA 1998 s 23 with effect from 31 July 1998.
⁴ Sub-s (3A) inserted by FA 1998 s 23 with effect from 31 July 1998.
⁵ Sub-s (3) substituted by FA 1999 s 15 with effect for the purposes of the making of any refund or repayment after 9 March 1999, but do not have effect in relation to anything received on or before that day.
⁶ Words in sub-s (5)(e) substituted by FA 1999 s 15 with effect from 27 July 1999.
⁷ Sub-ss (4A) and (5)(ea) repealed by FA 2002 ss 22(2), (3), 139, Sch 40 Pt 2(1) with effect for supplies made after 31 December 2002 (by virtue of SI 2002/3028).

[*Acquisitions*]

36A Relief from VAT on acquisition if importation would attract relief

(1) The Treasury may by order make provision for relieving from VAT the acquisition from another member State of any goods if, or to the extent that, relief from VAT would be given by an order under section 37 if the acquisition were an importation from a place outside the member States.

(2) An order under this section may provide for relief to be subject to such conditions as appear to the Treasury to be necessary or expedient.
These may—
- *(a) include conditions prohibiting or restricting the disposal of or dealing with the goods concerned;*
- *(b) be framed by reference to the conditions to which, by virtue of any order under section 37 in force at the time of the acquisition, relief under such an order would be subject in the case of an importation of the goods concerned.*

(3) Where relief from VAT given by an order under this section was subject to a condition that has been breached or not complied with, the VAT shall become payable at the time of the breach or, as the case may be, at the latest time allowed for compliance.][1] , [2]

Orders—See the VAT (Acquisitions) Relief Order, SI 2002/1935.
VAT (Relief for European Research Infrastructure Consortia) Order, SI 2012/2907.
Amendments—[1] This section inserted by FA 2002 s 25 with effect from 24 July 2002.
[2] Section 36A and preceding heading repealed by the Taxation (Cross-border Trade) Act 2018 s 43, Sch 8 paras 1, 38 with effect from IP completion day (11pm on 31 December 2020), by virtue of SI 2020/1642 reg 4(*b*).

Imports, overseas businesses etc

37 [VAT on importation of goods: reliefs etc]

[(A1) No VAT is chargeable on the importation of goods to which section 7(5B) applies.][2]
(1) The Treasury may by order make provision for giving relief from the whole or part of the VAT chargeable on the importation of goods . . . [1], subject to such conditions (including conditions prohibiting or restricting the disposal of or dealing with the goods) as may be imposed by or under the order . . . [1]
(2) In any case where—
  (*a*) it is proposed that goods which have been imported . . . [1] by any person ("the original importer") with the benefit of relief under subsection (1) above shall be transferred to another person ("the transferee"), and
  (*b*) on an application made by the transferee, the Commissioners direct that this subsection shall apply,
this Act shall have effect as if, on the date of the transfer of the goods (and in place of the transfer), the goods were exported by the original importer and imported by the transferee and, accordingly, where appropriate, provision made under subsection (1) above shall have effect in relation to the VAT chargeable on the importation of the goods by the transferee.
(3) The Commissioners may by regulations make provision for remitting or repaying, if they think fit, the whole or part of the VAT chargeable on the importation of any goods . . . [1] which are shown to their satisfaction to have been previously exported . . . [1].
(4) The Commissioners may by regulations make provision for remitting or repaying the whole or part of the VAT chargeable on the importation of any goods . . . [1] if they are satisfied that the goods have been or are to be re-exported . . . [1] and they think fit to do so in all the circumstances and having regard—
  (*a*) to the VAT chargeable on the supply of like goods in the United Kingdom;
  (*b*) . . . [1]

Commentary—*De Voil Indirect Tax Service* **V3.316**.
Northern Ireland—See Sch 9ZA para 18(2) (the Treasury may by order make provision for relieving from Northern Ireland acquisition VAT if, or to the extent that, relief from VAT would be given by an order under this section if the acquisition in question were an importation).
See Sch 9ZB para 13: this section is modified to have effect as follows—
  – as if any reference to the export of goods did not include the export of goods from Northern Ireland to a place in the member States;
  – in relation to a removal of goods from Northern Ireland to Great Britain (which is treated as an importation as a result of VATA 1994 Sch 9ZB para 3(3)) as if any reference to the export of goods included their removal from Great Britain to Northern Ireland; and
  – in relation to a removal of goods from Great Britain to Northern Ireland (which is treated as an importation as a result of VATA 1994 Sch 9ZB para 3(5)) as if any reference to the export of goods included their removal from Northern Ireland to Great Britain.
See also Sch 9ZB para 33(3) (modifications in relation to exports – goods removed to Isle of Man): this section has effect in relation to a removal of goods to Northern Ireland from the Isle of Man (which is treated as an importation as a result of Sch 9ZB paras 3(5) and 32(2)) as if any reference to the export of goods included their removal from Northern Ireland to the Isle of Man.
Regulations—See VAT Regulations, SI 1995/2518 regs 123–126.
VAT (Imported Gas, Electricity, Heat and Cooling) Relief Order, SI 2010/2924
Orders—See VAT (Imported Goods) Relief Order, SI 1984/746.
VAT (Small Non-commercial Consignments) Relief Order, SI 1986/939.
VAT (Imported Gold) Relief Order, SI 1992/3124.
VAT (Importation of Investment Gold) Relief Order, SI 1999/3115.
VAT (Relief for European Research Infrastructure Consortia) Order, SI 2012/2907.
VAT (Imported Goods) Relief (Amendment) Order, SI 2014/2364; VAT (Small Non-commercial Consignments) Relief (Amendment) Order, SI 2015/2015.
Value Added Tax (Small Non-Commercial Consignments) Relief (Amendment) Order, SI 2016/1199.
Amendments—[1] The following amendments made by the Taxation (Cross-border Trade) Act 2018 s 43, Sch 8 paras 1, 39 with effect from IP completion day (11pm on 31 December 2020), by virtue of SI 2020/1642 reg 4(*b*)—
  – in sub-s (1), words "from places outside the member States", and "if and so far as the relief appears to the Treasury to be necessary or expedient, having regard to any international agreement or arrangements", repealed;
  – in sub-s (2)(*a*), words "from a place outside the member States" repealed;
  – in sub-s (3), words "from places outside the member States" and "from the United Kingdom or removed from any member State" repealed;

- in sub-s (4)—
    (a) in opening words, words "from places outside the member States" and "or otherwise removed from the United Kingdom" repealed; and
    (b) para (*b*) repealed.
Sub-s (4)(*b*) previously read as follows—
    "   (b) to any VAT which may have become chargeable in another member State in respect of the goods".
2   Heading substituted (previously read: "Relief from VAT on importation of goods"), and sub-s (A1) inserted, by the Taxation (Post-transition Period) Act 2020 s 7, Sch 3 paras 1, 7 with effect from IP completion day (11pm on 31 December 2020), by virtue of SI 2020/1642 reg 9.

38 Importation of goods by taxable persons

The Commissioners may by regulations make provision for enabling goods imported . . . [1] by a taxable person in the course or furtherance of any business carried on by him to be delivered or removed, subject to such conditions or restrictions as the Commissioners may impose for the protection of the revenue, without payment of the VAT chargeable on the importation, and for that VAT to be accounted for together with the VAT chargeable on the supply of goods or services by him . . . [1].

Commentary—*De Voil Indirect Tax Service* **V5.115**.
Northern Ireland—See Sch 9ZA para 18(5) (Northern Ireland: this section has effect as if after "by him" there were inserted "or on the acquisition of goods by that person from member States").
Regulations—See VAT Regulations, SI 1995/2518 reg 122.
Amendments—[1] Words "from a place outside the member States" and "or on the acquisition of goods by him from other member States" repealed by the Taxation (Cross-border Trade) Act 2018 s 43, Sch 8 paras 1, 40 with effect from IP completion day (11pm on 31 December 2020), by virtue of SI 2020/1642 reg 4(*b*).

39 Repayment of VAT to those in business overseas

[(1) The Commissioners may, by means of a scheme embodied in regulations, provide for the repayment, to persons carrying on business wholly outside the United Kingdom, of VAT which would be input tax of theirs if they were taxable persons in the United Kingdom.
(2) The scheme may make different provision in relation to persons carrying on business in different places.][3]
(3) Repayment shall be made in such cases [and to such extent][1] only, and subject to such conditions, as the scheme may prescribe (being conditions specified in the regulations or imposed by the Commissioners either generally or in particular cases); and the scheme may provide—
   [(*za*) for claims to be made in such form and manner as may be specified in the scheme or by the Commissioners in accordance with the scheme;][2]
   (*a*) for claims and repayments to be made only through agents in the United Kingdom;
   (*b*) either generally or for specified purposes—
       (i) for the agents to be treated under this Act as if they were taxable persons; and
       (ii) for treating claims as if they were returns under this Act [in respect of such period as may be prescribed][1] and repayments as if they were repayments of input tax;
   [(*ba*) for and in connection with the payment of interest to or by the Commissioners (including in relation to the repayment of interest wrongly paid), and][1]
   [(*c*) for generally regulating—
       (i) the time by which claims must be made, and
       (ii) the methods by which the amount of any repayment is to be determined and the repayment is to be made.][2]

Commentary—*De Voil Indirect Tax Service* **V5.151A, V5.152**.
Regulations—See VAT Regulations, SI 1995/2518 regs 173–197.
VAT (Amendment) (No 2) Regulations, SI 2012/1899.
VAT (Amendment) (No 3) Regulations, SI 2014/2430.
Amendments—[1] In sub-s (3) words inserted, and para (*ba*) inserted by FA 2009 s 77 with effect from 21 July 2009.
2   In sub-s (3), para (*za*) inserted, and para (*c*) substituted, by FA 2012 s 204, Sch 29 paras 1, 5 with effect from 17 July 2012.
3   Sub-ss (1), (2) substituted by the Taxation (Cross-border Trade) Act 2018 s 43, Sch 8 paras 1, 41 with effect from IP completion day (11pm on 31 December 2020), by virtue of SI 2020/1642 reg 4(*b*). Note that, where these amendments remove a reference to the principal VAT Directive (2006/112/EC) or the Implementing VAT Regulation ((EU) No 282/2011), the removal is not to be taken as implying that the Directive or Regulation is no longer relevant for determining the meaning and effect of this section (Taxation (Cross-border Trade) Act 2018 Sch 8 para 99).
Sub-ss (1), (2) previously read as follows—
"(1) The Commissioners may, by means of a scheme embodied in regulations, provide for the repayment, to persons to whom this section applies, of VAT on supplies to them in the United Kingdom or on the importation of goods by them from places outside the member States which would be input tax of theirs if they were taxable persons in the United Kingdom.
    (2) This section—
        (*a*) applies to persons carrying on business in another member State, and
        (*b*) shall apply also to persons carrying on business in other countries, if, pursuant to any EU Directive, rules are adopted by the Council of the European Union about refunds of VAT to persons established elsewhere than in the member States,
but does not apply to persons carrying on business in the United Kingdom.".

[39A Applications for forwarding of VAT repayment claims to other member States
The Commissioners must make arrangements for dealing with applications made to the Commissioners by taxable persons, in accordance with Council Directive 2008/9/EC, for the forwarding to the tax authorities of another member State of claims for refunds of VAT on—
   (a) supplies to them in that member State, or
   (b) the importation of goods by them into that member State from places outside the member States.][1] , [2]

Amendments—[1] Section 39A inserted by FA 2009 s 77 with effect from 21 July 2009.
[2] Section 39A repealed by the Taxation (Cross-border Trade) Act 2018 s 43, Sch 8 paras 1, 42 with effect from IP completion day (11pm on 31 December 2020), by virtue of SI 2020/1642 reg 4(b). Note that, where the Commissioners receive a claim for repayment of VAT under SI 1995/2518 reg 173B or for an additional repayment under reg 173D(2), they must forward it on or before 30 April 2021 to the tax authorities of the member State from which the repayment or additional repayment is claimed and, to this extent, the repeal of s 39A does not have effect (see SI 2020/1495 reg 11(5)).

40 Refunds in relation to new means of transport supplied to other member States
(1) Subject to subsection (2) below, where a person who is not a taxable person makes such a supply of goods consisting in a new means of transport as involves the removal of the goods to another member State, the Commissioners shall, on a claim made in that behalf, refund to that person, as the case may be—
   (a) the amount of any VAT on the supply of that means of transport to that person, or
   (b) the amount of any VAT paid by that person on the acquisition of that means of transport from another member State or on its importation from a place outside the member States.
(2) The amount of VAT refunded under this section shall not exceed the amount that would have been payable on the supply involving the removal if it had been a taxable supply by a taxable person and had not been zero-rated.
(3) The Commissioners shall not be entitled to entertain a claim for refund of VAT under this section unless the claim—
   (a) is made within such time and in such form and manner;
   (b) contains such information; and
   (c) is accompanied by such documents, whether by way of evidence or otherwise,
as the Commissioners may by regulations prescribe.[1]

Commentary—*De Voil Indirect Tax Service* **V5.154**.
Regulations—See VAT Regulations, SI 1995/2518 regs 146, 149–154.
Amendments—[1] Section 40 repealed by the Taxation (Cross-border Trade) Act 2018 s 43, Sch 8 paras 1, 43 with effect from IP completion day (11pm on 31 December 2020), by virtue of SI 2020/1642 reg 4(b).

PART III
APPLICATION OF ACT IN PARTICULAR CASES

[40A Northern Ireland Protocol
(1) Schedule 9ZA—
   (a) makes provision about a charge to VAT on acquisitions of goods in Northern Ireland from a member State, and
   (b) contains modifications of the other provisions of this Act in connection with the movement of goods between Northern Ireland and member States.
(2) Schedule 9ZB—
   (a) makes provision about VAT charged on goods imported into the United Kingdom as a result of their entry into Northern Ireland,
   (b) makes provision about the treatment, for the purposes of VAT, of goods that are removed from Northern Ireland to Great Britain and goods that are removed from Great Britain to Northern Ireland, and
   (c) contains other provision relevant to the application of this Act in Northern Ireland.
[(3) Schedule 9ZC makes provision, as a result of the Protocol on Ireland/Northern Ireland in the EU withdrawal agreement, about the application of this Act in cases involving—
   (a) supplies of goods by persons established outside the United Kingdom that are facilitated by online marketplaces, and
   (b) the importation of goods of a low value.][2]][1]

Commentary—*De Voil Indirect Tax Service* **V3.360, V1.301, V1.308**.
Amendments—[1] Section 40A inserted by the Taxation (Post-transition Period) Act 2020 s 3(1) with effect from IP completion day (11pm on 31 December 2020) by virtue of SI 2020/1642 reg 9.
[2] Sub-s (3) inserted by the Taxation (Post-transition Period) Act 2020, s 7, Sch 3 paras 25, 26 with effect from IP completion day (11pm on 31 December 2020) by virtue of SI 2020/1642 reg 9.

41 Application to the Crown
(1) This Act shall apply in relation to taxable supplies by the Crown as it applies in relation to taxable supplies by taxable persons.

(2) Where the supply by a Government department of any goods or services does not amount to the carrying on of a business but it appears to the Treasury that similar goods or services are or might be supplied by taxable persons in the course or furtherance of any business, then, if and to the extent that the Treasury so direct, the supply of those goods or services by that department shall be treated for the purposes of this Act as a supply in the course or furtherance of any business carried on by it.[8]
(3) Where VAT is chargeable on the supply of goods or services to a Government department . . . [12] or on the importation of any goods by a Government department . . . [12] and the supply . . . [12] or importation is not for the purpose—
   (a) of any business carried on by the department, or
   (b) of a supply by the department which, by virtue of [section 41A,][8] is treated as a supply in the course or furtherance of a business,
then, if and to the extent that the Treasury so direct and subject to subsection (4) below, the Commissioners shall, on a claim made by the department at such time and in such form and manner as the Commissioners may determine, refund to it the amount of the VAT so chargeable.
(4) The Commissioners may make the refunding of any amount due under subsection (3) above conditional upon compliance by the claimant with requirements with respect to the keeping, preservation and production of records relating to the supply . . . [12] or importation in question.
(5) For the purposes of this section goods or services obtained by one Government department from another Government department shall be treated, if and to the extent that the Treasury so direct, as supplied by that other department and similarly as regards goods or services obtained by or from the Crown Estate Commissioners.
(6) In this section "Government department" includes [the Scottish Administration][2] [, the [Welsh Assembly Government][7]][1], a Northern Ireland department, a Northern Ireland health and social services body, any body of persons exercising functions on behalf of a Minister of the Crown, including . . . [4] and any part of a Government department (as defined in the foregoing) designated for the purposes of this subsection by a direction of the Treasury.
(7) For the purposes of subsection (6) [each of the following is to be regarded as a body of persons exercising functions on behalf of a Minister of the Crown][11][—
   [*(a)*] a health service body as defined in section 60(7) of the National Health Service and Community Care Act 1990,
   [*(b)*] a National Health Service trust established under Part I of that Act][4] or the National Health Service (Scotland) Act 1978[,
   [*(c)*] [an NHS foundation trust][6][,
   [*(d)*] [a Primary Care Trust][3][,
   [*(e)*] [a Local Health Board[,
   [*(f)*] [a clinical commissioning group,
   [*(g)*] the Health and Social Care Information Centre,
   [*(h)*] the National Health Service Commissioning Board[,
   [*(i)*] the National Institute for Health and Care Excellence][9][5][,
   [*(j)*] [Health Education England (established by the Care Act 2014), . . . [11]
   [*(k)*] the Health Research Authority (also established by that Act),][10]
   [*(l)*] a strategic highways company appointed under section 1 of the Infrastructure Act 2015.][11]
(8) In subsection (6) "a Northern Ireland health and social services body" means—
   (a) a health and social services body as defined in Article 7(6) of the Health and Personal Social Services (Northern Ireland) Order 1991; and
   (b) a Health and Social Services trust established under that Order.

Commentary—*De Voil Indirect Tax Service* **V5.161, V2.108**.
HMRC Manuals—VAT Government And Public Bodies VATGPB9310–VATGPB9350 (government department - definition, restrictions and VAT recovery).
VATGPB9650 (VAT refunds).
VAT Education Manual VATEDU39500 (public bodies).
Northern Ireland—See Sch 9ZA para 20 (sub-ss (3), (4) apply to Northern Ireland acquisition VAT as they apply to VAT chargeable on the supply of goods).
Amendments—[1] Words in sub-s (6) inserted by the Government of Wales Act 1998 Sch 12 para 35 with effect from 1 April 1999 by virtue of the Government of Wales Act 1998 (Commencement No 4) Order, SI 1999/782.
[2] Words in sub-s (6) inserted by the Scotland Act 1998 Sch 8 para 30, with effect from 6 May 1999 by virtue of the Scotland Act 1998 (Commencement) Order SI 1998/3178.
[3] Words in sub-s (7) inserted by the Health Act 1999 s 65 Sch 8 para 86 with effect from 1 April 2000 (by virtue of the Health Act 1999 (Commencement No 2) Order, SI 1999/2342 art 2(4)(b)(iii)).
[4] Words in sub-s (6) revoked and words in sub-s (7) substituted by the Health Act 1999 (Supplementary, Consequential etc Provisions) Order, SI 2000/90 art 3(1), Sch 1 para 29 with effect from 8 February 2000.
[5] Words inserted by the National Health Service Reform and Health Care Professions Act 2002 s 6(2), Sch 5 para 40 with effect from 10 October 2002 (by virtue of SI 2002/2532).
[6] Words in sub-s (7) inserted by the Health and Social Care (Community Health and Standards) Act 2003 s 33(3) with effect from 1 April 2004 (by virtue of SI 2004/759, art 2).
[7] Words in sub-s (6) substituted by the Government of Wales Act 2006, s 160(1), Sch 10, para 39 with effect from 25 May 2007, being the date on which the initial period ended (following the appointment of the First Minister) (Government of Wales Act 2006, ss 46, 161(4), (5)).

[8] Sub-s (2) repealed, and in sub-s (3)(b), words substituted for words "a direction under subsection (2) above,", by FA 2012 s 198(1), (2) with effect from 17 July 2012.
[9] Words in sub-s (7) inserted by FA 2013 s 191. This amendment is treated as having come into force on 1 April 2013.
[10] Sub-s (7) restructured into a list format, entries for "Health Education England" and "the Heath Research Authority" inserted, and in final sentence, words substituted for word "shall", by FA 2014 s 107 with effect from 17 July 2014.
[11] In sub-s (7), words inserted, word at the end of para (j) repealed, and para (l) inserted by FA 2015 s 67 with effect from 1 April 2015.
[12] The following amendments made by the Taxation (Cross-border Trade) Act 2018 s 43, Sch 8 paras 1, 44 with effect from IP completion day (11pm on 31 December 2020), by virtue of SI 2020/1642 reg 4(b)—
- in sub-s (3), the following words repealed—
  (a) ", on the acquisition of any goods by a Government department from another member State";
  (b) "from a place outside the member States"; and
  (c) ", acquisition"; and
- in sub-s (4), word ", acquisition" repealed.

Prospective amendments—In sub-s (7), words "section 18 of the National Health Service (Wales) Act 2006" to be substituted for words "Part I of that Act", by the Health and Social Care Act 2012 s 179, Sch 14 paras 65, 66 with effect from a date to be appointed.

[41A Supply of goods or services by public bodies

(1) This section applies where goods or services are supplied by a [public authority]² in the course of activities or transactions in which it is engaged as a public authority.

[(2) Unless the supply is on such a small scale as to be negligible, it is to be treated for the purposes of this Act as a supply in the course or furtherance of a business if it is in respect of any of the following activities—

(a) telecommunications services,
(b) supply of water, gas, electricity or thermal energy,
(c) transport of goods,
(d) port or airport services,
(e) passenger transport,
(f) supply of new goods manufactured for sale,
(g) engaging in transactions in respect of agricultural products in the exercise of regulatory functions,
(h) organisation of trade fairs or exhibitions,
(i) warehousing,
(j) activities of commercial publicity bodies,
(k) activities of travel agents,
(l) running of staff shops, cooperatives, industrial canteens, or similar institutions, or
(m) activities carried out by radio and television bodies which are of a commercial nature.]²

(3) If the supply is not in respect of such an activity, it is to be treated for the purposes of this Act as a supply in the course or furtherance of a business if (and only if) not charging VAT on the supply would lead to a significant distortion of competition.

(4) . . . ²]¹

Commentary—*De Voil Indirect Tax Service* **V2.213, V2.201B**.

HMRC Manuals—VAT Government and Public Bodies VATGPB8875 (other local authority activities: waste collection and disposal).

Amendments—[1] Section 41A inserted by FA 2012 s 198(1), (3) with effect from 17 July 2012.
[2] The following amendments made by the Taxation (Cross-border Trade) Act 2018 s 43, Sch 8 paras 1, 45 with effect from IP completion day (11pm on 31 December 2020) by virtue of SI 2020/1642 reg 4(b)).
- in sub-s (1), words substituted for words "body mentioned in Article 13(1) of the VAT Directive (status of public bodies as taxable persons)";
- sub-s (2) substituted; and
- sub-s (4) repealed.

Note that, where these amendments remove a reference to the principal VAT Directive (2006/112/EC) or the Implementing VAT Regulation ((EU) No 282/2011), the removal is not to be taken as implying that the Directive or Regulation is no longer relevant for determining the meaning and effect of this section (Taxation (Cross-border Trade) Act 2018 Sch 8 para 99).

Before these amendments, section 41A previously read as follows—

"(1) This section applies where goods or services are supplied by a body mentioned in Article 13(1) of the VAT Directive (status of public bodies as taxable persons) in the course of activities or transactions in which it is engaged as a public authority.

(2) If the supply is in respect of an activity listed in Annex I to the VAT Directive (activities in respect of which public bodies are to be taxable persons), it is to be treated for the purposes of this Act as a supply in the course or furtherance of a business unless it is on such a small scale as to be negligible.

(3) If the supply is not in respect of such an activity, it is to be treated for the purposes of this Act as a supply in the course or furtherance of a business if (and only if) not charging VAT on the supply would lead to a significant distortion of competition.

(4) In this section "the VAT Directive" means Council Directive 2006/112/ EC on the common system of value added tax.

42 Local authorities
A local authority which makes taxable supplies is liable to be registered under this Act, whatever the value of the supplies; and accordingly Schedule 1 shall apply, in a case where the value of the taxable supplies made by a local authority in any period of one year does not exceed the sum for the time being specified in paragraph 1(1)(*a*) of that Schedule, as if that value exceeded that sum.
Commentary—*De Voil Indirect Tax Service* **V2.108**.
HMRC Manuals—VAT Government And Public Bodies VATGPB4920 (Section 33 bodies: local authorities).

43 Groups of companies
(1) Where under [sections 43A to 43D][10] any [persons][14] are treated as members of a group, any business carried on by a member of the group shall be treated as carried on by the representative member, and—
   (*a*) any supply of goods or services by a member of the group to another member of the group shall be disregarded; and
   (*b*) any [supply which is a supply to which paragraph (*a*) above does not apply and is a supply][1] of goods or services by or to a member of the group shall be treated as a supply by or to the representative member; and
   [(*c*) any VAT paid or payable by a member of the group on the importation of goods shall be treated as paid or payable by the representative member and the goods shall be treated, for the purposes of sections 38 and 73(7), as imported by the representative member;][15]
and all members of the group shall be liable jointly and severally for any VAT due from the representative member.
[(1AA) Where—
   (*a*) it is material, for the purposes of any provision made by or under this Act ('the relevant provision'), whether the person by or to whom a supply is made, or the person by whom goods are . . . [15] imported, is a person of a particular description,
   (*b*) paragraph (*b*) or (*c*) of subsection (1) above applies to any supply . . . [15] or importation, and
   (*c*) there is a difference that would be material for the purposes of the relevant provision between—
      (i) the description applicable to the representative member, and
      (ii) the description applicable to the [person who][14] (apart from this section) would be regarded for the purposes of this Act as making the supply . . . [15] or importation or, as the case may be, as being the person to whom the supply is made.
the relevant provision shall have effect in relation to that supply . . . [15] or importation as if the only description applicable to the representative member were the description in fact applicable to that [person][14].][5]
[(1AB) Subsection (1AA) above does not apply to the extent that what is material for the purposes of the relevant provision is whether a person is a taxable person."][5]
[(1A) . . .][4]
(2) An order under section 5(5) or (6) may make provision for securing that any goods or services which, if all the members of the group were one person, would fall to be treated under that section as supplied to and by that person, are treated as supplied to and by the representative member [and may provide for that purpose that the representative member is to be treated as a person of such description as may be determined under the order][6].
[(2A) A supply made by a member of a group ('the supplier') to another member of the group ('the UK member') shall not be disregarded under subsection (*1*)(*a*) above if—
   (*a*) it would (if there were no group) be a supply of services [to which section 7A(2)(*a*) applies made][11] to a person belonging in the United Kingdom;
   (*b*) those services are not within any of the descriptions specified in Schedule 9;
   (*c*) the supplier has been supplied (whether or not by a person belonging in the United Kingdom) with [any services . . . [11] which do not fall within any of the descriptions specified in Schedule 9][8] [and section 7A(2)(*a*) applied to the supply][11];
   (*d*) the supplier belonged outside the United Kingdom when it was supplied with the services mentioned in paragraph (*c*) above; and
   (*e*) the services so mentioned have been used by the supplier for making the supply to the UK member.][7]
[(2B) Subject to subsection (2C) below, where a supply is excluded by virtue of subsection (2A) above from the supplies that are disregarded in pursuance of subsection (1)(*a*) above, all the same consequences shall follow under this Act as if that supply—
   (*a*) were a taxable supply in the United Kingdom by the representative member to itself, and
   (*b*) without prejudice to that, were made by the representative member in the course or furtherance of its business.][7]
[(2C) [Except in so far as the Commissioners may be regulations otherwise provide][9] a supply which is deemed by virtue of subsection (2B) above to be a supply by the representative member to itself—

(a) shall not be taken into account as a supply made by the representative member when determining any allowance of input tax under section 26(1) in the case of the representative member;
(b) shall be deemed for the purposes of paragraph 1 of Schedule 6 to be a supply in the case of which the person making the supply and the person supplied are connected within the meaning of [section 1122 of the Corporation Tax Act 2010][12] (connected persons); and
(c) subject to paragraph (b) above [and paragraph 8A of Schedule 6][13], shall be taken to be a supply the value and time of which are determined as if it were a supply of services which is treated by virtue of section 8 as made by the person by whom the services are received.][7]

[(2D) For the purposes of subsection (2A) above where—
(a) there has been a supply of the assets of a business of a person ('the transferor') to a person to whom the whole or any part of that business was transferred as a going concern ('the transferee'),
(b) that supply is either—
  (i) a supply falling to be treated, in accordance with an order under section 5(3), as being neither a supply of goods nor a supply of services, or
  (ii) a supply that would have fallen to be so treated if it had taken place in the United Kingdom,
and
(c) the transferor was supplied with services . . . [11] at a time before the transfer when the transferor belonged outside the United Kingdom [and section 7A(2)(a) applied to the supply][11],

those services, so far as they are used by the transferee for making any supply [to which section 7A(2)(a) applies][11], shall be deemed to have been supplied to the transferee at a time when the transferee belonged outside the United Kingdom.][7]

[(2E) Where, in the case of a supply of assets falling within paragraphs (a) and (b) of subsection (2D) above—
(a) the transferor himself acquired any of the assets in question by way of a previous supply of assets falling within those paragraphs, and
(b) [there is a supply to which section 7A(2)(a) applies] of services which, if used by the transferor for making such a supply][11], would be deemed by virtue of that subsection to have been supplied to the transferor at a time when he belonged outside the United Kingdom,

that subsection shall have effect, notwithstanding that the services have not been so used by the transferor, as if the transferor were a person to whom those services were supplied and as if he were a person belonging outside the United Kingdom at the time of their deemed supply to him; and this subsection shall apply accordingly through any number of successive supplies of assets falling within paragraphs (a) and (b) of that subsection.][7]

(3)–(8) . . . [2]

[(9) Schedule 9A (which makes provision for ensuring that this section is not used for tax avoidance) shall have effect.][3]

Commentary—*De Voil Indirect Tax Service* **V3.267, V2.190, V2.113**.
HMRC Manuals—VAT Groups VGROUPS08100 (why is this legislation required?).
VAT Refund Manual VRM4300 (VAT groups).
Northern Ireland—See VATA 1994 Sch 9ZA para 21: this section applies to an acquisition of goods from a member State as it would apply to an importation of those goods as if the reference in subsection (1)(c) to section 38 were omitted.
See Also VATA 1994 Sch 9ZB para 31: sub-s (1)(a) does not apply to a supply of goods if the goods are in Northern Ireland at the time they are supplied unless the supplier and the recipient each has a business establishment, or some other fixed establishment, in Northern Ireland.
Orders—See VAT (Self-supply of Construction Services) Order, SI 1989/472; VAT (Cars) Order, SI 1992/3122; VAT (Special Provisions) Order, SI 1995/1268.
Amendments—[1] Words in sub-s (1)(b) substituted by FA 1995 s 25(2), (5), with effect in relation to any supply made on or after 1 March 1995 and any supply made before that date in the case of which both the body making the supply and the body supplied continued to be members of the group in question until at least that date.
[2] Words in sub-ss (3) to (8) repealed by FA 1999 s 16, Sch 2 para 1 with effect from 27 July 1999, subject to FA 1999 Sch 2 para 6.
[3] Sub-s (9) added by FA 1996 s 31(1) with effect from 29 April 1996.
[4] Sub-s (1A) (inserted by FA 1995 s 25(2)) repealed by FA 1996 s 31(5), Sch 41 Pt IV(5) with effect in relation to supplies on or after 29 April 1996.
[5] Sub-ss (1AA) and (1AB) inserted by FA 1997 s 40(1) in relation to any supply made after 26 November 1996 and in relation to any acquisition or importation taking place after that date.
[6] Words in sub-s (2) inserted by FA 1997 s 40(2) with effect from 19 March 1997.
[7] Sub-ss (2A)–(2E) inserted by FA 1997 s 41 in relation to supplies made on or after 26 November 1996.
[8] Words in sub-s (2A) (c) substituted by FA 1997 s 41(3), (4) in relation to supplies made after 19 March 1997. In relation to supplies made after 25 November 1996 and before 20 March 1997, the substituted words read 'services falling within any of paragraphs 1 to 8 of Schedule 5'.
[9] Words in sub-s (2C) inserted by FA 1997 s 41 (4)(5) in relation to supplies made after 19 March 1997.
[10] Words in sub-s (1) substituted by FA 2004 s 20(3) with effect from 22 July 2004.

[11] In sub-s (2A)(a) words "falling within Schedule 5", in sub-s (2D) "falling within that Schedule", in sub-s (2E)(b) "there are services falling within paragraphs 1 to 8 of Schedule 5 which, if used by the transferor for making supplies falling within that Schedule" substituted, in sub-ss (2A)(c), (2D)(c) words inserted and "falling within paragraphs 1 to 8 of Schedule 5" repealed, by FA 2009 s 76, Sch 36 paras 1, 7, 14, with effect from 1 January 2010. The references to a supply to which s 7A(2) applies include a supply of services falling within Sch 5 paras 1 to 8 made before that date.
[12] In sub-s (2C)(b) words substituted for words "section 839 of the Taxes Act 1988" by CTA 2010 s 1177, Sch 1 para 285(a). CTA 2010 has effect for corporation tax purposes for accounting periods ending on or after 1 April 2010, and for income and capital gains tax purposes for the tax year 2010–11 and subsequent tax years.
[13] Words in sub-s (2C)(c) inserted by FA 2012 s 200(1), (2) with effect in relation to supplies made on or after 17 July 2012.
[14] In sub-s (1), word substituted for words "bodies corporate", in sub-s (1A), in para (c)(ii), words substituted for words "person who", and in the closing words, words substituted for words "person", by FA 2019 s 53, Sch 18 paras 3, 5 with effect from 1 November 2019 (see SI 2019/1348).
[15] The following amendments made by the Taxation (Cross-border Trade) Act 2018 s 43, Sch 8 paras 1, 46 with effect from IP completion day (11pm on 31 December 2020), by virtue of SI 2020/1642 reg 4(b)—
- sub-s (1)(c) substituted;
- in sub-s (1AA), the following words repealed—
  (a) in para (a), "acquired or"; and
  (b) in paras (b), (c)(ii), and in words after para (c), ", acquisition".

Sub-s (1)(c), as substituted, to read as follows—
"(c) any VAT paid or payable by a member of the group on the acquisition of goods from another member State or on the importation of goods from a place outside the member States shall be treated as paid or payable by the representative member and the goods shall be treated—
  (i) in the case of goods acquired from another member State, for the purposes of section 73(7); and
  (ii) in the case of goods imported from a place outside the member States, for those purposes and the purposes of section 38,
as acquired or, as the case may be, imported by the representative member;".

Sub-s (1AA) previously read as follows—
"(1AA) Where—
  (a) it is material, for the purposes of any provision made by or under this Act ('the relevant provision'), whether the person by or to whom a supply is made, or the person by whom goods are acquired or imported, is a person of a particular description,
  (b) paragraph (b) or (c) of subsection (1) above applies to any supply, acquisition or importation, and
  (c) there is a difference that would be material for the purposes of the relevant provision between—
    (i) the description applicable to the representative member, and
    (ii) the description applicable to the person who (apart from this section) would be regarded for the purposes of this Act as making the supply, acquisition or importation or, as the case may be, as being the person to whom the supply is made,
the relevant provision shall have effect in relation to that supply, acquisition or importation as if the only description applicable to the representative member were the description in fact applicable to that person.".

[43A Groups: eligibility

(1) Two or more [UK bodies corporate][2] are eligible to be treated as members of a group if . . .[2]—
  (a) one of them controls each of the others,
  (b) one person (whether a body corporate or an individual) controls all of them, or
  (c) two or more individuals carrying on a business in partnership control all of them.

(2), (3) . . .

[(4) An individual carrying on a business and one or more UK bodies corporate are eligible to be treated as members of a group if the individual—
  (a) controls the UK body corporate or all of the UK bodies corporate, and
  (b) is established, or has a fixed establishment, in the United Kingdom in relation to the business.

(5) Two or more relevant persons carrying on a business in partnership ("the partnership") and one or more UK bodies corporate are eligible to be treated as members of a group if the partnership—
  (a) controls the UK body corporate or all of the UK bodies corporate, and
  (b) is established, or has a fixed establishment, in the United Kingdom in relation to the business.

(6) In this section—
  (a) "UK body corporate" means a body corporate which is established or has a fixed establishment in the United Kingdom;
  (b) "relevant person" means an individual, a body corporate or a Scottish partnership.

(7) Section 43AZA contains provision for determining for the purposes of this section whether a body corporate, individual or partnership controls a UK body corporate.[2]][1]

Commentary—*De Voil Indirect Tax Service* **V2.189Y**.
HMRC Manuals—VAT Groups VGROUPS02150 (control conditions).
VGROUPS04450 (grounds for refusal of VAT group registration application).
Amendments—[1] This section inserted by FA 1999 s 16, Sch 2 para 2 with effect from 27 July 1999, subject to FA 1999 Sch 2 para 6.

[2] In sub-s (1), in the opening words, word substituted for words "bodies corporate", words "each is established or has a fixed establishment in the United Kingdom and" repealed, sub-ss (2), (3) repealed, and sub-ss (4)–(7) inserted, by FA 2019 s 53, Sch 18 para 1 with effect from 1 November 2019 (see SI 2019/1348).

[43AZA Section 43A: control test

(1) This section applies for the purposes of section 43A (and expressions used in this section have the same meaning as in that section).
(2) A body corporate ("X") controls a UK body corporate if—
   (a) X is empowered by statute to control the UK body corporate's activities, or
   (b) X is the UK body corporate's holding company.
(3) An individual ("Y") controls a UK body corporate if Y would, were Y a company, be the UK body corporate's holding company.
(4) Two or more relevant persons carrying on a business in partnership ("the partnership") control a UK body corporate if the partnership would, were it a company, be the UK body corporate's holding company.
(5) In this section "holding company" has the meaning given by section 1159 of, and Schedule 6 to, the Companies Act 2006.][1]

Commentary—*De Voil Indirect Tax Service* **V2.189Y**.
Amendments—[1] Section 43AZA inserted by FA 2019 s 53, Sch 18 paras 1, 2 with effect from 1 November 2019 (see SI 2019/1348).

[43AA Power to alter eligibility for grouping

(1) The Treasury may by order provide for [sections 43A and 43AZA][2] to have effect with specified modifications in relation to a specified class of person.
(2) An order under subsection (1) may, in particular—
   (a) make provision by reference to generally accepted accounting practice;
   (b) define generally accepted accounting practice for that purpose by reference to a specified document or instrument (and may provide for the reference to be read as including a reference to any later document or instrument that amends or replaces the first);
   (c) adopt any statutory or other definition of generally accepted accounting practice (with or without modification);
   (d) make provision by reference to what would be required or permitted by generally accepted accounting practice if accounts, or accounts of a specified kind, were prepared for a person.
(3) An order under subsection (1) may also, in particular, make provision by reference to—
   (a) the nature of a person;
   (b) past or intended future activities of a person;
   (c) the relationship between a number of persons;
   (d) the effect of including a person within a group or of excluding a person from a group.
(4) An order under subsection (1) may—
   (a) make provision which applies generally or only in specified circumstances;
   (b) make different provision for different circumstances;
   (c) include supplementary, incidental, consequential or transitional provision.][1]

Commentary—*De Voil Indirect Tax Service* **V2.189Y**.
HMRC Manuals—VAT Groups VGROUPS02300 (eligibility conditions for specified bodies).
Orders—See VAT (Groups: eligibility) Order, SI 2004/1931.
Amendments—[1] This section inserted by FA 2004 s 20(1) with effect from 22 July 2004.
[2] In sub-s (1), words substituted for words "section 43A" by FA 2019 s 53, Sch 18 paras 3, 6 with effect from 1 November 2019 (see SI 2019/1348).

[43B Groups: applications

(1) This section applies where an application is made to the Commissioners for two or more [persons, who][3] are eligible [by virtue of section 43A][2], to be treated as members of a group.
(2) This section also applies where two or more [persons][3] are treated as members of a group and an application is made to the Commissioners—
   (a) for another [person, who][3] is eligible [by virtue of section 43A][2] to be treated as a member of the group, to be treated as a member of the group,
   (b) for a [person][3] to cease to be treated as a member of the group,
   (c) for a member to be substituted as the group's representative member, or
   (d) for the [persons][3] no longer to be treated as members of a group.
(3) An application with respect to any [persons][3]—
   (a) must be made by one of them or by the person controlling them, and
   (b) in the case of an application for the [persons][3] to be treated as a group, must appoint one of them as the representative member.
(4) Where this section applies in relation to an application it shall, subject to subsection (6) below, be taken to be granted with effect from—
   (a) the day on which the application is received by the Commissioners, or
   (b) such earlier or later time as the Commissioners may allow.

(5) The Commissioners may refuse an application, within the period of 90 days starting with the day on which it was received by them, if it appears to them—
 (a) in the case of an application such as is mentioned in subsection (1) above, that the [persons][3] are not eligible [by virtue of section 43A][2] to be treated as members of a group,
 (b) in the case of an application such as is mentioned in subsection (2)(a) above, that the [person][3] is not eligible [by virtue of section 43A][2] to be treated as a member of the group, or
 (c) in any case, that refusal of the application is necessary for the protection of the revenue.
(6) If the Commissioners refuse an application it shall be taken never to have been granted.][1]

Amendments—[1] This section inserted by FA 1999 s 16, Sch 2 para 2 with effect from 27 July 1999, subject to FA 1999 Sch 2 para 6.
[2] Words in sub-ss (1), (2)(a), (5)(a) and (5)(b) substituted by FA 2004 s 20(4) with effect from 22 July 2004.
[3] In sub-s (1), words substituted for words "bodies corporate, which", in sub-s (2) in opening words, and in para (d), words substituted for words "bodies corporate", in para (a) words substituted for words "body corporate, which", in para (b) words substituted for words "body corporate", in sub-s (3) in opening words, words substituted for words "bodies corporate", in para (b) words substituted for word "bodies", in sub-s (5) in para (a) words substituted for words "bodies corporate", and in para (b) words substituted for words "body corporate", by FA 2019 s 53, Sch 18 paras 3, 7 with effect from 1 November 2019 (see SI 2019/1348).

[**43C Groups: termination of membership**
(1) The Commissioners may, by notice given to a [person][3], terminate its treatment as a member of a group from a date—
 (a) which is specified in the notice, and
 (b) which is, or falls after, the date on which the notice is given.
(2) The Commissioners may give a notice under subsection (1) above only if it appears to them to be necessary for the protection of the revenue.
(3) Where—
 (a) a [person][3] is treated as a member of a group, and
 (b) it appears to the Commissioners that the [person][3] is not, or is no longer, eligible [by virtue of section 43A][2] to be treated as a member of the group,
the Commissioners shall, by notice given to the [person][3], terminate its treatment as a member of the group from a date specified in the notice.
(4) The date specified in a notice under subsection (3) above may be earlier than the date on which the notice is given but shall not be earlier than—
 (a) the first date on which, in the opinion of the Commissioners, the [person][3] was not eligible to be treated as a member of the group, or
 (b) the date on which, in the opinion of the Commissioners, the [person][3] ceased to be eligible to be treated as a member of the group.][1]

Amendments—[1] This section inserted by FA 1999 s 16, Sch 2 para 2 with effect from 27 July 1999 subject to FA 1999 Sch 2 para 6.
[2] Words in sub-s (3)(b) substituted by FA 2004 s 20(4) with effect from 22 July 2004.
[3] In sub-s (1), words substituted for words "body corporate", in sub-s (3)(a), (b), and in closing words, words substituted for words "body", and in sub-s (4)(a), (b), words substituted for words "body", by FA 2019 s 53, Sch 18 paras 3, 8 with effect from 1 November 2019 (see SI 2019/1348).

[**43D Groups: duplication**
(1) A [person][2] may not be treated as a member of more than one group at a time.
(2) A [person who][2] is a member of one group is not eligible by virtue of section 43A to be treated as a member of another group.
(3) If—
 (a) an application under section 43B(1) would have effect from a time in accordance with section 43B(4), but
 (b) at that time one or more of the [persons][2] specified in the application is a member of a group (other than that to which the application relates),
the application shall have effect from that time, but with the exclusion of the [person or persons][2] mentioned in paragraph (b).
(4) If—
 (a) an application under section 43B(2)(a) would have effect from a time in accordance with section 43B(4), but
 (b) at that time the [person][2] specified in the application is a member of a group (other than that to which the application relates),
the application shall have no effect.
(5) Where a [person][2] is a subject of two or more applications under section 43B(1) or (2)(a) that have not been granted or refused, the applications shall have no effect.][1]

Commentary—*De Voil Indirect Tax Service* **V2.190AA**.
Amendments—[1] This section inserted by FA 2004 s 20(2) with effect from 22 July 2004.

[2] In sub-s (1), words substituted for words "body corporate", in sub-s (2) words substituted for words "body which", in sub-s (3)(b), words "bodies" and in closing words, words substituted for words "body or bodies", and in sub-ss (4)(b), (5), words substituted for words "body", by FA 2019 s 53, Sch 18 paras 3, 9 with effect from 1 November 2019 (see SI 2019/1348).

44 Supplies to groups
(1) Subject to subsections (2) to (4) below, subsection (5) below applies where—
- (a) a business, or part of a business, carried on by a taxable person is transferred as a going concern to a [person][1] treated as a member of a group under section 43;
- (b) on the transfer of the business or part, chargeable assets of the business are transferred to the [person][1]; and
- (c) the transfer of the assets is treated by virtue of section 5(3)(c) as neither a supply of goods nor a supply of services.

(2) Subsection (5) below shall not apply if the representative member of the group is entitled to credit for the whole of the input tax on supplies to it and . . . [2] importations by it—
- (a) during the prescribed accounting period in which the assets are transferred, and
- (b) during any longer period to which regulations under section 26(3)(b) relate and in which the assets are transferred.

(3) Subsection (5) below shall not apply if the Commissioners are satisfied that the assets were assets of the taxable person transferring them more than 3 years before the day on which they are transferred.

(4) Subsection (5) below shall not apply to the extent that the chargeable assets consist of capital items in respect of which regulations made under section 26(3) and (4), and in force when the assets are transferred, provide for adjustment to the deduction of input tax.

(5) The chargeable assets shall be treated for the purposes of this Act as being, on the day on which they are transferred, both supplied to the representative member of the group for the purpose of its business and supplied by that member in the course or furtherance of its business.

(6) A supply treated under subsection (5) above as made by a representative member shall not be taken into account as a supply made by him when determining the allowance of input tax in his case under section 26.

(7) The value of a supply treated under subsection (5) above as made to or by a representative member shall be taken to be the open market value of the chargeable assets.

(8) For the purposes of this section, the open market value of any chargeable assets shall be taken to be the price that would be paid on a sale (on which no VAT is payable) between a buyer and a seller who are not in such a relationship as to affect the price.

(9) The Commissioners may reduce the VAT chargeable by virtue of subsection (5) above in a case where they are satisfied that the person by whom the chargeable assets are transferred has not received credit for the full amount of input tax arising on the supply to or . . . [2] importation by him of the chargeable assets.

(10) For the purposes of this section, assets are chargeable assets if their supply in the United Kingdom by a taxable person in the course or furtherance of his business would be a taxable supply (and not a zero-rated supply).

Commentary—*De Voil Indirect Tax Service* V3.246.
Northern Ireland—See Sch 9ZA para 21(Northern Ireland: sub-ss (2), (9) apply to input tax on acquisitions as they applies to input tax on supplies).
Amendments—[1] In sub-ss (1)(a), (b), words substituted for words "body corporate" by FA 2019 s 53, Sch 18 paras 3, 10 with effect from 1 November 2019 (see SI 2019/1348).
[2] In sub-s (2) words "acquisitions and", and in sub-s (9) words "acquisition or", repealed, by the Taxation (Cross-border Trade) Act 2018 s 43, Sch 8 paras 1, 47 with effect from IP completion day (11pm on 31 December 2020), by virtue of SI 2020/1642 reg 4(b).

45 Partnerships
(1) The registration under this Act of persons—
- (a) carrying on a business in partnership, . . . [1]
- (b) . . . [1]

may be in the name of the firm; and no account shall be taken, in determining for any purpose of this Act whether goods or services are supplied to or by such persons . . . [1], of any change in the partnership.

(2) Without prejudice to section 36 of the Partnership Act 1890 (rights of persons dealing with firm against apparent members of firm), until the date on which a change in the partnership is notified to the Commissioners a person who has ceased to be a member of a partnership shall be regarded as continuing to be a partner for the purposes of this Act and, in particular, for the purpose of any liability for VAT on the supply of goods or services by the partnership . . . [1].

(3) Where a person ceases to be a member of a partnership during a prescribed accounting period (or is treated as so doing by virtue of subsection (2) above) any notice, whether of assessment or otherwise, which is served on the partnership and relates to, or to any matter arising in, that period or any earlier period during the whole or part of which he was a member of the partnership shall be treated as served also on him.

Application of Act in particular cases **VATA 1994 s 46**

(4) Without prejudice to section 16 of the Partnership Act 1890 (notice to acting partner to be notice to the firm) any notice, whether of assessment or otherwise, which is addressed to a partnership by the name in which it is registered by virtue of subsection (1) above and is served in accordance with this Act shall be treated for the purposes of this Act as served on the partnership and, accordingly, where subsection (3) above applies, as served also on the former partner.

(5) Subsections (1) and (3) above shall not affect the extent to which, under section 9 of the Partnership Act 1890, a partner is liable for VAT owed by the firm; but where a person is a partner in a firm during part only of a prescribed accounting period, his liability for VAT on the supply by the firm of goods or services during that accounting period . . . [1] shall be such proportion of the firm's liability as may be just.

Commentary—*De Voil Indirect Tax Service* **V2.110**.
HMRC Manuals—VAT Registration VATREG12750 (entity to be registered).
VAT Assessments and Error Correction VAEC6170 (assessments to partnerships).
Northern Ireland—See Sch 9ZA para 22 (Northern Ireland: sub-s (1) applies to persons carrying on in partnership activities, other than carrying on a business, in the course or furtherance of which they acquire goods from a member State as it apples to persons carrying on a business in partnership; sub-ss (2), (5) apply to a liability for Northern Ireland acquisition VAT as they apply to VAT on the supply of goods or services).
Amendments—[1] The following amendments made by the Taxation (Cross-border Trade) Act 2018 s 43, Sch 8 paras 1, 48 with effect from IP completion day (11pm on 31 December 2020), by virtue of SI 2020/1642 reg 4(b)—
- sub-s (1)(b) and preceding word "or" repealed;
- in words after sub-s (1)(b), words "or are acquired by such persons from another member State" repealed;
- in sub-s (2), words "or on the acquisition of goods by the partnership from another member State" repealed; and
- in sub-s (5), words "or on the acquisition during that period by the firm of any goods from another member State" repealed.

Sub-s (1)(b) previously read as follows—
"   (b)   carrying on in partnership any other activities in the course or furtherance of which they acquire goods from other member States,".

46 Business carried on in divisions or by unincorporated bodies, personal representatives etc

(1) The registration under this Act of a body corporate carrying on a business in several divisions may, if the body corporate so requests and the Commissioners see fit, be in the names of those divisions.

(2) The Commissioners may by regulations make provision for determining by what persons anything required by or under this Act to be done by a person carrying on a business is to be done where a business is carried on in partnership or by a club, association or organisation the affairs of which are managed by its members or a committee or committees of its members.

(3) The registration under this Act of any such club, association or organisation may be in the name of the club, association or organisation; and in determining whether goods or services are supplied to or by such a club, association or organisation . . . [2], no account shall be taken of any change in its members.

(4) The Commissioners may by regulations make provision for persons who carry on a business of a taxable person who has died or become bankrupt or has had his estate sequestrated or has become incapacitated to be treated for a limited time as taxable persons, and for securing continuity in the application of this Act in cases where persons are so treated.

(5) In relation to a company which is a taxable person, the reference in subsection (4) above to the taxable person having become bankrupt or having had his estate sequestrated or having become incapacitated shall be construed as a reference to its being in liquidation or receivership or [administration][1].

(6) . . . [2]

Commentary—*De Voil Indirect Tax Service* **V2.190A, V2.102**.
HMRC Manuals—VAT Registration VATREG11000 (entity to be registered).
VATREG11450 (unincorporated associations).
Northern Ireland—See Sch 9ZA para 23 (Northern Ireland: in this section any reference to "a business" includes any activity in the course or furtherance of which any body corporate or any club, association, organisation or other unincorporated body acquires goods from a member State. Sub-s (3) applies in relation to the determination of whether goods are acquired from a member State by a club, association or organization mentioned in that subsection as it applies in relation to the determination of whether goods or services are supplied by such a club, association or organisation).
Regulations—See VAT Regulations, SI 1995/2518 regs 8, 9.
Amendments—[1] Word in sub-s (5) substituted by the Enterprise Act 2002 (Insolvency) Order, SI 2003/2096 art 4, Schedule paras 24, 25 with effect from 15 September 2003. However, this amendment does not apply in any case where a petition for an administration order was presented before that date: SI 2003/2096 arts 1, 6.
[2] The following amendments made by the Taxation (Cross-border Trade) Act 2018 s 43, Sch 8 paras 1, 49 with effect from IP completion day (11pm on 31 December 2020), by virtue of SI 2020/1642 reg 4(b)—
- in sub-s (3), words "or whether goods are acquired by such a club, association or organisation from another member State" repealed; and
- sub-s (6) repealed.

Sub-s (6) previously read as follows—
"(6) References in this section to a business include references to any other activities in the course or furtherance of which any body corporate or any club, association, organisation or other unincorporated body acquires goods from another member State.".

47 Agents etc

[(1) Where goods are imported by a taxable person ("T") who supplies them as agent for a person who is not a taxable person, then, if T acts in relation to the supply in T's own name, the goods are to be treated for the purposes of this Act as imported and supplied by T as principal.][6]
(2) For the purposes of subsection (1) above a person who is not resident in the United Kingdom and whose place or principal place of business is outside the United Kingdom may be treated as not being a taxable person if as a result he will not be required to be registered under this Act.
[(2A) Where, in the case of any supply of goods to which subsection (1) above does not apply, goods are supplied through an agent who acts in his own name, the supply shall be treated both as a supply to the agent and as a supply by the agent.][2]
(3) Where . . . [3] services[, other than electronically supplied services and telecommunication services,][4] are supplied through an agent who acts in his own name the Commissioners may, if they think fit, treat the supply both as a supply to the agent and as a supply by the agent.
[(4) Where electronically supplied services or telecommunication services are supplied through an agent, [acting in the agent's own name,][6] the supply is to be treated both as a supply to the agent and as a supply by the agent.
(5) . . . [6]
(6) In this section "electronically supplied services" and "telecommunication services" have the same meaning as in Schedule 4A (see paragraph 9(3) and (4) and [paragraph 9E(2)][5] of that Schedule).][4]

Commentary—*De Voil Indirect Tax Service* **V3.221**.
HMRC Manuals—VAT Taxable person Manual VTAXPER37580 (agents - introduction).
VTAXPER37900 (agents - account for VAT).
VAT Time of Supply VATTOS8300 (agents).
Northern Ireland—See Sch 9ZA para 24 (Northern Ireland: this section has effect as if the reference in sub-s (2) to "subsection (1) above" were to "subsection (1) and paragraph 24(1) of Schedule 9ZA", and the reference in sub-s (2A) to "subsection (1) above" were to "subsection (1) or paragraph 24(1) of Schedule 9ZA").
Amendments—[2] Sub-s (2A) inserted by FA 1995 s 23(2), (4)(b) with effect in relation to any supply taking place on or after 1 May 1995.
[3] Words repealed by FA 1995 s 23(3), (4)(b), Sch 29 Pt VI(2) with effect in relation to any supply taking place on or after 1 May 1995.
[4] In sub-s (3), words inserted, and sub-ss (4)–(6) inserted, by FA 2014 s 106 with effect in relation to supplies made on or after 1 January 2015.
[5] In sub-para (6), words substituted for words "paragraph 8(2)" by the VAT (Place of Supply of Services) (Telecommunication Services) Order, SI 2017/778 art 5 with effect in relation to supplies of services made on or after 1 November 2017.
[6] The following amendments made by the Taxation (Cross-border Trade) Act 2018 s 43, Sch 8 paras 1, 50 with effect from IP completion day (11pm on 31 December 2020), by virtue of SI 2020/1642 reg 4(*b*)—
- sub-s (1) substituted;
- in sub-s (4), words inserted; and
- sub-s (5) repealed.

Note that, where these amendments remove a reference to the principal VAT Directive (2006/112/EC) or the Implementing VAT Regulation ((EU) No 282/2011), the removal is not to be taken as implying that the Directive or Regulation is no longer relevant for determining the meaning and effect of this section (Taxation (Cross-border Trade) Act 2018 Sch 8 para 99).
Sub-ss (1), (5) previously read as follows—
"(1) Where—
    (*a*)   goods are acquired from another member State by a person who is not a taxable person and a taxable person acts in relation to the acquisition, and then supplies the goods as agent for the person by whom they are so acquired; or
    (*b*)   goods are imported from a place outside the member States by a taxable person who supplies them as agent for a person who is not a taxable person,
then, if the taxable person acts in relation to the supply in his own name, the goods shall be treated for the purposes of this Act as acquired and supplied or, as the case may be, imported and supplied by the taxable person as principal.".
"(5) For the purposes of subsection (4) "agent" means a person ("A") who acts in A's own name but on behalf of another person within the meaning of Article 28 of Council Directive 2006/112/EC on the common system of value added tax.".

48 VAT representatives [and security][6]

(1) [Subsection (1ZA) applies where][6] any person—
    (*a*) is a taxable person for the purposes of this Act or, without being a taxable person, is a person who makes taxable supplies . . . [7];
    [(*b*) is not established, and does not have any fixed establishment, in the United Kingdom;][2]
    [(*ba*) is established in a country or territory in respect of which it appears to the Commissioners that the condition specified in subsection (1A) below is satisfied; and][2]
    (*c*) in the case of an individual, does not have his usual place of residence [or permanent address][6] in the United Kingdom.
. . . . [6]
[(1ZA) The Commissioners may direct the person to secure that there is a UK-established person who is—
    (*a*) appointed to act on the person's behalf in relation to VAT, and

(b) registered against the name of the person in accordance with any regulations under subsection (4).]⁶

[(1A) The condition mentioned in subsection (1)(*ba*) is that there are no arrangements in relation to the country or territory relating to VAT which—

(*a*) have effect by virtue of an Order in Council under section 173 of the Finance Act 2006, and

(*b*) contain provision of a kind mentioned in subsection (2)(*a*) and (*b*) of that section.]⁷

[(2) With the agreement of the Commissioners, a person—

(*a*) who has not been [given a direction under subsection (1ZA)]⁶, and

(*b*) in relation to whom the conditions specified in paragraphs (*a*), (*b*) and (*c*) of [subsection (1)]⁶ are satisfied,

may appoint [a UK-established]⁶ person to act on his behalf in relation to VAT.]²

[(2A) In this Act "VAT representative" means a person appointed under subsection [(1ZA)]⁶ or (2) above.]²

(3) Where any person is appointed by virtue of this section to be the VAT representative of another ("his principal"), then, subject to subsections (4) to (6) below, the VAT representative—

(*a*) shall be entitled to act on his principal's behalf for any of the purposes of this Act, of any other enactment (whenever passed) relating to VAT or of any subordinate legislation made under this Act or any such enactment;

(*b*) shall, subject to such provisions as may be made by the Commissioners by regulations, secure (where appropriate by acting on his principal's behalf) his principal's compliance with and discharge of the obligations and liabilities to which his principal is subject by virtue of this Act, any such other enactment or any such subordinate legislation; and

(*c*) shall be personally liable in respect of—

(i) any failure to secure his principal's compliance with or discharge of any such obligation or liability; and

(ii) anything done for purposes connected with acting on his principal's behalf,

as if the obligations and liabilities imposed on his principal were imposed jointly and severally on the VAT representative and his principal.

(4) A VAT representative shall not be liable by virtue of subsection (3) above himself to be registered under this Act, but regulations made by the Commissioners may—

(*a*) require the registration of the names of VAT representatives against the names of their principals in any register kept for the purposes of this Act; . . . ⁶

(*b*) make it the duty of a VAT representative, for the purposes of registration, to notify the Commissioners, within such period as may be prescribed, that his appointment has taken effect or has ceased to have effect;

[(*c*) give the Commissioners power to refuse to register a person as a VAT representative, or to cancel a person's registration as a VAT representative, in such circumstances as may be specified in the regulations.]⁶

[(4A) Regulations under subsection (4) may require a notification under that subsection to be made in such form and manner, and to contain such particulars, as may be specified in the regulations or by the Commissioners in accordance with the regulations.]⁴

(5) A VAT representative shall not by virtue of subsection (3) above be guilty of any offence except in so far as—

(*a*) the VAT representative has consented to, or connived in, the commission of the offence by his principal;

(*b*) the commission of the offence by his principal is attributable to any neglect on the part of the VAT representative; or

(*c*) the offence consists in a contravention by the VAT representative of an obligation which, by virtue of that subsection, is imposed both on the VAT representative and on his principal.

(6) The Commissioners may by regulations make provision as to the manner and circumstances in which a person is to be appointed, or is to be treated as having ceased to be, another's VAT representative; and regulations under this subsection may include such provision as the Commissioners think fit for the purposes of subsection (4) above with respect to the making or deletion of entries in any register.

(7) [The Commissioners may require a person in relation to whom the conditions specified in paragraphs (*a*), (*b*) and (*c*) of subsection (1) are satisfied]⁶ to provide such security, or further security, as they may think appropriate for the payment of any VAT which is or may become due from him.

[(7A) A sum required by way of security under subsection (7) above shall be deemed for the purposes of—

(*a*) section 51 of the Finance Act 1997 (enforcement [by taking control of goods or, in Northern Ireland,]⁵ by distress) and any regulations under that section, and

(*b*) section 52 of that Act (enforcement [by taking control of goods or, in Northern Ireland,]⁵ by diligence),

to be recoverable as if it were VAT due from the person who is required to provide it.]¹
[(7B) A direction under subsection (1ZA)—
(a) may specify a time by which it (or any part of it) must be complied with;
(b) may be varied;
(c) continues to have effect (subject to any variation) until it is withdrawn or the conditions specified in subsection (1) are no longer satisfied.
(7C) A requirement under subsection (7)—
(a) may specify a time by which it (or any part of it) must be complied with;
(b) may be varied;
(c) continues to have effect (subject to any variation) until it is withdrawn.]⁶
(8) For the purposes of this Act a person shall not be treated as having been directed to appoint a VAT representative, or as having been required to provide security under subsection (7) above, unless the Commissioners have either—
(a) served notice of the direction or requirement on him; or
(b) taken all such other steps as appear to them to be reasonable for bringing the direction or requirement to his attention.
[(8A) For the purposes of subsections (1ZA) and (2)—
(a) a person is UK-established if the person is established, or has a fixed establishment, in the United Kingdom, and
(b) an individual is also UK-established if the person's usual place of residence or permanent address is in the United Kingdom.]⁶
(9) . . . ⁷

Commentary—*De Voil Indirect Tax Service* **V2.115**.
HMRC Manuals—VAT Registration VATREG37400 (requirement to appoint a VAT representative).
VATREG37450 - 37600 (non-established taxable persons (Netps)).
Northern Ireland—See Sch 9ZA para 25 (Northern Ireland: sub-s (1)(a) applies to a person who, without being a taxable person, acquires goods in Northern Ireland from one or more member States as it applies to a person who, without being a taxable person, makes taxable supplies).
Regulations—See VAT Regulations, SI 1995/2518 reg 10.
VAT (Amendment) (No 2) Regulations, SI 2012/1899.
Value Added Tax (Amendment) Regulations, SI 2016/989.
Amendments—¹ Sub-s (7A) inserted by FA 1997 s 53 (6) with effect from 1 July 1997 (see SI 1997/1432).
² Sub-s (1)(b), (ba) substituted for original sub-s (1)(b), and sub-ss (2), (2A) substituted for original sub-s (2) by FA 2001 s 100 with effect from 31 December 2001.
⁴ Sub-s (4A) inserted by FA 2012 s 204, Sch 29 paras 1, 6 with effect from 17 July 2012.
⁵ In sub-s (7A) words inserted by the Tribunals, Courts and Enforcement Act 2007 s 62(3), Sch 13 paras 117, 118 with effect from 6 April 2014 (the date appointed by virtue of the Tribunals, Courts and Enforcement Act 2007 (Commencement No 11) Order, SI 2014/768 art 2(1)(b)).
⁶ The following amendments made by FA 2016 s 123(1)–(11) with effect from 15 September 2016—
- in heading and sub-s (1)(c), words inserted;
- sub-ss (1ZA), (4)(c), (7B), (7C), (8A) inserted;
- in sub-s (1), words substituted for word "Where", and words "the Commissioners may direct that person to appoint another person (in this Act referred to as a "VAT representative") to act on his behalf in relation to VAT" repealed;
- In sub-s (2)(a), words substituted for words "required under subsection (1) above to appoint another person to act on his behalf in relation to VAT", in sub-s (2)(b), words substituted for words "that subsection", and words at the end substituted for word "another";
- in sub-s (2A), reference substituted for reference "(1)";
- in sub-s (4)(a), word "and" repealed; and
- in sub-s (7), words substituted for words "Where a person fails to appoint a VAT representative in accordance with any direction under subsection (1) above, the Commissioners may require him".
⁷ The following amendments made by the Taxation (Cross-border Trade) Act 2018 s 43, Sch 8 paras 1, 51 with effect from IP completion day (11pm on 31 December 2020), by virtue of SI 2020/1642 reg 4(b)—
- in sub-s (1)(a), words "or who acquires goods in the United Kingdom from one or more other member States" repealed;
- sub-s (1A) substituted for previous sub-ss (1A), (1B); and
- sub-s (9) repealed.
Sub-ss (1A), (1B) previously read as follows—
"(1A) The condition mentioned in subsection (1)(ba) above is that—
(a) the country or territory is neither a member State nor a part of a member State, and
(b) there is no provision for mutual assistance between the United Kingdom and the country or territory similar in scope to the assistance provided for between the United Kingdom and each other member State by the mutual assistance provisions.
(1B) In subsection (1A) above "the mutual assistance provisions" means—
(a) section 87 of the Finance Act 2011 (mutual assistance for recovery of taxes etc) and Schedule 25 to that Act;
(b) section 173 of the Finance Act 2006 (international tax enforcement arrangements);
(c) Council Regulation (EC) No 904/2010 of 7 October 2010 on administrative cooperation and combating fraud in the field of value added tax.".
Sub-s (9) previously read as follows—
"(9) The Treasury may by order amend the definition of "the mutual assistance provisions" in subsection (1B) above.".

49 Transfers of going concerns

(1) Where a business[, or part of a business,][1] carried on by a taxable person is transferred to another person as a going concern, then—
   (a) for the purpose of determining whether the transferee is liable to be registered under this Act he shall be treated as having carried on the business [or part of the business][1] before as well as after the transfer and supplies by the transferor shall be treated accordingly; . . . [1]
   (b) . . . [1]

(2) Without prejudice to subsection (1) above, the Commissioners may by regulations make provision for securing continuity in the application of this Act in cases where a business[, or part of a business,][1] carried on by a taxable person is transferred to another person as a going concern and the transferee is registered under this Act in substitution for the transferor.

[(2A) Regulations under subsection (2) above may, in particular, provide for the duties under this Act of the transferor to preserve records relating to the business or part of the business for any period after the transfer to become duties of the transferee unless the Commissioners, at the request of the transferor, otherwise direct.][1]

(3) Regulations under subsection (2) above may, in particular, provide—
   (a) for liabilities and duties under this Act (excluding sections 59 to 70) of the transferor [(other than the duties mentioned in subsection (2A) above)][1] to become, to such extent as may be provided by the regulations, liabilities and duties of the transferee; and
   (b) for any right of either of them to repayment or credit in respect of VAT to be satisfied by making a repayment or allowing a credit to the other;

but no such provision as is mentioned in paragraph (a) or (b) of this subsection shall have effect in relation to any transferor and transferee unless an application in that behalf has been made by them under the regulations.

[(4) Subsection (5) below applies where—
   (a) a business, or part of a business, carried on by a taxable person is transferred to another person as a going concern, and
   (b) the transferor continues to be required under this Act to preserve for any period after the transfer any records relating to the business or part of the business.

(5) So far as is necessary for the purpose of complying with the transferee's duties under this Act, the transferee ("E") may require the transferor—
   (a) to give to E, within such time and in such form as E may reasonably require, such information contained in the records as E may reasonably specify,
   (b) to give to E, within such time and in such form as E may reasonably require, such copies of documents forming part of the records as E may reasonably specify, and
   (c) to make the records available for E's inspection at such time and place as E may reasonably require (and permit E to take copies of, or make extracts from, them).

(6) Where a business, or part of a business, carried on by a taxable person is transferred to another person as a going concern, the Commissioners may disclose to the transferee any information relating to the business when it was carried on by the transferor for the purpose of enabling the transferee to comply with the transferee's duties under this Act.][1]

Commentary—*De Voil Indirect Tax Service* **V2.226, V2.137, V2.131.**
HMRC Manuals—VAT Registration VATREG29250 (transfers of going concerns).
VATREG30700 (record keeping obligations).
VATREC3060 (transfer of a going concern and record keeping).
Regulations—See VAT Regulations, SI 1995/2518 reg 6.
VAT (Amendment) (No 2) Regulations, SI 2012/1899.
Amendments—[1] Words in sub-s (1) inserted and repealed, words in sub-ss (2), (3) and whole of sub-ss (2A), (4)–(6) inserted, by FA 2007 ss 100(1)–(6), 114, Sch 27 Pt 6(2) with effect in relation to transfers pursuant to contracts entered into on or after 1 September 2007.

50 Terminal markets

(1) The Treasury may by order make provision for modifying the provisions of this Act in their application to dealings on terminal markets and such persons ordinarily engaged in such dealings as may be specified in the order, subject to such conditions as may be so specified.

(2) Without prejudice to the generality of subsection (1) above, an order under this section may include provision—
   (a) for zero-rating the supply of any goods or services or for treating the supply of any goods or services as exempt;
   (b) for the registration under this Act of any body of persons representing persons ordinarily engaged in dealing on a terminal market and for disregarding such dealings by persons so represented in determining liability to be registered under this Act, and for disregarding such dealings between persons so represented for all the purposes of this Act;
   (c) for refunding, to such persons as may be specified by or under the order, input tax attributable to such dealings on a terminal market as may be so specified,

and may contain such incidental and supplementary provisions as appear to the Treasury to be necessary or expedient.

(3) An order under this section may make different provision with respect to different terminal markets and with respect to different commodities.
Commentary—*De Voil Indirect Tax Service* **V2.114**.
HMRC Manuals—VAT Registration VATREG16250 (terminal markets).
Orders—See VAT (Terminal Markets) Order, SI 1973/173.

[50A Margin schemes

(1) The Treasury may by order provide, in relation to any such description of supplies to which this section applies as may be specified in the order, for a taxable person to be entitled to opt that, where he makes supplies of that description, VAT is to be charged by reference to the profit margin on the supplies, instead of by reference to their value.
(2) This section applies to the following supplies, that is to say—
    (a) supplies of works of art, antiques or collectors' items;
    (b) supplies of motor vehicles;
    (c) supplies of second-hand goods; and
    (d) any supply of goods through a person who acts as an agent, but in his own name, in relation to the supply.
(3) An option for the purposes of an order under this section shall be exercisable, and may be withdrawn, in such manner as may be required by such an order.
(4) Subject to subsection (7) below, the profit margin on a supply to which this section applies shall be taken, for the purposes of an order under this section, to be equal to the amount (if any) by which the price at which the person making the supply obtained the goods in question is exceeded by the price at which he supplies them.
(5) For the purposes of this section the price at which a person has obtained any goods and the price at which he supplies them shall each be calculated in accordance with the provisions contained in an order under this section; and such an order may, in particular, make provision stipulating the extent to which any VAT charged on a supply . . . [2] or importation of any goods is to be treated as included in the price at which those goods have been obtained or are supplied.
(6) An order under this section may provide that the consideration for any services supplied in connection with a supply of goods by a person who acts as an agent, but in his own name, in relation to the supply of the goods is to be treated for the purposes of any such order as an amount to be taken into account in computing the profit margin on the supply of the goods, instead of being separately chargeable to VAT as comprised in the value of the services supplied.
(7) An order under this section may provide for the total profit margin on all the goods of a particular description supplied by a person in any prescribed accounting period to be calculated by—
    (a) aggregating all the prices at which that person obtained goods of that description in that period together with any amount carried forward to that period in pursuance of paragraph (d) below;
    (b) aggregating all the prices at which he supplies goods of that description in that period;
    (c) treating the total profit margin on goods supplied in that period as being equal to the amount (if any) by which, for that period, the aggregate calculated in pursuance of paragraph (a) above is exceeded by the aggregate calculated in pursuance of paragraph (b) above; and
    (d) treating any amount by which, for that period, the aggregate calculated in pursuance of paragraph (b) above is exceeded by the aggregate calculated in pursuance of paragraph (a) above as an amount to be carried forward to the following prescribed accounting period so as to be included, for the period to which it is carried forward, in any aggregate falling to be calculated in pursuance of paragraph (a) above.
(8) An order under this section may—
    (a) make different provision for different cases; and
    (b) make provisions of the order subject to such general or special directions as may, in accordance with the order, be given by the Commissioners with respect to any matter to which the order relates.][1]

Commentary—*De Voil Indirect Tax Service* **V3.531, V3.532, V3.534**.
HMRC Manuals—VAT Margin Schemes VATMARG01150 (introduction: law governing the scheme)
Northern Ireland—See Sch 9ZA para 26 (Northern Ireland: sub-s (5) has effect as if after "supply," there were inserted "acquisition").
Order—VAT (Special Provisions) Order, SI 1995/1268.
Amendments—[1] Section inserted by FA 1995 s 24(1).
[2] In sub-s (5), word ", acquisition" repealed by the Taxation (Cross-border Trade) Act 2018 s 43, Sch 8 paras 1, 52 with effect from IP completion day (11pm on 31 December 2020), by virtue of SI 2020/1642 reg 4(b).

51 Buildings and land

(1) Schedule 10 shall have effect with respect to buildings and land.
(2) The Treasury may by order amend Schedule 10.
Commentary—*De Voil Indirect Tax Service* **V4.111 – V4.115**.
Orders—VAT (Buildings and Land) Order, SI 2011/86.

[51A Co-owners etc of buildings and land
(1) This section applies to a supply consisting in the grant, assignment or surrender of any interest in or right over land in a case where there is more than one person by whom the grant, assignment or surrender is made or treated as made; and for this purpose—
 (a) a licence to occupy land, and
 (b) in relation to land in Scotland, a personal right to call for or be granted any interest or right in or over land,
shall be taken to be a right over land.
(2) The persons who make or are treated as making a supply to which this section applies ("the grantors") shall be treated, in relation to that supply and in relation to any other such supply with respect to which the grantors are the same, as a single person ("the property-owner") who is distinct from each of the grantors individually.
(3) Registration under this Act of the property-owner shall be in the name of the grantors acting together as a property-owner.
(4) The grantors shall be jointly and severally liable in respect of the obligations falling by virtue of this section on the property-owner.
(5) Any notice, whether of assessment or otherwise, which is addressed to the property-owner by the name in which the property-owner is registered and is served on any of the grantors in accordance with this Act shall be treated for the purposes of this Act as served on the property-owner.
(6) Where there is any change in some, but not all, of the persons who are for the time being to be treated as the grantors in relation to any supply to which this section applies—
 (a) that change shall be disregarded for the purposes of this section in relation to any prescribed accounting period beginning before the change is notified in the prescribed manner to the Commissioners; and
 (b) any notice (whether of assessment or otherwise) which is served, at any time after such a notification, on the property-owner for the time being shall, so far as it relates to, or to any matter arising in, such a period, be treated for the purposes of this Act as served on whoever was the property-owner in that period.][1, 2]

Commentary—*De Voil Indirect Tax Service* **V2.114**.
Definitions—"Assignment", s 96(1); "the Commissioners", s 96(1); "prescribed", s 96(1); "prescribed accounting period", s 25(1); "registered", s 3(3); "supply", s 5.
Amendments—[1] Section inserted by FA 1995 s 26(1), (4) with effect from a day to be appointed by order made by the Commissioners of Customs and Excise.
[2] This section repealed by the Value Added Tax (Buildings and Land) Order, SI 2008/1146 art 5(2) with effect in relation to supplies made on or after 1 June 2008, subject to savings in Sch 2 of the Order.

[51B Face-value vouchers [issued before 1 January 2019]
[(1)] Schedule 10A shall have effect with respect to face-value vouchers.
[(2) Schedule 10A does not have effect with respect to a face value voucher (within the meaning of that Schedule) issued on or after 1 January 2019.]²]¹

Commentary—*De Voil Indirect Tax Service* **V3.167**.
Amendments—[1] Section 51B inserted by FA 2003 s 19, Sch 1 para 1 with effect for supplies of tokens, stamps or vouchers issued after 8 April 2003.
[2] Words in heading inserted, sub-s (1) designated as such, and sub-s (2) inserted, by FA 2019 s 52, Sch 17 paras 1, 2 with effect from 12 February 2019.

[51C Vouchers issued on or after 1 January 2019
(1) Schedule 10B makes provision about the VAT treatment of vouchers.
(2) Schedule 10B has effect with respect to a voucher (within the meaning of that Schedule) issued on or after 1 January 2019.]¹

Commentary—*De Voil Indirect Tax Service* **V3.167**.
Amendments—[1] Sections 51C, 51D inserted by FA 2019 s 52, Sch 17 paras 1, 3 with effect from 12 February 2019.

[51D Postage stamps issued on or after 1 January 2019
(1) The issue of a postage stamp, and any subsequent transfer of it, is a supply of services for the purposes of this Act.
(2) The consideration for the issue or subsequent transfer of a postage stamp is to be disregarded for the purposes of this Act, except to the extent (if any) that it exceeds the face value of the stamp.
(3) The "face value" of the stamp is the amount stated on or recorded in the stamp or the terms and conditions governing its use.
(4) This section has effect with respect to postage stamps issued on or after 1 January 2019.]¹

Commentary—*De Voil Indirect Tax Service* **V4.126**.
Amendments—[1] Sections 51C, 51D inserted by FA 2019 s 52, Sch 17 paras 1, 3 with effect from 12 February 2019.

52 Trading stamp schemes
The Commissioners may by regulations modify [section 19 and Schedule 6]¹ for the purpose of providing (in place of the provision for the time being contained [in that section and Schedule)]¹ for the manner of determining for the purposes of this Act the value of—
 (a) a supply of goods, . . . ¹

(b) ... [1]

in a case where the goods are supplied ... [1] under a trading stamp scheme (within the meaning of the Trading Stamps Act 1964 or the Trading Stamps Act (Northern Ireland) 1965) ... [1].

Commentary—*De Voil Indirect Tax Service* **V3.167, V3.388**.
Regulations—See VAT Regulations, SI 1995/2518 regs 76–80.
Amendments—[1] The following amendments made by the Taxation (Cross-border Trade) Act 2018 s 43, Sch 8 paras 1, 53 with effect from IP completion day (11pm on 31 December 2020), by virtue of SI 2020/1642 reg 4(b)—
- in opening words, words substituted for words "sections 19 and 20 and Schedules 6 and 7" and "in those sections and Schedules)";
- para (b) and preceding word "or" repealed; and
- in words after para (b), words "or acquired" and "or under any scheme of an equivalent description which is in operation in another member State" repealed.

Before these amendments, section 52 read as follows—
"The Commissioners may by regulations modify sections 19 and 20 and Schedules 6 and 7 for the purpose of providing (in place of the provision for the time being contained in those sections and Schedules) for the manner of determining for the purposes of this Act the value of—
  (a) a supply of goods, or
  (b) a transaction in pursuance of which goods are acquired from another member State,
in a case where the goods are supplied or acquired under a trading stamp scheme (within the meaning of the Trading Stamps Act 1964 or the Trading Stamps Act (Northern Ireland) 1965) or under any scheme of an equivalent description which is in operation in another member State.".

53 Tour operators

(1) The Treasury may by order modify the application of this Act in relation to supplies of goods or services by tour operators or in relation to such of those supplies as may be determined by or under the order.

(2) Without prejudice to the generality of subsection (1) above, an order under this section may make provision—
  (a) for two or more supplies of goods or services by a tour operator to be treated as a single supply of services;
  (b) for the value of that supply to be ascertained, in such manner as may be determined by or under the order, by reference to the difference between sums paid or payable to and sums paid or payable by the tour operator;
  (c) for account to be taken, in determining the VAT chargeable on that supply, of the different rates of VAT that would have been applicable apart from this section;
  (d) excluding any [person][1] from the application of section 43;
  (e) as to the time when a supply is to be treated as taking place.

(3) In this section "tour operator" includes a travel agent acting as principal and any other person providing for the benefit of travellers services of any kind commonly provided by tour operators or travel agents.

(4) Section 97(3) shall not apply to an order under this section, notwithstanding that it makes provision for excluding any VAT from credit under section 25.

Commentary—*De Voil Indirect Tax Service* **V3.594**.
HMRC Manuals—VAT Supply And Consideration VATSC11112 (single and multiple supplies).
Orders—See VAT (Tour Operators) Order, SI 1987/1806.
Amendments—[1] In sub-s (2)(d), words substituted for words "body corporate" by FA 2019 s 53, Sch 18 paras 3, 10 with effect from 1 November 2019 (see SI 2019/1348).

54 Farmers etc

(1) The Commissioners may, in accordance with such provision as may be contained in regulations made by them, certify for the purposes of this section any person who satisfies them—
  (a) that he is carrying on a business involving one or more designated activities;
  (b) that he is of such a description and has complied with such requirements as may be prescribed; and
  (c) where an earlier certification of that person has been cancelled, that more than the prescribed period has elapsed since the cancellation or that such other conditions as may be prescribed are satisfied.

(2) Where a person is for the time being certified under this section, then (whether or not that person is a taxable person) so much of any supply by him of any goods or services as, in accordance with provision contained in regulations, is allocated to the relevant part of his business shall be disregarded for the purpose of determining whether he is, has become or has ceased to be liable or entitled to be registered under Schedule 1 [or is, has become or has ceased to be liable to be registered under Schedule 1A][1].

(3) The Commissioners may by regulations provide for an amount included in the consideration for any taxable supply which is made—
  (a) in the course or furtherance of the relevant part of his business by a person who is for the time being certified under this section;

(b) at a time when that person is not a taxable person; and
(c) to a taxable person,
to be treated, for the purpose of determining the entitlement of the person supplied to credit under sections 25 and 26, as VAT on a supply to that person.
(4) The amount which, for the purposes of any provision made under subsection (3) above, may be included in the consideration for any supply shall be an amount equal to such percentage as the Treasury may by order specify of the sum which, with the addition of that amount, is equal to the consideration for the supply.
(5) The Commissioners' power by regulations under section 39 to provide for the repayment to persons to whom that section applies of VAT which would be input tax of theirs if they were taxable persons in the United Kingdom includes power to provide for the payment to persons to whom that section applies of sums equal to the amounts which, if they were taxable persons in the United Kingdom, would be input tax of theirs by virtue of regulations under this section; and references in that section, or in any other enactment, to a repayment of VAT shall be construed accordingly.
(6) Regulations under this section may provide—
 (a) for . . . [2] an application for certification under this section, or for the cancellation of any such certification, [to be made in the form and manner specified in the regulations or by the Commissioners in accordance with the regulations][2];
 (b) for the cases and manner in which the Commissioners may cancel a person's certification;
 (c) for entitlement to a credit such as is mentioned in subsection (3) above to depend on the issue of an invoice containing such particulars as may be prescribed, or as may be notified by the Commissioners in accordance with provision contained in regulations; and
 (d) for the imposition on certified persons of obligations with respect to the keeping, preservation and production of such records as may be prescribed and of obligations to comply with such requirements with respect to any of those matters as may be so notified;
and regulations made by virtue of paragraph (b) above may confer on the Commissioners power, if they think fit, to refuse to cancel a person's certification, and to refuse to give effect to any entitlement of that person to be registered, until the end of such period after the grant of certification as may be prescribed.
(7) In this section references, in relation to any person, to the relevant part of his business are references—
 (a) where the whole of his business relates to the carrying on of one or more designated activities, to that business; and
 (b) in any other case, to so much of his business as does so relate.
[(8) In this section "designated activities" means activities relating to farming, fisheries or forestry which are designated in an order made by the Treasury.][3]

Commentary—*De Voil Indirect Tax Service* **V2.191**.
HMRC Manuals—VAT Agricultural Flat Rate Scheme VATAFRS0110 (introduction).
VAT Transfer Of A Going Concern VTOGC4250 (flat rate farmers scheme).
Regulations—See VAT Regulations, SI 1995/2518 regs 202–211.
VAT (Amendment) (No 2) Regulations, SI 2012/1899.
VAT (Amendment) Regulations, SI 2020/1384.
Orders—See VAT (Flat-rate Scheme for Farmers) (Designated Activities) Order, SI 1992/3220; VAT (Flat-rate Scheme for Farmers) (Percentage Addition) Order, SI 1992/3221.
Amendments—[1] In sub-s (2), words inserted by FA 2012 s 203, Sch 28 paras 2, 4 with effect in relation to supplies made or to be made on or after 1 December 2012.
[2] In sub-s (6)(a), words "the form and manner in which" repealed, and words substituted for words "is to be made", by FA 2012 s 204, Sch 29 paras 1, 7 with effect from 17 July 2012.
[3] Sub-s (8) substituted by the Taxation (Cross-border Trade) Act 2018 s 43, Sch 8 paras 1, 54 with effect from IP completion day (11pm on 31 December 2020), by virtue of SI 2020/1642 reg 4(b).
  Sub-s (8) previously read as follows—
"(8) In this section "designated activities" means such activities, being activities carried on by a person who, by virtue of carrying them on, falls to be treated as a farmer for the purposes of Article 25 of the directive of the Council of the European Communities dated 17th May 1977 No 77/388/EEC (common flat-rate scheme for farmers), as the Treasury may by order designate.".

55 Customers to account for tax on supplies of gold etc
(1) Where any person makes a supply of gold to another person and that supply is a taxable supply but not a zero rated supply, the supply shall be treated for purposes of [Schedules 1 and 1A[3]]—
 (a) as a taxable supply of that other person (as well as a taxable supply of the person who makes it); and
 (b) in so far as that other person is supplied in connection with the carrying on by him of any business, as a supply made by him in the course or furtherance of that business;
but nothing in paragraph (b) above shall require any supply to be disregarded for the purposes of [Schedule 1][3] on the grounds that it is a supply of capital assets of that other person's business.
(2) Where a taxable person makes a supply of gold to a person who—
 (a) is himself a taxable person at the time when the supply is made; and
 (b) is supplied in connection with the carrying on by him of any business,

it shall be for the person supplied, on the supplier's behalf, to account for and pay tax on the supply, and not for the supplier.

(3) So much of this Act and of any other enactment or any subordinate legislation as has effect for the purposes of or in connection with, the enforcement of any obligation to account for and pay VAT shall apply for the purposes of this section in relation to any person who is required under subsection (2) above to account for and pay any VAT as if that VAT were VAT on a supply made by him.

(4) Section 6(4) to (10) shall not apply for determining when any supply of gold is to be treated as taking place.

(5) References in this section to a supply of gold are references to—
- [(a) any supply of goods consisting in fine gold, in gold grain of any purity or in gold coins of any purity; . . . ²]¹
- (b) any supply of goods containing gold where the consideration for the supply (apart from any VAT) is, or is equivalent to, an amount which does not exceed, or exceeds by no more than a negligible amount, the open market value of the gold contained in the goods [; or
- (c) any supply of services consisting in the application to another person's goods of a treatment or process which produces goods a supply of which would fall within paragraph (a) above.]²

(6) The Treasury may by order provide for this section to apply, as it applies to the supplies specified in subsection (5) above, to such other supplies of—
- (a) goods consisting in or containing any precious or semi-precious metal or stones; or
- (b) services relating to, or to anything containing, any precious or semi-precious metal or stones,

as may be specified or described in the order.

Commentary—*De Voil Indirect Tax Service* **V5.143**.
HMRC Manuals—VAT Time Of Supply VATTOS9200 (gold).
Northern Ireland—See the Value Added Tax (Northern Ireland) (EU Exit) Regulations, SI 2020/1546 reg 3 (exceptions to liability for VAT on removals: movements between Great Britain and Northern Ireland)
Amendments—¹   Sub-s (5)(a) substituted by FA 1996 s 32 in relation to any supply after 28 November 1995.
²   Word omitted from sub-s (5) repealed and sub-s (5)(c) and word "; or" preceding it inserted by FA 1996 s 29(3), Sch 41 Pt IV(2), with effect in relation to supplies made after 31 December 1995.
³   In sub-s (1), words substituted for words "Schedule 1" and "that Schedule", by FA 2012 s 203, Sch 28 paras 2, 5 with effect in relation to supplies made or to be made on or after 1 December 2012.

[55A Customers to account for tax on supplies of goods [or services] of a kind used in missing trader . . . fraud

(1) Subsection (3) applies if—
- (a) a taxable (but not a zero-rated) supply of goods [or services]² ("the relevant supply") is made to a person ("the recipient"),
- (b) the relevant supply is of goods [or services]² to which this section applies (see subsection (9)),
- (c) the relevant supply is not an excepted supply (see subsection (10)), and
- (d) the total value of the relevant supply, and of corresponding supplies made to the recipient in the month in which the relevant supply is made, exceeds £1,000 ("the disregarded amount").

(2) For this purpose a "corresponding supply" means a taxable (but not a zero-rated) supply of goods [or services]² which—
- (a) is a supply of goods [or services]² to which this section applies, and
- (b) is not an excepted supply.

(3) The relevant supply, and the corresponding supplies made to the recipient in the month in which the relevant supply is made, are to be treated for the purposes of [Schedules 1 and 1A³]—
- (a) as taxable supplies of the recipient (as well as taxable supplies of the person making them), and
- (b) in so far as the recipient is supplied in connection with the carrying on by him of any business, as supplies made by him in the course or furtherance of that business,

but the relevant supply, and those corresponding supplies, are to be so treated only in so far as their total value exceeds the disregarded amount.

(4) Nothing in subsection (3)(b) requires any supply to be disregarded for the purposes of Schedule 1 on the grounds that it is a supply of capital assets of the recipient's business.

(5) For the purposes of subsections (1) and (3), the value of a supply is determined on the basis that no VAT is chargeable on the supply.

(6) If—
- (a) a taxable person makes a supply of goods [or services]² to a person ("the recipient") at any time,
- (b) the supply is of goods [or services]² to which this section applies and is not an excepted supply, and
- (c) the recipient is a taxable person at that time and is supplied in connection with the carrying on by him of any business,

it is for the recipient, on the supplier's behalf, to account for and pay tax on the supply and not for the supplier.

(7) The relevant enforcement provisions apply for the purposes of this section, in relation to any person required under subsection (6) to account for and pay any VAT, as if that VAT were VAT on a supply made by him.

(8) For this purpose "the relevant enforcement provisions" means so much of—
  (a) this Act and any other enactment, and
  (b) any subordinate legislation,
as has effect for the purposes of, or in connection with the enforcement of, any obligation to account for and pay VAT.

(9) For the purposes of this section, goods [or services][2] are goods [or services][2] to which this section applies if they are of a description specified in an order made by the Treasury.

[(9A) An order made under subsection (9) may modify the application of subsection (3) in relation to any description of goods or services specified in the order.][4]

(10) For the purposes of this section, an "excepted supply" means a supply which is of a description specified in, or determined in accordance with, provision contained in an order made by the Treasury.

(11) Any order made under subsection (10) may describe a supply of goods [or services][2] by reference to—
  (a) the use which has been made of the goods [or services][2], or
  (b) other matters unrelated to the characteristics of the goods [or services][2] themselves.

(12) The Treasury may by order substitute for the sum for the time being specified in subsection (1)(d) such greater sum as they think fit.

(13) The Treasury may by order make such amendments of any provision of this Act as they consider necessary or expedient for the purposes of this section or in connection with this section.

  An order under this subsection may confer power on the Commissioners to make regulations or exercise any other function, but no order may be made under this subsection on or after 22nd March 2009.

(14) Any order made under this section (other than one under subsection (12)) may—
  (a) make different provision for different cases, and
  (b) contain supplementary, incidental, consequential or transitional provisions.][1]

Commentary—*De Voil Indirect Tax Service* **V3.233, V5.273**.
HMRC Manuals—VAT Gold VGOLD1500 (the special accounting scheme).
Northern Ireland—See the Value Added Tax (Northern Ireland) (EU Exit) Regulations, SI 2020/1546 reg 5 (reverse charge where supply involves the removal of goods from Great Britain to Northern Ireland, or vice versa).
Orders—Value Added Tax (Section 55A) (Specified Goods and Services and Excepted Supplies) Order, SI 2010/2239 (specifies goods and services to which this section applies, and excepted supplies; this Order relates to supplies of mobile phones and integrated circuit devices (CPUs etc), and transfers of emissions allowances under the EU emission allowance trading scheme).
Value Added Tax (Section 55A) (Specified Goods and Excepted Supplies) Order, SI 2014/1458 (specifies goods to which this section applies, and excepted supplies; this Order relates to various supplies of gas and electricity).
Value Added Tax (Section 55A) (Specified Services and Excepted Supplies) Order, SI 2016/12 (specifies services to which this section applies, and excepted supplies; this Order relates to supplies of telecommunications to business customers).
Value Added Tax (Section 55A) (Specified Services and Excepted Supplies) Order, SI 2019/892 (specifies services to which this section applies, and excepted supplies; this Order relates to supplies of construction services together with any goods supplied with those services which fall to be treated as part of a single supply of services).
Value Added Tax (Section 55A) (Specified Services) Order, SI 2019/1015 (specifies services to which this section applies; this Order relates to supplies of gas and electricity certificates (also known as "renewable energy certificates")).
Value Added Tax (Section 55A) (Specified Services and Excepted Supplies) (Change of Commencement Day) Order, SI 2019/1240 (this Order changed the date on which SI 2019/892 comes into force from 1 October 2019 to 1 October 2020; this has been superseded by SI 2020/578).
Value Added Tax (Section 55A) (Specified Services and Excepted Supplies) (Change of Commencement Day and Amendment) (Coronavirus) Order, SI 2020/578 (further changes the date on which SI 2019/892 comes into force, from 1 October 2020 to 1 March 2021; this is the date from which the reverse charge for construction services is introduced).
Modifications—VAT (Section 55A) (Specified Services and Excepted Supplies) Order, SI 2019/892 art 10 (sub-s (3), which provides for reverse charge supplies to be treated as supplies made by the recipient for the purposes of VAT registration limits, does not apply in relation to construction services).
Amendments—[1] This section inserted by FA 2006 s 19(1), (8) in relation to supplies made on or after 1 June 2007 (by virtue of the Finance Act 2006, section 19, (Appointed Day) Order, SI 2007/1419).
[2] Words inserted in each place by FA 2010 s 50(1) with effect from 8 April 2010.
[3] In sub-s (3), words substituted for words "Schedule 1" by FA 2012 s 203, Sch 28 paras 2, 6 with effect in relation to supplies made or to be made on or after 1 December 2012.
[4] Sub-s (9A) inserted by FA 2019 s 51 with effect from 12 February 2019.
Other amendments—In heading, words "intra-community" repealed by the Taxation (Cross-border Trade) Act 2018 s 43, Sch 8 paras 1, 55 with effect from IP completion day (11pm on 31 December 2020), by virtue of SI 2020/1642 reg 4(b).

56 Fuel for private use

Note—See the VAT (Flat-rate Valuation of Supplies of Fuel for Private Use) Order, SI 2013/2911
HMRC's VAT fuel scale charge pages are available at: www.gov.uk/fuel-scale-charge.
Amendments—Sections 56, 57 repealed by FA 2013 s 192, Sch 38 paras 1, 4 with effect in relation to prescribed accounting periods beginning on or after 1 February 2014.

57 Determination of consideration for fuel supplied for private use
Note—See the VAT (Flat-rate Valuation of Supplies of Fuel for Private Use) Order, SI 2013/2911
HMRC's VAT fuel scale charge pages are available at: www.gov.uk/fuel-scale-charge.
Amendments—Sections 56, 57 repealed by FA 2013 s 192, Sch 38 paras 1, 4 with effect in relation to prescribed accounting periods beginning on or after 1 February 2014.

PART IV
ADMINISTRATION, COLLECTION AND ENFORCEMENT

General administrative provisions

58 General provisions relating to the administration and collection of VAT
Schedule 11 shall have effect, subject to section [58ZA(5)(*a*)][1], with respect to the administration, collection and enforcement of VAT.
Regulations—Value Added Tax (Amendment) (No 2) Regulations, SI 2010/2240.
Commentary—*De Voil Indirect Tax Service* **V5.404, V5.352**.
HMRC Manuals—VAT Assessments and Error Correction VAEC9620 (demand for VAT: recovery powers).
VAT Accounting Manual VATAC1570 (commissioners have yet to make a decision).
VAT Time Of Supply VATTOS2295 (self-billed invoices).
Amendments—[1] Reference "58ZA(5)(*a*)" substituted for reference "92(6)" by the Taxation (Cross-border Trade) Act 2018 s 43, Sch 8 paras 1, 56 with effect from IP completion day (11pm on 31 December 2020), by virtue of SI 2020/1642 reg 4(*b*).

[58ZA International VAT arrangements
(1) The Commissioners may make regulations imposing obligations on taxable persons for the purpose of giving effect to international VAT arrangements.
(2) The regulations may require the submission to the Commissioners by taxable persons of statements containing such particulars of—
 (*a*) relevant transactions in which the taxable persons are concerned, and
 (*b*) the persons concerned in those transactions,
as may be specified in the regulations.
(3) The regulations may provide for statements about relevant transactions to be submitted at such times and intervals, in such cases and in such form and manner as may be specified—
 (*a*) in the regulations, or
 (*b*) by the Commissioners in accordance with the regulations.
(4) A transaction is a "relevant transaction" for the purposes of this section if information about it could be relevant to any international VAT arrangements.
(5) If any international VAT arrangements have effect—
 (*a*) any Schedule 11 information power is exercisable with respect to matters that are relevant to those arrangements as it is exercisable with respect to matters that are relevant for any of the purposes of this Act, and
 (*b*) any power of an officer of Revenue and Customs to obtain information or documents under any enactment or subordinate legislation relating to VAT is exercisable in relation to matters which are relevant to those arrangements.
(6) The Commissioners may disclose information which is obtained as a result of subsection (5) (and no obligation of secrecy, whether imposed by statute or otherwise, prevents such disclosure) if—
 (*a*) the disclosure is required in accordance with the international VAT arrangements, and
 (*b*) the Commissioners are satisfied that the recipient is bound, or has undertaken, both to observe rules of confidentiality which are no less strict than those applying to the information in the United Kingdom and to use the information only for the purposes contemplated by the arrangements.
(7) Powers are exercisable as a result of subsection (5) only if the Commissioners have given (and not withdrawn) a direction in writing authorising their use (either generally or in relation to specified cases).
(8) The Commissioners may not make regulations under this section, or give a direction under subsection (7), unless they consider that making the regulations or giving the direction would facilitate the administration, collection or enforcement of VAT.
(9) In this section—
 "international VAT arrangements" means arrangements which—
  (*a*) have effect by virtue of an Order in Council under section 173 of the Finance Act 2006, and
  (*b*) relate to VAT or any tax corresponding to VAT imposed under the law of the territory, or any of the territories, in relation to which the arrangements have been made, and
 "Schedule 11 information power" means any power of the Commissioners under Schedule 11 relating to—
  (*a*) the keeping of accounts,
  (*b*) the making of returns and the submission of other documents to the Commissioners,
  (*c*) the production, use and contents of invoices,
  (*d*) the keeping and preservation of records, and

(e) the furnishing of information and the production of documents.]¹

Amendments—¹ Section 58ZA inserted by the Taxation (Cross-border Trade) Act 2018 s 43, Sch 8 paras 1, 57 with effect from IP completion day (11pm on 31 December 2020), by virtue of SI 2020/1642 reg 4(b).

Disclosure of avoidance schemes

[58B Payment by cheque
Regulations under section 95(1) of the Finance Act 2007 (payment by cheque) may, in particular, provide for a payment which is made by cheque in contravention of regulations under section 25(1) above to be treated as made when the cheque clears, as defined in the regulations under section 95(1) of that Act.]¹

Commentary—*De Voil Indirect Tax Service* **V5.108A.**
Amendments—¹ This section inserted by FA 2007 s 95(8) with effect from 19 July 2007.

Default surcharges and other penalties and criminal offences

59 The default surcharge

(1) [Subject to subsection (1A) below]¹ If, by the last day on which a taxable person is required in accordance with regulations under this Act to furnish a return for a prescribed accounting period—
 (a) the Commissioners have not received that return, or
 (b) the Commissioners have received that return but have not received the amount of VAT shown on the return as payable by him in respect of that period,
then that person shall be regarded for the purposes of this section as being in default in respect of that period.
[(1A) A person shall not be regarded for the purposes of this section as being in default in respect of any prescribed accounting period if that period is one in respect of which he is required by virtue of any order under section 28 to make any payment on account of VAT.]¹
(2) Subject to subsections (9) and (10) below, subsection (4) below applies in any case where—
 (a) a taxable person is in default in respect of a prescribed accounting period; and
 (b) the Commissioners serve notice on the taxable person (a "surcharge liability notice") specifying as a surcharge period for the purposes of this section a period ending on the first anniversary of the last day of the period referred to in paragraph (a) above and beginning, subject to subsection (3) below, on the date of the notice.
(3) If a surcharge liability notice is served by reason of a default in respect of a prescribed accounting period and that period ends at or before the expiry of an existing surcharge period already notified to the taxable person concerned, the surcharge period specified in that notice shall be expressed as a continuation of the existing surcharge period and, accordingly, for the purposes of this section, that existing period and its extension shall be regarded as a single surcharge period.
(4) Subject to subsections (7) to (10) below, if a taxable person on whom a surcharge liability notice has been served—
 (a) is in default in respect of a prescribed accounting period ending within the surcharge period specified in (or extended by) that notice, and
 (b) has outstanding VAT for that prescribed accounting period,
he shall be liable to a surcharge equal to whichever is the greater of the following, namely, the specified percentage of his outstanding VAT for that prescribed accounting period and £30.
(5) Subject to subsections (7) to (10) below, the specified percentage referred to in subsection (4) above shall be determined in relation to a prescribed accounting period by reference to the number of such periods in respect of which the taxable person is in default during the surcharge period and for which he has outstanding VAT, so that—
 (a) in relation to the first such prescribed accounting period, the specified percentage is 2 per cent;
 (b) in relation to the second such period, the specified percentage is 5 per cent;
 (c) in relation to the third such period, the specified percentage is 10 per cent; and
 (d) in relation to each such period after the third, the specified percentage is 15 per cent.
(6) For the purposes of subsections (4) and (5) above a person has outstanding VAT for a prescribed accounting period if some or all of the VAT for which he is liable in respect of that period has not been paid by the last day on which he is required (as mentioned in subsection (1) above) to make a return for that period; and the reference in subsection (4) above to a person's outstanding VAT for a prescribed accounting period is to so much of the VAT for which he is so liable as has not been paid by that day.
(7) If a person who, apart from this subsection, would be liable to a surcharge under subsection (4) above satisfies the Commissioners or, on appeal, a tribunal that, in the case of a default which is material to the surcharge—
 (a) the return or, as the case may be, the VAT shown on the return was despatched at such a time and in such a manner that it was reasonable to expect that it would be received by the Commissioners within the appropriate time limit, or
 (b) there is a reasonable excuse for the return or VAT not having been so despatched,

he shall not be liable to the surcharge and for the purposes of the preceding provisions of this section he shall be treated as not having been in default in respect of the prescribed accounting period in question (and, accordingly, any surcharge liability notice the service of which depended upon that default shall be deemed not to have been served).

(8) For the purposes of subsection (7) above, a default is material to a surcharge if—
   (a) it is the default which, by virtue of subsection (4) above, gives rise to the surcharge; or
   (b) it is a default which was taken into account in the service of the surcharge liability notice upon which the surcharge depends and the person concerned has not previously been liable to a surcharge in respect of a prescribed accounting period ending within the surcharge period specified in or extended by that notice.

(9) In any case where—
   (a) the conduct by virtue of which a person is in default in respect of a prescribed accounting period is also conduct falling within section 69(1), and
   (b) by reason of that conduct, the person concerned is assessed to a penalty under that section,
the default shall be left out of account for the purposes of subsections (2) to (5) above.

(10) If the Commissioners, after consultation with the Treasury, so direct, a default in respect of a prescribed accounting period specified in the direction shall be left out of account for the purposes of subsections (2) to (5) above.

[(11) For the purposes of this section references to a thing's being done by any day include references to its being done on that day.][1]

Commentary—*De Voil Indirect Tax Service* **V5.371–V5.376**.
HMRC Manuals—VAT Default Surcharge Officer's Guide VDSOG1000 (factors affecting default surcharge).
Amendments—[1] Words in sub-s (1), and sub-ss (1A), (11), inserted by FA 1996 s 35(3), (4), with effect in relation to any prescribed accounting period ending on or after 1 June 1996, but a liability to make a payment on account of VAT shall be disregarded for the purposes of the amendments made by FA 1996 s 35 if the payment is one becoming due before that date.

[59A Default surcharge: payments on account
(1) For the purposes of this section a taxable person shall be regarded as in default in respect of any prescribed accounting period if the period is one in respect of which he is required, by virtue of an order under section 28, to make any payment on account of VAT and either—
   (a) a payment which he is so required to make in respect of that period has not been received in full by the Commissioners by the day on which it became due; or
   (b) he would, but for section 59(1A), be in default in respect of that period for the purposes of section 59.

(2) Subject to subsections (10) and (11) below, subsection (4) below applies in any case where—
   (a) a taxable person is in default in respect of a prescribed accounting period; and
   (b) the Commissioners serve notice on the taxable person (a "surcharge liability notice") specifying as a surcharge period for the purposes of this section a period which—
      (i) begins, subject to subsection (3) below, on the date of the notice; and
      (ii) ends on the first anniversary of the last day of the period referred to in paragraph (a) above.

(3) If—
   (a) a surcharge liability notice is served by reason of a default in respect of a prescribed accounting period, and
   (b) that period ends at or before the expiry of an existing surcharge period already notified to the taxable person concerned,
the surcharge period specified in that notice shall be expressed as a continuation of the existing surcharge period; and, accordingly, the existing period and its extension shall be regarded as a single surcharge period.

(4) Subject to subsections (7) to (11) below, if—
   (a) a taxable person on whom a surcharge liability notice has been served is in default in respect of a prescribed accounting period,
   (b) that prescribed accounting period is one ending within the surcharge period specified in (or extended by) that notice, and
   (c) the aggregate value of his defaults in respect of that prescribed accounting period is more than nil,
that person shall be liable to a surcharge equal to whichever is the greater of £30 and the specified percentage of the aggregate value of his defaults in respect of that prescribed accounting period.

(5) Subject to subsections (7) to (11) below, the specified percentage referred to in subsection (4) above shall be determined in relation to a prescribed accounting period by reference to the number of such periods during the surcharge period which are periods in respect of which the taxable person is in default and in respect of which the value of his defaults is more than nil, so that—
   (a) in relation to the first such prescribed accounting period, the specified percentage is 2 per cent;
   (b) in relation to the second such period, the specified percentage is 5 per cent;
   (c) in relation to the third such period, the specified percentage is 10 per cent; and

(d) in relation to each such period after the third, the specified percentage is 15 per cent.

(6) For the purposes of this section the aggregate value of a person's defaults in respect of a prescribed accounting period shall be calculated as follows—
- (a) where the whole or any part of a payment in respect of that period on account of VAT was not received by the Commissioners by the day on which it became due, an amount equal to that payment or, as the case may be, to that part of it shall be taken to be the value of the default relating to that payment;
- (b) if there is more than one default with a value given by paragraph (a) above, those values shall be aggregated;
- (c) the total given by paragraph (b) above, or (where there is only one default) the value of the default under paragraph (a) above, shall be taken to be the value for that period of that person's defaults on payments on account;
- (d) the value of any default by that person which is a default falling within subsection (1)(b) above shall be taken to be equal to the amount of any outstanding VAT less the amount of unpaid payments on account; and
- (e) the aggregate value of a person's defaults in respect of that period shall be taken to be the aggregate of—
  - (i) the value for that period of that person's defaults (if any) on payments on account; and
  - (ii) the value of any default of his in respect of that period that falls within subsection (1)(b) above.

(7) In the application of subsection (6) above for the calculation of the aggregate value of a person's defaults in respect of a prescribed accounting period—
- (a) the amount of outstanding VAT referred to in paragraph (d) of that subsection is the amount (if any) which would be the amount of that person's outstanding VAT for that period for the purposes of section 59(4); and
- (b) the amount of unpaid payments on account referred to in that paragraph is the amount (if any) equal to so much of any payments on account of VAT (being payments in respect of that period) as has not been received by the Commissioners by the last day on which that person is required (as mentioned in section 59(1)) to make a return for that period.

(8) If a person who, apart from this subsection, would be liable to a surcharge under subsection (4) above satisfies the Commissioners or, on appeal, a tribunal—
- (a) in the case of a default that is material for the purposes of the surcharge and falls within subsection (1)(a) above—
  - (i) that the payment on account of VAT was despatched at such a time and in such a manner that it was reasonable to expect that it would be received by the Commissioners by the day on which it became due, or
  - (ii) that there is a reasonable excuse for the payment not having been so despatched,

or
- (b) in the case of a default that is material for the purposes of the surcharge and falls within subsection (1)(b) above, that the condition specified in section 59(7)(a) or (b) is satisfied as respects the default,

he shall not be liable to the surcharge and for the purposes of the preceding provisions of this section he shall be treated as not having been in default in respect of the prescribed accounting period in question (and, accordingly, any surcharge liability notice the service of which depended upon that default shall be deemed not to have been served).

(9) For the purposes of subsection (8) above, a default is material to a surcharge if—
- (a) it is the default which, by virtue of subsection (4) above, gives rise to the surcharge; or
- (b) it is a default which was taken into account in the service of the surcharge liability notice upon which the surcharge depends and the person concerned has not previously been liable to a surcharge in respect of a prescribed accounting period ending within the surcharge period specified in or extended by that notice.

10) In any case where—
- (a) the conduct by virtue of which a person is in default in respect of a prescribed accounting period is also conduct falling within section 69(1), and
- (b) by reason of that conduct, the person concerned is assessed to a penalty under section 69,

the default shall be left out of account for the purposes of subsections (2) to (5) above.

(11) If the Commissioners, after consultation with the Treasury, so direct, a default in respect of a prescribed accounting period specified in the direction shall be left out of account for the purposes of subsections (2) to (5) above.

(12) For the purposes of this section the Commissioners shall be taken not to receive a payment by the day on which it becomes due unless it is made in such a manner as secures (in a case where the payment is made otherwise than in cash) that, by the last day for the payment of that amount, all the transactions can be completed that need to be completed before the whole amount of the payment becomes available to the Commissioners.

(13) In determining for the purposes of this section whether any person would, but for section 59(1A), be in default in respect of any period for the purposes of section 59, subsection (12) above shall be deemed to apply for the purposes of section 59 as it applies for the purposes of this section.

(14) For the purposes of this section references to a thing's being done by any day include references to its being done on that day.][1]

Commentary—*De Voil Indirect Tax Service* **V5.381**.
HMRC Manuals—VAT Default Surcharge Officer's Guide VDSOG900 (movement into and out of the POA scheme).
Amendments—[1] Section inserted by FA 1996 s 35(2), with effect in relation to any prescribed accounting period ending on or after 1 June 1996, but a liability to make a payment on account of VAT shall be disregarded for the purposes of the amendments made by FA 1996 s 35 if the payment is one becoming due before that date.

[59B Relationship between sections 59 and 59A

(1) This section applies in each of the following cases, namely—
- (a) where a section 28 accounting period ends within a surcharge period begun or extended by the service on a taxable person (whether before or after the coming into force of section 59A) of a surcharge liability notice under section 59; and
- (b) where a prescribed accounting period which is not a section 28 accounting period ends within a surcharge period begun or extended by the service on a taxable person of a surcharge liability notice under section 59A.

(2) In a case falling within subsection (1)(a) above section 59A shall have effect as if—
- (a) subject to paragraph (b) below, the section 28 accounting period were deemed to be a period ending within a surcharge period begun or, as the case may be, extended by a notice served under section 59A; but
- (b) any question—
  - (i) whether a surcharge period was begun or extended by the notice, or
  - (ii) whether the taxable person was in default in respect of any prescribed accounting period which was not a section 28 accounting period but ended within the surcharge period begun or extended by that notice,

  were to be determined as it would be determined for the purposes of section 59.

(3) In a case falling within subsection (1)(b) above section 59 shall have effect as if—
- (a) subject to paragraph (b) below, the prescribed accounting period that is not a section 28 accounting period were deemed to be a period ending within a surcharge period begun or, as the case may be, extended by a notice served under section 59;
- (b) any question—
  - (i) whether a surcharge period was begun or extended by the notice, or
  - (ii) whether the taxable person was in default in respect of any prescribed accounting period which was a section 28 accounting period but ended within the surcharge period begun or extended by that notice,

  were to be determined as it would be determined for the purposes of section 59A; and
- (c) that person were to be treated as having had outstanding VAT for a section 28 accounting period in any case where the aggregate value of his defaults in respect of that period was, for the purposes of section 59A, more than nil.

(4) In this section "a section 28 accounting period", in relation to a taxable person, means any prescribed accounting period ending on or after the day on which the Finance Act 1996 was passed in respect of which that person is liable by virtue of an order under section 28 to make any payment on account of VAT.][1]

Commentary—*De Voil Indirect Tax Service* **V5.381**.
HMRC Manuals—VAT Default Surcharge Officer's Guide VDSOG900 (movement into and out of the POA scheme).
Amendments—[1] Section inserted by FA 1996 s 35(5), with effect in relation to any prescribed accounting period ending on or after 1 June 1996, but a liability to make a payment on account of VAT shall be disregarded for the purposes of the amendments made by FA 1996 s 35 if the payment is one becoming due before that date.

60 VAT evasion: conduct involving dishonesty

(1) In any case where—
- (a) *for the purpose of evading VAT, a person does any act or omits to take any action, and*
- (b) *his conduct involves dishonesty (whether or not it is such as to give rise to criminal liability),*

he shall be liable, subject to subsection (6) below, to a penalty equal to the amount of VAT evaded or, as the case may be, sought to be evaded, by his conduct.

(2) The reference in subsection (1)(a) above to evading VAT includes a reference to obtaining any of the following sums—
- (a) *a refund under any regulations made by virtue of section 13(5);*
- (b) *a VAT credit;*
- (c) *a refund under section 35, 36 or 40 of this Act or section 22 of the 1983 Act; and*
- (d) *a repayment under section 39,*

in circumstances where the person concerned is not entitled to that sum.

(3) The reference in subsection (1) above to the amount of the VAT evaded or sought to be evaded by a person's conduct shall be construed—
- (a) in relation to VAT itself or a VAT credit as a reference to the aggregate of the amount (if any) falsely claimed by way of credit for input tax and the amount (if any) by which output tax was falsely understated; and
- (b) in relation to the sums referred to in subsection (2)(a), (c) and (e) above, as a reference to the amount falsely claimed by way of refund or repayment.

(4) Statements made or documents produced by or on behalf of a person shall not be inadmissible in any such proceedings as are mentioned in subsection (5) below by reason only that it has been drawn to his attention—
- (a) that, in relation to VAT, the Commissioners may assess an amount due by way of a civil penalty instead of instituting criminal proceedings and, though no undertaking can be given as to whether the Commissioners will make such an assessment in the case of any person, it is their practice to be influenced by the fact that a person has made a full confession of any dishonest conduct to which he has been a party and has given full facilities for investigation, and
- (b) that the Commissioners or, on appeal, a tribunal have power under section 70 to reduce a penalty under this section,

and that he was or may have been induced thereby to make the statements or produce the documents.

(5) The proceedings mentioned in subsection (4) above are—
- (a) any criminal proceedings against the person concerned in respect of any offence in connection with or in relation to VAT, and
- (b) any proceedings against him for the recovery of any sum due from him in connection with or in relation to VAT.

(6) Where, by reason of conduct falling within subsection (1) above, a person is convicted of an offence (whether under this Act or otherwise), that conduct shall not also give rise to liability to a penalty under this section.

(7) On an appeal against an assessment to a penalty under this section, the burden of proof as to the matters specified in subsection (1)(a) and (b) above shall lie upon the Commissioners.[1]

Commentary—*De Voil Indirect Tax Service* V5.341.
Amendments—[1] This section repealed by FA 2007 ss 97, 114, Sch 24 para 29(d), Sch 27 Pt 5(5) with effect as follows (by virtue of SI 2008/568 art 2, and subject to transitional provisions and savings in arts 3, 4)—
- 1 April 2008 in relation to relevant documents relating to tax periods commencing on or after that date;
- 1 April 2008 in relation to assessments falling within Sch 24 para 2 for tax periods commencing on or after that date;
- 1 July 2008 in relation to relevant documents relating to claims under the Thirteenth Council Directive (arrangements for the refund of value added tax to persons not established in Community territory) for years commencing on or after that date;
- 1 January 2009 in relation to relevant documents relating to claims under the Eighth Council Directive (arrangements for the refund of value added tax to taxable persons not established in the territory of the country) for years commencing on or after that date;
- 1 April 2009 in relation to documents relating to all other claims for repayments of relevant tax made on or after 1 April 2009 which are not related to a tax period; and
- in any other case, 1 April 2009 in relation to documents given where a person's liability to pay relevant tax arises on or after that date.

Sections 60, 61 shall continue to have effect with respect to conduct involving dishonesty which does not relate to an inaccuracy in a document or a failure to notify HMRC of an under-assessment by HMRC (SI 2008/568 art 4). Notwithstanding FA 2007 Sch 24 para 29(d), ss 60 and 61 shall continue to have effect with respect to conduct involving dishonesty which does not relate to an inaccuracy in a document or a failure to notify HMRC of an under-assessment by HMRC (SI 2009/571 art 7).

61 VAT evasion: liability of directors etc

(1) Where it appears to the Commissioners—
- (a) that a body corporate is liable to a penalty under section 60, and
- (b) that the conduct giving rise to that penalty is, in whole or in part, attributable to the dishonesty of a person who is, or at the material time was, a director or managing officer of the body corporate (a "named officer"),

the Commissioners may serve a notice under this section on the body corporate and on the named officer.

(2) A notice under this section shall state—
- (a) the amount of the penalty referred to in subsection (1)(a) above ("the basic penalty"), and
- (b) that the Commissioners propose, in accordance with this section, to recover from the named officer such portion (which may be the whole) of the basic penalty as is specified in the notice.

(3) Where a notice is served under this section, the portion of the basic penalty specified in the notice shall be recoverable from the named officer as if he were personally liable under section 60 to a penalty which corresponds to that portion; and the amount of that penalty may be assessed and notified to him accordingly under section 76.

(4) Where a notice is served under this section—
   (a) the amount which, under section 76, may be assessed as the amount due by way of penalty from the body corporate shall be only so much (if any) of the basic penalty as is not assessed on and notified to a named officer by virtue of subsection (3) above; and
   (b) the body corporate shall be treated as discharged from liability for so much of the basic penalty as is so assessed and notified.
(5) No appeal shall lie against a notice under this section as such but—
   (a) where a body corporate is assessed as mentioned in subsection (4)(a) above, the body corporate may appeal against the Commissioners' decision as to its liability to a penalty and against the amount of the basic penalty as if it were specified in the assessment; and
   (b) where an assessment is made on a named officer by virtue of subsection (3) above, the named officer may appeal against the Commissioners' decision that the conduct of the body corporate referred to in subsection (1)(b) above is, in whole or part, attributable to his dishonesty and against their decision as to the portion of the penalty which the Commissioners propose to recover from him.
(6) In this section a "managing officer", in relation to a body corporate, means any manager, secretary or other similar officer of the body corporate or any person purporting to act in any such capacity or as a director; and where the affairs of a body corporate are managed by its members, this section shall apply in relation to the conduct of a member in connection with his functions of management as if he were a director of the body corporate.[1]

Commentary—*De Voil Indirect Tax Service* **V5.341**.
Amendments—[1]   This section repealed by FA 2007 ss 97, 114, Sch 24 para 29(d), Sch 27 Pt 5(5) with effect as follows (by virtue of SI 2008/568 art 2, and subject to transitional provisions and savings in arts 3, 4)—
   – 1 April 2008 in relation to relevant documents relating to tax periods commencing on or after that date;
   – 1 April 2008 in relation to assessments falling within Sch 24 para 2 for tax periods commencing on or after that date;
   – 1 July 2008 in relation to relevant documents relating to claims under the Thirteenth Council Directive (arrangements for the refund of value added tax to persons not established in Community territory) for years commencing on or after that date;
   – 1 January 2009 in relation to relevant documents relating to claims under the Eighth Council Directive (arrangements for the refund of value added tax to taxable persons not established in the territory of the country) for years commencing on or after that date;
   – 1 April 2009 in relation to documents relating to all other claims for repayments of relevant tax made on or after 1 April 2009 which are not related to a tax period; and
   – in any other case, 1 April 2009 in relation to documents given where a person's liability to pay relevant tax arises on or after that date.
   Sections 60, 61 shall continue to have effect with respect to conduct involving dishonesty which does not relate to an inaccuracy in a document or a failure to notify HMRC of an under-assessment by HMRC (SI 2008/568 art 4). Notwithstanding FA 2007 Sch 24 para 29(d), ss 60 and 61 shall continue to have effect with respect to conduct involving dishonesty which does not relate to an inaccuracy in a document or a failure to notify HMRC of an under-assessment by HMRC (SI 2009/571 art 7).

62 Incorrect certificates as to zero-rating etc

[(1) Subject to subsections (3) and (4) below, where—
   (a) a person to whom one or more supplies are, or are to be, made—
      (i) gives to the supplier a certificate that the supply or supplies fall, or will fall, wholly or partly within [any of the Groups of Schedule 7A][3], Group 5 or 6 of Schedule 8 or Group 1 of Schedule 9, or
      (ii) gives to the supplier a certificate for the purposes of section 18B(2)(*d*) or 18C(1)(*c*),
   and
   (b) the certificate is incorrect,
the person giving the certificate shall be liable to a penalty.
(1A)   . . .[5]
[(1B) Where—
   (a) a person gives a certificate for the purposes of Note (5R) to Group 12 of Schedule 8 with respect to a supply of a motor vehicle, and
   (b) the certificate is incorrect,
the person giving the certificate is to be liable to a penalty.][4]
(2) The amount of the penalty shall be equal to—
   (a) in a case where the penalty is imposed by virtue of subsection (1) above, the difference between—
      (i) the amount of the VAT which would have been chargeable on the supply or supplies if the certificate had been correct; and
      (ii) the amount of VAT actually chargeable;
   (*b*)   . . .[5]
   [(*c*) in a case where it is imposed by virtue of subsection (1B), the difference between—

(i) the amount of the VAT which would have been chargeable on the supply if the certificate had been correct, and
(ii) the amount of VAT actually chargeable.]⁴
(3) The giving [or preparing]¹ of a certificate shall not give rise to a penalty under this section if the person who gave [or prepared]¹ it satisfies the Commissioners or, on appeal, a tribunal that there is a reasonable excuse for his having given [or prepared]¹ it.
(4) Where by reason of giving [or preparing]¹ a certificate a person is convicted of an offence (whether under this Act or otherwise), the giving [or preparing]¹ of the certificate shall not also give rise to a penalty under this section.

Commentary—*De Voil Indirect Tax Service* **V5.340**.
HMRC Manuals—VAT Civil Penalties VAT11311-11312 (incorrect certificates to zero-rating).
Northern Ireland—See VATA 1994 Sch 9ZB para 24: in relation to incorrect Northern Ireland fiscal warehousing certificates, this section has effect as if in subsection (1)(*a*)(ii), after "18C(1)(*c*)" there were inserted "or paragraph 19(3)(*d*) of Schedule 9ZB (Northern Ireland fiscal warehouses)".
Amendments—¹ Words in sub-ss (3) and (4) inserted and word "or" at the end of sub-para (i) and word "and" at the end of sub-para (ii) of sub-s (1)(a) repealed by FA 1996 Sch 3 para 8, Sch 41 Pt IV(1), with effect from 1 June 1996 (see Finance Act 1996, Section 26, (Appointed Day) Order, SI 1996/1249), and applying to any acquisition of goods from another member State and any supply taking place on or after that day.
² Sub-ss (1) and (2) substituted by FA 1999 s 17 with effect in relation to certificates given or, as the case may be, prepared on or after 27 July 1999.
³ In sub-s (1)(*a*)(i), words substituted by FA 2001 s 99(6), Sch 31 para 3 with effect for supplies made, or to be made, after 31 October 2001.
⁴ Sub-ss (1B), (2)(*c*) inserted by FA 2017 s 16, Sch 7 para 3 with effect in relation to supplies made, and acquisitions and importations taking place, on or after 1 April 2017.
⁵ Sub-ss (1A), (2)(*b*) repealed by the Taxation (Cross-border Trade) Act 2018 s 43, Sch 8 paras 1, 58 with effect from IP completion day (11pm on 31 December 2020), by virtue of SI 2020/1642 reg 4(*b*).
Sub-s (1A) previously read as follows—
"(1A) Subject to subsections (3) and (4) below, where—
  (*a*) a person who makes, or is to make, an acquisition of goods from another member State prepares a certificate for the purposes of section 18B(1)(*d*), and
  (*b*) the certificate is incorrect,
the person preparing the certificate shall be liable to a penalty."
Sub-s (2)(*b*) previously read as follows—
  "(*b*) in a case where it is imposed by virtue of subsection (1A) above, the amount of VAT actually chargeable on the acquisition.".

63 Penalty for misdeclaration or neglect resulting in VAT loss for one accounting period equalling or exceeding certain amounts

(1) In any case where, for a prescribed accounting period—
  (*a*) a return is made which understates a person's liability to VAT or overstates his entitlement to a VAT credit, or
  (*b*) an assessment is made which understates a person's liability to VAT and, at the end of the period of 30 days beginning on the date of the assessment, he has not taken all such steps as are reasonable to draw the understatement to the attention of the Commissioners,
and the circumstances are as set out in subsection (2) below, the person concerned shall be liable, subject to subsections (10) and (11) below, to a penalty equal to 15 per cent of the VAT which would have been lost if the inaccuracy had not been discovered.
(2) The circumstances referred to in subsection (1) above are that the VAT for the period concerned which would have been lost if the inaccuracy had not been discovered equals or exceeds whichever is the lesser of £1,000,000 and 30 per cent of the relevant amount for that period.
(3) Any reference in this section to the VAT for a prescribed accounting period which would have been lost if an inaccuracy had not been discovered is a reference to the amount of the understatement of liability or, as the case may be, overstatement of entitlement referred to, in relation to that period, in subsection (1) above.
(4) In this section "the relevant amount", in relation to a prescribed accounting period, means—
  (*a*) for the purposes of a case falling within subsection (1)(*a*) above, the gross amount of VAT for that period; and
  (*b*) for the purposes of a case falling within subsection (1)(*b*) above, the true amount of VAT for that period.
(5) In this section "the gross amount of tax", in relation to a prescribed accounting period, means the aggregate of the following amounts, that is to say—
  (*a*) the amount of credit for input tax which (subject to subsection (8) below) should have been stated on the return for that period, and
  (*b*) the amount of output tax which (subject to that subsection) should have been so stated.
(6) In relation to any return which, in accordance with prescribed requirements, includes a single amount as the aggregate for the prescribed accounting period to which the return relates of—
  (*a*) the amount representing credit for input tax, and

(b) any other amounts representing refunds or repayments of VAT to which there is an entitlement,

references in this section to the amount of credit for input tax shall have effect (so far as they would not so have effect by virtue of subsection (9) below) as references to the amount of that aggregate.

(7) In this section "the true amount of VAT", in relation to a prescribed accounting period, means the amount of VAT which was due from the person concerned for that period or, as the case may be, the amount of the VAT credit (if any) to which he was entitled for that period.

(8) Where—
   (a) a return for any prescribed accounting period overstates or understates to any extent a person's liability to VAT or his entitlement to a VAT credit, and
   (b) that return is corrected, in such circumstances and in accordance with such conditions as may be prescribed, by a return for a later such period which understates or overstates, to the corresponding extent, that liability or entitlement,

it shall be assumed for the purposes of this section that the statements made by each of those returns (so far as they are not inaccurate in any other respect) are correct statements for the accounting period to which it relates.

(9) This section shall have effect in relation to a body which is registered and to which section 33 applies as if—
   (a) any reference to a VAT credit included a reference to a refund under that section, and
   (b) any reference to credit for input tax included a reference to VAT chargeable on supplies, acquisitions or importations which were not for the purposes of any business carried on by the body.

[(9A) This section shall have effect in relation to a body which is registered and to which section 33A applies as if—
   (a) any reference to a VAT credit included a reference to a refund under that section, and
   (b) any reference to credit for input tax included a reference to VAT chargeable on supplies, acquisitions or importations which were attributable to the provision by the body of free rights of admission to a museum or gallery that in relation to the body was a relevant museum or gallery for the purposes of section 33A.][1]

(10) Conduct falling within subsection (1) above shall not give rise to liability to a penalty under this section if—
   (a) the person concerned satisfies the Commissioners or, on appeal, a tribunal that there is a reasonable excuse for the conduct, or
   (b) at a time when he had no reason to believe that enquiries were being made by the Commissioners into his affairs, so far as they relate to VAT, the person concerned furnished to the Commissioners full information with respect to the inaccuracy concerned.

(11) Where, by reason of conduct falling within subsection (1) above—
   (a) a person is convicted of an offence (whether under this Act or otherwise), or
   (b) a person is assessed to a penalty under section 60,

that conduct shall not also give rise to liability to a penalty under this section.[2]

Commentary—De Voil Indirect Tax Service **V5.139**.
Amendments—[1] Sub-s (9A) inserted by FA 2001 s 98(1), (3) with effect from 1 September 2001.
[2] This section repealed by FA 2007 ss 97, 114, Sch 24 para 29(d), Sch 27 Pt 5(5) with effect as follows (by virtue of SI 2008/568 art 2, and subject to transitional provisions and savings in arts 3, 4)—
   – 1 April 2008 in relation to relevant documents relating to tax periods commencing on or after that date;
   – 1 April 2008 in relation to assessments falling within Sch 24 para 2 for tax periods commencing on or after that date;
   – 1 July 2008 in relation to relevant documents relating to claims under the Thirteenth Council Directive (arrangements for the refund of value added tax to persons not established in Community territory) for years commencing on or after that date;
   – 1 January 2009 in relation to relevant documents relating to claims under the Eighth Council Directive (arrangements for the refund of value added tax to taxable persons not established in the territory of the country) for years commencing on or after that date;
   – 1 April 2009 in relation to documents relating to all other claims for repayments of relevant tax made on or after 1 April 2009 which are not related to a tax period; and
   – in any other case, 1 April 2009 in relation to documents given where a person's liability to pay relevant tax arises on or after that date.

64 Repeated misdeclarations

(1) In any case where—
   (a) for a prescribed accounting period (including one beginning before the commencement of this section), a return has been made which understates a person's liability to VAT or overstates his entitlement to a VAT credit; and
   (b) the VAT for that period which would have been lost if the inaccuracy had not been discovered equals or exceeds whichever is the lesser of £500,000 and 10 per cent of the gross amount of tax for that period,

the inaccuracy shall be regarded, subject to subsections (5) and (6) below, as material for the purposes of this section.
(2) Subsection (3) below applies in any case where—
   (a) there is a material inaccuracy in respect of any prescribed accounting period;
   (b) the Commissioners serve notice on the person concerned (a "penalty liability notice") specifying a penalty period for the purposes of this section;
   (c) that notice is served before the end of 5 consecutive prescribed accounting periods beginning with the period in respect of which there was the material inaccuracy; and
   (d) the period specified in the penalty liability notice as the penalty period is the period of 8 consecutive prescribed accounting periods beginning with that in which the date of the notice falls.
(3) If, where a penalty liability notice has been served on any person, there is a material inaccuracy in respect of any of the prescribed accounting periods falling within the penalty period specified in the notice, that person shall be liable, except in relation to the first of those periods in respect of which there is a material inaccuracy, to a penalty equal to 15 per cent of the VAT for the prescribed accounting period in question which would have been lost if the inaccuracy had not been discovered.
(4) Subsections (3), (5), (8) and (9) of section 63 shall apply for the purposes of this section as they apply for the purposes of that section.
(5) An inaccuracy shall not be regarded as material for the purposes of this section if—
   (a) the person concerned satisfies the Commissioners or, on appeal, a tribunal that there is a reasonable excuse for the inaccuracy; or
   (b) at a time when he had no reason to believe that enquiries were being made by the Commissioners into his affairs, so far as they relate to VAT, the person concerned furnished to the Commissioners full information with respect to the inaccuracy.
[(6) Subject to subsection (6A) below, where by reason of conduct falling within subsection (1) above—
   (a) a person is convicted of an offence (whether under this Act or otherwise), or
   (b) a person is assessed to a penalty under section 60 or 63,
the inaccuracy concerned shall not be regarded as material for the purposes of this section.][1]
[(6A) Subsection (6) above shall not prevent an inaccuracy by reason of which a person has been assessed to a penalty under section 63—
   (a) from being regarded as a material inaccuracy in respect of which the Commissioners may serve a penalty liability notice under subsection (2) above; or
   (b) from being regarded for the purposes of subsection (3) above as a material inaccuracy by reference to which any prescribed accounting period falling within the penalty period is to be treated as the first prescribed accounting period so falling in respect of which there is a material inaccuracy.][1]
[(7) Where subsection (5) or (6) above requires any inaccuracy to be regarded as not material for the purposes of the serving of a penalty liability notice, any such notice served in respect of that inaccuracy shall be deemed not to have been served.] [1, 2]

Amendments—[1] Sub-ss (6), (6A), (7) substituted for sub-ss (6), (7) by FA 1996 s 36, with effect in relation to inaccuracies contained in returns made on or after 29 April 1996.
[2] This section repealed by FA 2007 ss 97, 114, Sch 24 para 29(d), Sch 27 Pt 5(5) with effect as follows (by virtue of SI 2008/568 art 2, and subject to transitional provisions and savings in arts 3, 4)—
  - 1 April 2008 in relation to relevant documents relating to tax periods commencing on or after that date;
  - 1 April 2008 in relation to assessments falling within Sch 24 para 2 for tax periods commencing on or after that date;
  - 1 July 2008 in relation to relevant documents relating to claims under the Thirteenth Council Directive (arrangements for the refund of value added tax to persons not established in Community territory) for years commencing on or after that date;
  - 1 January 2009 in relation to relevant documents relating to claims under the Eighth Council Directive (arrangements for the refund of value added tax to taxable persons not established in the territory of the country) for years commencing on or after that date;
  - 1 April 2009 in relation to documents relating to all other claims for repayments of relevant tax made on or after 1 April 2009 which are not related to a tax period; and
  - in any other case, 1 April 2009 in relation to documents given where a person's liability to pay relevant tax arises on or after that date.

65 [Inaccuracies in section 55A statements]
(1) Where—
   (a) [a section 55A statement][1] containing a material inaccuracy has been submitted by any person to the Commissioners;
   (b) the Commissioners have, within 6 months of discovering the inaccuracy, issued that person with a written warning identifying that statement and stating that future inaccuracies might result in the service of a notice for the purposes of this section;
   (c) [another section 55A statement][1] containing a material inaccuracy ("the second inaccurate statement") has been submitted by that person to the Commissioners;

(d) the submission date for the second inaccurate statement fell within the period of 2 years beginning with the day after the warning was issued;
(e) the Commissioners have, within 6 months of discovering the inaccuracy in the second inaccurate statement, served that person with a notice identifying that statement and stating that future inaccuracies will attract a penalty under this section;
(f) yet [another section 55A statement][1] containing a material inaccuracy is submitted by that person to the Commissioners; and
(g) the submission date for the statement falling within paragraph (f) above is not more than 2 years after the service of the notice or the date on which any previous statement attracting a penalty was submitted by that person to the Commissioners,

that person shall be liable to a penalty of £100 in respect of the statement so falling.

(2) Subject to subsections (3) and (4) below, [a section 55A statement][1] shall be regarded for the purposes of this section as containing a material inaccuracy if, having regard to the matters required to be included in the statement, the inclusion or omission of any information from the statement is misleading in any material respect.

(3) An inaccuracy contained in [a section 55A statement][1] shall not be regarded as material for the purposes of this section if—
  (a) the person who submitted the statement satisfies the Commissioners or, on appeal, a tribunal that there is a reasonable excuse for the inaccuracy; or
  (b) at a time when he had no reason to believe that enquiries were being made by the Commissioners into his affairs, that person furnished the Commissioners with full information with respect to the inaccuracy.

(4) Where, by reason of the submission of a statement containing a material inaccuracy by any person, that person is convicted of an offence (whether under this Act or otherwise), the inaccuracy to which the conviction relates shall be regarded for the purposes of this section as not being material.

(5) Where the only statement identified in a warning or notice served for the purposes of subsection (1)(b) or (e) above is one which (whether by virtue of either or both of subsections (3) and (4) above or otherwise) is regarded as containing no material inaccuracies, that warning or notice shall be deemed not to have been issued or served for those purposes.

[(6) In this section—

"section 55A statement" means a statement which is required to be submitted to the Commissioners in accordance with regulations under paragraph 2(3A) of Schedule 11; and

"submission date", in relation to a section 55A statement, means whichever is the earlier of the last day for the submission of the statement to the Commissioners in accordance with those regulations and the day on which it was in fact submitted to them.][1]

Commentary—*De Voil Indirect Tax Service* **V5.346**.
HMRC Manuals—VAT Reverse Charge VATREVCHG32000 (penalties for failure to submit and inaccuracies in an RCSL).
VAT Civil Penalties VCP11416 (the legal power to impose a penalty).
Northern Ireland—See Sch 9ZA para 73 (Northern Ireland: ss 55 and 56 apply to any statement which is required to be submitted to the Commissioners in accordance with regulations under Sch 9ZA para 73(1) as they apply to a s 55A statement).
Cross references—See the Taxation (Cross-border Trade) Act 2018 (Value Added Tax Transitional Provisions) (EU Exit) Regulations, SI 2019/105 reg 5 (as amended by SI 2020/1495 reg 21(5)) (any reference in this section to a s 55A statement is to be read after IP completion day as including a reference to a statement which in accordance with regulations under VATA 1994 Sch 11 para 2(3) was required to be submitted before IP completion day).
Amendments—[1] The following amendments made by the Taxation (Cross-border Trade) Act 2018 s 43, Sch 8 paras 1, 59 with effect from IP completion day (11pm on 31 December 2020), by virtue of SI 2020/1642 reg 4(b)—
  – in sub-s (1)—
    (a) in para (a), words substituted for words "an EC sales statement";
    (b) in paras (c), (f), words substituted for words "another EC sales statement";
  – in sub-ss (2), (3), words substituted for words "an EC sales statement";
  – sub-s (6) substituted for previous sub-ss (6), (7); and
  – heading to s 65 substituted.
Before these amendments, section 65 read as follows—

"**65 Inaccuracies in EC sales statements or in statements relating to section 55A**

(1) Where—
  (a) an EC sales statement containing a material inaccuracy has been submitted by any person to the Commissioners;
  (b) the Commissioners have, within 6 months of discovering the inaccuracy, issued that person with a written warning identifying that statement and stating that future inaccuracies might result in the service of a notice for the purposes of this section;
  (c) another EC sales statement containing a material inaccuracy ("the second inaccurate statement") has been submitted by that person to the Commissioners;
  (d) the submission date for the second inaccurate statement fell within the period of 2 years beginning with the day after the warning was issued;

(e) the Commissioners have, within 6 months of discovering the inaccuracy in the second inaccurate statement, served that person with a notice identifying that statement and stating that future inaccuracies will attract a penalty under this section;
(f) yet another EC sales statement containing a material inaccuracy is submitted by that person to the Commissioners; and
(g) the submission date for the statement falling within paragraph (f) above is not more than 2 years after the service of the notice or the date on which any previous statement attracting a penalty was submitted by that person to the Commissioners,

that person shall be liable to a penalty of £100 in respect of the statement so falling.

(2) Subject to subsections (3) and (4) below, an EC sales statement shall be regarded for the purposes of this section as containing a material inaccuracy if, having regard to the matters required to be included in the statement, the inclusion or omission of any information from the statement is misleading in any material respect.

(3) An inaccuracy contained in an EC sales statement shall not be regarded as material for the purposes of this section if—
(a) the person who submitted the statement satisfies the Commissioners or, on appeal, a tribunal that there is a reasonable excuse for the inaccuracy; or
(b) at a time when he had no reason to believe that enquiries were being made by the Commissioners into his affairs, that person furnished the Commissioners with full information with respect to the inaccuracy.

(4) Where, by reason of the submission of a statement containing a material inaccuracy by any person, that person is convicted of an offence (whether under this Act or otherwise), the inaccuracy to which the conviction relates shall be regarded for the purposes of this section as not being material.

(5) Where the only statement identified in a warning or notice served for the purposes of subsection (1)(b) or (e) above is one which (whether by virtue of either or both of subsections (3) and (4) above or otherwise) is regarded as containing no material inaccuracies, that warning or notice shall be deemed not to have been issued or served for those purposes.

(6) In this section—
"EC sales statement" means any statement which is required to be submitted to the Commissioners in accordance with regulations under paragraph 2(3) of Schedule 11; and
"submission date", in relation to such a statement, means whichever is the earlier of the last day for the submission of the statement to the Commissioners in accordance with those regulations and the day on which it was in fact submitted to the Commissioners.

(7) This section applies in relation to a statement which is required to be submitted to the Commissioners in accordance with regulations under paragraph 2(3A) of Schedule 11 as it applies in relation to an EC sales statement.".

66 [Failure to submit section 55A statement]

(1) If, by the last day on which a person is required in accordance with regulations under this Act to submit [a section 55A statement][2] for any prescribed period to the Commissioners, the Commissioners have not received that statement, that person shall be regarded for the purposes of this section as being in default in relation to that statement until it is submitted.

(2) Where any person is in default in respect of [any section 55A statement][2] the Commissioners may serve notice on him stating—
(a) that he is in default in relation to the statement specified in the notice;
(b) that (subject to the liability mentioned in paragraph (d) below) no action will be taken if he remedies the default before the end of the period of 14 days beginning with the day after the service of the notice;
(c) that if the default is not so remedied, that person will become liable in respect of his default to penalties calculated on a daily basis from the end of that period in accordance with the following provisions of this section; and
(d) that that person will become liable, without any further notices being served under this section, to penalties under this section if he commits any more defaults before a period of 12 months has elapsed without his being in default.

(3) Where a person has been served with a notice under subsection (2) above, he shall become liable under this section—
(a) if the statement to which the notice relates is not submitted before the end of the period of 14 days beginning with the day after the service of the notice, to a penalty in respect of that statement; and
(b) whether or not that statement is so submitted, to a penalty in respect of [any section 55A statement][2] the last day for the submission of which is after the service and before the expiry of the notice and in relation to which he is in default.

(4) For the purposes of this section a notice served on any person under subsection (2) above shall continue in force—
(a) except in a case falling within paragraph (b) below, until the end of the period of 12 months beginning with the day after the service of the notice; and
(b) where at any time in that period of 12 months that person is in default in relation to [any section 55A statement][2] other than one in relation to which he was in default when the notice was served, until a period of 12 months has elapsed without that person becoming liable to a penalty under this section in respect of [any section 55A statement][2].

(5) The amount of any penalty to which a person who has been served with a notice under subsection (2) above is liable under this section shall be whichever is the greater of £50 and—

(a) in the case of a liability in respect of the statement to which the notice relates, a penalty of £5 for every day for which the default continues after the end of the period of 14 days mentioned in subsection (3)(a) above, up to a maximum of 100 days; and

(b) in the case of a liability in respect of any other statement, a penalty of the relevant amount for every day for which the default continues, up to a maximum of 100 days.

(6) In subsection (5)(b) above "the relevant amount", in relation to a person served with a notice under subsection (2) above, means—

(a) £5, where (that person not having been liable to a penalty under this section in respect of the statement to which the notice relates) the statement in question is the first statement in respect of which that person has become liable to a penalty while the notice has been in force;

(b) £10 where the statement in question is the second statement in respect of which he has become so liable while the notice has been in force (counting the statement to which the notice relates where he has become liable in respect of that statement); and

(c) £15 in any other case.

(7) If a person who, apart from this subsection, would be liable to a penalty under this section satisfies the Commissioners or, on appeal a tribunal, that—

(a) [a section 55A statement][2] has been submitted at such a time and in such a manner that it was reasonable to expect that it would be received by the Commissioners within the appropriate time limit; or

(b) there is a reasonable excuse for such a statement not having been dispatched,

he shall be treated for the purposes of this section and sections 59 to 65 and 67 to 71, 73 . . . [2] and 76 [and Schedule 24 to the Finance Act 2007][1] as not having been in default in relation to that statement and, accordingly, he shall not be liable to any penalty under this section [or that Schedule][1] in respect of that statement and any notice served under subsection (2) above exclusively in relation to the failure to submit that statement shall have no effect for the purposes of this section.

(8) If it appears to the Treasury that there has been a change in the value of money since 1st January 1993 or, as the case may be, the last occasion when the sums specified in subsections (5) and (6) above were varied, they may by order substitute for the sums for the time being specified in those subsections such other sums as appear to them to be justified by the change; but an order under this section shall not apply to any default in relation to a statement the last day for the submission of which was before the order comes into force.

[(9) In this section, "section 55A statement" means a statement which is required to be submitted to the Commissioners in accordance with regulations under paragraph 2(3A) of Schedule 11.][2]

Commentary—*De Voil Indirect Tax Service* V5.355.

HMRC Manuals—VAT Civil Penalties VCP10947 (calculation and notification of the penalty: time limits). VCP10945 (issuing a penalty liability notice).
VCP11416 (the legal power to impose a penalty).

Cross references—See the Taxation (Cross-border Trade) Act 2018 (Value Added Tax Transitional Provisions) (EU Exit) Regulations, SI 2019/105 reg 5 (as amended by SI 2020/1495 reg 21(5)) (any reference in this section to a s 55A statement is to be read after IP completion day as including a reference to a statement which in accordance with regulations under VATA 1994 Sch 11 para 2(3) was required to be submitted before IP completion day).

Amendments—[1] Words in sub-s (7) inserted by the Finance Act 2008, Schedule 40 (Appointed Day, Transitional Provisions and Consequential Amendments) Order, SI 2009/571 art 8, Sch 1 paras 12, 13 with effect from 1 April 2009.

[2] The following amendments made by the Taxation (Cross-border Trade) Act 2018 s 43, Sch 8 paras 1, 60 with effect from IP completion day (11pm on 31 December 2020), by virtue of SI 2020/1642 reg 4(b)—

- in sub-ss (1), (7)(a), words substituted for words "an EC sales statement"
- in sub-ss (2), (3)(b), (4)(b), words substituted (in all places) for words "any EC sales statement";
- in sub-s (7), in words after para (b), reference ", 75" repealed;
- sub-s (9) substituted for previous sub-ss (9), (10); and
- heading to s 66 substituted.

Before these amendments, section 66 read as follows—

"66 Failure to submit EC sales statement or statement relating to section 55A

(1) If, by the last day on which a person is required in accordance with regulations under this Act to submit an EC sales statement for any prescribed period to the Commissioners, the Commissioners have not received that statement, that person shall be regarded for the purposes of this section as being in default in relation to that statement until it is submitted.

(2) Where any person is in default in respect of any EC sales statement the Commissioners may serve notice on him stating—

(a) that he is in default in relation to the statement specified in the notice;

(b) that (subject to the liability mentioned in paragraph (d) below) no action will be taken if he remedies the default before the end of the period of 14 days beginning with the day after the service of the notice;

(c) that if the default is not so remedied, that person will become liable in respect of his default to penalties calculated on a daily basis from the end of that period in accordance with the following provisions of this section; and

(d) that that person will become liable, without any further notices being served under this section, to penalties under this section if he commits any more defaults before a period of 12 months has elapsed without his being in default.

(3) Where a person has been served with a notice under subsection (2) above, he shall become liable under this section—

(a) if the statement to which the notice relates is not submitted before the end of the period of 14 days beginning with the day after the service of the notice, to a penalty in respect of that statement; and

(b) whether or not that statement is so submitted, to a penalty in respect of any EC sales statement the last day for the submission of which is after the service and before the expiry of the notice and in relation to which he is in default.

(4) For the purposes of this section a notice served on any person under subsection (2) above shall continue in force—

(a) except in a case falling within paragraph (b) below, until the end of the period of 12 months beginning with the day after the service of the notice; and

(b) where at any time in that period of 12 months that person is in default in relation to any EC sales statement other than one in relation to which he was in default when the notice was served, until a period of 12 months has elapsed without that person becoming liable to a penalty under this section in respect of any EC sales statement.

(5) The amount of any penalty to which a person who has been served with a notice under subsection (2) above is liable under this section shall be whichever is the greater of £50 and—

(a) in the case of a liability in respect of the statement to which the notice relates, a penalty of £5 for every day for which the default continues after the end of the period of 14 days mentioned in subsection (3)(a) above, up to a maximum of 100 days; and

(b) in the case of a liability in respect of any other statement, a penalty of the relevant amount for every day for which the default continues, up to a maximum of 100 days.

(6) In subsection (5)(b) above "the relevant amount", in relation to a person served with a notice under subsection (2) above, means—

(a) £5, where (that person not having been liable to a penalty under this section in respect of the statement to which the notice relates) the statement in question is the first statement in respect of which that person has become liable to a penalty while the notice has been in force;

(b) £10 where the statement in question is the second statement in respect of which he has become so liable while the notice has been in force (counting the statement to which the notice relates where he has become liable in respect of that statement); and

(c) £15 in any other case.

(7) If a person who, apart from this subsection, would be liable to a penalty under this section satisfies the Commissioners or, on appeal a tribunal, that—

(a) an EC sales statement has been submitted at such a time and in such a manner that it was reasonable to expect that it would be received by the Commissioners within the appropriate time limit; or

(b) there is a reasonable excuse for such a statement not having been dispatched,

he shall be treated for the purposes of this section and sections 59 to 65 and 67 to 71, 73, 75 and 76 and Schedule 24 to the Finance Act 2007 as not having been in default in relation to that statement and, accordingly, he shall not be liable to any penalty under this section or that Schedule in respect of that statement and any notice served under subsection (2) above exclusively in relation to the failure to submit that statement shall have no effect for the purposes of this section.

(8) If it appears to the Treasury that there has been a change in the value of money since 1st January 1993 or, as the case may be, the last occasion when the sums specified in subsections (5) and (6) above were varied, they may by order substitute for the sums for the time being specified in those subsections such other sums as appear to them to be justified by the change; but an order under this section shall not apply to any default in relation to a statement the last day for the submission of which was before the order comes into force.

(9) In this section "EC sales statement" means any statement which is required to be submitted to the Commissioners in accordance with regulations under paragraph 2(3) of Schedule 11.

(10) This section applies in relation to a statement which is required to be submitted to the Commissioners in accordance with regulations under paragraph 2(3A) of Schedule 11 as it applies in relation to an EC sales statement.".

68 Breaches of walking possession agreements

(1) This section applies where—

(a) in accordance with regulations under [section 51 of the Finance Act 1997 (enforcement by distress)][1], a distress is authorised to be levied on the goods and chattels of a person (a "person in default") who has refused or neglected to pay any VAT due or any amount recoverable as if it were VAT due, and

(b) the person levying the distress and the person in default have entered into a walking possession agreement, as defined in subsection (2) below.

(2) In this section a "walking possession agreement" means an agreement under which, in consideration of the property distrained upon being allowed to remain in the custody of the person in default and of the delaying of its sale, the person in default—

(a) acknowledges that the property specified in the agreement is under distraint and held in walking possession; and

(b) undertakes that, except with the consent of the Commissioners and subject to such conditions as they may impose, he will not remove or allow the removal of any of the specified property from the premises named in the agreement.

(3) Subject to subsection (4) below, if the person in default is in breach of the undertaking contained in a walking possession agreement, he shall be liable to a penalty equal to half of the VAT or other amount referred to in subsection (1)(a) above.

(4) The person in default shall not be liable to a penalty under subsection (3) above if he satisfies the Commissioners or, on appeal, a tribunal that there is a reasonable excuse for the breach in question.
[(5) This section extends only to Northern Ireland.][2]
Commentary—*De Voil Indirect Tax Service* **V5.351**.
HMRC Manuals—VAT Civil Penalties VCP11511 (arises: what is a breach of walking possession order).
VCP11541 (calculation of the penalty).
VAT Registration VATREG30100 (conditions of reallocation).
Amendments—[1] Words in sub-s (1)(a) substituted for the words "paragraph 5(4) of Schedule 11" by FA 1997 s 53(7) with effect from 1 July 1997 (see SI 1997/1432).
[2] Sub-s (5) substituted by the Tribunals, Courts and Enforcement Act 2007 s 62(3), Sch 13 paras 117, 120 with effect from 6 April 2014 (the date appointed by virtue of the Tribunals, Courts and Enforcement Act 2007 (Commencement No 11) Order, SI 2014/768 art 2(1)(*b*)).

69 Breaches of regulatory provisions

(1) If any person fails to comply with a regulatory requirement, that is to say, a requirement imposed under—
  (*a*) paragraph 11 or 12 of Schedule 1, [paragraph 7 of Schedule 1A][6] . . . [9] [or paragraph 5 of Schedule 3A][10]; or
  (*b*) any regulations made under section 48 requiring a VAT representative, for the purposes of registration, to notify the Commissioners that his appointment has taken effect or has ceased to have effect; or
  [(*ba*) paragraph 2(3B) of Schedule 11; or][4]
  (*c*) paragraph 6(1) or 7 of Schedule 11; or
  (*d*) any regulations or rules made under this Act, other than rules made under paragraph 9 of Schedule 12; or
  (*e*) any order made by the Treasury under this Act; or
  (*f*) any regulations made under the European Communities Act 1972 and relating to VAT [; or
  (*g*) section 18A in the form of a condition imposed by the Commissioners under subsection (1) or (6) of that section;][1] [or
  (*h*) section 77E (display of VAT registration numbers on online marketplaces),][7]
he shall be liable, subject to subsections (8) and (9) below and section 76(6), to a penalty equal to the prescribed rate multiplied by the number of days on which the failure continues (up to a maximum of 100) or, if it is greater, to a penalty of £50.
(2) If any person fails to comply with a requirement to preserve records imposed under . . . [10] paragraph 6(3) of Schedule 11, he shall be liable, subject to the following provisions of this section, to a penalty of £500.
(3) Subject to subsection (4) below, in relation to a failure to comply with any regulatory requirement, the prescribed rate shall be determined by reference to the number of occasions in the period of 2 years preceding the beginning of the failure in question on which the person concerned has previously failed to comply with that requirement and, subject to the following provisions of this section, the prescribed rate shall be—
  (*a*) if there has been no such previous occasion in that period, £5;
  (*b*) if there has been only one such occasion in that period, £10; and
  (*c*) in any other case, £15.
(4) For the purposes of subsection (3) above—
  (*a*) a failure to comply with any regulatory requirement shall be disregarded if, as a result of the failure, the person concerned became liable for a surcharge under section 59 [or 59A][2];
  (*b*) a continuing failure to comply with any such requirement shall be regarded as one occasion of failure occurring on the date on which the failure began;
  (*c*) if the same omission gives rise to a failure to comply with more than one such requirement, it shall nevertheless be regarded as the occasion of only one failure; and
  (*d*) in relation to a failure to comply with a requirement imposed by regulations as to the furnishing of a return or as to the payment of VAT, a previous failure to comply with such a requirement as to either of those matters shall be regarded as a previous failure to comply with the requirement in question.
(5) Where the failure referred to in subsection (1) above consists—
  (*a*) in not paying the VAT due in respect of any period within the time required by regulations under section 25(1), or
  (*b*) in not furnishing a return in respect of any period within the time required by regulations under paragraph 2(1) of Schedule 11,
the prescribed rate shall be whichever is the greater of that which is appropriate under subsection (3)(a) to (c) above and an amount equal to one-sixth, one-third or one-half of 1 per cent of the VAT due in respect of that period, the appropriate fraction being determined according to whether subsection (3)(a), (b) or (c) above is applicable.
(6) For the purposes of subsection (5) above, the VAT due—

(a) if the person concerned has furnished a return, shall be taken to be the VAT shown in the return as that for which he is accountable in respect of the period in question, and
(b) in any other case, shall be taken to be such VAT as has been assessed for that period and notified to him under section 73(1).

(7) If it appears to the Treasury that there has been a change in the value of money since 25th July 1985 or, as the case may be, the last occasion when the power conferred by this subsection was exercised, they may by order substitute for the sums for the time being specified in subsections (2) and (3)(a) to (c) above such other sums as appear to them to be justified by the change; but an order under this subsection shall not apply to a failure which began before the date on which the order comes into force.

(8) A failure by any person to comply with any regulatory requirement or the requirement referred to in subsection (2) above shall not give rise to liability to a penalty under this section if the person concerned satisfies the Commissioners or, on appeal, a tribunal that there is a reasonable excuse for the failure; and a failure in respect of which the Commissioners or tribunal have been so satisfied shall be disregarded for the purposes of subsection (3) above.

(9) Where, by reason of conduct falling within subsection (1) or (2) above—
(a) a person is convicted of an offence (whether under this Act or otherwise), or
(b) a person is assessed to a surcharge under section 59 [or 59A]², or
(c) a person is assessed to a penalty under section 60 or 63 [or a penalty under Schedule 24 to the Finance Act 2007]⁵,

that conduct shall not also give rise to liability to a penalty under this section.

(10) This section applies in relation to failures occurring before as well as after the commencement of this Act, and for that purpose any reference to any provision of this Act includes a reference to the corresponding provision of the enactments repealed by this Act.

Commentary—*De Voil Indirect Tax Service* **V5.352, V5.353, V5.354**.
HMRC Manuals—VAT Civil Penalties VCP11156 (action to take with regulatory penalties).
VCP11131 (what are regulatory penalties).
Northern Ireland—See Sch 9ZA para 27 (Northern Ireland: sub-s (1) applies to a failure to comply with a requirement imposed under Sch 9ZA paras 42, 52 or 65(1) or (2)(a) as it applies to a requirement imposed under the provisions mentioned in sub-s (1)(a); sub-s (2) has effect as if after "imposed under" there were inserted "paragraph 64 or 65(2)(b) of Schedule 9ZA or"). See also SI 2020/1546 regs 17, 18 (accounting for VAT on removals: penalties).
Amendments—¹ Words in sub-s (1) added by FA 1996 Sch 3 para 9, with effect from 1 June 1996 (see Finance Act 1996, Section 26, (Appointed Day) Order, SI 1996/1249), and applying to any acquisition of goods from another member State and any supply taking place on or after that day.
² Words in sub-ss (4), (9) inserted by FA 1996 s 35(6), with effect in relation to any prescribed accounting period ending on or after 1 June 1996, but a liability to make a payment on account of VAT shall be disregarded for the purposes of the amendments made by FA 1996 s 35 if the payment is one becoming due before that date.
⁴ Sub-s (1)(ba) inserted by FA 2006 s 19(5), (8) with effect for supplies made on or after 1 June 2007 (by virtue of the Finance Act 2006, section 19, (Appointed Day) Order, SI 2007/1419).
⁵ Words in sub-s (9)(c) inserted by the Finance Act 2008, Schedule 40 (Appointed Day, Transitional Provisions and Consequential Amendments) Order, SI 2009/571 art 8, Sch 1 paras 12, 14 with effect from 1 April 2009.
⁶ In sub-s (1)(a), words inserted by FA 2012 s 203, Sch 28 paras 2, 7 with effect in relation to supplies made or to be made on or after 1 December 2012.
⁷ Sub-s (1)(h) and preceding word inserted by FA 2018 s 38(1). (2) with effect from 15 March 2018.
⁹ In sub-s (1)(a), words ", paragraph 5 of Schedule 2, paragraph 5 of Schedule 3" repealed by the Taxation (Cross-border Trade) Act 2018 s 43, Sch 8 paras 1, 61 with effect from IP completion day (11pm on 31 December 2020), by virtue of SI 2020/1642 reg 4(b).
¹⁰ In sub-s (1)(a) words substituted for words ", paragraph 5 of Schedule 3A or paragraph 9(1) or (2)(a) of Schedule 4B", in sub-s (2) words "paragraph 8 or 9(2)(b) of Schedule 4B or" repealed, by the Taxation (Post-transition Period) Act 2020 s 3, Sch 2 para 7(2) with effect from IP completion day (11pm on 31 December 2020), by virtue of SI 2020/1642 reg 9

[69A Breach of record-keeping requirements etc in relation to transactions in gold
(1) This section applies where a person fails to comply with a requirement of regulations under section 13(5)(a) or (b) of the Finance Act 1999 (gold: duties to keep records or provide information). Where this section applies, the provisions of section 69 do not apply.

(2) A person who fails to comply with any such requirement is liable to a penalty not exceeding 17.5% of the value of the transactions to which the failure relates.

(3) For the purposes of assessing the amount of any such penalty, the value of the transactions to which the failure relates shall be determined by the Commissioners to the best of their judgement and notified by them to the person liable.

(4) No assessment of a penalty under this section shall be made more than 2 years after evidence of facts sufficient in the opinion of the Commissioners to justify the making of the assessment comes to their knowledge.

(5) The reference in subsection (4) above to facts sufficient to justify the making of the assessment is to facts sufficient—
(a) to indicate that there had been a failure to comply with any such requirement as is referred to in subsection (1) above, and
(b) to determine the value of the transactions to which the failure relates.

(6) A failure by any person to comply with any such requirement as is mentioned in subsection (1) above shall not give rise to a liability to a penalty under this section if the person concerned satisfies the Commissioners or, on appeal, a tribunal, that there is a reasonable excuse for the failure.
(7) Where by reason of conduct falling within subsection (1) above a person—
　(a) is assessed to a penalty under section 60 [or a penalty for a deliberate inaccuracy under Schedule 24 to the Finance Act 2007][2], or
　(b) is convicted of an offence (whether under this Act or otherwise),
that conduct shall not also give rise to a penalty under this section.][1]

Commentary—*De Voil Indirect Tax Service* **V5.334**.
HMRC Manuals—VAT Civil Penalties VCP11713 (what penalties can be mitigated).
Amendments—[1]　This section inserted by FA 2000 s 137(1), (2), with effect from 28 July 2000.
[2]　Words in sub-s (7)(b) inserted by the Finance Act 2008, Schedule 40 (Appointed Day, Transitional Provisions and Consequential Amendments) Order, SI 2009/571 art 8, Sch 1 paras 12, 15 with effect from 1 April 2009.

[69B Breach of record-keeping requirements imposed by directions
(1) If any person fails to comply with a requirement imposed under paragraph 6A(1) of Schedule 11, the person is liable to a penalty.
(2) The amount of the penalty is equal to £200 multiplied by the number of days on which the failure continues (up to a maximum of 30 days).
(3) If any person fails to comply with a requirement to preserve records imposed under paragraph 6A(6) of Schedule 11, the person is liable to a penalty of £500.
(4) If it appears to the Treasury that there has been a change in the value of money since—
　(a) the day on which the Finance Act 2006 is passed, or
　(b) (if later) the last occasion when the power conferred by this subsection was exercised,
they may by order substitute for the sums for the time being specified in subsections (2) and (3) such other sums as appear to them to be justified by the change.
(5) But any such order does not apply to a failure which began before the date on which the order comes into force.
(6) A failure by any person to comply with any requirement mentioned in subsection (1) or (3) does not give rise to a liability to a penalty under this section if the person concerned satisfies—
　(a) the Commissioners, or
　(b) on appeal, a tribunal,
that there is a reasonable excuse for the failure.
(7) If by reason of conduct falling within subsection (1) or (3) a person—
　(a) is assessed to a penalty under section 60 [or a penalty for a deliberate inaccuracy under Schedule 24 to the Finance Act 2007][2], or
　(b) is convicted of an offence (whether under this Act or otherwise),
that conduct does not also give rise to a penalty under this section.][1]

Commentary—*De Voil Indirect Tax Service* **V5.356A**.
HMRC Manuals—VAT Fraud VATF35520-355540 (making and issuing a notice of direction).
Amendments—[1]　Inserted by FA 2006 s 21(2) with effect from 19 July 2006.
[2]　Words in sub-s (7)(a) inserted by the Finance Act 2008, Schedule 40 (Appointed Day, Transitional Provisions and Consequential Amendments) Order, SI 2009/571 art 8, Sch 1 paras 12, 16 with effect from 1 April 2009.

[69C Transactions connected with VAT fraud
(1) A person (T) is liable to a penalty where—
　(a) T has entered into a transaction involving the making of a supply by or to T ("the transaction"), and
　(b) conditions A to C are satisfied.
(2) Condition A is that the transaction was connected with the fraudulent evasion of VAT by another person (whether occurring before or after T entered into the transaction).
(3) Condition B is that T knew or should have known that the transaction was connected with the fraudulent evasion of VAT by another person.
(4) Condition C is that HMRC have issued a decision ("the denial decision") in relation to the supply which—
　(a) prevents T from exercising or relying on a VAT right in relation to the supply,
　(b) is based on the facts which satisfy conditions A and B in relation to the transaction, and
　(c) applies a relevant principle of EU case law (whether or not in circumstances that are the same as the circumstances in which any relevant case was decided by the European Court of Justice).
(5) In this section "VAT right" includes the right to deduct input tax, the right to apply a zero rate to international supplies and any other right connected with VAT in relation to a supply.
(6) The relevant principles of EU case law for the purposes of this section are the principles established by the European Court of Justice in the following cases—
　(a) joined Cases C-439/04 and C-440/04 *Axel Kittel v. Belgian State*; *Belgium v. Recolta Recycling* (denial of right to deduct input tax), and

(b) Case C-273/11 Mecsek-Gabona Kft v Nemzeti Adó- és Vámhivatal Dél-dunántúli Regionális Adó Főigazgatósága (denial of right to zero rate),

as developed or extended by that Court [in any other cases][2] relating to the denial or refusal of a VAT right in order to prevent abuses of the VAT system [which were decided before the coming into force of section 42 of TCTA 2018][2].

(7) The penalty payable under this section is 30% of the potential lost VAT.

(8) The potential lost VAT is—
   (a) the additional VAT which becomes payable by T as a result of the denial decision,
   (b) the VAT which is not repaid to T as a result of that decision, or
   (c) in a case where as a result of that decision VAT is not repaid to T and additional VAT becomes payable by T, the aggregate of the VAT that is not repaid and the additional VAT.

(9) Where T is liable to a penalty under this section the Commissioners may assess the amount of the penalty and notify it to T accordingly.

(10) No assessment of a penalty under this section may be made more than two years after the denial decision is issued.

(11) The assessment of a penalty under this section may be made immediately after the denial decision is made (and notice of the assessment may be given to T in the same document as the notice of the decision).

(12) Where by reason of actions involved in making a claim to exercise or rely on a VAT right in relation to a supply T—
   (a) is liable to a penalty for an inaccuracy under paragraph 1 of Schedule 24 to the Finance Act 2007 for which T has been assessed (and the assessment has not been successfully appealed against by T or withdrawn), or
   (b) is convicted of an offence (whether under this Act or otherwise),
those actions do not give rise to liability to a penalty under this section.][1]

Commentary—*De Voil Indirect Tax Service* **V5.360I.**
HMRC Manuals—VAT Fraud VATF45131 (A penalty for transactions connected with VAT fraud).
Amendments—[1] Sections 69C–69E inserted by F(No 2)A 2017 s 68(1), (2) with effect from 16 November 2017. This section does not apply in relation to transactions entered into before that date (F(No 2)A 2017 s 68(7)).
[2] In sub-s (6), in words after para (b), words substituted for words "(whether before or after the coming into force of this section) in other cases", and words inserted, by the Taxation (Cross-border Trade) Act 2018 s 43, Sch 8 paras 1, 62 with effect from IP completion day (11pm on 31 December 2020), by virtue of SI 2020/1642 reg 4(b).

[69D Penalties under section 69C: officers' liability

(1) Where—
   (a) a company is liable to a penalty under section 69C, and
   (b) the actions of the company which give rise to that liability were attributable to an officer of the company ("the officer"),
the officer is liable to pay such portion of the penalty (which may be equal to or less than 100%) as HMRC may specify in a notice given to the officer (a "decision notice").

(2) Before giving the officer a decision notice HMRC must—
   (a) inform the officer that they are considering doing so, and
   (b) afford the officer the opportunity to make representations about whether a decision notice should be given or the portion that should be specified.

(3) A decision notice—
   (a) may not be given before the amount of the penalty due from the company has been assessed (but it may be given immediately after that has happened), and
   (b) may not be given more than two years after the denial decision relevant to that penalty was issued.

(4) Where the Commissioners have specified a portion of the penalty in a decision notice given to the officer—
   (a) section 70 applies to the specified portion as to a penalty under section 69C,
   (b) the officer must pay the specified portion before the end of the period of 30 days beginning with the day on which the notice is given,
   (c) section 76(9) applies as if the decision notice were an assessment notified under section 76, and
   (d) a further decision notice may be given in respect of a portion of any additional amount assessed in an additional assessment.

(5) HMRC may not recover more than 100% of the penalty through issuing decision notices in relation to two or more persons.

(6) A person is not liable to pay an amount by virtue of this section if the actions of the company concerned are attributable to the person by reference to conduct for which the person has been convicted of an offence.

In this subsection "conduct" includes omissions.

(7) In this section "company" means a body corporate or unincorporated association but does not include a partnership, a local authority or a local authority association.

(8) In its application to a body corporate other than a limited liability partnership "officer" means—
  (a) a director (including a shadow director within the meaning of section 251 of the Companies Act 2006),
  (b) a manager, or
  (c) a secretary.
(9) In in its application to a limited liability partnership "officer" means a member.
(10) In its application in any other case, "officer" means—
  (a) a director,
  (b) a manager,
  (c) a secretary, or
  (d) any other person managing or purporting to manage any of the company's affairs.][1]

Commentary—*De Voil Indirect Tax Service* **V5.360I**.
HMRC Manuals—VATF45131 (A penalty for transactions connected with VAT fraud).
Amendments—[1]   Sections 69C–69E inserted by F(No 2)A 2017 s 68(1), (2) with effect from 16 November 2017.

[69E Publication of details of persons liable to penalties under section 69C
(1) The Commissioners may publish information about a person if—
  (a) in consequence of an investigation the person has been found liable to one or more penalties under section 69C (the amount of which has been assessed), and
  (b) the potential lost VAT in relation to the penalty (or the aggregate of the potential lost VAT in relation to each of the penalties) exceeds £50,000.
(2) The information that may be published under subsection (1) is—
  (a) the person's name (including any trading name, previous name or pseudonym),
  (b) the person's address (or registered office),
  (c) the nature of any business carried on by the person,
  (d) the amount of the penalty or penalties in question,
  (e) the periods or times to which the actions giving rise to the penalty or penalties relate,
  (f) any other information that the Commissioners consider it appropriate to publish in order to make clear the person's identity.
(3) In a case where—
  (a) the requirements in subsection (1)(a) and (b) are met in relation to a penalty or penalties for which a company is liable,
  (b) information about the company is published by virtue of this section,
  (c) a person ("the officer") has been given a decision notice under section 69D specifying a portion of the penalty (or, if there is more than one penalty, of any of the penalties) payable by the company as a portion which the officer is liable to pay, and
  (d) the amount (or, if the decision notice specifies portions of more than one penalty, the aggregate amount) which the officer is liable to pay under the decision notice exceeds £25,000,
the Commissioners may publish information about the officer.
(4) The information that may be published under subsection (3) is—
  (a) the officer's name,
  (b) the officer's address,
  (c) the officer's position (or former position) in the company,
  (d) the amount of any penalty imposed on the company of which a portion is payable by the officer under the decision notice and the portion so payable,
  (e) the periods or times to which the actions giving rise to any such penalty relate,
  (f) any other information that the Commissioners consider it appropriate to publish in order to make clear the officer's identity.
(5) Information published under this section may be published in any manner that the Commissioners consider appropriate.
(6) Before publishing any information under this section the Commissioners must—
  (a) inform the person or officer to which it relates that they are considering doing so (in the case of an officer, on the assumption that they publish information about the company), and
  (b) afford the person or officer the opportunity to make representations about whether it should be published.
(7) No information may be published under subsection (1) before the day on which the penalty becomes final or, where more than one penalty is involved, the latest day on which any of the penalties becomes final.
(8) No information may be published under subsection (1) for the first time after the end of the period of one year beginning with that day.
(9) No information may be published under subsection (3) before whichever is the later of—
  (a) the day mentioned in subsection (7), and
  (b) the day on which the decision notice given to the officer becomes final.
(10) No information may be published under subsection (3) for the first time after the end of the period of one year beginning with the later of the two days mentioned in subsection (9).

(11) No information may be published (or continue to be published) under subsection (1) or (3) after the end of the period of three years beginning with the day mentioned in subsection (7).
(12) For the purposes of this section a penalty or a decision notice becomes final when the time for any appeal or further appeal relating to it expires or, if later, any appeal or final appeal relating to it is finally determined.
(13) The Treasury may by regulations made by statutory instrument—
   (a) amend subsection (1) to vary the amount for the time being specified in paragraph (b), or
   (b) amend subsection (3) to vary the amount for the time being specified in paragraph (d).
(14) A statutory instrument containing regulations under subsection (13) is subject to annulment in pursuance of a resolution of the House of Commons.]¹

Commentary—*De Voil Indirect Tax Service* **V5.360I**.
HMRC Manuals—VAT fraud VATF45131 (A penalty for transactions connected with VAT fraud).
Amendments—¹   Sections 69C–69E inserted by F(No 2)A 2017 s 68(1), (2) with effect from 16 November 2017.

70 Mitigation of penalties under sections 60, 63, 64[, 67, 69A and 69C]

(1) Where a person is liable to a penalty under section 60, 63, 64[, 67[, 69A or 69C]³]¹ [or under paragraph 10 of Schedule 11A]², the Commissioners or, on appeal, a tribunal may reduce the penalty to such amount (including nil) as they think proper.
(2) In the case of a penalty reduced by the Commissioners under subsection (1) above, a tribunal, on an appeal relating to the penalty, may cancel the whole or any part of the reduction made by the Commissioners.
(3) None of the matters specified in subsection (4) below shall be matters which the Commissioners or any tribunal shall be entitled to take into account in exercising their powers under this section.
(4) Those matters are—
   (a) the insufficiency of the funds available to any person for paying any VAT due or for paying the amount of the penalty;
   (b) the fact that there has, in the case in question or in that case taken with any other cases, been no or no significant loss of VAT;
   (c) the fact that the person liable to the penalty or a person acting on his behalf has acted in good faith.
[(5) In the application of subsections (3) and (4) in relation to a penalty under section 69C, subsection (4) has effect with the omission of paragraphs (b) and (c).]³

Commentary—*De Voil Indirect Tax Service* **V5.334**.
HMRC Manuals—VAT Civil Penalties VCP11253 (mitigation - penalties).
Amendments—¹   Words in sub-s (1) substituted for "or 67" by FA 2000 s 137(1), (3), with effect from 28 July 2000.
²   Words in sub-s (1) inserted by FA 2004 s 19, Sch 2 para 3 with effect from the passing of FA 2004, so far as is necessary for enabling the making of any orders or regulations by virtue of FA 2004 Sch 2, and otherwise with effect from such day as the Treasury may by order made by statutory instrument appoint.
³   In heading, words substituted for words "and 67", in sub-s (1), words substituted for words "or 69A", and sub-s (5) inserted, by F(No 2)A 2017 s 68(1), (3) with effect from 16 November 2017.

71 Construction of sections 59 to 70

(1) For the purpose of any provision of sections 59 to 70 which refers to a reasonable excuse for any conduct—
   (a) an insufficiency of funds to pay any VAT due is not a reasonable excuse; and
   (b) where reliance is placed on any other person to perform any task, neither the fact of that reliance nor any dilatoriness or inaccuracy on the part of the person relied upon is a reasonable excuse.
(2) In relation to a prescribed accounting period, any reference in sections 59 to 69 to credit for input tax includes a reference to any sum which, in a return for that period, is claimed as a deduction from VAT due.

Commentary—*De Voil Indirect Tax Service* **V5.335**.
HMRC Manuals—VAT Civil Penalties VCP10761 (Exclusions and general considerations for reasonable excuse).

72 Offences

(1) If any person is knowingly concerned in, or in the taking of steps with a view to, the fraudulent evasion of VAT by him or any other person, he shall be liable—
   (a) on summary conviction, to a penalty of the statutory maximum or of three times the amount of the VAT, whichever is the greater, or to imprisonment for a term not exceeding 6 months or to both; or
   (b) on conviction on indictment, to a penalty of any amount or to imprisonment for a term not exceeding 7 years or to both.
(2) Any reference in subsection (1) above or subsection (8) below to the evasion of VAT includes a reference to the obtaining of—
   (a) the payment of a VAT credit; or
   (b) a refund under section [35 or 36]³ of this Act or section 22 of the 1983 Act; or
   (c) . . . ³ or
   (d) a repayment under section 39;

and any reference in those subsections to the amount of the VAT shall be construed—
   (i) in relation to VAT itself or a VAT credit, as a reference to the aggregate of the amount (if any) falsely claimed by way of credit for input tax and the amount (if any) by which output tax was falsely understated, and
   (ii) in relation to a refund or repayment falling within paragraph [(b) or (d)]³ above, as a reference to the amount falsely claimed by way of refund or repayment.
(3) If any person—
   (a) with intent to deceive produces, furnishes or sends for the purposes of this Act or otherwise makes use for those purposes of any document which is false in a material particular; or
   (b) in furnishing any information for the purposes of this Act makes any statement which he knows to be false in a material particular or recklessly makes a statement which is false in a material particular,
he shall be liable—
   (i) on summary conviction, to a penalty of the statutory maximum or, where subsection (4) or (5) below applies, to the alternative penalty specified in that subsection if it is greater, or to imprisonment for a term not exceeding 6 months or to both; or
   (ii) on conviction on indictment, to a penalty of any amount or to imprisonment for a term not exceeding 7 years or to both.
(4) In any case where—
   (a) the document referred to in subsection (3)(a) above is a return required under this Act, or
   (b) the information referred to in subsection (3)(b) above is contained in or otherwise relevant to such a return,
the alternative penalty referred to in subsection (3)(i) above is a penalty equal to three times the aggregate of the amount (if any) falsely claimed by way of credit for input tax and the amount (if any) by which output tax was falsely understated.
(5) In any case where—
   (a) the document referred to in subsection (3)(a) above is a claim for a refund under section [35 or 36]³ of this Act or section 22 of the 1983 Act, . . . ³ or for a repayment under section 39, or
   (b) the information referred to in subsection (3)(b) above is contained in or otherwise relevant to such a claim,
the alternative penalty referred to in subsection (3)(i) above is a penalty equal to 3 times the amount falsely claimed.
(6) The reference in subsection (3)(a) above to furnishing, sending or otherwise making use of a document which is false in a material particular, with intent to deceive, includes a reference to furnishing, sending or otherwise making use of such a document, with intent to secure that a machine will respond to the document as if it were a true document.
(7) Any reference in subsection (3)(a) or (6) above to producing, furnishing or sending a document includes a reference to causing a document to be produced, furnished or sent.
(8) Where a person's conduct during any specified period must have involved the commission by him of one or more offences under the preceding provisions of this section, then, whether or not the particulars of that offence or those offences are known, he shall, by virtue of this subsection, be guilty of an offence and liable—
   (a) on summary conviction, to a penalty of the statutory maximum or, if greater, 3 times the amount of any VAT that was or was intended to be evaded by his conduct, or to imprisonment for a term not exceeding 6 months or to both, or
   (b) on conviction on indictment to a penalty of any amount or to imprisonment for a term not exceeding 7 years or to both.
(9) . . . ²
(10) If any person acquires possession of or deals with any goods, or accepts the supply of any services, having reason to believe that VAT on the supply of the goods or services . . . ³ or on the importation of the goods . . . ³ has been or will be evaded, he shall be liable on summary conviction to a penalty of level 5 on the standard scale or three times the amount of the VAT, whichever is the greater.
(11) If any person supplies [or is supplied with]¹ goods or services in contravention of paragraph 4(2) of Schedule 11, he shall be liable on summary conviction to a penalty of level 5 on the standard scale.
(12) Subject to subsection (13) below, sections 145 to 155 of the Management Act (proceedings for offences, mitigation of penalties and certain other matters) shall apply in relation to offences under this Act (which include any act or omission in respect of which a penalty is imposed) and penalties imposed under this Act as they apply in relation to offences and penalties under the customs and excise Acts as defined in that Act; and accordingly in section 154(2) as it applies by virtue of this subsection the reference to duty shall be construed as a reference to VAT.
(13) In subsection (12) above the references to penalties do not include references to penalties under sections 60 to 70.

Commentary—*De Voil Indirect Tax Service* **V5.311, V5.312**.
Northern Ireland—See Sch 9ZA para 28(1) (Northern Ireland: any reference in sub-ss (1) or (8) to the evasion of VAT includes a reference to the obtaining of a refund under regulations made under Sch 9ZA para 5(4) or under para 19, and any reference to the amount of VAT, in relation to such a refund, is to be construed as a reference to the amount falsely claimed by way of refund).
See Sch 9ZA para 28(2), (3) (Northern Ireland: sub-s (5) applies to a claim for a refund under regulations made under Sch 9ZA para 5(4) or under para 19 as it applies to a claim for a refund under the provisions mentioned in sub-s (5)(*a*); sub-s (10) applies where a person has reason to believe that NI acquisition VAT has been or will be evaded as it applies where a person has reason to believe that VAT on the supply of goods or services has been or will be evaded).
Amendments—[1] Words in sub-s (11) inserted by FA 2003 s 17(5) with effect from 10 April 2003.
[2] Sub-s (9) repealed by FA 2007 ss 84, 114, Sch 22 paras 3, 8(a), Sch 27 Pt 5(1) with effect from 1 December 2007 (by virtue of SI 2007/3166 art 3(a)).
[3] The following amendments made by the Taxation (Cross-border Trade) Act 2018 s 43, Sch 8 paras 1, 63 with effect from IP completion day (11pm on 31 December 2020), by virtue of SI 2020/1642 reg 4(*b*)—
- in sub-s (2)—
    (a) in para (*b*), words substituted for words "35, 36 or 40";
    (b) para (*c*) repealed; and
    (c) in para (ii), words substituted for words "(*b*), (*c*) or (*d*)";
- in sub-s (5)(*a*), words substituted for words "35, 36 or 40", and words "for a refund under any regulations made by virtue of section 13(5)" repealed; and
- in sub-s (10), words ", on the acquisition of the goods from another member State" and "from a place outside the member States" repealed.
Sub-s (2)(*c*) previously read as follows—
    "(*c*) a refund under any regulations made by virtue of section 13(5);".

Assessments of VAT and other payments due

73 Failure to make returns etc
(1) Where a person has failed to make any returns required under this Act (or under any provision repealed by this Act) or to keep any documents and afford the facilities necessary to verify such returns or where it appears to the Commissioners that such returns are incomplete or incorrect, they may assess the amount of VAT due from him to the best of their judgment and notify it to him.
(2) In any case where, for any prescribed accounting period, there has been paid or credited to any person—
   (*a*) as being a repayment or refund of VAT, or
   (*b*) as being due to him as a VAT credit,
an amount which ought not to have been so paid or credited, or which would not have been so paid or credited had the facts been known or been as they later turn out to be, the Commissioners may assess that amount as being VAT due from him for that period and notify it to him accordingly.
(3) An amount—
   (*a*) which has been paid to any person as being due to him as a VAT credit, and
   (*b*) which, by reason of the cancellation of that person's registration under paragraph 13(2) to (6) of Schedule 1, [paragraph 9 or 11 of Schedule 1A][4] . . . [6] [or paragraph 6(1) or (2) of Schedule 3A][2] ought not to have been so paid,
may be assessed under subsection (2) above notwithstanding that cancellation.
(4) Where a person is assessed under subsections (1) and (2) above in respect of the same prescribed accounting period the assessments may be combined and notified to him as one assessment.
(5) Where the person failing to make a return, or making a return which appears to the Commissioners to be incomplete or incorrect, was required to make the return as a personal representative, trustee in bankruptcy, [trustee in sequestration][5], receiver, liquidator or person otherwise acting in a representative capacity in relation to another person, subsection (1) above shall apply as if the reference to VAT due from him included a reference to VAT due from that other person.
(6) An assessment under subsection (1), (2) or (3) above of an amount of VAT due for any prescribed accounting period must be made within the time limits provided for in section 77 and shall not be made after the later of the following—
   (*a*) 2 years after the end of the prescribed accounting period; or
   (*b*) one year after evidence of facts, sufficient in the opinion of the Commissioners to justify the making of the assessment, comes to their knowledge,
but (subject to that section) where further such evidence comes to the Commissioners' knowledge after the making of an assessment under subsection (1), (2) or (3) above, another assessment may be made under that subsection, in addition to any earlier assessment.
[(6A) In the case of an assessment under subsection (2), the prescribed accounting period referred to in subsection (6)(*a*) and in section 77(1)(*a*) is the prescribed accounting period in which the repayment or refund of VAT, or the VAT credit, was paid or credited.][3]
(7) Where a taxable person—
   (*a*) has in the course or furtherance of a business carried on by him, been supplied with any goods . . . [6] or otherwise obtained possession or control of any goods, or
   (*b*) has, in the course or furtherance of such a business, imported any goods . . . [6],

the Commissioners may require him from time to time to account for the goods; and if he fails to prove that the goods have been or are available to be supplied by him or have been exported or otherwise removed from the United Kingdom without being exported or so removed by way of supply or have been lost or destroyed, they may assess to the best of their judgment and notify to him the amount of VAT that would have been chargeable in respect of the supply of the goods if they had been supplied by him.

[(7A) Where a fiscal warehousekeeper has failed to pay VAT required by the Commissioners under section 18E(2), the Commissioners may assess to the best of their judgment the amount of that VAT due from him and notify it to him.

(7B) Where it appears to the Commissioners that goods have been removed from a warehouse or fiscal warehouse without payment of the VAT payable under section 18(4) or section 18D on that removal, they may assess to the best of their judgment the amount of VAT due from the person removing the goods or other person liable and notify it to him][1].

(8) In any case where—
- (a) as a result of a person's failure to make a return for a prescribed accounting period, the Commissioners have made an assessment under subsection (1) above for that period,
- (b) the VAT assessed has been paid but no proper return has been made for the period to which the assessment related, and
- (c) as a result of a failure to make a return for a later prescribed accounting period, being a failure by a person referred to in paragraph (a) above or a person acting in a representative capacity in relation to him, as mentioned in subsection (5) above, the Commissioners find it necessary to make another assessment under subsection (1) above,

then, if the Commissioners think fit, having regard to the failure referred to in paragraph (a) above, they may specify in the assessment referred to in paragraph (c) above an amount of VAT greater than that which they would otherwise have considered to be appropriate.

(9) Where an amount has been assessed and notified to any person under subsection (1), (2), (3) [, (7), (7A) or (7B)][1] above it shall, subject to the provisions of this Act as to appeals, be deemed to be an amount of VAT due from him and may be recovered accordingly, unless, or except to the extent that, the assessment has subsequently been withdrawn or reduced.

(10) For the purposes of this section notification to a personal representative, trustee in bankruptcy, [trustee in sequestration][5], receiver, liquidator or person otherwise acting as aforesaid shall be treated as notification to the person in relation to whom he so acts.

Commentary—*De Voil Indirect Tax Service* **V5.132B**.
HMRC Manuals—VAT Assessments and Error Correction VAEC1130 (the law supporting time limits).
VAEC1160 (time limits for long first period return assessments).
Northern Ireland—See Sch 9ZA para 29 (Northern Ireland: sub-s (3) applies to an amount which by reason of the cancellation of a person's registration under Sch 9ZA para 43(2), 43(5) or 53(5) ought not to have been paid as it applies to an amount which ought not to have been paid by reason of the cancellation of a person's registration under any of the provisions mentioned in sub-s (3); sub-s (7) applies to the acquisition of goods from a member State by a taxable person as it applies to the supply of goods to a taxable person).
Modifications—VATA 1994 Sch 3BA para 20 (for the purposes of Sch 3BA, modification of this section so that sub-s (1) reads as if reference to returns required under this Act includes relevant non-UK returns, and references in this section to a prescribed accounting period include a tax period).
VATA 1994 Sch 3BA para 21(1)–(3): for the purposes of Sch 3BA, modification of this section as follows—
- sub-ss (3A)–(3C) inserted, and
- reference in sub-s (9) to sub-s (1) of this section includes a reference to sub-s (3A).

Sub-ss (3A)–(3C), for the purposes of this modification, read as follows—
"(3A) Where a person has failed to make an amendment or notification that the person is required to make under paragraph 31 of Schedule 3BA in respect of an increase in the consideration for a UK supply (as defined in paragraph 31(7)), the Commissioners may assess the amount of VAT due from the person as a result of the increase to the best of their judgement and notify it to the person.
(3B) An assessment under subsection (3A)—
(a) is of VAT due for the tax period mentioned in paragraph 31(1)(a) of Schedule 3BA;
(b) must be made within the time limits provided for in section 77, and must not be made after the later of—
(i) 2 years after the end of the tax period referred to in paragraph 31(1)(a);
(ii) one year after evidence of facts sufficient in the opinion of the Commissioners to justify making the assessment comes to their knowledge.
(3C) Subject to section 77, where further evidence such as is mentioned in subsection (3B)(b)(ii) comes to the Commissioners' knowledge after they have made an assessment under subsection (3A), another assessment may be made under that subsection, in addition to any earlier assessment.".

VATA 1994 Sch 3B para 16 (for the purposes of Sch 3B, modification of this section so that sub-s (1) reads as if reference to returns required under this Act includes relevant special scheme returns, and references in this section to a prescribed accounting period include a tax period).
VATA 1994 Sch 3B para 16A(1)–(3): for the purposes of Sch 3B, modification of this section as follows—
- sub-ss (3A)–(3C) inserted, and
- reference in sub-s (9) to sub-s (1) of this section includes a reference to sub-s (3A).

Sub-ss (3A)–(3C), for the purposes of this modification, read as follows—

Commentary—*De Voil Indirect Tax Service* **V5.132B, V5.136A**.
HMRC Manuals—VAT Assessments and Error Correction VAEC3730 (standard notice acquisition of certain goods non taxable person).
Amendments—[1] In sub-s (4), words substituted by the Bankruptcy (Scotland) Act 2016 (Consequential Provisions and Modifications) Order, SI 2016/1034 art 7(1), Sch 1 para 12(1), (3) with effect from 30 November 2016. Note that, as a consequence of the repeal of this section by TCBTA 2018 (see note below), SI 2016/1034 Sch 1 para 12(3) is revoked with effect from IP completion day.
[2] Section 75 repealed by the Taxation (Cross-border Trade) Act 2018 s 43, Sch 8 paras 1, 66 with effect from IP completion day (11pm on 31 December 2020), by virtue of SI 2020/1642 reg 4(b).

76 Assessment of amounts due by way of penalty, interest or surcharge

(1) Where any person is liable—
    (a) to a surcharge under section 59 [or 59A][10] or
    (b) to a penalty under any of sections 60 [to 69C[9], or
    (c) for interest under section 74, [or
    (d) a penalty under regulations made under section 135 of the Finance Act 2002 (mandatory electronic filing of returns) in connection with VAT,][6]
the Commissioners may, subject to subsection (2) below, assess the amount due by way of penalty, interest or surcharge, as the case may be, and notify it to him accordingly; and the fact that any conduct giving rise to a penalty under any of sections 60 [to 69C[9] [or the regulations][6] may have ceased before an assessment is made under this section shall not affect the power of the Commissioners to make such an assessment.

(2) Where a person is liable to a penalty under section 69 for any failure to comply with such a requirement as is referred to in subsection (1)(c) to (f) of that section, no assessment shall be made under this section of the amount due from him by way of such penalty unless, within the period of 2 years preceding the assessment, the Commissioners have issued him with a written warning of the consequences of a continuing failure to comply with that requirement.

(3) In the case of the penalties, interest and surcharge referred to in the following paragraphs, the assessment under this section shall be of an amount due in respect of the prescribed accounting period which in the paragraph concerned is referred to as "the relevant period"—
    (a) in the case of a surcharge under section 59 [or 59A][1], the relevant period is the prescribed accounting period in respect of which the taxable person is in default and in respect of which the surcharge arises;
    (b) in the case of a penalty under section 60 relating to the evasion of VAT, the relevant period is the prescribed accounting period for which the VAT evaded was due;
    (c) in the case of a penalty under section 60 relating to the obtaining of the payment of a VAT credit, the relevant period is the prescribed accounting period in respect of which the payment was obtained;
    (d) in the case of a penalty under section 63, the relevant period is the prescribed accounting period for which liability to VAT was understated or, as the case may be, for which entitlement to a VAT credit was overstated; . . . [6]
    (e) in the case of interest under section 74, the relevant period is the prescribed accounting period in respect of which the VAT (or amount assessed as VAT) was due[; and
    (f) in the case of a penalty under regulations made under section 135 of the Finance Act 2002, the relevant period is the prescribed accounting period in respect of which the contravention of, or failure to comply with, the regulations occurred.][6]

(3A) . . . [10]

(4) In any case where the amount of any penalty, interest or surcharge falls to be calculated by reference to VAT which was not paid at the time it should have been and that VAT (or the supply which gives rise to it) cannot be readily attributed to any one or more prescribed accounting periods, it shall be treated for the purposes of this Act as VAT due for such period or periods as the Commissioners may determine to the best of their judgement and notify to the person liable for the VAT and penalty, interest or surcharge.

(5) Where a person is assessed under this section to an amount due by way of any penalty, interest or surcharge falling within subsection (3) . . . [10] above and is also assessed under section 73(1), (2)[, (7), (7A) or (7B)][2] for the prescribed accounting period which is the relevant period under subsection (3) . . . [10] above, the assessments may be combined and notified to him as one assessment, but the amount of the penalty, interest or surcharge shall be separately identified in the notice.

(6) . . . [10]

(7) In the case of an amount due by way of penalty under section 66 or 69 or interest under section 74—
    (a) a notice of assessment under this section shall specify a date, being not later than the date of the notice, to which the aggregate amount of the penalty which is assessed or, as the case may be, the amount of interest is calculated; and
    (b) if the penalty or interest continues to accrue after that date, a further assessment or assessments may be made under this section in respect of amounts which so accrue.

(8) If, within such period as may be notified by the Commissioners to the person liable to a penalty under section 66 or 69 or for interest under section 74—
   (a) a failure or default falling within section 66(1) or 69(1) is remedied, or
   (b) the VAT or other amount referred to in section 74(1) is paid,
it shall be treated for the purposes of section 66 or 69 or, as the case may be, section 74 as paid or remedied on the date specified as mentioned in subsection (7)(a) above.
(9) If an amount is assessed and notified to any person under this section, then unless, or except to the extent that, the assessment is withdrawn or reduced, that amount shall be recoverable as if it were VAT due from him.
(10) For the purposes of this section, notification to a personal representative, trustee in bankruptcy, [trustee in sequestration][8], receiver, liquidator or person otherwise acting in a representative capacity in relation to [another][3] shall be treated as notification to the person in relation to whom he so acts.
Commentary—*De Voil Indirect Tax Service* **V5.333, V5.336, V5.379.**
HMRC Manuals—VAT Civil Penalties VCP11155 (issuing penalty warning letters).
VCP11167 (action to take with regulatory penalties - letter).
Northern Ireland—See SI 2020/1546 regs 17, 18 (accounting for VAT on removals: penalties).
Modifications—Recovery of Duties and Taxes Etc Due on Other Member States (Corresponding UK Claims, Procedure and Supplementary) (adaptation of this section with respect to VAT interest).
VATA 1994 Sch 3BA para 21(4) (for the purposes of Sch 3BA, modification of this section so that reference in sub-s (5) to s 73(1) includes a reference to s 73(3A)).
References to prescribed accounting periods in this section are to be read in accordance with the modifications made by VATA 1994 Sch 3BA paras 20 and 21, in relation to the use of non-UK special accounting schemes for supplies of e-services (VATA 1994 Sch 3BA para 22).
VATA 1994 Sch 3B para 16A(4) (for the purposes of Sch 3B, modification of this section so that reference in sub-s (5) to s 73(1) includes a reference to s 73(3A)).
References to prescribed accounting periods in this section are to be read in accordance with the modifications made by VATA 1994 Sch 3B paras 16 and 16A, in relation to returns under the non-Union scheme from 1 January 2015 (VATA 1994 Sch 3B para 16B).
Amendments—[1]   Words in sub-s (3) inserted by FA 1996 s 35(7), with effect in relation to any prescribed accounting period ending on or after 1 June 1996, but a liability to make a payment on account of VAT shall be disregarded for the purposes of the amendments made by FA 1996 s 35 if the payment is one becoming due before that date.
[2]   Words in sub-s (5) substituted by FA 1996 Sch 3 para 11, with effect from 1 June 1996 (see Finance Act 1996, Section 26, (Appointed Day) Order, SI 1996/1249), and applying to any acquisition of goods from another member State and any supply taking place on or after that day.
[3]   Word "another" in sub-s(10) substituted by FA 1997 s 45(6) and deemed always to have had effect.
[6]   Sub-s (1)(d) and preceding word "or", words in sub-s (1), and sub-s (3)(f) and preceding word "and", inserted, and in sub-s (3)(d) word "and" repealed, by FA 2007 ss 93(4)–(7), 114, Sch 27 Pt 5(4) with effect from 19 July 2007.
[8]   In sub-s (10), words substituted by the Bankruptcy (Scotland) Act 2016 (Consequential Provisions and Modifications) Order, SI 2016/1034 art 7(1), Sch 1 para 12(1), (4) with effect from 30 November 2016.
[9]   In sub-s (1), words substituted by F(No 2)A 2017 s 68(1), (4) with effect from 16 November 2017.
[10]   The following amendments made by the Taxation (Cross-border Trade) Act 2018 s 43, Sch 8 paras 1, 67 with effect from IP completion day (11pm on 31 December 2020), by virtue of SI 2020/1642 reg 4(b)—
   –   in sub-s (1)(a), words substituted for words ", section 59A, paragraph 16F of Schedule 3B or paragraph 26 of Schedule 3BA";
   –   sub-ss (3A), (6) repealed; and
   –   in sub-s (5), words "or (3A)" repealed (in both places).
Sub-ss (3A), (6) previously read as follows—
   "(3A) In the case of a surcharge under paragraph 16F of Schedule 3B or paragraph 26 of Schedule 3BA, the assessment under this section is of an amount due in respect of "the relevant period", that is to say, the tax period (see section 76A) in respect of which the person is in default and in respect of which the surcharge arises.".
   "(6) An assessment to a penalty under section 67 by virtue of subsection (1)(b) of that section may be combined with an assessment under section 75 and the 2 assessments notified together but the amount of the penalty shall be separately identified in the notice.".

[76A Section 76: cases involving special accounting schemes
(1) References in section 76 to a prescribed accounting period are to be read as including a tax period so far as that is necessary for the purposes of the references in section 76(1)(a) to paragraph 16F of Schedule 3B and paragraph 26 of Schedule 3BA (assessment of surcharge in certain cases involving special accounting schemes).
(2) References in section 77 to a prescribed accounting period are to be read accordingly.
(3) In this section and section 76 "tax period" means a tax period as defined in paragraph 23(1) of Schedule 3B or paragraph 38(1) of Schedule 3BA, as the case requires.][1], [2]
Amendments—[1]   Section 76A inserted by FA 2014 s 103, Sch 22 paras 11, 14 with effect in relation to supplies made on or after 1 January 2015.
[2]   Section 76A repealed by the Taxation (Cross-border Trade) Act 2018 s 43, Sch 8 paras 1, 68 with effect from IP completion day (11pm on 31 December 2020), by virtue of SI 2020/1642 reg 4(b).

77 Assessments: time limits and supplementary assessments
(1) Subject to the following provisions of this section, an assessment under section 73 . . .[6] or 76, shall not be made—

(a) more than [4 years]² after the end of the prescribed accounting period or importation . . . ⁶ concerned, or

(b) in the case of an assessment under section 76 of an amount due by way of a penalty which is not among those referred to in subsection (3) of that section, [4 years]² after the event giving rise to the penalty.

[(2) Subject to subsection (5) below, an assessment under section 76 of an amount due by way of any penalty, interest or surcharge referred to in subsection (3) . . . ⁶ of that section may be made at any time before the expiry of the period of 2 years beginning with the time when the amount of VAT due for the prescribed accounting period concerned has been finally determined.]¹

[(2A) Subject to subsection (5) below, an assessment under section 76 of a penalty under section 65 or 66 may be made at any time before the expiry of the period of 2 years beginning with the time when facts sufficient in the opinion of the Commissioners to indicate, as the case may be—
(a) that the statement in question contained a material inaccuracy, or
(b) that there had been a default within the meaning of section 66(1),
came to the Commissioners' knowledge.]¹

(3) In relation to an assessment under section 76, any reference in subsection (1) or (2) above to the prescribed accounting period concerned is a reference to that period which, in the case of the penalty, interest or surcharge concerned, is the relevant period referred to in subsection (3) . . . ⁶ of that section.

[(4) In any case falling within subsection (4A), an assessment of a person ("P"), or of an amount payable by P, may be made at any time not more than 20 years after the end of the prescribed accounting period or the importation . . . ⁶ or event giving rise to the penalty, as appropriate (subject to subsection (5)).

(4A) Those cases are—
(a) a case involving a loss of VAT brought about deliberately by P (or by another person acting on P's behalf),
(b) a case in which P has participated in a transaction knowing that it was part of arrangements of any kind (whether or not legally enforceable) intended to bring about a loss of VAT,
(c) a case involving a loss of VAT attributable to a failure by P to comply with a notification obligation, and
(d) a case involving a loss of VAT attributable to a scheme in respect of which P has failed to comply with an obligation under paragraph 6 of Schedule 11A [or an obligation under paragraph 17(2) or 18(2) of Schedule 17 to FA 2017]⁵.

(4B) In subsection (4A) the references to a loss of tax brought about deliberately by P or another person include a loss that arises as a result of a deliberate inaccuracy in a document given to Her Majesty's Revenue and Customs by that person.

(4C) In subsection (4A)(c) "notification obligation" means an obligation under—
(a) paragraph 5, 6, 7 or 14(2) or (3) of Schedule 1,
[(aa) paragraph 5, 6 or 13(3) of Schedule 1A,]³ [or]⁶
(b), (c) . . . ⁶
(d) paragraph 3, 4 or 7(2) or (3) of Schedule 3A, . . . ⁶
(e) . . . ⁶]²

(5) Where, after a person's death, the Commissioners propose to assess a sum as due by reason of some conduct (howsoever described) of the deceased, including a sum due by way of penalty, interest or surcharge—
(a) the assessment shall not be made more than [4 years]² after the death; . . . ²
(b) . . . ²

(6) If, otherwise than in circumstances falling within section 73(6)(b) . . . ⁶, it appears to the Commissioners that the amount which ought to have been assessed in an assessment under that section or under section 76 exceeds the amount which was so assessed, then—
(a) under the like provision as that assessment was made, and
(b) on or before the last day on which that assessment could have been made,
the Commissioners may make a supplementary assessment of the amount of the excess and shall notify the person concerned accordingly.

Commentary—*De Voil Indirect Tax Service* V5.134, V5.136, V5.136B.
HMRC Manuals—VAT Assessments and Error Correction VAEC6210 (when to use supplementary assessments).
VAEC1160 (time limits for long first period return assessments).
VAEC1360 (power of assessment: twenty year assessments).
Northern Ireland—See Sch 9ZA para 32 (Northern Ireland: this section has effect as if modified as follows—
- in sub-s (1), in the words before paragraph (a), after "or 76" there were inserted "or paragraph 31 of Schedule 9ZA";
- in sub-s (1)(a), after "importation" there were inserted "or acquisition";
- in sub-s (4), after "importation" there were inserted ", acquisition";
- in sub-s (4C) after paragraph (a) there were inserted—
    "(aza) paragraph 40 or 44(2) of Schedule 9ZA,
    (azb) paragraph 50 of that Schedule,
    (azc) regulations under paragraph 73(4) of that Schedule,";

- in sub-s (6), after "73(6)(b)" there were inserted "or paragraph 31(2)(b) of Schedule 9ZA".

Modifications—References to prescribed accounting periods in this section are to be read in accordance with the modifications made by VATA 1994 Sch 3BA paras 20 and 21, in relation to the use of non-UK special accounting schemes for supplies of e-services (VATA 1994 Sch 3BA para 22).

References to prescribed accounting periods in this section are to be read in accordance with the modifications made by VATA 1994 Sch 3B paras 16 and 16A, in relation to returns under the non-Union scheme from 1 January 2015 (VATA 1994 Sch 3B para 16B).

Amendments—[1] Sub-s (2) substituted and sub-s (2A) inserted by FA 1999 s 18 with effect in relation to any amount by way of penalty, interest or surcharge which becomes due on or after 27 July 1999.

[2] In sub-ss (1)(a), (b), (5)(a), words substituted, sub-ss (4)–(4C) substituted for previous sub-s (4), and sub-s (5)(b) and preceding word "and" repealed, by FA 2008 Sch 39 para 34 with effect from 1 April 2009 (by virtue of SI 2009/403 art 2(2)). FA 2008 Sch 39 para 34 is disregarded where—
- for the purposes of VATA 1994 s 77, the end of the prescribed accounting period or the importation, acquisition or event giving rise to the penalty, as appropriate, occurred on or before 31 March 2006; and
- after a person's death, a sum is assessed as due by reason of some conduct (however described) of the deceased, including a sum due by way of penalty, interest or surcharge, and the date of the death is on or before 31 March 2006 (SI 2009/403 art 4).Sub-s (4A)(c), (d) shall not apply where the end of the prescribed accounting period or the importation, acquisition or event giving rise to the penalty, as appropriate, occurred on or before 31 March 2010, except where VAT has been lost in circumstances giving rise to a penalty under VATA 1994 s 67 (SI 2009/403 art 9).

[3] Sub-s (4C)(aa) inserted by FA 2012 s 203, Sch 28 paras 2, 10 with effect in relation to supplies made or to be made on or after 1 December 2012.

[5] In sub-s (4A)(d), words inserted by F(No 2)A 2017 s 66, Sch 17 para 51 with effect from 1 January 2018.

[6] The following amendments made by the Taxation (Cross-border Trade) Act 2018 s 43, Sch 8 paras 1, 69 with effect from IP completion day (11pm on 31 December 2020), by virtue of SI 2020/1642 reg 4(b)—
- in sub-s (1), in opening words reference ", 75" repealed, and in para (a) words "or acquisition" repealed;
- in sub-ss (2), (3), words "or (3A)" repealed;
- in sub-s (4), word ", acquisition" repealed;
- in sub-s (4C), in para (aa) word "or" inserted, and paras (b), (c), (e) (including word "or" before paragraph (e)) repealed; and
- in sub-s (6), words "or 75(2)(b)" repealed.

Sub-s (4C)(b), (c), (e) previously read as follows—
  "(b)   paragraph 3 of Schedule 2,
  (c)   paragraph 3 or 8(2) of Schedule 3,".
  "(e)   regulations under paragraph 2(4) of Schedule 11.".

[Liability for unpaid VAT of another]

77A Joint and several liability of traders in supply chain where tax unpaid

(1) This section applies to goods [which fall within any one or more][2] of the following descriptions—

[(a) any equipment made or adapted for use as a telephone and any other equipment made or adapted for use in connection with telephones or telecommunication;

(b) any equipment made or adapted for use as a computer and any other equipment made or adapted for use in connection with computers or computer systems (including, in particular, positional determination devices for use with satellite navigation systems);

(c) any other electronic equipment made or adapted for use by individuals for the purposes of leisure, amusement or entertainment and any other equipment made or adapted for use in connection with any such electronic equipment;

and in this subsection "other equipment" includes parts, accessories and software.][2]

(2) Where—

(a) a taxable supply of goods to which this section applies has been made to a taxable person, and

(b) at the time of the supply the person knew or had reasonable grounds to suspect that some or all of the VAT payable in respect of that supply, or on any previous or subsequent supply of those goods, would go unpaid,

the Commissioners may serve on him a notice specifying the amount of the VAT so payable that is unpaid, and stating the effect of the notice.

(3) The effect of a notice under this section is that—

(a) the person served with the notice, and

(b) the person liable, apart from this section, for the amount specified in the notice,

are jointly and severally liable to the Commissioners for that amount.

(4) For the purposes of subsection (2) above the amount of VAT that is payable in respect of a supply is the lesser of—

(a) the amount chargeable on the supply, and

(b) the amount shown as due on the supplier's return for the prescribed accounting period in question (if he has made one) together with any amount assessed as due from him for that period (subject to any appeal by him).

(5) The reference in subsection (4)(b) above to assessing an amount as due from a person includes a reference to the case where, because it is impracticable to do so, the amount is not notified to him.

(6) For the purposes of subsection (2) above, a person shall be presumed to have reasonable grounds for suspecting matters to be as mentioned in paragraph (*b*) of that subsection if the price payable by him for the goods in question—
  (*a*) was less than the lowest price that might reasonably be expected to be payable for them on the open market, or
  (*b*) was less than the price payable on any previous supply of those goods.
(7) The presumption provided for by subsection (6) above is rebuttable on proof that the low price payable for the goods was due to circumstances unconnected with failure to pay VAT.
(8) Subsection (6) above is without prejudice to any other way of establishing reasonable grounds for suspicion.
[(9) The Treasury may by order amend subsection (1) above.
(9A) The Treasury may by order amend this section in order to extend or otherwise alter the circumstances in which a person shall be presumed to have reasonable grounds for suspecting matters to be as mentioned in subsection (2)(*b*) above.
(9B) Any order under this section may make such incidental, supplemental, consequential or transitional provision as the Treasury think fit.]³
(10) For the purposes of this section—
  (*a*) "goods" includes services;
  (*b*) an amount of VAT counts as unpaid only to the extent that it exceeds the amount of any refund due.]¹

Commentary—*De Voil Indirect Tax Service* **V3.502**.
HMRC Manuals—VAT Joint and Several Liability JSL2150 (what is meant by other equipment).
JSL2250 (presumption).
Amendments—¹ This section inserted by FA 2003 s 18(1) with effect from 10 April 2003.
² In sub-s (1) words substituted, and paras (*a*)–(*c*) substituted for original paras (*a*), (*b*), by the VAT (Amendment of section 77A of the VATA 1994) Order, SI 2007/939 reg 2 with effect from 1 May 2007.
³ Sub-ss (9)–(9B) substituted for original sub-s (9) by FA 2007 s 98(1) with effect from 19 July 2007.

[Online marketplaces]

[77B Joint and several liability: [sellers identified as non-compliant by the Commissioners]
(1) This section applies where a person ("P") . . . ²—
  (*a*) makes taxable supplies of goods through an online marketplace, and
  (*b*) fails to comply with any requirement imposed on P by or under this Act (whether or not it relates to those supplies).
(2) The Commissioners may give the person who is the operator of the online marketplace ("the operator") a notice—
  (*a*) stating that, unless the operator secures the result mentioned in subsection (3), subsection (5) will apply, and
  (*b*) explaining the effect of subsection (5).
(3) The result referred to in subsection (2)(*a*) is that P does not offer goods for sale through the online marketplace at any time between—
  (*a*) the end of such period as may be specified in the notice, and
  (*b*) the notice ceasing to have effect.
(4) If the operator does not secure the result mentioned in subsection (3), subsection (5) applies.
(5) The operator is jointly and severally liable to the Commissioners for the amount of VAT payable by P in respect of all taxable supplies of goods made by P through the online marketplace in the period for which the notice has effect.
(6) A notice under subsection (2) ("the liability notice") has effect for the period beginning with the day after the day on which it is given, and ending—
  (*a*) with the day specified in a notice given by the Commissioners under subsection (7), or
  (*b*) in accordance with subsection (8).
(7) The Commissioners may at any time give the operator a notice stating that the period for which the liability notice has effect ends with the day specified in the notice.
(8) If the person to whom the liability notice is given ceases to be the operator of the online marketplace, the liability notice ceases to have effect at the end of—
  (*a*) the day on which the person ceases to be the operator, or
  (*b*) (if later) the day on which the person notifies the Commissioners that the person is no longer the operator.
(9) . . . ³
(10) . . . ²
(11) The Treasury may by regulations provide that supplies made or goods offered for sale in circumstances specified in the regulations are, or are not, to be treated for the purposes of this section as having been made or offered through an online marketplace.
(12) . . . ³]¹

Commentary—*De Voil Indirect Tax Service* **V3.502**.
Amendments—¹ Sections 77B–77D inserted by FA 2016 s 124(1), (2) with effect from 15 September 2016.

[2] Crosshead inserted; in section heading, words substituted; in sub-s (1), words repealed; and sub-s (10) repealed; by FA 2018 s 38(1), (3), (4) with effect from 15 March 2018.
[3] Sub-ss (9), (12) repealed by the Taxation (Post-transition Period) Act 2020 s 7, Sch 3 paras 1, 8 with effect from IP completion day (11pm on 31 December 2020), by virtue of SI 2020/1642 reg 9. Those subsections previously read as follows—
"(9) In this section—
"online marketplace" means a website, or any other means by which information is made available over the internet, through which persons other than the operator are able to offer goods for sale (whether or not the operator also does so);
"operator", in relation to an online marketplace, means the person who controls access to, and the contents of, the online marketplace.".
"(12) The Treasury may by regulations amend this section so as to alter the meaning of—
"online marketplace",
"operator". ".

[77BA Joint and several liability: non-UK sellers in breach of Schedule 1A registration requirement

(1) This section applies where—
  (a) a person ("P") who makes taxable supplies of goods through an online marketplace is in breach of a Schedule 1A registration requirement, and
  (b) the operator of the online marketplace knows, or should know, that P is in breach of a Schedule 1A registration requirement.
(2) If the operator of the online marketplace does not secure the result in subsection (3), subsection (4) applies.
(3) The result referred to in subsection (2) is that P does not offer goods for sale through the online marketplace in any period between—
  (a) the end of the period of 60 days beginning with the day on which the operator first knew, or should have known, that P was in breach of a Schedule 1A registration requirement, and
  (b) P ceasing to be in breach of a Schedule 1A registration requirement.
(4) The operator is jointly and severally liable to the Commissioners for the amount of VAT payable by P in respect of all taxable supplies of goods made by P through the online marketplace in the relevant period.
(5) The relevant period is the period—
  (a) beginning with the day on which the operator first knew, or should have known, that P was in breach of a Schedule 1A registration requirement, and
  (b) ending with P ceasing to be in breach of a Schedule 1A registration requirement.
(6) But if the operator has been given a notice under section 77B in respect of P, the relevant period does not include—
  (a) any period for which the operator is jointly and severally liable for the amount mentioned in subsection (4) by virtue of section 77B, or
  (b) if the operator secures the result mentioned in section 77B(3), the period beginning with the day on which the operator is given the notice and ending with the day on which the operator secures that result.
(7) P is in breach of a Schedule 1A registration requirement if P is liable to be registered under Schedule 1A to this Act, but is not so registered.
(8) . . . [2]][1]

Commentary—*De Voil Indirect Tax Service* **V3.502**.
Amendments—[1] Section 77BA inserted by FA 2018 s 38(1), (5) with effect from 15 March 2018.
[2] Sub-s (8) repealed by the Taxation (Post-transition Period) Act 2020 s 7, Sch 3 paras 1, 9 with effect from IP completion day (11pm on 31 December 2020), by virtue of SI 2020/1642 reg 9.
Sub-s (8) previously read as follows—
"(8) In this section "online marketplace" and "operator", in relation to an online marketplace, have the same meaning as in section 77B.".

[77C Joint and several liability under section 77B [or 77BA]: assessments

(1) The Commissioners may assess the amount of VAT due from the operator of an online marketplace by virtue of section 77B [or 77BA][2] to the best of their judgment and notify it to the operator.
(2) Subject to subsections (3) to (6), an assessment may be made for such period or periods as the Commissioners consider appropriate.
(3) An assessment for any month may not be made after the end of—
  (a) 2 years after the end of that month, or
  (b) (if later) one year after evidence of facts, sufficient in the opinion of the Commissioners to justify the making of an assessment for that month, comes to their knowledge.
(4) Subsection (5) applies if, after the Commissioners have made an assessment for a period, evidence of facts sufficient in the opinion of the Commissioners to justify the making of a further assessment for that period comes to their knowledge.
(5) The Commissioners may, no later than one year after that evidence comes to their knowledge, make a further assessment for that period (subject to subsection (6)).

(6) An assessment or further assessment for a month may not be made more than 4 years after the end of the month.
(7) An amount which has been assessed and notified to a person under this section is deemed to be an amount of VAT due from the person and may be recovered accordingly (unless, or except to the extent that, the assessment is subsequently withdrawn or reduced).
(8) Subsection (7) is subject to the provisions of this Act as to appeals.
(9) . . . ³]¹

Commentary—*De Voil Indirect Tax Service* **V5.136A, V5.132B**.
Amendments—¹ Sections 77B–77D inserted by FA 2016 s 124(1), (2) with effect from 15 September 2016.
² In heading and sub-s (1), words inserted by FA 2018 s 38(1), (6) with effect from 15 March 2018.
³ Sub-s (9) repealed by the Taxation (Post-transition Period) Act 2020 s 7, Sch 3 paras 1, 10 with effect from IP completion day (11pm on 31 December 2020), by virtue of SI 2020/1642 reg 9. Sub-s (9) previously read as follows—
 "(9) In this section "online marketplace" and "operator", in relation to an online marketplace, have the same meaning as in section 77B.".

[77D Joint and several liability under section 77B [or 77BA]: interest
(1) If an amount assessed under section 77C is not paid before the end of the period of 30 days beginning with the day on which notice of the assessment is given, the amount assessed carries interest from the day on which the notice of assessment is given until payment.
(2) Interest under this section is payable at the rate applicable under section 197 of the Finance Act 1996.
(3) Where the operator of an online marketplace is liable for interest under this section the Commissioners may assess the amount due and notify it to the operator.
(4) A notice of assessment under this section must specify a date (not later than the date of the notice) to which the interest is calculated.
(5) A further assessment or assessments may be made under this section in respect of any interest accrued after that date.
(6) An amount of interest assessed and notified to the operator of an online marketplace under this section is recoverable as if it were VAT due from the operator (unless, or except to the extent that, the assessment is withdrawn or reduced).
(7) Interest under this section is to be paid without any deduction of income tax.
(8) . . . ³]¹

Commentary—*De Voil Indirect Tax Service* **V5.361, V5.364**.
Amendments—¹ Sections 77B–77D inserted by FA 2016 s 124(1), (2) with effect from 15 September 2016.
² In heading, words inserted by FA 2018 s 38(1), (7) with effect from 15 March 2018.
³ Sub-s (8) repealed by the Taxation (Post-transition Period) Act 2020 s 7, Sch 3 paras 1, 11 with effect from IP completion day (11pm on 31 December 2020), by virtue of SI 2020/1642 reg 9. Sub-s (8) previously read as follows—
 "(8) In this section "online marketplace" and "operator", in relation to an online marketplace, have the same meaning as in section 77B.".

[77E Display of VAT registration numbers
(1) This section applies where a person ("P") offers, or proposes to offer, goods for sale through an online marketplace.
(2) The operator of the online marketplace must take reasonable steps to check that—
 (a) any number provided to the operator (by P or another person) as P's VAT registration number is valid, and
 (b) any number displayed on the online marketplace as P's VAT registration number (under subsection (3) or otherwise) is valid.
(3) If a number is provided to the operator (by P or another person) as P's VAT registration number and the number is valid, the operator must secure that it is displayed on the online marketplace as P's VAT registration number no later than the time mentioned in subsection (4).
(4) The time is—
 (a) the end of the period of 10 days beginning with the day on which the operator is provided with the number, or
 (b) if the number is provided before P offers goods for sale through the online marketplace, the later of—
  (i) the end of the period in paragraph (a), and
  (ii) the end of the day on which P first offers goods for sale through the online marketplace.
(5) If the operator becomes aware that a number displayed on the online marketplace as P's VAT registration number (under subsection (3) or otherwise) is not valid, the operator must secure that it is removed from the online marketplace before the end of the relevant period.
(6) The relevant period is the period of 10 days beginning with the day on which the operator first became aware that the number was not valid.
(7) A number is provided or displayed as P's VAT registration number only if it is provided or displayed in connection with P offering, or proposing to offer, goods for sale through the online marketplace.
(8) A number provided or displayed as P's VAT registration number is valid only if—
 (a) P is registered under this Act, and

(b) the number is P's VAT registration number.
(9) In this section—
. . .²
"VAT registration number" means the number allocated by the Commissioners to a person registered under this Act.]¹

Commentary—*De Voil Indirect Tax Service* **V3.502**.
Cross-references—See s 95A below (meaning of "online marketplace" and "operator").
Amendments—¹ Section 77E inserted by FA 2018 s 38(1), (8) with effect from 15 March 2018.
² In sub-s (9) definition relating to "online marketplace and operator" repealed by the Taxation (Post-transition Period) Act 2020 s 7, Sch 3 paras 1, 12 with effect from IP completion day (11pm on 31 December 2020), by virtue of SI 2020/1642 reg 9. Definition previously read as follows—
" "online marketplace" and "operator", in relation to an online marketplace, have the same meaning as in section 77B;".

[Liability of operators of online marketplaces for VAT in cases of deemed supply
77F Exception from liability under section 5A
(1) This section applies where an amount of VAT is due from the operator of an online marketplace by virtue of section 5A.
(2) The operator is not liable for any amount of VAT in excess of the amount paid by R (as defined in section 5A) provided that the operator took—
   (a) all reasonable steps to ascertain the matters set out in subsection (3), and
   (b) all other reasonable steps to satisfy itself that the amount charged was correct.
(3) The matters are—
   (a) the place of establishment of the person making taxable supplies facilitated by the online marketplace;
   (b) the location of the goods at the time of their supply.]¹

Northern Ireland—See VATA 1994 Sch 9ZC para 2 (online sales by overseas persons and low value importations: modifications relating to the Northern Ireland Protocol): s 77F has effect as if—
- in the heading, after "section 5A" there were inserted "or Part 1 of Schedule 9ZC";
- in sub-s (1), after "section 5A" there were inserted "or Part 1 of Schedule 9ZC"; and
- in sub-s (2), after "(as defined in section 5A" there were inserted "or Part 1 of Schedule 9ZC, as the case may be".
Amendments—¹ Section 77F and preceding heading inserted by the Taxation (Post-transition Period) Act 2020 s 7, Sch 3 paras 1, 13 with effect from IP completion day (11pm on 31 December 2020), by virtue of SI 2020/1642 reg 9.

Interest, repayment supplements etc payable by Commissioners
78 Interest in certain cases of official error
(1) Where, due to an error on the part of the Commissioners, a person has—
   (a) accounted to them for an amount by way of output tax which was not output tax due from him [and, as a result, they are liable under section 80(2A) to pay (or repay) an amount to him,]⁵ or
   (b) failed to claim credit under section 25 for an amount for which he was entitled so to claim credit and which they are in consequence liable to pay to him, or
   (c) (otherwise than in a case falling within paragraph (a) or (b) above) paid to them by way of VAT an amount that was not VAT due and which they are in consequence liable to repay to him, or
   (d) suffered delay in receiving payment of an amount due to him from them in connection with VAT,
then, if and to the extent that they would not be liable to do so apart from this section, they shall pay interest to him on that amount for the applicable period, but subject to the following provisions of this section.
[(1A) In subsection (1) above—
   (a) references to an amount which the Commissioners are liable in consequence of any matter to pay or repay to any person are references, where a claim for the payment or repayment has to be made, to only so much of that amount as is the subject of a claim that the Commissioners are required to satisfy or have satisfied; and
   (b) the amounts referred to in paragraph (d) do not include any amount payable under this section.]²
(2) Nothing in subsection (1) above requires the Commissioners to pay interest—
   (a) on any amount which falls to be increased by a supplement under section 79; or
   (b) where an amount is increased under that section, on so much of the increased amount as represents the supplement.
(3) Interest under this section shall be payable at [the rate applicable under section 197 of the Finance Act 1996]¹.
(4) The "applicable period" in a case falling within subsection (1)(a) or (b) above is the period—
   (a) beginning with the appropriate commencement date, and
   (b) ending with the date on which the Commissioners authorise payment of the amount on which the interest is payable.
(5) In subsection (4) above, the "appropriate commencement date"—

(a) in a case where an amount would have been due from the person by way of VAT in connection with the relevant return, had his input tax and output tax been as stated in that return, means the date on which the Commissioners received payment of that amount; and
(b) in a case where no such payment would have been due from him in connection with that return, means the date on which the Commissioners would, apart from the error, have authorised payment of the amount on which the interest is payable;
and in this subsection "the relevant return" means the return in which the person accounted for, or (as the case may be) ought to have claimed credit for, the amount on which the interest is payable.
(6) The "applicable period" in a case falling within subsection (1)(c) above is the period—
(a) beginning with the date on which the payment is received by the Commissioners, and
(b) ending with the date on which they authorise payment of the amount on which the interest is payable.
(7) The "applicable period" in a case falling within subsection (1)(d) above is the period—
(a) beginning with the date on which, apart from the error, the Commissioners might reasonably have been expected to authorise payment of the amount on which the interest is payable, and
(b) ending with the date on which they in fact authorise payment of that amount.
[(8) In determining in accordance with subsection (4), (6) or (7) above the applicable period for the purposes of subsection (1) above, there shall be left out of account any period by which the Commissioners' authorisation of the payment of interest is delayed by the conduct of the person who claims the interest.][4]
[(8A) The reference in subsection (8) above to a period by which the Commissioners' authorisation of the payment of interest is delayed by the conduct of the person who claims it includes, in particular, any period which is referable to—
(a) any unreasonable delay in the making of the claim for interest or in the making of any claim for the payment or repayment of the amount on which interest is claimed;
(b) any failure by that person or a person acting on his behalf or under his influence to provide the Commissioners—
(i) at or before the time of the making of a claim, or
(ii) subsequently in response to a request for information by the Commissioners,

with all the information required by them to enable the existence and amount of the claimant's entitlement to a payment or repayment, and to interest on that payment or repayment, to be determined; and
(c) the making, as part of or in association with either—
(i) the claim for interest, or
(ii) any claim for the payment or repayment of the amount on which interest is claimed,

of a claim to anything to which the claimant was not entitled.][4]
[(9) In determining for the purposes of subsection (8A) above whether any period of delay is referable to a failure by any person to provide information in response to a request by the Commissioners, there shall be taken to be so referable, except so far as may be prescribed, any period which—
(a) begins with the date on which the Commissioners require that person to provide information which they reasonably consider relevant to the matter to be determined; and
(b) ends with the earliest date on which it would be reasonable for the Commissioners to conclude—
(i) that they have received a complete answer to their request for information;
(ii) that they have received all that they need in answer to that request; or
(iii) that it is unnecessary for them to be provided with any information in answer to that request.][4]
(10) The Commissioners shall only be liable to pay interest under this section on a claim made in writing for that purpose.
[(11) A claim under this section shall not be made more than [4 years][6] after the end of the applicable period to which it relates.][3]
(12) In this section—
(a) references to the authorisation by the Commissioners of the payment of any amount include references to the discharge by way of set-off (whether under section 81(3) or otherwise) of the Commissioners' liability to pay that amount; and][2]
(b) any reference to a return is a reference to a return required to be made in accordance with paragraph 2 of Schedule 11.

Commentary—*De Voil Indirect Tax Service* **V5.196, V7.289**.
HMRC Manuals—Statutory Interest Manual VSIM6100-6500 (for what period is statutory interest due).
CRG3225 (mistakes: VAT Act 1994 s 78: official error).
Modifications—VATA 1994 Sch 3BA para 28 (in relation to cases where, because of an error on the part of the Commissioners, a person has accounted under a non-UK special scheme for UK VAT that was not due, this section applies as if the condition in sub-s (1)(a) were met in relation to that person).

VATA 1994 Sch 3B para 16H (in relation to cases where, because of an error on the part of the Commissioners, a person has accounted under a special scheme for UK VAT that was not due, this section applies as if the condition in sub-s (1)(a) were met in relation to that person).
Orders—See VATA 1983 (Interest on Overpayments etc) (Prescribed Rate) Order, SI 1991/1754.
Cross references—See the VAT (Accounting Procedures for Import VAT for VAT Registered Persons and Amendment) (EU Exit) Regulations, SI 2019/60 reg 8: this section applies for the purposes of SI 2019/60 as if references to "output tax" in paras (1)(a) and (5)(a) include import VAT chargeable on the importation of relevant goods. See also the modifications of SI 2019/60 reg 8 in its application for the purposes of the VAT (Miscellaneous and Transitional Provisions, Amendment and Revocation) (EU Exit) Regulations, SI 2020/1495 Part 2 Chapter 2 (accounting for Import VAT by VAT registered persons making transitional simplified customs declarations using the EIDR procedure) (see SI 2020/1495 reg 8(a)).
Amendments—[1] Words in sub-s (3) substituted by FA 1996 s 197(6)(d) with effect for periods beginning on or after 1 April 1997 (see SI 1997/1015) and with effect in relation to interest running from before that day, as well as in relation to interest running from, or from after, that day.
[2] Sub-s (1A) inserted, and sub-s (12)(a) substituted, by FA 1997 s 44 (1), (3) and deemed always to have had effect.
[3] Sub-s (11) substituted by FA 1997 s 44 (2) in relation to claims made on or after 18 July 1996 and deemed always to have had effect in relation to such claims.
[4] Sub-s (8), (8A) and (9) substituted by FA 1997 s 44 (4), (5) for the purposes of determining whether any period beginning on or after 19 March 1997 is left out of account.
[5] In sub-s (1)(a), words substituted for the words "and which they are in consequence liable to repay to him" by F(No 2)A 2005 s 4(1), (2) with effect in any case where a claim under VATA 1994 s 80(2) is made on or after 26 May 2005, whenever the event occurred in respect of which the claim is made: F(No 2)A 2005 s 4(6).
[6] In sub-s (11), words substituted for words "three years" by FA 2008 Sch 39 para 35 with effect from 1 April 2009 (by virtue of SI 2009/403 art 2(2)). FA 2008 Sch 39 para 35 is disregarded where, for the purposes of a claim under VATA 1994 s 78, the end of the applicable period to which the claim relates was on or before 31 March 2006 (SI 2009/403 art 5).

[78A Assessment for interest overpayments
(1) Where—
  (a) any amount has been paid to any person by way of interest under section 78, but
  (b) that person was not entitled to that amount under that section,
the Commissioners may, to the best of their judgement, assess the amount so paid to which that person was not entitled and notify it to him.
(2) An assessment made under subsection (1) above shall not be made more than two years after the time when evidence of facts sufficient in the opinion of the Commissioners to justify the making of the assessment comes to the knowledge of the Commissioners.
(3) Where an amount has been assessed and notified to any person under subsection (1) above, that amount shall be deemed (subject to the provisions of this Act as to appeals) to be an amount of VAT due from him and may be recovered accordingly.
(4) Subsection (3) above does not have effect if or to the extent that the assessment in question has been withdrawn or reduced.
(5) An assessment under subsection (1) above shall be a recovery assessment for the purposes of section 84(3A).
(6) Sections 74 and 77(6) apply in relation to assessments under subsection (1) above as they apply in relation to assessments under section 73 but as if the reference in subsection (1) of section 74 to the reckonable date were a reference to the date on which the assessment is notified.
(7) Where by virtue of subsection (6) above any person is liable to interest under section 74—
  (a) section 76 shall have effect in relation to that liability with the omission of subsections (2) to [(5)][3]; and
  (b) section 77, except subsection (6), shall not apply to an assessment of the amount due by way of interest;
and (without prejudice to the power to make assessments for interest for later periods) the interest to which any assessment made under section 76 by virtue of paragraph (a) above may relate shall be confined to interest for a period of no more than two years ending with the time when the assessment to interest is made.
(8) For the purposes of this section notification to a personal representative, trustee in bankruptcy, [trustee in sequestration][2], receiver, liquidator or person otherwise acting in a representative capacity in relation to another shall be treated as notification to the person in relation to whom he so acts.][1]
Commentary—*De Voil Indirect Tax Service* V5.132B, V5.361.
HMRC Manuals—VAT Assessments and Error Correction VAEC4140 (recovery of statutory interest under section 78A).
Amendments—[1] This section inserted by FA 1997 s 45(1) and deemed to have come into force on 4 December 1996 in relation to amounts paid by way of interest on or after 18 July 1996.
[2] In sub-s (8), words substituted by the Bankruptcy (Scotland) Act 2016 (Consequential Provisions and Modifications) Order, SI 2016/1034 art 7(1), Sch 1 para 12(1), (5) with effect from 30 November 2016.
[3] In sub-s (7)(a), reference "(5)" substituted for reference "(6)" by the Taxation (Cross-border Trade) Act 2018 s 43, Sch 8 paras 1, 70 with effect from IP completion day (11pm on 31 December 2020), by virtue of SI 2020/1642 reg 4(b).

79 Repayment supplement in respect of certain delayed payments or refunds
(1) In any case where—
  (a) a person is entitled to a VAT credit, or
  (b) a body which is registered and to which section 33 applies is entitled to a refund under that section, [or

(c) a body which is registered and to which section 33A applies is entitled to a refund under that section,]² [or
(d) the proprietor of an Academy who is registered is entitled to a refund under section 33B, [or]³
(e) a charity which is registered is entitled to a refund under section 33C,]⁴
and the conditions mentioned in subsection (2) below are satisfied, the amount which, apart from this section, would be due by way of that payment or refund shall be increased by the addition of a supplement equal to 5 per cent of that amount or £50, whichever is the greater.
(2) The said conditions are—
  (a) that the requisite return or claim is received by the Commissioners not later than the last day on which it is required to be furnished or made, and
  (b) that a written instruction directing the making of the payment or refund is not issued by the Commissioners within [the relevant period]¹, and
  (c) that the amount shown on that return or claim as due by way of payment or refund does not exceed the payment or refund which was in fact due by more than 5 per cent of that payment or refund or £250, whichever is the greater.
[(2A) The relevant period in relation to a return or claim is the period of 30 days beginning with the later of—
  (a) the day after the last day of the prescribed accounting period to which the return or claim relates, and
  (b) the date of the receipt by the Commissioners of the return or claim.]¹
(3) Regulations may provide that, in computing the period of 30 days referred to in [subsection (2A)]¹ above, there shall be left out of account periods determined in accordance with the regulations and referable to—
  (a) the raising and answering of any reasonable inquiry relating to the requisite return or claim,
  (b) the correction by the Commissioners of any errors or omissions in that return or claim, and
  (c) in the case of a payment, the following matters, namely—
    (i) any such continuing failure to submit returns as is referred to in section 25(5), and
    (ii) compliance with any such condition as is referred to in paragraph 4(1) of Schedule 11.
(4) In determining for the purposes of regulations under subsection (3) above whether any period is referable to the raising and answering of such an inquiry as is mentioned in that subsection, there shall be taken to be so referable any period which—
  (a) begins with the date on which the Commissioners first consider it necessary to make such an inquiry, and
  (b) ends with the date on which the Commissioners—
    (i) satisfy themselves that they have received a complete answer to the inquiry, or
    (ii) determine not to make the inquiry or, if they have made it, not to pursue it further,
but excluding so much of that period as may be prescribed; and it is immaterial whether any inquiry is in fact made or whether it is or might have been made of the person or body making the requisite return or claim or of an authorised person or of some other person.
(5) Except for the purpose of determining the amount of the supplement—
  (a) a supplement paid to any person under subsection (1)(a) above shall be treated as an amount due to him by way of credit under section 25(3), and
  (b) a supplement paid to any body under subsection (1)(b) above shall be treated as an amount due to it by way of refund under section 33[, and
  (c) a supplement paid to any body under subsection (1)(c) shall be treated as an amount due to it by way of refund under section 33A]²[, and
  (d) a supplement paid to the proprietor of an Academy under subsection (1)(d) shall be treated as an amount due to that proprietor by way of refund under section 33B[, and]³
  (e) a supplement paid to a charity under subsection (1)(e) shall be treated as an amount due to the charity by way of refund under section 33C.]⁴
(6) In this section "requisite return or claim" means—
  (a) in relation to a payment, the return for the prescribed accounting period concerned which is required to be furnished in accordance with regulations under this Act, and
  (b) in relation to a refund, the claim for that refund which is required to be made in accordance with the Commissioners' determination under section 33 [or (as the case may be) the Commissioners' determination under, and the provisions of, section 33A[, 33B or 33C]⁴.]²
(7) If the Treasury by order so direct, any period specified in the order shall be disregarded for the purpose of calculating the period of 30 days referred to in [subsection (2A)]¹ above.

Commentary—*De Voil Indirect Tax Service* **V5.191, V5.192**.
HMRC Manuals—Statutory Interest Manual VSIM4500 (no liability to pay statutory interest - repayment supplement). VATA Repayment Supplement Manual VATRS10230 (timeliness - enquiries, correcting errors and amending details).
Regulations—See VAT Regulations, SI 1995/2518 regs 198, 199.

Amendments—[1] Words in sub-s (2)(*b*), (3) and (7) substituted, and sub-s (2A) inserted by FA 1999 s 19 with effect in relation to returns and claims received by the Commissioners on or after 9 March 1999.
[2] Sub-ss (1)(*c*), (5)(*c*) inserted by FA 2001 s 98(4)–(7) with effect from 1 September 2001.
[3] Sub-s (1)(*d*) and preceding word "or", and sub-s (5)(*d*) and preceding word "and", and words in sub-s (6)(*b*), inserted, by FA 2011 s 76(2) with effect in relation to supplies made, and acquisitions and importations taking place, on or after 1 April 2011. Words "or 33C" inserted by FA 2015 s 66(2)(c) with effect in relation to supplies made, and acquisitions and importations taking place, on or after 1 April 2015.
[4] Sub-ss (1)(*e*), (5)(*e*) and preceding word in each case inserted, and in sub-s (6)(*b*), words substituted, by FA 2015 s 66(1), (2) with effect in relation to supplies made, and acquisitions and importations taking place, on or after 1 April 2015.

80 [Credit for, or repayment of, overstated or overpaid VAT][4]

[(1) Where a person—
  (*a*) has accounted to the Commissioners for VAT for a prescribed accounting period (whenever ended), and
  (*b*) in doing so, has brought into account as output tax an amount that was not output tax due,
the Commissioners shall be liable to credit the person with that amount.][4]

[(1A) Where the Commissioners—
  (*a*) have assessed a person to VAT for a prescribed accounting period (whenever ended), and
  (*b*) in doing so, have brought into account as output tax an amount that was not output tax due,
they shall be liable to credit the person with that amount.][4]

[(1B) Where a person has for a prescribed accounting period (whenever ended) paid to the Commissioners an amount by way of VAT that was not VAT due to them, otherwise than as a result of—
  (*a*) an amount that was not output tax due being brought into account as output tax, or
  (*b*) an amount of input tax allowable under section 26 not being brought into account,
the Commissioners shall be liable to repay to that person the amount so paid.][4]

(2) The Commissioners shall only be liable to [credit or][4] repay an amount under this section on a claim being made for the purpose.

[(2A) Where—
  (*a*) as a result of a claim under this section by virtue of subsection (1) or (1A) above an amount falls to be credited to a person, and
  (*b*) after setting any sums against it under or by virtue of this Act, some or all of that amount remains to his credit,
the Commissioners shall be liable to pay (or repay) to him so much of that amount as so remains.][4]

(3) It shall be a defence, in relation to a claim [under this section by virtue of subsection (1) or (1A) above, that the crediting][4] of an amount would unjustly enrich the claimant.

[(3A) Subsection (3B) below applies for the purposes of subsection (3) above where—
  (*a*) an amount would (apart from subsection (3) above) fall to be credited under subsection (1) or (1A) above to any person ("the taxpayer"), and
  (*b*) the whole or a part of the amount brought into account as mentioned in paragraph (*b*) of that subsection has, for practical purposes, been borne by a person other than the taxpayer.][4]

[(3B) Where, in a case to which this subsection applies, loss or damage has been or may be incurred by the taxpayer as a result of mistaken assumptions made in his case about the operation of any VAT provisions, that loss or damage shall be disregarded, except to the extent of the quantified amount, in the making of any determination—
  (*a*) of whether or to what extent the [crediting][4] of an amount to the taxpayer would enrich him; or
  (*b*) of whether or to what extent any enrichment of the taxpayer would be unjust.][1]

[(3C) In subsection (3B) above —
  "the quantified amount" means the amount (if any) which is shown by the taxpayer to constitute the amount that would appropriately compensate him for loss or damage shown by him to have resulted, for any business carried on by him, from the making of the mistaken assumptions; and
  "VAT provisions" means the provisions of—
    (*a*) any enactment [or subordinate legislation][7] (whether or not still in force) which relates to VAT or to any matter connected with VAT; or
    (*b*) any notice published by the Commissioners under or for the purposes of any such enactment or subordinate legislation.][1]

[(4) The Commissioners shall not be liable on a claim under this section—
  (*a*) to credit an amount to a person under subsection (1) or (1A) above, or
  (*b*) to repay an amount to a person under subsection (1B) above,
if the claim is made more than [4 years][6] after the relevant date.][4]

[(4ZA) The relevant date is—
  (*a*) in the case of a claim by virtue of subsection (1) above, the end of the prescribed accounting period mentioned in that subsection, unless paragraph (*b*) below applies;
  (*b*) in the case of a claim by virtue of subsection (1) above in respect of an erroneous voluntary disclosure, the end of the prescribed accounting period in which the disclosure was made;

(c) in the case of a claim by virtue of subsection (1A) above in respect of an assessment issued on the basis of an erroneous voluntary disclosure, the end of the prescribed accounting period in which the disclosure was made;
(d) in the case of a claim by virtue of subsection (1A) above in any other case, the end of the prescribed accounting period in which the assessment was made;
(e) in the case of a claim by virtue of subsection (1B) above, the date on which the payment was made.

In the case of a person who has ceased to be registered under this Act, any reference in paragraphs (b) to (d) above to a prescribed accounting period includes a reference to a period that would have been a prescribed accounting period had the person continued to be registered under this Act.]⁴

[(4ZB) For the purposes of this section the cases where there is an erroneous voluntary disclosure are those cases where—
(a) a person discloses to the Commissioners that he has not brought into account for a prescribed accounting period (whenever ended) an amount of output tax due for the period;
(b) the disclosure is made in a later prescribed accounting period (whenever ended); and
(c) some or all of the amount is not output tax due.]⁴

[(4A) Where—
(a) an amount has been credited under subsection (1) or (1A) above to any person at any time on or after 26th May 2005, and
(b) the amount so credited exceeded the amount which the Commissioners were liable at that time to credit to that person,

the Commissioners may, to the best of their judgement, assess the excess credited to that person and notify it to him.]⁴

[(4AA) An assessment under subsection (4A) shall not be made more than 2 years after the later of—
(a) the end of the prescribed accounting period in which the amount was credited to the person, and
(b) the time when evidence of facts sufficient in the opinion of the Commissioners to justify the making of the assessment comes to the knowledge of the Commissioners.]⁵

(4B) . . . ⁴

[(4C) Subsections [(3)]⁵ to (8) of section 78A apply in the case of an assessment under subsection (4A) above as they apply in the case of an assessment under section 78A(1).]³

(5) . . . ²

(6) A claim under this section shall be made in such form and manner and shall be supported by such documentary evidence as the Commissioners prescribe by regulations; and regulations under this subsection may make different provision for different cases.

[(7) Except as provided by this section . . . ⁷, the Commissioners shall not be liable to credit or repay any amount accounted for or paid to them by way of VAT that was not VAT due to them.]⁴

Commentary—*De Voil Indirect Tax Service* **V3.519, V5.159B**.
HMRC Manuals—VAT Refund Manual VRM6000 (what can be claimed).
VRM8200 (time limits).
VAT Assessments And Error Correction VAEC4030 (time limits for section 80(4A)).
Statutory Interest Manual VSIM4200 (examples).
Northern Ireland—See Sch 9ZA para 33 (Northern Ireland: this section has effect as if in sub-s (3C) reference to VAT provisions included any provision of any EU instrument relating to VAT, or to any matter connected with VAT, that has effect in Northern Ireland as a result of the European Union (Withdrawal) Act 2018 s 7A (general implementation of withdrawal agreement)).
Modifications—VATA 1994 Sch 3BA para 30 (modification of this section in relation to claims for overpayments regarding the use of non-UK special accounting schemes).
VATA 1994 Sch 3B para 16J (modification of this section in relation to overpayment claims by participants in special schemes).
Regulations—See VAT Regulations, SI 1995/2518 reg 37.
VAT (Amendment) (No 3) Regulations, SI 2014/2430.
Amendments—¹ Sub-ss (3A)–(3C) inserted by FA 1997 s 46(1) with effect for the purposes of making any repayment on or after 19 March 1997, even if the claim for that repayment was made before that date.
² Sub-s (4) substituted for sub-ss (4), (5) by FA 1997 s 47(1) with effect from 18 July 1996, subject to transitional provisions in FA 1997 s 47(3)–(5).
³ Sub-ss (4A)–(4C) inserted by FA 1997 s 47(6) and deemed to have come into force on 4 December 1996.
⁴ Sub-s (1)–(1B) substituted for sub-s (1); words inserted in sub-s (2); sub-s (2A) inserted; in sub-s (3), words substituted for the words "under this section, that repayment"; sub-ss (3A), (7) substituted; in sub-s (3B)(a), word substituted for the word "repayment"; sub-ss (4)–(4ZB) substituted for sub-s (4); sub-s (4A) substituted for sub-ss (4A), (4B); and Heading substituted; by F(No 2)A 2005 s 3 with effect in any case where a claim under sub-s (2) above is made on or after 26 May 2005, whenever the event occurred in respect of which the claim is made: F(No 2)A 2005 s 4(6).
⁵ Sub-s (4AA) inserted, and reference in sub-s (4C) substituted by FA 2008 s 120(2)–(4). These amendments are treated as having come into force on 19 March 2008.
⁶ In sub-s (4) words substituted for words "3 years" by FA 2008 Sch 39 para 36 with effect from 1 April 2009 (by virtue of SI 2009/403 art 2(2)). FA 2008 Sch 39 para 36 is disregarded where, for the purposes of VATA 1994 s 80, the relevant date is on or before 31 March 2006 (SI 2009/403 art 6).
⁷ The following amendments made by the Taxation (Cross-border Trade) Act 2018 s 43, Sch 8 paras 1, 71 with effect from IP completion day (11pm on 31 December 2020), by virtue of SI 2020/1642 reg 4(b)—

- in sub-s (3C), in definition of "VAT provisions", in para (a), words substituted for words ", subordinate legislation or EU legislation"; and
- in sub-s (7), words "(and paragraph 16I of Schedule 3B and paragraph 29 of Schedule 3BA)".

[80A Arrangements for reimbursing customers

(1) The Commissioners may by regulations make provision for reimbursement arrangements made by any person to be disregarded for the purposes of section 80(3) except where the arrangements—
  (a) contain such provision as may be required by the regulations; and
  (b) are supported by such undertakings to comply with the provisions of the arrangements as may be required by the regulations to be given to the Commissioners.
(2) In this section 'reimbursement arrangements' means any arrangements for the purposes of a claim under section 80 which—
  (a) are made by any person for the purpose of securing that he is not unjustly enriched by the [crediting]² of any amount in pursuance of the claim; and
  (b) provide for the reimbursement of persons who have for practical purposes borne the whole or any part of [the amount brought into account as mentioned in paragraph (b) of subsection (1) or (1A) of that section]².
(3) Without prejudice to the generality of subsection (1) above, the provision that may be required by regulations under this section to be contained in reimbursement arrangements includes—
  (a) provision requiring a reimbursement for which the arrangements provide to be made within such period after the [crediting of the amount]² to which it relates as may be specified in the regulations;
  [(b) provision for cases where an amount is credited but an equal amount is not reimbursed in accordance with the arrangements;]²
  (c) provision requiring interest paid by the Commissioners on any amount [paid (or repaid)]² by them to be treated in the same way as that amount for the purposes of any requirement under the arrangements to make reimbursement or to repay the Commissioners;
  (d) provision requiring such records relating to the carrying out of the arrangements as may be described in the regulations to be kept and produced to the Commissioners, or to an officer of theirs.
(4) Regulations under this section may impose obligations on such persons as may be specified in the regulations—
  (a) [to make the repayments, or give the notifications, to the Commissioners that they are required to make or give]² in pursuance of any provisions contained in any reimbursement arrangements by virtue of subsection (3)(b) or (c) above;
  (b) to comply with any requirements contained in any such arrangements by virtue of subsection (3)(d) above.
(5) Regulations under this section may make provision for the form and manner in which, and the times at which, undertakings are to be given to the Commissioners in accordance with the regulations; and any such provision may allow for those matters to be determined by the Commissioners in accordance with the regulations.
(6) Regulations under this section may—
  (a) contain any such incidental, supplementary, consequential or transitional provision as appears to the Commissioners to be necessary or expedient; and
  (b) make different provision for different circumstances.
(7) Regulations under this section may have effect (irrespective of when the claim for [credit]² was made) for the purposes of [the crediting of any amount]² by the Commissioners after the time when the regulations are made; and, accordingly, such regulations may apply to arrangements made before that time.]¹

Commentary—*De Voil Indirect Tax Service* **V5.159B**.
HMRC Manuals—VAT Refunds Manual VRM12500 (reimbursement arrangements).
Regulations—VAT (Amendment) (No 3) Regulations, SI 2014/2430.
Amendments—¹ This section inserted by FA 1997 s 46(2).
² In sub-s (2)(a), (3)(a), (7), words substituted for the word "repayment"; in sub-s (2)(b), words substituted for the words "the cost of the original payment of that amount to the Commissioners"; sub-s (3)(b) substituted; in sub-s (3)(c), words substituted for the word "repaid"; in sub-s (4)(a), words substituted for the words "to make the repayments to the Commissioners that they are required to make"; in sub-s (7), words substituted for the words "the making of any repayment"; by F(No 2)A 2005 s 4(1), (3) with effect in any case where a claim under VATA 1994 s 80(2) is made on or after 26 May 2005, whenever the event occurred in respect of which the claim is made: F(No 2)A 2005 s 4(6).

[80B Assessments of amounts due under section 80A arrangements

(1) Where any person is liable to pay any amount to the Commissioners in pursuance of an obligation imposed by virtue of section 80A(4)(a), the Commissioners may, to the best of their judgement, assess the amount due from that person and notify it to him.
[(1A) Where—
  (a) an amount ("the gross credit") has been credited to any person under subsection (1) or (1A) of section 80,

(b) any sums were set against that amount, in accordance with subsection (2A) of that section, and
(c) the amount reimbursed in accordance with the reimbursement arrangements was less than the gross credit,
subsection (1B) below applies.]²
[(1B) In any such case—
  (a) the person shall cease to be entitled to so much of the gross credit as exceeds the amount so reimbursed, and
  (b) the Commissioners may, to the best of their judgement, assess the amount due from that person and notify it to him,
but an amount shall not be assessed under this subsection to the extent that the person is liable to pay it to the Commissioners as mentioned in subsection (1) above.]²
[(1C) In determining the amount that a person is liable to pay as mentioned in subsection (1) above, any amount reimbursed in accordance with the reimbursement arrangements shall be regarded as first reducing so far as possible the amount that he would have been liable so to pay, but for the reimbursement of that amount.]²
[(1D) For the purposes of this section, nil is an amount.]²
[(1E) Any reference in any other provision of this Act to an assessment under subsection (1) above includes, if the context so admits, a reference to an assessment under subsection (1B) above.]²
(2) Subsections (2) to (8) of section 78A apply in the case of an assessment under subsection (1) above as they apply in the case of an assessment under section 78A(1).]¹

Commentary—*De Voil Indirect Tax Service* **V5.132B**.
Amendments—¹ This section inserted by FA 1997 s 46(2).
² Sub-ss (1A)–(1E) inserted by F(No 2)A 2005 s 4(1), (4) with effect in any case where a claim under VATA 1994 s 80(2) is made on or after 26 May 2005, whenever the event occurred in respect of which the claim is made: F(No 2)A 2005 s 4(6).

81 Interest given by way of credit and set-off of credits

(1) Any interest payable by the Commissioners (whether under an enactment or instrument or otherwise) to a person on a sum due to him under or by virtue of any provision of this Act shall be treated as an amount due by way of credit under section 25(3).
(2) Subsection (1) above shall be disregarded for the purpose of determining a person's entitlement to interest or the amount of interest to which he is entitled.
(3) Subject to subsection (1) above, in any case where—
  (a) an amount is due from the Commissioners to any person under any provision of this Act, and
  (b) that person is liable to pay a sum by way of VAT, penalty, interest or surcharge,
the amount referred to in paragraph (a) above shall be set against the sum referred to in paragraph (b) above and, accordingly, to the extent of the set-off, the obligations of the Commissioners and the person concerned shall be discharged.
[(3A) Where—
  (a) the Commissioners are liable to pay or repay any amount to any person under this Act,
  (b) that amount falls to be paid or repaid in consequence of a mistake previously made about whether or to what extent amounts were payable under this Act to or by that person, and
  (c) by reason of that mistake a liability of that person to pay a sum by way of VAT, penalty, interest or surcharge was not assessed, was not enforced or was not satisfied,
any limitation on the time within which the Commissioners are entitled to take steps for recovering that sum shall be disregarded in determining whether that sum is required by subsection (3) above to be set against the amount mentioned in paragraph (a) above.]²
[(4A) Subsection (3) above shall not require any such amount as is mentioned in paragraph (a) of that subsection ("the credit") to be set against any such sum as is mentioned in paragraph (b) of that subsection ("the debit") in any case where—
  (a) an insolvency procedure has been applied to the person entitled to the credit;
  (b) the credit became due after that procedure was so applied; and
  (c) the liability to pay the debit either arose before that procedure was so applied or (having arisen afterwards) relates to, or to matters occurring in the course of, the carrying on of any business at times before the procedure was so applied.]¹
[(4B) Subject to subsection (4C) below, the following are the times when an insolvency procedure is to be taken, for the purposes of this section, to be applied to any person, that is to say—
  [(a) when a bankruptcy order or winding-up order or award of sequestration is made or an administrator is appointed in relation to that person;]³
  (b) when that person is put into administrative receivership;
  (c) when that person, being a corporation, passes a resolution for voluntary winding up;
  (d) when any voluntary arrangement approved in accordance with Part I or VIII of the Insolvency Act 1986 or Part II or Chapter II of Part VIII of the Insolvency (Northern Ireland) Order 1989 comes into force in relation to that person;
  (e) when a deed of arrangement registered in accordance with . . . ⁵ or Chapter I of Part VIII of that Order of 1989 takes effect in relation to that person;

(f) when that person's estate becomes vested in any other person as that person's trustee under a trust deed.][1]

[(4C) In this section, references to the application of an insolvency procedure to a person do not include—
  (a) the application of an insolvency procedure to a person at a time when another insolvency procedure applies to the person, or
  (b) the application of an insolvency procedure to a person immediately upon another insolvency procedure ceasing to have effect.][4]

[(4D) For the purposes of this section a person shall be regarded as being in administrative receivership throughout any continuous period for which (disregarding any temporary vacancy in the office of receiver) there is an administrative receiver of that person, and the reference in subsection (4B) above to a person being put into administrative receivership shall be construed accordingly.][1]

(5) In [this section[1]]—
  (a) *"administration order"* means an administration order under Part II of the Insolvency Act 1986 or an administration order within the meaning of Article 5(1) of the Insolvency (Northern Ireland) Order 1989; [4]
  (b) *"administrative receiver"* means an administrative receiver within the meaning of section 251 of [the Insolvency Act 1986][4] or Article 5(1) of [the Insolvency (Northern Ireland) Order 1989][4;]
  [(ba) *"administrator"* means a person appointed to manage the affairs, business and property of another person under Schedule B1 to that Act or to that Order;][4] and
  (c) *"trust deed"* has the same meaning as in the Bankruptcy (Scotland) Act [2016][6].

Commentary—*De Voil Indirect Tax Service* **V5.101A, V5.172, V5.196**.
HMRC Manuals—VAT Refunds Manual VRM7000 (what must be set-off in a claim).
Statutory Interest Manual VSIM4600 (interaction of statutory interest law and set off law).
VSIM4200 (examples).
Amendments—[1] Sub-ss (4A)–(4D) substituted for sub-s (4) as originally enacted, and words in sub-s (5) substituted by FA 1995 s 27 with effect in relation to amounts becoming due from the Commissioners of Customs and Excise at times on or after 1 May 1995.
[2] Sub-s (3A) inserted by FA 1997 s 48(1) and deemed to have come into force on 18 July 1996 for determining the amount of any payment or repayment by C&E on or after that date.
[3] Sub-ss (4B)(a) substituted, by the Enterprise Act 2002 (Insolvency) Order, SI 2003/2096 art 4, Schedule, paras 24, 26 with effect from 15 September 2003. However, this amendment does not apply in any case where a petition for an administration order was presented before that date: SI 2003/2096 arts 1, 6.
[4] Sub-s (4C) substituted, sub-s (5)(a) repealed, in sub-s (5)(b), words substituted for words "that Act of 1986", and "that Order of 1989", and sub-s (5)(ba) inserted, by FA 2008 s 132 with effect from 21 July 2008.
[5] In sub-s (4B)(e), words "the Deeds of Arrangement Act 1914 or" repealed by the Deregulation Act 2015 s 19, Sch 6 para 2(1), (13) with effect from 1 October 2015 (by virtue of SI 2015/1732 art 2(e)(i)). This repeal has no effect in relation to a deed of arrangement registered under the Deeds of Arrangement Act 1914 s 5 before 1 October 2015 if, immediately before that date, the estate of the debtor who executed the deed of arrangement has not been finally wound up (Deregulation Act Sch 6 para 3).
[6] In sub-s (5)(c), date substituted by the Bankruptcy (Scotland) Act 2016 (Consequential Provisions and Modifications) Order, SI 2016/1034 art 7(1), Sch 1 para 12(1), (6) with effect from 30 November 2016.

PART V
[REVIEWS AND APPEALS]

Cross reference—See the VAT (Accounting Procedures for Import VAT for VAT Registered Persons and Amendment) (EU Exit) Regulations, SI 2019/60 reg 10: application of Part 5 of this Act (and regulations and orders made under Part 5) to appeals made under SI 2019/60 reg 10. Note that SI 2019/60 reg 10 also applies for the purposes of the VAT (Miscellaneous and Transitional Provisions, Amendment and Revocation) (EU Exit) Regulations, SI 2020/1495 Part 2 Chapter 2 (accounting for Import VAT by VAT registered persons making transitional simplified customs declarations using the EIDR procedure) (see SI 2020/1495 reg 8(b)).
Amendments—Heading substituted for previous heading "Appeals" by the Transfer of Tribunal Functions and Revenue and Customs Appeals Order, SI 2009/56 art 3, Sch 1 para 217 with effect from 1 April 2009, subject to transitional and savings provisions in Sch 3 para 4.

[82 Meaning of "tribunal"
In this Act "tribunal" means the First-tier Tribunal or, where determined by or under Tribunal Procedure Rules, the Upper Tribunal.][1]

Commentary—*De Voil Indirect Tax Service* **V1.288**.
HMRC Manuals—Appeals, Reviews and Tribunals Manual ARTG1010 (tribunals : introduction).
ARTG8040 (FT and UT : matters that the tribunals may consider).
Amendments—[1] This section substituted by the Transfer of Tribunal Functions and Revenue and Customs Appeals Order, SI 2009/56 art 3, Sch 1 para 218 with effect from 1 April 2009, subject to transitional and savings provisions in Sch 3 para 4.

83 Appeals
[(1)] [21]Subject to [sections 83G and 84][21], an appeal shall lie to [the tribunal][21] with respect to any of the following matters—
  (a) the registration or cancellation of registration of any person under this Act;

(b) the VAT chargeable on the supply of any goods or services . . . [27] or, subject to section 84(9), on the importation of goods . . . [27];
(c) the amount of any input tax which may be credited to a person;
(d) . . . [27]
[(da) a decision of the Commissioners under section 18A—
   (i) as to whether or not a person is to be approved as a fiscal warehouse keeper or the conditions from time to time subject to which he is so approved;
   (ii) for the withdrawal of any such approval; or
   (iii) for the withdrawal of fiscal warehouse status from any premises;][1]
(e) the proportion of input tax allowable under section 26;
(f) a claim by a taxable person under section 27;
[(fza) a decision of the Commissioners—
   (i) refusing or withdrawing authorisation for a person's liability to pay VAT (or entitlement to credit for VAT) to be determined as mentioned in subsection (1) of section 26B;
   (ii) as to the appropriate percentage or percentages (within the meaning of that section) applicable in a person's case.][10]
[(fa) a decision contained in a notification under paragraph (4) of article 12A of the Value Added Tax (Payments on Account) Order 1993 that an election under paragraph (1) of that article shall cease to have effect;][6]
(g) the amount of any refunds under section 35;
(h) a claim for a refund under section 36 or section 22 of the 1983 Act;
[(ha) any decision of the Commissioners to refuse to make a repayment under a scheme under section 39;][22]
(j) . . . [27]
[(k) the refusal of an application such as is mentioned in section 43B(1) or (2);
(ka) the giving of a notice under section 43C(1) or (3);][7]
(l) the requirement of any security under section 48(7) or [paragraph 4(1A) or (2)][11] of Schedule 11;
(m) any refusal or cancellation of certification under section 54 or any refusal to cancel such certification;
(n) any liability to a penalty or surcharge by virtue of any of sections [59 to [69B][17]][8];
[(na) any liability to a penalty under section 69C, any assessment of a penalty under that section or the amount of such an assessment;
(nb) the giving of a decision notice under section 69D or the portion of a penalty assessed under section 69C which is specified in such a notice;][25]
(o) a decision of the Commissioners under section 61 (in accordance with section 61(5));
(p) an assessment—
   (i) under section 73(1) or (2) in respect of a period for which the appellant has made a return under this Act; or
   (ii) under [subsections (7), (7A) or (7B)][1] of that section; . . . [27]
   (iii) . . . [27]
or the amount of such an assessment;
(q) the amount of any penalty, interest or surcharge specified in an assessment under section 76;
(r) the making of an assessment on the basis set out in section 77(4);
[(ra) any liability arising by virtue of section 77A;][12]
[(rb) an assessment under section 77C or the amount of such an assessment;][24]
(s) any liability of the Commissioners to pay interest under section 78 or the amount of interest so payable;
[(sa) an assessment under section 78A(1) or the amount of such an assessment;][3]
(t) a claim for the [crediting or][16] repayment of an amount under section 80[, an assessment under subsection (4A) of that section or the amount of such an assessment;][5]
[(ta) an assessment under section 80B(1) [or (1B)][16] or the amount of such an assessment;][4]
(u) any direction or supplementary direction made under paragraph 2 of Schedule 1;
(v) any direction under paragraph 1[, 1A][15][, 2 or 8A][23] of Schedule 6 or under paragraph 2 of Schedule 4 to the 1983 Act;
(w) . . . [27]
[(wa) any direction or assessment under Schedule 9A;][2]
[(wb) any refusal of the Commissioners to grant any permission under, or otherwise to exercise in favour of a particular person any power conferred by, any provision of Part 1 of Schedule 10;][20]
(x) any refusal to permit the value of supplies to be determined by a method described in a notice published under paragraph 2(6) of Schedule 11;
(y) any refusal of authorisation or termination of authorisation in connection with the scheme made under paragraph 2(7) of Schedule 11;

[(z) any conditions imposed by the Commissioners in a particular case by virtue of paragraph 2B(2)(c) or 3(1) of Schedule 11][13]
[(zza) a direction under paragraph 6A of Schedule 11;][18]
[(za) a direction under paragraph 8 of Schedule 11A;][14]
[(zb) any liability to a penalty under paragraph 10(1) of Schedule 11A, any assessment under paragraph 12(1) of that Schedule or the amount of such an assessment;][14]
[(zc) a decision of the Commissioners about the application of any provision of regulations under paragraph 2 or 6 of Schedule 11, or of regulations under section 135 or 136 of the Finance Act 2002 relating to VAT, which—

(i) requires returns to be made or information to be submitted by electronic communications, or

(ii) requires records to be kept or preserved in electronic form,

(including in particular a decision as to whether such a requirement applies and a decision to impose a penalty).][26]

(zz) . . . [9]

[(2) In the following provisions of this Part, a reference to a decision with respect to which an appeal under this section lies, or has been made, includes any matter listed in subsection (1) whether or not described there as a decision.][21]

Commentary—*De Voil Indirect Tax Service* **V5.404**.
HMRC Manuals—Appeals, Reviews And Tribunals Manual ARTG3041 (Reviews and appeals for indirect taxes: appeals under specific provisions of the VAT Act 1994).
VAT Refund Manual VRM15000 (appeals against refusal of a claim).
Other Non-Statutory Clearance Guidance ONSCG9200 (VAT appealable decisions).
Statutory Interest Manual VSIM7300 (Appeals and reviews).
VAT Refund Supplement Manual VRS2400 (appeals against refusal of use).
Northern Ireland—See Sch 9ZA para 34 (Northern Ireland: matters to be treated as if included in the list of matters in sub-s (1)). See also SI 2020/1546 regs 17, 18 (accounting for VAT on removals: penalties).
Modifications—VATA 1994 Sch 3BA para 37 (where the Commissioners have made an assessment under s 73 in relation to a relevant non-UK return, sub-s (1)(p)(i) applies as if that return were a return under this Act).
Modifications—Money Laundering, Terrorist Financing and Transfer of Funds (Information on the Payer) Regulations, SI 2017/692 reg 99 (Part 5 applies in respect of appeals to the tribunal made under SI 2017/692 reg 99(1) as it applies in respect of appeals made to the tribunal under s 83, but as if ss 83A–84, 85A and 85B were revoked).
Cross references—See the Value Added Tax (Accounting Procedures for Import VAT for VAT Registered Persons and Amendment) (EU Exit) Regulations, SI 2019/60 art 10 (appeals relating to import VAT).
Amendments—[1] Para (da) inserted and words in para (p)(ii) substituted by FA 1996 Sch 3 para 12, with effect from 1 June 1996 (see Finance Act 1996, Section 26, (Appointed Day) Order SI 1996/1249), and applying to any acquisition of goods from another member State and any supply taking place on or after that day.
[2] Para (wa) inserted by FA 1996 s 31(3).
[3] Para (sa) inserted by FA 1997 s 45(2) and deemed to have come into force on 4 December 1996 in relation to assessments made on or after that date.
[4] Para (ta) inserted by FA 1997 s 46 (3).
[5] Words in para (t) inserted by FA 1997 s 47 (7) with effect from 4 December 1996.
[6] Para (fa) inserted by the VAT (Payments on Account) (Appeals) Order, SI 1997/2542 with effect from 1 December 1997.
[7] Para (k) substituted and para (ka) inserted by FA 1999 s 16, Sch 2 para 3 with effect from 27 July 1999 subject to FA 1999 Sch 2 para 6.
[8] Words in para (n) substituted for "59 to 69" by FA 2000 s 137(1), (5), with effect from 28 July 2000.
[9] Para (zz) (originally added by the Money Laundering Regulations 2001) repealed by the Money Laundering Regulations, SI 2007/2157 reg 51, Sch 6 para 1 with effect from 15 December 2007.
[10] Para (fza) inserted by FA 2002 s 23(2), (4) and deemed to have come into force on 24 April 2002.
[11] Words in para (l) substituted for the words "paragraph 4(2)" by FA 2003 s 17(6) with effect from 10 April 2003.
[12] Para (ra) inserted by FA 2003 s 18(2) with effect from 10 April 2003.
[13] Para (z) substituted by FA 2002 s 24(4)(b), (5), with effect from 1 December 2003 (by virtue of SI 2003/3043).
[14] Paras (za) and (zb) inserted by FA 2004 s 19, Sch 2 para 4 with effect from the passing of FA 2004, so far as is necessary for enabling the making of any orders or regulations by virtue of FA 2004 Sch 2, and otherwise with effect from such day as the Treasury may by order made by statutory instrument appoint.
[15] Words in para (v) inserted by FA 2004 s 22(3) with effect from 22 July 2004.
[16] Words in paras (t), (ta) inserted by F(No 2)A 2005 s 4(1), (5) with effect in any case where a claim under VATA 1994 s 80(2) is made on or after 26 May 2005, whenever the event occurred in respect of which the claim is made: F(No 2)A 2005 s 4(6).
[17] Words "69B" in para (n) substituted by FA 2006 s 21(4) with effect from 19 July 2006.
[18] Para (zza) inserted by FA 2006 s 21(4) with effect from 19 July 2006.
[19] Para (zc) inserted by FA 2007 s 93(8) with effect from 19 July 2007.
[20] Para (wb) inserted by the Value Added Tax (Buildings and Land) Order, SI 2008/1146, art 3(1), (2) with effect in relation to supplies made on or after 1 June 2008, subject to savings in Sch 2 of the Order.
[21] Sub-s (1) numbered as such; in new sub-s (1) words in the first place substituted for the words "section 84" and in the second place substituted for the words "a tribunal"; sub-s (2) inserted by the Transfer of Tribunal Functions and Revenue and Customs Appeals Order, SI 2009/56 art 3, Sch 1 para 219 with effect from 1 April 2009, subject to transitional and savings provisions in Sch 3 para 4.
[22] Para (ha) inserted by FA 2009 s 77 with effect from 21 July 2009.
[23] In sub-s (1)(v), words substituted for words "or 2" by FA 2012 s 200(1), (3) with effect in relation to supplies made on or after 17 July 2012.

[24] Sub-s (1)(*rb*) inserted by FA 2016 s 124(1), (3) with effect from 15 September 2016.
[25] Sub-s (1)(*na*), (*nb*) inserted by F(No 2)A 2017 s 68(1), (5) with effect from 15 November 2017.
[26] Sub-para (1)(*zc*) substituted by F(No 2)A 2017 s 62(1), (5) with effect from 15 November 2017. Regulations providing for digital record-keeping cannot come into force before 1 April 2019 (F(No 2)A 2017 s 62(7)).
[27] In sub-s (1), the following amendments made by the Taxation (Cross-border Trade) Act 2018 s 43, Sch 8 paras 1, 72 with effect from IP completion day (11pm on 31 December 2020), by virtue of SI 2020/1642 reg 4(*b*)—
- in para (*b*), words ", on the acquisition of goods from another member State" and "from a place outside the member States" repealed;
- paras (*d*), (*j*), (*w*) repealed; and
- in para (*p*), sub-para (iii) and preceding word "or" repealed.

Sub-s (1)(*d*), (*j*), (*w*) previously read as follows—
"(*d*) any claim for a refund under any regulations made by virtue of section 13(5);".
"(*j*) the amount of any refunds under section 40;".
"(*w*) any direction under paragraph 1 of Schedule 7;".

Sub-s (1)(*p*)(iii) previously read as follows—
"(iii) under section 75;".

[83A Offer of review
(1) HMRC must offer a person (P) a review of a decision that has been notified to P if an appeal lies under section 83 in respect of the decision.
(2) The offer of the review must be made by notice given to P at the same time as the decision is notified to P.
(3) This section does not apply to the notification of the conclusions of a review.][1]

Commentary—*De Voil Indirect Tax Service* **V5.407**.
HMRC Manuals—Securities Guidance Manual SG15115 (taxable person's right to a review).
Modifications—Money Laundering, Terrorist Financing and Transfer of Funds (Information on the Payer) Regulations, SI 2017/692 reg 99 (Part 5 applies in respect of appeals to the tribunal made under SI 2017/692 reg 99(1) as it applies in respect of appeals made to the tribunal under s 83, but as if ss 83A–84, 85A and 85B were revoked).
Amendments—[1] Sections 83A–83G inserted by the Transfer of Tribunal Functions and Revenue and Customs Appeals Order, SI 2009/56 art 3, Sch 1 para 220 with effect from 1 April 2009, subject to transitional and savings provisions in Sch 3 para 4.

[83B Right to require review
(1) Any person (other than P) who has the right of appeal under section 83 against a decision may require HMRC to review that decision if that person has not appealed to the tribunal under section 83G.
(2) A notification that such a person requires a review must be made within 30 days of that person becoming aware of the decision.][1]

Commentary—*De Voil Indirect Tax Service* **V5.407**.
Modifications—Money Laundering, Terrorist Financing and Transfer of Funds (Information on the Payer) Regulations, SI 2017/692 reg 99 (Part 5 applies in respect of appeals to the tribunal made under SI 2017/692 reg 99(1) as it applies in respect of appeals made to the tribunal under s 83, but as if ss 83A–84, 85A and 85B were revoked).
Amendments—[1] Sections 83A–83G inserted by the Transfer of Tribunal Functions and Revenue and Customs Appeals Order, SI 2009/56 art 3, Sch 1 para 220 with effect from 1 April 2009, subject to transitional and savings provisions in Sch 3 para 4.

[83C Review by HMRC
(1) HMRC must review a decision if—
  (*a*) they have offered a review of the decision under section 83A, and
  (*b*) P notifies HMRC accepting the offer within 30 days from the date of the document containing the notification of the offer.
(2) But P may not notify acceptance of the offer if P has already appealed to the tribunal under section 83G.
(3) HMRC must review a decision if a person other than P notifies them under section 83B.
(4) HMRC shall not review a decision if P, or another person, has appealed to the tribunal under section 83G in respect of the decision.][1]

Commentary—*De Voil Indirect Tax Service* **V5.407**.
HMRC Manuals—Securities Guidance Manual SG15115 (taxable person's right to a review).
Modifications—Money Laundering, Terrorist Financing and Transfer of Funds (Information on the Payer) Regulations, SI 2017/692 reg 99 (Part 5 applies in respect of appeals to the tribunal made under SI 2017/692 reg 99(1) as it applies in respect of appeals made to the tribunal under s 83, but as if ss 83A–84, 85A and 85B were revoked).
Amendments—[1] Sections 83A–83G inserted by the Transfer of Tribunal Functions and Revenue and Customs Appeals Order, SI 2009/56 art 3, Sch 1 para 220 with effect from 1 April 2009, subject to transitional and savings provisions in Sch 3 para 4.

[83D Extensions of time
(1) If under section 83A HMRC have offered P a review of a decision, HMRC may within the relevant period notify P that the relevant period is extended.
(2) If under section 83B another person may require HMRC to review a matter, HMRC may within the relevant period notify the other person that the relevant period is extended.
(3) If notice is given the relevant period is extended to the end of 30 days from—
  (*a*) the date of the notice, or
  (*b*) any other date set out in the notice or a further notice.
(4) In this section "relevant period" means—

(a) the period of 30 days referred to in—
   (i) section 83C(1)(b) (in a case falling within subsection (1)), or
   (ii) section 83B(2) (in a case falling within subsection (2)), or
(b) if notice has been given under subsection (1) or (2), that period as extended (or as most recently extended) in accordance with subsection (3).][1]

Commentary—*De Voil Indirect Tax Service* **V5.407**.
HMRC Manuals—Appeals, Reviews And Tribunals Manual ARTG3060 (extension of review acceptance or appeal period). ARTG3080 (customer rejects the offer and provides new information).
Modifications—Money Laundering, Terrorist Financing and Transfer of Funds (Information on the Payer) Regulations, SI 2017/692 reg 99 (Part 5 applies in respect of appeals to the tribunal made under SI 2017/692 reg 99(1) as it applies in respect of appeals made to the tribunal under s 83, but as if ss 83A–84, 85A and 85B were revoked).
Amendments—[1] Sections 83A–83G inserted by the Transfer of Tribunal Functions and Revenue and Customs Appeals Order, SI 2009/56 art 3, Sch 1 para 220 with effect from 1 April 2009, subject to transitional and savings provisions in Sch 3 para 4.

[83E Review out of time
(1) This section applies if—
   (a) HMRC have offered a review of a decision under section 83A and P does not accept the offer within the time allowed under section 83C(1)(b) or 83D(3); or
   (b) a person who requires a review under section 83B does not notify HMRC within the time allowed under that section or section 83D(3).
(2) HMRC must review the decision under section 83C if—
   (a) after the time allowed, P, or the other person, notifies HMRC in writing requesting a review out of time,
   (b) HMRC are satisfied that P, or the other person, had a reasonable excuse for not accepting the offer or requiring review within the time allowed, and
   (c) HMRC are satisfied that P, or the other person, made the request without unreasonable delay after the excuse had ceased to apply.
(3) HMRC shall not review a decision if P, or another person, has appealed to the tribunal under section 83G in respect of the decision.][1]

Commentary—*De Voil Indirect Tax Service* **V5.407**.
HMRC Manuals—Appeals, Reviews And Tribunals Manual ARTG3060 (extension of review acceptance or appeal period).
Modifications—Money Laundering, Terrorist Financing and Transfer of Funds (Information on the Payer) Regulations, SI 2017/692 reg 99 (Part 5 applies in respect of appeals to the tribunal made under SI 2017/692 reg 99(1) as it applies in respect of appeals made to the tribunal under s 83, but as if ss 83A–84, 85A and 85B were revoked).
Amendments—[1] Sections 83A–83G inserted by the Transfer of Tribunal Functions and Revenue and Customs Appeals Order, SI 2009/56 art 3, Sch 1 para 220 with effect from 1 April 2009, subject to transitional and savings provisions in Sch 3 para 4.

[83F Nature of review etc
(1) This section applies if HMRC are required to undertake a review under section 83C or 83E.
(2) The nature and extent of the review are to be such as appear appropriate to HMRC in the circumstances.
(3) For the purpose of subsection (2), HMRC must, in particular, have regard to steps taken before the beginning of the review—
   (a) by HMRC in reaching the decision, and
   (b) by any person in seeking to resolve disagreement about the decision.
(4) The review must take account of any representations made by P, or the other person, at a stage which gives HMRC a reasonable opportunity to consider them.
(5) The review may conclude that the decision is to be—
   (a) upheld,
   (b) varied, or
   (c) cancelled.
(6) HMRC must give P, or the other person, notice of the conclusions of the review and their reasoning within—
   (a) a period of 45 days beginning with the relevant date, or
   (b) such other period as HMRC and P, or the other person, may agree.
(7) In subsection (6) "relevant date" means—
   (a) the date HMRC received P's notification accepting the offer of a review (in a case falling within section 83A), or
   (b) the date HMRC received notification from another person requiring review (in a case falling within section 83B), or
   (c) the date on which HMRC decided to undertake the review (in a case falling within section 83E).
(8) Where HMRC are required to undertake a review but do not give notice of the conclusions within the time period specified in subsection (6), the review is to be treated as having concluded that the decision is upheld.
(9) If subsection (8) applies, HMRC must notify P or the other person of the conclusion which the review is treated as having reached.][1]

Commentary—*De Voil Indirect Tax Service* **V5.407**.

HMRC Manuals—Securities Guidance Manual SG15120 (time limits for review completion).
Modifications—Money Laundering, Terrorist Financing and Transfer of Funds (Information on the Payer) Regulations, SI 2017/692 reg 99 (Part 5 applies in respect of appeals to the tribunal made under SI 2017/692 reg 99(1) as it applies in respect of appeals made to the tribunal under s 83, but as if ss 83A–84, 85A and 85B were revoked).
Amendments—[1]   Sections 83A–83G inserted by the Transfer of Tribunal Functions and Revenue and Customs Appeals Order, SI 2009/56 art 3, Sch 1 para 220 with effect from 1 April 2009, subject to transitional and savings provisions in Sch 3 para 4.

[83G Bringing of appeals
(1) An appeal under section 83 is to be made to the tribunal before—
   (a) the end of the period of 30 days beginning with—
      (i) in a case where P is the appellant, the date of the document notifying the decision to which the appeal relates, or
      (ii) in a case where a person other than P is the appellant, the date that person becomes aware of the decision, or
   (b) if later, the end of the relevant period (within the meaning of section 83D).
(2) But that is subject to subsections (3) to (5).
(3) In a case where HMRC are required to undertake a review under section 83C—
   (a) an appeal may not be made until the conclusion date, and
   (b) any appeal is to be made within the period of 30 days beginning with the conclusion date.
[(4) In a case where HMRC are requested to undertake a review by virtue of section 83E—
   (a) an appeal may not be made—
      (i) unless HMRC have notified P, or the other person, as to whether or not a review will be undertaken, and
      (ii) if HMRC have notified P, or the other person, that a review will be undertaken, until the conclusion date;
   (b) any appeal where paragraph (a)(ii) applies is to be made within the period of 30 days beginning with the conclusion date;
   (c) if HMRC have notified P, or the other person, that a review will not be undertaken, an appeal may be made only if the tribunal gives permission to do so.][2]
(5) In a case where section 83F(8) applies, an appeal may be made at any time from the end of the period specified in section 83F(6) to the date 30 days after the conclusion date.
(6) An appeal may be made after the end of the period specified in subsection (1), (3)(b), (4)(b) or (5) if the tribunal gives permission to do so.
(7) In this section "conclusion date" means the date of the document notifying the conclusions of the review.][1]

Commentary—*De Voil Indirect Tax Service* **V1.406, V5.411**.
HMRC Manuals—Securities Guidance Manual SG15125 (timeline to appeal - independent tribunal).
Appeals, Reviews And Tribunals Manual ARTG7510 (application for a late indirect tax appeal).
Modifications—Money Laundering, Terrorist Financing and Transfer of Funds (Information on the Payer) Regulations, SI 2017/692 reg 99 (Part 5 applies in respect of appeals to the tribunal made under SI 2017/692 reg 99(1) as it applies in respect of appeals made to the tribunal under s 83, but as if ss 83A–84, 85A and 85B were revoked).
Amendments—[1]   Sections 83A–83G inserted by the Transfer of Tribunal Functions and Revenue and Customs Appeals Order, SI 2009/56 art 3, Sch 1 para 220 with effect from 1 April 2009, subject to transitional and savings provisions in Sch 3 para 4.
[2]   Sub-s (4) substituted by the Revenue and Customs (Amendment of Appeal Provisions for Out of Time Reviews) Order, SI 2014/1264 art 4 with effect in relation to requests for a review out of time notified to HMRC on or after 14 May 2014.

84 Further provisions relating to appeals
(1) References in this section to an appeal are references to an appeal under section 83.
(2) . . .[10]
[(3) Subject to subsections (3B) and (3C), where the appeal is against a decision with respect to any of the matters mentioned in section 83(1)(b), (n), (p), (q), (ra)[, (rb)][12] or (zb), it shall not be entertained unless the amount which HMRC have determined to be payable as VAT has been paid or deposited with them.][10]
[(3A) Subject to subsections (3B) and (3C), where the appeal is against an assessment which is a recovery assessment for the purposes of this subsection, or against the amount of such an assessment, it shall not be entertained unless the amount notified by the assessment has been paid or deposited with HMRC.][10]
[(3B) In a case where the amount determined to be payable as VAT or the amount notified by the recovery assessment has not been paid or deposited an appeal shall be entertained if—
   (a) HMRC are satisfied (on the application of the appellant), or
   (b) the tribunal decides (HMRC not being so satisfied and on the application of the appellant), that the requirement to pay or deposit the amount determined would cause the appellant to suffer hardship.
(3C) Notwithstanding the provisions of sections 11 and 13 of the Tribunals, Courts and Enforcement Act 2007, the decision of the tribunal as to the issue of hardship is final.][10]
(4) Subject to subsection (11) below, where—

(a) there is an appeal against a decision of [HMRC][10] with respect to, or to so much of any assessment as concerns, the amount of input tax that may be credited to any person or the proportion of input tax allowable under section 26, and
(b) that appeal relates, in whole or in part, to any determination by [HMRC[10]]—
  (i) as to the purposes for which any goods or services were or were to be used by any person, or
  (ii) as to whether or to what extent the matters to which any input tax was attributable were or included matters other than the making of supplies within section 26(2), and
(c) VAT for which, in pursuance of that determination, there is no entitlement to a credit is VAT on the supply . . . [13] or importation of something in the nature of a luxury, amusement or entertainment,

the tribunal shall not allow the appeal or, as the case may be, so much of it as relates to that determination unless it considers that the determination is one which it was unreasonable to make or which it would have been unreasonable to make if information brought to the attention of the tribunal that could not have been brought to the attention of [HMRC][10] had been available to be taken into account when the determination was made.

[(4ZA) Where an appeal is brought—
(a) against such a decision as is mentioned in section [83(1)][10](*fza*), or
(b) to the extent that it is based on such a decision, against an assessment,
the tribunal shall not allow the appeal unless it considers that [HMRC][10] could not reasonably have been satisfied that there were grounds for the decision.][4]

[(4A) Where an appeal is brought against the refusal of an application such as is mentioned in section 43B(1) or (2) on the grounds stated in section 43B(5)(*c*)—
(a) the tribunal shall not allow the appeal unless it considers that [HMRC][10] could not reasonably have been satisfied that there were grounds for refusing the application,
(b) the refusal shall have effect pending the determination of the appeal, and
(c) if the appeal is allowed, the refusal shall be deemed not to have occurred.

(4B) Where an appeal is brought against the giving of a notice under section 43C(1) or (3)—
(a) the notice shall have effect pending the determination of the appeal, and
(b) if the appeal is allowed, the notice shall be deemed never to have had effect.

(4C) Where an appeal is brought against the giving of a notice under section 43C(1), the tribunal shall not allow the appeal unless it considers that [HMRC][10] could not reasonably have been satisfied that there were grounds for giving the notice.

(4D) Where—
(a) an appeal is brought against the giving of a notice under section 43C(3), and
(b) the grounds of appeal relate wholly or partly to the date specified in the notice,
the tribunal shall not allow the appeal in respect of the date unless it considers that [HMRC][10] could not reasonably have been satisfied that it was appropriate.][3]

[(4E) Where an appeal is brought against a requirement imposed under paragraph 4(2)(*b*) of Schedule 11 that a person give security, the tribunal shall allow the appeal unless [HMRC satisfies][10] the tribunal that—
(a) there has been an evasion of, or an attempt to evade, VAT in relation to goods or services supplied to or by that person, or
(b) it is likely, or without the requirement for security it is likely, that VAT in relation to such goods or services will be evaded.

(4F) A reference in subsection (4E) above to evading VAT includes a reference to obtaining a VAT credit that is not due or a VAT credit in excess of what is due.][5]

(5) Where, on an appeal against a decision with respect to any of the matters mentioned in section [83(1)][10](*p*) [or (*rb*)[12]]—
(a) it is found that the amount specified in the assessment is less than it ought to have been, and
(b) the tribunal gives a direction specifying the correct amount,
the assessment shall have effect as an assessment of the amount specified in the direction, and that amount shall be deemed to have been notified to the appellant.

(6) Without prejudice to section 70, . . . [13] nothing in section [83(1)][10](*q*) shall be taken to confer on a tribunal any power to vary an amount assessed by way of penalty, interest or surcharge except in so far as it is necessary to reduce it to the amount which is appropriate under sections 59 to 70; and in this subsection "penalty" includes an amount assessed by virtue of section 61(3) or (4)(*a*).

[(6A) Without prejudice to section 70, nothing in section [83(1)][10](*zb*) shall be taken to confer on a tribunal any power to vary an amount assessed by way of penalty except in so far as it is necessary to reduce it to the amount which is appropriate under paragraph 11 of Schedule 11A.][6]

[(6B) Nothing in section [83(1)][10](*zc*) shall be taken to confer on a tribunal any power to vary an amount assessed by way of penalty except in so far as it is necessary to reduce it to the amount which is appropriate under regulations made under section 135 of the Finance Act 2002.][8]

(7) Where there is an appeal against a decision to make such a direction as is mentioned in section [83(1)]¹⁰(*u*), the tribunal shall not allow the appeal unless it considers that [HMRC]¹⁰ could not reasonably have been satisfied [that there were grounds for making the direction]².

[(7A) Where there is an appeal against a decision to make such a direction as is mentioned in section [83(1)]¹⁰(*wa*), the cases in which the tribunal shall allow the appeal shall include (in addition to the case where the conditions for the making of the direction were not fulfilled) the case where the tribunal are satisfied in relation to the relevant event by reference to which the direction was given, that—
  (*a*) the change in the treatment of the body corporate, or
  (*b*) the transaction in question,

  had as its main purpose or, as the case may be, as each of its main purposes a genuine commercial purpose unconnected with the fulfilment of the condition specified in paragraph 1(3) of Schedule 9A.]¹

[(7ZA) Where there is an appeal against such a refusal as is mentioned in section [83(1)]¹⁰(*wb*)—
  (*a*) the tribunal shall not allow the appeal unless it considers that [HMRC]¹⁰ could not reasonably have been satisfied that there were grounds for the refusal, and
  (*b*) the refusal shall have effect pending the determination of the appeal.]⁹

[(7B) Where there is an appeal against a decision to make such a direction as is mentioned in section [83(1)]¹⁰(*zza*)—
  (*a*) the tribunal shall not allow the appeal unless it considers that [HMRC]¹⁰ could not reasonably have been satisfied that there were grounds for making the direction;
  (*b*) the direction shall have effect pending the determination of the appeal.]⁷

(8) . . . ¹⁰

(9) No appeal shall lie under this section with respect to the subject-matter of any decision which by virtue of section 16 is a decision to which section 14 [or 15A]¹⁰ of the Finance Act 1994 (decisions subject to review) applies unless the decision—
  (*a*) relates exclusively to one or both of the following matters, namely whether or not section 30(3) applies in relation to the importation of the goods in question and (if it does not) the rate of tax charged on those goods; and
  (*b*) is not one in respect of which notice has been given to [HMRC]¹⁰ under section 14 of that Act requiring them to review it[; and
  (*c*) a review is not being undertaken following a request under section 14A of that Act; and
  (*d*) a review is not being undertaken under section 15 of that Act as a consequence of section 15B(3), 15C(3) or 15E(3) of that Act.]¹⁰

(10) Where an appeal is against [an HMRC decision]¹⁰ which depended upon a prior decision taken . . . ¹⁰ in relation to the appellant, the fact that the prior decision is not within section 83 shall not prevent the tribunal from allowing the appeal on the ground that it would have allowed an appeal against the prior decision.

(11) Subsection (4) above shall not apply in relation to any appeal relating to the input tax that may be credited to any person at the end of a prescribed accounting period beginning before 27th July 1993.

Commentary—*De Voil Indirect Tax Service* **V1.284, V5.424, V5.406**.
HMRC Manuals—Appeals, Reviews and Tribunals Manual ARTG3041 (appeals under specific provisions).
ARTG3330 (hardship applications).
VAT Input tax VIT43200 (business entertainment).
VIT43500 (appeals about business and staff entertainment).
Northern Ireland—See Sch 9ZA para 34(2) (Northern Ireland: this section has effect as if in sub-s (4)(*c*), after "supply" there were inserted ", acquisition").
Modifications—Money Laundering Regulations, SI 2007/2157 reg 44(3), Sch 5 para 1 (repeal of this section in relation to appeals to a VAT and duties tribunal made under SI 2007/2157 reg 44).
Transfer of Funds (Information on the Payer) Regulations, SI 2007/3298 reg 13(4), Sch 2 para 2 (repeal of this section in relation to appeals to a VAT and duties tribunal made under SI 2007/3298 reg 13).
Money Laundering, Terrorist Financing and Transfer of Funds (Information on the Payer) Regulations, SI 2017/692 reg 99 (Part 5 applies in respect of appeals to the tribunal made under SI 2017/692 reg 99(1) as it applies in respect of appeals made to the tribunal under s 83, but as if ss 83A–84, 85A and 85B were revoked).
Amendments—¹ Sub-s (7A) inserted by FA 1996 s 31(4).
² Words in sub-s (7) substituted for the words 'as to the matters in sub-paragraph (2)(a) to (d) of paragraph 2 of Schedule 1 or, as the case may be, as to the matters in sub-paragraph (4) of that paragraph" by FA 1997 s 31 in relation to directions made on or after the date of passing of FA 1997.
³ Sub-ss (4A)–(4D) inserted by FA 1999 s 16, Sch 2 para 4 with effect from 27 July 1999 subject to FA 1999 Sch 2 para 6.
⁴ Sub-s (4ZA) inserted by FA 2002 s 23(3), (4) and deemed to have come into force on 24 April 2002.
⁵ Sub-ss (4E), (4F) inserted by FA 2003 s 17(7) with effect from 10 April 2003.
⁶ Sub-s (6A) inserted, by FA 2004 s 19, Sch 2 para 5 with effect from the passing of FA 2004, so far as is necessary for enabling the making of any orders or regulations by virtue of FA 2004 Sch 2, and otherwise with effect from such day as the Treasury may by order made by statutory instrument appoint.
⁷ Sub-ss (7B) inserted by FA 2006 s 21(5) with effect from 19 July 2006.
⁸ Sub-s (6B) inserted by FA 2007 s 93(9) with effect from 19 July 2007.

[9] Sub-s (7ZA) inserted by the Value Added Tax (Buildings and Land) Order, SI 2008/1146, art 3(1), (3) with effect in relation to supplies made on or after 1 June 2008, subject to savings in Sch 2 of the Order.
[10] Amendments made by the Transfer of Tribunal Functions and Revenue and Customs Appeals Order, SI 2009/56 art 3, Sch 1 para 221 with effect from 1 April 2009, subject to transitional and savings provisions in Sch 3 para 4
[12] In sub-ss (3), (5), words inserted by FA 2016 s 124(1), (4) with effect from 15 September 2016.
[13] The following words repealed by the Taxation (Cross-border Trade) Act 2018 s 43, Sch 8 paras 1, 73 with effect from IP completion day (11pm on 31 December 2020), by virtue of SI 2020/1642 reg 4(b)—
- in sub-s (4)(c), word ", acquisition"; and
- in sub-s (6), words "or (as the case requires) paragraph 26 of Schedule 3BA or paragraph 16F of Schedule 3B".

85 Settling appeals by agreement

(1) Subject to the provisions of this section, where a person gives notice of appeal under section 83 and, before the appeal is determined by a tribunal, [HMRC][1] and the appellant come to an agreement (whether in writing or otherwise) under the terms of which the decision under appeal is to be treated—

(a) as upheld without variation, or

(b) as varied in a particular manner, or

(c) as discharged or cancelled,

the like consequences shall ensue for all purposes as would have ensued if, at the time when the agreement was come to, a tribunal had determined the appeal in accordance with the terms of the agreement . . . [1].

(2) Subsection (1) above shall not apply where, within 30 days from the date when the agreement was come to, the appellant gives notice in writing to [HMRC][1] that he desires to repudiate or resile for the agreement.

(3) Where an agreement is not in writing—

(a) the preceding provisions of this section shall not apply unless the fact that an agreement was come to, and the terms agreed, are confirmed by notice in writing given by [HMRC][1] to the appellant or by the appellant to [HMRC][1], and

(b) references in those provisions to the time when the agreement was come to shall be construed as references to the time of the giving of that notice of confirmation.

(4) Where—

(a) a person who has given a notice of appeal notifies [HMRC][1], whether orally or in writing, that he desires not to proceed with the appeal; and

(b) 30 days have elapsed since the giving of the notification without [HMRC][1] giving to the appellant notice in writing indicating that they are unwilling that the appeal should be treated as withdrawn,

the preceding provisions of this section shall have effect as if, at the date of the appellant's notification, the appellant and [HMRC][1] had come to an agreement, orally or in writing, as the case may be, that the decision under appeal should be upheld without variation.

(5) References in this section to an agreement being come to with an appellant and the giving of notice or notification to or by an appellant include references to an agreement being come to with, and the giving of notice or notification to or by, a person acting on behalf of the appellant in relation to the appeal.

Commentary—De Voil Indirect Tax Service **V5.461**.

HMRC Manuals—Appeals, Reviews And Tribunals Manual ARTG3420 (settlement by agreement).

Modifications—Customs Safety and Security (Penalty) Regulations, SI 2019/121 reg 15 (section 85 has effect as if the reference to VATA 1994, s 83 included a reference to Customs Safety and Security (Penalty) Regulations, SI 2019/121 reg 9 (Right to appeal)).

Amendments—[1] Word substituted in each place for the words "the Commissioners" and in sub-s (1) words "(including any terms as to costs)" at the end repealed by the Transfer of Tribunal Functions and Revenue and Customs Appeals Order, SI 2009/56 art 3, Sch 1 para 222 with effect from 1 April 2009, subject to transitional and savings provisions in Sch 3 para 4.

[85A Payment of tax on determination of appeal

(1) This section applies where the tribunal has determined an appeal under section 83.

(2) Where on the appeal the tribunal has determined that—

(a) the whole or part of any disputed amount paid or deposited is not due, or

(b) the whole or part of any VAT credit due to the appellant has not been paid,

so much of that amount, or of that credit, as the tribunal determines not to be due or not to have been paid shall be paid or repaid with interest at the rate applicable under section 197 of the Finance Act 1996.

(3) Where on the appeal the tribunal has determined that—

(a) the whole or part of any disputed amount not paid or deposited is due, or

(b) the whole or part of any VAT credit paid was not payable,

so much of that amount, or of that credit, as the tribunal determines to be due or not payable shall be paid or repaid to HMRC with interest at the rate applicable under section 197 of the Finance Act 1996.

(4) Interest under subsection (3) shall be paid without any deduction of income tax.

(5) Nothing in this section requires HMRC to pay interest—
   (a) on any amount which falls to be increased by a supplement under section 79 (repayment supplement in respect of certain delayed payments or refunds); or
   (b) where an amount is increased under that section, on so much of the increased amount as represents the supplement.]¹

Commentary—*De Voil Indirect Tax Service* **V5.461**.
HMRC Manuals—Statutory Interest Manual VDIM12060 (interest following HMRC's success at tribunal).
VSIM7600 (interest following HMRC loss at tribunal).
Compliance Handbook Manual CH146080 (repayment interest: when is interest not paid).
Modifications—Money Laundering, Terrorist Financing and Transfer of Funds (Information on the Payer) Regulations, SI 2017/692 reg 99 (Part 5 applies in respect of appeals to the tribunal made under SI 2017/692 reg 99(1) as it applies in respect of appeals made to the tribunal under s 83, but as if ss 83A–84, 85A and 85B were revoked).
Amendments—¹ Sections 85A–85B inserted by the Transfer of Tribunal Functions and Revenue and Customs Appeals Order, SI 2009/56 art 3, Sch 1 para 223 with effect from 1 April 2009, subject to transitional and savings provisions in Sch 3 para 4.

[85B Payment of tax where there is a further appeal
(1) Where a party makes a further appeal, notwithstanding that the further appeal is pending, value added tax or VAT credits, or a credit of overstated or overpaid value added tax shall be payable or repayable in accordance with the determination of the tribunal or court against which the further appeal is made.
(2) But if the amount payable or repayable is altered by the order or judgment of the tribunal or court on the further appeal—
   (a) if too much value added tax has been paid or the whole or part of any VAT credit due to the appellant has not been paid the amount overpaid or not paid shall be refunded with such interest, if any, as the tribunal or court may allow; and
   (b) if too little value added tax has been charged or the whole or part of any VAT credit paid was not payable so much of the amount as the tribunal or court determines to be due or not payable shall be due or repayable, as appropriate, at the expiration of a period of thirty days beginning with the date on which HMRC issue to the other party a notice of the total amount payable in accordance with the order or judgment of that tribunal or court.
(3) If, on the application of HMRC, the relevant tribunal or court considers it necessary for the protection of the revenue, subsection (1) shall not apply and the relevant tribunal or court may—
   (a) give permission to withhold any payment or repayment; or
   (b) require the provision of adequate security before payment or repayment is made.
(4) If, on the application of the original appellant, HMRC are satisfied that financial extremity might be reasonably expected to result if payment or repayment is required or withheld as appropriate, HMRC may do one or more of the things listed in subsection (6).
(5) If on the application of the original appellant, the relevant tribunal or court decides that—
   (a) the original appellant has applied to HMRC under subsection (4),
   (b) HMRC have decided that application,
   (c) financial extremity might be reasonably expected to result from that decision by HMRC,
the relevant tribunal or court may replace, vary or supplement the decision by HMRC by doing one or more of the things listed in subsection (6).
(6) These are the things which HMRC or the relevant tribunal or court may do under subsection (4) or (5)—
   (a) decide how much, if any, of the amount under appeal should be paid or repaid as appropriate,
   (b) require the provision of adequate security from the original appellant,
   (c) stay the requirement to pay or repay under subsection (1).
(7) Subsections (3) to (6) cease to have effect when the further appeal has been determined.
(8) In this section—
   "adequate security" means security that is of such amount and given in such manner—
      (a) as the tribunal or court may determine (in a case falling within subsection (3) or (5)), or
      (b) as HMRC consider adequate to protect the revenue (in a case falling within subsection (4));
   "further appeal" means an appeal against—
      (a) the tribunal's determination of an appeal under section 83, or
      (b) a decision of the Upper Tribunal or a court that arises (directly or indirectly) from that determination;
   "original appellant" means the person who made the appeal to the tribunal under section 83;
   "relevant tribunal or court" means the tribunal or court from which permission or leave to appeal is sought.]¹

Commentary—*De Voil Indirect Tax Service* **V5.461**.
HMRC Manuals—Appeals, Reviews And Tribunals Manual ARTG8930 (FTT and UT : outcome of the tribunal proceedings).
Modifications—Money Laundering, Terrorist Financing and Transfer of Funds (Information on the Payer) Regulations, SI 2017/692 reg 99 (Part 5 applies in respect of appeals to the tribunal made under SI 2017/692 reg 99(1) as it applies in respect of appeals made to the tribunal under s 83, but as if ss 83A–84, 85A and 85B were revoked).

Amendments—[1] Sections 85A–85B inserted by the Transfer of Tribunal Functions and Revenue and Customs Appeals Order, SI 2009/56 art 3, Sch 1 para 223 with effect from 1 April 2009, subject to transitional and savings provisions in Sch 3 para 4. If an appeal from a decision of a VAT and duties tribunal, or from a court, is made before 1 April 2009, this section does not apply in relation to that decision (SI 2009/56 Sch 3 para 10).

PART VI
SUPPLEMENTARY PROVISIONS

Change in rate of VAT etc and disclosure of information

88 Supplies spanning change of rate etc

(1) This section applies where there is a change in the rate of VAT in force under section 2 [or 29A][1] or in the descriptions of exempt[, zero-rated or reduced-rate][1] supplies . . . [3].

(2) Where—

    (*a*) a supply affected by the change would, apart from section 6(4), (5), (6) or (10), be treated under section 6(2) or (3) as made wholly or partly at a time when it would not have been affected by the change; or

    (*b*) a supply not so affected would apart from section 6(4), (5), (6) or (10) be treated under section 6(2) or (3) as made wholly or partly at a time when it would have been so affected,

the rate at which VAT is chargeable on the supply, or any question whether it is zero-rated or exempt [or a reduced-rate supply][1], shall if the person making it so elects be determined without regard to section 6(4), (5), (6) or (10).

(3) Any power to make regulations under this Act with respect to the time when a supply is to be treated as taking place shall include power to provide for this section to apply as if the references in subsection (2) above to section 6(4), (5), (6) or (10) included references to specified provisions of the regulations.

(4) . . . [3]

(5) Regulations under [paragraph 2A][2] of Schedule 11 may make provision for the replacement or correction of any VAT invoice which—

    (*a*) relates to a supply in respect of which an election is made under this section, but

    (*b*) was issued before the election was made.

(6) No election may be made under this section in respect of a supply to which [paragraph 7 of Schedule 4 or paragraph 2B(4) of Schedule 11][2] applies.

(7) . . . [3]

[(8) References in this section to a supply being a reduced-rate supply are references to a supply being one on which VAT is charged at the rate in force under section 29A.][3]

Commentary—*De Voil Indirect Tax Service* **V3.141.**

HMRC Manuals—VAT Time Of Supply VATTOS2280 (legislation: section 88 supplies spanning change of rate, etc).
VATTOS7210 (basic principles).
VATTOS7220 (adoption of the special rules).
VAT Traders' Records Manual VATREC13110 (liability incorrect and change in rate of VAT in force).

Regulations—See VAT Regulations, SI 1995/2518 reg 95.

Amendments—[1] In sub-s (1), "or 29A" inserted, and words substituted for "or zero-rated", and words in sub-s (2) inserted, by FA 2001 s 99(6), Sch 31 para 4 with effect from 11 May 2001.

[2] Words in sub-ss (5), (6) substituted by FA 2002 s 24(4)(c), (5) with effect from 1 December 2003 (by virtue of SI 2003/3043).

[3] The following amendments made by the Taxation (Cross-border Trade) Act 2018 s 43, Sch 8 paras 1, 74 with effect from IP completion day (11pm on 31 December 2020), by virtue of SI 2020/1642 reg 4(*b*)—

    – in sub-s (1), words "or exempt, zero-rated or reduced-rate acquisitions" repealed;

    – sub-ss (4), (7) repealed; and

    – sub-s (8) substituted.

Sub-ss (4), (7), (8) previously read as follows—

"(4) Where—

    (*a*) any acquisition of goods from another member State which is affected by the change would not have been affected (in whole or in part) if it had been treated as taking place at the time of the event which, in relation to that acquisition, is the first relevant event for the purposes of taxing the acquisition; or".

"(7) References in this section to an acquisition being zero-rated are references to an acquisition of goods from another member State being one in relation to which section 30(3) provides for no VAT to be chargeable.

    (*b*) any acquisition of goods from another member State which is not so affected would have been affected (in whole or in part) if it had been treated as taking place at the time of that event,

the rate at which VAT is chargeable on the acquisition, or any question whether it is zero-rated or exempt or a reduced-rate acquisition, shall, if the person making the acquisition so elects, be determined as at the time of that event.".

"(8) References in this section—

    (*a*) to a supply being a reduced-rate supply, or

    (*b*) to an acquisition being a reduced-rate acquisition,

are references to a supply, or (as the case may be) an acquisition, being one on which VAT is charged at the rate in force under section 29A.".

89 Adjustments of contracts on changes in VAT

(1) Where, after the making of a contract for the supply of goods or services and before the goods or services are supplied, there is a change in the VAT charged on the supply, then, unless the contract otherwise provided, there shall be added to or deducted from the consideration for the supply an amount equal to the change.

(2) Subsection (1) above shall apply in relation to a tenancy or lease as it applies in relation to a contract except that a term of a tenancy or lease shall not be taken to provide that the rule contained in that subsection is not to apply in the case of the tenancy or lease if the term does not [refer][1] specifically to VAT or this section.

(3) References in this section to a change in the VAT charged on a supply include references to a change to or from no VAT being charged on the supply (including a change attributable to the making of an [option to tax any land under Part 1 of Schedule 10][2]).

Commentary—*De Voil Indirect Tax Service* **V3.151**.

HMRC Manuals—VAT Time Of Supply VATTOS2285 (legislation: Section 89 adjustments of contracts on changes in VAT). VATTOS7230 (adjustment of contract prices).

Amendments—[1] The Commissioners have confirmed that the word "refer" has been accidentally omitted from s 89(2).
[2] In sub-s (3) words substituted by the Value Added Tax (Buildings and Land) Order, SI 2008/1146, art 6, Sch 1 paras 1, 2 with effect in relation to supplies made on or after 1 June 2008, subject to savings in Sch 2 of the Order.

90 Failure of resolution under Provisional Collection of Taxes Act 1968

(1) Where—
 (a) by virtue of a resolution having effect under the Provisional Collection of Taxes Act 1968 VAT has been paid at a rate specified in the resolution on the supply of any goods or services by reference to a value determined under section 19(2) . . . [4], and
 (b) by virtue of section 1(6) or (7) or 5(3) of that Act any of that VAT is repayable in consequence of the restoration in relation to that supply . . . [4] of a lower rate,
the amount repayable shall be the difference between the VAT paid by reference to that value at the rate specified in the resolution and the VAT that would have been payable by reference to that value at the lower rate.

(2) Where—
 (a) by virtue of such a resolution VAT is chargeable at a rate specified in the resolution on the supply of any goods or services by reference to a value determined under section 19(2) . . . [4], but
 (b) before the VAT is paid it ceases to be chargeable at that rate in consequence of the restoration in relation to that supply . . . [4] of a lower rate,
the VAT chargeable at the lower rate shall be charged by reference to the same value as that by reference to which VAT would have been chargeable at the rate specified in the resolution.

(3) The VAT that may be credited as input tax under section 25 or refunded under section 33, [or 33A,][1] [33B,][2] [33C][3] [or 35][4] does not include VAT that has been repaid by virtue of any of the provisions mentioned in subsection (1)(b) above or that would be repayable by virtue of any of those provisions if it had been paid.

Commentary—*De Voil Indirect Tax Service* **V1.131**.

Northern Ireland—See Sch 9ZA para 36 (Northern Ireland: failure of resolution under PCTA 1968: sub-s (3) has effect as if after "or 35" there were inserted "or paragraph 19 of Schedule 9ZA).

Amendments—[1] Words in sub-s (3) inserted by FA 2001 s 98(8) with effect from 1 September 2001.
[2] Words in sub-s (3) inserted by FA 2011 s 76(3) with effect in relation to supplies made, and acquisitions and importations taking place, on or after 1 April 2011.
[3] Words in sub-s (3)" inserted by FA 2015 s 66(1), (3) with effect in relation to supplies made, and acquisitions and importations taking place, on or after 1 April 2015.
[4] The following amendments made by the Taxation (Cross-border Trade) Act 2018 s 43, Sch 8 paras 1, 75 with effect from IP completion day (11pm on 31 December 2020), by virtue of SI 2020/1642 reg 4(b)—
  – in sub-ss (1), (2), the following words repealed—
   (a) in para (a), words "or on the acquisition of goods from another member State by reference to a value determined under section 20(3)"; and
   (b) in para (b), words "or acquisition"; and
  – in sub-s (3), words substituted for words ", 35 or 40".

91 Disclosure of information for statistical purposes

(1) For the purpose of the compilation or maintenance by the Department of Trade and Industry or the [Statistics Board][1] of a central register of businesses, or for the purpose of any statistical survey conducted or to be conducted by that Department [or Board][1], the Commissioners or an authorised officer of the Commissioners may disclose to an authorised officer of that Department [or Board][1] particulars of the following descriptions obtained or recorded by them in pursuance of this Act—
 (a) numbers allocated by the Commissioners on the registration of persons under this Act and reference numbers for members of a group;
 (b) names, trading styles and addresses of persons so registered or of members of groups and status and trade classifications of businesses; and
 (c) actual or estimated value of supplies.

(2) Subject to subsection (3) below, no information obtained by virtue of this section by an officer of the Department of Trade and Industry or the [Statistics Board][1] may be disclosed except to an officer of a Government department (including a Northern Ireland department [or to a member of the staff of the Scottish Administration][2]) for the purpose for which the information was obtained, or for a like purpose.

(3) Subsection (2) above does not prevent the disclosure—
   (a) of any information in the form of a summary so framed as not to enable particulars to be identified as particulars relating to a particular person or to the business carried on by a particular person; or
   (b) with the consent of any person, of any information enabling particulars to be identified as particulars relating only to him or to a business carried on by him.

(4) If any person who has obtained any information by virtue of this section discloses it in contravention of this section he shall be liable—
   (a) on summary conviction to a fine not exceeding the statutory maximum; and
   (b) on conviction on indictment to imprisonment for a term not exceeding 2 years or to a fine of any amount or to both.

(5) In this section, references to the Department of Trade and Industry or the [Statistics Board][1] include references to any Northern Ireland department [or to any part of the Scottish Administration][2] carrying out similar functions.

Commentary—*De Voil Indirect Tax Service* **V1.270, V5.315**.
Amendments—[1] Words in sub-ss (1), (2), (5) substituted by Statistics and Registration Service Act 2007 s 46, Sch 2 para 6 with effect from 1 April 2008, by virtue of SI 2008/839, art 2.
[2] Words in sub-ss (2), (5) inserted by The Scotland Act 1998 (Consequential Modifications) (No 2) Order, SI 1999/1820 s 114(2), which comes into force on the "principle appointed day", currently 1 July 1999, by virtue of the Scotland Act 1998 (Commencement) Order 1998/3178.

Interpretative provisions

92 Taxation under the laws of other member States etc

(1) Subject to the following provisions of this section, references in this Act, in relation to another member State, to the law of that member State shall be construed as confined to so much of the law of that member State as for the time being has effect for the purposes of any EU instrument relating to VAT.

(2) Subject to the following provisions of this section—
   (a) references in this Act to a person being taxable in another member State are references to that person being taxable under so much of the law of that member State as makes provision for purposes corresponding, in relation to that member State, to the purposes of so much of this Act as makes provision as to whether a person is a taxable person; and
   (b) references in this Act to goods being acquired by a person in another member State are references to goods being treated as so acquired in accordance with provisions of the law of that member State corresponding, in relation to that member State, to so much of this Act as makes provision for treating goods as acquired in the United Kingdom from another member State.

(3) Without prejudice to subsection (5) below, the Commissioners may by regulations make provision for the manner in which any of the following are to be or may be proved for any of the purposes of this Act, that is to say—
   (a) the effect of any provisions of the law of any other member State;
   (b) that provisions of any such law correspond or have a purpose corresponding, in relation to any member State, to or to the purpose of any provision of this Act.

(4) The Commissioners may by regulations provide—
   (a) for a person to be treated for prescribed purposes of this Act as taxable in another member State only where he has given such notification, and furnished such other information, to the Commissioners as may be prescribed;
   (b) for the form and manner in which any notification or information is to be given or furnished under the regulations and the particulars which it is to contain;
   (c) for the proportion of any consideration for any transaction which is to be taken for the purposes of this Act as representing a liability, under the law of another member State, for VAT to be conclusively determined by reference to such invoices or in such other manner as may be prescribed.

(5) In any proceedings (whether civil or criminal), a certificate of the Commissioners—
   (a) that a person was or was not, at any date, taxable in another member State; or
   (b) that any VAT payable under the law of another member State has or has not been paid,
shall be sufficient evidence of that fact until the contrary is proved, and any document purporting to be a certificate under this subsection shall be deemed to be such a certificate until the contrary is proved.

(6) Without prejudice to the generality of any of the powers of the Commissioners under the relevant information provisions, those powers shall, for the purpose of facilitating compliance with any EU obligations, be exercisable with respect to matters that are relevant to a charge to VAT under the law of another member State, as they are exercisable with respect to matters that are relevant for any of the purposes of this Act.
(7) The reference in subsection (6) above to the relevant information provisions is a reference to the provisions of section 73(7) and Schedule 11 relating to—
 (a) the keeping of accounts;
 (b) the making of returns and the submission of other documents to the Commissioners;
 (c) the production, use and contents of invoices;
 (d) the keeping and preservation of records; and
 (e) the furnishing of information and the production of documents.[1]

Commentary—*De Voil Indirect Tax Service* **V1.244**.
Amendments—[1]   Section 92 repealed by the Taxation (Cross-border Trade) Act 2018 s 43, Sch 8 paras 1, 76 with effect from IP completion day (11pm on 31 December 2020), by virtue of SI 2020/1642 reg 4(*b*).

93 Territories included in references to other member States etc
(1) The Commissioners may by regulations provide for the territory of the European Union, or for the member States, to be treated for any of the purposes of this Act as including or excluding such territories as may be prescribed.
(2) Without prejudice to the generality of the powers conferred by subsection (1) and section 16, the Commissioners may, for any of the purposes of this Act, by regulations provide for prescribed provisions of any customs and excise legislation to apply in relation to cases where any territory is treated under subsection (1) above as excluded from the territory of the European Union, with such exceptions and adaptations as may be prescribed.
(3) In subsection (2) above the reference to customs and excise legislation is a reference to any enactment or subordinate or EU legislation (whenever passed, made or adopted) which has effect in relation to, or to any assigned matter connected with, the importation or exportation of goods.
(4) In subsection (3) above "assigned matter" has the same meaning as in the Management Act.[1]

Commentary—*De Voil Indirect Tax Service* **V1.213**.
Regulations—See VAT Regulations, SI 1995/2518 regs 118–121, 136–145.
Value Added Tax (Amendment) (No 3) Regulations 2013/3211.
Amendments—[1]   Section 93 repealed by the Taxation (Cross-border Trade) Act 2018 s 43, Sch 8 paras 1, 77 with effect with effect from IP completion day (11pm on 31 December 2020), by virtue of SI 2020/1642 reg 4(*b*).

94 Meaning of "business" etc
(1) In this Act "business" includes any trade, profession or vocation.
(2) Without prejudice to the generality of anything else in this Act, the following are deemed to be the carrying on of a business—
 (a) the provision by a club, association or organisation (for a subscription or other consideration) of the facilities or advantages available to its members; and
 (b) the admission, for a consideration, of persons to any premises.
(3) . . .[1]
(4) Where a person, in the course or furtherance of a trade, profession or vocation, accepts any office, services supplied by him as the holder of that office are treated as supplied in the course or furtherance of the trade, profession or vocation.
(5) Anything done in connection with the termination or intended termination of a business is treated as being done in the course or furtherance of that business.
(6) The disposition of a business[, or part of a business,][2] as a going concern, or of [the assets or liabilities of the business or part of the business][2] (whether or not in connection with its reorganisation or winding up), is a supply made in the course or furtherance of the business.

Commentary—*De Voil Indirect Tax Service* **V2.201B, V2.211, V2.214, V3.125**.
HMRC Manuals—VAT Business and Non Business Activities VBNB24000 (business and non business activities). VBNB60410 (deemed business).
VBNB72400 (cases about section 94(2) activities).
Amendments—[1]   Sub-s (3) repealed by FA 1999 s 20 Sch 20 Pt II with effect from 1 December 1999 (by virtue of the Finance Act 1999, Section 20, (Appointed Day) Order, SI 1999/2769, art 2).
[2]   In sub-s (6) words inserted and substituted by FA 2007 s 100(7), (10) with effect in relation to transfers pursuant to contracts entered into on or after 1 September 2007.

95 Meaning of "new means of transport"
(1) In this Act "means of transport" in the expression "new means of transport" means, subject to subsection (2) below, any of the following, that is to say—
 (a) any ship exceeding 7.5 metres in length;
 (b) any aircraft the take-off weight of which exceeds 1550 kilograms;
 (c) any motorised land vehicle which—
  (i) has an engine with a displacement or cylinder capacity exceeding 48 cubic centimetres; or

(ii) is constructed or adapted to be electrically propelled using more than 7.2 kilowatts.
(2) A ship, aircraft or motorised land vehicle does not fall within subsection (1) above unless it is intended for the transport of persons or goods.
[(3) For the purposes of this Act a means of transport shall be treated as new, in relation to any supply or any acquisition from another member State, at any time unless at that time—
    (a) the period that has elapsed since its first entry into service is—
        (i) in the case of a ship or aircraft, a period of more than 3 months; and
        (ii) in the case of a land vehicle, a period of more than 6 months;
and][1]
    (b) it has, since its first entry into service, travelled under its own power—
        (i) in the case of a ship, for more than 100 hours;
        (ii) in the case of an aircraft, for more than 40 hours; and
        (iii) in the case of a land vehicle, for more than [6000 kilometres][1].
(4) The Treasury may by order vary this section—
    (a) by adding or deleting any ship, aircraft or vehicle of a description specified in the order to or from those which are for the time being specified in subsection (1) above; and
    (b) by altering, omitting or adding to the provisions of subsection (3) above for determining whether a means of transport is new.
(5) The Commissioners may by regulations make provision specifying the circumstances in which a means of transport is to be treated for the purposes of this section as having first entered into service.[1]

Commentary—*De Voil Indirect Tax Service* **V1.294**.
Regulations—See VAT Regulations, SI 1995/2518 reg 147.
Amendments—[1] Words in sub-s (3) substituted by the Value Added Tax (Means of Transport) Order, SI 1994/3128 with effect in relation to means of transport whose first entry into service is on or after 1 January 1995.
[2] Section 95 repealed by the Taxation (Cross-border Trade) Act 2018 s 43, Sch 8 paras 1, 78 with effect from IP completion day (11pm on 31 December 2020), by virtue of SI 2020/1642 reg 4(*b*).

[95A Meaning of "online marketplace" and "operator" etc

(1) In this Act—
"online marketplace" means a website, or any other means by which information is made available over the internet, which facilitates the sale of goods through the website or other means by persons other than the operator (whether or not the operator also sells goods through the marketplace);
"operator", in relation to an online marketplace, means the person who controls access to, and the contents of, the online marketplace provided that the person is involved in—
    (a) determining any terms or conditions applicable to the sale of goods,
    (b) processing, or facilitating the processing, of payment for the goods, and
    (c) the ordering or delivery, or facilitating the ordering or delivery, of the goods.
(2) For the purposes of subsection (1), an online marketplace facilitates the sale of goods if it allows a person to—
    (*a*) offer goods for sale, and
    (*b*) enter into a contract for the sale of those goods.
(3) The Treasury may by regulations amend this section so as to alter the meaning of—
    "online marketplace", and
    "operator".][1]

Commentary—*De Voil Indirect Tax Service* **V3.305, V1.306A**.
Amendments—[1] Section 95A inserted by the Taxation (Post-transition Period) Act 2020 s 7, Sch 3 paras 1, 14 with effect from IP completion day (11pm on 31 December 2020), by virtue of SI 2020/1642 reg 9.

96 Other interpretative provisions

(1) In this Act—
"the 1983 Act" means the Value Added Tax Act 1983;[14]
. . .
"assignment", in relation to Scotland, means assignation;
"authorised person" means any person acting under the authority of the Commissioners;
"the Commissioners" means the Commissioners of Customs and Excise;
["copy", in relation to a document, means anything onto which information recorded in the document has been copied, by whatever means and whether directly or indirectly;][2]
["document" means anything in which information of any description is recorded; and][2]
"fee simple"—
    (*a*) in relation to Scotland, means the . . . [8] interest of the owner;
    (*b*) in relation to Northern Ireland, includes the estate of a person who holds land under a fee farm grant;
["HMRC" means Her Majesty's Revenue and Customs;][10]
["import duty" means import duty charged in accordance with Part 1 of TCTA 2018;][14]

"invoice" includes any document similar to an invoice;
"input tax" has the meaning given by section 24;
. . . [13]
"local authority" has the meaning given by subsection (4) below;
"major interest", in relation to land, means the fee simple or a tenancy for a term certain exceeding 21 years, and in relation to Scotland means [the][8] interest of the owner, or the lessee's interest under a lease for a period [of not less than 20 years][5];
"the Management Act" means the Customs and Excise Management Act 1979;
"money" includes currencies other than sterling;
"output tax" has the meaning given by section 24;
. . . [13]
. . . [12]
["postal operator" means a person who provides—
  (a) the service of conveying postal packets from one place to another by post, or
  (b) any of the incidental services of receiving, collecting, sorting and delivering postal packets;][15]
["postal packet" means a letter, parcel, packet or other article transmissible by post;][15]
"prescribed" means prescribed by regulations;
"prescribed accounting period" has the meaning given by section 25(1);
"quarter" means a period of 3 months ending at the end of March, June, September or December;
"regulations" means regulations made by the Commissioners under this Act;
["relevant business person" has the meaning given by section 7A(4)][11];
"ship" includes hovercraft;
"subordinate legislation" has the same meaning as in the Interpretation Act 1978;
"tax" means VAT;
. . . [14]
"taxable person" means a person who is a taxable person under section 3;
"taxable supply" has the meaning given by section 4(2);
["TCTA 2018" means the Taxation (Cross-border Trade) Act 2018;][14]
"the Taxes Act" means the Income and Corporation Taxes Act 1988;
"tribunal" has the meaning given by section 82;
["trustee in sequestration" means a trustee (or interim trustee) in a sequestration under the Bankruptcy (Scotland) Act 2016;][13]
["VAT" means value added tax charged in accordance with this Act;][14]
"VAT credit" has the meaning given by section 25(3);
"VAT invoice" has the meaning given by section 6(15);
"VAT representative" has the meaning given by section 48;
and any reference to a particular section, Part or Schedule is a reference to that section or Part of, or Schedule to, this Act.
(2) Any reference in this Act to being registered shall be construed in accordance with section 3(3).
(4) In this Act "local authority" means the council of a county, [county borough,][1] district, London borough, parish or group of parishes (or, in Wales, community or group of communities), the Common Council of the City of London, the Council of the Isles of Scilly, and any joint committee or joint board established by two or more of the foregoing and, in relation to Scotland, a regional, islands or district council within the meaning of the Local Government (Scotland) Act 1973 any combination and any joint committee or joint board established by two or more of the foregoing and any joint board to which section 226 of that Act applies.
(5) Any reference in this Act to the amount of any duty of excise on any goods shall be taken to be a reference to the amount of duty charged on those goods with any addition or deduction falling to be made under section 1 of the Excise Duties (Surcharges or Rebates) Act 1979.
(6), (7) . . . [3]
(8) The question whether, in relation to any supply of services, the supplier or the recipient of the supply belongs in one country or another shall be determined . . . [11] in accordance with section 9.
(9) Schedules [7A,][6] 8 and 9 shall be interpreted in accordance with the notes contained in those Schedules; and accordingly the powers conferred by this Act to vary those Schedules include a power to add to, delete or vary those notes.
(10) The descriptions of Groups in those Schedules are for ease of reference only and shall not affect the interpretation of the descriptions of items in those Groups.
[(10A) Where—
  (a) the grant of any interest, right, licence or facilities gives rise for the purposes of this Act to supplies made at different times after the making of the grant, and
  (b) a question whether any of those supplies is zero-rated or exempt falls to be determined according to whether or not the grant is a grant of a description specified in Schedule 8 or 9 or [any of paragraphs 5 to 11 of Schedule 10][9],

that question shall be determined according to whether the description is applicable as at the time of supply, rather than by reference to the time of the grant.]⁴

[(10B) Notwithstanding subsection (10A) above—
(a) item 1 of Group 1 of Schedule 9 does not make exempt any supply that arises for the purposes of this Act from the prior grant of a fee simple falling within paragraph (a) of that item; and
(b) that paragraph does not prevent the exemption of a supply that arises for the purposes of this Act from the prior grant of a fee simple not falling within that paragraph.]⁷

(11) References in this Act to the United Kingdom include the territorial sea of the United Kingdom.

Commentary—*De Voil Indirect Tax Service* **V1.241, V3,512, V4.232G**.
HMRC Manuals—VAT Time Of Supply VATTOS2275 (meaning of a VAT invoice).
VAT Land And Property VATLP02800 (time of supply).
VAT Construction VCONST03210 (meaning of 'major interest').
VAT Government And Public Bodies VATGPB4860 (section 33 bodies: common errors).
Orders—Value Added Tax (Drugs and Medicines) Order, SI 2009/2972.
VAT (Relief for European Research Infrastructure Consortia) Order, SI 2012/2907.
Value Added Tax (Reduced Rate) (Cable-Suspended Passenger Transport Systems) Order, SI 2013/430.
Value Added Tax (Drugs and Medicines) Order, SI 2014/1111.
Value Added Tax (Sport) Order, SI 2014/3185.
Value Added Tax (Finance) (EU Exit) Order, SI 2019/43.
Value Added Tax (Finance) (EU Exit) (Revocation) Order, SI 2019/1014.
Value Added Tax (Finance) Order, SI 2020/209.
Value Added Tax (Drugs and Medicines) Order, SI 2020/250.
Value Added Tax (Zero Rate for Personal Protective Equipment) (Coronavirus) Order, SI 2020/458.
Value Added Tax (Extension of Zero-Rating to Electronically Supplied Books etc) (Coronavirus) Order, SI 2020/459.
VAT (Reduced Rate) (Hospitality and Tourism) (Coronavirus) Order, SI 2020/728.
Amendments—¹ Words in sub-s (4) inserted by the Local Government Reorganisation (Wales) (Consequential Amendments No 2) Order, SI 1995/1510 art 2 with effect from 16 June 1995.
² Definitions "document" and "copy" in sub-s (1) inserted by the Civil Evidence Act 1995 Sch 1 para 20 with effect from 31 January 1997 (see SI 1996/3217).
³ Sub-ss (6), (7) repealed by the Civil Evidence Act 1995 Sch 2 with effect from 31 January 1997 (see SI 1996/3217).
⁴ Sub-s (10A) inserted by FA 1997 s 35 and deemed always to have had effect.
⁵ Words in the definition of "major interest" in para (b) substituted by FA 1998 s 24 with effect from 31 July 1998.
⁶ In sub-s (9), "7A" inserted by FA 2001 s 99(6), Sch 31 para 5 with effect from 11 May 2001.
⁷ Sub-s (10B) inserted by FA 2003 s 20 with effect for any supply that arises for the purposes of VATA 1994 from the prior grant of a fee simple made after 8 April 2003.
⁸ In sub-s (1), words in definition of "fee simple" repealed and words in definition of "major interest" substituted by the Abolition of Feudal Tenure etc (Scotland) Act 2000 s 76(1), (2), Sch 12 Pt I para 57, Sch 13 Pt 1 with effect from 28 November 2004 (by virtue of SI 2003/456).
⁹ In sub-s (10A)(b), words substituted by the Value Added Tax (Buildings and Land) Order, SI 2008/1146, art 6, Sch 1 paras 1, 3 with effect in relation to supplies made on or after 1 June 2008, subject to savings in Sch 2 of the Order.
¹⁰ In sub-s (1) definition of "HMRC" inserted by the Transfer of Tribunal Functions and Revenue and Customs Appeals Order, SI 2009/56 art 3, Sch 1 para 225 with effect from 1 April 2009, subject to transitional and savings provisions in Sch 3 para 4.
¹¹ In sub-s (1) words inserted, in sub-s (8) words "(subject to any provision made under section 8(6))" repealed by FA 2009 s 76, Sch 36 paras 1, 8 with effect in relation to supplies made on or after 1 January 2010.
¹² In sub-s (1), definition of "the Post Office company" repealed by F(No 3)A 2010 s 22(3)(a) with effect in relation to supplies made on or after 31 January 2011.
¹³ In sub-s (1), definitions of "interim trustee" and "permanent trustee" revoked, and definition of "trustee in sequestration" inserted, by the Bankruptcy (Scotland) Act 2016 (Consequential Provisions and Modifications) Order, SI 2016/1034 art 7(1), Sch 1 para 12(1), (7) with effect from 30 November 2016.
¹⁴ The following amendments made by the Taxation (Cross-border Trade) Act 2018 s 43, Sch 8 paras 1, 79 with effect from IP completion day (11pm on 31 December 2020), by virtue of SI 2020/1642 reg 4(b)—
– in sub-s (1)—
  (a) definitions of "another member State" and "taxable acquisition" repealed;
  (b) definitions of "TCTA 2018" and "import duty" inserted; and
  (c) definition of "VAT" substituted; and
– sub-s (3) repealed.
Definitions previously read as follows—
" "another member State" means, subject to section 93(1), any member State other than the United Kingdom, and "other member States" shall be construed accordingly;".
" "taxable acquisition" has the meaning given by section 10(2);".
" "VAT" means value added tax charged in accordance with this Act or, where the context requires, with the law of another member State;".
Sub-s (3) previously read as follows—
"(3) Subject to section 93—
(a) the question whether or not goods have entered the territory of the European Union;
(b) the time when any EU customs debt in respect of duty on the entry of any goods into the territory of the European Union would be incurred; and
(c) the person by whom any such debt would fall to be discharged,
shall for the purposes of this Act be determined (whether or not the goods in question are themselves subject to any such duties) according to the EU legislation applicable to goods which are in fact subject to such duties.".

[15] In sub-s (1) definitions of "postal operator" and "postal packet" inserted by the Taxation (Post-transition Period) Act 2020 s 7, Sch 3 paras 1, 15 with effect from IP completion day (11pm on 31 December 2020), by virtue of SI 2020/1642 reg 9.

Supplementary provisions

97 Orders, rules and regulations

(1) Any order made by the Treasury . . . [12] under this Act and any regulations or rules under this Act shall be made by statutory instrument.

(2) . . . [12]

(3) An order to which this subsection applies shall be laid before the House of Commons; and unless it is approved by that House before the expiration of a period of 28 days beginning with the date on which it was made, it shall cease to have effect on the expiration of that period, but without prejudice to anything previously done thereunder or to the making of a new order.

In reckoning any such period no account shall be taken of any time during which Parliament is dissolved or prorogued or during which the House of Commons is adjourned for more than 4 days.

(4) Subject to section 53(4), subsection (3) above applies to—

(aa) . . . [1]

(a) an order under section 5(4)[, 7A(6)][14] or 28;

[(ab) an order under paragraph 5(7) of Schedule 4 substituting a lesser sum for the sum for the time being specified in paragraph 5(2)(a) of that Schedule;][2]

(b) . . . [3]

(c) an order under this Act making provision—
  (i) for increasing the rate of VAT in force [under section 2][4] at the time of the making of the order;
  (ii) for excluding any VAT from credit under section 25;
  [(iia) for varying Schedule 7A so as to cause VAT to be charged on a supply at the rate in force under section 2 instead of that in force under section 29A;][5]
  (iii) for varying Schedule 8 or 9 so as to abolish the zero-rating of a supply or to abolish the exemption of a supply without zero-rating it;

[(ca) an order under section 43AA(1) if as a result of the order any [persons][17] would cease to be eligible to be treated as members of a group;][8]

(d) an order under section 51, except one making only such amendments as are necessary or expedient in consequence of provisions of an order under this Act which—
  (i) vary Schedule [7A,][5] 8 or 9; but
  (ii) are not within paragraph (c) above;

(e) an order under section 54(4) or (8);

[(ea) an order under section 55A(13);][10]

[(eb) an order under section 77A(9) or (9A);][11]

[(f) an order under paragraph [B1, C1(4),][16] 1A(7)[, 2A(4)][16] [or 8A(7)][15] of Schedule 6;][6]

[(fa) an order under paragraph 3(4) of Schedule 10A);][9]

[(g) an order under paragraph 3 or 4 of Schedule 11A][7].

[(4A) Where an order under section 2(2) is in force, the reference in subsection (4)(c)(i) of this section to the rate of VAT in force under section 2 at the time of the making of an order is a reference to the rate which would be in force at that time if no such order had been made.][13]

(5) A statutory instrument made under any provision of this Act except—
  (a) an order made under section 79, or
  (b) an instrument as respects which any other Parliamentary procedure is expressly provided, or
  (c) an instrument containing an order appointing a day for the purposes of any provision of this Act, being a day as from which the provision will have effect, with or without amendments, or will cease to have effect,

shall be subject to annulment in pursuance of a resolution of the House of Commons.

Commentary—*De Voil Indirect Tax Service* **V1.236**.

Amendments—[1] Sub-s (4)(aa) inserted by FA 1995 s 21(4), (6), with effect in relation to any supply made after 31 March 1995 and any acquisition or importation taking place after that date, and repealed by FA 2001 s 110, Sch 33 Pt 3(1) with effect from 1 November 2001.

[2] Sub-s (4)(ab) inserted by FA 1996 s 33(3).

[3] Sub-s (4)(b) repealed by FA 1996 Sch 41 Pt IV(2).

[4] Words in sub-s (4)(c)(i) inserted by FA 2001 s 99(6), Sch 31 para 6(2) with effect in relation to orders under VATA 1994 s 2(2) that make changes only in the rate of VAT that is in force at times after 31 October 2001.

[5] Sub-s (4)(c)(iia) inserted, and words in sub-s (4)(d)(i) inserted, by FA 2001 s 99(6), Sch 31 para 6(3), (4) with effect from 11 May 2001.

[6] Sub-s (4)(f) inserted by FA 2004 s 22(4) with effect from 22 July 2004.

[7] Sub-s (4)(g) inserted by FA 2004 s 19, Sch 2 para 6 with effect from the passing of FA 2004, so far as is necessary for enabling the making of any orders or regulations by virtue of FA 2004 Sch 2, and otherwise with effect from such day as the Treasury may by order made by statutory instrument appoint.

[8] Sub-s (ca) inserted by FA 2004 s 20(5) with effect from 22 July 2004.

[9] Sub-s (4)(fa) inserted by FA 2006 s 22(2) with effect from 19 July 2006.

[10] Sub-s (4)(ea) inserted by FA 2006 s 19(6), (8) with effect for supplies made on or after 1 June 2007 (by virtue of the Finance Act 2006, Section 19, (Appointed Day) Order, SI 2007/1419).
[11] Sub-s (4)(eb) inserted by FA 2007 s 98(2) with effect from 19 July 2007.
[12] In sub-s (1) words "or the Lord Chancellor" repealed; sub-(2) repealed by the Transfer of Tribunal Functions and Revenue and Customs Appeals Order, SI 2009/56 art 3, Sch 1 para 226 with effect from 1 April 2009, subject to transitional and savings provisions in Sch 3 para 4.
[13] Sub-s (4A) inserted by FA 2009 Sch 3 para 25(3) with effect from 21 July 2009.
[14] Words in sub-s (4)(a) inserted by FA 2009 s 76, Sch 36 paras 1, 9 with effect in relation to supplies made on or after 1 January 2010.
[15] In sub-s (4)(f), words inserted by FA 2012 s 200(1), (4) with effect in relation to supplies made on or after 17 July 2012.
[16] Words inserted in sub-s (4)(f) by FA 2013 s 192, Sch 38 paras 1, 5 with effect from 17 July 2013.
[17] In sub-s (4)(ca), words substituted for words "bodies" by FA 2019 s 53, Sch 18 paras 3, 12 with effect from 1 November 2019 (see SI 2019/1348).

Prospective amendments—In sub-s (4)(a) words ", 28 or 40A" to be substituted for words "or 28", by the Taxation (Post-transition Period) Act 2020 s 3, Sch 2 para 7(3) with effect from a date to be appointed. Note that all other provisions of the TPTPA 2020 were brought into force with effect from IP completion day (11pm on 31 December 2020), by virtue of SI 2020/1642 reg 9.

[97A Place of supply orders: transitional provision.
(1) This section shall have effect for the purpose of giving effect to any order made [under section 7A(6)][2], if—
  (a) the order provides for services of a description specified in the order to be treated as supplied in the United Kingdom;
  (b) the services would not have fallen to be so treated apart from the order;
  (c) the services are not services that would have fallen to be so treated under any provision re-enacted in the order; and
  (d) the order is expressed to come into force in relation to services supplied on or after a date specified in the order ("the commencement date").
(2) Invoices and other documents provided to any person before the commencement date shall be disregarded in determining the time of the supply of any services which, if their time of supply were on or after the commencement date, would be treated by virtue of the order as supplied in the United Kingdom.
(3) If there is a payment in respect of any services of the specified description that was received by the supplier before the commencement date, so much (if any) of that payment as relates to times on or after that date shall be treated as if it were a payment received on the commencement date.
(4) If there is a payment in respect of services of the specified description that is or has been received by the supplier on or after the commencement date, so much (if any) of that payment as relates to times before that date shall be treated as if it were a payment received before that date.
(5) Subject to subsection (6) below, a payment in respect of any services shall be taken for the purposes of this section to relate to the time of the performance of those services.
(6) Where a payment is received in respect of any services the performance of which takes place over a period a part of which falls before the commencement date and a part of which does not—
  (a) an apportionment shall be made, on a just and reasonable basis, of the extent to which the payment is attributable to so much of the performance of those services as took place before that date;
  (b) the payment shall, to that extent, be taken for the purposes of this section to relate to a time before that date; and
  (c) the remainder, if any, of the payment shall be taken for those purposes to relate to times on or after that date.][1]

Commentary—*De Voil Indirect Tax Service* V3.133.
HMRC Manuals—VAT Time Of Supply VATTOS2290 (legislation: section 97A place of supply orders transitional provisions). VATTOS7300 (place of supply).
Amendments—[1] This section inserted by FA 1998 s 22 with effect from 17 March 1998.
[2] In sub-s (1) words "on or after 17th March 1998 under section 7(11)" substituted by FA 2009 s 76, Sch 36 paras 1, 10 with effect in relation to supplies made on or after 1 January 2010.

98 Service of notices

Any notice, notification, requirement or demand to be served on, given to or made of any person for the purposes of this Act may be served, given or made by sending it by post in a letter addressed to that person or his VAT representative at the last or usual residence or place of business of that person or representative.

Commentary—*De Voil Indirect Tax Service* V5.131, V5.137, V5.138, V5.373.

99 Refund of VAT to Government of Northern Ireland

The Commissioners shall refund to the Government of Northern Ireland the amount of the VAT charged on the supply of goods or services to that Government . . . [1] or on the importation of any goods by that Government . . . [1], after deducting therefrom so much of that amount as may be agreed between them and the Department of Finance and Personnel for Northern Ireland as attributable to supplies . . . [1] and importations for the purpose of a business carried on by the Government of Northern Ireland.

HMRC Manuals—VAT Government And Public Bodies VATGPB9350 (refund scheme).

Northern Ireland—See Sch 9ZA para 37 (Northern Ireland: this section applies to VAT charged on the acquisition of goods from a member State by the Government of Northern Ireland as it applies to VAT charged on the supply of goods or services to that Government, and to any amount attributable to acquisitions of goods from a member State for the purpose of a business carried on by the Government of Northern Ireland as it applies to supplies for that purpose).

Amendments—[1] The following words repealed by the Taxation (Cross-border Trade) Act 2018 s 43, Sch 8 paras 1, 80 with effect from IP completion day (11pm on 31 December 2020), by virtue of SI 2020/1642 reg 4(*b*)—
- ", on the acquisition of any goods by that Government from another member State";
- "from a place outside the member States"; and
- ", acquisitions".

100 Savings and transitional provisions, consequential amendments and repeals
(1) Schedule 13 (savings and transitional provisions) and Schedule 14 (consequential amendments) shall have effect.
(2) The enactments and Orders specified in Schedule 15 are hereby repealed to the extent mentioned in the third column of that Schedule.
(3) This section is without prejudice to the operation of sections 15 to 17 of the Interpretation Act 1978 (which relate to the effect of repeals).

101 Commencement and extent
(1) This Act shall come into force on 1st September 1994 and Part I shall have effect in relation to the charge to VAT on supplies, acquisitions and importations in prescribed accounting periods ending on or after that date.
(2) Without prejudice to section 16 of the Interpretation Act 1978 (continuation of proceedings under repealed enactments) except in so far as it enables proceedings to be continued under repealed enactments, section 72 shall have effect on the commencement of this Act to the exclusion of section 39 of the 1983 Act.
(3) This Act extends to Northern Ireland.
(4) Paragraph 23 of Schedule 13 and paragraph 7 of Schedule 14 shall extend to the Isle of Man but no other provision of this Act shall extend there.

102 Short title
This Act may be cited as the Value Added Tax Act 1994.

SCHEDULES

[SCHEDULE A1
CHARGE AT REDUCED RATE]

Section 2

Amendments—Sch A1 inserted by FA 1995 s 21(3), (6), with effect in relation to any supply made after 31 March 1995 and any acquisition or importation taking place after that date, and repealed by FA 2001 s 99(3) with effect for supplies made, and acquisitions and importations taking place, after 31 October 2001. See VATA 1994 Sch 7A for supplies, etc after 31 October 2001.

SCHEDULE 1
REGISTRATION IN RESPECT OF TAXABLE SUPPLIES[: UK ESTABLISHMENT]

Section 3(2)

Northern Ireland—See Sch 9ZA para 38 (Northern Ireland: liability to register for VAT in respect of acquisitions from member States).

See Sch 9ZA para 48 (Northern Ireland: liability to register in respect of distance sales from the EU to Northern Ireland).

See Sch 9ZC paras 6–13 (Northern Ireland: liability to register for those deemed to be the importer of goods under Sch 9ZC).

Liability to be registered

1—(1) Subject to sub-paragraphs (3) to (7) below, a person who makes taxable supplies but is not registered under this Act becomes liable to be registered under this Schedule—
   (*a*) at the end of any month, if [the person is UK-established and][4] the value of his taxable supplies in the period of one year then ending has exceeded [£85,000][5]; or
   (*b*) at any time, if [the person is UK-established and][4] there are reasonable grounds for believing that the value of his taxable supplies in the period of 30 days then beginning will exceed [£85,000][5].

(2) Where a business[, or part of a business,]³ carried on by a taxable person is transferred to another person as a going concern[, the transferee is UK-established at the time of the transfer and the transferee is not registered under this Act at that time]⁴, then, subject to sub-paragraphs (3) to (7) below, the transferee becomes liable to be registered under this Schedule at that time if—
- (a) the value of his taxable supplies in the period of one year ending at the time of the transfer has exceeded [£85,000]⁵; or
- (b) there are reasonable grounds for believing that the value of his taxable supplies in the period of 30 days beginning at the time of the transfer will exceed [£85,000]⁵.

[(2A) In determining the value of a person's supplies for the purposes of sub-paragraph (1)(a) or (2)(a), supplies are to be taken into account (subject to sub-paragraphs (3) to (7)) whether or not the person was UK-established when they were made.]⁴

(3) A person does not become liable to be registered by virtue of sub-paragraph (1)(a) or (2)(a) above if the Commissioners are satisfied that the value of his taxable supplies in the period of one year beginning at the time at which, apart from this sub-paragraph, he would become liable to be registered will not exceed [£83,000].

(4) In determining the value of a person's supplies for the purposes of sub-paragraph (1)(a) or (2)(a) above, supplies made at a time when he was previously registered under this Act shall be disregarded if—
- (a) his registration was cancelled otherwise than under paragraph 13(3) below, [paragraph 11 of Schedule 1A]⁴ . . . ⁶ [or paragraph 6(2) of Schedule 3A]², and
- (b) the Commissioners are satisfied that before his registration was cancelled he had given them all the information they needed in order to determine whether to cancel the registration.

(5) A person shall be treated as having become liable to be registered under this Schedule at any time when he would have become so liable under the preceding provisions of this paragraph but for any registration which is subsequently cancelled under paragraph 13(3) below, [paragraph 11 of Schedule 1A]⁴ . . . ⁶ [or paragraph 6(2) of Schedule 3A]².

(6) A person shall not cease to be liable to be registered under this Schedule except in accordance with paragraph 2(5), 3 or 4 below.

(7) In determining the value of a person's supplies for the purposes of sub-paragraph (1) or (2) above, supplies of goods or services that are capital assets of the business in the course or furtherance of which they are supplied . . . ⁶ shall be disregarded.

(8) Where, apart from this sub-paragraph, an interest in, right over or licence to occupy any land would under sub-paragraph (7) above be disregarded for the purposes of sub-paragraph (1) or (2) above, it shall not be if it is supplied on a taxable supply which is not zero-rated.

[(9) In determining the value of a person's supplies for the purposes of sub-paragraph (1) or (2) above, supplies to which section 18B(4) (last . . . ⁶ supply of goods before removal from fiscal warehousing) applies and supplies treated as made by him under section 18C(3) (self-supply of services on removal of goods from warehousing) shall be disregarded.]¹

[(10) A person is "UK-established" if the person has a business establishment, or some other fixed establishment, in the United Kingdom in relation to a business carried on by the person.]⁴

Commentary—*De Voil Indirect Tax Service* **V2.134, V2.135, V2.136.**

Northern Ireland—See Sch 9ZA para 66: Northern Ireland: this para has effect as if—
- the provisions mentioned in sub-paras (4)(a) and (5) included Sch 9ZA paras 43(5) and 53(5));
- in sub-para (7), after "are supplied" there were inserted "and any taxable supplies which would not be taxable supplies apart from paragraph 29(1) of Schedule 9ZB"; and
- in sub-para (9), after "section 18B(4)" there were inserted "or paragraph 19(5) of Schedule 9ZB", and after "supply" there were inserted "or acquisition".

See also Sch 9ZC para 6 (Northern Ireland: liability to register for those deemed to be the importer of goods under Sch 9ZC).

Amendments—¹ Sub-para (9) added by FA 1996 Sch 3 para 13, with effect from 1 June 1996 (see Finance Act 1996, Section 26, (Appointed Day) Order, SI 1996/1249), and applying to any acquisition of goods from another member State and any supply taking place on or after that day.
² Words in sub-paras (4)(a), (5) substituted by FA 2000 s 136(6), with effect for supplies made after 20 March 2000.
³ Words in sub-para (2) inserted by FA 2007 s 100(8), (10) with effect in relation to transfers pursuant to contracts entered into on or after 1 September 2007.
⁴ In sub-paras (1)(a), (b), (4)(a), (5) words inserted, in sub-para (2) words substituted for words "and the transferee is not registered under this Act at the time of the transfer", sub-paras (2A), (10) inserted, and words in Schedule heading inserted, by FA 2012 s 203, Sch 28 paras 2, 11, 13 with effect in relation to supplies made or to be made on or after 1 December 2012.
⁵ Sums in sub-paras (1)(a), (b), (2)(a), (b), (3) substituted by the VAT (Increase of Registration Limits) Order, SI 2017/290 arts 2, 3(a), (b) with effect from 1 April 2017. The VAT registration limit figure was previously £83,000 and the cancellation of registration figure £81,000 from 1 April 2015 to 31 March 2016.
⁶ The following words repealed by the Taxation (Cross-border Trade) Act 2018 s 43, Sch 8 paras 1, 81(1), (2) with effect from IP completion day (11pm on 31 December 2020), by virtue of SI 2020/1642 reg 4(b)—
- in sub-para (4)(a), ", paragraph 6(2) of Schedule 2, paragraph 6(3) of Schedule 3";
- in sub-para (5), ", paragraph 6(2) of Schedule 2, paragraph 6(3) of Schedule 3";
- in sub-para (7), "and any taxable supplies which would not be taxable supplies apart from section 7(4)"; and
- in sub-para (9), "acquisition or".

[1A—(1) Paragraph 2 below is for the purpose of preventing the maintenance or creation of any artificial separation of business activities carried on by two or more persons from resulting in an avoidance of VAT.
(2) In determining for the purposes of sub-paragraph (1) above whether any separation of business activities is artificial, regard shall be had to the extent to which the different persons carrying on those activities are closely bound to one another by financial, economic and organisational links.][1]

Amendments—[1] This paragraph inserted by FA 1997 s 31(1) in relation to directions made on or after 19 March 1997.

2—(1) Without prejudice to paragraph 1 above, if the Commissioners make a direction under this paragraph, the persons named in the direction shall be treated as a single taxable person carrying on the activities of a business described in the direction and that taxable person shall be liable to be registered under this Schedule with effect from the date of the direction or, if the direction so provides, from such later date as may be specified therein.
(2) The Commissioners shall not make a direction under this paragraph naming any person unless they are satisfied—
  (*a*) that he is making or has made taxable supplies; and
  (*b*) that the activities in the course of which he makes or made those taxable supplies form only part of certain activities . . . [1], the other activities being carried on concurrently or previously (or both) by one or more other persons; and
  (*c*) that, if all the taxable supplies [the business described in the direction][1] were taken into account, a person carrying on that business would at the time of the direction be liable to be registered by virtue of paragraph 1 above; . . . [1]
  (*d*) . . . [1]
(3) A direction made under this paragraph shall be served on each of the persons named in it.
(4) Where, after a direction has been given under this paragraph specifying a description of business, it appears to the Commissioners that a person who was not named in that direction is making taxable supplies in the course of activities which should . . . [1] be regarded as part of the activities of that business, the Commissioners may make and serve on him a supplementary direction referring to the earlier direction and the description of business specified in it and adding that person's name to those of the persons named in the earlier direction with effect from—
  (*a*) the date on which he began to make those taxable supplies, or
  (*b*) if it was later, the date with effect from which the single taxable person referred to in the earlier direction became liable to be registered under this Schedule.
(5) If, immediately before a direction (including a supplementary direction) is made under this paragraph, any person named in the direction is registered in respect of the taxable supplies made by him as mentioned in sub-paragraph (2) or (4) above, he shall cease to be liable to be so registered with effect from whichever is the later of—
  (*a*) the date with effect from which the single taxable person concerned became liable to be registered; and
  (*b*) the date of the direction.
(6) In relation to a business specified in a direction under this paragraph, the persons named in the direction, together with any person named in a supplementary direction relating to that business (being the persons who together are to be treated as the taxable person), are in sub-paragraphs (7) and (8) below referred to as "the constituent members".
(7) Where a direction is made under this paragraph then, for the purposes of this Act—
  (*a*) the taxable person carrying on the business specified in the direction shall be registrable in such name as the persons named in the direction may jointly nominate by notice in writing given to the Commissioners not later than 14 days after the date of the direction or, in default of such a nomination, in such name as may be specified in the direction;
  (*b*) any supply of goods or services by or to one of the constituent members in the course of the activities of the taxable person shall be treated as a supply by or to that person;
  (*c*) . . . [2]
  (*d*) each of the constituent members shall be jointly and severally liable for any VAT due from the taxable person;
  (*e*) without prejudice to paragraph (*d*) above, any failure by the taxable person to comply with any requirement imposed by or under this Act shall be treated as a failure by each of the constituent members severally; and
  (*f*) subject to paragraphs (*a*) to (*e*) above, the constituent members shall be treated as a partnership carrying on the business of the taxable person and any question as to the scope of the activities of that business at any time shall be determined accordingly.
(8) If it appears to the Commissioners that any person who is one of the constituent members should no longer be regarded as such for the purposes of paragraphs (*d*) and (*e*) of sub-paragraph (7) above and they give notice to that effect, he shall not have any liability by virtue of those paragraphs for anything done after the date specified in that notice and, accordingly, on that date he shall be treated as having ceased to be a member of the partnership referred to in paragraph (*f*) of that sub-paragraph.

Commentary—*De Voil Indirect Tax Service* **V2.190C**.
Northern Ireland—See Sch 9ZA para 66(2): Northern Ireland: this para has effect as if a new sub-para (*c*) were inserted, as follows—
"(*c*) any acquisition of goods from a member State by one of the constituent members in the course of the activities of the taxable person is to be treated as an acquisition by that person;".
Amendments—[1] Word in sub-para (2)(*b*), (4) and whole of sub-para (2)(*d*) and the word "and " preceding it repealed, and words in sub-para (2)(*c*) substituted by FA 1997 s 31(2), (4), Sch 18 Pt IV(1) with effect in relation to directions made after 18 March 1997.
[2] Sub-para (7)(*c*) repealed by the Taxation (Cross-border Trade) Act 2018 s 43, Sch 8 paras 1, 81(1), (3) with effect from IP completion day (11pm on 31 December 2020), by virtue of SI 2020/1642 reg 4(*b*).
Sub-para (7)(*c*) previously read as follows—
"(*c*) any acquisition of goods from another member State by one of the constituent members in the course of the activities of the taxable person shall be treated as an acquisition by that person;".

3 A person who has become liable to be registered under this Schedule shall cease to be so liable at any time if the Commissioners are satisfied in relation to that time that he—
  (*a*) has ceased to make taxable supplies; or
  (*b*) is not at that time a person in relation to whom any of the conditions specified in paragraphs 1(1)(*a*) and (*b*) and (2)(*a*) and (*b*) above is satisfied[; or
  (*c*) is not at that time UK-established (see paragraph 1(10)).][1]
Commentary—*De Voil Indirect Tax Service* **V2.151**.
Northern Ireland—See Sch 9ZC para 7 (Northern Ireland: conditions where a person liable to be registered as a deemed importer of goods under Sch 9ZC ceases to be so liable).
Amendments—[1] Para (*c*) inserted, by FA 2012 s 203, Sch 28 paras 2, 12 with effect in relation to supplies made or to be made on or after 1 December 2012.

4—(1) Subject to sub-paragraph (2) below, a person who has become liable to be registered under this Schedule shall cease to be so liable at any time after being registered if the Commissioners are satisfied that the value of his taxable supplies in the period of one year then beginning will not exceed [£83,000][1].
(2) A person shall not cease to be liable to be registered under this Schedule by virtue of sub-paragraph (1) above if the Commissioners are satisfied that the reason the value of his taxable supplies will not exceed [£83,000][1] is that in the period in question he will cease making taxable supplies, or will suspend making them for a period of 30 days or more.
(3) In determining the value of a person's supplies for the purposes of sub-paragraph (1) above, supplies of goods or services that are capital assets of the business in the course or furtherance of which they are supplied . . . [2] shall be disregarded.
(4) Where, apart from this sub-paragraph, an interest in, right over or licence to occupy any land would under sub-paragraph (3) above be disregarded for the purposes of sub-paragraph (1) above, it shall not be if it is supplied on a taxable supply which is not zero-rated.
Commentary—*De Voil Indirect Tax Service* **V2.151**.
Northern Ireland—See Sch 9ZA para 66(3): Northern Ireland: sub-para (3) has effect as if after "are supplied" there were inserted "and any taxable supplies which would not be taxable supplies apart from paragraph 29(1) of Schedule 9ZB".
Amendments—[1] Sums in sub-paras (1), (2) substituted by the VAT (Increase of Registration Limits) Order, SI 2017/290 arts 2, 3(*c*) with effect from 1 April 2017. Figures were previously £81,000 from 1 April 2016 to 31 March 2017.
[2] In sub-para (3), words "and any taxable supplies which would not be taxable supplies apart from section 7(4)" repealed by the Taxation (Cross-border Trade) Act 2018 s 43, Sch 8 paras 1, 81(1), (4) with effect from IP completion day (11pm on 31 December 2020), by virtue of SI 2020/1642 reg 4(*b*).

Notification of liability and registration

5—(1) A person who becomes liable to be registered by virtue of paragraph 1(1)(*a*) above shall notify the Commissioners of the liability within 30 days of the end of the relevant month.
(2) The Commissioners shall register any such person (whether or not he so notifies them) with effect from the end of the month following the relevant month or from such earlier date as may be agreed between them and him.
(3) In this paragraph "the relevant month", in relation to a person who becomes liable to be registered by virtue of paragraph 1(1)(*a*) above, means the month at the end of which he becomes liable to be so registered.
Commentary—*De Voil Indirect Tax Service* **V2.135**.
Northern Ireland—See Sch 9ZC para 8 (Northern Ireland: notification of liability and registration requirements for a person who becomes liable to be registered under Sch 9ZC).

6—(1) A person who becomes liable to be registered by virtue of paragraph 1(1)(*b*) above shall notify the Commissioners of the liability before the end of the period by reference to which the liability arises.
(2) The Commissioners shall register any such person (whether or not he so notifies them) with effect from the beginning of the period by reference to which the liability arises.
Commentary—*De Voil Indirect Tax Service* **V2.136**.

7—(1) A person who becomes liable to be registered by virtue of paragraph 1(2) above shall notify the Commissioners of the liability within 30 days of the time when the business is transferred.
(2) The Commissioners shall register any such person (whether or not he so notifies them) with effect from the time when the business is transferred.
Commentary—*De Voil Indirect Tax Service* **V5.352**.

8 Where a person becomes liable to be registered by virtue of paragraph 1(1)(*a*) above and by virtue of paragraph 1(1)(*b*) or 1(2) above at the same time, the Commissioners shall register him in accordance with paragraph 6(2) or 7(2) above, as the case may be, rather than paragraph 5(2) above.

Entitlement to be registered

9 Where a person who is not liable to be registered under this Act and is not already so registered satisfies the Commissioners that he—
(*a*) makes taxable supplies; or
(*b*) is carrying on a business and intends to make such supplies in the course or furtherance of that business,
they shall, if he so requests, register him with effect from the day on which the request is made or from such earlier date as may be agreed between them and him.
Commentary—*De Voil Indirect Tax Service* **V2.144**.
Northern Ireland—See Sch 9ZC para 9 (Northern Ireland: circumstances where a person deemed to have imported goods under Sch 9ZC, and who is not liable to be registered, is entitled to be registered).

10—(1) Where a person who is not liable to be registered under this Act and is not already so registered satisfies the Commissioners that he—
(*a*) makes supplies within sub-paragraph (2) below; or
(*b*) is carrying on a business and intends to make such supplies in the course or furtherance of that business,
and (in either case) is within sub-paragraph (3) below, they shall, if he so requests, register him with effect from the day on which the request is made or from such earlier date as may be agreed between them and him.
[(2) A supply is within this sub-paragraph if—
(*a*) it is made outside the United Kingdom but would be a taxable supply if made in the United Kingdom; or
(*b*) it is specified for the purposes of subsection (2) of section 26 in an order made under paragraph (*c*) of that subsection.][1]
(3) A person is within this sub-paragraph if—
(*a*) he has a business establishment in the United Kingdom or his usual place of residence is in the United Kingdom; and
(*b*) he does not make and does not intend to make taxable supplies.
(4) For the purposes of this paragraph—
(*a*) a person carrying on a business through a branch or agency in the United Kingdom shall be treated as having a business establishment in the United Kingdom, and
(*b*) "usual place of residence", in relation to a body corporate, means the place where it is legally constituted.
Commentary—*De Voil Indirect Tax Service* **V2.146**.
Amendments—[1] Sub-para (2) substituted by FA 1997 s 32 with effect from 19 March 1997.

Notification of end of liability or entitlement etc

11 A person registered under paragraph 5, 6 or 9 above who ceases to make or have the intention of making taxable supplies shall notify the Commissioners of that fact within 30 days of the day on which he does so unless he would, when he so ceases, be otherwise liable or entitled to be registered under this Act if his registration and any enactment preventing a person from being liable to be registered under different provisions at the same time were disregarded.
Commentary—*De Voil Indirect Tax Service* **V2.151**.
Northern Ireland—See Sch 9ZC para 10 (Northern Ireland: requirement to notify HMRC of matters affecting continuance of registration).

12 A person registered under paragraph 10 above who—
(*a*) ceases to make or have the intention of making supplies within sub-paragraph (2) of that paragraph; or
(*b*) makes or forms the intention of making taxable supplies,
shall notify the Commissioners of that fact within 30 days of the day on which he does so unless, in the case of a person ceasing as mentioned in sub-paragraph (a) above, he would, when he so ceases, be otherwise liable or entitled to be registered under this Act if his registration and any enactment

preventing a person from being liable to be registered under different provisions at the same time were disregarded.
Commentary—*De Voil Indirect Tax Service* **V2.153**.
Northern Ireland—See Sch 9ZC para 10 (Northern Ireland: requirement to notify HMRC of matters affecting continuance of registration).

Cancellation of registration

13—(1) Subject to sub-paragraph (4) below, where a registered person satisfies the Commissioners that he is not liable to be registered under this Schedule, they shall, if he so requests, cancel his registration with effect from the day on which the request is made or from such later date as may be agreed between them and him.
(2) Subject to sub-paragraph (5) below, where the Commissioners are satisfied that a registered person has ceased to be registrable, they may cancel his registration with effect from the day on which he so ceased or from such later date as may be agreed between them and him.
(3) Where the Commissioners are satisfied that on the day on which a registered person was registered he was not registrable, they may cancel his registration with effect from that day.
(4) The Commissioners shall not under sub-paragraph (1) above cancel a person's registration with effect from any time unless they are satisfied that it is not a time when that person would be subject to a requirement to be registered under this Act.
(5) The Commissioners shall not under sub-paragraph (2) above cancel a person's registration with effect from any time unless they are satisfied that it is not a time when that person would be subject to a requirement, or entitled, to be registered under this Act.
(6) In determining for the purposes of sub-paragraph (4) or (5) above whether a person would be subject to a requirement, or entitled, to be registered at any time, so much of any provision of this Act as prevents a person from becoming liable or entitled to be registered when he is already registered or when he is so liable under any other provision shall be disregarded.
(7) In this paragraph, any reference to a registered person is a reference to a person who is registered under this Schedule.
(8) . . . [1]

Commentary—*De Voil Indirect Tax Service* **V2.151, V2.152**.
Northern Ireland—See Sch 9ZC para 11 (Northern Ireland: cancellation of registration for person registered under Sch 9ZC).
Amendments—[1] Sub-para (8) repealed by the Taxation (Cross-border Trade) Act 2018 s 43, Sch 8 paras 1, 81(1), (5) with effect from IP completion day (11pm on 31 December 2020), by virtue of SI 2020/1642 reg 4(*b*).
Sub-para (8) previously read as follows—
"(8) This paragraph is subject to paragraph 18 of Schedule 3B (cancellation of registration under this Schedule of persons seeking to be registered under that Schedule, etc).".

Exemption from registration

14—(1) Notwithstanding the preceding provisions of this Schedule, where a person who makes or intends to make taxable supplies satisfies the Commissioners that any such supply is zero-rated or would be zero-rated if he were a taxable person, they may, if he so requests and they think fit, exempt him from registration under this Schedule until it appears to them that the request should no longer be acted upon or is withdrawn.
(2) Where there is a material change in the nature of the supplies made by a person exempted under this paragraph from registration under this Schedule, he shall notify the Commissioners of the change—
    (*a*) within 30 days of the date on which it occurred; or
    (*b*) if no particular day is identifiable as the day on which it occurred, within 30 days of the end of the quarter in which it occurred.
(3) Where there is a material alteration in any quarter in the proportion of taxable supplies of such a person that are zero-rated, he shall notify the Commissioners of the alteration within 30 days of the end of the quarter.
Commentary—*De Voil Indirect Tax Service* **V2.147**.

Power to vary specified sums by order

15 The Treasury may by order substitute for any of the sums for the time being specified in this Schedule such greater sums as they think fit.
Orders—VAT (Increase of Registration Limits) Order, SI 2014/703.
VAT (Increase of Registration Limits) Order, SI 2015/750.
VAT (Increase of Registration Limits) Order, SI 2016/365.
VAT (Increase of Registration Limits) Order, SI 2017/290.

Supplementary

16 The value of a supply of goods or services shall be determined for the purposes of this Schedule on the basis that no VAT is chargeable on the supply.

17 Any notification required under this Schedule shall be made in such form [and manner][1] and shall contain such particulars [as may be specified in regulations or by the Commissioners in accordance with regulations.][1]
Regulations—See VAT Regulations, SI 1995/2518 reg 5 Sch 1.
VAT (Amendment) (No 2) Regulations, SI 2012/1899.
Northern Ireland—See Sch 9ZC para 12 (Northern Ireland: equivalent provision for notifications required under Sch 9ZC).
Amendments—[1] Words inserted, and words substituted for words "as the Commissioners may by regulations prescribe", by FA 2012 s 204, Sch 29 paras 1, 8 with effect from 17 July 2012.

18 In this Schedule "registrable" means liable or entitled to be registered under this Schedule.

19 References in this Schedule to supplies are references to supplies made in the course or furtherance of a business.

[SCHEDULE 1A

REGISTRATION IN RESPECT OF TAXABLE SUPPLIES: NON-UK ESTABLISHMENT]

Northern Ireland—See Sch 9ZA para 38 (Northern Ireland: liability to register for VAT in respect of acquisitions from member States).

See Sch 9ZA para 48 (Northern Ireland: liability to register in respect of distance sales from the EU to Northern Ireland).

Amendments—Schedule 1A inserted by FA 2012 s 203, Sch 28 para 1 with effect in relation to supplies made or to be made on or after 1 December 2012.

[Liability to be registered]

1—(1) A person becomes liable to be registered under this Schedule at any time if conditions A to D are met.
(2) Condition A is that—
  (*a*) the person makes taxable supplies, or
  (*b*) there are reasonable grounds for believing that the person will make taxable supplies in the period of 30 days then beginning.
(3) Condition B is that those supplies (or any of them) are or will be made in the course or furtherance of a business carried on by the person.
(4) Condition C is that the person has no business establishment, or other fixed establishment, in the United Kingdom in relation to any business carried on by the person.
(5) Condition D is that the person is not registered under this Act.][1]
Amendments—[1] Schedule 1A inserted by FA 2012 s 203, Sch 28 para 1 with effect in relation to supplies made or to be made on or after 1 December 2012.

[**2**—(1) A person does not become liable to be registered by virtue of paragraph 1(2)(*b*) if the reason for believing that taxable supplies will be made in the 30-day period mentioned there is that a business, or part of a business, carried on by a taxable person is to be transferred to the person as a going concern in that period.
(2) But if the transfer takes place, the transferee becomes liable to be registered under this Schedule at the time of the transfer if conditions A to D in paragraph 1 are met in relation to the transferee at that time.
(3) In determining for the purposes of sub-paragraph (2) whether condition B is met, the reference in paragraph 1(3) to a business is to be read as a reference to the business, or part of the business, that is transferred to the transferee.][1]
Amendments—[1] Schedule 1A inserted by FA 2012 s 203, Sch 28 para 1 with effect in relation to supplies made or to be made on or after 1 December 2012.

[**3** A person is treated as having become liable to be registered under this Schedule at any time when the person would have become so liable under paragraph 1 or 2 but for any registration that is subsequently cancelled under—
  (*a*) paragraph 11,
  (*b*) paragraph 13(3) of Schedule 1,
  (*c*), (*d*) . . . [2]
  (*d*) paragraph 6(3) of Schedule 3, or
  (*e*) paragraph 6(2) of Schedule 3A.][1]
Northern Ireland—See Sch 9ZA para 67 (Northern Ireland: this para has effect as if the provisions mentioned in sub-paras (*a*)–(*e*) included Sch 9ZA paras 43(5) and 53(5)).
Amendments—[1] Schedule 1A inserted by FA 2012 s 203, Sch 28 para 1 with effect in relation to supplies made or to be made on or after 1 December 2012.
[2] Sub-paras (*c*), (*d*) repealed by the Taxation (Cross-border Trade) Act 2018 s 43, Sch 8 paras 1, 82(1), (2) with effect from IP completion day (11pm on 31 December 2020), by virtue of SI 2020/1642 reg 4(*b*).
Sub-paras (*c*), (*d*) previously read as follows—

"(c) paragraph 6(2) of Schedule 2,
(d) paragraph 6(3) of Schedule 3,".

[4—(1) A person does not cease to be liable to be registered under this Schedule except in accordance with sub-paragraph (2).
(2) A person who has become liable to be registered under this Schedule ceases to be so liable at any time if the Commissioners are satisfied that—
(a) the person has ceased to make taxable supplies in the course or furtherance of a business carried on by the person, or
(b) the person is no longer a person in relation to whom condition C in paragraph 1 is met.][1]

Amendments—[1] Schedule 1A inserted by FA 2012 s 203, Sch 28 para 1 with effect in relation to supplies made or to be made on or after 1 December 2012.

[Notification of liability and registration

5—(1) A person who becomes liable to be registered by virtue of paragraph 1(2)(a) or 2(2) must notify the Commissioners of the liability before the end of the period of 30 days beginning with the day on which the liability arises.
(2) The Commissioners must register any such person (whether or not the person so notifies them) with effect from the beginning of the day on which the liability arises.][1]

Amendments—[1] Schedule 1A inserted by FA 2012 s 203, Sch 28 para 1 with effect in relation to supplies made or to be made on or after 1 December 2012.

[6—(1) A person who becomes liable to be registered by virtue of paragraph 1(2)(b) must notify the Commissioners of the liability before the end of the period by reference to which the liability arises.
(2) The Commissioners must register any such person (whether or not the person so notifies them) with effect from the beginning of the period by reference to which the liability arises.][1]

Amendments—[1] Schedule 1A inserted by FA 2012 s 203, Sch 28 para 1 with effect in relation to supplies made or to be made on or after 1 December 2012.

[Notification of end of liability

7—(1) A person registered under paragraph 5 or 6 who, on any day, ceases to make or have the intention of making taxable supplies in the course or furtherance of a business carried on by that person must notify the Commissioners of that fact within 30 days beginning with that day.
(2) But the person need not notify the Commissioners if on that day the person would otherwise be liable or entitled to be registered under this Act (disregarding for this purpose the person's registration under this Schedule and any enactment that prevents a person from being liable to be registered under different provisions at the same time).][1]

Amendments—[1] Schedule 1A inserted by FA 2012 s 203, Sch 28 para 1 with effect in relation to supplies made or to be made on or after 1 December 2012.

[Cancellation of registration

8—(1) The Commissioners must cancel a person's registration under this Schedule if—
(a) the person satisfies them that the person is not liable to be registered under this Schedule, and
(b) the person requests the cancellation.
(2) The cancellation is to be made with effect from—
(a) the day on which the request is made, or
(b) such later day as may be agreed between the Commissioners and the person.
(3) But the Commissioners must not cancel the registration with effect from any time unless they are satisfied that it is not a time when the person would be subject to a requirement to be registered under this Act.][1]

Amendments—[1] Schedule 1A inserted by FA 2012 s 203, Sch 28 para 1 with effect in relation to supplies made or to be made on or after 1 December 2012.

[9—(1) The Commissioners may cancel a person's registration under this Schedule if they are satisfied that the person has ceased to be liable to be registered under this Schedule.
(2) The cancellation is to be made with effect from—
(a) the day on which the person ceased to be so liable, or
(b) such later day as may be agreed between the Commissioners and the person.
(3) But the Commissioners must not cancel the registration with effect from any time unless they are satisfied that it is not a time when the person would be subject to a requirement, or entitled, to be registered under this Act.][1]

Amendments—[1] Schedule 1A inserted by FA 2012 s 203, Sch 28 para 1 with effect in relation to supplies made or to be made on or after 1 December 2012.

[10 In determining for the purposes of paragraphs 8 and 9 whether a time is a time when a person would be subject to a requirement, or entitled, to be registered under this Act, so much of any provision of this Act as prevents a person from becoming liable or entitled to be registered when the person is already registered or when the person is so liable under any other provision must be disregarded.][1]

Amendments—[1] Schedule 1A inserted by FA 2012 s 203, Sch 28 para 1 with effect in relation to supplies made or to be made on or after 1 December 2012.

[11—(1) The Commissioners may cancel a person's registration under this Schedule if they are satisfied that the person was not liable to be registered under this Schedule on the day on which the person was registered.
(2) The cancellation is to be made with effect from the day on which the person was registered.][1]

Amendments—[1] Schedule 1A inserted by FA 2012 s 203, Sch 28 para 1 with effect in relation to supplies made or to be made on or after 1 December 2012.

[12 Paragraphs 8 to 11 are subject to paragraph 18 of Schedule 3B *[and paragraph 16 of Schedule 3BA][2] (cancellation of registration under this Schedule of persons seeking to be registered under [the Schedule concerned][2]).]*[1], [3]

Amendments—[1] Schedule 1A inserted by FA 2012 s 203, Sch 28 para 1 with effect in relation to supplies made or to be made on or after 1 December 2012.
[2] Words inserted, and words substituted for words "that Schedule etc", by FA 2014 s 103, Sch 22 para 18 with effect in relation to supplies made on or after 1 January 2015.
[3] Para 12 repealed by the Taxation (Cross-border Trade) Act 2018 s 43, Sch 8 paras 1, 82(1), (3) with effect from IP completion day (11pm on 31 December 2020), by virtue of SI 2020/1642 reg 4(*b*).

[Exemption from registration

13—(1) The Commissioners may exempt a person from registration under this Schedule if the person satisfies them that the taxable supplies that the person makes or intends to make—
 (*a*) are all zero-rated, or
 (*b*) would all be zero-rated if the person were a taxable person.
(2) The power in sub-paragraph (1) is exercisable only if the person so requests and the Commissioners think fit.
(3) If there is a material change in the nature of the supplies made by a person exempted under this paragraph, the person must notify the Commissioners of the change—
 (*a*) within 30 days beginning with the day on which the change occurred, or
 (*b*) if no particular day is identifiable as that day, within 30 days of the end of the quarter in which the change occurred.
(4) If it appears to the Commissioners that a request under this paragraph should no longer be acted upon on or after any day or has been withdrawn on any day, they must register the person who made the request with effect from that day.
(5) A reference in this paragraph to supplies is to supplies made in the course or furtherance of a business carried on by the person.]*[1]

Amendments—[1] Schedule 1A inserted by FA 2012 s 203, Sch 28 para 1 with effect in relation to supplies made or to be made on or after 1 December 2012.

[Supplementary

14 Any notification required under this Schedule must be made in such form and manner and must contain such particulars as may be specified in regulations or by the Commissioners in accordance with regulations.]*[1]

Regulations—VAT (Amendment) (No 2) Regulations, SI 2012/1899.
Amendments—[1] Schedule 1A inserted by FA 2012 s 203, Sch 28 para 1 with effect in relation to supplies made or to be made on or after 1 December 2012.

SCHEDULE 2
REGISTRATION IN RESPECT OF SUPPLIES FROM OTHER MEMBER STATES
Section 3(2)

Amendments—Schedule 2 repealed by the Taxation (Cross-border Trade) Act 2018 s 43, Sch 8 paras 1, 83 with effect from IP completion day (11pm on 31 December 2020), by virtue of SI 2020/1642 reg 4(*b*).

Liability to be registered

1—(*1*) A person who—
 (*a*) is not registered under this Act; and
 (*b*) is not liable to be registered under Schedule 1 *[or 1A]*[3],

becomes liable to be registered under this Schedule on any day if, in the period beginning with 1st January of the year in which that day falls, that person has made relevant supplies whose value exceeds £70,000.

(2) A person who is not registered or liable to be registered as mentioned in sub-paragraph (1)(a) and (b) above becomes liable to be registered under this Schedule where—
   (a) that person has exercised any option, in accordance with the law of any other member State where he is taxable, for treating relevant supplies made by him as taking place outside that member State;
   (b) the supplies to which the option relates involve the removal of goods from that member State and, apart from the exercise of the option, would be treated, in accordance with the law of that member State, as taking place in that member State; and
   (c) that person makes a relevant supply at a time when the option is in force in relation to him.

(3) A person who is not registered or liable to be registered as mentioned in sub-paragraph (1)(a) and (b) above becomes liable to be registered under this Schedule if he makes a supply in relation to which the following conditions are satisfied, that is to say—
   (a) it is a supply of goods subject to a duty of excise;
   (b) it involves the removal of the goods to the United Kingdom by or under the directions of the person making the supply;
   (c) it is a transaction in pursuance of which the goods are acquired in the United Kingdom from another member State by a person who is not a taxable person;
   (d) it is made on or after 1st January 1993 and in the course or furtherance of a business carried on by the supplier; and
   (e) it is not anything which is treated as a supply for the purposes of this Act by virtue only of paragraph 5(1) or 6 of Schedule 4.

(4) A person shall be treated as having become liable to be registered under this Schedule at any time when he would have become so liable under the preceding provisions of this paragraph but for any registration which is subsequently cancelled under paragraph 6(2) below, paragraph 13(3) of Schedule 1[, [paragraph 11 of Schedule 1A,]³ paragraph 6(3) of Schedule 3 or paragraph 6(2) of Schedule 3A]².

(5) A person shall not cease to be liable to be registered under this Schedule except in accordance with paragraph 2 below.

(6) In determining for the purposes of this paragraph the value of any relevant supplies, so much of the consideration for any supply as represents any liability of the supplier, under the law of another member State, for VAT on that supply shall be disregarded.

[(7) For the purposes of sub-paragraphs (1) and (2) above supplies to which section 18B(4) (last acquisition or supply of goods before removal from fiscal warehousing) applies shall be disregarded.]¹, ⁴

Commentary—De Voil Indirect Tax Service **V2.171**.
Amendments—¹ Sub-para (7) added by FA 1996 Sch 3 para 14, with effect for any supply taking place on or after 1 June 1996 (see Finance Act 1996, Section 26, (Appointed Day) Order, SI 1996/1249).
² Words in sub-para (4) substituted by FA 2000 s 136(6), with effect for supplies made after 20 March 2000.
³ In sub-paras (1)(b), (4), words inserted by FA 2012 s 203, Sch 28 paras 2, 14 with effect in relation to supplies made or to be made on or after 1 December 2012.
⁴ Schedule 2 repealed by the Taxation (Cross-border Trade) Act 2018 s 43, Sch 8 paras 1, 83 with effect from IP completion day (11pm on 31 December 2020), by virtue of SI 2020/1642 reg 4(b).

2—(1) Subject to sub-paragraph (2) below, a person who has become liable to be registered under this Schedule shall cease to be so liable if at any time—
   (a) the relevant supplies made by him in the year ending with 31st December last before that time did not have a value exceeding £70,000 and did not include any supply in relation to which the conditions mentioned in paragraph 1(3) above were satisfied; and
   (b) the Commissioners are satisfied that the value of his relevant supplies in the year immediately following that year will not exceed £70,000 and that those supplies will not include a supply in relation to which those conditions are satisfied.

(2) A person shall not cease to be liable to be registered under this Schedule at any time when such an option as is mentioned in paragraph 1(2) above is in force in relation to him.¹

Commentary—De Voil Indirect Tax Service **V2.151**.
Amendments—¹ Schedule 2 repealed by the Taxation (Cross-border Trade) Act 2018 s 43, Sch 8 paras 1, 83 with effect from IP completion day (11pm on 31 December 2020), by virtue of SI 2020/1642 reg 4(b).

Notification of liability and registration

3—(1) A person who becomes liable to be registered under this Schedule shall notify the Commissioners of the liability within the period of 30 days after the day on which the liability arises.

(2) The Commissioners shall register any such person (whether or not he so notifies them) with effect from the day on which the liability arose or from such earlier time as may be agreed between them and him.[1]

Commentary—*De Voil Indirect Tax Service* **V2.173**.

Amendments—[1] Schedule 2 repealed by the Taxation (Cross-border Trade) Act 2018 s 43, Sch 8 paras 1, 83 with effect from IP completion day (11pm on 31 December 2020), by virtue of SI 2020/1642 reg 4(*b*).

Request to be registered

4—*(1) Where a person who is not liable to be registered under this Act and is not already so registered—*
  (a) satisfies the Commissioners that he intends—
    (i) *to exercise an option such as is mentioned in paragraph 1(2) above and, from a specified date, to make relevant supplies to which that option will relate;*
    (ii) *from a specified date to make relevant supplies to which any such option that he has exercised will relate; or*
    (iii) *from a specified date to make supplies in relation to which the conditions mentioned in paragraph 1(3) above will be satisfied; and*
  (b) requests to be registered under this Schedule,
the Commissioners may, subject to such conditions as they think fit to impose, register him with effect from such date as may be agreed between them and him.
(2) Conditions imposed under sub-paragraph (1) above—
  (a) may be so imposed wholly or partly by reference to, or without reference to, any conditions prescribed for the purposes of this paragraph; and
  (b) may, whenever imposed, be subsequently varied by the Commissioners.
(3) Where a person who is entitled to be registered under paragraph 9 or 10 of Schedule 1 requests registration under this paragraph, he shall be registered under that Schedule, and not under this Schedule.[1]

Commentary—*De Voil Indirect Tax Service* **V2.174**.

Amendments—[1] Schedule 2 repealed by the Taxation (Cross-border Trade) Act 2018 s 43, Sch 8 paras 1, 83 with effect from IP completion day (11pm on 31 December 2020), by virtue of SI 2020/1642 reg 4(*b*).

Notification of matters affecting continuance of registration

5—*(1) Any person registered under this Schedule who ceases to be registrable under this Act shall notify the Commissioners of that fact within 30 days of the day on which he does so.*
(2) A person registered under paragraph 4 above by reference to any intention of his to exercise any option or to make supplies of any description shall notify the Commissioners within 30 days of exercising that option or, as the case may be, of the first occasion after his registration when he makes such a supply, that he has exercised the option or made such a supply.
(3) A person who has exercised such an option as is mentioned in paragraph 1(2) above which, as a consequence of its revocation or otherwise, ceases to have effect in relation to any relevant supplies by him shall notify the Commissioners, within 30 days of the option's ceasing so to have effect, that it has done so.
(4) For the purposes of this paragraph, a person ceases to be registrable under this Act where—
  (a) he ceases to be a person who would be liable or entitled to be registered under this Act if his registration and any enactment preventing a person from being liable to be registered under different provisions at the same time were disregarded; or
  (b) in the case of a person who (having been registered under paragraph 4 above) has not been such a person during the period of his registration, he ceases to have any such intention as is mentioned in sub-paragraph (1)(a) of that paragraph.[1]

Commentary—*De Voil Indirect Tax Service* **V2.176**.

Amendments—[1] Schedule 2 repealed by the Taxation (Cross-border Trade) Act 2018 s 43, Sch 8 paras 1, 83 with effect from IP completion day (11pm on 31 December 2020), by virtue of SI 2020/1642 reg 4(*b*).

Cancellation of registration

6—*(1) Subject to paragraph 7 below, where a person registered under this Schedule satisfies the Commissioners that he is not liable to be so registered, they shall, if he so requests, cancel his registration with effect from the day on which the request is made or from such later date as may be agreed between them and him.*
(2) Where the Commissioners are satisfied that, on the day on which a person was registered under this Schedule, he—
  (a) was not liable to be registered under this Schedule; and
  (b) in the case of a person registered under paragraph 4 above, did not have the intention by reference to which he was registered,

they may cancel his registration with effect from that day.

(3) Subject to paragraph 7 below, where the Commissioners are satisfied that a person who has been registered under paragraph 4 above and is not for the time being liable to be registered under this Schedule—
- (a) has not, by the date specified in his request to be registered, begun to make relevant supplies, exercised the option in question or, as the case may be, begun to make supplies in relation to which the conditions mentioned in paragraph 1(3) above are satisfied; or
- (b) has contravened any condition of his registration,

they may cancel his registration with effect from the date so specified or, as the case may be, the date of the contravention or from such later date as may be agreed between them and him.[1]

Commentary—*De Voil Indirect Tax Service* **V2.177**.
Amendments—[1]   Schedule 2 repealed by the Taxation (Cross-border Trade) Act 2018 s 43, Sch 8 paras 1, 83 with effect from IP completion day (11pm on 31 December 2020), by virtue of SI 2020/1642 reg 4(b).

Conditions of cancellation

7—(1) The Commissioners shall not, under paragraph 6(1) above, cancel a person's registration with effect from any time unless they are satisfied that it is not a time when that person would be subject to a requirement to be registered under this Act.

(2) The Commissioners shall not, under paragraph 6(3) above, cancel a person's registration with effect from any time unless they are satisfied that it is not a time when that person would be subject to a requirement, or entitled, to be registered under this Act.

(3) The registration of a person who has exercised such an option as is mentioned in paragraph 1(2) above shall not be cancelled with effect from any time before the 1st January which is, or next follows, the second anniversary of the date on which his registration took effect.

(4) In determining for the purposes of this paragraph whether a person would be subject to a requirement, or entitled, to be registered at any time, so much of any provision of this Act as prevents a person from becoming liable or entitled to be registered when he is already registered or when he is so liable under any other provision shall be disregarded.[1]

Commentary—*De Voil Indirect Tax Service* **V2.177**.
Amendments—[1]   Schedule 2 repealed by the Taxation (Cross-border Trade) Act 2018 s 43, Sch 8 paras 1, 83 with effect from IP completion day (11pm on 31 December 2020), by virtue of SI 2020/1642 reg 4(b).

Power to vary specified sums by order

8   The Treasury may by order substitute for any of the sums for the time being specified in this Schedule such greater sums as they think fit.[1]

Amendments—[1]   Schedule 2 repealed by the Taxation (Cross-border Trade) Act 2018 s 43, Sch 8 paras 1, 83 with effect from IP completion day (11pm on 31 December 2020), by virtue of SI 2020/1642 reg 4(b).

Supplementary

9   Any notification required under this Schedule shall be made in such form [and manner][1] and shall contain such particulars [as may be specified in regulations or by the Commissioners in accordance with regulations.][1], [2]

Regulations—VAT Regulations, SI 1995/2518 reg 5, Sch 1.
VAT (Amendment) (No 2) Regulations, SI 2012/1899.
Amendments—[1]   Words inserted, and words substituted for words "as the Commissioners may by regulations prescribe", by FA 2012 s 204, Sch 29 paras 1, 9 with effect from 17 July 2012.
[2]   Schedule 2 repealed by the Taxation (Cross-border Trade) Act 2018 s 43, Sch 8 paras 1, 83 with effect from IP completion day (11pm on 31 December 2020), by virtue of SI 2020/1642 reg 4(b).

10   For the purposes of this Schedule a supply of goods is a relevant supply where—
- (a) the supply involves the removal of the goods to the United Kingdom by or under the directions of the person making the supply;
- (b) the supply does not involve the installation or assembly of the goods at a place in the United Kingdom;
- (c) the supply is a transaction in pursuance of which goods are acquired in the United Kingdom from another member State by a person who is not a taxable person;
- (d) the supply is made on or after 1st January 1993 and in the course or furtherance of a business carried on by the supplier; and
- (e) the supply is neither an exempt supply nor a supply of goods which are subject to a duty of excise or consist in a new means of transport and is not anything which is treated as a supply for the purposes of this Act by virtue only of paragraph 5(1) or 6 of Schedule 4.[1]

Commentary—*De Voil Indirect Tax Service* **V3.172**.
Northern Ireland—See Sch 9ZC para 13 (Northern Ireland: meaning of "relevant supply" for the purposes of Sch 9ZC).

Amendments—[1] Schedule 2 repealed by the Taxation (Cross-border Trade) Act 2018 s 43, Sch 8 paras 1, 83 with effect from IP completion day (11pm on 31 December 2020), by virtue of SI 2020/1642 reg 4(b).

SCHEDULE 3
REGISTRATION IN RESPECT OF ACQUISITIONS FROM OTHER MEMBER STATES
Section 3(2)

Amendments—Schedule 3 repealed by the Taxation (Cross-border Trade) Act 2018 s 43, Sch 8 paras 1, 84 with effect from IP completion day (11pm on 31 December 2020), by virtue of SI 2020/1642 reg 4(b).

Liability to be registered

1—(1) A person who—
  (a) is not registered under this Act; and
  (b) is not liable to be registered under Schedule 1[, 1A][3] or 2,
becomes liable to be registered under this Schedule at the end of any month if, in the period beginning with 1st January of the year in which that month falls, that person had made relevant acquisitions whose value exceeds [£85,000][4].
(2) A person who is not registered or liable to be registered as mentioned in sub-paragraph (1)(a) and (b) above becomes liable to be registered under this Schedule at any time if there are reasonable grounds for believing that the value of his relevant acquisitions in the period of 30 days then beginning will exceed [£85,000][4].
(3) A person shall be treated as having become liable to be registered under this Schedule at any time when he would have become so liable under the preceding provisions of this paragraph but for any registration which is subsequently cancelled under paragraph 6(3) below, paragraph 13(3) of Schedule 1[, [paragraph 11 of Schedule 1A,][3] paragraph 6(2) of Schedule 2 or paragraph 6(2) of Schedule 3A][2].
(4) A person shall not cease to be liable to be registered under this Schedule except in accordance with paragraph 2 below.
(5) In determining the value of any person's relevant acquisitions for the purposes of this paragraph, so much of the consideration for any acquisition as represents any liability of the supplier, under the law of another member State, for VAT on the transaction in pursuance of which the acquisition is made, shall be disregarded.
[(6) In determining the value of a person's acquisitions for the purposes of sub-paragraph (1) or (2) above, acquisitions to which section 18B(4) (last acquisition or supply of goods before removal from fiscal warehousing) applies shall be disregarded.][1], [5]

Commentary—*De Voil Indirect Tax Service* **V2.181**.
Amendments—[1] Sub-para (6) inserted by FA 1996 Sch 3 para 15, with effect for any acquisition of goods from another member State taking place on or after 1 June 1996 (see Finance Act 1996, Section 26, (Appointed Day) Order, SI 1996/1249).
[2] Words in sub-para (3) substituted by FA 2000 s 136(7), with effect for supplies made after 20 March 2000.
[3] In sub-paras (1)(b), (3), words inserted by FA 2012 s 203, Sch 28 paras 2, 15 with effect in relation to supplies made or to be made on or after 1 December 2012.
[4] Sums in sub-paras (1), (2) substituted by the VAT (Increase of Registration Limits) Order, SI 2017/290 arts 2, 4(a) with effect from 1 April 2017. Figures were previously £83,000 from 1 April 2016 to 31 March 2017. Note that, as a consequence of the repeal of Sch 3 by TCBTA 2018 (see footnote below), SI 2017/290 art 4 is revoked by TCBTA 2018 s 43, Sch 8 para 132(o) with effect from IP completion day.
[5] Schedule 3 repealed by the Taxation (Cross-border Trade) Act 2018 s 43, Sch 8 paras 1, 84 with effect from IP completion day (11pm on 31 December 2020), by virtue of SI 2020/1642 reg 4(b).

2—(1) Subject to sub-paragraph (2) below, a person who has become liable to be registered under this Schedule shall cease to be so liable if at any time—
  (a) his relevant acquisitions in the year ending with 31st December last before that time did not have a value exceeding [£85,000][1]; and
  (b) the Commissioners are satisfied that the value of his relevant acquisitions in the year immediately following that year will not exceed [£85,000][1].
(2) A person shall not cease to be liable to be registered under this Schedule at any time if there are reasonable grounds for believing that the value of that person's relevant acquisitions in the period of 30 days then beginning will exceed [£85,000][1].[2]

Commentary—*De Voil Indirect Tax Service* **V2.188**.
Amendments—[1] Sums in sub-paras (1)(a), (b), (2) substituted by the VAT (Increase of Registration Limits) Order, SI 2017/290 arts 2, 4(a) with effect from 1 April 2017. Figures were previously £83,000 from 1 April 2016 to 31 March 2017. Note that, as a consequence of the repeal of Sch 3 by TCBTA 2018 (see footnote below), SI 2017/290 art 4 is revoked by TCBTA 2018 s 43, Sch 8 para 132(o) with effect from IP completion day.
[2] Schedule 3 repealed by the Taxation (Cross-border Trade) Act 2018 s 43, Sch 8 paras 1, 84 with effect from IP completion day (11pm on 31 December 2020), by virtue of SI 2020/1642 reg 4(b).

Notification of liability and registration

3—(1) A person who becomes liable to be registered under this Schedule shall notify the Commissioners of the liability—
  (a) in the case of a liability under sub-paragraph (1) of paragraph 1 above, within 30 days of the end of the month when he becomes so liable; and
  (b) in the case of a liability under sub-paragraph (2) of that paragraph, before the end of the period by reference to which the liability arises.
(2) The Commissioners shall register any such person (whether or not he so notifies them) with effect from the relevant time or from such earlier time as may be agreed between them and him.
(3) In this paragraph "the relevant time"—
  (a) in a case falling within sub-paragraph (1)(a) above, means the end of the month following the month at the end of which the liability arose; and
  (b) in a case falling within sub-paragraph (1)(b), means the beginning of the period by reference to which the liability arose.[1]

Commentary—*De Voil Indirect Tax Service* **V2.184**.
Amendments—[1] Schedule 3 repealed by the Taxation (Cross-border Trade) Act 2018 s 43, Sch 8 paras 1, 84 with effect from IP completion day (11pm on 31 December 2020), by virtue of SI 2020/1642 reg 4(b).

Entitlement to be registered etc

4—(1) Where a person who is not liable to be registered under this Act and is not already so registered satisfies the Commissioners that he makes relevant acquisitions, they shall, if he so requests, register him with effect from the day on which the request is made or from such earlier date as may be agreed between them and him.
(2) Where a person who is not liable to be registered under this Act and is not already so registered—
  (a) satisfies the Commissioners that he intends to make relevant acquisitions from a specified date; and
  (b) requests to be registered under this Schedule,
the Commissioners may, subject to such conditions as they think fit to impose, register him with effect from such date as may be agreed between them and him.
(3) Conditions imposed under sub-paragraph (2) above—
  (a) may be so imposed wholly or partly by reference to, or without reference to, any conditions prescribed for the purposes of this paragraph, and
  (b) may, whenever imposed, be subsequently varied by the Commissioners.
(4) Where a person who is entitled to be registered under paragraph 9 or 10 of Schedule 1 requests registration under this paragraph, he shall be registered under that Schedule, and not under this Schedule.[1]

Commentary—*De Voil Indirect Tax Service* **V2.181**.
Amendments—[1] Schedule 3 repealed by the Taxation (Cross-border Trade) Act 2018 s 43, Sch 8 paras 1, 84 with effect from IP completion day (11pm on 31 December 2020), by virtue of SI 2020/1642 reg 4(b).

Notification of matters affecting continuance of registration

5—(1) Any person registered under this Schedule who ceases to be registrable under this Act shall notify the Commissioners of that fact within 30 days of the day on which he does so.
(2) A person registered under paragraph 4(2) above shall notify the Commissioners, within 30 days of the first occasion after his registration when he makes a relevant acquisition, that he has done so.
(3) For the purposes of this paragraph a person ceases to be registrable under this Act where—
  (a) he ceases to be a person who would be liable or entitled to be registered under this Act if his registration and any enactment preventing a person from being liable to be registered under different provisions at the same time were disregarded; or
  (b) in the case of a person who (having been registered under paragraph 4(2) above) has not been such a person during the period of his registration, he ceases to have any intention of making relevant acquisitions.[1]

Commentary—*De Voil Indirect Tax Service* **V2.187**.
Amendments—[1] Schedule 3 repealed by the Taxation (Cross-border Trade) Act 2018 s 43, Sch 8 paras 1, 84 with effect from IP completion day (11pm on 31 December 2020), by virtue of SI 2020/1642 reg 4(b).

Cancellation of registration

6—(1) Subject to paragraph 7 below, where a person registered under this Schedule satisfies the Commissioners that he is not liable to be so registered, they shall, if he so requests, cancel his registration with effect from the day on which the request is made or from such later date as may be agreed between them and him.

(2) Subject to paragraph 7 below, where the Commissioners are satisfied that a person registered under this Schedule has ceased since his registration to be registrable under this Schedule, they may cancel his registration with effect from the day on which he so ceased or from such later date as may be agreed between them and him.
(3) Where the Commissioners are satisfied that, on the day on which a person was registered under this Schedule, he—
   (a) was not registrable under this Schedule; and
   (b) in the case of a person registered under paragraph 4(2) above, did not have the intention by reference to which he was registered,
they may cancel his registration with effect from that day.
(4) Subject to paragraph 7 below, where the Commissioners are satisfied that a person who has been registered under paragraph 4(2) above and is not for the time being liable to be registered under this Schedule—
   (a) has not begun, by the date specified in his request to be registered, to make relevant acquisitions; or
   (b) has contravened any condition of his registration,
they may cancel his registration with effect from the date so specified or, as the case may be, the date of the contravention or from such later date as may be agreed between them and him.
(5) For the purposes of this paragraph a person is registrable under this Schedule at any time when he is liable to be registered under this Schedule or is a person who makes relevant acquisitions.[1]

Commentary—*De Voil Indirect Tax Service* **V2.188**.
Amendments—[1]   Schedule 3 repealed by the Taxation (Cross-border Trade) Act 2018 s 43, Sch 8 paras 1, 84 with effect from IP completion day (11pm on 31 December 2020), by virtue of SI 2020/1642 reg 4(*b*).

Conditions of cancellation

7—*(1) The Commissioners shall not, under paragraph 6(1) above, cancel a person's registration with effect from any time unless they are satisfied that it is not a time when that person would be subject to a requirement to be registered under this Act.*
(2) The Commissioners shall not, under paragraph 6(2) or (4) above, cancel a person's registration with effect from any time unless they are satisfied that it is not a time when that person would be subject to a requirement, or entitled, to be registered under this Act.
(3) Subject to sub-paragraph (4) below, the registration of a person who—
   (a) is registered under paragraph 4 above; or
   (b) would not, if he were not registered, be liable or entitled to be registered under any provision of this Act except paragraph 4 above,
shall not be cancelled with effect from any time before the 1st January which is, or next follows, the second anniversary of the date on which his registration took effect.
(4) Sub-paragraph (3) above does not apply to cancellation under paragraph 6(3) or (4) above.
(5) In determining for the purposes of this paragraph whether a person would be subject to a requirement, or entitled, to be registered at any time, so much of any provision of this Act as prevents a person from becoming liable or entitled to be registered when he is already registered or when he is so liable under any other provision shall be disregarded.[1]

Commentary—*De Voil Indirect Tax Service* **V2.188**.
Amendments—[1]   Schedule 3 repealed by the Taxation (Cross-border Trade) Act 2018 s 43, Sch 8 paras 1, 84 with effect from IP completion day (11pm on 31 December 2020), by virtue of SI 2020/1642 reg 4(*b*).

Exemption from registration

8—*(1) Notwithstanding the preceding provisions of this Schedule, where a person who makes or intends to make relevant acquisitions satisfies the Commissioners that any such acquisition would be an acquisition in pursuance of a transaction which would be zero-rated if it were a taxable supply by a taxable person, they may, if he so requests and they think fit, exempt him from registration under this Schedule until it appears to them that the request should no longer be acted upon or is withdrawn.*
(2) Where a person who is exempted under this paragraph from registration under this Schedule makes any relevant acquisition in pursuance of any transaction which would, if it were a taxable supply by a taxable person, be chargeable to VAT otherwise than as a zero-rated supply, he shall notify the Commissioners of the change within 30 days of the date on which he made the acquisition.[1]

Commentary—*De Voil Indirect Tax Service* **V2.183**.
Amendments—[1]   Schedule 3 repealed by the Taxation (Cross-border Trade) Act 2018 s 43, Sch 8 paras 1, 84 with effect from IP completion day (11pm on 31 December 2020), by virtue of SI 2020/1642 reg 4(*b*).

Power to vary specified sums by order

9 The Treasury may by order substitute for any of the sums for the time being specified in this Schedule such greater sums as they think fit.[1]

Orders—VAT (Increase of Registration Limits) Order, SI 2014/703.
VAT (Increase of Registration Limits) Order, SI 2015/750.
VAT (Increase of Registration Limits) Order, SI 2016/365.
VAT (Increase of Registration Limits) Order, SI 2017/290.

Amendments—[1] Schedule 3 repealed by the Taxation (Cross-border Trade) Act 2018 s 43, Sch 8 paras 1, 84 with effect from IP completion day (11pm on 31 December 2020), by virtue of SI 2020/1642 reg 4(b).

Supplementary

10 Any notification required under this Schedule shall be made in such form [and manner][1] and shall contain such particulars [as may be specified in regulations or by the Commissioners in accordance with regulations.][1], [2]

Regulations—See VAT Regulations, SI 1995/2518 reg 5, Sch 1.
VAT (Amendment) (No 2) Regulations, SI 2012/1899.

Amendments—[1] Words inserted, and words substituted for words "as the Commissioners may by regulations prescribe", by FA 2012 s 204, Sch 29 paras 1, 10 with effect from 17 July 2012.
[2] Schedule 3 repealed by the Taxation (Cross-border Trade) Act 2018 s 43, Sch 8 paras 1, 84 with effect from IP completion day (11pm on 31 December 2020), by virtue of SI 2020/1642 reg 4(b).

11 For the purposes of this Schedule an acquisition of goods from another member State is a relevant acquisition where—
(a) it is a taxable acquisition of goods other than goods which are subject to a duty of excise or consist in a new means of transport;
(b) it is an acquisition otherwise than in pursuance of a taxable supply and is treated, for the purposes of this Act, as taking place in the United Kingdom; and
(c) the event which, in relation to that acquisition, is the first relevant event for the purposes of taxing that acquisition occurs on or after 1st January 1993.[1]

Amendments—[1] Schedule 3 repealed by the Taxation (Cross-border Trade) Act 2018 s 43, Sch 8 paras 1, 84 with effect from IP completion day (11pm on 31 December 2020), by virtue of SI 2020/1642 reg 4(b).

[SCHEDULE 3A

REGISTRATION IN RESPECT OF DISPOSALS OF ASSETS FOR WHICH A VAT REPAYMENT IS CLAIMED]

Section 3(2)

Amendments—Sch 3A inserted by FA 2000 s 136(8), Sch 36, with effect for relevant supplies (within the meaning of this Schedule) made after 20 March 2000.

Liability to be registered

[**1**—(1) A person who is not registered under this Act, and is not liable to be registered under [Schedule 1 or 1A][2], becomes liable to be registered under this Schedule at any time—
(a) if he makes relevant supplies; or
(b) if there are reasonable grounds for believing that he will make such supplies in the period of 30 days then beginning.
(2) A person shall be treated as having become liable to be registered under this Schedule at any time when he would have become so liable under sub-paragraph (1) above but for any registration which is subsequently cancelled under paragraph 6(2) below, paragraph 13(3) of Schedule 1 [or paragraph 11 of Schedule 1A][2]
(3) A person shall not cease to be liable to be registered under this Schedule except in accordance with paragraph 2 below.][1]

Northern Ireland—See Sch 9ZA para 68 (Northern Ireland: this para has effect as if in sub-para (1), after "or 1A" there were inserted "or Part 8 or 9 of Schedule 9ZA", and as if the provisions mentioned in sub-para (2) included Sch 9ZA paras 43(5) and 53(5)).

Amendments—[1] Sch 3A inserted by FA 2000 s 136(8), Sch 36, with effect for relevant supplies (within the meaning of this Schedule) made after 20 March 2000.
[2] The following amendments made by the Taxation (Cross-border Trade) Act 2018 s 43, Sch 8 paras 1, 85 with effect from IP completion day (11pm on 31 December 2020), by virtue of SI 2020/1642 reg 4(b)—
  – in sub-para (1), words substituted for words "Schedule 1, 1A, 2 or 3"; and
  – in sub-para (2), words substituted for words ", paragraph 11 of Schedule 1A, paragraph 6(2) of Schedule 2 or paragraph 6(3) of Schedule 3.".

[**2** A person who has become liable to be registered under this Schedule shall cease to be so liable at any time if the Commissioners are satisfied that he has ceased to make relevant supplies.][1]

Amendments—[1] Sch 3A inserted by FA 2000 s 136(8), Sch 36, with effect for relevant supplies (within the meaning of this Schedule) made after 20 March 2000.

Notification of liability and registration

[3—(1) A person who becomes liable to be registered by virtue of paragraph 1(1)(*a*) above shall notify the Commissioners of the liability before the end of the period of 30 days beginning with the day on which the liability arises.
(2) The Commissioners shall register any such person (whether or not he so notifies them) with effect from the beginning of the day on which the liability arises.][1]

Amendments—[1] Sch 3A inserted by FA 2000 s 136(8), Sch 36, with effect for relevant supplies (within the meaning of this Schedule) made after 20 March 2000.

[4—(1) A person who becomes liable to be registered by virtue of paragraph 1(1)(*b*) above shall notify the Commissioners of the liability before the end of the period by reference to which the liability arises.
(2) The Commissioners shall register any such person (whether or not he so notifies them) with effect from the beginning of the period by reference to which the liability arises.][1]

Amendments—[1] Sch 3A inserted by FA 2000 s 136(8), Sch 36, with effect for relevant supplies (within the meaning of this Schedule) made after 20 March 2000.

Notification of end of liability

[5—(1) Subject to sub-paragraph (2) below, a person registered under paragraph 3 or 4 above who ceases to make or have the intention of making relevant supplies shall notify the Commissioners of that fact within 30 days of the day on which he does so.
(2) Sub-paragraph (1) above does not apply if the person would, when he so ceases, be otherwise liable or entitled to be registered under this Act if his registration and any enactment preventing a person from being liable to be registered under different provisions at the same time were disregarded.][1]

Amendments—[1] Sch 3A inserted by FA 2000 s 136(8), Sch 36, with effect for relevant supplies (within the meaning of this Schedule) made after 20 March 2000.

Cancellation of registration

[6—(1) Subject to sub-paragraph (3) below, where the Commissioners are satisfied that a registered person has ceased to be liable to be registered under this Schedule, they may cancel his registration with effect from the day on which he so ceased or from such later date as may be agreed between them and him.
(2) Where the Commissioners are satisfied that on the day on which a registered person was registered he was not registrable, they may cancel his registration with effect from that day.
(3) The Commissioners shall not under sub-paragraph (1) above cancel a person's registration with effect from any time unless they are satisfied that it is not a time when that person would be subject to a requirement, or entitled, to be registered under this Act.
(4) In determining for the purposes of sub-paragraph (3) above whether a person would be subject to a requirement, or entitled, to be registered at any time, so much of any provision of this Act as prevents a person from becoming liable or entitled to be registered when he is already registered or when he is so liable under any other provision shall be disregarded.][1]

Amendments—[1] Sch 3A inserted by FA 2000 s 136(8), Sch 36, with effect for relevant supplies (within the meaning of this Schedule) made after 20 March 2000.

Exemption from registration

[7—(1) Notwithstanding the preceding provisions of this Schedule, where a person who makes or intends to make relevant supplies satisfies the Commissioners that any such supply is zero-rated or would be zero-rated if he were a taxable person, they may, if he so requests and they think fit, exempt him from registration under this Schedule.
(2) Where there is a material change in the nature of the supplies made by a person exempted under this paragraph from registration under this Schedule, he shall notify the Commissioners of the change—
  (*a*) within 30 days of the date on which the change occurred; or
  (*b*) if no particular date is identifiable as the day on which it occurred, within 30 days of the end of the quarter in which it occurred.
(3) Where there is a material alteration in any quarter in the proportion of relevant supplies of such a person that are zero-rated, he shall notify the Commissioners of the alteration within 30 days of the end of the quarter.
(4) If it appears to the Commissioners that a request under sub-paragraph (1) above should no longer have been acted upon on or after any day, or has been withdrawn on any day, they shall register the person who made the request with effect from that day.][1]

Commentary—*De Voil Indirect Tax Service* **V2.189A**.
Amendments—[1] Sch 3A inserted by FA 2000 s 136(8), Sch 36, with effect for relevant supplies (within the meaning of this Schedule) made after 20 March 2000.

Supplementary

[8 Any notification required under this Schedule shall be made in such form [and manner][2] and shall contain such particulars [as may be specified in regulations or by the Commissioners in accordance with regulations.]²]¹

Regulations—VAT (Amendment) (No 2) Regulations, SI 2012/1899.
Amendments—[1] Sch 3A inserted by FA 2000 s 136(8), Sch 36, with effect for relevant supplies (within the meaning of this Schedule) made after 20 March 2000.
[2] Words inserted, and words substituted for words "as the Commissioners may by regulations prescribe", by FA 2012 s 204, Sch 29 paras 1, 11 with effect from 17 July 2012.

[9—(1) For the purposes of this Schedule a supply of goods is a relevant supply where—
   (*a*) the supply is a taxable supply;
   (*b*) the goods are assets of the business in the course or furtherance of which they are supplied; and
   (*c*) the person by whom they are supplied, or a predecessor of his, has received or claimed, or is intending to claim, a repayment of VAT on the supply to him, or the importation by him, of the goods or of anything comprised in them.
(2) In relation to any goods, a person is the predecessor of another for the purposes of this paragraph if—
   (*a*) that other person is a person to whom he has transferred assets of his business by a transfer of that business, or part of it, as a going concern;
   (*b*) those assets consisted of or included those goods; and
   (*c*) the transfer of the assets is one falling by virtue of an order under section 5(3) (or under an enactment re-enacted in section 5(3)) to be treated as neither a supply of goods nor a supply of services;
and the reference in this paragraph to a person's predecessor includes references to the predecessors of his predecessor through any number of transfers.
(3) The reference in this paragraph to a repayment of VAT is a reference to such a repayment under a scheme embodied in regulations made under section 39.]¹

Amendments—[1] Sch 3A inserted by FA 2000 s 136(8), Sch 36, with effect for relevant supplies (within the meaning of this Schedule) made after 20 March 2000.

[SCHEDULE 3B

[ELECTRONIC, TELECOMMUNICATION AND BROADCASTING SERVICES: NON-UNION SCHEME]]

Section 3A

Amendments—Schedule 3B inserted by FA 2003 s 23, Sch 2 paras 1, 4 with effect for qualifying supplies made after 30 June 2003, see FA 2003 s 23(2).

In Schedule heading, words substituted for words "Supply of electronic services in member states: special accounting scheme" by FA 2014 s 103, Sch 22 paras 3, 5 with effect in relation to supplies made on or after 1 January 2015.

Schedule 3B repealed by the Taxation (Cross-border Trade) Act 2018 s 43, Sch 8 paras 1, 86 with effect from IP completion day (11pm on 31 December 2020), by virtue of SI 2020/1642 reg 4(*b*).

Saving provision—Schedule 3B continues to apply in relation to supplies made before IP completion day despite its repeal by TCTA 2018 Sch 8, para 86. To the extent that it continues to apply, Sch 3B has effect subject to such modifications as may be specified in a notice published by the Commissioners (see SI 2020/1495 reg 14).

Any references to VATA 1994, Schs 3B or 3BA (other than those mentioned above) that have been repealed by TCTA 2018 Sch 8 continue to apply in relation to supplies made before IP completion day as if they had not been repealed, but only to the extent that Schs 3B and 3BA continue to have effect in accordance with SI 2020/1495. To the extent that they continue to apply, references to VATA 1994, Schs 3B or 3BA have effect subject to such modifications as may be specified in a notice published by the Commissioners (see SI 2020/1495, reg 16).

PART 1
[NON-UNION SCHEME: REGISTRATION]

Amendments—In heading for Part 1, words substituted for word "Registration" by FA 2014 s 103, Sch 22 paras 3, 6(8) with effect in relation to supplies made on or after 1 January 2015.
Schedule 3B repealed by the Taxation (Cross-border Trade) Act 2018 s 43, Sch 8 paras 1, 86 with effect from IP completion day (11pm on 31 December 2020), by virtue of SI 2020/1642 reg 4(*b*).

Saving provision—Schedule 3B continues to apply in relation to supplies made before IP completion day despite its repeal by TCTA 2018 Sch 8, para 86. To the extent that it continues to apply, Sch 3B has effect subject to such modifications as may be specified in a notice published by the Commissioners (see SI 2020/1495, reg 14).
Any references to VATA 1994, Schs 3B or 3BA (other than those mentioned above) that have been repealed by TCTA 2018 Sch 8 continue to apply in relation to supplies made before IP completion day as if they had not been repealed, but only to the extent that Schs 3B and 3BA continue to have effect in accordance with SI 2020/1495. To the extent that they continue to apply, references to VATA 1994, Schs 3B or 3BA have effect subject to such modifications as may be specified in a notice published by the Commissioners (see SI 2020/1495, reg 16).

The register

[1 Persons registered under this Schedule are to be registered in a single register kept by the Commissioners for the purposes of this Schedule.][1], [2]
Commentary—*De Voil Indirect Tax Service* **V2.121**.
Amendments—[1]   Sch 3B inserted by FA 2003 s 23, Sch 2 paras 1, 4 with effect for qualifying supplies made after 30 June 2003, see FA 2003 s 23(2).
[2]   Sch 3B repealed by the Taxation (Cross-border Trade) Act 2018 s 43, Sch 8 paras 1, 86 with effect from IP completion day (11pm on 31 December 2020), by virtue of SI 2020/1642 reg 4(*b*).
Saving provision—Schedule 3B continues to apply in relation to supplies made before IP completion day despite its repeal by TCTA 2018 Sch 8, para 86. To the extent that it continues to apply, Sch 3B has effect subject to such modifications as may be specified in a notice published by the Commissioners (see SI 2020/1495, reg 14).
Any references to VATA 1994, Schs 3B or 3BA (other than those mentioned above) that have been repealed by TCTA 2018 Sch 8 continue to apply in relation to supplies made before IP completion day as if they had not been repealed, but only to the extent that Schs 3B and 3BA continue to have effect in accordance with SI 2020/1495. To the extent that they continue to apply, references to VATA 1994, Schs 3B or 3BA have effect subject to such modifications as may be specified in a notice published by the Commissioners (see SI 2020/1495, reg 16).

Persons who may be registered

[2—*(1) A person may be registered under this Schedule if he satisfies the following conditions.*
(2) Condition 1 is that the person makes or intends to make qualifying supplies in the course of a business carried on by him.
(3) Condition 2 is that the person has neither his business establishment nor a fixed establishment in the United Kingdom or in another member State in relation to any supply of goods or services.
(4) Condition 3 is that the person is not—
   (a) registered under this Act,
   (b) identified for the purposes of VAT in accordance with the law of another member State, or
   (c) registered under an Act of Tynwald for the purposes of any tax imposed by or under an Act of Tynwald which corresponds to VAT.[3]
(5) Condition 4 is that the person—
   (a) is not required to be registered or identified as mentioned in condition 3, or
   (b) is required to be so registered or identified, but solely by virtue of the fact that he makes or intends to make qualifying supplies.[3]
(6) [Condition 3][3] *is that the person is not identified under any provision of the law of another member State which implements [Section 2 of Chapter 6 of Title XII of the VAT Directive]*[2].
[(7) In this Schedule "the VAT Directive" means Directive 2006/112/EC (Title XII of which is amended by Council Directive 2008/8/EC [and Council Directive (EU) 2017/2455][3]*).]*[2]
(8) References in this Schedule to a person's being registered under this Act do not include a reference to that person's being registered under this Schedule.][1, 3, 4]
Amendments—[1]   Sch 3B inserted by FA 2003 s 23, Sch 2 paras 1, 4 with effect for qualifying supplies made after 30 June 2003, see FA 2003 s 23(2).
[2]   In sub-para (6), words substituted for words "Article 26c", and sub-para (7) substituted, by FA 2014 s 103, Sch 22 paras 3, 6(1), (2) with effect in relation to supplies made on or after 1 January 2015.
[3]   Sub-paras (4), (5) and (8) revoked, in sub-para (6) words substituted for words "Condition 5", and in sub-para (7) words inserted, by the Value Added Tax (Special Accounting Schemes) (Supplies of Electronic, Telecommunication and Broadcasting Services) Order, SI 2018/1197 arts 2, 3(*a*) with effect in relation to supplies made on or after 1 January 2019. Note that SI 2018/1197 is revoked by SI 2019/513 reg 16 with effect from IP completion day (11pm on 31 December 2020).
[4]   Sch 3B repealed by the Taxation (Cross-border Trade) Act 2018 s 43, Sch 8 paras 1, 86 with effect from IP completion day (11pm on 31 December 2020), by virtue of SI 2020/1642 reg 4(*b*). Note that, where these amendments remove a reference to the principal VAT Directive (2006/112/EC) or the Implementing VAT Regulation ((EU) No 282/2011), the removal is not to be taken as implying that the Directive or Regulation is no longer relevant for determining the meaning and effect of this para (Taxation (Cross-border Trade) Act 2018 Sch 8 para 99).
Saving provision—Schedule 3B continues to apply in relation to supplies made before IP completion day despite its repeal by TCTA 2018 Sch 8, para 86. To the extent that it continues to apply, Sch 3B has effect subject to such modifications as may be specified in a notice published by the Commissioners (see SI 2020/1495, reg 14).
Any references to VATA 1994, Schs 3B or 3BA (other than those mentioned above) that have been repealed by TCTA 2018 Sch 8 continue to apply in relation to supplies made before IP completion day as if they had not been repealed, but only to the extent that Schs 3B and 3BA continue to have effect in accordance with SI 2020/1495. To the extent that they continue to apply, references to VATA 1994, Schs 3B or 3BA have effect subject to such modifications as may be specified in a notice published by the Commissioners (see SI 2020/1495, reg 16).

Qualifying supplies

[3—(1) In this Schedule "qualifying supply" means a supply of electronically supplied services, telecommunication services or broadcasting services to a person who—
  (a) belongs in the United Kingdom or another member State, and
  (b) is not a relevant business person.
(2) In sub-paragraph (1)—
  "broadcasting services" means radio and television broadcasting services;
  "electronically supplied services" has the same meaning as in Schedule 4A (see paragraph 9(3) and (4) of that Schedule);
  "telecommunication services" has the same meaning as in Schedule 4A (see [paragraph 9E(2)]^2 of that Schedule).]^1, ^{3}

Amendments—^{1} Sch 3B inserted by FA 2003 s 23, Sch 2 paras 1, 4 with effect for qualifying supplies made after 30 June 2003, see FA 2003 s 23(2).
^{2} In sub-para (2), words substituted for words "paragraph 8(2)" by the VAT (Place of Supply of Services) (Telecommunication Services) Order, SI 2017/778 art 6 with effect in relation to supplies of services made on or after 1 November 2017.
^{3} Sch 3B repealed by the Taxation (Cross-border Trade) Act 2018 s 43, Sch 8 paras 1, 86 with effect from IP completion day (11pm on 31 December 2020), by virtue of SI 2020/1642 reg 4(b).
Saving provision—Schedule 3B continues to apply in relation to supplies made before IP completion day despite its repeal by TCTA 2018 Sch 8, para 86. To the extent that it continues to apply, Sch 3B has effect subject to such modifications as may be specified in a notice published by the Commissioners (see SI 2020/1495, reg 14).
Any references to VATA 1994, Schs 3B or 3BA (other than those mentioned above) that have been repealed by TCTA 2018 Sch 8 continue to apply in relation to supplies made before IP completion day as if they had not been repealed, but only to the extent that Schs 3B and 3BA continue to have effect in accordance with SI 2020/1495. To the extent that they continue to apply, references to VATA 1994, Schs 3B or 3BA have effect subject to such modifications as may be specified in a notice published by the Commissioners (see SI 2020/1495, reg 16).

Registration request

[4—(1) If a person—
  (a) satisfies the Commissioners that the conditions in paragraph 2 above are satisfied in his case, and
  (b) makes a request in accordance with this paragraph (a "registration request"),
the Commissioners must register him under this Schedule.
(2) Sub-paragraph (1) above is subject to [Article 58b of Implementing Regulation (EU) No 282/2011]^3.
(3) A registration request must contain the following particulars—
  (a) the name of the person making the request;
  (b) his postal address;
  (c) his electronic addresses (including any websites);
  (d) where he has been allocated a number by the tax authorities in the country in which he belongs, that number;
  (e) the date on which he began, or intends to begin, making qualifying supplies.
[(4) A registration request must include a statement that the person making the request has no business establishment, and no fixed establishment, in the United Kingdom or in another member State.]^4
[(5) A registration request—
  (a) must contain any further information, and any declaration about its contents, that the Commissioners may by regulations require;
  (b) must be made by such electronic means, and in such manner, as the Commissioners may direct or may by regulations require.]^2]^1, ^{5}

Commentary—De Voil Indirect Tax Service **V2.189G**.
Regulations—VAT (Amendment) (No 3) Regulations, SI 2014/2430.
Amendments—^{1} Sch 3B inserted by FA 2003 s 23, Sch 2 paras 1, 4 with effect for qualifying supplies made after 30 June 2003, see FA 2003 s 23(2).
^{2} Sub-para (5) substituted by FA 2014 s 103, Sch 22 para 6(1), (3)(b) with effect from 17 July 2014.
^{3} In sub-para (2), words substituted for words "paragraph 9 below" by FA 2014 s 103, Sch 22 para 6(1), (3)(a) with effect in relation to supplies made on or after 1 January 2015.
^{4} Sub-para (4) substituted by the Value Added Tax (Special Accounting Schemes) (Supplies of Electronic, Telecommunication and Broadcasting Services) Order, SI 2018/1197 arts 2, 3(b) with effect in relation to supplies made on or after 1 January 2019. Note that SI 2018/1197 is revoked by SI 2019/513 reg 16 with effect from IP completion day (11pm on 31 December 2020).
^{5} Sch 3B repealed by the Taxation (Cross-border Trade) Act 2018 s 43, Sch 8 paras 1, 86 with effect from IP completion day (11pm on 31 December 2020), by virtue of SI 2020/1642 reg 4(b).
Saving provision—Schedule 3B continues to apply in relation to supplies made before IP completion day despite its repeal by TCTA 2018 Sch 8, para 86. To the extent that it continues to apply, Sch 3B has effect subject to such modifications as may be specified in a notice published by the Commissioners (see SI 2020/1495, reg 14).

Any references to VATA 1994, Schs 3B or 3BA (other than those mentioned above) that have been repealed by TCTA 2018 Sch 8 continue to apply in relation to supplies made before IP completion day as if they had not been repealed, but only to the extent that Schs 3B and 3BA continue to have effect in accordance with SI 2020/1495. To the extent that they continue to apply, references to VATA 1994, Schs 3B or 3BA have effect subject to such modifications as may be specified in a notice published by the Commissioners (see SI 2020/1495, reg 16).

Registration number

[6 On registering a person under this Schedule, the Commissioners must—
(a) allocate a registration number to him, and
(b) notify him electronically of the number.]^1, ^{2}

Amendments—^{1} Sch 3B inserted by FA 2003 s 23, Sch 2 paras 1, 4 with effect for qualifying supplies made after 30 June 2003, see FA 2003 s 23(2).
^{2} Sch 3B repealed by the Taxation (Cross-border Trade) Act 2018 s 43, Sch 8 paras 1, 86 with effect from IP completion day (11pm on 31 December 2020), by virtue of SI 2020/1642 reg 4(b).

Saving provision—Schedule 3B continues to apply in relation to supplies made before IP completion day despite its repeal by TCTA 2018 Sch 8, para 86. To the extent that it continues to apply, Sch 3B has effect subject to such modifications as may be specified in a notice published by the Commissioners (see SI 2020/1495, reg 14).

Any references to VATA 1994, Schs 3B or 3BA (other than those mentioned above) that have been repealed by TCTA 2018 Sch 8 continue to apply in relation to supplies made before IP completion day as if they had not been repealed, but only to the extent that Schs 3B and 3BA continue to have effect in accordance with SI 2020/1495. To the extent that they continue to apply, references to VATA 1994, Schs 3B or 3BA have effect subject to such modifications as may be specified in a notice published by the Commissioners (see SI 2020/1495, reg 16).

Obligation to notify changes

[7—(1) . . .^{2}
(2) . . .^{2}
(3) A notification under [Article 57h of Implementing Regulation (EU) No 282/2011]^2 must be given by such electronic means, and in such manner, as the Commissioners may direct or may by regulations prescribe.]^1, ^{3}

Regulations—VAT (Amendment) (No 3) Regulations, SI 2014/2430.
Amendments—^{1} Sch 3B inserted by FA 2003 s 23, Sch 2 paras 1, 4 with effect for qualifying supplies made after 30 June 2003, see FA 2003 s 23(2).
^{2} Sub-paras (1), (2) repealed, and in sub-para (3), words substituted for words "this paragraph", by FA 2014 s 103, Sch 22 para 6(1), (5) with effect in relation to supplies made on or after 1 January 2015.
^{3} Sch 3B repealed by the Taxation (Cross-border Trade) Act 2018 s 43, Sch 8 paras 1, 86 with effect from IP completion day (11pm on 31 December 2020), by virtue of SI 2020/1642 reg 4(b).

Saving provision—Schedule 3B continues to apply in relation to supplies made before IP completion day despite its repeal by TCTA 2018 Sch 8, para 86. To the extent that it continues to apply, Sch 3B has effect subject to such modifications as may be specified in a notice published by the Commissioners (see SI 2020/1495, reg 14).

Any references to VATA 1994, Schs 3B or 3BA (other than those mentioned above) that have been repealed by TCTA 2018 Sch 8 continue to apply in relation to supplies made before IP completion day as if they had not been repealed, but only to the extent that Schs 3B and 3BA continue to have effect in accordance with SI 2020/1495. To the extent that they continue to apply, references to VATA 1994, Schs 3B or 3BA have effect subject to such modifications as may be specified in a notice published by the Commissioners (see SI 2020/1495, reg 16).

Cancellation of registration

[8—(1) The Commissioners must cancel a person's registration under this Schedule if—
(a) he notifies them that he has ceased to make, or to have the intention of making, qualifying supplies,
(b) they otherwise determine that he has ceased to make, or to have the intention of making, qualifying supplies,
(c) he notifies them that he has ceased to satisfy the conditions in any of sub-paragraphs (3) to (6) of paragraph 2 above,
(d) they otherwise determine that he has ceased to satisfy any of those conditions, or
(e) they determine that he has persistently failed to comply with his obligations under this Schedule [or Implementing Regulation (EU) No 282/2011]^2.
(2), (3) . . . ^{2}]^1, ^{3}

Commentary—*De Voil Indirect Tax Service* **V2.189J**.
Amendments—^{1} Sch 3B inserted by FA 2003 s 23, Sch 2 paras 1, 4 with effect for qualifying supplies made after 30 June 2003, see FA 2003 s 23(2).
^{2} In sub-para (1)(e), words inserted, and sub-paras (2), (3) repealed, by FA 2014 s 103, Sch 22 para 6(1), (6) with effect in relation to supplies made on or after 1 January 2015.
^{3} Sch 3B repealed by the Taxation (Cross-border Trade) Act 2018 s 43, Sch 8 paras 1, 86 with effect from IP completion day (11pm on 31 December 2020), by virtue of SI 2020/1642 reg 4(b).

Saving provision—Schedule 3B continues to apply in relation to supplies made before IP completion day despite its repeal by TCTA 2018 Sch 8, para 86. To the extent that it continues to apply, Sch 3B has effect subject to such modifications as may be specified in a notice published by the Commissioners (see SI 2020/1495, reg 14).

Any references to VATA 1994, Schs 3B or 3BA (other than those mentioned above) that have been repealed by TCTA 2018 Sch 8 continue to apply in relation to supplies made before IP completion day as if they had not been repealed, but only to the extent that Schs 3B and 3BA continue to have effect in accordance with SI 2020/1495. To the extent that they continue to apply, references to VATA 1994, Schs 3B or 3BA have effect subject to such modifications as may be specified in a notice published by the Commissioners (see SI 2020/1495, reg 16).

. . .

9—

Amendments—Para 9 and preceding heading repealed by FA 2014 s 103, Sch 22 para 6(1), (7) with effect in relation to supplies made on or after 1 January 2015.

PART 2
[NON-UNION SCHEME: LIABILITY, RETURNS, PAYMENT ETC]

Amendments—In heading to Part 2, words substituted for words "Obligations following registration, etc" by FA 2014 s 103, Sch 22 paras 3, 7(1), (8) with effect in relation to supplies made on or after 1 January 2015.
Sch 3B repealed by the Taxation (Cross-border Trade) Act 2018 s 43, Sch 8 paras 1, 86 with effect from IP completion day (11pm on 31 December 2020), by virtue of SI 2020/1642 reg 4(b).
Saving provision—Schedule 3B continues to apply in relation to supplies made before IP completion day despite its repeal by TCTA 2018 Sch 8, para 86. To the extent that it continues to apply, Sch 3B has effect subject to such modifications as may be specified in a notice published by the Commissioners (see SI 2020/1495, reg 14).
Any references to VATA 1994, Schs 3B or 3BA (other than those mentioned above) that have been repealed by TCTA 2018 Sch 8 continue to apply in relation to supplies made before IP completion day as if they had not been repealed, but only to the extent that Schs 3B and 3BA continue to have effect in accordance with SI 2020/1495. To the extent that they continue to apply, references to VATA 1994, Schs 3B or 3BA have effect subject to such modifications as may be specified in a notice published by the Commissioners (see SI 2020/1495, reg 16).

Liability for VAT

[10—(1) A person is liable to pay VAT under and in accordance with this Schedule if—
  (a) he makes a qualifying supply, and
  (b) he is registered under this Schedule when he makes the supply.
(2) The amount of VAT which a person is liable to pay by virtue of this Schedule on any qualifying supply is to be determined in accordance with sub-paragraphs (3) and (4) below [(and the VAT is to be paid without any deduction of VAT pursuant to Article 168 of Directive 2006/112/EC)]^2.
(3) If the qualifying supply is treated as made in the United Kingdom, the amount is the amount of VAT . . . ^{2} charged on the supply under this Act [(see paragraph 17(2))]^2.
(4) If the qualifying supply is treated as made in another member State, the amount is the amount of VAT . . . ^{2} charged on the supply in accordance with the law of that member State . . . ^{2}.
(5) Where a person is liable to pay VAT by virtue of this Schedule—
  (a) any amount falling to be determined in accordance with sub-paragraph (3) above is to be regarded for the purposes of this Act as VAT charged in accordance with this Act, . . . ^{2}
  (b) . . . ^{2}]^1, ^{3}

Amendments—[1] Sch 3B inserted by FA 2003 s 23, Sch 2 paras 1, 4 with effect for qualifying supplies made after 30 June 2003, see FA 2003 s 23(2).
[2] In sub-para (2), words inserted, in sub-para (3), words "that would have been" repealed and words substituted for words "if the person had been registered under this Act when he made the supply", in sub-para (4), words "that would have been" repealed and words "if the person had been identified for the purposes of VAT in that member State when he made the supply" repealed, and in sub-para (5), para (b) and preceding word "and" repealed, by FA 2014 s 103, Sch 22 paras 3, 7(1), (2) with effect in relation to supplies made on or after 1 January 2015.
[3] Sch 3B repealed by the Taxation (Cross-border Trade) Act 2018 s 43, Sch 8 paras 1, 86 with effect from IP completion day (11pm on 31 December 2020), by virtue of SI 2020/1642 reg 4(b). Note that, where these amendments remove a reference to the principal VAT Directive (2006/112/EC) or the Implementing VAT Regulation ((EU) No 282/2011), the removal is not to be taken as implying that the Directive or Regulation is no longer relevant for determining the meaning and effect of this para (Taxation (Cross-border Trade) Act 2018 Sch 8 para 99).
Saving provision—Schedule 3B continues to apply in relation to supplies made before IP completion day despite its repeal by TCTA 2018 Sch 8, para 86. To the extent that it continues to apply, Sch 3B has effect subject to such modifications as may be specified in a notice published by the Commissioners (see SI 2020/1495, reg 14).
Any references to VATA 1994, Schs 3B or 3BA (other than those mentioned above) that have been repealed by TCTA 2018 Sch 8 continue to apply in relation to supplies made before IP completion day as if they had not been repealed, but only to the extent that Schs 3B and 3BA continue to have effect in accordance with SI 2020/1495. To the extent that they continue to apply, references to VATA 1994, Schs 3B or 3BA have effect subject to such modifications as may be specified in a notice published by the Commissioners (see SI 2020/1495, reg 16).

Obligation to submit special accounting returns

[11—(1) A person who is, or has been, registered under this Schedule must submit a return (a "special accounting return") to the [Commissioners]^2 for each reporting period.
(2) Each quarter for the whole or any part of which a person is registered under this Schedule is a "reporting period" in the case of that person.

Supply of electronic services: non-Union scheme **VATA 1994 Sch 3B**

(3)–(7) . . . ²]¹, ³

Amendments—¹ Sch 3B inserted by FA 2003 s 23, Sch 2 paras 1, 4 with effect for qualifying supplies made after 30 June 2003, see FA 2003 s 23(2).
² In sub-para (1), word substituted for word "Controller", and sub-paras (3)–(7) repealed, by FA 2014 s 103, Sch 22 paras 3, 7(1), (3) with effect in relation to supplies made on or after 1 January 2015.
³ Sch 3B repealed by the Taxation (Cross-border Trade) Act 2018 s 43, Sch 8 paras 1, 86 with effect from IP completion day (11pm on 31 December 2020), by virtue of SI 2020/1642 reg 4(b).
Saving provision—Schedule 3B continues to apply in relation to supplies made before IP completion day despite its repeal by TCTA 2018 Sch 8, para 86. To the extent that it continues to apply, Sch 3B has effect subject to such modifications as may be specified in a notice published by the Commissioners (see SI 2020/1495, reg 14).
Any references to VATA 1994, Schs 3B or 3BA (other than those mentioned above) that have been repealed by TCTA 2018 Sch 8 continue to apply in relation to supplies made before IP completion day as if they had not been repealed, but only to the extent that Schs 3B and 3BA continue to have effect in accordance with SI 2020/1495. To the extent that they continue to apply, references to VATA 1994, Schs 3B or 3BA have effect subject to such modifications as may be specified in a notice published by the Commissioners (see SI 2020/1495, reg 16).

Further obligations with respect to special accounting returns

[12—(1) A special accounting return [is to be made out in sterling]².
(2) Any conversion from one currency into another for the purposes of sub-paragraph (1) above shall be made by using the exchange rates published by the European Central Bank—
   (a) for the last day of the reporting period to which the special accounting return relates, or
   (b) if no such rate is published for that day, for the next day for which such a rate is published.
(3) A special accounting return must be submitted to the [Commissioners]² within the period of 20 days after the last day of the reporting period to which it relates.
(4) A special accounting return must be submitted by such electronic means, and in such manner, as the Commissioners may direct or may by regulations prescribe.]¹, ³

Regulations—VAT (Amendment) (No 3) Regulations, SI 2014/2430.
Amendments—¹ Sch 3B inserted by FA 2003 s 23, Sch 2 paras 1, 4 with effect for qualifying supplies made after 30 June 2003, see FA 2003 s 23(2).
² In sub-para (1), words substituted for words "must set out in sterling the amounts referred to in paragraph 11 above", and in sub-para (3), word substituted for word "Controller", by FA 2014 s 103, Sch 22 paras 3, 7(1), (4) with effect in relation to supplies made on or after 1 January 2015.
³ Sch 3B repealed by the Taxation (Cross-border Trade) Act 2018 s 43, Sch 8 paras 1, 86 with effect from IP completion day (11pm on 31 December 2020), by virtue of SI 2020/1642 reg 4(b).
Saving provision—Schedule 3B continues to apply in relation to supplies made before IP completion day despite its repeal by TCTA 2018 Sch 8, para 86. To the extent that it continues to apply, Sch 3B has effect subject to such modifications as may be specified in a notice published by the Commissioners (see SI 2020/1495, reg 14).
Any references to VATA 1994, Schs 3B or 3BA (other than those mentioned above) that have been repealed by TCTA 2018 Sch 8 continue to apply in relation to supplies made before IP completion day as if they had not been repealed, but only to the extent that Schs 3B and 3BA continue to have effect in accordance with SI 2020/1495. To the extent that they continue to apply, references to VATA 1994, Schs 3B or 3BA have effect subject to such modifications as may be specified in a notice published by the Commissioners (see SI 2020/1495, reg 16).

Payment of VAT

[13—(1) A person who is required to submit a special accounting return must, [by the deadline for submitting the return, pay to the Commissioners the amount of VAT that the person is liable, in accordance with paragraph 10, to pay on qualifying supplies treated as made by the person in]² the reporting period to which the return relates.
(2) A payment under this paragraph must be made in such manner as the Commissioners may direct or may by regulations prescribe.]¹, ³

Amendments—¹ Sch 3B inserted by FA 2003 s 23, Sch 2 paras 1, 4 with effect for qualifying supplies made after 30 June 2003, see FA 2003 s 23(2).
² In sub-para (1), words substituted for words "at the same time as he submits the return, pay to the Controller in sterling the amount referred to in paragraph 11(5) above in respect of", by FA 2014 s 103, Sch 22 paras 3, 7(1), (5) with effect in relation to supplies made on or after 1 January 2015.
³ Sch 3B repealed by the Taxation (Cross-border Trade) Act 2018 s 43, Sch 8 paras 1, 86 with effect from IP completion day (11pm on 31 December 2020), by virtue of SI 2020/1642 reg 4(b).
Saving provision—Schedule 3B continues to apply in relation to supplies made before IP completion day despite its repeal by TCTA 2018 Sch 8, para 86. To the extent that it continues to apply, Sch 3B has effect subject to such modifications as may be specified in a notice published by the Commissioners (see SI 2020/1495, reg 14).
Any references to VATA 1994, Schs 3B or 3BA (other than those mentioned above) that have been repealed by TCTA 2018 Sch 8 continue to apply in relation to supplies made before IP completion day as if they had not been repealed, but only to the extent that Schs 3B and 3BA continue to have effect in accordance with SI 2020/1495. To the extent that they continue to apply, references to VATA 1994, Schs 3B or 3BA have effect subject to such modifications as may be specified in a notice published by the Commissioners (see SI 2020/1495, reg 16).

Obligations to keep and produce records

[14—(1) A person must keep records of the transactions which he enters into for the purposes of, or in connection with, qualifying supplies made by him at any time when he is registered under this Schedule.
(2) The records to be kept must be such as will enable the tax authorities for the member State in which a qualifying supply is treated as made to determine whether any special accounting return which is submitted in respect of that supply is correct.
(3) Any records required to be kept must be made available—
   (a) to the tax authorities for the member State in which the qualifying supply to which the records relate was treated as made, if they so request, or
   (b) to the Commissioners, if they so request.
(4) Records must be made available electronically under sub-paragraph (3) above.
(5) The records relating to a transaction must be maintained for a period of ten years beginning with the 1st January following the date on which the transaction was entered into.]^1, ^{2}

Commentary—*De Voil Indirect Tax Service* **V5.201**.
Amendments—^{1} Sch 3B inserted by FA 2003 s 23, Sch 2 paras 1, 4 with effect for qualifying supplies made after 30 June 2003, see FA 2003 s 23(2).
^{2} Sch 3B repealed by the Taxation (Cross-border Trade) Act 2018 s 43, Sch 8 paras 1, 86 with effect from IP completion day (11pm on 31 December 2020), by virtue of SI 2020/1642 reg 4(b).
Saving provision—Schedule 3B continues to apply in relation to supplies made before IP completion day despite its repeal by TCTA 2018 Sch 8, para 86. To the extent that it continues to apply, Sch 3B has effect subject to such modifications as may be specified in a notice published by the Commissioners (see SI 2020/1495, reg 14).
Any references to VATA 1994, Schs 3B or 3BA (other than those mentioned above) that have been repealed by TCTA 2018 Sch 8 continue to apply in relation to supplies made before IP completion day as if they had not been repealed, but only to the extent that Schs 3B and 3BA continue to have effect in accordance with SI 2020/1495. To the extent that they continue to apply, references to VATA 1994, Schs 3B or 3BA have effect subject to such modifications as may be specified in a notice published by the Commissioners (see SI 2020/1495, reg 16).

Commissioners' power to request production of records

[15—(1) The Commissioners may request a person to make available to them electronically records of the transactions entered into by him for the purposes of, or in connection with, qualifying supplies to which this paragraph applies.
(2) This paragraph applies to qualifying supplies which—
   (a) are treated as made in the United Kingdom, and
   (b) are made by the person while he is identified under any provision of the law of another member State which implements [Section 2 of Chapter 6 of Title XII of the VAT Directive]^2.]^1, ^{3}

Amendments—^{1} Sch 3B inserted by FA 2003 s 23, Sch 2 paras 1, 4 with effect for qualifying supplies made after 30 June 2003, see FA 2003 s 23(2).
^{2} In sub-para (2)(b), words substituted for words "Article 26c" by FA 2014 s 103, Sch 22 paras 3, 7(1), (6) with effect in relation to supplies made on or after 1 January 2015.
^{3} Sch 3B repealed by the Taxation (Cross-border Trade) Act 2018 s 43, Sch 8 paras 1, 86 with effect from IP completion day (11pm on 31 December 2020), by virtue of SI 2020/1642 reg 4(b). Note that, where these amendments remove a reference to the principal VAT Directive (2006/112/EC) or the Implementing VAT Regulation ((EU) No 282/2011), the removal is not to be taken as implying that the Directive or Regulation is no longer relevant for determining the meaning and effect of this para (Taxation (Cross-border Trade) Act 2018 Sch 8 para 99).
Saving provision—Schedule 3B continues to apply in relation to supplies made before IP completion day despite its repeal by TCTA 2018 Sch 8, para 86. To the extent that it continues to apply, Sch 3B has effect subject to such modifications as may be specified in a notice published by the Commissioners (see SI 2020/1495, reg 14).
Any references to VATA 1994, Schs 3B or 3BA (other than those mentioned above) that have been repealed by TCTA 2018 Sch 8 continue to apply in relation to supplies made before IP completion day as if they had not been repealed, but only to the extent that Schs 3B and 3BA continue to have effect in accordance with SI 2020/1495. To the extent that they continue to apply, references to VATA 1994, Schs 3B or 3BA have effect subject to such modifications as may be specified in a notice published by the Commissioners (see SI 2020/1495, reg 16).

[15A—Section 44 of the Commissioners for Revenue and Customs Act 2005 (requirement to pay receipts into the Consolidated Fund) does not apply to any money received for or on account of VAT that is required to be paid to another member State under Article 46 of Council Regulation (EU) No 904/2010.]^1, ^{2}

Amendments—^{1} Para 15A inserted by FA 2014 s 103, Sch 22 paras 3, 7(1), (7) with effect in relation to supplies made on or after 1 January 2015.
^{2} Sch 3B repealed by the Taxation (Cross-border Trade) Act 2018 s 43, Sch 8 paras 1, 86 with effect from IP completion day (11pm on 31 December 2020), by virtue of SI 2020/1642 reg 4(b).
Saving provision—Schedule 3B continues to apply in relation to supplies made before IP completion day despite its repeal by TCTA 2018 Sch 8, para 86. To the extent that it continues to apply, Sch 3B has effect subject to such modifications as may be specified in a notice published by the Commissioners (see SI 2020/1495, reg 14).
Any references to VATA 1994, Schs 3B or 3BA (other than those mentioned above) that have been repealed by TCTA 2018 Sch 8 continue to apply in relation to supplies made before IP completion day as if they had not been repealed, but only to the extent

that Schs 3B and 3BA continue to have effect in accordance with SI 2020/1495. To the extent that they continue to apply, references to VATA 1994, Schs 3B or 3BA have effect subject to such modifications as may be specified in a notice published by the Commissioners (see SI 2020/1495, reg 16).

[PART 3
SPECIAL SCHEMES: COLLECTION ETC OF UK VAT

Assessments: general modifications of section 73

16—*(1) For the purposes of this Schedule, section 73 (assessments: incorrect returns etc) is to be read as if—*
  (a) the reference in subsection (1) of that section to returns required under this Act included relevant special scheme returns, and
  (b) references in that section to a prescribed accounting period included a tax period.
(2) See also the modifications in paragraph 16A.
(3) In this Schedule "relevant special scheme return" means a special scheme return that is required to be made (wholly or partly) in respect of supplies of scheme services that are treated as made in the United Kingdom.][1], [2]

Commentary—*De Voil Indirect Tax Service* **V2.189L**.
Amendments—[1] Part 3 (paras 16–16N) substituted by FA 2014 s 103, Sch 22 paras 3, 8 with effect in relation to supplies made on or after 1 January 2015. Any amendment made by FA 2014 Sch 22 so far as it confers power to make regulations has effect from 17 July 2014 (FA 2014 Sch 22 para 23(2)(*b*)). Part 3, as it applied in relation to supplies made before 1 January 2015, is reproduced below after para 16N.
[2] Sch 3B repealed by the Taxation (Cross-border Trade) Act 2018 s 43, Sch 8 paras 1, 86 with effect from IP completion day (11pm on 31 December 2020), by virtue of SI 2020/1642 reg 4(*b*).
Saving provision—Schedule 3B continues to apply in relation to supplies made before IP completion day despite its repeal by TCTA 2018 Sch 8, para 86. To the extent that it continues to apply, Sch 3B has effect subject to such modifications as may be specified in a notice published by the Commissioners (see SI 2020/1495, reg 14).
Any references to VATA 1994, Schs 3B or 3BA (other than those mentioned above) that have been repealed by TCTA 2018 Sch 8 continue to apply in relation to supplies made before IP completion day as if they had not been repealed, but only to the extent that Schs 3B and 3BA continue to have effect in accordance with SI 2020/1495. To the extent that they continue to apply, references to VATA 1994, Schs 3B or 3BA have effect subject to such modifications as may be specified in a notice published by the Commissioners (see SI 2020/1495, reg 16).

[Assessment in connection with increase in consideration

16A—*(1) Sub-paragraphs (2) to (4) make modifications of sections 73 and 76 which—*
  (a) have effect for the purposes of this Schedule, and
  (b) are in addition to any other modifications of those sections made by this Schedule.
(2) Section 73 has effect as if the following were inserted after subsection (3) of that section—
  "(3A) Where a person has failed to make an amendment or notification that the person is required to make under paragraph 16K of Schedule 3B in respect of an increase in the consideration for a UK supply (as defined in paragraph 16K(7)), the Commissioners may assess the amount of VAT due from the person as a result of the increase to the best of their judgement and notify it to the person.
  (3B) An assessment under subsection (3A)—
    (a) is of VAT due for the tax period mentioned in paragraph 16K(1)(a) of Schedule 3B;
    (b) must be made within the time limits provided for in section 77, and must not be made after the later of—
      (i) 2 years after the end of the tax period referred to in paragraph 16K(1)(a);
      (ii) one year after evidence of facts sufficient in the opinion of the Commissioners to justify making the assessment comes to their knowledge.
  (3C) Subject to section 77, where further evidence such as is mentioned in subsection (3B)(b)(ii) comes to the Commissioners' knowledge after they have made an assessment under subsection (3A), another assessment may be made under that subsection, in addition to any earlier assessment."
(3) The reference in section 73(9) to subsection (1) of that section is taken to include a reference to section 73(3A) (as inserted by sub-paragraph (2)).
(4) Section 76 (assessment of amounts due by way of interest etc) is to be read as if the reference in subsection (5) of that section to section 73(1) included a reference to section 73(3A) (as inserted by sub-paragraph (2)).][1], [2]

Commentary—*De Voil Indirect Tax Service* **V2.189L**.
Amendments—[1] Part 3 (paras 16–16N) substituted by FA 2014 s 103, Sch 22 paras 3, 8 with effect in relation to supplies made on or after 1 January 2015. Any amendment made by FA 2014 Sch 22 so far as it confers power to make regulations has effect from 17 July 2014 (FA 2014 Sch 22 para 23(2)(*b*)). Part 3, as it applied in relation to supplies made before 1 January 2015, is reproduced below after para 16N.

² Sch 3B repealed by the Taxation (Cross-border Trade) Act 2018 s 43, Sch 8 paras 1, 86 with effect from IP completion day (11pm on 31 December 2020), by virtue of SI 2020/1642 reg 4(*b*).
Saving provision—Schedule 3B continues to apply in relation to supplies made before IP completion day despite its repeal by TCTA 2018 Sch 8, para 86. To the extent that it continues to apply, Sch 3B has effect subject to such modifications as may be specified in a notice published by the Commissioners (see SI 2020/1495, reg 14).
Any references to VATA 1994, Schs 3B or 3BA (other than those mentioned above) that have been repealed by TCTA 2018 Sch 8 continue to apply in relation to supplies made before IP completion day as if they had not been repealed, but only to the extent that Schs 3B and 3BA continue to have effect in accordance with SI 2020/1495. To the extent that they continue to apply, references to VATA 1994, Schs 3B or 3BA have effect subject to such modifications as may be specified in a notice published by the Commissioners (see SI 2020/1495, reg 16).

[Assessments: consequential modifications

16B *References to prescribed accounting periods in the following provisions are to be read in accordance with the modifications made by paragraphs 16 and 16A—*
  (a) *section 74 (interest on VAT recovered or recoverable by assessment);*
  (b) *section 76 (assessment of amounts due by way of penalty, interest or surcharge);*
  (c) *section 77 (assessment: time limits).]¹, ²*
Commentary—*De Voil Indirect Tax Service* **V2.189L**.
Amendments—¹ Part 3 (paras 16–16N) substituted by FA 2014 s 103, Sch 22 paras 3, 8 with effect in relation to supplies made on or after 1 January 2015. Any amendment made by FA 2014 Sch 22 so far as it confers power to make regulations has effect from 17 July 2014 (FA 2014 Sch 22 para 23(2)(*b*)). Part 3, as it applied in relation to supplies made before 1 January 2015, is reproduced below after para 16N.
² Sch 3B repealed by the Taxation (Cross-border Trade) Act 2018 s 43, Sch 8 paras 1, 86 with effect from IP completion day (11pm on 31 December 2020), by virtue of SI 2020/1642 reg 4(*b*).
Saving provision—Schedule 3B continues to apply in relation to supplies made before IP completion day despite its repeal by TCTA 2018 Sch 8, para 86. To the extent that it continues to apply, Sch 3B has effect subject to such modifications as may be specified in a notice published by the Commissioners (see SI 2020/1495, reg 14).
Any references to VATA 1994, Schs 3B or 3BA (other than those mentioned above) that have been repealed by TCTA 2018 Sch 8 continue to apply in relation to supplies made before IP completion day as if they had not been repealed, but only to the extent that Schs 3B and 3BA continue to have effect in accordance with SI 2020/1495. To the extent that they continue to apply, references to VATA 1994, Schs 3B or 3BA have effect subject to such modifications as may be specified in a notice published by the Commissioners (see SI 2020/1495, reg 16).

[Deemed amendments of relevant special scheme returns

16C—*(1) Where a person who has made a relevant special scheme return makes a claim under paragraph 16I(7)(b) (overpayments) in relation to an error in the return, the relevant special scheme return is taken for the purposes of this Act to have been amended by the information in the claim.*
(2) Where a person who has made a relevant special scheme return gives the Commissioners a notice relating to the return under paragraph 16K(2)(b) (increase or decrease in consideration), the relevant special scheme return is taken for the purposes of this Act to have been amended by that information.
(3) Where (in a case not falling within sub-paragraph (1) or (2)) a person who has made a relevant special scheme return notifies the Commissioners (after the expiry of the period during which the non-UK return may be amended under Article 61 of the Implementing Regulation) of a change that needs to be made to the return to correct an error, or rectify an omission, in it, the relevant special scheme return is taken for the purposes of this Act to have been amended by that information.
(4) The Commissioners may by regulations—
  (a) *specify within what period and in what form and manner notice may be given under sub-paragraph (3);*
  (b) *require notices to be supported by documentary evidence described in the regulations.]¹, ²*
Commentary—*De Voil Indirect Tax Service* **V2.189L**.
Regulations—VAT (Amendment) (No 3) Regulations, SI 2014/2430.
Amendments—¹ Part 3 (paras 16–16N) substituted by FA 2014 s 103, Sch 22 paras 3, 8 with effect in relation to supplies made on or after 1 January 2015. Any amendment made by FA 2014 Sch 22 so far as it confers power to make regulations has effect from 17 July 2014 (FA 2014 Sch 22 para 23(2)(*b*)). Part 3, as it applied in relation to supplies made before 1 January 2015, is reproduced below after para 16N.
² Sch 3B repealed by the Taxation (Cross-border Trade) Act 2018 s 43, Sch 8 paras 1, 86 with effect from IP completion day (11pm on 31 December 2020), by virtue of SI 2020/1642 reg 4(*b*).
Saving provision—Schedule 3B continues to apply in relation to supplies made before IP completion day despite its repeal by TCTA 2018 Sch 8, para 86. To the extent that it continues to apply, Sch 3B has effect subject to such modifications as may be specified in a notice published by the Commissioners (see SI 2020/1495, reg 14).
Any references to VATA 1994, Schs 3B or 3BA (other than those mentioned above) that have been repealed by TCTA 2018 Sch 8 continue to apply in relation to supplies made before IP completion day as if they had not been repealed, but only to the extent that Schs 3B and 3BA continue to have effect in accordance with SI 2020/1495. To the extent that they continue to apply, references to VATA 1994, Schs 3B or 3BA have effect subject to such modifications as may be specified in a notice published by the Commissioners (see SI 2020/1495, reg 16).

[Interest on VAT: "reckonable date"

16D—*(1) Sub-paragraph (2) states the "reckonable date" for the purposes of section 74(1) and (2) for any case where an amount carrying interest under that section—*
   (a) is an amount assessed under section 73(2) (refunds etc) in reliance on paragraph 16, or that could have been so assessed, and
   (b) was correctly paid or credited to the person, but would not have been paid or credited to the person had the facts been as they later turn out to be.
(2) The "reckonable date" is the first day after the end of the tax period in which the events occurred as a result of which the Commissioners were authorised to make the assessment (that was or could have been made) under section 73(2).
(3) Sub-paragraph (4) states the "reckonable date", for any other case where an amount carrying interest under section 74 is assessed under section 74(1) or (2) in reliance on paragraph 16, or could have been so assessed.
(4) The "reckonable date" is taken to be the latest date by which a non-UK return was required to be made for the tax period to which the amount assessed relates.
(5) Where section 74(1) or (2) (interest on VAT recovered or recoverable by assessment) applies in relation to an amount assessed under section 73(3A) (as inserted by paragraph 16A(2)), the "reckonable date" for the purposes of section 74(1) or (2) is taken to be the day after the end of the tax period referred to in paragraph 16K(2).][1], [2]

Commentary—*De Voil Indirect Tax Service* **V2.189L.**
Amendments—[1] Part 3 (paras 16–16N) substituted by FA 2014 s 103, Sch 22 paras 3, 8 with effect in relation to supplies made on or after 1 January 2015. Any amendment made by FA 2014 Sch 22 so far as it confers power to make regulations has effect from 17 July 2014 (FA 2014 Sch 22 para 23(2)(*b*)). Part 3, as it applied in relation to supplies made before 1 January 2015, is reproduced below after para 16N.
[2] Sch 3B repealed by the Taxation (Cross-border Trade) Act 2018 s 43, Sch 8 paras 1, 86 with effect from IP completion day (11pm on 31 December 2020), by virtue of SI 2020/1642 reg 4(*b*).

Saving provision—Schedule 3B continues to apply in relation to supplies made before IP completion day despite its repeal by TCTA 2018 Sch 8, para 86. To the extent that it continues to apply, Sch 3B has effect subject to such modifications as may be specified in a notice published by the Commissioners (see SI 2020/1495, reg 14).
Any references to VATA 1994, Schs 3B or 3BA (other than those mentioned above) that have been repealed by TCTA 2018 Sch 8 continue to apply in relation to supplies made before IP completion day as if they had not been repealed, but only to the extent that Schs 3B and 3BA continue to have effect in accordance with SI 2020/1495. To the extent that they continue to apply, references to VATA 1994, Schs 3B or 3BA have effect subject to such modifications as may be specified in a notice published by the Commissioners (see SI 2020/1495, reg 16).

[Default surcharge: notice of special surcharge period

16E—*(1) A person who is required to make a relevant special scheme return for a tax period is regarded for the purposes of this paragraph and paragraph 16F as being in default in respect of that period if either—*
   (a) conditions 1A and 2A are met, or
   (b) conditions 1B and 2B are met;
(but see also paragraph 16G).
(2) For the purposes of sub-paragraph (1)(a)—
   (a) condition 1A is that the tax authorities for the administering member State have not received the return by the deadline for submitting it;
   (b) condition 2A is that those tax authorities have, in accordance with Article 60a of the Implementing Regulation, issued a reminder of the obligation to submit the return.
(3) For the purposes of sub-paragraph (1)(b)—
   (a) condition 1B is that, by the deadline for submitting the return, the tax authorities for the administering member State have received the return but have not received the amount of VAT shown on the return as payable by the person in respect of the tax period;
   (b) condition 2B is that those tax authorities have, in accordance with Article 60a of the Implementing Regulation, issued a reminder of the VAT outstanding.
(4) The Commissioners may serve on a person who is in default in respect of a tax period a notice (a "special surcharge liability notice") specifying a period—
   (a) ending on the first anniversary of the last day of that tax period, and
   (b) beginning on the date of the notice.
(5) A period specified under sub-paragraph (4) is a "special surcharge period".
(6) If a special surcharge liability notice is served in respect of a tax period which ends at or before the end of an existing special surcharge period, the special surcharge period specified in that notice must be expressed as a continuation of the existing special surcharge period (so that the existing period and its extension are regarded as a single special surcharge period).][1], [2]

Commentary—*De Voil Indirect Tax Service* **V2.189L.**

Amendments—[1] Part 3 (paras 16–16N) substituted by FA 2014 s 103, Sch 22 paras 3, 8 with effect in relation to supplies made on or after 1 January 2015. Any amendment made by FA 2014 Sch 22 so far as it confers power to make regulations has effect from 17 July 2014 (FA 2014 Sch 22 para 23(2)(*b*)). Part 3, as it applied in relation to supplies made before 1 January 2015, is reproduced below after para 16N.
[2] Sch 3B repealed by the Taxation (Cross-border Trade) Act 2018 s 43, Sch 8 paras 1, 86 with effect from IP completion day (11pm on 31 December 2020), by virtue of SI 2020/1642 reg 4(*b*).
Saving provision—Schedule 3B continues to apply in relation to supplies made before IP completion day despite its repeal by TCTA 2018 Sch 8, para 86. To the extent that it continues to apply, Sch 3B has effect subject to such modifications as may be specified in a notice published by the Commissioners (see SI 2020/1495, reg 14).
Any references to VATA 1994, Schs 3B or 3BA (other than those mentioned above) that have been repealed by TCTA 2018 Sch 8 continue to apply in relation to supplies made before IP completion day as if they had not been repealed, but only to the extent that Schs 3B and 3BA continue to have effect in accordance with SI 2020/1495. To the extent that they continue to apply, references to VATA 1994, Schs 3B or 3BA have effect subject to such modifications as may be specified in a notice published by the Commissioners (see SI 2020/1495, reg 16).

[Further default after service of notice

16F—(*1*) *If a person on whom a special surcharge liability notice has been served—*
  (*a*) *is in default in respect of a tax period ending within the special surcharge period specified in (or extended by) that notice, and*
  (*b*) *has outstanding special scheme VAT for that tax period,*
the person is to be liable to a surcharge of the amount given by sub-paragraph (2).
(*2*) *The surcharge is equal to whichever is the greater of—*
  (*a*) *£30, and*
  (*b*) *the specified percentage of the person's outstanding special scheme VAT for the tax period.*
(*3*) *The specified percentage depends on whether the tax period is the first, second or third etc in the default period in respect of which the person is in default and has outstanding special scheme VAT, and is—*
  (*a*) *for the first such tax period, 2%;*
  (*b*) *for the second such tax period, 5%;*
  (*c*) *for the third such tax period, 10%;*
  (*d*) *for each such tax period after the third, 15%.*
(*4*) *"Special scheme VAT", in relation to a person, means VAT that the person is liable to pay to the tax authorities for the administering member State under a special scheme in respect of supplies of scheme services treated as made in the United Kingdom.*
(*5*) *A person has "outstanding special scheme VAT" for a tax period if some or all of the special scheme VAT for which the person is liable in respect of that period has not been paid by the deadline for the person to submit a special scheme return for that period (and the amount unpaid is referred to in sub-paragraph (2)(b) as "the person's outstanding special scheme VAT" for the tax period).]*[1],[2]

Commentary—*De Voil Indirect Tax Service* **V2.189L**.
Amendments—[1] Part 3 (paras 16–16N) substituted by FA 2014 s 103, Sch 22 paras 3, 8 with effect in relation to supplies made on or after 1 January 2015. Any amendment made by FA 2014 Sch 22 so far as it confers power to make regulations has effect from 17 July 2014 (FA 2014 Sch 22 para 23(2)(*b*)). Part 3, as it applied in relation to supplies made before 1 January 2015, is reproduced below after para 16N.
[2] Sch 3B repealed by the Taxation (Cross-border Trade) Act 2018 s 43, Sch 8 paras 1, 86 with effect from IP completion day (11pm on 31 December 2020), by virtue of SI 2020/1642 reg 4(*b*).
Saving provision—Schedule 3B continues to apply in relation to supplies made before IP completion day despite its repeal by TCTA 2018 Sch 8, para 86. To the extent that it continues to apply, Sch 3B has effect subject to such modifications as may be specified in a notice published by the Commissioners (see SI 2020/1495, reg 14).
Any references to VATA 1994, Schs 3B or 3BA (other than those mentioned above) that have been repealed by TCTA 2018 Sch 8 continue to apply in relation to supplies made before IP completion day as if they had not been repealed, but only to the extent that Schs 3B and 3BA continue to have effect in accordance with SI 2020/1495. To the extent that they continue to apply, references to VATA 1994, Schs 3B or 3BA have effect subject to such modifications as may be specified in a notice published by the Commissioners (see SI 2020/1495, reg 16).

[Default surcharge: exceptions for reasonable excuse etc

16G—(*1*) *A person who would otherwise have been liable to a surcharge under paragraph 16F(1) is not to be liable to the surcharge if the person satisfies the Commissioners or, on appeal, the tribunal that, in the case of a default which is material to the surcharge—*
  (*a*) *the special scheme return or, as the case may be, the VAT shown on that return, was despatched at such a time and in such manner that it was reasonable to expect that it would be received by the tax authorities for the administering member State within the appropriate time limit, or*
  (*b*) *there is a reasonable excuse for the return or the VAT not having been so despatched.*
(*2*) *Where sub-paragraph (1) applies to a person—*
  (*a*) *the person is treated as not having been in default in respect of the tax period in question, and*

(b) accordingly, any special surcharge liability notice the service of which depended on that default is regarded as not having been served.

(3) A default is "material" to a surcharge if—
  (a) it is the default which gives rise to the surcharge, under paragraph 16F(1), or
  (b) it is a default which was taken into account in the service of the special surcharge liability notice on which the surcharge depends and the person concerned has not previously been liable to a surcharge in respect of a tax period ending within the special surcharge period specified in or extended by that notice.

(4) A default is left out of account for the purposes of paragraphs 16E(4) and 16F(1) if—
  (a) the conduct by virtue of which the person is in default is also conduct falling within section 69(1) (breaches of regulatory provisions), and
  (b) by reason of that conduct the person concerned is assessed to a penalty under that section.

(5) If the Commissioners, after consultation with the Treasury, so direct, a default in respect of a tax period specified in the direction is to be left out of account for the purposes of paragraphs 16E(4) and 16F(1).

(6) Section 71(1) (meaning of "reasonable excuse") applies for the purposes of this paragraph as it applies for the purposes of sections 59 to 70.][1], [2]

Commentary—*De Voil Indirect Tax Service* **V2.189L**.
Amendments—[1] Part 3 (paras 16–16N) substituted by FA 2014 s 103, Sch 22 paras 3, 8 with effect in relation to supplies made on or after 1 January 2015. Any amendment made by FA 2014 Sch 22 so far as it confers power to make regulations has effect from 17 July 2014 (FA 2014 Sch 22 para 23(2)(*b*)). Part 3, as it applied in relation to supplies made before 1 January 2015, is reproduced below after para 16N.
[2] Sch 3B repealed by the Taxation (Cross-border Trade) Act 2018 s 43, Sch 8 paras 1, 86 with effect from IP completion day (11pm on 31 December 2020), by virtue of SI 2020/1642 reg 4(*b*).
Saving provision—Schedule 3B continues to apply in relation to supplies made before IP completion day despite its repeal by TCTA 2018 Sch 8, para 86. To the extent that it continues to apply, Sch 3B has effect subject to such modifications as may be specified in a notice published by the Commissioners (see SI 2020/1495, reg 14).
Any references to VATA 1994, Schs 3B or 3BA (other than those mentioned above) that have been repealed by TCTA 2018 Sch 8 continue to apply in relation to supplies made before IP completion day as if they had not been repealed, but only to the extent that Schs 3B and 3BA continue to have effect in accordance with SI 2020/1495. To the extent that they continue to apply, references to VATA 1994, Schs 3B or 3BA have effect subject to such modifications as may be specified in a notice published by the Commissioners (see SI 2020/1495, reg 16).

[Interest in certain cases of official error

16H—*(1)* Section 78 (interest in certain cases of official error) applies as follows in relation to a case where, due to an error on the part of the Commissioners—
  (a) a person has accounted, under a special scheme, for an amount by way of UK VAT that was not UK VAT due from the person, and as a result the Commissioners are liable under paragraph 16I to pay (or repay) an amount to the person, or
  (b) (in a case not falling within paragraph (*a*)), a person has paid, in accordance with an obligation under a special scheme, an amount by way of UK VAT that was not UK VAT due from the person and which the Commissioners are in consequence liable to repay to the person.

(2) Section 78 has effect as if the condition in section 78(1)(*a*) were met in relation to that person.

(3) In the application of section 78 as a result of this paragraph, section 78(12)(*b*) is read as providing that any reference in that section to a return is to a return required to be made under a special scheme.

(4) In section 78 in its application as a result of this section, "output tax" has the meaning that that expression would have if the reference in section 24(2) to a "taxable person" were to a "person".][1], [2]

Commentary—*De Voil Indirect Tax Service* **V2.189L**.
Amendments—[1] Part 3 (paras 16–16N) substituted by FA 2014 s 103, Sch 22 paras 3, 8 with effect in relation to supplies made on or after 1 January 2015. Any amendment made by FA 2014 Sch 22 so far as it confers power to make regulations has effect from 17 July 2014 (FA 2014 Sch 22 para 23(2)(*b*)). Part 3, as it applied in relation to supplies made before 1 January 2015, is reproduced below after para 16N.
[2] Sch 3B repealed by the Taxation (Cross-border Trade) Act 2018 s 43, Sch 8 paras 1, 86 with effect from IP completion day (11pm on 31 December 2020), by virtue of SI 2020/1642 reg 4(*b*).
Saving provision—Schedule 3B continues to apply in relation to supplies made before IP completion day despite its repeal by TCTA 2018 Sch 8, para 86. To the extent that it continues to apply, Sch 3B has effect subject to such modifications as may be specified in a notice published by the Commissioners (see SI 2020/1495, reg 14).
Any references to VATA 1994, Schs 3B or 3BA (other than those mentioned above) that have been repealed by TCTA 2018 Sch 8 continue to apply in relation to supplies made before IP completion day as if they had not been repealed, but only to the extent that Schs 3B and 3BA continue to have effect in accordance with SI 2020/1495. To the extent that they continue to apply, references to VATA 1994, Schs 3B or 3BA have effect subject to such modifications as may be specified in a notice published by the Commissioners (see SI 2020/1495, reg 16).

[Overpayments]

16I—*(1)* A person may make a claim if the person—
  (a) has made a special scheme return for a tax period relating wholly or partly to supplies of scheme services treated as made in the United Kingdom,
  (b) has accounted to the tax authorities for the administering member State (whether that is the United Kingdom or another member State) for VAT in respect of those supplies, and
  (c) in doing so has brought into account as UK VAT due to those authorities an amount ("the overpaid amount") that was not UK VAT due to them.
(2) A person may make a claim if the person has, as a participant in a special scheme, paid (to the tax authorities for the administering member State or to the Commissioners) an amount by way of UK VAT that was not UK VAT due ("the overpaid amount"), otherwise than in the circumstances mentioned in sub-paragraph (1)(c).
(3) A person who is or has been a participant in a special scheme may make a claim if the Commissioners—
  (a) have assessed the person to VAT for a tax period, and
  (b) in doing so, have brought into account as VAT an amount ("the amount not due") that was not VAT due.
(4) Where a person makes a claim under sub-paragraph (1) or (2), the Commissioners must repay the overpaid amount to the person.
(5) Where a person makes a claim under sub-paragraph (3), the Commissioners must credit the person with the amount not due.
(6) Where—
  (a) as a result of a claim under sub-paragraph (3) an amount is to be credited to a person, and
  (b) after setting any sums against that amount under or by virtue of this Act, some or all of the amount remains to the person's credit,
the Commissioners must pay (or repay) to the person so much of the amount as remains to the person's credit.
(7) The reference in sub-paragraph (1) to a claim is to a claim made—
  (a) by correcting, in accordance with Article 61 of the Implementing Regulation, the error in the non-UK return mentioned in sub-paragraph (1)(a), or
  (b) (after the expiry of the period during which the non-UK return may be amended under Article 61) to the Commissioners.
(8) Sub-paragraphs (1) and (2) do not require any amount to be repaid except so far as that is required by Article 63 of the Implementing Regulation.]![1], [2]

Commentary—*De Voil Indirect Tax Service* **V2.189L**.
Amendments—[1] Part 3 (paras 16–16N) substituted by FA 2014 s 103, Sch 22 paras 3, 8 with effect in relation to supplies made on or after 1 January 2015. Any amendment made by FA 2014 Sch 22 so far as it confers power to make regulations has effect from 17 July 2014 (FA 2014 Sch 22 para 23(2)(b)). Part 3, as it applied in relation to supplies made before 1 January 2015, is reproduced below after para 16N.
[2] Sch 3B repealed by the Taxation (Cross-border Trade) Act 2018 s 43, Sch 8 paras 1, 86 with effect from IP completion day (11pm on 31 December 2020), by virtue of SI 2020/1642 reg 4(b).
Saving provision—Schedule 3B continues to apply in relation to supplies made before IP completion day despite its repeal by TCTA 2018 Sch 8, para 86. To the extent that it continues to apply, Sch 3B has effect subject to such modifications as may be specified in a notice published by the Commissioners (see SI 2020/1495, reg 14).
Any references to VATA 1994, Schs 3B or 3BA (other than those mentioned above) that have been repealed by TCTA 2018 Sch 8 continue to apply in relation to supplies made before IP completion day as if they had not been repealed, but only to the extent that Schs 3B and 3BA continue to have effect in accordance with SI 2020/1495. To the extent that they continue to apply, references to VATA 1994, Schs 3B or 3BA have effect subject to such modifications as may be specified in a notice published by the Commissioners (see SI 2020/1495, reg 16).

[Overpayments: supplementary]

16J—*(1)* In section 80—
  (a) subsections (3) to (3C) (unjust enrichment), and
  (b) subsections (4A), (4C) and (6) (recovery by assessment of amounts wrongly credited),
have effect as if a claim under paragraph 16I(1) were a claim under section 80(1), a claim under paragraph 16I(2) were a claim under section 80(1B) and a claim under paragraph 16I(3) were a claim under section 80(1A).
(2) In section 80(3) to (3C), (4A), (4C) and (6), as applied by sub-paragraph (1)—
  (a) references to the crediting of amounts are to be read as including the payment of amounts;
  (b) references to a prescribed accounting period include a tax period.
(3) The Commissioners are not liable to repay the overpaid amount on a claim made—
  (a) under paragraph 16I(2),or
  (b) as mentioned in paragraph 16I(7)(b),
if the claim is made more than 4 years after the relevant date.

(4) On a claim made under paragraph 16I(3), the Commissioners are not liable to credit the amount not due if the claim is made more than 4 years after the relevant date.
(5) The "relevant date" is—
  (a) in the case of a claim under paragraph 16I(1), the end of the tax period mentioned in paragraph 16I(1)(a), except in the case of a claim resulting from an incorrect disclosure;
  (b) in the case of a claim under paragraph 16I(1) resulting from an incorrect disclosure, the end of the tax period in which the disclosure was made;
  (c) in the case of a claim under paragraph 16I(2), the date on which the payment was made;
  (d) in the case of a claim under paragraph 16I(3), the end of the quarter in which the assessment was made.
(6) A person makes an "incorrect disclosure" where—
  (a) the person discloses to the tax authorities in question (whether the Commissioners or the tax authorities for the administering member State) that the person has not brought into account for a tax period an amount of UK VAT due for the period ("the disclosed amount"),
  (b) the disclosure is made in a later tax period, and
  (c) some or all of the disclosed amount is not in fact VAT due.][1], [2]

Commentary—*De Voil Indirect Tax Service* **V2.189L**.
Regulations—VAT (Amendment) (No 3) Regulations, SI 2014/2430.
Amendments—[1] Part 3 (paras 16–16N) substituted by FA 2014 s 103, Sch 22 paras 3, 8 with effect in relation to supplies made on or after 1 January 2015. Any amendment made by FA 2014 Sch 22 so far as it confers power to make regulations has effect from 17 July 2014 (FA 2014 Sch 22 para 23(2)(*b*)). Part 3, as it applied in relation to supplies made before 1 January 2015, is reproduced below after para 16N.
[2] Sch 3B repealed by the Taxation (Cross-border Trade) Act 2018 s 43, Sch 8 paras 1, 86 with effect from IP completion day (11pm on 31 December 2020), by virtue of SI 2020/1642 reg 4(*b*).
Saving provision—Schedule 3B continues to apply in relation to supplies made before IP completion day despite its repeal by TCTA 2018 Sch 8, para 86. To the extent that it continues to apply, Sch 3B has effect subject to such modifications as may be specified in a notice published by the Commissioners (see SI 2020/1495, reg 14).
Any references to VATA 1994, Schs 3B or 3BA (other than those mentioned above) that have been repealed by TCTA 2018 Sch 8 continue to apply in relation to supplies made before IP completion day as if they had not been repealed, but only to the extent that Schs 3B and 3BA continue to have effect in accordance with SI 2020/1495. To the extent that they continue to apply, references to VATA 1994, Schs 3B or 3BA have effect subject to such modifications as may be specified in a notice published by the Commissioners (see SI 2020/1495, reg 16).

[Increase or decrease in consideration for a supply

16K—*(1) This paragraph applies where—*
  (a) a person makes a special scheme return for a tax period ("the affected tax period") relating (wholly or partly) to a UK supply, and
  (b) after the return has been made the amount of the consideration for the UK supply increases or decreases.
(2) The person must, in the tax period in which the increase or decrease is accounted for in the person's business accounts—
  (a) amend the special scheme return to take account of the increase or decrease, or
  (b) (if the period during which the person is entitled under Article 61 of the Implementing Regulation to amend the special scheme return has expired) notify the Commissioners of the adjustment needed to the figures in the special scheme return because of the increase or decrease.
(3) Where the change to which an amendment or notice under sub-paragraph (2) relates is an increase in the consideration for a UK supply, the person must pay to the tax authorities for the administering member State (in accordance with Article 62 of the Implementing Regulation) or, in a case falling within sub-paragraph (2)(b), the Commissioners, the difference between—
  (a) the amount of VAT that was chargeable on the supply before the increase in consideration, and
  (b) the amount of VAT that is chargeable in respect of the whole of the increased consideration for the supply.
(4) Where the change to which an amendment or notice under sub-paragraph (2) relates is a decrease in the consideration for a UK supply, the amendment or notice has effect as a claim; and where a claim is made the Commissioners must repay any VAT paid by the person that would not have been VAT due from the person had the consideration for the supply always been the decreased amount.
(5) The Commissioners may by regulations specify—
  (a) the latest time by which, and the form and manner in which, a claim or other notice under sub-paragraph (2)(b) must be given;
  (b) the latest time by which, and the form in which, a payment under sub-paragraph (3) must be made in a case within sub-paragraph (2)(b).

(6) A payment made under sub-paragraph (3) in a case within sub-paragraph (2)(a) must be made before the end of the tax period referred to in sub-paragraph (2).

(7) In this paragraph "UK supply" means a supply of scheme services that is treated as made in the United Kingdom.][1], [2]

Commentary—*De Voil Indirect Tax Service* **V2.189L**.
Regulations—VAT (Amendment) (No 3) Regulations, SI 2014/2430.
Amendments—[1] Part 3 (paras 16–16N) substituted by FA 2014 s 103, Sch 22 paras 3, 8 with effect in relation to supplies made on or after 1 January 2015. Any amendment made by FA 2014 Sch 22 so far as it confers power to make regulations has effect from 17 July 2014 (FA 2014 Sch 22 para 23(2)(b)). Part 3, as it applied in relation to supplies made before 1 January 2015, is reproduced below after para 16N.
[2] Sch 3B repealed by the Taxation (Cross-border Trade) Act 2018 s 43, Sch 8 paras 1, 86 with effect from IP completion day (11pm on 31 December 2020), by virtue of SI 2020/1642 reg 4(b).
Saving provision—Schedule 3B continues to apply in relation to supplies made before IP completion day despite its repeal by TCTA 2018 Sch 8, para 86. To the extent that it continues to apply, Sch 3B has effect subject to such modifications as may be specified in a notice published by the Commissioners (see SI 2020/1495, reg 14).
Any references to VATA 1994, Schs 3B or 3BA (other than those mentioned above) that have been repealed by TCTA 2018 Sch 8 continue to apply in relation to supplies made before IP completion day as if they had not been repealed, but only to the extent that Schs 3B and 3BA continue to have effect in accordance with SI 2020/1495. To the extent that they continue to apply, references to VATA 1994, Schs 3B or 3BA have effect subject to such modifications as may be specified in a notice published by the Commissioners (see SI 2020/1495, reg 16).

[Bad debts]

16L *Where a participant in a special scheme—*
   (a) has submitted a special scheme return to the tax authorities for the administering member State, and
   (b) amends the return to take account of the writing-off as a bad debt of the whole or part of the consideration for a supply of scheme services that is treated as made in the United Kingdom,

the amending of the return may be treated as the making of a claim to the Commissioners for the purposes of section 36(2) (bad debts: claim for refund of VAT).][1], [2]

Commentary—*De Voil Indirect Tax Service* **V2.189L**.
Regulations—VAT (Amendment) (No 3) Regulations, SI 2014/2430.
Amendments—[1] Part 3 (paras 16–16N) substituted by FA 2014 s 103, Sch 22 paras 3, 8 with effect in relation to supplies made on or after 1 January 2015. Any amendment made by FA 2014 Sch 22 so far as it confers power to make regulations has effect from 17 July 2014 (FA 2014 Sch 22 para 23(2)(b)). Part 3, as it applied in relation to supplies made before 1 January 2015, is reproduced below after para 16N.
[2] Sch 3B repealed by the Taxation (Cross-border Trade) Act 2018 s 43, Sch 8 paras 1, 86 with effect from IP completion day (11pm on 31 December 2020), by virtue of SI 2020/1642 reg 4(b).
Saving provision—Schedule 3B continues to apply in relation to supplies made before IP completion day despite its repeal by TCTA 2018 Sch 8, para 86. To the extent that it continues to apply, Sch 3B has effect subject to such modifications as may be specified in a notice published by the Commissioners (see SI 2020/1495, reg 14).
Any references to VATA 1994, Schs 3B or 3BA (other than those mentioned above) that have been repealed by TCTA 2018 Sch 8 continue to apply in relation to supplies made before IP completion day as if they had not been repealed, but only to the extent that Schs 3B and 3BA continue to have effect in accordance with SI 2020/1495. To the extent that they continue to apply, references to VATA 1994, Schs 3B or 3BA have effect subject to such modifications as may be specified in a notice published by the Commissioners (see SI 2020/1495, reg 16).

[Penalties for errors: disclosure]

16M *Where a person corrects a special scheme return in a way that constitutes telling the tax authorities for the administering member State about—*
   (a) an inaccuracy in the return,
   (b) a supply of false information, or
   (c) a withholding of information,

the person is regarded as telling HMRC about that for the purposes of paragraph 9 of Schedule 24 to the Finance Act 2007.][1], [2]

Commentary—*De Voil Indirect Tax Service* **V2.189L**.
Amendments—[1] Part 3 (paras 16–16N) substituted by FA 2014 s 103, Sch 22 paras 3, 8 with effect in relation to supplies made on or after 1 January 2015. Any amendment made by FA 2014 Sch 22 so far as it confers power to make regulations has effect from 17 July 2014 (FA 2014 Sch 22 para 23(2)(b)). Part 3, as it applied in relation to supplies made before 1 January 2015, is reproduced below after para 16N.
[2] Sch 3B repealed by the Taxation (Cross-border Trade) Act 2018 s 43, Sch 8 paras 1, 86 with effect from IP completion day (11pm on 31 December 2020), by virtue of SI 2020/1642 reg 4(b).
Saving provision—Schedule 3B continues to apply in relation to supplies made before IP completion day despite its repeal by TCTA 2018 Sch 8, para 86. To the extent that it continues to apply, Sch 3B has effect subject to such modifications as may be specified in a notice published by the Commissioners (see SI 2020/1495, reg 14).
Any references to VATA 1994, Schs 3B or 3BA (other than those mentioned above) that have been repealed by TCTA 2018 Sch 8 continue to apply in relation to supplies made before IP completion day as if they had not been repealed, but only to the extent

that Schs 3B and 3BA continue to have effect in accordance with SI 2020/1495. To the extent that they continue to apply, references to VATA 1994, Schs 3B or 3BA have effect subject to such modifications as may be specified in a notice published by the Commissioners (see SI 2020/1495, reg 16).

[Set-offs]

16N *Where a participant in a special scheme is liable to pay UK VAT to the tax authorities for the administering member State in accordance with the scheme, the UK VAT is regarded for the purposes of section 130(6) of the Finance Act 2008 (set-off: England, Wales and Northern Ireland) as payable to the Commissioners.]¹,²*

Commentary—*De Voil Indirect Tax Service* **V2.189L**.
Amendments—[1] Part 3 (paras 16–16N) substituted by FA 2014 s 103, Sch 22 paras 3, 8 with effect in relation to supplies made on or after 1 January 2015. Any amendment made by FA 2014 Sch 22 so far as it confers power to make regulations has effect from 17 July 2014 (FA 2014 Sch 22 para 23(2)(*b*)).
[2] Sch 3B repealed by the Taxation (Cross-border Trade) Act 2018 s 43, Sch 8 paras 1, 86 with effect from IP completion day (11pm on 31 December 2020), by virtue of SI 2020/1642 reg 4(*b*).
Saving provision—Schedule 3B continues to apply in relation to supplies made before IP completion day despite its repeal by TCTA 2018 Sch 8, para 86. To the extent that it continues to apply, Sch 3B has effect subject to such modifications as may be specified in a notice published by the Commissioners (see SI 2020/1495, reg 14).
Any references to VATA 1994, Schs 3B or 3BA (other than those mentioned above) that have been repealed by TCTA 2018 Sch 8 continue to apply in relation to supplies made before IP completion day as if they had not been repealed, but only to the extent that Schs 3B and 3BA continue to have effect in accordance with SI 2020/1495. To the extent that they continue to apply, references to VATA 1994, Schs 3B or 3BA have effect subject to such modifications as may be specified in a notice published by the Commissioners (see SI 2020/1495, reg 16).

PART 4
[OTHER PROVISIONS ABOUT SPECIAL SCHEMES]

Amendments—In heading to Part 4, words substituted for words "Application of provisions relating to VAT", by FA 2014 s 103, Sch 22 paras 3, 9(1), (8) with effect in relation to supplies made on or after 1 January 2015.
Sch 3B repealed by the Taxation (Cross-border Trade) Act 2018 s 43, Sch 8 paras 1, 86 with effect from IP completion day (11pm on 31 December 2020), by virtue of SI 2020/1642 reg 4(*b*).
Saving provision—Schedule 3B continues to apply in relation to supplies made before IP completion day despite its repeal by TCTA 2018 Sch 8, para 86. To the extent that it continues to apply, Sch 3B has effect subject to such modifications as may be specified in a notice published by the Commissioners (see SI 2020/1495, reg 14).
Any references to VATA 1994, Schs 3B or 3BA (other than those mentioned above) that have been repealed by TCTA 2018 Sch 8 continue to apply in relation to supplies made before IP completion day as if they had not been repealed, but only to the extent that Schs 3B and 3BA continue to have effect in accordance with SI 2020/1495. To the extent that they continue to apply, references to VATA 1994, Schs 3B or 3BA have effect subject to such modifications as may be specified in a notice published by the Commissioners (see SI 2020/1495, reg 16).

Registration under this Act

[17 [(1)] ²*Notwithstanding any provision in this Act to the contrary, a participant in the special scheme is not required to be registered under this Act by virtue of making qualifying supplies.*
[*(2) Where a participant in the special scheme ("the scheme participant") makes relevant supplies, it is to be assumed for all purposes of this Act relating to the determination of—*
   (a) *whether or not VAT is chargeable under this Act on those supplies,*
   (b) *how much VAT is chargeable under this Act on those supplies,*
   (c) *the time at which those supplies are treated as taking place, and*
   (d) *any other matter that the Commissioners may specify by regulations,*
that the scheme participant is registered under this Act.
(3) Supplies of scheme services made by the scheme participant are "relevant supplies" if—
   (a) *the value of the supplies must be accounted for in a special scheme return, and*
   (b) *the supplies are treated as made in the United Kingdom.]²*
[*(4) References in this Schedule to a person being registered under this Act do not include a reference to that person being registered under this Schedule.]³]¹,⁴*

Amendments—[1] Sch 3B inserted by FA 2003 s 23, Sch 2 paras 1, 4 with effect for qualifying supplies made after 30 June 2003, see FA 2003 s 23(2).
[2] Sub-para (1) numbered as such, and sub-paras (2), (3) inserted, by FA 2014 s 103, Sch 22 paras 3, 9(1)–(3) with effect in relation to supplies made on or after 1 January 2015.
[3] Sub-para (4) inserted by the Value Added Tax (Special Accounting Schemes) (Supplies of Electronic, Telecommunication and Broadcasting Services) Order, SI 2018/1197 arts 2, 4(*a*) with effect in relation to supplies made on or after 1 January 2019. Note that SI 2018/1197 is revoked by SI 2019/513 reg 16 with effect from IP completion day (11pm on 31 December 2020).
[4] Sch 3B repealed by the Taxation (Cross-border Trade) Act 2018 s 43, Sch 8 paras 1, 86 with effect from IP completion day (11pm on 31 December 2020), by virtue of SI 2020/1642 reg 4(*b*).
Saving provision—Schedule 3B continues to apply in relation to supplies made before IP completion day despite its repeal by TCTA 2018 Sch 8, para 86. To the extent that it continues to apply, Sch 3B has effect subject to such modifications as may be specified in a notice published by the Commissioners (see SI 2020/1495, reg 14).
Any references to VATA 1994, Schs 3B or 3BA (other than those mentioned above) that have been repealed by TCTA 2018 Sch 8 continue to apply in relation to supplies made before IP completion day as if they had not been repealed, but only to the extent

that Schs 3B and 3BA continue to have effect in accordance with SI 2020/1495. To the extent that they continue to apply, references to VATA 1994, Schs 3B or 3BA have effect subject to such modifications as may be specified in a notice published by the Commissioners (see SI 2020/1495, reg 16).

De-registration

[18 Where a person who is registered under Schedule 1 [or 1A][2] [solely by virtue of the fact he makes or intends to make qualifying supplies][4] satisfies the Commissioners that he intends to apply for—
- (a) registration under this Schedule, or
- (b) identification under any provision of the law of another member State which implements [Section 2 of Chapter 6 of Title XII of the VAT Directive,][3]

they may, if he so requests, cancel his registration under Schedule 1[or, as the case may be, 1A][2] with effect from the day on which the request is made or from such later date as may be agreed between him and the Commissioners.][1], [5]

Amendments—[1] Sch 3B inserted by FA 2003 s 23, Sch 2 paras 1, 4 with effect for qualifying supplies made after 30 June 2003, see FA 2003 s 23(2).
[2] Words inserted by FA 2012 s 203, Sch 28 paras 2, 17 with effect in relation to supplies made or to be made on or after 1 December 2012.
[3] In para (b), words substituted for words "Article 26c," by FA 2014 s 103, Sch 22 paras 3, 9(1), (4) with effect in relation to supplies made on or after 1 January 2015.
[4] Words inserted by the Value Added Tax (Special Accounting Schemes) (Supplies of Electronic, Telecommunication and Broadcasting Services) Order, SI 2018/1197 arts 2, 4(b) with effect in relation to supplies made on or after 1 January 2019. Note that SI 2018/1197 is revoked by SI 2019/513 reg 16 with effect from IP completion day (11pm on 31 December 2020).
[5] Sch 3B repealed by the Taxation (Cross-border Trade) Act 2018 s 43, Sch 8 paras 1, 86 with effect from IP completion day (11pm on 31 December 2020), by virtue of SI 2020/1642 reg 4(b). Note that, where these amendments remove a reference to the principal VAT Directive (2006/112/EC) or the Implementing VAT Regulation ((EU) No 282/2011), the removal is not to be taken as implying that the Directive or Regulation is no longer relevant for determining the meaning and effect of this para (Taxation (Cross-border Trade) Act 2018 Sch 8 para 99).
Saving provision—Schedule 3B continues to apply in relation to supplies made before IP completion day despite its repeal by TCTA 2018 Sch 8, para 86. To the extent that it continues to apply, Sch 3B has effect subject to such modifications as may be specified in a notice published by the Commissioners (see SI 2020/1495, reg 14).
Any references to VATA 1994, Schs 3B or 3BA (other than those mentioned above) that have been repealed by TCTA 2018 Sch 8 continue to apply in relation to supplies made before IP completion day as if they had not been repealed, but only to the extent that Schs 3B and 3BA continue to have effect in accordance with SI 2020/1495. To the extent that they continue to apply, references to VATA 1994, Schs 3B or 3BA have effect subject to such modifications as may be specified in a notice published by the Commissioners (see SI 2020/1495, reg 16).

[Scheme participants who are also registered under this Act

18ZA (1) A person who—
- (a) is a participant in a special scheme, and
- (b) is also registered, or required to be registered, under this Act,

is not required to discharge any obligation placed on the person as a taxable person, so far as the obligation relates to relevant supplies unless the obligation is an input tax obligation.
(2) The reference in sub-paragraph (1) to an obligation placed on the person as a taxable person is to an obligation—
- (a) to which the person is subject under or by virtue of this Act, and
- (b) to which the person would not be subject if the person were neither registered nor required to be registered under this Act.

(3) A supply made by a participant in a special scheme is a "relevant supply" if—
- (a) the value of the supply must be accounted for in a return required to be made by the participant under the special scheme, and
- (b) the supply is treated as made in the United Kingdom.

(4) In section 25(2) (deduction of input tax from output tax by a taxable person) the reference to output tax that is due from the taxable person does not include any VAT that the taxable person is liable under a special scheme to pay to the tax authorities for the administering member State.
(5) In this paragraph, "input tax obligation" means an obligation imposed on a taxable person relating to a claim to deduct under section 25(2) or to the payment of a VAT credit.][1], [2]

Amendments—[1] Para 18ZA inserted by the Value Added Tax (Special Accounting Schemes) (Supplies of Electronic, Telecommunication and Broadcasting Services) Order, SI 2018/1197 arts 2, 4(c) with effect in relation to supplies made on or after 1 January 2019. Note that SI 2018/1197 is revoked by SI 2019/513 reg 16 with effect from IP completion day (11pm on 31 December 2020).
[2] Sch 3B repealed by the Taxation (Cross-border Trade) Act 2018 s 43, Sch 8 paras 1, 86 with effect from IP completion day (11pm on 31 December 2020), by virtue of SI 2020/1642 reg 4(b).
Saving provision—Schedule 3B continues to apply in relation to supplies made before IP completion day despite its repeal by TCTA 2018 Sch 8, para 86. To the extent that it continues to apply, Sch 3B has effect subject to such modifications as may be specified in a notice published by the Commissioners (see SI 2020/1495, reg 14).

Any references to VATA 1994, Schs 3B or 3BA (other than those mentioned above) that have been repealed by TCTA 2018 Sch 8 continue to apply in relation to supplies made before IP completion day as if they had not been repealed, but only to the extent that Schs 3B and 3BA continue to have effect in accordance with SI 2020/1495. To the extent that they continue to apply, references to VATA 1994, Schs 3B or 3BA have effect subject to such modifications as may be specified in a notice published by the Commissioners (see SI 2020/1495, reg 16).

[Value of supplies to connected persons

18A *In paragraph 1 of Schedule 6 (valuation: supply to connected person at less than market value) the reference to a supply made by a taxable person is to be read as including a supply of scheme services that is made by a participant in the special scheme (and is treated as made in the United Kingdom).]*[1], [2]

Amendments—[1] Para 18A inserted by FA 2014 s 103, Sch 22 paras 3, 9(1), (5) with effect in relation to supplies made on or after 1 January 2015.
[2] Sch 3B repealed by the Taxation (Cross-border Trade) Act 2018 s 43, Sch 8 paras 1, 86 with effect from IP completion day (11pm on 31 December 2020), by virtue of SI 2020/1642 reg 4(b).
Saving provision—Schedule 3B continues to apply in relation to supplies made before IP completion day despite its repeal by TCTA 2018 Sch 8, para 86. To the extent that it continues to apply, Sch 3B has effect subject to such modifications as may be specified in a notice published by the Commissioners (see SI 2020/1495, reg 14).
Any references to VATA 1994, Schs 3B or 3BA (other than those mentioned above) that have been repealed by TCTA 2018 Sch 8 continue to apply in relation to supplies made before IP completion day as if they had not been repealed, but only to the extent that Schs 3B and 3BA continue to have effect in accordance with SI 2020/1495. To the extent that they continue to apply, references to VATA 1994, Schs 3B or 3BA have effect subject to such modifications as may be specified in a notice published by the Commissioners (see SI 2020/1495, reg 16).

VAT representatives

[19 Section 48[(1ZA)][2] *(VAT representatives) does not permit the Commissioners to direct a participant in the special scheme to appoint a VAT representative.]*[1], [3]

Amendments—[1] Sch 3B inserted by FA 2003 s 23, Sch 2 paras 1, 4 with effect for qualifying supplies made after 30 June 2003, see FA 2003 s 23(2).
[2] Reference "(1ZA)" substituted for reference "(1)" by FA 2016 s 123(1), (12) with effect from 15 September 2016.
[3] Sch 3B repealed by the Taxation (Cross-border Trade) Act 2018 s 43, Sch 8 paras 1, 86 with effect from IP completion day (11pm on 31 December 2020), by virtue of SI 2020/1642 reg 4(b).
Saving provision—Schedule 3B continues to apply in relation to supplies made before IP completion day despite its repeal by TCTA 2018 Sch 8, para 86. To the extent that it continues to apply, Sch 3B has effect subject to such modifications as may be specified in a notice published by the Commissioners (see SI 2020/1495, reg 14).
Any references to VATA 1994, Schs 3B or 3BA (other than those mentioned above) that have been repealed by TCTA 2018 Sch 8 continue to apply in relation to supplies made before IP completion day as if they had not been repealed, but only to the extent that Schs 3B and 3BA continue to have effect in accordance with SI 2020/1495. To the extent that they continue to apply, references to VATA 1994, Schs 3B or 3BA have effect subject to such modifications as may be specified in a notice published by the Commissioners (see SI 2020/1495, reg 16).

Appeals

[20—(1) An appeal shall lie to a tribunal with respect to any of the following—
(a) the registration or cancellation of the registration of any person under this Schedule;
[(b) a refusal to make a repayment under paragraph 16I (overpayments), or a decision by the Commissioners as to the amount of the repayment due under that provision;
(c) a refusal to make a repayment under paragraph 16K(4) (decrease in consideration);
(d) any liability to a surcharge under paragraph 16F (default surcharge).][3]
[(2) Part 5 (appeals), and any order or regulations under that Part, have effect as if an appeal under this paragraph were an appeal which lies to the tribunal under section 83(1) (but not under any particular paragraph of that subsection).][2]*]*[1]
[(3) Where the Commissioners have made an assessment under section 73 in reliance on paragraph 16 or 16A—
(a) section 83(1)(p)(i): (appeals against assessments under section 73(1) etc) applies as if the relevant special scheme return were a return under this Act, and
(b) the references in section 84(3) and (5) to the matters mentioned in section 83(1)(p) are to be read accordingly.][3], [4]

Amendments—[1] Sch 3B inserted by FA 2003 Sch 2 para 4 with effect in relation to qualifying supplies made after 30 June 2003, see FA 2003 s 23(2).
[2] Sub-para (2) substituted by the Transfer of Tribunal Functions and Revenue and Customs Appeals Order, SI 2009/56 art 3, Sch 1 para 227 with effect from 1 April 2009, subject to transitional and savings provisions in Sch 3 para 4.
[3] In sub-para (1), paras (b)–(d) substituted for previous paras (b), (c), and sub-para (3) inserted, by FA 2014 s 103, Sch 22 paras 3, 9(1), (6) with effect in relation to supplies made on or after 1 January 2015.
[4] Sch 3B repealed by the Taxation (Cross-border Trade) Act 2018 s 43, Sch 8 paras 1, 86 with effect from IP completion day (11pm on 31 December 2020), by virtue of SI 2020/1642 reg 4(b).
Saving provision—Schedule 3B continues to apply in relation to supplies made before IP completion day despite its repeal by TCTA 2018 Sch 8, para 86. To the extent that it continues to apply, Sch 3B has effect subject to such modifications as may be specified in a notice published by the Commissioners (see SI 2020/1495, reg 14).

Any references to VATA 1994, Schs 3B or 3BA (other than those mentioned above) that have been repealed by TCTA 2018 Sch 8 continue to apply in relation to supplies made before IP completion day as if they had not been repealed, but only to the extent that Schs 3B and 3BA continue to have effect in accordance with SI 2020/1495. To the extent that they continue to apply, references to VATA 1994, Schs 3B or 3BA have effect subject to such modifications as may be specified in a notice published by the Commissioners (see SI 2020/1495, reg 16).

Payments on account of non-UK VAT to other member States

[21—(1) Neither—
 (a) paragraph 1(2) of Schedule 11, nor
 [(b) section 44 of the Commissioners for Revenue and Customs Act 2005,][2]
applies to money or securities for money collected or received for or on account of VAT if required to be paid to another member State by virtue of the VAT Co-operation Regulation.
(2) In sub-paragraph (1) above, "the VAT Co-operation Regulation" means the Council Regulation of 27 January 1992 on administrative co-operation in the field of indirect taxation (VAT) (218/92/EEC), as amended by the Council Regulation of 7 May 2002 (792/2002/EC) (which temporarily amends the VAT Co-operation Regulation as regards additional measures regarding electronic commerce).][1], [3], [4]

Amendments—[1]   Sch 3B inserted by FA 2003 Sch 2 para 4 with effect in relation to qualifying supplies made after 30 June 2003, see FA 2003 s 23(2).
[2]   Sub-para (1)(b) substituted by Commissioners for Revenue and Customs Act 2005 s 50, Sch 4 para 55 with effect from 18 April 2005 by virtue of the Commissioners for Revenue and Customs Act 2005 (Commencement) Order, SI 2005/1126, art 2(2).
[3]   Para 21 and preceding heading repealed by FA 2014 s 103, Sch 22 paras 3, 9(1), (7) with effect in relation to supplies made on or after 1 January 2015. See also para 15A above as inserted by FA 2014 Sch 22 para 7(7)).
[4]   Sch 3B repealed by the Taxation (Cross-border Trade) Act 2018 s 43, Sch 8 paras 1, 86 with effect from IP completion day (11pm on 31 December 2020), by virtue of SI 2020/1642 reg 4(b).
Saving provision—Schedule 3B continues to apply in relation to supplies made before IP completion day despite its repeal by TCTA 2018 Sch 8, para 86. To the extent that it continues to apply, Sch 3B has effect subject to such modifications as may be specified in a notice published by the Commissioners (see SI 2020/1495, reg 14).
Any references to VATA 1994, Schs 3B or 3BA (other than those mentioned above) that have been repealed by TCTA 2018 Sch 8 continue to apply in relation to supplies made before IP completion day as if they had not been repealed, but only to the extent that Schs 3B and 3BA continue to have effect in accordance with SI 2020/1495. To the extent that they continue to apply, references to VATA 1994, Schs 3B or 3BA have effect subject to such modifications as may be specified in a notice published by the Commissioners (see SI 2020/1495, reg 16).

Refund of UK VAT

[22—(1) The provisions which give effect to the 1986 VAT Refund Directive in the United Kingdom have effect in relation to a participant in the special scheme, but with the following modifications.
(2) The provision which gives effect to Article 2(1) of the 1986 VAT Refund Directive (as at 9th April 2003, see regulation 186 of the Value Added Tax Regulations 1995) shall apply in relation to a participant in the special scheme, but only so as to entitle him to a refund of VAT charged on—
 (a) goods imported by him into the United Kingdom, and
 (b) supplies made to him in the United Kingdom,
in connection with the making by him of qualifying supplies while he is a participant in the special scheme.
(3) The following provisions shall be omitted.
(4) The first provision is that which gives effect to Article 1(1) of the 1986 VAT Refund Directive, so far as it requires a member State to prevent a person who is deemed to have supplied services in that member State during a period from being granted a refund of VAT for that period (as at 9th April 2003, see regulation 188(2)(b) of the Value Added Tax Regulations 1995).
(5) The second provision is that which gives effect to Article 2(2) of the 1986 VAT Refund Directive (which permits member States to make refunds conditional upon the granting by third States of comparable advantages regarding turnover taxes: as at 9th April 2003, see regulation 188(1) of the Value Added Tax Regulations 1995).
(6) The third provision is that which gives effect to Article 2(3) of the 1986 VAT Refund Directive (which permits member States to require the appointment of a tax representative: as at 9th April 2003, see regulation 187 of the Value Added Tax Regulations 1995).
(7) The fourth provision is that which gives effect to Article 4(2) of the 1986 VAT Refund Directive (which permits member States to provide for the exclusion of certain expenditure and to make refunds subject to additional conditions).
(8) In this paragraph "the 1986 VAT Refund Directive" means the Thirteenth Council Directive of 17th November 1986 on the harmonisation of the laws of the member States relating to turnover taxes—arrangements for the refund of value added tax to taxable persons not established in Community territory (86/560/EEC).][1], [2]

Amendments—[1]   Sch 3B inserted by FA 2003 s 23, Sch 2 paras 1, 4 with effect for qualifying supplies made after 30 June 2003, see FA 2003 s 23(2).

[2] Sch 3B repealed by the Taxation (Cross-border Trade) Act 2018 s 43, Sch 8 paras 1, 86 with effect from IP completion day (11pm on 31 December 2020), by virtue of SI 2020/1642 reg 4(*b*).

Saving provision—Schedule 3B continues to apply in relation to supplies made before IP completion day despite its repeal by TCTA 2018 Sch 8, para 86. To the extent that it continues to apply, Sch 3B has effect subject to such modifications as may be specified in a notice published by the Commissioners (see SI 2020/1495, reg 14).

Any references to VATA 1994, Schs 3B or 3BA (other than those mentioned above) that have been repealed by TCTA 2018 Sch 8 continue to apply in relation to supplies made before IP completion day as if they had not been repealed, but only to the extent that Schs 3B and 3BA continue to have effect in accordance with SI 2020/1495. To the extent that they continue to apply, references to VATA 1994, Schs 3B or 3BA have effect subject to such modifications as may be specified in a notice published by the Commissioners (see SI 2020/1495, reg 16).

PART 5
SUPPLEMENTARY

Interpretation

[**23**—(1) In this Schedule—

"the 1977 VAT Directive" means the Sixth Council Directive of 17 May 1977 on the harmonisation of the laws of the member States relating to turnover taxes—common system of value added tax: uniform basis of assessment (77/388/EEC);

"the 2002 VAT Directive" means the Council Directive of 7 May 2002 amending and amending temporarily the 1977 VAT Directive as regards the value added tax arrangements applicable to radio and television broadcasting services and certain electronically supplied services (2002/38/EC);

["administering member State", in relation to a special scheme, means the member State under whose law the scheme is established (whether that is the United Kingdom or another member State);

"the Implementing Regulation" means Implementing Regulation (EU) No 282/2011;][2]

["participant in the special scheme" means a person who—

    (*a*) is registered under this Schedule, or

    (*b*) is identified under any provision of the law of another member State which implements Section 2 of Chapter 6 of Title XII of the VAT Directive;][2]

"qualifying supply" has the meaning given by paragraph 3 above;

"registration number" means the number allocated to a person on his registration under this Schedule in accordance with paragraph 6(*a*) above;

"registration request" is to be construed in accordance with paragraph 4(1)(*b*) above;

["relevant special scheme return" has the meaning given by paragraph 16(3);][2]

"reporting period" is to be construed in accordance with paragraph 11(2) above;

["scheme services" means electronically supplied services, broadcasting services or telecommunication services (and in this definition "electronically supplied services", "broadcasting services" and

"telecommunication services" have the meaning given by paragraph 3(2));][2]

"special accounting return" is to be construed in accordance with paragraph 11(1) above.

["special scheme" means—

    (*a*) the accounting scheme under this Schedule, or

    [(*b*) any other scheme, under the law of another member State, implementing Section 2 of Chapter 6 of Title XII of the VAT Directive;][3]

"special scheme return" means—

    (*a*) a special accounting return, or

    (*b*) a value added tax return submitted to the tax authorities of another member State;

"tax period" means—

    (*a*) a reporting period (under the accounting scheme under this Schedule), or

    (*b*) any other period for which a person is required to make a return under a special scheme;

"UK VAT" means VAT which a person is liable to pay (whether in the United Kingdom or another member State) in respect of qualifying supplies treated as made in the United Kingdom at a time when the person is or was a participant in the special scheme;

"value added tax return", in relation to another member State, means any value added tax return required to be submitted under any provision of the law of that member State which implements Article 364 of the VAT Directive (as substituted by Article 5(11) of Council Directive 2008/8/EC);

"the VAT Directive" has the meaning given by paragraph 2(7);][2]

(2) References in this Schedule to a qualifying supply being "treated as made" in a member State are references to its being treated as made—

(a) in the United Kingdom, by [paragraph 15 of Schedule 4A (place of supply of electronic, telecommunication and broadcasting services),][2] or

(b) in another member State, by virtue of any provision of the law of that member State which gives effect to that Article.

(3) The provision which, as at 9th April 2003, is to give effect in the United Kingdom to Article 9(2)(f) of the 1977 VAT Directive (as mentioned in sub-paragraph (2)(a) above) is article 16A of the Value Added Tax (Place of Supply of Services) Order 1992 (which is prospectively inserted by article 3 of the Value Added Tax (Place of Supply of Services) (Amendment) Order 2003).][1], [4]

Amendments—[1] Sch 3B inserted by FA 2003 s 23, Sch 2 paras 1, 4 with effect for qualifying supplies made after 30 June 2003, see FA 2003 s 23(2).

[2] In sub-para (1) definitions substituted and inserted, in sub-para (2)(a), words substituted for words "virtue of any provision which gives effect in the United Kingdom to Article 9(2)(f) of the 1977 VAT Directive (which is inserted by Article 1(1)(b) of the 2002 VAT Directive),", and sub-para (3) repealed, by FA 2014 s 103, Sch 22 paras 3, 10 with effect in relation to supplies made on or after 1 January 2015.

[3] In sub-para (1), in definition of "special scheme", para (b) substituted by the Value Added Tax (Special Accounting Schemes) (Supplies of Electronic, Telecommunication and Broadcasting Services) Order, SI 2018/1197 arts 2, 5 with effect in relation to supplies made on or after 1 January 2019.

Note that SI 2018/1197 is revoked by SI 2019/513 reg 16 with effect from IP completion day (11pm on 31 December 2020).

[4] Sch 3B repealed by the Taxation (Cross-border Trade) Act 2018 s 43, Sch 8 paras 1, 86 with effect from IP completion day (11pm on 31 December 2020), by virtue of SI 2020/1642 reg 4(b). Note that, where these amendments remove a reference to the principal VAT Directive (2006/112/EC) or the Implementing VAT Regulation ((EU) No 282/2011), the removal is not to be taken as implying that the Directive or Regulation is no longer relevant for determining the meaning and effect of this para (Taxation (Cross-border Trade) Act 2018 Sch 8 para 99).

Saving provision—Schedule 3B continues to apply in relation to supplies made before IP completion day despite its repeal by TCTA 2018 Sch 8, para 86. To the extent that it continues to apply, Sch 3B has effect subject to such modifications as may be specified in a notice published by the Commissioners (see SI 2020/1495, reg 14).

Any references to VATA 1994, Schs 3B or 3BA (other than those mentioned above) that have been repealed by TCTA 2018 Sch 8 continue to apply in relation to supplies made before IP completion day as if they had not been repealed, but only to the extent that Schs 3B and 3BA continue to have effect in accordance with SI 2020/1495. To the extent that they continue to apply, references to VATA 1994, Schs 3B or 3BA have effect subject to such modifications as may be specified in a notice published by the Commissioners (see SI 2020/1495, reg 16).

[SCHEDULE 3BA

ELECTRONIC, TELECOMMUNICATION AND BROADCASTING SERVICES: UNION SCHEME

Amendments—Sch 3BA inserted by FA 2014 s 103, Sch 22 para 1 with effect in relation to supplies made on or after 1 January 2015, except in so far as it confers power to make regulations in which case it has effect from 17 July 2014.

No registration under Sch 3BA may take effect before 1 January 2015. A request for registration under Sch 3BA that is made before 1 October 2014 is to be treated for the purposes of Article 57d of Implementing Regulation (EU) No 282/2011 (registration to have effect from first day of subsequent quarter) as if it were made on that date (FA 2014 Sch 22 para 24).

Schedule 3BA repealed by the Taxation (Cross-border Trade) Act 2018 s 43, Sch 8 paras 1, 87 with effect from IP completion day (11pm on 31 December 2020), by virtue of SI 2020/1642 reg 4(b).

Saving provision—Schedule 3BA continues to apply in relation to supplies made before IP completion day despite its repeal by TCTA 2018 Sch 8, para 87. To the extent that it continues to apply, Sch 3BA has effect subject to such modifications as may be specified in a notice published by the Commissioners (see SI 2020/1495, reg 15).

Any references to VATA 1994, Schs 3B or 3BA (other than those mentioned above) that have been repealed by TCTA 2018 Sch 8 continue to apply in relation to supplies made before IP completion day as if they had not been repealed, but only to the extent that Schs 3B and 3BA continue to have effect in accordance with SI 2020/1495. To the extent that they continue to apply, references to VATA 1994, Schs 3B or 3BA have effect subject to such modifications as may be specified in a notice published by the Commissioners (see SI 2020/1495, reg 16).

PART 1
INTRODUCTION

Overview

1 *In this Schedule—*

(a) *Parts 2 and 3 establish a special accounting scheme (called the "Union scheme") which may be used by certain persons established in the United Kingdom who make supplies of electronically supplied, telecommunication or broadcasting services that are treated as made in other member States;*

(b) *Part 4 is about persons participating in schemes in other member States that correspond to the Union scheme;*

(c) *Part 5 is about appeals;*

(d) *Part 6 contains definitions for the Schedule.]¹, ²*

Amendments—¹ Sch 3BA inserted by FA 2014 s 103, Sch 22 para 1 with effect in relation to supplies made on or after 1 January 2015, except in so far as it confers power to make regulations in which case it has effect from 17 July 2014. No registration under Sch 3BA may take effect before 1 January 2015. A request for registration under Sch 3BA that is made before 1 October 2014 is to be treated for the purposes of Article 57d of Implementing Regulation (EU) No 282/2011 (registration to have effect from first day of subsequent quarter) as if it were made on that date (FA 2014 Sch 22 para 24).
² Schedule 3BA repealed by the Taxation (Cross-border Trade) Act 2018 s 43, Sch 8 paras 1, 87 with effect from IP completion day (11pm on 31 December 2020), by virtue of SI 2020/1642 reg 4(b).
Saving provision—Schedule 3BA continues to apply in relation to supplies made before IP completion day despite its repeal by TCTA 2018 Sch 8, para 87. To the extent that it continues to apply, Sch 3BA has effect subject to such modifications as may be specified in a notice published by the Commissioners (see SI 2020/1495, reg 15).
Any references to VATA 1994, Schs 3B or 3BA (other than those mentioned above) that have been repealed by TCTA 2018 Sch 8 continue to apply in relation to supplies made before IP completion day as if they had not been repealed, but only to the extent that Schs 3B and 3BA continue to have effect in accordance with SI 2020/1495. To the extent that they continue to apply, references to VATA 1994, Schs 3B or 3BA have effect subject to such modifications as may be specified in a notice published by the Commissioners (see SI 2020/1495, reg 16).

[Meaning of "scheme services"

2—*(1) In this Schedule "scheme services" means electronically supplied services, broadcasting services or telecommunication services.*
(2) In sub-paragraph (1)—
"broadcasting services" means radio and television broadcasting services;
"electronically supplied services" has the same meaning as in Schedule 4A (see paragraph 9(3) and (4) of that Schedule);
"telecommunication services" has the same meaning as in Schedule 4A (see [paragraph 9E(2)]² of that Schedule).]¹, ³

Amendments—¹ Sch 3BA inserted by FA 2014 s 103, Sch 22 para 1 with effect in relation to supplies made on or after 1 January 2015, except in so far as it confers power to make regulations in which case it has effect from 17 July 2014. No registration under Sch 3BA may take effect before 1 January 2015. A request for registration under Sch 3BA that is made before 1 October 2014 is to be treated for the purposes of Article 57d of Implementing Regulation (EU) No 282/2011 (registration to have effect from first day of subsequent quarter) as if it were made on that date (FA 2014 Sch 22 para 24).
² In sub-para (2), words substituted for words "paragraph 8(2)" by the VAT (Place of Supply of Services) (Telecommunication Services) Order, SI 2017/778 art 7 with effect in relation to supplies of services made on or after 1 November 2017.
³ Schedule 3BA repealed by the Taxation (Cross-border Trade) Act 2018 s 43, Sch 8 paras 1, 87 with effect from IP completion day (11pm on 31 December 2020), by virtue of SI 2020/1642 reg 4(b).
Saving provision—Schedule 3BA continues to apply in relation to supplies made before IP completion day despite its repeal by TCTA 2018 Sch 8, para 87. To the extent that it continues to apply, Sch 3BA has effect subject to such modifications as may be specified in a notice published by the Commissioners (see SI 2020/1495, reg 15).
Any references to VATA 1994, Schs 3B or 3BA (other than those mentioned above) that have been repealed by TCTA 2018 Sch 8 continue to apply in relation to supplies made before IP completion day as if they had not been repealed, but only to the extent that Schs 3B and 3BA continue to have effect in accordance with SI 2020/1495. To the extent that they continue to apply, references to VATA 1994, Schs 3B or 3BA have effect subject to such modifications as may be specified in a notice published by the Commissioners (see SI 2020/1495, reg 16).

[PART 2
UNION SCHEME: REGISTRATION

The register

3 *Persons registered under the scheme provided for by this Schedule ("the Union scheme") are to be registered in a single register kept by the Commissioners for the purposes of the scheme.]¹, ²*

Amendments—¹ Sch 3BA inserted by FA 2014 s 103, Sch 22 para 1 with effect in relation to supplies made on or after 1 January 2015, except in so far as it confers power to make regulations in which case it has effect from 17 July 2014. No registration under Sch 3BA may take effect before 1 January 2015. A request for registration under Sch 3BA that is made before 1 October 2014 is to be treated for the purposes of Article 57d of Implementing Regulation (EU) No 282/2011 (registration to have effect from first day of subsequent quarter) as if it were made on that date (FA 2014 Sch 22 para 24).
² Schedule 3BA repealed by the Taxation (Cross-border Trade) Act 2018 s 43, Sch 8 paras 1, 87 with effect from IP completion day (11pm on 31 December 2020), by virtue of SI 2020/1642 reg 4(b).
Saving provision—Schedule 3BA continues to apply in relation to supplies made before IP completion day despite its repeal by TCTA 2018 Sch 8, para 87. To the extent that it continues to apply, Sch 3BA has effect subject to such modifications as may be specified in a notice published by the Commissioners (see SI 2020/1495, reg 15).
Any references to VATA 1994, Schs 3B or 3BA (other than those mentioned above) that have been repealed by TCTA 2018 Sch 8 continue to apply in relation to supplies made before IP completion day as if they had not been repealed, but only to the extent that Schs 3B and 3BA continue to have effect in accordance with SI 2020/1495. To the extent that they continue to apply, references to VATA 1994, Schs 3B or 3BA have effect subject to such modifications as may be specified in a notice published by the Commissioners (see SI 2020/1495, reg 16).

[Persons who may be registered

4 *(1) A person may register under the Union scheme if all the following conditions are met—*

(a) the person makes or intends to make one or more qualifying supplies of scheme services in the course of a business that the person carries on;
(b) either the person's business is established in the United Kingdom or (if the person's business is not established in any member State) the person has a fixed establishment in the United Kingdom;
(c) the person is not barred from registering by sub-paragraph (3), by the second paragraph of Article 369a(2) of Directive 2006/112/EC or by any provision of the Implementing Regulation;
(d) the person is registered under Schedule 1.

(2) A supply of scheme services is a "qualifying supply of scheme services" if the following conditions are met.

1. The recipient of the services must belong in a member State other than the United Kingdom and must not be a relevant business person.
2. The person making the supply must not have a fixed establishment in the member State in which the recipient belongs.

(3) A person may not be registered under the Union scheme if the person is a participant in a non-UK special scheme (see paragraph 38(1)).]^1, ^{2}

Amendments—^{1} Sch 3BA inserted by FA 2014 s 103, Sch 22 para 1 with effect in relation to supplies made on or after 1 January 2015, except in so far as it confers power to make regulations in which case it has effect from 17 July 2014. No registration under Sch 3BA may take effect before 1 January 2015. A request for registration under Sch 3BA that is made before 1 October 2014 is to be treated for the purposes of Article 57d of Implementing Regulation (EU) No 282/2011 (registration to have effect from first day of subsequent quarter) as if it were made on that date (FA 2014 Sch 22 para 24).
^{2} Schedule 3BA repealed by the Taxation (Cross-border Trade) Act 2018 s 43, Sch 8 paras 1, 87 with effect from IP completion day (11pm on 31 December 2020), by virtue of SI 2020/1642 reg 4(b). Note that, where these amendments remove a reference to the principal VAT Directive (2006/112/EC) or the Implementing VAT Regulation ((EU) No 282/2011), the removal is not to be taken as implying that the Directive or Regulation is no longer relevant for determining the meaning and effect of this para (Taxation (Cross-border Trade) Act 2018 Sch 8 para 99).
Saving provision—Schedule 3BA continues to apply in relation to supplies made before IP completion day despite its repeal by TCTA 2018 Sch 8, para 87. To the extent that it continues to apply, Sch 3BA has effect subject to such modifications as may be specified in a notice published by the Commissioners (see SI 2020/1495, reg 15).
Any references to VATA 1994, Schs 3B or 3BA (other than those mentioned above) that have been repealed by TCTA 2018 Sch 8 continue to apply in relation to supplies made before IP completion day as if they had not been repealed, but only to the extent that Schs 3B and 3BA continue to have effect in accordance with SI 2020/1495. To the extent that they continue to apply, references to VATA 1994, Schs 3B or 3BA have effect subject to such modifications as may be specified in a notice published by the Commissioners (see SI 2020/1495, reg 16).

Becoming registered

5—(1) The Commissioners must register under the Union scheme any person who—
(a) satisfies them that the requirements for registration are met, and
(b) makes a request in accordance with this paragraph (a "registration request").

(2) A registration request made by a person must state the person's—
(a) name and postal address, and
(b) electronic addresses (including any websites).

(3) A registration request made by a person must also state—
(a) whether or not the person has begun to make qualifying supplies of scheme services, and
(b) (if applicable) the date on which the person began to do so.

(4) A registration request made by a person must also state—
(a) whether or not the person has previously been identified under a non-UK special scheme, and
(b) (if applicable) the date on which the person was first identified under the scheme concerned.

(5) A registration request—
(a) must contain any further information, and any declaration about its contents, that the Commissioners may by regulations require;
(b) must be made by such electronic means, and in such manner, as the Commissioners may direct or may by regulations require.]^1, ^{2}

Regulations—VAT (Amendment) (No 3) Regulations, SI 2014/2430.
Amendments—^{1} Sch 3BA inserted by FA 2014 s 103, Sch 22 para 1 with effect in relation to supplies made on or after 1 January 2015, except in so far as it confers power to make regulations in which case it has effect from 17 July 2014. No registration under Sch 3BA may take effect before 1 January 2015. A request for registration under Sch 3BA that is made before 1 October 2014 is to be treated for the purposes of Article 57d of Implementing Regulation (EU) No 282/2011 (registration to have effect from first day of subsequent quarter) as if it were made on that date (FA 2014 Sch 22 para 24).
^{2} Schedule 3BA repealed by the Taxation (Cross-border Trade) Act 2018 s 43, Sch 8 paras 1, 87 with effect from IP completion day (11pm on 31 December 2020), by virtue of SI 2020/1642 reg 4(b).
Saving provision—Schedule 3BA continues to apply in relation to supplies made before IP completion day despite its repeal by TCTA 2018 Sch 8, para 87. To the extent that it continues to apply, Sch 3BA has effect subject to such modifications as may be specified in a notice published by the Commissioners (see SI 2020/1495, reg 15).
Any references to VATA 1994, Schs 3B or 3BA (other than those mentioned above) that have been repealed by TCTA 2018 Sch 8 continue to apply in relation to supplies made before IP completion day as if they had not been repealed, but only to the extent

that Schs 3B and 3BA continue to have effect in accordance with SI 2020/1495. To the extent that they continue to apply, references to VATA 1994, Schs 3B or 3BA have effect subject to such modifications as may be specified in a notice published by the Commissioners (see SI 2020/1495, reg 16).

[*Notification of changes etc*]

6—*(1) A person registered under the Union scheme must inform the Commissioners of the date when the person first makes qualifying supplies of scheme services (unless the person has already given the Commissioners the information mentioned in paragraph 5(3)(b)).*
(2) That information, and any information a person is required to give under Article 57h of the Implementing Regulation (notification of certain changes), must be communicated by such electronic means, and in such manner, as the Commissioners may direct or may by regulations require.][1], [2]

Regulations—VAT (Amendment) (No 3) Regulations, SI 2014/2430.
Amendments—[1] Sch 3BA inserted by FA 2014 s 103, Sch 22 para 1 with effect in relation to supplies made on or after 1 January 2015, except in so far as it confers power to make regulations in which case it has effect from 17 July 2014. No registration under Sch 3BA may take effect before 1 January 2015. A request for registration under Sch 3BA that is made before 1 October 2014 is to be treated for the purposes of Article 57d of Implementing Regulation (EU) No 282/2011 (registration to have effect from first day of subsequent quarter) as if it were made on that date (FA 2014 Sch 22 para 24).
[2] Schedule 3BA repealed by the Taxation (Cross-border Trade) Act 2018 s 43, Sch 8 paras 1, 87 with effect from IP completion day (11pm on 31 December 2020), by virtue of SI 2020/1642 reg 4(*b*).
Saving provision—Schedule 3BA continues to apply in relation to supplies made before IP completion day despite its repeal by TCTA 2018 Sch 8, para 87. To the extent that it continues to apply, Sch 3BA has effect subject to such modifications as may be specified in a notice published by the Commissioners (see SI 2020/1495, reg 15).
Any references to VATA 1994, Schs 3B or 3BA (other than those mentioned above) that have been repealed by TCTA 2018 Sch 8 continue to apply in relation to supplies made before IP completion day as if they had not been repealed, but only to the extent that Schs 3B and 3BA continue to have effect in accordance with SI 2020/1495. To the extent that they continue to apply, references to VATA 1994, Schs 3B or 3BA have effect subject to such modifications as may be specified in a notice published by the Commissioners (see SI 2020/1495, reg 16).

[*Cancellation of registration*]

7 *The Commissioners must cancel the registration under the Union scheme of a person if—*
   (a) *the person has ceased to make, or no longer intends to make, supplies of scheme services and has notified them of that fact;*
   (b) *they otherwise determine that the person has ceased to make, or no longer intends to make, supplies of scheme services;*
   (c) *the person has ceased to satisfy any of the other conditions for registration in paragraph 4(1) and has notified them of that fact,*
   (d) *they otherwise determine that the person has ceased to satisfy any of those conditions, or*
   (e) *they determine that the person has persistently failed to comply with the person's obligations under this Schedule or the Implementing Regulation.]*[1], [2]

Amendments—[1] Sch 3BA inserted by FA 2014 s 103, Sch 22 para 1 with effect in relation to supplies made on or after 1 January 2015, except in so far as it confers power to make regulations in which case it has effect from 17 July 2014. No registration under Sch 3BA may take effect before 1 January 2015. A request for registration under Sch 3BA that is made before 1 October 2014 is to be treated for the purposes of Article 57d of Implementing Regulation (EU) No 282/2011 (registration to have effect from first day of subsequent quarter) as if it were made on that date (FA 2014 Sch 22 para 24).
[2] Schedule 3BA repealed by the Taxation (Cross-border Trade) Act 2018 s 43, Sch 8 paras 1, 87 with effect from IP completion day (11pm on 31 December 2020), by virtue of SI 2020/1642 reg 4(*b*).
Saving provision—Schedule 3BA continues to apply in relation to supplies made before IP completion day despite its repeal by TCTA 2018 Sch 8, para 87. To the extent that it continues to apply, Sch 3BA has effect subject to such modifications as may be specified in a notice published by the Commissioners (see SI 2020/1495, reg 15).
Any references to VATA 1994, Schs 3B or 3BA (other than those mentioned above) that have been repealed by TCTA 2018 Sch 8 continue to apply in relation to supplies made before IP completion day as if they had not been repealed, but only to the extent that Schs 3B and 3BA continue to have effect in accordance with SI 2020/1495. To the extent that they continue to apply, references to VATA 1994, Schs 3B or 3BA have effect subject to such modifications as may be specified in a notice published by the Commissioners (see SI 2020/1495, reg 16).

[PART 3
UNION SCHEME : LIABILITY, RETURNS, PAYMENT ETC

Liability to pay non-UK VAT to Commissioners

8—*(1) This paragraph applies where a person—*
   (a) *makes a qualifying supply of scheme services, and*
   (b) *is registered under the Union scheme when the supply is made.*
(2) The person is liable to pay to the Commissioners the gross amount of VAT on the supply.
(3) The reference in sub-paragraph (2) to the gross amount of VAT on the supply is to the amount of VAT charged on the supply in accordance with the law of the member State in which the supply is treated as made, without any deduction of VAT pursuant to Article 168 of Directive 2006/112/EC.][1], [2]

Amendments—[1] Sch 3BA inserted by FA 2014 s 103, Sch 22 para 1 with effect in relation to supplies made on or after 1 January 2015, except in so far as it confers power to make regulations in which case it has effect from 17 July 2014. No registration under Sch 3BA may take effect before 1 January 2015. A request for registration under Sch 3BA that is made before 1 October 2014 is to be treated for the purposes of Article 57d of Implementing Regulation (EU) No 282/2011 (registration to have effect from first day of subsequent quarter) as if it were made on that date (FA 2014 Sch 22 para 24).

[2] Schedule 3BA repealed by the Taxation (Cross-border Trade) Act 2018 s 43, Sch 8 paras 1, 87 with effect from IP completion day (11pm on 31 December 2020), by virtue of SI 2020/1642 reg 4(b). Note that, where these amendments remove a reference to the principal VAT Directive (2006/112/EC) or the Implementing VAT Regulation ((EU) No 282/2011), the removal is not to be taken as implying that the Directive or Regulation is no longer relevant for determining the meaning and effect of this para (Taxation (Cross-border Trade) Act 2018 Sch 8 para 99).

Saving provision—Schedule 3BA continues to apply in relation to supplies made before IP completion day despite its repeal by TCTA 2018 Sch 8, para 87. To the extent that it continues to apply, Sch 3BA has effect subject to such modifications as may be specified in a notice published by the Commissioners (see SI 2020/1495, reg 15).

Any references to VATA 1994, Schs 3B or 3BA (other than those mentioned above) that have been repealed by TCTA 2018 Sch 8 continue to apply in relation to supplies made before IP completion day as if they had not been repealed, but only to the extent that Schs 3B and 3BA continue to have effect in accordance with SI 2020/1495. To the extent that they continue to apply, references to VATA 1994, Schs 3B or 3BA have effect subject to such modifications as may be specified in a notice published by the Commissioners (see SI 2020/1495, reg 16).

[Union scheme returns

9—*(1) A person who is or has been registered under the Union scheme must submit a return (a "Union scheme return") to the Commissioners for each reporting period.*

(2) Each quarter for the whole or part of which a person is registered under the Union scheme is a "reporting period" for that person.][1], [2]

Amendments—[1] Sch 3BA inserted by FA 2014 s 103, Sch 22 para 1 with effect in relation to supplies made on or after 1 January 2015, except in so far as it confers power to make regulations in which case it has effect from 17 July 2014. No registration under Sch 3BA may take effect before 1 January 2015. A request for registration under Sch 3BA that is made before 1 October 2014 is to be treated for the purposes of Article 57d of Implementing Regulation (EU) No 282/2011 (registration to have effect from first day of subsequent quarter) as if it were made on that date (FA 2014 Sch 22 para 24).

[2] Schedule 3BA repealed by the Taxation (Cross-border Trade) Act 2018 s 43, Sch 8 paras 1, 87 with effect from IP completion day (11pm on 31 December 2020), by virtue of SI 2020/1642 reg 4(b).

Saving provision—Schedule 3BA continues to apply in relation to supplies made before IP completion day despite its repeal by TCTA 2018 Sch 8, para 87. To the extent that it continues to apply, Sch 3BA has effect subject to such modifications as may be specified in a notice published by the Commissioners (see SI 2020/1495, reg 15).

Any references to VATA 1994, Schs 3B or 3BA (other than those mentioned above) that have been repealed by TCTA 2018 Sch 8 continue to apply in relation to supplies made before IP completion day as if they had not been repealed, but only to the extent that Schs 3B and 3BA continue to have effect in accordance with SI 2020/1495. To the extent that they continue to apply, references to VATA 1994, Schs 3B or 3BA have effect subject to such modifications as may be specified in a notice published by the Commissioners (see SI 2020/1495, reg 16).

[Union scheme returns: further requirements

10—*(1) A Union scheme return is to be made out in sterling.*

(2) Any conversion from one currency into another for the purposes of sub-paragraph (1) is to be made using the exchange rates published by the European Central Bank—

(a) for the last day of the reporting period to which the Union scheme return relates, or

(b) if no such rate is published for that day, for the next day for which such a rate is published.

(3) A Union scheme return—

(a) must be submitted to the Commissioners within the 20 days after the last day of the reporting period to which it relates;

(b) must be submitted by such electronic means, and in such manner, as the Commissioners may direct or may by regulations require.][1], [2]

Regulations—VAT (Amendment) (No 3) Regulations, SI 2014/2430.

Amendments—[1] Sch 3BA inserted by FA 2014 s 103, Sch 22 para 1 with effect in relation to supplies made on or after 1 January 2015, except in so far as it confers power to make regulations in which case it has effect from 17 July 2014. No registration under Sch 3BA may take effect before 1 January 2015. A request for registration under Sch 3BA that is made before 1 October 2014 is to be treated for the purposes of Article 57d of Implementing Regulation (EU) No 282/2011 (registration to have effect from first day of subsequent quarter) as if it were made on that date (FA 2014 Sch 22 para 24).

[2] Schedule 3BA repealed by the Taxation (Cross-border Trade) Act 2018 s 43, Sch 8 paras 1, 87 with effect from IP completion day (11pm on 31 December 2020), by virtue of SI 2020/1642 reg 4(b).

Saving provision—Schedule 3BA continues to apply in relation to supplies made before IP completion day despite its repeal by TCTA 2018 Sch 8, para 87. To the extent that it continues to apply, Sch 3BA has effect subject to such modifications as may be specified in a notice published by the Commissioners (see SI 2020/1495, reg 15).

Any references to VATA 1994, Schs 3B or 3BA (other than those mentioned above) that have been repealed by TCTA 2018 Sch 8 continue to apply in relation to supplies made before IP completion day as if they had not been repealed, but only to the extent that Schs 3B and 3BA continue to have effect in accordance with SI 2020/1495. To the extent that they continue to apply, references to VATA 1994, Schs 3B or 3BA have effect subject to such modifications as may be specified in a notice published by the Commissioners (see SI 2020/1495, reg 16).

[Payment

11—*(1) A person who is required to submit a Union scheme return must pay, by the deadline for submitting the return, the amounts required in accordance with paragraph 8 in respect of qualifying supplies of scheme services made in the reporting period to which the return relates.*
(2) A payment under this paragraph must be made in such manner as the Commissioners may direct or may by regulations require.]¹, ²

Amendments—¹ Sch 3BA inserted by FA 2014 s 103, Sch 22 para 1 with effect in relation to supplies made on or after 1 January 2015, except in so far as it confers power to make regulations in which case it has effect from 17 July 2014. No registration under Sch 3BA may take effect before 1 January 2015. A request for registration under Sch 3BA that is made before 1 October 2014 is to be treated for the purposes of Article 57d of Implementing Regulation (EU) No 282/2011 (registration to have effect from first day of subsequent quarter) as if it were made on that date (FA 2014 Sch 22 para 24).
² Schedule 3BA repealed by the Taxation (Cross-border Trade) Act 2018 s 43, Sch 8 paras 1, 87 with effect from IP completion day (11pm on 31 December 2020), by virtue of SI 2020/1642 reg 4(*b*).
Saving provision—Schedule 3BA continues to apply in relation to supplies made before IP completion day despite its repeal by TCTA 2018 Sch 8, para 87. To the extent that it continues to apply, Sch 3BA has effect subject to such modifications as may be specified in a notice published by the Commissioners (see SI 2020/1495, reg 15).
Any references to VATA 1994, Schs 3B or 3BA (other than those mentioned above) that have been repealed by TCTA 2018 Sch 8 continue to apply in relation to supplies made before IP completion day as if they had not been repealed, but only to the extent that Schs 3B and 3BA continue to have effect in accordance with SI 2020/1495. To the extent that they continue to apply, references to VATA 1994, Schs 3B or 3BA have effect subject to such modifications as may be specified in a notice published by the Commissioners (see SI 2020/1495, reg 16).

[Availability of records

12 *(1) A person who is registered under the Union scheme must make available to the Commissioners, on request, any obligatory records the person is keeping of transactions entered into by the person while registered under the scheme.*
(2) The records must be made available by electronic means.
(3) In sub-paragraph (1) "obligatory records" means records kept in accordance with an obligation imposed in accordance with Article 369k of Directive 2006/112/EC.]¹, ²

Amendments—¹ Sch 3BA inserted by FA 2014 s 103, Sch 22 para 1 with effect in relation to supplies made on or after 1 January 2015, except in so far as it confers power to make regulations in which case it has effect from 17 July 2014. No registration under Sch 3BA may take effect before 1 January 2015. A request for registration under Sch 3BA that is made before 1 October 2014 is to be treated for the purposes of Article 57d of Implementing Regulation (EU) No 282/2011 (registration to have effect from first day of subsequent quarter) as if it were made on that date (FA 2014 Sch 22 para 24).
² Schedule 3BA repealed by the Taxation (Cross-border Trade) Act 2018 s 43, Sch 8 paras 1, 87 with effect from IP completion day (11pm on 31 December 2020), by virtue of SI 2020/1642 reg 4(*b*). Note that, where these amendments remove a reference to the principal VAT Directive (2006/112/EC) or the Implementing VAT Regulation ((EU) No 282/2011), the removal is not to be taken as implying that the Directive or Regulation is no longer relevant for determining the meaning and effect of this para (Taxation (Cross-border Trade) Act 2018 Sch 8 para 99).
Saving provision—Schedule 3BA continues to apply in relation to supplies made before IP completion day despite its repeal by TCTA 2018 Sch 8, para 87. To the extent that it continues to apply, Sch 3BA has effect subject to such modifications as may be specified in a notice published by the Commissioners (see SI 2020/1495, reg 15).
Any references to VATA 1994, Schs 3B or 3BA (other than those mentioned above) that have been repealed by TCTA 2018 Sch 8 continue to apply in relation to supplies made before IP completion day as if they had not been repealed, but only to the extent that Schs 3B and 3BA continue to have effect in accordance with SI 2020/1495. To the extent that they continue to apply, references to VATA 1994, Schs 3B or 3BA have effect subject to such modifications as may be specified in a notice published by the Commissioners (see SI 2020/1495, reg 16).

[Amounts required to be paid to other member States

13 *Section 44 of the Commissioners for Revenue and Customs Act 2005 (requirement to pay receipts into the Consolidated Fund) does not apply to any money received for or on account of VAT that is required to be paid to another member State under Article 46 of Council Regulation (EU) No 904/2010.]¹*

Amendments—¹ Sch 3BA inserted by FA 2014 s 103, Sch 22 para 1 with effect in relation to supplies made on or after 1 January 2015, except in so far as it confers power to make regulations in which case it has effect from 17 July 2014. No registration under Sch 3BA may take effect before 1 January 2015. A request for registration under Sch 3BA that is made before 1 October 2014 is to be treated for the purposes of Article 57d of Implementing Regulation (EU) No 282/2011 (registration to have effect from first day of subsequent quarter) as if it were made on that date (FA 2014 Sch 22 para 24).
² Schedule 3BA repealed by the Taxation (Cross-border Trade) Act 2018 s 43, Sch 8 paras 1, 87 with effect from IP completion day (11pm on 31 December 2020), by virtue of SI 2020/1642 reg 4(*b*).
Saving provision—Schedule 3BA continues to apply in relation to supplies made before IP completion day despite its repeal by TCTA 2018 Sch 8, para 87. To the extent that it continues to apply, Sch 3BA has effect subject to such modifications as may be specified in a notice published by the Commissioners (see SI 2020/1495, reg 15).
Any references to VATA 1994, Schs 3B or 3BA (other than those mentioned above) that have been repealed by TCTA 2018 Sch 8 continue to apply in relation to supplies made before IP completion day as if they had not been repealed, but only to the extent that Schs 3B and 3BA continue to have effect in accordance with SI 2020/1495. To the extent that they continue to apply, references to VATA 1994, Schs 3B or 3BA have effect subject to such modifications as may be specified in a notice published by the Commissioners (see SI 2020/1495, reg 16).

[PART 4
PERSONS REGISTERED UNDER NON-UK SPECIAL SCHEMES

Meaning of "non-UK special scheme"

14—*(1) In this Schedule "non-UK special scheme" means any provision of the law of a member State other than the United Kingdom which implements Section 3 of Chapter 6 of Title XII of Directive 2006/112/EC.*
(2) In relation to a non-UK special scheme, references to the "administering member State" are to the member State under whose law the scheme is established.][1], [2]

Amendments—[1] Sch 3BA inserted by FA 2014 s 103, Sch 22 para 1 with effect in relation to supplies made on or after 1 January 2015, except in so far as it confers power to make regulations in which case it has effect from 17 July 2014.
No registration under Sch 3BA may take effect before 1 January 2015. A request for registration under Sch 3BA that is made before 1 October 2014 is to be treated for the purposes of Article 57d of Implementing Regulation (EU) No 282/2011 (registration to have effect from first day of subsequent quarter) as if it were made on that date (FA 2014 Sch 22 para 24).
[2] Schedule 3BA repealed by the Taxation (Cross-border Trade) Act 2018 s 43, Sch 8 paras 1, 87 with effect from IP completion day (11pm on 31 December 2020), by virtue of SI 2020/1642 reg 4(b). Note that, where these amendments remove a reference to the principal VAT Directive (2006/112/EC) or the Implementing VAT Regulation ((EU) No 282/2011), the removal is not to be taken as implying that the Directive or Regulation is no longer relevant for determining the meaning and effect of this para (Taxation (Cross-border Trade) Act 2018 Sch 8 para 99).
Saving provision—Schedule 3BA continues to apply in relation to supplies made before IP completion day despite its repeal by TCTA 2018 Sch 8, para 87. To the extent that it continues to apply, Sch 3BA has effect subject to such modifications as may be specified in a notice published by the Commissioners (see SI 2020/1495, reg 15).
Any references to VATA 1994, Schs 3B or 3BA (other than those mentioned above) that have been repealed by TCTA 2018 Sch 8 continue to apply in relation to supplies made before IP completion day as if they had not been repealed, but only to the extent that Schs 3B and 3BA continue to have effect in accordance with SI 2020/1495. To the extent that they continue to apply, references to VATA 1994, Schs 3B or 3BA have effect subject to such modifications as may be specified in a notice published by the Commissioners (see SI 2020/1495, reg 16).

[Exemption from requirement to register under this Act

15—*(1) A participant in a non-UK special scheme is not required to be registered under this Act by virtue of making supplies of scheme services in respect of which the participant is required to make returns under that scheme.*
(2) Sub-paragraph (1) overrides any contrary provision in this Act.
(3) Where a participant in a non-UK special scheme who is not registered under this Act ("the unregistered person") makes relevant supplies, it is to be assumed for all purposes of this Act relating to the determination of—
  (a) whether or not VAT is chargeable under this Act on those supplies,
  (b) how much VAT is chargeable under this Act on those supplies,
  (c) the time at which those supplies are treated as taking place, and
  (d) any other matter that the Commissioners may specify by regulations,
that the unregistered person is registered under this Act.
(4) Supplies of scheme services made by the unregistered person are "relevant supplies" if—
  (a) the value of the supplies must be accounted for in a return required to be made by the unregistered person under the non-UK special scheme, and
  (b) the supplies are treated as made in the United Kingdom.][1], [2]

Amendments—[1] Sch 3BA inserted by FA 2014 s 103, Sch 22 para 1 with effect in relation to supplies made on or after 1 January 2015, except in so far as it confers power to make regulations in which case it has effect from 17 July 2014.
No registration under Sch 3BA may take effect before 1 January 2015. A request for registration under Sch 3BA that is made before 1 October 2014 is to be treated for the purposes of Article 57d of Implementing Regulation (EU) No 282/2011 (registration to have effect from first day of subsequent quarter) as if it were made on that date (FA 2014 Sch 22 para 24).
[2] Schedule 3BA repealed by the Taxation (Cross-border Trade) Act 2018 s 43, Sch 8 paras 1, 87 with effect from IP completion day (11pm on 31 December 2020), by virtue of SI 2020/1642 reg 4(b).
Saving provision—Schedule 3BA continues to apply in relation to supplies made before IP completion day despite its repeal by TCTA 2018 Sch 8, para 87. To the extent that it continues to apply, Sch 3BA has effect subject to such modifications as may be specified in a notice published by the Commissioners (see SI 2020/1495, reg 15).
Any references to VATA 1994, Schs 3B or 3BA (other than those mentioned above) that have been repealed by TCTA 2018 Sch 8 continue to apply in relation to supplies made before IP completion day as if they had not been repealed, but only to the extent that Schs 3B and 3BA continue to have effect in accordance with SI 2020/1495. To the extent that they continue to apply, references to VATA 1994, Schs 3B or 3BA have effect subject to such modifications as may be specified in a notice published by the Commissioners (see SI 2020/1495, reg 16).

[De-registration

16—*(1) Sub-paragraph (2) applies where a person who is registered under Schedule 1A—*
  (a) satisfies the Commissioners that the person intends to apply for identification under a non-UK special scheme, and
  (b) asks the Commissioners to cancel the person's registration under Schedule 1A.

(2) The Commissioners may cancel the person's registration under Schedule 1A with effect from—
  (a) the day on which the request is made, or
  (b) a later date agreed between the person and the Commissioners.][1], [2]

Amendments—[1] Sch 3BA inserted by FA 2014 s 103, Sch 22 para 1 with effect in relation to supplies made on or after 1 January 2015, except in so far as it confers power to make regulations in which case it has effect from 17 July 2014. No registration under Sch 3BA may take effect before 1 January 2015. A request for registration under Sch 3BA that is made before 1 October 2014 is to be treated for the purposes of Article 57d of Implementing Regulation (EU) No 282/2011 (registration to have effect from first day of subsequent quarter) as if it were made on that date (FA 2014 Sch 22 para 24).
[2] Schedule 3BA repealed by the Taxation (Cross-border Trade) Act 2018 s 43, Sch 8 paras 1, 87 with effect from IP completion day (11pm on 31 December 2020), by virtue of SI 2020/1642 reg 4(b).
Saving provision—Schedule 3BA continues to apply in relation to supplies made before IP completion day despite its repeal by TCTA 2018 Sch 8, para 87. To the extent that it continues to apply, Sch 3BA has effect subject to such modifications as may be specified in a notice published by the Commissioners (see SI 2020/1495, reg 15).
Any references to VATA 1994, Schs 3B or 3BA (other than those mentioned above) that have been repealed by TCTA 2018 Sch 8 continue to apply in relation to supplies made before IP completion day as if they had not been repealed, but only to the extent that Schs 3B and 3BA continue to have effect in accordance with SI 2020/1495. To the extent that they continue to apply, references to VATA 1994, Schs 3B or 3BA have effect subject to such modifications as may be specified in a notice published by the Commissioners (see SI 2020/1495, reg 16).

[Scheme participants who are also registered under this Act

17—(1) A person who—
  (a) is a participant in a non-UK special scheme, and
  (b) is also registered, or required to be registered, under this Act,
is not required to discharge any obligation placed on the person as a taxable person, so far as the obligation relates to relevant supplies.
(2) The reference in sub-paragraph (1) to an obligation placed on the person as a taxable person is to an obligation—
  (a) to which the person is subject under or by virtue of this Act, and
  (b) to which the person would not be subject if the person were neither registered nor required to be registered under this Act.
(3) A supply made by a participant in a non-UK special scheme is a "relevant supply" if—
  (a) the value of the supply must be accounted for in a return required to be made by the participant under the non-UK special scheme, and
  (b) the supply is treated as made in the United Kingdom.
(4) The Commissioners may by regulations specify cases in relation to which sub-paragraph (1) is not to apply.
(5) In section 25(2) (deduction of input tax from output tax by taxable person) the reference to output tax that is due from the taxable person does not include any VAT that the taxable person is liable under a non-UK special scheme to pay to the tax authorities for the administering member State.][1], [2]

Regulations—VAT (Amendment) (No 3) Regulations, SI 2014/2430.
Amendments—[1] Sch 3BA inserted by FA 2014 s 103, Sch 22 para 1 with effect in relation to supplies made on or after 1 January 2015, except in so far as it confers power to make regulations in which case it has effect from 17 July 2014. No registration under Sch 3BA may take effect before 1 January 2015. A request for registration under Sch 3BA that is made before 1 October 2014 is to be treated for the purposes of Article 57d of Implementing Regulation (EU) No 282/2011 (registration to have effect from first day of subsequent quarter) as if it were made on that date (FA 2014 Sch 22 para 24).
[2] Schedule 3BA repealed by the Taxation (Cross-border Trade) Act 2018 s 43, Sch 8 paras 1, 87 with effect from IP completion day (11pm on 31 December 2020), by virtue of SI 2020/1642 reg 4(b).
Saving provision—Schedule 3BA continues to apply in relation to supplies made before IP completion day despite its repeal by TCTA 2018 Sch 8, para 87. To the extent that it continues to apply, Sch 3BA has effect subject to such modifications as may be specified in a notice published by the Commissioners (see SI 2020/1495, reg 15).
Any references to VATA 1994, Schs 3B or 3BA (other than those mentioned above) that have been repealed by TCTA 2018 Sch 8 continue to apply in relation to supplies made before IP completion day as if they had not been repealed, but only to the extent that Schs 3B and 3BA continue to have effect in accordance with SI 2020/1495. To the extent that they continue to apply, references to VATA 1994, Schs 3B or 3BA have effect subject to such modifications as may be specified in a notice published by the Commissioners (see SI 2020/1495, reg 16).

[Value of supplies to connected persons

18 In paragraph 1 of Schedule 6 (valuation: supply to connected person at less than market value) the reference to a supply made by a taxable person is to be read as including a supply of scheme services that is made by a participant in a non-UK special scheme (and is treated as made in the United Kingdom).][1], [2]

Amendments—[1] Sch 3BA inserted by FA 2014 s 103, Sch 22 para 1 with effect in relation to supplies made on or after 1 January 2015, except in so far as it confers power to make regulations in which case it has effect from 17 July 2014. No registration under Sch 3BA may take effect before 1 January 2015. A request for registration under Sch 3BA that is made before 1 October 2014 is to be treated for the purposes of Article 57d of Implementing Regulation (EU) No 282/2011 (registration to have effect from first day of subsequent quarter) as if it were made on that date (FA 2014 Sch 22 para 24).

[2] Schedule 3BA repealed by the Taxation (Cross-border Trade) Act 2018 s 43, Sch 8 paras 1, 87 with effect from IP completion day (11pm on 31 December 2020), by virtue of SI 2020/1642 reg 4(*b*).
Saving provision—Schedule 3BA continues to apply in relation to supplies made before IP completion day despite its repeal by TCTA 2018 Sch 8, para 87. To the extent that it continues to apply, Sch 3BA has effect subject to such modifications as may be specified in a notice published by the Commissioners (see SI 2020/1495, reg 15).
Any references to VATA 1994, Schs 3B or 3BA (other than those mentioned above) that have been repealed by TCTA 2018 Sch 8 continue to apply in relation to supplies made before IP completion day as if they had not been repealed, but only to the extent that Schs 3B and 3BA continue to have effect in accordance with SI 2020/1495. To the extent that they continue to apply, references to VATA 1994, Schs 3B or 3BA have effect subject to such modifications as may be specified in a notice published by the Commissioners (see SI 2020/1495, reg 16).

[Refund of VAT on supplies of goods and services supplied to scheme participant

19 *The power of the Commissioners to make regulations under section 39 (repayment of VAT to those in business overseas) includes power to make provision for giving effect to the second sentence of Article 369j of Directive 2006/112/EC (which provides for VAT on certain supplies to participants in special accounting schemes to be refunded in accordance with Directive 2008/9/EC).]*[1], [2]
Regulations—VAT (Amendment) (No 3) Regulations, SI 2014/2430.
Amendments—[1] Sch 3BA inserted by FA 2014 s 103, Sch 22 para 1 with effect in relation to supplies made on or after 1 January 2015, except in so far as it confers power to make regulations in which case it has effect from 17 July 2014.
No registration under Sch 3BA may take effect before 1 January 2015. A request for registration under Sch 3BA that is made before 1 October 2014 is to be treated for the purposes of Article 57d of Implementing Regulation (EU) No 282/2011 (registration to have effect from first day of subsequent quarter) as if it were made on that date (FA 2014 Sch 22 para 24).
[2] Schedule 3BA repealed by the Taxation (Cross-border Trade) Act 2018 s 43, Sch 8 paras 1, 87 with effect from IP completion day (11pm on 31 December 2020), by virtue of SI 2020/1642 reg 4(*b*). Note that, where these amendments remove a reference to the principal VAT Directive (2006/112/EC) or the Implementing VAT Regulation ((EU) No 282/2011), the removal is not to be taken as implying that the Directive or Regulation is no longer relevant for determining the meaning and effect of this para (Taxation (Cross-border Trade) Act 2018 Sch 8 para 99).
Saving provision—Schedule 3BA continues to apply in relation to supplies made before IP completion day despite its repeal by TCTA 2018 Sch 8, para 87. To the extent that it continues to apply, Sch 3BA has effect subject to such modifications as may be specified in a notice published by the Commissioners (see SI 2020/1495, reg 15).
Any references to VATA 1994, Schs 3B or 3BA (other than those mentioned above) that have been repealed by TCTA 2018 Sch 8 continue to apply in relation to supplies made before IP completion day as if they had not been repealed, but only to the extent that Schs 3B and 3BA continue to have effect in accordance with SI 2020/1495. To the extent that they continue to apply, references to VATA 1994, Schs 3B or 3BA have effect subject to such modifications as may be specified in a notice published by the Commissioners (see SI 2020/1495, reg 16).

[Assessments: general modifications of section 73

20—*(1) For the purposes of this Schedule, section 73 (assessments: incorrect returns etc) is to be read as if—*
  (a) the reference in subsection (1) of that section to returns required under this Act included relevant non-UK returns, and
  (b) references in that section to a prescribed accounting period included a tax period.
(2) See also the modifications in paragraph 21.
(3) In this Schedule "relevant non-UK return" means a non-UK return (see paragraph 38(1)) that is required to be made (wholly or partly) in respect of supplies of scheme services that are treated as made in the United Kingdom.][1], [2]
Amendments—[1] Sch 3BA inserted by FA 2014 s 103, Sch 22 para 1 with effect in relation to supplies made on or after 1 January 2015, except in so far as it confers power to make regulations in which case it has effect from 17 July 2014.
No registration under Sch 3BA may take effect before 1 January 2015. A request for registration under Sch 3BA that is made before 1 October 2014 is to be treated for the purposes of Article 57d of Implementing Regulation (EU) No 282/2011 (registration to have effect from first day of subsequent quarter) as if it were made on that date (FA 2014 Sch 22 para 24).
[2] Schedule 3BA repealed by the Taxation (Cross-border Trade) Act 2018 s 43, Sch 8 paras 1, 87 with effect from IP completion day (11pm on 31 December 2020), by virtue of SI 2020/1642 reg 4(*b*).
Saving provision—Schedule 3BA continues to apply in relation to supplies made before IP completion day despite its repeal by TCTA 2018 Sch 8, para 87. To the extent that it continues to apply, Sch 3BA has effect subject to such modifications as may be specified in a notice published by the Commissioners (see SI 2020/1495, reg 15).
Any references to VATA 1994, Schs 3B or 3BA (other than those mentioned above) that have been repealed by TCTA 2018 Sch 8 continue to apply in relation to supplies made before IP completion day as if they had not been repealed, but only to the extent that Schs 3B and 3BA continue to have effect in accordance with SI 2020/1495. To the extent that they continue to apply, references to VATA 1994, Schs 3B or 3BA have effect subject to such modifications as may be specified in a notice published by the Commissioners (see SI 2020/1495, reg 16).

[Assessment in connection with increase in consideration

21—*(1) Sub-paragraphs (2) to (4) make modifications of sections 73 and 76 which—*
  (a) have effect for the purposes of this Schedule, and
  (b) are in addition to any other modifications of those sections made by this Schedule.
(2) Section 73 has effect as if the following were inserted after subsection (3) of that section—

"(3A) Where a person has failed to make an amendment or notification that the person is required to make under paragraph 31 of Schedule 3BA in respect of an increase in the consideration for a UK supply (as defined in paragraph 31(7)), the Commissioners may assess the amount of VAT due from the person as a result of the increase to the best of their judgement and notify it to the person.

(3B) An assessment under subsection (3A)—
> (a) is of VAT due for the tax period mentioned in paragraph 31(1)(a) of Schedule 3BA;
> (b) must be made within the time limits provided for in section 77, and must not be made after the later of—
>> (i) 2 years after the end of the tax period referred to in paragraph 31(1)(a);
>> (ii) one year after evidence of facts sufficient in the opinion of the Commissioners to justify making the assessment comes to their knowledge.

(3C) Subject to section 77, where further evidence such as is mentioned in subsection (3B)(b)(ii) comes to the Commissioners' knowledge after they have made an assessment under subsection (3A), another assessment may be made under that subsection, in addition to any earlier assessment."

(3) The reference in section 73(9) to subsection (1) of that section is taken to include a reference to section 73(3A) (as inserted by sub-paragraph (2)).

(4) Section 76 (assessment of amounts due by way of interest etc) is to be read as if the reference in subsection (5) of that section to section 73(1) included a reference to section 73(3A) (as inserted by sub-paragraph (2)).]¹, ²

Amendments—¹ Sch 3BA inserted by FA 2014 s 103, Sch 22 para 1 with effect in relation to supplies made on or after 1 January 2015, except in so far as it confers power to make regulations in which case it has effect from 17 July 2014. No registration under Sch 3BA may take effect before 1 January 2015. A request for registration under Sch 3BA that is made before 1 October 2014 is to be treated for the purposes of Article 57d of Implementing Regulation (EU) No 282/2011 (registration to have effect from first day of subsequent quarter) as if it were made on that date (FA 2014 Sch 22 para 24).
² Schedule 3BA repealed by the Taxation (Cross-border Trade) Act 2018 s 43, Sch 8 paras 1, 87 with effect from IP completion day (11pm on 31 December 2020), by virtue of SI 2020/1642 reg 4(b).

Saving provision—Schedule 3BA continues to apply in relation to supplies made before IP completion day despite its repeal by TCTA 2018 Sch 8, para 87. To the extent that it continues to apply, Sch 3BA has effect subject to such modifications as may be specified in a notice published by the Commissioners (see SI 2020/1495, reg 15).

Any references to VATA 1994, Schs 3B or 3BA (other than those mentioned above) that have been repealed by TCTA 2018 Sch 8 continue to apply in relation to supplies made before IP completion day as if they had not been repealed, but only to the extent that Schs 3B and 3BA continue to have effect in accordance with SI 2020/1495. To the extent that they continue to apply, references to VATA 1994, Schs 3B or 3BA have effect subject to such modifications as may be specified in a notice published by the Commissioners (see SI 2020/1495, reg 16).

[Assessments: consequential modifications

22 *References to prescribed accounting periods in the following provisions are to be read in accordance with the modifications made by paragraphs 20 and 21—*
> *(a) section 74 (interest on VAT recovered or recoverable by assessment);*
> *(b) section 76 (assessment of amounts due by way of penalty, interest or surcharge);*
> *(c) section 77 (assessment: time limits).]¹, ²*

Amendments—¹ Sch 3BA inserted by FA 2014 s 103, Sch 22 para 1 with effect in relation to supplies made on or after 1 January 2015, except in so far as it confers power to make regulations in which case it has effect from 17 July 2014. No registration under Sch 3BA may take effect before 1 January 2015. A request for registration under Sch 3BA that is made before 1 October 2014 is to be treated for the purposes of Article 57d of Implementing Regulation (EU) No 282/2011 (registration to have effect from first day of subsequent quarter) as if it were made on that date (FA 2014 Sch 22 para 24).
² Schedule 3BA repealed by the Taxation (Cross-border Trade) Act 2018 s 43, Sch 8 paras 1, 87 with effect from IP completion day (11pm on 31 December 2020), by virtue of SI 2020/1642 reg 4(b).

Saving provision—Schedule 3BA continues to apply in relation to supplies made before IP completion day despite its repeal by TCTA 2018 Sch 8, para 87. To the extent that it continues to apply, Sch 3BA has effect subject to such modifications as may be specified in a notice published by the Commissioners (see SI 2020/1495, reg 15).

Any references to VATA 1994, Schs 3B or 3BA (other than those mentioned above) that have been repealed by TCTA 2018 Sch 8 continue to apply in relation to supplies made before IP completion day as if they had not been repealed, but only to the extent that Schs 3B and 3BA continue to have effect in accordance with SI 2020/1495. To the extent that they continue to apply, references to VATA 1994, Schs 3B or 3BA have effect subject to such modifications as may be specified in a notice published by the Commissioners (see SI 2020/1495, reg 16).

[Deemed amendments of relevant non-UK returns

23 *(1) Where a person who has made a relevant non-UK return makes a claim under paragraph 29(7)(b) (overpayments) in relation to an error in the return, the relevant non-UK return is taken for the purposes of this Act to have been amended by the information in the claim.*

(2) Where a person who has made a relevant non-UK return gives the Commissioners a notice relating to the return under paragraph 31(2)(b) (increase or decrease in consideration), the relevant non- UK return is taken for the purposes of this Act to have been amended by that information.

(3) Where (in a case not falling within sub-paragraph (1) or (2)) a person who has made a relevant non-UK return notifies the Commissioners (after the expiry of the period during which the non-UK return may be amended under Article 61 of the Implementing Regulation) of a change that needs to be made to the return to correct an error, or rectify an omission, in it, the relevant non-UK return is taken for the purposes of this Act to have been amended by that information.

(4) The Commissioners may by regulations—
   (a) specify within what period and in what form and manner notice is to be given under sub-paragraph (3);
   (b) require notices to be supported by documentary evidence described in the regulations.][1], [2]

Regulations—VAT (Amendment) (No 3) Regulations, SI 2014/2430.

Amendments—[1] Sch 3BA inserted by FA 2014 s 103, Sch 22 para 1 with effect in relation to supplies made on or after 1 January 2015, except in so far as it confers power to make regulations in which case it has effect from 17 July 2014. No registration under Sch 3BA may take effect before 1 January 2015. A request for registration under Sch 3BA that is made before 1 October 2014 is to be treated for the purposes of Article 57d of Implementing Regulation (EU) No 282/2011 (registration to have effect from first day of subsequent quarter) as if it were made on that date (FA 2014 Sch 22 para 24).

[2] Schedule 3BA repealed by the Taxation (Cross-border Trade) Act 2018 s 43, Sch 8 paras 1, 87 with effect from IP completion day (11pm on 31 December 2020), by virtue of SI 2020/1642 reg 4(b).

Saving provision—Schedule 3BA continues to apply in relation to supplies made before IP completion day despite its repeal by TCTA 2018 Sch 8, para 87. To the extent that it continues to apply, Sch 3BA has effect subject to such modifications as may be specified in a notice published by the Commissioners (see SI 2020/1495, reg 15).

Any references to VATA 1994, Schs 3B or 3BA (other than those mentioned above) that have been repealed by TCTA 2018 Sch 8 continue to apply in relation to supplies made before IP completion day as if they had not been repealed, but only to the extent that Schs 3B and 3BA continue to have effect in accordance with SI 2020/1495. To the extent that they continue to apply, references to VATA 1994, Schs 3B or 3BA have effect subject to such modifications as may be specified in a notice published by the Commissioners (see SI 2020/1495, reg 16).

[Interest on VAT: "reckonable date"

24—(1) Sub-paragraph (2) states the "reckonable date" for the purposes of section 74(1) and (2) for any case where an amount carrying interest under that section—
   (a) is an amount assessed under section 73(2) (refunds etc) in reliance on paragraph 20, or that could have been so assessed, and
   (b) was correctly paid or credited to the person, but would not have been paid or credited to the person had the facts been as they later turn out to be.

(2) The "reckonable date" is the first day after the end of the tax period in which the events occurred as a result of which the Commissioners were authorised to make the assessment (that was or could have been made) under section 73(2).

(3) Sub-paragraph (4) states the "reckonable date" for any other case where an amount carrying interest under section 74 is assessed under section 74(1) or (2) in reliance on paragraph 20, or could have been so assessed.

(4) The "reckonable date" is taken to be the latest date by which a non- UK return was required to be made for the tax period to which the amount assessed relates.

(5) Where section 74(1) or (2) (interest on VAT recovered or recoverable by assessment) applies in relation to an amount assessed under section 73(3A) (as inserted by paragraph 21(2)), the "reckonable date" for the purposes of section 74(1) or (2) is taken to be the day after the end of the tax period referred to in paragraph 31(2).][1], [2]

Amendments—[1] Sch 3BA inserted by FA 2014 s 103, Sch 22 para 1 with effect in relation to supplies made on or after 1 January 2015, except in so far as it confers power to make regulations in which case it has effect from 17 July 2014. No registration under Sch 3BA may take effect before 1 January 2015. A request for registration under Sch 3BA that is made before 1 October 2014 is to be treated for the purposes of Article 57d of Implementing Regulation (EU) No 282/2011 (registration to have effect from first day of subsequent quarter) as if it were made on that date (FA 2014 Sch 22 para 24).

[2] Schedule 3BA repealed by the Taxation (Cross-border Trade) Act 2018 s 43, Sch 8 paras 1, 87 with effect from IP completion day (11pm on 31 December 2020), by virtue of SI 2020/1642 reg 4(b).

Saving provision—Schedule 3BA continues to apply in relation to supplies made before IP completion day despite its repeal by TCTA 2018 Sch 8, para 87. To the extent that it continues to apply, Sch 3BA has effect subject to such modifications as may be specified in a notice published by the Commissioners (see SI 2020/1495, reg 15).

Any references to VATA 1994, Schs 3B or 3BA (other than those mentioned above) that have been repealed by TCTA 2018 Sch 8 continue to apply in relation to supplies made before IP completion day as if they had not been repealed, but only to the extent that Schs 3B and 3BA continue to have effect in accordance with SI 2020/1495. To the extent that they continue to apply, references to VATA 1994, Schs 3B or 3BA have effect subject to such modifications as may be specified in a notice published by the Commissioners (see SI 2020/1495, reg 16).

Default surcharge: notice of special surcharge period

25 (1) A person who is required to make a relevant non-UK return for a tax period is regarded for the purposes of this paragraph and paragraph 26 as being in default in respect of that period if either—

(a) conditions 1A and 2A are met, or
(b) conditions 1B and 2B are met;
(but see also paragraph 27).
(2) For the purposes of sub-paragraph (1)(a)—
   (a) condition 1A is that the tax authorities for the administering member State have not received the return by the deadline for submitting it;
   (b) condition 2A is that those tax authorities have, in accordance with Article 60a of the Implementing Regulation, issued a reminder of the obligation to submit the return.
(3) For the purposes of sub-paragraph (1)(b)—
   (a) condition 1B is that, by the deadline for submitting the return, the tax authorities for the administering member State have received the return but have not received the amount of VAT shown on the return as payable by the person in respect of the tax period;
   (b) condition 2B is that those tax authorities have, in accordance with Article 60a of the Implementing Regulation, issued a reminder of the VAT outstanding.
(4) The Commissioners may serve on a person who is in default in respect of a tax period a notice (a "special surcharge liability notice") specifying a period—
   (a) ending on the first anniversary of the last day of that tax period, and
   (b) beginning on the date of the notice.
(5) A period specified under sub-paragraph (4) is a "special surcharge period".
(6) If a special surcharge liability notice is served in respect of a tax period which ends at or before the end of an existing special surcharge period, the special surcharge period specified in that notice must be expressed as a continuation of the existing special surcharge period (so that the existing period and its extension are regarded as a single special surcharge period).][1], [2]

Amendments—[1] Sch 3BA inserted by FA 2014 s 103, Sch 22 para 1 with effect in relation to supplies made on or after 1 January 2015, except in so far as it confers power to make regulations in which case it has effect from 17 July 2014. No registration under Sch 3BA may take effect before 1 January 2015. A request for registration under Sch 3BA that is made before 1 October 2014 is to be treated for the purposes of Article 57d of Implementing Regulation (EU) No 282/2011 (registration to have effect from first day of subsequent quarter) as if it were made on that date (FA 2014 Sch 22 para 24).
[2] Schedule 3BA repealed by the Taxation (Cross-border Trade) Act 2018 s 43, Sch 8 paras 1, 87 with effect from IP completion day (11pm on 31 December 2020), by virtue of SI 2020/1642 reg 4(b).
Saving provision—Schedule 3BA continues to apply in relation to supplies made before IP completion day despite its repeal by TCTA 2018 Sch 8, para 87. To the extent that it continues to apply, Sch 3BA has effect subject to such modifications as may be specified in a notice published by the Commissioners (see SI 2020/1495, reg 15).
Any references to VATA 1994, Schs 3B or 3BA (other than those mentioned above) that have been repealed by TCTA 2018 Sch 8 continue to apply in relation to supplies made before IP completion day as if they had not been repealed, but only to the extent that Schs 3B and 3BA continue to have effect in accordance with SI 2020/1495. To the extent that they continue to apply, references to VATA 1994, Schs 3B or 3BA have effect subject to such modifications as may be specified in a notice published by the Commissioners (see SI 2020/1495, reg 16).

[Further default after service of notice

26—(1) If a person on whom a special surcharge liability notice has been served—
   (a) is in default in respect of a tax period ending within the special surcharge period specified in (or extended by) that notice, and
   (b) has outstanding special scheme VAT for that tax period,
the person is to be liable to a surcharge of the amount given by sub-paragraph (2).
(2) The surcharge is equal to whichever is the greater of—
   (a) £30, and
   (b) the specified percentage of the person's outstanding special scheme VAT for the tax period.
(3) The specified percentage depends on whether the tax period is the first, second or third etc in the default period in respect of which the person is in default and has outstanding special scheme VAT, and is—
   (a) for the first such tax period, 2%;
   (b) for the second such tax period, 5%;
   (c) for the third such tax period, 10%;
   (d) for each such tax period after the third, 15%.
(4) "Special scheme VAT", in relation to a person, means VAT that the person is liable to pay to the tax authorities for the administering member State under a non-UK special scheme in respect of supplies of scheme services treated as made in the United Kingdom.
(5) A person has "outstanding special scheme VAT" for a tax period if some or all of the special scheme VAT for which the person is liable in respect of that period has not been paid by the deadline for the person to submit a non-UK return for that period (and the amount unpaid is referred to in sub-paragraph (2)(b) as "the person's outstanding special scheme VAT" for the tax period).][1], [2]

Amendments—[1] Sch 3BA inserted by FA 2014 s 103, Sch 22 para 1 with effect in relation to supplies made on or after 1 January 2015, except in so far as it confers power to make regulations in which case it has effect from 17 July 2014. No registration under Sch 3BA may take effect before 1 January 2015. A request for registration under Sch 3BA that is made before 1 October 2014 is to be treated for the purposes of Article 57d of Implementing Regulation (EU) No 282/2011 (registration to have effect from first day of subsequent quarter) as if it were made on that date (FA 2014 Sch 22 para 24).

² Schedule 3BA repealed by the Taxation (Cross-border Trade) Act 2018 s 43, Sch 8 paras 1, 87 with effect from IP completion day (11pm on 31 December 2020), by virtue of SI 2020/1642 reg 4(b).

Saving provision—Schedule 3BA continues to apply in relation to supplies made before IP completion day despite its repeal by TCTA 2018 Sch 8, para 87. To the extent that it continues to apply, Sch 3BA has effect subject to such modifications as may be specified in a notice published by the Commissioners (see SI 2020/1495, reg 15).

Any references to VATA 1994, Schs 3B or 3BA (other than those mentioned above) that have been repealed by TCTA 2018 Sch 8 continue to apply in relation to supplies made before IP completion day as if they had not been repealed, but only to the extent that Schs 3B and 3BA continue to have effect in accordance with SI 2020/1495. To the extent that they continue to apply, references to VATA 1994, Schs 3B or 3BA have effect subject to such modifications as may be specified in a notice published by the Commissioners (see SI 2020/1495, reg 16).

[Default surcharge: exceptions for reasonable excuse etc

27—(1) A person who would otherwise have been liable to a surcharge under paragraph 26(1) is not to be liable to the surcharge if the person satisfies the Commissioners or, on appeal, the tribunal that, in the case of a default which is material to the surcharge—
   (a) the non-UK return or, as the case may be, the VAT shown on that return, was despatched at such a time and in such manner that it was reasonable to expect that it would be received by the tax authorities for the administering member State within the appropriate time limit, or
   (b) there is a reasonable excuse for the return or the VAT not having been so despatched.
(2) Where sub-paragraph (1) applies to a person—
   (a) the person is treated as not having been in default in respect of the tax period in question, and
   (b) accordingly, any special surcharge liability notice the service of which depended on that default is regarded as not having been served.
(3) A default is "material" to a surcharge if—
   (a) it is the default which gives rise to the surcharge, under paragraph 26(1), or
   (b) it is a default which was taken into account in the service of the special surcharge liability notice on which the surcharge depends and the person concerned has not previously been liable to a surcharge in respect of a tax period ending within the special surcharge period specified in or extended by that notice.
(4) A default is left out of account for the purposes of paragraphs 25(4) and 26(1) if—
   (a) the conduct by virtue of which the person is in default is also conduct falling within section 69(1) (breaches of regulatory provisions), and
   (b) by reason of that conduct the person concerned is assessed to a penalty under that section.
(5) If the Commissioners, after consultation with the Treasury, so direct, a default in respect of a tax period specified in the direction is to be left out of account for the purposes of paragraphs 25(4) and 26(1).
(6) Section 71(1) (meaning of "reasonable excuse") applies for the purposes of this paragraph as it applies for the purposes of sections 59 to 70.]¹, ²

Amendments—¹ Sch 3BA inserted by FA 2014 s 103, Sch 22 para 1 with effect in relation to supplies made on or after 1 January 2015, except in so far as it confers power to make regulations in which case it has effect from 17 July 2014. No registration under Sch 3BA may take effect before 1 January 2015. A request for registration under Sch 3BA that is made before 1 October 2014 is to be treated for the purposes of Article 57d of Implementing Regulation (EU) No 282/2011 (registration to have effect from first day of subsequent quarter) as if it were made on that date (FA 2014 Sch 22 para 24).

² Schedule 3BA repealed by the Taxation (Cross-border Trade) Act 2018 s 43, Sch 8 paras 1, 87 with effect from IP completion day (11pm on 31 December 2020), by virtue of SI 2020/1642 reg 4(b).

Saving provision—Schedule 3BA continues to apply in relation to supplies made before IP completion day despite its repeal by TCTA 2018 Sch 8, para 87. To the extent that it continues to apply, Sch 3BA has effect subject to such modifications as may be specified in a notice published by the Commissioners (see SI 2020/1495, reg 15).

Any references to VATA 1994, Schs 3B or 3BA (other than those mentioned above) that have been repealed by TCTA 2018 Sch 8 continue to apply in relation to supplies made before IP completion day as if they had not been repealed, but only to the extent that Schs 3B and 3BA continue to have effect in accordance with SI 2020/1495. To the extent that they continue to apply, references to VATA 1994, Schs 3B or 3BA have effect subject to such modifications as may be specified in a notice published by the Commissioners (see SI 2020/1495, reg 16).

[Interest in certain cases of official error

28—(1) Section 78 (interest in certain cases of official error) applies as follows in relation to a case where, due to an error on the part of the Commissioners—
   (a) a person has accounted under a non-UK special scheme for an amount by way of UK VAT that was not UK VAT due from the person, and as a result the Commissioners are liable under paragraph 29 to pay (or repay) an amount to the person, or
   (b) (in a case not falling within paragraph (a)), a person has paid, in accordance with an obligation under a non-UK special scheme, an amount by way of UK VAT that was not UK VAT due from the person and which the Commissioners are in consequence liable to repay to the person.
(2) Section 78 has effect as if the condition in section 78(1)(a) were met in relation to that person.

(3) In the application of section 78 as a result of this paragraph, section 78(12)(b) is read as providing that any reference in that section to a return is to a return required to be made under a non-UK special scheme.

(4) In section 78, as it applies as a result of this section, *"output tax"* has the meaning that that expression would have if the reference in section 24(2) to a *"taxable person"* were to a *"person".]¹,* ²

Amendments—¹ Sch 3BA inserted by FA 2014 s 103, Sch 22 para 1 with effect in relation to supplies made on or after 1 January 2015, except in so far as it confers power to make regulations in which case it has effect from 17 July 2014. No registration under Sch 3BA may take effect before 1 January 2015. A request for registration under Sch 3BA that is made before 1 October 2014 is to be treated for the purposes of Article 57d of Implementing Regulation (EU) No 282/2011 (registration to have effect from first day of subsequent quarter) as if it were made on that date (FA 2014 Sch 22 para 24).

² Schedule 3BA repealed by the Taxation (Cross-border Trade) Act 2018 s 43, Sch 8 paras 1, 87 with effect from IP completion day (11pm on 31 December 2020), by virtue of SI 2020/1642 reg 4(b).

Saving provision—Schedule 3BA continues to apply in relation to supplies made before IP completion day despite its repeal by TCTA 2018 Sch 8, para 87. To the extent that it continues to apply, Sch 3BA has effect subject to such modifications as may be specified in a notice published by the Commissioners (see SI 2020/1495, reg 15).

Any references to VATA 1994, Schs 3B or 3BA (other than those mentioned above) that have been repealed by TCTA 2018 Sch 8 continue to apply in relation to supplies made before IP completion day as if they had not been repealed, but only to the extent that Schs 3B and 3BA continue to have effect in accordance with SI 2020/1495. To the extent that they continue to apply, references to VATA 1994, Schs 3B or 3BA have effect subject to such modifications as may be specified in a notice published by the Commissioners (see SI 2020/1495, reg 16).

[Overpayments

29—*(1) A person may make a claim if the person—*
  (a) has made a non-UK return for a tax period relating wholly or partly to supplies of scheme services treated as made in the United Kingdom,
  (b) has accounted to the tax authorities for the administering member State for VAT in respect of those supplies, and
  (c) in doing so has brought into account as UK VAT due to those authorities an amount ("the overpaid amount") that was not UK VAT due to them.
(2) A person may make a claim if the person has, as a participant in a non-UK special scheme, paid (to the tax authorities for the administering member State or to the Commissioners) an amount by way of UK VAT that was not UK VAT due ("the overpaid amount"), otherwise than in the circumstances mentioned in sub-paragraph (1)(c).
(3) A person who is or has been a participant in a non-UK special scheme may make a claim if the Commissioners—
  (a) have assessed the person to VAT for a tax period, and
  (b) in doing so, have brought into account as VAT an amount ("the amount not due") that was not VAT due.
(4) Where a person makes a claim under sub-paragraph (1) or (2), the Commissioners must repay the overpaid amount to the person.
(5) Where a person makes a claim under sub-paragraph (3), the Commissioners must credit the person with the amount not due.
(6) Where—
  (a) as a result of a claim under sub-paragraph (3) an amount is to be credited to a person, and
  (b) after setting any sums against that amount under or by virtue of this Act, some or all of the amount remains to the person's credit,
the Commissioners must pay (or repay) to the person so much of the amount as remains to the person's credit.
(7) The reference in sub-paragraph (1) to a claim is to a claim made—
  (a) by correcting, in accordance with Article 61 of the Implementing Regulation, the error in the non-UK return mentioned in sub-paragraph (1)(a), or
  (b) (after the expiry of the period during which the non-UK return may be amended under Article 61) to the Commissioners.
(8) Sub-paragraphs (1) and (2) do not require any amount to be repaid except so far as that is required by Article 63 of the Implementing Regulation.]¹, ²

Amendments—¹ Sch 3BA inserted by FA 2014 s 103, Sch 22 para 1 with effect in relation to supplies made on or after 1 January 2015, except in so far as it confers power to make regulations in which case it has effect from 17 July 2014. No registration under Sch 3BA may take effect before 1 January 2015. A request for registration under Sch 3BA that is made before 1 October 2014 is to be treated for the purposes of Article 57d of Implementing Regulation (EU) No 282/2011 (registration to have effect from first day of subsequent quarter) as if it were made on that date (FA 2014 Sch 22 para 24).

² Schedule 3BA repealed by the Taxation (Cross-border Trade) Act 2018 s 43, Sch 8 paras 1, 87 with effect from IP completion day (11pm on 31 December 2020), by virtue of SI 2020/1642 reg 4(b).

Saving provision—Schedule 3BA continues to apply in relation to supplies made before IP completion day despite its repeal by TCTA 2018 Sch 8, para 87. To the extent that it continues to apply, Sch 3BA has effect subject to such modifications as may be specified in a notice published by the Commissioners (see SI 2020/1495, reg 15).

Any references to VATA 1994, Schs 3B or 3BA (other than those mentioned above) that have been repealed by TCTA 2018 Sch 8 continue to apply in relation to supplies made before IP completion day as if they had not been repealed, but only to the extent that Schs 3B and 3BA continue to have effect in accordance with SI 2020/1495. To the extent that they continue to apply, references to VATA 1994, Schs 3B or 3BA have effect subject to such modifications as may be specified in a notice published by the Commissioners (see SI 2020/1495, reg 16).

[Overpayments: supplementary

30—*(1) In section 80—*
   (a) subsections (3) to (3C) (unjust enrichment), and
   (b) subsections (4A), (4C) and (6) (recovery by assessment of amounts wrongly credited),
have effect as if a claim under paragraph 29(1) were a claim under section 80(1), a claim under paragraph 29(2) were a claim under section 80(1B) and a claim under paragraph 29(3) were a claim under section 80(1A).
(2) In section 80(3) to (3C), (4A), (4C) and (6), as applied by sub-paragraph (1)—
   (a) references to the crediting of amounts are to be read as including the payment of amounts;
   (b) references to a prescribed accounting period include a tax period.
(3) The Commissioners are not liable to repay the overpaid amount on a claim made—
   (a) under paragraph 29(2),or
   (b) as mentioned in paragraph 29(7)(b),
if the claim is made more than 4 years after the relevant date.
(4) On a claim made under paragraph 29(3), the Commissioners are not liable to credit the amount not due if the claim is made more than 4 years after the relevant date.
(5) The "relevant date" is—
   (a) in the case of a claim under paragraph 29(1), the end of the tax period mentioned in paragraph 29(1)(a), except in the case of a claim resulting from an incorrect disclosure;
   (b) in the case of a claim under paragraph 29(1) resulting from an incorrect disclosure, the end of the tax period in which the disclosure was made;
   (c) in the case of a claim under paragraph 29(2), the date on which the payment was made;
   (d) in the case of a claim under paragraph 29(3), the end of the quarter in which the assessment was made.
(6) A person makes an "incorrect disclosure" where—
   (a) the person discloses to the tax authorities in question (whether the Commissioners or the tax authorities for the administering member State) that the person has not brought into account for a tax period an amount of UK VAT due for the period ("the disclosed amount"),
   (b) the disclosure is made in a later tax period, and
   (c) some or all of the disclosed amount is not in fact VAT due.][1], [2]

Regulations—VAT (Amendment) (No 3) Regulations, SI 2014/2430.
Amendments—[1] Sch 3BA inserted by FA 2014 s 103, Sch 22 para 1 with effect in relation to supplies made on or after 1 January 2015, except in so far as it confers power to make regulations in which case it has effect from 17 July 2014. No registration under Sch 3BA may take effect before 1 January 2015. A request for registration under Sch 3BA that is made before 1 October 2014 is to be treated for the purposes of Article 57d of Implementing Regulation (EU) No 282/2011 (registration to have effect from first day of subsequent quarter) as if it were made on that date (FA 2014 Sch 22 para 24).
[2] Schedule 3BA repealed by the Taxation (Cross-border Trade) Act 2018 s 43, Sch 8 paras 1, 87 with effect from IP completion day (11pm on 31 December 2020), by virtue of SI 2020/1642 reg 4(b).
Saving provision—Schedule 3BA continues to apply in relation to supplies made before IP completion day despite its repeal by TCTA 2018 Sch 8, para 87. To the extent that it continues to apply, Sch 3BA has effect subject to such modifications as may be specified in a notice published by the Commissioners (see SI 2020/1495, reg 15).
Any references to VATA 1994, Schs 3B or 3BA (other than those mentioned above) that have been repealed by TCTA 2018 Sch 8 continue to apply in relation to supplies made before IP completion day as if they had not been repealed, but only to the extent that Schs 3B and 3BA continue to have effect in accordance with SI 2020/1495. To the extent that they continue to apply, references to VATA 1994, Schs 3B or 3BA have effect subject to such modifications as may be specified in a notice published by the Commissioners (see SI 2020/1495, reg 16).

[Increase or decrease in consideration for a supply

31—*(1) This paragraph applies where—*
   (a) a person makes a non-UK return for a tax period ("the affected tax period") relating (wholly or partly) to a UK supply, and
   (b) after the return has been made the amount of the consideration for the UK supply increases or decreases.
(2) The person must, in the tax period in which the increase or decrease is accounted for in the person's business accounts—
   (a) amend the non-UK return to take account of the increase or decrease, or
   (b) (if the period during which the person is entitled under Article 61 of the Implementing Regulation to amend the non-UK return has expired) notify the Commissioners of the adjustment needed to the figures in the non-UK return because of the increase or decrease.

(3) Where the change to which an amendment or notice under sub-paragraph (2) relates is an increase in the consideration for a UK supply, the person must pay to the tax authorities for the administering member State (in accordance with Article 62 of the Implementing Regulation) or, in a case falling within sub-paragraph (2)(b), the Commissioners, the difference between—
  (a) the amount of VAT that was chargeable on the supply before the increase in consideration, and
  (b) the amount of VAT that is chargeable in respect of the whole of the increased consideration for the supply.
(4) Where the change to which an amendment or notice under sub-paragraph (2) relates is a decrease in the consideration for a UK supply, the amendment or notice has effect as a claim; and where a claim is made the Commissioners must repay any VAT paid by the person that would not have been VAT due from the person had the consideration for the supply always been the decreased amount.
(5) The Commissioners may by regulations specify—
  (a) the latest time by which, and the form and manner in which, a claim or other notice under sub-paragraph (2)(b) must be given;
  (b) the latest time by which, and the form in which, a payment under sub-paragraph (3) must be made in a case within sub-paragraph (2)(b).
(6) A payment made under sub-paragraph (3) in a case within sub-paragraph (2)(a) must be made before the end of the tax period referred to in sub-paragraph (2).
(7) In this paragraph "UK supply" means a supply of scheme services that is treated as made in the United Kingdom.]¹, ²

Regulations—VAT (Amendment) (No 3) Regulations, SI 2014/2430.
Amendments—¹ Sch 3BA inserted by FA 2014 s 103, Sch 22 para 1 with effect in relation to supplies made on or after 1 January 2015, except in so far as it confers power to make regulations in which case it has effect from 17 July 2014.
No registration under Sch 3BA may take effect before 1 January 2015. A request for registration under Sch 3BA that is made before 1 October 2014 is to be treated for the purposes of Article 57d of Implementing Regulation (EU) No 282/2011 (registration to have effect from first day of subsequent quarter) as if it were made on that date (FA 2014 Sch 22 para 24).
² Schedule 3BA repealed by the Taxation (Cross-border Trade) Act 2018 s 43, Sch 8 paras 1, 87 with effect from IP completion day (11pm on 31 December 2020), by virtue of SI 2020/1642 reg 4(b).
Saving provision—Schedule 3BA continues to apply in relation to supplies made before IP completion day despite its repeal by TCTA 2018 Sch 8, para 87. To the extent that it continues to apply, Sch 3BA has effect subject to such modifications as may be specified in a notice published by the Commissioners (see SI 2020/1495, reg 15).
Any references to VATA 1994, Schs 3B or 3BA (other than those mentioned above) that have been repealed by TCTA 2018 Sch 8 continue to apply in relation to supplies made before IP completion day as if they had not been repealed, but only to the extent that Schs 3B and 3BA continue to have effect in accordance with SI 2020/1495. To the extent that they continue to apply, references to VATA 1994, Schs 3B or 3BA have effect subject to such modifications as may be specified in a notice published by the Commissioners (see SI 2020/1495, reg 16).

[Bad debts

32 *Where a participant in a non-UK special scheme—*
  (a) has submitted a non-UK return to the tax authorities for the administering member State, and
  (b) amends the return to take account of the writing-off as a bad debt of the whole or part of the consideration for a supply of scheme services that is treated as made in the United Kingdom,
the amending of the return may be treated as the making of a claim to the Commissioners for the purposes of section 36(2) (bad debts: claim for refund of VAT).]¹, ²

Regulations—VAT (Amendment) (No 3) Regulations, SI 2014/2430.
Amendments—¹ Sch 3BA inserted by FA 2014 s 103, Sch 22 para 1 with effect in relation to supplies made on or after 1 January 2015, except in so far as it confers power to make regulations in which case it has effect from 17 July 2014.
No registration under Sch 3BA may take effect before 1 January 2015. A request for registration under Sch 3BA that is made before 1 October 2014 is to be treated for the purposes of Article 57d of Implementing Regulation (EU) No 282/2011 (registration to have effect from first day of subsequent quarter) as if it were made on that date (FA 2014 Sch 22 para 24).
² Schedule 3BA repealed by the Taxation (Cross-border Trade) Act 2018 s 43, Sch 8 paras 1, 87 with effect from IP completion day (11pm on 31 December 2020), by virtue of SI 2020/1642 reg 4(b).
Saving provision—Schedule 3BA continues to apply in relation to supplies made before IP completion day despite its repeal by TCTA 2018 Sch 8, para 87. To the extent that it continues to apply, Sch 3BA has effect subject to such modifications as may be specified in a notice published by the Commissioners (see SI 2020/1495, reg 15).
Any references to VATA 1994, Schs 3B or 3BA (other than those mentioned above) that have been repealed by TCTA 2018 Sch 8 continue to apply in relation to supplies made before IP completion day as if they had not been repealed, but only to the extent that Schs 3B and 3BA continue to have effect in accordance with SI 2020/1495. To the extent that they continue to apply, references to VATA 1994, Schs 3B or 3BA have effect subject to such modifications as may be specified in a notice published by the Commissioners (see SI 2020/1495, reg 16).

[Records relating to supplies in UK

33—*(1) A person who is a participant in a non-UK special scheme must keep records of the transactions which the person enters into for the purposes of, or in connection with, relevant supplies.*

(2) A supply made by a participant in a non-UK special scheme is a "relevant supply" if—
  (a) the value of the supply must be accounted for in a return required to be made by the participant under the non-UK special scheme, and
  (b) the supply is treated as made in the United Kingdom.
(3) The records must be sufficiently detailed to enable the Commissioners to determine whether any special scheme return submitted in respect of the supplies is correct.
(4) The records must be made available on request to the Commissioners by electronic means.
(5) Records must be kept for 10 years beginning with the 1 January following the date on which the transaction was entered into.]^1,^{2}

Amendments—^{1} Sch 3BA inserted by FA 2014 s 103, Sch 22 para 1 with effect in relation to supplies made on or after 1 January 2015, except in so far as it confers power to make regulations in which case it has effect from 17 July 2014.
No registration under Sch 3BA may take effect before 1 January 2015. A request for registration under Sch 3BA that is made before 1 October 2014 is to be treated for the purposes of Article 57d of Implementing Regulation (EU) No 282/2011 (registration to have effect from first day of subsequent quarter) as if it were made on that date (FA 2014 Sch 22 para 24).
^{2} Schedule 3BA repealed by the Taxation (Cross-border Trade) Act 2018 s 43, Sch 8 paras 1, 87 with effect from IP completion day (11pm on 31 December 2020), by virtue of SI 2020/1642 reg 4(b).
Saving provision—Schedule 3BA continues to apply in relation to supplies made before IP completion day despite its repeal by TCTA 2018 Sch 8, para 87. To the extent that it continues to apply, Sch 3BA has effect subject to such modifications as may be specified in a notice published by the Commissioners (see SI 2020/1495, reg 15).
Any references to VATA 1994, Schs 3B or 3BA (other than those mentioned above) that have been repealed by TCTA 2018 Sch 8 continue to apply in relation to supplies made before IP completion day as if they had not been repealed, but only to the extent that Schs 3B and 3BA continue to have effect in accordance with SI 2020/1495. To the extent that they continue to apply, references to VATA 1994, Schs 3B or 3BA have effect subject to such modifications as may be specified in a notice published by the Commissioners (see SI 2020/1495, reg 16).

[Penalties for errors: disclosure

34 Where a person corrects a non-UK return in a way that constitutes telling the tax authorities for the administering member State about—
  (a) an inaccuracy in the return,
  (b) a supply of false information, or
  (c) a withholding of information,
the person is regarded as telling HMRC about that for the purposes of paragraph 9 of Schedule 24 to the Finance Act 2007.]^1, ^{2}

Amendments—^{1} Sch 3BA inserted by FA 2014 s 103, Sch 22 para 1 with effect in relation to supplies made on or after 1 January 2015, except in so far as it confers power to make regulations in which case it has effect from 17 July 2014.
No registration under Sch 3BA may take effect before 1 January 2015. A request for registration under Sch 3BA that is made before 1 October 2014 is to be treated for the purposes of Article 57d of Implementing Regulation (EU) No 282/2011 (registration to have effect from first day of subsequent quarter) as if it were made on that date (FA 2014 Sch 22 para 24).
^{2} Schedule 3BA repealed by the Taxation (Cross-border Trade) Act 2018 s 43, Sch 8 paras 1, 87 with effect from IP completion day (11pm on 31 December 2020), by virtue of SI 2020/1642 reg 4(b).
Saving provision—Schedule 3BA continues to apply in relation to supplies made before IP completion day despite its repeal by TCTA 2018 Sch 8, para 87. To the extent that it continues to apply, Sch 3BA has effect subject to such modifications as may be specified in a notice published by the Commissioners (see SI 2020/1495, reg 15).
Any references to VATA 1994, Schs 3B or 3BA (other than those mentioned above) that have been repealed by TCTA 2018 Sch 8 continue to apply in relation to supplies made before IP completion day as if they had not been repealed, but only to the extent that Schs 3B and 3BA continue to have effect in accordance with SI 2020/1495. To the extent that they continue to apply, references to VATA 1994, Schs 3B or 3BA have effect subject to such modifications as may be specified in a notice published by the Commissioners (see SI 2020/1495, reg 16).

[Set-offs

35 Where a participant in a non-UK special scheme is liable to pay UK VAT to the tax authorities for the administering member State in accordance with the scheme, the UK VAT is regarded for the purposes of section 130(6) of the Finance Act 2008 (set-off: England, Wales and Northern Ireland) as payable to the Commissioners.]^1, ^{2}

Amendments—^{1} Sch 3BA inserted by FA 2014 s 103, Sch 22 para 1 with effect in relation to supplies made on or after 1 January 2015, except in so far as it confers power to make regulations in which case it has effect from 17 July 2014.
No registration under Sch 3BA may take effect before 1 January 2015. A request for registration under Sch 3BA that is made before 1 October 2014 is to be treated for the purposes of Article 57d of Implementing Regulation (EU) No 282/2011 (registration to have effect from first day of subsequent quarter) as if it were made on that date (FA 2014 Sch 22 para 24).
^{2} Schedule 3BA repealed by the Taxation (Cross-border Trade) Act 2018 s 43, Sch 8 paras 1, 87 with effect from IP completion day (11pm on 31 December 2020), by virtue of SI 2020/1642 reg 4(b).
Saving provision—Schedule 3BA continues to apply in relation to supplies made before IP completion day despite its repeal by TCTA 2018 Sch 8, para 87. To the extent that it continues to apply, Sch 3BA has effect subject to such modifications as may be specified in a notice published by the Commissioners (see SI 2020/1495, reg 15).
Any references to VATA 1994, Schs 3B or 3BA (other than those mentioned above) that have been repealed by TCTA 2018 Sch 8 continue to apply in relation to supplies made before IP completion day as if they had not been repealed, but only to the extent

that Schs 3B and 3BA continue to have effect in accordance with SI 2020/1495. To the extent that they continue to apply, references to VATA 1994, Schs 3B or 3BA have effect subject to such modifications as may be specified in a notice published by the Commissioners (see SI 2020/1495, reg 16).

[PART 5
APPEALS

36—*(1) An appeal lies to the tribunal with respect to any of the following—*
(a) a refusal to register a person under the Union scheme;
(b) the cancellation of the registration of any person under the Union scheme;
(c) a refusal to make a repayment under paragraph 29 (overpayments), or a decision by the Commissioners as to the amount of the repayment due under that provision;
(d) a refusal to make a repayment under paragraph 31(4) (decrease in consideration);
(e) any liability to a surcharge under paragraph 26 (default surcharge).
(2) Part 5 of this Act (appeals), and any order or regulations under that Part, have effect as if an appeal under this paragraph were an appeal which lies to the tribunal under section 83(1) (but not under any particular paragraph of that subsection).][1], [2]

Amendments—[1] Sch 3BA inserted by FA 2014 s 103, Sch 22 para 1 with effect in relation to supplies made on or after 1 January 2015, except in so far as it confers power to make regulations in which case it has effect from 17 July 2014. No registration under Sch 3BA may take effect before 1 January 2015. A request for registration under Sch 3BA that is made before 1 October 2014 is to be treated for the purposes of Article 57d of Implementing Regulation (EU) No 282/2011 (registration to have effect from first day of subsequent quarter) as if it were made on that date (FA 2014 Sch 22 para 24).
[2] Schedule 3BA repealed by the Taxation (Cross-border Trade) Act 2018 s 43, Sch 8 paras 1, 87 with effect from IP completion day (11pm on 31 December 2020), by virtue of SI 2020/1642 reg 4(b).
Saving provision—Schedule 3BA continues to apply in relation to supplies made before IP completion day despite its repeal by TCTA 2018 Sch 8, para 87. To the extent that it continues to apply, Sch 3BA has effect subject to such modifications as may be specified in a notice published by the Commissioners (see SI 2020/1495, reg 15).
Any references to VATA 1994, Schs 3B or 3BA (other than those mentioned above) that have been repealed by TCTA 2018 Sch 8 continue to apply in relation to supplies made before IP completion day as if they had not been repealed, but only to the extent that Schs 3B and 3BA continue to have effect in accordance with SI 2020/1495. To the extent that they continue to apply, references to VATA 1994, Schs 3B or 3BA have effect subject to such modifications as may be specified in a notice published by the Commissioners (see SI 2020/1495, reg 16).

[37 *Where the Commissioners have made an assessment under section 73 in reliance on paragraph 20 or 21—*
(a) section 83(1)(p)(i): (appeals against assessments under section 73(1) etc) applies as if the relevant non-UK return were a return under this Act, and
(b) the references in section 84(3) and (5) to the matters mentioned in section 83(1)(p) are to be read accordingly.][1], [2]

Amendments—[1] Sch 3BA inserted by FA 2014 s 103, Sch 22 para 1 with effect in relation to supplies made on or after 1 January 2015, except in so far as it confers power to make regulations in which case it has effect from 17 July 2014. No registration under Sch 3BA may take effect before 1 January 2015. A request for registration under Sch 3BA that is made before 1 October 2014 is to be treated for the purposes of Article 57d of Implementing Regulation (EU) No 282/2011 (registration to have effect from first day of subsequent quarter) as if it were made on that date (FA 2014 Sch 22 para 24).
[2] Schedule 3BA repealed by the Taxation (Cross-border Trade) Act 2018 s 43, Sch 8 paras 1, 87 with effect from IP completion day (11pm on 31 December 2020), by virtue of SI 2020/1642 reg 4(b).
Saving provision—Schedule 3BA continues to apply in relation to supplies made before IP completion day despite its repeal by TCTA 2018 Sch 8, para 87. To the extent that it continues to apply, Sch 3BA has effect subject to such modifications as may be specified in a notice published by the Commissioners (see SI 2020/1495, reg 15).
Any references to VATA 1994, Schs 3B or 3BA (other than those mentioned above) that have been repealed by TCTA 2018 Sch 8 continue to apply in relation to supplies made before IP completion day as if they had not been repealed, but only to the extent that Schs 3B and 3BA continue to have effect in accordance with SI 2020/1495. To the extent that they continue to apply, references to VATA 1994, Schs 3B or 3BA have effect subject to such modifications as may be specified in a notice published by the Commissioners (see SI 2020/1495, reg 16).

[PART 6
INTERPRETATION OF SCHEDULE

38—*(1) In this Schedule—*
"administering member State", in relation to a non-UK special scheme, has the meaning given by paragraph 14(2);
"the Implementing Regulation" means Council Implementing Regulation (EU) No 282/2011;
"non-UK return" means a return required to be made, for a tax period, under a non-UK special scheme;
"non-UK special scheme" has the meaning given by paragraph 14(1);
"participant", in relation to a non-UK special scheme, means a person who is identified under that scheme;
"qualifying supply of scheme services" has the meaning given by paragraph 4(2);

"relevant non-UK return" has the meaning given by paragraph 20(3);
"reporting period" is to be read in accordance with paragraph 9(2);
"scheme services" has the meaning given by paragraph 2;
"tax period" means a period for which a person is required to make a return under a non-UK special scheme;
"UK VAT" means VAT in respect of supplies of scheme services treated as made in the United Kingdom;
"Union scheme" has the meaning given by paragraph 3;
"Union scheme return" has the meaning given by paragraph 9(1).

(2) In relation to a non-UK special scheme (or a non-UK return), references in this Schedule to "the tax authorities" are to the tax authorities for the member State under whose law the non-UK special scheme is established.

(3) References in this Schedule to a supply of scheme services being "treated as made" in the United Kingdom are to its being treated as made in the United Kingdom by paragraph 15 of Schedule 4A.][1],[2]

Amendments—[1] Sch 3BA inserted by FA 2014 s 103, Sch 22 para 1 with effect in relation to supplies made on or after 1 January 2015, except in so far as it confers power to make regulations in which case it has effect from 17 July 2014.
No registration under Sch 3BA may take effect before 1 January 2015. A request for registration under Sch 3BA that is made before 1 October 2014 is to be treated for the purposes of Article 57d of Implementing Regulation (EU) No 282/2011 (registration to have effect from first day of subsequent quarter) as if it were made on that date (FA 2014 Sch 22 para 24).
[2] Schedule 3BA repealed by the Taxation (Cross-border Trade) Act 2018 s 43, Sch 8 paras 1, 87 with effect from IP completion day (11pm on 31 December 2020), by virtue of SI 2020/1642 reg 4(b).

Saving provision—Schedule 3BA continues to apply in relation to supplies made before IP completion day despite its repeal by TCTA 2018 Sch 8, para 87. To the extent that it continues to apply, Sch 3BA has effect subject to such modifications as may be specified in a notice published by the Commissioners (see SI 2020/1495, reg 15).

Any references to VATA 1994, Schs 3B or 3BA (other than those mentioned above) that have been repealed by TCTA 2018 Sch 8 continue to apply in relation to supplies made before IP completion day as if they had not been repealed, but only to the extent that Schs 3B and 3BA continue to have effect in accordance with SI 2020/1495. To the extent that they continue to apply, references to VATA 1994, Schs 3B or 3BA have effect subject to such modifications as may be specified in a notice published by the Commissioners (see SI 2020/1495, reg 16).

SCHEDULE 4
MATTERS TO BE TREATED AS SUPPLY OF GOODS OR SERVICES
Section 5

1—(1) Any transfer of the whole property in goods is a supply of goods; but, subject to sub-paragraph (2) below, the transfer—
 (a) of any undivided share of the property, or
 (b) of the possession of goods,
is a supply of services.
(2) If the possession of goods is transferred—
 (a) under an agreement for the sale of the goods, or
 (b) under agreements which expressly contemplate that the property also will pass at some time in the future (determined by, or ascertainable from, the agreements but in any case not later than when the goods are fully paid for),
it is then in either case a supply of the goods.

Commentary—*De Voil Indirect Tax Service* **V3.112, V3.113**.

3 The supply of any form of power, heat, refrigeration [or other cooling,][1] or ventilation is a supply of goods.

Commentary—*De Voil Indirect Tax Service* **V3.178**.
Amendments—[1] Words inserted by F(No 3)A 2010 s 20(2) with effect in relation to supplies made on or after 1 January 2011.

4 The grant, assignment or surrender of a major interest in land is a supply of goods.

Commentary—*De Voil Indirect Tax Service* **V3.140A**.

5—(1) Subject to sub-paragraph (2) below, where goods forming part of the assets of a business are transferred or disposed of by or under the directions of the person carrying on the business so as no longer to form part of those assets, whether or not for a consideration, that is a supply by him of goods.
(2) Sub-paragraph (1) above does not apply where the transfer or disposal is—
 [(a) a business gift the cost of which, together with the cost of any other business gifts made to the same person in the same year, was not more than £50;][6]
 [(b) the provision to a person, otherwise than for a consideration, of a sample of goods.][9]
[(2ZA) In sub-paragraph (2) above—

"business gift" means a gift of goods that is made in the course or furtherance of the business in question;
"cost", in relation to a gift of goods, means the cost to the donor of acquiring or, as the case may be, producing the goods;
"the same year", in relation to a gift, means any period of twelve months that includes the day on which the gift is made.][7]
[(2A) For the purposes of determining the cost to the donor of acquiring or producing goods of which he has made a gift, where—
   (a) the acquisition by the donor of the goods, or anything comprised in the goods, was by means of a transfer of a business, or a part of a business, as a going concern,
   (b) the assets transferred by that transfer included those goods or that thing, and
   (c) the transfer of those assets is one falling by virtue of an order under section 5(3) (or under an enactment re-enacted in section 5(3)) to be treated as neither a supply of goods nor a supply of services,
the donor and his predecessor or, as the case may be, all of his predecessors shall be treated as if they were the same person.][4]
(3) . . . [9]
(4) Where by or under the directions of a person carrying on a business goods held or used for the purposes of the business are put to any private use or are used, or made available to any person for use, for any purpose other than a purpose of the business, whether or not for a consideration, that is a supply of services.
[(4A) Sub-paragraph (4) does not apply (despite paragraph 9(1)) to—
   (a) any interest in land,
   (b) any building or part of a building,
   (c) any civil engineering work or part of such a work,
   (d) any goods incorporated or to be incorporated in a building or civil engineering work (whether by being installed as fixtures or fittings or otherwise),
   (e) any ship, boat or other vessel, or
   (f) any aircraft.][8]
(5) Neither sub-paragraph (1) nor [sub-paragraph (4) above][1] shall require anything which a person carrying on a business does otherwise than for a consideration in relation to any goods to be treated as a supply except in a case where that person [or any of his predecessors is a person who (disregarding this paragraph) has or will become][3] entitled—
   [(a) under sections 25 and 26, to credit for the whole or any part of the VAT on the supply . . . [10] or importation of those goods or of anything comprised in them; or
   (b) under a scheme embodied in regulations made under section 39, to a repayment of VAT on the supply or importation of those goods or of anything comprised in them.][5]
[(5A) In relation to any goods or anything comprised in any goods, a person is the predecessor of another for the purposes of this paragraph if—
   (a) that other person is a person to whom he has transferred assets of his business by a transfer of that business, or a part of it, as a going concern;
   (b) those assets consisted of or included those goods or that thing; and
   (c) the transfer of the assets is one falling by virtue of an order under section 5(3) (or under an enactment re-enacted in section 5(3)) to be treated as neither a supply of goods nor a supply of services;
and references in this paragraph to a person's predecessors include references to the predecessors of his predecessors through any number of transfers.][4]
(6) Anything which is a supply of goods or services by virtue of sub-paragraph (1) or (4) above is to be treated as made in the course or furtherance of the business (if it would not otherwise be so treated); and in the case of a business carried on by an individual—
   (a) sub-paragraph (1) above applies to any transfer or disposition of goods in favour of himself personally; and
   (b) [sub-paragraph (4) above][1] applies to goods used, or made available for use, by himself personally.
[(7) The Treasury may by order substitute for the sum for the time being specified in sub-paragraph (2)(a) above such sum, not being less than £10, as they think fit.][2]

Commentary—*De Voil Indirect Tax Service* **V3.211, V3.212**.
Amendments—[1]   Words in sub-paras (5), (6)(b) substituted by FA 1995 s 33(1), (3)(a) and are deemed to have always had effect.
[2]   Sub-para (7) added by FA 1996 s 33(2).
[3]   Words in sub-paras (2)(a), (5) inserted by FA 1998 s 21 with effect for goods transferred or disposed of, or put to use, used or made available for use after 16 March 1998.
[4]   Sub-paras (2A), (5A) inserted by FA 1998 s 21 with effect for goods transferred or disposed of, or put to use, used or made available for use after 16 March 1998.

5 Words in sub-para (5) substituted by FA 2000 s 136(9), with effect for supplies made after 20 March 2000.
6 Words in sub-para (2)(a) substituted by FA 2003 s 21(2) with effect for gifts made after 30 September 2003.
7 Sub-para (2ZA) inserted by FA 2003 s 21(3) with effect for gifts made after 30 September 2003.
8 Sub-para (4A) inserted by F(No 3)A 2010 s 19, Sch 8 para 3(1) with effect from 1 January 2011. Note that this amendment does not apply in relation to an asset in respect of which the person in question or any of that person's predecessors incurred VAT before 1 January 2011 but, where VAT is incurred by such a person before that date in respect of the asset, VAT incurred by such a person on or after that date in respect of the asset is not to be treated as referable to that person's business purposes by virtue of sub-paras (4) and (6) if, and to the extent that, the asset is used or to be used for that person's private use or the private use of that person's staff, or more generally for purposes other than those of that person's business (F(No 3)A 2010 Sch 8 para 3(3), (4)). See also definitions in relation to this note in F(No 3)A 2010 Sch 8 para 3(5).
9 Sub-para (2)(b) substituted and sub-para (3) repealed, by FA 2011 s 74(1)–(3) with effect from 19 July 2011.
10 In sub-para (5)(a), word ", acquisition" repealed by the Taxation (Cross-border Trade) Act 2018 s 43, Sch 8 paras 1, 88(1), (2) with effect from IP completion day (11pm on 31 December 2020), by virtue of SI 2020/1642 reg 4(b).

6—(1) Where, in a case not falling within paragraph 5(1) above, goods forming part of the assets of any business—
  (a) are removed from any member State by or under the directions of the person carrying on the business; and
  (b) are so removed in the course or furtherance of that business for the purpose of being taken to a place in a member State other than that from which they are removed,
then, whether or not the removal is or is connected with a transaction for a consideration, that is a supply of goods by that person.
(2) Sub-paragraph (1) above does not apply—
  (a) to the removal of goods from any member State in the course of their removal from one part of that member State to another part of the same member State; or
  (b) to goods which have been removed from a place outside the member States for entry into the territory of the European Union and are removed from a member State before the time when any EU customs debt in respect of any EU customs duty on their entry into that territory would be incurred.
[(3) Sub-paragraph (1) above is subject to paragraph 2 of Schedule 4B (call-off stock arrangements).][1], [2]

Commentary—De Voil Indirect Tax Service **V3.213**.

Amendments—[1] Sub-para (3) inserted by FA 2020 s 80(1), (4) with effect from 22 July 2020.
[2] Para 6 repealed by the Taxation (Cross-border Trade) Act 2018 s 43, Sch 8 paras 1, 88(1), (3) with effect from IP completion day (11pm on 31 December 2020), by virtue of SI 2020/1642 reg 4(b).

7 Where in the case of a business carried on by a taxable person goods forming part of the assets of the business are, under any power exercisable by another person, sold by the other in or towards satisfaction of a debt owed by the taxable person, they shall be deemed to be supplied by the taxable person in the course or furtherance of his business.

Commentary—De Voil Indirect Tax Service **V3.226**.

8—(1) Where a person ceases to be a taxable person, any goods then forming part of the assets of a business carried on by him shall be deemed to be supplied by him in the course or furtherance of his business immediately before he ceases to be a taxable person, unless—
  (a) the business is transferred as a going concern to another taxable person; or
  (b) the business is carried on by another person who, under regulations made under section 46(4), is treated as a taxable person; or
  (c) the VAT on the deemed supply would not be more than [£1,000][1].
(2) This paragraph does not apply to any goods in the case of which the taxable person can show to the satisfaction of the Commissioners—
  (a) that no credit for input tax has been allowed to him in respect of the supply of the goods [or their importation into the United Kingdom][3];
  (b) that the goods did not become his as part of the assets of a business[, or part of a business,][2] which was transferred to him as a going concern by another taxable person; and
  (c) that he has not obtained relief in respect of the goods under section 4 of the Finance Act 1973.
(3) This paragraph does not apply where a person ceases to be a taxable person in consequence of having been certified under section 54.
(4) The Treasury may by order increase or further increase the sum specified in sub-paragraph (1)(c) above.

Commentary—De Voil Indirect Tax Service **V3.261**.

Amendments—[1] Figure in para (1)(c) substituted by the VAT (Deemed Supply of Goods) Order, SI 2000/266, art 2 with effect from 1 April 2000.
[2] Words in sub-para (2)(b) inserted by FA 2007 s 100(9), (10) with effect in relation to transfers pursuant to contracts entered into on or after 1 September 2007.

[3] In sub-para (2)(a), words substituted for words ", their acquisition from another member State or their importation from a place outside the member States", by the Taxation (Cross-border Trade) Act 2018 s 43, Sch 8 paras 1, 88(1), (4) with effect from IP completion day (11pm on 31 December 2020), by virtue of SI 2020/1642 reg 4(b).

9—(1) Subject to sub-paragraphs (2) and (3) below, paragraphs 5 to 8 above have effect in relation to land forming part of the assets of, or held or used for the purposes of, a business as if it were goods forming part of the assets of, or held or used for the purposes of, a business.
(2) In the application of those paragraphs by virtue of sub-paragraph (1) above, references to transfer, disposition or sale shall have effect as references to the grant or assignment of any interest in, right over or licence to occupy the land concerned.
(3) Except in relation to—
   (a) the grant or assignment of a major interest; or
   (b) a grant or assignment otherwise than for a consideration,
in the application of paragraph 5(1) above by virtue of sub-paragraph (1) above the reference to a supply of goods shall have effect as a reference to a supply of services.
[(4) In this paragraph "grant" includes surrender.][1]
Commentary—*De Voil Indirect Tax Service* **V3.211**.
Amendments—[1] Sub-para (4) inserted by FA 2007 s 99(1), (3), (7) with effect for surrenders on or after 21 March 2007.

[SCHEDULE 4A
PLACE OF SUPPLY OF SERVICES: SPECIAL RULES][1]
Section 7A

Amendments—
[1] Sch 4A inserted by FA 2009 s 76, Sch 36 paras 1, 11 with effect in relation to supplies made on or after 1 January 2010.

PART 1
GENERAL EXCEPTIONS
Services relating to land

1—(1) A supply of services to which this paragraph applies is to be treated as made in the country in which the land in connection with which the supply is made is situated.
(2) This paragraph applies to—
   (a) the grant, assignment or surrender of any interest in or right over land,
   (b) the grant, assignment or surrender of a personal right to call for or be granted any interest in or right over land,
   (c) the grant, assignment or surrender of a licence to occupy land or any other contractual right exercisable over or in relation to land (including the provision of holiday accommodation, seasonal pitches for caravans and facilities at caravan parks for persons for whom such pitches are provided and pitches for tents and camping facilities),
   (d) the provision in an hotel, inn, boarding house or similar establishment of sleeping accommodation or of accommodation in rooms which are provided in conjunction with sleeping accommodation or for the purpose of a supply of catering,
   (e) any works of construction, demolition, conversion, reconstruction, alteration, enlargement, repair or maintenance of a building or civil engineering work, and
   (f) services such as are supplied by estate agents, auctioneers, architects, surveyors, engineers and others involved in matters relating to land.
(3) In sub-paragraph (2)(c) "holiday accommodation" includes any accommodation in a building, hut (including a beach hut or chalet), caravan, houseboat or tent which is advertised or held out as holiday accommodation or as suitable for holiday or leisure use.
(4) In sub-paragraph (2)(d) "similar establishment" includes premises in which there is provided furnished sleeping accommodation, whether with or without the provision of board or facilities for the preparation of food, which are used by, or held out as being suitable for use by, visitors or travellers.][1]
Commentary—*De Voil Indirect Tax Service* **V3.188**.
Amendments—[1] Sch 4A inserted by FA 2009 s 76, Sch 36 paras 1, 11 with effect in relation to supplies made on or after 1 January 2010.

[*Passenger transport*

2—(1) A supply of services consisting of the transportation of passengers (or of any luggage or motor vehicles accompanying passengers) is to be treated as made in the country in which the transportation takes place, and (in a case where it takes place in more than one country) in proportion to the distances covered in each.
(2) For the purposes of sub-paragraph (1) transportation which takes place partly outside the territorial jurisdiction of a country is to be treated as taking place wholly in the country if—

(a) it takes place in the course of a journey between two points in the country (whether or not as part of a longer journey involving travel to or from another country), and

(b) the means of transport used does not (except in an emergency or involuntarily) stop, put in or land in another country in the course of the journey between those two points.

(3) For the purposes of sub-paragraph (1) a pleasure cruise is to be regarded as the transportation of passengers (so that services provided as part of a pleasure cruise are to be treated as supplied in the same place as the transportation of the passengers).

(4) In sub-paragraph (3) "pleasure cruise" includes a cruise wholly or partly for education or training.]¹

Commentary—*De Voil Indirect Tax Service* **V3.189**.

Amendments—¹ Sch 4A inserted by FA 2009 s 76, Sch 36 paras 1, 11 with effect in relation to supplies made on or after 1 January 2010.

[Hiring of means of transport

3—(1) A supply of services consisting of the short-term hiring of a means of transport is to be treated as made in the country in which the means of transport is actually put at the disposal of the person by whom it is hired.

But this is subject to sub-paragraphs (3) and (4).

(2) For the purposes of this Schedule the hiring of a means of transport is "short-term" if it is hired for a continuous period not exceeding—

(a) if the means of transport is a vessel, 90 days, and

(b) otherwise, 30 days.

(3) Where—

(a) a supply of services consisting of the hiring of a means of transport would otherwise be treated as made in the United Kingdom, and

(b) the services are to any extent effectively used and enjoyed [outside the United Kingdom]²,

the supply is to be treated to that extent as made [outside the United Kingdom]².

(4) Where—

(a) a supply of services consisting of the hiring of a means of transport would otherwise be treated as made [outside the United Kingdom]², and

(b) the services are to any extent effectively used and enjoyed in the United Kingdom,

the supply is to be treated to that extent as made in the United Kingdom.]¹

Commentary—*De Voil Indirect Tax Service* **V3.194**.

Amendments—¹ Sch 4A inserted by FA 2009 s 76, Sch 36 paras 1, 11 with effect in relation to supplies made on or after 1 January 2010.

² In sub-paras (3)(b), (4)(a), words substituted for words "in a country which is not a member State", and in words following sub-para (3)(b), words substituted for words "in that country", by the Taxation (Cross-border Trade) Act 2018 s 43, Sch 8 paras 1, 89(1), (2) with effect from IP completion day (11pm on 31 December 2020), by virtue of SI 2020/1642 reg 4(b).

[Cultural, educational and entertainment services etc

4—(1) A supply of services to which this paragraph applies is to be treated as made in the country in which the services are physically carried out.

(2) This paragraph applies to the provision of—

(a) services relating to cultural, artistic, sporting, scientific, educational, entertainment or similar activities (including fairs and exhibitions), and

(b) ancillary services relating to such activities, including services of organisers of such activities.]¹, ²

Commentary—*De Voil Indirect Tax Service* **V3.192**.

Amendments—¹ Sch 4A inserted by FA 2009 s 76, Sch 36 paras 1, 11 with effect in relation to supplies made on or after 1 January 2010.

² Para 4 repealed by FA 2009 s 76, Sch 36 paras 1, 15(2) with effect in relation to supplies made on or after 1 January 2011.

[Restaurant and catering services . . .

[5 A supply of restaurant or catering services is to be treated as made in the country in which the services are physically carried out.]¹

Commentary—*De Voil Indirect Tax Service* **V3.198**.

Amendments—¹ In heading above para 5 word ": general" repealed, and para 5 substituted, by the Taxation (Cross-border Trade) Act 2018 s 43, Sch 8 paras 1, 89(1), (3), (4) with effect from IP completion day (11pm on 31 December 2020), by virtue of SI 2020/1642 reg 4(b). Para 5 previously read as follows—

> 5—
>
> "(1) A supply of services to which this paragraph applies is to be treated as made in the country in which the services are physically carried out.
>
> (2) This paragraph applies to the provision of restaurant services and the provision of catering services, other than the provision of services to which paragraph 6 applies.".

[EC on-board restaurant and catering services

6—(1) A supply of services consisting of
   (a) the provision of restaurant services, or
   (b) the provision of catering services,
on board a ship, aircraft or train in connection with the transportation of passengers during an intra-EC passenger transport operation is to be treated as made in the country in which the relevant point of departure is located.

(2) An intra-EC passenger transport operation is a passenger transport operation which, or so much of a passenger transport operation as,—
   (a) has as the first place at which passengers can embark a place which is within the EC,
   (b) has as the last place at which passengers who embarked in a member State can disembark a place which is within the EC, and
   (c) does not include a stop at a place which is not within the EC and at which passengers can embark or passengers who embarked in a member State can disembark.

(3) "Relevant point of departure", in relation to an intra-EC passenger transport operation, is the first place in the intra-EC passenger transport operation at which passengers can embark.

(4) A place is within the EC if it is within any member State.

(5) For the purposes of this paragraph the return stage of a return passenger transport operation is to be regarded as a separate passenger transport operation; and for this purpose—
   (a) a return passenger transport operation is one which takes place in more than one country but is expected to end in the country in which it begins, and
   (b) the return stage of a return passenger transport operation is the part of it which ends in the country in which it began and begins with the last stop at a place at which there has not been a previous stop during it.][1], [2]

Commentary—*De Voil Indirect Tax Service* **V3.198**.
Amendments—[1]   Sch 4A inserted by FA 2009 s 76, Sch 36 paras 1, 11 with effect in relation to supplies made on or after 1 January 2010.
[2]   Para 6 and preceding heading repealed by the Taxation (Cross-border Trade) Act 2018 s 43, Sch 8 paras 1, 89(1), (5) with effect from IP completion day (11pm on 31 December 2020), by virtue of SI 2020/1642 reg 4(b).

[Hiring of goods

7—(1) Where—
   (a) a supply of services consisting of the hiring of any goods other than a means of transport would otherwise be treated as made in the United Kingdom, and
   (b) the services are to any extent effectively used and enjoyed [outside the United Kingdom][2],
the supply is to be treated to that extent as made [outside the United Kingdom][2].

(2) Where—
   (a) a supply of services consisting of the hiring of any goods other than a means of transport would otherwise be treated as made [outside the United Kingdom][2], and
   (b) the services are to any extent effectively used and enjoyed in the United Kingdom,
the supply is to be treated to that extent as made in the United Kingdom.][1]

Amendments—[1]   Sch 4A inserted by FA 2009 s 76, Sch 36 paras 1, 11 with effect in relation to supplies made on or after 1 January 2010.
[2]   In sub-paras (1)(b), (2)(a), words substituted for words "in a country which is not a member State", and in words following sub-para (1)(b), words substituted for words "in that country", by the Taxation (Cross-border Trade) Act 2018 s 43, Sch 8 paras 1, 89(1), (6) with effect from IP completion day (11pm on 31 December 2020), by virtue of SI 2020/1642 reg 4(b).

[. . . broadcasting services

8—(1) This paragraph applies to a supply of services consisting of the provision of—
   (a)   . . .[2]
   (b) radio or television broadcasting services.

(2)   . . .[2]

(3) Where—
   (a) a supply of services to which this paragraph applies would otherwise be treated as made in the United Kingdom, and
   (b) the services are to any extent effectively used and enjoyed [outside the United Kingdom][3],
the supply is to be treated to that extent as made [outside the United Kingdom][3].

(4) Where—
   (a) a supply of services to which this paragraph applies would otherwise be treated as made [outside the United Kingdom][3], and
   (b) the services are to any extent effectively used and enjoyed in the United Kingdom,
the supply is to be treated to that extent as made in the United Kingdom.][1]

Amendments—[1] Sch 4A inserted by FA 2009 s 76, Sch 36 paras 1, 11 with effect in relation to supplies made on or after 1 January 2010.
[2] In heading to para 8, words "Telecommunication and" repealed, and sub-paras (1)(a), (2) repealed, by the Value Added Tax (Place of Supply of Services) (Telecommunication Services) Order, SI 2017/778 art 2 with effect in relation to supplies of services made on or after 1 November 2017.
[3] In sub-paras (3)(b), (4)(a), words substituted for words "in a country which is not a member State", and in words following sub-para (3)(b), words substituted for words "in that country", by the Taxation (Cross-border Trade) Act 2018 s 43, Sch 8 paras 1, 89(1), (7) with effect from IP completion day (11pm on 31 December 2020), by virtue of SI 2020/1642 reg 4(b).

[PART 2
EXCEPTIONS RELATING TO SUPPLIES MADE TO RELEVANT BUSINESS PERSON

Electronically-supplied services

9—(1) Where—
  (a) a supply of services consisting of the provision of electronically supplied services to a relevant business person would otherwise be treated as made in the United Kingdom, and
  (b) the services are to any extent effectively used and enjoyed [outside the United Kingdom]², the supply is to be treated to that extent as made [outside the United Kingdom]².
(2) Where—
  (a) a supply of services consisting of the provision of electronically supplied services to a relevant business person would otherwise be treated as made [outside the United Kingdom]², and
  (b) the services are to any extent effectively used and enjoyed in the United Kingdom, the supply is to be treated to that extent as made in the United Kingdom.
(3) Examples of what are electronically supplied services for the purposes of this Schedule include—
  (a) website supply, web-hosting and distance maintenance of programmes and equipment,
  (b) the supply of software and the updating of software,
  (c) the supply of images, text and information, and the making available of databases,
  (d) the supply of music, films and games (including games of chance and gambling games),
  (e) the supply of political, cultural, artistic, sporting, scientific, educational or entertainment broadcasts (including broadcasts of events), and
  (f) the supply of distance teaching.
(4) But where the supplier of a service and the supplier's customer communicate via electronic mail, this does not of itself mean that the service provided is an electronically supplied service for the purposes of this Schedule.]¹

Amendments—[1] Sch 4A inserted by FA 2009 s 76, Sch 36 paras 1, 11 with effect in relation to supplies made on or after 1 January 2010.
[2] In sub-paras (1)(b), (2)(a), words substituted for words "in a country which is not a member State", and in words following sub-para (1)(b), words substituted for words "in that country", by the Taxation (Cross-border Trade) Act 2018 s 43, Sch 8 paras 1, 89(1), (8) with effect from IP completion day (11pm on 31 December 2020), by virtue of SI 2020/1642 reg 4(b).

[Admission to cultural, educational and entertainment activities etc

9A—(1) A supply to a relevant business person of services to which this paragraph applies is to be treated as made in the country in which the events in question actually take place.
(2) This paragraph applies to the provision of—
  (a) services in respect of admission to cultural, artistic, sporting, scientific, educational, entertainment or similar events (including fairs and exhibitions), and
  (b) ancillary services relating to admission to such events.]¹

Amendments—[1] Para 9A inserted by FA 2009 s 76, Sch 36 paras 1, 15(3) with effect in relation to supplies made on or after 1 January 2011.

[Transport of goods

9B Where—
  (a) a supply of services to a relevant business person consisting of the transportation of goods would otherwise be treated as made in the United Kingdom, and
  (b) the transportation takes place wholly [outside the United Kingdom]², the supply is to be treated as made [outside the United Kingdom]².]¹

Amendments—[1] Paras 9B, 9C inserted by the Value Added Tax (Place of Supply of Services) (Transport of Goods) Order, SI 2012/2787 art 2 with effect in relation to supplies made on or after 20 December 2012.
[2] In sub-para (b), words substituted for words "outside the member States", and in words following sub-para (b), words substituted for words "wholly outside the member States", by the Taxation (Cross-border Trade) Act 2018 s 43, Sch 8 paras 1, 89(1), (9) with effect from IP completion day (11pm on 31 December 2020), by virtue of SI 2020/1642 reg 4(b).

[Ancillary transport services]

9C—(1) Where—
  (a) a supply of services to a relevant business person consisting of ancillary transport services would otherwise be treated as made in the United Kingdom, and
  (b) the services are physically performed wholly [outside the United Kingdom]²,
the supply is to be treated as made [outside the United Kingdom]².
(2) In sub-paragraph (1)(a) "ancillary transport services" means loading, unloading, handling and similar activities.]¹

Amendments—¹ Paras 9B, 9C inserted by the Value Added Tax (Place of Supply of Services) (Transport of Goods) Order, SI 2012/2787 art 2 with effect in relation to supplies made on or after 20 December 2012.
² In sub-para (1)(b), words substituted for words "outside the member States", and in words following sub-para (1)(b), words substituted for words "wholly outside the member States", by the Taxation (Cross-border Trade) Act 2018 s 43, Sch 8 paras 1, 89(1), (10) with effect from IP completion day (11pm on 31 December 2020), by virtue of SI 2020/1642 reg 4(b).

[Repair services: contracts of insurance]

9D—(1) This paragraph applies to a supply of services consisting of the repair of tangible movable property where—
  (a) the supply is pursuant to a claim made under a contract of insurance, and
  (b) the supply is made to a relevant business person who is not the person insured.
(2) Where—
  (a) a supply of services to which this paragraph applies would otherwise be treated as made in the United Kingdom, and
  (b) the services are effectively used and enjoyed [outside the United Kingdom]²,
the supply is to be treated as made [outside the United Kingdom]².
(3) Where—
  (a) a supply of services to which this paragraph applies would otherwise be treated as made [outside the United Kingdom]², and
  (b) the services are effectively used and enjoyed in the United Kingdom,
the supply is to be treated as made in the United Kingdom.]¹

Amendments—¹ Para 9D inserted by the Value Added Tax (Place of Supply of Services: Exceptions Relating to Supplies Made to Relevant Business Person) Order, SI 2016/726 art 2 with effect in relation to supplies made on or after 1 October 2016.
² In sub-paras (2)(b), (3)(a), words substituted for words "outside the territories of the member States", and in words following sub-para (2)(b), words substituted for words "where it is used and enjoyed", by the Taxation (Cross-border Trade) Act 2018 s 43, Sch 8 paras 1, 89(1), (11) with effect from IP completion day (11pm on 31 December 2020), by virtue of SI 2020/1642 reg 4(b).

[Telecommunication services]

9E—(1) This paragraph applies to a supply of services to a relevant business person consisting of the provision of telecommunication services.
(2) In this Schedule "telecommunication services" means services relating to the transmission, emission or reception of signals, writing, images and sounds or information of any nature by wire, radio, optical or other electromagnetic systems, including—
  (a) the related transfer or assignment of the right to use capacity for such transmission, emission or reception, and
  (b) the provision of access to global information networks.
(3) Where—
  (a) a supply of services to which this paragraph applies would otherwise be treated as made in the United Kingdom, and
  (b) the services are to any extent effectively used and enjoyed [outside the United Kingdom]²,
the supply is to be treated to that extent as made [outside the United Kingdom]².
(4) Where—
  (a) a supply of services to which this paragraph applies would otherwise be treated as made [outside the United Kingdom]², and
  (b) the services are to any extent effectively used and enjoyed in the United Kingdom, the supply is to be treated to that extent as made in the United Kingdom.]¹

Commentary—*De Voil Indirect Tax Service* **V3.193A**.
Amendments—¹ Para 9E inserted by the Value Added Tax (Place of Supply of Services) (Telecommunication Services) Order, SI 2017/778 art 3 with effect in relation to supplies of services made on or after 1 November 2017.
² In sub-paras (3)(b), (4)(a), words substituted for words "in a country which is not a member State", and in words following sub-para (3)(b), words substituted for words "in that country", by the Taxation (Cross-border Trade) Act 2018 s 43, Sch 8 paras 1, 89(1), (12) with effect from IP completion day (11pm on 31 December 2020), by virtue of SI 2020/1642 reg 4(b).

[PART 3]
EXCEPTIONS RELATING TO SUPPLIES NOT MADE TO RELEVANT BUSINESS PERSON

Intermediaries

10—(1) A supply of services to which this paragraph applies is to be treated as made in the same country as the supply to which it relates.
(2) This paragraph applies to a supply to a person who is not a relevant business person consisting of the making of arrangements for a supply by or to another person or of any other activity intended to facilitate the making of such a supply.][1]
Commentary—*De Voil Indirect Tax Service* **V3.195**.
Amendments—[1] Sch 4A inserted by FA 2009 s 76, Sch 36 paras 1, 11 with effect in relation to supplies made on or after 1 January 2010.

[Transport of goods . . .

11—(1) A supply of services to a person who is not a relevant business person consisting of the transportation of goods is to be treated as made in the country in which the transportation takes place, and (in a case where it takes place in more than one country) in proportion to the distances covered in each.
(2) For the purposes of sub-paragraph (1) transportation which takes place partly outside the territorial jurisdiction of a country is to be treated as taking place wholly in the country if—
    (*a*) it takes place in the course of a journey between two points in the country (whether or not as part of a longer journey involving travel to or from another country), and
    (*b*) the means of transport used does not (except in an emergency or involuntarily) stop, put in or land in another country in the course of the journey between those two points.
(3) . . . [2]][1]
Amendments—[1] Sch 4A inserted by FA 2009 s 76, Sch 36 paras 1, 11 with effect in relation to supplies made on or after 1 January 2010.
[2] In heading above para 11, word ": general" repealed, and sub-para (3) repealed, by the Taxation (Cross-border Trade) Act 2018 s 43, Sch 8 paras 1, 89(1), (13), (14) with effect from IP completion day (11pm on 31 December 2020), by virtue of SI 2020/1642 reg 4(*b*).
Sub-para (3) previously read as follows—
"(3) This paragraph does not apply to a transportation of goods beginning in one member State and ending in another (see paragraph 12).".

[Intra-Community transport of goods

12—A supply of services to a person who is not a relevant business person consisting of the transportation of goods which begins in one member State and ends in another is to be treated as made in the member State in which the transportation begins.][1], [2]
Commentary—*De Voil Indirect Tax Service* **V3.190**.
Amendments—[1] Sch 4A inserted by FA 2009 s 76, Sch 36 paras 1, 11 with effect in relation to supplies made on or after 1 January 2010.
[2] Para 12 and preceding heading repealed by the Taxation (Cross-border Trade) Act 2018 s 43, Sch 8 paras 1, 89(1), (15) with effect from IP completion day (11pm on 31 December 2020), by virtue of SI 2020/1642 reg 4(*b*).

[Ancillary transport services

13—(1) A supply to a person who is not a relevant business person of ancillary transport services is to be treated as made where the services are physically performed.
(2) "Ancillary transport services" means loading, unloading handling and similar activities.][1]
Commentary—*De Voil Indirect Tax Service* **V3.191**.
Amendments—[1] Sch 4A inserted by FA 2009 s 76, Sch 36 paras 1, 11 with effect in relation to supplies made on or after 1 January 2010.

[Long-term hiring of means of transport

13A—(1) A supply to a person who is not a relevant business person ("the recipient") of services consisting of the long-term hiring of a means of transport is to be treated as made in the country in which the recipient belongs.
But this is subject to sub-paragraph (2) and paragraph 3(3) and (4).
(2) A supply to a person who is not a relevant business person ("the recipient") of services consisting of the long-term hiring of a pleasure boat which is actually put at the disposal of the recipient at the supplier's business establishment, or some other fixed establishment of the supplier, is to be treated as made in the country where the pleasure boat is actually put at the disposal of the recipient.
(3) For the purposes of this Schedule, the hiring of a means of transport is "long-term" if it is not short-term (as to the meaning of which see paragraph 3(2)).][1]

Amendments—[1] This para inserted by FA 2009 s 76, Sch 36 paras 1, 17 with effect in relation to supplies made on or after 1 January 2013.

[Valuation services etc

14 A supply to a person who is not a relevant business person of services consisting of the valuation of, or carrying out of work on, goods is to be treated as made where the services are physically performed.][1]

Amendments—[1] Sch 4A inserted by FA 2009 s 76, Sch 36 paras 1, 11 with effect in relation to supplies made on or after 1 January 2010.

[Cultural, educational and entertainment services etc

14A—(1) A supply to a person who is not a relevant business person of services to which this paragraph applies is to be treated as made in the country in which the activities concerned actually take place.
(2) This paragraph applies to the provision of—
   (*a*) services relating to cultural, artistic, sporting, scientific, educational, entertainment or similar activities (including fairs and exhibitions), and
   (*b*) ancillary services relating to such activities, including services of organisers of such activities.][1]

Amendments—[1] Para 14A inserted by FA 2009 s 76, Sch 36 paras 1, 15(4) with effect in relation to supplies made on or after 1 January 2011.

[[Electronically supplied, telecommunication and broadcasting services]

[15—(1) A supply to a person who is not a relevant business person of services to which this paragraph applies is to be treated as made in the country in which the recipient belongs (but see . . . [4] paragraph 8).
(2) This paragraph applies to-
   (*a*) electronically supplied services (as to the meaning of which see paragraph 9(3) and (4)),
   (*b*) telecommunication services (as to the meaning of which see [paragraph 9E(2)][3]), and
   (*c*) radio and television broadcasting services.][2]
(3)–(7) . . . [4]

Commentary—*De Voil Indirect Tax Service* **V3.193B**.
Amendments—[1] Sch 4A inserted by FA 2009 s 76, Sch 36 paras 1, 11 with effect in relation to supplies made on or after 1 January 2010.
[2] Para 15 and preceding heading substituted by the VAT (Place of Supply of Services) (Exceptions Relating to Supplies Not Made to Relevant Business Person) Order, SI 2014/2726 arts 2, 3 with effect in relation to supplies made on or after 1 January 2015.
[3] In sub-para (2)(*b*), words substituted for words "paragraph 8(2)" by the VAT (Place of Supply of Services) (Telecommunication Services) Order, SI 2017/778 art 4 with effect in relation to supplies of services made on or after 1 November 2017.
[4] In sub-para (1) words "sub-paragraph (3) and" repealed, and sub-paras (3)–(7) repealed, by the Value Added Tax (Place of Supply of Services) (Supplies of Electronic, Telecommunication and Broadcasting Services) (Amendment and Revocation) (EU Exit) Order, SI 2019/404 art 3 with effect from IP completion day (11pm UK time on 31 December 2020). Sub-paras (3)–(7) previously read as follows—
"(3) Sub-paragraph (1) does not apply in relation to a supply of services where—
   (*a*) the supplier of the services belongs in only one member State,
   (*b*) the services are supplied to relevant EU persons,
   (*c*) the value of the supply, taken together with the value of relevant supplies already made by the supplier in the calendar year in which the supply is made, does not exceed £8,818, and
   (*d*) the value of relevant supplies made by the supplier in the calendar year preceding that in which the supply is made did not exceed £8,818,
unless the supplier has made an election under this paragraph or under the law of a member State in which the supplier belongs that the supply is to be treated as made in the country in which the recipient belongs.
   (4) An election may be made for the purposes of this paragraph by a supplier who belongs in the UK in relation to relevant supplies made by that supplier.
   (5) An election under this paragraph must—
      (*a*) be made by notice in writing,
      (*b*) specify the date on which the election is made, and
      (*c*) be received by the Commissioners no later than 30 days after that date.
   (6) An election made by a supplier under this paragraph has effect in relation to relevant supplies made by that supplier—
      (*a*) on the day on which the election is made,
      (*b*) on subsequent days in the same calendar year, and
      (*c*) in the next two calendar years.
   (7) For the purposes of this paragraph—
      "relevant EU persons" means persons belonging in a member State or member States other than that in which the supplier belongs, and

"relevant supplies" means supplies to relevant EU persons of services to which this paragraph applies; references to the value of supplies are to their value excluding VAT."

[Other services provided to recipient belonging outside [United Kingdom and the Isle of Man]

16—(1) A supply consisting of the provision to a person ("the recipient") who—
   (a) is not a relevant business person, and
   (b) belongs in a country [other than the United Kingdom or the Isle of Man][4],
of services to which this paragraph applies is to be treated as made in the country in which the recipient belongs.

(2) This paragraph applies to—
   (a) transfers and assignments of copyright, patents, licences, trademarks and similar rights,
   (b) the acceptance of any obligation to refrain from pursuing or exercising (in whole or in part) any business activity or any rights within paragraph (a),
   (c) advertising services,
   (d) services of consultants, engineers, consultancy bureaux, lawyers, accountants, and similar services, data processing and provision of information, other than any services relating to land,
   (e) banking, financial and insurance services (including reinsurance), other than the provision of safe deposit facilities,
   [(f) the provision of access to, or transmission or distribution through—
      (i) a natural gas system [in the United Kingdom][4] or any network connected to [a natural gas system in the United Kingdom][4], or
      (ii) an electricity system, or
      (iii) a network through which heat or cooling is supplied,
   and the provision of other directly linked services,][2]
   (g) the supply of staff, [and][3]
   (h) the letting on hire of goods other than means of transport,
   (i) . . . [3]
   (j) . . . [3]
   (k) . . . [3]][1]

Commentary—*De Voil Indirect Tax Service* V3.193A.
Amendments—[1] Sch 4A inserted by FA 2009 s 76, Sch 36 paras 1, 11 with effect in relation to supplies made on or after 1 January 2010.
[2] Sub-para (2)(f) substituted by the VAT (Exceptions Relating to Supplies not Made to Relevant Business Person) Order, SI 2010/3017 art 2 with effect in relation to supplies made on or after 1 January 2011.
[3] In sub-para (2), paras (i), (j), (k) repealed, and word inserted at end of para (g), by the VAT (Place of Supply of Services) (Exceptions Relating to Supplies Not Made to Relevant Business Person) Order, SI 2014/2726 arts 2, 4 with effect in relation to supplies made on or after 1 January 2015.
[4] The following amendments made by the Taxation (Cross-border Trade) Act 2018 s 43, Sch 8 paras 1, 89(1), (16), (17) with effect from IP completion day (11pm on 31 December 2020), by virtue of SI 2020/1642 reg 4(b)—
   – in heading above para 16, words substituted for words "EC";
   – in sub-para (1)(b), words substituted for words "which is not a member State (other than the Isle of Man)"; and
   – in sub-para (2)(f)(i)—
      – words substituted for words "situated within the territory of a member State"; and
      – words "a natural gas system in the United Kingdom" substituted for words "such a system".

[SCHEDULE 4B

CALL-OFF STOCK ARRANGEMENTS

Section 14A

Northern Ireland—See VATA Sch 9ZA Part 10 (paras 57–65): businesses moving own goods from Northern Ireland to EU member State or vice versa under call-off stock provisions.

See also VATA 1994 Sch 9ZB para 30: movements of own goods between Northern Ireland and EU member States.

Amendments—Section 14A and Schedule 4B repealed by the Taxation (Post-transition Period) Act 2020 s 3, Sch 2 para 7(1) with effect from IP completion day (11pm on 31 December 2020), by virtue of SI 2020/1642 reg 9. Schedule 4B continues to have effect in relation to goods to which Sch 4B applied (see Sch 4B para 1) immediately before its repeal (see Taxation (Post-transition Period) Act 2020 Sch 2 para 7(6)) subject to the transitional provisions in Sch 2 para 7(7)–(9).

Where this Schedule applies

1 (1) This Schedule applies where—
   (a) on or after 1 January 2020 goods forming part of the assets of any business are removed —
      (i) from the United Kingdom for the purpose of being taken to a place in a member State, or

(ii) *from a member State for the purpose of being taken to a place in the United Kingdom,*
(b) *the goods are removed in the course or furtherance of that business by or under the directions of the person carrying on that business ("the supplier"),*
(c) *the goods are removed with a view to their being supplied in the destination State, at a later stage and after their arrival there, to another person ("the customer"),*
(d) *at the time of the removal the customer is entitled to take ownership of the goods in accordance with an agreement existing between the customer and the supplier,*
(e) *at the time of the removal the supplier does not have a business establishment or other fixed establishment in the destination State,*
(f) *at the time of the removal the customer is identified for the purposes of VAT in accordance with the law of the destination State and both the identity of the customer and the number assigned to the customer for the purposes of VAT by the destination State are known to the supplier,*
(g) *as soon as reasonably practicable after the removal the supplier records the removal in the register provided for in Article 243(3) of Council Directive 2006/112/EC of 28 November 2006 on the common system of value added tax, and*
(h) *the supplier includes the number mentioned in paragraph (f) in the recapitulative statement provided for in Article 262(2) of Council Directive 2006/112/EC.*

(2) In this Schedule—
"the destination State" means—
(a) *in a case within paragraph (i) of sub-paragraph (1)(a), the member State concerned, and*
(b) *in a case within paragraph (ii) of sub-paragraph (1)(a), the United Kingdom, and*
"the origin State" means—
(a) *in a case within paragraph (i) of sub-paragraph (1)(a), the United Kingdom, and*
(b) *in a case within paragraph (ii) of sub-paragraph (1)(a), the member State concerned.]*[1], [2]

Amendments—[1] Sch 4B inserted by FA 2020 s 80(1), (5) with effect from 22 July 2020.
[2] Section 14A and Schedule 4B repealed by the Taxation (Post-transition Period) Act 2020 s 3, Sch 2 para 7(1) with effect from IP completion day (11pm on 31 December 2020), by virtue of SI 2020/1642 reg 9. Schedule 4B continues to have effect in relation to goods to which Sch 4B applied (see Sch 4B para 1) immediately before its repeal (see Taxation (Post-transition Period) Act 2020 Sch 2 para 7(6)) subject to the transitional provisions in Sch 2 para 7(7)–(9).

[Removal of the goods not to be treated as a supply

2 *The removal of the goods from the origin State is not to be treated by reason of paragraph 6(1) of Schedule 4 as a supply of goods by the supplier.]*[1], [2]

Amendments—[1] Sch 4B inserted by FA 2020 s 80(1), (5) with effect from 22 July 2020.
[2] Section 14A and Schedule 4B repealed by the Taxation (Post-transition Period) Act 2020 s 3, Sch 2 para 7(1) with effect from IP completion day (11pm on 31 December 2020), by virtue of SI 2020/1642 reg 9. Schedule 4B continues to have effect in relation to goods to which Sch 4B applied (see Sch 4B para 1) immediately before its repeal (see Taxation (Post-transition Period) Act 2020 Sch 2 para 7(6)) subject to the transitional provisions in Sch 2 para 7(7)–(9).

[Goods transferred to the customer within 12 months of arrival

3 *(1) The rules in sub-paragraph (2) apply if—*
(a) *during the period of 12 months beginning with the day the goods arrive in the destination State the supplier transfers the whole property in the goods to the customer, and*
(b) *during the period beginning with the day the goods arrive in the destination State and ending immediately before the time of that transfer no relevant event occurs.*
(2) The rules are that—
(a) *a supply of the goods in the origin State is deemed to be made by the supplier,*
(b) *the deemed supply is deemed to involve the removal of the goods from the origin State at the time of the transfer mentioned in sub-paragraph (1),*
(c) *the consideration given by the customer for the transfer mentioned in sub-paragraph (1) is deemed to have been given for the deemed supply, and*
(d) *an acquisition of the goods by the customer in pursuance of the deemed supply is deemed to take place in the destination State.*
(3) For the meaning of a "relevant event", see paragraph 7.][1], [2]

Amendments—[1] Sch 4B inserted by FA 2020 s 80(1), (5) with effect from 22 July 2020.
[2] Section 14A and Schedule 4B repealed by the Taxation (Post-transition Period) Act 2020 s 3, Sch 2 para 7(1) with effect from IP completion day (11pm on 31 December 2020), by virtue of SI 2020/1642 reg 9. Schedule 4B continues to have effect in relation to goods to which Sch 4B applied (see Sch 4B para 1) immediately before its repeal (see Taxation (Post-transition Period) Act 2020 Sch 2 para 7(6)) subject to the transitional provisions in Sch 2 para 7(7)–(9).

[Relevant event occurs within 12 months of arrival

4 *(1) The rules in sub-paragraph (2) apply (subject to paragraph 6) if—*

(a) during the period of 12 months beginning with the day the goods arrive in the destination State a relevant event occurs, and
(b) during the period beginning with the day the goods arrive in the destination State and ending immediately before the time that relevant event occurs the supplier does not transfer the whole property in the goods to the customer.
(2) The rules are that—
   (a) a supply of the goods in the origin State is deemed to be made by the supplier,
   (b) the deemed supply is deemed to involve the removal of the goods from the origin State at the time the relevant event occurs, and
   (c) an acquisition of the goods by the supplier in pursuance of the deemed supply is deemed to take place in the destination State.
(3) For the meaning of a "relevant event", see paragraph 7.]¹, ²

Amendments—¹ Sch 4B inserted by FA 2020 s 80(1), (5) with effect from 22 July 2020.
² Section 14A and Schedule 4B repealed by the Taxation (Post-transition Period) Act 2020 s 3, Sch 2 para 7(1) with effect from IP completion day (11pm on 31 December 2020), by virtue of SI 2020/1642 reg 9. Schedule 4B continues to have effect in relation to goods to which Sch 4B applied (see Sch 4B para 1) immediately before its repeal (see Taxation (Post-transition Period) Act 2020 Sch 2 para 7(6)) subject to the transitional provisions in Sch 2 para 7(7)–(9).

[Goods not transferred and no relevant event occurs within 12 months of arrival

5 (1) The rules in sub-paragraph (2) apply (subject to paragraph 6) if during the period of 12 months beginning with the day the goods arrive in the destination State the supplier does not transfer the whole property in the goods to the customer and no relevant event occurs.
(2) The rules are that—
   (a) a supply of the goods in the origin State is deemed to be made by the supplier,
   (b) the deemed supply is deemed to involve the removal of the goods from the origin State at the beginning of the day following the expiry of the period of 12 months mentioned in sub-paragraph (1), and
   (c) an acquisition of the goods by the supplier in pursuance of the deemed supply is deemed to take place in the destination State.
(3) For the meaning of a "relevant event", see paragraph 7.]¹, ²

Amendments—¹ Sch 4B inserted by FA 2020 s 80(1), (5) with effect from 22 July 2020.
² Section 14A and Schedule 4B repealed by the Taxation (Post-transition Period) Act 2020 s 3, Sch 2 para 7(1) with effect from IP completion day (11pm on 31 December 2020), by virtue of SI 2020/1642 reg 9. Schedule 4B continues to have effect in relation to goods to which Sch 4B applied (see Sch 4B para 1) immediately before its repeal (see Taxation (Post-transition Period) Act 2020 Sch 2 para 7(6)) subject to the transitional provisions in Sch 2 para 7(7)–(9).

[Exception to paragraphs 4 and 5: goods returned to origin State

6 The rules in paragraphs 4(2) and 5(2) do not apply if during the period of 12 months beginning with the day the goods arrive in the destination State—
   (a) the goods are returned to the origin State by or under the direction of the supplier, and
   (b) the supplier records the return of the goods in the register provided for in Article 243(3) of Council Directive 2006/112/EC.]¹, ²

Amendments—¹ Sch 4B inserted by FA 2020 s 80(1), (5) with effect from 22 July 2020.
² Section 14A and Schedule 4B repealed by the Taxation (Post-transition Period) Act 2020 s 3, Sch 2 para 7(1) with effect from IP completion day (11pm on 31 December 2020), by virtue of SI 2020/1642 reg 9. Schedule 4B continues to have effect in relation to goods to which Sch 4B applied (see Sch 4B para 1) immediately before its repeal (see Taxation (Post-transition Period) Act 2020 Sch 2 para 7(6)) subject to the transitional provisions in Sch 2 para 7(7)–(9).

[Meaning of "relevant event"

7 (1) For the purposes of this Schedule each of the following events is a relevant event—
   (a) the supplier forms an intention not to supply the goods to the customer (but see sub-paragraph (2)),
   (b) the supplier forms an intention to supply the goods to the customer otherwise than in the destination State,
   (c) the supplier establishes a business establishment or other fixed establishment in the destination State,
   (d) the customer ceases to be identified for the purposes of VAT in accordance with the law of the destination State,
   (e) the goods are removed from the destination State by or under the directions of the supplier otherwise than for the purpose of being returned to the origin State, or
   (f) the goods are destroyed, lost or stolen.
(2) But the event mentioned in paragraph (a) of sub-paragraph (1) is not a relevant event for the purposes of this Schedule if—

(a) at the time that the event occurs the supplier forms an intention to supply the goods to another person ("the substitute customer"),
(b) at that time the substitute customer is identified for the purposes of VAT in accordance with the law of the destination State,
(c) the supplier includes the number assigned to the substitute customer for the purposes of VAT by the destination State in the recapitulative statement provided for in Article 262(2) of Council Directive 2006/112/EC, and
(d) as soon as reasonably practicable after forming the intention to supply the goods to the substitute customer the supplier records that intention in the register provided for in Article 243(3) of Council Directive 2006/112/EC.

(3) In a case where sub-paragraph (2) applies, references in this Schedule to the customer are to be then read as references to the substitute customer.

(4) In a case where the goods are destroyed, lost or stolen but it is not possible to determine the date on which that occurred, the goods are to be treated for the purposes of this Schedule as having been destroyed, lost or stolen on the date on which they were found to be destroyed or missing.][1], [2]

Amendments—[1] Sch 4B inserted by FA 2020 s 80(1), (5) with effect from 22 July 2020.
[2] Section 14A and Schedule 4B repealed by the Taxation (Post-transition Period) Act 2020 s 3, Sch 2 para 7(1) with effect from IP completion day (11pm on 31 December 2020), by virtue of SI 2020/1642 reg 9. Schedule 4B continues to have effect in relation to goods to which Sch 4B applied (see Sch 4B para 1) immediately before its repeal (see Taxation (Post-transition Period) Act 2020 Sch 2 para 7(6)) subject to the transitional provisions in Sch 2 para 7(7)–(9).

[Record keeping by the supplier

8 *In a case where the origin State is the United Kingdom, any record made by the supplier in pursuance of paragraph 1(1)(g), 6(b) or 7(2)(d) must be preserved for such period not exceeding 6 years as the Commissioners may specify in writing.]*[1], [2]

Amendments—[1] Sch 4B inserted by FA 2020 s 80(1), (5) with effect from 22 July 2020.
[2] Section 14A and Schedule 4B repealed by the Taxation (Post-transition Period) Act 2020 s 3, Sch 2 para 7(1) with effect from IP completion day (11pm on 31 December 2020), by virtue of SI 2020/1642 reg 9. Schedule 4B continues to have effect in relation to goods to which Sch 4B applied (see Sch 4B para 1) immediately before its repeal (see Taxation (Post-transition Period) Act 2020 Sch 2 para 7(6)) subject to the transitional provisions in Sch 2 para 7(7)–(9).

[Record keeping by the customer

9 *(1) In a case where the destination State is the United Kingdom, the customer must as soon as is reasonably practicable make a record of the information relating to the goods that is specified in Article 54A(2) of Council Implementing Regulation (EU) No. 282/2011 of 15 March 2011 laying down implementing measures for Directive 2006/112/EC on the common system of value added tax.*
(2) A record made under this paragraph must—
   (a) be made in a register kept by the customer for the purposes of this paragraph, and
   (b) be preserved for such period not exceeding 6 years as the Commissioners may specify in writing.][1], [2]

Amendments—[1] Sch 4B inserted by FA 2020 s 80(1), (5) with effect from 22 July 2020.
[2] Section 14A and Schedule 4B repealed by the Taxation (Post-transition Period) Act 2020 s 3, Sch 2 para 7(1) with effect from IP completion day (11pm on 31 December 2020), by virtue of SI 2020/1642 reg 9. Schedule 4B continues to have effect in relation to goods to which Sch 4B applied (see Sch 4B para 1) immediately before its repeal (see Taxation (Post-transition Period) Act 2020 Sch 2 para 7(6)) subject to the transitional provisions in Sch 2 para 7(7)–(9).

SCHEDULE 5
SERVICES SUPPLIED WHERE RECEIVED
Section 8

Amendments—Sch 5 repealed by FA 2009 s 76, Sch 36 paras 1, 12 with effect in relation to supplies made on or after 1 January 2010.

[SCHEDULE 5A
GOODS ELIGIBLE TO BE FISCALLY WAREHOUSED
Section 18B

Description of goods	[customs tariff (within the meaning of TCTA 2018) code][2]
Tin	8001
Copper	7402
	7403
	7405
	7408

Description of goods	[customs tariff (within the meaning of TCTA 2018) code][2]
Zinc	7901
Nickel	7502
Aluminium	7601
Lead	7801
Indium	ex 811291
	ex 811299
Cereals	1001 to 1005
	1006: unprocessed rice only
	1007 to 1008
Oil seeds and oleaginous fruit	1201 to 1207
Coconuts, Brazil nuts and cashew nuts	0801
Other nuts	0502
Olives	071120
Grains and seeds (including soya beans)	1201 to 1207
Coffee, not roasted	0901 11 00
	0901 12 00
Tea	0902
Cocoa beans, whole or broken, raw or roasted	1801
Raw sugar	1701 11
	1701 12
Rubber, in primary forms or in plates, sheets or strip	4001
	4002
Wool	5101
Chemicals in bulk	Chapters 28 and 29
Mineral oils (including propane and butane; also including crude petroleum oils)	2709
	2710
	2711 12
	2711 13
Silver	7106
Platinum (palladium, rhodium)	7110 11 00
	7110 21 00
	7110 31 00
Potatoes	0701
Vegetable oils and fats and their fractions, whether or not refined, but not chemically modified	1507 to 1515][1]

Commentary—*De Voil Indirect Tax Service* **V3.176**.
Amendments—[1] Schedule inserted by FA 1996 Sch 3 para 18, with effect from 1 June 1996 (see Finance Act 1996, Section 26, (Appointed Day) Order, SI 1996/1249).
[2] In the Table, heading of the second column substituted by the Taxation (Cross-border Trade) Act 2018 s 43, Sch 8 paras 1, 90 with effect from IP completion day (11pm on 31 December 2020), by virtue of SI 2020/1642 reg 4(*b*). Heading previously read: "Combined nomenclature code of the European Communities".

SCHEDULE 6
VALUATION: SPECIAL CASES
Section 19

[PART 1
VALUATION OF SUPPLIES OF FUEL FOR PRIVATE USE

Option for valuation on flat-rate basis

A1— (1) This paragraph applies if, in a prescribed accounting period, supplies of goods by a taxable person ("P") arise by virtue of paragraph 5(1) of Schedule 4 (but otherwise than for a consideration) where road fuel which is or has previously been supplied to or imported or manufactured by P in the course of P's business is provided for, or appropriated to, private use.
(2) For this purpose "road fuel is provided for, or appropriated to, private use" if—
    (*a*) it is provided or to be provided by P—

(i) to an individual for private use in the individual's own car or a car allocated to the individual, and
(ii) by reason of the individual's employment,
(b) where P is an individual, it is appropriated or to be appropriated by P for private use in P's own car, or
(c) where P is a partnership, it is provided or to be provided to any of the individual partners for private use in that partner's own car.

(3) P may opt for all supplies of goods within sub-paragraph (1) made by P in the prescribed accounting period to be valued on the flat-rate basis.

(4) On the flat-rate basis, the value of all supplies made to any one individual in respect of any one car is that determined in accordance with an order under paragraph B1.]

Amendments—Part 1 (paras A1–C1), and heading to Part 2, inserted by FA 2013 s 192, Sch 38 paras 1, 2 with effect in relation to prescribed accounting periods beginning on or after 1 February 2014.

[**B1**—(1) The Treasury must, by order, make provision about the valuation of supplies on the flat-rate basis.

(2) In particular, an order under this paragraph must—
(a) set out a table ("the base valuation table") by reference to which the value of supplies is to be determined until such time as the base valuation table is replaced under paragraph (b),
(b) provide that at regular intervals—
(i) the amounts specified in the base valuation table are to be revalorised by the Commissioners in accordance with the order, and
(ii) a table (an "updated valuation table") containing the revalorised amounts is to take effect (and replace any existing table) in accordance with the order, and
(c) require the Commissioners to publish any updated valuation table before it takes effect, together with a statement specifying the date from which it has effect.

(3) An order under this paragraph may provide for the base valuation table and any updated valuation table to be implemented or supplemented by either or both of the following—
(a) rules set out in the order which explain how the value is to be determined by reference to any table;
(b) notes set out in the order with respect to the interpretation or application of any table or any rules or notes.

(4) Rules or notes may make different provision for different circumstances or cases.]

Orders—Value Added Tax (Flat-rate Valuation of Supplies of Fuel for Private Use) Order, SI 2013/2911.

Amendments—Part 1 (paras A1–C1), and heading to Part 2, inserted by FA 2013 s 192, Sch 38 paras 1, 2 with effect in relation to prescribed accounting periods beginning on or after 1 February 2014.

[Interpretation

C1—(1) For the purposes of this Part of this Schedule—
(a) any reference to an individual's own car is to be construed as including any car of which for the time being the individual has the use, other than a car allocated to the individual,
(b) subject to sub-paragraph (2), a car is at any time to be taken to be allocated to an individual if at that time it is made available (without any transfer of the property in it) either to the individual or to any other person, and is so made available by reason of the individual's employment and for private use, and
(c) fuel provided by an employer to an employee and fuel provided to any person for private use in a car which, by virtue of paragraph (b), is for the time being taken to be allocated to the employee is to be taken to be provided to the employee by reason of the employee's employment.

(2) For the purposes of this Part of this Schedule, in any prescribed accounting period a car is not regarded as allocated to an individual by reason of the individual's employment if—
(a) in that period it was made available to, and actually used by, more than one of the employees of one or more employers and, in the case of each of them, it—
(i) was made available to that employee by reason of the employment, but
(ii) was not in that period ordinarily used by any one of them to the exclusion of the others,
(b) in the case of each of the employees, any private use of the car made by the employee in that period was merely incidental to the employee's other use of it in that period, and
(c) in that period it was not normally kept overnight on or in the vicinity of any residential premises where any of the employees was residing, except while being kept overnight on premises occupied by the person making the car available to them.

(3) In this Part of this Schedule—
"employment" includes any office, and related expressions are to be construed accordingly;
"car" means a motor car as defined by paragraph 1A(4) and (5);

"road fuel" means hydrocarbon oil as defined by the Hydrocarbon Oil Duties Act 1979 (see section 1(2) of that Act) on which duty has been or is required to be paid in accordance with that Act.

(4) The Treasury may, by order, amend the definition of "road fuel" in sub-paragraph (3).]

Amendments—Part 1 (paras A1–C1), and heading to Part 2, inserted by FA 2013 s 192, Sch 38 paras 1, 2 with effect in relation to prescribed accounting periods beginning on or after 1 February 2014.

[PART 2
OTHER PROVISIONS]

Amendments—Part 1 (paras A1–C1), and heading to Part 2, inserted by FA 2013 s 192, Sch 38 paras 1, 2 with effect in relation to prescribed accounting periods beginning on or after 1 February 2014.

1—(1) Where—
   (a) the value of a supply made by a taxable person for a consideration in money is (apart from this paragraph) less than its open market value, and
   (b) the person making the supply and the person to whom it is made are connected, and
   (c) if the supply is a taxable supply, the person to whom the supply is made is not entitled under sections 25 and 26 to credit for all the VAT on the supply,

the Commissioners may direct that the value of the supply shall be taken to be its open market value.

(2) A direction under this paragraph shall be given by notice in writing to the person making the supply, but no direction may be given more than 3 years after the time of the supply.

(3) A direction given to a person under this paragraph in respect of a supply made by him may include a direction that the value of any supply—
   (a) which is made by him after the giving of the notice, or after such later date as may be specified in the notice, and
   (b) as to which the conditions in paragraphs (a) to (c) of sub-paragraph (1) above are satisfied,

shall be taken to be its open market value.

(4) For the purposes of this paragraph any question whether a person is connected with another shall be determined in accordance with [section 1122 of the Corporation Tax Act 2010][1].

(5) This paragraph does not apply to a supply to which paragraph [8A or][2] 10 below applies.

Commentary—*De Voil Indirect Tax Service* **V3.162**.

Amendments—[1] In sub-para (4) words substituted for words "section 839 of the Taxes Act 1988" by CTA 2010 s 1177, Sch 1 para 285(b). CTA 2010 has effect for corporation tax purposes for accounting periods ending on or after 1 April 2010, and for income and capital gains tax purposes for the tax year 2010–11 and subsequent tax years.

[2] Words in sub-para (5) inserted by FA 2012 s 200(1), (5), (6) with effect in relation to supplies made on or after 17 July 2012.

[**1A**—(1) Where—
   (a) the value of a supply made by a taxable person for a consideration is (apart from this sub-paragraph) less than its open market value,
   (b) the taxable person is a motor manufacturer or motor dealer,
   (c) the person to whom the supply is made is—
      (i) an employee of the taxable person,
      (ii) a person who, under the terms of his employment, provides services to the taxable person, or
      (iii) a relative of a person falling within sub-paragraph (i) or (ii) above,
   (d) the supply is a supply of services by virtue of sub-paragraph (4) of paragraph 5 of Schedule 4 (business goods put to private use etc),
   (e) the goods mentioned in that sub-paragraph consist of a motor car (whether or not any particular motor car) that forms part of the stock in trade of the taxable person, and
   (f) the supply is not one to which paragraph 1 above applies,

the Commissioners may direct that the value of the supply shall be taken to be its open market value.

(2) A direction under this paragraph shall be given by notice in writing to the person making the supply, but no direction may be given more than 3 years after the time of the supply.

(3) A direction given to a person under this paragraph in respect of a supply made by him may include a direction that the value of any supply—
   (a) which is made by him after the giving of the notice, or after such later date as may be specified in the notice, and
   (b) as to which the conditions in paragraphs (a) to (f) of sub-paragraph (1) above are satisfied,

shall be taken to be its open market value.

(4) In this paragraph—

"motor car" means any motor vehicle of a kind normally used on public roads which has three or more wheels and either—
   (a) is constructed or adapted solely or mainly for the carriage of passengers, or

(b) has to the rear of the driver's seat roofed accommodation which is fitted with side windows or which is constructed or adapted for the fitting of side windows,

but does not include any vehicle excluded by sub-paragraph (5) below;

"motor dealer" means a person whose business consists in whole or in part of obtaining supplies of, . . . [2] or importing, new or second-hand motor cars for resale with a view to making an overall profit on the sale of them (whether or not a profit is made on each sale);

"motor manufacturer" means a person whose business consists in whole or part of producing motor cars including producing motor cars by conversion of a vehicle (whether a motor car or not);

"relative" means husband, wife, brother, sister, ancestor or lineal descendant;

"stock in trade" means new or second-hand motor cars (other than second-hand motor cars which are not qualifying motor cars within sub-paragraph (6) below) which are—

produced by (a) motor manufacturer, or supplied to or imported by a motor dealer, for the purpose of resale, and

(b) intended to be sold within 12 months of their production, supply or importation (as the case may require),][2]

and such motor cars shall not cease to be stock in trade where they are temporarily put to a use in the motor manufacturer's or, as the case may be, the motor dealer's business which involves making them available for private use.

(5) The vehicles excluded by this sub-paragraph are—
(a) vehicles capable of accommodating only one person;
(b) vehicles which meet the requirements of Schedule 6 to the Road Vehicles (Construction and Use) Regulations 1986 and are capable of carrying twelve or more seated persons;
(c) vehicles of not less than three tonnes unladen weight (as defined in the Table to regulation 3(2) of the Road Vehicles (Construction and Use) Regulations 1986);
(d) vehicles constructed to carry a payload (the difference between—
(i) a vehicle's kerb weight (as defined in the Table to regulation 3(2) of the Road Vehicles (Construction and Use) Regulations 1986), and
(ii) its maximum gross weight (as defined in that Table)),

of one tonne or more;
(e) caravans, ambulances and prison vans;
(f) vehicles constructed for a special purpose other than the carriage of persons and having no other accommodation for carrying persons than such as is incidental to that purpose.

(6) For the purposes of this paragraph a motor car is a "qualifying motor car" if—
(a) it has never been supplied . . . [2] or imported in circumstances in which the VAT on that supply . . . [2] or importation was wholly excluded from credit as input tax by virtue of an order under section 25(7) (as at 17th March 2004 see article 7 of the Value Added Tax (Input Tax) Order 1992); or
(b) a taxable person has elected under such an order for it to be treated as such.

(7) The Treasury may by order amend any of the definitions in this paragraph.]][1]

Northern Ireland—See Sch 9ZA para 69: Northern Ireland: this para has effect as if—
- in sub-para (4), in the definition of "motor dealer", after "supplies of" there were inserted ", or acquiring in Northern Ireland from a member State";
- in sub-para (4), in the definition of "stock in trade", in para (a), after "supplied to" there were inserted "or acquired in Northern Ireland from a member State by", and in para (b), after "supply" there were inserted ", acquisition"; and
- in sub-para (6)(a), after "supplied" there were inserted ", acquired in Northern Ireland from a member State", and after "supply" there were inserted ", acquisition".

Commentary—*De Voil Indirect Tax Service* V3.162A.
Amendments—[1] This paragraph inserted by FA 2004 s 22(1), (2), (5), (6) in relation to any use or availability for use on or after such day as the Treasury may by order made by statutory instrument appoint, whatever the date of the directions mentioned in VATA 1994 Sch 4 para 5(4). The appointed date is 1 January 2005 (by virtue of SI 2004/3104).
[2] The following amendments made by the Taxation (Cross-border Trade) Act 2018 s 43, Sch 8 paras 1, 91(1), (2) with effect from IP completion day (11pm on 31 December 2020), by virtue of SI 2020/1642 reg 4(b)—
- in sub-para (4),
  - in definition of "motor dealer", words "or acquiring from another member State" repealed;
  - in definition of "stock in trade", paras (a), (b) substituted; and
- in sub-para (6)(a), words ", acquired from another member State," and ", acquisition" repealed.

In definition of "stock in trade", paras (a), (b) previously read as follows—

"(a) produced by a motor manufacturer or, as the case may require, supplied to or acquired from another member State or imported by a motor dealer, for the purpose of resale, and
(b) intended to be sold—
(i) by a motor manufacturer within 12 months of their production, or
(ii) by a motor dealer within 12 months of their supply, acquisition from another member State or importation, as the case may require,".

2 Where—
  (a) the whole or part of a business carried on by a taxable person consists in supplying to a number of persons goods to be sold, whether by them or others, by retail, and
  (b) those persons are not taxable persons,
the Commissioners may by notice in writing to the taxable person direct that the value of any such supply by him after the giving of the notice or after such later date as may be specified in the notice shall be taken to be its open market value on a sale by retail.
Commentary—*De Voil Indirect Tax Service* **V3.163**.

[**2A**—(1) This paragraph applies if—
  (a) a taxable person ("P") makes a supply of road fuel for a consideration,
  (b) the recipient of the supply is—
    (i) connected with P, or
    (ii) an employee or partner of P or a person who is connected with such an employee or partner,
  (c) the value of the supply would (in the absence of this paragraph) be less than its open market value, and
  (d) the recipient of the supply is not entitled to credit for the whole of the input tax arising on the supply.
(2) The value of the supply is to be taken to be an amount equal to its open market value.
(3) For the purposes of this paragraph—
  (a) "road fuel" means hydrocarbon oil as defined by the Hydrocarbon Oil Duties Act 1979 (see section 1(2) of that Act) on which duty has been or is required to be paid in accordance with that Act, and
  (b) any question whether a person is connected with another is to be determined in accordance with section 1122 of the Corporation Tax Act 2010.
(4) The Treasury may, by order, amend the definition of "road fuel" in sub-paragraph (3)(a).][1]
Amendments—[1] Para 2A inserted by FA 2013 s 192, Sch 38 paras 1, 6. This amendment is to be treated as coming into force on 11 December 2012 and has effect in relation to: (a) supplies of goods on or after the commencement day, and (b) supplies of goods in the period beginning with 11 December 2012 and ending immediately before the commencement day, if and to the extent that the goods are not made available before the end of that period to the person to whom they are supplied. The commencement day means 17 July 2013 (FA 2013 Sch 38 para 8(2)).

3—(1) Where—
  (a) any goods whose supply involves their removal to the United Kingdom—
    (i) are charged in connection with their removal to the United Kingdom with a duty of excise; or
    (ii) on that removal are subject, in accordance with any provision for the time being having effect for transitional purposes in connection with the accession of any State to the European Union, to any . . . [1] agricultural levy of the European Union; or
  (b) the time of supply of any dutiable goods, or of any goods which comprise a mixture of dutiable goods and other goods, is determined under section 18(4) to be the duty point,
then the value of the supply shall be taken for the purposes of this Act to be the sum of its value apart from this paragraph and the amount, so far as not already included in that value, of the duty or, as the case may be, agricultural levy which has been or is to be paid in respect of the goods.
(2) In this paragraph "dutiable goods" and "duty point" have the same meanings as in section 18.
Commentary—*De Voil Indirect Tax Service* **V5.141**.
Northern Ireland—See VATA 1994 Sch 9ZB para 26(1): para 3 has effect in relation to goods whose supply involves their removal to Northern Ireland from a place outside the United Kingdom as if—
  – in sub-para (1)(a)(ii), after "EU" there were inserted "customs duty or";
  – in sub-para (1)(b), for "section 18(4)" there were substituted "paragraph 16(7) of Schedule 9ZB"; and
  – in sub-para (2), for "section 18" there were substituted "paragraph 16 of Schedule 9ZB".
Amendments—[1] In sub-para (1)(a)(ii), words "EU customs duty or" repealed by the Taxation (Cross-border Trade) Act 2018 s 43, Sch 8 paras 1, 91(1), (3) with effect from IP completion day (11pm on 31 December 2020), by virtue of SI 2020/1642 reg 4(b).

[**4**—(1) Sub-paragraph (2) applies where—
  (a) goods or services are supplied for a consideration which is a price in money,
  (b) the terms on which those goods or services are so supplied allow a discount for prompt payment of that price,
  (c) payment of that price is not made by instalments, and
  (d) payment of that price is made in accordance with those terms so that the discount is realised in relation to that payment.
(2) For the purposes of section 19 (value of supply of goods or services) the consideration is the discounted price paid.][1]

Commentary—*De Voil Indirect Tax Service* **V3.157**.
Amendments—[1]   Paragraph substituted by FA 2014 s 108 with effect in relation to relevant supplies made on or after 1 May 2014.
Note that the Treasury may by order made by statutory instrument provide that the amendment has effect in relation to supplies of a description specified in the order made on or after a date so specified (being a date before 1 April 2015) (FA 2014 s 108(3). Subject to that, the amendment has effect in relation to supplies made on or after 1 April 2015.

6—(1) Where there is a supply of goods by virtue of—
  (*a*) a Treasury order under section 5(5); or
  (*b*) paragraph 5(1) or 6 of Schedule 4 but otherwise than for a consideration); or
  (*c*) paragraph 8 of that Schedule; . . . [2]
  (*d*) . . . [2]
then, except where [the person making the supply opts under paragraph A1(3) above for valuation on the flat-rate basis or][1] paragraph 10 below applies, the value of the supply shall be determined as follows.
(2) The value of the supply shall be taken to be—
  (*a*) such consideration in money as would be payable by the person making the supply if he were, at the time of the supply, to purchase goods identical in every respect (including age and condition) to the goods concerned; or
  (*b*) where the value cannot be ascertained in accordance with paragraph (*a*) above, such consideration in money as would be payable by that person if he were, at that time, to purchase goods similar to, and of the same age and condition as, the goods concerned; or
  (*c*) where the value can be ascertained in accordance with neither paragraph (*a*) nor paragraph (*b*) above, the cost of producing the goods concerned if they were produced at that time.
(3) For the purposes of sub-paragraph (2) above the amount of consideration in money that would be payable by any person if he were to purchase any goods shall be taken to be the amount that would be so payable after the deduction of any amount included in the purchase price in respect of VAT on the supply of the goods to that person.
Commentary—*De Voil Indirect Tax Service* **V3.211, V3.213, V3.242**.
Northern Ireland—See Sch 9ZA para 69(2): Northern Ireland: sub-para (1) has effect as if—
  –   in para (*b*), after "Schedule 4" there were inserted "or paragraph 30 of Schedule 9ZB";
  –   in para (*c*), for "that Schedule;" there were substituted "Schedule 4; or"; and
  –   new para (*d*) were inserted as follows:
      "(*d*) paragraph 60(2)(*a*) or 61(2)(*a*) of Schedule 9ZA,".
Amendments—[1]   In sub-para (1) words inserted by FA 2013 s 192, Sch 38 paras 1, 3 with effect in relation to prescribed accounting periods beginning on or after 1 February 2014.
[2]   Sub-para (1)(*d*), and preceding word "or" repealed by the Taxation (Post-transition Period) Act 2020 s 3, Sch 2 para 7(4) with effect from IP completion day (11pm on 31 December 2020), by virtue of SI 2020/1642 reg 9.
      "(*d*)   paragraph 4(2)(*a*) or 5(2)(*a*) of Schedule 4B,".

7—[(1)] [2] Where there is a supply of services by virtue of—
  (*a*) a Treasury order under section 5(4); or
  (*b*) [paragraph 5(4)][1] of Schedule 4 (but otherwise than for a consideration),
the value of the supply shall be taken to be the full cost to the taxable person of providing the services except where paragraph 10 below applies.
[(2) Regulations may, in relation to a supply of services by virtue of paragraph 5(4) of Schedule 4 (but otherwise than for a consideration), make provision for determining how the full cost to the taxable person of providing the services is to be calculated.
(3) The regulations may, in particular, make provision for the calculation to be made by reference to any prescribed period.
(4) The regulations may make—
  (*a*) different provision for different circumstances;
  (*b*) such incidental, supplementary, consequential or transitional provision as the Commissioners think fit.][2]
Commentary—*De Voil Indirect Tax Service* **V3.212**.
Amendments—[1]   Words in sub-para (b) substituted by FA 1995 s 33(1), (3)(b) and are deemed to have always had effect.
[2]   Sub-s (1) numbered as such, and sub-ss (2)–(4) inserted by FA 2007 s 99(4), (5) with effect from 19 July 2007.

8   Where any supply of services is treated by virtue of section 8[, or any supply of goods is treated by virtue of section 9A,][1] as made by the person by whom they are received, the value of the supply shall be taken—
  (*a*) in a case where the consideration for which the services [or goods][1] were in fact supplied to him was a consideration in money, to be such amount as is equal to that consideration; and
  (*b*) in a case where that consideration did not consist or not wholly consist of money, to be such amount in money as is equivalent to that consideration.
Commentary—*De Voil Indirect Tax Service* **V3.231**.

Amendments—[1] Words inserted by F(No 2)A 2005 s 5 with effect in relation to supplies made on or after 17 March 2005.

[**8A**—(1) This paragraph applies where—
- (*a*) a supply ("the intra-group supply") made by a member of a group ("the supplier") to another member of the group is, by virtue of section 43(2A), excluded from the supplies disregarded under section 43(1)(*a*), and
- (*b*) the representative member of the group satisfies the Commissioners as to the value of each bought-in supply.

(2) "Bought-in supply", in relation to the intra-group supply, means a supply of services to the supplier to which section 43(2A)(*c*) to (*e*) refers, so far as that supply is used by the supplier for making the intra-group supply.

(3) The value of the intra-group supply shall be taken to be the total of the relevant amounts in relation to the bought-in supplies.

(4) The relevant amount in relation to a bought-in supply is the value of the bought-in supply, unless a direction is made under subparagraph (5).

(5) If the value of a bought-in supply is less than its open market value, the Commissioners may direct that the relevant amount in relation to that supply is its open market value.

(6) A direction under this paragraph must be given by notice in writing to the representative member, but no direction may be given more than 3 years after the time of the intra-group supply.

(7) The Treasury may by order vary the provision made by this Schedule about the value of supplies of the kind mentioned in subparagraph (1)(*a*).

(8) An order under sub-paragraph (7) may include incidental, supplemental, consequential or transitional provision (including provision amending section 43 or 83).][1]

Amendments—[1] Para 8A inserted by FA 2012 s 200(1), (5), (7) with effect in relation to supplies made on or after 17 July 2012.

9—(1) This paragraph applies where a supply of services consists in the provision of accommodation falling within paragraph (*d*) of Item 1 of Group 1 in Schedule 9 and—
- (*a*) that provision is made to an individual for a period exceeding 4 weeks; and
- (*b*) throughout that period the accommodation is provided for the use of the individual either alone or together with one or more other persons who occupy the accommodation with him otherwise than at their own expense (whether incurred directly or indirectly).

(2) Where this paragraph applies—
- (*a*) the value of so much of the supply as is in excess of 4 weeks shall be taken to be reduced to such part thereof as is attributable to facilities other than the right to occupy the accommodation; and
- (*b*) that part shall be taken to be not less than 20 per cent.

Commentary—*De Voil Indirect Tax Service* **V3.166**.

10—(1) This paragraph applies to a supply of goods or services, whether or not for consideration, which is made by an employer and consists of—
- (*a*) the provision in the course of catering of food or beverages to his employees, or
- (*b*) the provision of accommodation for his employees in a hotel, inn, boarding house or similar establishment.

(2) The value of a supply to which this paragraph applies shall be taken to be nil unless the supply is for a consideration consisting wholly or partly of money, and in that case its value shall be determined without regard to any consideration other than money.

Commentary—*De Voil Indirect Tax Service* **V3.166**.

11—(1) Subject to the following provisions of this paragraph, where—
- (*a*) there is a supply of goods or services; and
- (*b*) any sum relevant for determining the value of the supply is expressed in a currency other than sterling,

then, for the purpose of valuing the supply, that sum is to be converted into sterling at the market rate which, on the relevant day, would apply in the United Kingdom to a purchase with sterling by the person to whom they are supplied of that sum in the currency in question.

(2) Where the Commissioners have published a notice which, for the purposes of this paragraph, specifies—
- (*a*) rates of exchange; or
- (*b*) methods of determining rates of exchange,

a rate specified in or determined in accordance with the notice, as for the time being in force, shall apply (instead of the rate for which sub-paragraph (1) above provides) in the case of any supply by a person who opts, in such manner as may be allowed by the Commissioners, for the use of that rate in relation to that supply.

(3) An option for the purposes of sub-paragraph (2) above for the use of a particular rate or method of determining a rate—

(a) shall not be exercised by any person except in relation to all such supplies by him as are of a particular description or after a particular date; and

(b) shall not be withdrawn or varied except with the consent of the Commissioners and in such manner as they may require.

(4) In specifying a method of determining a rate of exchange a notice published by the Commissioners under sub-paragraph (2) above may allow a person to apply to the Commissioners for the use, for the purpose of valuing some or all of his supplies, of a rate of exchange which is different from any which would otherwise apply.

(5) On an application made in accordance with provision contained in a notice under sub-paragraph (4) above, the Commissioners may authorise the use with respect to the applicant of such a rate of exchange, in such circumstances, in relation to such supplies and subject to such conditions as they think fit.

(6) A notice published by the Commissioners for the purposes of this paragraph may be withdrawn or varied by a subsequent notice published by the Commissioners.

(7) The time by reference to which the appropriate rate of exchange is to be determined for the purpose of valuing any supply is the time when the supply takes place; and, accordingly, the day on which it takes place is the relevant day for the purposes of sub-paragraph (1) above.

Commentary—*De Voil Indirect Tax Service* **V3.164**.

12 Regulations may require that in prescribed circumstances there is to be taken into account, as constituting part of the consideration for the purposes of section 19(2) (where it would not otherwise be so taken into account), money paid in respect of the supply by persons other than those to whom the supply is made.

Commentary—*De Voil Indirect Tax Service* **V3.153**.

13 A direction under paragraph 1 or 2 above may be varied or withdrawn by the Commissioners by a further direction given by notice in writing.

Commentary—*De Voil Indirect Tax Service* **V3.162, V3.163**.

SCHEDULE 7

VALUATION OF ACQUISITIONS FROM OTHER MEMBER STATES: SPECIAL CASES

Section 20

Amendments—Schedule 7 repealed by the Taxation (Cross-border Trade) Act 2018 s 43, Sch 8 paras 1, 92 with effect from IP completion day (11pm on 31 December 2020), by virtue of SI 2020/1642 reg 4(b).

1—*(1) Where, in the case of the acquisition of any goods from another member State—*

(a) *the relevant transaction is for a consideration in money;*

(b) *the value of the relevant transaction is (apart from this paragraph) less than the transaction's open market value;*

(c) *the supplier and the person who acquires the goods are connected; and*

(d) *that person is not entitled under sections 25 and 26 to credit for all the VAT on the acquisition,*

the Commissioners may direct that the value of the relevant transaction shall be taken to be its open market value.

(2) A direction under this paragraph shall be given by notice in writing to the person by whom the acquisition in question is made; but no direction may be given more than 3 years after the relevant time.

(3) A direction given to a person under this paragraph in respect of a transaction may include a direction that the value of any transaction—

(a) *in pursuance of which goods are acquired by him from another member State after the giving of the notice, or after such later date as may be specified in the notice; and*

(b) *as to which the conditions in paragraphs (a) to (d) of sub-paragraph (1) above are satisfied, shall be taken to be its open market value.*

(4) For the purposes of this paragraph the open market value of a transaction in pursuance of which goods are acquired from another member State shall be taken to be the amount which would fall to be taken as its value under section 20(3) if it were for such consideration in money as would be payable by a person standing in no such relationship with any person as would affect that consideration.

(5) For the purposes of this paragraph any question whether a person is connected with another shall be determined in accordance with [section 1122 of the Corporation Tax Act 2010][1]*.*

(6) A direction under this paragraph may be varied or withdrawn by the Commissioners by a further direction given by notice in writing.[2]

Commentary—*De Voil Indirect Tax Service* **V3.391**.

Amendments—[1] In sub-para (5) words substituted for words "section 839 of the Taxes Act 1988" by CTA 2010 s 1177, Sch 1 para 285(c). CTA 2010 has effect for corporation tax purposes for accounting periods ending on or after 1 April 2010, and for income and capital gains tax purposes for the tax year 2010–11 and subsequent tax years.
[2] Schedule 7 repealed by the Taxation (Cross-border Trade) Act 2018 s 43, Sch 8 paras 1, 92 with effect from IP completion day (11pm on 31 December 2020), by virtue of SI 2020/1642 reg 4(*b*).

2—*(1) Where, in such cases as the Commissioners may by regulations prescribe, goods acquired in the United Kingdom from another member State—*
  (a) are charged in connection with their removal to the United Kingdom with a duty of excise; or
  (b) on that removal are subject, in accordance with any provision for the time being having effect for transitional purposes in connection with the accession of any State to the European Union, to any EU customs duty or agricultural levy of the European Union,
then the value of the relevant transaction shall be taken for the purposes of this Act to be the sum of its value apart from this paragraph and the amount, so far as not already included in that value, of the duty or, as the case may be, agricultural levy which has been or is to be paid in respect of those goods.
(2) Sub-paragraph (1) above shall not require the inclusion of any amount of duty or agricultural levy in the value of a transaction in pursuance of which there is an acquisition of goods which, under subsection (4) of section 18, is treated as taking place before the time which is the duty point within the meaning of that section.[1]
Commentary—*De Voil Indirect Tax Service* **V3.390**.
Regulations—See VAT Regulations, SI 1995/2518 regs 96, 97.
Amendments—[1] Schedule 7 repealed by the Taxation (Cross-border Trade) Act 2018 s 43, Sch 8 paras 1, 92 with effect from IP completion day (11pm on 31 December 2020), by virtue of SI 2020/1642 reg 4(*b*).

3—*(1) Where goods are acquired from another member State in pursuance of anything which is treated as a supply for the purposes of this Act by virtue of paragraph 5(1) or 6 of Schedule 4, the value of the relevant transaction shall be determined, in a case where there is no consideration, as follows.*
(2) The value of the transaction shall be taken to be—
  (a) such consideration in money as would be payable by the supplier if he were, at the time of the acquisition, to purchase goods identical in every respect (including age and condition) to the goods concerned; or
  (b) where the value cannot be ascertained in accordance with paragraph (a) above, such consideration in money as would be payable by the supplier if he were, at that time, to purchase goods similar to, and of the same age and condition as, the goods concerned; or
  (c) where the value can be ascertained in accordance with neither paragraph (a) nor paragraph (b) above, the cost of producing the goods concerned if they were produced at that time.
(3) For the purposes of sub-paragraph (2) above the amount of consideration in money that would be payable by any person if he were to purchase any goods shall be taken to be the amount that would be so payable after the deduction of any amount included in the purchase price in respect of VAT on the supply of the goods to that person.[1]
Commentary—*De Voil Indirect Tax Service* **V3.390**.
Amendments—[1] Schedule 7 repealed by the Taxation (Cross-border Trade) Act 2018 s 43, Sch 8 paras 1, 92 with effect from IP completion day (11pm on 31 December 2020), by virtue of SI 2020/1642 reg 4(*b*).

4—*(1) Subject to the following provisions of this paragraph, where—*
  (a) goods are acquired from another member State; and
  (b) any sum relevant for determining the value of the relevant transaction is expressed in a currency other than sterling,
then, for the purpose of valuing the relevant transaction, that sum is to be converted into sterling at the market rate which, on the relevant day, would apply in the United Kingdom to a purchase with sterling by the person making the acquisition of that sum in the currency in question.
(2) Where the Commissioners have published a notice which, for the purposes of this paragraph, specifies—
  (a) rates of exchange; or
  (b) methods of determining rates of exchange,
a rate specified in or determined in accordance with the notice, as for the time being in force, shall apply (instead of the rate for which sub-paragraph (1) above provides) in the case of any transaction in pursuance of which goods are acquired by a person who opts, in such manner as may be allowed by the Commissioners, for the use of that rate in relation to that transaction.
(3) An option for the purposes of sub-paragraph (2) above for the use of a particular rate or method of determining a rate—
  (a) shall not be exercised by any person except in relation to all such transactions in pursuance of which goods are acquired by him from another member State as are of a particular description or after a particular date; and

(b) shall not be withdrawn or varied except with the consent of the Commissioners and in such manner as they may require.

(4) In specifying a method of determining a rate of exchange a notice published by the Commissioners under sub-paragraph (2) above may allow a person to apply to the Commissioners for the use, for the purpose of valuing some or all of the transactions in pursuance of which goods are acquired by him from another member State, of a rate of exchange which is different from any which would otherwise apply.

(5) On an application made in accordance with provision contained in a notice under sub-paragraph (4) above, the Commissioners may authorise the use with respect to the applicant of such a rate of exchange, in such circumstances, in relation to such transactions and subject to such conditions as they think fit.

(6) A notice published by the Commissioners for the purposes of this paragraph may be withdrawn or varied by a subsequent notice published by the Commissioners.

(7) Where goods are acquired from another member State, the appropriate rate of exchange is to be determined for the purpose of valuing the relevant transaction by reference to the relevant time; and, accordingly, the day on which that time falls is the relevant day for the purposes of sub-paragraph (1) above.[1]

Commentary—*De Voil Indirect Tax Service* **V3.393**.

Amendments—[1] Schedule 7 repealed by the Taxation (Cross-border Trade) Act 2018 s 43, Sch 8 paras 1, 92 with effect from IP completion day (11pm on 31 December 2020), by virtue of SI 2020/1642 reg 4(b).

5   In this Schedule—

"relevant transaction", in relation to any acquisition of goods from another member State, means the transaction in pursuance of which the goods are acquired;

"the relevant time", in relation to any such acquisition, means—

(a) if the person by whom the goods are acquired is not a taxable person and the time of acquisition does not fall to be determined in accordance with regulations made under section 12(3), the time of the event which, in relation to that acquisition, is the first relevant event for the purposes of taxing the acquisition; and

(b) in any other case, the time of acquisition.[1]

Amendments—[1] Schedule 7 repealed by the Taxation (Cross-border Trade) Act 2018 s 43, Sch 8 paras 1, 92 with effect from IP completion day (11pm on 31 December 2020), by virtue of SI 2020/1642 reg 4(b).

[SCHEDULE 7A
CHARGE AT REDUCED RATE]
Section 29A

Cross-references—See Sch 9ZA para 16 (reduced rate: application in relation to Northern Ireland acquisition VAT).

Amendments—This Schedule inserted by FA 2001 s 99(5), Sch 31 with effect for supplies made, and acquisitions and importations taking place, after 31 October 2001.

[PART I
INDEX TO REDUCED-RATE SUPPLIES OF GOODS AND SERVICES

[Cable-suspended passenger transport systems	Group 13][4]
[Caravans	Group 12][5]
Children's car seats	Group 5
[Contraceptive products	Group 8][2]
[Course of catering	Group 14][6]
Domestic fuel or power	Group 1
Energy-saving materials: installation	Group 2
Heating equipment, security goods and gas supplies: grant-funded installation or connection	Group 3
[Holiday accommodation etc	Group 15][6]
[Installation of mobility aids for the elderly	Group 10][3]
Residential renovations and alterations	Group 7
Residential conversions	Group 6
[Shows and certain other attractions	Group 16][6]
[Smoking cessation products	Group 11][3]
[Welfare advice or information	Group 9][2]
. . .[7]	. . .[7]][1]

Amendments—[1] This Schedule inserted by FA 2001 s 99(5), Sch 31 with effect for supplies made, and acquisitions and importations taking place, after 31 October 2001.

[2] Entries inserted by the Value Added Tax (Reduced Rate) Order, SI 2006/1472 arts 2, 3 with effect from 1 July 2006.
[3] Entries inserted by the Value Added Tax (Reduced Rate) Order, SI 2007/1601 arts 2, 3. Entry "Installation of mobility aids for the elderly" has effect in relation to supplies made on or after 1 July 2007. Entry "Smoking cessation products" has effect in relation to supplies made on or after 1 July 2007 but before 1 July 2008.
[4] Entry for "Cable-suspended passenger transport systems" (Group 13) inserted by the Value Added Tax (Reduced Rate) (Cable-Suspended Passenger Transport Systems) Order, SI 2013/430 art 2(1), (2) with effect from 1 April 2013.
[5] Entry for Caravans (Group 12) inserted by FA 2012 s 196, Sch 26 para 6(1), (2) with effect from 6 April 2013.
[6] Entries for supplies of catering, holiday accommodation and shows inserted by the Value Added Tax (Reduced Rate) (Hospitality and Tourism) (Coronavirus) Order, SI 2020/728 arts 2, 3. These changes have effect for the period beginning with 15 July 2020 and ending with 31 March 2021 (the end date was extended by SI 2020/1413; previously the temporary reduced rate had been due to end on 12 January 2021). Budget 2021 (3 March 2021) announced that the temporary 5% reduced rate will be extended until 30 September 2021. From 1 October 2021 until 31 March 2022 a new 12.5% rate will apply. See HMRC's Tax Information and Impact Note.
[7] Entry for "Women's sanitary products" (Group 4) repealed by FA 2016 s 126(1), (2)(*a*) with effect in relation to supplies made, and acquisitions and importations taking place on or after 11pm (UK time) on 31 December 2020 (by virtue of SI 2020/1642 reg 3). Note that, although the Taxation (Cross-border Trade) Act 2018 Sch 8 para 2 amends VATA 1994 s 1 to omit acquisitions from chargeable events for VAT purposes, acquisition tax continues to be charged in Northern Ireland by virtue of Sch 9ZB para 2 (as inserted by the Taxation (Post-transition Period) Act 2020 Sch 2 para 2).

[PART II
THE GROUPS

GROUP 1
SUPPLIES OF DOMESTIC FUEL OR POWER

Item No.

1 Supplies for qualifying use of—
  (*a*) coal, coke or other solid substances held out for sale solely as fuel;
  (*b*) coal gas, water gas, producer gases or similar gases;
  (*c*) petroleum gases, or other gaseous hydrocarbons, whether in a gaseous or liquid state;
  (*d*) fuel oil, gas oil or kerosene; or
  (*e*) electricity, heat or air-conditioning.

NOTES:

Matters included or not included in the supplies

1—(1) Item 1(*a*) shall be deemed to include combustible materials put up for sale for kindling fires but shall not include matches.
(2) Item 1(*b*) and (*c*) shall not include any road fuel gas (within the meaning of the Hydrocarbon Oil Duties Act 1979) on which a duty of excise has been charged or is chargeable.
(3) Item 1(*d*) shall not include hydrocarbon oil on which a duty of excise has been or is to be charged without relief from, or rebate of, such duty by virtue of the provisions of the Hydrocarbon Oil Duties Act 1979[, unless the oil is—
  (*a*) kerosene in respect of which a relevant declaration has been made under section 13AC(3) of that Act (use of rebated kerosene for private pleasure-flying); or
  (*b*) oil in respect of which a relevant declaration has been made under section 14E(3) of that Act (use of rebated heavy oil for private pleasure craft)][1].

Amendments—[1] In Note 1 para (3), words inserted at end by the Value Added Tax (Reduced Rate) (Supplies of Domestic Fuel or Power) Order, SI 2008/2676 art 2 with effect from 1 November 2008.

Prospective amendments—In Note 1 para (3), para (*b*) and preceding word "or" to be repealed by FA 2020 s 89, Sch 11 para 15 with effect from a date to be appointed.

Meaning of "fuel oil", "gas oil" and "kerosene"

2—(1) In this Group "fuel oil" means heavy oil which contains in solution an amount of asphaltenes of not less than 0.5 per cent. or which contains less than 0.5 per cent. but not less than 0.1 per cent. of asphaltenes and has a closed flash point not exceeding 150°C.
(2) In this Group "gas oil" means heavy oil of which not more than 50 per cent. by volume distils at a temperature not exceeding 240°C and of which more than 50 per cent. by volume distils at a temperature not exceeding 340°C.
(3) In this Group "kerosene" means heavy oil of which more than 50 per cent. by volume distils at a temperature not exceeding 240°C.
(4) In this paragraph "heavy oil" has the same meaning as in the Hydrocarbon Oil Duties Act 1979.

Meaning of "qualifying use"

3 In this Group "qualifying use" means—
  (*a*) domestic use; or

(b) use by a charity otherwise than in the course or furtherance of a business.

Supplies only partly for qualifying use

4 For the purposes of this Group, where there is a supply of goods partly for qualifying use and partly not—
(a) if at least 60 per cent. of the goods are supplied for qualifying use, the whole supply shall be treated as a supply for qualifying use; and
(b) in any other case, an apportionment shall be made to determine the extent to which the supply is a supply for qualifying use.

Supplies deemed to be for domestic use

5 For the purposes of this Group the following supplies are always for domestic use—
(a) a supply of not more than one tonne of coal or coke held out for sale as domestic fuel;
(b) a supply of wood, peat or charcoal not intended for sale by the recipient;
(c) a supply to a person at any premises of piped gas (that is, gas within item 1(b), or petroleum gas in a gaseous state, provided through pipes) where the gas (together with any other piped gas provided to him at the premises by the same supplier) was not provided at a rate exceeding 150 therms a month or, if the supplier charges for the gas by reference to the number of kilowatt hours supplied, 4397 kilowatt hours a month;
(d) a supply of petroleum gas in a liquid state where the gas is supplied in cylinders the net weight of each of which is less than 50 kilogrammes and either the number of cylinders supplied is 20 or fewer or the gas is not intended for sale by the recipient;
(e) a supply of petroleum gas in a liquid state, otherwise than in cylinders, to a person at any premises at which he is not able to store more than two tonnes of such gas;
(f) a supply of not more than 2,300 litres of fuel oil, gas oil or kerosene;
(g) a supply of electricity to a person at any premises where the electricity (together with any other electricity provided to him at the premises by the same supplier) was not provided at a rate exceeding 1000 kilowatt hours a month.

Other supplies that are for domestic use

6 For the purposes of this Group supplies not within paragraph 5 are for domestic use if and only if the goods supplied are for use in—
(a) a building, or part of a building, that consists of a dwelling or number of dwellings;
(b) a building, or part of a building, used for a relevant residential purpose;
(c) self-catering holiday accommodation;
(d) a caravan; or
(e) a houseboat.

Interpretation of paragraph 6

7—(1) For the purposes of this Group, "use for a relevant residential purpose" means use as—
(a) a home or other institution providing residential accommodation for children,
(b) a home or other institution providing residential accommodation with personal care for persons in need of personal care by reason of old age, disablement, past or present dependence on alcohol or drugs or past or present mental disorder,
(c) a hospice,
(d) residential accommodation for students or school pupils,
(e) residential accommodation for members of any of the armed forces,
(f) a monastery, nunnery or similar establishment, or
(g) an institution which is the sole or main residence of at least 90 per cent. of its residents,
except use as a hospital, a prison or similar institution or an hotel or inn or similar establishment.
(2) For the purposes of this Group "self-catering holiday accommodation" includes any accommodation advertised or held out as such.
(3) In paragraph 6 "houseboat" means a boat or other floating decked structure designed or adapted for use solely as a place of permanent habitation and not having means of, or capable of being readily adapted for, self-propulsion.][1]

Amendments—[1] This Schedule inserted by FA 2001 s 99(5), Sch 31 with effect for supplies made, and acquisitions and importations taking place, after 31 October 2001.

[GROUP 2
INSTALLATION OF ENERGY-SAVING MATERIALS

Item No.

[1 The supply of services of installing energy-saving materials in residential accommodation, where the energy-saving materials are not supplied by the person supplying the services.

2 The supply of services of installing energy-saving materials in residential accommodation, including the energy-saving materials installed, where—
- (a) the supply is made to a qualifying person and the residential accommodation is the qualifying person's sole or main residence,
- (b) the supply is made to a relevant housing association, or
- (c) the residential accommodation is a building, or part of a building, used solely for a relevant residential purpose.

3 The supply, in a case not falling within item 2, of services of installing energy-saving materials in residential accommodation, including the energy-saving materials installed (but see Note A1).][4]

NOTES:

[Restriction on item 3]

A1 (1) Item 3 does not apply to a supply so far as relating to the energy-saving materials installed if the open market value of the supply of the materials exceeds 60% of the cost of the total supply to the person to whom it is made.
(2) In this Note, the reference to cost is to cost net of VAT.][4]

Meaning of "energy-saving materials"

1 For the purposes of this Group "energy-saving materials" means any of the following—
- (a) insulation for walls, floors, ceilings, roofs or lofts or for water tanks, pipes or other plumbing fittings;
- (b) draught stripping for windows and doors;
- (c) central heating system controls (including thermostatic radiator valves);
- (d) hot water system controls;
- (e) solar panels;
- (f), (g) . . . [4]
- [(h) ground source heat pumps][1].
- [(i) air source heat pumps;
- (j) micro combined heat and power units;][2]
- [(k) boilers designed to be fuelled solely by wood, straw or similar vegetal matter.][3]

Amendments—[1] Note (1)(h) inserted by the VAT (Reduced Rate) Order, SI 2004/777 with effect from 1 June 2004.
[2] Note (1)(i), (j) inserted by the VAT (Reduced Rate) Order, SI 2005/726 with effect from 7 April 2005.
[3] Note (1)(k) inserted by the VAT (Reduced Rate) (No 2) Order, SI 2005/3329 with effect from 1 January 2006.
[4] Items 1–3 substituted for previous Items 1, 2, Note A1 inserted, and in Note 1 paras (f) (wind turbines) and (g) (water turbines) repealed, by the VAT (Reduced Rate) (Energy-Saving Materials) Order, SI 2019/958 arts 2–5 with effect in relation to supplies made on or after 1 October 2019, except for supplies paid for before that date, and supplies made pursuant to a contract entered into before that date. Items 1, 2 previously read as follows—

"1

Supplies of services of installing energy-saving materials in residential accommodation.

2

Supplies of energy-saving materials by a person who installs those materials in residential accommodation.".

Meaning of "residential accommodation"

2—(1) For the purposes of this Group "residential accommodation" means—
- (a) a building, or part of a building, that consists of a dwelling or a number of dwellings;
- (b) a building, or part of a building, used for a relevant residential purpose;
- (c) a caravan used as a place of permanent habitation; or
- (d) a houseboat.

(2) For the purposes of this Group "use for a relevant residential purpose" has the same meaning as it has for the purposes of Group 1 (see paragraph 7(1) of the Notes to that Group).
(3) In sub-paragraph (1)(d) "houseboat" has the meaning given by paragraph 7(3) of the Notes to Group 1.

Meaning of "use for a relevant charitable purpose"

3 For the purposes of this Group "use for a relevant charitable purpose" means use by a charity in either or both of the following ways, namely—
- (a) otherwise than in the course or furtherance of a business;

(*b*) as a village hall or similarly in providing social or recreational facilities for a local community.]¹, ²

[Meaning of "qualifying person"

4 For the purposes of this Group "qualifying person" has the same meaning as it has for the purposes of Group 3 (see paragraph 6 of the Notes to that Group).

Meaning of "relevant housing association"

5 For the purposes of this Group "relevant housing association" has the meaning given by Note (21) of Group 5 of Schedule 8 (zero-rating: construction of buildings etc.).]³

Amendments—¹ This Schedule inserted by FA 2001 s 99(5), Sch 31 with effect for supplies made, and acquisitions and importations taking place, after 31 October 2001.
² Note 3 repealed by FA 2013 s 193(1), (3) with effect in relation to supplies made on or after 1 August 2013.
³ Notes 4, 5 inserted by the VAT (Reduced Rate) (Energy-Saving Materials) Order, SI 2019/958 arts 2, 6 with effect in relation to supplies made on or after 1 October 2019, except for supplies paid for before that date, and supplies made pursuant to a contract entered into before that date.

[GROUP 3
GRANT-FUNDED INSTALLATION OF HEATING EQUIPMENT OR SECURITY GOODS OR CONNECTION OF GAS SUPPLY

Item No.

1 Supplies to a qualifying person of any services of installing heating appliances in the qualifying person's sole or main residence.

2 Supplies of heating appliances made to a qualifying person by a person who installs those appliances in the qualifying person's sole or main residence.

3 Supplies to a qualifying person of services of connecting, or reconnecting, a mains gas supply to the qualifying person's sole or main residence.

4 Supplies of goods made to a qualifying person by a person connecting, or reconnecting, a mains gas supply to the qualifying person's sole or main residence, being goods whose installation is necessary for the connection, or reconnection, of the mains gas supply.

5 Supplies to a qualifying person of services of installing, maintaining or repairing a central heating system in the qualifying person's sole or main residence.

6 Supplies of goods made to a qualifying person by a person installing, maintaining or repairing a central heating system in the qualifying person's sole or main residence, being goods whose installation is necessary for the installation, maintenance or repair of the central heating system.

7 Supplies consisting in the leasing of goods that form the whole or part of a central heating system installed in the sole or main residence of a qualifying person.

8 Supplies of goods that form the whole or part of a central heating system installed in a qualifying person's sole or main residence and that, immediately before being supplied, were goods leased under arrangements such that the consideration for the supplies consisting in the leasing of the goods was, in whole or in part, funded by a grant made under a relevant scheme.

[8A Supplies to a qualifying person of services of installing, maintaining or repairing a renewable source heating system in the qualifying person's sole or main residence.]¹

Amendments—¹ Items 8A, 8B inserted, words in Notes (1), (4) substituted, and Notes (4A), (4B) inserted, by the VAT (Reduced Rate) Order, SI 2002/1100 arts 2, 3 with effect from 1 June 2002.

[8B Supplies of goods made to a qualifying person by a person installing, maintaining or repairing a renewable source heating system in the qualifying person's sole or main residence, being goods whose installation is necessary for the installation, maintenance or repair of the system.]¹

Amendments—¹ Items 8A, 8B inserted, words in Notes (1), (4) substituted, and Notes (4A), (4B) inserted, by the VAT (Reduced Rate) Order, SI 2002/1100 arts 2, 3 with effect from 1 June 2002.

9 Supplies to a qualifying person of services of installing qualifying security goods in the qualifying person's sole or main residence.

10 Supplies of qualifying security goods made to a qualifying person by a person who installs those goods in the qualifying person's sole or main residence.

NOTES:

Supply only included so far as grant-funded

1—(1) Each of [items 1 to 7 and 8A to 10][1] applies to a supply only to the extent that the consideration for the supply is, or is to be, funded by a grant made under a relevant scheme.
(2) Item 8 applies to a supply only to the extent that the consideration for the supply—
  (*a*) is, or is to be, funded by a grant made under a relevant scheme; or
  (*b*) is a payment becoming due only by reason of the termination (whether by the passage of time or otherwise) of the leasing of the goods in question.

Amendments—[1] Words substituted by the VAT (Reduced Rate) Order, SI 2002/1100 arts 2, 3 with effect from 1 June 2002.

Meaning of "relevant scheme"

2—(1) For the purposes of this Group a scheme is a "relevant scheme" if it is one which satisfies the conditions specified in this paragraph.
(2) The first condition is that the scheme has as one of its objectives the funding of the installation of energy-saving materials in the homes of any persons who are qualifying persons.
(3) The second condition is that the scheme disburses, whether directly or indirectly, its grants in whole or in part out of funds made available to it in order to achieve that objective—
  (*a*) by the Secretary of State,
  (*b*) by the Scottish Ministers,
  (*c*) by the National Assembly for Wales,
  (*d*) by a Minister (within the meaning given by section 7(3) of the Northern Ireland Act 1998) or a Northern Ireland department,
  (*e*) . . . [1]
  (*f*) under an arrangement approved by the Gas and Electricity Markets Authority,
  (*g*) under an arrangement approved by the Director General of Electricity Supply for Northern Ireland, or
  (*h*) by a local authority.
(4) The reference in sub-paragraph (3)(*f*) to an arrangement approved by the Gas and Electricity Markets Authority includes a reference to an arrangement approved by the Director General of Electricity Supply, or the Director General of Gas Supply, before the transfer (under the Utilities Act 2000) of his functions to the Authority.

Amendments—[1] Sub-para (3)(*e*) repealed by the Taxation (Cross-border Trade) Act 2018 s 43, Sch 8 paras 1, 93 with effect from IP completion day (11pm on 31 December 2020), by virtue of SI 2020/1642 reg 4(*b*).
Sub-para (3)(*e*) previously read as follows—
  "(*e*) by the European Union,".

Apportionment of grants that also cover other supplies

3 Where a grant is made under a relevant scheme in order—
  (*a*) to fund a supply of a description to which any of items 1 to 10 applies ("the relevant supply"), and
  (*b*) also to fund a supply to which none of those items applies ("the non-relevant supply"),
the proportion of the grant that is to be attributed, for the purposes of paragraph 1, to the relevant supply shall be the same proportion as the consideration reasonably attributable to that supply bears to the consideration for that supply and for the non-relevant supply.

Meaning of "heating appliances"

4 For the purposes of items 1 and 2 "heating appliances" means any of the following—
  (*a*) gas-fired room heaters that are fitted with thermostatic controls;
  (*b*) electric storage heaters;
  (*c*) closed solid fuel fire cassettes;
  (*d*) electric dual immersion water heaters with [factory-insulated][1] hot water tanks;
  (*e*) gas-fired boilers;
  (*f*) oil-fired boilers;
  (*g*) radiators.

Amendments—[1] Words substituted by the VAT (Reduced Rate) Order, SI 2002/1100 arts 2, 3 with effect from 1 June 2002.

[Meaning of "central heating system"

4A For the purposes of items 5 to 8 "central heating system" includes a system which generates electricity.][1]

Amendments—[1] Notes (4A), (4B) inserted, by the VAT (Reduced Rate) Order, SI 2002/1100 arts 2, 3 with effect from 1 June 2002.

[Meaning of "renewable source heating system"

4B For the purposes of items 8A and 8B "renewable source heating system" means a space or water heating system which uses energy from—
  (*a*) renewable sources, including solar, wind and hydroelectric power; or
  (*b*) near renewable resources, including ground and air heat.]¹

Amendments—¹ Notes (4A), (4B) inserted, by the VAT (Reduced Rate) Order, SI 2002/1100 arts 2, 3 with effect from 1 June 2002.

Meaning of "qualifying security goods"

5 For the purposes of items 9 and 10 "qualifying security goods" means any of the following—
  (*a*) locks or bolts for windows;
  (*b*) locks, bolts or security chains for doors;
  (*c*) spy holes;
  (*d*) smoke alarms.

Meaning of "qualifying person"

6—(1) For the purposes of this Group, a person to whom a supply is made is "a qualifying person" if at the time of the supply he—
  (*a*) is aged 60 or over; or
  (*b*) is in receipt of one or more of the benefits mentioned in sub-paragraph (2).
(2) Those benefits are—
  (*a*) council tax benefit under Part VII of the Contributions and Benefits Act;
  (*b*) disability living allowance under Part III of the Contributions and Benefits Act or Part III of the Northern Ireland Act;
  (*c*) [any element of child tax credit other than the family element, working tax credit,]² housing benefit or income support under Part VII of the Contributions and Benefits Act or Part VII of the Northern Ireland Act;
  (*d*) an income-based jobseeker's allowance within the meaning of section 1(4) of the Jobseekers Act 1995 or Article 3(4) of the Jobseekers (Northern Ireland) Order 1995;
  (*e*) disablement pension under Part V of the Contributions and Benefits Act, or Part V of the Northern Ireland Act, that is payable at the increased rate provided for under section 104 (constant attendance allowance) of the Act concerned;
  (*f*) war disablement pension under the Naval, Military and Air Forces Etc. (Disablement and Death) Service Pensions Order 1983 that is payable at the increased rate provided for under article 14 (constant attendance allowance) or article 26A (mobility supplement) of that Order.
  [(*g*) personal independence payment under Part 4 of the Welfare Reform Act 2012 or the corresponding provision having effect in Northern Ireland;
  (*h*) armed forces independence payment under a scheme established under section 1 of the Armed Forces (Pensions and Compensation) Act 2004.]³
  [(*i*) universal credit under Part 1 of the Welfare Reform Act 2012.]⁴
(3) In sub-paragraph (2)—
  (*a*) "the Contributions and Benefits Act" means the Social Security Contributions and Benefits Act 1992; and
  (*b*) "the Northern Ireland Act" means the Social Security Contributions and Benefits (Northern Ireland) Act 1992.]¹

Amendments—¹ This Schedule inserted by FA 2001 s 99(5), Sch 31 with effect for supplies made, and acquisitions and importations taking place, after 31 October 2001.
² Words substituted by TCA 2002 s 47, Sch 3 paras 47, 48 with effect from 6 April 2003 (by virtue of SI 2003/962).
³ Paras (6)(*g*), (*h*) inserted by the Value Added Tax (Independence Payment) Order, SI 2013/601 art 2 with effect from 8 April 2013.
⁴ Para (2)(*i*) inserted by the Universal Credit (Consequential, Supplementary, Incidental and Miscellaneous Provisions) Regulations, SI 2013/630 reg 9 with effect from 29 April 2013.

Prospective amendments—In Note 6(2)(*b*), words "Part III of the Contributions and Benefits Act or" to be repealed by the Welfare Reform Act 2012 s 147, Sch 14 Part 9 with effect from a date to be appointed.
In Note 6(2)(*i*), words "or Part 2 of the Welfare Reform (Northern Ireland) Order 2015" to be inserted after words "Welfare Reform Act 2012" by the Universal Credit (Consequential, Supplementary, Incidental and Miscellaneous Provisions) Regulations (Northern Ireland), NISR 2016/236 art 5(1), (2) with effect from a date to be appointed.
Note 6(2)(*b*) to be repealed by the Welfare Reform (Northern Ireland) Order, SI 2015/2006 art 140 Sch 12 Pt 8 with effect from a date to be appointed. This amendment extends to Northern Ireland only (SI 2015/2006 art 3).

GROUP 4
WOMEN'S SANITARY PRODUCTS

Item No.

1 Supplies of women's sanitary products.
NOTES:

Meaning of "women's sanitary products"

1—(1) In this Group "women's sanitary products" means women's sanitary products of any of the following descriptions—
   (a) subject to sub-paragraph (2), products that are designed, and marketed, as being solely for use for absorbing, or otherwise collecting, lochia or menstrual flow;
   (b) panty liners, other than panty liners that are designed as being primarily for use as incontinence products;
   (c) sanitary belts.
(2) Sub-paragraph (1)(a) does not include protective briefs or any other form of clothing.[1]

Amendments—[1] Group 4 ("women's sanitary products") repealed by FA 2016 s 126(1), (2)(b) with effect in relation to supplies made, and acquisitions and importations taking place on or after 11pm (UK time) on 31 December 2020 (by virtue of SI 2020/1642 reg 3). Note that, although the Taxation (Cross-border Trade) Act 2018 Sch 8 para 2 amends VATA 1994 s 1 to omit acquisitions from chargeable events for VAT purposes, acquisition tax continues to be charged in Northern Ireland by virtue of Sch 9ZB para 2 (as inserted by the Taxation (Post-transition Period) Act 2020 Sch 2 para 2).

[GROUP 5
CHILDREN'S CAR SEATS

Item No.

1 Supplies of children's car seats.
NOTES:

Meaning of "children's car seats"

1—(1) For the purposes of this Group, the following are "children's car seats"—
   (a) a safety seat;
   [(aa) a related base unit for a safety seat;][1]
   (b) the combination of a safety seat and a related wheeled framework;
   (c) a booster seat;
   (d) a booster cushion.
(2) In this Group "child" means a person aged under 14 years.

Amendments—[1] In Note 1, para (1)(aa) inserted by the Value Added Tax (Reduced Rate) (Children's Car Seats) Order, SI 2009/1359 arts 2, 3 with effect in relation to supplies made, and acquisitions and importations taking place, on or after 1 July 2009.

Meaning of "safety seat"

2 In this Group "safety seat" means a seat—
   (a) designed to be sat in by a child in a road vehicle,
   [(b) designed so that, when in use in a road vehicle, it can be restrained in one or more of the following ways—
      (i) by a seat belt fitted in the vehicle, or
      (ii) by belts, or anchorages, that form part of the seat being attached to the vehicle, or
      (iii) by a related base unit, and][1]
   (c) incorporating an integral harness, or integral impact shield, for restraining a child seated in it.

Amendments—[1] Note 2 para (b) substituted, by the Value Added Tax (Reduced Rate) (Children's Car Seats) Order, SI 2009/1359 arts 2, 3 with effect in relation to supplies made, and acquisitions and importations taking place, on or after 1 July 2009.

[Meaning of "related base unit"

2A In this Group "related base unit" means a base unit which is designed solely for the purpose of attaching a safety seat securely in a road vehicle by means of anchorages that form part of the base unit and which, when in use in a road vehicle, can be restrained in one or more of the following ways—
   (a) by a seat belt fitted in the vehicle, or
   (b) by permanent anchorage points in the vehicle, or
   (c) by belts attached to permanent anchorage points in the vehicle.][1]

Amendments—[1] Note 2A inserted, by the Value Added Tax (Reduced Rate) (Children's Car Seats) Order, SI 2009/1359 arts 2, 3 with effect in relation to supplies made, and acquisitions and importations taking place, on or after 1 July 2009.

Meaning of "related wheeled framework"

3 For the purposes of this Group, a wheeled framework is "related" to a safety seat if the framework and the seat are each designed so that—
   (*a*) when the seat is not in use in a road vehicle it can be attached to the framework, and
   (*b*) when the seat is so attached, the combination of the seat and the framework can be used as a child's pushchair.

Meaning of "booster seat"

4 In this Group "booster seat" means a seat designed—
   (*a*) to be sat in by a child in a road vehicle, and
   (*b*) so that, when in use in a road vehicle, it and a child seated in it can be restrained by a seat belt fitted in the vehicle.

Meaning of "booster cushion"

5 In this Group "booster cushion" means a cushion designed—
   (*a*) to be sat on by a child in a road vehicle, and
   (*b*) so that a child seated on it can be restrained by a seat belt fitted in the vehicle.][1]

Amendments—[1] This Schedule inserted by FA 2001 s 99(5), Sch 31 with effect for supplies made, and acquisitions and importations taking place, after 31 October 2001.

[GROUP 6
RESIDENTIAL CONVERSIONS

Item No.

1 The supply, in the course of a qualifying conversion, of qualifying services related to the conversion.

2 The supply of building materials if—
   (*a*) the materials are supplied by a person who, in the course of a qualifying conversion, is supplying qualifying services related to the conversion, and
   (*b*) those services include the incorporation of the materials in the building concerned or its immediate site.

NOTES:

Supplies only partly within item 1

1—(1) Sub-paragraph (2) applies where a supply of services is only in part a supply to which item 1 applies.
(2) The supply, to the extent that it is one to which item 1 applies, is to be taken to be a supply to which item 1 applies.
(3) An apportionment may be made to determine that extent.

Meaning of "qualifying conversion"

2—(1) A "qualifying conversion" means—
   (*a*) a changed number of dwellings conversion (see paragraph 3);
   (*b*) a house in multiple occupation conversion (see paragraph 5); or
   (*c*) a special residential conversion (see paragraph 7).
(2) Sub-paragraph (1) is subject to paragraphs 9 and 10.

Meaning of "changed number of dwellings conversion"

3—(1) A "changed number of dwellings conversion" is—
   (*a*) a conversion of premises consisting of a building where the conditions specified in this paragraph are satisfied, or
   (*b*) a conversion of premises consisting of a part of a building where those conditions are satisfied.
(2) The first condition is that after the conversion the premises being converted contain a number of single household dwellings that is—
   (*a*) different from the number (if any) that the premises contain before the conversion, and
   (*b*) greater than, or equal to, one.
(3) The second condition is that there is no part of the premises being converted that is a part that after the conversion contains the same number of single household dwellings (whether zero, one or two or more) as before the conversion.

Meaning of "single household dwelling" and "multiple occupancy dwelling"

4—(1) For the purposes of this Group "single household dwelling" means a dwelling—
  (a) that is designed for occupation by a single household, and
  (b) in relation to which the conditions set out in sub-paragraph (3) are satisfied.
(2) For the purposes of this Group "multiple occupancy dwelling" means a dwelling—
  (a) that is designed for occupation by persons not forming a single household, . . .
  [(aa) that is not to any extent used for a relevant residential purpose, and][1]
  (b) in relation to which the conditions set out in sub-paragraph (3) are satisfied.
(3) The conditions are—
  (a) that the dwelling consists of self-contained living accommodation,
  (b) that there is no provision for direct internal access from the dwelling to any other dwelling or part of a dwelling,
  (c) that the separate use of the dwelling is not prohibited by the terms of any covenant, statutory planning consent or similar provision, and
  (d) that the separate disposal of the dwelling is not prohibited by any such terms.
(4) For the purposes of this paragraph, a dwelling "is designed" for occupation of a particular kind if it is so designed—
  (a) as a result of having been originally constructed for occupation of that kind and not having been subsequently adapted for occupation of any other kind, or
  (b) as a result of adaptation.

Amendments—[1] Note (4)(2)(aa) inserted by the VAT (Reduced Rate) Order, SI 2002/1100 arts 2, 4 with effect from 1 June 2002.

Meaning of "house in multiple occupation conversion"

5—(1) A "house in multiple occupation conversion" is—
  (a) a conversion of premises consisting of a building where the condition specified in sub-paragraph (2) below is satisfied, or
  (b) a conversion of premises consisting of a part of a building where that condition is satisfied.
(2) The condition is that—
  [(a) before the conversion the premises being converted do not contain any multiple occupancy dwellings,][1]
  (b) after the conversion those premises contain only a multiple occupancy dwelling or two or more such dwellings, and
  (c) the use to which those premises are intended to be put after the conversion is not to any extent use for a relevant residential purpose.

Amendments—[1] Note 5(2)(a) substituted by the VAT (Reduced Rate) Order, SI 2002/1100 arts 2, 4 with effect from 1 June 2002.

Meaning of "use for a relevant residential purpose"

6 For the purposes of this Group "use for a relevant residential purpose" means use as—
  (a) a home or other institution providing residential accommodation for children,
  (b) a home or other institution providing residential accommodation with personal care for persons in need of personal care by reason of old age, disablement, past or present dependence on alcohol or drugs or past or present mental disorder,
  (c) a hospice,
  (d) residential accommodation for students or school pupils,
  (e) residential accommodation for members of any of the armed forces,
  (f) a monastery, nunnery or similar establishment, or
  (g) an institution which is the sole or main residence of at least 90 per cent. of its residents,
except use as a hospital, prison or similar institution or an hotel, inn or similar establishment.

Meaning of "special residential conversion"

7—(1) A "special residential conversion" is a conversion of premises consisting of—
  (a) a building or two or more buildings,
  (b) a part of a building or two or more parts of buildings, or
  (c) a combination of—
    (i) a building or two or more buildings, and
    (ii) a part of a building or two or more parts of buildings,
  where the conditions specified in this paragraph are satisfied.
[(2) The first condition is that—

(a) the use to which the premises being converted were last put before the conversion was not to any extent use for a relevant residential purpose, and
(b) those premises are intended to be used solely for a relevant residential purpose after the conversion.]¹
(3)–(5) . . . ¹
(6) The [second]¹ condition is that, where the relevant residential purpose [for which the premises are intended to be used]¹ is an institutional purpose, the premises being converted must be intended to form after the conversion the entirety of an institution used for that purpose.
(7) In sub-paragraph (6) "institutional purpose" means a purpose within paragraph 6(a) to (c), (f) or (g).

Amendments—¹ Note 7(2) and words in Note 7(6) substituted, Notes 7(3)–(5) repealed, by the VAT (Reduced Rate) Order, SI 2002/1100 arts 2, 4 with effect from 1 June 2002.

Special residential conversions: reduced rate only for supplies made to intended user of converted accommodation

8—(1) This paragraph applies where the qualifying conversion concerned is a special residential conversion.
(2) Item 1 or 2 does not apply to a supply unless—
   (a) it is made to a person who intends to use the premises being converted for the relevant residential purpose, and
   (b) before it is made, the person to whom it is made has given to the person making it a certificate that satisfies the requirements in sub-paragraph (3).
(3) Those requirements are that the certificate—
   (a) is in such form as may be specified in a notice published by the Commissioners, and
   (b) states that the conversion is a special residential conversion.
(4) In sub-paragraph (2)(a) "the relevant residential purpose" means the purpose within paragraph 6 for which the premises being converted are intended to be used after the conversion.

"Qualifying conversion" includes related garage works

9—(1) A qualifying conversion includes any garage works related to the—
   (a) changed number of dwellings conversion,
   (b) house in multiple occupation conversion, or
   (c) special residential conversion,
concerned.
(2) In this paragraph "garage works" means—
   (a) the construction of a garage, or
   (b) a conversion of a non-residential building, or of a non-residential part of a building, that results in a garage.
(3) For the purposes of sub-paragraph (1), garage works are "related" to a conversion if—
   (a) they are carried out at the same time as the conversion, and
   (b) the resulting garage is intended to be occupied with—
      (i) where the conversion concerned is a changed number of dwellings conversion, a single household dwelling that will after the conversion be contained in the building, or part of a building, being converted,
      (ii) where the conversion concerned is a house in multiple occupation conversion, a multiple occupancy dwelling that will after the conversion be contained in the building, or part of a building, being converted, or
      (iii) where the conversion concerned is a special residential conversion, the institution or other accommodation resulting from the conversion.
(4) In sub-paragraph (2) "non-residential" means neither designed, nor adapted, for use—
   (a) as a dwelling or two or more dwellings, or
   (b) for a relevant residential purpose.

Conversion not "qualifying" if planning consent and building control approval not obtained

10—(1) A conversion is not a qualifying conversion if any statutory planning consent needed for the conversion has not been granted.
(2) A conversion is not a qualifying conversion if any statutory building control approval needed for the conversion has not been granted.

Meaning of "supply of qualifying services"

11—(1) In the case of a conversion of a building, "supply of qualifying services" means a supply of services that consists in—

(a) the carrying out of works to the fabric of the building, or
(b) the carrying out of works within the immediate site of the building that are in connection with—
  (i) the means of providing water, power, heat or access to the building,
  (ii) the means of providing drainage or security for the building, or
  (iii) the provision of means of waste disposal for the building.

(2) In the case of a conversion of part of a building, "supply of qualifying services" means a supply of services that consists in—
  (a) the carrying out of works to the fabric of the part, or
  (b) the carrying out of works to the fabric of the building, or within the immediate site of the building, that are in connection with—
    (i) the means of providing water, power, heat or access to the part,
    (ii) the means of providing drainage or security for the part, or
    (iii) the provision of means of waste disposal for the part.

(3) In this paragraph—
  (a) references to the carrying out of works to the fabric of a building do not include the incorporation, or installation as fittings, in the building of any goods that are not building materials;
  (b) references to the carrying out of works to the fabric of a part of a building do not include the incorporation, or installation as fittings, in the part of any goods that are not building materials.

Meaning of "building materials"

12 In this Group "building materials" has the meaning given by Notes (22) and (23) of Group 5 to Schedule 8 (zero-rating of construction and conversion of buildings).][1]

Amendments—[1] This Schedule inserted by FA 2001 s 99(5), Sch 31 with effect for supplies made, and acquisitions and importations taking place, after 31 October 2001.

[GROUP 7
[RESIDENTIAL RENOVATIONS AND ALTERATIONS]

Amendments—Title substituted, words in Items 1 and 2, Note (2) substituted, Notes (3) and (5) amended, and Notes (3A), (4A) inserted, by the VAT (Reduced Rate) Order, SI 2002/1100 arts 2, 5 with effect from 1 June 2002.

Item No.

1 The supply, in the course of the renovation or alteration of [qualifying residential premises][1], of qualifying services related to the renovation or alteration.

Amendments—[1] Words in Items 1 and 2 substituted by the VAT (Reduced Rate) Order, SI 2002/1100 arts 2, 5 with effect from 1 June 2002.

2 The supply of building materials if—
  (a) the materials are supplied by a person who, in the course of the renovation or alteration of a [qualifying residential premises], is supplying qualifying services related to the renovation or alteration, and
  (b) those services include the incorporation of the materials in [the premises concerned or their immediate site][1].

Amendments—[1] Words in Items 1 and 2 substituted by the VAT (Reduced Rate) Order, SI 2002/1100 arts 2, 5 with effect from 1 June 2002.

NOTES:

Supplies only partly within item 1

1—(1) Sub-paragraph (2) applies where a supply of services is only in part a supply to which item 1 applies.
(2) The supply, to the extent that it is one to which item 1 applies, is to be taken to be a supply to which item 1 applies.
(3) An apportionment may be made to determine that extent.

Meaning of "alteration" and "single household dwelling"

2—(1) For the purposes of this Group—
  "alteration" includes extension;
  "qualifying residential premises" means—
    (a) a single household dwelling,
    (b) a multiple occupancy dwelling, or

(c) a building, or part of a building, which, when it was last lived in, was used for a relevant residential purpose.

(2) Where a building, when it was last lived in, formed part of a relevant residential unit then, to the extent that it would not be so regarded otherwise, the building shall be treated as having been used for a relevant residential purpose.

(3) A building forms part of a relevant residential unit at any time when—
  (a) it is one of a number of buildings on the same site, and
  (b) the buildings are used together as a unit for a relevant residential purpose.

(4) The following expressions have the same meaning in this Group as they have in Group 6—
  "multiple occupancy dwelling" (paragraph 4(2) of the Notes to that Group);
  "single household dwelling" (paragraph 4(1) of the Notes);
  "use for a relevant residential purpose" (paragraph 6 of the Notes).]

Items 1 and 2 only apply where [premises have] been empty for at least [2 years]

3—[(1) Item 1 or 2 does not apply to a supply unless—
  (a) the first empty home condition is satisfied, or
  (b) if the premises are a single household dwelling, either of the empty home conditions is satisfied.]

[(2) The first "empty home condition" is that neither—
  (a) the premises concerned, nor
  (b) where those premises are a building, or part of a building, which, when it was last lived in, formed part of a relevant residential unit, any of the other buildings that formed part of the unit,
have been lived in during the period of [2 years] ending with the commencement of the relevant works.]

(3) The second "empty home condition" is that—
  (a) the dwelling was not lived in during a period of at least [2 years];
  (b) the person, or one the persons, whose beginning to live in the dwelling brought that period to an end was a person who (whether alone or jointly with another or others) acquired the dwelling at a time—
    (i) no later than the end of that period, and
    (ii) when the dwelling had been not lived in for at least [2 years];
  (c) no works by way of renovation or alteration were carried out to the dwelling during the period of [2 years] ending with the acquisition;
  (d) the supply is made to a person who is—
    (i) the person, or one of the persons, whose beginning to live in the property brought to an end the period mentioned in paragraph (a), and
    (ii) the person, or one of the persons, who acquired the dwelling as mentioned in paragraph (b); and
  (e) the relevant works are carried out during the period of one year beginning with the day of the acquisition.

(4) In this paragraph "the relevant works" means—
  (a) where the supply is of the description set out in item 1, the works that constitute the services supplied;
  (b) where the supply is of the description set out in item 2, the works by which the materials concerned are incorporated in [the premises concerned or their immediate site].

(5) In sub-paragraph (3), references to a person acquiring a dwelling are to that person having a major interest in the dwelling granted, or assigned, to him for a consideration.

[Items 1 and 2 apply to related garage works

3A—(1) For the purposes of this Group a renovation or alteration of any premises includes any garage works related to the renovation or alteration.

(2) In this paragraph "garage works" means—
  (a) the construction of a garage,
  (b) the conversion of a building, or of a part of a building, that results in a garage, or
  (c) the renovation or alteration of a garage.

(3) For the purposes of sub-paragraph (1), garage works are "related" to a renovation or alteration if—
  (a) they are carried out at the same time as the renovation or alteration of the premises concerned, and
  (b) the garage is intended to be occupied with the premises.]

Items 1 and 2 only apply if planning consent and building control approval obtained

4—(1) Item 1 or 2 does not apply to a supply unless any statutory planning consent needed for the renovation or alteration has been granted.
(2) Item 1 or 2 does not apply to a supply unless any statutory building control approval needed for the renovation or alteration has been granted.

[Items 1 and 2 only apply if building used for relevant residential purpose is subsequently used solely for that purpose

4A—(1) Item 1 or 2 does not apply to a supply if the premises in question are a building, or part of a building, which, when it was last lived in, was used for a relevant residential purpose unless—
   (a) the building or part is intended to be used solely for such a purpose after the renovation or alteration, and
   (b) before the supply is made the person to whom it is made has given to the person making it a certificate stating that intention.
(2) Where a number of buildings on the same site are—
   (a) renovated or altered at the same time, and
   (b) intended to be used together as a unit solely for a relevant residential purpose,
then each of those buildings, to the extent that it would not be so regarded otherwise, shall be treated as intended for use solely for a relevant residential purpose.]

Meaning of "supply of qualifying services"

5—(1) "Supply of qualifying services" means a supply of services that consists in—
   (a) the carrying out of works to the fabric of the [premises], or
   (b) the carrying out of works within the immediate site of the [premises] that are in connection with—
      (i) the means of providing water, power, heat or access to the [premises],
      (ii) the means of providing drainage or security for the [premises], or
      (iii) the provision of means of waste disposal for the [premises].
(2) In sub-paragraph (1)(a), the reference to the carrying out of works to the fabric of the [premises] does not include the incorporation, or installation as fittings, in the [premises] of any goods that are not building materials.

Meaning of "building materials"

6 In this Group "building materials" has the meaning given by Notes (22) and (23) of Group 5 to Schedule 8 (zero-rating of construction and conversion of buildings).]

Commentary—*De Voil Indirect Tax Service* **V4.413**.
Amendments—This Schedule inserted by FA 2001 s 99(5), Sch 31 with effect for supplies made, and acquisitions and importations taking place, after 31 October 2001.
Note (2) substituted, Notes (3) and (5) amended, and Notes (3A), (4A) inserted, by the VAT (Reduced Rate) Order, SI 2002/1100 arts 2, 5 with effect from 1 June 2002.
Words "2 years" in Note (3), and in heading to Note (3), substituted by the VAT (Reduced Rate) (No 2) Order, SI 2007/3448 regs 2–4 with effect from 1 January 2008: SI 2007/3448 reg 1.

[GROUP 8
CONTRACEPTIVE PRODUCTS

Item No

1 Supplies of contraceptive products, other than relevant exempt supplies.
NOTES:[1]

Meaning of "contraceptive products"

1 In this Group "contraceptive product" means any product designed for the purposes of human contraception, but does not include any product designed for the purpose of monitoring fertility.

Meaning of "relevant exempt supplies"

2 In this Group "relevant exempt supplies" means supplies which fall within item 4 of Group 7 of Schedule 9 (exempt supplies of goods in any hospital etc in connection with medical or surgical treatment).][1]

Amendments—[1] This Group inserted by the Value Added Tax (Reduced Rate) Order, SI 2006/1472 arts 2, 4, Schedule with effect from 1 July 2006.

[GROUP 9
WELFARE ADVICE OR INFORMATION

Item No

1 Supplies of welfare advice or information by—
(*a*) a charity, or
(*b*) a state-regulated private welfare institution or agency.

NOTES:

Meaning of "welfare advice or information"

1 In this Group "welfare advice or information" means advice or information which directly relates to—
(*a*) the physical or mental welfare of elderly, sick, distressed or disabled persons, or
(*b*) the care or protection of children and young persons.

Meaning of "state-regulated"

2 For the purposes of this Group "state-regulated" has the same meaning as in Group 7 (health and welfare) of Schedule 9 (see Note (8) of that Group).

Supplies not included in item 1

3 Item 1 does not include—
(*a*) supplies that would be exempt by virtue of Group 6 of Schedule 9 (education) if they were made by an eligible body within the meaning of that Group,
(*b*) supplies of goods, unless the goods are supplied wholly or almost wholly for the purpose of conveying the advice or information, or
(*c*) supplies of advice or information provided solely for the benefit of a particular individual or according to his personal circumstances.][1]

Amendments—[1] This Group inserted by the Value Added Tax (Reduced Rate) Order, SI 2006/1472 arts 2, 4, Schedule with effect from 1 July 2006.

[GROUP 10
INSTALLATION OF MOBILITY AIDS FOR THE ELDERLY

Item No

1 The supply of services of installing mobility aids for use in domestic accommodation by a person who, at the time of the supply, is aged 60 or over.

2 The supply of mobility aids by a person installing them for use in domestic accommodation by a person who, at the time of the supply, is aged 60 or over.

NOTES:

Meaning of "mobility aids"

1 For the purposes of this Group "mobility aids" means any of the following—
(*a*) grab rails;
(*b*) ramps;
(*c*) stair lifts;
(*d*) bath lifts;
(*e*) built-in shower seats or showers containing built-in shower seats;
(*f*) walk-in baths fitted with sealable doors.

Meaning of "domestic accommodation"

2 For the purposes of this Group "domestic accommodation" means a building, or part of a building, that consists of a dwelling or a number of dwellings.][1]

Amendments—[1] This Group inserted by the Value Added Tax (Reduced Rate) Order, SI 2007/1601 arts 2, 4, with effect in relation to supplies made on or after 1 July 2007.

[GROUP 11
SMOKING CESSATION PRODUCTS

Item No.

1 Supplies of pharmaceutical products designed to help people to stop smoking tobacco.][1]

Order—The Value Added Tax (Reduced Rate) (Smoking Cessation Products) Order, SI 2008/1410 arts 2, 3 (the reduced rate provided for in Group 11 shall have effect in relation to supplies made on or after 1 July 2008).

Amendments—[1] This Group inserted by the Value Added Tax (Reduced Rate) Order, SI 2007/1601 arts 2, 5, with effect in relation to supplies made on or after 1 July 2007 but before 1 July 2008. The reduced rate for smoking cessation products continues in relation to supplies made on or after 1 July 2008: see note above.

[GROUP 12
CARAVANS

Item No

1 Supplies of caravans which exceed the limits of size of a trailer for the time being permitted to be towed on roads by a motor vehicle having a maximum gross weight of 3,500 kilogrammes.

2 The supply of such services as are described in paragraph 1(1) or 5(4) of Schedule 4 in respect of a caravan within item 1.

NOTE:

This Group does not include—
- (a) removable contents other than goods of a kind mentioned in item 4 of Group 5 of Schedule 8, or
- (b) the supply of accommodation in a caravan.][1]

Amendments—[1] Group 12 inserted by FA 2012 s 196, Sch 26 para 6(1), (3) with effect from 6 April 2013.

[GROUP 13
CABLE-SUSPENDED PASSENGER TRANSPORT SYSTEMS

Item No

1 Transport of passengers by means of a cable-suspended chair, bar, gondola or similar vehicle designed or adapted to carry not more than 9 passengers.

NOTES:

Supplies not within item 1

1. Item 1 does not include the transport of passengers to, from or within—
   - (i) a place of entertainment, recreation or amusement; or
   - (ii) a place of cultural, scientific, historical or similar interest,

by the person, or a person connected with that person, who supplies a right of admission to, or a right to use facilities at, such a place.

2. For the purposes of Note 1 any question as to whether a person is connected with another shall be determined in accordance with section 1122 of the Corporation Tax Act 2010.][1]

Amendments—[1] Group 13 inserted by the Value Added Tax (Reduced Rate) (Cable-Suspended Passenger Transport Systems) Order, SI 2013/430 art 2(1), (3) with effect from 1 April 2013.

[GROUP 14
COURSE OF CATERING

Item No

1 Supplies in the course of catering of—
   - (a) any food or drink for consumption on the premises on which it is supplied, or
   - (b) any hot food or hot drink for consumption off those premises,

except supplies of alcoholic beverages.

NOTES

(1) Note (3A) to Group 1 (Food) of Schedule 8 applies in relation to this Group as it applies in relation to Note (3) in that Group.

(2) Notes (3B) to (3D) to Group 1 (Food) of Schedule 8 apply in relation to this Group as they apply in relation to that Group.

(3) "Alcoholic beverage" means a beverage within Item 3 in the list of excepted items in Group 1 of Schedule 8.][1]

Amendments—[1] Groups 14–16 inserted by the Value Added Tax (Reduced Rate) (Hospitality and Tourism) (Coronavirus) Order, SI 2020/728 arts 2, 4. These changes have effect for the period beginning with 15 July 2020 and ending with 31 March 2021 (the end date was extended by SI 2020/1413; previously the temporary reduced rate had been due to end on 12 January 2021). Budget 2021 (3 March 2021) announced that the temporary 5% reduced rate will be extended until 30 September 2021. From 1 October 2021 until 31 March 2022 a new 12.5% rate will apply. See HMRC's Tax Information and Impact Note.

[GROUP 15
HOLIDAY ACCOMMODATION ETC

Item No

1 Any supply which, because it falls within paragraph (*d*), (*e*) so far as the supply consists of the grant of a licence to occupy holiday accommodation, (*f*) or (*g*) of Item 1 in Group 1 (Land) of Schedule 9, is not an exempt supply by virtue of that Item.][1]

Amendments—[1] Groups 14–16 inserted by the Value Added Tax (Reduced Rate) (Hospitality and Tourism) (Coronavirus) Order, SI 2020/728 arts 2, 4. These changes have effect for the period beginning with 15 July 2020 and ending with 31 March 2021 (the end date was extended by SI 2020/1413; previously the temporary reduced rate had been due to end on 12 January 2021). Budget 2021 (3 March 2021) announced that the temporary 5% reduced rate will be extended until 30 September 2021. From 1 October 2021 until 31 March 2022 a new 12.5% rate will apply. See HMRC's Tax Information and Impact Note.

[GROUP 16
SHOWS AND CERTAIN OTHER ATTRACTIONS

Item No

1 Supplies of a right of admission to shows, theatres, circuses, fairs, amusement parks, concerts, museums, zoos, cinemas and exhibitions and similar cultural events and facilities but excluding any supplies that are exempt supplies by virtue of Items 1 or 2 in Group 13 of Schedule 9.][1]

Amendments—[1] Groups 14–16 inserted by the Value Added Tax (Reduced Rate) (Hospitality and Tourism) (Coronavirus) Order, SI 2020/728 arts 2, 4. These changes have effect for the period beginning with 15 July 2020 and ending with 31 March 2021 (the end date was extended by SI 2020/1413; previously the temporary reduced rate had been due to end on 12 January 2021). Budget 2021 (3 March 2021) announced that the temporary 5% reduced rate will be extended until 30 September 2021. From 1 October 2021 until 31 March 2022 a new 12.5% rate will apply. See HMRC's Tax Information and Impact Note.

SCHEDULE 8
ZERO-RATING
Section 30

PART I
INDEX TO ZERO-RATED SUPPLIES OF GOODS AND SERVICES

Subject matter	*Group Number*
Bank notes	Group 11
Books etc	Group 3
Caravans and houseboats	Group 9
Charities etc	Group 15
Clothing and footwear	Group 16
Construction of buildings etc	Group 5
Drugs, medicines, aids for the [disabled][4] etc	Group 12
. . .	. . . [2]
[European Research Infrastructure Consortia	Group 18][3]
Food	Group 1
Gold	Group 10
Imports, exports etc	Group 13
International services	Group 7
[Online marketplaces (deemed supply)	Group 21][7]
[Personal protective equipment (coronavirus)	Group 20][5]
Protected buildings	Group 6
Sewerage services and water	Group 2
Talking books for the blind and [disabled][4] and wireless sets for the blind	Group 4
[. . .][1]	
Transport	Group 8
[Women's sanitary products	Group 19][6]

Amendments—[1] Group 14 deleted by the Value Added Tax (Abolition of Zero-Rating for Tax Free Shops) Order, SI 1999/1642, with effect from 1 July 1999.
[2] Entry for "Emissions allowances" repealed by the Value Added Tax (Emissions Allowances) Order, SI 2010/2549 art 2(1), (2) with effect from 1 November 2010.
[3] Group 18 inserted by the Value Added Tax (Relief for European Research Infrastructure Consortia) Order, SI 2012/2907 art 3(1) with effect in relation to importations, acquisitions or supplies made on or after 1 January 2013. Note that this Group was to have been repealed by TCBTA 2018 s 43, Sch 8 para 94 with effect from IP completion day but para 94 was itself repealed before coming into force.
[4] In entries relating to Groups 4, 12, word substituted by FA 2017 s 16, Sch 7 paras 4, 5 with effect in relation to supplies made, and acquisitions and importations taking place, on or after 1 April 2017.

⁵ Entry for Group 20 inserted by the Value Added Tax (Zero Rate for Personal Protective Equipment) (Coronavirus) Order, SI 2020/458 arts 2, 3 with effect from 1 May 2020. The zero-rating of supplies of personal protective equipment (PPE) for protection from infection with coronavirus applies where the supplies are made in the period beginning with 1 May 2020 and ending with 31 October 2020 (see Group 20 below).

⁶ Entry inserted by FA 2016 s 126(1), (3) with effect in relation to supplies made, and acquisitions and importations taking place on or after 11pm (UK time) on 31 December 2020 (by virtue of SI 2020/1642 reg 3). Note that, although the Taxation (Cross-border Trade) Act 2018 Sch 8 para 2 amends VATA 1994 s 1 to omit acquisitions from chargeable events for VAT purposes, acquisition tax continues to be charged in Northern Ireland by virtue of Sch 9ZB para 2 (as inserted by the Taxation (Post-transition Period) Act 2020 Sch 2 para 2).

⁷ Entry for "Online marketplaces (deemed supply)" inserted by the Taxation (Post-transition Period) Act 2020 s 7, Sch 3 paras 1, 16(1), (2) with effect from IP completion day (11pm on 31 December 2020), by virtue of SI 2020/1642 reg 9.

PART II
THE GROUPS

GROUP 1
FOOD

The supply of anything comprised in the general items set out below, except—
  (*a*) a supply in the course of catering; and
  (*b*) a supply of anything comprised in any of the excepted items set out below, unless it is also comprised in any of the items overriding the exceptions set out below which relates to that excepted item.

General items

Item No

1   Food of a kind used for human consumption.

2   Animal feeding stuffs.

3   Seeds or other means of propagation of plants comprised in item 1 or 2.

4   Live animals of a kind generally used as, or yielding or producing, food for human consumption.

Excepted items

Item No

1   Ice cream, ice lollies, frozen yoghurt, water ices and similar frozen products, and prepared mixes and powders for making such products.

2   Confectionery, not including cakes or biscuits other than biscuits wholly or partly covered with chocolate or some product similar in taste and appearance.

3   Beverages chargeable with any duty of excise specifically charged on spirits, beer, wine or made-wine and preparations thereof.

4   Other beverages (including fruit juices and bottled waters) and syrups, concentrates, essences, powders, crystals or other products for the preparation of beverages.

[4A Sports drinks that are advertised or marketed as products designed to enhance physical performance, accelerate recovery after exercise or build bulk, and other similar drinks, including (in either case) syrups, concentrates, essences, powders, crystals or other products for the preparation of such drinks.]²

5   Any of the following when packaged for human consumption without further preparation, namely, potato crisps, potato sticks, potato puffs, and similar products made from the potato, or from potato flour, or from potato starch, and savoury food products obtained by the swelling of cereals or cereal products; and salted or roasted nuts other than nuts in shell.

6   Pet foods, canned, packaged or prepared; packaged foods (not being pet foods) for birds other than poultry or game; and biscuits and meal for cats and dogs.

7   Goods described in items 1, 2 and 3 of the general items which are canned, bottled, packaged or prepared for use—
  (*a*) in the domestic brewing of any beer;
  (*b*) in the domestic making of any cider or perry;
  (*c*) in the domestic production of any wine or made-wine.

Items overriding the exceptions

Item No

1 Yoghurt unsuitable for immediate consumption when frozen.
2 Drained cherries.
3 Candied peels.
4 Tea, maté, herbal teas and similar products, and preparations and extracts thereof.
5 Cocoa, coffee and chicory and other roasted coffee substitutes, and preparations and extracts thereof.
6 Milk and preparations and extracts thereof.
7 Preparations and extracts of meat, yeast or egg.

NOTES:
(1) "Food" includes drink.
(2) "Animal" includes bird, fish, crustacean and mollusc.
(3) A supply of anything in the course of catering includes—
   (a) any supply of it for consumption on the premises on which it is supplied; and
   (b) any supply of hot food for consumption off those premises;
. . . [2]
[(3A) For the purposes of Note (3), in the case of any supplier, the premises on which food is supplied include any area set aside for the consumption of food by that supplier's customers, whether or not the area may also be used by the customers of other suppliers.
(3B) "Hot food" means food which (or any part of which) is hot at the time it is provided to the customer and—
   (a) has been heated for the purposes of enabling it to be consumed hot,
   (b) has been heated to order,
   (c) has been kept hot after being heated,
   (d) is provided to a customer in packaging that retains heat (whether or not the packaging was primarily designed for that purpose) or in any other packaging that is specifically designed for hot food, or
   (e) is advertised or marketed in a way that indicates that it is supplied hot.
(3C) For the purposes of Note (3B)—
   (a) something is "hot" if it is at a temperature above the ambient air temperature, and
   (b) something is "kept hot" after being heated if the supplier stores it in an environment which provides, applies or retains heat, or takes other steps to ensure it remains hot or to slow down the natural cooling process.
(3D) In Notes (3B) and (3C), references to food being heated include references to it being cooked or reheated.][2]
(4) Item 1 of the items overriding the exceptions relates to item 1 of the excepted items.
(5) Items 2 and 3 of the items overriding the exceptions relate to item 2 of the excepted items; and for the purposes of item 2 of the excepted items "confectionery" includes chocolates, sweets and biscuits; drained, glacé or crystallised fruits; and any item of sweetened prepared food which is normally eaten with the fingers.
(6) Items 4 to 6 of the items overriding the exceptions relate to item 4 of the excepted items.
(7) Any supply described in this Group shall include a supply of services described in paragraph 1(1) of Schedule 4.

Commentary—*De Voil Indirect Tax Service* **V4.221, V4.226, V4.227**.
Amendments—[1] In Note (3), para (ii) substituted by the VAT (Food) Order, SI 2004/3343 with effect from 1 January 2005.
[2] Excepted item 4A inserted, in Note (3) words repealed, and Notes (3A)–(3D) inserted, by FA 2012 s 196, Sch 26 paras 1, 2 with effect from 1 October 2012.

GROUP 2
SEWERAGE SERVICES AND WATER

Item No

1 Services of—
   (a) reception, disposal or treatment of foul water or sewage in bulk, and
   (b) emptying of cesspools, septic tanks or similar receptacles which are used otherwise than in connection with the carrying on in the course of a business of a relevant industrial activity.

2 The supply, for use otherwise than in connection with the carrying on in the course of a business of a relevant industrial activity, of water other than—
   (a) distilled water, deionised water and water of similar purity, . . . [1]
   (b) water comprised in any of the excepted items set out in Group 1 [and

(c) water which has been heated so that it is supplied at a temperature higher than that at which it was before it was heated][1].

Note: "Relevant industrial activity" means any activity described in any of Divisions 1 to 5 of the 1980 edition of the publication prepared by the Central Statistical Office and known as the Standard Industrial Classification.

Commentary—*De Voil Indirect Tax Service* **V4.271**.
Amendments—[1] Word revoked from para (a) of item 2 and para (c) added to item 2 by the Value Added Tax (Anti-avoidance (Heating)) Order, SI 1996/1661 with effect from 27 June 1996.

GROUP 3
BOOKS, ETC

Item No

1 Books, booklets, brochures, pamphlets and leaflets.

2 Newspapers, journals and periodicals.

3 Children's picture books and painting books.

4 Music (printed, duplicated or manuscript).

5 Maps, charts and topographical plans.

6 Covers, cases and other articles supplied with items 1 to 5 and not separately accounted for.

[7 The publications listed in Items 1 to 3 when supplied electronically, but excluding publications which—
   (a) are wholly or predominantly devoted to advertising, or
   (b) consist wholly or predominantly of audio or video content.][2]

[Notes:
[(1) Items 1 to 7 do not include plans or drawings for industrial, architectural, engineering, commercial or similar purposes.
(1A) Items 1 to 6 include the supply of the services described in paragraph 1(1) of Schedule 4 in respect of goods comprised in the items.][2]
   (a)
   (b)
[(2) Items 1 to 6 do not include goods in circumstances where—
   (a) the supply of the goods is connected with a supply of services, and
   (b) those connected supplies are made by different suppliers.
[(2A) Item 7 does not include services in circumstances where—
   (a) the supply of the services is connected with a supply of goods or services; and
   (b) those connected supplies are made by different suppliers.][2]
(3) For the purposes of [Notes (2) and (2A)][2] [two supplies are connected with each other][2] if, had those two supplies been made by a single supplier—
   (a) they would have been treated as a single supply . . . [2], and
   (b) that single supply would have been a taxable supply (other than a zero-rated supply) or an exempt supply.][1]

Commentary—*De Voil Indirect Tax Service* **V4.273**.
Amendment—[1] Notes (2) and (3) inserted by FA 2011 s 75(1)–(3) with effect in relation to supplies made on or after 19 July 2011.
[2] Item 7 inserted, Notes (1), (1A) substituted for previous Note (1), Note (2A) inserted, and in Note (3) words substituted for words "Note (2)" and "a supply of goods is connected with a supply of services", and words "of services" repealed, by the Value Added Tax (Extension of Zero-Rating to Electronically Supplied Books etc) (Coronavirus) Order, SI 2020/459 with effect from 1 May 2020.

GROUP 4
TALKING BOOKS FOR THE BLIND AND [DISABLED] AND WIRELESS SETS FOR THE BLIND

Item No

1 The supply to the Royal National Institute for the Blind, the National Listening Library or other similar charities of—
   (a) magnetic tape specially adapted for the recording and reproduction of speech for the blind or severely [disabled][1];
   (b) apparatus designed or specially adapted for the making on a magnetic tape, by way of the transfer of recorded speech from another magnetic tape, of a recording described in paragraph (f) below;

(c) apparatus designed or specially adapted for transfer to magnetic tapes of a recording made by apparatus described in paragraph (b) above;
(d) apparatus for re-winding magnetic tape described in paragraph (f) below;
(e) apparatus designed or specially adapted for the reproduction from recorded magnetic tape of speech for the blind or severely [disabled][1] which is not available for use otherwise than by the blind or severely [disabled][1];
(f) magnetic tape upon which has been recorded speech for the blind or severely [disabled][1], such recording being suitable for reproduction only in the apparatus mentioned in paragraph (e) above;
(g) apparatus solely for the making on a magnetic tape of a sound recording which is for use by the blind or severely [disabled][1];
(h) parts and accessories (other than a magnetic tape for use with apparatus described in paragraph (g) above) for goods comprised in paragraphs (a) to (g) above;
(i) the supply of a service of repair or maintenance of any goods comprised in paragraphs (a) to (h) above.

2 The supply to a charity of—
(a) wireless receiving sets; or
(b) apparatus solely for the making and reproduction of a sound recording on a magnetic tape permanently contained in a cassette,
being goods solely for gratuitous loan to the blind.

Note: The supply mentioned in items 1 and 2 includes the letting on hire of goods comprised in the items.

Commentary—*De Voil Indirect Tax Service* **V4.262**.
Amendments—[1] In heading and in Item 1 in each place, word substituted by FA 2017 s 16, Sch 7 paras 4, 6 with effect in relation to supplies made, and acquisitions and importations taking place, on or after 1 April 2017.

[GROUP 5
CONSTRUCTION OF BUILDINGS, ETC

Item No

1 The first grant by a person—
(a) constructing a building—
(i) designed as a dwelling or number of dwellings; or
(ii) intended for use solely for a relevant residential or a relevant charitable purpose; or
(b) converting a non-residential building or a non-residential part of a building into a building designed as a dwelling or number of dwellings or a building intended for use solely for a relevant residential purpose,
of a major interest in, or in any part of, the building, dwelling or its site.

2 The supply in the course of the construction of—
(a) a building designed as a dwelling or number of dwellings or intended for use solely for a relevant residential purpose or a relevant charitable purpose; or
(b) any civil engineering work necessary for the development of a permanent park for residential caravans,
of any services related to the construction other than the services of an architect, surveyor or any person acting as a consultant or in a supervisory capacity.

3 The supply to a [relevant housing association][1] in the course of conversion of a non-residential building or a non-residential part of a building into—
(a) a building or part of a building designed as a dwelling or number of dwellings; or
(b) a building or part of a building intended for use solely for a relevant residential purpose,
of any services related to the conversion other than the services of an architect, surveyor or any person acting as a consultant or in a supervisory capacity.

Amendments—[1] Words in Item No 3 substituted by the VAT (Registered Social Landlords) (No 1) Order, SI 1997/50 with effect from 1 March 1997.

4 The supply of building materials to a person to whom the supplier is supplying services within item 2 or 3 of this Group which include the incorporation of the materials into the building (or its site) in question.

NOTES
(1) "Grant" includes an assignment or surrender.
(2) A building is designed as a dwelling or a number of dwellings where in relation to each dwelling the following conditions are satisfied—
(a) the dwelling consists of self-contained living accommodation;

(b) there is no provision for direct internal access from the dwelling to any other dwelling or part of a dwelling;
(c) the separate use, or disposal of the dwelling is not prohibited by the term of any covenant, statutory planning consent or similar provision; and
(d) statutory planning consent has been granted in respect of that dwelling and its construction or conversion has been carried out in accordance with that consent.

(3) The construction of, or conversion of a non-residential building to, a building designed as a dwelling or a number of dwellings includes the construction of, or conversion of a non-residential building to, a garage provided that—
 (a) the dwelling and the garage are constructed or converted at the same time; and
 (b) the garage is intended to be occupied with the dwelling or one of the dwellings.

(4) Use for a relevant residential purpose means use as—
 (a) a home or other institution providing residential accommodation for children;
 (b) a home or other institution providing residential accommodation with personal care for persons in need of personal care by reason of old age, disablement, past or present dependence on alcohol or drugs or past or present mental disorder;
 (c) a hospice;
 (d) residential accommodation for students or school pupils;
 (e) residential accommodation for members of any of the armed forces;
 (f) a monastery, nunnery or similar establishment; or
 (g) an institution which is the sole or main residence of at least 90 per cent of its residents,
except use as a hospital, prison or similar institution or an hotel, inn or similar establishment.

(5) Where a number of buildings are—
 (a) constructed at the same time and on the same site; and
 (b) are intended to be used together as a unit solely for a relevant residential purpose;
then each of those buildings, to the extent that they would not be so regarded but for this Note, are to be treated as intended for use solely for a relevant residential purpose.

(6) Use for a relevant charitable purpose means use by a charity in either or both the following ways, namely—
 (a) otherwise than in the course or furtherance of a business;
 (b) as a village hall or similarly in providing social or recreational facilities for a local community.

[(7) For the purposes of item 1(b), and for the purposes of these Notes so far as having effect for the purposes of item 1(b), a building or part of a building is "non-residential" if—
 (a) it is neither designed, nor adapted, for use—
  (i) as a dwelling or number of dwellings, or
  (ii) for a relevant residential purpose; or
 (b) it is designed, or adapted, for such use but—
  (i) it was constructed more than 10 years before the grant of the major interest; and
  (ii) no part of it has, in the period of 10 years immediately preceding the grant, been used as a dwelling or for a relevant residential purpose.]³

[(7A) For the purposes of item 3, and for the purposes of these Notes so far as having effect for the purposes of item 3, a building or part of a building is "non-residential" if—
 (a) it is neither designed, nor adapted, for use—
  (i) as a dwelling or number of dwellings, or
  (ii) for a relevant residential purpose; or
 (b) it is designed, or adapted, for such use but—
  (i) it was constructed more than 10 years before the commencement of the works of conversion, and
  (ii) no part of it has, in the period of 10 years immediately preceding the commencement of those works, been used as a dwelling or for a relevant residential purpose, and
  (iii) no part of it is being so used.]³

(8) References to a non-residential building or a non-residential part of a building do not include a reference to a garage occupied together with a dwelling.

(9) The conversion, other than to a building designed for a relevant residential purpose, of a non-residential part of a building which already contains a residential part is not included within items 1(b) or 3 unless the result of that conversion is to create an additional dwelling or dwellings.

(10) Where—
 (a) part of a building that is constructed is designed as a dwelling or number of dwellings or is intended for use solely for a relevant residential purpose or relevant charitable purpose (and part is not); or

(b) part of a building that is converted is designed as a dwelling or number of dwellings or is used solely for a relevant residential purpose (and part is not)—

then in the case of—
  (i) a grant or other supply relating only to the part so designed or intended for that use (or its site) shall be treated as relating to a building so designed or intended for such use;
  (ii) a grant or other supply relating only to the part neither so designed nor intended for such use (or its site) shall not be so treated; and
  (ii) any other grant or other supply relating to, or to any part of, the building (or its site), an apportionment shall be made to determine the extent to which it is to be so treated.

(11) Where, a service falling within the description in items 2 or 3 is supplied in part in relation to the construction or conversion of a building and in part for other purposes, an apportionment may be made to determine the extent to which the supply is to be treated as falling within items 2 or 3.

(12) Where all or part of a building is intended for use solely for a relevant residential purpose or a relevant charitable purpose—
  (a) a supply relating to the building (or any part of it) shall not be taken for the purposes of items 2 and 4 as relating to a building intended for such use unless it is made to a person who intends to use the building (or part) for such a purpose; and
  (b) a grant or other supply relating to the building (or any part of it) shall not be taken as relating to a building intended for such use unless before it is made the person to whom it is made has given to the person making it a certificate in such form as may be specified in a notice published by the Commissioners stating that the grant or other supply (or a specified part of it) so relates.

(13) The grant of an interest in, or in any part of—
  (a) a building designed as a dwelling or number of dwellings; or
  (b) the site of such a building,

is not within item 1 if—
  (i) the interest granted is such that the grantee is not entitled to reside in the building or part, throughout the year; or
  (ii) residence there throughout the year, or the use of the building or part as the grantee's principal private residence, is prevented by the terms of a covenant, statutory planning consent or similar permission.

(14) Where the major interest referred to in item 1 is a tenancy or lease—
  (a) if a premium is payable, the grant falls within that item-only to the extent that it is made for consideration in the form of the premium; and
  (b) if a premium is not payable, the grant falls within that item only to the extent that it is made for consideration in the form of the first payment of rent due under the tenancy or lease.

(15) The reference in item 2(b) of this Group to the construction of a civil engineering work does not include a reference to the conversion, reconstruction, alteration or enlargement of a work.

(16) For the purpose of this Group, the construction of a building does not include—
  (a) the conversion, reconstruction or alteration of an existing building; or
  (b) any enlargement of, or extension to, an existing building except to the extent the enlargement or extension creates an additional dwelling or dwellings; or
  (c) subject to Note (17) below, the construction of an annexe to an existing building.

(17) Note 16(c) above shall not apply [where the whole or a part of an annexe is intended for use solely for a relevant charitable purpose and][4]
  (a) [the annexe][4] is capable of functioning independently from the existing building; and
  (b) the only access or where there is more than one means of access, the main access to:
    (i) the annexe is not via the existing building; and
    (ii) the existing building is not via the annexe.

(18) A building only ceases to be an existing building when:
  (a) demolished completely to ground level; or
  (b) the part remaining above ground level consists of no more than a single facade or where a corner site, a double facade, the retention of which is a condition or requirement of statutory planning consent or similar permission.

(19) A caravan is not a residential caravan if residence in it throughout the year is prevented by the terms of a covenant, statutory planning consent or similar permission.

(20) Item 2 and Item 3 do not include the supply of services described in paragraph 1(1) or 5(4) of Schedule 4.

[(21) In Item 3 "relevant housing association" means—
  [(za) a private registered provider of social housing,][5]
  (a) a registered social landlord within the meaning of Part 1 of the Housing Act 1996 [(Welsh registered social landlords)][5],

[(b) a registered social landlord within the meaning of the Housing (Scotland) Act 2010 (asp 17) which is either—
  (i) a society registered under the Co-operative and Community Benefit Societies and Credit Unions Act 1965 (c 12), or
  (ii) a company within the meaning of the Companies Act 2006 (c 46), or][6]
(c) a registered housing association within the meaning of Part II of the Housing (Northern Ireland) Order 1992 (Northern Irish registered housing association).][2]

(22) "Building materials", in relation to any description of building, means goods of a description ordinarily incorporated by builders in a building of that description, (or its site), but does not include—
  (a) finished or prefabricated furniture, other than furniture designed to be fitted in kitchens;
  (b) materials for the construction of fitted furniture, other than kitchen furniture;
  (c) electrical or gas appliances, unless the appliance is an appliance which is—
    (i) designed to heat space or water (or both) or to provide ventilation, air cooling, air purification, or dust extraction; or
    (ii) intended for use in a building designed as a number of dwellings and is a door-entry system, a waste disposal unit or a machine for compacting waste; or
    (iii) a burglar alarm, a fire alarm, or fire safety equipment or designed solely for the purpose of enabling aid to be summoned in an emergency; or
    (iv) a lift or hoist;
  (d) carpets or carpeting material.

(23) For the purposes of Note (22) above the incorporation of goods in a building includes their installation as fittings.

(24) Section 30(3) does not apply to goods forming part of a description of supply in this Group.][1]

Amendments—[1] Group 5 substituted by the Value Added Tax (Construction of Buildings) Order, SI 1995/280 with effect from 1 March 1995.

[2] Words in Note (21) substituted by the VAT (Registered Social Landlords) (No 1) Order, SI 1997/50 with effect from 1 March 1997.

[3] Notes (7), (7A) substituted for Note (7) by the VAT (Conversion of Buildings) Order, SI 2001/2305 arts 1–3 with effect for supplies made after 31 July 2001.

[4] Words in Note (17) substituted and inserted by the VAT (Construction of Buildings) Order, SI 2002/1101 art 2 with effect from 1 June 2002.

[5] In Note (21), whole of para (za), and words in para (a), inserted by the VAT (Construction of Buildings) Order, SI 2010/486 art 2(1) with effect from 1 April 2010.
Note that until the coming into force of provision defining "private registered provider of social housing" in enactments and instruments generally, that expression in Note 21 means persons listed in the register of providers of social housing maintained under the Housing and Regeneration Act 2008 Part 2, Chapter 3 who are not local authorities within the meaning of the Housing Associations Act 1985.

[6] In Note (21) para (b) substituted by the Housing (Scotland) Act 2010 (Consequential Provisions and Modifications) Order, SI 2012/700 art 4, Schedule para 5(1), (2) with effect from 1 April 2012.

[GROUP 6
PROTECTED BUILDINGS

Item No

1 The first grant by a person substantially reconstructing a protected building, of a major interest in, or in any part of, the building or its site.

2 *The supply, in the course of an approved alteration of a protected building, of any services other than the services of an architect, surveyor or any person acting as consultant or in a supervisory capacity.*[4]

3 *The supply of building materials to a person to whom the supplier is supplying services within item 2 of this Group which include the incorporation of the materials into the building (or its site) in question.*[4]

NOTES

(1) "Protected building" means a building which is designed to remain as or become a dwelling or number of dwellings (as defined in Note (2) below) or is intended for use solely for a relevant residential purpose or a relevant charitable purpose after the reconstruction or alteration and which, in either case, is—
  (a) a listed building, within the meaning of—
    (i) the Planning (Listed Buildings and Conservation Areas) Act 1990; or
    (ii) [the Planning (Listed Buildings and Conservation Areas) (Scotland) Act 1997][3]; or
    (iii) the Planning (Northern Ireland) Order 1991; or
  (b) a scheduled monument, within the meaning of—
    (i) the Ancient Monuments and Archaeological Areas Act 1979; or

(ii) *[the Historic Monuments and Archaeological Objects (Northern Ireland) Order 1995.]²*
(2) *A building is designed to remain as or become a dwelling or number of dwellings where in relation to each dwelling the following conditions are satisfied—*
   (a) *the dwelling consists of self-contained living accommodation;*
   (b) *there is no provision for direct internal access from the dwelling to any other dwelling or part of a dwelling;*
   (c) *the separate use, or disposal of the dwelling is not prohibited by the terms of any covenant, statutory planning consent or similar provision,*
and includes a garage (occupied together with a dwelling) either constructed at the same time as the building or where the building has been substantially reconstructed at the same time as that reconstruction.
(3) *Notes (1), (4), (6), [and (12) to (14)]⁵ of Group 5 apply in relation to this Group as they apply in relation to that Group but subject to any appropriate modifications.*
[(4) For the purposes of item 1, a protected building is not to be regarded as substantially reconstructed unless, when the reconstruction is completed, the reconstructed building incorporates no more of the original building (that is to say, the building as it was before the reconstruction began) than the external walls, together with other external features of architectural or historic interest.]⁴
(5) *Where part of a protected building that is substantially reconstructed is designed to remain as or become a dwelling or a number of dwellings or is intended for use solely for a relevant residential or relevant charitable purpose (and part is not)—*
   (a) *a grant . . . ⁴ relating only to the part so designed or intended for such use (or its site) shall be treated as relating to a building so designed or intended for such use;*
   (b) *a grant . . . ⁴ relating only to the part neither so designed nor intended for such use (or its site) shall not be so treated; and*
   (c) *in the case of any other grant . . . ⁴ relating to, or to any part of, the building (or its site), an apportionment shall be made to determine the extent to which it is to be so treated.*
(6) *"Approved alteration" means—*
   (a) *in the case of a protected building which is an ecclesiastical building to which section 60 of the Planning (Listed Buildings and Conservation Areas) Act 1990 applies, any works of alteration; and*
   (b) *in the case of a protected building which is a scheduled monument within the meaning of the Historic Monuments Act (Northern Ireland) 1971 and in respect of which a protection order, within the meaning of that Act, is in force, works of alteration for which consent has been given under section 10 of that Act; and*
   (c) *in any other case, works of alteration which may not, or but for the existence of a Crown interest or Duchy interest could not, be carried out unless authorised under, or under any provision of—*
      (i) *Part I of the Planning (Listed Buildings and Conservation Areas) Act 1990,*
      (ii) *[Part I of the Planning (Listed Buildings and Conservation Areas) (Scotland) Act 1997]³,*
      (iii) *Part V of the Planning (Northern Ireland) Order 1991,*
      (iv) *Part I of the Ancient Monuments and Archaeological Areas Act 1979,*
   and for which, except in the case of a Crown interest or Duchy interest, consent has been obtained under any provision of that Part,
but does not include any works of repair or maintenance, or any incidental alteration to the fabric of a building which results from the carrying out of repairs, or maintenance work.⁴
(7) *For the purposes of paragraph (a) of Note (6), a building used or available for use by a minister of religion wholly or mainly as a residence from which to perform the duties of his office shall be treated as not being an ecclesiastical building.⁴*
(8) *For the purposes of paragraph (c) of Note (6) "Crown interest" and "Duchy interest" have the same meaning as in section 50 of the Ancient Monuments and Archaeological Areas Act 1979.⁴*
(9) *Where a service is supplied in part in relation to an approved alteration of a building, and in part for other purposes, an apportionment may be made to determine the extent to which the supply is to be treated as falling within item 2.⁴*
(10) *For the purposes of item 2 the construction of a building separate from, but in the curtilage of, a protected building does not constitute an alteration of the protected building.⁴*
(11) *Item 2 does not include the supply of services described in paragraph 1(1) or 5(4) of Schedule 4.⁴]¹*

Commentary—*De Voil Indirect Tax Service* **V4.232C, V4.235, V4.239**.
Amendments—¹ Group 6 substituted by the Value Added Tax (Protected Buildings) Order, SI 1995/283 with effect from 1 March 1995.
² Words in Note (1)(b)(ii) substituted by the Historic Monuments and Archaeological Objects (Northern Ireland) Order, SI 1995/1625 (NI 9) Sch 3 para 4 with effect from 29 August 1995.

[3] Words in notes (1)(a)(ii) and (6)(c)(ii) substituted by the Planning (Consequential Provisions) (Scotland) Act 1997, s 4, Sch 2, para 57(a).
[4] Items 2, 3 and Notes (6)–(11) repealed, in Note (3), words substituted for words "(12) to (14) and (22) to (24)", Note (4) substituted, and in Note (5), in paras (a), (b), (c), words "or other supply" repealed, by FA 2012 s 196, Sch 26 paras 1, 3 with effect, in relation to relevant supplies, from 1 October 2015, subject to transitional provisions in FA 2012 Sch 26 para 7(4)–(10).

Purported amendments—The following amendments were purportedly made to Note (4): para (b) and the word "or" at the end of para (c)(iii) are repealed, and in para (c), sub-para (v) and the word "or" immediately preceding it are inserted as follows by the Historic Objects (Northern Ireland) Order, SI 1995/1625 (NI 9) Sch 3 para 4, Sch 4, with effect from 29 August 1995:

"(v) Part II of the Historic Monuments and Archaeological Objects (Northern Ireland) Order 1995,".

This amendment relates to the text of this Group prior to its substitution by SI 1995/283 (see footnote 1 above) and it is submitted that Note (6), as so substituted, should be considered in the light of these amendments.

GROUP 7
INTERNATIONAL SERVICES

Item No

1 The supply of services of work carried out on goods which, for that purpose, have been obtained . . . [1] in, or imported into, [the United Kingdom][1] and which are intended to be, and in fact are, subsequently exported . . . [1]—

(a) by or on behalf of the supplier; or

(b) where the recipient of the services belongs in a place outside the [United Kingdom][1], by or on behalf of the recipient.

Amendments—[1] In opening words, words "or acquired" repealed, words substituted for words "any of the member States" and words "to a place outside the member States" repealed, and in para (b) words substituted for words "member States", by the Taxation (Cross-border Trade) Act 2018 s 43, Sch 8 paras 1, 94(1), (3)(a), (b) with effect from IP completion day (11pm on 31 December 2020) by virtue of SI 2020/1642 reg 4(b).

2 The supply of services consisting of the making of arrangements for—

(a) the export of any goods . . . [1];

(b) a supply of services of the description specified in item 1 of this Group; or

(c) any supply of services which is made outside the [United Kingdom][1].

NOTE

This Group does not include any services of a description specified in Group 2 or Group 5 of Schedule 9.

Commentary—*De Voil Indirect Tax Service* **V4.246**.
Amendments—[1] In para (a) words "to a place outside the member States" repealed, and in para (c) words substituted for words "member States", by the Taxation (Cross-border Trade) Act 2018 s 43, Sch 8 paras 1, 94(1), (3)(c) with effect from IP completion day (11pm on 31 December 2020) by virtue of SI 2020/1642 reg 4(b).

GROUP 8
TRANSPORT

Item No

[1 The supply, repair or maintenance of a qualifying ship or the modification or conversion of any such ship provided that when so modified or converted it will remain a qualifying ship.][1]

Amendments—[1] Items 1 and 2 substituted, by the Value Added Tax (Ships and Aircraft) Order, SI 1995/3039 with effect from 1 January 1996.

[2 The supply, repair or maintenance of a qualifying aircraft or the modification or conversion of any such aircraft provided that when so modified or converted it will remain a qualifying aircraft.][1]

Amendments—[1] Items 1 and 2 substituted, by the Value Added Tax (Ships and Aircraft) Order, SI 1995/3039 with effect from 1 January 1996.

[2A The supply of parts and equipment, of a kind ordinarily installed or incorporated in, and to be installed, or incorporated in,—

(a) the propulsion, navigation or communication systems; or

(b) the general structure,

of a qualifying ship or, as the case may be, aircraft.][1]

Amendments—[1] Items 2A, 2B inserted by the Value Added Tax (Ships and Aircraft) Order, SI 1995/3039 with effect from 1 January 1996.

[2B The supply of life jackets, life rafts, smoke hoods and similar safety equipment for use in a qualifying ship or, as the case may be, aircraft.][1]

Amendments—[1] Items 2A, 2B inserted by the Value Added Tax (Ships and Aircraft) Order, SI 1995/3039 with effect from 1 January 1996.

3
  (a) The supply to and repair or maintenance for a charity providing rescue or assistance at sea of—
    (i) any lifeboat;
    (ii) carriage equipment designed solely for the launching and recovery of lifeboats;
    (iii) tractors for the sole use of the launching and recovery of lifeboats;
    (iv) winches and hauling equipment for the sole use of the recovery of lifeboats.
  (b) The construction, modification, repair or maintenance for a charity providing rescue or assistance at sea of slipways used solely for the launching and recovery of lifeboats.
  (c) The supply of spare parts or accessories to a charity providing rescue or assistance at sea for use in or with goods comprised in paragraph (a) above or slipways comprised in paragraph (b) above.
  [(d) The supply to a charity providing rescue or assistance at sea of equipment that is to be installed, incorporated or used in a lifeboat and is of a kind ordinarily installed, incorporated or used in a lifeboat.][1]
  [(e) The supply of fuel to a charity providing rescue or assistance at sea where the fuel is for use in a lifeboat.][2]

Amendments—[1] Para (d) in item 3 added by the VAT (Equipment in Lifeboats) Order, SI 2002/456 with effect from 1 April 2002.
[2] Para (e) of item 3 inserted by the Value Added Tax (Lifeboats) Order, SI 2006/1750 arts 1, 2 with effect from 1 August 2006.

4 Transport of passengers—
  (a) in any vehicle . . . [3] designed or adapted to carry not less than [10][1] passengers;
  (b) by [a universal service provider][2];
  (c) on any scheduled flight; or
  (d) from a place within to a place outside the United Kingdom or vice versa, to the extent that those services are supplied in the United Kingdom.

Amendments—[1] Figure in item 4 substituted inserted by the Value Added Tax (Passenger Vehicles) Order, SI 2001/753 arts 2, 3 with effect for supplies made after 31 March 2001.
[2] In item 4, words substituted for words "the Post Office company", by F(No 3)A 2010 s 22(1) with effect in relation to supplies made on or after 31 January 2011.
[3] In para (a), words ", ship or aircraft" repealed by the Value Added Tax (Miscellaneous Amendments to Acts of Parliament) (EU Exit) Regulations, SI 2020/1312 regs 3, 4 with effect from IP completion day (11pm UK time on 31 December 2020) by virtue of SI 2020/1641 reg 2, Schedule para 9.

5 The transport of goods from a place within to a place outside the [United Kingdom][1] or vice versa, to the extent that those services are supplied within the United Kingdom.

Amendments—[1] Words substituted for words "member States" by the Taxation (Cross-border Trade) Act 2018 s 43, Sch 8 paras 1, 94(1), (4)(a) with effect from IP completion day (11pm on 31 December 2020) by virtue of SI 2020/1642 reg 4(b).

[6
  Any services provided for—
  (a) the handling of ships, aircraft or railway vehicles—
    (i) in a port, customs and excise airport or international railway area, or
    (ii) outside the United Kingdom;
  (b) the handling or storage—
    (i) in a port,
    (ii) on land adjacent to a port,
    (iii) in a customs and excise airport,
    (iv) in an international railway area, or
    (v) in a temporary storage facility, of goods carried in a ship, aircraft or railway vehicle.][1]

Amendments—[1] Item 6 substituted by the Value Added Tax (Miscellaneous Amendments to Acts of Parliament) (EU Exit) Regulations, SI 2020/1312 regs 3, 5 with effect from IP completion day (11pm UK time on 31 December 2020) by virtue of SI 2020/1641 reg 2, Schedule para 9. Item 6 previously read as follows—

  6
  Any services provided for—
    (a)   the handling of ships or aircraft in a port, customs and excise airport or outside the United Kingdom; or
    [(b) the handling or storage—
      (i)   in a port,
      (ii)   on land adjacent to a port,
      (iii) in a customs and excise airport, or
      (iv)   in a transit shed,
    of goods carried in a ship or aircraft.]

[6ZA Any services provided in an airport that is not a customs and excise airport for—
(a) the handling of an aircraft, or
(b) the handling or storage of goods carried in an aircraft,
provided that the aircraft is of a type mentioned in paragraph (b)(i) of Note (A1).][1]

Amendments—[1] Item 6ZA inserted by the Value Added Tax (Miscellaneous Amendments to Acts of Parliament) (EU Exit) Regulations, SI 2020/1312 regs 3, 6 with effect from IP completion day (11pm UK time on 31 December 2020) by virtue of SI 2020/1641 reg 2, Schedule para 9.

[6A Air navigation services.][1]

Amendments—[1] Item 6A inserted by the Value Added Tax (Transport) Order, SI 1995/653 with effect from 1 April 1995.

7 Pilotage services.

8 Salvage or towage services.

9 Any services supplied for or in connection with the surveying of any ship or aircraft or the classification of any ship or aircraft for the purposes of any register.

10 The making of arrangements for—
(a) the supply of, or of space in, any ship or aircraft; . . .
(b) the supply of any service included in [items 1 and 2, 3 to 9 and 11; or][1]
[(c) the supply of any goods of a description falling within items 2A or 2B][1][, or paragraph (d) of item 3.][2]

Amendments—[1] Words in item 10 substituted by the Value Added Tax (Ships and Aircraft) Order, SI 1995/3039 with effect from 1 January 1996.
[2] Words in item 10 added by the VAT (Equipment in Lifeboats) Order, SI 2002/456 with effect from 1 April 2002.

11 The supply—
(a) of services consisting of
[(i) the transport of goods to or from a place—
(a) from which they are to be exported, or
(b) to which they have been imported,
(ii) the handling or storage of those goods at that place, or
(iii) the handling or storage of those goods in connection with their transport to or from that place, or][2]
(b) to a person who receives the supply for the purpose of a business carried on by him and who belongs outside the United Kingdom, of services of a description specified in paragraph (a) of item 6, [item 6A,][1] item 9 or paragraph (a) of item 10 of this Group.

Amendments—[1] Words in item 11(b) inserted by the Value Added Tax (Transport) Order, SI 1995/653 with effect from 1 April 1995.
[2] In para (a), sub-paras (i)–(ii) substituted for previous sub-paras (i), (ii) by the Taxation (Cross-border Trade) Act 2018 s 43, Sch 8 paras 1, 94(1), (4)(b) with effect from IP completion day (11pm on 31 December 2020) by virtue of SI 2020/1642 reg 4(b). Those sub-paras previously read as follows—
   "(i) the handling or storage of goods at, or their transport to or from, a place at which they are to be exported to or have been imported from a place outside the member States; or
   (ii) the handling or storage of such goods in connection with such transport; or".

[12 The supply of a designated travel service to be enjoyed outside the United Kingdom, to the extent to which the supply is so enjoyed.][1]

Amendments—[1] Item 12 substituted by the Value Added Tax (Tour Operators) (Amendment) (EU Exit) Regulations, SI 2019/73 regs 5, 6 with effect from IP completion day (11pm on 31 December 2020), by virtue of SI 2020/1641 reg 2, Schedule para 3.
Item 12 previously read as follows—
"The supply of a designated travel service to be enjoyed outside the European Union, to the extent to which the supply is so enjoyed."
Note that the former wording was to have been amended by the Taxation (Cross-border Trade) Act 2018 Sch 8 para 94(4)(c), with the insertion of words "the United Kingdom or" after the words "enjoyed outside", with effect from IP completion day, but this amendment appears to have been superseded by SI 2020/1641.

13 Intra-Community transport services supplied in connection with the transport of goods to or from the Azores or Madeira or between those places, to the extent that the services are treated as supplied in the United Kingdom.[11]

NOTES
[(A1) In this Group—
(a) a "qualifying ship" is any ship of a gross tonnage of not less than 15 tons which is neither designed nor adapted for use for recreation or pleasure; and
[(b) a "qualifying aircraft" is any aircraft which—
(i) is used by an airline operating for reward chiefly on international routes, or

(ii) is used by a State institution and meets the condition in Note (B1).]⁸]³
[(B1) The condition is that the aircraft—
(a) is of a weight of not less than 8,000 kilograms, and
(b) is neither designed nor adapted for use for recreation or pleasure.
(C1) In Note (A1)(b)—
"airline" means an undertaking which provides services for the carriage by air of passengers or cargo (or both);
. . . ¹¹]⁸
(1) In items 1 and 2 the supply of a [qualifying]³ ship or, as the case may be, aircraft includes the supply of services under a charter of that ship or aircraft except where the services supplied under such a charter consist wholly of any one or more of the following—
(a) transport of passengers;
(b) accommodation;
(c) entertainment;
(d) education;
being services wholly performed in the United Kingdom.
(2) Items 1, 2 [, 2A, 2B]³ and 3 include the letting on hire of the goods specified in the items.
[(2A) Items 2A and 2B do not include the supply of parts and equipment to a Government department [or any part of the Scottish Administration]⁴ unless—
(a) they are installed or incorporated in the course of a supply which is treated as being made in the course of furtherance of a business carried on by the department; or
(b) the parts and equipment are to be installed or incorporated in ships or aircraft used for the purpose of providing rescue or assistance at sea.]³
(3) Item 3 shall not apply unless, before the supply is made, the recipient of the supply gives to the person making the supply a certificate stating—
(a) the name and address of the recipient;
(b) that the supply is of a description specified in item 3 of this Group.
(4) "Lifeboat" means any vessel used or to be used solely for rescue or assistance at sea.
[(4ZA) "Vehicle" has the same meaning as in the Management Act.]¹²
[(4A) Item 4 does not include the transport of passengers—
(a) in any vehicle to, from or within—
(i) a place of entertainment, recreation or amusement; or
(ii) a place of cultural, scientific, historical or similar interest,
by the person, or a person connected with him, who supplies a right of admission to, or a right to use facilities at, such a place;
(b) in any motor vehicle between a car park (or land adjacent thereto) and an airport passenger terminal (or land adjacent thereto) by the person, or a person connected with him, who supplies facilities for the parking of vehicles in that car park; or
(c) in an aircraft where the flight is advertised or held out to be for the purpose of—
(i) providing entertainment, recreation or amusement; or
(ii) the experience of flying, or the experience of flying in that particular aircraft,
and not primarily for the purpose of transporting passengers from one place to another.]¹
[(4B) For the purposes of Note (4A) any question whether a person is connected with another shall be determined in accordance with [section 1122 of the Corporation Tax Act 2010]⁷.]¹
[(4C) In Note (4A)(b) "motor vehicle" means a mechanically propelled vehicle intended or adapted for use on the roads.]¹
[(4D) Item 4(a) includes the transport of passengers in a vehicle—
(a) which is designed, or substantially and permanently adapted, for the safe carriage of a person in a wheelchair or two or more such persons, and
(b) which, if it were not so designed or adapted, would be capable of carrying no less than 10 persons.]⁵
[(4E) "Universal service provider" means a person who provides a universal postal service (within the meaning of [Part 3 of the Postal Services Act 2011]¹⁰), or part of such a service, in the United Kingdom.]⁹
(5) Item 6 does not include the letting on hire of goods.
(6) . . . ¹¹
[(6) In Item 6—
(a) "port" and "temporary storage facility" have the same meanings as in the Management Act;
(b) "international railway area" means— (i) any place which may be designated as a railway customs area by virtue of section 26(1ZB) of the Management Act, or (ii) such other place relating to international rail travel as may be specified in a notice published by the Commissioners;

(c) "railway vehicle" has the same meaning as in section 83 of the Railways Act 1993.][12]
[(6ZA) "Customs and excise airport" has the same meaning as in the Management Act.][12]
[(6A) "Air navigation services" has the same meaning as in the Civil Aviation Act 1982.][2]
(7) Except for the purposes of item 11, paragraph (a) of item 6, [item 6A,][2] item 9 and paragraph (a) of item 10 [only include supplies of services where the ships or aircraft referred to in those paragraphs are qualifying ships or, as the case may be, aircraft.][3]
(8) "Designated travel service" has the same meaning as in the Value Added Tax Tour Operators) Order 1987.
(9) . . . [11]

Commentary—*De Voil Indirect Tax Service* **V4.251, V6.377**.
Amendments—[1] Notes (4A)–(4C) inserted by the Value Added Tax (Transport) Order, SI 1994/3014 with effect from 1 April 1995.
[2] Item 6A and Note (6A) inserted, and words in item 11(b) and Note (7) inserted, by the Value Added Tax (Transport) Order, SI 1995/653 with effect from 1 April 1995.
[3] Items 1 and 2 substituted, items 2A, 2B inserted, words in item 10 substituted, Notes (A1), (2A) and words in Notes (1), (2) inserted and words in Note (7) substituted by the Value Added Tax (Ships and Aircraft) Order, SI 1995/3039 with effect from 1 January 1996.
[4] Words in Note (2A) inserted by The Scotland Act 1998 (Consequential Modifications) (No 2) Order, SI 1999/1820 s 114(2), which comes into force on the "principle appointed day", currently 1 July 1999, by virtue of the Scotland Act 1998 (Commencement) Order 1998/3178.
[5] Figure in item 4 substituted, and Note (4D) inserted by the Value Added Tax (Passenger Vehicles) Order, SI 2001/753 arts 2, 3 with effect for supplies made after 31 March 2001.
[6] Para (b) of item 6, and words in Note (6) substituted by the Value Added Tax (Transport) Order, SI 2002/1173 art 2 with effect from 1 June 2002.
[7] In Note (4B) words substituted for words "section 839 of the Taxes Act 1988" by CTA 2010 s 1177, Sch 1 para 285(d). CTA 2010 has effect for corporation tax purposes for accounting periods ending on or after 1 April 2010, and for income and capital gains tax purposes for the tax year 2010–11 and subsequent tax years.
[8] In Note (A1), para (b) substituted, and Notes (B1), (C1) inserted, by F(No 3)A 2010 s 21(1)–(3) with effect in relation to supplies made, and acquisitions and importations taking place, on or after 1 January 2011.
[9] Note (4E) inserted by F(No 3)A 2010 s 22(1) with effect in relation to supplies made on or after 31 January 2011.
[10] In Note (4E) words substituted by the Postal Services Act 2011 (Consequential Modifications and Amendments) Order, SI 2011/2085 art 5(1), Schedule para 28(1), (2) with effect from 1 October 2011.
[11] Item 13 and Note (9) repealed, and in Note (C1) definition of "State institution" repealed, by the Taxation (Cross-border Trade) Act 2018 s 43, Sch 8 paras 1, 94(1), (4)(d)–(f) with effect from IP completion day (11pm on 31 December 2020) by virtue of SI 2020/1642 reg 4(b).
Definition of "State institution" previously read as follows—
" "State institution" has the same meaning as in Part B of Annex X to the Council Directive 2006/112/EC on the common system of value added tax (transactions which member States may continue to exempt).".
Note (9) previously read as follows—
"(9) "Intra-Community transport services" means—
(a) the intra-Community transport of goods within the meaning of the Value Added Tax (Place of Supply of Services) Order 1992;
(b) ancillary transport services within the meaning of the Value Added Tax (Place of Supply of Services) Order 1992 which are provided in connection with the intra-Community transport of goods; or
(c) the making of arrangements for the supply by or to another person of a supply within (a) or (b) above or any other activity which is intended to facilitate the making of such a supply,
and, for the purpose of this Note only, the Azores and Madeira shall each be treated as a separate member State.".
[12] Notes (4ZA), (6ZA) inserted, and Note (6) substituted, by the Value Added Tax (Miscellaneous Amendments to Acts of Parliament) (EU Exit) Regulations, SI 2020/1312 regs 3, 7–9 with effect from IP completion day (11pm UK time on 31 December 2020) by virtue of SI 2020/1641 reg 2, Schedule para 9. Note (6) previously read as follows—
"(6) "Port"[,"customs and excise airport" and "transit shed"] have the same meanings as in the Management Act."

GROUP 9
CARAVANS AND HOUSEBOATS

Item No

[1 Caravans which exceed the limits of size of a trailer for the time being permitted to be towed on roads by a motor vehicle having a maximum gross weight of 3,500 kilogrammes and which—
(a) were manufactured to standard BS 3632:2005 [or BS 3632:2015][2] approved by the British Standards Institution, or
(b) are second hand, were manufactured to a previous version of standard BS 3632 approved by that Institution and were occupied before 6 April 2013.][1]

2 Houseboats being boats or other floating decked structures designed or adapted for use solely as places of permanent habitation and not having means of, or capable of being readily adapted for, self-propulsion.

3 The supply of such services as are described in paragraph 1(1) or [5(4)][1] of Schedule 4 in respect of a caravan comprised in item 1 or a houseboat comprised in item 2.

Note: This Group does not include—
  (a) removable contents other than goods of a kind mentioned in [item 4]¹ of Group 5; or
  (b) the supply of accommodation in a caravan or houseboat.

Commentary—*De Voil Indirect Tax Service* **V4.275**.
Amendments—¹   Item 1 substituted, and in item 3 and in the Note words substituted, by FA 2012 s 196, Sch 26 paras 1, 4 with effect from 6 April 2013.
² Words in Item 1(a) inserted by the Value Added Tax (Caravans) Order, SI 2015/1949 art 2 with effect from 2 December 2015.

GROUP 10
GOLD

Item No

1 The supply, by a Central Bank to another Central Bank or a member of the London Gold Market, of gold held in the United Kingdom.

2 The supply, by a member of the London Gold Market to a Central Bank, of gold held in the United Kingdom.

NOTES
(1) "Gold" includes gold coins.
(2) Section 30(3) does not apply to goods forming part of a description of supply in this Group.
(3) Items 1 and 2 include—
  (a) the granting of a right to acquire a quantity of gold; and
  (b) any supply described in those items which by virtue of paragraph 1 of Schedule 4 is a supply of services.

Commentary—*De Voil Indirect Tax Service* **V4.277**.

GROUP 11
BANK NOTES

Item No

1 The issue by a bank of a note payable to bearer on demand.

Commentary—*De Voil Indirect Tax Service* **V4.279**.

GROUP 12
DRUGS, MEDICINES, AIDS FOR THE [DISABLED,] ETC

Item No

[**1** The supply of any qualifying goods dispensed to an individual for that individual's personal use on the prescription of an appropriate practitioner where the dispensing is—
  (a) by a registered pharmacist, or
  (b) in accordance with a requirement or authorisation under a relevant provision.]¹

Amendments—¹   Item 1 substituted for previous Items 1, 1A, by the Value Added Tax (Drugs and Medicines) Order, SI 2009/2972 arts 2–7 with effect in relation to supplies made on or after 2 December 2009.
    Note that Item 1 is purported to be amended further by the Pharmacy Order, SI 2010/231 art 68, Sch 4 para 5(2) with effect from 27 September 2010 (by virtue of SI 2010/1621). However, the amendment made by Sch 4 para 5(2) appears to refer to the text of Item 1 prior to substitution by SI 2009/2972. This amendment has therefore not been carried through in the text.
² In heading, word substituted by FA 2017 s 16, Sch 7 para 7(c) with effect in relation to supplies made, and acquisitions and importations taking place, on or after 1 April 2017.

2 The supply to a [disabled]² person for domestic or his personal use, or to a charity for making available to [disabled]² persons by sale or otherwise, for domestic or their personal use, of—
  (a) medical or surgical appliances designed solely for the relief of a severe abnormality or severe injury;
  (b) electrically or mechanically adjustable beds designed for invalids;
  (c) commode chairs, commode stools, devices incorporating a bidet jet and warm air drier and frames or other devices for sitting over or rising from a sanitary appliance;
  (d) chair lifts or stair lifts designed for use in connection with invalid wheelchairs;
  (e) hoists and lifters designed for use by invalids;
  (f) motor vehicles designed or substantially and permanently adapted for the carriage of a person in a wheelchair or on a stretcher and of no more than [11]¹ other persons;
  (g) equipment and appliances not included in paragraphs (a) to (f) above designed solely for use by a [disabled]² person;
  (h) parts and accessories designed solely for use in or with goods described in paragraphs (a) to (g) above;
  (i) boats designed or substantially and permanently adapted for use by [disabled]² persons.

Amendments—[1] Figure substituted in Item 2(*f*) by SI 2001/754 arts 2, 4 and 5 with effect for supplies, acquisitions or importations made after 31 March 2001.
[2] Word substituted in each place by FA 2017 s 16, Sch 7 para 7(*a*) with effect in relation to supplies made, and acquisitions and importations taking place, on or after 1 April 2017.

[2A (1) The supply of a motor vehicle (other than a motor vehicle capable of carrying more than 12 persons including the driver) to a person ("P") if—
  (*a*) the motor vehicle is a qualifying motor vehicle by virtue of paragraph (2) or (3),
  (*b*) P is a disabled person to whom paragraph (4) applies, and
  (*c*) the vehicle is supplied for domestic or P's personal use.
(2) A motor vehicle is a "qualifying motor vehicle" by virtue of this paragraph if it is designed to enable a person to whom paragraph (4) applies to travel in it.
(3) A motor vehicle is a "qualifying motor vehicle" by virtue of this paragraph if—
  (*a*) it has been substantially and permanently adapted to enable a person to whom paragraph (4) applies to travel in it, and
  (*b*) the adaptation is necessary to enable P to travel in it.
(4) This paragraph applies to a disabled person—
  (*a*) who usually uses a wheelchair, or
  (*b*) who is usually carried on a stretcher.][1]
Commentary—*De Voil Indirect Tax Service* **V4.281**.
Amendments—[1] Items 2A, 2B substituted for previous Item 2A by FA 2017 s 16, Sch 7 para 1 with effect in relation to supplies made, and acquisitions and importations taking place, on or after 1 April 2017.

[2B (1) The supply of a qualifying motor vehicle (other than a motor vehicle capable of carrying more than 12 persons including the driver) to a charity for making available, by sale or otherwise to a person to whom paragraph (3) applies, for domestic or the person's personal use.
(2) A motor vehicle is a "qualifying motor vehicle" for the purposes of this item if it is designed or substantially and permanently adapted to enable a disabled person to whom paragraph (3) applies to travel in it.
(3) This paragraph applies to a disabled person—
  (*a*) who usually uses a wheelchair, or
  (*b*) who is usually carried on a stretcher.][1]
Commentary—*De Voil Indirect Tax Service* **V4.281**.
Amendments—[1] Items 2A, 2B substituted for previous Item 2A by FA 2017 s 16, Sch 7 para 1 with effect in relation to supplies made, and acquisitions and importations taking place, on or after 1 April 2017.

3 The supply to a [disabled][1] person of services of adapting goods to suit his condition.
Commentary—*De Voil Indirect Tax Service* **V4.281**.
Amendments—[1] Word substituted by FA 2017 s 16, Sch 7 para 7(*a*) with effect in relation to supplies made, and acquisitions and importations taking place, on or after 1 April 2017.

4 The supply to a charity of services of adapting goods to suit the condition of a [disabled][1] person to whom the goods are to be made available, by sale or otherwise, by the charity.
Commentary—*De Voil Indirect Tax Service* **V4.281**.
Amendments—[1] Word substituted by FA 2017 s 16, Sch 7 para 7(*a*) with effect in relation to supplies made, and acquisitions and importations taking place, on or after 1 April 2017.

5 The supply to a [disabled][2] person or to a charity of a service of repair or maintenance of any goods specified in item 2, [2A,][1] 6, 18 or 19 and supplied as described in that item.
Commentary—*De Voil Indirect Tax Service* **V4.281**.
Amendments—[1] Figure added in Item 5 by SI 2001/754 arts 2, 4 and 5 with effect for supplies, acquisitions or importations made after 31 March 2001.
[2] Word substituted by FA 2017 s 16, Sch 7 para 7(*a*) with effect in relation to supplies made, and acquisitions and importations taking place, on or after 1 April 2017.

6 The supply of goods in connection with a supply described in item 3, 4 or 5.

7 The supply to a [disabled][1] person or to a charity of services necessarily performed in the installation of equipment or appliances (including parts and accessories therefor) specified in item 2 and supplied as described in that item.
Commentary—*De Voil Indirect Tax Service* **V4.281**.
Amendments—[1] Word substituted by FA 2017 s 16, Sch 7 para 7(*a*) with effect in relation to supplies made, and acquisitions and importations taking place, on or after 1 April 2017.

8 The supply to a [disabled][1] person of a service of constructing ramps or widening doorways or passages for the purpose of facilitating his entry to or movement within his private residence.
Commentary—*De Voil Indirect Tax Service* **V4.281**.
Amendments—[1] Word substituted by FA 2017 s 16, Sch 7 para 7(*a*) with effect in relation to supplies made, and acquisitions and importations taking place, on or after 1 April 2017.

9 The supply to a charity of a service described in item 8 for the purpose of facilitating a [disabled][1] person's entry to or movement within any building.
Commentary—*De Voil Indirect Tax Service* **V4.281**.
Amendments—[1] Word substituted by FA 2017 s 16, Sch 7 para 7(*a*) with effect in relation to supplies made, and acquisitions and importations taking place, on or after 1 April 2017.

10 The supply to a [disabled][1] person of a service of providing, extending or adapting a bathroom, washroom or lavatory in his private residence where such provision, extension or adaptation is necessary by reason of his condition.
Commentary—*De Voil Indirect Tax Service* **V4.281**.
Amendments—[1] Word substituted by FA 2017 s 16, Sch 7 para 7(*a*) with effect in relation to supplies made, and acquisitions and importations taking place, on or after 1 April 2017.

[11 The supply to a charity of a service of providing, extending or adapting a bathroom, washroom or lavatory for use by [disabled][2] persons—
  (*a*) in residential accommodation, or
  (*b*) in a day-centre where at least 20 per cent of the individuals using the centre are [disabled][2] persons,
where such provision, extension or adaptation is necessary by reason of the condition of the [disabled][2] persons.][1]
Commentary—*De Voil Indirect Tax Service* **V4.281**.
Amendments—[1] Item 11 substituted by the VAT (Charities and Aids for the Handicapped) Order, SI 2000/805 arts 2, 3 with effect from 1 April 2000.
[2] Word substituted in each place by FA 2017 s 16, Sch 7 para 7(*a*) with effect in relation to supplies made, and acquisitions and importations taking place, on or after 1 April 2017.

12 The supply to a charity of a service of providing, extending or adapting a washroom or lavatory for use by [disabled][1] persons in a building, or any part of a building, used principally by a charity for charitable purposes where such provision, extension or adaptation is necessary to facilitate the use of the washroom or lavatory by [disabled][1] persons.
Commentary—*De Voil Indirect Tax Service* **V4.281**.
Amendments—[1] Word substituted in both places by FA 2017 s 16, Sch 7 para 7(*a*) with effect in relation to supplies made, and acquisitions and importations taking place, on or after 1 April 2017.

13 The supply of goods in connection with a supply described in items 8, 9, 10 or 11.

14 The letting on hire of a motor vehicle for a period of not less than 3 years to a [disabled][2] person in receipt of a disability living allowance by virtue of entitlement to the mobility component[, of a personal independence payment by virtue of entitlement to the mobility component, of an armed forces independence payment][1] or of mobility supplement where the lessor's business consists predominantly of the provision of motor vehicles to such persons.
Commentary—*De Voil Indirect Tax Service* **V4.281**.
Amendments—[1] Words inserted by the Value Added Tax (Independence Payment) Order, SI 2013/601 art 3(*a*) with effect from 8 April 2013.
[2] Word substituted by FA 2017 s 16, Sch 7 para 7(*a*) with effect in relation to supplies made, and acquisitions and importations taking place, on or after 1 April 2017.
Prospective amendments—Words "disability living allowance by virtue of entitlement to the mobility component or of" to be repealed by the Welfare Reform (Northern Ireland) Order, SI 2015/2006 art 140 Sch 12 Pt 8 with effect from a date to be appointed. This amendment extends to Northern Ireland only (SI 2015/2006 art 3).

15 The sale of a motor vehicle which had been let on hire in the circumstances described in item 14, where such sale constitutes the first supply of the vehicle after the end of the period of such letting.

16 The supply to a [disabled][1] person of services necessarily performed in the installation of a lift for the purpose of facilitating his movement between floors within his private residence.
Commentary—*De Voil Indirect Tax Service* **V4.281**.
Amendments—[1] Word substituted by FA 2017 s 16, Sch 7 para 7(*a*) with effect in relation to supplies made, and acquisitions and importations taking place, on or after 1 April 2017.

17 The supply to a charity providing a permanent or temporary residence or day-centre for [disabled][1] persons of services necessarily performed in the installation of a lift for the purpose of facilitating the movement of [disabled][1] persons between floors within that building.
Commentary—*De Voil Indirect Tax Service* **V4.281**.
Amendments—[1] Word substituted in both places by FA 2017 s 16, Sch 7 para 7(*a*) with effect in relation to supplies made, and acquisitions and importations taking place, on or after 1 April 2017.

18 The supply of goods in connection with a supply described in item 16 or 17.

19 The supply to a [disabled]¹ person for domestic or his personal use, or to a charity for making available to [disabled]¹ persons by sale or otherwise for domestic or their personal use, of an alarm system designed to be capable of operation by a [disabled]¹ person, and to enable him to alert directly a specified person or a control centre.

Commentary—*De Voil Indirect Tax Service* **V4.281**.
Amendments—¹ Word substituted in each place by FA 2017 s 16, Sch 7 para 7(a) with effect in relation to supplies made, and acquisitions and importations taking place, on or after 1 April 2017.

20 The supply of services necessarily performed by a control centre in receiving and responding to calls from an alarm system specified in item 19.

NOTES

(1) Section 30(3) does not apply to goods forming part of a description of supply in item 1 . . . ¹², nor to other goods forming part of a description of supply in this Group, except where those other goods are . . . ²³ imported . . . ²³ by a [disabled]²¹ person for domestic or his personal use, or by a charity for making available to [disabled]²¹ persons, by sale or otherwise, for domestic or their personal use.

(2) . . . ¹¹

[(2A) In [item 1]¹², 'qualifying goods' means any goods designed or adapted for use in connection with any medical or surgical treatment except—
  (a) hearing aids;
  (b) dentures; and
  (c) spectacles and contact lenses.]²

[(2B) In item 1 "appropriate practitioner" means—
  (a) a registered medical practitioner;
  (b) a person registered in the dentists' register under the Dentists Act 1984;
  [(ba) an approved country health professional within the meaning given by regulation 213 of the Human Medicines Regulations 2012;]²²
  (c) a community practitioner nurse prescriber;
  (d) a nurse independent prescriber;
  (e) an optometrist independent prescriber;
  (f) a pharmacist independent prescriber;
  [(fa) a physiotherapist independent prescriber;
  (fb) a podiatrist independent prescriber;]¹⁶
  (g) a supplementary prescriber.

For the purposes of this Note "community practitioner nurse prescriber", "nurse independent prescriber", "optometrist independent prescriber", "pharmacist independent prescriber"[, "physiotherapist independent prescriber", "podiatrist independent prescriber"]¹⁶ and "supplementary prescriber" have the meanings given in [regulation 8(1) of the Human Medicines Regulations 2012]¹⁴.

(2C) In item 1 "registered pharmacist" means a person who is registered in [the register maintained under article 19 of the Pharmacy Order 2010 or in the register of pharmaceutical chemists kept] under the Pharmacy (Northern Ireland) Order 1976.¹³

(2D) In item 1 "relevant provision" means—
  (a) article 57 of the Health and Personal Social Services (Northern Ireland) Order 1972;
  (b) regulation 20 of the National Health Service (Pharmaceutical Services) Regulations 1992;
  (c) regulation 12 of the Pharmaceutical Services Regulations (Northern Ireland) 1997;
  (d) . . . ¹⁸
  (e) paragraph 15 of Schedule 1 to the National Health Service (Primary Medical Services Section 17C Agreements) (Scotland) Regulations 2004;
  (f) paragraphs 47 and 49 of Schedule 6 to the National Health Service (General Medical Services Contracts) Regulations 2004;
  (g) paragraph 44 of Schedule 5 to the Health and Personal Social Services (General Medical Services Contracts) Regulations (Northern Ireland) 2004;
  (h) paragraphs 46, 48 and 49 of Schedule 5 to the National Health Service (Personal Medical Services Agreements) Regulations 2004;
  (i) . . . ¹⁷
  (j) regulation 60 of the National Health Service (Pharmaceutical Services) Regulations 2005.]¹²

[(3) Any person who is chronically sick or disabled is "disabled" for the purposes of this Group.]²¹

(4) Item 2 shall not include hearing aids (except hearing aids designed for the auditory training of deaf children), dentures, spectacles and contact lenses but shall be deemed to include—
  (a) clothing, footwear and wigs;
  (b) invalid wheelchairs, and invalid carriages [. . .]³; and

(c) renal haemodialysis units, oxygen concentrators, artificial respirators and other similar apparatus.

(5) The supplies described in Items 1[, 1A]¹ [, 2 and 2A]⁷ include supplies of services of letting on hire of the goods respectively comprised in those items.

[(5A) In item 1 the reference to personal use does not include any use which is, or involves, a use by or in relation to an individual while that individual, for the purposes of being provided (whether or not by the person making the supply) with medical or surgical treatment, or with any form of care—

(a) is an in-patient or resident in a relevant institution which is a hospital or nursing home; or

(b) is attending at the premises of a relevant institution which is a hospital or nursing home.

(5B) Subject to Notes (5C) and (5D), in item 2 the reference to domestic or personal use does not include any use which is, or involves, a use by or in relation to a [disabled]²¹ person while that person, for the purposes of being provided (whether or not by the person making the supply) with medical or surgical treatment, or with any form of care—

(a) is an in-patient or resident in a relevant institution; or

(b) is attending at the premises of a relevant institution.

(5C) Note (5B) does not apply for the purpose of determining whether any of the following supplies falls within item 2, that is to say—

(a) a supply to a charity;

(b) a supply by a person mentioned in any of paragraphs (a) to (g) of Note (5H) of an invalid wheelchair or invalid carriage;

(c) a supply by a person so mentioned of any parts or accessories designed solely for use in or with an invalid wheelchair or invalid carriage.

(5D) Note (5B) applies for the purpose of determining whether a supply of goods by a person not mentioned in any of paragraphs (a) to (g) of Note (5H) falls within item 2 only if those goods are—

(a) goods falling within paragraph (a) of that item;

(b) incontinence products and wound dressings; or

(c) parts and accessories designed solely for use in or with goods falling within paragraph (a) of this Note.

(5E) Subject to Note (5F), item 2 does not include—

(a) a supply made in accordance with any agreement, arrangement or understanding (whether or not legally enforceable) to which any of the persons mentioned in paragraphs (a) to (g) of Note (5H) is or has been a party otherwise than as the supplier; or

(b) any supply the whole or any part of the consideration for which is provided (whether directly or indirectly) by a person so mentioned.

(5F) A supply to a [disabled]²¹ person of an invalid wheelchair or invalid carriage is excluded from item 2 by Note (5E) only if—

(a) that Note applies in relation to that supply by reference to a person falling within paragraph (g) of Note (5H); or

(b) the whole of the consideration for the supply is provided (whether directly or indirectly) by a person falling within any of paragraphs (a) to (f) of Note (5H).

(5G) In Notes (4), (5C) and (5F), the references to an invalid wheelchair and to an invalid carriage do not include references to any mechanically propelled vehicle which is intended or adapted for use on roads.

(5H) The persons referred to in Notes (5C) to (5F) are—

[(a) a [the National Health Service Commissioning Board or a]¹⁸ Special Health Authority in England;]⁹

[(aa) a Health Authority, Special Health Authority or Local Health Board in Wales;]⁹

(b) a Health Board or Special Health Board in Scotland;

[(c) the Regional Health and Social Care Board established under section 7 of the Health and Social Care (Reform) Act (Northern Ireland) 2009 or a Local Commissioning Group in Northern Ireland appointed under section 9 of that Act;]¹⁹

(d) the Common Services Agency for the Scottish Health Service, [the Regional Business Services Organisation established under section 14 of the Health and Social Care (Reform) Act (Northern Ireland) 2009]¹⁹ and [the Isle of Man Department of Health and Social Care]¹⁹;

(e) a National Health Service trust established under Part I of the National Health Service and Community Care Act 1990 or the National Health Service (Scotland) Act 1978;

[(eaa) an NHS foundation trust;]¹⁰

[(ea) a clinical commissioning group established under section 14D of the National Health Service Act 2006;]⁴

[(f) a Health and Social Care trust established under the Health and Personal Social Services (Northern Ireland) Order 1991;]¹⁹ or

(g) any person not falling within any of paragraphs (a) to (f) above who is engaged in the carrying on of any activity in respect of which a relevant institution is required to be approved, licensed or registered or as the case may be, would be so required if not exempt.

(5I) In Notes (5A), (5B) and (5H), 'relevant institution' means any institution (whether a hospital, nursing home or other institution) which provides care or medical or surgical treatment and is either—

(a) approved, licensed or registered in accordance with the provisions of any enactment or Northern Ireland legislation; or

(b) exempted by or under the provisions of any enactment or Northern Ireland legislation from any requirement to be approved, licensed or registered;

and in this Note the references to the provisions of any enactment or Northern Ireland legislation include references only to provisions which, so far as relating to England, Wales, Scotland or Northern Ireland, have the same effect in every locality within that part of the United Kingdom.][2]

[(5J) For the purposes of item 11 "residential accommodation" means—

(a) a residential home, or

(b) self-contained living accommodation,

provided as a residence (whether on a permanent or temporary basis or both) for [disabled][21] persons, but does not include an inn, hotel, boarding house or similar establishment or accommodation in any such type of establishment.

(5K) In this Group "washroom" means a room that contains a lavatory or washbasin (or both) but does not contain a bath or a shower or cooking, sleeping or laundry facilities.][5]

[(5L) . . . [20]

[(5M) For the purposes of Notes (5N) to (5S), the supply of a motor vehicle is a "relevant supply" if it is a supply of goods (which is made in the United Kingdom).

(5N) In the case of a relevant supply of a motor vehicle to a disabled person ("the new supply"), items 2(f) and 2A do not apply if, in the period of 3 years ending with the day on which the motor vehicle is made available to the disabled person—

(a) a reckonable zero-rated supply of another motor vehicle has been made to that person, or

(b) that person has made a . . . [23] reckonable zero-rated importation, of another motor vehicle.

(5O) If a relevant supply of a motor vehicle is made to a disabled person and—

(a) any reckonable zero-rated supply of another motor vehicle has previously been made to the person, or

(b) any reckonable zero-rated . . . [23] importation of another motor vehicle has previously been made by the person,

the reckonable zero-rated supply or (as the case may be) reckonable zero-rated importation . . . [23] is treated for the purposes of Note (5N) as not having been made if either of the conditions in Note (5P) is met.

(5P) The conditions mentioned in Note (5O) are that—

(a) at the time of the new supply (see Note (5N)) the motor vehicle mentioned in Note (5O)(a) or (b) is unavailable for the disabled person's use because—

(i) it has been stolen, or

(ii) it has been destroyed or damaged beyond repair (accidentally, or otherwise in circumstances beyond the disabled person's control), or

(b) the Commissioners are satisfied that (at the time of the new supply) the motor vehicle mentioned in Note (5O)(a) or (b) has ceased to be suitable for the disabled person's use because of changes in the person's condition.

(5Q) In the case of a relevant supply of a motor vehicle to a disabled person, items 2(f) and 2A cannot apply unless the supplier—

(a) gives to the Commissioners, before the end of the period of 12 months beginning with the day on which the supply is made, any information and supporting documentary evidence that may be specified in a notice published by them, and

(b) in doing so complies with any requirements as to method set out in the notice.

(5R) In the case of a relevant supply of a motor vehicle to a disabled person, items 2(f) and 2A cannot apply unless, before the supply is made, the person making the supply has been given a certificate in the required form which—

(a) states that the supply will not fall within Note (5N), and

(b) sets out any other matters, and is accompanied by any supporting documentary evidence, that may be required under a notice published by the Commissioners for the purposes of this Note.

(5S) The information that may be required under Note (5Q)(a) includes—

(a) the name and address of the disabled person and details of the person's disability, and

(b) any other information that may be relevant for the purposes of that Note,

(and the matters that may be required under Note (5R)(*b*) include any information that may be required for the purposes of Note (5Q)).
(5T) In Notes (5N) to (5S)—
"in the required form" means complying with any requirements as to form that may be specified in a notice published by the Commissioners;
. . .[23]
"reckonable zero-rated importation", in relation to a motor vehicle, means an importation of the vehicle . . .[23] in a case where—
  (*a*) VAT is not chargeable on the importation as a result of item 2(*f*) or 2A, and
  (*b*) the importation takes place on or after 1 April 2017;
"reckonable zero-rated supply", in relation to a motor vehicle, means a supply of the vehicle which—
  (*a*) is a supply of goods,
  (*b*) is zero-rated as a result of item 2(*f*) or 2A, and
  (*c*) is made on or after 1 April 2017.
(5U) In items 2A and 2B references to design, or adaptation, of a motor vehicle to enable a person (or a person of any description) to travel in it are to be read as including a reference to design or, as the case may be, adaptation of the motor vehicle to enable the person (or persons of that description) to drive it.][20]
(6) Item 14 applies only—
  (*a*) where the vehicle is unused at the commencement of the period of letting; and
  (*b*) where the consideration for the letting consists wholly or partly of sums paid to the lessor by [the Department for Work and Pensions][8] or the Ministry of Defence on behalf of the lessee in respect of the mobility component of the disability living allowance[, the mobility component of the personal independence payment, armed forces independence payment][15] or mobility supplement to which he is entitled.
(7) In item 14—
  (*a*) "disability living allowance" is a disability living allowance within the meaning of section 71 of the Social Security Contributions and Benefits Act 1992 or section 71 of the Social Security Contributions and Benefits (Northern Ireland) Act 1992; . . .[15]
  [(*aa*) "personal independence payment" means a personal independence payment under Part 4 of the Welfare Reform Act 2012 or the corresponding provision having effect in Northern Ireland;
  (*ab*) "armed forces independence payment" means an armed forces independence payment under a scheme established under section 1 of the Armed Forces (Pensions and Compensation) Act 2004; and][15]
  (*b*) "mobility supplement" is a mobility supplement within the meaning of Article 26A of the Naval, Military and Air Forces etc (Disablement and Death Service Pensions Order 1983, Article 25A of the Personal Injuries (Civilians) Scheme 1983, Article 3 of the Motor Vehicles (Exemption from Vehicles Excise Duty) Order 1985 or Article 3 of the Motor Vehicles (Exemption from Vehicles Excise Duty) (Northern Ireland) Order 1985.
(8) Where in item 3 or 4 the goods are adapted in accordance with that item prior to their supply to the [disabled][21] person or the charity, an apportionment shall be made to determine the supply of services which falls within item 3 or 4.
(9) In item 19 or 20, a specified person or control centre is a person or centre who or which—
  (*a*) is appointed to receive directly calls activated by an alarm system described in that item, and
  (*b*) retains information about the [disabled][21] person to assist him in the event of illness, injury or similar emergency.
Commentary—*see De Voil Indirect Tax Service* **V4.281**.
Northern Ireland—See Sch 9ZA para 70: Northern Ireland: Group 12 has effect as if—
  – in Note (1), after "goods are" there were inserted "acquired from a member State";
  – in Note (5N), in para (*b*), after "made a" there were inserted "reckonable zero-rated acquisition, or";
  – in Note (5O), in para (*b*), after "zero-rated" there were inserted "acquisition or"; and
  – in Note (5T), after the definition of "in the required form" there were inserted—
    " "reckonable zero-rated acquisition", in relation to a motor vehicle, means an acquisition of the vehicle from a member State in a case where NI acquisition VAT is not chargeable as a result of item 2(*f*) or 2A.".
Modification—Pending amendment of Group 12 to take account of the repeal of the National Health Service (Pharmaceutical Services) Regulations 2005, the definition of "relevant provision" in Note (2D) shall apply in relation to supplies on or after 1 October 2010 as if for paragraph (j) there were substituted: "(j) Part 8 of the National Health Service (Pharmaceutical Services) Regulations 2012." (National Health Service (Pharmaceutical Services) Regulations, SI 2012/1909 reg 103, Sch 7 para 15 with effect from 1 September 2012).
Pending amendment of Group 12 to take account of to take account of the coming into force of the National Health Service (Pharmaceutical and Local Pharmaceutical Services) Regulations 2013, the definition of "relevant provision" in Note (2D) shall apply in relation to supplies on or after 1 April 2013 as if for paragraph (j) there were substituted: (*j*) "Part 8 of the National

Health Service (Pharmaceutical and Local Pharmaceutical Services) Regulations 2013." (National Health Service (Pharmaceutical and Local Pharmaceutical Services) Regulations, SI 2013/349, Sch 9 para 17 in relation to supplies on or after 1 April 2013).

Amendments—[1] Words in Notes (1), (5), inserted by the VAT (Supply of Pharmaceutical Goods) Order, SI 1995/652 with effect from 1 April 1995.

[2] Notes (2A), (5A), (5B), (5C), (5D), (5E), (5F), (5G), (5H), (5I), inserted by the VAT (Drugs, Medicines and Aids for the Handicapped) Order, SI 1997/2744 with effect from 1 January 1998.

[3] Words in Note (4)(*b*) revoked by the VAT (Drugs, Medicines and Aids for the Handicapped) Order, SI 1997/2744 with effect from 1 January 1998.

[4] Note (5H)(*ea*) inserted by the VAT (Drugs, Medicines, Aids for the Handicapped and Charities Etc) Order, SI 2000/503 arts 2, 3 with effect from 1 April 2000.

[5] Notes (5J), (5K) inserted by the VAT (Charities and Aids for the Handicapped) Order, SI 2000/805 arts 2, 3 with effect from 1 April 2000.

[7] Figure substituted in Item 2(*f*); "2A" added in Item 5, and words substituted in Note (5) by SI 2001/754 arts 2, 4 and 5 with effect for supplies, acquisitions or importations made after 31 March 2001.

[8] Words in Note (6)(*b*) substituted by the Secretaries of State for Education and Skills and for Work and Pensions Order, SI 2002/1397 art 12, Schedule para 11 with effect from 27 June 2002.

[9] Note (5H)(*a*), (*aa*) substituted for Note (5H)(a) as originally enacted, by the VAT (Drugs, Medicines, Aids for the Handicapped and Charities etc) Order, SI 2002/2813 arts 2, 3 with effect from 5 December 2002.

[10] In Note (5H), para (*eaa*) inserted by the Health and Social Care (Community Health and Standards) Act 2003 s 34, Sch 4 paras 97, 98 with effect, in relation to England and Wales, from 1 April 2004 (by virtue of SI 2004/759) and in relation to Scotland, from a date to be appointed.

[11] Note 2 revoked by the European Qualifications (Health and Social Care Professions) Regulations, SI 2007/3101 reg 65(*a*) with effect from 3 December 2007.

[12] In Note (1), words "or item 1A" repealed, in Note (2A), words substituted for words "items 1 and 1A", Notes (2B)–(2D) inserted, and in Note (5), reference "1A," repealed, by the Value Added Tax (Drugs and Medicines) Order, SI 2009/2972 arts 2–7 with effect in relation to supplies made on or after 2 December 2009.

[13] In Note (2C), words substituted by the Pharmacy Order, SI 2010/231, art 68, Sch 4 para 5(1), (2) with effect for the purpose only of the exercise of powers enabling rules or orders to be made or which enable standards or requirements to be set by the Council, from 10 February 2010 and for remaining purposes from 27 September 2010 (by virtue of SI 2010/1621, art 2(1), Schedule).

[14] In Note (2B), words substituted for words "article 1(2) of the Prescription Only Medicines (Human Use) Order 1997" by the Human Medicines Regulations, SI 2012/1916 reg 348, Sch 34 para 42(*a*) with effect from 14 August 2012.

[15] In Note (6), words in para (*b*) inserted; in Note (7), word "and" at end of para (*a*) repealed, and paras (*aa*), (*ab*) inserted, by the Value Added Tax (Independence Payment) Order, SI 2013/601 art 3(*b*), (*c*) with effect from 8 April 2013.

[16] In note (2B), paras (*fa*), (*fb*) inserted, and words in second sentence inserted, by the Value Added Tax (Drugs and Medicines) Order, SI 2014/1111 art 2 with effect in relation to supplies made on or after 21 May 2014.

[17] Note (2D), para (*d*) revoked by the National Health Service (Personal Medical Services Agreements) Regulations, SI 2015/1879 reg 90 Sch 4 with effect from 7 December 2015. **Publisher's note**: SI 2015/1879 reg 90, Sch 4 as published makes this amendment to "para 4 of Note (2D) of the inserted text". The Publisher contends that the intention was that this text should instead read "para (*d*) of Note (2D) of the inserted text". The above text incorporates this correction.

[18] Note (2D), para (*i*) revoked by the National Health Service (General Medical Services Contracts) Regulations, SI 2015/1862 reg 98 Sch 5 with effect from 7 December 2015.

[19] In Note (5H), in paras (*a*), (*d*), words substituted, and paras (*c*), (*ea*), (*f*) substituted, by the Value Added Tax (Drugs, Medicines, Aids and Charities, etc.) Order, SI 2016/620 art 2(1), (2) with effect from 28 June 2016.

[20] Note (5L) repealed, and Notes (5M)–(5U) inserted, by FA 2017 s 16, Sch 7 para 2 with effect in relation to supplies made, and acquisitions and importations taking place, on or after 1 April 2017.

[21] In Notes (1), (5B), (5F), (5J), (8), (9), word substituted in each place, and Note (3) substituted, by FA 2017 s 16, Sch 7 para 7(*a*), (*b*) with effect in relation to supplies made, and acquisitions and importations taking place, on or after 1 April 2017.

[22] In Note (2B), para (*ba*) inserted by the Value Added Tax (Drugs and Medicines) Order, SI 2020/250 art 3 with effect in relation to supplies made on or after IP completion day (11pm on 31 December 2020). Note that for supplies made on or after 1 April 2020 but before IP completion day para (*ca*) applied and read as follows—

"(*ca*) an EEA health professional within the meaning given by regulation 213 of the Human Medicines Regulations 2012;".

[23] In Note (1), words "acquired from another member State or" and "from a place outside the member States" repealed, in Note (5N)(*b*) words "reckonable zero-rated acquisition, or" repealed, in Note (5O) words "acquisition or" and "or acquisition" repealed, and in Note (5T) definition of "reckonable zero-rated acquisition" repealed, and in definition of "reckonable zero-rated importation" words "from a place outside the member States" repealed, by the Taxation (Cross-border Trade) Act 2018 s 43, Sch 8 paras 1, 94(1), (5) with effect from IP completion day (11pm on 31 December 2020) by virtue of SI 2020/1642 reg 4(*b*).

Definition of "reckonable zero-rated acquisition" previously read as follows—

" "reckonable zero-rated acquisition", in relation to a motor vehicle, means an acquisition of the vehicle from another member State in a case where—

(*a*) VAT is not chargeable on the acquisition as a result of item 2(*f*) or 2A, and

(*b*) the acquisition takes place on or after 1 April 2017;".

Prospective amendments—In Note (5H)(*e*), words "the National Health Service Act 2006 or" to be repealed by the Health and Social Care Act 2012 s 179, Sch 14 paras 65, 67(*a*) with effect from a date to be appointed.

In Note (7)(*a*) words "section 71 of the Social Security Contributions and Benefits Act 1992, or" to be repealed by the Welfare Reform Act 2012 s 147, Sch 14 Part 9 with effect from a date to be appointed.

The following amendments to be made by the Welfare Reform (Northern Ireland) Order, SI 2015/2006 art 140 Sch 12 Pt 8 with effect from a date to be appointed. These amendments extend to Northern Ireland only (SI 2015/2006 art 3)—

– in Note(6)(*b*), words "mobility component of the disability living allowance or" to be repealed; and

– Note (7)(*a*) to be repealed.

GROUP 13
IMPORTS, EXPORTS ETC

Item No

[1 The supply of imported goods before a Customs declaration has been made under Part 1 of TCTA 2018 in respect of those goods where the supplier and the purchaser of the goods have agreed that the purchaser will make the Customs declaration.][1]

Northern Ireland—Sch 9ZB para 7: Item 1 applies to a supply of goods which are removed from Great Britain to Northern Ireland as if the reference to a Customs declaration were to such a declaration made for the purposes of Union customs legislation (rather than under TCBTA 2018 Part 1); Item 1 does not apply to goods which are removed from Northern Ireland to Great Britain where no Customs declaration under TCBTA 2018 Part 1 is required to be made in respect of the removal of the goods.

Amendments—[1] Item 1 substituted by the Taxation (Cross-border Trade) Act 2018 s 43, Sch 8 paras 1, 94(1), (6)(*a*) with effect from IP completion day (11pm on 31 December 2020) by virtue of SI 2020/1642 reg 4(*b*).

Item 1 previously read as follows—

"The supply before the delivery of an entry (within the meaning of regulation 5 of the Customs Controls on Importation of Goods Regulations 1991)) under an agreement requiring the purchaser to make such entry of goods imported from a place outside the member States.".

2 The supply to or by an overseas authority, overseas body or overseas trader, charged with the management of any defence project which is the subject of an international collaboration arrangement or under direct contract with any government or government-sponsored international body participating in a defence project under such an arrangement, of goods or services in the course of giving effect to that arrangement.

3 The supply to an overseas authority, overseas body or overseas trader of jigs, patterns, templates, dies, punches and similar machine tools used in the United Kingdom solely for the manufacture of goods for export . . . .[1]

NORTHERN IRELAND—

See Sch 9ZB para 14(1): Item 3 has effect as if the reference to goods for export did not include goods for export from Northern Ireland to a place in the member States.

Amendments—[1] Words "to places outside the member States" repealed by the Taxation (Cross-border Trade) Act 2018 s 43, Sch 8 paras 1, 94(1), (6)(*b*) with effect from IP completion day (11pm on 31 December 2020), by virtue of SI 2020/1642 reg 4(*b*).

Notes

(1) An "international collaboration arrangement" means any arrangement which—

  (*a*) is made between the United Kingdom Government and the government of one or more other countries, or any government-sponsored international body for collaboration in a joint project of research, development or production; and

  (*b*) includes provision for participating governments to relieve the cost of the project from taxation.

(2) "Overseas authority" means any country other than the United Kingdom or any part of or place in such a country or the government of any such country, part or place.

(3) "Overseas body" means a body established outside the United Kingdom.

(4) "Overseas trader" means a person who carries on a business and has his principal place of business outside the United Kingdom.

(5) Item 3 does not apply where the overseas authority, overseas body or overseas trader is a taxable person . . . .[1]

Commentary—*De Voil Indirect Tax Service* **V.283**.

Amendments—[1] In Note (5), words ", another member State, any part of or place in another member State, the government of any such member State, part or place, a body established in another member State or a person who carries on business, or has a place of business, in another member State" repealed by the Taxation (Cross-border Trade) Act 2018 s 43, Sch 8 paras 1, 94(1), (6)(*c*) with effect from IP completion day (11pm on 31 December 2020) by virtue of SI 2020/1642 reg 4(*b*).

GROUP 15
CHARITIES ETC

NORTHERN IRELAND—

See Sch 9ZB para 14(2): Group 15 has effect as if any reference to the export of goods did not include the export of goods from Northern Ireland to a place in the member States, and as if any reference to the export of goods, other than the reference in item 3, included the removal of goods from Great Britain to Northern Ireland or vice versa.

See also Sch 9ZB para 33(4) (modifications in relation to exports – goods removed to Isle of Man): Group 15 has effect as if any reference to the export of goods, other than the reference in item 3, included the removal of goods from Northern Ireland to the Isle of Man, and as if the insertion of new item 3A (made by Sch 9ZB para 14(2)(*c*)) applied to the removal of goods to the Isle of Man from Northern Ireland as it applies to the removal of goods from Northern Ireland to Great Britain.

Item No

[1 The sale, or letting on hire, by a charity of any goods donated to it for—
   (a) sale,
   (b) letting,
   (c) sale or letting,
   (d) sale or export,
   (e) letting or export, or
   (f) sale, letting or export.

1A The sale, or letting on hire, by a taxable person of any goods donated to him for—
   (a) sale,
   (b) letting,
   (c) sale or letting,
   (d) sale or export,
   (e) letting or export, or
   (f) sale, letting or export,
if he is a profits-to-charity person in respect of the goods.

2 The donation of any goods for any one or more of the following purposes—
   (a) sale by a charity or a taxable person who is a profits-to-charity person in respect of the goods;
   (b) export by a charity or such a taxable person;
   (c) letting by a charity or such a taxable person.][1]

Amendments—[1] Items 1, 1A and 2 substituted for original items 1, 2 by the VAT (Charities and Aids for the Handicapped) Order, SI 2000/805 arts 5–9 with effect from 1 April 2000.

3 The export of any goods by a charity . . . [1].

Amendments—[1] Words "to a place outside the member States" repealed by the Taxation (Cross-border Trade) Act 2018 s 43, Sch 8 paras 1, 94(1), (7) with effect from IP completion day (11pm on 31 December 2020) by virtue of SI 2020/1642 reg 4(b).

NORTHERN IRELAND—

See Sch 9ZB para 14(2): Group 15 has effect as if—
   – any reference to the export of goods did not include the export of goods from Northern Ireland to a place in the member States;
   – any reference to the export of goods, other than the reference in item 3, included the removal of goods from Great Britain to Northern Ireland or vice versa; and
   – item 3A were inserted as follows—
"3A The removal by a charity of goods donated to it—
   (a) from Great Britain to Northern Ireland;
   (b) from Northern Ireland to Great Britain.".
See also Sch 9ZB para 33(4) (modifications in relation to exports – goods removed to Isle of Man): Group 15 has effect as if any reference to the export of goods, other than the reference in item 3, included the removal of goods from Northern Ireland to the Isle of Man, and as if the insertion of new item 3A applied to the removal of goods to the Isle of Man from Northern Ireland as it applies to the removal of goods from Northern Ireland to Great Britain.

4 The supply of any relevant goods for donation to a nominated eligible body where the goods are purchased with funds provided by a charity or from voluntary contributions.

5 The supply of any relevant goods to an eligible body which pays for them with funds provided by a charity or from voluntary contributions or to an eligible body which is a charitable institution providing care or medical or surgical treatment for [disabled][1] persons.

Amendments—[1] Word substituted by FA 2017 s 16, Sch 7 para 8(a) with effect in relation to supplies made, and acquisitions and importations taking place, on or after 1 April 2017.

6 Repair and maintenance of relevant goods owned by an eligible body.

7 The supply of goods in connection with the supply described in item 6.

[8 The supply to a charity of a right to promulgate an advertisement by means of a medium of communication with the public.

8A A supply to a charity that consists in the promulgation of an advertisement by means of such a medium.

8B The supply to a charity of services of design or production of an advertisement that is, or was intended to be, promulgated by means of such a medium.

8C The supply to a charity of goods closely related to a supply within item 8B.][1]

Amendments—[1] Items 8, 8A, 8B, 8C substituted for original item 8 by the VAT (Charities and Aids for the Handicapped) Order, SI 2000/805 arts 5–9 with effect from 1 April 2000.

9 The supply to a charity, providing care or medical or surgical treatment for human beings or animals, or engaging in medical or veterinary research, of a medicinal product [or veterinary medicinal product][1] where the supply is solely for use by the charity in such care, treatment or research.

Amendments—[1] Words in item 9 inserted by the Veterinary Medicines Regulations, SI 2006/2407, reg 44(3), Sch 9 para 10(*a*), (*b*) with effect from 1 October 2006.

10 The supply to a charity of a substance directly used for synthesis or testing in the course of medical or veterinary research.

NOTES

[(1) Item 1 or 1A does not apply unless the sale or letting—
  (*a*) takes place as a result of the goods having been made available—
    (i) to two or more specified persons, or
    (ii) to the general public,
for purchase or hire (whether so made available in a shop or elsewhere), and
  (*b*) does not take place as a result of any arrangements (whether legally binding or not) relating to the goods and entered into, before the goods were made so available, by—
    (i) each of the parties to the sale or letting, or
    (ii) the donor of the goods and either or both of those parties.
(1A) For the purposes of items 1, 1A and 2, goods are donated for letting only if they are donated for—
  (*a*) letting, and
  (*b*) re-letting after the end of any first or subsequent letting, and
  (*c*) all or any of—
    (i) sale,
    (ii) export, or
    (iii) disposal as waste,
if not, or when no longer, used for letting.
(1B) Items 1 and 1A do not include (and shall be treated as having not included) any sale, or letting on hire, of particular donated goods if the goods, at any time after they are donated but before they are sold, exported or disposed of as waste, are whilst unlet used for any purpose other than, or in addition to, that of being available for purchase, hire or export.
(1C) In Note (1) "specified person" means a person who—
  (*a*) is [disabled][10], or
  (*b*) is entitled to any one or more of the specified benefits, or
  (*c*) is both [disabled][10] and so entitled.
(1D) For the purposes of Note (1C) the specified benefits are—
  (*a*) income support under Part VII of the Social Security Contributions and Benefits Act 1992 or Part VII of the Social Security Contributions and Benefits (Northern Ireland) Act 1992;
  (*b*) housing benefit under Part VII of the Social Security Contributions and Benefits Act 1992 or Part VII of the Social Security Contributions and Benefits (Northern Ireland) Act 1992;
  (*c*) council tax benefit under Part VII of the Social Security Contributions and Benefits Act 1992;
  (*d*) an income-based jobseeker's allowance within the meaning of section 1(4) of the Jobseekers Act 1995 or article 3(4) of the Jobseekers (Northern Ireland) Order 1995;
  [(*e*) any element of child tax credit other than the family element; . . . [8]][5]
  [(*f*) working tax credit.][5] [and
  (*g*) universal credit under Part 1 of the Welfare Reform Act 2012.][8]
(1E) For the purposes of items 1A and 2 a taxable person is a "profits-to-charity" person in respect of any goods if—
  (*a*) he has agreed in writing (whether or not contained in a deed) to transfer to a charity his profits from supplies and lettings of the goods, or
  (*b*) his profits from supplies and lettings of the goods are otherwise payable to a charity.
(1F) In items 1, 1A and 2, and any Notes relating to any of those items, "goods" means goods (and, in particular, does not include anything that is not goods even though provision made by or under an enactment provides for a supply of that thing to be, or be treated as, a supply of goods).][3]
(2) "Animals" includes any species of the animal kingdom.
(3) "Relevant goods" means—
  (*a*) medical, scientific, computer, video, sterilising, laboratory or refrigeration equipment for use in medical or veterinary research, training, diagnosis or treatment;
  (*b*) ambulances;
  (*c*) parts or accessories for use in or with goods described in paragraph (*a*) or (*b*) above;
  (*d*) goods of a kind described in item 2 of Group 12 of this Schedule;

(e) motor vehicles (other than vehicles with more than 50 seats) designed or substantially and permanently adapted for the safe carriage of a [disabled][10] person in a wheelchair provided that—
  (i) in the case of vehicles with more than 16 but fewer than 27 seats, the number of persons for which such provision shall exist shall be at least 2;
  (ii) in the case of vehicles with more than 26 but fewer than 37 seats, the number of persons for which such provision shall exist shall be at least 3;
  (iii) in the case of vehicles with more than 36 but fewer than 47 seats, the number of persons for which such provision shall exist shall be at least 4;
  (iv) in the case of vehicles with more than 46 seats, the number of persons for which such provision shall exist shall be at least 5;
  (v) there is either a fitted electrically or hydraulically operated lift or, in the case of vehicles with fewer than 17 seats, a fitted ramp to provide access for a passenger in a wheelchair;
(f) motor vehicles (with more than 6 but fewer than 51 seats) for use by an eligible body providing care for blind, deaf, mentally[disabled][10] or terminally sick persons mainly to transport such persons;
(g) telecommunication, aural, visual, light enhancing or heat detecting equipment (not being equipment ordinarily supplied for private or recreational use) solely for use for the purpose of rescue or first aid services undertaken by a charitable institution providing such services.

(4) "Eligible body" means—
  [(a) [the National Health Service Commissioning Board or a][9] Special Health Authority in England;][4]
  [(aa) a Health Authority, Special Health Authority or Local Health Board in Wales;][4]
  (b) a Health Board in Scotland;
  [(c) the Regional Health and Social Care Board established under section 7 of the Health and Social Care (Reform) Act (Northern Ireland) 2009 or a Local Commissioning Group in Northern Ireland appointed under section 9 of that Act;][9]
  (d) a hospital whose activities are not carried on for profit;
  (e) a research institution whose activities are not carried on for profit;
  (f) a charitable institution providing care or medical or surgical treatment for [disabled][10] persons;
  (g) the Common Services Agency for the Scottish Health Service, [the Regional Business Services Organisation established under section 14 of the Health and Social Care (Reform) Act (Northern Ireland) 2009][9] or [the Isle of Man Department of Health and Social Care][9];
  (h) a charitable institution providing rescue or first-aid services;
  (i) a National Health Service trust established under Part I of the National Health Service and Community Care Act 1990 or the National Health Service (Scotland) Act 1978;
  [(j) a clinical commissioning group established under section 14D of the National Health Service Act 2006;][4]

[(4A) Subject to Note (5B), a charitable institution shall not be regarded as providing care or medical or surgical treatment for [disabled][10] persons unless—
  (a) it provides care or medical or surgical treatment in a relevant establishment; and
  (b) the majority of the persons who receive care or medical or surgical treatment in that establishment are [disabled][10] persons.][1]

[(4B) "Relevant establishment" means—
  (a) a day-centre, other than a day-centre which exists primarily as a place for activities that are social or recreational or both; or
  (b) an institution which is—
    (i) approved, licensed or registered in accordance with the provisions of any enactment or Northern Ireland legislation; or
    (ii) exempted by or under the provisions of any enactment or Northern Ireland legislation from any requirement to be approved, licensed or registered;
  and in paragraph (b) above the references to the provisions of any enactment or Northern Ireland legislation are references only to provisions which, so far as relating to England, Wales, Scotland or Northern Ireland, have the same effect in every locality within that part of the United Kingdom.][1]

[(5) Any person who is chronically sick or disabled is "disabled" for the purposes of this Group.][10]

[(5A) Subject to Note (5B), items 4 to 7 do not apply where the eligible body falls within Note (4)(f) unless the relevant goods are or are to be used in a relevant establishment in which that body provides care or medical or surgical treatment to persons the majority of whom are [disabled][10].][1]

[(5B) Nothing in Note (4A) or (5A) shall prevent a supply from falling within items 4 to 7 where—
  (a) the eligible body provides medical care to [disabled][10] persons in their own homes;

(b) the relevant goods fall within Note (3)(a) or are parts or accessories for use in or with goods described in Note (3)(a); and

(c) those goods are or are to be used in or in connection with the provision of that care.]¹

(6) Item 4 does not apply where the donee of the goods is not a charity and has contributed in whole or in part to the funds for the purchase of the goods.

(7) Item 5 does not apply where the body to whom the goods are supplied is not a charity and has contributed in whole or in part to the funds for the purchase of the goods.

(8) Items 6 and 7 do not apply unless—

(a) the supply is paid for with funds which have been provided by a charity or from voluntary contributions, and

(b) in a case where the owner of the goods repaired or maintained is not a charity, it has not contributed in whole or in part to those funds.

(9) Items 4 and 5 include the letting on hire of relevant goods; accordingly in items 4, 5 and 6 and the notes relating thereto, references to the purchase or ownership of goods shall be deemed to include references respectively to their hiring and possession.

(10) Item 5 includes computer services by way of the provision of computer software solely for use in medical research, diagnosis or treatment.

[(10A) Neither of items 8 and 8A includes a supply where any of the members of the public (whether individuals or other persons) who are reached through the medium are selected by or on behalf of the charity.

For this purpose "selected" includes selected by address (whether postal address or telephone number, e-mail address or other address for electronic communications purposes) or at random.

(10B) None of items 8 to 8C includes a supply used to create, or contribute to, a website that is the charity's own.

For this purpose a website is a charity's own even though hosted by another person.

(10C) Neither of items 8B and 8C includes a supply to a charity that is used directly by the charity to design or produce an advertisement.]³

(11) In item 9—

[(a) "medicinal product" has the meaning assigned to it by regulation 2(1) of the Human Medicines Regulations 2012;]⁷

(b) . . .⁷

(c) . . .⁷

[(d) "veterinary medicinal product" has the meaning assigned to it by regulation 2 of the Veterinary Medicines Regulations 2006.]⁶

(12) In items 9 and 10 "substance" and "ingredient" have the meanings assigned to them by section 132 of the Medicines Act 1968.

Commentary—*De Voil Indirect Tax Service* **V4.266**.

Amendments—¹ Notes (4A), (4B), (5A) and (5B) inserted by FA 1997 s 34 in relation to supplies made on or after 26 November 1996.

² Para (j) in Note (4) added by the VAT (Drugs, Medicines, Aids for the Handicapped and Charities Etc) Order, SI 2000/503 arts 2, 4 with effect from 1 April 2000.

³ Notes (1)–(1F) substituted for original Note (1) and Notes (10A)–(10C) inserted by the VAT (Charities and Aids for the Handicapped) Order, SI 2000/805 arts 5–9 with effect from 1 April 2000.

⁴ Note (4)(a), (aa) substituted for Note (4)(a) by the VAT (Drugs, Medicines, Aids for the Handicapped and Charities Etc) Order, SI 2002/2813 arts 2, 4 with effect from 5 December 2002.

⁵ Note (1D)(e), (f) substituted by TCA 2002 s 47, Sch 3 paras 47, 49 with effect from 6 April 2003 (by virtue of SI 2003/962).

⁶ Words in Note (11)(a), and Note (11)(d) inserted by the Veterinary Medicines Regulations, SI 2006/2407, reg 44(3), Sch 9 para 10(a), (b) with effect from 1 October 2006.

⁷ In note (11), para (a) substituted and paras (b), (c) repealed, by the Human Medicines Regulations, SI 2012/1916 reg 348, Sch 34 para 42(b) with effect from 14 August 2012.

⁸ In Note (1D), word "and" at the end of para (e) repealed, and para (g) and preceding word "and" inserted, by the Universal Credit (Consequential, Supplementary, Incidental and Miscellaneous Provisions) Regulations, SI 2013/630 reg 9 with effect from 29 April 2013.

⁹ In Note (4), in paras (a), (g), words substituted, and paras (c), (j) substituted, by the Value Added Tax (Drugs, Medicines, Aids and Charities, etc.) Order, SI 2016/620 art 2(1), (3) with effect from 28 June 2016.

¹⁰ In Notes (1C), (3), (4), (4A), (5A), (5B), word substituted, and Note (5) substituted, by FA 2017 s 16, Sch 7 para 8 with effect in relation to supplies made, and acquisitions and importations taking place, on or after 1 April 2017.

Prospective amendments—In Note (4)(i), words "section 18 of the National Health Service (Wales) Act 2006" to be substituted for words "Part I of the National Health Service and Community Care Act 1990" by the Health and Social Care Act 2012 s 179, Sch 14 paras 65, 67(b) with effect from a date to be appointed.

In Note (1D), words "or Part 2 of the Welfare Reform (Northern Ireland) Order 2015" to be inserted after words "Welfare Reform Act 2012" by the Universal Credit (Consequential, Supplementary, Incidental and Miscellaneous Provisions) Regulations (Northern Ireland), NISR 2016/236 art 5(1), (3) with effect from a date to be appointed.

GROUP 16
CLOTHING AND FOOTWEAR

Item No

1 Articles designed as clothing or footwear for young children and not suitable for older persons.

2 The supply to a person for use otherwise than by employees of his of protective boots and helmets for industrial use.

3 Protective helmets for wear by a person driving or riding a motor bicycle [or riding a pedal cycle]².

NOTES

(1) "Clothing" includes hats and other headgear.
(2) Item 1 does not include articles of clothing made wholly or partly of fur skin, except—
   (*a*) headgear;
   (*b*) gloves;
   (*c*) buttons, belts and buckles;
   (*d*) any garment merely trimmed with fur skin unless the trimming has an area greater than one-fifth of the area of the outside material or, in the case of a new garment, represents a cost to the manufacturer greater than the cost to him of the other components.
(3) "Fur skin" means any skin with fur, hair or wool attached except—
   (*a*) rabbit skin;
   (*b*) woolled sheep or lamb skin; and
   (*c*) the skin, if neither tanned nor dressed, of bovine cattle (including buffalo), equine animals, goats or kids (other than Yemen, Mongolian and Tibetan goats or kids), swine (including peccary), chamois, gazelles, deer or dogs.
(4) [Item 2 applies only where the goods to which it refers are—]¹
   (*a*) goods which—
      (i) are manufactured to standards approved by the British Standards Institution; and
      (ii) bear a marking indicating compliance with the specification relating to such goods; or
   (*b*) goods which—
      [(i) are manufactured to standards which satisfy the requirements of regulation 8(2) of the Personal Protective Equipment Regulations 2002, and
      (ii) bear the mark of conformity required by that regulation.]⁴
[(4A) Item 3 does not apply to a protective helmet unless—
   (*a*) it is of a type that on 30th June 2000 is prescribed by regulations made under section 17 of the Road Traffic Act 1988 (types of helmet recommended as affording protection to persons on or in motor cycles from injury in the event of accident); or
   (*b*) it is of a type that—
      [(i) is manufactured to standards which satisfy the requirements of regulation 8(2) of the Personal Protective Equipment Regulations 2002, and
      (ii) bears the mark of conformity required by that regulation.]⁴]³
(5) Items 1, 2 and 3 include the supply of the services described in paragraphs 1(1) and [5(4)]¹ of Schedule 4 in respect of goods comprised in the items, but, in the case of goods comprised in item 2, only if the goods are for use otherwise than by employees of the person to whom the services are supplied.

Commentary—*De Voil Indirect Tax Service* **V4.287**.
Amendments—¹ Words in Note (4), (5) substituted by the VAT (Protective Helmets) Order, SI 2000/1517 arts 2–5 with effect in relation to supplies made after 29 June 2000.
² Words in Item 3 inserted by the Value Added Tax (Protective Helmets) Order, SI 2001/732 art 3 with effect for supplies made after 31 March 2001
³ Note (4A) substituted by SI 2001/732 arts 4–6 with effect for supplies made after 31 March 2001.
⁴ In Notes (4)(*b*), (4A)(*b*), sub-paras (i), (ii) substituted by the Taxation (Cross-border Trade) Act 2018 s 43, Sch 8 paras 1, 94(1), (8) with effect from IP completion day (11pm on 31 December 2020)
Note (4)(*b*)(i), (ii) previously read as follows:
   "(i) are manufactured to standards which satisfy requirements imposed (whether under the law of the United Kingdom or the law of any other member State) for giving effect to the directive of the Council of the European Communities dated 21st December 1989 No 89/686/EEC or to that directive as amended by Council Directives 93/68/EEC of 22nd July 1993, 93/95/EEC of 29th October 1993 and 96/58/EC of 3rd September 1996; and
   (ii) bear any mark of conformity provided for by virtue of that directive, or (as the case may be) that directive as so amended, in relation to those goods.".
Note (4A)(*b*)(i), (ii) previously read as follows—
   "(i) is manufactured to a standard which satisfies requirements imposed (whether under the law of the United Kingdom or the law of any other member State) for giving effect to Council Directive 89/686/EEC of 21st December 1989 as amended by Council Directives 93/68/EEC of 22nd July 1993, 93/95/EEC of 29th October 1993 and 96/58/EC of 3rd September 1996; and
   (ii) bears any mark of conformity required by virtue of those directives.".

[GROUP 18
EUROPEAN RESEARCH INFRASTRUCTURE CONSORTIA

Item No

1 The supply of goods or services to an ERIC.

NOTES

(1) "ERIC" means a body set up as a European Research Infrastructure Consortium by a decision under Article 6(1)(*a*) of Council Regulation (EC) No 723/2009 on the Community legal framework for a European Research Infrastructure Consortium.

(2) Item 1 applies only where the following requirements are met—
- (*a*) the statutory seat of the ERIC referred to in Article 8(1) of Council Regulation (EC) No 723/2009 is located in [the United Kingdom, a member State or an associated country (within the meaning given by Article 2(*c*) of that Regulation)][2];
- (*b*) the goods or services are for the official use of the ERIC;
- (*c*) a certificate in writing has been given to the supplier on behalf of the ERIC that—
  - (i) the requirements in paragraphs (*a*) and (*b*) are met in relation to the supply, and
  - (ii) the relief is not precluded by the limitations and conditions referred to in Note (3); and
- (*d*) VAT would have been chargeable on the supply but for item 1.

(3) Item 1 is subject to the limitations and conditions laid down in the agreement between the members of the ERIC referred to in Article 5(1)(d) of Council Regulation (EC) No 723/2009.][1]

Note—Group 18 was to have been repealed by the Taxation (Cross-border Trade) Act 2018 s 43, Sch 8 paras 1, 94(1), (9) with effect from IP completion day (11pm on 31 December 2020) but para 94(9) was itself repealed before coming into force.

Amendments—[1] Group 18 inserted by the Value Added Tax (Relief for European Research Infrastructure Consortia) Order, SI 2012/2907 art 3(2) with effect in relation to importations, acquisitions or supplies made on or after 1 January 2013.

[2] In Note (2), in para (*a*), words substituted for words "a member State" by the Taxation (Post-transition Period) Act 2020 s 3, Sch 2 para 8 with effect from IP completion day (11pm on 31 December 2020), by virtue of SI 2020/1642 reg 9.

[GROUP 19
WOMEN'S SANITARY PRODUCTS

Item No

1 The supply of women's sanitary products.

NOTES

(1) In this Group "women's sanitary products" means women's sanitary products of any of the following descriptions—
- (*a*) subject to Note (2), products that are designed, and marketed, as being solely for use for absorbing, or otherwise collecting, lochia or menstrual flow;
- (*b*) panty liners, other than panty liners that are designed as being primarily for use as incontinence products;
- (*c*) sanitary belts.

(2) Note (1)(*a*) does not include protective briefs or any other form of clothing.][1]

Amendments—[1] Group 19 inserted by FA 2016 s 126(1), (4) with effect in relation to supplies made, and acquisitions and importations taking place on or after 11pm (UK time) on 31 December 2020 (by virtue of SI 2020/1642 reg 3). Note that, although the Taxation (Cross-border Trade) Act 2018 Sch 8 para 2 amends VATA 1994 s 1 to omit acquisitions from chargeable events for VAT purposes, acquisition tax continues to be charged in Northern Ireland by virtue of Sch 9ZB para 2 (as inserted by the Taxation (Post-transition Period) Act 2020 Sch 2 para 2).

[GROUP 20
PERSONAL PROTECTIVE EQUIPMENT (CORONAVIRUS)

Item No

1 The supply of equipment to provide protection from infection where the supply is made in the period beginning with 1st May 2020 and ending with [31st October 2020][2].

NOTES

(1) In this Group "equipment to provide protection from infection" means personal protective equipment recommended for use in connection with protection from infection with coronavirus in guidance published by Public Health England on 24th April 2020 titled "Guidance, COVID-19 personal protective equipment (PPE)" namely—
- (*a*) disposable gloves,
- (*b*) disposable plastic aprons,
- (*c*) disposable fluid-resistant coveralls or gowns,
- (*d*) surgical masks (including fluid-resistant type IIR surgical masks),
- (*e*) filtering face piece respirators, and
- (*f*) eye and face protection (including single or reusable full face visors or goggles).

(2) Item 1 does not include—

(a) any of the supplies described in Group 12 or Group 15 of this Schedule, or

(b) any of the supplies that would be exempt by virtue of Group 7 of Schedule 9.

(3) In this Group "coronavirus" means severe acute respiratory syndrome coronavirus 2 (SARS-CoV-2).][1]

Amendments—[1] Group 20 inserted by the Value Added Tax (Zero Rate for Personal Protective Equipment) (Coronavirus) Order, SI 2020/458 arts 2, 4 with effect from 1 May 2020.

[2] In item 1 words substituted for words "31st July 2020" by the Value Added Tax (Zero Rate for Personal Protective Equipment) (Extension) (Coronavirus) Order, SI 2020/698 arts 2, 3 with effect from 30 July 2020.

[GROUP 21
ONLINE MARKETPLACES (DEEMED SUPPLY)

Item No

1 A supply by a person established outside the United Kingdom that is deemed to be a supply to an operator of an online marketplace by virtue of section 5A, provided that the supply does not involve the goods being imported for the purposes of that section.][1]

Amendments—[1] Group 21 inserted by the Taxation (Post-transition Period) Act 2020 s 7, Sch 3 paras 1, 16(1), (3) with effect from IP completion day (11pm on 31 December 2020), by virtue of SI 2020/1642 reg 9.

SCHEDULE 9

EXEMPTIONS

Sections 8 and 31

PART I

INDEX TO EXEMPT SUPPLIES OF GOODS AND SERVICES

[Betting, gaming, dutiable machine games and lotteries][5]	Group 4
Burial and cremation	Group 8
[Cultural services etc	Group 13][1]
Education	Group 6
Finance	Group 5
Fund raising events by charities and other qualifying bodies	Group 12
Health and welfare	Group 7
Insurance	Group 2
[Investment gold	Group 15][2]
Land	Group 1
Postal services	Group 3
Sport, sports competitions and physical education	Group 10
[Subscriptions to trade unions, professional and other public interest bodies	Group 9][1]
[Supplies of goods where input tax cannot be recovered	Group 14][3]
[Supplies of services by groups involving cost sharing	Group 16][4]
Works of art etc	Group 11

Amendments—[1] Entry inserted and words substituted by the Value Added Tax (Subscriptions to Trade Unions, Professional and Other Public Interest Bodies) Order, SI 1999/2834, arts 2, 3, with effect from 1 December 1999.

[2] Entry inserted by the Value Added Tax (Investment Gold) Order, SI 1999/3116, art 2(1), (2), with effect from 1 January 2000.

[3] Entry inserted by the Value Added Tax (Supplies of Goods where Input Tax cannot be recovered) Order, SI 1999/2833, art 2(1), (2), with effect from 1 March 2000.

[4] Entry inserted by FA 2012 s 197(1) with effect from 17 July 2012.

[5] In entry for "Betting, gaming and lotteries", words substituted by FA 2012 s 191, Sch 24 para 64(1), (5)(b) with effect in relation to supplies made on or after 1 February 2013.

PART II

THE GROUPS

GROUP 1

LAND

Item No

1 The grant of any interest in or right over land or of any licence to occupy land, or, in relation to land in Scotland, any personal right to call for or be granted any such interest or right, other than—

(*a*) the grant of the fee simple in—
  (i) a building which has not been completed and which is neither designed as a dwelling or number of dwellings nor intended for use solely for a relevant residential purpose or a relevant charitable purpose;
  (ii) a new building which is neither designed as a dwelling or number of dwellings nor intended for use solely for a relevant residential purpose or a relevant charitable purpose after the grant;
  (iii) a civil engineering work which has not been completed;
  (iv) a new civil engineering work;
(*b*) a supply made pursuant to a developmental tenancy, developmental lease or developmental licence;[4]
(*c*) the grant of any interest, right or licence consisting of a right to take game or fish unless at the time of the grant the grantor grants to the grantee the fee simple of the land over which the right to take game or fish is exercisable;
(*d*) the provision in an hotel, inn, boarding house or similar establishment of sleeping accommodation or of accommodation in rooms which are provided in conjunction with sleeping accommodation or for the purpose of a supply of catering;
(*e*) the grant of any interest in, right over or licence to occupy holiday accommodation;
(*f*) the provision of seasonal pitches for caravans, and the grant of facilities at caravan parks to persons for whom such pitches are provided;
(*g*) the provision of pitches for tents or of camping facilities;
(*h*) the grant of facilities for parking a vehicle;
(*j*) the grant of any right to fell and remove standing timber;
(*k*) the grant of facilities for housing, or storage of, an aircraft or for mooring, or storage of, a ship, boat or other vessel;
[(*ka*) the grant of facilities for the self storage of goods;][3]
(*l*) the grant of any right to occupy a box, seat or other accommodation at a sports ground, theatre, concert hall or other place of entertainment;
(*m*) the grant of facilities for playing any sport or participating in any physical recreation; . . . [3]
[(*ma*) the grant of facilities to a person who uses the facilities wholly or mainly to supply hairdressing services; and][3]
(*n*) the grant of any right, including—
  (i) an equitable right,
  (ii) a right under an option or right of pre-emption, or
  (iii) in relation to land in Scotland, a personal right,
  to call for or be granted an interest or right which would fall within any of paragraphs (*a*) or (*c*) to [(*ma*)][3] above.

NOTES
[(1) "Grant" includes an assignment or surrender and the supply made by the person to whom an interest is surrendered when there is a reverse surrender.][1]
[(1A) A "reverse surrender" is one in which the person to whom the interest is surrendered is paid by the person by whom the interest is being surrendered to accept the surrender.][1]
(2) A building shall be taken to be completed when an architect issues a certificate of practical completion in relation to it or it is first fully occupied, whichever happens first; and a civil engineering work shall be taken to be completed when an engineer issues a certificate of completion in relation to it or it is first fully used, whichever happens first.
(3) [Notes (2) to (10) and (12)][1] to Group 5 of Schedule 8 apply in relation to this Group as they apply in relation to that Group.
(4) A building or civil engineering work is new if it was completed less than three years before the grant.
(5) Subject to Note (6), the grant of the fee simple in a building or work before 1st April 1989 is not excluded from this Group by paragraph (*a*) (ii) or (iv).
(6) Note (5) does not apply where the grant is the first grant of the fee simple made on or after 1st April 1989 and the building was not fully occupied, or the work not fully used, before that date.
(7) A tenancy of, lease of or licence to occupy a building or work is treated as becoming a developmental tenancy, developmental lease or developmental licence (as the case may be) when a tenancy of, lease of or licence to occupy a building or work, whose construction, reconstruction, enlargement or extension commenced on or after 1st January 1992, is treated as being supplied to and by the developer under paragraph 6(1) of Schedule 10 [(except where that paragraph applies by virtue of paragraph 5(1)(b) of that Schedule)][1].[4]
(8) Where a grant of an interest in, right over or licence to occupy land includes a valuable right to take game or fish, an apportionment shall be made to determine the supply falling outside this Group by virtue of paragraph (*c*).

(9) "Similar establishment" includes premises in which there is provided furnished sleeping accommodation, whether with or without the provision of board or facilities for the preparation of food, which are used by or held out as being suitable for use by visitors or travellers.

(10) "Houseboat" includes a houseboat within the meaning of Group 9 of Schedule 8.

(11) Paragraph (*e*) includes—
- (*a*) any grant excluded from item 1 of Group 5 of Schedule 8 by [Note (13)][1] in that Group;
- (*b*) any supply made pursuant to a tenancy, lease or licence under which the grantee is or has been permitted to erect and occupy holiday accommodation.

(12) Paragraph (*e*) does not include a grant in respect of a building or part which is not a new building of—
- (*a*) the fee simple, or
- (*b*) a tenancy, lease or licence to the extent that the grant is made for a consideration in the form of a premium.

(13) "Holiday accommodation" includes any accommodation in a building, hut (including a beach hut or chalet), caravan, houseboat or tent which is advertised or held out as holiday accommodation or as suitable for holiday or leisure use, but excludes any accommodation within paragraph (*d*).

[(14) A seasonal pitch for a caravan is—
- (a) a pitch on a holiday site other than an employee pitch, or
- (b) a non-residential pitch on any other site.

(14A) In this Note and in Note (14)—

"employee pitch" means a pitch occupied by an employee of the site operator as that person's principal place of residence during the period of occupancy;

"holiday site" means a site or part of a site which is operated as a holiday or leisure site;

"non-residential pitch" means a pitch which—
- (a) is provided for less than a year, or
- (b) is provided for a year or more and is subject to an occupation restriction,

and which is not intended to be used as the occupant's principal place of residence during the period of occupancy;

"occupation restriction" means any covenant, statutory planning consent or similar permission, the terms of which prevent the person to whom the pitch is provided from occupying it by living in a caravan at all times throughout the period for which the pitch is provided.][2]

(15) "Mooring" includes anchoring or berthing.

[(15A) In paragraph (*ka*)—

"facilities for the self storage of goods" means the use of a relevant structure for the storage of goods by the person (or persons) to whom the grant of facilities is made, and "goods" does not include live animals.

(15B) For the purposes of Note (15A), use by a person with the permission of the person (or any of the persons) to whom the grant of facilities is made counts as use by the person (or persons) to whom that grant is made.

(15C) A grant of facilities for the self storage of goods does not fall within paragraph (*ka*) if—
- (*a*) the person making the grant ("P")—
  - (i) is doing so in circumstances where the relevant structure used is, or forms part of, a relevant capital item, and
  - (ii) is connected with any person who uses that relevant structure for the self storage of goods,
- (*b*) the grant is made to a charity which uses the relevant structure solely otherwise than in the course of a business, or
- (*c*) in a case where the relevant structure is part of a building, its use for the storage of goods by the person (or persons) to whom the grant is made is ancillary to other use of the building by that person (or those persons).

(15D) In Notes (15A) and (15C) "relevant structure" means the whole or part of—
- (*a*) a container or other structure that is fully enclosed, or
- (*b*) a unit or building.

(15E) In Note (15C)(*a*)(i) "relevant capital item" means a capital item which—
- (*a*) is subject to adjustments of input tax deduction by P under regulations made under section 26(3), and
- (*b*) has not yet reached the end of its prescribed period of adjustment.][3]

(16) Paragraph (*m*) shall not apply where the grant of the facilities is for—
- (*a*) a continuous period of use exceeding 24 hours; or
- (*b*) a series of 10 or more periods, whether or not exceeding 24 hours in total, where the following conditions are satisfied—
  - (i) each period is in respect of the same activity carried on at the same place;

(ii) the interval between each period is not less than one day and not more than 14 days;
(iii) consideration is payable by reference to the whole series and is evidenced by written agreement;
(iv) the grantee has exclusive use of the facilities; and
(v) the grantee is a school, a club, an association or an organisation representing affiliated clubs or constituent associations.

[(17) Paragraph (*ma*) does not apply to a grant of facilities which provides for the exclusive use, by the person to whom the grant is made, of a whole building, a whole floor, a separate room or a clearly defined area, unless the person making the grant or a person connected with that person provides or makes available (directly or indirectly) services related to hairdressing for use by the person to whom the grant is made.

(18) For the purposes of Note (17)—
  (*a*) "services related to hairdressing" means the services of a hairdresser's assistant or cashier, the booking of appointments, the laundering of towels, the cleaning of the facilities subject to the grant, the making of refreshments and other similar services typically used in connection with hairdressing, but does not include the provision of utilities or the cleaning of shared areas in a building, and
  (*b*) it does not matter if the services related to hairdressing are shared with other persons.

(19) For the purposes of Notes (15C) and (17) any question whether a person is connected with any other person is to be determined in accordance with section 1122 of the Corporation Tax Act 2010 (connected person).][3]

Commentary—*De Voil Indirect Tax Service* **V3.140A**.
Amendments—[1] Note (1) and words in Notes (3), (11) substituted, Note (1A) inserted, and words in Note (7) added, by the Value Added Tax (Land) Order, SI 1995/282 with effect from 1 March 1995.
[2] Notes (14), (14A) substituted for previous Note (14) by the Value Added Tax (Land Exemption) Order, SI 2012/58 arts 2, 3 with effect from 1 March 2012.
[3] Item 1(*ka*), (*ma*) and Notes (15A)–(15E), (17)–(19) inserted; in Item 1, word "and" at the end of para (*m*) repealed, and in para (*n*), reference substituted for previous reference "(*m*)", by FA 2012 s 196, Sch 26 para 5 with effect from 1 October 2012.
[4] Item 1(*b*), and Note (7), repealed by the Value Added Tax (Buildings and Land) Order, SI 2008/1146 art 4 with effect in relation to supplies made on or after 1 June 2020. The fact that former VATA 1994 Sch 10 paras 5–7 are not rewritten by SI 2008/1146 art 2 is not to affect the continued operation of Sch 9 Group 1 item 1(*b*), as read with Note (7), in relation to supplies made before 1 June 2020.

[GROUP 2
INSURANCE

Item No.

[1 Insurance transactions and reinsurance transactions.][1]

Amendments—[1] Item 1 substituted for Items 1–3 by the VAT (Insurance) Order, SI 2004/3083 with effect from 1 January 2005.

4 The provision by an insurance broker or insurance agent of any of the services of an insurance intermediary in a case in which those services—
  (*a*) are related (whether or not [a contract of insurance][2] [or reinsurance][3] is finally concluded) to [an insurance transaction or a reinsurance transaction][3]; and
  (*b*) are provided by that broker or agent in the course of his acting in an intermediary capacity.

NOTES
  (A1)–(C1) . . . [3]

(1) For the purposes of item 4 services are services of an insurance intermediary if they fall within any of the following paragraphs—
  (*a*) the bringing together, with a view to the insurance or reinsurance of risks, of—
    (i) persons who are or may be seeking insurance or reinsurance, and
    (ii) persons who provide insurance or reinsurance;
  (*b*) the carrying out of work preparatory to the conclusion of contracts of insurance or reinsurance;
  (*c*) the provision of assistance in the administration and performance of such contracts, including the handling of claims;
  (*d*) the collection of premiums.

(2) For the purposes of item 4 an insurance broker or insurance agent is acting 'in an intermediary capacity' wherever he is acting as an intermediary, or one of the intermediaries, between—
  (*a*) a person who provides [insurance or reinsurance][3], and
  (*b*) a person who is or may be seeking insurance or reinsurance or is an insured person.

(3) Where—
  (*a*) a person ('the supplier') makes a supply of goods or services to another ('the customer'),
  (*b*) the supply of the goods or services is a taxable supply and is not a zero-rated supply,

(c) a transaction under which insurance is to be or may be arranged for the customer is entered into in connection with the supply of the goods or services,

(d) a supply of services which are related (whether or not a contract of insurance is finally concluded) to the provision of insurance in pursuance of that transaction is made by—

   (i) the person by whom the supply of the goods or services is made, or

   (ii) a person who is connected with that person and, in connection with the provision of that insurance, deals directly with the customer,

and

(e) the related services do not consist in the handling of claims under the contract for that insurance,

those related services do not fall within item 4 unless the relevant requirements are fulfilled.

(4) For the purposes of Note (3) the relevant requirements are—

(a) that a document containing the statements specified in Note (5) is prepared;

(b) that the matters that must be stated in the document have been disclosed to the customer at or before the time when the transaction mentioned in Note (3)(c) is entered into; and

(c) that there is compliance with all such requirements (if any) as to—

   (i) the preparation and form of the document,

   (ii) the manner of disclosing to the customer the matters that must be stated in the document, and

   (iii) the delivery of a copy of the document to the customer,

as may be set out in a notice that has been published by the Commissioners and has not been withdrawn.

(5) The statements referred to in Note (4) are—

(a) a statement setting out the amount of the premium under any contract of insurance that is to be or may be entered into in pursuance of the transaction in question; and

(b) a statement setting out every amount that the customer is, is to be or has been required to pay, otherwise than by way of such a premium, in connection with that transaction or anything that is to be, may be or has been done in pursuance of that transaction.

(6) For the purposes of Note (3) any question whether a person is connected with another shall be determined in accordance with [section 1122 of the Corporation Tax Act 2010][4].

(7) Item 4 does not include—

(a) the supply of any market research, product design, advertising, promotional or similar services; or

(b) the collection, collation and provision of information for use in connection with market research, product design, advertising, promotional or similar activities.

(8) Item 4 does not include the supply of any valuation or inspection services.

(9) Item 4 does not include the supply of any services by loss adjusters, average adjusters, motor assessors, surveyors or other experts except where—

(a) the services consist in the handling of a claim under a contract of insurance or reinsurance;

(b) the person handling the claim is authorised when doing so to act on behalf of the insurer or reinsurer; and

(c) that person's authority so to act includes written authority to determine whether to accept or reject the claim and, where accepting it in whole or in part, to settle the amount to be paid on the claim.

(10) Item 4 does not include the supply of any services which—

(a) are supplied in pursuance of a contract of insurance or reinsurance or of any arrangements made in connection with such a contract; and

(b) are so supplied either—

   (i) instead of the payment of the whole or any part of any indemnity for which the contract provides, or

   (ii) for the purpose, in any other manner, of satisfying any claim under that contract, whether in whole or in part.][1]

Commentary—*De Voil Indirect Tax Service* **V4.122, V4.123.**

Amendments—[1] This Group substituted by FA 1997 s 38 with effect in relation to supplies made on or after 19 March 1997.

[2] Item 2 substituted, words in Item 4 substituted by the Financial Services and Markets Act 2000 (Consequential Amendments and Repeals) Order, SI 2001/3649 art 347 with effect from 1 December 2001.

[3] Item 1 substituted for Items 1–3, words in Item 4(a) substituted and inserted, Notes (A1)–(C1) repealed, and words in Note (2)(a) substituted, by the VAT (Insurance) Order, SI 2004/3083 with effect from 1 January 2005.

[4] In Note (6) words substituted for words "section 839 of the Taxes Act 1988" by CTA 2010 s 1177, Sch 1 para 285(e)(i). CTA 2010 has effect for corporation tax purposes for accounting periods ending on or after 1 April 2010, and for income and capital gains tax purposes for the tax year 2010–11 and subsequent tax years.

[GROUP 3
POSTAL SERVICES

Item No

1 The supply of public postal services by a universal service provider.

2 The supply of goods by a universal service provider which is incidental to the supply of public postal services by that provider.

NOTES:
(1) . . . [2]
(2) Subject to the following Notes, "public postal services", in relation to a universal service provider, means any postal services which the provider is required to provide in the discharge of [a specified condition][2].
(3) Public postal services include postal services which a universal service provider provides to allow a person access to the provider's [postal network (within the meaning of section 38 of the Postal Services Act 2011) and which are required to be provided by a specified condition][2].
(4) Services are not "public postal services" if—
    (a) the price is not controlled by or under [a specified condition][2], or
    (b) any of the other terms on which the services are provided are freely negotiated.
(5) But Note (4) does not apply if [a specified condition][2] requires the universal service provider to make the services available to persons generally—
    (a) where the price is not controlled by or under [the condition][2], at the same price, or
    (b) where terms are freely negotiated as mentioned in Note (4)(b), on those terms.
[(6) In this Group "specified condition" means a designated USP condition, a USP access condition or a transitory condition under paragraph 5 of Schedule 9 to the Postal Services Act 2011 which is imposed only on a universal service provider.][1]
(7) Any expression which is used in this Group and in Part 3 of the Postal Services Act 2011 has the same meaning in this Group as in that Part.][2]

Commentary—*De Voil Indirect Tax Service* **V4.126**.
Amendments—[1] Group 3 substituted by F(No 3)A 2010 s 22(2) with effect in relation to supplies made on or after 31 January 2011.
[2] Note (1) repealed, in Notes (2)–(5) words substituted, and Notes (6), (7) substituted for previous Note (6) by the Postal Services Act 2011 (Consequential Modifications and Amendments) Order, SI 2011/2085 art 5(1), Sch 1 para 28(1), (3), art 5(2) Sch 2 with effect from 1 October 2011.

GROUP 4
BETTING, GAMING[, DUTIABLE MACHINE GAMES] AND LOTTERIES

Amendments—In heading to Group 4, words inserted by FA 2012 s 191, Sch 24 para 64(1), (5) with effect in relation to supplies made on or after 1 February 2013.

Item No

1 The provision of any facilities for the placing of bets [or for the playing of any games of chance for a prize][1].

Amendments—[1] Words in item 1 substituted by the Value Added Tax (Betting, Gaming and Lotteries) Order, SI 2006/2685 art 2, with effect from 1 November 2006.

[1A The provision of any facilities for the playing of dutiable machine games (as defined in Part 1 of Schedule 24 to the Finance Act 2012) but only to the extent that—
    (a) the facilities are used to play such games, and
    (b) the takings and payouts in respect of those games are taken into account in determining the charge to machine games duty.][1]

Amendments—[1] Item 1A inserted by FA 2012 s 191, Sch 24 para 64(1), (2) with effect in relation to supplies made on or after 1 February 2013.

2 The granting of a right to take part in a lottery.

NOTES
(1) [Items 1 and 1A do][3] not include—
    (a) admission to any premises; or
    (b) . . . [2]
    (c) the provision by a club of such facilities to its members as are available to them on payment of their subscription but without further charge; . . . [3]
    (d) . . . [3]
[(1A) Item 1 does not apply to the provision of facilities to the extent that the facilities are used to play a relevant machine game (as defined in section 23A).][3]
[(2) "Game of chance"—
    (a) includes—

(i) a game that involves both an element of chance and an element of skill,
(ii) a game that involves an element of chance that can be eliminated by superlative skill, and
(iii) a game that is presented as involving an element of chance, but
(b) does not include a sport.
(3) A person plays a game of chance if he participates in a game of chance—
(a) whether or not there are other participants in the game, and
(b) whether or not a computer generates images or data taken to represent the actions of other participants in the game.
(4) "Prize" does not include the opportunity to play the game again.][1]
(5)–(11) . . . [2]

Commentary—*De Voil Indirect Tax Service* **V4.131**.
Amendments—[1] Notes (2)–(4) substituted for Notes (2)–(8) as previously enacted, by the Value Added Tax (Betting, Gaming and Lotteries) Order, SI 2006/2685 art 2, with effect from 1 November 2006.
[2] Note (1)(b) and Notes (5)–(11) repealed by FA 2009 s 113 with effect from 27 April 2009.
[3] In Note (1), words substituted for words "Item 1 does", and para (d) and preceding word "or" repealed, and Note (1A) inserted, by FA 2012 s 191, Sch 24 para 64(1), (3), (4) with effect in relation to supplies made on or after 1 February 2013.

GROUP 5
FINANCE

Item No

1 The issue, transfer or receipt of, or any dealing with, money, any security for money or any note or order for the payment of money.

2 The making of any advance or the granting of any credit.

[2A The management of credit by the person granting it.][1]

Amendments—[1] Item 2A by the VAT (Finance) (No 2) Order, SI 2003/1569 with effect for any services performed after 31 July 2003.

3 The provision of the facility of instalment credit finance in a hire-purchase, conditional sale or credit sale agreement for which facility a separate charge is made and disclosed to the recipient of the supply of goods.

4 The provision of administrative arrangements and documentation and the transfer of title to the goods in connection with the supply described in item 3 if the total consideration therefor is specified in the agreement and does not exceed £10.

5 [The provision of intermediary services in relation to any transaction comprised in item 1, 2, 3, 4 or 6 (whether or not any such transaction is finally concluded) by a person acting in an intermediary capacity.][1]

Amendments—[1] Item 5 substituted and Item 5A inserted by the VAT (Finance) Order, SI 1999/594 art 3, with effect from 10 March 1999.

[5A—The underwriting of an issue within item 1 or any transaction within item 6.][1]

Amendments—[1] Item 5 substituted and Item 5A inserted by the VAT (Finance) Order, SI 1999/594 art 3, with effect from 10 March 1999.

6 The issue, transfer or receipt of, or any dealing with, any security or secondary security being—
(a) shares, stocks, bonds, notes (other than promissory notes), debentures, debenture stock or shares in an oil royalty; or
(b) any document relating to money, in any currency, which has been deposited with the issuer or some other person, being a document which recognises an obligation to pay a stated amount to bearer or to order, with or without interest, and being a document by the delivery of which, with or without endorsement, the right to receive that stated amount, with or without interest, is transferable; or
(c) any bill, note or other obligation of the Treasury or of a Government in any part of the world, being a document by the delivery of which, with or without endorsement, title is transferable, and not being an obligation which is or has been legal tender in any part of the world; or
(d) any letter of allotment or rights, any warrant conferring an option to acquire a security included in this item, any renounceable or scrip certificates, rights coupons, coupons representing dividends or interest on such a security, bond mandates or other documents conferring or containing evidence of title to or rights in respect of such a security; or
(e) units or other documents conferring rights under any trust established for the purpose, or having the effect of providing, for persons having funds available for investment, facilities for the participation by them as beneficiaries under the trust, in any profits or income arising from the acquisition, holding, management or disposal of any property whatsoever.

7 [. . .]¹
Amendments—¹ Item 7 repealed by the VAT (Finance) Order, SI 1999/594 arts 4, 5 and 6 respectively, with effect from 10 March 1999.

8 The operation of any current, deposit or savings account.

[**9** The management of—
(a) an authorised open-ended investment company; or
[(aa) an authorised contractual scheme; or]²
(b) an authorised unit trust scheme; or
(c) a Gibraltar collective investment scheme that is not an umbrella scheme; or
(d) a sub-fund of any other Gibraltar collective investment scheme; or
(e) an individually recognised overseas scheme that is not an umbrella scheme; or
(f) a sub-fund of any other individually recognised overseas scheme; or
(g) a recognised collective investment scheme authorised in a designated country or territory that is not an umbrella scheme; or
(h) a sub-fund of any other recognised collective investment scheme authorised in a designated country or territory; or³
(i), (j) . . .⁶
(k) a qualifying pension fund.]⁴]¹

Amendments—¹ Item 9 substituted by the Value Added Tax (Finance) (No 2) Order, SI 2008/2547 art 3 with effect from 1 October 2008.
Note that Item 9 was to be substituted by the Value Added Tax (Finance) Order, SI 2008/1892 art 2(1), (2) with effect from 1 October 2008. However, this Order was revoked, following further consultation, by the Value Added Tax (Finance) (No 2) Order, SI 2008/2547 art 2 with effect from 30 September 2008 and was therefore revoked before it was due to take effect.
² Para (aa) inserted by the Value Added Tax (Finance) Order, SI 2013/1402 art 2(2) with effect from 28 June 2013.
³ Paras (g), (h) repealed by the Alternative Investment Fund Managers Regulations, SI 2013/1773 reg 80, Sch 1 para 40 with effect from 22 July 2013.
⁴ Para (k) inserted by the Value Added Tax (Finance) Order, SI 2020/209 arts 2, 3 with effect from 1 April 2020.
⁵ In paras (i), (j), words substituted for words "another EEA state" by the Taxation (Cross-border Trade) Act 2018 s 43, Sch 8 paras 1, 95(1), (2)(a) with effect from IP completion day (11pm on 31 December 2020), by virtue of SI 2020/1642 reg 4(b).
⁶ Paras (i) and (j) repealed by the Value Added Tax (Miscellaneous Amendments and Transitional Provisions) (EU Exit) Regulations, SI 2019/1214 reg 2(1), (2) with effect from IP completion day (11pm on 31 December 2020), by virtue of SI 2020/1641 reg 2, Schedule para 8. Paras (i) and (j) previously read as follows—
"(i) a recognised collective investment scheme constituted in [an EEA state] that is not an umbrella scheme; or
(j) a sub-fund of any other recognised collective investment scheme constituted in [an EEA state]; or"

[**10** The management of a closed-ended collective investment undertaking.]⁷
NOTES
(1) Item 1 does not include anything included in item 6.
[(1A) Item 1 does not include a supply of services which is preparatory to the carrying out of a transaction falling within that item.]²
(2) This Group does not include the supply of a coin or a banknote as a collectors' piece or as an investment article.
(2A) . . .⁶
(2B) . . .⁵
(3) Item 2 includes the supply of credit by a person, in connection with a supply of goods or services by him, for which a separate charge is made and disclosed to the recipient of the supply of goods or services.
(4) This Group includes any supply by a person carrying on a credit card, charge card or similar payment card operation made in connection with that operation to a person who accepts the card used in the operation when presented to him in payment for goods or services.
[(5) For the purposes of item 5 "intermediary services" consist of bringing together, with a view to the provision of financial services—
(a) persons who are or may be seeking to receive financial services, and
(b) persons who provide financial services,
together with (in the case of financial services falling within item 1, 2, 3 or 4) the performance of work preparatory to the conclusion of contracts for the provision of those financial services, but do not include the supply of any market research, product design, advertising, promotional or similar services or the collection, collation and provision of information in connection with such activities.
(5A) For the purposes of item 5 a person is "acting in an intermediary capacity" wherever he is acting as an intermediary, or one of the intermediaries, between—
(a) a person who provides financial services, and
(b) a person who is or may be seeking to receive financial services . . .⁷
(5B) For the purposes of notes 5 and 5A "financial services" means the carrying out of any transaction falling within item 1, 2, 3, 4 or 6.]³

[(6) For the purposes of this Group—
"authorised open-ended investment company"[, "authorised contractual scheme"][8] and "authorised unit trust scheme" have the meaning given in section 237(3) of the Financial Services and Markets Act 2000;
"closed-ended collective investment undertaking" means an undertaking in relation to which the following conditions are satisfied—
   (a) its sole object is the investment of capital, raised from the public . . . [11]; and
   (b) it manages its assets on the principle of spreading investment risk; and
   (c) all of its ordinary shares (of each class if there is more than one) or equivalent units are included in the official list maintained by the [Financial Conduct Authority][9] pursuant to section 74(1) of the Financial Services and Markets Act 2000; and
   (d) all of its ordinary shares (of each class if there is more than one) or equivalent units are admitted to trading on a regulated market situated or operating in the United Kingdom;
"collective investment scheme" has the meaning given in section 235 of the Financial Services and Markets Act 2000;
"Gibraltar collective investment scheme" means—
   (a) a collective investment scheme to which section 264 of the Financial Services and Markets Act 2000 applies pursuant to an order made under section 409(1)(d) of that Act;
   (b) . . . [13]
"individually recognised overseas scheme" means a collective investment scheme declared by the [Financial Conduct Authority][9] Financial Services Authority to be a recognised scheme pursuant to section 272 of the Financial Services and Markets Act 2000;
["pension member" means, in relation to a qualifying pension fund, a person to or in respect of whom retirement benefits are to be paid from the fund;][11]
["qualifying pension fund" means a pension fund in relation to which all of the following conditions are satisfied—
   (a) it is solely funded, whether directly or indirectly, by pension members;
   (b) the pension members bear the investment risk;
   (c) the fund contains the pooled contributions of more than one pension member;
   (d) the risk borne by the pension members is spread over a range of investments; and
   (e) the fund is established in the United Kingdom . . . [14];][11]
"recognised collective investment scheme authorised in a designated country or territory" means a collective investment scheme recognised pursuant to section 270 of the Financial Services and Markets Act 2000;[10]
. . . [13]
"regulated market" has the meaning given in section 103(1) of the Financial Services and Markets Act 2000;
"sub-fund" means a separate part of the property of an umbrella scheme that is pooled separately;
"umbrella scheme" means a collective investment scheme under which the contributions of the participants in the scheme and the profits or income out of which payments are to be made to them are pooled separately in relation to separate parts of the scheme property.][7]
[(6A) A collective investment scheme, or sub-fund, that is not for the time being marketed in the United Kingdom is to be treated as not falling within item 9(c) [to (f)][13] if—
   (a) it has never been marketed in the United Kingdom, or
   (b) less than 5% of its shares or units are held by, or on behalf of, investors who are in the United Kingdom.][7]
[(6B) For the purposes of Note (6), a pension fund is funded indirectly where contributions are made by a third party on behalf of a pension member.][11]
(7) . . . [6]
(8) For the purposes of item 10 . . . [7], an open-ended investment company's scheme property is the property subject to the collective investment scheme constituted by that company.[7]
(9) . . . [6]
[(10) For the purposes of this Group—
   "collective investment scheme" has the meaning given in section 235 of the Financial Services and Markets Act 2000; and
   "open-ended investment company" has the meaning given in section 236 of that Act.] [4][1, 7]

Commentary—*De Voil Indirect Tax Service* **V4.136–V4.136F**.
Amendments—[1] Notes (7)–(10) inserted by the VAT (Finance) Order, SI 1997/510 art 2 with effect from 24 March 1997.
[2] Notes (1A), (2A), (2B) inserted by the VAT (Finance) Order, SI 1999/594 arts 4, 5 and 6 respectively, with effect from 10 March 1999.
[3] Note (5) substituted and Notes (5A), (5B) inserted by the VAT (Finance) Order, SI 1999/594 art 7, with effect from 10 March 1999.

[4] Note (10) substituted by the Financial Services and Markets Act 2000 (Consequential Amendments and Repeals) Order, SI 2001/3649 art 348 with effect from 1 December 2001.
[5] Note (2B) (inserted by SI 1999/594) repealed by the VAT (Finance) Order, SI 2003/1568 with effect for any services performed after 31 July 2003.
[6] Notes (2A), (7) and (9), words in Note (5A), and words in Note (8) repealed, by the VAT (Finance) (No 2) Order, SI 2003/1569 with effect for any services performed after 31 July 2003.
[7] Item 10 and Note (6) substituted, Note (6A) inserted, and Notes (8), (9) repealed by the Value Added Tax (Finance) (No 2) Order, SI 2008/2547 art 3 with effect from 1 October 2008.
Note that the intention appears to have been to repeal Note (10) rather than Note (9) which was already repealed as per footnote 7 above.
Note that Item 10, and Note (6) were to be substituted, and Notes (8), (10) were to be repealed, by the Value Added Tax (Finance) Order, SI 2008/1892 art 2(1), (2) with effect from 1 October 2008. However, this Order was revoked, following further consultation, by the Value Added Tax (Finance) (No 2) Order, SI 2008/2547 art 2 with effect from 30 September 2008 and was therefore revoked before it was due to take effect.
[8] In Note (6) words inserted by the Value Added Tax (Finance) Order, SI 2013/1402 art 2 with effect from 28 June 2013.
[9] In Note (6), in definitions of "closed-ended collective investment undertaking" and "individually-recognised overseas scheme", words substituted by the Financial Services Act 2012, s 114(1), Sch 18 para 81 with effect from 1 April 2013 (the appointed day for the coming into force of Sch 18 by virtue of SI 2013/423 art 3).
[10] In Note (6), definition of "recognised collective investment scheme authorised in a designated country or territory" repealed by the Alternative Investment Fund Managers Regulations, SI 2013/1773 reg 80, Sch 1 para 40 with effect from 22 July 2013.
[11] In Note (6), in definition of "closed-ended collective investment undertaking", in para (*a*), words ", wholly or mainly in securities" repealed, definitions of "pension member" and "qualifying pension fund" inserted, and Note (6B) inserted, by the Value Added Tax (Finance) Order, SI 2020/209 arts 2, 4, 5 with effect from 1 April 2020.
[12] In Note (6), in definition of "recognised collective investment scheme constituted in another EEA state", words substituted for words "another EEA state", by the Taxation (Cross-border Trade) Act 2018 s 43, Sch 8 paras 1, 95(1), (2)(*b*) with effect from IP completion day (11pm on 31 December 2020), by virtue of SI 2020/1642 reg 4(*b*).
[13] In Note (6) para (*b*) of the definition of "Gibraltar collective investment scheme" repealed, and the definition of "recognised collective investment scheme constituted in another EEA state" repealed, by the Value Added Tax (Miscellaneous Amendments and Transitional Provisions) (EU Exit) Regulations, SI 2019/1214 reg 2(1), (3), (4) with effect from IP completion day (11pm on 31 December 2020), by virtue of SI 2020/1641 reg 2, Schedule para 8. Para (*b*) of the definition of "Gibraltar collective investment scheme" previously read as follows—

"(*b*) a collective investment scheme to which the Financial Services and Markets Act 2000 applies pursuant to an order made under section 409(1)(*f*) of that Act;"

The definition of "recognised collective investment scheme constituted in another EEA state" previously read as follows—
""recognised collective investment scheme constituted in [an EEA state]" means a collective investment scheme which is recognised pursuant to section 264 of the Financial Services and Markets Act 2000;"
[13] In Note (6), in the definition of "qualifying pension fund", in para (e), words "or in a member State" repealed, by the VAT (Miscellaneous Amendments to Acts of Parliament) (EU Exit) Regulations, SI 2020/1312 reg 10 with effect from IP completion day (11pm on 31 December 2020) by virtue of SI 2020/1641 reg 2, Schedule para 9.

GROUP 6
EDUCATION

Item No

1 The provision by an eligible body of—
  (*a*) education;
  (*b*) *research, where supplied to an eligible body*[2]; or
  (*c*) vocational training.

2 The supply of private tuition, in a subject ordinarily taught in a school or university, by an individual teacher acting independently of an employer.

3 The provision of examination services—
  (*a*) by or to an eligible body; or
  (*b*) to a person receiving education or vocational training which is—
    (i) exempt by virtue of items 1, 2[, 5 or 5A][1]; or
    (ii) provided otherwise than in the course or furtherance of a business.

Amendments—[1] Words in Item 3(*b*)(i) substituted by the Learning and Skills Act 2000 Sch 9 para 47 with effect from 1 April 2001 (by virtue of SI 2001/654).
[2] In item 1, para (*b*) repealed by the Value Added Tax (Education) Order, SI 2013/1897 art 2 with effect from 1 August 2013. Note that this amendment does not apply in relation to a supply of services made pursuant to a written contract entered into before 1 August 2013 if the supply is within the scope of that contract as it stood immediately before that date (SI 2013/1897 art 1(2), (3)).

4 The supply of any goods or services (other than examination services) which are closely related to a supply of a description falling within item 1 (the principal supply) by or to the eligible body making the principal supply provided—
  (*a*) the goods or services are for the direct use of the pupil, student or trainee (as the case may be) receiving the principal supply; and

(b) where the supply is to the eligible body making the principal supply, it is made by another eligible body.

5 The provision of vocational training, and the supply of any goods or services essential thereto by the person providing the vocational training, to the extent that the consideration payable is ultimately a charge to funds provided pursuant to arrangements made under section 2 of the Employment and Training Act 1973, section 1A of the Employment and Training Act (Northern Ireland) 1950 or section 2 of the Enterprise and New Towns (Scotland) Act 1990.

[5A The provision of education or vocational training and the supply, by the person providing that education or training, of any goods or services essential to that provision, to the extent that the consideration payable is ultimately a charge to funds provided by—
 [(a) . . . [3]
 (b) . . . [4]
 (c)][2] the National Council for Education and Training for Wales under . . . [2] Part II of the Learning and Skills Act 2000.][1]

Amendments—[1] Item 5A and Note (5A) inserted by the Learning and Skills Act 2000 Sch 9 para 47 with effect from 1 April 2001 (by virtue of SI 2001/654).
[2] In Item 5A, words substituted for words "the Learning and Skills Council for England or", and words "Part 1 or" repealed, by the Apprenticeships, Skills, Children and Learning Act 2009 (Consequential Amendments) (England and Wales) Order, SI 2010/1080 art 2(1), Sch 1 paras 26, 94, Sch 2 Pt 1, with effect from 1 April 2010.
[3] In Item 5A, para (a) repealed and words in para (b) substituted by the Education Act 2011 s 67, Sch 16 para 9(1), (2) with effect from 1 April 2012 (by virtue of SI 2012/924, art 2).
[4] In Item 5A, para (b) repealed by the Deregulation Act 2015 s 64(3), Sch 14 paras 41(1), (2) with effect from 26 May 2015.

[5B The provision of education or vocational training and the supply, by the person providing that education or training, of any goods or services essential to that provision, to persons who are—
 (a) aged under 19,
 (b) aged 19 or over, in respect of education or training begun by them when they were aged under 19,
 [(ba) aged 19 or over and for whom an EHC plan is maintained,][2]
 (c) aged 19 or over but under 25 and subject to learning difficulty assessment, or
 (d) aged 25 or over, in respect of education or training begun by them when they were within paragraph [(ba) or][2] (c),
to the extent that the consideration payable is ultimately a charge to funds provided by the Secretary of State.][1]

Amendments—[1] Item 5B inserted by the Education Act 2011 s 67, Sch 16 para 9(1), (3) with effect from 1 April 2012 (by virtue of SI 2012/924, art 2).
[2] Para (ba), and words in para (d), inserted, by the Children and Families Act 2014 s 82, Sch 3 para 66 with effect from 1 September 2014 (by virtue of SI 2014/889 art 7(a))..

[5C The provision of education or vocational training and the supply, by the person providing that education or training, of any goods or services essential to that provision, to persons who are aged 19 or over, to the extent that the consideration payable is ultimately a charge to funds provided by the Secretary of State in exercise of functions under Part 4 of the Apprenticeships, Skills, Children and Learning Act 2009.][1]

Amendments—[1] Item 5C inserted by the Deregulation Act 2015 s 64(3), Sch 14 paras 41(1), (3) with effect from 26 May 2015.

6 The provision of facilities by—
 (a) a youth club or an association of youth clubs to its members; or
 (b) an association of youth clubs to members of a youth club which is a member of that association.

NOTES
(1) For the purposes of this Group an "eligible body" is—
 (a) a school within the meaning of [The Education Act 1996][2], the Education (Scotland) Act 1980 the Education and Libraries (Northern Ireland) Order 1986 or the Education Reform (Northern Ireland) Order 1989, which is—
  (i) provisionally or finally registered or deemed to be registered as a school within the meaning of the aforesaid legislation in a register of independent schools; or
  (ii) a school in respect of which grants are made by the Secretary of State to the proprietor or managers; or
  (iii) [[a community, foundation or voluntary school within the meaning of the School Standards and Framework Act 1998, a special school within the meaning of section 337 of the Education Act 1996][3] or a maintained school within the meaning of][2] the Education and Libraries (Northern Ireland) Order 1986; or

　　　　(iv) a public school within the meaning of section 135(1) of the Education (Scotland) Act 1980; or
　　　　(v) . . . ³; or
　　　　(vi) . . . ⁵
　　　　(vii) . . . ³; or
　　　　(viii) a grant-maintained integrated school within the meaning of Article 65 of the Education Reform (Northern Ireland) Order 1989;
　　(b) a United Kingdom university, and any college, institution, school or hall of such a university;
　　(c) an institution—
　　　　(i) falling within section 91(3)(a)[, (b) or (c)]⁶ or section 91(5)[(za)¹⁰, (b) or (c) of the Further and Higher Education Act 1992; or
　　　　(ii) which is a designated institution as defined in section 44(2) of the Further and Higher Education (Scotland) Act 1992; or
　　　　(iii) managed by a board of management as defined in section 36(1) of the Further and Higher Education (Scotland) Act 1992; or
　　　　(iv) to which grants are paid by the Department of Education for Northern Ireland under Article 66(2) of the Education and Libraries (Northern Ireland) Order 1986;
　　(d) a public body of a description in Note (5) to Group 7 below;
　　[(e) a body which—
　　　　(i) is precluded from distributing and does not distribute any profit it makes; and
　　　　(ii) applies any profits made from supplies of a description within this Group to the continuance or improvement of such supplies;]¹
　　[(f) a body not falling within paragraphs (a) to (e) above which provides the teaching of English as a foreign language.]¹
(2) A supply by a body, which is an eligible body only by virtue of falling within Note [(1)(f)]¹, shall not fall within this Group insofar as it consists of the provision of anything other than the teaching of English as a foreign language.
[(3) "Vocational training" means—
　　training, re-training or the provision of work experience for—
　　　　(a) any trade, profession or employment; or
　　　　(b) any voluntary work connected with—
　　　　　　(i) education, health, safety, or welfare; or
　　　　　　(ii) the carrying out of activities of a charitable nature.]¹
(4) "Examination services" include the setting and marking of examinations, the setting of educational or training standards, the making of assessments and other services provided with a view to ensuring educational and training standards are maintained.
(5) For the purposes of item 5 a supply of any goods or services shall not be taken to be essential to the provision of vocational training unless the goods or services in question are provided directly to the trainee.
[(5A) For the purposes of [items 5A [to 5C]⁹]⁷ a supply of any goods or services shall not be taken to be essential to the provision of education or vocational training unless—
　　(a) in the case of the provision of education, the goods or services are provided directly to the person receiving the education;
　　(b) in the case of the provision of vocational training, the goods or services are provided directly to the person receiving the training.]⁴
[(5B) In item 5B, ["EHC plan" and]⁸ "subject to learning difficulty assessment" [have the same meanings]⁸ as in the Education Act 1996.]⁷
(6) For the purposes of item 6 a club is a "youth club" if—
　　(a) it is established to promote the social, physical, educational or spiritual development of its members;
　　(b) its members are mainly under 21 years of age; and
　　(c) it satisfies the requirements of Note (1)(f)(i) and (ii).

Commentary—*De Voil Indirect Tax Service* **V4.141**.
Amendments—¹ Notes (1)(e), (f), (3) and the figure in note (2) substituted by the Value Added Tax (Education) (No 2) Order, SI 1994/2969 with effect from 1 January 1995.
² Words in Note (1)(a) substituted by Education Act 1996 s 582(1), Sch 37 Part I para 125.
³ Words in Note (1)(a)(iii) substituted and sub-paras (v) and (vii) omitted by School Standards and Framework Act 1998 Sch 30 para 51, with effect from 1 September 1999, by the School Standards and Framework Act 1998 (Commencement No 7 and Saving and Transitional Provisions) Order SI 1999/2323 para 2(1), Sch 1.
⁴ Note (5A) inserted by the Learning and Skills Act 2000 Sch 9 para 47 with effect from 1 April 2001 (by virtue of SI 2001/654).
⁵ Note (1)(a)(vi) repealed by the Standards in Scotland's Schools etc Act 2000 s 60(2), Sch 3 with effect from 31 December 2004 (by virtue of SSI 2004/528).

6   In Note (1)(c)(i) words substituted for words "or (b)", by the Apprenticeships, Skills, Children and Learning Act 2009 (Consequential Amendments) (England and Wales) Order, SI 2010/1080 art 2(1), Sch 1 paras 26, 94, Sch 2 Pt 1, with effect from 1 April 2010.
7   In Note (5A) words substituted and Note 5B inserted by the Education Act 2011 s 67, Sch 16 para 9(1), (4), (5) with effect from 1 April 2012 (by virtue of SI 2012/924, art 2).
8   In Note (5B), words inserted and substituted by the Children and Families Act 2014 s 82, Sch 3 para 66 with effect from 1 September 2014 (by virtue of SI 2014/889 art 7(a)).
9   In Note (5A) words substituted by the Deregulation Act 2015 s 64(3), Sch 14 paras 41(1), (4) with effect from 26 May 2015.
10 In Note (1)(c)(i) words "(za), " in square brackets inserted by SI 2019/1027, reg 5 with effect from 1 August 2019 (by virtue of SI 2019/1027, reg 1).

GROUP 7
HEALTH AND WELFARE

Item No

1 The supply of services [consisting in the provision of medical care][5] by a person registered or enrolled in any of the following—

(a) the register of medical practitioners or the register of medical practitioners with limited registration;

(b) either of the registers of ophthalmic opticians or the register of dispensing opticians kept under the Opticians Act 1989 or either of the lists kept under section 9 of that Act of bodies corporate carrying on business as ophthalmic opticians or as dispensing opticians;

[(c) the register kept under [the Health Professions Order 2001][9];][4]

[(ca) the register of osteopaths maintained in accordance with the provisions of the Osteopaths Act 1993;][2]

[(cb) the register of chiropractors maintained in accordance with the provisions of the Chiropractors Act 1994;][3]

[(d) the register of qualified [nurses, midwives and nursing associates][8] maintained under article 5 of the Nursing and Midwifery Order 2001][1]

(e) *the register of dispensers of hearing aids or the register of persons employing such dispensers maintained under section 2 of the Hearing Aid Council Act 1968.*[6]

Amendments—[1] Words in Item 1(d) substituted by the Nursing and Midwifery Order, SI 2002/253 art 54, Sch 5 para 12 with effect from 1 August 2004 (see the London Gazette, 21 July 2004).
2   Item 1(ca) inserted by Value Added Tax (Osteopaths) Order, SI 1998/1294 with effect from 12 June 1998.
3   Item 1 (cb) inserted by Value Added Tax (Chiropractors) Order, SI 1999/1575 with effect from 29 June 1999 (implements art 13A(1)(c) of the Sixth Council Directive, 77/388/EEC (OJ L145, 17.05.1977, p1)).
4   Item 1(c) substituted by the Health Professions Order, SI 2002/254 art 48, Sch 4 para 6 with effect from 9 July 2003 (see the London Gazette, 27 June 2003).
5   Words in item 1 inserted by the VAT (Health and Welfare) Order, SI 2007/206 arts 2–6 with effect from 1 May 2007.
6   Item 1(e) repealed by the Health and Social Care Act 2008 s 166, Sch 15 Pt 2 with effect from 1 April 2010 (by virtue of SI 2010/708 art 4(2)(d)(vi)).
8   Words in item 1(d) substituted for words "nurses and midwives" by the Nursing and Midwifery (Amendment) Order, SI 2018/838 art 2(3), Sch 3 para 2 with effect from 28 January 2019.
9   In Item 1(c), words substituted for words "the Health and Social Work Professions Order 2001" by the Children and Social Work Act 2017 s 62, Sch 5 para 47(f) with effect from 2 December 2019 (by virtue of SI 2019/1436 reg 2(s)).

2 [The supply of any services consisting in the provision of medical care, or the supply of dental prostheses, by][1] —

(a) a person registered in the dentists' register;

[(b) a person registered in the dental care professionals register established under section 36B of the Dentists Act 1984;][2] . . . [1]

Amendments—[1] Words in items 1, 3 inserted, words in item 2 substituted, item 2(c) and preceding word "or" repealed, and item 2A inserted, by the VAT (Health and Welfare) Order, SI 2007/206 arts 2–6 with effect from 1 May 2007.
2   Item 2(b) substituted by the Dentists Act 1984 (Amendment) Order, SI 2005/2011 art 49, Sch 6 para 3 with effect from 31 July 2006.

[2A The supply of any services or dental prostheses by a dental technician.][1]

Amendments—[1] Item 2A inserted by the VAT (Health and Welfare) Order, SI 2007/206 arts 2–6 with effect from 1 May 2007.

3 The supply of any services [consisting in the provision of medical care][1] by a person registered in the register of pharmaceutical chemists kept under the Pharmacy Act 1954 or the Pharmacy (Northern Ireland) Order 1976.

Amendments—[1] Words in item 3 inserted by the VAT (Health and Welfare) Order, SI 2007/206 arts 2–6 with effect from 1 May 2007.

4 The provision of care or medical or surgical treatment and, in connection with it, the supply of any goods, in any hospital [or state regulated institution][1].

Amendments—[1] Words in Item 4 substituted by the Value Added Tax (Health and Welfare) Order, SI 2002/762 with effect from 21 March 2002.

5 The provision of a deputy for a person registered in the register of medical practitioners or the register of medical practitioners with limited registration.

6 Human blood.

7 Products for therapeutic purposes, derived from human blood.

8 Human (including foetal) organs or tissue for diagnostic or therapeutic purposes or medical research.

[**9** The supply by—
  (a) a charity,
  (b) a state-regulated private welfare institution [or agency]², or
  (c) a public body,
of welfare services and of goods supplied in connection with those welfare services.]¹

Amendments—¹ Item 9 and Note (6) substituted by the Value Added Tax (Health and Welfare) Order, SI 2002/762 with effect from 21 March 2002.
² Words in Item 9(b) inserted by the VAT (Health and Welfare) Order, SI 2003/24 with effect from 31 January 2003.

10 The supply, otherwise than for profit, of goods and services incidental to the provision of spiritual welfare by a religious community to a resident member of that community in return for a subscription or other consideration paid as a condition of membership.

11 The supply of transport services for sick or injured persons in vehicles specially designed for that purpose.

NOTES
(1) Item 1 does not include the letting on hire of goods except where the letting is in connection with a supply of other services comprised in the item.
(2) Paragraphs (a) to (d) of item 1 and paragraphs (a) and (b) of item 2 include supplies of services made by a person who is not registered or enrolled in any of the registers or rolls specified in those paragraphs where the services are wholly performed or directly supervised by a person who is so registered or enrolled.
(2ZA) . . . ⁴
[(2A Item 3 includes supplies of services made by a person who is not registered in either of the registers specified in that item where the services are wholly performed by a person who is so registered.]¹
(3) Item 3 does not include the letting on hire of goods.
(4) . . . ³
(5) In item 9 "public body" means—
  (a) a Government department within the meaning of section 41(6);
  (b) a local authority;
  (c) a body which acts under any enactment or instrument for public purposes and not for its own profit and which performs functions similar to those of a Government department or local authority.
[(6) In item 9 "welfare services" means services which are directly connected with—
  (a) the provision of care, treatment or instruction designed to promote the physical or mental welfare of elderly, sick, distressed or disabled persons,
  (b) the care or protection of children and young persons, or
  (c) the provision of spiritual welfare by a religious institution as part of a course of instruction or a retreat, not being a course or a retreat designed primarily to provide recreation or a holiday,
and, in the case of services supplied by a state-regulated private welfare institution, includes only those services in respect of which the institution is so regulated.]²
(7) Item 9 does not include the supply of accommodation or catering except where it is ancillary to the provision of care, treatment or instruction.
[(8) In this Group "state-regulated" means approved, licensed, registered or exempted from registration by any Minister or other authority pursuant to a provision of a public general Act, other than a provision that is capable of being brought into effect at different times in relation to different local authority areas.
Here "Act" means—
  (a) an Act of Parliament;
  (b) an Act of the Scottish Parliament;
  (c) an Act of the Northern Ireland Assembly;
  (d) an Order in Council under Schedule 1 to the Northern Ireland Act 1974;
  (e) a Measure of the Northern Ireland Assembly established under section 1 of the Northern Ireland Assembly Act 1973;

(f) an Order in Council under section 1(3) of the Northern Ireland (Temporary Provisions) Act 1972;

(g) an Act of the Parliament of Northern Ireland.][2]

Commentary—*De Voil Indirect Tax Service* **V4.146**.

Amendments—[1] Note (2A) inserted by the VAT (Pharmaceutical Chemists) Order, SI 1996/2949 with effect from 1 January 1997.

[2] Note (6) substituted, and Note (8) added, by the Value Added Tax (Health and Welfare) Order, SI 2002/762 with effect from 21 March 2002.

[3] Note 4 repealed by the European Qualifications (Health and Social Care Professions) Regulations, SI 2007/3101 reg 65(b) with effect from 3 December 2007.

[4] Note (2ZA) repealed by the Children and Social Work Act 2017 s 62, Sch 5 para 5 with effect from 2 December 2019 (by virtue of SI 2019/1436 reg 2(s)).

GROUP 8
BURIAL AND CREMATION

Item No

1 The disposal of the remains of the dead.

2 The making of arrangements for or in connection with the disposal of the remains of the dead.

Commentary—*De Voil Indirect Tax Service* **V4.151**.

[GROUP 9
SUBSCRIPTIONS TO TRADE UNIONS, PROFESSIONAL AND OTHER PUBLIC INTEREST BODIES][1]

Item No

1 The supply to its members of such services and, in connection with those services, of such goods as are both referable only to its aims and available without payment other than a membership subscription by any of the following non-profit-making organisations—

    (a) a trade union or other organisation of persons having as its main object the negotiation on behalf of its members of the terms and conditions of their employment;

    (b) a professional association, membership of which is wholly or mainly restricted to individuals who have or are seeking a qualification appropriate to the practice of the profession concerned;

    (c) an association, the primary purpose of which is the advancement of a particular branch of knowledge, or the fostering of professional expertise, connected with the past or present professions or employments of its members;

    (d) an association, the primary purpose of which is to make representations to the Government on legislation and other public matters which affect the business or professional interests of its members.

    [(e) a body which has objects which are in the public domain and are of a political, religious, patriotic, philosophical, philanthropic or civic nature.][1]

NOTES

(1) Item 1 does not include any right of admission to any premises, event or performance, to which non-members are admitted for a consideration.

(2) "Trade union" has the meaning assigned to it by section 1 of the Trade Union and Labour Relations (Consolidation) Act 1992.

(3) Item 1 shall include organisations and associations the membership of which consists wholly or mainly of constituent or affiliated associations which as individual associations would be comprised in the item; and "member" shall be construed as including such an association and "membership subscription" shall include an affiliation fee or similar levy.

(4) Paragraph (c) does not apply unless the association restricts its membership wholly or mainly to individuals whose present or previous professions or employments are directly connected with the purposes of the association.

(5) Paragraph (d) does not apply unless the association restricts its membership wholly or mainly to individuals or corporate bodies whose business or professional interests are directly connected with the purposes of the association.

Commentary—*De Voil Indirect Tax Service* **V4.156**.

Amendments—[1] Group title substituted, and Item 1, para (e) inserted by the Value Added Tax (Subscriptions to Trade Unions, Professional and Other Public Interest Bodies) Order, SI 1999/2834, arts 2, 4.

GROUP 10
SPORT, SPORTS COMPETITIONS AND PHYSICAL EDUCATION

Item No

1   The grant of a right to enter a competition in sport or physical recreation where the consideration for the grant consists in money which is to be allocated wholly towards the provision of a prize or prizes awarded in that competition.

2   The grant, by a [an eligible body][1] established for the purposes of sport or physical recreation, of a right to enter a competition in such an activity.

Amendments—[1] Words in Items 2 and 3 substituted by the VAT (Sport, Sports Competitions and Physical Education) Order, SI 1999/1994, arts 2–5, with effect from 1 January 2000.

3   The supply by a [an eligible body][1] to an individual . . . [3] of services closely linked with and essential to sport or physical education in which the individual is taking part.

NOTES
(1) Item 3 does not include the supply of any services by a [an eligible body][1] of residential accommodation, catering or transport.
(2) . . . [3]
[(2A) Subject to Notes (2C) and (3), in this Group "eligible body" means a non-profit making body which—
   (a) is precluded from distributing any profit it makes, or is allowed to distribute any such profit by means only of distributions to a non-profit making body;
   (b) applies in accordance with Note (2B) any profits it makes from supplies of a description within Item 2 or 3; and
   (c) is not subject to commercial influence.
(2B) For the purposes of Note (2A)(b) the application of profits made by any body from supplies of a description within Item 2 or 3 is in accordance with this Note only if those profits are applied for one or more of the following purposes, namely—
   (a) the continuance or improvement of any facilities made available in or in connection with the making of the supplies of those descriptions made by that body;
   (b) the purposes of a non-profit making body.
(2C) In determining whether the requirements of Note (2A) for being an eligible body are satisfied in the case of any body, there shall be disregarded any distribution of amounts representing unapplied or undistributed profits that falls to be made to the body's members on its winding-up or dissolution.][1]
(3) In Item 3 a "[an eligible body[1]]" does not include—
   (a) a local authority;
   (b) a Government department within the meaning of section 41(6); or
   (c) a non-departmental public body which is listed in the 1993 edition of the publication prepared by the Office of Public Service and Science and known as Public Bodies.
[(4) For the purposes of this Group a body shall be taken, in relation to a sports supply, to be subject to commercial influence if, and only if, there is a time in the relevant period when—
   (a) a relevant supply was made to that body by a person associated with it at that time;
   (b) an emolument was paid by that body to such a person;
   (c) an agreement existed for either or both of the following to take place after the end of that period, namely—
      (i) the making of a relevant supply to that body by such a person; or
      (ii) the payment by that body to such a person of any emoluments.
(5) In this Group "the relevant period", in relation to a sports supply, means—
   (a) where that supply is one made before 1st January 2003, the period beginning with 14th January 1999 and ending with the making of that sports supply; and
   (b) where that supply is one made on or after 1st January 2003, the period of three years ending with the making of that sports supply.
(6) Subject to Note (7), in this Group "relevant supply", in relation to any body, means a supply falling within any of the following paragraphs—
   (a) the grant of any interest in or right over land which at any time in the relevant period was or was expected to become sports land;
   (b) the grant of any licence to occupy any land which at any such time was or was expected to become sports land;
   (c) the grant, in the case of land in Scotland, of any personal right to call for or be granted any such interest or right as is mentioned in paragraph (a) above;
   (d) a supply arising from a grant falling within paragraph (a), (b) or (c) above, other than a grant made before 1st April 1996;
   (e) the supply of any services consisting in the management or administration of any facilities provided by that body;
   (f) the supply of any goods or services for a consideration in excess of what would have been agreed between parties entering into a commercial transaction at arm's length.

(7) A supply which has been, or is to be or may be, made by any person shall not be taken, in relation to a sports supply made by any body, to be a relevant supply for the purposes of this Group if—
  (a) the principal purpose of that body is confined, at the time when the sports supply is made, to the provision for employees of that person of facilities for use for or in connection with sport or physical recreation, or both;
  (b) the supply in question is one made by a charity or local authority or one which (if it is made) will be made by a person who is a charity or local authority at the time when the sports supply is made;
  (c) the supply in question is a grant falling within Note (6)(a) to (c) which has been made, or (if it is made) will be made, for a nominal consideration;
  (d) the supply in question is one arising from such a grant as is mentioned in paragraph (c) above and is not itself a supply the consideration for which was, or will or may be, more than a nominal consideration; or
  (e) the supply in question—
    (i) is a grant falling within Note (6)(a) to (c) which is made for no consideration; but
    (ii) falls to be treated as a supply of goods or services, or (if it is made) will fall to be so treated, by reason only of the application, in accordance with paragraph 9 of Schedule 4, of paragraph 5 of that Schedule.
(8) Subject to Note (10), a person shall be taken, for the purposes of this Group, to have been associated with a body at any of the following times, that is to say—
  (a) the time when a supply was made to that body by that person;
  (b) the time when an emolument was paid by that body to that person; or
  (c) the time when an agreement was in existence for the making of a relevant supply or the payment of emoluments,
if, at that time, or at another time (whether before or after that time) in the relevant period, that person was an officer or shadow officer of that body or an intermediary for supplies to that body.
(9) Subject to Note (10), a person shall also be taken, for the purposes of this Group, to have been associated with a body at a time mentioned in paragraph (a), (b) or (c) of Note (8) if, at that time, he was connected with another person who in accordance with that Note—
  (a) is to be taken to have been so associated at that time; or
  (b) would be taken to have been so associated were that time the time of a supply by the other person to that body.
(10) Subject to Note (11), a person shall not be taken for the purposes of this Group to have been associated with a body at a time mentioned in paragraph (a), (b) or (c) of Note (8) if the only times in the relevant period when that person or the person connected with him was an officer or shadow officer of the body are times before 1st January 2000.
(11) Note (10) does not apply where (but for that Note) the body would be treated as subject to commercial influence at any time in the relevant period by virtue of—
  (a) the existence of any agreement entered into on or after 14th January 1999 and before 1st January 2000; or
  (b) anything done in pursuance of any such agreement.
(12) For the purposes of this Group a person shall be taken, in relation to a sports supply, to have been at all times in the relevant period an intermediary for supplies to the body making that supply if—
  (a) at any time in that period either a supply was made to him by another person or an agreement for the making of a supply to him by another was in existence; and
  (b) the circumstances were such that, if—
    (i) that body had been the person to whom the supply was made or (in the case of an agreement) the person to whom it was to be or might be made; and
    (ii) Note (7) above were to be disregarded to the extent (if at all) that it would prevent the supply from being a relevant supply, the body would have fallen to be regarded in relation to the sports supply as subject to commercial influence.
(13) In determining for the purposes of Note (12) or this Note whether there are such circumstances as are mentioned in paragraph (b) of that Note in the case of any supply, that Note and this Note shall be applied first for determining whether the person by whom the supply was made, or was to be or might be made, was himself an intermediary for supplies to the body in question, and so on through any number of other supplies or agreements.
(14) In determining for the purposes of this Group whether a supply made by any person was made by an intermediary for supplies to a body, it shall be immaterial that the supply by that person was made before the making of the supply or agreement by reference to which that person falls to be regarded as such an intermediary.
(15) Without prejudice to the generality of subsection (1AA) of section 43, for the purpose of determining—

(a) whether a relevant supply has at any time been made to any person;
(b) whether there has at any time been an agreement for the making of a relevant supply to any person; and
(c) whether a person falls to be treated as an intermediary for the supplies to any body by reference to supplies that have been, were to be or might have been made to him,

references in the preceding Notes to a supply shall be deemed to include references to a supply falling for other purposes to be disregarded in accordance with section 43(1)(a).

(16) In this Group—

"agreement" includes any arrangement or understanding (whether or not legally enforceable);

"emolument" means any emolument (within the meaning of the Income Tax Acts) the amount of which falls or may fall, in accordance with the agreement under which it is payable, to be determined or varied wholly or partly by reference—

(i) to the profits from some or all of the activities of the body paying the emolument; or
(ii) to the level of that body's gross income from some or all of its activities;

"employees", in relation to a person, includes retired employees of that person;

"grant" includes an assignment or surrender;

"officer", in relation to a body, includes—

(i) a director of a body corporate; and
(ii) any committee member or trustee concerned in the general control and management of the administration of the body;

"shadow officer", in relation to a body, means a person in accordance with whose directions or instructions the members or officers of the body are accustomed to act;

"sports land", in relation to any body, means any land used or held for use for or in connection with the provision by that body of facilities for use for or in connection with sport or physical recreation, or both;

"sports supply" means a supply which, if made by an eligible body, would fall within Item 2 or 3.

(17) For the purposes of this Group any question whether a person is connected with another shall be determined in accordance with [section 1122 of the Corporation Tax Act 2010][2] (connected persons).][1]

Commentary—*De Voil Indirect Tax Service* **V4.161**.
Amendments—[1] Words in Items 2 and 3 and words in Notes (1) and (3) substituted, and Notes (2A)–(2C) and (4)–(17) inserted, by the VAT (Sport, Sports Competitions and Physical Education) Order, SI 1999/1994, arts 2–5, with effect from 1 January 2000.
[2] In Note (17) words substituted for words "section 839 of the Taxes Act 1988" by CTA 2010 s 1177, Sch 1 para 285(e)(*ii*). CTA 2010 has effect for corporation tax purposes for accounting periods ending on or after 1 April 2010, and for income and capital gains tax purposes for the tax year 2010–11 and subsequent tax years.
[3] In Item 3, words ", except, where the body operates a membership scheme, an individual who is not a member," repealed, and Note (2) repealed, by the Value Added Tax (Sport) Order, SI 2014/3185 art 2 with effect from 1 January 2015.

GROUP 11
WORKS OF ART ETC

Item No

1 The disposal of an object with respect to which estate duty is not chargeable by virtue of section 30(3) of the Finance Act 1953, section 34(1) of the Finance Act 1956 or the proviso to section 40(2) of the Finance Act 1930.

2 The disposal of an object with respect to which inheritance tax is not chargeable by virtue of paragraph 1(3)(*a*) or (4), paragraph 3(4)(*a*), or the words following paragraph 3(4), of Schedule 5 to the Inheritance Tax Act 1984.

3 The disposal of property with respect to which inheritance tax is not chargeable by virtue of section 32(4) or 32A(5) or (7) of the Inheritance Tax Act 1984.

4 The disposal of an asset in a case in which any gain accruing on that disposal is not a chargeable gain by virtue of section 258(2) of the Taxation of Chargeable Gains Act 1992.

Commentary—*De Voil Indirect Tax Service* **V4.166**.

[GROUP 12
FUND-RAISING EVENTS BY CHARITIES AND OTHER QUALIFYING BODIES

Item No.

1 The supply of goods and services by a charity in connection with an event—
(*a*) that is organised for charitable purposes by a charity or jointly by more than one charity,

(b) whose primary purpose is the raising of money, and
(c) that is promoted as being primarily for the raising of money.

2   The supply of goods and services by a qualifying body in connection with an event—
(a) that is organised exclusively for the body's own benefit,
(b) whose primary purpose is the raising of money, and
(c) that is promoted as being primarily for the raising of money.

3   The supply of goods and services by a charity or a qualifying body in connection with an event—
(a) that is organised jointly by a charity, or two or more charities, and the qualifying body,
(b) that is so organised exclusively for charitable purposes or exclusively for the body's own benefit or exclusively for a combination of those purposes and that benefit,
(c) whose primary purpose is the raising of money, and
(d) that is promoted as being primarily for the raising of money.

NOTES
(1) For the purposes of this Group "event" includes an event accessed (wholly or partly) by means of electronic communications.
For this purpose "electronic communications" includes any communications by means of [an electronic communications network]^2.
(2) For the purposes of this Group "charity" includes a body corporate that is wholly owned by a charity if—
(a) the body has agreed in writing (whether or not contained in a deed) to transfer its profits (from whatever source) to a charity, or
(b) the body's profits (from whatever source) are otherwise payable to a charity.
(3) For the purposes of this Group "qualifying body means—
(a) any non-profit making organisation mentioned in item 1 of Group 9;
(b) any body that is an eligible body for the purposes of Group 10 and whose principal purpose is the provision of facilities for persons to take part in sport or physical education; or
(c) any body that is an eligible body for the purposes of item 2 of Group 13.
(4) Where in a financial year of a charity or qualifying body there are held at the same location more than 15 events involving the charity or body that are of the same kind, items 1 to 3 do not apply (or shall be treated as having not applied) to a supply in connection with any event involving the charity or body that is of that kind and is held in that financial year at that location.
(5) In determining whether the limit of 15 events mentioned in Note (4) has been exceeded in the case of events of any one kind held at the same location, disregard any event of that kind held at that location in a week during which the aggregate gross takings from events involving the charity or body that are of that kind and are held in that location do not exceed £1,000.
(6) In the case of a financial year that is longer or shorter than a year, Notes (4) and (5) have effect as if for "15" there were substituted the whole number nearest to the number obtained by—
(a) first multiplying the number of days in the financial year by 15, and
(b) then dividing the result by 365.
(7) For the purposes of Notes (4) and (5)—
(a) an event involves a charity if the event is organised by the charity or a connected charity;
(b) an event involves a qualifying body if the event is organised by the body.
In this Note "organised" means organised alone or jointly in any combination, and "organising" in Note (8) shall be construed accordingly.
(8) Items 1 to 3 do not include any supply in connection with an event if—
(a) accommodation in connection with the event is provided to a person by means of a supply, or in pursuance of arrangements, made by—
(i) the charity or any of the charities, or the qualifying body, organising the event, or
(ii) a charity connected with any charity organising the event,
and
(b) the provision of the accommodation is not incidental to the event.
(9) For the purposes of Note (8) the provision of accommodation is incidental to the event only if accommodation provided to the person by such means, or in pursuance of such arrangements, as are mentioned in paragraph (a) of that Note—
(a) does not exceed two nights in total (whether or not consecutive), and
(b) is not to any extent provided by means of a supply to which an order under section 53 applies.
(10) For the purposes of Notes (7)(a) and (8), two charities are connected if—
(a) one is a charity for the purposes of this Group only by virtue of Note (2) and the other is the charity that owns it, or

(b) each is a charity for the purposes of this Group only by virtue of Note (2) and the two of them are owned by the same charity.

(11) Items 1 to 3 do not include any supply the exemption of which would be likely to create distortions of competition such as to place a commercial enterprise carried on by a taxable person at a disadvantage.]¹

Commentary—*De Voil Indirect Tax Service* **V4.171**.
Amendments—¹ Group substituted by the Value Added Tax (Fund-Raising Events by Charities and Other Qualifying Bodies) Order, SI 2000/802 arts 2, 3 with effect in the case of supplies made from 1 April 2000.
² Words in Note (1) substituted by the Communications Act 2003 s 406, Sch 17 para 129(1), (3) with effect from 25 July 2003 to 29 December 2003 for certain purposes (see SI 2003/1900), 29 December 2003 for other purposes (see SI 2003/3142), and from a date to be appointed for remaining purposes.

[GROUP 13
CULTURAL SERVICES ETC

Item No

1 The supply by a public body of a right of admission to—
   (a) a museum, gallery, art exhibition or zoo; or
   (b) a theatrical, musical or choreographic performance of a cultural nature.

2 The supply by an eligible body of a right of admission to—
   (a) a museum, gallery, art exhibition or zoo; or
   (b) a theatrical, musical or choreographic performance of a cultural nature.

NOTES
(1) For the purposes of this Group "public body" means—
   (a) a local authority;
   (b) a government department within the meaning of section 41(6); or
   (c) a non-departmental public body which is listed in the 1995 edition of the publication prepared by the Office of Public Service and known as "Public Bodies".
(2) For the purposes of item 2 "eligible body" means any body (other than a public body) which—
   (a) is precluded from distributing, and does not distribute, any profit it makes;
   (b) applies any profits made from supplies of a description falling within item 2 to the continuance or improvement of the facilities made available by means of the supplies; and
   (c) is managed and administered on a voluntary basis by persons who have no direct or indirect financial interest in its activities.
(3) Item 1 does not include any supply the exemption of which would be likely to create distortions of competition such as to place a commercial enterprise carried on by a taxable person at a disadvantage
(4) Item 1(b) includes the supply of a right of admission to a performance only if the performance is provided exclusively by one or more public bodies, one or more eligible bodies or any combination of public bodies and eligible bodies.]¹

Commentary—*De Voil Indirect Tax Service* **V4.176**.
Amendments—¹ This group inserted by the VAT (Cultural Services) Order, SI 1996/1256, with effect from 1 June 1996.

[GROUP 14
SUPPLIES OF GOODS WHERE INPUT TAX CANNOT BE RECOVERED... . . . . *input tax*

Item No

1 A supply of goods in relation to which each of the following conditions is satisfied, that is to say—
   (a) there is input tax of the person making the supply ('the relevant supplier'), or of any predecessor of his, that has arisen or will arise on the supply to, . . . ⁸ or importation by, the relevant supplier or any such predecessor of goods used for the supply made by the relevant supplier;
   (b) the only such input tax is non-deductible input tax; and
   (c) the supply made by the relevant supplier is not a supply which would be exempt under Item 1 of Group 1 of Schedule 9 but for an [option to tax any land under Part 1 of Schedule 10]³.

NOTES
(1) Subject to Note (2) below, in relation to any supply of goods by the relevant supplier, the goods used for that supply are—
   (a) the goods supplied, and
   (b) any goods used in the process of producing the supplied goods so as to be comprised in them.
(2) In relation to a supply by any person consisting in or arising from the grant of a major interest in land ('the relevant supply')—

(a) any supply consisting in or arising from a previous grant of a major interest in the land is a supply of goods used for the relevant supply, and

(b) subject to paragraph (a) above, the goods used for the relevant supply are any goods used in the construction of a building or civil engineering work so as to become part of the land.

(3) Subject to Notes (7) to (10) below, non-deductible input tax is input tax to which Note (4) or (5) below applies.

(4) This Note applies to input tax which (disregarding this Group and regulation 106 of the Value Added Tax Regulations 1995 (*de minimis* rule)) is not, and will not become, attributable to supplies to which section 26(2) applies.

(5) This Note applies to input tax if—

(a) disregarding this Group and the provisions mentioned in Note (6) below, the relevant supplier or a predecessor of his has or will become entitled to credit for the whole or a part of the amount of that input tax; and

(b) the effect (disregarding this Group) of one or more of those provisions is that neither the relevant supplier nor any predecessor of his has or will become entitled to credit for any part of that amount.

(6) The provisions mentioned in Note (5) above are—

(a) Article 5 of the Value Added Tax (Input Tax) Order 1992 (no credit for input tax on goods or services used for business entertainment);

(b) Article 6 of that Order (no credit for input tax on non-building materials incorporated in building or site);

(c) Article 7 of that Order (no credit for input tax on motor cars);

(d) any provision directly or indirectly re-enacted (with or without modification) in a provision mentioned in paragraphs (a) to (c) above.

(7) For the purposes of this Group the input tax of a person shall be deemed to include any VAT which—

(a) has arisen or will arise on a supply to, . . . [8] or importation by, that person; and

(b) would fall to be treated as input tax of that person but for its arising when that person is not a taxable person.

(8) Subject to Note (9) below, the input tax that is taken to be non-deductible input tax shall include any VAT which—

(a) is deemed to be input tax of any person by virtue of Note (7) above; and

(b) would be input tax to which Note (4) or (5) above would apply if it were input tax of that person and, in the case of a person to whom section 39 applies, if his business were carried on in the United Kingdom.

(9) Non-deductible input tax does not include any VAT that has arisen or will arise on a supply to, . . . [8] or importation by, any person of any goods used for a supply of goods ('the relevant supply') if—

(a) that VAT; or

(b) any other VAT arising on the supply to, . . . [8] or importation by, that person or any predecessor of his of any goods used for the relevant supply,

has been or will be refunded under section 33, [33A,][2] [33B,][4] [33C,][5] 39 or 41.

(10) Input tax arising on a supply . . . [8] or importation of goods shall be disregarded for the purposes of determining whether the conditions in Item No 1(a) and (b) are satisfied if, at a time after that supply . . . [8] or importation but before the supply by the relevant supplier, a supply of the goods or of anything in which they are comprised is treated under or by virtue of any provision of this Act as having been made by the relevant supplier or any predecessor of his to himself.

(11) In relation to any goods or anything comprised in any goods, a person is a predecessor of another ('the putative successor') only if Note (12) or (13) below applies to him in relation to those goods or that thing; and references in this Group to a person's predecessors include references to the predecessors of his predecessors through any number of transfers and events such as are mentioned in Notes (12) and (13).

(12) This Note applies to a person in relation to any goods or thing if—

(a) the putative successor is a person to whom he has transferred assets of his business by a transfer of that business, or a part of it, as a going concern;

(b) those assets consisted of or included those goods or that thing; and

(c) the transfer of the assets is one falling by virtue of an Order under section 5(3) (or under an enactment re-enacted in section 5(3)) to be treated as neither a supply of goods nor a supply of services.

(13) This Note applies to a [person][6] in relation to any goods or thing if—

(a) those goods or that thing formed part of the assets of the business of that [person][6] at a time when it became a member of a group of which the putative successor was at that time the representative member;

(b) those goods or that thing formed part of the assets of the business of that [person, or of any other person who]⁶ was a member of the same group as that [person, at a time when that person]⁶ was succeeded as the representative member of the group by the putative successor; or
(c) those goods or that thing formed part of the assets of the putative successor at a time when it ceased to be a member of a group of which the [person]⁶ in question was at the time the representative member.
(14) References in Note (13) above to a [person's]⁷ being or becoming or ceasing to be a member of a group or the representative member of a group are references to its falling to be so treated for the purposes of section 43.
(15) In Notes (11) to (13) above the references to anything comprised in other goods shall be taken, in relation to any supply consisting in or arising from the grant of a major interest in land, to include anything the supply . . . ⁸ or importation of which is, by virtue of Note (2) above, taken to be a supply . . . ⁸ or importation of goods used for making the supply so consisting or arising.
(16) Notes (1) and (1A) to Group 1 shall apply for the purposes of this Group as they apply for the purposes of that Group.]¹

Commentary—*De Voil Indirect Tax Service* **V4.181**.
Northern Ireland—See Sch 9ZA para 71: Northern Ireland: Group 14 has effect as if—

- in para (a) of item 1, after "supply to" there were inserted "or acquisition";
- in Note (7)(a), after "supply to" there were inserted "or acquisition";
- in Note (9), in the words before paragraph (a), after "supply to" there were inserted "or acquisition", and in para (b), after "supply to" there were inserted "or acquisition";
- in Note (10), after "on a supply" there were inserted ", acquisition", and after "that supply", there were inserted ", acquisition"; and
- in Note (15), after "anything the supply" there were inserted ", acquisition", and after "be a supply" there were inserted ", acquisition".

Amendments—¹ This group inserted by the Value Added Tax (Supplies of Goods where Input Tax cannot be recovered) Order, SI 1999/2833, art 2(1), (3), with effect from 1 March 2000.
² In Note (9), "33A," inserted after "33," by FA 2001 s 98(9) with effect from 1 September 2001.
³ In Item 1(c) words substituted by the Value Added Tax (Buildings and Land) Order, SI 2008/1146, art 6, Sch 1 paras 1, 4 with effect in relation to supplies made on or after 1 June 2008, subject to savings in Sch 2 of the Order.
⁴ In Note (9), "33B," inserted after "33A," by FA 2011 s 76(4) with effect in relation to supplies made, and acquisitions and importations taking place, on or after 1 April 2011.
⁵ In Note (9), words inserted by FA 2015 s 66(1), (4) with effect in relation to supplies made, and acquisitions and importations taking place, on or after 1 April 2015.
⁶ In Note (13), in opening words, words substituted for words "body corporate", in para (a), words substituted for words "body", in para (b), words substituted for words "body corporate, or of any other body corporate which", and words substituted for words "body, at a time when that body", in para (c), words substituted for words "body corporate", by FA 2019 s 53, Sch 18 paras 3, 13(1), (2) with effect from 1 November 2019 (see SI 2019/1348).
⁷ In Note (14) words substituted for words "body corporate's" by FA 2019 s 53, Sch 18 paras 3, 13(1), (3) with effect from 1 November 2019 (see SI 2019/1348).
⁸ The following amendments made by the Taxation (Cross-border Trade) Act 2018 s 43, Sch 8 paras 1, 95(1), (3) with effect from IP completion day (11pm on 31 December 2020), by virtue of SI 2020/1642 reg 4(b)—
- in Item 1, in para (a), words "or acquisition" repealed;
- in Notes (7)(a), (9) words "or acquisition" repealed in all places; and
- in Notes (10), (15), words ", acquisition" repealed in all places.

[GROUP 15
INVESTMENT GOLD

Item no:

1 The supply of investment gold.

2 The grant, assignment or surrender of any right, interest, or claim in, over or to investment gold if the right, interest or claim is or confers a right to the transfer of the possession of investment gold.

3 The supply, by a person acting as agent for a disclosed principal, of services consisting of—
(a) the effecting of a supply falling within item 1 or 2 that is made by or to his principal, or
(b) attempting to effect a supply falling within item 1 or 2 that is intended to be made by or to his principal but is not in fact made.

NOTES:
(1) For the purposes of this Group "investment gold" means—
(a) gold of a purity not less than 995 thousandths that is in the form of a bar, or a wafer, of a weight accepted by the bullion markets;
(b) a gold coin minted after 1800 that—
(i) is of a purity of not less than 900 thousandths,
(ii) is, or has been, legal tender in its country of origin, and

(iii) is of a description of coin that is normally sold at a price that does not exceed 180% of the open market value of the gold contained in the coin; or

(c) a gold coin of a description specified in a notice that has been published by the Commissioners for the purposes of this Group and has not been withdrawn.

(2) A notice under Note (1)(c) may provide that a description specified in the notice has effect only for the purposes of supplies made at times falling within a period specified in the notice.

(3) Item 2 does not include—

(a) the grant of an option, or

(b) the assignment or surrender of a right under an option at a time before the option is exercised.

(4) This Group does not include a supply—

(a) between members of the London Bullion Market Association, or

(b) by a member of that Association to a taxable person who is not a member or by such a person to a member.][1]

Commentary—*De Voil Indirect Tax Service* **V4.186**.
Northern Ireland—See the Value Added Tax (Northern Ireland) (EU Exit) Regulations, SI 2020/1546 reg 4 (removals of investment gold: person to account is the person who would have accounted for VAT on the supply).
Amendments—[1] This group inserted by the Value Added Tax (Investment Gold) Order, SI 1999/3116, art 2(1), (3), with effect from 1 January 2000.

GROUP 16

SUPPLIES OF SERVICES BY GROUPS INVOLVING COST SHARING... . . . cost sharing

Item No

1 The supply of services by an independent group of persons where each of the following conditions is satisfied—

(a) each of those persons is a person who is carrying on an activity ("the relevant activity") which is exempt from VAT or [is not carried on in the course or furtherance of carrying on a business,][2]

(b) the supply of services is made for the purpose of rendering the members of the group the services directly necessary for the exercise of the relevant activity,

(c) the group merely claims from its members exact reimbursement of their share of the joint expenses, and

(d) the exemption of the supply is not likely to cause distortion of competition.][1]

Amendments—[1] Group 16 inserted by FA 2012 s 197(2) with effect from 17 July 2012.
[2] In para (a), words substituted for words "in relation to which the person is not a taxable person within the meaning of Article 9 of Council Directive 2006/112/EC,", by the Taxation (Cross-border Trade) Act 2018 s 43, Sch 8 paras 1, 95(1), (4) with effect from IP completion day (11pm on 31 December 2020), by virtue of SI 2020/1642 reg 4(b). Note that, where these amendments remove a reference to the principal VAT Directive (2006/112/EC) or the Implementing VAT Regulation ((EU) No 282/2011), the removal is not to be taken as implying that the Directive or Regulation is no longer relevant for determining the meaning and effect of this para (Taxation (Cross-border Trade) Act 2018 Sch 8 para 99).

[SCHEDULE 9ZA

VAT ON ACQUISITIONS IN NORTHERN IRELAND FROM MEMBER STATES

Section 40A(1)

PART 1

CHARGE TO VAT FOR ACQUISITIONS IN NORTHERN IRELAND FROM MEMBER STATES

Charge to VAT

1—(1) VAT is charged, in accordance with this Schedule, on the acquisition in Northern Ireland of goods from a member State—

(a) by reference to the value of the acquisition as determined under Part 2 of this Schedule, and

(b) subject to paragraph 16, at the rate of VAT for the time being in force under section 2.

(2) VAT charged on the acquisition of goods in Northern Ireland from a member State is a liability of the person who acquires the goods and (subject to provisions about accounting and payment) becomes due at the time of acquisition.

(3) VAT charged on the acquisition of goods in Northern Ireland from a member State in accordance with this Schedule is referred to in this Schedule as "NI acquisition VAT".

(4) References to VAT (without more) in this Act include NI acquisition VAT.

(5) The Commissioners may by regulations make provision about (including provision modifying) the application of provision that applies to value added tax made by or under any enactment (including provision made by or under this Act) to NI acquisition VAT or to goods acquired in Northern Ireland from a member State.][1]

Amendments—[1] Sch 9ZA inserted by the Taxation (Post-transition Period) Act 2020 s 3, Sch 2 paras 1, 2 with effect from IP completion day (11pm on 31 December 2020), by virtue of SI 2020/1642 reg 9.

[Scope of NI acquisition VAT

2—(1) NI acquisition VAT is charged on any acquisition from a member State of any goods where—
   (*a*) the acquisition is a taxable acquisition,
   (*b*) it takes place in Northern Ireland,
   (*c*) it is not in pursuance of a taxable supply (see section 4(2)), and
   (*d*) the person who makes it is a taxable person or the goods acquired are subject to a duty of excise or consist in a new means of transport.
(2) In this Act, a "taxable acquisition" means an acquisition of goods from a member State that—
   (*a*) is not an exempt acquisition (see paragraph 17(5)), and
   (*b*) falls within sub-paragraph (3) or is an acquisition of goods consisting in a new means of transport.
(3) An acquisition of goods from a member State falls within this subparagraph if—
   (*a*) the goods are acquired in the course or furtherance of—
      (i) any business carried on by any person, or
      (ii) any activities carried on otherwise than by way of business by any body corporate or by any club, association, organisation or other unincorporated body,
   (*b*) it is the person who carries on that business or those activities who acquires the goods, and
   (*c*) the supplier—
      (i) is taxable in a member State at the time of the transaction in pursuance of which the goods are acquired, and
      (ii) in participating in that transaction, acts in the course or furtherance of a business carried on by the supplier.][1]

Amendments—[1] Sch 9ZA inserted by the Taxation (Post-transition Period) Act 2020 s 3, Sch 2 paras 1, 2 with effect from IP completion day (11pm on 31 December 2020), by virtue of SI 2020/1642 reg 9.

[Meaning of acquisition of goods from a member State

3—(1) References in this Act to the acquisition of goods from a member State are to an acquisition of goods in pursuance of a transaction that—
   (*a*) is a supply of goods (including anything treated for the purposes of this Act as a supply of goods), and
   (*b*) involves the removal of the goods from a member State (whether by or under the direction of the supplier, the person who acquires the goods or any other person),
and references in this Act, in relation to such an acquisition, to the supplier are to be construed accordingly.
(2) Where the person with the property in any goods does not change in consequence of anything which is treated for the purposes of this Act as a supply of goods, that supply is to be treated for the purposes of this Act as a transaction in pursuance of which there is an acquisition by the person making the supply.
(3) The Treasury may by regulations make provision about the circumstances in which an acquisition of goods is not to be treated as an acquisition of goods from a member State.][1]

Amendments—[1] Sch 9ZA inserted by the Taxation (Post-transition Period) Act 2020 s 3, Sch 2 paras 1, 2 with effect from IP completion day (11pm on 31 December 2020), by virtue of SI 2020/1642 reg 9.

[Time of acquisition

4—(1) For the purposes of this Act, the normal rule for determining the time that goods were acquired from a member State is that they are treated as being acquired on the earlier of—
   (*a*) the 15th day of the month after the month in which the first removal of the goods occurs, and
   (*b*) the day a relevant invoice is issued in respect of the transaction in pursuance of which the goods were acquired.
(2) But—
   (*a*) different rules apply to acquisitions to which Part 4 of Schedule 9ZB applies (warehouses), and
   (*b*) the Commissioners may by regulations provide for different rules to apply in any case described in those regulations.
(3) Regulations under sub-paragraph (2)(*b*) may include provision treating an acquisition as a series of acquisitions taking place at different times.
(4) In sub-paragraph (1) "relevant invoice" means an invoice of a description prescribed by regulations made by the Commissioners.
(5) For the purposes of this Act "first removal", in relation to goods acquired, means the first removal of the goods in the course of the transaction in pursuance of which they are acquired.][1]

Cross-references—See SI 2020/1545 regs 115–118: transitional provisions in relation to transactions involving the removal of goods from a member State to the UK as a result of their entry into Northern Ireland
Amendments—[1] Sch 9ZA inserted by the Taxation (Post-transition Period) Act 2020 s 3, Sch 2 paras 1, 2 with effect from IP completion day (11pm on 31 December 2020), by virtue of SI 2020/1642 reg 9.

[Place of acquisition

5—(1) For the purposes of this Act, the normal rule for determining whether goods are acquired in Northern Ireland is that they are treated as being acquired in Northern Ireland if—
  (*a*) they are acquired in pursuance of a transaction which involves their removal from a member State to Northern Ireland and which does not involve their removal from Northern Ireland, or
  (*b*) they are acquired by a person who, for the purposes of their acquisition, makes use of a number assigned to the person for the purposes of VAT in the United Kingdom along with an NI VAT identifier (see paragraph 7).
(2) But—
  (*a*) goods are not treated as being acquired in Northern Ireland by virtue of sub-paragraph (1)(*b*) where it is established in accordance with regulations made by the Commissioners that VAT—
    (i) has been paid in a member State on the acquisition of those goods, and
    (ii) fell to be paid by virtue of provisions of the law of that member State corresponding, in relation to that member State, to the provision made by sub-paragraph (1)(*a*), and
  (*b*) different rules apply to acquisitions to which paragraph 16 or 17 of Schedule 9ZB applies.
(3) If an acquisition of goods is not treated, for the purposes of this Act, as taking place in Northern Ireland it is treated for those purposes as an acquisition taking place outside Northern Ireland.
(4) The Commissioners may by regulations make provision—
  (*a*) about the circumstances in which a person is to be treated as having made use of a number assigned to the person for the purposes of VAT in the United Kingdom along with an NI VAT identifier for the purposes of the acquisition of any goods, and
  (*b*) for the refund, in prescribed circumstances, of NI acquisition VAT paid on acquisitions of goods in relation to which the conditions in sub-paragraph (2)(*a*)(i) and (ii) are met.][1]

Amendments—[1] Sch 9ZA inserted by the Taxation (Post-transition Period) Act 2020 s 3, Sch 2 paras 1, 2 with effect from IP completion day (11pm on 31 December 2020), by virtue of SI 2020/1642 reg 9.

[Acquisitions from persons belonging in member States

6—(1) Sub-paragraph (2) applies where—
  (*a*) a person ("the original supplier") makes a supply of goods to a person who belongs in a member State ("the intermediate supplier"),
  (*b*) that supply involves the removal of the goods from a member State and their removal to Northern Ireland but does not involve the removal of the goods from Northern Ireland,
  (*c*) both that supply and the removal of the goods to Northern Ireland are for the purposes of the making of a supply by the intermediate supplier to another person ("the customer") who is registered under this Act,
  (*d*) neither of those supplies involves the removal of the goods from a member State in which the intermediate supplier is taxable at the time of the removal without also involving the previous removal of the goods to that member State, and
  (*e*) there would be a taxable acquisition by the customer if the supply to the customer involved the removal of goods from a member State to Northern Ireland.
(2) Where this sub-paragraph applies—
  (*a*) the supply by the original supplier to the intermediate supplier is ignored for the purposes of this Act, and
  (*b*) the supply by the intermediate supplier to the customer is treated for the purposes of this Act, other than for the purposes of Part 8 of this Schedule, as if it did involve the removal of the goods from a member State to Northern Ireland.
(3) For the purposes of this Act, other than for the purposes of Part 8 of this Schedule, a supply of goods is treated as involving their removal from a member State to Northern Ireland, and is treated as not being a taxable supply if—
  (*a*) the supply is made by a person belonging in a member State to a person who is registered under this Act,
  (*b*) the supply involves the installation or assembly of the goods at a place in Northern Ireland to which they are removed, and
  (*c*) were the supply to be treated as described in the words before paragraph (a), there would be a taxable acquisition by the registered person.
(4) But neither sub-paragraph (2) nor sub-paragraph (3) applies in relation to a supply unless—
  (*a*) in the case of sub-paragraph (2), the intermediate supplier, or

(*b*) in the case of sub-paragraph (3), the person making the supply,
complies with such requirements to provide information to the Commissioners or to the person supplied as may be specified in regulations made by the Commissioners.
(5) The requirements to provide information that may be specified in regulations include—
   (*a*) requirements to provide documents (for example, invoices);
   (*b*) requirements to provide information or documents before a supply is made (as well as after);
   (*c*) requirements as to the content and form of information or documents to be provided;
   (*d*) requirements as to the manner in which information or documents are to be provided.
(6) Where a taxable acquisition is treated as having been made by virtue of this paragraph, that acquisition is treated as taking place at the time referred to in paragraph 4(1)(*b*) (day on which invoice issued).
(7) For the purposes of this paragraph a person belongs in a member State if—
   (*a*) the person is taxable in a member State,
   (*b*) the person does not have any business establishment or other fixed establishment in Northern Ireland,
   (*c*) the person's usual place of residence is not in Northern Ireland,
   (*d*) the person is not identified for the purposes of VAT in Northern Ireland and is not required, as a result of regulations under paragraph 7, to make a request to be so identified, and
   (*e*) the person does not have a VAT representative who is identified for the purposes of VAT in Northern Ireland in connection with acting on the person's behalf, and is not for the time being required to appoint one who would be identified for those purposes.
(8) In determining, for the purposes of sub-paragraph (7)(*d*), whether a person is required to be registered under this Act, ignore any supplies made by the person that would be ignored for the purposes of this Act if the person belonged in a member State and complied with the information requirements that would apply by virtue of sub-paragraph (4).
(9) Where—
   (*a*) any goods are acquired from a member State in a case which corresponds, in relation to another member State, to the case described in sub-paragraph (1) in relation to Northern Ireland, and
   (*b*) the person who acquires the goods is registered under this Act, is identified for the purposes of VAT in Northern Ireland and would be the intermediate supplier in relation to that corresponding case,
the supply to that person of those goods and the supply by that person of those goods to the person who would be the customer in that corresponding case are to be ignored for the purposes of this Act.
(10) References in this paragraph to a person being taxable in a member State do not include references to a person who is so taxable by virtue only of provisions of the law of that member State corresponding to the provisions of this Act by virtue of which a person who is not registered under this Act is a taxable person if the person is required to be so registered.][1]

Cross-references—See SI 2020/1545 regs 115–118: transitional provisions in relation to transactions involving the removal of goods from a member State to the UK as a result of their entry into Northern Ireland
Amendments—[1]   Sch 9ZA inserted by the Taxation (Post-transition Period) Act 2020 s 3, Sch 2 paras 1, 2 with effect from IP completion day (11pm on 31 December 2020), by virtue of SI 2020/1642 reg 9.

[Identification of persons for the purposes of VAT in Northern Ireland

7—(1) The Commissioners may by regulations make provision for the identification of persons for the purposes of VAT in Northern Ireland.
(2) In this Act "identified for the purposes of VAT in Northern Ireland" means identified in accordance with regulations under this paragraph.
(3) A person may only be identified for the purposes of VAT in Northern Ireland if—
   (*a*) the person is registered under this Act, or
   (*b*) the person acts on behalf of a person in relation to VAT in Northern Ireland as a VAT representative.
(4) Regulations may make provision—
   (*a*) about the circumstances in which a person may request to be identified for the purposes of VAT in Northern Ireland;
   (*b*) for a person to be required to request to be identified for the purposes of Northern Ireland VAT;
   (*c*) about the circumstances in which the Commissioners may determine that a person is identified for the purposes of VAT in Northern Ireland otherwise than at the person's request;
   (*d*) requiring a person to notify the Commissioners of such matters as may be specified for the purpose of allowing the Commissioners to ascertain whether a person should be identified for the purposes VAT in Northern Ireland;

(e) about the circumstances in which a person is to be treated, for such purposes as may be specified, as if they were identified for the purposes of VAT in Northern Ireland (and which may include circumstances where the person is neither registered under this Act nor acting as a VAT representative);

(f) about the circumstances in which a person ceases to be identified for the purposes of VAT in Northern Ireland.

(5) Regulations may also make provision—

(a) about a specified means of communicating the fact of a person's identification for the purposes of VAT in Northern Ireland (and that means is referred to in this Act as an "NI VAT identifier");

(b) about the circumstances in which a person may use, or is required to use, an NI VAT identifier (for example, in connection with the making of a transaction or return).

(6) In this paragraph "specified" means specified in regulations.][1]

Amendments—[1] Sch 9ZA inserted by the Taxation (Post-transition Period) Act 2020 s 3, Sch 2 paras 1, 2 with effect from IP completion day (11pm on 31 December 2020), by virtue of SI 2020/1642 reg 9.

[PART 2
VALUATION OF ACQUISITIONS

Valuation of acquisitions from member States

8—(1) For the purposes of this Act the value of any acquisition of goods from a member State is taken to be the value of the transaction in pursuance of which they are acquired.

(2) Where goods are acquired from a member State otherwise than in pursuance of a taxable supply, the value of the transaction in pursuance of which they are acquired is to be determined for the purposes of sub-paragraph (1) in accordance with this Part, and for those purposes—

(a) sub-paragraphs (3) to (5) have effect subject to paragraphs 9 to 13, and

(b) section 19 and Schedule 6 do not apply in relation to the transaction.

(3) If the transaction is for a consideration in money, its value is taken to be such amount as is equal to the consideration.

(4) If the transaction is for a consideration not consisting or not wholly consisting of money, its value is taken to be such amount in money as is equivalent to the consideration.

(5) Where a transaction in pursuance of which goods are acquired from a member State is not the only matter to which a consideration in money relates, the transaction is deemed to be for such part of the consideration as is properly attributable to it.][1]

Amendments—[1] Sch 9ZA inserted by the Taxation (Post-transition Period) Act 2020 s 3, Sch 2 paras 1, 2 with effect from IP completion day (11pm on 31 December 2020), by virtue of SI 2020/1642 reg 9.

[Transactions below market value

9—(1) Where, in the case of the acquisition of any goods from a member State—

(a) the relevant transaction (see paragraph 13) is for a consideration in money,

(b) the value of the relevant transaction is (apart from this paragraph) less than the transaction's open market value,

(c) the supplier and the person who acquires the goods are connected, and

(d) that person is not entitled under sections 25 and 26 to credit for all the VAT on the acquisition,

the Commissioners may direct that the value of the relevant transaction is taken to be its open market value.

(2) A direction under this paragraph must be given—

(a) by notice in writing to the person by whom the acquisition in question is made, and

(b) within the period of 3 years commencing with the relevant time (see paragraph 13).

(3) A direction given to a person under this paragraph in respect of a transaction may include a direction that the value of any transaction—

(a) in pursuance of which goods are acquired by the person from a member State after the giving of the notice, or after such later date as may be specified in the notice, and

(b) as to which the conditions in paragraphs (a) to (d) of subparagraph (1) are satisfied,

is be taken to be its open market value.

(4) For the purposes of this paragraph, the open market value of a transaction in pursuance of which goods are acquired from a member State is to be taken to be the amount which would fall to be taken as its value under paragraph 8(3) if it were for such consideration in money as would be payable by a person standing in no such relationship with any person as would affect that consideration.

(5) Section 1122 of the Corporation Tax Act 2010 ("connected" persons) applies for the purpose of determining whether a person is connected with another for the purposes of this paragraph.

(6) A direction under this paragraph may be varied or withdrawn by the Commissioners by a further direction given by notice in writing.]¹

Amendments—¹ Sch 9ZA inserted by the Taxation (Post-transition Period) Act 2020 s 3, Sch 2 paras 1, 2 with effect from IP completion day (11pm on 31 December 2020), by virtue of SI 2020/1642 reg 9.

[Value where goods subject to excise duty etc

10 (1) This paragraph applies, in such cases as the Commissioners may by regulations prescribe, to an acquisition—
   (*a*) of goods acquired in Northern Ireland from a member State,
   (*b*) where those goods are charged with a relevant duty, and
   (*c*) that is not an acquisition that is treated, by virtue of paragraph 16(7) of Schedule 9ZB, as taking place before the time which is the duty point (within the meaning given by paragraph 16(11) of that Schedule).

(2) The value of the relevant transaction in relation to an acquisition to which this paragraph applies is the sum of the value of that transaction (apart from this paragraph) and the total amount of relevant duty charged that is not already reflected in the value of that transaction.

(3) In this paragraph "relevant duty" in relation to an acquisition means—
   (*a*) a duty of excise charged in connection with the removal of goods to Northern Ireland;
   (*b*) any EU customs duty or agricultural levy of the European Union charged on that removal in accordance with any provision for the time being having effect for transitional purposes in connection with the accession of any State to the European Union.]¹

Amendments—¹ Sch 9ZA inserted by the Taxation (Post-transition Period) Act 2020 s 3, Sch 2 paras 1, 2 with effect from IP completion day (11pm on 31 December 2020), by virtue of SI 2020/1642 reg 9.

[Transfer or disposal for no consideration

11—(1) Where goods are acquired from a member State in pursuance of anything which is treated as a supply for the purposes of this Act as a result of paragraph 5(1) of Schedule 4 or paragraph 30 of Schedule 9ZB and there is no consideration, sub-paragraph (3) applies for determining the value of the relevant transaction.

(2) Sub-paragraph (3) also applies for determining the value of the relevant transaction in the case of an acquisition by a supplier that is deemed to take place as a result of paragraph 60(2)(*c*) or 61(2)(*c*).

(3) The value of the relevant transaction is taken to be—
   (*a*) such consideration in money as would be payable by the supplier if the supplier were, at the time of the acquisition, to purchase goods identical in every respect (including age and condition) to the goods concerned,
   (*b*) where the value cannot be ascertained in accordance with paragraph (*a*), such consideration in money as would be payable by the supplier if the supplier were, at that time, to purchase goods similar to, and of the same age and condition as, the goods concerned, or
   (*c*) where the value cannot be ascertained in accordance with paragraph (*a*) or (*b*), the cost of producing the goods concerned if they were produced at that time.

(4) For the purposes of sub-paragraph (3), the amount of consideration in money that would be payable by any person if the person were to purchase any goods is taken to be the amount that would be so payable after the deduction of any amount included in the purchase price in respect of VAT on the supply of the goods to that person.]¹

Amendments—¹ Sch 9ZA inserted by the Taxation (Post-transition Period) Act 2020 s 3, Sch 2 paras 1, 2 with effect from IP completion day (11pm on 31 December 2020), by virtue of SI 2020/1642 reg 9.

[Foreign currency transactions

12—(1) Subject to the following provisions of this paragraph, where—
   (*a*) goods are acquired from a member State, and
   (*b*) any sum relevant for determining the value of the relevant transaction is expressed in a currency other than sterling,
then, for the purpose of valuing the relevant transaction, that sum is to be converted into sterling at the market rate which, on the relevant day, would apply in the United Kingdom to a purchase with sterling of that sum in the currency in question by the person making the acquisition.

(2) Where the Commissioners have published a notice which, for the purposes of this paragraph, specifies—
   (*a*) rates of exchange, or
   (*b*) methods of determining rates of exchange,
a rate specified in or determined in accordance with the notice, as for the time being in force, applies (instead of the rate for which sub-paragraph (1) provides) in the case of any transaction in pursuance of which goods are acquired by a person who opts, in such manner as may be allowed by the Commissioners, for the use of that rate in relation to that transaction.

(3) An option for the purposes of sub-paragraph (2) for the use of a particular rate or method of determining a rate—
- (a) may not be exercised by any person except in relation to all such transactions in pursuance of which goods are acquired by the person from a member State as are of a particular description or after a particular date, and
- (b) may not be withdrawn or varied except with the consent of the Commissioners and in such manner as they may require.

(4) In specifying a method of determining a rate of exchange, a notice published by the Commissioners under sub-paragraph (2) may allow a person to apply to the Commissioners for the use, for the purpose of valuing some or all of the transactions in pursuance of which goods are acquired by the person from a member State, of a rate of exchange which is different from any which would otherwise apply.

(5) On an application made in accordance with provision contained in a notice under sub-paragraph (4), the Commissioners may authorise the use with respect to the applicant of such a rate of exchange, in such circumstances, in relation to such transactions and subject to such conditions as they think fit.

(6) A notice published by the Commissioners for the purposes of this paragraph may be withdrawn or varied by a subsequent notice published by the Commissioners.

(7) Where goods are acquired from a member State, the appropriate rate of exchange is to be determined for the purpose of valuing the relevant transaction by reference to the relevant time; and, accordingly, the day on which that time falls is the relevant day for the purposes of sub-paragraph (1).][1]

Amendments—[1] Sch 9ZA inserted by the Taxation (Post-transition Period) Act 2020 s 3, Sch 2 paras 1, 2 with effect from IP completion day (11pm on 31 December 2020), by virtue of SI 2020/1642 reg 9.

[Meaning of "relevant transaction" and "relevant time"

13—In this Part of this Schedule—
"relevant transaction", in relation to any acquisition of goods from a member State, means the transaction in pursuance of which the goods are acquired;
"the relevant time", in relation to any such acquisition, means—
- (a) if the person by whom the goods are acquired is not a taxable person and the time of acquisition does not fall to be determined in accordance with regulations made under paragraph 4(2)(b), the time of the first removal of the goods (see paragraph 4(5)), and
- (b) in any other case, the time of acquisition.][1]

Amendments—[1] Sch 9ZA inserted by the Taxation (Post-transition Period) Act 2020 s 3, Sch 2 paras 1, 2 with effect from IP completion day (11pm on 31 December 2020), by virtue of SI 2020/1642 reg 9.

[PART 3
PAYMENT OF NI ACQUISITION VAT BY TAXABLE PERSONS

Input tax and output tax

14—(1) NI acquisition VAT is input tax in relation to the taxable person acquiring the goods in question if the goods are used or are to be used for the purpose of any business carried on or to be carried on by the person.

(2) NI acquisition VAT is output tax in relation to the taxable person acquiring the goods in question (including VAT which is also to be counted as input tax by virtue of sub-paragraph (1)).

(3) Subsections (5) to (6A) of section 24 (input tax and output tax) apply to NI acquisition VAT as they apply to VAT on the supply or importation of goods.][1]

Amendments—[1] Sch 9ZA inserted by the Taxation (Post-transition Period) Act 2020 s 3, Sch 2 paras 1, 2 with effect from IP completion day (11pm on 31 December 2020), by virtue of SI 2020/1642 reg 9.

[Payment of NI acquisition VAT

15—(1) A taxable person must account for and pay NI acquisition VAT by reference to prescribed accounting periods (see section 25(1)).

(2) Subsections (2) to (6) of section 25 (payment by reference to accounting period and credit for input tax against output tax) contain provision relevant to the payment of NI acquisition VAT.

(3) Subsection (7) of that section (power to make order excluding credit for VAT paid) applies to acquisitions in Northern Ireland from a member State as it applies to the supply of goods.

(4) Section 26(1) has effect as if the reference to "input tax on supplies and importations" included input tax on acquisitions in Northern Ireland from a member State.

(5) That section and sections 26A to 28 contain further provision relevant to the payment of NI acquisition VAT.][1]

Amendments—[1] Sch 9ZA inserted by the Taxation (Post-transition Period) Act 2020 s 3, Sch 2 paras 1, 2 with effect from IP completion day (11pm on 31 December 2020), by virtue of SI 2020/1642 reg 9.

[PART 4
RELIEFS ETC
Reduced rate

16—(1) NI acquisition VAT is charged at the rate of 5% (instead of at the rate provided by section 2) if—
   (*a*) the acquisition in question is of goods the supply of which would be a supply of a description for the time being specified in Schedule 7A (charge at reduced rate), or
   (*b*) the acquisition in question is of a description for the time being specified in regulations made by the Treasury for the purposes of this paragraph.
(2) Regulations under this paragraph may provide that subparagraph (1)(a) does not apply to a description of a supply specified in Schedule 7A that is specified in those regulations.
(3) The power to specify a description of an acquisition conferred by sub-paragraph (1)(b) may be exercised so as to describe an acquisition of goods by reference to matters unrelated to the characteristics of the goods.][1]

Amendments—[1] Sch 9ZA inserted by the Taxation (Post-transition Period) Act 2020 s 3, Sch 2 paras 1, 2 with effect from IP completion day (11pm on 31 December 2020), by virtue of SI 2020/1642 reg 9.

[Zero-rating and exempt acquisitions

17 (1) Section 30(3) (zero-rating) applies to an acquisition of goods in Northern Ireland from a member State as it would apply to an importation of those goods.
(2) The Treasury may by regulations provide—
   (*a*) that sub-paragraph (1) does not apply to an acquisition of goods specified or described in the regulations;
   (*b*) that no NI acquisition VAT is chargeable on an acquisition of goods specified or described in the regulations.
(3) The Commissioners may by regulations provide for the zero-rating of supplies of goods, or of such goods as may be specified in the regulations, in cases where—
   (*a*) the supply in question involves both the removal of the goods from Northern Ireland and their acquisition in a member State by a person who is liable for VAT on the acquisition in accordance with provisions of the law of that member State corresponding, in relation to that member State, to the provisions of paragraph 2, and
   (*b*) such other conditions, if any, as may be specified in the regulations or the Commissioners may impose are fulfilled.
(4) Section 30(10) applies to a supply of goods that has been zero-rated in pursuance of regulations made under sub-paragraph (3) as it applies to a supply of goods that has been zero-rated in pursuance of regulations made under section 30(8) or (9).
(5) An acquisition of goods from a member State is an exempt acquisition if the goods are acquired in pursuance of an exempt supply (see section 31).][1]

Amendments—[1] Sch 9ZA inserted by the Taxation (Post-transition Period) Act 2020 s 3, Sch 2 paras 1, 2 with effect from IP completion day (11pm on 31 December 2020), by virtue of SI 2020/1642 reg 9.

[Refunds and reliefs

18 (1) Sections 33 to 33C, 33E and 34 apply to an acquisition of goods from a member State as they apply to a supply of those goods.
(2) The Treasury may by order make provision for relieving from NI acquisition VAT if, or to the extent that, relief from VAT would be given by an order under section 37 (relief from VAT on importation) if the acquisition in question were an importation.
(3) An order under sub-paragraph (2) may provide for relief to be subject to such conditions as appear to the Treasury to be necessary or expedient, which may include conditions—
   (*a*) prohibiting or restricting the disposal of or dealing with the goods concerned;
   (*b*) framed by reference to the conditions to which, by virtue of any order under section 37 in force at the time of the acquisition, relief under such an order would be subject in the case of an importation of the goods concerned.
(4) Where relief from NI acquisition VAT given by an order under this paragraph was subject to a condition that has been breached or not complied with, the VAT becomes payable at the time of the breach or, as the case may be, at the latest time allowed for compliance.
(5) Section 38 has effect as if after "by him" there were inserted "or on the acquisition of goods by that person from member States".][1]

Amendments—[1] Sch 9ZA inserted by the Taxation (Post-transition Period) Act 2020 s 3, Sch 2 paras 1, 2 with effect from IP completion day (11pm on 31 December 2020), by virtue of SI 2020/1642 reg 9.

[Refund of NI acquisition VAT to persons constructing certain buildings

18A (1) Where—

(a) a person carries out works to which this paragraph applies, and
(b) the carrying out of the work by the person is lawful and otherwise than in the course or furtherance of any business, and
(c) NI acquisition VAT is chargeable on the acquisition from a member State of any goods used by the person for the purposes of the works

the Commissioners must, on a claim made in that behalf, refund to that person the a mount of NI acquisition VAT so chargeable.

(2) Where—
(a) a person carries out works to which this paragraph applies,
(b) the carrying out of the work by the person is lawful and otherwise than in the course or furtherance of any business, and
(c) VAT is chargeable in accordance with the law of a member State (see paragraph 80) on the supply of any goods used by the person for the purposes of the works,

the Commissioners must, on a claim made in that behalf, pay to that person an amount equal to that VAT so chargeable.

(3) The works to which this paragraph applies are—
(a) he construction of a building in Northern Ireland designed as a dwelling or a number of dwellings;
(b) the construction of a building in Northern Ireland for use solely for a relevant residential purpose or relevant charitable purpose;
(c) a residential conversion of a building, or a part of a building, in Northern Ireland.

(4) Subsections (1B) and (1D) of section 35 (refund of VAT to persons constructing certain buildings) apply for the purposes of this paragraph as they apply for the purposes of that section.
(5) Subsection (2) of that section applies to a refund under subparagraph (1) or (2) as it applies to a refund of VAT under that section.
(6) Subsections (4) and (4A) of that section apply for the purpose of construing this paragraph.
(7) Subsection (5) of that section has effect as if in paragraphs (a) and (b), after "this section" there were inserted "or paragraph 18A of Schedule 9ZA".
(8) The provisions made by or under this Act or any other enactment (whenever passed or made) that apply to a refund under section 35 apply to a refund under sub-paragraph (2) a s if references in those provisions (however framed)—
(a) to VAT chargeable on the supply of goods were to VAT chargeable under the law of a member State;
(b) to refunding VAT to a person were to paying a person in accordance with that sub-paragraph.][1]

Amendments—[1] Para 18A inserted by the Value Added Tax (Miscellaneous Amendments to the Value Added Tax Act 1994 and Revocation) (EU Exit) Regulations, SI 2020/1544 regs 2, 3(1), (2) with effect from IP completion day (11pm UK time on 31 December 2020) by virtue of SI 2020/1641 reg 2, Schedule para 13.

[Refunds in relation to new means of transport supplied to member States

19—(1) Where a person who is not a taxable person makes such a supply of goods consisting in a new means of transport that involves the removal of the goods to a member State from Northern Ireland, the Commissioners must, on a claim made in that behalf, refund to that person, as the case may be—
(a) the amount of any VAT on the supply of that means of transport to that person, or
(b) the amount of any VAT paid by that person on the acquisition of that means of transport from a member State or on its importation into the United Kingdom as a result of its entry into Northern Ireland.

(2) But the amount of VAT that is to be refunded under this paragraph is not to exceed the amount that would have been payable on the supply involving the removal if it had been a taxable supply by a taxable person and had not been zero-rated.
(3) A claim for refund of VAT under this paragraph must—
(a) be made within such time and in such form and manner as may be specified in regulations made by the Commissioners,
(b) contain such information as may be specified in those regulations, and
(c) be accompanied by such documents as may be specified in those regulations.][1]

Amendments—[1] Sch 9ZA inserted by the Taxation (Post-transition Period) Act 2020 s 3, Sch 2 paras 1, 2 with effect from IP completion day (11pm on 31 December 2020), by virtue of SI 2020/1642 reg 9.

[PART 5
APPLICATION OF ACT TO ACQUISITIONS IN PARTICULAR CASES
Crown application

20—Subsections (3) and (4) of section 41 (application to the Crown) apply to NI acquisition VAT as they apply to VAT chargeable on the supply of goods.][1]

Amendments—[1] Sch 9ZA inserted by the Taxation (Post-transition Period) Act 2020 s 3, Sch 2 paras 1, 2 with effect from IP completion day (11pm on 31 December 2020), by virtue of SI 2020/1642 reg 9.

[Groups of companies

21—(1) Section 43 (groups of companies) applies to an acquisition of goods from a member State as it would apply to an importation of those goods as if the reference in subsection (1)(c) to section 38 were omitted.
(2) Subsections (2) and (9) of section 44 (supplies to groups) apply to input tax on acquisitions as they applies to input tax on supplies.][1]

Amendments—[1] Sch 9ZA inserted by the Taxation (Post-transition Period) Act 2020 s 3, Sch 2 paras 1, 2 with effect from IP completion day (11pm on 31 December 2020), by virtue of SI 2020/1642 reg 9.

[Partnerships

22—(1) Subsection (1) of section 45 (partnerships) applies to persons carrying on in partnership activities, other than carrying on a business, in the course or furtherance of which they acquire goods from a member State as it apples to persons carrying on a business in partnership.
(2) Subsections (2) and (5) of that section apply to a liability for NI acquisition VAT as they apply to VAT on the supply of goods or services.][1]

Amendments—[1] Sch 9ZA inserted by the Taxation (Post-transition Period) Act 2020 s 3, Sch 2 paras 1, 2 with effect from IP completion day (11pm on 31 December 2020), by virtue of SI 2020/1642 reg 9.

[Unincorporated bodies, personal representative etc

23—(1) In section 46 (business carried on in divisions or by unincorporated bodies, personal representatives etc) any reference to "a business" includes any activity in the course or furtherance of which any body corporate or any club, association, organisation or other unincorporated body acquires goods from a member State.
(2) Subsection (3) of that section (no account to be taken in change of members of a club, association or organisation) applies in relation to the determination of whether goods are acquired from a member State by a club, association or organization mentioned in that subsection as it applies in relation to the determination of whether goods or services are supplied by such a club, association or organisation.][1]

Amendments—[1] Sch 9ZA inserted by the Taxation (Post-transition Period) Act 2020 s 3, Sch 2 paras 1, 2 with effect from IP completion day (11pm on 31 December 2020), by virtue of SI 2020/1642 reg 9.

[Agents

24—(1) Where goods are acquired from a member State by a person who is not a taxable person ("N") and a taxable person ("T") acts in relation to the acquisition and then supplies the goods in T's own name as agent of N, the goods are to be treated for the purposes of this Act as acquired and supplied by T as principal.
(2) Section 47 (agents) has effect as if—
  (*a*) the reference in subsection (2) to "subsection (1) above" were to "subsection (1) and paragraph 24(1) of Schedule 9ZA";
  (*b*) the reference in subsection (2A) to "subsection (1) above" were to "subsection (1) or paragraph 24(1) of Schedule 9ZA".][1]

Amendments—[1] Sch 9ZA inserted by the Taxation (Post-transition Period) Act 2020 s 3, Sch 2 paras 1, 2 with effect from IP completion day (11pm on 31 December 2020), by virtue of SI 2020/1642 reg 9.

[VAT representatives

25—Subsection (1)(*a*) of section 48 (VAT representatives and security) applies to a person who, without being a taxable person, acquires goods in Northern Ireland from one or more member States as it applies to a person who, without being a taxable person, makes taxable supplies.][1]

Amendments—[1] Sch 9ZA inserted by the Taxation (Post-transition Period) Act 2020 s 3, Sch 2 paras 1, 2 with effect from IP completion day (11pm on 31 December 2020), by virtue of SI 2020/1642 reg 9.

[Margin schemes

26—Section 50A(5) (margin schemes) has effect as if after "supply," there were inserted "acquisition".][1]

Amendments—[1] Sch 9ZA inserted by the Taxation (Post-transition Period) Act 2020 s 3, Sch 2 paras 1, 2 with effect from IP completion day (11pm on 31 December 2020), by virtue of SI 2020/1642 reg 9.

[PART 6
ADMINISTRATION, COLLECTION AND ENFORCEMENT

Breaches of regulatory provisions

27—(1) Section 69(1) (breaches of regulatory provisions) applies to a failure to comply with a requirement imposed under paragraph 42, 52 or 65(1) or (2)(*a*) of this Schedule as it applies to a requirement imposed under the provisions mentioned in subsection (1)(*a*) of that section.
(2) Section 69(2) has effect as if after "imposed under" there were inserted "paragraph 64 or 65(2)(*b*) of Schedule 9ZA or".][1]
Amendments—[1] Sch 9ZA inserted by the Taxation (Post-transition Period) Act 2020 s 3, Sch 2 paras 1, 2 with effect from IP completion day (11pm on 31 December 2020), by virtue of SI 2020/1642 reg 9.

[Offences

28—(1) Any reference in section 72(1) or (8) (offences)—
 (*a*) to the evasion of VAT includes a reference to the obtaining of a refund under regulations made under paragraph 5(4) or under paragraph [18A or][2] 19, and
 (*b*) to the amount of VAT, in relation to such a refund, is to be construed as a reference to the amount falsely claimed by way of refund.
(2) Subsection (5) of section 72 applies to a claim for a refund under regulations made under paragraph 5(4) or under paragraph [18A or][2] 19 as it applies to a claim for a refund under the provisions mentioned in paragraph (*a*) of that subsection.
(3) Subsection (10) of that section applies where a person has reason to believe that NI acquisition VAT has been or will be evaded as it applies where a person has reason to believe that VAT on the supply of goods or services has been or will be evaded.][1]
Amendments—[1] Sch 9ZA inserted by the Taxation (Post-transition Period) Act 2020 s 3, Sch 2 paras 1, 2 with effect from IP completion day (11pm on 31 December 2020), by virtue of SI 2020/1642 reg 9.
[2] In sub-paras (1)(a), (2) words inserted by the Value Added Tax (Miscellaneous Amendments to the Value Added Tax Act 1994 and Revocation) (EU Exit) Regulations, SI 2020/1544 regs 2, 3(1), (3) with effect from IP completion day (11pm UK time on 31 December 2020) by virtue of SI 2020/1641 reg 2, Schedule para 13.

[Failure to make returns

29—(1) Subsection (3) of section 73 (failure to make returns etc) applies to an amount which by reason of the cancellation of a person's registration under paragraph 43(2), 43(5) or 53(5) ought not to have been paid as it applies to an amount which ought not to have been paid by reason of the cancellation of a person's registration under any of the provisions mentioned in that subsection.
(2) Subsection (7) of that section applies to the acquisition of goods from a member State by a taxable person as it applies to the supply of goods to a taxable person.][1]
Amendments—[1] Sch 9ZA inserted by the Taxation (Post-transition Period) Act 2020 s 3, Sch 2 paras 1, 2 with effect from IP completion day (11pm on 31 December 2020), by virtue of SI 2020/1642 reg 9.

[Interest on VAT

30—Paragraph (*c*) of Section 74(1) applies to a person who was, but should no longer have been, exempted from registration (under Part 8 of this Schedule) under paragraph 44 as it applies to a person who was, but should no longer have been, exempted from registration under any of the provisions mentioned in that paragraph.][1]
Amendments—[1] Sch 9ZA inserted by the Taxation (Post-transition Period) Act 2020 s 3, Sch 2 paras 1, 2 with effect from IP completion day (11pm on 31 December 2020), by virtue of SI 2020/1642 reg 9.

[Assessment in cases of acquisitions of certain goods by non-taxable persons

31—(1) Where a person who has, at a time when the person was not a taxable person, acquired in Northern Ireland from a member State any goods subject to a duty of excise or consisting in a new means of transport and—
 (*a*) notification of that acquisition has not been given to the Commissioners by the person who is required to give one by regulations under paragraph 73(4) (whether before or after this paragraph comes into force),
 (*b*) the Commissioners are not satisfied that the particulars relating to the acquisition in any notification given to them are accurate and complete, or
 (*c*) there has been a failure to supply the Commissioners with the information necessary to verify the particulars contained in any such notification,
the Commissioners may assess the amount of VAT due on the acquisition to the best of their judgment and notify their assessment to that person.

(2) An assessment under this paragraph must be made within the time limits provided for in section 77 and may not be made after the later of—
   (a) 2 years after the time when a notification of the acquisition of the goods in question is given to the Commissioners by the person who is required to give one by regulations under paragraph 73(4), and
   (b) one year after evidence of the facts, sufficient in the opinion of the Commissioners to justify the making of the assessment, comes to their knowledge,
but (subject to section 77) where further such evidence comes to the Commissioners' knowledge after the making of an assessment under this section, another assessment may be made under this paragraph, in addition to any earlier assessment.
(3) Where an amount has been assessed and notified to any person under this paragraph, it is, subject to the provisions of this Act as to appeals, deemed to be an amount of VAT due from the person and may be recovered accordingly, unless, or except to the extent that, the assessment has subsequently been withdrawn or reduced.
(4) For the purposes of this paragraph, notification to a personal representative, trustee in bankruptcy, trustee in sequestration, receiver, liquidator or person otherwise acting in a representative capacity in relation to the person who made the acquisition in question is to be treated as notification to that person.][1]

Amendments—[1] Sch 9ZA inserted by the Taxation (Post-transition Period) Act 2020 s 3, Sch 2 paras 1, 2 with effect from IP completion day (11pm on 31 December 2020), by virtue of SI 2020/1642 reg 9.

[Assessment of amounts due

32—Section 77 (time limits and supplementary assessments) has effect as if—
   (a) in subsection (1), in the words before paragraph (a), after "or 76" there were inserted "or paragraph 31 of Schedule 9ZA";
   (b) in paragraph (a) of that subsection, after "importation" there were inserted "or acquisition";
   (c) in subsection (4), after "importation" there were inserted ", acquisition";
   (d) in subsection (4C) after paragraph (a) there were inserted—
      "(aza) paragraph 40 or 44(2) of Schedule 9ZA,
      (azb)   paragraph 50 of that Schedule,
      (azc)   regulations under paragraph 73(4) of that Schedule,";
   (e) in subsection (6), after "73(6)(b)" there were inserted "or paragraph 31(2)(b) of Schedule 9ZA".][1]

Amendments—[1] Sch 9ZA inserted by the Taxation (Post-transition Period) Act 2020 s 3, Sch 2 paras 1, 2 with effect from IP completion day (11pm on 31 December 2020), by virtue of SI 2020/1642 reg 9.

[Credit for, or repayment of, overstated or overpaid VAT

33—In section 80 (credit for, or repayment of, overstated or overpaid VAT) has effect as if in subsection (3C) reference to VAT provisions included any provision of any EU instrument relating to VAT, or to any matter connected with VAT, that has effect in Northern Ireland as a result of section 7A of the European Union (Withdrawal) Act 2018 (general implementation of withdrawal agreement).][1]

Amendments—[1] Sch 9ZA inserted by the Taxation (Post-transition Period) Act 2020 s 3, Sch 2 paras 1, 2 with effect from IP completion day (11pm on 31 December 2020), by virtue of SI 2020/1642 reg 9.

[PART 7
APPEALS AND SUPPLEMENTARY PROVISION

Appeals

34 (1) The following matters are to be treated as if they were included in the list of matters in subsection (1) of section 83 (matters subject to appeal to the tribunal)—
   (a) the VAT chargeable on the acquisition of goods from a member State;
   (b) any claim for a refund under any regulations made by virtue of paragraph 5(4) of this Schedule;
   (c) any direction under paragraph 9 of this Schedule;
   (d) the amount of any refunds under paragraph [18A or][2] 19 of this Schedule;
   (e) an assessment under paragraph 31 of this Schedule, or the amount of such an assessment;
   (f) a decision of the Commissioners under paragraph 17 of Schedule 9ZB—
      (i) as to whether or not a person is to be approved as a Northern Ireland fiscal warehousekeeper or the conditions from time to time subject to which the person is so approved,
      (ii) for the withdrawal of any such approval, or

(iii) for the withdrawal of Northern Ireland fiscal warehouse status from any premises.

(2) Section 84 (further provisions relating to appeals) has effect as if in subsection (4)(c), after "supply" there were inserted ", acquisition".][1]

Amendments—[1] Sch 9ZA inserted by the Taxation (Post-transition Period) Act 2020 s 3, Sch 2 paras 1, 2 with effect from IP completion day (11pm on 31 December 2020), by virtue of SI 2020/1642 reg 9.

[2] In sub-para (1)(d) words inserted by the Value Added Tax (Miscellaneous Amendments to the Value Added Tax Act 1994 and Revocation) (EU Exit) Regulations, SI 2020/1544 regs 2, 3(1), (4) with effect from IP completion day (11pm UK time on 31 December 2020) by virtue of SI 2020/1641 reg 2, Schedule para 13.

[Supplies spanning change of rate etc

35—(1) This paragraph applies where there is a change in the rate of VAT in force under section 2 or paragraph 16 of this Schedule or in the descriptions of exempt, zero-rated or reduced-rate acquisitions.

(2) Where—
- (a) any acquisition of goods from a member State which is affected by the change would not have been affected (in whole or in part) if it had been treated as taking place at the time of the first removal of the goods (see paragraph 4(5)), or
- (b) any acquisition of goods from a member State which is not so affected would have been affected (in whole or in part) if it had been treated as taking place at the time of that removal,

the rate at which VAT is chargeable on the acquisition, or any question of whether it is an exempt, zero-rated or reduced-rate acquisition, is to be determined as at the time of the first removal of the goods, if the person making the acquisition so elects.

(3) References in this paragraph to a zero-rated acquisition is to an acquisition on which no NI acquisition VAT is charged as a result of provision made by or under paragraph 17 (zero-rating).

(4) Reference in this paragraph to a reduced rate acquisition is to an acquisition on which NI acquisition VAT is charged at the rate in force under paragraph 16(1).][1]

Amendments—[1] Sch 9ZA inserted by the Taxation (Post-transition Period) Act 2020 s 3, Sch 2 paras 1, 2 with effect from IP completion day (11pm on 31 December 2020), by virtue of SI 2020/1642 reg 9.

[Failure of resolution under Provisional Collection of Taxes Act 1968

36—(1) Where—
- (a) by virtue of a resolution having effect under the Provisional Collection of Taxes Act 1968 NI acquisition VAT has been paid at a rate specified in the resolution by reference to a value determined under paragraph 8(3) of this Schedule, and
- (b) by virtue of section 1(6) or (7) or 5(3) of that Act any of that VAT is repayable in consequence of the restoration of a lower rate,

the amount repayable is to be the difference between the VAT paid by reference to that value at the rate specified in the resolution and the VAT that would have been payable by reference to that value at the lower rate.

(2) Where—
- (a) by virtue of such a resolution NI acquisition VAT is chargeable at a rate specified in the resolution by reference to a value determined under paragraph 8(3) of this Schedule, but
- (b) before the VAT is paid it ceases to be chargeable at that rate in consequence of the restoration of a lower rate,

the VAT chargeable at the lower rate is to be charged by reference to the same value as that by reference to which NI acquisition VAT would have been chargeable at the rate specified in the resolution.

(3) Section 90(3) (failure of resolution under Provisional Collection of Taxes Act 1968) has effect as if after "or 35" there were inserted "or paragraph [18A or][2] 19 of Schedule 9ZA".][1]

Amendments—[1] Sch 9ZA inserted by the Taxation (Post-transition Period) Act 2020 s 3, Sch 2 paras 1, 2 with effect from IP completion day (11pm on 31 December 2020), by virtue of SI 2020/1642 reg 9.

[2] In sub-para (3) words inserted by the Value Added Tax (Miscellaneous Amendments to the Value Added Tax Act 1994 and Revocation) (EU Exit) Regulations, SI 2020/1544 regs 2, 3(1), (5) with effect from IP completion day (11pm UK time on 31 December 2020) by virtue of SI 2020/1641 reg 2, Schedule para 13.

[Refund of VAT to Government of Northern Ireland

37—(1) Section 99 (refund of VAT to Government of Northern Ireland) applies to—
- (a) VAT charged on the acquisition of goods from a member State by the Government of Northern Ireland as it applies to VAT charged on the supply of goods or services to that Government, and
- (b) any amount attributable to acquisitions of goods from a member State for the purpose of a business carried on by the Government of Northern Ireland as it applies to supplies for that purpose.][1]

Amendments—[1] Sch 9ZA inserted by the Taxation (Post-transition Period) Act 2020 s 3, Sch 2 paras 1, 2 with effect from IP completion day (11pm on 31 December 2020), by virtue of SI 2020/1642 reg 9.

][1]PART 8

REGISTRATION IN RESPECT OF ACQUISITIONS FROM MEMBER STATES

Liability to be registered

38—(1) A person who—

(*a*) is not registered under this Act, and

(*b*) is not liable to be registered under Schedule 1 or 1A or Part 9 of this Schedule,

becomes liable to be registered under this Part of this Schedule at the end of any month if, in the period beginning with 1 January of the year in which that month falls, that person had made relevant acquisitions whose value exceeds £85,000.

(2) A person who is not registered or liable to be registered as mentioned in sub-paragraph (1)(*a*) and (*b*) becomes liable to be registered under this Part of this Schedule at any time if there are reasonable grounds for believing that the value of the person's relevant acquisitions in the following 30 days will exceed £85,000.

(3) A person is treated as having become liable to be registered under this Part of this Schedule at any time when the person would have become so liable under the preceding provisions of this paragraph but for any registration which is subsequently cancelled under paragraph 43(2) or 53(5) of this Schedule, paragraph 13(3) of Schedule 1, paragraph 11 of Schedule 1A or paragraph 6(2) of Schedule 3A.

(4) A person does not cease to be liable to be registered under this Part of this Schedule except in accordance with paragraph 39.

(5) In determining the value of any person's relevant acquisitions for the purposes of this paragraph, so much of the consideration for any acquisition as represents any liability of the supplier, under the law of a member State, for VAT on the transaction in pursuance of which the acquisition is made, is to be disregarded.

(6) In determining the value of a person's acquisitions for the purposes of sub-paragraph (1) or (2), acquisitions to which paragraph 19(6) of Schedule 9ZB (last acquisition or supply of goods before removal from Northern Ireland fiscal warehousing) applies are to be disregarded.][1]

Amendments—[1] Sch 9ZA inserted by the Taxation (Post-transition Period) Act 2020 s 3, Sch 2 paras 1, 2 with effect from IP completion day (11pm on 31 December 2020), by virtue of SI 2020/1642 reg 9.

[**39—**(1) A person who has become liable to be registered under this Part of this Schedule ceases to be so liable if at any time—

(*a*) the person's relevant acquisitions in the year ending with 31 December last before that time did not have a value exceeding £85,000, and

(*b*) the Commissioners are satisfied that the value of the person's relevant acquisitions in the year immediately following that year will not exceed £85,000.

(2) But a person does not cease to be liable to be registered under this Part of this Schedule at any time if there are reasonable grounds for believing that the value of that person's relevant acquisitions in the following 30 days will exceed £85,000.][1]

Amendments—[1] Sch 9ZA inserted by the Taxation (Post-transition Period) Act 2020 s 3, Sch 2 paras 1, 2 with effect from IP completion day (11pm on 31 December 2020), by virtue of SI 2020/1642 reg 9.

[Notification of liability and registration

40—(1) A person who becomes liable to be registered under this Part of this Schedule must notify the Commissioners of the liability—

(*a*) in the case of a liability under sub-paragraph (1) of paragraph 38, within 30 days of the end of the month when the person becomes so liable, and

(*b*) in the case of a liability under sub-paragraph (2) of that paragraph, before the end of the period by reference to which the liability arises.

(2) The Commissioners must register any such person (whether or not the person notifies them) with effect from the relevant time or from such earlier time as may be agreed between the Commissioners and the person.

(3) In this paragraph "the relevant time"—

(*a*) in a case falling within sub-paragraph (1)(*a*), means the end of the month following the month at the end of which the liability arose, and

(*b*) in a case falling within sub-paragraph (1)(*b*), means the beginning of the period by reference to which the liability arose.][1]

Amendments—[1] Sch 9ZA inserted by the Taxation (Post-transition Period) Act 2020 s 3, Sch 2 paras 1, 2 with effect from IP completion day (11pm on 31 December 2020), by virtue of SI 2020/1642 reg 9.

[Entitlement to be registered etc

41—(1) Where a person who is not liable to be registered under this Act and is not already so registered satisfies the Commissioners that the person makes relevant acquisitions, the Commissioners must, if the person so requests, register the person with effect from the day on which the request is made or from such earlier date as may be agreed between the Commissioners and the person.

(2) Where a person who is not liable to be registered under this Act and is not already so registered—
   (*a*) satisfies the Commissioners that the person intends to make relevant acquisitions from a specified date, and
   (*b*) requests to be registered under this Part of this Schedule,
the Commissioners may, subject to such conditions as they think fit to impose, register the person with effect from such date as may be agreed between the Commissioners and the person.

(3) Conditions imposed under sub-paragraph (2) may—
   (*a*) be so imposed wholly or partly by reference to, or without reference to, any conditions prescribed for the purposes of this paragraph, and
   (*b*) be subsequently varied by the Commissioners (whenever the conditions were imposed).

(4) Where a person who is entitled to be registered under paragraph 9 or 10 of Schedule 1 requests registration under this paragraph, the person is to be registered under that Schedule, and not under this Part of this Schedule.][1]

Amendments—[1] Sch 9ZA inserted by the Taxation (Post-transition Period) Act 2020 s 3, Sch 2 paras 1, 2 with effect from IP completion day (11pm on 31 December 2020), by virtue of SI 2020/1642 reg 9.

[Notification of matters affecting continuance of registration

42—(1) Any person registered under this Part of this Schedule who ceases to be registrable under this Act must notify the Commissioners of that fact within 30 days of the day on which the person ceases to be registrable.

(2) A person registered under paragraph 41(2) must notify the Commissioners, within 30 days of the first occasion after the person's registration when the person makes a relevant acquisition, that the person has made that acquisition.

(3) For the purposes of this paragraph a person ceases to be registrable under this Act where—
   (*a*) the person ceases to be a person who would be liable or entitled to be registered under this Act if the person's registration and any enactment preventing a person from being liable to be registered under different provisions at the same time were disregarded, or
   (*b*) in the case of a person who (having been registered under paragraph 41(2)) has not been such a person during the period of the person's registration, the person ceases to have any intention of making relevant acquisitions.][1]

Amendments—[1] Sch 9ZA inserted by the Taxation (Post-transition Period) Act 2020 s 3, Sch 2 paras 1, 2 with effect from IP completion day (11pm on 31 December 2020), by virtue of SI 2020/1642 reg 9.

[Cancellation of registration

43—(1) Where a person registered under this Part of this Schedule satisfies the Commissioners that the person is not liable to be so registered, the Commissioners must, if the person so requests, cancel that registration with effect from the day on which the request is made or from such later date as may be agreed between the Commissioners and the person.

(2) Where the Commissioners are satisfied that a person registered under this Part of this Schedule has ceased since the person's registration to be registrable under this Part of this Schedule, they may cancel that registration with effect from the day on which the person so ceased or from such later date as may be agreed between the Commissioners and the person.

(3) Where the Commissioners are satisfied that a person who has been registered under paragraph 41(2) and is not for the time being liable to be registered under this Part of this Schedule—
   (*a*) has not begun, by the date specified in the person's request to be registered, to make relevant acquisitions, or
   (*b*) has contravened any condition of the person's registration,
the Commissioners may cancel the person's registration with effect from the date so specified or, as the case may be, the date of the contravention or from such later date as may be agreed between the Commissioners and the person.

(4) But the Commissioners may not, under sub-paragraph (1), (2) or (3), cancel a person's registration with effect from any time unless the Commissioners are satisfied that it is not a time when that person would be subject to a requirement, or in a case falling under sub-paragraph (2) or (3) a requirement or entitlement, to be registered under this Act.

(5) Where the Commissioners are satisfied that, on the day on which a person was registered under this Part of this Schedule, the person—
   (*a*) was not registrable under this Part of this Schedule, and

(*b*) in the case of a person registered under paragraph 41(2), did not have the intention by reference to which the person was registered,
the Commissioners may cancel that registration with effect from that day.
(6) The registration of a person who—
(*a*) is registered under paragraph 41, or
(*b*) would not, if the person were not registered, be liable or entitled to be registered under any provision of this Act except that paragraph,
may not be cancelled with effect from any time before 1 January which is, or next follows, the second anniversary of the date on which the person's registration took effect.
(7) But sub-paragraph (6) does not apply to cancellation under subparagraph (3) or (5).
(8) In determining, for the purposes of sub-paragraphs (4) and (6), whether a person would be subject to a requirement, or would be entitled, to be registered at any time, so much of any provision of this Act as prevents a person from becoming liable or entitled to be registered when the person is already registered or when the person is so liable under any other provision is to be disregarded.
(9) For the purposes of this paragraph, a person is registrable under this Part of this Schedule at any time when the person is liable to be registered under this Part of this Schedule or is a person who makes relevant acquisitions.][1]

Amendments—[1]   Sch 9ZA inserted by the Taxation (Post-transition Period) Act 2020 s 3, Sch 2 paras 1, 2 with effect from IP completion day (11pm on 31 December 2020), by virtue of SI 2020/1642 reg 9.

[Exemption from registration

44—(1) Where a person who makes or intends to make relevant acquisitions satisfies the Commissioners that any such acquisition would be an acquisition in pursuance of a transaction which would be zero-rated if it were a taxable supply by a taxable person, the Commissioners may, if the person so requests and the Commissioners think fit, exempt the person from registration under this Part of this Schedule until it appears to the Commissioners that the request should no longer be acted upon or is withdrawn.
(2) Where a person who is exempted under this paragraph from registration under this Part of this Schedule makes any relevant acquisition in pursuance of any transaction which would, if it were a taxable supply by a taxable person, be chargeable to VAT otherwise than as a zero-rated supply, the person must notify the Commissioners of the change within 30 days of the date the acquisition was made.][1]

Amendments—[1]   Sch 9ZA inserted by the Taxation (Post-transition Period) Act 2020 s 3, Sch 2 paras 1, 2 with effect from IP completion day (11pm on 31 December 2020), by virtue of SI 2020/1642 reg 9.

[Power to vary specified sums by regulations

45—The Treasury may by regulations substitute for any of the sums for the time being specified in this Part of this Schedule such greater sums as the Treasury consider appropriate.][1]

Amendments—[1]   Sch 9ZA inserted by the Taxation (Post-transition Period) Act 2020 s 3, Sch 2 paras 1, 2 with effect from IP completion day (11pm on 31 December 2020), by virtue of SI 2020/1642 reg 9.

[Notifications

46—Any notification required under this Part of this Schedule must be made in such form and manner and must contain such particulars as may be specified in regulations or by the Commissioners in accordance with regulations.][1]

Amendments—[1]   Sch 9ZA inserted by the Taxation (Post-transition Period) Act 2020 s 3, Sch 2 paras 1, 2 with effect from IP completion day (11pm on 31 December 2020), by virtue of SI 2020/1642 reg 9.

[Meaning of relevant supply

47—For the purposes of this Part of this Schedule "relevant acquisition" means an acquisition that—
(*a*) is a taxable acquisition (see paragraph 2(2)) of goods other than goods which are subject to a duty of excise or consist in a new means of transport, and
(*b*) is otherwise than in pursuance of a taxable supply and is treated, for the purposes of this Act, as taking place in Northern Ireland.][1]

Amendments—[1]   Sch 9ZA inserted by the Taxation (Post-transition Period) Act 2020 s 3, Sch 2 paras 1, 2 with effect from IP completion day (11pm on 31 December 2020), by virtue of SI 2020/1642 reg 9.

[PART 9
REGISTRATION IN RESPECT OF DISTANCE SALES FROM THE EU TO NORTHERN IRELAND

Liability to be registered

48—(1) A person who—

(a) is not registered under this Act, and

(b) is not liable to be registered under Schedule 1 or 1A,

becomes liable to be registered under this Part of this Schedule on any day if, in the period beginning with 1 January of the year in which that day falls, that person has made relevant supplies whose value exceeds £70,000.

(2) A person who is not registered or liable to be registered as mentioned in sub-paragraph (1)(a) and (b) becomes liable to be registered under this Part of this Schedule where—

(a) the person has exercised any option, in accordance with the law of any member State where the person is taxable, for treating relevant supplies made by that person as taking place outside that member State,

(b) the supplies to which the option relates involve the removal of goods from that member State and, apart from the exercise of the option, would be treated, in accordance with the law of that member State, as taking place in that member State, and

(c) the person makes a relevant supply at a time when the option is in force in relation to that person.

(3) A person who is not registered or liable to be registered as mentioned in sub-paragraph (1)(a) and (b) above becomes liable to be registered under this Part of this Schedule if the person makes a supply that—

(a) is a supply of goods subject to a duty of excise,

(b) involves the removal of the goods to Northern Ireland by or under the directions of the person making the supply,

(c) is a transaction in pursuance of which the goods are acquired in Northern Ireland from a member State by a person who is not a taxable person,

(d) is made in the course or furtherance of a business carried on by the supplier, and

(e) is not anything which is treated as a supply for the purposes of this Act by virtue only of paragraph 5(1) of Schedule 4 or paragraph 30 of Schedule 9ZB.

(4) A person is treated as having become liable to be registered under this Part of this Schedule at any time when the person would have become so liable under the preceding provisions of this paragraph but for any registration which is subsequently cancelled under paragraph 43(3) or 53(5) of this Schedule, paragraph 13(3) of Schedule 1, paragraph 11 of Schedule 1A, or paragraph 6(2) of Schedule 3A.

(5) A person does not cease to be liable to be registered under this Part of this Schedule except in accordance with paragraph 49.

(6) In determining for the purposes of this paragraph the value of any relevant supplies, so much of the consideration for any supply as represents any liability of the supplier, under the law of a member State, for VAT on that supply is to be disregarded.

(7) For the purposes of sub-paragraphs (1) and (2), supplies to which section 18B(4) or paragraph 19(6) of Schedule 9ZB (last supply of goods before removal from fiscal warehousing) apply are to be disregarded.][1]

Amendments—[1] Sch 9ZA inserted by the Taxation (Post-transition Period) Act 2020 s 3, Sch 2 paras 1, 2 with effect from IP completion day (11pm on 31 December 2020), by virtue of SI 2020/1642 reg 9.

[**49**—(1) A person who has become liable to be registered under this Part of this Schedule ceases to be so liable if at any time—

(a) the relevant supplies made by the person in the year ending with 31 December last before that time did not have a value exceeding £70,000 and did not include any supply in relation to which the conditions mentioned in paragraph 48(3) were satisfied, and

(b) the Commissioners are satisfied that the value of the person's relevant supplies in the year immediately following that year will not exceed £70,000 and that those supplies will not include a supply in relation to which those conditions are satisfied.

(2) But a person does not cease to be liable to be registered under this Part of this Schedule at any time when such an option as is mentioned in paragraph 48(2) above is in force in relation to that person.][1]

Amendments—[1] Sch 9ZA inserted by the Taxation (Post-transition Period) Act 2020 s 3, Sch 2 paras 1, 2 with effect from IP completion day (11pm on 31 December 2020), by virtue of SI 2020/1642 reg 9.

[Notification of liability and registration]

50—(1) A person who becomes liable to be registered under this Part of this Schedule must notify the Commissioners of the liability within the period of 30 days after the day on which the liability arises.

(2) The Commissioners must register any such person (whether or not the person has notified them) with effect from the day on which the liability arose or from such earlier time as may be agreed between the Commissioners and the person.][1]

[Request to be registered

51—(1) Where a person who is not liable to be registered under this Act and is not already so registered—
  (a) satisfies the Commissioners that the person intends—
    (i) to exercise an option such as is mentioned in paragraph 48(2) and, from a specified date, to make relevant supplies to which that option will relate,
    (ii) from a specified date to make relevant supplies to which any such option that the person has exercised will relate, or
    (iii) from a specified date to make supplies in relation to which the conditions mentioned in paragraph 48(3) will be satisfied, and
  (b) requests to be registered under this Part of this Schedule,
the Commissioners may, subject to such conditions as they think fit to impose, register the person with effect from such date as may be agreed between the Commissioners and the person.
(2) Conditions imposed under sub-paragraph (1) may—
  (a) be imposed wholly or partly by reference to, or without reference to, any conditions prescribed for the purposes of this paragraph, and
  (b) be subsequently varied by the Commissioners (whenever the conditions were imposed).
(3) Where a person who is entitled to be registered under paragraph 9 or 10 of Schedule 1 requests registration under this paragraph, the person is to be registered under that Schedule, and not under this Part of this Schedule.][1]

Amendments—[1] Sch 9ZA inserted by the Taxation (Post-transition Period) Act 2020 s 3, Sch 2 paras 1, 2 with effect from IP completion day (11pm on 31 December 2020), by virtue of SI 2020/1642 reg 9.

[Notification of matters affecting continuance of registration

52—(1) Any person registered under this Part of this Schedule who ceases to be registrable under this Act must notify the Commissioners of that fact within 30 days of the day on which the person ceases to be registrable.
(2) A person registered under paragraph 51 by reference to any intention to exercise any option or to make supplies of any description must notify the Commissioners within 30 days of exercising that option or, as the case may be, of the first occasion after registration when the person makes such a supply, that the person has exercised the option or made such a supply.
(3) A person who has exercised an option mentioned in paragraph 48(2) which, as a consequence of the option's revocation or otherwise, ceases to have effect in relation to any relevant supplies by the person must notify the Commissioners, within 30 days of the option's ceasing so to have effect, that it has done so.
(4) For the purposes of this paragraph, a person ceases to be registrable under this Act where—
  (a) the person ceases to be a person who would be liable or entitled to be registered under this Act if the person's registration and any enactment preventing a person from being liable to be registered under different provisions at the same time were disregarded, or
  (b) in the case of a person who (having been registered under paragraph 51) has not been such a person during the period of the person's registration, the person ceases to have any such intention as is mentioned in sub-paragraph (1)(a) of that paragraph.][1]

Amendments—[1] Sch 9ZA inserted by the Taxation (Post-transition Period) Act 2020 s 3, Sch 2 paras 1, 2 with effect from IP completion day (11pm on 31 December 2020), by virtue of SI 2020/1642 reg 9.

[Cancellation of registration

53 (1) Where a person registered under this Part of this Schedule satisfies the Commissioners that the person is not liable to be so registered, the Commissioners must, if the person so requests, cancel that registration with effect from the day on which the request is made or from such later date as may be agreed between the Commissioners and the person.
(2) Where the Commissioners are satisfied that a person who has been registered under paragraph 51 and is not for the time being liable to be registered under this Part of this Schedule—
  (a) has not, by the date specified in the person's request to be registered, begun to make relevant supplies, exercised the option in question or, as the case may be, begun to make supplies in relation to which the conditions mentioned in paragraph 48(3) are satisfied, or
  (b) has contravened any condition of the person's registration,
the Commissioners may cancel the person's registration with effect from the date so specified or, as the case may be, the date of the contravention or from such later date as may be agreed between the Commissioners and the person.

(3) But the Commissioners may not, under sub-paragraph (1) or (2), cancel a person's registration with effect from any time unless the Commissioners are satisfied that it is not a time when that person would be subject to a requirement, or in a case falling under subparagraph (2) a requirement or entitlement, to be registered under this Act.

(4) In determining for the purposes of sub-paragraph (3) whether a person would be subject to a requirement, or would be entitled, to be registered at any time, so much of any provision of this Act as prevents a person from becoming liable or entitled to be registered when the person is already registered or when the person is so liable under any other provision is to be disregarded.

(5) Where the Commissioners are satisfied that, on the day on which a person was registered under this Part of this Schedule, the person—
- (a) was not liable to be registered under this Part of this Schedule, and
- (b) in the case of a person registered under paragraph 51, did not have the intention by reference to which the person was registered,

the Commissioners may cancel that registration with effect from that day.

(6) The registration of a person who has exercised an option mentioned in paragraph 48(2) may not be cancelled with effect from any time before the 1 January which is, or next follows, the second anniversary of the date on which the person's registration took effect.][1]

Amendments—[1] Sch 9ZA inserted by the Taxation (Post-transition Period) Act 2020 s 3, Sch 2 paras 1, 2 with effect from IP completion day (11pm on 31 December 2020), by virtue of SI 2020/1642 reg 9.

[Power to vary specified sums by regulations

54 The Treasury may by regulations substitute for any of the sums for the time being specified in this Part of this Schedule such greater sums as the Treasury consider appropriate.][1]

Amendments—[1] Sch 9ZA inserted by the Taxation (Post-transition Period) Act 2020 s 3, Sch 2 paras 1, 2 with effect from IP completion day (11pm on 31 December 2020), by virtue of SI 2020/1642 reg 9.

[Notifications

55 Any notification required under this Part of this Schedule must be made in such form and manner and must contain such particulars as may be specified in regulations or by the Commissioners in accordance with regulations.][1]

Amendments—[1] Sch 9ZA inserted by the Taxation (Post-transition Period) Act 2020 s 3, Sch 2 paras 1, 2 with effect from IP completion day (11pm on 31 December 2020), by virtue of SI 2020/1642 reg 9.

[Meaning of relevant supply

56—For the purposes of this Part of this Schedule "relevant supply" means a supply of goods that—
- (a) involves the removal of the goods to Northern Ireland from a place outside the United Kingdom by or under the directions of the person making the supply,
- (b) does not involve the installation or assembly of the goods at a place in Northern Ireland,
- (c) is a transaction in pursuance of which goods are acquired in Northern Ireland from a member State by a person who is not a taxable person,
- (d) is made in the course or furtherance of a business carried on by the supplier, and
- (e) is neither an exempt supply nor a supply of goods which are subject to a duty of excise or consist in a new means of transport and is not anything which is treated as a supply for the purposes of this Act by virtue only of paragraph 5(1) of Schedule 4 or paragraph 30 of Schedule 9ZB.][1]

Amendments—[1] Sch 9ZA inserted by the Taxation (Post-transition Period) Act 2020 s 3, Sch 2 paras 1, 2 with effect from IP completion day (11pm on 31 December 2020), by virtue of SI 2020/1642 reg 9.

[PART 10
CALL-OFF STOCK ARRANGEMENTS]

Note—Part 10 does not apply to goods in respect of which the savings provisions in Taxation (Post-transition Period) Act 2020 Sch 2 para 7(6) and (7) apply (see Taxation (Post-transition Period) Act 2020 Sch 2 para 7(10)).

[Where this Part of this Schedule applies

57—(1) This Part of this Schedule applies where—
- (a) goods forming part of the assets of any business are removed—
  - (i) from Northern Ireland for the purpose of being taken to a place in a member State, or
  - (ii) from a member State for the purpose of being taken to a place in Northern Ireland,
- (b) the goods are removed in the course or furtherance of that business by or under the directions of the person carrying on that business ("the supplier"),
- (c) the goods are removed with a view to their being supplied in the destination territory, at a later stage and after their arrival there, to another person ("the customer"),

(d) at the time of the removal the customer is entitled to take ownership of the goods in accordance with an agreement existing between the customer and the supplier,
(e) at the time of the removal the supplier does not have a business establishment or other fixed establishment in the destination territory,
(f) at the time of the removal the customer is identified for the purposes of VAT in accordance with the law of the destination territory and both the identity of the customer and the number assigned to the customer for the purposes of VAT by the destination territory are known to the supplier,
(g) as soon as reasonably practicable after the removal the supplier records the removal in the register provided for in Article 243(3) of Council Directive 2006/112/EC of 28 November 2006 on the common system of value added tax, and
(h) the supplier includes the number mentioned in paragraph (f) in the recapitulative statement provided for in Article 262(2) of Council Directive 2006/112/EC.
(2) For the purposes of this Part of this Schedule, where the destination territory is Northern Ireland, a customer is identified for the purposes of VAT in accordance with the law of the destination territory if the customer is registered under this Act and is identified for the purposes of VAT in Northern Ireland.
(3) In this Part of this Schedule—
"the destination territory" means—
(a) in a case within paragraph (i) of sub-paragraph (1)(a), the member State concerned, and
(b) in a case within paragraph (ii) of sub-paragraph (1)(a), Northern Ireland, and
"the origin territory" means—
(a) in a case within paragraph (i) of sub-paragraph (1)(a), Northern Ireland, and
(b) in a case within paragraph (ii) of sub-paragraph (1)(a), the member State concerned.][1]

Note—Part 10 does not apply to goods in respect of which the savings provisions in Taxation (Post-transition Period) Act 2020 Sch 2 para 7(6) and (7) apply (see Taxation (Post-transition Period) Act 2020 Sch 2 para 7(10)).

Amendments—[1] Sch 9ZA inserted by the Taxation (Post-transition Period) Act 2020 s 3, Sch 2 paras 1, 2 with effect from IP completion day (11pm on 31 December 2020), by virtue of SI 2020/1642 reg 9.

[Removal of the goods not to be treated as a supply

58 The removal of the goods from the origin territory is not to be treated by reason of paragraph 30 of Schedule 9ZB as a supply of goods by the supplier.][1]

Note—Part 10 does not apply to goods in respect of which the savings provisions in Taxation (Post-transition Period) Act 2020 Sch 2 para 7(6) and (7) apply (see Taxation (Post-transition Period) Act 2020 Sch 2 para 7(10)).

Amendments—[1] Sch 9ZA inserted by the Taxation (Post-transition Period) Act 2020 s 3, Sch 2 paras 1, 2 with effect from IP completion day (11pm on 31 December 2020), by virtue of SI 2020/1642 reg 9.

[Goods transferred to the customer within 12 months of arrival

59—(1) The rules in sub-paragraph (2) apply if—
(a) during the period of 12 months beginning with the day the goods arrive in the destination territory the supplier transfers the whole property in the goods to the customer, and
(b) during the period beginning with the day the goods arrive in the destination territory and ending immediately before the time of that transfer no relevant event occurs.
(2) The rules are that—
(a) a supply of the goods in the relevant territory is deemed to be made by the supplier,
(b) the deemed supply is deemed to involve the removal of the goods from the origin territory at the time of the transfer mentioned in sub-paragraph (1),
(c) the consideration given by the customer for the transfer mentioned in sub-paragraph (1) is deemed to have been given for the deemed supply, and
(d) an acquisition of the goods by the customer in pursuance of the deemed supply is deemed to take place in the destination territory.
(3) In sub-paragraph (2) and in paragraphs 60(2) and 61(2) "the relevant territory" means—
(a) where the origin territory is Northern Ireland, the United Kingdom, or
(b) where the origin territory is a member State, that member State.
(4) For the meaning of a "relevant event", see paragraph 63.][1]

Note—Part 10 does not apply to goods in respect of which the savings provisions in Taxation (Post-transition Period) Act 2020 Sch 2 para 7(6) and (7) apply (see Taxation (Post-transition Period) Act 2020 Sch 2 para 7(10)).

Amendments—[1] Sch 9ZA inserted by the Taxation (Post-transition Period) Act 2020 s 3, Sch 2 paras 1, 2 with effect from IP completion day (11pm on 31 December 2020), by virtue of SI 2020/1642 reg 9.

[Relevant event occurs within 12 months of arrival

60—(1) The rules in sub-paragraph (2) apply (subject to paragraph 62) if—

(a) during the period of 12 months beginning with the day the goods arrive in the destination territory a relevant event occurs, and
(b) during the period beginning with the day the goods arrive in the destination territory and ending immediately before the time that relevant event occurs the supplier does not transfer the whole property in the goods to the customer.

(2) The rules are that—
   (a) a supply of the goods in the relevant territory (see paragraph 59(3)) is deemed to be made by the supplier,
   (b) the deemed supply is deemed to involve the removal of the goods from the origin territory at the time the relevant event occurs, and
   (c) an acquisition of the goods by the supplier in pursuance of the deemed supply is deemed to take place in the destination territory.

(3) For the meaning of a "relevant event", see paragraph 63.][1]

Note—Part 10 does not apply to goods in respect of which the savings provisions in Taxation (Post-transition Period) Act 2020 Sch 2 para 7(6) and (7) apply (see Taxation (Post-transition Period) Act 2020 Sch 2 para 7(10)).

Cross-references—See Sch 9ZA para 11 above (determining the value of the relevant transaction in the case of an acquisition by a supplier that is deemed to take place as a result of sub-para (2)(c)).

Amendments—[1] Sch 9ZA inserted by the Taxation (Post-transition Period) Act 2020 s 3, Sch 2 paras 1, 2 with effect from IP completion day (11pm on 31 December 2020), by virtue of SI 2020/1642 reg 9.

[Goods not transferred and no relevant event occurs within 12 months of arrival

61—(1) The rules in sub-paragraph (2) apply (subject to paragraph 62) if during the period of 12 months beginning with the day the goods arrive in the destination territory the supplier does not transfer the whole property in the goods to the customer and no relevant event occurs.

(2) The rules are that—
   (a) a supply of the goods in the relevant territory (see paragraph 59(3)) is deemed to be made by the supplier,
   (b) the deemed supply is deemed to involve the removal of the goods from the origin territory at the beginning of the day following the expiry of the period of 12 months mentioned in sub-paragraph (1), and
   (c) an acquisition of the goods by the supplier in pursuance of the deemed supply is deemed to take place in the destination territory.

(3) For the meaning of a "relevant event", see paragraph 63.][1]

Note—Part 10 does not apply to goods in respect of which the savings provisions in Taxation (Post-transition Period) Act 2020 Sch 2 para 7(6) and (7) apply (see Taxation (Post-transition Period) Act 2020 Sch 2 para 7(10)).

Cross-references—See Sch 9ZA para 11 above (determining the value of the relevant transaction in the case of an acquisition by a supplier that is deemed to take place as a result of sub-para (2)(c)).

Amendments—[1] Sch 9ZA inserted by the Taxation (Post-transition Period) Act 2020 s 3, Sch 2 paras 1, 2 with effect from IP completion day (11pm on 31 December 2020), by virtue of SI 2020/1642 reg 9.

[Exception to paragraphs 60 and 61: goods returned to origin territory

62 The rules in paragraphs 60(2) and 61(2) do not apply if during the period of 12 months beginning with the day the goods arrive in the destination territory—
   (a) the goods are returned to the origin territory by or under the direction of the supplier, and
   (b) the supplier records the return of the goods in the register provided for in Article 243(3) of Council Directive 2006/112/EC.][1]

Note—Part 10 does not apply to goods in respect of which the savings provisions in Taxation (Post-transition Period) Act 2020 Sch 2 para 7(6) and (7) apply (see Taxation (Post-transition Period) Act 2020 Sch 2 para 7(10)).

Amendments—[1] Sch 9ZA inserted by the Taxation (Post-transition Period) Act 2020 s 3, Sch 2 paras 1, 2 with effect from IP completion day (11pm on 31 December 2020), by virtue of SI 2020/1642 reg 9.

[Meaning of "relevant event"

63—(1) For the purposes of this Part of this Schedule each of the following events is a relevant event—
   (a) the supplier forms an intention not to supply the goods to the customer (but see sub-paragraph (2)),
   (b) the supplier forms an intention to supply the goods to the customer otherwise than in the destination territory,
   (c) the supplier establishes a business establishment or other fixed establishment in the destination territory,
   (d) the customer ceases to be identified for the purposes of VAT in accordance with the law of the destination territory,
   (e) the goods are removed from the destination territory by or under the directions of the supplier otherwise than for the purpose of being returned to the origin territory, or

(*f*) the goods are destroyed, lost or stolen.

(2) But the event mentioned in paragraph (*a*) of sub-paragraph (1) is not a relevant event for the purposes of this Part of this Schedule if—

(*a*) at the time that the event occurs the supplier forms an intention to supply the goods to another person ("the substitute customer"),

(*b*) at that time the substitute customer is identified for the purposes of VAT in accordance with the law of the destination territory,

(*c*) the supplier includes the number assigned to the substitute customer for the purposes of VAT by the destination territory in the recapitulative statement provided for in Article 262(2) of Council Directive 2006/112/EC, and

(*d*) as soon as reasonably practicable after forming the intention to supply the goods to the substitute customer the supplier records that intention in the register provided for in Article 243(3) of Council Directive 2006/112/EC.

(3) Where the destination territory is Northern Ireland, the reference in sub-paragraph (2)(c) to the number assigned to the substitute customer for the purposes of VAT is to the number assigned to the substitute customer for the purposes of VAT in the United Kingdom along with an NI VAT identifier.

(4) In a case where sub-paragraph (2) applies, references in this Part of this Schedule to the customer are to be then read as references to the substitute customer.

(5) In a case where the goods are destroyed, lost or stolen but it is not possible to determine the date on which that occurred, the goods are to be treated for the purposes of this Part of this Schedule as having been destroyed, lost or stolen on the date on which they were found to be destroyed or missing.][1]

Note—Part 10 does not apply to goods in respect of which the savings provisions in Taxation (Post-transition Period) Act 2020 Sch 2 para 7(6) and (7) apply (see Taxation (Post-transition Period) Act 2020 Sch 2 para 7(10)).

Amendments—[1] Sch 9ZA inserted by the Taxation (Post-transition Period) Act 2020 s 3, Sch 2 paras 1, 2 with effect from IP completion day (11pm on 31 December 2020), by virtue of SI 2020/1642 reg 9.

[Record keeping by the supplier

64 In a case where the origin territory is Northern Ireland, any record made by the supplier in pursuance of paragraph 57(1)(*g*), 62(*b*) or 63(2)(*d*) must be preserved for such period not exceeding 6 years as the Commissioners may specify in writing.][1]

Note—Part 10 does not apply to goods in respect of which the savings provisions in Taxation (Post-transition Period) Act 2020 Sch 2 para 7(6) and (7) apply (see Taxation (Post-transition Period) Act 2020 Sch 2 para 7(10)).

Amendments—[1] Sch 9ZA inserted by the Taxation (Post-transition Period) Act 2020 s 3, Sch 2 paras 1, 2 with effect from IP completion day (11pm on 31 December 2020), by virtue of SI 2020/1642 reg 9.

[Record keeping by the customer

65—(1) In a case where the destination territory is Northern Ireland, the customer must as soon as is reasonably practicable make a record of the information relating to the goods that is specified in Article 54A(2) of Council Implementing Regulation (EU) No. 282/2011 of 15 March 2011 laying down implementing measures for Directive 2006/112/EC on the common system of value added tax.

(2) A record made under this paragraph must—

(*a*) be made in a register kept by the customer for the purposes of this paragraph, and

(*b*) be preserved for such period not exceeding 6 years as the Commissioners may specify in writing.][1]

Note—Part 10 does not apply to goods in respect of which the savings provisions in Taxation (Post-transition Period) Act 2020 Sch 2 para 7(6) and (7) apply (see Taxation (Post-transition Period) Act 2020 Sch 2 para 7(10)).

Amendments—[1] Sch 9ZA inserted by the Taxation (Post-transition Period) Act 2020 s 3, Sch 2 paras 1, 2 with effect from IP completion day (11pm on 31 December 2020), by virtue of SI 2020/1642 reg 9.

[PART 11
MODIFICATION OF OTHER SCHEDULES

Registration in respect of taxable supplies: UK establishment (Schedule 1)

66—(1) Paragraph 1 of Schedule 1 (registration in respect of taxable supplies: UK establishment) has effect as if—

(*a*) the provisions mentioned in sub-paragraphs (4)(*a*) and (5) included paragraphs 43(5) and 53(5) of this Schedule (cancellation of registration);

(*b*) in sub-paragraph (7), after "are supplied" there were inserted "and any taxable supplies which would not be taxable supplies apart from paragraph 29(1) of Schedule 9ZB";

(*c*) in sub-paragraph (9)—

(i) after "section 18B(4)" there were inserted "or paragraph 19(5) of Schedule 9ZB";

(ii) after "supply" there were inserted "or acquisition".

(2) Paragraph 2 of that Schedule has effect as if in sub-paragraph (7), after paragraph (*b*) there were inserted—

"(*c*) any acquisition of goods from a member State by one of the constituent members in the course of the activities of the taxable person is to be treated as an acquisition by that person;".

(3) Paragraph 4(3) of that Schedule has effect as if after "are supplied" there were inserted "and any taxable supplies which would not be taxable supplies apart from paragraph 29(1) of Schedule 9ZB".][1]

Amendments—[1] Sch 9ZA inserted by the Taxation (Post-transition Period) Act 2020 s 3, Sch 2 paras 1, 2 with effect from IP completion day (11pm on 31 December 2020), by virtue of SI 2020/1642 reg 9.

[Registration in respect of taxable supplies: non-UK establishment (Schedule 1A)]

67 Paragraph 3 of Schedule 1A (registration in respect of taxable supplies: non-UK establishment) has effect as if the provisions mentioned in paragraphs (*a*) to (*e*) of that paragraph included paragraphs 43(5) and 53(5) of this Schedule.][1]

Amendments—[1] Sch 9ZA inserted by the Taxation (Post-transition Period) Act 2020 s 3, Sch 2 paras 1, 2 with effect from IP completion day (11pm on 31 December 2020), by virtue of SI 2020/1642 reg 9.

[Registration: disposals of assets where repayment is claimed (Schedule 3A)]

68 Paragraph 1 of Schedule 3A (registration in respect of disposals of assets for which a VAT repayment is claimed) has effect as if—

(*a*) in sub-paragraph (1), after "or 1A" there were inserted "or Part 8 or 9 of Schedule 9ZA", and
(*b*) the provisions mentioned in sub-paragraph (2) included paragraphs 43(5) and 53(5) of this Schedule.][1]

Amendments—[1] Sch 9ZA inserted by the Taxation (Post-transition Period) Act 2020 s 3, Sch 2 paras 1, 2 with effect from IP completion day (11pm on 31 December 2020), by virtue of SI 2020/1642 reg 9.

[Valuation of supplies: special cases (Schedule 6)]

69 (1) Paragraph 1A of Schedule 6 (valuation: special cases) has effect as if—
(*a*) in sub-paragraph (4), in the definition of "motor dealer", after "supplies of" there were inserted ", or acquiring in Northern Ireland from a member State";
(*b*) in that sub-paragraph, in the definition of "stock in trade"—
 (i) in paragraph (*a*) of that definition, after "supplied to" there were inserted "or acquired in Northern Ireland from a member State by";
 (ii) in paragraph (*b*) of that definition, after "supply" there were inserted ", acquisition";
(*c*) in sub-paragraph (6)(*a*)—
 (i) after "supplied" there were inserted ", acquired in Northern Ireland from a member State";
 (ii) after "supply" there were inserted ", acquisition".
(2) In paragraph 6(1) of that Schedule—
(*a*) in paragraph (*b*), after "Schedule 4" there were inserted "or paragraph 30 of Schedule 9ZB";
(*b*) in paragraph (*c*), for "that Schedule;" there were substituted "Schedule 4; or";
(*c*) after that paragraph there were inserted—

"(*d*) paragraph 60(2)(*a*) or 61(2)(*a*) of Schedule 9ZA,".][1]

Amendments—[1] Sch 9ZA inserted by the Taxation (Post-transition Period) Act 2020 s 3, Sch 2 paras 1, 2 with effect from IP completion day (11pm on 31 December 2020), by virtue of SI 2020/1642 reg 9.

[Zero-rating (Schedule 8)]

70 Group 12 in Part 2 of Schedule 8 (zero-rating: drugs etc) has effect as if—
(*a*) in Note (1), after "goods are" there were inserted "acquired from a member State";
(*b*) in Note (5N), in paragraph (*b*), after "made a" there were inserted "reckonable zero-rated acquisition, or";
(*c*) in Note (5O), in paragraph (*b*), after "zero-rated" there were inserted "acquisition or";
(*d*) in Note (5T), after the definition of "in the required form" there were inserted—

""reckonable zero-rated acquisition", in relation to a motor vehicle, means an acquisition of the vehicle from a member State in a case where NI acquisition VAT is not chargeable as a result of item 2(*f*) or 2A."][1]

Amendments—[1] Sch 9ZA inserted by the Taxation (Post-transition Period) Act 2020 s 3, Sch 2 paras 1, 2 with effect from IP completion day (11pm on 31 December 2020), by virtue of SI 2020/1642 reg 9.

[Exempt supplies (Schedule 9)]

71 Group 14 in Part 2 of Schedule 9 (exemptions: supplies of goods where input tax cannot be recovered) has effect as if—
- (*a*) in paragraph (*a*) of item 1, after "supply to" there were inserted "or acquisition";
- (*b*) in Note (7)(*a*), after "supply to" there were inserted "or acquisition";
- (*c*) in Note (9)—
    - (i) in the words before paragraph (*a*), after "supply to" there were inserted "or acquisition";
    - (ii) in paragraph (*b*), after "supply to" there were inserted "or acquisition";
- (*d*) in Note (10)—
    - (i) after "on a supply" there were inserted ", acquisition";
    - (ii) after "that supply", there were inserted ", acquisition";
- (*e*) in Note (15)—
    - (i) after "anything the supply" there were inserted ", acquisition";
    - (ii) after "be a supply" there were inserted ", acquisition".][1]

Amendments—[1] Sch 9ZA inserted by the Taxation (Post-transition Period) Act 2020 s 3, Sch 2 paras 1, 2 with effect from IP completion day (11pm on 31 December 2020), by virtue of SI 2020/1642 reg 9.

[Avoidance (Schedules 9A and 11A)]

72—(1) Paragraph 1(5) of Schedule 9A (anti-avoidance provisions: groups) has effect as if, in paragraph (a), after "importation" there were inserted "or acquisition".
(2) Schedule 11A (disclosure of avoidance schemes) has effect as if the reference to VAT "incurred" by a taxable person in paragraph 2A(1)(*b*) included VAT on the acquisition by the person of any goods from a member State.][1]

Amendments—[1] Sch 9ZA inserted by the Taxation (Post-transition Period) Act 2020 s 3, Sch 2 paras 1, 2 with effect from IP completion day (11pm on 31 December 2020), by virtue of SI 2020/1642 reg 9.

[Accounting for VAT and payment of VAT (Schedule 11)]

73—(1) Regulations under this paragraph may require the submission to the Commissioners by taxable persons, at such times and intervals, in such cases and in such form and manner as may be—
- (*a*) specified in the regulations, or
- (*b*) specified by the Commissioners in accordance with the regulations,

of statements containing such particulars of transactions in which the taxable persons are concerned and to which this subparagraph applies, and of the persons concerned in those transactions, as may be so specified.
(2) Sub-paragraph (1) applies to transactions involving the movement of goods between a member State and Northern Ireland, or between member States.
(3) Sections 65 and 66 (inaccuracies in, or and failure to submit, section 55A statements) apply to any statement which is required to be submitted to the Commissioners in accordance with regulations under sub-paragraph (1) as they apply to a section 55A statement.
(4) Regulations under this paragraph may make provision in relation to cases where—
- (*a*) any goods which are subject to a duty of excise or consist in a new means of transport are acquired in Northern Ireland from a member State by any person,
- (*b*) the acquisition of the goods is a taxable acquisition and is not in pursuance of a taxable supply, and
- (*c*) that person is not a taxable person at the time of the acquisition,

for requiring the person who acquires the goods to give to the Commissioners such notification of the acquisition, and for requiring any VAT on the acquisition to be paid, at such time and in such form or manner as may be specified in the regulations or (in the case of the notification requirement) by the Commissioners in accordance with the regulations.
(5) Regulations under this paragraph may provide for a notification required by virtue of sub-paragraph (4)—
- (*a*) to contain such particulars relating to the notified acquisition and any VAT chargeable in relation to it as may be specified in the regulations or by the Commissioners in accordance with the regulations, and
- (*b*) to be given, in prescribed cases, by the personal representative, trustee in bankruptcy, trustee in sequestration, receiver, liquidator or person otherwise acting in a representative capacity in relation to the person who makes that acquisition.

(6) Regulations under this paragraph may provide for—
- (*a*) the time when any invoice described in regulations under paragraph 4(1)(*b*) of this Schedule or paragraph 28(2)(*b*) of Schedule 9ZB is to be treated as having been issued;

(b) VAT accounted for and paid by reference to the date of issue of such an invoice to be confined to VAT on so much of the value of the supply or acquisition as is shown on the invoice.

(7) Sub-paragraphs (1) to (4), (5) and (6) are to be treated, for the purposes of this Act, as if they were contained in paragraph 2 of Schedule 11.]¹

Amendments—¹ Sch 9ZA inserted by the Taxation (Post-transition Period) Act 2020 s 3, Sch 2 paras 1, 2 with effect from IP completion day (11pm on 31 December 2020), by virtue of SI 2020/1642 reg 9.

[Administration, collection and enforcement (Schedule 11)]

74 (1) Paragraph 2 of Schedule 11 has effect as if—
- (a) in sub-paragraph (5A)(b), after "transport" there were inserted "acquired from a member State, or";
- (b) in sub-paragraph (5B)(a), after "chargeable on its" there were inserted "acquisition or";
- (c) in sub-paragraph (5D) in the definition of "relevant person"—
  - (i) before paragraph (b) there were inserted—
    "(a) where the means of transport has been acquired in Northern Ireland from a member State, the person who so acquires it,";
  - (ii) after paragraph (b) there were inserted—
    "(c) in any other case—
      (i) the owner of the means of transport at the time of its arrival in the United Kingdom, or
      (ii) where it is subject to a lease or hire agreement, the lessee or hirer of the means of transport at that time."

(2) Paragraph 2(8) of Schedule 11 applies to NI acquisition VAT in respect of an acquisition by any person from a member State of dutiable goods as it applies to VAT in respect of any supply by a taxable person of dutiable goods.

(3) Invoices described in regulations under paragraph 4(2)(b) of this Schedule or paragraph 28(2)(b) of Schedule 9ZB are items to which paragraph 3 of Schedule 11 applies (in addition to the items described in paragraph 3(2)(a) and (b) of that Schedule).

(4) Paragraph 6 of Schedule 11 has effect as if—
(a) after sub-paragraph (1) there were inserted—
"(1A) Every person who, at a time when the person is not a taxable person, acquires in Northern Ireland from a member State any goods which are subject to a duty of excise or consist in a new means of transport must keep such records with respect to the acquisition (if it is a taxable acquisition and is not in pursuance of a taxable supply) as the Commissioners may by regulations require.";
(b) in sub-paragraph (2), after "sub-paragraph (1)" there were inserted "or (1A)".

(5) Paragraph 8(1) of Schedule 11 applies—
- (a) to goods in the possession of a person who acquires goods in Northern Ireland from a member State as it applies to goods in the possession of a person who supplies goods, and
- (b) to goods in the possession of a Northern Ireland fiscal warehousekeeper as it applies to goods in the possession of a fiscal warehousekeeper.

(6) Paragraph 14(1) has effect as if in paragraph (c), after "paragraph 5A" there were inserted "or paragraph 73(1) or (4) of Schedule 9ZA".]¹

Amendments—¹ Sch 9ZA inserted by the Taxation (Post-transition Period) Act 2020 s 3, Sch 2 paras 1, 2 with effect from IP completion day (11pm on 31 December 2020), by virtue of SI 2020/1642 reg 9.

[PART 12
MODIFICATION OF OTHER ACTS

Diplomatic privileges etc

75—(1) The following provisions apply to NI acquisition VAT as they apply to value added tax charged in accordance with section 1(1)(c) of this Act—
- (a) section 2(5A) of the Diplomatic Privileges Act 1964 (application of Vienna Convention);
- (b) paragraph 10(1A) of the Schedule to the Commonwealth Secretariat Act 1966 (immunities and privileges);
- (c) section 1(8A) of the Consular Relations Act 1968 (application of Vienna Convention);
- (d) paragraph 19(c) of Schedule 1 to the International Organisations Act 1968 (privileges and immunities);
- (e) section 1(5) of the Diplomatic and other Privileges Act 1971 (refund of customs duties on hydrocarbon oil used for diplomatic or Commonwealth Secretariat purposes).

(2) Section 8 of the Consular Relations Act 1968 applies to VAT charged on the acquisition of oil in Northern Ireland from a member State as it applies to VAT charged on the importation of oil.]¹

Amendments—[1] Sch 9ZA inserted by the Taxation (Post-transition Period) Act 2020 s 3, Sch 2 paras 1, 2 with effect from IP completion day (11pm on 31 December 2020), by virtue of SI 2020/1642 reg 9.

[Customs and Excise Duties (General Reliefs) Act 1979

76 Section 13 of the Customs and Excise Duties (General Reliefs) Act 1979 (power to provide reliefs for VAT etc) has effect as if, in subsection (4), in the definition of "value added tax" after "goods" there were inserted "or on the acquisition of goods from a member State".][1]

Amendments—[1] Sch 9ZA inserted by the Taxation (Post-transition Period) Act 2020 s 3, Sch 2 paras 1, 2 with effect from IP completion day (11pm on 31 December 2020), by virtue of SI 2020/1642 reg 9.

[Vehicle Excise and Registration Act 1994

77 Section 8 of the Vehicle Excise and Registration Act 1994 (vehicles removed into UK) has effect as if, in subsection (2)—
   (*a*) in paragraph (*a*), after "United Kingdom" there were inserted ", or on the acquisition of the vehicle from a member State,";
   (*b*) in paragraph (*c*), after "charged on the" there were inserted "acquisition or".][1]

Amendments—[1] Sch 9ZA inserted by the Taxation (Post-transition Period) Act 2020 s 3, Sch 2 paras 1, 2 with effect from IP completion day (11pm on 31 December 2020), by virtue of SI 2020/1642 reg 9.

[Finance Act 2008

78 (1) Paragraph 11 of Schedule 36 to the Finance Act 2008 (information and inspection powers) has effect as if—
   (*a*) in sub-paragraph (1), after paragraph (*a*) there were inserted—
      "(*b*) premises are used in connection with the acquisition of goods from member States under taxable acquisitions and goods to be so acquired or documents relating to such goods are on those premises,";
   (*b*) in sub-paragraph (2), in paragraph (*c*), after "taxable supplies" there were inserted ", the acquisition of goods from member States under taxable acquisitions".
(2) Paragraph 34 of that Schedule has effect as if—
   (*a*) in sub-paragraph (1), after paragraph (*a*) there were inserted—
      "(*b*) the acquisition of goods from a member State,";
   (*b*) in sub-paragraph (4), after "Schedule 4" there were inserted "and paragraph 3 of Schedule 9ZA".
(3) Paragraph 1 of Schedule 41 to that Act has effect as if in the table there were inserted the following entries—

"Value added tax	Obligations under paragraphs 40 and 44(2) of Schedule 9ZA to VATA 1994 (obligations to notify liability to register and notify acquisition affecting exemption from registration).
Value added tax	Obligation under paragraph 50 of Schedule 9ZA to VATA 1994 (obligation to notify liability to register).
Value added tax	Obligation under regulations under paragraph 73(4) of Schedule 9ZA to VATA 1994 (obligation to give notification of acquisition of goods from a member State)."

(4) For the purposes of paragraph 7 of that Schedule—
   (*a*) in a case of a failure to comply with an obligation under regulations under paragraph 73(4) of this Schedule, the "potential lost revenue" is the value added tax on the acquisition to which the failure relates (instead of as provided for by paragraph 7(6) of that Schedule), and
   (*b*) the "relevant period" in relation to a failure to comply with paragraph 44(2) of this Schedule is the period beginning on the date of the change or alteration concerned and ending on the date on which HMRC received notification of, or otherwise became fully aware of, that change or alteration.
(5) In a case to which sub-paragraph (6) of paragraph 7 of that Schedule applies (whether as a result of sub-paragraph (3) of this paragraph or otherwise), the amount of the "potential lost revenue" as determined in accordance with that sub-paragraph is—

(a) if the amount of the tax mentioned in that sub-paragraph includes tax on an acquisition of goods from a member State, to be reduced by the amount of any VAT which HMRC are satisfied has been paid on the supply in pursuance of which the goods were acquired under the law of that member State, and

(b) if the amount of that tax includes tax chargeable as a result of paragraph 29 of Schedule 9ZB on a supply, to be reduced by the amount of any VAT which HMRC are satisfied has been paid on that supply under the law of a member State.]¹

Amendments—¹ Sch 9ZA inserted by the Taxation (Post-transition Period) Act 2020 s 3, Sch 2 paras 1, 2 with effect from IP completion day (11pm on 31 December 2020), by virtue of SI 2020/1642 reg 9.

[Finance Act 2016

79 Schedule 18 to the Finance Act 2016 (serial tax avoidance) has effect as if—

(a) in paragraph 5(4), after paragraph (a) there were inserted—

"(b) VAT on the acquisition by the person of any goods from a member State,";

(b) the references to VAT "incurred" by a taxable person in paragraphs 6(1)(b) and 36(7)(b) included VAT on the acquisition by the person of any goods from a member State.]¹

Amendments—¹ Sch 9ZA inserted by the Taxation (Post-transition Period) Act 2020 s 3, Sch 2 paras 1, 2 with effect from IP completion day (11pm on 31 December 2020), by virtue of SI 2020/1642 reg 9.

[Finance (No. 2) Act 2017

80 Schedule 17 to the Finance (No 2) Act 2017 (disclosure of tax avoidance schemes: VAT and other indirect taxes) has effect as if—

(a) the reference in paragraph 6(2)(b) to VAT "incurred" by a taxable person included VAT on the acquisition by the person of any goods from a member State;

(b) in paragraph 6(5), after paragraph (a) there were inserted—

"(b) VAT on the acquisition by the person of any goods from a member State,".]¹

Amendments—¹ Sch 9ZA inserted by the Taxation (Post-transition Period) Act 2020 s 3, Sch 2 paras 1, 2 with effect from IP completion day (11pm on 31 December 2020), by virtue of SI 2020/1642 reg 9.

[PART 13
INTERPRETIVE PROVISIONS

Taxation under the laws of member States etc

81 (1) References in this Act, in relation to a member State, to the law of that member State are to be construed as confined to so much of the law of that member State as for the time being has effect for the purposes of any EU instrument relating to VAT.

(2) References in this Act to a person being taxable in a member State are references to that person being taxable under so much of the law of that member State as makes provision for purposes corresponding, in relation to that member State, to the purposes of so much of this Act as makes provision as to whether a person is a taxable person.

(3) The Commissioners may by regulations make provision for the manner in which any of the following are to be or may be proved for any of the purposes of this Act—

(a) the effect of any provisions of the law of any member State;

(b) that provisions of any such law correspond, in relation to any member State, to any provision of this Act;

(c) that provisions of any such law have a purpose corresponding, in relation to any member State, to the purpose of any provision of this Act.

(4) The Commissioners may by regulations provide—

(a) for a person to be treated for prescribed purposes of this Act as taxable in a member State only where the person has given such notification, and furnished such other information, to the Commissioners as may be prescribed;

(b) for the form and manner in which any notification or information is to be given or furnished under the regulations and what the notification or information must contain;

(c) for the proportion of any consideration for any transaction which is to be taken for the purposes of this Act as representing a liability, under the law of a member State, for VAT to be conclusively determined by reference to such invoices or in such other manner as may be prescribed.

(5) In any proceedings (whether civil or criminal), a certificate of the Commissioners—

(a) that a person was or was not, at any date, taxable in a member State, or

(b) that any VAT payable under the law of a member State has or has not been paid,

is sufficient evidence of that fact until the contrary is proved, and any document purporting to be a certificate under this subsection is deemed to be such a certificate until the contrary is proved.

[(6) Without prejudice to the generality of any of the powers of the Commissioners under the relevant information provisions, those powers are, for the purpose of facilitating compliance with any obligation of the United Kingdom under the EU withdrawal agreement, exercisable with respect to matters that are relevant to a charge to VAT under the law of a member State, as they are exercisable with respect to matters that are relevant for any of the purposes of this Act.
(7) The reference in subsection (6) to the relevant information provisions is a reference to the provisions of section 73(7) and Schedule 11 (see also paragraph 73 which contains provision treated as if contained within that Schedule)relating to—
   (a) the keeping of accounts;
   (b) the making of returns and the submission of other documents to the Commissioners;
   (c) the production, use and contents of invoices;
   (d) the keeping and preservation of records;
   (e) the furnishing of information and the production of documents.][2]][1]

Amendments— [1] Sch 9ZA inserted by the Taxation (Post-transition Period) Act 2020 s 3, Sch 2 paras 1, 2 with effect from IP completion day (11pm on 31 December 2020), by virtue of SI 2020/1642 reg 9.
[2] Sub-paras (6) and (7) inserted by the Value Added Tax (Miscellaneous Amendments to the Value Added Tax Act 1994 and Revocation) (EU Exit) Regulations, SI 2020/1544 regs 2, 4 with effect from IP completion day (11pm UK time on 31 December 2020) by virtue of SI 2020/1641 reg 2, Schedule para 13.

[Territories included in references to member States etc

82 (1) The Commissioners may by regulations provide for the territory of the European Union, or for the member States, to be treated for any of the purposes of this Act as including or excluding such territories as may be prescribed.
(2) Without prejudice to the generality of the powers conferred by sub-paragraph (1) and section 16, the Commissioners may, for any of the purposes of this Act, by regulations provide for prescribed provisions of any customs and excise legislation to apply in relation to cases where any territory is treated under subparagraph (1) as excluded from the territory of the European Union, with such exceptions and adaptations as may be prescribed.
(3) In sub-paragraph (2) the reference to customs and excise legislation is a reference to any provision (whenever passed, made or adopted) which has effect in relation to, or to any assigned matter connected with, the importation or exportation of goods or movements of goods between Northern Ireland and Great Britain.
(4) In sub-paragraph (3) "assigned matter" has the same meaning as in the Management Act.][1]

Amendments— [1] Sch 9ZA inserted by the Taxation (Post-transition Period) Act 2020 s 3, Sch 2 paras 1, 2 with effect from IP completion day (11pm on 31 December 2020), by virtue of SI 2020/1642 reg 9.

[Meaning of "new means of transport"

83 (1) In this Act "means of transport" in the expression "new means of transport" means any of the following if they are intended for the transport of persons or goods—
   (a) any ship exceeding 7.5 metres in length;
   (b) any aircraft the take-off weight of which exceeds 1550 kilograms;
   (c) any motorized land vehicle which—
      (i) has an engine with a displacement or cylinder capacity exceeding 48 cubic centimetres, or
      (ii) is constructed or adapted to be electrically propelled using more than 7.2 kilowatts.
(2) For the purposes of this Schedule a means of transport is to be treated as new, in relation to any supply or any acquisition from a member State, at any time unless at that time—
   (a) the period that has elapsed since its first entry into service is—
      (i) in the case of a ship or aircraft, a period of more than 3 months, and
      (ii) in the case of a land vehicle, a period of more than 6 months. and
   (b) it has, since its first entry into service, travelled under its own power—
      (i) in the case of a ship, for more than 100 hours,
      (ii) in the case of an aircraft, for more than 40 hours, and
      (iii) in the case of a land vehicle, for more than 6000 kilometres.
(3) The Treasury may by order vary this paragraph—
   (a) by adding or deleting any ship, aircraft or vehicle of a description specified in the order to or from those which are for the time being specified in sub-paragraph (1);
   (b) by altering, omitting or adding to the provisions of subparagraph (2) for determining whether a means of transport is new.
(4) The Commissioners may by regulations make provision specifying the circumstances in which a means of transport is to be treated for the purposes of this paragraph as having first entered into service.][1]

Amendments—[1] Sch 9ZA inserted by the Taxation (Post-transition Period) Act 2020 s 3, Sch 2 paras 1, 2 with effect from IP completion day (11pm on 31 December 2020), by virtue of SI 2020/1642 reg 9.

[VAT charged in a member State

84 Where the context requires it, references in this Schedule to VAT means value added tax charged in accordance with the law of a member State (instead of in accordance with this Act).][1]

Amendments—[1] Sch 9ZA inserted by the Taxation (Post-transition Period) Act 2020 s 3, Sch 2 paras 1, 2 with effect from IP completion day (11pm on 31 December 2020), by virtue of SI 2020/1642 reg 9.

[SCHEDULE 9ZB

GOODS REMOVED TO OR FROM NORTHERN IRELAND AND SUPPLY RULES

Section 40A(2)

PART 1
IMPORTATIONS

Importations

1—(1) The importation of Union goods into the United Kingdom as a result of their entry into Northern Ireland is not an importation for the purposes of value added tax.
(2) Accordingly, no charge to VAT occurs on the importation of Union goods into the United Kingdom as a result of their entry into Northern Ireland (but see paragraph 1 of Schedule 9ZA, which imposes a charge to VAT on the acquisition of goods in Northern Ireland from a member State).
(3) VAT on the importation of any other goods imported into the United Kingdom as a result of their entry into Northern Ireland is to be charged and payable as if it were relevant NI import duty (instead of as provided under section 1(4)).
(4) Sub-paragraph (3) is to be taken as applying, in relation to any VAT chargeable on the importation of such goods—
  (*a*) any provision of Union customs legislation that is relevant to the charging of relevant NI import duty, and
  (*b*) any provision made by or under Part 1 of TCTA 2018 that is relevant to the charging of that duty.
(5) Section 15 (meaning of "importation of goods" into the United Kingdom) applies to the importation of such goods as if—
  (*a*) any reference to import duty were to relevant NI import duty;
  (*b*) the references in subsections (2) and (3) to a Customs, storage, transit or inward processing procedure were to a procedure corresponding to such a procedure under Union customs legislation, and
  (*c*) the reference in subsection (3)(b) to section 5(1) of, or paragraph 1(5) or 3(4) of Schedule 1 to, that Act included any provision (including any provision of Union customs legislation) corresponding to those provisions that may apply to those goods.
(6) In section 16 (application of customs enactments)—
  (*a*) subsection (1) applies to the importation of such goods as if the reference to "other enactments for the time being having effect generally in relation to duties of customs and excise charged by reference to the importation of goods into the United Kingdom" included any provision of Union customs legislation that applies in relation to relevant NI import duty, and
  (*b*) subsections (3) and (4) apply to sub-paragraph (4) of this paragraph as they apply to subsection (2) of that section.
(7) The Commissioners may by regulations—
  (*a*) supplement or modify any provision made by provision that applies to value added tax made by or under any enactment (including provision made by or under this Act or TCTA 2018) so far as it applies to VAT charged on the importation of goods into the United Kingdom as a result of their entry into Northern Ireland;
  (*b*) supplement or modify any provision of Union customs legislation so far as it applies to VAT charged on such an importation.
(8) In this Schedule—
  "relevant NI import duty" means duty charged under section 30A(3) of TCTA 2018 (importation of goods: Northern Ireland), and in relation to goods of a description specified in regulations under section 30B(1) of that Act, means that duty as it would be charged if that description were not specified;

"Union customs legislation" means provisions contained in "customs legislation" within the meaning of Regulation (EU) No 952/2013 of the European Parliament and of the Council of 9 October 2013 laying down the Union Customs Code (see Article 5(2) of that Regulation), so far as they apply by virtue of section 7A of the European Union (Withdrawal) Act 2018);
"Union goods" has the meaning it has in that Regulation.
[(9) This paragraph is subject to paragraph 4 of Schedule 9ZC.]²]¹

Amendments—¹ Sch 9ZB inserted by the Taxation (Post-transition Period) Act 2020 s 3, Sch 2 para 2 with effect from IP completion day (11pm on 31 December 2020), by virtue of SI 2020/1642 reg 9.
² Sub-para (9) inserted by the Taxation (Post-transition Period) Act 2020, s 7, Sch 3 paras 25, 27(1), (2) with effect from IP completion day (11pm on 31 December 2020), by virtue of SI 2020/1642 reg 9.

[Valuation of imports

2—(1) For the purposes of this Act, the value of goods imported into the United Kingdom as a result of their entry into Northern Ireland is their value as if determined for the purposes of relevant NI import duty, whether or not the goods are subject to that duty.
(2) Accordingly, section 21(1) (value of imported goods) does not apply in relation to such goods.
(3) Subsections (2) to (7) of section 21 apply in relation to such goods (and sub-paragraph (1) is subject to those subsections) as if—
   (*a*) the reference in subsection (2) to the rules mentioned in subsection (1) of that section were to the rules mentioned in sub-paragraph (1);
   (*b*) in subsection (2)(c), after "United Kingdom" there were inserted "or a member State";
   (*c*) the reference in subsection (2A) to the temporary admission procedure under Part 1 of TCTA 2018 were to the procedure that corresponds to that procedure under Union customs legislation.]¹

Amendments—¹ Sch 9ZB inserted by the Taxation (Post-transition Period) Act 2020 s 3, Sch 2 para 2 with effect from IP completion day (11pm on 31 December 2020), by virtue of SI 2020/1642 reg 9.

[PART 2
MOVEMENTS BETWEEN NORTHERN IRELAND AND GREAT BRITAIN

Movements between Northern Ireland and Great Britain

3—(1) A supply of goods that involves the removal of goods from Northern Ireland to Great Britain or vice versa is zero-rated (see section 30(1)) if such other conditions, if any, as may be specified in regulations or imposed by the Commissioners are fulfilled.
(2) Where goods are removed from Northern Ireland to Great Britain, VAT is charged on the entry of those goods into Great Britain as if those goods had been imported into the United Kingdom.
(3) Accordingly, any provision made by or under any enactment—
   (*a*) that is relevant to the charging of VAT on the importation of goods applies in relation to VAT charged as a result of sub-paragraph (2);
   (*b*) that applies to an importation of goods for the purpose of value added tax applies to such a removal (and references in any such provision to imported goods are to be read as including goods that have been so removed).
(4) Where goods are removed from Great Britain to Northern Ireland, VAT is charged on the entry of those goods into Northern Ireland as if those goods had been imported into the United Kingdom as a result of their entry (from a place outside the United Kingdom) into Northern Ireland.
(5) Accordingly, any provision made by or under any enactment—
   (*a*) that is relevant to the charging of VAT on the importation of goods applies (as modified by or under Part 1 of this Schedule) in relation to VAT charged as a result of subparagraph (4);
   (*b*) that applies to an importation of goods for the purposes of VAT applies (as modified by or under that Part) to such a removal (and references in this Act to imported goods are to be read as including goods that have been so removed).
(6) Sub-paragraphs (3) and (5)—
   (*a*) do not apply so far as the context otherwise requires, and
   (*b*) are subject to the other provisions of this Part of this Schedule.
(7) The Treasury may by regulations—
   (*a*) supplement or modify any provision that applies to value added tax made by or under any enactment (including provision made by or under this Act or TCTA 2018) so far as it applies to VAT charged as a result of sub-paragraph (2) or (4);
   (*b*) supplement or modify any provision of Union customs legislation so far as it applies to VAT charged as a result of sub-paragraph (4).]¹

CROSS-REFERENCES—
See Sch 9ZB para 32: application of this para to goods removed from Northern Ireland to the Isle of Man.

See SI 2020/1545 reg 119: transitional provisions in relation to the movement of goods between Great Britain and Northern Ireland.
See SI 2020/1546 regs 15, 16 (VAT on removals to be payable by a taxable person as if it were VAT on a supply) and reg 17 (requirement to produce import document).
Amendments—[1] Sch 9ZB inserted by the Taxation (Post-transition Period) Act 2020 s 3, Sch 2 para 2 with effect from IP completion day (11pm on 31 December 2020), by virtue of SI 2020/1642 reg 9.

[*Liability for VAT on movements between Great Britain and Northern Ireland*

4—(1) This paragraph applies to a removal of goods from Northern Ireland to Great Britain or vice versa, instead of section 15 (general provision relating to imported goods).
(2) Goods are treated as imported—
  (*a*) in the case of goods removed from Northern Ireland to Great Britain, when a liability to pay duty under section 30C of TCTA 2018 (duty on potentially imported goods) in respect of those goods is, or on the relevant assumptions would be, incurred, and
  (*b*) in the case of goods removed from Great Britain to Northern Ireland, when a liability to pay duty under section 40A of TCTA 2018 (duty on certain goods removed to Northern Ireland) in respect of those goods is, or on the relevant assumptions would be, incurred.
(3) Where the removal is made in the course of a taxable supply made by a taxable person, the taxable person is the person who is treated as having imported the goods.
(4) Otherwise, each person who—
  (*a*) in the case of goods removed from Northern Ireland to Great Britain, is, or on the relevant assumptions would be, liable to pay duty under section 30C of TCTA 2018 in respect of those goods, or
  (*b*) in the case of goods removed from Great Britain to Northern Ireland, is, or on the relevant assumptions would be, liable to pay duty under section 40A of TCTA 2018 in respect of those goods,
is a person who is treated as having imported the goods.
(5) For the purposes of this paragraph "the relevant assumptions" are—
  (*a*) in the case of goods removed from Northern Ireland to Great Britain, an assumption that duty under section 30C of TCTA 2018 is chargeable in respect of those goods,
  (*b*) in the case of goods removed from Great Britain to Northern Ireland, an assumption that duty under section 40A of TCTA 2018 is chargeable in respect of those goods,
  (*c*) in a case where there is no obligation to present the goods to customs on their arrival in the part of the United Kingdom to which they are removed, an assumption that there is such an obligation,
  (*d*) an assumption that a liability to duty at a nil rate is replaced by a liability to duty at a higher rate, and
  (*e*) an assumption that no relief from duty is available.
(6) The Commissioners may by regulations make provision—
  (*a*) for any other person to be treated as importing the goods (instead of, or as well as, any person treated as importing the goods as a result of sub-paragraph (3) or (4));
  (*b*) relation to such a person, of any provision made by or under any enactment that has effect for the purposes of, or in connection with the enforcement of, any obligation to account for and pay VAT;
  (*c*) for requiring any relevant person liable to VAT as a result of provision made by or under this paragraph to give to the Commissioners such notification of the removal of goods in question, and for such VAT to be paid, in such form or manner as may be specified in the regulations or by the Commissioners in accordance with the regulations.
(7) A person is "relevant" for the purposes of sub-paragraph (6)(c) if the person was not a taxable person at the time they became liable to the VAT in question.
(8) If two or more persons are treated as having imported goods those persons are jointly and severally liable to any VAT that is payable on the removal that is treated as an importation as a result of paragraph 3.
(9) The preceding provisions of this paragraph, and any provision made under sub-paragraph (6)(a), are to be ignored in reading any reference to importation or to an importer in anything applied for the purposes of this Act by section 16(1) or (2).
(10) But sub-paragraph (9) does not apply so far as the context otherwise requires or provision to the contrary is contained in regulations under section 16(3).
[(11) Sub-paragraphs (3) and (4) are subject to paragraph 4A of Schedule 9ZC.][2]][1]

CROSS-REFERENCES—
See Sch 9ZB para 32(3): application of this para to goods removed from Northern Ireland to the Isle of Man.

See also Sch 9ZC para 4A (online sales by overseas persons and low value importations: modifications relating to the Northern Ireland Protocol): in the circumstances set out in Sch 9ZC para 4A(1), in relation to a removal of goods from Northern Ireland to Great Britain or vice versa, the operator of the online marketplace is the person who is treated as having imported the goods (subject to certain exceptions).

See the Value Added Tax (Northern Ireland) (EU Exit) Regulations, SI 2020/1546 reg 6 (removals where goods declared to special customs procedure), reg 7 (movement of own goods and on behalf of third party: remover to account), regs 8–11 (removals from Northern Ireland to Great Britain: zero-rating of supplies for export), reg 12 (gifts from Great Britain to Northern Ireland: sender to account), reg 13 (other removals by non-taxable persons), reg 15 (VAT on removals to be payable by a taxable person as if it were VAT on a supply), reg 17 (requirement to produce import document).

Amendments—[1] Sch 9ZB inserted by the Taxation (Post-transition Period) Act 2020 s 3, Sch 2 para 2 with effect from IP completion day (11pm on 31 December 2020), by virtue of SI 2020/1642 reg 9.

[2] Para (11) inserted by the Taxation (Post-transition Period) Act 2020 s 7, Sch 3 paras 25, 27(1), (3) with effect from IP completion day (11pm on 31 December 2020), by virtue of SI 2020/1642 reg 9.

[*Valuation of goods removed from Northern Ireland to Great Britain*

5—(1) This paragraph applies where goods are removed from Northern Ireland to Great Britain and—

   (*a*) the removal is in the course of a supply, or

   (*b*) the last supply of those goods before their removal is zero-rated as a result of that removal.

(2) Where this paragraph applies—

   (*a*) section 21 (value of imported goods) does not apply for the purpose of determining the value of those goods, and

   (*b*) the value of those goods is to be treated as—

      (i) in a case falling within sub-paragraph (1)(*a*), the value of the supply in accordance with section 19 and Schedule 6 (value of supply of goods), and

      (ii) in a case falling within sub-paragraph (1)(*b*), the value of the last supply of those goods before their removal as determined in accordance with that section and that Schedule.][1]

Amendments—[1] Sch 9ZB inserted by the Taxation (Post-transition Period) Act 2020 s 3, Sch 2 para 2 with effect from IP completion day (11pm on 31 December 2020), by virtue of SI 2020/1642 reg 9.

[*Relief for qualifying Northern Ireland goods*

6—(1) No VAT is to be charged on the removal of qualifying Northern Ireland goods from Northern Ireland to Great Britain as a result of paragraph 3(2) unless the removal is made in the course of a taxable supply made by a taxable person.

(2) But the relief provided by sub-paragraph (1) does not apply to a removal of qualifying goods from Northern Ireland to Great Britain if—

   (*a*) the last supply of those goods before their removal is zero-rated as a result of [that removal, or][2]

   [(*b*) duty under section 30C of TCTA 2018 is charged on that removal as a result of subsection (2) of that section (duty on goods removed for an avoidance purpose).][2]

(3) Any VAT that is chargeable as a result of sub-paragraph [(2)(*a*)][2] becomes chargeable from the later of—

   (*a*) the time when the goods were treated as having been imported as a result of the removal, and

   (*b*) the time at which that last supply becomes zero-rated.

(4) In this paragraph "qualifying Northern Ireland goods" has the meaning it has in the European Union (Withdrawal) Act 2018 (see section 8C(6) of that Act).][1]

Amendments—[1] Sch 9ZB inserted by the Taxation (Post-transition Period) Act 2020 s 3, Sch 2 para 2 with effect from IP completion day (11pm on 31 December 2020), by virtue of SI 2020/1642 reg 9.

[2] In sub-para (2), para (*a*) designated as such, and words in para (*a*) substituted for words "that removal", and para (*b*) inserted, and in para (3) reference substituted for reference "(2)", by the Value Added Tax (Miscellaneous Amendments to the Value Added Tax Act 1994 and Revocation) (EU Exit) Regulations, SI 2020/1544 regs 2, 5 with effect from IP completion day (11pm UK time on 31 December 2020) by virtue of SI 2020/1641 reg 2, Schedule para 13.

[*Zero-rating of supplies made before declaration on removal*

7—(1) Item 1 of Group 13 of Schedule 8 (zero-rating)—

   (*a*) applies to a supply of goods which are removed from Great Britain to Northern Ireland as if the reference to a Customs declaration were to such a declaration made for the purposes of Union customs legislation (rather than under Part 1 of TCTA 2018);

   (*b*) does not apply to goods which are removed from Northern Ireland to Great Britain where no Customs declaration under Part 1 of TCTA 2018 is required to be made in respect of the removal of the goods.][1]

CROSS-REFERENCES—

See Sch 9ZB para 32(4): application of this para to goods removed from Northern Ireland to the Isle of Man.

Amendments—[1] Sch 9ZB inserted by the Taxation (Post-transition Period) Act 2020 s 3, Sch 2 para 2 with effect from IP completion day (11pm on 31 December 2020), by virtue of SI 2020/1642 reg 9.

[PART 3
MODIFICATIONS IN RELATION TO EXPORTS
Movements of goods by charities

8—Subsection (5) of Section 30 (export by charities treated as supply in United Kingdom) has effect as if the reference to the export of goods—
   (*a*) included the removal of goods from Great Britain to Northern Ireland, and
   (*b*) did not include the export of goods from Northern Ireland to a place in the member States.][1]
Amendments—[1] Sch 9ZB inserted by the Taxation (Post-transition Period) Act 2020 s 3, Sch 2 para 2 with effect from IP completion day (11pm on 31 December 2020), by virtue of SI 2020/1642 reg 9.

[Goods exported from Northern Ireland

9—Section 30(6) (zero-rating of exports by supplier) has effect as if reference to the export of goods did not include the export of goods from Northern Ireland to a place in the member States.][1]
Amendments—[1] Sch 9ZB inserted by the Taxation (Post-transition Period) Act 2020 s 3, Sch 2 para 2 with effect from IP completion day (11pm on 31 December 2020), by virtue of SI 2020/1642 reg 9.

[Zero-rating regulations

10—Subsection (8) of section 30 (power to zero-rate supplies where goods have been or are to be exported) has effect as if reference to the export of goods—
   (*a*) included the removal of goods from Northern Ireland to Great Britain, or vice versa, and
   (*b*) did not include the export of goods from Northern Ireland to a place in the member States.][1]
Amendments—[1] Sch 9ZB inserted by the Taxation (Post-transition Period) Act 2020 s 3, Sch 2 para 2 with effect from IP completion day (11pm on 31 December 2020), by virtue of SI 2020/1642 reg 9.

[Zero-rating of supply of exported goods let on hire

11—Section 30(9) (zero-rating of supply of exported goods let on hire) has effect as if the reference to the export of goods did not include the export of goods from Northern Ireland to a place in the member States.][1]
Amendments—[1] Sch 9ZB inserted by the Taxation (Post-transition Period) Act 2020 s 3, Sch 2 para 2 with effect from IP completion day (11pm on 31 December 2020), by virtue of SI 2020/1642 reg 9.

[Application of section 30(10)

12—(1) Where a supply of goods has been zero-rated under paragraph 3(1), or as a result of regulations under section 30(8), on the basis that the goods have been or are to be removed from Northern Ireland to Great Britain, section 30(10) (forfeiture of goods found in the United Kingdom) applies in relation to that supply as if any reference to the United Kingdom were to Northern Ireland.
(2) Where a supply of goods has been zero-rated under paragraph 3(1) [or 31A(3)][2], or as a result of regulations under section 30(8), on the basis that the goods have been or are to be removed from Great Britain to Northern Ireland, section 30(10) applies in relation to that supply as if any reference to the United Kingdom were to Great Britain.][1]
Amendments—[1] Sch 9ZB inserted by the Taxation (Post-transition Period) Act 2020 s 3, Sch 2 para 2 with effect from IP completion day (11pm on 31 December 2020), by virtue of SI 2020/1642 reg 9.
[2] Words in sub-para (2) inserted by the Value Added Tax (Miscellaneous Amendments to the Value Added Tax Act 1994 and Revocation) (EU Exit) Regulations, SI 2020/1544 regs 2, 7 with effect from IP completion day (11pm UK time on 31 December 2020) by virtue of SI 2020/1641 reg 2, Schedule para 13.

[Relief from VAT on importation of goods

13—(1) Section 37 (relief from VAT on importation of goods) has effect as if any reference to the export of goods did not include the export of goods from Northern Ireland to a place in the member States.
(2) That section has effect in relation to a removal of goods from Northern Ireland to Great Britain (which is treated as an importation as a result of paragraph 3(3)) as if any reference to the export of goods included their removal from Great Britain to Northern Ireland.
(3) That section has effect in relation to a removal of goods from Great Britain to Northern Ireland (which is treated as an importation as a result of paragraph 3(5)) as if any reference to the export of goods included their removal from Northern Ireland to Great Britain.][1]
Amendments—[1] Sch 9ZB inserted by the Taxation (Post-transition Period) Act 2020 s 3, Sch 2 para 2 with effect from IP completion day (11pm on 31 December 2020), by virtue of SI 2020/1642 reg 9.

[Schedule 8: modifications to Group 13 and 15

14—(1) Item 3 of Group 13 of Schedule 8 (zero-rating) has effect as if the reference to goods for export did not include goods for export from Northern Ireland to a place in the member States.

(2) Group 15 of that Schedule has effect as if—
  (a) any reference to the export of goods did not include the export of goods from Northern Ireland to a place in the member States;
  (b) any reference to the export of goods, other than the reference in item 3, included the removal of goods from Great Britain to Northern Ireland or vice versa;
  (c) after item 3 there were inserted—
"3A The removal by a charity of goods donated to it—
  (a) from Great Britain to Northern Ireland;
  (b) from Northern Ireland to Great Britain."][1]

Amendments—[1] Sch 9ZB inserted by the Taxation (Post-transition Period) Act 2020 s 3, Sch 2 para 2 with effect from IP completion day (11pm on 31 December 2020), by virtue of SI 2020/1642 reg 9.

[PART 4
WAREHOUSES

Northern Ireland—See Sch 9ZB para 34 below: Part 4 of this Schedule has effect as if any reference to Great Britain included the Isle of Man (see also the Value Added Tax (Isle of Man) Order, SI 1982/1067 art 2 which provides that this Act has effect as if the Isle of Man were part of the United Kingdom subject to the provisions of that Order).

Modification of sections 18 and 18A

15—(1) Section 18 (place and time of supply) has effect as if—
  (a) every reference to the United Kingdom were to Great Britain, other than the references—
    (i) in the phrases "taking place outside the United Kingdom" and "taking place in the United Kingdom", and
    (ii) in the definition of "warehouse" in subsection (6);
  (b) in subsection (6)—
    (i) in the definition of "the duty point", in paragraph (b), after "import duty" there were inserted "or duty under section 30C of TCTA 2018";
    (ii) in the definition of "warehouse", in paragraph (a), after "import duty" there were inserted "or duty under section 30C of TCTA 2018".
(2) Section 18A (fiscal warehousing) has effect as if the reference to "such place in the United Kingdom" in subsection (3) were to "such place in Great Britain".][1]

Amendments—[1] Sch 9ZB inserted by the Taxation (Post-transition Period) Act 2020 s 3, Sch 2 para 2 with effect from IP completion day (11pm on 31 December 2020), by virtue of SI 2020/1642 reg 9.

[*Place and time of supply: Northern Ireland warehouses*

16—(1) A supply of goods, or an acquisition of goods in Northern Ireland from a member State, is treated as taking place outside the United Kingdom where—
  (a) the goods are subject to a Northern Ireland warehousing regime,
  (b) they have been removed—
    (i) from a place outside the member States, other than Northern Ireland, and have entered the territory of the European Union, or
    (ii) from a place outside the member States and have entered Northern Ireland (which includes goods removed to Northern Ireland from Great Britain),
  (c) the material time for their supply, or their acquisition in Northern Ireland, is while they are subject to that regime and before the duty point, and
  (d) those goods are not, or are not mixed with, any dutiable goods which were produced or manufactured in Northern Ireland or acquired from a member State.
(2) The Commissioners may by regulations provide that subparagraph (1) does not apply in circumstances specified or described in the regulations.
(3) A supply of dutiable goods which were produced or manufactured in Northern Ireland or acquired from a member State, or a supply of a mixture of such goods and other goods, is treated as taking place outside the United Kingdom where the conditions in sub-paragraph (5) are met.
(4) An acquisition in Northern Ireland from a member State of dutiable goods is treated as taking place outside the United Kingdom where those conditions are met.
(5) Those conditions are—
  (a) that the goods are subject to a Northern Ireland warehousing regime,
  (b) that the material time for the supply mentioned in subparagraph (3), or the acquisition mentioned in subparagraph (4), is while the goods are subject to that regime and before the duty point, and
  (c) that the material time for any subsequent supply of those goods is also while the goods are subject to that regime and before the duty point.
(6) Where—

(a) the conditions in sub-paragraph (5)(a) and (b) are met in relation to a supply of goods mentioned in sub-paragraph (3) or an acquisition of goods mentioned in sub-paragraph (4),
(b) the condition in sub-paragraph (5)(c) is not met in relation to that supply or acquisition, and
(c) the supply or acquisition is treated as taking place within the United Kingdom,

sub-paragraph (7) applies to the supply or acquisition.

(7) Where this sub-paragraph applies to a supply or acquisition of goods, the supply or acquisition is treated as taking place at the earlier of—
 (a) the time when the goods are removed from the Northern Ireland warehousing regime, and
 (b) the duty point.

(8) Where sub-paragraph (7) applies to a supply of goods, any VAT payable on the supply must be paid—
 (a) at the time when the supply is treated as taking place, and
 (b) by—
  (i) the person who removed the goods from the Northern Ireland warehousing regime, or
  (ii) the person who is required to pay any duty or agricultural levy in respect of the goods.

(9) The Commissioners may by regulations make provision for enabling a taxable person to pay the VAT the person is required to pay by virtue of sub-paragraph (8) at a time later than that provided for by that sub-paragraph.

(10) Regulations under sub-paragraph (9) may in particular make provision for either or both of the following—
 (a) for the taxable person to pay the VAT together with the VAT chargeable on other supplies by the person of goods and services;
 (b) for the taxable person to pay the VAT together with any duty of excise deferment of which has been granted to the person under section 127A of the Customs and Excise Management Act 1979,

and the regulations may make different provision for different descriptions of taxable person and for different descriptions of goods.

(11) In this paragraph—
 "dutiable goods" means any goods which are subject—
  (a) to a duty of excise, or
  (b) in accordance with any provision for the time being having effect for transitional purposes in connection with the accession of any State to the European Union, to any EU customs duty or agricultural levy of the European Union;
 "the duty point", in relation to any goods, means—
  (a) in the case of goods which are subject to a duty of excise, the time when the requirement to pay the duty on those goods takes effect, and
  (b) in the case of goods which are not so subject—
   (i) the time when the requirement to pay duty charged under section 30A(3) of TCTA 2018 (importation of goods: Northern Ireland) on those goods takes effect,
   (ii) the time when the requirement to pay duty charged under section 40A of TCTA 2018 (duty on goods potentially for export from Northern Ireland) on those goods takes effect, or
   (iii) the time when any Community customs debt in respect of duty on the entry of the goods into the territory of the European Union would be incurred or, as the case may be, the corresponding time in relation to any such duty or levy as is mentioned in paragraph (b) of the definition of dutiable goods;
 "Northern Ireland warehouse" means any warehouse where goods may be stored in the United Kingdom or a member State without payment of any one or more of the following—
  (a) duty charged under section 30A(3) of TCTA 2018 (importation of goods: Northern Ireland) or under section 40A of TCTA 2018 (duty on goods potentially for export from Northern Ireland);
  (b) EU customs duty;
  (c) any agricultural levy of the European Union;
  (d) VAT on the importation of the goods into any member State;
  (e) VAT on the importation of goods into the United Kingdom as a result of their entry into Northern Ireland;
  (f) any duty of excise or any duty which is equivalent in a member State to a duty of excise.

(12) References in this paragraph to goods being subject to a Northern Ireland warehousing regime are to goods being kept in a Northern Ireland warehouse or being transported between Northern Ireland warehouses (whether in the same country or different countries) without the payment in a country of any duty, levy or VAT; and references to the removal of goods from a warehousing regime are to be construed accordingly.][1]

Amendments—[1] Sch 9ZB inserted by the Taxation (Post-transition Period) Act 2020 s 3, Sch 2 para 2 with effect from IP completion day (11pm on 31 December 2020), by virtue of SI 2020/1642 reg 9.

[Northern Ireland fiscal warehouses

17—(1) The Commissioners may, if it appears to them proper, upon application approve any registered person as a Northern Ireland fiscal warehousekeeper, and such approval is subject to such conditions as the Commissioners impose.
(2) Subject to those conditions and to regulations made under paragraph 25(6), such a person is entitled to keep a Northern Ireland fiscal warehouse.
(3) "Northern Ireland fiscal warehouse" means a place in Northern Ireland in the occupation or under the control of a Northern Ireland fiscal warehousekeeper that the warehousekeeper has notified to the Commisioners as a Northern Ireland fiscal warehouse.
(4) Retail premises may not be notified as a Northern Ireland fiscal warehouse.
(5) A place notified under sub-paragraph (3) is a Northern Ireland fiscal warehouse from the later of—
   (*a*) the date the Commissioners received the notification, and
   (*b*) the date specified in the notice from which the notification is to have effect.
(6) A place ceases to be a Northern Ireland fiscal warehouse—
   (*a*) if that place ceases to be in the occupation or under the control of the Northern Ireland fiscal warehousekeeper, or
   (*b*) if the Northern Ireland fiscal warehousekeeper notifies the Commissioners that the place is to cease to be a Northern Ireland fiscal warehouse.
(7) The Commissioners may in considering an application by a person to be a Northern Ireland fiscal warehousekeeper take into account any matter which they consider relevant, and may without prejudice to the generality of that provision take into account all or any one or more of the following—
   (*a*) the person's record of compliance and ability to comply with the provisions made by or under this Act;
   (*b*) the person's record of compliance and ability to comply with the provisions made by or under the customs and excise Acts (as defined in the Management Act);
   (*c*) the person's record of compliance and ability to comply with Union customs legislation;
   (*d*) the person's record of compliance and ability to comply with the requirements of member States relating to VAT and duties equivalent to duties of excise;
   (*e*) if the applicant is a company, the records of compliance and ability to comply with the matters set out in paragraphs (a) to (d) of its directors, persons connected with its directors, its managing officers, any shadow directors or any of those persons, and, if it is a close company, the records of compliance and ability to comply with the matters set out in those paragraphs of the beneficial owners of the shares of the company or any of them;
   (*f*) if the applicant is an individual, the records of compliance and ability to comply with the matters set out in those paragraphs of any company of which the applicant is or has been a director, managing officer or shadow director or, in the case of a close company, a shareholder or the beneficial owner of shares.
(8) For the purposes of paragraphs (e) and (f) of sub-paragraph (7)—
   (*a*) a person is "connected" with a director if that person is the director's spouse or civil partner, or is a relative, or the spouse or civil partner of a relative, of the director or of the director's spouse or civil partner;
   (*b*) "managing officer" in relation to a body corporate, means any manager, secretary or other similar officer of the body corporate or any person purporting to act in any such capacity or as a director;
   (*c*) "shadow director" has the meaning given by section 251 of the Companies Act 2006;
   (*d*) "close company" has the meaning it has in the Corporation Tax Acts (see Chapter 2 of Part 10 of the Corporation Tax Act 2010).
(9) Subject to sub-paragraph (10), a person approved under subparagraph (1) remains a Northern Ireland fiscal warehousekeeper until the person—
   (*a*) ceases to be a registered person, or
   (*b*) notifies the Commissioners in writing that the person is to cease to be a Northern Ireland fiscal warehousekeeper.
(10) The Commissioners may if they consider it appropriate from time to time—
   (*a*) impose conditions on a Northern Ireland fiscal warehousekeeper in addition to those conditions, if any, imposed under sub-paragraph (1);
   (*b*) vary or revoke any conditions previously imposed;
   (*c*) withdraw approval of any person as a Northern Ireland fiscal warehousekeeper;
   (*d*) withdraw Northern Ireland fiscal warehouse status from any premises.

(11) Any application by or on behalf of a person to be a Northern Ireland fiscal warehousekeeper must be in writing and in such form as the Commissioners may direct and must be accompanied by such information as the Commissioners require.
(12) Any approval by the Commissioners under sub-paragraph (1), and any withdrawal of approval or other act by them under subparagraph (10), must be notified to the fiscal warehousekeeper in writing and takes effect on such notification being made or on any later date specified for the purpose in the notification.
(13) Without prejudice to the provisions of section 43 concerning liability for VAT, "registered person", for the purposes of this paragraph, includes any person who under that section is for the time being treated as a member of a group.][1]

Amendments—[1] Sch 9ZB inserted by the Taxation (Post-transition Period) Act 2020 s 3, Sch 2 para 2 with effect from IP completion day (11pm on 31 December 2020), by virtue of SI 2020/1642 reg 9.

[Conversion of relevant fiscal warehouses etc

18—(1) Sub-paragraph (2) applies to any place in Northern Ireland that was a fiscal warehouse immediately before the coming into force of paragraph 17.
(2) On the coming into force of that paragraph, a place to which this sub-paragraph applies becomes a Northern Ireland fiscal warehouse (and may cease to be in accordance with that paragraph).
(3) On the coming into force of that paragraph, any fiscal warehousekeeper in relation to such a place immediately before the coming into force of that paragraph becomes a Northern Ireland warehousekeeper (and may cease to be in accordance with that paragraph).
(4) But a person does not cease to be a fiscal warehousekeeper in relation to a place in Great Britain as a result of sub-paragraph (3).
(5) Sub-paragraph (6) applies to a fiscal warehousekeeper who becomes a Northern Ireland fiscal warehousekeeper as a result of sub-paragraph (3).
(6) Any condition imposed under section 18A(1) or (6) that, immediately before the coming into force of paragraph 17, applied to a fiscal warehousekeeper to whom this sub-paragraph applies, applies to that person as a Northern Ireland fiscal warehousekeeper as if imposed under paragraph 17 (and may be varied or revoked accordingly).
(7) In this paragraph "fiscal warehouse" and "fiscal warehousekeeper" have the meaning they have in sections 18A to 18F (see section 18F).][1]

Amendments—[1] Sch 9ZB inserted by the Taxation (Post-transition Period) Act 2020 s 3, Sch 2 para 2 with effect from IP completion day (11pm on 31 December 2020), by virtue of SI 2020/1642 reg 9.

[Northern Ireland fiscal warehouses: relief]

19—(1) Sub-paragraphs (5) and (6) apply where—
  (a) there is an acquisition of goods in Northern Ireland from a member State,
  (b) those goods are eligible goods,
  (c) either—
    (i) the acquisition takes place while the goods are subject to a Northern Ireland fiscal warehousing regime, or
    (ii) after the acquisition but before the supply, if any, of those goods which next occurs, the acquirer causes the goods to be placed in a Northern Ireland fiscal warehousing regime, and
  (d) the acquirer, not later than the time of the acquisition, prepares and keeps a certificate that the goods are subject to a fiscal warehousing regime, or (as the case may be) that the acquirer will cause paragraph (c)(ii) to be satisfied.
(2) A certificate prepared for the purposes of sub-paragraph (1)(d) must be kept for such period as the Commissioners may by regulations specify.
(3) Sub-paragraphs (5) and (6) also apply where—
  (a) there is a supply of goods,
  (b) those goods are eligible goods,
  (c) either—
    (i) that supply takes place while the goods are subject to a Northern Ireland fiscal warehousing regime, or
    (ii) after that supply but before the supply, if any, of those goods which next occurs, the person to whom the former supply is made causes the goods to be placed in a Northern Ireland fiscal warehousing regime,
  (d) in a case falling within paragraph (c)(ii), the person to whom the supply is made gives the supplier, not later than the time of the supply, a certificate that the person will cause paragraph (c)(ii) to be satisfied, and
  (e) the supply is not a retail transaction.
(4) A certificate under sub-paragraph (1)(d) or (3)(d) must be in such form as may be specified by regulations or by the Commissioners in accordance with regulations.

(5) An acquisition or supply to which this sub-paragraph applies is treated for the purposes of this Act as taking place outside the United Kingdom if any subsequent supply of those goods is while they are subject to the Northern Ireland fiscal warehousing regime.

(6) Where an acquisition or supply to which this sub-paragraph applies falls, for the purposes of this Act, to be treated as taking place in the United Kingdom that acquisition or supply is treated for the purposes of this Act as taking place when the goods are removed from the Northern Ireland fiscal warehousing regime.

(7) Where—
- (*a*) sub-paragraph (6) applies to an acquisition or a supply,
- (*b*) the acquisition or supply is taxable and not zero-rated, and
- (*c*) the acquirer or supplier is not a taxable person but would be were it not for paragraph 1(9) of Schedule 1 and paragraphs 38(6) and 48(7) of Schedule 9ZA, or any of those provisions,

VAT is chargeable on that acquisition or supply notwithstanding that the acquirer or the supplier is not a taxable person.

(8) For the purposes of this paragraph, apart from sub-paragraph (6), an acquisition or supply is treated as taking place at the material time for the acquisition or supply.

(9) In this paragraph "eligible goods" has the meaning it has in section 18B, but as if in section 18B(6)(b)—
- (*a*) in sub-paragraph (i)—
  - (i) after "import duty" there were inserted ", and any duty under section 30A(3) of TCTA 2018,";
  - (ii) after "those Acts" there were inserted "or Union customs legislation";
- (*b*) in sub-paragraph (ii), after "section 1(1)(c)" there were inserted "(including any VAT chargeable on the movement of goods from Great Britain to Northern Ireland as a result of paragraph 3(4))".

(10) The Commissioners may by regulations provide that goods of a description specified in regulations are, for the purposes of this paragraph, to be treated—
- (*a*) where such goods are not of a description falling within Schedule 5A (goods eligible to be fiscally warehoused), as if they were;
- (*b*) where such goods are of a description falling within that Schedule, as if they were not.

(11) The Commissioners may by regulations provide for the zero-rating of supplies of goods, or of such goods as may be specified in regulations, in cases where—
- (*a*) the Commissioners are satisfied that the supply in question involves both—
  - (i) the removal of the goods from a Northern Ireland fiscal warehousing regime, and
  - (ii) their being placed in a warehousing regime in a member State, or in such member State or States as may be prescribed, where that regime is established by provisions of the law of that member State corresponding, in relation to that member State, to the provisions of this paragraph and paragraph 17, and
- (*b*) such other conditions, if any, as may be specified in the regulations or the Commissioners may impose are fulfilled.

(12) Section 30(10) (zero-rating) applies in relation to regulations made under sub-paragraph (11) as it applies to regulations made under section 30(8) or (9).][1]

Cross-references—The certificates referred to in sub-paras (1)(*d*) and (3)(*d*) must contain the information indicated in the form specified in a notice published by the Commissioners. A certificate prepared under sub-para (1)(*d*) by an acquirer who is not a taxable person must be kept by that person for a period of six years commencing on the day the certificate is prepared; and the person must produce it to a proper officer when that officer requests the person to do so.
See VAT Regs, SI 1995/2518 reg 145S, as inserted by SI 2020/1545 reg 79.
Amendments—[1] Sch 9ZB inserted by the Taxation (Post-transition Period) Act 2020 s 3, Sch 2 para 2 with effect from IP completion day (11pm on 31 December 2020), by virtue of SI 2020/1642 reg 9.

[Modification of section 18B]

20—Section 18B(5) (fiscally warehoused goods: relief) has effect as if after "Schedule 1" there were inserted "and paragraphs 38(6) and 48(7) of Schedule 9ZA, or any of those provisions".][1]

Amendments—[1] Sch 9ZB inserted by the Taxation (Post-transition Period) Act 2020 s 3, Sch 2 para 2 with effect from IP completion day (11pm on 31 December 2020), by virtue of SI 2020/1642 reg 9.

[Northern Ireland warehouses and fiscal warehouses: services]

21—(1) Section 18C has effect as if any reference to—
- (*a*) "a warehousing or fiscal warehousing regime" were to "a warehousing, Northern Ireland warehousing, fiscal warehousing, or Northern Ireland fiscal warehousing regime";
- (*b*) "a warehouse or a fiscal warehousekeeper" were to "a warehouse, Northern Ireland warehouse, fiscal or Northern Ireland fiscal warehousekeeper";
- (*c*) "a warehousing regime" were to "a warehousing or Northern Ireland warehousing regime";

(d) "a fiscal warehousing regime" were to "a fiscal or Northern Ireland fiscal warehousing regime".

(2) Subsection (2) of that section has effect in relation to goods subject to a Northern Ireland warehousing or Northern Ireland fiscal warehousing regime as if the term "material time" had the meaning it has in this Part of this Schedule.

(3) Subsection (3) of that section has effect in relation to goods subject to a Northern Ireland warehousing or Northern Ireland fiscal warehousing regime as if the term "duty point" had the meaning it has in paragraph 16.

(4) Subsection (4)(b) of that section has effect in relation to goods subject to a Northern Ireland fiscal warehousing regime as if after "carried out under" there were inserted "Union customs legislation (within the meaning of Schedule 9ZB) or under".][1]

Amendments—[1] Sch 9ZB inserted by the Taxation (Post-transition Period) Act 2020 s 3, Sch 2 para 2 with effect from IP completion day (11pm on 31 December 2020), by virtue of SI 2020/1642 reg 9.

[Removal from warehousing: accountability

22—(1) This paragraph applies to any supply to which paragraph 19(6) applies (supply treated as taking place on removal or duty point) and any acquisition to which paragraph 19(7) applies (acquisition treated as taking place on removal where acquirer not a taxable person).

(2) Any VAT payable on the supply or acquisition must (subject to any regulations under sub-paragraph (3)) be paid—
   (a) at the time when the supply or acquisition is treated as taking place under the paragraph in question, and
   (b) by the person by whom the goods are removed or, as the case may be, together with the excise duty, by the person who is required to pay that duty.

(3) The Commissioners may by regulations make provision for enabling a taxable person to pay the VAT the person is required to pay by virtue of sub-paragraph (2) at a time later than that provided by that sub-paragraph.

(4) Regulations may make different provisions for different descriptions of taxable persons and for different descriptions of goods and services.][1]

Amendments—[1] Sch 9ZB inserted by the Taxation (Post-transition Period) Act 2020 s 3, Sch 2 para 2 with effect from IP completion day (11pm on 31 December 2020), by virtue of SI 2020/1642 reg 9.

[Deficiency in Northern Ireland fiscally warehoused goods

23—(1) Section 18E applies—
   (a) to goods which have been subject to a Northern Ireland fiscal warehousing regime as it applies to goods which have been subject to a fiscal warehousing regime, and
   (b) to a Northern Ireland fiscal warehousekeeper as it applies to a fiscal warehousekeeper.

(2) In this paragraph "fiscal warehousekeeper" has the meaning it has in sections 18A to 18F (see section 18F).][1]

Amendments—[1] Sch 9ZB inserted by the Taxation (Post-transition Period) Act 2020 s 3, Sch 2 para 2 with effect from IP completion day (11pm on 31 December 2020), by virtue of SI 2020/1642 reg 9.

[Incorrect Northern Ireland fiscal warehousing certificates

24—(1) Where—
   (a) a person who makes, or is to make, an acquisition of goods in Northern Ireland from a member State prepares a certificate for the purposes of paragraph 19(1)(d), and
   (b) the certificate is incorrect,
the person preparing the certificate is liable to a penalty.

(2) The amount of the penalty is the amount of VAT actually chargeable on the acquisition.

(3) A person is not liable to a penalty under sub-paragraph (1) if the person satisfies the Commissioners or, on appeal, a tribunal that there is a reasonable excuse for having prepared the certificate in question.

(4) If a person is convicted of an offence (whether under this Act or otherwise) by reason of preparing an incorrect certificate for the purposes of paragraph 19(1)(d), the person is not liable to a penalty under sub-paragraph (1).

(5) A penalty under sub-paragraph (1) is to be treated, for the purposes of sections 76 and 83 (assessments and appeals), as if it were a penalty under section 62 (incorrect certificates).

(6) Section 62 has effect as if in subsection (1)(a)(ii), after "18C(1)(c)" there were inserted "or paragraph 19(3)(d) of Schedule 9ZB (Northern Ireland fiscal warehouses)".][1]

Amendments—[1] Sch 9ZB inserted by the Taxation (Post-transition Period) Act 2020 s 3, Sch 2 para 2 with effect from IP completion day (11pm on 31 December 2020), by virtue of SI 2020/1642 reg 9.

[Supplementary provision]

25—(1) In this Part of this Schedule—
"eligible goods" is to be construed in accordance with paragraph 19(9) and (10);
"material time"—
- (a) in relation to any acquisition or supply the time of which is determined in accordance with regulations under section 6(14) or paragraph 4(2)(b) of Schedule 9ZA, means such time as may be prescribed for the purpose of this paragraph by those regulations,
- (b) in relation to any other acquisition, means the time of the first removal of the goods (see paragraph 4(5) of that Schedule), and
- (c) in relation to any other supply, means the time when the supply would be treated as taking place in accordance with subsection (2) of section 6 if paragraph (c) of that subsection were omitted;

"Northern Ireland fiscal warehouse" is to be construed in accordance with paragraph 17;
"Northern Ireland fiscal warehousekeeper" is to be construed in accordance with that paragraph;
"Northern Ireland warehouse" has the meaning given by paragraph 16(11).

(2) Any reference in this Part of this Schedule to goods being subject to a Northern Ireland fiscal warehousing regime is, subject to any regulations made under sub-paragraph (6), a reference to eligible goods being kept in a Northern Ireland fiscal warehouse or being transferred between Northern Ireland fiscal warehouses in accordance with such regulations; and any reference to the removal of goods from a Northern Ireland fiscal warehousing regime are to be construed accordingly.

(3) Where as a result of an operation on eligible goods subject to a Northern Ireland fiscal warehousing regime they change their nature but the resulting goods are also eligible goods, the provisions of this Part of this Schedule apply as if the resulting goods were the original goods.

(4) Where as a result of an operation on eligible goods subject to a Northern Ireland fiscal warehousing regime they cease to be eligible goods, on their ceasing to be so this Part applies as if they had at that time been removed from the regime; and for that purpose the proprietor of the goods is treated as if that person were the person removing them.

(5) Where—
- (*a*) any person ceases to be a Northern Ireland fiscal warehousekeeper, or
- (*b*) any premises cease to have Northern Ireland fiscal warehouse status,

this Part of this Schedule applies as if the goods of which the person is the fiscal warehousekeeper, or the goods in the fiscal warehouse, as the case may be, had at that time been removed from the fiscal warehousing regime; and for that purpose the proprietor of the goods is to be treated as if the proprietor were the person removing them.

(6) The Commissioners may make regulations governing the deposit, keeping, securing and treatment of goods in a Northern Ireland fiscal warehouse, and the removal of goods from a Northern Ireland fiscal warehouse.

(7) Regulations may, without prejudice to the generality of subparagraph (6), include provision—
- (*a*) in relation to—
  - (i) goods which are, have been or are to be subject to a Northern Ireland fiscal warehousing regime,
  - (ii) other goods which are, have been or are to be kept in Northern Ireland fiscal warehouses,
  - (iii) Northern Ireland fiscal warehouse premises, and
  - (iv) Northern Ireland fiscal warehousekeepers and their businesses,

  as to the keeping, preservation and production of records and the furnishing of returns and information by Northern Ireland fiscal warehousekeepers and any other persons;
- (*b*) requiring goods deposited in a fiscal warehouse to be produced to or made available for inspection by an authorised person on the request of that authorised person;
- (*c*) prohibiting the carrying out on Northern Ireland fiscally warehoused goods of such operations as the Commissioners may prescribe;
- (*d*) regulating the transfer of goods from one Northern Ireland fiscal warehouse to another;
- (*e*) concerning goods which, though kept in a Northern Ireland fiscal warehouse, are not eligible goods or are not intended by a relevant person to be goods in respect of which reliefs are to be enjoyed under this Part of this Schedule;
- (*f*) prohibiting a Northern Ireland fiscal warehousekeeper from allowing goods to be removed from a Northern Ireland fiscal warehousing regime without payment of any VAT payable under paragraph 22 on or by reference to that removal and, if in breach of that prohibition the warehousekeeper allows goods to be so removed, making the warehousekeeper liable for the VAT jointly and severally with the remover,

and may contain such incidental or supplementary provisions as the Commissioners think necessary or expedient.

(8) Regulations may make different provision for different cases, including different provision for different Northern Ireland fiscal warehousekeepers or descriptions of Northern Ireland fiscal warehousekeeper, for Northern Ireland fiscal warehouses of different descriptions or for goods of different classes or descriptions or of the same class or description in different circumstances.][1]

Amendments—[1] Sch 9ZB inserted by the Taxation (Post-transition Period) Act 2020 s 3, Sch 2 para 2 with effect from IP completion day (11pm on 31 December 2020), by virtue of SI 2020/1642 reg 9.

[Modification of other provisions

26—(1) Paragraph 3 of Schedule 6 (valuation: special cases) has effect in relation to goods whose supply involves their removal to Northern Ireland from a place outside the United Kingdom as if—
  (a) in sub-paragraph (1)(a)(ii), after "EU" there were inserted "customs duty or";
  (b) in sub-paragraph (1)(b), for "section 18(4)" there were substituted "paragraph 16(7) of Schedule 9ZB";
  (c) in sub-paragraph (2), for "section 18" there were substituted "paragraph 16 of Schedule 9ZB".
(2) Paragraph 2(8) of Schedule 11 has effect as if after "section 18" there were inserted "in relation to goods other than goods in Northern Ireland, or paragraph 16 of Schedule 9ZB in relation to goods in Northern Ireland".
(3) Section 702 of the Income Tax (Earnings and Pensions) Act 2003 (meaning of "readily convertible asset") has effect as if in subsection (6)(a), in the definition of "warehousing regime", after "Value Added Tax Act 1994 (c23))" there were inserted "or a Northern Ireland warehousing or Northern Ireland fiscal warehousing regime (within the meaning of paragraphs 16 to 25 of Schedule 9ZB to that Act)".
(4) Paragraph 11 of Schedule 36 to the Finance Act 2008 (power to inspect premises) has effect as if—
  (a) in sub-paragraph (1)(c), after "warehouse" there were inserted "or Northern Ireland fiscal warehouse";
  (b) in sub-paragraph (2)(c), after "warehousing" there were inserted "or Northern Ireland fiscal warehousing".][1]

Amendments—[1] Sch 9ZB inserted by the Taxation (Post-transition Period) Act 2020 s 3, Sch 2 para 2 with effect from IP completion day (11pm on 31 December 2020), by virtue of SI 2020/1642 reg 9.

[PART 5
RULES RELATING TO PARTICULAR SUPPLIES

Supplies of gas, electricity or heat

27—(1) Paragraph 3(1) (zero-rating of supplies involving removal of goods from Northern Ireland to Great Britain or vice versa) does not apply to a supply of relevant goods.
(2) In this paragraph "relevant goods" has the meaning it has in section 9A (reverse charge on gas, electricity, heat or cooling).][1]

Amendments—[1] Sch 9ZB inserted by the Taxation (Post-transition Period) Act 2020 s 3, Sch 2 para 2 with effect from IP completion day (11pm on 31 December 2020), by virtue of SI 2020/1642 reg 9.

[Time of supply involving both a supply and an acquisition

28—(1) Where any supply of goods involves both—
  (a) the removal of the goods from Northern Ireland, and
  (b) their acquisition in a member State by a person who is liable for VAT on the acquisition in accordance with provisions of the law of that member State corresponding, in relation to that member State, to the provisions of paragraph 2,
subsections (2), (4) to (6) and (10) to (12) of section 6 (time of supply) do not apply and the supply is treated for the purposes of this Act as taking place on whichever is the earlier of the days specified in sub-paragraph (2).
(2) The days mentioned in sub-paragraph (1) are—
  (a) the 15th day of the month following that in which the removal in question takes place, and
  (b) the day of the issue, in respect of the supply, of a VAT invoice or of an invoice of such other description as the Commissioners may by regulations prescribe.
(3) Section 6(14) has effect as if after "section 55(4)" there were inserted "or paragraph 28 of Schedule 9ZB".][1]

Amendments—[1] Sch 9ZB inserted by the Taxation (Post-transition Period) Act 2020 s 3, Sch 2 para 2 with effect from IP completion day (11pm on 31 December 2020), by virtue of SI 2020/1642 reg 9.

[Distance selling between EU and Northern Ireland: place of supply]

29—(1) Goods whose place of supply is not determined under subsection (2) or (3) of section 7 (place of supply of goods) are treated as supplied in the United Kingdom where—
  (*a*) the supply involves the removal of the goods to Northern Ireland by or under the directions of the person who supplies them,
  (*b*) the supply is a transaction in pursuance of which the goods are acquired in Northern Ireland from a member State by a person who is not a taxable person,
  (*c*) the supplier—
    (i) is liable to be registered under Part 9 of Schedule 9ZA, or
    (ii) would be so liable if the supplier were not already registered under this Act or liable to be registered under Schedule 1 or 1A, and
  (*d*) the supply is neither a supply of goods consisting in a new means of transport nor anything which is treated as a supply for the purposes of this Act by virtue only of paragraph 5(1) of Schedule 4 or paragraph 30 of Schedule 9ZB.
(2) Goods whose place of supply is not determined under subparagraph (1) or subsection (2) or (3) of section 7 and which do not consist in a new means of transport are treated as supplied outside the United Kingdom where—
  (*a*) the supply involves the removal of the goods from Northern Ireland, by or under the directions of the person who supplies them, to a member State,
  (*b*) the person who makes the supply is taxable in a member State, and
  (*c*) provisions of the law of that member State corresponding, in relation to that member State, to the provisions made by sub-paragraph (1) make that person liable to VAT on the supply.
(3) But sub-paragraph (2) does not apply in relation to any supply in a case where the liability mentioned in sub-paragraph (2)(c) depends on the exercise by any person of an option in the United Kingdom corresponding to such an option as is mentioned in paragraph 48(2) unless that person has given, and has not withdrawn, a notification to the Commissioners that the person wishes supplies by that person to be treated as taking place outside the United kingdom where they are supplies in relation to which the other requirements of sub-paragraph (2) are satisfied.
(4) The Commissioners may by regulations provide that a notification for the purposes of sub-paragraph (3) is not to be given or withdrawn except in such circumstances, and in such form and manner, as may be prescribed.
(5) For the purposes of this paragraph—
  (*a*) where goods, in the course of their removal from a place in Northern Ireland to another place in Northern Ireland leave and re-enter Northern Ireland the removal is not to be treated as a removal from or to Northern Ireland, and
  (*b*) where goods, in the course of their removal from a place in Northern Ireland to another place in the United Kingdom leave and re-enter the United Kingdom the removal is not to be treated as a removal from Northern Ireland.
(6) Section 7 has effect as if the references in subsections (5A) to (7) to "the preceding provisions of this section" included subparagraphs (1) and (2) of this paragraph.][1]

Amendments—[1] Sch 9ZB inserted by the Taxation (Post-transition Period) Act 2020 s 3, Sch 2 para 2 with effect from IP completion day (11pm on 31 December 2020), by virtue of SI 2020/1642 reg 9.

[Removal of business assets to be treated as a supply of goods]

30—(1) A person carrying on a business makes a supply of goods where—
  (*a*) the goods form part of the assets of that business,
  (*b*) they are removed from Northern Ireland or a member State under the directions of that person, and
  (*c*) the removal is in the course or furtherance of that business for the purpose of being taken to a place in—
    (i) in the case of goods removed from Northern Ireland, a member State, or
    (ii) in the case of goods removed from a member State, to another member State or to Northern Ireland.
(2) Sub-paragraph (1) applies to the removal of goods, whether or not that removal of the goods is, or is connected with, a transaction for consideration.
(3) Sub-paragraph (1) does not apply—
  (*a*) to a case falling within paragraph 5(1) of Schedule 4 (matters to be treated as supply of goods or services),
  (*b*) to the removal of goods from Northern Ireland where that removal is in the course of their removal from one part of Northern Ireland to another part of Northern Ireland,
  (*c*) to the removal of goods from a member State where that removal is in the course of their removal from one part of a member State to another part of that member State,

(d) to goods which have been removed from a place outside the member States for entry into the territory of the European Union and are removed from a member State before the time when any Community customs debt in respect of any EU customs duty on their entry into that territory would be incurred,

(e) to goods which have been removed from a place outside the United Kingdom and the member States for entry into Northern Ireland and are removed from Northern Ireland before any duty under section 30A(3) of TCTA 2018 on their entry into Northern Ireland would be incurred, or

(f) to goods which have been removed from Great Britain to Northern Ireland and are removed from Northern Ireland before any duty under section 40A of TCTA 2018 on their entry into Northern Ireland would be incurred.

(4) Sub-paragraph (1) is subject to paragraph 58 of Schedule 9ZA (call-off stock arrangements).][1]

Cross-references—See Sch 9ZA para 58 (the removal of the goods from the origin territory is not to be treated by reason of this para as a supply of goods by the supplier).

Amendments—[1] Sch 9ZB inserted by the Taxation (Post-transition Period) Act 2020 s 3, Sch 2 para 2 with effect from IP completion day (11pm on 31 December 2020), by virtue of SI 2020/1642 reg 9.

[Application of section 43 (company groups) to goods in Northern Ireland

31—Subsection (1)(a) of Section 43 (disregard of supplies between members of groups) does not apply to a supply of goods if the goods are in Northern Ireland at the time they are supplied unless the supplier and the recipient each has a business establishment, or some other fixed establishment, in Northern Ireland.][1]

Amendments—[1] Sch 9ZB inserted by the Taxation (Post-transition Period) Act 2020 s 3, Sch 2 para 2 with effect from IP completion day (11pm on 31 December 2020), by virtue of SI 2020/1642 reg 9.

[Partially exempt supplies

31A—(1) A removal of goods from Great Britain to Northern Ireland to which this subparagraph applies is to be treated as a taxable supply of goods made in the course or furtherance of a business carried on by the person who removes the goods.

(2) Sub-paragraph (1) applies to a removal of goods if—

(a) the removal is not (ignoring sub-paragraph (1)) made in the course of a taxable supply,

(b) before the removal the goods were supplied to, or were imported by, the person who removed them ("P"),

(c) P is, at the time of that supply or importation and at the time of the removal, a taxable person,

(d) P has incurred VAT on that supply or importation,

(e) the removal takes place within 12 months of P becoming liable to that VAT

(f) some, or all, of the VAT incurred on the supply or importation has not been credited as input tax in relation to P because it has, before the removal, been attributed to—

(i) both taxable and exempt supplies, or

(ii) exempt supplies, and

(g) either—

(i) P has not used the goods before their removal, or

(ii) P meets the condition in sub-paragraph (3).

(3) That condition is that P uses the goods, after their removal, exclusively for the purpose of making—

(a) in a case falling within sub-paragraph (2)(f)(i), both taxable and exempt supplies, or

(b) in a case falling within sub-paragraph (2)(f)(ii), exempt supplies.

(4) A supply of goods which is treated as arising under sub-paragraph (1)is zero-rated.

(5) VAT incurred by P on the removal of the goods from Great Britain to Northern Ireland (see paragraph 3(4))is not to be treated as attributable (for the purposes of section 26) to the supply treated as arising under sub-paragraph (1).][1]

Amendments—[1] Para 31A inserted by the Value Added Tax (Miscellaneous Amendments to the Value Added Tax Act 1994 and Revocation) (EU Exit) Regulations, SI 2020/1544 regs 2, 6 with effect from IP completion day (11pm UK time on 31 December 2020) by virtue of SI 2020/1641 reg 2, Schedule para 13.

[PART 6
NORTHERN IRELAND AND THE ISLE OF MAN

Application of Part 2 of this Schedule

32—(1) Paragraph 3(1) (zero-rating of supply of goods removed from Great Britain to Northern Ireland and vice versa) applies to goods removed from Northern Ireland to the Isle of Man as they apply to goods removed from Northern Ireland to Great Britain.

(2) The following provisions apply to goods removed to Northern Ireland from the Isle of Man as they apply to goods removed from Great Britain to Northern Ireland—
   (a) sub-paragraphs (4) and (5) of paragraph 3 (charge on goods removed from Great Britain to Northern Ireland);
   (b) sub-paragraphs (6) and (7) of that paragraph (so far as they relate to sub-paragraph (4) or (5)).
(3) Paragraph 4 (liability for VAT on movements between Great Britain and Northern Ireland) applies to goods removed to Northern Ireland from the Isle of Man as they apply to goods removed from Great Britain to Northern Ireland as if the references to a "taxable person" included a person who is, or is required to be, registered under an Act of Tynwald for the purposes of any tax imposed by or under an Act of Tynwald which corresponds to VAT.
(4) Paragraph 7 (zero-rating of supplies made before declaration on removal) applies to goods removed to Northern Ireland from the Isle of Man as it applies to goods removed from Great Britain to Northern Ireland.][1]

Amendments—[1] Sch 9ZB inserted by the Taxation (Post-transition Period) Act 2020 s 3, Sch 2 para 2 with effect from IP completion day (11pm on 31 December 2020), by virtue of SI 2020/1642 reg 9.

[Modifications in relation to exports: goods removed to Isle of Man

33—(1) Subsection (8) of section 30 (power to zero-rate supplies where goods have been or are to be exported) has effect as if reference to the export of goods included the removal of goods from Northern Ireland to the Isle of Man.
(2) Where a supply of goods has been zero-rated as a result of paragraph 3(1) or regulations under section 30(8), on the basis that the goods have been or are to be removed from Northern Ireland to the Isle of Man, section 30(10) applies in relation to that supply as if any reference to the United Kingdom were to Northern Ireland.
(3) Section 37 (relief from VAT on importation of goods) has effect in relation to a removal of goods to Northern Ireland from the Isle of Man (which is treated as an importation as a result of paragraphs 3(5) and 32(2)) as if any reference to the export of goods included their removal from Northern Ireland to the Isle of Man.
(4) Group 15 of Schedule 8 (zero-rating) has effect as if—
   (a) any reference to the export of goods, other than the reference in item 3, included the removal of goods from Northern Ireland to the Isle of Man;
   (b) the modification made by paragraph 14(2)(c) applied to the removal of goods to the Isle of Man from Northern Ireland as it applies to the removal of goods from Northern Ireland to Great Britain.][1]

Amendments—[1] Sch 9ZB inserted by the Taxation (Post-transition Period) Act 2020 s 3, Sch 2 para 2 with effect from IP completion day (11pm on 31 December 2020), by virtue of SI 2020/1642 reg 9.

[Warehouses

34—Part 4 (warehouses) has effect as if any reference to Great Britain included the Isle of Man (see also article 2 of the Value Added Tax (Isle of Man) Order 1982 which provides that this Act has effect as if the Isle of Man were part of the United Kingdom subject to the provisions of that Order).][1]

Amendments—[1] Sch 9ZB inserted by the Taxation (Post-transition Period) Act 2020 s 3, Sch 2 para 2 with effect from IP completion day (11pm on 31 December 2020), by virtue of SI 2020/1642 reg 9.

[Extent

35—Nothing in this Part of this Schedule is to be taken as extending to the Isle of Man.][1]

Amendments—[1] Sch 9ZB inserted by the Taxation (Post-transition Period) Act 2020 s 3, Sch 2 para 2 with effect from IP completion day (11pm on 31 December 2020), by virtue of SI 2020/1642 reg 9.

[SCHEDULE 9ZC

ONLINE SALES BY OVERSEAS PERSONS AND LOW VALUE IMPORTATIONS: MODIFICATIONS RELATING TO THE NORTHERN IRELAND PROTOCOL

Section 40A(3)

PART 1
MODIFICATION OF THIS ACT

1—References in the following provisions of this Act to goods being imported do not include goods imported into the United Kingdom as a result of their entry into Northern Ireland or goods treated as having been imported into the United Kingdom as a result of their being removed from Northern Ireland to Great Britain—
   (a) section 5A(3) (the imported consignment condition);
   (b) section 7(5B)(b) (place of supply of goods);

(c) section 7AA(1)(c) (reverse charge on goods supplied from abroad).][1]

Amendments—[1] Sch 9ZC inserted by the Taxation (Post-transition Period) Act 2020 s 7, Sch 3 paras 25, 28 with effect from IP completion day (11pm on 31 December 2020), by virtue of SI 2020/1642 reg 9.

[1A—Section 5A has effect as if in subsection (1)(c)(ii) after "outside the United Kingdom" there were inserted "and prior to the supply the goods were located in Great Britain".][1]

Amendments—[1] Para 1A inserted by the Taxation (Post-transition Period) Act 2020 s 7, Sch 3 paras 25, 29(1), (2) with effect from IP completion day (11pm on 31 December 2020), by virtue of SI 2020/1642 reg 9.

[2—Section 77F (exception from liability under section 5A) has effect as if—
(a) in the heading, after "section 5A" there were inserted "or Part 1 of Schedule 9ZC";
(b) in subsection (1), after "section 5A" there were inserted "or Part 1 of Schedule 9ZC";
(c) in subsection (2), after "(as defined in section 5A" there were inserted "or Part 1 of Schedule 9ZC, as the case may be".][1]

Amendments—[1] Sch 9ZC inserted by the Taxation (Post-transition Period) Act 2020 s 7, Sch 3 paras 25, 28 with effect from IP completion day (11pm on 31 December 2020), by virtue of SI 2020/1642 reg 9.

[3—(1) In Schedule 11, paragraph 6 has effect subject to the following modifications.
(2) Sub-paragraph (4C) has effect as if—
(a) the "or" at the end of paragraph (a) were omitted;
(b) after paragraph (b) there were inserted ", or
(c) Part 1 of Schedule 9ZC makes provision about who is treated as having imported those goods."
(3) Sub-paragraph (4D) has effect as if—
(a) the "or" at the end of paragraph (b) were omitted;
(b) after paragraph (c) there were inserted ", or
(d) is treated as having imported goods under Part 1 of Schedule 9ZC."][1]

Amendments—[1] Sch 9ZC inserted by the Taxation (Post-transition Period) Act 2020 s 7, Sch 3 paras 25, 28 with effect from IP completion day (11pm on 31 December 2020), by virtue of SI 2020/1642 reg 9.

[4—(1) Sub-paragraph (2) applies, instead of section 15(4) and (5) (as modified by paragraph 1 of Schedule 9ZB), where—
(a) goods are imported into the United Kingdom as a result of their entry into Northern Ireland in the course or furtherance of a business by a person ("P"),
(b) that importation is in the course of a taxable supply to a person ("R") who—
(i) is not registered under this Act, or
(ii) is registered under this Act but who has not provided P or, where the supply is facilitated by an online marketplace, the operator of that marketplace, with R's VAT registration number,
(c) the intrinsic value of the consignment of which the goods are part is not more than £135, and
(d) the consignment of which the goods are part—
(i) does not contain excepted goods, and
(ii) is not a consignment in relation to which a postal operator established outside the United Kingdom has an obligation under an agreement with the Commissioners to pay any import VAT that is chargeable on the importation of that consignment into the United Kingdom.
(2) The person who is treated as having imported the goods is—
(a) in a case where the supply is facilitated by an online marketplace, the operator of the online marketplace, or
(b) in any other case, P.
(3) In sub-paragraph (1)(b)(ii), "VAT registration number" means the number allocated by the Commissioners to a person registered under this Act.
(4) For the purposes of sub-paragraph (1)(d)(i), "excepted goods" means goods of a class or description subject to any duty of excise whether or not those goods are in fact chargeable with that duty, and whether or not that duty has been paid on the goods.
(5) The Commissioners may by regulations substitute a different figure for a figure that is at any time specified in sub-paragraph (1)(c).][1]

Cross-references—See SI 2020/1546 regs 33, 34 (accounting for import VAT on low value importations).

Amendments—[1] Sch 9ZC inserted by the Taxation (Post-transition Period) Act 2020 s 7, Sch 3 paras 25, 28 with effect from IP completion day (11pm on 31 December 2020), by virtue of SI 2020/1642 reg 9.

[4A—(1) Sub-paragraph (2) applies, instead of paragraph 4(3) and (4) of Schedule 9ZB, in relation to a removal of goods from Northern Ireland to Great Britain or, as the case may be, vice versa where—
(a) the removal is in the course of a supply by a person established outside of the United Kingdom ("P"), and

(b) the supply is facilitated by an online marketplace.
(2) The operator of the online marketplace is the person who is treated as having imported the goods.
(3) But sub-paragraph (2) does not apply where the person to whom the goods are supplied ("R")—
   (a) is registered under this Act,
   (b) has provided the operator of the online marketplace with R's VAT registration number, and
   (c) the operator of the online marketplace has provided P with that number and details of the supply before the end of the relevant period.
(4) In sub-paragraph (3)—
   "relevant period" means the period of 7 days beginning with the day on which the supply is treated as taking place under section 6 or such longer period as the Commissioners may allow in general or specific directions;
   "VAT registration number" means the number allocated by the Commissioners to a person registered under this Act.
(5) The Commissioners may by regulations specify the details that must be provided for the purposes of sub-paragraph (3)(c).]

Cross-references—See the Value Added Tax (Northern Ireland) (EU Exit) Regulations, SI 2020/1546 reg 15 (VAT on removals to be payable by a taxable person as if it were VAT on a supply).
Amendments—[1] Para 4A inserted by the Taxation (Post-transition Period) Act 2020 s 7, Sch 3 paras 25, 29(1), (3) with effect from IP completion day (11pm on 31 December 2020), by virtue of SI 2020/1642 reg 9.

[PART 2
MODIFICATION OF THE VALUE ADDED TAX (IMPORTED GOODS) RELIEF ORDER 1984

5—(1) In Schedule 2 to the Value Added Tax (Imported Goods) Relief Order 1984 (S.I. 1984/746) (reliefs for goods of certain descriptions), Group 8 (articles sent for miscellaneous purposes) has effect subject to the following modifications.
(2) That Group has effect as if after item 7 there were inserted—
   "8   Any consignment of goods imported into the United Kingdom as a result of their entry into Northern Ireland (other than alcoholic beverages, tobacco products, perfumes or toilet waters) not exceeding £15 in value."
(3) That Group has effect as if after note (1) there were inserted—
   "(2)   Item 8 does not apply in relation to any goods imported on mail order.
   (3)   For the purposes of note (2)—
   "mail order" in relation to any goods means any transaction or series of transactions under which a seller (S) sends goods in fulfilment of an order placed remotely,
   "remotely" means by any means that do not involve the simultaneous physical presence of S and the person placing the order, and
   "seller" does not include any person acting otherwise than in a commercial or professional capacity."][1]

Amendments—[1] Sch 9ZC inserted by the Taxation (Post-transition Period) Act 2020 s 7, Sch 3 paras 25, 28 with effect from IP completion day (11pm on 31 December 2020), by virtue of SI 2020/1642 reg 9.

[PART 3
REGISTRATION

Liability to be registered

6—(1) A person who is treated as having imported goods under Part 1 of this Schedule and—
   (a) is not registered under this Act, and
   (b) is not liable to be registered under Schedule 1, 1A or 9ZA to this Act,
becomes liable to be registered under this Schedule at the point they are so treated.
(2) A person who is not registered or liable to be registered as mentioned in sub-paragraph (1)(a) and (b) becomes liable to be registered under this Schedule at any time if there are reasonable grounds for believing that the person will be treated as having imported goods under Part 1 of this Schedule in the following 30 days.
(3) A person is treated as having become liable to be registered under this Schedule at any time when the person would have become so liable under the preceding provisions of this paragraph but for any registration which is subsequently cancelled under paragraph 11(2) of this Schedule, paragraph 13(3) of Schedule 1, paragraph 11 of Schedule 1A, paragraph 6(2) of Schedule 3A or paragraph 43 or 53 of Schedule 9ZA.
(4) A person does not cease to be liable to be registered under this Schedule except in accordance with paragraph 7.][1]

Amendments—[1] Sch 9ZC inserted by the Taxation (Post-transition Period) Act 2020 s 7, Sch 3 paras 25, 28 with effect from IP completion day (11pm on 31 December 2020), by virtue of SI 2020/1642 reg 9.

[7—(1) A person who has become liable to be registered under this Schedule ceases to be so liable at any time if the Commissioners are satisfied that the person is no longer a person who is, or will be, treated as having imported goods under Part 1 of this Schedule.
(2) But a person does not cease to be liable to be registered under this Schedule at any time if there are reasonable grounds for believing that the person will be treated as having imported goods under Part 1 of this Schedule in the following 30 days.][1]

Amendments—[1] Sch 9ZC inserted by the Taxation (Post-transition Period) Act 2020 s 7, Sch 3 paras 25, 28 with effect from IP completion day (11pm on 31 December 2020), by virtue of SI 2020/1642 reg 9.

[Notification of liability and registration

8—(1) A person who becomes liable to be registered under this Schedule must notify the Commissioners of the liability—
   (*a*) in the case of a liability under sub-paragraph (1) of paragraph 6, within 30 days of the person becoming so liable, and
   (*b*) in the case of a liability under sub-paragraph (2) of that paragraph, before the end of the period by reference to which the liability arises.
(2) The Commissioners must register any such person (whether or not the person notifies them) with effect from the relevant time.
(3) In this paragraph "the relevant time"—
   (*a*) in a case falling within sub-paragraph (1)(*a*), means the beginning of the day on which the liability arose, and
   (*b*) in a case falling within sub-paragraph (1)(*b*), means the beginning of the period by reference to which the liability arose.][1]

Amendments—[1] Sch 9ZC inserted by the Taxation (Post-transition Period) Act 2020 s 7, Sch 3 paras 25, 28 with effect from IP completion day (11pm on 31 December 2020), by virtue of SI 2020/1642 reg 9.

[Entitlement to be registered etc

9—(1) Where a person who is not liable to be registered under this Act and is not already so registered—
   (*a*) satisfies the Commissioners that the person intends to make or facilitate a relevant supply from a specified date, and
   (*b*) requests to be registered under this Schedule,
the Commissioners may, subject to such conditions as they think fit to impose, register the person with effect from such date as may be agreed between the Commissioners and the person.
(2) Conditions imposed under sub-paragraph (1) may—
   (*a*) be so imposed wholly or partly by reference to, or without reference to, any conditions prescribed for the purposes of this paragraph, and
   (*b*) be subsequently varied by the Commissioners (whenever the conditions were imposed).
(3) Where a person who is entitled to be registered under paragraph 9 or 10 of Schedule 1 requests registration under this paragraph, the person is to be registered under that Schedule, and not under this Schedule.][1]

Amendments—[1] Sch 9ZC inserted by the Taxation (Post-transition Period) Act 2020 s 7, Sch 3 paras 25, 28 with effect from IP completion day (11pm on 31 December 2020), by virtue of SI 2020/1642 reg 9.

[Notification of matters affecting continuance of registration

10—(1) Any person registered under this Schedule who ceases to be registrable under this Act must notify the Commissioners of that fact within 30 days of the day on which the person ceases to be registrable.
(2) A person registered under paragraph 9(1) must notify the Commissioners, within 30 days of the first occasion after the person's registration when the person makes or facilitates a relevant supply, that the person has made or facilitated that supply.
(3) For the purposes of this paragraph a person ceases to be registrable under this Act where—
   (*a*) the person ceases to be a person who would be liable or entitled to be registered under this Act if the person's registration and any enactment preventing a person from being liable to be registered under different provisions at the same time were disregarded, or
   (*b*) in the case of a person who (having been registered under paragraph 9(1)) has not been such a person during the period of the person's registration, the person ceases to have any intention of making or facilitating relevant supplies.][1]

Amendments—[1] Sch 9ZC inserted by the Taxation (Post-transition Period) Act 2020 s 7, Sch 3 paras 25, 28 with effect from IP completion day (11pm on 31 December 2020), by virtue of SI 2020/1642 reg 9.

[Cancellation of registration]

11—(1) Where a person registered under this Schedule satisfies the Commissioners that the person is not liable to be so registered, the Commissioners must, if the person so requests, cancel that registration with effect from the day on which the request is made or from such later date as may be agreed between the Commissioners and the person.
(2) Where the Commissioners are satisfied that a person registered under this Schedule has ceased since the person's registration to be registrable under this Schedule, they may cancel that registration with effect from the day on which the person so ceased or from such later date as may be agreed between the Commissioners and the person.
(3) Where the Commissioners are satisfied that a person who has been registered under paragraph 9(1) and is not for the time being liable to be registered under this Schedule—
   (*a*) has not begun, by the date specified in the person's request to be registered, to make or facilitate relevant supplies, or
   (*b*) has contravened any condition of the person's registration,
the Commissioners may cancel the person's registration with effect from the date so specified or, as the case may be, the date of the contravention or from such later date as may be agreed between the Commissioners and the person.
(4) But the Commissioners may not, under sub-paragraph (1), (2) or (3), cancel a person's registration with effect from any time unless the Commissioners are satisfied that it is not a time when that person would be subject to a requirement, or in a case falling under sub-paragraph (2) or (3) a requirement or entitlement, to be registered under this Act.
(5) Where the Commissioners are satisfied that, on the day on which a person was registered under this Schedule, the person—
   (*a*) was not registrable under this Schedule, and
   (*b*) in the case of a person registered under paragraph 9(1), did not have the intention by reference to which the person was registered,
the Commissioners may cancel that registration with effect from that day.
(6) In determining, for the purposes of sub-paragraph (4), whether a person would be subject to a requirement, or would be entitled, to be registered at any time, so much of any provision of this Act as prevents a person from becoming liable or entitled to be registered when the person is already registered or when the person is so liable under any other provision is to be disregarded.
(7) For the purposes of this paragraph, a person is registrable under this Schedule at any time when the person is liable to be registered under this Schedule or is a person who makes or facilitates relevant supplies.][1]

Amendments—[1] Sch 9ZC inserted by the Taxation (Post-transition Period) Act 2020 s 7, Sch 3 paras 25, 28 with effect from IP completion day (11pm on 31 December 2020), by virtue of SI 2020/1642 reg 9.

[Notifications

12—Any notification required under this Part of this Schedule must be made in such form and manner and must contain such particulars as may be specified in regulations or by the Commissioners in accordance with regulations.][1]

Amendments—[1] Sch 9ZC inserted by the Taxation (Post-transition Period) Act 2020 s 7, Sch 3 paras 25, 28 with effect from IP completion day (11pm on 31 December 2020), by virtue of SI 2020/1642 reg 9.

[Meaning of relevant supply

13—For the purposes of this Part of this Schedule a supply is a "relevant supply" if the person making or facilitating it would be treated as having imported goods under Part 1 of this Schedule.][1]

Amendments—[1] Sch 9ZC inserted by the Taxation (Post-transition Period) Act 2020 s 7, Sch 3 paras 25, 28 with effect from IP completion day (11pm on 31 December 2020), by virtue of SI 2020/1642 reg 9.

[Modification of the Finance Act 2008

14—Paragraph 1 of Schedule 41 to the Finance Act 2008 (penalties: failure to notify etc) has effect as if in the table there were inserted the following entry—

"Value added tax	Obligation under paragraph 8 of Schedule 9ZC to VATA 1994 (obligations to notify liability to register and notify matters affecting continuance of registration)."][1]

Amendments—[1] Sch 9ZC inserted by the Taxation (Post-transition Period) Act 2020 s 7, Sch 3 paras 25, 28 with effect from IP completion day (11pm on 31 December 2020), by virtue of SI 2020/1642 reg 9.

[SCHEDULE 9A

ANTI-AVOIDANCE PROVISIONS: GROUPS]

Section 43(9)

Commentary—*De Voil Indirect Tax Service* **V2.190B**.
Amendments—This Schedule inserted by FA 1996 s 31(2), Sch 4.

Power to give directions

[1—(1) Subject to paragraph 2 below, the Commissioners may give a direction under this Schedule if, in any case—
- (*a*) a relevant event has occurred;
- (*b*) the condition specified in sub-paragraph (3) below is fulfilled;
- (*c*) that condition would not be fulfilled apart from the occurrence of that event; and
- (*d*) in the case of an event falling within sub-paragraph (2)(*b*) below, the transaction in question is not a supply which is the only supply by reference to which the case falls within paragraphs (*a*) to (*c*) above.

(2) For the purposes of this Schedule, a relevant event occurs when a [person]² —
- (*a*) begins to be, or ceases to be, treated as a member of a group; or
- (*b*) enters into any transaction.

(3) The condition mentioned in sub-paragraph (1) above is that—
- (*a*) there has been, or will or may be, a taxable supply on which VAT has been, or will or may be, charged otherwise than by reference to the supply's full value;
- (*b*) there is at least a part of the supply which is not or, as the case may be, would not be zero-rated; and
- (*c*) the charging of VAT on the supply otherwise than by reference to its full value gives rise or, as the case may be, would give rise to a tax advantage.

(4) For the purposes of this paragraph the charging of VAT on a supply ("the undercharged supply") otherwise than by reference to its full value shall be taken to give rise to a tax advantage if, and only if, a person has become entitled—
- (*a*) to credit for input tax allowable as attributable to that supply or any part of it, or
- (*b*) in accordance with regulations under section 39, to any repayment in respect of that supply or any part of it.

(5) The case where a person shall be taken for the purposes of sub-paragraph (4) above to have become entitled to a credit for input tax allowable as attributable to the undercharged supply, or to a part of it, shall include any case where—
- (*a*) a person has become entitled to a credit for any input tax on the supply to him, or the . . . ³ importation by him, of any goods or services; and
- (*b*) whatever the supplies to which the credit was treated as attributable when the entitlement to it arose, those goods or services are used by him in making the undercharged supply, or a part of it.

(6) For the purposes of sub-paragraphs (4) and (5) above where—
- (*a*) there is a supply of any of the assets of a business of a person ("the transferor") to a person to whom the whole or any part of that business is transferred as a going concern ("the transferee"), and
- (*b*) that supply is treated, in accordance with an order under section 5(3), as being neither a supply of goods nor a supply of services,

the question, so far as it falls to be determined by reference to those assets, whether a credit for input tax to which any person has become entitled is one allowable as attributable to the whole or any part of a supply shall be determined as if the transferor and the transferee were the same person.

(7) Where, in a case to which sub-paragraph (6) above applies, the transferor himself acquired any of the assets in question by way of a supply falling within paragraphs (*a*) and (*b*) of that sub-paragraph, that sub-paragraph shall have the effect, as respects the assets so acquired, of requiring the person from whom those assets were acquired to be treated for the purposes of sub-paragraphs (4) and (5) above as the same person as the transferor and the transferee, and so on in the case of any number of successive supplies falling within those paragraphs.

(8) For the purposes of this paragraph any question—
- (*a*) whether any credit for input tax to which a person has become entitled was, or is to be taken to have been, a credit allowable as attributable to the whole or any part of a supply, or
- (*b*) whether any repayment is a repayment in respect of the whole or any part of a supply,

shall be determined, in relation to a supply of a right to goods or services or to a supply of goods or services by virtue of such a right, as if the supply of the right and supplies made by virtue of the right were a single supply of which the supply of the right and each of those supplies constituted different parts.

(9) References in this paragraph to the full value of a supply are references to the amount which (having regard to any direction under paragraph 1 of Schedule 6) would be the full value of that supply for the purposes of the charge to VAT if that supply were not a supply falling to be disregarded, to any extent, in pursuance of section 43(1)(a).
(10) References in this paragraph to the supply of a right to goods or services include references to the supply of any right, option or priority with respect to the supply of goods or services, and to the supply of an interest deriving from any right to goods or services.][1]

Northern Ireland—See Sch 9ZA para 72(1) (Northern Ireland: sub-para (5) has effect as if, in para (a), after "importation" there were inserted "or acquisition").
Amendments—[1] This Schedule inserted by FA 1996 s 31(2), Sch 4.
[2] In sub-para (2), words substituted for words "body corporate" by FA 2019 s 53, Sch 18 paras 3, 14(1), (2) with effect from 1 November 2019 (see SI 2019/1348).
[3] In para (a), words "acquisition or" repealed by the Taxation (Cross-border Trade) Act 2018 s 43, Sch 8 paras 1, 96(1), (2) with effect from IP completion day (11pm on 31 December 2020), by virtue of SI 2020/1642 reg 4(b).

Restrictions on giving directions

[2—[(1)] [2] The Commissioners shall not give a direction under this Schedule by reference to a relevant event if they are satisfied that—
  (a) the change in the treatment of the [person][3], or
  (b) the transaction in question,
had as its main purpose or, as the case may be, as each of its main purposes a genuine commercial purpose unconnected with the fulfilment of the condition specified in paragraph 1(3) above.][1]
[(2) This paragraph shall not apply where the relevant event is the termination of a [person's][3] treatment as a member of a group by a notice under section 43C(1) or (3).][2]

Amendments—[1] This Schedule inserted by FA 1996 s 31(2), Sch 4.
[2] Para 2 amended to renumber existing text as sub-para (1), and sub-para (2) inserted by FA 1999 s 16, Sch 2 para 5 with effect from 27 July 1999 subject to FA 1999 Sch 2 para 6.
[3] In sub-para (1)(a), words substituted for words "body corporate", and in sub-para (2), words substituted for words "body corporate's", by FA 2019 s 53, Sch 18 paras 3, 14(1), (3) with effect from 1 November 2019 (see SI 2019/1348).

Form of directions under Schedule

[3—(1) The directions that may be given by the Commissioners under this Schedule are either—
  (a) a direction relating to any supply of goods or services that has been made, in whole or in part, by one [person][3] to another; or
  (b) a direction relating to a particular [person][3].
(2) A direction under this Schedule relating to a supply shall require it to be assumed (where it would not otherwise be the case) that, to the extent described in the direction, the supply was not a supply falling to be disregarded in pursuance of section 43(1)(a).
(3) A direction under this Schedule relating to a [person][3] shall require it to be assumed (where it would not otherwise be the case) that, for such period (comprising times before the giving of the direction or times afterwards or both) as may be described in the direction, the [person][3]—
  (a) did not fall to be treated, or is not to be treated, as a member of a group, or of a particular group so described; or
  (b) fell to be treated, or is to be treated, as a member of any group so described of which, for that period, it was or is eligible to be a member.
(4) Where a direction under this Schedule requires any assumptions to be made, then—
  (a) so far as the assumptions relate to times on or after the day on which the direction is given, this Act shall have effect in relation to such times in accordance with those assumptions; and
  (b) paragraph 6 below shall apply for giving effect to those assumptions in so far as they relate to earlier times.
(5) A direction falling within sub-paragraph (3)(b) above may identify in relation to any times or period the [person who][3] is to be assumed to have been, or to be, the representative member of the group at those times or for that period.
(6) A direction under this Schedule may vary the effect of a previous direction under this Schedule.
(7) The Commissioners may at any time, by notice in writing to the person to whom it was given, withdraw a direction under this Schedule.
(8) The refusal or non-refusal by the Commissioners of an application [such as is mentioned in section 43B][2] shall not prejudice the power of the Commissioners to give a direction under this Schedule requiring any case to be assumed to be what it would have been had the application not been refused or, as the case may be, had it been refused.][1]

Amendments—[1] This Schedule inserted by FA 1996 s 31(2), Sch 4.
[2] Words in sub-para (8) substituted by FA 1999 s 16, Sch 2 para 5 with effect from 27 July 1999 subject to FA 1999 Sch 2 para 6.

³ In sub-paras (1)(*a*), (*b*), and (3) words substituted for words "body corporate", and in sub-para (5), words substituted for words "body corporate which", by FA 2019 s 53, Sch 18 paras 3, 14(1), (4) with effect from 1 November 2019 (see SI 2019/1348).

Time limit on directions

[**4**—(1) A direction under this Schedule shall not be given more than six years after whichever is the later of—
  (*a*) the occurrence of the relevant event by reference to which it is given; and
  (*b*) the time when the relevant entitlement arose.
(2) A direction under this Schedule shall not be given by reference to a relevant event occurring on or before 28th November 1995.
(3) Subject to sub-paragraphs (1) and (2) above, a direction under this Schedule—
  (*a*) may be given by reference to a relevant event occurring before the coming into force of this Schedule; and
  (*b*) may require assumptions to be made in relation to times (including times before 29th November 1995) falling before the occurrence of the relevant event by reference to which the direction is given, or before the relevant entitlement arose.
(4) For the purposes of this paragraph the reference, in relation to the giving of a direction, to the relevant entitlement is a reference to the entitlement by reference to which the requirements of paragraph 1(4) above are taken to be satisfied for the purposes of that direction.]¹
Amendments—¹ This Schedule inserted by FA 1996 s 31(2), Sch 4.

Manner of giving directions

[**5**—(1) A direction under this Schedule relating to a supply may be given to—
  (*a*) the person who made the supply to which the direction relates; or
  (*b*) any [person who]² which, at the time when the direction is given, is the representative member of a group of which [the person mentioned in paragraph (a)]² was treated as being a member at the time of the supply.
(2) A direction under this Schedule relating to a [person ("the relevant person")]² may be given to [that person or to any person who]² at the time when the direction is given is, or in pursuance of the direction is to be treated as, the representative member of a group of which [the relevant person]²—
  (*a*) is treated as being a member;
  (*b*) was treated as being a member at a time to which the direction relates; or
  (*c*) is to be treated as being, or having been, a member at any such time.
(3) A direction given to any person under this Schedule shall be given to him by notice in writing.
(4) A direction under this Schedule must specify the relevant event by reference to which it is given.]¹
Amendments—¹ This Schedule inserted by FA 1996 s 31(2), Sch 4.
² In sub-para (1)(*b*), words substituted for words "body corporate which", and words substituted for words "that person"; in sub-para (2) words substituted for words "body corporate ("the relevant body")", words substituted for words "that body or to any body corporate which", and words substituted for words "the relevant body", by FA 2019 s 53, Sch 18 paras 3, 14(1), (5) with effect from 1 November 2019 (see SI 2019/1348).

Assessment in consequence of a direction

[**6**—(1) Subject to sub-paragraph (3) below, where—
  (*a*) a direction is given under this Schedule, and
  (*b*) there is an amount of VAT ("the unpaid tax") for which a relevant person would have been liable before the giving of the direction if the facts had accorded with the assumptions specified in the direction,
the Commissioners may, to the best of their judgment, assess the amount of unpaid tax as tax due from the person to whom the direction was given or another relevant person and notify their assessment to that person.
(2) In sub-paragraph (1) above the reference to an amount of VAT for which a person would, on particular assumptions, have been liable before the giving of a direction under this Schedule is a reference to the aggregate of the following—
  (*a*) any amount of output tax which, on those assumptions but not otherwise, would have been due from a relevant person at the end of a prescribed accounting period ending before the giving of the direction;
  (*b*) the amount of any credit for input tax to which a relevant person is treated as having been entitled at the end of such an accounting period but to which he would not have been entitled on those assumptions; and
  (*c*) the amount of any repayment of tax made to a relevant person in accordance with regulations under section 39 but to which he would not have been entitled on those assumptions.

(3) Where any assessment falls to be made under this paragraph in a case in which the Commissioners are satisfied that the actual revenue loss is less than the unpaid tax, the total amount to be assessed under this paragraph shall not exceed what appears to them, to the best of their judgement, to be the amount of that loss.

(4) For the purposes of the making of an assessment under this paragraph in relation to any direction, the actual revenue loss shall be taken to be equal to the amount of the unpaid tax less the amount given by aggregating the amounts of every entitlement—

(a) to credit for input tax, or

(b) to a repayment in accordance with regulations under section 39,

which (whether as an entitlement of the person in relation to whom the assessment is made or as an entitlement of any other person) would have arisen on the assumptions contained in the direction, but not otherwise.

(5) An assessment under this paragraph relating to a direction may be notified to the person to whom that direction is given by being incorporated in the same notice as that direction.

(6) An assessment under this paragraph shall not be made—

(a) more than one year after the day on which the direction to which it relates was given, or

(b) in the case of any direction that has been withdrawn.

(7) Where an amount has been assessed on any person under this paragraph and notified to him—

(a) that amount shall be deemed (subject to the provisions of this Act as to appeals) to be an amount of VAT due from him;

(b) that amount may be recovered accordingly, either from that person or, in the case of a [person who]² is for the time being treated as a member of a group, from the representative member of that group; and

(c) to the extent that more than one person is liable by virtue of any assessment under this paragraph in respect of the same amount of unpaid tax, those persons shall be treated as jointly and severally liable for that amount.

(8) Sub-paragraph (7) above does not have effect if or to the extent that the assessment in question has been withdrawn or reduced.

(9) Sections 74 and 77(6) apply in relation to assessments under this paragraph as they apply in relation to assessments under section 73 but as if the reference in subsection (1) of section 74 to the reckonable date were a reference to the date on which the assessment is notified.

(10) Where by virtue of sub-paragraph (9) above any person is liable to interest under section 74—

(a) section 76 shall have effect in relation to that liability with the omission of subsections (2) to [(5)]³; and

(b) section 77, except subsection (6), shall not apply to an assessment of the amount due by way of interest;

and (without prejudice to the power to make assessments for interest for later periods) the interest to which any assessment made under section 76 by virtue of paragraph (a) above may relate shall be confined to interest for a period of no more than two years ending with the time when the assessment to interest is made.

(11) In this paragraph "a relevant person", in relation to a direction, means—

(a) the person to whom the direction is given;

(b) the [person who]² was the representative member of any group of which [the person mentioned in paragraph (a)]² was treated as being, or in pursuance of the direction is to be treated as having been, a member at a time to which the assumption specified in the direction relates; or

(c) any [person who]², in pursuance of the direction, is to be treated as having been the representative member of such a group.]¹

Amendments—¹   This Schedule inserted by FA 1996 s 31(2), Sch 4.

²   In sub-para (7)(b), words substituted for words "body corporate that", in sub-para (11)(b), words substituted for words "body corporate which", and words substituted for words "that person", and in sub-para (11)(c), words substituted for words "body corporate which", by FA 2019 s 53, Sch 18 paras 3, 14(1), (6) with effect from 1 November 2019 (see SI 2019/1348).

³   In para (10)(a), "5" substituted for "6" by the Taxation (Cross-border Trade) Act 2018 s 43, Sch 8 paras 1, 96(1), (3) with effect from IP completion day (11pm on 31 December 2020), by virtue of SI 2020/1642 reg 4(b).

Interpretation of Schedule etc

[**7**—(1) References in this Schedule to being treated as a member of a group and to being eligible to be treated as a member of a group shall be construed in accordance with [sections 43 to 43C]².

(2) For the purposes of this Schedule the giving of any notice or notification to any receiver, liquidator or person otherwise acting in a representative capacity in relation to another shall be treated as the giving of a notice or, as the case may be, notification to the person in relation to whom he so acts.]¹

¹   This Schedule inserted by FA 1996 s 31(2), Sch 4.

[2] Words in sub-para (1) substituted by FA 1999 s 16, Sch 2 para 5 with effect from 27 July 1999 subject to FA 1999 Sch 2 para 6.

[SCHEDULE 10
BUILDINGS AND LAND
Section 51]

Commentary—De Voil Indirect Tax Service **V4.116**.
Amendment—Schedule 10 substituted by the Value Added Tax (Buildings and Land) Order, SI 2008/1146, art 2 with effect in relation to supplies made on or after 1 June 2008, subject to savings in Sch 2 of the Order.

[PART 1
THE OPTION TO TAX LAND

INTRODUCTION

Overview of the option to tax

1—(1) This Part of the Schedule makes provision for a person to opt to tax any land.
(2) The effect of the option to tax is dealt with in paragraph 2 (exempt supplies become taxable), as read with paragraph 3.
(3) Grants are excluded from the effect of paragraph 2 by—
  (a) paragraph 5 (dwellings designed or adapted, and intended for use, as dwelling etc),
  (b) paragraph 6 (conversion of buildings for use as dwelling etc),
  (c) paragraph 7 (charities),
  (d) paragraph 8 (residential caravans),
  (e) paragraph 9 (residential houseboats),
  (f) paragraph 10 (relevant housing associations), and
  (g) paragraph 11 (grant to individual for construction of dwelling).
(4) Paragraphs 12 to 17 (anti-avoidance: developers of land etc) provide for certain supplies to which any grant gives rise to be excluded from the effect of paragraph 2.
(5) Paragraphs 18 to 30 deal with—
  (a) the scope of the option to tax,
  (b) the day from which the option to tax has effect,
  (c) notification requirements,
  (d) elections to opt to tax land subsequently acquired,
  (e) the revocation of the option,
  (f) the effect of the option to tax in relation to new buildings, and
  (g) requirements for prior permission in the case of exempt grants made before the exercise of an option to tax.
(6) Paragraphs 31 to 34 deal with definitions which apply for the purposes of this Part, as well as other supplemental matters.][1]

Commentary—De Voil Indirect Tax Service **V3.248, V4.113**.
Amendments—[1] Schedule 10 substituted by the Value Added Tax (Buildings and Land) Order, SI 2008/1146, art 2 with effect in relation to supplies made on or after 1 June 2008, subject to savings in Sch 2 of the Order.

[THE OPTION TO TAX

Effect of the option to tax: exempt supplies become taxable

2—(1) This paragraph applies if—
  (a) a person exercises the option to tax any land under this Part of this Schedule, and
  (b) a grant is made in relation to the land at any time when the option to tax it has effect.
(2) If the grant is made—
  (a) by the person exercising that option, or
  (b) by a relevant associate (if that person is a body corporate),
the grant does not fall within Group 1 of Schedule 9 (exemptions for land).
(3) For the meaning of "relevant associate", see paragraph 3.][1]

Commentary—De Voil Indirect Tax Service **V4.115**.
Amendments—[1] Schedule 10 substituted by the Value Added Tax (Buildings and Land) Order, SI 2008/1146, art 2 with effect in relation to supplies made on or after 1 June 2008, subject to savings in Sch 2 of the Order.

[Meaning of "relevant associate"

3—(1) This paragraph explains for the purposes of this Part of this Schedule what is meant by a "relevant associate" in a case where a [person][3] ("the opter") exercises an option to tax in relation to any building or land.

(2) A [person]³ is a relevant associate of the opter if under sections 43A to 43D (groups of companies) the [person]³—
  (a) was treated as a member of the same group as the opter at the time when the option first had effect,
  (b) has been so treated at any later time when the opter had a relevant interest in the building or land, or
  (c) has been treated as a member of the same group as a [person]³ within paragraph (a) or (b) or this paragraph at a time when [that person]³ had a relevant interest in the building or land.
(3) But a body corporate ceases to be a relevant associate of the opter in relation to the building or land in the following circumstances.
(4) [P]³ ceases to be a relevant associate of the opter in relation to the building or land at the time when all of the following conditions are first met—
  (a) [P]³ has no relevant interest in the building or land [,
  (aa) where [P]³ has disposed of such an interest, it is not the case that a supply for the purposes of the charge to VAT in respect of the disposal—
    (i) is yet to take place, or
    (ii) would be yet to take place if one or more conditions (such as the happening of an event or the doing of an act) were to be met,]²
  (b) [P]³ or the opter is not treated under sections 43A to 43D as a member of the group mentioned above, and
  (c) [P]³ is not connected with any person who has a relevant interest in the building or land where that person is the opter or another relevant associate of the opter.
(5) [P]³ also ceases to be a relevant associate of the opter in relation to the building or land if [P]³—
  (a) meets conditions specified in a public notice (see paragraph 4), or
  (b) gets the prior permission of the Commissioners (also, see that paragraph).
The time when [P]³ ceases to be a relevant associate of the opter is determined in accordance with that paragraph.
(6) In this paragraph "relevant interest in the building or land" means an interest in, right over or licence to occupy the building or land (or any part of it).]¹

Commentary—*De Voil Indirect Tax Service* **V4.115**.
Amendments—¹ Schedule 10 substituted by the Value Added Tax (Buildings and Land) Order, SI 2008/1146, art 2 with effect in relation to supplies made on or after 1 June 2008, subject to savings in Sch 2 of the Order.
² In sub-para (4), words substituted for words "and no part of any consideration payable in respect of any disposal by the body corporate of such a interest is unpaid,", by the Value Added Tax (Buildings and Land) Order, SI 2009/1966 arts 2, 3 with effect in relation to supplies made on or after 1 August 2009.
³ In sub-para (1), words substituted for words "body corporate", in sub-para (2) in opening words (in both places), and in para (c), words substituted for words "body corporate", in para (c), words substituted for words "that body", in sub-para (3), words substituted for words "body corporate", in sub-para (4) in opening words, words substituted for words "The body corporate", in paras (a), (aa), (b), (c), words substituted for words "the body corporate", in sub-para (5) in opening words, words substituted for words "The body corporate" and "the body corporate" and in closing words, words substituted for words "the body corporate", by FA 2019 s 53, Sch 18 paras 3, 15(1), (2) with effect from 1 November 2019 (see SI 2019/1348).

[Permission for a body corporate to cease to be a relevant associate of the opter]

4—(1) This paragraph applies for the purposes of paragraph 3(5) in relation to a [person ("P") who]² has been a relevant associate of the opter.
(2) If the conditions specified in the public notice under paragraph 3(5)(a) are met in relation to [P, P]² ceases to be a relevant associate of the opter only if notification of those conditions being met is given to the Commissioners.
(3) The notification must—
  (a) be made in a form specified in a public notice,
  (b) state the day from which [P]² is to cease to be a relevant associate of the opter (which may not be before the day on which the notification is given),
  (c) contain a statement by [P]² certifying that, on that day, the conditions specified in the public notice under paragraph 3(5)(a) are met in relation to [P]², and
  (d) contain other information specified in a public notice.
(4) An application for the prior permission of the Commissioners must—
  (a) be made in a form specified in a public notice,
  (b) contain a statement by [P]² certifying which (if any) of the conditions specified in the public notice under paragraph 3(5)(a) are met in relation to [P]², and
  (c) contain other information specified in a public notice.
(5) If [P]² gets the prior permission of the Commissioners, [P]² ceases to be a relevant associate of the opter from—
  (a) the day on which the Commissioners give their permission, or
  (b) such earlier or later day as they specify in their permission.

(6) The Commissioners may specify an earlier day only if—
  (a) [P]² has purported to give a notification of [P's]² ceasing to be a relevant associate of the opter,
  (b) the conditions specified in the public notice are not, in the event, met in relation to [P]², and
  (c) the Commissioners consider that the grounds on which those conditions are not so met are insignificant.
(7) The day specified may be the day from which [P]² would have ceased to be a relevant associate of the opter if those conditions had been so met.
(8) The Commissioners may specify conditions subject to which their permission is given and, if any of those conditions are broken, they may treat the application as if it had not been made.]¹

Amendments—¹ Schedule 10 substituted by the Value Added Tax (Buildings and Land) Order, SI 2008/1146, art 2 with effect in relation to supplies made on or after 1 June 2008, subject to savings in Sch 2 of the Order.
² In sub-para (1), words substituted for words "body corporate which", in sub-para (2), words substituted for words "the body corporate, it", in sub-paras (3)(b), (6)(b), (7), words substituted for words "the body corporate", in sub-paras (3)(c), (4)(b), (5), words substituted for words "the body corporate" and "it", and in sub-para (6)(a), words substituted for words "the body corporate", and words substituted for word "its", by FA 2019 s 53, Sch 18 paras 3, 15(1), (3) with effect from 1 November 2019 (see SI 2019/1348).

[EXCLUSIONS FROM EFFECT OF OPTION TO TAX

Dwellings designed or adapted, and intended for use, as dwelling etc

5—(1) An option to tax has no effect in relation to any grant in relation to a building or part of a building if the building or part of the building is designed or adapted, and is intended, for use—
  (a) as a dwelling or number of dwellings, or
  (b) solely for a relevant residential purpose.
(2) In relation to the expression "relevant residential purpose", see the certification requirement imposed as a result of the application of Note (12) of Group 5 of Schedule 8 by paragraph 33 of this Schedule.]¹

Commentary—*De Voil Indirect Tax Service* **V4.116**.
Amendments—¹ Schedule 10 substituted by the Value Added Tax (Buildings and Land) Order, SI 2008/1146, art 2 with effect in relation to supplies made on or after 1 June 2008, subject to savings in Sch 2 of the Order.

[Conversion of buildings for use as dwelling etc

6—(1) An option to tax has no effect in relation to any grant made to a person ("the recipient") in relation to a building or part of a building if the recipient certifies that the building or part of the building is intended for use—
  (a) as a dwelling or number of dwellings, or
  (b) solely for a relevant residential purpose.
(2) The recipient must give the certificate to the person making the grant ("the seller")—
  (a) within the period specified in a public notice, or
  (b) if the seller agrees, at any later time before the seller makes a supply to which the grant gives rise.
(3) The recipient may give the certificate to the seller only if the recipient—
  (a) intends to use the building or part of the building as mentioned above,
  (b) has the relevant conversion intention, or
  (c) is a relevant intermediary.
(4) The recipient is a relevant intermediary if—
  (a) the recipient intends to dispose of the relevant interest to another person, and
  (b) that other person gives the recipient a certificate stating that the other person has the relevant conversion intention or the relevant disposal intention.
(5) For this purpose a person has the relevant disposal intention if—
  (a) the person intends to dispose of the relevant interest to a third person, and
  (b) the third person gives a qualifying certificate to the person.
(6) A person (P) gives a qualifying certificate to another if P gives a certificate to that other person stating that P has the relevant conversion intention or intends to dispose of the relevant interest to another person (Q) who has given a certificate to P stating—
  (a) that Q has the relevant conversion intention, or
  (b) that Q intends to dispose of the relevant interest to another person who has given a qualifying certificate to Q,
and so on (in the case of further disposals of the relevant interest).
(7) In this paragraph—
  "the relevant conversion intention", in relation to a person, means an intention of the person to convert the building or part of the building with a view to its being used as mentioned above, and

"the relevant interest", in relation to any interest in the building or part of the building to which the grant gives rise, means the whole of that interest.

(8) For the purposes of this paragraph a building or part of a building is not to be regarded as intended for use as a dwelling or number of dwellings at any time if there is intended to be a period before that time during which it will not be so used (but disregarding use for incidental or other minor purposes).

(9) For the purposes of this paragraph the reference to use solely for a relevant residential purpose is to be read without regard to Note (12) of Group 5 of Schedule 8 (which would otherwise apply as a result of paragraph 33 of this Schedule).

(10) The Commissioners may publish a notice for the purposes of this paragraph—
   (a) preventing a person from giving any certificate under this paragraph unless the person meets conditions specified in the notice,
   (b) specifying the form in which any certificate under this paragraph must be made, and
   (c) specifying any information which any certificate under this paragraph must contain.][1]

Commentary—*De Voil Indirect Tax Service* **V4.116**.
Amendments—[1]   Schedule 10 substituted by the Value Added Tax (Buildings and Land) Order, SI 2008/1146, art 2 with effect in relation to supplies made on or after 1 June 2008, subject to savings in Sch 2 of the Order.

[Charities

7—(1) An option to tax has no effect in relation to any grant made to a person in relation to a building or part of a building intended by the person for use—
   (a) solely for a relevant charitable purpose, but
   (b) not as an office.

(2) In relation to the expression "relevant charitable purpose", see the certification requirement imposed as a result of the application of Note (12) of Group 5 of Schedule 8 by paragraph 33 of this Schedule.][1]

Commentary—*De Voil Indirect Tax Service* **V4.113**.
Amendments—[1]   Schedule 10 substituted by the Value Added Tax (Buildings and Land) Order, SI 2008/1146, art 2 with effect in relation to supplies made on or after 1 June 2008, subject to savings in Sch 2 of the Order.

Residential caravans

8—(1) An option to tax has no effect in relation to any grant made in relation to a pitch for a residential caravan.

(2) A caravan is not a residential caravan if residence in it throughout the year is prevented by the terms of a covenant, statutory planning consent or similar permission.][1]

Amendments—[1]   Schedule 10 substituted by the Value Added Tax (Buildings and Land) Order, SI 2008/1146, art 2 with effect in relation to supplies made on or after 1 June 2008, subject to savings in Sch 2 of the Order.

[Residential houseboats

9—(1) An option to tax has no effect in relation to any grant made in relation to facilities for the mooring of a residential houseboat.

"Mooring" includes anchoring or berthing.

(2) In this paragraph—
   (a) "houseboat" means a houseboat within the meaning of Group 9 of Schedule 8, and
   (b) a houseboat is not a residential houseboat if residence in it throughout the year is prevented by the terms of a covenant, statutory planning consent or similar permission.][1]

Amendments—[1]   Schedule 10 substituted by the Value Added Tax (Buildings and Land) Order, SI 2008/1146, art 2 with effect in relation to supplies made on or after 1 June 2008, subject to savings in Sch 2 of the Order.

[Relevant housing associations

10—(1) An option to tax has no effect in relation to any grant made to a relevant housing association in relation to any land if the association certifies that the land is to be used (after any necessary demolition work) for the construction of a building or buildings intended for use—
   (a) as a dwelling or number of dwellings, or
   (b) solely for a relevant residential purpose.

(2) The association must give the certificate to the person making the grant ("the seller")—
   (a) within the period specified in a public notice, or
   (b) if the seller agrees, at any later time before the seller makes a supply to which the grant gives rise.

(3) In this paragraph "relevant housing association" means—
   [(za) a private registered provider of social housing,][2]
   (a) a registered social landlord within the meaning of Part 1 of the Housing Act 1996 (. . . [2] Welsh registered social landlords),

[(*b*) a registered social landlord within the meaning of the Housing (Scotland) Act 2010 (asp 17) which is either—
  (i) a society registered under the Co-operative and Community Benefit Societies and Credit Unions Act 1965 (c 12), or
  (ii) a company within the meaning of the Companies Act 2006 (c 46), or][3]
(*c*) a registered housing association within the meaning of Part 2 of the Housing (Northern Ireland) Order 1992 (Northern Irish registered housing associations).

(4) For the purposes of this paragraph the reference to use solely for a relevant residential purpose is to be read without regard to Note (12) of Group 5 of Schedule 8 (which would otherwise apply as a result of paragraph 33 of this Schedule).

(5) The Commissioners may publish a notice for the purposes of this paragraph—
  (*a*) specifying the form in which any certificate under this paragraph must be made, and
  (*b*) specifying any information which any certificate under this paragraph must contain.][1]

Amendments—[1] Schedule 10 substituted by the Value Added Tax (Buildings and Land) Order, SI 2008/1146, art 2 with effect in relation to supplies made on or after 1 June 2008, subject to savings in Sch 2 of the Order.

[2] In sub-para (3), para (*za*) inserted, and in para (*a*) words "English or" repealed, by the VAT (Buildings and Land) Order, SI 2010/485 arts 3, 4(1) with effect from 1 April 2010. Note that until the coming into force of provision defining "private registered provider of social housing" in enactments and instruments generally, that expression in para 10(3) means persons listed in the register of providers of social housing maintained under the Housing and Regeneration Act 2008 Part 2, Chapter 3 who are not local authorities within the meaning of the Housing Associations Act 1985 (SI 2010/485 art 4(2)).

[3] Sub-para (3)(*b*) substituted by the Housing (Scotland) Act 2010 (Consequential Provisions and Modifications) Order, SI 2012/700 art 4, Schedule para 5(1), (3) with effect from 1 April 2012.

[Grant to individual for construction of dwelling]

11 An option to tax has no effect in relation to any grant made to an individual if—
  (*a*) the land is to be used for the construction of a building intended for use by the individual as a dwelling, and
  (*b*) the construction is not carried out in the course or furtherance of a business carried on by the individual.][1]

Amendments—[1] Schedule 10 substituted by the Value Added Tax (Buildings and Land) Order, SI 2008/1146, art 2 with effect in relation to supplies made on or after 1 June 2008, subject to savings in Sch 2 of the Order.

[ANTI-AVOIDANCE

Developers of exempt land

12—(1) A supply is not, as a result of an option to tax, a taxable supply if—
  (*a*) the grant giving rise to the supply was made by a person ("the grantor") who was a developer of the land, and
  (*b*) the exempt land test is met.

(2) The exempt land test is met if, at the time when the grant was made (or treated for the purposes of this paragraph as made), the relevant person intended or expected that the land—
  (*a*) would become exempt land (whether immediately or eventually and whether or not as a result of the grant), or
  (*b*) would continue, for a period at least, to be exempt land.

(3) "The relevant person" means—
  (*a*) the grantor, or
  (*b*) a development financier.

(4) For the meaning of a development financier, see paragraph 14.

(5) For the meaning of "exempt land", see paragraphs 15 and 16.

(6) If a supply is made by a person other than the person who made the grant giving rise to it—
  (*a*) the person making the supply is treated for the purposes of this paragraph as the person who made the grant giving rise to it, and
  (*b*) the grant is treated for the purposes of this paragraph as made at the time when that person made the first supply arising from the grant.

(7) For a special rule in the case of a grant made on or after 19th March 1997 and before 10th March 1999, see paragraph 17.

(8) Nothing in this paragraph applies in relation to a supply arising from—
  (*a*) a grant made before 26th November 1996, or
  (*b*) a grant made on or after that date but before 30th November 1999, in pursuance of a written agreement entered into before 26th November 1996, on terms which (as terms for which provision was made by that agreement) were fixed before 26th November 1996.][1]

Commentary—*De Voil Indirect Tax Service* **V4.116**.

Amendments—[1] Schedule 10 substituted by the Value Added Tax (Buildings and Land) Order, SI 2008/1146, art 2 with effect in relation to supplies made on or after 1 June 2008, subject to savings in Sch 2 of the Order.

[Meaning of grants made by a developer]

13—(1) This paragraph applies for the purposes of paragraph 12.
(2) A grant made by any person ("the grantor") in relation to any land is made by a developer of the land if—
- (*a*) the land is, or was intended or expected to be, a relevant capital item (see sub-paragraphs (3) to (5)), and
- (*b*) the grant is made at an eligible time as respects that capital item (see sub-paragraph (6)).

(3) The land is a relevant capital item if—
- (*a*) the land, or
- (*b*) the building or part of a building on the land,

is a capital item in relation to the grantor.

(4) The land was intended or expected to be a relevant capital item if the grantor, or a development financier, intended or expected that—
- (*a*) the land, or
- (*b*) a building or part of a building on, or to be constructed on, the land,

would become a capital item in relation to the grantor or any relevant transferee.

(5) A person is a relevant transferee if the person is someone to whom the land, building or part of a building was to be transferred—
- (*a*) in the course of a supply, or
- (*b*) in the course of a transfer of a business or part of a business as a going concern.

(6) A grant is made at an eligible time as respects a capital item if it is made before the end of the period provided in the relevant regulations for the making of adjustments relating to the deduction of input tax as respects the capital item.

(7) But if—
- (*a*) a person other than the grantor is treated by paragraph 12(6) as making the grant of the land, and
- (*b*) the grant is consequently treated as made at what would otherwise be an ineligible time,

the grant is treated instead as if were not made at an ineligible time.

(8) In this paragraph a "capital item", in relation to any person, means an asset falling, in relation to the person, to be treated as a capital item for the purposes of the relevant regulations.

(9) In this paragraph "the relevant regulations", as respects any item, means regulations under section 26(3) and (4) providing for adjustments relating to the deduction of input tax to be made as respects that item.][1]

Amendments—[1] Schedule 10 substituted by the Value Added Tax (Buildings and Land) Order, SI 2008/1146, art 2 with effect in relation to supplies made on or after 1 June 2008, subject to savings in Sch 2 of the Order.

[Meaning of "development financier"]

14—(1) This paragraph explains for the purposes of paragraphs 12 to 17 what is meant, in relation to the grantor of any land, by a development financier.
(2) A "development financier" means a person who—
- (*a*) has provided finance for the grantor's development of the land, or
- (*b*) has entered into any arrangement to provide finance for the grantor's development of the land,

with the intention or in the expectation that the land will become exempt land or continue (for a period at least) to be exempt land.

(3) For the purposes of this paragraph references to finance being provided for the grantor's development of the land are to doing (directly or indirectly) any one or more of the following—
- (*a*) providing funds for meeting the whole or any part of the cost of the grantor's development of the land,
- (*b*) procuring the provision of such funds by another,
- (*c*) providing funds for discharging (in whole or in part) any liability that has been or may be incurred by any person for or in connection with the raising of funds to meet the cost of the grantor's development of the land, and
- (*d*) procuring that any such liability is or will be discharged (in whole or in part) by another.

(4) For the purposes of this paragraph references to providing funds for a particular purpose are to—
- (*a*) the making of a loan of funds that are or are to be used for that purpose,
- (*b*) the provision of any guarantee or other security in relation to such a loan,
- (*c*) the provision of any of the consideration for the issue of any shares or other securities issued wholly or partly for raising those funds,
- (*d*) the provision of any consideration for the acquisition by any person of any shares or other securities issued wholly or partly for raising those funds, or

(e) any other transfer of assets or value as a consequence of which any of those funds are made available for that purpose.

(5) For the purposes of this paragraph references to the grantor's development of the land are to the acquisition by the grantor of the asset which—

(a) consists in the land or a building or part of a building on the land, and

(b) is, or (as the case may be) was intended or expected to be, a relevant capital item in relation to the grantor (within the meaning of paragraph 13).

(6) For this purpose the reference to the acquisition of the asset includes—

(a) its construction or reconstruction, and

(b) the carrying out in relation to it of any other works by reference to which it is, or was intended or expected to be, a relevant capital item (within the meaning of paragraph 13).

(7) In this paragraph "arrangement" means any agreement, arrangement or understanding (whether or not legally enforceable).][1]

Amendments—[1] Schedule 10 substituted by the Value Added Tax (Buildings and Land) Order, SI 2008/1146, art 2 with effect in relation to supplies made on or after 1 June 2008, subject to savings in Sch 2 of the Order.

[Meaning of "exempt land": basic definition

15—(1) This paragraph explains for the purposes of paragraphs 12 to 17 what is meant by exempt land.

(2) Land is exempt land if, at any time before the end of the relevant adjustment period as respects that land—

(a) a relevant person is in occupation of the land, and

(b) that occupation is not wholly, or substantially wholly, for eligible purposes.

(3) Each of the following is a relevant person—

(a) the grantor,

(b) a person connected with the grantor,

(c) a development financier, and

(d) a person connected with a development financier.

[(3A) Where a person ("P") is in occupation of the land at any time before the end of the relevant adjustment period as respects that land, P is treated for the purposes of sub-paragraph (2) as not in occupation of the land at that time if—

(a) the building occupation conditions are met at that time, or

(b) P's occupation of the land arises solely by reference to any automatic teller machine of P.][2]

(4) The relevant adjustment period as respects any land is the period provided in the relevant regulations (within the meaning of paragraph 13) for the making of adjustments relating to the deduction of input tax as respects the land.

(5) For the purposes of this paragraph any question whether a person's occupation of any land is "wholly, or substantially wholly," for eligible purposes is to be decided by reference to criteria specified in a public notice.][1]

Commentary—*De Voil Indirect Tax Service* **V4.116**.

Amendments—[1] Schedule 10 substituted by the Value Added Tax (Buildings and Land) Order, SI 2008/1146, art 2 with effect in relation to supplies made on or after 1 June 2008, subject to savings in Sch 2 of the Order.

[2] Sub-para (3A) substituted by the VAT (Buildings and Land) Order, SI 2011/86 arts 4, 5 with effect in relation to supplies made on or after 1 March 2011 other than a supply arising from a grant made before 1 March 2011 (SI 2011/86 art 2). Sub-para (3A) was originally inserted by SI 2010/485 arts 3, 5 with effect in relation to supplies made on or after 1 April 2010 other than a supply arising from a grant made before 1 April 2010.

[Meaning of "exempt land": the building occupation conditions

15A (1) For the purposes of paragraph 15(3A), the building occupation conditions are met at any time ("the time in question") if—

(a) the grant consists of or includes the grant of a relevant interest in a building, and

(b) P does not, at the time in question, occupy—

(i) any part of the land that is not a building, or

(ii) more than [the maximum allowable percentage][2] of any relevant building.

(2) For the purposes of sub-paragraph (1)(b)(i) and (ii) occupation by a person connected with P is treated as occupation by P [if that occupation is not wholly, or substantially wholly, for eligible purposes][2].

(3) For the purposes of sub-paragraph (1)(b)(i) occupation by a person of—

(a) land used for the parking of cars or other vehicles, or

(b) land that is within the curtilage of a building,

is disregarded if the occupation is ancillary to the occupation by that person of a building.

[(4) In sub-paragraph (1)(b)(ii)—

"the maximum allowable percentage" means—

(a) 2% where P is the grantor or a person connected with the grantor, and
(b) 10% where P is a development financier or a person connected with a development financier (but not also the grantor or a person connected with the grantor), and

"relevant building"—
(a) means a building any relevant interest in which is included in the grant, other than any part of such a building in which, immediately before the grant, neither the grantor nor any person connected with the grantor held a relevant interest, but
(b) does not include any building P's occupation of which arises solely by reference to any automatic teller machine of P.][2]

(5) The way in which occupation by a person of a building is measured for the purposes of sub-paragraph (1)(b)(ii) is to be determined in accordance with conditions specified in a public notice.
(6) In this paragraph "relevant interest", in relation to a building or part of a building, means any interest in, right over or licence to occupy the building or part.
[(6A) Sub-paragraph (5) of paragraph 15 (determination of whether occupation "wholly, or substantially wholly" for eligible purposes to be by reference to criteria in public notice) applies for the purposes of this paragraph.][2]
(7) Sub-paragraphs (4) to (7) of paragraph 18 (meaning of "building") apply for the purposes of this paragraph.][1]

Amendments—[1] Para 15A inserted by the VAT (Buildings and Land) Order, SI 2010/485 arts 3, 6 with effect in relation to supplies made on or after 1 April 2010 other than a supply arising from a grant made before 1 April 2010.
[2] In sub-para (1)(b)(ii) words substituted for figure "10%", in sub-para (2) words inserted, sub-para (4) substituted, and sub-para (6A) inserted, by the VAT (Buildings and Land) Order, SI 2011/86 arts 4, 6 with effect in relation to supplies made on or after 1 March 2011 other than a supply arising from a grant made before 1 March 2011 (SI 2011/86 art 2).

[Meaning of "exempt land": eligible purposes

16—(1) This paragraph explains what is meant for the purposes of paragraph 15 by a person occupying land for eligible purposes.
(2) A person cannot occupy land at any time for eligible purposes unless the person is a taxable person at that time (but this rule is qualified by sub-paragraphs (5) and (6)).
(3) A taxable person occupies land for eligible purposes so far as the occupation is for the purpose of making creditable supplies (but this rule is qualified by sub-paragraphs (5) to (7)).
(4) "Creditable supplies" means supplies which—
(a) are or are to be made in the course or furtherance of a business carried on by the person, and
(b) are supplies of such a description that the person would be entitled to a credit for any input tax wholly attributable to those supplies.
(5) Any occupation of land by a body to which section 33 applies (local authorities etc) is occupation of the land for eligible purposes so far as the occupation is for purposes other than those of a business carried on by the body.
(6) Any occupation of land by a Government department (within the meaning of section 41) is occupation of the land for eligible purposes.
(7) . . .[2]
(8) If a person occupying land—
(a) holds the land in order to put it to use for particular purposes, and
(b) does not occupy it for any other purpose,
the person is treated for the purposes of this paragraph, for so long as the conditions in paragraphs (a) and (b) continue to be met, as occupying the land for the purposes for which the person proposes to use it.
(9) If land is in the occupation of a person ("A") who—
(a) is not a taxable person, but
(b) is a person whose supplies are treated for the purposes of this Act as made by another person ("B") who is a taxable person,
the land is treated for the purposes of this paragraph as if A and B were a single taxable person.
(10) For the purposes of this paragraph a person occupies land—
(a) whether the person occupies it alone or together with one or more other persons, and
(b) whether the person occupies all of the land or only part of it.][1]

Commentary—*De Voil Indirect Tax Service* **V4.116**.
Amendments—[1] Schedule 10 substituted by the Value Added Tax (Buildings and Land) Order, SI 2008/1146, art 2 with effect in relation to supplies made on or after 1 June 2008, subject to savings in Sch 2 of the Order.
[2] Sub-para (7) revoked by the VAT (Buildings and Land) Order, SI 2011/86 arts 4, 7 with effect in relation to supplies made on or after 1 March 2011 other than a supply arising from a grant made before 1 March 2011 (SI 2011/86 art 2).

[Paragraph 12: grants made on or after 19th March 1997 and before 10th March 1999

17—(1) A grant in relation to land which was made—
(a) on or after 19th March 1997, and

(b) before 10th March 1999,
is treated for the purposes of paragraph 12 as made on 10th March 1999 if, at the time of the grant, the capital item test was met.
(2) The capital item test was met if the person making the grant, or a development financier, intended or expected that—
  (a) the land, or
  (b) a building or part of a building on, or to be constructed on, the land,
would become a capital item in relation to the grantor or any relevant transferee but it had not become such an item.
(3) For the purposes of that test "capital item" and "relevant transferee" have the meaning given by paragraph 13.][1]

Amendments—[1] Schedule 10 substituted by the Value Added Tax (Buildings and Land) Order, SI 2008/1146, art 2 with effect in relation to supplies made on or after 1 June 2008, subject to savings in Sch 2 of the Order.

[SCOPE OF THE OPTION, ITS DURATION, NOTIFICATION ETC

Scope of the option

18—(1) An option to tax has effect in relation to the particular land specified in the option.
(2) If an option to tax is exercised in relation to—
  (a) a building, or
  (b) part of a building,
the option has effect in relation to the whole of the building and all the land within its curtilage.
(3) If an option to tax—
  (a) is exercised in relation to any land, but
  (b) is not exercised by reference to a building or part of a building,
the option is nonetheless taken to have effect in relation to any building which is (or is to be) constructed on the land (as well as in relation to land on which no building is constructed).
(4) For the purposes of this paragraph—
  (a) buildings linked internally or by a covered walkway, and
  (b) complexes consisting of a number of units grouped around a fully enclosed concourse,
are treated as a single building.
(5) But for those purposes—
  (a) buildings which are linked internally are not treated as a single building if the internal link is created after the buildings are completed, and
  (b) buildings which are linked by a covered walkway are not treated as a single building if the walkway starts to be constructed after the buildings are completed.
(6) In this paragraph a "building" includes—
  (a) an enlarged or extended building,
  (b) an annexe to a building, and
  (c) a planned building.
(7) In this paragraph "covered walkway" does not include a covered walkway to which the general public has reasonable access.][1]

Commentary—*De Voil Indirect Tax Service* **V4.116**.
Amendments—[1] Schedule 10 substituted by the Value Added Tax (Buildings and Land) Order, SI 2008/1146, art 2 with effect in relation to supplies made on or after 1 June 2008, subject to savings in Sch 2 of the Order.

[*The day from which the option has effect*

19—(1) An option to tax has effect from—
  (a) the start of the day on which it is exercised, or
  (b) the start of any later day specified in the option.
(2) But if, when an option to tax is exercised, the person exercising the option intends to revoke it in accordance with paragraph 23 (revocation of option: the "cooling off" period), the option is treated for the purposes of this Act as if it had never been exercised.
(3) An option to tax may be revoked in accordance with paragraph 22(2) or (3) and any of paragraphs 23 to 25, but not otherwise.
(4) This paragraph needs to be read with—
  (a) paragraph 20 (requirement to notify the option), and
  (b) paragraph 29(3) (application for prior permission in the case of an exempt grant before the exercise of an option to tax).][1]

Amendments—[1] Schedule 10 substituted by the Value Added Tax (Buildings and Land) Order, SI 2008/1146, art 2 with effect in relation to supplies made on or after 1 June 2008, subject to savings in Sch 2 of the Order.

[Requirement to notify the option

20—(1) An option to tax has effect only if—
   (*a*) notification of the option is given to the Commissioners within the allowed time, and
   (*b*) that notification is given together with such information as the Commissioners may require.
(2) Notification of an option is given within the allowed time if (and only if) it is given—
   (*a*) before the end of the period of 30 days beginning with the day on which the option was exercised, or
   (*b*) before the end of such longer period beginning with that day as the Commissioners may in any particular case allow.
(3) The Commissioners may publish a notice for the purposes of this paragraph specifying—
   (*a*) the form in which a notification under this paragraph must be made, and
   (*b*) the information which a notification under this paragraph must contain.
(4) Notification of an option to tax does not need to be given under this paragraph if the option is treated as exercised in accordance with paragraph 29(3).][1]
Commentary—*De Voil Indirect Tax Service* **V4.116**.
Amendments—[1]   Schedule 10 substituted by the Value Added Tax (Buildings and Land) Order, SI 2008/1146, art 2 with effect in relation to supplies made on or after 1 June 2008, subject to savings in Sch 2 of the Order.

[Real estate elections: elections to opt to tax land subsequently acquired

21—(1) A person (E) may make an election (a "real estate election") for this paragraph to have effect in relation to—
   (*a*) relevant interests in any building or land which E acquires after the election is made, and
   (*b*) relevant interests in any building or land which a [person][3] acquires after the election is made at a time when [the person][3] is a relevant group member.
(2) If E makes a real estate election—
   (*a*) E is treated for the purposes of this Part of this Schedule as if E had exercised an option to tax in relation to the building or land in which the relevant interest is acquired,
   (*b*) that option is treated for those purposes as if it had been exercised on the day on which the acquisition was made and as if it had effect from the start of that day, and
   (*c*) paragraph 20 does not apply in relation to that option,
but this sub-paragraph is subject to sub-paragraphs (3) to (5).
(3) A person (P) is not to be treated as a result of this paragraph as exercising an option to tax in relation to any building or land where at any time—
   (*a*) P, or any [person who][3] was a relevant group member at that time, exercises an option to tax in relation to the building (or part of the building) or land apart from this paragraph, and
   (*b*) that option has effect from a time earlier than the time from which an option to tax exercised by P in relation to the building or land would otherwise have been treated as having effect as a result of this paragraph.
(4) A person (P) is not to be treated as a result of this paragraph as exercising an option to tax in relation to any building or land in which a relevant interest is acquired ("the later interest") if—
   (*a*) the person making the acquisition in question held another relevant interest in that building or land before P makes a real estate election, and
   (*b*) the person making the acquisition in question continues to hold that other relevant interest at the time when the later interest is acquired.
(5) A person is not to be treated as a result of this paragraph as exercising an option to tax in relation to any building or land if—
   (*a*) a relevant interest in the building or land is acquired as mentioned in sub-paragraph (1), and
   (*b*) on the relevant assumptions the case would fall within paragraph 28 (pre-option exempt grants: requirement for prior permission before exercise of option to tax).
(6) The relevant assumptions are that—
   (*a*) the effect of this paragraph is disregarded, and
   (*b*) the day from which the person would want the option to tax to have effect for the purposes of paragraphs 28 or 29(3) is the day on which the relevant interest is acquired.
(7) A real estate election has effect only if—
   (*a*) notification of the election is given to the Commissioners before the end of the period of 30 days beginning with the day on which it was made or such longer period as the Commissioners may in any particular case allow,
   (*b*) the notification is made in a form specified in a public notice, and
   (*c*) the notification contains information so specified.
(8) The Commissioners may at any time require a person who has made a real estate election to give to the Commissioners information specified in a public notice before the end of—
   (*a*) the period of 30 days beginning with that time, or

(b) such longer period as the Commissioners may in any particular case allow.
(9) If a person (P) does not comply with that requirement—
  (a) the Commissioners may revoke the election, and
  (b) that revocation has effect in relation to relevant interests in any building or land acquired after the notified time by P or a [person who]³ is a relevant group member at the time of acquisition.
    "The notified time" means the time specified in a notification given by the Commissioners to P (which may not be before the notification is given).
(10) A real estate election may not be revoked except in accordance with sub-paragraph (9).
(11) If a real estate election made by a person (P) is revoked in accordance with that sub-paragraph, another real estate election may be made at any subsequent time by—
  (a) P, or
  (b) any [person who]³ is a relevant group member at that subsequent time,
but only with the prior permission of the Commissioners.
(12) In this paragraph—
  "relevant group member", in relation to any person [("P")]³ making a real estate election and any time, means a [person who]³ is treated under sections 43A to 43D as a member of the same group as [P]³ at that time, and
  "relevant interest", in relation to any building or land, means any interest in, right over or licence to occupy the building or land (or any part of it).]¹
[(13) For the purposes of this paragraph, the time at which a relevant interest in any building or land is acquired is—
  (a) the time at which a supply is treated as taking place for the purposes of the charge to VAT in respect of the acquisition, or
  (b) if there is more than one such time, the earliest of them.
(14) For the purposes of sub-paragraph (13)(a), any order under section 5(3)(c) that would otherwise have the effect that the acquisition in question is to be treated as neither a supply of goods nor a supply of services is to be disregarded.]²

Amendments—¹ Schedule 10 substituted by the Value Added Tax (Buildings and Land) Order, SI 2008/1146, art 2 with effect in relation to supplies made on or after 1 June 2008, subject to savings in Sch 2 of the Order.
² Sub-paras (13), (14) inserted by the Value Added Tax (Buildings and Land) Order, SI 2009/1966 arts 2, 4 with effect in relation to supplies made on or after 1 August 2009.
³ In sub-para (1)(b), words substituted for words "body corporate", and words substituted for words "the body", in sub-paras (3)(a), (9)(b), (11)(b) words substituted for words "body corporate which", in sub-para (12), in definition of "relevant group member", words inserted, words e substituted for words "body corporate which", and words substituted for words "that person", by FA 2019 s 53, Sch 18 paras 3, 15(1), (4) with effect from 1 November 2019 (see SI 2019/1348).

[Real estate elections: supplementary

22—(1) This paragraph applies if, at any time ("the relevant time"), a person (e) makes a real estate election under paragraph 21.
(2) An option to tax exercised in relation to any building or part of any building before the relevant time by—
  (a) E, or
  (b) any relevant group member,
is treated for the purposes of this Part of this Schedule as if it had been revoked from the relevant time if, at that time, neither E nor any relevant group member has a relevant interest in that building.
(3) An option to tax exercised in relation to any land (otherwise than by reference to any building or part of a building) before the relevant time by—
  (a) E, or
  (b) any relevant group member,
is treated for the purposes of this Part of this Schedule as if it had been revoked in accordance with sub-paragraph (4) from the relevant time if, at that time, neither E nor any relevant group member has a relevant interest in that land, or E or any relevant group member has a relevant interest in only some of it.
(4) The option is treated for the purposes of this Part of this Schedule as if it had been revoked in relation to—
  (a) that land, or
  (b) the parts of that land in which neither E nor any relevant group member has a relevant interest at the relevant time,
as the case may be.
(5) Sub-paragraphs (2) and (3) are subject to paragraph 26 (anti-avoidance).
(6) An option to tax ("the original option") exercised in relation to any land (otherwise than by reference to any building or part of a building) before the relevant time by—

(a) E, or

(b) any relevant group member,

may, in circumstances specified in a public notice, be converted by E into separate options to tax if, at the relevant time, E or any relevant group member has a relevant interest in the land or any part of it.

(7) The original option is converted into separate options to tax different parcels of land comprised in that land or part.

(8) Those separate options to tax are treated for the purposes of this Part of this Schedule—

(a) as if they had been exercised by E, and

(b) as if they had effect from the time from which the original option had effect.

(9) But—

(a) those separate options to tax are treated for the purposes of paragraph 3(2) as if they had effect from the relevant time, and

(b) paragraph 23 (revocation of an option: the "cooling off" period) does not apply to those separate options to tax.

(10) The notification of the election given by E must identify—

(a) the separate options to tax treated as exercised by E as a result of sub-paragraphs (6) to (8), and

(b) the different parcels of land in relation to which those separate options to tax are treated as having effect.

(11) In this paragraph—

(a) any reference to any relevant group member is to a body corporate which is a relevant group member at the relevant time, and

(b) any reference to any relevant group member, in relation to any relevant interest in any building or land (or any part of it), is to any relevant group member regardless of whether it has exercised an option to tax the building or land (or any part of it).

(12) In this paragraph "relevant group member" and "relevant interest", have the meaning given by paragraph 21.

(13) In this paragraph any reference to a real estate election under paragraph 21 does not include an election which is made under sub-paragraph (11) of that paragraph.][1]

Amendments—[1] Schedule 10 substituted by the Value Added Tax (Buildings and Land) Order, SI 2008/1146, art 2 with effect in relation to supplies made on or after 1 June 2008, subject to savings in Sch 2 of the Order.

[Revocation of option: the "cooling off" period

23—(1) An option to tax any land exercised by any person ("the taxpayer") may be revoked with effect from the day on which it was exercised if—

(a) the time that has lapsed since the day on which the option had effect is less than 6 months,

(b) the taxpayer has not used the land since the option had effect,[2]

(c) no tax has become chargeable as a result of the option,

(d) there is no relevant transfer of a business as a going concern (see sub-paragraph (2)), and

(e) notification of the revocation is given to the Commissioners (see sub-paragraph (3)).

(2) There is no relevant transfer of a business as a going concern if, since the option had effect, no grant in relation to the land has been made which is treated as neither a supply of goods nor a supply of services because—

(a) the supply is a supply of the assets of a business by the taxpayer to a person to whom the business (or part of it) is transferred as a going concern, or

(b) the supply is a supply of assets of a business by a person to the taxpayer to whom the business (or part of it) is so transferred.

(3) The notification of the revocation must—

(a) be made in a form specified in a public notice, and

(b) contain information so specified.

(4) The Commissioners may publish a notice for the purposes of this paragraph providing that a revocation under this paragraph is effective only if—

(a) the conditions specified in the notice are met in relation to the option, or

(b) the taxpayer gets the prior permission of the Commissioners on an application made to them before the end of the 6 month period mentioned above.

(5) A notice under sub-paragraph (4) may—

(a) provide that, in a case falling with paragraph (a) of that sub-paragraph, the taxpayer must certify that the conditions specified under that paragraph are met in relation to the option,

(b) specify the form in which an application under paragraph (b) of that sub-paragraph must be made,

(c) provide that an application under that paragraph must contain a statement by the taxpayer certifying which (if any) of the conditions specified under sub-paragraph (4)(a) are met in relation to the option,
(d) specify other information which an application under sub-paragraph (4)(a) must contain, and
(e) provide that the Commissioners may specify conditions subject to which their permission is given and, if any of those conditions are broken, the Commissioners may treat the revocation as if it had not been made.][1]

Amendments—[1] Schedule 10 substituted by the Value Added Tax (Buildings and Land) Order, SI 2008/1146, art 2 with effect in relation to supplies made on or after 1 June 2008, subject to savings in Sch 2 of the Order.
[2] Sub-para (1)(b) repealed by the VAT (Buildings and Land) Order, SI 2010/485 arts 3, 7 with effect from 1 April 2010.

[Revocation of option: lapse of 6 years since having a relevant interest

24—(1) An option to tax exercised by any person in relation to any building or land is treated for the purposes of this Part of this Schedule as revoked if the person does not have a relevant interest in the building or land throughout any continuous period of 6 years beginning at any time after the option has effect.
(2) The option to tax is treated for the purposes of this Part of this Schedule as revoked from the end of that period.
(3) In this paragraph "a relevant interest in the building or land" means an interest in, right over or licence to occupy the building or land (or any part of it).
(4) This paragraph is subject to paragraph 26 (anti-avoidance).][1]

Amendments—[1] Schedule 10 substituted by the Value Added Tax (Buildings and Land) Order, SI 2008/1146, art 2 with effect in relation to supplies made on or after 1 June 2008, subject to savings in Sch 2 of the Order.

[Revocation of option: lapse of more than 20 years since option had effect

25—(1) An option to tax any land exercised by any person ("the taxpayer") may be revoked if the time that has lapsed since the day on which the option had effect is more than 20 years and—
(a) at the time when the option is to be revoked the conditions specified in a public notice are met in relation to the option (in which case, see sub-paragraphs (2) to (4)), or
(b) the taxpayer gets the prior permission of the Commissioners (in which case, see the remaining sub-paragraphs).
(2) If the conditions specified in the public notice are met in relation to the option, the revocation has effect only if notification of the revocation is given to the Commissioners.
(3) The notification must—
(a) be made in the specified form,
(b) state the day from which the option is to be revoked (which may not be before the day on which the notification is given),
(c) contain a statement by the taxpayer certifying that, on that day, the conditions specified in the public notice are met in relation to the option, and
(d) contain other information specified in a public notice.
(4) If—
(a) notification of the revocation of an option is given to the Commissioners on the basis that the conditions specified in the public notice were met in relation to the option, but
(b) it is subsequently discovered that those conditions were not met in relation to the option,
the Commissioners may nonetheless treat the option as if it had been validly revoked in accordance with this paragraph.
(5) An application for the prior permission of the Commissioners must—
(a) be made in a form specified in a public notice,
(b) contain a statement by the taxpayer certifying which (if any) of the conditions specified in the public notice under sub-paragraph (1)(a) are met in relation to the option, and
(c) contain other information specified in a public notice.
(6) If the taxpayer gets the prior permission of the Commissioners for the revocation of an option, the option is revoked from—
(a) the day on which the Commissioners give their permission, or
(b) such earlier or later day [or time as they may][2] specify in their permission.
(7) The Commissioners may specify an earlier day [or time][2] only if—
(a) the taxpayer has purported to give a notification of the revocation of the option,
(b) the conditions specified in the public notice are not, in the event, met in relation to the option, and
(c) the Commissioners consider that the grounds on which those conditions are not so met are insignificant.
[(8) The Commissioners may specify a day or time under sub-paragraph (6)(b) by reference to the happening of an event or the meeting of a condition.][2]

(9) The Commissioners may specify conditions subject to which their permission is given and, if any of those conditions are broken, they may treat the revocation as if it had not been made.][1]

Amendments—[1] Schedule 10 substituted by the Value Added Tax (Buildings and Land) Order, SI 2008/1146, art 2 with effect in relation to supplies made on or after 1 June 2008, subject to savings in Sch 2 of the Order.
[2] In sub-para (6)(b), words substituted for words "as they", in sub-para (7), words inserted, and sub-para (8) substituted, by the Value Added Tax (Buildings and Land) Order, SI 2009/1966 arts 2, 4 with effect in relation to supplies made on or after 1 August 2009.

[**26**—(1) Sub-paragraphs (2) and (3) of paragraph 22 (revocation of option to tax where a real estate election is made) do not apply if condition A or B is met.
(2) Paragraph 24 (lapse of option to tax) does not apply if condition A, B or C is met.
(3) Condition A is that—
  (a) the opter, or a relevant associate of the opter, disposes of a relevant interest in the building or land before the relevant time, and
  (b) at the relevant time, a supply for the purposes of the charge to VAT in respect of the disposal—
    (i) is yet to take place, or
    (ii) would be yet to take place if one or more conditions (such as the happening of an event or the doing of an act) were to be met.
(4) Condition B is that—
  (a) the opter is a body corporate that was, at any time before the relevant time, treated under sections 43A to 43D as a member of a group ("the group"), and
  (b) before the relevant time, a relevant associate of the opter in relation to the building or land ceased to be treated under those sections as a member of the group without at the same time meeting the conditions in sub-paragraph (5).
(5) A person ("A") meets the conditions in this sub-paragraph if—
  (a) A has no relevant interest in the building or land,
  (b) where A has disposed of such an interest, it is not the case that a supply for the purposes of the charge to VAT in respect of the disposal—
    (i) is yet to take place, or
    (ii) would be yet to take place if one or more conditions (such as the happening of an event or the doing of an act) were to be met, and
  (c) A is not connected with any person who has a relevant interest in the building or land where that person is the opter or another relevant associate of the opter.
(6) Condition C is that the opter is a body corporate and, at the relevant time, a relevant associate of the opter in relation to the building or land—
  (a) is treated under sections 43A to 43D as a member of the same group as the opter, and
  (b) holds a relevant interest in the building or land or has held such an interest at any time within the previous 6 years.
(7) In this paragraph—
  "relevant interest in the building or land" means an interest in, right over or license to occupy the building or land (or any part of it);
  "the relevant time", in relation to any option to tax, means the time from which the option would (but for this paragraph) have been treated as revoked as a result of paragraph 22(2) or (3) or 24;
  "opter" means the person who exercised the option to tax in question.][1]

Amendments—[1] This para substituted, by the Value Added Tax (Buildings and Land) Order, SI 2009/1966 arts 2, 6 with effect in relation to supplies made on or after 1 August 2009.

[Exclusion of new building from effect of an option

27—(1) This paragraph applies if—
  (a) a person ("the taxpayer") has at any time opted to tax any land,
  (b) at any subsequent time the construction of a building ("the new building") on the land begins, and
  (c) no land within the curtilage of the new building is within the curtilage of an existing building.
(2) The taxpayer may exclude—
  (a) the whole of the new building, and
  (b) all the land within its curtilage,
from the effect of the option if notification of that exclusion is given to the Commissioners.
(3) The exclusion has effect from the earliest of the following times—
  (a) the time when a grant of an interest in, or in any part of, the new building is first made,
  (b) the time when the new building, or any part of it, is first used,
  (c) the time when the new building is completed.
(4) The notification of the exclusion must—

[(za) be given before the end of the period of 30 days beginning with the day on which it is to have effect or such longer period as the Commissioners may in any case allow,]²
(a) be made in a form specified in a public notice,
[(b) state the time from which it is to have effect, and]²
(c) contain other information so specified.
(5) Sub-paragraphs (4) to (6) of paragraph 18 (meaning of "building") apply for the purposes of this paragraph as they apply for the purposes of that paragraph.
(6) For the purposes of this paragraph the reference to the construction of a building is to be read without regard to Note (17) or (18)(b) of Group 5 of Schedule 8 (which would otherwise apply as a result of paragraph 33 of this Schedule).
(7) The Commissioners may publish a notice for determining the time at which the construction of a building on any land is to be taken to begin for the purposes of this paragraph.]¹

Amendments—¹ Schedule 10 substituted by the Value Added Tax (Buildings and Land) Order, SI 2008/1146, art 2 with effect in relation to supplies made on or after 1 June 2008, subject to savings in Sch 2 of the Order.
² In sub-para (4), para (za) inserted and para (b) substituted, by the Value Added Tax (Buildings and Land) Order, SI 2009/1966 arts 2, 7 with effect in relation to supplies made on or after 1 August 2009.

[Pre-option exempt grants: requirement for prior permission before exercise of option to tax

28—(1) This paragraph applies if—
(a) a person wants to exercise an option to tax any land with effect from a particular day,
(b) at any time ("the relevant time") before that day the person has made, makes or intends to make an exempt supply to which any grant in relation to the land gives rise, and
(c) the relevant time is within the period of 10 years ending with that day.
(2) The person may exercise the option to tax the land only if—
(a) the conditions specified in a public notice are met in relation to the land, or
(b) the person gets the prior permission of the Commissioners (but see also paragraph 30).
(3) The Commissioners must refuse their permission if they are not satisfied that there would be a fair and reasonable attribution of relevant input tax to relevant supplies.
(4) For this purpose—
"relevant input tax" means input tax incurred, or likely to be incurred, in relation to the land, and
"relevant supplies" means supplies to which any grant in relation to the land gives rise which would be taxable (if the option has effect).
(5) In deciding whether there would be a fair and reasonable attribution of relevant input tax to relevant supplies, the Commissioners must have regard to all the circumstances of the case.
(6) But they must have regard in particular to—
(a) the total value of any exempt supply to which any grant in relation to the land gives rise and which is made or to be made before the day from which the person wants the option to have effect,
(b) the expected total value of any supply to which any grant in relation to the land gives rise that would be taxable (if the option has effect), and
(c) the total amount of input tax incurred, or likely to be incurred, in relation to the land.]¹

Amendments—¹ Schedule 10 substituted by the Value Added Tax (Buildings and Land) Order, SI 2008/1146, art 2 with effect in relation to supplies made on or after 1 June 2008, subject to savings in Sch 2 of the Order.

[Paragraph 28: application for prior permission

29—(1) An application for the prior permission of the Commissioners under paragraph 28 must—
(a) be made in a form specified in a public notice,
(b) contain a statement by the applicant certifying which (if any) of the conditions specified in the public notice under paragraph 28(2)(a) are met in relation to the land, and
(c) contain other information specified in a public notice.
(2) The Commissioners may specify conditions subject to which their permission is given and, if any of those conditions are broken, they may treat the application as if it had not been made.
(3) If the applicant (a) gets the prior permission of the Commissioners, A is, as a result of this sub-paragraph, treated for the purposes of this Part of this Schedule as if A had exercised the option to tax the land with effect from—
(a) the start of the day on which the application was made, or
(b) the start of any later day specified in the application.]¹

Amendments—¹ Schedule 10 substituted by the Value Added Tax (Buildings and Land) Order, SI 2008/1146, art 2 with effect in relation to supplies made on or after 1 June 2008, subject to savings in Sch 2 of the Order.

[Paragraph 28: purported exercise where prior permission not obtained

30—(1) This paragraph applies if—

(*a*) an option to tax was purportedly exercised in a case where, before the option could be exercised, the prior permission of the Commissioners was required under paragraph 28, and
(*b*) notification of the purported option was purportedly given to the Commissioners in accordance with paragraph 20.
(2) The Commissioners may, in the case of any such option, subsequently dispense with the requirement for their prior permission to be given under paragraph 28.
(3) If the Commissioners dispense with that requirement, a purported option—
(*a*) is treated for the purposes of this Part of this Schedule as if it had instead been validly exercised, and
(*b*) has effect in accordance with paragraph 19.]¹

Amendments—¹ Schedule 10 substituted by the Value Added Tax (Buildings and Land) Order, SI 2008/1146, art 2 with effect in relation to supplies made on or after 1 June 2008, subject to savings in Sch 2 of the Order.

[SUPPLEMENTARY PROVISIONS]

Timing of grant and supplies

31—(1) This paragraph applies if—
(*a*) an option to tax is exercised in relation to any land,
(*b*) a grant in relation to the land would otherwise be taken to have been made (whether in whole or in part) before the time when the option has effect, and
(*c*) the grant gives rise to supplies which are treated for the purposes of this Act as taking place after that time.
(2) For the purposes of this Part of this Schedule, the option to tax has effect, in relation to those supplies, as if the grant had been made after that time.]¹

Amendments—¹ Schedule 10 substituted by the Value Added Tax (Buildings and Land) Order, SI 2008/1146, art 2 with effect in relation to supplies made on or after 1 June 2008, subject to savings in Sch 2 of the Order.

[Supplies in relation to a building where part designed or intended for residential or charitable use and part designed or intended for other uses

32 Note (10) of Group 5 of Schedule 8 applies for the purposes of this Part of this Schedule.]¹

Amendments—¹ Schedule 10 substituted by the Value Added Tax (Buildings and Land) Order, SI 2008/1146, art 2 with effect in relation to supplies made on or after 1 June 2008, subject to savings in Sch 2 of the Order.

[Definitions in Schedules 8 or 9 that are applied for the purposes of this Schedule

33 In this Part of this Schedule, references to the expressions listed in the first column are to be read in accordance with the provisions listed in the second column—

Expression	Provision
building designed or adapted for use as a dwelling or a number of dwellings	Note (2) to Group 5 of Schedule 8
completion of a building	Note (2) to Group 1 of Schedule 9
Construction of a building	Notes (16) to (18) to Group 5 of Schedule 8 (but see paragraph 27(6) of this Schedule)
Construction of a building intended for use as a dwelling or a number of dwellings	Note (3) to Group 5 of Schedule 8
Grant	Note (1) to Group 5 of Schedule 8/ Notes (1) and (1A) to Group 1 of Schedule 9
use for a relevant charitable purpose	Notes (6) and (12) to Group 5 of Schedule 8
use for a relevant residential purpose	Notes (4), (5) and (12) to Group 5 of Schedule 8 (but see paragraphs 6(9) and 10(4) of this Schedule)]¹

Amendments—¹ Schedule 10 substituted by the Value Added Tax (Buildings and Land) Order, SI 2008/1146, art 2 with effect in relation to supplies made on or after 1 June 2008, subject to savings in Sch 2 of the Order.

[Other definitions etc

34—(1) In this Part of this Schedule—
"notification" means written notification, and
"permission" means written permission.
(2) For the purposes of this Part of this Schedule any question whether a person is connected with another person is to be decided in accordance with [section 1122 of the Corporation Tax Act 2010]³[; but this is subject to sub-paragraph (2A)]².
[(2A) For the purposes of this Part of this Schedule, a company is not connected with another company only because both are under the control of—

(a) the Crown,
(b) a Minister of the Crown,
(c) a government department, or
(d) a Northern Ireland department.

(2B) In sub-paragraph (2A) "company" and "control" have the same meaning as in section 839 of the Taxes Act.][2]

(3) Any reference in any provision of this Part of this Schedule to a public notice is to a notice published by the Commissioners for the purposes of that provision.]][1]

Amendments—[1] Schedule 10 substituted by the Value Added Tax (Buildings and Land) Order, SI 2008/1146, art 2 with effect in relation to supplies made on or after 1 June 2008, subject to savings in Sch 2 of the Order.
[2] In sub-para (2), words inserted and sub-paras (2A), (2B) inserted, by the Value Added Tax (Buildings and Land) Order, SI 2009/1966 arts 2, 8 with effect in relation to supplies made on or after 1 August 2009.
[3] In sub-para (2) words substituted for words "section 839 of the Taxes Act 1988" by CTA 2010 s 1177, Sch 1 para 285(f). CTA 2010 has effect for corporation tax purposes for accounting periods ending on or after 1 April 2010, and for income and capital gains tax purposes for the tax year 2010–11 and subsequent tax years. Note that the reference to TA 1988 s 839 in sub-para (2B) is not expressly substituted by CTA 2010.

[PART 2
RESIDENTIAL AND CHARITABLE BUILDINGS: CHANGE OF USE ETC

[Introductory]

35—(1) This Part of this Schedule applies where one or more relevant zero-rated supplies relating to a building (or part of a building) have been made to a person ("P").
(2) In this Part of this Schedule—
"relevant zero-rated supply" means a grant or other supply which relates to a building (or part of a building) intended for use solely for—
(a) a relevant residential purpose, or
(b) a relevant charitable purpose,
and which, as a result of Group 5 of Schedule 8, is zero-rated (in whole or in part);
"relevant premises" means the building (or part of a building) in relation to which a relevant zero-rated supply has been made to P;
"relevant period", in relation to relevant premises, means 10 years beginning with the day on which the relevant premises are completed.
(3) Where P is a [person][2] treated as a member of a group under sections 43A to 43D, any reference in this Part of this Schedule to P includes a reference to any member of that group.][1]
Commentary—*De Voil Indirect Tax Service* V3.248, V4.113.
Amendments—[1] Paras 35–37 substituted by the VAT (Buildings and Land) Order, SI 2011/86 arts 4, 8 with effect in relation to buildings that are completed on or after 1 March 2011.
[2] In sub-para (3), words substituted for words "body corporate" by FA 2019 s 53, Sch 18 paras 3, 15(1), (5) with effect from 1 November 2019 (see SI 2019/1348).

[Disposal of interest or change of use following relevant zero-rated supply]

36—(1) Paragraph 37 applies on each occasion during the relevant period when—
(a) there is an increase in the proportion of the relevant premises falling within sub-paragraph (2) or (3), and
(b) as a result, the proportion of the relevant premises so falling ("R2") exceeds the maximum proportion of those premises so falling at any earlier time in the relevant period ("R1").
(2) The relevant premises fall (or part of the relevant premises falls) within this sub-paragraph if P has, since the beginning of the relevant period, disposed of P's entire interest in the relevant premises (or part).
(3) The relevant premises fall (or a part of the relevant premises falls) within this sub-paragraph if—
(a) those premises do not (or that part does not) fall within sub-paragraph (2), and
(b) those premises are (or that part is) being used for a purpose that is neither a relevant residential purpose nor a relevant charitable purpose.
(4) Sub-paragraph (5) applies where—
(a) only a proportion of the use of the relevant premises (or the use of a part of those premises) is for a relevant residential purpose or a relevant charitable purpose, and
(b) that use is not confined to a part of those premises (or of that part) which is used solely for a relevant residential purpose or a relevant charitable purpose.
(5) Where this sub-paragraph applies, sub-paragraph (3) applies as if—
(a) the same proportion of the relevant premises (or part) were being used for a relevant residential purpose or a relevant charitable purpose, and
(b) the remainder of the relevant premises (or part) were being used for a purpose that is neither a relevant residential purpose nor a relevant charitable purpose.

(6) Where P is a charity using the relevant premises (or a part of the relevant premises) as a village hall or similarly in providing social or recreational facilities for a local community the premises are (or the part is) treated as being used for a relevant charitable purpose whether or not any person in occupation is using the premises (or part) for a relevant charitable purpose.][1]

Commentary—*De Voil Indirect Tax Service* **V3.248, V4.113**.
Amendments—[1]   Paras 35–37 substituted by the VAT (Buildings and Land) Order, SI 2011/86 arts 4, 8 with effect in relation to buildings that are completed on or after 1 March 2011.

[Charge to VAT

37—(1) Where this paragraph applies, P's interest, right or licence in the relevant premises held immediately prior to the time when the increase referred to in paragraph 36(1) occurs is treated for the purposes of this Part of this Schedule as—
(*a*) supplied to P for the purposes of a business which P carries on, and
(*b*) supplied by P in the course or furtherance of that business
immediately prior to the time of that increase.
(2) The supply is taken to be a taxable supply which is not zero-rated as a result of Group 5 of Schedule 8.
(3) The value of the supply is taken to be—
(*a*) in the case of the first deemed supply under this paragraph, the amount obtained by the formula—
$R\ 2 \times Y \times ((120 - Z) / 120)$, and
(*b*) in the case of any subsequent deemed supply under this paragraph, the amount obtained by the formula—
$(R\ 2 - R\ 1) \times Y \times ((120 - Z) / 120)$
(4) For the purpose of sub-paragraph (3)—
(*a*) R1 and R2 have the meaning given by paragraph 36(1)(*b*),
(*b*) Y is the amount that yields an amount of VAT chargeable on it equal to—
(i) the VAT which would have been chargeable on the relevant zero-rated supply, or
(ii) if there was more than one supply, the aggregate amount of the VAT which would have been chargeable on the supplies,
had the relevant premises not been intended for use solely for a relevant residential
purpose or a relevant charitable purpose, and
(*c*) Z is the number of whole months since the day on which the relevant premises were completed.][1]

Commentary—*De Voil Indirect Tax Service* **V3.248**.
Amendments—[1]   Paras 35–37 substituted by the VAT (Buildings and Land) Order, SI 2011/86 arts 4, 8 with effect in relation to buildings that are completed on or after 1 March 2011.

[Supplies in relation to a building where part designed for residential or charitable use and part designed for other uses

38   Note (10) of Group 5 of Schedule 8 applies for the purposes of this Part of this Schedule.][1]
Amendments—[1]   Schedule 10 substituted by the Value Added Tax (Buildings and Land) Order, SI 2008/1146, art 2 with effect in relation to supplies made on or after 1 June 2008, subject to savings in Sch 2 of the Order.

[Definitions

39   In this Part of this Schedule, references to the expressions listed in the first column are to be read in accordance with the provisions listed in the second column—

Expression	Provision
completion of a building	Note (2) to Group 1 of Schedule 9
Grant	Note (1) to Group 5 of Schedule 8/ Notes (1) and (1A) to Group 1 of Schedule 9
use for a relevant charitable purpose	Notes (6) and (12) to Group 5 of Schedule 8
use for a relevant residential purpose	Notes (4), (5) and (12) to Group 5 of Schedule 8][1]

Amendments—[1]   Schedule 10 substituted by the Value Added Tax (Buildings and Land) Order, SI 2008/1146, art 2 with effect in relation to supplies made on or after 1 June 2008, subject to savings in Sch 2 of the Order.

[PART 3
GENERAL

Benefit of consideration for grant accruing to a person other than the grantor

40—(1) This paragraph applies if the benefit of the consideration for the grant of an interest in, right over or licence to occupy land accrues to a person ("the beneficiary") other than the person making the grant.
(2) The beneficiary is to be treated for the purposes of this Act as the person making the grant.
(3) So far as any input tax of the person actually making the grant is attributable to the grant, it is to be treated for the purposes of this Act as input tax of the beneficiary.][1]

Amendments—[1] Schedule 10 substituted by the Value Added Tax (Buildings and Land) Order, SI 2008/1146, art 2 with effect in relation to supplies made on or after 1 June 2008, subject to savings in Sch 2 of the Order.

[SCHEDULE 10A
FACE-VALUE VOUCHERS [ISSUED BEFORE 1 JANUARY 2019]]
Section 51B

Amendments—This Schedule inserted by FA 2003 s 19, Sch 1 para 2 with effect for supplies of tokens, stamps or vouchers issued after 8 April 2003.

Words in heading inserted by FA 2019 s 52, Sch 17 paras 1, 4 with effect from 12 February 2019.

Meaning of "face-value voucher" etc

[**1**—(1) In this Schedule "face-value voucher" means a token, stamp or voucher (whether in physical or electronic form) that represents a right to receive goods or services to the value of an amount stated on it or recorded in it.
(2) References in this Schedule to the "face value" of a voucher are to the amount referred to in sub-paragraph (1) above.][1]

Amendments—[1] Schedule inserted by FA 2003 Sch 1 para 2 in relation to supplies of tokens, stamps or vouchers issued after 8 April 2003.

Nature of supply

[**2** The issue of a face-value voucher, or any subsequent supply of it, is a supply of services for the purposes of this Act.][1]

Amendments—[1] Schedule inserted by FA 2003 Sch 1 para 2 in relation to supplies of tokens, stamps or vouchers issued after 8 April 2003.

Treatment of credit vouchers

[**3**—(1) This paragraph applies to a face-value voucher issued by a person who—
   (*a*) is not a person from whom goods or services may be obtained by the use of the voucher, and
   (*b*) undertakes to give complete or partial reimbursement to any such person from whom goods or services are so obtained.
Such a voucher is referred to in this Schedule as a "credit voucher".
(2) The consideration for any supply of a credit voucher shall be disregarded for the purposes of this Act except to the extent (if any) that it exceeds the face value of the voucher.
(3) Sub-paragraph (2) above does not apply if any of the persons from whom goods or services are obtained by the use of the voucher fails to account for any of the VAT due on the supply of those goods or services to the person using the voucher to obtain them.][1]
[(4) The Treasury may by order specify other circumstances in which sub-paragraph (2) above does not apply.][2]

Amendments—[1] Schedule inserted by FA 2003 Sch 1 para 2 in relation to supplies of tokens, stamps or vouchers issued after 8 April 2003.
[2] Sub-para (4) inserted by FA 2006 s 22(3) with effect from 19 July 2006.

Treatment of retailer vouchers

[**4**—(1) This paragraph applies to a face-value voucher issued by a person who—
   (*a*) is a person from whom goods or services may be obtained by the use of the voucher, and
   (*b*) if there are other such persons, undertakes to give complete or partial reimbursement to those from whom goods or services are so obtained.
Such a voucher is referred to in this Schedule as a "retailer voucher".
(2) The consideration for the issue of a retailer voucher shall be disregarded for the purposes of this Act except to the extent (if any) that it exceeds the face value of the voucher.
(3) Sub-paragraph (2) above does not apply if—

(*a*) the voucher is used to obtain goods or services from a person other than the issuer, and
(*b*) that person fails to account for any of the VAT due on the supply of those goods or services to the person using the voucher to obtain them.
(4) Any supply of a retailer voucher subsequent to the issue of it shall be treated in the same way as the supply of a voucher to which paragraph 6 applies.][1]

Amendments—[1] Schedule inserted by FA 2003 Sch 1 para 2 in relation to supplies of tokens, stamps or vouchers issued after 8 April 2003.

Treatment of postage stamps

[5— The consideration for the supply of a face-value voucher that is a postage stamp shall be disregarded for the purposes of this Act except to the extent (if any) that it exceeds the face value of the stamp.][1]

Amendments—[1] Schedule inserted by FA 2003 Sch 1 para 2 in relation to supplies of tokens, stamps or vouchers issued after 8 April 2003.

Treatment of other kinds of face-value voucher

[6— (1) This paragraph applies to a face-value voucher that is not a credit voucher, a retailer voucher or a postage stamp.
(2) A supply of such a voucher is chargeable at the rate in force under section 2(1) (standard rate) except where sub-paragraph (3), (4) or (5) below applies.
(3) Where the voucher is one that can only be used to obtain goods or services in one particular non-standard rate category, the supply of the voucher falls in that category.
(4) Where the voucher is used to obtain goods or services all of which fall in one particular non-standard rate category, the supply of the voucher falls in that category.
(5) Where the voucher is used to obtain goods or services in a number of different rate categories—
  (*a*) the supply of the voucher shall be treated as that many different supplies, each falling in the category in question, and
  (*b*) the value of each of those supplies shall be determined on a just and reasonable basis.][1]

Amendments—[1] Schedule inserted by FA 2003 Sch 1 para 2 in relation to supplies of tokens, stamps or vouchers issued after 8 April 2003.

Vouchers supplied free with other goods or services

[7 Where—
  (*a*) a face-value voucher (other than a postage stamp) and other goods or services are supplied to the same person in a composite transaction, and
  (*b*) the total consideration for the supplies is no different, or not significantly different, from what it would be if the voucher were not supplied, the supply of the voucher shall be treated as being made for no consideration.][1]

Amendments—[1] Schedule inserted by FA 2003 Sch 1 para 2 in relation to supplies of tokens, stamps or vouchers issued after 8 April 2003.

[Exclusion of single purpose vouchers

7A Paragraphs 2 to 4, 6 and 7 do not apply in relation to the issue, or any subsequent supply, of a face-value voucher that represents a right to receive goods or services of one type which are subject to a single rate of VAT.][1]

Amendments—[1] This para inserted by FA 2012 s 201 with effect in relation to supplies of face-value vouchers issued on or after 10 May 2012, subject to provisions relating to vouchers issued before 10 May 2012 and used after that date: see FA 2012 s 201(3), (4).

Interpretation

[8— (1) In this Schedule—
  "credit voucher" has the meaning given by paragraph 3(1) above;
  "face value" has the meaning given by paragraph 1(2) above;
  "face value voucher" has the meaning given by paragraph 1(1) above;
  "retailer voucher" has the meaning given by paragraph 4(1) above.
(2) For the purposes of this Schedule—
  (*a*) the "rate categories" of supplies are—
    (i) supplies chargeable at the rate in force under section 2(1) (standard rate),
    (ii) supplies chargeable at the rate in force under section 29A (reduced rate),
    (iii) zero-rated supplies, and
    (iv) exempt supplies and other supplies that are not taxable supplies;

(b) the "non-standard rate categories" of supplies are those in sub-paragraphs (ii), (iii) and (iv) of paragraph (a) above;
(c) goods or services are in a particular rate category if a supply of those goods or services falls in that category.
(3) A reference in this Schedule to a voucher being used to obtain goods or services includes a reference to the case where it is used as part-payment for those goods or services.][1]

Amendments—[1] Schedule inserted by FA 2003 Sch 1 para 2 in relation to supplies of tokens, stamps or vouchers issued after 8 April 2003.

[SCHEDULE 10B

VAT TREATMENT OF VOUCHERS ISSUED ON OR AFTER 1 JANUARY 2019
Section 51C

Meaning of "voucher"

1 (1) In this Schedule "voucher" means an instrument (in physical or electronic form) in relation to which the following conditions are met.
(2) The first condition is that one or more persons are under an obligation to accept the instrument as consideration for the provision of goods or services.
(3) The second condition is that either or both of—
  (a) the goods and services for the provision of which the instrument may be accepted as consideration, and
  (b) the persons who are under the obligation to accept the instrument as consideration for the provision of goods or services,
are limited and are stated on or recorded in the instrument or the terms and conditions governing the use of the instrument.
(4) The third condition is that the instrument is transferable by gift (whether or not it is transferable for consideration).
(5) The following are not vouchers—
  (a) an instrument entitling a person to a reduction in the consideration for the provision of goods or services;
  (b) an instrument functioning as a ticket, for example for travel or for admission to a venue or event;
  (c) postage stamps.][1]

Amendments—[1] Schedule 10B inserted by FA 2019 s 52, Sch 17 paras 1, 5 with effect in relation to vouchers issued on or after 1 January 2019 (VATA 1994 s 51C(2)).

[Meaning of related expressions

2 (1) This paragraph gives the meaning of other expressions used in this Schedule.
(2) "Relevant goods or services", in relation to a voucher, are any goods or services for the provision of which the voucher may be accepted as consideration.
(3) References in this Schedule to the transfer of a voucher do not include the voucher being offered and accepted as consideration for the provision of relevant goods or services.
(4) References in this Schedule to a voucher being offered or accepted as consideration for the provision of relevant goods or services include references to the voucher being offered or accepted as part consideration for the provision of relevant goods or services.][1]

Amendments—[1] Schedule 10B inserted by FA 2019 s 52, Sch 17 paras 1, 5 with effect in relation to vouchers issued on or after 1 January 2019 (VATA 1994 s 51C(2)).

[VAT treatment of vouchers: general rule

3 (1) The issue, and any subsequent transfer, of a voucher is to be treated for the purposes of this Act as a supply of relevant goods or services.
(2) References in this Schedule to the "paragraph 3 supply", in relation to the issue or transfer of a voucher, are to the supply of relevant goods or services treated by this paragraph as having been made on the issue or transfer of the voucher.][1]

Amendments—[1] Schedule 10B inserted by FA 2019 s 52, Sch 17 paras 1, 5 with effect in relation to vouchers issued on or after 1 January 2019 (VATA 1994 s 51C(2)).

[Single purpose vouchers: special rules

4 (1) A voucher is a single purpose voucher if, at the time it is issued, the following are known—
  (a) the place of supply of the relevant goods or services, and
  (b) that any supply of relevant goods or services falls into a single supply category (and what that supply category is).

(2) The supply categories are—
   (*a*) supplies chargeable at the rate in force under section 2(1) (standard rate),
   (*b*) supplies chargeable at the rate in force under section 29A (reduced rate),
   (*c*) zero-rated supplies, and
   (*d*) exempt supplies and other supplies that are not taxable supplies.
(3) For the purposes of this paragraph, assume that the supply of relevant goods or services is the provision of relevant goods or services for which the voucher may be accepted as consideration (rather than the supply of relevant goods or services treated as made on the issue or transfer of the voucher).][1]

Amendments—[1] Schedule 10B inserted by FA 2019 s 52, Sch 17 paras 1, 5 with effect in relation to vouchers issued on or after 1 January 2019 (VATA 1994 s 51C(2)).

[**5** (1) This paragraph applies where a single purpose voucher is accepted as consideration for the provision of relevant goods or services.
(2) The provision of the relevant goods or services is not a supply of goods or services for the purposes of this Act.
(3) But where the person who provides the relevant goods or services (the "provider") is not the person who issued the voucher (the "issuer"), for the purposes of this Act the provider is to be treated as having made a supply of those goods or services to the issuer.][1]

Amendments—[1] Schedule 10B inserted by FA 2019 s 52, Sch 17 paras 1, 5 with effect in relation to vouchers issued on or after 1 January 2019 (VATA 1994 s 51C(2)).

[Multi-purpose vouchers: special rules

6 A voucher is a multi-purpose voucher if it is not a single purpose voucher.][1]

Amendments—[1] Schedule 10B inserted by FA 2019 s 52, Sch 17 paras 1, 5 with effect in relation to vouchers issued on or after 1 January 2019 (VATA 1994 s 51C(2)).

[**7** (1) Any consideration for the issue or subsequent transfer of a multi-purpose voucher is to be disregarded for the purposes of this Act.
(2) The paragraph 3 supply made on the issue or subsequent transfer of a multi-purpose voucher is to be treated as not being a supply within section 26(2).][1]

Amendments—[1] Schedule 10B inserted by FA 2019 s 52, Sch 17 paras 1, 5 with effect in relation to vouchers issued on or after 1 January 2019 (VATA 1994 s 51C(2)).

[**8** (1) Where a multi-purpose voucher is accepted as consideration for the provision of relevant goods or services, for the purposes of this Act—
   (*a*) the provision of the relevant goods or services is to be treated as a supply, and
   (*b*) the value of the supply treated as having been made by paragraph (*a*) is determined as follows.
(2) If the consideration for the most recent transfer of the voucher for consideration is known to the supplier, the value of the supply is such amount as, with the addition of the VAT chargeable on the supply, is equal to that consideration.
(3) If the consideration for the most recent transfer of the voucher for consideration is not known to the supplier, the value of the supply is such amount as, with the addition of the VAT chargeable on the supply, is equal to the face value of the voucher.
(4) The "face value" of a voucher is the monetary value stated on or recorded in—
   (*a*) the voucher, or
   (*b*) the terms and conditions governing the use of the voucher.][1]

Amendments—[1] Schedule 10B inserted by FA 2019 s 52, Sch 17 paras 1, 5 with effect in relation to vouchers issued on or after 1 January 2019 (VATA 1994 s 51C(2)).

[Intermediaries

9 (1) This paragraph applies where—
   (*a*) a voucher is issued or transferred by an agent who acts in their own name, and
   (*b*) the paragraph 3 supply is a supply of services to which section 47(3) would apply (apart from this paragraph).
(2) Section 47(3) does not apply.
(3) The paragraph 3 supply is treated as both a supply to the agent and a supply by the agent.][1]

Amendments—[1] Schedule 10B inserted by FA 2019 s 52, Sch 17 paras 1, 5 with effect in relation to vouchers issued on or after 1 January 2019 (VATA 1994 s 51C(2)).

[**10** Nothing in this Schedule affects the application of this Act to any services provided, by a person who issues or transfers a voucher, in addition to the issue or transfer of the voucher.][1]

Amendments—[1] Schedule 10B inserted by FA 2019 s 52, Sch 17 paras 1, 5 with effect in relation to vouchers issued on or after 1 January 2019 (VATA 1994 s 51C(2)).

[Composite transactions

11 (1) This paragraph applies where, as part of a composite transaction—
  (*a*) goods or services are supplied to a person, and
  (*b*) a voucher is issued or transferred to that person.
(2) If the total consideration for the transaction is not different, or not significantly different, from what it would be if the voucher were not issued or transferred, the paragraph 3 supply is to be treated as being made for no consideration.]¹

Amendments—¹ Schedule 10B inserted by FA 2019 s 52, Sch 17 paras 1, 5 with effect in relation to vouchers issued on or after 1 January 2019 (VATA 1994 s 51C(2)).

SCHEDULE 11
ADMINISTRATION, COLLECTION AND ENFORCEMENT
Section 58

Cross references—See VATA 1994 Sch 9ZA para 73 (Northern Ireland: accounting for VAT and payment of VAT).

General

[**1**—The Commissioners for Her Majesty's Revenue and Customs shall be responsible for the collection and management of VAT.]¹

Amendments—¹ Para substituted by the Commissioners for Revenue and Customs Act 2005 s 50, Sch 4 para 56 with effect from 18 April 2005 by virtue of the Commissioners for Revenue and Customs Act 2005 (Commencement) Order, SI 2005/1126, art 2(2).

Accounting for VAT . . . and payment of VAT

2—(1) Regulations under this paragraph may require the keeping of accounts[, the making of returns and the submission of information]⁹ in such form and manner as may be specified in the regulations . . . ² [or by the Commissioners in accordance with the regulations.]⁸
(2), (2A) . . . ²
(3), (3ZA) . . . ¹⁰
[(3A) Regulations under this paragraph may require the submission to the Commissioners by taxable persons, at such times and intervals, in such cases and in such form and manner as may be—
  (*a*) specified in the regulations, or
  (*b*) determined by the Commissioners in accordance with powers conferred by the regulations,
of statements containing such particulars of supplies to which section 55A(6) applies in which the taxable persons are concerned, and of the persons concerned in those supplies, as may be [so specified]⁸.
[(3B) Regulations under this paragraph may make provision for requiring—
  (*a*) a person who first makes a supply of goods [or services]⁶ to which section 55A(6) applies (a "reverse charge supply"),
  (*b*) a person who ceases making reverse charge supplies without intending subsequently to make such supplies, or
  (*c*) a person who has fallen within paragraph (*b*) above but who nonetheless starts to make reverse charge supplies again,
to give to the Commissioners such notification of that fact at such time and in such form and manner as may be specified in the regulations or [by the Commissioners in accordance with the regulations]⁸.]⁴.]³
(4), (5) . . . ¹⁰
[(5A) Regulations under this paragraph may make provision—
  (*a*) for requiring the relevant person to give to the Commissioners such notification of the arrival in the United Kingdom of goods consisting of a means of transport, at such time and in such form and manner, as may be specified in the regulations or by the Commissioners in accordance with the regulations, and
  [(*b*) where notification of the arrival of a means of transport imported into the United Kingdom is required by virtue of paragraph (*a*), for requiring any VAT on its importation to be paid at such time and in such manner as may be specified in the regulations.]¹⁰
(5B) The provision that may be made by regulations made by virtue of sub-paragraph (5A) includes—
  (*a*) provision for a notification required by virtue of that subparagraph to contain such particulars relating to the notified arrival of the means of transport and any VAT chargeable on its . . . ¹⁰ importation as may be specified in the regulations or by the Commissioners in accordance with the regulations,
  (*b*) provision for such a notification to be given by a person who is not the relevant person and is so specified, or is of a description so specified,

(c) provision for such a notification to contain a declaration, given in such form and by such person as may be so specified, as to the information contained in the notification, and

(d) supplementary, incidental, consequential or transitional provision (including provision amending any provision made by or under this Act or any other enactment).

(5C) Subsection (3) of section 97 (orders subject to Commons approval) applies to a statutory instrument containing any regulations made by virtue of sub-paragraph (5A) which amend an enactment as it applies to an order within subsection (4) of that section.

(5D) For the purposes of sub-paragraph (5A)—

. . .[10]

"relevant person", in relation to the arrival of a means of transport in the United Kingdom, means—

(a) . . .[10]

(b) where it has been imported . . .[10], the person liable to pay VAT on the importation, . . .

(c) . . .[10]

[(5E) For the purposes of sub-paragraphs (5A) to (5D) "means of transport" means—

(a) any ship which exceeds 7.5 metres in length,

(b) any aircraft the take-off weight of which exceeds 1550 kilograms, or

(c) any motorised land vehicle which—

(i) has an engine with a displacement or cylinder capacity exceeding 48 cubic centimetres, or

(ii) is constructed or adapted to be electrically propelled using more than 7.2 kilowatts,

but only if the ship, aircraft or vehicle is intended for the transport of persons or goods.

(5F) The Treasury may by order vary sub-paragraph (5E) by adding or deleting any ship, aircraft or vehicle of a description specified in the order to or from those which are for the time being specified there.][10]

(6) Regulations under this paragraph may make special provision for such taxable supplies by retailers of any goods or of any description of goods or of services or any description of services as may be determined by or under the regulations and, in particular—

(a) for permitting the value which is to be taken as the value of the supplies in any prescribed accounting period or part thereof to be determined, subject to any limitations or restrictions, by such method or one of such methods as may have been described in any notice published by the Commissioners in pursuance of the regulations and not withdrawn by a further notice or as may be agreed with the Commissioners; and

(b) for determining the proportion of the value of the supplies which is to be attributed to any description of supplies; and

(c) for adjusting that value and proportion for periods comprising two or more prescribed accounting periods or parts thereof.

(7) Regulations under this paragraph may make provision whereby, in such cases and subject to such conditions as may be determined by or under the regulations, VAT in respect of a supply may be accounted for and paid by reference to the time when consideration for the supply is received; and any such regulations may make such modifications of the provisions of this Act (including in particular, but without prejudice to the generality of the power, the provisions as to the time when, and the circumstances in which, credit for input tax is to be allowed) as appear to the Commissioners necessary or expedient.

(8) Regulations under this paragraph may make provision whereby, in such cases and subject to such conditions as may be determined by or under the regulations—

(a) VAT in respect of any supply by a taxable person of dutiable goods, . . .[10]

(b) . . .[10]

may be accounted for and paid, and any question as to the inclusion of any duty or agricultural levy in the value of the supply . . .[10] determined, by reference to the duty point or by reference to such later time as the Commissioners may allow.

In this sub-paragraph "dutiable goods" and "duty point" have the same meanings as in section 18.

(9) . . .[10]

(10) Regulations under this paragraph may make provision—

(a) for treating VAT chargeable in one prescribed accounting period as chargeable in another such period; and

(b) with respect to the making of entries in accounts for the purpose of making adjustments, whether for the correction of errors or otherwise; and

(c) for the making of financial adjustments in connection with the making of entries in accounts for the purpose mentioned in paragraph (b) above [and (*d*) for a person, for purposes connected with the making of any such entry or financial adjustment, to be required to provide to any prescribed person, or to retain, a document in the prescribed form containing prescribed particulars of the matters to which the entry or adjustment relates; and

(*e*) for enabling the Commissioners, in such cases as they may think fit, to dispense with or relax a requirement imposed by regulations made by virtue of paragraph (*d*) above.]¹

(11) Regulations under this paragraph may make different provision for different circumstances and may provide for different dates as the commencement of prescribed accounting periods applicable to different persons.

[(11A) Regulations under this paragraph may include incidental, supplemental, consequential, saving, transitional or transitory provision.]⁹

(12) The provisions made by regulations under this paragraph for cases where goods are treated as supplied by a taxable person by virtue of paragraph 7 of Schedule 4 may require VAT chargeable on the supply to be accounted for and paid, and particulars thereof to be provided, by such other person and in such manner as may be specified by the regulations.

(13) Where, at the end of a prescribed accounting period, the amount of VAT due from any person or the amount of any VAT credit would be less than £1, that amount shall be treated as nil.

Northern Ireland—See Sch 9ZA para 73 (Northern Ireland: for the purposes of this Act, Sch 9ZA para 73(1)–(4), (5), (6) are to be treated as if they were contained in para 2).

See Sch 9ZA para 74 (Northern Ireland: para 2 has effect as if—
- in sub-para (5A)(*b*), after "transport" there were inserted "acquired from a member State, or";
- in sub-para (5B)(*a*), after "chargeable on its" there were inserted "acquisition or"; and
- in sub-para (5D) in the definition of "relevant person"—
  - (i) before paragraph (*b*) there were inserted—
    "(*a*) where the means of transport has been acquired in Northern Ireland from a member State, the person who so acquires it,"; and
  - (ii) after paragraph (*b*) there were inserted—
    "(*c*) in any other case—
    (i) the owner of the means of transport at the time of its arrival in the United Kingdom, or
    (ii) where it is subject to a lease or hire agreement, the lessee or hirer of the means of transport at that time."

Sub-para (8) applies to NI acquisition VAT in respect of an acquisition by any person from a member State of dutiable goods as it applies to VAT in respect of any supply by a taxable person of dutiable goods (Sch 9ZA para 74(2)).

See also VATA 1994 Sch 9ZB para 26(2): sub-para (8) has effect as if after "section 18" there were inserted "in relation to goods other than goods in Northern Ireland, or paragraph 16 of Schedule 9ZB in relation to goods in Northern Ireland".

Regulations—See VAT Regulations, SI 1995/2518 regs 13–20 (VAT and other invoices); regs 21–23 (EC sales statements); regs 24–42 (accounting and records); regs 49–55 (annual accounting scheme); regs 56–65 (cash accounting scheme); regs 66–75 (retail schemes); regs 146–155 (new means of transport).

Value Added Tax (Amendment) (No 2) Regulations, SI 2010/2240.
VAT (Amendment) Regulations, SI 2012/33
VAT (Amendment) (No 2) Regulations, SI 2012/1899.
VAT (Amendment) Regulations, SI 2013/701.
Value Added Tax (Amendment) Regulations, SI 2014/548.
Value Added Tax (Amendment) (No 2) Regulations, SI 2014/1497.
VAT (Amendment) Regulations, SI 2018/261.
VAT (Amendment) Regulations, SI 2019/1048.

Amendments—¹ Sub-para (2A) and sub-para (10)(*d*), (*e*) inserted by FA 1996 s 38.
² Words in Heading and sub-para (1) repealed, and sub-paras (2), (2A) repealed by FA 2002 ss 24(1)(*b*), (5), 139, Sch 40 Pt 2(2) with effect 1 December 2003 (by virtue of SI 2003/3043).
³ Sub-paras (3A), (3B) inserted by FA 2006 s 19(7), (8) with effect for supplies made on or after 1 June 2007 (by virtue of the Finance Act 2006, Section 19, (Appointed Day) Order, SI 2007/1419).
⁴ Sub-para (3B) substituted by the VAT (Administration, Collection and Enforcement) Order, SI 2007/1421 art 2 with effect from 1 June 2007.
⁶ Words in sub-para (3B) inserted by FA 2010 s 50(2) with effect from 8 April 2010.
⁷ Sub-paras (5A)–(5D) inserted by FA 2012 s 202 with effect from 17 July 2012.
⁸ In sub-paras (1), (5)(*a*), words inserted; in sub-para (3A), para (*b*) substituted and words substituted for word "prescribed"; and in sub-para (3B), words substituted for words "determined by the Commissioners in accordance with powers conferred by the regulations"; by FA 2012 s 204, Sch 29 paras 1, 12 with effect from 17 July 2012.
⁹ In sub-para (1), words substituted for words "and the making of returns", and sub-para (11A) inserted, by F(No 2)A 2017 s 62(1), (2) with effect from 15 November 2017.
¹⁰ The following amendments made by the Taxation (Cross-border Trade) Act 2018 s 43, Sch 8 paras 1, 97(1), (2) with effect from IP completion day (11pm on 31 December 2020), by virtue of SI 2020/1642 reg 4(*b*)—
- sub-paras (3), (3ZA), (4), (5), (9) repealed;
- sub-para (5A)(*b*) substituted;
- in sub-para (5B)(*a*), words "acquisition or" repealed;
- in sub-para (5D), definition of "means of transport" repealed;
- in sub-para (5D) in definition of "relevant person", the following repealed: para (*a*), in para (*b*) words "from a place outside the member States", and para (*c*);
- sub-paras (5E), (5F) inserted; and
- in sub-para (8), the following repealed: para (*b*) and preceding word "or", and in words following para (*b*) words "or acquisition".

Note that, where these amendments remove a reference to the principal VAT Directive (2006/112/EC) or the Implementing VAT Regulation ((EU) No 282/2011), the removal is not to be taken as implying that the Directive or Regulation is no longer relevant for determining the meaning and effect of this para (Taxation (Cross-border Trade) Act 2018 Sch 8 para 99). Before these amendments, para 2 read as follows—

"2—

(1) Regulations under this paragraph may require the keeping of accounts, the making of returns and the submission of information in such form and manner as may be specified in the regulations or by the Commissioners in accordance with the regulations.

(2), (2A)

(3) Regulations under this paragraph may require the submission to the Commissioners by taxable persons, at such times and intervals, in such cases and in such form and manner as may be—
  (a) specified in the regulations; or
  (b) specified by the Commissioners in accordance with the regulations,

of statements containing such particulars of transactions in which the taxable persons are concerned and to which this sub-paragraph applies, and of the persons concerned in those transactions, as may be so specified.

  (3ZA) Sub-paragraph (3) above applies to—
  (a) transactions involving the movement of goods between member States, and
  (b) transactions involving the supply of services to a person in a member State other than the United Kingdom who is required to pay VAT on the supply in accordance with provisions of the law of that other member State giving effect to Article 196 of Council Directive 2006/112/EC.

  (3A) Regulations under this paragraph may require the submission to the Commissioners by taxable persons, at such times and intervals, in such cases and in such form and manner as may be—
  (a) specified in the regulations, or
  (b) determined by the Commissioners in accordance with powers conferred by the regulations,

of statements containing such particulars of supplies to which section 55A(6) applies in which the taxable persons are concerned, and of the persons concerned in those supplies, as may be so specified.

  (3B) Regulations under this paragraph may make provision for requiring—
  (a) a person who first makes a supply of goods or services to which section 55A(6) applies (a "reverse charge supply"),
  (b) a person who ceases making reverse charge supplies without intending subsequently to make such supplies, or
  (c) a person who has fallen within paragraph (b) above but who nonetheless starts to make reverse charge supplies again,

to give to the Commissioners such notification of that fact at such time and in such form and manner as may be specified in the regulations or by the Commissioners in accordance with the regulations.

  (4) Regulations under this paragraph may make provision in relation to cases where—
  (a) any goods which are subject to a duty of excise or consist in a new means of transport are acquired in the United Kingdom from another member State by any person;
  (b) the acquisition of the goods is a taxable acquisition and is not in pursuance of a taxable supply; and
  (c) that person is not a taxable person at the time of the acquisition,

for requiring the person who acquires the goods to give to the Commissioners such notification of the acquisition, and for requiring any VAT on the acquisition to be paid, at such time and in such form or manner as may be specified in the regulations or (in the case of the notification requirement) by the Commissioners in accordance with the regulations.

  (5) Regulations under this paragraph may provide for a notification required by virtue of sub-paragraph (4) above—
  (a) to contain such particulars relating to the notified acquisition and any VAT chargeable thereon as may be specified in the regulations or by the Commissioners in accordance with the regulations; and
  (b) to be given, in prescribed cases, by the personal representative, trustee in bankruptcy, trustee in sequestration, receiver, liquidator or person otherwise acting in a representative capacity in relation to the person who makes that acquisition.

  (5A) Regulations under this paragraph may make provision—
  (a) for requiring the relevant person to give to the Commissioners such notification of the arrival in the United Kingdom of goods consisting of a means of transport, at such time and in such form and manner, as may be specified in the regulations or by the Commissioners in accordance with the regulations, and
  (b) where notification of the arrival of a means of transport acquired from another member State, or imported from a place outside the member States, is required by virtue of paragraph (a), for requiring any VAT on the acquisition or importation to be paid at such time and in such manner as may be specified in the regulations.

  (5B) The provision that may be made by regulations made by virtue of sub-paragraph (5A) includes—
  (a) provision for a notification required by virtue of that subparagraph to contain such particulars relating to the notified arrival of the means of transport and any VAT chargeable on its acquisition or importation as may be specified in the regulations or by the Commissioners in accordance with the regulations,
  (b) provision for such a notification to be given by a person who is not the relevant person and is so specified, or is of a description so specified,
  (c) provision for such a notification to contain a declaration, given in such form and by such person as may be so specified, as to the information contained in the notification, and

(d) supplementary, incidental, consequential or transitional provision (including provision amending any provision made by or under this Act or any other enactment).

(5C) Subsection (3) of section 97 (orders subject to Commons approval) applies to a statutory instrument containing any regulations made by virtue of sub-paragraph (5A) which amend an enactment as it applies to an order within subsection (4) of that section.

(5D) For the purposes of sub-paragraph (5A)—

"means of transport" has the same meaning as it has in this Act in the expression "new means of transport" (see section 95);

"relevant person", in relation to the arrival of a means of transport in the United Kingdom, means—

    (a) where the means of transport has been acquired in the United Kingdom from another member State, the person who so acquires it,

    (b) where it has been imported from a place outside the member States, the person liable to pay VAT on the importation, and

    (c) in any other case—

        (i) the owner of the means of transport at the time of its arrival in the United Kingdom, or

        (ii) where it is subject to a lease or hire agreement, the lessee or hirer of the means of transport at that time.

(6) Regulations under this paragraph may make special provision for such taxable supplies by retailers of any goods or of any description of goods or of services or any description of services as may be determined by or under the regulations and, in particular—

    (a) for permitting the value which is to be taken as the value of the supplies in any prescribed accounting period or part thereof to be determined, subject to any limitations or restrictions, by such method or one of such methods as may have been described in any notice published by the Commissioners in pursuance of the regulations and not withdrawn by a further notice or as may be agreed with the Commissioners; and

    (b) for determining the proportion of the value of the supplies which is to be attributed to any description of supplies; and

    (c) for adjusting that value and proportion for periods comprising two or more prescribed accounting periods or parts thereof.

(7) Regulations under this paragraph may make provision whereby, in such cases and subject to such conditions as may be determined by or under the regulations, VAT in respect of a supply may be accounted for and paid by reference to the time when consideration for the supply is received; and any such regulations may make such modifications of the provisions of this Act (including in particular, but without prejudice to the generality of the power, the provisions as to the time when, and the circumstances in which, credit for input tax is to be allowed) as appear to the Commissioners necessary or expedient.

(8) Regulations under this paragraph may make provision whereby, in such cases and subject to such conditions as may be determined by or under the regulations—

    (a) VAT in respect of any supply by a taxable person of dutiable goods, or

    (b) VAT in respect of an acquisition by any person from another member State of dutiable goods,

may be accounted for and paid, and any question as to the inclusion of any duty or agricultural levy in the value of the supply or acquisition determined, by reference to the duty point or by reference to such later time as the Commissioners may allow.

In this sub-paragraph "dutiable goods" and "duty point" have the same meanings as in section 18.

(9) Regulations under this paragraph may provide for the time when any invoice described in regulations made for the purposes of section 6(8)(b) or 12(1)(b) is to be treated as having been issued and provide for VAT accounted for and paid by reference to the date of issue of such an invoice to be confined to VAT on so much of the value of the supply or acquisition as is shown on the invoice.

(10) Regulations under this paragraph may make provision—

    (a) for treating VAT chargeable in one prescribed accounting period as chargeable in another such period; and

    (b) with respect to the making of entries in accounts for the purpose of making adjustments, whether for the correction of errors or otherwise; and

    (c) for the making of financial adjustments in connection with the making of entries in accounts for the purpose mentioned in paragraph (b) above and

    (d) for a person, for purposes connected with the making of any such entry or financial adjustment, to be required to provide to any prescribed person, or to retain, a document in the prescribed form containing prescribed particulars of the matters to which the entry or adjustment relates; and

    (e) for enabling the Commissioners, in such cases as they may think fit, to dispense with or relax a requirement imposed by regulations made by virtue of paragraph (d) above.

(11) Regulations under this paragraph may make different provision for different circumstances and may provide for different dates as the commencement of prescribed accounting periods applicable to different persons.

(11A) Regulations under this paragraph may include incidental, supplemental, consequential, saving, transitional or transitory provision.

(12) The provisions made by regulations under this paragraph for cases where goods are treated as supplied by a taxable person by virtue of paragraph 7 of Schedule 4 may require VAT chargeable on the supply to be accounted for and paid, and particulars thereof to be provided, by such other person and in such manner as may be specified by the regulations.

(13) Where, at the end of a prescribed accounting period, the amount of VAT due from any person or the amount of any VAT credit would be less than £1, that amount shall be treated as nil.".

[VAT invoices

2A—(1) Regulations may require a taxable person supplying goods or services to provide an invoice (a "VAT invoice") to the person supplied.
(2) A VAT invoice must give—
  (a) such particulars as may be prescribed of the supply, the supplier and the person supplied;
  (b) such an indication as may be prescribed of whether VAT is chargeable on the supply under this Act . . . [2];
  (c) such particulars of any VAT that is so chargeable as may be prescribed.
(3) Regulations may confer power on the Commissioners to allow the requirements of any regulations as to the information to be given in a VAT invoice to be relaxed or dispensed with.
(4) Regulations may—
  (a) provide that the VAT invoice that is required to be provided in connection with a particular description of supply must be provided within a prescribed time after the supply is treated as taking place, or at such time before the supply is treated as taking place as may be prescribed;
  (b) allow for the invoice to be issued later than required by the regulations where it is issued in accordance with general or special directions given by the Commissioners.
(5) Regulations may—
  (a) make provision about the manner in which a VAT invoice may be provided, including provision prescribing conditions that must be complied with in the case of an invoice issued by a third party on behalf of the supplier;
  (b) prescribe conditions that must be complied with in the case of a VAT invoice that relates to more than one supply;
  (c) make, in relation to a document that refers to a VAT invoice and is intended to amend it, such provision corresponding to that which may be made in relation to a VAT invoice as appears to the Commissioners to be appropriate.
(6) Regulations may confer power on the Commissioners to require a person who has received in the United Kingdom a VAT invoice that is (or part of which is) in a language other than English to provide them with an English translation of the invoice (or part).
(7) Regulations under this paragraph—
  (a) may be framed so as to apply only in prescribed cases or only in relation to supplies made to persons of prescribed descriptions;
  (b) may make different provision for different circumstances.][1]

Regulations—VAT (Amendment) (No 2) Regulations, SI 2012/1899.
VAT (Amendment) (No 3) Regulations, SI 2012/2951.
Amendments—[1] Para 2A inserted by FA 2002 s 24(2), (5) with effect from 1 December 2003 (by virtue of SI 2003/3043).
[2] In sub-para (2)(b), words "or the law of another member State" repealed by the Taxation (Cross-border Trade) Act 2018 s 43, Sch 8 paras 1, 97(1), (3) with effect from IP completion day (11pm on 31 December 2020), by virtue of SI 2020/1642 reg 4(b).

[Self-billed invoices

2B—(1) This paragraph applies where a taxable person provides to himself a document (a "self-billed invoice") that purports to be a VAT invoice in respect of a supply of goods or services to him by another taxable person.
(2) Subject to compliance with such conditions as may be—
  (a) prescribed,
  (b) specified in a notice published by the Commissioners, or
  (c) imposed in a particular case in accordance with regulations,
a self-billed invoice shall be treated as the VAT invoice required by regulations under paragraph 2A above to be provided by the supplier.
(3) For the purposes of section 6(4) (under which the time of supply can be determined by the prior issue of an invoice) a self-billed invoice shall not be treated as issued by the supplier.
(4) For the purposes of section 6(5) and (6) (under which the time of supply can be determined by the subsequent issue of an invoice) a self-billed invoice in relation to which the conditions mentioned in sub-paragraph (2) are complied with shall, subject to compliance with such further conditions as may be prescribed, be treated as issued by the supplier.
In such a case, any notice of election given or request made for the purposes of section 6(5) or (6) by the person providing the self-billed invoice shall be treated for those purposes as given or made by the supplier.
(5) Regulations under this paragraph—
  (a) may be framed so as to apply only in prescribed cases or only in relation to supplies made to persons of prescribed descriptions;
  (b) may make different provision for different circumstances.][1]

Regulations—VAT (Amendment) (No 3) Regulations, SI 2012/2951.
Amendments—[1] Para 2B inserted by FA 2002 s 24(2), (5) with effect 1 December 2003 (by virtue of SI 2003/3043).

[Electronic communication and storage of VAT invoices etc

3—(1) Regulations may prescribe, or provide for the Commissioners to impose in a particular case, conditions that must be complied with in relation to—
   (a) the provision by electronic means of any item to which this paragraph applies;
   (b) the preservation by electronic means of any such item or of information contained in any such item.
(2) The items to which this paragraph applies are—
   (a) any VAT invoice;
   (b) any document that refers to a VAT invoice and is intended to amend it;
   (c) . . . [2]
(3) Regulations under this paragraph may make different provision for different circumstances.][1]

Northern Ireland—See Sch 9ZA para 73(3) (Northern Ireland: invoices described in regulations under Sch 9ZA para 4(2)(b) or Sch 9ZB para 28(2)(b) are items to which this para applies (in addition to the items described in sub-para (2)(a) and (b)).
Regulations—VAT (Amendment) (No 3) Regulations, SI 2012/2951.
Amendments—[1] This paragraph substituted by FA 2002 s 24(3), (5) with effect from 1 December 2003 (by virtue of SI 2003/3043).
[2] Para (2)(c) repealed by the Taxation (Cross-border Trade) Act 2018 s 43, Sch 8 paras 1, 97(1), (4) with effect from IP completion day (11pm on 31 December 2020), by virtue of SI 2020/1642 reg 4(b).
Para (2)(c) previously read as follows—
   "(c) any invoice described in regulations made for the purposes of section 6(8)(b) or 12(1)(b).".

Power to require security and production of evidence

4—[(1) The Commissioners may, as a condition of allowing or repaying input tax to any person, require the production of such evidence relating to VAT as they may specify.
(1A) If they think it necessary for the protection of the revenue, the Commissioners may require, as a condition of making any VAT credit, the giving of such security for the amount of the payment as appears to them appropriate.][1]
[(2) If they think it necessary for the protection of the revenue, the Commissioners may require a taxable person, as a condition of his supplying or being supplied with goods or services under a taxable supply, to give security, or further security, for the payment of any VAT that is or may become due from—
   (a) the taxable person, or
   (b) any person by or to whom relevant goods or services are supplied.
(3) In sub-paragraph (2) above "relevant goods or services" means goods or services supplied by or to the taxable person.
(4) Security under sub-paragraph (2) above shall be of such amount, and shall be given in such manner, as the Commissioners may determine.
(5) The powers conferred on the Commissioners by sub-paragraph (2) above are without prejudice to their powers under section 48(7).][2]

Amendments—[1] Sub-paras (1), (1A) substituted for sub-para (1) by FA 2003 s 17(3) with effect from 10 April 2003.
[2] Sub-paras (2)–(5) substituted for sub-s (2) by FA 2003 s 17(4) with effect from 10 April 2003.

Recovery of VAT, etc

5—(1) VAT due from any person shall be recoverable as a debt due to the Crown.
(2) Where an invoice shows a supply of goods or services as taking place with VAT chargeable on it, there shall be recoverable from the person who issued the invoice an amount equal to that which is shown on the invoice as VAT or, if VAT is not separately shown, to so much of the total amount shown as payable as is to be taken as representing VAT on the supply.
(3) Sub-paragraph (2) above applies whether or not—
   (a) the invoice is a VAT invoice issued in pursuance of paragraph 2(1) above; or
   (b) the supply shown on the invoice actually takes or has taken place, or the amount shown as VAT, or any amount of VAT, is or was chargeable on the supply; or
   (c) the person issuing the invoice is a taxable person;
and any sum recoverable from a person under the sub-paragraph shall, if it is in any case VAT be recoverable as such and shall otherwise be recoverable as a debt due to the Crown.
(4)–(10) . . . [1]

Regulations—See VAT Regulations, SI 1995/2518 regs 212, 213.
Amendments—[1] Sub-paras (4)–(10) repealed by FA 1997 Sch 18(2) Part V(2) with effect from 1 July 1997 (see SI 1997/1433).

Duty to keep records

6—(1) Every taxable person shall keep such records as the Commissioners may by regulations require . . . [4]

(2) Regulations under sub-paragraph (1) above may make different provision for different cases and may be framed by reference to such records as may be specified in any notice published by the Commissioners in pursuance of the regulations and not withdrawn by a further notice.
(3) The Commissioners may require any records kept in pursuance of this paragraph to be preserved for such period not exceeding 6 years as they may [specify in writing (and different periods may be specified for different cases)]¹.
(4) . . . ³
[(4A) In relation to a relevant taxable person, a duty under this paragraph to preserve records relating to a relevant taxable supply must be discharged by at least preserving the information contained in the records electronically.
(4B) A relevant taxable person must make available to the Commissioners electronically on request any records preserved in accordance with sub-paragraph (4A).
(4C) In sub-paragraph (4A) "relevant taxable supply" means a supply of goods where—
  (a) that supply is deemed to be a supply by an operator of an online marketplace by virtue of section 5A, or
  (b) the place of supply of those goods is determined by section 7(5B).
(4D) In sub-paragraphs (4A) and (4B) "relevant taxable person" means a person who is a taxable person and who—
  (a) is the operator of an online marketplace,
  (b) is a person making taxable supplies of goods facilitated by an online marketplace, or
  (c) makes taxable supplies, the place of supply of which is determined by section 7(5B).]⁵
[(5) The Commissioners may by regulations make [further]⁵ provision about the form in which, and means by which, records are to be kept and preserved.
(6) Regulations under sub-paragraph (5) may—
  (a) make different provision for different cases;
  (b) provide for any provision of the regulations to be subject to conditions or exceptions specified in writing by the Commissioners;
  (c) include incidental, supplemental, consequential, saving, transitional or transitory provision.
(7) If regulations under sub-paragraph (5) make provision requiring records to be kept or preserved in electronic form they must make provision for a taxable person to be exempt from those requirements for any month ("the current month") if—
  (a) the value of the person's taxable supplies, in the period of one year ending with the month before the current month, was less than the VAT threshold, and
  (b) the person was not subject to those requirements in the month before the current month.
(8) The regulations may modify the exemption for cases where a business or part of a business carried on by a taxable person is transferred to another person as a going concern.
(9) The "VAT threshold" means the amount specified in paragraph 1(1)(a) of Schedule 1 on the first day of the current month.
(10) Regulations under sub-paragraph (5) requiring records to be kept or preserved in electronic form may (among other things) make provision—
  (a) as to the electronic form in which records are to be kept or preserved,
  (b) for the production of the contents of records kept or preserved in accordance with the regulations,
  (c) as to conditions that must be complied with in connection with the keeping or preservation of electronic records,
  (d) for treating records as not having been kept or preserved unless conditions are complied with,
  (e) for authenticating records,
  (f) about the manner of proving for any purpose the contents of any records (including provision for the application of conclusive or other presumptions).
(11) Regulations under sub-paragraph (5) requiring records to be kept or preserved in electronic form may—
  (a) allow any authorisation or requirement for which the regulations may provide to be given by means of a specific or general direction given by the Commissioners,
  (b) provide that the conditions of an authorisation or requirement are to be taken to be satisfied only where the Commissioners are satisfied as to specified matters.]²

Northern Ireland—See Sch 9ZA para 73(4): this para has effect as if a new sub-para (1A) were inserted (as below), and as if in sub–para (2) after "sub-paragraph (1)" there were inserted "or (1A)"—
"(1A) Every person who, at a time when the person is not a taxable person, acquires in Northern Ireland from a member State any goods which are subject to a duty of excise or consist in a new means of transport must keep such records with respect to the acquisition (if it is a taxable acquisition and is not in pursuance of a taxable supply) as the Commissioners may by regulations require.".
See also VATA 1994 Sch 9ZC para 3 (online sales by overseas persons and low value importations: modifications relating to the Northern Ireland Protocol): para 6 has effect subject to the following modifications—
  – Sub-para (4C) has effect as if—

(i) the "or" at the end of para (a) were omitted; and
(ii) after para (b) there were inserted ", or
(c) Part 1 of Schedule 9ZC makes provision about who is treated as having imported those goods."
– Sub-para (4D) has effect as if—
(i) the "or" at the end of para (b) were omitted; and
(ii) after para (c) there were inserted ", or
(d) is treated as having imported goods under Part 1 of Schedule 9ZC.".

Regulations—See VAT Regulations, SI 1995/2518 regs 31, 33.
VAT (Amendment) (No 3) Regulations, SI 2012/2951.
VAT (Amendment) Regulations, SI 2018/261.
Amendments—[1] In sub-para (3), words substituted for word "require", and sub-para (4) substituted, by FA 2008 s 115, Sch 37 paras 4, 5 with effect from 1 April 2009 (by virtue of SI 2009/402).
[2] Sub-paras (5)–(11) inserted by F(No 2)A 2017 s 62(1), (3)(b) with effect from 15 November 2017.
[3] Sub-para (4) repealed by F(No 2)A 2017 s 62(1), (3)(a) with effect from 1 April 2019 (the date on which the first regulations to be made under sub-para (5) came into force; those regulations are the VAT (Amendment) Regulations, SI 2018/261). Sub-para (4) previously read as follows—
"(4) The duty under this paragraph to preserve records may be discharged—
(a) by preserving them in any form and by any means, or
(b) by preserving the information contained in them in any form and by any means,
subject to any conditions or exceptions specified in writing by the Commissioners for Her Majesty's Revenue and Customs.".
[4] In sub-para (1), words ", and every person who, at a time when he is not a taxable person, acquires in the United Kingdom from another member State any goods which are subject to a duty of excise or consist in a new means of transport shall keep such records with respect to the acquisition (if it is a taxable acquisition and is not in pursuance of a taxable supply) as the Commissioners may so require." repealed by the Taxation (Cross-border Trade) Act 2018 s 43, Sch 8 paras 1, 97(1), (5) with effect from IP completion day (11pm on 31 December 2020), by virtue of SI 2020/1642 reg 4(b).
[5] Sub-paras (4A)–(4D) inserted, and in sub-para (5) word inserted, by the Taxation (Post-transition Period) Act 2020 s 7, Sch 3 paras 1, 17 with effect from IP completion day (11pm on 31 December 2020), by virtue of SI 2020/1642 reg 9.

[6A—(1) The Commissioners may direct any taxable person named in the direction to keep such records as they specify in the direction in relation to such goods as they so specify.
(2) A direction under this paragraph may require the records to be compiled by reference to VAT invoices or any other matter.
(3) The Commissioners may not make a direction under this paragraph unless they have reasonable grounds for believing that the records specified in the direction might assist in identifying taxable supplies in respect of which the VAT chargeable might not be paid.
(4) The taxable supplies in question may be supplies made by—
(a) the person named in the direction, or
(b) any other person.
(5) A direction under this paragraph—
(a) must be given by notice in writing to the person named in it,
(b) must warn that person of the consequences under section 69B of failing to comply with it, and
(c) remains in force until it is revoked or replaced by a further direction.
(6) The Commissioners may require any records kept in pursuance of this paragraph to be preserved for such period not exceeding 6 years as they may require.
[(7) Regulations under paragraph 6(5) apply for the purposes of this paragraph as they apply for the purposes of paragraph 6.][2]
(8) This paragraph is without prejudice to the power conferred by paragraph 6(1) to make regulations requiring records to be kept.
(9) Any records required to be kept by virtue of this paragraph are in addition to any records required to be kept by virtue of paragraph 6.][1]

[1] Para 6A inserted by FA 2006 s 21(6) with effect from 19 July 2006.
[2] Sub-para (7) substituted by F(No 2)A 2017 s 62(1), (4) with effect from 1 April 2019 (the date on which the first regulations to be made under sub-para (5) came into force; those regulations are the VAT (Amendment) Regulations, SI 2018/261). Sub-para (7) previously read as follows—
"(7) Sub-paragraph (4) of paragraph 6 (preservation of information) applies for the purposes of this paragraph as it applies for the purposes of that paragraph.".

Furnishing of information and production of documents

7—(1) The Commissioners may by regulations make provision for requiring taxable persons to notify to the Commissioners such particulars of changes in circumstances relating to those persons or any business carried on by them as appear to the Commissioners required for the purpose of keeping the register kept under this Act up to date.
(2)–(9) . . .[1]

Regulations—See VAT Regulations, SI 1995/2518 regs 31, 33.
VAT (Amendment) (No 2) Regulations, SI 2012/1899.

Amendments—[1] Sub-paras (2)–(9) repealed by FA 2008 s 113, Sch 36 para 87 with effect from 1 April 2009 (by virtue of SI 2009/404 art 2).

Power to take samples

8—[(1) An authorised person may take samples from goods that are in the possession of either a person who supplies goods or a fiscal warehousekeeper if it appears necessary to do so—
   (a) to protect the revenue against mistake or fraud, and
   (b) to determine how the goods, or the material of which they are made, ought to be or to have been treated for the purposes of VAT.][1]
(2) Any sample taken under this paragraph shall be disposed of and accounted for in such manner as the Commissioners may direct.
(3) Where a sample is taken under this paragraph from the goods in any person's possession and is not returned to him within a reasonable time and in good condition the Commissioners shall pay him by way of compensation a sum equal to the cost of the sample to him or such larger sum as they may determine.

Northern Ireland—See Sch 9ZA para 73(5): Northern Ireland: sub-para (1) applies to goods in the possession of a person who acquires goods in Northern Ireland from a member State as it applies to goods in the possession of a person who supplies goods, and to goods in the possession of a Northern Ireland fiscal warehousekeeper as it applies to goods in the possession of a fiscal warehousekeeper.

Amendments—[1] Sub-para (1) substituted by the Taxation (Cross-border Trade) Act 2018 s 43, Sch 8 paras 1, 97(1), (6) with effect from IP completion day (11pm on 31 December 2020), by virtue of SI 2020/1642 reg 4(b).
   Para (1) previously read as follows—
   "(1) An authorised person, if it appears to him necessary for the protection of the revenue against mistake or fraud, may at any time take, from the goods in the possession of any person who supplies goods or acquires goods from another member State, or in the possession of a fiscal warehouse keeper, such samples as the authorised person may require with a view to determining how the goods or the materials of which they are made ought to be or to have been treated for the purposes of VAT.".

Power to require opening of [machines on which relevant machine games are played][1]

9 An authorised person may at any reasonable time require a person making such a supply as is referred to in section 23(1) or any person acting on his behalf—
   [(a) to open any machine on which relevant machine games (as defined in section 23A) are capable of being played; and][1]
   (b) to carry out any other operation which may be necessary to enable the authorised person to ascertain the amount which, in accordance with [section 23(3)][1], is to be taken as the value of supplies made in the circumstances mentioned in subsection (1) of that section in any period.

Amendments—[1] Para (a) substituted, and in para (b) and in italic heading, words substituted by FA 2012 s 191, Sch 24 para 64(1), (5)(b) with effect in relation to supplies made on or after 1 February 2013.

Entry and search of premises and persons

10—(1)–(2A) . . .[2]
(3)–(6) . . .[1]

Amendments—[1] Sub-paras (3)–(6) repealed by FA 2007 ss 84, 114, Sch 22 paras 3, 8(b), Sch 27 Pt 5(1) with effect from 1 December 2007 (by virtue of SI 2007/3166 art 3(a)).
[2] Sub-paras (1)–(2A) repealed by FA 2008 s 113, Sch 36 para 87 with effect from 1 April 2009 (by virtue of SI 2009/404 art 2).

Order for access to recorded information etc

11—(1) Where, on an application by an authorised person, a justice of the peace or, in Scotland, a justice (within the meaning of [section 308 of the Criminal Procedure (Scotland) Act 1975][1]) is satisfied that there are reasonable grounds for believing—
   (a) that an offence in connection with VAT is being, has been or is about to be committed, and
   (b) that any recorded information (including any document of any nature whatsoever) which may be required as evidence for the purpose of any proceedings in respect of such an offence is in the possession of any person,
he may make an order under this paragraph.
(2) An order under this paragraph is an order that the person who appears to the justice to be in possession of the recorded information to which the application relates shall—
   (a) give an authorised person access to it, and
   (b) permit an authorised person to remove and take away any of it which he reasonably considers necessary,
not later than the end of the period of 7 days beginning on the date of the order or the end of such longer period as the order may specify.
(3) The reference in sub-paragraph (2)(a) above to giving an authorised person access to the recorded information to which the application relates includes a reference to permitting the authorised person to take copies of it or to make extracts from it.

(4) Where the recorded information consists of information [stored in any electronic form][2], an order under this paragraph shall have effect as an order to produce the information in a form in which it is visible and legible [or from which it can readily be produced in a visible and legible form][2] and, if the authorised person wishes to remove it, in a form in which it can be removed.

(5) This paragraph is without prejudice to paragraphs 7 and 10 above.

Amendments—[1]   Words in sub-para (1) substituted, subject to transitional provisions and savings by Criminal Procedure (Consequential Provisions) (Scotland) Act 1995 Sch 3, Sch 4 para 91(b).
[2]   Words in sub-para (4) substituted and inserted by Criminal Justice and Police Act 2001 ss 70, 138, Sch 2 Pt 2 para 13 with effect from 1 April 2003 (by virtue of SI 2003/708).

Procedure where documents etc are removed

12—(1) An authorised person who removes anything in the exercise of a power conferred by or under paragraph 10 or 11 above shall, if so requested by a person showing himself—
  (*a*) to be the occupier of premises from which it was removed, or
  (*b*) to have had custody or control of it immediately before the removal,
provide that person with a record of what he removed.

(2) The authorised person shall provide the record within a reasonable time from the making of the request for it.

(3) Subject to sub-paragraph (7) below, if a request for permission to be granted access to anything which—
  (*a*) has been removed by an authorised person, and
  (*b*) is retained by the Commissioners for the purposes of investigating an offence,
is made to the officer in overall charge of the investigation by a person who had custody or control of the thing immediately before it was so removed or by someone acting on behalf of such a person, the officer shall allow the person who made the request access to it under the supervision of an authorised person.

(4) Subject to sub-paragraph (7) below, if a request for a photograph or copy of any such thing is made to the officer in overall charge of the investigation by a person who had custody or control of the thing immediately before it was so removed, or by someone acting on behalf of such a person, the officer shall—
  (*a*) allow the person who made the request access to it under the supervision of an authorised person for the purpose of photographing it or copying it, or
  (*b*) photograph or copy it, or cause it to be photographed or copied.

(5) Where anything is photographed or copied under sub-paragraph (4)(*b*) above the photograph or copy shall be supplied to the person who made the request.

(6) The photograph or copy shall be supplied within a reasonable time from the making of the request.

(7) There is no duty under this paragraph to grant access to, or to supply a photograph or copy of, anything if the officer in overall charge of the investigation for the purposes of which it was removed has reasonable grounds for believing that to do so would prejudice—
  (*a*) that investigation;
  (*b*) the investigation of an offence other than the offence for the purposes of the investigation of which the thing was removed; or
  (*c*) any criminal proceedings which may be brought as a result of—
    (i) the investigation of which he is in charge, or
    (ii) any such investigation as is mentioned in paragraph (*b*) above.

(8) Any reference in this paragraph to the officer in overall charge of the investigation is a reference to the person whose name and address are endorsed on the warrant or order concerned as being the officer so in charge.

13—(1) Where, on an application made as mentioned in sub-paragraph (2) below, the appropriate judicial authority is satisfied that a person has failed to comply with a requirement imposed by paragraph 12 above, the authority may order that person to comply with the requirement within such time and in such manner as may be specified in the order.

(2) An application under sub-paragraph (1) above shall be made—
  (*a*) in the case of a failure to comply with any of the requirements imposed by paragraph 12(1) and (2) above, by the occupier of the premises from which the thing in question was removed or by the person who had custody or control of it immediately before it was so removed, and
  (*b*) in any other case, by the person who had such custody or control.

(3) In this paragraph "the appropriate judicial authority" means—
  (*a*) in England and Wales, a magistrates' court;
  (*b*) in Scotland, the sheriff; and
  (*c*) in Northern Ireland, a court of summary jurisdiction.

(4) In England and Wales and Northern Ireland, an application for an order under this paragraph shall be made by way of complaint; and sections 21 and 42(2) of the Interpretation Act (Northern Ireland) 1954 shall apply as if any reference in those provisions to any enactment included a reference to this paragraph.

Evidence by certificate, etc

14—(1) A certificate of the Commissioners—
  (*a*) that a person was or was not, at any date, registered under this Act; or
  (*b*) that any return required by or under this Act has not been made or had not been made at any date; or
  (*c*) that any statement or notification required to be submitted or given to the Commissioners in accordance with any regulations under paragraph [2(5A)][2] above has not been submitted or given or had not been submitted or given at any date; [. . .][1]
  (*d*) . . . [1]
shall be sufficient evidence of that fact until the contrary is proved.
(2) A photograph of any document furnished to the Commissioners for the purposes of this Act and certified by them to be such a photograph shall be admissible in any proceedings, whether civil or criminal, to the same extent as the document itself.
(3) Any document purporting to be a certificate under sub-paragraph (1) or (2) above shall be deemed to be such a certificate until the contrary is proved.
Northern Ireland—See Sch 9ZA para 73(6): Northern Ireland: sub-para (1) has effect as if in para (*c*), after "paragraph 5A" there were inserted "or paragraph 73(1) or (4) of Schedule 9ZA".
Amendments—[1] Sub-para (1)(d) and preceding word "or" repealed by FA 2008 s 138, Sch 44 para 6 with effect from 21 July 2008.
[2] In sub-para (1)(*c*), "2(5A)" substituted for "2(3) or (4)" by the Taxation (Cross-border Trade) Act 2018 s 43, Sch 8 paras 1, 97(1), (7) with effect from IP completion day (11pm on 31 December 2020), by virtue of SI 2020/1642 reg 4(*b*).

[SCHEDULE 11A

DISCLOSURE OF AVOIDANCE SCHEMES][1], [2]

Section 58A

Commentary—*De Voil Indirect Tax Service* **V5.213, 358**.
Amendments—[1] Schedule inserted by FA 2004 s 19, Sch 2 para 2 with effect from the passing of FA 2004 so far as is necessary for enabling the making of any orders or regulations by virtue of FA 2004 Sch 2, and otherwise with effect from 1 August 2004 (by virtue of SI 2004/1934).
[2] This Schedule repealed by F(No 2)A 2017 s 66(2) with effect from 1 January 2018. In consequence of provision made by F(No 2)A 2017 Sch 17, it ceases to have effect to require a person to disclose any scheme which: (a) is first entered into by that person on or after 1 January 2018; (b) is first entered into by that person on or after 1 January 2018; (c) implements proposals which are notifiable proposals under Schedule 17.

[Interpretation

1 In this Schedule—
  "designated scheme" has the meaning given by paragraph 3(4);
  [*"non-deductible tax", in relation to a taxable person, has the meaning given by paragraph 2A;*][2]
  "notifiable scheme" has the meaning given by paragraph 5(1);
  "scheme" includes any arrangements, transaction or series of transactions;
  "tax advantage" is to be read in accordance with paragraph 2.][1], [3]
Amendments—[1] Schedule inserted by FA 2004 s 19, Sch 2 para 2 with effect from the passing of FA 2004, so far as is necessary for enabling the making of any orders or regulations by virtue of FA 2004 Sch 2, and otherwise with effect from 1 August 2004 (by virtue of SI 2004/1934).
[2] Definition of "non-deductible tax" inserted by F(No 2)A 2005 s 6, Sch 1 paras 1, 2 with effect from 1 August 2005, by virtue of SI 2005/2010 art 2, subject to savings in arts 3, 4.
[3] This Schedule repealed by F(No 2)A 2017 s 66(2) with effect from 1 January 2018. In consequence of provision made by F(No 2)A 2017 Sch 17, it ceases to have effect to require a person to disclose any scheme which: (a) is first entered into by that person on or after 1 January 2018; (b) is first entered into by that person on or after 1 January 2018; (c) implements proposals which are notifiable proposals under Schedule 17.

[Obtaining a tax advantage

[**2**—(1) For the purposes of this Schedule, a taxable person obtains a tax advantage if—
  (*a*) in any prescribed accounting period, the amount by which the output tax accounted for by him exceeds the input tax deducted by him is less than it would otherwise be,
  (*b*) he obtains a VAT credit when he would not otherwise do so, or obtains a larger VAT credit or obtains a VAT credit earlier than would otherwise be the case,
  (*c*) in a case where he recovers input tax as a recipient of a supply before the supplier accounts for the output tax, the period between the time when the input tax is recovered and the time when the output tax is accounted for is greater than would otherwise be the case, or

(d) in any prescribed accounting period, the amount of his non-deductible tax is less than it would otherwise be.

(2) For the purposes of this Schedule, a person who is not a taxable person obtains a tax advantage if his non-refundable tax is less than it would otherwise be.

(3) In sub-paragraph (2), "non-refundable tax", in relation to a person who is not a taxable person, means—

(a) VAT on the supply to him of any goods or services,
(b) VAT on the acquisition by him from another member State of any goods, and
(c) VAT paid or payable by him on the importation of any goods from a place outside the member States,

but excluding (in each case) any VAT in respect of which he is entitled to a refund from the Commissioners by virtue of any provision of this Act.]²]¹, ³

Amendments—¹ Schedule inserted by FA 2004 s 19, Sch 2 para 2 with effect from the passing of FA 2004, so far as is necessary for enabling the making of any orders or regulations by virtue of FA 2004 Sch 2, and otherwise with effect from 1 August 2004 (by virtue of SI 2004/1934).
² This paragraph substituted by F(No 2)A 2005 s 6, Sch 1 paras 1, 3 with effect from 1 August 2005 (by virtue of SI 2005/2010 art 2, subject to savings in arts 3, 4).
³ This Schedule repealed by F(No 2)A 2017 s 66(2) with effect from 1 January 2018. In consequence of provision made by F(No 2)A 2017 Sch 17, it ceases to have effect to require a person to disclose any scheme which: (a) is first entered into by that person on or after 1 January 2018; (b) is first entered into by that person on or after 1 January 2018; (c) implements proposals which are notifiable proposals under Schedule 17.

[Meaning of "non-deductible tax"]

2A—(1) In this Schedule "non-deductible tax", in relation to a taxable person, means—

(a) input tax for which he is not entitled to credit under section 25, and
(b) any VAT incurred by him which is not input tax and in respect of which he is not entitled to a refund from the Commissioners by virtue of any provision of this Act.

(2) For the purposes of sub-paragraph (1)(b), the VAT "incurred" by a taxable person is—

(a) VAT on the supply to him of any goods or services,
(b) . . . ³ and
(c) VAT paid or payable by him on the importation of any goods . . . ³.]¹, ²

Northern Ireland—See Sch 9ZA para 72(2) (Northern Ireland: this Schedule has effect as if the reference to VAT "incurred" by a taxable person in sub-para (1)(b) included VAT on the acquisition by the person of any goods from a member State).

Amendments—¹ Paragraph 2A inserted by F(No 2)A 2005 s 6, Sch 1 paras 1, 4 with effect from 1 August 2005 (by virtue of SI 2005/2010 art 2, subject to savings in arts 3, 4).
² This Schedule repealed by F(No 2)A 2017 s 66(2) with effect from 1 January 2018. In consequence of provision made by F(No 2)A 2017 Sch 17, it ceases to have effect to require a person to disclose any scheme which: (a) is first entered into by that person on or after 1 January 2018; (b) is first entered into by that person on or after 1 January 2018; (c) implements proposals which are notifiable proposals under Schedule 17.
³ In sub-para (2), para (b) repealed, and in para (c) words "from a place outside the member States" repealed, by the Taxation (Cross-border Trade) Act 2018 s 43, Sch 8 paras 1, 98 with effect from IP completion day (11pm on 31 December 2020), by virtue of SI 2020/1642 reg 4(b).
Sub-para (2)(b) previously read as follows—
"(b) VAT on the acquisition by him from another member State of any goods,".

[Designation by order of avoidance schemes]

3—(1) If it appears to the Treasury—

(a) that a scheme of a particular description has been, or might be, entered into for the purpose of enabling any person to obtain a tax advantage, and
(b) that it is unlikely that persons would enter into a scheme of that description unless the main purpose, or one of the main purposes, of doing so was the obtaining by any person of a tax advantage,

the Treasury may by order designate that scheme for the purposes of this paragraph.

(2) A scheme may be designated for the purposes of this paragraph even though the Treasury are of the opinion that no scheme of that description could as a matter of law result in the obtaining by any person of a tax advantage.

(3) The order must allocate a reference number to each scheme.

(4) In this Schedule "designated scheme" means a scheme of a description designated for the purposes of this paragraph.]¹, ²

Orders—See VAT (Disclosure of Avoidance Schemes) (Designations) Order, SI 2004/1933.

Amendments—¹ Schedule inserted by FA 2004 s 19, Sch 2 para 2 with effect from the passing of FA 2004, so far as is necessary for enabling the making of any orders or regulations by virtue of FA 2004 Sch 2, and otherwise with effect from 1 August 2004 (by virtue of SI 2004/1934).

[2] This Schedule repealed by F(No 2)A 2017 s 66(2) with effect from 1 January 2018. In consequence of provision made by F(No 2)A 2017 Sch 17, it ceases to have effect to require a person to disclose any scheme which: (a) is first entered into by that person on or after 1 January 2018; (b) is first entered into by that person on or after 1 January 2018; (c) implements proposals which are notifiable proposals under Schedule 17.

[Designation by order of provisions included in or associated with avoidance schemes

4—(1) If it appears to the Treasury that a provision of a particular description is, or is likely to be, included in or associated with schemes that are entered into for the purpose of enabling any person to obtain a tax advantage, the Treasury may by order designate that provision for the purposes of this paragraph.
(2) A provision may be designated under this paragraph even though it also appears to the Treasury that the provision is, or is likely to be, included in or associated with schemes that are not entered into for the purpose of obtaining a tax advantage.
(3) In this paragraph "provision" includes any agreement, transaction, act or course of conduct.][1], [2]

Orders—See VAT (Disclosure of Avoidance Schemes) (Designations) Order, SI 2004/1933.
Amendments—[1] Schedule inserted by FA 2004 s 19, Sch 2 para 2 with effect from the passing of FA 2004, so far as is necessary for enabling the making of any orders or regulations by virtue of FA 2004 Sch 2, and otherwise with effect from 1 August 2004 (by virtue of SI 2004/1934).
[2] This Schedule repealed by F(No 2)A 2017 s 66(2) with effect from 1 January 2018. In consequence of provision made by F(No 2)A 2017 Sch 17, it ceases to have effect to require a person to disclose any scheme which: (a) is first entered into by that person on or after 1 January 2018; (b) is first entered into by that person on or after 1 January 2018; (c) implements proposals which are notifiable proposals under Schedule 17.

[Meaning of "notifiable scheme"

5—(1) For the purposes of this Schedule, a scheme is a "notifiable scheme" if—
  (*a*) it is a designated scheme, or
  (*b*) although it is not a designated scheme, conditions A and B below are met in relation to it.
(2) Condition A is that the scheme includes, or is associated with, a provision of a description designated under paragraph 4.
(3) Condition B is that the scheme has as its main purpose, or one of its main purposes, the obtaining of a tax advantage by any person.][1], [2]

Amendments—[1] Schedule inserted by FA 2004 s 19, Sch 2 para 2 with effect from the passing of FA 2004, so far as is necessary for enabling the making of any orders or regulations by virtue of FA 2004 Sch 2, and otherwise with effect from 1 August 2004 (by virtue of SI 2004/1934).
[2] This Schedule repealed by F(No 2)A 2017 s 66(2) with effect from 1 January 2018. In consequence of provision made by F(No 2)A 2017 Sch 17, it ceases to have effect to require a person to disclose any scheme which: (a) is first entered into by that person on or after 1 January 2018; (b) is first entered into by that person on or after 1 January 2018; (c) implements proposals which are notifiable proposals under Schedule 17.

[Duty to notify Commissioners

6—(1) This paragraph applies in relation to a taxable person where—
  (*a*) the amount of VAT shown in a return in respect of a prescribed accounting period as payable by or to him is less than or greater than it would be but for any notifiable scheme to which he is party, . . . [2]
  (*b*) he makes a claim for the repayment of output tax or an increase in credit for input tax in respect of any prescribed accounting period in respect of which he has previously delivered a return and the amount claimed is greater than it would be but for such a scheme[, or
  (*c*) the amount of his non-deductible tax in respect of any prescribed accounting period is less than it would be but for such a scheme.][2]
(2) Where the scheme is a designated scheme, the taxable person must notify the Commissioners within the prescribed time, and in such form and manner as may be required by or under regulations, of the reference number allocated to the scheme under paragraph 3(3).
[(2A) Sub-paragraph (2) does not apply to a taxable person in relation to any scheme if he has on a previous occasion—
  (*a*) notified the Commissioners under that sub-paragraph in relation to the scheme, or
  (*b*) provided the Commissioners with prescribed information under sub-paragraph (3) (as it applied before the scheme became a designated scheme) in relation to the scheme.][2]
(3) Where the scheme is not a designated scheme, the taxable person must, subject to sub-paragraph (4), provide the Commissioners within the prescribed time, and in such form and manner as may be required by or under regulations, with prescribed information relating to the scheme.
(4) Sub-paragraph (3) does not apply where the scheme is one in respect of which any person has previously—
  (*a*) provided the Commissioners with prescribed information under paragraph 9, and
  (*b*) provided the taxable person with a reference number notified to him by the Commissioners under paragraph 9(2)(*b*).

[(5) Sub-paragraph (3) also does not apply where the scheme is one in respect of which the taxable person has on a previous occasion provided the Commissioners with prescribed information under that sub-paragraph.][2]

(6) This paragraph has effect subject to paragraph 7.][1], [3]

Orders—See VAT (Disclosure of Avoidance Schemes) Regulations, SI 2004/1929.

Amendments—[1] Schedule inserted by FA 2004 s 19, Sch 2 para 2 with effect from the passing of FA 2004, so far as is necessary for enabling the making of any orders or regulations by virtue of FA 2004 Sch 2, and otherwise with effect from 1 August 2004 (by virtue of SI 2004/1934).

[2] Word "or" in sub-para (1)(a) repealed; sub-paras (1)(c), (2A) inserted; and sub-para (5) substituted; by F(No 2)A 2005 ss 6, 70, Sch 1 paras 1, 5, Sch 11 Pt 1 with effect from 1 August 2005 (by virtue of SI 2005/2010 art 2, subject to savings in arts 3, 4). Paragraph 6(1)(c) shall not apply in relation to any prescribed accounting period beginning before 1 August 2005.

[3] This Schedule repealed by F(No 2)A 2017 s 66(2) with effect from 1 January 2018. In consequence of provision made by F(No 2)A 2017 Sch 17, it ceases to have effect to require a person to disclose any scheme which: (a) is first entered into by that person on or after 1 January 2018; (b) is first entered into by that person on or after 1 January 2018; (c) implements proposals which are notifiable proposals under Schedule 17.

[Exemptions from duty to notify under paragraph 6

7—(1) Paragraph 6 does not apply to a taxable person in relation to a scheme—
(a) where the taxable person is not a group undertaking in relation to any other undertaking and conditions A and B below, as they have effect in relation to the scheme, are met in relation to the taxable person, or
(b) where the taxable person is a group undertaking in relation to any other undertaking and conditions A and B below, as they have effect in relation to the scheme, are met in relation to the taxable person and every other group undertaking.

(2) Condition A is that the total value of the person's taxable supplies and exempt supplies in the period of twelve months ending immediately before the beginning of the relevant period is less than the minimum turnover.

(3) Condition B is that the total value of the person's taxable supplies and exempt supplies in the prescribed accounting period immediately preceding the relevant period is less than the appropriate proportion of the minimum turnover.

(4) In sub-paragraphs (2) and (3) "the minimum turnover" means—
(a) in relation to a designated scheme, £600,000, and
(b) in relation to any other notifiable scheme, £10,000,000.

(5) In sub-paragraph (3) "the appropriate proportion" means the proportion which the length of the prescribed accounting period bears to twelve months.

(6) The value of a supply of goods or services shall be determined for the purposes of this paragraph on the basis that no VAT is chargeable on the supply.

(7) The Treasury may by order substitute for the sum for the time being specified in sub-paragraph (4)(a) or (b) such other sum as they think fit.

(8) This paragraph has effect subject to paragraph 8.

(9) In this paragraph—

"relevant period" means the prescribed accounting period referred to in paragraph [6(1)(a), (b) or (c)][2];

"undertaking" and "group undertaking" have the same meanings as in [section 1161 of the Companies Act 2006][3].][1], [4]

Amendments—[1] Schedule inserted by FA 2004 s 19, Sch 2 para 2 with effect from the passing of FA 2004, so far as is necessary for enabling the making of any orders or regulations by virtue of FA 2004 Sch 2, and otherwise with effect from 1 August 2004 (by virtue of SI 2004/1934).

[2] In the definition of "relevant period", words substituted for the words "6(1)(a) or (b)" by F(No 2)A 2005 s 6, Sch 1 paras 1, 6 with effect from 1 August 2005 (by virtue of SI 2005/2010 art 2, subject to savings in arts 3, 4).

[3] Words in sub-para (9) substituted by the Companies Act 2006 (Consequential Amendments) (Taxes and National Insurance) Order, SI 2008/954 art 20 with effect from 6 April 2008.

[4] This Schedule repealed by F(No 2)A 2017 s 66(2) with effect from 1 January 2018. In consequence of provision made by F(No 2)A 2017 Sch 17, it ceases to have effect to require a person to disclose any scheme which: (a) is first entered into by that person on or after 1 January 2018; (b) is first entered into by that person on or after 1 January 2018; (c) implements proposals which are notifiable proposals under Schedule 17.

[Power to exclude exemption

8—(1) The purpose of this paragraph is to prevent the maintenance or creation of any artificial separation of business activities carried on by two or more persons from resulting in an avoidance of the obligations imposed by paragraph 6.

(2) In determining for the purposes of sub-paragraph (1) whether any separation of business activities is artificial, regard shall be had to the extent to which the different persons carrying on those activities are closely bound to one another by financial, economic and organisational links.

(3) If the Commissioners make a direction under this section—

(a) the persons named in the direction shall be treated for the purposes of paragraph 7 as a single taxable person carrying on the activities of a business described in the direction with effect from the date of the direction or, if the direction so provides, from such later date as may be specified in the direction, and

(b) if paragraph 7 would not exclude the application of paragraph 6, in respect of any notifiable scheme, to that single taxable person, it shall not exclude the application of paragraph 6, in respect of that scheme, to the persons named in the direction.

(4) The Commissioners shall not make a direction under this section naming any person unless they are satisfied—

(a) that he is making or has made taxable or exempt supplies,

(b) that the activities in the course of which he makes those supplies form only part of certain activities, the other activities being carried on concurrently or previously (or both) by one or more other persons, and

(c) that, if all the taxable and exempt supplies of the business described in the direction were taken into account, conditions A and B in paragraph 7(2) and (3), as those conditions have effect in relation to designated schemes, would not be met in relation to that business.

(5) A direction under this paragraph shall be served on each of the persons named in it.

(6) A direction under this paragraph remains in force until it is revoked or replaced by a further direction.][1], [2]

Amendments—[1] Schedule inserted by FA 2004 s 19, Sch 2 para 2 with effect from the passing of FA 2004, so far as is necessary for enabling the making of any orders or regulations by virtue of FA 2004 Sch 2, and otherwise with effect from 1 August 2004 (by virtue of SI 2004/1934).

[2] This Schedule repealed by F(No 2)A 2017 s 66(2) with effect from 1 January 2018. In consequence of provision made by F(No 2)A 2017 Sch 17, it ceases to have effect to require a person to disclose any scheme which: (a) is first entered into by that person on or after 1 January 2018; (b) is first entered into by that person on or after 1 January 2018; (c) implements proposals which are notifiable proposals under Schedule 17.

[Voluntary notification of avoidance scheme that is not designated scheme

9—(1) Any person may, at any time, provide the Commissioners with prescribed information relating to a scheme or proposed scheme of a particular description which is (or, if implemented, would be) a notifiable scheme by virtue of paragraph 5(1)(b).

(2) On receiving the prescribed information, the Commissioners may—

(a) allocate a reference number to the scheme (if they have not previously done so under this paragraph), and

(b) notify the person who provided the information of the number allocated.][1], [2]

Orders—See VAT (Disclosure of Avoidance Schemes) Regulations, SI 2004/1929.

Amendments—[1] Schedule inserted by FA 2004 s 19, Sch 2 para 2 with effect from the passing of FA 2004, so far as is necessary for enabling the making of any orders or regulations by virtue of FA 2004 Sch 2, and otherwise with effect from 1 August 2004 (by virtue of SI 2004/1934).

[2] This Schedule repealed by F(No 2)A 2017 s 66(2) with effect from 1 January 2018. In consequence of provision made by F(No 2)A 2017 Sch 17, it ceases to have effect to require a person to disclose any scheme which: (a) is first entered into by that person on or after 1 January 2018; (b) is first entered into by that person on or after 1 January 2018; (c) implements proposals which are notifiable proposals under Schedule 17.

No scheme or proposed scheme may be notified to the Commissioners under this para on or after 1 January 2018 (F(No 2)A 2017 s 66(3).

[Penalty for failure to notify use of notifiable scheme

10—(1) A person who fails to comply with paragraph 6 shall be liable, subject to sub-paragraphs (2) and (3), to a penalty of an amount determined under paragraph 11.

(2) Conduct falling within sub-paragraph (1) shall not give rise to liability to a penalty under this paragraph if the person concerned satisfies the Commissioners or, on appeal, a tribunal that there is a reasonable excuse for the failure.

(3) Where, by reason of conduct falling within sub-paragraph (1)—

(a) a person is convicted of an offence (whether under this Act or otherwise), or

(b) a person is assessed to a penalty under section 60 [or a penalty for a deliberate inaccuracy under Schedule 24 to the Finance Act 2007][2],

that conduct shall not give rise to a penalty under this paragraph.][1], [3]

Amendments—[1] Schedule inserted by FA 2004 s 19, Sch 2 para 2 with effect from the passing of FA 2004, so far as is necessary for enabling the making of any orders or regulations by virtue of FA 2004 Sch 2, and otherwise with effect from 1 August 2004 (by virtue of SI 2004/1934).

[2] Words in sub-para (3)(b) inserted by the Finance Act 2008, Schedule 40 (Appointed Day, Transitional Provisions and Consequential Amendments) Order, SI 2009/571 art 8, Sch 1 paras 12, 17 with effect from 1 April 2009.

[2] This Schedule repealed by F(No 2)A 2017 s 66(2) with effect from 1 January 2018. In consequence of provision made by F(No 2)A 2017 Sch 17, it ceases to have effect to require a person to disclose any scheme which: (a) is first entered into by that person on or after 1 January 2018; (b) is first entered into by that person on or after 1 January 2018; (c) implements proposals which are notifiable proposals under Schedule 17.

[Amount of penalty]

11—(1) Where the failure mentioned in paragraph 10(1) relates to a notifiable scheme that is not a designated scheme, the amount of the penalty is £5,000.
(2) Where the failure mentioned in paragraph 10(1) relates to a designated scheme, the amount of the penalty is 15 per cent. of the VAT saving (as determined under sub-paragraph (3)).
(3) For this purpose the VAT saving is—
- (a) to the extent that the case falls within paragraph 6(1)(a), the aggregate of—
  - (i) the amount by which the amount of VAT that would, but for the scheme, have been shown in returns in respect of the relevant periods as payable by the taxable person exceeds the amount of VAT that was shown in those returns as payable by him, and
  - (ii) the amount by which the amount of VAT that was shown in such returns as payable to the taxable person exceeds the amount of VAT that would, but for the scheme, have been shown in those returns as payable to him, . . . [2]
- (b) to the extent that the case falls within paragraph 6(1)(b), the amount by which the amount claimed exceeds the amount which the taxable person would, but for the scheme, have claimed[, and
- (c) to the extent that—
  - (i) the case falls within paragraph 6(1)(c), and
  - (ii) the excess of the notional non-deductible tax of the taxable person for the relevant periods over his non-deductible tax for those periods is not represented by a corresponding amount which by virtue of paragraph (a) or (b) is part of the VAT saving, the amount of the excess.][2]

(4) In sub-paragraph (3)(a) [and (c)][2] "the relevant periods" means the prescribed accounting periods beginning with that in respect of which the duty to comply with paragraph 6 first arose and ending with the earlier of the following—
- (a) the prescribed accounting period in which the taxable person complied with that paragraph, and
- (b) the prescribed accounting period immediately preceding the notification by the Commissioners of the penalty assessment.][1]

[(5) In sub-paragraph (3)(c), "notional non-deductible tax", in relation to a taxable person, means the amount that would, but for the scheme, have been the amount of his non-deductible tax.][2], [3]

Amendments—[1] Schedule inserted by FA 2004 s 19, Sch 2 para 2 with effect from the passing of FA 2004, so far as is necessary for enabling the making of any orders or regulations by virtue of FA 2004 Sch 2, and otherwise with effect from 1 August 2004 (by virtue of SI 2004/1934).
[2] Word "and" in sub-para (3)(a) repealed; sub-para (3)(c) inserted; words in sub-para (4) inserted; and sub-para (5) inserted; by F(No 2)A 2005 ss 6, 70, Sch 1 paras 1, 7, Sch 11 Pt 1 with effect from 1 August 2005 (by virtue of SI 2005/2010 art 2, subject to savings in arts 3, 4).
[3] This Schedule repealed by F(No 2)A 2017 s 66(2) with effect from 1 January 2018. In consequence of provision made by F(No 2)A 2017 Sch 17, it ceases to have effect to require a person to disclose any scheme which: (a) is first entered into by that person on or after 1 January 2018; (b) is first entered into by that person on or after 1 January 2018; (c) implements proposals which are notifiable proposals under Schedule 17.

[Penalty assessments]

12—(1) Where any person is liable under paragraph 10 to a penalty of an amount determined under paragraph 11, the Commissioners may, subject to sub-paragraph (3), assess the amount due by way of penalty and notify it to him accordingly.
(2) The fact that any conduct giving rise to a penalty under paragraph 10 may have ceased before an assessment is made under this paragraph shall not affect the power of the Commissioners to make such an assessment.
[(3) In a case where—
- (a) the penalty falls to be calculated by reference to the VAT saving as determined under paragraph 11(3), and
- (b) the notional tax cannot readily be attributed to any one or more prescribed accounting periods,

the notional tax shall be treated for the purposes of this Schedule as attributable to such period or periods as the Commissioners may determine to the best of their judgment and notify to the person liable for the penalty.][2]

[(3A) In sub-paragraph (3) "the notional tax" means—
- (a) the VAT that would, but for the scheme, have been shown in returns as payable by or to the taxable person, or
- (b) any amount that would, but for the scheme, have been the amount of the non-deductible tax of the taxable person.][2]

(4) No assessment to a penalty under this paragraph shall be made more than two years from the time when facts sufficient, in the opinion of the Commissioners, to indicate that there has been a failure to comply with paragraph 6 in relation to a notifiable scheme came to the Commissioners' knowledge.
(5) Where the Commissioners notify a person of a penalty in accordance with sub-paragraph (1), the notice of assessment shall specify—
   (*a*) the amount of the penalty,
   (*b*) the reasons for the imposition of the penalty,
   (*c*) how the penalty has been calculated, and
   (*d*) any reduction of the penalty in accordance with section 70.
(6) Where a person is assessed under this paragraph to an amount due by way of penalty and is also assessed under section 73(1), (2), (7), (7A) or (7B) for any of the prescribed accounting periods to which the assessment under this paragraph relates, the assessments may be combined and notified to him as one assessment, but the amount of the penalty shall be separately identified in the notice.
(7) If an amount is assessed and notified to any person under this paragraph, then unless, or except to the extent that, the assessment is withdrawn or reduced, that amount shall be recoverable as if it were VAT due from him.
(8) Subsection (10) of section 76 (notification to certain persons acting for others) applies for the purposes of this paragraph as it applies for the purposes of that section.][1], [3]

Amendments—[1]   Schedule inserted by FA 2004 s 19, Sch 2 para 2 with effect from the passing of FA 2004, so far as is necessary for enabling the making of any orders or regulations by virtue of FA 2004 Sch 2, and otherwise with effect from 1 August 2004 (by virtue of SI 2004/1934).
[2]   Sub-paras (3), (3A) substituted for sub-para (3) by F(No 2)A 2005 s 6, Sch 1 paras 1, 8 with effect from 1 August 2005 (by virtue of SI 2005/2010 art 2, subject to savings in arts 3, 4).
[3]   This Schedule repealed by F(No 2)A 2017 s 66(2) with effect from 1 January 2018. In consequence of provision made by F(No 2)A 2017 Sch 17, it ceases to have effect to require a person to disclose any scheme which: (a) is first entered into by that person on or after 1 January 2018; (b) is first entered into by that person on or after 1 January 2018; (c) implements proposals which are notifiable proposals under Schedule 17.

[**13**—Regulations under this Schedule—
   (*a*) may make different provision for different circumstances, and
   (*b*) may include transitional provisions or savings.] [1], [2]

Orders—See VAT (Disclosure of Avoidance Schemes) Regulations, SI 2004/1929.
Amendments—[1]   Schedule inserted by FA 2004 s 19, Sch 2 para 2 with effect from the passing of FA 2004, so far as is necessary for enabling the making of any orders or regulations by virtue of FA 2004 Sch 2, and otherwise with effect from 1 August 2004 (by virtue of SI 2004/1934).
[2]   This Schedule repealed by F(No 2)A 2017 s 66(2) with effect from 1 January 2018. In consequence of provision made by F(No 2)A 2017 Sch 17, it ceases to have effect to require a person to disclose any scheme which: (a) is first entered into by that person on or after 1 January 2018; (b) is first entered into by that person on or after 1 January 2018; (c) implements proposals which are notifiable proposals under Schedule 17.

SCHEDULE 12
CONSTITUTION AND PROCEDURE OF TRIBUNALS
Section 61

Amendments—This schedule repealed by the Transfer of Tribunal Functions and Revenue and Customs Appeals Order, SI 2009/56 art 3, Sch 1 para 228 with effect from 1 April 2009, subject to transitional and savings provisions in Sch 3 para 4.

SCHEDULE 13
TRANSITIONAL PROVISIONS AND SAVINGS
Section 100

General provisions

1—(1) The continuity of the law relating to VAT shall not be affected by the substitution of this Act for the enactments repealed by this Act and earlier enactments repealed by and corresponding to any of those enactments ("the repealed enactments").
(2) Any reference, whether express or implied, in any enactment, instrument or document (including this Act or any Act amended by this Act) to, or to things done falling to be done under or for the purposes of, any provision of this Act shall, if and so far as the nature of the reference permits, be construed as including, in relation to the times, years or periods, circumstances or purposes in relation to which the corresponding provision in the repealed enactments has or had effect, a reference to, or as the case may be, to things done or falling to be done under or for the purposes of, that corresponding provision.
(3) Any reference, whether express or implied, in any enactment, instrument or document (including the repealed enactments and enactments, instruments and documents passed or made or otherwise coming into existence after the commencement of this Act) to, or to things done or falling to be done

under or for the purposes of, any of the repealed enactments shall, if and so far as the nature of the reference permits, be construed as including, in relation to the times, years or periods, circumstances or purposes in relation to which the corresponding provision of this Act has effect, a reference to, or as the case may be to things done or falling to be done under or for the purposes of, that corresponding provision.

(4) Without prejudice to paragraphs (1) to (3) above, in any case where as respects the charge to VAT on any supply, acquisition or importation made at a time before 1st September 1994 but falling in a prescribed accounting period to which Part I applies

(a) an enactment applicable to that charge to VAT is not re-enacted in this Act or is re-enacted with amendments which came into force after that time, or

(b) a repealed enactment corresponding to an enactment in this Act did not apply to that charge to VAT,

any question arising under Part I and relating to that charge to VAT shall continue to be determined in accordance with the law in force at that time.

Validity of subordinate legislation

2 So far as this Act re-enacts any provision contained in a statutory instrument made in exercise of powers conferred by any Act, it shall be without prejudice to the validity of that provision, and any question as to its validity shall be determined as if the re-enacted provision were contained in a statutory instrument made under those powers.

Provisions related to the introduction of VAT

3 Where a vehicle in respect of which purchase tax was remitted under section 23 of the Purchase Tax Act 1963 (vehicles for use outside the United Kingdom) is brought back to the United Kingdom the vehicle shall not, when brought back, be treated as imported for the purpose of VAT chargeable on the importation of goods.

Supply in accordance with pre-21.4.75 arrangements

4 Where there were in force immediately before 21st April 1975 arrangements between the Commissioners and any taxable person for supplies made by him (or such supplies made by him as were specified in the arrangements) to be treated as taking place at times or on dates which, had section 6(10) been in force when the arrangements were made, could have been provided for by a direction under that section, he shall be treated for the purposes of that section as having requested the Commissioners to give a direction thereunder to the like effect, and the Commissioners may give a direction (or a general direction applying to cases of any class or description specified in the direction) accordingly.

President, chairmen etc of tribunals

5—(1) Any appointment to a panel of chairmen of the tribunals current at the commencement of this Act and made by the Treasury before the passing of the 1983 Act shall not be affected by the repeal by this Act of paragraph 8 of Schedule 10 to that Act.

(2) The terms of appointment of any person who was appointed to the office of President of the tribunal or chairman or other member of the tribunals before 1st April 1986 and holds that office on the coming into force of this Act shall continue to have effect notwithstanding the re-enactment, as Schedule 12 to this Act, of Schedule 8 to the 1983 Act as amended by Schedule 8 to the Finance Act 1985.

Overseas suppliers accounting through their customers

6 Notwithstanding the repeal by this Act of section 32B of the 1983 Act, that section shall continue to apply in relation to any supply in relation to which section 14 does not apply by virtue of section 14(8), and for the purposes to this paragraph section 32B shall have effect as if it were included in Part III of this Act, any reference in section 32B to any enactment repealed by this Act being read as a reference to the corresponding provision of this Act.

Zero-rated supplies of goods and services

8—(1) A supply of services made after the commencement of this Act in pursuance of a legally binding obligation incurred before 21st June 1988 shall if—

(a) the supply fell within item 2 of Group 8A of Schedule 5 to the 1983 Act immediately before 1st April 1989, and

(b) it was by virtue of paragraph 13(1) of Schedule 3 to the Finance Act 1989 a zero-rated supply,

be a zero-rated supply for the purposes of this Act.

(2) Where a grant, assignment or other supply is zero-rated by virtue of this paragraph, it is not a relevant zero-rated supply for the purposes of [Part 2 of Schedule 10][1].

Amendments—[1] In sub-para (2), words substituted by the Value Added Tax (Buildings and Land) Order, SI 2008/1146, art 6, Sch 1 paras 1, 5(a) with effect in relation to supplies made on or after 1 June 2008, subject to savings in Sch 2 of the Order.

Bad debt relief

9—(1) . . . [2]

[(2) Claims for refunds of VAT shall not be made in accordance with section 36 of this Act in relation to—

(a) any supply made before 1st April 1989; or

(b) any supply as respects which a claim is or has been made under section 22 of the 1983 Act.][1]

Commentary—*De Voil Indirect Tax Service* **V5.156**.

Amendments—[1] Sub-para (2) substituted by FA 1995 s 33(1), (4) and is deemed to have always had effect.
[2] Sub-para (1) repealed by FA 1997 Sch 18 Part IV(3) in relation to claims made after 19 March 1997.

Supplies during construction of buildings and works

10—(1) Nothing in paragraphs 5 and 6 of Schedule 10 shall apply—

(a) in relation to a person who has constructed a building if he incurred before 21st June 1988 a legally binding obligation to make a grant or assignment of a major interest in, or in any part of, the building or its site;

(b) in relation to a building or work if there was incurred before that date a legally binding obligation to make in relation to the building or work a supply within item 2 of Group 8 of Schedule 5 to the 1983 Act;

(c) in relation to a person who has constructed a building if—

(i) he incurred before that date a legally binding obligation to construct the building or any development of which it forms part, and

(ii) planning permission for the construction of the building was granted before that date, and

(iii) he has made a grant or assignment of a major interest in, or in any part of, the building or its site before 21st June 1993.

(2) Sub-paragraph (1) above shall not apply in any case where the Commissioners required proof of any of the matters specified in paragraph (a), (b) or (c)(i) above to be given to their satisfaction by the production of documents made before 21st June 1988 and that requirement was not complied with.[1]

Amendments—[1] Para 10 repealed by the Value Added Tax (Buildings and Land) Order, SI 2008/1146, art 6, Sch 1 paras 1, 5(b) with effect in relation to supplies made on or after 1 June 2008, subject to savings in Sch 2 of the Order.

Offences and Penalties

11 Where an offence for the continuation of which a penalty was provided has been committed under an enactment repealed by this Act, proceedings may be taken under this Act in respect of the continuance of the offence after the commencement of this Act in the same manner as if the offence had been committed under the corresponding provision of this Act.

12 Part IV of this Act, except section 72, shall not apply in relation to any act done or omitted to be done before 25th July 1985, and the following provision of this Schedule shall have effect accordingly.

13—(1) Section 72 shall have effect in relation to any offence committed or alleged to have been committed at any time ("the relevant time") before the commencement of this Act subject to the following provisions of this paragraph.

(2) Where the relevant time falls between 25th July 1983 and 26th July 1985 (the dates of passing of the 1983 and 1985 Finance Acts respectively), section 72 shall apply—

(a) with the substitution in subsection (1)(b), (3)(ii) and (8)(b) of "2 years" for "7 years";

(b) with the omission of subsections (2) and (4) to (7).

14—(1) The provisions of this paragraph have effect in relation to section 59.

(2) Section 59 shall apply in any case where a person is in default in respect of a prescribed accounting period which has ended before the commencement of this Act, but shall have effect in any case where the last day referred to in subsection (1) of that section falls before 1st October 1993 subject to the following modifications—

(a) for the words "a prescribed accounting period" in subsection (2)(a) there shall be substituted "any two prescribed accounting periods";

(b) with the addition of the following paragraph in subsection (2)—

"(aa) the last day of the later one of those periods falls on or before the first anniversary of the last day of the earlier one; and";

(c) for the words "period referred to in paragraph (a)" in subsection (2)(b) there shall be substituted "later period referred to in paragraph (aa)"; and

(d) for the words "a default in respect of a prescribed accounting period and that period" in subsection (3) there shall be substituted "defaults in respect of two prescribed accounting periods and the second of those periods".

(3) Section 59 shall have effect, in any case where a person has been served with a surcharge liability notice and that person is in default in respect of a prescribed accounting period because of a failure of the Commissioners to receive a return or an amount of VAT on or before a day falling before 30th September 1993 with the omission of—

(a) subsection (4)(b);

(b) the words in subsection (5) "and for which he has outstanding VAT"; and

(c) subsection (6).

15—(1) Section 63 does not apply in relation to returns and assessments made for prescribed accounting periods beginning before 1st April 1990 but subject to that shall have effect in relation to the cases referred to in the following sub-paragraphs subject to the modifications there specified.

(2) Subsection (1) shall have effect in a case falling within paragraph (b) of that subsection where the assessment was made on or before 10th March 1992 with the substitution of "20 per cent" for "15 per cent".

(3) In relation to any prescribed accounting period beginning before 1st December 1993 section 63 shall have effect with the substitution—

(a) for the words in subsection (2) following "exceeds" of "either 30 per cent of the true amount of the VAT for that period or whichever is the greater of £10,000 and 5 per cent of the true amount of VAT for that period." and with the omission of subsections (4) to (6); and

(b) for the words in subsection (8) from "subsections" to "statements" of "subsection (7) that the statement by each of those returns is a correct statement".

(4) In relation to any prescribed accounting period beginning before 1st June 1994 section 63 shall have effect with the substitution for subsection (3) of the following subsection—

"(3) Any reference in this section to the VAT for a prescribed accounting period which would have been lost if an inaccuracy had not been discovered is a reference to the aggregate of—

(a) the amount (if any) by which credit for input tax for that period was overstated; and

(b) the amount (if any) by which output tax for that period was understated;

but if for any period there is an understatement of credit for input tax or an overstatement of output tax, allowance shall be made for that error in determining the VAT for that period which would have been so lost."

and in subsection (8) for "this section" there shall be substituted "subsections (5) and (7) above".

16—(1) In relation to any prescribed accounting period beginning before 1st December 1993 section 64 shall have effect subject to the following modifications—

(a) in subsection (1)(b) for the words from "whichever" to "period" there shall be substituted "whichever is the greater of £100 and 1 per cent of the true amount of VAT for that period";

(b) for subsections (2) and (3) there shall be substituted—

"(2) Subsection (3) below applies in any case where—

(a) there is a material inaccuracy in respect of any two prescribed accounting periods, and

(b) the last day of the later one of those periods falls on or before the second anniversary of the last day of the earlier one, and

(c) after 29th July 1988 the Commissioners serve notice on the person concerned ("a penalty liability notice") specifying as a penalty period for the purposes of this section a period beginning on the date of the notice and ending on the second anniversary of that date.

(3) If there is a material inaccuracy in respect of a prescribed accounting period ending within the penalty period specified in a penalty liability notice served on the person concerned that person shall be liable to a penalty equal to 15 per cent of the VAT for that period which would have been lost if the inaccuracy had not been discovered.";

(c) in subsection (4) for "(5)" there shall be substituted "(7)"; and

(d) in subsection (6) the words from "except" to the end shall be omitted.

(2) A penalty liability notice shall not be served under section 64 by reference to any material inaccuracy in respect of a prescribed accounting period beginning before 1st December 1993, and the penalty period specified in any penalty liability notice served before that day shall be deemed to end with the day before that day.

17 Section 70 shall not apply in relation to any penalty to which a person has been assessed before 27th July 1993 and in the case of any penalty in relation to which that section does not apply by virtue of this paragraph, section 60 shall have effect subject to the following modifications—
   (*a*) in subsection (1) for "subsection (6)" there shall be substituted "subsections (3A) and (6)";
   (*b*) after subsection (3) there shall be inserted—
"(3A) If a person liable to a penalty under this section has co-operated with the Commissioners in the investigation of his true liability to tax or, as the case may be, of his true entitlement to any payment, refund or repayment, the Commissioners or, on appeal, a tribunal may reduce the penalty to an amount which is not less than half what it would have been apart from this subsection; and in determining the extent of any reduction under this subsection, the Commissioners or tribunal shall have regard to the extent of the co-operation which the person concerned has given to the Commissioners in their investigation.";
   (*c*) in subsection (4)(*b*) for the words from "under" to "this section" there shall be substituted "to reduce a penalty under this section, as provided in subsection (4) above, and, in determining the extent of such a reduction in the case of any person, the Commissioners or tribunal will have regard to the extent of the co-operation which he has given to the Commissioners in their investigation";
and in section 61(6) for "70" there shall be substituted "60(3A)".
Commentary—*De Voil Indirect Tax Service* **V5.334**.

18 Section 74 shall not apply in relation to prescribed accounting periods beginning before 1st April 1990 and subsection (3) of that section shall not apply in relation to interest on amounts assessed or, as the case may be, paid before 1st October 1993.

Importation of goods

19 Nothing in this Act shall prejudice the effect of the Finance (No 2) Act 1992 (Commencement No 4 and Transitional Provisions) Order 1992 and accordingly—
   (*a*) where Article 4 of that Order applies immediately before the commencement of this Act in relation to any importation of goods, that Article and the legislation repealed by this Act shall continue to apply in relation to that importation as if this Act had not been enacted, and
   (*b*) where Article 5 of that Order applies in relation to any goods, this Act shall apply in relation to those goods in accordance with that Article and Article 6 of that Order.

Assessments

20 An assessment may be made under section 73 in relation to amounts paid or credited before the commencement of this Act but—
   (*a*) in relation to an amount paid or credited before 30th July 1990 section 73(2) shall have effect with the omission of the words from "or which" to "out to be", and
   (*b*) in relation to amounts repaid or paid to any person before the passing of the Finance Act 1982 section 73 shall have effect with the omission of subsection (2).

Set-off of credits

21 Section 81 shall have effect in relation to amounts becoming due before 10th May 1994 with the omission of subsections (4) and (5).

VAT tribunals

22—(1) Without prejudice to paragraph 1 above, section 83 applies to things done or omitted to be done before the coming into force of this Act and accordingly references in Part V to any provision of this Act includes a reference to the corresponding provision of the enactments repealed by this Act or by any enactment repealed by such an enactment.
(2) Section 84 shall have effect before such day as may be appointed for the purposes of section 18(3) of the Finance Act 1994 with the substitution for subsection (5) of the following subsection—
"(5) No appeal shall lie with respect to any matter that has been or could have been referred to arbitration under section 127 of the Management Act as applied by section 16."

Isle of Man

23 Nothing in paragraph 7 of Schedule 14 shall affect the validity of any Order made under section 6 of the Isle of Man Act 1979 and, without prejudice to section 17 of the Interpretation Act 1978 for any reference in any such Order to any enactment repealed by this Act there shall be substituted a reference to the corresponding provision of this Act.

SCHEDULE 14
CONSEQUENTIAL AMENDMENTS

1–5 (*amend* provisions outside the scope of this Publication).

Customs and Excise Management Act 1979 c 2

6 (*amends* CEMA 1979 s 1(1)).

Isle of Man Act 1979 c 58

7 (*amends* IOM 1979 ss 1(1), 6(1), 14(4)).

Insolvency Act 1986 c 45

8 (*amended* Sch 6, *repealed by* the Enterprise Act 2002 s 278, Sch 26).

Bankruptcy (Scotland) Act 1985 c 66

9 (*amended* Sch 3 para 8; *revoked by* the Bankruptcy (Scotland) Act 2016 (Consequential Provisions and Modifications) Order, SI 2016/1034 art 7(2), Sch 2 Pt 1 with effect from 30 November 2016)).

Income and Corporation Taxes Act 1988 c 1

10 (*amends* TA 1988 s 827).

Capital Allowances Act 1990 c 1

11 (*amended* s 159A, *repealed by* CAA 2001 s 580, Sch 4 with effect in accordance with CAA 2001 s 579).

Tribunals and Inquiries Act 1992 c 53

[12 (*amends* Sch 1).]¹

[1] This para repealed by the Transfer of Tribunal Functions and Revenue and Customs Appeals Order, SI 2009/56 art 3, Sch 1 para 229 with effect from 1 April 2009, subject to transitional and savings provisions in Sch 3 para 4.

Finance Act 1994 c 9

13 (*amends* s 7(4), (5) (and is *amended* by FA 1995 s 33(1), (5), this amendment being deemed to have always had effect)).

Vehicle Excise and Registration Act 1994 c 22

14 (*amends* Sch 2 para 23).

FINANCE ACT 2003
(2003 Chapter 14)
ARRANGEMENT OF SECTIONS

PART 3
TAXES AND DUTIES ON IMPORTATION AND EXPORTATION: PENALTIES
Preliminary

24	Introductory

The penalties

25	Penalty for evasion
26	Penalty for contravention of relevant rule
27	Exceptions from section 26
28	Liability of directors etc where body corporate liable to penalty for evasion

Reduction of amount of penalty

29	Reduction of penalty under section 25 or 26

Demand notices

30	Demands for penalties
31	Time limits for demands for penalties
32	No prosecution after demand notice for penalty under section 26

Appeals and reviews

33	Right to appeal against certain decisions
33A	Offer of review
33B	Review by HMRC
33C	Extensions of time
33D	Review out of time
33E	Nature of review
33F	Bringing of appeals
34	*Time limit and right to further review* (repealed)
35	*Powers of Commissioners on a review* (repealed)

Appeals

36	Appeals to a tribunal
37	Appeal tribunals

Evidence

38	Admissibility of certain statements and documents

Miscellaneous and supplementary

39	Service of notices
40	Penalties not to be deducted for income tax or corporation tax purposes
41	Regulations and orders

PART 3
TAXES AND DUTIES ON IMPORTATION AND EXPORTATION: PENALTIES

Commentary—*De Voil Indirect Tax Service* **V3.311, V5.301, V5.331.**

Preliminary

24 Introductory

(1) This Part makes provision for and in connection with the imposition of liability to a penalty where a person—
    (*a*) engages in any conduct for the purpose of evading any relevant tax or duty, or
    (*b*) engages in any conduct by which he contravenes a duty, obligation, requirement or condition imposed by or under legislation relating to any relevant tax or duty.

(2) For the purposes of this Part "relevant tax or duty" means any of the following—
    (*a*) customs duty;
    (*b*) . . .[3]
    (*c*) . . .[3]
    (*d*) import VAT;
    (*e*) . . .[3]

(3) In this Part—
    "appeal tribunal" means [the First-tier Tribunal or, where determined by or under Tribunal Procedure Rules, the Upper Tribunal][1];

"the Commissioners" means the Commissioners of Customs and Excise;
. . . ²

"contravene" includes fail to comply with;
. . . ³

"demand notice" means a demand notice within the meaning of section 30;
["HMRC" means "Her Majesty's Revenue and Customs."]¹
"import VAT" means value added tax chargeable by virtue of section 1(1)(c) of the Value Added Tax Act 1994 (c 23) (importation of goods [into the United Kingdom]⁴);
"notice" means notice in writing;
. . . ³

"prescribed" means specified in, or determined in accordance with, regulations made by the Treasury;
"relevant rule", in relation to any relevant tax or duty, has the meaning given by subsection (8) of section 26 (as read with subsection (9) of that section);
"representative", in relation to any person, means—
  (a) his personal representative,
  (b) his trustee in bankruptcy or interim or permanent trustee,
  (c) any receiver or liquidator appointed in relation to that person or any of his property,
or any other person acting in a representative capacity in relation to that person.
. . . ³

(4)–(6) . . . ³

(7) Except for this subsection and section 41 (which accordingly come into force on the passing of this Act), this Part comes into force on such day as the Treasury may by order appoint.

Regulations—Finance Act 2003, Part 3, (Appointed Day) Order 2003, SI 2003/2985 (appoints 27 November 2003 as the date for Part 3 to come into force).
Customs (Contravention of a Relevant Rule) (Amendment) Regulations, SI 2015/636.
Taxation (Cross-border Trade) (Miscellaneous Provisions) (EU Exit) Regulations, SI 2019/486.
Taxation (Cross-border Trade) (Miscellaneous Provisions) (EU Exit) (No 2) Regulations, SI 2019/1346.
Customs (Reliefs from a Liability to Import Duty and Miscellaneous Amendments) (EU Exit) Regulations, SI 2020/1431.
Amendment—¹ In sub-s (3), words in the definition of "appeal tribunal" substituted, and definition of "HMRC" inserted, by the Transfer of Tribunal Functions and Revenue and Customs Appeals Order, SI 2009/56 art 3, Sch 1 para 360 with effect from 1 April 2009.
² In sub-s (3), entries for "the Community Customs Code", "Community export duty" and "Community import duty" repealed by the Finance Act 2003, Part 3 (Amendment) Order, SI 2018/461 arts 3, 4 with effect in respect of conduct which begins on or after 30 March 2018.
³ Sub-s (2)(b), (c), (e) repealed, in sub-s (3) definitions of "the European Union Customs Code", "Community export duty", "Community import duty", "customs duty of a preferential tariff country" and "preferential tariff country" repealed, and sub-ss (4)–(6) repealed, by the Taxation (Cross-border Trade) Act 2018 s 29, Sch 7 para 148 with effect from IP completion day (11pm on 31 December 2020), by virtue of SI 2020/1642 reg 4(a).
See TCBTA 2018 Sch 7 para 158(7): Part 3 of FA 2003 continues to have effect, for any purpose in connection with duty under TCBTA 2018 ss 30A(3) or 40A as if sub-ss (4)–(6) were not made.
Before these amendments, section 24 read as follows—

"24 Introductory

(1) This Part makes provision for and in connection with the imposition of liability to a penalty where a person—
  (a) engages in any conduct for the purpose of evading any relevant tax or duty, or
  (b) engages in any conduct by which he contravenes a duty, obligation, requirement or condition imposed by or under legislation relating to any relevant tax or duty.

(2) For the purposes of this Part "relevant tax or duty" means any of the following—
  (a) customs duty;
  (b) [Union export duty;
  (c) Union import duty;
  (d) import VAT;
  (e) customs duty of a preferential tariff country.

(3) In this Part—
"appeal tribunal" means the First-tier Tribunal or, where determined by or under Tribunal Procedure Rules, the Upper Tribunal;
"the Commissioners" means the Commissioners of Customs and Excise;
. . .

"contravene" includes fail to comply with;
"customs duty of a preferential tariff country" includes a reference to any charge imposed by a preferential tariff country and having an equivalent effect to customs duty payable on the importation of goods into the territory of that country;
"demand notice" means a demand notice within the meaning of section 30;
"HMRC" means "Her Majesty's Revenue and Customs.
"import VAT" means value added tax chargeable by virtue of section 1(1)(c) of the Value Added Tax Act 1994 (c 23) (importation of goods from places outside the member States);

"notice" means notice in writing;

"preferential tariff country" means a country outside the European Community which is, or is a member of a group of countries which is, party to an agreement falling within Article 56(2)(d) of the Union Customs Code (preferential tariff agreements with the Community);

"prescribed" means specified in, or determined in accordance with, regulations made by the Treasury;

"relevant rule", in relation to any relevant tax or duty, has the meaning given by subsection (8) of section 26 (as read with subsection (9) of that section);

"representative", in relation to any person, means—
- (a) his personal representative,
- (b) his trustee in bankruptcy or interim or permanent trustee,
- (c) any receiver or liquidator appointed in relation to that person or any of his property,

or any other person acting in a representative capacity in relation to that person.

"Union Customs Code" means Regulation (EU) No 952/2013 of the European Parliament and of the Council of 9 October 2013 laying down the Union Customs Code;

"Union export duty" means export duty, as defined in Article 5(21) of the Union Customs Code;

"Union import duty" means import duty, as defined in Article 5(20) of the Union Customs Code.

(4) References in this Part to the Union Customs Code are references to that Code as from time to time amended, whether before or after the coming into force of this Part.

(5) The Treasury may by order amend this Part for the purpose of replacing any reference to, or to a provision of,—
- (a) the Union Customs Code, or
- (b) any instrument referred to in this Part by virtue of an order under this subsection,

with a reference to, or (as the case may be) to a provision of, a different instrument.

(6) A statutory instrument containing an order under subsection (5) may not be made unless a draft of the instrument has been laid before, and approved by a resolution of, the House of Commons.

(7) Except for this subsection and section 41 (which accordingly come into force on the passing of this Act), this Part comes into force on such day as the Treasury may by order appoint.".

[4] In sub-s (3), in definition of "import VAT", words substituted for words "from places outside the member States" by the Taxation (Cross-border Trade) Act 2018 s 43, Sch 8 para 109 with effect from IP completion day (11pm on 31 December 2020), by virtue of SI 2020/1642 reg 4(b).

The penalties

25 Penalty for evasion

(1) In any case where—
- (a) a person engages in any conduct for the purpose of evading any relevant tax or duty, and
- (b) his conduct involves dishonesty (whether or not such as to give rise to any criminal liability),

that person is liable to a penalty of an amount equal to the amount of the tax or duty evaded or, as the case may be, sought to be evaded.

(2) Subsection (1) is subject to the following provisions of this Part.

(3) . . . [1]

(4) Any reference in this section to a person's "evading" any relevant tax or duty includes a reference to his obtaining or securing, without his being entitled to it,—
- (a) any repayment, rebate or drawback of any relevant tax or duty,
- (b) any relief or exemption from, or any allowance against, any relevant tax or duty, or
- (c) any deferral or other postponement of his liability to pay any relevant tax or duty or of the discharge by payment of any such liability,

and also includes a reference to his evading the cancellation of any entitlement to, or the withdrawal of, any such repayment, rebate, drawback, relief, exemption or allowance.

(5) In relation to any such evasion of any relevant tax or duty as is mentioned in subsection (4), the reference in subsection (1) to the amount of the tax or duty evaded or sought to be evaded is a reference to the amount of—
- (a) the repayment, rebate or drawback,
- (b) the relief, exemption or allowance, or
- (c) the payment which, or the liability to make which, is deferred or otherwise postponed,

as the case may be.

(6) Where, by reason of conduct falling within subsection (1) in the case of any relevant tax or duty, a person—
- (a) is convicted of an offence,
- (b) is given, and has not had withdrawn, a demand notice in respect of a penalty to which he is liable under section 26, or
- (c) is liable to a penalty imposed upon him under any other provision of the law relating to that relevant tax or duty,

that conduct does not also give rise to liability to a penalty under this section in respect of that relevant tax or duty.

Amendments—[1] Sub-s (3) repealed by the Taxation (Cross-border Trade) Act 2018 s 29, Sch 7 para 149 with effect from IP completion day (11pm on 31 December 2020), by virtue of SI 2020/1642 reg 4(a).

Sub-s (3) previously read as follows—
   "(3) Nothing in this section applies in relation to any customs duty of a preferential tariff country.".

26 Penalty for contravention of relevant rule

(1) If, in the case of any relevant tax or duty, a person of a prescribed description engages in any conduct by which he contravenes—
   (a) a prescribed relevant rule, or
   (b) a relevant rule of a prescribed description,
he is liable to a penalty under this section of a prescribed amount.
(2) Subsection (1) is subject to the following provisions of this Part.
(3) The power conferred by subsection (1) to prescribe a description of person includes power to prescribe any person (without further qualification) as such a description.
(4) Different penalties may be prescribed under subsection (1) for different cases or different circumstances.
(5) Any amount prescribed under subsection (1) as the amount of a penalty must not be more than £2,500.
[(5A) Where the conduct constituting a contravention of a relevant rule is a contravention of a condition imposed under regulations under section 20(1A), 22(1A) or 25(1A) of the Customs and Excise Management Act 1979—
   (a) the Treasury may by regulations provide that, in prescribed circumstances, there are to be deemed for the purposes of subsection (1) of this section to be further separate contraventions of the rule, and
   (b) the provision that may be made by the regulations includes provision replicating or applying, with or without modifications, any provision made by section 20A(1A) or (1B), 22A(1A) or (1B) or 25A(1A) or (1B) of the Customs and Excise Management Act 1979.][2]
(6) The Treasury may by order amend subsection (5) by substituting a different amount for the amount for the time being specified in that subsection.
(7) A statutory instrument containing an order under subsection (6) may not be made unless a draft of the instrument has been laid before, and approved by a resolution of, the House of Commons.
(8) In this Part "relevant rule", in relation to any relevant tax or duty, means any duty, obligation, requirement or condition imposed by or under any of the following—
   [(za) Part 1 and sections 40A and 40B of the Taxation (Cross-border Trade) Act 2018, as they apply in relation to the relevant tax or duty;][2]
   (a) the Customs and Excise Management Act 1979 (c 2), as it applies in relation to the relevant tax or duty;
   (b) any other Act, or any statutory instrument, as it applies in relation to the relevant tax or duty;
   [(c) . . .][2]
   (d) . . .[3]
   (e) . . .[2]
   (f) any relevant international rules applying in relation to the relevant tax or duty.
(9) In subsection (8)—
   . . .[1]
   "relevant international rules" means international agreements so far as applying in relation to a relevant tax or duty and having effect as part of the law of any part of the United Kingdom by virtue of—
      (a) any Act or statutory instrument . . .[2]
   ["Union customs legislation" means customs legislation, as defined in Article 5(2) of the Union Customs Code.][1]

Regulations—Customs (Contravention of a Relevant Rule) Regulations, SI 2003/3113.
Customs (Contravention of a Relevant Rule) (Amendment) Regulations, SI 2015/636.
Customs (Contravention of a Relevant Rule) (Amendment) (EU Exit) Regulations, SI 2019/148.
Taxation (Cross-border Trade) (Miscellaneous Provisions) (EU Exit) Regulations, SI 2019/486.
Customs (Managed Transition Procedure) (EU Exit) Regulations, SI 2019/487.
Taxation (Cross-border Trade) (Miscellaneous Provisions) (EU Exit) (No 2) Regulations, SI 2019/1346.
Customs (Reliefs from a Liability to Import Duty and Miscellaneous Amendments) (EU Exit) Regulations, SI 2020/1431.
Amendments—[1] In sub-s (9), definition of "Community customs rules" repealed, and definition of "Union customs legislation" inserted by the Finance Act 2003, Part 3 (Amendment) Order, SI 2018/461 arts 3, 5 with effect in respect of conduct which begins on or after 30 March 2018.
[2] Sub-ss (5A), (8)(za) inserted, sub-s (8)(c), (e) repealed, and in sub-s (9) in the definition of "relevant international rules", para (b) and preceding word "or" repealed, by the Taxation (Cross-border Trade) Act 2018 s 29, Sch 7 para 150 (as amended by the Taxation (Post-transition Period) Act 2020 Sch 1 para 10(4)) with effect from IP completion day (11pm on 31 December 2020), by virtue of SI 2020/1642 reg 4(a).
See TCBTA 2018 Sch 7 para 158(7): Part 3 of FA 2003 continues to have effect, for any purpose in connection with duty under TCBTA 2018 ss 30A(3) or 40A as if these amendments (except for the insertion of sub-s (8)(za)) were not made, and as if in the preserved sub-s (8)(c), the words "Union export duty or Union import duty," were repealed.
Sub-s (8)(c), (e) previously read as follows—
   "(c) in the case of customs duty, Union export duty or Union import duty, Union customs legislation;".
   "(e) any directly applicable Community legislation relating to the relevant tax or duty;".

Para (*b*) in definition of "relevant international rules" previously read as follows—
"(*b*) any directly applicable Community legislation.".
3 Sub-s (8)(*d*) repealed by the Taxation (Cross-border Trade) Act 2018 s 43, Sch 8 para 110 with effect from IP completion day (11pm on 31 December 2020), by virtue of SI 2020/1642 reg 4(*b*).
Sub-s (8)(*d*) previously read as follows—
"(*d*) in the case of import VAT, Union customs legislation as it applies in relation to import VAT;".

27 Exceptions from section 26
(1) A person is not liable to a penalty under section 26 if he satisfies—
 (*a*) the Commissioners, or
 (*b*) on appeal, an appeal tribunal,
that there is a reasonable excuse for his conduct.
(2) For the purposes of subsection (1) none of the following is a reasonable excuse—
 (*a*) an insufficiency of funds available to any person for paying any relevant tax or duty or any penalty due;
 (*b*) that reliance was placed by any person on another to perform any task;
 (*c*) that the contravention is attributable, in whole or in part, to the conduct of a person on whom reliance to perform any task was so placed.
(3) Where, by reason of conduct falling within subsection (1) of section 26 in the case of any relevant tax or duty, a person—
 (*a*) is prosecuted for an offence,
 (*b*) is given, and has not had withdrawn, a demand notice in respect of a penalty to which he is liable under section 25, or
 (*c*) is liable to a penalty imposed upon him under any other provision of the law relating to that relevant tax or duty,
that conduct does not also give rise to liability to a penalty under section 26 in respect of that relevant tax or duty.
(4) A person is not liable to a penalty under section 26 in respect of any conduct, so far as relating to import VAT, if in respect of that conduct—
 (*a*) he is liable to a penalty under any of sections 62 to 69A of the Value Added Tax Act 1994 (c 23) (penalty for contravention of statutory requirements as to VAT), or
 (*b*) he would be so liable but for section 62(4), 63(11), 64(6), 67(9), 69(9) or 69A(7) of that Act (conduct resulting in conviction, different penalty etc).

28 Liability of directors etc where body corporate liable to penalty for evasion
(1) Where it appears to the Commissioners—
 (*a*) that a body corporate is liable to a penalty under section 25, and
 (*b*) that the conduct giving rise to the penalty is, in whole or in part, attributable to the dishonesty of a person who is, or at the material time was, a director or managing officer of the body corporate (a "relevant officer"),
the Commissioners may give a notice under this section to the body corporate (or its representative) and to the relevant officer (or his representative).
(2) A notice under this section must state—
 (*a*) the amount of the penalty referred to in subsection (1)(*a*) (the "basic penalty"), and
 (*b*) that the Commissioners propose, in accordance with this section, to recover from the relevant officer such portion (which may be the whole) of the basic penalty as is specified in the notice.
(3) If a notice is given under this section, this Part shall apply in relation to the relevant officer as if he were personally liable under section 25 to a penalty which corresponds to that portion of the basic penalty specified in the notice.
(4) If a notice is given under this section—
 (*a*) the amount which may be recovered from the body corporate under this Part is limited to so much (if any) of the basic penalty as is not recoverable from the relevant officer by virtue of subsection (3), and
 (*b*) the body corporate is to be treated as discharged from liability for so much of the basic penalty as is so recoverable from the relevant officer.
(5) In this section "managing officer", in relation to a body corporate, means—
 (*a*) a manager, secretary or other similar officer of the body corporate, or
 (*b*) a person purporting to act in any such capacity or as a director.
(6) Where the affairs of a body corporate are managed by its members, this section applies in relation to the conduct of a member in connection with his functions of management as if he were a director of the body corporate.

Reduction of amount of penalty

29 Reduction of penalty under section 25 or 26
(1) Where a person is liable to a penalty under section 25 or 26—

(*a*) the Commissioners (whether originally or on review) or, on appeal, an appeal tribunal may reduce the penalty to such amount (including nil) as they think proper; and
(*b*) the Commissioners on a review, or an appeal tribunal on an appeal, relating to a penalty reduced by the Commissioners under this subsection may cancel the whole or any part of the reduction previously made by the Commissioners.
(2) In exercising their powers under subsection (1), neither the Commissioners nor an appeal tribunal are entitled to take into account any of the matters specified in subsection (3).
(3) Those matters are—
(*a*) the insufficiency of the funds available to any person for paying any relevant tax or duty or the amount of the penalty,
(*b*) the fact that there has, in the case in question or in that case taken with any other cases, been no or no significant loss of any relevant tax or duty,
(*c*) the fact that the person liable to the penalty, or a person acting on his behalf, has acted in good faith.

Demand notices

30 Demands for penalties

(1) Where a person is liable to a penalty under this Part, the Commissioners may give to that person or his representative a notice in writing (a "demand notice") demanding payment of the amount due by way of penalty.
(2) An amount demanded as due from a person or his representative in accordance with subsection (1) is recoverable as if it were an amount due from the person or, as the case may be, the representative as an amount of customs duty.
This subsection is subject to—
(*a*) any appeal under section [33][1] (appeals to tribunal); and
(*b*) subsection (3).
(3) An amount so demanded is not recoverable if or to the extent that—
(*a*) the demand has subsequently been withdrawn; or
(*b*) the amount has been reduced under section 29.

Amendments—[1] In sub-s (2) figure substituted for the figure "36"; definition of "HMRC" inserted by the Transfer of Tribunal Functions and Revenue and Customs Appeals Order, SI 2009/56 art 3, Sch 1 para 361 with effect from 1 April 2009.

31 Time limits for demands for penalties

(1) A demand notice may not be given—
(*a*) in the case of a penalty under section 25, more than 20 years after the conduct giving rise to the liability to the penalty ceased, or
(*b*) in the case of a penalty under section 26, more than 3 years after the conduct giving rise to the liability to the penalty ceased.
(2) A demand notice may not be given more than 2 years after there has come to the knowledge of the Commissioners evidence of facts sufficient in the opinion of the Commissioners to justify the giving of the demand notice.
(3) A demand notice—
(*a*) may be given in respect of a penalty to which a person was liable under section 25 or 26 immediately before his death, but
(*b*) in the case of a penalty to which the deceased was so liable under section 25, may not be given more than 3 years after his death.

32 No prosecution after demand notice for penalty under section 26

[(1)] Where a demand notice is given demanding payment of an amount due by way of penalty under section 26 in respect of any conduct of a person, no proceedings may be brought against that person for any offence constituted by that conduct (whether or not the demand notice is subsequently withdrawn).
[(2) Nothing in subsection (1) prevents the bringing of proceedings against a person for an offence under section 20A(1A), 22A(1A) or 25A(1A) of the Customs and Excise Management Act 1979 in circumstances where it is alleged that the person is liable to a penalty of an enhanced amount.][1]

Amendments—[1] Sub-s (1) numbered as such, and sub-s (2) inserted, by the Taxation (Cross-border Trade) Act 2018 s 29, Sch 7 para 151 with effect from IP completion day (11pm on 31 December 2020), by virtue of SI 2020/1642 reg 4(*a*).
See TCBTA 2018 Sch 7 para 158(7): Part 3 of FA 2003 continues to have effect, for any purpose in connection with duty under TCBTA 2018 ss 30A(3) or 40A as if these amendments were not made.

[Appeals and reviews]

Amendments—Cross-head substituted for "Reviews" by the Transfer of Tribunal Functions and Revenue and Customs Appeals Order, SI 2009/56 art 3, Sch 1 para 363 with effect from 1 April 2009, subject to transitional and savings provisions in Sch 3 paras 2, 3.

(i) the conclusion date (if HMRC decide to undertake a review), or

(ii) the date on which HMRC decide not to undertake a review.

(5) In a case where section 33E(8) applies, an appeal may be made at any time from the end of the period specified in section 33E(6) to the date 30 days after the conclusion date.

(6) An appeal may be made after the end of the period specified in subsection (1), (3)(*b*), (4)(*b*) or (5) if an appeal tribunal gives permission to do so.

(7) In this section "conclusion date" means the date of the document notifying the conclusions of the review.][1]

Amendments—[1] Sections 33A–33F inserted by the Transfer of Tribunal Functions and Revenue and Customs Appeals Order, SI 2009/56 art 3, Sch 1 para 364 with effect from 1 April 2009.

[37 Appeal tribunals

Section 85 of the Value Added Tax Act 1994 (settling appeals by agreement) has effect as if the reference to section 83 of that Act included a reference to section 33 above.][1]

Amendments—[1] Sections 37 substituted by the Transfer of Tribunal Functions and Revenue and Customs Appeals Order, SI 2009/56 art 3, Sch 1 para 366 with effect from 1 April 2009, subject to transitional and savings provisions in Sch 3 paras 2, 3.

Evidence

38 Admissibility of certain statements and documents

(1) Statements made or documents produced by or on behalf of a person are not inadmissible in—

(*a*) any criminal proceedings against that person in respect of any offence in connection with or in relation to any relevant tax or duty, or

(*b*) any proceedings against that person for the recovery of any sum due from him in connection with or in relation to any relevant tax or duty,

by reason only that any of the matters specified in subsection (2) has been drawn to his attention and that he was, or may have been, induced by that matter having been brought to his attention to make the statements or produce the documents.

(2) The matters mentioned in subsection (1) are—

(*a*) that the Commissioners have power, in relation to any relevant tax or duty, to demand by means of a written notice an amount by way of a civil penalty, instead of instituting criminal proceedings;

(*b*) that it is the Commissioners' practice, without being able to give an undertaking as to whether they will make such a demand in any case, to be influenced in determining whether to make such a demand by the fact (where it is the case) that a person has made a full confession of any dishonest conduct to which he has been a party and has given full facilities for an investigation;

(*c*) that the Commissioners or, on appeal, an appeal tribunal have power to reduce a penalty under section 25, as provided in subsection (1) of section 29; and

(*d*) that, in determining the extent of such a reduction in the case of any person, the Commissioners or tribunal will have regard to the extent of the co-operation which he has given to the Commissioners in their investigation.

(3) . . . [1]

Amendments—[1] Sub-s (3) repealed by the Taxation (Cross-border Trade) Act 2018 s 29, Sch 7 para 152 with effect from IP completion day (11pm on 31 December 2020), by virtue of SI 2020/1642 reg 4(*a*).

Sub-s (3) previously read as follows—

"(3) References in this section to a relevant tax or duty do not include a reference to customs duty of a preferential tariff country.".

Miscellaneous and supplementary

39 Service of notices

Any notice to be given to any person for the purposes of this Part may be given by sending it by post in a letter addressed to that person or his representative at the last or usual residence or place of business of that person or representative.

40 Penalties not to be deducted for income tax or corporation tax purposes

(*inserts* TA 1988 s 827(1E); *repealed* by CTA 2009 s 1326, Sch 3 Pt 1).

41 Regulations and orders

(1) Any power conferred on the Treasury by this Part to make regulations or an order includes power—

(*a*) to make different provision for different cases, and

(*b*) to make incidental, consequential, supplemental or transitional provision or savings.

(2) Any power conferred on the Treasury by this Part to make regulations or an order shall be exercisable by statutory instrument.

(3) Any statutory instrument containing regulations under this Part shall be subject to annulment in pursuance of a resolution of the House of Commons.

Regulations—Customs (Contravention of a Relevant Rule) Regulations, SI 2003/3113.
Customs (Contravention of a Relevant Rule) (Amendment) Regulations, SI 2015/636.
Taxation (Cross-border Trade) (Miscellaneous Provisions) (EU Exit) Regulations, SI 2019/486.
Order—Finance Act 2003, Part 3 (Appointed Day) Order, SI 2003/2985.

FINANCE ACT 2007

(2007 Chapter 11)

CONTENTS

Schedule 24—Penalties for errors

SCHEDULES

SCHEDULE 24

PENALTIES FOR ERRORS

Section 97

HMRC Manuals—Compliance Handbook Manual, CH81000–84974 (HMRC Compliance Handbook Manual chapter on penalties for inaccuracies).
Orders—The Finance Act 2007, Schedule 24 (Commencement And Transitional Provisions) Order, SI 2008/568: this Schedule has effect as follows—

(a) 1 April 2008 in relation to relevant documents relating to tax periods commencing on or after that date;
(b) 1 April 2008 in relation to assessments falling within Sch 24 para 2 for tax periods commencing on or after that date;
(c) 1 July 2008 in relation to relevant documents relating to claims under the Thirteenth Council Directive (arrangements for the refund of value added tax to persons not established in Community territory) for years commencing on or after that date;
(d) 1 January 2009 in relation to relevant documents relating to claims under the Eighth Council Directive (arrangements for the refund of value added tax to taxable persons not established in the territory of the country) for years commencing on or after that date;
(e) 1 April 2009 in relation to documents relating to all other claims for repayments of relevant tax made on or after 1 April 2009 which are not related to a tax period; and
(f) in any other case, 1 April 2009 in relation to documents given where a person's liability to pay relevant tax arises on or after that date.

PART 1

LIABILITY FOR PENALTY

Error in taxpayer's document

1—(1) A penalty is payable by a person (P) where—
 (a) P gives HMRC a document of a kind listed in the Table below, and
 (b) Conditions 1 and 2 are satisfied.
(2) Condition 1 is that the document contains an inaccuracy which amounts to, or leads to—
 (a) an understatement of [a][1] liability to tax,
 (b) a false or inflated statement of a loss . . . [1], or
 (c) a false or inflated claim to repayment of tax.
(3) Condition 2 is that the inaccuracy was [careless (within the meaning of paragraph 3) or deliberate on P's part][1].
(4) Where a document contains more than one inaccuracy, a penalty is payable for each inaccuracy.

Tax	Document
Income tax or capital gains tax	Return under section 8 of TMA 1970 (personal return).
Income tax or capital gains tax	Return under section 8A of TMA 1970 (trustee's return).
Income tax or capital gains tax	Return, statement or declaration in connection with a claim for an allowance, deduction or relief.
Income tax or capital gains tax	Accounts in connection with ascertaining liability to tax.
Income tax or capital gains tax	Partnership return.
Income tax or capital gains tax	Statement or declaration in connection with a partnership return.
Income tax or capital gains tax	Accounts in connection with a partnership return.

Tax	Document
[Apprenticeship levy	Return under regulations under section 105 of FA 2016.][7]
[Capital gains tax	Return under [Schedule 2 to FA 2019][9].][6]
[Income tax	Return under section 254 of FA 2004.][1]
Income tax	Return for the purposes of PAYE regulations.
Construction industry deductions	Return for the purposes of regulations under section 70(1)(a) of FA 2004 in connection with deductions on account of tax under the Construction Industry Scheme.
Corporation tax	Company tax return under paragraph 3 of Schedule 18 to FA 1998.
Corporation tax	Return, statement or declaration in connection with a claim for an allowance, deduction or relief.
Corporation tax	Accounts in connection with ascertaining liability to tax.
[Digital services tax	DST return under paragraph 2 of Schedule 8 to FA 2020.][10]
VAT	VAT return under regulations made under paragraph 2 of Schedule 11 to VATA 1994.
VAT	Return, statement or declaration in connection with a claim.
. . .[11]	. . .[11]
[Insurance premium tax	Return under regulations under section 54 of FA 1994.
Insurance premium tax	Return, statement or declaration in connection with a claim.
Inheritance tax	Account under section 216 or 217 of IHTA 1984.
Inheritance tax	Information or document under regulations under section 256 of IHTA 1984.
Inheritance tax	Statement or declaration in connection with a deduction, exemption or relief.
Stamp duty land tax	Return under section 76 of FA 2003.
Stamp duty reserve tax	Return under regulations under section 98 of FA 1986.
[Annual tax on enveloped dwellings	Annual tax on enveloped dwellings return.
Annual tax on enveloped dwellings	Return of adjusted chargeable amount.][4]
Petroleum revenue tax	Return under paragraph 2 of Schedule 2 to the Oil Taxation Act 1975.
[Petroleum revenue tax	Statement or declaration in connection with a claim under paragraph 13A of Schedule 2 to the Oil Taxation Act 1975.][2]
Petroleum revenue tax	Statement or declaration in connection with a claim under Schedule 5, 6, 7 or 8 to the Oil Taxation Act 1975.
Petroleum revenue tax	Statement under section 1(1)(a) of the Petroleum Revenue Tax Act 1980.
[Soft drinks industry levy	Return under regulations under section 52 of FA 2017][8]
Aggregates levy	Return under regulations under section 25 of FA 2001.
Climate change levy	Return under regulations under paragraph 41 of Schedule 6 to FA 2000.
Landfill tax	Return under regulations under section 49 of FA 1996.
Air passenger duty	Return under section 38 of FA 1994.
Alcoholic liquor duties	Return under regulations under section 13, 49, 56 or 62 of the Alcoholic Liquor Duties Act 1979.
Alcoholic liquor duties	Statement or declaration in connection with a claim for repayment of duty under section 4(4) of FA 1995.
Tobacco products duty	Return under regulations under section 7 of the Tobacco Products Duties Act 1979.
Hydrocarbon oil duties	Return under regulations under section 21 of the Hydrocarbon Oil Duties Act 1979.
Excise duties	Return under regulations under section 93 of CEMA 1979.
Excise duties	Return under regulations under section 100G or 100H of CEMA 1979.

Tax	Document
Excise duties	Statement or declaration in connection with a claim.
General betting duty	Return under regulations under paragraph 2 of Schedule 1 to BGDA 1981.
Pool betting duty	Return under regulations under paragraph 2A of Schedule 1 to BGDA 1981.
Bingo duty	Return under regulations under paragraph 9 of Schedule 3 to BGDA 1981.
Lottery duty	Return under regulations under section 28(2) of FA 1993.
Gaming duty	Return under directions under paragraph 10 of Schedule 1 to FA 1997.
Remote gaming duty	Return under regulations under section 26K of BGDA 1981.][1]
[Machine games duty]	Return under regulations under paragraph 18 of Schedule 24 to FA 2012.][3]
[Any of the taxes mentioned above][1]	Any document which is likely to be relied upon by HMRC to determine, without further inquiry, a question about— (a) P's liability to tax, (b) payments by P by way of or in connection with tax, (c) any other payment by P (including penalties), or (d) repayments, or any other kind of payment or credit, to P.

(4A)–(4C) . . . [11]

(5) In relation to a return under paragraph 2 of Schedule 2 to the Oil Taxation Act 1975 [or a statement or declaration under paragraph 13A of that Schedule][2], references in this Schedule to P include any person who, after the giving of the return for a taxable field (within the meaning of that Act), becomes the responsible person for the field (within the meaning of that Act).][1]

HMRC Manuals—Compliance Handbook Manual, CH81011–81013 (penalties for inaccuracies: commencement date for penalties).
CH81060 (penalties for inaccuracies: which documents do penalties for inaccuracies apply to).
CH81070 (conditions for penalty for inaccuracy).
Modifications—FA 2007 Sch 24 has effect as if, in the Table in this para, the list of taxes included bank payroll tax and the list of documents included a bank payroll tax return (FA 2010 s 22, Sch 1 para 37(1)).
Amendments—[1] In sub-para (2), word substituted and words repealed, in sub-para (3), words substituted, in the table, entries inserted, in the last entry in column 1 words substituted, and sub-para (5) inserted, by FA 2008 s 122, Sch 40 paras 1, 2 with effect from 1 April 2009 (by virtue of SI 2009/571 art 2). In their application in relation to penalties payable under paras 1, 1A of this Schedule, the entries inserted in the table (by FA 2008 Sch 40 para 2(4), (5)) shall have effect in relation to—
    (a)   relevant documents—
        (i)   which relate to tax periods commencing on or after 1 April 2009, and
        (ii)   for which the filing date is on or after 1 April 2010;
    (b)   relevant documents relating to all claims for repayments of relevant tax made on or after 1 April 2010 which are not related to a tax period;
    (c)   relevant documents produced under regulations under IHTA 1984 s 256 where the date of death is on or after 1 April 2009; and
    (d)   in any other case, relevant documents given where a person's liability to pay relevant tax arises on or after 1 April 2010 (SI 2009/571 arts 3, 4).
In their application in relation to assessments falling within para 2 of this Schedule, the entries inserted in the table (by FA 2008 Sch 40 para 2(4), (5)) shall have effect in relation to tax periods commencing on or after 1 April 2009, where the filing date for the relevant document is on or after 1 April 2010 (SI 2009/571 art 5).
[2] In table, entry inserted, and in sub-para (5) words inserted, by F(No 3)A 2010 s 28, Sch 12 Pt 2 para 12 with effect in relation to claims made on or after 1 April 2011.
[3] In table, entry inserted by FA 2012 s 191, Sch 24 para 29 with effect in relation to the playing of machine games on or after 1 February 2013
[4] In table, entries inserted by FA 2013 s 164, Sch 34 para 6 with effect from 17 July 2013.
[6] In table, entry inserted by FA 2015 s 37, Sch 7 para 56(1), (2) with effect in relation to disposals made on or after 6 April 2015.
[7] In table, entry inserted by FA 2016 s 113(1), (2) with effect from 6 April 2017 (by virtue of SI 2017/355).
[8] In table, entry relating to soft drinks industry inserted by FA 2017 s 56, Sch 11 para 3 with effect from 6 April 2018 (by virtue of SI 2018/467).
[9] In table, in entry relating to capital gains tax, words substituted for words "section 12ZB of TMA 1970 (NRCGT return)" by FA 2019 s 14, Sch 2 para 27(1), (2) with effect in relation to disposals made on or after 6 April 2019.
[10] In table, entry relating to digital services tax inserted by FA 2020 s 70, Sch 10 para 3 with effect from 22 July 2020.
[11] In the table, the third entry relating to VAT (return under a special scheme) repealed, and sub-paras (4A)–(4C) repealed, by the Taxation (Cross-border Trade) Act 2018 s 43, Sch 8 para 111 with effect from IP completion day (11pm on 31 December 2020), by virtue of SI 2020/1642 reg 4(b).

Sub-paras (4A)–(4C) previously read as follows—
"(4A) In this paragraph "return under a special scheme" means any of the following, so far as relating to supplies of services treated as made in the United Kingdom—
   (a) a special accounting return under paragraph 11 of Schedule 3B;
   (b) a value added tax return submitted under any provision of the law of a member State other than the United Kingdom which implements Article 364 of the VAT Directive (as substituted by Article 5(11) of the Amending Directive);
   (c) a value added tax return submitted under any provision of the law of a member State other than the United Kingdom which implements Article 369f of the VAT Directive (as inserted by Article 5(15) of the Amending Directive).
(4B) A value added tax return mentioned in paragraph (b) or (c) of subparagraph (4A) is regarded for the purposes of sub-paragraph (1) as given to HMRC when it is submitted to the authority to whom it is required to be submitted.
(4C) In sub-paragraph (4A)—
   "the VAT Directive" means Directive 2006/112/EC;
   "the Amending Directive" means Council Directive 2008/8/EC.".

FINANCE ACT 2008

(2008 Chapter 9)

CONTENTS

Schedules:
Schedule 36—Information and inspection powers
Schedule 41—Penalties: failure to notify and certain VAT and excise wrongdoing

SCHEDULES

SCHEDULE 36

INFORMATION AND INSPECTION POWERS

Section 113

Commentary—*Simon's Taxes* **A6.301A**.
HMRC Manuals—Compliance Handbook Manual, CH275000–285000 (HMRC inspection powers – compliance check).

CH20150–27200 (HMRC information and inspection powers).
Modifications—See F(No 2)A 2017 Sch 16 para 41 (application of this Schedule in relation to penalties for enablers of defeated tax avoidance).

PART 1
POWERS TO OBTAIN INFORMATION AND DOCUMENTS

Power to obtain information and documents from taxpayer

1—(1) An officer of Revenue and Customs may by notice in writing require a person ("the taxpayer")—
   (a) to provide information, or
   (b) to produce a document,
if the information or document is reasonably required by the officer for the purpose of checking the taxpayer's tax position.
(2) In this Schedule, "taxpayer notice" means a notice under this paragraph.
Commentary—*Simon's Taxes* **A6.301A**.
HMRC Manuals—Compliance Handbook Manual, CH23060 and 23080 (HMRC inspection powers: three types of information notice and approval thereof).
CH23520 (HMRC inspection powers: specific rules regarding taxpayer notice).
CH221000–223200 (HMRC inspection powers – how to do a compliance check: taxpayer notice).
CH223400 (tribunal approval).

Power to obtain information and documents from third party

2—(1) An officer of Revenue and Customs may by notice in writing require a person—
   (a) to provide information, or
   (b) to produce a document,
if the information or document is reasonably required by the officer for the purpose of checking the tax position of another person whose identity is known to the officer ("the taxpayer").
(2) A third party notice must name the taxpayer to whom it relates, unless the [tribunal][1] has approved the giving of the notice and disapplied this requirement under paragraph 3.
(3) In this Schedule, "third party notice" means a notice under this paragraph.

Commentary—*Simon's Taxes* **A6.301A**.
HMRC Manuals—Compliance Handbook Manual, CH23060 and 23080 (HMRC inspection powers: three types of information notice and approval thereof).
CH23620 (HMRC inspection powers: specific rules regarding third party notice).
CH225050 (HMRC inspection powers – how to do a compliance check: what is a third party notice).
CH225100 (persons on whom a third party notice can be served).
CH225150 (considerations prior to issue).
CH225200 (restrictions on third party notices).
Amendments—[1] In sub-para (2) word substituted for the words "First-tier Tribunal" by the Transfer of Tribunal Functions and Revenue and Customs Appeals Order, SI 2009/56 art 3, Sch 1 para 471 with effect from 1 April 2009.

Approval etc of taxpayer notices and third party notices

3—(1) An officer of Revenue and Customs may not give a third party notice without—
  (a) the agreement of the taxpayer, or
  (b) the approval of the [tribunal][1].
(2) An officer of Revenue and Customs may ask for the approval of the [tribunal][1] to the giving of any taxpayer notice or third party notice (and for the effect of obtaining such approval see paragraphs 29, 30 and 53 (appeals against notices and offence)).
[(2A) An application for approval under this paragraph may be made without notice (except as required under sub-paragraph (3)).][2]
(3) The [tribunal][1] may not approve the giving of a taxpayer notice or third party notice unless—
  (a) an application for approval is made by, or with the agreement of, an authorised officer of Revenue and Customs,
  (b) the [tribunal][1] is satisfied that, in the circumstances, the officer giving the notice is justified in doing so,
  (c) the person to whom the notice is [to be][2] addressed has been told that the information or documents referred to in the notice are required and given a reasonable opportunity to make representations to an officer of Revenue and Customs,
  (d) the [tribunal][1] has been given a summary of any representations made by that person, and
  (e) in the case of a third party notice, the taxpayer has been given a summary of the reasons why an officer of Revenue and Customs requires the information and documents.
(4) Paragraphs (c) to (e) of sub-paragraph (3) do not apply to the extent that the [tribunal][1] is satisfied that taking the action specified in those paragraphs might prejudice the assessment or collection of tax.
(5) Where the [tribunal][1] approves the giving of a third party notice under this paragraph, it may also disapply the requirement to name the taxpayer in the notice if it is satisfied that the officer has reasonable grounds for believing that naming the taxpayer might seriously prejudice the assessment or collection of tax.

Commentary—*Simon's Taxes* **A6.301A**.
HMRC Manuals—Compliance Handbook Manual, CH23060 and 23080 (HMRC inspection powers: three types of information notice and approval thereof).
CH23520 (HMRC inspection powers: specific rules regarding taxpayer notice).
CH23620 (HMRC inspection powers: specific rules regarding third party notice).
CH24100 (HMRC inspection powers: the Tribunal).
CH24120–24180 (taxpayer and third party notices).
CH25450 (Tribunal approval).
CH225310–225320 (where no approval is required).
CH225410 (where approval is required).
CH225420 (taxpayer agreement).
CH225430–225440 (summary of reasons and reasons not be given).
CH225460 (opportunity letter requirements).
Amendments—[1] Word substituted for the words "First-tier Tribunal" in each place; in sub-para (4) word substituted for the word "Tribunal" by the Transfer of Tribunal Functions and Revenue and Customs Appeals Order, SI 2009/56 art 3, Sch 1 para 471 with effect from 1 April 2009.
[2] Sub-para (2A), and words in sub-para (3)(c), inserted, by FA 2009 s 95, Sch 47 para 2 with effect from 21 July 2009.

Copying third party notice to taxpayer

4—(1) An officer of Revenue and Customs who gives a third party notice must give a copy of the notice to the taxpayer to whom it relates, unless the [tribunal][1] has disapplied this requirement.
(2) The [tribunal][1] may not disapply that requirement unless—
  (a) an application for approval is made by, or with the agreement of, an authorised officer of Revenue and Customs, and
  (b) the [tribunal][1] is satisfied that the officer has reasonable grounds for believing that giving a copy of the notice to the taxpayer might prejudice the assessment or collection of tax.

Commentary—*Simon's Taxes* **A6.301A**.
HMRC Manuals—Compliance Handbook Manual, CH23620 (HMRC inspection powers: specific rules regarding third party notice).

CH23640–23660 (HMRC inspection powers: copy of the notice to the named person).
CH225250 (HMRC inspection powers – how to do a compliance check: copying notice to taxpayer).
Amendments—[1]   Word substituted for the words "First-tier Tribunal" in each place; in sub-para (2)(b) word substituted for the word "Tribunal" by the Transfer of Tribunal Functions and Revenue and Customs Appeals Order, SI 2009/56 art 3, Sch 1 para 471 with effect from 1 April 2009.

Power to obtain information and documents about persons whose identity is not known

5—(1) An authorised officer of Revenue and Customs may by notice in writing require a person—
   (a) to provide information, or
   (b) to produce a document,
if the condition in sub-paragraph (2) is met.
(2) That condition is that the information or document is reasonably required by the officer for the purpose of checking the . . . [4] tax position of—
   (a) a person whose identity is not known to the officer, or
   (b) a class of persons whose individual identities are not known to the officer.
(3) An officer of Revenue and Customs may not give a notice under this paragraph without the approval of the [tribunal][1].
[(3A) An application for approval under this paragraph may be made without notice.][2]
(4) The [tribunal][1] may not [approve the giving of a notice under][2] this paragraph unless it is satisfied that—
   (a) the notice would meet the condition in sub-paragraph (2),
   (b) there are reasonable grounds for believing that the person or any of the class of persons to whom the notice relates may have failed or may fail to comply with any provision of [the law (including the law of a territory outside the United Kingdom) relating to tax,][4][3],
   (c) any such failure is likely to have led or to lead to serious prejudice to the assessment or collection of . . . [4] tax, and
   (d) the information or document to which the notice relates is not readily available from another source.
(5) . . . [4]
Commentary—*Simon's Taxes* A6.301A.
HMRC Manuals—Compliance Handbook Manual, CH23900 (HMRC inspection powers: identity unknown notice).
CH24200 (HMRC inspection powers: Tribunal approval of identity unknown notice).
CH227100–227200 (HMRC inspection powers – how to do a compliance check: identity unknown notice).
Amendments—[1]   In sub-paras (3), (4) word substituted for the words "First-tier Tribunal" by the Transfer of Tribunal Functions and Revenue and Customs Appeals Order, SI 2009/56 art 3, Sch 1 para 471 with effect from 1 April 2009.
[2] Sub-para (3A) inserted, in sub-para (4) words substituted for words "give its approval for the purpose of", by FA 2009 s 95, Sch 47 para 3 with effect from 21 July 2009.
[3] In sub-para (4)(b) words substituted for words ", VATA 1994 or any other enactment relating to value added tax charged in accordance with that Act", by FA 2009 s 96, Sch 48 para 2 with effect from 1 April 2010 (by virtue of SI 2009/3054 art 2.
[4] In sub-paras (2), (4)c), word repealed, in sub-para (4)(b) words substituted, and sub-para (5) repealed, by FA 2011 s 86(2), Sch 24 paras 1, 2 with effect from 1 April 2012 and from then on in relation to tax regardless of when the tax became due (whether before, on or after that date).

[Power to obtain information about persons whose identity can be ascertained

5A—(1) An authorised officer of Revenue and Customs may by notice in writing require a person to provide relevant information about another person ("the taxpayer") if conditions A to D are met.
(2) Condition A is that the information is reasonably required by the officer for the purpose of checking the tax position of the taxpayer.
(3) Condition B is that—
   (a) the taxpayer's identity is not known to the officer, but
   (b) the officer holds information from which the taxpayer's identity can be ascertained.
(4) Condition C is that the officer has reason to believe that—
   (a) the person will be able to ascertain the taxpayer's identity from the information held by the officer, and
   (b) the person obtained relevant information about the taxpayer in the course of carrying on a business.
(5) Condition D is that the taxpayer's identity cannot readily be ascertained by other means from the information held by the officer.
(6) "Relevant information" means all or any of the following—
   (a) name,
   (b) last known address, and
   (c) date of birth (in the case of an individual).
(7) This paragraph applies for the purpose of checking the tax position of a class of persons as for the purpose of checking the tax position of a single person (and references to "the taxpayer" are to be read accordingly).][1]

Amendments—[1] This para inserted by FA 2012 s 224(1), (2) with effect for the purpose of checking the tax position of a taxpayer as regards periods or tax liabilities whenever arising (whether before, on or after 17 July 2012).

Notices

6—(1) In this Schedule, "information notice" means a notice under paragraph 1, 2[, 5 or 5A][3].
(2) An information notice may specify or describe the information or documents to be provided or produced.
(3) If an information notice is given with the approval of the [tribunal][1], it must state that it is given with that approval.
[(4) A decision of the tribunal under paragraph 3, 4 or 5 is final (despite the provisions of sections 11 and 13 of the Tribunals, Courts and Enforcement Act 2007).][2]

Commentary—*Simon's Taxes* **A6.301A**.
HMRC Manuals—Compliance Handbook Manual, CH229300–229900 (HMRC inspection powers – how to do a compliance check: rules that apply to all notices).
Amendments—[1]   In sub-para (3) word substituted for the words "First-tier Tribunal" by the Transfer of Tribunal Functions and Revenue and Customs Appeals Order, SI 2009/56 art 3, Sch 1 para 471 with effect from 1 April 2009.
[2]   Sub-para (4) inserted by FA 2009 s 95, Sch 47 para 4 with effect from 21 July 2009.
[3]   In sub-para (1) words substituted by FA 2012 s 224(1), (3) with effect for the purpose of checking the tax position of a taxpayer as regards periods or tax liabilities whenever arising (whether before, on or after 17 July 2012).

Complying with notices

7—(1) Where a person is required by an information notice to provide information or produce a document, the person must do so—
    (*a*) within such period, and
    (*b*) at such time, by such means and in such form (if any),
as is reasonably specified or described in the notice.
(2) Where an information notice requires a person to produce a document, it must be produced for inspection—
    (*a*) at a place agreed to by that person and an officer of Revenue and Customs, or
    (*b*) at such place as an officer of Revenue and Customs may reasonably specify.
(3) An officer of Revenue and Customs must not specify a place that is used solely as a dwelling.
(4) The production of a document in compliance with an information notice is not to be regarded as breaking any lien claimed on the document.

Producing copies of documents

8—(1) Where an information notice requires a person to produce a document, the person may comply with the notice by producing a copy of the document, subject to any conditions or exceptions set out in regulations made by the Commissioners.
(2) Sub-paragraph (1) does not apply where—
    (*a*) the notice requires the person to produce the original document, or
    (*b*) an officer of Revenue and Customs subsequently makes a request in writing to the person for the original document.
(3) Where an officer of Revenue and Customs requests a document under sub-paragraph (2)(*b*), the person to whom the request is made must produce the document—
    (*a*) within such period, and
    (*b*) at such time and by such means (if any),
as is reasonably requested by the officer.

Restrictions and special cases

9 This Part of this Schedule has effect subject to Parts 4 and 6 of this Schedule.

PART 2
POWERS TO INSPECT [PREMISES AND OTHER PROPERTY][1]

Amendments—[1]   Words in heading substituted for words "Businesses etc" by the Finance Act 2009, Section 96 and Schedule 48 (Appointed Day, Savings and Consequential Amendments) Order, SI 2009/3054 art 3, Schedule para 15 with effect from 1 April 2010.

Power to inspect business premises etc

10—(1) An officer of Revenue and Customs may enter a person's business premises and inspect—
    (*a*) the premises,
    (*b*) business assets that are on the premises, and
    (*c*) business documents that are on the premises,

if the inspection is reasonably required for the purpose of checking that person's tax position.
(2) The powers under this paragraph do not include power to enter or inspect any part of the premises that is used solely as a dwelling.
(3) In this Schedule—
"business assets" means assets that an officer of Revenue and Customs has reason to believe are owned, leased or used in connection with the carrying on of a business by any person [(but see sub-paragraph (4))][1],
"business documents" means documents (or copies of documents)—
  (a) that relate to the carrying on of a business by any person, and
  (b) that form part of any person's statutory records, and
"business premises", in relation to a person, means premises (or any part of premises) that an officer of Revenue and Customs has reason to believe are (or is) used in connection with the carrying on of a business by or on behalf of the person.
[(4) For the purposes of this Schedule, "business assets" does not include documents, other than—
  (a) documents that are trading stock for the purposes of Chapter 11A of Part 2 of ITTOIA 2005 (see section 172A of that Act), and
  (b) documents that are plant for the purposes of Part 2 of CAA 2001.][1]
[(5) In sub-paragraph (1), the reference to a person's tax position does not include a reference to a person's position as regards soft drinks industry levy.][2]

Commentary—*Simon's Taxes* A6.301A.
HMRC Manuals—Compliance Handbook Manual, CH25120 (HMRC inspection powers: meaning of "enter").
CH25140–25160 (meaning of "inspect" with examples).
CH25180 (meaning of "business premises").
CH25220–25240 (inspecting business premises that are a home).
CH25260 and 25280 (meaning of "business assets" and "business documents").
CH25420 (HMRC inspection powers: start and end of an inspection).
CH25460 (when to carry out an inspection).
CH25480 (HMRC inspection powers: announced and unannounced inspection).
CH25540 (Tribunal approval).
CH25560 (wording of inspection notices).
Amendments—[1] In sub-para (3) in the definition of "business assets" words substituted for words ", excluding documents", and sub-para (4) inserted by FA 2009 s 95, Sch 47 para 5 with effect from 21 July 2009.
[2] Sub-para (5) inserted by FA 2017 s 56, Sch 11 para 1(1), (2) with effect from 6 April 2018 (by virtue of SI 2018/464). The charge to soft drinks industry levy arises on chargeable events which occur on or after 6 April 2018 (FA 2017 s 31(1)).

[Power to inspect business premises etc of involved third parties

10A—(1) An officer of Revenue and Customs may enter business premises of an involved third party (see paragraph 61A) and inspect—
  (a) the premises,
  (b) business assets that are on the premises, and
  (c) relevant documents that are on the premises,
if the inspection is reasonably required by the officer for the purpose of checking the position of any person or class of persons as regards a relevant tax.
(2) The powers under this paragraph may be exercised whether or not the identity of that person is, or the individual identities of those persons are, known to the officer.
(3) The powers under this paragraph do not include power to enter or inspect any part of the premises that is used solely as a dwelling.
(4) In relation to an involved third party, "relevant documents" and "relevant tax" are defined in paragraph 61A.]

Amendments—Para 10A inserted by FA 2009 s 96, Sch 48 para 3 with effect from 1 April 2010 (by virtue of SI 2009/3054 art 2).

Power to inspect premises used in connection with taxable supplies etc

11—(1) This paragraph applies where an officer of Revenue and Customs has reason to believe that—
  (a) premises are used in connection with the supply of goods under taxable supplies and goods to be so supplied [or documents relating to such goods][1] are on those premises,
  (b) . . .[2] or
  (c) premises are used as [or in connection with][1] a fiscal warehouse.
(2) An officer of Revenue and Customs may enter the premises and inspect—
  (a) the premises,
  (b) any goods that are on the premises, and
  (c) any documents on the premises that appear to the officer to relate to [the supply of goods under taxable supplies . . .[2] or fiscal warehousing][1].

(3) The powers under this paragraph do not include power to enter or inspect any part of the premises that is used solely as a dwelling.
(4) Terms used both in [this paragraph][1] and in VATA 1994 have the same meaning [here][1] as they have in that Act.

Commentary—*Simon's Taxes* A6.301A.
Northern Ireland—See Sch 9ZA para 78: this para has effect in relation to NI acquisition VAT as if new sub-para (1)(b) were inserted, and in sub-para (2)(c) after "taxable supplies" there were inserted ", the acquisition of goods from member States under taxable acquisitions". New sub-para (1)(b) reads as follows—
"(b) premises are used in connection with the acquisition of goods from member States under taxable acquisitions and goods to be so acquired or documents relating to such goods are on those premises,".
See also VATA 1994 Sch 9ZB para 26(4): this para has effect in relation to goods whose supply involves their removal to Northern Ireland from a place outside the United Kingdom as if in sub-para (1)(c), after "warehouse" there were inserted "or Northern Ireland fiscal warehouse", and in sub-para (2)(c), after "warehousing" there were inserted "or Northern Ireland fiscal warehousing".
HMRC Manuals—Compliance Handbook Manual, CH25420 (HMRC inspection powers: start and end of an inspection).
CH25460 (when to carry out an inspection).
CH25480 (HMRC inspection powers: announced and unannounced inspection).
CH25540 (Tribunal approval).
CH25560 (wording of inspection notices).
Amendments—[1] In sub-para (1)(a), (c) words inserted; in sub-para (2)(c) words substituted for words "such goods"; in sub-para (4) words substituted in the first place for words "sub-paragraph (1)" and in the second place for words "in that sub-paragraph", by FA 2009 s 95, Sch 47 para 6 with effect from 21 July 2009.
[2] Sub-para (1)(b), repealed, and in sub-para (2)(c), words "the acquisition of goods from other member States under taxable acquisitions" repealed, by the Taxation (Cross-border Trade) Act 2018 s 43, Sch 8 paras 112, 113(1), (2) with effect from IP completion day (11pm on 31 December 2020), by virtue of SI 2020/1642 reg 4(b).
Sub-para (1)(b) previously read as follows—
"(b) premises are used in connection with the acquisition of goods from other member States under taxable acquisitions and goods to be so acquired or documents relating to such goods are on those premises,".

Carrying out inspections [under paragraph 10, 10A or 11]

12—(1) An inspection under [paragraph 10, 10A or 11][3] may be carried out only—
   (a) at a time agreed to by the occupier of the premises, or
   (b) if sub-paragraph (2) is satisfied, at any reasonable time.
(2) This sub-paragraph is satisfied if—
   (a) the occupier of the premises has been given at least 7 days' notice of the time of the inspection (whether in writing or otherwise), or
   (b) the inspection is carried out by, or with the agreement of, an authorised officer of Revenue and Customs.
(3) An officer of Revenue and Customs seeking to carry out an inspection under sub-paragraph (2)(b) must provide a notice in writing as follows—
   (a) if the occupier of the premises is present at the time the inspection is to begin, the notice must be provided to the occupier,
   (b) if the occupier of the premises is not present but a person who appears to the officer to be in charge of the premises is present, the notice must be provided to that person, and
   (c) in any other case, the notice must be left in a prominent place on the premises.
(4) The notice referred to in sub-paragraph (3) must state the possible consequences of obstructing the officer in the exercise of the power.
(5) If a notice referred to in sub-paragraph (3) is given [in respect of an inspection approved by][2] the [tribunal][1] (see paragraph 13), it must state that [the inspection has been so approved][2].

Amendments—[1] In sub-para (5) word substituted for the words "First-tier Tribunal" by the Transfer of Tribunal Functions and Revenue and Customs Appeals Order, SI 2009/56 art 3, Sch 1 para 471 with effect from 1 April 2009.
[2] In sub-para (5) words substituted in the first place for the words "with the approval of" and in the second place for the words "it is given with that approval", by FA 2009 s 95, Sch 47 para 7 with effect from 21 July 2009.
[3] In heading words inserted, in sub-para (1) words substituted for words "this Part of this Schedule", by FA 2009 s 96, Sch 48 para 4 with effect from 1 April 2010 (by virtue of SI 2009/3054 art 2).

[Powers to inspect property for valuation etc

12A—(1) An officer of Revenue and Customs may enter and inspect premises for the purpose of valuing the premises if the valuation is reasonably required for the purpose of checking any person's position as regards income tax or corporation tax.
(2) An officer of Revenue and Customs may enter premises and inspect—
   (a) the premises, and
   (b) any other property on the premises,
for the purpose of valuing, measuring or determining the character of the premises or property.
(3) Sub-paragraph (2) only applies if the valuation, measurement or determination is reasonably required for the purpose of checking any person's position as regards—
   (a) capital gains tax,

(b) corporation tax in respect of chargeable gains,
(c) inheritance tax,
(d) stamp duty land tax, ... [2]
(e) stamp duty reserve tax[, or
(f) annual tax on enveloped dwellings.][2]
(4) A person who the officer considers is needed to assist with the valuation, measurement or determination may enter and inspect the premises or property with the officer.][1]

Amendments—[1] Paras 12A, 12B inserted by FA 2009 s 96, Sch 48 para 5 with effect from 1 April 2010 (by virtue of SI 2009/3054 art 2).
[2] In sub-para (3), word "or" in para (d) repealed, and para (f) and preceding word "or" inserted by FA 2013 s 164, Sch 34 paras 1, 2 with effect from 17 July 2013.

[Carrying out inspections under paragraph 12A

12B—(1) An inspection under paragraph 12A may be carried out only if condition A or B is satisfied.
(2) Condition A is that—
 (a) the inspection is carried out at a time agreed to by a relevant person, and
 (b) the relevant person has been given notice in writing of the agreed time of the inspection.
(3) "Relevant person" means—
 (a) the occupier of the premises, or
 (b) if the occupier cannot be identified or the premises are vacant, a person who controls the premises.
(4) Condition B is that—
 (a) the inspection has been approved by the tribunal, and
 (b) any relevant person specified by the tribunal has been given at least 7 days' notice in writing of the time of the inspection.
(5) A notice under sub-paragraph (4)(b) must state the possible consequences of obstructing the officer in the exercise of the power.
(6) If a notice is given under this paragraph in respect of an inspection approved by the tribunal (see paragraph 13), it must state that the inspection has been so approved.
(7) An officer of Revenue and Customs seeking to carry out an inspection under paragraph 12A must produce evidence of authority to carry out the inspection if asked to do so by—
 (a) the occupier of the premises, or
 (b) any other person who appears to the officer to be in charge of the premises or property.]

Amendments—Paras 12A, 12B inserted by FA 2009 s 96, Sch 48 para 5 with effect from 1 April 2010 (by virtue of SI 2009/3054 art 2).

Approval of [tribunal]

13—(1) An officer of Revenue and Customs may ask the [tribunal][1] to approve an inspection under this Part of this Schedule [(and for the effect of obtaining such approval see paragraph 39 (penalties))][3].
[(1A) An application for approval under this paragraph may be made without notice [(except as required under sub-paragraph (2A))][3].][2]
(2) The [tribunal][1] may not approve an inspection [under paragraph 10, 10A or 11][3] unless—
 (a) an application for approval is made by, or with the agreement of, an authorised officer of Revenue and Customs, and
 (b) the [tribunal][1] is satisfied that, in the circumstances, the inspection is justified.
[(2A) The tribunal may not approve an inspection under paragraph 12A unless—
 (a) an application for approval is made by, or with the agreement of, an authorised officer of Revenue and Customs,
 (b) the person whose tax position is the subject of the proposed inspection has been given a reasonable opportunity to make representations to the officer of Revenue and Customs about that inspection,
 (c) the occupier of the premises has been given a reasonable opportunity to make such representations,
 (d) the tribunal has been given a summary of any representations made, and
 (e) the tribunal is satisfied that, in the circumstances, the inspection is justified.
(2B) Paragraph (c) of sub-paragraph (2A) does not apply if the tribunal is satisfied that the occupier of the premises cannot be identified.][3]
[(3) A decision of the tribunal under this paragraph is final (despite the provisions of sections 11 and 13 of the Tribunals, Courts and Enforcement Act 2007).][2]

Amendments—[1] Word substituted for the words "First-tier Tribunal" in the heading and in each place; in sub-para (2)(*b*) word substituted for the word "Tribunal" by the Transfer of Tribunal Functions and Revenue and Customs Appeals Order, SI 2009/56 art 3, Sch 1 para 471 with effect from 1 April 2009.
[2] Sub-paras (1A), (3) inserted by FA 2009 s 95, Sch 47 para 8 with effect from 21 July 2009.
[3] In sub-paras (1), (1A), (2), words inserted, and whole of sub-paras (2A), (2B) inserted, by FA 2009 s 96, Sch 48 para 6 with effect from 1 April 2010 (by virtue of SI 2009/3054 art 2).

Restrictions and special cases

14 This Part of this Schedule has effect subject to Parts 4 and 6 of this Schedule.

PART 3
FURTHER POWERS

Power to copy documents

15 Where a document (or a copy of a document) is produced to, or inspected by, an officer of Revenue and Customs, such an officer may take copies of, or make extracts from, the document.

Power to remove documents

16—(1) Where a document is produced to, or inspected by, an officer of Revenue and Customs, such an officer may—
   (*a*) remove the document at a reasonable time, and
   (*b*) retain it for a reasonable period,
if it appears to the officer to be necessary to do so.
(2) Where a document is removed in accordance with sub-paragraph (1), the person who produced the document may request—
   (*a*) a receipt for the document, and
   (*b*) if the document is reasonably required for any purpose, a copy of the document,
and an officer of Revenue and Customs must comply with such a request without charge.
(3) The removal of a document under this paragraph is not to be regarded as breaking any lien claimed on the document.
(4) Where a document removed under this paragraph is lost or damaged, the Commissioners are liable to compensate the owner of the document for any expenses reasonably incurred in replacing or repairing the document.
(5) In this paragraph references to a document include a copy of a document.

Power to mark assets and to record information

17 The powers under Part 2 of this Schedule include—
   (*a*) power to mark business assets, and anything containing business assets, for the purpose of indicating that they have been inspected, and
   (*b*) power to obtain and record information (whether electronically or otherwise) relating to the premises, [property, goods,][1] assets and documents that have been inspected.

Amendments—[1] In para (*b*) words inserted by FA 2009 s 96, Sch 48 para 7 with effect from 1 April 2010 (by virtue of SI 2009/3054 art 2).

PART 4
RESTRICTIONS ON POWERS

Documents not in person's possession or power

18 An information notice only requires a person to produce a document if it is in the person's possession or power.

Commentary—*Simon's Taxes* **A6.301A.**
HMRC Manuals—Compliance Handbook Manual, CH22120 (HMRC inspection powers: meaning of possession and power).
Modification—See FA 2016 Sch 20 para 19 (application of this para in relation to penalties for enablers of offshore tax evasion or non-compliance).

Types of information

19—(1) An information notice does not require a person to provide or produce—
   (*a*) information that relates to the conduct of a pending appeal relating to tax or any part of a document containing such information, or
   [(*aa*) information that relates to the conduct of a pending appeal under the Savings (Government Contributions) Act 2017 or any part of a document containing such information,][1] or

(b) journalistic material (as defined in section 13 of the Police and Criminal Evidence Act 1984 (c 60)) or information contained in such material.
(2) An information notice does not require a person to provide or produce personal records (as defined in section 12 of the Police and Criminal Evidence Act 1984) or information contained in such records, subject to sub-paragraph (3).
(3) An information notice may require a person—
  (a) to produce documents, or copies of documents, that are personal records, omitting any information whose inclusion (whether alone or with other information) makes the original documents personal records ("personal information"), and
  (b) to provide any information contained in such records that is not personal information.
[(4) An information notice does not require a telecommunications operator or postal operator to provide or produce communications data.
(5) In sub-paragraph (4) "communications data", "postal operator" and "telecommunications operator" have the same meanings as in the Investigatory Powers Act 2016 (see sections 261 and 262 of that Act).][2]
Commentary—*Simon's Taxes* **A6.301A**.
HMRC Manuals—Compliance Handbook Manual, CH22160 (HMRC inspection powers: appeal material, with example). CH22180 and 22200 (personal records, with example).
Amendments—[1] Sub-para (1)(aa) inserted by the Savings (Government Contributions) Act 2017 s 5(3) with effect from 17 January 2017.
[2] Sub-paras (4), (5) inserted by the Investigatory Powers Act 2016 s 12(1), Sch 2 para 10 with effect from 22 July 2020 (by virtue of SI 2020/766 reg 2).

Old documents

20 An information notice may not require a person to produce a document if the whole of the document originates more than 6 years before the date of the notice, unless the notice is given by, or with the agreement of, an authorised officer.
Commentary—*Simon's Taxes* **A6.301A**.
HMRC Manuals—Compliance Handbook Manual, CH22140 (HMRC inspection powers: old documents).

Taxpayer notices [following tax return]

21—(1) Where a person has made a tax return in respect of a chargeable period under section 8, 8A or 12AA of TMA 1970 (returns for purpose of income tax and capital gains tax), a taxpayer notice may not be given for the purpose of checking that person's income tax position or capital gains tax position in relation to the chargeable period.
(2) Where a person has made a tax return in respect of a chargeable period under paragraph 3 of Schedule 18 to FA 1998 (company tax returns), a taxpayer notice may not be given for the purpose of checking that person's corporation tax position in relation to the chargeable period.
(3) Sub-paragraphs (1) and (2) do not apply where, or to the extent that, any of conditions A to D is met.
(4) Condition A is that a notice of enquiry has been given in respect of—
  (a) the return, or
  (b) a claim or election (or an amendment of a claim or election) made by the person in relation to the chargeable period in respect of the tax (or one of the taxes) to which the return relates ("relevant tax"),
and the enquiry has not been completed [so far as relating to the matters to which the taxpayer notice relates][3].
(5) In sub-paragraph (4), "notice of enquiry" means a notice under—
  (a) section 9A or 12AC of, or paragraph 5 of Schedule 1A to, TMA 1970, or
  (b) paragraph 24 of Schedule 18 to FA 1998.
(6) Condition B is that an officer of Revenue and Customs has reason to suspect that[, as regards the person,][1]
  (a) an amount that ought to have been assessed to relevant tax for the chargeable period may not have been assessed,
  (b) an assessment to relevant tax for the chargeable period may be or have become insufficient, or
  (c) relief from relevant tax given for the chargeable period may be or have become excessive.
(7) Condition C is that the notice is given for the purpose of obtaining any information or document that is also required for the purpose of checking [the][1] person's [position as regards any tax other than income tax, capital gains tax or corporation tax][2].
(8) Condition D is that the notice is given for the purpose of obtaining any information or document that is required (or also required) for the purpose of checking the person's position as regards any deductions or repayments [of tax or withholding of income][1] referred to in paragraph 64(2) [or (2A)][1] (PAYE etc).

[(9) In this paragraph, references to the person who made the return are only to that person in the capacity in which the return was made.]¹

Modification—See FA 2010 Sch 1 para 36 (modification of this para in relation to bank payroll tax).
Amendments—¹ In sub-paras (6), (8) in both places, words inserted; in sub-para (7) word substituted for the word "that"; and sub-para (9) inserted, by FA 2009 s 95, Sch 47 para 9 with effect from 21 July 2009.
² In the cross-heading words inserted, and in sub-para (7) words substituted for words "VAT position", by FA 2009 s 95, Sch 48 para 8 with effect from 1 April 2010 (by virtue of SI 2009/3054 art 2).
³ In sub-para (4), words inserted by F(No 2)A 2017 s 63, Sch 15 para 36 with effect in relation to an enquiry under TMA 1970 ss 9A, 12ZM or 12AC or FA 1998 Sch 18 where notice of the enquiry is given on or after 16 November 2017 or the enquiry is in progress immediately before that day.
Prospective amendments—In sub-para (1), words ", or regulations under paragraph 10 of Schedule A1 to," to be inserted after words "12AA of" by F(No 2)A 2017 s 61(1), Sch 14 para 38(1), (2) with effect from a day to be appointed.

[Application of paragraph 21 in case of returns under Schedule 2 to FA 2019]

21ZA (1) For the purposes of paragraph 21 any reference to the making by a person of a return under section 8 or 8A of TMA 1970 includes the making by the person of a return under Schedule 2 to FA 2019.
(2) In the application of paragraph 21 in relation to a return under Schedule 2 to FA 2019, the return is to be treated as if it required a self-assessment of an amount of capital gains tax.
(3) For the purposes of paragraph 21, the definition of "the notice of enquiry" in its application to a return under Schedule 2 to FA 2019 needs to be read in the light of the provision made by paragraph 20 of that Schedule.]¹

Amendments—¹ Para 21ZA substituted by FA 2019 s 14, Sch 2 para 28 with effect in relation to disposals made on or after 6 April 2019.

[Taxpayer notices following land transaction return]

21A—(1) Where a person has delivered a land transaction return under section 76 of FA 2003 (returns for purposes of stamp duty land tax) in respect of a transaction, a taxpayer notice may not be given for the purpose of checking that person's stamp duty land tax position in relation to that transaction.
(2) Sub-paragraph (1) does not apply where, or to the extent that, any of conditions A to C is met.
(3) Condition A is that a notice of enquiry has been given in respect of—
   (*a*) the return, or
   (*b*) a claim (or an amendment of a claim) made by the person in connection with the transaction, and the enquiry has not been completed.
(4) In sub-paragraph (3) "notice of enquiry" means a notice under paragraph 12 of Schedule 10, or paragraph 7 of Schedule 11A, to FA 2003.
(5) Condition B is that, as regards the person, an officer of Revenue and Customs has reason to suspect that—
   (*a*) an amount that ought to have been assessed to stamp duty land tax in respect of the transaction may not have been assessed,
   (*b*) an assessment to stamp duty land tax in respect of the transaction may be or have become insufficient, or
   (*c*) relief from stamp duty land tax in respect of the transaction may be or have become excessive.
(6) Condition C is that the notice is given for the purpose of obtaining any information or document that is also required for the purpose of checking that person's position as regards a tax other than stamp duty land tax.]

Amendments—Para 21A inserted by FA 2009 s 96, Sch 48 para 9 with effect from 1 April 2010 (by virtue of SI 2009/3054 art 2).

[Annual tax on enveloped dwellings: taxpayer notices following return]

21B—(1) Where a person has delivered, for a chargeable period with respect to a single-dwelling interest—
   (*a*) an annual tax on enveloped dwellings return, or
   (*b*) a return of the adjusted chargeable amount,
a taxpayer notice may not be given for the purpose of checking the person's annual tax on enveloped dwellings position as regards the matters dealt with in that return.
(2) Sub-paragraph (1) does not apply where, or to the extent that, any of conditions A to C is met.
(3) Condition A is that notice of enquiry has been given in respect of—
   (*a*) the return, or
   (*b*) a claim (or an amendment of a claim) made by the person in relation to the chargeable period, and the enquiry has not been completed.

(4) In sub-paragraph (3) "notice of enquiry" means a notice under paragraph 8 of Schedule 33 to FA 2013 or paragraph 7 of Schedule 11A to FA 2003 (as applied by paragraphs 28(2) and 31(3) of Schedule 33 to FA 2013).
(5) Condition B is that, as regards the person, an officer of Revenue and Customs has reason to suspect that—
- (a) an amount that ought to have been assessed to annual tax on enveloped dwellings for the chargeable period may not have been assessed,
- (b) an assessment to annual tax on enveloped dwellings for the chargeable period may be or have become insufficient, or
- (c) relief from annual tax on enveloped dwellings for the chargeable period may be or have become excessive.

(6) Condition C is that the notice is given for the purpose of obtaining any information or document that is also required for the purpose of checking that person's position as regards a tax other than annual tax on enveloped dwellings.
(7) In this Schedule references to a "single-dwelling interest" are to be read in accordance with section 108 of FA 2013.][1]

Amendments—[1] Para 21B inserted by FA 2013 s 164, Sch 34 paras 1, 3 with effect from 17 July 2013.

Deceased persons

22 An information notice given for the purpose of checking the tax position of a person who has died may not be given more than 4 years after the person's death.

Privileged communications between professional legal advisers and clients

23—(1) An information notice does not require a person—
- (a) to provide privileged information, or
- (b) to produce any part of a document that is privileged.

(2) For the purpose of this Schedule, information or a document is privileged if it is information or a document in respect of which a claim to legal professional privilege, or (in Scotland) to confidentiality of communications as between client and professional legal adviser, could be maintained in legal proceedings.
(3) The Commissioners may by regulations make provision for the resolution by the [tribunal][1] of disputes as to whether any information or document is privileged.
(4) The regulations may, in particular, make provision as to—
- (a) the custody of a document while its status is being decided, . . . [1]
- (b) . . . [1]

Commentary—*Simon's Taxes* **A6.301A**.
HMRC Manuals—Compliance Handbook Manual, CH22240 (HMRC restrictions on inspection powers: legal professional privilege).
Regulations—Information Notice: Resolution of Disputes as to Privileged Communications Regulations, SI 2009/1916.
Amendments—[1] In sub-para (3) word substituted for the words "First-tier Tribunal"; sub-para (4)(b) and the word "and" immediately preceding it repealed by the Transfer of Tribunal Functions and Revenue and Customs Appeals Order, SI 2009/56 art 3, Sch 1 para 471 with effect from 1 April 2009.

Auditors

24—(1) An information notice does not require a person who has been appointed as an auditor for the purpose of an enactment—
- (a) to provide information held in connection with the performance of the person's functions under that enactment, or
- (b) to produce documents which are that person's property and which were created by that person or on that person's behalf for or in connection with the performance of those functions.

(2) Sub-paragraph (1) has effect subject to paragraph 26.
Commentary—*Simon's Taxes* **A6.301A, A6.310**.
Modification—See FA 2016 Sch 20 para 20(a) (disapplication of this para in relation to penalties for enablers of offshore tax evasion or non-compliance).

Tax advisers

25—(1) An information notice does not require a tax adviser—
- (a) to provide information about relevant communications, or
- (b) to produce documents which are the tax adviser's property and consist of relevant communications.

(2) Sub-paragraph (1) has effect subject to paragraph 26.
(3) In this paragraph—
"relevant communications" means communications between the tax adviser and—

(a) a person in relation to whose tax affairs he has been appointed, or
(b) any other tax adviser of such a person,

the purpose of which is the giving or obtaining of advice about any of those tax affairs, and "tax adviser" means a person appointed to give advice about the tax affairs of another person (whether appointed directly by that person or by another tax adviser of that person).

Commentary—*Simon's Taxes* **A6.301A, A6.310**.
HMRC Manuals—Compliance Handbook Manual, CH22240 and 22320 (HMRC restrictions on inspection powers: tax advisers' papers).
Modification—See FA 2016 Sch 20 para 20(b) (disapplication of this para in relation to penalties for enablers of offshore tax evasion or non-compliance).

Auditors and tax advisers: supplementary

26—(1) Paragraphs 24(1) and 25(1) do not have effect in relation to—
(a) information explaining any information or document which the person to whom the notice is given has, as tax accountant, assisted any client in preparing for, or delivering to, HMRC, or
(b) a document which contains such information.
(2) In the case of a notice given under paragraph 5, paragraphs 24(1) and 25(1) do not have effect in relation to—
(a) any information giving the identity or address of a person to whom the notice relates or of a person who has acted on behalf of such a person, or
(b) a document which contains such information.
(3) Paragraphs 24(1) and 25(1) are not disapplied by sub-paragraph (1) or (2) if the information in question has already been provided, or a document containing the information in question has already been produced, to an officer of Revenue and Customs.

Commentary—*Simon's Taxes* **A6.301A, A6.310**.
HMRC Manuals—Compliance Handbook Manual, CH22340 (HMRC restrictions on inspection powers: exceptions for auditors' and tax advisers' papers).
Modification—See FA 2016 Sch 20 para 20(c) (disapplication of this para in relation to penalties for enablers of offshore tax evasion or non-compliance).

27—(1) This paragraph applies where paragraph 24(1) or 25(1) is disapplied in relation to a document by paragraph 26(1) or (2).
(2) An information notice that requires the document to be produced has effect as if it required any part or parts of the document containing the information mentioned in paragraph 26(1) or (2) to be produced.

Modification—See FA 2016 Sch 20 para 20(c) (disapplication of this para in relation to penalties for enablers of offshore tax evasion or non-compliance).

Corresponding restrictions on inspection of . . . documents

28 An officer of Revenue and Customs may not inspect a business document under Part 2 of this Schedule if or to the extent that, by virtue of this Part of this Schedule, an information notice given at the time of the inspection to the occupier of the premises could not require the occupier to produce the document.

Amendments—In the heading, word "business" repealed by FA 2009 s 96, Sch 48 para 10 with effect from 1 April 2010 (by virtue of SI 2009/3054 art 2).

PART 5
APPEALS AGAINST INFORMATION NOTICES

Right to appeal against taxpayer notice

29—(1) Where a taxpayer is given a taxpayer notice, the taxpayer may appeal . . . [1] against the notice or any requirement in the notice.
(2) Sub-paragraph (1) does not apply to a requirement in a taxpayer notice to provide any information, or produce any document, that forms part of the taxpayer's statutory records.
(3) Sub-paragraph (1) does not apply if the [tribunal][1] approved the giving of the notice in accordance with paragraph 3.

Commentary—*Simon's Taxes* **A6.301A**.
HMRC Manuals—Compliance Handbook Manual, CH23520 (HMRC inspection powers: specific rules regarding taxpayer notice).
CH24100 (HMRC inspection powers: appealing against a taxpayer notice).
Amendments—[1] In sub-para (1) words "to the First-tier Tribunal" repealed; in sub-para (3) word substituted for the words "First-tier Tribunal" by the Transfer of Tribunal Functions and Revenue and Customs Appeals Order, SI 2009/56 art 3, Sch 1 para 471 with effect from 1 April 2009.

Right to appeal against third party notice

30—(1) Where a person is given a third party notice, the person may appeal . . . [1] against the notice or any requirement in the notice on the ground that it would be unduly onerous to comply with the notice or requirement.
(2) Sub-paragraph (1) does not apply to a requirement in a third party notice to provide any information, or produce any document, that forms part of the taxpayer's statutory records.
(3) Sub-paragraph (1) does not apply if the [tribunal][1] approved the giving of the notice in accordance with paragraph 3.
Commentary—*Simon's Taxes* **A6.301A**.
HMRC Manuals—Compliance Handbook Manual, CH23620 (HMRC inspection powers: specific rules regarding third party notice).
CH24100 (HMRC inspection powers: appealing against a third party notice).
CH24420 (meaning of "unduly onerous").
Amendments—[1] In sub-para (1) words "to the First-tier Tribunal" repealed; in sub-para (3) word substituted for the words "First-tier Tribunal" by the Transfer of Tribunal Functions and Revenue and Customs Appeals Order, SI 2009/56 art 3, Sch 1 para 471 with effect from 1 April 2009.

Right to appeal against notice given under paragraph 5 [or 5A]

31 Where a person is given a notice under paragraph 5 [or 5A][2], the person may appeal . . . [1] against the notice or any requirement in the notice on the ground that it would be unduly onerous to comply with the notice or requirement.
Amendments—[1] In sub-para (1) words "to the First-tier Tribunal" repealed by the Transfer of Tribunal Functions and Revenue and Customs Appeals Order, SI 2009/56 art 3, Sch 1 para 471 with effect from 1 April 2009.
[2] Words inserted by FA 2012 s 224(1), (4), (5) with effect for the purpose of checking the tax position of a taxpayer as regards periods or tax liabilities whenever arising (whether before, on or after 17 July 2012).

Procedure

32—(1) Notice of an appeal under this Part of this Schedule must be given—
  (*a*) in writing,
  (*b*) before the end of the period of 30 days beginning with the date on which the information notice is given, and
  (*c*) to the officer of Revenue and Customs by whom the information notice was given.
(2) Notice of an appeal under this Part of this Schedule must state the grounds of appeal.
(3) On an appeal the [that is notified to the tribunal, the tribunal][1] may—
  (*a*) confirm the information notice or a requirement in the information notice,
  (*b*) vary the information notice or such a requirement, or
  (*c*) set aside the information notice or such a requirement.
(4) Where the [tribunal][1] confirms or varies the information notice or a requirement, the person to whom the information notice was given must comply with the notice or requirement—
  (*a*) within such period as is specified by the [tribunal][1], or
  (*b*) if the [tribunal][1] does not specify a period, within such period as is reasonably specified in writing by an officer of Revenue and Customs following the [tribunal's][1] decision.
[(5) Notwithstanding the provisions of sections 11 and 13 of the Tribunals, Courts and Enforcement Act 2007 a decision of the tribunal on an appeal under this Part of this Schedule is final.][1]
(6) Subject to this paragraph, the provisions of Part 5 of TMA 1970 relating to appeals have effect in relation to appeals under this Part of this Schedule as they have effect in relation to an appeal against an assessment to income tax.
Commentary—*Simon's Taxes* **A6.301A**.
HMRC Manuals—Compliance Handbook Manual, CH24340 (HMRC inspection powers: appeal procedures).
CH24440 (what the first-tier Tribunal can decide).
Amendments—[1] In sub-paras (3), (4) word substituted for the words "First-tier Tribunal"; in sub-para (4)(*a*), (*b*) word substituted for word "Tribunal" and "Tribunal's"; sub-para (5) substituted by the Transfer of Tribunal Functions and Revenue and Customs Appeals Order, SI 2009/56 art 3, Sch 1 para 471 with effect from 1 April 2009.

Special cases

33 This Part of this Schedule has effect subject to Part 6 of this Schedule.

PART 6
SPECIAL CASES

Supply of goods or services etc

34—(1) This paragraph applies to a taxpayer notice or third party notice that refers only to information or documents that form part of any person's statutory records and relate to—

(a) the supply of goods or services,
(b) ... [2] or
(c) the importation of goods ... [2] in the course of carrying on a business.

(2) Paragraph 3(1) (requirement for consent to, or approval of, third party notice) does not apply to such a notice.

(3) Where a person is given such a notice, the person may not appeal ... [1] against the notice or any requirement in the notice.

(4) Sections 5, 11 and 15 of, and Schedule 4 to, VATA 1994, and any orders made under those provisions, apply for the purposes of this paragraph as if it were part of that Act.

Northern Ireland—See Sch 9ZA para 78(2) (Northern Ireland: this para has effect in relation to NI acquisition VAT as if new sub-para (1)(b) were inserted, and in sub-para (4), after "Schedule 4" there were inserted "and paragraph 3 of Schedule 9ZA". Sub-para (1)(b) reads as follows—

"(b) the acquisition of goods from a member State,".

HMRC Manuals—Compliance Handbook Manual, CH23520 (HMRC inspection powers: specific rules regarding taxpayer notice).
CH23620 (HMRC inspection powers: specific rules regarding third party notice).

Amendments—[1] In sub-para (3) words "to the First-tier Tribunal" repealed by the Transfer of Tribunal Functions and Revenue and Customs Appeals Order, SI 2009/56 art 3, Sch 1 para 471 with effect from 1 April 2009.

[2] Sub-para (1)(b) repealed, in sub-para (1)(c), words "from a place outside the member States" repealed, and in sub-para (4) word ", 11" repealed, by the Taxation (Cross-border Trade) Act 2018 s 43, Sch 8 paras 112, 113(1), (3) with effect from IP completion day (11pm on 31 December 2020), by virtue of SI 2020/1642 reg 4(b).
Sub-para (1)(b) previously read as follows—
"(b) the acquisition of goods from another member State,".

[Registered pension schemes etc

34B—(1) This paragraph applies to a third party notice or a notice under paragraph 5 if it refers only to information or documents that relate to any pensions matter.

(2) "Pensions matter" means any matter relating to—
(a) a registered pension scheme,
(b) an annuity purchased with sums or assets held for the purposes of a registered pension scheme or a pre-2006 pension scheme, ... [2]
(c) an employer-financed retirement benefits scheme,
[(d) a QROPS or former QROPS, or
(e) an annuity purchased with sums or assets held for the purposes of a QROPS or former QROPS.][2]

(3) In relation to such a third party notice—
(a) paragraph 3(1) (approval etc of third party notices) does not apply,
(b) paragraph 4(1) (copying third party notices to taxpayer) does not apply, and
(c) paragraph 30(1) (appeal) has effect as if it permitted an appeal on any grounds.

(4) In relation to such a notice under paragraph 5—
(a) sub-paragraphs (3) and (4) of that paragraph (approval of tribunal) have effect as if they permitted, but did not require, an authorised officer of Revenue and Customs to obtain the approval of the tribunal, and
(b) paragraph 31 (appeal) has effect as if it permitted an appeal on any grounds.

[(4A) In relation to a notice to which this paragraph applies that refers only to information or documents relating to a matter within sub-paragraph (2)(d) or (e), paragraph 20 (old documents) has effect as if the reference to 6 years were to 10 years.][2]

(5) A person may not appeal against a requirement in the notice to provide any information, or produce any document, that forms part of any person's statutory records.

(6) Where the notice relates to a matter within sub-paragraph (2)(a) or (b), the officer of Revenue and Customs who gives the notice must give a copy of the notice to the scheme administrator in relation to the pension scheme.

(7) Where the notice relates to a matter within sub-paragraph (2)(c), the officer of Revenue and Customs who gives the notice must give a copy of the notice to the responsible person in relation to the employer-financed retirement benefits scheme.

[(7A) Where the notice relates to a matter within sub-paragraph (2)(d) or (e), the officer of Revenue and Customs who gives the notice must give a copy of the notice to the scheme manager in relation to the pension scheme.][2]

(8) Sub-paragraphs (6) [to (7A)][2] do not apply if the notice is given to a person who, in relation to the scheme or annuity to which the notice relates, is a prescribed description of person.][1]

Amendments—[1] Paras 34A–34C inserted by FA 2009 s 96, Sch 48 para 11 with effect from 1 April 2010 (by virtue of SI 2009/3054 art 2).

[2] In sub-para (2), word "or" at end of para (b) repealed, and paras (d), (e) inserted; sub-paras (4A), (7A) inserted; and in sub-para (8), words substituted for words "and (7)"; by FA 2013 s 54(1), (2) with effect from 17 July 2013.

(4) In relation to such a notice [given to a person other than one of the partners][1]
  (a) in paragraphs 3 and 4 (approval etc of notices and copying third party notices to taxpayer), the references to the taxpayer have effect as if they were references to at least one of the partners, and
  (b) in paragraph 30(2) (no appeal in relation to taxpayer's statutory records), the reference to the taxpayer has effect as if it were a reference to [any of the partners in the partnership][1] [, or
  (c) section 733 of CTA 2010 (company liable to counteraction of corporation tax advantage).][3]
[(5) In relation to a third party notice given to one of the partners for the purpose of checking the tax position of one or more of the other partners (in their capacity as such)—
  (a) in paragraph 3 (approval etc of notices), sub-paragraphs (1) and (3)(e) do not apply,
  (b) paragraph 4(1) (copying third party notices to taxpayer) does not apply,
  (c) paragraph 30(1) (appeal) has effect as if it permitted an appeal on any grounds, and
  (d) in paragraph 30(2) (no appeal in relation to taxpayer's statutory records), the reference to the taxpayer has effect as if it were a reference to any of the partners in the partnership.][1]
(6) Where a notice is given under paragraph 5 to one of the partners for the purpose of checking the tax position of one or more of the other partners whose identities are not known to the officer giving the notice[—
  (a) sub-paragraphs (3) and (4) of that paragraph (approval of tribunal) have effect as if they permitted, but did not require, the officer to obtain the approval of the tribunal, and
  (b) paragraph 31 (appeal) has effect as if it permitted an appeal on any grounds, but the partner to whom the notice is given may not appeal against a requirement in the notice to produce any document that forms part of that partner's statutory records.][1]
(7) Where a third party notice or a notice under paragraph 5 is given to one of the partners for the purpose of checking the tax position of one or more of the other partners, that partner may not appeal against a requirement in the notice to produce any document that forms part of that partner's statutory records.[1]

Amendments—[1]   The following amendments made by FA 2009 s 95, Sch 47 para 11 with effect from 21 July 2009—
  – sub-paras (2), (5) substituted;
  – in sub-para (3) words "to any person (other than one of the partners)" repealed, words substituted for the words "paragraph 2", and para (b) and the preceding word "and" inserted;
  – in sub-para (4) words inserted, and words substituted for the words "each of the partners";
  – in sub-para (6) words substituted for the words ", sub-paragraph (3) of that paragraph (approval of tribunal) does not apply";
  – sub-para (7) repealed.
[2] Sub-para (2A) inserted by FA 2009 s 96, Sch 48 para 13 with effect from 1 April 2010 (by virtue of SI 2009/3054 art 2).
[3] Sub-para (3)(a) repealed and (3)(c) inserted by CTA 2010 s 1177, Sch 1 paras 576, 582(1),(3), Sch 3 Pt 1. CTA 2010 has effect for corporation tax purposes for accounting periods ending on or after 1 April 2010, and for income and capital gains tax purposes for the tax year 2010–11 and subsequent tax years.
[4] Sub-para (2B) inserted by FA 2013 s 164, Sch 34 paras 1, 4 with effect from 17 July 2013.

Prospective amendments—In sub-para (2)(a), words ", or regulations under paragraph 10 of Schedule A1 to," to be inserted after words "section 12AA of" by F(No 2)A 2017 s 61(1), Sch 14 para 38(1), (3) with effect from a day to be appointed.

[Information in connection with herd basis election

37A—(1) This paragraph applies to a taxpayer notice given to a person carrying on a trade in relation to which a herd basis election is made if the notice refers only to information or documents that relate to—
  (a) the animals kept for the purposes of the trade, or
  (b) the products of those animals.
(2) Paragraph 21 (restrictions on giving taxpayer notice where taxpayer has made tax return) does not apply in relation to the notice.
(3) "Herd basis election" means an election under Chapter 8 of Part 2 of ITTOIA 2005 or Chapter 8 of Part 3 of CTA 2009.][1]

Amendments—[1]   Paras 37A, 37B inserted by FA 2009 s 95, Sch 47 para 12 with effect from 21 July 2009.

[Information from persons liable to counteraction of tax advantage

37B—(1) This paragraph applies to a taxpayer notice given to a person if—
  (a) it appears to an officer of Revenue and Customs that a counteraction provision may apply to the person by reason of one or more transactions, and
  (b) the notice refers only to information or documents relating to the transaction (or, if there are two or more transactions, any of them).
(2) Paragraph 21 (restrictions on giving taxpayer notice where taxpayer has made tax return) does not apply in relation to the notice.
(3) "Counteraction provision" means—
  (a) *section 703 of ICTA (company liable to counteraction of corporation tax advantage), or*[2]
  (b) *section 684 of ITA 2007 (person liable to counteraction of income tax advantage)*[1] [, or

(c) section 733 of CTA 2010 (company liable to counteraction of corporation tax advantage).][2]

Amendments—[1] Paras 37A, 37B inserted by FA 2009 s 94, Sch 47 para 12 with effect from 21 July 2009.
[2] Sub-s (3)(a) repealed and sub-para (3)(c) inserted by CTA 2010 ss 1177, 1181, Sch 1 paras 576, 582 (1) ,(3), Sch 3 Pt 1. CTA 2010 has effect for corporation tax purposes for accounting periods ending on or after 1 April 2010, and for income and capital gains tax purposes for the tax year 2010–11 and subsequent tax years.

Application to the Crown

38 This Schedule (other than Part 8) applies to the Crown, but not to Her Majesty in Her private capacity (within the meaning of the Crown Proceedings Act 1947 (c 44)).

PART 7
PENALTIES

. . . *Penalties [for failure to comply or obstruction]*

39—(1) This paragraph applies to a person who—
  (a) fails to comply with an information notice, or
  (b) deliberately obstructs an officer of Revenue and Customs in the course of an inspection under Part 2 of this Schedule that has been approved by the [tribunal][1].
(2) [The person][2] is liable to a penalty of £300.
(3) The reference in this paragraph to a person who fails to comply with an information notice includes a person who conceals, destroys or otherwise disposes of, or arranges for the concealment, destruction or disposal of, a document in breach of paragraph 42 or 43.

Commentary—*Simon's Taxes* **A6.301A**.
HMRC Manuals—Compliance Handbook Manual, CH25700 (HMRC inspection powers: information and deliberate obstruction of an inspection).
CH26220 (penalties: failure to comply with an information notice).
CH26240 (deliberate obstruction of a Tribunal approved inspection).
CH26260 (concealing, destroying or disposing of a document).
CH26640 (details of standard penalty).
CH26760 (HMRC inspection powers: two examples relating to penalties).
Amendments—[1] In sub-para (1)(b) word substituted for the words "First-tier Tribunal" by the Transfer of Tribunal Functions and Revenue and Customs Appeals Order, SI 2009/56 art 3, Sch 1 para 471 with effect from 1 April 2009.
[2] In heading, word "Standard" at the start repealed and words at the end inserted, and in sub-para (2) words substituted for the words "A person to whom this paragraph applies", by FA 2009 s 95, Sch 47 para 13 with effect from 21 July 2009.

Daily default penalties [for failure to comply or obstruction]

40—(1) This paragraph applies if the failure or obstruction mentioned in paragraph 39(1) continues after the date on which a penalty is imposed under that paragraph in respect of the failure or obstruction.
(2) The person is liable to a further penalty or penalties not exceeding £60 for each subsequent day on which the failure or obstruction continues.

Commentary—*Simon's Taxes* **A6.301A**.
HMRC Manuals—Compliance Handbook Manual, CH26660–26680 (HMRC inspection powers: details regarding daily penalties).
CH26760 (HMRC inspection powers: two examples relating to penalties).
Amendments—In heading words at the end inserted by FA 2009 s 95, Sch 47 para 14 with effect from 21 July 2009.

[Penalties for inaccurate information and documents

40A—(1) This paragraph applies if—
  (a) in complying with an information notice, a person provides inaccurate information or produces a document that contains an inaccuracy, and
  (b) condition [A, B or C][2] is met.
(2) Condition A is that the inaccuracy is careless or deliberate.
(3) An inaccuracy is careless if it is due to a failure by the person to take reasonable care.
[(3A) Condition B is that the person knows of the inaccuracy at the time the information is provided or the document produced but does not inform HMRC at that time.][2]
(4) Condition [C][2] is that the person—
  (a) discovers the inaccuracy some time later, and
  (b) fails to take reasonable steps to inform HMRC.
(5) The person is liable to a penalty not exceeding £3,000.
(6) Where the information or document contains more than one inaccuracy, a penalty is payable for each inaccuracy.][1]

Amendments—[1] Para 40A inserted by FA 2009 s 95, Sch 47 para 15 with effect from 21 July 2009.
[2] In sub-para (1)(b), words substituted, sub-para (3A) inserted, and in sub-para (4), letter substituted, by FA 2011 s 86(2), Sch 24 paras 1, 3 with effect in relation to any inaccuracy in information provided, or in documents produced, on or after 1 April 2012.

Power to change amount of . . . penalties

41—(1) If it appears to the Treasury that there has been a change in the value of money since the last relevant date, they may by regulations substitute for the sums for the time being specified in paragraphs 39(2)[, 40(2) and 40A(5)][1] such other sums as appear to them to be justified by the change.
(2) In sub-paragraph (1)[, in relation to a specified sum,][1] "relevant date" means—
   (*a*) the date on which this Act is passed, and
   (*b*) each date on which the power conferred by that sub-paragraph has been exercised [in relation to that sum][1].
(3) Regulations under this paragraph do not apply to[—
   (*a*)] [1]any failure or obstruction which began before the date on which they come into force[, or
   (*b*) an inaccuracy in any information or document provided to HMRC before that date.][1]

Amendments—[1] In cross-heading words "standard and daily default" repealed; in sub-para (1) words substituted for the words "and 40(2)"; in sub-para (2) words inserted in both places; in sub-para (3) words inserted, and para (*b*) and the preceding word "or" inserted; by FA 2009 s 95, Sch 47 para 16 with effect from 21 July 2009.

Concealing, destroying etc documents following information notice

42—(1) A person must not conceal, destroy or otherwise dispose of, or arrange for the concealment, destruction or disposal of, a document that is the subject of an information notice addressed to the person (subject to sub-paragraphs (2) and (3)).
(2) Sub-paragraph (1) does not apply if the person acts after the document has been produced to an officer of Revenue and Customs in accordance with the information notice, unless an officer of Revenue and Customs has notified the person in writing that the document must continue to be available for inspection (and has not withdrawn the notification).
(3) Sub-paragraph (1) does not apply, in a case to which paragraph 8(1) applies, if the person acts after the expiry of the period of 6 months beginning with the day on which a copy of the document was produced in accordance with that paragraph unless, before the expiry of that period, an officer of Revenue and Customs made a request for the original document under paragraph 8(2)(*b*).

Concealing, destroying etc documents following informal notification

43—(1) A person must not conceal, destroy or otherwise dispose of, or arrange for the concealment, destruction or disposal of, a document if an officer of Revenue and Customs has informed the person that the document is, or is likely, to be the subject of an information notice addressed to that person (subject to sub-paragraph (2)).
(2) Sub-paragraph (1) does not apply if the person acts after—
   (*a*) at least 6 months has expired since the person was, or was last, so informed, or
   (*b*) an information notice has been given to the person requiring the document to be produced.

Failure to comply with time limit

44 A failure by a person to do anything required to be done within a limited period of time does not give rise to liability to a penalty under paragraph 39 or 40 if the person did it within such further time, if any, as an officer of Revenue and Customs may have allowed.

Commentary—*Simon's Taxes* **A6.301A**.

Reasonable excuse

45—(1) Liability to a penalty under paragraph 39 or 40 does not arise if the person satisfies HMRC or [(on an appeal notified to the tribunal) the tribunal][1] that there is a reasonable excuse for the failure or the obstruction of an officer of Revenue and Customs.
(2) For the purposes of this paragraph—
   (*a*) an insufficiency of funds is not a reasonable excuse unless attributable to events outside the person's control,
   (*b*) where the person relies on any other person to do anything, that is not a reasonable excuse unless the first person took reasonable care to avoid the failure or obstruction, and
   (*c*) where the person had a reasonable excuse for the failure or obstruction but the excuse has ceased, the person is to be treated as having continued to have the excuse if the failure is remedied, or the obstruction stops, without unreasonable delay after the excuse ceased.

Commentary—*Simon's Taxes* **A6.301A**.
HMRC Manuals—Compliance Handbook Manual, CH26320–26440 (HMRC inspection powers: what is and is not a reasonable excuse, with example at CH26420).
Amendments—[1] In sub-para (1) words substituted for the words "(on appeal) the First-tier Tribunal" by the Transfer of Tribunal Functions and Revenue and Customs Appeals Order, SI 2009/56 art 3, Sch 1 para 471 with effect from 1 April 2009.

Assessment of . . . penalty

46—(1) Where a person becomes liable for a penalty under paragraph 39[, 40 or 40A][1], . . . [1]
   (*a*) [HMRC may][1] assess the penalty, and
   (*b*) [if they do so, they must][1] notify the person.
(2) An assessment of a penalty under paragraph 39 or 40 must be made [within the period of 12 months beginning with the date on which the person became liable to the penalty, subject to sub-paragraph (3)][1].
[(3) In a case involving an information notice against which a person may appeal, an assessment of a penalty under paragraph 39 or 40 must be made within the period of 12 months beginning with the latest of the following—
   (*a*) the date on which the person became liable to the penalty,
   (*b*) the end of the period in which notice of an appeal against the information notice could have been given, and
   (*c*) if notice of such an appeal is given, the date on which the appeal is determined or withdrawn.
(4) An assessment of a penalty under paragraph 40A must be made—
   (*a*) within the period of 12 months beginning with the date on which the inaccuracy first came to the attention of an officer of Revenue and Customs, and
   (*b*) within the period of 6 years beginning with the date on which the person became liable to the penalty.][1]

Modifications—Delivery of Tax Information through Software (Ancillary Metadata) Regulations, SI 2019/360 reg 4: this para applies to a penalty under SI 2019/360 reg 4(1) (penalty for non-compliance with relevant ancillary metadata obligation) as it applies to a penalty under para 39(1)(*a*) for failure to comply with an information notice, as if (a) in sub-para (2) the words "subject to sub-paragraph (3)", and (b) the whole of sub-para (3), were revoked.
Amendments—[1] In the cross-heading, words "standard penalty or daily default" repealed; in sub-para (1) words substituted for the words "or 40"; words "HMRC may" repealed and words at the beginning of paras (*a*), (*b*) inserted; in sub-para (2), words substituted for the words "within 12 months of the relevant date"; and sub-paras (3), (4) substituted for previous sub-para (3), by FA 2009 s 95, Sch 47 para 17 with effect from 21 July 2009.

Right to appeal against . . . penalty

47 A person may appeal . . . [1] against any of the following decisions of an officer of Revenue and Customs—
   (*a*) a decision that a penalty is payable by that person under paragraph 39[, 40 or 40A][2], or
   (*b*) a decision as to the amount of such a penalty.

Commentary—*Simon's Taxes* A6.301A.
HMRC Manuals—Compliance Handbook Manual, CH26900 (HMRC inspection powers (penalties): types of appeal and procedures).
Modifications—F(No 2)A 2017 Sch 16 para 42(3) (application of this para in relation to penalties for enablers of defeated tax avoidance).
Delivery of Tax Information through Software (Ancillary Metadata) Regulations, SI 2019/360 reg 4: this para applies to a penalty under SI 2019/360 reg 4(1) (penalty for non-compliance with relevant ancillary metadata obligation) as it applies to a penalty under para 39(1)(*a*) for failure to comply with an information notice, as if (a) the word "or" at the end of sub-para (*a*), and (b) the whole of sub-para (*b*), were revoked.
Amendments—[1] Words "to the First-tier Tribunal" repealed by the Transfer of Tribunal Functions and Revenue and Customs Appeals Order, SI 2009/56 art 3, Sch 1 para 471 with effect from 1 April 2009.
[2] In the cross-heading, words "standard penalty or daily default" repealed, in sub-para (*a*) words substituted for the words "or 40", by FA 2009 s 95, Sch 47 para 18 with effect from 21 July 2009.

Procedure on appeal against . . . penalty

48—(1) Notice of an appeal under paragraph 47 must be given—
   (*a*) in writing,
   (*b*) before the end of the period of 30 days beginning with the date on which the notification under paragraph 46 was issued, and
   (*c*) to HMRC.
(2) Notice of an appeal under paragraph 47 must state the grounds of appeal.
(3) On an appeal under paragraph 47(*a*), [that is notified to the tribunal, the tribunal][1] may confirm or cancel the decision.
(4) On an appeal under paragraph 47(*b*), [that is notified to the tribunal, the tribunal][1] may—
   (*a*) confirm the decision, or
   (*b*) substitute for the decision another decision that the officer of Revenue and Customs had power to make.
(5) Subject to this paragraph and paragraph 49, the provisions of Part 5 of TMA 1970 relating to appeals have effect in relation to appeals under this Part of this Schedule as they have effect in relation to an appeal against an assessment to income tax.

Modifications—Delivery of Tax Information through Software (Ancillary Metadata) Regulations, SI 2019/360 reg 4: this para applies to a penalty under SI 2019/360 reg 4(1) (penalty for non-compliance with relevant ancillary metadata obligation) as it applies to a penalty under para 39(1)(*a*) for failure to comply with an information notice, as if sub-para (4), were revoked.
Amendments—In the heading, words "standard penalty or daily default" repealed by FA 2009 s 95, Sch 47 para 19 with effect from 21 July 2009.
[1] In sub-paras (3), 4) words substituted for the words "First-tier Tribunal" by the Transfer of Tribunal Functions and Revenue and Customs Appeals Order, SI 2009/56 art 3, Sch 1 para 471 with effect from 1 April 2009.

Enforcement of . . . penalty

49—(1) A penalty under paragraph 39[, 40 or 40A][1] must be paid—
 (*a*) before the end of the period of 30 days beginning with the date on which the notification under paragraph 46 was issued, or
 (*b*) if a notice of an appeal against the penalty is given, before the end of the period of 30 days beginning with the date on which the appeal is determined or withdrawn.
(2) A penalty under paragraph 39[, 40 or 40A][1] may be enforced as if it were income tax charged in an assessment and due and payable.
Commentary—*Simon's Taxes* A6.301A.
HMRC Manuals—Compliance Handbook Manual, CH26880 (HMRC inspection powers: when is the penalty payable).
Amendments—[1] In the heading, words "standard penalty or daily default" repealed, in sub-paras (1), (2) words substituted for the words "or 40", by FA 2009 s 95, Sch 47 para 20 with effect from 21 July 2009.

[Increased daily default penalty

49A (1) This paragraph applies if—
 (*a*) a penalty under paragraph 40 is assessed under paragraph 46 in respect of a person's failure to comply with a notice under paragraph 5,
 (*b*) the failure continues for more than 30 days beginning with the date on which notification of that assessment was issued, and
 (*c*) the person has been told that an application may be made under this paragraph for an increased daily penalty to be imposed.
(2) If this paragraph applies, an officer of Revenue and Customs may make an application to the tribunal for an increased daily penalty to be imposed on the person.
(3) If the tribunal decides that an increased daily penalty should be imposed, then for each applicable day (see paragraph 49B) on which the failure continues—
 (*a*) the person is not liable to a penalty under paragraph 40 in respect of the failure, and
 (*b*) the person is liable instead to a penalty under this paragraph of an amount determined by the tribunal.
(4) The tribunal may not determine an amount exceeding £1,000 for each applicable day.
(5) But subject to that, in determining the amount the tribunal must have regard to—
 (*a*) the likely cost to the person of complying with the notice,
 (*b*) any benefits to the person of not complying with it, and
 (*c*) any benefits to anyone else resulting from the person's non-compliance.
(6) Paragraph 41 applies in relation to the sum specified in sub-paragraph (4) as it applies in relation to the sums mentioned in paragraph 41(1).][1]
Modification—See F(No 2)A 2017 Sch 16 para 42(4) (application of this para in relation to penalties for enablers of defeated tax avoidance).
Amendments—[1] Paras 49A–49C inserted by FA 2011 s 86(2), Sch 24 paras 1, 4 with effect in relation to failures to comply with a notice under FA 2008 Sch 36 para 5 that begin on or after 1 April 2012.

[49B (1) If a person becomes liable to a penalty under paragraph 49A, HMRC must notify the person.
(2) The notification must specify the day from which the increased penalty is to apply.
(3) That day and any subsequent day is an "applicable day" for the purposes of paragraph 49A(3).][1]
Modification—See F(No 2)A 2017 Sch 16 para 42(5) (application of this para in relation to penalties for enablers of defeated tax avoidance).
Amendments—[1] Paras 49A–49C inserted by FA 2011 s 86(2), Sch 24 paras 1, 4 with effect in relation to failures to comply with a notice under FA 2008 Sch 36 para 5 that begin on or after 1 April 2012.

[49C (1) A penalty under paragraph 49A must be paid before the end of the period of 30 days beginning with the date on which the notification under paragraph 49B is issued.
(2) A penalty under paragraph 49A may be enforced as if it were income tax charged in an assessment and due and payable.][1]
Modification—See F(No 2)A 2017 Sch 16 para 42(6) (disapplication of this para in relation to penalties for enablers of defeated tax avoidance).
Amendments—[1] Paras 49A–49C inserted by FA 2011 s 86(2), Sch 24 paras 1, 4 with effect in relation to failures to comply with a notice under FA 2008 Sch 36 para 5 that begin on or after 1 April 2012.

Tax-related penalty

50—(1) This paragraph applies where—
  (*a*) a person becomes liable to a penalty under paragraph 39,
  (*b*) the failure or obstruction continues after a penalty is imposed under that paragraph,
  (*c*) an officer of Revenue and Customs has reason to believe that, as a result of the failure or obstruction, the amount of tax that the person has paid, or is likely to pay, is significantly less than it would otherwise have been,
  (*d*) before the end of the period of 12 months beginning with the relevant date . . . [1], an officer of Revenue and Customs makes an application to the Upper Tribunal for an additional penalty to be imposed on the person, and
  (*e*) the Upper Tribunal decides that it is appropriate for an additional penalty to be imposed.
(2) The person is liable to a penalty of an amount decided by the Upper Tribunal.
(3) In deciding the amount of the penalty, the Upper Tribunal must have regard to the amount of tax which has not been, or is not likely to be, paid by the person.
(4) Where a person becomes liable to a penalty under this paragraph, HMRC must notify the person.
(5) Any penalty under this paragraph is in addition to the penalty or penalties under paragraph 39 or 40.
(6) In the application of the following provisions, no account shall be taken of a penalty under this paragraph—
  (*a*) section 97A of TMA 1970 (multiple penalties),
  (*b*) paragraph 12(2) of Schedule 24 to FA 2007 (interaction with other penalties), and
  (*c*) paragraph 15(1) of Schedule 41 (interaction with other penalties).
[(7) In sub-paragraph (1)(*d*) "the relevant date" means—
  (*a*) in a case involving an information notice against which a person may appeal, the latest of—
    (i) the date on which the person became liable to the penalty under paragraph 39,
    (ii) the end of the period in which notice of an appeal against the information notice could have been given, and
    (iii) if notice of such an appeal is given, the date on which the appeal is determined or withdrawn, and
  (*b*) in any other case, the date on which the person became liable to the penalty under paragraph 39.][1]

Commentary—*Simon's Taxes* **A6.301A**.
HMRC Manuals—Compliance Handbook Manual, CH26720 (HMRC inspection powers: details regarding tax related penalty). CH26760 (HMRC inspection powers: two examples relating to penalties).
Modification—See FA 2016 Sch 20 para 20(*d*) (disapplication of this para in relation to penalties for enablers of offshore tax evasion or non-compliance).
See F(No 2)A 2017 Sch 16 para 43 (disapplication of this para in relation to penalties for enablers of defeated tax avoidance).
Amendments—[1] In sub-para (1)(*d*) words "(within the meaning of paragraph 46)" repealed, and sub-para (7) inserted, by FA 2011 s 86(2), Sch 24 paras 1, 5(1)–(3) with effect where a person becomes liable to a penalty under FA 2008 Sch 36 para 39 on or after 19 July 2011.

Enforcement of tax-related penalty

51—(1) A penalty under paragraph 50 must be paid before the end of the period of 30 days beginning with the date on which the notification of the penalty is issued.
(2) A penalty under paragraph 50 may be enforced as if it were income tax charged in an assessment and due and payable.

Commentary—*Simon's Taxes* **A6.301A**.
Modification—See FA 2016 Sch 20 para 20(*d*) (disapplication of this para in relation to penalties for enablers of offshore tax evasion or non-compliance).
See F(No 2)A 2017 Sch 16 para 43 (disapplication of this para in relation to penalties for enablers of defeated tax avoidance).

Double jeopardy

52 A person is not liable to a penalty under this Schedule in respect of anything in respect of which the person has been convicted of an offence.

Commentary—*Simon's Taxes* **A6.301A**.

PART 8
OFFENCE

Concealing etc documents following information notice

53—(1) A person is guilty of an offence (subject to sub-paragraphs (2) and (3)) if—
  (*a*) the person is required to produce a document by an information notice,
  (*b*) the [tribunal][1] approved the giving of the notice in accordance with paragraph 3 or 5, and

(c) the person conceals, destroys or otherwise disposes of, or arranges for the concealment, destruction or disposal of, that document.
(2) Sub-paragraph (1) does not apply if the person acts after the document has been produced to an officer of Revenue and Customs in accordance with the information notice, unless an officer of Revenue and Customs has notified the person in writing that the document must continue to be available for inspection (and has not withdrawn the notification).
(3) Sub-paragraph (1) does not apply, in a case to which paragraph 8(1) applies, if the person acts after the expiry of the period of 6 months beginning with the day on which a copy of the document was so produced unless, before the expiry of that period, an officer of Revenue and Customs made a request for the original document under paragraph 8(2)(*b*).

Amendments—[1] In sub-para (1)(*b*) word substituted for the words "First-tier Tribunal" by the Transfer of Tribunal Functions and Revenue and Customs Appeals Order, SI 2009/56 art 3, Sch 1 para 471 with effect from 1 April 2009.

Concealing etc documents following informal notification

54—(1) A person is also guilty of an offence (subject to sub-paragraph (2)) if the person conceals, destroys or otherwise disposes of, or arranges for the concealment, destruction or disposal of a document after the person has been informed by an officer of Revenue and Customs in writing that—
(*a*) the document is, or is likely, to be the subject of an information notice addressed to that person, and
(*b*) an officer of Revenue and Customs intends to seek the approval of the [tribunal][1] to the giving of the notice under paragraph 3 or 5 in respect of the document.
(2) A person is not guilty of an offence under this paragraph if the person acts after—
(*a*) at least 6 months has expired since the person was, or was last, so informed, or
(*b*) an information notice has been given to the person requiring the document to be produced.

Amendments—[1] In sub-para (1)(*b*) word substituted for the words "First-tier Tribunal" by the Transfer of Tribunal Functions and Revenue and Customs Appeals Order, SI 2009/56 art 3, Sch 1 para 471 with effect from 1 April 2009.

Fine or imprisonment

55 A person who is guilty of an offence under this Part of this Schedule is liable—
(*a*) on summary conviction, to a fine not exceeding the statutory maximum, and
(*b*) on conviction on indictment, to imprisonment for a term not exceeding 2 years or to a fine, or both.

PART 9
MISCELLANEOUS PROVISIONS AND INTERPRETATION

Application of provisions of TMA 1970

56 Subject to the provisions of this Schedule, the following provisions of TMA 1970 apply for the purposes of this Schedule as they apply for the purposes of the Taxes Acts—
(*a*) section 108 (responsibility of company officers),
(*b*) section 114 (want of form), and
(*c*) section 115 (delivery and service of documents).

Regulations under this Schedule

57—(1) Regulations made by the Commissioners or the Treasury under this Schedule are to be made by statutory instrument.
(2) A statutory instrument containing regulations under this Schedule is subject to annulment in pursuance of a resolution of the House of Commons.

General interpretation

58 In this Schedule—
"checking" includes carrying out an investigation or enquiry of any kind,
"the Commissioners" means the Commissioners for Her Majesty's Revenue and Customs,
"document" includes a part of a document (except where the context otherwise requires),
"enactment" includes subordinate legislation (within the meaning of the Interpretation Act 1978 (c 30)),
"HMRC" means Her Majesty's Revenue and Customs,
"premises" includes—
(*a*) any building or structure,
(*b*) any land, and
(*c*) any means of transport,

"the Taxes Acts" means—
  (a) TMA 1970,
  (b) the Tax Acts, and
  (c) TCGA 1992 and all other enactments relating to capital gains tax, . . . [1]
"taxpayer", in relation to a taxpayer notice or a third party notice, has the meaning given in paragraph 1(1) or 2(1) (as appropriate) [and][1]
["tribunal" means the First-tier Tribunal or, where determined by or under Tribunal Procedure Rules, the Upper Tribunal.][1]

Amendments—[1] In sub-para (c) in the definition of "the Taxes Acts" word "and" at the end repealed; definition of "tribunal" and the preceding word "and" inserted by the Transfer of Tribunal Functions and Revenue and Customs Appeals Order, SI 2009/56 art 3, Sch 1 para 471 with effect from 1 April 2009.

Authorised officer of Revenue and Customs

59 A reference in a provision of this Schedule to an authorised officer of Revenue and Customs is a reference to an officer of Revenue and Customs who is, or is a member of a class of officers who are, authorised by the Commissioners for the purpose of that provision.

Business

60—(1) In this Schedule (subject to regulations under this paragraph), references to carrying on a business include—
  (a) the letting of property,
  (b) the activities of a charity, and
  (c) the activities of a government department, a local authority, a local authority association and any other public authority.
[(1A) A person who under section 41 of FA 1996 is liable to pay landfill tax charged on a taxable disposal is treated for the purposes of this Schedule (subject to regulations under this paragraph) as carrying on a business.][2]
(2) In sub-paragraph (1)—
  . . . [1]
  "local authority" has the meaning given in section 999 of ITA 2007, and
  "local authority association" has the meaning given in section 1000 of that Act.
(3) The Commissioners may by regulations provide that for the purposes of this Schedule—
  (a) the carrying on of an activity specified in the regulations, or
  (b) the carrying on of such an activity (or any activity) by a person specified in the regulations,
is or is not to be treated as the carrying on of a business.

Amendments—[1] In sub-s (2) definition of "charity" repealed by FA 2010 s 30, Sch 6 para 24 with effect from 1 April 2012 (SI 2012/736 art 19).
[2] Sub-para (1A) inserted by FA 2018 s 42(1), Sch 12 para 26(1), (2) with effect in relation to disposals made, or treated as made, on or after 1 April 2018, subject to transitional arrangements relating to disposals before April 2018 at places other than landfill sites (FA 2018 Sch 12 paras 31, 32). This amendment has effect in relation to disposals made in England or Northern Ireland only.

Chargeable period

61 In this Schedule "chargeable period" means—
  (a) in relation to income tax or capital gains tax, a tax year, and
  (b) in relation to corporation tax, an accounting period.

[Involved third parties

61A—(1) In this Schedule, "involved third party" means a person described in the first column of the Table below.
(2) In this Schedule, in relation to an involved third party, . . . [3] "relevant document" and "relevant tax" have the meaning given in the corresponding entries in that Table.

	Involved third party	Relevant . . . [3] documents	Relevant tax
1	A body approved by an officer of Revenue and Customs for the purpose of paying donations within the meaning of Part 12 of ITEPA 2003 (donations to charity: payroll giving) (see section 714 of that Act)	[Documents][3] relating to the donations	Income tax

	Involved third party	Relevant . . . ³ documents	Relevant tax
2	A plan manager (see section 696 of ITTOIA 2005 (managers of individual investment plans))	[Documents]³ relating to the plan, including investments which are or have been held under the plan	Income tax
3	An account provider in relation to a child trust fund (as defined in section 3 of the Child Trust Funds Act 2004)	[Documents]³ relating to the fund, including investments which are or have been held under the fund	Income tax
4	A person who is or has been registered as a managing agent at Lloyd's in relation to a syndicate of underwriting members of Lloyd's	[Documents]³ relating to, and to the activities of, the syndicate	Income tax Capital gains tax Corporation tax
5	A person involved (in any capacity) in an insurance business (as defined for the purposes of Part 3 of FA 1994)	[Documents]³ relating to contracts of insurance entered into in the course of the business	Insurance premium tax
6	A person who makes arrangements for persons to enter into contracts of insurance	[Documents]³ relating to the contracts	Insurance premium tax
7	A person who— (a) is concerned in a business that is not an insurance business (as defined for the purposes of Part 3 of FA 1994), and (b) has been involved in the entry into a contract of insurance providing cover for any matter associated with that business	[Documents]³ relating to the contracts	Insurance premium tax
8	A person who, in relation to a charge to stamp duty reserve tax on an agreement, transfer, issue, appropriation or surrender, is an accountable person (as defined in regulation 2 of the Stamp Duty Reserve Tax Regulations SI 1986/1711 (as amended from time to time))	[Documents]³ relating to the agreement, transfer, issue, appropriation or surrender	Stamp duty reserve tax
9	A responsible person in relation to an oil field (as defined for the purposes of Part 1 of OTA 1975)	[Documents]³ relating to the oil field	Petroleum revenue tax
10	A person involved (in any capacity) in subjecting aggregate to exploitation in the United Kingdom (as defined for the purposes of Part 2 of FA 2001) or in connected activities	[Documents]³ relating to matters in which the person is or has been involved	Aggregates levy
11	A person involved (in any capacity) in making or receiving [supplies of]² taxable commodities (as defined for the purposes of Schedule 6 to FA 2000) or in connected activities	[Documents]³ relating to matters in which the person is or has been involved	Climate change levy
12	A person involved (in any capacity) with any [disposal of material]⁴ (as defined for the purposes of Part 3 of FA 1996)	[Documents]³ relating to the disposal	Landfill tax]¹

Amendments— ¹ Para 61A inserted by FA 2009 s 96, Sch 48 para 14 with effect from 1 April 2010 (by virtue of SI 2009/3054 art 2).
² In Table, words in item 11 inserted by FA 2011 s 86(2), Sch 24 paras 1, 6 with effect from 19 July 2011.
³ In sub-para (2) words ""relevant information"," repealed, in each entry in second column of the Table word substituted for words "Information and documents", and in heading of that column words "information and relevant" repealed, by FA 2011 s 86(1), Sch 23 paras 60, 62(1), (3) with effect from 1 April 2012 in relation to relevant data with a bearing on any period (whether before, on or after 1 April 2012) subject to FA 2011 Sch 23 para 3(2). This para will continue to have effect in relation to notices given, or requests made, under any of the provisions repealed by FA 2011 Sch 23 Pt 6 before 1 April 2012 as if the amendments had not been made (FA 2011 Sch 23 para 65(2)).
⁴ In Table, words in item 12 substituted for words "landfill disposal" by FA 2018 s 42(1), Sch 12 para 26(1), (3) with effect in relation to disposals made, or treated as made, on or after 1 April 2018, subject to transitional arrangements relating to disposals before April 2018 at places other than landfill sites (FA 2018 Sch 12 paras 31, 32). This amendment has effect in relation to disposals made in England or Northern Ireland only.

Statutory records

62—(1) For the purposes of this Schedule, information or a document forms part of a person's statutory records if it is information or a document which the person is required to keep and preserve under or by virtue of—
  (a) the Taxes Acts, or
  [(b) any other enactment relating to a tax,][1]
subject to the following provisions of this paragraph.
(2) To the extent that any information or document that is required to be kept and preserved under or by virtue of the Taxes Acts—
  (a) does not relate to the carrying on of a business, and
  (b) is not also required to be kept or preserved under or by virtue of [any other enactment relating to a tax][1],
it only forms part of a person's statutory records to the extent that the chargeable period or periods to which it relates has or have ended.
(3) Information and documents cease to form part of a person's statutory records when the period for which they are required to be preserved by the enactments mentioned in sub-paragraph (1) has expired.

Amendments—[1] Sub-para (1)(b) substituted, and in sub-para (2) words substituted for words "VATA 1994 or any other enactment relating to value added tax", by FA 2009 s 95, Sch 48 para 15 with effect from 1 April 2010 (by virtue of SI 2009/3054 art 2).

Tax

63—(1) In this Schedule, except where the context otherwise requires, "tax" means all or any of the following—
  (a) income tax,
  (b) capital gains tax,
  (c) corporation tax,
  [(ca) diverted profits tax,][5]
  [(cb) apprenticeship levy,][6]
  [(cc) digital services tax,][8]
  (d) VAT, and
  [(e) insurance premium tax,
  (f) inheritance tax,
  (g) stamp duty land tax,
  (h) stamp duty reserve tax,
  [(ha) annual tax on enveloped dwellings,][3]
  (i) petroleum revenue tax,
  [(ia soft drinks industry levy,][7]
  (j) aggregates levy,
  (k) climate change levy,
  (l) landfill tax, and
  (m) relevant foreign tax,][2]
and references to "a tax" are to be interpreted accordingly.
(2) In this Schedule "corporation tax" includes any amount assessable or chargeable as if it were corporation tax.
(3) In this Schedule "VAT" means—
  (a) value added tax charged in accordance with VATA 1994, . . . [1]
  (b) . . . [9] [and
  (c) amounts listed in sub-paragraph (3A).][1]
[(3A) Those amounts are—
  (a) any amount that is recoverable under paragraph 5(2) of Schedule 11 to VATA 1994 (amounts shown on invoices as VAT), and
  (b) any amount that is treated as VAT by virtue of regulations under section 54 of VATA 1994 (farmers etc).][1]
(4) In this Schedule "relevant foreign tax" means—
  (a) a tax of a member State, other than the United Kingdom, which is covered by the provisions for the exchange of information under [Council Directive 2011/16/EU of 15 February 2011 on administrative cooperation in the field of taxation][4] (as amended from time to time), and
  (b) any tax or duty which is imposed under the law of a territory in relation to which arrangements having effect by virtue of section 173 of FA 2006 (international tax enforcement arrangements) have been made and which is covered by the arrangements.

Modification—See FA 2010 Sch 1 para 36 (modification of this para in relation to bank payroll tax).
Amendments—[1] In sub-para (3)(*a*) word "and" repealed, sub-para (3)(*c*) and the preceding word "and" substituted for the words "and includes any amount that is recoverable under paragraph 5(2) of Schedule 11 to VATA 1994 (amounts shown on invoices as VAT)", and sub-para (3A) inserted, by FA 2009 s 95, Sch 47 para 21 with effect from 21 July 2009.
[2] In sub-para (1), paras (*e*)–(*m*) substituted for previous para (*e*) and preceding word "and" by FA 2009 s 96(1) with effect from 1 April 2010 (by virtue of SI 2009/3054 art 2).
[3] Sub-para (1)(*ha*) inserted by FA 2013 s 164, Sch 34 paras 1, 5 with effect from 17 July 2013.
[4] In sub-para (4)(*a*), words substituted by the European Administrative Co-operation (Taxation) Regulations, SI 2012/3062 reg 6 with effect from 1 January 2013.
[5] Sub-para (1)(*ca*) inserted by FA 2015 s 105(2) with effect in relation to accounting periods beginning on or after 1 April 2015. For accounting periods that straddle that date, see FA 2015 s 116(2).
[6] Sub-para (1)(*cb*) inserted by FA 2016 s 112 with effect from 15 September 2016. The apprenticeship levy applies in relation to 2017–18 and subsequent tax years.
[7] Sub-para (1)(*ia*) inserted by FA 2017 s 56, Sch 11 para 1(1), (3) with effect from 6 April 2018 (by virtue of SI 2018/464). The charge to soft drinks industry levy arises on chargeable events which occur on or after 6 April 2018 (FA 2017 s 31(1)).
[8] Sub-para (1)(*cc*) inserted by FA 2020 s 70, Sch 10 paras 4, 5 with effect from 22 July 2020.
[9] Sub-para (3)(*b*) repealed by the Taxation (Cross-border Trade) Act 2018 s 43, Sch 8 paras 112, 113(1), (4) with effect from IP completion day (11pm on 31 December 2020), by virtue of SI 2020/1642 reg 4(*b*).
Sub-para (3)(*b*) previously read as follows—
   "(*b*)   value added tax charged in accordance with the law of another member State,".

Tax position

64—(1) In this Schedule, except as otherwise provided, "tax position", in relation to a person, means the person's position as regards any tax, including the person's position as regards—
   (*a*) past, present and future liability to pay any tax,
   (*b*) penalties and other amounts that have been paid, or are or may be payable, by or to the person in connection with any tax, and
   (*c*) claims, elections, applications and notices that have been or may be made or given in connection with [the person's liability to pay]¹ any tax,
and references to a person's position as regards a particular tax (however expressed) are to be interpreted accordingly.
(2) References in this Schedule to a person's tax position include, where appropriate, a reference to the person's position as regards any deductions or repayments of tax, or of sums representing tax, that the person is required to make—
   (*a*) under PAYE regulations,
   (*b*) under Chapter 3 of Part 3 of FA 2004 or regulations made under that Chapter (construction industry scheme), or
   (*c*) by or under any other provision of the Taxes Acts.
[(2A) References in this Schedule to a person's tax position also include, where appropriate, a reference to the person's position as regards the withholding by the person of another person's PAYE income (as defined in section 683 of ITEPA 2003).]¹
(3) References in this Schedule to the tax position of a person include the tax position of—
   (*a*) a company that has ceased to exist, and
   (*b*) an individual who has died.
(4) References in this Schedule to a person's tax position are to the person's tax position at any time or in relation to any period, unless otherwise stated.
Amendments—[1] In sub-para (1)(*c*) words inserted, and sub-para (2A) inserted, by FA 2009 s 95, Sch 47 para 22 with effect from 21 July 2009.

PART 10
CONSEQUENTIAL PROVISIONS

TMA 1970

65   TMA 1970 is amended as follows.

66   Omit section 19A (power to call for documents for purposes of enquiries).

67   Omit section 20 (power to call for documents of taxpayer and others).

68—(1) Section 20B (restrictions on powers to call for documents under ss 20 and 20A) is amended as follows.
(2) In the heading, for "**ss 20 and**" substitute "**section**".
(3) In subsection (1)—
   (*a*) omit "under section 20(1), (3) or (8A), or",
   (*b*) omit "(or, in the case of section 20(3), to deliver or make available)",
   (*c*) omit ", or to furnish the particulars in question", and
   (*d*) omit "section 20(7) or (8A) or, as the case may be,".

(4) Omit subsections (1A) and (1B).
(5) In subsection (2), omit from the beginning to "taxpayer; and".
(6) In subsection (3)—
   (a) omit "under section 20(1) or (3) or", and
   (b) omit "section 20(3) and (4) and".
(7) In subsection (4)—
   (a) omit "section 20(1) or", and
   (b) omit ", and as an alternative to delivering documents to comply with a notice under section 20(3) or (8A)".
(8) Omit subsections (5), (6) and (7).
(9) In subsection (8), omit "section 20(3) or (8A) or".
(10) Omit subsections (9) to (14).

69—(1) Section 20BB (falsification etc of documents) is amended as follows.
(2) In subsection (1)(a), omit "20 or".
(3) In subsection (2)(b), omit "or, in a case within section 20(3) or (8A) above, inspected".

70—(1) Section 20D (interpretation) is amended as follows.
(2) In subsection (2), for "sections 20 and" substitute "section".
(3) Omit subsection (3).

71 In section 29(6)(c) (assessment where loss of tax discovered), omit ", whether in pursuance of a notice under section 19A of this Act or otherwise".

72 Omit section 97AA (failure to produce documents under section 19A).

73 In section 98 (penalties), in the Table—
   (a) in the first column, omit the entry for section 767C of ICTA, and
   (b) in the second column, omit the entry for section 28(2) of F(No 2)A 1992.

75 (1) Section 107A (relevant trustees) is amended as follows.
(2) In subsection (2)(a), for ", 95 or 97AA" substitute 'or 95'.
(3) In subsection (3)(a), omit "or 97AA(1)(b)".

76 In section 118 (interpretation), in the definition of "tax", omit "20,".

77 In Schedule 1A (claims etc not included in returns), omit paragraphs 6 and 6A (power to call for documents for purposes of enquiries and power to appeal against notice to produce documents).

National Savings Bank Act 1971 (c 29)

78 In section 12(3) (secrecy), for the words from "and of section 20(3)" to the end substitute "and of Schedule 36 to the Finance Act 2008 (powers of officers of Revenue and Customs to obtain information and documents and inspect business premises)".

ICTA

79 ICTA is amended as follows.

81 Omit section 767C (change in company ownership: information).

FA 1990

83 In section 125 of FA 1990 (information for tax authorities in other member States)—
   (a) omit subsections (1) and (2),
   (b) in subsection (3), for "the Directive mentioned in subsection (1) above" substitute "the Directive of the Council of the European Communities dated 19 December 1977 No 77/799/EEC (the "1977 Directive")",[1]
   (c) in subsection (4), for "such as is mentioned in subsection (1) above" substitute "which is covered by the provisions for the exchange of information under the 1977 Directive", and[1]
   (d) in subsection (6), omit the words from the beginning to "passed,".[1]

Amendments—[1] Sub-paras (b)–(d) repealed by Finance Act 2009 Schedule 47 (Consequential Amendments) Order, SI 2009/2035, Art 2 Schedule, para 60(p) with effect from 13 August 2009.

Social Security Administration Act 1992 (c 5)

84 In section 110ZA of the Social Security Administration Act 1992 (Class 1, 1A, 1B or 2 contributions: powers to call for documents etc), for subsections (1) and (2) substitute—
   "(1) Schedule 36 to the Finance Act 2008 (information and inspection powers) applies for the purpose of checking a person's position as regards relevant contributions as it applies for the purpose of checking a person's tax position, subject to the modifications in subsection (2).

(2) That Schedule applies as if—
  (a) references to any provision of the Taxes Acts were to any provision of this Act or the Contributions and Benefits Act relating to relevant contributions,
  (b) references to prejudice to the assessment or collection of tax were to prejudice to the assessment of liability for, and payment of, relevant contributions,
  (c) the reference to information relating to the conduct of a pending appeal relating to tax were a reference to information relating to the conduct of a pending appeal relating to relevant contributions, and
  (d) paragraphs 21, 35(4)(b), 36 and 37(2) of that Schedule (restrictions on giving taxpayer notice where taxpayer has made tax return) were omitted."

Social Security Administration (Northern Ireland) Act 1992 (c 8)

85 In section 104ZA of the Social Security Administration (Northern Ireland) Act 1992 (Class 1, 1A, 1B or 2 contributions: powers to call for documents etc), for subsections (1) and (2) substitute—
"(1) Schedule 36 to the Finance Act 2008 (information and inspection powers) applies for the purpose of checking a person's position as regards relevant contributions as it applies for the purpose of checking a person's tax position, subject to the modifications in subsection (2).
(2) That Schedule applies as if—
  (a) references to any provision of the Taxes Acts were to any provision of this Act or the Contributions and Benefits Act relating to relevant contributions,
  (b) references to prejudice to the assessment or collection of tax were to prejudice to the assessment of liability for, and payment of, relevant contributions,
  (c) the reference to information relating to the conduct of a pending appeal relating to tax were a reference to information relating to the conduct of a pending appeal relating to relevant contributions, and
  (d) paragraphs 21, 35(4)(b), 36 and 37(2) of that Schedule (restrictions on giving taxpayer notice where taxpayer has made tax return) were omitted."

F(No 2)A 1992

86 Omit section 28(1) to (3) (powers of inspection).

VATA 1994

87 (*amends* VATA 1994 Sch 11)

FA 1998

88 In Schedule 18 to FA 1998 (company tax returns), omit paragraphs 27, 28 and 29 (notice to produce documents etc for purposes of enquiry into company tax return, power to appeal against such notices and penalty for failure to produce documents etc).

FA 1999

89 In section 13(5) (gold), omit paragraph (c).

Tax Credits Act 2002 (c 21)

90 In section 25 of the Tax Credits Act 2002 (payments of working tax credit by employers), omit subsections (3) and (4).

FA 2006

91 Omit section 174 of FA 2006 (international tax enforcement arrangements: information powers).

Other repeals

92 In consequence of the preceding provisions of this Part of this Schedule, omit the following—
  (a) section 126 of FA 1988,
  (b) sections 142(2), (3), (4), (6)(a), (7), (8) and (9) and 144(3), (5) and (7) of FA 1989,
  (c) sections 187 and 255 of, and paragraph 29 of Schedule 19 to, FA 1994,
  (d) paragraph 6 of Schedule 1 to the Civil Evidence Act 1995 (c 38),
  (e) paragraph 17 of Schedule 3, paragraph 3 of Schedule 19 and paragraph 2 of Schedule 22 to FA 1996,

(f) paragraph 17 of Schedule 3, paragraph 3 of Schedule 19 and paragraph 2 of Schedule 22 to FA 1996,
(g) section 115 of, and paragraphs 36 and 42(6) and (7) of Schedule 19 to, FA 1998,
(h) section 15(3) of FA 1999,
(i) paragraphs 21 and 38(4) of Schedule 29 to FA 2001,
(j) section 20 of FA 2006, and
(k) paragraph 350 of Schedule 1 to ITA 2007.

SCHEDULE 41

PENALTIES: FAILURE TO NOTIFY AND CERTAIN VAT AND EXCISE WRONGDOING

Section 123

Commentary—*Simon's Taxes* **Division A4.5**.

Failure to notify etc

1 A penalty is payable by a person (P) where P fails to comply with an obligation specified in the Table below (a "relevant obligation").

Tax to which obligation relates	Obligation
Income tax and capital gains tax	Obligation under section 7 of TMA 1970 (obligation to give notice of liability to income tax or capital gains tax).
Corporation tax	Obligation under paragraph 2 of Schedule 18 to FA 1998 (obligation to give notice of chargeability to corporation tax).
[Diverted profits tax	Obligation under section 92 of FA 2015 (duty to notify if within scope of diverted profits tax).][8]
[Digital services tax	Obligation under section 54 of FA 2020 (obligation to notify HMRC when threshold conditions for digital services tax are met).][11]
Value added tax	Obligations under paragraphs 5, 6, 7 and 14(2) and (3) of Schedule 1 to VATA 1994 (obligations to notify liability to register and notify material change in nature of supplies made by person exempted from registration).
[Value added tax	Obligations under paragraphs 5, 6 and 13(3) of Schedule 1A to VATA 1994 (obligations to notify liability to register and notify material change in nature of supplies made by person exempted from registration).][2]
. . .[12]	. . .[12]
. . .[12]	. . .[12]
Value added tax	Obligations under paragraphs 3, 4 and 7(2) and (3) of Schedule 3A to VATA 1994 (obligations to notify liability to register and notify relevant change in supplies made by person exempted from registration).
. . .[12]	. . .[12]
Insurance premium tax	Obligations under section 53(1) and (2) of FA 1994 (obligations to register in respect of receipt of premiums in course of taxable business and notify intended receipt of premiums in course of taxable business).
Insurance premium tax	Obligations under section 53AA(1) and (3) of FA 1994 (obligations to register as taxable intermediary and notify intention to charge taxable intermediary's fees).
[soft drinks industry levy	Obligation under section 44 of FA 2017 (obligation to give notice of liability to be registered).][10]
Aggregates levy	Obligations under section 24(2) of, and paragraph 1 of Schedule 4 to, FA 2001 (obligations to register in respect of carrying out of taxable activities and notify intention of carrying out such activities).
Climate change levy	Obligations under paragraphs 53 and 55 of Schedule 6 to FA 2000 (obligations to register in respect of taxable supplies and notify intention to make, or have made, taxable supply).
Landfill tax	Obligations under [section 47(2), (3) and (3A)][9] of FA 1996 (obligations to register in respect of carrying out of taxable activities and notify intention of carrying out such activities).
Air passenger duty	Obligation under section 33(4) [or 33A(4)][3] of FA 1994 (obligation to give notice of liability to register to operate chargeable aircraft).
[Alcohol liquor duties	Obligation to be authorised and registered to obtain and use duty stamps under regulations under paragraph 4 of Schedule 2A to ALDA 1979 (duty stamps).

Tax to which obligation relates	Obligation
Alcohol liquor duties	Obligations under sections 12(1), 47(1), 54(2), 55(2) and 62(2) of ALDA 1979 (obligations to hold licence to manufacture spirits, register to brew beer, hold licence to produce wine or made-wine and register to make cider).
Alcohol liquor duties	Obligation to have plant and processes approved for the manufacture of spirits under regulations under section 15(6) of ALDA 1979 (distillers' warehouses).
Tobacco products duty	Obligation to manufacture tobacco products only on premises registered under regulations under section 7 of TPDA 1979 (management of tobacco products duty).
Hydrocarbon oil duties	Obligation to make entry of premises intended to be used for production of oil under regulations under section 21 of HODA 1979 (administration and enforcement).
Excise duties	Obligation to receive, deposit or hold duty suspended excise goods only in premises approved under regulations under section 92 of CEMA 1979 (approval of warehouses).
Excise duties	Obligation to receive duty suspended excise goods only if approved or registered (or approved and registered) as a [Registered Consignee] under regulations under section 100G or 100H of CEMA 1979 (registered excise dealers and shippers etc).
Excise duties	Obligation to receive, deposit or hold duty suspended excise goods only if approved or registered (or approved and registered) as a registered owner, a duty representative, a registered mobile operator or a fiscal representative of a registered mobile operator or an authorised warehousekeeper under regulations under section 100G or 100H of CEMA 1979 (registered excise dealers and shippers etc).
[Excise duties	Obligation to dispatch excise goods under duty suspension arrangements upon their release for free circulation in accordance with [Part 1 of the Taxation (Cross-border Trade) Act 2018][13] only if approved and registered (or approved and registered) as a Registered Consignor under regulations under section 100G or 100H of CEMA 1979 (registered excise dealers and shippers etc).][1]
[General betting duty	Obligation to register under section 164(2) of FA 2014 (registration of persons liable etc for general betting duty).[3]
Pool betting duty	Obligation to register under section 164(2) of FA 2014 (registration of persons liable etc for pool betting duty).][7]
Bingo duty	Obligations under paragraph 10(1) and (1A) of Schedule 3 to BGDA 1981 (obligation to notify and register in respect of bingo-promotion).
Lottery duty	Obligation under section 29(1) of FA 1993 (obligation to register in respect of promotion of lotteries).
Gaming duty	Obligations under paragraphs 3 and 6 of Schedule 1 to FA 1997 (obligations to register in respect of gaming and to notify premises).
[Remote gaming duty	Obligation to register under section 164(2) of FA 2014 (registration of persons liable etc for remote gaming duty).][7]
[Machine games duty	Obligation under paragraph 20(3) of Schedule 24 to FA 2012 (obligation to register in respect of premises).][5]
. . .	. . .][6]

Northern Ireland—See Sch 9ZA para 78(3) (Northern Ireland: this para has effect in relation to NI acquisition VAT as if the following table entries were inserted—

"Value added tax	Obligations under paragraphs 40 and 44(2) of Schedule 9ZA to VATA 1994 (obligations to notify liability to register and notify acquisition affecting exemption from registration).
Value added tax	Obligation under paragraph 50 of Schedule 9ZA to VATA 1994 (obligation to notify liability to register).
Value added tax	Obligation under regulations under paragraph 73(4) of Schedule 9ZA to VATA 1994 (obligation to give notification of acquisition of goods from a member State).".

See Sch 9ZC para 14 (Northern Ireland: this para has effect in relation to the obligation to notify liability to register and notify matters affecting continuance of registration under Sch 9ZC as if the following table entry were inserted—

"Value added tax	Obligation under paragraph 8 of Schedule 9ZC to VATA 1994 (obligations to notify liability to register and notify matters affecting continuance of registration).".

Modifications—FA 2018 Sch 12 paras 32, 33(*a*) (application of Table in para (1) to obligations in connection with a disposal made before 1 April 2018 at a place other than a landfill site).

Amendments—[1] In second entry for excise duties, in second column words substituted for words "REDS or an Occasional Importer", and entry inserted, by the Excise Goods (Holding, Movement and Duty Point) Regulations, SI 2010/593 reg 90, Sch 2 para 22 with effect from 1 April 2010.

[2] Entry inserted by FA 2012 s 203, Sch 28 para 18 with effect in relation to supplies made or to be made on or after 1 December 2012.

[3] In entry for air passenger duty, words in column 2 inserted by FA 2012 s 190, Sch 23 para 15 with effect from 17 July 2012.

[5] Entry inserted by FA 2012 s 191, Sch 24 para 30 with effect in relation to the playing of machine games on or after 1 February 2013.

[5] Entry relating to amusement machine licence duty repealed by FA 2012 s 191, Sch 24 para 57 with effect in relation to the provision of amusement machines on or after 1 February 2013. That definition to continue to have effect (with necessary modifications) on and after that date in relation to the provision of amusement machines before that date (FA 2012 Sch 24 para 62).

[7] Entries for general betting duty, pool betting duty and remote gaming duty substituted by FA 2014 s 196, Sch 28 para 27 with effect from 1 December 2014 (FA 2014 s 198(2)), subject to the transitional provisions and savings in FA 2014 Sch 29.

[8] Entry for diverted profits tax inserted by FA 2015 s 104(4), (5) with effect in relation to accounting periods beginning on or after 1 April 2015. For accounting periods that straddle that date, see FA 2015 s 116(2).

[9] In entry for "landfill tax", words substituted for words "section 47(2) and (3)" by FA 2018 s 42(1), Sch 12 para 27(1), (2) with effect in relation to disposals made, or treated as made, on or after 1 April 2018, subject to transitional arrangements relating to disposals before April 2018 at places other than landfill sites (FA 2018 Sch 12 paras 31, 32). This amendment has effect in relation to disposals made in England or Northern Ireland only.

[10] Entry for soft drinks industry levy inserted by FA 2017 s 56, Sch 11 para 2(1), (2) with effect from 6 April 2018 (by virtue of SI 2018/464). The charge to soft drinks industry levy arises on chargeable events which occur on or after 6 April 2018 (FA 2017 s 31(1)).

[11] Entry for digital services tax inserted by FA 2020 s 70, Sch 10 paras 4, 6(1), (2) with effect from 22 July 2020.

[12] In the table, third, fourth and fifth entries relating to Value Added Tax repealed by the Taxation (Cross-border Trade) Act 2018 s 43, Sch 8 paras 112, 114(1), (2) with effect from IP completion day (11pm on 31 December 2020), by virtue of SI 2020/1642 reg 4(*b*).

Those entries previously read as follows—
"Obligation under paragraph 3 of Schedule 2 to VATA 1994 (obligation to notify liability to register).
Obligations under paragraphs 3 and 8(2) of Schedule 3 to VATA 1994 (obligations to notify liability to register and notify acquisition affecting exemption from registration).
Obligation under regulations under paragraph 2(4) of Schedule 11 to VATA 1994 (obligation to give notification of acquisition of goods from another member State).".

[13] In the table, in final entry relating to excise duties, words substituted for words "Article 79 of Council Regulation 2913/92/EEC" by the Taxation (Cross-border Trade) Act 2018 s 50, Sch 9 para 9 with effect from IP completion day (11pm on 31 December 2020), by virtue of SI 2020/1642 reg 4(*d*).

Note that Sch 41 para 1 continues to have effect for any purpose in connection with duty charged as a result of the Taxation (Post-transition Period) Act 2020 s 4(1), and in relation to goods in Northern Ireland, as if these amendments had not been made (see TCBTA 2018 Sch 9 para 10).

Note also that, where the direct EU legislation referred to in TCBTA 2018 Sch 7 para 1(1) (or any part of it) continues to have effect in relation to a release for free circulation in accordance with Title II of Part 3 of the Agreement on the Withdrawal of the UK from the European Union and the European Atomic Energy Community, this amendment is to be read as if for "Part 1 of the Taxation (Cross-border Trade) Act 2018" there were substituted "Article 201 of Regulation (EU) No 952/2013 of the European Parliament and of the Council of 9 October 2013 laying down the Union Customs Code" (see SI 2020/1642 reg 8).

Issue of invoice showing VAT by unauthorised person

2—(1) A penalty is payable by a person (P) where P makes an unauthorised issue of an invoice showing VAT.

(2) P makes an unauthorised issue of an invoice showing VAT if P—

(*a*) is an unauthorised person, and

(*b*) issues an invoice showing an amount as being value added tax or as including an amount attributable to value added tax.

(3) In sub-paragraph (2)(*a*) "an unauthorised person" means anyone other than—

(*a*) a person registered under VATA 1994,

(*b*) a body corporate treated for the purposes of section 43 of that Act as a member of a group,

(*c*) a person treated as a taxable person under regulations under section 46(4) of that Act,

(*d*) a person authorised to issue an invoice under regulations under paragraph 2(12) of Schedule 11 to that Act, or

(e) a person acting on behalf of the Crown.
(4) This paragraph has effect in relation to any invoice which—
  (a) for the purposes of any provision made under subsection (3) of section 54 of VATA 1994 shows an amount as included in the consideration for any supply, and
  (b) either fails to comply with the requirements of any regulations under that section or is issued by a person who is not for the time being authorised to do so for the purposes of that section,
as if the person issuing the invoice were an unauthorised person and that amount were shown on the invoice as an amount attributable to value added tax.

Putting product to use that attracts higher duty

3—(1) A penalty is payable by a person ("P") where P does an act which enables HMRC to assess an amount as duty due from P under any of the provisions in the Table below (a "relevant excise provision").

Provision under which assessment may be made	Subject-matter of provision
ALDA 1979 section 8(4)	Spirits for use for medical or scientific purposes.
ALDA 1979 section 10(4)	Spirits for use in art or manufacture.
ALDA 1979 section 11(3)	Imported goods not for human consumption containing spirits.
HODA 1979 section 10(3)	Duty-free oil.
HODA 1979 section 13(1A)	Rebated heavy oil.
HODA 1979 section 13AB(1)(a) or (2)(a)	Kerosene.
HODA 1979 section 13AD(2)	Kerosene.
HODA 1979 section 13ZB(1)	Heating oil etc
HODA 1979 section 14(4)	Light oil for use as furnace oil.
HODA 1979 section 14D(1)	Rebated biodiesel or bioblend.
HODA 1979 section 14F(2)	Rebated heavy oil or bioblend.
HODA 1979 section 23(1B)	Road fuel gas on which no duty paid.
HODA 1979 section 24(4A)	Duty-free and rebated oil.

(2) A penalty is payable by a person ("P") where P supplies a product knowing that it will be used in a way which enables HMRC to assess an amount as duty due from another person under a relevant excise provision.

Prospective amendments—Entry relating to section 14F(2) of HODA 1979 to be substituted by FA 2020 s 89, Sch 11, para 16 with effect from a date to be appointed. Substituted entry to read as follows—

| "HODA 1979 section 14F(8) | Rebated heavy oil, biodiesel or bioblend". |

[Involvement in landfill disposal by unregistered person

3A A penalty is payable by a person ("P") where P does an act which enables HMRC to assess an amount as landfill tax due from P under section 50A of FA 1996. This is subject to paragraph 6CA(2).][1]

Amendments—[1] Paragraph 3A inserted by FA 2018 s 42(1), Sch 12 para 27(1), (3) with effect in relation to disposals made, or treated as made, on or after 1 April 2018, subject to transitional arrangements relating to disposals before April 2018 at places other than landfill sites (FA 2018 Sch 12 paras 31, 32). This amendment has effect in relation to disposals made in England or Northern Ireland only.

Handling goods subject to unpaid excise duty [etc]

4—(1) A penalty is payable by a person (P) where—
  (a) after the excise duty point for any goods which are chargeable with a duty of excise, P acquires possession of the goods or is concerned in carrying, removing, depositing, keeping or otherwise dealing with the goods, and
  (b) at the time when P acquires possession of the goods or is so concerned, a payment of duty on the goods is outstanding and has not been deferred.
[(1A) A penalty is payable by a person (P) where—
  (a) after a charge to soft drinks industry levy has arisen in respect of chargeable soft drinks, P acquires possession of them or is concerned with carrying, removing, depositing, keeping or otherwise dealing with them, and

(b) at the time when P acquires possession of the chargeable soft drinks or is so concerned, a payment of soft drinks industry levy in respect of the chargeable soft drinks is due or payable and has not been paid.]¹

(2) In [this paragraph]¹—

"excise duty point" has the meaning given by section 1 of F(No 2)A 1992, and

"goods" has the meaning given by section 1(1) of CEMA 1979.

["chargeable soft drinks" has the same meaning as in Part 2 of FA 2017.]¹

Amendments—¹ Word inserted at end of heading, sub-para (1A) inserted, and in sub-para (2), words substituted for words "sub-paragraph (1)" and words inserted, by FA 2017 s 56, Sch 11 para 2(1), (3)–(5) with effect from 6 April 2018 (by virtue of SI 2018/464). The charge to soft drinks industry levy arises on chargeable events which occur on or after 6 April 2018 (FA 2017 s 31(1)).

Degrees of culpability

5—(1) A failure by P to comply with a relevant obligation is—
   (a) "deliberate and concealed" if the failure is deliberate and P makes arrangements to conceal the situation giving rise to the obligation, and
   (b) "deliberate but not concealed" if the failure is deliberate but P does not make arrangements to conceal the situation giving rise to the obligation.

(2) The making by P of an unauthorised issue of an invoice showing VAT is—
   (a) "deliberate and concealed" if it is done deliberately and P makes arrangements to conceal it, and
   (b) "deliberate but not concealed" if it is done deliberately but P does not make arrangements to conceal it.

(3) The doing by P of an act which enables HMRC to assess an amount of duty as due from P under a relevant excise provision[, or to assess an amount of landfill tax as due from P under section 50A of FA 1996,]¹ is—
   (a) "deliberate and concealed" if it is done deliberately and P makes arrangements to conceal it, and
   (b) "deliberate but not concealed" if it is done deliberately but P does not make arrangements to conceal it.

(4) P's acquiring possession of, or being concerned in dealing with, goods on which a payment of duty is outstanding and has not been deferred [or (as the case may be) chargeable soft drinks in respect of which a payment of soft drinks industry levy is due and payable and has not been paid]² is—
   (a) "deliberate and concealed" if it is done deliberately and P makes arrangements to conceal it, and
   (b) "deliberate but not concealed" if it is done deliberately but P does not make arrangements to conceal it.

Amendments—¹ In sub-para (3), words inserted by FA 2018 s 42(1), Sch 12 para 27(1), (4) with effect in relation to disposals made, or treated as made, on or after 1 April 2018, subject to transitional arrangements relating to disposals before April 2018 at places other than landfill sites (FA 2018 Sch 12 paras 31, 32). This amendment has effect in relation to disposals made in England or Northern Ireland only.
² In sub-para (4), words inserted by FA 2017 s 56, Sch 11 para 2(1), (6) with effect from 6 April 2018 (by virtue of SI 2018/464). The charge to soft drinks industry levy arises on chargeable events which occur on or after 6 April 2018 (FA 2017 s 31(1)).

Amount of penalty: standard amount

[**6**—(1) This paragraph sets out the penalty payable under paragraph 1.

(2) If the failure is in category 1, the penalty is—
   (a) for a deliberate and concealed failure, 100% of the potential lost revenue,
   (b) for a deliberate but not concealed failure, 70% of the potential lost revenue, and
   (c) for any other case, 30% of the potential lost revenue.

(3) If the failure is in category 2, the penalty is—
   (a) for a deliberate and concealed failure, 150% of the potential lost revenue,
   (b) for a deliberate but not concealed failure, 105% of the potential lost revenue, and
   (c) for any other case, 45% of the potential lost revenue.

(4) If the failure is in category 3, the penalty is—
   (a) for a deliberate and concealed failure, 200% of the potential lost revenue,
   (b) for a deliberate but not concealed failure, 140% of the potential lost revenue, and
   (c) for any other case, 60% of the potential lost revenue.

(5) Paragraph 6A explains the 3 categories of failure.]¹

Amendments—¹ Paras 6–6D substituted for previous para 6 by FA 2010 s 35 Sch 10 paras 7, 8 with effect from 6 April 2011 (by virtue of SI 2011/975 art 2(1)). Note that (by virtue of SI 2011/975 art 4) these changes do not have effect in relation to—

- any relevant obligation arising under TMA 1970 s 7, FA 1998 Sch 18 para 2, and VATA 1994 Sch 1 paras 5, 6, 14(2), (3), Sch 3 para 3, Sch 3A paras 4, 7(2), (3), in relation to a tax period commencing on or before 5 April 2011;
- all other relevant obligations arising on or before 5 April 2011;
- any unauthorised issue of an invoice taking place on or before 5 April 2011;
- any act which enables HMRC to assess an amount as duty under a relevant excise provision and which is done on or before 5 April 2011; and
- any act giving rise to a penalty under FA 2008 Sch 41 para 4 which is done on or before 5 April 2011.

Prospective amendments—Sub-para (1A) to be inserted, in sub-para (2), "125%" to be substituted for "100%", "87.5%" to be substituted for "70%" and "37.5%" to be substituted for "30%", and in sub-para (5), figure "4" to be substituted for figure "3", by FA 2015 s 120, Sch 20 paras 9, 10 with effect from a day to be appointed. Sub-para (1A) as inserted to read as follows—

"(1A) If the failure is in category 0, the penalty is—

for a deliberate and concealed failure, 100% of the potential lost revenue,

for a deliberate but not concealed failure, 70% of the potential lost revenue, and

for any other case, 30% of the potential lost revenue.".

[6A—(1) A failure is in category 1 if—
  (a) it involves a domestic matter, or
  (b) it involves an offshore matter and—
    (i) the territory in question is a category 1 territory, or
    (ii) the tax at stake is a tax other than income tax or capital gains tax.
(2) A failure is in category 2 if—
  (a) it involves an offshore matter [or an offshore transfer]²,
  (b) the territory in question is a category 2 territory, and
  (c) the tax at stake is income tax or capital gains tax.
(3) A failure is in category 3 if—
  (a) it involves an offshore matter [or an offshore transfer]²,
  (b) the territory in question is a category 3 territory, and
  (c) the tax at stake is income tax or capital gains tax.
(4) A failure "involves an offshore matter" if it results in a potential loss of revenue that is charged on or by reference to—
  (a) income arising from a source in a territory outside the UK,
  (b) assets situated or held in a territory outside the UK,
  (c) activities carried on wholly or mainly in a territory outside the UK, or
  (d) anything having effect as if it were income, assets or activities of a kind described above.
[(4A) A failure "involves an offshore transfer" if—
  (a) it does not involve an offshore matter,
  (b) it is deliberate (whether or not concealed) and results in a potential loss of revenue,
  (c) the tax at stake is income tax or capital gains tax, and
  (d) the applicable condition in paragraph 6AA is satisfied.]²
(5) A failure "involves a domestic matter" if it results in a potential loss of revenue [and does not involve either an offshore matter or an offshore transfer]².
(6) If a single failure is in more than one category (each referred to as a "relevant category")—
  (a) it is to be treated for the purposes of this Schedule as if it were separate failures, one in each relevant category according to the matters [or transfers]² that it involves, and
  (b) the potential lost revenue in respect of each separate failure is taken to be such share of the potential lost revenue in respect of the single failure (see paragraphs 7 and 11) as is just and reasonable.
(7) For the purposes of this Schedule—
  (a) paragraph 21A of Schedule 24 to FA 2007 (classification of territories) has effect, but
  (b) an order under that paragraph does not apply to relevant obligations that are to be complied with by a date before the date on which the order comes into force.
(8) . . .²
(9) In this paragraph [and paragraph 6AA²]—

"assets" has the meaning given in section 21(1) of TCGA 1992, but also includes sterling;

"UK" means the United Kingdom, including the territorial sea of the United Kingdom.]¹

Amendments—¹ Paras 6–6D substituted for previous para 6 by FA 2010 s 35 Sch 10 paras 7, 8 with effect from 6 April 2011 (by virtue of SI 2011/975 art 2(1)). Note that (by virtue of SI 2011/975 art 4) these changes do not have effect in relation to—
- any relevant obligation arising under TMA 1970 s 7, FA 1998 Sch 18 para 2, and VATA 1994 Sch 1 paras 5, 6, 14(2), (3), Sch 3 para 3, Sch 3A paras 4, 7(2), (3), in relation to a tax period commencing on or before 5 April 2011;
- all other relevant obligations arising on or before 5 April 2011;
- any unauthorised issue of an invoice taking place on or before 5 April 2011;
- any act which enables HMRC to assess an amount as duty under a relevant excise provision and which is done on or before 5 April 2011; and

- any act giving rise to a penalty under FA 2008 Sch 41 para 4 which is done on or before 5 April 2011.
[2] In sub-paras (2)(a), (3)(a), (6)(a), (9)(a), words inserted, sub-para (4A), inserted, in sub-para (5), words substituted, and sub-para (8) repealed by FA 2015 s 120, Sch 20 paras 9, 11(3)–(9) with effect from 6 April 2016 in relation to an obligation arising under TMA 1970 s 7 in respect of a tax year commencing on or after that date (by virtue of SI 2016/456 art 4).
Prospective amendments—Sub-paras (A1), (1) to be substituted for sub-para (1) by FA 2015 s 120, Sch 20 paras 9, 11(1), (2) with effect from a day to be appointed. Sub-paragraphs (A1), (1) as substituted to read as follows—

"(A1) A failure is in category 0 if—

it involves a domestic matter,

it involves an offshore matter or an offshore transfer, the territory in question is a category 0 territory and the tax at stake is income tax or capital gains tax, or

it involves an offshore matter and the tax at stake is a tax other than income tax or capital gains tax.

(1) A failure is in category 1 if—

it involves an offshore matter or an offshore transfer,

the territory in question is a category 1 territory, and

the tax at stake is income tax or capital gains tax.".

[**6AA** (1) This paragraph makes provision in relation to offshore transfers.
(2) Where the tax at stake is income tax, the applicable condition is satisfied if the income on or by reference to which the tax is charged, or any part of the income—
 (a) is received in a territory outside the UK, or
 (b) is transferred before the calculation date to a territory outside the UK.
(3) Where the tax at stake is capital gains tax, the applicable condition is satisfied if the proceeds of the disposal on or by reference to which the tax is charged, or any part of the proceeds—
 (a) are received in a territory outside the UK, or
 (b) are transferred before the calculation date to a territory outside the UK.
(4) In the case of a transfer falling within sub-paragraph (2)(b) or (3)(b), references to the income or proceeds transferred are to be read as including references to any assets derived from or representing the income or proceeds.
(5) In relation to an offshore transfer, the territory in question for the purposes of paragraph 6A is the highest category of territory by virtue of which the failure involves an offshore transfer.
(6) In this paragraph "calculation date" means the date by reference to which the potential lost revenue is to be calculated (see paragraph 7).][1]
Amendments—[1] Paragraphs 6AA, 6AB inserted by FA 2015 s 120, Sch 20 paras 9, 12 with effect from 6 April 2016 in relation to an obligation arising under TMA 1970 s 7 in respect of a tax year commencing on or after that date (by virtue of SI 2016/456 art 4).

[**6AB** Regulations under paragraph 21B of Schedule 24 to FA 2007 (location of assets etc) apply for the purposes of paragraphs 6A and 6AA of this Schedule as they apply for the purposes of paragraphs 4A and 4AA of that Schedule.][1]
Amendments—[1] Paragraphs 6AA, 6AB inserted by FA 2015 s 120, Sch 20 paras 9, 12 with effect from 6 April 2016 in relation to an obligation arising under TMA 1970 s 7 in respect of a tax year commencing on or after that date (by virtue of SI 2016/456 art 4).

[**6B** The penalty payable under any of paragraphs 2, 3(1) and 4 is—
 (a) for a deliberate and concealed act or failure, 100% of the potential lost revenue,
 (b) for a deliberate but not concealed act or failure, 70% of the potential lost revenue, and
 (c) for any other case, 30% of the potential lost revenue.][1]
Amendments—[1] Paras 6–6D substituted for previous para 6 by FA 2010 s 35 Sch 10 paras 7, 8 with effect from 6 April 2011 (by virtue of SI 2011/975 art 2(1)). Note that (by virtue of SI 2011/975 art 4) these changes do not have effect in relation to—
- any relevant obligation arising under TMA 1970 s 7, FA 1998 Sch 18 para 2, and VATA 1994 Sch 1 paras 5, 6, 14(2), (3), Sch 3 para 3, Sch 3A paras 4, 7(2), (3), in relation to a tax period commencing on or before 5 April 2011;
- all other relevant obligations arising on or before 5 April 2011;
- any unauthorised issue of an invoice taking place on or before 5 April 2011;
- any act which enables HMRC to assess an amount as duty under a relevant excise provision and which is done on or before 5 April 2011; and
- any act giving rise to a penalty under FA 2008 Sch 41 para 4 which is done on or before 5 April 2011.

[**6C** The penalty payable under paragraph 3(2) is 100% of the potential lost revenue.][1]
Amendments—[1] Paras 6–6D substituted for previous para 6 by FA 2010 s 35 Sch 10 paras 7, 8 with effect from 6 April 2011 (by virtue of SI 2011/975 art 2(1)). Note that (by virtue of SI 2011/975 art 4) these changes do not have effect in relation to—
- any relevant obligation arising under TMA 1970 s 7, FA 1998 Sch 18 para 2, and VATA 1994 Sch 1 paras 5, 6, 14(2), (3), Sch 3 para 3, Sch 3A paras 4, 7(2), (3), in relation to a tax period commencing on or before 5 April 2011;
- all other relevant obligations arising on or before 5 April 2011;
- any unauthorised issue of an invoice taking place on or before 5 April 2011;
- any act which enables HMRC to assess an amount as duty under a relevant excise provision and which is done on or before 5 April 2011; and

- any act giving rise to a penalty under FA 2008 Sch 41 para 4 which is done on or before 5 April 2011.

[6CA (1) The penalty payable under paragraph 3A is—
   (a) for a deliberate and concealed act or failure, 100% of the potential lost revenue, and
   (b) for a deliberate but not concealed act or failure, 70% of the potential lost revenue.
(2) No penalty is payable under paragraph 3A in any other case.][1]

Amendments—[1] Paragraph 6CA inserted by FA 2018 s 42(1), Sch 12 para 27(1), (5) with effect in relation to disposals made, or treated as made, on or after 1 April 2018, subject to transitional arrangements relating to disposals before April 2018 at places other than landfill sites (FA 2018 Sch 12 paras 31, 32). This amendment has effect in relation to disposals made in England or Northern Ireland only.

[6D Paragraphs 7 to 11 define "potential lost revenue".][1]

Amendments—[1] Paras 6–6D substituted for previous para 6 by FA 2010 s 35 Sch 10 paras 7, 8 with effect from 6 April 2011 (by virtue of SI 2011/975 art 2(1)). Note that (by virtue of SI 2011/975 art 4) these changes do not have effect in relation to—
- any relevant obligation arising under TMA 1970 s 7, FA 1998 Sch 18 para 2, and VATA 1994 Sch 1 paras 5, 6, 14(2), (3), Sch 3 para 3, Sch 3A paras 4, 7(2), (3), in relation to a tax period commencing on or before 5 April 2011;
- all other relevant obligations arising on or before 5 April 2011;
- any unauthorised issue of an invoice taking place on or before 5 April 2011;
- any act which enables HMRC to assess an amount as duty under a relevant excise provision and which is done on or before 5 April 2011; and
- any act giving rise to a penalty under FA 2008 Sch 41 para 4 which is done on or before 5 April 2011.

Potential lost revenue

7—(1) "The potential lost revenue" in respect of a failure to comply with a relevant obligation is as follows.
[(1A) In the case of an obligation under section 7 of TMA 1970 which arises by virtue of subsection (1B) of that section, the potential lost revenue is so much of any income tax or capital gains tax to which P is liable in respect of the tax year in question as is, by reason of the failure to comply with the obligation—
   (a) where the period specified in subsection (1C)(b)(ii) of that section applies and ends after the relevant date, unpaid at the end of that period, or
   (b) in any other case, unpaid on the relevant date.
(1B) For the purposes of sub-paragraph (1A) the relevant date is—
   (a) 31 January following the tax year, or
   (b) if, after that date, HMRC refund a payment on account in respect of the tax year to P, the day after the refund is issued.][2]
(2) In the case of a relevant obligation relating to income tax or capital gains tax and a tax year [(not falling within subparagraph (1A))][2], the potential lost revenue is so much of any income tax or capital gains tax to which P is liable in respect of the tax year as by reason of the failure is unpaid on 31 January following the tax year.
(3) In the case of a relevant obligation relating to corporation tax and an accounting period, the potential lost revenue is (subject to sub-paragraph (4)) so much of any corporation tax to which P is liable in respect of the accounting period as by reason of the failure is unpaid 12 months after the end of the accounting period.
(4) In computing the amount of that tax no account shall be taken of any relief under [section 458 of CTA 2010][1] (relief in respect of repayment etc of loan) which is deferred under [subsection (5)][1] of that section.
[(4A) In the case of a relevant obligation relating to diverted profits tax, the potential lost revenue is the amount of diverted profits tax for which P would be liable at the end of the period of 6 months beginning immediately after the accounting period assuming—
   (a) a charge to diverted profits tax had been imposed on P on the taxable diverted profits arising to P for the accounting period, and
   (b) that tax was required to be paid before the end of that period of 6 months.][3]
[(4B) In the case of a relevant obligation relating to digital services tax and an accounting period, the potential lost revenue is so much of any digital services tax payable by members of the group for the accounting period as by reason of the failure is unpaid 12 months after the end of the accounting period.][5]
(5) . . . [6]
(6) In the case of [a][6] relevant obligation relating to value added tax, the potential lost revenue is the amount of the value added tax (if any) for which P is, or but for any exemption from registration would be, liable for the relevant period (see sub-paragraph (7)) . . . [6].
(7) "The relevant period" is—
   (a) in relation to a failure to comply with paragraph 14(2) or (3) of Schedule 1 to VATA 1994 . . . [6] or paragraph 7(2) or (3) of Schedule 3A to that Act, the period beginning on the date of the change or alteration concerned and ending on the date on which HMRC received notification of, or otherwise became fully aware of, that change or alteration, and

(b) in relation to a failure to comply with an obligation under any other provision, the period beginning on the date with effect from which P is required in accordance with that provision to be registered and ending on the date on which HMRC received notification of, or otherwise became fully aware of, P's liability to be registered.

(8) . . . [6]

[(8A) In the case of a relevant obligation under section 47 of FA 1996 (which relates to landfill tax), the potential lost revenue is the amount of tax (if any) for which P is liable for the period—
  (a) beginning with the date with effect from which P is required in accordance with that section to be registered or (as the case may be) from which the Commissioners may register P under that section, and
  (b) ending with the day on which HMRC received notification of, or otherwise became fully aware of, P's liability to be registered or (as the case may be) the Commissioners' power to register P.][4]

(9) In the case of a relevant obligation under any provision relating to insurance premium tax, aggregates levy, climate change levy . . . [4] or air passenger duty, the potential lost revenue is the amount of the tax (if any) for which P is liable for the period—
  (a) beginning on the date with effect from which P is required in accordance with that provision to be registered, and
  (b) ending on the date on which HMRC received notification of, or otherwise became fully aware of, P's liability to be registered.

(10) In the case of a failure to comply with a relevant obligation relating to any other tax, the potential lost revenue is the amount of any tax which is unpaid by reason of the failure.

Northern Ireland—See Sch 9ZA para 78(4): Northern Ireland: in relation to NI acquisition VAT, for the purposes of para 7—
  – in a case of a failure to comply with an obligation under regulations under Sch 9ZA para 73(4), the "potential lost revenue" is the VAT on the acquisition to which the failure relates (instead of as provided for by sub-para (6) of this para); and
  – the "relevant period" in relation to a failure to comply with Sch 9ZA para 44(2) is the period beginning on the date of the change or alteration concerned and ending on the date on which HMRC received notification of, or otherwise became fully aware of, that change or alteration.

See Sch 9ZA para 78(5): Northern Ireland: in relation to NI acquisition VAT, in a case to which sub-para (6) of this para applies, the amount of the "potential lost revenue" as determined in accordance with sub-para (6) is—
  – if the amount of the tax mentioned in that sub-para includes tax on an acquisition of goods from a member State, to be reduced by the amount of any VAT which HMRC are satisfied has been paid on the supply in pursuance of which the goods were acquired under the law of that member State; and
  – if the amount of that tax includes tax chargeable as a result of Sch 9ZB para 29 on a supply, to be reduced by the amount of any VAT which HMRC are satisfied has been paid on that supply under the law of a member State.

Amendments—[1] In sub-para (4) words "subsection (4) of section 419 of ICTA" and "subsection (4A)" substituted by CTA 2010 s 1177, Sch 1 paras 576, 583. CTA 2010 has effect for corporation tax purposes for accounting periods ending on or after 1 April 2010, and for income and capital gains tax purposes for the tax year 2010–11 and subsequent tax years.

[2] Sub-paras (1A), (1B) inserted, and words in sub-s (2) inserted, by FA 2013 s 233, Sch 51 paras 1, 6 with effect in relation to a return—
  (a) under TMA 1970 s 12AA for a partnership which includes one or more companies, for a relevant period beginning on or after 6 April 2012; and
  (b) under TMA 1970 s 12AA for any other partnership, or a return under TMA 1970 s 8 or s 8A, for a year of assessment beginning on or after 6 April 2012.

A "relevant period" means a period in respect of which a return is required: FA 2013 Sch 51 para 9(2).

[3] Sub-para (4A) inserted by FA 2015 s 104(4), (6) with effect in relation to accounting periods beginning on or after 1 April 2015. For accounting periods that straddle that date, see FA 2015 s 116(2).

[4] Sub-para (8A) inserted, and in sub-para (9), words ", landfill tax" repealed, by FA 2018 s 42(1), Sch 12 para 27(1), (6) with effect in relation to disposals made, or treated as made, on or after 1 April 2018, subject to transitional arrangements relating to disposals before April 2018 at places other than landfill sites (FA 2018 Sch 12 paras 31, 32). This amendment has effect in relation to disposals made in England or Northern Ireland only.

[5] Sub-para (4B) inserted by FA 2020 s 70, Sch 10 paras 4, 6(1), (3) with effect from 22 July 2020.

[6] Sub-paras (5), (8) repealed, in sub-para (6) word substituted for words "any other" and words ", but subject to sub-paragraph (8)" repealed, and in sub-para (7)(a) words ", paragraph 8(2) of Schedule 3 to that Act" repealed, by the Taxation (Cross-border Trade) Act 2018 s 43, Sch 8 paras 112, 114(1), (3) with effect from IP completion day (11pm on 31 December 2020), by virtue of SI 2020/1642 reg 4(b).

Sub-paras (5), (8) previously read as follows—
  "(5) In any case where the failure is a failure to comply with the obligation under paragraph 2(4) of Schedule 11 to VATA 1994, the potential lost revenue is the value added tax on the acquisition to which the failure relates.".
  "(8) But the amount mentioned in sub-paragraph (6) is reduced—
    (a) if the amount of the tax mentioned in that sub-paragraph includes tax on an acquisition of goods from another member State, by the amount of any VAT which HMRC are satisfied has been paid on the supply in pursuance of which the goods were acquired under the law of that member State, and
    (b) if the amount of that tax includes tax chargeable by virtue of section 7(4) of VATA 1994 on a supply, by the amount of any VAT which HMRC are satisfied has been paid on that supply under the law of another member State.".

8 In the case of the making of an unauthorised issue of an invoice showing VAT, the potential lost revenue is the amount shown on the invoice as value added tax or the amount to be taken as representing value added tax.

9 In the case of—
  (*a*) the doing of an act which enables HMRC to assess an amount of duty as due under a relevant excise provision, or
  (*b*) supplying a product knowing that it will be used in a way which enables HMRC to assess an amount as duty due from another person under a relevant excise provision,
the potential lost revenue is the amount of the duty which may be assessed as due.

[9A In the case of the doing of an act which enables HMRC to assess an amount of landfill tax as due under section 50A of FA 1996, the potential lost revenue is the amount of the tax which may be assessed as due.][1]

Amendments—[1] Paragraph 9A inserted by FA 2018 s 42(1), Sch 12 para 27(1), (7) with effect in relation to disposals made, or treated as made, on or after 1 April 2018, subject to transitional arrangements relating to disposals before April 2018 at places other than landfill sites (FA 2018 Sch 12 paras 31, 32). This amendment has effect in relation to disposals made in England or Northern Ireland only.

10 In the case of acquiring possession of, or being concerned in dealing with, goods the payment of duty on which is outstanding and has not been deferred [or (as the case may be) chargeable soft drinks in respect of which a payment of soft drinks industry levy is due and payable and has not been paid][1], the potential lost revenue is an amount equal to the amount of duty due on the goods.

Amendments—[1] Words inserted by FA 2017 s 56, Sch 11 para 2(1), (7) with effect from 6 April 2018 (by virtue of SI 2018/464). The charge to soft drinks industry levy arises on chargeable events which occur on or after 6 April 2018 (FA 2017 s 31(1)).

11—(1) In calculating potential lost revenue in respect of a relevant act or failure on the part of P no account is to be taken of the fact that a potential loss of revenue from P is or may be balanced by a potential over-payment by another person (except to the extent that an enactment requires or permits a person's tax liability to be adjusted by reference to P's).
(2) In this Schedule "a relevant act or failure" means—
  (*a*) a failure to comply with a relevant obligation,
  (*b*) the making of an unauthorised issue of an invoice showing VAT,
  (*c*) the doing of an act which enables HMRC to assess an amount of duty as due under a relevant excise provision or supplying a product knowing that it will be used in a way which enables HMRC to assess an amount as duty due from another person under a relevant excise provision, or
  (*d*) acquiring possession of, or being concerned in dealing with, goods the payment of duty on which is outstanding and has not been deferred [or (as the case may be) chargeable soft drinks in respect of which a payment of soft drinks industry levy is due and payable and has not been paid][1].

Amendments—[1] In sub-para (2), words inserted by FA 2017 s 56, Sch 11 para 2(1), (8) with effect from 6 April 2018 (by virtue of SI 2018/464). The charge to soft drinks industry levy arises on chargeable events which occur on or after 6 April 2018 (FA 2017 s 31(1)).

Reductions for disclosure

12—[(1) Paragraph 13 provides for reductions in penalties—
  (*a*) under paragraph 1 where P discloses a relevant failure that involves a domestic matter, and
  (*b*) under paragraphs 2 to 4 where P discloses a relevant act or failure.
(1A) Paragraph 13A provides for reductions in penalties under paragraph 1 where P discloses a relevant failure that involves an offshore matter or an offshore transfer.
(1B) Sub-paragraph (2) applies where P discloses—
  (*a*) a relevant failure that involves a domestic matter,
  (*b*) a non-deliberate relevant failure that involves an offshore matter, or
  (*c*) a relevant act or failure giving rise to a penalty under any of paragraphs 2 to 4.][1]
(2) P discloses [the][1] relevant act or failure by—
  (*a*) telling HMRC about it,
  (*b*) giving HMRC reasonable help in quantifying the tax unpaid by reason of it, and
  (*c*) allowing HMRC access to records for the purpose of checking how much tax is so unpaid.
[(2A) Sub-paragraph (2B) applies where P discloses—
  (*a*) a deliberate relevant failure (whether concealed or not) that involves an offshore matter, or
  (*b*) a relevant failure that involves an offshore transfer.
(2B) P discloses the failure by—
  (*a*) telling HMRC about it,

(b) giving HMRC reasonable help in quantifying the tax unpaid by reason of it,
(c) allowing HMRC access to records for the purpose of checking how much tax is so unpaid, and
(d) providing HMRC with additional information.
(2C) The Treasury must make regulations setting out what is meant by "additional information" for the purposes of sub-paragraph (2B)(d).
(2D) Regulations under sub-paragraph (2C) are to be made by statutory instrument.
(2E) An instrument containing regulations under sub-paragraph (2C) is subject to annulment in pursuance of a resolution of the House of Commons.]¹
(3) Disclosure of a relevant act or failure—
  (a) is "unprompted" if made at a time when the person making it has no reason to believe that HMRC have discovered or are about to discover the relevant act or failure, and
  (b) otherwise, is "prompted".
(4) In relation to disclosure "quality" includes timing, nature and extent.
[(5) Paragraph 6A(4) to (5) applies to determine whether a failure involves an offshore matter, an offshore transfer or a domestic matter for the purposes of this paragraph.
(6) In this paragraph "relevant failure" means a failure to comply with a relevant obligation.]¹

Regulations—Penalties Relating to Offshore Matters and Offshore Transfers (Additional Information) Regulations, SI 2017/345.
Amendments—¹ Sub-paras (1)–(1B) substituted for sub-para (1); in sub-para (2), word substituted; and sub-paras (2A)–(2E), (5), (6) inserted; by FA 2016 s 163, Sch 21 paras 5, 6 with effect, by virtue of SI 2017/259 regs 2, 3—
  – for inheritance tax purposes, in relation to transfers of value made on or after 1 April 2017;
  – for income tax and capital gains tax purposes, in relation to any tax year commencing on or after 6 April 2016; and
  – for the purpose of making regulations, from 8 March 2017.

[13 (1) If a person who would otherwise be liable to a penalty of a percentage shown in column 1 of the Table (a "standard percentage") has made a disclosure, HMRC must reduce the standard percentage to one that reflects the quality of the disclosure.
(2) But the standard percentage may not be reduced to a percentage that is below the minimum shown for it—
  (a) for a prompted disclosure, in column 2 of the Table, and
  (b) for an unprompted disclosure, in column 3 of the Table.
(3) Where the Table shows a different minimum for case A and case B—
  (a) the case A minimum applies if—
    (i) the penalty is one under paragraph 1, and
    (ii) HMRC become aware of the failure less than 12 months after the time when the tax first becomes unpaid by reason of the failure, and
  (b) otherwise, the case B minimum applies.¹

[Standard %	Minimum % for prompted disclosure	Minimum % for unprompted disclosure
30%	Case A: 10% Case B: 20%	Case A: 0% Case B: 10%
70%	35%	20%
100%	50%	30%]²

Amendments—¹ This para substituted by FA 2010 s 35 Sch 10 paras 7, 9 with effect from 6 April 2011 (by virtue of SI 2011/975 art 2(1)). Note that (by virtue of SI 2011/975 art 4) these changes do not have effect in relation to—
  – any relevant obligation arising under TMA 1970 s 7, FA 1998 Sch 18 para 2, and VATA 1994 Sch 1 paras 5, 6, 14(2), (3), Sch 3 para 3, Sch 3A paras 4, 7(2), (3), in relation to a tax period commencing on or before 5 April 2011;
  – all other relevant obligations arising on or before 5 April 2011;
  – any unauthorised issue of an invoice taking place on or before 5 April 2011;
  – any act which enables HMRC to assess an amount as duty under a relevant excise provision and which is done on or before 5 April 2011; and
  – any act giving rise to a penalty under FA 2008 Sch 41 para 4 which is done on or before 5 April 2011.
² In sub-para (3), Table substituted by FA 2016 s 163, Sch 21 paras 5, 7 with effect, by virtue of SI 2017/259 regs 2, 3—
  – for inheritance tax purposes, in relation to transfers of value made on or after 1 April 2017; and
  – for income tax and capital gains tax purposes, in relation to any tax year commencing on or after 6 April 2016.
Prospective amendments—In sub-para (3), the following Table entries to be inserted at the appropriate places by FA 2015 s 120, Sch 20 paras 9, 13 with effect from a day to be appointed—

"37.5%	case A: 12.5% case B: 25%	case A: 0% case B: 12.5%"

| "87.5% | 43.75% | 25%" |

| "125% | 62.5% | 40%" |

[**13A** (1) If a person who would otherwise be liable to a penalty of a percentage shown in column 1 of the Table (a "standard percentage") has made a disclosure, HMRC must reduce the standard percentage to one that reflects the quality of the disclosure.
(2) But the standard percentage may not be reduced to a percentage that is below the minimum shown for it—
    (*a*) for a prompted disclosure, in column 2 of the Table, and
    (*b*) for an unprompted disclosure, in column 3 of the Table.
(3) Where the Table shows a different minimum for case A and case B—
    (*a*) the case A minimum applies if HMRC becomes aware of the failure less than 12 months after the time when the tax first becomes unpaid by reason of the failure;
    (*b*) otherwise, the case B minimum applies.

Standard %	Minimum % for prompted disclosure	Minimum % for unprompted disclosure
30%	Case A: 10% Case B: 20%	Case A: 0% Case B: 10%
37.5%	Case A: 12.5% Case B: 25%	Case A: 0% Case B: 12.5%
45%	Case A: 15% Case B: 30%	Case A: 0% Case B: 15%
60%	Case A: 20% Case B: 40%	Case A: 0% Case B: 20%
70%	45%	30%
87.5%	53.75%	35%
100%	60%	40%
105%	62.5%	40%
125%	72.5%	50%
140%	80%	50%
150%	85%	55%
200%	110%	70%][1]

Amendments—[1] Paragraph 13A inserted by FA 2016 s 163, Sch 21 paras 5, 8 with effect, by virtue of SI 2017/259 regs 2, 3—
  – for inheritance tax purposes, in relation to transfers of value made on or after 1 April 2017; and
  – for income tax and capital gains tax purposes, in relation to any tax year commencing on or after 6 April 2016.

Special reduction

14—(1) If HMRC think it right because of special circumstances, they may reduce a penalty under any of paragraphs 1 to 4.
(2) In sub-paragraph (1) "special circumstances" does not include—
    (*a*) ability to pay, or
    (*b*) the fact that a potential loss of revenue from one taxpayer is balanced by a potential overpayment by another.
(3) In sub-paragraph (1) the reference to reducing a penalty includes a reference to—
    (*a*) staying a penalty, and
    (*b*) agreeing a compromise in relation to proceedings for a penalty.

Interaction with other penalties and late payment surcharges

15—(1) The amount of a penalty for which P is liable under any of paragraphs 1 to 4 shall be reduced by the amount of any other penalty incurred by P, or any surcharge for late payment of tax imposed on P, if the amount of the penalty or surcharge is determined by reference to the same tax liability.
[(1A) In sub-paragraph (2) "any other penalty" does not include a penalty under Part 4 of FA 2014 (penalty where corrective action not taken after follower notice etc) [or Schedule 22 to FA 2016 (asset-based penalty)][2].][1]
(2) If P is liable to a penalty under section 9 of FA 1994 in respect of a failure to comply with a relevant obligation, the amount of any penalty payable under paragraph 1 in respect of the failure is to be reduced by the amount of the penalty under that section.

(3) Where penalties are imposed under paragraph 3(1) and (2) in respect of the same act or use, the aggregate of the amounts of the penalties must not exceed 100% of the potential lost revenue.

Amendments—[1]   Sub-para (1A) inserted by FA 2014 s 233, Sch 33 para 4 with effect from 17 July 2014.
[2]   In sub-para (1A), words inserted by FA 2016 Sch 22 para 20(4) with effect—
- for inheritance tax purposes, in relation to transfers of value (within the meaning of IHTA 1984 s 3) made on or after that day; and
- for income tax and capital gains tax purposes, in relation to any tax year commencing on or after 6 April 2016.

Assessment

16—(1) Where P becomes liable for a penalty under any of paragraphs 1 to 4 HMRC shall—
   (*a*) assess the penalty,
   (*b*) notify P, and
   (*c*) state in the notice the period in respect of which the penalty is assessed.
(2) A penalty under any of paragraphs 1 to 4 must be paid before the end of the period of 30 days beginning with the day on which notification of the penalty is issued.
(3) An assessment—
   (*a*) shall be treated for procedural purposes in the same way as an assessment to tax (except in respect of a matter expressly provided for by this Act),
   (*b*) may be enforced as if it were an assessment to tax, and
   (*c*) may be combined with an assessment to tax.
(4) An assessment of a penalty under any of paragraphs 1 to 4 must be made before the end of the period of 12 months beginning with—
   (*a*) the end of the appeal period for the assessment of tax unpaid by reason of the relevant act or failure in respect of which the penalty is imposed, or
   (*b*) if there is no such assessment, the date on which the amount of tax unpaid by reason of the relevant act or failure is ascertained.
(5) In sub-paragraph (4)(*a*) "appeal period" means the period during which—
   (*a*) an appeal could be brought, or
   (*b*) an appeal that has been brought has not been determined or withdrawn.
(6) Subject to sub-paragraph (4), a supplementary assessment may be made in respect of a penalty if an earlier assessment operated by reference to an underestimate of potential lost revenue.
(7) The references in this paragraph to "an assessment to tax" are, in relation to a penalty under paragraph 2, a demand for recovery.

Appeal

17—(1) P may appeal against a decision of HMRC that a penalty is payable by P.
(2) P may appeal against a decision of HMRC as to the amount of a penalty payable by P.
Commentary—*Simon's Taxes* E5.203A.

[**18**—(1) An appeal shall be treated in the same way as an appeal against an assessment to the tax concerned (including by the application of any provision about bringing the appeal by notice to HMRC, about HMRC review of the decision or about determination of the appeal by the First-tier Tribunal or the Upper Tribunal).
[(2) Sub-paragraph (1) does not apply—
   (*a*) so as to require P to pay a penalty before an appeal against the assessment of the penalty is determined, or
   (*b*) in respect of any other matter expressly provided for by this Act.]²]¹
Commentary—*Simon's Taxes* E5.203A.
Amendments—[1]   This para substituted by the Transfer of Tribunal Functions and Revenue and Customs Appeals Order, SI 2009/56 art 3, Sch 1 para 473 with effect from 1 April 2009.
[2]   Sub-para (2) substituted by FA 2009 s 109, Sch 57 para 11 with effect from 21 July 2009.

19—(1) On an appeal under paragraph 17(1) the [tribunal]¹ may affirm or cancel HMRC's decision.
(2) On an appeal under paragraph 17(2) the [tribunal]¹ may—
   (*a*) affirm HMRC's decision, or
   (*b*) substitute for HMRC's decision another decision that HMRC had power to make.
(3) If the First-tier [tribunal]¹ substitutes its decision for HMRC's, the [tribunal]¹ may rely on paragraph 14—
   (*a*) to the same extent as HMRC (which may mean applying the same percentage reduction as HMRC to a different starting point), or
   (*b*) to a different extent, but only if the [tribunal]¹ thinks that HMRC's decision in respect of the application of paragraph 14 was flawed.
(4) In sub-paragraph (3)(*b*) "flawed" means flawed when considered in the light of the principles applicable in proceedings for judicial review.

[(5) In this paragraph, "tribunal" means the First-tier Tribunal or Upper Tribunal (as appropriate by virtue of paragraph 18(1)).][1]

Amendments—[1] In sub-paras (1), (2) word substituted for the words "First-tier Tribunal"; in sub-para (3) word substituted for the word "Tribunal" in each place; sub-para (5) inserted by the Transfer of Tribunal Functions and Revenue and Customs Appeals Order, SI 2009/56 art 3, Sch 1 para 473 with effect from 1 April 2009.

Reasonable excuse

20—(1) Liability to a penalty under any of paragraphs 1, 2, 3(1) and 4 does not arise in relation to an act or failure which is not deliberate if P satisfies HMRC or [(on an appeal notified to the tribunal) the tribunal][1] that there is a reasonable excuse for the act or failure.

(2) For the purposes of sub-paragraph (1)—

(a) an insufficiency of funds is not a reasonable excuse unless attributable to events outside P's control,

(b) where P relies on any other person to do anything, that is not a reasonable excuse unless P took reasonable care to avoid the relevant act or failure, and

(c) where P had a reasonable excuse for the relevant act or failure but the excuse has ceased, P is to be treated as having continued to have the excuse if the relevant act or failure is remedied without unreasonable delay after the excuse ceased.

Amendments—[1] In sub-para (1) words substituted for the words "[on appeal) the First-tier Tribunal" by the Transfer of Tribunal Functions and Revenue and Customs Appeals Order, SI 2009/56 art 3, Sch 1 para 473 with effect from 1 April 2009.

Agency

21—(1) In paragraph 1 the reference to a failure by P includes a failure by a person who acts on P's behalf; but P is not liable to a penalty in respect of any failure by P's agent where P satisfies HMRC or [(on an appeal notified to the tribunal) the tribunal][1] that P took reasonable care to avoid the failure.

(2) In paragraph 2 the reference to the making by P of an unauthorised issue of an invoice showing VAT includes the making of such an unauthorised issue by a person who acts on P's behalf; but P is not liable to a penalty in respect of any action by P's agent where P satisfies HMRC or (on appeal) the First-tier Tribunal that P took reasonable care to avoid it.

(3) In paragraph 3(1) the reference to the doing by P of an act which enables HMRC to assess an amount as duty due from P under a relevant excise provision includes the doing of such an act by a person who acts on P's behalf; but P is not liable to a penalty in respect of any action by P's agent where P satisfies HMRC or (on appeal) the First-tier Tribunal that P took reasonable care to avoid it.

(4) In [paragraph 4(1)][2] the reference to P acquiring possession of, or being concerned in dealing with, goods the payment of duty on which is outstanding and has not been deferred includes a person who acts on P's behalf doing so; but P is not liable to a penalty in respect of any action by P's agent where P satisfies HMRC or (on appeal) the First-tier Tribunal that P took reasonable care to avoid it.

[(5) In paragraph 4(1A) the reference to P acquiring possession of, or being concerned in dealing with, chargeable soft drinks in respect of which a payment of soft drinks industry levy is payable but has not been paid includes a person who acts on P's behalf in doing so; but P is not liable to a penalty in respect of any action by P's agent where P satisfies HMRC or (on appeal) the First-tier Tribunal that P took reasonable care to avoid it.][2]

Amendments—[1] In sub-para (1) words substituted for the words "[on appeal) the First-tier Tribunal" by the Transfer of Tribunal Functions and Revenue and Customs Appeals Order, SI 2009/56 art 3, Sch 1 para 473 with effect from 1 April 2009.
[2] In sub-para (4), words substituted for words "paragraph (4)", and sub-para (5) inserted, by FA 2017 s 56, Sch 11 para 2(1), (9) with effect from 6 April 2018 (by virtue of SI 2018/464). The charge to soft drinks industry levy arises on chargeable events which occur on or after 6 April 2018 (FA 2017 s 31(1)).

Companies: officers' liability

22—(1) Where a penalty under any of paragraphs 1, 2, 3(1) and 4 is payable by a company for a deliberate act or failure which was attributable to an officer of the company, the officer is liable to pay such portion of the penalty (which may be 100%) as HMRC may specify by written notice to the officer.

(2) Sub-paragraph (1) does not allow HMRC to recover more than 100% of a penalty.

(3) In the application of sub-paragraph (1) to a body corporate [other than a limited liability partnership][1] "officer" means—

(a) a director (including a shadow director within the meaning of section 251 of the Companies Act 2006 (c 46)), . . . [1]

[(aa) a manager, and][1]

(b) a secretary.

[(3A) In the application of sub-paragraph (1) to a limited liability partnership, "officer" means a member.][1]

(4) In the application of sub-paragraph (1) in any other case "officer" means—

(a) a director,
(b) a manager,
(c) a secretary, and
(d) any other person managing or purporting to manage any of the company's affairs.
(5) Where HMRC have specified a portion of a penalty in a notice given to an officer under sub-paragraph (1)—
  (a) paragraph 14 applies to the specified portion as to a penalty,
  (b) the officer must pay the specified portion before the end of the period of 30 days beginning with the day on which the notice is given,
  (c) paragraph 16(3) to (5) and (7) apply as if the notice were an assessment of a penalty,
  (d) a further notice may be given in respect of a portion of any additional amount assessed in a supplementary assessment in respect of the penalty under paragraph 16(6),
  (e) paragraphs 17 to 19 apply as if HMRC had decided that a penalty of the amount of the specified portion is payable by the officer, and
  (f) paragraph 23 applies as if the officer were liable to a penalty.
[(6) In this paragraph "company" means any body corporate or unincorporated association, but does not include a partnership, a local authority or a local authority association.][1]

Amendments—[1] In sub-para (3) words inserted, word "or" repealed and para (aa) inserted, sub-paras (3A), (6) inserted, by FA 2009 s 109, Sch 57 para 12 with effect from 21 July 2009.

Double jeopardy

23 P is not liable to a penalty under any of paragraphs 1 to 4 in respect of a failure or action in respect of which P has been convicted of an offence.

Commentary—*Simon's Taxes* A4.530.

Interpretation

24—(1) This paragraph applies for the construction of this Schedule
(2) "HMRC" means Her Majesty's Revenue and Customs.
(3) "Tax", without more, includes duty.
(4) An expression used in relation to value added tax has the same meaning as in VATA 1994.

Consequential repeals

25 In consequence of this Schedule the following provisions are omitted—
  (a) in TMA 1970—
    (i) section 7(8), and
    (ii) in the table in section 98, in the second column, the entry relating to section 55 of FA 2004,
  (b) section 170A of CEMA 1979,
  (c) in ALDA 1979—
    (i) in section 47(5), "which shall be calculated by reference to the amount of duty charged on the beer produced",
    (ii) in section 54(5), "which shall be calculated by reference to the amount of duty charged on the wine produced",
    (iii) in section 55(6), "which shall be calculated by reference to the amount of duty charged on the made-wine produced", and
    (iv) in section 62(4), "which shall be calculated by reference to the amount of duty charged on the cider made",
  (d) in HODA 1979—
    (i) section 13AD(4)(a) and (b), and
    (ii) section 14F(4)(a) and (b),
  (e) in FA 1994—
    (i) section 33(6),
    (ii) paragraph 13 of Schedule 4, and
    (iii) paragraph 14 of Schedule 7,
  (f) section 67 of VATA 1994,
  (g) section 32 of FA 1995,
  (h) in FA 1996—
    (i) section 37, and
    (ii) paragraph 21(1), (2) and (4) of Schedule 5,
  (i) section 27(11) of FA 1997,
  (j) paragraph 2(3) and (4) of Schedule 18 to FA 1998,

(k) in FA 2000—
  (i) section 136(2), and
  (ii) paragraph 55(2) to (6) of Schedule 6, and
(l) paragraph 1(2) to (6) of Schedule 4 to FA 2001.

FINANCE ACT 2009

(2009 Chapter 10)

PART 7 ADMINISTRATION

Interest

101   Late payment interest on sums due to HMRC

Penalties

108   Suspension of penalties during currency of agreement for deferred payment

PART 7
ADMINISTRATION

Interest

101 Late payment interest on sums due to HMRC

(1) This section applies to any amount that is payable by a person to HMRC under or by virtue of an enactment.

(2) But this section does not apply to—
  (a) an amount of corporation tax,
  (b) an amount of petroleum revenue tax, or
  (c) an amount of any description specified in an order made by the Treasury.

(3) An amount to which this section applies carries interest at the late payment interest rate from the late payment interest start date until the date of payment.

(4) The late payment interest start date in respect of any amount is the date on which that amount becomes due and payable.

(5) In Schedule 53—
  (a) Part 1 makes special provision as to the amount on which late payment interest is calculated,
  (b) Part 2 makes special provision as to the late payment interest start date,
  (c) Part 3 makes special provision as to the date to which late payment interest runs, and
  (d) Part 4 makes provision about the effect that the giving of a relief has on late payment interest.

(6) Subsection (3) applies even if the late payment interest start date is a non-business day within the meaning of section 92 of the Bills of Exchange Act 1882.

(7) Late payment interest is to be paid without any deduction of income tax.

(8) Late payment interest is not payable on late payment interest.

(9) For the purposes of this section any reference to the payment of an amount to HMRC includes a reference to its being set off against an amount payable by HMRC (and, accordingly, the reference to the date on which an amount is paid includes a reference to the date from which the set-off takes effect).

(10), (11) . . . [1]

Commentary—*Simon's Taxes* **A4.620, A4.629, A4.621**.

HMRC Manuals—Compliance Handbook Manual CH140100 (late payment interest).
CH141120 (general rule).
CH142100 (late payment overview).

Regulations—Taxes and Duties, etc (Interest Rate) Regulations, SI 2011/2446 (formula for calculating late payment interest rate for the purposes of this section).

Amendments—[1] Sub-ss (10), (11) repealed by the Taxation (Cross-border Trade) Act 2018 s 43, Sch 8 para 115, 116 with effect from IP completion day (11pm on 31 December 2020), by virtue of SI 2020/1642 reg 4(b). Those subsections previously read as follows—

"(10) The reference in subsection (1) to amounts payable to HMRC includes—
  (a) amounts of UK VAT payable under a non-UK special scheme;
  (b) amounts of UK VAT payable under a special scheme;

and references in Schedule 53 to amounts due or payable to HMRC are to be read accordingly.

(11) In subsection (10)—
  (a) expressions used in paragraph (a) have the meaning given by paragraph 23(1) of Schedule 3B to VATA 1994 (non- Union scheme);
  (b) expressions used in paragraph (b) have the meaning given by paragraph 38(1) of Schedule 3BA to VATA 1994 (Union scheme).".

Prospective amendment—Sub-s (2)(a), (b) to be repealed by F(No 3)A 2010 s 25, Sch 9 Pt 1 paras 1, 2, Pt 2 paras 13, 14 with effect from a day to be appointed by Treasury order (F(No 3)A 2010 s 25).

Penalties

108 Suspension of penalties during currency of agreement for deferred payment
(1) This section applies if—
- (a) a person ("P") fails to pay an amount of tax falling within the Table in subsection (5) when it becomes due and payable,
- (b) P makes a request to an officer of Revenue and Customs that payment of the amount of tax be deferred, and
- (c) an officer of Revenue and Customs agrees that payment of that amount may be deferred for a period ("the deferral period").

(2) P is not liable to a penalty for failing to pay the amount mentioned in subsection (1) if—
- (a) the penalty falls within the Table, and
- (b) P would (apart from this subsection) become liable to it between the date on which P makes the request and the end of the deferral period.

(3) But if—
- (a) P breaks the agreement (see subsection (4)), and
- (b) an officer of Revenue and Customs serves on P a notice specifying any penalty to which P would become liable apart from subsection (2),

P becomes liable, at the date of the notice, to that penalty.

(4) P breaks an agreement if—
- (a) P fails to pay the amount of tax in question when the deferral period ends, or
- (b) the deferral is subject to P complying with a condition (including a condition that part of the amount be paid during the deferral period) and P fails to comply with it.

(5) The taxes and penalties referred to in subsections (1) and (2) are—

Tax	Penalty
Income tax or capital gains tax	Surcharge under section 59C(2) or (3) of TMA 1970[1]
Value added tax	Surcharge under section 59(4) or 59A(4) of VATA 1994 . . .[2]
Aggregates levy	Penalty interest under paragraph 5 of Schedule 5 to FA 2001
Climate change levy	Penalty interest under paragraph 82 of Schedule 6 to FA 2000
Landfill tax	Penalty interest under paragraph 27(2) of Schedule 5 to FA 1996
Insurance premium tax	Penalty under paragraph 15(2) or (3) of Schedule 7 to FA 1994 which is payable by virtue of paragraph 15(1)(a) of that Schedule.
Any duty of excise	Penalty under section 9(2) or (3) of FA 1994 which is imposed for a failure to pay an amount of any duty of excise or an amount payable on account of any such duty.

(6) If the agreement mentioned in subsection (1)(c) is varied at any time by a further agreement between P and an officer of Revenue and Customs, this section applies from that time to the agreement as varied.
(7) The Treasury may by order amend the Table by adding or removing a tax or a penalty.
(8) An order under subsection (7) is to be made by statutory instrument.
(9) A statutory instrument containing an order under subsection (7) is subject to annulment in pursuance of a resolution of the House of Commons.
(10) In this section, except in the entries in the Table, "penalty" includes surcharge and penalty interest.
(11) This section has effect where the agreement mentioned in subsection (1)(c) is made on or after 24 November 2008.

Commentary—*Simon's Taxes* **A4.565**.
HMRC Manuals—Compliance Handbook Manual CH150500 (overview).
Modification—Social Security (Contributions) Regulations, SI 2001/1004 reg 90K(8) (this section modified in relation to a surcharge payable under SI 2001/1004 reg 90K).
Income Tax (Pay As You Earn) Regulations, SI 2003/2682 reg 203(8) (this section modified in relation to a surcharge payable under SI 2003/2682 reg 203).
Income Tax (Construction Industry Scheme) (Amendment) Regulations, SI 2009/2030 reg 2 (this section modified in relation to a surcharge payable under SI 2009/2030 reg 2).
Amendments—[1] In sub-s (5), first row of Table repealed by the Finance Act 2009, Schedules 55 and 56 (Income Tax Self Assessment and Pension Schemes) (Appointed Days and Consequential and Savings Provisions) Order, SI 2011/702 art 15(b) with effect from 1 April 2011. This amendment has no effect in relation to a return or other document which is required to be made or delivered to HMRC or an amount of tax which is payable in relation to the tax year 2009–10 or any previous tax year (SI 2011/702 art 20).

2 In sub-s (5), in Table, in the entry relating to value added tax, words "or under paragraph 16F of Schedule 3B, or paragraph 26 of Schedule 3BA, to that Act" repealed by the Taxation (Cross-border Trade) Act 2018 s 43, Sch 8 paras 115, 117 with effect from IP completion day (11pm on 31 December 2020), by virtue of SI 2020/1642 reg 4(b).

FINANCE ACT 2011

(2011 Chapter 11)

[19 July 2011]

SCHEDULE 23
DATA-GATHERING POWERS

Section 86(1)

Commentary—*Simon's Taxes* **A4.150**.
HMRC Manuals—Compliance Handbook, CH271400 (amount of penalty).

PART 1
POWER TO OBTAIN DATA

Power to give notice

1 (1) An officer of Revenue and Customs may by notice in writing require a relevant data-holder to provide relevant data.
(2) Part 2 of this Schedule sets out who is a relevant data-holder.
(3) In relation to a relevant data-holder, "relevant data" means data of a kind specified for that type of data-holder in regulations made by the Treasury.
(4) The data that a relevant data-holder may be required to provide—
   (a) may be general data or data relating to particular persons or matters, and
   (b) may include personal data (such as names and addresses of individuals).
(5) A notice under this paragraph is referred to as a data-holder notice.

Regulations—Data-gathering Powers (Relevant Data) Regulations, SI 2012/847.
Data-gathering Powers (Relevant Data) (Amendment) Regulations, SI 2015/672.
Data-gathering Powers (Relevant Data) (Amendment) Regulations, SI 2016/979.
Data-gathering Powers (Relevant Data) (Amendment) Regulations, SI 2017/1175.
Data-gathering Powers (Relevant Data) (Amendment) (EU Exit) Regulations, SI 2019/1221.
Value Added Tax (Miscellaneous and Transitional Provisions, Amendment and Revocation) (EU Exit) Regulation, SI 2020/1495.

Purpose of power

2 (1) The power in paragraph 1(1) is exercisable to assist with the efficient and effective discharge of HMRC's tax functions—
   (a) whether a particular function or more generally, and
   (b) whether involving a particular taxpayer or taxpayers generally.
(2) It is additional to and is not limited by other powers that HMRC may have to obtain data (for example, in Schedule 36 to FA 2008).
(3) But it may not be used (in place of the power in paragraph 1 of that Schedule) to obtain data required for the purpose of checking the relevant data-holder's own tax position.
(4) Sub-paragraph (3) does not prevent use of the power in paragraph 1(1) of this Schedule to obtain data about a matter mentioned in paragraph 14(3)(a) (beneficial ownership of certain payments etc).
(5) Nothing in this paragraph limits the use that may be made of data that have been obtained under this Schedule (see section 17(1) of CRCA 2005).

Specifying relevant data

3 (1) A data-holder notice must specify the relevant data to be provided.
(2) Relevant data may not be specified in a data-holder notice unless an officer of Revenue and Customs has reason to believe that the data could have a bearing on chargeable or other periods ending on or after the applicable day.
(3) The applicable day is the first day of the period of 4 years ending with the day on which the notice is given.

Compliance

4 (1) Relevant data specified in a data-holder notice must be provided by such means and in such form as is reasonably specified in the notice.
(2) If the notice specifies that the data are to be provided by sending them somewhere, the data must be sent to such address and within such period as is reasonably specified in the notice.

(3) If the notice specifies that the data are to be provided by making documents available for inspection somewhere, the documents must be made available for inspection at such place and time as is—
   (a) reasonably specified in the notice, or
   (b) agreed between an officer of Revenue and Customs and the data-holder.
(4) A place used solely as a dwelling may not be specified under sub-paragraph (3)(a).
(5) A data-holder notice requiring the provision of specified documents requires the documents to be provided only if they are in the data-holder's possession or power.
(6) A power in this paragraph to specify something in a notice includes power to specify it in a document referred to in the notice.

Approval by tribunal

5 (1) An officer of Revenue and Customs may ask for the approval of the tribunal before giving a data-holder notice.
(2) This does not require an officer to do so (but see paragraph 28(3) for the effect of obtaining approval).
(3) An application for approval under this paragraph may be made without notice (except as required under sub-paragraph (4)).
(4) The tribunal may not approve the giving of a data-holder notice unless—
   (a) the application for approval is made by, or with the agreement of, an authorised officer,
   (b) the tribunal is satisfied that, in the circumstances, the officer giving the notice is justified in doing so,
   (c) the data-holder has been told that the data are to be required and given a reasonable opportunity to make representations to an officer of Revenue and Customs, and
   (d) the tribunal has been given a summary of any representations made by the data-holder.
(5) Paragraphs (c) and (d) of sub-paragraph (4) do not apply to the extent that the tribunal is satisfied that taking the action specified in those paragraphs might prejudice any purpose for which the data are required.
(6) A decision by the tribunal under this paragraph is final (despite the provisions of sections 11 and 13 of the Tribunals, Courts and Enforcement Act 2007).
(7) "Authorised officer" means an officer of Revenue and Customs who is, or is a member of a class of officers who are, authorised by the Commissioners for the purposes of this paragraph.

Power to copy documents

6 An officer of Revenue and Customs may take copies of or make extracts from any document provided pursuant to a data-holder notice.

Power to retain documents

7 (1) If an officer of Revenue and Customs thinks it reasonable to do so, HMRC may retain documents provided pursuant to a data-holder notice for a reasonable period.
(2) While a document is being retained, the data-holder may, if the document is reasonably required for any purpose, request a copy of it.
(3) The retention of a document under this paragraph is not to be regarded as breaking any lien claimed on the document.
(4) If a document retained under this paragraph is lost or damaged, the Commissioners are liable to compensate the owner of the document for any expenses reasonably incurred in replacing or repairing the document.

PART 2
RELEVANT DATA-HOLDERS

Introduction

8 (1) This Part of this Schedule sets out who is a relevant data-holder for the purposes of this Schedule.
(2) Descriptions of the various types of data-holder are to be read as including anyone who was previously of such a description.

Salaries, fees, commission etc

9 (1) Each of the following is a relevant data-holder—
   (a) an employer,
   (b) a person who is concerned in making payments to or in respect of another person's employees with respect to their employment with that other person,

(c) an approved agent within the meaning of section 714 of ITEPA 2003 (which relates to payroll giving), and
(d) a person who carries on a business in connection with which relevant payments are or are likely to be made.

(2) Relevant payments are—
   (a) payments for or in connection with services provided by persons who are not employed in the business, or
   (b) periodical or lump sum payments in respect of any copyright, public lending right, right in a registered design or design right.

(3) Payments are taken to be made in connection with a business if they are made—
   (a) in the course of carrying on the business or a part of it, or
   (b) in connection with the formation, acquisition, development or disposal of the business or a part of it.

(4) Sub-paragraph (1)(d) applies to the carrying on of any other kind of activity as it applies to the carrying on of a business, but only if the activity is being carried on by a body of persons (and references in sub-paragraphs (2) and (3) to the business are to be read accordingly).

(5) A reference in this paragraph to the making of payments includes—
   (a) the provision of benefits, and
   (b) the giving of any other valuable consideration.

10 (1) This paragraph applies if—
   (a) services that an individual provides or is obliged to provide under an agency contract are treated under section 44(2) of ITEPA 2003 as the duties of an employment held by the individual with the agency, or
   (b) remuneration receivable under or in consequence of arrangements falling within section 45 of that Act is treated as earnings from an employment held by an individual with the agency.

(2) For the purposes of paragraph 9—
   (a) the individual is treated as being employed by the agency, and
   (b) payments made to the individual under or in consequence of the agency contract, or treated as earnings under section 45 of ITEPA 2003, do not count as "relevant payments".

(3) "Agency contract" and "remuneration" have the same meaning as in Chapter 7 of Part 2 of ITEPA 2003.

11 (1) This paragraph applies if—
   (a) a person ("A") performs in the United Kingdom duties of an employment,
   (b) the employment is under or with a person resident outside and not resident in the United Kingdom,
   (c) the duties performed in the United Kingdom are performed for a continuous period of not less than 30 days, and
   (d) those duties are performed for the benefit of a person ("B") resident or carrying on a trade, profession or vocation in the United Kingdom.

(2) For the purposes of paragraph 9—
   (a) B is treated as if B were an employer, but
   (b) only the name and place of residence of A may be specified for a relevant data-holder of B's type in regulations made under paragraph 1(3).

Interest etc

12 (1) A person by or through whom interest is paid or credited is a relevant data-holder.

(2) For the purposes of this paragraph, the following are to be treated as interest—
   (a) a dividend in respect of a share in a building society,
   (b) an amount to which a person holding a deeply discounted security is entitled on the redemption of that security,
   (c) a foreign dividend, and
   (d) an alternative finance return.

(3) In sub-paragraph (2)—
   "alternative finance return" means—
      (a) an alternative finance return within the meaning of Part 10A of ITA 2007, and
      (b) an alternative finance return within the meaning of Part 6 of CTA 2009;
   "building society" means a building society within the meaning of the Building Societies Act 1986;
   "deeply discounted security" has the same meaning as in Chapter 8 of Part 4 of ITTOIA 2005;
   "foreign dividend" means any annual payment, interest or dividend payable out of, or in respect of the funds or securities of—

(a) a body of persons that is not resident in the United Kingdom, or

(b) a government or public or local authority in a country outside the United Kingdom.

Income, assets etc belonging to others

13 A person who (in whatever capacity) is in receipt of money or value of or belonging to another is a relevant data-holder.

[Merchant acquirers etc

13A—(1) A person who has a contractual obligation to make payments to retailers in settlement of payment card transactions is a relevant data-holder.
(2) In this paragraph—
"payment card" includes a credit card, a charge card and a debit card;
"payment card transaction" means any transaction in which a payment card is accepted as payment;
"retailer" means a person who accepts a payment card as payment for any transaction.
(3) In this paragraph any reference to a payment card being accepted as payment includes a reference to any account number or other indicators associated with a payment card being accepted as payment.][1]
Amendments—[1] Para 13A inserted by FA 2013 s 228 with effect in relation to relevant data with a bearing on any period (whether before, on or after 17 July 2013).

[Providers of electronic stored-value payment services

13B (1) A person who provides electronic stored-value payment services is a relevant data-holder.
(2) In this paragraph "electronic stored-value payment services" means services by means of which monetary value is stored electronically for the purpose of payments being made in respect of transactions to which the provider of those services is not a party.][1]
Amendments—[1] Paragraphs 13B, 13C inserted by FA 2016 s 176 with effect in relation to relevant data with a bearing on any period (whether before, on or after 15 September 2016).

[Business intermediaries

13C (1) A person who—
(a) provides services to enable or facilitate transactions between suppliers and their customers or clients (other than services provided solely to enable payments to be made), and
(b) receives information about such transactions in the course of doing so,
is a relevant data-holder.
(2) In this paragraph "suppliers" means persons supplying goods or services in the course of business.
(3) For the purposes of this paragraph, information about transactions includes information that is capable of indicating the likely quantity or value of transactions.][1]
Amendments—[1] Paragraphs 13B, 13C inserted by FA 2016 s 176 with effect in relation to relevant data with a bearing on any period (whether before, on or after 15 September 2016).

[Money service businesses

13D (1) A person is a relevant data-holder if the person—
(a) carries on any of the activities in sub-paragraph (2) by way of business,
(b) is a relevant person within the meaning of regulation 8(1) of the Money Laundering, Terrorist Financing and Transfer of Funds (Information on the Payer) Regulations 2017 (SI 2017/692), and
(c) is not an excluded credit institution.
(2) The activities referred to in sub-paragraph (1)(a) are—
(a) operating a currency exchange office;
(b) transmitting money (or any representation of monetary value) by any means;
(c) cashing cheques which are made payable to customers.
(3) An excluded credit institution is a credit institution which has permission to carry on the regulated activity of accepting deposits—
(a) under Part 4A of the Financial Services and Markets Act 2000 (permission to carry on regulated activities), . . . [2]
(b) . . . [2]
(4) Sub-paragraph (3) is to be read with section 22 of and Schedule 2 to the Financial Services and Markets Act 2000, and any order under that section (classes of regulated activities).

(5) In this paragraph "credit institution" has the meaning given by Article 4.1(1) of Regulation (EU) No 575/2013 of the European Parliament and of the Council of 26 June 2013 on prudential requirements for credit institutions and investment firms.]¹

Amendments— [1] Paragraph 13D inserted by F(No 2)A 2017 s 69 with effect in relation to relevant data with a bearing on any period (whether before, on or after 16 November 2017).

[2] In sub-para (3)(*a*) word ", or" repealed, and sub-para (3)(*b*) repealed, by the Taxes (Amendments) (EU Exit) Regulations, SI 2019/689 reg 20(1), (3)(*a*) with effect from Implementation Period completion day (11pm on 31 December 2020) (see EU(WA)A 2020 Sch 5 para 1(1)). These amendments to do not apply where a person qualifies for authorisation under FSMA 2000 Sch 3 by virtue of SI 2001/3084 (see SI 2019/689 reg 41(*i*)). Sub-para (3)(*b*) previously read as follows—

"(*b*) resulting from Part 2 of Schedule 3 to that Act (exercise of passport rights by EEA firms).".

Payments derived from securities

14 (1) Each of the following is a relevant data-holder—
  (*a*) a person who is the registered or inscribed holder of securities,
  (*b*) a person who receives a payment derived from securities or would be entitled to do so if a payment were made,
  (*c*) a person who receives a payment treated by the company that makes it as a payment to which section 1033 of CTA 2010 applies (purchase by unquoted trading company of own shares), and
  (*d*) a person who receives a chargeable payment within the meaning of Chapter 5 of Part 23 of CTA 2010 (company distributions: demergers).
(2) But, for a relevant data-holder of a type described in this paragraph, data may only be specified in regulations under paragraph 1(3) if the data concern a matter mentioned in sub-paragraph (3).
(3) The matters are—
  (*a*) whether the relevant data-holder is the beneficial owner (or sole beneficial owner) of the securities or payment in question,
  (*b*) if not—
    (i) details of the beneficial owner (or other beneficial owners), and
    (ii) if those details are not known or if different, details of the person for whom the securities are held or to whom the payment is or may be paid on, and
  (*c*) if there is more than one beneficial owner or more than one person of the kind mentioned in paragraph (*b*)(ii), their respective interests in the securities or payment.
(4) "Payment derived from securities" includes in particular—
  (*a*) an amount (whether of income or capital) that is payable out of or in respect of securities or rights attaching to securities, and
  (*b*) a payment that is representative of any such amount.

15 (1) A person who makes a payment derived from securities that has been received from or is paid on behalf of another is a relevant data-holder.
(2) "Payment derived from securities" has the same meaning as in paragraph 14.

Grants and subsidies out of public funds

16 (1) A person by whom a payment out of public funds is made by way of grant or subsidy is a relevant data-holder.
(2) For these purposes, a payment is a payment out of public funds if it is provided directly or indirectly by—
  (*a*) the Crown,
  (*b*) any government, public or local authority whether in the United Kingdom or elsewhere, or
  (*c*) any EU institution.

Licences, approvals etc

17 (1) A person by whom licences or approvals are issued or a register is maintained is a relevant data-holder.
(2) "Register" includes—
  (*a*) any record or list that a local authority maintains, and
  (*b*) any record or list that any other person is required or permitted to maintain by or under an enactment.

Rent and other payments arising from land

18 (1) Each of the following is a relevant data-holder—
  (*a*) a lessee (or successor in title of a lessee),
  (*b*) an occupier of land,
  (*c*) a person having the use of land, and

(d) a person who, as agent, manages land or is in receipt of rent or other payments arising from land.

(2) The reference to a person who manages land includes a person who markets property to potential tenants, searches for tenants or provides similar services.

Dealing etc in securities

19 (1) Each of the following is a relevant data-holder—
  (a) a person who effects or is a party to securities transactions wholly or partly on behalf of others (whether as agent or principal),
  (b) a person who, in the course of business, acts as registrar or administrator in respect of securities transactions (including a person who manages a clearing house [or a central securities depository as defined in point (1) of Article 2(1) of Regulation (EU) No 909/2014 of the European Parliament and of the Council of 23 July 2014 on improving securities settlement in the European Union and on central securities depositories][1] for any terminal market in securities),
  (c) a person who makes a payment derived from securities to anyone other than the registered or inscribed holder of the securities,
  (d) a person who makes a payment derived from bearer securities, and
  (e) an accountable person within the meaning of the Stamp Duty Reserve Tax Regulations 1986 (S.I. 1986/1711).

(2) "Payment derived from securities" has the same meaning as in paragraph 14 (and "payment derived from bearer securities" is to be read accordingly).

(3) "Securities transactions" means—
  (a) transactions in securities,
  (b) transactions under which a representative payment has been, is to be or may be made, or
  (c) the making or receipt of a representative payment.

(4) In sub-paragraph (3)—
  "representative payment" means a payment that is representative of an amount payable out of or in respect of securities or rights attaching to securities;
  "transactions in securities" means transactions, of whatever description, relating to securities, and includes in particular—
    (a) the purchase, sale or exchange of securities,
    (b) issuing or securing the issue of new securities,
    (c) applying or subscribing for new securities, and
    (d) altering or securing the alteration of rights attached to securities.

Amendments—[1] In sub-para (1)(b) words inserted by the Central Securities Depositories Regulations, SI 2017/1064 reg 10, Sch para 15(a) with effect from 28 November 2017.

Dealing in other property

20 Each of the following is a relevant data-holder—
  (a) the committee or other person or body of persons responsible for managing a clearing house [or a central securities depository (as defined in paragraph 19)][1] for any terminal market in commodities,
  (b) an auctioneer,
  (c) a person carrying on a business of dealing in any description of tangible movable property, and
  (d) a person carrying on a business of acting as an agent or intermediary in dealings in any description of tangible movable property.

Amendments—[1] In sub-para (a) words inserted by the Central Securities Depositories Regulations, SI 2017/1064 reg 10, Sch para 15(b) with effect from 28 November 2017.

Lloyd's

21 A person who is registered as managing agent at Lloyd's in relation to a syndicate of underwriting members of Lloyd's is a relevant data-holder.

Investment plans etc

22 Each of the following is a relevant data-holder—
  (a) a plan manager (see section 696 of ITTOIA 2005), and
  (b) an account provider in relation to a child trust fund (as defined in section 3 of the Child Trust Funds Act 2004).

Petroleum activities

23 Each of the following is a relevant data-holder—
  (*a*) the holder of a licence granted under Part 1 of the Petroleum Act 1998, and
  (*b*) the responsible person in relation to an oil field (within the meaning of Part 1 of OTA 1975).

Insurance activities

24 Each of the following is a relevant data-holder—
  (*a*) a person who is involved (in any capacity) in an insurance business (as defined for the purposes of Part 3 of FA 1994),
  (*b*) a person who makes arrangements for persons to enter into contracts of insurance, and
  (*c*) a person who is concerned in a business that is not an insurance business and who has been involved in the entering into of a contract of insurance that provides cover for any matter associated with the business.

[Chargeable soft drinks

24A (1) A person who is involved (in any capacity) in any of the following activities is a relevant data-holder—
  (*a*) producing chargeable soft drinks;
  (*b*) packaging chargeable soft drinks;
  (*c*) carrying on a business involving the sale of chargeable soft drinks.
(2) For the purposes of sub-paragraph (1), "chargeable soft drinks", "producing" and "packaging" have the same meaning as in Part 3 of FA 2017.]

Prospective amendments—Paragraph 24A and preceding cross-head to be inserted by FA 2017 s 56, Sch 11 para 6(1), (2) with effect from a date to be appointed. The charge to soft drinks industry levy arises on chargeable events which occur on or after 6 April 2018 (FA 2017 s 31(1)).

Environmental activities

25 A person who is involved (in any capacity) in any of the following activities is a relevant data-holder—
  (*a*) subjecting aggregate to exploitation in the United Kingdom (as defined for the purposes of Part 2 of FA 2001) or connected activities,
  (*b*) making or receiving supplies of taxable commodities (as defined for the purposes of Schedule 6 to FA 2000) or connected activities, and
  (*c*) [disposal of material][1] (as defined for the purposes of Part 3 of FA 1996).

Amendments—[1] In sub-para (*c*), words substituted for words "landfill tax" by FA 2018 s 42(1), Sch 12 para 28 with effect in relation to disposals made, or treated as made, on or after 1 April 2018, subject to transitional arrangements relating to disposals before April 2018 at places other than landfill sites (FA 2018 Sch 12 paras 31, 32). This amendment has effect in relation to disposals made in England or Northern Ireland only.

Prospective amendments—In para (*a*), words "England, Wales or Northern Ireland" to be substituted for words "the United Kingdom" by the Scotland Act 2016 s 18(3), Sch 1 para 13 with effect from a date to be appointed.

Settlements

26 (1) Each of the following is a relevant data-holder—
  (*a*) a person who makes a settlement,
  (*b*) the trustees of a settlement,
  (*c*) a beneficiary under a settlement, and
  (*d*) any other person to whom income is payable under a settlement.
(2) Section 620 of ITTOIA 2005 (meaning of "settlement" etc) applies for the purposes of this paragraph.

Charities

27 A charity is a relevant data-holder.

PART 3
APPEALS AGAINST DATA-HOLDER NOTICES

Right of appeal

28 (1) The data-holder may appeal against a data-holder notice, or any requirement in such a notice, on any of the following grounds—
  (*a*) it is unduly onerous to comply with the notice or requirement,

(b) the data-holder is not a relevant data-holder, or
   (c) data specified in the notice are not relevant data.
(2) Sub-paragraph (1)(a) does not apply to a requirement to provide data that form part of the data-holder's statutory records.
(3) Sub-paragraph (1) does not apply if the tribunal approved the giving of the notice in accordance with paragraph 5.

Procedure for appeal

29 (1) Notice of an appeal under paragraph 28 must be given—
   (a) in writing,
   (b) before the end of the period of 30 days beginning with the date on which the data-holder notice was given, and
   (c) to the officer of Revenue and Customs by whom the data-holder notice was given.
(2) It must state the grounds of appeal.
(3) On an appeal that is notified to the tribunal, the tribunal may confirm, vary or set aside the data-holder notice or a requirement in it.
(4) If the tribunal confirms or varies the notice or a requirement in it, the data-holder must comply with the notice or requirement—
   (a) within such period as is specified by the tribunal, or
   (b) if the tribunal does not specify a period, within such period as is reasonably specified in writing by an officer of Revenue and Customs following the tribunal's decision.
(5) A decision by the tribunal under this Part is final (despite the provisions of sections 11 and 13 of the Tribunals, Courts and Enforcement Act 2007).
(6) Subject to this paragraph, the provisions of Part 5 of TMA 1970 relating to appeals have effect in relation to appeals under paragraph 28 as they have effect in relation to an appeal against an assessment to income tax.

PART 4
PENALTIES

Penalties for failure to comply

30 (1) If the data-holder fails to comply with a data-holder notice, the data-holder is liable to a penalty of £300.
(2) A reference in this Schedule to failing to comply with a data-holder notice includes—
   (a) concealing, destroying or otherwise disposing of a material document, or
   (b) arranging for any such concealment, destruction or disposal.
(3) A document is a material document if, at the time when the data-holder acts—
   (a) the data-holder has received a data-holder notice requiring the data-holder to provide the document or data contained in the document, or
   (b) the data-holder has not received such a notice but has been informed by an officer of Revenue and Customs that the data-holder will do so or is likely to do so.
(4) A document is not a material document by virtue of sub-paragraph (3)(a) if the data-holder notice has already been complied with, unless—
   (a) the data-holder has been notified in writing by an officer of Revenue and Customs that the data-holder must continue to preserve the document, and
   (b) the notification has not been withdrawn.
(5) A document is not a material document by virtue of sub-paragraph (3)(b) if more than 6 months have elapsed since the data-holder was (or was last) informed.

Daily default penalties for failure to comply

31 If—
   (a) a penalty under paragraph 30 is assessed, and
   (b) the failure in question continues after the data-holder has been notified of the assessment,
the data-holder is liable to a further penalty, for each subsequent day on which the failure continues, of an amount not exceeding £60 for each such day.

Penalties for inaccurate information or documents

32 (1) This paragraph applies if—
   (a) in complying with a data-holder notice, the data-holder provides inaccurate data, and
   (b) condition A, B or C is met.
(2) Condition A is that the inaccuracy is—
   (a) due to a failure by the data-holder to take reasonable care, or

(*b*) deliberate on the data-holder's part.
(3) Condition B is that the data-holder knows of the inaccuracy at the time the data are provided but does not inform HMRC at that time.
(4) Condition C is that the data-holder—
   (*a*) discovers the inaccuracy some time later, and
   (*b*) fails to take reasonable steps to inform HMRC.
(5) If this paragraph applies, the data-holder is liable to a penalty not exceeding £3,000.

Failure to comply with time limit

33 A failure to do anything required to be done within a limited period of time does not give rise to liability under paragraph 30 or 31 if the thing was done within such further time (if any) as an officer of Revenue and Customs may have allowed.

Reasonable excuse

34 (1) Liability to a penalty under paragraph 30 or 31 does not arise if the data-holder satisfies HMRC or (on an appeal notified to the tribunal) the tribunal that there is a reasonable excuse for the failure.
(2) For the purposes of this paragraph—
   (*a*) an insufficiency of funds is not a reasonable excuse unless attributable to events outside the data-holder's control,
   (*b*) if the data-holder relies on another person to do anything, that is not a reasonable excuse unless the data-holder took reasonable care to avoid the failure,
   (*c*) if the data-holder had a reasonable excuse for the failure but the excuse has ceased, the data-holder is to be treated as having continued to have the excuse if the failure is remedied without unreasonable delay after the excuse ceased.

Assessment of penalties

35 (1) If the data-holder becomes liable to a penalty under paragraph 30, 31 or 32, HMRC may assess the penalty.
(2) If they do so, they must notify the data-holder.
(3) An assessment of a penalty under paragraph 30 or 31 must be made within the period of 12 months beginning with the latest of the following—
   (*a*) the date on which the data-holder became liable to the penalty,
   (*b*) the end of the period in which notice of an appeal against the data-holder notice (or a requirement in it) could have been given, and
   (*c*) if notice of such an appeal is given, the date on which the appeal is determined or withdrawn.
(4) An assessment of a penalty under paragraph 32 must be made—
   (*a*) within the period of 12 months beginning with the date on which the inaccuracy first came to the attention of an officer of Revenue and Customs, and
   (*b*) within the period of 6 years beginning with the date on which the data-holder became liable to the penalty.

Right to appeal against penalty

36 [(1)] The data-holder may appeal against a decision by an officer of Revenue and Customs—
   (*a*) that a penalty is payable under paragraph 30, 31 or 32, or
   (*b*) as to the amount of such a penalty.
   [(2) But sub-paragraph (1)(*b*) does not give a right of appeal against the amount of an increased daily penalty payable by virtue of paragraph 38.][2]

Amendments—[1] Sub-s (1) numbered as such, and sub-s (2) inserted, by FA 2016 s 177(1), (5) with effect from 15 September 2016.

Procedure on appeal against penalty

37 (1) Notice of an appeal under paragraph 36 must be given—
   (*a*) in writing,
   (*b*) before the end of the period of 30 days beginning with the date on which notification under paragraph 35 was given, and
   (*c*) to HMRC.
(2) It must state the grounds of appeal.
(3) On an appeal under paragraph 36(*a*) that is notified to the tribunal, the tribunal may confirm or cancel the decision.
(4) On an appeal under paragraph 36(*b*) that is notified to the tribunal, the tribunal may—

(a) confirm the decision, or
(b) substitute for the decision another decision that the officer of Revenue and Customs had power to make.
(5) Subject to this paragraph and paragraph 40, the provisions of Part 5 of TMA 1970 relating to appeals have effect in relation to appeals under paragraph 36 as they have effect in relation to an appeal against an assessment to income tax.

Increased daily default penalty

38 (1) This paragraph applies if—
   (a) a penalty under paragraph 31 is assessed under paragraph 35,
   (b) the failure in respect of which that assessment is made continues for more than 30 days beginning with the date on which notification of that assessment is given, and
   (c) the data-holder has been told that an application may be made under this paragraph for an increased daily penalty to be [assessable]¹.
(2) If this paragraph applies, an officer of Revenue and Customs may make an application to the tribunal for an increased daily penalty to be [assessable]¹ on the data-holder.
[(3) If the tribunal decides that an increased daily penalty should be assessable—
   (a) the tribunal must determine the day from which the increased daily penalty is to apply and the maximum amount of that penalty ("the new maximum amount");
   (b) from that day, paragraph 31 has effect in the data-holder's case as if "the new maximum amount" were substituted for "£60".
(4) The new maximum amount may not be more than £1,000.]¹
(5) But subject to that, in determining [the new maximum amount]¹ the tribunal must have regard to—
   (a) the likely cost to the data-holder of complying with the data-holder notice,
   (b) any benefits to the data-holder of not complying with it, and
   (c) any benefits to anyone else resulting from the data-holder's non-compliance.
Amendments—¹ In sub-paras (1)(c), (2), word substituted for word "imposed", sub-paras (3), (4) substituted, and in sub-para (5), words substituted for words "the amount", by FA 2016 s 177(1), (2) with effect from 15 September 2016.

39 (1) If [the tribunal makes a determination]¹ under paragraph 38, HMRC must notify the data-holder.
(2) The notification must specify [new maximum amount and the day from which it applies]¹.
(3) . . . ¹
Amendments—¹ In sub-para (1), words substituted for words "a data-holder becomes liable to a penalty", in sub-para (2), words substituted for words "the day from which the increased penalty is to apply", and sub-para (3) repealed, by FA 2016 s 177(1), (3) with effect from 15 September 2016.

Enforcement of penalties

40 (1) A penalty under this Schedule must be paid before the end of the period of 30 days beginning with the date mentioned in sub-paragraph (2).
(2) That date is—
   (a) the date on which notification under paragraph 35 . . . ¹ is given in respect of the penalty, or
   (b) if (in the case of a penalty under paragraph 30, 31 or 32) a notice of appeal under paragraph 36 is given, the date on which the appeal is finally determined or withdrawn.
(3) A penalty under this Schedule may be enforced as if it were income tax charged in an assessment and due and payable.
Amendments—¹ In sub-para (2)(a), words "or 39" repealed by FA 2016 s 177(1), (4) with effect from 15 September 2016.

Power to change amount of penalties

41 (1) If it appears to the Treasury that there has been a change in the value of money since the last relevant date, they may by regulations substitute for the sums for the time being specified in paragraphs 30(1), 31, 32(5) and 38(4) such other sums as appear to them to be justified by the change.
(2) "Relevant date", in relation to a specified sum, means—
   (a) the day on which this Act is passed, and
   (b) each date on which the power conferred by sub-paragraph (1) has been exercised in relation to that sum.
(3) Regulations under this paragraph do not apply to—
   (a) a failure which began before the date on which they come into force, or
   (b) an inaccuracy in any data or document provided to HMRC before that date.

Double jeopardy

42 The data-holder is not liable to a penalty under this Schedule in respect of anything in respect of which the data-holder has been convicted of an offence.

PART 5
MISCELLANEOUS PROVISION AND INTERPRETATION

Application of provisions of TMA 1970

43 Subject to the provisions of this Schedule, the following provisions of TMA 1970 apply for the purposes of this Schedule as they apply for the purposes of the Taxes Acts—
- (*a*) section 108 (responsibility of company officers),
- (*b*) section 114 (want of form), and
- (*c*) section 115 (delivery and service of documents).

Regulations

44 (1) Regulations under this Schedule are to be made by statutory instrument.
(2) The first regulations to be made under paragraph 1(3) may not be made unless the instrument containing them has been laid in draft before, and approved by a resolution of, the House of Commons.
(3) Subject to sub-paragraph (2), a statutory instrument containing regulations under this Schedule is subject to annulment in pursuance of a resolution of the House of Commons.

Tax

45 (1) In this Schedule "tax" means any or all of the following—
- (*a*) income tax,
- (*b*) capital gains tax,
- (*c*) corporation tax,
- [(*ca*) diverted profits tax,][2]
- (*d*) VAT,
- (*e*) insurance premium tax,
- (*f*) inheritance tax,
- (*g*) stamp duty land tax,
- (*h*) stamp duty reserve tax,
- (*i*) petroleum revenue tax,
- (*j*) aggregates levy,
- (*k*) climate change levy,
- (*l*) landfill tax, and
- (*m*) relevant foreign tax.

(2) "Corporation tax" includes any amount assessable or chargeable as if it were corporation tax.
(3) "VAT" means—
- (*a*) value added tax charged in accordance with VATA 1994, . . . [4]
- (*b*) . . . [4]

and includes any amount that is recoverable under paragraph 5(2) of Schedule 11 to VATA 1994 (amounts shown on invoices as VAT).
(4) "Relevant foreign tax" means—
- (*a*) a tax of a member State . . . [3] which is covered by the provisions for the exchange of information under the [Council Directive 2011/16/EU of 15 February 2011 on administrative cooperation in the field of taxation][1] (as amended from time to time), and
- (*b*) any tax or duty which is imposed under the law of a territory in relation to which arrangements having effect by virtue of section 173 of FA 2006 (international tax enforcement arrangements) have been made and which is covered by the arrangements.

Amendments—[1] In sub-para (4), words substituted by the European Administrative Co-operation (Taxation) Regulations, SI 2012/3062 reg 6(2) with effect from 1 January 2013.
[2] Sub-para (1)(*ca*) inserted by FA 2015 s 105(1) with effect in relation to accounting periods beginning on or after 1 April 2015. For accounting periods that straddle that date, see FA 2015 s 116(2).
[3] In sub-para (4)(*a*) words ", other than the United Kingdom," repealed by the Taxes (Amendments) (EU Exit) Regulations, SI 2019/689 reg 20(1), (3)(*b*) with effect from Implementation Period completion day (11pm on 31 December 2020) (see EU(WA)A 2020 Sch 5 para 1(1)).
[4] Sub-para(3)(*b*), and preceding word "and" repealed by the Taxation (Cross-border Trade) Act 2018 s 43, Sch 8 para 120 with effect from IP completion day (11pm on 31 December 2020), by virtue of SI 2020/1642 reg 4(*b*). Sub-para(3)(*b*) previously read as follows—
  "(*b*) value added tax charged in accordance with the law of another member State,".

Prospective amendments—Sub-para (1)(*ia*) to be inserted by FA 2017 s 56, Sch 11 para 6(1), (3) with effect from a date to be appointed. The charge to soft drinks industry levy arises on chargeable events which occur on or after 6 April 2018 (FA 2017 s 31(1)).Sub-para (1)(*ia*) as inserted to read as follows—

"(*ia*) soft drinks industry levy,".

Statutory records

46 (1) For the purposes of this Schedule data form part of a data-holder's statutory records if they are data that the data-holder is required to keep and preserve under or by virtue of any enactment relating to tax.

(2) Data cease to form part of a data-holder's statutory records when the period for which the data are required to be preserved under or by virtue of that enactment has expired.

General interpretation

47 In this Schedule—

"address" includes an electronic address;

"body of persons" has the same meaning as in TMA 1970;

"chargeable period" means a tax year, accounting period or other period for which a tax is charged;

"charity" has the meaning given by paragraph 1(1) of Schedule 6 to FA 2010;

"the Commissioners" means the Commissioners for Her Majesty's Revenue and Customs;

"company" has the meaning given by section 288(1) of TCGA 1992;

"data" includes information held in any form;

"the data-holder", in relation to a data-holder notice, means the person to whom the notice is addressed;

"data-holder notice" is defined in paragraph 1;

"dividend" includes any kind of distribution;

"document" includes a copy of a document (see also section 114 of FA 2008);

"employment", "employee" and "employer" have the same meaning as in Parts 2 to 7 of ITEPA 2003 (see, in particular, sections 4 and 5 of that Act);

"HMRC" means Her Majesty's Revenue and Customs;

"local authority" has the meaning given in section 999 of ITA 2007;

"provide" includes make available for inspection;

"specify" includes describe;

"securities" includes—

(*a*) shares and stock,

(*b*) debentures, including debenture stock, loan stock, bonds, certificates of deposit and other instruments creating or acknowledging indebtedness, and

(*c*) warrants or other instruments entitling the holder to subscribe for or otherwise acquire anything within paragraph (*a*) or (*b*),

issued by or on behalf of a person resident in, or a government or public or local authority of, any country (including a country outside the United Kingdom);

"shares" is to be construed in accordance with [section 99][1] of TCGA 1992;

"tax functions" means functions relating to tax;

"the tribunal" means the First-tier Tribunal or, where determined by or under the Tribunal Procedure Rules, the Upper Tribunal.

Amendments—[1] In definition of "shares", words substituted for words "sections 99 and 103A" by the Collective Investment Schemes and Offshore Funds (Amendment of the Taxation of Chargeable Gains Act 1992) Regulations, SI 2017/1204 regs 2, 15 with effect in relation to disposals on or after 1 January 2018.

48 A reference in this Schedule to providing data includes—

(*a*) preparing and delivering a return, statement or declaration, and

(*b*) providing documents.

49 (1) A reference in this Schedule to the carrying on of a business also includes—

(*a*) the letting of property,

(*b*) the activities of a charity, and

(*c*) the activities of a government department, a local authority, a local authority association or any other public authority.

(2) "Local authority association" has the meaning given in section 1000 of ITA 2007.

Crown application

50 This Schedule applies to the Crown but not to Her Majesty in Her private capacity (within the meaning of the Crown Proceedings Act 1947).

PART 6
CONSEQUENTIAL PROVISIONS

TMA 1970

51 (1) TMA 1970 is amended as follows.
(2) (*repeals* TMA 1970 ss 13–19, 21, 23–27, 76, 77I)
(3), (4) (*amend* TMA 1970 s 98, Table)
(5) (*inserts* TMA 1970 s 103ZA(*f*))

FA 1973

52 (*repeals* FA 1973 Sch 15 para 2)

FA 1974

53 (1) (*amends* FA 1974 s 24)
(2) Sub-paragraph (1) applies so far as section 24 of FA 1974 continues to have effect (see section 381 of TIOPA 2010).

FA 1986

54 (*repeals* FA 1986 Sch 18 para 8(4), (5))

ICTA

55 (*repeals* TA 1988 ss 42(7), 217(4), 226(4), 768(9), 816(3))

FA 1989

56 (*repeals* FA 1989 Sch 12 para 3)

ITTOIA 2005

57 (*repeals* ITTOIA 2005 ss 302B(3), (4), 647)

FA 2005

58 (*repeals* FA 2005 Sch 2 para 2)

CRCA 2005

59 (*repeals* CRCA 2005 Sch 2 para 2)

FA 2008

60 FA 2008 is amended as follows.

61 (*repeals* FA 2008 s 39(1)(*a*))

62 (1) Schedule 36 (information and inspection powers) is amended as follows.
(2) (*repeals* FA 2008 Sch 36 para 34A)
(3) (*amends* FA 2008 Sch 36 para 61A)

CTA 2009

63 (*repeals* CTA 2009 s 241(3), (4))

CTA 2010

64 (1), (2) (*repeal* CTA 2010 ss 31(1), 465(1), 728, 1046(5)–(7), 1097, 1102(2))
(3) (*amended* CTA 2010 s 1109; *repealed* by FA 2016 s 5, Sch 1 para 69(*a*))

PART 7
APPLICATION OF THIS SCHEDULE

65 (1) This Schedule—

(a) comes into force on 1 April 2012, and
(b) applies from then on to relevant data with a bearing on any period (whether before, on or after that date), subject to paragraph 3(2).
(2) The provisions repealed or otherwise amended by Part 6 of this Schedule continue to have effect in relation to notices given, or requests made, pursuant to any of the repealed provisions before 1 April 2012 as if the repeals and other amendments had not been made.

SCHEDULE 25
MUTUAL ASSISTANCE FOR RECOVERY OF TAXES ETC
Section 87

MARD

1   In this Schedule "MARD" means Council Directive 2010/24/EU.

HMRC functions

2   (1) The Commissioners are a competent authority in the United Kingdom for the purposes of all matters under MARD.
(2) HMRC is designated as the central liaison office in the United Kingdom for the purposes of all matters under MARD.

Exchange of information

3   (1) No obligation of secrecy imposed by statute or otherwise precludes a public authority (or anyone acting on behalf of a public authority) from disclosing information if the disclosure is made for the purpose of giving effect, or enabling effect to be given, to MARD or a MARD-related instrument.
(2) Sub-paragraph (1) applies, in particular, to any disclosure (to persons in the United Kingdom or elsewhere) in connection with a request or proposed request by or on behalf of an applicant authority [of the United Kingdom or][1] of any member State for assistance in accordance with MARD.
(3) Sub-paragraph (2) is not to be taken to limit sub-paragraph (1).

Amendments—[1] In sub-para (2) words inserted after words "applicant authority" by the MARD (Amendment) (EU Exit) Regulations, SI 2020/996 reg 2(1), (2) with effect from IP completion day (11pm on 31 December 2020).

Onward disclosure of information received from HMRC

4   (1) A public authority commits an offence if—
(a) it discloses relevant information, and
(b) the disclosure is not permitted by sub-paragraph (3).
(2) "Relevant information" is information that—
(a) the public authority has received from HMRC by virtue of paragraph 3, and
(b) relates to a person whose identity is specified in the disclosure or can be deduced from it.
(3) A disclosure is permitted by this sub-paragraph if it is made—
(a) in accordance with paragraph 3,
(b) in accordance with another enactment (or an instrument made under an enactment) permitting the disclosure,
(c) in pursuance of an order of a court,
(d) for the purposes of civil proceedings (whether or not within the United Kingdom),
(e) for the purposes of a criminal investigation or criminal proceedings (whether or not within the United Kingdom),
(f) with the consent of each person to whom the information relates, or
(g) with the consent of the Commissioners.
(4) Sub-paragraph (1) applies to each of the following as it applies to a public authority—
(a) an employee or agent of the public authority;
(b) anyone providing services or exercising functions on behalf of the public authority;
(c) anyone authorised by the public authority to receive information on its behalf.

5   (1) It is a defence for a person charged with an offence under paragraph 4 to prove that the person reasonably believed—
(a) that the disclosure was lawful, or
(b) that the information had already and lawfully been made available to the public.
(2) A person guilty of an offence under paragraph 4 is liable—
(a) on conviction on indictment, to imprisonment for a term not exceeding 2 years or a fine, or both;
(b) on summary conviction, to imprisonment for a term not exceeding 12 months or a fine not exceeding the statutory maximum, or both.

(3) A prosecution for an offence under paragraph 4 may be instituted in England and Wales [only by or with the consent of the Director of Public Prosecutions.][1]
(4) A prosecution for an offence under paragraph 4 may be instituted in Northern Ireland only—
  (a) by the Commissioners, or
  (b) with the consent of the Director of Public Prosecutions for Northern Ireland.
(5) In the application of this paragraph—
  (a) in England and Wales, in relation to an offence committed before the commencement of [paragraph 24(2) of Schedule 22 to the Sentencing Act 2020][2], or
  (b) in Northern Ireland,
the reference in sub-paragraph (2)(b) to 12 months is to be read as a reference to 6 months.

Amendments—[1] Words in sub-para (3) substituted by the Public Bodies (Merger of the Director of Public Prosecutions and the Director of Revenue and Customs Prosecutions) Order, SI 2014/834 art 3(3), Sch 2 para 75 with effect from 27 March 2014.
[2] In sub-para (5)(a), words substituted for words "section 154(1) of the Criminal Justice Act 2003" by the Sentencing Act 2020 s 410, Sch 24 para 443(1) with effect from 1 December 2020 (see s 416(1) of that Act, as amended by SI 2020/1236 regs 3, 4(5)).

Enforcement of foreign claims in the UK

6 (1) This paragraph applies if an applicant authority of [a][1] member State makes a request in accordance with MARD for the recovery in the United Kingdom of a claim.
(2) The claim in relation to which such a request is made is referred to as "the foreign claim".
(3) Such steps may be taken by or on behalf of the relevant UK authority to enforce the foreign claim as might be taken (whether or not by the relevant UK authority) to enforce a corresponding UK claim.
(4) "Steps" includes any legal or administrative steps, whether by way of legal proceedings, distress, diligence or otherwise.
(5) See paragraphs 7 and 8 for the meaning of "the relevant UK authority" and "corresponding UK claim".
(6) The steps mentioned in sub-paragraph (3) include exercising any powers of set-off that the relevant UK authority would have been entitled to exercise if the foreign claim had been payable to it under an enactment.
(7) Any enactment or rule of law relating to a corresponding UK claim is to apply, with any necessary adaptations, in relation to the foreign claim.
(8) The enactments applied by sub-paragraph (7) include in particular those relating to the recovery of penalties and to the charging and recovery of interest on unpaid amounts.

Amendments—[1] In sub-para (1) word substituted for word "another" by the MARD (Amendment) (EU Exit) Regulations, SI 2020/996 reg 2(1), (3) with effect from IP completion day (11pm on 31 December 2020).

The relevant UK authority

7 (1) "The relevant UK authority" is—
  (a) if the foreign claim relates to anything other than an agricultural levy, the Commissioners;
  (b) if the foreign claim relates to an agricultural levy and the steps are ones to be taken in or in relation to England, the Commissioners concurrently with the Secretary of State;
  (c) if the foreign claim relates to an agricultural levy and the steps are ones to be taken in or in relation to Wales, the Commissioners concurrently with the Welsh Ministers;
  (d) if the foreign claim relates to an agricultural levy and the steps are ones to be taken in or in relation to Scotland, the Commissioners concurrently with the Scottish Ministers;
  (e) if the foreign claim relates to an agricultural levy and the steps are ones to be taken in or in relation to Northern Ireland, the Commissioners concurrently with the Department of Agriculture and Rural Development.
(2) A reference in this paragraph to claims relating to an agricultural levy includes claims for penalties, fees, surcharges, interest or costs arising in connection with an agricultural levy.

Corresponding UK claim

8 (1) In relation to a foreign claim, "corresponding UK claim" means a claim in the United Kingdom of a kind that appears to the relevant UK authority to correspond most closely to the kind of foreign claim to which the foreign claim belongs.
(2) But if the relevant UK authority concludes that there is nothing in the United Kingdom of a kind that is similar to that kind of foreign claim, "corresponding UK claim" is taken to mean a claim for income tax charged in an assessment and due and payable.

Application of relevant enactments

9 (1) In relation to any kind of foreign claim, the relevant UK authority may by regulations make provision as to the application, non-application or adaptation of any enactment or rule of law relating to corresponding UK claims.
(2) Paragraph 6(7) is subject to any provision so made.

Power to make further provision

10 The Treasury may by regulations make provision about procedural or other supplementary matters for the purpose of giving effect to MARD and any MARD-related instrument.

Contested claims

11 (1) The taking or continuation of steps against a person under paragraph 6(3) must be suspended if the person shows that relevant proceedings are pending, or about to be instituted, before a court, tribunal or other competent body in the member State in question.
(2) "Relevant proceedings" are proceedings relevant to the person's liability on the foreign claim.
(3) Relevant proceedings are "pending" so long as an appeal may be brought against any decision in the proceedings.
(4) Sub-paragraph (1) does not apply to steps that may be taken or continued against the person by the application (by virtue of paragraphs 6(7) and 9) of an enactment or rule of law that permits such steps to be taken or continued in similar circumstances in the case of a corresponding UK claim.
(5) Sub-paragraph (1) ceases to apply if the relevant proceedings are not prosecuted or instituted with reasonable speed.

Claims determined in taxpayer's favour

12 (1) Steps under paragraph 6(3) must not be taken or continued against a person if a final decision on the foreign claim has been given in the person's favour by a court, tribunal or other competent body in the member State in question.
(2) For this purpose, a final decision is one against which no appeal lies or against which an appeal lies within a period that has expired without an appeal having been brought.
(3) If the person shows that such a decision has been given in respect of part of the foreign claim, steps under paragraph 6(3) must not be taken or continued in relation to that part.

Liability to pay

13 In relation to any steps against a person under paragraph 6(3), no question may be raised as to the person's liability on the foreign claim except as mentioned in paragraph 12.

Presumption of validity

14 For the purposes of any steps under paragraph 6(3), a request made by an applicant authority in [a][1] member State is taken to be duly made in accordance with MARD unless the contrary is proved.
Amendments—[1] Word substituted for word "another" by the MARD (Amendment) (EU Exit) Regulations, SI 2020/996 reg 2(1), (4) with effect from IP completion day (11pm on 31 December 2020).

Regulations

15 (1) Regulations under this Schedule are to be made by statutory instrument.
(2) A statutory instrument containing regulations under this Schedule is subject to annulment in pursuance of a resolution of the House of Commons.

Interpretation

16 In this Schedule—
"agricultural levy" has the meaning given by section 6 of the European Communities Act 1972;
"applicant authority" has the same meaning as in MARD;
"the Commissioners" means the Commissioners for Her Majesty's Revenue and Customs;
"enactment" includes—
    (*a*) an Act of the Scottish Parliament,
    (*b*) a Measure or Act of the National Assembly for Wales, and
    (*c*) any Northern Ireland legislation as defined by section 24(5) of the Interpretation Act 1978;
"HMRC" means Her Majesty's Revenue and Customs;
"MARD-related instrument" means any EU instrument (including one made after the passing of this Act) that lays down detailed rules for implementing MARD;

"public authority" means a person with functions of a public nature;
"requested authority" has the same meaning as in MARD.

Consequential amendments etc

17 (1) Section 134 of and Schedule 39 to FA 2002 (which concern Council Directive 2008/55/EC) are repealed with effect from 1 January 2012.
(2) Any outstanding request for assistance made in accordance with Council Directive 2008/55/EC before that date is to be treated on and after that date for the purposes of this Schedule as if it had been made in accordance with MARD.

18 (1) Section 322 of FA 2004 (mutual assistance: customs union with the Principality of Andorra) is amended as follows.
(2), (3) (*amend* FA 2004 s 322(2))
(4) (*substitutes* FA 2004 s 322(3))
(5) (*amends* FA 2004 s 322(4))
(6) The amendments made by this paragraph have effect from 1 January 2012.
(7) Any regulations made by virtue of subsection (4) of section 322 of FA 2004 and in force immediately before 1 January 2012 are to have effect on and after that date as if made by virtue of that subsection as amended by sub-paragraph (5).

Application

19 This Schedule has effect in relation to the recovery of sums becoming due at any time, whether before or after this Act is passed.

FINANCE ACT 2016

2016 Chapter 24

CONTENTS

Schedules
Schedule 18 — Serial tax avoidance

SCHEDULE 18
SERIAL TAX AVOIDANCE

Section 159

PART 1
CONTENTS OF SCHEDULE

1 In this Schedule—
  (a) Part 2 provides for HMRC to give warning notices to persons who incur relevant defeats and includes—
    (i) provision about the duration of warning periods under warning notices (see paragraph 3), and
    (ii) definitions of "relevant defeat" and other key terms;
  (b) Part 3 contains provisions about persons to whom a warning notice has been given, and in particular—
    (i) imposes a duty to give information notices, and
    (ii) allows the Commissioners to publish information about such persons in certain cases involving repeated relevant defeats;
  (c) Part 4 contains provision about the restriction of reliefs;
  (d) Part 5 imposes liability to penalties on persons who incur relevant defeats in relation to arrangements used in warning periods;
  (e) Part 6 contains provisions about corporate groups, associated persons and partnerships;
  (f) Part 7 contains definitions and other supplementary provisions.

PART 2
ENTRY INTO THE REGIME AND BASIC CONCEPTS

Duty to give warning notice

2 (1) This paragraph applies where a person incurs a relevant defeat in relation to any arrangements.
(2) HMRC must give the person a written notice (a "warning notice").
(3) The notice must be given within the period of 90 days beginning with the day on which the relevant defeat is incurred.
(4) The notice must—
  (a) set out when the warning period begins and ends (see paragraph 3),
  (b) specify the relevant defeat to which the notice relates, and
  (c) explain the effect of paragraphs 3 and 17 to 46.
(5) A warning notice given by virtue of paragraph 49 must also explain the effect of paragraph 51 (information in certain cases involving partnerships).
(6) In this Schedule "arrangements" includes any agreement, understanding, scheme, transaction or series of transactions (whether or not legally enforceable).
(7) For the meaning of "relevant defeat" and provision about when a relevant defeat is incurred see paragraph 11.

Warning period

3 (1) If a person is given a warning notice with respect to a relevant defeat (and sub-paragraph (2) does not apply) the period of 5 years beginning with the day after the day on which the notice is given is a "warning period" in relation to that person.
(2) If a person incurs a relevant defeat in relation to arrangements during a period which is a warning period in relation to that person, the warning period is extended to the end of the 5 years beginning with the day after the day on which the relevant defeat occurs.
(3) In relation to a warning period which has been extended under this Schedule, references in this Schedule (including this paragraph) to the warning period are to be read as references to the warning period as extended.

Meaning of "tax"

4 [(1)] [1]In this Schedule "tax" includes any of the following taxes—
  (*a*) income tax,
  (*b*) corporation tax, including any amount chargeable as if it were corporation tax or treated as if it were corporation tax,
  (*c*) capital gains tax,
  (*d*) petroleum revenue tax,
  (*e*) diverted profits tax,
  (*f*) apprenticeship levy,
  (*g*) inheritance tax,
  (*h*) stamp duty land tax,
  (*i*) annual tax on enveloped dwellings,
  (*j*) VAT [and indirect taxes][1], and
  (*k*) national insurance contributions.
[(2) For the purposes of this Schedule "indirect tax" means any of the following—
  insurance premium tax
  general betting duty
  pool betting duty
  remote gaming duty
  machine games duty
  gaming duty
  lottery duty
  bingo duty
  air passenger duty
  hydrocarbon oils duty
  tobacco products duty
  duties on spirits, beer, wine, made-wine and cider
  soft drinks industry levy
  aggregates levy
  landfill tax
  climate change levy
  customs duties.][1]

Amendments—[1] Sub-para (1) numbered as such, in sub-para (1)(*j*), words inserted, and sub-para (2) inserted, by F(No 2)A 2017 s 66, Sch 17 para 55(1), (2) with effect from 1 January 2018.

Meaning of "tax advantage" in relation to VAT

5 (1) In this Schedule "tax advantage", in relation to VAT, is to be read in accordance with sub-paragraphs (2) to (4).
(2) A taxable person obtains a tax advantage if—
  (*a*) in any prescribed accounting period, the amount by which the output tax accounted for by the person exceeds the input tax deducted by the person is less than it would otherwise be,
  (*b*) the person obtains a VAT credit when the person would not otherwise do so, or obtains a larger VAT credit or obtains a VAT credit earlier than would otherwise be the case,
  (*c*) in a case where the person recovers input tax as a recipient of a supply before the supplier accounts for the output tax, the period between the time when the input tax is recovered and the time when the output tax is accounted for is greater than would otherwise be the case, or
  (*d*) in any prescribed accounting period, the amount of the person's non-deductible tax is less than it would otherwise be.
(3) A person who is not a taxable person obtains a tax advantage if the person's non-refundable tax is less than it otherwise would be.
(4) In sub-paragraph (3) "non-refundable tax", in relation to a person who is not a taxable person, means—
  (*a*) VAT on the supply to the person of any goods or services,
  (*b*) . . . [1] and
  (*c*) VAT paid or payable by the person on the importation of any goods . . . [1],
but excluding (in each case) any VAT in respect of which the person is entitled to a refund from the Commissioners by virtue of any provision of VATA 1994.

Northern Ireland—See Sch 9ZA para 79(*a*) (Northern Ireland: this para has effect in relation to NI acquisition VAT as if new sub-para (4)(*b*) were inserted as follows—
"(*b*) VAT on the acquisition by the person of any goods from a member State,".

Amendments—[1] Sub-para (4)(*b*), repealed, and in sub-para (4)(*c*) words "from a place outside the member States" repealed, by the Taxation (Cross-border Trade) Act 2018 s 43, Sch 8 para 121(*a*) with effect from IP completion day (11pm on 31 December 2020), by virtue of SI 2020/1642 reg 4(*b*).
Sub-para (4)(*b*) previously read as follows—
"(*b*) VAT on the acquisition by the person from another member State of any goods,".

Meaning of "non-deductible tax"

6 (1) In this Schedule "non-deductible tax", in relation to a taxable person, means—
   (*a*) input tax for which the person is not entitled to credit under section 25 of VATA 1994, and
   (*b*) any VAT incurred by the person which is not input tax and in respect of which the person is not entitled to a refund from the Commissioners by virtue of any provision of VATA 1994.
(2) For the purposes of sub-paragraph (1)(*b*), the VAT "incurred" by a taxable person is—
   (*a*) VAT on the supply to the person of any goods or services,
   (*b*) . . . [1] and
   (*c*) VAT paid or payable by the person on the importation of any goods . . . [1].

Northern Ireland—See Sch 9ZA para 79(*b*) (Northern Ireland: this para has effect in relation to NI acquisition VAT as if the reference to VAT "incurred" by a taxable person in sub-para (1)(*b*) included VAT on the acquisition by the person of any goods from a member State).
Amendments—[1] Sub-para (2)(*b*) repealed, and in sub-para (2)(*c*) words "from a place outside the member States" repealed, by the Taxation (Cross-border Trade) Act 2018 s 43, Sch 8 para 121(*b*) with effect from IP completion day (11pm on 31 December 2020), by virtue of SI 2020/1642 reg 4(*b*).
Sub-para (2)(*b*) previously read as follows—
"(*b*) VAT on the acquisition by the person from another member State of any goods,".

"Tax advantage": other taxes

7 In relation to taxes other than VAT, "tax advantage" includes—
   (*a*) relief or increased relief from tax,
   (*b*) repayment or increased repayment of tax,
   (*c*) receipt, or advancement of a receipt, of a tax credit,
   (*d*) avoidance or reduction of a charge to tax, an assessment of tax or a liability to pay tax,
   (*e*) avoidance of a possible assessment to tax or liability to pay tax,
   (*f*) deferral of a payment of tax or advancement of a repayment of tax, and
   (*g*) avoidance of an obligation to deduct or account for tax.

"DOTAS arrangements"

8 (1) For the purposes of this Schedule arrangements are "DOTAS arrangements" at any time if they are notifiable arrangements at the time in question and a person—
   (*a*) has provided information in relation to the arrangements under section 308(3), 309 or 310 of FA 2004, or
   (*b*) has failed to comply with any of those provisions in relation to the arrangements.
(2) But for the purposes of this Schedule "DOTAS arrangements" does not include arrangements in respect of which HMRC has given notice under section 312(6) of FA 2004 (notice that promoters not under duty to notify client of reference number).
(3) For the purposes of sub-paragraph (1) a person who would be required to provide information under subsection (3) of section 308 of FA 2004—
   (*a*) but for the fact that the arrangements implement a proposal in respect of which notice has been given under subsection (1) of that section, or
   (*b*) but for subsection (4A), (4C) or (5) of that section,
is treated as providing the information at the end of the period referred to in subsection (3) of that section.
(4) In this paragraph "notifiable arrangements" has the same meaning as in Part 7 of FA 2004.

"Disclosable [Schedule 11A] VAT arrangements"

[8A (1) For the purposes of this Schedule arrangements are "disclosable VAT arrangements" at any time if at that time sub-paragraph (2) or (3) applies.
(2) This sub-paragraph applies if the arrangements are disclosable Schedule 11A VAT arrangements (see paragraph 9).
(3) This paragraph applies if—
   (*a*) the arrangements are notifiable arrangements for the purposes of Schedule 17 to FA 2017,
   (*b*) the main benefit, or one of the main benefits that might be expected to arise from the arrangements is the obtaining of a tax advantage in relation to VAT (within the meaning of paragraph 6 of that Schedule), and

(c) a person—
   (i) has provided information about the arrangements under paragraph 12(1), 17(2) or 18(2) of that Schedule, or
   (ii) has failed to comply with any of those provisions in relation to the arrangements.

(4) But for the purposes of this Schedule arrangements in respect of which HMRC have given notice under paragraph 23(6) of Schedule 17 (notice that promoters not under duty to notify client of reference number) are not to be regarded as "disclosable VAT arrangements".

(5) For the purposes of sub-paragraph (3)(c) a person who would be required to provide information under paragraph 12(1) of Schedule 17 to FA 2017—
   (a) but for the fact that the arrangements implement a proposal in respect of which notice has been given under paragraph 11(1) of that Schedule, or
   (b) but for paragraph 13, 14 or 15 of that Schedule,
is treated as providing the information at the end of the period referred to in paragraph 12(1).][1]

Amendments—[1] In heading, words inserted, and para 8A inserted, by F(No 2)A 2017 s 66, Sch 17 para 55(1), (3), (4) with effect from 1 January 2018.

9 For the purposes of [paragraph 8A][1] arrangements are "disclosable [Schedule 11A][1] VAT arrangements" at any time if at that time—
   (a) a person has complied with paragraph 6 of Schedule 11A to VATA 1994 in relation to the arrangements (duty to notify Commissioners),
   (b) a person under a duty to comply with that paragraph in relation to the arrangements has failed to do so, or
   (c) a reference number has been allocated to the scheme under paragraph 9 of that Schedule (voluntary notification of avoidance scheme which is not a designated scheme).

Amendments—[1] In opening words, words substituted for words "this Schedule", and words inserted, by F(No 2)A 2017 s 66, Sch 17 para 55(1), (5) with effect from 1 January 2018.

["Disclosable indirect tax arrangements"

9A (1) For the purposes of this Schedule arrangements are "disclosable indirect tax arrangements" at any time if at that time—
   (a) the arrangements are notifiable arrangements for the purposes of Schedule 17 to FA 2017,
   (b) the main benefit, or one of the main benefits that might be expected to arise from the arrangements is the obtaining of a tax advantage in relation to an indirect tax other than VAT (within the meaning of paragraph 7 of that Schedule), and
   (c) a person—
      (i) has provided information about the arrangements under paragraph 12(1), 17(2) or 18(2) of that Schedule, or
      (ii) has failed to comply with any of those provisions in relation to the arrangements.

(2) But for the purposes of this Schedule arrangements in respect of which HMRC have given notice under paragraph 23(6) of Schedule 17 to FA 2016 (notice that promoters not under duty to notify client of reference number) are not to be regarded as "disclosable indirect tax arrangements".

(3) For the purposes of sub-paragraph (1)(c) a person who would be required to provide information under paragraph 12(1) of Schedule 17—
   (a) but for the fact that the arrangements implement a proposal in respect of which notice has been given under paragraph 11(1) of that Schedule, or
   (b) but for paragraph 13, 14 or 15 of that Schedule,
is treated as providing the information at the end of the period referred to in paragraph 12(1).][1]

Amendments—[1] Paragraph 9A inserted by F(No 2)A 2017 s 66, Sch 17 para 55(1), (6) with effect from 1 January 2018.

Paragraphs 8 [to 9A]: "failure to comply"

10 (1) A person "fails to comply" with any provision mentioned in paragraph 8(1)[, 8A(2)(c), 9(a) or 9A(1)(c)][1] if and only if any of the conditions in sub-paragraphs (2) to (4) is met.

(2) The condition in this sub-paragraph is that—
   (a) the tribunal has determined that the person has failed to comply with the provision concerned,
   (b) the appeal period has ended, and
   (c) the determination has not been overturned on appeal.

(3) The condition in this sub-paragraph is that—
   (a) the tribunal has determined for the purposes of section 118(2) of TMA 1970 that the person is to be deemed not to have failed to comply with the provision concerned as the person had a reasonable excuse for not doing the thing required to be done,
   (b) the appeal period has ended, and
   (c) the determination has not been overturned on appeal.

(4) The condition in this sub-paragraph is that the person admitted in writing to HMRC that the person has failed to comply with the provision concerned.
(5) In this paragraph "the appeal period" means—
- (a) the period during which an appeal could be brought against the determination of the tribunal, or
- (b) where an appeal mentioned in paragraph (a) has been brought, the period during which that appeal has not been finally determined, withdrawn or otherwise disposed of.

(6) In this paragraph "the tribunal" means the First-tier tribunal or, where determined by or under Tribunal Procedure Rules, the Upper Tribunal.

Amendments—[1] In heading, words substituted for words "and 9", and in sub-para (1), words substituted for words "or 9(a)", by F(No 2)A 2017 s 66, Sch 17 para 55(1), (7), (8) with effect from 1 January 2018.

"Relevant defeat"

11 (1) A person ("P") incurs a "relevant defeat" in relation to arrangements if any of Conditions A to [F][1] is met in relation to P and the arrangements.
(2) The relevant defeat is incurred when the condition in question is first met.

Amendments—[1] In sub-para (1), letter substituted for letter "E" by F(No 2)A 2017 s 66, Sch 17 para 55(1), (9) with effect from 1 January 2018.

Condition A

12 (1) Condition A is that—
- (a) P has been given a notice under paragraph 12 of Schedule 43 to FA 2013 (general anti-abuse rule: notice of final decision), paragraph 8 or 9 of Schedule 43A to that Act (pooling and binding of arrangements: notice of final decision) or paragraph 8 of Schedule 43B to that Act (generic referrals: notice of final decision) stating that a tax advantage arising from the arrangements is to be counteracted,
- (b) that tax advantage has been counteracted under section 209 of FA 2013, and
- (c) the counteraction is final.

(2) For the purposes of this paragraph the counteraction of a tax advantage is "final" when the adjustments made to effect the counteraction, and any amounts arising as a result of those adjustments, can no longer be varied, on appeal or otherwise.

Condition B

13 (1) Condition B is that (in a case not falling within Condition A above) a follower notice has been given to P by reference to the arrangements (and not withdrawn) and—
- (a) the necessary corrective action for the purposes of section 208 of FA 2014 has been taken in respect of the denied advantage, or
- (b) the denied advantage has been counteracted otherwise than as mentioned in paragraph (a) and the counteraction of the denied advantage is final.

(2) In sub-paragraph (1) the reference to giving a follower notice to P includes a reference to giving a partnership follower notice in respect of a partnership return in relation to which P is a relevant partner (as defined in paragraph 2(5) of Schedule 31 to FA 2014).
(3) For the purposes of this paragraph it does not matter whether the denied advantage has been dealt with—
- (a) wholly as mentioned in one or other of paragraphs (a) and (b) of sub-paragraph (1), or
- (b) partly as mentioned in one and partly as mentioned in the other of those paragraphs.

(4) In this paragraph "the denied advantage" has the same meaning as in Chapter 2 of Part 4 of FA 2014 (see section 208(3) of and paragraph 4(3) of Schedule 31 to that Act).
(5) For the purposes of this paragraph the counteraction of a tax advantage is "final" when the adjustments made to effect the counteraction, and any amounts arising as a result of those adjustments, can no longer be varied, on appeal or otherwise.
(6) In this Schedule "follower notice" means a follower notice under Chapter 2 of Part 4 of FA 2014.
(7) For the purposes of this paragraph a partnership follower notice is given "in respect of" the partnership return mentioned in paragraph (a) or (b) of paragraph 2(2) of Schedule 31 to FA 2014.

Condition C

14 (1) Condition C is that (in a case not falling within Condition A or B)—
- (a) the arrangements are DOTAS arrangements,
- (b) P has relied on the arrangements (see sub-paragraph (2))—
- (c) the arrangements have been counteracted, and
- (d) the counteraction is final.

(2) For the purposes of sub-paragraph (1), P "relies on the arrangements" if—

(a) P makes a return, claim or election, or a partnership return is made, on the basis that a relevant tax advantage arises, or

(b) P fails to discharge a relevant obligation ("the disputed obligation") and there is reason to believe that P's failure to discharge that obligation is connected with the arrangements.

(3) For the purposes of sub-paragraph (2) "relevant tax advantage" means a tax advantage which the arrangements might be expected to enable P to obtain.

(4) For the purposes of sub-paragraph (2) an obligation is a "relevant obligation" if the arrangements might be expected to have the result that the obligation does not arise.

(5) For the purposes of this paragraph the arrangements are "counteracted" if—
- (a) adjustments, other than taxpayer emendations, are made in respect of P's tax position—
  - (i) on the basis that the whole or part of the relevant tax advantage mentioned in sub-paragraph (2)(a) does not arise, or
  - (ii) on the basis that the disputed obligation does (or did) arise, or
- (b) an assessment to tax other than a self-assessment is made, or any other action is taken by HMRC, on the basis mentioned in paragraph (a)(i) or (ii) (otherwise than by way of an adjustment).

(6) For the purposes of this paragraph a counteraction is "final" when the assessment, adjustments or action in question, and any amounts arising from the assessment, adjustments or action, can no longer be varied, on appeal or otherwise.

(7) For the purposes of sub-paragraph (1) the time at which it falls to be determined whether or not the arrangements are DOTAS arrangements is when the counteraction becomes final.

(8) The following are "taxpayer emendations" for the purposes of sub-paragraph (5)—
- (a) an adjustment made by P at a time when P had no reason to believe that HMRC had begun or were about to begin enquiries into P's affairs relating to the tax in question;
- (b) an adjustment (by way of an assessment or otherwise) made by HMRC with respect to P's tax position as a result of a disclosure made by P which meets the conditions in sub-paragraph (9).

For the purposes of paragraph (a) a payment in respect of a liability to pay national insurance contributions is not an adjustment unless it is a payment in full.

(9) The conditions are that the disclosure—
- (a) is a full and explicit disclosure of an inaccuracy in a return or other document or of a failure to comply with an obligation, and
- (b) was made at a time when P had no reason to believe that HMRC were about to begin enquiries into P's affairs relating to the tax in question.

(10) For the purposes of this paragraph a contract settlement which HMRC enters into with P is treated as an assessment to tax (other than a self-assessment); and in relation to contract settlements references in sub-paragraph (5) to the basis on which any assessment or adjustments are made, or any other action is taken, are to be read with any necessary modifications.

Condition D

15 (1) Condition D is that—
- (a) P is a taxable person;
- (b) the arrangements are disclosable VAT arrangements to which P is a party,
- (c) P has relied on the arrangements (see sub-paragraph (2));
- (d) the arrangements have been counteracted, and
- (e) the counteraction is final.

(2) For the purposes of sub-paragraph (1) P "relies on the arrangements" if—
- (a) P makes a return or claim on the basis that a relevant tax advantage arises, or
- b) P fails to discharge a relevant obligation ("the disputed obligation") and there is reason to believe that P's failure to discharge that obligation is connected with those arrangements.

(3) For the purposes of sub-paragraph (2) "relevant tax advantage" means a tax advantage which the arrangements might be expected to enable P to obtain.

(4) For the purposes of sub-paragraph (2) an obligation is a "relevant obligation" if the arrangements might be expected to have the result that the obligation does not arise.

(5) For the purposes of this paragraph the arrangements are "counteracted" if—
- (a) adjustments, other than taxpayer emendations, are made in respect of P's tax position—
  - (i) on the basis that the whole or part of the relevant tax advantage mentioned in sub-paragraph (2)(a) does not arise, or
  - (ii) on the basis that the disputed obligation does (or did) arise, or
- (b) an assessment to tax is made, or any other action is taken by HMRC, on the basis mentioned in paragraph (a)(i) or (ii) (otherwise than by way of an adjustment).

(6) For the purposes of this paragraph a counteraction is "final" when the assessment, adjustments or action in question, and any amounts arising from the assessment, adjustments or action, can no longer be varied, on appeal or otherwise.
(7) For the purposes of sub-paragraph (1) the time at which it falls to be determined whether or not the arrangements are disclosable VAT arrangements is when the counteraction becomes final.
(8) The following are "taxpayer emendations" for the purposes of sub-paragraph (5)—
  (a) an adjustment made by P at a time when P had no reason to believe that HMRC had begun or were about to begin enquiries into P's affairs relating to VAT;
  (b) an adjustment made by HMRC with respect to P's tax position (by way of an assessment or otherwise) as a result of a disclosure made by P which meets the conditions in sub-paragraph (9).
(9) The conditions are that the disclosure—
  (a) is a full and explicit disclosure of an inaccuracy in a return or other document or of a failure to comply with an obligation, and
  (b) was made at a time when P had no reason to believe that HMRC were about to begin enquiries into P's affairs relating to VAT.

Condition E

16 (1) Condition E is that the arrangements are disclosable VAT arrangements to which P is a party and—
  (a) the arrangements relate to the position with respect to VAT of a person other than P ("S") who has made supplies of goods or services to P,
  (b) the arrangements might be expected to enable P to obtain a tax advantage in connection with those supplies of goods or services,
  (c) the arrangements have been counteracted, and
  (d) the counteraction is final.
(2) For the purposes of this paragraph the arrangements are "counteracted" if—
  (a) HMRC assess S to tax or take any other action on a basis which prevents P from obtaining (or obtaining the whole of) the tax advantage in question, or
  (b) adjustments, other than taxpayer emendations, are made in relation to S's VAT affairs on a basis such as is mentioned in paragraph (a).
(3) For the purposes of this paragraph a counteraction is "final" when the assessment, adjustments or action in question, and any amounts arising from the assessment, adjustments or action, can no longer be varied, on appeal or otherwise.
(4) For the purposes of sub-paragraph (1) the time when it falls to be determined whether or not the arrangements are disclosable VAT arrangements is when the counteraction becomes final.
(5) The following are "taxpayer emendations" for the purposes of sub-paragraph (2)—
  (a) an adjustment made by S at a time when neither P nor S had reason to believe that HMRC had begun or were about to begin enquiries into the affairs of S or P relating to VAT;
  (b) an adjustment (by way of an assessment or otherwise) made by HMRC with respect to S's tax position as a result of a disclosure made by S which meets the conditions in sub-paragraph (6).
(6) The conditions are that the disclosure—
  (a) is a full and explicit disclosure of an inaccuracy in a return or other document or of a failure to comply with an obligation, and
  (b) was made at a time when neither S nor P had reason to believe that HMRC were about to begin enquiries into the affairs of S or P relating to VAT.

[Condition F

16A (1) Condition F is that—
  (a) the arrangements are indirect tax arrangements,
  (b) P has relied on the arrangements (see sub-paragraph (2)),
  (c) the arrangements have been counteracted, and
  (d) the counteraction is final.
(2) For the purpose of sub-paragraph (1) P relies on the arrangements if—
  (a) P makes a return, claim, declaration or application for approval on the basis that a relevant tax advantage arises, or
  (b) P fails to discharge a relevant obligation ("the disputed obligation") and there is reason to believe that P's failure to discharge that obligation is connected with the arrangements.
(3) For the purposes of sub-paragraph (2) "relevant tax advantage" means a tax advantage which the arrangements might be expected to enable P to obtain.
(4) For the purposes of sub-paragraph (2) an obligation is a relevant obligation if the arrangements might be expected to have the result that the obligation does not arise.

(5) For the purposes of this paragraph the arrangements are "counteracted" if—
  (a) adjustments, other than taxpayer emendations, are made in respect of P's tax position —
    (i) on the basis that the whole or part of the relevant tax advantage mentioned in sub-paragraph (2)(a) does not arise, or
    (ii) on the basis that the disputed obligation does (or did) arise, or
  (b) an assessment to tax is made, or any other action is taken by HMRC, on the basis mentioned in paragraph (a)(i) or (ii) (otherwise than by way of an adjustment).
(6) For the purposes of this paragraph a "counteraction" is final when the adjustments, assessment or action in question, and any amounts arising from the adjustments, assessment or action, can no longer be varied, on appeal or otherwise.
(7) For the purposes of sub-paragraph (1) the time at which it falls to be determined whether or not the arrangements are disclosable indirect tax arrangements is when the counteraction becomes final.
(8) The following are "taxpayer emendations" for the purposes of sub-paragraph (5)—
  (a) an adjustment made by P at a time when P had no reason to believe that HMRC had begun or were about to begin enquiries into P's affairs in relation to the tax in question;
  (b) an adjustment made by HMRC with respect to P's tax position (whether by way of an assessment or otherwise) as a result of a disclosure by P which meets the conditions in sub-paragraph (9).
(9) The conditions are that the disclosure—
  (a) is a full and explicit disclosure of an inaccuracy in a return or other document or of a failure to comply with an obligation, and
  (b) was made at a time when P had no reason to believe that HMRC were about to begin enquiries into P's affairs in relation to the tax in question.][1]

Amendments—[1] Paragraph 16A inserted by F(No 2)A 2017 s 66, Sch 17 para 55(1), (10) with effect from 1 January 2018.

PART 3
ANNUAL INFORMATION NOTICES AND NAMING

Annual information notices

17 (1) A person ("P") who has been given a warning notice under this Schedule must give HMRC a written notice (an "information notice") in respect of each reporting period in the warning period (see sub-paragraph (11)).
(2) An information notice must be given not later than the 30th day after the end of the reporting period to which it relates.
(3) An information notice must state whether or not P—
  (a) has in the reporting period delivered a return, or made a claim[, election, declaration or application for approval,][1] on the basis that a relevant tax advantage arises, or has since the end of the reporting period delivered on that basis a return which P was required to deliver before the end of that period,
  (b) has in the reporting period failed to take action which P would be required to take under or by virtue of an enactment relating to tax but for particular [disclosable][1] arrangements to which P is a party,
  (c) has in the reporting period become a party to arrangements which—
    (i) relate to the position with respect to VAT of another person ("S") who has made supplies of goods or services to P, and
    (ii) might be expected to enable P to obtain a relevant tax advantage ("the expected tax advantage") in connection with those supplies of goods or services,
  (d) has failed to deliver a return which P was required to deliver by a date falling in the reporting period.
(4) In this paragraph "relevant tax advantage" means a tax advantage which particular [disclosable][1] arrangements enable, or might be expected to enable, P to obtain.
(5) If P has, in the reporting period concerned, made a return, claim[, election, declaration or application for approval,][1] on the basis mentioned in sub-paragraph (3)(a) or failed to take action as mentioned in sub-paragraph (3)(b) the information notice must—
  (a) explain (on the assumptions made by P in so acting or failing to act) how the [disclosable][1] arrangements enable P to obtain the tax advantage, or (as the case may be) have the result that P is not required to take the action in question, and
  (b) state (on the same assumptions) the amount of the relevant tax advantage mentioned in sub-paragraph (3)(a) or (as the case may be) the amount of any tax advantage which arises in connection with the absence of a requirement to take the action mentioned in sub-paragraph (3)(b).
(6) If P has, in the reporting period, become a party to arrangements such as are mentioned in sub-paragraph (3)(c), the information notice—
  (a) must state whether or not it is P's view that the expected tax advantage arises to P, and

(b) if that is P's view, must explain how the arrangements enable P to obtain the tax advantage and state the amount of the tax advantage.

(7) If the time by which P must deliver a return falls within a reporting period and P fails to deliver the return by that time, HMRC may require P to give HMRC a written notice (a "supplementary information notice") setting out any matters which P would have been required to set out in an information notice had P delivered the return in that reporting period.

(8) A requirement under sub-paragraph (7) must be made by a written notice which states the period within which P must comply with the notice.

(9) If P fails to comply with a requirement of (or imposed under) this paragraph HMRC may by written notice extend the warning period to the end of the period of 5 years beginning with—
- (a) the day by which the information notice or supplementary information notice should have been given (see sub-paragraphs (2) and (8)) or, as the case requires,
- (b) the day on which P gave the defective information notice or supplementary information notice to HMRC,

or, if earlier, the time when the warning period would have expired but for the extension.

(10) HMRC may permit information notices given by members of the same group of companies (as defined in paragraph 46(9)) to be combined.

(11) For the purposes of this paragraph—
- (a) the first reporting period in any warning period begins with the first day of the warning period and ends with a day specified by HMRC ("the specified day"),
- (b) the remainder of the warning period is divided into further reporting periods each of which begins immediately after the end of the preceding reporting period and is twelve months long or (if that would be shorter) ends at the end of the warning period.

[(12) In this paragraph "disclosable arrangements" means any of the following—
- (a) DOTAS arrangements,
- (b) disclosable VAT arrangements, and
- (c) disclosable indirect tax arrangements.][1]

Amendments—[1] In sub-paras (3)(a), (5), words substituted for words "or election", in sub-paras (3)(b), (4), (5)(a), word substituted for words "DOTAS arrangements or VAT", and sub-para 12 inserted, by F(No 2)A 2017 s 66, Sch 17 para 55(1), (11) with effect from 1 January 2018.

Naming

18 (1) The Commissioners may publish information about a person if the person—
- (a) incurs a relevant defeat in relation to arrangements which the person has used in a warning period, and
- (b) has been given at least two warning notices in respect of other defeats of arrangements which were used in the same warning period.

(2) Information published for the first time under sub-paragraph (1) must be published within the 12 months beginning with the day on which the most recent of the warning notices falling within that sub-paragraph has been given to the person.

(3) No information may be published (or continue to be published) after the end of the period of 12 months beginning with the day on which it is first published.

(4) The information that may be published is—
- (a) the person's name (including any trading name, previous name or pseudonym),
- (b) the person's address (or registered office),
- (c) the nature of any business carried on by the person,
- (d) information about the fiscal effect of the defeated arrangements (had they not been defeated), for instance information about total amounts of tax understated or total amounts by which claims, or statements of losses, have been adjusted,
- (e) the amount of any penalty to which the person is liable under paragraph 30 in respect of the relevant defeat of any defeated arrangements,
- (f) the periods in which or times when the defeated arrangements were used, and
- (g) any other information the Commissioners may consider it appropriate to publish in order to make clear the person's identity.

(5) If the person mentioned in sub-paragraph (1) is a member of a group of companies (as defined in paragraph 46(9)), the information which may be published also includes—
- (a) any trading name of the group, and
- (b) information about other members of the group of the kind described in sub-paragraph (4)(a), (b) or (c).

(6) If the person mentioned in sub-paragraph (1) is a person carrying on a trade or business in partnership, the information which may be published also includes—
- (a) any trading name of the partnership, and

(b) information about other members of the partnership of the kind described in sub-paragraph (4)(a) or (b).

(7) The information may be published in any manner the Commissioners may consider appropriate.

(8) Before publishing any information the Commissioners—
 (a) must inform the person that they are considering doing so, and
 (b) afford the person reasonable opportunity to make representations about whether or not it should be published.

(9) Arrangements are "defeated arrangements" for the purposes of sub-paragraph (4) if the person used them in the warning period mentioned in sub-paragraph (1) and a warning notice specifying the defeat of those arrangements has been given to the person before the information is published.

(10) If a person has been given a single warning notice in relation to two or more relevant defeats, the person is treated for the purposes of this paragraph as having been given a separate warning notice in relation to each of those relevant defeats.

(11) Nothing in this paragraph prevents the power under sub-paragraph (1) from being exercised on a subsequent occasion in relation to arrangements used by the person in a different warning period.

PART 4
RESTRICTION OF RELIEFS

Duty to give a restriction relief notice

19 (1) HMRC must give a person a written notice (a "restriction of relief notice") if—
 (a) the person incurs a relevant defeat in relation to arrangements which the person has used in a warning period,
 (b) the person has been given at least two warning notices in respect of other relevant defeats of arrangements which were used in that same warning period, and
 (c) the defeats mentioned in paragraphs (a) and (b) meet the conditions in sub-paragraph (2).

(2) The conditions are—
 (a) that each of the relevant defeats is by virtue of Condition A, B or C,
 (b) that each of the relevant defeats relates to the misuse of a relief (see sub-paragraph (5)), and
 (c) in the case of each of the relevant defeats, either—
  (i) that the relevant counteraction (see sub-paragraph (7)) was made on the basis that a particular avoidance-related rule applies in relation to a person's affairs, or
  (ii) that the misused relief is a loss relief.

(3) In sub-paragraph (2)(c)—
 (a) the "misused relief" means the relief mentioned in sub-paragraph (5), and
 (b) "loss relief" means any relief under Part 4 of ITA 2007 or Part 4 or 5 of CTA 2010.

(4) A restriction of relief notice must—
 (a) explain the effect of paragraphs 20, 21 and 22, and
 (b) set out when the restricted period is to begin and end.

(5) For the purposes of this Part of this Schedule, a relevant defeat by virtue of Condition A, B or C "relates to the misuse of a relief" if—
 (a) the tax advantage in question, or part of the tax advantage in question, is or results from (or would but for the counteraction be or result from) a relief or increased relief from tax, or
 (b) it is reasonable to conclude that the making of a particular claim for relief, or the use of a particular relief, is a significant component of the arrangements in question.

(6) In sub-paragraph (5) "the tax advantage in question" means—
 (a) in relation to a defeat by virtue of Condition A, the tax advantage mentioned in paragraph 12(1)(a),
 (b) in relation to a defeat by virtue of Condition B, the denied advantage (as defined in paragraph 13(4)), or
 (c) in relation to a defeat by virtue of Condition C—
  (i) the tax advantage mentioned in paragraph 14(2)(a), or, as the case requires,
  (ii) the absence of the relevant obligation (as defined in paragraph 14(4)).

(7) In this paragraph "the relevant counteraction", in relation to a relevant defeat means—
 (a) in the case of a defeat by virtue of Condition A, the counteraction referred to in paragraph 12(1)(c);
 (b) in the case of a defeat by virtue of Condition B, the action referred to in paragraph 13(1);
 (c) in the case of a defeat by virtue of Condition C, the counteraction referred to in paragraph 14(1)(d).

(8) If a person has been given a single warning notice in relation to two or more relevant defeats, the person is treated for the purposes of this paragraph as having been given a separate warning notice in relation to each of those relevant defeats.

Restriction of relief

20 (1) Sub-paragraphs (2) to (15) have effect in relation to a person to whom a relief restriction notice has been given.
(2) The person may not, in the restricted period, make any claim for relief.
(3) Sub-paragraph (2) does not have effect in relation to—
 (a) a claim for relief under Schedule 8 to FA 2003 (stamp duty land tax: charities relief);
 (b) a claim for relief under Chapter 3 of Part 8 of ITA 2007 (gifts of shares, securities and real property to charities etc);
 (c) a claim for relief under Part 10 of ITA 2007 (special rules about charitable trusts etc);
 (d) a claim for relief under double taxation arrangements;
 (e) an election under section 426 of ITA 2007 (gift aid: election to treat gift as made in previous year).
(4) Claims under the following provisions in Part 4 of FA 2004 (registered pension schemes: tax reliefs etc) do not count as claims for relief for the purposes of this paragraph—
 section 192(4) (increase of basic rate limit and higher rate limit);
 section 193(4) (net pay arrangements: excess relief);
 section 194(1) (relief on making of a claim).
(5) The person may not, in the restricted period, surrender group relief under Part 5 of CTA 2010.
(6) No deduction is to be made under section 83 of ITA 2007 (carry forward against subsequent trade profits) in calculating the person's net income for a relevant tax year.
(7) No deduction is to be made under section 118 of ITA 2007 (carry-forward property loss relief) in calculating the person's net income for a relevant tax year.
(8) The person is not entitled to relief under section 448 (annual payments: relief for individuals) or 449 (annual payments: relief for other persons) of ITA 2007 for any payment made in the restricted period.
(9) No deduction of expenses referable to a relevant accounting period is to be made under section 1219(1) of CTA 2009 (expenses of management of a company's investment business).
(10) No reduction is to be made under section 45(4) of CTA 2010 (carry-forward of trade loss relief) in calculating the profits for a relevant accounting period of a trade carried on by the person.
(11) In calculating the total amount of chargeable gains accruing to a person in a relevant tax year (or part of a relevant tax year), no losses are to be deducted under subsections (2) to (2B) of section 2 of TCGA 1992 (persons and gains chargeable to capital gains tax, and allowable losses).
(12) In calculating the total amount of ATED-related chargeable gains accruing to a person in a relevant tax year, no losses are to be deducted under subsection (3) of section 2B of TCGA 1992 (persons chargeable to capital gains tax on ATED-related gains).
(13) In calculating the total amount of chargeable NRCGT gains accruing to a person in a relevant tax year on relevant high value disposals, no losses are to be deducted under subsection (2) of section 14D of TCGA 1992 (persons chargeable to capital gains tax on NRCGT gains).
(14) If the person is a company, no deduction is to be made under section 62 of CTA 2010 (relief for losses made in UK property business) from the company's total profits of a relevant accounting period.
(15) No deduction is to be made under regulation 18 of the Unauthorised Unit Trusts (Tax) Regulations 2013 (S.I. 2013/2819) (relief for deemed payments by trustees of an exempt unauthorised unit trust) in calculating the person's net income for a relevant tax year.
(16) In this paragraph "relevant tax year" means any tax year the first day of which is in the restricted period.
(17) In this paragraph "relevant accounting period" means an accounting period the first day of which is in the restricted period.
(18) In this paragraph "double taxation arrangements" means arrangements which have effect under section 2(1) of TIOPA 2010 (double taxation relief by agreement with territories outside the UK).

The restricted period

21 (1) In paragraphs 19 and 20 (and this paragraph) "the restricted period" means the period of 3 years beginning with the day on which the relief restriction notice is given.
(2) If during the restricted period (or the restricted period as extended under this sub-paragraph) the person to whom a relief restriction notice has been given incurs a further relevant defeat meeting the conditions in sub-paragraph (4), HMRC must give the person a written notice (a "restricted period extension notice").
(3) A restricted period extension notice extends the restricted period to the end of the period of 3 years beginning with the day on which the further relevant defeat occurs.
(4) The conditions mentioned in sub-paragraph (2) are that—
 (a) the relevant defeat is incurred by virtue of Condition A, B or C in relation to arrangements which the person used in the warning period mentioned in paragraph 19(1)(a), and

(b) the warning notice given to the person in respect of the relevant defeat relates to the misuse of a relief.
(5) If the person to whom a relief restriction notice has been given incurs a relevant defeat which meets the conditions in sub-paragraph (4) after the restricted period has expired but before the end of a concurrent warning period, HMRC must give the person a restriction of relief notice.
(6) In sub-paragraph (5) "concurrent warning period" means a warning period which at some time ran concurrently with the restricted period.

Reasonable excuse

22 (1) If a person who has incurred a relevant defeat satisfies HMRC or, on an appeal under paragraph 24, the First-tier Tribunal or Upper Tribunal that the person had a reasonable excuse for the matters to which that relevant defeat relates, then—
    (a) for the purposes of paragraph 19(1)(a) and 21(2) and (5), the person is treated as not having incurred that relevant defeat, and
    (b) for the purposes of paragraph 19(1)(b) and (c) any warning notice given to the person which relates to that relevant defeat is treated as not having been given to the person.
(2) For the purposes of this paragraph, in the case of a person ("P")—
    (a) an insufficiency of funds is not a reasonable excuse unless attributable to events outside P's control,
    (b) where P relies on another person to do anything, that is not a reasonable excuse unless P took reasonable care to avoid the relevant failure, and
    (c) where P had reasonable excuse for the relevant failure but the excuse had ceased, P is to be treated as having continued to have the excuse if the failure is remedied without unreasonable delay after the excuse ceased.
(3) In determining for the purposes of this paragraph whether or not a person ("P") had a reasonable excuse for any action, failure or inaccuracy, reliance on advice is to be taken automatically not to constitute a reasonable excuse if the advice is addressed to, or was given to, a person other than P or takes no account of P's individual circumstances.
(4) In this paragraph "relevant failure", in relation to a relevant defeat, is to be interpreted in accordance with sub-paragraphs (2) to (7) of paragraph 43.

Mitigation of restriction of relief

23 (1) The Commissioners may mitigate the effects of paragraph 20 in relation to a person ("P") so far as it appears to them that there are exceptional circumstances such that the operation of that paragraph would otherwise have an unduly serious impact with respect to the tax affairs of P or another person.
(2) For the purposes of sub-paragraph (1) the Commissioners may modify the effects of paragraph 20 in any way they think appropriate, including by allowing P access to the whole or part of a relief to which P would otherwise not be entitled as a result of paragraph 20.

Appeal

24 (1) A person may appeal against—
    (a) a relief restriction notice, or
    (b) a restricted period extension notice.
(2) An appeal under this paragraph must be made within the period of 30 days beginning with the day on which the notice is given.
(3) An appeal under this paragraph is to be treated in the same way as an appeal against an assessment to income tax (including by the application of any provision about bringing the appeal by notice to HMRC, about HMRC's review of the decision or about determination of the appeal by the First-tier Tribunal or Upper Tribunal).
(4) On an appeal the tribunal may—
    (a) cancel HMRC's decision, or
    (b) affirm that decision with or without any modifications in accordance with sub-paragraph (5).
(5) On an appeal the tribunal may rely on paragraph 23 (mitigation of restriction of relief)—
    (a) to the same extent as HMRC (which may mean applying the same mitigation as HMRC to a different starting point), or
    (b) to a different extent, but only if the tribunal thinks that HMRC's decision in respect of the application of paragraph 23 was flawed.
(6) In this paragraph "tribunal" means the First-tier Tribunal or Upper Tribunal (as appropriate by virtue of sub-paragraph (3)).

Meaning of "avoidance-related rule"

25 (1) In this Part of this Schedule "avoidance-related rule" means a rule in Category 1 or 2.
(2) A rule is in Category 1 if it refers (in whatever terms)—
 (*a*) to the purpose or main purpose or purposes of a transaction, arrangements or any other action or matter, and
 (*b*) to whether or not the purpose in question is or involves the avoidance of tax or the obtaining of any advantage in relation to tax (however described).
(3) A rule is also in Category 1 if it refers (in whatever terms) to—
 (*a*) expectations as to what are, or may be, the expected benefits of a transaction, arrangements or any other action or matter, and
 (*b*) whether or not the avoidance of tax or the obtaining of any advantage in relation to tax (however described) is such a benefit.
For the purposes of paragraph (*b*) it does not matter whether the reference is (for instance) to the "sole or main benefit" or "one of the main benefits" or any other reference to a benefit.
(4) A rule falls within Category 2 if as a result of the rule a person may be treated differently for tax purposes depending on whether or not purposes referred to in the rule (for instance the purposes of an actual or contemplated action or enterprise) are (or are shown to be) commercial purposes.
(5) For example, a rule in the following form would fall within Category 1 and within Category 2—

"Example rule
 Section X does not apply to a company in respect of a transaction if the company shows that the transaction meets Condition A or B.
 Condition A is that the transaction is effected—
  (*a*) for genuine commercial reasons, or
  (*b*) in the ordinary course of managing investments.
 Condition B is that the avoidance of tax is not the main object or one of the main objects of the transaction."

Meaning of "relief"

26 The following are "reliefs" for the purposes of this Part of this Schedule—
 (*a*) any relief from tax (however described) which must be claimed, or which is not available without making an election,
 (*b*) relief under section 1219 of CTA 2009 (expenses of management of a company's investment business),
 (*c*) any relief (not falling within paragraph (*a*)) under Part 4 of ITA 2007 (loss relief) or Part 4 or 5 of CTA 2010 (loss relief and group relief), and
 (*d*) any relief (not falling within paragraph (*a*) or (*b*)) under a provision listed in section 24 of ITA 2007 (reliefs deductible at Step 2 of the calculation of income tax liability).

"Claim" for relief

27 In this Part of this Schedule "claim for relief" includes any election or other similar action which is in substance a claim for relief.

VAT [and indirect taxes]

28 In this Part of this Schedule "tax" does not include VAT [or any other indirect tax][1].
Amendments—[1] In heading and text, words inserted by F(No 2)A 2017 s 66, Sch 17 para 55(1), (12), (13) with effect from 1 January 2018.

Power to amend

29 (1) The Treasury may by regulations—
 (*a*) amend paragraph 20;
 (*b*) amend paragraph 26.
(2) Regulations under sub-paragraph (1)(*a*) may, in particular, alter the application of paragraph 20 in relation to any relief, exclude any relief from its application or extend its application to further reliefs.
(3) Regulations under sub-paragraph (1)(*b*) may amend the meaning of "relief" in any way (including by extending or limiting the meaning).
(4) Regulations under this paragraph may—
 (*a*) make supplementary, incidental and consequential provision;
 (*b*) make transitional provision.
(5) Regulations under this paragraph are to be made by statutory instrument.

PART 5
PENALTY

Penalty

30 (1) A person is liable to pay a penalty if the person incurs a relevant defeat in relation to any arrangements which the person has used in a warning period.
(2) The penalty is 20% of the value of the counteracted advantage if neither sub-paragraph (3) nor sub-paragraph (4) applies.
(3) The penalty is 40% of the value of the counteracted advantage if before the relevant defeat is incurred the person has been given, or become liable to be given, one (but not more than one) relevant prior warning notice.
(4) The penalty is 60% of the value of the counteracted advantage if before the current defeat is incurred the person has been given, or become liable to be given, two or more relevant prior warning notices.
(5) In this paragraph "relevant prior warning notice" means a warning notice in relation to the defeat of arrangements which the person has used in the warning period mentioned in sub-paragraph (1).
(6) For the meaning of "the value of the counteracted advantage" see paragraphs 32 to 37.

Simultaneous defeats etc

31 (1) If a person incurs simultaneously two or more relevant defeats in relation to different arrangements, sub-paragraphs (2) to (4) of paragraph 30 have effect as if the relevant defeat with the lowest value was incurred last, the relevant defeat with the next lowest value immediately before it, and so on.
(2) For this purpose the "value" of a relevant defeat is taken to be equal to the value of the counteracted advantage.
(3) If a person has been given a single warning notice in relation to two or more relevant defeats, the person is treated for the purposes of paragraph 30 as having been given a separate warning notice in relation to each of those relevant defeats.

Value of the counteracted advantage: basic rule for taxes other than VAT

32 (1) In relation to a relevant defeat incurred by virtue of Condition A, B[, C or F][1], the "value of the counteracted advantage" is—
  (a) in the case of a relevant defeat incurred by virtue of Condition A, the additional amount due or payable in respect of tax as a result of the counteraction mentioned in paragraph 12(1)(c);
  (b) in the case of a relevant defeat incurred by virtue of Condition B, the additional amount due or payable in respect of tax as a result of the action mentioned in paragraph 13(1);
  (c) in the case of a relevant defeat incurred by virtue of Condition C, the additional amount due or payable in respect of tax as a result of the counteraction mentioned in paragraph 14(1)(d);
  [(d) in the case of a relevant defeat incurred by virtue of Condition F, the additional amount due or payable in respect of tax as a result of the counteraction mentioned in paragraph 16A(1)(d).][1]
(2) The reference in sub-paragraph (1) to the additional amount due and payable includes a reference to—
  (a) an amount payable to HMRC having erroneously been paid by way of repayment of tax, and
  (b) an amount which would be repayable by HMRC if the counteraction mentioned in paragraph (a)[, (c) or (d)][1] of sub-paragraph (1) were not made or the action mentioned in paragraph (b) of that sub-paragraph were not taken (as the case may be).
(3) The following are ignored in calculating the value of the counteracted advantage—
  (a) group relief, and
  (b) any relief under section 458 of CTA 2010 (relief in respect of repayment etc of loan) which is deferred under subsection (5) of that section.
(4) This paragraph is subject to paragraphs 33 and 34.

Amendments—[1] In sub-para (1), words substituted for words "or C", sub-para (1)(d) inserted, and in sub-para (2)(b), words substituted for words "or c" by F(No 2)A 2017 s 66, Sch 17 para 55(1), (14) with effect from 1 January 2018.

Value of counteracted advantage: losses for purposes of direct tax

33 (1) This paragraph has effect in relation to relevant defeats incurred by virtue of Condition A, B or C.

(2) To the extent that the counteracted advantage (see paragraph 35) has the result that a loss is wrongly recorded for the purposes of direct tax and the loss has been wholly used to reduce the amount due or payable in respect of tax, the value of the counteracted advantage is determined in accordance with paragraph 32.
(3) To the extent that the counteracted advantage has the result that a loss is wrongly recorded for purposes of direct tax and the loss has not been wholly used to reduce the amount due or payable in respect of tax, the value of the counteracted advantage is—
 (a) the value under paragraph 32 of so much of the counteracted advantage as results from the part (if any) of the loss which is used to reduce the amount due or payable in respect of tax, plus
 (b) 10% of the part of the loss not so used.
(4) Sub-paragraphs (2) and (3) apply both—
 (a) to a case where no loss would have been recorded but for the counteracted advantage, and
 (b) to a case where a loss of a different amount would have been recorded (but in that case sub-paragraphs (2) and (3) apply only to the difference between the amount recorded and the true amount).
(5) To the extent that a counteracted advantage creates or increases an aggregate loss recorded for a group of companies—
 (a) the value of the counteracted advantage is calculated in accordance with this paragraph, and
 (b) in applying paragraph 32 in accordance with sub-paragraphs (2) and (3), group relief may be taken into account (despite paragraph 32(3)).
(6) To the extent that the counteracted advantage results in a loss, the value of it is nil where, because of the nature of the loss or the person's circumstances, there is no reasonable prospect of the loss being used to support a claim to reduce a tax liability (of any person).

Value of counteracted advantage: deferred tax

34 (1) To the extent that the counteracted advantage (see paragraph 35) is a deferral of tax (other than VAT), the value of that advantage is—
 (a) 25% of the amount of the deferred tax for each year of the deferral, or
 (b) a percentage of the amount of the deferred tax, for each separate period of deferral of less than a year, equating to 25% per year,
or, if less, 100% of the amount of the deferred tax.
(2) This paragraph does not apply to a case to the extent that paragraph 33 applies.

Meaning of "the counteracted advantage" in paragraphs 33 and 34

35 (1) In paragraphs 33 and 34 "the counteracted advantage" means—
 (a) in relation to a relevant defeat incurred by virtue of Condition A, the tax advantage mentioned in paragraph 12(1)(b);
 (b) in relation to a relevant defeat incurred by virtue of Condition B, the denied advantage in relation to which the action mentioned in paragraph 13(1) is taken;
 (c) in relation to a relevant defeat incurred by virtue of Condition C, means any tax advantage in respect of which the counteraction mentioned in paragraph 14(1)(c) is made;
 [(d) in relation to a relevant defeat incurred by virtue of Condition F, means any tax advantage in respect of which the counteraction mentioned in paragraph 16A(1)(c) is made.][1]
(2) In sub-paragraph (1)(c) "counteraction" is to be interpreted in accordance with paragraph 14(5).
Amendments—[1]   Sub-para (1)(d) inserted by F(No 2)A 2017 s 66, Sch 17 para 55(1), (15) with effect from 1 January 2018.

Value of the counteracted advantage: Conditions D and E

36 (1) In relation to a relevant defeat incurred by a person by virtue of Condition D or E, the "value of the counteracted advantage" is equal to the sum of any counteracted tax advantages determined under sub-paragraphs (3) to (6). But see also paragraph 37.
(2) In this paragraph "the counteraction" means the counteraction mentioned in paragraph 15(1) or 16(1) (as the case may be).
(3) If the amount of VAT due or payable by the person in respect of any prescribed accounting period (X) exceeds the amount (Y) that would have been so payable but for the counteraction, the amount by which X exceeds Y is a counteracted tax advantage.
(4) If the person obtains no VAT credit for a particular prescribed accounting period, the amount of any VAT credit which the person would have obtained for that period but for the counteraction is a counteracted tax advantage.
(5) If for a prescribed accounting period the person obtains a VAT credit of an amount (Y) which is less than the amount (X) of the VAT credit which the person would have obtained but for the counteraction, the amount by which X exceeds Y is a counteracted tax advantage.

(6) If the amount (X) of the person's non-deductible tax for any prescribed accounting period is greater than Y, where Y is what would be the amount of the person's non-deductible tax for that period but for the counteraction, then the amount by which X exceeds Y is a counteracted tax advantage, but only to the extent that amount is not represented by a corresponding amount which is the whole or part of a counteracted tax advantage by virtue of sub-paragraphs (3) to(5).
(7) In this paragraph "non-deductible tax", in relation to the person who incurred the relevant defeat, means—
   (a) input tax for which the person is not entitled to credit under section 25 of VATA 1994, and
   (b) any VAT incurred by the person which is not input tax and in respect of which the person is not entitled to a refund from the Commissioners by virtue of any provision of VATA 1994.
(8) For the purposes of sub-paragraph (7)(b) the VAT "incurred" by a taxable person is—
   (a) VAT on the supply to the person of any goods or services,
   (b) . . . [1]
   (c) VAT on the importation of any goods . . . [1].
(9) References in sub-paragraph (3) to amounts due and payable by the person in respect of a prescribed accounting period include references to—
   (a) amounts payable to HMRC having erroneously been paid by way of repayment of tax, and
   (b) amounts which would be repayable by HMRC if the counteraction mentioned in sub-paragraph (3) were not made.

Northern Ireland—See Sch 9ZA para 79(b) (Northern Ireland: this para has effect in relation to NI acquisition VAT as if the reference to VAT "incurred" by a taxable person in sub-para (7)(b) included VAT on the acquisition by the person of any goods from a member State).

Amendments—[1] Sub-para (8)(b) repealed, and in sub-para (8)(c) words "from a place outside the member States" repealed, by the Taxation (Cross-border Trade) Act 2018 s 43, Sch 8 para 121(c) with effect from IP completion day (11pm on 31 December 2020), by virtue of SI 2020/1642 reg 4(b).
Sub-para (8)(b) previously read as follows—
   "(b) VAT on the acquisition by the person from another member State of any goods;".

Value of counteracted advantage: delayed VAT

37 (1) Sub-paragraph (3) of paragraph 36 has effect as follows so far as the tax advantage which is counteracted as mentioned in that sub-paragraph is in the nature of a delay in relation to the person's obligations with respect to VAT.
(2) That sub-paragraph has effect as if for "the amount by which X exceeds Y is a counteracted tax advantage" there were substituted, "there is a counteracted tax advantage of—
   (d) 25% of the amount of the delayed VAT for each year of the delay, or
   (e) a percentage of the amount of the delayed VAT, for each separate period of delay of less than a year, equating to 25% per year,
or, if less, 100% of the amount of the delayed VAT".

Assessment of penalty

38 (1) Where a person is liable for a penalty under paragraph 30, HMRC must assess the penalty.
(2) Where HMRC assess the penalty, HMRC must—
   (a) notify the person who is liable for the penalty, and
   (b) state in the notice a tax period in respect of which the penalty is assessed.
(3) A penalty under this paragraph must be paid before the end of the period of 30 days beginning with the day on which the person is notified of the penalty under sub-paragraph (2).
(4) An assessment—
   (a) is to be treated for procedural purposes as if it were an assessment to tax,
   (b) may be enforced as if it were an assessment to tax, and
   (c) may be combined with an assessment to tax.
(5) An assessment of a penalty under this paragraph must be made before the end of the period of 12 months beginning with the date of the defeat mentioned in paragraph 30(1).

Alteration of assessment of penalty

39 (1) After notification of an assessment has been given to a person under paragraph 38(2), the assessment may not be altered except in accordance with this paragraph or on appeal.
(2) A supplementary assessment may be made in respect of a penalty if an earlier assessment operated by reference to an underestimate of the value of the counteracted advantage.
(3) An assessment may be revised as necessary if operated by reference to an overestimate of the value of the counteracted advantage.

Aggregate penalties

40 (1) The amount of a penalty for which a person is liable under paragraph 30 is to be reduced by the amount of any other penalty incurred by the person, or any surcharge for late payment of tax imposed on the person, if the amount of the penalty or surcharge is determined by reference to the same tax liability.
(2) In sub-paragraph (1) "any other penalty" does not include a penalty under section 212A of FA 2013 (GAAR penalty) or Part 4 of FA 2014 (penalty where corrective action not taken after follower notice etc).
(3) In the application of section 97A of TMA 1970 (multiple penalties) no account shall be taken of a penalty under paragraph 30.

Appeal against penalty

41 (1) A person may appeal against a decision of HMRC that a penalty is payable under paragraph 30.
(2) A person may appeal against a decision of HMRC as to the amount of a penalty payable by P under paragraph 30.
(3) An appeal under this paragraph must be made within the period of 30 days beginning with the day on which notification of the penalty is given under paragraph 38.
(4) An appeal under this paragraph is to be treated in the same way as an appeal against an assessment to the tax concerned (including by the application of any provision about bringing the appeal by notice to HMRC, about HMRC's review of the decision or about determination of the appeal by the First-tier Tribunal or Upper Tribunal).
(5) Sub-paragraph (4) does not apply—
  (*a*) so as to require a person to pay a penalty before an appeal against the assessment of the penalty is determined, or
  (*b*) in respect of any other matter expressly provided for by this Part of this Schedule.
(6) On an appeal under sub-paragraph (1) or (2) the tribunal may—
(*a*) affirm HMRC's decision, or
(*b*) substitute for HMRC's decision another decision that HMRC has power to make.
(7) In this paragraph "tribunal" means the First-tier Tribunal or Upper Tribunal (as appropriate by virtue of sub-paragraph (4)).

Penalties: reasonable excuse

42 (1) A person is not liable to a penalty under paragraph 30 in respect of a relevant defeat if the person satisfies HMRC or (on appeal) the First-tier Tribunal or Upper Tribunal that the person had a reasonable excuse for the relevant failure to which that relevant defeat relates (see paragraph 43).
(2) Sub-paragraph (3) applies if—
  (*a*) a person has incurred a relevant defeat in respect of which the person is liable to a penalty under paragraph 30, and
  (*b*) before incurring that defeat the person had been given, or become liable to be given, an excepted warning notice.
(3) The person is treated for the purposes of sub-paragraphs (2) to (4) of paragraph 30 (rate of penalty) as not having been given, and not having become liable to be given, the excepted notice (so far as it relates to the relevant defeat in respect of which the person had a reasonable excuse).
(4) A warning notice is "excepted" for the purposes of this paragraph if the person was not liable to a penalty in respect of the defeat specified in it because the person had a reasonable excuse for the relevant failure in question.
(5) For the purposes of this paragraph, in the case of a person ("P")—
  (*a*) an insufficiency of funds is not a reasonable excuse unless attributable to events outside P's control,
  (*b*) where P relies on another person to do anything, that is not a reasonable excuse unless P took reasonable care to avoid the relevant failure, and
  (*c*) where P had a reasonable excuse for the relevant failure but the excuse had ceased, P is to be treated as having continued to have the excuse if the failure is remedied without unreasonable delay after the excuse ceased.
(6) In determining for the purposes of this paragraph whether or not a person ("P") had a reasonable excuse for any action, failure or inaccuracy, reliance on advice is to be taken automatically not to constitute a reasonable excuse if the advice is addressed to, or was given to, a person other than P or takes no account of P's individual circumstances.

Paragraph 42: meaning of "the relevant failure"

43 (1) In paragraph 42 "the relevant failure", in relation to a relevant defeat, is to be interpreted in accordance with sub-paragraphs (2) to (7).

(2) In relation to a relevant defeat incurred by virtue of Condition A, "the relevant failure" means the failures or inaccuracies as a result of which the counteraction under section 209 of FA 2013 was necessary
(3) In relation to a relevant defeat incurred by virtue of Condition B, "the relevant failure" means the failures or inaccuracies in respect of which the action mentioned in paragraph 13(1) was taken.
(4) In relation to a relevant defeat incurred by virtue of Condition C, "the relevant failure" means the failures of inaccuracies as a result of which the adjustments, assessments, or other action mentioned in paragraph 14(5) are required.
(5) In relation to a relevant defeat incurred by virtue of Condition D, "the relevant failure" means the failures or inaccuracies as a result of which the adjustments, assessments or other action mentioned in paragraph 15(5) are required.
(6) In relation to a relevant defeat incurred by virtue of Condition E, "the relevant failure" means P's actions (and failures to act), so far as they are connected with matters in respect of which the counteraction mentioned in paragraph 16(1) is required.
(7) In sub-paragraph (6) "counteraction" is to be interpreted in accordance with paragraph 16(2).
[(8) In relation to a relevant defeat incurred by virtue of Condition F, "the relevant failure" means the failures or inaccuracies as a result of which the adjustments, assessments, or other actions mentioned in paragraph 16A(5) are required.][1]
Amendments—[1] Sub-para (8) inserted by F(No 2)A 2017 s 66, Sch 17 para 55(1), (16) with effect from 1 January 2018.

Mitigation of penalties

44 (1) The Commissioners may in their discretion mitigate a penalty under paragraph 30, or stay or compound any proceedings for such a penalty.
(2) They may also, after judgment, further mitigate or entirely remit the penalty.

PART 6
CORPORATE GROUPS, ASSOCIATED PERSONS AND PARTNERSHIPS

Representative member of a VAT group

45 (1) Where a body corporate ("R") is the representative member of a group (and accordingly is treated for the purposes of this Schedule as mentioned in section 43(1) of VATA 1994), anything which has been done by or in relation to another body corporate ("B") in B's capacity as representative member of that group is treated for the purposes of this Schedule as having been done by or in relation to R in R's capacity as representative member of the group. Accordingly paragraph 3 (warning period) operates as if the successive representative members of a group were a single person.
(2) This Schedule has effect as if the representative member of a group, so far as acting in its capacity as such, were a different person from that body corporate so far as acting in any other capacity.
(3) In this paragraph the reference to a "group" is to be interpreted in accordance with sections 43A to 43D of VATA 1994.

Corporate groups

46 (1) Sub-paragraphs (2) and (3) apply if HMRC has a duty under paragraph 2 to give a warning notice to a company ("C") which is a member of a group.
(2) That duty has effect as a duty to give a warning notice to each current group member (see sub-paragraph (8)).
(3) Any warning notice which has been given (or is treated as having been given) previously to any current group member is treated as having been given to each current group member (and any provision in this Schedule which refers to a "warning period" in relation to a person is to be interpreted accordingly).
But see sub-paragraphs (4) and (5).
(4) In relation to a company which incurs a relevant defeat, paragraph 19(1) (duty to give relief restriction notice) does not have effect unless the warning period mentioned in that sub-paragraph would be a warning period in relation to the company regardless of sub-paragraph (3).
(5) A company which incurs a relevant defeat is not liable to pay a penalty under paragraph 30 unless the warning period mentioned in sub-paragraph (1) of that paragraph would be a warning period in relation to the company regardless of sub-paragraph (3).
(6) HMRC may discharge any duty to give a warning notice to a current group member in accordance with sub-paragraph (2) by delivering the notice to C (and if it does so may combine one or more warning notices in a single notice).
(7) If a company ceases to be a member of a group, and—
   (*a*) immediately before it ceases to be a member of the group, a warning period has effect in relation to the company, but

(b) no warning period would have effect in relation to the company at that time but for sub-paragraph (2) or (3),

that warning period ceases to have effect in relation to the company when it ceases to be a member of that group.

(8) In this paragraph "current group member" means a company which is a member of the group concerned at the time when the warning notice mentioned in sub-paragraph (1) is given.

(9) For the purposes of this paragraph two companies are members of the same group of companies if—

(a) one is a 75% subsidiary of the other, or

(b) both are 75% subsidiaries of a third company.

(10) In this paragraph "75% subsidiary" has the meaning given by section 1154 of CTA 2010.

(11) In this paragraph "company" has the same meaning as in the Corporation Tax Acts (see section 1121 of CTA 2010).

Associated persons treated as incurring relevant defeats

47 (1) Sub-paragraph (2) applies if a person ("P") incurs a relevant defeat in relation to any arrangements (otherwise than by virtue of this paragraph).

(2) Any person ("S") who is associated with P at the relevant time is also treated for the purposes of paragraphs 2 (duty to give warning notice) and 3(2) (warning period) as having incurred that relevant defeat in relation to those arrangements (but see sub-paragraph (3)).

For the meaning of "associated" see paragraph 48.

(3) Sub-paragraph (2) does not apply if P and S are members of the same group of companies (as defined in paragraph 46(9)).

(4) In relation to a warning notice given to S by virtue of sub-paragraph (2), paragraph 2(4)(c) (certain information to be included in warning notice) is to be read as referring only to paragraphs 3, 17 and 18.

(5) A warning notice which is given to a person by virtue of sub-paragraph (2) is treated for the purposes of paragraphs 19(1) (duty to give relief restriction notice) and 30 (penalty) as not having been given to that person.

(6) In sub-paragraph (2) "the relevant time" means the time when P is given a warning notice in respect of the relevant defeat.

Meaning of "associated"

48 (1) For the purposes of paragraph 47 two persons are associated with one another if—

(a) one of them is a body corporate which is controlled by the other, or

(b) they are bodies corporate under common control.

(2) Two bodies corporate are under common control if both are controlled—

(a) by one person,

(b) by two or more, but fewer than six, individuals, or

(c) by any number of individuals carrying on business in partnership.

(3) For the purposes of this section a body corporate ("H") is taken to control another body corporate ("B") if—

(a) H is empowered by statute to control B's activities, or

(b) H is B's holding company within the meaning of section 1159 of and Schedule 6 to the Companies Act 2006.

(4) For the purposes of this section an individual or individuals are taken to control a body corporate ("B") if the individual or individuals, were they a body corporate, would be B's holding company within the meaning of those provisions.

Partners treated as incurring relevant defeats

49 (1) Where paragraph 50 applies in relation to a partnership return, each relevant partner is treated for the purposes of this Schedule as having incurred the relevant defeat mentioned in paragraph 50(1)(b), (2) or (3)(b) (as the case may be).

(2) In this paragraph "relevant partner" means any person who was a partner in the partnership at any time during the relevant reporting period (but see sub-paragraph (3)).

(3) The "relevant partners" do not include—

(a) the person mentioned in sub-paragraph (1)(b), (2) or (3)(b) (as the case may be) of paragraph 50, or

(b) any other person who would, apart from this paragraph, incur a relevant defeat in connection with the subject matter of the partnership return mentioned in sub-paragraph (1).

(4) In this paragraph the "relevant reporting period" means the period in respect of which the partnership return mentioned in sub-paragraph (1), (2) or (3) of paragraph 50 was required.

Partnership returns to which this paragraph applies

50 (1) This paragraph applies in relation to a partnership return if—
   (a) that return has been made on the basis that a tax advantage arises to a partner from any arrangements, and
   (b) that person has incurred, in relation to that tax advantage and those arrangements, a relevant defeat by virtue of Condition A (final counteraction of tax advantage under general anti-abuse rule).

(2) Where a person has incurred a relevant defeat by virtue of sub-paragraph (2) of paragraph 13 (Condition B: case involving partnership follower notice) this paragraph applies in relation to the partnership return mentioned in that sub-paragraph.

(3) This paragraph applies in relation to a partnership return if—
   (a) that return has been made on the basis that a tax advantage arises to a partner from any arrangements, and
   (b) that person has incurred, in relation to that tax advantage and those arrangements, a relevant defeat by virtue of Condition C (return, claim or election made in reliance on DOTAS arrangements).

(4) The references in this paragraph to a relevant defeat do not include a relevant defeat incurred by virtue of paragraph 47(2).

Partnerships: information

51 (1) If paragraph 50 applies in relation to a partnership return, the appropriate partner must give HMRC a written notice (a "partnership information notice") in respect of each sub-period in the information period.

(2) The "information period" is the period of 5 years beginning with the day after the day of the relevant defeat mentioned in paragraph 50.

(3) If, in the case of a partnership, a new information period (relating to another partnership return) begins during an existing information period, those periods are treated for the purposes of this paragraph as a single period (which includes all times that would otherwise fall within either period).

(4) An information period under this paragraph ends if the partnership ceases.

(5) A partnership information notice must be given not later than the 30th day after the end of the sub-period to which it relates.

(6) A partnership information notice must state—
   (a) whether or not any relevant partnership return which was, or was required to be, delivered in the sub-period has been made on the basis that a relevant tax advantage arises, and
   (b) whether or not there has been a failure to deliver a relevant partnership return in the sub-period.

(7) In this paragraph—
   (a) "relevant partnership return" means a partnership return in respect of the partnership's trade, profession or business;
   (b) "relevant tax advantage" means a tax advantage which particular DOTAS arrangements enable, or might be expected to enable, a person who is or has been a partner in the partnership to obtain.

(8) If a partnership information notice states that a relevant partnership return has been made on the basis mentioned in sub-paragraph (6)(a) the notice must—
   (a) explain (on the assumptions made for the purposes of the return) how the DOTAS arrangements enable the tax advantage concerned to be obtained, and
   (b) describe any variation in the amounts required to be stated in the return under section 12AB(1) of TMA 1970 which results from those arrangements.

(9) HMRC may require the appropriate partner to give HMRC a notice (a "supplementary information notice") setting out further information in relation to a partnership information notice. In relation to a partnership information notice "further information" means information which would have been required to be set out in the notice by virtue of sub-paragraph (6)(a) or (8) had there not been a failure to deliver a relevant partnership return.

(10) A requirement under sub-paragraph (9) must be made by a written notice and the notice must state the period within which the notice must be complied with.

(11) If a person fails to comply with a requirement of (or imposed under) this paragraph, HMRC may by written notice extend the information period concerned to the end of the period of 5 years beginning with—
   (a) the day by which the partnership information notice or supplementary information notice was required to be given to HMRC or, as the case requires,
   (b) the day on which the person gave the defective notice to HMRC,

or, if earlier, the time when the information period would have expired but for the extension.

(12) For the purposes of this paragraph—

(a) the first sub-period in an information period begins with the first day of the information period and ends with a day specified by HMRC,

(b) the remainder of the information period is divided into further sub-periods each of which begins immediately after the end of the preceding sub-period and is twelve months long or (if that would be shorter) ends at the end of the information period.

(13) In this paragraph "the appropriate partner" means the partner in the partnership who is for the time being nominated by HMRC for the purposes of this paragraph.

Prospective amendments—In sub-para (8)(*b*), words ", or under equivalent provision made by regulations under paragraph 10 of Schedule A1 to that Act," to be inserted after words "TMA 1970" by F(No 2)A 2017 s 61(1), Sch 14 paras 47, 48(1), (2) with effect from a day to be appointed.

Partnerships: special provision about taxpayer emendations

52 (1) Sub-paragraph (2) applies if a partnership return is amended at any time under section 12ABA of TMA 1970 (amendment of partnership return by representative partner etc) on a basis that—

(a) results in an increase or decrease in, or

(b) otherwise affects the calculation of,

any amount stated under subsection (1)(*b*) of section 12AB of that Act (partnership statement) as a partner's share of any income, loss, consideration, tax or credit for any period.

(2) For the purposes of paragraph 14 (Condition C: counteraction of DOTAS arrangements), the partner is treated as having at that time amended—

(a) the partner's return under section 8 or 8A of TMA 1970, or

(b) the partner's company tax return,

so as to give effect to the amendments of the partnership return.

(3) Sub-paragraph (4) applies if a partnership return is amended at any time by HMRC as a result of a disclosure made by the representative partner or that person's successor on a basis that—

(a) results in an increase or decrease in, or

(b) otherwise affects the calculation of,

any amount stated under subsection (1)(*b*) of section 12AB of TMA 1970 (partnership statement) as the share of a particular partner (P) of any income, loss, consideration, tax or credit for any period.

(4) If the conditions in sub-paragraph (5) are met, P is treated for the purposes of paragraph 14 as having at that time amended—

(a) P's return under section 8 or 8A of TMA 1970, or

(b) P's company tax return,

so as to give effect to the amendments of the partnership return.

(5) The conditions are that the disclosure—

(a) is a full and explicit disclosure of an inaccuracy in the partnership return, and

(b) was made at a time when neither the person making the disclosure nor P had reason to believe that HMRC was about to begin enquiries into the partnership return.

Prospective amendments—The following amendments to be made by F(No 2)A 2017 s 61(1), Sch 14 paras 47, 48(1), (3) with effect from a day to be appointed—

– in sub-para (1), words "section 12AB(1)(*b*) of that Act or under equivalent provision made by regulations under paragraph 10 of Schedule A1 to that Act (partnership statement)" to be substituted for words "subsection (1)(*b*) of section 12AB of that Act (partnership statement)"; and

– in sub-para (3), in words at the beginning, words "(in the case of a section 12AA partnership return) or the nominated partner (in the case of a Schedule A1 partnership return)" to be inserted after words "that person's successor", and in words at the end, words "section 12AB(1)(*b*) of TMA 1970 or under equivalent provision made by regulations under paragraph 10 of Schedule A1 to that Act (partnership statement)" to be substituted for words "subsection (1)(*b*) of section 12AB of TMA 1970 (partnership statement)".

Supplementary provision relating to partnerships

53 (1) In paragraphs 49 to 52 and this paragraph—

"partnership" is to be interpreted in accordance with section 12AA of TMA 1970 (and includes a limited liability partnership);

"the representative partner", in relation to a partnership return, means the person who was required by a notice served under or for the purposes of section 12AA(2) or (3) of TMA 1970 to deliver the return;

"successor", in relation to a person who is the representative partner in the case of a partnership return, has the same meaning as in TMA 1970 (see section 118(1) of that Act).

(2) For the purposes of this Part of this Schedule a partnership is treated as the same partnership notwithstanding a change in membership if any person who was a member before the change remains a member after the change.

Prospective amendments—In sub-s (1), in definition of "the representative partner", words "section 12AA" to be inserted after words "in relation to a", and definition of "the nominated partner" to be inserted after definition of "successor", by F(No 2)A 2017 s 61(1), Sch 14 paras 47, 48(1), (4) with effect from a day to be appointed. Definition as inserted to read as follows—
> ""the nominated partner", in relation to a Schedule A1 partnership return, has the meaning given by paragraph 5 of Schedule A1 to TMA 1970.".

PART 7
SUPPLEMENTAL

Meaning of "adjustments"

54 (1) In this Schedule "adjustments" means any adjustments, whether by way of an assessment, the modification of an assessment or return, amendment or disallowance of a claim, a payment, the entering into of a contract settlement, or otherwise (and references to "making" adjustments accordingly include securing that adjustments are made by entering into a contract settlement).
(2) "Adjustments" also includes a payment in respect of a liability to pay national insurance contributions.

Time of "use" of defeated arrangements

55 (1) With reference to a particular relevant defeat incurred by a person in relation to arrangements, the person is treated as having "used" the arrangements on the dates set out in this paragraph.
(2) If the person incurs the relevant defeat by virtue of Condition A, the person is treated as having "used" the arrangements on the following dates—
  (*a*) the filing date of any return made by the person on the basis that the tax advantage mentioned in paragraph 12(1)(*a*) arises from the arrangements;
  (*b*) the date on which the person makes any claim or election on that basis;
  (*c*) the date of any relevant failure by the person to comply with an obligation.
(3) For the purposes of sub-paragraph (2) a failure to comply with an obligation is a "relevant failure" if the whole or part of the tax advantage mentioned in paragraph 12(1)(*b*) arose as a result of, or in connection with, that failure.
(4) If the person incurs the relevant defeat by virtue of Condition B, the person is treated as having "used" the arrangements on the following dates—
  (*a*) the filing date of any return made by the person on the basis that the asserted advantage (see section 204(3) of FA 2014) results from the arrangements,
  (*b*) the date on which any claim is made by the person on that basis,
  (*c*) the date of any failure by the person to comply with a relevant obligation.
In this sub-paragraph "relevant obligation" means an obligation which would not have fallen on the person (or might have been expected not to do so), had the denied advantage arisen (see section 208(3) of FA 2014).
(5) If the person incurs the relevant defeat by virtue of Condition C, the person is treated as having "used" the arrangements on the following dates—
  (*a*) the filing date of any return made by the person on the basis mentioned in paragraph 14(2)(*a*);
  (*b*) the date on which the person makes any claim or election on that basis;
  (*c*) the date of any failure by the person to comply with a relevant obligation (as defined in paragraph 14(4)).
(6) If the person incurs the relevant defeat by virtue of Condition D, the person is treated as having "used" the arrangements on the following dates—
  (*a*) the filing date of any return made by the person on the basis mentioned in paragraph 15(2)(*a*);
  (*b*) the date on which the person makes any claim on that basis;
  (*c*) the date of any failure by the person to comply with a relevant obligation (as defined in paragraph 15(4)).
(7) If the person incurs the relevant defeat by virtue of Condition E, the person is treated as having "used" the arrangements on the following dates—
  (*a*) the filing date of any return made by S to which the counteraction mentioned in paragraph 16(1)(*c*) relates;
  (*b*) the date on which S made any claim to which that counteraction relates;
  (*c*) the date of any relevant failure by S to which that counteraction relates.
(8) In sub-paragraph (7) "relevant failure" means a failure to comply with an obligation relating to VAT.
[(8A) If the person incurs the relevant defeat by virtue of Condition F, the person is treated as having "used" the arrangements on the following dates—
  (*a*) the filing date of any return made by the person on the basis mentioned in paragraph 16A(2)(*a*);
  (*b*) the date on which the person makes any claim, declaration or application for approval;

(c) the date of any failure by the person to comply with a relevant obligation (as defined in paragraph 16A(4)).][1]

(9) In this paragraph "filing date", in relation to a return, means the earlier of—
   (a) the day on which the return is delivered, or
   (b) the last day of the period within which the return must be delivered.

(10) References in this paragraph to the date on which a person fails to comply with an obligation are to the date on which the person is first in breach of the obligation.

Amendments—[1] Sub-para (8A) inserted by F(No 2)A 2017 s 66, Sch 17 para 55(1), (17) with effect from 1 January 2018.

Inheritance tax

56 (1) In the case of inheritance tax, each of the following is treated as a return for the purposes of this Schedule—
   (a) an account delivered by a person under section 216 or 217 of IHTA 1984 (including an account delivered in accordance with regulations under section 256 of that Act);
   (b) a statement or declaration which amends or is otherwise connected with such an account produced by the person who delivered the account;
   (c) information or a document provided by a person in accordance with regulations under section 256 of that Act;
and such a return is treated as made by the person in question.

(2) In this Schedule (except where the context requires otherwise) "assessment", in relation to inheritance tax, includes a determination.

National insurance contributions

57 (1) In this Schedule references to an assessment to tax include a NICs decision relating to a person's liability for relevant contributions.

(2) In this Schedule a reference to a provision of Part 7 of FA 2004 (disclosure of tax avoidance schemes) (a "DOTAS provision") includes a reference to—
   (a) that DOTAS provision as applied by regulations under section 132A of the Social Security Administration Act 1992 (disclosure of contributions avoidance arrangements);
   (b) any provision of regulations under that section that corresponds to that DOTAS provision, whenever the regulations are made.

(3) Regulations under section 132A of that Act may disapply, or modify the effect of, sub-paragraph (2).

(4) In this paragraph "NICs decision" means a decision under section 8 of the Social Security Contributions (Transfer of Functions, etc) Act 1999 or Article 7 of the Social Security Contributions (Transfer of Functions, etc) (Northern Ireland) Order 1999 (S.I. 1999/671).

General interpretation

58 (1) In this Schedule—
"arrangements" has the meaning given by paragraph 2(6);
"the Commissioners" means the Commissioners for Her Majesty's Revenue and Customs;
"contract settlement" means an agreement in connection with a person's liability to make a payment to the Commissioners under or by virtue of an enactment;
["disclosable indirect tax arrangements" is to be interpreted in accordance with paragraph 9A;
"disclosable Schedule 11A VAT arrangements" is to be interpreted in accordance with paragraph 9;][1]
"disclosable VAT arrangements" is to be interpreted in accordance with paragraph [8A][1];
"DOTAS arrangements" is to be interpreted in accordance with paragraph 8 (and see also paragraph 57(2));
"follower notice" has the meaning given by paragraph 13(6);
"HMRC" means Her Majesty's Revenue and Customs;
["indirect tax" has the meaning given by paragraph 4(2);][1]
"national insurance contributions" means contributions under Part 1 of the Social Security Contributions and Benefits Act 1992 or Part 1 of the Social Security Contributions and Benefits (Northern Ireland) Act 1992;
"net income" has the meaning given by section 23 of ITA 2007 (see Step 2 of that section);
"partnership follower notice" has the meaning given by paragraph 2(2) of Schedule 31 to FA 2014;
"partnership return" means a return under section 12AA of TMA 1970;

"relevant contributions" means the following contributions under Part 1 of the Social Security Contributions and Benefits Act 1992 or Part 1 of the Social Security Contributions and Benefits (Northern Ireland) Act 1992—
- (a) Class 1 contributions;
- (b) Class 1A contributions;
- (c) Class 1B contributions;
- (d) Class 2 contributions which must be paid but in relation to which section 11A of the Act in question (application of certain provisions of the Income Tax Acts in relation to Class 2 contributions under section 11(2) of that Act) does not apply;

"relevant defeat" is to be interpreted in accordance with paragraph 11;
"tax" has the meaning given by paragraph [4(1)][1];
"tax advantage" has the meaning given by paragraph 7;
"warning notice" has the meaning given by paragraph 2.

(2) In this Schedule an expression used in relation to VAT has the same meaning as in VATA 1994.

(3) In this Schedule (except where the context requires otherwise) references, however expressed, to a person's affairs in relation to tax include the person's position as regards deductions or repayments of, or of sums representing, tax that the person is required to make by or under an enactment.

(4) For the purposes of this Schedule a partnership return is regarded as made on the basis that a particular tax advantage arises to a person from particular arrangements if—
- (a) it is made on the basis that an increase or reduction in one or more of the amounts mentioned in section 12AB(1) of TMA 1970 (amounts in the partnership statement in a partnership return) results from those arrangements, and
- (b) that increase or reduction results in that tax advantage for the person.

Amendments—[1] In sub-para (1), definitions of "disclosable indirect tax arrangements", "disclosable Schedule 11A VAT arrangements" and "indirect tax" inserted; in definition of "disclosable VAT arrangements", reference substituted for reference "9"; and in definition of "tax", reference substituted for reference "4", by F(No 2)A 2017 s 66, Sch 17 para 55(1), (18) with effect from 1 January 2018.

Prospective amendments—In sub-s (1), definition of "partnership return" to be substituted by F(No 2)A 2017 s 61(1), Sch 14 paras 47, 48(1), (5) with effect from a day to be appointed. Definition as substituted to read as follows—

"""partnership return" means a return—
under section 12AA of TMA 1970 (a "section 12AA partnership return"), or
required by regulations made under paragraph 10 of Schedule A1 to TMA 1970 (a "Schedule A1 partnership return");".

Consequential amendments

59 In section 103ZA of TMA 1970 (disapplication of sections 100 to 103 in the case of certain penalties)—
- (a) omit "or" at the end of paragraph (ga), and
- (b) after paragraph (h) insert "or
    - (i) Part 5 of Schedule 18 to the Finance Act 2016 (serial tax avoidance)."

60 In section 212 of FA 2014 (follower notices: aggregate penalties), in subsection (4)—
- (a) omit "or" at the end of paragraph (b), and
- (b) after paragraph (c) insert ", or
    - (d) Part 5 of Schedule 18 to FA 2016 (serial tax avoidance)."

61 (1) The Social Security Contributions and Benefits Act 1992 is amended as follows.
(2) In section 11A (application of certain provisions of the Income Tax Acts in relation to Class 2 contributions under section 11(2)), in subsection (1), at the end of paragraph (e) insert—
"(ea) the provisions of Schedule 18 to the Finance Act 2016 (serial tax avoidance);".
(3) In section 16 (application of Income Tax Acts and destination of Class 4 contributions), in subsection (1), at the end of paragraph (d) insert "and
"(e) the provisions of Schedule 18 to the Finance Act 2016 (serial tax avoidance),".

62 In the Social Security Contributions and Benefits (Northern Ireland) Act 1992, in section 11A (application of certain provisions of the Income Tax Acts in relation to Class 2 contributions under section 11(2)), in subsection (1), at the end of paragraph (e) insert—
"(ea) the provisions of Schedule 18 to the Finance Act 2016 (serial tax avoidance);".

Commencement

63 Subject to paragraphs 64 and 65, paragraphs 1 to 62 of this Schedule have effect in relation to relevant defeats incurred after the day on which this Act is passed.

64 (1) A relevant defeat is to be disregarded for the purposes of this Schedule if it is incurred before 6 April 2017 in relation to arrangements which the person has entered into before the day on which this Act is passed.

(2) A relevant defeat incurred on or after 6 April 2017 is to be disregarded for the purposes of this Schedule if—
   (a) the person entered into the arrangements concerned before the day on which this Act is passed, and
   (b) before 6 April 2017—
       (i) the person incurring the defeat fully discloses to HMRC the matters to which the relevant counteraction relates, or
       (ii) that person gives HMRC notice of a firm intention to make a full disclosure of those matters and makes such a full disclosure within any time limit set by HMRC.

(3) In sub-paragraph (2) "the relevant counteraction" means—
   (a) in a case within Condition A, the counteraction mentioned in paragraph 12(1)(c);
   (b) in a case within Condition B, the action mentioned in paragraph 13(1);
   (c) in a case within Condition C, the counteraction mentioned in paragraph 14(1)(c);
   (d) in a case within Condition D, the counteraction mentioned in paragraph 15(1)(d);
   (e) in a case within Condition E, the counteraction mentioned in paragraph 16(1)(c).

(4) In sub-paragraph (3)—
   (a) in paragraph (c) "counteraction" is to be interpreted in accordance with paragraph 14(5);
   (b) in paragraph (d) "counteraction" is to be interpreted in accordance with paragraph 15(5);
   (c) in paragraph (e) "counteraction" is to be interpreted in accordance with paragraph 16(2).

(5) See paragraph 11(2) for provision about when a relevant defeat is incurred. 65 (1) A warning notice given to a person is to be disregarded for the purposes of—
   (a) paragraph 18 (naming), and
   (b) Part 4 of this Schedule (restriction of reliefs), if the relevant defeat specified in the notice relates to arrangements which the person has entered into before the day on which this Act is passed.

(2) Where a person has entered into any arrangements before the day on which this Act is passed—
   (a) a relevant defeat incurred by a person in relation to the arrangements, and
   (b) any warning notice specifying such a relevant defeat, is to be disregarded for the purposes of paragraph 30 (penalty).

65 (1) A warning notice given to a person is to be disregarded for the purposes of—
   (a) paragraph 18 (naming), and
   (b) Part 4 of this Schedule (restriction of reliefs),
if the relevant defeat specified in the notice relates to arrangements which the person has entered into before the day on which this Act is passed.

(2) Where a person has entered into any arrangements before the day on which this Act is passed—
   (a) a relevant defeat incurred by a person in relation to the arrangements, and
   (b) any warning notice specifying such a relevant defeat,
is to be disregarded for the purposes of paragraph 30 (penalty).

FINANCE (NO 2) ACT 2017

CONTENTS

PART 3
FULFILMENT BUSINESSES

48	Carrying on a third country goods fulfilment business
49	Requirement for approval
50	Register of approved persons
51	Regulations relating to approval, registration etc.
52	Disclosure of information by HMRC
53	Offence
54	Forfeiture
55	Penalties
56	Appeals
57	Regulations
58	Interpretation
59	Commencement
	Schedules

Schedule 13 — Third country goods fulfilment businesses: penalty
Schedule 17 — Disclosure of tax avoidance schemes: VAT and other indirect taxes

PART 3
FULFILMENT BUSINESSES

48 Carrying on [an imported goods] fulfilment business

(1) For the purposes of this Part a person carries on [an imported goods][1] fulfilment business if the person, by way of business—
   (a) stores [imported goods][1] which are owned by a person who is not [UK-established][1], or
   (b) stores [imported goods][1] on behalf of a person who is not [UK-established][1],
at a time when the conditions in subsection (2) are met in relation to the goods.
(2) The conditions are that—
   (a) there has been no supply of the goods in the United Kingdom for the purposes of VATA 1994, and
   (b) the goods are being offered for sale in the United Kingdom or elsewhere.
(3) But a person does not carry on [an imported goods][1] fulfilment business if the person's activities within subsection (1) are incidental to the carriage of the goods.
[(4) Goods are "imported goods" if they have been imported into the United Kingdom for the purposes of VATA 1994 (as to which, see section 15 [and paragraph 1 of Schedule 9ZB][2]).
[(4A) But goods that are treated as imported for the purposes of VATA 1994 as a result of paragraph 3 of Schedule 9ZB are not imported goods for the purposes of this Part.][2]
(5) A person is "UK-established" if the person's business establishment is in the United Kingdom as determined for the purposes of section 9 of VATA 1994.][1]

Commentary—*De Voil Indirect Tax Service* **V3.304A**.
Amendments—[1] In the heading and in sub-ss (1), (3), words substituted for words "a third country goods"; in sub-s (1)(a), (b), words substituted for words "third country goods" and "established in a Member State"; and sub-ss (4), (5) substituted; by the Taxation (Cross-border Trade) Act 2018 s 43, Sch 8 paras 122, 123 with effect from IP completion day (11pm on 31 December 2020), by virtue of SI 2020/1642 reg 4(b).
Sub-ss (4), (5) previously read as follows—
  "(4) Goods are "third country" goods if they have been imported from a place outside the Member States within the meaning of section 15 of VATA 1994.
  (5) Whether a person is established in a Member State is to be determined in accordance with Article 10 of Council Implementing Regulation (EU) No 282/2011 of 15 March 2011 laying down implementing measures for Directive 2006/112/EC on the common system of value added tax.".
[2] In sub-s (4), words inserted, and sub-s (4A) inserted, by the Taxation (Post-transition Period) Act 2020 s 3, Sch 2 para 9 with effect from IP completion day (11pm on 31 December 2020), by virtue of SI 2020/1642 reg 9.

49 Requirement for approval

(1) A person may not carry on [an imported goods][1] fulfilment business otherwise than in accordance with an approval given by the Commissioners under this section.
(2) The Commissioners may approve a person to carry on [an imported goods][1] fulfilment business only if they are satisfied that the person is a fit and proper person to carry on the business.
(3) The Commissioners may approve a person to carry on [an imported goods][1] fulfilment business for such periods and subject to such conditions or restrictions as they may think fit or as they may by regulations made by them prescribe.
(4) The Commissioners may at any time for reasonable cause vary the terms of, or revoke, an approval under this section.
(5) In this Part "approved person" means a person approved under this section to carry on [an imported goods][1] fulfilment business.

Regulations—Fulfilment Businesses Regulations, SI 2018/326.
Commentary—*De Voil Indirect Tax Service* **V3.304A**.
Amendments—[1] In sub-ss (1)–(3), (5), words substituted for words "a third country goods" by the Taxation (Cross-border Trade) Act 2018 s 43, Sch 8 paras 122, 124 with effect from IP completion day (11pm on 31 December 2020), by virtue of SI 2020/1642 reg 4(b).

50 Register of approved persons

(1) The Commissioners must maintain a register of approved persons.
(2) The register is to contain such information relating to approved persons as the Commissioners consider appropriate.
(3) The Commissioners may make publicly available such information contained in the register as they consider necessary to enable those who deal with a person who carries on [an imported goods][1] fulfilment business to determine whether the person in question is an approved person in relation to that activity.
(4) The information may be made available by such means (including the internet) as the Commissioners consider appropriate.

Commentary—*De Voil Indirect Tax Service* **V3.304A**.
Amendments—[1] In sub-s (3) words substituted for words "a third country goods" by the Taxation (Cross-border Trade) Act 2018 s 43, Sch 8 paras 122, 125 with effect from IP completion day (11pm on 31 December 2020), by virtue of SI 2020/1642 reg 4(b).

51 Regulations relating to approval, registration etc.

(1) The Commissioners may by regulations make provision—
  (a) regulating the approval and registration of persons under this Part,
  (b) regulating the variation or revocation of any such approval or registration, or of any condition or restriction to which such an approval or registration is subject,
  (c) about the register maintained under section 50,
  (d) regulating the carrying on of [an imported goods][1] fulfilment business, and
  (e) imposing obligations on approved persons.

(2) The regulations may, in particular, make provision—
  (a) requiring applications, and other communications with the Commissioners, to be made electronically;
  (b) as to the procedure for the approval and registration of bodies corporate which are members of the same group;
  (c) requiring approved persons to keep and make available for inspection such records as may be prescribed by or under the regulations.

Commentary—*De Voil Indirect Tax Service* **V3.304A**.
Regulations—Fulfilment Businesses (Approval Scheme) Regulations, SI 2018/299.
Fulfilment Businesses Regulations, SI 2018/326.
Amendments—[1] In sub-s (1)(d) words substituted for words "a third country goods" by the Taxation (Cross-border Trade) Act 2018 s 43, Sch 8 paras 122, 126 with effect from IP completion day (11pm on 31 December 2020), by virtue of SI 2020/1642 reg 4(b).

52 Disclosure of information by HMRC

(1) The Commissioners may disclose to an approved person information held by Her Majesty's Revenue and Customs in connection with a function of Her Majesty's Revenue and Customs, but only for the purpose mentioned in subsection (2).

(2) The purpose is to assist the approved person in complying with obligations imposed on that person by virtue of section 51.

(3) An approved person to whom information is disclosed under subsection (1)—
  (a) may use the information only for the purpose of complying with obligations imposed on that person by virtue of section 51, and
  (b) may not further disclose the information except with the consent of the Commissioners.

(4) Section 19 of the Commissioners for Revenue and Customs Act 2005 (offence) applies to a disclosure in contravention of subsection (3)(b) as it applies to a disclosure, in contravention of section 20(9) of that Act, of revenue and customs information relating to a person whose identity is specified in the disclosure or can be deduced from it.

Commentary—*De Voil Indirect Tax Service* **V3.304A**.

53 Offence

(1) A person who—
  (a) carries on [an imported goods][1] fulfilment business, and
  (b) is not an approved person,
commits an offence.

(2) In proceedings for an offence under subsection (1) it is a defence to show that the person did not know, and had no reasonable grounds to suspect, that the person—
  (a) was carrying on [an imported goods][1] fulfilment business, or
  (b) was not an approved person.

(3) A person is taken to have shown the fact mentioned in subsection (2) if—
  (a) sufficient evidence of that fact is adduced to raise an issue with respect to it, and
  (b) the contrary is not proved beyond reasonable doubt.

(4) A person guilty of an offence under this section is liable on summary conviction—
  (a) in England and Wales, to imprisonment for a term not exceeding 12 months, or a fine, or both;
  (b) in Scotland, to imprisonment for a term not exceeding 12 months, or a fine not exceeding the statutory maximum, or both;
  (c) in Northern Ireland, to imprisonment for a term not exceeding 6 months, or a fine not exceeding the statutory maximum, or both.

(5) A person guilty of an offence under this section is liable on conviction on indictment to—
  (a) imprisonment for a period not exceeding 7 years,
  (b) a fine, or
  (c) both.

(6) In relation to an offence committed before the commencement of [paragraph 24(2) of Schedule 22 to the Sentencing Act 2020][2] the reference in subsection (4)(a) to 12 months is to be read as a reference to 6 months.

Commentary—*De Voil Indirect Tax Service* **V3.304A**.

Amendments—[1] In sub-ss (1)(*a*), (2)(*a*), words substituted for words "a third country goods", by the Taxation (Cross-border Trade) Act 2018 s 43, Sch 8 paras 122, 127 with effect from IP completion day (11pm on 31 December 2020), by virtue of SI 2020/1642 reg 4(*b*).
[2] In sub-s (6) words substituted for words "section 154(1) of the Criminal Justice Act 2003" by the Sentencing Act 2020 s 410, Sch 24 para 443(1) with effect from 1 December 2020 (see s 416(1) of that Act, as amended by SI 2020/1236 regs 3, 4(5)).

54 Forfeiture
(1) If a person—
  (*a*) carries on [an imported goods][1] fulfilment business, and
  (*b*) is not an approved person,
any goods within subsection (2) are liable to forfeiture under CEMA 1979.
(2) Goods are within this subsection if—
  (*a*) they are stored by the person, and
  (*b*) their storage by the person constitutes, or has constituted, the carrying on of [an imported goods][1] fulfilment business by the person.

Commentary—*De Voil Indirect Tax Service* **V3.304A**.
Amendments—[1] In sub-ss (1)(*a*), (2)(*b*) words substituted for words "a third country goods", by the Taxation (Cross-border Trade) Act 2018 s 43, Sch 8 paras 122, 128 with effect from IP completion day (11pm on 31 December 2020), by virtue of SI 2020/1642 reg 4(*b*).

55 Penalties
(1) Schedule 13 provides for a penalty to be payable by a person who carries on [an imported goods][1] fulfilment business and is not an approved person.
(2) The Commissioners may make regulations ("penalty regulations") imposing a penalty for the contravention of—
  (*a*) any condition or restriction imposed under this Part;
  (*b*) regulations under this Part.
(3) The amount of a penalty imposed by the penalty regulations is to be specified in the regulations, but must not exceed £3,000.
(4) The penalty regulations may make provision for the assessment and recovery of a penalty imposed by the regulations.
(5) The Commissioners may by regulations make provision for corporate bodies which are members of the same group to be jointly and severally liable for any penalties imposed under—
  (*a*) Schedule 13;
  (*b*) penalty regulations.

Commentary—*De Voil Indirect Tax Service* **V3.304A**.
Regulations—Fulfilment Businesses (Approval Scheme) Regulations, SI 2018/299.
Fulfilment Businesses Regulations, SI 2018/326.
Amendments—[1] In sub-s (1) words substituted for words "a third country goods" by the Taxation (Cross-border Trade) Act 2018 s 43, Sch 8 paras 122, 129 with effect from IP completion day (11pm on 31 December 2020), by virtue of SI 2020/1642 reg 4(*b*).

56 Appeals
(1) FA 1994 is amended as follows.
(2) In section 13A(2) (customs and excise reviews and appeals: relevant decisions) after paragraph (gb) insert—
  "(gc) any decision by HMRC that a person is liable to a penalty, or as to the amount of a person's liability, under—
    (i) regulations under section 55 of the Finance (No. 2) Act 2017, or
    (ii) Schedule 13 to that Act;".
(3) In Schedule 5 to that Act (decisions subject to review and appeal) after paragraph 9A insert—

"The Finance (No 2) Act 2017

9B

Any decision for the purposes of Part 3 of the Finance (No. 2) Act 2017 (third country goods fulfilment businesses) as to—
  (*a*) whether or not, and in which respects, any person is to be, or to continue to be, approved and registered, or
  (*b*) the conditions or restrictions subject to which any person is approved and registered."

Commentary—*De Voil Indirect Tax Service* **V3.304A**.

57 Regulations
(1) Regulations under this Part may—
  (*a*) make provision which applies generally or only for specified cases or purposes;
  (*b*) make different provision for different cases or purposes;

(c) include incidental, consequential, transitional or transitory provision;
(d) confer a discretion on the Commissioners;
(e) make provision by reference to a notice to be published by the Commissioners.
(2) Regulations under this Part are to be made by statutory instrument.
(3) A statutory instrument containing regulations under this Part is subject to annulment in pursuance of a resolution of the House of Commons.
(4) This section does not apply to regulations under section 59 (commencement).
Commentary—*De Voil Indirect Tax Service* **V3.304A**.
Regulations—Fulfilment Businesses (Approval Scheme) Regulations, SI 2018/299.
Fulfilment Businesses Regulations, SI 2018/326.

58 Interpretation

(1) In this Part—
"approved person" has the meaning given by section 49(5);
"the Commissioners" means the Commissioners for Her Majesty's Revenue and Customs.
(2) For the purposes of this Part two or more bodies corporate are members of a group if—
(a) one of them controls each of the others,
(b) one person (whether a body corporate or an individual) controls all of them, or
(c) two or more individuals carrying on a business in partnership control all of them.
(3) A body corporate is to be taken to control another body corporate if—
(a) it is empowered by or under legislation to control that body's activities, or
(b) it is that body's holding company within the meaning of section 1159 of, and Schedule 6 to, the Companies Act 2006.
(4) An individual or individuals are to be taken to control a body corporate if the individual or individuals (were the individual or individuals a company) would be that body's holding company within the meaning of section 1159 of, and Schedule 6 to, the Companies Act 2006.
Commentary—*De Voil Indirect Tax Service* **V3.304A**.

59 Commencement

(1) This Part comes into force—
(a) so far as it confers powers to make regulations, on the day on which this Act is passed, and
(b) for all other purposes, on such day as the Commissioners may by regulations made by statutory instrument appoint.
(2) Regulations under subsection (1)(b) may appoint different days for different purposes.
Commentary—*De Voil Indirect Tax Service* **V3.304A**.

SCHEDULE 13

[IMPORTED GOODS] FULFILMENT BUSINESSES: PENALTY

Section 55

Commentary—*De Voil Indirect Tax Service* **V3.304A**.
amendments—In the heading, words substituted for words "Third country goods" by the Taxation (Cross-border Trade) Act 2018 s 43, Sch 8 paras 122, 130(1), (3) with effect from IP completion day (11pm on 31 December 2020), by virtue of SI 2020/1642 reg 4(b).

Liability to penalty

1 (1) A penalty is payable by a person ("P") who—
(a) carries on [an imported goods][1] fulfilment business, and
(b) is not an approved person.
(2) In this Schedule references to a "contravention" are to acting as mentioned in sub-paragraph (1).

Amendments—[1] In sub-para (1)(a) words substituted for words "a third country goods", by the Taxation (Cross-border Trade) Act 2018 s 43, Sch 8 paras 122, 130(1), (2) with effect from IP completion day (11pm on 31 December 2020), by virtue of SI 2020/1642 reg 4(b).

Amount of penalty

2 (1) If the contravention is deliberate and concealed, the amount of the penalty is the maximum amount (see paragraph 10).
(2) If the contravention is deliberate but not concealed, the amount of the penalty is 70% of the maximum amount.
(3) In any other case, the amount of the penalty is 30% of the maximum amount.
(4) The contravention is—
(a) "deliberate and concealed" if the contravention is deliberate and P makes arrangements to conceal the contravention, and
(b) "deliberate but not concealed" if the contravention is deliberate but P does not make arrangements to conceal the contravention.

Reductions for disclosure

3 (1) Paragraph 4 provides for reductions in penalties under this Schedule where P discloses a contravention.
(2) P discloses a contravention by—
  (a) telling the Commissioners about it,
  (b) giving the Commissioners reasonable help in identifying any other contraventions of which P is aware, and
  (c) allowing the Commissioners access to records for the purpose of identifying such contraventions.
(3) Disclosure of a contravention—
  (a) is "unprompted" if made at a time when P has no reason to believe that the Commissioners have discovered or are about to discover the contravention, and
  (b) otherwise, is "prompted".
(4) In relation to disclosure, "quality" includes timing, nature and extent.
Regulations—Indirect Taxes (Notifiable Arrangements) Regulations, SI 2017/1216.

4 (1) Where P discloses a contravention, the Commissioners must reduce the penalty to one that reflects the quality of the disclosure.
(2) If the disclosure is prompted, the penalty may not be reduced below—
  (a) in the case of a contravention that is deliberate and concealed, the maximum amount,
  (b) in the case of a contravention that is deliberate but not concealed, 35% of the maximum amount, and
  (c) in any other case, 20% of the maximum amount.
(3) If the disclosure is unprompted, the penalty may not be reduced below—
  (a) in the case of a contravention that is deliberate and concealed, 30% of the maximum amount,
  (b) in the case of a contravention that is deliberate but not concealed, 20% of the maximum amount, and
  (c) in any other case, 10% of the maximum amount.

Special reduction

5 (1) If the Commissioners think it right because of special circumstances, they may reduce a penalty under this Schedule.
(2) In sub-paragraph (1) "special circumstances" does not include ability to pay.
(3) In sub-paragraph (1) the reference to reducing a penalty includes a reference to—
  (a) staying a penalty, and
  (b) agreeing a compromise in relation to proceedings for a penalty.

Assessment

6 (1) Where P becomes liable for a penalty under this Schedule, the Commissioners must—
  (a) assess the penalty,
  (b) notify P, and
  (c) state in the notice the contravention in respect of which the penalty is assessed.
(2) A penalty under this Schedule must be paid before the end of the period of 30 days beginning with the day on which notification of the penalty is issued.
(3) A penalty under this Schedule is recoverable as a debt due to the Crown.
(4) An assessment of a penalty under this Schedule may not be made later than one year after evidence of facts sufficient in the opinion of the Commissioners to indicate the contravention comes to their knowledge.
(5) Two or more contraventions may be treated by the Commissioners as a single contravention for the purposes of assessing a penalty under this Schedule.

Reasonable excuse

7 (1) Liability to a penalty does not arise under this Schedule in respect of a contravention which is not deliberate if P satisfies the Commissioners or (on an appeal made to the appeal tribunal) the tribunal that there is a reasonable excuse for the contravention.
(2) For the purposes of sub-paragraph (1), where P relies on any other person to do anything, that is not a reasonable excuse unless P took reasonable care to avoid the contravention.

Companies: officer's liability

8 (1) Where a penalty under this Schedule is payable by a company in respect of a contravention which was attributable to an officer of the company, the officer is liable to pay such portion of the penalty (which may be 100%) as the Commissioners may specify by written notice to the officer.

(2) Sub-paragraph (1) does not allow the Commissioners to recover more than 100% of a penalty.
(3) In the application of sub-paragraph (1) to a body corporate other than a limited liability partnership, "officer" means—
   (a) a director (including a shadow director within the meaning of section 251 of the Companies Act 2006),
   (b) a manager, and
   (c) a secretary.
(4) In the application of sub-paragraph (1) to a limited liability partnership, "officer" means a member.
(5) In the application of sub-paragraph (1) in any other case, "officer" means—
   (a) a director,
   (b) a manager,
   (c) a secretary, and
   (d) any other person managing or purporting to manage any of the company's affairs.
(6) Where the Commissioners have specified a portion of a penalty in a notice given to an officer under sub-paragraph (1)—
   (a) paragraph 5 applies to the specified portion as to a penalty,
   (b) the officer must pay the specified portion before the end of the period of 30 days beginning with the day on which the notice is given,
   (c) sub-paragraphs (3) to (5) of paragraph 6 apply as if the notice were an assessment of a penalty, and
   (d) paragraph 9 applies as if the officer were liable to a penalty.
(7) In this paragraph "company" means any body corporate or unincorporated association, but does not include a partnership.

Double jeopardy

9 P is not liable to a penalty under this Schedule in respect of a contravention in respect of which P has been convicted of an offence.

The maximum amount

10 (1) In this Schedule "the maximum amount" means £10,000.
(2) If it appears to the Treasury that there has been a change in the value of money since the last relevant date, they may by regulations substitute for the sum for the time being specified in sub-paragraph (1) such other sum as appears to them to be justified by the change.
(3) In sub-paragraph (2), "relevant date" means—
   (a) the date on which this Act is passed, and
   (b) each date on which the power conferred by that sub-paragraph has been exercised.
(4) Regulations under this paragraph do not apply to any contravention which occurs wholly before the date on which they come into force.

Appeal tribunal

11 In this Schedule "appeal tribunal" has the same meaning as in Chapter 2 of Part 1 of the Finance Act 1994.

SCHEDULE 17
DISCLOSURE OF TAX AVOIDANCE SCHEMES: VAT AND OTHER INDIRECT TAXES
Section 66

Commentary—*De Voil Indirect Tax Service* **V5.213A, V5.358A**.

PART 1
DUTIES TO DISCLOSE AVOIDANCE SCHEMES ETC

Preliminary: application of definitions

1 The definitions in paragraphs 2, 3, and 7 to 10 apply for the purposes of this Schedule.

"Indirect tax"

2 (1) "Indirect tax" means any of the following—
   VAT
   insurance premium tax
   general betting duty

pool betting duty
remote gaming duty
machine games duty
gaming duty
lottery duty
bingo duty
air passenger duty
hydrocarbon oils duty
tobacco products duty
duties on spirits, beer, wine, made-wine and cider
soft drinks industry levy
aggregates levy
landfill tax
climate change levy
customs duties.

(2) The Treasury may by regulations amend the list in sub-paragraph (1) by adding, varying or omitting an entry for a tax.

Commentary—*De Voil Indirect Tax Service* **V5.213A, V5.358A.**

"Notifiable arrangements" and "notifiable proposal"

3 (1) "Notifiable arrangements" means any arrangements not excluded by sub-paragraph (2) which—
  (*a*) fall within any description prescribed by the Treasury by regulations,
  (*b*) enable, or might be expected to enable, any person to obtain a tax advantage in relation to any indirect tax that is so prescribed in relation to arrangements of that description, and
  (*c*) are such that the main benefit, or one of the main benefits, that might be expected to arise from the arrangements is the obtaining of that tax advantage.

(2) Arrangements that meet the requirements in paragraphs (*a*) to (*c*) of sub-paragraph (1) are not notifiable arrangements if they implement a proposal which is excluded from being a notifiable proposal by sub-paragraph (4).

(3) "Notifiable proposal" means a proposal for arrangements which, if entered into, would be notifiable arrangements (whether the proposal relates to a particular person or to any person who may seek to take advantage of it).

(4) A proposal is not a notifiable proposal if any of the following occur before 1 January 2018—
  (*a*) a promoter first makes a firm approach to another person in relation to the proposal,
  (*b*) a promoter makes the proposal available for implementation by any other person, or
  (*c*) a promoter first becomes aware of any transaction forming part of arrangements implementing the proposal.

Commentary—*De Voil Indirect Tax Service* **V5.213A, V5.358A.**

4 (1) HMRC may apply to the tribunal for an order that—
  (*a*) a proposal is notifiable, or
  (*b*) arrangements are notifiable.

(2) An application must specify—
  (*a*) the proposal or arrangements in respect of which the order is sought, and
  (*b*) the promoter.

(3) On an application the tribunal may make the order only if satisfied that paragraph 3(1)(*a*) to (*c*) applies to the relevant arrangements and that they are not excluded from being notifiable by paragraph 3(2).

Commentary—*De Voil Indirect Tax Service* **V5.213A, V5.358A.**

5 (1) HMRC may apply to the tribunal for an order that—
  (*a*) a proposal is to be treated as notifiable, or
  (*b*) arrangements are to be treated as notifiable.

(2) An application must specify—
  (*a*) the proposal or arrangements in respect of which the order is sought, and
  (*b*) the promoter.

(3) On an application the tribunal may make the order only if satisfied that HMRC—
  (*a*) have taken all reasonable steps to establish whether the proposal or arrangements are notifiable, and
  (*b*) have reasonable grounds for suspecting that the proposal or arrangements may be notifiable.

(4) Reasonable steps under sub-paragraph (3)(*a*) may (but need not) include taking action under paragraph 29 or 30.
(5) Grounds for suspicion under sub-paragraph (3)(*b*) may include—
   (*a*) the fact that the relevant arrangements fall within a description prescribed under paragraph 3(1)(*a*),
   (*b*) an attempt by the promoter to avoid or delay providing information or documents about the proposal or arrangements under or by virtue of paragraph 29 or 30,
   (*c*) the promoter's failure to comply with a requirement under or by virtue of paragraph 29 or 30 in relation to another proposal or other arrangements.
(6) Where an order is made under this paragraph in respect of a proposal or arrangements, the relevant period for the purposes of sub-paragraph (1) of paragraph 11 or 12 in so far as it applies by virtue of the order is the period of 11 days beginning with the day on which the order is made.
(7) An order under this paragraph in relation to a proposal or arrangements is without prejudice to the possible application of any of paragraphs 11 to 15, other than by virtue of this paragraph, to the proposal or arrangements.
Commentary—*De Voil Indirect Tax Service* **V5.213A**, **V5.358A**.

"Tax advantage" in relation to VAT

6 (1) A person (P) obtains a tax advantage in relation to VAT if—
   (*a*) in any prescribed accounting period, the amount by which the output tax accounted for by P exceeds the input tax deducted by P is less than it would otherwise be;
   (*b*) P obtains a VAT credit when P would otherwise not do so, or obtains a larger credit or obtains a credit earlier than would otherwise be the case;
   (*c*) in a case where P recovers input tax as a recipient of a supply before the supplier accounts for the output tax, the period between the time when the input tax is recovered and the time when the output tax is accounted for is greater than would otherwise be the case;
   (*d*) in any prescribed accounting period, the amount of P's non-deductible tax is less than it otherwise would be;
   (*e*) P avoids an obligation to account for tax.
(2) In sub-paragraph (1)(*d*) "non-deductible tax", in relation to a taxable person, means—
   (*a*) input tax for which the person is not entitled to credit under section 25 of VATA 1994,
   (*b*) any VAT incurred by the person which is not input tax and in respect of which the person is not entitled to a refund from the Commissioners by virtue of any provision of VATA 1994.
(3) For the purposes of sub-paragraph (2)(*b*), the VAT "incurred" by a taxable person is—
   (*a*) VAT on the supply to the person of any goods or services,
   (*b*) . . . [1]
   (*c*) VAT paid or payable by the person on the importation of any goods . . . [1],
(4) A person who is not a taxable person obtains a tax advantage in relation to VAT if that person's non-refundable tax is less that it otherwise would be.
(5) In sub-paragraph (4) "non-refundable tax" means—
   (*a*) VAT on the supply to the person of any goods or services,
   (*b*) . . . [1]
   (*c*) VAT paid or payable by the person on the importation of any goods . . . [1],
but excluding (in each case) any VAT in respect of which the person is entitled to a refund from the Commissioners by virtue of any provision of VATA 1994.
(6) Terms used in this paragraph which are defined in section 96 of VATA 1994 have the meanings given by that section.
Commentary—*De Voil Indirect Tax Service* **V5.213A**, **V5.358A**.
Northern Ireland—See Sch 9ZA para 80 (Northern Ireland: this para has effect in relation to NI acquisition VAT as if the reference in sub-para (2)(*b*) to VAT "incurred" by a taxable person included VAT on the acquisition by the person of any goods from a member State, and new sub-para (5)(*b*) were inserted as follows—
"(*b*) VAT on the acquisition by the person of any goods from a member State,".
Amendments—[1] Sub-paras (3)(*b*), (5)(*b*) repealed, and in sub-paras (3)(*c*), (5)(*c*), words "from a place outside the member States" repealed, by the Taxation (Cross-border Trade) Act 2018 s 43, Sch 8 paras 122, 131 with effect from IP completion day (11pm on 31 December 2020), by virtue of SI 2020/1642 reg 4(*b*).
   Sub-para (3)(*b*) previously read as follows—
      "(*b*) VAT on the acquisition by the person from another member State of any goods,".
   Sub-para (5)(*b*) previously read as follows—
      "(*b*) VAT on the acquisition by the person from another member State of goods,".

"Tax advantage" in relation to taxes other than VAT

7 "Tax advantage", in relation to an indirect tax other than VAT, means—
   (*a*) relief or increased relief from tax,
   (*b*) repayment or increased repayment of tax,

(c) avoidance or reduction of a charge to tax, an assessment of tax or a liability to pay tax,
(d) avoidance of a possible assessment to tax or liability to pay tax,
(e) deferral of a payment of tax or advancement of a repayment of tax, or
(f) avoidance of an obligation to deduct or account for tax.

Commentary—*De Voil Indirect Tax Service* **V5.213A, V5.358A**.

"Promoter"

8 (1) This paragraph describes when a person (P) is a promoter in relation to a notifiable proposal or notifiable arrangements.
(2) P is a promoter in relation to a notifiable proposal if, in the course of a relevant business, P—
   (a) is to any extent responsible for the design of the proposed arrangements,
   (b) makes a firm approach to another person (c) in relation to the proposal with a view to P making the proposal available for implementation by C or any other person, or
   (c) makes the proposal available for implementation by other persons.
(3) P is a promoter in relation to notifiable arrangements if—
   (a) P is by virtue of sub-paragraph (2)(b) or (c) a promoter in relation to a notifiable proposal which is implemented by the arrangements, or
   (b) if in the course of a relevant business, P is to any extent responsible for—
      (i) the design of the arrangements, or
      (ii) the organisation or management of the arrangements.
(4) In this paragraph "relevant business" means any trade, profession or business which—
   (a) involves the provision to other persons of services relating to taxation, or
   (b) is carried on by a bank or securities house.
(5) In sub-paragraph (4)(b)—
   "bank" has the meaning given by section 1120 of CTA 2010, and
   "securities house" has the meaning given by section 1009(3) of that Act.
(6) For the purposes of this paragraph anything done by a company is to be taken to be done in the course of a relevant business if it is done for the purposes of a relevant business falling within sub-paragraph (4)(b) carried on by another company which is a member of the same group.
(7) Section 170 of the TCGA 1992 has effect for determining for the purposes of sub-paragraph (6) whether two companies are members of the same group, but as if in that section—
   (a) for each of the references to a 75 per cent subsidiary there were substituted a reference to a 51 per cent subsidiary, and
   (b) subsection (3)(b) and subsections (6) to (8) were omitted.
(8) A person is not to be treated as a promoter by reason of anything done in prescribed circumstances.
(9) In the application of this Schedule to a proposal or arrangements which are not notifiable, a reference to a promoter is a reference to a person who would be a promoter under this paragraph if the proposal or arrangements were notifiable.

Regulations—Indirect Taxes (Disclosure of Avoidance Schemes) Regulations, SI 2017/1215.
Commentary—*De Voil Indirect Tax Service* **V5.213A, V5.358A**.

"Introducer"

9 (1) A person is an introducer in relation to a notifiable proposal if the person makes a marketing contact with another person in relation to the proposal.
(2) A person is not to be treated as an introducer by reason of anything done in prescribed circumstances.
(3) In the application of this Schedule to a proposal or arrangements which are not notifiable, a reference to an introducer is a reference to a person who would be an introducer under this paragraph if the proposal or arrangements were notifiable.

"Makes a firm approach" and "marketing contact"

10 (1) A person makes a firm approach to another person in relation to a notifiable proposal if the person makes a marketing contact with the other person in relation to the proposal at a time when the proposed arrangements have been substantially designed.
(2) A person makes a marketing contact with another person in relation to a notifiable proposal if—
   (a) the person communicates information about the proposal to the other person,
   (b) the communication is made with a view to that other person, or any other person, entering into transactions forming part of the proposed arrangements, and
   (c) the information communicated includes an explanation of the tax advantage that might be expected to be obtained from the proposed arrangements.

(3) For the purposes of sub-paragraph (1) proposed arrangements have been substantially designed at any time if by that time the nature of the transactions to form part of them has been sufficiently developed for it to be reasonable to believe that a person who wished to obtain the tax advantage mentioned in sub-paragraph (2)(*c*) might enter into—
- (*a*) transactions of the nature developed, or
- (*b*) transactions not substantially different from transactions of that nature.

Commentary—*De Voil Indirect Tax Service* **V5.213A, V5.358A**.

Duties of promoter in relation to notifiable proposals or notifiable arrangements

11 (1) A person who is a promoter in relation to a notifiable proposal must, within the relevant period, provide HMRC with prescribed information relating to the proposal.
(2) In sub-paragraph (1) "the relevant period" is the period of 31 days beginning with the relevant date.
(3) In sub-paragraph (2) "the relevant date" is the earliest of the following—
- (*a*) the date on which the promoter first makes a firm approach to another person in relation to the proposal,
- (*b*) the date on which the promoter makes the proposal available for implementation by any other person, or
- (*c*) the date on which the promoter first becomes aware of any transaction forming part of notifiable arrangements implementing the proposal.

Regulations—Indirect Taxes (Disclosure of Avoidance Schemes) Regulations, SI 2017/1215.
Commentary—*De Voil Indirect Tax Service* **V5.213A, V5.358A**.

12 (1) A person who is a promoter in relation to notifiable arrangements must, within the relevant period after the date on which the person first becomes aware of any transaction forming part of the arrangements, provide HMRC with prescribed information relating to the arrangements.
(2) In sub-paragraph (1) "the relevant period" is the period of 31 days beginning with that date.
(3) The duty under sub-paragraph (1) does not apply if the notifiable arrangements implement a proposal in respect of which notice has been given to HMRC under paragraph 11(1).

Regulations—Indirect Taxes (Disclosure of Avoidance Schemes) Regulations, SI 2017/1215.
Commentary—*De Voil Indirect Tax Service* **V5.213A, V5.358A**.

13 (1) This paragraph applies where a person complies with paragraph 11(1) in relation to a notifiable proposal for arrangements and another person is—
- (*a*) also a promoter in relation to the proposal or is a promoter in relation to a notifiable proposal for arrangements which are substantially the same as the proposed arrangements (whether they relate to the same or different parties), or
- (*b*) a promoter in relation to notifiable arrangements implementing the proposal or notifiable arrangements which are substantially the same as notifiable arrangements implementing the proposal (whether they relate to the same or different parties).

(2) Any duty of the other person under paragraph 11(1) or 12(1) in relation to the notifiable proposal or notifiable arrangements is discharged if—
- (*a*) the person who complied with paragraph 11(1) has notified the identity and address of the other person to HMRC or the other person holds the reference number allocated to the proposed notifiable arrangements under paragraph 22(1), and
- (*b*) the other person holds the information provided to HMRC in compliance with paragraph 11(1).

Commentary—*De Voil Indirect Tax Service* **V5.213A, V5.358A**.

14 (1) This paragraph applies where a person complies with paragraph 12(1) in relation to notifiable arrangements and another person is—
- (*a*) a promoter in relation to a notifiable proposal for arrangements which are substantially the same as the notifiable arrangements (whether they relate to the same or different parties), or
- (*b*) also a promoter in relation to the notifiable arrangements or notifiable arrangements which are substantially the same (whether they relate to the same or different parties).

(2) Any duty of the other person under paragraph 11(1) or 12(1) in relation to the notifiable proposal or notifiable arrangements is discharged if—
- (*a*) the person who complied with paragraph 12(1) has notified the identity and address of the other person to HMRC or the other person holds the reference number allocated to the notifiable arrangements under paragraph 22(1), and
- (*b*) the other person holds the information provided to HMRC in compliance with paragraph 12(1).

Commentary—*De Voil Indirect Tax Service* **V5.213A, V5.358A**.

15 Where a person is a promoter in relation to two or more notifiable proposals or sets of notifiable arrangements which are substantially the same (whether they relate to the same parties or different parties) the person need not provide information under paragraph 11(1) or 12(1) if the person has already provided information under either of those paragraphs in relation to any of the other proposals or arrangements.

Commentary—*De Voil Indirect Tax Service* **V5.213A, V5.358A.**

Duty of promoter: supplemental information

16 (1) This paragraph applies where—
- (a) a promoter (P) has provided information in purported compliance with paragraph 11(1) or 12(1), but
- (b) HMRC believe that P has not provided all the prescribed information.

(2) HMRC may apply to the tribunal for an order requiring P to provide specified information about, or documents relating to, the notifiable proposal or arrangements.

(3) The tribunal may make an order under sub-paragraph (2) in respect of information or documents only if satisfied that HMRC have reasonable grounds for suspecting that the information or documents—
- (a) form part of the prescribed information, or
- (b) will support or explain the prescribed information.

(4) A requirement by virtue of sub-paragraph (2) is to be treated as part of P's duty under paragraph 11(1) or 12(1).

(5) In so far as P's duty under sub-paragraph (1) of paragraph 11 or 12 arises out of an order made by virtue of sub-paragraph (2) above the relevant period for the purposes of that sub-paragraph (1) is—
- (a) the period of 11 days beginning with the date of the order, or
- (b) such longer period as HMRC may direct.

Commentary—*De Voil Indirect Tax Service* **V5.213A, V5.358A.**

Duty of person dealing with promoter outside United Kingdom

17 (1) This paragraph applies where a person enters into any transaction forming part of any notifiable arrangements in relation to which—
- (a) a promoter is resident outside the United Kingdom, and
- (b) no promoter is resident in the United Kingdom.

(2) The person must, within the relevant period, provide HMRC with prescribed information relating to the arrangements.

(3) In sub-paragraph (2) "the relevant period" is the period of 6 days beginning with the day on which the person enters into the first transaction forming part of the arrangements.

(4) Compliance with paragraph 11(1) or 12(1) by any promoter in relation to the arrangements discharges the person's duty under sub-paragraph (1).

Regulations—Indirect Taxes (Disclosure of Avoidance Schemes) Regulations, SI 2017/1215.
Commentary—*De Voil Indirect Tax Service* **V5.213A, V5.358A.**

Duty of parties to notifiable arrangements not involving promoter

18 (1) This paragraph applies to any person who enters into any transaction forming part of notifiable arrangements as respects which neither that person nor any other person in the United Kingdom is liable to comply with paragraph 11(1), 12(1) or 17(2).

(2) The person must at the prescribed time provide HMRC with prescribed information relating to the arrangements.

Regulations—Indirect Taxes (Disclosure of Avoidance Schemes) Regulations, SI 2017/1215.
Commentary—*De Voil Indirect Tax Service* **V5.213A, V5.358A.**

Duty to provide further information requested by HMRC

19 (1) This paragraph applies where—
- (a) a person has provided the prescribed information about notifiable proposals or arrangements in compliance with paragraph 11(1), 12(1), 17(2) or 18(2), or
- (b) a person has provided information in purported compliance with paragraph 17(2) or 18(2) but HMRC believe that the person has not provided all the prescribed information.

(2) HMRC may require the person to provide—
- (a) further specified information about the notifiable proposals or arrangements (in addition to the prescribed information under paragraph 11(1), 12(1), 17(2) or 18(2));
- (b) documents relating to the notifiable proposals or arrangements.

(3) Where HMRC impose a requirement on a person under this paragraph, the person must comply with the requirement within—

(a) the period of 10 working days beginning with the day on which HMRC imposed the requirement, or
(b) such longer period as HMRC may direct.
Commentary—*De Voil Indirect Tax Service* **V5.213A, V5.358A**.

20 (1) This paragraph applies where HMRC—
(a) have required a person to provide information or documents under paragraph 19, but
(b) believe that the person has failed to provide the information or documents required.
(2) HMRC may apply to the tribunal for an order requiring the person to provide the information or documents required.
(3) The tribunal may make an order imposing such a requirement only if satisfied that HMRC have reasonable grounds for suspecting that the information or documents will assist HMRC in considering the notifiable proposals or arrangements.
(4) Where the tribunal makes an order imposing such a requirement, the person must comply with the requirement within—
(a) the period of 10 working days beginning with the day on which the tribunal made the order, or
(b) such longer period as HMRC may direct.
Commentary—*De Voil Indirect Tax Service* **V5.213A, V5.358A**.

Duty of promoters to provide updated information

21 (1) This paragraph applies where—
(a) information has been provided under paragraph 11(1), or 12(1) about any notifiable arrangements, or proposed notifiable arrangements, to which a reference number is allocated under paragraph 22, and
(b) after the provision of the information, there is a change in relation to the arrangements of a kind mentioned in sub-paragraph (2).
(2) The changes referred to in sub-paragraph (1)(b) are—
(a) a change in the name by which the notifiable arrangements, or proposed notifiable arrangements, are known;
(b) a change in the name or address of any person who is a promoter in relation to the arrangements or, in the case of proposed arrangements, the notifiable proposal.
(3) A person who is a promoter in relation to the notifiable arrangements or, in the case of proposed notifiable arrangements, the notifiable proposal must inform HMRC of the change mentioned in sub-paragraph (1)(b) within 30 days after it is made.
(4) Sub-paragraphs (5) and (6) apply for the purposes of sub-paragraph (3) where there is more than one person who is a promoter in relation to the notifiable arrangements or proposal.
(5) If the change in question is a change in the name or address of a person who is a promoter in relation to the notifiable arrangements or proposal, it is the duty of that person to comply with sub-paragraph (3).
(6) If a person provides information in compliance with sub-paragraph (3), the duty imposed by that sub-paragraph on any other person, so far as relating to the provision of that information, is discharged.
Commentary—*De Voil Indirect Tax Service* **V5.213A, V5.358A**.

Arrangements to be given reference number

22 (1) Where a person (P) complies or purports to comply with paragraph 11(1), 12(1), 17(2) or 18(2) in relation to any notifiable proposal or notifiable arrangements, HMRC may within 90 days allocate a reference number to the notifiable arrangements or, in the case of a notifiable proposal, to the proposed notifiable arrangements.
(2) If HMRC do so it must notify the number to P and (where the person is one who has complied or purported to comply with paragraph 11(1) or 12(1)), to any other person—
(a) who is a promoter in relation to—
(i) the notifiable proposal (or arrangements implementing the notifiable proposal), or
(ii) the notifiable arrangements (or proposal implemented by the notifiable arrangements), and
(b) whose identity and address has been notified to HMRC by P.
(3) The allocation of a reference number to any notifiable arrangements (or proposed notifiable arrangements) is not to be regarded as constituting any indication by HMRC that the arrangements would or could as a matter of law result in the obtaining by any person of a tax advantage.
(4) In this Part of this Schedule "reference number", in relation to any notifiable arrangements, means the reference number allocated under this paragraph.
Commentary—*De Voil Indirect Tax Service* **V5.213A, V5.358A**.

Duty of promoter to notify client of number

23 (1) This paragraph applies where a person who is a promoter in relation to notifiable arrangements is providing (or has provided) services to any person ("the client") in connection with the arrangements.

(2) The promoter must, within 30 days after the relevant date, provide the client with prescribed information relating to any reference number (or, if more than one, any one reference number) that has been notified to the promoter (whether by HMRC or any other person) in relation to—
   (a) the notifiable arrangements, or
   (b) any arrangements substantially the same as the notifiable arrangements (whether involving the same or different parties).

(3) In sub-paragraph (2) "the relevant date" means the later of—
   (a) the date on which the promoter becomes aware of any transaction which forms part of the notifiable arrangements, and
   (b) the date on which the reference number is notified to the promoter.

(4) But where the conditions in sub-paragraph (5) are met the duty imposed on the promoter under sub-paragraph (2) to provide the client with information in relation to notifiable arrangements is discharged

(5) Those conditions are—
   (a) that the promoter is also a promoter in relation to a notifiable proposal and provides services to the client in connection with them both,
   (b) the notifiable proposal and the notifiable arrangements are substantially the same, and
   (c) the promoter has provided to the client, in a form and manner specified by HMRC, prescribed information relating to the reference number that has been notified to the promoter in relation to the proposed notifiable arrangements.

(6) HMRC may give notice that, in relation to notifiable arrangements specified in the notice, promoters are not under the duty under sub-paragraph (2) after the date specified in the notice.

Regulations—Indirect Taxes (Disclosure of Avoidance Schemes) Regulations, SI 2017/1215.
Commentary—*De Voil Indirect Tax Service* **V5.213A, V5.358A**.

Duty of client to notify parties of number

24 (1) In this paragraph "client" means a person to whom a person who is a promoter in relation to notifiable arrangements or a notifiable proposal is providing (or has provided) services in connection with the arrangements or proposal.

(2) Sub-paragraph (3) applies where the client receives prescribed information relating to the reference number allocated to the arrangements or proposed arrangements,

(3) The client must, within the relevant period, provide prescribed information relating to the reference number to any other person—
   (a) who the client might reasonably be expected to know is or is likely to be a party to the arrangements or proposed arrangements, and
   (b) who might reasonably be expected to gain a tax advantage in relation to any relevant tax by reason of the arrangements or proposed arrangements.

(4) In sub-paragraph (3) "the relevant period" is the period of 30 days beginning with the later of—
   (a) the day on which the client first becomes aware of any transaction forming part of the notifiable arrangements or proposed notifiable arrangements, and
   (b) the day on which the prescribed information is notified to the client by the promoter under paragraph 23.

(5) HMRC may give notice that, in relation to notifiable arrangements or a notifiable proposal specified in the notice, persons are not under the duty under sub-paragraph (3) after the date specified in the notice.

(6) The duty under sub-paragraph (3) does not apply in prescribed circumstances.

(7) For the purposes of this paragraph a tax is a "relevant tax", in relation to arrangements or arrangements proposed in a proposal of any description, if it is prescribed in relation to arrangements or proposals of that description by regulations under paragraph 3(1).

Regulations—Indirect Taxes (Disclosure of Avoidance Schemes) Regulations, SI 2017/1215.
Commentary—*De Voil Indirect Tax Service* **V5.213A, V5.358A**.

Duty of client to provide information to promoter

25 (1) This paragraph applies where a person who is a promoter in relation to notifiable arrangements has provided a person ("the client") with the information prescribed under paragraph 23(2).

(2) The client must, within the relevant period, provide the promoter with prescribed information relating to the client.

(3) In sub-paragraph (2) "the relevant period" is the period of 11 days beginning with the later of—

(*a*) the date the client receives the reference number for the arrangements, and
(*b*) the date the client first enters into a transaction which forms part of the arrangements.
(4) The duty under sub-paragraph (2) is subject to any exceptions that may be prescribed.
Regulations—Indirect Taxes (Disclosure of Avoidance Schemes) Regulations, SI 2017/1215.
Commentary—*De Voil Indirect Tax Service* **V5.213A, V5.358A.**

Duty of parties to notifiable arrangements to notify HMRC of number, etc

26 (1) Any person (P) who is a party to any notifiable arrangements must provide HMRC with prescribed information relating to—
  (*a*) any reference number notified to P under paragraph 23 or 24, and
  (*b*) the time when P obtains or expects to obtain by virtue of the arrangements a tax advantage in relation to any relevant tax.
(2) For the purposes of sub-paragraph (1) a tax is a "relevant tax" in relation to any notifiable arrangements if it is prescribed in relation to arrangements of that description by regulations under paragraph 3(1).
(3) Regulations made by the Commissioners may—
  (*a*) in prescribed cases, require the information prescribed under sub-paragraph (1) to be given to HMRC—
    (i) in the prescribed manner,
    (ii) in the prescribed form,
    (iii) at the prescribed time, and
  (*b*) in prescribed cases, require the information prescribed under sub-paragraph (1) and such other information as is prescribed to be provided separately to HMRC at the prescribed time or times.
(4) In sub-paragraph (3) "prescribed" includes being prescribed in a document made under a power conferred by regulations made by the Commissioners.
(5) HMRC may give notice that, in relation to notifiable arrangements specified in the notice, persons are not under the duty under sub-paragraph (1) after the date specified in the notice.
(6) The duty under sub-paragraph (1) does not apply in prescribed circumstances.
Regulations—Indirect Taxes (Disclosure of Avoidance Schemes) Regulations, SI 2017/1215.
Commentary—*De Voil Indirect Tax Service* **V5.213A, V5.358A.**

Duty of promoter to provide details of clients

27 (1) This paragraph applies where a person who is a promoter in relation to notifiable arrangements is providing (or has provided) services to any person ("the client") in connection with the arrangements and either—
  (*a*) the promoter is subject to the reference number information requirement, or
  (*b*) the promoter has failed to comply with paragraph 11(1) or 12(1) in relation to the arrangements (or the notifiable proposal for them) but would be subject to the reference number information requirement if a reference number had been allocated to the arrangements.
(2) For the purposes of this paragraph "the reference number information requirement" is the requirement under paragraph 23(2) to provide to the client prescribed information relating to the reference number allocated to the notifiable arrangements.
(3) The promoter must, within the prescribed period after the end of the relevant period, provide HMRC with prescribed information in relation to the client.
(4) In sub-paragraph (3) "the relevant period" means such period (during which the promoter is or would be subject to the reference number information requirement) as is prescribed.
(5) The promoter need not comply with sub-paragraph (3) in relation to any notifiable arrangements at any time after HMRC have given notice under paragraph 23(6) in relation to the arrangements.
Regulations—Indirect Taxes (Disclosure of Avoidance Schemes) Regulations, SI 2017/1215.
Commentary—*De Voil Indirect Tax Service* **V5.213A, V5.358A.**

Enquiry following disclosure of client details

28 (1) This paragraph applies where—
  (*a*) a person who is a promoter in relation to notifiable arrangements has provided HMRC with information in relation to a person ("the client") under paragraph 27(3) (duty to provide client details), and
  (*b*) HMRC suspect that a person other than the client is or is likely to be a party to the arrangements.
(2) HMRC may by written notice require the promoter to provide prescribed information in relation to any person other than the client who the promoter might reasonably be expected to know is or is likely to be a party to the arrangements.

(3) The promoter must comply with a requirement under or by virtue of sub-paragraph (2) within—
   (a) the relevant period, or
   (b) such longer period as HMRC may direct.
(4) In sub-paragraph (3) "the relevant period" is the period of 11 days beginning with the day on which the promoter receives the notice under sub-paragraph (2).

Regulations—Indirect Taxes (Disclosure of Avoidance Schemes) Regulations, SI 2017/1215.
Commentary—*De Voil Indirect Tax Service* **V5.213A, V5.358A.**

Pre-disclosure enquiry

29 (1) Where HMRC suspect that a person (P) is the promoter or introducer of a proposal, or the promoter of arrangements, which may be notifiable, they may by written notice require P to state—
   (a) whether in P's opinion the proposal or arrangements are notifiable by P, and
   (b) if not, the reasons for P's opinion.
(2) The notice must specify the proposal or arrangements to which it relates.
(3) For the purposes of sub-paragraph (1)(b)—
   (a) it is not sufficient to refer to the fact that a lawyer or other professional has given an opinion,
   (b) the reasons must show, by reference to this Part of this Schedule and regulations under it, why P thinks the proposal or arrangements are not notifiable by P, and
   (c) in particular, if P asserts that the arrangements do not fall within any description prescribed under paragraph 3(1)(a), the reasons must provide sufficient information to enable HMRC to confirm the assertion.
(4) P must comply with a requirement under or by virtue of sub-paragraph (1) within—
   (a) the relevant period, or
   (b) such longer period as HMRC may direct.
(5) In sub-paragraph (4) "the relevant period" is the period of 11 days beginning with the day on which the notice under sub-paragraph (1) is issued.

Commentary—*De Voil Indirect Tax Service* **V5.213A, V5.358A.**

Reasons for non-disclosure: supporting information

30 (1) Where HMRC receive from a person (P) a statement of reasons why a proposal or arrangements are not notifiable by P, HMRC may apply to the tribunal for an order requiring P to provide specified information or documents in support of the reasons.
(2) P must comply with a requirement under or by virtue of sub-paragraph (1) within—
   (a) the relevant period, or
   (b) such longer period as HMRC may direct.
(3) In sub-paragraph (2) "the relevant period" is the period of 15 days beginning with the day on which the order concerned is made.
(4) The power under sub-paragraph (1)—
   (a) may be exercised more than once, and
   (b) applies whether or not the statement of reasons was received under paragraph 29(1)(b).

Commentary—*De Voil Indirect Tax Service* **V5.213A, V5.358A.**

Provision of information to HMRC by introducers

31 (1) This paragraph applies where HMRC suspect—
   (a) that a person (P) is an introducer in relation to a proposal, and
   (b) that the proposal may be notifiable.
(2) HMRC may by written notice require P to provide HMRC with one or both of the following—
   (a) prescribed information in relation to each person who has provided P with any information relating to the proposal,
   (b) prescribed information in relation to each person with whom P has made a marketing contact in relation to the proposal.
(3) A notice must specify the proposal to which it relates.
(4) P must comply with a requirement under or sub-paragraph(2) within—
   (a) the relevant period, or
   (b) such longer period as HMRC may direct.
(5) In sub-paragraph (4) "the relevant period" is the period of 11 days beginning with the day on which the notice under sub-paragraph (2) is given.

Regulations—Indirect Taxes (Disclosure of Avoidance Schemes) Regulations, SI 2017/1215.
Commentary—*De Voil Indirect Tax Service* **V5.213A, V5.358A.**

Legal professional privilege

32 (1) Nothing in this Part of this Schedule requires any person to disclose to HMRC any privileged information.
(2) In this Part of this Schedule "privileged information" means information with respect to which a claim to legal professional privilege, or, in Scotland, to confidentiality of communications, could be maintained in legal proceedings.
Commentary—*De Voil Indirect Tax Service* **V5.213A, V5.358A.**

Information

33 (1) This paragraph applies where a person is required to provide information under paragraph 23(2) or 24(3).
(2) HMRC may specify additional information which must be provided by that person to the recipients under paragraph 23(2) or 24(3) at the same time as the information referred to in sub-paragraph (1).
(3) HMRC may specify the form and manner in which the additional information is to be provided.
(4) For the purposes of this paragraph "additional information" means information supplied by HMRC which relates to notifiable proposals or notifiable arrangements in general.
Commentary—*De Voil Indirect Tax Service* **V5.213A, V5.358A.**

34 (1) HMRC may specify the form and manner in which information required to be provided by or under any of the information provisions must be provided if the provision is to be complied with.
(2) The "information provisions" are paragraphs 11(1), 12(1), 17(2), 18(2), 19(2), 21(3), 23(2), 24(3), 26(1) and (3), 27(3), 28(2), 29(1), 31(2) and 33(2).
Commentary—*De Voil Indirect Tax Service* **V5.213A, V5.358A.**

35 No duty of confidentiality or other restriction on disclosure (however imposed) prevents the voluntary disclosure by any person to HMRC of information or documents which the person has reasonable grounds for suspecting will assist HMRC in determining whether there has been a breach of any requirement imposed by or under this Part of this Schedule.
Commentary—*De Voil Indirect Tax Service* **V5.213A, V5.358A.**

36 (1) HMRC may publish information about—
   (*a*) any notifiable arrangements, or proposed notifiable arrangements, to which a reference number is allocated under paragraph 22;
   (*b*) any person who is a promoter in relation to the notifiable arrangements or, in the case of proposed notifiable arrangements, the notifiable proposal.
(2) The information that may be published is (subject to sub-paragraph (4))—
   (*a*) any information relating to arrangements within sub-paragraph (1)(*a*), or a person within sub-paragraph (1)(*b*), that is prescribed information for the purposes of paragraph 11, 12, 17 or 18;
   (*b*) any ruling of a court or tribunal relating to any such arrangements or person (in that person's capacity as a promoter in relation to a notifiable proposal or arrangements);
   (*c*) the number of persons in any period who enter into transactions forming part of notifiable arrangements within sub-paragraph (1)(*a*);
   (*d*) any other information that HMRC considers it appropriate to publish for the purpose of identifying arrangements within sub-paragraph (1)(*a*) or a person within sub-paragraph (1)(*b*).
(3) The information may be published in any manner that HMRC considers appropriate.
(4) No information may be published under this paragraph that identifies a person who enters into a transaction forming part of notifiable arrangements within sub-paragraph (1)(*a*).
(5) But where a person who is a promoter within sub-paragraph (1)(*b*) is also a person mentioned in sub-paragraph (4), nothing in sub-paragraph (4) is to be taken as preventing the publication under this paragraph of information so far as relating to the person's activities as a promoter.
(6) Before publishing any information under this paragraph that identifies a person as a promoter within sub-paragraph (1)(*b*), HMRC must—
   (*a*) inform the person that they are considering doing so, and
   (*b*) give the person reasonable opportunity to make representations about whether it should be published.
Commentary—*De Voil Indirect Tax Service* **V5.213A, V5.358A.**

37 (1) This paragraph applies if—
   (*a*) information about notifiable arrangements, or proposed notifiable arrangements, is published under paragraph 36,
   (*b*) at any time after the information is published, a ruling of a court or tribunal is made in relation to tax arrangements, and

(c) HMRC is of the opinion that the ruling is relevant to the arrangements mentioned in paragraph (a)

(2) A ruling is "relevant" to the arrangements if—
  (a) the principles laid down, or reasoning given, in the ruling would, if applied to the arrangements, allow the purported advantage arising from the arrangements in relation to tax, and
  (b) the ruling is final.

(3) HMRC must publish information about the ruling.

(4) The information must be published in the same manner as HMRC published the information mentioned in sub-paragraph (1)(a) (and may also be published in any other manner that HMRC considers appropriate).

(5) A ruling is "final" if it is—
  (a) a ruling of the Supreme Court, or
  (b) a ruling of any other court or tribunal in circumstances where—
    (i) no appeal may be made against the ruling,
    (ii) if an appeal may be made against the ruling with permission, the time limit for applications has expired and either no application has been made or permission has been refused,
    (iii) if such permission to appeal against the ruling has been granted or is not required, no appeal has been made within the time limit for appeals, or
    (iv) if an appeal was made, it was abandoned or otherwise disposed of before it was determined by the court or tribunal to which it was addressed.

(6) Where a ruling is final by virtue of sub-paragraph (ii), (iii) or (iv) of sub-paragraph (5)(b), the ruling is to be treated as made at the time when the sub-paragraph in question is first satisfied.

(7) In this paragraph "tax arrangements" means arrangements in respect of which it would be reasonable to conclude (having regard to all the circumstances) that the main purpose, or one of the main purposes, was the obtaining of a tax advantage.

Commentary—*De Voil Indirect Tax Service* **V5.213A, V5.358A**.

Power to vary certain relevant periods

38 The Commissioners may by regulations amend this Part of this Schedule with a view to altering the definition of "the relevant period" for the purposes of—

  paragraph 5(6)
  paragraph 11(1)
  paragraph 12(1)
  paragraph 16(5)
  paragraph 17(2)
  paragraph 24(3)
  paragraph 25(2)
  paragraph 27(3)
  paragraph 28(3)
  paragraph 29(4)
  paragraph 30(2))
  paragraph 31(4).

PART 2
PENALTIES

Penalty for failure to comply with duties under Part 1 (apart from paragraph 26)

39 (1) A person who fails to comply with any of the provisions of Part 1 of this Schedule mentioned in sub-paragraph (2) is liable—
  (a) to a penalty not exceeding—
    (i) in the case of a failure to comply with paragraph 11(1), 12(1), 17(2), 18(2) or 19, £600 for each day during the initial period for which the failure continues (but see also paragraphs 40(4) and 41), and
    (ii) in any other case, £5,000, and
  (b) if the failure continues after a penalty is imposed under paragraph (a), to a further penalty or penalties not exceeding £600 for each day on which the failure continues after the day on which the penalty under paragraph (a) was imposed (but excluding any day for which a penalty under this paragraph has already been imposed).

(2) Those provisions are—
  (a) paragraph 11(1) (duty of promoter in relation to notifiable proposal),

(b) paragraph 12(1) (duty of promoter in relation to notifiable arrangements),
(c) paragraph 17(2) (duty of person dealing with promoter outside United Kingdom),
(d) paragraph 18(2) (duty of parties to notifiable arrangements not involving promoter),
(e) paragraph 19 (duty to provide further information requested by HMRC),
(f) paragraph 21 (duty of promoters to provide updated information),
(g) paragraph 23(2) (duty of promoter to notify client of reference number),
(h) paragraph 24(3) (duty of client to notify parties of reference number),
(i) paragraph 25(2) (duty of client to provide information to promoter),
(j) paragraph 27(3) (duty of promoter to provide details of clients),
(k) paragraph 28(3) (enquiry following disclosure of client details),
(l) paragraphs 29(4) and 30(2) (duty of promoter to respond to inquiry)
(m) paragraph 31(4) (duty of introducer to give details of persons who have provided information or have been provided with information, and
(n) paragraph 33 (duty to provide additional information).

(3) In this paragraph "the initial period" means the period—
(a) beginning with the relevant day, and
(b) ending with the earlier of the day on which the penalty under sub-paragraph (1)(a)(i) is determined and the last day before the failure ceases.

(4) For the purposes of sub-paragraph (3)(a) "the relevant day" is the day specified in relation to the failure in the following table—

Failure	Relevant day
A failure to comply with paragraph 11(1) or 12(1) in so far as it applies by virtue of an order under paragraph 5	The first day after the end of the relevant period described in paragraph 5(6)
A failure to comply with paragraph 11(1) or 12(1) in so far as it applies by virtue of an order under paragraph 16(2)	The first day after the end of the relevant period (whether that is the period described in sub-paragraph 16(5)(a) or that period as extended by a direction under paragraph 16(5)(b))
Any other failure to comply with sub-paragraph (1) of paragraph 11	The first day after the end of the relevant period described in paragraph 11(2)
Any other failure to comply with sub-paragraph (1) of paragraph 12	The first day after the end of the relevant period described in paragraph 12(2)
A failure to comply with paragraph 17(2)	The first day after the end of the relevant period described in paragraph 17(3)
A failure to comply with paragraph 18(2)	The first day after the latest time by which paragraph 18(2) should have been complied with in the case concerned
A failure to comply with paragraph 19	The first day after the end of the period within which the person must comply with paragraph 19

Commentary—*De Voil Indirect Tax Service* **V5.213A, V5.358A**.

40 (1) In the case of a failure to comply with paragraph 11(1), 12(1), 17(2), 18(2) or 19, the amount of the penalty under paragraph 39(1)(a)(i) is to be arrived at after taking account of all relevant considerations.

(2) Those considerations include the desirability of the penalty being set at a level which appears appropriate for deterring the person, or other persons, from similar failures to comply on future occasions having regard (in particular)—
(a) in the case of a penalty for a promoter's failure to comply with paragraph 11(1), 12(1) or 19, to the amount of any fees received, or likely to have been received, by the promoter in connection with the notifiable proposal (or arrangements implementing the notifiable proposal), or with the notifiable arrangements, and
(b) in the case of a penalty for a relevant person's failure to comply with paragraph 17(2), 18(2) or 19, to the amount of any advantage gained, or sought to be gained, by the person in relation to any tax prescribed under paragraph 3(1)(b) in relation to the notifiable arrangements

(3) In sub-paragraph (2)(b) "relevant person" means a person who enters into any transaction forming part of notifiable arrangements.

(4) If the maximum penalty under paragraph 39(1)(a)(i) appears inappropriately low after taking account of all relevant considerations, the penalty is to be of such amount not exceeding £1 million as appears appropriate having regard to those considerations.

Commentary—*De Voil Indirect Tax Service* **V5.213A, V5.358A**.

41 (1) This paragraph applies where a failure to comply with a provision mentioned in paragraph 39(2) concerns a proposal or arrangements in respect of which an order has been made under paragraph 4 or 5.
(2) The amounts specified in paragraph 39(1)(*a*)(i) and (*b*) are increased to £5,000 in relation to days falling after the end of the period of 11 days beginning with the day on which the order is made.
Commentary—*De Voil Indirect Tax Service* **V5.213A, V5.358A**.

42 (1) The Treasury may by regulations vary—
 (*a*) any of the sums for the time being specified in paragraph 39(1);
 (*b*) the sum for the time being specified in paragraph 40(4);
 (*c*) the period for the time being specified in paragraph 41(2);
 (*d*) the sum for the time being specified in paragraph 41(2).
(2) Regulations under this paragraph may include incidental or transitional provision.
Commentary—*De Voil Indirect Tax Service* **V5.213A, V5.358A**.

43 Where it appears to an officer of Revenue and Customs that—
 (*a*) a penalty under paragraph 39(1)(*a*) has been imposed in a case where the maximum penalty is set by paragraph 39(1)(*a*)(i), and
 (*b*) the maximum penalty was calculated on the basis that the initial period began with a day later than that which the officer considers to be the relevant day,
an officer of Revenue and Customs may commence proceedings for a re-determination of the penalty.
Commentary—*De Voil Indirect Tax Service* **V5.213A, V5.358A**.

Penalty for failure to comply with duties under paragraph 26

44 (1) A person who fails to comply with—
 (*a*) paragraph 26(1), or
 (*b*) regulations under paragraph 26(3),
is liable to a penalty not exceeding the relevant sum.
(2) The relevant sum is £5,000 in respect of each scheme to which the failure relates unless the person falls within sub-paragraph (3) or (4).
(3) If the person has previously failed to comply with paragraph 26(1) or regulations under paragraph 26(3) on one (and only one) occasion during the period of 36 months ending with the date on which the current failure began, the relevant sum is £7,500 in respect of each scheme to which the current failure relates (whether or not the same as any scheme to which the previous failure relates).
(4) If the person has previously failed to comply with paragraph 26(1) or regulations under paragraph 26(3) on two or more occasions during the period of 36 months ending with the date on which the current failure began, the relevant sum is £10,000 in respect of each scheme to which the current failure relates (whether or not the same as any scheme to which any of the previous failures relates).
(5) In this paragraph "scheme" means any notifiable arrangements.
Commentary—*De Voil Indirect Tax Service* **V5.213A, V5.358A**.

Penalty proceedings before First-tier tribunal

45 (1) An authorised officer may commence proceedings before the First-tier Tribunal for any penalty under paragraph 39(1)(*a*).
(2) In sub-paragraph (1) "authorised officer" means an officer of Revenue and Customs authorised by HMRC for the purposes of this paragraph.
(3) Proceedings for a penalty may not be commenced more than 12 months after evidence of facts sufficient to justify the bringing of proceedings comes to the knowledge of HMRC.
(4) If the First-tier Tribunal decide that the penalty is payable by the person—
 (*a*) the penalty is for all purposes to be treated as if it were tax charged in an assessment and due and payable,
 (*b*) the person may appeal to the Upper Tribunal against the decision that the penalty is payable, and
 (*c*) the person may appeal to the Upper Tribunal against the decision as to the amount of the penalty.
(5) On an appeal under sub-paragraph (4)(*b*) the Upper Tribunal may, if it appears that no penalty has been incurred, cancel the decision of the First-tier Tribunal.
(6) On an appeal under sub-paragraph (4)(*c*) the Upper Tribunal may—
 (*a*) affirm the decision of the First-tier Tribunal as to the amount of the penalty, or
 (*b*) substitute for that decision a decision that the First-tier Tribunal had power to make.
Commentary—*De Voil Indirect Tax Service* **V5.213A, V5.358A**.

Assessment of penalties under paragraph 39(1)(b) or 44

46 (1) Where a person is liable to a penalty under paragraph 39(1)(*b*) or 44 an authorised officer may assess the amount due by way of a penalty.
(2) An assessment may not be made more than 12 months after evidence of facts sufficient to justify the making of the assessment first comes to the knowledge of HMRC.
(3) A notice of an assessment under sub-paragraph (1) stating—
  (*a*) the date on which it is issued, and
  (*b*) the time within which an appeal against the assessment may be made,
must be served on the person liable to the penalty.
(4) After the notice has been served the assessment may not be altered except in accordance with this paragraph or on appeal.
(5) If it is discovered by an authorised officer that the amount of a penalty assessed under this paragraph is or has become insufficient the officer may make an assessment in a further amount so that the penalty is set at the amount which, in the officer's opinion, is correct or appropriate.
(6) A penalty imposed by a decision under this paragraph—
  (*a*) is due and payable at the end of the period of 30 days beginning with the date of the issue of the notice of the decision, and
  (*b*) is to be treated for all purposes as if it were tax charged in an assessment and due and payable.
(7) In this paragraph "authorised officer" means an officer of Revenue and Customs authorised by HMRC for the purposes of this paragraph.
Commentary—*De Voil Indirect Tax Service* **V5.213A, V5.358A.**

47 (1) Where a person (P) is served with notice of an assessment under paragraph 46—
  (*a*) P may appeal against the decision that a penalty is payable by P, and
  (*b*) P may appeal against the decision as to the amount of the penalty.
(2) An appeal under sub-paragraph (1) is to be treated for procedural purposes in the same way as an appeal against an assessment to the relevant tax (including by the application of any provision about the bringing of an appeal by notice to HMRC, about HMRC review of the decision or about determination of the appeal by the First-tier Tribunal or Upper Tribunal)
(3) Sub-paragraph (2) does not apply—
  (*a*) so as to require P to pay a penalty before an appeal under sub-paragraph (1) is determined, or
  (*b*) in respect of any other matter expressly provided for by this Schedule.
(4) On an appeal under sub-paragraph (1)(*a*) the tribunal may affirm or cancel the decision that a penalty is payable by P.
(5) On an appeal under sub-paragraph (1)(*b*) the tribunal may—
  (*a*) affirm the decision as to the amount of the penalty, or
  (*b*) substitute for that decision another decision that the authorised officer had power to make.
(6) In this paragraph "tribunal" means the First-tier Tribunal or Upper Tribunal (as appropriate by virtue of sub-paragraph (2)).
Commentary—*De Voil Indirect Tax Service* **V5.213A, V5.358A.**

Reasonable excuse

48 (1) Liability to a penalty under this Part of this Schedule does not arise in relation to a particular failure to comply if the person concerned (P) satisfies HMRC or the relevant tribunal (as the case may be) that there is a reasonable excuse for the failure.
(2) For this purpose—
  (*a*) an insufficiency of funds is not a reasonable excuse, unless attributable to events outside P's control,
  (*b*) where P relied on any other person to do anything, that cannot be a reasonable excuse unless P took reasonable care to avoid the failure,
  (*c*) where P had a reasonable excuse but the excuse has ceased, P is to be treated as continuing to have the excuse if the failure is remedied without unreasonable delay after the excuse ceased, and
  (*d*) reliance on advice is to be taken automatically not to be a reasonable excuse if the advice was addressed to, or was given to, a person other than P or takes no account of P's individual circumstances.
Commentary—*De Voil Indirect Tax Service* **V5.213A, V5.358A.**

49 (1) The making of an order under paragraph 4 or 5 against P does not of itself mean that P either did or did not have a reasonable excuse for non- compliance before the order was made.
(2) Where an order is made under paragraph 4 or 5 then for the purposes of paragraph 48—

(*a*) the person identified in the order as the promoter of the proposal or arrangements cannot, in respect of any time after the end of the prescribed period mentioned in paragraph 41, rely on doubt as to notifiability as a reasonable excuse for failure to comply with paragraph 11(1) or 12(1), and

(*b*) any delay in compliance with that provision after the end of that period is not capable of being a reasonable excuse unless attributable to something other than doubt as to notifiability.

Commentary—*De Voil Indirect Tax Service* **V5.213A, V5.358A.**

50 (1) Where a person fails to comply with—

(*a*) paragraph 17(2) and the promoter for the purposes of paragraph 17 is a monitored promoter, or

(*b*) paragraph 18(2) and the arrangements for the purposes of paragraph 18 are arrangements of a monitored promoter,

then for the purposes of paragraph 48 legal advice which the person took into account is to be disregarded in determining whether the person had a reasonable excuse, if the advice was given or procured by that monitored promoter.

(2) In determining for the purpose of paragraph 48 whether or not a person who is a monitored promoter had a reasonable excuse for a failure to do something, reliance on legal advice is to be taken automatically not to constitute a reasonable excuse if either—

(*a*) the advice was not based on a full and accurate description of the facts, or

(*b*) the conclusions in the advice that the person relied on were unreasonable.

(3) In this paragraph "monitored promoter" means a person who is a monitored promoter for the purposes of Part 5 of FA 2014

Commentary—*De Voil Indirect Tax Service* **V5.213A, V5.358A.**

PART 3
CONSEQUENTIAL AMENDMENTS

VATA 1994

51 In section 77(4A) of VATA 1994 (cases in which the time allowed for assessment is 20 years), in paragraph (*d*) after "11A" insert "or an obligation under paragraph 17(2) or 18(2) of Schedule 17 to FA 2017".

Promoters of tax avoidance schemes

52 Part 5 of FA 2014 (promoters of tax avoidance schemes) is amended as follows.

53 (1) Section 281A (VAT: meaning of "tax advantage") is amended as follows.
(2) In the heading after "VAT" insert "and other indirect taxes".
(3) In subsection (1)—
   (*a*) in paragraph (*a*) after "VAT" insert "and other indirect taxes", and
   (*b*) in paragraph (*b*) for the words from "in paragraph 1" to the end substitute "for VAT in paragraph 6, and for other indirect taxes in paragraph 7, of Schedule 17 to FA 2017 (disclosure of tax avoidance schemes: VAT and other indirect taxes)."
(4) In subsection (3) after "value added tax" (in both places) insert "or other indirect taxes".
(5) After subsection (3) insert—
   "(4) In this section "indirect tax" has the same meaning as in Schedule 17 to FA 2017."

54 (1) Schedule 34A (defeated arrangements) is amended as follows.
(2) In paragraph 2(4) after ""schemes)" insert "or paragraph 22 of Schedule 17 to FA 2017 (disclosure of avoidance schemes: VAT and other indirect taxes).
(3) In paragraph 14—
   (*a*) in sub-paragraph (1)(*a*) after "VAT" insert "or other indirect tax", and
   (*b*) in sub-paragraphs (1)(*a*) and (*b*), (2) and (3) omit "taxable".
(4) Para 26A inserted.
(5) In the heading before paragraph 27, after ""disclosable" insert "Schedule 11A".
(6) In paragraph 27—
   (*a*) for "this Schedule" substitute "paragraph 26A", and
   (*b*) after ""disclosable" insert "Schedule 11A".
(7) In the heading before paragraph 28 for "and 27" substitute "to 27".
(8) In paragraph 28(1) after "26(1)(*a*)" insert "26A(2)(*a*)"

Serial tax avoidance

55 (1) Schedule 18 to FA 2016 (serial tax avoidance) is amended as follows.
(2) In paragraph 4 (meaning of "tax")—

(a) number the current text as sub-paragraph (1) of that paragraph,
(b) in that sub-paragraph (1), in paragraph (j) after "VAT" insert" "and indirect taxes", and
(c) after that sub-paragraph (1) insert—
"(2) For the purposes of this Schedule "indirect tax" means any of the following—
insurance premium tax
general betting duty
pool betting duty
remote gaming duty
machine games duty
gaming duty
lottery duty
bingo duty
air passenger duty
hydrocarbon oils duty
tobacco products duty
duties on spirits, beer, wine, made-wine and cider
soft drinks industry levy
aggregates levy
landfill tax
climate change levy
customs duties.
(3) Para 8A inserted.
(4) In the heading before paragraph 9 after ""Disclosable" insert "Schedule 11A".
(5) In paragraph 9—
 (a) for "this Schedule" substitute "paragraph 8A", and
 (b) after ""disclosable" insert "Schedule 11A".
(6) Para 9A inserted.
(7) In the heading before paragraph 10 (meaning of "failure to comply") for "and 9" substitute "to 9A".
(8) In paragraph 10(1) for "or 9(a)" substitute ", 8A(2)(c), 9(a) or 9A(1)(c)".
(9) In paragraph 11(1) (meaning of "relevant defeat") for "E" substitute "F".
(10) Para 16A inserted.
(11) In paragraph 17 (annual information notices)—
 (a) in sub-paragraph (3)(a) for "or election," insert "election, declaration or application for approval,",
 (b) in sub-paragraphs (3)(b), (4) and (5)(a) for "DOTAS arrangements or VAT" substitute "disclosable",
 (c) in sub-paragraph (5) for "or election" insert "election, declaration or application for approval", and
 (d) after sub-paragraph (11) insert—
 "(12) In this paragraph "disclosable arrangements" means any of the following—
   (a) DOTAS arrangements,
   (b) disclosable VAT arrangements, and
   (c) disclosable indirect tax arrangements.
(12) In the heading before paragraph 28 (exclusion of VAT from Part 4 of Schedule) after "VAT" insert "and indirect taxes".
(13) In paragraph 28 after "VAT" insert "or any other indirect tax".
(14) In paragraph 32 (value of counteracted advantage: basic rule for taxes other than VAT)—
 (a) in sub-paragraph (1) for "or C" substitute "C or F" and after paragraph (c) insert ";
   (d) in the case of a relevant defeat incurred by virtue of Condition F, the additional amount due or payable in respect of tax as a result of the counteraction mentioned in paragraph 16A(1)(d).", and
 (b) in sub-paragraph (2)(b) for "or (c)" substitute "(c) or (d)".
(15) In paragraph 35 (meaning of "the counteracted advantage" in paragraphs 33 and 34) in sub-paragraph (1) after paragraph (c) insert ";
   "(d) in relation to a relevant defeat incurred by virtue of Condition F, means any tax advantage in respect of which the counteraction mentioned in paragraph 16A(1)(c) is made."
(16) In paragraph 43 (paragraph 42: meaning of "the relevant failure") after sub-paragraph (7) insert—

"(8) In relation to a relevant defeat incurred by virtue of Condition F, "the relevant failure" means the failures or inaccuracies as a result of which the adjustments, assessments, or other actions mentioned in paragraph 16A(5) are required."

(17) In paragraph 55 (time of "use" of defeated arrangements) after sub-paragraph (8) insert—

"(8A) If the person incurs the relevant defeat by virtue of Condition F, the person is treated as having "used" the arrangements on the following dates—

 (a) the filing date of any return made by the person on the basis mentioned in paragraph 16A(2)(a);

 (b) the date on which the person makes any claim, declaration or application for approval;

 (c) the date of any failure by the person to comply with a relevant obligation (as defined in paragraph 16A(4))."

(18) In paragraph 58(1) (interpretation)—

 (a) after the definition of "contract settlement" insert—

""disclosable indirect tax arrangements" is to be interpreted in accordance with paragraph 9A;
"disclosable Schedule 11A VAT arrangements is to be interpreted in accordance with paragraph 9;",

 (b) after the definition of "HMRC" insert—

""indirect tax" has the meaning given by paragraph 4(2);",

 (c) in the definition of "disclosable VAT arrangements" for "9" substitute "8A", and

 (d) in the definition of "tax" for "4" substitute "4(1)".

PART 4
SUPPLEMENTAL

Regulations

56 (1) Any power of the Treasury or the Commissioners to make regulations under this Schedule is exercisable by statutory instrument.

(2) Regulations made under any such power may make different provision for different cases and may contain transitional provisions and savings.

(3) A statutory instrument containing regulations made by the Treasury under paragraph 2(2) or 42(1) may not be made unless a draft of the instrument has been laid before and approved by a resolution of the House of Commons.

(4) Any other statutory instrument containing regulations made under this Schedule, if made without a draft having been approved by a resolution of the House of Commons, is subject to annulment in pursuance of a resolution of the House of Commons.

Regulations—Indirect Taxes (Disclosure of Avoidance Schemes) Regulations, SI 2017/1215.
Indirect Taxes (Notifiable Arrangements) Regulations, SI 2017/1216.

Interpretation

57 In this Schedule—

"arrangements" includes any scheme, transaction or series of transactions;
"the Commissioners" means the Commissioners for Her Majesty's Revenue and Customs;
"company" has the meaning given by section 1121 of the Corporation Tax Act 2010;
"HMRC" means Her Majesty's Revenue and Customs;
"indirect tax" has the meaning given by paragraph 2(1);
"introducer" is to be construed in accordance with paragraph 9;
"makes a firm approach" has the meaning given by paragraph 10(1);
"makes a marketing contact" has the meaning given by paragraph 10(2);
"marketing contact" has the meaning give by paragraph 10(2);
"notifiable arrangements" has the meaning given by paragraph 3(1);
"notifiable proposal" has the meaning given by paragraph 3(3);
"prescribed" (except in or in references to paragraph 3(1)(a)), means prescribed by regulations made by HMRC;
"promoter" is to be construed in accordance with paragraph 8;
"reference number", in relation to notifiable arrangements, has the meaning given by paragraph 22(4);
"TCEA 2007" means the Tribunals, Courts and Enforcement Act 2007;
"tax advantage" means a tax advantage within the meaning of—

 (a) paragraph 6 (in relation to VAT), or

(b) paragraph 7 (in relation to indirect taxes other than VAT);
"trade" includes every venture in the nature of a trade;
"tribunal" means the First-tier tribunal, or where determined by or under Tribunal Procedure Rules, the Upper Tribunal;
"working day" means a day which is not a Saturday or a Sunday, Christmas Day, Good Friday or a bank holiday under the Banking and Financial Dealings Act 1971 in any part of the United Kingdom.

Regulations—Indirect Taxes (Disclosure of Avoidance Schemes) Regulations, SI 2017/1215.

TAXATION (CROSS-BORDER TRADE) ACT 2018

2018 Chapter 22

CONTENTS

PART 3
VALUE ADDED TAX

41	Abolition of acquisition VAT and extension of import VAT
42	EU law relating to VAT
43	Other VAT amendments connected with withdrawal from EU

PART 5
OTHER PROVISION CONNECTED WITH WITHDRAWAL FROM EU

51	Power to make provision in relation to VAT or duties of customs or excise
52	Subordinate legislation relating to VAT or duties of customs or excise

PART 6
FINAL PROVISIONS

54	Prohibition on collection of certain taxes or duties on behalf of country or territory without reciprocity
55	Single United Kingdom customs territory
56	Consequential and transitional provision
57	Commencement
58	Short title

Schedules
Schedule 7—Import duty: consequential amendments
Schedule 8—VAT amendments connected with withdrawal from EU

PART 3
VALUE ADDED TAX

Cross-references See the Taxation (Cross-border Trade) Act 2018 (Value Added Tax Transitional Provisions) (EU Exit) Regulations, SI 2019/105 (as amended by SI 2020/1495 reg 21) which provide as follows—
- reg 3: the amendments made by Part 3 of this Act do not have effect in relation to supplies made, and acquisitions taking place, before IP completion day (11pm UK time on 31 December 2020).
- reg 4: the amendments made by Part 3 of this Act do not have effect in relation to a supply of goods dispatched or transported from the territory of the UK to the territory of a member State of the EU, or vice versa, provided that the dispatch or transport started before IP completion day and ended thereafter.

See also SI 2020/1545 reg 110 (transitional provision in relation to acquisition VAT): where the time that an acquisition in the UK of goods from a member state is treated as taking place (as determined by VATA 1994 s 12 (as it had effect immediately before IP completion day)), falls on or after IP completion day and the goods enter the territory of the UK before IP completion day, acquisition VAT is charged, and the person who is liable for the acquisition VAT must account for it, as if amendments made by TCBTA 2018 Part 3 or any regulations relating to the UK's withdrawal from the EU, so far as they relate to acquisition VAT, had no effect.

SI 2020/1545 reg 111 provides similar transitional provisions where the acquisition in the UK of goods from a member state is treated as taking place before IP completion day and the goods enter the territory of the UK on or after IP completion day.

SI 2020/1545 regs 112–114 for further transitional provisions.

SI 2020/1545 regs 115–118 set out transitional provisions in relation to transactions involving the removal of goods from a member State to the UK as a result of their entry into Northern Ireland. See also VATA 1994 Sch 9ZA for provisions relating to VAT on acquisitions in Northern Ireland from member states.

41 Abolition of acquisition VAT and extension of import VAT
(1) The Value Added Tax Act 1994 is amended as follows.
(2) In section 1 (imposition of charge to value added tax), in subsection (1)—
    (a) omit paragraph (b) (which charges VAT on the acquisition in the United Kingdom of goods from other member States), and

    (b) for paragraph (c) substitute—
        "(c)   on the importation of goods into the United Kingdom,".
(3) Section 15 substituted.
Commencement—Taxation (Cross-border Trade) Act 2018 (Appointed day No 3) and the Value Added Tax (Postal Packets and Amendment) (EU Exit) Regulations 2018 (Appointed day) (EU Exit) Regulations, SI 2019/104 reg 2: 28 January 2019 is appointed as the day on which sub-s (2)(b) comes into force, but only to the extent that it relates to, and for the purpose of, the interpretation of the definition of "import VAT" in the Value Added Tax (Postal Packets and Amendment) (EU Exit) Regulations, SI 2018/1376 reg 2.
Finance Act 2016, Section 126 (Appointed Day), the Taxation (Cross-border Trade) Act 2018 (Appointed Day No 8, Transition and Saving Provisions) and the Taxation (Post-transition Period) Act 2020 (Appointed Day No 1) (EU Exit) Regulations, SI 2020/1642 reg 4(b): 11pm UK time on 31 December 2020 (IP completion day) is appointed for the coming into force of Part 3 so far as not already in force.

42 EU law relating to VAT

(1) Any EU regulation so far as applying in relation to value added tax, and any direct EU legislation so far as relevant to any such regulation, that form part of the law of the United Kingdom as a result of section 3 of the European Union (Withdrawal) Act 2018 cease to have effect (but, in the case of the implementing VAT regulation, see also subsection (5)).
(2) In the application of section 4(1) of that Act (saving for EU rights, powers, liabilities, obligations, restrictions, remedies and procedures) in relation to value added tax, the rights, powers, liabilities, obligations, restrictions, remedies and procedures mentioned there are subject to any exclusions or other modifications made by regulations made by the Treasury by statutory instrument.
(3) Further provision relevant to the law relating to value added tax is made by the European Union (Withdrawal) Act 2018: see, for example, section 6 of that Act (interpretation of retained EU law).
(4) One of the consequences of the provision made by that Act is that the principle of EU law preventing the abuse of the VAT system (see, for example, the cases of *Halifax* and *Kittel*) continues to be relevant, in accordance with that Act, for the purposes of the law relating to value added tax.
(5) Where the principal VAT directive remains relevant for determining the meaning and effect of the law relating to value added tax, that directive is to be read for that purpose in the light of the provision made by the implementing VAT regulation but ignoring such of its provisions as are excluded by regulations made by the Treasury by statutory instrument.
(6) No regulations may be made under this section on or after 1 April 2023.
(7) A statutory instrument containing regulations under this section must be laid before the House of Commons, and, unless approved by that House before the end of the period of 28 days beginning with the date on which the instrument is made, ceases to have effect at the end of that period.
(8) The fact that a statutory instrument ceases to have effect as mentioned in subsection (7) does not affect—
    (a) anything previously done under the instrument, or
    (b) the making of a new statutory instrument.
(9) In calculating the period for the purposes of subsection (7), no account is to be taken of any time—
    (a) during which Parliament is dissolved or prorogued, or
    (b) during which the House of Commons is adjourned for more than 4 days.
(10) Regulations under this section—
    (a) may make different provision for different purposes or areas,
    (b) may contain supplementary, incidental and consequential provision, and
    (c) may contain transitional or transitory provision and savings.
(11) In this section—
    "the implementing VAT regulation" means Council Implementing Regulation (EU) No 282/2011, and
    "the principal VAT directive" means Council Directive 2006/112/EC on the common system of value added tax.
Commencement—Finance Act 2016, Section 126 (Appointed Day), the Taxation (Cross-border Trade) Act 2018 (Appointed Day No 8, Transition and Saving Provisions) and the Taxation (Post-transition Period) Act 2020 (Appointed Day No 1) (EU Exit) Regulations, SI 2020/1642 reg 4(b): 11pm UK time on 31 December 2020 (IP completion day) is appointed for the coming into force of Part 3 so far as not already in force.

43 Other VAT amendments connected with withdrawal from EU

Schedule 8 makes amendments of the Value Added Tax Act 1994, and other enactments relating to VAT, in consequence of the provision made by this Part or otherwise in connection with the withdrawal of the United Kingdom from the EU.
Commencement—Taxation (Cross-border Trade) Act 2018 (Appointed day No 1) (EU Exit) Regulations, SI 2018/1362: section 43 came into force on 16 December 2018 but only insofar as it relates to Sch 8 para 14.
Finance Act 2016, Section 126 (Appointed Day), the Taxation (Cross-border Trade) Act 2018 (Appointed Day No 8, Transition and Saving Provisions) and the Taxation (Post-transition Period) Act 2020 (Appointed Day No 1) (EU Exit) Regulations, SI 2020/1642 reg 4(b): 11pm UK time on 31 December 2020 (IP completion day) is appointed for the coming into force of Part 3 so far as not already in force.

Excise Duties (Miscellaneous Amendments) (EU Exit) (No 2) Regulations, SI 2019/15.
Value Added Tax (Miscellaneous Amendments and Revocations) (EU Exit) Regulations, SI 2019/59.
Value Added Tax (Accounting Procedures for Import VAT for VAT Registered Persons and Amendment) (EU Exit) Regulations, SI 2019/60.
Value Added Tax (Tour Operators) (Amendment) (EU Exit) Regulations, SI 2019/73.
Value Added Tax and Excise Personal Reliefs (Special Visitors and Goods Permanently Imported) (Amendment) (EU Exit) Regulations, SI 2019/91.
Taxation (Cross-border Trade) Act 2018 (Appointed day No 3) and the Value Added Tax (Postal Packets and Amendment) (EU Exit) Regulations 2018 (Appointed day) (EU Exit) Regulations, SI 2019/104.
Taxation (Cross-border Trade) Act 2018 (Value Added Tax Transitional Provisions) (EU Exit) Regulations, SI 2019/105.
Customs (Export) (EU Exit) Regulations, SI 2019/108.
Customs (Contravention of a Relevant Rule) (Amendment) (EU Exit) Regulations, SI 2019/148.
Value Added Tax (Input Tax) (Specified Supplies) (EU Exit) Regulations, SI 2019/175.
Customs (Import Duty, Transit and Miscellaneous Amendments) (EU Exit) Regulations, SI 2019/326.
Customs (Crown Dependencies Customs Union) (EU Exit) Regulations, SI 2019/385.
Value Added Tax (Place of Supply of Services) (Supplies of Electronic, Telecommunication and Broadcasting Services) (Amendment and Revocation) (EU Exit) Order, SI 2019/404.
Value Added Tax (Input Tax) (Specified Supplies) (EU Exit) (No 2) Regulations, SI 2019/408.
Excise Duties (Miscellaneous Amendments) (EU Exit) (No 3) Regulations, SI 2019/474.
Taxation (Cross-border Trade) (Miscellaneous Provisions) (EU Exit) Regulations, SI 2019/486.
Customs (Managed Transition Procedure) (EU Exit) Regulations, SI 2019/487.
Value Added Tax (Miscellaneous Amendments, Revocation and Transitional Provisions) (EU Exit) Regulations, SI 2019/513.
Taxation (Cross-border Trade) Act 2018 (Appointed Day No 5 and Miscellaneous Commencements) (EU Exit) Regulations, SI 2019/819.
Value Added Tax (Miscellaneous Amendments and Transitional Provisions) (EU Exit) Regulations, SI 2019/1214.
Customs and Excise (Miscellaneous Provisions and Amendments) (EU Exit) Regulations, SI 2019/1215.
Excise Duties (Miscellaneous Amendments) (EU Exit) (No 4) Regulations, SI 2019/1216.
Data-gathering Powers (Relevant Data) (Amendment) (EU Exit) Regulations, SI 2019/1221.
Customs (Import Duty) (EU Exit) Regulations 2018 and the Customs (Export) (EU Exit) Regulations 2019 (Appointed Day) (EU Exit) Regulations, SI 2019/1282.
Taxation (Cross-border Trade) (Miscellaneous Provisions) (EU Exit) (No 2) Regulations, SI 2019/1346.
Value Added Tax (Miscellaneous Amendments, Revocation and Transitional Provisions) (EU Exit) Regulations 2019 (Appointed Day No 1) (EU Exit) Regulations, SI 2020/87.
Customs (Bulk Customs Declaration and Miscellaneous Amendments) (EU Exit) Regulations, SI 2020/967.
Customs (Transitional Arrangements) (EU Exit) Regulations, SI 2020/1088.
Customs (Declarations) (Amendment and Modification) (EU Exit) Regulations, SI 2020/1234.
Value Added Tax (Miscellaneous Amendments to Acts of Parliament) (EU Exit) Regulations, SI 2020/1312.
Value Added Tax (Disclosure of Information Relating to VAT Registration) (Appointed Day) (EU Exit) Regulations, SI 2020/1333.
Taxation (Cross-border Trade) (Miscellaneous Provisions) (EU Exit) (No 2) Regulations, SI 2019/1346.
Value Added Tax (Disclosure of Information Relating to VAT Registration) (Appointed Day) (EU Exit) Regulations, SI 2020/1333.
Customs (Reliefs from a Liability to Import Duty and Miscellaneous Amendments) (EU Exit) Regulations, SI 2020/1431.
Customs (Origin of Chargeable Goods) (EU Exit) Regulations, SI 2020/1433.
Customs (Origin of Chargeable Goods: Trade Preference Scheme) (EU Exit) Regulations, SI 2020/1436.
Trade Preference Scheme (EU Exit) Regulations, SI 2020/1438.
Taxation Cross-border Trade (Special Procedures Supplementary and General Provision etc) (EU Exit) Regulations, SI 2020/1439.

Customs (Transitional) (EU Exit) Regulations, SI 2020/1449.
Customs Transit Procedures (Amendment, etc) (EU Exit) Regulations, SI 2020/1491.
Value Added Tax (Miscellaneous and Transitional Provisions, Amendment and Revocation) (EU Exit) Regulation, SI 2020/1495.
Value Added Tax (Miscellaneous Amendments to the Value Added Tax Act 1994 and Revocation) (EU Exit) Regulations, SI 2020/1544.
Value Added Tax (Miscellaneous Amendments, Northern Ireland Protocol and Savings and Transitional Provisions) (EU Exit) Regulations, SI 2020/1545.
Value Added Tax (Northern Ireland) (EU Exit) Regulations, SI 2020/1546.
Customs (Amendment) (EU Exit) Regulations, SI 2020/1552.
Customs (Northern Ireland) (EU Exit) Regulations, SI 2020/1605.
Customs (Modification and Amendment) (EU Exit) Regulations, SI 2020/1629.
Excise Duties (Appointed Day) (EU Exit) Regulations, SI 2020/1640.
Value Added Tax and Excise Duties (Appointed Day) (EU Exit) Regulations, SI 2020/1641.
Customs and Tariff (Appointed Day) (EU Exit) Regulations, SI 2020/1643.

PART 6
FINAL PROVISIONS

54 Prohibition on collection of certain taxes or duties on behalf of country or territory without reciprocity

(1) Subject to subsection (2), it shall be unlawful for HMRC to account for any duty of customs or VAT or excise duty collected by HMRC to the government of a country or territory outside the United Kingdom.

(2) Subsection (1) shall not apply if the Treasury declare by Order that arrangements have been entered into by Her Majesty's Government and that government under which that government will account to HMRC for those duties and taxes collected in that country or territory on a reciprocal basis.
Commencement—Part 6 of this Act came into force on 13 September 2018 (see s 57(1)(e)).

55 Single United Kingdom customs territory
(1) It shall be unlawful for Her Majesty's Government to enter into arrangements under which Northern Ireland forms part of a separate customs territory to Great Britain.
(2) For the purposes of this section "customs territory" shall have the same meaning as in the General Agreement on Tariffs and Trade 1947 as amended.
Commencement—Part 6 of this Act came into force on 13 September 2018 (see s 57(1)(e)).

56 Consequential and transitional provision
(1) The appropriate Minister may by regulations made by statutory instrument make such provision as the appropriate Minister considers appropriate in consequence of this Act.
(2) The power to make regulations under subsection (1) may (among other things) be exercised by amending or repealing any Act of Parliament other than this Act or one passed after the end of the Session in which this Act is passed.
(3) The power to make regulations under subsection (1) includes power to make transitional or transitory provision and savings.
(4) The appropriate Minister may by regulations made by statutory instrument make such transitional, transitory or saving provision as the appropriate Minister considers appropriate in connection with the coming into force of any provision of this Act.
(5) In this section "the appropriate Minister" means—
  (a) in any case where the provision relates to any provision mentioned in section 57(2), the Secretary of State or the Treasury, and
  (b) in any other case, the Treasury.
(6) Any power to make regulations under this section may be exercised so as to make different provision for different purposes or areas.
(7) Any power to make regulations under this section includes—
  (a) power conferring a discretion on any specified person to do anything under, or for the purposes of, the regulations,
  (b) power to make provision by reference to things specified in a notice published in accordance with the regulations, and
  (c) power to make supplementary, incidental and consequential provision.
(8) A statutory instrument containing regulations under subsection (1) that amends or repeals any Act of Parliament must be laid before the House of Commons, and, unless approved by that House before the end of the period of 28 days beginning with the date on which the instrument is made, ceases to have effect at the end of that period.
(9) The fact that a statutory instrument ceases to have effect as mentioned in subsection (8) does not affect—
  (a) anything previously done under the instrument, or
  (b) the making of a new statutory instrument.
(10) In calculating the period for the purposes of subsection (8), no account is to be taken of any time—
  (a) during which Parliament is dissolved or prorogued, or
  (b) during which the House of Commons is adjourned for more than 4 days.
(11) A statutory instrument containing regulations under subsection (1) to which subsection (8) does not apply is subject to annulment in pursuance of a resolution of the House of Commons.
(12) If—
  (a) a statutory instrument contains provision relating to excise duty under subsection (1) and provision relating to excise duty under another enactment (and "excise duty" has the same meaning in this paragraph as in Part 5), and
  (b) the Parliamentary procedure applicable to a statutory instrument containing provision under the other enactment does not require House of Commons approval (within the meaning of section 48(7)),
the only Parliamentary procedure that is to apply to the instrument mentioned in paragraph (a) is that given by this section.
(13) After it is established, the appropriate Minister must consult the Trade Remedies Authority before including in regulations under this section provision relating to Schedule 4 or 5.
Commencement—Part 6 of this Act came into force on 13 September 2018 (see s 57(1)(e)).
Regulations—Customs (Import Duty) (EU Exit) Regulations, SI 2018/1248.
Value Added Tax (Miscellaneous Amendments and Revocations) (EU Exit) Regulations, SI 2019/59.
Value Added Tax (Accounting Procedures for Import VAT for VAT Registered Persons and Amendment) (EU Exit) Regulations, SI 2019/60.

Value Added Tax and Excise Personal Reliefs (Special Visitors and Goods Permanently Imported) (Amendment) (EU Exit) Regulations, SI 2019/91.
Taxation (Cross-border Trade) Act 2018 (Value Added Tax Transitional Provisions) (EU Exit) Regulations, SI 2019/105.
Customs (Export) (EU Exit) Regulations, SI 2019/108.
Customs (Consequential Amendments) (EU Exit) Regulations, SI 2019/140.
Customs (Import Duty, Transit and Miscellaneous Amendments) (EU Exit) Regulations, SI 2019/326.
Taxation (Cross-border Trade) Act 2018 (Appointed Days No 4 and Transitional Provisions) (Modification) (EU Exit) Regulations, SI 2019/429.
Trade Remedies (Dumping and Subsidisation) (EU Exit) Regulations, SI 2019/450.
Taxation (Cross-border Trade) Act 2018 (Appointed Day No 6 and Transitional Provisions) (Modification) (EU Exit) Regulations, SI 2019/914.
Value Added Tax (Miscellaneous Amendments and Transitional Provisions) (EU Exit) Regulations, SI 2019/1214.
Customs and Excise (Miscellaneous Provisions and Amendments) (EU Exit) Regulations, SI 2019/1215.
Taxation (Cross-border Trade) (Miscellaneous Provisions) (EU Exit) (No 2) Regulations, SI 2019/1346.
Taxation (Cross-border Trade) Act 2018 (Appointed Day No. 7 and Transitory Provisions) (EU Exit) Regulations, SI 2020/97.
Customs (Transitional) (EU Exit) Regulations, SI 2020/1449.
Value Added Tax (Miscellaneous and Transitional Provisions, Amendment and Revocation) (EU Exit) Regulation, SI 2020/1495.
Customs (Northern Ireland) (EU Exit) Regulations, SI 2020/1605.
Customs (Modification and Amendment) (EU Exit) Regulations, SI 2020/1629.
Finance Act 2016, Section 126 (Appointed Day), the Taxation (Cross-border Trade) Act 2018 (Appointed Day No 8, Transition and Saving Provisions) and the Taxation (Post-transition Period) Act 2020 (Appointed Day No 1) (EU Exit) Regulations, SI 2020/1642.

57 Commencement

(1) The following provisions come into force on the day on which this Act is passed—
   (a) Part 1 (other than the provisions mentioned in subsection (2)) so far as making provision for anything to be done by regulations or public notice,
   (b) Part 2,
   (c) sections 44 to 46 and sections 48 and 49,
   (d) Part 5, and
   (e) this Part.
(2) The following provisions come into force on such day as the Secretary of State may by regulations under this section appoint—
   (a) section 10 and Schedule 3 (import duty: preferential rates given unilaterally),
   (b) section 13 and Schedules 4 and 5 (import duty: dumping of goods, foreign subsidies, etc),
   (c) section 15 (import duty: international disputes etc), and
   (d) paragraph 1 of Schedule 7 (replacement of EU customs duties) so far as relating to EU trade duties.
(3) The remaining provisions of this Act come into force on such day as the Treasury may by regulations under this section appoint.
(4) Any power of the Treasury or Secretary of State to appoint a day under this section includes—
   (a) a power to appoint different days for different purposes or areas, and
   (b) a power to appoint a time on a day if the person exercising the power considers it appropriate to do so (including a time that has effect by reference to the coming into force of any other enactment).
(5) Regulations under this section are to be made by statutory instrument.

Commencement—Part 6 of this Act came into force on 13 September 2018 (see s 57(1)(e)).
Regulations—Taxation (Cross-border Trade) Act 2018 (Appointed day No 1) (EU Exit) Regulations, SI 2018/1362.
Taxation (Cross-border Trade) Act 2018 (Appointed Day No 2) (EU Exit) Regulations, SI 2019/69.
Taxation (Cross-border Trade) Act 2018 (Appointed day No 3) and the Value Added Tax (Postal Packets and Amendment) (EU Exit) Regulations 2018 (Appointed day) (EU Exit) Regulations, SI 2019/104.
Taxation (Cross-border Trade) Act 2018 (Appointed Days No 4 and Transitional Provisions) (Modification) (EU Exit) Regulations, SI 2019/429.
Taxation (Cross-border Trade) Act 2018 (Appointed Day No 5 and Miscellaneous Commencements) (EU Exit) Regulations, SI 2019/819.
Taxation (Cross-border Trade) Act 2018 (Appointed Day No 6 and Transitional Provisions) (Modification) (EU Exit) Regulations, SI 2019/914.
Taxation (Cross-border Trade) Act 2018 (Appointed Day No. 7 and Transitory Provisions) (EU Exit) Regulations, SI 2020/97.
Finance Act 2016, Section 126 (Appointed Day), the Taxation (Cross-border Trade) Act 2018 (Appointed Day No 8, Transition and Saving Provisions) and the Taxation (Post-transition Period) Act 2020 (Appointed Day No 1) (EU Exit) Regulations, SI 2020/1642.

58 Short title

This Act may be cited as the Taxation (Cross-border Trade) Act 2018.

SCHEDULE 7

IMPORT DUTY: CONSEQUENTIAL AMENDMENTS

Section 29

Commencement—So far as not already in force, Schedule 7 was brought into force with effect from IP completion day (11pm on 31 December 2020) by the Finance Act 2016, Section 126 (Appointed Day), the Taxation

(Cross-border Trade) Act 2018 (Appointed Day No 8, Transition and Saving Provisions) and the Taxation (Post-transition Period) Act 2020 (Appointed Day No 1) (EU Exit) Regulations, SI 2020/1642 reg 4(a).

Previous commencement provisions affecting Sch 7 are as follows—

Taxation (Cross-border Trade) Act 2018 (Appointed Days No 4 and Transitional Provisions) (Modification) (EU Exit) Regulations, 2019/429 (brought para 1 info force so far as it relates to EU trade duties, immediately after the coming into force of EUWA 2018 s 3 (s 3 came into force on IP completion day, by virtue of SI 2020/1622 reg 3(b))).

Taxation (Cross-border Trade) Act 2018 (Appointed Day No 5 and Miscellaneous Commencements) (EU Exit) Regulations, SI 2019/819 (brought paras 3 and 16 partially into force from 8 April 2019; those paras amend CEMA 1979 s 25).

PART 1
REPLACEMENT OF EU CUSTOMS DUTIES

1 (1) Any direct EU legislation, so far as imposing or otherwise applying in relation to any EU customs duty, that forms part of the law of the United Kingdom as a result of section 3 of the European Union (Withdrawal) Act 2018 (incorporation of direct EU legislation) ceases to have effect.
(2) Nothing in—
   (a) any direct EU legislation, or
   (b) section 4(1) of the European Union (Withdrawal) Act 2018 (saving for EU rights, powers, liabilities, obligations, restrictions, remedies and procedures),
is to have effect in relation to import duty.
(3) Part 1 of this Act—
   (a) contains provisions replacing EU customs duties,
   (b) is not retained EU law, and
   (c) so far as it contains powers to make or give regulations or public notices, enables provision to be made of a kind corresponding to that which could previously have been made by the legislation ceasing to have effect as a result of sub-paragraph (1).
(4) In this paragraph—
   (a) any reference to EU customs duty includes any EU trade duty,
   (b) the reference to EU trade duty is to anti-dumping duty, countervailing duty, safeguard duty and any duty imposed in consequence of an international dispute, and
   (c) the reference to Part 1 of this Act does not include section 29 or this Schedule.

Regulations—Customs (Import Duty) (EU Exit) Regulations, SI 2018/1248.
Customs (Export) (EU Exit) Regulations, SI 2019/108.
Taxation (Cross-border Trade) (Miscellaneous Provisions) (EU Exit) Regulations, SI 2019/486.
Customs and Excise (Miscellaneous Provisions and Amendments) (EU Exit) Regulations, SI 2019/1215.
Taxation (Cross-border Trade) (Miscellaneous Provisions) (EU Exit) (No 2) Regulations, SI 2019/1346.
Customs Tariff (Establishment) (EU Exit) Regulations, SI 2020/1430.
Customs (Reliefs from a Liability to Import Duty and Miscellaneous Amendments) (EU Exit) Regulations, SI 2020/1431.
Customs (Origin of Chargeable Goods) (EU Exit) Regulations , SI 2020/1433.
Customs (Origin of Chargeable Goods: Trade Preference Scheme) (EU Exit) Regulations, SI 2020/1436.
Customs Tariff (Establishment and Suspension of Import Duty) (EU Exit) (Amendment) Regulations, SI 2021/63.

2 Provision relevant to the law relating to duties of customs and other customs matters is made by the European Union (Withdrawal) Act 2018: see, for example, section 2 of that Act (which, among other things, provides for CEMA 1979 to continue to have effect in the law of the United Kingdom).

PART 2
AMENDMENTS OF CEMA 1979

3–117 *(Relevant amendments have been made in CEMA 1979 above and are therefore not reproduced here.)*

PART 3
AMENDMENTS OF OTHER ENACTMENTS

118–157 *(Relevant amendments have been made in the substantive legislation above and are therefore not reproduced here.)*

[PART 4
SAVINGS AND MODIFICATIONS IN RELATION TO NORTHERN IRELAND

Application of CEMA 1979 etc

158 (1) CEMA 1979—

(a) continues to have effect, for any purpose in connection with duty under section 30A(3), as if the amendments made by Part 2 of this Schedule, other than the amendments made by paragraphs 4(4), 93 and 114, were not made, and
(b) applies for any such purpose as if—
  (i) references to an exportation of goods (however framed) included the exit of goods from Northern Ireland that are being removed to Great Britain,
  (ii) references to the departure (however framed) of any goods, person or vehicle from the United Kingdom included a departure of those goods or that person or vehicle from Northern Ireland that is not also a departure from the United Kingdom,
  (iii) references to "the customs territory of the European Union", other than the reference in section 21(2), were to "Northern Ireland or the customs territory of the European Union",
  (iv) references to "EU customs duties" were to "duty under section 30A(3) of the Taxation (Cross-border Trade) Act 2018",
  (v) in section 63(1) and (2), after "place outside" there were inserted "Northern Ireland and" (and the reference to "those States" in section 63(1) included Northern Ireland),
  (vi) in section 78(1B)—
    (a) in the words before paragraph (a), for "another" there were substituted "a", and
    (b) in paragraphs (a) and (b)(ii) after "place outside" there were inserted "Northern Ireland and",
  (vii) in section 92(4)(a) and (b), before "member States" there were inserted "Northern Ireland or the",
  (viii) in section 125(1), for "an EU customs duty" there were substituted "a duty of customs",
  (ix) in subsection (1A) and (2)(a) of section 157, the words "other than the United Kingdom" were omitted,
  (x) the following references to the United Kingdom were to Northern Ireland—
    (a) the references in the definitions of "Community transit goods" and "transit or transhipment" in section 1(1);
    (b) the references in sections 36(1), 55(4)(a), 63(2) to (4), 74, 78(1)(a) and (b), 96(4) and 134(2);
    (c) the reference in the words after paragraph (b) of section 58C(3);
    (d) the second reference in sections 67(1) and 78(2A);
    (e) the first reference in sections 69(1) and 70(3), and
  (xi) the following were omitted—
    (a) sections 21(8), 35(9), 61(9), 63(7), 70(5), 74(5) and 78(1A);
    (b) the words after paragraph (b) of the definition of "Community transit goods" in section 1;
    (c) the words "and the Isle of Man" in sections 34(1), 36(1), 53(1), 64(1) and 66(1)(a) and (d);
    (d) the words "or the Isle of Man" in section 43(5);
    (e) the words "or between a place in the United Kingdom and a place in the Isle of Man" in section 69(1) and (3);
    (f) the words "subject to subsection (1A) above," in section 78(2A).
(2) CEMA 1979 applies, for any purpose in connection with duty under section 30C, as if—
  (a) references to an importation of goods (however framed) included the entry of goods in Great Britain in the course of a removal of those goods to Great Britain from Northern Ireland,
  (b) references to an exportation of goods (however framed) included the exit of goods from Great Britain that are being removed to Northern Ireland,
  (c) references to the departure (however framed) of any goods, person or vehicle from the United Kingdom included a departure of those goods or that person or vehicle from Great Britain that is not also a departure from the United Kingdom, and
  (d) references to the arrival of any goods, person or vehicle from a place outside the United Kingdom (however framed) included the arrival of those goods or that person or vehicle in Great Britain.
(3) CEMA 1979—
  (a) continues to have effect, for any purpose in connection with duty under section 40A, as if the amendments made by Part 2 of this Schedule, other than the amendments made by paragraphs 4(4), 93 and 114, were not made, and
  (b) applies for any such purpose as if—

(i) references to an importation of goods (however framed) included the entry of goods in Northern Ireland in the course of a removal of those goods to Northern Ireland from Great Britain,
(ii) references to an exportation of goods (however framed) included the exit of goods from Northern Ireland that are being removed to Great Britain,
(iii) references to the departure (however framed) of any goods, person or vehicle from the United Kingdom included a departure of those goods or that person or vehicle from Northern Ireland that is not also a departure from the United Kingdom,
(iv) references to the arrival of any goods, person or vehicle from a place outside the United Kingdom (however framed), except in section 78(2A), were to the arrival of those goods or that person or vehicle in Northern Ireland,
(v) references to "the customs territory of the European Union", other than the reference in section 21(2), were to "Northern Ireland or the Customs territory of the European Union",
(vi) references to "EU customs duties" were to "duty under section 40A of the Taxation (Cross-border Trade) Act 2018",
(vii) in section 63(1) and (2), after "place outside" there were inserted "Northern Ireland and" (and the reference to "those States" in section 63(1) included Northern Ireland),
(viii) in section 78(1B)—
 (a) in the words before paragraph (a), for "another" there were substituted "a", and
 (b) in paragraphs (a) and (b)(ii) after "place outside" there were inserted "Northern Ireland and",
(ix) in section 92(4)(a) and (b), before "member States" there were inserted "Northern Ireland or the",
(x) in section 125(1), for "an EU customs duty" there were substituted "a duty of customs",
(xi) in subsection (1A) and (2)(a) of section 157, the words "other than the United Kingdom" were omitted,
(xii) the following references to "the United Kingdom" were to "Northern Ireland"—
 (a) the references in the definitions of "Community transit goods" and "transit or transhipment" in section 1(1);
 (b) the references in sections 36(1), 55(4)(a), 63(2) to (4), 74, 78(1)(a) and (b), 96(4) and 134(2);
 (c) the reference in the words after paragraph (b) of section 58C(3);
 (d) the second reference in sections 67(1) and 78(2A);
 (e) the first reference in sections 69(1) and 70(3), and
(xiii) the following were omitted—
 (a) sections 21(8), 35(9), 61(9), 63(7), 70(5), 74(5) and 78(1A);
 (b) the words after paragraph (b) of the definition of "Community transit goods" in section 1;
 (c) the words "and the Isle of Man" in sections 34(1), 36(1), 53(1), 64(1) and 66(1)(a) and (d);
 (d) the words "or the Isle of Man" in section 43(5);
 (e) the words "or between a place in the United Kingdom and a place in the Isle of Man" in section 69(1) and (3);
 (f) the words "subject to subsection (1A) above," in section 78(2A).
(4) The Customs and Excise Duties (General Reliefs) Act 1979—
 (a) continues to have effect, for any purpose in connection with duty under section 30A(3) or 40A, as if the amendments made by Part 3 of this Schedule, other than the amendments made by paragraphs 123, 135 and 138(3)(b), were not made, and
 (b) applies for any such purpose as if—
  (i) references to an EU instrument or an EU obligation were to the provisions of Union customs legislation,
  (ii) references to an importation of goods (however framed) included the entry of those goods in Northern Ireland in the course of a removal of those goods to Northern Ireland from Great Britain,
  (iii) references to an exportation of goods (however framed) included the exit of goods from Northern Ireland that are being removed to Great Britain,
  (iv) references to the entry of any person or vehicle into the United Kingdom (however framed) included the arrival of that person or vehicle in Northern Ireland, and
  (v) in section 2 (reliefs from customs duty referable to Community practices), for "other" there were substituted "the".

(5) Part 1 of the Finance Act 1994—
 (a) continues to have effect, for any purpose in connection with duty under section 30A(3) or 40A, as if the amendments made by Part 3 of this Schedule, other than the amendments made by paragraphs 144(b) and 145(3)(d), (f) and (i), were not made,
 (b) applies for any such purpose as if—
  (i) references to an importation of goods (however framed) included the entry of goods in Northern Ireland in the course of a removal of those goods to Northern Ireland from Great Britain,
  (ii) references to an exportation of goods (however framed) included the exit of goods from Northern Ireland that are being removed to Great Britain,
  (iii) any reference to the Community Customs Code were to Union customs legislation, and
  (iv) in section 12B(2)(a) (relevant time in case of assessment under section 61 of CEMA 1979) the reference to the United Kingdom were to Northern Ireland, and
 (c) applies for any purpose in connection with duty under section 30C as if—
  (i) references to an importation of goods (however framed) included the entry of goods in Great Britain in the course of a removal of those goods to Great Britain from Northern Ireland, and
  (ii) references to an exportation of goods (however framed) included the exit of goods from Great Britain that are being removed to Northern Ireland.
(6) Item 6 of Group 8 of Schedule 8 to the Value Added Tax Act 1994 has effect as if the reference to a temporary storage facility included a transit shed (within the meaning of CEMA 1979 as it has effect as a result of sub-paragraphs (1) and (3)).
(7) Part 3 of the Finance Act 2003 continues to have effect, for any purpose in connection with duty under section 30A(3) or 40A, as if—
 (a) the amendments made by Part 3 of this Schedule, other than the amendments made by paragraphs 148(2) and (3), 149, 150(3)(a) and 152, were not made, and
 (b) in section 26(8)(c), the words "Union export duty or Union import duty," were omitted.
(8) This paragraph is subject to any provision made by regulations under section 30B(3), 30C(5) or 40B(2) about the application of the customs and excise Acts (which may, for example, include provision for the application of provisions of the customs and excise Acts either as amended or unamended by Parts 2 and 3 of this Schedule).][1]

Modifications—See the Customs (Modification and Amendment) (EU Exit) Regulations, SI 2020/1629 reg 2: any reference in this para to "vehicle" includes a ship, an aircraft and a railway vehicle.
Amendments—[1] Part 4 (para 158) inserted by the Taxation (Post-transition Period) Act 2020 s 2(5), Sch 1 paras 1, 10(1), (6) with effect from IP completion day (11pm on 31 December 2020), by virtue of SI 2020/1642 reg 9.

SCHEDULE 8
VAT AMENDMENTS CONNECTED WITH WITHDRAWAL FROM EU
Section 43

Commencement—So far as not already in force, Schedule 8 was brought into force with effect from IP completion day (11pm on 31 December 2020) by the Finance Act 2016, Section 126 (Appointed Day), the Taxation (Cross-border Trade) Act 2018 (Appointed Day No 8, Transition and Saving Provisions) and the Taxation (Post-transition Period) Act 2020 (Appointed Day No 1) (EU Exit) Regulations, SI 2020/1642 reg 4(b).

Para 14 (which inserted s 16A "postal packets" into VATA 1994) was brought into force by SI 2018/1362 reg 2 with effect from 16 December 2018.

PART 1
AMENDMENTS OF VALUE ADDED TAX ACT 1994

(these amendments have been noted up accordingly alongside the relevant provisions of VATA 1994 and therefore are not reproduced here)

Effect of amendments made by this Part of this Schedule

99 (1) If an amendment made by this Part of this Schedule to a provision of the Value Added Tax Act 1994 has the effect of removing a reference to the principal VAT directive or the implementing VAT regulation, the removal is not to be taken as implying that the directive or regulation is no longer relevant for determining the meaning and effect of that provision.
(2) In this paragraph "the principal VAT directive" and "the implementing VAT regulation" have the same meaning as in section 42.

PART 2
AMENDMENTS OF OTHER ENACTMENTS

(these amendments have been noted up accordingly alongside the relevant provisions and therefore are not reproduced here)

TAXATION (POST-TRANSITION PERIOD) ACT 2020
2020 Chapter 26

An Act to make provision (including the imposition and regulation of new duties of customs) in connection with goods in Northern Ireland and their movement into or out of Northern Ireland; to make provision amending certain enactments relating to value added tax, excise duty or insurance premium tax; to make provision in connection with the recovery of unlawful state aid in relation to controlled foreign companies; and for connected purposes.

17 December 2020

Commencement—The day appointed for the coming into force of this Act, so far as not already in force (and other than Sch 2 para 7(3)), is IP completion day (11pm on 31 December 2020): Finance Act 2016, Section 126 (Appointed Day), the Taxation (Cross-border Trade) Act 2018 (Appointed Day No 8, Transition and Saving Provisions) and the Taxation (Post-transition Period) Act 2020 (Appointed Day No 1) (EU Exit) Regulations, SI 2020/1642 reg 9.

CONTENTS

Northern Ireland Protocol

1   Duty on goods removed to Northern Ireland
2   Duty on goods imported into or removed from Northern Ireland
3   Value added tax in Northern Ireland
4   Excise duty on the removal of goods to Northern Ireland
5   Duty under section 4: supplementary
6   Rate of fuel duty on aviation gasoline

Other provision about value added tax

7   Online sales by overseas persons and low value importations

Insurance premium tax

8   Liability of insured in certain cases

Controlled foreign companies

9   Recovery of unlawful state aid

Final provisions

10   Interpretation
11   Commencement
12   Short title
    Schedules
    Schedule 1—Customs duties etc: amendments relating to the Northern Ireland Protocol
    Schedule 2—Value added tax: amendments relating to the Northern Ireland Protocol etc
    Schedule 3—Online sales by overseas persons and low value importations
    Schedule 4—Recovery of unlawful state aid

Northern Ireland Protocol

1 Duty on goods removed to Northern Ireland

After section 40 of TCTA 2018 insert—

"40A Removal to Northern Ireland of at risk goods etc

(1) A duty of customs is charged on the removal of goods to Northern Ireland from Great Britain if the goods—
    (a) are not domestic goods, or
    (b) are at risk of subsequently being moved into the European Union.

(2) For the purposes of this section "at risk of subsequently being moved into the European Union" has the meaning given by regulations made by the Treasury.

(3) Duty under this section is charged in accordance with Union customs legislation as if the goods subject to the charge were brought into the customs territory of the European Union.

40B Duty under section 40A: supplementary

(1) The Treasury may by regulations provide that, in relation to goods of a specified description, the following matters are to be determined in accordance with provision made by or under this Act (instead of in accordance with Union customs legislation)—
    (a) whether goods in particular circumstances are chargeable to duty under section 40A;
    (b) the amount of duty charged under that section;
    (c) such other matters relating to the charging of duty under section 40A as may be specified.

(2) The Treasury may by regulations make provision generally for the purposes of duty under section 40A.

(3) The following are examples of provision that regulations under subsection (2) may make for the purposes of that duty—

    (a) that section 40A(1) does not apply to goods of a specified description;

    (b) provision about reliefs, repayment and remission (including provision for the recovery of amounts where any condition in connection with any relief, repayment or remission is not met);

    (c) provision about (including provision modifying) the application of provision made by or under the customs and excise Acts (including provision made by or under this Act) to duty under section 40A or to goods removed to Northern Ireland from Great Britain;

    (d) provision supplementing or modifying provisions of Union customs legislation that apply to that duty or to those goods;

    (e) provision imposing checks, controls or administrative processes in connection with the removal of goods to Northern Ireland from Great Britain;

    (f) provision regulating the unloading, landing, movement and removal of goods on their removal to Northern Ireland from Great Britain (including provision restricting the places in which such goods may enter Northern Ireland).

(4) Regulations under this section that specify a description of goods may do so by reference to any matter or circumstance (including, for example, any matter or circumstance relating to any person concerned with the removal of such goods).

(5) Section 40 (regulations) applies to regulations under this section and section 40A as it applies to regulations under section 39 other than the first regulations under that section.

(6) In this section and in section 40A, reference to "Great Britain" is to be treated as including the territorial sea of the United Kingdom.

(7) Expressions used in provision made by or under this section or section 40A that are defined for the purposes of Part 1 have the same meaning they have in that Part."

Commencement—The day appointed for the coming into force of this Act, so far as not already in force (and other than Sch 2 para 7(3)), is IP completion day (11pm on 31 December 2020): SI 2020/1642 reg 9.

2 Duty on goods imported into or removed from Northern Ireland

(1) Part 1 of TCTA 2018 is amended as follows.

(2) In section 1 (charge to import duty)—

    (a) the existing text becomes subsection (1);

    (b) after that subsection insert—

"(2) Sections 30A and 30B make provision about the application of this Part to goods imported into the United Kingdom as a result of their entry into Northern Ireland."

(3) In section 2 (chargeable goods)—

    (a) the existing text becomes subsection (1);

    (b) after that subsection insert—

"(2) But subsection (1) is subject to section 30A(4) (importation of goods: Northern Ireland)."

(4) After section 30 insert—

"Northern Ireland

30A Importation of goods: Northern Ireland

(1) Union goods imported into the United Kingdom as a result of their entry into Northern Ireland are to be treated for the purposes of this Part as if they were domestic goods.

(2) Accordingly, such goods are not chargeable to import duty (but see section 30C).

(3) Other goods imported into the United Kingdom as a result of their entry into Northern Ireland are not chargeable to import duty, but are chargeable to duty under this subsection.

(4) Except as may be provided for by regulations made by the Treasury, such goods are not chargeable goods for the purposes of this Part.

(5) Duty under subsection (3) is chargeable in accordance with Union customs legislation as if the goods subject to the charge were brought into the customs territory of the European Union.

(6) Duty under subsection (3) is a duty of customs, and accordingly the revenues of that duty (as with import duty) are revenues of customs that HMRC Commissioners are responsible for collecting and managing.

30B Duty under section 30A(3): supplementary

(1) The Treasury may by regulations provide that, in relation to goods of a specified description, the following matters are to be determined in accordance with provision made by or under this Act (instead of in accordance with Union customs legislation)—
- (a) whether goods in particular circumstances are chargeable to duty under section 30A(3);
- (b) the amount of duty charged under that subsection;
- (c) such other matters relating to the charging of duty under that subsection as may be specified.

(2) Regulations under subsection (1) may specify a description of goods by reference to any matter or circumstance (including, for example, any matter or circumstance relating to any person concerned with the importation of such goods).

(3) The Treasury may by regulations make provision generally for the purposes of duty under section 30A(3).

(4) The following are examples of provision that regulations under subsection (3) may make for the purposes of that duty—
- (a) provision about reliefs, repayment and remission in relation to duty under section 30A(3) (including provision for the recovery of amounts where any condition in connection with any relief, repayment or remission is not met);
- (b) provision about (including provision modifying) the application of provision made by or under the customs and excise Acts (including provision made by or under this Act) to duty under section 30A(3) or to goods imported into the United Kingdom as a result of their entry into the Northern Ireland;
- (c) provision supplementing or modifying provisions of Union customs legislation that apply to that duty or to those goods.

30C Duty on potentially imported goods

(1) A duty of customs is charged on the removal of goods to Great Britain from Northern Ireland if the goods are not qualifying Northern Ireland goods.

(2) A duty of customs is charged on the removal of other goods to Great Britain from Northern Ireland if the main purpose, or one of the main purposes, of the removal is to—
- (a) avoid any other duty chargeable as a result of this Act, or
- (b) avoid any obligation in connection with such a duty.

(3) The relevant import duty provisions apply for the purposes of duty charged under this section as if—
- (a) any reference to chargeable goods were to goods removed to Great Britain from Northern Ireland,
- (b) any reference to the importation of goods were to their removal to Great Britain from Northern Ireland,
- (c) in section 6(2), for "the United Kingdom" there were substituted "Great Britain", and
- (d) in section 16(2), for "export to the United Kingdom" there were substituted "removal to Great Britain".

(4) A provision is a "relevant import duty provision" if it is provision made by or under any of sections 3 to 28 and 34 and Schedules 1 to 6.

(5) The Treasury may by regulations make provision generally for the purposes of duty under this section.

(6) The following are examples of provision that regulations under subsection (5) may make for the purposes of that duty—
- (a) that subsection (1) does not to apply to goods of a specified description (and if it does not, whether such goods are to be treated as "other goods" for the purposes of subsection (2));
- (b) that subsection (3) does not apply, to such extent as may be specified, to goods of a specified description;
- (c) that any reference in this Part to Great Britain is to be treated as including the territorial sea, or any specified area of the territorial sea, of the United Kingdom;
- (d) provision about (including provision modifying) the application of provision made by or under the customs and excise Acts (including provision made by or under this Act) to duty under this section or to goods removed from Northern Ireland to Great Britain;

(e) provision imposing checks, controls or administrative processes in connection with the removal of goods to Great Britain from Northern Ireland (and such checks, controls and processes may be imposed for any purpose in connection with duty under this section despite any provision of any enactment whenever passed);
(f) provision regulating the unloading, landing, movement and removal of goods on their removal to Great Britain from Northern Ireland (including provision restricting the places in which such goods may enter Great Britain).

(7) Regulations under this section that specify a description of goods may do so by reference to any matter or circumstance (including, for example, any matter or circumstance relating to any person concerned with the removal of such goods)."

(5) Schedule 1 contains amendments to TCTA 2018 and other Acts in connection with the provisions of the Protocol on Ireland/Northern Ireland in the EU withdrawal agreement that concern tax.

Commencement—The day appointed for the coming into force of this Act, so far as not already in force (and other than Sch 2 para 7(3)), is IP completion day (11pm on 31 December 2020): SI 2020/1642 reg 9.

3 Value added tax in Northern Ireland

(1) In VATA 1994, before section 41 insert—

"**40A Northern Ireland Protocol**
(1) Schedule 9ZA—
 (a) makes provision about a charge to VAT on acquisitions of goods in Northern Ireland from a member State, and
 (b) contains modifications of the other provisions of this Act in connection with the movement of goods between Northern Ireland and member States.
(2) Schedule 9ZB—
 (a) makes provision about VAT charged on goods imported into the United Kingdom as a result of their entry into Northern Ireland,
 (b) makes provision about the treatment, for the purposes of VAT, of goods that are removed from Northern Ireland to Great Britain and goods that are removed from Great Britain to Northern Ireland, and
 (c) contains other provision relevant to the application of this Act in Northern Ireland."

(2) Part 1 of Schedule 2 inserts the Schedules referred to in the amendment made by subsection (1) into VATA 1994 and contains further amendments of that Act (as amended by TCTA 2018).
(3) Part 2 of that Schedule makes amendments to other legislation in connection with the amendments made by Part 1.
(4) Where a provision inserted into VATA 1994 as a result of Schedule 2 re-enacts (with or without modifications) provision repealed by TCTA 2018 (or by that Schedule), unless the contrary intention appears—
 (a) any reference in any provision made by or under an enactment to the repealed provision is to be construed as a reference to the re-enacted provision;
 (b) any order or regulations that would otherwise cease to have effect as a result of the repeal continues to have effect as if made under the re-enacted provision (subject to any modifications made to that provision, and with such modifications to that order or those regulations as may be necessary).

Commencement—The day appointed for the coming into force of this Act, so far as not already in force (and other than Sch 2 para 7(3)), is IP completion day (11pm on 31 December 2020): SI 2020/1642 reg 9.

4 Excise duty on the removal of goods to Northern Ireland

(1) Where goods to which a relevant excise duty provision applies are removed to Northern Ireland from Great Britain, excise duty is charged on those goods under that provision.
(2) Each of the following is a "relevant excise duty provision"—
 (a) section 5 of ALDA 1979 (spirits);
 (b) section 36 of that Act (beer);
 (c) section 37 of that Act (high strength beer);
 (d) section 54 of that Act (wine);
 (e) section 55 of that Act (made-wine);
 (f) section 62 of that Act (cider);
 (g) section 6 of HODA 1979 (hydrocarbon oil);
 (h) section 6AA of that Act (biodiesel);
 (i) section 6AB of that Act (bioblend);
 (j) section 6AD of that Act (bioethanol);
 (k) section 6AE of that Act (bioethanol blend);
 (l) section 6AG of that Act (aqua methanol);
 (m) section 6A of that Act (fuel substitutes);
 (n) section 8 of that Act (road fuel gas);

(o) section 2 of TPDA 1979 (tobacco products).

(3) Subsection (1) does not apply to a removal of goods to which a relevant excise duty provision mentioned in paragraph (h), (j), (l) or (m) applies unless, prior to their removal, the goods were set aside for, or put to, a chargeable use (within the meaning of the relevant excise duty provision in question) by any person.

(4) Subsection (1) does not apply to a removal of road fuel gas (within the meaning given by section 5 of HODA 1979) unless, prior to its removal from Great Britain the gas was—
  (a) sent out from the premises of a person producing or dealing in road fuel gas, or
  (b) set aside for use, or put to use, as fuel for a road vehicle (within the meaning of that Act) by any person.

(5) Goods are removed to Northern Ireland when their entry in Northern Ireland would amount to an importation of excise goods within the meaning of Article 4 of the Union excise directive if—
  (a) any reference in that Article to "excise goods" included any goods to which a relevant excise duty provision applies,
  (b) the references in point 8 of that Article to "the territory of the Community" and "the Community" were to Northern Ireland, and
  (c) the reference in point 6 of that Article to "special procedures as provided for under Regulation (EEC) No 2913/92" were to the procedures under Union customs legislation that correspond to those procedures.

(6) In subsection (5)—
  "the Union excise directive" means Council Directive 2008/118/EC of 16 December 2008 concerning the general arrangements for excise duty and repealing Directive 92/12/EEC;
  "Union customs legislation" means provisions contained in "customs legislation" within the meaning of Regulation (EU) No 952/2013 of the European Parliament and of the Council of 9 October 2013 laying down the Union Customs Code (see Article 5(2) of that Regulation), as they have effect as a result of section 7A of the European Union (Withdrawal) Act 2018.

Commencement—The day appointed for the coming into force of this Act, so far as not already in force (and other than Sch 2 para 7(3)), is IP completion day (11pm on 31 December 2020): SI 2020/1642 reg 9.

5 Duty under section 4: supplementary

(1) Any provision made by or under the customs and excise Acts that applies to, or in connection with, duty under a relevant excise duty provision by reference to the importation of goods applies to duty charged as a result of section 4(1) as if—
  (a) any reference to the importation of goods (however framed) were to their removal to Northern Ireland from Great Britain, and
  (b) any reference to the entry of any person or vehicle into the United Kingdom (however framed) were to the arrival of that person or vehicle in Northern Ireland.

(2) The Treasury may by regulations made by statutory instrument make provision, for the purposes of duty charged as a result of section 4(1), about (including provision modifying) the application of the customs and excise Acts (including this section and section 4) to that duty or to goods that are, or may be, subject to that duty.

(3) A statutory instrument containing regulations made under subsection (2) is subject to annulment in pursuance of a resolution of the House of Commons.

(4) In this section—
  "the customs and excise Acts" has the meaning it has in CEMA 1979 (see section 1(1) of that Act);
  "relevant excise duty provision" is to be construed in accordance with section 4(2).

(5) This section and section 4 have effect in relation to any removal of goods to Northern Ireland from Great Britain that commences on or after IP completion day.

(6) For the purposes of subsection (5), a removal of goods commences—
  (a) in the case of goods carried by (which for these purposes includes where the goods constitute, or are within, accompanying baggage of) a person travelling from Great Britain to Northern Ireland on an aircraft or vessel, when the aircraft or vessel is scheduled to depart from the airport or port in Great Britain from which it departs, and
  (b) in any other case, when the goods are dispatched from the place in Great Britain from which they are removed.

Commencement—The day appointed for the coming into force of this Act, so far as not already in force (and other than Sch 2 para 7(3)), is IP completion day (11pm on 31 December 2020): SI 2020/1642 reg 9.

6 Rate of fuel duty on aviation gasoline

In section 6(1A)(aa) of HODA 1979 (rate of fuel duty on aviation gasoline), for "£0.3770" substitute "£0.3820".

Commencement—Section 6 came into force on 1 January 2021 (see s 11(2)).

Other provision about value added tax

7 Online sales by overseas persons and low value importations

Schedule 3 makes provision for the purposes of value added tax in cases involving—

(a) supplies of goods by persons established outside the United Kingdom that are facilitated by online marketplaces;
(b) the importation into the United Kingdom of goods of a low value.

Commencement—The day appointed for the coming into force of this Act, so far as not already in force (and other than Sch 2 para 7(3)), is IP completion day (11pm on 31 December 2020): SI 2020/1642 reg 9.

Insurance premium tax

8 Liability of insured in certain cases

In section 65 of FA 1994 (insurance premium tax: liability of insured in certain cases), for subsections (1A) and (1B) substitute—

"(1A) The condition mentioned in subsection (1)(b) above is that there are no arrangements in relation to the country or territory relating to insurance premium tax which—
 (a) have effect by virtue of an Order in Council under section 173 of the Finance Act 2006, and
 (b) contain provision of a kind mentioned in subsection (2)(a) and (b) of that section."

Commencement—The day appointed for the coming into force of this Act, so far as not already in force (and other than Sch 2 para 7(3)), is IP completion day (11pm on 31 December 2020): SI 2020/1642 reg 9.

Controlled foreign companies

9 Recovery of unlawful state aid

Schedule 4 makes provision in connection with the charging of amounts under Part 9A of TIOPA 2010 (the CFC charge in relation to controlled foreign companies) as if one of the exemptions in Chapter 9 of that Part (exemptions for profits from qualifying loan relationships) had not applied, in order to comply with Commission Decision (EU) 2019/1352 of 2 April 2019 on the state aid SA.44896 implemented by the United Kingdom concerning the CFC Group Financing Exemption (referred to in that Schedule as "the Commission Decision").

Commencement—Section 9 came into force on 17 December 2020 (see s 11(1)(a)).
The day appointed for the coming into force of this Act, so far as not already in force (and other than Sch 2 para 7(3)), is IP completion day (11pm on 31 December 2020): SI 2020/1642 reg 9.

Final provisions

10 Interpretation

In this Act the following abbreviations are references to the following Acts—

ALDA 1979	Alcoholic Liquor Duties Act 1979
CEMA 1979	Customs and Excise Management Act 1979
FA, followed by a year	Finance Act of that year
F(No 2)A, followed by a year	Finance (No 2) Act of that year
HODA 1979	Hydrocarbon Oil Duties Act 1979
TCTA 2018	Taxation (Cross-border Trade) Act 2018
TIOPA 2010	Taxation (International and Other Provisions) Act 2010
TPDA 1979	Tobacco Products Duty Act 1979
VATA 1994	Value Added Tax Act 1994

Commencement—Section 10 came into force on 17 December 2020 (see s 11(1)(b)).
The day appointed for the coming into force of this Act, so far as not already in force (and other than Sch 2 para 7(3)), is IP completion day (11pm on 31 December 2020): SI 2020/1642 reg 9.

11 Commencement

(1) The following provisions come into force on the day on which this Act is passed—
 (a) section 9 and Schedule 4,
 (b) section 10,
 (c) this section,
 (d) section 12, and
 (e) the remaining provisions of this Act so far as making provision for anything to be done by regulations or order.
(2) Section 6 comes into force on 1 January 2021.
(3) The remaining provisions of this Act come into force on such day as the Treasury may by regulations made by statutory instrument appoint.
(4) The power of the Treasury to appoint a day under subsection (3) includes—
 (a) a power to appoint different days for different purposes or areas, and
 (b) a power to appoint a time on a day if the Treasury consider it appropriate to do so (including a time that has effect by reference to the coming into force of any other enactment).

(5) The Treasury may by regulations made by statutory instrument make such consequential, supplementary, incidental, transitional, transitory or saving provision as the Treasury consider appropriate in connection with the coming into force of any provision of this Act.
(6) Regulations under subsection (5) may make different provision for different purposes or areas.

Commencement—The day appointed for the coming into force of this Act, so far as not already in force (and other than Sch 2 para 7(3)), is IP completion day (11pm on 31 December 2020): SI 2020/1642 reg 9.

Regulations—Customs (Modification and Amendment) (EU Exit) Regulations, SI 2020/1629.

Finance Act 2016, Section 126 (Appointed Day), the Taxation (Cross-border Trade) Act 2018 (Appointed Day No 8, Transition and Saving Provisions) and the Taxation (Post-transition Period) Act 2020 (Appointed Day No 1) (EU Exit) Regulations, SI 2020/1642.

12 Short title

This Act may be cited as the Taxation (Post-transition Period) Act 2020.

SCHEDULE 1
CUSTOMS DUTIES ETC: AMENDMENTS RELATING TO THE NORTHERN IRELAND PROTOCOL

Section 2

Commencement—The day appointed for the coming into force of this Act, so far as not already in force (and other than Sch 2 para 7(3)), is IP completion day (11pm on 31 December 2020): SI 2020/1642 reg 9.

Amendments of TCTA 2018

1   TCTA 2018 is amended in accordance with paragraphs 2 to 11.

2   In section 3 (obligation to declare goods for a customs procedure on import), in subsection (3)(a) for "the United Kingdom" substitute "Great Britain".

3   In section 32 (regulations), in subsection (9)(a) after "Part" insert "or under section 40A or 40B".

4   (1) Section 33 (meaning of "domestic goods") is amended as follows.
(2) In subsection (2)—
  (a) omit the "or" after paragraph (a);
  (b) in paragraph (b) for "discharged." substitute "discharged, or";
  (c) after that paragraph insert—
    "(c)   the goods—
      (i)   are not Union goods and were removed to Northern Ireland (in the course of their importation into the United Kingdom or otherwise), and
      (ii)   were declared, in accordance with Union customs legislation, for a procedure corresponding to the free-circulation procedure or the authorised use procedure and that corresponding procedure has been discharged, while the goods were in Northern Ireland, in accordance with that legislation."
(3) In subsection (3)—
  (a) in paragraph (a), after "the United Kingdom" insert "as a result of the removal of the goods from Great Britain";
  (b) in the words after paragraph (b), after "then" insert "(subject to section 30A)".
(4) In subsection (4), after "goods" insert "resulting from the removal of the goods from Great Britain".
(5) After that subsection insert—
  "(4A) Goods also cease to be domestic goods if they—
    (a) are exported from the United Kingdom as a result of their removal from Northern Ireland, and
    (b) are not of a description specified in regulations made by the Treasury,
  and the goods are then (subject to section 30A) chargeable goods until such time (if any) as they are next subject to a chargeable Customs procedure.
  (4B) Regulations under subsection (4A)(b) may specify a description of goods by reference to any matter or circumstance (including, for example, any matter or circumstance relating to any person concerned with the export of such goods)."
(6) In subsection (5), for "goods exported from the United Kingdom in accordance with the applicable export provisions" substitute "relevant exported goods".
(7) After that subsection insert—
  "(5A) For the purposes of subsection (5), exported goods are "relevant" if—
    (a) they were exported as a result of their removal from Northern Ireland, or
    (b) they were exported as a result of their removal from Great Britain and were so exported in accordance with the applicable export provisions."

5 In section 36 (outward processing procedure), in subsection (2)—
   (a) in paragraph (a), after "the United Kingdom", in the first place it occurs, insert "as a result of the removal of the goods from Great Britain";
   (b) in paragraph (b), after "the United Kingdom" insert "and removed to Great Britain (whether in the course of that importation or otherwise)".

6 In section 37 (minor definitions), in subsection (1), at the appropriate places insert—
   ""the customs and excise Acts" has the meaning it has in CEMA 1979 (see section 1(1) of that Act);";
   ""qualifying Northern Ireland goods" has the meaning it has in the European Union (Withdrawal) Act 2018 (see section 8C(6) of that Act);";
   ""Union customs legislation" means provisions contained in "customs legislation" within the meaning of Regulation (EU) No 952/2013 of the European Parliament and of the Council of 9 October 2013 laying down the Union Customs Code (see Article 5(2) of that Regulation), as they have effect as a result of section 7A of the European Union (Withdrawal) Act 2018;";
   ""Union goods" has the meaning it has in that Regulation;".

7 In section 38 (table of definitions), in the table, at the appropriate places insert—

"the customs and excise Acts	section 37(1)"
"qualifying Northern Ireland goods	section 37(1)"
"Union goods	section 37(1)"
"Union customs legislation	section 37(1)"

8 (1) Schedule 1 (customs declarations) is amended as follows.
(2) In paragraph 1(4)—
   (a) in paragraph (a), after "United Kingdom" insert ", or removed to Northern Ireland,";
   (b) in paragraph (b), before "the export" insert "in the case of goods exported from the United Kingdom,".
(3) In paragraph 2(2)—
   (a) in paragraph (a), for the words from "in the United Kingdom" to the end substitute "in, or outside, a specified place";
   (b) in paragraph (b)—
      (i) after "have" insert ", or do not have,";
      (ii) for "the United Kingdom or to a specified place outside the United Kingdom" substitute "a specified place".

9 (1) Schedule 2 (special customs procedures) is amended as follows.
(2) In paragraph 1(2)(a) for the words from "in the United Kingdom" to the end substitute "in, or outside, a specified place".
(3) In paragraph 5(1), for "the United Kingdom", in each place it occurs, substitute "Great Britain".
(4) In paragraph 9—
   (a) in sub-paragraph (1)(a), for "there" substitute "in Great Britain";
   (b) in sub-paragraph (5)—
      (i) after "provisions" insert ", or removed to Northern Ireland,";
      (ii) for "the United Kingdom" substitute "Great Britain";
   (c) in sub-paragraph (6)(a), for "the United Kingdom" substitute "Great Britain".
(5) In paragraph 11—
   (a) in paragraph (a), for "the United Kingdom, or" substitute "Great Britain,";
   (b) after that paragraph insert—
      "(aa) that the goods are to be subject to any operation designed to secure that they comply with requirements that must be met before the goods can lawfully be released in accordance with Union customs legislation to a procedure corresponding to the free-circulation procedure, or".
(6) In paragraph 15, in paragraph (b), after "provisions" insert "or are removed to Northern Ireland".

(7) In paragraph 19, in sub-paragraph (3)(a) after "provisions" insert "or are removed to Northern Ireland".

10 (1) Schedule 7 (import duty: consequential amendments) is amended as follows.
(2) In paragraph 114, after "Part 1" insert "or section 40A or 40B".
(3) In paragraph 146—
   (a) the existing text becomes sub-paragraph (1);
   (b) after that sub-paragraph insert—
   "(2) Where the provisions of CEMA 1979 relating to transit sheds continue to have effect for any purpose (see paragraph 158), the provision amended by sub-paragraph (1) continues to have effect, for that purpose, as if the amendments made by that sub-paragraph were not made."
(4) In paragraph 150(3)(a)—
   (a) after "Part 1" insert "and sections 40A and 40B";
   (b) for "it applies" substitute "they apply".
(5) In paragraph 156—
   (a) for sub-paragraph (2) substitute—
   "(2)   In subsection (2)—
       (a)   in paragraph (b), for "of Council Regulation (EC) No 384/96, as amended from time to time" substitute "it has in Union customs legislation";
       (b)   in paragraph (c) for "of Council Regulation (EC) No 2026/97, as amended from time to time" substitute "it has in Union customs legislation".";
   (b) in sub-paragraph (3)(b), after "Part 1" insert "and sections 40A and 40B";
   (c) for sub-paragraph (4) substitute—
   "(4)   In subsection (9), in paragraph (c), for "EU law" substitute "retained EU law, or Union customs legislation,".
   (5)   After that subsection insert—
   "(10)   In this section "Union customs legislation" has the meaning it has in Part 1 of the Taxation (Cross-border Trade) Act 2018.""
(6) After paragraph 157 insert—

"PART 4
SAVINGS AND MODIFICATIONS IN RELATION TO NORTHERN IRELAND

Application of CEMA 1979 etc

158
(1)   CEMA 1979—
      (a)   continues to have effect, for any purpose in connection with duty under section 30A(3), as if the amendments made by Part 2 of this Schedule, other than the amendments made by paragraphs 4(4), 93 and 114, were not made, and
      (b)   applies for any such purpose as if—
            (i)   references to an exportation of goods (however framed) included the exit of goods from Northern Ireland that are being removed to Great Britain,
            (ii)   references to the departure (however framed) of any goods, person or vehicle from the United Kingdom included a departure of those goods or that person or vehicle from Northern Ireland that is not also a departure from the United Kingdom,
            (iii) references to "the customs territory of the European Union", other than the reference in section 21(2), were to "Northern Ireland or the customs territory of the European Union",
            (iv)   references to "EU customs duties" were to "duty under section 30A(3) of the Taxation (Cross-border Trade) Act 2018",
            (v)   in section 63(1) and (2), after "place outside" there were inserted "Northern Ireland and" (and the reference to "those States" in section 63(1) included Northern Ireland),
            (vi)   in section 78(1B)—
                   (a) in the words before paragraph (a), for "another" there were substituted "a", and
                   (b) in paragraphs (a) and (b)(ii) after "place outside" there were inserted "Northern Ireland and",
            (vii) in section 92(4)(a) and (b), before "member States" there were inserted "Northern Ireland or the",

(viii) in section 125(1), for "an EU customs duty" there were substituted "a duty of customs",
(ix) in subsection (1A) and (2)(a) of section 157, the words "other than the United Kingdom" were omitted,
(x) the following references to the United Kingdom were to Northern Ireland—
(a) the references in the definitions of "Community transit goods" and "transit or transhipment" in section 1(1);
(b) the references in sections 36(1), 55(4)(a), 63(2) to (4), 74, 78(1)(a) and (b), 96(4) and 134(2);
(c) the reference in the words after paragraph (b) of section 58C(3);
(d) the second reference in sections 67(1) and 78(2A);
(e) the first reference in sections 69(1) and 70(3), and
(xi) the following were omitted—
(a) sections 21(8), 35(9), 61(9), 63(7), 70(5), 74(5) and 78(1A);
(b) the words after paragraph (b) of the definition of "Community transit goods" in section 1;
(c) the words "and the Isle of Man" in sections 34(1), 36(1), 53(1), 64(1) and 66(1)(a) and (d);
(d) the words "or the Isle of Man" in section 43(5);
(e) the words "or between a place in the United Kingdom and a place in the Isle of Man" in section 69(1) and (3);
(f) the words "subject to subsection (1A) above," in section 78(2A).

(2) CEMA 1979 applies, for any purpose in connection with duty under section 30C, as if—
(a) references to an importation of goods (however framed) included the entry of goods in Great Britain in the course of a removal of those goods to Great Britain from Northern Ireland,
(b) references to an exportation of goods (however framed) included the exit of goods from Great Britain that are being removed to Northern Ireland,
(c) references to the departure (however framed) of any goods, person or vehicle from the United Kingdom included a departure of those goods or that person or vehicle from Great Britain that is not also a departure from the United Kingdom, and
(d) references to the arrival of any goods, person or vehicle from a place outside the United Kingdom (however framed) included the arrival of those goods or that person or vehicle in Great Britain.

(3) CEMA 1979—
(a) continues to have effect, for any purpose in connection with duty under section 40A, as if the amendments made by Part 2 of this Schedule, other than the amendments made by paragraphs 4(4), 93 and 114, were not made, and
(b) applies for any such purpose as if—
(i) references to an importation of goods (however framed) included the entry of goods in Northern Ireland in the course of a removal of those goods to Northern Ireland from Great Britain,
(ii) references to an exportation of goods (however framed) included the exit of goods from Northern Ireland that are being removed to Great Britain,
(iii) references to the departure (however framed) of any goods, person or vehicle from the United Kingdom included a departure of those goods or that person or vehicle from Northern Ireland that is not also a departure from the United Kingdom,
(iv) references to the arrival of any goods, person or vehicle from a place outside the United Kingdom (however framed), except in section 78(2A), were to the arrival of those goods or that person or vehicle in Northern Ireland,
(v) references to "the customs territory of the European Union", other than the reference in section 21(2), were to "Northern Ireland or the Customs territory of the European Union",
(vi) references to "EU customs duties" were to "duty under section 40A of the Taxation (Cross-border Trade) Act 2018",
(vii) in section 63(1) and (2), after "place outside" there were inserted "Northern Ireland and" (and the reference to "those States" in section 63(1) included Northern Ireland),
(viii) in section 78(1B)—

(a) in the words before paragraph (a), for "another" there were substituted "a", and
(b) in paragraphs (a) and (b)(ii) after "place outside" there were inserted "Northern Ireland and",
   (ix) in section 92(4)(a) and (b), before "member States" there were inserted "Northern Ireland or the",
   (x) in section 125(1), for "an EU customs duty" there were substituted "a duty of customs",
   (xi) in subsection (1A) and (2)(a) of section 157, the words "other than the United Kingdom" were omitted,
   (xii) the following references to "the United Kingdom" were to "Northern Ireland"—
      (a) the references in the definitions of "Community transit goods" and "transit or transhipment" in section 1(1);
      (b) the references in sections 36(1), 55(4)(a), 63(2) to (4), 74, 78(1)(a) and (b), 96(4) and 134(2);
      (c) the reference in the words after paragraph (b) of section 58C(3);
      (d) the second reference in sections 67(1) and 78(2A);
      (e) the first reference in sections 69(1) and 70(3), and
   (xiii) the following were omitted—
      (a) sections 21(8), 35(9), 61(9), 63(7), 70(5), 74(5) and 78(1A);
      (b) the words after paragraph (b) of the definition of "Community transit goods" in section 1;
      (c) the words "and the Isle of Man" in sections 34(1), 36(1), 53(1), 64(1) and 66(1)(a) and (d);
      (d) the words "or the Isle of Man" in section 43(5);
      (e) the words "or between a place in the United Kingdom and a place in the Isle of Man" in section 69(1) and (3);
      (f) the words "subject to subsection (1A) above," in section 78(2A).
(4) The Customs and Excise Duties (General Reliefs) Act 1979—
   (a) continues to have effect, for any purpose in connection with duty under section 30A(3) or 40A, as if the amendments made by Part 3 of this Schedule, other than the amendments made by paragraphs 123, 135 and 138(3)(b), were not made, and
   (b) applies for any such purpose as if—
      (i) references to an EU instrument or an EU obligation were to the provisions of Union customs legislation,
      (ii) references to an importation of goods (however framed) included the entry of those goods in Northern Ireland in the course of a removal of those goods to Northern Ireland from Great Britain,
      (iii) references to an exportation of goods (however framed) included the exit of goods from Northern Ireland that are being removed to Great Britain,
      (iv) references to the entry of any person or vehicle into the United Kingdom (however framed) included the arrival of that person or vehicle in Northern Ireland, and
      (v) in section 2 (reliefs from customs duty referable to Community practices), for "other" there were substituted "the".
(5) Part 1 of the Finance Act 1994—
   (a) continues to have effect, for any purpose in connection with duty under section 30A(3) or 40A, as if the amendments made by Part 3 of this Schedule, other than the amendments made by paragraphs 144(b) and 145(3)(d), (f) and (i), were not made,
   (b) applies for any such purpose as if—
      (i) references to an importation of goods (however framed) included the entry of goods in Northern Ireland in the course of a removal of those goods to Northern Ireland from Great Britain,
      (ii) references to an exportation of goods (however framed) included the exit of goods from Northern Ireland that are being removed to Great Britain,
      (iii) any reference to the Community Customs Code were to Union customs legislation, and

(iv) in section 12B(2)(a) (relevant time in case of assessment under section 61 of CEMA 1979) the reference to the United Kingdom were to Northern Ireland, and

(c) applies for any purpose in connection with duty under section 30C as if—
  (i) references to an importation of goods (however framed) included the entry of goods in Great Britain in the course of a removal of those goods to Great Britain from Northern Ireland, and
  (ii) references to an exportation of goods (however framed) included the exit of goods from Great Britain that are being removed to Northern Ireland.

(6) Item 6 of Group 8 of Schedule 8 to the Value Added Tax Act 1994 has effect as if the reference to a temporary storage facility included a transit shed (within the meaning of CEMA 1979 as it has effect as a result of sub-paragraphs (1) and (3)).

(7) Part 3 of the Finance Act 2003 continues to have effect, for any purpose in connection with duty under section 30A(3) or 40A, as if—
  (a) the amendments made by Part 3 of this Schedule, other than the amendments made by paragraphs 148(2) and (3), 149, 150(3)(a) and 152, were not made, and
  (b) in section 26(8)(c), the words "Union export duty or Union import duty," were omitted.

(8) This paragraph is subject to any provision made by regulations under section 30B(3), 30C(5) or 40B(2) about the application of the customs and excise Acts (which may, for example, include provision for the application of provisions of the customs and excise Acts either as amended or unamended by Parts 2 and 3 of this Schedule)."

11 In Schedule 9 (excise duty amendments connected with withdrawal from EU), after paragraph 9 insert—

"Savings in relation to Northern Ireland

10

The provisions amended by this Schedule continue to have effect—
  (a) for any purpose in connection with duty charged as a result of section 4(1) of the Taxation (Post-transition Period) Act 2020, and
  (b) in relation to goods in Northern Ireland,
as if those provisions were not so amended."

Isle of Man Act 1979

12 (1) The Isle of Man Act 1979 is amended as follows.
(2) In section 8 (removal of goods from Isle of Man to United Kingdom), in subsection (2), before paragraph (a) insert—
  "(za) goods removed to Northern Ireland from the Isle of Man;".
(3) In section 9 (removal of goods from United Kingdom to Isle of Man), after subsection (1) insert—
  "(1A) Subsection (1) does not apply to goods removed from Northern Ireland to the Isle of Man."

Finance (No 2) Act 1992

13 (1) Section 4 of F(No 2)A 1992 is amended as follows.
(2) In subsection (1)—
  (a) for "the United Kingdom" substitute "Northern Ireland";
  (b) for "different" substitute "Northern Ireland and a member State or between".
(3) In subsection (1A), for "different" substitute "Northern Ireland and a member State or between".
(4) In subsection (2)—
  (a) in paragraph (a)—
    (i) omit "EU" in the first place it occurs;
    (ii) for "EU legislation" substitute "Union customs legislation (within the meaning of Part 1 of the Taxation (Cross-border Trade) Act 2018);
  (b) in paragraph (b), for "EU legislation" substitute "provision of Union customs legislation".
(5) In subsection (5), omit the definition of "EU customs duty".

SCHEDULE 2
VALUE ADDED TAX: AMENDMENTS RELATING TO THE NORTHERN IRELAND PROTOCOL ETC

Section 3

Commencement—The day appointed for the coming into force of this Act, so far as not already in force (and other than Sch 2 para 7(3)), is IP completion day (11pm on 31 December 2020): SI 2020/1642 reg 9.

PART 1
AMENDMENTS OF VATA 1994

1 VATA 1994 is amended as follows.

New Schedules: VAT in Northern Ireland

2 After Schedule 9 insert—

"SCHEDULE 9ZA
VAT ON ACQUISITIONS IN NORTHERN IRELAND FROM MEMBER STATES

Section 40A(1)

PART 1
CHARGE TO VAT FOR ACQUISITIONS IN NORTHERN IRELAND FROM MEMBER STATES

Charge to VAT

1

(1) VAT is charged, in accordance with this Schedule, on the acquisition in Northern Ireland of goods from a member State—
   (a) by reference to the value of the acquisition as determined under Part 2 of this Schedule, and
   (b) subject to paragraph 16, at the rate of VAT for the time being in force under section 2.

(2) VAT charged on the acquisition of goods in Northern Ireland from a member State is a liability of the person who acquires the goods and (subject to provisions about accounting and payment) becomes due at the time of acquisition.

(3) VAT charged on the acquisition of goods in Northern Ireland from a member State in accordance with this Schedule is referred to in this Schedule as "NI acquisition VAT".

(4) References to VAT (without more) in this Act include NI acquisition VAT.

(5) The Commissioners may by regulations make provision about (including provision modifying) the application of provision that applies to value added tax made by or under any enactment (including provision made by or under this Act) to NI acquisition VAT or to goods acquired in Northern Ireland from a member State.

Scope of NI acquisition VAT

2

(1) NI acquisition VAT is charged on any acquisition from a member State of any goods where—
   (a) the acquisition is a taxable acquisition,
   (b) it takes place in Northern Ireland,
   (c) it is not in pursuance of a taxable supply (see section 4(2)), and
   (d) the person who makes it is a taxable person or the goods acquired are subject to a duty of excise or consist in a new means of transport.

(2) In this Act, a "taxable acquisition" means an acquisition of goods from a member State that—
   (a) is not an exempt acquisition (see paragraph 17(5)), and
   (b) falls within sub-paragraph (3) or is an acquisition of goods consisting in a new means of transport.

(3) An acquisition of goods from a member State falls within this sub-paragraph if—

(a) the goods are acquired in the course or furtherance of—
    (i) any business carried on by any person, or
    (ii) any activities carried on otherwise than by way of business by any body corporate or by any club, association, organisation or other unincorporated body,
(b) it is the person who carries on that business or those activities who acquires the goods, and
(c) the supplier—
    (i) is taxable in a member State at the time of the transaction in pursuance of which the goods are acquired, and
    (ii) in participating in that transaction, acts in the course or furtherance of a business carried on by the supplier.

Meaning of acquisition of goods from a member State

3

(1) References in this Act to the acquisition of goods from a member State are to an acquisition of goods in pursuance of a transaction that—
(a) is a supply of goods (including anything treated for the purposes of this Act as a supply of goods), and
(b) involves the removal of the goods from a member State (whether by or under the direction of the supplier, the person who acquires the goods or any other person),

and references in this Act, in relation to such an acquisition, to the supplier are to be construed accordingly.

(2) Where the person with the property in any goods does not change in consequence of anything which is treated for the purposes of this Act as a supply of goods, that supply is to be treated for the purposes of this Act as a transaction in pursuance of which there is an acquisition by the person making the supply.

(3) The Treasury may by regulations make provision about the circumstances in which an acquisition of goods is not to be treated as an acquisition of goods from a member State.

Time of acquisition

4

(1) For the purposes of this Act, the normal rule for determining the time that goods were acquired from a member State is that they are treated as being acquired on the earlier of—
(a) the 15th day of the month after the month in which the first removal of the goods occurs, and
(b) the day a relevant invoice is issued in respect of the transaction in pursuance of which the goods were acquired.

(2) But—
(a) different rules apply to acquisitions to which Part 4 of Schedule 9ZB applies (warehouses), and
(b) the Commissioners may by regulations provide for different rules to apply in any case described in those regulations.

(3) Regulations under sub-paragraph (2)(b) may include provision treating an acquisition as a series of acquisitions taking place at different times.

(4) In sub-paragraph (1) "relevant invoice" means an invoice of a description prescribed by regulations made by the Commissioners.

(5) For the purposes of this Act "first removal", in relation to goods acquired, means the first removal of the goods in the course of the transaction in pursuance of which they are acquired.

Place of acquisition

5

(1) For the purposes of this Act, the normal rule for determining whether goods are acquired in Northern Ireland is that they are treated as being acquired in Northern Ireland if—

        (a)   they are acquired in pursuance of a transaction which involves their removal from a member State to Northern Ireland and which does not involve their removal from Northern Ireland, or
        (b)   they are acquired by a person who, for the purposes of their acquisition, makes use of a number assigned to the person for the purposes of VAT in the United Kingdom along with an NI VAT identifier (see paragraph 7).
  (2)   But—
        (a)   goods are not treated as being acquired in Northern Ireland by virtue of sub-paragraph (1)(b) where it is established in accordance with regulations made by the Commissioners that VAT—
               (i)   has been paid in a member State on the acquisition of those goods, and
               (ii)   fell to be paid by virtue of provisions of the law of that member State corresponding, in relation to that member State, to the provision made by sub-paragraph (1)(a), and
        (b)   different rules apply to acquisitions to which paragraph 16 or 17 of Schedule 9ZB applies.
  (3)   If an acquisition of goods is not treated, for the purposes of this Act, as taking place in Northern Ireland it is treated for those purposes as an acquisition taking place outside Northern Ireland.
  (4)   The Commissioners may by regulations make provision—
        (a)   about the circumstances in which a person is to be treated as having made use of a number assigned to the person for the purposes of VAT in the United Kingdom along with an NI VAT identifier for the purposes of the acquisition of any goods, and
        (b)   for the refund, in prescribed circumstances, of NI acquisition VAT paid on acquisitions of goods in relation to which the conditions in sub-paragraph (2)(a)(i) and (ii) are met.

                         Acquisitions from persons belonging in member States

6
  (1)   Sub-paragraph (2) applies where—
        (a)   a person ("the original supplier") makes a supply of goods to a person who belongs in a member State ("the intermediate supplier"),
        (b)   that supply involves the removal of the goods from a member State and their removal to Northern Ireland but does not involve the removal of the goods from Northern Ireland,
        (c)   both that supply and the removal of the goods to Northern Ireland are for the purposes of the making of a supply by the intermediate supplier to another person ("the customer") who is registered under this Act,
        (d)   neither of those supplies involves the removal of the goods from a member State in which the intermediate supplier is taxable at the time of the removal without also involving the previous removal of the goods to that member State, and
        (e)   there would be a taxable acquisition by the customer if the supply to the customer involved the removal of goods from a member State to Northern Ireland.
  (2)   Where this sub-paragraph applies—
        (a)   the supply by the original supplier to the intermediate supplier is ignored for the purposes of this Act, and
        (b)   the supply by the intermediate supplier to the customer is treated for the purposes of this Act, other than for the purposes of Part 8 of this Schedule, as if it did involve the removal of the goods from a member State to Northern Ireland.
  (3)   For the purposes of this Act, other than for the purposes of Part 8 of this Schedule, a supply of goods is treated as involving their removal from a member State to Northern Ireland, and is treated as not being a taxable supply if—
        (a)   the supply is made by a person belonging in a member State to a person who is registered under this Act,
        (b)   the supply involves the installation or assembly of the goods at a place in Northern Ireland to which they are removed, and
        (c)   were the supply to be treated as described in the words before paragraph (a), there

would be a taxable acquisition by the registered person.

(4) But neither sub-paragraph (2) nor sub-paragraph (3) applies in relation to a supply unless—
- (a) in the case of sub-paragraph (2), the intermediate supplier, or
- (b) in the case of sub-paragraph (3), the person making the supply,

complies with such requirements to provide information to the Commissioners or to the person supplied as may be specified in regulations made by the Commissioners.

(5) The requirements to provide information that may be specified in regulations include—
- (a) requirements to provide documents (for example, invoices);
- (b) requirements to provide information or documents before a supply is made (as well as after);
- (c) requirements as to the content and form of information or documents to be provided;
- (d) requirements as to the manner in which information or documents are to be provided.

(6) Where a taxable acquisition is treated as having been made by virtue of this paragraph, that acquisition is treated as taking place at the time referred to in paragraph 4(1)(b) (day on which invoice issued).

(7) For the purposes of this paragraph a person belongs in a member State if—
- (a) the person is taxable in a member State,
- (b) the person does not have any business establishment or other fixed establishment in Northern Ireland,
- (c) the person's usual place of residence is not in Northern Ireland,
- (d) the person is not identified for the purposes of VAT in Northern Ireland and is not required, as a result of regulations under paragraph 7, to make a request to be so identified, and
- (e) the person does not have a VAT representative who is identified for the purposes of VAT in Northern Ireland in connection with acting on the person's behalf, and is not for the time being required to appoint one who would be identified for those purposes.

(8) In determining, for the purposes of sub-paragraph (7)(d), whether a person is required to be registered under this Act, ignore any supplies made by the person that would be ignored for the purposes of this Act if the person belonged in a member State and complied with the information requirements that would apply by virtue of sub-paragraph (4).

(9) Where—
- (a) any goods are acquired from a member State in a case which corresponds, in relation to another member State, to the case described in sub-paragraph (1) in relation to Northern Ireland, and
- (b) the person who acquires the goods is registered under this Act, is identified for the purposes of VAT in Northern Ireland and would be the intermediate supplier in relation to that corresponding case,

the supply to that person of those goods and the supply by that person of those goods to the person who would be the customer in that corresponding case are to be ignored for the purposes of this Act.

(10) References in this paragraph to a person being taxable in a member State do not include references to a person who is so taxable by virtue only of provisions of the law of that member State corresponding to the provisions of this Act by virtue of which a person who is not registered under this Act is a taxable person if the person is required to be so registered.

Identification of persons for the purposes of VAT in Northern Ireland

7

(1) The Commissioners may by regulations make provision for the identification of persons for the purposes of VAT in Northern Ireland.

(2) In this Act "identified for the purposes of VAT in Northern Ireland" means identified in accordance with regulations under this paragraph.

(3) A person may only be identified for the purposes of VAT in Northern Ireland if—
- (a) the person is registered under this Act, or
- (b) the person acts on behalf of a person in relation to VAT in Northern Ireland as a VAT

representative.

(4) Regulations may make provision—
- (a) about the circumstances in which a person may request to be identified for the purposes of VAT in Northern Ireland;
- (b) for a person to be required to request to be identified for the purposes of Northern Ireland VAT;
- (c) about the circumstances in which the Commissioners may determine that a person is identified for the purposes of VAT in Northern Ireland otherwise than at the person's request;
- (d) requiring a person to notify the Commissioners of such matters as may be specified for the purpose of allowing the Commissioners to ascertain whether a person should be identified for the purposes VAT in Northern Ireland;
- (e) about the circumstances in which a person is to be treated, for such purposes as may be specified, as if they were identified for the purposes of VAT in Northern Ireland (and which may include circumstances where the person is neither registered under this Act nor acting as a VAT representative);
- (f) about the circumstances in which a person ceases to be identified for the purposes of VAT in Northern Ireland.

(5) Regulations may also make provision—
- (a) about a specified means of communicating the fact of a person's identification for the purposes of VAT in Northern Ireland (and that means is referred to in this Act as an "NI VAT identifier");
- (b) about the circumstances in which a person may use, or is required to use, an NI VAT identifier (for example, in connection with the making of a transaction or return).

(6) In this paragraph "specified" means specified in regulations.

PART 2
VALUATION OF ACQUISITIONS

Valuation of acquisitions from member States

8

(1) For the purposes of this Act the value of any acquisition of goods from a member State is taken to be the value of the transaction in pursuance of which they are acquired.

(2) Where goods are acquired from a member State otherwise than in pursuance of a taxable supply, the value of the transaction in pursuance of which they are acquired is to be determined for the purposes of sub-paragraph (1) in accordance with this Part, and for those purposes—
- (a) sub-paragraphs (3) to (5) have effect subject to paragraphs 9 to 13, and
- (b) section 19 and Schedule 6 do not apply in relation to the transaction.

(3) If the transaction is for a consideration in money, its value is taken to be such amount as is equal to the consideration.

(4) If the transaction is for a consideration not consisting or not wholly consisting of money, its value is taken to be such amount in money as is equivalent to the consideration.

(5) Where a transaction in pursuance of which goods are acquired from a member State is not the only matter to which a consideration in money relates, the transaction is deemed to be for such part of the consideration as is properly attributable to it.

Transactions below market value

9

(1) Where, in the case of the acquisition of any goods from a member State—
- (a) the relevant transaction (see paragraph 13) is for a consideration in money,
- (b) the value of the relevant transaction is (apart from this paragraph) less than the transaction's open market value,
- (c) the supplier and the person who acquires the goods are connected, and
- (d) that person is not entitled under sections 25 and 26 to credit for all the VAT on the acquisition,

the Commissioners may direct that the value of the relevant transaction is taken to be its open market value.

(2) A direction under this paragraph must be given—
　(a)　by notice in writing to the person by whom the acquisition in question is made, and
　(b)　within the period of 3 years commencing with the relevant time (see paragraph 13).

(3) A direction given to a person under this paragraph in respect of a transaction may include a direction that the value of any transaction—
　(a)　in pursuance of which goods are acquired by the person from a member State after the giving of the notice, or after such later date as may be specified in the notice, and
　(b)　as to which the conditions in paragraphs (a) to (d) of sub-paragraph (1) are satisfied,
is be taken to be its open market value.

(4) For the purposes of this paragraph, the open market value of a transaction in pursuance of which goods are acquired from a member State is to be taken to be the amount which would fall to be taken as its value under paragraph 8(3) if it were for such consideration in money as would be payable by a person standing in no such relationship with any person as would affect that consideration.

(5) Section 1122 of the Corporation Tax Act 2010 ("connected" persons) applies for the purpose of determining whether a person is connected with another for the purposes of this paragraph.

(6) A direction under this paragraph may be varied or withdrawn by the Commissioners by a further direction given by notice in writing.

Value where goods subject to excise duty etc

10

(1) This paragraph applies, in such cases as the Commissioners may by regulations prescribe, to an acquisition—
　(a)　of goods acquired in Northern Ireland from a member State,
　(b)　where those goods are charged with a relevant duty, and
　(c)　that is not an acquisition that is treated, by virtue of paragraph 16(7) of Schedule 9ZB, as taking place before the time which is the duty point (within the meaning given by paragraph 16(11) of that Schedule).

(2) The value of the relevant transaction in relation to an acquisition to which this paragraph applies is the sum of the value of that transaction (apart from this paragraph) and the total amount of relevant duty charged that is not already reflected in the value of that transaction.

(3) In this paragraph "relevant duty" in relation to an acquisition means—
　(a)　a duty of excise charged in connection with the removal of goods to Northern Ireland;
　(b)　any EU customs duty or agricultural levy of the European Union charged on that removal in accordance with any provision for the time being having effect for transitional purposes in connection with the accession of any State to the European Union.

Transfer or disposal for no consideration

11

(1) Where goods are acquired from a member State in pursuance of anything which is treated as a supply for the purposes of this Act as a result of paragraph 5(1) of Schedule 4 or paragraph 30 of Schedule 9ZB and there is no consideration, sub-paragraph (3) applies for determining the value of the relevant transaction.

(2) Sub-paragraph (3) also applies for determining the value of the relevant transaction in the case of an acquisition by a supplier that is deemed to take place as a result of paragraph 60(2)(c) or 61(2)(c).

(3) The value of the relevant transaction is taken to be—
　(a)　such consideration in money as would be payable by the supplier if the supplier were, at the time of the acquisition, to purchase goods identical in every respect (including age and condition) to the goods concerned,

(b) where the value cannot be ascertained in accordance with paragraph (a), such consideration in money as would be payable by the supplier if the supplier were, at that time, to purchase goods similar to, and of the same age and condition as, the goods concerned, or

(c) where the value cannot be ascertained in accordance with paragraph (a) or (b), the cost of producing the goods concerned if they were produced at that time.

(4) For the purposes of sub-paragraph (3), the amount of consideration in money that would be payable by any person if the person were to purchase any goods is taken to be the amount that would be so payable after the deduction of any amount included in the purchase price in respect of VAT on the supply of the goods to that person.

Foreign currency transactions

12

(1) Subject to the following provisions of this paragraph, where—
   (a) goods are acquired from a member State, and
   (b) any sum relevant for determining the value of the relevant transaction is expressed in a currency other than sterling,

then, for the purpose of valuing the relevant transaction, that sum is to be converted into sterling at the market rate which, on the relevant day, would apply in the United Kingdom to a purchase with sterling of that sum in the currency in question by the person making the acquisition.

(2) Where the Commissioners have published a notice which, for the purposes of this paragraph, specifies—
   (a) rates of exchange, or
   (b) methods of determining rates of exchange,

a rate specified in or determined in accordance with the notice, as for the time being in force, applies (instead of the rate for which sub-paragraph (1) provides) in the case of any transaction in pursuance of which goods are acquired by a person who opts, in such manner as may be allowed by the Commissioners, for the use of that rate in relation to that transaction.

(3) An option for the purposes of sub-paragraph (2) for the use of a particular rate or method of determining a rate—
   (a) may not be exercised by any person except in relation to all such transactions in pursuance of which goods are acquired by the person from a member State as are of a particular description or after a particular date, and
   (b) may not be withdrawn or varied except with the consent of the Commissioners and in such manner as they may require.

(4) In specifying a method of determining a rate of exchange, a notice published by the Commissioners under sub-paragraph (2) may allow a person to apply to the Commissioners for the use, for the purpose of valuing some or all of the transactions in pursuance of which goods are acquired by the person from a member State, of a rate of exchange which is different from any which would otherwise apply.

(5) On an application made in accordance with provision contained in a notice under sub-paragraph (4), the Commissioners may authorise the use with respect to the applicant of such a rate of exchange, in such circumstances, in relation to such transactions and subject to such conditions as they think fit.

(6) A notice published by the Commissioners for the purposes of this paragraph may be withdrawn or varied by a subsequent notice published by the Commissioners.

(7) Where goods are acquired from a member State, the appropriate rate of exchange is to be determined for the purpose of valuing the relevant transaction by reference to the relevant time; and, accordingly, the day on which that time falls is the relevant day for the purposes of sub-paragraph (1).

Meaning of "relevant transaction" and "relevant time"

13

In this Part of this Schedule—

"relevant transaction", in relation to any acquisition of goods from a member State, means the transaction in pursuance of which the goods are acquired;

"the relevant time", in relation to any such acquisition, means—
> (a) if the person by whom the goods are acquired is not a taxable person and the time of acquisition does not fall to be determined in accordance with regulations made under paragraph 4(2)(b), the time of the first removal of the goods (see paragraph 4(5)), and
> (b) in any other case, the time of acquisition.

PART 3
PAYMENT OF NI ACQUISITION VAT BY TAXABLE PERSONS

Input tax and output tax

14

(1) NI acquisition VAT is input tax in relation to the taxable person acquiring the goods in question if the goods are used or are to be used for the purpose of any business carried on or to be carried on by the person.

(2) NI acquisition VAT is output tax in relation to the taxable person acquiring the goods in question (including VAT which is also to be counted as input tax by virtue of sub-paragraph (1)).

(3) Subsections (5) to (6A) of section 24 (input tax and output tax) apply to NI acquisition VAT as they apply to VAT on the supply or importation of goods.

Payment of NI acquisition VAT

15

(1) A taxable person must account for and pay NI acquisition VAT by reference to prescribed accounting periods (see section 25(1)).

(2) Subsections (2) to (6) of section 25 (payment by reference to accounting period and credit for input tax against output tax) contain provision relevant to the payment of NI acquisition VAT.

(3) Subsection (7) of that section (power to make order excluding credit for VAT paid) applies to acquisitions in Northern Ireland from a member State as it applies to the supply of goods.

(4) Section 26(1) has effect as if the reference to "input tax on supplies and importations" included input tax on acquisitions in Northern Ireland from a member State.

(5) That section and sections 26A to 28 contain further provision relevant to the payment of NI acquisition VAT.

PART 4
RELIEFS ETC

Reduced rate

16

(1) NI acquisition VAT is charged at the rate of 5% (instead of at the rate provided by section 2) if—
> (a) the acquisition in question is of goods the supply of which would be a supply of a description for the time being specified in Schedule 7A (charge at reduced rate), or
> (b) the acquisition in question is of a description for the time being specified in regulations made by the Treasury for the purposes of this paragraph.

(2) Regulations under this paragraph may provide that sub-paragraph (1)(a) does not apply to a description of a supply specified in Schedule 7A that is specified in those regulations.

(3) The power to specify a description of an acquisition conferred by sub-paragraph (1)(b) may be exercised so as to describe an acquisition of goods by reference to matters unrelated to the characteristics of the goods.

Zero-rating and exempt acquisitions

17

(1) Section 30(3) (zero-rating) applies to an acquisition of goods in Northern Ireland from a member State as it would apply to an importation of those goods.

(2) The Treasury may by regulations provide—
  (a) that sub-paragraph (1) does not apply to an acquisition of goods specified or described in the regulations;
  (b) that no NI acquisition VAT is chargeable on an acquisition of goods specified or described in the regulations.

(3) The Commissioners may by regulations provide for the zero-rating of supplies of goods, or of such goods as may be specified in the regulations, in cases where—
  (a) the supply in question involves both the removal of the goods from Northern Ireland and their acquisition in a member State by a person who is liable for VAT on the acquisition in accordance with provisions of the law of that member State corresponding, in relation to that member State, to the provisions of paragraph 2, and
  (b) such other conditions, if any, as may be specified in the regulations or the Commissioners may impose are fulfilled.

(4) Section 30(10) applies to a supply of goods that has been zero-rated in pursuance of regulations made under sub-paragraph (3) as it applies to a supply of goods that has been zero-rated in pursuance of regulations made under section 30(8) or (9).

(5) An acquisition of goods from a member State is an exempt acquisition if the goods are acquired in pursuance of an exempt supply (see section 31).

Refunds and reliefs

18

(1) Sections 33 to 33C, 33E and 34 apply to an acquisition of goods from a member State as they apply to a supply of those goods.

(2) The Treasury may by order make provision for relieving from NI acquisition VAT if, or to the extent that, relief from VAT would be given by an order under section 37 (relief from VAT on importation) if the acquisition in question were an importation.

(3) An order under sub-paragraph (2) may provide for relief to be subject to such conditions as appear to the Treasury to be necessary or expedient, which may include conditions—
  (a) prohibiting or restricting the disposal of or dealing with the goods concerned;
  (b) framed by reference to the conditions to which, by virtue of any order under section 37 in force at the time of the acquisition, relief under such an order would be subject in the case of an importation of the goods concerned.

(4) Where relief from NI acquisition VAT given by an order under this paragraph was subject to a condition that has been breached or not complied with, the VAT becomes payable at the time of the breach or, as the case may be, at the latest time allowed for compliance.

(5) Section 38 has effect as if after "by him" there were inserted "or on the acquisition of goods by that person from member States".

Refunds in relation to new means of transport supplied to member States

19

(1) Where a person who is not a taxable person makes such a supply of goods consisting in a new means of transport that involves the removal of the goods to a member State from Northern Ireland, the Commissioners must, on a claim made in that behalf, refund to that person, as the case may be—
  (a) the amount of any VAT on the supply of that means of transport to that person, or
  (b) the amount of any VAT paid by that person on the acquisition of that means of transport from a member State or on its importation into the United Kingdom as a result of its entry into Northern Ireland.

(2) But the amount of VAT that is to be refunded under this paragraph is not to exceed the amount that would have been payable on the supply involving the removal if it had been a taxable supply by a taxable person and had not been zero-rated.

(3) A claim for refund of VAT under this paragraph must—
  (a) be made within such time and in such form and manner as may be specified in regulations made by the Commissioners,
  (b) contain such information as may be specified in those regulations, and

(c) be accompanied by such documents as may be specified in those regulations.

PART 5
APPLICATION OF ACT TO ACQUISITIONS IN PARTICULAR CASES

Crown application

20

Subsections (3) and (4) of section 41 (application to the Crown) apply to NI acquisition VAT as they apply to VAT chargeable on the supply of goods.

Groups of companies

21

(1) Section 43 (groups of companies) applies to an acquisition of goods from a member State as it would apply to an importation of those goods as if the reference in subsection (1)(c) to section 38 were omitted.

(2) Subsections (2) and (9) of section 44 (supplies to groups) apply to input tax on acquisitions as they applies to input tax on supplies.

Partnerships

22

(1) Subsection (1) of section 45 (partnerships) applies to persons carrying on in partnership activities, other than carrying on a business, in the course or furtherance of which they acquire goods from a member State as it apples to persons carrying on a business in partnership.

(2) Subsections (2) and (5) of that section apply to a liability for NI acquisition VAT as they apply to VAT on the supply of goods or services.

Unincorporated bodies, personal representative etc

23

(1) In section 46 (business carried on in divisions or by unincorporated bodies, personal representatives etc) any reference to "a business" includes any activity in the course or furtherance of which any body corporate or any club, association, organisation or other unincorporated body acquires goods from a member State.

(2) Subsection (3) of that section (no account to be taken in change of members of a club, association or organisation) applies in relation to the determination of whether goods are acquired from a member State by a club, association or organization mentioned in that subsection as it applies in relation to the determination of whether goods or services are supplied by such a club, association or organisation.

Agents

24

(1) Where goods are acquired from a member State by a person who is not a taxable person ("N") and a taxable person ("T") acts in relation to the acquisition and then supplies the goods in T's own name as agent of N, the goods are to be treated for the purposes of this Act as acquired and supplied by T as principal.

(2) Section 47 (agents) has effect as if—
    (a) the reference in subsection (2) to "subsection (1) above" were to "subsection (1) and paragraph 24(1) of Schedule 9ZA";
    (b) the reference in subsection (2A) to "subsection (1) above" were to "subsection (1) or paragraph 24(1) of Schedule 9ZA".

VAT representatives

25

Subsection (1)(a) of section 48 (VAT representatives and security) applies to a person who, without being a taxable person, acquires goods in Northern Ireland from one or more member States as it applies to a person who, without being a taxable person, makes taxable supplies.

Margin schemes

26

Section 50A(5) (margin schemes) has effect as if after "supply," there were inserted "acquisition".

PART 6
ADMINISTRATION, COLLECTION AND ENFORCEMENT

Breaches of regulatory provisions

27

(1) Section 69(1) (breaches of regulatory provisions) applies to a failure to comply with a requirement imposed under paragraph 42, 52 or 65(1) or (2)(a) of this Schedule as it applies to a requirement imposed under the provisions mentioned in subsection (1)(a) of that section.

(2) Section 69(2) has effect as if after "imposed under" there were inserted "paragraph 64 or 65(2)(b) of Schedule 9ZA or".

Offences

28

(1) Any reference in section 72(1) or (8) (offences)—
    (a) to the evasion of VAT includes a reference to the obtaining of a refund under regulations made under paragraph 5(4) or under paragraph 19, and
    (b) to the amount of VAT, in relation to such a refund, is to be construed as a reference to the amount falsely claimed by way of refund.

(2) Subsection (5) of section 72 applies to a claim for a refund under regulations made under paragraph 5(4) or under paragraph 19 as it applies to a claim for a refund under the provisions mentioned in paragraph (a) of that subsection.

(3) Subsection (10) of that section applies where a person has reason to believe that NI acquisition VAT has been or will be evaded as it applies where a person has reason to believe that VAT on the supply of goods or services has been or will be evaded.

Failure to make returns

29

(1) Subsection (3) of section 73 (failure to make returns etc) applies to an amount which by reason of the cancellation of a person's registration under paragraph 43(2), 43(5) or 53(5) ought not to have been paid as it applies to an amount which ought not to have been paid by reason of the cancellation of a person's registration under any of the provisions mentioned in that subsection.

(2) Subsection (7) of that section applies to the acquisition of goods from a member State by a taxable person as it applies to the supply of goods to a taxable person.

Interest on VAT

30

Paragraph (c) of Section 74(1) applies to a person who was, but should no longer have been, exempted from registration (under Part 8 of this Schedule) under paragraph 44 as it applies to a person who was, but should no longer have been, exempted from registration under any of the provisions mentioned in that paragraph.

Assessment in cases of acquisitions of certain goods by non-taxable persons

31

(1) Where a person who has, at a time when the person was not a taxable person, acquired in Northern Ireland from a member State any goods subject to a duty of excise or consisting in a new means of transport and—
- (a) notification of that acquisition has not been given to the Commissioners by the person who is required to give one by regulations under paragraph 73(4) (whether before or after this paragraph comes into force),
- (b) the Commissioners are not satisfied that the particulars relating to the acquisition in any notification given to them are accurate and complete, or
- (c) there has been a failure to supply the Commissioners with the information necessary to verify the particulars contained in any such notification,

the Commissioners may assess the amount of VAT due on the acquisition to the best of their judgment and notify their assessment to that person.

(2) An assessment under this paragraph must be made within the time limits provided for in section 77 and may not be made after the later of—
- (a) 2 years after the time when a notification of the acquisition of the goods in question is given to the Commissioners by the person who is required to give one by regulations under paragraph 73(4), and
- (b) one year after evidence of the facts, sufficient in the opinion of the Commissioners to justify the making of the assessment, comes to their knowledge,

but (subject to section 77) where further such evidence comes to the Commissioners' knowledge after the making of an assessment under this section, another assessment may be made under this paragraph, in addition to any earlier assessment.

(3) Where an amount has been assessed and notified to any person under this paragraph, it is, subject to the provisions of this Act as to appeals, deemed to be an amount of VAT due from the person and may be recovered accordingly, unless, or except to the extent that, the assessment has subsequently been withdrawn or reduced.

(4) For the purposes of this paragraph, notification to a personal representative, trustee in bankruptcy, trustee in sequestration, receiver, liquidator or person otherwise acting in a representative capacity in relation to the person who made the acquisition in question is to be treated as notification to that person.

Assessment of amounts due

32

Section 77 (time limits and supplementary assessments) has effect as if—
- (a) in subsection (1), in the words before paragraph (a), after "or 76" there were inserted "or paragraph 31 of Schedule 9ZA";
- (b) in paragraph (a) of that subsection, after "importation" there were inserted "or acquisition";
- (c) in subsection (4), after "importation" there were inserted ", acquisition";
- (d) in subsection (4C) after paragraph (a) there were inserted—
- "(aza) paragraph 40 or 44(2) of Schedule 9ZA,
- (azb) paragraph 50 of that Schedule,
- (azc) regulations under paragraph 73(4) of that Schedule,";
- (e) in subsection (6), after "73(6)(b)" there were inserted "or paragraph 31(2)(b) of Schedule 9ZA".

Credit for, or repayment of, overstated or overpaid VAT

33

In section 80 (credit for, or repayment of, overstated or overpaid VAT) has effect as if in subsection (3C) reference to VAT provisions included any provision of any EU instrument relating to VAT, or to any matter connected with VAT, that has effect in Northern Ireland as a result of section 7A of the European Union (Withdrawal) Act 2018 (general implementation of withdrawal agreement).

PART 7

APPEALS AND SUPPLEMENTARY PROVISION

Appeals

34

(1) The following matters are to be treated as if they were included in the list of matters in subsection (1) of section 83 (matters subject to appeal to the tribunal)—

    (a)   the VAT chargeable on the acquisition of goods from a member State;

    (b)   any claim for a refund under any regulations made by virtue of paragraph 5(4) of this Schedule;

    (c)   any direction under paragraph 9 of this Schedule;

    (d)   the amount of any refunds under paragraph 19 of this Schedule;

    (e)   an assessment under paragraph 31 of this Schedule, or the amount of such an assessment;

    (f)   a decision of the Commissioners under paragraph 17 of Schedule 9ZB—

        (i)   as to whether or not a person is to be approved as a Northern Ireland fiscal warehousekeeper or the conditions from time to time subject to which the person is so approved,

        (ii)   for the withdrawal of any such approval, or

        (iii)   for the withdrawal of Northern Ireland fiscal warehouse status from any premises.

(2) Section 84 (further provisions relating to appeals) has effect as if in subsection (4)(c), after "supply" there were inserted ", acquisition".

Supplies spanning change of rate etc

35

(1) This paragraph applies where there is a change in the rate of VAT in force under section 2 or paragraph 16 of this Schedule or in the descriptions of exempt, zero-rated or reduced-rate acquisitions.

(2) Where—

    (a)   any acquisition of goods from a member State which is affected by the change would not have been affected (in whole or in part) if it had been treated as taking place at the time of the first removal of the goods (see paragraph 4(5)), or

    (b)   any acquisition of goods from a member State which is not so affected would have been affected (in whole or in part) if it had been treated as taking place at the time of that removal,

the rate at which VAT is chargeable on the acquisition, or any question of whether it is an exempt, zero-rated or reduced-rate acquisition, is to be determined as at the time of the first removal of the goods, if the person making the acquisition so elects.

(3) References in this paragraph to a zero-rated acquisition is to an acquisition on which no NI acquisition VAT is charged as a result of provision made by or under paragraph 17 (zero-rating).

(4) Reference in this paragraph to a reduced rate acquisition is to an acquisition on which NI acquisition VAT is charged at the rate in force under paragraph 16(1).

Failure of resolution under Provisional Collection of Taxes Act 1968

36

(1) Where—

    (a)   by virtue of a resolution having effect under the Provisional Collection of Taxes Act 1968 NI acquisition VAT has been paid at a rate specified in the resolution by reference to a value determined under paragraph 8(3) of this Schedule, and

    (b)   by virtue of section 1(6) or (7) or 5(3) of that Act any of that VAT is repayable in consequence of the restoration of a lower rate,

the amount repayable is to be the difference between the VAT paid by reference to that value at the rate specified in the resolution and the VAT that would have been payable by reference to that value at the lower rate.

(2) Where—
  (a) by virtue of such a resolution NI acquisition VAT is chargeable at a rate specified in the resolution by reference to a value determined under paragraph 8(3) of this Schedule, but
  (b) before the VAT is paid it ceases to be chargeable at that rate in consequence of the restoration of a lower rate,

the VAT chargeable at the lower rate is to be charged by reference to the same value as that by reference to which NI acquisition VAT would have been chargeable at the rate specified in the resolution.

(3) Section 90(3) (failure of resolution under Provisional Collection of Taxes Act 1968) has effect as if after "or 35" there were inserted "or paragraph 19 of Schedule 9ZA".

Refund of VAT to Government of Northern Ireland

37

(1) Section 99 (refund of VAT to Government of Northern Ireland) applies to—
  (a) VAT charged on the acquisition of goods from a member State by the Government of Northern Ireland as it applies to VAT charged on the supply of goods or services to that Government, and
  (b) any amount attributable to acquisitions of goods from a member State for the purpose of a business carried on by the Government of Northern Ireland as it applies to supplies for that purpose.

PART 8

REGISTRATION IN RESPECT OF ACQUISITIONS FROM MEMBER STATES

Liability to be registered

38

(1) A person who—
  (a) is not registered under this Act, and
  (b) is not liable to be registered under Schedule 1 or 1A or Part 9 of this Schedule,

becomes liable to be registered under this Part of this Schedule at the end of any month if, in the period beginning with 1 January of the year in which that month falls, that person had made relevant acquisitions whose value exceeds £85,000.

(2) A person who is not registered or liable to be registered as mentioned in sub-paragraph (1)(a) and (b) becomes liable to be registered under this Part of this Schedule at any time if there are reasonable grounds for believing that the value of the person's relevant acquisitions in the following 30 days will exceed £85,000.

(3) A person is treated as having become liable to be registered under this Part of this Schedule at any time when the person would have become so liable under the preceding provisions of this paragraph but for any registration which is subsequently cancelled under paragraph 43(2) or 53(5) of this Schedule, paragraph 13(3) of Schedule 1, paragraph 11 of Schedule 1A or paragraph 6(2) of Schedule 3A.

(4) A person does not cease to be liable to be registered under this Part of this Schedule except in accordance with paragraph 39.

(5) In determining the value of any person's relevant acquisitions for the purposes of this paragraph, so much of the consideration for any acquisition as represents any liability of the supplier, under the law of a member State, for VAT on the transaction in pursuance of which the acquisition is made, is to be disregarded.

(6) In determining the value of a person's acquisitions for the purposes of sub-paragraph (1) or (2), acquisitions to which paragraph 19(6) of Schedule 9ZB (last acquisition or supply of goods before removal from Northern Ireland fiscal warehousing) applies are to be disregarded.

39

(1) A person who has become liable to be registered under this Part of this Schedule ceases to be so liable if at any time—
  (a) the person's relevant acquisitions in the year ending with 31 December last before that time did not have a value exceeding £85,000, and

(b) the Commissioners are satisfied that the value of the person's relevant acquisitions in the year immediately following that year will not exceed £85,000.

(2) But a person does not cease to be liable to be registered under this Part of this Schedule at any time if there are reasonable grounds for believing that the value of that person's relevant acquisitions in the following 30 days will exceed £85,000.

Notification of liability and registration

40

(1) A person who becomes liable to be registered under this Part of this Schedule must notify the Commissioners of the liability—
- (a) in the case of a liability under sub-paragraph (1) of paragraph 38, within 30 days of the end of the month when the person becomes so liable, and
- (b) in the case of a liability under sub-paragraph (2) of that paragraph, before the end of the period by reference to which the liability arises.

(2) The Commissioners must register any such person (whether or not the person notifies them) with effect from the relevant time or from such earlier time as may be agreed between the Commissioners and the person.

(3) In this paragraph "the relevant time"—
- (a) in a case falling within sub-paragraph (1)(a), means the end of the month following the month at the end of which the liability arose, and
- (b) in a case falling within sub-paragraph (1)(b), means the beginning of the period by reference to which the liability arose.

Entitlement to be registered etc

41

(1) Where a person who is not liable to be registered under this Act and is not already so registered satisfies the Commissioners that the person makes relevant acquisitions, the Commissioners must, if the person so requests, register the person with effect from the day on which the request is made or from such earlier date as may be agreed between the Commissioners and the person.

(2) Where a person who is not liable to be registered under this Act and is not already so registered—
- (a) satisfies the Commissioners that the person intends to make relevant acquisitions from a specified date, and
- (b) requests to be registered under this Part of this Schedule,

the Commissioners may, subject to such conditions as they think fit to impose, register the person with effect from such date as may be agreed between the Commissioners and the person.

(3) Conditions imposed under sub-paragraph (2) may—
- (a) be so imposed wholly or partly by reference to, or without reference to, any conditions prescribed for the purposes of this paragraph, and
- (b) be subsequently varied by the Commissioners (whenever the conditions were imposed).

(4) Where a person who is entitled to be registered under paragraph 9 or 10 of Schedule 1 requests registration under this paragraph, the person is to be registered under that Schedule, and not under this Part of this Schedule.

Notification of matters affecting continuance of registration

42

(1) Any person registered under this Part of this Schedule who ceases to be registrable under this Act must notify the Commissioners of that fact within 30 days of the day on which the person ceases to be registrable.

(2) A person registered under paragraph 41(2) must notify the Commissioners, within 30 days of the first occasion after the person's registration when the person makes a relevant acquisition, that the person has made that acquisition.

(3) For the purposes of this paragraph a person ceases to be registrable under this Act where—

(a) the person ceases to be a person who would be liable or entitled to be registered under this Act if the person's registration and any enactment preventing a person from being liable to be registered under different provisions at the same time were disregarded, or

(b) in the case of a person who (having been registered under paragraph 41(2)) has not been such a person during the period of the person's registration, the person ceases to have any intention of making relevant acquisitions.

Cancellation of registration

43

(1) Where a person registered under this Part of this Schedule satisfies the Commissioners that the person is not liable to be so registered, the Commissioners must, if the person so requests, cancel that registration with effect from the day on which the request is made or from such later date as may be agreed between the Commissioners and the person.

(2) Where the Commissioners are satisfied that a person registered under this Part of this Schedule has ceased since the person's registration to be registrable under this Part of this Schedule, they may cancel that registration with effect from the day on which the person so ceased or from such later date as may be agreed between the Commissioners and the person.

(3) Where the Commissioners are satisfied that a person who has been registered under paragraph 41(2) and is not for the time being liable to be registered under this Part of this Schedule—

(a) has not begun, by the date specified in the person's request to be registered, to make relevant acquisitions, or

(b) has contravened any condition of the person's registration,

the Commissioners may cancel the person's registration with effect from the date so specified or, as the case may be, the date of the contravention or from such later date as may be agreed between the Commissioners and the person.

(4) But the Commissioners may not, under sub-paragraph (1), (2) or (3), cancel a person's registration with effect from any time unless the Commissioners are satisfied that it is not a time when that person would be subject to a requirement, or in a case falling under sub-paragraph (2) or (3) a requirement or entitlement, to be registered under this Act.

(5) Where the Commissioners are satisfied that, on the day on which a person was registered under this Part of this Schedule, the person—

(a) was not registrable under this Part of this Schedule, and

(b) in the case of a person registered under paragraph 41(2), did not have the intention by reference to which the person was registered,

the Commissioners may cancel that registration with effect from that day.

(6) The registration of a person who—

(a) is registered under paragraph 41, or

(b) would not, if the person were not registered, be liable or entitled to be registered under any provision of this Act except that paragraph,

may not be cancelled with effect from any time before 1 January which is, or next follows, the second anniversary of the date on which the person's registration took effect.

(7) But sub-paragraph (6) does not apply to cancellation under sub-paragraph (3) or (5).

(8) In determining, for the purposes of sub-paragraphs (4) and (6), whether a person would be subject to a requirement, or would be entitled, to be registered at any time, so much of any provision of this Act as prevents a person from becoming liable or entitled to be registered when the person is already registered or when the person is so liable under any other provision is to be disregarded.

(9) For the purposes of this paragraph, a person is registrable under this Part of this Schedule at any time when the person is liable to be registered under this Part of this Schedule or is a person who makes relevant acquisitions.

Exemption from registration

44

(1) Where a person who makes or intends to make relevant acquisitions satisfies the Commissioners that any such acquisition would be an acquisition in pursuance of a transaction which would be zero-rated if it were a taxable supply by a taxable person, the Commissioners may, if the person so requests and the Commissioners think fit, exempt the person from registration under this Part of this Schedule until it appears to the Commissioners that the request should no longer be acted upon or is withdrawn.

(2) Where a person who is exempted under this paragraph from registration under this Part of this Schedule makes any relevant acquisition in pursuance of any transaction which would, if it were a taxable supply by a taxable person, be chargeable to VAT otherwise than as a zero-rated supply, the person must notify the Commissioners of the change within 30 days of the date the acquisition was made.

Power to vary specified sums by regulations

45

The Treasury may by regulations substitute for any of the sums for the time being specified in this Part of this Schedule such greater sums as the Treasury consider appropriate.

Notifications

46

Any notification required under this Part of this Schedule must be made in such form and manner and must contain such particulars as may be specified in regulations or by the Commissioners in accordance with regulations.

Meaning of relevant supply

47

For the purposes of this Part of this Schedule "relevant acquisition" means an acquisition that—
  (a) is a taxable acquisition (see paragraph 2(2)) of goods other than goods which are subject to a duty of excise or consist in a new means of transport, and
  (b) is otherwise than in pursuance of a taxable supply and is treated, for the purposes of this Act, as taking place in Northern Ireland.

PART 9
REGISTRATION IN RESPECT OF DISTANCE SALES FROM THE EU TO NORTHERN IRELAND

Liability to be registered

48

(1) A person who—
  (a) is not registered under this Act, and
  (b) is not liable to be registered under Schedule 1 or 1A,
becomes liable to be registered under this Part of this Schedule on any day if, in the period beginning with 1 January of the year in which that day falls, that person has made relevant supplies whose value exceeds £70,000.

(2) A person who is not registered or liable to be registered as mentioned in sub-paragraph (1)(a) and (b) becomes liable to be registered under this Part of this Schedule where—
  (a) the person has exercised any option, in accordance with the law of any member State where the person is taxable, for treating relevant supplies made by that person as taking place outside that member State,
  (b) the supplies to which the option relates involve the removal of goods from that member State and, apart from the exercise of the option, would be treated, in accordance with the law of that member State, as taking place in that member State, and
  (c) the person makes a relevant supply at a time when the option is in force in relation to that person.

(3) A person who is not registered or liable to be registered as mentioned in sub-paragraph (1)(a) and (b) above becomes liable to be registered under this Part of this Schedule if the person makes a supply that—
    (a) is a supply of goods subject to a duty of excise,
    (b) involves the removal of the goods to Northern Ireland by or under the directions of the person making the supply,
    (c) is a transaction in pursuance of which the goods are acquired in Northern Ireland from a member State by a person who is not a taxable person,
    (d) is made in the course or furtherance of a business carried on by the supplier, and
    (e) is not anything which is treated as a supply for the purposes of this Act by virtue only of paragraph 5(1) of Schedule 4 or paragraph 30 of Schedule 9ZB.

(4) A person is treated as having become liable to be registered under this Part of this Schedule at any time when the person would have become so liable under the preceding provisions of this paragraph but for any registration which is subsequently cancelled under paragraph 43(3)or 53(5) of this Schedule, paragraph 13(3) of Schedule 1, paragraph 11 of Schedule 1A, or paragraph 6(2) of Schedule 3A.

(5) A person does not cease to be liable to be registered under this Part of this Schedule except in accordance with paragraph 49.

(6) In determining for the purposes of this paragraph the value of any relevant supplies, so much of the consideration for any supply as represents any liability of the supplier, under the law of a member State, for VAT on that supply is to be disregarded.

(7) For the purposes of sub-paragraphs (1) and (2), supplies to which section 18B(4) or paragraph 19(6) of Schedule 9ZB (last supply of goods before removal from fiscal warehousing) apply are to be disregarded.

49

(1) A person who has become liable to be registered under this Part of this Schedule ceases to be so liable if at any time—
    (a) the relevant supplies made by the person in the year ending with 31 December last before that time did not have a value exceeding £70,000 and did not include any supply in relation to which the conditions mentioned in paragraph 48(3) were satisfied, and
    (b) the Commissioners are satisfied that the value of the person's relevant supplies in the year immediately following that year will not exceed £70,000 and that those supplies will not include a supply in relation to which those conditions are satisfied.

(2) But a person does not cease to be liable to be registered under this Part of this Schedule at any time when such an option as is mentioned in paragraph 48(2) above is in force in relation to that person.

Notification of liability and registration

50

(1) A person who becomes liable to be registered under this Part of this Schedule must notify the Commissioners of the liability within the period of 30 days after the day on which the liability arises.

(2) The Commissioners must register any such person (whether or not the person has notified them) with effect from the day on which the liability arose or from such earlier time as may be agreed between the Commissioners and the person.

Request to be registered

51

(1) Where a person who is not liable to be registered under this Act and is not already so registered—
    (a) satisfies the Commissioners that the person intends—
        (i) to exercise an option such as is mentioned in paragraph 48(2) and, from a specified date, to make relevant supplies to which that option will relate,
        (ii) from a specified date to make relevant supplies to which any such option that the person has exercised will relate, or

    (iii) from a specified date to make supplies in relation to which the conditions mentioned in paragraph 48(3) will be satisfied, and
  (b) requests to be registered under this Part of this Schedule,

the Commissioners may, subject to such conditions as they think fit to impose, register the person with effect from such date as may be agreed between the Commissioners and the person.

(2) Conditions imposed under sub-paragraph (1) may—
  (a) be imposed wholly or partly by reference to, or without reference to, any conditions prescribed for the purposes of this paragraph, and
  (b) be subsequently varied by the Commissioners (whenever the conditions were imposed).

(3) Where a person who is entitled to be registered under paragraph 9 or 10 of Schedule 1 requests registration under this paragraph, the person is to be registered under that Schedule, and not under this Part of this Schedule.

Notification of matters affecting continuance of registration

52

(1) Any person registered under this Part of this Schedule who ceases to be registrable under this Act must notify the Commissioners of that fact within 30 days of the day on which the person ceases to be registrable.

(2) A person registered under paragraph 51 by reference to any intention to exercise any option or to make supplies of any description must notify the Commissioners within 30 days of exercising that option or, as the case may be, of the first occasion after registration when the person makes such a supply, that the person has exercised the option or made such a supply.

(3) A person who has exercised an option mentioned in paragraph 48(2) which, as a consequence of the option's revocation or otherwise, ceases to have effect in relation to any relevant supplies by the person must notify the Commissioners, within 30 days of the option's ceasing so to have effect, that it has done so.

(4) For the purposes of this paragraph, a person ceases to be registrable under this Act where—
  (a) the person ceases to be a person who would be liable or entitled to be registered under this Act if the person's registration and any enactment preventing a person from being liable to be registered under different provisions at the same time were disregarded, or
  (b) in the case of a person who (having been registered under paragraph 51) has not been such a person during the period of the person's registration, the person ceases to have any such intention as is mentioned in sub-paragraph (1)(a) of that paragraph.

Cancellation of registration

53

(1) Where a person registered under this Part of this Schedule satisfies the Commissioners that the person is not liable to be so registered, the Commissioners must, if the person so requests, cancel that registration with effect from the day on which the request is made or from such later date as may be agreed between the Commissioners and the person.

(2) Where the Commissioners are satisfied that a person who has been registered under paragraph 51 and is not for the time being liable to be registered under this Part of this Schedule—
  (a) has not, by the date specified in the person's request to be registered, begun to make relevant supplies, exercised the option in question or, as the case may be, begun to make supplies in relation to which the conditions mentioned in paragraph 48(3) are satisfied, or
  (b) has contravened any condition of the person's registration,

the Commissioners may cancel the person's registration with effect from the date so specified or, as the case may be, the date of the contravention or from such later date as may be agreed between the Commissioners and the person.

(3) But the Commissioners may not, under sub-paragraph (1) or (2), cancel a person's registration with effect from any time unless the Commissioners are satisfied that it is not a time when that person would be subject to a requirement, or in a case falling under sub-paragraph (2) a requirement or entitlement, to be registered under this Act.

(4) In determining for the purposes of sub-paragraph (3) whether a person would be subject to a requirement, or would be entitled, to be registered at any time, so much of any provision of this Act as prevents a person from becoming liable or entitled to be registered when the person is already registered or when the person is so liable under any other provision is to be disregarded.

(5) Where the Commissioners are satisfied that, on the day on which a person was registered under this Part of this Schedule, the person—
- (a) was not liable to be registered under this Part of this Schedule, and
- (b) in the case of a person registered under paragraph 51, did not have the intention by reference to which the person was registered,

the Commissioners may cancel that registration with effect from that day.

(6) The registration of a person who has exercised an option mentioned in paragraph 48(2) may not be cancelled with effect from any time before the 1 January which is, or next follows, the second anniversary of the date on which the person's registration took effect.

Power to vary specified sums by regulations

54

The Treasury may by regulations substitute for any of the sums for the time being specified in this Part of this Schedule such greater sums as the Treasury consider appropriate.

Notifications

55

Any notification required under this Part of this Schedule must be made in such form and manner and must contain such particulars as may be specified in regulations or by the Commissioners in accordance with regulations.

Meaning of relevant supply

56

For the purposes of this Part of this Schedule "relevant supply" means a supply of goods that—
- (a) involves the removal of the goods to Northern Ireland from a place outside the United Kingdom by or under the directions of the person making the supply,
- (b) does not involve the installation or assembly of the goods at a place in Northern Ireland,
- (c) is a transaction in pursuance of which goods are acquired in Northern Ireland from a member State by a person who is not a taxable person,
- (d) is made in the course or furtherance of a business carried on by the supplier, and
- (e) is neither an exempt supply nor a supply of goods which are subject to a duty of excise or consist in a new means of transport and is not anything which is treated as a supply for the purposes of this Act by virtue only of paragraph 5(1) of Schedule 4 or paragraph 30 of Schedule 9ZB.

PART 10
CALL-OFF STOCK ARRANGEMENTS

Where this Part of this Schedule applies

57

(1) This Part of this Schedule applies where—
- (a) goods forming part of the assets of any business are removed—
  - (i) from Northern Ireland for the purpose of being taken to a place in a member State, or
  - (ii) from a member State for the purpose of being taken to a place in Northern Ireland,
- (b) the goods are removed in the course or furtherance of that business by or under the directions of the person carrying on that business ("the supplier"),

(c) the goods are removed with a view to their being supplied in the destination territory, at a later stage and after their arrival there, to another person ("the customer"),
(d) at the time of the removal the customer is entitled to take ownership of the goods in accordance with an agreement existing between the customer and the supplier,
(e) at the time of the removal the supplier does not have a business establishment or other fixed establishment in the destination territory,
(f) at the time of the removal the customer is identified for the purposes of VAT in accordance with the law of the destination territory and both the identity of the customer and the number assigned to the customer for the purposes of VAT by the destination territory are known to the supplier,
(g) as soon as reasonably practicable after the removal the supplier records the removal in the register provided for in Article 243(3) of Council Directive 2006/112/EC of 28 November 2006 on the common system of value added tax, and
(h) the supplier includes the number mentioned in paragraph (f) in the recapitulative statement provided for in Article 262(2) of Council Directive 2006/112/EC.

(2) For the purposes of this Part of this Schedule, where the destination territory is Northern Ireland, a customer is identified for the purposes of VAT in accordance with the law of the destination territory if the customer is registered under this Act and is identified for the purposes of VAT in Northern Ireland.

(3) In this Part of this Schedule—
"the destination territory" means—
(a) in a case within paragraph (i) of sub-paragraph (1)(a), the member State concerned, and
(b) in a case within paragraph (ii) of sub-paragraph (1)(a), Northern Ireland, and
"the origin territory" means—
(a) in a case within paragraph (i) of sub-paragraph (1)(a), Northern Ireland, and
(b) in a case within paragraph (ii) of sub-paragraph (1)(a), the member State concerned.

Removal of the goods not to be treated as a supply

58

The removal of the goods from the origin territory is not to be treated by reason of paragraph 30 of Schedule 9ZB as a supply of goods by the supplier.

Goods transferred to the customer within 12 months of arrival

59

(1) The rules in sub-paragraph (2) apply if—
(a) during the period of 12 months beginning with the day the goods arrive in the destination territory the supplier transfers the whole property in the goods to the customer, and
(b) during the period beginning with the day the goods arrive in the destination territory and ending immediately before the time of that transfer no relevant event occurs.

(2) The rules are that—
(a) a supply of the goods in the relevant territory is deemed to be made by the supplier,
(b) the deemed supply is deemed to involve the removal of the goods from the origin territory at the time of the transfer mentioned in sub-paragraph (1),
(c) the consideration given by the customer for the transfer mentioned in sub-paragraph (1) is deemed to have been given for the deemed supply, and
(d) an acquisition of the goods by the customer in pursuance of the deemed supply is deemed to take place in the destination territory.

(3) In sub-paragraph (2) and in paragraphs 60(2) and 61(2) "the relevant territory" means—
(a) where the origin territory is Northern Ireland, the United Kingdom, or
(b) where the origin territory is a member State, that member State.

(4) For the meaning of a "relevant event", see paragraph 63.

Relevant event occurs within 12 months of arrival

60

(1) The rules in sub-paragraph (2) apply (subject to paragraph 62) if—
  (a) during the period of 12 months beginning with the day the goods arrive in the destination territory a relevant event occurs, and
  (b) during the period beginning with the day the goods arrive in the destination territory and ending immediately before the time that relevant event occurs the supplier does not transfer the whole property in the goods to the customer.

(2) The rules are that—
  (a) a supply of the goods in the relevant territory (see paragraph 59(3)) is deemed to be made by the supplier,
  (b) the deemed supply is deemed to involve the removal of the goods from the origin territory at the time the relevant event occurs, and
  (c) an acquisition of the goods by the supplier in pursuance of the deemed supply is deemed to take place in the destination territory.

(3) For the meaning of a "relevant event", see paragraph 63.

Goods not transferred and no relevant event occurs within 12 months of arrival

61

(1) The rules in sub-paragraph (2) apply (subject to paragraph 62) if during the period of 12 months beginning with the day the goods arrive in the destination territory the supplier does not transfer the whole property in the goods to the customer and no relevant event occurs.

(2) The rules are that—
  (a) a supply of the goods in the relevant territory (see paragraph 59(3)) is deemed to be made by the supplier,
  (b) the deemed supply is deemed to involve the removal of the goods from the origin territory at the beginning of the day following the expiry of the period of 12 months mentioned in sub-paragraph (1), and
  (c) an acquisition of the goods by the supplier in pursuance of the deemed supply is deemed to take place in the destination territory.

(3) For the meaning of a "relevant event", see paragraph 63.

Exception to paragraphs 60 and 61: goods returned to origin territory

62

The rules in paragraphs 60(2) and 61(2) do not apply if during the period of 12 months beginning with the day the goods arrive in the destination territory—
  (a) the goods are returned to the origin territory by or under the direction of the supplier, and
  (b) the supplier records the return of the goods in the register provided for in Article 243(3) of Council Directive 2006/112/EC.

Meaning of "relevant event"

63

(1) For the purposes of this Part of this Schedule each of the following events is a relevant event—
  (a) the supplier forms an intention not to supply the goods to the customer (but see sub-paragraph (2)),
  (b) the supplier forms an intention to supply the goods to the customer otherwise than in the destination territory,
  (c) the supplier establishes a business establishment or other fixed establishment in the destination territory,
  (d) the customer ceases to be identified for the purposes of VAT in accordance with the law of the destination territory,

(e) the goods are removed from the destination territory by or under the directions of the supplier otherwise than for the purpose of being returned to the origin territory, or

(f) the goods are destroyed, lost or stolen.

(2) But the event mentioned in paragraph (a) of sub-paragraph (1) is not a relevant event for the purposes of this Part of this Schedule if—

(a) at the time that the event occurs the supplier forms an intention to supply the goods to another person ("the substitute customer"),

(b) at that time the substitute customer is identified for the purposes of VAT in accordance with the law of the destination territory,

(c) the supplier includes the number assigned to the substitute customer for the purposes of VAT by the destination territory in the recapitulative statement provided for in Article 262(2) of Council Directive 2006/112/EC, and

(d) as soon as reasonably practicable after forming the intention to supply the goods to the substitute customer the supplier records that intention in the register provided for in Article 243(3) of Council Directive 2006/112/EC.

(3) Where the destination territory is Northern Ireland, the reference in sub-paragraph (2)(c) to the number assigned to the substitute customer for the purposes of VAT is to the number assigned to the substitute customer for the purposes of VAT in the United Kingdom along with an NI VAT identifier.

(4) In a case where sub-paragraph (2) applies, references in this Part of this Schedule to the customer are to be then read as references to the substitute customer.

(5) In a case where the goods are destroyed, lost or stolen but it is not possible to determine the date on which that occurred, the goods are to be treated for the purposes of this Part of this Schedule as having been destroyed, lost or stolen on the date on which they were found to be destroyed or missing.

Record keeping by the supplier

64

In a case where the origin territory is Northern Ireland, any record made by the supplier in pursuance of paragraph 57(1)(g), 62(b) or 63(2)(d) must be preserved for such period not exceeding 6 years as the Commissioners may specify in writing.

Record keeping by the customer

65

(1) In a case where the destination territory is Northern Ireland, the customer must as soon as is reasonably practicable make a record of the information relating to the goods that is specified in Article 54A(2) of Council Implementing Regulation (EU) No 282/2011 of 15 March 2011 laying down implementing measures for Directive 2006/112/EC on the common system of value added tax.

(2) A record made under this paragraph must—

(a) be made in a register kept by the customer for the purposes of this paragraph, and

(b) be preserved for such period not exceeding 6 years as the Commissioners may specify in writing.

PART 11
MODIFICATION OF OTHER SCHEDULES

Registration in respect of taxable supplies: UK establishment (Schedule 1)

66

(1) Paragraph 1 of Schedule 1 (registration in respect of taxable supplies: UK establishment) has effect as if—

(a) the provisions mentioned in sub-paragraphs (4)(a) and (5) included paragraphs 43(5) and 53(5) of this Schedule (cancellation of registration);

(b)　　in sub-paragraph (7), after "are supplied" there were inserted "and any taxable supplies which would not be taxable supplies apart from paragraph 29(1) of Schedule 9ZB";
　　　(c)　　in sub-paragraph (9)—
　　　　　　(i)　　after "section 18B(4)" there were inserted "or paragraph 19(5) of Schedule 9ZB";
　　　　　　(ii)　　after "supply" there were inserted "or acquisition".
(2)　Paragraph 2 of that Schedule has effect as if in sub-paragraph (7), after paragraph (b) there were inserted—
　　　"(c)　　any acquisition of goods from a member State by one of the constituent members in the course of the activities of the taxable person is to be treated as an acquisition by that person;".
(3)　Paragraph 4(3) of that Schedule has effect as if after "are supplied" there were inserted "and any taxable supplies which would not be taxable supplies apart from paragraph 29(1) of Schedule 9ZB".

Registration in respect of taxable supplies: non-UK establishment (Schedule 1A)

67

Paragraph 3 of Schedule 1A (registration in respect of taxable supplies: non-UK establishment) has effect as if the provisions mentioned in paragraphs (a) to (e) of that paragraph included paragraphs 43(5) and 53(5) of this Schedule.

Registration: disposals of assets where repayment is claimed (Schedule 3A)

68

Paragraph 1 of Schedule 3A (registration in respect of disposals of assets for which a VAT repayment is claimed) has effect as if—In a case where the origin territory is Northern Ireland, any record made by the supplier in pursuance of paragraph 57(1)(g), 62(b) or 63(2)(d) must be preserved for such period not exceeding 6 years as the Commissioners may specify in writing.
　　　(a)　　in sub-paragraph (1), after "or 1A" there were inserted "or Part 8 or 9 of Schedule 9ZA", and
　　　(b)　　the provisions mentioned in sub-paragraph (2) included paragraphs 43(5) and 53(5) of this Schedule.

Valuation of supplies: special cases (Schedule 6)

69

(1)　Paragraph 1A of Schedule 6 (valuation: special cases) has effect as if—
　　　(a)　　in sub-paragraph (4), in the definition of "motor dealer", after "supplies of" there were inserted ", or acquiring in Northern Ireland from a member State";
　　　(b)　　in that sub-paragraph, in the definition of "stock in trade"—
　　　　　　(i)　　in paragraph (a) of that definition, after "supplied to" there were inserted "or acquired in Northern Ireland from a member State by";
　　　　　　(ii)　　in paragraph (b) of that definition, after "supply" there were inserted ", acquisition";
　　　(c)　　in sub-paragraph (6)(a)—
　　　　　　(i)　　after "supplied" there were inserted ", acquired in Northern Ireland from a member State";
　　　　　　(ii)　　after "supply" there were inserted ", acquisition".
(2)　In paragraph 6(1) of that Schedule—
　　　(a)　　in paragraph (b), after "Schedule 4" there were inserted "or paragraph 30 of Schedule 9ZB";
　　　(b)　　in paragraph (c), for "that Schedule;" there were substituted "Schedule 4; or";
　　　(c)　　after that paragraph there were inserted—
　　　"(d)　　paragraph 60(2)(a) or 61(2)(a) of Schedule 9ZA,".

Zero-rating (Schedule 8)

70

Group 12 in Part 2 of Schedule 8 (zero-rating: drugs etc) has effect as if—
- (a) in Note (1), after "goods are" there were inserted "acquired from a member State";
- (b) in Note (5N), in paragraph (b), after "made a" there were inserted "reckonable zero-rated acquisition, or";
- (c) in Note (5O), in paragraph (b), after "zero-rated" there were inserted "acquisition or";
- (d) in Note (5T), after the definition of "in the required form" there were inserted—

""reckonable zero-rated acquisition", in relation to a motor vehicle, means an acquisition of the vehicle from a member State in a case where NI acquisition VAT is not chargeable as a result of item 2(f) or 2A."

Exempt supplies (Schedule 9)

71

Group 14 in Part 2 of Schedule 9 (exemptions: supplies of goods where input tax cannot be recovered) has effect as if—
- (a) in paragraph (a) of item 1, after "supply to" there were inserted "or acquisition";
- (b) in Note (7)(a), after "supply to" there were inserted "or acquisition";
- (c) in Note (9)—
  - (i) in the words before paragraph (a), after "supply to" there were inserted "or acquisition";
  - (ii) in paragraph (b), after "supply to" there were inserted "or acquisition";
- (d) in Note (10)—
  - (i) after "on a supply" there were inserted ", acquisition";
  - (ii) after "that supply", there were inserted ", acquisition";
- (e) in Note (15)—
  - (i) after "anything the supply" there were inserted ", acquisition";
  - (ii) after "be a supply" there were inserted ", acquisition".

Avoidance (Schedules 9A and 11A)

72

(1) Paragraph 1(5) of Schedule 9A (anti-avoidance provisions: groups) has effect as if, in paragraph (a), after "importation" there were inserted "or acquisition".

(2) Schedule 11A (disclosure of avoidance schemes) has effect as if the reference to VAT "incurred" by a taxable person in paragraph 2A(1)(b) included VAT on the acquisition by the person of any goods from a member State.

Accounting for VAT and payment of VAT (Schedule 11)

73

(1) Regulations under this paragraph may require the submission to the Commissioners by taxable persons, at such times and intervals, in such cases and in such form and manner as may be—
- (a) specified in the regulations, or
- (b) specified by the Commissioners in accordance with the regulations,

of statements containing such particulars of transactions in which the taxable persons are concerned and to which this sub-paragraph applies, and of the persons concerned in those transactions, as may be so specified.

(2) Sub-paragraph (1) applies to transactions involving the movement of goods between a member State and Northern Ireland, or between member States.

(3) Sections 65 and 66 (inaccuracies in, or and failure to submit, section 55A statements) apply to any statement which is required to be submitted to the Commissioners in accordance with regulations under sub-paragraph (1) as they apply to a section 55A statement.

(4) Regulations under this paragraph may make provision in relation to cases where—

(a) any goods which are subject to a duty of excise or consist in a new means of transport are acquired in Northern Ireland from a member State by any person,
(b) the acquisition of the goods is a taxable acquisition and is not in pursuance of a taxable supply, and
(c) that person is not a taxable person at the time of the acquisition,

for requiring the person who acquires the goods to give to the Commissioners such notification of the acquisition, and for requiring any VAT on the acquisition to be paid, at such time and in such form or manner as may be specified in the regulations or (in the case of the notification requirement) by the Commissioners in accordance with the regulations.

(5) Regulations under this paragraph may provide for a notification required by virtue of sub-paragraph (4)—
(a) to contain such particulars relating to the notified acquisition and any VAT chargeable in relation to it as may be specified in the regulations or by the Commissioners in accordance with the regulations, and
(b) to be given, in prescribed cases, by the personal representative, trustee in bankruptcy, trustee in sequestration, receiver, liquidator or person otherwise acting in a representative capacity in relation to the person who makes that acquisition.

(6) Regulations under this paragraph may provide for—
(a) the time when any invoice described in regulations under paragraph 4(1)(b) of this Schedule or paragraph 28(2)(b) of Schedule 9ZB is to be treated as having been issued;
(b) VAT accounted for and paid by reference to the date of issue of such an invoice to be confined to VAT on so much of the value of the supply or acquisition as is shown on the invoice.

(7) Sub-paragraphs (1) to (4), (5) and (6) are to be treated, for the purposes of this Act, as if they were contained in paragraph 2 of Schedule 11.

Administration, collection and enforcement (Schedule 11)

74

(1) Paragraph 2 of Schedule 11 has effect as if—
(a) in sub-paragraph (5A)(b), after "transport" there were inserted "acquired from a member State, or";
(b) in sub-paragraph (5B)(a), after "chargeable on its" there were inserted "acquisition or";
(c) in sub-paragraph (5D) in the definition of "relevant person"—
(i) before paragraph (b) there were inserted—
"(a) where the means of transport has been acquired in Northern Ireland from a member State, the person who so acquires it,";
(ii) after paragraph (b) there were inserted—
"(c) in any other case—
(i) the owner of the means of transport at the time of its arrival in the United Kingdom, or
(ii) where it is subject to a lease or hire agreement, the lessee or hirer of the means of transport at that time."

(2) Paragraph 2(8) of Schedule 11 applies to NI acquisition VAT in respect of an acquisition by any person from a member State of dutiable goods as it applies to VAT in respect of any supply by a taxable person of dutiable goods.

(3) Invoices described in regulations under paragraph 4(2)(b) of this Schedule or paragraph 28(2)(b) of Schedule 9ZB are items to which paragraph 3 of Schedule 11 applies (in addition to the items described in paragraph 3(2)(a) and (b) of that Schedule).

(4) Paragraph 6 of Schedule 11 has effect as if—
(a) after sub-paragraph (1) there were inserted—

"(1A) Every person who, at a time when the person is not a taxable person, acquires in Northern Ireland from a member State any goods which are subject to a duty of excise or consist in a new means of transport must keep such records with respect to the acquisition (if it is a taxable acquisition and is not in pursuance of a taxable supply) as the Commissioners may by regulations require.";

(a) in sub-paragraph (2), after "sub-paragraph (1)" there were inserted "or (1A)".

(5) Paragraph 8(1) of Schedule 11 applies—
- (a) to goods in the possession of a person who acquires goods in Northern Ireland from a member State as it applies to goods in the possession of a person who supplies goods, and
- (b) to goods in the possession of a Northern Ireland fiscal warehousekeeper as it applies to goods in the possession of a fiscal warehousekeeper.

(6) Paragraph 14(1) has effect as if in paragraph (c), after "paragraph 5A" there were inserted "or paragraph 73(1) or (4) of Schedule 9ZA".

PART 12

MODIFICATION OF OTHER ACTS

Diplomatic privileges etc

75

(1) The following provisions apply to NI acquisition VAT as they apply to value added tax charged in accordance with section 1(1)(c) of this Act—
- (a) section 2(5A) of the Diplomatic Privileges Act 1964 (application of Vienna Convention);
- (b) paragraph 10(1A) of the Schedule to the Commonwealth Secretariat Act 1966 (immunities and privileges);
- (c) section 1(8A) of the Consular Relations Act 1968 (application of Vienna Convention);
- (d) paragraph 19(c) of Schedule 1 to the International Organisations Act 1968 (privileges and immunities);
- (e) section 1(5) of the Diplomatic and other Privileges Act 1971 (refund of customs duties on hydrocarbon oil used for diplomatic or Commonwealth Secretariat purposes).

(2) Section 8 of the Consular Relations Act 1968 applies to VAT charged on the acquisition of oil in Northern Ireland from a member State as it applies to VAT charged on the importation of oil.

Customs and Excise Duties (General Reliefs) Act 1979

76

Section 13 of the Customs and Excise Duties (General Reliefs) Act 1979 (power to provide reliefs for VAT etc) has effect as if, in subsection (4), in the definition of "value added tax" after "goods" there were inserted "or on the acquisition of goods from a member State".

Vehicle Excise and Registration Act 1994

77

Section 8 of the Vehicle Excise and Registration Act 1994 (vehicles removed into UK) has effect as if, in subsection (2)—
- (a) in paragraph (a), after "United Kingdom" there were inserted ", or on the acquisition of the vehicle from a member State,";
- (b) in paragraph (c), after "charged on the" there were inserted "acquisition or".

Finance Act 2008

78

(1) Paragraph 11 of Schedule 36 to the Finance Act 2008 (information and inspection powers) has effect as if—
- (a) in sub-paragraph (1), after paragraph (a) there were inserted—

"(b) premises are used in connection with the acquisition of goods from member States under taxable acquisitions and goods to be so acquired or documents relating to such goods are on those premises,";
- (b) in sub-paragraph (2), in paragraph (c), after "taxable supplies" there were inserted ",

the acquisition of goods from member States under taxable acquisitions".

(2) Paragraph 34 of that Schedule has effect as if—
    (a)   in sub-paragraph (1), after paragraph (a) there were inserted—
"(b)   the acquisition of goods from a member State,";
    (b)   in sub-paragraph (4), after "Schedule 4" there were inserted "and paragraph 3 of Schedule 9ZA".

(3) Paragraph 1 of Schedule 41 to that Act has effect as if in the table there were inserted the following entries—

"Value added tax	Obligations under paragraphs 40 and 44(2) of Schedule 9ZA to VATA 1994 (obligations to notify liability to register and notify acquisition affecting exemption from registration).
Value added tax	Obligation under paragraph 50 of Schedule 9ZA to VATA 1994 (obligation to notify liability to register).
Value added tax	Obligation under regulations under paragraph 73(4) of Schedule 9ZA to VATA 1994 (obligation to give notification of acquisition of goods from a member State)."

(4) For the purposes of paragraph 7 of that Schedule—
    (a)   in a case of a failure to comply with an obligation under regulations under paragraph 73(4) of this Schedule, the "potential lost revenue" is the value added tax on the acquisition to which the failure relates (instead of as provided for by paragraph 7(6) of that Schedule), and
    (b)   the "relevant period" in relation to a failure to comply with paragraph 44(2) of this Schedule is the period beginning on the date of the change or alteration concerned and ending on the date on which HMRC received notification of, or otherwise became fully aware of, that change or alteration.

(5) In a case to which sub-paragraph (6) of paragraph 7 of that Schedule applies (whether as a result of sub-paragraph (3) of this paragraph or otherwise), the amount of the "potential lost revenue" as determined in accordance with that sub-paragraph is—
    (a)   if the amount of the tax mentioned in that sub-paragraph includes tax on an acquisition of goods from a member State, to be reduced by the amount of any VAT which HMRC are satisfied has been paid on the supply in pursuance of which the goods were acquired under the law of that member State, and
    (b)   if the amount of that tax includes tax chargeable as a result of paragraph 29 of Schedule 9ZB on a supply, to be reduced by the amount of any VAT which HMRC are satisfied has been paid on that supply under the law of a member State.

Finance Act 2016

79

Schedule 18 to the Finance Act 2016 (serial tax avoidance) has effect as if—
    (a)   in paragraph 5(4), after paragraph (a) there were inserted—
"(b)   VAT on the acquisition by the person of any goods from a member State,";
    (b)   the references to VAT "incurred" by a taxable person in paragraphs 6(1)(b) and 36(7)(b) included VAT on the acquisition by the person of any goods from a member State.

Finance (No 2) Act 2017

80

Schedule 17 to the Finance (No 2) Act 2017 (disclosure of tax avoidance schemes: VAT and other indirect taxes) has effect as if—
    (a)   the reference in paragraph 6(2)(b) to VAT "incurred" by a taxable person included VAT on the acquisition by the person of any goods from a member State;
    (b)   in paragraph 6(5), after paragraph (a) there were inserted—

"(b) VAT on the acquisition by the person of any goods from a member State,".

PART 13
INTERPRETIVE PROVISIONS

Taxation under the laws of member States etc

81

(1) References in this Act, in relation to a member State, to the law of that member State are to be construed as confined to so much of the law of that member State as for the time being has effect for the purposes of any EU instrument relating to VAT.

(2) References in this Act to a person being taxable in a member State are references to that person being taxable under so much of the law of that member State as makes provision for purposes corresponding, in relation to that member State, to the purposes of so much of this Act as makes provision as to whether a person is a taxable person.

(3) The Commissioners may by regulations make provision for the manner in which any of the following are to be or may be proved for any of the purposes of this Act—
   (a) the effect of any provisions of the law of any member State;
   (b) that provisions of any such law correspond, in relation to any member State, to any provision of this Act;
   (c) that provisions of any such law have a purpose corresponding, in relation to any member State, to the purpose of any provision of this Act.

(4) The Commissioners may by regulations provide—
   (a) for a person to be treated for prescribed purposes of this Act as taxable in a member State only where the person has given such notification, and furnished such other information, to the Commissioners as may be prescribed;
   (b) for the form and manner in which any notification or information is to be given or furnished under the regulations and what the notification or information must contain;
   (c) for the proportion of any consideration for any transaction which is to be taken for the purposes of this Act as representing a liability, under the law of a member State, for VAT to be conclusively determined by reference to such invoices or in such other manner as may be prescribed.

(5) In any proceedings (whether civil or criminal), a certificate of the Commissioners—
   (a) that a person was or was not, at any date, taxable in a member State, or
   (b) that any VAT payable under the law of a member State has or has not been paid,
is sufficient evidence of that fact until the contrary is proved, and any document purporting to be a certificate under this subsection is deemed to be such a certificate until the contrary is proved.

Territories included in references to member States etc

82

(1) The Commissioners may by regulations provide for the territory of the European Union, or for the member States, to be treated for any of the purposes of this Act as including or excluding such territories as may be prescribed.

(2) Without prejudice to the generality of the powers conferred by sub-paragraph (1) and section 16, the Commissioners may, for any of the purposes of this Act, by regulations provide for prescribed provisions of any customs and excise legislation to apply in relation to cases where any territory is treated under sub-paragraph (1) as excluded from the territory of the European Union, with such exceptions and adaptations as may be prescribed.

(3) In sub-paragraph (2) the reference to customs and excise legislation is a reference to any provision (whenever passed, made or adopted) which has effect in relation to, or to any assigned matter connected with, the importation or exportation of goods or movements of goods between Northern Ireland and Great Britain.

(4) In sub-paragraph (3) "assigned matter" has the same meaning as in the Management Act.

Meaning of "new means of transport"

83

(1) In this Act "means of transport" in the expression "new means of transport" means any of the following if they are intended for the transport of persons or goods—
    (a)   any ship exceeding 7.5 metres in length;
    (b)   any aircraft the take-off weight of which exceeds 1550 kilograms;
    (c)   any motorized land vehicle which—
        (i)   has an engine with a displacement or cylinder capacity exceeding 48 cubic centimetres, or
        (ii)   is constructed or adapted to be electrically propelled using more than 7.2 kilowatts.

(2) For the purposes of this Schedule a means of transport is to be treated as new, in relation to any supply or any acquisition from a member State, at any time unless at that time—
    (a)   the period that has elapsed since its first entry into service is—
        (i)   in the case of a ship or aircraft, a period of more than 3 months, and
        (ii)   in the case of a land vehicle, a period of more than 6 months. and
    (b)   it has, since its first entry into service, travelled under its own power—
        (i)   in the case of a ship, for more than 100 hours,
        (ii)   in the case of an aircraft, for more than 40 hours, and
        (iii)   in the case of a land vehicle, for more than 6000 kilometres.

(3) The Treasury may by order vary this paragraph—
    (a)   by adding or deleting any ship, aircraft or vehicle of a description specified in the order to or from those which are for the time being specified in sub-paragraph (1);
    (b)   by altering, omitting or adding to the provisions of sub-paragraph (2) for determining whether a means of transport is new.

(4) The Commissioners may by regulations make provision specifying the circumstances in which a means of transport is to be treated for the purposes of this paragraph as having first entered into service.

VAT charged in a member State

84

Where the context requires it, references in this Schedule to VAT means value added tax charged in accordance with the law of a member State (instead of in accordance with this Act).

SCHEDULE 9ZB
GOODS REMOVED TO OR FROM NORTHERN IRELAND AND SUPPLY RULES

Section 40A(2)

PART 1
IMPORTATIONS

Importations

1

(1) The importation of Union goods into the United Kingdom as a result of their entry into Northern Ireland is not an importation for the purposes of value added tax.

(2) Accordingly, no charge to VAT occurs on the importation of Union goods into the United Kingdom as a result of their entry into Northern Ireland (but see paragraph 1 of Schedule 9ZA, which imposes a charge to VAT on the acquisition of goods in Northern Ireland from a member State).

(3) VAT on the importation of any other goods imported into the United Kingdom as a result of their entry into Northern Ireland is to be charged and payable as if it were relevant NI import duty (instead of as provided under section 1(4)).

(4) Sub-paragraph (3) is to be taken as applying, in relation to any VAT chargeable on the importation of such goods—
    (a)   any provision of Union customs legislation that is relevant to the charging of relevant NI import duty, and
    (b)   any provision made by or under Part 1 of TCTA 2018 that is relevant to the charging of that duty.

(5) Section 15 (meaning of "importation of goods" into the United Kingdom) applies to the importation of such goods as if—
- (a) any reference to import duty were to relevant NI import duty;
- (b) the references in subsections (2) and (3) to a Customs, storage, transit or inward processing procedure were to a procedure corresponding to such a procedure under Union customs legislation, and
- (c) the reference in subsection (3)(b) to section 5(1) of, or paragraph 1(5) or 3(4) of Schedule 1 to, that Act included any provision (including any provision of Union customs legislation) corresponding to those provisions that may apply to those goods.

(6) In section 16 (application of customs enactments)—
- (a) subsection (1) applies to the importation of such goods as if the reference to "other enactments for the time being having effect generally in relation to duties of customs and excise charged by reference to the importation of goods into the United Kingdom" included any provision of Union customs legislation that applies in relation to relevant NI import duty, and
- (b) subsections (3) and (4) apply to sub-paragraph (4) of this paragraph as they apply to subsection (2) of that section.

(7) The Commissioners may by regulations—
- (a) supplement or modify any provision made by provision that applies to value added tax made by or under any enactment (including provision made by or under this Act or TCTA 2018) so far as it applies to VAT charged on the importation of goods into the United Kingdom as a result of their entry into Northern Ireland;
- (b) supplement or modify any provision of Union customs legislation so far as it applies to VAT charged on such an importation.

(8) In this Schedule—

"relevant NI import duty" means duty charged under section 30A(3) of TCTA 2018 (importation of goods: Northern Ireland), and in relation to goods of a description specified in regulations under section 30B(1) of that Act, means that duty as it would be charged if that description were not specified;

"Union customs legislation" means provisions contained in "customs legislation" within the meaning of Regulation (EU) No 952/2013 of the European Parliament and of the Council of 9 October 2013 laying down the Union Customs Code (see Article 5(2) of that Regulation), so far as they apply by virtue of section 7A of the European Union (Withdrawal) Act 2018);

"Union goods" has the meaning it has in that Regulation.

Valuation of imports

2

(1) For the purposes of this Act, the value of goods imported into the United Kingdom as a result of their entry into Northern Ireland is their value as if determined for the purposes of relevant NI import duty, whether or not the goods are subject to that duty.

(2) Accordingly, section 21(1) (value of imported goods) does not apply in relation to such goods.

(3) Subsections (2) to (7) of section 21 apply in relation to such goods (and sub-paragraph (1) is subject to those subsections) as if—
- (a) the reference in subsection (2) to the rules mentioned in subsection (1) of that section were to the rules mentioned in sub-paragraph (1);
- (b) in subsection (2)(c), after "United Kingdom" there were inserted "or a member State";
- (c) the reference in subsection (2A) to the temporary admission procedure under Part 1 of TCTA 2018 were to the procedure that corresponds to that procedure under Union customs legislation.

PART 2
MOVEMENTS BETWEEN NORTHERN IRELAND AND GREAT BRITAIN

Movements between Northern Ireland and Great Britain

3

(1) A supply of goods that involves the removal of goods from Northern Ireland to Great Britain or vice versa is zero-rated (see section 30(1)) if such other conditions, if any, as may be specified in regulations or imposed by the Commissioners are fulfilled.

(2) Where goods are removed from Northern Ireland to Great Britain, VAT is charged on the entry of those goods into Great Britain as if those goods had been imported into the United Kingdom.

(3) Accordingly, any provision made by or under any enactment—
   (a) that is relevant to the charging of VAT on the importation of goods applies in relation to VAT charged as a result of sub-paragraph (2);
   (b) that applies to an importation of goods for the purpose of value added tax applies to such a removal (and references in any such provision to imported goods are to be read as including goods that have been so removed).

(4) Where goods are removed from Great Britain to Northern Ireland, VAT is charged on the entry of those goods into Northern Ireland as if those goods had been imported into the United Kingdom as a result of their entry (from a place outside the United Kingdom) into Northern Ireland.

(5) Accordingly, any provision made by or under any enactment—
   (a) that is relevant to the charging of VAT on the importation of goods applies (as modified by or under Part 1 of this Schedule) in relation to VAT charged as a result of sub-paragraph (4);
   (b) that applies to an importation of goods for the purposes of VAT applies (as modified by or under that Part) to such a removal (and references in this Act to imported goods are to be read as including goods that have been so removed).

(6) Sub-paragraphs (3) and (5)—
   (a) do not apply so far as the context otherwise requires, and
   (b) are subject to the other provisions of this Part of this Schedule.

(7) The Treasury may by regulations—
   (a) supplement or modify any provision that applies to value added tax made by or under any enactment (including provision made by or under this Act or TCTA 2018) so far as it applies to VAT charged as a result of sub-paragraph (2) or (4);
   (b) supplement or modify any provision of Union customs legislation so far as it applies to VAT charged as a result of sub-paragraph (4).

Cross-references—See para 27 below (sub-para (1) does not apply to a supply of "relevant goods" as defined in VATA 1994 s 9A (reverse charge on gas, electricity, heat or cooling).

Liability for VAT on movements between Great Britain and Northern Ireland

4

(1) This paragraph applies to a removal of goods from Northern Ireland to Great Britain or vice versa, instead of section 15 (general provision relating to imported goods).

(2) Goods are treated as imported—
   (a) in the case of goods removed from Northern Ireland to Great Britain, when a liability to pay duty under section 30C of TCTA 2018 (duty on potentially imported goods) in respect of those goods is, or on the relevant assumptions would be, incurred, and
   (b) in the case of goods removed from Great Britain to Northern Ireland, when a liability to pay duty under section 40A of TCTA 2018 (duty on certain goods removed to Northern Ireland) in respect of those goods is, or on the relevant assumptions would be, incurred.

(3) Where the removal is made in the course of a taxable supply made by a taxable person, the taxable person is the person who is treated as having imported the goods.

(4) Otherwise, each person who—

    (a)   in the case of goods removed from Northern Ireland to Great Britain, is, or on the relevant assumptions would be, liable to pay duty under section 30C of TCTA 2018 in respect of those goods, or

    (b)   in the case of goods removed from Great Britain to Northern Ireland, is, or on the relevant assumptions would be, liable to pay duty under section 40A of TCTA 2018 in respect of those goods,

is a person who is treated as having imported the goods.

(5) For the purposes of this paragraph "the relevant assumptions" are—

    (a)   in the case of goods removed from Northern Ireland to Great Britain, an assumption that duty under section 30C of TCTA 2018 is chargeable in respect of those goods,

    (b)   in the case of goods removed from Great Britain to Northern Ireland, an assumption that duty under section 40A of TCTA 2018 is chargeable in respect of those goods,

    (c)   in a case where there is no obligation to present the goods to customs on their arrival in the part of the United Kingdom to which they are removed, an assumption that there is such an obligation,

    (d)   an assumption that a liability to duty at a nil rate is replaced by a liability to duty at a higher rate, and

    (e)   an assumption that no relief from duty is available.

(6) The Commissioners may by regulations make provision—

    (a)   for any other person to be treated as importing the goods (instead of, or as well as, any person treated as importing the goods as a result of sub-paragraph (3) or (4));

    (b)   about (including provision modifying) the application, in relation to such a person, of any provision made by or under any enactment that has effect for the purposes of, or in connection with the enforcement of, any obligation to account for and pay VAT;

    (c)   for requiring any relevant person liable to VAT as a result of provision made by or under this paragraph to give to the Commissioners such notification of the removal of goods in question, and for such VAT to be paid, in such form or manner as may be specified in the regulations or by the Commissioners in accordance with the regulations.

(7) A person is "relevant" for the purposes of sub-paragraph (6)(c) if the person was not a taxable person at the time they became liable to the VAT in question.

(8) If two or more persons are treated as having imported goods those persons are jointly and severally liable to any VAT that is payable on the removal that is treated as an importation as a result of paragraph 3.

(9) The preceding provisions of this paragraph, and any provision made under sub-paragraph (6)(a), are to be ignored in reading any reference to importation or to an importer in anything applied for the purposes of this Act by section 16(1) or (2).

(10) But sub-paragraph (9) does not apply so far as the context otherwise requires or provision to the contrary is contained in regulations under section 16(3).

Valuation of goods removed from Northern Ireland to Great Britain

5

(1) This paragraph applies where goods are removed from Northern Ireland to Great Britain and—

    (a)   the removal is in the course of a supply, or

    (b)   the last supply of those goods before their removal is zero-rated as a result of that removal.

(2) Where this paragraph applies—

    (a)   section 21 (value of imported goods) does not apply for the purpose of determining the value of those goods, and

    (b)   the value of those goods is to be treated as—

        (i)   in a case falling within sub-paragraph (1)(a), the value of the supply in accordance with section 19 and Schedule 6 (value of supply of goods), and

        (ii)   in a case falling within sub-paragraph (1)(b), the value of the last supply of those goods before their removal as determined in accordance with that section and that Schedule.

Relief for qualifying Northern Ireland goods

6

(1) No VAT is to be charged on the removal of qualifying Northern Ireland goods from Northern Ireland to Great Britain as a result of paragraph 3(2) unless the removal is made in the course of a taxable supply made by a taxable person.

(2) But the relief provided by sub-paragraph (1) does not apply to a removal of qualifying goods from Northern Ireland to Great Britain if the last supply of those goods before their removal is zero-rated as a result of that removal.

(3) Any VAT that is chargeable as a result of sub-paragraph (2) becomes chargeable from the later of—

    (a) the time when the goods were treated as having been imported as a result of the removal, and

    (b) the time at which that last supply becomes zero-rated.

(4) In this paragraph "qualifying Northern Ireland goods" has the meaning it has in the European Union (Withdrawal) Act 2018 (see section 8C(6) of that Act).

Zero-rating of supplies made before declaration on removal

7

Item 1 of Group 13 of Schedule 8 (zero-rating)—

    (a) applies to a supply of goods which are removed from Great Britain to Northern Ireland as if the reference to a Customs declaration were to such a declaration made for the purposes of Union customs legislation (rather than under Part 1 of TCTA 2018);

    (b) does not apply to goods which are removed from Northern Ireland to Great Britain where no Customs declaration under Part 1 of TCTA 2018 is required to be made in respect of the removal of the goods.

PART 3
MODIFICATIONS IN RELATION TO EXPORTS

Movements of goods by charities

8

Subsection (5) of Section 30 (export by charities treated as supply in United Kingdom) has effect as if the reference to the export of goods—

    (a) included the removal of goods from Great Britain to Northern Ireland, and

    (b) did not include the export of goods from Northern Ireland to a place in the member States.

Goods exported from Northern Ireland

9

Section 30(6) (zero-rating of exports by supplier) has effect as if reference to the export of goods did not include the export of goods from Northern Ireland to a place in the member States.

Zero-rating regulations

10

Subsection (8) of section 30 (power to zero-rate supplies where goods have been or are to be exported) has effect as if reference to the export of goods—

    (a) included the removal of goods from Northern Ireland to Great Britain, or vice versa, and

    (b) did not include the export of goods from Northern Ireland to a place in the member States.

Zero-rating of supply of exported goods let on hire

11

Section 30(9) (zero-rating of supply of exported goods let on hire) has effect as if the reference to the export of goods did not include the export of goods from Northern Ireland to a place in the member States.

Application of section 30(10)

12

(1) Where a supply of goods has been zero-rated under paragraph 3(1), or as a result of regulations under section 30(8), on the basis that the goods have been or are to be removed from Northern Ireland to Great Britain, section 30(10) (forfeiture of goods found in the United Kingdom) applies in relation to that supply as if any reference to the United Kingdom were to Northern Ireland.

(2) Where a supply of goods has been zero-rated under paragraph 3(1), or as a result of regulations under section 30(8), on the basis that the goods have been or are to be removed from Great Britain to Northern Ireland, section 30(10) applies in relation to that supply as if any reference to the United Kingdom were to Great Britain.

Relief from VAT on importation of goods

13

(1) Section 37 (relief from VAT on importation of goods) has effect as if any reference to the export of goods did not include the export of goods from Northern Ireland to a place in the member States.

(2) That section has effect in relation to a removal of goods from Northern Ireland to Great Britain (which is treated as an importation as a result of paragraph 3(3)) as if any reference to the export of goods included their removal from Great Britain to Northern Ireland.

(3) That section has effect in relation to a removal of goods from Great Britain to Northern Ireland (which is treated as an importation as a result of paragraph 3(5)) as if any reference to the export of goods included their removal from Northern Ireland to Great Britain.

Schedule 8: modifications to Group 13 and 15

14

(1) Item 3 of Group 13 of Schedule 8 (zero-rating) has effect as if the reference to goods for export did not include goods for export from Northern Ireland to a place in the member States.

(2) Group 15 of that Schedule has effect as if—
    (a) any reference to the export of goods did not include the export of goods from Northern Ireland to a place in the member States;
    (b) any reference to the export of goods, other than the reference in item 3, included the removal of goods from Great Britain to Northern Ireland or vice versa;
    (c) after item 3 there were inserted—

"3A

The removal by a charity of goods donated to it—
    (a) from Great Britain to Northern Ireland;
    (b) from Northern Ireland to Great Britain."

PART 4
WAREHOUSES

Modification of sections 18 and 18A

15

(1) Section 18 (place and time of supply) has effect as if—
    (a) every reference to the United Kingdom were to Great Britain, other than the references—

        (i) in the phrases "taking place outside the United Kingdom" and "taking place in the United Kingdom", and
        (ii) in the definition of "warehouse" in subsection (6);
    (b) in subsection (6)—
        (i) in the definition of "the duty point", in paragraph (b), after "import duty" there were inserted "or duty under section 30C of TCTA 2018";
        (ii) in the definition of "warehouse", in paragraph (a), after "import duty" there were inserted "or duty under section 30C of TCTA 2018".

(2) Section 18A (fiscal warehousing) has effect as if the reference to "such place in the United Kingdom" in subsection (3) were to "such place in Great Britain".

Place and time of supply: Northern Ireland warehouses

16

(1) A supply of goods, or an acquisition of goods in Northern Ireland from a member State, is treated as taking place outside the United Kingdom where—
    (a) the goods are subject to a Northern Ireland warehousing regime,
    (b) they have been removed—
        (i) from a place outside the member States, other than Northern Ireland, and have entered the territory of the European Union, or
        (ii) from a place outside the member States and have entered Northern Ireland (which includes goods removed to Northern Ireland from Great Britain),
    (c) the material time for their supply, or their acquisition in Northern Ireland, is while they are subject to that regime and before the duty point, and
    (d) those goods are not, or are not mixed with, any dutiable goods which were produced or manufactured in Northern Ireland or acquired from a member State.

(2) The Commissioners may by regulations provide that sub-paragraph (1) does not apply in circumstances specified or described in the regulations.

(3) A supply of dutiable goods which were produced or manufactured in Northern Ireland or acquired from a member State, or a supply of a mixture of such goods and other goods, is treated as taking place outside the United Kingdom where the conditions in sub-paragraph (5) are met.

(4) An acquisition in Northern Ireland from a member State of dutiable goods is treated as taking place outside the United Kingdom where those conditions are met.

(5) Those conditions are—
    (a) that the goods are subject to a Northern Ireland warehousing regime,
    (b) that the material time for the supply mentioned in sub-paragraph (3), or the acquisition mentioned in sub-paragraph (4), is while the goods are subject to that regime and before the duty point, and
    (c) that the material time for any subsequent supply of those goods is also while the goods are subject to that regime and before the duty point.

(6) Where—
    (a) the conditions in sub-paragraph (5)(a) and (b) are met in relation to a supply of goods mentioned in sub-paragraph (3) or an acquisition of goods mentioned in sub-paragraph (4),
    (b) the condition in sub-paragraph (5)(c) is not met in relation to that supply or acquisition, and
    (c) the supply or acquisition is treated as taking place within the United Kingdom,
sub-paragraph (7) applies to the supply or acquisition.

(7) Where this sub-paragraph applies to a supply or acquisition of goods, the supply or acquisition is treated as taking place at the earlier of—
    (a) the time when the goods are removed from the Northern Ireland warehousing regime, and
    (b) the duty point.

(8) Where sub-paragraph (7) applies to a supply of goods, any VAT payable on the supply must be paid—
    (a) at the time when the supply is treated as taking place, and
    (b) by—

(i) the person who removed the goods from the Northern Ireland warehousing regime, or
(ii) the person who is required to pay any duty or agricultural levy in respect of the goods.

(9) The Commissioners may by regulations make provision for enabling a taxable person to pay the VAT the person is required to pay by virtue of sub-paragraph (8) at a time later than that provided for by that sub-paragraph.

(10) Regulations under sub-paragraph (9) may in particular make provision for either or both of the following—
(a) for the taxable person to pay the VAT together with the VAT chargeable on other supplies by the person of goods and services;
(b) for the taxable person to pay the VAT together with any duty of excise deferment of which has been granted to the person under section 127A of the Customs and Excise Management Act 1979,

and the regulations may make different provision for different descriptions of taxable person and for different descriptions of goods.

(11) In this paragraph—
"dutiable goods" means any goods which are subject—
(a) to a duty of excise, or
(b) in accordance with any provision for the time being having effect for transitional purposes in connection with the accession of any State to the European Union, to any EU customs duty or agricultural levy of the European Union;

"the duty point", in relation to any goods, means—
(a) in the case of goods which are subject to a duty of excise, the time when the requirement to pay the duty on those goods takes effect, and
(b) in the case of goods which are not so subject—
  (i) the time when the requirement to pay duty charged under section 30A(3) of TCTA 2018 (importation of goods: Northern Ireland) on those goods takes effect,
  (ii) the time when the requirement to pay duty charged under section 40A of TCTA 2018 (duty on goods potentially for export from Northern Ireland) on those goods takes effect, or
  (iii) the time when any Community customs debt in respect of duty on the entry of the goods into the territory of the European Union would be incurred or, as the case may be, the corresponding time in relation to any such duty or levy as is mentioned in paragraph (b) of the definition of dutiable goods;

"Northern Ireland warehouse" means any warehouse where goods may be stored in the United Kingdom or a member State without payment of any one or more of the following—
(a) duty charged under section 30A(3) of TCTA 2018 (importation of goods: Northern Ireland) or under section 40A of TCTA 2018 (duty on goods potentially for export from Northern Ireland);
(b) EU customs duty;
(c) any agricultural levy of the European Union;
(d) VAT on the importation of the goods into any member State;
(e) VAT on the importation of goods into the United Kingdom as a result of their entry into Northern Ireland;
(f) any duty of excise or any duty which is equivalent in a member State to a duty of excise.

(12) References in this paragraph to goods being subject to a Northern Ireland warehousing regime are to goods being kept in a Northern Ireland warehouse or being transported between Northern Ireland warehouses (whether in the same country or different countries) without the payment in a country of any duty, levy or VAT; and references to the removal of goods from a warehousing regime are to be construed accordingly.

Northern Ireland fiscal warehouses

17

(1) The Commissioners may, if it appears to them proper, upon application approve any registered person as a Northern Ireland fiscal warehousekeeper, and such approval is subject to

such conditions as the Commissioners impose.

(2) Subject to those conditions and to regulations made under paragraph 25(6), such a person is entitled to keep a Northern Ireland fiscal warehouse.

(3) "Northern Ireland fiscal warehouse" means a place in Northern Ireland in the occupation or under the control of a Northern Ireland fiscal warehousekeeper that the warehousekeeper has notified to the Commisioners as a Northern Ireland fiscal warehouse.

(4) Retail premises may not be notified as a Northern Ireland fiscal warehouse.

(5) A place notified under sub-paragraph (3) is a Northern Ireland fiscal warehouse from the later of—
- (a) the date the Commissioners received the notification, and
- (b) the date specified in the notice from which the notification is to have effect.

(6) A place ceases to be a Northern Ireland fiscal warehouse—
- (a) if that place ceases to be in the occupation or under the control of the Northern Ireland fiscal warehousekeeper, or
- (b) if the Northern Ireland fiscal wareshousekeeper notifies the Commissioners that the place is to cease to be a Northern Ireland fiscal warehouse.

(7) The Commissioners may in considering an application by a person to be a Northern Ireland fiscal warehousekeeper take into account any matter which they consider relevant, and may without prejudice to the generality of that provision take into account all or any one or more of the following—
- (a) the person's record of compliance and ability to comply with the provisions made by or under this Act;
- (b) the person's record of compliance and ability to comply with the provisions made by or under the customs and excise Acts (as defined in the Management Act);
- (c) the person's record of compliance and ability to comply with Union customs legislation;
- (d) the person's record of compliance and ability to comply with the requirements of member States relating to VAT and duties equivalent to duties of excise;
- (e) if the applicant is a company, the records of compliance and ability to comply with the matters set out in paragraphs (a) to (d) of its directors, persons connected with its directors, its managing officers, any shadow directors or any of those persons, and, if it is a close company, the records of compliance and ability to comply with the matters set out in those paragraphs of the beneficial owners of the shares of the company or any of them;
- (f) if the applicant is an individual, the records of compliance and ability to comply with the matters set out in those paragraphs of any company of which the applicant is or has been a director, managing officer or shadow director or, in the case of a close company, a shareholder or the beneficial owner of shares.

(8) For the purposes of paragraphs (e) and (f) of sub-paragraph (7)—
- (a) a person is "connected" with a director if that person is the director's spouse or civil partner, or is a relative, or the spouse or civil partner of a relative, of the director or of the director's spouse or civil partner;
- (b) "managing officer" in relation to a body corporate, means any manager, secretary or other similar officer of the body corporate or any person purporting to act in any such capacity or as a director;
- (c) "shadow director" has the meaning given by section 251 of the Companies Act 2006;
- (d) "close company" has the meaning it has in the Corporation Tax Acts (see Chapter 2 of Part 10 of the Corporation Tax Act 2010).

(9) Subject to sub-paragraph (10), a person approved under sub-paragraph (1) remains a Northern Ireland fiscal warehousekeeper until the person—
- (a) ceases to be a registered person, or
- (b) notifies the Commissioners in writing that the person is to cease to be a Northern Ireland fiscal warehousekeeper.

(10) The Commissioners may if they consider it appropriate from time to time—
- (a) impose conditions on a Northern Ireland fiscal warehousekeeper in addition to those conditions, if any, imposed under sub-paragraph (1);
- (b) vary or revoke any conditions previously imposed;

  (c) withdraw approval of any person as a Northern Ireland fiscal warehousekeeper;
  (d) withdraw Northern Ireland fiscal warehouse status from any premises.

(11) Any application by or on behalf of a person to be a Northern Ireland fiscal warehousekeeper must be in writing and in such form as the Commissioners may direct and must be accompanied by such information as the Commissioners require.

(12) Any approval by the Commissioners under sub-paragraph (1), and any withdrawal of approval or other act by them under sub-paragraph (10), must be notified to the fiscal warehousekeeper in writing and takes effect on such notification being made or on any later date specified for the purpose in the notification.

(13) Without prejudice to the provisions of section 43 concerning liability for VAT, "registered person", for the purposes of this paragraph, includes any person who under that section is for the time being treated as a member of a group.

Conversion of relevant fiscal warehouses etc

18

(1) Sub-paragraph (2) applies to any place in Northern Ireland that was a fiscal warehouse immediately before the coming into force of paragraph 17.

(2) On the coming into force of that paragraph, a place to which this sub-paragraph applies becomes a Northern Ireland fiscal warehouse (and may cease to be in accordance with that paragraph).

(3) On the coming into force of that paragraph, any fiscal warehousekeeper in relation to such a place immediately before the coming into force of that paragraph becomes a Northern Ireland warehousekeeper (and may cease to be in accordance with that paragraph).

(4) But a person does not cease to be a fiscal warehousekeeper in relation to a place in Great Britain as a result of sub-paragraph (3).

(5) Sub-paragraph (6) applies to a fiscal warehousekeeper who becomes a Northern Ireland fiscal warehousekeeper as a result of sub-paragraph (3).

(6) Any condition imposed under section 18A(1) or (6) that, immediately before the coming into force of paragraph 17, applied to a fiscal warehousekeeper to whom this sub-paragraph applies, applies to that person as a Northern Ireland fiscal warehousekeeper as if imposed under paragraph 17 (and may be varied or revoked accordingly).

(7) In this paragraph "fiscal warehouse" and "fiscal warehousekeeper" have the meaning they have in sections 18A to 18F (see section 18F).

Northern Ireland fiscal warehouses: relief

19

(1) Sub-paragraphs (5) and (6) apply where—
  (a) there is an acquisition of goods in Northern Ireland from a member State,
  (b) those goods are eligible goods,
  (c) either—
    (i) the acquisition takes place while the goods are subject to a Northern Ireland fiscal warehousing regime, or
    (ii) after the acquisition but before the supply, if any, of those goods which next occurs, the acquirer causes the goods to be placed in a Northern Ireland fiscal warehousing regime, and
  (d) the acquirer, not later than the time of the acquisition, prepares and keeps a certificate that the goods are subject to a fiscal warehousing regime, or (as the case may be) that the acquirer will cause paragraph (c)(ii) to be satisfied.

(2) A certificate prepared for the purposes of sub-paragraph (1)(d) must be kept for such period as the Commissioners may by regulations specify.

(3) Sub-paragraphs (5) and (6) also apply where—
  (a) there is a supply of goods,
  (b) those goods are eligible goods,
  (c) either—

    (i) that supply takes place while the goods are subject to a Northern Ireland fiscal warehousing regime, or
    (ii) after that supply but before the supply, if any, of those goods which next occurs, the person to whom the former supply is made causes the goods to be placed in a Northern Ireland fiscal warehousing regime,
  (d) in a case falling within paragraph (c)(ii), the person to whom the supply is made gives the supplier, not later than the time of the supply, a certificate that the person will cause paragraph (c)(ii) to be satisfied, and
  (e) the supply is not a retail transaction.

(4) A certificate under sub-paragraph (1)(d) or (3)(d) must be in such form as may be specified by regulations or by the Commissioners in accordance with regulations.

(5) An acquisition or supply to which this sub-paragraph applies is treated for the purposes of this Act as taking place outside the United Kingdom if any subsequent supply of those goods is while they are subject to the Northern Ireland fiscal warehousing regime.

(6) Where an acquisition or supply to which this sub-paragraph applies falls, for the purposes of this Act, to be treated as taking place in the United Kingdom that acquisition or supply is treated for the purposes of this Act as taking place when the goods are removed from the Northern Ireland fiscal warehousing regime.

(7) Where—
  (a) sub-paragraph (6) applies to an acquisition or a supply,
  (b) the acquisition or supply is taxable and not zero-rated, and
  (c) the acquirer or supplier is not a taxable person but would be were it not for paragraph 1(9) of Schedule 1 and paragraphs 38(6) and 48(7) of Schedule 9ZA, or any of those provisions,

VAT is chargeable on that acquisition or supply notwithstanding that the acquirer or the supplier is not a taxable person.

(8) For the purposes of this paragraph, apart from sub-paragraph (6), an acquisition or supply is treated as taking place at the material time for the acquisition or supply.

(9) In this paragraph "eligible goods" has the meaning it has in section 18B, but as if in section 18B(6)(b)—
  (a) in sub-paragraph (i)—
    (i) after "import duty" there were inserted ", and any duty under section 30A(3) of TCTA 2018,";
    (ii) after "those Acts" there were inserted "or Union customs legislation";
  (b) in sub-paragraph (ii), after "section 1(1)(c)" there were inserted "(including any VAT chargeable on the movement of goods from Great Britain to Northern Ireland as a result of paragraph 3(4))".

(10) The Commissioners may by regulations provide that goods of a description specified in regulations are, for the purposes of this paragraph, to be treated—
  (a) where such goods are not of a description falling within Schedule 5A (goods eligible to be fiscally warehoused), as if they were;
  (b) where such goods are of a description falling within that Schedule, as if they were not.

(11) The Commissioners may by regulations provide for the zero-rating of supplies of goods, or of such goods as may be specified in regulations, in cases where—
  (a) the Commissioners are satisfied that the supply in question involves both—
    (i) the removal of the goods from a Northern Ireland fiscal warehousing regime, and
    (ii) their being placed in a warehousing regime in a member State, or in such member State or States as may be prescribed, where that regime is established by provisions of the law of that member State corresponding, in relation to that member State, to the provisions of this paragraph and paragraph 17, and
  (b) such other conditions, if any, as may be specified in the regulations or the Commissioners may impose are fulfilled.

(12) Section 30(10) (zero-rating) applies in relation to regulations made under sub-paragraph (11) as it applies to regulations made under section 30(8) or (9).

Modification of section 18B

20

Section 18B(5) (fiscally warehoused goods: relief) has effect as if after "Schedule 1" there were inserted "and paragraphs 38(6) and 48(7) of Schedule 9ZA, or any of those provisions".

Northern Ireland warehouses and fiscal warehouses: services

21

(1) Section 18C has effect as if any reference to—
- (a) "a warehousing or fiscal warehousing regime" were to "a warehousing, Northern Ireland warehousing, fiscal warehousing, or Northern Ireland fiscal warehousing regime";
- (b) "a warehouse or a fiscal warehousekeeper" were to "a warehouse, Northern Ireland warehouse, fiscal or Northern Ireland fiscal warehousekeeper";
- (c) "a warehousing regime" were to "a warehousing or Northern Ireland warehousing regime";
- (d) "a fiscal warehousing regime" were to "a fiscal or Northern Ireland fiscal warehousing regime".

(2) Subsection (2) of that section has effect in relation to goods subject to a Northern Ireland warehousing or Northern Ireland fiscal warehousing regime as if the term "material time" had the meaning it has in this Part of this Schedule.

(3) Subsection (3) of that section has effect in relation to goods subject to a Northern Ireland warehousing or Northern Ireland fiscal warehousing regime as if the term "duty point" had the meaning it has in paragraph 16.

(4) Subsection (4)(b) of that section has effect in relation to goods subject to a Northern Ireland fiscal warehousing regime as if after "carried out under" there were inserted "Union customs legislation (within the meaning of Schedule 9ZB) or under".

Removal from warehousing: accountability

22

(1) This paragraph applies to any supply to which paragraph 19(6) applies (supply treated as taking place on removal or duty point) and any acquisition to which paragraph 19(7) applies (acquisition treated as taking place on removal where acquirer not a taxable person).

(2) Any VAT payable on the supply or acquisition must (subject to any regulations under sub-paragraph (3)) be paid—
- (a) at the time when the supply or acquisition is treated as taking place under the paragraph in question, and
- (b) by the person by whom the goods are removed or, as the case may be, together with the excise duty, by the person who is required to pay that duty.

(3) The Commissioners may by regulations make provision for enabling a taxable person to pay the VAT the person is required to pay by virtue of sub-paragraph (2) at a time later than that provided by that sub-paragraph.

(4) Regulations may make different provisions for different descriptions of taxable persons and for different descriptions of goods and services.

Deficiency in Northern Ireland fiscally warehoused goods

23

(1) Section 18E applies—
- (a) to goods which have been subject to a Northern Ireland fiscal warehousing regime as it applies to goods which have been subject to a fiscal warehousing regime, and
- (b) to a Northern Ireland fiscal warehousekeeper as it applies to a fiscal warehousekeeper.

(2) In this paragraph "fiscal warehousekeeper" has the meaning it has in sections 18A to 18F (see section 18F).

Incorrect Northern Ireland fiscal warehousing certificates

24

(1) Where—
- (a) a person who makes, or is to make, an acquisition of goods in Northern Ireland from a member State prepares a certificate for the purposes of paragraph 19(1)(d), and
- (b) the certificate is incorrect,

the person preparing the certificate is liable to a penalty.

(2) The amount of the penalty is the amount of VAT actually chargeable on the acquisition.

(3) A person is not liable to a penalty under sub-paragraph (1) if the person satisfies the Commissioners or, on appeal, a tribunal that there is a reasonable excuse for having prepared the certificate in question.

(4) If a person is convicted of an offence (whether under this Act or otherwise) by reason of preparing an incorrect certificate for the purposes of paragraph 19(1)(d), the person is not liable to a penalty under sub-paragraph (1).

(5) A penalty under sub-paragraph (1) is to be treated, for the purposes of sections 76 and 83 (assessments and appeals), as if it were a penalty under section 62 (incorrect certificates).

(6) Section 62 has effect as if in subsection (1)(a)(ii), after "18C(1)(c)" there were inserted "or paragraph 19(3)(d) of Schedule 9ZB (Northern Ireland fiscal warehouses)".

Supplementary provision

25

(1) In this Part of this Schedule—

"eligible goods" is to be construed in accordance with paragraph 19(9) and (10);

"material time"—
- (a) in relation to any acquisition or supply the time of which is determined in accordance with regulations under section 6(14) or paragraph 4(2)(b) of Schedule 9ZA, means such time as may be prescribed for the purpose of this paragraph by those regulations,
- (b) in relation to any other acquisition, means the time of the first removal of the goods (see paragraph 4(5) of that Schedule), and
- (c) in relation to any other supply, means the time when the supply would be treated as taking place in accordance with subsection (2) of section 6 if paragraph (c) of that subsection were omitted;

"Northern Ireland fiscal warehouse" is to be construed in accordance with paragraph 17;

"Northern Ireland fiscal warehousekeeper" is to be construed in accordance with that paragraph;

"Northern Ireland warehouse" has the meaning given by paragraph 16(11).

(2) Any reference in this Part of this Schedule to goods being subject to a Northern Ireland fiscal warehousing regime is, subject to any regulations made under sub-paragraph (6), a reference to eligible goods being kept in a Northern Ireland fiscal warehouse or being transferred between Northern Ireland fiscal warehouses in accordance with such regulations; and any reference to the removal of goods from a Northern Ireland fiscal warehousing regime are to be construed accordingly.

(3) Where as a result of an operation on eligible goods subject to a Northern Ireland fiscal warehousing regime they change their nature but the resulting goods are also eligible goods, the provisions of this Part of this Schedule apply as if the resulting goods were the original goods.

(4) Where as a result of an operation on eligible goods subject to a Northern Ireland fiscal warehousing regime they cease to be eligible goods, on their ceasing to be so this Part applies as if they had at that time been removed from the regime; and for that purpose the proprietor of the goods is treated as if that person were the person removing them.

(5) Where—
- (a) any person ceases to be a Northern Ireland fiscal warehousekeeper, or
- (b) any premises cease to have Northern Ireland fiscal warehouse status,

this Part of this Schedule applies as if the goods of which the person is the fiscal warehousekeeper, or the goods in the fiscal warehouse, as the case may be, had at that time been removed from the fiscal warehousing regime; and for that purpose the proprietor of the goods is to be treated as if the proprietor were the person removing them.

(6) The Commissioners may make regulations governing the deposit, keeping, securing and treatment of goods in a Northern Ireland fiscal warehouse, and the removal of goods from a Northern Ireland fiscal warehouse.

(7) Regulations may, without prejudice to the generality of sub-paragraph (6), include provision—

    (a) in relation to—
- (i) goods which are, have been or are to be subject to a Northern Ireland fiscal warehousing regime,
- (ii) other goods which are, have been or are to be kept in Northern Ireland fiscal warehouses,
- (iii) Northern Ireland fiscal warehouse premises, and
- (iv) Northern Ireland fiscal warehousekeepers and their businesses,

as to the keeping, preservation and production of records and the furnishing of returns and information by Northern Ireland fiscal warehousekeepers and any other persons;

    (b) requiring goods deposited in a fiscal warehouse to be produced to or made available for inspection by an authorised person on the request of that authorised person;

    (c) prohibiting the carrying out on Northern Ireland fiscally warehoused goods of such operations as the Commissioners may prescribe;

    (d) regulating the transfer of goods from one Northern Ireland fiscal warehouse to another;

    (e) concerning goods which, though kept in a Northern Ireland fiscal warehouse, are not eligible goods or are not intended by a relevant person to be goods in respect of which reliefs are to be enjoyed under this Part of this Schedule;

    (f) prohibiting a Northern Ireland fiscal warehousekeeper from allowing goods to be removed from a Northern Ireland fiscal warehousing regime without payment of any VAT payable under paragraph 22 on or by reference to that removal and, if in breach of that prohibition the warehousekeeper allows goods to be so removed, making the warehousekeeper liable for the VAT jointly and severally with the remover,

and may contain such incidental or supplementary provisions as the Commissioners think necessary or expedient.

(8) Regulations may make different provision for different cases, including different provision for different Northern Ireland fiscal warehousekeepers or descriptions of Northern Ireland fiscal warehousekeeper, for Northern Ireland fiscal warehouses of different descriptions or for goods of different classes or descriptions or of the same class or description in different circumstances.

Modification of other provisions

26

(1) Paragraph 3 of Schedule 6 (valuation: special cases) has effect in relation to goods whose supply involves their removal to Northern Ireland from a place outside the United Kingdom as if—

    (a) in sub-paragraph (1)(a)(ii), after "EU" there were inserted "customs duty or";

    (b) in sub-paragraph (1)(b), for "section 18(4)" there were substituted "paragraph 16(7) of Schedule 9ZB";

    (c) in sub-paragraph (2), for "section 18" there were substituted "paragraph 16 of Schedule 9ZB".

(2) Paragraph 2(8) of Schedule 11 has effect as if after "section 18" there were inserted "in relation to goods other than goods in Northern Ireland, or paragraph 16 of Schedule 9ZB in relation to goods in Northern Ireland".

(3) Section 702 of the Income Tax (Earnings and Pensions) Act 2003 (meaning of "readily convertible asset") has effect as if in subsection (6)(a), in the definition of "warehousing regime", after "Value Added Tax Act 1994 (c23))" there were inserted "or a Northern Ireland warehousing or Northern Ireland fiscal warehousing regime (within the meaning of paragraphs 16 to 25 of Schedule 9ZB to that Act)".

(4) Paragraph 11 of Schedule 36 to the Finance Act 2008 (power to inspect premises) has effect as if—

    (a) in sub-paragraph (1)(c), after "warehouse" there were inserted "or Northern Ireland fiscal warehouse";

(b) in sub-paragraph (2)(c), after "warehousing" there were inserted "or Northern Ireland fiscal warehousing".

PART 5
RULES RELATING TO PARTICULAR SUPPLIES

Supplies of gas, electricity or heat

27

(1) Paragraph 3(1) (zero-rating of supplies involving removal of goods from Northern Ireland to Great Britain or vice versa) does not apply to a supply of relevant goods.

(2) In this paragraph "relevant goods" has the meaning it has in section 9A (reverse charge on gas, electricity, heat or cooling).

Time of supply involving both a supply and an acquisition

28

(1) Where any supply of goods involves both—
  (a) the removal of the goods from Northern Ireland, and
  (b) their acquisition in a member State by a person who is liable for VAT on the acquisition in accordance with provisions of the law of that member State corresponding, in relation to that member State, to the provisions of paragraph 2,
subsections (2), (4) to (6) and (10) to (12) of section 6 (time of supply) do not apply and the supply is treated for the purposes of this Act as taking place on whichever is the earlier of the days specified in sub-paragraph (2).

(2) The days mentioned in sub-paragraph (1) are—
  (a) the 15th day of the month following that in which the removal in question takes place, and
  (b) the day of the issue, in respect of the supply, of a VAT invoice or of an invoice of such other description as the Commissioners may by regulations prescribe.

(3) Section 6(14) has effect as if after "section 55(4)" there were inserted "or paragraph 28 of Schedule 9ZB".

Distance selling between EU and Northern Ireland: place of supply

29

(1) Goods whose place of supply is not determined under subsection (2) or (3) of section 7 (place of supply of goods) are treated as supplied in the United Kingdom where—
  (a) the supply involves the removal of the goods to Northern Ireland by or under the directions of the person who supplies them,
  (b) the supply is a transaction in pursuance of which the goods are acquired in Northern Ireland from a member State by a person who is not a taxable person,
  (c) the supplier—
    (i) is liable to be registered under Part 9 of Schedule 9ZA, or
    (ii) would be so liable if the supplier were not already registered under this Act or liable to be registered under Schedule 1 or 1A, and
  (d) the supply is neither a supply of goods consisting in a new means of transport nor anything which is treated as a supply for the purposes of this Act by virtue only of paragraph 5(1) of Schedule 4 or paragraph 30 of Schedule 9ZB.

(2) Goods whose place of supply is not determined under sub-paragraph (1) or subsection (2) or (3) of section 7 and which do not consist in a new means of transport are treated as supplied outside the United Kingdom where—
  (a) the supply involves the removal of the goods from Northern Ireland, by or under the directions of the person who supplies them, to a member State,
  (b) the person who makes the supply is taxable in a member State, and
  (c) provisions of the law of that member State corresponding, in relation to that member State, to the provisions made by sub-paragraph (1) make that person liable to VAT on the supply.

(3) But sub-paragraph (2) does not apply in relation to any supply in a case where the liability mentioned in sub-paragraph (2)(c) depends on the exercise by any person of an option in the United Kingdom corresponding to such an option as is mentioned in paragraph 48(2) unless that person has given, and has not withdrawn, a notification to the Commissioners that the person wishes supplies by that person to be treated as taking place outside the United kingdom where they are supplies in relation to which the other requirements of sub-paragraph (2) are satisfied.

(4) The Commissioners may by regulations provide that a notification for the purposes of sub-paragraph (3) is not to be given or withdrawn except in such circumstances, and in such form and manner, as may be prescribed.

(5) For the purposes of this paragraph—
- (a) where goods, in the course of their removal from a place in Northern Ireland to another place in Northern Ireland leave and re-enter Northern Ireland the removal is not to be treated as a removal from or to Northern Ireland, and
- (b) where goods, in the course of their removal from a place in Northern Ireland to another place in the United Kingdom leave and re-enter the United Kingdom the removal is not to be treated as a removal from Northern Ireland.

(6) Section 7 has effect as if the references in subsections (5A) to (7) to "the preceding provisions of this section" included sub-paragraphs (1) and (2) of this paragraph.

Removal of business assets to be treated as a supply of goods

30

(1) A person carrying on a business makes a supply of goods where—
- (a) the goods form part of the assets of that business,
- (b) they are removed from Northern Ireland or a member State under the directions of that person, and
- (c) the removal is in the course or furtherance of that business for the purpose of being taken to a place in—
  - (i) in the case of goods removed from Northern Ireland, a member State, or
  - (ii) in the case of goods removed from a member State, to another member State or to Northern Ireland.

(2) Sub-paragraph (1) applies to the removal of goods, whether or not that removal of the goods is, or is connected with, a transaction for consideration.

(3) Sub-paragraph (1) does not apply—
- (a) to a case falling within paragraph 5(1) of Schedule 4 (matters to be treated as supply of goods or services),
- (b) to the removal of goods from Northern Ireland where that removal is in the course of their removal from one part of Northern Ireland to another part of Northern Ireland,
- (c) to the removal of goods from a member State where that removal is in the course of their removal from one part of a member State to another part of that member State,
- (d) to goods which have been removed from a place outside the member States for entry into the territory of the European Union and are removed from a member State before the time when any Community customs debt in respect of any EU customs duty on their entry into that territory would be incurred,
- (e) to goods which have been removed from a place outside the United Kingdom and the member States for entry into Northern Ireland and are removed from Northern Ireland before any duty under section 30A(3) of TCTA 2018 on their entry into Northern Ireland would be incurred, or
- (f) to goods which have been removed from Great Britain to Northern Ireland and are removed from Northern Ireland before any duty under section 40A of TCTA 2018 on their entry into Northern Ireland would be incurred.

(4) Sub-paragraph (1) is subject to paragraph 58 of Schedule 9ZA (call-off stock arrangements).

Application of section 43 (company groups) to goods in Northern Ireland

31

Subsection (1)(a) of Section 43 (disregard of supplies between members of groups) does not apply to a supply of goods if the goods are in Northern Ireland at the time they are supplied unless the supplier and the recipient each has a business establishment, or some other fixed establishment, in Northern Ireland.

PART 6
NORTHERN IRELAND AND THE ISLE OF MAN

Application of Part 2 of this Schedule

32

(1) Paragraph 3(1) (zero-rating of supply of goods removed from Great Britain to Northern Ireland and vice versa) applies to goods removed from Northern Ireland to the Isle of Man as they apply to goods removed from Northern Ireland to Great Britain.

(2) The following provisions apply to goods removed to Northern Ireland from the Isle of Man as they apply to goods removed from Great Britain to Northern Ireland—
- (a) sub-paragraphs (4) and (5) of paragraph 3 (charge on goods removed from Great Britain to Northern Ireland);
- (b) sub-paragraphs (6) and (7) of that paragraph (so far as they relate to sub-paragraph (4) or (5)).

(3) Paragraph 4 (liability for VAT on movements between Great Britain and Northern Ireland) applies to goods removed to Northern Ireland from the Isle of Man as they apply to goods removed from Great Britain to Northern Ireland as if the references to a "taxable person" included a person who is, or is required to be, registered under an Act of Tynwald for the purposes of any tax imposed by or under an Act of Tynwald which corresponds to VAT.

(4) Paragraph 7 (zero-rating of supplies made before declaration on removal) applies to goods removed to Northern Ireland from the Isle of Man as it applies to goods removed from Great Britain to Northern Ireland.

Modifications in relation to exports: goods removed to Isle of Man

33

(1) Subsection (8) of section 30 (power to zero-rate supplies where goods have been or are to be exported) has effect as if reference to the export of goods included the removal of goods from Northern Ireland to the Isle of Man.

(2) Where a supply of goods has been zero-rated as a result of paragraph 3(1) or regulations under section 30(8), on the basis that the goods have been or are to be removed from Northern Ireland to the Isle of Man, section 30(10) applies in relation to that supply as if any reference to the United Kingdom were to Northern Ireland.

(3) Section 37 (relief from VAT on importation of goods) has effect in relation to a removal of goods to Northern Ireland from the Isle of Man (which is treated as an importation as a result of paragraphs 3(5) and 32(2)) as if any reference to the export of goods included their removal from Northern Ireland to the Isle of Man.

(4) Group 15 of Schedule 8 (zero-rating) has effect as if—
- (a) any reference to the export of goods, other than the reference in item 3, included the removal of goods from Northern Ireland to the Isle of Man;
- (b) the modification made by paragraph 14(2)(c) applied to the removal of goods to the Isle of Man from Northern Ireland as it applies to the removal of goods from Northern Ireland to Great Britain.

Warehouses

34

Part 4 (warehouses) has effect as if any reference to Great Britain included the Isle of Man (see also article 2 of the Value Added Tax (Isle of Man) Order 1982 which provides that this Act has effect as if the Isle of Man were part of the United Kingdom subject to the provisions of that Order).

Extent

35

Nothing in this Part of this Schedule is to be taken as extending to the Isle of Man."

Other amendments of VATA 1994

3 In section 3 (taxable persons)—
  (a) in subsection (2), after "registration" insert "(and see also Parts 8 and 9 of Schedule 9ZA which contain further provisions about registration)";
  (b) in subsection (3)—
    (i) after "Schedules", in the first place it occurs, insert "and Part 8 and 9 of Schedule 9ZA";
    (ii) after "Schedules", in the second place it occurs, insert "or those Parts".

4 In section 5 (meaning of supply), after subsection (3) insert—
"(3A) An order under subsection (3) may provide that paragraph 30 of Schedule 9ZB does not apply, in such circumstances as may be described in the order, so as to make a removal of assets a supply of goods under that paragraph."

5 (1) Section 9A (reverse charge on gas, electricity, heat or cooling supplied by persons outside the United Kingdom) is amended as follows.
(2) In the heading, omit "supplied by persons outside the United Kingdom".
(3) After subsection (1) insert—
"(1A) This section also applies if relevant goods are supplied by a person ("A") to another person ("B") for the purposes of any business carried on by B and—
  (a) A is in Great Britain and B is registered under this Act and is identified for the purposes of VAT in Northern Ireland, or
  (b) A is in Northern Ireland and B is so registered but is not so identified."
(4) In subsection (5)—
  (a) in paragraph (a), for "the United Kingdom", in both places it occurs, substitute "Great Britain",
  (b) after that paragraph insert—
    "(aa) gas supplied through a natural gas system situated within Northern Ireland or the territory of a member State or any network connected to such a system,".
(5) In subsection (6), after "United Kingdom" insert ", in Great Britain or in Northern Ireland".

6 In section 18A (fiscal warehousing)—
  (a) in subsection (4), omit the words after paragraph (f);
  (b) after that subsection insert—
"(4A) For the purposes of paragraphs (e) and (f) of subsection (4)—
  (a) a person is "connected" with a director if that person is the director's spouse or civil partner, or is a relative, or the spouse or civil partner of a relative, of the director or of the director's spouse or civil partner;
  (b) "managing officer" in relation to a body corporate, means any manager, secretary or other similar officer of the body corporate or any person purporting to act in any such capacity or as a director;
  (c) "shadow director" has the meaning given by section 251 of the Companies Act 2006;
  (d) "close company" has the meaning it has in the Corporation Tax Acts (see Chapter 2 of Part 10 of the Corporation Tax Act 2010)."

7 (1) Omit section 14A and Schedule 4B (call-off stock arrangements).
(2) In section 69 (breaches of regulatory provisions)—
  (a) in subsection (1)(a) for ", paragraph 5 of Schedule 3A or paragraph 9(1) or (2)(a) of Schedule 4B" substitute "or paragraph 5 of Schedule 3A";
  (b) in subsection (2) omit "paragraph 8 or 9(2)(b) of Schedule 4B or".

(3) In section 97 (orders, rule and regulations), in subsection (4), in paragraph (a) for "or 28" substitute ", 28 or 40A".

(4) In Schedule 6 (valuation of supplies: special cases), in paragraph 6(1) omit paragraph (d) (and the "or" before it).

(5) In consequence of the amendment made by sub-paragraph (1), the Value Added Tax Regulations 1995 (SI 1995/2518) are amended as follows—
   (a) in regulation 21 (interpretation of Part 4), omit paragraph (2);
   (b) omit regulation 22ZA;
   (c) in regulation 22B (EC sales statements: supplementary)—
      (i) in paragraph (1), for "more than one statement is to be submitted under regulations 22 to" substitute "statements are to be submitted under regulation 22 and 22A";
      (ii) in paragraphs (2) and (3) omit ", 22ZA".

(6) Schedule 4B continues to have effect in relation to goods to which Schedule 4B applied (see paragraph 1 of that Schedule) immediately before its repeal.

(7) Any other provision repealed, revoked or amended by or under this Act or TCTA 2018 at the same time as, or after, the repeal of Schedule 4B continues to have effect in relation to any deemed acquisition or supply of such goods arising as a result of that Schedule (as saved by paragraph (6)) as if the provision had not been so repealed, revoked or amended.

(8) The savings in sub-paragraphs (6) and (7) do not apply to the provisions mentioned in sub-paragraph (9) in relation to goods to which Schedule 4B applied as a result of their removal from Great Britain for the purpose of being taken to a place in a member State.

(9) Those provisions are—
   (a) paragraph 7(2)(c) of that Schedule;
   (b) the provisions of Part 4 of the Value Added Tax Regulations 1994 (SI 1994/2518) (EC sales statements).

(10) Part 10 of Schedule 9ZA of VATA 1994 (as inserted by this Schedule) does not apply to goods in respect of which the savings in sub-paragraph (6) and (7) apply.

Commencement—The day appointed for the coming into force of the provisions of this Act, so far as not already in force, is IP completion day, other than Sch 2 para 7(3) (Finance Act 2016, Section 126 (Appointed Day), the Taxation (Cross-border Trade) Act 2018 (Appointed Day No 8, Transition and Saving Provisions) and the Taxation (Post-transition Period) Act 2020 (Appointed Day No 1) (EU Exit) Regulations, SI 2020/1642).

8 In Schedule 8 (zero-rating), in Group 18, in Note (2), in paragraph (a), for "a member State" substitute "the United Kingdom, a member State or an associated country (within the meaning given by Article 2(c) of that Regulation)".

PART 2
AMENDMENTS OF OTHER LEGISLATION

F(No 2)A 2017

9 In section 48 of F(No 2)A 2017 (carrying on an imported goods fulfilment business)—
   (a) in subsection (4) (as amended by TCTA 2018), after "section 15" insert "and paragraph 1 of Schedule 9ZB";
   (b) after that subsection insert—

"(4A) But goods that are treated as imported for the purposes of VATA 1994 as a result of paragraph 3 of Schedule 9ZB are not imported goods for the purposes of this Part."

TCTA 2018

10 (1) Schedule 8 to TCTA 2018 (VAT amendments connected with withdrawal from EU) is amended as follows.

(2) In paragraph 64(3)—
   (a) at the end of paragraph (a) insert "and";
   (b) omit paragraph (c) (and the "and" before it).

(3) In paragraph 94, omit sub-paragraphs (2) and (9).

(4) In paragraph 114, in sub-paragraph (2)—
   (a) in paragraph (a), for "second" substitute "third";
   (b) in paragraph (b), for "third" substitute "fourth";
   (c) in paragraph (c), for "fifth" substitute "sixth".

(5) In paragraph 132, omit paragraph (k).

Value Added Tax (Place of Supply of Goods) Order 2004

11 (1) The Value Added Tax (Place of Supply of Goods) Order 2004 (SI 2004/3148) is amended as follows.

(2) In article 9, in the definition of "relevant goods"—
   (a) in paragraph (i), after "within" insert "Northern Ireland or";
   (b) after that paragraph insert—
>"(ia) gas supplied through a natural gas system situated within Great Britain or any network connected to such a system,".

(3) In article 14—
   (a) the existing text becomes paragraph (1);
   (b) after that paragraph insert—
>"(2) For the purposes of that section a person is in Great Britain if—
>   (a) the person has established their business or has a fixed establishment in Great Britain, or
>   (b) in the absence of such a place of business or fixed establishment, the place where the person has their permanent address, or the place where they usually reside, is in Great Britain.
>(3) For the purposes of that section a person is in Northern Ireland if—
>   (a) the person has established their business or has a fixed establishment in Northern Ireland, or
>   (b) in the absence of such a place of business or fixed establishment, the place where the person has their permanent address, or the place where they usually reside, is in Northern Ireland."

Value Added Tax (Relief for European Research Infrastructure Consortia) Order 2012

12 In article 2 of the Value Added Tax (Relief for European Research Infrastructure Consortia) Order 2012 (SI 2012/2907)—
   (a) in paragraph (1)—
      (i) omit "from a place outside the member States";
      (ii) for "another" substitute "a";
   (b) in paragraph (2)(a) for "a member State" substitute "the United Kingdom, a member State or an associated country (within the meaning given by Article 2(c) of that Regulation)".

Value Added Tax (Miscellaneous Amendments, Revocation and Transitional Provisions) (EU Exit) Regulations 2019

13 In the Value Added Tax (Miscellaneous Amendments, Revocation and Transitional Provisions) (EU Exit) Regulations 2019 (SI 2019/513), omit regulation 7.

SCHEDULE 3
ONLINE SALES BY OVERSEAS PERSONS AND LOW VALUE IMPORTATIONS
Section 7

Commencement—The day appointed for the coming into force of this Act, so far as not already in force (and other than Sch 2 para 7(3)), is IP completion day (11pm on 31 December 2020): SI 2020/1642 reg 9.

PART 1
MAIN AMENDMENTS

Amendments to the Value Added Tax Act 1994

1 VATA 1994 is amended as follows.

2 After section 5 insert—

>**"5A Supplies of goods facilitated by online marketplaces: deemed supply**
>(1) This section applies where—
>   (a) a person ("P") makes a taxable supply of goods in the course or furtherance of a business to another person ("R"),
>   (b) that supply is facilitated by an online marketplace, and
>   (c) the imported consignment condition is met.
>(2) For the purposes of this Act—
>   (a) P is to be treated as having supplied the goods to the operator of the online marketplace, and
>   (b) the operator is to be treated as having supplied the goods to R in the course or furtherance of a business carried on by the operator.
>(3) The imported consignment condition is met where—

(a) the supply of the goods to R involves those goods being imported,
(b) the intrinsic value of the consignment of which the goods are part is not more than £135, and
(c) the consignment of which the goods are part—
 (i) does not contain excepted goods, and
 (ii) is not a consignment in relation to which a postal operator established outside the United Kingdom has an obligation under an agreement with the Commissioners to pay any import VAT that is chargeable on the importation of that consignment into the United Kingdom.
(4) For the purposes of subsection (3)(c)(i), "excepted goods" means goods of a class or description subject to any duty of excise whether or not those goods are in fact chargeable with that duty, and whether or not that duty has been paid on the goods.
(5) The Commissioners may by regulations substitute a different figure for a figure that is at any time specified in subsection (3)(b)."

3 (1) Section 5A (supplies of goods facilitated by online marketplaces: deemed supply) (inserted by paragraph 2 of this Schedule) is amended as follows.
(2) In subsection (1), for paragraph (c) substitute—
"(c) one of the following applies—
 (i) the imported consignment condition is met, or
 (ii) the supply of goods to R does not involve those goods being imported, but P is established outside the United Kingdom."
(3) After subsection (1) insert—
"(1A) But this section does not apply in a case where P is established outside the United Kingdom and the imported consignment condition is not met if—
(a) R is registered under this Act,
(b) R has provided the operator of the online marketplace with R's VAT registration number, and
(c) the operator of the online marketplace has provided P with that number and details of the supply before the end of the relevant period."
(4) In subsection (5), after "regulations" insert "—
(a) specify the details that must be provided for the purposes of subsection (1A)(c);
(b) ".
(5) After subsection (5) insert—
"(6) In this section—
"relevant period" means the period of 7 days beginning with the day on which the supply is treated as taking place under section 6 or such longer period as the Commissioners may allow in general or specific directions;
"VAT registration number" means the number allocated by the Commissioners to a person registered under this Act."

4 (1) Section 7 (place of supply of goods) is amended as follows.
(2) Before subsection (6) insert—
"(5A) Goods whose place of supply is not determined under any of the preceding provisions of this section shall be treated as supplied outside the United Kingdom where the supply—
(a) meets the imported consignment condition in section 5A; and
(b) is deemed to be to the operator of an online marketplace.
(5B) Goods whose place of supply is not determined under any of the preceding provisions of this section shall be treated as supplied in the United Kingdom where—
(a) they are supplied by a person in the course or furtherance of a business carried on by that person;
(b) the supply involves the goods being imported;
(c) the intrinsic value of the consignment of which the goods are part is not more than £135; and
(d) the consignment of which the goods are part—
 (i) does not contain goods of a class or description subject to any duty of excise whether or not those goods are in fact chargeable with that duty, and whether or not that duty has been paid on the goods; and
 (ii) is not a consignment in relation to which a postal operator established outside the United Kingdom has an obligation under an agreement with

the Commissioners to pay any import VAT that is chargeable on the importation of that consignment into the United Kingdom."

(3) After subsection (9) insert—

"(9A) The Commissioners may by regulations substitute a different figure for a figure that is at any time specified in subsection (5B)(c)."

5 After section 7 insert—

"**7AA Reverse charge on goods supplied from abroad**

(1) This section applies where—
 (a) goods are supplied by a person ("A") to another person ("B"),
 (b) B is registered under this Act,
 (c) the supply involves the goods being imported,
 (d) the intrinsic value of the consignment of which the goods are part is not more than £135, and
 (e) the consignment of which the goods are part—
  (i) does not contain goods of a class or description subject to any duty of excise whether or not those goods are in fact chargeable with that duty, and whether or not that duty has been paid on the goods, and
  (ii) is not a consignment in relation to which a postal operator established outside the United Kingdom has an obligation under an agreement with the Commissioners to pay any import VAT that is chargeable on the importation of that consignment into the United Kingdom.

(2) This Act has effect as if, instead of there being a supply of the goods by A to B—
 (a) there were a supply of the goods by B in the course of furtherance of a business carried on by B, and
 (b) that supply were a taxable supply.

(3) The Commissioners may by regulations substitute a different figure for a figure that is at any time specified in subsection (1)(d)."

6 In section 16A(1) (postal packets) omit "(within the meaning of the Postal Services Act 2000)".

7 (1) Section 37 (relief from VAT on importation of goods) is amended as follows.
(2) For the heading, substitute "VAT on importation of goods: reliefs etc".
(3) Before subsection (1) insert—

"(A1) No VAT is chargeable on the importation of goods to which section 7(5B) applies."

8 In section 77B (joint and several liability: sellers identified as non-compliant by the Commissioners) omit subsections (9) and (12).

9 In section 77BA (joint and several liability: non-UK sellers in breach of Schedule 1A registration requirement) omit subsection (8).

10 In section 77C (joint and several liability under section 77B or 77BA: assessments) omit subsection (9).

11 In section 77D (joint and several liability under section 77B or 77BA: interest) omit subsection (8).

12 In section 77E (display of VAT registration numbers), in subsection (9) omit the definition of "online marketplace" and "operator".

13 After section 77E insert—

"*Liability of operators of online marketplaces for VAT in cases of deemed supply*

77F Exception from liability under section 5A

(1) This section applies where an amount of VAT is due from the operator of an online marketplace by virtue of section 5A.

(2) The operator is not liable for any amount of VAT in excess of the amount paid by R (as defined in section 5A) provided that the operator took—
 (a) all reasonable steps to ascertain the matters set out in subsection (3), and
 (b) all other reasonable steps to satisfy itself that the amount charged was correct.

(3) The matters are—
 (a) the place of establishment of the person making taxable supplies facilitated by the online marketplace;
 (b) the location of the goods at the time of their supply."

14 Before section 96 insert—

"95A Meaning of "online marketplace" and "operator" etc
(1) In this Act—
"online marketplace" means a website, or any other means by which information is made available over the internet, which facilitates the sale of goods through the website or other means by persons other than the operator (whether or not the operator also sells goods through the marketplace);
"operator", in relation to an online marketplace, means the person who controls access to, and the contents of, the online marketplace provided that the person is involved in—
  (a) determining any terms or conditions applicable to the sale of goods,
  (b) processing, or facilitating the processing, of payment for the goods, and
  (c) the ordering or delivery, or facilitating the ordering or delivery, of the goods.
(2) For the purposes of subsection (1), an online marketplace facilitates the sale of goods if it allows a person to—
  (a) offer goods for sale, and
  (b) enter into a contract for the sale of those goods.
(3) The Treasury may by regulations amend this section so as to alter the meaning of—
"online marketplace", and
"operator"."

15 In section 96(1) (other interpretative provisions), at the appropriate places insert—
""postal operator" means a person who provides—
  (a) the service of conveying postal packets from one place to another by post, or
  (b) any of the incidental services of receiving, collecting, sorting and delivering postal packets;";
""postal packet" means a letter, parcel, packet or other article transmissible by post;"."

16 (1) Schedule 8 (zero-rating) is amended as follows.
(2) In Part 1 (index to zero-rated supplies of goods and services), at the appropriate place insert—

"Online marketplaces (deemed supply) | Group 21"

(3) In Part 2 (the groups), after Group 20 insert—

"GROUP 21
ONLINE MARKETPLACES (DEEMED SUPPLY)
Item No.

1
A supply by a person established outside the United Kingdom that is deemed to be a supply to an operator of an online marketplace by virtue of section 5A, provided that the supply does not involve the goods being imported for the purposes of that section."

17 (1) In Schedule 11 (administration, collection and enforcement), paragraph 6 (record keeping) is amended as follows.
(2) Before sub-paragraph (5) insert—
"(4A) In relation to a relevant taxable person, a duty under this paragraph to preserve records relating to a relevant taxable supply must be discharged by at least preserving the information contained in the records electronically.
(4B) A relevant taxable person must make available to the Commissioners electronically on request any records preserved in accordance with sub-paragraph (4A).
(4C) In sub-paragraph (4A) "relevant taxable supply" means a supply of goods where—
  (a) that supply is deemed to be a supply by an operator of an online marketplace by virtue of section 5A, or
  (b) the place of supply of those goods is determined by section 7(5B).
(4D) In sub-paragraphs (4A) and (4B) "relevant taxable person" means a person who is a taxable person and who—
  (a) is the operator of an online marketplace,
  (b) is a person making taxable supplies of goods facilitated by an online marketplace, or
  (c) makes taxable supplies, the place of supply of which is determined by section 7(5B)."

(3) In sub-paragraph (5), after "may by regulations make" insert "further".

Amendment to the Value Added Tax (Imported Goods) Relief Order 1984

18 In Schedule 2 to the Value Added Tax (Imported Goods) Relief Order 1984 (SI 1984/746) (reliefs for goods of certain descriptions), omit Item 8 and Notes (2) and (3) in Group 8 (low value consignment relief).

Amendments to the Value Added Tax Regulations 1995

19 The Value Added Tax Regulations 1995 (SI 1995/2518) are amended as follows.

20 In regulation 13(1) (obligation to supply a VAT invoice), before sub-paragraph (2) insert—
"(1C) Save as otherwise provided in these Regulations, where a registered person makes a taxable supply of goods to a person who is not a taxable person, if—
    (a)   that supply is deemed to be a supply by an operator of an online marketplace by virtue of section 5A of the Act, or
    (b)   the place of supply of those goods is determined by section 7(5B) of the Act,
the registered person must provide the other person with a VAT invoice."

21 (1) Regulation 13A (electronic invoicing) is amended as follows.
(2) In paragraph (1) for "goods or services" substitute "services or relevant goods".
(3) After paragraph (4) insert—
"(5) In this regulation, "relevant goods" means all goods other than goods—
    (a)   the supply of which is deemed to be a supply by an operator of an online marketplace by virtue of section 5A of the Act, or
    (b)   the place of supply of which is determined by section 7(5B) of the Act."

22 (1) Regulation 15 (change of rate, credit notes) is amended as follows.
(2) The existing text becomes paragraph (1).
(3) In that paragraph, after "relates to a" insert "relevant".
(4) After that paragraph insert—
"(2) In this regulation, "relevant supply" means a supply of goods or services other than a supply of goods to a person who is not a taxable person."

23 (1) Regulation 15C (changes in consideration: debit notes and credit notes) is amended as follows.
(2) In paragraph (1), at the end insert ", subject to paragraph (1A)".
(3) After paragraph (1) insert—
"(1A) This regulation does not apply in relation to a case where the original supply was a supply of goods to a person who was not a taxable person."

24 After regulation 16A insert—

"**16B Retailers' and simplified invoices: exceptions**
Regulations 16 and 16A do not apply in relation to a supply of goods if—
    (a)   that supply is deemed to be a supply by an operator of an online marketplace by virtue of section 5A of the Act, or
    (b)   the place of supply of those goods is determined by section 7(5B) of the Act."

PART 2
AMENDMENTS AND MODIFICATIONS RELATING TO THE NORTHERN IRELAND PROTOCOL

Amendments to the Value Added Tax Act 1994

25 VATA 1994 is amended as follows.

26 In section 40A (Northern Ireland Protocol) (inserted by section 3 of this Act), after subsection (2) insert—
"(3) Schedule 9ZC makes provision, as a result of the Protocol on Ireland/Northern Ireland in the EU withdrawal agreement, about the application of this Act in cases involving—
    (a)   supplies of goods by persons established outside the United Kingdom that are facilitated by online marketplaces, and
    (b)   the importation of goods of a low value."

27 (1) Schedule 9ZB (inserted by paragraph 2 of Schedule 2 to this Act) is amended as follows.
(2) After paragraph 1(8) insert—

"(9) This paragraph is subject to paragraph 4 of Schedule 9ZC.";

(3) After paragraph 4(10) insert—

"(11) Sub-paragraphs (3) and (4) are subject to paragraph 4A of Schedule 9ZC."

28 After that Schedule insert—

"SCHEDULE 9ZC

ONLINE SALES BY OVERSEAS PERSONS AND LOW VALUE IMPORTATIONS: MODIFICATIONS RELATING TO THE NORTHERN IRELAND PROTOCOL

Section 40A(3)

PART 1
MODIFICATION OF THIS ACT

1

References in the following provisions of this Act to goods being imported do not include goods imported into the United Kingdom as a result of their entry into Northern Ireland or goods treated as having been imported into the United Kingdom as a result of their being removed from Northern Ireland to Great Britain—

    (a)   section 5A(3) (the imported consignment condition);
    (b)   section 7(5B)(b) (place of supply of goods);
    (c)   section 7AA(1)(c) (reverse charge on goods supplied from abroad).

2

Section 77F (exception from liability under section 5A) has effect as if—

    (a)   in the heading, after "section 5A" there were inserted "or Part 1 of Schedule 9ZC";
    (b)   in subsection (1), after "section 5A" there were inserted "or Part 1 of Schedule 9ZC";
    (c)   in subsection (2), after "(as defined in section 5A" there were inserted "or Part 1 of Schedule 9ZC, as the case may be".

3

(1) In Schedule 11, paragraph 6 has effect subject to the following modifications.

(2) Sub-paragraph (4C) has effect as if—

    (a)   the "or" at the end of paragraph (a) were omitted;
    (b)   after paragraph (b) there were inserted ", or
    (c)   Part 1 of Schedule 9ZC makes provision about who is treated as having imported those goods."

(3) Sub-paragraph (4D) has effect as if—

    (a)   the "or" at the end of paragraph (b) were omitted;
    (b)   after paragraph (c) there were inserted ", or
    (d)   is treated as having imported goods under Part 1 of Schedule 9ZC."

4

(1) Sub-paragraph (2) applies, instead of section 15(4) and (5) (as modified by paragraph 1 of Schedule 9ZB), where—

    (a)   goods are imported into the United Kingdom as a result of their entry into Northern Ireland in the course or furtherance of a business by a person ("P"),
    (b)   that importation is in the course of a taxable supply to a person ("R") who—
        (i)   is not registered under this Act, or
        (ii)   is registered under this Act but who has not provided P or, where the supply is facilitated by an online marketplace, the operator of that marketplace, with R's VAT registration number,
    (c)   the intrinsic value of the consignment of which the goods are part is not more than £135, and
    (d)   the consignment of which the goods are part—
        (i)   does not contain excepted goods, and
        (ii)   is not a consignment in relation to which a postal operator established outside the United Kingdom has an obligation under an agreement with the Commissioners to pay any import VAT that is chargeable on the importation of that consignment into the United Kingdom.

(2) The person who is treated as having imported the goods is—
   (a) in a case where the supply is facilitated by an online marketplace, the operator of the online marketplace, or
   (b) in any other case, P.

(3) In sub-paragraph (1)(b)(ii), "VAT registration number" means the number allocated by the Commissioners to a person registered under this Act.

(4) For the purposes of sub-paragraph (1)(d)(i), "excepted goods" means goods of a class or description subject to any duty of excise whether or not those goods are in fact chargeable with that duty, and whether or not that duty has been paid on the goods.

(5) The Commissioners may by regulations substitute a different figure for a figure that is at any time specified in sub-paragraph (1)(c).

PART 2

MODIFICATION OF THE VALUE ADDED TAX (IMPORTED GOODS) RELIEF ORDER 1984

5

(1) In Schedule 2 to the Value Added Tax (Imported Goods) Relief Order 1984 (SI 1984/746) (reliefs for goods of certain descriptions), Group 8 (articles sent for miscellaneous purposes) has effect subject to the following modifications.

(2) That Group has effect as if after item 7 there were inserted—

"8

Any consignment of goods imported into the United Kingdom as a result of their entry into Northern Ireland (other than alcoholic beverages, tobacco products, perfumes or toilet waters) not exceeding £15 in value."

(3) That Group has effect as if after note (1) there were inserted—

"(2) Item 8 does not apply in relation to any goods imported on mail order.

(3) For the purposes of note (2)—

"mail order" in relation to any goods means any transaction or series of transactions under which a seller (S) sends goods in fulfilment of an order placed remotely,

"remotely" means by any means that do not involve the simultaneous physical presence of S and the person placing the order, and

"seller" does not include any person acting otherwise than in a commercial or professional capacity."

PART 3

REGISTRATION

Liability to be registered

6

(1) A person who is treated as having imported goods under Part 1 of this Schedule and—
   (a) is not registered under this Act, and
   (b) is not liable to be registered under Schedule 1, 1A or 9ZA to this Act,
becomes liable to be registered under this Schedule at the point they are so treated.

(2) A person who is not registered or liable to be registered as mentioned in sub-paragraph (1)(a) and (b) becomes liable to be registered under this Schedule at any time if there are reasonable grounds for believing that the person will be treated as having imported goods under Part 1 of this Schedule in the following 30 days.

(3) A person is treated as having become liable to be registered under this Schedule at any time when the person would have become so liable under the preceding provisions of this paragraph but for any registration which is subsequently cancelled under paragraph 11(2) of this Schedule, paragraph 13(3) of Schedule 1, paragraph 11 of Schedule 1A, paragraph 6(2) of Schedule 3A or paragraph 43 or 53 of Schedule 9ZA.

(4) A person does not cease to be liable to be registered under this Schedule except in accordance with paragraph 7.

7

(1) A person who has become liable to be registered under this Schedule ceases to be so liable at any time if the Commissioners are satisfied that the person is no longer a person who is, or will be, treated as having imported goods under Part 1 of this Schedule.

(2) But a person does not cease to be liable to be registered under this Schedule at any time if there are reasonable grounds for believing that the person will be treated as having imported goods under Part 1 of this Schedule in the following 30 days.

Notification of liability and registration

8

(1) A person who becomes liable to be registered under this Schedule must notify the Commissioners of the liability—
    (a) in the case of a liability under sub-paragraph (1) of paragraph 6, within 30 days of the person becoming so liable, and
    (b) in the case of a liability under sub-paragraph (2) of that paragraph, before the end of the period by reference to which the liability arises.

(2) The Commissioners must register any such person (whether or not the person notifies them) with effect from the relevant time.

(3) In this paragraph "the relevant time"—
    (a) in a case falling within sub-paragraph (1)(a), means the beginning of the day on which the liability arose, and
    (b) in a case falling within sub-paragraph (1)(b), means the beginning of the period by reference to which the liability arose.

Entitlement to be registered etc

9

(1) Where a person who is not liable to be registered under this Act and is not already so registered—
    (a) satisfies the Commissioners that the person intends to make or facilitate a relevant supply from a specified date, and
    (b) requests to be registered under this Schedule,
the Commissioners may, subject to such conditions as they think fit to impose, register the person with effect from such date as may be agreed between the Commissioners and the person.

(2) Conditions imposed under sub-paragraph (1) may—
    (a) be so imposed wholly or partly by reference to, or without reference to, any conditions prescribed for the purposes of this paragraph, and
    (b) be subsequently varied by the Commissioners (whenever the conditions were imposed).

(3) Where a person who is entitled to be registered under paragraph 9 or 10 of Schedule 1 requests registration under this paragraph, the person is to be registered under that Schedule, and not under this Schedule.

Notification of matters affecting continuance of registration

10

(1) Any person registered under this Schedule who ceases to be registrable under this Act must notify the Commissioners of that fact within 30 days of the day on which the person ceases to be registrable.

(2) A person registered under paragraph 9(1) must notify the Commissioners, within 30 days of the first occasion after the person's registration when the person makes or facilitates a relevant supply, that the person has made or facilitated that supply.

(3) For the purposes of this paragraph a person ceases to be registrable under this Act where—
    (a) the person ceases to be a person who would be liable or entitled to be registered under this Act if the person's registration and any enactment preventing a person from being liable to be registered under different provisions at the same time were disregarded, or

(b) in the case of a person who (having been registered under paragraph 9(1)) has not been such a person during the period of the person's registration, the person ceases to have any intention of making or facilitating relevant supplies.

Cancellation of registration

11

(1) Where a person registered under this Schedule satisfies the Commissioners that the person is not liable to be so registered, the Commissioners must, if the person so requests, cancel that registration with effect from the day on which the request is made or from such later date as may be agreed between the Commissioners and the person.

(2) Where the Commissioners are satisfied that a person registered under this Schedule has ceased since the person's registration to be registrable under this Schedule, they may cancel that registration with effect from the day on which the person so ceased or from such later date as may be agreed between the Commissioners and the person.

(3) Where the Commissioners are satisfied that a person who has been registered under paragraph 9(1) and is not for the time being liable to be registered under this Schedule—
- (a) has not begun, by the date specified in the person's request to be registered, to make or facilitate relevant supplies, or
- (b) has contravened any condition of the person's registration,

the Commissioners may cancel the person's registration with effect from the date so specified or, as the case may be, the date of the contravention or from such later date as may be agreed between the Commissioners and the person.

(4) But the Commissioners may not, under sub-paragraph (1), (2) or (3), cancel a person's registration with effect from any time unless the Commissioners are satisfied that it is not a time when that person would be subject to a requirement, or in a case falling under sub-paragraph (2) or (3) a requirement or entitlement, to be registered under this Act.

(5) Where the Commissioners are satisfied that, on the day on which a person was registered under this Schedule, the person—
- (a) was not registrable under this Schedule, and
- (b) in the case of a person registered under paragraph 9(1), did not have the intention by reference to which the person was registered,

the Commissioners may cancel that registration with effect from that day.

(6) In determining, for the purposes of sub-paragraph (4), whether a person would be subject to a requirement, or would be entitled, to be registered at any time, so much of any provision of this Act as prevents a person from becoming liable or entitled to be registered when the person is already registered or when the person is so liable under any other provision is to be disregarded.

(7) For the purposes of this paragraph, a person is registrable under this Schedule at any time when the person is liable to be registered under this Schedule or is a person who makes or facilitates relevant supplies.

Notifications

12

Any notification required under this Part of this Schedule must be made in such form and manner and must contain such particulars as may be specified in regulations or by the Commissioners in accordance with regulations.

Meaning of relevant supply

13

For the purposes of this Part of this Schedule a supply is a "relevant supply" if the person making or facilitating it would be treated as having imported goods under Part 1 of this Schedule.

Modification of the Finance Act 2008

14

Paragraph 1 of Schedule 41 to the Finance Act 2008 (penalties: failure to notify etc) has effect as if in the table there were inserted the following entry—

"Value added tax	Obligation under paragraph 8 of Schedule 9ZC to VATA 1994 (obligations to notify liability to register and notify matters affecting continuance of registration).'"

29 (1) Part 1 of Schedule 9ZC (inserted by paragraph 28) is amended as follows.
(2) After paragraph 1 insert—

"**1A**

Section 5A has effect as if in subsection (1)(c)(ii) after "outside the United Kingdom" there were inserted "and prior to the supply the goods were located in Great Britain"."
(3) After paragraph 4 insert—

"**4A**

(1) Sub-paragraph (2) applies, instead of paragraph 4(3) and (4) of Schedule 9ZB, in relation to a removal of goods from Northern Ireland to Great Britain or, as the case may be, vice versa where—
    (a) the removal is in the course of a supply by a person established outside of the United Kingdom ("P"), and
    (b) the supply is facilitated by an online marketplace.
(2) The operator of the online marketplace is the person who is treated as having imported the goods.
(3) But sub-paragraph (2) does not apply where the person to whom the goods are supplied ("R")—
    (a) is registered under this Act,
    (b) has provided the operator of the online marketplace with R's VAT registration number, and
    (c) the operator of the online marketplace has provided P with that number and details of the supply before the end of the relevant period.
(4) In sub-paragraph (3)—
"relevant period" means the period of 7 days beginning with the day on which the supply is treated as taking place under section 6 or such longer period as the Commissioners may allow in general or specific directions;
"VAT registration number" means the number allocated by the Commissioners to a person registered under this Act.
(5) The Commissioners may by regulations specify the details that must be provided for the purposes of sub-paragraph (3)(c)."

SCHEDULE 4

RECOVERY OF UNLAWFUL STATE AID

Section 9

Commencement—The day appointed for the coming into force of this Act, so far as not already in force (and other than Sch 2 para 7(3)), is IP completion day (11pm on 31 December 2020): SI 2020/1642 reg 9.

TIOPA 2010 has effect as if—
    (a) after Chapter 21 of Part 9A there were inserted—

"CHAPTER 21A

RECOVERY OF UNLAWFUL STATE AID

371UFA Recovery of unlawful state aid
Schedule 7ZA makes provision in connection with Commission Decision (EU) 2019/1352 of 2 April 2019 on the state aid SA.44896 implemented by the United Kingdom concerning the CFC Group Financing Exemption (referred to in that Schedule as "the Commission Decision").", and
    (b) after Schedule 7 there were inserted—

"SCHEDULE 7ZA

RECOVERY OF UNLAWFUL STATE AID

Section 371UFA

Recovery of unlawful state aid

1

(1) Any amount that would have been chargeable on a company as if it were corporation tax for a relevant accounting period of the company by virtue of this Part, if the company had not benefited from the unlawful state aid identified in the Commission Decision, is to be treated as chargeable on that company as if it were corporation tax for that relevant accounting period by virtue of this Part.

(2) In this Schedule, such an amount is referred to as an "additional amount".

Charging notice

2

(1) This paragraph applies where an officer of HMRC has reason to believe that an additional amount is chargeable on a company in respect of one or more of the company's relevant accounting periods.

(2) The officer may—

    (a) make an assessment of the additional amounts which ought in their opinion to be charged on the company for each relevant accounting period, and

    (b) give a notice (a "charging notice") to that company requiring it to pay those amounts.

(3) More than one charging notice may be given to a company in respect of a relevant accounting period.

(4) A charging notice must—

    (a) state the relevant accounting periods to which the notice applies,

    (b) state the additional amounts required to be paid by the notice for each of those relevant accounting periods,

    (c) set out the basis on which the officer has calculated the additional amounts,

    (d) state the period within which payment must be made, and

    (e) explain how interest is to be calculated in accordance with paragraph 8.

(5) Where a charging notice is given to a company, the company must pay the additional amounts specified in the notice within the period of 30 days beginning with the day on which the notice is given to the company.

(6) The payment of the amounts specified in the notice may not be postponed on any grounds, and so the amounts charged by the charging notice remain due and payable despite any appeal in respect of the notice.

Charging period

3

(1) No charging notice may be given after the end of the charging period.

(2) The charging period is the period of 12 months beginning with the day on which Schedule 4 to the Taxation (Post-transition Period) Act 2020 comes into force.

(3) The Treasury may by regulations amend sub-paragraph (2) so as to extend the charging period if they consider it necessary to do so in order to give effect to the Commission Decision.

(4) The power in sub-paragraph (3) may be exercised more than once.

Consequential claims etc

4

(1) An officer of HMRC may by notice (a "consequential amendment notice") given to a company make any adjustment or amendment, in relation to the company, to any company tax return, self-assessment, discovery assessment, claim, election, application or notice (including a

charging notice) relating to any accounting period which the officer considers is appropriate in consequence of—
- (a) a charging notice,
- (b) any claim, election, application, notice or other representation relating to a charging notice, or
- (c) anything done by the Tribunal under paragraph 6(4) (powers of the Tribunal on an appeal).

(2) More than one consequential amendment notice may be given to a company in respect of an accounting period.

(3) Adjustments or amendments made in reliance on sub-paragraph (1) may (among other things) relate to—
- (a) an additional amount charged on a company in a charging notice,
- (b) any other part of the CFC charge charged on the company (if any),
- (c) any other tax payable by the company, or
- (d) any claim, election, application or notice relating to a matter within paragraph (a), (b) or (c).

(4) In sub-paragraphs (1)(b) and (3)(d), the references to "any claim" include any claim for relief which a company may make in respect of an additional amount.

(5) Where a consequential amendment notice reduces the amount which is chargeable on a company as the additional amount for a relevant accounting period—
- (a) an officer of HMRC must exercise the power in sub-paragraph (1) so as to secure, so far as reasonably practicable, that relevant reliefs are treated in the same way as they were treated before any steps were taken under this Schedule in relation to them, and
- (b) any amount which was overpaid must be repaid.

(6) In sub-paragraph (5), "relevant reliefs" means so much of any reliefs previously taken into account in calculating the additional amount chargeable on the company for the relevant accounting period in question as are referable to the amount by which that additional amount is reduced.

(7) Subject to sub-paragraph (8), paragraphs 61 to 64 of Schedule 18 to FA 1998 apply in relation to the following as they apply in relation to a discovery assessment—
- (a) a charging notice, and
- (b) a consequential amendment notice.

(8) Paragraph 62(1)(a) of that Schedule is to be read as if the reference to one year from the end of the relevant accounting period were a reference to the period of 60 days beginning with the day on which the charging notice or consequential amendment notice is given.

Interaction with enquiries etc

5

(1) This Schedule applies in respect of an additional amount whether or not any functions in or under Schedule 18 to FA 1998 (company tax returns, assessments etc) have been exercised, or any other steps have been taken, in relation to that amount.

(2) Where a company is required to pay an additional amount for a relevant accounting period in accordance with a charging notice—
- (a) any discovery assessment ceases to have effect so far as it relates to that additional amount, and
- (b) any claim, election, application or notice ceases to have effect so far as it relates to that discovery assessment.

(3) Nothing in sub-paragraph (2)(b) prevents a company making or giving a new claim, election, application or notice, including in relation to any matter referred to in the discovery assessment mentioned in that sub-paragraph.

(4) When giving a partial or final closure notice to a company in relation to an enquiry into the company's tax return relating to a relevant accounting period, an officer of HMRC must take into account—
- (a) any charging notice given to the company,
- (b) any claim, election, application or notice relating to such a charging notice, and

        (c) any consequential amendment notice given to the company.

Appeals

6 (1) A company may appeal against any of the following—
    (a) a charging notice, and
    (b) a consequential amendment notice.

(2) Notice of an appeal must be given to HMRC, in writing, within the period of 30 days beginning with the day on which the notice is given.

(3) The notice of appeal must specify the grounds of appeal.

(4) On an appeal under this paragraph, the Tribunal may—
    (a) confirm the notice to which the appeal relates,
    (b) amend the notice, or
    (c) cancel the notice.

(5) References in Part 5 of TMA 1970 (appeals etc) to an assessment are to be read as including a charging notice or a consequential amendment notice, unless the context requires otherwise.

Payment of interest

7 (1) An officer of HMRC may give a notice (an "interest charging notice") to a company requiring it to pay an amount of interest in relation to one or more additional amounts after they have been paid.

(2) The amount of interest to be paid in relation to an additional amount is to be calculated in accordance with paragraph 8 (and not in accordance with provision made in or under section 87A of TMA 1970 (interest on overdue corporation tax etc) or section 178 of FA 1989 (setting of rates of interest)).

(3) An interest charging notice must—
    (a) state the additional amount to which each amount of interest relates,
    (b) explain how each amount of interest has been calculated, and
    (c) state the period within which payment must be made.

(4) An officer of HMRC may vary or cancel an interest charging notice.

(5) Where an interest charging notice is given to a company, the company must pay the amounts specified in the notice within the period of 30 days beginning with the day on which the notice is given to the company.

(6) The payment of those amounts may not be postponed on any grounds.

Calculation of interest payable in relation to an additional amount

8 (1) The interest which an additional amount carries is to be calculated in accordance with Chapter 5 of the Commission Regulation.

(2) For the purposes of Article 11(1) of the Commission Regulation—
    (a) the reference to the date on which unlawful aid was first put at the disposal of the beneficiary is to be read as a reference to the date when an additional amount would have become due and payable by the company on which it is chargeable if the company had not benefited from the unlawful state aid identified in the Commission Decision, and
    (b) the reference to the date of recovery of the aid is to be read as a reference to the date on which that additional amount is paid.

(3) In this paragraph, "the Commission Regulation" means Commission Regulation (EC) No 794/2004 of 21 April 2004 implementing Council Regulation (EC) No 659/1999 laying down detailed rules for the application of Article 93 of the EC Treaty.

Liability of related company

9

(1) This paragraph applies where the company on which an additional amount is (or would be) chargeable for a relevant accounting period in accordance with paragraph 1(1) (the "original company")—

    (a) does not fully pay the additional amount before the date on which it must be paid in accordance with paragraph 2(5),

    (b) does not fully pay any interest on an additional amount before the date on which that interest must be paid in accordance with paragraph 7(5),

    (c) is in liquidation, in administration or in receivership, or

    (d) has been dissolved.

(2) Where this paragraph applies by virtue of sub-paragraph (1)(a) or (c), each related company of the original company is jointly and severally liable with the original company for—

    (a) the additional amounts which are chargeable on the original company for each of its relevant accounting periods, and

    (b) interest on those amounts.

(3) Where this paragraph applies by virtue of sub-paragraph (1)(b), each related company of the original company is jointly and severally liable with the original company for interest on the additional amounts which are chargeable on the original company for each of its relevant accounting periods.

(4) Where this paragraph applies by virtue of sub-paragraph (1)(d), each related company of the original company is jointly and severally liable for—

    (a) the additional amounts which would have been chargeable on the original company for each of its relevant accounting periods if it had not been dissolved, and

    (b) interest on those amounts.

(5) Where a related company is liable for an additional amount or interest on an additional amount, an officer of HMRC may, for the purposes of giving effect to the Commission Decision, exercise any function under this Schedule in relation to the related company as if it were the original company in respect of which it is a related company.

(6) In applying paragraphs 2 to 5 of this Schedule for the purposes of sub-paragraph (5), references to a relevant accounting period of a company are to be read as references to a relevant accounting period of the original company.

(7) Where this paragraph applies by virtue of sub-paragraph (1)(a), sub-paragraphs (2) to (6) have effect only in relation to so much of the additional amount as was not paid by the original company before the date on which it had to be paid in accordance with paragraph 2(5).

(8) Where this paragraph applies by virtue of sub-paragraph (1)(b), sub-paragraphs (2) to (6) have effect only in relation to so much of any interest on the additional amount as was not paid by the original company before the date on which it had to be paid in accordance with paragraph 7(5).

(9) Where this paragraph applies by virtue of sub-paragraph (1)(c) or (d), sub-paragraphs (2) to (6) have effect only in relation to so much of the additional amount, or so much of any interest on the additional amount, as was not paid by the original company before the date on which sub-paragraph (1)(c) or (d) began to apply.

(10) For the purposes of sub-paragraph (1)(c)—

    (a) a company is "in liquidation" if it is in liquidation within the meaning of section 247 of the Insolvency Act 1986 or Part 3 of the Insolvency (Northern Ireland) Order 1989 (SI 1989/2405 (NI 19)), or a corresponding situation under the law of a country or territory outside the United Kingdom exists in relation to the company;

    (b) a company is "in administration" if it is in administration within the meaning of Schedule B1 to the Insolvency Act 1986 or Schedule B1 to the Insolvency (Northern Ireland) Order 1989, or there is in force in relation to it under the law of a country or territory outside the United Kingdom any appointment corresponding to the appointment of an administrator under either of those Schedules;

(c) a company is "in receivership" if there is in force in relation to it an order for the appointment of an administrative receiver, a receiver and manager or a receiver under Chapter 1 or 2 of Part 3 of the Insolvency Act 1986 or Part 4 of the Insolvency (Northern Ireland) Order 1989, or any corresponding order under the law of a country or territory outside the United Kingdom.

(11) In this paragraph, a company is a "related company" of an original company if—
- (a) at any time when the original company benefited from the unlawful state aid identified in the Commission Decision, it was a member—
  - (i) of the same group as the original company,
  - (ii) of a consortium which at that time owned the original company, or
  - (iii) of the same group as a company which at that time was a member of a consortium owning the original company, and
- (b) an officer of HMRC has given the company a notice informing the company that it is a related company for the purposes of this paragraph.

(12) For the purposes of sub-paragraph (11)(a)—
- (a) a company is a member of a consortium if it is a member of a consortium within the meaning of Part 5 of CTA 2010, and
- (b) a company is owned by a consortium if it is owned by a consortium within the meaning of that Part.

(13) For the purposes of sub-paragraph (11)(a)(i), two companies are members of the same group if—
- (a) one is the 51% subsidiary of the other, or
- (b) both are 51% subsidiaries of a third company.

(14) For the purposes of sub-paragraph (11)(a)(iii), two companies are members of the same group if they are members of the same group of companies within the meaning of Part 5 of CTA 2010 (group relief).

(15) An officer of HMRC may give a notice to a company for the purposes of sub-paragraph (11)(b) only if the officer considers that the company, by virtue of its relationship or a transaction with the original company, received a benefit or experienced an advantage, whether directly or indirectly, as a result of the unlawful state aid identified in the Commission Decision.

Variation of the Commission Decision

10

(1) If the Commission Decision is revoked or annulled, the Treasury must by regulations make such provision as they consider appropriate for the purposes of securing, so far as reasonably practicable, that any company affected by this Schedule is put into the position it would have been in if—
- (a) the Commission Decision had not been made, and
- (b) this Schedule had not had effect.

(2) The duty in sub-paragraph (1) does not apply if there is, or the Treasury consider that there may be, a further decision within the meaning of Article 288 of the Treaty on the Functioning of the European Union which is to the same or similar effect as the Commission Decision.

(3) The Treasury may by regulations make such provision as they consider appropriate to take account of—
- (a) any variation of the Commission Decision, or
- (b) any further decision within the meaning of Article 288 of the Treaty on the Functioning of the European Union which is to the same or similar effect as the Commission Decision.

(4) The power to make regulations under this paragraph may (among other things) be exercised by modifying—
- (a) this Part;
- (b) provision made under this Part.

(5) In sub-paragraph (4), "modify" includes amend, repeal or revoke.

Consequential modifications

11

Section 371UE (appeal affecting more than one person) has effect as if an appeal against a charging notice or a consequential amendment notice by virtue of paragraph 6(1) of this Schedule were a "relevant appeal" for the purposes of that section.

Management of the CFC charge for the purposes of the Commission Decision

12

(1) The application to the CFC charge of enactments applying generally to corporation tax by section 371UB (application of the Taxes Acts to the CFC charge) has effect subject to—
    (a) this Schedule, and
    (b) any other modifications that are necessary to give effect to the Commission Decision.

(2) Any relevant time limit is disapplied so far as necessary to give effect to the Commission Decision.

(3) A time limit is relevant if it would otherwise have applied or had effect, by or under an enactment (apart from this Schedule), in connection with—
    (a) the CFC charge charged on a company,
    (b) any other tax payable by that company,
    (c) the tax liability of another company, or
    (d) any adjustment, amendment, claim, election, application or notice relating to a matter within paragraphs (a) to (c).

Interpretation

13

(1) For the purposes of this Schedule, a relevant accounting period of a company is any accounting period of the company for corporation tax purposes during some or all of which the unlawful state aid identified in the Commission Decision was available (whether or not the company considers that it benefited from it).

(2) Terms used in this Schedule which are defined or explained in Schedule 18 to FA 1998 have the same meaning in this Schedule as in that Schedule.

(3) In this Schedule—
"additional amount" has the meaning given by paragraph 1(2);
"charging notice" has the meaning given by paragraph 2(2)(b);
the "Commission Decision" means Commission Decision (EU) 2019/1352 of 2 April 2019 on the state aid SA.44896 implemented by the United Kingdom concerning the CFC Group Financing Exemption;
"consequential amendment notice" has the meaning given by paragraph 4(1);
"HMRC" means Her Majesty's Revenue and Customs;
"interest charging notice" has the meaning given by paragraph 7(1);
"officer of HMRC" means an officer of Revenue and Customs."

EUROPEAN UNION (FUTURE RELATIONSHIP) ACT 2020
2020 Chapter 29

An Act to make provision to implement, and make other provision in connection with, the Trade and Cooperation Agreement; to make further provision in connection with the United Kingdom's future relationship with the EU and its member States; to make related provision about passenger name record data, customs and privileges and immunities; and for connected purposes.

31 December 2020

PART 2
TRADE AND OTHER MATTERS
Customs and tax

22 Administrative co-operation on VAT and mutual assistance on tax debts
(1) The arrangements contained in the Protocol have effect (and do so in spite of anything in any enactment).
(2) The Commissioners for Her Majesty's Revenue and Customs are the competent authority in the United Kingdom responsible for the application of the Protocol.
(3) A reference in any enactment to arrangements having effect by virtue of, or by virtue of an Order in Council under, section 173 of the Finance Act 2006 (international tax enforcement arrangements) includes a reference to arrangements having effect by virtue of this section.
(4) In this section "the Protocol" means—
   (a) the protocol, contained in the Trade and Cooperation Agreement, on administrative co-operation and combating fraud in the field of Value Added Tax and on mutual assistance for the recovery of claims relating to taxes and duties, and
   (b) any decision or recommendation adopted by the Specialised Committee in accordance with that protocol.
(5) In subsection (4)—
   (a) a reference to the Trade and Cooperation Agreement or to any provision of it is to that agreement or provision as it has effect at the relevant time;
   (b) a reference to a decision or recommendation adopted by the Specialised Committee in accordance with any provision is to a decision or recommendation so adopted at or before the relevant time.
(6) In subsection (5) "the relevant time" means the time at which the protocol mentioned in subsection (4)(a) comes into effect (or, if it comes into effect at different times for different purposes, the earliest such time).
(7) The Commissioners for Her Majesty's Revenue and Customs may by regulations amend subsection (6) so as to substitute a later time for that for the time being specified there.

Commencement—European Union (Future Relationship) Act 2020 (Commencement No 1) Regulations, SI 2020/1662 reg 2(t) (the appointed day for the purposes of this section is IP completion day (11pm UK time on 31 December 2020)).

PART 3
GENERAL IMPLEMENTATION
General implementation of agreements

29 General implementation of agreements
(1) Existing domestic law has effect on and after the relevant day with such modifications as are required for the purposes of implementing in that law the Trade and Cooperation Agreement or the Security of Classified Information Agreement so far as the agreement concerned is not otherwise so implemented and so far as such implementation is necessary for the purposes of complying with the international obligations of the United Kingdom under the agreement.
(2) Subsection (1)—
   (a) is subject to any equivalent or other provision—
      (i) which (whether before, on or after the relevant day) is made by or under this Act or any other enactment or otherwise forms part of domestic law, and
      (ii) which is for the purposes of (or has the effect of) implementing to any extent the Trade and Cooperation Agreement, the Security of Classified Information Agreement or any other future relationship agreement, and
   (b) does not limit the scope of any power which is capable of being exercised to make any such provision.
(3) The references in subsection (1) to the Trade and Cooperation Agreement or the Security of Classified Information Agreement are references to the agreement concerned as it has effect on the relevant day.
(4) In this section—
   "domestic law" means the law of England and Wales, Scotland or Northern Ireland;
   "existing domestic law" means—
      (a) an existing enactment, or

(b) any other domestic law as it has effect on the relevant day;
"existing enactment" means an enactment passed or made before the relevant day;
"modifications" does not include any modifications of the kind which would result in a public bill in Parliament containing them being treated as a hybrid bill;
"relevant day", in relation to the Trade and Cooperation Agreement or the Security of Classified Information Agreement or any aspect of either agreement, means—
- (a) so far as the agreement or aspect concerned is provisionally applied before it comes into force, the time and day from which the provisional application applies, and
- (b) so far as the agreement or aspect concerned is not provisionally applied before it comes into force, the time and day when it comes into force;

and references to the purposes of (or having the effect of) implementing an agreement include references to the purposes of (or having the effect of) making provision consequential on any such implementation.

Commencement—European Union (Future Relationship) Act 2020 (Commencement No 1) Regulations, SI 2020/1662 reg 2(z) (the appointed day for the purposes of this section is IP completion day (11pm UK time on 31 December 2020)).

30 Interpretation of agreements

A court or tribunal must have regard to Article COMPROV.13 of the Trade and Cooperation Agreement (public international law) when interpreting that agreement or any supplementing agreement.

Commencement—Section 30 came into effect on 31 December 2020 (s 40(6)(d) of this Act).

SCHEDULE 5
REGULATIONS UNDER THIS ACT
Section 38

PART 1
PROCEDURE

Criminal records

Administrative co-operation on VAT and mutual assistance on tax debts

3 A statutory instrument containing regulations under section 22(7) may not be made unless a draft of the instrument has been laid before, and approved by a resolution of, the House of Commons.

Commencement—Schedule 5 came into effect on 31 December 2020 (s 40(6)(e) of this Act).

Part 2

Value Added Tax Statutory Instruments

Contents

Chronological list of printed Statutory Instruments

SI 1984/746 VAT (Imported Goods) Relief Order 1984
SI 1984/1176 Control of Movement of Goods Regulations 1984
SI 1986/939 VAT (Small Non-Commercial Consignments) Relief Order 1986
SI 1987/1806 VAT (Tour Operators) Order 1987
SI 1988/809 Excise Warehousing (Etc) Regulations 1988
SI 1990/2167 Channel Tunnel (Customs and Excise) Order 1990
SI 1991/2724 Customs Controls on Importation of Goods Regulations 1991
SI 1992/2790 Statistics of Trade (Customs and Excise) Regulations 1992
SI 1992/3111 VAT (Removal of Goods) Order 1992
SI 1992/3122 VAT (Cars) Order 1992
SI 1992/3124 VAT (Imported Gold) Relief Order 1992
SI 1992/3130 VAT (Supply of Temporarily Imported Goods) Order 1992
SI 1992/3132 VAT (Treatment of Transactions) (No 2) Order 1992
SI 1992/3156 Customs and Excise (Personal Reliefs for Special Visitors) Order 1992
SI 1992/3193 Customs and Excise Duties (Personal Reliefs for Goods Permanently Imported) Order 1992
SI 1992/3222 VAT (Input Tax) Order 1992
SI 1993/2001 VAT (Payments on Account) Order 1993
SI 1994/955 Travellers' Allowances Order 1994
SI 1995/958 VAT (Treatment of Transactions) Order 1995
SI 1995/1268 VAT (Special Provisions) Order 1995
SI 1995/2518 VAT Regulations 1995
SI 1996/1255 VAT (Fiscal Warehousing) (Treatment of Transactions) Order 1996
SI 1999/3115 VAT (Importation of Investment Gold) Relief Order 1999
SI 1999/3121 VAT (Input Tax) (Specified Supplies) Order 1999
SI 2002/1935 VAT (Acquisitions) Relief Order 2002
SI 2003/3113 Customs (Contravention of a Relevant Rule) Regulations 2003
SI 2004/3148 VAT (Place of Supply of Goods) Order 2004
SI 2010/2239 VAT (Section 55A) (Specified Goods and Services and Excepted Supplies) Order 2010
SI 2010/2924 VAT (Imported Gas, Electricity, Heat and Cooling) Relief Order 2010
SI 2010/2925 VAT (Removal of Gas, Electricity, Heat and Cooling) Order 2010
SI 2011/2931 MARD Regulations 2011
SI 2011/3036 Postal Packets (Revenue and Customs) Regulations 2011
SI 2012/2907 VAT (Relief for European Research Infrastructure Consortia) Order 2012
SI 2014/1458 VAT (Section 55A) (Specified Goods and Excepted Supplies) Order 2014
SI 2016/12 Value Added Tax (Section 55A) (Specified Services and Excepted Supplies) Order 2016
SI 2017/1216 Indirect Taxes (Notifiable Arrangements) Regulations 2017
SI 2018/326 Fulfilment Businesses Regulations 2018
SI 2018/1228 Value Added Tax (Disclosure of Information Relating to VAT Registration) (EU Exit) Regulations 2018
SI 2018/1376 Value Added Tax (Postal Packets and Amendment) (EU Exit) Regulations 2018
SI 2019/60 Value Added Tax (Accounting Procedures for Import VAT for VAT Registered Persons and Amendment) (EU Exit) Regulations 2019
SI 2019/105 Taxation (Cross-border Trade) Act 2018 (Value Added Tax Transitional Provisions) (EU Exit) Regulations 2019
SI 2019/385 Customs (Crown Dependencies Customs Union) (EU Exit) Regulations 2019

SI 2019/429 Taxation (Cross-border Trade) Act 2018 (Appointed Days No 4 and Transitional Provisions) (Modification) (EU Exit) Regulations 2019

SI 2019/1015 Value Added Tax (Section 55A) (Specified Services) Order 2019

SI 2020/1454 Definition of Qualifying Northern Ireland Goods (EU Exit) Regulations 2020

SI 2020/1495 Value Added Tax (Miscellaneous and Transitional Provisions Amendment and Revocation) (EU Exit) Regulations 2020

SI 2020/1525 European Union (Withdrawal) Act 2018 (Relevant Court) (Retained EU Case Law) Regulations 2020

SI 2020/1545 Value Added Tax (Miscellaneous Amendments, Northern Ireland Protocol and Savings and Transitional Provisions) (EU Exit) Regulations 2020

SI 2020/1546 Value Added Tax (Northern Ireland) (EU Exit) Regulations 2020

SI 2020/1622 European Union (Withdrawal) Act 2018 and European Union (Withdrawal Agreement) Act 2020 (Commencement, Transitional and Savings Provisions) Regulations 2020

SI 2020/1642 Finance Act 2016, Section 126 (Appointed Day), the Taxation (Cross-border Trade) Act 2018 (Appointed Day No 8, Transition and Saving Provisions) and the Taxation (Post-transition Period) Act 2020 (Appointed Day No 1) (EU Exit) Regulations 2020

VAT Statutory Instruments

1984/746

VALUE ADDED TAX (IMPORTED GOODS) RELIEF ORDER 1984

Made by the Treasury under VATA 1983 ss 19(1) and 45(1) and (2) (see now VATA 1994 ss 37(1), 97(1), (5))

Made . . . . .23 May 1984
Laid before the House of Commons . . . . .5 June 1984
Coming into Operation . . . . .1 July 1984

1 Citation and commencement
This Order may be cited as the Value Added Tax (Imported Goods) Relief Order 1984 and shall come into operation on 1st July 1984.

2 Interpretation
(1) In this Order—
    ["abroad" means a place outside [the United Kingdom]⁵;]³
    "alcoholic beverages" means beverages falling within headings 22.03 to [22.08]²;
    "approved" means approved by the Secretary of State;
    ["exported" means exported to a place outside [the United Kingdom]⁵ and "exportation" shall be construed accordingly;]³
    ["importation" is to be interpreted in accordance with the provisions of the Value Added Tax Act 1994;]⁶
    ["sent" means sent from a place outside [the United Kingdom]⁵;]³
    . . . ⁵
    "tobacco products" has the same meaning as in section 1 of the Tobacco Products Duty Act 1979.
[(2) In this Order, references to a heading or sub-heading are references to a heading or sub-heading of the customs tariff (within the meaning of the Taxation (Cross-border Trade) Act 2018) code.]⁵
(3) Section 48(4) of the Value Added Tax Act 1983⁴ (definition of "document" etc) shall not apply for the purposes of this Order.
(4), (5) . . . ⁵

Notes—¹ Words in para (2) substituted by the VAT (Imported Goods) Relief (Amendment) (No 2) Order, SI 1987/2108 art 3 with effect from 1 January 1988.
² Figure substituted for the figure "22.09" by the VAT (Imported Goods) Relief (Amendment) Order, SI 1988/1193 with effect from 1 August 1988.
³ Definition of "abroad" in para (1) substituted and definitions of "exported", "exportation", "sent" and "third country" and paras (4), (5) inserted by the VAT (Imported Goods) Relief (Amendment) Order, SI 1992/3120 arts 1–3 with effect from 1 January 1993.
⁴ VATA 1994 s 96(6), (7).
⁵ In para (1), in the definitions of "abroad", "exported" and "sent" words substituted for words "the member States", the definition of "import" inserted, the definition of "third country" revoked, para (2) substituted, and paras (4), (5) revoked, by the Value Added Tax (Miscellaneous Amendments and Revocations) (EU Exit) Regulations, SI 2019/59 reg 3(1), (2) with effect from IP completion day (11pm UK time on 31 December 2020). Para (2) previously read as follows—
    "(2) In this Order, references to a heading or sub-heading are references to a heading or sub-heading of the Combined Nomenclature of the European Economic Community."
The definition of "third country" previously read as follows—
    ""third country" means a place outside the member States;"
Paras (4), (5) previously read as follows—
    "(4) Except where it appears in Article 3(2) "import" means import from a place outside the member States and "importation" and "imported" shall be construed accordingly.
    (5) Except where it appears in Note (3) to Group 7 of Schedule 2, for "United Kingdom" there shall be substituted "member States"."
⁶ The definition of "import" substituted by the Value Added Tax (Miscellaneous Amendments, Northern Ireland Protocol and Savings and Transitional Provisions) (EU Exit) Regulations, SI 2020/1545 reg 104(1), (2) with effect from IP completion day (11pm UK time on 31 December 2020). The definition of "import" was to have read as follows—
    ""import" means import into the United Kingdom and "imported" and "importation" are to be construed accordingly;"

3 Application
(1) This Order shall apply without prejudice to relief from tax on the importation of goods afforded under or by virtue of any other enactment.
[(2) Nothing in this Order shall be construed as authorising a person to import anything . . . ² in contravention of any prohibition or restriction for the time being in force with respect thereto under or by virtue of any enactment.]¹

Amendments—¹ Para (2) substituted by the VAT (Imported Goods) Relief (Amendment) Order, SI 1992/3120 arts 1, 2, 4 with effect from 1 January 1993.

[2] In para (2) words "from a place outside or within the member States" revoked by the Value Added Tax (Miscellaneous Amendments and Revocations) (EU Exit) Regulations, SI 2019/59 reg 3(1), (3) with effect from IP completion day (11pm UK time on 31 December 2020).

[3A Application to importations into Northern Ireland
(1) This article applies where goods are imported into the United Kingdom as a result of their entry into Northern Ireland.
(2) Where this article applies this Order has effect with the following modifications—
  (a) article 2(1) is to be read as if the following definitions were substituted for their equivalents—
    ""abroad" means a place outside Northern Ireland and the member States;";
    ""exported" means exported to a place outside Northern Ireland and the member States, and "exportation" shall be construed accordingly;";
    ""sent" means sent from a place outside Northern Ireland and the member States;";
  (b) article 2(2) does not apply and instead references to a heading or sub-heading are to be read as references to a heading or sub-heading of the Combined Nomenclature of the European Union which is contained in Commission Implementing Regulation (EU) 2019/1776 of 9 October 2019 amending Annex I to Council Regulation (EEC) No 2658/87 on the tariff and statistical nomenclature and on the Common Customs Tariff as it has effect in Northern Ireland as a result of section 7A of the European Union (Withdrawal) Act 2020;
  (c) article 2(5) does not apply and instead, except where it appears in Note (3) to Group 7 of Schedule 2 and Items 3 and 4 of Group 6 of Schedule 2, references to "United Kingdom" are to be read as references to "member States";
  (d) Note 2 of Group 5 of Schedule 2 does not apply and instead Item 3 of that Group applies only where the goods fulfil the conditions laid down under or by virtue of Article 53 of Council Regulation (EC) No 1186/2009 of 16 November 2009 setting up a Community system of reliefs from customs duty as it has effect in Northern Ireland as a result of section 7A of the European Union (Withdrawal) Act 2020;
  (e) in Group 6 of Schedule 2—
    (i) in Items 3 and 4, for "United Kingdom" read "one or more member States"; and
    (ii) in Note 5, for "HM Treasury" read "the Commission of the European Union".
(3) The modifications provided for in this article are subject to the modifications provided for in paragraph 5 of Schedule 9ZC to the Value Added Tax Act 1994.][1]

Amendments—[1] Articles 3A and 3B inserted by the Value Added Tax (Miscellaneous Amendments, Northern Ireland Protocol and Savings and Transitional Provisions) (EU Exit) Regulations, SI 2020/1545 reg 2 with effect from IP completion day (11pm UK time on 31 December 2020).

[3B (1) This article applies where goods are imported pursuant to paragraph 3(2) of Schedule 9ZB to the Value Added Tax Act 1994.
(2) Where this article applies this Order has effect with the following modifications—
  (a) article 2(1) is to be read as if the following definitions were substituted for their equivalents—
    ""abroad" means a place outside Great Britain;";
    ""exported" means exported to a place outside Great Britain, and "exported" shall be construed accordingly;";
    ""sent" means sent from a place outside Great Britain;";
  (b) article 2(5) does not apply and instead, except where it appears in Note (3) to Group 7 of Schedule 2, for "United Kingdom" read "Great Britain".][1]

Amendments—[1] Articles 3A and 3B inserted by the Value Added Tax (Miscellaneous Amendments, Northern Ireland Protocol and Savings and Transitional Provisions) (EU Exit) Regulations, SI 2020/1545 reg 2 with effect from IP completion day (11pm UK time on 31 December 2020) by virtue of SI 2020/1641 reg 2, Schedule para 11.

4 Relief for United Nations goods
No tax shall be payable on the importation, for whatever purpose, of goods produced by the United Nations or by a United Nations organisation, being goods—
  (*a*) of a description specified in Part I of Schedule 1 to this Order, or
  (*b*) classified under any heading or sub-heading specified in column 1 of Part II of Schedule 1 to this Order and within the limits of relief specified in column 2 thereof in relation to such heading or sub-heading.

5 Relief for goods of other descriptions
(1) Subject to the provisions of this Order, no tax shall be payable on the importation of goods of a description specified in any item in Schedule 2 to this Order.
(2) Schedule 2 shall be interpreted in accordance with the notes therein contained, except that the descriptions of Groups in that Schedule are for ease of reference only and shall not affect the interpretation of the descriptions of items in those Groups.

6 Condition as to use or purpose of goods in Schedule 2

(1) Where relief has been afforded in respect of any goods by virtue of an item comprised in Schedule 2 which describes the goods by reference to a use or purpose, it shall be a condition of the relief that the goods are put to such use or the purpose fulfilled in the United Kingdom.

(2) Without prejudice to paragraph (1) above, where relief has been afforded by virtue of item 5, 6 or 7 of Group 3 of Schedule 2 in respect of goods for demonstration or use, it shall be a condition of the relief that, in the course of, or as a result of, such demonstration or use, the goods are consumed or destroyed or rendered incapable of being used again for the same purpose.

(3) Without prejudice to paragraph (1) above, where relief has been afforded by virtue of item 1 of Group 4 of Schedule 2 in respect of goods for examination, analysis or testing, the relief shall be subject to the following conditions:

(*a*) the examination, analysis or testing shall be completed within such time as the Commissioners may require; and

(*b*) any goods not completely used up or destroyed in the course of, or as a result of, such examination, analysis or testing, and any products resulting therefrom, shall forthwith be destroyed or rendered commercially worthless, or exported.

7 Restriction on disposal of goods in Schedule 2, Group 6

(1) Without prejudice to article 6(1) above and subject to paragraph (2) below, where relief is afforded in respect of any goods by virtue of Group 6 of Schedule 2, it shall be a condition of the relief that the goods are not lent, hired-out or transferred, except in accordance with the provisions of that Group relating to those goods.

(2) Paragraph (1) above shall not apply and relief shall continue to be afforded where goods are lent, hired-out or transferred to an organisation which would be entitled to relief by virtue of Group 6 of Schedule 2, if importing the goods on that date, on condition that—

(*a*) prior notification in writing is received by the Commissioners; and

(*b*) the goods are used solely in accordance with the provisions of Group 6 relating thereto.

8 Supplementary provisions as to goods in Schedule 2, Group 6

Where any goods in respect of which relief has been afforded by virtue of Group 6 of Schedule 2—

(*a*) are to be lent, hired-out, transferred or used except in accordance with the provisions of this Order relating to those goods; or

(*b*) remain in the possession of an organisation which has ceased to fulfil any condition subject to which it is approved,

and written notification thereof is given to the Commissioners, the tax payable on the goods shall be determined as if the goods had been imported on the date when the tax becomes due, provided that where the amount of the tax first relieved is less, such lesser amount shall become payable.

9 Revocation

The Value Added Tax (Imported Goods) Relief (No 1) Order 1973 and the Value Added Tax (Health) Order 1983 are hereby revoked.

SCHEDULE 1

RELIEF FOR GOODS PRODUCED BY THE UNITED NATIONS OR A UNITED NATIONS ORGANISATION

Article 4

PART I

1 Holograms for laser projection.

2 Multi-media kits.

3 Materials for programmed instruction, including materials in kit form, with the corresponding printed materials.

[PART II

Column 1 Heading or sub-heading	Column 2 Limits of Relief
370400 10	Limited to films of an educational, scientific or cultural character.
37 05	Limited to films of an educational, scientific or cultural character.
370690 51	Limited to newsreels (with or without soundtrack) depicting events of current news value at the time of importation and, in the case of each importer, not exceeding two copies of each subject for copying.

370610 99	
370690 91	Limited to—
370690 99	(i) archival film material (with our without soundtrack) intended for use in connection with newsreel films;
	(ii) recreational film particularly suited for children and young people, and
	(iii) other films of an educational, scientific or cultural character.
49 11	Limited to—
	(i) microcards or other information storage media required in computerised information and documentation services of an educational, scientific or cultural character; and
	(ii) wall charts designed solely for demonstration and education.
85 24	Limited to those of an educational, scientific or cultural character.
90 23	Limited to—
	(i) patterns, models and wall charts of an educational, scientific or cultural character, designed solely for demonstration and education; and
	(ii) mock-ups or visualisations of abstract concepts such as molecular structures or mathematical formulae.][1]

Amendments—[1] Pt II substituted by the VAT (Imported Goods) Relief (Amendment) (No 2) Order, SI 1987/2108 art 4 with effect from 1 January 1988.

SCHEDULE 2
RELIEF FOR GOODS OF OTHER DESCRIPTIONS
Article 5

GROUP 1
CAPITAL GOODS AND EQUIPMENT ON TRANSFER OF ACTIVITIES

Item No

1 Capital goods and equipment imported by a person for the purposes of a business he has ceased to carry on abroad and which he has notified the Commissions is to be carried on by him in the United Kingdom and concerned exclusively with making taxable supplies.

2 . . .[1]

Notes:

(1) "Capital goods and equipment" includes livestock other than livestock in the possession of dealers, but does not include—

(*a*) food of a kind used for human consumption or animal feeding stuffs;

(*b*) fuel;

(*c*) stocks of raw materials and finished or semi-finished products; or

(*d*) any motor vehicle in respect of which deduction of input tax is disallowed by article 4 of the Value Added Tax (Cars) Order 1980.

(2) For the purposes of item 1, a person is not to be treated as intending to carry on a business in the United Kingdom if such business is to be merged with, or absorbed by, another business already carried on there.

(3) Item 1 applies only where the goods—

(*a*) have been used in the course of the business for at least twelve months before it ceased to be carried on abroad;

(*b*) are imported within twelve months of the date on which such business ceased to be carried on abroad, or within such longer period as the Commissioners allow; and

(*c*) are appropriate both to the nature and size of the business to be carried on in the United Kingdom.

(4) . . .[1]

Amendments—[1] Item 2 and Note (4) revoked by the VAT (Imported Goods) Relief (Amendment) Order, SI 1992/3120 arts 1, 2, 5(*a*) with effect from 1 January 1993.

GROUP 3
PROMOTION OF TRADE

Item No

1 Articles of no intrinsic commercial value sent free of charge by suppliers of goods and services for the sole purpose of advertising.

2 Samples of negligible value of a kind and in quantities capable of being used solely for soliciting orders for goods of the same kind.

[3 Printed advertising matter, including catalogues, price lists, directions for use or brochures, which relates to goods for sale or hire by a person established outside the United Kingdom, . . . [2], or to transport, commercial insurance or banking services offered by a person established [abroad][3], and which clearly displays the name of the person by whom such goods or services are offered.][1]

4 Goods to be distributed free of charge at an event, as small representative samples, for use or consumption by the public.

5 Goods imported solely for the purpose of being demonstrated at an event.

6 Goods imported solely for the purpose of being used in the demonstration of any machine or apparatus displayed at an event.

7 Paints, varnishes, wallpaper and other materials of low value to be used in the building, fitting-out and decoration of a temporary stand at an event.

8 Catalogues, prospectuses, price lists, advertising posters, calendars (whether or not illustrated) unframed photographs and other printed matter or articles advertising goods displayed at an event, supplied without charge for the purpose of distribution free of charge to the public at such event.

Notes:

(1) Where the Commissioners so require, item 2 applies only to goods which are rendered permanently unusable, except as samples, by being torn, perforated, clearly and indelibly marked, or by any other process.

(2) [Save in the case of imported printed matter intended for distribution free of charge and relating to either goods for sale or hire . . . [2], item 3 does not apply to—][1]

(a) any consignment containing two or more copies of different documents;

(b) any consignment containing two or more copies of the same document, unless the total gross weight of such consignment does not exceed one kilogram; or

(c) any goods which are the subject of grouped consignments from the same consignor to the same consignee.

(3) "Event" means any of the following—

(a) any trade, industrial, agricultural or craft exhibition, fair or similar show or display, not being an exhibition, fair, show or display organised for private purposes in a shop or on business premises with a view to the sale of the goods displayed;

(b) any exhibition or meeting which is primarily organised—

(i) for a charitable purpose, or

(ii) to promote any branch of learning, art, craft, sport or scientific, technical, educational, cultural or trade union activity, or tourism, or

(iii) to promote friendship between peoples, or

(iv) to promote religious knowledge or worship;

(c) any meeting of representatives of any international organisation or international group of organisations; and

(d) any representative meeting or ceremony of an official or commemorative character.

(4) In item 4, "representative samples" means goods which are—

(a) imported free of charge or obtained at such event from goods imported in bulk;

(b) identifiable as advertising samples of low value;

(c) not easily marketable and, where appropriate, packaged in quantities which are less than the lowest quantity of the same goods as marketed; and

(d) intended to be consumed at such event, where the goods comprise foodstuffs or beverages not packaged as described in paragraph (c) above.

(5) Items 4, 5 and 6 do not apply to fuels, alcoholic beverages or tobacco products.

(6) Items 4 to 8 apply only where the aggregate value and quantity thereof is appropriate to the nature of the event, the number of visitors and the extent of the exhibitor's participation in it.

Amendments— [1] Item 3 and words at the beginning of Note (2) substituted by the VAT (Imported Goods) Relief (Amendment) (No 2) Order, SI 1988/2212 art 4 with effect from 1 January 1989.

[2] Words in item 3 and Note (2) deleted by the VAT (Imported Goods) Relief (Amendment) Order, SI 1992/3120 arts, 1, 2, 5 with effect from 1 January 1993.

[3] In Item 3, word " words "in a third country" substituted by the Value Added Tax (Miscellaneous Amendments and Revocations) (EU Exit) Regulations, SI 2019/59 reg 3(1), (4)(a) with effect from IP completion day (11pm UK time on 31 December 2020).

GROUP 4
GOODS FOR TESTING, ETC

Item No

1 Goods imported for the purpose of examination, analysis or testing to determine their composition, quality or other technical characteristics, to provide information or for industrial or commercial research.

Note:

Item 1 does not apply to goods exceeding the quantities necessary for such purposes or where the examination, analysis or testing, itself constitutes a sales promotion.

GROUP 5
HEALTH

Item No
1 Animals specially prepared for laboratory use and sent free of charge to a relevant establishment.
2 ... [2]
3 Biological or chemical substances sent to a relevant establishment ... [3].
4 Human blood.
5 Products for therapeutic purposes, derived from human blood.
6 Human (including foetal) organs or tissue for diagnostic or therapeutic purposes or medical research.
7 Reagents for use in blood type grouping or for the detection of blood grouping incompatibilities, by approved institutions or laboratories, exclusively for non-commercial medical or scientific purposes.
8 Reagents for use in the determination of human tissue types by approved institutions or laboratories, exclusively for non-commercial medical or scientific purposes.
9 Pharmaceutical products imported by or on behalf of persons or animals for their use while visiting the United Kingdom to participate in an international sporting event.
[10 Samples of reference substances approved by the World Health Organisation for the quality control of materials used in the manufacture of medicinal products.][1]

Notes:

(1) In items 1, ... [2] and 3, "relevant establishment" means—
   (a) a public establishment, or a department of such establishment, principally engaged in education or scientific research; or
   (b) a private establishment so engaged, which is approved.

[(2) Item 3 applies only to the extent that conditions for the equivalent import duty relief are met.][3]

(3) Items 4, 5, 6, 7 and 8 include special packaging essential for transport of the goods and any solvents or accessories necessary for their use.

(4) In items 7 and 8, "reagents" means all reagents, whether of human, animal, plant, or other, origin.

[(5) Item 10 applies only to samples addressed to consignees authorised to receive them free of tax.][2]

Cross-references—See Arts 3A and 3B of this Order: application of this Order to importations into Northern Ireland.

Amendments—[1] Item 10 and Note (5) added and words in Note (2) substituted by the VAT (Imported Goods) Relief (Amendment) (No 2) Order, SI 1988/2212 art 5 with effect from 1 January 1989.

[2] Words in item 3 substituted and Item 2 and figure in Note (1) revoked by the VAT (Imported Goods) Relief (Amendment) Order SI 1992/3120 arts 1, 2, 5 with effect from 1 January 1993.

[3] In Item 3 words "from a place outside the member States" revoked, and Note (2) substituted, by the Value Added Tax (Miscellaneous Amendments and Revocations) (EU Exit) Regulations, SI 2019/59 reg 3(1), (4)(b) with effect from IP completion day (11pm UK time on 31 December 2020). Note (2) previously read as follows—

"(2) Item 3 applies only where the goods fulfil the conditions laid down under or by virtue of [Article 60] of Council Regulation (EEC) No 918/83."

GROUP 6
CHARITIES, ETC

Item No
1 Basic necessities obtained without charge for distribution free of charge to the needy by a relevant organisation.
2 Goods donated by a person established abroad to a relevant organisation for use to raise funds at occasional charity events for the benefit of the needy.
3 Equipment and office materials donated by a person established abroad to a relevant organisation for meeting its operating needs or carrying out its charitable aims.
4 Goods imported by a relevant organisation for distribution or loan, free of charge, to victims of a disaster affecting the territory of [the United Kingdom][1].
5 Goods imported by a relevant organisation for meeting its operating needs in the relief of a disaster affecting the territory of [the United Kingdom][1].
6 Articles donated to and imported by a relevant organisation for supply to blind or other physically or mentally handicapped persons and which are specially designed for the education, employment or social advancement of such persons.
7 Spare parts, components or accessories for any article of a kind mentioned in item 6, including tools for its maintenance, checking, calibration or repair.

Notes:

(1) In items 1 to 5, "relevant organisation" means a State organisation or other approved charitable or philanthropic organisation.
(2) In item 1, "basic necessities" means food, medicines, clothing, blankets, orthopaedic equipment and crutches, required to meet a person's immediate needs.
(3) Items 1, 2 and 3 do not include alcoholic beverages, tobacco products, coffee, tea or motor vehicles other than ambulances.
(4) Items 2, 3 and 6 do not apply where there is any commercial intent on the part of the donor.
(5) Items 4 and 5 apply only where the [HM Treasury][1] has made a Decision authorising importation of the goods.
(6) In item 6, "relevant organisation" means an approved organisation principally engaged in the education of, or the provision of assistance to, blind or other physically or mentally handicapped persons.
(7) In item 6, "supply" means any loan, hiring-out or transfer, for consideration or free of charge, other than on a profit-making basis.
(8) Item 7 applies only where the goods are imported with an article of a kind mentioned in item 6 to which they relate, or, if imported subsequently, are identifiable as being intended for that article, where relief from tax on that article has been afforded by virtue of item 6, or would have been so afforded if such article were imported with the goods which relate to it.

Cross-references—See Arts 3A and 3B of this Order: application of this Order to importations into Northern Ireland.
Amendments—[1] In Items 4 and 5, words "one or more member States" substituted in both places, and in Note (5), words "the Commission of the European Union" substituted, by the Value Added Tax (Miscellaneous Amendments and Revocations) (EU Exit) Regulations, SI 2019/59 reg 3(1), (4)(c) with effect from IP completion day (11pm UK time on 31 December 2020).

GROUP 7
PRINTED MATTER, ETC

Item No
1 Documents sent free of charge to public services in the United Kingdom.
2 Foreign government publications and publications of official international bodies intended for free distribution.
3 Ballot papers for elections organised by bodies abroad.
4 Specimen signatures and printed circulars concerning signatures, forming part of exchanges of information between bankers or public services.
5 Official printed matter sent to a Central Bank in the United Kingdom.
6 Documents sent by companies incorporated abroad to bearers of, or subscribers to, securities issued by such companies.
7 Files, archives and other documents for use at international meetings, conferences or congresses and reports of such gatherings.
8 Plans, technical drawings, traced designs and other documents sent by any person for the purpose of participating in a competition in the United Kingdom or to obtain or fulfil an order executed abroad.
9 Documents to be used in examinations held in the United Kingdom on behalf of institutions established abroad.
10 Printed forms to be used as official documents in the international movement of vehicles or goods pursuant to international conventions.
11 Printed forms, labels, tickets and similar documents sent to travel agents in the United Kingdom by transport and tourist undertakings abroad.
12 Used commercial documents.
13 Official printed forms from national or international authorities.
14 Printed matter conforming to international standards, for distribution by an association in the United Kingdom and sent by a corresponding association abroad.
15 Documents sent for the purpose of free distribution to encourage persons to visit foreign countries, in particular to attend cultural, tourist, sporting, religious, trade or professional meetings or events.
16 Foreign hotel lists and yearbooks published by or on behalf of official tourist agencies and timetables for foreign transport services, for free distribution.
17 Yearbooks, lists of telephone and telex numbers, hotel lists, catalogues for fairs, specimens of craft goods of negligible value and literature on museums, universities, spas or other similar establishments, supplied as reference material to accredited representatives or correspondents appointed by official national tourist agencies and not intended for distribution.
[18 Official publications issued under the authority of the country of exportation, international institutions, regional or local authorities and bodies governed by public law established in the country of exportation.][1]

[19 Printed matter distributed by foreign political organisations on the occasion of elections to the European Parliament or national elections in the country in which the printed matter originates.][1]

Notes:

[(1) Items 15 and 16 do not apply where the goods contain more than 25 per cent of private commercial advertising.][1]

[(2) Items 18 and 19 apply only to publications or printed matter on which value added tax or any other tax has been paid in the . . . [3] country from which they have been exported and which have not benefited, by virtue of their exportation, from any relief from payment thereof.][2]

[(3) In Item 19, "foreign political organisations" means those which are officially recognised as such in the United Kingdom.][1]

[(4) In Item 11 "travel agent" includes airlines, national railway undertakings, ferry operators and similar organisations.

(5) In Items 2, 15, 16 and 19 "foreign" means from a country other than the United Kingdom.][2]

Amendments—[1] Items 18 and 19 added and Notes (1)–(3) substituted for the original Note by the VAT (Imported Goods) Relief (Amendment) (No 2) Order, SI 1988/2212 art 6 with effect from 1 January 1989.
[2] Note (2) substituted and Notes (4), (5) inserted by the VAT (Imported Goods) Relief (Amendment) Order, SI 1992/3120 arts 1, 2, 5 with effect from 1 January 1993.
[3] In Note (2), word "third" revoked by the Value Added Tax (Miscellaneous Amendments and Revocations) (EU Exit) Regulations, SI 2019/59 reg 3(1), (4)(d) with effect from IP completion day (11pm UK time on 31 December 2020).

GROUP 8
ARTICLES SENT FOR MISCELLANEOUS PURPOSES

Item No

1 Material relating to trademarks, patterns or designs and supporting documents and applications for patents, imported for the purpose of being submitted to bodies competent to deal with protection of copyright or industrial or commercial patent rights.

2 Objects imported for the purpose of being submitted as evidence, or for a like purpose, to a court or other official body in the United Kingdom.

3 Photographs, slides and stereotype mats for photographs, whether or not captioned, sent to press agencies and publishers of newspapers or magazines.

4 Recorded media, including punched cards, sound recordings and microfilm, sent free of charge for the transmission of information.

5 Any honorary decoration conferred by a government or Head of State abroad on a person resident in the United Kingdom and imported on his behalf.

6 Any cup, medal or similar article of an essentially symbolic nature, intended as a tribute to activities in the arts, sciences, sport, or the public service, or in recognition of merit at a particular event, which is either—

(a) donated by an authority or person established abroad for the purpose of being presented in the United Kingdom, or

(b) awarded abroad to a person resident in the United Kingdom and imported on his behalf.

7 Goods (other than alcoholic beverages or tobacco products) sent on an occasional basis as gifts in token of friendship or goodwill between bodies, public authorities or groups carrying on an activity in the public interest.

8 . . . [3]

[9 Awards, trophies and souvenirs of a symbolic nature and of limited value intended for distribution free of charge at business conferences or similar events to persons normally resident in a country other than the United Kingdom.][1]

Notes:

[(1)] [2] Items 5, 6, 7 and 9 do not apply to any importation of a commercial character.][1]

(2), (3) . . . [3]

Northern Ireland—See VATA 1994 Sch 9ZC para 5: modification of Group 8 so that provisions relating to low-value consignment relief which were revoked by Sch 9ZC Part 1 continue to apply for goods imported into the UK as a result of their entry into Northern Ireland. Those modifications are: insertion of item 8 and Notes (2) and (3), as follows—

"8 Any consignment of goods imported into the United Kingdom as a result of their entry into Northern Ireland (other than alcoholic beverages, tobacco products, perfumes or toilet waters) not exceeding £15 in value.".

"(2) Item 8 does not apply in relation to any goods imported on mail order.

(3) For the purposes of note (2)—

"mail order" in relation to any goods means any transaction or series of transactions under which a seller (S) sends goods in fulfilment of an order placed remotely,

"remotely" means by any means that do not involve the simultaneous physical presence of S and the person placing the order, and

"seller" does not include any person acting otherwise than in a commercial or professional capacity.".

Amendments—[1] Item 9 inserted and Note (1) substituted by the VAT (Imported Goods) Relief (Amendment) (No 2) Order, SI 1988/2212 art 7 with effect from 1 January 1989.
[2] Note (1) numbered as such by FA 2012 s 199 with effect in relation to goods imported on or after 1 April 2012.

³ Item 8 and Notes (2), (3) revoked by the Taxation (Post-transition Period) Act 2020, s 7, Sch 3 para 18 with effect from IP completion day (11pm on 31 December 2020), by virtue of SI 2020/1642 reg 9. See also modifications above in relation to Northern Ireland.

Item 8 previously read as follows—

"8 Any consignment of goods (other than alcoholic beverages, tobacco products, perfumes or toilet waters) not exceeding £15 in value,".

Notes (2), (3) previously read as follows—

"(2) Item 8 does not apply in relation to any goods imported on mail order from the Channel Islands.

(3) For the purposes of note (2)—

"mail order" in relation to any goods means any transaction or series of transactions under which a seller (S) sends goods in fulfilment of an order placed remotely,

"remotely" means by any means that do not involve the simultaneous physical presence of S and the person placing the order, and

"seller" does not include any person acting otherwise than in a commercial or professional capacity.".

GROUP 9
WORKS OF ART AND COLLECTORS' PIECES

Item No

1 Works of art and collectors' pieces imported by approved museums, galleries or other institutions for a purpose other than sale.

Note: Item 1 applies only where the goods are—

(*a*) of an educational, scientific or cultural character; and

(*b*) imported free of charge or, if for a consideration, are not supplied to the importer in the course or furtherance of any business.

[GROUP 10
TRANSPORT][1]

[Item No

1 Fuel contained in the standard tanks of a vehicle or of a special container, for use exclusively by such vehicle or such special container.

2 Fuel, not exceeding 10 litres for each vehicle, contained in portable tanks carried by a vehicle, for use exclusively by such vehicle.

3 Lubricants contained in a vehicle, for use exclusively by such vehicle.

4 Litter, fodder and feeding stuffs contained in any means of transport carrying animals, for the use of such animals during their journey.

5 Disposable packings for the stowage and protection of goods during their transportation to the United Kingdom.

Notes:

(1) "Standard tanks" means any of the following—

(*a*) tanks permanently fitted to a vehicle and which are fitted to all vehicles of that type by the manufacturer, to supply directly fuel for the purpose of propulsion and, where appropriate, for the operation, during transport, of refrigeration systems and other systems;

(*b*) gas tanks fitted to vehicles designed for the direct use of gas as a fuel;

(*c*) tanks fitted to ancillary systems with which a vehicle is equipped; and

(*d*) tanks permanently fitted to a special container and which are fitted to all special containers of that type by the manufacturer, to supply directly fuel for the operation, during transport, of refrigeration systems and other systems with which special containers are equipped.

(2) "Vehicle" means any motor road vehicle.

(3) "Special container" means any container fitted with specially designed apparatus for refrigeration systems, oxygenation systems, thermal insulation systems and other systems.

(4) Item 2 does not apply in the case of any special purpose vehicle or a vehicle which, by its type of construction and equipment, is designed for and capable of transporting goods or more than nine persons including the driver.

(5) Item 3 applies only to lubricants necessary for the normal operation of the vehicle during its journey.

(6) Item 5 applies only where the cost of the packings is included in the consideration for the goods transported.][1]

Amendments—[1] This group substituted by the VAT (Imported Goods) Relief (Amendment) (No 2) Order, SI 1988/2212 art 8 with effect from 1 January 1989.

GROUP 11
WAR GRAVES, FUNERALS, ETC

Item No

1 Goods imported by an approved organisation for use in the construction, upkeep or ornamentation of cemeteries, tombs and memorials in the United Kingdom which commemorate war victims of other countries.

2 Coffins containing human remains.

3 Urns containing human ashes.

4 Flowers, wreaths and other ornamental objects accompanying goods described in items 2 or 3.

5 Flowers, wreaths and other ornamental objects, imported without any commercial intent by a person resident abroad, for use at a funeral or to decorate a grave.

1984/1176

CONTROL OF MOVEMENT OF GOODS REGULATIONS 1984

Made by the Commissioners of Customs and Excise under the Customs and Excise Management Act 1979 s 31 and all other enabling powers

Made . . . .*1 August 1984*
Laid before Parliament . . . .*3 August 1984*
Coming into Operation . . . .*6 August 1984*

1 Citation and commencement

These Regulations may be cited as the Control of Movement of Goods Regulations 1984 and shall come into operation on 6th August 1984.

2 Revocation

The Control of Movement of Goods Regulations 1981 are hereby revoked.

3 Interpretation

In these Regulations—

"the Act" means the Customs and Excise Management Act 1979;

"approved place"—

    (a) in relation to imported goods means a place approved by the Commissioners under section 20 or 25 of the Act for [facilitating the administration, collection or enforcement of any duty of customs][2], and

    (b) in relation to goods intended for export means a place appointed under section 159 of the Act for the examination of goods which is approved by the Commissioners under section 31 of the Act for the examination of such goods before their movement to a place of exportation;

"the loader" [means][2] the owner of the [vehicle][2] in which the goods are to be exported or a person appointed by him;

"place of importation" and "place of exportation" shall, where appropriate, include a free zone;

"removal" means a movement of goods which is authorised under these Regulations and "remove" and "removed" shall be construed accordingly;

"removal document" means a document to be obtained from or approved by the Commissioners made in such form and containing such particulars as the Commissioners may direct under section 31(2A) of the Act and for the purpose of regulation 16 shall include a copy of the application referred to in regulations 5, . . . [1] and 7 stamped by the proper officer.

Amendments—[1]   In the definition of "removal document" word ", 6" revoked by the Taxation (Cross-border Trade) (Miscellaneous Provisions) (EU Exit) Regulations, SI 2019/486 reg 4(1), (2) with effect from IP completion day (11pm UK time on 31 December 2020).

[2]   In the definition of "approved place" words substituted for words "the clearance out of charge of such goods", and in the definition of "the loader" word substituted for words "shall have the same meaning as in section 57 of the Act; that is to say", and word substituted for words "ship or aircraft", by the Customs (Temporary Storage Facilities Approval Conditions and Miscellaneous Amendments) (EU Exit) Regulations, SI 2018/1247 reg 5(1), (2) with effect from IP completion day (11pm on 31 December 2020) by virtue of SI 2020/1643 reg 2, Schedule.

4—(1) These Regulations shall not apply where any goods are moved under the [common transit procedure as defined in paragraph 1(2) of Schedule 1 to the Customs Transit Procedures (EU Exit) Regulations 2018][1].

(2) The application of regulations 11 and 13 of these Regulations to goods carried under the provisions of an international convention having effect in the United Kingdom shall be without prejudice to any such provisions.

Amendments—[1]   In sub-para (1) words substituted for words "internal or external Community transit procedure" by the Taxation (Cross-border Trade) (Miscellaneous Provisions) (EU Exit) Regulations, SI 2019/486 reg 4(1), (3) with effect from IP completion day (11pm UK time on 31 December 2020).

5 Restrictions on the movement of goods

Subject to regulation 10, no imported goods [subject to the control of any officer of Revenue and Customs as a result of Part 1 of the Taxation (Cross-border Trade) Act 2018][1] shall be moved between their place of importation and . . . [1] an approved place . . . [1] unless the movement is authorised by the proper officer upon application made to him.

Amendments—[1] Words substituted for words "not yet cleared from customs and excise charge" and word "either", and words "or a free zone and, in the case of transit goods, between their place of importation and a place of exportation" revoked, by the Customs (Temporary Storage Facilities Approval Conditions and Miscellaneous Amendments) (EU Exit) Regulations, SI 2018/1247 reg 5(1), (3) with effect from IP completion day (11pm on 31 December 2020) by virtue of SI 2020/1643 reg 2, Schedule. These changes incorporate an amendment made to SI 2018/1247 reg 5(3) by SI 2019/1215 reg 10(1), (3)(b) also with effect from IP completion day.

6 Subject to regulation 10, no goods shall be moved between—
   (a) a free zone and a place approved for the clearance out of charge of such goods,
   (b) such a place and a free zone, and
   (c) a free zone and another free zone,
unless the movement is authorised by the proper officer upon application made to him.[1]

Amendments—[1] Reg 6 revoked by the Customs (Temporary Storage Facilities Approval Conditions and Miscellaneous Amendments) (EU Exit) Regulations, SI 2018/1247 reg 5(1), (4) with effect from IP completion day (11pm on 31 December 2020) by virtue of SI 2020/1643 reg 2, Schedule.

7 Subject to regulations 9 and 10, no goods intended for export and made available at [an appropriate place as required by regulation 40 of the Customs (Export) (EU Exit) Regulations 2019][1] for the purposes of examination shall be moved between any such place and a place of exportation unless the movement is authorised by the proper officer upon application made to him.

Amendments—[1] Words substituted for words "an approved place or a place designated by the proper officer under section 53(4) or 58(3) of the Act" by the Taxation (Cross-border Trade) (Miscellaneous Provisions) (EU Exit) Regulations, SI 2019/486 reg 4(1), (4) with effect from IP completion day (11pm UK time on 31 December 2020).

8 Save as the Commissioners may otherwise allow, the applications referred to in regulations 5 . . . [1] and 7 above shall be made in [an electronic form specified in a public notice given by HMRC Commissioners][1] and shall be made—
   (a) . . . [1] by the importer or the person in charge of the goods,
   (b) in the case of goods intended for export, by the exporter or the person in charge of the goods,
   . . .
   (c) . . . [1]

Amendments—[1] Word ", 6" revoked, words substituted for words "writing on a document obtained from or approved by the Commissioners for that purpose", in sub-para (a) words "in the case of imported goods," revoked, and sub-para (c) revoked, by the Customs (Temporary Storage Facilities Approval Conditions and Miscellaneous Amendments) (EU Exit) Regulations, SI 2018/1247 reg 5(1), (5) with effect from IP completion day (11pm on 31 December 2020) by virtue of SI 2020/1643 reg 2, Schedule. SI 2018/1247 reg 5(5) is itself amended by the Customs and Excise (Miscellaneous Provisions and Amendments) (EU Exit) Regulations, SI 2019/1215 also with effect from IP completion day and these changes have been incorporated.

Para (c) previously read as follows—
   "(c) in any other case, by the proprietor of the goods or the person in charge of the goods.".

9 Local export control

(1) Where a notice under section 58A(3)(a)(i) of the Act is delivered by the exporter such notice shall replace the application required under regulation 7.
(2) Where the notice is for a single movement of goods, if the authority of the proper officer, required under regulation 7, is neither given nor refused by the date and time for the movement specified in that notice, it shall be deemed to be given on the date and immediately before the time so specified.
(3) Where the notice is for more than one movement of goods, if the authority of the proper officer, required under regulation 7, is neither given nor refused, it shall be deemed to be given immediately before each movement commences.[1]

Amendments—[1] Reg 9 revoked by the Customs (Temporary Storage Facilities Approval Conditions and Miscellaneous Amendments) (EU Exit) Regulations, SI 2018/1247 reg 5(1), (6) with effect from IP completion day (11pm on 31 December 2020) by virtue of SI 2020/1643 reg 2, Schedule.

10 Standing permission to remove

Where the Commissioners so permit, during a period specified by them, goods may be moved as contemplated in regulations 5 . . . [1] and 7 without an application to the proper officer; and, unless the proper officer previously gives or refuses his authority, it shall be deemed to be given immediately before the movement commences.

Amendments—[1] Word ", 6" revoked by the Customs (Temporary Storage Facilities Approval Conditions and Miscellaneous Amendments) (EU Exit) Regulations, SI 2018/1247 reg 5(1), (7) with effect from IP completion day (11pm on 31 December 2020) by virtue of SI 2020/1643 reg 2, Schedule.

11 Requirement for removal document
Before any removal commences the person by whom, or on whose behalf, the goods are being moved shall be in possession of a removal document.

12 Specification of vehicles etc
(1) The Commissioners may, in respect of any class or description of goods, require that vehicles or containers in which goods of a particular class or description are removed shall be of a type specified by them for the removal of such goods.
(2) Save as provided by paragraph (3) below, no person shall remove any goods in respect of which a requirement under paragraph (1) above has been imposed unless the vehicle or container in which they are carried conforms to such requirement.
(3) The proper officer, upon application made to him by the person in charge of goods to be removed, may for the purposes of the removal in question relax any requirement imposed under paragraph (1) above.

13 Specification of routes
Vehicles and containers proceeding under a removal shall be moved by such routes as the Commissioners may specify.

14 Security of goods, vehicles and containers
(1) Before any goods are removed they or the vehicle or container carrying them shall be secured or identified by any such seals, locks or marks as the Commissioners may specify.
(2) Where in the United Kingdom, seals, locks or marks are affixed for any customs or excise purpose in order to secure or identify the goods to be removed or the vehicles or containers carrying the goods, they shall be so affixed by the proper officer or by such other person as the Commissioners may authorise.

15—(1) Save in the circumstances hereunder mentioned, no person shall at any time during a removal—
   (a) wilfully break, open or remove any seal, lock or mark affixed for any customs or excise purpose on any goods or to a vehicle or container; or
   (b) load or unload or assist in the loading or unloading of a vehicle or container.
(2) The circumstances referred to in paragraph (1) above are—
   (a) where authorisation has been given by the proper officer; or
   (b) in accordance with any general or special permission given by the Commissioners; or
   (c) in an emergency in order to safeguard the goods or to protect life or property.

16 Completion of removals, time limits and accidents
(1) Save as the Commissioners otherwise allow, the person in charge of goods proceeding under a removal shall complete the removal by producing the goods, together with the vehicle or container in which they are carried if such vehicle or container has been secured or identified, and delivering a removal document to the proper officer at the approved place or, in the case of goods intended for export, at the place of exportation.
(2) The Commissioners may allow the removal of goods intended for export to be completed by the person in charge of the goods placing them, together with any container in which they are carried if such container has been secured or identified, under the control of the loader and delivering the removal document to him.

17 The person in charge of goods proceeding under a removal shall complete the removal within such period as the Commissioners may specify.

18 Where as a result of an accident or other occurrence arising during a removal a vehicle or container is delayed or diverted from a specified route the person in charge of the goods shall as soon as practicable give sufficient notification of the accident or occurrence as required by the Commissioners to the local office of customs and excise.

1986/939

VALUE ADDED TAX (SMALL NON-COMMERCIAL CONSIGNMENTS) RELIEF ORDER 1986

Made by the Treasury under VATA 1983 s 19(1) (see now VATA 1994 s 37(1))

Made . . . .*3 June 1986*
Laid before the House of Commons . . . .*9 June 1986*
Coming into Operation . . . .*1 July 1986*

1 Citation and commencement

This Order may be cited as the Value Added Tax (Small Non-Commercial Consignments) Relief Order 1986 and shall come into operation on 1st July 1986.

2 Revocation

The Value Added Tax (Imported Goods) Relief Order 1980 and the Value Added Tax (Imported Goods) Relief (Amendment) Order 1985 are hereby revoked.

3 Relief from value added tax

(1) Subject to the provisions of this Order, no tax is payable on the importation . . . [2] of goods forming part of a small consignment of a non-commercial character.

(2) In this Order "small consignment" means a consignment (not forming part of a larger consignment) containing goods with a value for customs purposes not exceeding [£39][1].

(3) For the purposes of this Order a consignment is of a non-commercial character only if the following requirements are met, namely—

(a) it is consigned by one private individual to another;

(b) it is not imported for any consideration in money or money's worth;

(c) it is intended solely for the personal use of the consignee or that of his family and not for any commercial purpose.

Amendments—[1] Figure in para (2) substituted by the VAT (Small Non-Commercial Consignments) Relief (Amendment) Order, SI 2016/1199 arts 2, 3 with effect from 1 January 2017. Figure was previously £34 (with effect from 1 January 2016).
[2] In para (1) words "from a place outside the member States" revoked by the Value Added Tax (Miscellaneous Amendments and Revocations) (EU Exit) Regulations, SI 2019/59 reg 4 with effect from IP completion day (11pm on 31 December 2020).

[4 Conditions of relief

No relief shall be given under this Order unless the consignment is of an occasional nature.][1]

Amendments—[1] This article substituted by the VAT (Small Non-Commercial Consignments) Relief (Amendment) Order, SI 1992/3118 with effect from 1 January 1993.

5 Quantitative restriction on relief for certain goods

Where a small consignment of a non-commercial character contains goods of any of the following descriptions, namely—

(a) tobacco products (being cigarettes, cigars or smoking tobacco);

(b) alcohol and alcoholic beverages (being spirits or wine), tafia and saké; or

(c) perfumes or toilet waters,

in excess of the quantity shown in relation to goods of that description in the Schedule to this Order, no relief under this Order shall be given in respect of any goods of that description contained in that consignment.

6 Relief not applicable to travellers' baggage

This Order does not apply to goods contained in the baggage of a person entering the United Kingdom or carried with such a person.

SCHEDULE
Article 5

(1) Tobacco products—	
Cigarettes	50
Or	
cigarillos (cigars with a maximum weight each of 3 grammes)	25
Or	
Cigars	10
Or	
smoking tobacco	50 grammes
(2) Alcohol and alcoholic beverages—	
distilled beverages and spirits of an alcoholic strength exceeding 22% by volume; undenatured ethyl alcohol of 80% by volume and over	1 litre
Or	
distilled beverages and spirits, and aperitifs with a wine or alcohol base, tafia, saké or similar beverages of an alcoholic strength of 22% by volume or less; sparkling wines and fortified wines	1 litre
Or	
still wines	2 litres

(3) Perfumes Or	50 grammes
toilet waters	[250 millilitres][1]

Amendments—[1] Words in para (3) substituted by the VAT (Small Non-Commercial Consignments) Relief (Amendment) Order, SI 1991/2535 arts 1, 2 with effect from 30 November 1991.

1987/1806

VALUE ADDED TAX (TOUR OPERATORS) ORDER 1987

Made by the Treasury under VATA 1983 ss 3(3), 6(6), 16(4), 37A(1)–(2), 48(6) (see now VATA 1994 ss 5(3), 7(11), 30(4), 53(1), (2), 96(9))

Made . . . . .14 October 1987
Laid before the House of Commons . . . . .21 October 1987
Coming into force . . . . .1 April 1988

1 Citation and Commencement
This Order may be cited as the Value Added Tax (Tour Operators) Order 1987 and shall come into force on 1st April 1988.

2 Supplies to which this Order applies
This Order shall apply to any supply of goods or services by a tour operator where the supply is for the benefit of travellers.

3 Meaning of "designated travel service"
(1) Subject to paragraphs (2) . . . [1] and (4) of this article, a "designated travel service" is a supply of goods or services—
  (a) acquired for the purposes of his business; and
  (b) supplied for the benefit of a traveller without material alteration or further processing;
by a tour operator [who has a business establishment, or some other fixed establishment, in the United Kingdom][2].
(2) The supply of one or more designated travel services, as part of a single transaction, shall be treated as a single supply of services.
(3) . . . [1]
(4) The supply of goods and services of such description as the Commissioners of Customs and Excise may specify shall be deemed not to be a designated travel service.

Amendments—[1] Reference in sub-para (1) and whole of sub-para (3) revoked by the Value Added Tax (Tour Operators) (Amendment) Order, SI 2009/3166 arts 2, 3 with effect in relation to supplies made on or after 1 January 2010.
[2] In sub-para (1) words substituted for words "in a member State of the European Union in which he has established his business or has a fixed establishment" by the Value Added Tax (Tour Operators) (Amendment) (EU Exit) Regulations, SI 2019/73 regs 2, 3 with effect from IP completion day (11pm UK time on 31 December 2020).

4 Time of supply
(1) Sections 4 and 5 of the Value Added Tax Act 1983[1] shall not apply to any supply comprising in whole or in part a designated travel service.
(2) Subject to paragraphs (3) and (4) of this article, all supplies comprising in whole or in part a designated travel service shall, at the election of the tour operator making the supplies, be treated as taking place either—
  (a) when the traveller commences a journey or occupies any accommodation supplied, whichever is the earlier; or
  (b) when any payment is received by the tour operator in respect of that supply which, when aggregated with any earlier such payment, exceeds 20 per cent of the total consideration, to the extent covered by that and any earlier such payment, save in so far as any earlier such payment has already been treated as determining the time of part of that supply.
(3) Save as the Commissioners of Customs and Excise may otherwise allow, all supplies comprising in whole or in part a designated travel service made by the same tour operator shall, subject to paragraph (4) of this article, be treated as taking place at the time determined under one only of the methods specified in paragraph (2) of this article.
(4) Where—
  (a) a tour operator uses the method specified in paragraph (2)(b) to determine the time of a supply; and
  (b) payment is not received in respect of all or part of the supply;
notwithstanding paragraph (3), the time of any part of that supply, which has not already been determined under paragraph (2)(b), shall be determined in accordance with paragraph (2)(a).

Note—[1] VATA 1994 s 6.

[5 A designated travel service shall be treated for the purposes of the Value Added Tax Act 1994 as supplied in the United Kingdom regardless of the place where it is to be enjoyed.][1]

Amendments—[1]   Article 5 substituted by the Value Added Tax (Tour Operators) (Amendment) (EU Exit) Regulations, SI 2019/73 regs 2, 4 with effect from IP completion day (11pm UK time on 31 December 2020). Article 5 previously read as follows—

> "**5 Place of supply**
>
> (1) . . .
>
> (2) A designated travel service shall be treated [for the purposes of this Act] as supplied in the member State in which the tour operator has established his business or, if the supply was made from a fixed establishment, in the member State in which the fixed establishment is situated."

7   Value of a designated travel service
Subject to articles [8, 9 and 9A][1] of this Order, the value of a designated travel service shall be determined by reference to the difference between sums paid or payable to and sums paid or payable by the tour operator in respect of that service, calculated in such manner as the Commissioners of Customs and Excise shall specify.

Amendments—[1]   Words substituted by the Value Added Tax (Tour Operators) (Amendment) Order, SI 2009/3166 arts 2, 4 with effect in relation to supplies made on or after 1 January 2010.

8—(1) Where—
  (a) a supply of goods or services is acquired for a consideration in money by a tour operator, for the purpose of supplying a designated travel service, and
  (b) the value of the supply is (apart from this article) greater than its open market value, and
  (c) the person making the supply and the tour operator to whom it is made are connected,
the Commissioners of Customs and Excise may direct that the value of the supply shall be deemed to be its open market value for the purpose of calculating the value of the designated travel service.
(2) A direction under this article shall be given by notice in writing to the tour operator acquiring the supply, but no direction may be given more than three years after the time of the supply.
(3) A direction given to a tour operator under this paragraph, in respect of a supply acquired by him, may include a direction that the value of any supply—
  (a) which is acquired by him after the giving of the notice, or after such later date as may be specified in the notice, and
  (b) as to which the conditions in sub-paragraph (a) to (c) of paragraph (1) above are satisfied,
shall be deemed to be its open market value for the purpose of calculating the value of the designated travel service.
(4) For the purposes of this article any question whether a person is connected with another shall be determined in accordance with section 533 of the Income and Corporation Taxes Act 1970[1].

Note—[1]   TA 1988 s 839.

9—(1) Where—
  (a) goods and services have been acquired prior to the commencement of this Order; and
  (b) input tax credit has been claimed in respect of those goods and services; and
  (c) the goods and services are supplied as a designated travel service or as part of a designated travel service after the commencement of this Order;
article 7 of this Order shall not apply in determining the value of that part of a designated travel service referable to goods and services on which input tax has been claimed.
(2) The value of that part of the designated travel service to which, by virtue of paragraph (1) of this article, article 7 of this Order does not apply shall be calculated in accordance with section 10 of the Value Added Tax Act 1983[1].

Note—[1]   VATA 1994 s 19.

[**9A**—(1) Where—
  (a) goods or services have been supplied to a tour operator by a taxable person before 1st January 2010,
  (b) the tour operator claims input tax in respect of those goods or services, and
  (c) the tour operator supplies those goods or services on or after 1st January 2010 as a designated travel service, or as part of a designated travel service, without material alteration or further processing, to a taxable person who ordered the supply for use in the United Kingdom by that person for the purpose of that person's business other than by way of re-supply,
article 7 of this Order shall not apply in determining the value of that part of the designated travel service which is referable to the goods or services in respect of which input tax is claimed.
(2) The value of that part of a designated travel service to which, by virtue of paragraph (1), article 7 of this Order does not apply, shall be calculated in accordance with section 19 of the Value Added Tax Act 1994.][1]

Amendments—[1]   This article inserted by the Value Added Tax (Tour Operators) (Amendment) Order, SI 2009/3166 arts 2, 5 with effect in relation to supplies made on or after 1 January 2010.

12 Disallowance of input tax

[Subject to article 9A of this Order,][2] input tax on goods or services acquired by a tour operator for re-supply as a designated travel service shall be excluded from credit under sections 14 and 15 of the Value Added Tax Act 1983[1].

Note—[1] VATA 1994 ss 24–26.
Amendments—[2] Words inserted by the Value Added Tax (Tour Operators) (Amendment) Order, SI 2009/3166 arts 2, 6 with effect in relation to supplies made on or after 1 January 2010.

13 Disqualification from membership of group of companies

A tour operator shall not be eligible to be treated as a member of a group for the purposes of section 29 of the Value Added Tax Act 1983[1] if any other member of the proposed or existing group—
  (a) has an overseas establishment;
  (b) makes supplies outside the United Kingdom which would be taxable supplies if made within the United Kingdom; and
  (c) supplies goods or services which will become, or are intended to become, a designated travel service.

Note—[1] VATA 1994 s 43.

14 Option not to treat supply as designated travel service

(1) Where a tour operator supplies a designated travel service he may treat that supply as not being a designated travel service if:
  (a) there are reasonable grounds for believing that the value of all such supplies in the period of one year then beginning will not exceed one per cent of all supplies made by him during that period; and
  (b) he makes no supplies of designated travel services consisting of accommodation or transport.
(2) For the purposes of this article the value of any supplies shall be calculated in accordance with section 10 of the Value Added Tax Act 1983[1].

Note—[1] VATA 1994 s 19.

1988/809

EXCISE WAREHOUSING (ETC) REGULATIONS 1988

Made by the Commissioners of Customs and Excise under CEMA 1979 s 93 and ALDA 1979 ss 2(3A), 15 and 56(1)

> Made . . . . .29 April 1988
> Laid before Parliament . . . . .9 May 1988
> Coming into force . . . . .1 June 1988

ARRANGEMENT OF REGULATIONS

1	Citation and commencement
2	Interpretation
3	Application
4	Designated file
5	Variation of provisions at request of occupier or proprietor
6	Limitation of penalties (revoked)
7	Manner of Commissioners' directions etc
8	Form of entries etc
9	Revocation
	PART II PROCEDURES FOR EXCISE WAREHOUSES AND WAREHOUSED GOODS
10	Time of warehousing
10A	*Goods to which section 46 of the Customs and Excise Management Act 1979 applies* (revoked)
11	Receipt of goods into warehouse
12	Securing, marking and taking stock of warehoused goods
13	Proprietor's examination of goods
14	Operations
15	Removal from warehouse—occupier's responsibilities
16	Removal from warehouse—entry
17	Removal from warehouse—general
18	Entry of goods not in warehouse
19	Samples

PART III RETURNS AND RECORDS

20	Returns
21	Records to be kept
22	Preservation of records
23	Production of records
24	Information for the protection of the revenue
25	Further provision as to records

PART IV DUTY CHARGEABLE ON WAREHOUSED GOODS

26	Duty chargeable on goods removed for home use
27	Duty chargeable on goods diverted to home use after removal without payment of duty
28	Duty chargeable on missing or deficient goods
29	Calculation of duty
30	Ascertainment of quantity by taking an account

PART V ASCERTAINMENT OF DUTY BY REFERENCE TO LABELS ETC

31	Ascertainment of duty by reference to labels etc

Schedules:
Schedule 1—Operations which may be permitted on warehoused goods
Schedule 2—Records to be kept by the occupier
Schedule 3—Records which the proprietor may be required to keep

PART I
PRELIMINARY

1 Citation and commencement
These Regulations may be cited as the Excise Warehousing (Etc) Regulations 1988 and shall come into force on 1st June 1988, but the Commissioners may give consent and agree conditions, restrictions or requirements under regulation 5 (variation of provisions at request of occupier or proprietor) before that date.

2 Interpretation
In these Regulations, unless the context otherwise requires—
 "duty" means excise duty;
 "occupier" means the occupier of an excise warehouse, and in the case of a distiller's warehouse means the distiller;
 "package" includes any bundle, case, carton, cask, or other container whatsoever;
 "proprietor" means the proprietor of goods in an excise warehouse or of goods which have been in, or are to be deposited in, or are treated as being in, an excise warehouse, and "proprietorship" shall be construed accordingly;
 "warehoused" means warehoused or rewarehoused in an excise warehouse, and
 "warehousing" and "rewarehousing" shall be construed accordingly.

3 Application
(1) Except as provided by or under the Hydrocarbon Oil Duties Act 1979 Parts I to IV of these Regulations apply to all goods chargeable with a duty of excise.
(2) Part V of these Regulations applies for all purposes of the Alcoholic Liquor Duties Act 1979.

4 Designated file
(1) For the purposes of these Regulations delivery to the proper officer of anything in writing—
 (a) shall be effected by placing it in the relevant designated file; and
 (b) the time of such delivery shall be when it is placed in that designated file,
but the proper officer may direct that delivery shall be effected in another manner.
(2) Nothing in a designated file shall be removed without the permission of the proper officer.
(3) Nothing in a designated file shall be altered in any way, and an amendment to anything in it shall be made by depositing a notice of amendment in the designated file.
(4) The designated file shall be kept at such place as the Commissioners direct and, if kept at the excise warehouse, shall be provided by the occupier.
(5) The designated file shall be a receptacle approved by the Commissioners for the secure keeping of written material, and different files may be approved for different purposes.
(6) For the purposes of these Regulations delivery to the proper officer of anything not in writing shall be effected in such manner, and be subject to such conditions, as the Commissioners direct.

5 Variation of provisions at request of occupier or proprietor

(1) The Commissioners may, if they see fit, consent in writing to an application by an occupier or proprietor for variation of any condition, restriction or requirement contained in or arising under regulations 11 to 24 below, and may make that consent subject to compliance with such other condition, restriction or requirement (as the case may be) as may be agreed by them and the applicant in writing.

(2) Where under paragraph (1) above any condition or restriction is varied or another is substituted for it, then, if the varied or substituted condition or restriction is one—

(a) subject to which goods may be deposited in, secured in, kept in or removed from an excise warehouse or made available there to their owner for any prescribed purpose; or

(b) subject to which an operation may be carried out on goods in an excise warehouse,

breach of the varied or substituted condition or restriction shall give rise to forfeiture of those goods, provided that breach of the original condition or restriction would have given rise to forfeiture.

7 Manner of Commissioners' directions etc

(1) Where, by or under these Regulations, it is provided that the Commissioners may—

(a) make a direction or requirement;
(b) give their permission or consent;
(c) grant approval; or
(d) impose a condition or restriction,

then they may do so only in writing; and they may make a direction or requirement or impose a condition or restriction by means of a public notice.

(2) Any request for the proper officer to give his permission or grant approval under these Regulations shall, if he or the Commissioners direct, be made in writing.

(3) Any right granted to the Commissioners or the proper officer by these Regulations to—

(a) make a direction or requirement;
(b) give permission or consent;
(c) grant approval; or
(d) impose a condition or restriction,

shall include a right to revoke, vary or replace any such direction, requirement, permission, consent, approval, condition or restriction.

8 Form of entries etc

(1) Except as the Commissioners otherwise allow, and subject to paragraph (2) below, any entry, account, notice, specification, record or return required by or under these Regulations shall be in writing.

(2) This regulation does not apply to the records referred to in regulation 22(3) and (4) below (records kept for the purposes of any relevant business or activity).

9 Revocation

The Excise Warehousing (Etc) Regulations 1982 and the Excise Warehousing (Etc) (Amendment) Regulations 1986 are hereby revoked.

PART II
PROCEDURES FOR EXCISE WAREHOUSES AND WAREHOUSED GOODS

10 Time of warehousing

Goods brought to an excise warehouse for warehousing shall be deemed to be warehoused when they are put in the excise warehouse.

11 Receipt of goods into warehouse

(1) Subject to paragraph (6) below, when goods are warehoused the occupier shall immediately deliver to the proper officer an entry of the goods in such form and containing such particulars as the Commissioners direct.

(2) When goods are warehoused the occupier shall take account of the goods and deliver a copy of that account to the proper officer by the start of business on the next day after warehousing that the warehouse is open.

(3) The occupier shall, if there is any indication that the goods may have been subject to loss or tampering in the course of removal to the excise warehouse, immediately inform the proper officer and retain the goods intact for his examination.

(4) [Except in any case to which the Excise Goods (Holding, Movement and Duty Point) Regulations 2010 apply], the occupier shall, within 5 days of goods being warehoused, send a certificate of receipt for the goods to the person from whom they were received identifying the goods and stating the quantity which has been warehoused.][2]

[(4A) Where goods are warehoused in circumstances where duty may be drawn back the certificate of receipt mentioned in paragraph (4) above shall—

(a) be in such form and contain such particulars as the Commissioners may require, and
(b) be endorsed on one of the copies of the warehousing advice note that accompanied the goods,

and in this paragraph "warehousing advice note" means a document (in such form and containing such particulars as the Commissioners may require) drawn up by the person to whom the certificate of receipt will be sent.]¹
(5) Except as the proper officer otherwise allows the occupier shall give only one receipt required by paragraph (4) above for each lot or parcel of goods warehoused.
(6) In the case of spirits warehoused at the distillery where they were produced satisfaction of the requirements of regulation 21 of the Spirits Regulations 1982 shall be deemed to be compliance with the requirements of entry and account in paragraphs (1) and (2) above.
(7) Should the occupier fail to comply with any condition or restriction imposed by or under paragraphs (1), (2), (3) or (6) above any goods in respect of which the failure occurred shall be liable to forfeiture.

Amendments—[1] Para (4A) inserted by Excise Goods (Drawback) Regulations, SI 1995/1046, Pt V, reg 15(b) with effect from 1 June 1995.
[2] In para (4), words substituted for words "Except as the proper officer may otherwise allow," by the Excise Goods (Holding, Movement and Duty Point) Regulations, SI 2010/593 reg 90, Sch 2 paras 1, 2 with effect from 1 April 2010.

12 Securing, marking and taking stock of warehoused goods
(1) The occupier shall take all necessary steps to ensure that no access is had to warehoused goods other than as allowed by or under these Regulations.
(2) Goods shall be warehoused in the packages and lots in which they were first entered for warehousing.
(3) The occupier shall—
  (a) legibly and uniquely mark and keep marked warehoused goods so that at any time they can be identified in the stock records; and
  (b) stow warehoused goods so that safe and easy access may be had to each package or lot.
(4) The occupier shall, when required by the proper officer to do so, promptly produce to him any warehoused goods which have not lawfully been removed from the warehouse.
(5) The occupier shall take stock of all goods in the warehouse—
  (a) monthly in the case of bulk goods in vats or in storage tanks; and
  (b) annually in the case of all other goods,
and shall take stock at such other times and to such extent as the Commissioners may for reasonable cause require.
(6) In accordance with the Commissioners' directions the occupier shall—
  (a) balance his stock accounts and reconcile the quantities of those balances with his Excise Warehouse Returns; and
  (b) balance his stock accounts so that they can be compared with the result of any stock-taking.
(7) The occupier shall notify the proper officer immediately in writing of any deficiency, surplus or other discrepancy concerning stocks or records of stocks whenever or however discovered.
(8) Any goods—
  (a) found not to be marked in accordance with paragraph (3) above; or
  (b) found to be in excess of the relevant stock account and not immediately notified to the proper officer,
shall be liable to forfeiture.

13 Proprietor's examination of goods
The proprietor of warehoused goods may, provided that the occupier has first given his consent and has given at least 6 hours' notice to the proper officer—
  (a) examine the goods and their packaging;
  (b) take any steps necessary to prevent any loss therefrom; or
  (c) display them for sale.

14 Operations
(1) Except as provided by or under this regulation or by or under sections 57 and 58 of the Alcoholic Liquor Duties Act 1979 (mixing of spirits with made-wine or wine), no operation shall be carried out on warehoused goods.
(2) The Commissioners may allow the operations described in Schedule 1 to these Regulations to be carried out on warehoused goods, and may allow other operations if they are satisfied that the control of the goods and the security and collection of the revenue will not be prejudiced.
(3) Save as the proper officer may allow in cases of emergency for the preservation of the goods, no operation shall be commenced unless the occupier has delivered to the proper officer a notice of the proposed operation with a specification of the goods involved, and 24 hours have elapsed following the delivery of that notice.
(4) Before commencing any operation on goods the occupier shall ensure that an account is taken of those goods and that immediately after completion of the operation an account is taken of the out-turn quantities.

(5) The occupier shall deliver to the proper officer a notice containing such detail of the accounts required by paragraph (4) above as the proper officer requires.

(6) The occupier shall ensure that—
  (a) any operation is carried out in part of the warehouse approved by the Commissioners for that purpose, or in such other part as the proper officer allows; and
  (b) such other requirements as the proper officer may impose in any particular circumstances are observed.

(7) Any goods in respect of which this regulation is not observed shall be liable to forfeiture.

(8) Nothing in paragraph (2) above shall permit the mixing of spirits with wine or made-wine while that operation is excluded from the provisions of section 93(2)(c) of the Customs and Excise Management Act 1979.

15 Removal from warehouse—occupier's responsibilities

The occupier shall ensure that—
  (a) notice of intention to remove the goods is given to the proper officer in accordance with any directions made by the Commissioners;
  (b) an entry of the goods is delivered to the proper officer in such form and containing such particulars as the Commissioners may direct;
  (c) no goods are removed until any duty chargeable has been paid, secured, or otherwise accounted for;
  (d) no goods are removed contrary to any condition or restriction imposed by the proper officer;
  (e) an account of the goods is taken in such manner and to such extent as the proper officer requires and a copy of the account is delivered to the proper officer; . . . [2]
  (f) [except in any case to which the Excise Goods (Holding, Movement and Duty Point) Regulations 2010 apply,][1] when goods are removed other than for home use, a certificate of receipt is obtained showing that all the goods arrived at the place to which they were entered on removal and, if no such receipt is obtained within 21 days of the removal, notice of that fact is given to the proper officer for the excise warehouse from which the goods were removed[; and
  (g) in any case where, in accordance with regulations made under section 60A of the Customs and Excise Management Act 1979, authorisation is required to ship goods as stores without payment of duty, a copy of the authorisation is obtained before the goods are removed.][2]

Amendments—[1] In para (f), words inserted by the Excise Goods (Holding, Movement and Duty Point) Regulations, SI 2010/593 reg 90, Sch 2 paras 1, 2 with effect from 1 April 2010.

[2] In para (e), word revoked, in para (f), word substituted for full stop, and para (g) inserted by the Excise Goods (Aircraft and Ship's Stores) Regulations, SI 2015/368 regs 13, 14 with effect in relation to excise goods: (a) supplied to be shipped as stores on or after 1 April 2015; (b) shipped as stores on or after 1 April 2015; or (c) carried as stores on or after 1 April 2015, where they were shipped on or after that date.

16 Removal from warehouse—entry

(1) Goods may be entered for removal from warehouse for—
  (a) home use, if so eligible;
  (b) exportation;
  (c) shipment as stores; or
  (d) removal to the Isle of Man [;

provided that, where goods are warehoused in circumstances where duty may be drawn back they may not, under this paragraph, be entered for removal from warehouse for any purpose that may result in their being consumed in the United Kingdom or the Isle of Man][1].

(2) The Commissioners may allow goods to be entered for removal from warehouse for—
  (a) rewarehousing in another excise warehouse;
  (b) temporary removal for such purposes and such periods as they may allow;
  (c) scientific research and testing;
  (d) removal to premises where goods of the same class or description may, by or under the customs and excise Acts, be kept without payment of excise duty;
  (e) denaturing or destruction; or
  (f) such other purpose as they permit,

and may by direction impose conditions and restrictions on the entry of goods or classes of goods for any of the above purposes.

(3) Save as the Commissioners direct no goods may be removed from warehouse unless they have been entered in accordance with this regulation.

(4), (5) . . .

[(6) In any case where, in accordance with regulations made under section 60A of the Customs and Excise Management Act 1979, authorisation is required to ship goods as stores without payment of duty, goods entered for shipment as stores may be removed from warehouse without payment of duty only if a copy of the authorisation has been given to the occupier.][2]

Amendments—[1] Words in para (1) inserted by Excise Goods (Drawback) Regulations, SI 1995/1046, Pt V, reg 15(c) with effect from 1 June 1995.

[2] Para 6 inserted by the Excise Goods (Aircraft and Ship's Stores) Regulations, SI 2015/368 regs 13, 15 with effect in relation to excise goods: (a) supplied to be shipped as stores on or after 1 April 2015; (b) shipped as stores on or after 1 April 2015; or (c) carried as stores on or after 1 April 2015, where they were shipped on or after that date.

17 Removal from warehouse—general

(1) Any goods removed from an excise warehouse without payment of duty as samples or for scientific research and testing and which are no longer required for the purpose for which they were removed shall be—
   (a) destroyed to the satisfaction of the proper officer;
   (b) rewarehoused in an excise warehouse; or
   (c) diverted to home use on payment of the duty chargeable thereon.

(2) The proper officer may require any goods entered for removal from an excise warehouse for any purpose, other than home use, to be secured or identified by the use of a seal, lock or mark, and any such requirement may continue after the goods have been removed.

(3) In such cases as the Commissioners may direct the proper officer may impose conditions and restrictions on the removal of goods from an excise warehouse in addition to those imposed elsewhere in these Regulations.

(4) Any goods in respect of which any of the provisions of these Regulations relating to removal of goods from an excise warehouse (other than regulation 15(f)) is contravened shall be liable to forfeiture.

(5) The Commissioners may direct that any provision of these Regulations relating to removal of goods from an excise warehouse shall not apply in the case of hydrocarbon oils.

[(6) Subject to paragraph (7) below, goods entered for removal from an excise warehouse for any of the purposes set out in regulation 16 above shall be accompanied by an accompanying document that has been completed and is used in accordance with the instructions for completion and use set out on the reverse of copy 1 of that document.

(7) Paragraph (6) above does not apply to—
   (a) goods entered for removal for home use, shipment as stores or denaturing;
   (b) goods entered for removal for use by a person to whom section 13A of the Customs and Excise Duties (General Reliefs) Act 1979 (reliefs from duties and taxes for persons enjoying certain immunities and privileges) applies;
   (c) goods entered for removal that are, in accordance with regulations made under section 12(1) of the Customs and Excise Duties (General Reliefs) Act 1979 (supply of duty-free goods to Her Majesty's ships), to be treated as exported;
   (d) spirits entered for removal for use by a person authorised to receive them in accordance with section 8 of the Alcoholic Liquor Duties Act 1979 (remission of duty in respect of spirits used for medical or scientific purposes);
   (e), (ea) . . . [3]
   (eb) goods entered for removal in circumstances to which Part 8 of the Excise Goods (Holding, Movement and Duty Point) Regulations 2010 apply;][2]
   (f) goods that are being lawfully moved under the cover of a single administrative document; or
   (g) any goods that are entered for removal from an excise warehouse for any of the purposes set out in regulation 16 above before 1st October 2002 if those goods are accompanied by a document that has been approved by the Commissioners for that purpose.

(8) If there is a contravention of, or failure to comply with, paragraph (6) above, the excise duty point for excise goods that are required by this regulation to be accompanied by an accompanying document is the time those goods were removed from the excise warehouse.

(9) The person liable to pay the excise duty at the excise duty point is—
   (a) the person who arranged for the security required by regulation 16(5) above, or
   (b) if regulation 16(5) above was not complied with, the authorized warehousekeeper.

(10) Any person whose conduct caused a contravention of, or failure to comply with, paragraph (6) above is jointly and severally liable to pay the excise duty with the person specified in paragraph (9) above.

(11) Any excise duty that any person is liable to pay by virtue of this regulation must be paid immediately.

(12) In this regulation—
   ["single administrative document" means the single administrative document provided for in a public notice made by the Commissioners under paragraph 5 of Schedule 1 to the Taxation (Cross-border Trade) Act 2018;][3]
   "accompanying document" means the document set out in Schedule 4 below.][1]

Amendments—[1] Paras (6)–(12) inserted by the Excise Goods (Accompanying Documents) Regulations, SI 2002/501 reg 27(1), (3) with effect from 1 April 2002.
[2] Sub-para (7)(eb) inserted by the Excise Goods (Holding, Movement and Duty Point) Regulations, SI 2010/593 reg 90, Sch 2 paras 1, 2 with effect from 1 April 2010.
[3] Sub-paras (7)(e), (ea) revoked, and definition of "single administrative document" substituted, by the Excise Duties (Miscellaneous Amendments) (EU Exit) (No 2) Regulations, SI 2019/15 reg 2 with effect from IP completion day (11pm on 31 December 2020) by virtue of SI 2020/1640 reg 2, Schedule.

Definition previously read as follows—
" "single administrative document" has the same meaning as in Commission Regulation (EEC) No 2454/93;".
Sub-paras (7)(*e*), (*ea*) previously read as follows—
- (*e*) goods entered for removal for exportation in circumstances to which Part II of the Excise Goods (Accompanying Documents) Regulations 2002 apply;
- (*ea*) goods entered for removal for exportation in circumstances to which Part 6 of the Excise Goods (Holding, Movement and Duty Point) Regulations 2010 apply;".

18 Entry of goods not in warehouse

Except in such cases as the Commissioners direct, goods which are to be warehoused and goods which have been lawfully removed from an excise warehouse without payment of duty may, with the permission of the proper officer, be entered or further entered by their proprietor for any of the purposes referred to in paragraphs (1) and (2) of regulation 16 above as if they were to be removed from the excise warehouse:

Provided that where any such goods are packaged and part only is to be further entered, that part shall consist of one or more complete packages.

19 Samples

(1) The Commissioners may make directions—
- (*a*) allowing the proprietor of warehoused goods to draw samples thereof for such purposes and subject to such conditions as they specify; and
- (*b*) . . .

and no sample shall be drawn or removed except as allowed by, and in accordance with directions and conditions under, this regulation.
(2) Any samples drawn or removed in breach of this regulation shall be liable to forfeiture.

PART III
RETURNS AND RECORDS

20 Returns

(1) The occupier shall complete and sign an Excise Warehouse Return and shall deliver such return to the proper officer within 14 days of the end of the stock period to which it relates.
(2) A return shall be in such form and contain such particulars of goods received into, stored in and delivered from an excise warehouse as the Commissioners direct, and different provisions may be made for goods of different classes or descriptions.
(3) The Commissioners may direct that separate returns be made in respect of goods of different classes or descriptions.
(4) The occupier shall support each return with such schedules and further information relating to the goods as the Commissioners may require.
(5) "Stock period" means one calendar month or such other period, not exceeding 5 weeks, as the proper officer, at the request of the occupier, allows.

21 Records to be kept

(1) The occupier shall, in relation to goods in an excise warehouse, keep the records prescribed by Schedule 2 to these Regulations.
(2) The proprietor of goods in an excise warehouse, or of goods which have been removed from an excise warehouse without payment of duty, or which are to be warehoused, may be required by the proper officer to keep the records prescribed by Schedule 3 to these Regulations in so far as they relate to his proprietorship of the goods.
(3) In addition to the other records required by this regulation the occupier shall, in relation to his occupation of the warehouse, keep such records of the receipt and use of goods received into the excise warehouse other than for warehousing therein as the proper officer requires.
(4) Records required by or under this regulation shall—
- (*a*) be entered up promptly;
- (*b*) identify the goods to which they relate;
- (*c*) in the case of an occupier be kept at the warehouse;
- (*d*) in the case of a proprietor be kept at his principal place of business in the United Kingdom, or at such other place as the proper officer allows; and
- (*e*) be kept in such form and manner and contain such information as the Commissioners direct.

22 Preservation of records

(1) The occupier shall preserve, for not less than 3 years from the lawful removal of the goods or such shorter period as the Commissioners direct, all records which he is required to keep by virtue of regulation 21(1) above, but no record shall be destroyed until the relevant stock accounts have been balanced and any discrepancy reconciled.
(2) The proprietor shall preserve, for not less than 3 years from when he ceased to be the proprietor of the goods, or for such shorter period as the Commissioners direct, all records which he is required to keep by virtue of regulation 21(2) above.

(3) Each occupier and proprietor shall preserve all records (other than those referred to in paragraphs (1) and (2) above) kept by him for the purposes of any relevant business or activity for not less than 3 years from the events recorded in them, except that such records need not be preserved if they are records which (or records of a class which) the Commissioners have directed as not needing preservation.

(4) The requirements to preserve records imposed by paragraph (3) above may be discharged by the preservation in a form approved by the Commissioners of the information contained in those records.

23 Production of records

(1) The occupier or the proprietor shall, when required by the Commissioners, produce or cause to be produced to the proper officer any records, copy records or information which he was required by these Regulations to preserve.

(2) Production under paragraph (1) above shall—
   (a) take place at such reasonable time as the proper officer requires; and
   (b) take place at the excise warehouse or at such other place as the proper officer may reasonably require.

(3) The proper officer may inspect, copy or take extracts from and may remove at a reasonable time and for a reasonable period any record produced or required to be produced to him under this regulation, and the occupier and proprietor shall permit such inspection, copying, extraction and removal.

(4) Where the records required to be produced by this regulation are preserved in a form which is not readily legible, or which is legible only with the aid of equipment, the occupier or proprietor shall, if the proper officer so requires, produce a transcript or other permanently legible reproduction of the records and shall permit the proper officer to retain that reproduction.

24 Information for the protection of the revenue

(1) The occupier or the proprietor shall furnish the Commissioners with any information relating to any relevant business or activity of his which they specify as information which they think it is necessary or expedient for them to be given for the protection of the revenue.

(2) Such information shall be furnished to the Commissioners within such time, and at such place and in such form as they may reasonably require.

25 Further provision as to records

For the purposes of regulations 21 to 24 above, in relation to a proprietor—
   (a) goods which are to be warehoused shall be treated as if they were warehoused in the warehouse to which they are being removed; and
   (b) goods which have been removed from warehouse without payment of duty shall be treated as if they were warehoused in the warehouse from which they have been removed.

PART IV
DUTY CHARGEABLE ON WAREHOUSED GOODS

26 Duty chargeable on goods removed for home use

The duty and the rate thereof chargeable on any warehoused goods removed from an excise warehouse for home use shall be those in force for goods of that class or description at the time of their removal.

27 Duty chargeable on goods diverted to home use after removal without payment of duty

(1) The duty and the rate thereof chargeable on any goods removed from an excise warehouse without payment of duty and in respect of which duty is payable under regulation 17(1)(c) above shall be those in force for goods of that class or description at the time of payment of the duty.

(2) The duty and the rate thereof chargeable on any goods which have been entered for home use under regulation 18 above shall be those in force for goods of that class or description—
   (a) where removal for home use is allowed under section 119 of the Customs and Excise Management Act 1979 on the giving of security for the duty chargeable thereon, at the time of giving of the security, or
   (b) in any other case, at the time of payment.

28 Duty chargeable on missing or deficient goods

The duty and the rate thereof chargeable on any goods found to be missing or deficient and upon which duty is payable under section 94 of the Customs and Excise Management Act 1979 shall be those in force for goods of that class or description at the time the loss or deficiency occurred:

Provided that where that time cannot be ascertained to the proper officer's satisfaction, the rate of duty chargeable on such goods shall be the highest rate applicable thereto from the time of their deposit in the excise warehouse, or, where appropriate, from the time that the last account of them was taken, until the loss or deficiency came to the notice of the proper officer.

29 Calculation of duty

(1) Where duty is charged on any such goods as are referred to in regulation 26 above, the quantity of those goods shall be ascertained by reference to any account taken in accordance with these Regulations at the time of their removal from the excise warehouse or, if no account is taken, the quantity declared to and accepted by the proper officer as the quantity of goods being removed or, if greater, the actual quantity of goods being removed.

(2) Where duty is charged on any such goods as are referred to in regulations 27 or 28 above the quantity of such goods shall be ascertained by reference to the last account taken in accordance with these Regulations, or, if no account has been taken, the quantity declared to and accepted by the proper officer as the quantity of goods on which duty is to be charged, or, if greater, the actual quantity of goods.

30 Ascertainment of quantity by taking an account

(1) Where the quantity of warehoused goods is to be ascertained by taking an account thereof, it shall be ascertained for the purposes of these Regulations by reference to weight, measure, strength, original gravity or number as the case may require.

(2) Where under these Regulations an occupier is required to deliver a copy of an account of goods he shall deliver to the proper officer a notice giving such details of the account as the proper officer requires, and the taking of the account shall not be complete until that notice has been delivered.

PART V
ASCERTAINMENT OF DUTY BY REFERENCE TO LABELS ETC

31 Ascertainment of duty by reference to labels etc

(1) Subject to paragraph (2) of this regulation, for the purpose of charging duty on any spirits, wine or made-wine contained in any bottle or other container the strength, weight and volume of the spirits, wine or made-wine shall be ascertained conclusively by reference to any information given on the bottle or other container by means of a label, or otherwise, or by reference to any documents relating to the bottle or other container, notwithstanding any other legal provision.

(2) The method of ascertaining the strength, weight or volume, or any of them, referred to in paragraph (1) above shall not be used if another method would produce a result upon which a greater amount of duty would be charged than would be the case if the method in paragraph (1) above were used.

SCHEDULE 1
OPERATIONS WHICH MAY BE PERMITTED ON WAREHOUSED GOODS
(Regulation 14(2))

1 Sorting, separating, packing or repacking and such other operations as are necessary for the preservation, sale, shipment or disposal of the goods.
2 The rectifying and compounding of spirits.
3 The rendering sparkling of wine and made-wine.
4 The mixing of a fermented liquor or a liquor derived from a fermented liquor with any other liquor or substance so as to produce made-wine.
5 The mixing of lime or lemon juice with spirits for shipment as stores or for exportation.
6 Denaturing.
7 Reducing.
8 Marrying.
9 Blending.

SCHEDULE 2
RECORDS TO BE KEPT BY THE OCCUPIER
(Regulation 21(1))

Records of—
- (*a*) goods deposited in the excise warehouse, from where and from whom received, and date of warehousing;
- [(*aa*) any certificate or other document that accompanied beer that contained a statement of the amount of beer produced in the brewery where the beer was produced;][1]
- (*b*) goods removed from the excise warehouse, the purpose of the removal, date of removal and (if the purpose of the removal is other than for home use) the place to which the goods are removed;
- (*c*) stock of warehoused goods;
- (*d*) deficiencies and increases in stock;
- (*e*) operations performed;
- (*f*) deficiencies and increases in operation;

(g) accounts taken of goods deposited in the excise warehouse, removed from the excise warehouse, put into operation, received from operation, and of stocks in the excise warehouse;

(h) samples drawn from warehoused goods, samples removed from warehouse, and the person to whom samples are delivered;

(i) the manner in which duty is paid or accounted for when goods chargeable with duty are removed for home use;

(j) the manner in which security is given when goods chargeable with duty are removed for purposes other than home use, and the dates when certificates of receipt or shipment are received;

[(jj) a copy of any authorisation which is required, in accordance with regulations made under section 60A of the Customs and Excise Management Act 1979, to ship goods as stores without payment of duty;][2]

(k) notices delivered to the proper officer and of the manner and time of delivery;

(l) times when the excise warehouse is opened and closed;

(m) names and titles of keyholders to the excise warehouse;

(n) the name and address of the proprietor of each lot or parcel of goods, and of changes of proprietorship.

Amendments—[1] Paragraph (aa) inserted by the Beer and Excise Warehousing (Amendment) Regulations, SI 2002/1265 reg 3(1), (2) with effect from 1 June 2002.

[2] Paragraph (jj) inserted by the Excise Goods (Aircraft and Ship's Stores) Regulations, SI 2015/368 regs 13, 16 with effect in relation to excise goods: (a) supplied to be shipped as stores on or after 1 April 2015; (b) shipped as stores on or after 1 April 2015; or (c) carried as stores on or after 1 April 2015, where they were shipped on or after that date.

SCHEDULE 3
RECORDS WHICH THE PROPRIETOR MAY BE REQUIRED TO KEEP
(Regulation 21(2))

Records of

(a) goods which are to be warehoused in an excise warehouse;

(b) goods which have been warehoused in an excise warehouse;

(c) goods which have been removed from an excise warehouse otherwise than for home use on payment of the duty chargeable, and all movements of such goods;

(d) his stock of goods in each excise warehouse;

(e) operations performed;

(f) samples drawn, removed from warehouse and, where that removal is other than on payment of the duty chargeable, their use, location and disposal;

(g) the time and manner in which the duty chargeable on goods to which regulation 21(2) relates is paid, secured or accounted for.

[SCHEDULE 5
PARTICULARS WHICH MUST BE CONTAINED IN A DOCUMENT
Regulation 10A

1 Date of entry of the goods and their entry number.

2 Importer's name and address.

3 The name, address and approval number of the excise warehouse to which the goods are to be moved.

4 A description of the goods and their quantity.]

Amendments—This Schedule inserted by the Excise Warehousing (Etc) (Amendment) Regulations, SI 2008/2832 regs 2, 3(2) with effect from 1 December 2008.

Schedule revoked by the Excise Goods (Holding, Movement and Duty Point) Regulations, SI 2010/593 reg 91, Sch 3 with effect from 1 January 2011.

1990/2167

CHANNEL TUNNEL (CUSTOMS AND EXCISE) ORDER 1990

Made by the Commissioners of Customs and Excise under the Channel Tunnel Act 1987 ss 11(1)(a), (c), (d), (g), (h), 11(2), 11(3)(a), (d), 13(1) and (2) and all other enabling powers

Made . . . .*1 November 1990*
Laid before Parliament . . . .*9 November 1990*
Coming into force . . . .*1 December 1990*

1 Citation and commencement

This Order may be cited as the Channel Tunnel (Customs and Excise) Order 1990 and shall come into force on 1st December 1990.

2 Interpretation

(1) In this Order—
"the Act of 1979" means the Customs and Excise Management Act 1979;
"the Act of 1987" means the Channel Tunnel Act 1987;
"customs approved area" has the meaning given by article 3(1) below;
"the tunnel" except in the expression "tunnel system" means that part of the tunnel system comprising the tunnels specified in section 1(7)(a) of the Act 1987 or any of those tunnels.

(2) In this Order the following expressions have the meanings assigned to them by section 1 of the Act of 1979:
"approved wharf";
"the boundary";
"commander";
"the Commissioners";
"the customs and excise Acts";
"customs and excise airport";
"goods";
"officer";
"owner";
"port";
["proper";][1]
"ship";
"shipped" and cognate expressions.

(3)–(5) . . .

Amendments—[1] Words in para (2) inserted by Channel Tunnel (International Arrangements) Order, SI 1993/1813 art 8 Sch 5 Pt II paras 7, 8(a) with effect from 2 August 1993.

4 Modification of the Act of 1979

The Act of 1979 shall be modified in accordance with the provisions of the Schedule to this Order.

SCHEDULE
MODIFICATIONS OF THE ACT OF 1979
Article 4

[Part II of the Act of 1979: Administration

A1 In section 17(1) (disposal of duties, etc) the reference to Great Britain shall be construed as including a reference to a control zone in France [or Belgium][2].][1]

Amendments—[1] Paras A1, A2 inserted by Channel Tunnel (International Agreements) Order, SI 1993/1813 art 8 Sch 5 Pt II para 11 with effect from 2 August 1993.
[2] Words in para A1 inserted by Channel Tunnel (Miscellaneous Provisions) Order, SI 1994/1405 art 8 Sch 4 para 7 with effect from 1 December 1997.

Prospective amendments—Words "a Designated State" to be substituted for words "France of Belgium" by the Channel Tunnel (International Arrangements and Miscellaneous Provisions) (Amendment) Order, SI 2020/915 art 14(2)(c) with effect from a date to be appointed. The effective date is dependent on the entering into force of the Agreement of 7 July 2020 between France, Belgium, Netherlands and UK on rail travel between Belgium and the UK using the Channel Fixed Link (Treaty CP 283)

Part III of the Act of 1979: Customs and Excise Control Areas

[**A2—**(1) For the purposes of section 21 (control of movement of aircraft, etc, into and out of the United Kingdom) references to an aircraft shall be treated as including references to a through train, and in relation to such trains section 21 shall be construed in accordance with sub-paragraphs (2) to (5).

(2) References to a customs and excise airport shall be construed as references to a terminal control point or a place which is a customs approved area.

(3) References to a flight shall be construed as references to a journey, and the reference in section 21(4) to flying shall be construed accordingly.

(4) References to landing shall be construed as references to stopping for the purpose of enabling passengers or crew to board or leave the train or goods to be loaded onto or unloaded from it.

(5) References to the commander of an aircraft shall be construed as references to the train manager of a train.][1]

Amendments—[1] Paras A1, A2 inserted by Channel Tunnel (International Agreements) Order, SI 1993/1813 art 8 Sch 5 Pt II para 11 with effect from 2 August 1993.

Part IV of the Act of 1979: Control of Importation

6 In section 42(1)(*a*) (power to regulate the unloading, removal, etc of imported goods) the reference to a [vehicle entering the United Kingdom][2] shall be construed as including a reference to a vehicle arriving [at a place which is a customs approved area either in France or through the tunnel from France][1] at a customs approved area through the tunnel from France.

Amendments—[1] Words in para 6 inserted by Channel Tunnel (International Arrangements) Order, SI 1993/1813 arts 1, 8 Sch 5 Pt II paras 19–21, 32, 33, with effect from 2 August 1993.
[2] Words substituted for words "ship arriving at a port" by the Customs (Temporary Storage Facilities Approval Conditions and Miscellaneous Amendments) (EU Exit) Regulations, SI 2018/1247 reg 9(1), (5) with effect from IP completion day (11pm on 31 December 2020) by virtue of SI 2020/1643.

[**7** In section 49(1) (forfeiture of goods improperly imported)—
  (*a*) the reference in paragraph (*a*)(ii) to goods unloaded from any aircraft in the United Kingdom shall be construed as including a reference to goods unloaded from a through train or shuttle train which has brought them into the United Kingdom and a reference to goods otherwise brought through the tunnel into the United Kingdom; and
  (*b*) the reference in paragraph (*c*) to goods found to have been concealed on board any aircraft shall be construed as including references to goods found concealed—
    (i) on a through train or shuttle train has brought them into the United Kingdom,
    (ii) on a through train while it constitutes a control zone in France [or Belgium][2], or
    (iii) in a road vehicle in a control zone in France within the tunnel system.]][1]

Amendments—[1] Para 7 substituted by Channel Tunnel (International Arrangements) Order, SI 1993/1813 arts 1, 8 Sch 5 Pt II paras 19–21, 32, 33, with effect from 2 August 1993.
[2] Words in paras 7(*b*)(ii) inserted by Channel Tunnel (Miscellaneous Provisions) Order, SI 1994/1405 arts 1, 8 Sch 4 para 7 with effect from 1 December 1997.

8 Section 50(2) (penalty for improper importation of goods) shall have effect as if—
  (*a*) any person who unloads or assists or is otherwise concerned in the unloading of those goods mentioned in section 50(1) from any vehicle which has arrived from France [or Belgium][2] through the tunnel[, or who brings or assists or is otherwise concerned in the bringing of such goods into a control zone in France [or Belgium][2],][1] were a person who unships such goods in a port; and[3]
  (*b*) any person who removes or assists or is otherwise concerned in the removal of such goods from any customs approved area were a person who removes such goods from an approved wharf.

Amendments—[1] Words in para 8(*a*) inserted by Channel Tunnel (International Arrangements) Order, SI 1993/1813 arts 1, 8 Sch 5 Pt II paras 19–21, 32, 33, with effect from 2 August 1993.
[2] Words in para 8(*a*) inserted by Channel Tunnel (Miscellaneous Provisions) Order, SI 1994/1405 arts 1, 8 Sch 4 para 7 with effect from 1 December 1997.
[3] Sub-para (*a*) revoked by the Customs (Temporary Storage Facilities Approval Conditions and Miscellaneous Amendments) (EU Exit) Regulations, SI 2018/1247 reg 9(1), (6) with effect from IP completion day (11pm on 31 December 2020) by virtue of SI 2020/1643 reg 2, Schedule.

Prospective amendments—Words "a Designated State" to be substituted for words "France of Belgium" by the Channel Tunnel (International Arrangements and Miscellaneous Provisions) (Amendment) Order, SI 2020/915 art 14(2)(*c*) with effect from a date to be appointed. The effective date is dependent on the entering into force of the Agreement of 7 July 2020 between France, Belgium, Netherlands and UK on rail travel between Belgium and the UK using the Channel Fixed Link (Treaty CP 283)

Part XI of the Act of 1979: Detention of Persons, Forfeiture and Legal Proceedings

22 In section 146(1) (service of process) the reference in paragraph (*c*) to an aircraft shall be construed as including a reference to a vehicle which has arrived from or is departing to France through the tunnel[, and in relation to such a vehicle the second reference to the United Kingdom shall be construed as including a reference to a control zone in France within the tunnel system][1].

Amendments—[1] Words in para 22 inserted by Channel Tunnel (International Arrangements) Order, SI 1993/1813 arts 1, 8 Sch 5 Pt II paras 19–21, 32, 33, with effect from 2 August 1993.

23 *In section 154(2) (proof of certain other matters) any reference to goods loaded or to be loaded into or unloaded from an aircraft shall be construed respectively as including references to goods loaded or to be loaded onto or unloaded from a vehicle which is departing to or has arrived from France through the tunnel.*[1]

Amendments—[1] Para 23 revoked by the Customs (Temporary Storage Facilities Approval Conditions and Miscellaneous Amendments) (EU Exit) Regulations, SI 2018/1247 reg 9(1), (8) with effect from IP completion day (11pm on 31 December 2020) by virtue of SI 2020/1643 reg 2, Schedule.

24 In section 159(1) (power to examine and take account of goods) the reference in paragraph (*c*) to goods which have been loaded into a ship shall be construed as including a reference to goods which have been loaded onto a vehicle for exportation through the tunnel.

[25 The persons to whom section 164 (search of persons) applies shall be taken to include any person who is—
(a) in the tunnel system in the United Kingdom;
(b) in a through train in the United Kingdom;
(c) in, entering or leaving a customs approved area in the United Kingdom; or
(d) in a control zone in France [or Belgium][2]].[1]

Amendments—[1] Para 25 substituted by Channel Tunnel (International Arrangements) Order, SI 1993/1813 arts 1, 8 Sch 5 Pt II paras 19–21, 32, 33, with effect from 2 August 1993.
[2] Words in para 25(d) inserted by Channel Tunnel (Miscellaneous Provisions) Order, SI 1994/1405 arts 1, 8 Sch 4 para 7 with effect from 1 December 1997.

1991/2724

CUSTOMS CONTROLS ON IMPORTATION OF GOODS REGULATIONS 1991

Made by the Commissioners of Customs and Excise under the European Communities Act 1972 s 2(2) and all other enabling powers

Made . . . . .4 December 1991
Laid before the House of Commons . . . . .11 December 1991
Coming into force . . . . .1 January 1992

Note—Amending provisions and provisions outside the scope of this Handbook have not been reproduced.
Amendments—These regulations are revoked by the Customs (Temporary Storage Facilities Approval Conditions and Miscellaneous Amendments) (EU Exit) Regulations, SI 2018/1247 reg 6 with effect from IP completion day (11pm on 31 December 2020) by virtue of SI 2020/1643 reg 2, Schedule.

1 Citation and commencement

These Regulations may be cited as the Customs Controls on Importation of Goods Regulations 1991 and shall come into force on 1st January 1992.[1]

Amendments—[1] These regulations are revoked by the Customs (Temporary Storage Facilities Approval Conditions and Miscellaneous Amendments) (EU Exit) Regulations, SI 2018/1247 reg 6 with effect from IP completion day (11pm on 31 December 2020) by virtue of SI 2020/1643 reg 2, Schedule.

2 Interpretation

In these Regulations—
"the Act" means the Customs and Excise Management Act 1979;
"the Commissioners" means the Commissioners of Customs and Excise;
"the Council Regulation" means [Council Regulation (EEC) No 2913/92][1];
["the Commission Regulation" means the Commission Regulation (EEC) No 2454/93][1]
"the customs and excise Acts" has the same meaning as in section 1(1) of the Act.[2]

Amendments—[1] Words substituted and definition "the Commission Regulation" inserted by Community Customs Code (Consequential Amendment of References) Regulations, SI 1993/3014 reg 4(1), (2) with effect from 1 January 1994.
[2] These regulations are revoked by the Customs (Temporary Storage Facilities Approval Conditions and Miscellaneous Amendments) (EU Exit) Regulations, SI 2018/1247 reg 6 with effect from IP completion day (11pm on 31 December 2020) by virtue of SI 2020/1643 reg 2, Schedule.

3 Presentation

(1) Notification to the Commissioners of the arrival of goods as required by [Article 40][1], of the Council Regulation shall be made in the form prescribed in Schedule 1 or a form to the like effect approved by the Commissioners.
(2) Where a computerised inventory system has been approved by the Commissioners presentation may consist in a computerised record capable of being printed out.
(3) Within three hours of its arrival at the wharf or airport at which a ship or aircraft carrying the goods is to unload them, notification of such arrival, as required by [Article 40][1], of the Council Regulation shall be made at the customs office for the wharf or airport; should such notification be impossible due to the office being closed during that period, the period shall end at the expiration of one hour following the re-opening of the office.[2]

Amendments—[1] Words in paras (1), (3) substituted by Community Customs Code (Consequential Amendment of References) Regulations, SI 1993/3014 reg 4(1), (3), (4) with effect from 1 January 1994.
[2] These regulations are revoked by the Customs (Temporary Storage Facilities Approval Conditions and Miscellaneous Amendments) (EU Exit) Regulations, SI 2018/1247 reg 6 with effect from IP completion day (11pm on 31 December 2020) by virtue of SI 2020/1643 reg 2, Schedule.

4 Summary declaration

The summary declaration required under [Article 43][1] of the Council Regulation shall be in the form prescribed in Schedule 2 or a form to the like effect approved by the Commissioners.[2]

Amendments—[1] Words substituted by Community Customs Code (Consequential Amendment of References) Regulations, SI 1993/3014 reg 4(1), (5) with effect from 1 January 1994.

[2] These regulations are revoked by the Customs (Temporary Storage Facilities Approval Conditions and Miscellaneous Amendments) (EU Exit) Regulations, SI 2018/1247 reg 6 with effect from IP completion day (11pm on 31 December 2020) by virtue of SI 2020/1643 reg 2, Schedule.

5 Entry

(1) For the purposes of [Article 49][2] of the Council Regulation the goods shall be entered not later than—

(a) [forty-five][1] *days from the date on which the summary declaration is lodged in the case of goods carried by sea; or*

(b) [twenty][1] *days from the date on which the summary declaration is lodged in the case of goods carried otherwise than by sea.*

(2) The entry shall be delivered by the importer to the proper officer . . . [1]

(3) Except with the permission of the Commissioners no entry shall be delivered before the goods have been presented at the proper office of customs and excise.

(4) Where the Commissioners permit an entry to be delivered before presentation of the goods, the goods must be presented to the proper office of customs and excise within such time as the Commissioners may allow; and if the goods are not so presented the entry shall be treated as not having been delivered.

(5) Acceptance of an entry by the proper officer shall be signified in such manner as the Commissioners may direct.[3]

Amendments—[1] Word in paras (1)(*a*), (*b*) substituted and words in para (2) revoked by Customs and Excise (Single Market etc) Regulations, SI 1992/3095 reg 7(*a*) with effect from 1 January 1993.
[2] Words in para (1) substituted by Community Customs Code (Consequential Amendment of References) Regulations, SI 1993/3014 reg 4(1), (6) with effect from 1 January 1994.
[3] These regulations are revoked by the Customs (Temporary Storage Facilities Approval Conditions and Miscellaneous Amendments) (EU Exit) Regulations, SI 2018/1247 reg 6 with effect from IP completion day (11pm on 31 December 2020) by virtue of SI 2020/1643 reg 2, Schedule.

1992/2790

STATISTICS OF TRADE (CUSTOMS AND EXCISE) REGULATIONS 1992

Made by the Commissioners of Customs and Excise under the European Communities Act 1972 s 2(2) and all other enabling powers

> Made . . . . .6 November 1992
> Laid before parliament . . . . .10 November 1992
> Coming into force . . . . .1 December 1992

Commentary—*De Voil Indirect Tax Service* **V5.276**.

1 Citation, commencement and interpretation

(1) These Regulations may be cited as the Statistics of Trade (Customs and Excise) Regulations 1992 and shall come into force on 1st December 1992.

(2) In these Regulations—

"the Act" means the Customs and Excise Management Act 1979;[1]
. . . [3]

"authorised person" means any person acting under the authority of the Commissioners;[1]
. . . [3]

"document" includes in addition to a document in writing—

(*a*) any photograph;

(*b*) any disc, tape, sound track or other device in which sounds or other data (not being visual images) are recorded so as to be capable (with or without the aid of some other equipment) of being reproduced therefrom; and

(*c*) any film, negative, tape or other device in which one or more visual images are recorded so as to be capable (as aforesaid) of being reproduced therefrom;

"film" includes a microfilm;
. . . [3]

["Intrastat" refers to the data collection system established and implemented by [as when the Statistics of Trade (Amendment etc) (EU Exit) Regulations 2019, regulation 6 comes into force][4]—

(*a*) Council and European Parliament Regulation (EC) No 638/2004 ("establishing Regulation"); and

(*b*) Commission Regulation (EC) No 1982/2004 ("implementing Regulation");][2]

. . .

["periodic declaration" refers to the means of providing the simplified information in regulations 3(1) and 3(2) (VAT return) or to a supplementary declaration in regulation 4;][2]

. . .³
. . .¹
. . .³

(3) In these Regulations, unless defined above, words and expressions shall have the meanings assigned to them by section 1 of the Act [or have the same meaning as in the establishing or implementing Regulation]².

Amendments—¹ Definitions in para (2) revoked by Statistics of Trade (Customs and Excise) (Amendment) Regulations, SI 1997/2864 with effect from 1 January 1998 (previously inserted by Statistics of Trade (Customs and Excise) (Amendment) Regulations, SI 1993/541 reg 3).
² In para (2), definition of "Intrastat" substituted for that of "Intrastat system", and definition of "periodic declaration" substituted; and words in para (3) inserted; by the Statistics of Trade (Customs and Excise) (Amendment) Regulations, SI 2004/3284 regs 1(3), 2 with effect from 1 January 2005.
³ Definitions revoked by SI 2004/3284 regs 1(3), 5, Schedule with effect from 1 January 2005. The revoked definitions are those of "arrival stage", "assimilation threshold", "dispatch stage", "goods", "Member State", "Principal Regulation", "reference period", "register of intra-Community operators", "supplementary declaration" and "Threshold Regulation".
⁴ In para (2), in the meaning of "Intrastat", words inserted by the Statistics of Trade (Amendment etc) (EU Exit) Regulations, SI 2019/47 reg 6(1), (2). This amendment came into force immediately before IP completion day (11pm on 31 December 2020) (see SI 2019/47 reg 1 and EU(WA)A 2020 Sch 5 para 1(1)). Note that this amendment does not apply in relation to a dispatch from, or an arrival to, a place in Northern Ireland (SI 2019/47 reg 6(11), as inserted by SI 2020/1624 reg 8(5)).

2 [Application of Intrastat

(1) For the purposes of the United Kingdom's statistical territory [(the United Kingdom)]², Intrastat is under the care and management of the Commissioners of Customs and Excise (the "Commissioners").

(2)–(4) . . .²

(5) For the purposes of Article 9 of the establishing Regulation (information that must or may be collected), the Commissioners must only collect information in accordance with Regulations 3, 4 and 4A (simplified information and supplementary declaration).]¹

Amendments—¹ Regulations 2–4A substituted for regulations 2–4 by the Statistics of Trade (Customs and Excise) (Amendment) Regulations, SI 2004/3284 regs 1(3), 3 with effect from 1 January 2005.
² In para (1) words substituted for words "(see Article 4(1) of the establishing Regulation)", and paras (2)–(4) revoked, by the Statistics of Trade (Amendment etc) (EU Exit) Regulations, SI 2019/47 reg 6(1), (3), (4). These amendments came into force immediately before IP completion day (11pm on 31 December 2020) (see SI 2019/47 reg 1 and EU(WA)A 2020 Sch 5 para 1(1)). Note that these amendments do not apply in relation to a dispatch from, or an arrival to, a place in Northern Ireland (SI 2019/47 reg 6(11), as inserted by SI 2020/1624 reg 8(5)).
Paras (2)–(4) previously read as follows—
"(2) For the purposes mentioned in paragraph (1), the Commissioners are—
 (a) "customs" within Article 5(2) of the establishing Regulation (provision to national authority of statistical information on other goods at least once a month);
 (b) the "national authority" within—
  (i) Articles 5(2), 8(1), 8(2), 9(1) and 11 of the establishing Regulation (other goods, etc; register of intra-Community operators; identification of parties responsible for providing information; information that must be collected; statistical confidentiality); and
  (ii) Articles 5, 13(4), 17(4), 21(4), 22(4) and 23(2) of the implementing Regulation (identification of persons who have declared goods for fiscal purposes; simplification for certain individual transactions; access to additional data sources in the case of vessels and aircraft, sea products, spacecraft and electricity);
 (c) the "tax administration" within—
  (i) Articles 8(2) and 8(3) of the establishing Regulation (duty to furnish lists of persons who have declared that they have supplied goods to or acquired goods from other Member States; duty to furnish information provided for fiscal purposes which could improve quality of statistics; duty to bring the Intrastat obligations to the attention of VAT-registered traders); and
  (ii) Article 5 of the implementing Regulation (duty to provide specified information to identify persons who have declared goods for fiscal purposes).
(3) Also, for the purposes mentioned in paragraph (1), the duties or discretions expressed in the following Articles as those of the "Member States" must be performed or exercised by the Commissioners—
 (a) Articles 10(6), 12 and 13 of the establishing Regulation (sending information on thresholds to Commission; transmission of that data; quality of that data and yearly quality report to Commission); and
 (b) Articles 10, 16(2), 18, 19(3), 20(3), 23(3), 24(2), 25(2), 25(4) to 25(7) and 26(1) of the implementing Regulation (reporting nature of transaction; application of specific rules for staggered consignments, motor vehicle and aircraft parts, goods delivered to vessels and aircraft, offshore installations, electricity, military goods; transmission of data to Commission; yearly quality report to Commission).
(4) The Commissioners may do anything necessary for and reasonably incidental to any Article mentioned in paragraphs (2) and (3).
This paragraph is additional to any other basis for their doing so.".

[3 [Information collected on the value added tax return]

[(1) The Commissioners may treat the following information collected in accordance with regulations made under section 58 of, and Schedule 11 paragraphs 2(1) and 2(11) to, the Value Added Tax Act 1994 (information collected on the VAT return) for Intrastat purposes (see Article 10(1) of the establishing Regulation)—

 (a) information about the value of [exports]⁵ of goods and related costs to . . .⁵ Member States;

(b) information about the value of [imports]⁵ of goods and related costs from . . . ⁵ Member States.]²

[(2) If the annual value of . . . ⁵ 'dispatches' (see Articles 3, 7, and 10(2) of the establishing Regulation) of a party is at or below £250,000, that party may be treated as exempt from providing Intrastat information concerning dispatches, and therefore that party is not subject to regulation 4 (supplementary declarations) in respect of such information.

(3) If the annual value of . . . ⁵ 'arrivals' (see Articles 3, 7, and 10(2) of the establishing Regulation) of a party is at or below [£1,500,000]⁴, that party may be treated as exempt from providing Intrastat information concerning arrivals, and therefore that party is not subject to regulation 4 (supplementary declarations) in respect of such information.]³]¹

Amendments—¹ Regulations 2–4A substituted for regulations 2–4 by the Statistics of Trade (Customs and Excise) (Amendment) Regulations, SI 2004/3284 regs 1(3), 3 with effect from 1 January 2005.
² Heading, and para (1) substituted by the Statistics of Trade (Customs and Excise) (Amendment) Regulations, SI 2006/3216 regs 2, 3 with effect from 1 January 2007.
³ Paras (2), (3) substituted by the Statistics of Trade (Customs and Excise) (Amendment) Regulations, SI 2009/2974, reg 2(1) with effect from 1 January 2010.
⁴ In para (3), figure substituted by the Statistics of Trade (Customs and Excise) (Amendment) Regulations, SI 2014/3135, reg 2 with effect from 1 January 2015.
⁵ In para (1) words substituted for words "supplies" and "imports", and word "other" revoked in both places, and in paras (2), (3) words "intra-EU" revoked, by the Statistics of Trade (Amendment etc) (EU Exit) Regulations, SI 2019/47 reg 6(1), (5), (6). These amendments came into force immediately before IP completion day (11pm on 31 December 2020) (see SI 2019/47 reg 1 and EU(WA)A 2020 Sch 5 para 1(1)). Note that the substitutions of words "supplies" and "acquisitions" do not apply in relation to a dispatch from, or an arrival to, a place in Northern Ireland (SI 2019/47 reg 6(11), as inserted by SI 2020/1624 reg 8(5)).

[4 [Supplementary declarations
(1) A party that in relation to the United Kingdom is responsible for providing the information (see Article 7 of the establishing Regulation) must provide it to the Commissioners by means of electronic communication in the appropriate form specified in a current Commissioners' direction.
(2) That party must provide all the information sought by the appropriate form, in accordance with the establishing and implementing Regulations.
(3) But that party need provide the "delivery terms" information sought by the appropriate form only if that party's annual value of . . . ³ trade relevant to that form (namely, value of "arrivals" or value of "dispatches") exceeds [£24,000,000]².
(4) That party must use the coding mentioned in Article 11 of the implementing Regulation in providing any "delivery terms" information pursuant to paragraph (1) and this paragraph (and see also Article 9(2)(d) of the establishing Regulation).
(5) That party must deliver the completed supplementary declaration to the Commissioners no later than the 21st day of the month following the end of the reference period to which it relates.
(6) Only the reference period in Article [6(a)]³ of the establishing Regulation applies in relation to the supplementary declaration ("calendar month of dispatch or arrival of the goods".)
(7) . . . ³
(8) direction under paragraph (1) . . . ⁵ is not current for the purposes of the relevant paragraph to the extent that it is varied, replaced or revoked by another Commissioners' direction.]¹

Amendments—¹ Regulation 4 substituted by the Statistics of Trade (Customs and Excise) (Amendment) Regulations, SI 2012/532 reg 3 with effect from 1 April 2012.
² In para (3) amount substituted for previous amount "£16,000,000" by SI 2013/3043, reg 2(1), (3) with effect from 1 January 2014.
³ In para (3) words "intra-EU" revoked, in para (6) "6(a)" substituted for "6(1)", para (7) revoked, and in para (8) words "or (5)" revoked, by the Statistics of Trade (Amendment etc) (EU Exit) Regulations, SI 2019/47 reg 6(1), (6)–(9). These amendments came into force immediately before IP completion day (11pm on 31 December 2020) (see SI 2019/47 reg 1 and EU(WA)A 2020 Sch 5 para 1(1)).
Para (7) previously read as follows—
"(7) But the reference periods in Article 3 of the Implementing Regulation may be used instead if a current Commissioners' direction so permits in the interests of better administration ("calendar month" of "chargeable event" or in which "declaration is accepted").".

4A [Administration of rules concerning specific goods and movements
(1) The Commissioners must give directions as to matters of administration for the proper application of these Regulations in the case of the rules set out in Articles 16, 17, 19, 20, 21, 22, 23 and 24 of the implementing Regulation (rules concerning specific goods and movements – staggered consignments, vessels and aircraft, goods delivered to vessels and aircraft, offshore installations, sea products, spacecraft, electricity, military goods).
(2) The Commissioners may give such a direction in the case of the rules set out in Articles 15 and 18 of that Regulation (industrial plant, motor vehicle and aircraft parts).
(3) Regulation 4 (supplementary declarations) is subject to every current direction under this regulation.
(4) A direction is not current for the purposes of paragraph (3) to the extent that it is varied, replaced or revoked by another such direction.]¹

Amendments—[1] Regulations 2–4A substituted for regulations 2–4 by the Statistics of Trade (Customs and Excise) (Amendment) Regulations, SI 2004/3284 regs 1(3), 3 with effect from 1 January 2005.

5 Duty to keep and retain records

(1) Every person who is mentioned in the register of intra-Community operators, shall—
  (a) keep a copy of every periodic declaration . . . [1] he makes [or delivers or which is made or delivered][2] on his behalf;
  (b) keep copies of all documents which he or anyone acting on his behalf used for the purpose of compiling [his periodic declarations][1];
  (c) produce or cause to be produced [periodic declarations and documents][1] mentioned in paragraphs (a) and (b) above when required to do so by an authorised person;
  (d) permit an authorised person exercising the powers mentioned in paragraph (c) above to make [copies or extracts of those periodic declarations and documents][1] or to remove them for a reasonable period.

(2) The Commissioners may require [periodic declarations and documents][1] mentioned in paragraph (1) above to be preserved for such period not exceeding six years as they may require.

(3) For the purpose of exercising any powers granted by this regulation an authorised person may at any reasonable time enter premises used in connection with the carrying on of a business by a person mentioned in the register of intra-Community operators or another person compiling periodic declarations on his behalf.

Amendments—[1] Words in para (1)(a) revoked and words in paras (1)(b), (c), (d), (2) substituted by Statistics of Trade (Customs and Excise) (Amendment) Regulations, SI 1997/2864 reg 6 with effect from 1 January 1998.
[2] Words in para (1)(a) substituted by the Statistics of Trade (Customs and Excise) (Amendment) Regulations, SI 2004/3284 regs 1(3), 4(1) with effect from 1 January 2005.

6 Offences and evidence

(1) If any person required to [deliver][2] a supplementary declaration in accordance with [these Regulations][2] fails to do so he shall be liable on summary conviction to a penalty not exceeding level 4 on the standard scale.

(2) Any failure to [deliver][2] a supplementary declaration includes a failure to [provide][2] such supplementary declaration in the form and manner required by these Regulations . . . [3].

(3) Subject to paragraph (4) below, for the purpose of the rules against charging more than one offence in the same information—
  (a) failure to [deliver][2] one or more supplementary declarations of trade in goods dispatched to . . . [5] Member States for any given reference period shall constitute one offence; and
  (b) failure to [deliver][2] one or more supplementary declarations of trade in goods [arriving][2] from . . . [5] Member States for any given reference period shall constitute one offence.

(4) If the failure in respect of which a person is convicted under paragraph (1) above is continued after the conviction he shall be guilty of a further offence and may on summary conviction thereof be punished accordingly.

(5) . . . [3]

(5A) . . . [1]

(6) . . . [3]

(7) In any proceedings for an offence mentioned in this regulation it shall be a defence for the accused to prove that he took all reasonable precautions and exercised all due diligence to avoid the commission of such an offence by himself, any person under his control or any person to whom he transferred the task of providing information in accordance with [and subject to Article 7(2) of the establishing Regulation][2].

[(8) Liability to a penalty under paragraphs (1) and (2) does not arise in relation to a failure under paragraph (1) of regulation 4 if a party satisfies the Commissioners that there is a reasonable excuse for the failure.

(9) For the purposes of paragraph (8), where a party relies on any other person to do anything, that is not a reasonable excuse unless that party took reasonable care to avoid the relevant act or failure.][4]

Amendments—[1] Para (5A) and words in para (6) revoked by Statistics of Trade (Customs and Excise) (Amendment) Regulations, SI 1997/2864 reg 7 with effect from 1 January 1998.
[2] Words in paras (1), (2), (3), (7) substituted by the Statistics of Trade (Customs and Excise) (Amendment) Regulations, SI 2004/3284 regs 1(3), 4(2)–(6) with effect in relation to acts, or omissions, occurring after 31 December 2004.
[3] Words in para (2) revoked, and paras (5), (6) revoked, by SI 2004/3284 regs 1(3), 5, Schedule with effect from 1 January 2005.
[4] Paras (8), (9) inserted by the Statistics of Trade (Customs and Excise) (Amendment) Regulations, SI 2012/532 reg 4 with effect from 1 April 2012.
[5] In sub-para (3)(a), (b) word "other" revoked by the Statistics of Trade (Amendment etc) (EU Exit) Regulations, SI 2019/47 reg 6(1), (10). This amendment came into force immediately before IP completion day (11pm on 31 December 2020) (see SI 2019/47 reg 1 and EU(WA)A 2020 Sch 5 para 1(1)).

7—

(1) In any legal proceedings, whether civil or criminal, where any question arises concerning a document furnished[, provided, delivered][2] or created for the purposes of the Intrastat system this regulation shall apply.

(2) Where any document does not consist of legible visual images its . . . [1] content may be proved in any proceedings by production of a copy of the information in the form of legible visual images.

Amendments—[1] Words in para (2) revoked by Statistics of Trade (Customs and Excise) (Amendment) Regulations, SI 1993/541 reg 7 with effect from 1 April 1993.
[2] Words in para (1) inserted by the Statistics of Trade (Customs and Excise) (Amendment) Regulations, SI 2004/3284 regs 1(3), 4(7) with effect in relation to acts, or omissions, occurring after 31 December 2004.

8—(1) A certificate of the Commissioners—
   (a) that a person was or was not a party responsible for providing information in accordance with the Intrastat system;
   (b) that a person was or was not mentioned in the register of intra-Community operators;
   (c) that any information required for purposes connected with the Intrastat system has not been given or had not been given at any date;
   (d) that a copy produced in accordance with paragraph (2) of regulation 7 above is, both as to form and content, identical to that received by electronic means in accordance with [regulation 4(1)][2] above

shall be sufficient evidence of that fact until the contrary is proved.
(2) A photograph of any document furnished[, provided or delivered][1] to the Commissioners for the purposes of these Regulations and certified by them to be such a photograph shall be admissible in any proceedings, whether civil or criminal, to the same extent as the document itself.
(3) Any document purporting to be a certificate under paragraph (1) or (2) above shall be deemed to be such a certificate until the contrary is proved.

Amendments—[1] Words in para (2) inserted, by the Statistics of Trade (Customs and Excise) (Amendment) Regulations, SI 2004/3284 regs 1(3), 4(8), (9) with effect in relation to acts, or omissions, occurring after 31 December 2004.
[2] Words in para (1)(d) substituted by the Statistics of Trade (Customs and Excise) (Amendment) Regulations, SI 2012/532 reg 5 with effect from 1 April 2012.

9   Access to recorded information
(1) Where, on an application by an authorised person, a justice of the peace or, in Scotland, a justice (within the meaning of section 462 of the Criminal Procedure (Scotland) Act 1975) is satisfied that there are reasonable grounds for believing—
   (a) that an offence in connection with the Intrastat system is being, has been or is about to be committed, and
   (b) that any recorded information (including any document of any nature whatsoever) which may be required as evidence for the purpose of any proceedings in respect of such an offence is in the possession of any person,

he may make an order in accordance with this regulation.
(2) An order made in accordance with this regulation is an order that the person who appears to the justice to be in possession of the recorded information to which the application relates shall—
   (a) give an authorised person access to it, and
   (b) permit an authorised person to remove and take away any of it which he reasonably considers necessary,

not later than the end of the period of seven days beginning on the date of the order or the end of such longer period as the order may specify.
(3) The reference in sub-paragraph (2)(a) above to giving an authorised person access to the recorded information to which the application relates includes a reference to permitting the authorised person to take copies of it or to make extracts from it.
(4) Where the recorded information consists of information contained in a computer, an order made in accordance with this regulation shall have effect as an order to produce the information in a form in which it is visible and legible and, if the authorised person wishes to remove it, in a form in which it can be removed.

10—(1) An authorised person who removes anything in the exercise of a power conferred by or under regulation 9 above shall, if so requested by a person showing himself—
   (a) to be the occupier of premises from which it was removed, or
   (b) to have had custody or control of it immediately before the removal,

provide that person with a record of what he removed.
(2) The authorised person shall provide the record within a reasonable time from the making of the request for it.
(3) Subject to paragraph (7) below, if a request for permission to be granted access to anything which—
   (a) has been removed by an authorised person, and
   (b) is retained by the Commissioners for the purpose of investigating an offence,

is made to the officer in overall charge of the investigation by a person who had custody or control of the thing immediately before it was so removed or by someone acting on behalf of such a person, the officer shall allow the person who made the request access to it under the supervision of an authorised person.

(4) Subject to paragraph (7) below, if a request for a photograph or copy of any such thing is made to the officer in overall charge of the investigation by a person who had custody or control of the thing immediately before it was so removed, or by someone acting on behalf of such a person, the officer shall—
    (a) allow the person who made the request access to it under the supervision of an authorised person for the purpose of photographing it or copying it; or
    (b) photograph or copy it, or cause it to be photographed or copied.
(5) Where anything is photographed or copied under sub-paragraph (4)(b) above the photograph or copy shall be supplied to the person who made the request.
(6) The photograph or copy shall be supplied within a reasonable time from the making of the request.
(7) There is no duty under this regulation to grant access to, or to supply a photograph or copy of, anything if the officer in overall charge of the investigation for the purposes of which it was removed has reasonable grounds for believing that to do so would prejudice—
    (a) that investigation;
    (b) the investigation of an offence other than the offence for the purposes of the investigation of which the thing was removed; or
    (c) any criminal proceedings which may be brought as a result of—
        (i) the investigation of which he is in charge, or
        (ii) any such investigation as is mentioned in sub-paragraph (b) above.
(8) Any reference in this regulation to the officer in overall charge of the investigation is a reference to the person whose name and address are endorsed on the order concerned as being the officer so in charge.

11—(1) Where, on an application made as mentioned in paragraph (2) below, the appropriate judicial authority is satisfied that a person has failed to comply with a requirement imposed by regulation 10 above, the authority may order that person to comply with the requirement within such time and in such manner as may be specified in the order.
(2) An application under paragraph (1) above shall be made—
    (a) in the case of a failure to comply with any of the requirements imposed by paragraphs (1) and (2) of regulation 10 above, by the occupier of the premises from which the thing in question was removed or by the person who had custody or control of it immediately before it was so removed, and
    (b) in any other case, by the person who has such custody or control.
(3) In this regulation "the appropriate judicial authority" means—
    (a) in England and Wales, a magistrates' court;
    (b) in Scotland, the sheriff; and
    (c) in Northern Ireland, a court of summary jurisdiction, as defined in Article 2 (2) (a) of the Magistrates' Court (Northern Ireland) Order 1981.
(4) In England and Wales and Northern Ireland, an application for an order under this regulation shall be made by way of complaint; and sections 21 and 42(2) of the Interpretation Act (Northern Ireland) 1954 shall apply as if any reference in those provisions to any enactment included a reference to this regulation.

12 Supplementary
Where in connection with the operation of the Intrastat system a person is convicted of an offence contrary to section 167(1) or section 168(1) of the Act, section 167(2)(a) and section 168(2)(a) of the Act shall have effect as if, in each case, for the words "6 months" there were substituted the words "3 months".

[**13** The following provisions of the Act shall apply to these Regulations as they apply to the customs and excise Acts—
    Sections 145 to 148 (proceedings for offences, etc);
    Sections 150 to 154 (incidental provisions as to legal proceedings, mitigation of penalties, proof and other matters).][1]

Amendments—[1] This regulation added by Statistics of Trade (Customs and Excise) (Amendment No 2) Regulations, SI 1993/3015 regs 2, 4 with effect from 1 January 1994.

1992/3111

VALUE ADDED TAX (REMOVAL OF GOODS) ORDER 1992

Made by the Treasury under VATA 1983 s 3(3) (see now VATA 1994 s 5(3)) and all other enabling powers

Made . . . . .9 December 1992
Laid before the House of Commons . . . . .11 December 1992

Coming into force .... *1 January 1993*

1 This Order may be cited as the Value Added Tax (Removal of Goods) Order 1992 and shall come into force on 1st January 1993.

2 In this Order—
"the Act" means the Value Added Tax Act [1994][1];
["departure country" means the member State or Northern Ireland (as the case may be) from which the goods mentioned in paragraph 30 of Schedule 9ZB to the Act are removed;
"destination country" means the member State or Northern Ireland (as the case may be) to which the goods mentioned in paragraph 30 of Schedule 9ZB to the Act are removed;][1]
. . . [1]
. . . [1]
"the owner" means the person [referred to in paragraph 30(1) of Schedule 9ZB to the Act][1] who is carrying on the business of which the goods form part of the assets;
. . . [1]
"temporary importation relief" means relief [under the temporary admission procedure provided for in Union customs legislation][1], other than partial relief, from payment of any duty incurred on the entry of goods into the territory of [Northern Ireland or a member State;][1]
["Union customs legislation" has the same meaning as in paragraph 1(8) of Schedule 9ZB to the Act.][1]

Amendments—[1] In the definition of "the Act" year substituted for "1983", definitions "departure country", "destination country" and "Union customs legislation" inserted, definitions "the member State of arrival", "the member State of dispatch" and "registered" revoked, in definition of "the owner" words inserted, in definition of "temporary importation relief" words inserted and substituted by the Value Added Tax (Miscellaneous Amendments, Northern Ireland Protocol and Savings and Transitional Provisions) (EU Exit) Regulations, SI 2020/1545 regs 3, 4 with effect from IP completion day (11pm UK time on 31 December 2020) by virtue of SI 2020/1641 reg 2, Schedule para 11.
The definitions "the member State of arrival", "the member State of dispatch" and "registered" previously read as follows—
""the member State of arrival" means the member State to which the goods are removed;
"the member State of dispatch" means the member State from which the goods are removed;
"registered" means either registered under the Act or registered under the provisions of the law of another member State corresponding thereto;"

3 For the purposes of this Order, a person is treated as being established in a [Northern Ireland or a member State (as the case may be)][1] if he has there a business establishment or some other fixed establishment or carries on a business there through a branch or agency.

Amendments—[1] Words substituted for words "a member State" by the Value Added Tax (Miscellaneous Amendments, Northern Ireland Protocol and Savings and Transitional Provisions) (EU Exit) Regulations, SI 2020/1545 regs 3, 5 with effect from IP completion day (11pm UK time on 31 December 2020) by virtue of SI 2020/1641 reg 2, Schedule para 11.

4 Subject to article 5 below, [paragraph 30(1) and (2) of Schedule 9ZB][5] to the Act[1] shall not apply to the following removals of goods from a member State to a place in any other member State—
   (*a*) where the supply of the goods would be treated as having been made [in a place][5] other than the [departure country][5] by virtue of [section 7(3) of, or paragraph 29 of Schedule 9ZB to,][5] the Act;[2]
   (*b*) where the supply of the goods would be treated as having been made in the [departure country][5] by virtue of the Value Added Tax (Place of Supply of Goods) Order [2004][5];
   (*c*) where the goods have been removed by or under the directions of the owner for the purpose of—
      (i) his delivering them to a person to whom he is supplying those goods; or
      (ii) his taking possession of them from a person who is supplying those goods to him,
      and that supply is or will be zero-rated by virtue of [section 30(6) to (8) of, or paragraph 17(3) of Schedule 9ZA to,][5] the Act;[3]
   (*d*) . . . [4]
   [(*e*) where—
      (i) the goods have been removed [to a place in the destination country][5] for the purpose of delivering them to a person (other than the owner) who is to value or carry out any work on them [in that place][5]; and
      (ii) the owner intends that the goods will be returned to him by their removal to the [departure country][5] upon completion of the valuation or work;][4]
   (*f*) where—
      (i) the owner is established in the [departure country][5] and is not established in the [destination country][5];
      (ii) they are removed for the sole purpose of their being used by the owner in the course of a supply of services to be made by him;

(iii) at the time of their removal there exists a legally binding obligation to make that supply of services; and

(iv) the owner intends to remove them to the [departure country]⁵ upon his ceasing to use them in the course of making the supply;

(g) where—

(i) temporary importation relief would have been afforded had the goods been imported from a place outside the member States [and Northern Ireland]⁵; and

[(ii) the owner intends, before the end of the period of two years beginning with the day on which the goods were removed, to—

(aa) export the goods to a place outside the EU and Northern Ireland,

(bb) remove the goods from Northern Ireland to Great Britain, or

(cc) remove the goods to a place in Northern Ireland or a member State (as the case may be) other than the destination country;]⁵

(h) where the goods are removed in accordance with an intention described in paragraph [(e)]⁴, (f)(iv) or (g)(ii) above;

(i) . . . ⁴

Amendments—¹ VATA 1994 Sch 4 para 6.
2   VATA 1994 s 7(3)–(5).
3   VATA 1994 s 30(6), (8).
4   Paras (d), (i) revoked, para (e) substituted, and in para (h) reference substituted for reference "(d)(iii)", by the VAT (Removal of Goods) (Amendment) Order, SI 2012/2953 art 2(1), (2) with effect from 1 January 2013.
5   The following amendments made by the Value Added Tax (Miscellaneous Amendments, Northern Ireland Protocol and Savings and Transitional Provisions) (EU Exit) Regulations, SI 2020/1545 regs 3, 6 with effect from IP completion day (11pm UK time on 31 December 2020) by virtue of SI 2020/1641 reg 2, Schedule para 11:
- Words substituted for words "paragraph 5A of Schedule 2"
- in para (a) words substituted for words "in a member State", "member State of dispatch", and "section 6(2A), (2B) or (2C) of"
- in para (b) words substituted for words "member State of dispatch" and "1992,"
- in para (c) words substituted for words "section 16(6) or (7) of"
- in para (e) words substituted for words "to another member State", "in that member State" and "member State of dispatch"
- in para (f) words substituted for words "member State of dispatch", in both places, and "member State of arrival"
- in para (g) words inserted and sub-para (ii) substituted.

Sub-para (g)(ii) previously read as follows—

"(ii) the owner intends to export the goods to a place outside the member States or remove them to a member State other than the member State of arrival, in either case, not later than 2 years after the day upon which the goods were removed;"

5 In the case of a removal falling within paragraph [(e)]¹, (f) or (g) above, it shall be a condition of [paragraph 30(1) and (2) of Schedule 9ZB]³ to the Act² not applying that the relevant intention of the owner is fulfilled.

Amendments—¹ Reference substituted for reference "(d)" by the VAT (Removal of Goods) (Amendment) Order, SI 2012/2953 art 2(1), (3) with effect from 1 January 2013.
2   VATA 1994 Sch 4 para 6.
3   Words substituted for words "paragraph 5A of Schedule 2" by the Value Added Tax (Miscellaneous Amendments, Northern Ireland Protocol and Savings and Transitional Provisions) (EU Exit) Regulations, SI 2020/1545 regs 3, 7 with effect from IP completion day (11pm UK time on 31 December 2020) by virtue of SI 2020/1641 reg 2, Schedule para 11.

SCHEDULE
COMMUNITY LEGISLATION RELATING TO TEMPORARY IMPORTATION RELIEF

Article 2

Amendments—Schedule revoked by the Value Added Tax (Miscellaneous Amendments, Northern Ireland Protocol and Savings and Transitional Provisions) (EU Exit) Regulations, SI 2020/1545 regs 3, 8 with effect from IP completion day (11pm UK time on 31 December 2020) by virtue of SI 2020/1641 reg 2, Schedule para 11.

Council Regulation (EEC) No 3599/82
Council Regulation (EEC) No 1855/89
Council Regulation (EEC) No 3312/89
Commission Regulation (EEC) No 2249/91.

1992/3122

VALUE ADDED TAX (CARS) ORDER 1992

Made by the Treasury under VATA 1983 ss 3(3), 3(5), 18(1), 18(2), 18(3), 18(4), 18(5), 18(6) and 29(2) (see now VATA 1994 ss 5(3), (5), 32(1)–(6), 43(2)) and all other enabling powers

Made . . . . 9 December 1992
Laid before the House of Commons . . . . 11 December 1992

(2) The condition referred to in paragraph (1)(*b*) and (*c*) above is that the tax on the supply to, ...³ or importation by, the taxable person of the motor car or the vehicle from which it was converted, as the case may be, was not wholly excluded from credit under section 25 of the Act.
[(2A) For the purposes of paragraph (1)(*d*) above a person is a predecessor of a transferor if—
  (*a*) he transferred the motor car as an asset of a business or part of a business which he transferred as a going concern—
    (i) to the transferor, or
    (ii) where the motor car has been the subject of more than one such transfer, to a person who made one of those transfers; and
  (*b*) the transfer of the motor car was treated as neither a supply of goods nor a supply of services by virtue of any Order made or having effect as if made under section 5(3) of the Act.]²
[(3) Where a motor car to which this article applies—
  (*a*) has not been supplied by the taxable person in the course or furtherance of a business carried on by him; and
  (*b*) is used by him such that had it been supplied to, or imported ...³ by him at that time, his entitlement to credit under section 25 of the Act in respect of the VAT chargeable on such a supply [or importation]³ would have been wholly excluded by virtue of article 7 of the Value Added Tax (Input Tax) Order 1992,
it shall be treated for the purposes of the Act as both supplied to him for the purposes of a business carried on by him and supplied by him for the purposes of that business.]²]¹

Amendments—¹ This article substituted by the VAT (Cars) (Amendment) (No 2) Order, SI 1995/1667 arts 2, 5 with effect from 1 August 1995.
² Word "or" at end of para (1)(*b*) revoked, words at end of para (1), and para (3), substituted, and para (2A) inserted, by the VAT (Cars) (Amendment) Order, SI 1999/2832, arts 2, 5, 6, 7, with effect from 1 December 1999.
³ In para (1)(*c*) words "or acquired from another member State" revoked, in para (2) words "or acquisition" revoked, in para (3)(*b*) words "or acquired from another member State" revoked and words " ", importation or acquisition from another member State" substituted, by the Value Added Tax (Miscellaneous Amendments and Revocations) (EU Exit) Regulations, SI 2019/59 reg 5(1), (3) with effect from IP completion day (11pm UK time on 31 December 2020).

7 [Article 5]² above shall apply in relation to any bodies corporate which are treated for the purposes of section [43]¹ of the Act as members of a group as if those bodies were one person, but any motor car which would fall to be treated as supplied to and by that person shall be treated as supplied to and by the representative member.

Amendments—¹ Figure substituted for the figure "29" by the VAT (Cars) (Amendment) Order, SI 1995/1269 art 6 with effect from 1 June 1995.
² Words substituted by the VAT (Cars) (Amendment) Order, SI 1999/2832, arts 2, 9, with effect from 1 December 1999.

[8 Relief for second-hand motor cars
(1) Subject to complying with such conditions (including the keeping of such records and accounts) as the Commissioners may direct in a notice published by them for the purposes of this Order or may otherwise direct, and subject to paragraph (3) below, where a person supplies a used motor car which he took possession of in any of the circumstances set out in paragraph (2) below, he may opt to account for the VAT chargeable on the supply on the profit margin on the supply instead of by reference to its value.
(2) The circumstances referred to in paragraph (1) above are that the taxable person took possession of the motor car pursuant to—
  (*a*) a supply in respect of which no VAT was chargeable under the Act or under Part I of the Manx Act;
  (*b*) a supply on which VAT was chargeable on the profit margin in accordance with paragraph (1) above, ...⁶ [or a corresponding provision of the law of a member State where the motor car is removed to Northern Ireland]⁷;
  [(*bb*) a supply [received before 1 March 2000]³ to which the provisions of article 7(4) of the Value Added Tax (Input Tax) Order 1992 applied;]²
  [(*c*) a de-supplied transaction, other than an article 5 transaction;
  (*d*) subject to paragraph (2A) below, an article 5 transaction.]⁵
[(2A) An article 5 transaction does not fall within sub-paragraph (*d*) of paragraph (2) above unless the taxable person has a relevant predecessor in title.]⁵
(3) This article does not apply to—
  (*a*) a supply which is a letting on hire;
  (*b*) the supply by any person of a motor car which was produced by him, if it was neither previously supplied by him in the course or furtherance of any business carried on by him nor treated as so supplied by virtue of article 5 above;
  (*c*) any supply if an invoice or similar document showing an amount as being VAT or as being attributable to VAT is issued in respect of the supply;
  (*d*) ...²
  [(*e*) the supply by any person of a used motor car if the person took possession of that motor car in Great Britain, or the Isle of Man, and it is removed to Northern Ireland.]⁷

(4) . . .²

(5) Subject to paragraph (6) below, for the purposes of determining the profit margin—
   (a) the price at which the motor car was obtained shall be calculated as follows—
      (i) (where the taxable person took possession of the used motor car pursuant to a supply) in the same way as the consideration for the supply would be calculated for the purposes of the Act;
      (ii) (where the taxable person is a sole proprietor and the used motor car was supplied to him in his private capacity) in the same way as the consideration for the supply to him as a private individual would be calculated for the purposes of the Act;
      [(iii) (where the taxable person took possession of the motor car pursuant to a de-supplied transaction, other than an article 5 transaction) by taking the price he paid pursuant to the transaction;
      (iv) (where the taxable person took possession of the motor car pursuant to an article 5 transaction) by taking the price at which his relevant predecessor in title obtained the motor car;]⁵
   (b) the price at which the motor car is sold shall be calculated in the same way as the consideration for the supply would be calculated for the purposes of the Act;
   (c) . . .⁵

(6) Subject to paragraph (7) below, where the taxable person is an agent acting in his own name the price at which the motor car was obtained shall be calculated in accordance with paragraph 5(a) above but the selling price calculated in accordance with paragraph 5(b) above shall be increased by the amount of any consideration payable to the taxable person in respect of services supplied by him to the purchaser in connection with the supply of the motor car.

(7) Instead of calculating the price at which the motor car was obtained or supplied in accordance with paragraph (6) above, an auctioneer acting in his own name may—
   [(a) calculate the price at which the motor car was obtained by deducting from the successful bid the amount of the commission payable to him under his contract with the vendor for the sale of the motor car;]⁴
   (b) calculate the price at which the motor car was supplied by adding to the successful bid the consideration for any supply of services by him to the purchaser in connection with the sale of the motor car,

in either (or both) cases excluding the consideration for supplies of services that are not chargeable to VAT.]¹.

[(8) For the purposes of this article—
   "article 5 transaction" means a transaction which is a de-supplied transaction by virtue of a provision of article 5 of the Value Added Tax (Special Provisions) Order 1995 or a corresponding provision made under the Manx Act;
   "de-supplied transaction" means a transaction which was treated by virtue of any Order made or having effect as if made under section 5(3) of the Act or under the corresponding provisions of the Manx Act as being neither a supply or goods nor a supply of services.]⁵

[(9) For the purposes of this article a person is a relevant predecessor in title of a taxable person if—
   (a) he is the person from whom the taxable person took possession of the motor car and himself took possession of it pursuant to a transaction within any of sub-paragraphs (a) to (c) of sub-paragraph (2) above; or
   (b) where the motor car has been the subject of a succession of two or more article 5 transactions (culminating in the article 5 transaction to which the taxable person was a party), he was a party to one of those transactions and himself took possession of the motor car pursuant to a transaction within any of sub-paragraphs (a) to (c) of sub-paragraph (2) above.]⁵

Amendments—¹ This article substituted by the VAT (Cars) (Amendment) Order, SI 1995/1269 art 7 with effect from 1 June 1995.
² Para (2)(bb) inserted and paras (3)(d), (4) revoked by the VAT (Cars) (Amendment) (No 2) Order, SI 1995/1667 art 8 with effect from 1 August 1995.
³ In para 8(2)(bb) words inserted by the VAT (Cars) (Amendment) Order, SI 1999/2832, arts 2, 10, with effect from 1 March 2000.
⁴ Para (7)(a) substituted by the VAT (Cars) (Amendment) Order, SI 2001/3754 art 3 with effect from 2 January 2002.
⁵ Sub-paras (2)(c), (d) substituted, sub-paras (5)(a)(iii), (iv) substituted for sub-para (5)(a)(iii), sub-para (5)(c) revoked, and paras (8), (9) added, by the VAT (Cars) (Amendment) Order, SI 2002/1502 with effect from 1 July 2002. For further provisions as to the effect of that Order see SI 2002/1502 art 1(2).
⁶ In para (2)(b) words "or a corresponding provision of the law of another member State" revoked by the Value Added Tax (Miscellaneous Amendments and Revocations) (EU Exit) Regulations, SI 2019/59 reg 5(1), (4) with effect from IP completion day (11pm UK time on 31 December 2020).
⁷ In para (2)(b) words inserted, and sub-para (3)(e) inserted, by the Value Added Tax (Miscellaneous Amendments, Northern Ireland Protocol and Savings and Transitional Provisions) (EU Exit) Regulations, SI 2020/1545 regs 9, 11 with effect from IP completion day (11pm UK time on 31 December 2020) by virtue of SI 2020/1641 reg 2, Schedule para 11.
Sub-para (3)(e) does not apply where—

(a) a person ("P") took possession of the used motor car in Great Britain or the Isle of Man before IP completion day and P would have been eligible to opt to account for the VAT chargeable on a supply of the motor car on the profit margin in accordance with article 8 had it been so supplied before IP completion day; and

(b) the ownership of the used motor car remained with P from the time P took possession of it under paragraph (a) to the time of the supply of the motor car on which P elects to account for the VAT chargeable on that supply on the profit margin in accordance with article 8 (see SI 2020/1545 reg 121).

[8A Relief for second-hand motor cars removed from Northern Ireland to Great Britain
Article 8 has effect as if in paragraph (1)—

(1) after "in any of the circumstances set out in paragraph (2) below" there were inserted "and the supply involves the removal of a motor car from Northern Ireland to Great Britain"; and

(2) for "VAT chargeable on the supply" there were substituted "VAT chargeable on the removal".][1]

Amendments—[1] Article 8A inserted by the Value Added Tax (Miscellaneous Amendments, Northern Ireland Protocol and Savings and Transitional Provisions) (EU Exit) Regulations, SI 2020/1545 regs 9, 12 with effect from IP completion day (11pm UK time on 31 December 2020) by virtue of SI 2020/1641 reg 2, Schedule para 11.

1992/3124

VALUE ADDED TAX (IMPORTED GOLD) RELIEF ORDER 1992

Made by the Treasury under VATA 1983 s 19(1) (see now VATA 1994 s 37(1)) and all other enabling powers

Made . . . . 9 December 1992
Laid before the House of Commons . . . . 11 December 1992
Coming into force . . . . 1 January 1993

1 This Order may be cited as the Value Added Tax (Imported Gold) Relief Order 1992 and shall come into force on 1st January 1993.

2 The tax chargeable upon the importation of gold (including gold coins) . . . [1] shall not be payable where the importation is by a Central Bank.

Amendments—[1] Words "from a place outside the Member States" revoked by the Value Added Tax (Miscellaneous Amendments and Revocations) (EU Exit) Regulations, SI 2019/59 reg 6 with effect from IP completion day (11pm UK time on 31 December 2020).

3 The Value Added Tax (Imported Goods) Relief Order 1977 is hereby revoked.

1992/3130

VALUE ADDED TAX (SUPPLY OF TEMPORARILY IMPORTED GOODS) ORDER 1992

Made by the Treasury under VATA 1983 s 3(3) (see now VATA 1994 s 5(3)) and all other enabling powers

Made . . . . 9 December 1992
Laid before the House of Commons . . . . 11 December 1992
Coming into force . . . . 1 January 1993

1 This Order may be cited as the Value Added Tax (Supply of Temporarily Imported Goods) Order 1992 and shall come into force on 1st January 1993.

2—(1) Where goods held under [a temporary admission procedure][1] [in Great Britain][2] are supplied, that supply shall be treated as neither a supply of goods nor a supply of services provided that—

[(a) the conditions for getting full relief from import duty under regulation 40 of the Customs (Special Procedures and Outward Processing) (EU Exit) Regulations 2018 continue to be met; and][1]

(b) the supply is to a person established outside [Great Britain][2].

[(2) "Goods held under a temporary admission procedure" means goods declared for a temporary admission procedure under Part 1 of the Taxation (Cross-border Trade) Act 2018, for which full relief from a liability to import duty is to be given under regulation 40 of the Customs (Special Procedures and Outward Processing) (EU Exit) Regulations 2018.][1]

Amendments—[1] In para (1) words "temporary importation arrangements" substituted, para (1)(a) substituted, in para (1)(b) words "member States" substituted, and para (2) substituted, by the Value Added Tax (Miscellaneous Amendments and Revocations) (EU Exit) Regulations, SI 2019/59 reg 7 with effect from IP completion day (11pm UK time on 31 December 2020). Para (1)(a) previously read as follows—

"(a) the goods remain eligible for temporary importation arrangements; and"
Para (2) previously read as follows—
"(2) "Goods held under temporary importation arrangements" means goods placed under customs arrangements with total relief from customs duty within the meaning of Council Regulation (EEC) No 3599/82, whether or not the goods are subject to customs duty."
2 In para (1) words inserted and words substituted for words "the United Kingdom" by the Value Added Tax (Miscellaneous Amendments, Northern Ireland Protocol and Savings and Transitional Provisions) (EU Exit) Regulations, SI 2020/1545 regs 13, 14 with effect from IP completion day (11pm UK time on 31 December 2020) by virtue of SI 2020/1641 reg 2, Schedule para 11.

[3—(1) Where goods held under temporary importation arrangements in Northern Ireland are supplied, that supply shall be treated as neither a supply of goods nor a supply of services provided that—
(a) the goods remain eligible for temporary importation arrangements; and
(b) the supply is to a person established outside Northern Ireland and the member States.
(2) In this article—
"goods held under temporary importation arrangements" means goods placed under the temporary admission procedure provided for in Union customs legislation, with total relief from customs duty, whether or not the goods are subject to customs duty.
"Union customs legislation" has the same meaning as in paragraph 1(8) of Schedule 9ZB to the Value Added Tax Act 1994.][1]
Amendments—[1] Article 3 inserted by the Value Added Tax (Miscellaneous Amendments, Northern Ireland Protocol and Savings and Transitional Provisions) (EU Exit) Regulations, SI 2020/1545 regs 13, 15 with effect from IP completion day (11pm UK time on 31 December 2020) by virtue of SI 2020/1641 reg 2, Schedule para 11.

1992/3132

VALUE ADDED TAX (TREATMENT OF TRANSACTIONS) (NO 2) ORDER 1992

Made by the Treasury under VATA 1983 s 8A(4) (see now VATA 1994 s 11(4)) and all other enabling powers

Made . . . . .9 December 1992
Laid before the House of Commons . . . . .11 December 1992
Coming into force . . . . .1 January 1993

1 This Order may be cited as the Value Added Tax (Treatment of Transactions) (No 2) Order 1992, and shall come into force on 1st January 1993.

2—[(1) Where gold is supplied to a Central Bank by a supplier, and the transaction involves the removal of the gold from a member State to Northern Ireland, the taking possession of the gold by the Central Bank concerned is not to be treated for the purposes of the Value Added Tax Act 1994 as the acquisition in Northern Ireland of goods from a member State.][1]
(2) For the purposes of this article, gold includes gold coins.
Transitional provision—Where there is a removal of gold as described in SI 1992/3132 art 2, and acquisition VAT would (but for the provisions made in SI 1992/3132) be charged on or after IP completion day, in accordance with transitional provision made in SI 2020/1545 or other regulations made under TCTA 2018, the treatment of the acquisition of gold specified continues to apply as if the SI 1992/3132 had not been amended by SI 2020/1545 (see the Value Added Tax (Miscellaneous Amendments, Northern Ireland Protocol and Savings and Transitional Provisions) (EU Exit) Regulations, SI 2020/1545 reg 122).
Amendments—[1] Para (1) substituted by the Value Added Tax (Miscellaneous Amendments, Northern Ireland Protocol and Savings and Transitional Provisions) (EU Exit) Regulations, SI 2020/1545 reg 16 with effect from IP completion day (11pm UK time on 31 December 2020) by virtue of SI 2020/1641 reg 2, Schedule para 11. Para (1) previously read as follows—
"(1) Where gold is supplied to a Central Bank by a supplier in another member State, and the transaction involves the removal of the gold from that or some other member State to the United Kingdom, the taking possession of the gold by the Central Bank concerned is not to be treated for the purposes of the Value Added Tax Act 1983 as the acquisition of goods from another member State."

1992/3156

CUSTOMS AND EXCISE (PERSONAL RELIEFS FOR SPECIAL VISITORS) ORDER 1992

Made by the Commissioners of Customs and Excise under the Customs and Excise Duties (General Reliefs) Act 1979 s 13A and all other enabling powers

Made . . . . .10 December 1992
Laid before the House of Commons . . . . .11 December 1992
Coming into force . . . . .1 January 1993

PART I
PRELIMINARY

1 This Order may be cited as the Customs and Excise (Personal Reliefs for Special Visitors) Order 1992 and shall come into force on 1st January 1993.

PART II
INTERPRETATION

2 In this Order—

["acquisition" means an acquisition of goods from a member State within the meaning given in paragraph 3 of Schedule 9ZA to the Value Added Tax Act 1994 and "acquired" shall be construed accordingly;][4]

"duty" means any duty of customs or duty of excise;

"importation" means an importation from a place outside the [United Kingdom][3], and "imported" shall be construed accordingly;

"relief" means the remission of any duty or tax which is chargeable and which a person, whether the person upon whom the relief is conferred or some other person, would be liable to pay were it not for the relief conferred;

"supply" means a supply within the meaning of section 3 of the Value Added Tax Act 1983[1] and "supplied" shall be construed accordingly;

"tax" means value added tax;

"United Kingdom national" means a British citizen, a British Dependent Territories citizen, a British National (Overseas) or a British Overseas citizen;

"used", in relation to a person's use of consumable property, includes having the property at his disposal;

"warehouse" means a warehouse within the meaning of section 1(1) of the Customs and Excise Management Act 1979 [the premises in respect of which a person is registered under section 41A, 47, or 62(2) of the Alcoholic Liquor Duties Act 1979, the premises in respect of which a person holds an excise licence under section 54(2) or 55(2) of that Act, or premises registered for the safe storage of tobacco products in accordance with regulations made under section 7(1)(b) of the Tobacco Products Duty Act 1979;][2] and "removal from warehouse" shall be construed accordingly.

Notes—[1] VATA 1994 s 5.
[2] Words in definition of "warehouse" inserted by the Customs and Excise (Personal Reliefs for Special Visitors) (Amendment) Order, SI 2007/5 arts 1, 2 with effect from 1 February 2007.
[3] In the definition of "importation," words substituted for words "member States" by the Value Added Tax and Excise Personal Reliefs (Special Visitors and Goods Permanently Imported) (Amendment) (EU Exit) Regulations, SI 2019/91 regs 2, 3 with effect from IP completion day (11pm UK time on 31 December 2020) by virtue of SI 2020/1641 reg 2, Schedule para 4.
[4] The definition of "acquisition" substituted by the Value Added Tax (Miscellaneous Amendments, Northern Ireland Protocol and Savings and Transitional Provisions) (EU Exit) Regulations, SI 2020/1545 reg 17(1), (2) with effect from IP completion day (11pm UK time on 31 December 2020) by virtue of SI 2020/1641 reg 2, Schedule para 11. The definition of "acquisition" previously read as follows—

"'acquisition" means an acquisition of goods from another member State within the meaning of section 2A of the Value Added Tax Act 1983 and "acquired" shall be construed accordingly;"

PART III
CONDITIONS ATTACHING TO PART VI RELIEFS

3 In this Part—

"entitled person" means an entitled person for the purposes of Part VI.

4 It shall be a condition of the relief conferred under article 16 below that the entitled person deliver or cause to be delivered to the supplier of the motor vehicle a certificate in the form numbered 1 in the Schedule to this Order—

(*a*) containing full information in respect of the matters specified therein; and

(*b*) signed—

   (i) as to Part A, by the entitled person upon whom the relief is conferred;

   (ii) as to Part B, by the head of the mission or other body or organisation of which the entitled person is a member;

   (iii) as to Part C, by the Secretary of State or a person authorised to sign on his behalf; and

   (iv) as to Part D, by the supplier,

before the supply is made.

PART IV
CONDITIONS ATTACHING TO PART VII RELIEFS

5—(1) In this Part—
"entitled person" means an entitled person for the purposes of Part VII.
(2) For the purposes of articles 6 and 7 below, any reference to a certificate shall be construed as including a reference to a copy of such a certificate.

6—(1) It shall be a condition of relief conferred under article 19 below that the entitled person deliver or cause to be delivered in accordance with paragraph (2) below five certificates in the form numbered 2 in the Schedule to this Order—
   (*a*) containing full information in respect of the matters specified therein; and
   (*b*) signed—
      (i) as to Part A, by the entitled person upon whom the relief is conferred; and
      (ii) as to Part B, by the officer commanding the visiting force or other body or organisation of which the entitled person is a member or by a person authorised to sign on his behalf.
(2) The certificates referred to in paragraph (1) above shall be delivered before the supply is made as follows:
   (*a*) two certificates shall be delivered to the visiting force or other body or organisation of which the entitled person is a member;
   (*b*) two certificates shall be delivered to the proper officer; and
   (*c*) one certificate shall be delivered to the supplier of the motor vehicle.

7—(1) It shall be a condition of relief conferred under article 20 below in respect of a motor vehicle that the entitled person deliver or cause to be delivered in accordance with paragraph (2) below four certificates in the form numbered 3 in the Schedule to this Order—
   (*a*) containing full information in respect of the matters specified therein; and
   (*b*) signed—
      (i) as to Part A, by the entitled person upon whom the relief is conferred; and
      (ii) as to Part B, by the officer commanding the visiting force or other body or organisation of which the entitled person is a member or by a person authorised to sign on his behalf.
(2) The certificates referred to in paragraph (1) above shall be delivered before the goods are removed by or on behalf of the entitled person as follows:
   (*a*) one certificate shall be delivered to the visiting force or other body or organisation of which the entitled person is a member; and
   (*b*) three certificates shall be delivered to the proper officer.

[7A Nothing in this Order affords any relief from VAT charged under paragraph 3(2) of Schedule 9ZB(b) to the Value Added Tax Act 1994.[1]
Amendments—[1] Articles 7A and 7B inserted by the Value Added Tax (Miscellaneous Amendments, Northern Ireland Protocol and Savings and Transitional Provisions) (EU Exit) Regulations, SI 2020/1545 reg 17(1), (3) with effect from IP completion day (11pm UK time on 31 December 2020) by virtue of SI 2020/1641 reg 2, Schedule para 11.

[7B Article 21 applies in respect of tax where a gift of goods, other than tobacco products or beverages containing alcohol, is made to an entitled person by dispatching them to that person in Northern Ireland from Great Britain or the Isle of Man, as it applies where a gift of goods is made to an entitled person by dispatching them to the person from a place outside the United Kingdom.][1]
Amendments—[1] Articles 7A and 7B inserted by the Value Added Tax (Miscellaneous Amendments, Northern Ireland Protocol and Savings and Transitional Provisions) (EU Exit) Regulations, SI 2020/1545 reg 17(1), (3) with effect from IP completion day (11pm UK time on 31 December 2020) by virtue of SI 2020/1641 reg 2, Schedule para 11.

PART V
CONDITIONS ATTACHING TO ALL RELIEFS

8 In this Part—
"entitled person" means an entitled person for the purposes of either Part VI or Part VII of this Order.

9 An entitled person upon whom any relief is conferred under any Part of this Order shall be bound by the conditions described in the following provisions of this Part and in Part III or IV above, as the case may be.

10—(1) It shall be a condition of the relief that the goods shall not be lent, hired-out, given as security or transferred by the entitled person or any other person without the prior authorisation in writing of the Commissioners.

(2) Where the Commissioners authorise such disposal as is mentioned in paragraph (1) above, they may discharge the relief and the entitled person to whom the relief was afforded shall forthwith pay the duty or tax at the rate then in force, provided that where a lower rate was in force when relief was afforded the amount payable shall be determined by reference to the lower rate.

11 It shall be a condition of the relief that the goods are used exclusively by the entitled person or members of his family forming part of his household.

12 Where relief has been afforded and subsequently the Commissioners are not satisfied that any condition attaching to such relief, whether by virtue of a provision of this Order or otherwise, has been complied with, then, unless the Commissioners sanction the non-compliance in writing, the duty or tax shall become payable forthwith and the goods shall be liable to forfeiture.

13 Where relief has been afforded, but any duty or tax subsequently becomes payable by virtue of article 12 above, the following persons shall be jointly and severally liable to pay it—
(*a*) the entitled person upon whom the relief was conferred;
(*b*) any person who, at or after the time of the non-compliance with the condition which has caused the duty or tax to become payable, has been in possession of the goods.

PART VI
DIPLOMATS ETC

[**14** In this Part—
"entitled person" means any person who is neither a United Kingdom national nor a permanent resident of the United Kingdom and:
  (*a*) who enjoys any privilege or immunity by virtue of that person being –
    (i) a diplomatic agent for the purposes of the Diplomatic Privileges Act 1964,
    (ii) a senior officer of the Commonwealth Secretariat for the purposes of the Commonwealth Secretariat Act 1966
    (iii) a consular officer for the purposes of the Consular Relations Act 1968
    (iv) a representative or a person recognised as holding a rank equivalent to a diplomatic agent for the purposes of the International Organisations Act 1968, or
  (*b*) whose circumstances, at the time the duty or tax in respect of which relief is sought would otherwise become due, are such that had those circumstances existed immediately before exit day, that person would have enjoyed, under or by virtue of section 2 of the European Communities Act 1972, any privilege or immunity similar to those enjoyed under or by virtue of the enactments specified in paragraph (a) above by the persons therein specified.][1]

14 In this Part—
"entitled person" means:
  (*a*) any person enjoying any privilege or immunity by virtue of his being—
    (i) a diplomatic agent for the purposes of the Diplomatic Privileges Act 1964
    (ii) a senior officer of the Commonwealth Secretariat for the purposes of the Commonwealth Secretariat Act 1966
    (iii) a consular officer for the purposes of the Consular Relations Act 1968
    (iv) a representative or a person recognised as holding a rank equivalent to a diplomatic agent for the purposes of the International Organisations Act 1968 or
  (*b*) any person enjoying, under or by virtue of section 2 of the European Communities Act 1972 any privilege or immunity similar to those enjoyed under or by virtue of the enactments referred to in paragraph (*a*) above by the persons therein specified,
who is neither a United Kingdom national nor a permanent resident of the United Kingdom.

[1] Article 14 substituted by the Value Added Tax and Excise Personal Reliefs (Special Visitors and Goods Permanently Imported) (Amendment) (EU Exit) Regulations, SI 2019/91 regs 2, 4 with effect from IP completion day (11pm UK time on 31 December 2020) by virtue of SI 2020/1641 reg 2, Schedule para 4. Article 14 previously read as follows—

"**14**

In this Part—
"entitled person" means:
  (*a*) any person enjoying any privilege or immunity by virtue of his being—
    (i) a diplomatic agent for the purposes of the Diplomatic Privileges Act 1964
    (ii) a senior officer of the Commonwealth Secretariat for the purposes of the Commonwealth Secretariat Act 1966
    (iii) a consular officer for the purposes of the Consular Relations Act 1968

(iv) a representative or a person recognised as holding a rank equivalent to a diplomatic agent for the purposes of the International Organisations Act 1968 or

(b) any person enjoying, under or by virtue of section 2 of the European Communities Act 1972 any privilege or immunity similar to those enjoyed under or by virtue of the enactments referred to in paragraph (a) above by the persons therein specified,

who is neither a United Kingdom national nor a permanent resident of the United Kingdom."

15 Where any tobacco product or beverage containing alcohol is removed from warehouse in the course of its being supplied to an entitled person, payment of any duty or tax chargeable in respect of the removal from warehouse or supply shall not be required.

16—(1) Subject to the following provisions of this article, where an entitled person purchases a motor vehicle which has been manufactured in a country . . . [2] which is—
 (a) a member State; or
 (b) a member of the European Free Trade Association,
payment of any tax chargeable in respect of the supply shall not be required.
(2) No relief shall be afforded under paragraph (1) above if the entitled person has previously been afforded relief in respect of any other motor vehicle, whether under paragraph (1) above or otherwise, unless he has disposed of all previous motor vehicles in respect of which relief has been so afforded and paid any duty or tax which was required to be paid under article 10(2) above.
(3) Where the spouse [or civil partner][1] of the entitled person is present in the United Kingdom, paragraph (2) above shall apply as if the words "(or all but one)" were inserted after the words "motor vehicles".

Amendment—[1] Words in para (3) inserted by the Civil Partnership Act 2004 (Amendments to Subordinate Legislation) Order, SI 2005/2114 art 2(1), Sch 1 para 5 with effect from 5 December 2005.
[2] In para (1) words ", other than the United Kingdom," revoked by the Value Added Tax and Excise Personal Reliefs (Special Visitors and Goods Permanently Imported) (Amendment) (EU Exit) Regulations, SI 2019/91 regs 2, 5 with effect from IP completion day (11pm UK time on 31 December 2020) by virtue of SI 2020/1641 reg 2, Schedule para 4.

17 Nothing in this Part of this Order shall be taken as conferring relief in respect of any duty or tax which is subject to remission or refund by or under any of the enactments referred to in article 14 above.

PART VII
VISITING FORCES AND HEADQUARTERS

18 In this Part—
 "entitled person" means a person who is—
 (a) for the purposes of any provision of the Visiting Forces Act 1952 a serving member of a visiting force of a country, other than the United Kingdom, which is a party to the North Atlantic Treaty, or a person recognised by the Secretary of State as a member of a civilian component of such a force, or
 (b) a person who is a military or civilian member of a headquarters or organisation designated for the purposes of any provision of the International Headquarters and Defence Organisations Act 1964
 who is neither a United Kingdom national nor a permanent resident of the United Kingdom.

19 Subject to article 22 below, where an entitled person purchases a motor vehicle which has been manufactured in a country which is—
 (a) a member State; or
 (b) a member of the European Free Trade Association,
payment of any tax in respect of the supply shall not be required.

20 Subject to article 22 below, where an entitled person imports, acquires or removes from warehouse any goods, payment of any duty or tax chargeable in respect of the importation, acquisition or removal from warehouse shall not be required.

21 Subject to article 22 below, where a gift of goods, other than tobacco products or beverages containing alcohol, is made to an entitled person by dispatching them to him from a place outside the United Kingdom, payment of any duty or tax chargeable in respect of their acquisition or importation shall not be required.

22—(1) No relief shall be afforded under this Part of this Order in respect of a motor vehicle if the entitled person has previously been afforded relief under this Order in respect of any other motor vehicle, unless he has disposed of all previous motor vehicles in respect of which relief has been so afforded and paid any duty or tax which was required to be paid under article 10(2) above.

(2) Where the spouse [or civil partner]¹ of the entitled person is present in the United Kingdom, paragraph (1) above shall apply as if the words "(or all but one)" were inserted after the words "motor vehicles".

Amendment—¹ Words in para (2) inserted by the Civil Partnership Act 2004 (Amendments to Subordinate Legislation) Order, SI 2005/2114 art 2(1), Sch 1 para 5 with effect from 5 December 2005.

SCHEDULE
FORM NO 1—CERTIFICATE FOR USE IN CONNECTION WITH THE PURCHASE OF AN EC (NOT UK) OR EFTA ORIGIN VEHICLE FREE OF VALUE ADDED TAX (C 428) (ARTICLE 4).
FORM NO 2—VISITING FORCES' CERTIFICATE OF ENTITLEMENT TO RELIEF FROM DUTY AND VAT ON THE PURCHASE OF A MOTOR VEHICLE (C&E 941A) (ARTICLE 6(1)).
FORM NO 3—VISITING FORCES' CERTIFICATE OF ENTITLEMENT TO RELIEF FROM DUTY AND VAT ON THE IMPORT/WITHDRAWAL FROM WAREHOUSE OF A MOTOR VEHICLE (C 941) (ARTICLE 7(1)).

Note—Forms C428, C&E 941A, C941 not reproduced. These forms are available at www.legislation.gov.uk/uksi/1992/3156/schedule/made.

1992/3193

CUSTOMS AND EXCISE DUTIES (PERSONAL RELIEFS FOR GOODS PERMANENTLY IMPORTED) ORDER 1992

Made by the Commissioners of Customs and Excise under CED(GR)A 1979 ss 7, 13.

Made . . . . 16 December 1992
Laid before the House of Commons . . . . 17 December 1992
Coming into force . . . . 1 January 1993

PART I
PRELIMINARY

1 Citation and commencement
This order may be cited as the Customs and Excise Duties (Personal Reliefs for Goods Permanently Imported) Order 1992 and shall come into force on 1st January 1993.

2 Interpretation
In this Order—
["another country" means a country other than the United Kingdom]²
["customs procedure" has the meaning given by section 3(3) of the Taxation (Cross-border) Trade Act 2018.]²
"declared for relief" has the meaning assigned to it by article 8 below;
"household effects" means furnishing and equipment for personal household use;
"motor vehicle" shall include a trailer;
"normal residence" means a person's principal place of abode situated in the country where he is normally resident;
"normally resident" has the meaning assigned to it by article 3 below;
"occupational ties" shall not include attendance by a pupil or student at a school, college or university;
"personal ties" shall mean family or social ties to which a person devotes most of his time not devoted to occupational ties;
"property" means any personal property intended for personal use or for meeting household needs and shall include household effects, household provisions, household pets and riding animals, cycles, motor vehicles, caravans, pleasure boats and private aircraft, provided that there shall be excluded any goods which, by their nature or quantity, indicate that they are being imported for a commercial purpose;
["relevant NI import duty" has the meaning given in paragraph 1(8) of Schedule 9ZB to the Value Added Tax Act 1994"]¹
. . .¹
"used", in relation to a person's use of consumable property, shall include having the property at his disposal.

Amendments—¹ The definition of "relevant NI import duty" inserted, and the definition of "third country" revoked, by the Value Added Tax (Miscellaneous Amendments, Northern Ireland Protocol and Savings and Transitional Provisions) (EU Exit) Regulations, SI 2020/1545 reg 18(1), (2) with effect from IP completion day (11pm UK time on 31 December 2020) by virtue of SI 2020/1641 reg 2, Schedule para 11. The definition of "third country" previously read as follows—
""third country", shall have the meaning given by Article 3.1 of Council Directive 77/388/EEC;"

[2] The definitions of "another country" and "customs procedure" inserted by the Value Added Tax and Excise Personal Reliefs (Special Visitors and Goods Permanently Imported) (Amendment) (EU Exit) Regulations, SI 2019/91 regs 8, 9 with effect from IP completion day (11pm UK time on 31 December 2020) by virtue of SI 2020/1641 reg 2, Schedule para 4.

3 Rules for determining where a person is normally resident

(1) This article shall apply for the purpose of determining, in relation to this Order, where a person is normally resident.
(2) A person shall be treated as being normally resident in the country where he usually lives—
   (a) for a period of, or periods together amounting to, at least 185 days in a period of twelve months;
   (b) because of his occupational ties; and
   (c) because of his personal ties.
(3) In the case of a person with no occupational ties, paragraph (2) above shall apply with the omission of sub-paragraph (b), provided his personal ties show close links with that country.
(4) Where a person has his occupational ties in one country and his personal ties in [a different][1] country, he shall be treated as being normally resident in the latter country provided that either—
   (a) his stay in the former country is in order to carry out a task of a definite duration, or
   (b) he returns regularly to the country where he has his personal ties.
(5) Notwithstanding paragraph (4) above, a United Kingdom citizen whose personal ties are in the United Kingdom but whose occupational ties are in [another country][2] may for the purposes of relief under this Order be treated as normally resident in the country of his occupational ties, provided he has lived there for a period of, or periods together amounting to, at least 185 days in a period of twelve months.

Amendments—[1] Words substituted for words "another" by the Value Added Tax and Excise Personal Reliefs (Special Visitors and Goods Permanently Imported) (Amendment) (EU Exit) Regulations, SI 2019/91 regs 8, 10 with effect from IP completion day (11pm UK time on 31 December 2020) by virtue of SI 2020/1641 reg 2, Schedule para 4.
[2] In para (4) words substituted for words "another", and in para (5) words substituted for words "a third country", by the Value Added Tax and Excise Personal Reliefs (Special Visitors and Goods Permanently Imported) (Amendment) (EU Exit) Regulations, SI 2019/91 regs 8, 10 and 13 with effect from IP completion day (11pm UK time on 31 December 2020) by virtue of SI 2020/1641 reg 2, Schedule para 4.

4 Supplementary

For the purposes of this Order—
   (a) any reference to a person who has been normally resident in [another country][1] and who intends to become normally resident in the United Kingdom shall be taken as a reference to a person who intends to comply with the requirements of paragraphs (2), (3) or (4) of article 3 above, as the case may be, for being treated as normally resident in the United Kingdom;
   (b) the date on which a person becomes normally resident in the United Kingdom shall be the date when having given up his normal residence in [another country][1] he is in the United Kingdom for the purpose of fulfilling such intention as is mentioned in paragraph (a) above.

Amendments—[1] In paras (a) and (b) words substituted for words "a third country", by the Value Added Tax and Excise Personal Reliefs (Special Visitors and Goods Permanently Imported) (Amendment) (EU Exit) Regulations, SI 2019/91 regs 8, 13 with effect from IP completion day (11pm UK time on 31 December 2020) by virtue of SI 2020/1641 reg 2, Schedule para 4.

[4A Modifications for certain movements of goods involving Northern Ireland

(1) Nothing in this Order affords relief from tax charged under paragraph 3(2) of Schedule 9ZB to the Value Added Tax Act 1994 ("VATA").
(2) Paragraphs (3) to (13) of this article apply in respect of tax charged under paragraph 3(4) of Schedule 9ZB to VATA and where this article modifies the provisions of this Order, relief shall be afforded from such tax in accordance with such provisions only as modified.
(3) Where under this Order relief from tax applies to a movement of goods from Great Britain or the Isle of Man to Northern Ireland, Great Britain or the Isle of Man shall be treated as a country and Northern Ireland as a different country, including for the purposes of determining under this Order whether and when a person is normally resident in Great Britain or the Isle of Man and whether and when a person becomes or intends to become normally resident in Northern Ireland.
(4) Where it is necessary to determine for the purposes of relief under this Order where a person is normally resident, a United Kingdom citizen whose personal ties are in Northern Ireland but whose occupational ties are in Great Britain or the Isle of Man may be treated as normally resident in Great Britain or the Isle of Man if the person has lived there for a period of, or periods together amounting to, at least 185 days in a period of twelve months.
(5) In this Order—
   (a) any reference to a person who has been normally resident in Great Britain or the Isle of Man and who intends to become normally resident in Northern Ireland shall be taken as a reference to a person who intends to comply with the requirements of paragraph (2), (3) or (4) of article 3, as the case may be, for being treated as normally resident in Northern Ireland;

(b) the date on which a person becomes normally resident in Northern Ireland shall be the date when having given up the person's normal residence in Great Britain or the Isle of Man, the person is in Northern Ireland for the purposes of fulfilling such intention as is mentioned in paragraph (a).

(6) Article 6 applies in respect of tax where goods enter Northern Ireland from Great Britain or the Isle of Man as though the reference in that article to the United Kingdom were a reference to Northern Ireland.

(7) Article 8(2) applies as if the expression "declared for relief" refers to the act by which a person applies for relief on entry of goods to Northern Ireland from Great Britain or the Isle of Man or on their removal from another customs procedure, where customs procedure means a customs procedure for the purposes of Union customs legislation as defined in paragraph 1(8) of Schedule 9ZB to the VATA.

(8) Article 9 applies where relief from tax has been afforded subject to an intention of a person in relation to becoming normally resident in Northern Ireland as it applies where relief has been afforded subject to an intention of a person in relation to becoming normally resident in the United Kingdom.

(9) Articles 7, 11, 12, 13, 14, 16 and 17 apply as though references to the United Kingdom were references to Northern Ireland, as though references to importation into the United Kingdom were references to entry to Northern Ireland, as though references to property imported into the United Kingdom were references to property which entered Northern Ireland and as though references to another country were references to Great Britain or the Isle of Man.

(10) For the purposes of affording relief from tax under article 14 a wedding gift shall be treated as if it were liable to relevant NI import duty and valued in accordance with the rules applicable to such duty.

(11) Articles 18 and 19 do not apply in relation to tax charged under paragraph 3(4) of Schedule 9ZB to VATA.

(12) Article 21 applies to a person who has become entitled as legatee to property situated in Great Britain or the Isle of Man and the entry of such property to Northern Ireland as it applies to a person who has become entitled as legatee to property situated in another country and the importation of such property to the United Kingdom, on the following conditions (which apply instead of the conditions in sub-paragraphs (a) to (c) of article 21(1))—
- (a) the person is either—
    - (i) normally resident in Northern Ireland; or
    - (ii) a secondary resident who is not normally resident in Great Britain, the Isle of Man or a country which is not a member State; or
    - (iii) an eligible body;
- (b) the person furnishes proof to the officer of the person's entitlement as legatee to the property; and
- (c) save as the Commissioners otherwise allow, the property is imported by or for such person not later than two years from the date on which the person's entitlement as legatee is finally determined.

(13) In paragraph (12)—
"eligible body" means a body solely concerned with carrying on a non-profit making activity and has a business establishment or other fixed establishment in Northern Ireland; and
"secondary resident" means a person who, without being normally resident in Northern Ireland has a home situated in Northern Ireland which the person owns or is renting for at least twelve months.

(14) Paragraphs (15) to (20) of this article apply in respect of tax charged on the importation of goods into the United Kingdom as a result of their entry to Northern Ireland from a country other than Great Britain or the Isle of Man, and where those paragraphs modify the provisions of this Order, relief shall be afforded from such tax in accordance with such provisions only as modified.

(15) Northern Ireland shall be treated as a country for the purposes of determining under this Order whether and when a person becomes or intends to become normally resident in Northern Ireland.

(16) Where it is necessary to determine for the purposes of relief under this Order where a person is normally resident, a United Kingdom citizen whose personal ties are in Northern Ireland but whose occupational ties are in Great Britain, the Isle of Man or a country which is not a member State may be treated as normally resident in the country of his occupational ties if the person has lived there for a period of, or periods together amounting to, at least 185 days in a period of twelve months.

(17) Articles 4, 6, 7,11, 12, 13, 14, 16, 17, 18 and 19 apply as though references to the United Kingdom were references to Northern Ireland, as though references to importation into the United Kingdom were references to entry to Northern Ireland, as though references to property imported into the United Kingdom were references to property which entered Northern Ireland and as though references to another country mean a country other than Great Britain or the Isle of Man and other than a member State.

(18) Article 8(2) applies as if the expression "declared for relief" refers to the act by which a person applies for relief on entry of goods to Northern Ireland, where customs procedure means a customs procedure for the purposes of Union customs legislation as defined in paragraph 1(8) of Schedule 9ZB to VATA.

(19) For the purposes of affording relief from tax under article 14 a wedding gift shall be treated as if it were liable to relevant NI import duty and valued in accordance with the rules applicable to such duty.

(20) Article 21 applies to a person who has become entitled as legatee to property situated in Great Britain, the Isle of Man or a country which is not a member State and the entry of such property to Northern Ireland as it applies to a person who has become entitled as legatee to property situated in another country and the importation of such property to the United Kingdom on the conditions set out in sub-paragraphs (a) to (c) of article 4A(12) which apply instead of the conditions in sub-paragraphs (a) to (c) of article 21(1).][1]

Amendments—[1] Article 4A inserted by the Value Added Tax (Miscellaneous Amendments, Northern Ireland Protocol and Savings and Transitional Provisions) (EU Exit) Regulations, SI 2020/1545 reg 18(1), (3) with effect from IP completion day (11pm UK time on 31 December 2020) by virtue of SI 2020/1641 reg 2, Schedule para 11.

PART II
PROVISIONS COMMON TO CERTAIN RELIEFS

5 Property may be in separate consignments

Except as otherwise provided by this Order, where property in respect of which relief is afforded is permitted to be imported over a period it may be imported in more than one consignment during such period.

6 Condition as to security for certain importations

Where any goods are declared for relief under this Order—
   (*a*) before the date on which a person becomes normally resident in the United Kingdom, or
   (*b*) if he intends to become so resident on the occasion of his marriage before such marriage has taken place,
the relief shall be subject to the condition that there is furnished to the Commissioners such security as they may require.

7 Restriction on disposal without authorisation

(1) Except as provided by or under this Order, where relief is afforded under any Part of this Order, it shall be a condition of the relief that the goods are not lent, hired-out, given as security or transferred in the United Kingdom within a period of twelve months from the date on which relief was afforded, unless such disposal is authorised by the Commissioners.

(2) Where the Commissioners authorise any such disposal as is mentioned in paragraph (1) above, they may discharge the relief and the person to whom the relief was afforded shall forthwith pay tax at the rate then in force, provided that where a lower rate was in force when relief was afforded the amount payable shall be determined by reference to the lower rate.

PART III
PROVISIONS COMMON TO ALL RELIEFS

8 Goods to be declared for relief

(1) A person shall not be entitled to relief from payment of duty or tax in respect of any goods under any Part of this Order unless the goods are declared for relief to the proper officer.

(2) For the purposes of this Order, the expression "declared for relief" shall refer to the act by which a person applies for relief on importation of the goods or on their removal from another customs procedure . . . [1]

Amendments—[1] In para (2) words "and includes, as the case may be, any declaration under section 78 of the Customs and Excise Management Act 1979 or any entry under the Postal Packets (Customs and Excise) Regulations 1986, the Excise Warehousing (Etc) Regulations 1988, or regulation 5 of the Customs Controls on Importation of Goods Regulations 1991, or any entry required by Article 40 of Commission Regulation (EEC) No 2561/90." revoked by the Value Added Tax and Excise Personal Reliefs (Special Visitors and Goods Permanently Imported) (Amendment) (EU Exit) Regulations, SI 2019/91 regs 8, 11 with effect from IP completion day (11pm UK time on 31 December 2020) by virtue of SI 2020/1641 reg 2, Schedule para 4.

9 Fulfilment of intention to be a condition

Where relief from payment of duty or tax is afforded under any Part of this Order subject to a specified intention on the part of a person in relation to his becoming normally resident in the United Kingdom, or the use of the goods in respect of which relief is afforded, it shall be a condition of the relief that such intention be fulfilled.

10 Enforcement
Where relief from payment of duty or tax has been afforded under any Part of this Order and subsequently the Commissioners are not satisfied that any condition subject to which such relief was afforded has been complied with, then, unless the Commissioners sanction the non-compliance, the duty or tax shall become payable forthwith by the person to whom relief was afforded (except to the extent that the Commissioners may see fit to waive payment of the whole or any part thereof) and the goods shall be liable to forfeiture.

PART IV

11 Persons Transferring Their Normal Residence From [another country][1]
(1) Subject to the provisions of this Part, a person entering the United Kingdom shall not be required to pay any duty or tax chargeable in respect of property imported into the United Kingdom on condition that—
- (a) he has been normally resident in [another country][1] for a continuous period of at least twelve months;
- (b) he intends to become normally resident in the United Kingdom;
- (c) the property has been in his possession and used by him in the country where he has been normally resident, for a period of at least six months before its importation;
- (d) the property is intended for his personal or household use in the United Kingdom; and
- (e) the property is declared for relief—
  - (i) not earlier than six months before the date on which he becomes normally resident in the United Kingdom, and
  - (ii) not later than twelve months following that date.

(2) A person shall not be afforded relief under this Part unless the Commissioners are satisfied that the goods have borne, in their country of origin or exportation, the customs or other duties and taxes to which goods of that class or description are normally liable and that such goods have not, by reason of their exportation, been subject to any exemption from, or refund of, such duties and taxes as aforesaid, or any turnover tax, excise duty or other consumption tax.

(3) For the purposes of this Part, "property" shall not include—
- (a) beverages containing alcohol;
- (b) tobacco products;
- (c) any motor road vehicle which by its type of construction and equipment is designed for and capable of transporting more than nine persons including the driver, or goods, or any special purpose vehicle or mobile workshop; and
- (d) articles for use in the exercise of a trade or profession, other than portable instruments of the applied or liberal arts.

Amendments—[1] In the heading to Part IV, and in para (1)(a) words substituted for words "a third country", by the Value Added Tax and Excise Personal Reliefs (Special Visitors and Goods Permanently Imported) (Amendment) (EU Exit) Regulations, SI 2019/91 regs 8, 13 with effect from IP completion day (11pm UK time on 31 December 2020) by virtue of SI 2020/1641 reg 2, Schedule para 4.

12 Supplementary
Where the Commissioners are satisfied that a person has given up his normal residence in [another country][1] but is prevented by occupational ties from becoming normally resident in the United Kingdom immediately, they may allow property to be declared for relief earlier than as prescribed in article 11(1)(e)(i) above, subject to such conditions and restrictions as they think fit.

Amendments—[1] Words substituted for words "a third country", by the Value Added Tax and Excise Personal Reliefs (Special Visitors and Goods Permanently Imported) (Amendment) (EU Exit) Regulations, SI 2019/91 regs 8, 13 with effect from IP completion day (11pm UK time on 31 December 2020) by virtue of SI 2020/1641 reg 2, Schedule para 4.

PART V
ADDITIONAL RELIEF FOR PROPERTY IMPORTED ON MARRIAGE FROM [ANOTHER COUNTRY][1]

13 Relief
(1) Subject to the provisions of this article, in addition to the relief afforded by Part IV, a person entering the United Kingdom shall not be required to pay any duty or tax chargeable in respect of property imported into the United Kingdom on condition that—
- (a) he has been normally resident in [another country][1] for a continuous period of at least twelve months;
- (b) he intends to become normally resident in the United Kingdom on the occasion of his marriage; and
- (c) the property is declared for relief within the period provided by article 15 below.

(2) In this article "property" shall be limited to household effects and trousseaux, other than tobacco products and beverages containing alcohol.

Amendments—[1] In the heading to Part V, and in para (1)(a) words substituted for words "a third country", by the Value Added Tax and Excise Personal Reliefs (Special Visitors and Goods Permanently Imported) (Amendment) (EU Exit) Regulations, SI 2019/91 regs 8, 13 with effect from IP completion day (11pm UK time on 31 December 2020) by virtue of SI 2020/1641 reg 2, Schedule para 4.

14 Wedding gifts

(1) Subject to the provisions of this article, a person to whom article 13(1) above applies shall not be required to pay any duty or tax chargeable in respect of any wedding gift imported into the United Kingdom by him or on his behalf on condition that such wedding gift is—
  (a) given or intended to be given to him on the occasion of his marriage by a person who is normally resident in [another country][1];
  (b) declared for relief within the period provided by article 15 below.

(2) Relief shall not be afforded under this article in respect of any wedding gift the value of which exceeds £800.

(3) For the purpose of affording relief from any duty or tax under this article, a wedding gift shall be treated as if it were liable to [import duty, charged by provision made in accordance with or under Part 1 of the Taxation (Cross-border Trade) Act 2018][1] and valued in accordance with the rules applicable to such duty.

(4) In this article "wedding gift" means any property customarily given on the occasion of a marriage, other than tobacco products or beverages containing alcohol.

Amendments—[1] In para (1)(a) words substituted for words "a third country", and in para (3) substituted for words "EU customs duty", by the Value Added Tax and Excise Personal Reliefs (Special Visitors and Goods Permanently Imported) (Amendment) (EU Exit) Regulations, SI 2019/91 regs 8, 12, 13 with effect from IP completion day (11pm UK time on 31 December 2020) by virtue of SI 2020/1641 reg 2, Schedule para 4.

15 Time limit for relief

The property to which this Part applies shall be declared for relief—
  (a) not earlier than two months before the date fixed for the solemnisation of the marriage; and
  (b) not later than four months following the date of the marriage.

PART VI
PUPILS AND STUDENTS

16 Relief for scholastic equipment

(1) Without prejudice to relief afforded under any other Part of this Order and subject to the provisions of this article, a person entering the United Kingdom shall not be required to pay any duty or tax chargeable in respect of scholastic equipment imported into the United Kingdom on condition that—
  (a) he is a pupil or student normally resident in [another country][1] who has been accepted to attend a full-time course at a school, college or university in the United Kingdom; and
  (b) such equipment belongs to him and is intended for his personal use during the period of his studies.

(2) For the purposes of this article, "scholastic equipment" shall mean household effects which represent the normal furnishings for the room of a pupil or student, clothing, uniforms, and articles or instruments normally used by pupils or students for the purpose of their studies, including calculators or typewriters.

(3) The provisions of article 7 above shall not apply to relief afforded under this Part.

Amendments—[1] In para (1)(a) words substituted for words "a third country" by the Value Added Tax and Excise Personal Reliefs (Special Visitors and Goods Permanently Imported) (Amendment) (EU Exit) Regulations, SI 2019/91 regs 8, 12, 13 with effect from IP completion day (11pm UK time on 31 December 2020) by virtue of SI 2020/1641 reg 2, Schedule para 4.

PART VII
HONORARY DECORATIONS, AWARDS AND GOODWILL GIFTS

17 Relief for honorary decorations and awards

Subject to article 20 below, a person entering the United Kingdom shall not be required to pay any duty or tax chargeable on the importation into the United Kingdom of any goods on condition that—
  (a) he is normally resident in the United Kingdom; and
  (b) such goods comprise—
    (i) any honorary decoration which has been conferred on him by a government in [another country][1] or
    (ii) any cup, medal or similar article of an essentially symbolic nature which has been awarded to him in [another country][1] as a tribute to his activities in the arts, sciences, sport, or the public service, or in recognition of merit at a particular event.

Amendments—[1]   In para (b)(i), (ii) words substituted for words "a third country" by the Value Added Tax and Excise Personal Reliefs (Special Visitors and Goods Permanently Imported) (Amendment) (EU Exit) Regulations, SI 2019/91 regs 8, 12, 13 with effect from IP completion day (11pm UK time on 31 December 2020) by virtue of SI 2020/1641 reg 2, Schedule para 4.

18   Relief for gifts received by official visitors in [another country][1]
Subject to article 20 below, a person entering the United Kingdom shall not be required to pay any duty or tax chargeable on the importation into the United Kingdom of any goods on condition that—
   (*a*) he is normally resident in the United Kingdom;
   (*b*) he is returning from an official visit to [another country][1];
   (*c*) the goods were given to him by the host authorities of such country on the occasion of his visit; and
   (*d*) the goods are not intended for a commercial purpose.

Amendments—[1]   In the heading, and in para (*b*) words substituted for words "a third country" by the Value Added Tax and Excise Personal Reliefs (Special Visitors and Goods Permanently Imported) (Amendment) (EU Exit) Regulations, SI 2019/91 regs 8, 12, 13 with effect from IP completion day (11pm UK time on 31 December 2020) by virtue of SI 2020/1641 reg 2, Schedule para 4.

19   Relief for gifts brought by official visitors
Subject to article 20 below, a person entering the United Kingdom shall not be required to pay any duty or tax chargeable on the importation into the United Kingdom of any goods on condition that—
   (*a*) he is normally resident in [another country][1];
   (*b*) he is paying an official visit to the United Kingdom;
   (*c*) the goods are in the nature of an occasional gift which he intends to offer to the host authorities during his visit; and
   (*d*) the goods are not intended for a commercial purpose.

Amendments—[1]   In para (*a*) words substituted for words "a third country" by the Value Added Tax and Excise Personal Reliefs (Special Visitors and Goods Permanently Imported) (Amendment) (EU Exit) Regulations, SI 2019/91 regs 8, 12, 13 with effect from IP completion day (11pm UK time on 31 December 2020) by virtue of SI 2020/1641 reg 2, Schedule para 4.

20   Supplementary
(1) Part II shall not apply to relief afforded under this Part.
(2) No relief shall be afforded under this Part in respect of beverages containing alcohol, tobacco products or importations having a commercial character.

PART VIII
PERSONAL PROPERTY ACQUIRED BY INHERITANCE

21   Relief for legacies imported from [another country][1]
(1) Without prejudice to relief afforded under any other Part of this Order and subject to the provisions of this article, a person who has become entitled as a legatee to property situated in [another country][1] shall not be required to pay any duty or tax chargeable on the importation thereof into the United Kingdom, on condition that—
   (*a*) he is either—
      (i) normally resident in the United Kingdom or the Isle of Man; or
      (ii) a secondary resident who is not normally resident in [another country][1]; or
      (iii) an eligible body;
   (*b*) he furnishes proof to the officer of his entitlement as legatee to the property; and
   (*c*) save as the Commissioners otherwise allow, the property is imported by or for such person not later than two years from the date on which his entitlement as legatee is finally determined.
(2) No relief shall be afforded under paragraph (1) above in respect of goods specified in the Schedule to this Order.
(3) For the purposes of this Part—
   "eligible body" means a body solely concerned with carrying on a non-profit making activity and which is incorporated in the United Kingdom or the Isle of Man;
   "secondary resident" means a person who, without being normally resident in the United Kingdom or the Isle of Man has a home situated in the United Kingdom which he owns or is renting for at least twelve months.

Amendments—[1]   In the heading, and in para (1) in both places, words substituted for words "a third country" by the Value Added Tax and Excise Personal Reliefs (Special Visitors and Goods Permanently Imported) (EU Exit) Regulations, SI 2019/91 regs 8, 12, 13 with effect from IP completion day (11pm UK time on 31 December 2020) by virtue of SI 2020/1641 reg 2, Schedule para 4.

SCHEDULE
Article 21(2)

1 Beverages contain alcohol.
2 Tobacco products.

3 Any motor road vehicle which, by its type of construction and equipment, is designed for and capable of transporting more than nine persons including the driver, or goods, or any special purpose vehicle or mobile workshop.

4 Articles, other than portable instruments of the applied or liberal arts, used in the exercise of a trade or profession before his death by the person from whom the legatee has acquired them.

5 Stocks of new materials and finished or semi-finished products.

6 Livestock and stocks of agricultural products exceeding the quantities appropriate to normal family requirements.

1992/3222

VALUE ADDED TAX (INPUT TAX) ORDER 1992

Made by the Treasury under VATA 1983 s 14(10) (see now VATA 1994 s 25(7)) and all other enabling powers

Made . . . .*16 December 1992*
Laid before the House of Commons . . . .*17 December 1992*
Coming into force . . . .*1 January 1993*

1 Citation and commencement
This Order may be cited as the Value Added Tax (Input Tax) Order 1992, and shall come into force on 1st January 1993.

2 Interpretation
In this Order—
"the Act" means the Value Added Tax Act [1994][1];
"the Manx Act" means the Value Added Tax and Other Taxes Act 1973;
["antiques" means objects other than works of art or collectors' items, which are more than 100 years old;][2]
["collectors' items" means any collection or collector's piece falling within section 21(5) of the Act but excluding investment gold coins within the meaning of Note 1(*b*) and (*c*) to Group 15 of Schedule 9 to the Act;][4]
["building materials" means any goods the supply of which would be zero-rated if supplied by a taxable person to a person to whom he is also making a supply of a description within either item 2 or item 3 of Group 5, or item 2 of Group 6, of Schedule 8 to the Act][1]
. . .[2]
["Motor car" means any motor vehicle of a kind normally used on public roads which has three or more wheels and either—

(*a*) is constructed or adapted solely or mainly for the carriage of passengers; or

(*b*) has to the rear of the driver's seat roofed accommodation which is fitted with side windows or which is constructed or adapted for the fitting of side windows;

but does not include—

(i) vehicles capable of accommodating only one person;

(ii) vehicles which meet the requirements of Schedule 6 to the Road Vehicles (Construction and Use) Regulations 1986 and are capable of carrying [12][5] or more seated persons;

[(ii *a*) vehicles which would otherwise meet the requirements of sub-paragraph (ii) but which can carry fewer than 12 seated persons solely because they have been adapted for wheelchair users;][5]

(iii) vehicles of not less than three tonnes unladen weight (as defined in the Table to regulation 3(2) of the Road Vehicles (Construction and Use) Regulations 1986);

(iv) vehicles constructed to carry a payload (the difference between a vehicle's kerb weight (as defined in the Table to regulation 3(2) of the Road Vehicles (Construction and Use) Regulations 1986) and its maximum gross weight (as defined in that Table) of one tonne or more;

(v) caravans, ambulances and prison vans;

(vi) vehicles constructed for a special purpose other than the carriage of persons and having no other accommodation for carrying persons than such as is incidental to that purpose;][3]

["motor dealer" means a person whose business consists in whole or in part of obtaining supplies of, [or acquiring in Northern Ireland from a member State][7] . . .[6] or importing, new or second-hand motor cars for resale with a view to making an overall profit on the sale of them (whether or not a profit is made on each sale);

"motor manufacturer" means a person whose business consists in whole or part of producing motor cars including producing motors cars by conversion of a vehicle (whether a motor car or not);][3]

         . . .²
         . . .³
         . . .²
["Second-hand goods" means tangible moveable property (including motor cars) that is suitable for further use as it is or after repair other than works of art, collectors' items or antiques and other than precious metals and precious stones;]²

["stock in trade" means new or second-hand motor cars (other than second-hand motor cars which are not qualifying motor cars within the meaning of article 7(2A) below [or paragraph 4(3) of Schedule 2 to this Order]⁷) which are—

   (a) produced by a motor manufacturer or, as the case may require, supplied to [or acquired in Northern Ireland from a member State]⁷ . . . ⁶ or imported by a motor dealer, for the purpose of resale, and
   (b) are intended to be sold by—
       (i) a motor manufacturer within 12 months of their production, or
       (ii) by a motor dealer within 12 months of their supply[, acquisition in Northern Ireland from a member State]⁷ . . . ⁶ or importation, as the case may require,

and such motor cars shall not cease to be stock in trade where they are temporarily put to a use in the motor manufacturer's or, as the case may be, the motor dealer's business which involves making them available for private use;]³

["work of art" has the same meaning as in section 21 of the Act.]⁴

Amendments—¹ Word in the definition "the Act" substituted, and the definition "building materials" inserted, by the VAT (Input Tax) (Amendment) Order, SI 1995/281 art 3 with effect from 1 March 1995.
² Definitions of "caravan", "firearms", "motorcycle", "works of art", "antiques" and "collectors' pieces" revoked and the definitions of "antiques", and "Second-hand goods" inserted by the VAT (Input Tax) (Amendment) (No 2) Order, SI 1995/1267 art 3 with effect from 1 June 1995.
³ Definition of "motor car" substituted, definitions of "motor dealer", "motor manufacturer" and "stock in trade" inserted, and definition of "printed matter" revoked, by the VAT (Input Tax) (Amendment) Order, SI 1999/2930, arts 2, 3 with effect from 1 December 1999.
⁴ Definitions of "collectors' items" and "work of art" substituted (both definitions originally inserted by SI 1995/1267) by the VAT (Input Tax) (Amendment) (No 2) Order, SI 1999/3118, arts 2, 3, with effect from 1 January 2000.
⁵ In definition of "motor car", figure "12" substituted for word "twelve" and sub-para (b)(ii a) inserted, by the VAT (Input Tax) (Amendment) Order, SI 2009/217 art 2 with effect from 6 April 2009.
⁶ In the definition of "motor dealer" words "or acquiring from another member State" revoked, in the definition of "stock in trade", in para (a) words "or acquired from another member State" revoked and in para (b)(ii) words ", acquisition from another member State" revoked, by the Value Added Tax (Miscellaneous Amendments and Revocations) (EU Exit) Regulations, SI 2019/59 reg 8(1), (2) with effect from IP completion day (11pm UK time on 31 December 2020).
⁷ In the definitions of "motor dealer" and "stock in trade", words inserted by the Value Added Tax (Miscellaneous Amendments, Northern Ireland Protocol and Savings and Transitional Provisions) (EU Exit) Regulations, SI 2020/1545 regs 19, 20 with effect from IP completion day (11pm UK time on 31 December 2020) by virtue of SI 2020/1641 reg 2, Schedule para 11.

3 Revocations
The provisions specified in the first column of [Schedule 1]¹ to this Order are hereby revoked to the extent specified in the second column of that Schedule.

Amendments—¹ Words substituted for words "the Schedule" by the Value Added Tax (Miscellaneous Amendments, Northern Ireland Protocol and Savings and Transitional Provisions) (EU Exit) Regulations, SI 2020/1545 regs 19, 21 with effect from IP completion day (11pm UK time on 31 December 2020) by virtue of SI 2020/1641 reg 2, Schedule para 11.

[4 Disallowance of input tax
(1) Subject to paragraph (4) below, tax charged on the—
   (a) supply;
       . . .³ or
   (c) importation,
of any goods such as are described in paragraph (2) below which are supplied to, . . .³ or imported by, a taxable person in the circumstances described in paragraph (3) below shall be excluded from any credit under section 25 of the Act.
(2) The goods referred to in paragraph (1) above are—
   (a) works of art, antiques and collectors' items;
   (b) second-hand goods.
(3) The circumstances of the supply . . .³ or importation referred to in paragraph (1) above are—
   (a) a supply on which, by virtue of an Order made under Section 50A of the Act or a corresponding provision of the Manx Act . . .³, VAT was chargeable on the profit margin;
   [(aa) . . .]²
   (b) (if the goods are a work of art, an antique or a collectors' item) the taxable person imported it himself;
   (c) (if the goods are a work of art) it was supplied to the taxable person by, . . .³ from its creator or his successor in title;

(4) Paragraph (1) above shall only apply to exclude from credit, tax chargeable on a supply of goods to ... ³ or importation of goods by a taxable person in the circumstances set out in paragraph (3)(*b*) and (*c*) above if the taxable person—
  (*a*) has opted to account for VAT chargeable on his supplies of such goods on the profit margin and
  (*b*) has not elected to account for VAT chargeable on his supply of the goods by reference to its value, in accordance with the provisions of an Order made under section 50A of the Act.]¹

Amendments—¹ This article substituted by the VAT (Input Tax) (Amendment) (No 2) Order, SI 1995/1267 art 4 with effect from 1 June 1995.
² Para (3)(*aa*) revoked by the VAT (Input Tax) (Amendment) Order, SI 1999/2930, arts 2, 4, with effect from 1 March 2000 (previously inserted by the VAT (Input Tax) (Amendment) (No 3) Order, SI 1995/1666 art 3).
³ Para (1)(*b*) (but not the final "or") revoked, in the words after para (1)(*c*) words "or acquired from another member State" revoked, in para (3) words ", acquisition from another member State" revoked, in sub-para (3)(*a*) words "or by virtue of a corresponding provision of the law of another member State" revoked, in para (3)(*c*) words ", or acquired from another member State by him from" revoked, and in para (4) words "or an acquisition" revoked, by the Value Added Tax (Miscellaneous Amendments and Revocations) (EU Exit) Regulations, SI 2019/59 reg 8(1), (3) with effect from IP completion day (11pm UK time on 31 December 2020). Para (1)(*b*) previously read as follows—
  "(*b*) acquisition from another member State; or"

5—(1) Tax charged on any goods or services supplied to a taxable person, ... ⁴ or on any goods imported by a taxable person, is to be excluded from any credit under section [25]¹ of the Act, where the goods or services in question are used or to be used by the taxable person for the purposes of business entertainment [unless the entertainment is provided for an overseas customer of the taxable person and is of a kind and on a scale which is reasonable, having regard to all the circumstances]³.
(2) Where, by reason of the operation of paragraph (1) above, a taxable person has claimed no input tax on ... ²a supply of any services, tax shall be charged on a supply by him of the goods in question not being a letting on hire or on a supply by him of the services in question, as if that supply were for a consideration equal to the excess of—
  [(*a*) the consideration for which the services are supplied by him, over
  (*b*) the consideration for which the services were supplied to him,]²
and accordingly shall not be charged unless there is such an excess.
(3) For the purposes of this article, "business entertainment" means entertainment including hospitality of any kind provided by a taxable person in connection with a business carried on by him, but does not include the provision of any such entertainment for either or both—
  (*a*) employees of the taxable person;
  (*b*) if the taxable person is a body corporate, its directors or persons otherwise engaged in its management,
unless the provision of entertainment for persons such as are mentioned in sub-paragraph (a) and (b) above is incidental to its provisions for others.
[(4) For the purposes of this article "overseas customer", in relation to a taxable person, means—
  (*a*) any person who is not ordinarily resident nor carrying on a business in the United Kingdom or the Isle of Man and avails himself or herself, or may be expected to avail himself or herself, in the course of a business carried on by that person outside the United Kingdom and the Isle of Man, of any goods or services the supply of which forms part of the taxable person's business; and
  (*b*) any person who is not ordinarily resident in the United Kingdom or the Isle of Man and is acting, in relation to such goods or services, on behalf of an overseas customer as defined in paragraph (a) above or on behalf of any government or public authority outside the United Kingdom and the Isle of Man.]³

Amendments—¹ Figure in para (1) substituted by the VAT (Input Tax) (Amendment) Order, SI 1995/281 art 5 with effect from 1 March 1995.
² Words in para (2) revoked, and paras (2)(*a*), (*b*) substituted, by the VAT (Input Tax) (Amendment) Order, SI 1999/2930, arts 2, 5, with effect from 1 March 2000.
³ Words in para (1), and whole of para (4), inserted, by the VAT (Input Tax) (Amendment) Order, SI 2011/1071 art 2 with effect from 1 May 2011.
⁴ In para (1) words "or on any goods acquired by a taxable person," revoked, by the Value Added Tax (Miscellaneous Amendments and Revocations) (EU Exit) Regulations, SI 2019/59 reg 8(1), (4) with effect from IP completion day (11pm UK time on 31 December 2020).

[**6** Where a taxable person constructing, or effecting any works to a building, in either case for the purpose of making a grant of a major interest in it or any part of it or its site which is of a description in Schedule 8 to the Act, incorporates goods other than building materials in any part of the building or its site, input tax on the supply ... ² or importation of the goods shall be excluded from credit under section 25 of the Act.]¹

Amendments—¹ Substituted by the VAT (Input Tax) (Amendment) Order, SI 1995/281 art 6 with effect from 1 March 1995.
² Word ", acquisition" revoked by the Value Added Tax (Miscellaneous Amendments and Revocations) (EU Exit) Regulations, SI 2019/59 reg 8(1), (5) with effect from IP completion day (11pm UK time on 31 December 2020).

7—(1) Subject to paragraph (2) [to (2H)]² below tax charged on—
  (a) the supply [(including a letting on hire)]² to a taxable person;
  ... ⁶ or
  (c) the importation by a taxable person,
of a motor car shall be excluded from any credit under section [25]¹ of the Act.
[(2) Paragraph (1) above does not apply where—
  (a) the motor car is—
    (i) a qualifying motor car;
    (ii) [supplied (including on a letting on hire) to]³, ... ⁶ or imported by, a taxable person; and
    (iii) the relevant condition is satisfied;
  [(aa) the motor car forms part of the stock in trade of a motor manufacturer or a motor dealer;]⁴

  (b) the supply is a letting on hire of a motor car which is not a qualifying motor car [(other than a supply on a letting on hire of a motor car which is not a qualifying motor car by virtue only of the application of paragraph (2C) below, to a person whose supply on a letting on hire prior to 1st August 1995 resulted in the application of that paragraph)]³;
  (c) the motor car is unused and is supplied to a taxable person whose only taxable supplies are concerned with the letting of motor cars on hire to another taxable person whose business consists predominantly of making supplies of a description falling within item 14 of Group 12 of Schedule 8 to the Act; or
  (d) the motor car is unused and is supplied on a letting on hire to a taxable person whose business consists predominantly of making supplies of a description falling within item 14 of Group 12 of Schedule 8 to the Act, by a taxable person whose only taxable supplies are concerned with the letting on hire of motor cars to such a taxable person.]²

[(2A) Subject to paragraph (2B) and (2C) below, for the purposes of paragraph (2)(a) [and (b)]⁴ above a motor car is a qualifying motor car if—
  (a) it has never been supplied ... ⁶, or imported in circumstances in which the VAT on that supply ... ⁶ or importation was wholly excluded from credit as input tax by virtue of paragraph (1) above; or
  (b) a taxable person has elected for it to be treated as such.
(2B) A taxable person may only elect for a motor car to be treated as a qualifying motor car if it—
  (a) is first registered on or after 1st August 1995;
  (b) was supplied to, ... ⁶ or imported by, him prior to that date in circumstances in which the VAT on that supply ... ⁶ or importation was wholly excluded from credit as input tax by virtue of paragraph (1) above; and
  (c) had not been supplied on a letting on hire by him prior to 1st August 1995.
(2C) A motor car that is supplied ... ⁶ or imported on or after 1st August 1995 and which would, apart from this paragraph, be a qualifying motor car by virtue of sub-paragraph (a) of paragraph (2A) above shall not be such a car if it was supplied on a letting on hire prior to that date by the person to whom it is supplied or by whom it is ... ⁶ imported (as the case may be).
(2D) References in this article to registration of a motor car mean registration in accordance with section 21 of the Vehicle Excise and Registration Act 1994.
(2E) For the purposes of paragraph (2)(a) above the relevant condition is that the letting on hire, supply ... ⁶ or importation (as the case may be) is to a taxable person who intends to use the motor car either—
  (a) exclusively for the purposes of a business carried on by him, but this is subject to paragraph (2G) below; or
  (b) primarily for a relevant purpose.
(2F) For the purposes of paragraph (2E) above a relevant purpose, in relation to a motor car which is let on hire or supplied to ... ⁶ or imported by, a taxable person (as the case may be), is any of the following purposes—
  (a) to provide it on hire with the services of a driver for the purpose of carrying passengers;
  (b) to provide it for self-drive hire; or
  (c) to use it as a vehicle in which instruction in the driving of a motor car is to be given by him.
(2G) A taxable person shall not be taken to intend to use a motor car exclusively for the purposes of a business carried on by him if he intends to—
  (a) let it on hire to any person either for no consideration or for a consideration which is less than that which would be payable in money if it were a commercial transaction conducted at arms length; or
  (b) make it available (otherwise than by letting it on hire) to any person (including, where the taxable person is an individual, himself, or where the taxable person is a partnership, a partner) for private use, whether or not for a consideration.

(2H) Where paragraph (1) above applies to a supply of a motor car on a letting on hire it shall apply to the tax charged on that supply as if for the word "tax" there were substituted "one half of the tax".][2]

(3) In this article—
  (a) ...[2]
  (b) "self-drive hire" means hire where the hirer is the person normally expected to drive the motor car and the period of hire to each hirer, together with the period of hire of any other motor car expected to be hired to him by the taxable person—
    (i) will normally be less than 30 consecutive days; and
    (ii) will normally be less than 90 days in any period of 12 months.

(4), (5) ...[5]

Commentary—De Voil Indirect Tax Service **V3.449**.

Amendments—[1] Words in paras (1), (2)(d), (f), (4), (5)(b) substituted by the VAT (Input Tax) (Amendment) Order, SI 1995/281 art 7 with effect from 1 March 1995.
[2] Words in para (1), and paras (2A)–(2H) inserted, words in para (1), para (2) and the words in para (4) substituted, and para (3)(a) revoked by the VAT (Input Tax) (Amendment) (No 3) Order, SI 1995/1666 arts 4–8 with effect from 1 August 1995.
[3] Words in paras (2)(a)(ii) substituted and (2)(b) inserted by the VAT (Input Tax) (Amendment) Order, SI 1998/2767 with effect from 13 November 1998.
[4] Para (2)(aa), and words in para (2A), inserted by the VAT (Input Tax) (Amendment) Order, SI 1999/2930, arts 2, 6(a), (b), with effect from 1 December 1999.
[5] Paras (4), (5) revoked by the VAT (Input Tax) (Amendment) Order, SI 1999/2930, arts 2, 6(c), with effect from 1 March 2000.
[6] Para (1)(b) (but not the final "or") revoked, in para (2)(a)(ii) words "or acquired from another member State" revoked, in para (2A)(a) words ", acquired from another member State," and ", acquisition" revoked, in para (2B)(b) words "or acquired from another member State," and ", acquisition" revoked, in para (2C) words ", acquired from another member State," and "acquired or" revoked, in para (2E) word ", acquisition" revoked, and in para (2F) words "or acquired" revoked, by the Value Added Tax (Miscellaneous Amendments and Revocations) (EU Exit) Regulations, SI 2019/59 reg 8(1), (6) with effect from IP completion day (11pm UK time on 31 December 2020). Para (1)(b) previously read as follows—
  "(b) the acquisition by a taxable person from another member State; or".

[**8 Application of this Order in relation to Northern Ireland**
(1) In this Order, references to VAT charged on the importation of goods includes VAT charged under the following provisions of Schedule 9ZB (goods removed to or from Northern Ireland etc) to the Act—
  (a) paragraph 1(3);
  (b) paragraph 3(2); and
  (c) paragraph 3(4).
(2) Schedule 2 to this Order makes separate provision for the disallowance of input tax in relation to acquisitions in Northern Ireland from the EU.][1]

Amendments—[1] Article 8 inserted by the Value Added Tax (Miscellaneous Amendments, Northern Ireland Protocol and Savings and Transitional Provisions) (EU Exit) Regulations, SI 2020/1545 regs 19, 22 with effect from IP completion day (11pm UK time on 31 December 2020) by virtue of SI 2020/1641 reg 2, Schedule para 11.

1993/2001

VALUE ADDED TAX (PAYMENTS ON ACCOUNT) ORDER 1993

Made by the Treasury under VATA 1983 s 38C(1)–(2), (4), (5) (see now VATA 1994 s 28(1), (2), (4), (5)) and all other enabling powers

Made .... 9 August 1993
Laid before the House of Commons .... 9 August 1993
Coming into force .... 2 September 1993

1 Citation and commencement
This Order may be cited as the Value Added Tax (Payments on Account) Order 1993 and shall come into force on 2nd September 1993.

2 Interpretation
(1) In this Order—
  "the Act" means the Value Added Tax Act [1994][1];
  "the basic period" means, in relation to a taxable person falling within article 5 or 6 below, the period of one year in which there ended the prescribed accounting periods in respect of which his liability to pay a total amount of tax exceeding [the figure specified in article 5(1) or 6(1)][3] caused him to become such a taxable person;
  "Controller" means the Controller, Customs and Excise, Value Added Tax Central Unit;
  ...[2]
  "reference period" has the meaning ascribed to it in article 11(1) below.

(2) Any reference in articles 13 to 15 below to the total amount of tax by reference to which a taxable person's payments on account fall to be calculated being "reduced accordingly" or "increased accordingly" is in each case a reference to a reduction or increase of the same proportion as the difference between the total amount of tax by reference to which his payments on account are currently calculated and the total amount of tax, . . . [4] which he was, or (as the case may be) which the Commissioners are satisfied that he will be, liable to pay in respect of the prescribed accounting periods the ends of which fall within the year referred to in the relevant provision of the article in question.

[(3) The last reference in paragraph (2) to the "total amount of tax" includes only tax that is required to be, or has been, accounted for on a return for a prescribed accounting period.][4]

Amendments—[1] Substituted by SI 1996/1196 art 3 with effect from 1 June 1996.
[2] Definition of "credit transfer" revoked by SI 1996/1196 with effect from 1 June 1996.
[3] In para (1), in definition of "the basic period", words substituted for figure "£2,000,000" by the VAT (Payments on Account) (Amendment) Order, SI 2011/21 art 2(a) with effect from 1 June 2011.
[4] In para (2), words "excluding the tax on goods imported from countries other than member States," revoked, and para (3) inserted, by the Value Added Tax (Miscellaneous Amendments, Northern Ireland Protocol and Savings and Transitional Provisions) (EU Exit) Regulations, SI 2020/1545 reg 25(1)–(3) with effect from IP completion day (11pm UK time on 31 December 2020) by virtue of SI 2020/1641 reg 2, Schedule para 11.

2A [Supplies to which section 55A(6) of the Act applies (customers to account for tax on supplies of a kind used in missing trader . . . [2] fraud)

Where, on application, a taxable person satisfies the Commissioners that, by reason solely of any amount that he is liable to pay by virtue of section 55A(6) of the Act—

(a) he falls within article 5 or 6 below, or

(b) the amount of each of his payments on account is increased,

then, with effect from the date of the approval by the Commissioners of the application, any amount that he is so liable to pay by virtue of that section shall be disregarded for the purposes of those articles or, as the case may be, the calculation of the amount of each of his payments on account.][1]

Amendments—[1] Article 2A inserted by the VAT (Payments on Account) (Amendment) Order, SI 2007/1420 art 2 with effect from 1 June 2007.
[2] In the heading words "intra-community" revoked by the Value Added Tax (Miscellaneous Amendments and Revocations) (EU Exit) Regulations, SI 2019/59 reg 9(1), (3) with effect from IP completion day (11pm UK time on 31 December 2020).

3 Revocation

(1) Subject to paragraph (2) below, the Value Added Tax (Payments on Account) (No 2) Order 1992 is hereby revoked.

(2) The duty under the Value Added Tax (Payments on Account) (No 2) Order 1992 of any taxable person to make a payment on account in respect of a prescribed accounting period beginning before 2nd September 1993 shall not be affected by the revocation of that Order which shall continue to have effect in relation to any such payment on account.

4 Payments on account

(1) A taxable person falling within article 5 or 6 below shall be under a duty to pay, on account of any tax he may become liable to pay in respect of each prescribed accounting period exceeding one month beginning on or after [1st April each year][1] amounts (in this Order referred to as "payments on account") determined in accordance with this Order at times so determined, provided that in the case of a taxable person falling within article 6 below there shall be no duty to pay such amounts in respect of a prescribed accounting period other than one beginning after the basic period.

[(2) Where such a taxable person has a prescribed accounting period exceeding one month which begins on or after 2nd March each year and ends on or before 30th June each year, he shall be under a like duty to make payments on account also in respect of that prescribed accounting period.][1]

Note—The UK Government announced on 20 March 2020 the deferral of the 30 June 2020 quarter 1 VAT payments until 31 March 2021. No interest or surcharges arise on those deferred payments during the deferral period (see SI 2020/934).

Amendments—[1] Words in para (1) and whole of para (2) substituted by the VAT (Payments on Account) (Amendment) Order, SI 1995/291 arts 3, 4 with effect from 2 March 1995.

[5 Persons to whom this Order applies

(1) Subject to paragraph (2) below and article 16 below, a taxable person falls within this article in any year if the total amount of tax which he was liable to pay in respect of the prescribed accounting periods the ends of which fell within the period of one year ending on the last day of his last prescribed accounting period ending before the previous 1st December exceeded [£2,300,000][2].

(2) Where in any year ending 30th November a prescribed accounting period of the taxable person did not begin on the first day or did not end on the last day of a month, the period of one year shall, for the purpose of this article, be regarded as having comprised those prescribed account periods which related to the tax periods ending within the year ending 30th November of that year to which references are shown in the certificate of registration issued to him][1].

Amendments—[1] Substituted by the VAT (Payments on Account) (Amendment) Order, SI 1995/291 art 5 with effect from 2 March 1995.

² In para (1), figure "£2,300,000" substituted for figure "£2,000,000" by the VAT (Payments on Account) (Amendment) Order, SI 2011/21 art 2(b) with effect from 1 December 2011.

6—(1) Subject to paragraph (2) below and article 16 below, a taxable person who does not fall within article 5 above shall fall within this article if the total amount of tax which he was liable to pay in respect of the prescribed accounting periods the ends of which fell within any one period of one year ending on the last day of a prescribed accounting period of his ending after [30th November of the previous year]¹ exceeded [£2,300,000]².

(2) Where in the period of the year referred to in paragraph (1) above a prescribed accounting period of the taxable person did not begin on the first day or did not end on the last day of a month, that period of one year shall, for the purpose of this article, be regarded as having comprised those prescribed accounting periods which related to the tax periods ending within that period of one year to which references are shown in the certificate of registration issued to him.

Amendments—¹ Words in para (1) substituted by the VAT (Payments on Account) (Amendment) Order, SI 1995/291 art 6 with effect from 2 March 1995.
² In para (1), figure substituted for figure "£2,000,000" by the VAT (Payments on Account) (Amendment) Order, SI 2011/21 art 2(c) with effect from 1 June 2011.

7 Cessation of duty to make payments on account
If the total amount of tax which a taxable person who is under a duty to make payments on account was liable to pay in respect of the prescribed accounting periods the ends of which fell within any one period of one year ending after the end of the basic period was less than [£1,800,000]¹, then, with effect from the date of the written approval by the Commissioners of a written application by the taxable person to that effect, he shall not be under a duty to make payments on account.

Amendments—¹ Figure substituted for figure "£1,600,000" by the VAT (Payments on Account) (Amendment) Order, SI 2011/21 art 2(d) with effect from 1 June 2011.

8 Time for payment
[Subject to article 9 below]¹, in respect of each prescribed accounting period a payment on account shall be made to the Controller not later than—
   (a) the last day of the month next following the end of the first complete month included therein, and
   (b) the last day of the month next following the end of the second complete month included therein.

Amendments—¹ Words substituted by the VAT (Payments on Account) (Amendment) Order, SI 1996/1196 art 4 with effect from 1 June 1996.

9 . . . ¹ where a prescribed accounting period does not begin on the first day or does not end on the last day of a month—
   (a) the first payment on account shall be made not later than the last day of the month next following the end of the first complete month included therein, and
   (b) the second payment on account shall be made not later than the last day of the month next following the end of the second complete month included therein.
except that where—
   (i) a prescribed accounting period does not comprise more complete months than one, the first payment on account shall be made not later than the last day of that month and the second payment on account shall be made not later than the end of the prescribed accounting period, or
   (ii) a prescribed accounting period comprises an incomplete month followed by two complete months, the first payment on account shall be made not later than the end of the first complete month and the second payment on account shall be made not later than the end of the second complete month, or
   (iii) a prescribed accounting period comprises an incomplete month followed by two complete months and an incomplete month, the first payment on account shall be made not later than the end of the first complete month and the second payment on account shall be made not later than the end of the second complete month.

Amendments—¹ Words deleted by the VAT (Payments on Account) (Amendment) Order, SI 1996/1196 art 5 with effect from 1 June 1996.

10 . . .

Amendments—This article deleted by the VAT (Payments on Account) (Amendment) Order, SI 1996/1196 art 6 with effect from 1 June 1996.

11 Calculation of the payments on account
(1) Subject to paragraph (2) below and articles [12A,]², 13, 14 and 15 below, the amount of each payment on account to be made by a taxable person who falls within article 5 above shall equal [one twenty-fourth]³ of the total amount of tax, . . . ⁴ which he was liable to pay in respect of the prescribed accounting periods the ends of which fell within the period (in this Order referred to as "the reference period")—

[(a) 1st October to 30th September in the basic period where he has a prescribed accounting period beginning in April in any year in which he is under a duty to make payments on account,]¹
[(b) 1st November to 31st October in the basic period where he has a prescribed accounting period beginning in May in any year in which he is under a duty to make payments on account, and]¹
[(c) 1st December to 30th November in the basic period where he has a prescribed accounting period beginning in June in any year in which he is under a duty to make payments on account.]¹

[(1A) The reference in paragraph (1) to the "total amount of tax" includes only tax that is required to be, or has been, accounted for on a return for a prescribed accounting period.]⁴

(2) Where in the period of the year mentioned in sub-paragraph (a), (b) or (c) of paragraph (1) above a prescribed accounting period of the taxable person did not begin on the first day or did not end on the last day of a month, the reference period shall, for the purpose of paragraph (1), be regarded as having comprised those prescribed accounting periods which related to the tax periods ending within the period of the year mentioned in sub-paragraph (a), (b) or (c) of paragraph (1) as appropriate to which references are shown in the certificate of registration issued to him.

Amendments—¹ Para (1) (a)–(c) substituted by the VAT (Payments on Account) (Amendment) Order, SI 1995/291 arts 7–9 with effect from 2 March 1995.
² Words inserted by the VAT (Payments on Account) (Amendment) Order, SI 1996/1196 art 7 with effect from 1 June 1996.
³ Words substituted by the VAT (Payments on Account) (Amendment) Order, SI 1996/1196 art 7 with effect from 1 June 1996.
⁴ In para (1), words "excluding the tax on goods imported from countries other than member States," revoked, and para (1A) inserted, by the Value Added Tax (Miscellaneous Amendments, Northern Ireland Protocol and Savings and Transitional Provisions) (EU Exit) Regulations, SI 2020/1545 reg 25(1), (2) and (4) with effect from IP completion day (11pm UK time on 31 December 2020) by virtue of SI 2020/1641 reg 2, Schedule para 11.

12 [(1)] Subject to articles [12A]¹, 13, 14 and 15 below, the amount of each payment on account to be made by a taxable person who falls within article 6 above shall equal [one twenty-fourth]² of the total amount of tax, . . . ³ which he was liable to pay in respect of the prescribed accounting periods the ends of which fell within the basic period.

[(2) The reference in paragraph (1) to the "total amount of tax" includes only tax that is required to be, or has been, accounted for on a return for a prescribed accounting period.]³

Amendments—¹ Words inserted by the VAT (Payments on Account) (Amendment) Order, SI 1996/1196 art 8 with effect from 1 June 1996.
² Words substituted by the VAT (Payments on Account) (Amendment) Order, SI 1996/1196 art 8 with effect from 1 June 1996.
³ Para (1) numbered as such, words "excluding the tax on goods imported from countries other than member States," revoked, and para (2) inserted, by the Value Added Tax (Miscellaneous Amendments, Northern Ireland Protocol and Savings and Transitional Provisions) (EU Exit) Regulations, SI 2020/1545 reg 25(1), (2) and (5) with effect from IP completion day (11pm UK time on 31 December 2020) by virtue of SI 2020/1641 reg 2, Schedule para 11.

[12A—(1) Subject to paragraph (5) below a taxable person who is under a duty to make payments on account may instead of paying the amount calculated in accordance with paragraphs 11 or 12 above elect to pay an amount equal to his liability to VAT . . . ² for the preceding month.

[(1A) The reference in paragraph (1) to "liability to VAT for the preceding month" includes only tax that is required to be, or has been, accounted for on a return for a prescribed accounting period.]²

(2) A person making an election under paragraph (1) above shall notify the Commissioners in writing of—
 (a) the election, and
 (b) the date (being a date not less than 30 days after the date of the notification) on which it is to take effect.

(3) Subject to paragraph (4) below, an election under paragraph (1) above shall continue to have effect until a date notified by the taxable person in writing to the Commissioners, which date shall not be earlier than the first anniversary of the date on which the election took effect.

(4) Where the Commissioners are satisfied that an amount paid by a person who has elected in accordance with paragraph (1) above is less than the amount required to be paid by virtue of that paragraph the Commissioners may notify the taxable person in writing that his election shall cease to have effect from a date specified in the notification.

(5) A person may not make an election under paragraph (1) above within 12 months of the date on which any previous election made by him ceased to have effect by virtue of paragraph (4) above.]¹

Amendments—¹ This article inserted by the VAT (Payments on Account) (Amendment) Order, SI 1996/1196 art 10 with effect from 1 June 1996.
² In para (1) words "excluding the tax on goods imported from countries other than member States," revoked, and para (1A) inserted, by the Value Added Tax (Miscellaneous Amendments, Northern Ireland Protocol and Savings and Transitional Provisions) (EU Exit) Regulations, SI 2020/1545 reg 25(1), (2) and (6) with effect from IP completion day (11pm UK time on 31 December 2020) by virtue of SI 2020/1641 reg 2, Schedule para 11.

13 [(1)] If—
 (a) the total amount of tax, . . . ² which the taxable person was liable to pay in respect of the prescribed accounting periods the ends of which fell within any one period of one year—

(i) in the case of a taxable person who falls within article 5 above, ending after the end of his reference period was less than 80 per cent of the total amount of tax relevant in his case under article 11 above, or

(ii) in the case of a taxable person who falls within article 6 above, ending after the end of the basic period was less than 80 per cent of the total amount of tax referred to in article 12, or

(b) where such a period of one year has not ended, the Commissioners are satisfied that the total amount of tax, . . . [2] which the taxable person will be liable to pay in respect of the prescribed accounting periods the ends of which fall within that year will be less than 80 per cent of the total amount of tax referred to in sub-paragraph (i) or (ii) (as the case may be) of paragraph (a) above,

then, with effect from the date of the written approval by the Commissioners of a written application by the taxable person to that effect, but subject to article 14 below, the total amount of tax by reference to which his payments on account fall to be calculated shall be reduced accordingly and the amount of each payment on account beginning with the first payment on account which falls to be made after the date of that approval shall equal [one twenty-fourth][1] of the reduced amount.

[(2) In paragraph (1), the first reference to the "total amount of tax" in each of subparagraphs (a) and (b) includes only tax that is required to be, or has been, accounted for on a return for a prescribed accounting period.][2]

Amendments—[1] Words substituted by the VAT (Payments on Account) (Amendment) Order, SI 1996/1196 art 9 with effect from 1 June 1996.

[2] Para (1) numbered as such, in paras (1)(a) and (b) words "excluding the tax on goods imported from countries other than member States," revoked, and para (2) inserted, by the Value Added Tax (Miscellaneous Amendments, Northern Ireland Protocol and Savings and Transitional Provisions) (EU Exit) Regulations, SI 2020/1545 reg 25(1), (2) and (7) with effect from IP completion day (11pm UK time on 31 December 2020) by virtue of SI 2020/1641 reg 2, Schedule para 11.

14 [(1)] If the total amount of tax, . . . [2] which the taxable person was liable to pay in respect of the prescribed accounting periods the ends of which fell within any one period of one year—

(a) in the case of a taxable person who falls within article 5 above, ending after the end of his reference period exceeded by 20 per cent. or more the total amount of tax by reference to which his payments on account are currently calculated, or

(b) in the case of a taxable person who falls within article 6 above, ending after the end of the basic period exceeded by 20 per cent. or more the total amount of tax by reference to which his payments on account are currently calculated,

then, with effect from the end of the period of one year first mentioned, but subject to article 15 below, the total amount of tax by reference to which his payments on account fall to be calculated shall be increased accordingly and the amount of each payment on account beginning with the first payment on account which falls to be made after the end of that period of one year shall equal [one twenty-fourth][1] of the increased amount.

[(2) The first reference to the "total amount of tax" in paragraph (1) includes only tax that is required to be, or has been, accounted for on a return for a prescribed accounting period.][2]

Amendments—[1] Words substituted by the VAT (Payments on Account) (Amendment) Order, SI 1996/1196 art 9 with effect from 1 June 1996.

[2] Para (1) numbered as such, words "excluding the tax on goods imported from countries other than member States," revoked, and para (2) inserted, by the Value Added Tax (Miscellaneous Amendments, Northern Ireland Protocol and Savings and Transitional Provisions) (EU Exit) Regulations, SI 2020/1545 reg 25(1), (2) and (8) with effect from IP completion day (11pm UK time on 31 December 2020) by virtue of SI 2020/1641 reg 2, Schedule para 11.

15 [(1)] Where the payments on account payable by a taxable person have been increased by virtue of article 14 above and—

(a) the total amount of tax, . . . [2] which he was liable to pay in respect of the prescribed accounting periods the ends of which fell within any one period of one year ending after such increase has taken effect was less than 80 per cent of the total amount of tax by reference to which his payments on account are currently calculated, or

(b) where such a period of one year has not ended, the Commissioners are satisfied that the total amount of tax, . . . [2] which he will be liable to pay in respect of the prescribed accounting periods the ends of which fall within that year will be less than 80 per cent of the total amount of tax by reference to which his payments on account are currently calculated.

then, with effect from the date of the written approval by the Commissioners of a written application by the taxable person to that effect, the total amount of tax by reference to which his payments on account fall to be calculated shall be reduced accordingly and the amount of each payment on account beginning with the first payment on account which falls to be made after the date of that approval shall equal [one twenty-fourth][1] of the reduced amount.

[(2) In paragraph (1), the references to the "total amount of tax" in each of sub-paragraphs (a) and (b) includes only tax that is required to be, or has been, accounted for on a return for a prescribed accounting period.][2]

Amendments—[1] Words substituted by the VAT (Payments on Account) (Amendment) Order, SI 1996/1196 art 9 with effect from 1 June 1996.
[2] Para (1) numbered as such, in paras (1)(a) and (b) words "excluding the tax on goods imported from countries other than member States," revoked, and para (2) inserted, by the Value Added Tax (Miscellaneous Amendments, Northern Ireland Protocol and Savings and Transitional Provisions) (EU Exit) Regulations, SI 2020/1545 reg 25(1), (2) and (9) with effect from IP completion day (11pm UK time on 31 December 2020) by virtue of SI 2020/1641 reg 2, Schedule para 11.

16 Business carried on in divisions

(1) Subject to paragraph (3) below, where the registration under the Act of a body corporate is and was throughout the prescribed accounting periods mentioned in article 5(1) or 6(1) above in the names of divisions under section 31(1) of the Act[3] and those divisions are the same divisions, that body corporate shall not be under a duty to make payments on account by virtue of falling within article 5 or 6 above but shall be under a duty to make payments on account by reference to the business of any division if the total amount of tax which it was liable to pay in respect of the prescribed accounting periods of that division the ends of which fell within the period of one year ending on the last day of—
  (a) that division's last prescribed accounting period ending before [1st December of the previous year][1], or
  (b) a prescribed accounting period of that division ending after [30th November of the previous year][1],
and which was referable to the business of that division exceeded [the figure specified in article 5(1) or 6(1) respectively][2].
[(2) Where a relevant division has a prescribed accounting period exceeding one month which begins on or after 2nd March each year and ends on or before 30th June each year, the body corporate shall be under a like duty to make payments on account also in respect of that prescribed accounting period.][1]
(3) Articles 5(2) and 6(2) above shall apply for the purposes of this article as if for the references therein to the taxable person there were substituted references to a relevant division.
(4) Where payments on account fall to be made under this article, they shall be calculated and made separately in the case of each relevant division as if it were a taxable person and shall be remitted to the Controller through that division.
(5) In relation to a body corporate to which this article applies, references in articles 7, 13, 14 and 15 above to—
  (a) the total amount of tax which a taxable person was or will be liable to pay shall be construed as references to the total amount of such tax referable to the business of a relevant division; and
  (b) an application by the taxable person shall be construed as references to an application by the division in respect of which the application is made.
(6) In this article "relevant division" means a division by reference to the business of which a body corporate is under a duty to make payments on account by virtue of paragraph (1) above.

Notes—[1] Words in para (1) and whole of para (2) substituted by the VAT (Payments on Account) (Amendment) Order, SI 1995/291 arts 11, 12 with effect from 2 March 1995.
[2] In para (1), words substituted for figure "£2,000,000" by the VAT (Payments on Account) (Amendment) Order, SI 2011/21 art 2(e) with effect from 1 June 2011.
[3] VATA 1994 s 46(1).

17 Groups of companies

This Order shall apply in relation to any bodies corporate which are treated as members of a group under [section 43][1] of the Act as if those bodies were one taxable person; and where there is a duty to make a payment on account it shall be the responsibility of the representative member, except that in default of payment by the representative member it shall be the joint and several responsibility of each member of the group.

Amendments—[1] Words substituted by the VAT (Payments on Account) (Amendment) Order, SI 1996/1196 art 11 with effect from 1 June 1996.

1994/955

TRAVELLERS' ALLOWANCES ORDER 1994

Made by the Commissioners of Customs and Excise under CED(GR)A 1979 s 13(1) and (3)

Made .... 28 March 1994
Laid before the House of Commons .... 29 March 1994
Coming into force .... 1 April 1994

1 This Order may be cited as the Travellers' Allowances Order 1994 and shall come into force on 1st April 1994.

[Interpretation

1A (1) In this Order "excise goods" means any goods chargeable with excise duty by virtue of any provision of—

    (*a*) the Alcoholic Liquor Duties Act 1979; or

    (*b*) the Tobacco Products Duty Act 1979.

(2) For the purposes of this Order, goods shall be treated as contained in a person's personal luggage where they are carried with or accompanied by that person or, if intended to accompany that person, were at the time of that person's departure for the UK consigned by that person as personal luggage to the transport operator with whom that person travelled.][1]

Amendments—[1] Article 1A inserted by the Travellers' Allowances and Miscellaneous Provisions (EU Exit) Regulations, SI 2020/1412 regs 2, 3 with effect from IP completion day (11pm UK time on 31 December 2020).

Transitional provisions—The Travellers' Allowances Order 1994 as it had effect immediately before IP completion day continues to have effect in relation to persons who are travelling on a voyage, flight or railway journey to the United Kingdom that is scheduled to depart before IP completion day (see the Travellers' Allowances and Miscellaneous Provisions (EU Exit) Regulations, SI 2020/1412 reg 22).

[Travellers' reliefs – Great Britain][2]

2—(1) Subject to the following provisions of this Order a person . . . [2] shall on entering the United Kingdom [at a place in Great Britain][2] be relieved from payment of value added tax and excise duty on goods of the descriptions and in the quantities shown in [Schedule 1][2] to this Order . . . [1] contained in his personal luggage.

. . . [2]

Amendments—[1] Words in para (1) revoked, para (2)(*c*) substituted, and para (3) inserted, by the Travellers' Allowances (Amendment) Order, SI 2008/3058 art 2, Sch paras 1–3 with effect from 1 December 2008.

[2] Heading inserted, in para (1) words revoked, inserted, and substituted, and paras (2) and (3) revoked, by the Travellers' Allowances and Miscellaneous Provisions (EU Exit) Regulations, SI 2020/1412 regs 2–4 with effect from IP completion day (11pm UK time on 31 December 2020). Paras (2) and (3) previously read as follows—

"(2) For the purposes of this article—

    (*a*) goods shall be treated as contained in a person's personal luggage where they are carried with or accompanied by the person or, if intended to accompany him, were at the time of his departure for the United Kingdom consigned by him as personal luggage to the transport operator with whom he travelled;

    (*b*) a person shall not be treated as having travelled from a third country by reason only of his having arrived from its territorial waters or air space;

    [(*c*) "third country"—

        (i) shares the definition that applies to that expression for the purposes of Council Directive 2007/74/EC (this is termed "outside country" below) (see both indents of Article 3(1) of the Directive) (value added tax and excise duty exemptions for travellers from outside the Member States of the European Union, etc); but

        (ii) it incorporates the definition that applies for the purposes of that Directive to "territory where the Community provisions on VAT or excise duty, or both do not apply" (this is termed "outside territory" below) (see both indents of Article 3(2) of that Directive); but

        (iii) any outside territory where those "Community provisions on VAT" do apply (or where that Directive regards them as applying) is not a third country for value added tax purposes; and

        (iv) any outside territory where those "Community provisions on . . . excise duty" do apply (or where that Directive regards them as applying) is not a third country for excise duty purposes.]

[(3) Where the person's journey involved transit through an outside country, or began in outside territory, this Order applies if that person is unable to establish to an officer of Revenue and Customs that the goods contained in that person's personal luggage were acquired subject to the general conditions governing taxation on the domestic market of a member State and do not qualify for any refunding of value added tax or excise duty."

Transitional provisions—The Travellers' Allowances Order 1994 as it had effect immediately before IP completion day continues to have effect in relation to persons who are travelling on a voyage, flight or railway journey to the United Kingdom that is scheduled to depart before IP completion day (see the Travellers' Allowances and Miscellaneous Provisions (EU Exit) Regulations, SI 2020/1412 reg 22).

3 The reliefs afforded under this Order are subject to the condition that the goods in question, as indicated by their nature or quantity or otherwise, are not imported for a commercial purpose nor are used for such purpose; and if that condition is not complied with in relation to any goods, those goods shall, unless the non-compliance was sanctioned by the Commissioners, be liable to forfeiture. . . . [1]

Amendments—[1] Words revoked by the Travellers' Allowances and Miscellaneous Provisions (EU Exit) Regulations, SI 2020/1412 regs 2 and 5 with effect from IP completion day (11pm UK time on 31 December 2020). Revoked words previously read as follows—

"That condition is complied with, for example, where an occasional importation consists exclusively of goods intended as presents, or of goods for the personal or family use of the person in question.

(See Article 6 of Council Directive 2007/74/EC (non-commercial imports).)"

Transitional provisions—The Travellers' Allowances Order 1994 as it had effect immediately before IP completion day continues to have effect in relation to persons who are travelling on a voyage, flight or railway journey to the United Kingdom that is scheduled to depart before IP completion day (see the Travellers' Allowances and Miscellaneous Provisions (EU Exit) Regulations, SI 2020/1412 reg 22).

4 No relief shall be afforded under this Order to any person under the age of 17 in respect of tobacco products[, alcoholic beverages and alcohol][1].

Amendments—[1] Words substituted, by the Travellers' Allowances (Amendment) Order, SI 2008/3058 art 2, Sch para 5 with effect from 1 December 2008.

[Simplified calculation of excise duty

6 (1) This article has effect for the purposes of calculating the excise duty payable by a person entering the United Kingdom at a place in Great Britain on excise goods contained in the person's personal luggage.

(2) The person may elect for paragraph (3) to apply provided that the upper threshold given in column B of the Table in Schedule 2 and applicable to any of the goods is not exceeded.

(3) Where this paragraph applies, the sum calculated by applying the rate specified in column A of that Table in respect of a description of goods is treated as the amount of excise duty payable on any goods of that description.][1]

Amendments—[1] Article 6 inserted by the Travellers' Allowances and Miscellaneous Provisions (EU Exit) Regulations, SI 2020/1412 regs 2, 6 with effect from IP completion day (11pm UK time on 31 December 2020).

Transitional provisions—The Travellers' Allowances Order 1994 as it had effect immediately before IP completion day continues to have effect in relation to persons who are travelling on a voyage, flight or railway journey to the United Kingdom that is scheduled to depart before IP completion day (see the Travellers' Allowances and Miscellaneous Provisions (EU Exit) Regulations, SI 2020/1412 reg 22).

SCHEDULE [1][3]
Article 2

[Description	Quantity
Goods other than fuel and those described below	Total value [£390][2] or less, if the person [travelled by air, sea or rail][3]. Total value [£270][2] or less, if the person [travelled by way of private pleasureflying or private pleasure-sea-navigation][3]. Notes: (a) . . .[2] (b) Private pleasure-flying or private pleasure-sea-navigation . . .[3] refers to the use of an aircraft or a sea-going vessel by its owner or the person who enjoys its use either through hire or through any other means, for purposes other than commercial and in particular other than for the carriage of passengers or goods or for the supply of services for consideration or for the purposes of public authorities. (c) The value of an individual item must not be split up. (d) The value of the person's personal luggage if imported temporarily or re-imported following its temporary export, and of medicinal products required to meet the person's personal needs, is excluded from consideration. (e) . . .[3]
Alcoholic beverages and alcohol, other than beer and still wine	[4 litres][3] of alcohol and alcoholic beverages of an alcoholic strength exceeding 22% by volume, or undenatured ethyl alcohol of 80% by volume and over; or [9 litres][3] of alcohol and alcoholic beverages of an alcoholic strength not exceeding 22% by volume. Notes: (f) Each respective amount represents 100% of the total relief afforded for alcohol and alcoholic beverages. (g) For any one person, the relief applies to any combination of the types of alcohol and alcoholic beverage described, provided that the aggregate of the percentages used up from the relief the person is afforded for such alcohol and alcoholic beverage does not exceed 100%. (h) . . .[3]
Beer	[42 litres][3] or less Notes: (i) . . .
Still wine	[18 litres][3] or less Notes: (j) . . .[3]

[Description	Quantity
Tobacco products	200 cigarettes, or 100 cigarillos, or 50 cigars, or 250 grams of smoking tobacco[, or 200 sticks of tobacco for heating]³.
	Notes:
	(k) Each respective amount represents 100% of the total relief afforded for tobacco products.
	(l) For any one person, the relief applies to any combination of tobacco products provided that the aggregate of the percentages used up from the relief the person is afforded for such products does not exceed 100%.
	(m) A cigarillo is a cigar of maximum weight 3 grams.
	(n) . . . ³]¹

Amendments—¹ Table substituted, and words in previous table heading revoked, by the Travellers' Allowances (Amendment) Order, SI 2008/3058 art 2, Sch para 6 with effect from 1 December 2008.
² In column 2, figures substituted and Note (a) revoked, by the Travellers' Allowances (Amendment) Order, SI 2009/3172 arts 2, 3 with effect where the person in question enters the UK on or after 1 January 2010.
³ Schedule 1 numbered as such, tables entries amended, words in note (b) revoked, and notes (e), (h), (i), (j) and (n) revoked, by the Travellers' Allowances (Amendment) Order, SI 2009/3172 arts 2, 7 with effect where the person in question enters the UK on or after 1 January 2010.
Transitional provisions—The Travellers' Allowances Order 1994 as it had effect immediately before IP completion day continues to have effect in relation to persons who are travelling on a voyage, flight or railway journey to the United Kingdom that is scheduled to depart before IP completion day (see the Travellers' Allowances and Miscellaneous Provisions (EU Exit) Regulations, SI 2020/1412 reg 22).

[SCHEDULE 2

SIMPLIFIED CALCULATION OF EXCISE DUTY (GREAT BRITAIN)

Article 6

Description	A: Rate of Excise Duty	B: Upper threshold
Alcoholic beverages and alcohol—		
Beer	£0.80 per litre	110 litres
Still wine	£2.97 per litre	90 litres
Sparkling wine	£3.81 per litre	60 litres
Cider	£0.40 per litre	20 litres
Sparkling cider of an alcoholic strength not exceeding 5.5% by volume	£0.40 per litre	20 litres
Made-wine	£2.97 per litre	20 litres
Spirits	£10.77 per litre	10 litres
Tobacco products—		
Cigarettes	£320.90 per 1000 cigarettes	800 cigarettes
Hand rolling tobacco	£271.40 per kilogram	1 kilogram
Other smoking tobacco and chewing tobacco	£134.24 per kilogram	1 kilogram
Cigars	£305.32 per kilogram	200 cigars
Cigarillos (a cigarillo is a cigar weighing no more than 3 grams each)	£305.32 per kilogram	400 cigarillos
Tobacco for heating	£75.48 per 1000 sticks	800 sticks]¹

Amendments—¹ Schedule 2 inserted by the Travellers' Allowances (Amendment) Order, SI 2009/3172 arts 2, 8 with effect where the person in question enters the UK on or after 1 January 2010.
Transitional provisions—The Travellers' Allowances Order 1994 as it had effect immediately before IP completion day continues to have effect in relation to persons who are travelling on a voyage, flight or railway journey to the United Kingdom that is scheduled to depart before IP completion day (see the Travellers' Allowances and Miscellaneous Provisions (EU Exit) Regulations, SI 2020/1412 reg 22).

1995/958

VALUE ADDED TAX (TREATMENT OF TRANSACTIONS) ORDER 1995

Made by the Treasury under VATA 1994 s 5(3)

Made . . . . .30 March 1995
Laid before the House of Commons .31 March 1995
Coming into force in accordance with article 1 . . . . .1 May 1995

1 This Order may be cited as the Value Added Tax (Treatment of Transactions) Order 1995 and shall come into force on the day that the Finance Bill 1995 is passed.

[**2** In this Order—
"temporary admission with full customs duty relief" means—
(a) in Great Britain, the temporary admission procedure under Part 1 of the Taxation (Cross-border Trade) Act 2018, where full relief from a liability to import duty is to be given under regulation 40 of the Customs (Special Procedures and Outward Processing) (EU Exit) Regulations 2018;
(b) in Northern Ireland, the customs procedure for temporary importation with total relief from import duties provided for in Articles 250, 251 and 253 of Regulation (EU) No 952/2013 of the European Parliament and of the Council of 9 October 2013 laying down the Union Customs Code as it has effect in Northern Ireland as a result of section 7A of the European Union (Withdrawal) Act 2020;
"work of art" has the same meaning as in section 21 of the Value Added Tax Act 1994.][1]

Amendments—[1] Article 2 substituted by the Value Added Tax (Miscellaneous Amendments, Northern Ireland Protocol and Savings and Transitional Provisions) (EU Exit) Regulations, SI 2020/1545 regs 26, 27 with effect from IP completion day (11pm UK time on 31 December 2020) by virtue of SI 2020/1641 reg 2, Schedule para 11. Article 2 previously read as follows—

"**2**

In this Order "work of art" has the same meaning as in section 21 of the Value Added Tax Act 1994."

3—(1) Subject to paragraph (3) below, the transfer of ownership in—
(a) second-hand goods imported [into the United Kingdom][2] with a view to their sale by auction;
(b) works of art imported [into the United Kingdom][2] for the purposes of exhibition, with a view to possible sale,
at a time when the second-hand goods or works of art, as the case may be, are still subject to arrangements for [temporary admission with full customs duty relief][3] . . . [1], shall be treated as neither a supply of goods nor a supply of services.

(2) Subject to paragraph (3) [and article 4][1] below, the provision of any services relating to a transfer of ownership falling within paragraph (1)(a) or (b) above shall be treated as neither a supply of goods nor a supply of services.

(3) Paragraphs (1) and (2) above shall not apply in relation to any transfer of ownership in second-hand goods which is effected otherwise than by sale by auction.

Amendments—[1] Words in art 3(1) revoked, words in 3(2), and whole of new art 4 inserted, by the Value Added Tax (Treatment of Transactions and Special Provisions) (Amendment) Order, SI 2006/2187, art 2(1)–(3), with effect from 1 September 2006.
[2] In para (1)(a), (b) words substituted for words "from a place outside the member States" by the Value Added Tax (Miscellaneous Amendments and Revocations) (EU Exit) Regulations, SI 2019/59 reg 10(1), (2) with effect from IP completion day (11pm UK time on 31 December 2020).
[3] In the words after para (1)(b), words substituted for words "temporary importation with total exemption from import duty in accordance with Articles 137 to 141 and paragraph 1 of Article 144 of Council Regulation (EEC) No 2913/92" by the Value Added Tax (Miscellaneous Amendments, Northern Ireland Protocol and Savings and Transitional Provisions) (EU Exit) Regulations, SI 2020/1545 regs 26, 28 with effect from IP completion day (11pm UK time on 31 December 2020) by virtue of SI 2020/1641 reg 2, Schedule para 11.

[**4**—(1) Article 3(1) does not apply where—
(a) any goods falling within paragraph (2) are sold by auction at a time when they are subject to the procedure specified in paragraph (3), and
(b) arrangements made by or on behalf of the purchaser of the goods following the sale by auction result in the importation of the goods [into the United Kingdom][2].
(See section 21(2A) of the Value Added Tax Act 1994.)

(2) The goods that fall within this paragraph are—
(a) any work of art;
(b) any antique, not falling within sub-paragraph (a) or (c), that is more than one hundred years old;
(c) any collection or collector's piece that is of zoological, botanical, mineralogical, anatomical, historical, archaeological, palaeontological, ethnographic, numismatic or philatelic interest.
(See sections 21(5) to 21(6C) of the Value Added Tax Act 1994.)

[(3) That procedure is the temporary admission with full customs duty relief procedure.][3]

Amendments—[1] Words in art 3(1) revoked, words in 3(2), and whole of new art 4 inserted, by the Value Added Tax (Treatment of Transactions and Special Provisions) (Amendment) Order, SI 2006/2187, art 2(1)–(3), with effect from 1 September 2006.
[2] In para (1)(b) words substituted for words "from a place outside the member States" by the Value Added Tax (Miscellaneous Amendments and Revocations) (EU Exit) Regulations, SI 2019/59 reg 10(1), (3) with effect from IP completion day (11pm UK time on 31 December 2020).

[3] Para (3) substituted by the Value Added Tax (Miscellaneous Amendments, Northern Ireland Protocol and Savings and Transitional Provisions) (EU Exit) Regulations, SI 2020/1545 regs 26, 29 with effect from IP completion day (11pm UK time on 31 December 2020) by virtue of SI 2020/1641 reg 2, Schedule para 11. Para (3) previously read as follows—
"(3) That procedure is the customs procedure for temporary importation with total relief from import duties provided for in Articles 137 to 141 of Council Regulation (EEC) No 2913/92 establishing the Community Customs Code.
(See section 21(2B) of the Value Added Tax Act 1994.)"

1995/1268

VALUE ADDED TAX (SPECIAL PROVISIONS) ORDER 1995

Made by the Treasury under VATA 1994 ss 5(3), (5), 11(4), 43(2), 50A

Made . . . . .10 May 1995
Laid before the House of Commons . . . . .10 May 1995
Coming into force . . . . .1 June 1995

1 Citation and commencement
This Order may be cited as the Value Added Tax (Special provisions) Order 1995, and shall come into force on 1st June 1995.

2[Interpretation
(1)] [4] In this Order—
"finance agreement" means an agreement for the sale of goods whereby the property in those goods is not to be transferred until the whole of the price has been paid and the seller retains the right to repossess the goods;
. . .[6]
"marine mortgage" means a mortgage which is registered in accordance with the [Merchant Shipping Act 1995][7] and by virtue of which a boat (but not any share thereof) is made a security for a loan;
"aircraft mortgage" means a mortgage which is registered in accordance with the Mortgaging of Aircraft Order 1972 and by virtue of which an aircraft is made security for a loan;
"the Act" means the Value Added Tax Act 1994;
"the Manx Act" means [the Value Added Tax Act 1996][1];
["work of art" has the same meaning as in section 21 of the Act.][3]
"antiques" means objects other than works of art or collectors' items, which are more than 100 years old;
["collectors' items" means any collection or collector's piece falling within section 21(5) of the Act but excluding investment gold coins within the meaning of Note 1(b) and (c) to Group 15 of Schedule 9 to the Act;][3]
["Motor car" means any motor vehicle of a kind normally used on public roads which has three or more wheels and either—
  (a) is constructed or adapted solely or mainly for the carriage of passengers; or
  (b) has to the rear of the driver's seat roofed accommodation which is fitted with side windows or which is constructed or adapted for the fitting of side windows;
  but does not include—
  (i) vehicles capable of accommodating only one person;
  (ii) vehicles which meet the requirements of Schedule 6 to the Road Vehicles (Construction and Use) Regulations 1986 and are capable of carrying twelve or more seated persons;
  (iii) vehicles of not less than three tonnes unladen weight (as defined in the Table to regulation 3(2) of the Road Vehicles (Construction and Use) Regulations 1986);
  (iv) vehicles constructed to carry a payload (the difference between a vehicle's kerb weight (as defined in the Table to regulation 3(2) of the Road Vehicles (Construction and Use) Regulations 1986) and its maximum gross weight (as defined in that Table)) of one tonne or more;
  (v) caravans, ambulances and prison vans;
  (vi) vehicles constructed for a special purpose other than the carriage of persons and having no other accommodation for carrying persons than such as is incidental to that purpose;][2]
"second-hand goods" means tangible movable property that is suitable for further use as it is or after repair, other than motor cars, works of art, collectors' items or antiques and other than precious metals and precious stones;
"printed matter" includes printed stationery but does not include anything produced by typing, duplicating or photo-copying;[5]
"auctioneer" means a person who sells or offers for sale goods at any public sale where persons become purchasers by competition, being the highest bidders.
(2) . . .[6]

9 The following description of transaction shall be treated as neither a supply of goods nor a supply of services—

services in connection with a supply of goods provided by an agent acting in his own name to the purchaser of the goods the consideration for which is taken into account by virtue of article 12(6) below in calculating the price at which the agent obtained the goods.

10 The following description of transaction shall be treated as neither a supply of goods nor a supply of services—

services in connection with the sale of goods provided by an auctioneer acting in his own name to the vendor or the purchaser of the goods the consideration for which is taken into account by virtue of article 12(7) below in calculating the price at which the auctioneer obtained (or as the case may be) sold the goods.

10A [**Goods put to private use or used, or made available for use, for non-business purposes** Paragraph 5(4) of Schedule 4 to the Act shall not apply to goods (including land treated as goods for the purposes of that paragraph by virtue of paragraph 9 of that Schedule) which have no economic life for the purposes of Part 15A of the Value Added Tax Regulations 1995 at the time when they are used or made available for use.][1]
Amendments—[1] Para 10A inserted by the VAT (Special Provisions) (Amendment) Order, SI 2007/2923 arts 2, 3 with effect from 1 November 2007 in relation to the use, on or after that date, of goods or land held or used for the purposes of a business: SI 2007/2923 art 1.

11 Self-supply
(1) Where a person in the course or furtherance of any business carried on by him produces printed matter and the printed matter—
   (a) is not supplied to another person or incorporated in other goods produced in the course or furtherance of that business; but
   (b) is used by him for the purpose of a business carried on by him,
then, subject to paragraph (2) below, the printed matter shall be treated for the purposes of the Act as both supplied to him for the purpose of that business and supplied by him in the course or furtherance of that business.
(2) Paragraph (1) of this article does not apply if—
   (a) the person is a fully taxable person;
   (b) the value of the supplies falling to be treated as made by and to that person would not, if those were the only supplies made or to be made by that person, make him liable to be registered for VAT pursuant to the provisions of Schedule 1 to the Act; or
   (c) the Commissioners, being satisfied that the VAT (if any) which would be attributable to the supplies after allowing for any credit under sections 25 and 26 of the Act would be negligible, have given, and have not withdrawn, a direction that the paragraph is not to apply.
(3) For the purposes of paragraph (2)(a) above, a person is a fully taxable person if the only input tax of his to which he is not entitled to credit at the end of any prescribed accounting period or longer period is input tax which is excluded from any credit under section 25 of the Act by virtue of any Order made under sub-section (7) of that section.
(4) The preceding provisions of this article shall apply in relation to any bodies corporate which are treated for the purposes of section 43 of the Act as members of a group as if those bodies were one person, but any printed matter which would fall to be treated as supplied to and by that person shall be treated as supplied to and by the representative member.
Amendment—Revoked by the VAT (Special Provisions) (Amendment) Order, SI 2002/1280 arts 2, 3 with effect from 1 June 2002. See SI 2002/1280 art 1(2) for circumstances in which this amendment shall not have effect.

12 Relief for certain goods
(1) Without prejudice to article 13 below and subject to complying with such conditions as the Commissioners may direct in a notice published by them for the purposes of this Order or may otherwise direct and subject to paragraph (4) below, where a person supplies goods of a description in paragraph (2) below, of which he took possession in any of the circumstances set out in paragraph (3) below, he may opt to account for the VAT chargeable on the supply on the profit margin on the supply instead of by reference to its value.
(2) The supplies referred to in paragraph (1) above are supplies of—
   (a) works of art, antiques and collectors' items;
   (b) second-hand goods.
(3) The circumstances mentioned in paragraph (1) above are—
   [(a) [subject to paragraph (aa),][6] that the taxable person took possession of the goods pursuant to—
      (i) a supply in respect of which no VAT was chargeable under the Act or under Part I of the Manx Act;

(ii) a supply on which VAT was chargeable on the profit margin in accordance with paragraph (1) above or a corresponding provision made under the Manx Act or a corresponding provision of the law of [a member State][6] [where the goods are removed to Northern Ireland][6];
[(iii) a de-supplied transaction, other than an article 5 transaction;
(iv) subject to paragraph (3A) below, an article 5 transaction;][4]
(v) (if the goods are a work of art) a supply to the taxable person by, or an acquisition from [a member State][6] by him from its creator or his successor in title;][1]
[(aa) but the circumstances in sub-paragraph (a) do not apply if the person took possession of the goods in Great Britain or the Isle of Man and the goods are removed to Northern Ireland.][6]
(b) (if the goods are a work of art, an antique or a collectors' item) that they were imported by the taxable person himself[, which includes – if the taxable person is an auctioneer – the auctioneer having placed them in][5][—
(i) a temporary admission procedure under Part 1 of the Taxation (Cross-border Trade) Act 2018, where full relief from a liability to import duty is to be given under regulation 40 of the Customs (Special Procedures and Outward Processing) (EU Exit) Regulations 2018;
(ii) the customs procedure for temporary importation with total relief from import duties provided for in Articles 250, 251 and 253 of Regulation (EU) No 952/2013 of the European Parliament and of the Council of 9 October 2013 laying down the Union Customs Code as it has effect in Northern Ireland as a result of section 7A of the European Union (Withdrawal) Act 2020.][6]
[(3A) An article 5 transaction does not fall within paragraph (iv) of paragraph (3)(a) above unless the taxable person has a relevant predecessor in title.][4]
(4) A taxable person—
(a) may not opt under paragraph (1) above where—
(i) the supply is a letting on hire;
(ii) an invoice or similar document showing an amount as being VAT or as being attributable to VAT is issued in respect of the supply;
(iii) the supply is of an air gun unless the taxable person is registered for the purposes of the Firearms Act 1968; or
(iv) the supply is of goods which are being disposed of in the circumstances mentioned in article 4(1)(a)(b)(c) or (d) above but which is not disregarded by virtue of that article;
(b) may only exercise the option under paragraph (1) above in relation to supplies of—
(i) works of art of which he took possession in the circumstances mentioned in paragraph [(3)(a)(v)][2] above, or
(ii) works of art, antiques or collectors' items of which he took possession in circumstances set out in paragraph (3)(b) above,
if at the same time he exercises the option in relation to the other.
(5) Subject to paragraph (6) below, for the purposes of determining the profit margin—
(a) the price at which goods were obtained shall be calculated as follows—
(i) (where the taxable person took possession of the goods pursuant to a supply) in the same way as the consideration for the supply would be calculated for the purposes of the Act;
(ii) (where the taxable person is a sole proprietor and the goods were supplied to him in his private capacity) in the same way as the consideration for the supply to him as a private individual would be calculated for the purposes of the Act;
(iii) (where the goods are a work of art which was acquired from [a member State][6] by the taxable person pursuant to a supply to him by the creator of the item or his successor in title) in the same way as the value of the acquisition would be calculated for the purposes of the Act plus the VAT chargeable on the acquisition;
(iv) (where the goods are a work of art, an antique or a collectors' item which the taxable person has imported himself[, which includes – if the taxable person is an auctioneer – the auctioneer having placed them in][5] [a temporary admission procedure mentioned in article 12(3)(b)(i) or the customs procedure for temporary importation mentioned in article 12(3)(b)(ii) as the case may be][6]) in the same way as the value of the goods for the purpose of charging VAT on their importation would be calculated for the purposes of the Act plus any VAT chargeable on their importation;
[(v) (where the taxable person took possession of the goods pursuant to a de-supplied transaction, other than an article 5 transaction) by taking the price he paid pursuant to the transaction;
(vi) (where the taxable person took possession of the goods pursuant to an article 5 transaction) by taking the price at which his relevant predecessor in title obtained the goods;][4]

(b) the price at which goods are sold shall be calculated in the same way as the consideration for the supply would be calculated for the purposes of the Act[;
(c) . . . ⁴
(6) Subject to paragraph (7) below, where the taxable person is an agent acting in his own name the price at which the goods were obtained shall be calculated in accordance with paragraph (5)(a) above, but the selling price calculated in accordance with paragraph (5)(b) above shall be increased by the amount of any consideration payable to the taxable person in respect of services supplied by him to the purchaser in connection with the supply of the goods.
(7) Instead of calculating the price at which goods were obtained or supplied in accordance with paragraph (6) above an auctioneer acting in his own name may—
- [(a) calculate the price at which they were obtained by deducting from the successful bid the amount of the commission payable to him under his contract with the vendor for the sale of the goods;]³
- (b) calculate the price at which they were supplied by adding to the successful bid the consideration for any supply of services by him to the purchaser in connection with the sale of the goods,

in either (or both) cases excluding the consideration for supplies of services that are not chargeable to VAT.
(8) Where a taxable person opts under paragraph (1) above in respect of goods of which he took possession in the circumstances set out in paragraph [(3)(a)(v)]² and (b) above, the exercise of the option shall—
- (a) be notified by him to the Commissioners in writing;
- (b) have effect from the date of that notification or such later date as may be specified therein;
- (c) subject to paragraph (9) below, apply to all supplies of such goods made by the taxable person in the period ending 2 years after the date on which it first had effect or the date on which written notification of its revocation is given to the Commissioners, whichever is the later.

(9) Notwithstanding paragraph (8)(c) above a taxable person may elect to account for VAT chargeable on any particular supply of such goods by reference to the value of that supply.
[(10) For the purposes of this article—
"article 5 transaction" means a transaction which is a de-supplied transaction by virtue of a provision of article 5 above or a corresponding provision made under the Manx Act;
"de-supplied transaction" means a transaction which was treated by virtue of any Order made or having effect as if made under section 5(3) of the Act or under the corresponding provisions of the Manx Act as being neither a supply of goods nor a supply of services.
(11) For the purposes of this article a person is a relevant predecessor in title of a taxable person if—
- (a) he is the person from whom the taxable person took possession of the goods and himself took possession of them in any of the circumstances described in paragraph (3) above, but not pursuant to an article 5 transaction; or
- (b) where the goods have been the subject of a succession of two or more article 5 transactions (culminating in the article 5 transaction to which the taxable person was a party), he was a party to one of those transactions and himself took possession of the goods in any of the circumstances described in paragraph (3) above, but not pursuant to an article 5 transaction.]⁴

Amendments—[1] Para (3)(a) substituted by the VAT (Special Provisions) (Amendment) Order SI 1997/1616 with effect from 3 July 1997.
[2] Words in paras (4)(b)(i), (8) substituted, by the VAT (Special Provisions) (Amendment) Order, SI 1998/760 with effect from 18 March 1998.
[3] Para (7)(a) substituted by the VAT (Special Provisions) (Amendment) Order, SI 2001/3753 art 3 with effect from 2 January 2002.
[4] Sub-paras (3)(a)(iii), (iv) substituted, para (3A) inserted, sub-paras (5)(a)(v), (vi) substituted for sub-para (5)(a)(v), sub-para (5)(c) revoked, and paras (10), (11) added, by the VAT (Special Provisions) (Amendment) (No 2) Order, SI 2002/1503 with effect from 1 July 2002. For further provisions as to the effect of that Order see SI 2002/1503 art 1(2).
[5] Words in paras (3)(b) and (5)(a)(iv) inserted by the Value Added Tax (Tax Treatment of Transactions and Special Provisions) (Amendment) Order, SI 2006/2187, art 3(2), (3), with effect from 1 September 2006.
[6] Words substituted for words "another member State" in each place, in para (3)(a) words inserted, para (3)(aa) inserted, and in paras (3)(b) and (5)(a)(iv) words substituted, by the Value Added Tax (Miscellaneous Amendments, Northern Ireland Protocol and Savings and Transitional Provisions) (EU Exit) Regulations, SI 2020/1545 reg 30(1), (2) and (5) with effect from IP completion day (11pm UK time on 31 December 2020). by virtue of SI 2020/1641 reg 2, Schedule para 11. Paras (3)(b) and (5)(a)(iv) previously read as follows—

"(b) (if the goods are a work of art, an antique or a collectors' item) that they were imported by the taxable person himself, which includes – if the taxable person is an auctioneer – the auctioneer having placed them in the customs procedure for temporary importation with total relief from import duties provided for in Articles 137 to 141 of Council Regulation (EEC) No 2913/92 establishing the Community Customs Code.".

"(iv) (where the goods are a work of art, an antique or a collectors' item which the taxable person has imported himself, which includes – if the taxable person is an auctioneer – the auctioneer having placed them in the customs procedure for temporary importation with total relief from import duties mentioned in article 12(3)(*b*)) in the same way as the value of the goods for the purpose of charging VAT on their importation would be calculated for the purposes of the Act plus any VAT chargeable on their importation;".

Para (3)(*aa*) does not apply where—
- (a) a person ("P") took possession of the goods in Great Britain or the Isle of Man before IP completion day and P would have been eligible to opt to account for the VAT chargeable on a supply of the goods on the profit margin in accordance with article 12 of the Order had they been so supplied before IP completion day; and
- (b) the ownership of the goods remained with P from the time P took possession of the goods under paragraph (a) to the time of the supply of the goods on which P elects to account for the VAT chargeable on that supply on the profit margin in accordance with article 12 of the Order.

See SI 2020/1545 reg 124.

[12A Relief for certain goods removed from Northern Ireland to Great Britain

Article 12 has effect as if in paragraph (1)—
- (*a*) after "in any of the circumstances set out in paragraph (3) below," there were inserted "and the supply involves the removal of the goods from Northern Ireland to Great Britain,"; and
- (*b*) for "VAT chargeable on the supply" there were substituted "VAT chargeable on the removal".][1]

Amendments—[1] Article 12A inserted by the Value Added Tax (Miscellaneous Amendments, Northern Ireland Protocol and Savings and Transitional Provisions) (EU Exit) Regulations, SI 2020/1545 reg 30(1) and (6) with effect from IP completion day (11pm UK time on 31 December 2020) by virtue of SI 2020/1641 reg 2, Schedule para 11.

13 Global Accounting

(1) Subject to complying with such conditions as the Commissioners may direct in a notice published by them for the purposes of this Order or may otherwise direct, and subject to paragraph (2) below, a taxable person who has opted under article 12(1) above may account for VAT on the total profit margin on goods supplied by him during a prescribed accounting period, calculated in accordance with paragraph (3) below, instead of the profit margin on each supply.

(2) Paragraph (1) above does not apply to supplies of—
- (*a*) motor vehicles;
- (*b*) aircraft;
- (*c*) boats and outboard motors;
- (*d*) caravans and motor caravans;
- (*e*) horses and ponies;
- (*f*) any other individual items whose value calculated in accordance with article 12(5)(*a*) above, exceeds £500.

[(3) The total profit margin for a prescribed accounting period shall be the amount (if any) by which the total selling price calculated in accordance with paragraph (4) below, exceeds the total purchase price calculated in accordance with paragraph (5) below.][1]

(4) For the purposes of paragraph (3) above the total selling price shall be calculated by aggregating for all goods sold during the period the prices (calculated in accordance with article 12(5) or (6) above as appropriate) for which they were sold.

(5) For the purposes of paragraph (3) above the total purchase price shall be calculated by aggregating for all goods obtained during the period the prices (calculated in accordance with article 12(5) above) at which they were obtained and adding to that total the amount (if any) carried forward from the previous period in accordance with paragraph (6) below.

(6) If in any prescribed accounting period the total purchase price calculated in accordance with paragraph (5) above exceeds the total selling price, the excess amount shall be carried forward to the following prescribed accounting period for inclusion in the calculation of the total purchase price for that period.

Amendments—[1] Para (3) substituted by the VAT (Special Provisions) (Amendment) (No 2) Order, SI 1999/3120, arts 2, 4, with effect from 1 January 2000.

1995/2518

VALUE ADDED TAX REGULATIONS 1995

Made by the Commissioners of Customs and Excise under VATA 1994 ss 3(4), 6(14), 7(9), 8(4), 12(3), 14(3), 16(1) and (2), 18(5), (5A), 24(3), (4), (6), 25(1), (4), (6), 26(1), (3), (4), 28(3), (4) and (5), 30(8), 35(2), 36(5), 37(3) and (4), 38, 39(1), 40(3), 46(2), (4), 48(3)(b), (4), (6), 49(2), (3), 52, 54(1), (2), (3), (6), 58, 79(3), 80(6), 88(3), (5), 92(4), 93(1), (2), 95(5), 97(1) and Sch 1 para 17, Sch 2 para 9, Sch 3 para 10, Sch 7 paras 2(1)–(2), and Sch 11 paras 2(1)–(12), 5(4), (9), 6(1)–(2) and 7(1)

Made . . . . .27 September 1995
Laid before the House of Commons . . . . .28 September 1995
Coming into force . . . . .20 October 1995

ARRANGEMENT OF REGULATIONS

PART I PRELIMINARY

1	Citation and commencement.
2	Interpretation—general.
3	Revocations and savings.
4	Requirement, direction, demand or permission.
4A, 4B	Electronic communication.

PART II REGISTRATION AND PROVISIONS FOR SPECIAL CASES

5	Registration and notification.
6	Transfer of a going concern.
7	Notice by partnership.
8	Representation of club, association or organisation.
9	Death, bankruptcy or incapacity of taxable person.
10	VAT representatives.
11	Notification of intended section 14(1) supplies by intermediate suppliers.
12	Notification of intended section 14(2) supplies by persons belonging in other member States.

PART III VAT INVOICES AND OTHER INVOICING REQUIREMENTS

A13	*Interpretation of Part 3* (revoked).
13	Obligation to provide a VAT invoice.
13A, 13B	Electronic invoicing.
14	Contents of VAT invoice.
15	Change of rate, credit notes.
15A	Change of rate, supplementary charge invoices.
15B	Change of liability: anti-forestalling invoices.
15C	Changes in consideration: debit notes and credit notes.
16	Retailers' invoices.
16A	Simplified invoices.
16B	Retailers' and simplified invoices: exceptions.
17	Section 14(6) supplies to persons belonging in other member States.
18	Section 14(1) supplies by intermediate suppliers.
19	Section 14(2) supplies by persons belonging in other member States.
20	General.

PART IV EC SALES STATEMENTS

21	Interpretation of Part IV.
22–22C	Submission of statements.
23	*Final statements.* (revoked)

PART IVA REVERSE CHARGE SALES STATEMENTS

23A	Interpretation of Part 4A
23B	Notification of first relevant supply
23C	Submission of Statements
23D	Notification of cessation and recommencement of relevant supplies

PART 4B PROVISION OF INFORMATION RELATING TO ARRIVALS AND DISPATCHES.

23E, 23F	Interpretation of Part 4B.

PART V ACCOUNTING, PAYMENT AND RECORDS

24, 24A, 24B, 24C	Interpretation of Part V.
25, 25A	Making of returns.
26	Accounting for VAT on an acquisition by reference to the value shown on an invoice.
27	Supplies under Schedule 4, paragraph 7.
28	Estimation of output tax.
29	Claims for input tax.
30	Persons acting in a representative capacity.
31	Records.
31AA	Preservation of records.
31A, 31B, 31C	Records.
32	The VAT account.
32A	Recording and keeping of information in electronic form.
32B	Exemption from the electronic recording requirements.
32C	Election not to be exempt
33, 33A, 33B	The register of temporary movement of goods to and from other member States.
34–35	Correction of errors.
36	Notification of acquisition of goods subject to excise duty by non-taxable persons and payment of VAT.
37	Claims for credit for, or repayment of, overstated or overpaid VAT.
38, 38ZA	Adjustments in the course of business.
38A	Adjustments where a supply becomes, or ceases to be, a supply to which section 55A(6) of the Act applies (customers to account for tax on supplies of goods or services of a kind used in missing trader intra-community fraud).
39	Calculation of returns.
40, 40A	VAT to be accounted for on returns and payment of VAT.
41	Accounting etc by reference to the duty point, and prescribed accounting period in which VAT on certain supplies is to be treated as being chargeable.
42	Accounting for VAT on the removal of goods.
43	Goods removed from warehousing regime.

PART VA REIMBURSEMENT ARRANGEMENTS

43A	Interpretation of Part VA.
43B	Reimbursement arrangements—general.
43C	Reimbursement arrangements—provisions to be included.
43D	Notifications and repayments to the Commissioners.
43E	Records.
43F	Production of records.
43G	Undertakings.
43H	*Reimbursement arrangements made before 11 February 1998.* (revoked)

PART VI PAYMENTS ON ACCOUNT

44	Interpretation of Part VI.
45–48	Payments on account.

PART VII ANNUAL ACCOUNTING

49	Interpretation of Part VII.
50–51	Annual accounting scheme.
52–55	Admission to the scheme.

PART VIIA FLAT-RATE SCHEME FOR SMALL BUSINESSES

55A	Interpretation of Part VIIA.
55B	Flat-rate scheme for small businesses.
55C	Relevant supplies and purchases.
55D	Method of accounting.
55E	Input tax.
55F	Exceptional claims for VAT relief.
55G	Determining relevant turnover.
55H, 55J	Appropriate percentage.
55JA	Appropriate percentage.
55JB	Reduced appropriate percentage for newly registered period.
55K	Category of business.
55KA	Appropriate percentage for limited-cost traders.
55L	Admission to Scheme.

55M	Withdrawal from the scheme.
55N	Notification.
55P	Termination by the Commissioners.
55Q	Date of withdrawal from the scheme.
55R	Self-supply on withdrawal from scheme.
55S	Adjustments in respect of stock on hand at withdrawal from scheme.
55T	Amendment by Notice.
55U	Reverse charges.
55V	Bad Debt Relief.

PART VIII CASH ACCOUNTING

56	Interpretation of Part VIII.
57, 57A	Cash accounting scheme.
58–63	Admission to the scheme.
64	Withdrawal from the scheme.
64A	Bad debt relief
65	Accounting.

PART IX SUPPLIES BY RETAILERS

66	Interpretation of Part IX.
67–69A	Retail schemes.
70	Notification of use of a scheme.
71	Changing schemes.
72	Ceasing to use scheme.
73	*Supplies under Schedule 8, Group 1* (revoked).
74	*Supplies under Schedule 8, Group 12* (revoked).
75	Change in VAT.

PART X TRADING STAMPS

76	*Interpretation of Part X (revoked as from 1 June 1996)* (revoked).
77–80	*Trading stamp scheme (revoked as from 1 June 1996)* (revoked).

PART XI TIME OF SUPPLY AND TIME OF ACQUISITION

81	Goods for private use and free supplies of services.
82	Services from outside the United Kingdom.
82A	Goods supplied by persons outside the United Kingdom.
83	Time of acquisition.
84	Supplies of land—special cases.
85	Leases treated as supplies of goods.
86	Supplies of water, gas or any form of power, heat, refrigeration or ventilation.
87	Acquisitions of water, gas or any form of power, heat, refrigeration or ventilation.
88	Supplier's goods in possession of buyer.
89	Retention payments.
90–90B	Continuous supplies of services.
91	Royalties and similar payments.
92	Supplies of services by barristers and advocates.
93	Supplies in the construction industry.
94–94B	General.
95	Supplies spanning change of rate etc.

PART XII VALUATION OF ACQUISITIONS

96	Interpretation of Part XII.
97	Valuation of acquisitions.

PART XIII PLACE OF SUPPLY

98	Distance sales from the United Kingdom.

PART XIV INPUT TAX AND PARTIAL EXEMPTION

99–100	Interpretation of Part XIV and longer periods.
101	Attribution of input tax to taxable supplies.
102–102C	Use of other methods.
103	Attribution of input tax to foreign and specified supplies.
103A	Attribution of input tax to investment gold.
103B, 104	Attribution of input tax incurred on services and related goods used to make financial supplies

105–106A	Treatment of input tax attributable to exempt supplies as being attributable to taxable supplies.
107–110	Adjustment of attribution.
111	Exceptional claims for VAT relief.

PART XV ADJUSTMENTS TO THE DEDUCTION OF INPUT TAX ON CAPITAL ITEMS

112	Interpretation of Part XV.
113, 113A	Capital items to which this Part applies.
114	Period of adjustment.
115	Method of adjustment.
116	Ascertainment of taxable use of a capital item.

PART 15A GOODS USED FOR NON-BUSINESS PURPOSES DURING THEIR ECONOMIC LIFE

116A	Application.
116B	Interpretation of this Part.
116C–116D	Economic life of goods.
116E–116F	Value of a relevant supply.
116G	Later increase in the full cost of goods.
116H	Value of relevant supplies made during a new economic life.
116I	Value of relevant supplies of goods which have two or more economic lives.
116J–116N	Transitional provisions

PART XVI IMPORTATIONS, EXPORTATIONS AND REMOVALS

116O	Application of this Part.
117	Interpretation of Part XVI.
118	Enactments excepted.
119	Regulations excepted.
120	Community legislation.
121–121C	Adaptations.
121D	Adaptations and exceptions for the application of returned goods relief.
122	Postal importations by registered persons in the course of business.
123	Temporary importations.
124	*Reimportation of certain goods by non-taxable persons.* (revoked)
125	*Reimportation of certain goods by taxable persons.* (revoked)
126	Reimportation of goods exported for treatment or process.
127	*Supplies to export houses* (revoked).
128	Export of freight containers.
129	Supplies to overseas persons.
130–133	*Supplies to persons departing from the member States* (revoked).

PART 16ZA IMPORTATIONS, EXPORTATIONS AND REMOVALS IN RESPECT OF NORTHERN IRELAND

133A	Interpretation
133B	Supplies to persons outside the relevant states
133C	VAT Retail Export Scheme
133D–133E	Supplies to persons departing from the relevant states
133F–133G	Supplies to persons taxable in a member State
133H	Additional provision in relation to importations, exportations and removals in respect of Northern Ireland
134, 134A	Supplies to persons taxable in another member State.
135	Supplies of goods subject to excise duty to persons who are not taxable in another member State.
136–139	Territories to be treated as excluded from or included in the territory of the Community and of the member States.
140	Entry and exit formalities.
141	Use of the internal Community transit procedure.
142–145	Customs and excise legislation to be applied.

PART XVI(A) FISCAL AND OTHER WAREHOUSING REGIMES

145A	Interpretation of Part XVI(A).
145B	Fiscal warehousing certificates.
145C	Certificates connected with services in fiscal or other warehousing regimes.
145D	VAT invoices relating to services performed in fiscal or other warehousing regimes.
145E	Fiscal warehousing regimes.
145F	The fiscal warehousing record and stock control.
145G	Fiscal warehousing transfers in the United Kingdom.

145H, 145I	Removal of goods from a fiscal warehousing regime and transfers overseas.
145J	Payment on removal of goods from a fiscal warehousing regime.
145K	Place of supply of goods subject to warehousing regime.

PART XVII NEW MEANS OF TRANSPORT

146	Interpretation of Part XVII.
147	First entry into service of a means of transport.
148	Notification of acquisition of new means of transport by non-taxable persons and payment of VAT.
149–154	Refunds in relation to new means of transport.
155	Supplies of new means of transport to persons departing to another member State.

PART XVIII BAD DEBT RELIEF (THE OLD SCHEME)

156–164	[Revoked]

PART XIX BAD DEBT RELIEF (THE NEW SCHEME)

165	Interpretation of Part XIX.
165A	Time within which a claim must be made.
166	The making of a claim to the Commissioners.
166AA	*The making of a claim to the Commissioners: special accounting schemes* (revoked).
166A	Notice to purchaser of claim.
167	Evidence required of the claimant in support of the claim.
168	Records required to be kept by the claimant.
169	Preservation of documents and records and duty to produce.
170	Attribution of payments.
170A	Attribution of payments received under certain credit agreements.
171	Repayment of a refund.
171A	*Calculation of repayment where reduction in consideration: special accounting schemes* (revoked).
171B	*Timing and method of repayments: special accounting schemes* (revoked).
172	Writing off debts.
172A	Writing off debts—margin schemes.
172B	Writing off debts—tour operators margin scheme.

PART XIXA REPAYMENT OF INPUT TAX WHERE CLAIM MADE UNDER PART XIX

172ZC	Application.
172C	Interpretation of Part XIXA.
172D	Repayment of input tax.
172E	Restoration of an entitlement to credit for input tax.

PART XIXB REPAYMENT OF INPUT TAX WHERE CONSIDERATION NOT PAID

172F	Application.
172G	Interpretation.
172H	Repayment of input tax.
172I	Restoration of an entitlement to credit for input tax.
172J	Attribution of payments.

PART XIXC ADJUSTMENT OF OUTPUT TAX IN RESPECT OF SUPPLIES TO WHICH SECTION 55A(6) OF THE ACT APPLIES

172K	
172L	Adjustment of output tax.
172M, 172N	Readjustment of output tax.

PART XX REPAYMENTS TO COMMUNITY TRADERS (REVOKED)

173	Interpretation of Part XX .
173A–173D	Repayments of VAT.
173E	Persons to whom this Part applies.
173F	Time when VAT is incurred.
173G	Repayment period.
173H	Minimum total claim for a repayment period.
173I–173O	Requirements for a claim for repayment of VAT.
173P	Day by which a claim under this Part must be made.
173Q	Notification of entitlement to repayment.
173R	Requests for further information or a document.
173S	Relevant period applicable to any VAT for which repayment is claimed.

173T	Extension of the relevant period by virtue of the making of a request for information or a document.
173U	Extension of the relevant period where more than one request for information or a document is made in relation to the same VAT.
173V	Time when a repayment of VAT must be made.
173W, 173X	Interest on late payments.
174	*Repayment of VAT.* (revoked)
175	*Persons to whom this Part applies.* (revoked)
176	*Supplies and importations to which this Part applies.* (revoked)
177	*VAT which will not be repaid.* (revoked)
178	*Method of claiming.* (revoked)
179	*Time within which a claim must be made.* (revoked)
180	Deduction of bank charges .
181,182	Treatment of claim.
183, 184	incorrect claims.

PART XXI REPAYMENTS TO THIRD COUNTRY TRADERS

185	Interpretation of Part XXI.
186	Repayments of VAT.
187	VAT representatives.
188	Persons to whom this Part applies.
189	Supplies and importations to which this Part applies.
190	VAT which will not be repaid.
191	Method of claiming.
192	Time within which a claim must be made.
193	Deduction of bank charges.
194, 195	Treatment of claim (195 — revoked)
196, 197	False, altered or incorrect claims.

PART XXII REPAYMENT OF SUPPLEMENT

198	Computation of period.
199	Duration of period.

PART XXIII REFUNDS TO "DO-IT-YOURSELF" BUILDERS

200	Interpretation of Part XXIII.
201, 201A	Method and time for making claim.

PART XXIV FLAT-RATE SCHEME FOR FARMERS

202	Interpretation of Part XXIV.
203	Flat-rate scheme.
204	Admission to the scheme.
205	Certification.
206	Cancellation of certificates.
206A	Notification to Commissioners.
207	Death, bankruptcy or incapacity of certified person.
208	Further certification.
209	Claims by taxable persons for amounts to be treated as credits for input tax.
210	Duty to keep records.
211	Production of records.

PART XXV DISTRESS AND DILIGENCE

A212	[Untitled].
212	Distress (revoked)
213	Diligence.

PART XXVI UK UNION AND NON-UNION SPECIAL ACCOUNTING SCHEMES: REGISTRATION (REVOKED)

214	*Interpretation* (revoked).
215	*Registration requests: Non-Union scheme* (revoked).
216	*Registration requests: Union scheme* (revoked).
217	*Registration requests: declaration* (revoked).
218	*Communications with the Commissioners* (revoked).

PART XXVII NON-UK UNION AND NON-UNION SPECIAL ACCOUNTING SCHEMES: ADJUSTMENTS, CLAIMS AND ERROR CORRECTION (REVOKED).

219	*[Untitled]* (revoked).

220	*Correction of errors on non-UK and special scheme returns more than 3 years after the date the original return was required to be made* (revoked).
221	*Claims in respect of overpaid VAT* (revoked).
222	*Increases or decreases in consideration occurring more than 3 years after the end of the affected tax period* (revoked).
223	*Scheme participants who are also taxable persons: disapplication of paragraph 17(1)* (revoked).

Schedules:
Schedule 1—Forms (revoked).
Schedule 1A—[Untitled].
Schedule 2—revocations.

PART I
PRELIMINARY

1 Citation and commencement

These Regulations may be cited as the Value Added Tax Regulations 1995 and shall come into force on 20th October 1995.

Former regulation—VAT (General) Regulations, SI 1985/886 reg 1.

2 Interpretation—general

(1) In these Regulations unless the context otherwise requires—
"alphabetical code" means the alphabetical prefix as set out below which shall be used to identify the [relevant territory][8]—

Austria—AT
Belgium—BE
[Bulgaria—BG]
Cyprus—CY
Czech Republic—CZ
Denmark—DK
Estonia—EE
Finland—FI
France—FR
Germany—DE
Greece—EL
Hungary—HU
Ireland—IE
Italy—IT
Latvia—LV
Lithuania—LT
Luxembourg—LU
Malta—MT
Netherlands—NL
Poland—PL
Portugal—PT
[Romania—RO]
Slovakia—SK
Slovenia—SI
Spain—ES
Sweden—SE
United Kingdom—[XI][8];

"the Act" means the Value Added Tax Act 1994 and any reference to a Schedule to the Act includes a reference to a Schedule as amended from time to time by Order of the Treasury;
. . .[8]
"Collector" includes Deputy Collector and Assistant Collector;
"the Community" means the European Community;
"continental shelf" means a designated area within the meaning of the Continental Shelf Act 1964;
"Controller" means the Controller, Customs and Excise Value Added Tax Central Unit;
. . .[7]
["fiscal or other warehousing regime" means "fiscal warehousing regime or warehousing regime"][1] [, and "Northern Ireland fiscal or other Northern Ireland warehousing regime" means "Northern Ireland fiscal warehousing regime or Northern Ireland warehousing regime";][8]

["identified for the purposes of VAT in Northern Ireland" has the meaning given by paragraph 7 of Schedule 9ZA to the Act;
"Northern Ireland fiscal warehouse" and "Northern Ireland fiscal warehousing regime" have the meanings given by sub-paragraphs (1) and (2) respectively of paragraph 25 (supplementary provision) of Schedule 9ZB to the Act;
"Northern Ireland warehouse" and "Northern Ireland warehousing regime" have the meanings given by sub-paragraphs (11) and (12) respectively of paragraph 16 (place and time of supply: Northern Ireland warehouses) of Schedule 9ZB to the Act;][8]

. . .[6]

. . .[7]

. . .[7]

"prescribed accounting period", subject to regulation 99(I), means a period such as is referred to in regulation 25;

"proper officer" means the person appointed or authorised by the Commissioners to act in respect of any matter in the course of his duties;

"registered person" means a person registered by the Commissioners under [Schedule 1, [1A][5], 2, 3, [3A or 9ZC][8]][2] to the Act;

"registration number" means the number allocated by the Commissioners to a taxable person in the certificate of registration issued to him;

["relevant territory" means, except where otherwise provided, a member State or the United Kingdom;][8]

"return" means a return which is required to be made in accordance with regulation 25;

"specified date" means the date specified in a person's application for registration for the purpose of VAT as that on which he expects to make his first taxable supply.

. . .[7]

(2) A reference in these Regulations to "this Part" is a reference to the Part of these Regulations in which that reference is made.

(3) In these Regulations any reference to a form [specified in a notice published by the Commissioners] shall include a reference to a form which the Commissioners are satisfied is a form to the like effect.

[(4) A reference in these Regulations to "another member State" is to be read as a reference to "a member State", and "other member State" and "other member States" are to be interpreted accordingly.][8]

Commentary—*De Voil Indirect Tax Service* **V5.108A, V3.421**.

Note—Although Croatia joined the EU in 2013, it appears that Croatia has not so far been added to the list of alphabetical codes in para (1).

Former regulations—Para (1): VAT (General) Regulations, SI 1985/886 reg 2(1); VAT (General) (Amendment) Regulations, SI 1992/3102 regs 1, 3, SI 1993/1941 regs 2, 3, SI 1995/152 reg 3.

Para (2): None.

Para (3): VAT (General) Regulations, SI 1985/886 reg 2(2).

Amendments—[1] Definition of "fiscal or other warehousing regime" inserted by the VAT (Amendment) (No 3) Regulations, SI 1996/1250 reg 4 with effect from 1 June 1996.

[2] Words in definition of "registered person" substituted by the VAT (Amendment) (No 3) Regulations, SI 2000/794 regs 2, 3 with effect from 22 March 2000.

[3] Definition of "alphabetical code" substituted by the VAT (Amendment) (No 2) Regulations, SI 2004/1082 regs 2, 3 with effect from 1 May 2004.

[4] In para (1) entries inserted by the VAT (Amendment) (No 3) Regulations, SI 2006/3292 regs 2, 3 with effect from 1 January 2007.

[5] In para (1), in definition of "registered person", reference inserted, and in para (3), words substituted for words "prescribed in Schedule 1 to these Regulations", by the VAT (Amendment) (No 2) Regulations, SI 2012/1899 regs 3, 4 with effect from 15 October 2012.

[6] In para (1) words in the definition of "datapost packet" substituted, definitions inserted, and definition of "the Post office Company" revoked by the Postal Services Act 2011 (Consequential Modifications and Amendments) Order, SI 2011/2085 art 5(1), Sch 16 para 31 with effect from 1 October 2011.

[7] In para (1), definitions of "datapost packet", "post office", "postal packet" and "universal service provider" revoked by the Value Added Tax (Accounting Procedures for Import VAT for VAT Registered Persons and Amendment) (EU Exit) Regulations, SI 2019/60 reg 12(1), (2) with effect from IP completion day (11pm UK time on 31 December 2020). Definitions of "datapost packet", "post office", "postal packet" and "universal service provider" previously read as follows—

"'"datapost packet" means a postal packet containing goods which is posted in the United Kingdom as a datapost packet for transmission to a place outside the United Kingdom in accordance with the terms of a contract entered into between [a universal service provider] and the sender of the packet; or which is received at a post office [a universal service provider] in the United Kingdom from a place outside the United Kingdom for transmission and delivery in the United Kingdom [by that universal service provider] as if it were a datapost packet;

["post office" has the same meaning as in section 125(1) of the Postal Services Act 2000]

["postal packet" has the same meaning as in Part 3 of the Postal Services Act 2011]

["universal service provider" means a person who provides a universal postal service (within the meaning of Part 3 of the Postal Services Act 2011) or part of such a service, in the United Kingdom]"

[8] In para (1), in the definition of "alphabetical code" words substituted for words "member State", and in the entry for the United Kingdom, "XI" substituted for "GB", in the definition of "fiscal or other warehousing regime" words inserted, definitions "identified for the purposes of VAT in Northern Ireland", "Northern Ireland fiscal warehouse", "Northern Ireland warehouse" and "relevant territory" inserted, in the definition of "registered person", words substituted for words "or 3A", and para (4) inserted, by the Value Added Tax (Miscellaneous Amendments, Northern Ireland Protocol and Savings and Transitional Provisions) (EU Exit) Regulations, SI 2020/1545 regs 31 and 32 with effect from IP completion day (11pm UK time on 31 December 2020) by virtue of SI 2020/1641 reg 2, Schedule para 11.

3 Revocations and savings
(1) The Regulations described in Schedule 2 to these Regulations are hereby revoked.
(2) Anything begun under or for the purpose of any Regulations revoked by these Regulations shall be continued under or, as the case may be, for the purpose of the corresponding provision of these Regulations.
(3) Where any document used or required for the purpose of VAT refers to a provision of a regulation revoked by these Regulations, such reference shall, unless the context otherwise requires, be construed as a reference to the corresponding provision of these Regulations.

4 Requirement, direction, demand or permission
Any requirement, direction, demand or permission by the Commissioners, under or for the purposes of these Regulations, may be made or given by a notice in writing, or otherwise.

4A [Electronic communication
(1) A specified communication may be made to the Commissioners using an electronic communications system.
(2) Where an electronic communications system is used it must take a form approved by the Commissioners in a specific or general direction.
(3) A direction under paragraph (2) may in particular—
   (*a*) modify or dispense with any requirement of a form mentioned in regulation 2(3) used to make a specified communication;
   (*b*) specify different forms of electronic communications system for different cases; and
   (*c*) specify different circumstances in which the electronic communications system may be used, or not used, by or on behalf of the person required to make the communication and specify different circumstances for different cases.
(4) An electronic communications system shall incorporate an electronic validation process.
(5) Subject to paragraph (6) below and unless the contrary is proved—
   (*a*) the use of an electronic communications system shall be presumed to have resulted in the making of a communication to the Commissioners only if this has been successfully recorded as such by the relevant electronic validation process;
   (*b*) the time of making a communication to the Commissioners using an electronic communications system shall be presumed to be the time recorded as such by the relevant electronic validation process; and
   (*c*) the person delivering a communication to the Commissioners shall be presumed to be the person identified as such by any relevant feature of the electronic communications system.
(6) No communication shall be treated as having been made using an electronic communications system unless it is in the form required by paragraph (2).
(7) A communication made using an electronic communications system carries the same consequences as a communication made in paper form.
(8) In paragraph (2) "direction" refers only to a current direction, and a direction is not current to the extent that it is varied, replaced or revoked by another Commissioners' direction.][1]
Commentary—*De Voil Indirect Tax Service* **V2.126**.
Amendments—[1] Regs 4A, 4B inserted by the VAT (Amendment) (No 2) Regulations, SI 2012/1899 regs 3, 5 with effect from 15 October 2012.

[4B—(1) A specified communication is—
   (*a*) an application under section 43B(1), (2)(d) or (3) of the Act (Groups: applications);
   (*b*) a notification under regulation 5(1), (2) or (3) (registration and notification);
   (*c*) an application under regulation 6(1)(d) (transfer of a going concern);
   (*d*) a notification under regulation 10(1) or (4) (VAT representatives);
   (*e*) an application under regulation 52(1) (annual accounting scheme: eligibility);
   (*f*) a notification under regulation 54(2) (annual accounting scheme: termination);
   (*g*) a notification under regulation 55(1)(d) (annual accounting scheme: termination);
   (*h*) a notification under regulation 55B(1)(a) (flat-rate scheme for small businesses: notification of desire to join the scheme); . . . [2]
   (*i*) a notification under regulation 55Q(1)(e) (flat-rate scheme for small businesses: notification of decision to withdraw from the scheme); [and
   (*j*) a notification under paragraph (3)[, (3A) or (4)][3] of regulation 148A (notification of the arrival in the United Kingdom of motorised land vehicles and payment of VAT).][2][1]
Commentary—*De Voil Indirect Tax Service* **V2.126**.

Amendments—[1] Regs 4A, 4B inserted by the VAT (Amendment) (No 2) Regulations, SI 2012/1899 regs 3, 5 with effect from 15 October 2012.
[2] In para (h), word "and" revoked, and para (j) and preceding word "and" inserted, by the VAT (Amendment) Regulations, SI 2013/701 regs 3, 4 with effect from 15 April 2013.
[3] Words in para (j) inserted by the Value Added Tax (Amendment) Regulations, SI 2014/548 regs 2, 3 with effect from 1 April 2014.

PART II
REGISTRATION AND PROVISIONS FOR SPECIAL CASES

[5 Registration and notification
(1) Where any person is required under paragraph 5(1)[, 6(1) or 7(1)][2] of Schedule 1, [paragraph 5(1), 6(1) or (13)(3) of Schedule 1A][3] paragraph 3(1) of Schedule 2, paragraph 3(1) of Schedule 3 or paragraph 3(1) or 4(1) of Schedule 3A[, or paragraph 8 of Schedule 9ZC][4] to the Act to notify the Commissioners of his liability to be registered, the notification shall contain the particulars (including the declaration) set out [in the relevant form specified in a notice published by the Commissioners and shall be made in that form][3]; provided that, where the notification is made by a partnership, the notification shall also contain the particulars set out in [the relevant form specified in a notice published by the Commissioners][3].
(2) Every registered person except one to whom paragraph 11, 12, 13(1), (2) or (3) of Schedule 1, [paragraph 7, 8 or 9(1) of Schedule 1A,][3] paragraph 5 of Schedule 2, paragraph 5 of Schedule 3 or paragraph 5 of Schedule 3A[, or paragraph 10 of Schedule 9ZC][4] of the Act applies, shall, within 30 days of any changes being made in the name, constitution or ownership of his business, or of any other event occurring which may necessitate the variation of the register or cancellation of his registration, notify the Commissioners . . . [3] of such change or event and furnish them with full particulars thereof.
(3) Every notification by a registered person under paragraph 11 or 12 of Schedule 1, paragraph 5 of Schedule 2, paragraph 5 of Schedule 3 or paragraph 5 of Schedule 3A[, or paragraph 10 of Schedule 9ZC][4] to the Act . . . [3] shall state—
   (a) the date on which he ceased to make, or have the intention of making, taxable supplies; or
   (b) where paragraph 12(a) of Schedule 1 to the Act applies, the date on which he ceased to make, or have the intention of making, supplies within paragraph 10(2) of that Schedule; or
   (c) where paragraph 12(b) of Schedule 1 to the Act applies, the date on which he made, or formed the intention of making, taxable supplies; or
   (d) where paragraph 5(1) of Schedule 2 to the Act applies, the date on which he ceased to be registrable by virtue of paragraph 5(4) of that Schedule; or
   (e) where paragraph 5(1) of Schedule 3 to the Act applies, the date on which he ceased to be registrable by virtue of paragraph 5(3) of that Schedule; or
   (f) where paragraph 5(1) of Schedule 3A to the Act applies, the date on which he ceased to make, or have the intention of making, relevant supplies within the meaning of paragraph 9 of that [Schedule; or][4][1]
   [(g) where paragraph 10(1) of Schedule 9ZC to the Act applies, the date on which the person ceased to be registrable under the Act; or
   (h) where paragraph 10(2) of Schedule 9ZC to the Act applies, the date on which the person made or facilitated a relevant supply within that paragraph.][4]
(4)–(14) . . . [3]
Commentary—*De Voil Indirect Tax Service* **V2.126**.
HMRC Manuals—VAT Registration VATREG03100 (how notification must be made).
Amendments—[1] This regulation substituted by the VAT (Amendment) (No 3) Regulations, SI 2000/794 regs 2, 4 with effect from 22 March 2000.
[2] Words in para (1) substituted for the words "or 6(1)", and paras (4)–(14) inserted, by the VAT (Amendment) (No 3) Regulations, SI 2004/1675 regs 1, 2 with effect from 22 July 2004.
[3] In para (1), words inserted, and words substituted for words "in forms numbered 1, 6, 7 and 7A respectively in Schedule 1 to these Regulations and shall be made in those forms" and words "the form numbered 2 in that Schedule", in para (2), words inserted and words "in writing" revoked, in para (3), words "shall be made in writing to the Commissioners and" revoked, and paras (4)–(14) revoked, by the VAT (Amendment) (No 2) Regulations, SI 2012/1899 regs 3, 6 with effect from 15 October 2012.
[4] In paras (1)–(3) words inserted, in para (3)(f) words substituted for word "Schedule.", and paras (3)(g), (h) inserted, by the Value Added Tax (Miscellaneous Amendments, Northern Ireland Protocol and Savings and Transitional Provisions) (EU Exit) Regulations, SI 2020/1545 regs 31 and 33 with effect from IP completion day (11pm UK time on 31 December 2020) by virtue of SI 2020/1641 reg 2, Schedule para 11.

6 Transfer of a going concern
(1) Where—
   (a) a business [or part of a business][3] is transferred as a going concern,
   (b) the registration under Schedule 1 [or 1A][4] to the Act of the transferor has not already been cancelled,

(c) on the transfer of the business [or part of it][3] the registration of the transferor [under either Schedule][4] is to be cancelled and either the transferee becomes liable to be registered [under either Schedule][4] or the Commissioners agree to register him [under paragraph 9 of Schedule 1 to the Act][4], and

(d) an application is made in [the form specified in a notice published by the Commissioners][4] by or on behalf of both the transferor and the transferee of that business [or the part transferred][3],

the Commissioners may as from the date of the said transfer [cancel the registration under Schedule 1 or 1A to the Act of the transferor and register the transferee under Schedule 1 or 1A to the Act as appropriate with the registration number previously allocated to the transferor][4]

(2) An application under paragraph (1) above shall constitute notification for the purposes of paragraph 11 of Schedule 1 [or paragraph 7 of Schedule 1A][4] to the Act.

(3) Where the transferee of a business [or part of a business][3] has under paragraph (1) above been registered under Schedule 1 [or 1A][4] to the Act in substitution for the [transferor of it][3], and with the transferor's registration number—

(a) any liability of the transferor existing at the date of the transfer to make a return or to account for or pay VAT under regulation 25 or [40][2] shall become the liability of the transferee,

(b) any right of the transferor, whether or not existing at the date of the transfer, to credit for, or to repayment of, input tax shall become the right of the transferee, . . . [1]

(c) any right of either the transferor, whether or not existing at the date of the transfer, or the transferee to payment by the Commissioners under section 25(3) of the Act shall be satisfied by payment to either of them.

[(d) any right of the transferor, whether or not existing at the date of the transfer, to claim a refund under section 36 of the Act shall become the right of the transferee, . . . [3]

(e) any liability of the transferor, whether or not existing at the date of the transfer, to account for an amount under Part XIXA of these Regulations, shall become that of the transferee][1][, and

(f) any records relating to the business which, by virtue of these Regulations or a direction made by the Commissioners, are required to be preserved for any period after the transfer shall be preserved by the transferee unless the Commissioners, at the request of the transferor, otherwise direct.][3]

(4) In addition to the provisions set out in paragraph (3) above, where the transferee of a business [or part of a business][3] has been registered in substitution for, and with the registration number of, the transferor during a prescribed accounting period [subsequent to that in which the transfer took place][3] but with effect from [the date of the transfer][3], and any—

(a) return has been made,

(b) VAT has been accounted for and paid, or

(c) right to credit for input tax has been claimed,

either by or in the name of the transferee or the transferor, it shall be treated as having been done by the transferee.

Commentary—*De Voil Indirect Tax Service* **V5.103, V2.131**.
HMRC Manuals—VAT Registration VATREG29900 (transfers of going concerns: registration and deregistration). VATREG29950 (transfers of going concerns : : accounting for tax).
Amendments—[1] Word "and" in para (3)(b) deleted and paras (3)(d), (e) inserted by the VAT (Amendment) Regulations, SI 1997/1086 reg 3 with effect from 1 May 1997.
[2] In para (3)(a), figure substituted for "41" by the VAT (Amendment) (No 3) Regulations, SI 2004/1675 regs 1(1), (3), 3 with effect from 22 July 2004.
[3] Words in sub-s (1) inserted, words in sub-ss (3), (4) inserted and substituted, and sub-s (3)(f) and preceding word "and" inserted, by the Value Added Tax (Amendment) (No 5) Regulations, SI 2007/2085 regs 2–5 with effect from 1 September 2007, in relation to transfers of going concerns pursuant to contracts entered into on or after that date.
[4] In para (1), in sub-para (b) words inserted, in sub-para (c), words substituted for words "under that Schedule" and "under paragraph 9 of that Schedule", in sub-para (d) words substituted for words "the form numbered 3 in Schedule 1 to these Regulations", and words "cancel the registration under Schedule 1 to the Act of the transferor and register the transferee under that Schedule with the registration number previously allocated to the transferor." revoked, and words in paras (2), (3) inserted, by the VAT (Amendment) (No 2) Regulations, SI 2012/1899 regs 3, 7 with effect from 15 October 2012.

7 Notice by partnership

(1) Where any notice is required to be given for the purposes of the Act or these Regulations by a partnership, it shall be the joint and several liability of all the partners to give such notice, provided that a notice given by one partner shall be a sufficient compliance with any such requirement.

(2) Where, in Scotland, a body of persons carrying on a business which includes the making of taxable supplies is a partnership required to be registered, any notice shall be given and signed in the manner indicated in section 6 of the Partnership Act 1890.

Commentary—*De Voil Indirect Tax Service* **V2.110**.

8 Representation of club, association or organisation

Anything required to be done by or under the Act, these regulations or otherwise by or on behalf of a club, association or organisation, the affairs of which are managed by its members or a committee or committees of its members, shall be the joint and several responsibility of—

(a) every member holding office as president, chairman, treasurer, secretary or any similar office; or in default of any thereof,
(b) every member holding office as a member of a committee; or in default of any thereof,
(c) every member,

provided that if it is done by any official, committee member or member referred to above, that shall be sufficient compliance with any such requirement.

HMRC Manuals—VAT Registration VATREG10950 (clubs and associations: entity to be registered: law).

9 Death, bankruptcy or incapacity of taxable person

(1) If a taxable person dies or becomes bankrupt or incapacitated, the Commissioners may, from the date on which he died or became bankrupt or incapacitated treat as a taxable person any person carrying on that business until some other person is registered in respect of the taxable supplies made or intended to be made by that taxable person in the course or furtherance of his business or the incapacity ceases, as the case may be; and the provisions of the Act and of any Regulations made thereunder shall apply to any person so treated as though he were a registered person.

(2) Any person carrying on such business shall, within 21 days of commencing to do so, inform the Commissioners in writing of that fact and of the date of the death, [the date of the bankruptcy order][1] or of the nature of the incapacity and the date on which it began.

(3) In relation to a company which is a taxable person, the references in paragraph (1) above to the taxable person becoming bankrupt or incapacitated shall be construed as references to the company going into liquidation or receivership or [entering administration][2].

Commentary—*De Voil Indirect Tax Service* **V5.187, V2.102**.

HMRC Manuals—VAT Registration VATREG42300 (the effects of death, insolvency and Incapacity on registration: regulation 9).

Amendments—[1] Words in square brackets inserted by the VAT (Amendment) (No 3) Regulations, SI 1996/1250 reg 5 with effect from 1 June 1996.
[2] Words in para (3) substituted by the Enterprise Act 2002 (Insolvency) Order, SI 2003/2096 art 5, Schedule paras 55, 56 with effect from 15 September 2003. However, this amendment does not apply in any case where a petition for an administration order was presented before that date: SI 2003/2096 arts 1, 6.

10 VAT representatives

(1) Where any person is appointed by virtue of section 48 of the Act to be the VAT representative of another (in this regulation referred to as "his principal"), the VAT representative shall notify the Commissioners of his appointment [in the form specified in a notice published by the Commissioners][2] within 30 days of the date on which his appointment became effective and the notification shall contain the particulars (including the declaration) set out [in that notice][2].

(2) The notification referred to in this regulation shall be accompanied by evidence of the VAT representative's appointment.

(3) [Subject to paragraphs (3A) and (3B), where][3] a person is appointed by virtue of section 48 of the Act to be a VAT representative, the Commissioners shall register the name of that VAT representative against the name of his principal in the register kept for the purposes of the Act.

[(3A) The Commissioners may refuse to register a person in accordance with paragraph (3) if they are satisfied that the person is not a fit and proper person to act in that capacity.

(3B) Where a person is registered as a VAT representative in accordance with paragraph (3) the Commissioners may cancel that person's registration if they are satisfied that the person is not, or is no longer, a fit and proper person to act in that capacity.][3]

(4) Every VAT representative who is registered in accordance with this regulation shall, within 30 days of any changes being made in the name, constitution or ownership of his business or of his ceasing to be a person's VAT representative, or of any other event occurring which may necessitate the variation of the register, notify the Commissioners in writing of such change, cessation or event and furnish them with full particulars thereof.

(5) For the purposes of this regulation the date upon which the appointment of a VAT representative ("the first VAT representative") shall be regarded as having ceased shall be treated as being whichever is the earliest of the following times—
(a) when the Commissioners receive any notification in accordance with regulation 5(2), or
(b) when the Commissioners receive a notification of appointment in accordance with paragraph (1) above of a person other than the first VAT representative, or
(c) when the Commissioners receive a notification of cessation in accordance with regulation 5(2), or
(d) when the Commissioners receive a notification of cessation in accordance with paragraph (4) above, or
(e) when a VAT representative dies, becomes insolvent or becomes incapacitated, [or
(f) when the Commissioners cancel a VAT representative's registration in accordance with paragraph (3B),][3]

provided that if the Commissioners have not received a notification such as is mentioned in all or any of sub-paragraphs (a), (c) or (d) above and another person has been appointed as a VAT representative by virtue of section 48 of the Act, the Commissioners may treat the date of cessation as the date of appointment of that other person.

(6) In relation to a company which is a VAT representative, the references in paragraph (5)(e) above to the VAT representative becoming insolvent or incapacitated shall be construed as references to its going into liquidation or receivership or [entering administration][1].

Commentary—*De Voil Indirect Tax Service* **V2.126, V2.115**.

Amendments—[1] Words in para (6) substituted by the Enterprise Act 2002 (Insolvency) Order, SI 2003/2096 art 5, Schedule paras 55, 57 with effect from 15 September 2003. However, this amendment does not apply in any case where a petition for an administration order was presented before that date: SI 2003/2096 arts 1, 6.

[2] In para (1), words substituted for words "on the form numbered 8 in Schedule 1 to these Regulations" and words "in that form", by the VAT (Amendment) (No 2) Regulations, SI 2012/1899 regs 3, 8 with effect from 15 October 2012.

[3] In para (3), words substituted for word for "Where", paras (3A), (3B) inserted, and para (5)(f) and preceding word inserted, by the Value Added Tax (Amendment) Regulations, SI 2016/989 reg 2 with effect from 7 November 2016.

11 Notification of intended section 14(1) supplies by intermediate suppliers

(1) An intermediate supplier who has made or intends to make a supply to which he wishes section 14(1) of the Act to apply shall notify the Commissioners and the customer in writing of his intention to do so.

(2) A notification under this regulation shall contain the following particulars—
   (a) the name and address of the intermediate supplier,
   (b) the number including the alphabetical code, by which the intermediate supplier is identified for VAT purposes, which was used or is to be used for the purpose of the supply to him by the original supplier,
   (c) the date upon which the goods were first delivered or are intended to be first delivered, and
   (d) the name, address and registration number of the customer to whom the goods have been supplied or are to be supplied.

(3) A notification under this regulation shall be made no later than the provision, in accordance with regulation 18, of the first invoice in relation to the supply to which it relates, and sent to—
   (a) the office designated by the Commissioners for the receipt of such notifications, and
   (b) the customer.

(4) Notifications under this regulation shall be made separately in relation to each customer to whom it is intended to make supplies to which the intermediate supplier wishes section 14(1) of the Act to apply.

(5) Where an intermediate supplier has complied with the requirements of this regulation in relation to the first supply to a customer to which section 14(1) of the Act applies, those requirements shall be deemed to have been satisfied in relation to all subsequent supplies to that customer while the intermediate supplier continues to belong in another member State.

12 Notification of intended section 14(2) supplies by persons belonging in other member States

(1) A person belonging in another member State who has made or who intends to make a supply to which he wishes section 14(2) of the Act to apply shall notify the Commissioners and the registered person in writing of his intention to do so.

(2) A notification under this regulation shall contain the following particulars—
   (a) the name and address of the person belonging in another member State,
   (b) the number including the alphabetical code by which the person belonging in another member State is identified for VAT purposes in the member State in which he belongs,
   (c) the date upon which the installation or assembly of the goods was commenced or is intended to commence, and
   (d) the name, address and registration number of the registered person to whom the goods have been supplied or are to be supplied.

(3) A notification under this regulation shall be made no later than the provision, in accordance with regulation 19, of the first invoice in relation to the supply to which it relates, and sent to—
   (a) the office designated by the Commissioners for the receipt of such notifications, and
   (b) the registered person to whom the goods are to be supplied.

(4) Notifications under this regulation shall be made separately in relation to each registered person to whom it is intended to make supplies to which the person belonging in another member State wishes section 14(2) of the Act to apply.

(5) Where a person belonging in another member State has complied with the requirements of this regulation in relation to the first supply to a registered person to which section 14(2) of the Act applies, those requirements shall be deemed to have been satisfied in relation to all subsequent supplies to that registered person while the person making the supply continues to belong in another member State.

PART III
VAT INVOICES AND OTHER INVOICING REQUIREMENTS
13 Obligation to provide a VAT invoice
[(1) Save as otherwise provided in these Regulations, where a registered person (P)—
   (a) makes a taxable supply in the United Kingdom to a taxable person, or
   (b) makes a supply of goods to a person in a member State for the purpose of any business activity carried out by that person and P is identified for the purposes of VAT in Northern Ireland; or
   (c) receives a payment on account in respect of a supply of goods that P has made or intends to make from a person in a member State and P is identified for the purposes of VAT in Northern Ireland,

P must, unless paragraph (1ZA) applies, provide such persons as are mentioned above with a VAT invoice.][5]

[(1ZA) This paragraph applies where P, in relation to the description of supply mentioned in paragraph (1), is entitled to issue and issues a VAT invoice pursuant to section 18C(1)(d) of the Act and regulation 145D(1) in relation to the supply by P of specified services performed on or in relation to goods while those goods are subject to a fiscal or other warehousing regime, or to a Northern Ireland fiscal or other Northern Ireland warehousing regime.][5]

[(1A) Paragraph (1)(b) above shall not apply where the supply is an exempt supply which is made to a person in a member State which does not require an invoice to be issued for the supply.][3]

[(1B) Paragraph (1)(b) shall not apply in the case of a supply which falls within Group 2 or Group 5 of Schedule 9 to the Act.][4]

[(1C) Save as otherwise provided in these Regulations, where a registered person makes a taxable supply of goods to a person who is not a taxable person, if—
   (a) that supply is deemed to be a supply by an operator of an online marketplace by virtue of section 5A of the Act, or
   (b) the place of supply of those goods is determined by section 7(5B) of the Act,

the registered person must provide the other person with a VAT invoice.][6]

(2) The particulars of the VAT chargeable on a supply of goods described in paragraph 7 of Schedule 4 to the Act shall be provided, on a sale by auction, by the auctioneer, and, where the sale is otherwise than by auction, by the person selling the goods, on a document containing the particulars prescribed in regulation 14(1); and such a document issued to the buyer shall be treated for the purposes of paragraph (1)(a) above as a VAT invoice provided by the person by whom the goods are deemed to be supplied in accordance with the said paragraph 7.

[(3) Where a registered person provides a document to himself ("a self-billed invoice") that purports to be a VAT invoice in respect of a supply of goods or services to him by another registered person, that document shall be treated as the VAT invoice required to be provided by the supplier under paragraph (1)(a) if it complies with the conditions set out in paragraph (3A) and with any further conditions that may be contained in a notice published by the Commissioners or may be imposed in a particular case.][2]

[(3A) The following conditions must be complied with if a self-billed invoice is to be treated as a VAT invoice—
   (a) it must have been provided pursuant to a prior agreement ("a self-billing agreement") entered into between the supplier of the goods or services to which it relates and the recipient of the goods or services ("the customer") and which satisfies the requirements in paragraph (3B);
   (b) it must contain the particulars required under regulation 14(1) or (2);
   (c) it must relate to a supply or supplies made by a supplier who is a taxable person.][1]

[(3B) A self-billing agreement must—
   (a) authorise the customer to produce self-billed invoices in respect of supplies made by the supplier for a specified period . . . [4];
   (b) specify that the supplier will not issue VAT invoices in respect of supplies covered by the agreement;
   (c) specify that the supplier will accept each self-billed invoice created by the customer in respect of supplies made to him by the supplier;
   (d) specify that the supplier will notify the customer if he ceases to be a taxable person or if he changes his registration number.][1]

[(3C) Without prejudice to any term of a self-billing agreement, it shall be treated as having expired when—
   (a) the business of the supplier is transferred as a going concern;
   (b) the business of the customer is transferred as a going concern;
   (c) the supplier ceases to be registered for VAT.][1]

[(3D) In addition to the matters set out in paragraph (3B)—

(a) conditions that must be complied with may be set out in a notice published by the Commissioners;

(b) the Commissioners may impose further conditions in particular cases.]¹

[(3E) Where a customer (C) in a member State provides a document to C in respect of a supply of goods to C by a registered person who is identified for the purposes of VAT in Northern Ireland, that document is to be treated as the VAT invoice required to be provided by the supplier under paragraph (1)(b) or (c) if it complies with the conditions set out in paragraph (3A).]⁵

[(3F) For the purposes of the following, a self-billed invoice will not be treated as issued by the supplier (however the supplier may be described in the provision concerned)—

(a) regulation 84(2)(b)(ii);
(b) regulation 85(1)(b);
(c) regulation 85(2);
(d) regulation 86(1);
(e) regulation 86(2)(b);
(f) regulation 86(3);
(g) regulation 88(1)(b);
(h) regulation 89(b)(ii);
(i) regulation 90(1)(b);
(j) regulation 90(2);
(k) regulation 91;
(l) regulation 92(b);
(m) regulation 93(1)(b);
(n) regulation 94B(6)(a).]²

(4) Where the person who makes a supply to which regulation 93 relates gives an authenticated receipt containing the particulars required under regulation 14(1) to be specified in a VAT invoice in respect of that supply, that document shall be treated as the VAT invoice required to be provided under paragraph (1)(a) above on condition that no VAT invoice or similar document which was intended to be or could be construed as being a VAT invoice for the supply to which the receipt relates is issued.

(5) [With the exception of the supplies referred to in paragraph (6),]⁴ the documents specified in paragraphs (1), (2), (3) and (4) above shall be provided within 30 days of the time when the supply is treated as taking place under section 6 of the Act, or within such longer period as the Commissioners may allow in general or special directions.

[(6) The documents specified in paragraphs (1), (2), (3) and (4) shall—

(a) in the case of a supply of goods falling within section 6(7) of the Act, be provided by the 15th day of the month following that in which the removal in question takes place; and

(b) in the case of a supply of services falling within regulation 82, be provided by the 15th day of—

(i) the month following the month in which the services are treated as being performed under regulation 82(2),

(ii) the month following the month during which the services are treated as separately and successively made as a result of payments being made under regulation 82(4), or

(iii) the January following the 31st December on which the services are treated as being supplied under regulation 82(6).

(7) Both the supplier and the customer shall ensure the authenticity of the origin, the integrity of the content and the legibility of an invoice for such time as the invoice is required to be preserved.

(8) In this regulation—

(a) "authenticity of the origin" of an invoice means the assurance of either the identity of the supplier of the underlying goods or services or the issuer of that invoice;

(b) "integrity of the content" of an invoice means that the content required by regulation 14 has not been altered.]⁴

Commentary—*De Voil Indirect Tax Service* **V3.523, V3.140B.**
HMRC Manuals—VAT Traders' Records Manual VATREC4020 (when is a VAT Invoice not required?).
Amendments—² Para (3) substituted, paras (3A)–(3F) inserted, by the VAT (Amendment) (No 6) Regulations, SI 2003/3220 regs 1(1)(b), 2, 4 with effect from 1 January 2004.

³ Para (1A) inserted by the Value Added Tax (Amendment) (No 5) Regulations, SI 2007/2085 regs 2, 6 with effect from 1 October 2007.

⁴ Paras (1B), (6)–(8) inserted, in para (3B)(a) words revoked, and words in para (5) inserted, by the VAT (Amendment) (No 3) Regulations, SI 2012/2951 reg 2(1), (3) with effect from 1 January 2013.

⁵ Paras (1) and (3E) substituted, and para (1ZA) inserted, by the Value Added Tax (Miscellaneous Amendments, Northern Ireland Protocol and Savings and Transitional Provisions) (EU Exit) Regulations, SI 2020/1545 regs 31 and 34 with effect from IP completion day (11pm UK time on 31 December 2020) by virtue of SI 2020/1641 reg 2, Schedule para 11.

Para (1) previously read as follows—

"(1) Save as otherwise provided in these Regulations, where a registered person—

(a) makes a taxable supply in the United Kingdom to a taxable person, or

(b) makes a supply of goods or services . . . to a person in another member State for the purpose of any business activity carried out by that person, or

(c) receives a payment on account in respect of a supply he has made or intends to make from a person in another member State,

he shall provide such persons as are mentioned above with a VAT invoice (unless, in the case of that supply, he is entitled to issue and issues a VAT invoice pursuant to section 18C(1)(e) of the Act and regulation 145D(1) below in relation to the supply by him of specified services performed on or in relation to goods while those goods are subject to a fiscal or other warehousing regime)."

Para (3E) previously read as follows—
"(3E) Where a customer in another member State provides a document to himself in respect of a supply of goods or services to him by a registered person, that document shall be treated as the VAT invoice required to be provided by the supplier under paragraph 1(b) or (c) if it complies with the conditions set out in paragraph (3A)."

[6] Para (1C) inserted by the Taxation (Post-transition Period) Act 2020 s 7, Sch 3 paras 19, 20 with effect from IP completion day (11pm on 31 December 2020), by virtue of SI 2020/1642 reg 9.

[13A Electronic invoicing

(1) This regulation applies where a document is provided by a registered person [in any electronic format][2] that purports to be a VAT invoice in respect of a supply of [services or relevant goods][3].

[(2) The document is not to be treated as the VAT invoice required to be provided by the supplier under regulation 13(1) unless the use of the electronic invoice is accepted by the customer.

(3) When the document is a self-billed invoice that purports to be a VAT invoice, paragraph (2) applies as if the reference to the supplier is to the customer and the reference to the customer is to the supplier.

(4) In this regulation "electronic invoice" means an invoice that contains the particulars required by regulation 14 and which has been issued and received in any electronic format.][2]

[(5) In this regulation, "relevant goods" means all goods other than goods—
 (a) the supply of which is deemed to be a supply by an operator of an online marketplace by virtue of section 5A of the Act, or
 (b) the place of supply of which is determined by section 7(5B) of the Act.][3]][1]

Commentary—*De Voil Indirect Tax Service* **V3.516, V5.202**.
Amendments—[1] Inserted by the VAT (Amendment No 6) Regulations, SI 2003/3220 regs 1(1)(b), 2, 5 with effect from 1 January 2004.
[2] In para (1), words substituted for words "by electronic transmission", and paras (2)–(4) substituted, by the VAT (Amendment) (No 3) Regulations, SI 2012/2951 reg 2(1), (4) with effect from 1 January 2013.
[3] In para (1) words substituted for words "goods or services", and para (5) inserted by the Taxation (Post-transition Period) Act 2020 s 7, Sch 3 paras 19, 21 with effect from IP completion day (11pm on 31 December 2020), by virtue of SI 2020/1642 reg 9.

[13B Where a VAT invoice or part of a VAT invoice is in a language other than English the Commissioners may, by notice in writing, require that an English translation of the invoice is provided to them by a person who has received such an invoice in the United Kingdom within 30 days of the date of the notice.][1]

Commentary—*De Voil Indirect Tax Service* **V5.234, V3.511**.
HMRC Manuals—VAT Traders' Records Manual VATREC5070 (invoicing in a foreign language).
Amendments—[1] Inserted by the VAT (Amendment) (No 6) Regulations, SI 2003/3220 regs 1(1)(b), 2, 6 with effect from 1 January 2004.

14 Contents of VAT invoice

(1) Subject to paragraph (2) below and regulation 16 [and save as the Commissioners may otherwise allow][2], a registered person providing a VAT invoice in accordance with regulation 13 shall state thereon the following particulars—
 (a) [a sequential number based on one or more series which uniquely identifies the document][6],
 (b) the time of the supply,
 (c) the date of the issue of the document,
 (d) the name, address and registration number of the supplier,
 (e) the name and address of the person to whom the goods or services are supplied,
 (f) . . .[3]
 (g) a description sufficient to identify the goods or services supplied,
 (h) for each description, the quantity of the goods or the extent of the services, and the rate of VAT and the amount payable, excluding VAT, expressed in [any currency][3],
 (i) the gross total amount payable, excluding VAT, expressed in [any currency][3],
 (j) the rate of any cash discount offered,
 (k) . . .[3]
 (l) the total amount of VAT chargeable, expressed in sterling,
 [(m) the unit price.][3]
 [(n) where a margin scheme is applied under section 50A or section 53 of the Act, [the reference "margin scheme: works of art", "margin scheme: antiques or collectors' items", "margin scheme: second-hand goods", or "margin scheme: tour operators" as appropriate][7]
 (o) where a VAT invoice relates in whole or part to a supply where the person supplied is liable to pay the tax, [the reference "reverse charge"][7]][6]

(2) [Save as the Commissioners may otherwise allow, where a registered person [who is identified for the purposes of VAT in Northern Ireland][8] provides a person in another member State with a VAT invoice or any document that refers to a VAT invoice and is intended to amend it, he must ensure that it states thereon the following particulars—][4]
  (a) the information specified in sub-paragraphs [(a) to (e), (g), [(j), (m), (n) and (o)][6]][4] of paragraph (1) above,
  (b) the letters "[XI][8]" as a prefix to his registration number,
  (c) the registration number, if any, of the recipient of the supply of goods . . . [8] and which registration number, if any, shall contain the alphabetical code of the [relevant territory][8] in which that recipient is registered,
  (d) the gross amount payable, excluding VAT,
  (e) where the supply is of a new means of transport (as defined in section 95 of the Act) a description sufficient to identify it as such,
  (f) for each description, the quantity of the goods . . . [8], and where a positive rate of VAT is chargeable, the rate of VAT and the amount payable, excluding VAT, expressed in sterling, . . . [6]
  (g) where the supply of goods is a taxable supply, the information as specified in [sub-paragraph (l)][4] of paragraph (1) above[, and
  (h) where the supply is an exempt or zero-rated supply, a relevant reference or any indication that the supply is exempt or zero-rated as appropriate][6].
(3) Where a taxable supply takes place as described in section 6(2)(c) or section 6(5) of the Act, any consignment or delivery note or similar document or any copy thereof issued by the supplier before the time of supply shall not, notwithstanding that it may contain all the particulars set out in paragraph (1) above, be treated as a VAT invoice provided it is endorsed "This is not a VAT invoice".
(4) Where a registered person provides an invoice containing the particulars specified in paragraphs (1) and (3) above, and specifies thereon any goods or services which are the subject of an exempt or zero-rated supply, he shall distinguish on the invoice between the goods or services which are the subject of an exempt, zero-rated or other supply and state separately the gross total amount payable in respect of each supply and rate.
(5) . . . [6]
[(6) Where a registered person provides a VAT invoice relating in whole or in part to a supply of the letting on hire of a motor car other than for self-drive hire, he shall state on the invoice whether that motor car is a qualifying vehicle under article 7(2A) of the Value Added Tax (Input Tax) Order 1992.][1]
[(7) Where a registered person provides documents in batches to the same recipient [in any electronic format][7] that purport to be VAT invoices in respect of supplies of goods or services made to, or received by, him, as an exception to the requirements in regulation 14(1) and 14(2), details common to each such document need only be stated once for each batch file.][5]
[(8) In this regulation, a "relevant reference" is—
  (a) a reference to the appropriate provision of Council Directive 2006/112/EC, or
  (b) a reference to the corresponding provision of the Act.][6]

Commentary—*De Voil Indirect Tax Service* **V3.514, V3.515**.
HMRC Manuals—VAT Input Tax VIT11500 (UK law).
VAT Traders' Records Manual VATREC5010 (details which must be shown on a full VAT invoice).
Amendments—[1] Para (6) inserted by the VAT (Amendment) Regulations, SI 1995/3147 reg 3, with effect from 1 January 1996.
[2] Words in paras (1) and (2) inserted by the VAT (Amendment) (No 3) Regulations, SI 1996/1250 reg 7 with effect from 1 June 1996.
[3] In para (1), sub-paras (f) and (k) revoked, words in sub-paras (h) and (i) substituted, and sub-para (m) inserted, by the VAT (Amendment) (No 6) Regulations, SI 2003/3220 regs 1(1)(b), 2, 7 with effect from 1 January 2004.
[4] Words at beginning of sub-para (2), and in sub-paras (2)(a), (g) substituted by SI 2003/3220 regs 1(1)(b), 2, 8 with effect from 1 January 2004.
[5] Sub-para (7) inserted by SI 2003/3220 regs 1(1)(b), 2, 9 with effect from 1 January 2004.
[6] Words in paras (1), (2) substituted and inserted, para (5) revoked, and para (8) inserted, by the Value Added Tax (Amendment) (No 5) Regulations, SI 2007/2085 regs 2, 7 with effect from 1 October 2007.
[7] In para (1)(n), words substituted for words "a relevant reference or any indication that a margin scheme has been applied,", in para (1)(o), words substituted for words "a relevant reference or any indication that the supply is one where the customer is liable to pay the tax.", and in para (7), words substituted for words "by electronic transmission", by the VAT (Amendment) (No 3) Regulations, SI 2012/2951 reg 2(1), (5) with effect from 1 January 2013.
[8] In para (2), words inserted in the opening paragraph, in sub-para (b) "XI" substituted for "GB", in sub-para (c) words "or services" revoked and words substituted for words "member State", and in sub-para (f) words "or the extent of the services" revoked, by the Value Added Tax (Miscellaneous Amendments, Northern Ireland Protocol and Savings and Transitional Provisions) (EU Exit) Regulations, SI 2020/1545 regs 31 and 35 with effect from IP completion day (11pm UK time on 31 December 2020) by virtue of SI 2020/1641 reg 2, Schedule para 11.

15 Change of rate, credit notes
[(1)] Where there is a change in the rate of VAT in force under section 2 [or 29A][1] of the Act or in the descriptions of exempt[, zero-rated or reduced-rate][1] supplies, and a VAT invoice which relates to a [relevant][3] supply in respect of which an election is made under section 88 of the Act was issued

before the election was made, the person making the supply shall, within [45 days]² after any such change, [or within such longer period as the Commissioners may allow in general or special directions,]² provide the person to whom the supply was made with a credit note headed "Credit note-change of VAT rate" and containing the following particulars—
   (a) the identifying number and date of issue of the credit note,
   (b) the name, address and registration number of the supplier,
   (c) the name and address of the person to whom the supply is made,
   (d) the identifying number and date of issue of the VAT invoice,
   (e) a description sufficient to identify the goods or services supplied, and
   (f) the amount being credited in respect of VAT.
[(2) In this regulation, "relevant supply" means a supply of goods or services other than a supply of goods to a person who is not a taxable person.]³

Commentary—*De Voil Indirect Tax Service* **V3.519, V3.520**.
Amendments—¹ Words inserted, and words substituted for the words "or zero-rated", by the VAT (Amendment) (No 4) Regulations, SI 2003/1485 regs 2, 3 with effect from 1 July 2003.
² Figure substituted and words inserted, by the VAT (Amendment) (No 2) Regulations, SI 2008/3021 regs 2, 3 with effect from 1 December 2008.
³ Para (1) numbered as such and word inserted, and para (2) inserted, by the Taxation (Post-transition Period) Act 2020 s 7, Sch 3 paras 19, 22 with effect from IP completion day (11pm on 31 December 2020), by virtue of SI 2020/1642 reg 9.

15A [Change of rate, supplementary charge invoices
Where a supplementary charge is due under Schedule 3 to the Finance Act 2009 [or Schedule 2 to the Finance (No 2) Act 2010]² in respect of a supply and a VAT invoice has been issued in relation to that supply which invoice does not include the supplementary charge, the person making the supply shall, within 45 days after the date when the supplementary charge becomes due, provide the person to whom the supply is made with an invoice headed "Supplementary charge invoice" and containing the following particulars—
   (a) the identifying number and date of issue of the supplementary charge invoice,
   (b) the amount of the supplementary charge to VAT,
   (c) the name, address and registration number of the supplier,
   (d) the name and address of the person to whom the supply is made, and
   (e) the identifying number and date of issue of the VAT invoice.]¹

Commentary—*De Voil Indirect Tax Service* **V3.142A**.
Amendments—¹ Reg 15A inserted by the VAT (Amendment) (No 5) Regs, SI 2009/3241, regs 2, 3 with effect from 1 January 2010.
² Words inserted by the VAT (Amendment) (No 3) Regulations, SI 2010/2940 regs 2, 3 with effect from 4 January 2011.

15B [Change of liability: anti-forestalling invoices
(1) Where—
   (a) an anti-forestalling charge is due under Schedule 27 to the Finance Act 2012 in relation to any supply,
   (b) the person making the supply ("the supplier") would have been required to provide the person to whom the supply is made ("the recipient") with a VAT invoice under regulation 13 in respect of the supply at the time it was made had the supply been subject to the standard rate of VAT at that time, and
   (c) where the supply has been included in a VAT invoice, the supplier has not included the anti-forestalling charge in that VAT invoice,
the supplier shall, within 45 days after the date when the anti-forestalling charge becomes due, provide the recipient with an invoice headed "Anti-forestalling charge invoice" and containing the particulars specified in paragraph (2) or (3) as appropriate.
(2) Where the supply has not been included in a VAT invoice, the particulars are the particulars required in regulation 14.
(3) Where the supply has been included in a VAT invoice which does not include the anti-forestalling charge, the particulars are—
   (a) the identifying number and date of issue of the anti-forestalling charge invoice,
   (b) the amount of the anti-forestalling charge to VAT,
   (c) the name, address and registration number of the supplier,
   (d) the name and address of the recipient, and
   (e) the identifying number and date of issue of the VAT invoice in which the supply was previously included.]¹

Commentary—*De Voil Indirect Tax Service* **V3.515B**.
Amendments—¹ Reg 15B inserted by the VAT (Amendment) (No 2) Regulations, SI 2012/1899 regs 3, 9 with effect from 1 October 2012.

[15C Changes in consideration: debit notes and credit notes
(1) This regulation applies to increases and decreases in consideration as described in regulation 24A[, subject to paragraph (1A)]².

[(1A) This regulation does not apply in relation to a case where the original supply was a supply of goods to a person who was not a taxable person.]²

(2) Where there is an increase in consideration, the supplier must, no later than the end of the period of 14 days beginning with the day on which the increase occurs, provide to the recipient of the supply a debit note as specified in paragraph (3).

(3) For the purposes of this regulation, a "debit note" is a document which includes the following particulars—
- (a) the identifying number of the document,
- (b) the date of issue of the document,
- (c) the name, address and registration number of the supplier,
- (d) the name and address of the recipient of the supply,
- (e) the identifying number and date of issue of the VAT invoice or invoices relating to the supply for which there is an increase in consideration,
- (f) a description sufficient to identify the goods or services supplied,
- (g) the amount of the increase in consideration excluding VAT,
- (h) the rate and the amount (expressed in sterling) of the VAT chargeable in respect of the increase in consideration.

(4) The requirement in paragraph (2) to provide a debit note does not apply in cases where, in relation to the increase in consideration, a document having the same purpose as a debit note has been provided by the supplier to the recipient of the supply before 1st September 2019.

(5) Where there is a decrease in consideration, the supplier must, no later than the end of the period of 14 days beginning with the day on which the decrease occurs, provide to the recipient of the supply a credit note as specified in paragraph (6).

(6) For the purposes of this regulation, a "credit note" is a document which includes the following particulars—
- (a) the identifying number of the document,
- (b) the date of issue of the document,
- (c) the name, address and registration number of the supplier,
- (d) the name and address of the recipient of the supply,
- (e) the identifying number and date of issue of the VAT invoice or invoices relating to the supply for which there is a decrease in consideration,
- (f) a description sufficient to identify the goods or services supplied,
- (g) the amount of the decrease in consideration excluding VAT,
- (h) the rate and the amount (expressed in sterling) of the VAT credited in respect of the decrease in consideration.

(7) The requirement in paragraph (5) to provide a credit note does not apply in cases where, in relation to the decrease in consideration, a document having the same purpose as a credit note has been provided by the supplier to the recipient of the supply before 1st September 2019.

(8) In cases where a supplier was not required by these regulations to provide a VAT invoice in relation to the original supply, the requirement in paragraph (2) to provide a debit note and the requirement in paragraph (5) to provide a credit note do not apply unless the recipient of the supply is a taxable person and requests a debit note or a credit note (as the case may be) from the supplier.

(9) Where a request described in paragraph (8) has been made—
- (a) the period specified in paragraph (2) or (5) (as the case may be) begins with the day on which the request is made; and
- (b) paragraph (3)(e) or (6)(e) (as the case may be) does not apply.

(10) In relation to any increase or decrease in consideration for supplies to which regulation 16A applies, paragraph (3)(a), (d) and (e) or (6)(a), (d) and (e) (as the case may be) does not apply.

(11) Where there is a decrease in consideration to which regulation 38ZA applies—
- (a) paragraphs (5) to (10) do not apply; and
- (b) if the final consumer requests an accounting document in relation to the decrease in consideration, the first supplier must, no later than the end of the period of 14 days beginning with the day on which the request is made, provide to the final consumer a document which includes the following particulars—
  - (i) the date of issue of the document,
  - (ii) the name, address and registration number of the person issuing the document,
  - (iii) a description sufficient to identify the goods supplied,
  - (iv) the amount of the decrease in consideration excluding VAT,
  - (v) the rate and the amount (expressed in sterling) of the VAT credited in respect of the decrease in consideration.

(12) Where the recipient of the supply or, in cases where it is applicable, the final consumer agrees, the documents described in paragraphs (3), (6) and (11)(b) may be provided in electronic format.

(13) For the purposes of this regulation—
- (a) an increase or decrease in consideration occurs at the time specified in regulation 24B; and
- (b) "final consumer" and "first supplier" have the meanings given by regulation 38ZA(2).

(14) The Commissioners may, in such cases as they think fit, dispense with or relax the requirements in this regulation in such manner as they think fit.]¹
Commentary—*De Voil Indirect Tax Service* **V3.518, V3.519**.
HMRC Manuals—VAT Traders' Records Manual VATREC13040 (what are the conditions of a valid credit note?).
Amendments—¹ Regulation 15C inserted by the VAT (Amendment) Regulations, SI 2019/1048 regs 3, 4 with effect in relation to supplies for which there is an increase or decrease in consideration that occurs on or after 1 September 2019. An increase or decrease in consideration means an increase or decrease in consideration as described in reg 24A which occurs at the time specified in reg 24B.
² In para (1) words inserted, and para (1A) inserted, by the Taxation (Post-transition Period) Act 2020 s 7, Sch 3 paras 19, 23 with effect from IP completion day (11pm on 31 December 2020), by virtue of SI 2020/1642 reg 9.

16 Retailers' invoices

(1) Subject to paragraph (2) below, a registered person who is a retailer shall not be required to provide a VAT invoice, except that he shall provide such an invoice at the request of a customer who is a taxable person in respect of any supply to him; but, in that event, if, but only if, the consideration for the supply does not exceed [£250]¹ and[, where the retailer is identified for the purposes of VAT in Northern Ireland,]² the supply is other than to a person in another member State, the VAT invoice need contain only the following particulars—
   (a) the name, address and registration number of the retailer,
   (b) the time of the supply,
   (c) a description sufficient to identify the goods or services supplied,
   (d) the total amount payable including VAT, and
   (e) for each rate of VAT chargeable, the gross amount payable including VAT, and the VAT rate applicable.
(2) Where a registered person provides an invoice in accordance with this regulation, the invoice shall not contain any reference to any exempt supply.
Commentary—*De Voil Indirect Tax Service* **V3.513, V3.555**.
HMRC Manuals—VAT Traders' Records Manual VATREC16041 (other invoicing retailers: general).
Amendments—¹ Figure substituted by the VAT (Amendment) (No 6) Regulations, SI 2003/3220 regs 1(1)(b), 2, 10 with effect from 1 January 2004.
² In para (1) words inserted by the Value Added Tax (Miscellaneous Amendments, Northern Ireland Protocol and Savings and Transitional Provisions) (EU Exit) Regulations, SI 2020/1545 regs 31 and 36 with effect from IP completion day (11pm UK time on 31 December 2020) by virtue of SI 2020/1641 reg 2, Schedule para 11.

[16A Simplified invoices

In any case where the consideration for a supply does not exceed £250 and[, where the registered person is identified for the purposes of VAT in Northern Ireland,]² the supply is other than to a person in another member State, the VAT invoice that a registered person is required to provide need contain only the following particulars—
   (a) the name, address and registration number of the supplier;
   (b) the time of the supply;
   (c) a description sufficient to identify the goods or services supplied;
   (d) the total amount payable including VAT; and
   (e) for each rate of VAT chargeable, the gross amount payable including VAT, and the VAT rate applicable.]¹
Commentary—*De Voil Indirect Tax Service* **V3.514**.
HMRC Manuals—VAT Traders' Records Manual VATREC16042 (other invoicing retailers: less detailed VAT invoices).
Amendments—¹ Regulation 16A inserted by the VAT (Amendment) (No 3) Regulations, SI 2012/2951 reg 2(1), (6) with effect from 1 January 2013.
² Words inserted by the Value Added Tax (Miscellaneous Amendments, Northern Ireland Protocol and Savings and Transitional Provisions) (EU Exit) Regulations, SI 2020/1545 regs 31 and 37 with effect from IP completion day (11pm UK time on 31 December 2020) by virtue of SI 2020/1641 reg 2, Schedule para 11.

[16B Retailers' and simplified invoices: exceptions

Regulations 16 and 16A do not apply in relation to a supply of goods if—
   (a) that supply is deemed to be a supply by an operator of an online marketplace by virtue of section 5A of the Act, or
   (b) the place of supply of those goods is determined by section 7(5B) of the Act.]¹
Amendments—¹ Regulation 16B inserted by the Taxation (Post-transition Period) Act 2020 s 7, Sch 3 paras 19, 24 with effect from IP completion day (11pm on 31 December 2020), by virtue of SI 2020/1642 reg 9.

17 Section 14(6) supplies to persons belonging in other member States

(1) Where a registered person makes a supply such as is mentioned in section 14(6) of the Act he shall provide the person supplied with an invoice in respect of that supply.
[(2) An invoice provided under this regulation shall comply with the requirements of regulations 13 and 14.]¹
Commentary—*De Voil Indirect Tax Service* **V3.388A**.
Amendments—¹ Para (2) substituted by the Value Added Tax (Amendment) (No 5) Regulations, SI 2007/2085 regs 2, 8 with effect from 1 October 2007.

18 Section 14(1) supplies by intermediate suppliers
(1) On each occasion that an intermediate supplier makes or intends to make a supply to which he wishes section 14(1) of the Act to apply he shall, subject to paragraph (3) below, provide the customer with an invoice.
(2) An invoice provided under this regulation by an intermediate supplier shall—
   (a) comply with the provisions of the law corresponding, in relation to the member State which provided the intermediate supplier with the identification number for VAT purposes used or to be used by him for the purpose of the supply to him by the original supplier of the goods which were subsequently removed to the United Kingdom, to regulation 17,
   (b) be provided no later than 15 days after the time that the supply of the goods would, but for section 14(1) of the Act, have been treated as having taken place by or under section 6 of the Act,
   (c) cover no less than the extent of the supply which would, but for section 14(1) of the Act, have been treated as having taken place by or under section 6 of the Act at the time that such an invoice is provided, . . . [1]
   (d) . . . [1]
(3) Where an intermediate supplier makes a supply such as is mentioned in paragraph (1) above, and he has already provided the customer with an invoice that complies with the requirements of sub-paragraphs (a), (c) and (d) of paragraph (2) above, he shall not be required to provide the customer with a further invoice in relation to that supply.
(4) Where an intermediate supplier makes a supply such as is mentioned in paragraph (1) above and he provides the customer with an invoice such as is described in paragraphs (2) and (3) above, that invoice shall be treated as if it were an invoice for the purpose of regulation 83.
(5) Where an intermediate supplier makes a supply such as is mentioned in paragraph (1) above and he provides the customer with an invoice that complies only with the requirements of paragraph (2)(a) above, that invoice shall, for the purposes of this regulation only, be treated as if it were a VAT invoice.
Amendments—[1] Para (2)(d) and preceding word "and" revoked by the Value Added Tax (Amendment) (No 5) Regulations, SI 2007/2085 regs 2, 9 with effect from 1 October 2007.

19 Section 14(2) supplies by persons belonging in other member States
(1) On each occasion that a person belonging in another member State makes or intends to make a supply to which he wishes section 14(2) of the Act to apply he shall, subject to paragraph (3) below, provide the registered person with an invoice.
(2) An invoice provided under this regulation by a person belonging in another member State shall—
   (a) comply with the provisions of the law of the member State in which he belongs corresponding in relation to that member State to the provisions of regulation 14,
   (b) be provided no later than 15 days after the time that the supply of the goods would, but for section 14(2) of the Act, have been treated as having taken place by or under section 6 of the Act,
   (c) cover no less than the extent of the supply which would, but for section 14(2) of the Act, have been treated as having taken place by or under section 6 of the Act at the time that such an invoice is provided, . . . [1]
   (d) . . . [1]
(3) Where a person belonging in another member State makes a supply such as is mentioned in paragraph (1) above, and he has already provided the registered person with an invoice that complies with the requirements of sub-paragraphs (a), (c) and (d) of paragraph (2) above, he shall not be required to provide the registered person with a further invoice in relation to that supply.
(4) Where a person belonging in another member State makes a supply such as is mentioned in paragraph (1) above and he provides the registered person with an invoice such as is described in paragraphs (2) and (3) above, that invoice shall be treated as if it were an invoice for the purpose of regulation 83.
(5) Where a person belonging in another member State makes a supply such as is mentioned in paragraph (1) above, and he provides the registered person with an invoice that complies only with the requirements of paragraph (2)(a) above, that invoice shall, for the purposes of this regulation only, be treated as if it were a VAT invoice.
Commentary—*De Voil Indirect Tax Service* **V3.388AA**.
Amendments—[1] Para (2)(d) and preceding word "and" revoked by the Value Added Tax (Amendment) (No 5) Regulations, SI 2007/2085 regs 2, 10 with effect from 1 October 2007.

20 General
Regulations 13, 14, 15, 16, 17, 18 and 19 shall not apply to the following supplies made in the United Kingdom—
   (a) any zero-rated supply other than a supply for the purposes of an acquisition in another member State,
   (b) any supply to which an order made under section 25(7) of the Act applies,
   (c) any supply on which VAT is charged although it is not made for consideration, or

(d) any supply to which an order made under section 32 of the Act applies.

Commentary—*De Voil Indirect Tax Service* **V3.513**.

PART IV
EC SALES STATEMENTS

[21 Interpretation of Part IV
[(1)] In this Part—
. . .³
. . .³

"first relevant figure" means, up to and including 31st December 2011, £70,000 excluding VAT and thereafter £35,000 excluding VAT;
["new means of transport" has the same meaning as in paragraph 83(1) and (2) of Schedule 9ZA to the Act;]³
"NMT supply of goods" means a supply falling within paragraph 22C(1) and "NMT supplies of goods" shall be construed accordingly;
. . .³
["registered in a member State" means registered in accordance with the measures adopted by the competent authority in a member State for the purposes of the EU common system of VAT and "registered in that member State", "registered in another member State" and "registered in member States" shall be construed accordingly;]³
["relevant supply of goods" means a supply falling within regulation 22(1) and "relevant supplies of goods" shall be construed accordingly;]³
"second relevant figure" means the sum of the amount mentioned in paragraph 1(1)(*a*) of Schedule 1 to the Act as that paragraph has effect from time to time and £25,500;
"supply of goods" does not include either a supply of gas supplied through the natural gas distribution network or a supply of electricity;
["value" in the phrases "value of relevant supplies", "value of the taxable person's taxable supplies" and "value of the taxable person's supplies" means the consideration for the supplies and includes the costs of any freight transport services and services ancillary to the transport of the goods charged by the supplier to the customer.]³
[(1A) For the purposes of this Part—
  (*a*) goods are removed from Northern Ireland under call-off stock arrangements if they are removed in circumstances where the conditions in paragraphs (a) to (g) of paragraph 57(1) of Schedule 9ZA to the Act are met,
  (*b*) references to "the customer" or "the destination territory", in relation to goods removed from Northern Ireland under call-off stock arrangements, are to be construed in accordance with Part 10 of Schedule 9ZA to the Act, and
  (*c*) "call-off stock goods", in relation to a taxable person, means goods that have been removed from Northern Ireland under call-off stock arrangements by or under the directions of the taxable person.]³
(2) . . .⁴]¹

Commentary—*De Voil Indirect Tax Service* **V5.271A**.
Amendments—¹ Reg 21 substituted by the VAT (Amendment) (No 5) Regs, SI 2009/3241, regs 2, 4 with effect from 1 January 2010.
² Para (1) numbered as such by FA 2020 s 80(7), (8) with effect from 22 July 2020.
³ The definitions "EU supply of goods", "EU supply of services" and "registered in another member State" revoked, the definition of "value" substituted, the definitions of "new means of transport", "relevant supply of goods", and "registered in a member State" inserted, and para (1A) inserted by the Value Added Tax (Miscellaneous Amendments, Northern Ireland Protocol and Savings and Transitional Provisions) (EU Exit) Regulations, SI 2020/1545 regs 31 and 38 with effect from IP completion day (11pm UK time on 31 December 2020) by virtue of SI 2020/1641 reg 2, Schedule para 11. These amendments are to be treated for the purposes of VATA 1994 as if they were made under VATA 1994 Sch 9ZA para 73(1) (see SI 2020/1545 reg 44).
The definitions previously read as follows—
  ""EU supply of goods" means a supply falling within paragraph 22(1) and "EU supplies of goods" shall be construed accordingly;
  "EU supply of services" means a supply falling within paragraph 22A(1) and "EU supplies of services" shall be construed accordingly;
  "registered in another member State" means registered in accordance with the measures adopted by the competent authority in another member State for the purposes of the common system of VAT and "registered in that member State" and "registered in other member States" shall be construed accordingly;
  "value" in the phrases "value of EU supplies", "value of the taxable person's taxable supplies" and "value of the taxable person's supplies" means the consideration for the supplies and includes, if the supply is a supply of goods, the costs of any freight transport services and services ancillary to the transport of the goods charged by the supplier to the customer."
⁴ Sub-para (2) revoked by the Taxation (Post-transition Period) Act 2020 s 3, Sch 2 para 7(5)(*a*) with effect from IP completion day (11pm on 31 December 2020), by virtue of SI 2020/1642 reg 9.
Sub-para (2) previously read as follows—

"(2) For the purposes of this Part—
  (a) goods are removed from the United Kingdom under call-off stock arrangements if they are removed from the United Kingdom in circumstances where the conditions in paragraphs (a) to (g) of paragraph 1(1) of Schedule 4B to the Act are met,
  (b) references to "the customer" or "the destination State", in relation to goods removed from the United Kingdom under call-off stock arrangements, are to be construed in accordance with paragraph 1 of Schedule 4B to the Act, and
  (c) "call-off stock goods", in relation to a taxable person, means goods that have been removed from the United Kingdom under call-off stock arrangements by or under the directions of the taxable person.".

[22 **Submission of statements**
(1) Every taxable person [who is identified for the purposes of VAT in Northern Ireland][3] who makes a supply of goods—
  (a) to a person who, at the time of the supply, was registered [in a member State and those goods were dispatched or transported to that or a different member State, or][3]
  (b) to which section 14(6) of the Act applies, or
  (c) which falls within paragraph 6 of Schedule 4 to the Act to a person who, at the time of the supply, was registered in another member State,
shall submit a statement to the Commissioners.
(2) The statement shall—
  [(a) be made in the form specified in a notice published by the Commissioners,][2]
  (b) contain, in respect of the [relevant][3] supplies of goods which have been made within the period in respect of which the statement is made, such information as the Commissioners shall from time to time prescribe, and
  (c) contain a declaration that the information provided in the statement is true and complete.
(3)
  (a) Subject to paragraphs (4) to (6) below, the statement shall be submitted in respect of the month in which the [relevant][3] supply of goods is made.
  (b) Where during the period specified in sub-paragraph (a) above the taxable person—
    (i) ceases to be registered under Schedule 1 to the Act, and
    (ii) no other person has been registered with the registration number of and in substitution for A,
  the last day of that period is to be treated as being the same date as the effective date of A's deregistration.
(4)
  (a) This sub-paragraph applies where, in each of the four quarters preceding the quarter in which the supply is made ("the relevant quarter"), the total value of [relevant][3] supplies of goods made by the taxable person (a) did not exceed the first relevant figure.
  (b) This sub-paragraph applies where, in the relevant quarter, the total value of [relevant][3] supplies of goods made by A did not exceed the first relevant figure.
  (c) Where sub-paragraphs (a) and (b) above apply, A may submit the statement in respect of the relevant quarter.
  (d) Where—
    (i) sub-paragraph (a) above applies, and
    (ii) sub-paragraph (b) above does not apply,
  A may submit a statement in respect of the period beginning with the first day of the relevant quarter and ending on the last day of the month in which the total value of [relevant][3] supplies of goods made by A in that quarter first exceeded the relevant figure.
  (e) Where during the relevant quarter specified in sub-paragraph (c) above A—
    (i) ceases to be registered under Schedule 1 to the Act, and
    (ii) no other person has been registered with the registration number of and in substitution for A,
  the last day of that period is to be treated as being the same date as the effective date of A's deregistration.
(5)
  (a) A statement may be submitted in respect of the year mentioned in sub-paragraphs (i) to (iv) below provided that the taxable person making the statement (a) has not, during that year, made a supply of a new means of transport [that involved the removal of those goods from Northern Ireland to a member State][3] and the Commissioners are satisfied either that—
    (i) at the end of any month, the value of A's taxable supplies in the period of one year then ending is less than the second relevant figure, or
    (ii) at any time there are reasonable grounds for believing that the value of A's taxable supplies in the period of one year beginning at that or any later time will not exceed the second relevant figure,

and either that—
  (iii) at the end of any month, the value of A's supplies to persons registered in other member States in the period of one year then ending is less than £11,000, or
  (iv) at any time, there are reasonable grounds for believing that the value of A's supplies to persons registered in other member States in the period of one year beginning at that or any later time will not exceed £11,000.
  (b) Where during a period specified in sub-paragraph (a) above A—
    (i) ceases to be registered under Schedule 1 to the Act, and
    (ii) no other person has been registered with the registration number of and in substitution for A,
  the last day of that period is to be treated as being the same date as the effective date of A's deregistration.
(6) A taxable person (a) who is permitted under regulation 25 to make a return in respect of a period longer than 3 months may submit a statement under paragraph (1) above in respect of a period identical to the period permitted for the making of the return provided that A has not, during that period, made a supply of a new means of transport [that involved the removal of those goods from Northern Ireland to a member State][3] and the Commissioners are satisfied either that—
  (a) at the end of any month, the value of A's taxable supplies in the period of one year then ending is less than £145,000, or
  (b) at any time, there are reasonable grounds for believing that the value of A's taxable supplies in the period of one year beginning at that or any later time will not exceed £145,000,
and either that—
  (c) at the end of any month, the value of A's supplies to persons registered in other member States in the period of one year then ending is less than £11,000, or
  (d) at any time, there are reasonable grounds for believing that the value of A's supplies to persons registered in other member States in the period of one year beginning at that or any later time will not exceed £11,000.][1]

Amendments—[1] Reg 22 substituted by the VAT (Amendment) (No 5) Regs, SI 2009/3241, regs 2, 5 with effect from 1 January 2010.
[2] Para (2)(a) substituted by the VAT (Amendment) (No 2) Regulations, SI 2012/1899 regs 3, 10 with effect from 15 October 2012.
[3] In para (1) words inserted and words substituted for words "in another member State and those goods were dispatched or transported to that or another member State, or", in paras (2)–(4) words substituted for words "EU", and in paras (5)(a) and (6) words inserted, by the Value Added Tax (Miscellaneous Amendments, Northern Ireland Protocol and Savings and Transitional Provisions) (EU Exit) Regulations, SI 2020/1545 regs 31 and 39 with effect from IP completion day (11pm UK time on 31 December 2020) by virtue of SI 2020/1641 reg 2, Schedule para 11. These amendments are to be treated for the purposes of VATA 1994 as if they were made under VATA 1994 Sch 9ZA para 73(1) (see SI 2020/1545 reg 44).

[22ZZA (1) A taxable person must submit a statement to the Commissioners if any of the following events occurs—
  (a) goods are removed from Northern Ireland under call-off stock arrangements by or under the directions of the taxable person;
  (b) call-off stock goods are returned to Northern Ireland by or under the directions of the taxable person at any time during the period of 12 months beginning with their arrival in the destination territory;
  (c) the taxable person forms an intention to supply call-off stock goods to a person ("the substitute") other than the customer in circumstances where—
    (i) the taxable person forms that intention during the period of 12 months beginning with the arrival of the goods in the destination territory, and
    (ii) the substitute is identified for VAT purposes in accordance with the law of the destination territory.
(2) The statement must—
  (a) be made in the form specified in a notice published by the Commissioners,
  (b) contain, in respect of each event mentioned in paragraph (1) which has occurred within the period in respect of which the statement is made, such information as may from time to time be specified in a notice published by the Commissioners, and
  (c) contain a declaration that the information provided in the statement is true and complete.
(3) Paragraphs (3), (4) and (6) of regulation 22 have effect for the purpose of determining the period in respect of which the statement must be made, but as if—
  (a) in paragraph (3)(a) of that regulation—
    (i) for "paragraphs (4) to (6)" there were substituted "paragraphs (4) and (6)", and
    (ii) for "the relevant supply of goods is made" there were substituted "the event occurs";
  (c) in paragraph (4)(a) of that regulation, for "the supply is made" there were substituted "the event occurs", and

(d) in paragraph (6) of that regulation, the reference to paragraph (1) were a reference to paragraph (1) of this regulation.

(4) In determining the period in respect of which the statement must be made, the time at which an event mentioned in paragraph (1)(a) of this regulation is to be taken to occur is the time the goods concerned are removed from Northern Ireland rather than the time the condition mentioned in paragraph (g) of paragraph 57(1) to Schedule 9ZA to the Act is met in respect of the removal.][1]

Amendments—[1] Reg 22ZZA inserted by the Value Added Tax (Miscellaneous Amendments, Northern Ireland Protocol and Savings and Transitional Provisions) (EU Exit) Regulations, SI 2020/1545 regs 31 and 40 with effect from IP completion day (11pm UK time on 31 December 2020) by virtue of SI 2020/1641 reg 2, Schedule para 11. This amendment is to be treated for the purposes of VATA 1994 as if it were made under VATA 1994 Sch 9ZA para 73(1) (see SI 2020/1545 reg 44)

[22ZA (1) A taxable person must submit a statement to the Commissioners if any of the following events occurs—
  (a) goods are removed from the United Kingdom under call-off stock arrangements by or under the directions of the taxable person;
  (b) call-off stock goods are returned to the United Kingdom by or under the directions of the taxable person at any time during the period of 12 months beginning with their arrival in the destination State;
  (c) the taxable person forms an intention to supply call-off stock goods to a person ("the substitute") other than the customer in circumstances where—
    (i) the taxable person forms that intention during the period of 12 months beginning with the arrival of the goods in the destination State, and
    (ii) the substitute is identified for VAT purposes in accordance with the law of the destination State.
(2) The statement must—
  (a) be made in the form specified in a notice published by the Commissioners,
  (b) contain, in respect of each event mentioned in paragraph (1) which has occurred within the period in respect of which the statement is made, such information as may from time to time be specified in a notice published by the Commissioners, and
  (c) contain a declaration that the information provided in the statement is true and complete.
(3) Paragraphs (3), (4) and (6) of regulation 22 have effect for the purpose of determining the period in respect of which the statement must be made, but as if—
  (a) in paragraph (3)(a) of regulation 22, for "paragraphs (4) to (6)" there were substituted "paragraphs (4) and (6)",
  (b) in paragraph (3)(a) of regulation 22, for "the EU supply of goods is made" there were substituted "the event occurs",
  (c) in paragraph (4)(a) of regulation 22, for "the supply is made" there were substituted "the event occurs", and
  (d) in paragraph (6) of regulation 22, the reference to paragraph (1) of that regulation were a reference to paragraph (1) of this regulation.
(4) In determining the period in respect of which the statement must be made, the time at which an event mentioned in paragraph (1)(a) of this regulation is to be taken to occur is the time the goods concerned are removed from the United Kingdom (rather than the time the condition mentioned in paragraph (g) of paragraph 1(1) to Schedule 4B to the Act is met in respect of the removal).][1], [2]

Amendments—[1] Reg 22ZA inserted by FA 2020 s 80(7), (9) with effect from 22 July 2020. Note that, for the purposes of VATA 1994 ss 65 and 66, this reg is treated as having been made under VATA 1994 Sch 11 para 2(3) (requirement to submit EC sales statement) (FA 2020 s 80(11)).

[2] Reg 22ZA revoked by the Taxation (Post-transition Period) Act 2020 s 3, Sch 2 para 7(5)(b) with effect from IP completion day (11pm on 31 December 2020), by virtue of SI 2020/1642 reg 9.

[22A (1) Every taxable person who has made a supply of services to a person in a member State other than the United Kingdom in circumstances where the recipient is required to pay VAT on the supply in accordance with the provisions of the law of that other member State giving effect to Article 196 of Council Directive 2006/112/EC shall submit a statement to the Commissioners.
(2) The statement shall be—
  [(a) made in the form specified in a notice published by the Commissioners,][2]
  (b) contain, in respect of the EU supplies of services which have been made within the period to which the statement relates, such information as the Commissioners shall from time to time prescribe, and
  (c) contain a declaration that the information provided in the statement is true and complete.
(3)
  (a) Subject to paragraph (4) below the statement may be submitted in respect of the period of the month or the quarter in which the EU supply of services has been made.
  (b) Where during a period mentioned in sub-paragraph (a) above the taxable person (a)—
    (i) ceases to be registered under Schedule 1 to the Act, and
    (ii) no other person has been registered with the registration number of and in substitution for A,

the last day of that period is to be treated as being the same date as the effective date of A's deregistration.

(4) A taxable person *(a)* who is permitted under regulation 25 to make a return in respect of a period longer than 3 months may make a statement under paragraph (1) above in respect of a period identical to the period permitted for the making of the return provided that A has not, during that period, made a supply of a new means of transport and the Commissioners are satisfied either that—
- *(a)* at the end of any month, the value of A's taxable supplies in the period of one year then ending is less than £145,000, or
- *(b)* at any time, there are reasonable grounds for believing that the value of A's taxable supplies in the period of one year beginning at that or any later time will not exceed £145,000,

and either that—
- *(c)* at the end of any month, the value of A's supplies to persons registered in other member States in the period of one year then ending is less than £11,000, or
- *(d)* at any time, there are reasonable grounds for believing that the value of A's supplies to persons registered in other member States in the period of one year beginning at that or any later time will not exceed £11,000.]^1, ^{3}

Amendments—[1] Regs 22A–22C inserted by the VAT (Amendment) (No 5) Regs, SI 2009/3241, regs 2, 6 with effect from 1 January 2010.
[2] Para (2)(a) substituted by the VAT (Amendment) (No 2) Regulations, SI 2012/1899 regs 3, 11 with effect from 15 October 2012.
[3] Reg 22A revoked by the Value Added Tax (Miscellaneous Amendments, Northern Ireland Protocol and Savings and Transitional Provisions) (EU Exit) Regulations, SI 2020/1545 regs 31 and 41 with effect from IP completion day (11pm UK time on 31 December 2020) by virtue of SI 2020/1641 reg 2, Schedule para 11. This amendment is to be treated for the purposes of VATA 1994 as if it were made under VATA 1994 Sch 9ZA para 73(1) (see SI 2020/1545 reg 44).

[22B—(1) Where [statements are to be submitted under regulation 22 and]^3 [22ZZA]^2 in respect of periods ending on the same day, the statements may be submitted on a single form.
(2) A taxable person may submit a statement under regulation [22 or 22ZZA]^2 on paper or on-line using an electronic portal provided by the Commissioners for that purpose.
(3) A taxable person who is required to submit a statement under regulation [22 or 22ZZA]^2 must do so—
- *(a)* where the statement is submitted on-line, not later than 21 days from the end of the period to which the statement relates,
- *(b)* in every other case, not later than 14 days from the end of the period to which the statement relates.]^1

Amendments—[1] Regs 22A–22C inserted by the VAT (Amendment) (No 5) Regs, SI 2009/3241, regs 2, 6 with effect from 1 January 2010.
[2] In para (1) words substituted for word "22A", and in paras (2) and (3) words substituted for words "22 or 22A", by the Value Added Tax (Miscellaneous Amendments, Northern Ireland Protocol and Savings and Transitional Provisions) (EU Exit) Regulations, SI 2020/1545 regs 31 and 42 with effect from IP completion day (11pm UK time on 31 December 2020) by virtue of SI 2020/1641 reg 2, Schedule para 11. These amendments are to be treated for the purposes of VATA 1994 as if they were made under VATA 1994 Sch 9ZA para 73(1) (see SI 2020/1545 reg 44).
[3] In para (1) words substituted for words "more than one statement is to be submitted under regulations 22 to" by the Taxation (Post-transition Period) Act 2020 s 3, Sch 2 para 7(5)(c) with effect from IP completion day (11pm on 31 December 2020), by virtue of SI 2020/1642 reg 9.

[22C—(1) Every taxable person who in any quarter makes a supply of a new means of transport [which involves the removal of those goods from Northern Ireland to a member State]^3 to a person ("the acquirer")—
- *(a)* for the purposes of acquisition by that acquirer in another member State, and
- *(b)* where the acquirer is not, at the time of the acquisition, registered in that member State,

shall submit a statement to the Commissioners.
(2)
- *(a)* The statement shall be submitted in respect of the quarter in which the NMT supply of goods is made.
- *(b)* Where during the period mentioned in sub-paragraph *(a)* above the taxable person *(a)*—
  - (i) ceases to be registered under Schedule 1 to the Act, and
  - (ii) no other person has been registered with the registration number of and in substitution for A,

  the last day of that period is to be treated as being the same date as the effective date of A's deregistration.
(3) The statement shall—
- [*(a)* be made in the form specified in a notice published by the Commissioners,]^2
- *(b)* contain, in respect of the NMT supplies of goods which have been made within the period in respect of which the statement is made, such information as the Commissioners shall from time to time prescribe,
- *(c)* contain a declaration that the information provided in the statement is true and complete, and

(*d*) be submitted within 42 days of the end of the period to which it relates.]¹

Amendments—¹ Regs 22A–22C inserted by the VAT (Amendment) (No 5) Regs, SI 2009/3241, regs 2, 6 with effect from 1 January 2010.
² Para (3)(a) substituted by the VAT (Amendment) (No 2) Regulations, SI 2012/1899 regs 3, 12 with effect from 15 October 2012.
³ In para (1) words inserted by the Value Added Tax (Miscellaneous Amendments, Northern Ireland Protocol and Savings and Transitional Provisions) (EU Exit) Regulations, SI 2020/1545 regs 31 and 43 with effect from IP completion day (11pm UK time on 31 December 2020) by virtue of SI 2020/1641 reg 2, Schedule para 11. This amendment is to be treated for the purposes of VATA 1994 as if it were made under VATA 1994 Sch 9ZA para 73(1) (see SI 2020/1545 reg 44).

[PART 4A
REVERSE CHARGE SALES STATEMENTS

23A Interpretation of Part 4A

In this Part—

"relevant supply" means a supply of goods to which section 55A(6) of the Act applies (customers to account for tax on supplies of goods of a kind used in missing trader . . . ³ fraud) [other than a supply of gas or electricity]²;

"statement" means the statement which a taxable person is required to submit in accordance with this Part of these Regulations.]¹

HMRC Manuals—VAT Reverse Charge VATREVCHG31000 (the reverse charge sales list (RCSL): the legal obligation to submit an RCSL).

Amendments—¹ Regs 23A–23C inserted by the VAT (Amendment) (No 3) Regulations, SI 2007/1418 regs 2, 3 with effect from 1 June 2007.
² In definition of "relevant supply" words inserted by the VAT (Amendment) (No 2) Regulations, SI 2014/1497 reg 3 with effect in relation to supplies made on or after 1 July 2014 and returns required by reg 25 below made for any prescribed accounting period which commences on or after that date.
³ In the definition of "relevant supply" words "intra-community" revoked, by the Value Added Tax (Miscellaneous Amendments and Revocations) (EU Exit) Regulations, SI 2019/59 regs 12, 26 with effect from IP completion day (11pm UK time on 31 December 2020).

[23B Notification of first relevant supply

(1) On the first occasion on which a person makes a relevant supply, he must notify the Commissioners of that fact within 30 days of the day on which the supply is made.
(2) The notification referred to in paragraph (1) must be made on-line by using a portal provided by the Commissioners.
(3) If the portal referred to in paragraph (2) is unavailable for any reason, the Commissioners may allow the notification to be made by email.]¹

Commentary—*De Voil Indirect Tax Service* **V5.273, V5.352**.
HMRC Manuals—VAT Reverse Charge VATREVCHG31000 (the reverse charge sales list (RCSL): the legal obligation to submit an RCSL).
Amendments—¹ Regs 23A–23C inserted by the VAT (Amendment) (No 3) Regulations, SI 2007/1418 regs 2, 3 with effect from 1 June 2007.

[23C Submission of Statements

(1) Every taxable person who, in any prescribed accounting period, has made a relevant supply must, in relation to that period, submit to the Commissioners, no later than the day by which he is required to make a return for that period and in such a form and manner as may be determined by the Commissioners in a notice published by them (or otherwise), a statement containing the following prescribed particulars—
   (*a*) his registration number;
   (*b*) the registration number of each person to whom he has made a relevant supply; and
   (*c*) for each month falling within the prescribed accounting period, the total value of the relevant supplies made to each person mentioned in sub-paragraph (*b*).
(2) If, in any prescribed accounting period, no relevant supplies are made, a statement to that effect must be submitted to the Commissioners in such form and manner as may be determined by them in a notice published by them (or otherwise).
(3) Sub-paragraph (2) does not apply where a taxable person has notified the Commissioners that he has ceased making relevant supplies without intending subsequently to make such supplies.
(4) A statement must contain a declaration made by the taxable person that it is true and complete.]¹

Commentary—*De Voil Indirect Tax Service* **V5.273, V5.346**.
HMRC Manuals—VAT Reverse Charge VATREVCHG31000 (the reverse charge sales list (RCSL): the legal obligation to submit an RCSL).
Amendments—¹ Regs 23A–23C inserted by the VAT (Amendment) (No 3) Regulations, SI 2007/1418 regs 2, 3 with effect from 1 June 2007.

23D [Notification of cessation and recommencement of relevant supplies

Where a person—
   (*a*) ceases making relevant supplies without intending subsequently to make such supplies, or
   (*b*) has fallen within paragraph (*a*) above but nonetheless starts to make relevant supplies again,

he shall, within 30 days of so ceasing or, as the case may be, of so recommencing, notify the Commissioners of that fact in such form and manner as may be determined in a notice published by them (or otherwise).][1]

Commentary—*De Voil Indirect Tax Service* **V5.273, V3.233**.
HMRC Manuals—VAT Reverse Charge VATREVCHG31000 (the reverse charge sales list (RCSL): the legal obligation to submit an RCSL).
Amendments—[1] Regulation inserted by the VAT (Amendment) (No 4) Regulations, SI 2007/1599 regs 2, 3 with effect from 1 July 2007.

[PART 4B
PROVISION OF INFORMATION RELATING TO ARRIVALS AND DISPATCHES

23E Interpretation of Part 4B

(1) In this Part—
"establishing Regulation" means the Council and European Parliament Regulation (EC) No 638/2004;
"implementing Regulation" means the Commission Regulation (EC) N. 1982/2004;
"statistics Regulations" means the Statistics of Trade (Customs and Excise) Regulations 1992;
(2) In this Part—
"arrivals and dispatches" means those arrivals and dispatches for which a responsible party is required to provide information under the establishing Regulation, implementing Regulation and the statistics Regulations;
"for Intrastat purposes" means for any purpose under the establishing Regulation, implementing Regulation or the statistics Regulations;
"reference period" means the period applicable under Article 6(1) of the establishing Regulation or such other period directed by the Commissioners pursuant to regulation 4(3) of the statistics Regulations;
"responsible party" means a taxable person who is required by Article 7 of the establishing Regulation and regulation 3 of the statistics Regulations to provide information in relation to arrivals and dispatches;
"supplementary declaration" means the relevant form set out in the Schedule to the statistics Regulations;
"delivery terms", "nature of the transaction", "partner Member State", "quantity of the goods" and "value of the goods" shall have the same meaning as in the establishing Regulation and implementing Regulation.][1]

Commentary—*De Voil Indirect Tax Service* **V5.276**.
Amendments—[1] Part 4B inserted by VAT (Amendment) Regulations, SI 2008/556 reg 2 with effect from 1 April 2008.

23F—(1) A responsible party shall provide the information in paragraph (2) relating to arrivals and dispatches to the Commissioners.
(2) The information is—
   (*a*) the registration number of the responsible party,
   (*b*) the reference period,
   (*c*) whether the information relates to arrival or dispatch,
   (*d*) the commodity, identified by the eight digit code of the Combined Nomenclature as defined in Council Regulation (EEC) No 2658/87 of 23 July 1987 as amended on the tariff and statistical nomenclature and the Common Customs Tariff,
   (*e*) the partner Member State,
   (*f*) the value of the goods,
   (*g*) the quantity of the goods,
   (*h*) the nature of the transaction.
(3) A responsible party to whom regulation 4(2) of the statistics Regulations applies shall also provide the delivery terms relating to arrivals and dispatches to the Commissioners.
(4) The information required by paragraphs (2) and (3) shall be provided in the supplementary declaration in which, and for the same reference period as, information is provided relating to those arrivals and dispatches for Intrastat purposes.]

Commentary—*De Voil Indirect Tax Service* **V5.276**.
Amendments—[1] Part 4B inserted by VAT (Amendment) Regulations, SI 2008/556 reg 2 with effect from 1 April 2008.

PART V
ACCOUNTING, PAYMENT AND RECORDS

24 Interpretation of Part V

In this Part—

["API platform" means the application programming interface that enables electronic communication with HMRC, as specified by the Commissioners in a specific or general direction;

"functional compatible software" means a software program or set of compatible software programs the functions of which include—
   (a) recording and preserving electronic records in an electronic form;
   (b) providing information to HMRC from the electronic records and returns in an electronic form and by using the API platform; and
   (c) receiving information from HMRC using the API platform in relation to a person's compliance with obligations under these Regulations which are required to be met by use of the software;][4]

. . .[5]

"insolvent person" means—
   (a) an individual who has been adjudged bankrupt;
   (b) a company in relation to which—
      (i) a voluntary arrangement under Part I of the Insolvency Act 1986 has been approved,
      (ii) [an administrator has been appointed][3],
      (iii) an administrative receiver has been appointed,
      (iv) a resolution for voluntary winding up has been passed, or
      (v) an order for its winding-up has been made by the court at a time when it had not already gone into liquidation by passing a resolution for voluntary winding-up;

["investment gold" has the same meaning as that expression has for the purposes of Group 15 of Schedule 9 to the Act;][1]

"negative entry" means an amount entered into the VAT account as a negative amount;

"positive entry" means an amount entered into the VAT account as a positive amount;

"VAT allowable portion", "VAT payable portion" and "VAT account" have the meanings given in regulation [32][2];

"the Removal Order" means the Value Added Tax (Removal of Goods) Order 1992;

"the owner" has the same meaning as in article 2 of the Removal Order.

Commentary—*De Voil Indirect Tax Service* **V3.419, V3.519**.
Amendments—[1] Definition of "investment gold" inserted by the VAT (Amendment) (No 4) Regulations, SI 1999/3114, regs 2, 3, with effect from 1 January 2000.
[2] In the definition of "VAT allowable portion", "VAT payable portion" and "VAT account", figure "32" substituted for "33" by the VAT (Amendment) (No 4) Regulations, SI 2003/1485 regs 2,4 with effect from 1 July 2003.
[3] Words in definition of "insolvent person" substituted by the Enterprise Act 2002 (Insolvency) Order, SI 2003/2096 art 5, Schedule paras 55, 58 with effect from 15 September 2003. However, this amendment does not apply in any case where a petition for an administration order was presented before that date: SI 2003/2096 arts 1, 6.
[4] Definitions of "API platform" and "functional compatible software" inserted by the Value Added Tax (Amendment) Regulations, SI 2018/261 regs 2, 3 with effect from 1 April 2019 where a taxpayer has a prescribed accounting period which begins on that date, and otherwise from the first day of a taxpayer's first prescribed accounting period beginning after the 1 April 2019.
[5] Definition of "increase in consideration" and "decrease in consideration" revoked by the VAT (Amendment) Regulations, SI 2019/1048 regs 3, 5 with effect in relation to supplies for which there is an increase or decrease in consideration that occurs on or after 1 September 2019. An increase or decrease in consideration means an increase or decrease in consideration as described in reg 24A which occurs at the time specified in reg 24B.

[24A For the purposes of this Part—
   (a) an increase in consideration is an increase in the consideration for a supply made by a taxable person in respect of which the recipient of the supply or another person acting on behalf of, or pursuant to an arrangement with, the recipient of the supply pays or becomes liable to pay the amount of the increase to the supplier;
   (b) a decrease in consideration is a decrease in the consideration for a supply made by a taxable person in respect of which the supplier pays the amount of the decrease to the recipient of the supply or to any other person entitled to receive the payment;
   (c) where there is a decrease in consideration in respect of which the supplier makes a part payment on account to the recipient of the supply (or to any other person entitled to receive the part payment)—
      (i) the decrease is to be treated as a decrease in consideration only to the extent covered by the part payment; and
      (ii) each part payment on account is to be treated as being made in relation to a separate decrease in consideration.][1]

Commentary—*De Voil Indirect Tax Service* **V3.518, V3.519**.
Amendments—[1] Regulations 24A–24C inserted by the VAT (Amendment) Regulations, SI 2019/1048 regs 3, 6 with effect in relation to supplies for which there is an increase or decrease in consideration that occurs on or after 1 September 2019. An increase or decrease in consideration means an increase or decrease in consideration as described in reg 24A which occurs at the time specified in reg 24B.

[**24B** For the purposes of this Part—
  (a) an increase in consideration occurs when it is agreed by the supplier and the recipient of the supply; and
  (b) a decrease in consideration occurs when the supplier pays the amount of the decrease to the recipient of the supply or to any other person who is entitled to receive the payment.]¹

Commentary—*De Voil Indirect Tax Service* **V3.518, V3.519**.
Amendments—¹ Regulations 24A–24C inserted by the VAT (Amendment) Regulations, SI 2019/1048 regs 3, 6 with effect in relation to supplies for which there is an increase or decrease in consideration that occurs on or after 1 September 2019. An increase or decrease in consideration means an increase or decrease in consideration as described in reg 24A which occurs at the time specified in reg 24B.

[**24C** (1) For the purposes of regulations 24A and 24B, "payment"—
  (a) means a payment in money and "pay" and "pays" are to be construed accordingly; and
  (b) includes cases where a person—
    (i) sets off an amount against a corresponding monetary liability of another person; or
    (ii) makes a "relevant payment" as defined in regulation 38ZA(2).
(2) For the purposes of applying regulation 38ZA, the reference in regulation 24A(b) and (c) and in regulation 24B(b) to—
  (a) "the supplier" includes a reference to the "first supplier" as defined in regulation 38ZA(2); and
  (b) "the recipient of the supply" includes a reference to the "final consumer" as defined in regulation 38ZA(2).]¹

Commentary—*De Voil Indirect Tax Service* **V3.518, V3.519**.
Amendments—¹ Regulations 24A–24C inserted by the VAT (Amendment) Regulations, SI 2019/1048 regs 3, 6 with effect in relation to supplies for which there is an increase or decrease in consideration that occurs on or after 1 September 2019. An increase or decrease in consideration means an increase or decrease in consideration as described in reg 24A which occurs at the time specified in reg 24B.

25 Making of returns
(1) Every person who is registered or was or is required to be registered shall, in respect of every period of a quarter or in the case of a person who is registered, every period of 3 months ending on the dates notified either in the certificate of registration issued to him or otherwise, not later than the last day of the month next following the end of the period to which it relates, make to the Controller a return [in the manner prescribed in regulation 25A]³ showing the amount of VAT payable by or to him and containing full information in respect of the other matters specified in the form and a declaration, [signed by that person or by a person authorised to sign on that person's behalf]³, that the return is [correct]³ and complete;
provided that—
  (a) the Commissioners may allow or direct a person to make returns in respect of periods of one month and to make those returns within one month of the periods to which they relate;
  (b) the first return shall be for the period which includes the effective date determined in accordance with [Schedules 1, [1A,]¹ 2, 3[, 3A and 9ZC]⁴]² to the Act upon which the person was or should have been registered, and the said period shall begin on that date;
  (c) where the Commissioners consider it necessary in any particular case to vary the length of any period or the date on which any period begins or ends or by which any return shall be made, they may allow or direct any person to make returns accordingly, whether or not the period so varied has ended;
  (d) where the Commissioners consider it necessary in any particular case, they may allow or direct a person to make returns to a specified address.
(2) Any person to whom the Commissioners give any direction in pursuance of the proviso to paragraph (1) above shall comply therewith.
(3) Where for the purposes of this Part the Commissioners have made a requirement of any person pursuant to regulation 30—
  (a) the period in respect of which taxable supplies were being made by the person who died or became incapacitated shall end on the day previous to the date when death or incapacity took place; and
  (b) subject to sub-paragraph (1)(c) above, a return made on his behalf shall be made in respect of that period no later than the last day of the month next following the end of that period; and
  (c) the next period shall start on the day following the aforesaid period and it shall end, and all subsequent periods shall begin and end, on the dates previously determined under paragraph (1) above.
(4) Any person who—
  (a) ceases to be liable to be registered, or
  (b) ceases to be entitled to be registered under either or both of paragraphs 9 and 10 of Schedule 1[, paragraph 4 of Schedule 2 or paragraph 4 of Schedule 3 [or Schedule 9ZC]⁴]¹ to the Act,
shall, unless another person has been registered with his registration number in substitution for him under regulation 6, make to the Controller a final return [in the manner prescribed in

regulation 25A][3] and any such return shall contain full information in respect of the matters specified in the form and a declaration, [signed by that person or by a person authorised to sign on that person's behalf][3], that the return is [correct][3] and complete and shall be made, in the case of a person who was or is registered, within one month of the effective date for cancellation of his registration, and in the case of any other person, within one month of the date upon which he ceases to be liable to be registered, and in either case shall be in respect of the final period ending on the date aforementioned and be in substitution for the return for the period in which such date occurs.
(4A)–(4M) . . . [3]
(5) The Commissioners may allow VAT chargeable in any period to be treated as being chargeable in such later period as they may specify.

Commentary—*De Voil Indirect Tax Service* **V5.102, V5.103**.
HMRC Manuals—VAT Accounting Manual VATAC1100 (VAT returns - legal position).
Amendments—[1] In paras (1)(*b*), (4)(*b*) words inserted, by the VAT (Amendment) (No 2) Regulations, SI 2012/1899 regs 3, 13 with effect from 15 October 2012.
[2] Words in para (1)(*b*) substituted by the VAT (Amendment) (No 3) Regulations, SI 2000/794 regs 2, 5 with effect from 22 March 2000.
[3] In para (1), words substituted for words "on the form numbered 4 in Schedule 1 to these Regulations ("Form 4")", "signed by him" and "true", in para (4), words substituted for words "on the form numbered 5 in Schedule 1 to these Regulations ("Form 5")", "signed by him" and "true", and paras (4A)–(4M) revoked, by the Value Added Tax (Amendment) (No 4) Regulations, SI 2009/2978 regs 2, 3 with effect from 1 December 2009.
[4] In para (1)(*b*) words substituted for words "and 3A", and in para (4)(*b*) words inserted, by the Value Added Tax (Miscellaneous Amendments, Northern Ireland Protocol and Savings and Transitional Provisions) (EU Exit) Regulations, SI 2020/1545 regs 31 and 45 with effect from IP completion day (11pm UK time on 31 December 2020) by virtue of SI 2020/1641 reg 2, Schedule para 11.

[25A—[(A1) Where a person makes a return required by regulation 25 by means of electronic communications using functional compatible software, such a method of making a return shall be referred to in this Part as a "compatible software return system".][6]
(1) Where a person makes a return required by regulation 25 using electronic communications [other than functional compatible software][6], such a method of making a return shall be referred to in this Part as an "electronic return system".
(2) Where a person makes a return [or a final return on the relevant form specified in a notice published by the Commissioners][4], such a method of making a return shall be referred to in this Part as a "paper return system".
[(2A) A person who is subject to the requirements of regulation 32A, including by virtue of an election in accordance with regulation 32C, must make a return required by regulation 25 using a compatible software return system.][6]
[(3) Subject to [paragraphs (2A) above and (6) below][6], a person who is registered for VAT must make a return required by regulation 25 using an electronic return system [that that person is required or authorised to use][5] whether or not such a person is registered in substitution for another person under regulation 6 (transfer of a going concern).][3]
(4) In any case where an electronic return system [or a compatible software return system][6] is not used, a return must be made using a paper return system.
(5) . . . [3]
(6) . . . [3] A person—
  (*a*) who the Commissioners are satisfied is a practising member of a religious society or order whose beliefs are incompatible with the use of electronic communications, or
  (*b*) to whom an insolvency procedure as described in any of paragraphs (*a*) to (*f*) of section 81(4B) of the Act is applied . . . [3][, or
  (*c*) for whom the Commissioners are satisfied that it is not reasonably practicable to make a return using an electronic return system (including any electronic return system that that person is authorised to use) for reasons of disability, age, remoteness of location or any other reason][5],
[is not required to make a return required by regulation 25 using an electronic return system][3].
(7) . . . [3]
(8) Where an electronic return system [or a compatible software return system][6] is used, it must take a form approved by the Commissioners in a specific or general direction.
(9) Where a paper return system is used, a return required by regulation 25(1) [or 25(4) must be made on the relevant form specified in a notice published by the Commissioners][4].
(10) A direction under paragraph (8) above may in particular—
  (*a*) modify or dispense with any requirement of [the relevant form specified in a notice published by the Commissioners][4],
  (*b*) specify circumstances in which the electronic return system [or a compatible software return system][6] may be used, or not used, by or on behalf of the person required to make the return,
  [(*c*) approve telephone filing as a form of electronic return system for use by specified categories of persons.][5]

For the purposes of sub-paragraph (b), the direction may specify different circumstances for different cases.

(11) An electronic return system [or a compatible software return system]⁶ shall incorporate an electronic validation process.

(12) Subject to paragraph (13) below and unless the contrary is proved—
- (a) the use of an electronic return system [or a compatible software return system]⁶ shall be [presumed]² to have resulted in the making of the return to the Controller only if this has been successfully recorded as such by the relevant electronic validation process,
- (b) the time of making the return to the Controller using an electronic return system [or a compatible software return system]⁶ shall be . . . ² presumed to be the time recorded as such by the relevant electronic validation process, and
- (c) the person delivering the return to the Controller shall be presumed to be the person identified as such by any relevant feature of the electronic return system [or a compatible software return system]⁶.

(13) No return shall be treated as having been made using an electronic return system [or a compatible software return system]⁶ unless it is in the form required by paragraph (8) above. The requirement in paragraph (8) above incorporates the matters mentioned in paragraph (10) above.

(14) A return made using an electronic return system [or a compatible software return system]⁶ carries the same consequences as a return made using a paper return system, except in relation to any matter for which alternative or additional provision is made by or under this regulation.

(15) [Subject to paragraph (15A)]³ in relation to returns made for prescribed accounting periods which end on or after 31 March 2011, a . . . ³ person who fails to comply with paragraph [(2A) or]⁶ (3) above is liable to a penalty.

[(15A) A person who—
- (a) on 31 March 2012 was registered for VAT with an effective date of registration before that date,
- (b) was not as at 31 March 2012 required to make a return required by regulation 25 using an electronic return system, and
- (c) fails to comply with paragraph (3),

is only liable to a penalty in relation to returns made for prescribed accounting periods which end on or after 31 March 2013.]³

(16) But a . . . ³ person who has a reasonable excuse for so failing to comply is not liable to a penalty.

(17) The table below sets out the penalties depending on the level of turnover.

Annual VAT exclusive turnover	Penalty
£22,800,001 and above	£400
£5,600,001 to £22,800,000	£300
£100,001 to £5,600,000	£200
£100,000 and under	£100

(18) A person may appeal against the Commissioners' decision to impose a penalty only on the ground that—
- (a) that person is not [a person required to make a return required by regulation 25 using an electronic return system]³ [or a compatible software return system]⁶,
- (b) the amount of the penalty is incorrect,
- (c) paragraph (3) above was complied with, or
- (d) paragraph (16) above applies.

(19) In calculating a person's annual VAT exclusive turnover for the purposes of . . . ³ the table in paragraph (17) above, the Commissioners shall use any available figures which they determine to be fair and reasonable in the circumstances and such figures shall be taken to be the correct figures for the purposes of the calculation.

(20) Additional time is allowed to make—
- (a) a return using an electronic return system[, a compatible software return system]⁶ or a paper return system for which any related payment is made solely by means of electronic communications (see regulation 25(1)—time for making return, and regulations 40(2) to 40(4)—payment of VAT), or
- (b) a return using an electronic return system [or a compatible software return system]⁶ for which no payment is required to be made.

That additional time is only as the Commissioners may allow in a specific or general direction, and such a direction may allow different times for different means of payment.

The Commissioners need not give a direction pursuant to this paragraph.

(21) Where a corporate body is registered in the names of its divisions pursuant to section 46(1) of the Act, each such separately registered division is "a person" for the purposes of paragraphs . . . [3] (12) and (19) above.

(22) In this regulation—
  (a) . . . [3]
  (b) a reference to an appeal is a reference to an appeal made under section 83(1)(zc) of the Act,
  (c) "reasonable excuse" shall have the same limitation as it does in section 71(1)(b) of the Act.

(23) In paragraphs (8) and (20) above "direction" and "direct" refer only to a current direction, and a direction is not current to the extent that it is varied, replaced or revoked by another Commissioners' direction.][1]

Commentary—*De Voil Indirect Tax Service* **V5.101A, V5.103**.
HMRC Manuals—VAT Accounting Manual VATAC1200 (online VAT returns).
VATAC1250 (online VAT returns - exemptions).
Amendments—[1] Reg 25A inserted by the Value Added Tax (Amendment) (No 4) Regulations, SI 2009/2978 regs 2, 4 with effect from 1 December 2009.
[2] Word in para (12)(a), substituted, and word in para (12)(b) revoked, by the Value Added Tax (Amendment) Regulations, SI 2010/559 reg 2, 3 with effect from 1 April 2010.
[3] Para (3) substituted, paras (5), (7) revoked, in para (6) words revoked and substituted, in para (15) words inserted and word revoked, para (15A) inserted, in para (16) word revoked, in para (18)(a) words substituted, in paras (19), (21) words revoked, and para (22)(a) revoked, by the VAT (Amendment) Regulations, SI 2012/33 regs 3–14 with effect in relation to returns required by reg 25 of these regulations made for any prescribed accounting period which commences on or after 1 April 2012.
[4] In para (2), words substituted for words "on the form numbered 4 in Schedule 1 to these Regulations ("Form 4") or, in the case of a final return, on the form numbered 5 in Schedule 1 to these Regulations ("Form 5")", in para (9), words substituted for words "must be made on Form 4 and a return required by regulation 25(4) must be made on Form 5.", and in para (10)(a), words substituted for words "Form 4 or Form 5 (as appropriate)", by the VAT (Amendment) (No 2) Regulations, SI 2012/1899 regs 3, 14 with effect from 15 October 2012.
[5] Words in para (3) inserted, para (6)(c) and preceding word "or" inserted, and para (10)(c) inserted, VAT (Amendment) (No 2) Regulations, SI 2014/1497 reg 4 with effect in relation to supplies made on or after 1 July 2014 and returns required by reg 25 below made for any prescribed accounting period which commences on or after that date.
[6] Amendments made by the Value Added Tax (Amendment) Regulations, SI 2018/261 regs 2, 3 with effect from 1 April 2019 where a taxpayer has a prescribed accounting period which begins on that date, and otherwise from the first day of a taxpayer's first prescribed accounting period beginning after the 1 April 2019

26 Accounting for VAT on an acquisition by reference to the value shown on an invoice

Where the time of the acquisition of any goods from another member State is determined by reference to the issue of an invoice such as is described in regulation 83, VAT shall be accounted for and paid in respect of the acquisition only on so much of its value as is shown on that invoice.

27 Supplies under Schedule 4, paragraph 7

Where goods are deemed to be supplied by a taxable person by virtue of paragraph 7 of Schedule 4 to the Act, the auctioneer on a sale by auction or, where the sale is otherwise than by auction, the person selling the goods, shall, whether or not registered under the Act, within 21 days of the sale—
  (a) furnish to the Controller a statement showing—
    (i) his name and address and, if registered, his registration number,
    (ii) the name, address and registration number of the person whose goods were sold,
    (iii) the date of the sale,
    (iv) the description and quantity of goods sold at each rate of VAT, and
    (v) the amount for which they were sold and the amount of VAT charged at each rate,
  (b) pay the amount of VAT due, and
  (c) send to the person whose goods were sold a copy of the statement referred to in sub-paragraph (a) above, and the auctioneer or person selling the goods, as the case may be, and the person whose goods were sold shall exclude the VAT chargeable on that supply of those goods from any return made under these Regulations.

Commentary—*De Voil Indirect Tax Service* **V5.142, V3.522**.

28 Estimation of output tax

Where the Commissioners are satisfied that a person is not able to account for the exact amount of output tax chargeable in any period, he may estimate a part of his output tax for that period, provided that any such estimated amount shall be adjusted and exactly accounted for as VAT chargeable in the next prescribed accounting period or, if the exact amount is still not known and the Commissioners are satisfied that it could not with due diligence be ascertained, in the next but one prescribed accounting period.

Commentary—*De Voil Indirect Tax Service* **V3.505**.
HMRC Manuals—VAT Accounting Manual VATAC2200 (legal basis for estimation).
Modification—By virtue of the VAT (Miscellaneous and Transitional Provisions, Amendment and Revocation) (EU Exit) Regulations, SI 2020/1495 reg 9(a), where SI 2020/1495 Pt 2 Ch 2 applies, reg 28 is to be read as if the reference to "output tax" includes import VAT chargeable on goods comprising a relevant importation; and the words from "in the next prescribed accounting period" to the end were "in the prescribed accounting period in which the Commissioners make available to the

person details of the amount of import duty due from the person on goods comprising a relevant importation (and in this regulation "import duty" means import duty charged under section 1 of the Taxation (Cross-border Trade) Act 2018).".

29 Claims for input tax

(1) [Subject to paragraph (1A) below][2], and save as the Commissioners may otherwise allow or direct either generally or specially, a person claiming deduction of input tax under section 25(2) of the Act shall do so on a return made by him for the prescribed accounting period in which the VAT became chargeable [save that, where he does not at that time hold the document or invoice required by paragraph (2) below, he shall make his claim on the return for the first prescribed accounting period in which he holds that document or invoice][2].

[(1A) [Subject to paragraph (1B)][2] the Commissioners shall not allow or direct a person to make any claim for deduction of input tax in terms such that the deduction would fall to be claimed more than [4 years][2] after the date by which the return for [the first prescribed accounting period in which he was entitled to claim that input tax in accordance with paragraph (1) above][2] is required to be made.][1]

[(1B) The Commissioners shall not allow or direct a person to make any claim for deduction of input tax where the return for the first prescribed accounting period in which the person was entitled to claim that input tax in accordance with paragraph (1) above was required to be made on or before 31st March 2006.][2]

(2) At the time of claiming deduction of input tax in accordance with paragraph (1) above, a person shall, if the claim is in respect of—
- (a) a supply from another taxable person, hold the document which is required to be provided under regulation 13;
- (b) a supply under section 8(1) of the Act, hold the relative invoice from the supplier;
- (c) an importation of goods, hold a document authenticated or issued by the proper officer, showing the claimant as importer, consignee or owner and showing the amount of VAT charged on the goods;
- (d) goods which have been removed from warehouse [or Northern Ireland warehouse][3], hold a document authenticated or issued by the proper officer showing the claimant's particulars and the amount of VAT charged on the goods;
- (e) an acquisition by him from another member State of any goods other than a new means of transport, hold a document required by the authority in that other member State to be issued showing his registration number including the prefix ["XI"][3], the registration number of the supplier including the alphabetical code of the member State in which the supplier is registered, the consideration for the supply exclusive of VAT, the date of issue of the document and description sufficient to identify the goods supplied; or
- (f) an acquisition by him from another member State of a new means of transport, hold a document required by the authority in that other member State to be issued showing his registration number including the prefix ["XI"][3], the registration number of the supplier including the alphabetical code of the member State in which the supplier is registered, the consideration for the supply exclusive of VAT, the date of issue of the document and description sufficient to identify the acquisition as a new means of transport as specified in section 95 of the Act;

provided that where the Commissioners so direct, either generally or in relation to particular cases or classes of cases, a claimant shall hold [or provide][1] such other . . . [1] evidence of the charge to VAT as the Commissioners may direct.

(3) Where the Commissioners are satisfied that a person is not able to claim the exact amount of input tax to be deducted by him in any period, he may estimate a part of his input tax for that period, provided that any such estimated amount shall be adjusted and exactly accounted for as VAT deductible in the next prescribed accounting period or, if the exact amount is still not known and the Commissioners are satisfied that it could not with due diligence be ascertained, in the next but one prescribed accounting period.

[(4) Nothing in this regulation shall entitle a taxable person to deduct more than once input tax incurred on goods imported or acquired by him or on goods or services supplied to him.][2]

Commentary—*De Voil Indirect Tax Service* **V3.415, V3.418.**
HMRC Manuals—VAT Input Tax VIT11500 (UK law).
VAT Accounting Manual VATAC2200 (legal basis for estimation).
VAT refunds Manual VRM8300 (VAT regulations 1995 - overview).
Modification—By virtue of the VAT (Miscellaneous and Transitional Provisions, Amendment and Revocation) (EU Exit) Regulations, SI 2020/1495 reg 9(b), where SI 2020/1495 Pt 2, Ch 2 applies, reg 29(3) is to be read as if the words from "in the next prescribed accounting period" to the end read "in the prescribed accounting period in which the Commissioners make available to the person details of the amount of import duty due from the person in that prescribed accounting period on goods comprising a relevant importation (and "import duty" in this regulation means import duty charged under section 1 of the Taxation (Cross-border Trade) Act 2018).".
Amendments—[1] Words in para (2) substituted, and word revoked, by the VAT (Amendment) (No 3) Regulations, SI 2003/1114 with effect from 16 April 2003.

[2] In paras (1), words substituted for words "Subject to paragraphs (1A) and (2) below", and words inserted, in para (1A), words inserted and words substituted for words "3 years" and "the prescribed accounting period in which the VAT became chargeable" respectively, and paras (1B), (4) inserted, by the VAT (Amendment) Regulations, SI 2009/586 regs 2, 3 with effect from 1 April 2009.
[3] In para (2)(d) words inserted, and in paras (2)(e) and (f) "XI" substituted for "GB", by the Value Added Tax (Miscellaneous Amendments, Northern Ireland Protocol and Savings and Transitional Provisions) (EU Exit) Regulations, SI 2020/1545 regs 31 and 46 with effect from IP completion day (11pm UK time on 31 December 2020) by virtue of SI 2020/1641 reg 2, Schedule para 11.

30 Persons acting in a representative capacity

Where any person subject to any requirements under this Part dies or becomes incapacitated and control of his assets passes to another person, being a personal representative, trustee in bankruptcy, receiver, liquidator or person otherwise acting in a representative capacity, that other person shall, if the Commissioners so require and so long as he has such control, comply with these requirements, provided that any requirement to pay VAT shall only apply to that other person to the extent of the assets of the deceased or incapacitated person over which he has control; and save to the extent aforesaid this Part shall apply to such a person, so acting, in the same way as it would have applied to the deceased or incapacitated person had that person not been deceased or incapacitated.

Commentary—*De Voil Indirect Tax Service* **V5.101, V5.132A**.

31 Records

(1) Every taxable person shall, for the purpose of accounting for VAT, keep the following records—
   (a) his business and accounting records,
   (b) his VAT account,
   (c) copies of all VAT invoices issued by him,
   (d) all VAT invoices received by him,
   [(da) all certificates—
     (i) prepared by him relating to acquisitions by him of goods from other member States, or
     (ii) given to him relating to supplies by him of goods or services,][1]

     provided that, owing to provisions in force which concern fiscal or other warehousing regimes, [or Northern Ireland fiscal or other Northern Ireland warehousing regimes,][5] those acquisitions or supplies are either zero-rated or treated for the purposes of the Act as taking place outside the United Kingdom,
   (e) documentation received by him relating to acquisitions by him of any goods from other member States,
   (f) copy documentation issued by him relating to the transfer, dispatch or transportation of goods by him to other member States,
   (g) documentation received by him relating to the transfer, dispatch or transportation of goods by him to other member States,
   (h) documentation relating to importations and exportations by him, . . .[4]
   [(i) all documents received in accordance with regulation 15C and copies of such documents provided in accordance with that regulation,][4]
   [(j) a copy of any self-billing agreement within regulation 13(3A) to which he is a party;][2]
   [(k) where he is a customer, party to a self-billing agreement within regulation 13(3A), the name, address and VAT registration number of each supplier with whom he has entered into a self-billing agreement.][2]
   [(l) where the taxable person is subject to the requirements of regulation 32A, the electronic account required by that regulation.][3]
(2) The Commissioners may—
   (a) in relation to a trade or business of a description specified by them, or
   (b) for the purposes of any scheme established by, or under, Regulations made under the Act,
supplement the list of records required in paragraph (1) above by a notice published by them for that purpose.
(3) Every person who, at a time when he is not a taxable person, acquires in the United Kingdom from another member State any goods which are subject to a duty of excise or consist of a new means of transport shall, for the purposes of accounting for VAT, keep such records with respect to the acquisition as may be specified in any notice published by the Commissioners in pursuance of this regulation.

Commentary—*De Voil Indirect Tax Service* **V1.272, V5.201**.
HMRC Manuals—VAT Traders' Records Manual VATREC2020 (what records must a trader keep?).
VATREC2030 (are there any other rules for particular trades?).
Amendments—[1] Para (1)(da) inserted by the VAT (Amendment) (No 3) Regulations, SI 1996/1250 reg 8 with effect from 1 June 1996.
[2] Para (1)(j), (k) inserted by the VAT (Amendment) (No 6) Regulations, SI 2003/3220 regs 1(1)(b), 2, 11 with effect from 1 January 2004.

[3] Para (1)(*l*) inserted by the Value Added Tax (Amendment) Regulations, SI 2018/261 regs 2, 5 with effect from 1 April 2019 where a taxpayer has a prescribed accounting period which begins on that date, and otherwise from the first day of a taxpayer's first prescribed accounting period beginning after the 1 April 2019.
[4] In para (1), word "and" at end of sub-para (*h*) revoked, and sub-para (*i*) substituted, by the VAT (Amendment) Regulations, SI 2019/1048 regs 3, 7 with effect in relation to supplies for which there is an increase or decrease in consideration that occurs on or after 1 September 2019. An increase or decrease in consideration means an increase or decrease in consideration as described in reg 24A which occurs at the time specified in reg 24B.
[5] In para (1)(*da*) words inserted by the Value Added Tax (Miscellaneous Amendments, Northern Ireland Protocol and Savings and Transitional Provisions) (EU Exit) Regulations, SI 2020/1545 regs 31 and 47 with effect from IP completion day (11pm UK time on 31 December 2020) by virtue of SI 2020/1641 reg 2, Schedule para 11.

[31AA Preservation of records
(1) Subject to paragraph (2) the electronic account required to be kept pursuant to regulation 31(1)(*l*) must be preserved using functional compatible software.
(2) The obligation under paragraph (1) does not apply to a person to whom the requirements of regulation 32A have ceased to apply.
(3) Subject to paragraph (1) the duty to preserve records required to be kept pursuant to regulations 31 and 31A may be discharged by—
 (*a*) preserving them in any form or by any means; or
 (*b*) preserving the information in them by any means,
subject to any conditions or exceptions specified in writing by the Commissioners.
(4) The functional compatible software must take a form approved by the Commissioners in a specific or general direction.
(5) A direction under paragraph (4) may also specify the circumstances in which functional compatible software may be used or not used.][1]

Commentary—*De Voil Indirect Tax Service* **V5.202, V5.211.**
Amendments—[1] Regulation 31AA inserted by the Value Added Tax (Amendment) Regulations. SI 2018/261 regs 2, 6 with effect from 1 April 2019 where a taxpayer has a prescribed accounting period which begins on that date, and otherwise from the first day of a taxpayer's first prescribed accounting period beginning after the 1 April 2019.

[31A—(1) This regulation applies where a person—
 (*a*) makes a supply of investment gold of a description falling within item 1 of Group 15 of Schedule 9 to the Act, or
 (*b*) makes a supply of a description falling within item 2 of Group 15 of Schedule 9 to the Act, which subsequently results in the transfer of the possession of the investment gold.
(2) Subject to paragraph (6) below (and save as the Commissioners may otherwise allow in relation to supplies where the value is less than an amount equivalent to [£13,000][2] at a rate specified in any notice published by the Commissioners for the purposes of this regulation) in addition to the requirements upon every taxable person under this Part, a person making a supply of a description falling within paragraph (1) above shall—
 (*a*) without prejudice to regulations 13 and 14, issue an invoice in respect of the supply containing such details as may be specified in a notice published by the Commissioners for the purposes of this regulation;
 (*b*) keep and maintain a record of the supply containing such details as may be specified in a notice published by the Commissioners for the purposes of this regulation;
 (*c*) retain such documents in relation to the supply as may be specified in a notice published by the Commissioners for the purposes of this regulation;
 (*d*) keep and maintain a record of the recipient of the supply containing such particulars pertaining to the recipient as may be specified in a notice published by the Commissioners for the purposes of this regulation;
 (*e*) keep and maintain such other records and documents as may be specified in a notice published by the Commissioners for the purposes of this regulation to allow the proper identification of each recipient of the supply;
 (*f*) notify the Commissioners in writing that he is making such supplies within 28 days of the first supply;
 (*g*) furnish to the Commissioners such information in relation to his making of the supply as may be specified in a notice published by them.
(3) A taxable person shall keep and maintain, together with the account he is required to keep and maintain under regulation 32 below, a record of exempt supplies of a description falling within item 1 or 2 of Group 15 of Schedule 9 to the Act, that he makes to another taxable person.
(4) Where there is a sale of investment gold, which would if that person were supplying investment gold in the course or furtherance of any business, fall within item 1 or 2 of Group 15 of Schedule 9 to the Act, by a person who is not trading in investment gold, to a person who is so trading, the purchaser shall issue on behalf of the seller an invoice containing such particulars as may be set out in a notice published by the Commissioners for the purposes of this regulation and the seller shall sign such form of declaration as may be set out in a notice published by the Commissioners for the purposes of this regulation.

(5) The records required to be kept and the documents required to be retained under paragraphs (1) to (4) above shall be preserved for a minimum period of 6 years.
(6) Paragraphs (2) to (5) above shall not apply to any person in respect of a supply by him of a description falling within item 1 or 2 of Group 15 of Schedule 9 to the Act the value of which does not exceed £5,000, unless the total value of those supplies to any person over the last 12 months exceeds £10,000.][1]

Commentary—De Voil Indirect Tax Service **V5.201**.
Amendments—[1] This Regulation inserted by the VAT (Amendment) (No 4) Regulations, SI 1999/3114, regs 2, 4, with effect from 1 January 2000.
[2] In para (2), words "15,000 euro" substituted by the Value Added Tax (Miscellaneous Amendments and Revocations) (EU Exit) Regulations, SI 2019/59 regs 12, 32 with effect from IP completion day (11pm UK time on 31 December 2020).

[31B Where a person receives a supply of a description falling within article 31A(1) above that person shall retain the purchase invoice in relation to that supply for a minimum period of 6 years.][1]

Amendments—[1] This Regulation inserted by the VAT (Amendment) (No 4) Regulations, SI 1999/3114, regs 2, 4, with effect from 1 January 2000.

[31C Paragraph 10(2) of Schedule 11 to the Act shall apply in relation to supplies of a description falling within items 1 and 2 of Group 15 of Schedule 9 to the Act as it applies in relation to the supply of goods under taxable supplies.][1]

Amendments—[1] This Regulation inserted by the VAT (Amendment) (No 4) Regulations, SI 1999/3114, regs 2, 4, with effect from 1 January 2000.

32 The VAT account

(1) Every taxable person shall keep and maintain, in accordance with this regulation, an account to be known as the VAT account.
(2) The VAT account shall be divided into separate parts relating to the prescribed accounting periods of the taxable person and each such part shall be further divided into 2 portions to be known as "the VAT payable portion" and "the VAT allowable portion".
(3) The VAT payable portion for each prescribed accounting period shall comprise—
   (*a*) a total of the output tax due from the taxable person for that period,
   (*b*) a total of the output tax due on acquisitions from other member States by the taxable person for that period,
   [(*ba*) a total of the tax which the taxable person is required to account for and pay on behalf of the supplier,][1]
   [(*baa*) a total of the import VAT which the taxable person is accounting for on his return for that period in accordance with the Value Added Tax (Accounting Procedures for Import VAT for VAT Registered Persons and Amendment) (EU Exit) Regulations 2019,][2]
   (*c*) every correction or adjustment to the VAT payable portion which is required or allowed by regulation 34, 35[, 38, or 38A][1], and
   (*d*) every adjustment to the amount of VAT payable by the taxable person for that period which is required, or allowed, by or under any Regulations made under the Act.
(4) The VAT allowable portion for each prescribed period shall comprise—
   (*a*) a total of the input tax allowable to the taxable person for that period by virtue of section 26 of the Act,
   (*b*) a total of the input tax allowable in respect of acquisitions from other member States by the taxable person for that period by virtue of section 26 of the Act,
   (*c*) every correction or adjustment to the VAT allowable portion which is required or allowed by regulation 34, 35 or 38, and
   (*d*) every adjustment to the amount of input tax allowable to the taxable person for that period which is required, or allowed, by or under any Regulations made under the Act.

Commentary—De Voil Indirect Tax Service **V5.211**.
HMRC Manuals—VAT Traders' Records Manual VATREC2050 (the VAT account).
Modification—By virtue of the VAT (Miscellaneous and Transitional Provisions, Amendment and Revocation) (EU Exit) Regulations, SI 2020/1495 reg 9(c), where SI 2020/1495 Pt 2 Ch 2 applies, regs 32(3)(baa) and 40(1)(ba) are to be read as if after "2019" were added "or Chapter 2 of Part 2 of the Value Added Tax (Miscellaneous and Transitional Provisions, Amendment and Revocation) (EU Exit) Regulations 2020,".
Amendments—[1] Words in para (3)(*b*) inserted, and words in para (3)(*c*) substituted, by the VAT (Amendment) (No 3) Regulations, SI 2007/1418 regs 2, 4 with effect from 1 June 2007.
[2] Para (3)(*baa*) inserted, by the Value Added Tax (Accounting Procedures for Import VAT for VAT Registered Persons and Amendment) (EU Exit) Regulations, SI 2019/60 reg 12(1), (3) with effect from IP completion day (11pm UK time on 31 December 2020).

[32A Recording and keeping of information in electronic form

(1) Subject to regulation 32B a taxable person shall keep and maintain the information specified in paragraphs (2) and (3) in an electronic form ("the electronic account").
(2) The information specified for the purposes of paragraph (1) is—
   (*a*) the name of the taxable person;
   (*b*) the address of the taxable person's principal place of business;

(c) the taxable person's VAT registration number; and
(d) any VAT accounting schemes used by the taxable person.
(3) Subject to paragraph (4) the information specified for the purposes of paragraph (1) for each accounting period is—
- (a) subject to sub-paragraph (c), for each supply made within the period—
  - (i) the time of supply,
  - (ii) the value of the supply, and
  - (iii) the rate of VAT charged;
- (b) subject to sub-paragraph (c), for each supply received within the period—
  - (i) the time of supply,
  - (ii) the value of the supply, and
  - (iii) the total amount of input tax for which credit is allowable under section 26 of the Act;
- (c) where more than one supply is recorded on a tax invoice and those supplies are either—
  - (i) supplies made which are required to be accounted for in respect of the same prescribed accounting period and are subject to the same rate of VAT, or
  - (ii) supplies received for which credit is allowable in the same prescribed accounting period,

  they may be treated as a single supply for the purposes of either sub-paragraph (a) or b), whichever is relevant;
- (d) the information specified in each sub-paragraph of paragraphs (3) and (4) of regulation 32;
- (e) where adjustment or correction is made to the VAT account which is required or allowed by any provision of the Act, or any regulations made under the Act, the total amount adjusted or corrected for the period pursuant to that provision or those regulations;
- (f) the proportions of the total of the VAT exclusive value of all outputs for the period which are attributable in each case to standard rated, reduced rated, zero-rated, exempt or outside the scope outputs.

(4) The information specified in paragraph (3) may be varied by direction of the Commissioners to make provision about—
- (a) supplies of investment gold which are subject to the provisions of regulation 31A;
- (b) the operation of the flat-rate scheme under Part 7A of these Regulations (flat-rate scheme for small businesses);
- (c) the operation of retail schemes under Part 9 of these Regulations (supplies by retailers);
- (d) cases where the Commissioners are satisfied that keeping and maintaining information as specified in this regulation is likely to be impossible, impractical or unduly onerous.

(5) The electronic account must be kept and maintained using functional compatible software.
(6) The functional compatible software must take a form approved by the Commissioners in a specific or general direction.
(7) A direction under paragraph (6) may also specify the circumstances in which functional compatible software may be used or not used.
(8) The information specified in paragraph (3) must be entered in the electronic account for the relevant prescribed accounting period no later than the earlier of the date by which the taxable person is required to make the return or the date the return is made for that prescribed accounting period.
(9) Changes to the information specified in paragraph (2) must be made no later than the end of the prescribed accounting period in which those changes occur.
(10) Where a taxable person discovers an error or omission in the electronic account that person must correct the electronic account as soon as possible but in any event no later than the end of the prescribed accounting period in which the error is discovered.]

Commentary—*De Voil Indirect Tax Service* **V5.101B, V5.201**.
Amendments—Regulations 32A–32C inserted by the Value Added Tax (Amendment) Regulations, SI 2018/261 regs 2, 7 with effect from 1 April 2019 where a taxpayer has a prescribed accounting period which begins on that date, and otherwise from the first day of a taxpayer's first prescribed accounting period beginning after the 1 April 2019.

[32B Exemption from the electronic recording requirements
(1) The requirements imposed by regulation 32A do not apply to a person—
- (a) who the Commissioners are satisfied is a practising member of a religious society or order whose beliefs are incompatible with the use of electronic communications, or
- (b) for whom an insolvency procedure as described in any of paragraphs (a) to (f) of section 81(4B) of the Act is applied, or
- (c) for whom the Commissioners are satisfied that it is not reasonably practicable to make a return using a compatible software return system for reasons of disability, age, remoteness of location or any other reason.

(2) This paragraph applies if, for any month ("the current month"), the value of a taxable person's taxable supplies, in the period of one year ending with the month before the current month, was less than the VAT threshold. The "VAT threshold" has the meaning given in paragraph 6(9) of Schedule 11 to the Act.

(3) Where paragraph (2) applies to a taxable person for the current month and has not ceased to apply for any month prior to the current month then the requirements of regulation 32A shall not apply to that person.
(4) In a case where paragraph (2) ceases to apply to a taxable person, the requirements of regulation 32A shall apply from the beginning of that person's next taxable period falling on or after the day on which that application ceases.
(5) Where a business or a part of a business carried on by a taxable person is transferred to another person as a going concern then, for the purposes of determining whether paragraph (2) applies to the transferee, the transferee shall be treated as having carried on the business or part of the business before as well as after the transfer and the supplies by the transferor shall be treated accordingly.
(6) The exemptions under paragraphs (1)(b) and (3) do not apply if a person has elected not to be exempt in accordance with regulation 32C.]

Commentary—*De Voil Indirect Tax Service* **V7.300A**.
Amendments—Regulations 32A–32C inserted by the Value Added Tax (Amendment) Regulations, SI 2018/261 regs 2, 7 with effect from 1 April 2019 where a taxpayer has a prescribed accounting period which begins on that date, and otherwise from the first day of a taxpayer's first prescribed accounting period beginning after the 1 April 2019.

[32C Election not to be exempt
(1) An election not to be exempt under regulation 32B must—
  (a) be made before the start of the next prescribed accounting period ("the period") in which the exemption would otherwise apply, and
  (b) specify the date that the next period begins.
(2) An election has effect for the next period referred to in paragraph (1)(b) and for subsequent periods in which the exemption would otherwise apply.
(3) An election may be withdrawn and the withdrawal shall have effect for the period which immediately follows the period in which it is notified and for subsequent periods.
(4) An election and withdrawal of an election must be made by notice to the Commissioners.]

Amendments—Regulations 32A–32C inserted by the Value Added Tax (Amendment) Regulations, SI 2018/261 regs 2, 7 with effect from 1 April 2019 where a taxpayer has a prescribed accounting period which begins on that date, and otherwise from the first day of a taxpayer's first prescribed accounting period beginning after the 1 April 2019.

33 The register of temporary movement of goods to and from other member States
(1) Every taxable person shall keep and maintain, in accordance with this regulation, a register to be known as the register of temporary movement of goods to and from other member States.
(2) Where goods have been moved to or received from another member State and they are to be returned within a period of 2 years of the date of their first removal or receipt, as the case may be, the register shall contain the following information—
  (a) the date of removal of goods to another member State,
  (b) the date of receipt of the goods mentioned in sub-paragraph (a) above when they are returned from the member State mentioned in that sub-paragraph or [a different member State][1],
  (c) the date of receipt of goods from another member State,
  (d) the date of removal of the goods mentioned in sub-paragraph (c) above when they are returned to the member State mentioned in that sub-paragraph or another member State,
  (e) a description of the goods sufficient to identify them
  (f) a description of any process, work or other operation carried out on the goods either in the United Kingdom or in another member State,
  (g) the consideration for the supply of the goods, and
  (h) the consideration for the supply of any processing, work or other operation carried out on the goods either in the United Kingdom or another member State.
(3) The Commissioners may in relation to a trade or business of a description specified by them supplement the list of information required in paragraph (2) above by a notice published by them for that purpose.

Commentary—*De Voil Indirect Tax Service* **V5.212**.
Amendments—[1] In para (2)(b) words substituted for words "another member State" by the Value Added Tax (Miscellaneous Amendment, Northern Ireland Protocol and Savings and Transitional Provisions) (EU Exit) Regulations, SI 2020/1545 regs 31 and 48 with effect from IP completion day (11pm UK time on 31 December 2020) by virtue of SI 2020/1641 reg 2, Schedule para 11.

[33A A person making supplies of a description falling within article 4 of the Value Added Tax (Terminal Markets) Order 1973 shall not be required to keep in relation to those supplies the records specified in regulations 31 (save for paragraph (1)(a) of that regulation), 31A, 32 and 33 of these Regulations.][4]

Amendments— This Regulation inserted by the VAT (Amendment) (No 4) Regulations, SI 1999/3114, regs 2, 5, with effect from 1 January 2000.

[33B Where a person of a description in article 6 of the Value Added Tax (Terminal Markets) Order 1973 who makes or receives supplies of a description falling within that article, the following Parts of these Regulations shall not apply in relation to those supplies, that is to say—]

(a) Part IV;
(b) Part V.]¹

Amendments—¹ This Regulation inserted by the VAT (Amendment) (No 4) Regulations, SI 1999/3114, regs 2, 5, with effect from 1 January 2000.

34 Correction of errors

(1) [Subject to paragraph (1A) below]¹ this regulation applies where a taxable person has made a return, or returns, to the Controller which overstated or understated his liability to VAT or his entitlement to a payment under section 25(3) of the Act.

[(1A) Subject to paragraph (1B) [and (1C)]³ below, any overstatement or understatement in a return where—
   (a) a period of [4 years]³ has elapsed since the end of the prescribed accounting period for which the return was made; and
   (b) the taxable person has not (in relation to that overstatement or understatement) corrected his VAT account in accordance with this regulation before the end of the prescribed accounting period during which that period of [4 years]³ has elapsed,
shall be disregarded for the purposes of this regulation; and in paragraphs (2) to (6) of this regulation "overstatement", "understatement" and related expressions shall be construed accordingly.]¹

[(1B) Paragraph (1A) above does not apply where—
   (a) the overstatement or understatement is discovered in a prescribed accounting period which begins before 1st May 1997; and
   (b) the return for that prescribed accounting period has not been made, and was not required to have been made, before that date.]¹

[(1C) Where paragraph (1B) above does not apply, any overstatement or understatement in a return shall be disregarded for the purposes of this regulation where the prescribed accounting period for which the return was made or required to be made ended on or before 31st March 2006.]³

(2) In this regulation—
   (a) "under-declarations of liability" means the aggregate of—
      (i) the amount (if any) by which credit for input tax was overstated in any return, and
      (ii) the amount (if any) by which output tax was understated in any return;
   (b) "over-declarations of liability" means the aggregate of—
      (i) the amount (if any) by which credit for input tax was understated in any return, and
      (ii) the amount (if any) by which output tax was overstated in any return.

(3) Where, in relation to all such overstatements or understatements discovered by the taxable person during a prescribed accounting period, the difference between—
   (a) under-declarations of liability, and
   (b) over-declarations of liability,
does not exceed [£50,000]², the taxable person may correct his VAT account in accordance with this regulation.

[But if Box 6 of the taxable person's return for the prescribed accounting period must contain a total less than £5,000,000, the difference must not for these purposes exceed 1% of that total [unless the difference is £10,000 or less]³.

(Box 6 must contain the total value of sales and all other outputs excluding any VAT – [see regulations 25 and 25A and the relevant forms specified in a notice published by the Commissioners]⁴.)]²

(4) In the VAT payable portion—
   (a) where the amount of any overstatements of output tax is greater than the amount of any understatements of output tax a negative entry shall be made for the amount of the excess; or
   (b) where the amount of any understatements of output tax is greater than the amount of any overstatements of output tax a positive entry shall be made for the amount of the excess.

(5) In the VAT allowable portion—
   (a) where the amount of any overstatements of credit for input tax is greater than the amount of any understatements of credit for input tax a negative entry shall be made for the amount of the excess; or
   (b) where the amount of any understatements of credit for input tax is greater than the amount of any overstatements of credit for input tax a positive entry shall be made for the amount of the excess.

(6) Every entry required by this regulation shall—
   (a) be made in that part of the VAT account which relates to the prescribed accounting period in which the overstatements or understatements in any earlier returns were discovered;
   (b) make reference to the returns to which it applies, and
   (c) make reference to any documentation relating to the overstatements or understatements.

(7) Where the conditions referred to in paragraph (3) above do not apply, the VAT account may not be corrected by virtue of this regulation.

Commentary—*De Voil Indirect Tax Service* **V3.419, V3.506** .

HMRC Manuals—VAT Assessments And Error Correction VAEC7410 (error correction for VAT returns: time limits: introduction).
VAT Input Tax VIT11500 (UK law).
Amendments—[1] Words in para (1), and paras (1A) and (1B), inserted by the VAT (Amendment) Regulations, SI 1997/1086 reg 5 with effect from 1 May 1997.
[2] In para (3) figure substituted for figure "£2,000", and final two sentences inserted, by the Value Added Tax, etc (Correction of Errors, etc) Regulations, SI 2008/1482 reg 2(1) with effect from 1 July 2008. These amendments only have effect in relation to the overstatements or understatements of liability to VAT in reg 34(3) which taxable persons first discover during their prescribed accounting periods that begin on 1 July 2008 or later: SI 2008/1482 reg 2(2).
[3] In para (1A), words inserted and words substituted for words "3 years", para (1C) inserted, and words in para (3) substituted for words "unless the difference is less than £10,000", by the VAT (Amendment) Regulations, SI 2009/586 regs 2, 4 with effect from 1 April 2009.
[4] In para (3), words substituted for words "see regulation 25 and Schedule 1 Forms 4 and 5", by the VAT (Amendment) (No 2) Regulations, SI 2012/1899 regs 3, 15 with effect from 15 October 2012.

35 Where a taxable person has made an error—
  (a) in accounting for VAT, or
  (b) in any return made by him,
then, unless he corrects that error in accordance with regulation 34, he shall correct it in such manner and within such time as the Commissioners may require.
Commentary—*De Voil Indirect Tax Service* **V3.419**.
HMRC Manuals—VAT Assessments And Error Correction VAEC7410 (error correction for VAT returns: time limits: introduction).
VAT Input Tax VIT11500 (UK law)

36 Notification of acquisition of goods subject to excise duty by non-taxable persons and payment of VAT
(1) Where—
  (a) a taxable acquisition of goods subject to excise duty takes place in the United Kingdom,
  (b) the acquisition is not in pursuance of a taxable supply, and
  (c) the person acquiring the goods is not a taxable person at the time of the acquisition,
the person acquiring the goods shall notify the Commissioners of the acquisition at the time of the acquisition or the arrival of the goods in the United Kingdom, whichever is the later.
(2) The notification shall be in writing in the English language and shall contain the following particulars—
  (a) the name and current address of the person acquiring the goods,
  (b) the time of the acquisition,
  (c) the date when the goods arrived in the United Kingdom,
  (d) the value of the goods including any excise duty payable, and
  (e) the VAT due upon the acquisition.
(3) The notification shall include a declaration, signed by the person who is required to make the notification, that all the information entered in it is true and complete.
(4) Any person required to notify the Commissioners of an acquisition of goods subject to excise duty shall pay the VAT due upon the acquisition at the time of notification and, in any event, no later than the last day on which he is required by this regulation to make such notification.
(5) Where a person required to make notification dies or becomes incapacitated and control of his assets passes to another person, being a personal representative, trustee in bankruptcy, receiver, liquidator or person otherwise acting in a representative capacity, that other person shall, so long as he has such control, be required to make the notification referred to in this regulation, provided that the requirement to pay the VAT due upon the acquisition shall apply to that other person only to the extent of the assets of the deceased or incapacitated person over which he has control and, save to the extent aforesaid, this regulation shall apply to such person so acting in the same way as it would have applied to the deceased or incapacitated person had that person not been deceased or incapacitated.
Commentary—*De Voil Indirect Tax Service* **V5.125**.

37 [Claims for credit for, or repayment of, overstated or overpaid VAT]
Any claim under section 80 of the Act shall be made in writing to the Commissioners and shall, by reference to such documentary evidence as is in the possession of the claimant, state the amount of the claim and the method by which that amount was calculated.
Commentary—*De Voil Indirect Tax Service* **V5.159B**.
HMRC Manuals—VAT Retail Schemes Guidance VRS3480 (retrospective change of scheme allowed).
Amendments—Heading substituted by the VAT (Amendment) (No 2) Regulations, SI 2005/2231 reg 2 with effect from 1 September 2005 in relation to claims made under VATA 1994 s 80 on or after that date.

38 Adjustments in the course of business
(1) . . . [3] This regulation applies where—
  (a) there is an increase in consideration for a supply, or
  (b) there is a decrease in consideration for a supply,

which includes an amount of VAT and the increase or decrease occurs after the end of the prescribed accounting period in which the original supply took place.

[(1A) Subject to paragraph (1B) below, this regulation does not apply to any increase or decrease in consideration which occurs more than 3 years after the end of the prescribed accounting period in which the original supply took place.][1, 3]

[(1B) Paragraph (1A) above does not apply where—
- (a) the increase or decrease takes place during a prescribed accounting period beginning before 1st May 1997; and
- (b) the return for the prescribed accounting period in which effect is given to the increase or decrease in the business records of the taxable person has not been made, and was not required to have been made, before that date.][1, 3]

[(1C) Where an increase or decrease in consideration relates to a supply in respect of which it is for the recipient, on the supplier's behalf, to account for and pay the tax, the prescribed accounting period referred to in paragraph (1) is that of the recipient, and not the maker, of the supply. But this paragraph does not apply to the circumstances referred to in regulation 38A.][2]

[Where this regulation applies, both the taxable person who makes the supply and a taxable person who receives the supply shall adjust their respective VAT accounts in accordance with the provisions of this regulation.][3]

(3) [Subject to paragraph (3A) below,][2] the maker of the supply shall—
- (a) in the case of an increase in consideration, make a positive entry; or
- (b) in the case of a decrease in consideration, make a negative entry,

for the relevant amount of VAT in the VAT payable portion of his VAT account.

[(3A) Where an increase or decrease in consideration relates to a supply on which the VAT has been accounted for and paid by the recipient of the supply, any entry required to be made under paragraph (3) shall be made in the recipient's VAT account and not that of the supplier.][2]

(4) The recipient of the supply, if he is a taxable person, shall—
- (a) in the case of an increase in consideration, make a positive entry; or
- (b) in the case of a decrease in consideration, make a negative entry,

for the relevant amount of VAT in the VAT allowable portion of his VAT account.

[(4A) In the case of an increase in consideration, no entry may be made under paragraph (4) unless the recipient of the supply holds the debit note which the supplier is required to provide under regulation 15C(2).][4]

[(5) Every entry required by this regulation must be made in that part of the VAT account which relates to the prescribed accounting period in which the increase in consideration or decrease in consideration occurs.][4]

(6) . . . [4]

(7) None of the circumstances to which this regulation applies is to be regarded as giving rise to any application of regulations 34 and 35 [except insofar as there is an error arising from a failure to make any entry required by this regulation][4].

[(8) Paragraphs (4A) and (5) do not apply in cases where an adjustment in relation to an increase or decrease in consideration has been made in accordance with this regulation before 1st September 2019.][4]

Commentary—*De Voil Indirect Tax Service* **V3.518, V3.519**.
HMRC Manuals—VAT Traders' Records Manual VATREC13070 (regulation 38 - increase/decrease in consideration).
VAT Supply And Consideration VATSC06620 (consideration: change in consideration: law).
VAT refunds Manual VRM8300 (VAT regulations 1995 - overview).
Amendments—[1] Words in paras (1A) and (1B), inserted by the VAT (Amendment) Regulations, SI 1997/1086 reg 6 with effect from 1 May 1997.
[2] Paras (1C), (3A), and words in para (3) inserted, by the VAT (Amendment) (No 3) Regulations, SI 2007/1418 regs 2, 4(b) with effect from 1 June 2007.
[3] In para (1), words "Subject to paragraph (1A) below," revoked, paras (1A), (1B) revoked, and para (2) substituted, by the VAT (Amendment) Regulations, SI 2009/586 regs 2, 5 with effect from 1 April 2009.
[4] Paras (4A), (8) inserted, para (5) substituted, para (6) revoked, and words in para (7) inserted, by the VAT (Amendment) Regulations, SI 2019/1048 regs 3, 8 with effect in relation to supplies for which there is an increase or decrease in consideration that occurs on or after 1 September 2019. An increase or decrease in consideration means an increase or decrease in consideration as described in reg 24A which occurs at the time specified in reg 24B.

[**38ZA**—(1) Where—
- (a) there is a decrease in consideration for a supply of goods which includes an amount of VAT and the decrease occurs after the end of the prescribed accounting period in which the original supply took place,
- (b) the supply is the final supply in a chain of supplies made by taxable persons which relates to the same goods,
- (c) the decrease in consideration is as a result of a relevant payment (which may form part of a larger payment that includes an element of compensation) that reduces the taxable amount which serves as a basis for determination of the VAT payable by the first supplier, and

(d) the amount of the relevant payment equates to the whole, or a proportion, of the price paid for the goods by the final consumer to the final supplier and does not exceed the amount so paid,
then, in regulation 38(2), the reference to "the taxable person who makes the supply" shall include a reference to the first supplier and the reference to "a taxable person who receives the supply" shall include a reference to a final consumer who is a taxable person.

(2) In this regulation—
"cash refund" includes a payment made by cheque or equivalent but does not include the provision of a face-value voucher falling within Schedule 10A to the Act [or a voucher falling within Schedule 10B to the Act]²;
"final consumer" means the recipient of the supply referred to in paragraph (1)(b);
"final supplier" means the person who makes the supply referred to in paragraph (1)(b);
"first supplier" means the first person in the chain of supplies that ends with the final consumer;
"relevant payment" means—
   (a) a cash refund made by the first supplier direct to the final consumer—
       (i) to reflect the reduced value (including a reduction to nil) of goods which are faulty, damaged or otherwise do not fully meet expectations of the final consumer,
       (ii) as a result of a product recall, or
       (iii) in accordance with the terms of a sales promotion scheme operated by the first supplier under the terms of which the final consumer is required to provide proof of purchase of specified goods to the first supplier; or
   (b) a reimbursement made by the first supplier direct to the final supplier—
       (i) which equates to the redemption value of a money-off coupon issued by the first supplier and used by the final consumer in part payment for goods purchased from the final supplier, or
       (ii) to redeem a money-off coupon issued by the first supplier in any of the circumstances specified in sub-paragraph (a)(i) or (ii) and used by the final consumer in full or part payment for goods purchased from the final supplier.

(3) Where the rate of VAT applicable to the supply made by the first supplier differs from the rate of VAT applicable to the supply made by the final supplier, the adjustment made by the first supplier shall be at the rate of VAT applied by the final supplier.]¹

Commentary—*De Voil Indirect Tax Service* **V3.518, V3.519**.
HMRC Manuals—VAT Supply And Consideration VATSC06620 (consideration: change in consideration: law).
Amendments—¹ Reg 38ZA inserted by the Value Added Tax (Amendment) Regulations, SI 2014/548 regs 2, 4 with effect from 1 April 2014.
² In para (2), in definition of "cash refund", words inserted by FA 2019 s 52, Sch 17 para 6 with effect from 12 February 2019.

[38A Adjustments where a supply becomes, or ceases to be, a supply to which section 55A(6) of the Act applies (customers to account for tax on supplies of goods [or services]² of a kind used in missing trader . . . ⁴ fraud)

(1) Where regulation 38 applies and—
   (a) as a result of an increase in consideration for a supply it becomes one to which section 55A(6) of the Act applies; or
   (b) as a result of a decrease in consideration for a supply it ceases to be one to which that section applies,
both the maker, and the recipient, of the supply shall make such entries in the VAT payable portion of their VAT accounts as are necessary to account for that fact.

(2) [Paragraph (5) of regulation 38 applies]³ to any entry required by this regulation as [it applies]³ to any entry required by that regulation.

(3) None of the circumstances to which this regulation applies is to be regarded as giving rise to any application of regulations 34 and 35 [except insofar as there is an error arising from a failure to make any entry required by this regulation]³.]¹

Commentary—*De Voil Indirect Tax Service* **V3.518, V3.519**.
Amendments—¹ Regulation 38A inserted by the VAT (Amendment) (No 3) Regulations, SI 2007/1418 regs 2, 4(c) with effect from 1 June 2007.
² Words in heading inserted by the VAT (Amendment) (No 2) Regulations, SI 2010/2240 regs 2, 3(1) with effect from 1 November 2010.
³ In para (2) words substituted for words "Paragraphs (5) and (6) of regulation 38 shall apply" and "they apply", and in para (3) words inserted, by the VAT (Amendment) Regulations, SI 2019/1048 regs 3, 9 with effect in relation to supplies for which there is an increase or decrease in consideration that occurs on or after 1 September 2019. An increase or decrease in consideration means an increase or decrease in consideration as described in reg 24A which occurs at the time specified in reg 24B.
⁴ In the heading words "intra-community" revoked by the Value Added Tax (Miscellaneous Amendments and Revocations) (EU Exit) Regulations, SI 2019/59 regs 12, 37 with effect from IP completion day (11pm UK time on 31 December 2020).

39 Calculation of returns

(1) Where a person is required by regulations made under the Act to make a return to the Controller, the amounts to be entered on that return shall be determined in accordance with this regulation.

(2) In the box opposite the legend "VAT due in this period on sales and other outputs" shall be entered the aggregate of all the entries in the VAT payable portion of that part of the VAT account which relates to the prescribed accounting period for which the return is made . . . [1] [except that the total of the output tax due in that period on acquisitions in Northern Ireland from member States shall be entered instead in the box opposite the legend "VAT due in this period on acquisitions from other EC member States"].[2]

(3) In the box opposite the legend "VAT reclaimed in this period on purchases and other inputs" (including acquisitions from other member States) shall be entered the aggregate of all the entries in the VAT allowable portion of that part of the VAT account which relates to the prescribed accounting period for which the return is made.

(4) Where any correction has been made and a return calculated in accordance with these Regulations then any such return shall be regarded as correcting any earlier returns to which regulations 34 and 35 apply.

Commentary—*De Voil Indirect Tax Service* **V5.103**.

Amendments—[1] In para (2) words ", except that the total of the output tax due in that period on acquisitions from other member States shall be entered instead in the box opposite the legend "VAT due in this period on acquisitions from other EC member States" revoked by the Value Added Tax (Accounting Procedures for Import VAT for VAT Registered Persons and Amendment) (EU Exit) Regulations, SI 2019/60 reg 12(1), (4) (as amended by SI 2020/1495 reg 20(1), (4) and SI 2020/1545 reg 105(1), (5)) with effect from IP completion day (11pm UK time on 31 December 2020) by virtue of SI 2020/1641 reg 2, Schedule para 11.

[2] In para (2), words inserted by the Value Added Tax (Miscellaneous Amendments, Northern Ireland Protocol and Savings and Transitional Provisions) (EU Exit) Regulations, SI 2020/1545 regs 31, 49 with effect from IP completion day (11pm UK time on 31 December 2020) by virtue of SI 2020/1641 reg 2, Schedule para 11

40 VAT to be accounted for on returns and payment of VAT

[(1) Any person making a return shall in respect of the period to which the return relates account in that return for—

(a) all his output tax,

[(aa) all VAT which he is required to pay on behalf of the supplier.][4]

(b) all VAT for which he is accountable by virtue of Part XVI of these Regulations,

[(ba) all import VAT for which he is accounting on that return in accordance with the Value Added Tax (Accounting Procedures for Import VAT for VAT Registered Persons and Amendment) (EU Exit) Regulations 2019][7]

(c) all VAT which he is required to pay as a result of the removal of goods from a fiscal warehousing regime, [or Northern Ireland fiscal warehousing regime,][8] and

(d) all VAT which he is required to pay as a result of a supply of specified services (performed on or in relation to goods at a time when they are subject to a warehousing regime [or Northern Ireland warehousing regime][8]) being zero-rated under section 18C(1) of the Act where—

  (i) that warehousing regime [or Northern Ireland warehousing regime][8] is one where goods are stored without payment of any duty of excise,

  (ii) those goods are subject to a duty of excise,

  (iii) those goods have been the subject of an acquisition from another member State and the material time for that acquisition was while those goods were subject to that warehousing regime [or Northern Ireland warehousing regime][8], and,

  (iv) there was no supply of those goods while they were subject to that warehousing regime [or Northern Ireland warehousing regime][8].

The amounts to be entered on that return shall be determined in accordance with these Regulations.

(2) Any person required to make a return shall pay to the Controller such amount of VAT as is payable by him in respect of the period to which the return relates not later than the last day on which he is required to make that return.

[(2A) Where a return is made [or is required to be made][5] in accordance with [regulations 25 and 25A][5] above using an electronic return system [or a compatible software return system][6], the relevant payment to the Controller required by paragraph (2) above shall be made solely by means of electronic communications that are acceptable to the Commissioners for this purpose.][2]

[(2B) With effect from 1st April 2010, where a person makes any payment to the Controller required by paragraph (2) above by cheque (whether or not in contravention of paragraph (2A) above)—

(a) the payment shall be treated as made on the day when the cheque clears to the account of the Controller, and

(b) that shall be the day when payment of any VAT shown as due on the return is to be treated as received by the Commissioners for the purposes of section 59 of the Act.

(2C) For the purposes of this regulation, the day on which a cheque clears to the account of the Controller is the second business day following but not including the date of its receipt.

(2D) In this regulation a "business day" is any day except—

(a) Saturday Sunday, Good Friday or Christmas Day;
(b) a bank holiday under the Banking and Financial Dealings Act 1971;
(c) a day appointed by Royal proclamation as a public fast or thanksgiving day;
(d) a day declared by an order under section 2(1) of the Banking and Financial Dealings Act 1971 to be a non-business day.][5]
(3) The requirements of paragraphs (1) or (2) above shall not apply where the Commissioners allow or direct otherwise.][1]
[(4) A direction under paragraph (3) may in particular allow additional time for a payment mentioned in paragraph (2) that is made by means of electronic communications.
The direction may allow different times for different means of payment.][3]
[(5) Later payment so allowed does not of itself constitute a default for the purposes of section 59 of the Act (default surcharge).][3]

Commentary—*De Voil Indirect Tax Service* **V5.108A**.
HMRC Manuals—VAT Accounting Manual VATAC1300 (due date for returns and payments).
Modification—By virtue of the VAT (Miscellaneous and Transitional Provisions, Amendment and Revocation) (EU Exit) Regulations, SI 2020/1495 reg 9(c), where SI 2020/1495 Pt 2, Ch 2 applies, regs 32(3)(baa) and 40(1)(ba) are to be read as if after "2019" were added "or Chapter 2 of Part 2 of the Value Added Tax (Miscellaneous and Transitional Provisions, Amendment and Revocation) (EU Exit) Regulations 2020,".
Note—The UK Government announced on 20 March 2020 the deferral of the 30 June 2020 quarter 1 VAT payments until 31 March 2021. No interest or surcharges arise on those deferred payments during the deferral period (see SI 2020/934).
Amendments—[1] This Regulation substituted by the VAT (Amendment) (No 3) Regulations, SI 1996/1250 reg 9 with effect from 1 June 1996.
[2] Para (2A) inserted by the VAT (Amendment) Regulations, SI 2000/258 regs 2, 4 with effect from 1 March 2000.
[3] Paras (4), (5) inserted by the VAT (Amendment) (No 3) Regulations, SI 2004/1675 regs 1(1), (3), 5 with effect from 22 July 2004.
[4] Para (1)(aa) inserted by the VAT (Amendment) (No 3) Regulations, SI 2007/1418 regs 2, 4(d) with effect from 1 June 2007.
[5] In para (2A), words inserted and words substituted for words "regulation 25", and paras (2B)–(2D) inserted, by the Value Added Tax (Amendment) (No 4) Regulations, SI 2009/2978 regs 2, 5 with effect from 1 December 2009.
[6] In para (2A), words inserted by the Value Added Tax (Amendment) Regulations, SI 2018/261 regs 2, 8 with effect from 1 April 2019 where a taxpayer has a prescribed accounting period which begins on that date, and otherwise from the first day of a taxpayer's first prescribed accounting period beginning after the 1 April 2019.
[7] Para (1)(ba) inserted by the Value Added Tax (Accounting Procedures for Import VAT for VAT Registered Persons and Amendment) (EU Exit) Regulations, SI 2019/60 reg 12(1), (5) (as amended by SI 2020/1545 reg 105(1), (5)) with effect from IP completion day (11pm UK time on 31 December 2020) by virtue of SI 2020/1641 reg 2, Schedule para 11.
[8] In para (1)(c) and (d) words inserted by the Value Added Tax (Miscellaneous Amendments, Northern Ireland Protocol and Savings and Transitional Provisions) (EU Exit) Regulations, SI 2020/1545 regs 31 and 50 with effect from IP completion day (11pm UK time on 31 December 2020) by virtue of SI 2020/1641 reg 2, Schedule para 11.

[**40A**— Where the Commissioners in exercise of their power under section 28(2A) of the Act have directed the manner in which payments on account under section 28 of the Act are to be made, a person who is liable to make such payments shall also pay any amount of VAT payable in respect of a return for any prescribed accounting period in the like manner.][1]
Amendments—[1] This Regulation inserted by the VAT (Amendment) (No 2) Regulations, SI 1996/1198 reg 3 with effect from 1 June 1996.

41 Accounting etc by reference to the duty point, and prescribed accounting period in which VAT on certain supplies is to be treated as being chargeable
(1) Where in respect of—
(a) any supply by a taxable person of dutiable goods, or
(b) an acquisition by any person from another member State of dutiable goods,
the time of supply or acquisition, as the case may be, precedes the duty point in relation to those goods, the VAT in respect of that supply or acquisition shall be accounted for and paid, and any question as to the inclusion of any duty in the value of the supply or acquisition shall be determined, by reference to the duty point or by reference to such later time as the Commissioners may allow.
(2) . . . [1]

Commentary—*De Voil Indirect Tax Service* **V3.503**.
Amendments—[1] Paras (2) and (3) deleted by the VAT (Amendment) (No 3) Regulations, SI 1996/1250 reg 10 with effect from 1 June 1996 except that where 28 April 1996 fell within a taxable person's prescribed accounting period which ended on or after 1 June 1996, the amendment had effect in relation to that taxable person from the day after the end of that prescribed accounting period.

42 Accounting for VAT on the removal of goods
[(1) This regulation applies—
(a) where goods have been removed—
(i) from Northern Ireland to a member State, or
(ii) from a member State to a different Member State or to Northern Ireland; and
(b) the removal falls within paragraph (f) or (g) of article 4 of the Removal Order.][1]

(2) Except where paragraph (3) below applies in respect of the same prescribed accounting period, the owner shall not make any entry in the VAT payable portion of that part of his VAT account which relates to the prescribed accounting period in which he would be liable to account for any VAT chargeable in respect of the removal.

(3) Where—
  (a) the condition described in article 5 of the Removal Order has not been complied with, and
  (b) an amount of VAT has become payable,

the owner shall make a positive entry for the relevant amount of VAT in the VAT payable portion of that part of his VAT account which relates to the prescribed accounting period in which the condition was not complied with.

Commentary—*De Voil Indirect Tax Service* **V3.213A**.
Amendments—[1]   Para (1) substituted by the Value Added Tax (Miscellaneous Amendments, Northern Ireland Protocol and Savings and Transitional Provisions) (EU Exit) Regulations, SI 2020/1545 regs 31 and 51 with effect from IP completion day (11pm UK time on 31 December 2020) by virtue of SI 2020/1641 reg 2, Schedule para 11. Para (1) previously read as follows—
  "(1) This regulation applies where goods have been removed from a member State to a place in any other member State, and that removal falls within any of paragraphs (d), (f) or (g) of article 4 of the Removal Order."

43 Goods removed from warehousing regime
(1) This regulation applies to a registered person who is an approved person within the meaning of the Excise Duties (Deferred Payment) Regulations 1992 in respect of goods which are at a specified warehouse [or Northern Ireland warehouse][2].

(2) [Where a person to whom this regulation applies is—
  (a) the person who is liable under section 18(4)(b) of[, or paragraph 16(8) of Schedule 9ZB to,][2] the Act to pay VAT on a supply of goods while the goods are subject to a warehousing regime [or Northern Ireland warehousing regime, as the case may be][2], or
  (b) liable under section 18D(2) of the Act to pay VAT on a supply of services to which section 18C(3) of the Act applies (specified services performed on or in relation to goods which are subject to a warehousing regime),

he may pay that VAT at or before the relevant time determined in accordance with paragraph (3) below instead of at the time provided for by sections 18(4)(b) [or 18D(2)(a) of, or paragraph 16(8) of Schedule 9ZB to, the Act][2]][1]

(3) For the purposes of paragraph (2) above the relevant time means—
  (a) in relation to hydrocarbon oils, the 15th day of the month immediately following the month in which the hydrocarbon oils were removed from the warehousing regime;
  (b) in relation to any other goods subject to a duty of excise, the day (payment day) on which the registered person is required to pay the excise duty on the goods in accordance with regulation 5 of the Excise Duties (Deferred Payment) Regulations 1992.

(4) Where any goods of a kind chargeable to a duty of excise qualify for any relief of that duty, that relief shall be disregarded for the purposes of determining the relevant time under paragraph (3) above.

Commentary—*De Voil Indirect Tax Service* **V5.141**.
Amendments—[1]   Para (2) substituted by the VAT (Amendment) (No 3) Regulations, SI 1996/1250 reg 11 with effect from 1 June 1996.
[2]   In para (1) words inserted, in para (2) words inserted and words substituted for words "or 18D(2)(a) of the Act", by the Value Added Tax (Miscellaneous Amendments, Northern Ireland Protocol and Savings and Transitional Provisions) (EU Exit) Regulations, SI 2020/1545 regs 31 and 52 with effect from IP completion day (11pm UK time on 31 December 2020) by virtue of SI 2020/1641 reg 2, Schedule para 11.

[PART VA
REIMBURSEMENT ARRANGEMENTS]

Commentary—*De Voil Indirect Tax Service* **V5.159**.
Note—Part VA inserted after Part V by the VAT (Amendment) (No 5) Regulations, SI 1998/59 with effect from 11 February 1998. Regulations 37A to 37H within Part VA were incorrectly numbered. An amending statutory instrument, SI 1999/438, has now been issued. Regulations 37A to 37H have been renumbered in sequence, from 43A to 43H, with effect from 1 April 1999.

[43A Interpretation of Part VA
In this Part—
  ["claim" means—
    (a) a claim made under section 80 of the Act for credit of an amount accounted for to the Commissioners or assessed by them as output tax which was not output tax due to them; . . .[4]

  and "claimed" and "claimant" are to be construed accordingly;][3]

  "reimbursement arrangements" means any arrangements (whether made before, on or after 30th January 1998) for the purposes of a claim which—
    (a) are made by a claimant for the purpose of securing that he is not unjustly enriched by the [crediting][2] of any amount in pursuance of the claim; and

(b) provide for the reimbursement of persons (consumers) who have, for practical purposes, borne the whole or any part of the [original amount brought into account as output tax that was not output tax due]²;

"relevant amount" means that part (which may be the whole) of the amount of a claim which the claimant has reimbursed or intends to reimburse to consumers.]¹

Commentary—*De Voil Indirect Tax Service* **V5.159B, V5.159BA.**
HMRC Manuals—VAT Refunds Manual VRM12800 (reimbursement procedures).
VRM12500 (reimbursement arrangements).
Amendments—¹ This regulation inserted by the VAT (Amendment) (No 5) Regulations, SI 1998/59 with effect from 11 February 1998.
² In the definition of "reimbursement arrangements", words substituted, by the VAT (Amendment) (No 2) Regulations, SI 2005/2231 reg 3 with effect from 1 September 2005 in relation to claims made under VATA 1994 s 80 on or after that date.
³ Definition of "claim" substituted by the VAT (Amendment) (No 3) Regulations, SI 2014/2430 regs 2, 3 with effect from 1 January 2015.
⁴ In the definition of "claim" para (b) and the preceding "or" revoked by the Value Added Tax (Miscellaneous Amendments and Revocations) (EU Exit) Regulations, SI 2019/59 regs 12, 40 with effect from IP completion day (11pm UK time on 31 December 2020). Para (b) previously read as follows—
 "(b) a claim made under paragraph 16I of Schedule 3B, or paragraph 29 of Schedule 3BA, to the Act (claims which have effect for the purpose of section 80(3) of the Act as if they were section 80 claims),"

[43B Reimbursement arrangements—general

Without prejudice to regulation 43H below, for the purposes of section 80(3) of the Act (defence by the Commissioners that [crediting]² by them of an amount claimed would unjustly enrich the claimant) reimbursement arrangements made by a claimant shall be disregarded except where they—
 (a) include the provisions described in regulation 43C below; and
 (b) are supported by the undertakings described in regulation 43G below.]¹

Commentary—*De Voil Indirect Tax Service* **V5.159BA.**
HMRC Manuals—VAT Refunds Manual VRM12800 (reimbursement procedures).
Amendments—¹ This regulation inserted by the VAT (Amendment) (No 5) Regulations, SI 1998/59 with effect from 11 February 1998.
² Word substituted by the VAT (Amendment) (No 2) Regulations, SI 2005/2231 reg 4 with effect from 1 September 2005 in relation to claims made under VATA 1994 s 80 on or after that date.

[43C Reimbursement arrangements—provisions to be included

The provisions referred to in regulation 43B(a) above are that—
 (a) reimbursement for which the arrangements provide will be completed by no later than 90 days after the [crediting of the amount]² to which it relates;
 (b) no deduction will be made from the relevant amount by way of fee or charge (howsoever expressed or effected);
 (c) reimbursement will be made only in cash or by cheque;
 [(d) any part of the relevant amount credited to the claimant that is not reimbursed by the time mentioned in paragraph (a) above will be notified by the claimant to the Commissioners;]²
 [(da) any part of the relevant amount paid (or repaid) to the claimant that is not reimbursed by the time mentioned in paragraph (a) above will be repaid by the claimant to the Commissioners;]²
 (e) any interest paid by the Commissioners on any relevant amount [paid (or repaid)]² by them will also be treated by the claimant in the same way as the relevant amount falls to be treated under paragraphs (a) and (b) above; and
 (f) the records described in regulation 43E below will be kept by the claimant and produced by him to the Commissioners, or to an officer of theirs in accordance with regulation 43F below.]¹

Commentary—*De Voil Indirect Tax Service* **V5.159BA.**
HMRC Manuals—VAT Refunds Manual VRM12800 (reimbursement procedures).
Amendments—¹ This regulation inserted by the VAT (Amendment) (No 5) Regulations, SI 1998/59 with effect from 11 February 1998.
² Words substituted, and paras (d), (da) substituted for para (d) by the VAT (Amendment) (No 2) Regulations, SI 2005/2231 reg 5 with effect from 1 September 2005 in relation to claims made under VATA 1994 s 80 on or after that date.

43D [Notifications and repayments to the Commissioners

The claimant shall give any notification to the Commissioners that he is required to give by virtue of regulation 43C(d) above and, without any prior demand, make any repayment to the Commissioners that he is required to make by virtue of regulation 43C(da) and (e) above within 14 days of the expiration of the 90 days referred to in regulation 43C(a) above.]¹

Commentary—*De Voil Indirect Tax Service* **V5.159BA.**
HMRC Manuals—VAT Refunds Manual VRM12800 (reimbursement procedures).
Amendments—¹ This regulation substituted by the VAT (Amendment) (No 2) Regulations, SI 2005/2231 reg 6 with effect from 1 September 2005 in relation to claims made under VATA 1994 s 80 on or after that date.

[43E Records

The claimant shall keep records of the following matters—

(a) the names and addresses of those consumers whom he has reimbursed or whom he intends to reimburse;
(b) the total amount reimbursed to each such consumer;
(c) the amount of interest included in each total amount reimbursed to each consumer;
(d) the date that each reimbursement is made.][1]

Commentary—*De Voil Indirect Tax Service* **V5.159BA**.
HMRC Manuals—VAT Refunds Manual VRM12800 (reimbursement procedures).
Amendments—[1] This regulation inserted by the VAT (Amendment) (No 5) Regulations, SI 1998/59 with effect from 11 February 1998.

[43F Production of records

(1) Where a claimant is given notice in accordance with paragraph (2) below, he shall, in accordance with such notice produce to the Commissioners, or to an officer of theirs, the records that he is required to keep pursuant to regulation 43E above.
(2) A notice given for the purposes of paragraph (1) above shall—
   (a) be in writing;
   (b) state the place and time at which, and the date on which the records are to be produced; and
   (c) be signed and dated by the Commissioners, or by an officer of theirs,
and may be given before or after, or both before and after the Commissioners have [credited][2] the relevant amount to the claimant.][1]

Commentary—*De Voil Indirect Tax Service* **V5.159BA**.
HMRC Manuals—VAT Refunds Manual VRM12800 (reimbursement procedures).
Amendments—[1] This regulation inserted by the VAT (Amendment) (No 5) Regulations, SI 1998/59 with effect from 11 February 1998.
[2] Word in para (2) substituted by the VAT (Amendment) (No 2) Regulations, SI 2005/2231 reg 7 with effect from 1 September 2005 in relation to claims made under VATA 1994 s 80 on or after that date.

[43G Undertakings

(1) Without prejudice to regulation 43H(b) below, the undertakings referred to in regulation 43B(b) above shall be given to the Commissioners by the claimant no later than the time at which he makes the claim for which the reimbursement arrangements have been made.
(2) The undertakings shall be in writing, shall be signed and dated by the claimant, and shall be to the effect that—
   (a) at the date of the undertakings he is able to identify the names and addresses of those consumers whom he has reimbursed or whom he intends to reimburse;
   (b) he will apply the whole of the relevant amount [credited][2] to him, without any deduction by way of fee or charge or otherwise, to the reimbursement in cash or by cheque, of such consumers by no later than 90 days after his receipt of that amount (except insofar as he has already so reimbursed them);
   (c) he will apply any interest paid to him on the relevant amount [paid (or repaid)][2] to him wholly to the reimbursement of such consumers by no later than 90 days after his receipt of that interest;
   [(d) he will notify the Commissioners of the whole or such part of the relevant amount credited to him as he fails to apply in accordance with the undertakings mentioned in sub-paragraphs (b) and (c) above;][2]
   [(da) he will repay to the Commissioners without demand the whole or such part of the relevant amount paid (or repaid) to him or of any interest paid to him as he fails to apply in accordance with the undertakings mentioned in sub-paragraphs (b) and (c) above;][2]
   (e) he will keep the records described in regulation 43E above; and
   (f) he will comply with any notice given to him in accordance with regulation 43F above concerning the production of such records.][1]

Commentary—*De Voil Indirect Tax Service* **V5.159BA**.
HMRC Manuals—VAT Refunds Manual VRM12800 (reimbursement procedures).
Amendments—[1] This regulation inserted by the VAT (Amendment) (No 5) Regulations, SI 1998/59 with effect from 11 February 1998.
[2] In para (2), words substituted, and sub-paras (d), (da) substituted for sub-para (d), by the VAT (Amendment) (No 2) Regulations, SI 2005/2231 reg 8 with effect from 1 September 2005 in relation to claims made under VATA 1994 s 80 on or after that date.

43H Reimbursement arrangements made before 11th February 1998

Amendment—This regulation revoked by the VAT (Amendment) (No 2) Regulations, SI 2005/2231 reg 9 with effect from 1 September 2005 in relation to claims made under VATA 1994 s 80 on or after that date.

PART VI
PAYMENTS ON ACCOUNT

44 Interpretation of Part VI
In this Part—

"body corporate" means a body corporate which is under a duty to make payments on account by virtue of the Value Added Tax (Payments on Account) Order 1993 and "relevant division" means a division of a body corporate by reference to the business of which that body corporate is under such a duty;
"payments on account" has the same meaning as in the Value Added Tax (Payments on Account) Order 1993.

45 Payments on Account
Save in a case to which regulation 48 applies, the Commissioners shall give to a taxable person who is under a duty to make payments on account notification in writing of—
(a) the amounts that he is under a duty to pay,
(b) how those amounts have been calculated, and
(c) the times for payment of those amounts.

46 Save in a case to which regulation 48 applies, if in respect of a prescribed accounting period the total amount of the payment on account made by the taxable person exceeds the amount of VAT due from him in respect of that period, the amount of excess shall be paid to him by the Commissioners if and to the extent that it is not required by section 81 of the Act to be set against any sum which he is liable to pay to them.

[46A—(1) A payment on account and a payment in respect of a return to which regulation 40A above applies shall not be treated as having been made by the last day on which it is required to be made unless it is made in such a manner as secures that all the transactions can be completed that need to be completed before the whole of the amount becomes available to the Commissioners.
(2) For the purposes of this regulation and regulation 47 below, references to a payment being made by any day include references to its being made on that day.][1]
Commentary—De *Voil Indirect Tax Service* **V5.110**.
Amendments—[1] This regulation inserted by the VAT (Amendment) (No 2) Regulations, SI 1996/1198 reg 4 with effect from 1 June 1996.

47 Where a taxable person fails to make a payment on account by the last day by which he is required to make it, that payment on account shall be recoverable as if it were VAT due from him.
Commentary—De *Voil Indirect Tax Service* **V5.110, V5.171**.

48—(1) The Commissioners shall notify a relevant division in writing of—
(a) the amounts of the payments on account that the body corporate is under a duty to make by reference to the business of that division,
(b) how those amounts have been calculated, and
(c) the times for payment of those amounts.
(2) If in respect of a prescribed accounting period the total amount of the payments on account made by a body corporate by reference to the business of a particular relevant division exceeds the amount of VAT due from the body corporate in respect of that period by reference to that business, the amount of the excess shall be paid to the body corporate through that division by the Commissioners if and to the extent that it is not required by section 81 of the Act to be set against any sum which the body corporate is liable to pay to them.
(3) Section 81 of the Act shall not require any amount which is due to be paid by the Commissioners to a body corporate under paragraph (2) above by reference to the business of a particular relevant division to be set against any sum due from the body corporate otherwise than by reference to that business or to the liabilities of the body corporate arising in connection with that division.

[PART VII
ANNUAL ACCOUNTING][1]

Amendments—[1] This Part (regs 49–55) substituted by the VAT (Annual Accounting) Regulations, SI 1996/542 with effect, in the case of a taxable person who was on 31 March 1996 authorised to use the annual accounting scheme under the VAT Regulations, SI 1995/2518 reg 50, from the first day of his next current accounting year, and in respect of any other taxable person, from 1 April 1996.

[49 Interpretation of Part VII
In this Part—
"authorised person" means a person who has been authorised by the Commissioners in accordance with regulation 50(1), and "authorised" and "authorisation" shall be construed accordingly;
"transitional accounting period" means the period commencing on the first day of a person's prescribed accounting period in which the Commissioners authorise him to use the scheme, and ending on the day immediately preceding the first day of that person's first current accounting year, and is a prescribed accounting period within the meaning of section 25(1) of the Act;

"current accounting year" means the period of 12 months commencing on a date indicated by the Commissioners in their notification of authorisation of a person, or while a person remains authorised the most recent anniversary thereof, and is a prescribed accounting period within the meaning of section 25(1) of the Act;
"the scheme" means the annual accounting scheme established by regulations 50 and 51;
"credit transfer" means the transfer of funds from one bank account to another under a mandate given by the payer to the bank making the transfer;
["the quarterly sum" means—
   (a) in the case of a taxable person who has been registered for at least 12 months—
      (i) immediately preceding the first day of his current accounting year, or
      (ii) for the purposes of regulation 51, immediately preceding the first day of his transitional accounting period,
    a sum equal to 25 per cent. of the total amount of VAT that he was liable to pay to the Commissioners in respect of those 12 months; or
   (b) in any other case, a sum equal to 25 per cent of the total amount of VAT that the Commissioners are satisfied he will be liable to pay to the Commissioners in respect of the next 12 months;]²
"the agreed quarterly sum" means a sum agreed with the Commissioners, not being less than [25 per cent]² of a taxable person's estimated liability for VAT in his current accounting year;
["the monthly sum" means—
   (a) in the case of a taxable person who has been registered for at least 12 months—
      (i) immediately preceding the first day of his current accounting year, or
      (ii) for the purposes of regulation 51, immediately preceding the first day of his transitional accounting period,
    a sum equal to 10 per cent of the total amount of VAT that he was liable to pay to the Commissioners in respect of those 12 months; or
   (b) in any other case, a sum equal to 10 per cent. of the total amount of VAT that the Commissioners are satisfied he will be liable to pay to the Commissioners in respect of the next 12 months;]²
"the agreed monthly sum" means a sum agreed with the Commissioners, not being less than 10 per cent of a taxable person's estimated liability for VAT, in his current accounting year;
"working day" means any day of the week other than Saturday, Sunday, a bank holiday or a public holiday;
"relevant quarterly date" means the last working day of the fourth and, where a period has such months, the seventh and the tenth months of a transitional accounting period;
"relevant monthly date" means the last working day of the fourth and each successive month of a transitional accounting period.]¹

Commentary—*De Voil Indirect Tax Service* **V2.199A, V5.108A**.
Amendments—¹ This regulation substituted by the VAT (Annual Accounting) Regulations, SI 1996/542 with effect, in the case of a taxable person who was on 31 March 1996 authorised to use the annual accounting scheme under the VAT Regulations, SI 1995/2518 reg 50, from the first day of his next current accounting year, and in respect of any other taxable person, from 1 April 1996.
² Definitions of "the quarterly sum" and "the monthly sum" substituted, and definition of "the agreed monthly sum" amended, by the VAT (Amendment) (No 2) Regulations, SI 2002/1142 regs 1–3 with effect—
   (a) in the case of a taxable person who is on 24 April 2002 authorised under the Value Added Tax Regulations, SI 1995/2518 reg 50, from the first day of his next prescribed accounting period beginning after that date; and
   (b) in the case of any other taxable person, from 25 April 2002.

[50 Annual accounting scheme

(1) The Commissioners may, subject to the requirements of this Part, authorise a taxable person to pay and account for VAT by reference to any transitional accounting period, and any subsequent current accounting year at such times, and for such amounts, as may be determined in accordance with the scheme.
(2) A taxable person authorised to pay and account for VAT in accordance with the scheme shall—
   (a) pay to the Commissioners by credit transfer—
      [(i) where the taxable person and Commissioners agree to such payment pattern, the quarterly sum, or as the case may be the agreed quarterly sum, no later than the last working day of each of the fourth, seventh and tenth months of his current accounting year;]²
      (ii) in all other cases, the monthly sum, or as the case may be, the agreed monthly sum, in nine equal monthly instalments, commencing on the last working day of the fourth month of his current accounting year; and
   (b) make by the last working day of the second month following the end of that current accounting year a return in respect of that year, together with any outstanding payment due to the Commissioners in respect of his liability for VAT for the current accounting year declared on that return.

(3) . . . ²]¹

Commentary—*De Voil Indirect Tax Service* **V2.199A, V5.108A**.
HMRC Manuals—VAT Annual Accounting Scheme VATAAS5100 (conditions for continuing use of the scheme).
Note—The UK Government announced on 20 March 2020 the deferral of the 30 June 2020 quarter 1 VAT payments until 31 March 2021. No interest or surcharges arise on those deferred payments during the deferral period (see SI 2020/934).
Amendments—¹ This regulation substituted by the VAT (Annual Accounting) Regulations, SI 1996/542 with effect, in the case of a taxable person who was on 31 March 1996 authorised to use the annual accounting scheme under the VAT Regulations, SI 1995/2518 reg 50, from the first day of his next current accounting year, and in respect of any other taxable person, from 1 April 1996.
² Para (2)(*a*)(i) substituted, and para (3) revoked, by the VAT (Amendment) (No 2) Regulations, SI 2002/1142 regs 1, 2, 4 with effect—
   (a) in the case of a taxable person who is on 24 April 2002 authorised under the Value Added Tax Regulations, SI 1995/2518 reg 50, from the first day of his next prescribed accounting period beginning after that date; and
   (b) in the case of any other taxable person, from 25 April 2002.

[51 An authorised person shall, where in any given case the transitional accounting period is—
  (*a*) 4 months or more—
    [(i) where the taxable person and Commissioners agree to such payment pattern, pay to the Commissioners by credit transfer on each relevant quarterly date the quarterly sum;]²
    or
    (ii) in all other cases, pay to the Commissioners by credit transfer on each relevant monthly date the monthly sum; and
    (iii) make by the last working day of the second month following the end of his transitional accounting period a return in respect of that period, together with any outstanding payment due to the Commissioners in respect of his liability for VAT declared on that return; or
  (*b*) less than 4 months, make by the last working day of the first month following the end of his transitional accounting period a return in respect of that period, together with any outstanding payment due to the Commissioners in respect of his liability for VAT declared on that return. ¹

Commentary—*De Voil Indirect Tax Service* **V2.199A, V5.108A**.
Amendments—¹ This regulation substituted by the VAT (Annual Accounting) Regulations, SI 1996/542 with effect, in the case of a taxable person who was on 31 March 1996 authorised to use the annual accounting scheme under the VAT Regulations, SI 1995/2518 reg 50, from the first day of his next current accounting year, and in respect of any other taxable person, from 1 April 1996
² Para (*a*)(i) substituted by the VAT (Amendment) (No 2) Regulations, SI 2002/1142 regs 1, 2, 5 with effect—
   (a) in the case of a taxable person who is on 24 April 2002 authorised under the Value Added Tax Regulations, SI 1995/2518 reg 50, from the first day of his next prescribed accounting period beginning after that date; and
   (b) in the case of any other taxable person, from 25 April 2002.

[52 Admission to the scheme
(1) A taxable person shall be eligible to apply for authorisation under regulation 50(1) if—
  (*a*) . . . ²
  (*b*) he has reasonable grounds for believing that the value of taxable supplies made or to be made by him in the period of 12 months beginning on the date of his application for authorisation will not exceed [£1,350,000]²;
  (*c*) his registration is not in the name of a group under section 43(1) of the Act;
  (*d*) his registration is not in the name of a division under section 46(1) of the Act; and
  (*e*) he has not in the 12 months preceding the date of his application for authorisation ceased to operate the scheme.
(1A) . . . ²
(2) The Commissioners may refuse to authorise a person under regulation 50(1) where they consider it necessary to do so for the protection of the revenue.]¹

Commentary—*De Voil Indirect Tax Service* **V2.199A**.
HMRC Manuals—VAT Annual Accounting Scheme VATAAS2100 (conditions of entry).
VATAAS2200 (rejected applications).
Amendments—¹ This regulation substituted by the VAT (Annual Accounting) Regulations, SI 1996/542 with effect, in the case of a taxable person who was on 31 March 1996 authorised to use the annual accounting scheme under the VAT Regulations, SI 1995/2518 reg 50, from the first day of his next current accounting year, and in respect of any other taxable person, from 1 April 1996.
² Paras (1)(*a*), (1A) revoked, and figure in para (1)(*b*) substituted, by the VAT (Amendment) Regulations, SI 2006/587 regs 1(2), (5), 2 with effect from 1 April 2006.

[53—(1) An authorised person shall continue to account for VAT in accordance with the scheme until he ceases to be authorised.
(2) An authorised person ceases to be authorised when—
  (*a*) at the end of any [transitional accounting period]³ or current accounting year the value of taxable supplies made by him in that period or, as the case may be, year has exceeded [£1,600,000]²; or
  (*b*) his authorisation is terminated in accordance with regulation 54 below;

(c) he—
  (i) becomes insolvent and ceases to trade, other than for the purpose of disposing of stocks and assets; or
  (ii) ceases business or ceases to be registered; or
  (iii) dies, becomes bankrupt or incapacitated;
(d) he ceases to operate the scheme of his own volition.][1]

Commentary—*De Voil Indirect Tax Service* **V2.199A, V5.103**.
HMRC Manuals—VAT Annual Accounting Scheme VATAAS7300 (removal through default or change in circumstance—law).
Amendments—[1] This regulation substituted by the VAT (Annual Accounting) Regulations, SI 1996/542 with effect, in the case of a taxable person who was on 31 March 1996 authorised to use the annual accounting scheme under the VAT Regulations, SI 1995/2518 reg 50, from the first day of his next current accounting year, and in respect of any other taxable person, from 1 April 1996.
[2] Figure in sub-para (2)(a) substituted by the VAT (Amendment) Regulations, SI 2006/587 regs 1(2), (5), 3 with effect from 1 April 2006.
[3] In sub-para (2)(a), words substituted by the VAT (Amendment) (No 2) Regulations, SI 2003/1069 regs 1(1), 2, 4 with effect from 10 April 2003.

[**54**—(1) The Commissioners may terminate an authorisation in any case where—
  (a) a false statement has been made by or on behalf of an authorised person in relation to his application for authorisation; or
  (b) an authorised person fails to make by the due date a return in accordance with regulation 50(2)(b) or regulation 51(a)(iii) or (b); or
  (c) an authorised person fails to make any payment prescribed in regulation 50 or 51; or
  (d) where they receive a notification in accordance with paragraph (2) below; or
  (e) at any time during an authorised person's transitional accounting period or current accounting year they have reason to believe, that the value of taxable supplies he will make during the period or as the case may be year, will exceed [£1,600,000][2]; or
  (f) it is necessary to do so for the protection of the revenue; or
  (g) an authorised person has not, in relation to a return made by him prior to authorisation, paid to the Commissioners all such sums shown as due thereon; or
  (h) an authorised person has not, in relation to any assessment made under either section 73 or section 76 of the Act, paid to the Commissioners all such sums shown as due thereon.
(2) Where an authorised person has reason to believe that the value of taxable supplies made by him during a transitional accounting period or current accounting year will exceed [£1,600,000][2], he shall within 30 days notify the Commissioners in writing.][1]

Commentary—*De Voil Indirect Tax Service* **V2.199A**.
HMRC Manuals—VAT Annual Accounting Scheme VATAAS7300 (removal through default or change in circumstance—law).
Amendments—[1] This regulation substituted by the VAT (Annual Accounting) Regulations, SI 1996/542 with effect, in the case of a taxable person who was on 31 March 1996 authorised to use the annual accounting scheme under the VAT Regulations, SI 1995/2518 reg 50, from the first day of his next current accounting year, and in respect of any other taxable person, from 1 April 1996.
[2] Figures in paras (1)(e), (2) substituted by the VAT (Amendment) Regulations, SI 2006/587 regs 1(2), (5), 3 with effect from 1 April 2006.

[**55**—(1) The date from which an authorised person ceases to be authorised in accordance with Regulation 53(2) shall be—
  (a) where regulation 53(2)(a) applies, the day following the last day of the relevant transitional accounting period or current accounting year;
  (b) where regulation 53(2)(b) applies, the day on which the Commissioners terminate his authorisation;
  (c) where regulation 53(2)(c) applies, the day on which any one of the events mentioned in that paragraph occurs; and
  (d) where regulation 53(2)(d) applies, the date on which the Commissioners are notified in writing of the authorised persons decision to cease using the scheme.
(2) Where an authorised person ceases to be authorised, he or as the case may be, his representative, shall—
  (a) if his authorisation ceases before the end of his transitional accounting period or current accounting year, make a return within 2 months of the date specified in paragraph (1)(b), (1)(c) or (1)(d) above, together with any outstanding payment due to the Commissioners in respect of his liability for VAT for that part of the period or year arising before the date he ceased to be authorised; or
  (b) if his authorisation ceases at the end of his transitional accounting period or current accounting year, make a return together with any outstanding payment due to the Commissioners in respect of his liability for VAT in accordance with regulation 51 or 50 above; and
in either case, from the day following the day on which he ceases to be authorised, account for and pay VAT as provided for otherwise than under this Part.][1]

Commentary—*De Voil Indirect Tax Service* **V2.199A, V5.103**.
Amendments—[1] This regulation substituted by the VAT (Annual Accounting) Regulations, SI 1996/542 with effect, in the case of a taxable person who was on 31 March 1996 authorised to use the annual accounting scheme under the VAT Regulations, SI 1995/2518 reg 50, from the first day of his next current accounting year, and in respect of any other taxable person, from 1 April 1996.

[PART VIIA
FLAT-RATE SCHEME FOR SMALL BUSINESSES

55A Interpretation of Part VIIA
(1) In this Part—
...[2]
"capital expenditure goods" means any goods of a capital nature but does not include any goods acquired by a flat-rate trader (whether before he is a flat-rate trader or not)—
  (a) for the purpose of resale or incorporation into goods supplied by him,
  (b) for consumption by him within one year, or
  (c) to generate income by being leased, let or hired;
...[2]
["EDR" means the day with effect from which a person is registered under the Act;][2]
"end date" has the meaning given in regulation 55Q(2);
"flat-rate trader" means a person who is, for the time being, authorised by the Commissioners in accordance with regulation 55B(1);
"relevant purchase" has the meaning given in regulation 55C;
"start date" has the meaning given in regulation 55B(2);
"the scheme" means the flat-rate scheme for small businesses established by this Part;
"the Table" means the table set out in regulation 55K.
(2) For the purposes of this Part, a person is associated with another person at any time if that other person makes supplies in the course or furtherance of a business carried on by him, and—
  (a) the business of one is under the dominant influence of the other, or
  (b) the persons are closely bound to one another by financial, economic and organisational links.][1]
[(3) For the purposes of this Part, "relevant date", in relation to a flat-rate trader, means any of the following—
  (a) his start date;
  (b) the first day of the prescribed accounting period current at any anniversary of his start date;
  (c) any day on which he first carries on a new business activity;
  (d) any day on which he no longer carries on an existing business activity;
  (e) any day with effect from which the Table is amended in relation to him;
  (f) where regulation 55JB (reduced rate for newly registered period) applies—
    (i) the day that his newly registered period begins, and
    (ii) the first anniversary of his EDR.][2]
[(4) For the purposes of this Part, "limited-cost trader" is a flat-rate trader whose expenditure on relevant goods in any prescribed accounting period, together with any VAT chargeable on that expenditure, is less than the specified amount, and—
  (a) "relevant goods" are goods used or to be used by a flat-rate trader exclusively for the purposes of the trader's business but excluding the following—
    (i) vehicles, vehicle parts and fuel except where the category of business applicable to the flat-rate trader in the Table is, in that prescribed accounting period, "Transport or storage, including couriers, freight, removals and taxis" and the flat-rate trader owns or leases a vehicle for that business;
    (ii) food or beverages for consumption by the flat-rate trader or employees of the flat-rate trader;
    (iii) capital expenditure goods;
    (iv) goods for the purpose of resale, leasing, letting or hiring out except where the main business activity of the flat-rate trader ordinarily consists of selling, leasing, letting or hiring out such goods;
    (v) goods for disposal as promotional items, gifts or donations;
  (b) "specified amount" is the higher of—
    (i) per cent of the trader's relevant turnover in the prescribed accounting period; and
    (ii) where the prescribed accounting period is one year, £1000, and, in any other case, such proportion of £1000 as the length of the accounting period bears to the period of one year.][3]

Commentary—*De Voil Indirect Tax Service* **V2.199B, V2.199D**.
HMRC Manuals—VAT Flat Rate Scheme FRS6200 (anti-avoidance rules: what is the definition of an associated business?)
Amendments— This Part inserted by the VAT (Amendment) (No 2) Regulations, SI 2002/1142 regs 1, 7 with effect from 25 April 2002.

[2] Definition of "amendment date" and "change date" revoked, definition of "EDR" inserted, and para (3) inserted, by the VAT (Amendment) (No 6) Regulations, SI 2003/3220 regs 1(1)(*b*), 2, 18(1) with effect from 1 January 2004.
[3] Para (4) inserted by the Value Added Tax (Amendment) Regulations, SI 2017/295 regs 2, 3 with effect in relation to prescribed accounting periods commencing on or after 1st April 2017, subject to transitional provisions in respect of accounting periods straddling that date (SI 2017/295 regs 2(*b*), 3).

55B [Flat-rate scheme for small businesses

(1) The Commissioners may, subject to the requirements of this Part, authorise a taxable person to account for and pay VAT in respect of his relevant supplies in accordance with the scheme with effect from—
    (*a*) the beginning of his next prescribed accounting period after the date on which the Commissioners are notified . . . [2] of his desire to be so authorised, or
    (*b*) such earlier or later date as may be agreed between him and the Commissioners.
(2) The date with effect from which a person is so authorised shall be known as his start date.
(3) The Commissioners may refuse to so authorise a person if they consider it is necessary for the protection of the revenue that he is not so authorised.
(4) A flat-rate trader shall continue to account for VAT in accordance with the scheme until his end date.][1]

Commentary—*De Voil Indirect Tax Service* **V2.199B**.
HMRC Manuals—VAT Flat Rate Scheme FRS3200 (can HMRC allow a retrospective start date for FRS?).
Amendments—[1] This Part inserted by the VAT (Amendment) (No 2) Regulations, SI 2002/1142 regs 1, 7 with effect from 25 April 2002.
[2] Words revoked by the VAT (Amendment) (No 6) Regulations, SI 2003/3220 regs 1(1)(*b*), 2, 17 with effect from 1 January 2004.

55C [Relevant supplies and purchases

(1) Subject to paragraphs (3)[, (5) and (6)][2], any—
    (*a*) supply of any goods or services to,
    (*b*) acquisition of any goods from another member State by, or
    (*c*) importation of any goods . . . [4] by,
a flat-rate trader is a relevant purchase of his.
(2) Subject to the following provisions of this regulation, any supply made by a person when he is not a flat-rate trader is not a relevant supply of his.
(3) Subject to [paragraphs (4) and (6)][2] below, where—
    (*a*) a supply is made to, or made by, a person at a time when he is not a flat-rate trader, and
    (*b*) the operative date for VAT accounting purposes is, by virtue of regulation 57 (cash accounting scheme), a date when he is a flat-rate trader,
that supply is a relevant supply or a relevant purchase of his, as the case may be, if otherwise it would not be by virtue of paragraph (2) above.
(4) Where a person—
    (*a*) is entitled to any credit for input tax in respect of the supply to, or acquisition or importation by, him of capital expenditure goods,
    (*b*) claims any such credit, and
    (*c*) makes a supply of those capital expenditure goods,
the supply made by him is not a relevant supply of his, if otherwise it would be.
(5) Where by virtue of any provision of, or made under, the Act a supply is treated as made by a flat-rate trader, whether to himself or otherwise, that supply is neither a relevant supply nor a relevant purchase of his.][1]
[(6) Where a supply of goods [or services][3] to which section 55A(6) of the Act applies (customers to account for tax on supplies of goods [or services][3] of a kind used in missing trader . . . [4] fraud) is made to, or made by, a flat rate trader, that supply is neither a relevant purchase nor a relevant supply of his.][2]

Commentary—*De Voil Indirect Tax Service* **V2.199B, V2.199D**.
Amendments—[1] This Part inserted by the VAT (Amendment) (No 2) Regulations, SI 2002/1142 regs 1, 7 with effect from 25 April 2002.
[2] Words in paras (1), (3) substituted, and para (6) inserted, by the VAT (Amendment) (No 3) Regulations, SI 2007/1418 regs 2, 5 with effect from 1 June 2007.
[3] Words in para (6) inserted by the VAT (Amendment) (No 2) Regulations, SI 2010/2240 regs 2, 3(2) with effect from 1 November 2010.
[4] In para (1)(*c*) words "from a place outside the member States" revoked, and in para (6) words "intra-Community" revoked, by the Value Added Tax (Miscellaneous Amendments, Northern Ireland Protocol and Savings and Transitional Provisions) (EU Exit) Regulations, SI 2020/1545 regs 31 and 53 with effect from IP completion day (11pm UK time on 31 December 2020) by virtue of SI 2020/1641 reg 2, Schedule para 11.

55D [Method of accounting

Subject to [regulations [55H, 55JB and 55KA][3]][2] below, for any prescribed accounting period of a flat-rate trader, the output tax due from him in respect of his relevant supplies shall be deemed to be the appropriate percentage of his relevant turnover for that period][1]

Commentary—*De Voil Indirect Tax Service* **V2.199B**.

Amendments—[1] This regulation inserted by the VAT (Amendment) (No 2) Regulations, SI 2002/1142 regs 1, 7 with effect from 25 April 2002.
[2] Words substituted by the VAT (Amendment) (No 6) Regulations, SI 2003/3220 regs 1(1)(b), 2, 18(2) with effect from 1 January 200=.
[3] Words substituted for words "55H and 55JB" by the Value Added Tax (Amendment) Regulations, SI 2017/295 regs 2, 4 with effect in relation to prescribed accounting periods commencing on or after 1st April 2017, subject to transitional provisions in respect of accounting periods straddling that date (SI 2017/295 regs 2(b), 3).

55E [Input tax
(1) For any prescribed accounting period of a flat-rate trader, he is entitled to credit for input tax in respect of any relevant purchase of his of capital expenditure goods with a value, together with the VAT chargeable, of more than £2,000.
(2) Where paragraph (1) above applies, the whole of the input tax on the goods concerned shall be regarded as used or to be used by the flat-rate trader exclusively in making taxable supplies.
(3) Section 26B(5) of the Act shall not apply to prevent a taxable person from being entitled to credit for input tax in respect of any supply, acquisition or importation by him that is not a relevant purchase of his.
(4) Nothing in this regulation gives an entitlement to credit for input tax where such entitlement is excluded by virtue of any order made under section 25(7) of the Act.][1]
Commentary—De Voil Indirect Tax Service **V2.199D**.
HMRC Manuals—VAT Flat Rate Scheme FRS6500 (anti-avoidance rules: how is VAT reclaimed on 'capital expenditure goods'?).
Amendments—[1] This Part inserted by the VAT (Amendment) (No 2) Regulations, SI 2002/1142 regs 1, 7 with effect from 25 April 2002.

55F [Exceptional claims for VAT relief
(1) This regulation applies where—
  (a) the first prescribed accounting period for which a taxable person is authorised to account for and pay VAT in accordance with the scheme is the first prescribed accounting period for which he is, or is required to be, registered under the Act, and
  (b) the taxable person makes a claim in accordance with regulation 111 (exceptional claims for VAT relief).
(2) Where this regulation applies, section 26B(5) of the Act shall not apply to prevent the taxable person from being entitled to credit for input tax in relation to the matters for which he makes the claim described in paragraph (1)(b) above.
(3) Where—
  (a) this regulation applies, and
  (b) the Commissioners authorise the claim described in paragraph (1)(b) above,
the whole of the input tax on the goods or services concerned shall be regarded as used or to be used by the taxable person exclusively in making taxable supplies.][1]
Commentary—De Voil Indirect Tax Service **V2.199D**.
Amendments—[1] This Part inserted by the VAT (Amendment) (No 2) Regulations, SI 2002/1142 regs 1, 7 with effect from 25 April 2002.

55G [Determining relevant turnover
(1) The Commissioners shall prescribe, in a notice published by them, three methods to determine when supplies are to be treated as taking place for the purpose of ascertaining the relevant turnover of a flat-rate trader for a particular period, as follows—
  (a) "the basic turnover method", which shall be a method based on consideration for supplies taking place in a period;
  (b) "the cash turnover method", which shall be a method based on the actual consideration received in a period;
  (c) "the retailer's turnover method", which shall be a method based on the daily gross takings of a retailer.
(2) When exercising their power to prescribe these methods, the Commissioners shall prescribe what rules are to apply when a flat-rate trader ceases to use one of the methods and begins to use a different method.
(3) In any prescribed accounting period, a flat-rate trader must use one of the methods to determine the value of his relevant turnover.][1]
Commentary—De Voil Indirect Tax Service **V2.199B**.
Amendments—[1] This Part inserted by the VAT (Amendment) (No 2) Regulations, SI 2002/1142 regs 1, 7 with effect from 25 April 2002.

[**55H**—(1) [Subject to regulation 55KA, the appropriate percentage][2] to be applied by a flat-rate trader for any prescribed accounting period, or part of a prescribed accounting period (as the case may be), shall be determined in accordance with this regulation and regulations 55JB and 55K.
(2) For any prescribed accounting period—

(a) [not falling within (b)]², the appropriate percentage shall be that specified in the Table for the category of business that he is expected, [on the first day of the period]², on reasonable grounds, to carry on in that period;
(b) current at his start date but not beginning with his start date, the appropriate percentage shall be that specified in the Table for the category of business that he is expected, at his start date, on reasonable grounds, to carry on in the remainder of the period;
(c) *not falling within* (a) or (b), the appropriate percentage shall be that applicable to his relevant turnover at the end of the previous prescribed accounting period.²

(3) Except that, where a relevant date other than his start date occurs on a day other than the first day of a prescribed accounting period, the following rules shall apply for the remainder of that prescribed accounting period—
(a) for the remaining portion, the appropriate percentage shall be that specified in the Table for the category of business that he is expected, at the relevant date, on reasonable grounds, to carry on in that period;
(b) "remaining portion" means that part of the prescribed accounting period in which the relevant date occurs—
  (i) starting with the relevant date, and
  (ii) ending on the last day of that prescribed accounting period;
(c) the appropriate percentage specified in sub-paragraph (a) shall be applied to his relevant turnover in the remaining portion described;
(d) if the rules set out in paragraphs (a) to (c) apply and then another relevant date occurs in the same prescribed accounting period, then—
  (i) the existing remaining portion ends on the day before the latest relevant date,
  (ii) another remaining portion begins on the latest relevant date, and
  (iii) the rules in paragraph (a) to (c) shall be applied again in respect of the latest remaining portion.]¹

Commentary—*De Voil Indirect Tax Service* **V2.199C**.
Amendments—¹ Substituted for regulations 55H–55JA by the VAT (Amendment) (No 6) Regulations, SI 2003/3220 regs 1(1)(b), 2, 19(1) with effect from 1 January 2004.
² In para (1), words substituted for words "The appropriate percentage"; in para (2)(a), words substituted for words "beginning with a relevant date" and words substituted for words "at the relevant date"; and para (2)(c) revoked, by the Value Added Tax (Amendment) Regulations, SI 2017/295 regs 2, 5 with effect in relation to prescribed accounting periods commencing on or after 1st April 2017, subject to transitional provisions in respect of accounting periods straddling that date (SI 2017/295 regs 2(b), 3).

55JB [Reduced appropriate percentage for newly registered period
(1) This regulation applies where a flat-rate trader's start date falls within one year of his EDR.
(2) Except that this regulation does not apply where—
(a) the Commissioners received notification of, or otherwise became fully aware of, his liability to be registered more than one year after his EDR, or
(b) his end date or the first anniversary of his EDR falls before 1st January 2004.
(3) [Subject to regulation 55KA, at any relevant date]² on or after 1st January 2004 falling within his newly registered period, the Table shall be read as if each percentage specified in the right-hand column were reduced by one.
(4) A flat-rate trader's "newly registered period" is the period—
(a) beginning with the later of—
  (i) his start date; and
  (ii) the day the Commissioners received notification of, or otherwise became fully aware of, his liability to be registered under the Act, and
(b) ending on the day before the first anniversary of his EDR.]¹

Commentary—*De Voil Indirect Tax Service* **V2.199C**.
HMRC Manuals—VAT Flat Rate Scheme FRS7100 (flat rate scheme guidance: reduction during the first year of VAT registration).
Amendments—¹ Inserted by the VAT (Amendment) (No 6) Regulations, SI 2003/3220 regs 1(1)(b), 2, 19(2) with effect from 1 January 2004.
² In para (3), words substituted for words "At any relevant date" by the Value Added Tax (Amendment) Regulations, SI 2017/295 regs 2, 6 with effect in relation to prescribed accounting periods commencing on or after 1st April 2017, subject to transitional provisions in respect of accounting periods straddling that date (SI 2017/295 regs 2(b), 3).

55K [Category of business
(1) Where, at a relevant date, a flat-rate trader is expected, on reasonable grounds, to carry on business in more than one category in the period concerned, paragraph (3) below shall apply.
(2) . . .²
(3) He shall be regarded as being expected, on reasonable grounds, to carry on that category of business which is expected, on reasonable grounds, to be his main business activity in that period.

(4) In paragraph (3) above, his main business activity in a period is to be determined by reference to the respective proportions of his relevant turnover expected, on reasonable grounds, to be generated by each business activity expected, on reasonable grounds, to be carried on in the period.][1]

[Table

Category of business	Appropriate percentage
Accountancy or book-keeping	14.5
Advertising	11
Agricultural services	11
Any other activity not listed elsewhere	12
Architect, civil and structural engineer or surveyor	14.5
Boarding or care of animals	12
Business services that are not listed elsewhere	12
Catering services including restaurants and takeaways	12.5 [4.5][4]
Computer and IT consultancy or data processing	14.5
Computer repair services	10.5
Dealing in waste or scrap	10.5
Entertainment or journalism	12.5
Estate agency or property management services	12
Farming or agriculture that is not listed elsewhere	6.5
Film, radio, television or video production	13
Financial services	13.5
Forestry or fishing	10.5
General building or construction services*	9.5
Hairdressing or other beauty treatment services	13
Hiring or renting goods	9.5
Hotel or accommodation	10.5 [0][4]
Investigation or security	12
Labour-only building or construction services*	14.5
Laundry or dry-cleaning services	12
Lawyer or legal services	14.5
Library, archive, museum or other cultural activity	9.5
Management consultancy	14
Manufacturing fabricated metal products	10.5
Manufacturing food	9
Manufacturing that is not listed elsewhere	9.5
Manufacturing yarn, textiles or clothing	9
Membership organisation	8
Mining or quarrying	10
Packaging	9
Photography	11
Post offices	5
Printing	8.5
Publishing	11
Pubs	6.5 [1][4]
Real estate activity not listed elsewhere	14
Repairing personal or household goods	10
Repairing vehicles	8.5
Retailing food, confectionary, tobacco, newspapers or children's clothing	4
Retailing pharmaceuticals, medical goods, cosmetics or toiletries	8
Retailing that is not listed elsewhere	7.5
Retailing vehicles or fuel	6.5
Secretarial services	13

Category of business	Appropriate percentage
Social work	11
Sport or recreation	8.5
Transport or storage, including couriers, freight, removals and taxis	10
Travel agency	10.5
Veterinary medicine	11
Wholesaling agricultural products	8
Wholesaling food	7.5
Wholesaling that is not listed elsewhere	8.5

(1) * "Labour-only building or construction services" means building or construction services where the value of materials supplied is less than 10 per cent of relevant turnover from such services; any other building or construction services are "general building or construction services]³

Commentary—*De Voil Indirect Tax Service* **V2.199C**.
HMRC Manuals—VAT Flat Rate Scheme FRS7300 (A to Z of flat rate percentages by sector).
Amendments—[1] This Part inserted by the VAT (Amendment) (No 2) Regulations, SI 2002/1142 regs 1, 7 with effect from 25 April 2002.
[2] Para (2) revoked by the VAT (Amendment) (No 6) Regulations, SI 2003/3220 regs 1(1)(*b*), 2, 18(3) with effect from 1 January 2004.
[3] Table substituted by the VAT (Amendment) (No 3) Regulations, SI 2010/2940 regs 2, 4 with effect from 4 January 2011.
[4] In Table, in second column, rates substituted by the Value Added Tax (Reduced Rate) (Hospitality and Tourism) (Coronavirus) Order, SI 2020/728 arts 2, 5 as set out below. These changes have effect for the period beginning with 15 July 2020 and ending with 31 March 2021 (the end date was extended by SI 2020/1413; previously the temporary reduced rate had been due to end on 12 January 2021). Budget 2021 (3 March 2021) announced that the temporary 5% reduced rate will be extended until 30 September 2021. From 1 October 2021 until 31 March 2022 a new 12.5% rate will apply. See HMRC's Tax Information and Impact Note.
– in entry for "Catering services including restaurants and takeaways", "4.5" substituted for "12.5";
– in entry for "Hotel or accommodation", "0" substituted for "10.5"; and
– in entry for "Pubs", "1" substituted for "6.5".

[55KA Appropriate percentage for limited-cost traders
(1) This regulation applies for determining the appropriate percentage to be applied for a prescribed accounting period in which a flat-rate trader is a limited-cost trader.
(2) Where this regulation applies, the appropriate percentage is that specified in the Table for the category of business carried on by the trader in that prescribed accounting period but the number in the right-hand column is to be read as "16.5".
(3) Except that, where regulation 55JB also applies, the number in the right-hand column is to be read as "15.5".][1]

Commentary—*De Voil Indirect Tax Service* **V2.199C**.
Amendments—[1] Regulation 55KA inserted by the Value Added Tax (Amendment) Regulations, SI 2017/295 regs 2, 7 with effect in relation to prescribed accounting periods commencing on or after 1st April 2017, subject to transitional provisions in respect of accounting periods straddling that date (SI 2017/295 regs 2(*b*), 3).

55L [Admission to Scheme
(1) A taxable person shall be eligible to be authorised to account for VAT in accordance with the scheme at any time if—
    (*a*) there are reasonable grounds for believing that—
        (i) the value of taxable supplies to be made by him in the period of one year then beginning will not exceed [£150,000][2], and
        (ii) . . . [3]
    (*b*) he—
        (i) is not a tour operator,
        (ii) is not required to carry out adjustments in relation to a capital item under Part XV, or
        (iii) does not intend to opt to account for the VAT chargeable on a supply made by him by reference to the profit margin on the supply, in accordance with the provisions of any Order made under section 50A of the Act,
    (*c*) he has not, in the period of one year preceding that time—
        (i) been convicted of any offence in connection with VAT,
        (ii) made any payment to compound proceedings in respect of VAT under section 152 of the Customs and Excise Management Act 1979,
        (iii) been assessed to a penalty under section 60 of the Act, or
        (iv) ceased to operate the scheme, and
    (*d*) he is not, and has not been within the past 24 months—
        (i) eligible to be registered for VAT in the name of a group under section 43A of the Act,
        (ii) registered for VAT in the name of a division under section 46(1) of the Act, or

(iii) associated with another person.
(2) In determining the value of a person's taxable supplies ...³ for the purposes of paragraph (1)(a)—
   (a) any supply of goods or services that are capital assets of the business in the course or furtherance of which they are supplied, and
   (b) any supply of services treated as made by the recipient by virtue of section 8 of the Act (reverse charge on supplies from abroad),
shall be disregarded.
(3) Notwithstanding the above, where a person has been—
   (a) eligible to be registered for VAT in the name of a group under section 43A of the Act,
   (b) registered for VAT in the name of a division under section 46(1) of the Act, or
   (c) associated with another person,
in the period of 24 months before the date of his application, he shall not be authorised, unless the Commissioners are satisfied that such authorisation poses no risk to the revenue.]¹

Commentary—*De Voil Indirect Tax Service* **V2.199B, V2.199D**.
HMRC Manuals—VAT Flat Rate Scheme FRS3600 (why are there so many exclusions?).
FRS6400 (anti-avoidance rules: are there any circumstances in which HMRC can allow associated businesses to join or remain in the scheme?).
Amendments—¹ This Part inserted by the VAT (Amendment) (No 2) Regulations, SI 2002/1142 regs 1, 7 with effect from 25 April 2002
² In sub-para (1)(a)(i), "£150,000" substituted for "£100,000", by the VAT (Amendment) (No 2) Regulations, SI 2003/1069 regs 1(1), 2, 7 1) with effect from 10 April 2003.
³ Para (1)(a)(ii) revoked, and in para (2) words "or income" revoked, by the VAT (Amendment) Regulations, SI 2009/586 regs 2, 6 with effect from 1 April 2009.

55M [Withdrawal from the scheme
(1) Subject to paragraph (2) below, a flat-rate trader ceases to be eligible to be authorised to account for VAT in accordance with the scheme where—
   (a) at any anniversary of his start date, the total value of his income in the period of one year then ending is more than [£230,000]³,
   (b) there are reasonable grounds to believe that the total value of his income in the period of 30 days then beginning will exceed [£230,000]³,
   (c) he becomes a tour operator,
   (d) he intends to acquire, construct or otherwise obtain a capital item within the meaning of regulation 112(2),
   (e) he opts to account for the VAT chargeable on a supply made by him by reference to the profit margin on the supply, in accordance with the provisions of any Order made under section 50A of the Act,
   (f) he becomes—
      (i) eligible to be registered for VAT in the name of a group under section 43A of the Act,
      (ii) registered for VAT in the name of a division under section 46(1) of the Act, or
      (iii) associated with another person,
   (g) he opts to withdraw from the scheme, or
   (h) his authorisation is terminated in accordance with regulation 55P below.
(2) A flat-rate trader does not cease to be eligible to be authorised by virtue of paragraph (1)(a) above if the Commissioners are satisfied that the total value of his income in the period of one year then beginning will not exceed [£191,500]³.
(3) In determining the value of a flat-rate trader's income for the purposes of paragraphs (1)(a) and (b) and (2) above, any supply of goods or services that are capital assets of the business in the course or furtherance of which they are supplied, shall be disregarded.
[(4) For the purposes of this regulation, "income" shall be calculated in accordance with the method specified in regulation 55G(1) (determining relevant turnover) used by the business to determine the value of its turnover whilst accounting for VAT under the scheme.
(5) Where a business has used more than one method to determine the value of its turnover whilst accounting for VAT under the scheme, the method referred to in paragraph (4) above shall be the most recent method used.]²]¹

Commentary—*De Voil Indirect Tax Service* **V2.199D**.
HMRC Manuals—VAT Flat Rate Scheme FRS4100 (can HMRC allow a business to leave the scheme retrospectively?).
Amendments—¹ This Part inserted by the VAT (Amendment) (No 2) Regulations, SI 2002/1142 regs 1, 7 with effect from 25 April 2002.
² Paras (4), (5) inserted by the VAT (Amendment) Regulations, SI 2009/586 regs 2, 7 with effect from 1 April 2009.
³ In para (1)(e), (b) "£230,000" substituted for "£225,000", in para (2) "£191,500" substituted for "£187,500" by the VAT (Amendment) (No 3) Regulations, SI 2010/2940 regs 2, 5 with effect from 4 January 2011.

55N [Notification
[(1) [Subject to paragraph (1A), where—]³
   (a) at the first day of the prescribed accounting period current at any anniversary of his start date,

(b) the appropriate percentage to be applied by a flat-rate trader in accordance with regulation 55H(2)(a) for the prescribed accounting period just beginning differs from that applicable to his relevant turnover at the end of the previous prescribed accounting period,

he must notify the Commissioners of that fact within 30 days of the first day of the prescribed accounting period current at the anniversary of his start date.]²

[(1A) Paragraph (1) shall not apply where a difference in the appropriate percentage arises only because of the application of regulation 55KA.]³

[(2) Where a flat-rate trader begins to carry on a new business activity or ceases to carry on an existing business activity, he must notify the Commissioners of—
 (a) that fact,
 (b) the date that is the relevant date described by regulation 55A(3)(c) or (d) (as the case may be), and
 (c) the appropriate percentage to be applied to the period immediately before that relevant date and immediately after it,
within 30 days of that relevant date.]²

(3) Where any of sub-paragraphs (a) to (g) of regulation 55M(1) apply, the flat-rate trader shall notify the Commissioners of that fact within 30 days.

(4) Any notification required by this regulation shall be given in writing.]¹

Commentary—*De Voil Indirect Tax Service* **V2.199C, V2.199D**.
Amendments—¹ This Part inserted by the VAT (Amendment) (No 2) Regulations, SI 2002/1142 regs 1, 7 with effect from 25 April 2002.
² Paras (1), (2) substituted by the VAT (Amendment) (No 6) Regulations, SI 2003/3220 regs 1(1)(b), 2, 18(4) with effect from 1 January 2004.
³ In para (1), words substituted for words "Where—", and para (1A) inserted, by the Value Added Tax (Amendment) Regulations, SI 2017/295 regs 2, 8 with effect in relation to prescribed accounting periods commencing on or after 1st April 2017, subject to transitional provisions in respect of accounting periods straddling that date (SI 2017/295 regs 2(b), 3).

55P [Termination by the Commissioners
The Commissioners may terminate the authorisation of a flat-rate trader at any time if—
 (a) they consider it necessary to do so for the protection of the revenue, or
 (b) a false statement was made by, or on behalf of, him in relation to his application for authorisation.]¹

Commentary—*De Voil Indirect Tax Service* **V2.199D, V5.108A**.
HMRC Manuals—VAT Flat Rate Scheme FRS4300 (can HMRC withdraw use of the flat rate scheme?).
Amendments—¹ This Part inserted by the VAT (Amendment) (No 2) Regulations, SI 2002/1142 regs 1, 7 with effect from 25 April 2002.

55Q [Date of withdrawal from the scheme
(1) The date on which a flat-rate trader ceases to be authorised to account for VAT in accordance with the scheme shall be—
 (a) where regulation 55M(1)(a) applies—
  (i) in the case of a person who is authorised in accordance with regulation 50(1) (annual accounting scheme), the end of the prescribed accounting period in which the relevant anniversary occurred, or the end of the month next following, whichever is the earlier, or
  (ii) in all other cases, the end of the prescribed accounting period in which the relevant anniversary occurred,
 (b) where regulation 55M(1)(b) applies, the beginning of the period of 30 days in question,
 (c) where regulation 55M(1)(c), (d), or (f) applies, the date the event occurred,
 (d) where regulation 55M(1)(e) applies, the beginning of the prescribed accounting period for which he makes the election described by that provision,
 (e) where regulation 55M(1)(g) applies, the date on which the Commissioners are notified in writing of his decision to cease using the scheme, or such earlier or later date as may be agreed between them and him, and
 (f) where regulation 55M(1)(h) applies, the date of issue of a notice of termination by the Commissioners or such earlier or later date as may be directed in the notification.
(2) The date with effect from which a person ceases to be so authorised shall be known as his end date.]¹

Commentary—*De Voil Indirect Tax Service* **V2.199D**.
HMRC Manuals—VAT Flat Rate Scheme FRS4100 (can HMRC allow a business to leave the scheme retrospectively?). FRS4200 (what is the leaving date for businesses using both the FRS and the annual accounting schemes?).
Amendments—¹ This Part inserted by the VAT (Amendment) (No 2) Regulations, SI 2002/1142 regs 1, 7 with effect from 25 April 2002.

55R [Self-supply on withdrawal from scheme
(1) This regulation applies where—
 (a) a person continues to be a taxable person after his end date,
 (b) for any prescribed accounting period for which he was a flat-rate trader, he was entitled to, and claimed, credit for input tax in respect of any capital expenditure goods, and

(c) he did not, whilst he was a flat-rate trader, make a supply of those goods.

(2) Where this regulation applies, those goods shall be treated for the purposes of the Act as being, on the day after his end date, both supplied to him for the purpose of his business and supplied by him in the course or furtherance of his business.

(3) The value of a supply of goods treated under paragraph (2) above as made to or by a person shall be determined as though it were a supply falling within paragraph 6(1) of Schedule 6 to the Act.][1]

Commentary—*De Voil Indirect Tax Service* **V2.199D, V3.255**.

HMRC Manuals—VAT Flat Rate Scheme FRS6600 (anti-avoidance rules: what is the treatment of capital assets on leaving the flat rate scheme.

Amendments—[1] This Part inserted by the VAT (Amendment) (No 2) Regulations, SI 2002/1142 regs 1, 7 with effect from 25 April 2002.

55S [Adjustments in respect of stock on hand at withdrawal from scheme

(1) This regulation applies where—
  (a) a person continues to be a taxable person after his end date,
  (b) at his end date, he has stock on hand in respect of which he is not entitled to credit for input tax, and
  (c) the value of the stock on hand referred to in sub-paragraph (b) above exceeds the value of his stock on hand in respect of which he was entitled to credit for input tax, at his start date.

(2) Where this regulation applies, the taxable person, for the prescribed accounting period following that in which his end date falls, is entitled to credit for input tax in respect of his stock on hand in such amount as may be determined in accordance with a notice published by the Commissioners.][1]

Commentary—*De Voil Indirect Tax Service* **V2.199D**.

Amendments—[1] This Part inserted by the VAT (Amendment) (No 2) Regulations, SI 2002/1142 regs 1, 7 with effect from 25 April 2002

55T [Amendment by Notice

The Commissioners may vary the terms of any method prescribed by them for the purposes of regulations 55G or 55S by publishing a fresh notice or publishing a notice that amends an existing notice.][1]

Amendments—[1] This Part inserted by the VAT (Amendment) (No 2) Regulations, SI 2002/1142 regs 1, 7 with effect from 25 April 2002.

55U [Reverse charges

Section 8 of the Act (reverse charge on supplies from abroad) shall not apply to any relevant supply or relevant purchase of a flat-rate trader.][1]

Commentary—*De Voil Indirect Tax Service* **V2.199B, V2.199D**.

Amendments—[1] This Part inserted by the VAT (Amendment) (No 2) Regulations, SI 2002/1142 regs 1, 7 with effect from 25 April 2002.

55V [Bad Debt Relief

(1) This regulation applies where—
  (a) a person has made a relevant supply,
  (b) he has used the cash turnover method to determine the value of his relevant turnover for the prescribed accounting period in which the relevant supply was made,
  (c) he has not accounted for and paid VAT on the supply,
  (d) the whole or any part of the consideration for the supply has been written off in his accounts as a bad debt, and
  (e) a period of 6 months (beginning with the date of the supply) has elapsed.

(2) Where this regulation applies—
  (a) section 36 of the Act (bad debts) and any regulations made thereunder shall apply as if the conditions set out in subsection (1) of that section are satisfied, and
  (b) the amount of refund of VAT to which the person is entitled under that section shall be the VAT chargeable on the relevant supply described in paragraph (1) above less the flat-rate amount.

(3) In paragraph (2)(b) above, the flat-rate amount is—

$$A \times B$$

where—
  A is the appropriate percentage applicable for the prescribed accounting period, or part thereof, in which the relevant supply was made, and
  B is the value of the relevant supply together with the VAT chargeable thereon.][1]

Commentary—*De Voil Indirect Tax Service* **V2.199D**.

Amendments—[1] This Part inserted by the VAT (Amendment) (No 2) Regulations, SI 2002/1142 regs 1, 7 with effect from 25 April 2002.

PART VIII
CASH ACCOUNTING

56 Interpretation of Part VIII
In this Part—
"money" means banknotes or coins;
"notice" means any notice published pursuant to this Part.
Commentary—*De Voil Indirect Tax Service* **V3.514**.

57 Cash accounting scheme
A taxable person may, subject to this Part and to such conditions as are described in a notice published by the Commissioners, account for VAT in accordance with a scheme (hereinafter referred to in this Part as "the scheme") by which the operative dates for VAT accounting purposes shall be—
- (a) for output tax, the day on which payment or other consideration is received or the date of any cheque, if later; and
- (b) for input tax, the date on which payment is made or other consideration is given, or the date of any cheque, if later.

Commentary—*De Voil Indirect Tax Service* **V2.199, V3.503**.
HMRC Manuals—VAT Cash Accounting Scheme Manual VCAS1150 (cash accounting scheme: introduction: law).
Former regulations—VAT (Cash Accounting) Regulations, SI 1987/1427 reg 3; VAT (Cash Accounting) (Amendment) Regulations, SI 1993/762 reg 4.

[**57A**—(1) A person shall not account for VAT in accordance with the scheme in respect of any relevant supplies or relevant purchases of his.
(2) In this regulation, "relevant supplies" and "relevant purchases" have the same meanings as in Part VIIA (flat-rate scheme for small businesses).][1]
Amendments—[1] Regulation inserted by the VAT (Amendment) (No 2) Regulations, SI 2002/1142 regs 1, 8 with effect from 25 April 2002.

[58 Admission to the scheme
(1) Without prejudice to paragraph (4) below, a taxable person shall be eligible to begin to operate the scheme from the beginning of any prescribed accounting period if—
- (a) he has reasonable grounds for believing that the value of taxable supplies to be made by him in the period of one year then beginning will not exceed [£1,350,000][2],
- (b) he has made all returns which he is required to make, and has—
  - (i) paid to the Commissioners all such sums shown as due on those returns and on any assessments made either under section 76 of, or Schedule 11 to, the Act, or
  - (ii) agreed an arrangement with the Commissioners for any outstanding amount of such sums as are referred to in sub-paragraph (i) above to be paid in instalments over a specific period, and
- (c) he has not in the period of one year preceding that time—
  - (i) been convicted of any offence in connection with VAT,
  - (ii) made any payment to compound proceedings in respect of VAT under section 152 of the Customs and Excise Management Act 1979(c),
  - (iii) been assessed to a penalty under section 60 of the Act, or
  - (iv) by virtue of regulation 64(1), ceased to be entitled to continue to operate the scheme.
(2) The scheme shall not apply to—
- (a) lease purchase agreements;
- (b) hire purchase agreements;
- (c) conditional sale agreements;
- (d) credit sale agreements;
- (e) supplies where a VAT invoice is issued and full payment of the amount shown on the invoice is not due for a period in excess of 6 months from the date of the issue of the invoice; ... [3]
- (f) supplies of goods or services in respect of which a VAT invoice is issued in advance of the delivery or making available of the goods or the performance of the services as the case may be[; or
- (g) supplies of goods [or services][4] in respect of which it is for the recipient, on the supplier's behalf, to account for and pay the VAT.][3].
(3) Sub-paragraph (2)(f) above shall not apply where goods have been delivered or made available in part or where services have been performed in part and the VAT invoice in question relates solely to that part of the goods which have been delivered or made available or that part of the services which have been performed.
(4) A person shall not be entitled to begin to operate the scheme if the Commissioners consider it is necessary for the protection of the revenue that he shall not be so entitled.][1]

Commentary—*De Voil Indirect Tax Service* **V2.199**.
HMRC Manuals—VAT Cash Accounting Scheme Manual VCAS2050 (cash accounting scheme: conditions for entry). VCAS2200 (cash accounting scheme: transactions excluded from the scheme).

Amendments—[1] This regulation substituted by the VAT (Amendment) (No 3) Regulations, SI 1997/1614 reg 3 with effect from 3 July 1997.
[2] Figure in sub-para (1)(a) substituted by the VAT (Amendment) (No 2) Regulations, SI 2007/768 regs 2, 3 with effect from 1 April 2007.
[3] Words in sub-para (2)(f) revoked, and sub-para (2)(g) and preceding word "or" inserted, by the VAT (Amendment) (No 3) Regulations, SI 2007/1418 regs 2, 6 with effect from 1 June 2007.
[4] Words in para (2)(g) inserted by the VAT (Amendment) (No 2) Regulations, SI 2010/2240 regs 2, 3(3) with effect from 1 November 2010.

59 Without prejudice to the right of a person to withdraw from the scheme, the Commissioners may vary the terms of the scheme by publishing a fresh notice [or publishing a notice which amends an existing notice][1].

Commentary—De Voil Indirect Tax Service **V2.199**.
HMRC Manuals—VAT Cash Accounting Scheme Manual VCAS1200 (cash accounting scheme: introduction: public notice 731 cash accounting .
Amendments—[1] Words inserted by the VAT (Amendment) (No 3) Regulations, SI 1997/1614 reg 3 with effect from 3 July 1997.

[**60**—(1) Without prejudice to regulation 64 below, a person shall withdraw from the scheme immediately at the end of a prescribed accounting period of his if the value of taxable supplies made by him in the period of one year ending at the end of the prescribed accounting period in question has exceeded [£1,500,000][2].
(2) Subject to regulations 61 to 63 below a person may withdraw from the scheme at the end of any prescribed accounting period.
(3) The requirements in paragraph (1) above shall not apply where the Commissioners allow or direct otherwise.][1]

Commentary—De Voil Indirect Tax Service **V2.199**.
HMRC Manuals—VAT Cash Accounting Scheme Manual VCAS6050 (cash accounting scheme: withdrawing from the scheme voluntarily).
VCAS6100 (cash accounting scheme: compulsory withdrawal).
Amendments—[1] This regulation substituted by the VAT (Amendment) (No 3) Regulations, SI 1997/1614 reg 5 with effect from 3 July 1997.
[2] Figure in sub-s (1) substituted by the VAT (Amendment) (No 2) Regulations, SI 2007/768 regs 2, 4 with effect from 1 April 2007.

[**61**—(1) Subject to paragraph (2), a person who ceases to operate the scheme, either of his own volition or because the value of taxable supplies made by him exceeds the level provided for in regulation 60(1), must—
   (a) settle up, or
   (b) apply transitional arrangements.
(2) Where the value of taxable supplies made by a person in the period of three months ending at the end of the prescribed accounting period in which he ceased to operate the scheme has exceeded [£1,350,000][2], he may not apply transitional arrangements.
(3) In paragraph (1)(a), "settle up" means account for and pay on a return made for the prescribed accounting period in which he ceased to operate the scheme—
   (a) all VAT that he would have been required to pay to the Commissioners during the time when he operated the scheme, if he had not then been operating the scheme, minus
   (b) all VAT accounted for and paid to the Commissioners in accordance with the scheme, subject to any adjustment for credit for input tax.
(4) In paragraph (1)(b), "apply transitional arrangements" means continue to operate the scheme in respect of his scheme supplies for 6 months after the end of the prescribed accounting period in which he ceased to operate the scheme.
(5) In paragraph (4), "scheme supplies" means supplies made and received while he operated the scheme that are not excluded from the scheme by virtue of regulation 57A or 58 or conditions described in a notice.
(6) Where a person chooses to apply transitional arrangements, he shall account for and pay on a return made for the first prescribed accounting period that ends 6 months or more after the end of the prescribed accounting period in which he ceased to operate the scheme—
   (a) all VAT that he would have been required to pay to the Commissioners during the time when he operated the scheme, if he had not then been operating the scheme, minus
   (b) all VAT accounted for and paid to the Commissioners in accordance with the scheme (including any VAT accounted for and paid because he applied transitional arrangements), subject to any adjustment for credit for input tax.][1]

Commentary—De Voil Indirect Tax Service **V5.103, V5.108A**.
HMRC Manuals—VAT Cash Accounting Scheme Manual VCAS6200 (cash accounting scheme: accounting for VAT on leaving the scheme).
Amendments—[1] This regulation substituted by the VAT (Amendment) Regulations, SI 2004/767 regs 3, 9 with effect from 1 April 2004.

[2] Figure in sub-s (2) substituted by the VAT (Amendment) (No 2) Regulations, SI 2007/768 regs 2, 5 with effect from 1 April 2007.

[62 Where a person operating the scheme becomes insolvent he shall within 2 months of the date of insolvency account for VAT due on all supplies made and received up to the date of insolvency which has not otherwise been accounted for, subject to any credit for input tax.][1]
Commentary—*De Voil Indirect Tax Service* **V3.503, V5.103**.
HMRC Manuals—VAT Cash Accounting Scheme Manual VCAS3150 (cash accounting scheme: insolvency).
Amendments—[1] This regulation substituted by the VAT (Amendment) (No 3) Regulations, SI 1997/1614 reg 7 with effect from 3 July 1997.

63—[(1) Where a person operating the scheme ceases business or ceases to be registered he shall within 2 months or such longer period as the Commissioners may allow, make a return accounting for, and pay, VAT due on all supplies made and received up to the date of cessation which has not otherwise been accounted for, subject to any adjustment for credit for input tax.
(2) Where a business or part of a business carried on by a person operating the scheme is transferred as a going concern and regulation 6(1) does not apply, the transferor shall within 2 months or such longer period as the Commissioners may allow, make a return accounting for, and pay, VAT due on all supplies made and received which has not otherwise been accounted for, subject to credit for input tax.][1]
(3) Where a business carried on by a person operating the scheme is transferred in circumstances where regulation [6(1)][2] applies, the transferee shall continue to account for and pay VAT as if he were a person operating the scheme on supplies made and received by the transferor prior to the date of transfer.
Commentary—*De Voil Indirect Tax Service* **V3.503, V5.103**.
HMRC Manuals—VAT Cash Accounting Scheme Manual VCAS6550 (cash accounting scheme: accounting for tax on deregistration).
VCAS6600 (cash accounting scheme: transfer of a going concern).
Amendments—[1] Paras (1) and (2) substituted by the VAT (Amendment) (No 3) Regulations, SI 1997/1614 reg 8 with effect from 3 July 1997.
[2] Number substituted for "6(2)" by the VAT (Amendment) (No 3) Regulations, SI 1997/1614 reg 8 with effect from 3 July 1997.

[64 Withdrawal from the scheme
(1) A person shall not be entitled to continue to operate the scheme where—
  (*a*) he has, while operating the scheme, been convicted of an offence in connection with VAT or has made a payment to compound such proceedings under section 152 of the Customs and Excise Management Act 1979,
  (*b*) he has while operating the scheme been assessed to a penalty under section 60 of the Act,
  (*c*) he has failed to leave the scheme as required by regulation 60(1) above, or
  (*d*) the Commissioners consider it necessary for the protection of the revenue that he shall not be so entitled.
(2) A person who, by virtue of paragraph (1) above, ceases to be entitled to continue to operate the scheme shall account for and pay on a return made for the prescribed accounting period in which he ceased to be so entitled—
  (*a*) all VAT which he would have been required to pay to the Commissioners during the time when he operated the scheme, if he had not then been operating the scheme, less
  (*b*) all VAT accounted for and paid to the Commissioners in accordance with the scheme, subject to any adjustment for credit for input tax.][1]
Commentary—*De Voil Indirect Tax Service* **V3.503, V5.103**.
HMRC Manuals—VAT Cash Accounting Scheme Manual VCAS6100 (cash accounting scheme: compulsory withdrawal).
Amendments—[1] This regulation substituted by the VAT (Amendment) (No 3) Regulations, SI 1997/1614 reg 9 with effect from 3 July 1997.

64A [Bad debt relief
Where a person accounts for and pays VAT in relation to a supply in accordance with regulation 61(3) or (6) or 64(2), he shall be treated for the purposes of section 36(1)(*a*) of the Act as having accounted for and paid VAT on the supply in the prescribed accounting period in which he ceased to operate the scheme.][1]
Commentary—*De Voil Indirect Tax Service* **V3.503, V5.103**.
HMRC Manuals—VAT Cash Accounting Scheme Manual VCAS6300 (cash accounting scheme: claiming bad debt relief).
Amendments—[1] This regulation inserted by the VAT (Amendment) Regulations, SI 2004/767 regs 3, 10 with effect from 1 April 2004.

65 Accounting
(1) Except in the circumstances set out in regulations 61 to 63, VAT shall be accounted for and paid to the Commissioners by the due date prescribed for the accounting period in which payment or other consideration for the supply is received.
(2) Input tax may be credited either in the prescribed accounting period in which payment or consideration for a supply is given, or in such later period as may be agreed with the Commissioners.

(3) A person operating the scheme shall obtain and keep for a period of 6 years, or such lesser period as the Commissioners may allow, a receipted and dated VAT invoice from any taxable person to whom he has made a payment in money in respect of a taxable supply, and in such circumstances a taxable person must on request provide such a receipted and dated VAT invoice.
(4) A person operating the scheme shall keep for a period of 6 years, or such lesser period as the Commissioners may allow, a copy of any receipt which he gives under paragraph (3) above.
Commentary—*De Voil Indirect Tax Service* **V3.418, V5.202.**
HMRC Manuals—VAT Cash Accounting Scheme Manual VCAS5050 (cash accounting scheme: receipted VAT invoices).

PART IX
SUPPLIES BY RETAILERS

66 Interpretation of Part IX
In this Part—
["flat-rate trader" has the meaning given in regulation 55A;][1]
"notice" means any notice or leaflet published by the Commissioners pursuant to this Part;
"scheme" means a method as referred to in regulation 67.
Amendments—[1] Definition of "flat-rate trader" inserted by the VAT (Amendment) (No 2) Regulations, SI 2002/1142 regs 1, 9(a) with effect from 25 April 2002.

67 Retail schemes
(1) The Commissioners may permit the value which is to be taken as the value, in any prescribed accounting period or part thereof, of supplies by a retailer which are taxable at other than the zero rate to be determined by a method agreed with that retailer or by any method described in a notice published by the Commissioners for that purpose; and they may publish any notice accordingly.
(2) The Commissioners may vary the terms of any method by—
   (a) publishing a fresh notice,
   (b) publishing a notice which amends an existing notice, or
   (c) adapting any method by agreement with any retailer.
Commentary—*De Voil Indirect Tax Service* **V3.551, V3.552.**
HMRC Manuals—VAT Retail Schemes Guidance VRS1150 (introduction: the law governing retail schemes).

68
The Commissioners may refuse to permit the value of taxable supplies to be determined in accordance with a scheme if it appears to them—
   (a) that the use of any particular scheme does not produce a fair and reasonable valuation during any period,
   (b) that it is necessary to do so for the protection of the revenue, or
   (c) that the retailer could reasonably be expected to account for VAT in accordance with regulations made under paragraph 2(1) of Schedule 11 to the Act.
HMRC Manuals—VAT Retail Schemes Guidance VRS2355 (the power to refuse use of a retail scheme: general).

69
No retailer may at any time use more than one scheme except as provided for in any notice or as the Commissioners may otherwise allow.
HMRC Manuals—VAT Retail Schemes Guidance VRS3300 (issue of best judgement assessments to businesses operating retail schemes).

[69A
No retailer may use a scheme at any time for which he is a flat-rate trader.][1]
Amendments—[1] Regulation inserted by the VAT (Amendment) (No 2) Regulations, SI 2002/1142 regs 1, 9(b) with effect from 25 April 2002.

71[Changing schemes
(1)][1] Save as the Commissioners may otherwise allow, a retailer who accounts for VAT on the basis of taxable supplies valued in accordance with any scheme shall, so long as he remains a taxable person, continue to do so for a period of not less than one year from the adoption of that scheme by him, and any change by a retailer from one scheme to another shall be made at the end of any complete year reckoned from the beginning of the prescribed accounting period in which he first adopted the scheme.
[(2) Paragraph (1) shall not apply where a retailer ceases to operate a scheme solely because he becomes a flat-rate trader.][1]
Commentary—*De Voil Indirect Tax Service* **V3.563.**
HMRC Manuals—VAT Retail Schemes Guidance VRS3400 (changing retail schemes prospectively).
Amendments—[1] Para (1) numbered as such, and para (2) added, by the VAT (Amendment) (No 2) Regulations, SI 2002/1142 regs 1, 9(c) with effect from 25 April 2002.

72 Ceasing to use a scheme
(1) A retailer shall notify the Commissioners before ceasing to account for VAT on the basis of taxable supplies valued in accordance with these regulations.

(2) A retailer may be required to pay VAT on such proportion as the Commissioners may consider fair and reasonable of any sums due to him at the end of the prescribed accounting period in which he last used a scheme.
Commentary—*De Voil Indirect Tax Service* **V3.563**.
HMRC Manuals—VAT Retail Schemes Guidance VRS3500 (ceasing use of a retail scheme).

75 Change in VAT
Where pursuant to any enactment there is a change in the VAT charged on any supply, including a change to or from no VAT being charged on such supply, a retailer using any scheme shall take such steps relating to that scheme as are directed in any notice applicable to him or as may be agreed between him and the Commissioners.

PART XI
TIME OF SUPPLY AND TIME OF ACQUISITION

81 Goods for private use and free supplies of services
(1) Where the services referred to in paragraph 5(4) of Schedule 4 to the Act are supplied for any period, they shall be treated as being supplied on the last day of the supplier's prescribed accounting period, or of each such accounting period, in which the goods are made available or used.
(2) Where services specified in an order made by the Treasury under section 5(4) of the Act are supplied for any period, they shall be treated as being supplied on the last day of the supplier's prescribed accounting period, or of each such accounting period, in which the services are performed.
Commentary—*De Voil Indirect Tax Service* **V3.212**.
HMRC Manuals—VAT Time of Supply VATTOS2315 (legislation: regulation 81 goods for private use and free supply of services).

[82 Services from outside the United Kingdom
(1) This paragraph applies to services which are treated as being made by a person under section 8(1) of the Act which are not services to which paragraph (3) below applies.
(2) Subject to paragraphs (5) and (7) below, the services to which paragraph (1) above applies shall be treated as being made when they are performed.
(3) This paragraph applies to services which are treated as being made by a person under section 8(1) of the Act and which are supplied for a period for a consideration the whole or part of which is determined or payable periodically or from time to time.
(4) Subject to paragraphs (5), (6) and (7) below, services to which paragraph (3) above applies shall be treated as separately and successively made at the end of the periods in respect of which payments are made or invoices issued and to the extent covered by the relevant payment or invoice.
(5) Where—
    (*a*) in the case of a supply of services to which paragraph (1) above applies, a payment is made in respect of the supply before the time applicable under paragraph (2) above, or
    (*b*) in the case of services to which paragraph (3) above applies, either—
        (i) a payment is made at a time that is earlier than the end of the period to which it relates, or
        (ii) a payment is made which is not made in respect of any identified period, or
    (*c*) a payment is made in respect of services—
        (i) which are performed on or before 31stDecember 2009, or
        (ii) in respect of which a period as described in paragraph (4) above has ended on or before that date, or
        (iii) which the recipient has received the benefit of on or before that date,
the services shall be treated as being made at the time the payment is made.
(6) Where the supply of services to which paragraph (3) above applies—
    (*a*) commences before 1st January and continues after 31st December of any year, and
    (*b*) during that year no invoice is issued that has effect for the purposes of paragraph (4) above, and
    (*c*) no payment is made in respect of that supply,
the services supplied during that year shall be treated as being supplied on the 31st December of that year to the extent that the recipient has received the benefit of them.
(7) Services for which the consideration is not in money and which have been supplied during a period which—
    (*a*) commences on the day following the last day of the last complete prescribed accounting period in 2009 which is applicable to the recipient of the services, and
    (*b*) ends on 31st December 2009,
shall be treated as being supplied on 31st December 2009.][1]
Commentary—*De Voil Indirect Tax Service* **V3.231, V3.267**.
HMRC Manuals—VAT Time of Supply VATTOS2320 (legislation: regulation 82 services from outside the UK).

Amendments—[1]   Reg 82 substituted by the VAT (Amendment) (No 5) Regs, SI 2009/3241, regs 2, 10 with effect from 1 January 2010.

82A [Goods supplied by persons outside the United Kingdom

Goods which are treated as supplied by a person under section 9A of the Act shall be treated as being supplied when the goods are paid for or, if the consideration is not in money, on the last day of the prescribed accounting period in which the goods are removed or made available.][1]

Commentary—De Voil Indirect Tax Service V3.232.
HMRC Manuals—VAT Time of Supply VATTOS2325 (legislation: regulation 82A goods supplied by persons outside the UK).
Amendments—[1]   Regulation 82A inserted by the VAT (Amendment) (No 4) Regulations, SI 2004/3140 reg 4 with effect from 1 January 2005 in relation to supplies made on or after that date: SI 2004/3140 reg 2(1).

83 Time of acquisition

Where the time that goods are acquired from another member State falls to be determined in accordance with section 12(1)(b) of the Act by reference to the day of the issue, in respect of the transaction in pursuance of which the goods are acquired, of an invoice of such description as the Commissioners may by regulations prescribe, the invoice shall be one which is issued by the supplier [or the customer and which, in either case, is issued under the provisions of the law of the member State where the goods were supplied, corresponding in relation to that member State to the provisions of regulations 13, 13A and 14.][1]

Commentary—De Voil Indirect Tax Service V3.388.
Amendments—[1]   Words substituted by the VAT (Amendment) (No 6) Regulations, SI 2003/3220 regs 1(1)(b), 2, 12 with effect from 1 January 2004.

84 Supplies of land—special cases

(1) Where by or under any enactment an interest in, or right over, land is compulsorily purchased and, at the time determined in accordance with section 6(2) or (3) of the Act, the person (the grantor) from whom it is purchased does not know the amount of payment that he is to receive in respect of the purchase then goods or, as the case may require, services shall be treated as supplied each time the grantor receives any payment for the purchase.

(2) [[Subject to paragraphs (3) to (5)][2] below,][1] where a person (the grantor) grants or assigns the fee simple in any land, and at the time of the grant or assignment, the total consideration for it is not determinable, then goods shall be treated as separately and successively supplied at the following times—
  (a) the time determined in accordance with section 6(2), (4), (5), (6) . . .[4] or (10) of the Act, as the case may require, and
  (b) the earlier of the following times—
    (i) each time that any part of the consideration which was not determinable at the time mentioned in sub-paragraph (a) above is received by the grantor, or
    (ii) each time that the grantor issues a VAT invoice in respect of such a part.

[(3) Paragraph (2) above shall not apply in relation to a grant or assignment falling within item 1(a) of Group 1 of Schedule 9 to the Act where any of the persons specified in paragraph (4) below intend or expect to occupy the land on a date before a date ten years after completion of the building or civil engineering work on the land, without being in occupation of it [wholly, or substantially wholly,][5] for eligible purposes.][3]

[(4) The persons referred to in paragraph (3) above are—
  (a) the grantor;
  (b) any person who, with the intention or in the expectation that occupation of the land on a date before a date ten years after completion of the building or civil engineering work would not be [wholly, or substantially wholly,][5] for eligible purposes—
    (i) provides finance for the grantor's development of the land, or
    (ii) has entered into any agreement arrangement or understanding (whether or not legally enforceable) to provide finance for the grantor's development of the land;
  (c) any person who is connected with any person of a description within sub-paragraph (a) or (b) above.][3]

[(5) For the purposes of this regulation—
  (a) Note (2) to Group 1 of Schedule 9 to the Act shall apply in determining when a building or civil engineering work is completed;
  [(b) paragraph 16 of Schedule 10 to the Act shall have effect for determining the meaning of "eligible purposes" and "occupation";
  (ba) whether a person's occupation is "wholly, or substantially wholly," for eligible purposes shall be determined in the same way as it is for the purposes of paragraph 15 of that Schedule;][5]
  (c) "the grantor's development of the land" means any acquisition by the grantor of an interest in the land, building or civil engineering work and includes the construction of the building or civil engineering work;

(d) "providing finance" has the same meaning as in [paragraph 14(3) of Schedule 10][5] to the Act, subject to any appropriate modifications, but does not include paying the consideration for the grantor's grant or assignment within paragraph (3) above;
(e) any question whether one person is connected with another shall be determined in accordance with section 839 [of the Taxes Act; but this is subject to sub-paragraph (f);
(f) a company is not connected with another company only because both are under the control of—
  (i) the Crown,
  (ii) a Minister of the Crown,
  (iii) a government department, or
  (iv) a Northern Ireland department;
(g) "company" and "control" have the same meaning as in section 839 of the Taxes Act.][6][3]

Commentary—*De Voil Indirect Tax Service* **V3.140A**.
HMRC Manuals—VAT Time of Supply VATTOS2330 (legislation: regulation 84 supplies of land (special cases)).
Former regulations—VAT (General) Regulations, SI 1985/886 reg 18B; VAT (General) (Amendment) Regulations, SI 1992/3102 reg 12.
Amendments—[1] Words in para (2) inserted, and paras (3)–(9) inserted, by the VAT (Amendment) (No 3) Regulations, SI 2002/2918 with effect from 28 November 2002 in relation to grants or assignments made after 27 November 2002.
[2] Words in para (2) substituted by the VAT (Amendment) (No 2) Regulations, SI 2003/1069 regs 1(3), 2, 8 in relation to grants or assignments made after 9 April 2003.
[3] Paras (3)–(5) substituted for paras (3)–(9) by the VAT (Amendment) (No 2) Regulations, SI 2003/1069 regs 1(3), 2, 9 in relation to grants or assignments made after 9 April 2003.
[4] Reference revoked by the VAT (Amendment) (No 6) Regulations, SI 2003/3220 regs 1(1)(b), 2, 13 with effect from 1 January 2004.
[5] Words in paras (3), (4)(b) substituted, in para (5) sub-paras (b), (ba) substituted for previous sub-para (b), and words in para (5)(d) substituted, by the Value Added Tax (Buildings and Land) Order, SI 2008/1146, art 6, Sch 1 paras 16, 17 with effect in relation to supplies made on or after 1 June 2008, subject to savings in Sch 2 of the Order.
[6] Words in para (5)(e) substituted for words "of the Income and Corporation Taxes Act 1988." by the Value Added Tax (Amendment) (No 3) Regulations, SI 2009/1967 regs 2, 3 with effect from 15 August 2009.

85 Leases treated as supplies of goods
(1) Subject to paragraph (2) below, where the grant of a tenancy or lease is a supply of goods by virtue of paragraph 4 of Schedule 4 to the Act, and the whole or part of the consideration for that grant is payable periodically or from time to time, goods shall be treated as separately and successively supplied at the earlier of the following times—
  (a) each time that a part of the consideration is received by the supplier, or
  (b) each time that the supplier issues a VAT invoice relating to the grant.
(2) Where in respect of the grant of a tenancy or lease such as is mentioned in paragraph (1) above the supplier, at or about the beginning of any period not exceeding one year, issues a VAT invoice containing, in addition to the particulars specified in regulation 14, the following particulars—
  (a) the dates on which any parts of the consideration are to become due for payment in the period,
  (b) the amount payable (excluding VAT) on each such date, and
  (c) the rate of VAT in force at the time of the issue of the VAT invoice and the amount of VAT chargeable in accordance with that rate on each of such payments,
goods shall be treated as separately and successively supplied each time that a payment in respect of the tenancy or lease becomes due or is received by the supplier, whichever is the earlier.
(3) Where, on or before any of the dates that a payment is due as stated on an invoice issued as described in paragraph (2) above, there is a change in the VAT chargeable on supplies of the description to which the invoice relates, that invoice shall cease to be treated as a VAT invoice in respect of any such supplies for which payments are due after the change (and not received before the change).

Commentary—*De Voil Indirect Tax Service* **V3.140A**.
HMRC Manuals—VAT Time of Supply VATTOS2335 (legislation: regulation 85 leases treated as supplies of goods).

86 Supplies of water, gas or any form of power, heat, refrigeration [or other cooling,]or ventilation
(1) Except in relation to a supply to which subsections (7) and (8) of section 6 of the Act apply, and subject to paragraphs (2) and (3) below, a supply of—
  (a) water other than—
    (i) distilled water, deionised water and water of similar purity, and
    (ii) water comprised in any of the excepted items set out in Group 1 of Schedule 8 to the Act, or
  (b) coal gas, water gas, producer gases or similar gases, or
  (c) petroleum gases, or other gaseous hydrocarbons, in a gaseous state, or
  (d) any form of power, heat, refrigeration [or other cooling,][1] or ventilation,

shall be treated as taking place each time that a payment in respect of the supply is received by the supplier, or a VAT invoice relating to the supply is issued by the supplier, whichever is the earlier.
(2) Subject to paragraph (3) below, where the whole or part of the consideration for a supply such as is described in paragraph (1)(*a*), (*b*) or (*c*) above or of power in the form of electricity is determined or payable periodically or from time to time, goods shall be treated as separately and successively supplied at the earlier of the following times—
   (*a*) each time that a part of the consideration is received by the supplier, or
   (*b*) each time that the supplier issues a VAT invoice relating to the supply.
(3) Where separate and successive supplies as described in paragraph (2) above are made under an agreement which provides for successive payments, and the supplier at or about the beginning of any period not exceeding one year, issues a VAT invoice containing, in addition to the particulars specified in regulation 14, the following particulars—
   (*a*) the dates on which payments under the agreement are to become due in the period,
   (*b*) the amount payable (excluding VAT) on each such date, and
   (*c*) the rate of VAT in force at the time of issue of the VAT invoice and the amount of VAT chargeable in accordance with that rate on each of such payments,
goods shall be treated as separately and successively supplied each time that payment in respect of the supply becomes due or is received by the supplier, whichever is the earlier.
(4) Where, on or before any of the dates that a payment is due as stated on an invoice issued as described in paragraph (3) above, there is a change in the VAT chargeable on supplies of the description to which the invoice relates, that invoice shall cease to be treated as a VAT invoice in respect of any such supplies for which payments are due after the change (and not received before the change).
(5) A supply mentioned in paragraph (1)(a), (b), (c) or (d) above to which subsections (7) and (8) of section 6 of the Act apply shall be treated as taking place on the day of the issue of a VAT invoice in respect of the supply.[2]

Commentary—*De Voil Indirect Tax Service* **V3.137, V3.140B**.
HMRC Manuals—VAT Time of Supply VATTOS2340 (legislation: regulation 86 supplies of water, gas or any form of power, heat, refrigeration or other cooling, or ventilation).
Amendments—[1]   Words in heading and in para (1)(*d*) inserted by the VAT (Amendment) (No 4) Regulations, SI 2010/3022 regs 2, 3 with effect in relation to supplies made on or after 1 January 2011.
[2]   Para (5) revoked by the VAT (Amendment) (No 3) Regulations, SI 2012/2951 reg 2(1), (7) with effect from 1 January 2013.

87 Acquisitions of water, gas or any form of power, heat, refrigeration [or other cooling] or ventilation

Where goods described in regulation 86(1)(*a*), (*b*), (*c*) or (*d*) are acquired from another member State and the whole or part of any consideration comprised in the transaction in pursuance of which the goods are acquired is payable periodically, or from time to time, goods shall be treated as separately and successively acquired on each occasion that [an invoice such as is described in regulation 83 is issued.][1], [2]

Amendments—[1]   Words substituted by the VAT (Amendment) (No 6) Regulations, SI 2003/3220 regs 1(1)(*b*), 2, 14 with effect from 1 January 2004.
[2]   Regulation 87 revoked by the VAT (Amendment) (No 3) Regulations, SI 2012/2951 reg 2(1), (8) with effect from 1 January 2013.

Words in heading inserted by the VAT (Amendment) (No 4) Regulations, SI 2010/3022 regs 2, 4 with effect in relation to supplies made on or after 1 January 2011.

88 Supplier's goods in possession of buyer

(1) Except in relation to a supply mentioned in section 6(2)(*c*) of the Act, or to a supply to which subsections (7) and (8) of section 6 of the Act apply, where goods are supplied under an agreement whereby the supplier retains the property therein until the goods or part of them are appropriated under the agreement by the buyer and in circumstances where the whole or part of the consideration is determined at that time, a supply of any of the goods shall be treated as taking place at the earliest of the following dates—
   (*a*) the date of appropriation by the buyer,
   (*b*) the date when a VAT invoice is issued by the supplier, or
   (*c*) the date when a payment is received by the supplier.
(2) If, within 14 days after appropriation of the goods or part of them by the buyer as mentioned in paragraph (1) above, the supplier issues a VAT invoice in respect of goods appropriated [or a self-billed invoice fulfilling the conditions in regulation 13(3A) is issued by the customer][1], the provisions of section 6(5) of the Act shall apply to that supply.

Commentary—*De Voil Indirect Tax Service* **V3.140B**.
HMRC Manuals—VAT Time of Supply VATTOS2345 (legislation: regulation 88 supplier's goods in possession of buyer).
Amendments—[1]   Words inserted by the VAT (Amendment) (No 6) Regulations, SI 2003/3220 regs 1(1)(*b*), 2, 15 with effect from 1 January 2004.

89 Retention payments

Where any contract [other than one of a description falling within regulation 93 below][1] for the supply of goods (other than for a supply to which subsections (7) and (8) of section 6 of the Act apply) or for the supply of services provides for the retention of any part of the consideration by a person pending full and satisfactory performance of the contract, or any part of it, by the supplier, goods or services (as the case may require) shall be treated as separately and successively supplied at the following times—
- (a) the time determined in accordance with section 6(2), (3), (4), (5), (6), . . . [2] (10) or (13) of the Act, as the case may require, and
- (b) the earlier of the following times—
  - (i) the time that a payment in respect of any part of the consideration which has been retained, pursuant to the terms of the contract, is received by the supplier, or
  - (ii) the time that the supplier issues a VAT invoice relating to any such part.

Commentary—*De Voil Indirect Tax Service* **V3.140B, V3.140C**.
HMRC Manuals—VAT Time of Supply VATTOS2350 (legislation: regulation 89 retention payments).
Amendments—[1] Words inserted by the VAT (Amendment) (No 5) Regulations, SI 1997/2887 with effect from 1 January 1998.
[2] Reference revoked by the VAT (Amendment) (No 6) Regulations, SI 2003/3220 regs 1(1)(b), 2, 16 with effect from 1 January 2004.

90 Continuous supplies of services

(1) Subject to paragraph (2) below, where services[, except those to which regulation 93 applies,][2] are supplied for a period for a consideration the whole or part of which is determined or payable periodically or from time to time, they shall be treated as separately and successively supplied at the earlier of the following times—
- (a) each time that a payment in respect of the supplies is received by the supplier, or
- (b) each time that the supplier issues a VAT invoice relating to the supplies.

(2) Where separate and successive supplies of services as described in paragraph (1) above are made under an agreement which provides for successive payments, and the supplier at or about the beginning of any period not exceeding one year, issues a VAT invoice containing, in addition to the particulars specified in regulation 14, the following particulars—
- (a) the dates on which payments under the agreement are to become due in the period,
- (b) the amount payable (excluding VAT) on each such date, and
- (c) the rate of VAT in force at the time of issue of the VAT invoice and the amount of VAT chargeable in accordance with that rate on each of such payments,

services shall be treated as separately and successively supplied each time that a payment in respect of them becomes due or is received by the supplier, whichever is the earlier.

(3) Where, on or before any of the dates that a payment is due as stated on an invoice issued as described in paragraph (2) above, there is a change in the VAT chargeable on supplies of the description to which the invoice relates, that invoice shall cease to be treated as a VAT invoice in respect of any such supplies for which payments are due after the change (and not received before the change).

[(4) This regulation shall not apply to any relevant services—
- (a) where the period to which a payment falling within paragraph (1), (2) or (3) above relates, ends before 1st July 1997; or
- (b) which are treated as supplied on 1st July 1997 by virtue of regulation 90A below.][1]

[(5) In this regulation and in regulations 90A and 90B below, "relevant services" means services within the description contained in paragraph 7A of Schedule 5 to the Act (c) which are treated as supplied in the United Kingdom by virtue of [article 18][3] of the Value Added Tax (Place of Supply of Services) Order 1992.][1]

Commentary—*De Voil Indirect Tax Service* **V3.140C**.
HMRC Manuals—VAT Time of Supply VATTOS2355 (legislation: regulations 90, 90A and 90B continuous supplies of services).
Amendments—[1] Paras (4) and (5) inserted by the VAT (Amendment) (No 2) Regulations, SI 1997/1525 with effect from 1 July 1997.
[2] Words inserted by the VAT (Amendment) (No 5) Regulations, SI 1997/2887 with effect from 1 January 1998.
[3] Words amended by the VAT (Amendment) (No 2) Regulations, SI 1998/765 with effect from 18 March 1998.

[90A Where—
- (a) relevant services are supplied for a period for a consideration the whole or part of which is determined or payable periodically or from time to time;
- (b) the period covered by the payment referred to in sub-paragraph (c) below ends on or after 1st July 1997; and
- (c) a payment in respect of the services was made before 1st July 1997,

the services shall be treated as supplied on 1st July 1997.][1]

HMRC Manuals—VAT Time of Supply VATTOS2355 (legislation: regulations 90, 90A and 90B continuous supplies of services).

Amendments—[1] This regulation inserted by the VAT (Amendment) (No 2) Regulations, SI 1997/1525 with effect from 1 July 1997.

[**90B** Where relevant services are treated as supplied on or after 1st July 1997 by virtue of regulation 90 or 90A above, the supply shall be treated as taking place only to the extent covered by the lower of—
  (a) the payment; and
  (b) so much of the payment as is properly attributable to such part of the period covered by the payment as falls after 30th June 1997.][1]

HMRC Manuals—VAT Time of Supply VATTOS2355 (legislation: regulations 90, 90A and 90B continuous supplies of services).
Amendments—[1] This regulation inserted by the VAT (Amendment) (No 2) Regulations, SI 1997/1525 with effect from 1 July 1997.

91 Royalties and similar payments

Where the whole amount of the consideration for a supply of services was not ascertainable at the time when the services were performed and subsequently the use of the benefit of those services by a person other than the supplier gives rise to any payment of consideration for that supply which is—
  (a) in whole or in part determined or payable periodically or from time to time or at the end of any period,
  (b) additional to the amount, if any, already payable for the supply, and
  (c) not a payment to which regulation 90 applies,
a further supply shall be treated as taking place each time that a payment in respect of the use of the benefit of those services is received by the supplier or a VAT invoice is issued by the supplier, whichever is the earlier.

Commentary—*De Voil Indirect Tax Service* **V3.140C**.
HMRC Manuals—VAT Time of Supply VATTOS2360 (legislation: regulation 91 royalties and similar payments).

92 Supplies of services by barristers and advocates

Services supplied by a barrister, or in Scotland, by an advocate, acting in that capacity, shall be treated as taking place at whichever is the earliest of the following times—
  (a) when the fee in respect of those services is received by the barrister or advocate,
  (b) when the barrister or advocate issues a VAT invoice in respect of them, or
  (c) the day when the barrister or advocate ceases to practise as such.

Commentary—*De Voil Indirect Tax Service* **V3.140C, V3.503**.
HMRC Manuals—VAT Time of Supply VATTOS2365 (legislation: regulation 92 supplies of services by barristers and advocates).

[93 Supplies in the construction industry

(1) Where services, or services together with goods, are supplied in the course of the construction, alteration, demolition, repair or maintenance of a building or any civil engineering work under a contract which provides for payment for such supplies to be made periodically or from time to time, those services or goods and services shall be treated as separately and successively supplied at the earliest of the following times—
  (a) each time that a payment is received by the supplier,
  (b) each time that the supplier issues a VAT invoice, or
  (c) where the services are services to which paragraph (2) below applies, to the extent that they have not already been treated as supplied by virtue of sub-paragraphs (a) and (b) above—
    (i) if the services were performed on or after 9th December 1997 and before 9th June 1999, the day which falls eighteen months after the date on which those services were performed, or
    (ii) if the services are performed on or after 9th June 1999, the day on which the services are performed.

(2) This paragraph applies if, at the time the services were, or as the case may require, are performed—
  (a) it was, or as the case may require, is the intention or expectation of—
    (i) the supplier, or
    (ii) a person responsible for financing the supplier's cost of supplying the services or services together with goods,
    that relevant land would, or as the case may require, will become (whether immediately or eventually) exempt land or, as the case may be, continue (for a period at least) to be such land, or
  (b) the supplier had, or as the case may require, has received (and used in making his supply) any supply of services or of services together with goods the time of supply of which—
    (i) was, or
    (ii) but for the issue by the supplier of those services or services together with goods of a VAT invoice (other than one which has been paid in full), would have been,

determined by virtue of paragraph (1)(c) above.
(3) For the purposes of this regulation "relevant land" is land on which the building or civil engineering work to which the construction services relate is, or as the case may be, was situated.
(4) In this regulation references to a person's being responsible for financing the supplier's cost of supplying the services or goods and services are references to his being a person who, with the intention or in the expectation that relevant land will become, or continue (for a period at least) to be, exempt land—
    (*a*) has provided finance for the supplier's cost of supplying the services or services together with goods, or
    (*b*) has entered into any agreement, arrangement or understanding (whether or not legally enforceable) to provide finance for the supplier's cost of supplying the services or services together with goods.
(5) In this regulation references to providing finance for the supplier's cost of supplying services or services together with goods are references to doing any one or more of the following, that is to say—
    (*a*) directly or indirectly providing funds for meeting the whole or any part of the supplier's cost of supplying the services or services together with goods,
    (*b*) directly or indirectly procuring the provision of such funds by another,
    (*c*) directly or indirectly providing funds for discharging, in whole or in part any liability that has been or may be incurred by any person for or in connection with the raising of funds to meet the supplier's cost of supplying the services or services together with goods,
    (*d*) directly or indirectly procuring that any such liability is or will be discharged, in whole or in part, by another.
(6) The references in paragraph (5) above to the provision of funds for a purpose referred to in that paragraph include references to—
    (*a*) the making of a loan of funds that are or are to be used for that purpose,
    (*b*) the provision of any guarantee or other security in relation to such a loan,
    (*c*) the provision of any of the consideration for the issue of any shares or other securities issued wholly or partly for raising those funds, or
    (*d*) any other transfer of assets or value as a consequence of which any of those funds are made available for that purpose,

but do not include references to funds made available to the supplier by paying to him the whole or any part of the consideration payable for the supply of the services or services together with goods.

(7) In this regulation references to the supplier's cost of supplying the services or services together with goods are to—
    (*a*) amounts payable by the supplier for supplies to him of services or of goods used or to be used by him in making the supply of services or of services together with goods, and
    (*b*) the supplier's staff and other internal costs of making the supply of services or of services together with goods.
(8) For the purposes of this regulation relevant land is exempt land if—
    (*a*) the supplier,
    (*b*) a person responsible for financing the supplier's cost of supplying the services or goods and services, or
    (*c*) a person connected with the supplier or with a person responsible for financing the supplier's cost of supplying the services or goods and services,

is in occupation of the land without being in occupation of it wholly or mainly for eligible purposes.

(9) For the purposes of this regulation, but subject to paragraphs (11) and (13) below, a person's occupation at any time of any land is not capable of being occupation for eligible purposes unless he is a taxable person at that time.
(10) Subject to paragraphs (11) and (13) below, a taxable person in occupation of any land shall be taken for the purposes of this regulation to be in occupation of that land for eligible purposes to the extent only that his occupation of that land is for the purpose of making supplies which—
    (*a*) are or are to be made in the course or furtherance of a business carried on by him, and
    (*b*) are supplies of such a description that any input tax of his which was wholly attributable to those supplies would be input tax for which he would be entitled to credit.
(11) For the purposes of this regulation—
    (*a*) occupation of land by a body to which section 33 of the Act applies is occupation of the land for eligible purposes to the extent that the body occupies the land for purposes other than those of a business carried on by that body, and
    (*b*) any occupation of land by a government department (within the meaning of section 41 of the Act) is occupation of the land for eligible purposes.
(12) For the purposes of this regulation, where land of which a person is in occupation—
    (*a*) is being held by that person in order to be put to use by him for particular purposes, and

(b) is not land of which he is in occupation for any other purpose,

that person shall be deemed, for so long as the conditions in sub-paragraphs (a) and (b) above are satisfied, to be in occupation of the land for the purposes for which he proposes to use it.

(13) Paragraphs (9) to (12) above shall have effect where land is in the occupation of a person who—
   (a) is not a taxable person, but
   (b) is a person whose supplies are treated for the purposes of the Act as supplies made by another person who is a taxable person,

as if the person in occupation of the land and that other person were a single taxable person.

(14) For the purposes of this regulation a person shall be taken to be in occupation of any land whether he occupies it alone or together with one or more other persons and whether he occupies all of that land or only part of it.

(15) For the purposes of this regulation, any question as to whether one person is connected with another shall be determined in accordance with section 839 of the Taxes Act[; but this is subject to paragraph (16)]².

[(16) For the purposes of this regulation—
   (a) a company is not connected with another company only because both are under the control of—
      (i) the Crown,
      (ii) a Minister of the Crown,
      (iii) a government department, or
      (iv) a Northern Ireland department; and
   (b) "company" and "control" have the same meaning as in section 839 of the Taxes Act]².]¹

Commentary—*De Voil Indirect Tax Service* **V3.140, V3.140D**.
HMRC Manuals—VAT Time of Supply VATTOS2370 (legislation: regulation 93 supplies in the construction industry).
Amendments—¹ Para substituted by the VAT (Amendment) (No 3) Regulations, SI 1999/1374 with effect from 9 June 1999.
² Words in para (15), and whole of para (16), inserted, by the Value Added Tax (Amendment) (No 3) Regulations, SI 2009/1967 regs 2, 4, 5 with effect from 15 August 2009.

94 General

[Subject to regulation 90B above, where under this Part]¹ of these Regulations a supply is treated as taking place each time that a payment (however expressed) is received or an invoice is issued, the supply is to be treated as taking place only to the extent covered by the payment or invoice.

HMRC Manuals—VAT Time of Supply VATTOS2380 time of supply: legislation UK secondary law: regulation 94A general).
Amendments—¹ Words substituted for the words "Where under this Part" by the VAT (Amendment) (No 2) Regulations, SI 1997/1525 with effect from 1 July 1997.

[94A In this Part a reference to receipt of payment (however expressed) includes a reference to receipt by a person to whom a right to receive it has been assigned.]¹

Commentary—*De Voil Indirect Tax Service* **V3.133, V3.140E**.
HMRC Manuals—VAT Time of Supply VATTOS2380 time of supply: legislation UK secondary law: regulation 94A general).
Amendments—¹ This regulation inserted by the VAT (Amendment) (No 2) Regulations, SI 1999/599 reg 3, and shall have effect in respect of payments received on or after 10 March 1999.

[94B—(1) This regulation applies in relation to the following supplies where they are provided in the circumstances referred to in paragraph (2) below—
   (a) supplies falling within regulation 85 above (leases treated as supplies of goods) other than any supply which is exempt by virtue of Group 1 of Schedule 9 to the Act or would be exempt but for the operation of [Part 1 of Schedule 10]² to the Act;
   (b) supplies falling within regulation 86(1) to (4) above (supplies of water, gas or any form of power, heat, refrigeration or ventilation);
   (c) supplies falling within regulation 90 above (continuous supplies of services) other than any supply which is exempt by virtue of Group 1 of Schedule 9 to the Act or would be exempt but for the operation of [Part 1 of Schedule 10]² to the Act.

(2) The circumstances referred to in paragraph (1) above are—
   (a) that the person making the supply and the person to whom it is made are connected with each other, or
   (b) one of those persons is an undertaking in relation to which the other is a group undertaking (except where both undertakings are treated under sections 43A to 43C of the Act as members of the same group), and
   (c) the supply is subject to the rates of VAT prescribed in section 2 or section 29A of the Act.

(3) But this regulation does not apply where a person can show that a person to whom he has made a supply of a description falling within paragraph (1) above is entitled under sections 25 and 26 of the Act to credit for all of the VAT on that supply.

[(4) For the purposes of paragraph (2)—
   (a) any question whether one person is connected with another shall be determined in accordance with section 839 of the Taxes Act;

(b) a company is not connected with another company only because both are under the control of—
  (i) the Crown,
  (ii) a Minister of the Crown,
  (iii) a government department, or
  (iv) a Northern Ireland department;
(c) "company" and "control" have the same meaning as in section 839 of the Taxes Act; and
(d) "undertaking" and "group undertaking" have the same meaning as in section 1161 of the Companies Act 2006.]³

(5) Where this regulation applies, goods or services shall, to the extent that they have not already been treated as supplied by virtue of the regulations specified in paragraph (1) above (or any provision of the Act or other regulations made under the Act), and to the extent that they have been provided, be treated as separately and successively supplied—
  (a) in the case of supplies the provision of which commenced on or before 1st October 2003, at the end of the period of twelve months after that date;
  (b) in the case of supplies the provision of which commenced after 1st October 2003, at the end of the period of twelve months after the supplies commenced; or
  (c) where the Commissioners are satisfied that each category of supply has been adequately identified, on such other period end date nominated for each category and falling within the period specified in sub-paragraph (5)(a) or (b) above as may be notified by the taxable person to the Commissioners in writing,
and thereafter at the end of each subsequent period of twelve months.

(6) But where the person making the supply, within the period of six months after the time applicable under paragraph (5) above either—
  (a) issues a VAT invoice in respect of it, or
  (b) receives a payment in respect of it,
the supply shall, to the extent that it has not been treated as taking place at some other time by virtue of the regulations specified in paragraph (1) above (or any provision of the Act or other regulations made under the Act), be treated as taking place at the time the invoice is issued or the payment is received, unless the person making the supply has notified the Commissioners in writing that he elects not to avail himself of this paragraph.

(7) The Commissioners may, at the request of a taxable person, allow paragraph (6) above to apply in relation to supplies made by him (or such supplies as may be specified) as if for the period of six months there were substituted such other period as may be prescribed by them.

(8) A taxable person may after the start of any period to be established under paragraph (5) above—
  (a) in relation to some or all of his supplies, and
  (b) where the Commissioners give their approval,
select an alternative period end date falling before the end of that period (which end date but for this paragraph would be established under paragraph (5) above), from which date subsequent periods of twelve months will end.

(9) A date selected and approved under paragraph (8) above shall be the date which establishes the end of the taxable person's current period.

(10) For the purposes of paragraph (8) above, a reference to a period end established under paragraph (5) above includes a reference to a period end established by an earlier application of paragraph (8) above.

(11) Where the supply is one of the leasing of assets, and that leasing depends on one or more other leases of those assets (the superior lease or leases), then the reference in paragraph (2) above to the person making the supply includes a reference to any lessor of a superior lease.

(12) For the purposes of paragraph (11) above, a reference to the leasing of assets includes a reference to any letting, hiring or rental of assets however described, and "lessor" shall be construed accordingly.

(13) For the purposes of this regulation, goods or services are provided at the time when and to the extent that, the recipient receives the benefit of them.

(14) Where this regulation applies, the regulations specified in paragraph (1) above shall not apply to the extent that supplies have been treated as having taken place under this regulation.]¹

Commentary—*De Voil Indirect Tax Service* **V3.140A, V3.140B, V3.140C.**
HMRC Manuals—VAT Time of Supply VATTOS2385 (legislation: regulation 94B further rules for certain on-going supplies).
Amendments—¹ Regulation 94B inserted by the VAT (Amendment) (No 5) Regulations, SI 2003/2318 regs 2, 3 with effect from 1 October 2003. This insertion has effect for supplies of goods or services the benefit of which was received after the coming into force of SI 2003/2318.
² Words in para (1)(a), (c) substituted by the Value Added Tax (Buildings and Land) Order, SI 2008/1146, art 6, Sch 1 paras 16, 18 with effect in relation to supplies made on or after 1 June 2008, subject to savings in Sch 2 of the Order.
³ Para (4) substituted by the Value Added Tax (Amendment) (No 3) Regulations, SI 2009/1967 regs 2, 6 with effect from 15 August 2009.

95 Supplies spanning change of rate etc
Section 88 of the Act shall apply as if the references in subsection (2) of that section to section 6(4), (5), (6) and (11) of the Act included references to regulations 81, 82, [82A,]² 84, 85, 86(1) to (4) . . . [,]¹ 88 to 93 [and 94B]¹ of these Regulations.
Commentary—De Voil Indirect Tax Service **V3.141**.
HMRC Manuals—VAT Time of Supply VATTOS2390 (legislation: regulation 95 supplies spanning a change of rate).
Amendments—¹ This regulation amended by the VAT (Amendment) (No 5) Regulations, SI 2003/2318 regs 2, 4 with effect from 1 October 2003. The amendments have effect for supplies of goods or services the benefit of which was received after the coming into force of SI 2003/2318.
² Reference inserted by the VAT (Amendment) (No 4) Regulations, SI 2004/3140 reg 5 with effect from 1 January 2005 in relation to supplies made on or after that date: SI 2004/3140 reg 2(1).

PART XII
VALUATION OF ACQUISITIONS

96 Interpretation of Part XII
In this Part—
"relevant transaction", in relation to any acquisition of goods from another member State, and "relevant time" in relation to any such acquisition, have the meanings given in paragraph 5 of Schedule 7 to the Act.
HMRC Manuals—VAT Valuation Manual VATVAL10300 (special valuation rules for acquisitions - schedule 7, VATA 1994).

97 Valuation of acquisitions
(1) Subject to paragraph (2) below, the value of the relevant transaction in relation to any goods acquired in [Northern Ireland from a member State]¹ where—
   (a) the goods are charged in connection with their removal to [Northern Ireland]¹ with a duty of excise; or
   (b) on that removal are subject, in accordance with any provision for the time being having effect for transitional purposes in connection with the accession of any State to the European Communities, to any Community customs duty or agricultural levy of the [EU]¹,
shall be taken, for the purposes of the Act, to be the sum of its value apart from paragraph 2 of Schedule 7 to the Act and the amount, so far as not already included in that value, of the excise duty, Community customs duty or, as the case may be, agricultural levy which has been or is to be paid in respect of those goods.
(2) Paragraph (1) above does not apply to a transaction in pursuance of which there is an acquisition of goods which, under subsection (4) of section 18 of the Act, is treated as taking place before the duty point within the meaning of that section.
HMRC Manuals—VAT Valuation Manual VATVAL10300 (special valuation rules for acquisitions - schedule 7, VATA 1994).
Amendments—¹ In para (1) words substituted for words "the United Kingdom from another member State", in para (1)(a) words substituted for words "the United Kingdom", and in para (1)(b) words substituted for words "Economic Community", by the Value Added Tax (Miscellaneous Amendments, Northern Ireland Protocol and Savings and Transitional Provisions) (EU Exit) Regulations, SI 2020/1545 regs 31 and 54 with effect from IP completion day (11pm UK time on 31 December 2020) by virtue of SI 2020/1641 reg 2, Schedule para 11.

PART XIII
PLACE OF SUPPLY

98 Distance sales from [Northern Ireland to the EU]¹
(1) Where a person has exercised an option in the United Kingdom corresponding to an option mentioned in paragraph 1(2) of Schedule 2 to the Act, in respect of supplies involving the removal of goods [from Northern Ireland to a member State]¹, he shall notify the Commissioners in writing of the exercise of that option not less than 30 days before the date on which the first supply to which the option relates is made,
(2) The notification referred to in paragraph (1) above shall contain the name of the member State to which the goods have been, or are to be, removed under the direction or control of the person making the supply.
(3) Any person who has notified the Commissioners in accordance with paragraph (1) above shall within 30 days of the date of the first supply as is mentioned in that paragraph furnish to the Commissioners documentary evidence that he has notified the member State of the exercise of his option,
(4) Where a person has notified the Commissioners in accordance with paragraph (1) above he may withdraw his notification by giving a further written notification but that further notification must specify the date upon which the first notification is to be withdrawn, which date must not be earlier than—
   (a) the 1st January which is, or next follows, the second anniversary of the date of the making of the first supply mentioned above to which the option relates, and

(b) the day 30 days after the receipt by the Commissioners of the further notification, and not later than 30 days before the date of the first supply which he intends to make after the withdrawal.

Commentary—*De Voil Indirect Tax Service* **V3.172**.
Amendments—[1] In the heading words substituted for words "the United Kingdom", and in para (1) words substituted for words "to another member State", by the Value Added Tax (Miscellaneous Amendments, Northern Ireland Protocol and Savings and Transitional Provisions) (EU Exit) Regulations, SI 2020/1545 regs 31 and 55 with effect from IP completion day (11pm UK time on 31 December 2020) by virtue of SI 2020/1641 reg 2, Schedule para 11.

PART XIV
INPUT TAX AND PARTIAL EXEMPTION

99 Interpretation of Part XIV and longer periods

(1) In this Part—
  [(a) "exempt input tax" means input tax incurred by a taxable person on goods imported or acquired by, or goods or services supplied to, him in so far as they are used by him or are to be used by him, or a successor of his, in making exempt supplies, or supplies outside the United Kingdom which would be exempt if made in the United Kingdom, other than any input tax which is allowable under regulation [101][5] [[102,][4] 103, 103A or 103B][3]; and "successor" in this paragraph has the same meaning as in regulation 107D;][2]
  (b) "prescribed accounting period" means—
    (i) a prescribed accounting period such as is referred to in regulation 25, or
    (ii) a special accounting period, where the first prescribed accounting period would otherwise be 6 months or longer, save that this paragraph shall not apply where the reference to the prescribed accounting period is used solely in order to identify a particular return;
  (c) "special accounting period" means each of a succession of periods of the same length as the next prescribed accounting period which does not exceed 3 months, and—
    (i) the last such period shall end on the day before the commencement of that next prescribed accounting period, and
    (ii) the first such period shall commence on the effective date of registration determined in accordance with Schedule 1[, [1A,][7] 2, 3 or 3A][1] to the Act and end on the day before the commencement of the second such period;
  (d) the "tax year" of a taxable person means—
    (i) the first period of 12 calendar months commencing on the first day of April, May or June, according to the prescribed accounting periods allocated to him, next following his effective date of registration determined in accordance with Schedule 1[, [1A,][7] 2, 3 or 3A][1] to the Act, or
    (ii) any subsequent period of 12 calendar months commencing on the day following the end of his first, or any subsequent, tax year,

    save that the Commissioners may approve or direct that a tax year shall be a period of other than 12 calendar months or that it shall commence on a date other than that determined in accordance with paragraph (i) or (ii) above;
  (e) the "registration period" of a taxable person means the period commencing on his effective date of registration determined in accordance with Schedule 1[, [1A,][7] 2, 3 or 3A][1] to the Act and ending on the day before the commencement of his first tax year.

[(1A) In this Part "non-business VAT" has the meaning given in section 24(5)(b) of the Act.][6]

(2) In this Part, any reference to goods or services shall be construed as including a reference to anything which is supplied by way of a supply of goods or a supply of services respectively.

(3) The provisions of paragraphs (4), (5), (6) and (7) below shall be used for determining the longer period applicable to taxable persons under this Part.

(4) A taxable person who incurs exempt input tax during any tax year shall have applied to him a longer period which shall correspond with that tax year unless he did not incur exempt input tax during his immediately preceding tax year or registration period, in which case his longer period shall—
  (a) begin on the first day of the first prescribed accounting period in which he incurs exempt input tax, and
  (b) end on the last day of that tax year,
except where he incurs exempt input tax only in the last prescribed accounting period of his tax year, in which case no longer period shall be applied to him in respect of that tax year.

(5) A taxable person who incurs exempt input tax during his registration period shall have applied to him a longer period which shall begin on the first day on which he incurs exempt input tax and end on the day before the commencement of his first tax year.

(6) In the case of a taxable person ceasing to be taxable during a longer period applicable to him, that longer period shall end on the day when he ceases to be taxable.

(7) The Commissioners may approve in the case of a taxable person who incurs exempt input tax, or a class of such persons, that a longer period shall apply which need not correspond with a tax year.

Commentary—*De Voil Indirect Tax Service* **V3.465, V3.466**.
HMRC Manuals—VAT Partial Exemption Guidance PE12000 (partly exempt businesses and exempt input tax).
Amendments—[1] Words in para (1)(*c*), (*d*), (*e*) inserted by the VAT (Amendment) (No 3) Regulations, SI 2000/794 regs 2, 6 with effect from 22 March 2000.
[2] Para (1)(*a*) substituted by the VAT (Amendment) Regulations, SI 2002/1074 regs 2, 3, with effect for input tax incurred by a taxable person on goods imported or acquired by, or goods or services supplied to, him after 17 April 2002.
[3] In sub-para (1)(*a*), references substituted by the VAT (Amendment) (No 4) Regulations, SI 2004/3140 reg 9 with effect from 3 December 2004: SI 2004/3140 reg 2(3).
[4] Reference in para (1)(*a*) inserted by the VAT (Amendment) (No 2) Regulations, SI 2007/768 regs 2, 6 with effect from 1 April 2007.
[5] Reference in para (1)(*a*) inserted by the VAT (Amendment) (No 2) Regulations, SI 2009/820 regs 2, 3 with effect in relation to input tax incurred by a taxable person on goods imported or acquired by, or goods or services supplied to, him on or after 1 April 2009. Where 31 March 2009 falls within the prescribed accounting period of a taxable person, the amendments made by SI 2009/820 shall not, in relation to that taxable person, have effect until the day after the end of that prescribed accounting period (SI 2009/820reg 1(2)).
[6] Para (1A) inserted by the VAT (Amendment) (No 4) Regulations, SI 2010/3022 regs 2, 5 with effect from 1 January 2011.
[7] In para (1), words inserted by the VAT (Amendment) (No 2) Regulations, SI 2012/1899 regs 3, 16 with effect from 15 October 2012.

100 Nothing in this Part shall be construed as allowing a taxable person to deduct the whole or any part of VAT on the importation or acquisition by him of goods or the supply to him of goods or services where those goods or services are not used or to be used by him in making supplies in the course or furtherance of a business carried on by him.

101 Attribution of input tax to taxable supplies
(1) Subject to regulation regulations [102, 103A, 105A and 106ZA][2], the amount of input tax which a taxable person shall be entitled to deduct provisionally shall be that amount which is attributable to taxable supplies in accordance with this regulation.
(2) [Subject to paragraph (8) below and regulation 107(1)(*g*)(ii),][5] in respect of each prescribed accounting period—
  (*a*) goods imported or acquired by and . . . [1] goods or services supplied to, the taxable person in the period shall be identified,
  (*b*) there shall be attributed to taxable supplies the whole of the input tax on such of those goods or services as are used or to be used by him exclusively in making taxable supplies,
  (*c*) no part of the input tax on such of those goods or services as are used or to be used by him exclusively in making exempt supplies, or in carrying on any activity other than the making of taxable supplies, shall be attributed to taxable supplies, . . . [5]
  (*d*) [where a taxable person does not have an immediately preceding longer period and subject to subparagraph (*e*) below,][5] there shall be attributed to taxable supplies such proportion of the [residual input tax][5] as bears the same ratio to the total of such input tax as the value of taxable supplies made by him bears to the value of all supplies made by him in the period,
  [(*e*) the attribution required by subparagraph (*d*) above may be made on the basis of the extent to which the goods or services are used or to be used by him in making taxable supplies,
  (*f*) where a taxable person has an immediately preceding longer period and subject to subparagraph (*g*) below, his residual input tax shall be attributed to taxable supplies by reference to the percentage recovery rate for that immediately preceding longer period, and
  (*g*) the attribution required by subparagraph (*f*) above may be made using the calculation specified in subparagraph (*d*) above provided that that calculation is used for all the prescribed accounting periods which fall within any longer period applicable to a taxable person.][5]
(3) In calculating the proportion under paragraph (2)(*d*) [or (*g*)][5] above, there shall be excluded—
  (*a*) any sum receivable by the taxable person in respect of any supply of capital goods used by him for the purposes of his business,
  (*b*) any sum receivable by the taxable person in respect of any of the following descriptions of supplies made by him, where such supplies are incidental to one or more of his business activities—
    [(i) any supply of a description falling within Group 5 of Schedule 9 to the Act,
    (ii) any other financial transaction, and
    (iii) any real estate transaction,][4]
  (*c*) that part of the value of any supply of goods on which output tax is not chargeable by virtue of any order made by the Treasury under section 25(7) of the Act unless the taxable person has imported, acquired or been supplied with the goods for the purpose of selling them,
    . . . [5]

(d) the value of any supply which, under or by virtue of any provision of the Act, the taxable person makes to himself, [. . . [6]
(e) supplies of a description falling within paragraph (8) below[and][5]
(f) the value of supplies made from an establishment situated outside the United Kingdom.][6]
[(g) where a removal of goods is treated as a taxable supply by virtue of paragraph 31B(1) of Schedule 9ZB to the Act, the value of that supply.][7]
(4) The ratio calculated for the purpose of paragraph (2)(d)[, (e) or (g)][5] above shall be expressed as a percentage and, if that percentage is not a whole number, it shall be rounded up [as specified in paragraph (5) below][3].
[(5) The percentage shall be rounded up—
(a) where in any prescribed accounting period or longer period which is applied the amount of input tax which is available for attribution under paragraph 2(d)[, (e) or (g)][5] above prior to any such attribution being made does not amount to more than £400,000 per month on average, to the next whole number, and
(b) in any other case, to two decimal places.][3]
[(6) For the purposes of this regulation, a "real estate transaction" includes any grant, assignment (including any transfer, disposition or sale), surrender or reverse surrender of any interest in, right over or licence to occupy land.][4]
[(7) In this regulation "taxable supplies" include supplies of a description falling within regulation 103.
(8) Input tax incurred on goods or services acquired by or supplied to a taxable person which are used or to be used by him in whole or in part in making—
(a) supplies falling within either item 1 or item 6 of Group 5 of Schedule 9 to the Act; . . . [6]
(b) *supplies made from an establishment situated outside the United Kingdom,*[6]
shall, whether the supply in question is made within or outside the United Kingdom, be attributed to taxable supplies on the basis of the extent to which the goods or services are used or to be used by him in making taxable supplies.
(9) For the purposes of this regulation in relation to a taxable person—
(a) "immediately preceding longer period" means the longer period applicable to him which ends immediately before the longer period in which the prescribed accounting period in respect of which he is making the attribution required by paragraph (2)(d) to (g) above falls;
(b) "percentage recovery rate" means the amount of relevant residual input tax which he was entitled to attribute to taxable supplies under regulation 107(1)(a) to (d), expressed as a percentage of the total amount of the residual input tax which fell to be so attributed and rounded up in accordance with paragraphs (4) and (5) above;
(c) "relevant residual input tax" means all residual input tax other than that which falls to be attributed under paragraph (8) above.
(10) In this regulation "residual input tax" means input tax incurred by a taxable person on goods or services which are used or to be used by him in making both taxable and exempt supplies.][5]

Commentary—*De Voil Indirect Tax Service* **V3.461, V3.461B**.
HMRC Manuals—VAT Partial Exemption Guidance PE30500 (the standard method).
Amendments—[1] Words in para (2)(a) deleted by the VAT (Amendment) (No 3) Regulations, SI 1996/1250 reg 14, with effect from 1 June 1996 except that where 28 April 1996 fell within a taxable person's prescribed accounting period which ended on or after 1 June 1996, the Amendment has effect in relation to that taxable person from the day after the end of that prescribed accounting period.
[2] In para (1), reference substituted for "regulation 102 and 103A" by the VAT (Amendment) Regulations, SI 2010/559 regs 2, 4 with effect from 1 April 2010.
[3] Words in para (4) substituted for words "to the whole next number", and para (5) inserted, by the VAT (Amendment) Regulations, SI 2005/762 reg 3 with effect from 1 April 2005. Where 31 March 2005 falls within the prescribed accounting period of a taxable person, the amendments shall not, in relation to that taxable person, have effect until the day after the end of that prescribed accounting period: SI 2005/762 reg 1.
[4] In para (3) sub-paras (i)–(iii) substituted for original sub-paras (i)–(v), and para (6) inserted, by the VAT (Amendment) (No 2) Regulations, SI 2007/768 regs 2, 7 with effect from 1 April 2007.
[5] In para (2), words inserted at beginning, at end of sub-para (c) word "and" revoked, in sub-para (d) words inserted at beginning and words substituted for words "input tax on such of those goods or services as are used or to be used by him in making both taxable and exempt supplies", and sub-paras (e)–(g) inserted, in para (3), words inserted, in sub-para (c) word "and" revoked, sub-para (e) and preceding word "and" inserted, in paras (4), (5), words inserted, and paras (7)–(10) inserted, by the VAT (Amendment) (No 2) Regulations, SI 2009/820 regs 2, 4 with effect in relation to input tax incurred by a taxable person on goods imported or acquired by, or goods or services supplied to, him on or after 1 April 2009. Where 31 March 2009 falls within the prescribed accounting period of a taxable person, the amendments made by SI 2009/820 shall not, in relation to that taxable person, have effect until the day after the end of that prescribed accounting period (SI 2009/820 reg 1(2)).
[6] In para (3)(d), word "and" revoked, and para (3)(f) and preceding word "and " inserted, and para (8)(b) and preceding word "or" revoked by the VAT (Amendment) Regulations, SI 2015/1978 regs 3, 4 with effect in relation to longer periods commencing on or after 1 January 2016. "Longer periods" means the longer period determined under the Value Added Tax Regulations 1995 Pt 14 (SI 2015/1978 reg 2(2)).
[7] Sub-para (3)(g) inserted by the Value Added Tax (Miscellaneous Amendments, Northern Ireland Protocol and Savings and Transitional Provisions) (EU Exit) Regulations, SI 2020/1545 regs 31 and 56 with effect from IP completion day (11pm UK time on 31 December 2020) by virtue of SI 2020/1641 reg 2, Schedule para 11.

102 Use of other methods

(1) Subject to [paragraphs (2) and (9)]³ below and [regulations 103, 103A[, 103B, 105A and 106ZA]⁵]¹, the Commissioners may approve or direct the use by a taxable person of a method other than that specified in regulation 101 . . . .

[(1A) A method approved or directed under paragraph (1) above—
   (a) shall be in writing,
   (b) may attribute input tax which would otherwise fall to be attributed under regulation 103 provided that, where it attributes any such input tax, it shall attribute it all, . . . ⁶
   (c) shall identify the supplies in respect of which it attributes input tax by reference to the relevant paragraph or paragraphs of section 26(2) of the Act.]³
   [(d) may be based on sectors provided that the method reflects the use made of the goods and services in the business and each sector reflects—
       (i) the use made of the goods and services in that sector,
       (ii) the structure of the business, and
       (iii) the type of activity undertaken by that sector, and
   (e) must exclude the value of supplies made from an establishment situated outside the United Kingdom where the method is not based on sectors.]⁶

(2) Notwithstanding any provision of any method approved or directed to be used under this regulation which purports to have the contrary effect, in calculating the proportion of any input tax on goods or services used or to be used by the taxable person in making both taxable and exempt supplies which is to be treated as attributable to taxable supplies, the value of any supply [of a description falling within regulation [101(3)(a) to (d)] [and (g)]⁷⁴ whether made within or outside the United Kingdom]³ shall be excluded.

[(2A) Notwithstanding any provision of any method approved or directed to be used under this regulation which purports to have the contrary effect, where the method attributes input tax to exempt supplies specified by the Treasury in an order made under section 26(2)(c) of the Act—
   (a) no attribution is to be made in relation to any supplies that are made within the United Kingdom unless—
       (i) the supply is directly linked to the export of goods and the recipient of the goods is located outside the United Kingdom, or
       (ii) the supply is between a United Kingdom based intermediary and a United Kingdom based service provider and the recipient of any supply being arranged by the intermediary is located outside the United Kingdom, and
   (b) attribution may be made in relation to any supplies that are made within the European Union]⁷

(3) A taxable person using a method as approved or directed to be used by the Commissioners under paragraph (1) above shall continue to use that method unless the Commissioners approve or direct the termination of its use.

(4) Any direction under paragraph (1) or (3) above shall take effect from the date upon which the Commissioners give such direction or from such later date as they may specify.

[(5) Any approval given or direction made under this regulation shall only have effect if it is in writing in the form of a document which identifies itself as being such an approval or direction.]²

[(6) Where a taxable person who is using a method which has been approved or directed under this regulation incurs input tax of the description in paragraph (7) below, that input tax shall be attributed to taxable supplies to the extent that the goods or services are used or to be used in making taxable supplies expressed as a proportion of the whole use or intended use.]²

[(7) The input tax referred to in paragraph (6) above is input tax—
   (a) the attribution of which to taxable supplies is not prescribed in whole or in part by the method referred to in paragraph (6) above, and
   (b) which does not fall to be attributed to taxable or other supplies as specified under regulations 103, 103A or 103B.]²

[(8) Where the input tax specified in paragraph (7)(a) above is input tax the attribution of which to taxable supplies is only in part not prescribed by the method, only that part the attribution of which is not so prescribed shall fall within that paragraph.]²

[(9) With effect from 1st April 2007 the Commissioners shall not approve the use of a method under this regulation unless the taxable person has made a declaration to the effect that to the best of his knowledge and belief the method fairly and reasonably represents the extent to which goods or services are used by or are to be used by him in making taxable supplies.

(10) The declaration referred to in paragraph (9) above shall—
   (a) be in writing,
   (b) be signed by the taxable person or by a person authorised to sign it on his behalf, and
   (c) include a statement that the person signing it has taken reasonable steps to ensure that he is in possession of all relevant information.

(11) Where it appears to the Commissioners that a declaration made under this regulation is incorrect in that—

(a) the method does not fairly and reasonably represent the extent to which goods or services are used by or are to be used by the taxable person in making taxable supplies, and
(b) the person who signed the declaration knew or ought reasonably to have known this at the time when the declaration was made by the taxable person,

they may subject to paragraph (12) below serve on the taxable person a notice to that effect setting out their reasons in support of that notification and stating the effect of the notice.

(12) The Commissioners shall not serve a notice under this regulation unless they are satisfied that the overall result of the application of the method is an over-deduction of input tax by the taxable person.

(13) Subject to paragraph (14) below, the effect of a notice served under this regulation is that regulation 102B(1) shall apply to the person served with the notice in relation to—
(a) prescribed accounting periods commencing on or after the effective date of the method, and
(b) longer periods to the extent of that part of the longer period falling on or after the effective date of the method, save that no adjustment shall be required in relation to any part of any prescribed accounting period,

unless or until the method is terminated under regulation 102(3).

(14) In relation to any past prescribed accounting periods, the Commissioners may assess the amount of VAT due to the best of their judgement and notify it to the taxable person unless they allow him to account for the difference in such manner and within such time as they may require.

(15) The service of a notice on a taxable person under this regulation shall be without prejudice to the Commissioners' powers to serve a notice on him under regulation 102A and any notice served under regulation 102A shall take priority in relation to the periods which it covers.

(16) In this regulation "the effective date of the method" is the date when the method to which the declaration relates first takes effect and may predate the date when the declaration was made.

(17) In this regulation and in regulations 102A, 102B, 102C and 107, where paragraph (1A)(b) above applies, "taxable supplies" includes supplies of a description falling within regulation 103.][3]

Commentary—*De Voil Indirect Tax Service* **V3.461C, V3.462.**
HMRC Manuals—VAT Partial Exemption Guidance PE33000 (introduction to special methods).
Amendments—[1] In para (1), references substituted by the VAT (Amendment) (No 4) Regulations, SI 2004/3140 reg 11 with effect from 3 December 2004: SI 2004/3140 reg 2(3).
[2] Paras (5)–(8) inserted by the VAT (Amendment) Regulations, SI 2005/762 reg 4 with effect from 1 April 2005.
[3] Words in para (1) substituted and omitted, paras (1A) and (9)–(17) inserted, and words in para (2) substituted, by the VAT (Amendment) (No 2) Regulations, SI 2007/768 regs 2, 8 with effect from 1 April 2007.
[4] In para (2), words substituted for words "101(3)" by the VAT (Amendment) (No 2) Regulations, SI 2009/820 regs 2, 5 with effect in relation to input tax incurred by a taxable person on goods imported or acquired by, or goods or services supplied to, him on or after 1 April 2009. Where 31 March 2009 falls within the prescribed accounting period of a taxable person, the amendments made by SI 2009/820 shall not, in relation to that taxable person, have effect until the day after the end of that prescribed accounting period (SI 2009/820 reg 1(2)).
[5] In para (1), reference substituted for "and 103B" by the VAT (Amendment) Regulations, SI 2010/559 regs 2, 5 with effect from 1 April 2010.
[6] In para (1A)(b), word "and" revoked, and para (1A)(d), (e) inserted, by the VAT (Amendment) Regulations, SI 2015/1978 regs 3, 5 with effect in relation to methods approved or directed under this regulation on or after 1 January 2016.
[7] In para (2) words inserted, and para (2A) inserted, by the Value Added Tax (Miscellaneous Amendments, Northern Ireland Protocol and Savings and Transitional Provisions) (EU Exit) Regulations, SI 2020/1545 regs 31 and 57 with effect from IP completion day (11pm UK time on 31 December 2020) by virtue of SI 2020/1641 reg 2, Schedule para 11.

[102ZA (1) A taxable person who is required to make an apportionment under section 24(5) of the Act in relation to goods or services which are used or are to be used partly for business purposes and partly for other purposes may effect that apportionment using a method provided for in regulation 102(1).

(2) Where the taxable person referred to in paragraph (1) is not a fully taxable person, the method used shall be the only method used to calculate that person's deductible input tax.

(3) Where a person who was a fully taxable person at the time when the method was approved subsequently incurs exempt input tax, regulation 102B shall apply from the date on which that person first incurs such exempt input tax.

(4) Where a person effects the apportionment referred to in paragraph (1) using a method provided for in regulation 102(1)—
(a) regulations 102(1A) to (17) and 102A to 102C shall apply;
(b) regulations 105A, 106 and 106ZA shall not apply; and
(c) for the purposes of defining a longer period and determining an adjustment of attribution under regulation 107, "exempt input tax" shall include non-business VAT.

(5) In this regulation, a fully taxable person is a person who, disregarding paragraph (4)(c), has not incurred any exempt input tax in that person's current or immediately preceding (if any) tax year or registration period.][1]

Commentary—*De Voil Indirect Tax Service* **V3.462, V3.462A.**
Amendments—[1] Reg 102ZA inserted by the VAT (Amendment) (No 4) Regulations, SI 2010/3022 regs 2, 6 with effect from 1 January 2011.

[102A—(1) [Notwithstanding the Commissioners' powers to serve a notice under regulation 102,][2] where a taxable person—
  (a) is for the time being using a method approved or directed under regulation 102, and
  (b) that method does not fairly and reasonably represent the extent to which goods or services are used by him or are to be used by him in making taxable supplies,
the Commissioners may serve on him a notice to that effect, setting out their reasons in support of that notification and stating the effect of the notice.
(2) The effect of a notice served under this regulation is that regulation 102B shall apply to the person served with the notice in relation to—
  (a) prescribed accounting periods commencing on or after the date of the notice or such later date as may be specified in the notice, and
  (b) longer periods to the extent of that part of the longer period falling on or after the date of the notice or such later date as may be specified in the notice.][1]
[(2A) Notwithstanding any provision of any method approved or directed to be used under this regulation which purports to have the contrary effect, where the method attributes input tax to exempt supplies specified by the Treasury in an order made under section 26(2)(c) of the Act, no attribution is to be made in relation to any supplies that are made within the United Kingdom unless—
  (a) the supply is directly linked to the export of goods and the recipient of the goods is located outside both the United Kingdom and the EU, or
  (b) the supply is between a United Kingdom based intermediary and a United Kingdom based service provider and the recipient of any supply being arranged by the intermediary is located outside both the United Kingdom and the EU.][3]

Commentary—De Voil Indirect Tax Service **V3.462A**.
HMRC Manuals—VAT Partial Exemption Guidance PE51300 (example of a special method override notice).
PE51900 (the special method override notice regulations).
Amendments—[1] Regulations 102A–102C inserted by the VAT (Amendment) (No 6) Regulations, SI 2003/3220 regs 1(1)(b), (2), 2, 21 with effect for input tax incurred by a taxable person on goods imported or acquired by, or goods or services supplied to, him after 31 December 2003.
[2] Words in para (1) inserted by the VAT (Amendment) (No 2) Regulations, SI 2007/768 regs 2, 9 with effect from 1 April 2007.
[3] Para (2A) inserted by the VAT (Miscellaneous Amendments, Revocation and Transitional Provisions) (EU Exit) Regulations, SI 2019/513 regs 2, 4(1), (2) with effect from Exit Day (11pm on 31 January 2020) by virtue of SI 2020/87 reg 2. Note that this commencement provision explicitly refers to Exit Day and is excluded from the general "IP completion day" implementing provision in the EU (Withdrawal Agreement) Act 2020 Sch 5 para 1(1)).

[102B—(1) Where this regulation applies, a taxable person shall calculate the difference between—
  (a) the attribution made by him in any prescribed accounting period or longer period, and
  (b) an attribution which represents the extent to which the goods or services are used by him or are to be used by him in making taxable supplies,
and account for the difference on the return for that prescribed accounting period or on the return on which that longer period adjustment is required to be made, except where the Commissioners allow another return to be used for this purpose.
(2) This regulation shall apply from the date prescribed under regulation 102A(2) or 102C(2), unless or until the method referred to in regulation 102A(1)(a) or 102C(1)(a) is terminated under regulation 102(3).][1]

Commentary—De Voil Indirect Tax Service **V3.462A**.
HMRC Manuals—VAT Partial Exemption Guidance PE51300 (example of a special method override notice).
PE51900 (the special method override notice regulations).
Amendments—[1] Regulations 102A–102C inserted by the VAT (Amendment) (No 6) Regulations, SI 2003/3220 regs 1(1)(b), (2), 2, 21 with effect for input tax incurred by a taxable person on goods imported or acquired by, or goods or services supplied to, him after 31 December 2003.

[102C—(1) Subject to regulation 102A, where a taxable person—
  (a) is for the time being using a method approved or directed under regulation 102, and
  (b) that method does not fairly and reasonably represent the extent to which goods or services are used by him or are to be used by him in making taxable supplies,
the taxable person may serve on the Commissioners a notice to that effect, setting out his reasons in support of that notification.
(2) Where the Commissioners approve a notice served under this regulation, the effect is that regulation 102B shall apply to the person serving the notice in relation to—
  (a) prescribed accounting periods commencing on or after the date of the notice or such later date as may be specified in the notice, and
  (b) longer periods to the extent of that part of the longer period falling on or after the date of the notice or such later date as may be specified in the notice.][1]

Commentary—Le Voil Indirect Tax Service **V3.462A**.
HMRC Manuals—VAT Partial Exemption Guidance PE51900 (the special method override notice regulations).
Amendments—[1] Regulations 102A–102C inserted by the VAT (Amendment) (No 6) Regulations, SI 2003/3220 regs 1(1)(b), (2), 2, 21 with effect for input tax incurred by a taxable person on goods imported or acquired by, or goods or services supplied to, him after 31 December 2003.

103 Attribution of input tax to foreign and specified supplies

[(1)] [5]Other than where it falls to be attributed under [regulation 101 or][4] a method approved or directed by the Commissioners under regulation 102,] [subject to paragraph (1A)][5] [3] . . . [2] Input tax incurred by a taxable person in any prescribed accounting period on goods imported or acquired by, or goods or services supplied to, him which are used or to be used by him in whole or in part in making—

(a) supplies outside the United Kingdom which would be taxable supplies if made in the United Kingdom, or

(b) supplies specified in an Order under section 26(2)(c) of the Act, [other than supplies of a description falling within regulation 103A below,][1]

shall be attributed to taxable supplies to the extent that the goods or services are so used or to be used expressed as a proportion of the whole use or intended use.

[(1A) In calculating the proportion of any input tax incurred on goods or services used or to be used by a taxable person in making both taxable and exempt supplies which is to be attributed or treated as attributed to taxable supplies, the calculation—

(a) may be based on sectors provided that the calculation reflects the use made of the goods and services in the business and each sector reflects—

(i) the use made of the goods and services in that sector,

(ii) the structure of the business, and

(iii) the type of activity undertaken by that sector; and

(b) must exclude the value of supplies made from an establishment situated outside the United Kingdom where the calculation is not based on sectors.][5]

(2), (3) . . . [2]

Commentary—*De Voil Indirect Tax Service* **V3.464, V3.464A**.
HMRC Manuals—VAT Partial Exemption Guidance PE34000 (regulation 103 - recovery of input tax attributable to foreign and specified supplies).
Amendments—[1] Words inserted by the VAT (Amendment) (No 4) Regulations, SI 1999/3114, regs 2, 7, with effect from 1 January 2000.
[2] Paragraph numbering and paras (2), (3) revoked by the VAT (Amendment) (No 4) Regulations, SI 2004/3140 reg 7 with effect from 3 December 2004: SI 2004/3140 reg 2(3).
[3] Words inserted by the VAT (Amendment) (No 2) Regulations, SI 2007/768 regs 2, 10 with effect from 1 April 2007.
[4] Words inserted by the VAT (Amendment) (No 2) Regulations, SI 2009/820 regs 2, 6 with effect in relation to input tax incurred by a taxable person on goods imported or acquired by, or goods or services supplied to, him on or after 1 April 2009. Where 31 March 2009 falls within the prescribed accounting period of a taxable person, the amendments made by SI 2009/820 shall not, in relation to that taxable person, have effect until the day after the end of that prescribed accounting period (SI 2009/820 reg 1(2)).
[5] Para (1) numbered as such and words inserted, and para (1A) inserted, by the VAT (Amendment) Regulations, SI 2015/1978 regs 3, 6 with effect in relation to prescribed accounting periods commencing on or after 1 January 2016. "Prescribed accounting periods" means the prescribed accounting period determined under the Value Added Tax Regulations 1995 Pt 14 (SI 2015/1978 reg 2(2)).

[103A [Attribution of input tax to investment gold]

(1) This regulation applies to a taxable person who makes supplies of a description falling within item 1 or 2 of Group 15 of Schedule 9 to the Act.]

(2) Input tax incurred by him in any prescribed accounting period in respect of supplies by him of a description falling within paragraph (1) above shall be allowable as being attributable to those supplies only to the following extent, that is to say where it is incurred—

(a) on investment gold supplied to him which but for an election made under the Value Added Tax (Investment Gold) Order 1999, or but for Note 4(b) to Group 15 of Schedule 9 to the Act would have fallen within item 1 or 2 of that Group, or on investment gold acquired by him;

(b) on a supply to him, an acquisition by him, or on an importation by him of gold other than investment gold which is to be transformed by him or on his behalf into investment gold;

(c) on services supplied to him comprising a change of form, weight or purity of gold.

(3) Where a taxable person produces investment gold or transforms any gold into investment gold he shall also be entitled to credit for input tax incurred by him on any goods or services supplied to him, any acquisitions of goods by him or any importations of goods by him, but only to the extent that they are linked to the production or transformation of that gold into investment gold.

(4) Where input tax has been incurred on goods or services which are used or to be used in making supplies of a description falling within item 1 or 2 of Group 15 of Schedule 9 to the Act and any other supply, that input tax shall be attributed to the supplies falling within item 1 or 2 to the extent that the goods or services are so used or to be used, expressed as a proportion of the whole use or intended use.

(5) Where input tax is attributed to supplies of a description falling within item 1 or 2 of Group 15 to Schedule 9 to the Act under paragraph (4) above, the taxable person shall be entitled to credit for only so much input tax as is reasonably allowable under paragraph (2) or (3) above.

(6) For the purpose of attributing input tax to supplies of a description falling within item 1 or 2 of Group 15 of Schedule 9 to the Act under paragraph (4) above, any input tax of the description in that paragraph shall be deemed to be the only input tax incurred by the taxable person in the prescribed accounting period concerned.]

Commentary—*De Voil Indirect Tax Service* **V3.464B**.
Amendments—This Regulation inserted by the VAT (Amendment) (No 4) Regulations, SI 1999/3114, regs 2, 8, with effect from 1 January 2000.
Heading inserted by the VAT (Amendment) (No 2) Regulations, SI 2007/768 regs 2, 11 with effect from 1 April 2007.

103B [Attribution of input tax incurred on services and related goods used to make financial supplies
(1) This regulation applies to a taxable person who incurs input tax in the circumstances specified in paragraph (2) below.
(2) [Other than where it falls to be attributed under regulation 101,]² where—
  (a) input tax has been incurred by a taxable person in any prescribed accounting period on supplies to him of any of the services specified in paragraph (4) below and of any related goods, and
  (b) those services and related goods are used or to be used by the taxable person in making both a relevant supply and any other supply, and
  (c) the relevant supply is incidental to one or more of the taxable person's business activities,
that input tax shall be attributed to taxable supplies to the extent that the services or related goods are so used or to be used expressed as a proportion of the whole use or intended use, notwithstanding any provision of any input tax attribution method that the taxable person is required or allowed to use which purports to have the contrary effect.
(3) In this regulation—
  (a) "relevant supply" means a supply of a description falling within item 1 or 6 of Group 5 of Schedule 9 to the Act . . . ³; and
  (b) "taxable supplies" includes supplies of a description falling within regulation 103.
(4) The services referred to in paragraph (2)(a) above are services supplied by—
  (a) accountants;
  (b) advertising agencies;
  (c) bodies which provide listing and registration services;
  (d) financial advisers;
  (e) lawyers;
  (f) marketing consultants;
  (g) persons who prepare and design documentation; and
  (h) any person or body which provides similar services to those specified in sub-paragraphs (a) to (g) above.]¹

Commentary—*De Voil Indirect Tax Service* **V3.464**, **V3.464A**.
HMRC Manuals—VAT Partial Exemption Guidance PE35000 (regulation 103B).
Amendments—¹ Regulation 103B inserted by the VAT (Amendment) (No 4) Regulations, SI 2004/3140 reg 8 with effect from 3 December 2004 in relation to input tax incurred by a taxable person on goods imported or acquired by, or goods and services supplied to, him on or after that date: SI 2004/3140 reg 2(2).
² Words inserted in para (2) by the VAT (Amendment) (No 2) Regulations, SI 2009/820 regs 2, 7 with effect in relation to input tax incurred by a taxable person on goods imported or acquired by, or goods or services supplied to, him on or after 1 April 2009. Where 31 March 2009 falls within the prescribed accounting period of a taxable person, the amendments made by SI 2009/820 shall not, in relation to that taxable person, have effect until the day after the end of that prescribed accounting period (SI 2009/820 reg 1(2)).
³ In para (3)(a) words "and any supply of the same description which is made in another member State" revoked by the Value Added Tax (Miscellaneous Amendments, Northern Ireland Protocol and Savings and Transitional Provisions) (EU Exit) Regulations, SI 2020/1545 regs 31 and 58 with effect from IP completion day (11pm UK time on 31 December 2020) by virtue of SI 2020/1641 reg 2, Schedule para 11.

104 Attribution of input tax on self-supplies
Where under or by virtue of any provision of the Act a person makes a supply to himself, the input tax on that supply shall not be allowable as attributable to that supply.

Commentary—*De Voil Indirect Tax Service* **V3.424**.
Former regulation—VAT (General) Regulations, SI 1985/886 reg 32A; VAT (General) (Amendment) Regulations, SI 1992/645 regs 1–3.

[105A—(1) Subject to regulation 106ZA(1), where, in relation to a taxable person, total input tax incurred less any input tax incurred on goods or services used or to be used exclusively in making taxable supplies—
  (a) in any prescribed accounting period, or
  (b) in any applicable longer period,
does not amount to more than £625 per month on average, all input tax incurred in that period shall be treated as attributable to taxable supplies provided that the value of exempt supplies does not exceed one half of the value of all supplies.

(2) In the application of paragraph (1) above to a longer period—
  (a) any treatment of input tax as attributable to taxable supplies in any prescribed accounting period shall be disregarded, and
  (b) the amount of input tax incurred on goods or services used or to be used exclusively in making taxable supplies must reflect any changes in use or intention during that period.
(3) In this regulation—
  (a) "taxable supplies" includes supplies of a description falling within regulation 103, and
  (b) "exempt supplies" means any supplies that are not taxable supplies.][1]

Commentary—*De Voil Indirect Tax Service* **V3.465**.
Amendments—[1] Reg 105A inserted by the VAT (Amendment) Regulations, SI 2010/559, regs 2, 6 with effect from 1 April 2010.

[106—(1) [Where regulation 105A does not apply then, subject to regulations 106A and 106ZA(1)][3], where relevant input tax—
  (a) in any prescribed accounting period, or
  (b) in the case of a longer period, taken together with the amount of any adjustment in respect of that period under regulation 107B—
     (i) does not amount to more than £625 per month on average, and
     (ii) does not exceed one half of all his input tax for the period concerned,
all such input tax in that period shall be treated as attributable to taxable supplies.
(2) In the application of paragraph (1) above to a longer period—
  (a) any treatment of relevant input tax as attributable to taxable supplies in any prescribed accounting period shall be disregarded, and
  (b) no account shall be taken of any amount or amounts which may be deductible or payable under regulation 115.
(3) For the purposes of this regulation, relevant input tax is input tax attributed under regulations 101, 102, 103, 103A[, 103B][2] and, where the case arises, regulation 107, to exempt supplies or to supplies outside the United Kingdom which would be exempt if made in the United Kingdom (not being supplies specified in an Order made under section 26(2)(c) of the Act).][1]

Commentary—*De Voil Indirect Tax Service* **V3.465**.
HMRC Manuals—VAT Groups VGROUPS09400 (exempt input tax).
Amendments—[1] Regulation substituted by the VAT (Amendment) Regulations, SI 2002/1074 regs 2, 4 with effect for input tax incurred by a taxable person on goods imported or acquired by, or goods or services supplied to, him after 17 April 2002.
[2] In para (3), reference inserted by the VAT (Amendment) (No 4) Regulations, SI 2004/3140 reg 12 with effect from 3 December 2004: SI 2004/3140 reg 2(3).
[3] Words in para (1) substituted for "Subject to regulation 106A" by the VAT (Amendment) Regulations, SI 2010/559, regs 2, 7 with effect from 1 April 2010.

[106ZA (1) A taxable person who—
  (a) was entitled to attribute his input tax to taxable supplies under regulation 105A(1)(b) or regulation 106(1)(b) in his immediately preceding longer period, and
  (b) does not expect to incur more than £1,000,000 input tax in his current longer period,
may treat input tax incurred in each prescribed accounting period within his current longer period as attributable to taxable supplies, provided that he does so for all of the prescribed accounting periods that fall within that longer period.
(2) For the purposes of this regulation in relation to a taxable person, "immediately preceding longer period" means the longer period applicable to that person which ends immediately before the longer period in which the prescribed accounting period in respect of which he is making the attribution under paragraph (1) above falls.][1]

Commentary—*De Voil Indirect Tax Service* **V3.465**.
Amendments—[1] Reg 106ZA inserted by the VAT (Amendment) Regulations, SI 2010/559, regs 2, 8 with effect from 1 April 2010.

[106A—(1) This regulation applies where regulation 107A applies.
(2) Where, taken together with the amount of any adjustment under regulation 107A, input tax attributed under regulations 101, 103[, 103A and 103B][2] to exempt supplies, or to supplies outside the United Kingdom which would be exempt if made in the United Kingdom (in each case not being supplies specified in an Order made under section 26(2)(c) of the Act)—
  (a) does not amount to more than £625 per month on average, and
  (b) does not exceed one half of all his input tax for the period concerned,
all such input tax in that period shall be treated as attributable to taxable supplies.
(3) Where, in accordance with regulations 101, 103[, 103A and 103B][2], a taxable person has attributed an amount of input tax to exempt supplies, or to supplies outside the United Kingdom which would be exempt if made in the United Kingdom (in each case not being supplies specified in an Order made under section 26(2)(c) of the Act) and, after applying regulation 107A, he is entitled to treat all his input tax as attributable to taxable supplies under paragraph (2) above, he shall—
  (a) calculate the difference between—

(i) the total amount of input tax for that prescribed accounting period, and
(ii) the amount of input tax deducted in that prescribed accounting period, taken together with the amount of any adjustment under regulation 107A, and
(b) include this difference as an under-deduction in a return for the first prescribed accounting period next following the prescribed accounting period referred to in regulation 107A(1), except where the Commissioners allow another return to be used for this purpose.

(4) Where in a prescribed accounting period a taxable person has treated input tax as attributable to taxable supplies under regulation 106(1) but is not entitled to do so because of the operation of paragraph (2) above, he shall include the amount so treated as an over-deduction in a return for the first prescribed accounting period next following the prescribed accounting period referred to in regulation 107A(1), except where the Commissioners allow another return to be used for this purpose.

(5) But where a registered person has his registration cancelled at or before the end of the prescribed accounting period referred to in regulation 107A(1), he shall account for any adjustment under this regulation on his final return.]¹

Commentary—*De Voil Indirect Tax Service* **V3.465, V3.466**.
Amendments—¹ Regulation inserted by the VAT (Amendment) Regulations, SI 2002/1074 regs 2, 5 with effect for input tax incurred by a taxable person on goods imported or acquired by, or goods or services supplied to, him after 17 April 2002.
² In paras (2), (3), reference substituted by the VAT (Amendment) (No 4) Regulations, SI 2004/3140 reg 13 with effect from 3 December 2004: SI 2004/3140 reg 2(3).

107 Adjustment of attribution

(1) [Subject to regulation 105A(1)(b),]³ Where a taxable person to whom a longer period is applicable has provisionally attributed an amount of input tax to taxable supplies in accordance with a method [or treated an amount of input tax as attributable to taxable supplies under regulation 105A(1)(a) or regulation 106ZA(1)]³ . . . ² and save as the Commissioners may dispense with the following requirement to adjust, he² . . . —

[(a) shall, subject to [subparagraphs (b), (c), (d) and (da) below]³, determine for the longer period the amount of input tax which is attributable to taxable supplies according to the method used in the prescribed accounting periods,
(b) shall, where he has provisionally attributed input tax in accordance with regulation 101(2)(e) in any prescribed accounting period, determine for the longer period the amount of residual input tax which is attributable to taxable supplies on the basis of the extent to which the goods or services are used or to be used by him in making taxable supplies,
(c) may, where he has not provisionally attributed input tax in accordance with regulation 101(2)(e) but was nevertheless entitled to do so, determine for the longer period the amount of residual input tax which is attributable to taxable supplies on the basis of the extent to which the goods or services are used or to be used by him in making taxable supplies,
(d) shall, where he has provisionally attributed residual input tax under regulation 101(2)(f), determine for the longer period the amount of residual input tax which is attributable to taxable supplies using the calculation specified in regulation 101(2)(d) subject to the provisions of regulation 101(3) to (5),
[(da) shall where he has treated an amount of input tax as attributable to taxable supplies under regulation 105A(1)(a) or regulation 106ZA(1), determine for the longer period the amount of input tax that is attributable to taxable supplies in accordance with sub-paragraphs (a) to (d) above as appropriate,]³
(e) shall[, except where a taxable person is using a method provided for in regulation 102(1) to make the apportionment referred to in regulation 102ZA(1),]⁴ apply the tests set out in regulation 106 to determine whether all input tax in the longer period in question shall be treated as attributable to taxable supplies,
(f) shall calculate the difference between the amount of input tax determined to be attributable to taxable supplies under subparagraphs (a) to (e) above and the amounts of input tax, if any, which were deducted in the returns for the prescribed accounting periods, and
(g) shall include any such amount of over-deduction or under-deduction in a return for—
(i) the first prescribed accounting period next following the longer period, or
(ii) the last prescribed accounting period in the longer period,
except where the Commissioners allow another return to be used.]²

[(2) Where a taxable person makes no adjustment as required by paragraph (1) above, the requirement shall be that the adjustment is made in the return for the first prescribed accounting period next following the longer period.]²
[(3) But where a registered person has his registration cancelled at or before the end of a longer period, he shall account for any adjustment under this regulation on his final return.]¹
[(4) In this regulation "residual input tax" has the same meaning as in regulation 101(10).]²

Commentary—*De Voil Indirect Tax Service* **V3.465, V3.466**.
HMRC Manuals—VAT Civil Penalties VCP11118 (why a penalty arises: regulatory breaches - partial exemption).

Amendments—[1]   Para (3) added by the VAT (Amendment) Regulations, SI 2002/1074 regs 2, 6 with effect for input tax incurred by a taxable person on goods imported or acquired by, or goods or services supplied to, him after 17 April 2002.
[2]   In para (1), words ", and where all his exempt input tax in that longer period cannot be treated as attributable to taxable supplies under regulation 106," and "shall" revoked, and sub-paras (a)–(g) substituted for previous sub-paras (a)–(c), para (2) substituted, and para (4) inserted, by the VAT (Amendment) (No 2) Regulations, SI 2009/820 regs 2, 8 with effect in relation to input tax incurred by a taxable person on goods imported or acquired by, or goods or services supplied to, him on or after 1 April 2009. Where 31 March 2009 falls within the prescribed accounting period of a taxable person, the amendments made by SI 2009/820 shall not, in relation to that taxable person, have effect until the day after the end of that prescribed accounting period (SI 2009/820 reg 1(2)).
[3]   Words in para (1) inserted, words in para (1)(a) substituted and para (da) inserted, by the VAT (Amendment) Regulations, SI 2010/559, regs 2, 9 with effect from 1 April 2010.
[4]   Words in para (1)(e) inserted by the VAT (Amendment) (No 4) Regulations, SI 2010/3022 regs 2, 7 with effect from 1 January 2011.

[107A—(1) This regulation applies where a taxable person has made an attribution under regulation 101(2)(b) and (d) and the prescribed accounting period does not form part of a longer period, and the attribution differs substantially from one which represents the extent to which the goods or services are used by him or are to be used by him, or a successor of his, in making taxable supplies.
(2) Where this regulation applies, the taxable person shall calculate the difference and account for it on the return for the first prescribed accounting period next following the prescribed accounting period referred to in paragraph (1) above, except where the Commissioners allow another return to be used for this purpose.
(3) But where a registered person has his registration cancelled at or before the end of the prescribed accounting period referred to in paragraph (1) above, he shall account for any adjustment under this regulation on his final return.][1]
Commentary—*De Voil Indirect Tax Service* **V3.461C**.
Amendments—[1]   Regulations 107A–107E inserted by the VAT (Amendment) Regulations, SI 2002/1074 regs 2, 7 with effect for input tax incurred by a taxable person on goods imported or acquired by, or goods or services supplied to, him after 17 April 2002.

[107B—(1) [Other than where input tax falls to be attributed under regulation 101(8) or regulation 107(1)(b) or (c),][2] this regulation applies where a taxable person has made an attribution under [regulation 107(1)(a) or (d)][2] according to the method specified in regulation 101 and that attribution differs substantially from one which represents the extent to which the goods or services are used by him or are to be used by him, or a successor of his, in making taxable supplies.
(2) Where this regulation applies the taxable person shall—
   (a) calculate the difference, and
   (b) in addition to any amount required to be included under [regulation 107(1)(g)][2], account for the amount so calculated on the return for the first prescribed accounting period next following the longer period [or the return for the last prescribed accounting period in the longer period if applicable][2], except where the Commissioners allow another return to be used for this purpose.
(3) But where a registered person has his registration cancelled at or before the end of a longer period, he shall account for any adjustment under this regulation on his final return.][1]
Commentary—*De Voil Indirect Tax Service* **V3.461C**.
Amendments—[1]   Regulations 107A–107E inserted by the VAT (Amendment) Regulations, SI 2002/1074 regs 2, 7 with effect for input tax incurred by a taxable person on goods imported or acquired by, or goods or services supplied to, him after 17 April 2002.
[2]   In para (1), words inserted and words substituted for words "regulation 107(1)(a)", in para (2)(b), words substituted for words "regulation 107(1)(c)" and words inserted, by the VAT (Amendment) (No 2) Regulations, SI 2009/820 regs 2, 9 with effect in relation to input tax incurred by a taxable person on goods imported or acquired by, or goods or services supplied to, him on or after 1 April 2009. Where 31 March 2009 falls within the prescribed accounting period of a taxable person, the amendments made by SI 2009/820 shall not, in relation to that taxable person, have effect until the day after the end of that prescribed accounting period (SI 2009/820reg 1(2)).

[107C   For the purposes of regulations 107A and 107B, a difference is substantial if it exceeds—
   (a) £50,000; or
   (b) 50% of the amount of input tax falling to be apportioned under regulation 101(2)(d) within the prescribed accounting period referred to in regulation 107A(1), or longer period, as the case may be, but is not less than £25,000.][1]
Commentary—*De Voil Indirect Tax Service* **V3.461C**.
Amendments—[1]   Regulations 107A–107E inserted by the VAT (Amendment) Regulations, SI 2002/1074 regs 2, 7 with effect for input tax incurred by a taxable person on goods imported or acquired by, or goods or services supplied to, him after 17 April 2002.

[107D   For the purposes of regulations 107A and 107B a person is the successor of another if he is a person to whom that other person has—
   (a) transferred assets of his business by a transfer of that business, or part of it, as a going concern; and

(b) the transfer of the assets is one falling by virtue of an Order under section 5(3) of the Act to be treated as neither a supply of goods nor a supply of services;
and the reference in this regulation to a person's successor includes references to the successors of his successors through any number of transfers.][1]

Commentary—*De Voil Indirect Tax Service* **V3.461C**.
Amendments—[1] Regulations 107A–107E inserted by the VAT (Amendment) Regulations, SI 2002/1074 regs 2, 7 with effect for input tax incurred by a taxable person on goods imported or acquired by, or goods or services supplied to, him after 17 April 2002.

[107E—(1) Regulations 107A and 107B shall not apply where the amount of input tax falling to be apportioned under regulation 101(2)(d) within the prescribed accounting period referred to in regulation 107A(1), or longer period, as the case may be, does not exceed—
(a) in the case of a person who is a group undertaking in relation to one or more other undertakings (other than undertakings which are treated under sections 43A to 43C of the Act as members of the same group as the person), £25,000 per annum, adjusted in proportion for a period that is not 12 months; or
(b) in the case of any other person, £50,000 per annum, adjusted in proportion for a period that is not 12 months.
(2) For the purposes of paragraph (1) above, "undertaking" and "group undertaking" have the same meaning as in [section 1161 of the Companies Act 2006][2].][1]

Commentary—*De Voil Indirect Tax Service* **V3.461C**.
Amendments—[1] Regulations 107A–107E inserted by the VAT (Amendment) Regulations, SI 2002/1074 regs 2, 7 with effect for input tax incurred by a taxable person on goods imported or acquired by, or goods or services supplied to, him after 17 April 2002.
[2] Words in sub-para (2) substituted by the Companies Act 2006 (Consequential Amendments) (Taxes and National Insurance) Order, SI 2008/954 arts 43, 45 with effect from 6 April 2008.

[107F The references in regulations 107C and 107E to an apportionment under regulation 101(2)(d) in relation to a longer period include cases where the apportionment is made under regulation 107(1)(a) or (d) using the calculation specified in regulation 101(2)(d).][1]
Amendments—[1] This para inserted by the VAT (Amendment) (No 2) Regulations, SI 2009/820 regs 2, 10 with effect in relation to input tax incurred by a taxable person on goods imported or acquired by, or goods or services supplied to, him on or after 1 April 2009. Where 31 March 2009 falls within the prescribed accounting period of a taxable person, the amendments made by SI 2009/820 shall not, in relation to that taxable person, have effect until the day after the end of that prescribed accounting period (SI 2009/820reg 1(2)).

108—(1) This regulation applies where a taxable person has deducted an amount of input tax which has been attributed to taxable supplies because he intended to use the goods or services in making either—
(a) taxable supplies, or
(b) both taxable and exempt supplies,
and during a period of 6 years commencing on the first day of the prescribed accounting period in which the attribution was determined and before that intention is fulfilled, he uses or forms an intention to use the goods or services concerned in making exempt supplies or, in the case of an attribution within sub-paragraph (a) above, in making both taxable and exempt supplies.
(2) Subject to regulation 110 and save as the Commissioners otherwise allow, where this regulation applies the taxable person shall on the return for the prescribed accounting period in which the use occurs or the intention is formed, as the case may be, account for an amount equal to the input tax which has ceased to be attributable to taxable supplies in accordance with the method which he was required to use when the input tax was first attributed and he shall repay the said amount to the Commissioners.
(3) For the purposes of this regulation any question as to the nature of any supply shall be determined in accordance with the provisions of the Act and any Regulations or Orders made thereunder in force at the time when the input tax was first attributed.

Commentary—*De Voil Indirect Tax Service* **V3.467**.
HMRC Manuals—VAT input tax VIT25600 (is it input tax: changes in the use of goods).

109—(1) This regulation applies where a taxable person has incurred an amount of input tax which has not been attributed to taxable supplies because he intended to use the goods or services in making either—
(a) exempt supplies, or
(b) both taxable and exempt supplies,
and during a period of 6 years commencing on the first day of the prescribed accounting period in which the attribution was determined and before that intention is fulfilled, he uses or forms an intention to use the goods or services concerned in making taxable supplies or, in the case of an attribution within sub-paragraph (a) above, in making both taxable and exempt supplies.

(2) Subject to regulation 110 and where this regulation applies, the Commissioners shall, on receipt of an application made by the taxable person in such form and manner and containing such particulars as they may direct, pay to him an amount equal to the input tax which has become attributable to taxable supplies in accordance with the method which he was required to use when the input tax was first attributed.
(3) For the purposes of this regulation any question as to the nature of any supply shall be determined in accordance with the provisions of the Act and any Regulations or Orders made thereunder in force at the time when the input tax was first attributed.

Commentary—*De Voil Indirect Tax Service* **V3.467**.
HMRC Manuals—VAT Partial exemption guidance PE61100 (background and legal basis).
PE61600 (abortive costs).

[**109A** (1) This regulation applies where a taxable person—
  (a) has incurred an amount of input tax in relation to goods which has not been attributed to taxable supplies because the person has used the goods in making either—
    (i) exempt supplies, or
    (ii) both taxable supplies and exempt supplies,
  (b) is treated as having made a taxable supply of those goods ("the deemed supply") in accordance with paragraph 31B of Schedule 9ZB to the Act, and
  (c) the deemed supply is made in a subsequent tax year to the tax year in which the input tax was incurred.
(2) Subject to regulation 110 and where this regulation applies, the Commissioners shall, on receipt of an application made by the taxable person in such form and manner and containing such particulars as they may direct, pay to the person an amount equal to the input tax which has become attributable to the deemed supply in accordance with the method which the person was required to use when the input tax was first attributed.
(3) For the purposes of this regulation any question as to the nature of any supply shall be determined in accordance with the provisions of the Act or any Regulations or Orders made thereunder in force at the time when the input tax was first attributed.][1]

Amendments—[1] Reg 109A inserted by the Value Added Tax (Miscellaneous Amendments, Northern Ireland Protocol and Savings and Transitional Provisions) (EU Exit) Regulations, SI 2020/1545 regs 31 and 59 with effect from IP completion day (11pm UK time on 31 December 2020) by virtue of SI 2020/1641 reg 2, Schedule para 11.

[**110**—(1) Subject to paragraph (2) below, in this regulation, in regulations [103B,][2] 108 and 109 above and in Part XV of these Regulations—
  (a) "exempt supplies" includes supplies outside the United Kingdom which would be exempt if made in the United Kingdom, other than supplies of a description falling within subparagraph (b) below; and
  (b) "taxable supplies" includes supplies of a description falling within regulation [103][2] above.
(2) Subject to paragraph (3) below, for the purposes of identifying the use, or intended use, of goods and services in regulations 108 and 109 above and in Part XV of these Regulations—
  (a) "exempt supplies" shall be construed as including supplies of a description falling within regulation 103A(1) above, but only to the extent that there is, or would be, no credit for input tax on goods and services under that regulation; and
  (b) "taxable supplies" shall be construed as including supplies of a description falling within regulation 103A(1) above, but only to the extent that there is, or would be, credit for input tax on goods and services under that regulation.
(3) Any adjustment under regulations 108 and 109 above shall not cause any more or any less input tax to be credited, as the case may be, in respect of supplies of a description falling within regulation 103A(1) above than would be allowed or required under that regulation.
(4) Subject to [regulations 103 and 103B][2], where—
  (a) regulation 108 or 109 applies,
  (b) the use to which the goods or services concerned are put, or to which they are intended to be put, includes the making of any supplies outside the United Kingdom, and
  (c) at the time when the taxable person was first required to attribute the input tax he was not required to use a method approved or directed under regulation 102 or that method did not provide expressly for the attribution of input tax attributable to supplies outside the United Kingdom,
the amount for which the taxable person shall be liable to account under regulation 108 or the amount which he is entitled to be paid under regulation 109, as the case may be, shall be calculated by reference to the extent to which the goods or services concerned are used or intended to be used in making taxable supplies, expressed as a proportion of the whole use or intended use.
[(5) In regulations 108 and 109 a reference to—
  (a) "exempt supplies" includes a reference to non-business activities that give rise to an amount of non-business VAT;

(b) a method which a taxable person is required to use includes a reference to an apportionment which a taxable person is required to make under section 24(5) of the Act.]³]¹

Commentary—*De Voil Indirect Tax Service* **V3.467**.
HMRC Manuals—VAT input tax VIT25600 (is it input tax: changes in the use of goods).
VAT Partial exemption guidance PE61100 (background and legal basis).
Amendments—¹ This Regulation substituted by the VAT (Amendment) (No 4) Regulations, SI 1999/3114, regs 2, 9, with effect from 1 January 2000.
² Reference inserted in para (1), and references substituted in paras (1)(b), (4), by the VAT (Amendment) (No 4) Regulations, SI 2004/3140 reg 14 with effect from 3 December 2004: SI 2004/3140 reg 2(3).
³ Para (5) inserted by the VAT (Amendment) (No 4) Regulations, SI 2010/3022 regs 2, 8 with effect in relation to input tax incurred by a taxable person on goods imported or acquired by, or goods or services supplied to, that taxable person on or after 1 January 2011.

111 Exceptional claims for VAT relief

(1) Subject to paragraphs (2) and (4) below, on a claim made in accordance with paragraph (3) below, the Commissioners may authorise a taxable person to treat as if it were input tax—
  (a) VAT on the supply of goods or services to the taxable person before the date with effect from which he was, or was required to be, registered, or paid by him on the importation or acquisition of goods before that date, for the purpose of a business which either was carried on or was to be carried on by him at the time of such supply or payment, and
  (b) in the case of a body corporate, VAT on goods obtained for it before its incorporation, or on the supply of services before that time for its benefit or in connection with its incorporation, provided that the person to whom the supply was made or who paid VAT on the importation or acquisition—
    (i) became a member, officer or employee of the body and was reimbursed, or has received an undertaking to be reimbursed, by the body for the whole amount of the price paid for the goods or services,
    (ii) was not at the time of the importation, acquisition or supply a taxable person, and
    (iii) imported, acquired or was supplied with the goods, or received the services, for the purpose of a business to be carried on by the body and has not used them for any purpose other than such a business,
[(2) No VAT may be treated as if it were input tax under paragraph (1) above—
  (a) in respect of—
    (i) goods or services which had been supplied, or
    (ii) save as the Commissioners may otherwise allow, goods which had been consumed,
  by the relevant person before the date with effect from which the taxable person was, or was required to be, registered;
  (b) subject to paragraph (2A)[, (2C) and (2D)]³ below, in respect of goods which had been supplied to, or imported or acquired by, the relevant person more than [4 years]³ before the date with effect from which the taxable person was, or was required to be, registered;
  (c) in respect of services performed upon goods to which sub-paragraph (a) or (b) above applies;
     . . .⁴
  (d) in respect of services which had been supplied to the relevant person more than 6 months before the date with effect from which the taxable person was, or was required to be, registered; [or
  (e) in respect of capital items of a description falling within regulation 113.]⁴]¹
[(2A) Paragraph (2)(b) above does not apply where—
  (a) the taxable person was registered before 1st May 1997; and
  (b) he did not make any returns before that date.
(2B) In paragraph (2) above references to the relevant person are references to—
  (a) the taxable person; or
  (b) in the case of paragraph (1)(b) above, the person to whom the supply had been made, or who had imported or acquired the goods, as the case may be.]¹
[(2C) Where the relevant person was, or was required to be, registered on or before 1st April 2009, no VAT may be treated as if it were input tax under paragraph (1) above in respect of goods which were supplied to, or imported or acquired by the relevant person more than 3 years before the date with effect from which that person was, or was required to be, registered.
(2D) Where the relevant person was or was required to be registered on or before 31st March 2010 and paragraph (2C) above does not apply, no VAT may be treated as if it were input tax under paragraph (1) above in respect of goods which were supplied to, or imported or acquired by, the relevant person on or before 31st March 2006.]³
(3) [Subject to paragraph (3A) and (3B) below, a]¹ claim under paragraph (1) above shall, save as the Commissioners may otherwise allow, be made on [the first return the taxable person is required to make]² and, as the Commissioners may require, be supported by invoices and other evidence.

[(3A) Where the taxable person was registered before 1st May 1997 and has not made any returns before that date paragraph (3) above shall have effect as if for the words "the first return the taxable person is required to make" there were substituted the words "the first return the taxable person makes".
(3B) [Subject to paragraph (3C)]³ the Commissioners shall not allow a person to make any claim under paragraph (3) above in terms such that the VAT concerned would fall to be claimed as if it were input tax more than [4 years]³ after the date by which the first return he is required to make is required to be made.]¹
[(3C) The Commissioners shall not allow a person to make any claim under paragraph (3) above in the circumstances where the first return the taxable person was required to make was required to be made on or before 31st March 2006.]³
(4) A taxable person making a claim under paragraph (1) above shall compile and preserve for such period as the Commissioners may require—
    (a) in respect of goods, a stock account showing separately quantities purchased, quantities used in the making of other goods, date of purchase and date and manner of subsequent disposals of both such quantities, and
    (b) in respect of services, a list showing their description, date of purchase and date of disposal, if any.
(5) [Subject to paragraph (6) below]¹ if a person who has been, but is no longer, a taxable person makes a claim in such manner and supported by such evidence as the Commissioners may require, they may pay to him the amount of any VAT on the supply of services to him after the date with effect from which he ceased to be, or to be required to be, registered and which was attributable to any taxable supply made by him in the course or furtherance of any business carried on by him when he was, or was required to be, registered.
[(6) Subject to paragraph (7) [and (8)]³ below, no claim under paragraph (5) above may be made more than [4 years]³ after the date on which the supply of services was made.
(7) Paragraph (6) above does not apply where—
    (a) the person ceased to be, or ceased to be required to be, registered before 1st May 1997; and
    (b) the supply was made before that date.]¹
[(8) No claim may be made under paragraph (5) above in relation to a supply of services which was made on or before 31st March 2006.]³

Commentary—*De Voil Indirect Tax Service* **V3.431, V3.432**.
HMRC Manuals—VAT Land And Property VATLP22595 (option to tax: input tax and the option to tax: can pre-registration input tax be claimed?).
VAT Input Tax VIT11500 (UK law).
VIT32000 (pre-registration, pre-incorporation and post-deregistration claims to input tax under regulation 111).
VAT Refunds Manual VRM8300 (pre-registration input tax).
Amendments—¹ Para (2) substituted and paras (2A), (2B), (3A), (3B), (6), (7) and words in paras (3), (5) inserted by the VAT (Amendment) Regulations, SI 1997/1086 reg 7 with effect from 1 May 1997.
² Words in para (3) substituted by SI 1997/1086 reg 7 with effect from 1 May 1997.
³ In paras (2)(b), (3B), (6), words inserted and words substituted for words "3 years", paras (2C), (2D), (3C), (8) inserted, by the VAT (Amendment) Regulations, SI 2009/586 regs 2, 8 with effect from 1 April 2009.
⁴ In para (2)(c), word "or" revoked, and para (2)(e) and preceding word "or" inserted, by the VAT (Amendment) (No 4) Regulations, SI 2010/3022 regs 2, 9 with effect in relation to any person registering for VAT on or after 1 January 2011.

PART XV

ADJUSTMENTS TO THE DEDUCTION OF INPUT TAX
ON CAPITAL ITEMS

112 Interpretation of Part XV

(1) Any expression used in this Part to which a meaning is given in Part XIV of these Regulations shall, unless the contrary intention appears, have the same meaning in this Part as it has in that Part [and in particular, exempt supplies and taxable supplies shall be accorded the same meanings as defined in regulation 110 above]¹.
(2) Any reference in this Part to a capital item shall be construed as a reference to a capital item to which this Part applies by virtue of regulation 113, being an item which a person [who has or acquires an interest in the item in question]² (hereinafter referred to as "the owner") uses in the course or furtherance of a business carried on by him, and for the purpose of that business, otherwise than solely for the purpose of selling the item.
[(3) In this regulation and in regulation 114, an interest includes an interest which is treated as being supplied to a person under [paragraph 37(1)]³ of Schedule 10 to the Act provided that the numerator of the fraction in [paragraph 37(3)]³ of that Schedule is [36]³ or more.
(4) The reference to "owner" in paragraph (2) shall be taken to refer to—
    (a) subject to sub-paragraph (b), the transferee where the whole or part of a capital item is transferred from one person to another and that transfer is not treated as a supply for the purposes of VAT; and

(b) the representative member of a group under section 43 of the Act if the capital item is owned by a member of the group.

(5) Where the owner is a transferee or representative member, that person shall be treated as having done everything that the transferor or group member (as may be the case) has done in respect of the capital item.]²

Commentary—De Voil Indirect Tax Service **V3.470**.
Amendments—[1]   Words in para (1) inserted by the VAT (Amendment) (No 4) Regulations, SI 1999/3114, regs 2, 10, with effect from 1 January 2000.
[2]   Words in para (2), and whole of paras (3)–(5), inserted, by the VAT (Amendment) (No 4) Regulations, SI 2010/3022 regs 2, 10 with effect from 1 January 2011.
[3]   In para (3), words substituted for words "paragraph 37(3)", "paragraph 37(5)" and "3", by the VAT (Amendment) Regulations, SI 2011/254 regs 2, 3 with effect in relation to supplies treated as made under VATA 1994 Sch 10 where the building that is supplied was completed on or after 1 March 2011.

[113   Capital items to which this Part applies

(1) The capital items to which this Part applies are any of the items specified in paragraph (2) on or in relation to which the owner incurs VAT bearing capital expenditure of a type specified in paragraph (3), the value of which is not less than that specified in paragraph (4).
(2) The items are—
   (a) land;
   (b) a building or part of a building;
   (c) a civil engineering work or part of a civil engineering work;
   (d) a computer or an item of computer equipment;
   (e) an aircraft;
   (f) a ship, boat or other vessel.
(3) The expenditure—
   (a) in the case of an item falling within paragraph (2)(a) or (d), is the expenditure relating to its acquisition;
   (b) in the case of an item falling within paragraph (2)(b), (c), (e) or (f), is the expenditure relating to its—
      (i) acquisition,
      (ii) construction (including where appropriate manufacture),
      (iii) refurbishment,
      (iv) fitting out,
      (v) alteration, or
      (vi) extension (including the construction of an annex).
(4) The value for the purposes of paragraph (3) is—
   (a) not less than £250,000 where the item falls within paragraph (2)(a), (b) or (c);
   (b) not less than £50,000 where the item falls within paragraph (2)(d), (e) or (f).][1]

Commentary—De Voil Indirect Tax Service **V3.470**.
HMRC Manuals—VAT Partial Exemption Guidance PE67100 (The Capital Goods Scheme: legal basis).
VAT Supply and Consideration VATSC03360 (goods which are business assets on hand at deregistration).
Amendments—[1]   Reg 113 substituted by the VAT (Amendment) (No 4) Regulations, SI 2010/3022 regs 2, 11 with effect in relation to input tax incurred by a taxable person on goods imported or acquired by, or goods or services supplied to, that taxable person on or after 1 January 2011.

[113A—(1) This regulation applies where—
   (a) the owner of an item described by regulation 113(2)(a) to (c) ("O") (or a person to whom O has granted an interest in that item) uses that item to make a grant that falls within item 1(ka) of Group 1 of Schedule 9 to the Act,
   (b) apart from this regulation, the item would not be a capital item to which this Part applies,
   (c) O has, no later than 31st March 2013, decided to treat the item as a capital item for the purposes of this Part, and
   (d) O has made a written record of that decision specifying the date that it was made.
(2) Where this regulation applies, for the item in question—
   (a) for "£250,000" in regulation 113(4)(a) substitute "£1", but
   (b) no adjustment of deductions of input tax shall be made under this Part for any intervals ending before 1st October 2012 that fall within the period of adjustment for the capital item as prescribed in regulation 114.][1]

Commentary—De Voil Indirect Tax Service **V3.470**.
Amendments—[1]   Reg 113A inserted by the VAT (Amendment) (No 2) Regulations, SI 2012/1899 regs 3, 17 with effect from 1 October 2012.

114   Period of adjustment

(1) The proportion (if any) of the total input tax on a capital item which may be deducted under Part XIV shall be subject to adjustments in accordance with the provisions of this Part.
(2) Adjustments shall be made over a period determined in accordance with the following paragraphs of this regulation.

[(3) Subject to paragraphs (3A) and (3B), the period of adjustment is—
  (a) 10 successive intervals in the case of a capital item of a description falling within regulation 113(2)(a) to (c);
  (b) 5 successive intervals in the case of a capital item of a description falling within regulation 113(2)(d) to (f),
determined in accordance with paragraphs (4) to (5B) and (7).
(3A) If, at the time of the owner's first use, the number of intervals specified in paragraph (3)(a) or (b) (as may be the case) exceeds the number of complete years that the owner's interest in the capital item has to run by more than one, the number of intervals shall be reduced to one more than the number of complete years that the owner's interest has to run calculated from the date of the owner's first use of the item (but not to less than three intervals).
(3B) Where the owner's interest falls within regulation 112(3), the number of intervals shall be the same as the numerator of the fraction in [paragraph 37(5)][4] of Schedule 10 to the Act [divided by 12 and rounded up to the next whole number][4].
(3C) Where paragraph (3A) or (3B) applies, the relevant denominator in regulation 115(1) shall be adjusted accordingly.
(3D) Where a person who registers for VAT already owns an item of a description falling within regulation 113, for the purposes of calculating the period of adjustment—
  (a) one complete interval shall be deducted for each complete year which has elapsed since the date of that person's first use of the capital item prior to the date of VAT registration, and
  (b) the first interval applicable to the capital item which ends after the date of VAT registration shall be treated as a subsequent interval for the purposes of regulation 115(1).
(4) Subject to paragraphs (5A), (5B) and (7), the first interval applicable to a capital item shall commence on the day on which the owner first uses the capital item and shall end on the day before the start of his next tax year whether or not this is his first tax year.][3]
(5) Subject to [paragraphs (5A), (5B) and (7)][2] below, each subsequent interval applicable to a capital item shall correspond with a longer period applicable to the owner, or if no longer period applies to him, a tax year of his.
[(5A) On the first occasion during the period of adjustment applicable to a capital item that the owner of the item—
  (a) being a registered person subsequently becomes a member of a group under section 43 of the Act;
  (b) being a member of a group under section 43 ceases to be a member of that group (whether or not he becomes a member of another such group immediately thereafter); or
  (c) transfers the item in the course of the transfer of his business or part of his business as a going concern (the item therefore not being treated as supplied) in circumstances where the new owner is not, under regulation 6(1) above, registered with the registration number of and in substitution for the transferor,
the interval then applying shall end on the day before he becomes a member of a group or the day that he ceases to be a member of the group or transfers the business or part of the business (as the case may require) and thereafter each subsequent interval (if any) applicable to the capital item shall end on the successive anniversaries of that day..][1]
[(5B) Where the extent to which a capital item is used in making taxable supplies does not change between what would, but for this paragraph, have been the first interval and the first subsequent interval applicable to it and the length of the two intervals taken together does not exceed 12 months the first interval applicable to the capital item shall end on what would have been the day that the first subsequent interval expired.][1]
(6) . . .[2]
[(7) Where the owner of a capital item transfers it during the period of adjustment applicable to it in the course of the transfer of his business or a part of his business as a going concern (the item therefore not being treated as supplied) and the new owner is, under regulation 6(1) above, registered with the registration number of, and in substitution for the transferor, the interval applying to the capital item at the time of the transfer shall end on the last day of the longer period applying to the new owner immediately after the transfer or, if no longer period then applies to him, shall end on the last day of his tax year following the day of transfer.][2]

Commentary—*De Voil Indirect Tax Service* **V3.432, V3.470**.
Amendments—[1]   Paras (5A) and (5B), inserted by the VAT (Amendment) (No 3) Regulations, SI 1997/1614 reg 11 with effect from 3 July 1997.
[2]   Words in para (5) substituted, para (6) deleted and para (7) substituted by SI 1997/1614 reg 11 with effect from 3 July 1997.
[3]   Paras (3)–(4) substituted for previous paras (3), (4) by the VAT (Amendment) (No 4) Regulations, SI 2010/3022 regs 2, 12 with effect in relation to any capital item where the first interval of its adjustment period (as determined under the law prior to SI 2010/3022 regs 5 to 15 coming into force) has not started before 1 January 2011.
[4]   In para (3B), words substituted for words "paragraph 37(5)", and words inserted, by the VAT (Amendment) Regulations, SI 2011/254 regs 2, 4 with effect in relation to supplies treated as made under VATA 1994 Sch 10 where the building that is supplied was completed on or after 1 March 2011.

115 Method of adjustment

(1) Where in a subsequent interval applicable to a capital item, the extent to which it is used in making taxable supplies increases from the extent to which it was so used [or to be used at the time that the original entitlement to deduction of the input tax was determined][3], the owner may deduct for that subsequent interval an amount calculated as follows—
   (a) where the capital item falls within [regulation 114(3)(b)][3]

$$\frac{\text{the total input tax on the capital sum}}{5} \times \text{the adjustment percentage;}$$

   (b) where the capital item falls within [regulation 114(3)(a)][3]

$$\frac{\text{the total input tax on the capital sum}}{10} \times \text{the adjustment percentage;}$$

(2) Where in a subsequent interval applicable to a capital item, the extent to which it is used in making taxable supplies decreases from the extent to which it was so used [or to be used at the time that the original entitlement to deduction of the input tax was determined][3], the owner shall pay to the Commissioners for that subsequent interval an amount calculated in the manner described in paragraph (1) above.

[(3) Paragraph (3ZA) applies where, during an interval other than the last interval applicable to a capital item, the owner—
   (a) supplies the whole or part of his interest in the capital item, or
   (b) is deemed to supply the whole or part of his interest in the capital item, or
   (c) would have been deemed to supply the whole of his interest in the capital item but for the fact that the VAT on the deemed supply (whether by virtue of its value or because it is zero-rated or exempt) would not have exceeded the sum specified in paragraph 8(1)(c) of Schedule 4 to the Act.

(3ZA) If the supply (or deemed supply) of the capital item referred to in paragraph (3) is—
   (a) a taxable supply, the owner shall be treated as using the whole or part (as may be the case) of the capital item for each of the remaining complete intervals applicable to it wholly in making taxable supplies, or
   (b) an exempt supply, the owner shall be treated as not using the whole or part (as may be the case) of the capital item for any of the remaining complete intervals applicable to it in making any taxable supplies,

and, in each case, the owner shall, except where paragraph (3A) applies, calculate for each of the remaining complete intervals applicable to the capital item, in accordance with paragraph (1) or (2) as the case may require, such amount as the owner may deduct or be liable to pay to the Commissioners.][4]

[(3A) This paragraph applies if the total amount of input tax deducted or deductible by the owner of a capital item as a result of the initial deduction, any adjustments made under paragraph (1) or (2) above and the adjustment which would apart from this paragraph fall to be made under [paragraph (3ZA)][3] above would exceed the output tax chargeable by him [on the supply of the whole or part of that capital item][4].][2]

[(3B) Save as the Commissioners may otherwise allow, where paragraph (3A) above applies the owner may deduct, or as the case may require, shall pay to the Commissioners such amount as results in the total amount of input tax deducted or deductible being equal to the output tax chargeable by him [on the supply of the whole or part of the capital item][5].][2]

[(4) If a capital item is irretrievably lost or stolen or is totally destroyed, no further adjustment shall be made in respect of any remaining complete intervals applicable to it.][3]

[(5) Subject to paragraph (5A), for the purposes of this Part—
   "the adjustment percentage" means the difference (if any) between the extent, expressed as a percentage, to which the whole or part as appropriate of the capital item was used or to be used for the making of taxable supplies at the time the original entitlement to deduction of the input tax was determined and the extent to which the whole or part of it as appropriate is so used, or is treated under paragraph (3ZA) as being so used, in the subsequent interval in question;
   "the original entitlement to deduction" means the entitlement to deduction under sections 24 to 26 of the Act and regulations made under those sections;
   "the total input tax on the capital item" means—
      in relation to any capital item, all VAT incurred by the owner on the capital expenditure on that item (whether or not the person incurring it is VAT registered at the time that it is incurred) including any non-business VAT; and
      where a person is treated as making a supply to himself under [paragraph 37(1)][5] of Schedule 10 to the Act, the VAT charged on that supply;

"VAT bearing capital expenditure" means capital expenditure on which VAT is charged at the standard rate or at a reduced rate.]⁴

[(5A) Where paragraph (3ZA) applies in respect of part of a capital item, for the remaining complete intervals the total VAT incurred on the capital item as defined in paragraph (5) shall be reduced accordingly.

(5B) The person responsible for making an adjustment under paragraph (1), (2) or (3ZA) shall be the person who is treated as the owner of the capital item under regulation 112 at the point immediately prior to the end of the interval in question or, in the case of an adjustment under paragraph (3ZA), the event specified in paragraph (3).]³

(6) [Subject to [paragraphs (9) and (11)]³ below]¹ a taxable person claiming any amount pursuant to paragraph (1) above, or liable to pay any amount pursuant to paragraph (2) above, shall include such amount in a return for the second prescribed accounting period next following the interval to which that amount relates, except where the Commissioners allow another return to be used for this purpose . . .³

(7) [Subject to [paragraphs (9) and (11)]³ below]¹ a taxable person claiming any amount or amounts, or liable to pay any amount or amounts, pursuant to paragraph [(3ZA)]³ above, shall include such amount or amounts in a return for the second prescribed accounting period next following the interval in which the supply (or deemed supply) in question takes place except where the Commissioners allow another return to be used for this purpose.

[(8) For the purposes of paragraph (9), a "specified return" means a return specified in paragraph (6) or (7).]³

(9) . . .³ The Commissioners shall not allow the taxable person to use a return other than a specified return unless it is the return for a prescribed accounting period commencing within 4 years of the end of the prescribed accounting period to which the specified return relates.

(10) . . .³]

[(11) Where a person is required to make an adjustment under paragraph [(1), (2) or (3ZA) at a time when he is no longer registered for VAT, he shall make the required adjustment in his final VAT return.]³

Commentary—*De Voil Indirect Tax Service* **V3.470**.
HMRC Manuals—VAT refunds Manual VRM8300 (VAT regulations 1995 - overview).
VAT Supply and Consideration VATSC03360 (goods which are business assets on hand at deregistration).
Amendments—¹ Words in paras (6) and (7) inserted by the VAT (Amendment) Regulations, SI 1997/1086 reg 8 with effect from 1 May 1997.
² Paras (3A), (3B), inserted by the VAT (Amendment) (No 3) Regulations, SI 1997/1614 reg 12 with effect from 3 July 1997.
³ In paras (1)(a), (b), (3A), (3B), (7) words substituted, paras (3), (3ZA) substituted for previous para (3), paras (4), (8) substituted, paras (5A), (5B) inserted, in para (6) words substituted and revoked, in para (9) words revoked, para (10) revoked, and para (11) inserted, by the VAT (Amendment) (No 4) Regulations, SI 2010/3022 regs 2, 13(a)–(f), (h)–(n) with effect from 1 January 2011.
⁴ Para (5) substituted by the VAT (Amendment) (No 4) Regulations, SI 2010/3022 regs 2, 13(g) with effect in relation to input tax incurred by a taxable person on goods imported or acquired by, or goods or services supplied to, that taxable person on or after 1 January 2011.
⁵ In para (5), words substituted for words "paragraph 37(3)" by the VAT (Amendment) Regulations, SI 2011/254 regs 2, 5 with effect in relation to supplies treated as made under VATA 1994 Sch 10 where the building that is supplied was completed on or after 1 March 2011.

116 Ascertainment of taxable use of a capital item

(1) Subject to regulation 115(3) [and (3B)]² and paragraphs (2)[, (A2)]² and (3) below, for the purposes of this Part, an attribution of the total input tax on the capital item shall be determined for each subsequent interval applicable to it [in accordance with the provisions of sections 24 to 26 of the Act and regulations made under those sections as they apply to that interval]³ and the proportion of the input tax thereby determined to be attributable to taxable supplies shall be treated as being the extent to which the capital item is used in making taxable supplies in that subsequent interval.

[(A2) Subject to paragraph (2) below, the attribution of the total input tax on a capital item for subsequent intervals determined in accordance with regulation 114(5A) above shall be determined by such method as is agreed with the Commissioners.]²

(2) In any particular case the Commissioners may allow another method by which, or may direct the manner in which, the extent to which a capital item is used in making taxable supplies in any subsequent interval applicable to it is to be ascertained.

(3) Where the owner of a building which is a capital item of his grants or assigns a tenancy or lease in the whole or any part of that building and that grant or assignment is a zero-rated supply to the extent only as provided by—
  (a) note [(14)]¹ to Group 5 of Schedule 8 to the Act, or
  (b) that note as applied to Group 6 of that Schedule by note [(3)]¹ to Group 6, or
  (c) paragraph 8 of Schedule 13 to the Act,
any subsequent exempt supply of his arising directly from that grant or assignment shall be disregarded in determining the extent to which the capital item is used in making taxable supplies in any interval applicable to it.

Commentary—*De Voil Indirect Tax Service* **V3.470**.
HMRC Manuals—VAT Partial Exemption Guidance PE67150 (The Capital Goods Scheme: calculating taxable use). PE66300 (capital goods scheme (CGS) considerations).
Amendments—[1] Figures in para (3) substituted by the VAT (Amendment) Regulations, SI 1995/3147 reg 5, with effect from 1 January 1996.
[2] Words in para (1) above, and para (A2) above, inserted by the VAT (Amendment) (No 3) Regulations, SI 1997/1614 reg 13 with effect from 3 July 1997.
[3] In para (1), words substituted by the VAT (Amendment) (No 4) Regulations, SI 2010/3022 regs 2, 14 with effect from 1 January 2011.

[PART 15A
GOODS USED FOR NON-BUSINESS PURPOSES DURING THEIR ECONOMIC LIFE][1]

Note—The VAT (Amendment) (No 7) Regulations, SI 2007/3099 revoke and replace the VAT (Amendment) (No 6) Regulations, SI 2007/2922. This revocation was necessary owing to a typographical error in the recital powers pursuant to which the No 6 Regulations were made. The No 7 Regulations make the amendments to the VAT Regulations, SI 2003/2518, which were intended to be made by the No 6 Regulations.
Amendments—[1] Part 15A (regs 116A–116N) inserted by the VAT (Amendment) (No 7) Regulations, SI 2007/3099 regs 3, 4 with effect from 1 November 2007: SI 2007/3099 reg 1(2)(*b*).

116A [Application
This Part makes provision for calculating the full cost to a person of providing the supply of services ("relevant supply") that is treated as made pursuant to paragraph 5(4) of Schedule 4 to the Act where goods that are held or used for the purposes of a business are used for private or non-business purposes. Where goods that are held or used for the purposes of a business have an economic life (see regulations 116C, 116D, 116G and 116L) at the time when they are used for private or non-business purposes, the value or part of the value of the relevant supply which is referable to that use on or after 1st November 2007 shall be calculated in accordance with the regulations in this Part.][1]

Commentary—*De Voil Indirect Tax Service* **V3.212**.
HMRC Manuals—VAT Input Tax VIT25600 (temporary/partial private use).
Amendments—[1] Part 15A (regs 116A–116N) inserted by the VAT (Amendment) (No 7) Regulations, SI 2007/3099 regs 3, 4 with effect from 1 November 2007: SI 2007/3099 reg 1(2)(*b*).

116B Interpretation of this Part
(1) In this Part—
"full cost of the goods" means the full cost of the goods to the person (being the person making the relevant supply or any of his predecessors) who, in relation to the VAT on the goods mentioned in paragraph 5(5) of Schedule 4 to the Act, is described in that paragraph as being entitled to—
   (*a*) credit under sections 25 and 26 of the Act; or
   (*b*) a repayment under the scheme made under section 39 of the Act;
[but, in relation to any goods which are relevant assets, the full cost shall exclude any costs on which VAT was incurred on or after 1 January 2011;][2]
"goods" includes land forming part of the assets of, or held or used for the purposes of, a business which is treated as goods for the purposes of paragraph 5 of Schedule 4 to the Act by virtue of paragraph 9 of that Schedule and references to goods being held or used for the purposes of a business shall be construed accordingly;
"predecessor" has the same meaning as it does in paragraph 5 of Schedule 4 to the Act.
["relevant asset" has the same meaning as it has in section 24(5B) of the Act.][2]
(2) In this Part, references to a period of time comprising a number of months shall be computed to two decimal places where that period does not comprise a whole number of months.][1]

Commentary—*De Voil Indirect Tax Service* **V3.212**.
Amendments—[1] Part 15A (regs 116A–116N) inserted by the VAT (Amendment) (No 7) Regulations, SI 2007/3099 regs 3, 4 with effect from 1 November 2007: SI 2007/3099 reg 1(2)(*b*).
[2] In para (1), in definition of "the full cost of the goods", words inserted, and definition of "relevant asset" inserted, by the VAT (Amendment) (No 4) Regulations, SI 2010/3022 regs 2, 15 with effect from 1 January 2011.

116C [Economic life of goods
Goods held or used for the purposes of a business have an economic life being (subject to regulations 116G and 116L) the period of time commencing on the day when they are first used for any purpose after they have been supplied to, or acquired or imported by, a person or any of his predecessors and lasting for a period of—
   (*a*) 120 months in the case of land, a building or part of a building (but this is subject to regulation 116D);
   (*b*) 60 months for all other goods.][1]

Commentary—*De Voil Indirect Tax Service* **V3.212**.
Amendments—[1] Part 15A (regs 116A–116N) inserted by the VAT (Amendment) (No 7) Regulations, SI 2007/3099 regs 3, 4 with effect from 1 November 2007: SI 2007/3099 reg 1(2)(*b*).

[**116D** Where the economic life of the interest of a person, or any of his predecessors, in land, a building or part of a building commences at a time when that interest has less than 120 months to run at that time, it shall be limited to the number of months remaining before expiry of that interest and element B of the formula in regulation 116E and element D of the formula in regulation 116L shall be construed accordingly.][1]

Commentary—*De Voil Indirect Tax Service* **V3.212**.
Amendments—[1] Part 15A (regs 116A–116N) inserted by the VAT (Amendment) (No 7) Regulations, SI 2007/3099 regs 3, 4 with effect from 1 November 2007: SI 2007/3099 reg 1(2)(*b*).

116E [Value of a relevant supply
Subject to regulations 116F, 116H and 116I, the value of a relevant supply is the amount determined using the formula—

$$\frac{A}{B} \times (C \times U\%)$$

where—
    A is the number of months in the prescribed accounting period during which the relevant supply occurs which fall within the economic life of the goods concerned;
    B is the number of months of the economic life of the goods concerned or, in the case of an economic life commencing on 1st November 2007 by virtue of regulation 116L, what would have been its duration if it had been determined according to regulation 116C or 116G as appropriate;
    C is the full cost of the goods excluding any increase resulting from a supply of goods or services giving rise to a new economic life; and
    U% is the extent, expressed as a percentage, to which the goods are put to any private use or used, or made available for use, for non-business purposes as compared with the total use made of the goods during the part of the prescribed accounting period occurring within the economic life of the goods.][1]

Commentary—*De Voil Indirect Tax Service* **V3.212**.
Amendments—[1] Part 15A (regs 116A–116N) inserted by the VAT (Amendment) (No 7) Regulations, SI 2007/3099 regs 3, 4 with effect from 1 November 2007: SI 2007/3099 reg 1(2)(*b*).

[**116F** Where a prescribed accounting period in which a relevant supply occurs immediately follows a prescribed accounting period during which the goods whose use gives rise to that supply were not used or made available for use for any purpose, element "A" of the formula in regulation 116E shall (without prejudice to any other element of the formula) comprise the total number of months falling within the economic life concerned covered by—
    (*a*) the prescribed accounting period in which the relevant supply occurs; and
    (*b*) all preceding prescribed accounting periods which commence after the end of the prescribed accounting period during which the goods were last used or made available for use for any purpose before the prescribed accounting period in which the relevant supply occurs.][1]

Commentary—*De Voil Indirect Tax Service* **V3.212**.
HMRC Manuals—VAT Input Tax VIT25540 (periods of no use after the start of the economic life of goods).
Amendments—[1] Part 15A (regs 116A–116N) inserted by the VAT (Amendment) (No 7) Regulations, SI 2007/3099 regs 3, 4 with effect from 1 November 2007: SI 2007/3099 reg 1(2)(*b*).

116G [Later increase in the full cost of goods
Where—
    (*a*) a supply of goods or services is made to a person or any of his predecessors in respect of any goods held or used for the purposes of a business (whether or not the goods have an economic life in relation to that person at that time);
    (*b*) VAT is chargeable on that supply which is eligible (in whole or part) for credit under sections 25 and 26 of the Act or repayment under section 39 of the Act; and
    (*c*) by virtue of that supply, the full cost of the goods is greater than their full cost immediately before that supply,
a new economic life shall, without prejudice to any other economic life having effect in relation to those goods, be treated as commencing in respect of them in accordance with regulation 116C as if they had been supplied, acquired or imported at the time when the supply of goods or services is made.][1]

Commentary—*De Voil Indirect Tax Service* **V3.212**.
Amendments—[1] Part 15A (regs 116A–116N) inserted by the VAT (Amendment) (No 7) Regulations, SI 2007/3099 regs 3, 4 with effect from 1 November 2007: SI 2007/3099 reg 1(2)(*b*).

116H [Value of relevant supplies made during a new economic life
Subject to regulation 116I, the calculation of the value of a relevant supply made during a new economic life in accordance with the formula in regulation 116E is varied so that—

C is the increase in the full cost of the goods resulting from the supply of the goods or services giving rise to the new economic life; and

U% is the extent, expressed as a percentage, to which the goods are put to any private use or used, or made available for use, for non-business purposes as compared with the total use made of the goods during the part of the prescribed accounting period occurring during the new economic life of the goods.][1]

Commentary—*De Voil Indirect Tax Service* **V3.212**.
Amendments—[1] Part 15A (regs 116A–116N) inserted by the VAT (Amendment) (No 7) Regulations, SI 2007/3099 regs 3, 4 with effect from 1 November 2007: SI 2007/3099 reg 1(2)(*b*).

116I [Value of relevant supplies of goods which have two or more economic lives
Where a relevant supply occurs in relation to goods that have two or more economic lives at the time when they are put to private use or used, or made available for use, for non-business purposes, the value of that supply shall be such amount as represents the total of the amounts calculated in accordance with regulation 116E (as varied by regulation 116H as appropriate) in respect of those economic lives.][1]

Commentary—*De Voil Indirect Tax Service* **V3.212**.
Amendments—[1] Part 15A (regs 116A–116N) inserted by the VAT (Amendment) (No 7) Regulations, SI 2007/3099 regs 3, 4 with effect from 1 November 2007: SI 2007/3099 reg 1(2)(*b*).

116J [Transitional provisions
Regulation 116L applies to an economic life that—
  (*a*) would be treated as commencing before 1st November 2007 if that regulation did not apply; and
  (*b*) relates to goods that, before that day, have been put to any private use or used, or made available for use, for non-business purposes by the person described in regulation 116K or any of his predecessors (whether or not a relevant supply arising from that use has been treated as made before that day).][1]

Commentary—*De Voil Indirect Tax Service* **V3.212**.
Amendments—[1] Part 15A (regs 116A–116N) inserted by the VAT (Amendment) (No 7) Regulations, SI 2007/3099 regs 3, 4 with effect from 1 November 2007: SI 2007/3099 reg 1(2)(*b*).

[116K The person referred to in regulation 116J(b) is the person who holds or uses the goods concerned for the purposes of his business on 1st November 2007.][1]

Commentary—*De Voil Indirect Tax Service* **V3.212**.
Amendments—[1] Part 15A (regs 116A–116N) inserted by the VAT (Amendment) (No 7) Regulations, SI 2007/3099 regs 3, 4 with effect from 1 November 2007: SI 2007/3099 reg 1(2)(*b*).

[116L An economic life of goods to which this regulation applies shall be treated as commencing on 1st November 2007 and lasting for the period of time determined using the formula—

$$D \times \frac{(E - F)}{E}$$

where—
  D is the number of months which would have been the duration of the economic life concerned if it had commenced in accordance with regulation 116C or had been treated as having commenced in accordance with that regulation by virtue of regulation 116G;
  E is the value of element "C" of the formula contained in regulation 116E (as varied where appropriate in relation to that economic life by regulation 116H) for the purpose of determining the whole or, where the use occurs at a time when the goods have two or more economic lives at that time, part of the value of a relevant supply arising from the use of the goods during the economic life concerned;
  F is the value determined using the formula—

$$\frac{(G \times 100)}{(X\% \times 100)}$$

where—
  G is the total value of relevant supplies of the goods on which VAT has been or will be accounted for in respect of such relevant supplies arising from the goods being put to any private use or used, or made available for use, for non-business purposes before 1st November 2007 (whether or not such supplies are treated as made before or after that day) to the extent that the value of the relevant supplies comprised in the total value was determined by reference to the value of element "E" of the formula used in this regulation in respect of the economic life concerned; and

X% is the extent, expressed as a percentage, to which the goods have been put to any private use or used, or made available for use, for non-business purposes during the period described in regulation 116M as compared with the total use made of the goods in that period.]¹
Commentary—*De Voil Indirect Tax Service* **V3.212**.
Amendments—¹ Part 15A (regs 116A–116N) inserted by the VAT (Amendment) (No 7) Regulations, SI 2007/3099 regs 3, 4 with effect from 1 November 2007: SI 2007/3099 reg 1(2)(*b*).

[116M The period referred to in regulation 116L is the period of time commencing at the time when the economic life concerned would have commenced if it had commenced in accordance with regulation 116C or had been treated as having commenced in accordance with that regulation by virtue of regulation 116G and ending immediately before 1st November 2007.]¹
Commentary—*De Voil Indirect Tax Service* **V3.212**.
Amendments—¹ Part 15A (regs 116A–116N) inserted by the VAT (Amendment) (No 7) Regulations, SI 2007/3099 regs 3, 4 with effect from 1 November 2007: SI 2007/3099 reg 1(2)(*b*).

[116N Where a person has claimed deduction of input tax on goods which was incurred within the period of two years ending on 21st March 2007, he may withdraw that claim in whole or part as if it were made in error (but not so as to render him liable to any penalty or payment of interest in respect of that claim) provided that
  (*a*) the goods have not been used for any purpose before the claim is withdrawn;
  (*b*) he intends or expects that the goods will be put to private or non-business purposes during their economic life;
  (*c*) the withdrawal is in respect of—
    (i) all of the input tax claimed on the goods; or
    (ii) the part of the input tax claimed on the goods which is referable to his intended use of those goods for purposes other than those of his business; and
  (*d*) the withdrawal is made in accordance with regulation 35 (whatever the amount of the claim that is withdrawn) before 1st February 2008.]¹
Commentary—*De Voil Indirect Tax Service* **V3.212**.
Amendments—¹ Part 15A (regs 116A–116N) inserted by the VAT (Amendment) (No 7) Regulations, SI 2007/3099 regs 3, 4 with effect from 1 November 2007: SI 2007/3099 reg 1(2)(*b*).

PART XVI
IMPORTATIONS, EXPORTATIONS AND REMOVALS [IN RESPECT OF GREAT BRITAIN]

Amendments—In the heading, words inserted by the Value Added Tax (Miscellaneous Amendments, Northern Ireland Protocol and Savings and Transitional Provisions) (EU Exit) Regulations, SI 2020/1545 regs 31 and 60 with effect from IP completion day (11pm UK time on 31 December 2020) by virtue of SI 2020/1641 reg 2, Schedule para 11.

[116O Application of this Part
This Part applies to importations, exportations and removals in respect of Great Britain.]¹
Amendments—¹ Reg 116O inserted by the Value Added Tax (Miscellaneous Amendments, Northern Ireland Protocol and Savings and Transitional Provisions) (EU Exit) Regulations, SI 2020/1545 regs 31 and 61 with effect from IP completion day (11pm UK time on 31 December 2020) by virtue of SI 2020/1641 reg 2, Schedule para 11.

117 Interpretation of Part XVI
(1) In regulation 127 "approved inland clearance depot" means any inland premises approved by the Commissioners for the clearance of goods for customs and excise purposes.
(2) For the purposes of regulation 128 "container" means an article of transport equipment (lift-van, moveable tank or other similar structure)—
  (*a*) fully or partially enclosed to constitute a compartment intended for containing goods,
  (*b*) of a permanent character and accordingly strong enough to be suitable for repeated use,
  (*c*) specially designed to facilitate the carriage of goods, by one or more modes of transport, without intermediate reloading,
  (*d*) designed for ready handling, particularly when being transferred from one mode of transport to another,
  (*e*) designed to be easy to fill and to empty, and
  (*f*) having an internal volume of one cubic metre or more,
and the term "container" shall include the accessories and equipment of the container, appropriate for the type concerned, provided that such accessories and equipment are carried with the container, but shall not include vehicles, accessories or spare parts of vehicles, or packaging.
(3) [. . .]²
(4) . . . ⁵
(5), (6) . . . ¹
(7) For the purposes of regulation 129 "overseas authority" means any country other than the United Kingdom or any part of or place in such a country or the government of any such country, part or place.
(7A)–(7D) . . . ⁵

(8) In [regulation 132]² "overseas visitor" means a person who, during the 2 years immediately preceding . . . ² the date of the application mentioned in regulation 132, has not been in [Great Britain]⁷ for more than 365 days, or who, . . . ² during the 6 years immediately preceding the date of the application has not been in [Great Britain]⁷ for more than 1,095 days.
(9) . . . ³
(10), (11) . . . ⁶
[(12) In regulations 119 and 121D "UK Reliefs document" has the same meaning as in regulation 2 of the Customs (Reliefs from a Liability to Import Duty and Miscellaneous Amendments) (EU Exit) Regulations 2020.
(13) Unless otherwise specified, in this Part—
  (a) "importation" means—
    (i) the importation of goods from outside the United Kingdom (but not the Isle of Man) as a result of their entry into Great Britain; and
    (ii) the entry of goods into Great Britain following their removal from Northern Ireland,
  and related expressions are to be interpreted accordingly.
  (b) "export" means—
    (i) the export of goods from Great Britain to a place outside the United Kingdom (but not the Isle of Man); and
    (ii) the removal of goods from Great Britain to Northern Ireland,
  and related expressions are to be interpreted accordingly.]⁷

Commentary—*De Voil Indirect Tax Service* **V4.305, V4.306**.
HMRC Manuals—Insurance Premium Tax Manual IPT04630 (goods in foreign or international transit: definition of container). VAT Personal Exports: Retail Exports VATRES1150 (personal exports - retail exports: introduction: the law).
Amendments—¹ Para (4) substituted and paras (5), (6) revoked by the VAT (Amendment) Regulations, SI 1996/210 regs 8, 9, with effect from 1 March 1996.
² Para (3) revoked, paras (7A) to (7D) inserted and words in para (8) substituted and revoked by the VAT (Amendment) Regulations, SI 1999/438 reg 10, with effect from 1 April 1999.
³ Word in para. (4), (7A) substituted for the words "regulations 130 and" and "regulations 130(*a*)(i) and" respectively, and para (9) revoked, by the VAT (Amendment) (No 4) Regulations, SI 2003/1485 regs 2, 5 with effect for supplies made after 30 June 2003
⁴ Para (11) substituted by the VAT (Amendment) (No 3) Regulations, SI 2006/3292 regs 2, 4 with effect from 1 January 2007.
⁵ Paras (4) and (7A)–(7D) revoked by the Travellers' Allowances and Miscellaneous Provisions (EU Exit) Regulations, SI 2020/1412 reg 11(1), (2) with effect from IP completion day (11pm UK time on 31 December 2020). These amendments do not have effect in relation to goods that were purchased before IP completion day (see SI 2020/1412 reg 23). Para (4) previously read as follows—
  "(4) In [regulation] 131 "goods" does not include—
    (*a*)   a motor-vehicle, or
    (*b*)   a boat intended to be exported under its own power."
Paras (7A)–(7D). previously read as follows—
  "(7A) In [regulation] 131 the words "overseas visitor" refer to a traveller who is not established within the member States.
  (7B) For the purposes of paragraph (7A) above, a traveller is not established within the member States only if that traveller's domicile or habitual residence is situated outside the member States.
  (7C) Solely for the purposes of paragraph (7B) above, the traveller's domicile or habitual residence is the place entered as such in a valid—
    (*a*)   identity document,
    (*b*)   identity card, or
    (*c*)   passport.
  (7D) A document referred to in subparagraph (*a*), (*b*) or (*c*) of paragraph (7C) above is valid for the purposes of that paragraph only if—
    (*a*)   it is so recognised by the Commissioners; and
    (*b*)   it is not misleading as to the traveller's true place of domicile or habitual residence."
⁶ Paras (10) and (11) revoked by the VAT (Miscellaneous Amendments, Revocation and Transitional Provisions) (EU Exit) Regulations, SI 2019/513 regs 2, 5(1), (2) with effect from IP completion day (11pm UK time on 31 December 2020). Paras (10) and (11 previously read as follows—
  "(10) In regulations 140 and 144 "customs territory of the Community" has the same meaning as it has for the purposes of Council Regulation (EEC) No 2913 No 92.
  (11) In this Part references to Council Regulation (EEC) No 2913/92 (the Community Customs Code) and Commission Regulation (EEC) No 2454/93 (which contains provisions implementing the Community Customs Code) shall be read as references to those instruments as—
    (*a*)   amended by the Act concerning the accession of the Czech Republic, the Republic of Estonia, the Republic of Cyprus, the Republic of Latvia, the Republic of Lithuania, the Republic of Hungary, the Republic of Malta, the Republic of Poland, the Republic of Slovenia and the Slovak Republic, signed at Athens on 16th April 2003,
    (*b*)   amended, modified or otherwise affected by the Act concerning the conditions of Accession of the Republic of Bulgaria and Romania and the adjustments to the Treaties on which the European Union is founded, signed at Luxembourg on 25th April 2005 and Council Regulation (EC) No 1791/2006 (which contains consequential amendments to the Customs Code)."

[7] In para (8), in both places, words substituted for words "the United Kingdom", and paras (12) and (13) inserted, by the Value Added Tax (Miscellaneous Amendments, Northern Ireland Protocol and Savings and Transitional Provisions) (EU Exit) Regulations, SI 2020/1545 regs 31 and 62 with effect from IP completion day (11pm UK time on 31 December 2020) by virtue of SI 2020/1641 reg 2, Schedule para 11.

118 Enactments excepted

There shall be excepted from the enactments which are to apply [to importations][2] as mentioned in section 16(1) of the Act—
  (a) the Alcoholic Liquor Duties Act 1979—
    (i) section 7 (exemption from duty on spirits in articles used for medical purposes),
    (ii) section 8 (repayment of duty on spirits for medical or scientific purposes),
    (iii) section 9 (remission of duty on spirits for methylation),
    (iv) section 10 (remission of duty on spirits for use in art or manufacture),
    (v) section 22(4) (drawback on exportation of tinctures or spirits of wine), and
    (vi) sections 42 and 43 (drawback on exportation and warehousing of beer),
  (b) the Hydrocarbon Oil Duties Act 1979—
    (i) section 9 (relief for certain industrial uses),
    (ii) section 15 (drawback of duty on exportation etc of certain goods),
    (iii) section 16 (drawback of duty on exportation etc of power methylated spirits),
    (iv) section 17 (repayment of duty on heavy oil used by horticultural producers),
    (v) section 18 (repayment of duty on fuel for ships in home waters),
    (vi) section 19 (repayment of duty on fuel used in fishing boats etc),
    (vii) section 20 (relief from duty on oil contaminated or accidentally mixed in warehouse), and
    (viii) section 20AA (power to allow reliefs),
  (c) the Customs and Excise Management Act 1979—
    (i), (ii) . . . [2]
    (ii) section 125(1) and (2) (valuation of goods for the purpose of ad valorem duties),
    (iii) section 126 (charge of excise duty on manufactured or composite imported articles), and
    (iv) section 127(1)(b) (determination of disputes as to duties on imported goods),
  [(ca) the Taxation (Cross-border Trade) Act 2018—
    (i) section 16 (value of chargeable goods),
    (ii) section 36 (outward processing procedure),
    (iii) Schedule 2, Part 5 (authorised use procedure), except to the extent that it relates to the matters referred to in regulation 119(2)(a), and
    (iv) Schedule 2, Part 6 (temporary admission procedure), except to the extent that it relates to full relief from a liability to import duty in relation to a temporary admission procedure,][3]
  (d) the Customs and Excise Duties (General Reliefs) Act 1979 other than sections 8 and 9(b),
  (e) the Isle of Man Act 1979, sections 8 and 9 (removal of goods from Isle of Man to United Kingdom), . . . [1]
  (f) the Tobacco Products Duty Act 1979, section 2(2) (remission or repayment of duty on tobacco products)[, and
  (g) the Finance Act 1999, sections 126 and 127 (interest on unpaid customs debts and on certain repayments relating to customs duty)][1].

Commentary—*De Voil Indirect Tax Service* **V1.236, V3.322**.
HMRC Manuals—Imports Manual IMPS01200 (secondary law).
Amendments—[1] Word "and" at end of para (e) revoked, and para (g) and the word "and" immediately preceding it added by the VAT (Amendment) (No 2) Regulations, SI 2000/634 regs 2, 3 with effect from 1 April 2000.
[2] Sub-paras (c)(i) and (ii) revoked by the VAT (Miscellaneous Amendments, Revocation and Transitional Provisions) (EU Exit) Regulations, SI 2019/513 regs 2, 5(1), (3)(a) with effect from IP completion day (11pm UK time on 31 December 2020).
[3] Words inserted in the opening words, and para (ca) inserted, by the Value Added Tax (Miscellaneous Amendments, Northern Ireland Protocol and Savings and Transitional Provisions) (EU Exit) Regulations, SI 2020/1545 regs 31 and 63 with effect from IP completion day (11pm UK time on 31 December 2020) by virtue of SI 2020/1641 reg 2, Schedule para 11.

[119 Regulations excepted

(1) The provision made by or under the following subordinate legislation is excepted from applying to importations—
  (a) regulations 16(4) and (5) and 19(1)(b) of the Excise Warehousing (Etc) Regulations 1988 (certain removals from warehouse);
  (b) any regulations made under section 197(2)(f) of the Finance Act 1996 (rate of interest on overdue customs duty and on repayments of amounts paid by way of customs duty);
  (c) any regulation made under section 19 of the Taxation (Cross-border Trade) Act 2018 conferring full or partial relief from a liability to import duty; and
  (d) regulations 45 (interest on late payment of import duty) and 68 (interest payable by HMRC) of the Customs (Import Duty) (EU Exit) Regulations 2018.

(2) But paragraph (1)(c) does not include the following—
   (a) regulations 32 and 33 (authorised use procedure) of the Customs (Special Procedures and Outward Processing) (EU Exit) Regulations 2018 and regulation 20 of the Customs (Reliefs from a Liability to Import Duty and Miscellaneous Amendments) (EU Exit) Regulations 2020 including the authorised use rates document referred to in that regulation, in so far as these regulations relate to relief from import duty in respect of goods admitted into territorial waters—
      (i) in order to be incorporated into drilling or production platforms as part of the process of constructing, repairing, maintaining, altering or fitting-out of such platforms, or in order to link such platforms to the mainland of the United Kingdom; or
      (ii) for the fuelling and provisioning of drilling or production platforms;
   (b) regulations 35 to 40 (temporary admission procedure) of the Customs (Special Procedures and Outward Processing) (EU Exit) Regulations 2018, in so far as these regulations confer full relief from a liability to import duty in relation to a temporary admission procedure; and
   (c) the Customs (Reliefs from a Liability to Import Duty and Miscellaneous Amendments) (EU Exit) Regulations 2020, in so far as these Regulations confer a relief from import duty in relation to returned goods relief, as detailed at sections 37 to 39 of the UK Reliefs document, subject to the modifications and exceptions set out in regulation 121D.][1]

Commentary—*De Voil Indirect Tax Service* **V1.236**.
HMRC Manuals—Imports Manual IMPS01200 (secondary law).
Amendments—[1] Reg 119 substituted by the Value Added Tax (Miscellaneous Amendments, Northern Ireland Protocol and Savings and Transitional Provisions) (EU Exit) Regulations, SI 2020/1545 regs 31 and 64 with effect from IP completion day (11pm UK time on 31 December 2020) by virtue of SI 2020/1641 reg 2, Schedule para 11. Reg 119 previously read as follows—

"**119 Regulations excepted**

The provision made by or under the following subordinate legislation shall be excepted from applying as mentioned in section 16(1) of the Act—

   (a)   regulations 16(4) and (5) and 19(1)(b) of the Excise Warehousing (Etc) Regulations 1988 (certain removals from warehouse);
   (b)   any regulations made under section 197(2)(f) of the Finance Act 1996 (rate of interest on overdue customs duty and on repayments of amounts paid by way of customs duty)."

Commentary—*De Voil Indirect Tax Service* **V1.236**.
HMRC Manuals—Imports Manual IMPS01200 (secondary law).

120 Community legislation excepted

(1) Council Regulation (EEC) No 918/83 on conditional reliefs from duty on the final importation of goods, and any implementing Regulations made thereunder shall be excepted from the Community legislation which is to apply as mentioned in section 16(1) of the Act.

(2) The following Articles shall be excepted from the Community legislation which is to apply as mentioned in section 16(1) of the Act—
   (a) in Council Regulation (EEC) No 2913/92 establishing the Community Customs Code—
      (i) Articles 126 to 128 (drawback system of inward processing relief),
      (ii) . . . [2]
      (iii) Article 137 so far as it relates to partial relief on temporary importation, and Article 142,
      (iv) Articles 145 to 160 (outward processing),
      (v) . . . [4] . . . [1]
      (vi) Article 229(b) (interest payable on a customs debt),
      [(vii) Articles 232(1)(b), (2) and (3) (interest on arrears of duty), and
      (viii) Article 241, second and third sentences only (interest on certain repayments by the authorities),][1]
   [(b) in Commission Regulation (EEC) No 2454/93 which contains provisions implementing the Community Customs Code—
      (i) Articles 496 to 523, Articles 536 to 544 and Article 550 (but only to the extent that these Articles apply to the drawback system of inward processing relief),
      (ii) Article 519 (compensatory interest),
      (iii) Articles 585 to 592 (outward processing) (and Articles 496 to 523 to the extent that they are relevant to outward processing),
      (iv) . . . [4]][3]

(3) Council Regulation (EEC) No 2658/87 on the tariff and statistical nomenclature and on the Common Customs Tariff and implementing Regulations made thereunder (end use relief), save and in so far as the said Regulations apply to goods admitted into territorial waters—
   (a) in order to be incorporated into drilling or production platforms, for purposes of the construction, repair, maintenance, alteration or fitting-out of such platforms, or to link such drilling or production platforms to the mainland of the United Kingdom, or
   (b) for the fuelling and provisioning of drilling or production platforms,

shall be excepted from the Community legislation which is to apply as mentioned in section 16(1) of the Act.[5]

Commentary—*De Voil Indirect Tax Service* **V1.225**.
HMRC Manuals—Imports Manual IMPS01200 (secondary law).
Amendments—[1]   Words in para (2)(*a*)(v) revoked and para (2)(*a*)(vii), (viii) added by the VAT (Amendment) (No 2) Regulations, SI 2000/634 regs 2, 5 with effect from 1 April 2000.
[2]   In para (2), sub-paras (*a*)(ii), (*b*)(ii) revoked by the VAT (Amendment) Regulations, SI 2001/630 reg 3 with effect for goods imported after 31 March 2001.
[3]   Sub-para (2)(*b*) substituted by the VAT (Amendment)(No 5) Regulations, SI 2003/2318 regs 2, 5 with effect from 1 October 2003. This substitution has effect for supplies of goods or services the benefit of which was received after the coming into force of SI 2003/2318.
[4]   Paras (2)(*a*)(v), (2)(*b*)(iv) revoked by the VAT (Amendment) Regulations, SI 2006/587 regs 1(3), (5), 5 with effect from 6 April 2006.
[5]   Regulation 120 revoked by the VAT (Miscellaneous Amendments, Revocation and Transitional Provisions) (EU Exit) Regulations, SI 2019/513 regs 2, 5(1), (5) with effect from IP completion day (11pm UK time on 31 December 2020).

[121   Adaptations
(1) The provision made by the following enactments shall apply [to importations][3], as mentioned in section 16(1) of the Act, subject to the adaptations prescribed by this regulation.
(2) . . .[2]
(3) Section 129 of the Finance Act 1999 (recovery of certain amounts by the Commissioners) shall be regarded as providing for the recovery of a repayment of any relevant VAT (import VAT).][1]

Commentary—*De Voil Indirect Tax Service* **V1.236, V5.132B**.
HMRC Manuals—Imports Manual IMPS01200 (secondary law).
Amendments—[1]   This regulation substituted by the VAT (Amendment) (No 2) Regulations, SI 2000/634 regs 2, 6 with effect from 1 April 2000.
[2]   Para (2) revoked by the VAT (Miscellaneous Amendments, Revocation and Transitional Provisions) (EU Exit) Regulations, SI 2019/513 regs 2, 5(1), (6) with effect from IP completion day (11pm UK time on 31 December 2020). Para (2) previously read as follows—
"(2) Section 125(3) of the Customs and Excise Management Act 1979 (valuation of goods) shall have effect as if the reference to the preceding subsections of that section included a reference to section 21 of the Act.".
[3]   Words inserted by the Value Added Tax (Miscellaneous Amendments, Northern Ireland Protocol and Savings and Transitional Provisions) (EU Exit) Regulations, SI 2020/1545 regs 31 and 65 with effect from IP completion day (11pm UK time on 31 December 2020) by virtue of SI 2020/1641 reg 2, Schedule para 11.

[121A—In the Customs (Import Duty) (EU Exit) Regulations 2018, Part 10 (guarantees), in regulation 98(1), regard there being a third sub-paragraph as follows—
"(c)   relation to the VAT chargeable on the importation of goods into [Great Britain, from any territory not including Northern Ireland][2], the specified amount may be nil where in the opinion of an HMRC officer there is no risk to the payment."][1]

Amendments—[1]   Regulation 121A substituted by the VAT (Miscellaneous Amendments, Revocation and Transitional Provisions) (EU Exit) Regulations, SI 2019/513 regs 2, 5(1), (7) with effect from IP completion day (11pm UK time on 31 December 2020). Regulation 121A previously read as follows—

"121A—
(1) The application of the Customs Duties (Deferred Payment) Regulations 1976 in relation to any VAT chargeable on the importation of goods from places outside the member States is subject to the following prescribed adaptations.
(2) In regulation 4(1) (application for approval), regard "security" as being "appropriate security (which may be nil if there is no risk to the payment)".
(3) In regulation 4(2) (security and payment arrangements), regard there being a second sub-paragraph as follows—
"Provided that the amount in question may exceed that of the security in the case of nil security.".
(4) For regulation 4(3) (variations and revocations of approval), regard any Commissioners' variation consequent on the adaptations prescribed by this regulation as only being able to have effect after 30th November 2003.
(5) Before "and" at the end of regulation 8(*a*) (deemed payment for certain purposes at time deferment granted), regard there being—
"(*aa*)   Article 74(1) of Council Regulation (EEC) No 2913/92 (Community Customs Code) (no release of goods unless customs debt paid or secured);"."

[2]   Words substituted for words "the United Kingdom" by the Value Added Tax (Miscellaneous Amendments, Northern Ireland Protocol and Savings and Transitional Provisions) (EU Exit) Regulations, SI 2020/1545 regs 31 and 66 with effect from IP completion day (11pm UK time on 31 December 2020) by virtue of SI 2020/1641 reg 2, Schedule para 11.

[121B—*(1)* The application of Council Regulation (EEC) No 2913/92 (Community Customs Code) in relation to any VAT chargeable on the importation of goods from places outside the member States is subject to the following prescribed adaptations.
(2) But the adaptation in paragraph (5) only applies to the extent that the Commissioners grant deferment of payment of the relevant VAT with nil security.
(3) In Article 218(1) second sub-paragraph (single entry in the accounts), after "secured" regard there being "if required".

(4) In Article 225 first sub-paragraph (deferment of payment conditional on security), after "applicant" regard there being "(but the customs authorities may waive this condition if there is no risk to the payment)".
(5) Regard Article 225 as not being subject to Article 192 (fixing amount of security).][1], [2]

Amendments—[1] This regulation inserted by the VAT (Amendment) (No 5) Regulations, SI 2003/2318 regs 2, 6 with effect from 1 October 2003. This insertion has effect for supplies of goods or services the benefit of which was received after the coming into force of SI 2003/2318.
[2] Regulations 121B and 121C revoked by the VAT (Miscellaneous Amendments, Revocation and Transitional Provisions) (EU Exit) Regulations, SI 2019/513 regs 2, 5(1), (8) with effect from IP completion day (11pm UK time on 31 December 2020).

[121C—(1) The application of Commission Regulation (EEC) No 2454/93 (implementation of Community Customs Code) in relation to any VAT chargeable on the importation of goods from places outside the member States is subject to the following prescribed adaptations.
(2) But the adaptations in paragraphs (3) and (4) only apply to the extent that the Commissioners grant deferment of payment of the relevant VAT with nil security.
(3) Regard Articles 244, 248(1), 257(3), 257(4), 258, 262(1) and 876a(1) (circumstances in which duties have to be or are taken as having to be secured) as providing that the provision of security is at the discretion of the customs authorities.
(4) Regard Articles 244, 248(1), 257(3), 257(4) and 876a(1) (circumstances in which duties have to be secured) as not being subject to Article 192 of Council Regulation (EEC) No 2913/92 (Community Customs Code) (fixing amount of security).][1], [2]

Amendments—[1] This regulation substituted by the VAT (Amendment) (No 5) Regulations, SI 2003/2318 regs 2, 6 with effect from 1 October 2003.
[2] Regulations 121B and 121C revoked by the VAT (Miscellaneous Amendments, Revocation and Transitional Provisions) (EU Exit) Regulations, SI 2019/513 regs 2, 5(1), (8) with effect from IP completion day (11pm UK time on 31 December 2020).

[121D Modifications and exceptions for the application of returned goods relief

(1) For the purposes of relief from import VAT incurred on the importation of goods into Great Britain from outside the United Kingdom, the provisions of the Customs (Reliefs from a Liability to Import Duty and Miscellaneous Amendments) (EU Exit) Regulations 2020 are to be read as if the UK Reliefs document referred to in those Regulations was modified as follows.
(2) Regard sections 37 to 39 (returned goods relief) of the UK Reliefs document as requiring that the goods are re-imported into Great Britain by the same person who originally exported or re-exported the goods.
(3) Regard the amount of relief mentioned in sections 37 to 39 of the UK Reliefs document as reduced by the amount of any unpaid VAT.
(4) Regard the amount of import VAT in regulation 23 of the Customs (Special Procedures and Outward Processing) (EU Exit) Regulations 2018 as reduced by the amount of any paid VAT.
(5) For the purposes of paragraphs (3) and (4)—
  (a) "unpaid" refers to any part of the VAT charged and due on—
    (i) a supply of the goods in the United Kingdom before the re-importation, or
    (ii) an importation of the goods from outside the United Kingdom before the re-importation,
    which has been repaid, remitted or otherwise not paid;
  (b) "paid" refers to any part of the VAT charged, due and paid on—
    (i) a supply of the goods in the United Kingdom before the re-importation, or
    (ii) an importation of the goods from outside the United Kingdom before the re-importation,
    in circumstances where there is no actual, or no prospect of, repayment or remission;
  (c) a sum for which there is or was an entitlement or right to a deduction or refund within section 24 of the Act (input tax and output tax) is neither "unpaid" nor "paid".
(6) In the circumstances described in paragraph (7) or (8), the provisions of the Customs (Reliefs from a Liability to Import Duty and Miscellaneous Amendments) (EU Exit) Regulations 2020 are excepted from the legislation which is to apply as mentioned in section 16(1) of the Act (application of customs enactments).
(7) The circumstances are that—
  (a) the re-importer contemplated by sections 37 to 39 of the UK Reliefs document makes a supply of, or concerning, the goods whilst those goods are under the inward processing procedure or in the course of, or after, the relevant exportation, re-exportation or re-importation of the goods,
  (b) the place of supply for the purposes of VAT is determined by or under section 7 of the Act (place of supply of goods) as being outside the United Kingdom, and
  (c) the goods nevertheless are, or may be, stored or physically used in the United Kingdom by or under the direction of that re-importer or the person to whom that supply is made ("recipient");

and for these purposes "re-importer" and "recipient" include someone connected with either person or both persons as determined in accordance with sections 1122 and 1123 of the Corporation Tax Act 2010.

(8) The circumstances are that the goods in question were supplied at any time to any person pursuant to regulations 132 to 133 or pursuant to any corresponding provisions of the Isle of Man.][1]

Commentary—*De Voil Indirect Tax Service* **V3.322, V3.351**.

Transitional provisions—(1) Subject to para (2), reg 121D additionally applies to goods that are: (a) transported from the UK to a member State prior to IP completion day, and remain located in a member State as at IP completion day; or (b) exported from a member State prior to IP completion day and remain located outside the member States as at IP completion day.

(2) For the purposes of para (1), the terms "unpaid" and "paid" in reg 121D(5) also refer to: (a) an acquisition of goods in the UK before the re-importation; (b) an importation of the goods from outside the member States before the re-importation; (c) a supply or acquisition of the goods in a member State before the re-importation.

In the application of reg 121D to goods which are in the UK as at IP completion day, the terms "unpaid" and "paid" in reg 121D(5) are to have the additional meanings given in reg 125(2). Regulation 121D does not apply to goods supplied at any time to any person pursuant to reg 131 of the VAT Regulations.

(See SI 2020/1545 regs 125–127)

Amendments—[1] Reg 121D substituted by the Value Added Tax (Miscellaneous Amendments, Northern Ireland Protocol and Savings and Transitional Provisions) (EU Exit) Regulations, SI 2020/1545 regs 31 and 67 with effect from IP completion day (11pm UK time on 31 December 2020) by virtue of SI 2020/1641 reg 2, Schedule para 11. Reg 121D previously read as follows—

"**121D Adaptations and exceptions for the application of returned goods relief**

(1) The application of Council Regulation (EEC) No 2913/92 (Community Customs Code) and Commission Regulation (EEC) No 2454/93 (implementation Regulation) in relation to any VAT chargeable on the importation of goods from places outside the member States is subject to the following prescribed adaptations.

(2) Regard—
  (a) Articles 185 to 187 of the Community Customs Code (returned Community goods and returned compensating products), and
  (b) Articles 844 to 856 and Article 882 of the implementation Regulation (returned Community goods and returned compensating products),

as only applying in the case and to the extent of a reimportation to the United Kingdom by the person who originally exported or re-exported the relevant Community goods or compensating products from the VAT territory of the Community.

That VAT territory is the territorial application of Council Directive 77/388/EEC in accordance with Title III of that Directive (territorial application).

(3) Regard the amount of the relief mentioned in Article 186 of the Community Customs Code (returned Community goods) as reduced by the amount of any unpaid VAT.

(4) Regard the amount legally owed under Article 187 of the Community Customs Code (returned compensating products) as reduced by the amount of any paid VAT.

(5) For the purposes of paragraphs (3) and (4)—
  (a) "VAT" includes value added tax charged in accordance with the law of another member State (see sections 92(1), 92(2) and 96(1) of the Act);
  (b) "unpaid" refers to any part of the VAT charged and due on—
    (i) a supply or acquisition of the goods in a member State before the reimportation, or
    (ii) an importation of the goods from outside the member States before the reimportation,

  but repaid, remitted or otherwise not paid;
  (c) "paid" refers to any part of the VAT charged, due and paid on—
    (i) a supply or acquisition of the goods in a member State before the reimportation, or
    (ii) an importation of the goods from outside the member States before the reimportation,

  and without any actual, or prospect of, repayment or remission;
  (d) a sum for which there is or was under the law of a member State an entitlement or right to a deduction or refund within Article 17 of Council Directive 77/388/EEC (origin and scope of the right to deduct) is neither "unpaid" nor "paid".

(6) In the circumstances described by paragraph (7) or (8)—
  (a) Articles 185 to 187 of the Community Customs Code (returned goods), and
  (b) Articles 844 to 856 and Article 882 of the implementation Regulation (returned goods),

are excepted from the Community legislation which is to apply as mentioned in section 16(1) of the Act (application of customs legislation in relation to import VAT).

(7) These circumstances are that—
  (a) the reimporter contemplated by those Articles makes a supply of, or concerning, the goods whilst under the inward processing procedure or in the course of, or after, the relevant exportation, re-exportation or reimportation,
  (b) the place of that supply for the purposes of VAT is determined by or under section 7 of the Act (place of supply) as being outside the United Kingdom, and
  (c) the goods nevertheless are or may be stored or physically used in the United Kingdom by or under the direction of that reimporter or the person to whom that supply is made ("recipient").

For these purposes, "reimporter" and "recipient" include someone connected with either person or both persons as determined in accordance with section 839 of the Taxes Act.

(8) These circumstances are that the goods in question were supplied at any time to any person pursuant to regulations 131 to 133 (supplies to persons departing from the member States) or pursuant to any corresponding provision of the Isle of Man.

(9) For the purposes of the Articles of the Community Customs Code and implementation Regulation mentioned in paragraph (2)—
- (*a*) regard the description of the customs territory of the Community in Article 3 of the Community Customs Code as being substituted with a description of the VAT territory (see paragraph (2));
- (*b*) regard the following references as including a reference to the completion of the formalities referred to in Article 33a(1)(*a*) of Council Directive 77/388/EEC (formalities relating to entry of goods into VAT territory from territory considered a third territory)—
  - (i) "released for free circulation" in the definition of "Community goods" in Article 4(7), second indent and Article 185(1) of the Community Customs Code;
  - (ii) "entered" and "declared" for "release for free circulation" in, or for the purposes of, Articles 844(4), 848(1), 848(2), 849(1) and 849(5) of the implementation Regulation;
- (*c*) regard the following references as including a reference to the completion of the formalities referred to in Article 33a(2)(*a*) of Council Directive 77/388/EEC (or to a declaration under those formalities) (formalities relating to dispatch or transport of goods from Member State to territory considered a third territory)—
  - (i) "customs export formalities" in Articles 844(1), 849(1), 849(2) and 849(3) of the implementation Regulation;
  - (ii) "export declaration" in Article 848(1) of that Regulation;
  - (iii) "customs formalities relating to their exportation" in Articles 844(4) and 849(1) of that Regulation;
- (*d*) regard—
  - (i) the definition of "import duties" in Article 4(10) of the Community Customs Code as defining instead VAT charged on the importation of goods from places outside the member States in accordance with the Act; and
  - (ii) the references to "import duty" and "duty" in Article 185(1), second sub-paragraph, second indent and Article 187 of the Community Customs Code as references to such VAT.

(10) The references to Council Directive 77/388/EEC in paragraphs (2), (5)(*d*), (9)(*b*) and (9)(*c*) embrace relevant amendments up to and including 6th April 2006 only."

122 Postal importations by registered persons in the course of business

Goods imported by post from places outside the member States, other than by datapost packet, not exceeding £2,000 in value, or such greater sum as is determined for the time being by the Commissioners, by a registered person in the course of a business carried on by him may, with the authority of the proper officer, be delivered without payment of VAT if—
- (*a*) the registered person has given such security as the Commissioners may require, and
- (*b*) his registration number is shown on the customs declaration attached to or accompanying the package,

and save as the Commissioners may otherwise allow he shall account for VAT chargeable on the goods on their importation together with any VAT chargeable on the supply of goods or services by him or on the acquisition of goods by him from another member State in a return furnished by him in accordance with these Regulations for the prescribed accounting period during which the goods were imported.[1]

Commentary—*De Voil Indirect Tax Service* **V5.115, V5.211**.
HMRC Manuals—Imports Manual IMPS07300 (UK law).
Amendments—[1] Regulation 122 revoked by the Value Added Tax (Accounting Procedures for Import VAT for VAT Registered Persons and Amendment) (EU Exit) Regulations, SI 2019/60 reg 12(1), (6) with effect from IP completion day (11pm UK time on 31 December 2020).

123 Temporary importations

(1) Subject to such conditions as the Commissioners may impose, the VAT chargeable on the importation of goods from a place outside the member States shall not be payable where—
- (*a*) *a taxable person makes a supply of goods which is to be zero-rated in accordance with sub-paragraphs (a)(i) and (ii), and (b) of section 30(8) of the Act,*
- (*b*) *the goods so imported are the subject of that supply, and*
- (*c*) *the Commissioners are satisfied that—*
  - (i) *the importer intends to remove the goods to another member State, and*
  - (ii) *the importer is importing the goods in the course of a supply by him of those goods in accordance with the provisions of sub-paragraphs (a)(i) and (ii), and (b) of section 30(8) of the Act and any Regulations made thereunder.*

(2) As a condition of granting the relief afforded by paragraph (1) above the Commissioners may require the deposit of security, the amount of which shall not exceed the amount of VAT chargeable on the importation.

(3) The relief afforded by paragraph (1) above shall continue to apply provided that the importer—
- (*a*) *removes the goods to another member State within one month of the date of importation or within such longer period as the Commissioners may allow, and*
- (*b*) *supplies the goods in accordance with sub-paragraphs (a)(i) and (ii), and (b) of section 30(8) of the Act and any Regulations made thereunder.*[1]

Commentary—*De Voil Indirect Tax Service* **V3.320**.

Amendments—[1] Regulation 123 revoked by the VAT (Miscellaneous Amendments, Revocation and Transitional Provisions) (EU Exit) Regulations, SI 2019/513 regs 2, 5(1), (9) with effect from IP completion day (11pm UK time on 31 December 2020).

126 Reimportation of goods exported for treatment or process

[[(1)] Subject to such conditions as the Commissioners may impose, VAT chargeable on the importation of goods which have been temporarily exported and are re-imported after having undergone repair, process or adaptation outside [Great Britain][2], or after having been made up or reworked outside [Great Britain][2], shall be payable as if such treatment or process had been carried out in [Great Britain][2], if the Commissioners are satisfied that—
   (a) at the time of exportation the goods were intended to be re-imported after completion of the treatment or process outside [Great Britain][2], and
   (b) the ownership in the goods was not transferred to any other person at exportation or during the time they were abroad.
[(2) For the purposes of this regulation—
   (a) the reference to the importation of goods does not include the removal of goods from Northern Ireland to Great Britain, and related expressions are to be interpreted accordingly;
   (b) any reference to the exportation of goods does not include the removal of goods from Great Britain to Northern Ireland, and related expressions are to be interpreted accordingly.][2]][1]

Commentary—*De Voil Indirect Tax Service* **V3.306**.
HMRC Manuals—Import Manaul IMPS06100 (re-imports: introduction).
IMPS06600 (film re-importation after exposure abroad).
Amendments—[1] Regulation 126 substituted by the VAT (Miscellaneous Amendments, Revocation and Transitional Provisions) (EU Exit) Regulations, SI 2019/513 regs 2, 5(1), (10) with effect from IP completion day (11pm UK time on 31 December 2020). Regulation 126 previously read as follows—

> "126 Reimportation of goods exported for treatment or process
>
> Subject to such conditions as the Commissioners may impose, VAT chargeable on the importation of goods from a place outside the member States which have been temporarily exported from the member States and are reimported after having undergone repair, process or adaptation outside the member States, or after having been made up or reworked outside the member States, shall be payable as if such treatment or process had been carried out in the United Kingdom, if the Commissioners are satisfied that—
>   (a) at the time of exportation the goods were intended to be reimported after completion of the treatment or process outside the member States, and
>   (b) the ownership in the goods was not transferred to any other person at exportation or during the time they were abroad."

[2] Para (1) numbered as such, and words substituted for words "the United Kingdom", and para (2) inserted, by the Value Added Tax (Miscellaneous Amendments, Northern Ireland Protocol and Savings and Transitional Provisions) (EU Exit) Regulations, SI 2020/1545 regs 31 and 68 with effect from IP completion day (11pm UK time on 31 December 2020) by virtue of SI 2020/1641 reg 2, Schedule para 11.

128 Export of freight containers

Where the Commissioners are satisfied that a container is to be exported to a place outside [Great Britain][1], its supply, subject to such conditions as they may impose, shall be zero-rated.

Commentary—*De Voil Indirect Tax Service* **V4.207, V4.304**.
HMRC Manuals—VAT Export And Removal of Goods from the UK VEXP10530 (UK secondary law).
Amendments—[1] Words substituted for words "the United Kingdom" by the Value Added Tax (Miscellaneous Amendments, Northern Ireland Protocol and Savings and Transitional Provisions) (EU Exit) Regulations, SI 2020/1545 regs 31 and 69 with effect from IP completion day (11pm UK time on 31 December 2020) by virtue of SI 2020/1641 reg 2, Schedule para 11.

129 Supplies to overseas persons

(1) Where the Commissioners are satisfied that—
   (a) goods intended for export to a place outside the member States have been supplied [at a time when they were located in Great Britain][4] . . . [2] to—
      (i) a person not resident in [Great Britain][4],
      (ii) a trader who has no business establishment in [Great Britain][4] from which taxable supplies are made, or
      (iii) an overseas authority, . . . [3]
   (b) the goods were exported to a place outside [Great Britain][4], [and][3]
   [(c) the goods are not personal gifts on export as defined in regulation 2 of the Customs (Export) (EU Exit) Regulations 2019,][3] [and][4]
   [(d) any conditions that may be specified by the Commissioners in a notice published by them have been met,][4]
the supply, subject to such [other][4] conditions as they may impose, shall be zero-rated.
(2) . . . [1]

Commentary—*De Voil Indirect Tax Service* **V4.207, V4.306**.
HMRC Manuals—VAT Export And Removal Of Goods From The UK VEXP20300 (direct and indirect exports).
VEXP10530 (UK secondary law).
Amendments—[1] Para (2) revoked by the VAT (Amendment) (No 4) Regulations, SI 2003/1485 regs 2, 6 with effect for supplies made after 30 June 2003.

[2] In para (1)(a), words ", otherwise than to a taxable person," revoked by the VAT (Amendment) (No 2) Regulations, SI 2013/2241 regs 2, 3 with effect in relation to supplies made on or after 1 October 2013.
[3] The "and" at the end of sub-para (a)(iii) revoked, "and" at the end of sub-para (b) inserted, and sub-para (c) inserted by the Travellers' Allowances and Miscellaneous Provisions (EU Exit) Regulations, SI 2020/1412 reg 11(1), (3) with effect from IP completion day (11pm UK time on 31 December 2020).
[4] Words substituted for words "the United Kingdom", in sub-paras (a) and (c) words inserted, sub-para (d) inserted, and word "other" inserted into the text before para (2), by the Value Added Tax (Miscellaneous Amendments, Northern Ireland Protocol and Savings and Transitional Provisions) (EU Exit) Regulations, SI 2020/1545 regs 31 and 70 with effect from IP completion day (11pm UK time on 31 December 2020) by virtue of SI 2020/1641 reg 2, Schedule para 11.

131—(1) Where the Commissioners are satisfied that—
(a) goods have been supplied to a person who is an overseas visitor and who, at the time of the supply, intended to depart from the member States [before the end of the third month following that in which the supply is effected][1] and that the goods should accompany him,
(b) save as they may allow, the goods were produced to the competent authorities for the purposes of the common system of VAT in the member State from which the goods were finally exported to a place outside the member States, and
(c) the goods were exported to a place outside the member States,
the supply, subject to such conditions as they may impose, shall be zero-rated.
(2) [2] . . . [3]

Amendments—[1] Words in para (1)(a) substituted by the VAT (Amendment) Regulations, SI 1995/3147 reg 6, with effect from 1 January 1996.
[2] Para (2) revoked by the VAT (Amendment) (No 4) Regulations, SI 2003/1485 regs 2, 6 with effect for supplies made after 30 June 2003.
[3] Regulation 131 revoked by the Travellers' Allowances and Miscellaneous Provisions (EU Exit) Regulations, SI 2020/1412 reg 11(1), (5) with effect from IP completion day (11pm UK time on 31 December 2020). These amendments do not have effect in relation to goods that were purchased before IP completion day (see SI 2020/1412 reg 23).

132 [Supplies to persons departing from Great Britain][3]
[(1)] The Commissioners may, on application by an overseas visitor who intends to depart from [Great Britain][2] within 15 months and remain outside [Great Britain][2] for a period of at least 6 months, permit him within 12 months of his intended departure to purchase, from a registered person, a . . . [1] motor vehicle [located in Great Britain at the time of its purchase][2] without payment of VAT, for subsequent export, and its supply, subject to such conditions as they may impose, shall be zero-rated.
[(2) The conditions that the Commissioners may impose under paragraph (1) may be specified in a notice published by them.][2]

Commentary—*De Voil Indirect Tax Service* **V4.207**.
HMRC Manuals—VAT Personal Exports VEXMOTORS1200 (introduction),
VEXP30310 (exports/removals affected by the COVID19 emergency).
Amendments—[1] Word revoked by the VAT (Amendment) Regulations, SI 2000/258 regs 2, 6 with effect from 1 April 2000.
[2] Para (1) numbered as such, and words substituted for words "the United Kingdom" and words inserted, and para (2) inserted, by the Value Added Tax (Miscellaneous Amendments, Northern Ireland Protocol and Savings and Transitional Provisions) (EU Exit) Regulations, SI 2020/1545 regs 31 and 71 with effect from IP completion day (11pm UK time on 31 December 2020) by virtue of SI 2020/1641 reg 2, Schedule para 11.
[3] Heading inserted by the Value Added Tax (Miscellaneous Amendments, Northern Ireland Protocol and Savings and Transitional Provisions) (EU Exit) Regulations, SI 2020/1545 regs 31 and 72 with effect from IP completion day (11pm UK time on 31 December 2020) by virtue of SI 2020/1641 reg 2, Schedule para 11.

133 [(1)] The Commissioners may, on application by any person who intends to depart from [Great Britain][2] within 9 months and remain outside [Great Britain][2] for a period of at least 6 months, permit him within 6 months of his intended departure to purchase, from a registered person, a . . . [1] motor vehicle [located in Great Britain at the time of its purchase][2] without payment of VAT, for subsequent export, and its supply, subject to such conditions as they may impose, shall be zero-rated.
[(2) The conditions that the Commissioners may impose under paragraph (1) may be specified in a notice published by them.][2]

Commentary—*De Voil Indirect Tax Service* **V4.207**.
HMRC Manuals—VAT Personal Exports VEXMOTORS1200 (introduction),
VEXP30310 (exports/removals affected by the COVID19 emergency).
Amendments—[1] Word revoked by the VAT (Amendment) Regulations, SI 2000/258 regs 2, 6 with effect from 1 April 2000.
[2] Para (1) numbered as such, words substituted for words "the United Kingdom" and words inserted, and para (2) inserted, by the Value Added Tax (Miscellaneous Amendments, Northern Ireland Protocol and Savings and Transitional Provisions) (EU Exit) Regulations, SI 2020/1545 regs 31 and 73 with effect from IP completion day (11pm UK time on 31 December 2020) by virtue of SI 2020/1641 reg 2, Schedule para 11.

[PART 16ZA
IMPORTATIONS, EXPORTATIONS AND REMOVALS IN RESPECT OF
NORTHERN IRELAND

133A Interpretation
(1) This Part applies to importations, exportations and removals in respect of Northern Ireland.
(2) In this Part—
"container" has the same meaning as in Part 16;
"export" means—
  (i) the export of goods from Northern Ireland to a place outside the member States; and
  (ii) the removal of goods from Northern Ireland to Great Britain or the Isle of Man, and
  related expressions are to be interpreted accordingly.
"importation" means—
  (i) the importation of goods from outside the United Kingdom as a result of their entry into Northern Ireland; and
  (ii) the entry of goods into Northern Ireland following their removal from Great Britain or the Isle of Man,
  and related expressions are to be interpreted accordingly;
"overseas authority" means any country other than the United Kingdom or any part of or place in such a country or the government of any such country, part or place;
"relevant state" and "relevant states" means the member States and Northern Ireland;
"Union customs legislation" has the meaning given by paragraph 1(8) of Schedule 9ZB to the Act.][1]

Amendments—[1] Part 16ZA (regs 133A–133H) inserted by the Value Added Tax (Miscellaneous Amendments, Northern Ireland Protocol and Savings and Transitional Provisions) (EU Exit) Regulations, SI 2020/1545 regs 31 and 74 with effect from IP completion day (11pm UK time on 31 December 2020) by virtue of SI 2020/1641 reg 2, Schedule para 11.

[133B Supplies to persons outside the relevant states
Where the Commissioners are satisfied that—
(1) goods intended for export to a place outside the relevant states have been supplied at a time when they were located in Northern Ireland to—
  (a) a person not resident in Northern Ireland,
  (b) a trader who has no business establishment in Northern Ireland from which taxable supplies are made, or
  (c) an overseas authority, and
(2) the goods were exported to a place outside the relevant states;
(3) the goods are not personal gifts on export as defined in regulation 9 of the Customs (Export) (EU Exit) Regulations 2019; and
(4) any conditions that may be specified by the Commissioners in a notice published by them have been met,
the supply, subject to such other conditions as they may impose, shall be zero-rated.][1]

Amendments—[1] Part 16ZA (regs 133A–133H) inserted by the Value Added Tax (Miscellaneous Amendments, Northern Ireland Protocol and Savings and Transitional Provisions) (EU Exit) Regulations, SI 2020/1545 regs 31 and 74 with effect from IP completion day (11pm UK time on 31 December 2020) by virtue of SI 2020/1641 reg 2, Schedule para 11.

[133C VAT Retail Export Scheme
(1) Where the Commissioners are satisfied that—
  (a) goods, which at the time of the supply were located in Northern Ireland, have been supplied to a person who is an overseas visitor and who, at the time of the supply, intended to depart from the relevant states before the end of the third month following that in which the supply is effected and that the goods should accompany him,
  (b) save as they may allow, the goods were produced to the competent authorities for the purposes of the common system of VAT in the relevant state from which the goods were finally exported to a place outside the relevant states, and
  (c) the goods were exported to a place outside the relevant states,
the supply, subject to such conditions as they may impose, shall be zero-rated.
(2) In this regulation—
  (a) "goods" does not include—
    (i) a motor-vehicle, or
    (ii) a boat intended to be exported under its own power,
  (b) the words "overseas visitor" refer to a traveller who is not established within the relevant states,
  (c) for the purposes of paragraph (b) above, a traveller is not established within the relevant states only if that traveller's domicile or habitual residence is situated outside the relevant states,

(d) solely for the purposes of paragraph (c) above, the traveller's domicile or habitual residence is the place entered as such in a valid—
   (i) identity document,
   (ii) identity card, or
   (iii) passport,
(e) a document referred to in sub-paragraph (i), (ii) or (iii) of paragraph (d) is valid for the purposes of that paragraph only if—
   (i) it is so recognised by the Commissioners, and
   (ii) it is not misleading as to the traveller's true place of domicile or habitual residence.][1]

Amendments—[1] Part 16ZA (regs 133A–133H) inserted by the Value Added Tax (Miscellaneous Amendments, Northern Ireland Protocol and Savings and Transitional Provisions) (EU Exit) Regulations, SI 2020/1545 regs 31 and 74 with effect from IP completion day (11pm UK time on 31 December 2020) by virtue of SI 2020/1641 reg 2, Schedule para 11.

[133D Supplies to persons departing from the relevant states
(1) The Commissioners may, on application by an overseas visitor who intends to depart from the relevant states within 15 months and remain outside the relevant states for a period of at least 6 months, permit that person within 12 months of the person's intended departure to purchase, from a registered person, a motor vehicle located in Northern Ireland at the time of purchase without payment of VAT, for subsequent export, and its supply, subject to such conditions as they may impose, shall be zero-rated.
(2) The conditions that the Commissioners may impose under paragraph (1) may be specified in a notice published by them.
(3) In this regulation, "overseas visitor" means a person who, during the 2 years immediately preceding the date of the application has not been in Northern Ireland for more than 365 days, or who, during the 6 years immediately preceding the date of the application has not been in Northern Ireland for more than 1,095 days.][1]

Amendments—[1] Part 16ZA (regs 133A–133H) inserted by the Value Added Tax (Miscellaneous Amendments, Northern Ireland Protocol and Savings and Transitional Provisions) (EU Exit) Regulations, SI 2020/1545 regs 31 and 74 with effect from IP completion day (11pm UK time on 31 December 2020) by virtue of SI 2020/1641 reg 2, Schedule para 11.

[133E (1) The Commissioners may, on application by any person who intends to depart from the relevant states within 9 months and remain outside the relevant states for a period of at least 6 months, permit that person within 6 months of the person's intended departure to purchase, from a registered person, a motor vehicle located in Northern Ireland at the time of purchase without payment of VAT, for subsequent export, and its supply, subject to such conditions as they may impose, shall be zero-rated.
(2) The conditions that the Commissioners may impose under paragraph (1) may be specified in a notice published by them.
(3) In this regulation, "overseas visitor" means a person who, during the 2 years immediately preceding the date of the application has not been in Northern Ireland for more than 365 days, or who, during the 6 years immediately preceding the date of the application has not been in Northern Ireland for more than 1,095 days.][1]

Amendments—[1] Part 16ZA (regs 133A–133H) inserted by the Value Added Tax (Miscellaneous Amendments, Northern Ireland Protocol and Savings and Transitional Provisions) (EU Exit) Regulations, SI 2020/1545 regs 31 and 74 with effect from IP completion day (11pm UK time on 31 December 2020) by virtue of SI 2020/1641 reg 2, Schedule para 11.

133F Supplies to persons taxable in a member State
(1) Subject to regulation 133G, where the Commissioners are satisfied that—
   (a) a supply of goods by a taxable person involves their removal from Northern Ireland;
   (b) the supply is to a person ("P") who is registered for VAT in a member State and has provided the supplier with the VAT identification number issued to P by that member State,
   (c) the goods have been removed to a member State, and
   (d) the goods are not goods in relation to whose supply the taxable person has opted, pursuant to section 50A of the Act, for VAT to be charged by reference to the profit margin on the supply,
the supply, subject to such conditions as they may impose, shall be zero-rated.][1]

Amendments—[1] Part 16ZA (regs 133A–133H) inserted by the Value Added Tax (Miscellaneous Amendments, Northern Ireland Protocol and Savings and Transitional Provisions) (EU Exit) Regulations, SI 2020/1545 regs 31 and 74 with effect from IP completion day (11pm UK time on 31 December 2020) by virtue of SI 2020/1641 reg 2, Schedule para 11.

[133G The zero-rating provided for by regulation 133F shall be revoked where, in relation to a supply,—
   (a) the taxable person who makes the supply fails to comply with the obligation to submit a statement under regulation 22; or
   (b) the statement submitted by that taxable person does not set out the correct information as required by or under regulation 22, unless the taxable person can satisfy the Commissioners that there was a reasonable excuse for the failure to comply or the failure to provide the correct information, as appropriate.][1]

Amendments—[1] Part 16ZA (regs 133A–133H) inserted by the Value Added Tax (Miscellaneous Amendments, Northern Ireland Protocol and Savings and Transitional Provisions) (EU Exit) Regulations, SI 2020/1545 regs 31 and 74 with effect from IP completion day (11pm UK time on 31 December 2020) by virtue of SI 2020/1641 reg 2, Schedule para 11.

[133H Additional provision in relation to importations, exportations and removals in respect of Northern Ireland

(1) The Commissioners may make additional provision in relation to importation, exportation and removals so far as concerning value added tax in respect of Northern Ireland in a notice published by them.

(2) A notice made under this regulation may include provision for the following—
   (a) enactments, regulations and Union customs legislation which are to be excepted or adapted in relation to importations in, or exports from, Northern Ireland;
   (b) treatment of supplies made to persons taxable in a member State or supplies of goods subject to excise duty to persons who are not taxable in a member State;
   (c) reimportation of goods exported for treatment or process, temporary importations and export of freight containers;
   (d) territories to be treated as excluded from or included in the territory of the Community and of the member States, related entry and exit formalities and use of the internal transit procedure under Union customs legislation and Union customs legislation which will apply.][1]

Amendments—[1] Part 16ZA (regs 133A–133H) inserted by the Value Added Tax (Miscellaneous Amendments, Northern Ireland Protocol and Savings and Transitional Provisions) (EU Exit) Regulations, SI 2020/1545 regs 31 and 74 with effect from IP completion day (11pm UK time on 31 December 2020) by virtue of SI 2020/1641 reg 2, Schedule para 11.

REGULATIONS 134–145 [REVOKED]

Note—Regulations 134–145 were previously within Part 16 as it applied before IP completion day.

134 Supplies to persons taxable in another member State

[Subject to regulation 134A, where][1] the Commissioners are satisfied that—
   (a) a supply of goods by a taxable person involves their removal from the United Kingdom,
   (b) the supply is to [a person ("P") who is registered for VAT in another member State and has provided the supplier with the VAT identification number issued to P by that other member State][1],
   (c) the goods have been removed to another member State, and
   (d) the goods are not goods in relation to whose supply the taxable person has opted, pursuant to section 50A of the Act, for VAT to be charged by reference to the profit margin on the supply,

the supply, subject to such conditions as they may impose, shall be zero-rated.[2]

Commentary—*De Voil Indirect Tax Service* **V4.207, V4.311**.
HMRC Manuals—VAT Export And Removal Of Goods From The UK VEXP20400 (basic conditions for zero rating intra-EU removals).
Former regulations—VAT (General) Regulations, SI 1985/886 reg 57A; VAT (General) (Amendment) Regulations, SI 1992/3102 reg 44, SI 1995/1280 reg 3.
Simon's Tax Cases—*McMahon (trading as Irish Cottage Trading Co) v R&C Comrs* [2012] UKUT 106 (TCC), [2012] STC 1859 .
Amendments—[1] Words substituted for word "Where", and in para (b) words substituted for words "a person taxable in another member State" by the VAT (Amendment) (No 2) Regulations, SI 2019/1509 regs 2, 3 with effect from 1 January 2020.
[2] Regulations 134–145 revoked by the VAT (Miscellaneous Amendments, Revocation and Transitional Provisions) (EU Exit) Regulations, SI 2019/513 regs 2, 5(15) with effect from IP completion day (11pm UK time on 31 December 2020).

[134A The zero-rating provided for by regulation 134 shall be revoked where, in relation to a supply,—
   (a) the taxable person who makes the supply fails to comply with the obligation to submit a statement under regulation 22; or
   (b) the statement submitted by that taxable person does not set out the correct information as required by or under regulation 22, unless the taxable person can satisfy the Commissioners that there was a reasonable excuse for the failure to comply or the failure to provide the correct information, as appropriate.][1], [2]

Commentary—*De Voil Indirect Tax Service* **V4.311**.
Amendments—[1] Regulation 134A inserted by the VAT (Amendment) (No 2) Regulations, SI 2019/1509 regs 2, 4 with effect from 1 January 2020.
[2] Regulations 134–145 revoked by the VAT (Miscellaneous Amendments, Revocation and Transitional Provisions) (EU Exit) Regulations, SI 2019/513 regs 2, 5(15) with effect from IP completion day (11pm UK time on 31 December 2020).

135 Supplies of goods subject to excise duty to persons who are not taxable in another member State

Where the Commissioners are satisfied that—
   (a) a supply by a taxable person of goods subject to excise duty involves their removal from the United Kingdom to another member State,
   (b) that supply is other than to a person taxable in another member State and the place of supply is not, by virtue of section 7(5) of the Act, treated as outside the United Kingdom,

(c) the goods have been removed to another member State in accordance with the provisions of the [Excise Goods (Holding, Movement and Duty Point) Regulations 2010][1], and
(d) the goods are not goods in relation to whose supply the taxable person has opted, pursuant to section 50A of the Act, for VAT to be charged by reference to the profit margin on the supply,

the supply, subject to such conditions as they may impose, shall be zero-rated.[1]

Commentary—*De Voil Indirect Tax Service* **V4.207, V4.312**.
Amendments—[1] Regulations 134–145 revoked by the VAT (Miscellaneous Amendments, Revocation and Transitional Provisions) (EU Exit) Regulations, SI 2019/513 regs 2, 5(15) with effect from IP completion day (11pm UK time on 31 December 2020).

136 Territories to be treated as excluded from or included in the territory of the Community and of the member States

For the purposes of the Act the following territories shall be treated as excluded from the territory of the Community—
(a) the Channel Islands,
(b) Andorra,
(c) San Marino, and
(d) the Aland Islands.[1]

Commentary—*De Voil Indirect Tax Service* **V1.213**.
Amendments—[1] Regulations 134–145 revoked by the VAT (Miscellaneous Amendments, Revocation and Transitional Provisions) (EU Exit) Regulations, SI 2019/513 regs 2, 5(15) with effect from IP completion day (11pm UK time on 31 December 2020).

137 For the purposes of the Act the following territories shall be treated as excluded from the territory of the member States and the territory of the Community—
(a) the Canary Islands (Kingdom of Spain),
[(b) Guadeloupe, French Guiana, Martinique, Mayotte, Réunion and Saint-Martin (French Republic), and][1]
(c) Mount Athos (Hellenic Republic).[1]

Commentary—*De Voil Indirect Tax Service* **V1.213**.
Amendments—[1] Regulations 134–145 revoked by the VAT (Miscellaneous Amendments, Revocation and Transitional Provisions) (EU Exit) Regulations, SI 2019/513 regs 2, 5(15) with effect from IP completion day (11pm UK time on 31 December 2020).

138—[(1) For the purposes of the Act the territory of the Community shall be treated as excluding—
(a) Austria, Finland and Sweden ("the 1995 acceding States"),
(b) the Czech Republic, Estonia, Cyprus, Latvia, Lithuania, Hungary, Malta, Poland, Slovakia and Slovenia ("the 2004 acceding States"), and
(c) Bulgaria and Romania ("the 2007 acceding states")
in relation to goods to which this regulation applies.]
(2) Subject to [paragraph 4] below, the goods to which this regulation applies are—
(a) goods which are the subject of a supply made in an acceding State before [the date specified in paragraph (5)][1] and which in pursuance of that supply are removed to the United Kingdom on or after [the date specified in paragraph (6)][1] being goods in the case of which provisions of the law of the acceding State in question having effect for purposes corresponding to those of subsection (6)(a) or (so far as it applies to exportations) subsection (8) of section 30 of the Act have prevented VAT from being charged on that supply, and
(b) goods which were subject to a suspension regime before 1st January 1995, which by virtue of any Community legislation were to remain, for VAT purposes only, subject to that regime for a period beginning with that date and which cease to be subject to that regime on or after 20th October 1995.
(3) For the purposes of paragraph (2)(b) above, goods shall be treated as having become subject to a suspension regime if—
(a) on their entry into the territory of the Community—
 (i) they were placed under a temporary admission procedure with full exemption from import duties, in temporary storage, in a free zone, or under customs warehousing arrangements or inward processing arrangements, or
 (ii) they were admitted into the territorial waters of the United Kingdom for the purpose of being incorporated into drilling or production platforms, for the purposes of the construction, repair, maintenance, alteration or fitting-out of such platforms, for the purpose of linking such platforms to the mainland of the United Kingdom, or for the purpose of fuelling or provisioning such platforms, or
(b) they were placed under any customs transit procedure in pursuance of a supply made in the course of a business,
and (in the case in question) the time that any Community customs debt in relation to the goods would be incurred in the United Kingdom if the accession to the European Union of the

acceding States were disregarded would fall to be determined by reference to the matters mentioned in sub-paragraph (a) or (b) above.

(4) This regulation does not apply to the following goods—
  (a) goods which are exported on or after [the date specified in paragraph (6)] to a place outside the member States,
  (b) goods which are not means of transport and are removed on or after [the date specified in paragraph (6)] from a temporary admission procedure such as is referred to in paragraph (3)(a)(i) above, in order to be returned to the person in an acceding State who had exported them from that State,
  (c) means of transport which are removed on or after [the date specified in paragraph (6)] from a temporary admission procedure such as is referred to in paragraph (3)(a)(i) above and which—
    (i) were first brought into service before [the date specified in paragraph (7)], or
    (ii) have a value not exceeding £4,000, or
    (iii) have been charged in an acceding State with VAT which has not been remitted or refunded by reason of their exportation and to such other tax (if any) to which means of transport of that class or description are normally chargeable.
[(5) For the purposes of paragraphs (2) and (4) the specified date—
  (a) in relation to the 1995 acceding states is 1st January 1995;
  (b) in relation to the 2004 acceding states is 1st May 2004; and
  (c) in relation to the 2007 acceding states is 1st January 2007.
(6) For the purposes of paragraphs (2) and (4) the specified date—
  (a) in relation to the 1995 acceding states is 20th October 1995;
  (b) in relation to the 2004 acceding states 1st May 2004; and
  (c) in relation to the 2007 acceding states 1st January 2007.
(7) For the purposes of paragraph (4)(c)(i) the specified date—
  (a) in relation to the 1995 acceding states is 1st January 1987;
  (b) in relation to the 2004 acceding states is 1st May 2006; and
  (c) in relation to the 2007 acceding states is 1st January 1999.][1]

Commentary—*De Voil Indirect Tax Service* **V1.213**.
Amendments—[1] Regulations 134–145 revoked by the VAT (Miscellaneous Amendments, Revocation and Transitional Provisions) (EU Exit) Regulations, SI 2019/513 regs 2, 5(15) with effect from IP completion day (11pm UK time on 31 December 2020).

139 For the purposes of the Act the following territories shall be treated as included in the territory of the member States and the territory of the Community—
  (i) *the Principality of Monaco (French Republic),* . . .
  (ii) *the Isle of Man (United Kingdom)[, and*
  (iii) *the United Kingdom Sovereign Base Areas of Akrotiri and Dhekelia (Cyprus).]*[1]

Commentary—*De Voil Indirect Tax Service* **V1.213, V3.193A**.
Amendments—[1] Regulations 134–145 revoked by the VAT (Miscellaneous Amendments, Revocation and Transitional Provisions) (EU Exit) Regulations, SI 2019/513 regs 2, 5(15) with effect from IP completion day (11pm UK time on 31 December 2020).

140 Entry and exit formalities
(1) Where goods enter the United Kingdom from the territories prescribed in regulation 136 or 137 the formalities relating to the entry of goods into the customs territory of the Community contained in Council Regulation (EEC) No 2913/92, Commission Regulation (EEC) No 2454/93 and the Customs Controls on Importation of Goods Regulations 1991, shall be completed.
(2) Where goods are exported from the United Kingdom to the territories prescribed in regulation 136 or 137 the formalities relating to the export of goods to a place outside the customs territory of the Community contained in Council Regulation (EEC) No 2913/92 and Commission Regulation (EEC) No 2454/93 shall be completed.[1]

Amendments—[1] Regulations 134–145 revoked by the VAT (Miscellaneous Amendments, Revocation and Transitional Provisions) (EU Exit) Regulations, SI 2019/513 regs 2, 5(15) with effect from IP completion day (11pm UK time on 31 December 2020).

141 Use of the internal Community transit procedure
Where goods enter the United Kingdom from the territories prescribed in regulation 136 or 137 and the said goods are intended for another member State, or other destination outside the United Kingdom transport of the goods to which destination involves their passage through another member State, the internal Community transit procedure described in Council Regulation (EEC) No 2913/92 and Commission Regulation (EEC) No 2454/93 shall apply.[1]

Amendments—[1] Regulations 134–145 revoked by the VAT (Miscellaneous Amendments, Revocation and Transitional Provisions) (EU Exit) Regulations, SI 2019/513 regs 2, 5(15) with effect from IP completion day (11pm UK time on 31 December 2020).

142 Customs and excise legislation to be applied

Subject to regulation 143, where goods are imported into the United Kingdom from the territories prescribed in regulation 136 or 137 customs and excise legislation shall apply (so far as relevant) in relation to any VAT chargeable upon such importation with the same exception and adaptations as are prescribed in regulations 118, 119, 120 and 121 in relation to the application of section 16(1) of the Act.[1]

Commentary—*De Voil Indirect Tax Service* **V1.236**.
HMRC Manuals—Imports Manual IMPS01200 (secondary law).
Amendments—[1] Regulations 134–145 revoked by the VAT (Miscellaneous Amendments, Revocation and Transitional Provisions) (EU Exit) Regulations, SI 2019/513 regs 2, 5(15) with effect from IP completion day (11pm UK time on 31 December 2020).

143

Where goods are imported into the United Kingdom from the territories prescribed in regulation 137, section 4 of the Finance (No 2) Act 1992 (enforcement powers) shall apply in relation to any VAT chargeable upon such importation as if references in that section to "member States" excluded the territories prescribed in regulation 137.[1]

Amendments—[1] Regulations 134–145 revoked by the VAT (Miscellaneous Amendments, Revocation and Transitional Provisions) (EU Exit) Regulations, SI 2019/513 regs 2, 5(15) with effect from IP completion day (11pm UK time on 31 December 2020).

144

Where goods are exported from the United Kingdom to the territories prescribed in regulation 136 or 137 the provisions relating to the export of goods to a place outside the customs territory of the Community contained in Council Regulation (EEC) No 2913/92 and Commission Regulation (EEC) No 2454/93 shall apply for the purpose of ensuring the correct application of the zero rate of VAT to such goods.[1]

Amendments—[1] Regulations 134–145 revoked by the VAT (Miscellaneous Amendments, Revocation and Transitional Provisions) (EU Exit) Regulations, SI 2019/513 regs 2, 5(15) with effect from IP completion day (11pm UK time on 31 December 2020).

145—

(1) Subject to paragraph (2) below, where goods are exported from the United Kingdom to the territories prescribed in regulation 136 or 137 the provisions made by or under the Customs and Excise Management Act 1979 in relation to the exportation of goods to places outside the member States shall apply (so far as relevant) for the purpose of ensuring the correct application of the zero rate of VAT to such goods.
(2) Where goods are being exported from the United Kingdom to the territories prescribed in regulation 137, section 4 of the Finance (No 2) Act 1992 (enforcement powers) shall apply to such goods as if references in that section to "member States" excluded the territories prescribed in regulation 137.[1]

Amendments—[1] Regulations 134–145 revoked by the VAT (Miscellaneous Amendments, Revocation and Transitional Provisions) (EU Exit) Regulations, SI 2019/513 regs 2, 5(15) with effect from IP completion day (11pm UK time on 31 December 2020).

[PART XVI(A)][1]
FISCAL AND OTHER WAREHOUSING REGIMES

Northern Ireland—Part 16A and Sch 1A apply to Northern Ireland warehouses and Northern Ireland fiscal warehouses as they apply to warehouses and fiscal warehouses as if any reference to "fiscal warehouse", "warehouse", "fiscal warehousing regime" and "warehousing regime" were a reference respectively to "Northern Ireland fiscal warehouse", "Northern Ireland warehouse", "Northern Ireland fiscal warehousing regime" and "Northern Ireland warehousing regime"; and with the modifications set out in regs 145M–145R in respect of Part 16A, and in reg 145T in respect of Sch 1A (see VAT Regs, SI 1995/2518 reg 145L, as inserted by SI 2020/1545 reg 79).

Amendments—[1] This Part inserted by the VAT (Amendment) (No 3) Regulations, SI 1996/1250 reg 13 with effect from 1 June 1996.

145A Interpretation of Part XVI(A)

(1) In this Part unless the context otherwise requires—
   "eligible goods" has the meaning given by section 18B(6);
   "fiscal warehouse" includes all fiscal warehouses kept by the same fiscal warehousekeeper;
   "material time" has the meaning given by section 18F(1) in the case of a fiscal warehousing regime and section 18(6) in the case of a warehousing regime;
   "regulation" or "regulations" refers to the relevant regulation or regulations of these Regulations; and
   "section" or "sections" refers to the relevant section or sections of the Act.
(2) For the purposes of this Part, where a fiscal warehousekeeper keeps one or more fiscal warehouses there shall be associated with him a single fiscal warehousing regime; and "relevant fiscal warehousekeeper", "relevant fiscal warehouse", "relevant fiscal warehousing regime", "his fiscal warehouse", "his fiscal warehousing regime" and similar expressions shall be construed in this light.

Northern Ireland—In the definition of "eligible goods", read the words after "by" as "paragraph 25(1) of Schedule 9ZB to the Act(a) (supplementary provision)"; and in the definition of "material time", read the words after "by" as "paragraph 25(1) of Schedule 9ZB to the Act except in regulation 145D where "material time" means the time the services are performed." (see VAT Regs, SI 1995/2518 reg 145M, as inserted by SI 2020/1545 reg 79).

145B Fiscal warehousing certificates
(1) . . . [2] The certificate referred to in section 18B(2)(d) (supplies of goods intended for fiscal warehousing) shall contain the information indicated [in the form specified in a notice published by the Commissioners][1].
(2) . . . [2]

Amendments—[1] In para (1), words substituted for words "in the form numbered 17 in Schedule 1 to these Regulations", by the VAT (Amendment) (No 2) Regulations, SI 2012/1899 regs 3, 18 with effect from 15 October 2012.
[2] In para (1) words "The certificate referred to in section 18B(1)(d) (certificate relating to acquisitions in or intended for fiscal warehousing) and" revoked, and para (2) revoked, by the Value Added Tax (Miscellaneous Amendments, Northern Ireland Protocol and Savings and Transitional Provisions) (EU Exit) Regulations, SI 2020/1545 regs 31 and 75 with effect from IP completion day (11pm UK time on 31 December 2020) by virtue of SI 2020/1641 reg 2, Schedule para 11. Para (2) previously read as follows—

"(2) A certificate prepared under section 18B(1)(d) by an acquirer who is not a taxable person shall be kept by him for a period of six years commencing on the day the certificate is prepared; and he shall produce it to a proper officer when that officer requests him to do so."

145C Certificates connected with services in fiscal or other warehousing regimes
The certificate referred to in section 18C(1)(c) (certificate required for the zero-rating of certain services performed on or in relation to goods while those goods are subject to a fiscal or other warehousing regime) shall contain the information indicated [in the form specified in a notice published by the Commissioners][1].

Commentary—*De Voil Indirect Tax Service* **V4.209**.
Amendments—[1] Words substituted for words "in the form numbered 18 in Schedule 1 to these Regulations", by the VAT (Amendment) (No 2) Regulations, SI 2012/1899 regs 3, 19 with effect from 15 October 2012.

145D VAT invoices relating to services performed in fiscal or other warehousing regimes
(1) This regulation applies to the invoice referred to in section 18C(1)(e) (invoice required for the zero-rating of the supply of certain services performed on or in relation to goods while those goods are subject to a fiscal or other warehousing regime).
(2) The invoice shall be known as a VAT invoice and shall state the following particulars (unless the Commissioners allow any requirement of this paragraph to be relaxed or dispensed with)—
  (*a*) an identifying number,
  (*b*) the material time of the supply of the services in question,
  (*c*) the date of the issue of the invoice,
  (*d*) the name, an address and the registration number of the supplier,
  (*e*) the name and an address of the person to whom the services are supplied,
  (*f*) a description sufficient to identify the nature of the services supplied,
  (*g*) the extent of the services and the amount payable, excluding VAT, expressed in sterling,
  (*h*) the rate of any cash discount offered,
  (*i*) the rate of VAT as zero per cent, and
  (*j*) a declaration that in respect of the supply of services in question, the requirements of section 18C(1) will be or have been satisfied.
(3) The supplier of the services in question shall issue the invoice to the person to whom the supply is made within thirty days of the material time of that supply of services (or within such longer period as the Commissioners may allow in general or special directions).

Commentary—*De Voil Indirect Tax Service* **V3.515A, V4.209, V3.513**.

145E Fiscal warehousing regimes
(1) Upon any eligible goods entering a fiscal warehouse the relevant fiscal warehousekeeper shall record their entry in his relevant fiscal warehousing record.
(2) Eligible goods shall only be subject to or in a fiscal warehousing regime at any time—
  (*a*) while they are allocated to that regime in the relevant fiscal warehousing record;
  (*b*) while they are not identified in that record as having been transferred; or,
  (*c*) prior to their removal from that regime.

145F The fiscal warehousing record and stock control
(1) In addition to the records referred to in regulation 31, a fiscal warehousekeeper shall maintain a fiscal warehousing record for any fiscal warehouse in respect of which he is the relevant fiscal warehousekeeper.
(2) The fiscal warehousing record may be maintained in any manner acceptable to the Commissioners. In particular, it shall be capable of—
  (*a*) ready use by any proper officer in the course of his duties; and
  (*b*) reproduction into a form suitable for any proper officer to readily use at a place other than the relevant fiscal warehouse.

(3) Subject to paragraph (4) below, the fiscal warehousing record shall have the features and shall comply with the requirements set out in Schedule 1A to these Regulations.
(4) In respect of any goods the relevant fiscal warehousing record shall not be required to record events more than six years following—
   (a) the transfer or removal of those goods from the relevant fiscal warehousing regime; or,
   (b) the exit of those goods from the relevant fiscal warehouse (in the case of goods which were not allocated to the relevant fiscal warehousing regime).
(5) A fiscal warehousekeeper, upon receiving a request to do so from any proper officer, shall—
   (a) produce his fiscal warehousing record to that officer and permit him to inspect or take copies of it or of any part of it (as that officer shall require); or,
   (b) facilitate and permit that officer to inspect any goods which are stored or deposited in his fiscal warehouse (whether or not those goods are allocated to the relevant fiscal warehousing regime).

Commentary—*De Voil Indirect Tax Service* **V5.201**.

145G [Fiscal warehousing transfers in Great Britain][1]
(1) Subject to paragraphs (2) and (3) below, a fiscal warehousekeeper ("the original fiscal warehousekeeper") may permit eligible goods which are subject to his fiscal warehousing regime ("the original regime") to be transferred to another fiscal warehousing regime ("the other regime") without those goods being treated as removed from the original regime.
(2) The original fiscal warehousekeeper shall not allow eligible goods to exit from his fiscal warehouse in pursuance of this regulation before he receives a written undertaking from the fiscal warehousekeeper in relation to that other fiscal warehousing regime ("the other fiscal warehousekeeper") that, in respect of those eligible goods, the other fiscal warehousekeeper will comply with the requirements of paragraph (3) below.
(3) The other fiscal warehousekeeper, upon the entry of the goods to his fiscal warehouse, shall—
   (a) record that entry in his fiscal warehousing record; and,
   (b) allocate those goods to his fiscal warehousing regime.
Furthermore, within 30 days commencing with the day on which those goods left the original fiscal warehouse, he shall—
   (c) deliver or cause to be delivered to the original fiscal warehousekeeper a certificate in a form acceptable to the Commissioners confirming that he has recorded the entry of those goods to his fiscal warehouse and allocated them to his fiscal warehousing regime; and,
   (d) retain a copy of that certificate as part of his fiscal warehousing record.

Northern Ireland—Read the heading to reg 145G as "Fiscal warehousing transfers in Northern Ireland" (see VAT Regs, SI 1995/2518 reg 145N, as inserted by SI 2020/1545 reg 79).
Amendments—[1]   In the heading words substituted for words "Fiscal warehousing transfers in the United Kingdom" by the Value Added Tax (Miscellaneous Amendments, Northern Ireland Protocol and Savings and Transitional Provisions) (EU Exit) Regulations, SI 2020/1545 regs 31 and 76 with effect from IP completion day (11pm UK time on 31 December 2020) by virtue of SI 2020/1641 reg 2, Schedule para 11.

145H Removal of goods from a fiscal warehousing regime and transfers [outside Great Britain][1]
(1) Without prejudice to sections 18F(5), 18F(6) and the following paragraphs of this regulation, eligible goods which are allocated to a fiscal warehousing regime shall only be removed from that regime at the time and in any of the following circumstances—
   (a) when an entry in respect of those eligible goods is made in the relevant fiscal warehousing record which indicates the time and date of their removal from that regime;
   (b) when the eligible goods are moved outside the fiscal warehouse in respect of which they are allocated to a fiscal warehousing regime (except in the case of movements between fiscal warehouses kept by the same fiscal warehousekeeper); or,
   (c) at the time immediately preceding a retail sale of those eligible goods.
The person who shall be treated as the person who removes or causes the removal of the relevant goods from the relevant fiscal warehousing regime in any of the circumstances described above shall be, as the case requires, either the person who causes any of those circumstances to occur or, in the case of sub-paragraph (c), the person who makes the retail sale referred to there.
(2) Subject to paragraph (3) below, eligible goods which are subject to a fiscal warehousing regime shall not be treated as removed from that regime but shall be treated as transferred or as being in the process of transfer, as the case requires, in any of the following circumstances—
   (a) where the goods in question are transferred or are in the process of transfer to another fiscal warehousing regime in pursuance of regulation 145G(1) above;
   (b) . . . [1]
   (c) where the goods in question are exported or are in the process of being exported to a place outside [Great Britain][1]; or,
   (d) where the goods in question are moved temporarily to a place other than the relevant fiscal warehouse for repair, processing, treatment or other operations (subject to the prior agreement of and to conditions to be imposed by the Commissioners).

(3) Where any relevant document referred to in paragraph (4) below is not received by the relevant fiscal warehousekeeper within the time period indicated there (commencing on the day on which the relevant eligible goods leave his fiscal warehouse), he shall—
   (a) make an entry by way of adjustment to his fiscal warehousing record to show the relevant goods as having been removed from his fiscal warehousing regime at the time and on the day when they left;
   (b) identify in his fiscal warehousing record the person on whose instructions he allowed the goods to leave his fiscal warehouse as the person removing those goods and that person's address and registration number (if any); and,
   (c) notify the person on whose instructions he allowed the goods to leave his fiscal warehouse that the relevant document has not been received by him in time.
(4) The document and time period referred to in paragraph (3) above is, as the case requires, either—
   (a) the certificate referred to in regulation 145G(3)(c) confirming the completion of a transfer of eligible goods from the relevant fiscal warehousing regime to another fiscal warehousing regime (30 days);
   (b) . . .[1] or,
   (c) a document evidencing the export of the eligible goods from the relevant fiscal warehousing regime to a place outside [Great Britain][1] (60 days).

Northern Ireland—In the heading to reg 145H, read "Great Britain" as "Northern Ireland".
In para (1), read "sections 18F(5), 18F(6)" as "paragraph 25(4), 25(5) of Schedule 9ZB to the Act".
In para (2) read as there being a sub-para (bb) before sub-para (c)—
   "(bb)   where the goods in question are transferred or are in the process of transfer to arrangements which correspond in effect, under the law of a member State, to paragraph 19(5) (Northern Ireland fiscal warehouses: relief) of Schedule 9ZB to the Act whether or not those arrangements also correspond in effect to section 18C(1) (zero-rating of certain specified services performed in a fiscal or other warehousing regime) as applied by paragraph 21 (Northern Ireland warehouses and fiscal warehouses: services) of Schedule 9ZB to the Act"
In sub-para (c), read "Great Britain" as "Northern Ireland and the member States".
In para (4) read as there being a sub-para (bb) before sub-para (c)—
   "(bb)   a document evidencing the completion of the transfer of the eligible goods from the relevant Northern Ireland fiscal warehousing regime directly to arrangements which correspond, in a member state, to Northern Ireland (60 days); or"
In para (4)(c), read "Great Britain" as "Northern Ireland and the member States".
(see VAT Regs, SI 1995/2518 reg 145O, as inserted by SI 2020/1545 reg 79).
Amendments—[1] In the heading words substituted for word "overseas", sub-para (2)(b) revoked, in sub-para (2)(c) words substituted for words "the member States", sub-para (4)(b) revoked, and in sub-para (4)(c) words substituted for words "the member States", by the Value Added Tax (Miscellaneous Amendments, Northern Ireland Protocol and Savings and Transitional Provisions) (EU Exit) Regulations, SI 2020/1545 regs 31 and 77 with effect from IP completion day (11pm UK time on 31 December 2020) by virtue of SI 2020/1641 reg 2, Schedule para 11. Sub-para (2)(b) previously read as follows—
   "(b)   where the goods in question are transferred or are in the process of transfer to arrangements which correspond in effect, under the law of another member State, to section 18B(3) (fiscal warehousing) whether or not those arrangements also correspond in effect to section 18C(1) (zero-rating of certain specified services performed in a fiscal or other warehousing regime);"
Sub-para (4)(b) previously read as follows—
   "(b)   a document evidencing the completion of the transfer of the eligible goods from the relevant fiscal warehousing regime directly to arrangements which correspond, in another member State, to fiscal warehousing (60 days); or,"

145I—(1) A fiscal warehousekeeper shall not remove or allow the removal of any eligible goods from his fiscal warehousing regime at any time before—
   (a) he has inspected and placed on his fiscal warehousing record a copy of the relevant document issued by the Commissioners under regulation 145J(1) (removal document); or,
   (b) he is provided with the registration number of a person registered under the Act and a written undertaking from that person that any VAT payable by that person as the result of any removal of eligible goods from that fiscal warehousing regime will be accounted for on that person's return in accordance with regulation 40(1)(c).
(2) Without prejudice to section 18E, where a fiscal warehousekeeper allows the removal of any eligible goods to take place from his fiscal warehousing regime otherwise than in accordance with this regulation, he shall be jointly and severally liable with the person who removes the goods for the payment of the VAT payable under section 18D(2) to the Commissioners.
(3) Paragraphs (1) and (2) above shall not apply to a removal which is the result of an entry in the relevant fiscal warehousing record made by the relevant fiscal warehousekeeper in compliance with regulation 145H(3)(a) (non-receipt of a document following transfer or export).

Commentary—*De Voil Indirect Tax Service* **V5.141A**.
Northern Ireland—In para (2) read the reference to section 18D(2) as a reference to VATA 1994 Sch 9ZB, para 22(2) (removal from warehousing: accountability) (see VAT Regs, SI 1995/2518 reg 145P, as inserted by SI 2020/1545 reg 79).

145J—(1) The Commissioners may, in respect of a person who is seeking to remove or cause the removal of eligible goods from a fiscal warehousing regime,—

(a) accept from or on behalf of that person payment of the VAT payable (if any) as a result of that removal, and

(b) issue to that person a document bearing a reference or identification number.

(2) The Commissioners need not act in accordance with paragraph (1) above unless, as the case requires, they are satisfied as to—

(a) the value and material time of any supply of the relevant goods in the fiscal warehousing regime which is treated as taking place in the United Kingdom under section 18B(4) and the status of the person who made that supply;

(b) the nature and quantity of the relevant eligible goods;

(c) the value of any relevant self-supplies of specified services treated as made under section 18C(3) in the course or furtherance of his business by the person who is to remove the relevant goods, or by the person on whose behalf the goods are to be removed, at the time they are removed from the fiscal warehousing regime; and

(d) the nature and material time of any relevant supplies of specified services in respect of which the self-supplies referred to in sub-paragraph (c) above are treated as being identical (certain supplies of services on or in relation to goods while those goods are subject to the fiscal warehousing regime).

[(3) In paragraph (2)(a) "status" is a reference to whether the person in question is or is required to be registered under the Act or would be required to register under the Act were it not for paragraph 1(9) of Schedule 1, paragraph 38(6) or paragraph 48(7) of Schedule 9ZA, to the Act.][1]

Commentary—*De Voil Indirect Tax Service* **V5.141A**.

Northern Ireland—In sub-para (2)(a), read the reference to section 18B(4) as a reference to VATA 1994 Sch 9ZB para 19(6) (see VAT Regs, SI 1995/2518 reg 145Q, as inserted by SI 2020/1545 reg 79).

Amendments—[1] Sub-para (3) substituted by the Value Added Tax (Miscellaneous Amendments, Northern Ireland Protocol and Savings and Transitional Provisions) (EU Exit) Regulations, SI 2020/1545 regs 31 and 78 with effect from IP completion day (11pm UK time on 31 December 2020) by virtue of SI 2020/1641 reg 2, Schedule para 11. Sub-para (3) previously read as follows—

"(3) In paragraph (2)(a) above 'status' is a reference to whether the person in question—
  (a) is or is required to be registered under the Act, or
  (b) would be required to be registered under the Act were it not for paragraph 1(9) of Schedule 1 to the Act, paragraph 1(7) of Schedule 2 to the Act, paragraph 1(6) of Schedule 3 to the Act, or any of those provisions."

[145K Place of supply of goods subject to warehousing regime

(1) Section 18(1) (supply of goods subject to warehousing regime and before duty point treated as taking place outside the United Kingdom) shall not apply in the following prescribed circumstances.

(2) The circumstances are—

(a) that there is a supply of goods that would but for this regulation be treated for the purposes of the Act as taking place outside the United Kingdom by virtue of section 18(1);

(b) the whole or part of the business carried on by the supplier of those goods consists in supplying to a number of persons goods to be sold, by them or others, by retail;

(c) that supplier is a taxable person (or would be a taxable person but for section 18(1)); and

(d) that supply is to a person who is not a taxable person, and
  (i) consists in a supply of goods to that person to be sold, by that person, by retail, or
  (ii) consists in a supply of goods to that person by retail.][1]

Commentary—*De Voil Indirect Tax Service* **V5.141, V3.176**.

HMRC Manuals—VAT Supplies in Warehouse And Fiscal Warehousing VWRHS2030 (disapplication of section 18(1) Of VAT Act 1994).

Northern Ireland—Read "section 18(1)" in each place it occurs as "paragraph 16(1) of Schedule 9ZB to the Act" (see VAT Regs, SI 1995/2518 reg 145R, as inserted by SI 2020/1545 reg 79).

Amendments—[1] This regulation inserted by the VAT (Amendment) (No 2) Regulations, SI 2005/2231 reg 10 with effect from 1 September 2005.

[PART 16B

NORTHERN IRELAND FISCAL AND OTHER NORTHERN IRELAND WAREHOUSING REGIMES

Amendments—Part 16B (regs 145L–145U) inserted by the Value Added Tax (Miscellaneous Amendments, Northern Ireland Protocol and Savings and Transitional Provisions) (EU Exit) Regulations, SI 2020/1545 regs 31 and 79 with effect from IP completion day (11pm UK time on 31 December 2020) by virtue of SI 2020/1641 reg 2, Schedule para 11.

[145L Northern Ireland warehouses and fiscal warehouses: application of Part 16A with modifications

Part 16A and Schedule 1A apply to Northern Ireland warehouses and Northern Ireland fiscal warehouses as they apply to warehouses and fiscal warehouses—

(a) as if any reference to "fiscal warehouse", "warehouse", "fiscal warehousing regime" and "warehousing regime" were a reference respectively to "Northern Ireland fiscal warehouse", "Northern Ireland warehouse", "Northern Ireland fiscal warehousing regime" and "Northern Ireland warehousing regime"; and

(b) with the modifications set out in regulations 145M to 145R in respect of Part 16A, and in regulation 145T in respect of Schedule 1A.][1]

Amendments—[1] Part 16B (regs 145L–145U) inserted by the Value Added Tax (Miscellaneous Amendments, Northern Ireland Protocol and Savings and Transitional Provisions) (EU Exit) Regulations, SI 2020/1545 regs 31 and 79 with effect from IP completion day (11pm UK time on 31 December 2020) by virtue of SI 2020/1641 reg 2, Schedule para 11.

[**145M Interpretation**
In regulation 145A(1) (interpretation)—
   (a) in the definition of "eligible goods", read the words after "by" as "paragraph 25(1) of Schedule 9ZB to the Act (supplementary provision)";
   (b) in the definition of "material time", read the words after "by" as "paragraph 25(1) of Schedule 9ZB to the Act except in regulation 145D where "material time" means the time the services are performed.".][1]

Amendments—[1] Part 16B (regs 145L–145U) inserted by the Value Added Tax (Miscellaneous Amendments, Northern Ireland Protocol and Savings and Transitional Provisions) (EU Exit) Regulations, SI 2020/1545 regs 31 and 79 with effect from IP completion day (11pm UK time on 31 December 2020) by virtue of SI 2020/1641 reg 2, Schedule para 11.

[**145N Northern Ireland fiscal warehousing transfers**
Read the heading to regulation 145G (fiscal warehousing transfers in Great Britain) as "Fiscal warehousing transfers in Northern Ireland".][1]

Amendments—[1] Part 16B (regs 145L–145U) inserted by the Value Added Tax (Miscellaneous Amendments, Northern Ireland Protocol and Savings and Transitional Provisions) (EU Exit) Regulations, SI 2020/1545 regs 31 and 79 with effect from IP completion day (11pm UK time on 31 December 2020) by virtue of SI 2020/1641 reg 2, Schedule para 11.

[**145O Removal of goods from a Northern Ireland fiscal warehousing regime and transfers**
(1) In the heading to regulation 145H (removal of goods from a fiscal warehousing regime and transfers outside Great Britain), read "Great Britain" as "Northern Ireland".
(2) In regulation 145H(1), read "sections 18F(5), 18F(6)" as "paragraph 25(4), 25(5) of Schedule 9ZB to the Act";
(3) In regulation 145H(2)—
   (a) read there as being before sub-paragraph (c)—
      "(bb) where the goods in question are transferred or are in the process of transfer to arrangements which correspond in effect, under the law of a member State, to paragraph 19(5) (Northern Ireland fiscal warehouses: relief) of Schedule 9ZB to the Act whether or not those arrangements also correspond in effect to section 18C(1) (zero-rating of certain specified services performed in a fiscal or other warehousing regime) as applied by paragraph 21 (Northern Ireland warehouses and fiscal warehouses: services) of Schedule 9ZB to the Act";
   (b) in sub-paragraph (c), read "Great Britain" as "Northern Ireland and the member States";
(4) In regulation 145H(4)—
   (a) read there as being before sub-paragraph (c)—
      "(bb) a document evidencing the completion of the transfer of the eligible goods from the relevant Northern Ireland fiscal warehousing regime directly to arrangements which correspond, in a member state, to Northern Ireland (60 days); or";
   (b) in sub-paragraph (c), read "Great Britain" as "Northern Ireland and the member States".][1]

Amendments—[1] Part 16B (regs 145L–145U) inserted by the Value Added Tax (Miscellaneous Amendments, Northern Ireland Protocol and Savings and Transitional Provisions) (EU Exit) Regulations, SI 2020/1545 regs 31 and 79 with effect from IP completion day (11pm UK time on 31 December 2020) by virtue of SI 2020/1641 reg 2, Schedule para 11.

[**145P** In regulation 145I(2), read the reference to section 18D(2) as a reference to paragraph 22(2) (removal from warehousing: accountability) of Schedule 9ZB to the Act.][1]

Amendments—[1] Part 16B (regs 145L–145U) inserted by the Value Added Tax (Miscellaneous Amendments, Northern Ireland Protocol and Savings and Transitional Provisions) (EU Exit) Regulations, SI 2020/1545 regs 31 and 79 with effect from IP completion day (11pm UK time on 31 December 2020) by virtue of SI 2020/1641 reg 2, Schedule para 11.

[**145Q Payment on removal of goods from a Northern Ireland fiscal warehousing regime**
In regulation 145J(2)(a) (payment on removal of goods from a fiscal warehousing regime), read the reference to section 18B(4) as a reference to paragraph 19(6) of Schedule 9ZB to the Act.][1]

Amendments—[1] Part 16B (regs 145L–145U) inserted by the Value Added Tax (Miscellaneous Amendments, Northern Ireland Protocol and Savings and Transitional Provisions) (EU Exit) Regulations, SI 2020/1545 regs 31 and 79 with effect from IP completion day (11pm UK time on 31 December 2020) by virtue of SI 2020/1641 reg 2, Schedule para 11.

[**145R Place of supply of goods subject to a Northern Ireland warehousing regime**
In regulation 145K (place of supply of goods subject to a warehousing regime), read "section 18(1)" in each place it occurs as "paragraph 16(1) of Schedule 9ZB to the Act".][1]

Amendments—[1] Part 16B (regs 145L–145U) inserted by the Value Added Tax (Miscellaneous Amendments, Northern Ireland Protocol and Savings and Transitional Provisions) (EU Exit) Regulations, SI 2020/1545 regs 31 and 79 with effect from IP completion day (11pm UK time on 31 December 2020) by virtue of SI 2020/1641 reg 2, Schedule para 11.

[**145S Fiscal warehousing certificates**
(1) The certificate referred to in paragraph 19(1)(d) of Schedule 9ZB to the Act (certificate relating to acquisitions in or intended for fiscal warehousing) and the certificate referred to in paragraph 19(3)(d) of Schedule 9ZB to the Act (supplies of goods intended for fiscal warehousing) must contain the information indicated in the form specified in a notice published by the Commissioners
(2) A certificate prepared under paragraph 19(1)(d) of Schedule 9ZB by an acquirer who is not a taxable person must be kept by that person for a period of six years commencing on the day the certificate is prepared; and the person must produce it to a proper officer when that officer requests the person to do so.][1]

Amendments—[1] Part 16B (regs 145L–145U) inserted by the Value Added Tax (Miscellaneous Amendments, Northern Ireland Protocol and Savings and Transitional Provisions) (EU Exit) Regulations, SI 2020/1545 regs 31 and 79 with effect from IP completion day (11pm UK time on 31 December 2020) by virtue of SI 2020/1641 reg 2, Schedule para 11.

[**145T Northern Ireland: modification of Schedule 1A**
In Schedule 1A (fiscal warehousing)—
  (a) in paragraph 1—
      (i) read there as being before sub-paragraph (f)—
      "(ea) It must accurately identify as "transferred goods" all eligible goods which are transferred directly from the Northern Ireland fiscal warehousing regime to corresponding arrangements in a member State under regulation 145H(2)(bb), the date and time when the transfer starts, and the address of the place in the member State to which the goods in question are transferred.";
      (ii) in sub-paragraph (f), read "Great Britain" in both places it occurs as "Northern Ireland and the member States;";
  (b) in paragraph 3—
      (i) read there as being before sub-paragraph (d)—
      "(ca) It must include the document relating to the completion of a transfer to corresponding arrangements in a member State referred to in regulation 145H(4)(bb) and it must relate that document to the relevant transfer.";
      (ii) in sub-paragraph (d), read "Great Britain" as "Northern Ireland and the member States" ;
  (c) read paragraph 4(b) as—
      "(b) It shall be adjusted to show a removal (and not a transfer) where the document referred to in regulations 145H(4)(bb) or 145H(4)(c) concerning goods which have been transferred to corresponding arrangements in a member State or which have been exported to a place outside Northern Ireland and the member States, is not received in time.".][1]

Amendments—[1] Part 16B (regs 145L–145U) inserted by the Value Added Tax (Miscellaneous Amendments, Northern Ireland Protocol and Savings and Transitional Provisions) (EU Exit) Regulations, SI 2020/1545 regs 31 and 79 with effect from IP completion day (11pm UK time on 31 December 2020) by virtue of SI 2020/1641 reg 2, Schedule para 11.

[**145U Modification of the Value Added Tax (Fiscal Warehousing) (Treatment of Transactions) Order 1996**
(1) The Value Added Tax (Fiscal Warehousing) (Treatment of Transactions) Order 1996 applies with the modifications set out in paragraph (2) to goods subject to, or to be placed in, a Northern Ireland fiscal warehousing regime as it applies to goods subject to, or to be placed in, a fiscal warehousing regime.
(2) The modifications are—
  (a) in article 2, read "eligible goods" and "material time" as having the meanings given by paragraph 25(1) of Schedule 9ZB to the Act (supplementary provision);
  (b) in article 3(2)(a) and (b), read "fiscal warehousing regime" as "Northern Ireland fiscal warehousing regime".][1]

Amendments—[1] Part 16B (regs 145L–145U) inserted by the Value Added Tax (Miscellaneous Amendments, Northern Ireland Protocol and Savings and Transitional Provisions) (EU Exit) Regulations, SI 2020/1545 regs 31 and 79 with effect from IP completion day (11pm UK time on 31 December 2020) by virtue of SI 2020/1641 reg 2, Schedule para 11.

PART XVII
[MEANS OF TRANSPORT]

146 Interpretation of Part XVII
In this Part—
  "claim" means a claim for a refund of VAT made pursuant to section 40 of the Act and "claimant" shall be construed accordingly;
  "competent authority" means an authority having powers under the laws in force [in a relevant territory][1] to register a vehicle for road use [in that territory][1];

"first entry into service" in relation to a new means of transport means the time determined in relation to that means of transport under regulation 147;
["new means of transport" has the meaning given by paragraph 83 of Schedule 9ZA to the Act;][1]
"registration" means registration for road use in a member State corresponding in relation to that member State to registration in accordance with the Vehicles Excise and Registration Act 1994.
["relevant territory" means a member State or Northern Ireland.][1]

Commentary—*De Voil Indirect Tax Service* **V1.294**.
Amendments—Heading to Part 17 substituted by the VAT (Amendment) Regulations, SI 2013/701 regs 3, 5 with effect from 15 April 2013. Heading previously read "New Means of Transport".

[1] In the definition of "competent authority", words substituted for words "in any member State" and "in that member State", and the definitions of "new means of transport" and "relevant territory" inserted, by the Value Added Tax (Miscellaneous Amendments, Northern Ireland Protocol and Savings and Transitional Provisions) (EU Exit) Regulations, SI 2020/1545 regs 31 and 80 with effect from IP completion day (11pm UK time on 31 December 2020) by virtue of SI 2020/1641 reg 2, Schedule para 11.

147 First entry into service of a means of transport
(1) For the purposes of section 95 of the Act a means of transport is to be treated as having first entered into service—
  (a) in the case of a ship or aircraft—
    (i) when it is delivered from its manufacturer to its first purchaser or owner, or on its first being made available to its first purchaser or owner, whichever is the earlier, or
    (ii) if its manufacturer takes it into use for demonstration purposes, on its being first taken into such use, and
  (b) in the case of a motorised land vehicle—
    (i) on its first registration for road use by the competent authority [in the relevant territory][1] of its manufacture or when a liability to register for road use is first incurred [in the relevant territory][1] of its manufacture, whichever is the earlier,
    (ii) if it is not liable to be registered for road use [in the relevant territory][1] of its manufacture, on its removal by its first purchaser or owner, or on its first delivery or on its being made available to its first purchaser, whichever is the earliest, or
    (iii) if its manufacturer takes it into use for demonstration purposes, on its first being taken into such use.
(2) Where the times specified in paragraph (1) above cannot be established to the Commissioners' satisfaction, a means of transport is to be treated as having first entered into service on the issue of an invoice relating to the first supply of the means of transport.

Commentary—*De Voil Indirect Tax Service* **V1.294**.
HMRC Manuals—VAT New Means of Transport VATNMT300 (definitions).
VAT Civil penalties VCP11432 (definition of date of first entry into service).
Amendments—[1] In para (1)(b) words substituted for words "in the member State", in each place, by the Value Added Tax (Miscellaneous Amendments, Northern Ireland Protocol and Savings and Transitional Provisions) (EU Exit) Regulations, SI 2020/1545 regs 31 and 81 with effect from IP completion day (11pm UK time on 31 December 2020) by virtue of SI 2020/1641 reg 2, Schedule para 11.

148 Notification of acquisition of new [ships or new aircraft] by non-taxable persons and payment of VAT
(1) Where—
  (a) a taxable acquisition of a new [ship or new aircraft][1] takes place in the United Kingdom,
  (b) the acquisition is not in pursuance of a taxable supply, and
  (c) the person acquiring the goods is not a taxable person at the time of the acquisition,
the person acquiring the goods shall notify the Commissioners of the acquisition within [14][1] days of the time of the acquisition or the arrival of the goods in the United Kingdom, whichever is the later.
(2) The notification shall be in writing in the English language and shall contain the following particulars—
  (a) the name and current address of the person acquiring the new [ship or new aircraft][1],
  (b) the time of the acquisition,
  (c) the date when the new [ship or new aircraft][1] arrived in the United Kingdom,
  (d) a full description of the new [ship or new aircraft][1] which shall include any . . . [1] hull or airframe identification number and engine number,
  (e) the consideration for the transaction in pursuance of which the new [ship or new aircraft][1] was acquired,
  (f) the name and address of the supplier in the member State from which the new [ship or new aircraft][1] was acquired,
  (g) the place where the new [ship or new aircraft][1] can be inspected, and
  (h) the date of notification.
(3) The notification shall include a declaration, signed by the person who is required to make the notification or a person authorised in that behalf in writing, that all the information entered in it is true and complete.

(4) The notification shall be made at, or sent to, any office designated by the Commissioners for the receipt of such notifications.
(5) Any person required to notify the Commissioners of an acquisition of a new [ship or new aircraft][1] shall pay the VAT due upon the acquisition at the time of notification or within 30 days of the Commissioners issuing a written demand to him detailing the VAT due and requesting payment.

Commentary—*De Voil Indirect Tax Service* **V5.125**.
HMRC Manuals—VAT New Means of Transport VATNMT5300 (acquisition by unregistered persons).
Amendments—[1] In heading to s 148 and throughout s 148 itself, words substituted for words "means of transport', in para (1), figure substituted for figure "7", and in para (2)(*d*) words "registration mark allocated to it by any competent authority in another member State prior to its arrival in the United Kingdom and any chassis," revoked, by the VAT (Amendment) Regulations, SI 2013/701 regs 3, 6 with effect from 15 April 2013. Note that these amendments do not have effect in relation to the arrival in the UK on or before 14 April 2013 of a new means of transport that is a motorised land vehicle (SI 2013/701 reg 6(3)).

[148A Notification of the arrival in the United Kingdom of motorised land vehicles and payment of VAT
[(1) This regulation applies to a means of transport that is a motorised land vehicle as described by paragraph 2(5E) of Schedule 11 to the Act (a "land vehicle").][3]
(2) In this regulation an "excepted relevant person" means a relevant person [(see paragraph (5A)][3] who is—
  (*a*) bringing a land vehicle into the United Kingdom which that person has the approval of the Secretary of State to register and license in the United Kingdom in accordance with Parts 1 and 2 of the Vehicle Excise and Registration Act 1994 using a secure registration and licensing system (whether automated or paper based);
  (*b*) importing a land vehicle into the United Kingdom and who is not a taxable person acting as such in relation to the arrival of the land vehicle in the United Kingdom;
  (*c*) bringing a land vehicle into the United Kingdom which—
    (i) is not required to be registered for road use in the United Kingdom, and
    (ii) is to remain in the United Kingdom for a period (continuous or otherwise) of not more than 6 months in any 12 months; or
  (*d*) bringing a land vehicle into the United Kingdom which has remained registered for road use in the United Kingdom during the period when it has been outside the United Kingdom.
(3) A relevant person other than an excepted relevant person must notify the Commissioners of the arrival in the United Kingdom of a land vehicle within 14 days of the date of the arrival.
[(3A) Where a person falling within paragraph (2)(*a*) makes a decision that the land vehicle in question will not be registered using the secure registration and licensing system (whether because it is not required to be registered for road use in the United Kingdom or for any other reason), that person must notify the Commissioners of the arrival of that land vehicle in the United Kingdom within 14 days of the date of that decision.][2]
[(4) Where a person falling within paragraph (2)(*c*) makes a decision—
  (*a*) to register the land vehicle in question for road use in the United Kingdom, or
  (*b*) to keep the land vehicle in the United Kingdom for a period longer than that specified in sub-paragraph (*c*)(ii) in circumstances where that land vehicle is not required to be registered for road use in the United Kingdom,
that person must notify the Commissioners of the arrival in the United Kingdom of that land vehicle within 14 days of the date of that decision.][2]
[(4A) No obligation arises under paragraph (3) or (4) by reason of the removal of a land vehicle from Northern Ireland to Great Britain or vice versa.][3]
(5) In this regulation "registered for road use in the United Kingdom" means registered for such use in accordance with the Vehicle Excise and Registration Act 1994 and "register for road use in the United Kingdom" is to be construed accordingly.
[(5A) In this regulation "relevant person" has the meaning given by paragraph 2(5D) of Schedule 11 to the Act with the modification applied by paragraph 74(1)(c) of Schedule 9ZA to the Act.][3]
(6) A person required to notify under paragraph (3) or (4) may authorise a third party to notify on that person's behalf.
(7) The notification shall be made in the English language.
(8) A notification under paragraph (3) or (4) must—
  (*a*) contain the particulars listed in paragraph (9);
  (*b*) include a declaration by the person required to notify the arrival in the United Kingdom of a land vehicle or a person authorised on that person's behalf that all the information entered in it is true and complete; and
  (*c*) when made in paper form, be made at or sent to any office designated by the Commissioners for the receipt of such notifications.
(9) The particulars referred to in paragraph (8)(*a*) are—
  (*a*) the name and current address of the person bringing the land vehicle into the United Kingdom;

(b) the date when the land vehicle arrived in the United Kingdom;
(c) . . .²
(d) a full description of the land vehicle which shall include any vehicle registration mark allocated to it by any competent authority in another member State prior to its arrival and any chassis identification number;
(e) where applicable, the registration number of the person bringing the land vehicle into the United Kingdom;
(f) the date of the notification;
(g) in the case of an acquisition arising from a deemed supply under paragraph 6 of Schedule 4 to the Act—
  (i) the value of the transaction determined in accordance with paragraph 3 of Schedule 7 to the Act, and
  (ii) details of any relief claimed or to be claimed in relation to the acquisition under Item 2(f) of Group 12 of Schedule 8 to the Act (zero rating: drugs, medicines, aids for the handicapped etc);
(h) in the case of any other acquisition—
  (i) the consideration for the transaction in pursuance of which the land vehicle was acquired,
  (ii) the name and address of the supplier in the member State from which the land vehicle was acquired, and
  (iii) details of any relief claimed or to be claimed in relation to the acquisition under Item 2(f) of Group 12 of Schedule 8 to the Act;
(i) in the case of an import—
  (i) the price actually paid or payable for the land vehicle including any deposit, commission and fees,
  [(ii) any identifying number contained in a customs declaration made for the purposes of Part 1 of the Taxation (Cross-border Trade) Act 2018 or, in Northern Ireland, for the purposes of the corresponding provision of Union customs legislation as defined by paragraph 1(8) of Schedule 9ZB to the Act, and]³
  (iii) the relevant commodity code entered on the Customs declaration; and
(j) any other particulars specified in a notice published by the Commissioners (which includes such a notice as revised or replaced from time to time).

[(9A) In any case falling within paragraph (3A) or (4), the date of the relevant decision is to be treated as the date of the arrival in the United Kingdom of the land vehicle in question for the purposes of paragraph (9)(b).]²

(10) Any person required under paragraph (3) or (4) to notify the Commissioners of an arrival which is an acquisition must pay any VAT due on the acquisition at the time and in the manner prescribed in paragraphs (12) to (16) as appropriate.

(11) In the case of an import of a land vehicle, any requirements to notify the importation and pay any tax, duty of customs or duty of excise due as may be prescribed in any of the enactments referred to in section 16(1)(a) and (b) of the Act shall apply in addition to any requirements imposed by or under this regulation.

(12) Where—
  (a) the arrival is a taxable acquisition which takes place in the United Kingdom, and
  (b) the person acquiring the land vehicle is not a taxable person acting as such in relation to the acquisition of the land vehicle,
payment shall be made at the time of notification.

(13) Where—
  (a) the arrival is a taxable acquisition which takes place in the United Kingdom, and
  (b) the person acquiring the land vehicle is a taxable person acting as such in relation to the acquisition of the land vehicle,
payment shall be made in accordance with paragraph (15).

(14) Where the arrival is an acquisition arising from a deemed supply under paragraph 6 of Schedule 4 to the Act, payment shall be made in accordance with paragraph (15).

(15) Where this paragraph applies, payment shall be made in accordance with regulation 40 having been accounted for in the appropriate return required by regulation 25.

(16) In any case where—
  (a) VAT due is required to be paid at the time of notification under paragraph (12), and
  (b) notification is made under regulation 4A,
the relevant payment shall be made solely by means of electronic communications that are acceptable to the Commissioners for this purpose.]¹

Commentary—*De Voil Indirect Tax Service* **V5.125, V3.396A, V3.396**.

Amendments—¹ Reg 148A inserted by the VAT (Amendment) Regulations, SI 2013/701 regs 3, 7 with effect from 15 April 2013. Note that this amendment does not have effect in relation to the arrival in the UK on or before 14 April 2013 of a new means of transport that is a motorised land vehicle (SI 2013/701 reg 6(3)).

[2] Paras (3A), (9A) inserted, para (4) substituted, and para (9)(c) revoked, by the Value Added Tax (Amendment) Regulations, SI 2014/548 regs 2, 5 with effect from 1 April 2014.
[3] Para (1) substituted, in para (2) words substituted for words "(see paragraph 2(5D) of Schedule 11 to the Act)", paras (4A) and (5A) inserted, and sub-para (9)(i)(ii) substituted, by the Value Added Tax (Miscellaneous Amendments, Northern Ireland Protocol and Savings and Transitional Provisions) (EU Exit) Regulations, SI 2020/1545 regs 31 and 82 with effect from IP completion day (11pm UK time on 31 December 2020) by virtue of SI 2020/1641 reg 2, Schedule para 11. Para (1) previously read as follows—

"(1) This regulation applies to a means of transport that is a motorised land vehicle (see section 95 of, and paragraph 2(5D) of Schedule 11 to, the Act) (a "land vehicle")."

Sub-para (9)(i)(ii) previously read as follows—

"(ii) the entry number of the Customs declaration as defined in paragraph 17 of Article 4 of Council Regulation (EEC) No 2913/92 of 12 October 1992 establishing the Community Customs Code, and"

149 Refunds in relation to new means of transport

A claimant shall make his claim in writing no earlier than one month and no later than 14 days prior to making the supply of the new means of transport by virtue of which the claim arises.

Commentary—*De Voil Indirect Tax Service* **V5.154**.
HMRC Manuals—VAT New Means of Transport VATNMT4400 (a refund of VAT for a removed vehicle).

150

The claim shall be made at, or sent to, any office designated by the Commissioners for the receipt of such claims.

Commentary—*De Voil Indirect Tax Service* **V5.154**.
HMRC Manuals—VAT New Means of Transport VATNMT4400 (a refund of VAT for a removed vehicle).

151

The claim shall contain the following information—
(a) the name, current address and telephone number of the claimant,
(b) the place where the new means of transport is kept and the times when it may be inspected,
(c) the name and address of the person who supplied the new means of transport to the claimant,
(d) the price paid by the claimant for the supply to him of the new means of transport excluding any VAT,
(e) the amount of any VAT paid by the claimant on the supply to him of the new means of transport,
(f) the amount of any VAT paid by the claimant on the acquisition of the new means of transport from another member State or on its importation . . . [1],
(g) the name and address of the proposed purchaser, the member State to which the new means of transport is to be removed, and the date of the proposed purchase,
(h) the price to be paid by the proposed purchaser,
(i) a full description of the new means of transport including, in the case of motorised land vehicles, its mileage since its first entry into service and, in the case of ships and aircraft, its hours of use since its first entry into service,
(j) in the case of a ship, its length in metres,
(k) in the case of an aircraft, its take-off weight in kilograms,
(l) in the case of a motorised land vehicle powered by a combustion engine, its displacement or cylinder capacity in cubic centimetres, and in the case of an electrically propelled motorised land vehicle, its maximum power output in kilowatts, described to the nearest tenth of a kilowatt, and
(m) the amount of the refund being claimed.

Commentary—*De Voil Indirect Tax Service* **V5.154**.
Amendments—[1] In para (f) words "from a place outside the member States" revoked by the Value Added Tax (Miscellaneous Amendments, Northern Ireland Protocol and Savings and Transitional Provisions) (EU Exit) Regulations, SI 2020/1545 regs 31 and 83 with effect from IP completion day (11pm UK time on 31 December 2020) by virtue of SI 2020/1641 reg 2, Schedule para 11.

152

The claim shall be accompanied by the following documents—
(a) the invoice issued by the person who supplied the new means of transport to the claimant or such other documentary evidence of purchase as is satisfactory to the Commissioners,
(b) in respect of a new means of transport imported . . . [1] by the claimant, documentary evidence of its importation and of the VAT paid thereon, and
(c) in respect of a new means of transport acquired by the claimant from another member State, documentary evidence of the VAT paid thereon.

Commentary—*De Voil Indirect Tax Service* **V5.154**.
Amendments—[1] In para (b) words "from a place outside the member States" revoked by the Value Added Tax (Miscellaneous Amendments, Northern Ireland Protocol and Savings and Transitional Provisions) (EU Exit) Regulations, SI 2020/1545 regs 31 and 84 with effect from IP completion day (11pm UK time on 31 December 2020) by virtue of SI 2020/1641 reg 2, Schedule para 11.

153

The claim shall include a declaration, signed by the claimant or a person authorised by him in that behalf in writing, that all the information entered in or accompanying it is true and complete.

Commentary—*De Voil Indirect Tax Service* **V5.154**.

154 The claim shall be completed by the submission to the Commissioners of—
(a) the sales invoice or similar document identifying the new means of transport and showing the price paid by the claimant's customer, and
(b) documentary evidence that the new means of transport has been removed to another member State.

Commentary—*De Voil Indirect Tax Service* **V5.154**.

155 Supplies of new means of transport to persons [departing Northern Ireland for a member State][1]

The Commissioners may, on application by a person who is not taxable in [a member State][1] and who intends—
(a) to purchase a new means of transport in [Northern Ireland][1], and
(b) to remove that new means of transport [from Northern Ireland][1] to [a member State][1],

permit that person to purchase a new means of transport without payment of VAT, for subsequent removal to [a member State][1] within 2 months of the date of supply and its supply, subject to such conditions as they may impose, shall be zero-rated.

Commentary—*De Voil Indirect Tax Service* **V4.207, V4.312**.
HMRC Manuals—VAT New Means of Transport VATNMT4050 (purchasing a new means of transport - another member-State). VAT Export/Removal of Goods From the UK VEXP30310 (exports/removals affected by the COVID19 emergency).
Amendments—[1] In the heading, words substituted for words "departing to another member State", words substituted for words "in another member State" in each place, in sub-para (a) words substituted for words "the United Kingdom", and in sub-para (b) words inserted, by the Value Added Tax (Miscellaneous Amendments, Northern Ireland Protocol and Savings and Transitional Provisions) (EU Exit) Regulations, SI 2020/1545 regs 31 and 85 with effect from IP completion day (11pm UK time on 31 December 2020) by virtue of SI 2020/1641 reg 2, Schedule para 11.

PART XIX
BAD DEBT RELIEF (THE NEW SCHEME)

Note—With effect for the purposes of the making of any refund or repayment after 9 March 1999, but not anything received on or before that day, Part XIX, other than reg 171, of these regulations shall, subject to provisions made under VATA 1994 s 36, be read as if a reference to a payment being received by the claimant includes a payment received by a person to whom a right to receive it has been assigned by virtue of FA 1999 s 12(4).

165 Interpretation of Part XIX
In this Part—
"claim" means a claim in accordance with regulations 166 . . . [3] and 167 for a refund of VAT to which a person is entitled by virtue of section 36 of the Act and "claimant" shall be construed accordingly;
"payment" means any payment or part-payment which is made by any person . . . [1] by way of consideration for a supply regardless of whether such payment extinguishes the purchaser's debt to the claimant or not;
"purchaser" means a person to whom the claimant made a relevant supply;
"refunds for bad debts account" has the meaning given in regulation 168;
"relevant supply" means any taxable supply upon which a claim is based;
"return" means the return which the claimant is required to make in accordance with regulation 25 . . . [32];
"security" means—
(a) in relation to England, Wales and Northern Ireland, any mortgage, charge, lien or other security, and
(b) in relation to Scotland, any security (whether heritable or moveable), any floating charge and any right of lien or preference and right of retention (other than a right of compensation or set-off).
. . . [3]

Commentary—*De Voil Indirect Tax Service* **V5.156**.
HMRC Manuals—VAT Bad Debt Relief VBDR2100 (payments: what constitutes a payment)?.
Amendments—[1] In definition of "payment" words revoked by the VAT Regulations, SI 1999/3029, regs 2, 3 with effect from 1 December 1999.
[2] In definitions of "claim" and "return" words inserted, and definition of "tax period" inserted, by the VAT (Amendment) (No 3) Regulations, SI 2014/2430 regs 2, 4 with effect from 1 January 2015.
[3] In the definition of "claim" words "or 166AA" revoked, in the definition of "return" the words "but "*relevant non-UK return*" has the meaning given by paragraph 20(3) of Schedule 3BA to the Act and "relevant special scheme return" has the meaning given by paragraph 16(3) of Schedule 3B to the Act" revoked, and the definition of "tax period" revoked, by the Value Added Tax (Miscellaneous Amendments and Revocations) (EU Exit) Regulations, SI 2019/59 regs 12, 65 with effect from IP completion day (11pm UK time on 31 December 2020). The definition of "tax period" previously read as follows—
""tax period" has the meaning given by paragraph 23(1) of Schedule 3B or paragraph 38(1) of Schedule 3BA (as the case may require) to the Act."

165A [Time within which a claim must be made
(1) Subject to paragraph (3) [and (4)][2] below, a claim shall be made within the period of [4 years and 6 months][2] following the later of—

(a) the date on which the consideration (or part) which has been written off as a bad debt becomes due and payable to or to the order of the person who made the relevant supply; and
(b) the date of the supply.
(2) A person who is entitled to a refund by virtue of section 36 of the Act, but has not made a claim within the period specified in paragraph (1) shall be regarded for the purposes of this Part as having ceased to be entitled to a refund accordingly.
(3) This regulation does not apply insofar as the date mentioned at sub-paragraph (a) or (b) of paragraph (1) above, whichever is the later, falls before 1st May 1997.
[(4) A person shall be regarded for the purposes of this Part as having ceased to be entitled to a refund where the date mentioned at subparagraph (a) or (b) of paragraph (1) above, whichever is the later, is on or before 30th September 2005.]²]¹

Commentary—*De Voil Indirect Tax Service* **V5.156, V5.156C**.
HMRC Manuals—VAT refunds Manual VRM8300 (timeline to make a claim).
Amendments—¹ This regulation inserted by the VAT (Amendment) Regulations, SI 1997/1086 reg 10 with effect from 1 May 1997.
² In para (1), words inserted and words substituted for words "3 years and 6 months", and para (4) inserted, by the VAT (Amendment) Regulations, SI 2009/586 regs 2, 10 with effect from 1 April 2009.

166 The making of a claim to the Commissioners
(1) . . . ² save as the Commissioners may otherwise allow or direct, the claimant shall make a claim to the Commissioners by including the correct amount of the refund in the box opposite the legend "VAT reclaimed in this period on purchases and other inputs" on his return [for the prescribed accounting period in which he becomes entitled to make the claim or, subject to regulation 165A, any later return]¹.
(2) If at a time the claimant becomes entitled to a refund he is no longer required to make returns to the Commissioners he shall make a claim to the Commissioners in such form and manner as they may direct.

Commentary—*De Voil Indirect Tax Service* **V5.156**.
Amendments—¹ Words in para (1) inserted by the VAT (Amendment) Regulations, SI 1997/1086 reg 11 with effect from 1 May 1997.
² In para (1) words "Subject to regulation 166AA, and" revoked by the Value Added Tax (Miscellaneous Amendments and Revocations) (EU Exit) Regulations, SI 2019/59 regs 12, 66 with effect from IP completion day (11pm UK time on 31 December 2020).

[166AA The making of a claim to the Commissioners: special accounting schemes
(1) This regulation applies where the VAT on the relevant supply was accounted for on a relevant non-UK return or a relevant special scheme return.
(2) Where this regulation applies, the claimant must make the claim by—
   (a) amending, in accordance with Article 61 of the Implementing Regulation, that relevant non-UK return or relevant special scheme return; or
   (b) (where the period during which a person is entitled to make such an amendment has expired) notifying the Commissioners of the claim in writing in the English language.²]¹

Amendments—¹ Reg 166AA inserted by the VAT (Amendment) (No 3) Regulations, SI 2014/2430 regs 2, 5(2) with effect from 1 January 2015.
² Regulation 166AA revoked by the Value Added Tax (Miscellaneous Amendments and Revocations) (EU Exit) Regulations, SI 2019/59 regs 12, 67 with effect from IP completion day (11pm UK time on 31 December 2020).

166A [Notice to purchaser of claim
Where the purchaser is a taxable person[, and the relevant supply was made before 1st January 2003]² the claimant shall not before, but within 7 days from, the day he makes a claim give to the purchaser a notice in writing containing the following information—
   (a) the date of issue of the notice;
   (b) the date of the claim;
   (c) the date and number of any VAT invoice issued in relation to each relevant supply;
   (d) the amount of the consideration for each relevant supply which the claimant has written off as a bad debt;
   (e) the amount of the claim.]¹

Commentary—*De Voil Indirect Tax Service* **V5.156**.
Amendments—¹ This regulation inserted by the VAT (Amendment) Regulations, SI 1997/1086 reg 12 with effect from 1 May 1997.
² Words inserted by the VAT (Amendment) (No 4) Regulations, SI 2002/3027 regs 2, 3 with effect from 1 January 2003.

167 Evidence required of the claimant in support of the claim
Save as the Commissioners may otherwise allow, the claimant, before he makes a claim, shall hold in respect of each relevant supply—
   (a) either—
      (i) a copy of any VAT invoice which was provided in accordance with Part III of these Regulations, or

(ii) where there was no obligation to provide a VAT invoice, a document which shows the time, nature and purchaser of the relevant goods and services, and the consideration therefore,
   (b) records or any other documents showing that he has accounted for and paid the VAT thereon, and
   (c) records or any other documents showing that the consideration has been written off in his accounts as a bad debt.

Commentary—*De Voil Indirect Tax Service* **V5.156**.
HMRC Manuals—VAT Cash Accounting Scheme VCAS6300 (claiming bad debt relief).

168 Records required to be kept by the claimant

(1) Any person who makes a claim to the Commissioners shall keep a record of that claim.
(2) Save as the Commissioners may otherwise allow, the record referred to in paragraph (1) above shall consist of the following information in respect of each claim made—
   (a) in respect of each relevant supply for that claim—
      (i) the amount of VAT chargeable,
      (ii) the prescribed accounting period in which the VAT chargeable was accounted for and paid to the Commissioners,
      (iii) the date and number of any invoice issued in relation thereto or, where there is no such invoice, such information as is necessary to identify the time, nature and purchaser thereof, and
      (iv) any payment received therefor,
   (b) the outstanding amount to which the claim relates,
   (c) the amount of the claim, . . . [1]
   (d) the prescribed accounting period in which the claim was made[, and
   (e) a copy of the notice required to be given in accordance with regulations 166A.][1]
(3) Any records created in pursuance of this regulation shall be kept in a single account to be known as the "refunds for bad debts account".
(4) . . . [2]

Commentary—*De Voil Indirect Tax Service* **V5.156, V5.201**.
HMRC Manuals—Compliance Handbook Manaul CH12200 (specific records to be kept).
Amendments—[1] Word "and" in para 2(c) deleted and para (2)(e) and word "and" at end of para (2)(d) inserted by the VAT (Amendment) Regulations, SI 1997/1086 reg 13 with effect from 1 May 1997.
[2] Para (4) revoked by the Value Added Tax (Miscellaneous Amendments and Revocations) (EU Exit) Regulations, SI 2019/59 regs 12, 68 with effect from IP completion day (11pm UK time on 31 December 2020). Para (4) previously read as follows—
"(4) Where regulation 166AA applies, 'prescribed accounting period" in this regulation is to be read as "tax period".".

169 Preservation of documents and records and duty to produce

(1) Save as the Commissioners may otherwise allow, the claimant shall preserve the documents, invoices and records which he holds in accordance with regulations 167 and 168 for a period of 4 years from the date of the making of the claim.
(2) Upon demand made by an authorised person the claimant shall produce or cause to be produced any such documents, invoices and records for inspection by the authorised person and permit him to remove them at a reasonable time and for a reasonable period.

Commentary—*De Voil Indirect Tax Service* **V5.202, V5.234**.
HMRC Manuals—VAT Traders Records Manual VATREC3024 (preservation of parts of records).

170 Attribution of payments

(1) [Subject to regulation 170A below, where[1]]—
   (a) the claimant made more than one supply (whether taxable or otherwise) to the purchaser, and
   (b) a payment is received in relation to those supplies,
the payment shall be attributed to each such supply in accordance with the rules set out in paragraphs (2) and (3) below.
(2) The payment shall be attributed to the supply which is the earliest in time and, if not wholly attributed to that supply, thereafter to supplies in the order of the dates on which they were made, except that attribution under this paragraph shall not be made to any supply if the payment was allocated to that supply by the purchaser at the time of payment and the consideration for that supply was paid in full.
(3) Where—
   (a) the earliest supply and other supplies to which the whole of the payment could be attributed under this regulation occur on one day, or
   (b) the supplies to which the balance of the payment could be attributed under this regulation occur on one day,
the payment shall be attributed to those supplies by multiplying, for each such supply, the payment received by a fraction of which the numerator is the outstanding consideration for that supply and the denominator is the total outstanding consideration for those supplies.

Commentary—*De Voil Indirect Tax Service* **V5.156**.

HMRC Manuals—VAT Bad Debt Relief VBDR2200 (payments: how are payments attributed)?.
VBDR2600 (VAT groups containing a supplier of goods or services and a finance company).
VAT Retail Schemes Guidance VRS9270 (part-payment of debts).
Amendments—[1]   Words substituted by the VAT (Amendment) (No 4) Regulations, SI 2002/3027 regs 2, 4 with effect from 1 January 2003.

[170A   [Attribution of payments received under certain credit agreements
(1) This regulation applies where—
  (a) the claimant made a supply of goods and, in connection with that supply, a supply of credit;
  (b) those supplies were made under a hire purchase, conditional sale or credit sale agreement; and
  (c) a payment is received in relation to those supplies (other than a payment of an amount upon which interest is not charged).
(2) Where the supply of goods was made before 1st September 2006 the payment shall be attributed in accordance with the rule set out in paragraph (5).
(3) Where the supply of goods was made on or after 1st September 2006 and before 1st September 2007 the payment may be attributed in accordance with the rule set out in paragraph (5) or (6).
(4) Where the supply of goods was made on or after 1st September 2007 the payment shall be attributed in accordance with the rule set out in paragraph (6).
(5) Where this paragraph applies, the payment shall be attributed—
  (a) as to the amount obtained by multiplying it by the fraction A/B, to the supply of credit; and
  (b) as to the balance, to the supply of goods,
where—
  A is the total of the interest on the credit provided under the agreement under which the supplies are made (determined as at the date of the making of the agreement); and
  B is the total amount payable under the agreement, less any amount upon which interest is not charged.
(6) Where this paragraph applies, the payment shall be attributed—
  (a) in respect of payments made on or before termination of the agreement,
    (i) as to the amount obtained by multiplying it by the fraction A/B, to the supply of credit; and
    (ii) as to the balance, to the supply of goods,
where—
  A is the total of the interest on the credit provided under the agreement, less any rebate of interest granted, less any interest attributable to any unpaid instalments prior to the termination; and
  B is the total amount payable under the agreement being the total of A plus the total for the goods.
  "Total for the goods" means the amount due for the goods under the agreement, less any reduction as a consequence of termination, less any amount upon which interest is not charged, less any part of the total due for the goods which is unpaid at the time of termination.
  (b) in respect of payments made after termination of the agreement, between the supply of goods and the supply of credit according to the proportion of the balances due at the time the payment is made.
(7) Where an agreement provides for a variation of the rate of interest after the date of the making of the agreement then, for the purposes of the calculation in paragraph (5), it shall be assumed that the rate is not varied.][1]
Commentary—*De Voil Indirect Tax Service* **V5.156**.
HMRC Manuals—VAT Bad Debt Relief VBDR2410 (introduction).
VBDR2430 (the new method).
VBDR3600 (Abbey National plc- case).
VBDR2600 (VAT groups containing a supplier of goods or services and a finance company).
Amendments—[1]   This regulation substituted by the VAT (Amendment) Regulations, SI 2007/313 regs 2, 3 with effect from 1 March 2007.

[171   Repayment of a refund
(1) . . . [5] where a claimant—
  (a) has received a refund upon a claim, and
  (b) either—
    (i) a payment for the relevant supply is subsequently received, or
    (ii) a payment is, by virtue of regulation 170 or 170A, treated as attributed to the relevant supply, or
    (iii) the consideration for any relevant supply upon which the claim to refund is based is reduced after the claim is made,
he shall repay to the Commissioners such an amount as equals the amount of the refund, or the balance thereof, multiplied by a fraction of which the numerator is the amount so received or attributed, and the denominator is the amount of the outstanding consideration, or such an amount as

is equal to the negative entry made in the VAT allowable portion of his VAT account as provided for in regulation 38.][4]

(2) . . . [5] the claimant shall repay to the Commissioners the amount referred to in paragraph (1) above by including that amount in the box opposite the legend "VAT due in this period on sales and other outputs" on his return for the prescribed accounting period in which the payment is received.

(3) . . . [5] save as the Commissioners may otherwise allow, where the claimant fails to comply with the requirements of regulation 167, 168, 169[, 170 or 170A][2] he shall repay to the Commissioners the amount of the refund obtained by the claim to which the failure to comply relates; and he shall repay the amount by including that amount in the box opposite the legend "VAT due in this period on sales and other outputs" on his return for the prescribed accounting period which the Commissioners shall designate for that purpose.

(4) If at the time the claimant is required to repay any amount, he is no longer required to make returns to the Commissioners, he shall repay such amount to the Commissioners at such time and in such form and manner as they may direct.

[(5) For the purposes of this regulation[, but subject to paragraph (6) below,][3] a reference to payment shall not include a reference to a payment received by a person to whom a right to receive it has been assigned.][1]

[(6) Paragraph (5) above does not apply where any person to whom the right to receive a payment has been assigned (whether by the claimant or any other person) is connected to the claimant.][3]

[(7) Any question for the purposes of paragraph (6) above whether any person is connected to the claimant shall be determined in accordance with section 839 of the Taxes Act.][3]

[(8) Paragraphs (6) and (7) above apply where the right to receive a payment is assigned on or after 11th December 2003.][3]

Commentary—*De Voil Indirect Tax Service* **V5.156, V1.296**.
HMRC Manuals—VAT Bad Debt Relief VBDR4100 (repayment of relief when subsequent payments received).
Amendments—[1] Para (5) added by the VAT Regulations, SI 1999/3029, regs 2, 4 with effect from 1 December 1999.
[2] Words substituted by the VAT (Amendment) (No 4) Regulations, SI 2002/3027 regs 2, 6 with effect from 1 January 2003.
[3] 3 Words in para (5) inserted, and paras (6)–(8), inserted by the VAT (Amendment) (No 6) Regulations, SI 2003/3220 regs 1(1)(*a*), 2, 22, 23 with effect from 11 December 2003.
[4] Para (1) substituted by the VAT (Amendment) Regulations, SI 2007/313 regs 2, 4 with effect from 1 March 2007.
[5] In para (1) words "Subject to regulation 171A," revoked, in para (2) words "Subject to regulation 171B," revoked, and in para (3) words "Subject to regulation 171B and," revoked, by the Value Added Tax (Miscellaneous Amendments and Revocations) (EU Exit) Regulations, SI 2019/59 regs 12, 69 with effect from IP completion day (11pm UK time on 31 December 2020).

[171A Calculation of repayment where reduction in consideration: special accounting schemes
In a case falling within sub-paragraph (*b*)(iii) of regulation 171(1) where the VAT on the relevant supply was accounted for on a relevant non-UK return or a relevant special scheme return, the amount to be repaid is such an amount as is equal to the amount by which the VAT chargeable on the relevant supply is reduced.[2]][1]

Amendments—[1] Regs 171A, 171B inserted by the VAT (Amendment) (No 3) Regulations, SI 2014/2430 regs 2, 7(4) with effect from 1 January 2015.
[2] Regulations 171A, 171B revoked by the Value Added Tax (Miscellaneous Amendments and Revocations) (EU Exit) Regulations, SI 2019/59 regs 12, 70 with effect from IP completion day (11pm UK time on 31 December 2020).

[171B Timing and method of repayments: special accounting schemes
(1) Where—
   (a) the VAT on the relevant supply was accounted for on a relevant non-UK return or a relevant special scheme return, and
   (b) a repayment is required by regulation 171(1),
that repayment must be made no later than twenty days after the end of the tax period in which the payment for the relevant supply is received or the reduction in consideration is accounted for in the claimant's business accounts.
(2) Where—
   (a) the VAT on the relevant supply was accounted for on a relevant non-UK return or a relevant special scheme return, and
   (b) a repayment is required by regulation 171(3),
that repayment must be made no later than twenty days after the end of the tax period in which the failure to comply first occurred.
(3) In either case the repayment must be made by—
   (a) amending (in accordance with Article 61 of the Implementing Regulation) the relevant non-UK return or the relevant special scheme return for the tax period in which the VAT on the relevant supply was brought into account, or
   (b) (where the period during which a person is entitled to make such an amendment has expired) sending the sum due to the Commissioners.]*[1]*

Amendments—[1] Regs 171A, 171B inserted by the VAT (Amendment) (No 3) Regulations, SI 2014/2430 regs 2, 7(4) with effect from 1 January 2015.

[2] Regulations 171A, 171B revoked by the Value Added Tax (Miscellaneous Amendments and Revocations) (EU Exit) Regulations, SI 2019/59 regs 12, 70 with effect from IP completion day (11pm UK time on 31 December 2020).

172 Writing off debts

(1) This regulation shall apply for the purpose of ascertaining whether, and to what extent, the consideration is to be taken to have been written off as a bad debt.
[(1A) Neither the whole nor any part of the consideration for a supply shall be taken to have been written off in accounts as a bad debt until a period of not less than six months has elapsed from the time when such whole or part first became due and payable to or to the order of the person who made the [relevant supply][2].][1]
[(2) Subject to paragraph (1A) the whole or any part of the consideration for a [relevant supply][2] shall be taken to have been written off as a bad debt when an entry is made in relation to that supply in the refunds for bad debt account in accordance with regulation 168.][1]
(3) Where the claimant owes an amount of money to the purchaser which can be set off, the consideration written off in the accounts shall be reduced by the amount so owed.
(4) Where the claimant holds in relation to the purchaser an enforceable security, the consideration written off in the accounts of the claimant shall be reduced by the value of that security.

Commentary—*De Voil Indirect Tax Service* **V5.156**.
HMRC Manuals—VAT Bad Debt Relief VBDR1700 (when can a debt be written off)?
Amendments—[1] Para (1A) inserted by, and para (2) substituted by, VAT (Amendment) (No 5) Regulations, SI 1996/2960 with effect from 17 December 1996.
[2] Words in paras (1A) and (2) substituted by the VAT (Amendment) Regulations, SI 1997/1086 reg 14 with effect from 1 May 1997.

172A [Writing off debts—margin schemes

(1) This regulation applies where, by virtue of the claimant's having exercised an option under an order made under section 50A of the Act, the VAT chargeable on the relevant supply is charged by reference to the profit margin.
(2) Where this regulation applies the consideration for the relevant supply which is to be taken to have been written off as a bad debt shall not exceed the relevant amount.
(3) For the purposes of paragraph (2) above the relevant amount is—
   (*a*) where either—
      (i) no payment has been received in relation to the relevant supply, or
      (ii) the total of such payments as have been received does not exceed the non-profit element,
      the profit margin; or
   (*b*) where the total of such payments as have been received exceeds the non-profit element, the amount (if any) by which the consideration for the relevant supply exceeds that total.
(4) In paragraph (3) above—
   "non-profit element" means the consideration for the relevant supply less the profit margin.][1]

Commentary—*De Voil Indirect Tax Service* **V5.156**.
Amendments—[1] This regulation inserted by the VAT (Amendment) Regulations, SI 1997/1086 reg 15 with effect from 1 May 1997.

172B [Writing off debts—tour operators margin scheme

(1) This regulation applies where, by virtue of an order under section 53 of the Act, the value of the relevant supply falls to be determined otherwise than in accordance with section 19 of the Act.
(2) Where this regulation applies the consideration for the relevant supply which is to be taken to have been written off as a bad debt shall not exceed the relevant amount.
(3) For the purposes of paragraph (2) above the relevant amount is—
   (*a*) where either—
      (i) no payment has been received in relation to the relevant supply, or
      (ii) the total of any such payments as have been received does not exceed the non-profit element,
      the profit element; or
   (*b*) where the total of such payments as have been received exceeds the non-profit element, the amount (if any) by which the consideration for the relevant supply exceeds that total.
(4) In this regulation—
   "non-profit element" means the consideration for the relevant supply less the profit element;
   "profit element" means the sum of—
      (*a*) the value of the relevant supply; and
      (*b*) the VAT chargeable on the relevant supply.][1]

Commentary—*De Voil Indirect Tax Service* **V5.156**.
Amendments—[1] This regulation inserted by the VAT (Amendment) Regulations, SI 1997/1086 reg 15 with effect from 1 May 1997.

[PART XIXA
REPAYMENT OF INPUT TAX WHERE CLAIM MADE
UNDER PART XIX][1]

Amendments—[1] This part inserted by the VAT (Amendment) Regulations, SI 1997/1086 reg 16 with effect from 1 May 1997.

172ZC [Application
This Part applies where the relevant supply was made before 1st January 2003.][1]

Amendments—[1] This regulation inserted by the VAT (Amendment) (No 4) Regulations, SI 2002/3027 regs 2, 7 with effect from 1 January 2003.

172C [Interpretation of Part XIXA
Any expression used in this Part to which a meaning is given in Part XIX of these Regulations shall, unless the contrary intention appears, have the same meaning in this Part as it has in that Part.][1]

Amendments—[1] This regulation inserted by the VAT (Amendment) Regulations, SI 1997/1086 reg 16 with effect from 1 May 1997.

172D [Repayment of input tax
(1) Where—
   (a) a claim has been made; and
   (b) the purchaser has claimed deduction of the whole or part of the VAT on the relevant supply as input tax ('the deduction'),
the purchaser shall make an entry in his VAT account in accordance with paragraphs (2) and (3) below.
(2) The purchaser shall make a negative entry in the VAT allowable portion of that part of his VAT account which relates to the prescribed accounting period of his in which the claim has been made.
(3) The amount of the negative entry referred to in paragraph (2) above shall be such amount as is found by multiplying the amount of the deduction by a fraction of which the numerator is the amount of the claim and the denominator is the total VAT chargeable on the relevant supply.
(4) None of the circumstances to which this regulation applies is to be regarded as giving rise to any application of regulations 34 and 35.][1]

Amendments—[1] This regulation inserted by the VAT (Amendment) Regulations, SI 1997/1086 reg 15 with effect from 1 May 1997.

172E [Restoration of an entitlement to credit for input tax
(1) Where—
   (a) the purchaser has made an entry in his VAT account in accordance with regulation 172D ("the input tax repayment");
   (b) he has made the return for the prescribed accounting period concerned, and has paid any VAT payable by him in respect of that period; and
   (c) the claimant has made a repayment in accordance with regulation 171 in relation to the claim concerned,
the purchaser shall make an entry in his VAT account in accordance with paragraphs (2) and (3) below.
(2) The purchaser shall make a positive entry in the VAT allowable portion of that part of his VAT account which relates to the prescribed accounting period of his in which the repayment has been made.
(3) The amount of the positive entry referred to in paragraph (2) above shall be such amount as is found by multiplying the amount of the input tax repayment by a fraction of which the numerator is the amount repaid by the claimant and the denominator is the total amount of the claim.
(4) None of the circumstances to which this regulation applies is to be regarded as giving rise to any application of regulations 34 and 35.][1]

Amendments—[1] This regulation inserted by the VAT (Amendment) Regulations, SI 1997/1086 reg 16 with effect from 1 May 1997.

[PART XIXB
REPAYMENT OF INPUT TAX WHERE CONSIDERATION NOT PAID][1]

Amendments—[1] This Part inserted by the VAT (Amendment) (No 4) Regulations, SI 2002/3027 regs 2, 8 with effect from 1 January 2003.

172F [Application
This Part applies where the supply in relation to which a person has claimed credit for input tax was made on or after 1st January 2003.][1]

Commentary—*De Voil Indirect Tax Service* **V3.450**.
HMRC Manuals—VAT Bad Debt Relief VBDR5000 (repayment of input tax).
Amendments—[1] This regulation inserted by the VAT (Amendment) (No 4) Regulations, SI 2002/3027 regs 2, 8 with effect from 1 January 2003.

172G [Interpretation

In this Part—
"relevant period" means 6 months following—
(i) the date of the supply, or
(ii) if later, the date on which the consideration for the supply, or (as the case may be) the unpaid part of it, became payable.][1]

Commentary—*De Voil Indirect Tax Service* **V3.450**.
Amendments—[1] This regulation inserted by the VAT (Amendment) (No 4) Regulations, SI 2002/3027 regs 2, 8 with effect from 1 January 2003.

172H [Repayment of input tax

(1) Subject to [paragraphs (5) and (6)][2] below, where a person—
  (*a*) has not paid the whole or any part of the consideration for a supply by the end of the relevant period; and
  (*b*) has claimed deduction of the whole or part of the VAT on the supply as input tax ("the deduction"),
he shall make an entry in his VAT account in accordance with paragraphs (2) and (3) below.
(2) The person shall make a negative entry in the VAT allowable portion of that part of his VAT account which relates to the prescribed accounting period of his in which the end of the relevant period falls.
(3) The amount of the negative entry referred to in paragraph (2) above shall be such amount as is found by multiplying the amount of the deduction by a fraction of which the numerator is the amount of the consideration for the supply which has not been paid before the end of the relevant period and the denominator is the total consideration for the supply.
(4) None of the circumstances to which this regulation applies is to be regarded as giving rise to any application of regulations 34 and 35.
(5) This regulation does not apply where, for input tax, the operative date for VAT accounting purposes is the date mentioned in regulation 57(*b*) above.
[(6) This regulation does not apply in so far as a person is entitled under section 26AA of the Act to credit for input tax in relation to the supply.][2][1]

Commentary—*De Voil Indirect Tax Service* **V3.450**.
HMRC Manuals—VAT Bad Debt Relief VBDR5600 (how and when is input tax repaid?).
Amendments—[1] This regulation inserted by the VAT (Amendment) (No 4) Regulations, SI 2002/3027 regs 2, 8 with effect from 1 January 2003.
[2] In para (1), words substituted, and para (6) inserted, by the Enactment of Extra-Statutory Concessions Order, SI 2017/495 art 8 with effect in relation to supplies made on or after 6 April 2017.

172I [Restoration of an entitlement to credit for input tax

(1) Where a person—
  (*a*) has made an entry in his VAT account in accordance with regulation 172H ("the input tax repayment");
  (*b*) has made the return for the prescribed accounting period concerned, and has paid any VAT payable by him in respect of that period; and
  (*c*) after the end of the relevant period, has paid the whole or part of the consideration for the supply in relation to which the input tax repayment was made,
he shall make an entry in his VAT account in accordance with paragraphs (2) and (3) below in respect of each such payment made.
(2) The person shall make a positive entry in the VAT allowable portion of that part of his VAT account which relates to the prescribed accounting period of his in which payment of the whole or part of the consideration was made.
(3) The amount of the positive entry referred to in paragraph (2) above shall be such amount as is found by multiplying the amount of the input tax repayment by a fraction of which the numerator is the amount of the payment referred to in paragraph (1) (*c*) above and the denominator is [that consideration for the supply which was not paid before the end of the relevant period][2].
(4) None of the circumstances to which this regulation applies is to be regarded as giving rise to any application of regulations 34 and 35.
(5) . . . [2][1]

Commentary—*De Voil Indirect Tax Service* **V3.450**.
HMRC Manuals—VAT Bad Debt Relief VBDR6000 (how is the restored amount of input tax calculated?).
Amendments—[1] This regulation inserted by the VAT (Amendment) (No 4) Regulations, SI 2002/3027 regs 2, 8 with effect from 1 January 2003.
[2] Words in para (3) substituted, and para (5) revoked, by the VAT (Amendment) Regulations, SI 2003/532 with effect from 1 April 2003.

172J [Attribution of payments

The rules on the attribution of payments in regulation 170 and, as the case may be, [170A(5)][2] above shall apply for determining whether anything paid is to be taken as paid by way of consideration for a particular supply.][1]

Commentary—*De Voil Indirect Tax Service* **V3.450**.
Amendments—[1] This regulation inserted by the VAT (Amendment) (No 4) Regulations, SI 2002/3027 regs 2, 8 with effect from 1 January 2003.
[2] Figure substituted by the VAT (Amendment) Regulations, SI 2007/313 regs 2, 5 with effect from 1 March 2007.

[PART 19C
ADJUSTMENT OF OUTPUT TAX IN RESPECT OF SUPPLIES TO WHICH SECTION 55A (6) OF THE ACT APPLIES

172K This Part applies where a person is entitled, by virtue of section 26AB(2) of the Act, to make an adjustment to the amount of VAT which he is required to account for and pay under section 55A(6) of the Act ("the adjustment").][1]
HMRC Manuals—VAT Input Tax Basics VIT11500 (UK law).
VAT Traders' Records Manual VATREC13080 (when do regulation 38 adjustments need to be made to the VAT account?).
Amendments—[1] Regs 172K–172N inserted by the VAT (Amendment) (No 3) Regulations, SI 2007/1418 regs 2, 7 with effect from 1 June 2007.

[172L Adjustment of output tax
(1) The person must make the adjustment by making a negative entry in the VAT payable portion of that part of his VAT account which relates to the same prescribed accounting period of his as that in which he is required to make an entry in accordance with regulation 172H(2).
(2) The amount of the negative entry referred to in paragraph (1) above must be equal to the amount of the entry that is required to be made in accordance with regulation 172H(2).][1]
Amendments—[1] Regs 172K–172N inserted by the VAT (Amendment) (No 3) Regulations, SI 2007/1418 regs 2, 7 with effect from 1 June 2007.

[172M Readjustment of output tax
(1) Where a person—
   (*a*) has made an entry in his VAT account in accordance with regulation 172L; and
   (*b*) in relation to the same supply, he subsequently makes an entry in his VAT account in accordance with regulation 172I,
he must make an entry in his VAT account in accordance with paragraphs (2) and (3) below.
(2) The person must make a positive entry in the VAT payable portion of that part of his VAT account which relates to the same prescribed accounting period of his as that in which he makes an entry in accordance with regulation 172I.
(3) The amount of the positive entry referred to in paragraph (2) above must be equal to the amount of the entry he makes in accordance with regulation 172I.][1]
Amendments—[1] Regs 172K–172N inserted by the VAT (Amendment) (No 3) Regulations, SI 2007/1418 regs 2, 7 with effect from 1 June 2007.

[172N None of the circumstances to which this Part applies is to be regarded as giving rise to any application of regulations 34 and 35.][1]
Amendments—[1] Regs 172K–172N inserted by the VAT (Amendment) (No 3) Regulations, SI 2007/1418 regs 2, 7 with effect from 1 June 2007.

PART XX
REPAYMENTS TO COMMUNITY TRADERS

Saving and Transitional Provisions—Note that the revocation of Part 20 by SI 2019/59 reg 71 shall not have effect where a relevant claim is made on or after IP completion day or is made before that day but is still being processed by the Commissioners as at that day, or where a claimant who has made a claim for repayment of VAT under reg 173B is required to repay an amount to the Commissioners under reg 173D(3) on or after IP completion day (see the VAT (Miscellaneous and Transitional Provisions, Amendment and Revocation) (EU Exit) Regulations, SI 2020/1495 reg 11).
Where a relevant claim is made for the period from 1 January to 31 December 2019, and that claim was based on a provisional attribution of input tax under Directive 2006/112/EC Art 175(2) of as applied in the claimant's member State, the subsequent adjustment to the attribution of input tax under Directive 2006/112/EC Art 175(3) must be made on or before 31 March 2021 (see SI 2020/1495 reg 11(8)).
Where a relevant claim is made for the period from 1 January 2020 to IP completion day, and the claim is based on a provisional attribution of input tax under Directive 2006/112/EC Art 175(2) as applied in the claimant's member State, any subsequent adjustment to the attribution of input tax must be made under SI 2020/1495 reg 12 (see SI 2020/1495 reg 11(9)).
Where reg 11(9) applies and a person is required or wishes to make an adjustment to a provisional attribution of input tax for the period from 1 January 2020 to IP completion day, they must make a claim using the procedure in the VAT Regulations, Pt 21 as it has effect on and after IP completion day. The claim must be made on or before 31 December 2021.
Northern Ireland—See VAT Regs, SI 1995/2518 reg 184A: Part 20 of these Regulations as it had effect immediately before IP completion day continues to have effect subject to the modifications set out in regs 184B–184K.
Amendments—Part 20 revoked by the Value Added Tax (Miscellaneous Amendments and Revocations) (EU Exit) Regulations, SI 2019/59 regs 12, 71 with effect from IP completion day (11pm UK time on 31 December 2020).

173 Interpretation of Part XX
(1) In this Part—
   . . .[1]

"claimant" means a person making a claim under this Part or a person on whose behalf such a claim is made;
["claimant's member State" means the member State in which the claimant is established;][1]
...[1]
["principal VAT Directive" means Council Directive 2006/112/EC;
"refund Directive" means Council Directive 2008/9/EC;
"repayment period" means a period of time falling within one of the periods described in regulation 173G;
"repayment year" means the period of 12 calendar months commencing on 1st January.][1]
[(2) For the purposes of this Part, a person (P) is treated as being established in a country if—
   (a) P has there a business establishment or some other fixed establishment from which business transactions are effected; or
   (b) P's usual place of residence is there where P has no such establishment as is described in sub-paragraph (a) above in that country or elsewhere.][1]
(3) For the purposes of this Part—
   (a) a person carrying on business through a branch or agency in any country is treated as having there an establishment from which business transactions are effected, ...[1]
   (b) "usual place of residence", in relation to a body corporate, means the place where it is legally constituted.
   [(c) a reference to Article 170 of the principal VAT Directive is a reference to that Article—
      (i) as amended by Article 2(3) of the Council Directive 2008/8/EC, and
      (ii) as applied in the claimant's member State;
   (d) a reference to Article 214 of the principal VAT Directive is a reference to that Article—
      (i) as amended by Article 2(8) of Council Directive 2008/8/EC, and
      (ii) as applied in the claimant's member State;
   (e) a reference to any other Article in the principal VAT Directive or to any Article in the refund Directive is a reference to such Article as applied in the claimant's member State; and
   (f) a reference to Council Regulation (EC) No 1798/2003 is a reference to that Regulation as amended by Council Regulations (EC) No 885/2004, (EC) No 1791/2006, (EC) No 143/2008 and (EC) No 37/2009.[2]][1]

Commentary—*De Voil Indirect Tax Service* V5.151A.
Northern Ireland—See VAT Regs, SI 1995/2518 reg 184B: in relation repayments to EU traders incurring VAT on goods in Northern Ireland, this regulation continues to have effect as it had immediately before IP completion day but as if a para (4) were inserted, as follows—
   "(4) For the purposes of this Part, a supply is a supply of goods made to a claimant in Northern Ireland only where—
      (a) the goods are located in Northern Ireland at the time that they are supplied; and
      (b) the invoice required by regulation 13 to be provided to the claimant by the supplier in respect of that supply—
         (i) describes the supply as being a supply of goods; and
         (ii) does not contain particulars of any supply other than a supply of goods of the description set out in sub-paragraph (a)."
Saving and Transitional Provisions—Note that the revocation of Part 20 by SI 2019/59 reg 71 shall not have effect where a relevant claim is made on or after IP completion day or is made before that day but is still being processed by the Commissioners as at that day, or where a claimant who has made a claim for repayment of VAT under reg 173B is required to repay an amount to the Commissioners under reg 173D(3) on or after IP completion day (see the VAT (Miscellaneous and Transitional Provisions, Amendment and Revocation) (EU Exit) Regulations, SI 2020/1495 reg 11).
Where a relevant claim is made for the period from 1 January to 31 December 2019, and that claim was based on a provisional attribution of input tax under Directive 2006/112/EC Art 175(2) of as applied in the claimant's member State, the subsequent adjustment to the attribution of input tax under Directive 2006/112/EC Art 175(3) must be made on or before 31 March 2021 (see SI 2020/1495 reg 11(8)).
Where a relevant claim is made for the period from 1 January 2020 to IP completion day, and the claim is based on a provisional attribution of input tax under Directive 2006/112/EC Art 175(2) as applied in the claimant's member State, any subsequent adjustment to the attribution of input tax must be made under SI 2020/1495 reg 12 (see SI 2020/1495 reg 11(9)).
Where reg 11(9) applies and a person is required or wishes to make an adjustment to a provisional attribution of input tax for the period from 1 January 2020 to IP completion day, they must make a claim using the procedure in the VAT Regulations, Pt 21 as it has effect on and after IP completion day. The claim must be made on or before 31 December 2021.
Amendments—[1] Definitions "calendar year" and "official authority" substituted, definitions inserted, para (2) substituted, word "and" deleted and paras 3(c)–(f) inserted, by the VAT (Amendment) (No 5) Regs, SI 2009/3241, regs 2, 11 with effect from 1 January 2010.
Note that a claim for repayment of VAT in accordance with Part 20 made before 1 January 2010 shall be determined and, if appropriate, repayment made in accordance with this Part as it stood before the amendments made by SI 2009/3241 (see reg 18).
[2] Part 20 revoked by the Value Added Tax (Miscellaneous Amendments and Revocations) (EU Exit) Regulations, SI 2019/59 regs 12, 71 with effect from IP completion day (11pm UK time on 31 December 2020).

[173A Repayments of VAT
(1) The Commissioners shall make a repayment of VAT described in regulation 173B in accordance with this Part if—
   (a) the VAT is incurred in the repayment period covered by a repayment application;
   (b) the claimant is a person to whom this Part applies;

(c) the claimant makes a claim for repayment of the VAT in accordance with this Part; and
(d) the Commissioners are satisfied that the claimant is entitled to the repayment.
(2) Where—
  (a) a repayment application covering a repayment period has been submitted in accordance with this Part; and
  (b) a claim for repayment of VAT incurred in the repayment period covered by that repayment application is omitted from the repayment application,
the claim for repayment of that VAT may be made by means of a repayment application covering a later repayment period falling within the repayment year in which the VAT was incurred.²]¹

Saving and Transitional Provisions—Note that the revocation of Part 20 by SI 2019/59 reg 71 shall not have effect where a relevant claim is made on or after IP completion day or is made before that day but is still being processed by the Commissioners as at that day, or where a claimant who has made a claim for repayment of VAT under reg 173B is required to repay an amount to the Commissioners under reg 173D(3) on or after IP completion day (see the VAT (Miscellaneous and Transitional Provisions, Amendment and Revocation) (EU Exit) Regulations, SI 2020/1495 reg 11).
Where a relevant claim is made for the period from 1 January to 31 December 2019, and that claim was based on a provisional attribution of input tax under Directive 2006/112/EC Art 175(2) of as applied in the claimant's member State, the subsequent adjustment to the attribution of input tax under Directive 2006/112/EC Art 175(3) must be made on or before 31 March 2021 (see SI 2020/1495 reg 11(8)).
Where a relevant claim is made for the period from 1 January 2020 to IP completion day, and the claim is based on a provisional attribution of input tax under Directive 2006/112/EC Art 175(2) as applied in the claimant's member State, any subsequent adjustment to the attribution of input tax must be made under SI 2020/1495 reg 12 (see SI 2020/1495 reg 11(9)).
Where reg 11(9) applies and a person is required or wishes to make an adjustment to a provisional attribution of input tax for the period from 1 January 2020 to IP completion day, they must make a claim using the procedure in the VAT Regulations, Pt 21 as it has effect on and after IP completion day. The claim must be made on or before 31 December 2021.
Amendments—¹ Regs 173A–173X inserted by the VAT (Amendment) (No 5) Regs, SI 2009/3241, regs 2, 12 with effect from 1 January 2010. Note that a claim for repayment of VAT in accordance with Part 20 made before 1 January 2010 shall be determined and, if appropriate, repayment made in accordance with this Part as it stood before the amendments made by SI 2009/3241 (see reg 18).
² Part 20 revoked by the Value Added Tax (Miscellaneous Amendments and Revocations) (EU Exit) Regulations, SI 2019/59 regs 12, 71 with effect from IP completion day (11pm UK time on 31 December 2020).

[173B—(1) The VAT referred to in regulation 173A is VAT charged on—
  (a) an importation of goods by the claimant from a place outside the member States; and
  (b) supplies of goods or services made to the claimant in the United Kingdom if that VAT would be input tax of the claimant if the claimant were a taxable person.
(2) A claim for repayment may not be made in respect of VAT charged on—
  (a) an importation of goods in respect of which the VAT charged is eligible for other relief;
  (b) a supply or importation of goods which the claimant has removed or intends to remove to another member State, or which the claimant has exported or intends to export to a place outside the member States;
  (c) a supply or importation of goods or a supply of services which the claimant has used or intends to use for the purpose of any supply by the claimant in the United Kingdom other than a supply described in regulation 173E(b)(i), (ii)[, (iii) or (iv)]²;
  (d) a supply or importation of goods or a supply of services which if made to a taxable person would be excluded from credit under section 25 of the Act (payment of VAT by reference to accounting periods and credit for input tax against output tax); or
  (e) a supply or importation of goods or a supply of services to a travel agent which is for the direct benefit of a traveller other than the travel agent or the travel agent's employee.
(3) In this regulation "travel agent" includes a tour operator and any person who purchases and re-supplies services of a kind enjoyed by travellers.³]¹

Northern Ireland—See VAT Regs, SI 1995/2518 regs 184C, 184D: in relation repayments to EU traders incurring VAT on goods in Northern Ireland, this regulation continues to have effect as it had immediately before IP completion day but as if paras (1) and (2) were substituted, as follows—
  "(1) The VAT referred to in regulation 173A is VAT charged on—
    (a) an importation of goods into Northern Ireland; and
    (b) a supply of goods made to the claimant in Northern Ireland if that VAT would be, or would be treated as, input tax of the claimant if the claimant were a taxable person."
  "(2) A claim for repayment may not be made in respect of VAT charged on—
    (a) an importation of goods in respect of which the VAT charged is eligible for other relief;
    (b) a supply or importation of goods which the claimant has removed or intends to remove from Northern Ireland to a member State, or which the claimant has exported or intends to export to a place outside the member States or to remove to Great Britain;
    (c) a supply or importation of goods which the claimant has used or intends to use for the purpose of any supply made in the course of a business activity carried on by the claimant in Northern Ireland;
    (d) a supply or importation of goods which if made to a taxable person would be excluded from credit under section 25 of the Act (payment of VAT by reference to accounting periods and credit for input tax against output tax); or
    (e) the supply or importation of goods to a travel agent which is for the direct benefit of a traveller other than the travel agent or the travel agent's employee."

Saving and Transitional Provisions—Note that the revocation of Part 20 by SI 2019/59 reg 71 shall not have effect where a relevant claim is made on or after IP completion day or is made before that day but is still being processed by the Commissioners as at that day, or where a claimant who has made a claim for repayment of VAT under reg 173B is required to repay an amount to the Commissioners under reg 173D(3) on or after IP completion day (see the VAT (Miscellaneous and Transitional Provisions, Amendment and Revocation) (EU Exit) Regulations, SI 2020/1495 reg 11).

Where a relevant claim is made for the period from 1 January to 31 December 2019, and that claim was based on a provisional attribution of input tax under Directive 2006/112/EC Art 175(2) of as applied in the claimant's member State, the subsequent adjustment to the attribution of input tax under Directive 2006/112/EC Art 175(3) must be made on or before 31 March 2021 (see SI 2020/1495 reg 11(8)).

Where a relevant claim is made for the period from 1 January 2020 to IP completion day, and the claim is based on a provisional attribution of input tax under Directive 2006/112/EC Art 175(2) as applied in the claimant's member State, any subsequent adjustment to the attribution of input tax must be made under SI 2020/1495 reg 12 (see SI 2020/1495 reg 11(9)).

Where reg 11(9) applies and a person is required or wishes to make an adjustment to a provisional attribution of input tax for the period from 1 January 2020 to IP completion day, they must make a claim using the procedure in the VAT Regulations, Pt 21 as it has effect on and after IP completion day. The claim must be made on or before 31 December 2021.

Amendments—[1] Regs 173A–173X inserted by the VAT (Amendment) (No 5) Regs, SI 2009/3241, regs 2, 12 with effect from 1 January 2010. Note that a claim for repayment of VAT in accordance with Part 20 made before 1 January 2010 shall be determined and, if appropriate, repayment made in accordance with this Part as it stood before the amendments made by SI 2009/3241 (see reg 18).

[2] In para (2)(c), words substituted for words "or (iii)" by the VAT (Amendment) (No 3) Regulations, SI 2014/2430 regs 2, 8(1)(a) with effect from 1 January 2015.

[3] Part 20 revoked by the Value Added Tax (Miscellaneous Amendments and Revocations) (EU Exit) Regulations, SI 2019/59 regs 12, 71 with effect from IP completion day (11pm UK time on 31 December 2020).

[173C—(1) This regulation applies to VAT charged on the goods or services described in regulation 173B(1) which—
 (a) are not goods or services described in regulation 173B(2); and
 (b) are used by the claimant both for transactions—
  (i) giving rise to a right of deduction as required by Articles 168, 169 and 170 of the principal VAT Directive, and
  (ii) transactions that do not give rise to a right of deduction.
(2) The VAT to which this regulation applies is repayable only to the extent of the deductible proportion of that VAT.
(3) The deductible proportion of any VAT is the proportion of that VAT that the claimant would be entitled to deduct in accordance with Articles 173, 174 and 175 of the principal VAT Directive if the VAT were chargeable in the claimant's member State.[2]][1]

Northern Ireland—See VAT Regs, SI 1995/2518 reg 184E: in relation repayments to EU traders incurring VAT on goods in Northern Ireland, this regulation continues to have effect as it had immediately before IP completion day but as if "goods or services" in both places were read as "goods".

Saving and Transitional Provisions—Note that the revocation of Part 20 by SI 2019/59 reg 71 shall not have effect where a relevant claim is made on or after IP completion day or is made before that day but is still being processed by the Commissioners as at that day, or where a claimant who has made a claim for repayment of VAT under reg 173B is required to repay an amount to the Commissioners under reg 173D(3) on or after IP completion day (see the VAT (Miscellaneous and Transitional Provisions, Amendment and Revocation) (EU Exit) Regulations, SI 2020/1495 reg 11).

Where a relevant claim is made for the period from 1 January to 31 December 2019, and that claim was based on a provisional attribution of input tax under Directive 2006/112/EC Art 175(2) of as applied in the claimant's member State, the subsequent adjustment to the attribution of input tax under Directive 2006/112/EC Art 175(3) must be made on or before 31 March 2021 (see SI 2020/1495 reg 11(8)).

Where a relevant claim is made for the period from 1 January 2020 to IP completion day, and the claim is based on a provisional attribution of input tax under Directive 2006/112/EC Art 175(2) as applied in the claimant's member State, any subsequent adjustment to the attribution of input tax must be made under SI 2020/1495 reg 12 (see SI 2020/1495 reg 11(9)).

Where reg 11(9) applies and a person is required or wishes to make an adjustment to a provisional attribution of input tax for the period from 1 January 2020 to IP completion day, they must make a claim using the procedure in the VAT Regulations, Pt 21 as it has effect on and after IP completion day. The claim must be made on or before 31 December 2021.

Amendments—[1] Regs 173A–173X inserted by the VAT (Amendment) (No 5) Regs, SI 2009/3241, regs 2, 12 with effect from 1 January 2010. Note that a claim for repayment of VAT in accordance with Part 20 made before 1 January 2010 shall be determined and, if appropriate, repayment made in accordance with this Part as it stood before the amendments made by SI 2009/3241 (see reg 18).

[2] Part 20 revoked by the Value Added Tax (Miscellaneous Amendments and Revocations) (EU Exit) Regulations, SI 2019/59 regs 12, 71 with effect from IP completion day (11pm UK time on 31 December 2020).

[173D—(1) This regulation applies where—
 (a) a claim ("the original claim") for repayment of VAT to the extent of the deductible proportion of that VAT described in regulation 173C has been made; and
 (b) the deductible proportion used in making the claim was determined on a provisional basis as described in Article 175(2) of the principal VAT Directive.
(2) Where the amount of VAT claimed in the original claim is less than the VAT that would have been repayable if the deductible proportion had been determined by reference to the final proportion described in Article 175(3) of the principal VAT Directive, the VAT representing the difference

between the two amounts may be claimed by means of a repayment application submitted during the adjustment year as if that VAT had been incurred during the repayment period covered by that repayment application.

(3) Where the amount of VAT claimed in the original claim is more than the VAT that would have been repayable if the deductible proportion had been determined by reference to the final proportion described in Article 175(3) of the principal VAT Directive, the VAT representing the difference between the two amounts must be repaid to the Commissioners—
   (a) by way of adjustment of a repayment claim made by means of a repayment application submitted in the adjustment year, or
   (b) if no repayment claim is made as described in sub-paragraph (a) above, the payment back to the Commissioners must be made pursuant to a declaration submitted using the electronic portal set up by the claimant's member State for the purpose of facilitating repayments of VAT in accordance with the refund Directive before the expiry of the adjustment year.

(4) In this regulation "adjustment year" means the repayment year beginning immediately after the repayment year in which the repayment period of the original claim occurred or would have occurred if the original claim had been made in respect of the repayment period when the VAT was incurred.^{2}]^1

Saving and Transitional Provisions—Note that the revocation of Part 20 by SI 2019/59 reg 71 shall not have effect where a relevant claim is made on or after IP completion day or is made before that day but is still being processed by the Commissioners as at that day, or where a claimant who has made a claim for repayment of VAT under reg 173B is required to repay an amount to the Commissioners under reg 173D(3) on or after IP completion day (see the VAT (Miscellaneous and Transitional Provisions, Amendment and Revocation) (EU Exit) Regulations, SI 2020/1495 reg 11).

Where a relevant claim is made for the period from 1 January to 31 December 2019, and that claim was based on a provisional attribution of input tax under Directive 2006/112/EC Art 175(2) of as applied in the claimant's member State, the subsequent adjustment to the attribution of input tax under Directive 2006/112/EC Art 175(3) must be made on or before 31 March 2021 (see SI 2020/1495 reg 11(8)).

Where a relevant claim is made for the period from 1 January 2020 to IP completion day, and the claim is based on a provisional attribution of input tax under Directive 2006/112/EC Art 175(2) as applied in the claimant's member State, any subsequent adjustment to the attribution of input tax must be made under SI 2020/1495 reg 12 (see SI 2020/1495 reg 11(9)).

Where reg 11(9) applies and a person is required or wishes to make an adjustment to a provisional attribution of input tax for the period from 1 January 2020 to IP completion day, they must make a claim using the procedure in the VAT Regulations, Pt 21 as it has effect on and after IP completion day. The claim must be made on or before 31 December 2021.

Amendments—[1]   Regs 173A–173X inserted by the VAT (Amendment) (No 5) Regs, SI 2009/3241, regs 2, 12 with effect from 1 January 2010. Note that a claim for repayment of VAT in accordance with Part 20 made before 1 January 2010 shall be determined and, if appropriate, repayment made in accordance with this Part as it stood before the amendments made by SI 2009/3241 (see reg 18).

[2]   Part 20 revoked by the Value Added Tax (Miscellaneous Amendments and Revocations) (EU Exit) Regulations, SI 2019/59 regs 12, 71 with effect from IP completion day (11pm UK time on 31 December 2020).

[173E   Persons to whom this Part applies

This Part applies to a person who is established in and who carries on business in a member State other than the United Kingdom for the whole of a repayment period other than a person who—
   (a) is established in the United Kingdom during any part of the repayment period;
   (b) makes supplies in the United Kingdom of goods or services during any part of the repayment period other than—
      (i) transport of freight outside the United Kingdom or to or from a place outside the United Kingdom or services ancillary thereto,
      (ii) services where the VAT on the supply is payable solely by the person to whom the services are supplied in accordance with the provisions of section 8 of the Act (reverse charge on supplies received from abroad), and
      (iii) goods where the VAT on the supply is payable solely by the person to whom they are supplied as provided for in section 9A (reverse charge on gas and electricity supplied by persons outside the United Kingdom) or 14 (acquisitions from persons belonging in other member States) of the Act;
      [(iv) scheme services within paragraph 2 of Schedule 3BA to the Act supplied by a person who—
         (a) is required to account for the VAT on those supplies on a non-UK return; and
         (b) is not a registered person.]^2
   (c) during any part of the repayment period, does not undertake or intend to undertake transactions in the member State where that person is established which afford that person a right of deduction in accordance with Articles 168 and 169 of the principal VAT Directive as applied in the member State where that person is established;
   (d) makes or intends to make supplies in the repayment period upon which VAT was not or would not be charged by virtue of their being within the exemption afforded to small enterprises under Articles 284, 285, 286 and 287 of the principal VAT Directive as applied in the member State in which that person is established; or

(*e*) makes or intends to make supplies in the repayment period which are covered by the flat-rate scheme for farmers provided for in Articles 295 to 305 of the principal VAT Directive as applied in the member State in which that person is established.³]¹

Northern Ireland—See VAT Regs, SI 1995/2518 reg 184F: in relation repayments to EU traders incurring VAT on goods in Northern Ireland, this regulation continues to have effect as it had immediately before IP completion day but in the following modified form—

"**173E**

This Part applies to a person who is established in and who carries on business in a member State for the whole of a repayment period other than a person who—

(*a*) is established in Northern Ireland during any part of the repayment period; or
(*b*) is registered or required to be registered for VAT in the United Kingdom during any part of the repayment period."

Saving and Transitional Provisions—Note that the revocation of Part 20 by SI 2019/59 reg 71 shall not have effect where a relevant claim is made on or after IP completion day or is made before that day but is still being processed by the Commissioners as at that day, or where a claimant who has made a claim for repayment of VAT under reg 173B is required to repay an amount to the Commissioners under reg 173D(3) on or after IP completion day (see the VAT (Miscellaneous and Transitional Provisions, Amendment and Revocation) (EU Exit) Regulations, SI 2020/1495 reg 11).
Where a relevant claim is made for the period from 1 January to 31 December 2019, and that claim was based on a provisional attribution of input tax under Directive 2006/112/EC Art 175(2) of as applied in the claimant's member State, the subsequent adjustment to the attribution of input tax under Directive 2006/112/EC Art 175(3) must be made on or before 31 March 2021 (see SI 2020/1495 reg 11(8)).
Where a relevant claim is made for the period from 1 January 2020 to IP completion day, and the claim is based on a provisional attribution of input tax under Directive 2006/112/EC Art 175(2) as applied in the claimant's member State, any subsequent adjustment to the attribution of input tax must be made under SI 2020/1495 reg 12 (see SI 2020/1495 reg 11(9)).
Where reg 11(9) applies and a person is required or wishes to make an adjustment to a provisional attribution of input tax for the period from 1 January 2020 to IP completion day, they must make a claim using the procedure in the VAT Regulations, Pt 21 as it has effect on and after IP completion day. The claim must be made on or before 31 December 2021.
Amendments—¹ Regs 173A–173X inserted by the VAT (Amendment) (No 5) Regs, SI 2009/3241, regs 2, 12 with effect from 1 January 2010. Note that a claim for repayment of VAT in accordance with Part 20 made before 1 January 2010 shall be determined and, if appropriate, repayment made in accordance with this Part as it stood before the amendments made by SI 2009/3241 (see reg 18).
² Para (*b*)(iv) inserted by the VAT (Amendment) (No 3) Regulations, SI 2014/2430 regs 2, 8(2) with effect from 1 January 2015.
³ Part 20 revoked by the Value Added Tax (Miscellaneous Amendments and Revocations) (EU Exit) Regulations, SI 2019/59 regs 12, 71 with effect from IP completion day (11pm UK time on 31 December 2020).

[173F Time when VAT is incurred

(1) Paragraphs (2) to (4) below apply for determining the time when VAT is incurred for the purposes of a claim under this Part.
(2) VAT charged on the importation of goods is treated as incurred at the time when the VAT becomes chargeable.
(3) Where a supply of goods or services is treated as made at or before the time when the VAT invoice relating to it is issued, the VAT on that supply will be treated as incurred at the time when the VAT invoice is issued.
(4) Where a supply of goods or services is treated as made after the time when the VAT invoice relating to it is issued, the VAT will be treated as incurred at the time when the supply is treated as made.²]¹

Northern Ireland—See VAT Regs, SI 1995/2518 reg 184G: in relation repayments to EU traders incurring VAT on goods in Northern Ireland, this regulation continues to have effect as it had immediately before IP completion day but as if "supply of goods or services" in both places were read as "supply of goods".
Saving and Transitional Provisions—Note that the revocation of Part 20 by SI 2019/59 reg 71 shall not have effect where a relevant claim is made on or after IP completion day or is made before that day but is still being processed by the Commissioners as at that day, or where a claimant who has made a claim for repayment of VAT under reg 173B is required to repay an amount to the Commissioners under reg 173D(3) on or after IP completion day (see the VAT (Miscellaneous and Transitional Provisions, Amendment and Revocation) (EU Exit) Regulations, SI 2020/1495 reg 11).
Where a relevant claim is made for the period from 1 January to 31 December 2019, and that claim was based on a provisional attribution of input tax under Directive 2006/112/EC Art 175(2) of as applied in the claimant's member State, the subsequent adjustment to the attribution of input tax under Directive 2006/112/EC Art 175(3) must be made on or before 31 March 2021 (see SI 2020/1495 reg 11(8)).
Where a relevant claim is made for the period from 1 January 2020 to IP completion day, and the claim is based on a provisional attribution of input tax under Directive 2006/112/EC Art 175(2) as applied in the claimant's member State, any subsequent adjustment to the attribution of input tax must be made under SI 2020/1495 reg 12 (see SI 2020/1495 reg 11(9)).
Where reg 11(9) applies and a person is required or wishes to make an adjustment to a provisional attribution of input tax for the period from 1 January 2020 to IP completion day, they must make a claim using the procedure in the VAT Regulations, Pt 21 as it has effect on and after IP completion day. The claim must be made on or before 31 December 2021.
Amendments—¹ Regs 173A–173X inserted by the VAT (Amendment) (No 5) Regs, SI 2009/3241, regs 2, 12 with effect from 1 January 2010. Note that a claim for repayment of VAT in accordance with Part 20 made before 1 January 2010 shall be determined and, if appropriate, repayment made in accordance with this Part as it stood before the amendments made by SI 2009/3241 (see reg 18).
² Part 20 revoked by the Value Added Tax (Miscellaneous Amendments and Revocations) (EU Exit) Regulations, SI 2019/59 regs 12, 71 with effect from IP completion day (11pm UK time on 31 December 2020).

[173G Repayment period

A repayment period may be for a period of time covering—
  (a) a repayment year;
  (b) three or more consecutive months occurring wholly within a repayment year; or
  (c) the remainder of a repayment year where the period commences after 30th September in that year.[2]][1]

Saving and Transitional Provisions—Note that the revocation of Part 20 by SI 2019/59 reg 71 shall not have effect where a relevant claim is made on or after IP completion day or is made before that day but is still being processed by the Commissioners as at that day, or where a claimant who has made a claim for repayment of VAT under reg 173B is required to repay an amount to the Commissioners under reg 173D(3) on or after IP completion day (see the VAT (Miscellaneous and Transitional Provisions, Amendment and Revocation) (EU Exit) Regulations, SI 2020/1495 reg 11).

Where a relevant claim is made for the period from 1 January to 31 December 2019, and that claim was based on a provisional attribution of input tax under Directive 2006/112/EC Art 175(2) of as applied in the claimant's member State, the subsequent adjustment to the attribution of input tax under Directive 2006/112/EC Art 175(3) must be made on or before 31 March 2021 (see SI 2020/1495 reg 11(8)).

Where a relevant claim is made for the period from 1 January 2020 to IP completion day, and the claim is based on a provisional attribution of input tax under Directive 2006/112/EC Art 175(2) as applied in the claimant's member State, any subsequent adjustment to the attribution of input tax must be made under SI 2020/1495 reg 12 (see SI 2020/1495 reg 11(9)).

Where reg 11(9) applies and a person is required or wishes to make an adjustment to a provisional attribution of input tax for the period from 1 January 2020 to IP completion day, they must make a claim using the procedure in the VAT Regulations, Pt 21 as it has effect on and after IP completion day. The claim must be made on or before 31 December 2021.

Amendments—[1] Regs 173A–173X inserted by the VAT (Amendment) (No 5) Regs, SI 2009/3241, regs 2, 12 with effect from 1 January 2010. Note that a claim for repayment of VAT in accordance with Part 20 made before 1 January 2010 shall be determined and, if appropriate, repayment made in accordance with this Part as it stood before the amendments made by SI 2009/3241 (see reg 18).
[2] Part 20 revoked by the Value Added Tax (Miscellaneous Amendments and Revocations) (EU Exit) Regulations, SI 2019/59 regs 12, 71 with effect from IP completion day (11pm UK time on 31 December 2020).

[173H Minimum total claim for a repayment period

(1) A claim for a repayment period must not be made unless the total amount claimed for the period is equal to or exceeds the minimum amount specified in paragraph (2) below.
(2) The minimum amount specified for a repayment period is—
  (a) £35 in respect of the repayment period described in regulation 173G(a);
  (b) £295 in respect of the repayment period described in regulation 173G(b); and
  (c) £35 in respect of the repayment period described in regulation 173G(c).[2]][1]

Saving and Transitional Provisions—Note that the revocation of Part 20 by SI 2019/59 reg 71 shall not have effect where a relevant claim is made on or after IP completion day or is made before that day but is still being processed by the Commissioners as at that day, or where a claimant who has made a claim for repayment of VAT under reg 173B is required to repay an amount to the Commissioners under reg 173D(3) on or after IP completion day (see the VAT (Miscellaneous and Transitional Provisions, Amendment and Revocation) (EU Exit) Regulations, SI 2020/1495 reg 11).

Where a relevant claim is made for the period from 1 January to 31 December 2019, and that claim was based on a provisional attribution of input tax under Directive 2006/112/EC Art 175(2) of as applied in the claimant's member State, the subsequent adjustment to the attribution of input tax under Directive 2006/112/EC Art 175(3) must be made on or before 31 March 2021 (see SI 2020/1495 reg 11(8)).

Where a relevant claim is made for the period from 1 January 2020 to IP completion day, and the claim is based on a provisional attribution of input tax under Directive 2006/112/EC Art 175(2) as applied in the claimant's member State, any subsequent adjustment to the attribution of input tax must be made under SI 2020/1495 reg 12 (see SI 2020/1495 reg 11(9)).

Where reg 11(9) applies and a person is required or wishes to make an adjustment to a provisional attribution of input tax for the period from 1 January 2020 to IP completion day, they must make a claim using the procedure in the VAT Regulations, Pt 21 as it has effect on and after IP completion day. The claim must be made on or before 31 December 2021.

Amendments—[1] Regs 173A–173X inserted by the VAT (Amendment) (No 5) Regs, SI 2009/3241, regs 2, 12 with effect from 1 January 2010. Note that a claim for repayment of VAT in accordance with Part 20 made before 1 January 2010 shall be determined and, if appropriate, repayment made in accordance with this Part as it stood before the amendments made by SI 2009/3241 (see reg 18).
[2] Part 20 revoked by the Value Added Tax (Miscellaneous Amendments and Revocations) (EU Exit) Regulations, SI 2019/59 regs 12, 71 with effect from IP completion day (11pm UK time on 31 December 2020).

[173I Requirements for a claim for repayment of VAT

A claim for repayment of VAT under this Part must be made by means of a repayment application that—
  (a) is addressed to the United Kingdom;
  (b) contains the information required in regulations 173L and 173M completed in the English language;
  (c) is submitted at any time before the day specified in regulation 173P using the electronic portal set up by the claimant's member State for the purpose of facilitating repayments of VAT in accordance with the refund Directive.[2]][1]

Saving and Transitional Provisions—Note that the revocation of Part 20 by SI 2019/59 reg 71 shall not have effect where a relevant claim is made on or after IP completion day or is made before that day but is still being processed by the Commissioners as at that day, or where a claimant who has made a claim for repayment of VAT under reg 173B is required to repay an amount to the Commissioners under reg 173D(3) on or after IP completion day (see the VAT (Miscellaneous and Transitional Provisions, Amendment and Revocation) (EU Exit) Regulations, SI 2020/1495 reg 11).

Where a relevant claim is made for the period from 1 January to 31 December 2019, and that claim was based on a provisional attribution of input tax under Directive 2006/112/EC Art 175(2) of as applied in the claimant's member State, the subsequent adjustment to the attribution of input tax under Directive 2006/112/EC Art 175(3) must be made on or before 31 March 2021 (see SI 2020/1495 reg 11(8)).

Where a relevant claim is made for the period from 1 January 2020 to IP completion day, and the claim is based on a provisional attribution of input tax under Directive 2006/112/EC Art 175(2) as applied in the claimant's member State, any subsequent adjustment to the attribution of input tax must be made under SI 2020/1495 reg 12 (see SI 2020/1495 reg 11(9)).

Where reg 11(9) applies and a person is required or wishes to make an adjustment to a provisional attribution of input tax for the period from 1 January 2020 to IP completion day, they must make a claim using the procedure in the VAT Regulations, Pt 21 as it has effect on and after IP completion day. The claim must be made on or before 31 December 2021.

Amendments—[1] Regs 173A–173X inserted by the VAT (Amendment) (No 5) Regs, SI 2009/3241, regs 2, 12 with effect from 1 January 2010. Note that a claim for repayment of VAT in accordance with Part 20 made before 1 January 2010 shall be determined and, if appropriate, repayment made in accordance with this Part as it stood before the amendments made by SI 2009/3241 (see reg 18).

[2] Part 20 revoked by the Value Added Tax (Miscellaneous Amendments and Revocations) (EU Exit) Regulations, SI 2019/59 regs 12, 71 with effect from IP completion day (11pm UK time on 31 December 2020).

[173J] Where a claim for repayment of VAT under this Part comprises or includes a claim made in respect of a supply or importation described in regulation 173K, copies of such documentary evidence of an entitlement to deduct VAT as could be required of a taxable person claiming deduction of input tax in accordance with regulation 29 (requirements in connection with making claims for deduction of input tax) must be submitted using the electronic portal described in regulation 173I(*c*) at the same time as the repayment application in respect of that VAT.[2]][1]

Saving and Transitional Provisions—Note that the revocation of Part 20 by SI 2019/59 reg 71 shall not have effect where a relevant claim is made on or after IP completion day or is made before that day but is still being processed by the Commissioners as at that day, or where a claimant who has made a claim for repayment of VAT under reg 173B is required to repay an amount to the Commissioners under reg 173D(3) on or after IP completion day (see the VAT (Miscellaneous and Transitional Provisions, Amendment and Revocation) (EU Exit) Regulations, SI 2020/1495 reg 11).

Where a relevant claim is made for the period from 1 January to 31 December 2019, and that claim was based on a provisional attribution of input tax under Directive 2006/112/EC Art 175(2) of as applied in the claimant's member State, the subsequent adjustment to the attribution of input tax under Directive 2006/112/EC Art 175(3) must be made on or before 31 March 2021 (see SI 2020/1495 reg 11(8)).

Where a relevant claim is made for the period from 1 January 2020 to IP completion day, and the claim is based on a provisional attribution of input tax under Directive 2006/112/EC Art 175(2) as applied in the claimant's member State, any subsequent adjustment to the attribution of input tax must be made under SI 2020/1495 reg 12 (see SI 2020/1495 reg 11(9)).

Where reg 11(9) applies and a person is required or wishes to make an adjustment to a provisional attribution of input tax for the period from 1 January 2020 to IP completion day, they must make a claim using the procedure in the VAT Regulations, Pt 21 as it has effect on and after IP completion day. The claim must be made on or before 31 December 2021.

Amendments—[1] Regs 173A–173X inserted by the VAT (Amendment) (No 5) Regs, SI 2009/3241, regs 2, 12 with effect from 1 January 2010. Note that a claim for repayment of VAT in accordance with Part 20 made before 1 January 2010 shall be determined and, if appropriate, repayment made in accordance with this Part as it stood before the amendments made by SI 2009/3241 (see reg 18).

[2] Part 20 revoked by the Value Added Tax (Miscellaneous Amendments and Revocations) (EU Exit) Regulations, SI 2019/59 regs 12, 71 with effect from IP completion day (11pm UK time on 31 December 2020).

[173K] The supplies or importations referred to in regulation 173J are—
(*a*) a supply of goods or services of a value equal to or exceeding £750;
(*b*) an importation of goods of a value equal to or exceeding £750; and
(*c*) a supply or importation of fuel of a value equal to or exceeding £200.[2]][1]

Northern Ireland—See VAT Regs, SI 1995/2518 reg 184H: in relation repayments to EU traders incurring VAT on goods in Northern Ireland, this regulation continues to have effect as it had immediately before IP completion day but as if "supply of goods or services" were read as "supply of goods".

Saving and Transitional Provisions—Note that the revocation of Part 20 by SI 2019/59 reg 71 shall not have effect where a relevant claim is made on or after IP completion day or is made before that day but is still being processed by the Commissioners as at that day, or where a claimant who has made a claim for repayment of VAT under reg 173B is required to repay an amount to the Commissioners under reg 173D(3) on or after IP completion day (see the VAT (Miscellaneous and Transitional Provisions, Amendment and Revocation) (EU Exit) Regulations, SI 2020/1495 reg 11).

Where a relevant claim is made for the period from 1 January to 31 December 2019, and that claim was based on a provisional attribution of input tax under Directive 2006/112/EC Art 175(2) of as applied in the claimant's member State, the subsequent adjustment to the attribution of input tax under Directive 2006/112/EC Art 175(3) must be made on or before 31 March 2021 (see SI 2020/1495 reg 11(8)).

Where a relevant claim is made for the period from 1 January 2020 to IP completion day, and the claim is based on a provisional attribution of input tax under Directive 2006/112/EC Art 175(2) as applied in the claimant's member State, any subsequent adjustment to the attribution of input tax must be made under SI 2020/1495 reg 12 (see SI 2020/1495 reg 11(9)).

Where reg 11(9) applies and a person is required or wishes to make an adjustment to a provisional attribution of input tax for the period from 1 January 2020 to IP completion day, they must make a claim using the procedure in the VAT Regulations, Pt 21 as it has effect on and after IP completion day. The claim must be made on or before 31 December 2021.

Amendments—[1] Regs 173A–173X inserted by the VAT (Amendment) (No 5) Regs, SI 2009/3241, regs 2, 12 with effect from 1 January 2010. Note that a claim for repayment of VAT in accordance with Part 20 made before 1 January 2010 shall be determined and, if appropriate, repayment made in accordance with this Part as it stood before the amendments made by SI 2009/3241 (see reg 18).

² Part 20 revoked by the Value Added Tax (Miscellaneous Amendments and Revocations) (EU Exit) Regulations, SI 2019/59 regs 12, 71 with effect from IP completion day (11pm UK time on 31 December 2020).

[173L Contents of a repayment application
(1) A repayment application must contain the following information—
   (a) the claimant's name and full address;
   (b) an address for contact by electronic means;
   (c) a description of the claimant's business activity for which the goods or services were acquired by reference to the appropriate harmonised code contained in revision 2 of the common statistical classification of economic activities referred to as "NACE Rev. 2" established by the European Parliament and Council Regulation (EC) No 1983/2006;
   (d) the repayment period covered by the application;
   (e) a declaration that the claimant has made no supply falling within paragraph (2) below during any part of the repayment period;
   (f) the VAT identification number or tax reference number by which the claimant is identified for VAT purposes in the claimant's member State in accordance with Articles 214, 239 or 240 of the principal VAT Directive;
   (g) the details of the bank account to which the claimant requests the Commissioners to repay the VAT claimed; and
   (h) the information described in regulation 173M in relation to every importation of goods or supply in respect of which repayment of VAT charged thereon is claimed in the repayment application.
(2) A supply is within this paragraph if it is a supply of goods or services made in the United Kingdom other than a supply mentioned in regulation 173E(b)(i), (ii)[, (iii) or (iv)³]².]¹

Northern Ireland—See VAT Regs, SI 1995/2518 reg 184I: in relation repayments to EU traders incurring VAT on goods in Northern Ireland, this regulation continues to have effect as it had immediately before IP completion day but as if para (2) were substituted, as follows—

"(2) A supply is within this paragraph if it is a supply made in the course of a business activity carried on by the claimant in Northern Ireland."

Saving and Transitional Provisions—Note that the revocation of Part 20 by SI 2019/59 reg 71 shall not have effect where a relevant claim is made on or after IP completion day or is made before that day but is still being processed by the Commissioners as at that day, or where a claimant who has made a claim for repayment of VAT under reg 173B is required to repay an amount to the Commissioners under reg 173D(3) on or after IP completion day (see the VAT (Miscellaneous and Transitional Provisions, Amendment and Revocation) (EU Exit) Regulations, SI 2020/1495 reg 11).
Where a relevant claim is made for the period from 1 January to 31 December 2019, and that claim was based on a provisional attribution of input tax under Directive 2006/112/EC Art 175(2) of as applied in the claimant's member State, the subsequent adjustment to the attribution of input tax under Directive 2006/112/EC Art 175(3) must be made on or before 31 March 2021 (see SI 2020/1495 reg 11(8)).
Where a relevant claim is made for the period from 1 January 2020 to IP completion day, and the claim is based on a provisional attribution of input tax under Directive 2006/112/EC Art 175(2) as applied in the claimant's member State, any subsequent adjustment to the attribution of input tax must be made under SI 2020/1495 reg 12 (see SI 2020/1495 reg 11(9)).
Where reg 11(9) applies and a person is required or wishes to make an adjustment to a provisional attribution of input tax for the period from 1 January 2020 to IP completion day, they must make a claim using the procedure in the VAT Regulations, Pt 21 as it has effect on and after IP completion day. The claim must be made on or before 31 December 2021.

Amendments—¹ Regs 173A–173X inserted by the VAT (Amendment) (No 5) Regs, SI 2009/3241, regs 2, 12 with effect from 1 January 2010. Note that a claim for repayment of VAT in accordance with Part 20 made before 1 January 2010 shall be determined and, if appropriate, repayment made in accordance with this Part as it stood before the amendments made by SI 2009/3241 (see reg 18).
² In para (2), words substituted for words "or (iii)" by the VAT (Amendment) (No 3) Regulations, SI 2014/2430 regs 2, 8(1)(b) with effect from 1 January 2015.
³ Part 20 revoked by the Value Added Tax (Miscellaneous Amendments and Revocations) (EU Exit) Regulations, SI 2019/59 regs 12, 71 with effect from IP completion day (11pm UK time on 31 December 2020).

[173M In respect of every importation of goods or supply in respect of which repayment of VAT charged thereon is claimed, a repayment application must contain the following information—
   (a) the full name and address of the supplier;
   (b) except in the case of an importation of goods, the registration number of the supplier and the prefix "GB" or such other prefix by which the United Kingdom is identified in accordance with the requirements of Article 215 of the principal VAT Directive;
   (c) the date of issue of, and the unique sequential number identifying, the document authenticated or issued by a proper officer in respect of the importation of goods or the VAT invoice issued in respect of the supply;
   (d) the value of the supply or of the imported goods (expressed in sterling) as determined under the Act but excluding the VAT chargeable on the supply or importation;
   (e) the amount (expressed in sterling) of VAT chargeable on the supply or importation;
   (f) the amount of VAT on the supply or importation eligible for repayment under this Part expressed in sterling;
   (g) where applicable, the fraction described in regulation 173N, expressed as a percentage; and
   (h) the nature of goods and services acquired, described in accordance with regulation 173O.²]¹

Northern Ireland—See VAT Regs, SI 1995/2518 reg 184J: in relation repayments to EU traders incurring VAT on goods in Northern Ireland, this regulation continues to have effect as it had immediately before IP completion day but as if paras (*b*) and (*c*) were substituted (as below), and as if in para (*h*) "goods and services" read as "goods"—

"(*b*)   except in the case of an importation of goods, the registration number of the supplier and the prefix "XI";
(*c*)   the date of issue of, and the unique sequential number identifying, the import document required to be produced by regulation 17 of the Value Added Tax (Northern Ireland) (EU Exit) Regulations 2020(a) or the document authenticated or issued by a proper officer in respect of an importation of goods or the VAT invoice issued in respect of the supply;".

Saving and Transitional Provisions—Note that the revocation of Part 20 by SI 2019/59 reg 71 shall not have effect where a relevant claim is made on or after IP completion day or is made before that day but is still being processed by the Commissioners as at that day, or where a claimant who has made a claim for repayment of VAT under reg 173B is required to repay an amount to the Commissioners under reg 173D(3) on or after IP completion day (see the VAT (Miscellaneous and Transitional Provisions, Amendment and Revocation) (EU Exit) Regulations, SI 2020/1495 reg 11).

Where a relevant claim is made for the period from 1 January to 31 December 2019, and that claim was based on a provisional attribution of input tax under Directive 2006/112/EC Art 175(2) of as applied in the claimant's member State, the subsequent adjustment to the attribution of input tax under Directive 2006/112/EC Art 175(3) must be made on or before 31 March 2021 (see SI 2020/1495 reg 11(8)).

Where a relevant claim is made for the period from 1 January 2020 to IP completion day, and the claim is based on a provisional attribution of input tax under Directive 2006/112/EC Art 175(2) as applied in the claimant's member State, any subsequent adjustment to the attribution of input tax must be made under SI 2020/1495 reg 12 (see SI 2020/1495 reg 11(9)).

Where reg 11(9) applies and a person is required or wishes to make an adjustment to a provisional attribution of input tax for the period from 1 January 2020 to IP completion day, they must make a claim using the procedure in the VAT Regulations, Pt 21 as it has effect on and after IP completion day. The claim must be made on or before 31 December 2021.

Amendments—[1]   Regs 173A–173X inserted by the VAT (Amendment) (No 5) Regs, SI 2009/3241, regs 2, 12 with effect from 1 January 2010. Note that a claim for repayment of VAT in accordance with Part 20 made before 1 January 2010 shall be determined and, if appropriate, repayment made in accordance with this Part as it stood before the amendments made by SI 2009/3241 (see reg 18).

[2]   Part 20 revoked by the Value Added Tax (Miscellaneous Amendments and Revocations) (EU Exit) Regulations, SI 2019/59 regs 12, 71 with effect from IP completion day (11pm UK time on 31 December 2020).

[173N   The fraction referred to in regulation 173M(*g*) is the fraction described in Article 174(1) of the principal VAT Directive that would determine the deductible proportion of the VAT that the claimant would be entitled to deduct in accordance with Articles 173, 174 and 175 of that Directive if the VAT were chargeable in the claimant's member State.[2]][1]

Saving and Transitional Provisions—Note that the revocation of Part 20 by SI 2019/59 reg 71 shall not have effect where a relevant claim is made on or after IP completion day or is made before that day but is still being processed by the Commissioners as at that day, or where a claimant who has made a claim for repayment of VAT under reg 173B is required to repay an amount to the Commissioners under reg 173D(3) on or after IP completion day (see the VAT (Miscellaneous and Transitional Provisions, Amendment and Revocation) (EU Exit) Regulations, SI 2020/1495 reg 11).

Where a relevant claim is made for the period from 1 January to 31 December 2019, and that claim was based on a provisional attribution of input tax under Directive 2006/112/EC Art 175(2) of as applied in the claimant's member State, the subsequent adjustment to the attribution of input tax under Directive 2006/112/EC Art 175(3) must be made on or before 31 March 2021 (see SI 2020/1495 reg 11(8)).

Where a relevant claim is made for the period from 1 January 2020 to IP completion day, and the claim is based on a provisional attribution of input tax under Directive 2006/112/EC Art 175(2) as applied in the claimant's member State, any subsequent adjustment to the attribution of input tax must be made under SI 2020/1495 reg 12 (see SI 2020/1495 reg 11(9)).

Where reg 11(9) applies and a person is required or wishes to make an adjustment to a provisional attribution of input tax for the period from 1 January 2020 to IP completion day, they must make a claim using the procedure in the VAT Regulations, Pt 21 as it has effect on and after IP completion day. The claim must be made on or before 31 December 2021.

Amendments—[1]   Regs 173A–173X inserted by the VAT (Amendment) (No 5) Regs, SI 2009/3241, regs 2, 12 with effect from 1 January 2010. Note that a claim for repayment of VAT in accordance with Part 20 made before 1 January 2010 shall be determined and, if appropriate, repayment made in accordance with this Part as it stood before the amendments made by SI 2009/3241 (see reg 18).

[2]   Part 20 revoked by the Value Added Tax (Miscellaneous Amendments and Revocations) (EU Exit) Regulations, SI 2019/59 regs 12, 71 with effect from IP completion day (11pm UK time on 31 December 2020).

[173O—(1) The nature of the goods or services in respect of which repayment of VAT under this Part is claimed must be described by reference to—
   (*a*) the harmonised numerical codes in paragraph (2) below; and
   (*b*) where paragraph (3) below applies, the harmonised numerical codes for the goods and services concerned referred to in paragraph (4) below.

(2) The harmonised numerical codes referred to in paragraph (1) above are—
   (*a*) code 1 in respect of fuel;
   (*b*) code 2 in respect of hiring of means of transport;
   (*c*) code 3 in respect of expenditure relating to means of transport (other than the goods and services referred to by codes 1 and 2);
   (*d*) code 4 in respect of road tolls and road user charges;
   (*e*) code 5 in respect of travel expenses, such as taxi fares and public transport fares;
   (*f*) code 6 in respect of accommodation;
   (*g*) code 7 in respect of food, drink and restaurant services;
   (*h*) code 8 in respect of admissions to fairs and exhibitions;

(i) code 9 in respect of expenditures on luxuries, amusements and entertainment;
(j) code 10 in respect of other goods and services.
(3) This paragraph applies where the goods or services in respect of which repayment of VAT under this Part is claimed fall within any of the descriptions of goods or services represented by such of the harmonised numerical codes contained in the annex to Commission Regulation (EC) No 1174/2009 as listed in paragraph (4) below.
(4) The harmonised numerical codes referred to in paragraph (3) above are codes 1.6, 2.2, 2.4, 2.5.1, 2.5.2, 2.6.1, 2.6.2, 2.7, 2.9.1, 2.9.2, 3.2.1, 3.2.2, 3.2.3, 3.4.1, 3.4.2, 3.5.1, 3.5.2, 3.6.1, 3.6.2, 3.7.1, 3.7.2, 3.8.1, 3.8.2, 3.9, 3.10, 3.12, 5.1, 5.2, 5.3.1, 5.3.2, 6.1, 6.2, 6.4.1, 6.4.2, 6.6, 7.1.1, 7.1.2, 7.2.1, 7.2.2, 7.4, 8.1, 8.2, 9.1, 9.2, 9.3.1, 9.3.2, 9.4, 9.5, 9.6, 9.7, 10,1, 10.2, 10.3, 10.4.1, 10.4.2, 10.4.3, 10.5.1, 10.5.2, 10.5.3, 10.6, 10.7, 10.8, 10.9.1, 10.9.2, 10.9.3, 10.9.4, 10.10, 10.11, 10.12, 10.13, 10.14, 10.15, 10.16.1, 10.16.2, 10.16.3, 10.16.4, 10.17.1 and 10.17.2.
(5) Goods or services which fall within harmonised numerical code 10 in paragraph (2)(j) above but which do not fall within any of the harmonised numerical codes specified in paragraph (4) above must be expressly described in addition to their description by reference to harmonised code 10.[3]][1]

Northern Ireland—See VAT Regs, SI 1995/2518 reg 184K: in relation repayments to EU traders incurring VAT on goods in Northern Ireland, this regulation continues to have effect as it had immediately before IP completion day but in the following modified form—

"173O

The nature of the goods in respect of which repayment of VAT under this Part is claimed must be described in accordance with numerical codes specified for this purpose in a notice published by the Commissioners in accordance with this regulation."

Saving and Transitional Provisions—Note that the revocation of Part 20 by SI 2019/59 reg 71 shall not have effect where a relevant claim is made on or after IP completion day or is made before that day but is still being processed by the Commissioners as at that day, or where a claimant who has made a claim for repayment of VAT under reg 173B is required to repay an amount to the Commissioners under reg 173D(3) on or after IP completion day (see the VAT (Miscellaneous and Transitional Provisions, Amendment and Revocation) (EU Exit) Regulations, SI 2020/1495 reg 11).

Where a relevant claim is made for the period from 1 January to 31 December 2019, and that claim was based on a provisional attribution of input tax under Directive 2006/112/EC Art 175(2) of as applied in the claimant's member State, the subsequent adjustment to the attribution of input tax under Directive 2006/112/EC Art 175(3) must be made on or before 31 March 2021 (see SI 2020/1495 reg 11(8)).

Where a relevant claim is made for the period from 1 January 2020 to IP completion day, and the claim is based on a provisional attribution of input tax under Directive 2006/112/EC Art 175(2) as applied in the claimant's member State, any subsequent adjustment to the attribution of input tax must be made under SI 2020/1495 reg 12 (see SI 2020/1495 reg 11(9)).

Where reg 11(9) applies and a person is required or wishes to make an adjustment to a provisional attribution of input tax for the period from 1 January 2020 to IP completion day, they must make a claim using the procedure in the VAT Regulations, Pt 21 as it has effect on and after IP completion day. The claim must be made on or before 31 December 2021.

Amendments—[1] Regs 173A–173X inserted by the VAT (Amendment) (No 5) Regs, SI 2009/3241, regs 2, 12 with effect from 1 January 2010. Note that a claim for repayment of VAT in accordance with Part 20 made before 1 January 2010 shall be determined and, if appropriate, repayment made in accordance with this Part as it stood before the amendments made by SI 2009/3241 (see reg 18).
[2] Part 20 revoked by the Value Added Tax (Miscellaneous Amendments and Revocations) (EU Exit) Regulations, SI 2019/59 regs 12, 71 with effect from IP completion day (11pm UK time on 31 December 2020).

[173P Day by which a claim under this Part must be made
(1) [Subject to paragraph (1A),][2] the day before which a repayment application in respect of a repayment period must be submitted in accordance with regulation 173I(c) is 1st October of the repayment year immediately following the repayment year in which the repayment period covered by the repayment application falls.
[(1A) A repayment application in respect of a repayment period falling within the repayment year commencing on 1st January 2009 must be submitted in accordance with regulation 173I(c) before 1st April 2011.][2]
(2) A repayment application will be treated as having been submitted in accordance with regulation 173I(c) only if its submission is successfully recorded by the validation process of the electronic portal described in that regulation.
(3) The time of submission of a repayment application will be conclusively presumed to be the time recorded as such by the electronic portal.
(4) The Commissioners must, by electronic means, notify a claimant of the day on which the claimant's repayment application is received by the Commissioners.[3]][1]

Saving and Transitional Provisions—Note that the revocation of Part 20 by SI 2019/59 reg 71 shall not have effect where a relevant claim is made on or after IP completion day or is made before that day but is still being processed by the Commissioners as at that day, or where a claimant who has made a claim for repayment of VAT under reg 173B is required to repay an amount to the Commissioners under reg 173D(3) on or after IP completion day (see the VAT (Miscellaneous and Transitional Provisions, Amendment and Revocation) (EU Exit) Regulations, SI 2020/1495 reg 11).

Where a relevant claim is made for the period from 1 January to 31 December 2019, and that claim was based on a provisional attribution of input tax under Directive 2006/112/EC Art 175(2) of as applied in the claimant's member State, the subsequent adjustment to the attribution of input tax under Directive 2006/112/EC Art 175(3) must be made on or before 31 March 2021 (see SI 2020/1495 reg 11(8)).

Where a relevant claim is made for the period from 1 January 2020 to IP completion day, and the claim is based on a provisional attribution of input tax under Directive 2006/112/EC Art 175(2) as applied in the claimant's member State, any subsequent adjustment to the attribution of input tax must be made under SI 2020/1495 reg 12 (see SI 2020/1495 reg 11(9)).

Where reg 11(9) applies and a person is required or wishes to make an adjustment to a provisional attribution of input tax for the period from 1 January 2020 to IP completion day, they must make a claim using the procedure in the VAT Regulations, Pt 21 as it has effect on and after IP completion day. The claim must be made on or before 31 December 2021.

Amendments—[1]   Regs 173A–173X inserted by the VAT (Amendment) (No 5) Regs, SI 2009/3241, regs 2, 12 with effect from 1 January 2010. Note that a claim for repayment of VAT in accordance with Part 20 made before 1 January 2010 shall be determined and, if appropriate, repayment made in accordance with this Part as it stood before the amendments made by SI 2009/3241 (see reg 18).

[2]   Words in para (1), and whole of para (1A), inserted, by the VAT (Amendment) (No 3) Regulations, SI 2010/2940 regs 2, 6 with effect from 4 January 2011.

[3]   Part 20 revoked by the Value Added Tax (Miscellaneous Amendments and Revocations) (EU Exit) Regulations, SI 2019/59 regs 12, 71 with effect from IP completion day (11pm UK time on 31 December 2020).

[173Q   Notification of entitlement to repayment

(1) The Commissioners must notify a claimant whether they are satisfied that the claimant is entitled to repayment of VAT claimed under this Part before the expiry of the relevant period applicable to the VAT in question.

(2) If the Commissioners are not satisfied that the claimant is entitled to repayment of any VAT claimed, they must state their reasons in the notification.

(3) If the Commissioners do not, in relation to any VAT claimed for repayment under this Part, notify a claimant in accordance with paragraph (1) above, they shall be deemed to have refused to make payment of the VAT in question for the purposes of section 83(1)(ha) of the Act (appeals against refusal by the Commissioners to make repayment).[2]][1]

Saving and Transitional Provisions—Note that the revocation of Part 20 by SI 2019/59 reg 71 shall not have effect where a relevant claim is made on or after IP completion day or is made before that day but is still being processed by the Commissioners as at that day, or where a claimant who has made a claim for repayment of VAT under reg 173B is required to repay an amount to the Commissioners under reg 173D(3) on or after IP completion day (see the VAT (Miscellaneous and Transitional Provisions, Amendment and Revocation) (EU Exit) Regulations, SI 2020/1495 reg 11).

Where a relevant claim is made for the period from 1 January to 31 December 2019, and that claim was based on a provisional attribution of input tax under Directive 2006/112/EC Art 175(2) of as applied in the claimant's member State, the subsequent adjustment to the attribution of input tax under Directive 2006/112/EC Art 175(3) must be made on or before 31 March 2021 (see SI 2020/1495 reg 11(8)).

Where a relevant claim is made for the period from 1 January 2020 to IP completion day, and the claim is based on a provisional attribution of input tax under Directive 2006/112/EC Art 175(2) as applied in the claimant's member State, any subsequent adjustment to the attribution of input tax must be made under SI 2020/1495 reg 12 (see SI 2020/1495 reg 11(9)).

Where reg 11(9) applies and a person is required or wishes to make an adjustment to a provisional attribution of input tax for the period from 1 January 2020 to IP completion day, they must make a claim using the procedure in the VAT Regulations, Pt 21 as it has effect on and after IP completion day. The claim must be made on or before 31 December 2021.

Amendments—[1]   Regs 173A–173X inserted by the VAT (Amendment) (No 5) Regs, SI 2009/3241, regs 2, 12 with effect from 1 January 2010. Note that a claim for repayment of VAT in accordance with Part 20 made before 1 January 2010 shall be determined and, if appropriate, repayment made in accordance with this Part as it stood before the amendments made by SI 2009/3241 (see reg 18).

[2]   Part 20 revoked by the Value Added Tax (Miscellaneous Amendments and Revocations) (EU Exit) Regulations, SI 2019/59 regs 12, 71 with effect from IP completion day (11pm UK time on 31 December 2020).

[173R   Requests for further information or a document

(1) This regulation applies where, in order for the Commissioners to satisfy themselves whether a claimant is entitled to a repayment of VAT under this Part, information or the production of a document is requested by means of—
   (a) a notice pursuant to Schedule 36 of the Finance Act 2008 (information and inspection powers); or
   (b) a request to the competent authority of another member State in accordance with Council Regulation (EC) No 1798/2003 and Commission Regulation (EC) No 1925/2004.

(2) A request for information or the production of a document made to a claimant or competent authority of a member State must be made by electronic means.

(3) In any other case, a request for information or a document must be made by—
   (a) electronic means if such means are available to the recipient of the request; or
   (b) such other means as are expedient.

(4) A request for information or a document must be made before the expiry of the relevant period applicable to the VAT in question.

(5) There is no limit on the number of requests for information or documents that may be made before the expiry of relevant period applicable to the VAT in question.

(6) The question whether a request for information or the production of a document has been made before the expiry of a relevant period applicable to any VAT shall take account of any extension of the 4-month period mentioned in regulation 173S by virtue of regulations 173T and 173U resulting from a request that has already been made but no account shall be taken of any further extension to the relevant period that would arise if the request in question were to be made.

(7) In this regulation, references to the competent authority of a member State are references to the authorities listed as competent authorities in relation to the member States in Article 2 of Council Regulation (EC) No 1798/2003.²]¹

Saving and Transitional Provisions—Note that the revocation of Part 20 by SI 2019/59 reg 71 shall not have effect where a relevant claim is made on or after IP completion day or is made before that day but is still being processed by the Commissioners as at that day, or where a claimant who has made a claim for repayment of VAT under reg 173B is required to repay an amount to the Commissioners under reg 173D(3) on or after IP completion day (see the VAT (Miscellaneous and Transitional Provisions, Amendment and Revocation) (EU Exit) Regulations, SI 2020/1495 reg 11).

Where a relevant claim is made for the period from 1 January to 31 December 2019, and that claim was based on a provisional attribution of input tax under Directive 2006/112/EC Art 175(2) of as applied in the claimant's member State, the subsequent adjustment to the attribution of input tax under Directive 2006/112/EC Art 175(3) must be made on or before 31 March 2021 (see SI 2020/1495 reg 11(8)).

Where a relevant claim is made for the period from 1 January 2020 to IP completion day, and the claim is based on a provisional attribution of input tax under Directive 2006/112/EC Art 175(2) as applied in the claimant's member State, any subsequent adjustment to the attribution of input tax must be made under SI 2020/1495 reg 12 (see SI 2020/1495 reg 11(9)).

Where reg 11(9) applies and a person is required or wishes to make an adjustment to a provisional attribution of input tax for the period from 1 January 2020 to IP completion day, they must make a claim using the procedure in the VAT Regulations Pt 21 as it has effect on and after IP completion day. The claim must be made on or before 31 December 2021 (see SI 2020/1495 reg 12).

Amendments—¹ Regs 173A–173X inserted by the VAT (Amendment) (No 5) Regs, SI 2009/3241, regs 2, 12 with effect from 1 January 2010. Note that a claim for repayment of VAT in accordance with Part 20 made before 1 January 2010 shall be determined and, if appropriate, repayment made in accordance with this Part as it stood before the amendments made by SI 2009/3241 (see reg 18).

² Part 20 revoked by the Value Added Tax (Miscellaneous Amendments and Revocations) (EU Exit) Regulations, SI 2019/59 regs 12, 71 with effect from IP completion day (11pm UK time on 31 December 2020).

[173S Relevant period applicable to any VAT for which repayment is claimed
The relevant period applicable to any VAT for which repayment is claimed in this Part is the period which—

(a) commences on the day when the Commissioners receive the repayment application in respect of the VAT claimed, and

(b) ends 4 months after that day unless the end of that period is determined in accordance with regulations 173T or 173U.²]¹

Saving and Transitional Provisions—Note that the revocation of Part 20 by SI 2019/59 reg 71 shall not have effect where a relevant claim is made on or after IP completion day or is made before that day but is still being processed by the Commissioners as at that day, or where a claimant who has made a claim for repayment of VAT under reg 173B is required to repay an amount to the Commissioners under reg 173D(3) on or after IP completion day (see the VAT (Miscellaneous and Transitional Provisions, Amendment and Revocation) (EU Exit) Regulations, SI 2020/1495 reg 11).

Where a relevant claim is made for the period from 1 January to 31 December 2019, and that claim was based on a provisional attribution of input tax under Directive 2006/112/EC Art 175(2) of as applied in the claimant's member State, the subsequent adjustment to the attribution of input tax under Directive 2006/112/EC Art 175(3) must be made on or before 31 March 2021 (see SI 2020/1495 reg 11(8)).

Where a relevant claim is made for the period from 1 January 2020 to IP completion day, and the claim is based on a provisional attribution of input tax under Directive 2006/112/EC Art 175(2) as applied in the claimant's member State, any subsequent adjustment to the attribution of input tax must be made under SI 2020/1495 reg 12 (see SI 2020/1495 reg 11(9)).

Where reg 11(9) applies and a person is required or wishes to make an adjustment to a provisional attribution of input tax for the period from 1 January 2020 to IP completion day, they must make a claim using the procedure in the VAT Regulations, Pt 21 as it has effect on and after IP completion day. The claim must be made on or before 31 December 2021.

Amendments—¹ Regs 173A–173X inserted by the VAT (Amendment) (No 5) Regs, SI 2009/3241, regs 2, 12 with effect from 1 January 2010. Note that a claim for repayment of VAT in accordance with Part 20 made before 1 January 2010 shall be determined and, if appropriate, repayment made in accordance with this Part as it stood before the amendments made by SI 2009/3241 (see reg 18).

² Part 20 revoked by the Value Added Tax (Miscellaneous Amendments and Revocations) (EU Exit) Regulations, SI 2019/59 regs 12, 71 with effect from IP completion day (11pm UK time on 31 December 2020).

[173T Extension of the relevant period by virtue of the making of a request for information or a document
(1) Where a request for information or the production of a document as described in regulation 173R is made, then, subject to paragraphs (2), (3) and (4) below and regulation 173U, the relevant period applicable to the VAT in question shall end on the expiry of 2 months from the day on which the Commissioners receive the information or document requested.

(2) Where, by virtue of paragraph (1) above, the relevant period applicable to any VAT would end before the expiry of 6 months from the date on which the Commissioners received the repayment application for the VAT in question, the relevant period shall end on the expiry of that 6-month period.

(3) Where, by virtue of paragraph (1) above, the relevant period applicable to any VAT would end after the expiry of 8 months from the day on which the Commissioners received the repayment application for the VAT in question, the relevant period shall end on the expiry of that 8 month period.

(4) Where the Commissioners do not receive the information or a document requested before the expiry of 1 month from the date on which the request reaches the intended recipient of it, the end of the relevant period shall be determined in accordance with this regulation as if the Commissioners had received the requested information or document upon the expiry of that 1-month period.²]¹

Saving and Transitional Provisions—Note that the revocation of Part 20 by SI 2019/59 reg 71 shall not have effect where a relevant claim is made on or after IP completion day or is made before that day but is still being processed by the Commissioners as at that day, or where a claimant who has made a claim for repayment of VAT under reg 173B is required to repay an amount to the Commissioners under reg 173D(3) on or after IP completion day (see the VAT (Miscellaneous and Transitional Provisions, Amendment and Revocation) (EU Exit) Regulations, SI 2020/1495 reg 11).

Where a relevant claim is made for the period from 1 January to 31 December 2019, and that claim was based on a provisional attribution of input tax under Directive 2006/112/EC Art 175(2) of as applied in the claimant's member State, the subsequent adjustment to the attribution of input tax under Directive 2006/112/EC Art 175(3) must be made on or before 31 March 2021 (see SI 2020/1495 reg 11(8)).

Where a relevant claim is made for the period from 1 January 2020 to IP completion day, and the claim is based on a provisional attribution of input tax under Directive 2006/112/EC Art 175(2) as applied in the claimant's member State, any subsequent adjustment to the attribution of input tax must be made under SI 2020/1495 reg 12 (see SI 2020/1495 reg 11(9)).

Where reg 11(9) applies and a person is required or wishes to make an adjustment to a provisional attribution of input tax for the period from 1 January 2020 to IP completion day, they must make a claim using the procedure in the VAT Regulations, Pt 21 as it has effect on and after IP completion day. The claim must be made on or before 31 December 2021.

Amendments—¹ Regs 173A–173X inserted by the VAT (Amendment) (No 5) Regs, SI 2009/3241, regs 2, 12 with effect from 1 January 2010. Note that a claim for repayment of VAT in accordance with Part 20 made before 1 January 2010 shall be determined and, if appropriate, repayment made in accordance with this Part as it stood before the amendments made by SI 2009/3241 (see reg 18).
² Part 20 revoked by the Value Added Tax (Miscellaneous Amendments and Revocations) (EU Exit) Regulations, SI 2019/59 regs 12, 71 with effect from IP completion day (11pm UK time on 31 December 2020).

[173U Extension of the relevant period where more than one request for information or a document is made in relation to the same VAT

(1) This regulation applies to determine the end of the relevant period applicable to any VAT where more than one request for information or the production of a document as described in regulation 173R is made in relation to that VAT.

(2) Where the requests are—
   (a) made on different days; or
   (b) received by the recipients of the requests on different days,

the end of the relevant period shall be determined in accordance with regulation 173T as if all of the requests were comprised in a single request ("composite request") made on the latest day when a request forming part of the composite request was made.

(3) The question whether information or a document requested by a composite request has been provided to the Commissioners within the 1-month period mentioned in regulation 173T(4) shall be determined as if the composite request had been received on the latest day on which any of the requests forming part of the composite request is received.²]¹

Saving and Transitional Provisions—Note that the revocation of Part 20 by SI 2019/59 reg 71 shall not have effect where a relevant claim is made on or after IP completion day or is made before that day but is still being processed by the Commissioners as at that day, or where a claimant who has made a claim for repayment of VAT under reg 173B is required to repay an amount to the Commissioners under reg 173D(3) on or after IP completion day (see the VAT (Miscellaneous and Transitional Provisions, Amendment and Revocation) (EU Exit) Regulations, SI 2020/1495 reg 11).

Where a relevant claim is made for the period from 1 January to 31 December 2019, and that claim was based on a provisional attribution of input tax under Directive 2006/112/EC Art 175(2) of as applied in the claimant's member State, the subsequent adjustment to the attribution of input tax under Directive 2006/112/EC Art 175(3) must be made on or before 31 March 2021 (see SI 2020/1495 reg 11(8)).

Where a relevant claim is made for the period from 1 January 2020 to IP completion day, and the claim is based on a provisional attribution of input tax under Directive 2006/112/EC Art 175(2) as applied in the claimant's member State, any subsequent adjustment to the attribution of input tax must be made under SI 2020/1495 reg 12 (see SI 2020/1495 reg 11(9)).

Where reg 11(9) applies and a person is required or wishes to make an adjustment to a provisional attribution of input tax for the period from 1 January 2020 to IP completion day, they must make a claim using the procedure in the VAT Regulations, Pt 21 as it has effect on and after IP completion day. The claim must be made on or before 31 December 2021.

Amendments—¹ Regs 173A–173X inserted by the VAT (Amendment) (No 5) Regs, SI 2009/3241, regs 2, 12 with effect from 1 January 2010. Note that a claim for repayment of VAT in accordance with Part 20 made before 1 January 2010 shall be determined and, if appropriate, repayment made in accordance with this Part as it stood before the amendments made by SI 2009/3241 (see reg 18).
² Part 20 revoked by the Value Added Tax (Miscellaneous Amendments and Revocations) (EU Exit) Regulations, SI 2019/59 regs 12, 71 with effect from IP completion day (11pm UK time on 31 December 2020).

[173V Time when a repayment of VAT must be made

(1) VAT to which a claimant is entitled to repayment under this Part must be paid by the Commissioners within 10 business days of the expiry of the relevant period in relation to that VAT.

(2) For these purposes, a "business day" is any day except—
   (a) Saturday, Sunday, Good Friday or Christmas Day;
   (b) a bank holiday under the Banking and Financial Dealings Act 1971;
   (c) a day appointed by Royal proclamation as a public fast or thanksgiving day; or

(d) a day declared by an order under section 2(1) of the Banking and Financial Dealings Act 1971 to be a non-business day.²]¹

Saving and Transitional Provisions—Note that the revocation of Part 20 by SI 2019/59 reg 71 shall not have effect where a relevant claim is made on or after IP completion day or is made before that day but is still being processed by the Commissioners as at that day, or where a claimant who has made a claim for repayment of VAT under reg 173B is required to repay an amount to the Commissioners under reg 173D(3) on or after IP completion day (see the VAT (Miscellaneous and Transitional Provisions, Amendment and Revocation) (EU Exit) Regulations, SI 2020/1495 reg 11).

Where a relevant claim is made for the period from 1 January to 31 December 2019, and that claim was based on a provisional attribution of input tax under Directive 2006/112/EC Art 175(2) of as applied in the claimant's member State, the subsequent adjustment to the attribution of input tax under Directive 2006/112/EC Art 175(3) must be made on or before 31 March 2021 (see SI 2020/1495 reg 11(8)).

Where a relevant claim is made for the period from 1 January 2020 to IP completion day, and the claim is based on a provisional attribution of input tax under Directive 2006/112/EC Art 175(2) as applied in the claimant's member State, any subsequent adjustment to the attribution of input tax must be made under SI 2020/1495 reg 12 (see SI 2020/1495 reg 11(9)).

Where reg 11(9) applies and a person is required or wishes to make an adjustment to a provisional attribution of input tax for the period from 1 January 2020 to IP completion day, they must make a claim using the procedure in the VAT Regulations, Pt 21 as it has effect on and after IP completion day. The claim must be made on or before 31 December 2021.

Amendments—¹ Regs 173A–173X inserted by the VAT (Amendment) (No 5) Regs, SI 2009/3241, regs 2, 12 with effect from 1 January 2010. Note that a claim for repayment of VAT in accordance with Part 20 made before 1 January 2010 shall be determined and, if appropriate, repayment made in accordance with this Part as it stood before the amendments made by SI 2009/3241 (see reg 18).

² Part 20 revoked by the Value Added Tax (Miscellaneous Amendments and Revocations) (EU Exit) Regulations, SI 2019/59 regs 12, 71 with effect from IP completion day (11pm UK time on 31 December 2020).

[173W Interest on late payments
(1) Where the Commissioners fail to repay VAT to which a claimant is entitled to repayment under this Part before the expiry of the period described in regulation 173V, they must pay interest on that amount to the claimant for the applicable period.
(2) The "applicable period" is the period—
   (a) beginning upon the expiry of the period described in regulation 173V, and
   (b) ending on the day on which the Commissioners authorise the repayment to the claimant.
(3) Interest under this regulation shall be payable at the same rate as would have been payable if the Commissioners had been required to pay interest to the claimant pursuant to section 78 of the Act during the applicable period.
(4) Where—
   (a) a claimant is requested to provide information or produce a document by a notice described in regulation 173R, and
   (b) the claimant fails to provide the information or to produce the document within 1 month of receiving the notice,
the Commissioners shall not be liable to pay any interest under this regulation in respect of the VAT in relation to which the request was made even if the claimant provides the information or produces the document requested at a later time.
(5) The Commissioners shall not be liable to pay interest under this regulation during any period where a claimant has not provided to the Commissioners the documents described in regulation 173J that are required to be submitted at the same time as a repayment application in respect of supplies or importations described in regulation 173K.²]¹

Saving and Transitional Provisions—Note that the revocation of Part 20 by SI 2019/59 reg 71 shall not have effect where a relevant claim is made on or after IP completion day or is made before that day but is still being processed by the Commissioners as at that day, or where a claimant who has made a claim for repayment of VAT under reg 173B is required to repay an amount to the Commissioners under reg 173D(3) on or after IP completion day (see the VAT (Miscellaneous and Transitional Provisions, Amendment and Revocation) (EU Exit) Regulations, SI 2020/1495 reg 11).

Where a relevant claim is made for the period from 1 January to 31 December 2019, and that claim was based on a provisional attribution of input tax under Directive 2006/112/EC Art 175(2) of as applied in the claimant's member State, the subsequent adjustment to the attribution of input tax under Directive 2006/112/EC Art 175(3) must be made on or before 31 March 2021 (see SI 2020/1495 reg 11(8)).

Where a relevant claim is made for the period from 1 January 2020 to IP completion day, and the claim is based on a provisional attribution of input tax under Directive 2006/112/EC Art 175(2) as applied in the claimant's member State, any subsequent adjustment to the attribution of input tax must be made under SI 2020/1495 reg 12 (see SI 2020/1495 reg 11(9)).

Where reg 11(9) applies and a person is required or wishes to make an adjustment to a provisional attribution of input tax for the period from 1 January 2020 to IP completion day, they must make a claim using the procedure in the VAT Regulations, Pt 21 as it has effect on and after IP completion day. The claim must be made on or before 31 December 2021.

Amendments—¹ Regs 173A–173X inserted by the VAT (Amendment) (No 5) Regs, SI 2009/3241, regs 2, 12 with effect from 1 January 2010. Note that a claim for repayment of VAT in accordance with Part 20 made before 1 January 2010 shall be determined and, if appropriate, repayment made in accordance with this Part as it stood before the amendments made by SI 2009/3241 (see reg 18).

² Part 20 revoked by the Value Added Tax (Miscellaneous Amendments and Revocations) (EU Exit) Regulations, SI 2019/59 regs 12, 71 with effect from IP completion day (11pm UK time on 31 December 2020).

[173X Where—
   (a) any amount has been paid to any person by way of interest under regulation 173W, but

(ii) does not contain particulars of any supply other than a supply of goods of the description set out in sub-paragraph (a).".][1]

Amendments—[1] Part 20A (regs 184A–184K) inserted by the Value Added Tax (Miscellaneous Amendments, Northern Ireland Protocol and Savings and Transitional Provisions) (EU Exit) Regulations, SI 2020/1545 regs 31 and 86 with effect from IP completion day (11pm UK time on 31 December 2020) by virtue of SI 2020/1641 reg 2, Schedule para 11.

[184C For paragraph (1) of regulation 173B read—
"(1) The VAT referred to in regulation 173A is VAT charged on—
    (a) an importation of goods into Northern Ireland; and
    (b) a supply of goods made to the claimant in Northern Ireland if that VAT would be, or would be treated as, input tax of the claimant if the claimant were a taxable person.".][1]

Amendments—[1] Part 20A (regs 184A–184K) inserted by the Value Added Tax (Miscellaneous Amendments, Northern Ireland Protocol and Savings and Transitional Provisions) (EU Exit) Regulations, SI 2020/1545 regs 31 and 86 with effect from IP completion day (11pm UK time on 31 December 2020) by virtue of SI 2020/1641 reg 2, Schedule para 11.

[184D For paragraph (2) of regulation 173B read—
"(2) A claim for repayment may not be made in respect of VAT charged on—
    (a) an importation of goods in respect of which the VAT charged is eligible for other relief;
    (b) a supply or importation of goods which the claimant has removed or intends to remove from Northern Ireland to a member State, or which the claimant has exported or intends to export to a place outside the member States or to remove to Great Britain;
    (c) a supply or importation of goods which the claimant has used or intends to use for the purpose of any supply made in the course of a business activity carried on by the claimant in Northern Ireland;
    (d) a supply or importation of goods which if made to a taxable person would be excluded from credit under section 25 of the Act (payment of VAT by reference to accounting periods and credit for input tax against output tax); or
    (e) the supply or importation of goods to a travel agent which is for the direct benefit of a traveller other than the travel agent or the travel agent's employee.".][1]

Amendments—[1] Part 20A (regs 184A–184K) inserted by the Value Added Tax (Miscellaneous Amendments, Northern Ireland Protocol and Savings and Transitional Provisions) (EU Exit) Regulations, SI 2020/1545 regs 31 and 86 with effect from IP completion day (11pm UK time on 31 December 2020) by virtue of SI 2020/1641 reg 2, Schedule para 11.

[184E In regulation 173C, read "goods or services" in both places it occurs as "goods".][1]

Amendments—[1] Part 20A (regs 184A–184K) inserted by the Value Added Tax (Miscellaneous Amendments, Northern Ireland Protocol and Savings and Transitional Provisions) (EU Exit) Regulations, SI 2020/1545 regs 31 and 86 with effect from IP completion day (11pm UK time on 31 December 2020) by virtue of SI 2020/1641 reg 2, Schedule para 11.

[184F For regulation 173E (persons to whom this Part applies), read—
"**173E** This Part applies to a person who is established in and who carries on business in a member State for the whole of a repayment period other than a person who—
    (a) is established in Northern Ireland during any part of the repayment period; or
    (b) is registered or required to be registered for VAT in the United Kingdom during any part of the repayment period.".][1]

Amendments—[1] Part 20A (regs 184A–184K) inserted by the Value Added Tax (Miscellaneous Amendments, Northern Ireland Protocol and Savings and Transitional Provisions) (EU Exit) Regulations, SI 2020/1545 regs 31 and 86 with effect from IP completion day (11pm UK time on 31 December 2020) by virtue of SI 2020/1641 reg 2, Schedule para 11.

[184G In regulation 173F (time when VAT is incurred), read "supply of goods or services" in both places it occurs as "supply of goods".][1]

Amendments—[1] Part 20A (regs 184A–184K) inserted by the Value Added Tax (Miscellaneous Amendments, Northern Ireland Protocol and Savings and Transitional Provisions) (EU Exit) Regulations, SI 2020/1545 regs 31 and 86 with effect from IP completion day (11pm UK time on 31 December 2020) by virtue of SI 2020/1641 reg 2, Schedule para 11.

[184H In regulation 173K, read "supply of goods or services" as "supply of goods".][1]

Amendments—[1] Part 20A (regs 184A–184K) inserted by the Value Added Tax (Miscellaneous Amendments, Northern Ireland Protocol and Savings and Transitional Provisions) (EU Exit) Regulations, SI 2020/1545 regs 31 and 86 with effect from IP completion day (11pm UK time on 31 December 2020) by virtue of SI 2020/1641 reg 2, Schedule para 11.

[184I For paragraph (2) of regulation 173L (contents of a repayment application) read—
"(2) A supply is within this paragraph if it is a supply made in the course of a business activity carried on by the claimant in Northern Ireland.".][1]

Amendments—[1] Part 20A (regs 184A–184K) inserted by the Value Added Tax (Miscellaneous Amendments, Northern Ireland Protocol and Savings and Transitional Provisions) (EU Exit) Regulations, SI 2020/1545 regs 31 and 86 with effect from IP completion day (11pm UK time on 31 December 2020) by virtue of SI 2020/1641 reg 2, Schedule para 11.

[184J In regulation 173M—
(a) for paragraphs (b) and (c) read—
"(b) except in the case of an importation of goods, the registration number of the supplier and the prefix "XI";
(c) the date of issue of, and the unique sequential number identifying, the import document required to be produced by regulation 17 of the Value Added Tax (Northern Ireland) (EU Exit) Regulations 2020 or the document authenticated or issued by a proper officer in respect of an importation of goods or the VAT invoice issued in respect of the supply;".]¹
(b) in paragraph (h), read "goods and services" as "goods".]¹

Amendments—¹ Part 20A (regs 184A–184K) inserted by the Value Added Tax (Miscellaneous Amendments, Northern Ireland Protocol and Savings and Transitional Provisions) (EU Exit) Regulations, SI 2020/1545 regs 31 and 86 with effect from IP completion day (11pm UK time on 31 December 2020) by virtue of SI 2020/1641 reg 2, Schedule para 11.

[184K For regulation 173O read—
"**173O** The nature of the goods in respect of which repayment of VAT under this Part is claimed must be described in accordance with numerical codes specified for this purpose in a notice published by the Commissioners in accordance with this regulation.]¹

Amendments—¹ Part 20A (regs 184A–184K) inserted by the Value Added Tax (Miscellaneous Amendments, Northern Ireland Protocol and Savings and Transitional Provisions) (EU Exit) Regulations, SI 2020/1545 regs 31 and 86 with effect from IP completion day (11pm UK time on 31 December 2020) by virtue of SI 2020/1641 reg 2, Schedule para 11.

[PART 20B
OBLIGATION ON COMMISSIONERS TO FORWARD CLAIMS TO MEMBER STATES

184L The Commissioners must make arrangements for dealing with applications made to them by taxable persons for the forwarding, in accordance with the obligations of the United Kingdom under the EU withdrawal agreement, to the tax authorities of a member State of claims for refunds of VAT on—
(a) supplies to them in that member State, or
(b) the importation of goods by them into that member State from places outside the member States and Northern Ireland.]¹

Amendments—¹ Part 20B (reg 184L) inserted by the Value Added Tax (Miscellaneous Amendments, Northern Ireland Protocol and Savings and Transitional Provisions) (EU Exit) Regulations, SI 2020/1545 regs 31 and 86 with effect from IP completion day (11pm UK time on 31 December 2020) by virtue of SI 2020/1641 reg 2, Schedule para 11.

PART XXI
REPAYMENTS TO [TRADERS OUTSIDE THE UNITED KINGDOM]

Amendments—In the heading words "third country traders" substituted by the Value Added Tax (Miscellaneous Amendments and Revocations) (EU Exit) Regulations, SI 2019/59 regs 12, 72 with effect from IP completion day (11pm UK time on 31 December 2020).

185 Interpretation of Part XXI
(1) In this Part—
"claimant" means a person making a claim under this Part or a person on whose behalf a claim is made and any agent acting on his behalf as his VAT representative;
"official authority" means any-government body or agency in any country which is recognised by the Commissioners as having authority to act for the purposes of this Part;
"prescribed year" means the period of 12 months beginning on the first day of July in any year;
"VAT representative" means any person established in the United Kingdom and registered for VAT purposes in accordance with the provisions of Schedule 1 to the Act who acts as agent on behalf of a claimant;
. . .¹
"trader" means a person carrying on a business who is established [outside the United Kingdom]¹ and who is not a taxable person in the United Kingdom.
(2) For the purposes of this Part, a person is treated as being established in a country if—
(*a*) he has there a business establishment, or
(*b*) he has no such establishment (there or elsewhere) but his permanent address or usual place of residence is there.
(3) For the purposes of this Part—
(*a*) a person carrying on business through a branch or agency in any country is treated as being established there, and
(*b*) where the person is a body corporate its usual place of residence shall be the place where it is legally constituted.

Commentary—*De Voil Indirect Tax Service* **V5.152.**

Amendments—[1]   In para (1) the definition of "third country" revoked, and in the definition of "trader", words "in a third country" substituted, by the Value Added Tax (Miscellaneous Amendments and Revocations) (EU Exit) Regulations, SI 2019/59 regs 12, 73 with effect from IP completion day (11pm UK time on 31 December 2020). The definition of "third country" previously read as follows—

""third country" means a country other than those comprising the member States of the European Community;"

186 Repayments of VAT

Subject to the other provisions of this Part a trader shall be entitled to be repaid VAT charged on goods imported by him into the United Kingdom in respect of which no other relief is available or on supplies made to him in the United Kingdom if that VAT would be[, or would be treated as,][1] input tax of his were he a taxable person in the United Kingdom.

Commentary—*De Voil Indirect Tax Service* **V5.152**.
Amendments—[1]   Words inserted by the Value Added Tax (Miscellaneous Amendments, Northern Ireland Protocol and Savings and Transitional Provisions) (EU Exit) Regulations, SI 2020/1545 regs 31 and 87 with effect from IP completion day (11pm UK time on 31 December 2020) by virtue of SI 2020/1641 reg 2, Schedule para 11.

187 VAT representatives

The Commissioners may, as a condition of allowing a repayment under this Part, require a trader to appoint a VAT representative to act on his behalf.

188 Persons to whom this Part applies

(1) Save as the Commissioners may otherwise allow, a trader to whom this Part applies who is established in a . . . [1] country having a comparable system of turnover taxes will not be entitled to any refunds under this Part unless that country provides reciprocal arrangements for refunds to be made to taxable persons who are established in the United Kingdom.

(2) This Part shall apply to any trader but not if during any period determined under regulation 192—
   (a) . . . [1]
   (b) he made supplies in the United Kingdom of goods or services other than—
      (i) transport of freight outside the United Kingdom to or from a place outside the United Kingdom or services ancillary thereto,
      (ii) services where the VAT on the supply is payable solely by the person to whom they are supplied in accordance with the provisions of section 8 of the Act, and
      (iii) goods where the VAT on the supply is payable solely by the person to whom they are supplied.

Commentary—*De Voil Indirect Tax Service* **V5.152, V2.189M**.
Amendments—[1]   In para (1) word "third" revoked, and para (2)(a) revoked, by the Value Added Tax (Miscellaneous Amendments and Revocations) (EU Exit) Regulations, SI 2019/59 regs 12, 74 with effect from IP completion day (11pm UK time on 31 December 2020). Para (2)(a) previously read as follows—

"(a) he was established in any of the member States of the European Community, or"

189 Supplies and importations to which this Part applies

This Part applies to any supply of goods or services made in the United Kingdom or to any importation of goods into the United Kingdom on or after 1st July 1994 but does not apply to any supply or importation which—
   (a) the trader has used or intends to use for the purpose of any supply by him in the United Kingdom, or
   (b) has been exported or is intended for exportation from the United Kingdom by or on behalf of the trader.

190 VAT which will not be repaid

(1) The following VAT shall not be repaid—
   [(za) VAT which the Commissioners would be obliged to repay if it was the subject of a claim made in accordance with Part 20 or Part 20A;][2]
   (a) VAT charged on a supply which if made to a taxable person would be excluded from any credit under section 25 of the Act,
   (b) VAT charged on a supply to a travel agent which is for the direct benefit of a traveller other than the travel agent or his employee,
   [(c) VAT charged on a supply used or to be used in making supplies of a description falling within article 3 of the Value Added Tax (Input Tax) (Specified Supplies) Order 1999.][1]

(2) In this regulation a travel agent includes a tour operator or any person who purchases and resupplies services of a kind enjoyed by travellers.

Commentary—*De Voil Indirect Tax Service* **V5.152**.
Amendments—[1]   Sub-para (1)(c) inserted by the VAT (Amendment) (No 4) Regulations, SI 2004/3140 reg 15 with effect from 3 December 2004 in relation to VAT charged on or after that date: SI 2004/3140 reg 2(4).
[2]   Sub-para (1)(za) inserted by the Value Added Tax (Miscellaneous Amendments, Northern Ireland Protocol and Savings and Transitional Provisions) (EU Exit) Regulations, SI 2020/1545 regs 31 and 88 with effect from IP completion day (11pm UK time on 31 December 2020) by virtue of SI 2020/1641 reg 2, Schedule para 11.

191 Method of claiming

(1) A person claiming a repayment of VAT under this Part shall—
  (a) complete in the English language and send to the Commissioners either [the form specified in a notice published by the Commissioners][1], or a like form produced by any official authority, containing full information in respect of all the matters specified in the said form and a declaration as therein set out, and
  (b) at the same time furnish—
    (i) a certificate of status issued by the official authority of the . . . [2] country in which the trader is established either on [the form specified in a notice published by the Commissioners][1] or on a like form produced by the official authority, and
    (ii) such documentary evidence of an entitlement to deduct input tax as may be required of a taxable person claiming a deduction of input tax in accordance with the provisions of regulation 29.

(2) Where the Commissioners are in possession of a certificate of status issued not more than 12 months before the date of the claim, the claimant shall not be required to furnish a further such certificate.

(3) The Commissioners shall refuse to accept any document referred to in paragraph (1)(b)(ii) above if it bears an official stamp indicating that it had been furnished in support of an earlier claim.

Commentary—*De Voil Indirect Tax Service* **V5.152**.
Amendments—[1] In para (1)(a), words substituted for words "the form numbered 9 in Schedule 1 to these Regulations", and in para (1)(b), words substituted for words "the form numbered 10 in Schedule 1 to these Regulations", by the VAT (Amendment) (No 2) Regulations, SI 2012/1899 regs 3, 20 with effect from 15 October 2012.
[2] In para (1)(b)(i) word "third" revoked by the Value Added Tax (Miscellaneous Amendments and Revocations) (EU Exit) Regulations, SI 2019/59 regs 12, 75 with effect from IP completion day (11pm UK time on 31 December 2020).

192 Time within which a claim must be made

(1) A claim shall be made not later than 6 months after the end of the prescribed year in which the VAT claimed was charged and shall be in respect of VAT charged on supplies or on importations made during a period of not less than 3 months and not more than 12 months, provided that a claim may be made in respect of VAT charged on supplies or on importations made during a period of less than 3 months where that period represents the final part of the prescribed year.

(2) No claim shall be made for less than £16.

(3) No claim shall be made for less than £130 in respect of VAT charged on supplies or on importations made during a period of less than the prescribed year except where that period represents the final part of the prescribed year.

Commentary—*De Voil Indirect Tax Service* **V5.152**.

193 Deduction of bank charges

Where any repayment is to be made to a claimant in the country in which he is established, the Commissioners may reduce the amount of the repayment by the amount of any bank charges or costs incurred as a result thereof.

194 Treatment of claim

For the purposes of section 73 of the Act any claim made under this Part shall be treated as a return required under paragraph 2 of Schedule 11 to the Act [made in respect of a prescribed accounting period].

Commentary—*De Voil Indirect Tax Service* **V5.152, V5.132A**.
Amendment—Words "and repayment claimed" omitted from cross heading, and words inserted in reg 194, by the VAT (Amendment) (No 5) Regs, SI 2009/3241, regs 2, 17 with effect from 1 January 2010.

196 False, altered or incorrect claims

If any claimant furnishes or sends to the Commissioners for the purposes of this Part any document which is false or which has been altered after issue to that person the Commissioners may refuse to repay any VAT claimed by that claimant for the period of 2 years from the date when the claim in respect of which the false or altered documents were furnished or sent, was made.

Commentary—*De Voil Indirect Tax Service* **V5.152**.

197

Where any sum has been repaid to a claimant as a result of an incorrect claim, the amount of any subsequent repayment to that claimant may be reduced by the said sum.

Commentary—*De Voil Indirect Tax Service* **V5.152**.

PART XXII
REPAYMENT SUPPLEMENT

198 Computation of period

In computing the period of 30 days referred to in section 79(2)(b) of the Act, periods referable to the following matters shall be left out of account—
  (a) the raising and answering of any reasonable inquiry relating to the requisite return or claim,

(b) the correction by the Commissioners of any errors or omissions in that requisite return or claim, and
(c) in any case to which section 79(1)(a) of the Act applies, the following matters, namely—
  (i) any such continuing failure to submit returns as is referred to in section 25(5) of the Act, and
  (ii) compliance with any such condition as is referred to in paragraph 4(1) of Schedule 11 to the Act.

Commentary—*De Voil Indirect Tax Service* **V5.191**.

199 Duration of period

For the purpose of determining the duration of the periods referred to in regulation 198, the following rules shall apply—
(a) in the case of the period mentioned in regulation 198(a), it shall be taken to have begun on the date when the Commissioners first raised the inquiry and it shall be taken to have ended on the date when they received a complete answer to their inquiry;
(b) in the case of the period mentioned in regulation 198(b), it shall be taken to have begun on the date when the error or omission first came to the notice of the Commissioners and it shall be taken to have ended on the date when the error or omission was corrected by them;
(c) in the case of the period mentioned in regulation 198(c)(i), it shall be determined in accordance with a certificate of the Commissioners under paragraph 14(1)(b) of Schedule 11 to the Act;
(d) in the case of the period mentioned in regulation 198(c)(ii), it shall be taken to have begun on the date of the service of the written notice of the Commissioners which required the production of documents or the giving of security, and it shall be taken to have ended on the date when they received the required documents or the required security.

Commentary—*De Voil Indirect Tax Service* **V5.191**.

PART XXIII
REFUNDS TO "DO-IT-YOURSELF" BUILDERS

200 Interpretation of Part XXIII

In this Part—
"claim" means a claim for refund of VAT made pursuant to section 35 of[, or paragraph 18A of Schedule 9ZA to,][1] the Act, and
"claimant" shall be construed accordingly;
"relevant building" means a building in respect of which a claimant makes a claim.

Amendments—[1] Words inserted by the Value Added Tax (Miscellaneous Amendments, Northern Ireland Protocol and Savings and Transitional Provisions) (EU Exit) Regulations, SI 2020/1545 regs 31 and 89 with effect from IP completion day (11pm UK time on 31 December 2020) by virtue of SI 2020/1641 reg 2, Schedule para 11.

201 Method and time for making claim

A claimant shall make his claim in respect of a relevant building by—
(a) furnishing to the Commissioners no later than 3 months after the completion of the building [the relevant form for the purposes of the claim][1] containing the full particulars required therein, and
(b) at the same time furnishing to them—
  (i) a certificate of completion obtained from a local authority or such other documentary evidence of completion of the building as is satisfactory to the Commissioners,
  (ii) an invoice showing the registration number of the person supplying the goods, whether or not such an invoice is a VAT invoice, in respect of each supply of goods on which VAT has been paid which have been incorporated into the building or its site,
  (iii) in respect of imported goods which have been incorporated into the building or its site, documentary evidence of their importation and of the VAT paid thereon,
  (iv) documentary evidence that planning permission for the building had been granted, and
  (v) a certificate signed by a quantity surveyor or architect that the goods shown in the claim were or, in his judgement, were likely to have been, incorporated into the building or its site.

Commentary—*De Voil Indirect Tax Service* **V5.164**.
Amendments—[1] In para (a), words substituted for words "the form numbered 11 in Schedule 1 to these Regulations", by the Value Added Tax (Amendment) (No 3) Regulations, SI 2009/1967 regs 2, 7 with effect from 15 August 2009.

[**201A**—The relevant form for the purposes of a claim is—
(a) form VAT 431NB where the claim relates to works described in section 35(1A)(a) or (b) of the Act; and
(b) form VAT 431C where the claim relates to works described in section 35(1A)(c) of the Act.][1]

Commentary—*De Voil Indirect Tax Service* **V5.164**.

Amendments—[1] Section 201A substituted by the VAT (Amendment) (No 2) Regulations, SI 2012/1899 regs 3, 21 with effect from 15 October 2012.

PART XXIV
FLAT-RATE SCHEME FOR FARMERS

202 Interpretation of Part XXIV
[(1) In this Part—
["certification anniversary" means, in relation to a person, an anniversary of the date on which that person's certification takes effect pursuant to regulation 205;][1]
"certified person" means a person certified as a flat-rate farmer for the purposes of the flat-rate scheme under regulation 203 and "certified" and "certification" shall be construed accordingly.
[(2) For the purposes of this Part, a person is associated with another person at any time if that other person makes supplies in the course or furtherance of a business carried on by the other person and—
 (a) the business of one is under the dominant influence of the other, or
 (b) the persons are closely bound to one another by financial, economic and organisational links.][1]
Commentary—*De Voil Indirect Tax Service* **V2.196, V2.192**.
Amendments—[1] Para (1) numbered as such, and definition of "certification money" and para (2) inserted, by the Value Added Tax (Amendment) Regulations, SI 2020/1384 reg 2(1), (2) with effect from 1 January 2021.

203 Flat-rate scheme
(1) The Commissioners shall, if the conditions mentioned in regulation 204 are satisfied, certify that a person is a flat-rate farmer for the purposes of the flat-rate scheme (hereinafter in this Part referred to as "the scheme").
(2) Where a person is for the time being certified in accordance with this regulation, then (whether or not that person is a taxable person) any supply of goods or services made by him in the course or furtherance of the relevant part of his business shall be disregarded for the purpose of determining whether he is, has become or has ceased to be liable or entitled to be registered under Schedule 1 [or 1A][1] to the Act.
Commentary—*De Voil Indirect Tax Service* **V3.433**.
HMRC Manuals—VAT Agricultural Flat Rate Scheme VATAFRS0110 (purpose and outline of the scheme).
Amendments—[1] In para (2), words inserted by the VAT (Amendment) (No 2) Regulations, SI 2012/1899 regs 3, 22 with effect from 15 October 2012.

204 Admission to the scheme
The conditions mentioned in regulation 203 are that—
 (a) the person satisfies the Commissioners that he is carrying on a business involving one or more designated activities,
 (b) he has not in the 3 years preceding the date of his application for certification—
   (i) been convicted of any offence in connection with VAT,
   (ii) made any payment to compound proceedings in respect of VAT under section 152 of the Customs and Excise Management Act 1979 as applied by section 72(12) of the Act,
   (iii) been assessed to a penalty under section 60 of the Act,
 (c) he makes an application for certification on the form [specified in a notice published by the Commissioners][1], . . . [2]
 [(d) he satisfies the Commissioners that the total value of taxable supplies made by him in the course or furtherance of the relevant part of his business in the period of one year ending with the date of the application is £150,000 or less, and
 (e) he is not, and has not been within the past 24 months—
   (i) eligible to be registered for VAT in the name of a group under section 43A of the Act,
   (ii) registered for VAT in the name of a division under section 46(1) of the Act, or
   (iii) associated with another person.][2]
Commentary—*De Voil Indirect Tax Service* **V2.192, V2.193**.
HMRC Manuals—VAT Agricultural Flat Rate Scheme VATAFRS0205 (entitlement to join the scheme).
Amendments—[1] In para (c), words substituted for words "numbered 14 in Schedule 1 to these Regulations", by the VAT (Amendment) (No 2) Regulations, SI 2012/1899 regs 3, 23 with effect from 15 October 2012.
[2] Word "and" at end of para (c) revoked, and paras (d), (e) substituted for previous para (d), by the Value Added Tax (Amendment) Regulations, SI 2020/1384 reg 2(1), (3) with effect from 1 January 2021.
Para (d) previously read as follows—
 "*d*) he satisfies the Commissioners that he is a person in respect of whom the total of the amounts as are mentioned in regulation 209 relating to supplies made in the year following the date of his certification will not exceed £3,000 or more the amount of input tax to which he would otherwise be entitled to credit in that year.".

205 Certification
Where the Commissioners certify that a person is a flat-rate farmer for the purposes of the scheme, the certificate issued by the Commissioners shall be effective from—
 (a) the date on which the application for certification is received by the Commissioners,

(b) with the agreement of the Commissioners, an earlier date to that mentioned in sub-paragraph (a) above, or
(c) if the person so requests, a later date which is no more than 30 days after the date mentioned in sub-paragraph (a) above,

provided that any certificate shall not be effective from a date before the date when the person's registration under Schedule 1[, 1A][1] or 3 to the Act is cancelled and a certificate shall not be effective from a date earlier than 1st January 1993.

Commentary—*De Voil Indirect Tax Service* **V2.196, V2.192**.
Amendments—[1] Words inserted by the VAT (Amendment) (No 2) Regulations, SI 2012/1899 regs 3, 24 with effect from 15 October 2012.

206 Cancellation of certificates

(1) The Commissioners may cancel a person's certificate in any case where—
   (a) a statement false in a material particular was made by him or on his behalf in relation to his application for certification,
   (b) he has been convicted of an offence in connection with VAT or has made a payment to compound such proceedings under section 152 of the Customs and Excise Management Act 1979 as applied by section 72(12) of the Act,
   (c) he has been assessed to a penalty under section 60 of the Act,
   (d) he ceases to be involved in designated activities,
   (e) he dies, becomes bankrupt or incapacitated,
   (f) he is liable to be registered under Schedule 1[, 1A][1] or 3 to the Act,
   (g) he makes an application in writing for cancellation,
   (h) he makes an application in writing for registration under Schedule 1 or 3 to the Act, and such application shall be deemed to be an application for cancellation of his certificate,
   [(i) the total value of taxable supplies made by him in the course or furtherance of the relevant part of his business in the period of one year ending on a certification anniversary is more than £230,000,
   (ia) at the end of any month, the total value of taxable supplies made by him in the course or furtherance of the relevant part of his business in the period of 30 days then ending is more than £230,000,
   (ib) he becomes—
      (i) eligible to be registered for VAT in the name of a group under section 43A of the Act,
      (ii) registered for VAT in the name of a division under section 46(1) of the Act, or
      (iii) associated with another person, or][2]
   (j) they are not satisfied that any of the grounds for cancellation of a certificate mentioned in sub-paragraphs (a) to [(ib)][2] above do not apply.

(2) Where the Commissioners cancel a person's certificate in accordance with paragraph (1) above, the effective date of the cancellation shall be for each of the cases mentioned respectively in that paragraph as follows—
   (a) the date when the Commissioners discover that such a statement has been made,
   (b) the date of his conviction or the date on which a sum is paid to compound proceedings,
   (c) 30 days after the date when the assessment is notified,
   (d) the date of the cessation of designated activities,
   (e) the date on which he died, became bankrupt or incapacitated,
   (f) the effective date of registration,
   (g) not less than one year after the effective date of his certificate or such earlier date as the Commissioners may agree,
   (h) not less than one year after the effective date of his certificate or such earlier date as the Commissioners may agree,
   [(i) the certification anniversary on which the total value of taxable supplies made by him in the course or furtherance of the relevant part of his business for a period of one year then ending is more than £230,000,
   (ia) the date on which the total value of taxable supplies made by him in the course or furtherance of the relevant part of his business in the period of 30 days then ending is more than £230,000,
   (ib) the date he becomes—
      (i) eligible to be registered for VAT in the name of a group under section 43A of the Act,
      (ii) registered for VAT in the name of a division under section 46(1) of the Act, or
      (iii) associated with another person, or][2]
   (j) the date mentioned in sub-paragraphs (a) to [(ib)][2] above as appropriate.

Commentary—*De Voil Indirect Tax Service* **V2.196**.
HMRC Manuals—VAT Agricultural Flat Rate Scheme VATAFRS0400 (cancellation of certificates).
Amendments—[1] Words inserted in para (1)(f) by the VAT (Amendment) (No 2) Regulations, SI 2012/1899 regs 3, 25 with effect from 15 October 2012.

[2] In paras (1) and (2): sub-paras (*i*)–(*ib*) substituted for sub-para (*i*), and in sub-para (*j*) reference substituted for reference "(*h*)", by the Value Added Tax (Amendment) Regulations, SI 2020/1384 reg 2(1), (3) with effect from 1 January 2021.
Para (1)(*i*) previously read a follows—
"(*i*) they consider it is necessary to do so for the protection of the revenue, or".
Para (2)(*i*) previously read a follows—
"(*i*) the date on which the Commissioners consider a risk to the revenue arises, or".

[206A Notification to Commissioners
(1) A person must notify the Commissioners in writing if—
   (*a*) on any certification anniversary, the total value of taxable supplies made in the course or furtherance of the relevant part of that person's business in the period of one year then ending is more than £230,000,
   (*b*) at the end of any month, the total value of taxable supplies made in the course or furtherance of the relevant part of that person's business in the period of 30 days then ending is more than £230,000, or
   (*c*) that person becomes—
      (i) eligible to be registered for VAT in the name of a group under section 43A of the Act,
      (ii) registered for VAT in the name of a division under section 46(1) of the Act, or
      (iii) associated with another person.
(2) If a person is required to notify the Commissioners under this regulation, that person must do so within 30 days of—
   (*a*) in the case of paragraph (1)(*a*), the relevant certification anniversary,
   (*b*) in the case of paragraph (1)(*b*), the end of the relevant month, or
   (*c*) in the case of paragraph (1)(*c*), the date on which the relevant event occurs.][1]

Commentary—*De Voil Indirect Tax Service* **V2.196**.
Amendments—[1] Reg 206A inserted by the Value Added Tax (Amendment) Regulations, SI 2020/1384 reg 2(1), (5) with effect from 1 January 2021.

207 Death, bankruptcy or incapacity of certified person
(1) If a certified person dies or becomes bankrupt or incapacitated, the Commissioners may, from the date on which he died or became bankrupt or incapacitated treat as a certified person any person carrying on those designated activities until some other person is certified in respect of the designated activities or the incapacity ceases, as the case may be; and the provisions of the Act and of any Regulations made thereunder shall apply to any person so treated as though he were a certified person.
(2) Any person carrying on such designated activities shall, within 30 days of commencing to do so, inform the Commissioners in writing of that fact and of the date of the death, or of the nature of the incapacity and the date on which it began.
(3) In relation to a company which is a certified person, the references in regulation 206(1)(*e*) and (2)(*e*) and in paragraph (1) above to the certified person becoming bankrupt or incapacitated shall be construed as references to its going into liquidation or receivership or [entering administration][1].

Commentary—*De Voil Indirect Tax Service* **V2.196**.
HMRC Manuals—VAT Agricultural Flat Rate Scheme VATAFRS0600 (death, insolvency and incapacity).
Amendments—[1] Words in para (3) substituted by the Enterprise Act 2002 (Insolvency) Order, SI 2003/2096 art 5, Schedule paras 55, 59 with effect from 15 September 2003. However, this amendment does not apply in any case where a petition for an administration order was presented before that date: SI 2003/2096 arts 1, 6.

208 Further certification
Where a person who has been certified and is no longer so certified makes a further application under regulation 204, that person shall not be certified for a period of 3 years from the date of the cancellation of his previous certificate except—
   (*a*) the Commissioners may certify from the date of his further application a person who has not been registered under Schedule 1[, 1A][1] or 3 to the Act at any time since the cancellation of his previous certificate; and
   (*b*) where the circumstances as are mentioned in paragraph 8(1)(*c*) of Schedule 4 to the Act apply, the Commissioners may certify the person mentioned in that paragraph on a date after the expiry of one year from the date of the cancellation of his previous certificate.

Commentary—*De Voil Indirect Tax Service* **V2.192**.
Amendments—[1] Words inserted in para (*a*) by the VAT (Amendment) (No 2) Regulations, SI 2012/1899 regs 3, 25 with effect from 15 October 2012.

209 Claims by taxable persons for amounts to be treated as credits for input tax
(1) The amount referred to in section 54(4) of the Act and included in the consideration for any taxable supply which is made—
   (*a*) in the course or furtherance of the relevant part of his business by a person who is for the time being certified under this part,
   (*b*) at a time when that person is not a taxable person, and
   (*c*) to a taxable person,

shall be treated, for the purpose of determining the entitlement of the person supplied to credit under sections 25 and 26 of the Act, as VAT on a supply to that person.

(2) Subject to paragraph (3) below and save as the Commissioners may otherwise allow or direct generally or specially, a taxable person claiming entitlement to a credit of an amount as is mentioned in paragraph (1) above shall do so on the return made by him for the prescribed accounting period in which the invoice specified in paragraph (3) below is issued by a certified person.

(3) A taxable person shall not be entitled to credit as is mentioned in paragraph (1) above unless there has been issued an invoice containing the following particulars—
- (a) an identifying number,
- (b) the name, address and certificate number of the certified person by whom the invoice is issued,
- (c) the name and address of the person to whom the goods or services are supplied,
- (d) the time of the supply,
- (e) a description of the goods or services supplied,
- (f) the consideration for the supply or, in the case of any increase or decrease in the consideration, the amount of that increase or decrease excluding the amount as is mentioned in paragraph (1) above, and
- (g) the amount as is mentioned in paragraph (1) above which amount shall be entitled "Flat-rate Addition" or "FRA".

Commentary—*De Voil Indirect Tax Service* **V3.433, V2.194, V5.350**.

210 Duty to keep records

(1) Every certified person shall, for the purposes of the scheme, keep and preserve the following records—
- (a) his business and accounting records, and
- (b) copies of all invoices specified in regulation 209(3) issued by him or on his behalf.

(2) Every certified person shall comply with such requirements with respect to the keeping, preservation and production of records as the Commissioners may notify to him.

(3) Every certified person shall keep and preserve such records as are required by paragraph (1) above or by notification for a period of 6 years or such lesser period as the Commissioners may allow.

Commentary—*De Voil Indirect Tax Service* **V5.201, V5.202, V2.197**.
HMRC Manuals—VAT Agricultural Flat Rate Scheme VATAFRS0270 (records to be kept by the farmer).

211 Production of records

(1) Every certified person shall—
- (a) upon demand made by an authorised person, produce or cause to be produced for inspection by that person—
  - (i) at the principal place of business of the person upon whom the demand is made or at such other place as the authorised person may reasonably require, and
  - (ii) at such time as the authorised person may reasonably require,

  any documents specified in regulation 210(1), and
- (b) permit an authorised person to take copies of, or make extracts from, or remove at a reasonable time and for a reasonable period, any document produced under paragraph (1)(a) above.(2) Where a document removed by an authorised person under paragraph (1)(b) above is reasonably required for the proper conduct of a business, he shall, as soon as practicable, provide a copy of that document, free of charge, to the person by whom it was produced or caused to be produced.

(3) Where any documents removed under paragraph (1)(b) above are lost or damaged, the Commissioners shall be liable to compensate their owner for any expenses reasonably incurred by him in replacing or repairing the documents.

PART XXV
DISTRESS AND DILIGENCE

[A212 In this Part—
"Job Band" followed by a number between "1" and "12" means the band for the purposes of pay and grading in which the job an officer performs is ranked in the system applicable to Customs and Excise.][1]

Amendments—[1] This Regulation inserted by the VAT (Amendment) (No 4) Regulations, SI 1996/2098 with effect from 2 September 1996.

212 Distress

. . .

Amendments—This regulation revoked by the Customs and Excise Duties and Other Indirect Taxes Regulations, SI 1997/1431 with effect from 1 July 1997. See SI 1997/1431 for the replacement provisions.

213 Diligence

In Scotland, the following provisions shall have effect—

(a) where the Commissioners are empowered to apply to the Sheriff for a warrant to authorise a Sheriff Officer to recover any amount of VAT or any sum recoverable as if it were VAT remaining due and unpaid, any application, and any certificate required to accompany that application, may be made on their behalf by a Collector of Customs and Excise or an officer of rank not below that of [Job Band 7][1];

(b) where, during the course of a poinding and sale in accordance with Schedule 5 to the Debtors (Scotland) Act 1987 the Commissioners are entitled as a creditor to do any acts, then any such acts, with the exception of the exercise of the power contained in paragraph 18(3) of that Schedule, may be done on their behalf by a Collector of Customs and Excise or an officer of rank not below that of [Job Band 7][1].

Commentary—*De Voil Indirect Tax Service* **V5.173**.
Amendments—[1] Words in (a) and (b) above substituted by the VAT (Amendment) (No 4) Regulations, SI 1996/2098 with effect from 2 September 1996.

[PART 26
[UK UNION AND NON-UNION SPECIAL ACCOUNTING SCHEMES: REGISTRATION, NOTIFICATION OF CHANGES, AND RETURNS]]

Saving provision—Part 26 continues to apply in relation to supplies made before IP completion day. To the extent that it continues to apply, Part 26 has effect subject to such modifications as may be specified in a notice published by the Commissioners (see SI 2020/1495, reg 17).
AmendmentsPart 26 (regs 214–218) inserted by the VAT (Amendment) (No 3) Regulations, SI 2014/2430 regs 2, 9 with effect from 1 October 2014.
Heading to Part 26 substituted by the VAT (Amendment) (No 3) Regulations, SI 2014/2430 regs 2, 10(2) with effect from 1 January 2015.
Part 26 revoked by the Value Added Tax (Miscellaneous Amendments and Revocations) (EU Exit) Regulations, SI 2019/59 regs 12, 79 with effect from IP completion day (11pm UK time on 31 December 2020).

[214 Interpretation

(1) In this Part—

'applicant' means a person making a registration request under paragraph 4 of Schedule 3B or paragraph 5 of Schedule 3BA to the Act;

'principal VAT Directive' means Council Directive 2006/112/EC.

(2) In regulations 215 and 216, references to a number allocated under Article 362 of the principal VAT Directive mean a number allocated at any time under that Article.[2]][1]

Saving provision—Part 26 continues to apply in relation to supplies made before IP completion day. To the extent that it continues to apply, Part 26 has effect subject to such modifications as may be specified in a notice published by the Commissioners (see SI 2020/1495, reg 17).
Amendments[1] Part 26 (regs 214–218) inserted by the VAT (Amendment) (No 3) Regulations, SI 2014/2430 regs 2, 9 with effect from 1 October 2014.
[2] Part 26 revoked by the Value Added Tax (Miscellaneous Amendments and Revocations) (EU Exit) Regulations, SI 2019/59 regs 12, 79 with effect from IP completion day (11pm UK time on 31 December 2020).

[215 Registration requests: Non-Union scheme

A registration request under paragraph 4 of Schedule 3B to the Act must contain details of—

(a) any VAT identification number or tax reference number by which the applicant is identified for VAT purposes by any member State in accordance with Article 214, Article 239 or Article 240 of the principal VAT Directive, and the name of that member State;

(b) any number previously allocated to the applicant by any member State under Article 362 of the principal VAT Directive, or otherwise for the purposes of Article 369d of the principal VAT Directive, and the name of that member State.[2]][1]

Commentary—*De Voil Indirect Tax Service* **V2.189G**.
Saving provision—Part 26 continues to apply in relation to supplies made before IP completion day. To the extent that it continues to apply, Part 26 has effect subject to such modifications as may be specified in a notice published by the Commissioners (see SI 2020/1495, reg 17).
Amendments[1] Part 26 (regs 214–218) inserted by the VAT (Amendment) (No 3) Regulations, SI 2014/2430 regs 2, 9 with effect from 1 October 2014.
[2] Part 26 revoked by the Value Added Tax (Miscellaneous Amendments and Revocations) (EU Exit) Regulations, SI 2019/59 regs 12, 79 with effect from IP completion day (11pm UK time on 31 December 2020).

[216 Registration requests: Union scheme

A registration request under paragraph 5 of Schedule 3BA to the Act must contain the following information—

(a) any VAT identification number or tax reference number by which the applicant is identified for VAT purposes by any member State in accordance with Article 214, Article 239 or Article 240 of the principal VAT Directive, and the name of that member State;

(b) any number previously allocated to the applicant by any member State under Article 362 of the principal VAT Directive, or otherwise for the purposes of Article 369d of the principal VAT Directive, and the name of that member State;

(c) where the applicant has previously been identified under a non-UK special scheme, the date the applicant ceased to be so identified;

(d) whether the applicant is treated as a member of a group under any of sections 43A to 43D of the Act; and

(e) the name of any member States in which the applicant has a fixed establishment, and the address of each such fixed establishment.²]¹

Commentary—*De Voil Indirect Tax Service* **V2.189Q**.
Saving provision—Part 26 continues to apply in relation to supplies made before IP completion day. To the extent that it continues to apply, Part 26 has effect subject to such modifications as may be specified in a notice published by the Commissioners (see SI 2020/1495, reg 17).
Amendments¹ Part 26 (regs 214–218) inserted by the VAT (Amendment) (No 3) Regulations, SI 2014/2430 regs 2, 9 with effect from 1 October 2014.
² Part 26 revoked by the Value Added Tax (Miscellaneous Amendments and Revocations) (EU Exit) Regulations, SI 2019/59 regs 12, 79 with effect from IP completion day (11pm UK time on 31 December 2020).

[217 Registration requests: declaration
A registration request under paragraph 4 of Schedule 3B or paragraph 5 of Schedule 3BA to the Act must also contain a declaration by the applicant that the information the applicant has provided in the registration request is accurate and complete to the best of the applicant's knowledge.²]¹

Commentary—*De Voil Indirect Tax Service* **V2.189G, V2.189Q**.
Saving provision—Part 26 continues to apply in relation to supplies made before IP completion day. To the extent that it continues to apply, Part 26 has effect subject to such modifications as may be specified in a notice published by the Commissioners (see SI 2020/1495, reg 17).
Amendments¹ Part 26 (regs 214–218) inserted by the VAT (Amendment) (No 3) Regulations, SI 2014/2430 regs 2, 9 with effect from 1 October 2014.
² Part 26 revoked by the Value Added Tax (Miscellaneous Amendments and Revocations) (EU Exit) Regulations, SI 2019/59 regs 12, 79 with effect from IP completion day (11pm UK time on 31 December 2020).

[218 The following communications must be made by using the electronic portal set up by the Commissioners for the purpose of implementing Sections 2 and 3 of Chapter 6 of Title XII to the principal VAT Directive—

(a) a registration request under paragraph 4 of Schedule 3B or paragraph 5 of Schedule 3BA to the Act;

(b) the information required by paragraph 7 of Schedule 3B or paragraph 6 of Schedule 3BA to the Act;

(c) a return required under paragraph 11 of Schedule 3B or paragraph 9 of Schedule 3BA to the Act.²]¹

Commentary—*De Voil Indirect Tax Service* **V2.189G**.
Saving provision—Part 26 continues to apply in relation to supplies made before IP completion day. To the extent that it continues to apply, Part 26 has effect subject to such modifications as may be specified in a notice published by the Commissioners (see SI 2020/1495, reg 17).
Amendments¹ Reg 218 substituted by the VAT (Amendment) (No 3) Regulations, SI 2014/2430 regs 2, 10(1) with effect from 1 January 2015.
² Part 26 revoked by the Value Added Tax (Miscellaneous Amendments and Revocations) (EU Exit) Regulations, SI 2019/59 regs 12, 79 with effect from IP completion day (11pm UK time on 31 December 2020).

[PART 27

NON-UK UNION AND NON-UNION SPECIAL ACCOUNTING SCHEMES: ADJUSTMENTS, CLAIMS AND ERROR CORRECTION

Saving provision—Part 27 continues to apply in relation to supplies made before IP completion day. To the extent that it continues to apply, Part 27 has effect subject to such modifications as may be specified in a notice published by the Commissioners (see SI 2020/1495, reg 18).
Amendments—Part 27 revoked by the Value Added Tax (Miscellaneous Amendments and Revocations) (EU Exit) Regulations, SI 2019/59 regs 12, 80 with effect from IP completion day (11pm UK time on 31 December 2020).

219 In this Part, 'tax period' has the meaning given by paragraph 23(1) of Schedule 3B or paragraph 38(1) of Schedule 3BA (as the case may require) to the Act.²]¹

Saving provision—Part 27 continues to apply in relation to supplies made before IP completion day. To the extent that it continues to apply, Part 27 has effect subject to such modifications as may be specified in a notice published by the Commissioners (see SI 2020/1495, reg 18).
Amendments—¹ Part 27 (regs 219–223) inserted by the VAT (Amendment) (No 3) Regulations, SI 2014/2430 regs 2, 11 with effect from 1 January 2015.
² Part 27 revoked by the Value Added Tax (Miscellaneous Amendments and Revocations) (EU Exit) Regulations, SI 2019/59 regs 12, 80 with effect from IP completion day (11pm UK time on 31 December 2020).

[220 Correction of errors on non-UK and special scheme returns more than 3 years after the date the original return was required to be made

(1) In this regulation 'notice' means a notice given under paragraph 16C(3) of Schedule 3B or paragraph 23(3) of Schedule 3BA to the Act.

(2) A person giving a notice (P) must do so—
  (*a*) no later than 4 years after the end of the tax period in respect of which the return identified in the notice was required to be made; and
  (*b*) in writing in the English language.

(3) P must also provide such documentary evidence in support of the notice as P possesses.[2]][1]

Saving provision—Part 27 continues to apply in relation to supplies made before IP completion day. To the extent that it continues to apply, Part 27 has effect subject to such modifications as may be specified in a notice published by the Commissioners (see SI 2020/1495, reg 18).

Amendments—[1] Part 27 (regs 219–223) inserted by the VAT (Amendment) (No 3) Regulations, SI 2014/2430 regs 2, 11 with effect from 1 January 2015.
[2] Part 27 revoked by the Value Added Tax (Miscellaneous Amendments and Revocations) (EU Exit) Regulations, SI 2019/59 regs 12, 80 with effect from IP completion day (11pm UK time on 31 December 2020).

[221 Claims in respect of overpaid VAT

(1) A person making a claim under paragraph 16I(1) of Schedule 3B, or paragraph 29(1) of Schedule 3BA, to the Act must provide to the Commissioners at the time of making the claim a statement in writing in the English language explaining how the claim is calculated.

(2) A person making a claim under any other provision of paragraph 16I of Schedule 3B, or paragraph 29 of Schedule 3BA, to the Act must—
  (i) make that claim to the Commissioners; and
  (ii) provide to the Commissioners at the time of making the claim a statement in writing in the English language explaining how the claim is calculated.[2]][1]

Saving provision—Part 27 continues to apply in relation to supplies made before IP completion day. To the extent that it continues to apply, Part 27 has effect subject to such modifications as may be specified in a notice published by the Commissioners (see SI 2020/1495, reg 18).

Amendments—[1] Part 27 (regs 219–223) inserted by the VAT (Amendment) (No 3) Regulations, SI 2014/2430 regs 2, 11 with effect from 1 January 2015.
[2] Part 27 revoked by the Value Added Tax (Miscellaneous Amendments and Revocations) (EU Exit) Regulations, SI 2019/59 regs 12, 80 with effect from IP completion day (11pm UK time on 31 December 2020).

[222 Increases or decreases in consideration occurring more than 3 years after the end of the affected tax period

(1) A claim or other notice made under paragraph 16K(2)(*b*) of Schedule 3B or paragraph 31(2)(*b*) of Schedule 3BA to the Act must be made in writing in the English language.

(2) A person making a payment—
  (*a*) under paragraph 16K(3) of Schedule 3B to the Act in a case falling within paragraph 16K(2)(*b*) of that Schedule; or
  (*b*) under paragraph 31(3) of Schedule 3BA to the Act in a case falling within paragraph 31(2)(*b*) of that Schedule,

must do so no later than twenty days after the end of the tax period in which the increase in consideration is accounted for in the person's business accounts.[2]][1]

Saving provision—Part 27 continues to apply in relation to supplies made before IP completion day. To the extent that it continues to apply, Part 27 has effect subject to such modifications as may be specified in a notice published by the Commissioners (see SI 2020/1495, reg 18).

Amendments—[1] Part 27 (regs 219–223) inserted by the VAT (Amendment) (No 3) Regulations, SI 2014/2430 regs 2, 11 with effect from 1 January 2015.
[2] Part 27 revoked by the Value Added Tax (Miscellaneous Amendments and Revocations) (EU Exit) Regulations, SI 2019/59 regs 12, 80 with effect from IP completion day (11pm UK time on 31 December 2020).

[223 Scheme participants who are also taxable persons: disapplication of paragraph 17(1)

(1) Paragraph 17(1) of Schedule 3BA to the Act is not to apply in the case of an input tax obligation.

(2) In this regulation 'input tax obligation' means an obligation imposed on a taxable person relating to a claim to deduction under section 25(2) of the Act or to payment of a VAT credit.[2]][1]

Saving provision—Part 27 continues to apply in relation to supplies made before IP completion day. To the extent that it continues to apply, Part 27 has effect subject to such modifications as may be specified in a notice published by the Commissioners (see SI 2020/1495, reg 18).

Amendments—[1] Part 27 (regs 219–223) inserted by the VAT (Amendment) (No 3) Regulations, SI 2014/2430 regs 2, 11 with effect from 1 January 2015.
[2] Part 27 revoked by the Value Added Tax (Miscellaneous Amendments and Revocations) (EU Exit) Regulations, SI 2019/59 regs 12, 80 with effect from IP completion day (11pm UK time on 31 December 2020).

[SCHEDULE 1A

Regulation 145F

Northern Ireland—Part 16A and Sch 1A apply to Northern Ireland warehouses and Northern Ireland fiscal warehouses as they apply to warehouses and fiscal warehouses as if any reference to "fiscal warehouse",

"warehouse", "fiscal warehousing regime" and "warehousing regime" were a reference respectively to "Northern Ireland fiscal warehouse", "Northern Ireland warehouse", "Northern Ireland fiscal warehousing regime" and "Northern Ireland warehousing regime"; and with the modifications set out in regs 145M–145R in respect of Part 16A, and in reg 145T in respect of Sch 1A (see VAT Regs, SI 1995/2518 reg 145L, as inserted by SI 2020/1545 reg 79).

Amendments—This Schedule inserted by the VAT (Amendment) (No 3) Regulations, SI 1996/1250 reg 16, with effect from 1 June 1996.

The fiscal warehousing record which is referred to in paragraph (3) of regulation 145F shall have the features and comply with the requirements set out below.

1

Goods in and out of a fiscal warehouse and its regime

(a) It shall accurately identify any eligible goods which enter or exit the fiscal warehouse, their nature and quantity, and the time and date when they so enter or exit.

(b) It shall accurately identify any goods which are not eligible goods and which enter or exit the fiscal warehouse for storage (other than goods which enter for purposes wholly incidental to such storage), their nature and quantity, and time and date when they so enter or exit.

(c) It shall accurately identify all eligible goods which are allocated to or removed from the fiscal warehousing regime associated with the relevant fiscal warehousekeeper, the time and date when the allocation or removal takes place, and the location of the eligible goods while they are allocated to the relevant regime.

(d) It shall accurately identify as "transferred goods" all eligible goods which are transferred directly from the fiscal warehousing regime to another fiscal warehousing regime, the time and date when the transfer starts, and the address of the fiscal warehouse to which the goods in question are transferred.

(e) . . .[1]

(f) It shall accurately identify as "transferred goods (by reason of export)" all eligible goods which are directly exported from the fiscal warehousing regime to a place outside [Great Britain][1] under regulation 145H(2)(c), the date and time when the movement of the goods which is directly associated with the export starts, and the address of the place outside [Great Britain][1] to which the goods in question are consigned.

Northern Ireland—See VAT Regs, SI 1995/2518 reg 145T(a) (as inserted by SI 2020/1545 reg 79): in this para, the following sub-para to be read as being inserted before sub-para (f)—

"(ea) It must accurately identify as "transferred goods" all eligible goods which are transferred directly from the Northern Ireland fiscal warehousing regime to corresponding arrangements in a member State under regulation 145H(2)(bb), the date and time when the transfer starts, and the address of the place in the member State to which the goods in question are transferred.";

and in sub-para (f), "Great Britain" in both places to be read as "Northern Ireland and the member States;".

Amendments—[1] Sub-para (e) revoked, and in sub-para (f) words substituted for words "the member States", by the Value Added Tax (Miscellaneous Amendments, Northern Ireland Protocol and Savings and Transitional Provisions) (EU Exit) Regulations, SI 2020/1545 regs 31 and 90(a) with effect from IP completion day (11pm UK time on 31 December 2020) by virtue of SI 2020/1641 reg 2, Schedule para 11. Sub-para (e) previously read as follows—

"(e) It shall accurately identify as "transferred goods" all eligible goods which are transferred directly from the fiscal warehousing regime to corresponding arrangements in another member State under regulation 145H(2)(b), the date and time when the transfer starts, and the address of the place in the other member State to which the goods in question are transferred."

2

Specified services performed in a fiscal warehouse

It shall accurately identify the nature of any services which are performed on or in relation to eligible goods while those goods are allocated to the relevant fiscal warehousing regime, the date when the services are performed, the particular eligible goods on or in relation to which they are performed, and the name, address and registration number (if any) of the supplier of those services.

3

Documents relating to transfers and specified services

(a) It shall include the written undertaking from the other fiscal warehousekeeper relating to a transfer made within the United Kingdom referred to in regulation 145G(2), the certificate from the other fiscal warehousekeeper confirming a transfer made within the United Kingdom referred to in regulation 145G(3)(c), and it shall relate them to the relevant transfer.

(b) It shall include the copy of the certificate relating to a transfer received by the relevant fiscal warehousekeeper from another fiscal warehousing regime within the United Kingdom referred to in regulation 145G(3)(d) and it shall relate that copy to the relevant allocation to his relevant fiscal warehousing regime.

(c) . . .[1]

(d) It shall include the document relating to the completion of an export to a place outside [Great Britain]¹ referred to in regulation 145H(4)(c) and it shall relate that document to the export in question.

Northern Ireland—See VAT Regs, SI 1995/2518 reg 145T(b) (as inserted by SI 2020/1545 reg 79): in this para, the following sub-para to be read as being inserted before sub-para (d)—

"(ca) It must include the document relating to the completion of a transfer to corresponding arrangements in a member State referred to in regulation 145H(4)(bb) and it must relate that document to the relevant transfer."

and in sub-para (d), "Great Britain" to be read as "Northern Ireland and the member States;".

Amendments—¹ Sub-para (c) revoked, in sub-para (d) words substituted for words "the member States", by the Value Added Tax (Miscellaneous Amendments, Northern Ireland Protocol and Savings and Transitional Provisions) (EU Exit) Regulations, SI 2020/1545 regs 31 and 90(b) with effect from IP completion day (11pm UK time on 31 December 2020) by virtue of SI 2020/1641 reg 2, Schedule para 11. Sub-para (c) previously read as follows—

"(c) It shall include the document relating to the completion of a transfer to corresponding arrangements in another member State referred to in regulation 145H(4)(b) and it shall relate that document to the relevant transfer."

4

Procedures where transfers are not completed

(a) It shall be adjusted to show a removal (and not a transfer) where the certificate of transfer within the United Kingdom referred to in regulation 145G(3)(c) is not received in time from the other fiscal warehousekeeper.

(b) It shall be adjusted to show a removal (and not a transfer) where the document referred to in [regulation]¹ 145H(4)(c) concerning goods which have been transferred to corresponding arrangements in [Great Britain]¹, or which have been exported to a place outside [Great Britain]¹, is not received in time.

(c) It shall evidence any notification made under regulation 145H(3)(c) to the person on whose instructions the goods were allowed to leave the fiscal warehouse.

Northern Ireland—See VAT Regs, SI 1995/2518 reg 145T(c) (as inserted by SI 2020/1545 reg 79): sub-para (b) to be read as follows—

"(b) It shall be adjusted to show a removal (and not a transfer) where the document referred to in regulations 145H(4)(bb) or 145H(4)(c) concerning goods which have been transferred to corresponding arrangements in a member State or which have been exported to a place outside Northern Ireland and the member States, is not received in time."

Amendments—¹ In sub-para (b) words substituted for words "articles 145H(4)(b) or", "another member State" and "the member States", by the Value Added Tax (Miscellaneous Amendments, Northern Ireland Protocol and Savings and Transitional Provisions) (EU Exit) Regulations, SI 2020/1545 regs 31 and 90(b) with effect from IP completion day (11pm UK time on 31 December 2020) by virtue of SI 2020/1641 reg 2, Schedule para 11.

5

Removals from a fiscal warehousing regime

(a) It shall identify the name and address of any person who at any time removes or causes the removal of any goods from the fiscal warehousing regime and that person's registration number if he is registered under the Act.

(b) It shall include a copy of the removal document issued by the Commissioners under regulation 145J(1) and shall relate it to the relevant removal.

6

Miscellaneous

(a) It shall incorporate any modifications to the features or requirements set out in paragraphs 1 to 5 above which the Commissioners may require in respect of the relevant fiscal warehousekeeper.

(b) A fiscal warehousekeeper may, with the prior agreement of the Commissioners, maintain a fiscal warehousing record in which any of the features or requirements set out in paragraphs 1 to 5 above are relaxed or dispensed with.

1996/1255

VALUE ADDED TAX (FISCAL WAREHOUSING) (TREATMENT OF TRANSACTIONS) ORDER 1996

Made by the Treasury under VATA 1994 s 5(3)

Made . . . . .8 May 1996
Laid before the House of Commons . . . . .9 May 1996
Coming into force . . . . .1 June 1996

1 This Order may be cited as the Value Added Tax (Fiscal Warehousing) (Treatment of Transactions) Order 1996 and shall come into force on 1st June 1996.

2—(1) In this Order—
"eligible goods" has the meaning given by section 18B(6) of the Act;
"material time" has the meaning given by section 18F(1) of the Act;
"supply" means a supply for the purposes of section 5(2)(*a*) of the Act; and,
"the Act" means the Value Added Tax Act 1994.
(2) In construing article 3(2) below any supply referred to in that article must be treated as taking place at the material time for that supply.
Northern Ireland—Article 2 applies to goods subject to, or to be placed in, a Northern Ireland fiscal warehousing regime as it applies to goods subject to, or to be placed in, a fiscal warehousing regime, with the following modification: "eligible goods" and "material time" are to be read as having the meanings given by VATA 1994 Sch 9ZB para 25(1).

3—(1) A transaction fulfilling the description set out in paragraph (2) below shall be treated as a supply of goods and not as a supply of services.
(2) The description referred to in paragraph (1) above is that there is a supply (which is not a retail transaction) involving the transfer of any undivided share of property in eligible goods and either—
   (*a*) that supply takes place while the goods in question are subject to a fiscal warehousing regime, or
   (*b*) the transferee causes the goods in question to be placed in a fiscal warehousing regime after receiving that supply but before the supply, if any, which next occurs involving the transfer of any property in those goods.
Northern Ireland—Article 3 applies to goods subject to, or to be placed in, a Northern Ireland fiscal warehousing regime as it applies to goods subject to, or to be placed in, a fiscal warehousing regime, with the following modification: in paras (2)(*a*), (*b*), "fiscal warehousing regime" to be read as "Northern Ireland fiscal warehousing regime".

1999/3115

VALUE ADDED TAX (IMPORTATION OF INVESTMENT GOLD) RELIEF ORDER 1999

Made by the Treasury under VATA 1994 s 37(1) and FA 1999 s 13(3) and (4)

Made . . . . .19 November 1999
Laid before the House of Commons . . . . .22 November 1999
Coming into force . . . . .1 January 2000

1 This Order may be cited as the Value Added Tax (Importation of Investment Gold) Relief Order 1999 and shall come into force on 1st January 2000.

2 In this Order—
"Investment gold" has the same meaning as in Group 15 of Schedule 9 to the Value Added Tax Act 1994.

3 VAT shall not be chargeable on the importation of investment gold . . . . [1].
Amendments—[1] Words "from places outside the member States" revoked by the Value Added Tax (Miscellaneous Amendments and Revocations) (EU Exit) Regulations, SI 2019/59 reg 82 with effect from IP completion day (11pm UK time on 31 December 2020).

1999/3121

VALUE ADDED TAX (INPUT TAX) (SPECIFIED SUPPLIES) ORDER 1999

Made by the Treasury under VATA 1994 s 26(2)(c)

Made .... 19 November 1999
Laid before the House of Commons .... 22 November 1999
Coming into force .... 1 January 2000

1 This Order may be cited as the Value Added Tax (Input Tax) (Specified Supplies) Order 1999 and shall come into force on 1st January 2000 and shall have effect in relation to supplies made on or after that date.

2 The supplies described in articles 3 [,3A][1] and 4 below are hereby specified for the purposes of section 26(2)(c) of the Value Added Tax Act 1994.

Amendments—[1] Reference inserted by the Value Added Tax (Input Tax) (Specified Supplies) (Amendment) Order, SI 2018/1328 arts 2, 3 with effect in relation to supplies of services made on or after 1 March 2019.

3 Services—
   (a) which are supplied to a person who belongs outside the [United Kingdom][1];
   (b) which are directly linked to the export of goods to a place outside the [United Kingdom][1]; or
   (c) which consist of the provision of intermediary services within the meaning of item 4 of Group 2, or item 5 of Group 5, of Schedule 9 to the Value Added Tax Act 1994 in relation to any transaction specified in paragraph (a) or (b) above,

provided the supply is exempt, or would have been exempt if made in the United Kingdom, by virtue of any item of Group 2, or any of items 1 to 6 and item 8 of Group 5, of Schedule 9 to the Value Added Tax Act 1994.

Amendments—[1] In paras (a) and (b), words substituted for words "member States" by the Value Added Tax (Miscellaneous Amendments, Northern Ireland Protocol and Savings and Transitional Provisions) (EU Exit) Regulations, SI 2020/1545 regs 91, 92 with effect from IP completion day (11pm UK time on 31 December 2020) by virtue of SI 2020/1641 reg 2, Schedule para 11.

[3A Any services that are included within article 3 above by virtue of the fact that the supply is exempt, or would have been exempt if made in the United Kingdom, by virtue of item 4 of Group 2 of Schedule 9 to the Value Added Tax Act 1994 must be related to an insurance transaction or a reinsurance transaction where the party to be insured under the contract of insurance or reinsurance (whether or not a contract of insurance or reinsurance is finally concluded) is a person who belongs outside the United Kingdom.][1]

Amendments—[1] Art 3A inserted by the Value Added Tax (Input Tax) (Specified Supplies) (Amendment) Order, SI 2018/1328 arts 2, 4 with effect in relation to supplies of services made on or after 1 March 2019.

4 Supplies made either in or outside the United Kingdom which fall, or would fall, within item 1 or 2 of Group 15 of Schedule 9 to the Value Added Tax Act 1994 (investment gold).

5 (Revokes the Value Added Tax (Input Tax) (Specified Supplies) Order 1992, SI 1992/3123.)

2002/1935

VALUE ADDED TAX (ACQUISITIONS) RELIEF ORDER 2002

Made by the Treasury under VATA 1994 s 36A

Made .... 25 July 2002
Laid before the House of Commons .... 25 July 2002
Coming into force .... 15 August 2002

1 This Order may be cited as the Value Added Tax (Acquisitions) Relief Order 2002 and comes into force on 15th August 2002.

2 Subject to article 3 below, [NI acquisition VAT, as defined in paragraph 1(3) of Schedule 9ZA to the Value Added Tax Act 1994, shall not be charged on the acquisition in Northern Ireland of goods from a member State][1] where, if they were imported from a place outside the member States, relief from payment of VAT would be given by the Value Added Tax (Imported Goods) Relief Order 1984 (as amended from time to time).

Transitional provisions—Where acquisition VAT would, but for the provisions made in the SI 2002/1935, be charged on or after IP completion day (in accordance with transitional provision made in SI 2020/1545 or other regulations made under TCTA 2018), the relief from acquisition VAT provided for continues to apply as if SI 2002/1935 had not been amended by SI 2020/1545 (see SI 2020/1545 reg 128).

Amendments—[1] Words substituted for words "no VAT shall be payable on any acquisition from another member State of any goods" by the Value Added Tax (Miscellaneous Amendments, Northern Ireland Protocol and Savings and Transitional Provisions) (EU Exit) Regulations, SI 2020/1545 regs 93, 94 with effect from IP completion day (11pm UK time on 31 December 2020) by virtue of SI 2020/1641 reg 2, Schedule para 11.

3 The relief given by this Order in respect of the acquisition of any goods shall be subject to the same conditions as those to which, by virtue of the Value Added Tax (Imported Goods) Relief Order 1984 (as amended from time to time), relief under that Order would be subject in the case of an importation of those goods.

2003/3113

CUSTOMS (CONTRAVENTION OF A RELEVANT RULE) REGULATIONS 2003

Made by the Treasury under FA 2003 s 26(1), (2), (3), (4), (41)

Made . . . . .2 December 2003
Laid before the House of Commons . . . . .2 December 2003
Coming into force . . . . .23 December 2003

1 Citation and Commencement

These Regulations may be cited as the Customs (Contravention of a Relevant Rule) Regulations 2003 and shall come into force on 23rd December 2003.

2 Interpretation

In these Regulations—
"the Act" means the Customs and Excise Management Act 1979;
. . .[2]
. . .[2]
"the 1994 Act" means the Finance Act 1994;
["the 2018 Act" means the Taxation (Cross-border Trade) Act 2018;][3]
. . .[3]
["Customs" means Her Majesty's Revenue and Customs, the Secretary of State by whom customs functions are exercisable or the Director of Border Revenue;][1]
[functions exercised under these Regulations by the Secretary of State by whom customs functions are exercisable are general customs functions in accordance with the Borders, Citizenship and Immigration Act 2009 and those exercised by the Director of Border Revenue are customs revenue functions in accordance with the same Act;][1]
. . .[1]
. . .[2]
. . .[3]

Amendments—[1] Definition of "Customs" substituted and following words inserted, definition of "Customs authority of the United Kingdom" and following words, and definition of "the Transit Regulations", revoked, by the Customs (Contravention of a Relevant Rule) (Amendment) Regulations, SI 2009/3164 regs 2, 3 with effect from 24 December 2009.
[2] Definitions revoked by the Customs (Contravention of a Relevant Rule) (Amendment) Regulations, SI 2015/636 regs 2, 3 with effect from 2 April 2015.
[3] Definitions "the Code", "customs territory", "Delegated Regulation", "the Implementing Regulation", and "the Importation Regulations" revoked, and definition "the 2018 Act" inserted, by the Customs (Contravention of a Relevant Rule) (Amendment) (EU Exit) Regulations, SI 2018/1260 regs 2, 3 with effect from IP completion day (11pm UK time on 31 December 2020). The revoked definitions previously read as follows—
 ""the Code" means [Regulation (EU) No 952/2013 of the European Parliament and of the Council of 9 October 2013 laying down the Union Customs Code;
 "customs territory" has the meaning given by Article 3 of the Code to "customs territory of the Community";
 "Delegated Regulation" means Commission Delegated Regulation (EU) 2015/2446 of 28 July 2015 supplementing the Code as regards certain provisions of the Code;
 "the Implementing Regulation" means [Commission Implementing Regulation (EU) 2015/2447 of 24 November 2015] as it implements the Code;
 "the Importation Regulations" means the Customs Controls on Importation of Goods Regulations 1991;"

3 Relevant Rule and Amount of Penalty

(1) The Schedule to these regulations shall have effect.
(2) An entry in Column 1 of the Schedule specifies the relevant rule or the description of a relevant rule in the case of any relevant tax or duty to which it applies for the purposes of section 26(1) of the Finance Act 2003 (Penalty for contravention of relevant rule).
(3) An entry in Column 2 of the Schedule adjacent to an entry in Column 1 specifies a person, of the description there laid out, who shall be liable to a penalty under section 26 of the Finance Act 2003 (where his conduct contravenes the relevant rule or a relevant rule of the description specified for the purposes of that section).
(4) An entry in Column 3 of the Schedule adjacent to an entry in Columns 1 and 2 specifies for the purposes of section 26(1) of the Finance Act 2003 the maximum amount of the penalty which may be imposed upon a person specified for the purposes of that section as liable for that contravention of that specified relevant rule.
. . .[3]

[(7) [Where as a consequence of these Regulations, a person is liable to a penalty under section 26 of the Finance Act 2003][3] and the conduct giving rise to the liability continues after the date specified in a notice in writing given to that person by the Commissioners, that continuation of the conduct—
   (a) shall constitute a further contravention of the same rule; and
   (b) shall make that person liable to a separate penalty accordingly.][2]

Amendments—[1]   Para (7) inserted by the Customs (Contravention of a Relevant Rule) (Amendment) Regulations, SI 2011/2534, regs 2, 4 with effect from 15 November 2011.
[2]   In para (7), words substituted by the Customs (Contravention of a Relevant Rule) (Amendment) Regulations, SI 2015/636 regs 2, 4 with effect from 2 April 2015.
[3]   Paras (5), (6) revoked by the Customs (Contravention of a Relevant Rule) (Amendment) (EU Exit) Regulations, SI 2018/1260 regs 2, 4 with effect from IP completion day (11pm UK time on 31 December 2020). Paras (5), (6) previously read as follows—
   "(5) Any description of a relevant rule specified in Column 1 and any description of a person prescribed in Column 2 of the Schedule is without prejudice to the effect of any directly applicable [EU][1] provision so described or description of a person responsible contained in that provision so described.
   (6) A specified relevant rule or description of a person shall be construed in accordance with the effect and scope of that directly applicable [EU] provision referred to in Column 1."

SCHEDULE
Regulation 3

Column 1	Column 2	Column 3
Description of relevant Rule/Relevant Rule of a description	Person of a description	Penalty for contravention
Report		
[Section 20(1B), 22(1B) and 25(1B) of the Act		
Section 20(1A) and 22(1A) of the Act		
Any pre-approval conditions specified in regulations made under section 20(1) or 22(1A) of the Act.	The approved person.	£2,500.
Any conditions or restrictions attaching to any approval given under the provisions of section 20(1B), 22(1B) or 25(1B) of the Act.	The approved person.	£1,000.
The Customs (Temporary Storage Facilities Approval Conditions and Miscellaneous Amendments) (EU Exit) Regulations 2018		
Any pre-approval conditions contained in Schedule 1 to the Regulations or specified by an officer of HMRC under Schedule 2 to the Regulations.	The approved person.	£2,500.][5]
Section 21(1) and (3)(b) of the Act		
Except where permitted, not to cause, or permit, to land an aircraft other than at a customs and excise airport (which, in the case of flights departing the UK, must be as specified in the clearance application), except with Customs' permission or for unavoidable cause.	The commander of the aircraft.	£2,500.
Section 21(2) of the Act		
Except as permitted by Customs, not to bring into the United Kingdom, in an aircraft, at any place other than a customs and excise airport, goods being imported from . . . [5].	The person bringing in the goods.	£2,500.
Section 21(3)(a) of the Act		
Except where permitted, not to depart on a flight to a place or area outside the United Kingdom from any place in the United Kingdom other than a customs and excise airport.	The person departing.	£2,500.
Section 21(4)(a) of the Act		
In the case of landing other than as permitted under sections 21(1) or (3), (a) to make immediate report (b) not to permit goods to be unloaded from the aircraft (c) not to permit any crew or passengers to leave its vicinity (d) to comply with any directions given by an officer.	The commander of the aircraft.	£2,500.
Section 21(4)(b) of the Act		
In the case of landing other than as permitted under sections 21(1) or (3), no passenger or crew member to leave the immediate vicinity of the aircraft without the consent of an officer or constable.	The passenger or crew member in question.	£2,500.
Section 33(1) of the Act		
To allow an officer to board and inspect [a vehicle which is an aircraft or railway vehicle][5] and all goods and documents carried in and relating to it.	The [vehicle operator][5].	£2,500.
Section 33(2) of the Act		
To permit an officer to enter and inspect an aerodrome [or railway customs area] and all buildings and goods thereon][5].	The person in control of the aerodrome [or railway customs area][5].	£2,500.
Section 33(3) of the Act		

Column 1	Column 2	Column 3
Description of relevant Rule/Relevant Rule of a description	*Person of a description*	*Penalty for contravention*
[Obligation to comply with any record keeping requirements contained in section 33(3)(a), (b) and (c) of the Act.]⁵	The person in control of the aerodrome.	£2,500.
[Section 33(3A) of the Act		
Obligation to comply with any record keeping requirements contained in section 33(3A)(a), (b) and (c) of the Act.	The person in control of the railway customs area.	£2,500]⁵
Section 34(1) of the Act		
Any instructions given under section 34(1) of the Act.	The commander of the aircraft.	£2,500.
	The owner of the aircraft.	£2,500.]²
[Section 34(1A) of the Act		
Obligation to comply with any instructions given under section 34(1A) of the Act.	The railway vehicle operator, or the owner of the railway customs area.	£2,500]⁵
Section 35(1) of the Act		
To report in such form and manner containing such particulars as Customs direct.	[The vehicle operator.	£1,000]⁵
[Ship's Report, Importation and Exportation by Sea Regulations 1981]²:		
Regulation 3		
Completion of the forms directed by Customs under s 35(1) by the master, or a person authorised by him (as Customs permit).	The master	£1,000
	Person authorised by the master.	£1,000
Regulation 4		
Delivery of a duly completed report:	The master.	£1,000
(a) to a boarding officer immediately on request;	Person authorised by the master.	£1,000
(b) to the place designated within three hours of the ship having reached its place of loading or unloading; or		
(c) on the expiration of twenty four hours following arrival within the limits of the port when a ship has not arrived at its place of loading or unloading.		
Regulation 5		
To retain on board as long as the ship remains within the limits of the port a copy of the form of report for inspection by an officer.	The master.	£1,000
[Aircraft (Customs and Excise) Regulations 1981]²:		
Regulation 4(1)		
Delivery to the proper officer of:	Commander of the aircraft.	£1,000
(a) a General Declaration;		
(b) particulars of the goods on the aircraft; and		
(c) a list in duplicate of the stores on board the aircraft.		
Section 35(6) of the Act		
To answer all such question relating to:	[The vehicle operator.	£1,000]⁵
(a) the [vehicle]⁵;		
(b) the goods carried therein;		
(c) the crew; and		
(d) the voyage[, flight or journey]⁵		
as put to him by the proper officer.		
Section 35(7) of the Act		
Where prior to report:	[The vehicle operator.	£1,000]⁵
(a) bulk is broken;		
(b) stowage of any goods is altered to facilitate unloading of any part thereof before making report;		
(c) any part of the goods are staved, destroyed, thrown overboard; or		
(d) a container opened		
and no proper explanation is given to the satisfaction of Customs.		
[Section 35A of the Act		

Column 1	Column 2	Column 3
Description of relevant Rule/Relevant Rule of a description	Person of a description	Penalty for contravention
To provide confirmation of a Customs declaration as required in accordance with regulations made under section 35A.	The vehicle operator.	£1,000.][5]
[Section 64(1) and (1A) of the Act		
Except as otherwise provided for in regulations made under section 64(1A), no vehicle other than a road vehicle is to depart from the United Kingdom until clearance for departure has been obtained from the proper officer.	The vehicle operator.	£1,000.][5]
	The commander of the aircraft.	£1,000.
Section 71(1) of the Act		
To deliver a report to the proper officer as directed.	The master of the ship.	£500.
Section 72(2) and (3)(b) of the Act		
Any requirement made under section 72(2) or (3)(b) of the Act.	The master of the ship.	£500.
Section 77(1) of the Act		
Any requirement made under section 77(1) of the Act.	The person of whom the requirement is made.	£1,000.
Section 78(1) of the Act		
(a) A person (P) entering the United Kingdom must, at such place and in such manner as Customs may direct, declare any thing contained in P's baggage or carried with P which P has obtained outside the United Kingdom and in respect of which P is not entitled to exemption from duty and tax by virtue of any order under section 13 of the Customs and Excise Duties (General Reliefs) Act 1979 (personal reliefs) [or any regulations made under section 19(1) of the Taxation (Cross-border Trade) Act 2018][5].	Any person.	£1,000.
(b) A person (P) entering the United Kingdom must, at such place and in such manner as Customs may direct, declare any thing contained in P's baggage or carried with P which, being dutiable goods or chargeable goods, P has obtained in the United Kingdom without payment of duty or tax and in respect of which P is not entitled to exemption from duty and tax by virtue of any order under section 13 of the Customs and Excise Duties (General Reliefs) Act 1979 [or any regulations made under section 19(1) of the Taxation (Cross-border Trade) Act 2018][5].	Any person.	£1,000.
Section 158(1) and (3) of the Act		
Provision and maintenance of appliances, facilities and fittings; keeping the appliances in an approved place; allowing use of the same at any time to a proper officer; all necessary assistance to be given.	The person on whom the obligation falls.	£1,000.
The Control of Movement of Goods Regulations 1984		
Not to move or interfere with goods to which the Regulations apply other than in accordance with the Regulations.	The person moving or interfering with the goods.	£2,500.][2]
. . .[5]		
Presentation of Goods to Customs		
. . .[3]	. . .[3]	. . .[3]
. . .[5]		
[Directions made on 2 August 2011 under section 30 of the Act		
No goods to which section 30 applies to be moved except:	The declarant.	£1,000
(a) on the instructions of a proper officer;		
(b) in the manner and under the conditions specified by a proper officer.	The person who moves the goods.	£1,000][3]
[The Customs (Import Duty) (EU Exit) Regulations 2018		
Regulation 4(1) and (2)		
Obligation to give notification to HMRC of the importation of goods into the United Kingdom.	The person responsible for giving the notification.	£2,500.
Regulation 4(3)		
Notification of importation: Obligation to comply with any of the requirements in regulation 4(3)(a), (b) or (c).	The person giving the notification.	£1,000.][5]
[Regulation 4(3C) Notification of arrival:		
Where a person is deemed to have notified HMRC under regulation 4(3A) [, (3AB) or (3AC)][16] and the Customs declaration in respect of the goods was not made using the EIDR procedure [or the transitional EIDR procedure], the person must give a notification to HMRC that the goods have arrived in the United Kingdom which meets the requirements in regulation 4(3D).	The person responsible for giving the notification.	£2,500.][10]

Column 1	Column 2	Column 3
Description of relevant Rule/Relevant Rule of a description	*Person of a description*	*Penalty for contravention*
. . .[5]		
[Authorisations and Approvals		
The Customs (Import Duty) (EU Exit) Regulations 2018		
Regulation 89(5) The approved person must comply with any conditions specified in or under the Regulations relating to the approval or the notification of the approval.	The approved person.	£2,500.
Regulation 90 The approved person must notify HMRC if they cease to satisfy eligibility criteria for approval or they fail to meet any condition to which their approval is subject or there are material changes to the information [specified in a notice published by HMRC under paragraph (*ba*) of regulation 90 or] given in their application.	The approved person.	£2,500.
Customs Declarations		
Section 3(1) of the 2018 Act and paragraph 1(1) of Schedule 1 to the 2018 Act Chargeable goods which are presented to Customs on import must be declared for a Customs procedure by the making of a Customs declaration.	The person responsible for making the Customs declaration.	£2,500.
Section 6(4)(a) of the 2018 Act Persons providing false information in connection with a chargeable Customs declaration where the person knew or ought reasonably to have known that the information was false.	The person providing the false information.	£2,500.
The Customs (Import Duty) (EU Exit) Regulations 2018		
Regulation 8(2) Requirement to make a temporary storage declaration in accordance with paragraph (5).	The person who notifies the importation of the goods.	£1,000.
Regulation 12(1) Carrying out activity in relation to goods in temporary storage other than that described in paragraph (2).	The approved person.	£1,000.
Regulation 12(3) and (4) Requirement to keep a record. The approved person must keep a record, in the specified form and for a period of 3 years beginning with the date of any handling whilst the goods are in temporary storage.	The approved person.	£1,000.
[Regulation 29C(2) Requirement to comply with the transitional EIDR simplified Customs declaration process as required by regulation 29C(2).	The primary declarant	£2,500.
Regulation 29C(8) A primary declarant must make available for inspection by an HMRC officer by the end of the applicable period, any documents required to accompany the transitional simplified Customs declaration.	The primary declarant	£2,500.
Regulation 29C(9) An authorised declarant must make available for inspection by an HMRC officer by the end of the applicable period, any documents required to accompany the transitional supplementary Customs declaration.	The authorised declarant.	£2,500.
Regulation 29E(1) Requirement to allow access to transitional EIDR electronic system or provide information. An eligible person who makes a transitional simplified Customs declaration must, when required to do so by an HMRC officer— (a) allow access by the officer to the transitional EIDR electronic system operated by the person; or (b) provide to the officer from that system such information, as the officer reasonably requires in order to verify transitional EIDR records or records showing whether or not any goods have been imported which are subject to a prohibition or restriction on import imposed under an enactment.	The eligible person	£2,500.][15]
Regulation 32(1) Requirement to comply with the simplified customs declaration process as required by regulation 32(1).	The authorised declarant.	£2,500.
Regulation 32(2) An authorised declarant must make available for inspection by an HMRC officer by the end of the applicable period, any documents required to accompany the Customs declaration in question.	The authorised declarant.	£2,500.

Column 1	Column 2	Column 3
Description of relevant Rule/Relevant Rule of a description	Person of a description	Penalty for contravention
Regulation 37(5) Requirement to allow access to EIDR electronic system or provide information. An authorised EIDR declarant must, when required to do so by an HMRC officer— (a) allow access by the officer to the EIDR electronic system operated by the declarant; or (b) provide to the officer from that system such information, as the officer reasonably requires in order to verify EIDR records or records showing whether or not any goods have been imported which are subject to a prohibition or restriction on import imposed under an enactment.	The authorised EIDR declarant.	£2,500.][5]
Information and Records		
. . . [5] **[Section 23][5] of the 1994 Act**		
Any obligation to provide, furnish, or produce information or documents to Customs (whether subject to time limit or reasonable demand) in such form as may reasonably be required for examination, copying or making extracts or removal for such purposes and whether for a reasonable or specified period.	The person directly or indirectly involved in the customs operation concerned for the purposes of trade in goods.	£1,000
	Any person carrying on a trade or business within the meaning of section 20 of the 1994 Act.	£1,000
[The Customs (Records) (EU Exit) Regulations 2019		
Regulation 3(1) A person who is subject to a Customs obligation, or who carries out an act in pursuance of a Customs obligation, must keep and preserve such records, in such form and for such period as specified in a notice published by HMRC.	The person required to keep and preserve records.	£1,000.
Regulation 4(2) Where the regulation applies, a person referred to in regulation 4(1) must keep documents and information in accordance with Article 51 of Regulation (EU) No 952/2013 of the European Parliament and of the Council of 9 October 2013 laying the Union Customs Code ("the UCC") as saved by regulation 4(2).	The person who was immediately before exit day, subject to an obligation under Article 51 of the UCC to keep documents and information.	£1,000.][6]
. . . [5] **[The Customs][5] Traders (Accounts and Records) Regulations 1995**		
To keep and preserve records [as required by . . . [5] the Regulations.	The person upon whom the obligation falls.	£1,000.][2]
Assistance in Examination of goods		
. . . [5]		
[The Postal Packets (Revenue and Customs) Regulations 2011 Regulations 17, 18(1) and 19		
All foreign postal packets	The sender.	£1,000.
(a) to be accompanied by a customs declaration in the appropriate form, completed in one of the permitted languages, legibly, accurately and in full, and	The postal operator.	£2,500.
(b) in the cases to which regulation 18(1) applies, to be labelled or distinguished as required by that regulation.		
Regulation 18(2)		
On accepting a packet satisfying the requirements of regulation 18(1) to give the sender a duly endorsed certificate of sending.	The postal operator.	£2,500.
Regulation 21		
When so requested by a customs officer, to produce any packet to that officer or open it for that officer's examination.	The postal operator.	£2,500.
Regulation 22(3)		
To return, destroy or deliver up to Customs goods for which no proper account is given within the requisite period.	The postal operator.	£2,500.
Regulation 23		
To pay over to Customs any sums due to them recovered under section 105(3) of the Postal Services Act 2000.	The postal operator.	£2,500.][2]
Preference		
Section 80 of the Act		

Column 1	Column 2	Column 3
Description of relevant Rule/Relevant Rule of a description	Person of a description	Penalty for contravention
(a) To furnish information in such form and within such time as may be specified;	Any person appearing to the Customs or an officer to have been concerned in any way with the goods, or with any goods from which directly or indirectly they have been produced or manufactured, or to have been concerned with the obtaining or furnishing of the certificate or evidence.	£1,000
(b) To produce for inspection, copying or the taking of extracts, invoices, bills of lading, books or documents specified; as Customs or an officer may require for the purpose of verifying or investigating any certificate or other evidence under any Community requirement;		
	The exporter	£1,000
(i) as to the origin of goods; or		
(ii) as to payments made or relief from duty allowed in any country or territory.		
. . . [5]		

Column 1	Column 2	Column 3
Description of relevant Rule/Relevant Rule of a description	Person of a description	Penalty for contravention
[Reliefs][5]		
The Customs and Excise (Personal Reliefs for Special Visitors) Order 1992		
The conditions for relief set out in the Order.	The entitled person.	£1,000.][2]
[RoRo Vehicles		
The Customs (Import Duty) (EU Exit) Regulations 2018 Chargeable goods destined for RoRo listed locations		
Regulation 131(1) and (2) Where chargeable goods to be imported are carried by a RoRo vehicle which is boarded onto a train or vessel destined for a RoRo listed destination, a declaration in respect of the goods must be made in accordance with regulation 131(2).	The person responsible for making the declaration.	£1,000.
Regulation 131(3) The Customs declaration or temporary storage declaration must not be amended or withdrawn save as provided for in the paragraph.	The declarant.	£1,000
Regulation 131(4) Evidence of compliance with regulation 131(2) must be produced to an HMRC officer when required.	The person in possession or control of the RoRo vehicle.	£1,000.
Regulation 131(6) When required to do so by an HMRC officer, the person who is responsible for providing the service of operating a train or vessel destined for a RoRo listed location on to which a RoRo vehicle carrying goods is boarded ("the responsible person") must produce to the officer evidence that the person reasonably believed that paragraph (2) of the regulation had been complied with in respect of every RoRo vehicle carrying goods on board the train or vessel.	The responsible person.	£1,000.
Special Procedures		
The Customs (Special Procedures and Outward Processing) (EU Exit) Regulations 2018.		
Regulation 8 Declarations treated as application for authorisation. Requirement to comply with any conditions set out in a notice published by HMRC under paragraph (4) of regulation 8.	The authorised person.	£2,500.
Regulation 42(7) Requirement to comply with an obligation that has been transferred as specified in an approval notification under paragraph (7) of regulation 42.	Any person to whom rights and obligations in relation to a relevant non-transit Part 1 procedure are transferred under regulation 42.	£2,500.
Regulation 44 Requirement to keep and preserve records in a form specified in a notice by HMRC and update such records within a specified period after the occurrence of a specified event if required to do so by a notice published under paragraph (3) of regulation 44.	The person specified in paragraph (2) of regulation 44.	£1,000.

Column 1	Column 2	Column 3
Description of relevant Rule/Relevant Rule of a description	Person of a description	Penalty for contravention
Regulation 17 Goods not to be removed from a customs warehouse save as permitted under the Regulations.	The person who removed the goods in contravention of regulation 17.	£2,500.
	The holder of the procedure.	£2,500.
	The person approved by HMRC to operate premises as a place to keep goods declared for a storage procedure.	£2,500.
CTC, TIR and UK Transit [The Customs (Reliefs from a Liability to Import Duty and Miscellaneous Amendments) (EU Exit) Regulations 2020		
Regulation 7(1) Requirement to comply with a relief condition contained in the section of the UK Reliefs document (as defined in regulation 2(1) of the Customs (Reliefs from a Liability to Import Duty and Miscellaneous Amendments) (EU Exit) Regulations 2020) in relation to which a claim for relief is granted.	The person to whom the described condition is stated to apply.	£1,000.
Regulation 18 Where a claim for relief is granted and a relief condition applies to a person, if a breach of the condition occurs, the person must notify HMRC as soon as possible of details of the breach including when it occurred or first commenced to occur and make the notification in such form and accompany it with such additional information as HMRC may provide by notice.	The person required to make the notification.	£2,500.][12]
The Customs Transit Procedures (EU Exit) Regulations 2018 [Paragraphs 2(A1) and (4) and 27(A1) and (3) of Schedule 1.		
Requirement to provide, in specified cases, the Master Reference Number (MRN) of the declaration of goods to be brought into the United Kingdom, any transit accompanying document and vehicle registration number of any vehicle in which the goods are carried before the goods enter, or reenter, the United Kingdom.	The carrier.	£2,500.][9]
Paragraphs 4(1)(c), 29(1)(c) of Schedule 1 and paragraph 4(1) of Schedule 3. Requirement to provide a guarantee.	The holder of the procedure.	£2,500.
Paragraphs 4(1)(a) and 29(1)(a) of Schedule 1 and paragraph (8)(1) of Schedule 3. Requirement to present the goods intact and with the required information at the HMRC customs office of destination in the United Kingdom within the applicable time-limit and in compliance with the measures taken by HMRC and other customs authorities to ensure their identification.	The holder of the procedure.	£2,500.
Paragraphs 6(1) and 18(1) of Schedule 2. Where goods are moved under a TIR transit procedure, requirement to present on arrival at the HMRC customs office of destination: the goods together with the road vehicle, the combination of vehicles or the container; the TIR Carnet; any information required by HMRC.	The carrier.	£2,500.
	The TIR carnet holder.	£2,500
Paragraphs 3(2), 4(1) and 14(1) of Schedule 2. The TIR Carnet holder is required to submit without delay, goods and the TIR Carnet for the TIR transit procedure at the HMRC customs office of entry or customs office departure, as the case may be.	The TIR carnet holder.	£2,500.
Paragraphs 4(4) and 29(3) of Schedule 1 and paragraph 8(1) of Schedule 3. A carrier or recipient of goods who accepts goods knowing that they are moving under a common or UK transit procedure is also responsible for presentation of the goods intact at the customs office of destination within the time-limit set by the HMRC customs office of departure and in compliance with the measures taken by HMRC and other customs authorities to ensure their identification	A carrier or recipient of goods who accepts the goods knowing they are moving under a common or UK transit procedure.	£2,500.
Paragraphs 4(1)(b) and 29(1)(b) of Schedule 1 and paragraph 8(1) of Schedule 3. Requirement to observe the customs provisions relating to the procedure.	The holder of the procedure.	£2,500.
Paragraph 61(6) of Schedule 1 Requirement to meet the obligation that T2L or T2LF data drawn up in accordance with paragraph 61 must contain the endorsement: "signature waived" in place of the authorised issuer's signature.	The authorised issuer.	£2,500.

Column 1	Column 2	Column 3
Description of relevant Rule/Relevant Rule of a description	Person of a description	Penalty for contravention
Paragraphs 4(8) and 29(7) of Schedule 1 and paragraph 8(1) of Schedule 3. Requirement to notify all offences and irregularities related to the common or UK transit procedure to the HMRC customs office of destination.	The holder of the procedure	£2,500.
Paragraphs 2(1) [and (4)][11] and 27(1) [and (3)][11] of Schedule 1. Requirement to present the goods together with the Master Reference Number (MRN) of the declaration [and any transit accompanying document][11] at each HMRC customs office of transit.	The carrier.	£2,500.
Paragraphs 3(1) and 28(1) of Schedule 1 and paragraph 7 of Schedule 3. Other than where this requirement is waived or not required under these regulations, the carrier must present goods together with the MRN to HMRC under the circumstances described in paragraph 3(1) or 28(1) of Schedule 1 or paragraph 7 of Schedule 3.	The carrier.	£2,500.
Paragraphs 6(1) and 18(1) of Schedule 2. In the circumstances described in paragraph 8(1) or paragraph 18(1) of Schedule 2, requirement to present to the HMRC customs office within official opening hours unless otherwise agreed by HMRC: the goods together with the road vehicle, the combination of vehicles or the container, the TIR Carnet and any information required by HMRC.	The carrier.	£2,500.
Paragraphs 5(1), 30(1) of Schedule 1 and paragraph 8(2) of Schedule 3. Requirement to present the goods, the MRN of the declaration and any information required by HMRC or other customs authority at the HMRC office of destination during the official opening hours; or, where allowed by the office of destination and at the request of the person concerned, outside the official opening hours or at any other place.	The carrier.	£2,500.
	The holder of the procedure.	£2,500.
Paragraphs 7(1), 31(1) of Schedule 1, paragraphs 8(1) and 20(1) of Schedule 2 and paragraph 8(3) of Schedule 3. Requirement to: immediately notify the HMRC customs office of destination of the arrival of the goods and inform them of any irregularities or incidents that occurred during transport; wait for permission from the HMRC customs office of destination before unloading the goods; enter, after unloading, the results of the inspection and any other relevant information relating to the unloading into the authorised consignee's records without delay; notify HMRC at that HMRC customs office of destination of the results of the inspection of the goods and inform them of any irregularities no later than the third day following the day on which permission was received to unload the goods.	The authorised consignee.	£2,500
Paragraphs 8(2) and 20(2) of Schedule 2. The authorised consignee must ensure that the TIR Carnet for the TIR transit procedure is presented, within the time-limit laid down in the authorisation, at the HMRC customs office of destination for the purposes of terminating the TIR transit procedure in accordance with paragraph 7(1) of Schedule 2.	The authorised consignee.	£2,500.
Paragraph 63 of Schedule 1. Requirement to comply with business continuity procedure in a public notice made under paragraph 63 of Schedule 1.	The holder of the procedure,	
	the authorised consignee, or	£2,500.]
	the consignee.	
[The Customs (Northern Ireland) (EU Exit) Regulations 2020		
Regulation 16M Where a claim for relief is granted and the claimant becomes aware of the eligibility criterion in regulation 16E(1)(b) not having been met at the time of the grant of the claim, or an error, the claimant must notify HMRC as soon as practicable in accordance with regulation 16M of the Customs (Northern Ireland) (EU Exit) Regulations 2020.	The person required to make the notification.	£2,500.
Regulation 16S Requirement to keep and preserve records, in a form, and for a period, specified in a notice by HMRC.	The claimant and, where relevant, the principal.	£1,000.][17]
[**Unaccompanied Goods**		
The Customs (Import Duty) (EU Exit) Regulations 2018		
Regulation 131C(1)	The person responsible for making the declaration.	£1,000.

Column 1	Column 2	Column 3
Description of relevant Rule/Relevant Rule of a description	Person of a description	Penalty for contravention
Where unaccompanied goods are to be imported on a through train destined for St Pancras International, a declaration in respect of the goods must be made in accordance with regulation 131C(1).		
Regulation 131C(2) The Customs declaration or temporary storage declaration must not be amended or withdrawn save as provided for in the paragraph.	The declarant.	£1,000.
Regulation 131C(4) When required to do so by an HMRC officer, the person who is responsible for providing the service of operating a through train onto which the goods are loaded must produce to the officer evidence that the person took reasonable steps to ensure that paragraph (1) of the regulation had been, or would be, complied with in respect of the goods.	The responsible person.	£1,000.]
[Export declarations		
The Customs (Export) (EU Exit) Regulations 2019		
Regulation 10 For goods intended to be exported in accordance with a procedure for the purposes of the applicable export provisions, an export declaration must be made in accordance with Part 4 of those Regulations.	The person responsible for making the export declaration.	£2,500.
Regulation 11 Where the requirement to make an export declaration under regulation 10 is not met before exportation of the goods, a declaration in accordance with Part 4 of the Regulations must be made as soon the person who exported the goods becomes aware or is notified of the requirement.	The person who exported the goods.	£1,000.
Regulation 30 An export declaration must meet the requirements set out in regulation 30.	The person responsible for making the export declaration.	£2,500.
Simplified export declaration process		
The Customs (Export) (EU Exit) Regulations 2019		
Regulation 32(6) The simplified declaration process must be used in compliance with any condition contained in the authorisation as required by regulation 32(6).	The authorised declarant.	£2,500.
Regulation 33(1), (5) and (6) To comply with the simplified export declaration process an authorised declarant must make the export declaration, in respect of the goods in two parts, comprising— (a) a simplified export declaration, and (b) a supplementary export declaration. Each part must be made within the applicable timescale set out in regulation (5) and (6) as the case may be.	The authorised declarant	£2,500.
Regulation 33(8) An authorised declarant by the end of the period which applies to each respective part must make available for inspection by an HMRC officer any documents required to accompany each respective part.	The authorised declarant.	£2,500.
Regulation 38(1) Requirement to allow access to EIDR electronic system or provide information. An authorised EIDR export declarant must, when required to do so by an HMRC officer: (a) allow an officer access to the EIDR electronic system operated by the declarant; or (b) provide to the officer, from that system, information which the officer reasonably requires in order to verify EIDR records, or other records showing whether or not any goods have been exported which are subject to a prohibition or restriction on export imposed under an enactment.	The authorised EIDR export declarant.	£2,500.
Regulation 40(1), (3), (4) and (5) Save where regulation 40(1) is disapplied by regulation 40(2), goods, in respect of which an export declaration has been made, must be made available, by the person specified in regulation 40(3) ("A") or (where applicable) the person required to do so in regulation 40(4) ("B"), for examination at an appropriate place within a period of 30 days beginning with the day on which the declaration was made and A or (where applicable) B, must give HMRC a notification setting out when and where the goods are to be made so available.	A or (where applicable) B.	£2,500.

Column 1	Column 2	Column 3
Description of relevant Rule/Relevant Rule of a description	Person of a description	Penalty for contravention
Regulation 41(3) To comply immediately or at a specified time with the requirements to: (a) provide information (and documents) to the officer as specified by the officer; (b) handle goods, or otherwise deal with them, in accordance with instructions given by the officer (whether given orally or in any other way), or (c) keep the goods in any place specified by the officer.	The person required by an HMRC officer to comply with the requirement.	£1,000.
[Discharge from a common export procedure		
Regulation 50(3) and (4) A person who exported goods that have been presented to Customs on export is required to inform HMRC that the goods have been exported except if they secure that another person ("P") is to do it on their behalf.	The person who exported the goods or (where applicable) P.	£2,500]
Presentation of goods on export		
The Customs (Export) (EU Exit) Regulations 2019		
Regulation 51(1), (2) and (3) A person mentioned in regulation 51(2) must give a notification of export of goods to HMRC, except where another person mentioned in regulation 51(2) has given it, or is deemed to have given it, prior to the export of the goods and in compliance with regulation 51(4) to (6).	A person mentioned in regulation 51(2) who is required to give the notification.	£2,500.
Goods exported from RoRo listed locations		
The Customs (Export) (EU Exit) Regulations 2019		
Regulation 54(2) Where goods are carried by RoRo vehicles to, and are exported on RoRo vehicles from, RoRo listed locations goods must be made available for examination— (a) in cases specified in a notice which may be given by HMRC; or (b) if an HMRC officer requires that the goods are available for examination . . .	The person who made the export declaration (E) or (where applicable) a person who has been secured by E to make the goods available for examination on E's behalf.	£2,500.
[Unaccompanied goods		
The Customs (Export) (EU Exit) Regulations 2019		
Regulation 54B(1) Where goods are exported on a through train from St Pancras International goods must be made available for examination— (a) in cases specified in a notice which may be given by HMRC; or (b) if an HMRC officer requires that the goods are available for examination.	The person who made the export declaration (E) or (where applicable) a person who has been secured by E to make the goods available for examination on E's behalf.	£2,500.]
[Chargeable goods Destined for Other Listed Locations		
The Customs (Import Duty) (EU Exit) Regulations 2018		
Regulation 131F(3) Where unaccompanied chargeable goods to be imported are carried by a relevant vehicle which is destined for an other listed location, a declaration in respect of the goods must be made in accordance with regulation 131F(3).	Person responsible for making a declaration	£1,000.
Regulation 131F(4) When required to do so by an HMRC officer, the person who is in possession or control of the goods must produce to the officer evidence that the person took reasonable steps to ensure that regulation 131F(3) had been or would be complied with in respect of the goods.	Person in control or possession of goods	£1,000.][13]
[Goods intended to be carried in a shuttle train		
The Customs (Import Duty) (EU Exit) Regulations 2018		
Regulation 131H(1) Where goods are imported under the circumstances described in regulation 131G, a declaration in respect of the goods must be made in accordance with regulation 131H(1).	Person responsible for making a declaration	£1,000.][14]
Customs agents		
The Customs (Export) (EU Exit) Regulations 2019		
Regulation 57(1) Save where regulation 57(1) is disapplied by regulation 57(2), where a person ("P") appoints another person ("A") to act on P's behalf as a Customs agent, A must disclose that agency in each export declaration which is made by A as agent for P.	A.	£2,500.

Column 1	Column 2	Column 3
Description of relevant Rule/Relevant Rule of a description	Person of a description	Penalty for contravention
Regulation 58(2) Where a person's appointment as a Customs agent is required to be disclosed in an export declaration by regulation 57(1) and the appointment is withdrawn, the principal must disclose the withdrawal by amending each export declaration in which disclosure of the appointment was required to be given.	The principal who was required to disclose the withdrawal of the appointment.	£1,000.
Regulation 58(4) Where an appointment in respect of an export declaration is withdrawn and the principal appoints another person ("C") as a Customs agent in respect of the export declaration, C must comply with regulation 58(2) instead of the principal and disclose with the amendment to the export declaration that C is acting as a Customs agent in respect of the export declaration.	C	£1,000.
Regulation 58(6) Where a Customs agent originally acting in the capacity of— (a) a direct agent becomes an agent acting in the capacity of an indirect agent, or (b) an indirect agent becomes an agent acting in the capacity of a direct agent, the Customs agent must comply with regulation 58(2) instead of the principal and disclose with the amendment to the export declaration the agent's new capacity.	The customs agent to whom regulation 58(6) applies.	£1,000.][7]
[The Customs (Managed Transition Procedure) (EU Exit) Regulations 2019 Regulation 5 Completion of the Customs declaration. Where goods are declared for the free-circulation procedure, the declaration must be completed by the provision to HMRC of further information in respect of the importation of the goods that is specified in a public notice given by HMRC Commissioners, in the manner specified in and otherwise in accordance with provision made in a public notice given by HMRC Commissioners and within the time limit specified in paragraph (4).	The eligible person.	£2,500.
Regulation 10 Completion of the export declaration. Where goods are declared for a common export procedure, the declaration must be completed by the provision to HMRC of further information in respect of the export of the goods that is specified in a public notice given by HMRC Commissioners, in the manner specified in and otherwise in accordance with provision made in a public notice given by HMRC Commissioners and before the end of the period specified in a public notice given by HMRC	The eligible person.	£2,500.][8]

Amendments—[1] After the last entry under the heading "Customs Declarations", entries inserted, entries under heading "Transit" substituted, entries under heading "Provisions concerning bananas" inserted, and entry relating to "Preference" beginning "Article 199" substituted, by the Customs (Contravention of a Relevant Rule) (Amendment) Regulations, SI 2009/3164 regs 2, 4–7 with effect from 24 December 2009.

[2] Entries revoked, substituted and inserted, and in column 1, words substituted and revoked by the Customs (Contravention of a Relevant Rule) (Amendment) Regulations, SI 2015/636 regs 2, 5 with effect from 2 April 2015.

[3] In entries in columns 1 and 2, words substituted; under the heading "Goods brought into the customs territory of the Community (United Kingdom)" entries inserted; under the heading "Presentation of Goods to Customs" entry revoked and entries inserted; under heading "Customs Declarations" entry inserted; and under the heading "Simplified Procedures" entries substituted and entry revoked, by the Customs (Contravention of a Relevant Rule) (Amendment) Regulations, SI 2011/2534 regs 2, 5–12 with effect from 15 November 2011.

[5] The following amendments are made by the Customs (Contravention of a Relevant Rule) (Amendment) (EU Exit) Regulations, SI 2018/1260 regs 2, 5 with effect from IP completion day (11pm UK time on 31 December 2020). Note that the amendments below incorporate the changes made to SI 2018/1260 by SI 2019/148 with effect from 19 February 2019 and by SI 2019/1346 and SI 2020/1088 reg 5.

- The entry headed "sections 20, 22 and 25 of the Act" substituted for entry "Section 20(1B), 22(1B) and 25(1B) of the Act".
- In the entry "section 21(2) of the Act" in column 1, words "from within the customs territory" revoked.
- In the entry headed "section 33(1) of the Act", in column 1, words "an aircraft" substituted and in column 2, words "commander of the aircraft" substituted.
- In the entry headed "section 33(2) of the Act", in column 1, words "or railway customs area and all buildings and goods thereon" inserted, and in column 2, words "or railway customs area" inserted.
- In the entry headed "section 33(3) of the Act", "Obligation to comply with any record keeping requirements contained in section 33(3)(a), (b) and (c) of the Act." substituted for column 1.
- After the entry headed "section 33(3) of the Act", the entry for "Section 33(3A) of the Act" inserted.
- After the entry headed "section 34(1) of the Act", the entry for "Section 34(1A) of the Act" inserted.
- In the entry headed "section 35(1) of the Act", columns 2 and 3 substituted.
- In the entry headed "section 35(6) of the Act", in para (a) in column 1, words "ship or aircraft" substituted, in para (d) in column 1, words "or flight" substituted, and entries in column 2 and 3 substituted.

- In the entry headed "section 35(7) of the Act" entries in column 2 and 3 substituted.
- After the entry headed "section 35(7) of the Act" the entry "Section 35A of the Act" inserted.
- The entry headed "section 64(1) the Act" substituted.
- In the entry headed "section 78(1) of the Act", in column 1, at the end of both paras (a) and (b), words "or any regulations made under section 19(1) of the Taxation (Cross-border Trade) Act 2018" inserted.
- Heading "Goods brought into the customs territory (United Kingdom)" and the entries listed under that heading up to and including the entry headed "Article 137 of the Code" revoked.
- Under the heading "Presentation of Goods to Customs", entries from the entry headed "Regulation 3 of the Importation Regulations" up to and including the entry headed "Article 139(7) of the Code" revoked, after the entry headed "directions made on 2 August 2011 under section 30 of the Act" entry heading "The Customs (Import Duty) (EU Exit) Regulations 2018" inserted, and headings "Article 149 of the Code", "Article 51 of the Code" and "Article 147 of the Code" and the entries listed under those headings revoked.
- Headings "Customs Declarations", "Authorised economic operators", "Simplified and Local Procedures", "Customs Procedure with Economic Impact", "End Use" and "Free Zones" and the entries listed under those headings substituted.
- Heading "Transit, Customs status of goods and Community transit" and the entries under it revoked.
- Heading "Provisions concerning bananas" and the entry under it revoked.
- In the entries under the heading "Information and records", in column 1 of the entry headed "Article 15 of the Code and section 23 of the 1994 Act", words "Article 15 of the Code and" revoked, and words "section 23" substituted, and in column 1 of the entry headed "Article 51 of the Code, the Customs Traders (Accounts and Records) Regulations 1995", in the heading words "Article 51 of the Code," revoked, words "the Customs" substituted and words "Article 51(1) of the Code and by" revoked.
- In the entries under the heading "Assistance in examination of goods", entry headed "articles 239 and 240 of the Implementing Regulation" revoked.
- In the entries under the heading "Preference", entries commencing with the entry headed "articles 64 and 56(2)(d) and (e) of the Code" up to and including the entry headed "articles 52, 65 and 80 of the Council Regulation 1168/2009" revoked.
- Before the entry headed "The Customs and Excise (Personal Reliefs for Special Visitors) Order 1992", the heading "Reliefs" inserted.
- After the entry headed "The Customs and Excise (Personal Reliefs for Special Visitors) Order 1992", the heading "RoRo Vehicles" and the material below it inserted.

Note: Under the heading "RoRo vehicles", new entries were to have been inserted after the entry for regulation 131(6), by the Customs and Excise (Miscellaneous Provisions and Amendments) (EU Exit) Regulations, SI 2019/1215 reg 18. Reg 18 is revoked by the Customs (Transitional Arrangements) (EU Exit) Regulations, SI 2020/1088 reg 9(5) with effect from 29 October 2020 (before the amendments made by reg 18 had come into force).
The table entries revoked previously read as follows—

"Sections 20, 22 and 25 of the Act		
Any condition or restriction attaching to any approval given under section 20, 22 or 25 of the Act.	The approved person.	£1,000."

"Section 64(1) of the Act		
Except as permitted by Customs, no ship or aircraft requiring clearance under this section should depart from a port or customs and excise airport to a destination outside the member States and the Isle of Man, without a valid clearance.	The master of the ship.	£1,000.
	The commander of the aircraft.	£1,000.
Sections 20, 22 and 25 of the Act		
Any condition or restriction attaching to any approval given under section 20, 22 or 25 of the Act.	The approved person.	£1,000."

"Goods brought into the customs territory (United Kingdom)		
Articles 16 and 127 of the Code and Articles 182 and 183 of the Implementing Regulation		
Goods brought into the customs territory to be covered by an entry summary declaration, lodged electronically within the applicable time-limits laid down in Articles 105 to 110 of the Delegated Regulation, at the customs office of entry unless otherwise permitted, containing the particulars set out in Annex B to the Delegated Regulation, and completed in accordance with the explanatory notes to that Annex.	The carrier (as defined in Article 5(40) of the Code) or a person mentioned in paragraph (a) or (b) of Article 127(4) of the Code.	£1,000.
	The person on whom the obligation to provide particulars falls under Article 112 or 113 of the Delegated Regulation.	£1,000.
Article 189 of the Implementing Regulation		

Where an active means of transport entering the customs territory is diverted and is expected to arrive first at a customs office in a member State not indicated in the entry summary declaration, the operator of that means of transport must inform the customs office indicated in the entry summary declaration at the customs office of the first entry of that diversion.	The operator of the active means of transport.	£2,500
Article 133 of the Code and Article 189 of the Implementing Regulation		
The diversion notification must contain the particulars set out in Annex B (dataset G1) to the Delegated Regulation.	The operator of the active means of transport.	£1,000
Article 133 of the Code		
The operator of an active means of transport entering the customs territory or his agent must notify Customs of its arrival at the office of entry.	The operator of the active means of transport.	£2,500
Article 133 of the Code		
The notification of arrival must contain the particulars set out in Annex B (dataset G2) to the Delegated Regulation.	The operator of the active means of transport.	£1,000
Article 145 of the Code		
Non-Union goods presented to Customs must be covered by a temporary storage declaration containing all necessary particulars by the time of presentation of the goods to Customs.	The person who presents the goods.	£1,000
Article 135 of the Code		
Goods must be conveyed without delay to the customs office or other place designated or approved by Customs, or into a free zone, by the route specified and in accordance with any instructions of Customs.	Person bringing the goods into the customs territory.	£1,000
	Any person who assumes responsibility for the carriage of the goods after they have been brought into the customs territory.	£1,000
Article 137 of the Code		
Pursuant to Article 137, to inform without delay the Customs of:		
(a) the inability to comply with Article 135(1) due to unforeseen circumstances or force majeure; and	In respect of Article 137(1) the person bringing the goods into the customs territory or any person acting on behalf of that person.	£1,000
(b) the precise location of the goods where the unforeseen circumstances or force majeure does not result in the total loss of the goods.	In respect of Article 137(2), the person bringing the vessel or aircraft into the customs territory, or in the case of a vessel or aircraft covered by Article 135(6).	£1,000"

"Regulation 3 of the Importation Regulations		
To notify Customs:		
(a) of the arrival of goods in the prescribed form or where approved, by computerised record capable of being printed out; and	The person who brought the goods into the customs territory.	£1,000
(b) to make such notification within three hours of the arrival of the ship at the wharf or aircraft at the airport, or if the customs office is closed within one hour following the reopening of the office.	The person who assumes responsibility for carriage of the goods following entry.	£1,000
Article 134(2) of the Code		
To seek permission of the Customs before examination or sampling of goods in order to determine their tariff classification, customs value or customs status	The person authorised to assign the goods a customs approved treatment or use.	£1,000
	Any person able to present the goods or to have them presented. A person subject to a specific obligation in relation to goods being assigned to a customs approved treatment or use.	£1,000
	Any person doing so on his behalf.	£1,000
Article 140 of the Code		
Goods shall:		

(a) except in the event of imminent danger, only be unloaded or transhipped from the means of transport with the permission of Customs and in places designated or approved or;	The person who brought the goods into the customs territory.	£1,000
	The person who assumes responsibility for the carriage of the goods following entry into the Customs territory.	£1,000
(b) be unloaded and unpacked as required by Customs for the purposes of inspecting the goods and means of transport.	The person responsible for the contravention of the Importation Regulations.	£1,000
Where permission is not required, Customs must immediately be informed accordingly.		
Article 139(7) of the Code		
Goods must not be removed from the place where they have been presented without permission of Customs.	The person who brought the goods into the customs territory.	£1,000
	The person in whose name or on whose behalf the person who brought the goods into that territory acts.	£1,000
	The person who assumed responsibility for carriage of the goods after they were brought into that territory.	£1,000"

"Article 149 of the Code		
Non-Union goods in temporary storage must be placed under a customs procedure or re-exported within 90 days	The person who brought the goods into the customs territory.	£1,000
	The person in whose name or on whose behalf the person who brought the goods into that territory acts.	£1,000
	The person who assumed responsibility for carriage of the goods after they were brought into that territory.	£1,000
Article 147 of the Code		
Goods in temporary storage must be stored only in temporary storage facilities or in other places designated or approved by Customs.	The person bringing the goods into the customs territory	£1,000
	The person who removed the goods from customs supervision.	£1,000
	The person who participated in such removal.	£1,000
	The person required to fulfil the obligations arising from temporary storage.	£1,000"

"Customs Declarations		
Article 158 of the Code		
Goods intended to be placed under a customs procedure, except for the free zone procedure, must be covered by a declaration.	Any person who is able to present the goods in question together with the documents required for the application of the rules governing the procedure.	£2,500

	A specific person (where acceptance of a declaration imposes particular obligations on that specific person).	£2,500
	An agent acting on his behalf.	£2,500
	By a direct agent in the case of a specific person.	£2,500
Articles 162 and 163 of the Code and section 167(3) of the Act		
Declarations must contain all the particulars necessary, and be accompanied by all the documents required, for the application of the provisions governing the customs procedure for which the goods are declared.	Any person who is able to present the goods in question together with the documents required for the application of the rules governing the customs procedure.	£2,500
	A specific person (where acceptance of a declaration imposes particular obligations on that specific person).	£2,500
	By an agent on his behalf.	£2,500
	By a direct agent in the case of a specific person.	£2,500
Article 127(3) of the Code		
The entry summary declaration must be lodged at the customs office of first entry, within a specific time limit, before the goods are brought into the customs territory.	The declarant.	£1,000
Authorised economic operators		
Articles 23(2) and 38 of the Code		
Customs must be informed of any factors, arising after the grant of the status of authorised economic operator, which may influence the continuation or content of the decision to grant that status.	The authorised economic operator.	£2,500.
Simplified and Local Procedures		
Articles 23(1) & 23(2) of the Code and Articles 145 and 150 of the Delegated Regulation		
A person authorised under Article 166(2) of the Code for the regular use of a simplified declaration must: (a) comply with the relevant conditions, meet the relevant criteria and comply with the relevant obligations; (b) inform Customs of all factors arising after authorisation has been granted which may influence its continuation or content.	The authorised person.	£2,500
Article 166 of the Code		
The simplified declaration or the document or documents permitted in lieu of it must: (a) contain at least the particulars for a simplified declaration set out in Chapter 1 of Title XII of Annex A to the Delegated Regulation; (b) be accompanied by all documents which may be required to secure the release of the goods to free circulation; (c) bear a reference to any general release authorisation; (d) where the goods are entered for the relevant procedure by means of an entry in the records, bear the date of such entry. A supplementary declaration must be furnished.	The declarant	£2,500
Customs Procedure with Economic Impact		
Articles 211, 218, 219 and 254 of the Code, Articles 265 to 266 of the Implementing Regulation and Articles 166 to 173 and 239 of the Delegated Regulation	The person to whom the authorisation for use of any customs procedure with economic impact is issued.	£2,500
To comply with a condition (including special conditions governing the procedure in question) of an immediately enforceable binding decision of Customs, in respect of an authorisation or transferred obligations for use of any special procedure referred to in Article 211(1) of the Code. To notify Customs of all factors arising after the authorisation is granted and which may influence its continuation or content.	Any person to whom the conditions or obligations of a customs procedure with economic impact are transferred.	£2,500
	Any authorised person.	£2,500
Article 214 of the Code and Article 178 of the Delegated Regulation		
Appropriate records for goods placed under a special procedure must be kept in a form approved by Customs.	The holder of the authorisation.	£1,000

	The holder of the procedure.	£1,000
	Any person carrying on an activity involving the storage, working or processing of goods, or the sale or purchase of goods in a free zone.	£1,000
End Use		
Article 254 of the Code and Article 239 of the Delegated Regulation		
To comply with a condition of an immediately enforceable binding decision of Customs in respect of an authorisation or a transferred obligation under the end-use procedure referred to in Article 254 of the Code.	The person to whom the authorisation for End Use is issued.	£2,500
Free Zones		
Articles 22, 23, 243 and 244 to 249 of the Code		
To comply with a condition of an immediately enforceable binding decision of Customs in respect of an approval for a free zone.	The person to whom the approval for a free zone has been granted.	£2,500
To keep stock records in the form approved by Customs.	The designated person.	£1,000.
Transit		
Customs status of goods and Community transit		
Article 233(1)(c) of the Code		
To provide a guarantee.	The holder of the transit procedure.	£2,500.
Article 233(1)(a) and (b) and (3) of the Code		
Obligation to:		
(a) present the goods intact and the required information at the customs office of destination within the prescribed time-limit and in compliance with the measures taken by Customs to ensure their identification;	The holder of the transit procedure	£2,500.
	A carrier or recipient of goods who accepts the goods knowing they are moving under Union transit.	£2,500.
(b) observe the provisions relating to the Union transit procedure.	The holder of the transit procedure.	£2,500.
Article 153(2) of the Code and paragraph 25 of Annex 72-04 to the Implementing Regulation		
Obligation for T2L or other commercial documents to contain the endorsement "signature waived" in place of the authorised consignor's signature.	The authorised consignor.	£2,500.
Article 320(4) of the Implementing Regulation as it applies to Article 204 of that Regulation		
Obligation to notify all offences and irregularities to the customs authorities.	The shipping company.	£2,500.
Article 304(1) of the Implementing Regulation		
The goods together with the Movement Reference Number (MRN) of the transit declaration must be presented at each customs office of transit.]	The carrier.	£2,500.
Article 305(1) of the Implementing Regulation		
In the circumstances described in Article 305(1)(a) to (e) (prescribed itinerary changed, seals broken, goods transferred to another means of transport, goods unloaded, or an incident which may affect the ability of the holder of the procedure or carrier to comply with his obligations) of the Implementing Regulation, to present the goods together with the Movement Reference Number (MRN) of the transit declaration to the nearest customs authority of the Member State in whose territory the means of transport is located.	The carrier.	£2,500.
Article 306(1) of the Implementing Regulation		
To present the goods, the Movement Reference Number (MRN) and any information required by Customs at the office of destination during the official opening hours; or, where allowed by the office of destination and at the request and expense of the party concerned, outside the official opening hours or at any other place.	The holder of the transit procedure	£2,500.
	The carrier.	£2,500.
Articles 22 and 233(4) of the Code and Articles 313 to 320 of the Implementing Regulation		

To comply with conditions of authorisation set out by Customs (including conditions for operation and control methods) for the use of simplifications regarding the placing of goods under the Union transit procedure.	The holder of the transit procedure.	£2,500.
	The consignee.	
Article 23(2) of the Code		
Customs must be informed of any factors arising after the decision was taken which may influence its continuation or content.	The authorisation holder.	£2,500.
Article 315 of the Implementing Regulation		
Obligation to:		
(a) notify immediately the customs office of destination of the arrival of the goods and inform it of any irregularities or incidents that occurred during transport;	The authorised consignee.	£2,500.
(b) wait for permission from the customs office of destination before unloading the goods;	The authorised consignee.	£2,500.
(c) enter, after unloading, the results of the inspection and any other relevant information relating to the unloading into the consignee's records without delay;	The authorised consignee.	£2,500.
(d) notify the customs office of destination of the results of the inspection of the goods and inform it of any irregularities no later than the third day following the day on which the consignee receives permission to unload the goods.	The authorised consignee.	£2,500.
Article 291(2) of the Implementing Regulation		
The approval of Customs must be obtained for the acceptance of a paper based transit declaration in the event of a temporary failure within Article 291(1)(b) or (c) of the Implementing Regulation.	The holder of the transit procedure.	£2,500.
Paragraph 4 of Annex 72-04 to the Implementing Regulation		
Following unavailability of the computerised system used by the holder of the procedure for lodging the Union transit declaration data by means of electronic data-processing techniques, or of the electronic connection between that computerised system and the electronic transit system, Customs must be informed when it becomes available again.	The holder of the transit procedure	£2,500.
Paragraph 12 of Annex 72-04 to the Implementing Regulation		
Under the business continuity procedure, to present a transit advice note in the required form to each office of transit.	The carrier.	£2,500.
Paragraph 26 of Annex 72-04 to the Implementing Regulation		
Under the business continuity procedure: (a) the customs office of destination must be informed of the arrival of the goods; (b) copies 4 and 5 of the SAD that accompanied the goods, or the copy of the TAD/TSAD that accompanied the goods, indicating the date of arrival, the condition of any seals affixed and any irregularity, must be delivered to the customs office of destination.	The authorised consignee.	£2,500.
Provisions concerning bananas		
Article 163(3) of the Code, Article 251 of the Implementing Regulation and Article 155 of the Delegated Regulation		
To draw up a banana weighing certificate in accordance with the required procedure and in the required form.	Authorised weigher.	£2,500."

"Assistance in Examination of goods		
Articles 239 and 240 of the Implementing Regulation		
To render Customs:	The declarant.	£1,000
(a) satisfactory assistance to facilitate examination or sampling of goods; and	The person designated by the declarant to be present at the examination of the goods.	£1,000
(b) where necessary, by a deadline set by that authority."		

Articles 64 and 56(2)(d) and (e) of the Code and the agreements therein referred to, which the Union has concluded with certain countries or groups of countries and which provide for the granting of preferential tariff treatment and which require that penalties shall be imposed on any person who draws up or causes to be drawn up a document which contains incorrect information for the purpose of obtaining preferential treatment for products		
Not to draw up, or cause to be drawn up, a document which contains incorrect information for the purpose of obtaining a preferential treatment for products.	Any person drawing up or causing to be drawn up such a document.	£2,500.

Articles 15(2), 18, 19, 162 and 163 of the Code		
Submission of an accurate, authentic proof of origin or equivalent declaration with attached documents in compliance with any obligation under a particular international agreement entered into by the Union applying as part of the law of the United Kingdom in relation to a relevant tax or duty by virtue of directly applicable EU legislation.	The declarant or representative lodging the proof of origin or equivalent declaration with Customs.	£2,500.
Reliefs from customs duty and import VAT		
Articles 8, 16, 33, 48, 52, 64, 71, 72, 78, 79 of Council Regulation 1186/2009		
Not to lend, hire out, transfer or (in the case of Articles 8, 16 and 33) give as security goods admitted duty-free under the Regulation without (a) prior notification to Customs; and (b) payment of any import duties arising.	In respect of non-notification: the person lending, hiring, transferring the goods or giving them as security.	£1,000.
	In respect of non-payment of duties: the person to whom the relief has been given.	£1,000.
Articles 52, 65 and 80 of Council Regulation 1186/2009		
To inform Customs where the conditions for entitlement cease to be fulfilled or where the goods are to be used other than for the permitted purposes.	The institution or organisation in question.	£1,000."

[6] Under the heading "Information and Records" the entry "The Customs (Records) (EU Exit) Regulations 2019" inserted by the Customs (Contravention of a Relevant Rule) (Amendment) (EU Exit) Regulations, SI 2019/148 reg 2(1)-(3) with effect from IP completion day (11pm UK time on 31 December 2020).

[7] At the end of the Schedule, after the entries under the heading "CTC, TIR and UK Transit" the entry "Export declarations" inserted by the Customs (Contravention of a Relevant Rule) (Amendment) (EU Exit) Regulations, SI 2019/148 reg 2(1), (2), (4) with effect from IP completion day (11pm UK time on 31 December 2020). Note that the amendments incorporate the changes made to SI 2019/148 by SI 2019/486 reg 12 with effect from 29 March 2019.
Note: the amendments above incorporate the following amendment of SI 2019/148 regulation 2(4) by SI 2019/1346. In the entry under the heading "Goods exported from RoRo listed locations", words "at a place specified in a notice by HMRC" revoked, and the entry "Unaccompanied goods" inserted, by SI 2019/1346 reg 8 with effect from IP completion day (11pm UK time on 31 December 2020).

[8] Under the heading "Customs agents" the entry "The Customs (Managed Transition Procedure) (EU Exit) Regulations 2019" inserted by the Customs (Managed Transition Procedure) (EU Exit) Regulations, SI 2019/487 reg 12 with effect from IP completion day (11pm UK time on 31 December 2020).

[9] Under the heading "The Customs Transit Procedures (EU Exit) Regulations 2018" the entry "Paragraphs 2(A1) and (4) and 27(A1) and (3) of Schedule 1" inserted by the Customs (Import Duty, Transit and Miscellaneous Amendments) (EU Exit) Regulations, SI 2019/326 reg 4(1), (2)(a) with effect from IP completion day (11pm UK time on 31 December 2020).

[10] Under the heading "Presentation of Goods to Customs", after the entries relating to regulation 4(1), (2) and (3) of the Customs (Import) (EU Exit) Regulations 2018, the entry "Regulation 4(3C) Notification of arrival" inserted by the Taxation (Cross-border Trade) (Miscellaneous Provisions) (EU Exit) Regulations, SI 2019/486 reg 10 with effect from IP completion day (11pm UK time on 31 December 2020). Note that the wording incorporates an amendment made by the Customs (Transitional Arrangements) (EU Exit) Regulations, SI 2020/1088 reg 7(1), (3) with effect from 29 October 2020.

[11] In the entry headed "Paragraphs 2(1) and 27(1) of Schedule 1", in the heading, after "2(1)" words "and (4) inserted, after "27(1)" words "and (3)" inserted, and after "declaration" words "and any transit accompanying document" inserted, by the Customs (Import Duty, Transit and Miscellaneous Amendments) (EU Exit) Regulations, SI 2019/326 reg 4(1), (b) with effect from IP completion day (11pm UK time on 31 December 2020).

[12] Under the heading "reliefs", after the entry for "CTC, TIR and UK Transit", entry "The Customs (Reliefs from a Liability to Import Duty and Miscellaneous Amendments) (EU Exit) Regulations 2020" inserted, by the Customs (Reliefs from a Liability to Import Duty and Miscellaneous Amendments) (EU Exit) Regulations, SI 2020/1431 reg 21 with effect from IP completion day (11pm UK time on 31 December 2020).

[13] Entry "Chargeable goods Destined for Other Listed Locations" inserted by the Customs (Declarations) (Amendment and Modification) (EU Exit) Regulations, SI 2020/1234 reg 5 with effect from IP completion day (11pm UK time on 31 December 2020).

[14] Entry "Goods intended to be carried in a shuttle train" inserted by the Customs (Amendment) (EU Exit) Regulations, SI 2020/1552 reg 9 with effect from IP completion day (11pm UK time on 31 December 2020).

[15] Under the heading "Customs Declarations", after the entry for regulation 12(3) and (4), Entries "Regulation 29C(2)" to "Regulation 29C(9)" inserted, and in the entries for "regulation 32(1)", "regulation 32(2)", and "regulation 37(5) or 37A(8)" words revoked, by the Customs (Transitional Arrangements) (EU Exit) Regulations, SI 2020/1088 reg 5, with effect from 29 October 2020.

[16] Under the heading "Presentation of Goods to Customs", in the entry "Regulation 4(3C)", words substituted for words "or (3AA)", by the Taxation (Cross-border Trade) (Miscellaneous Provisions) (EU Exit) Regulations, SI 2019/486 reg 10(2) (as amended the Customs (Declarations) (Amendment and Modification) (EU Exit) Regulations, SI 2020/1234 reg 6(1), (3)), with effect from IP completion day (11pm UK time on 31 December 2020).

[17] Under the heading "reliefs", entries for The Customs (Northern Ireland) (EU Exit) Regulations 2020 inserted by the Customs (Modification and Amendment) (EU Exit) Regulations, SI 2020/1629 reg 7 with effect from IP completion day (11pm on 31 December 2020).

2004/3148

VALUE ADDED TAX (PLACE OF SUPPLY OF GOODS) ORDER 2004

Made . . . . .30 November 2004
Laid before the House of Commons . . . . .2 December 2004
Coming into force . . . . .1 January 2005

The Treasury, in exercise of the powers conferred on them by sections 7(11) and 9A of the Value Added Tax Act 1994, hereby make the following Order:

PART 1
PRELIMINARY

1 Citation and commencement
(1) This Order may be cited as the Value Added Tax (place of supply of goods) Order 2004 and shall come into force on 1 January 2005.
(2) Part 3 (supplies of gas and electricity) has effect in relation to supplies made on or after 1 January 2005.

2 Rules for determining place of supply
The rules for determining where a supply of goods is made shall be varied in accordance with the following provisions of this Order.

3 Revocation
The Value Added Tax (Place of Supply of Goods) Order 1992 is hereby revoked.

PART 2
GOODS SUPPLIED ON BOARD SHIPS, AIRCRAFT AND TRAINS

4 Interpretation of Part 2
In this Part—
. . .[1]
"homeward stage" means that part of the return trip which ends at the first stop in the country in which the return trip commenced and which involves only such other stops, if any, as are in [relevant countries][1] where there have previously been stops (in the course of that return trip)
"pleasure cruise" includes a cruise wholly or partly for the purposes of education or training
"point of arrival" means the last place [in a relevant country][1] where it is expected that passengers who have commenced their journey at a place [in a relevant country][1] will terminate their journey or, where there is to follow a leg which will involve a stop in a place [other than in a relevant country][1], the last such place before such leg is undertaken
"point of departure" means the first place [in a relevant country][1] where it is expected that passengers will commence their journey or, where there has been a leg which involved a stop in a place [other than in a relevant country][1], the first such place after such leg has been completed
["relevant country" means Northern Ireland or a member State;][1]
["relevant NI transport" means the transportation of passengers between the point of departure and the point of arrival in the course of which—

   (a) there is a stop in a relevant country other than that in which lies the point of departure; and

   (b) there is no stop in a country which is not a relevant country;][1]
"return trip" means any journey involving two or more countries where it is expected that the means of transport will stop in the country from which it originally departed.

Transitional provisions—Where the Community transport mentioned in SI 2004/3148, Pt 2 (as it had effect immediately before IP completion day) begins before IP completion day; and the goods to which SI 2004/3148 applies are supplied on or after IP completion day, the provisions in SI 2004/3148 concerning the place where the supply of goods is treated as taking place, continue to apply as if that Part had not been amended by SI 2020/1545 (see SI 2020/1545 reg 129).

Amendments—[1] The definition of "Community transport" revoked, in the definition of "homeward stage", words substituted for words "member States", in the definition of "point of arrival" words substituted for words "in the member States", "in a member State" and "outside the member States", in the definition of "point of departure" words substituted for words "in the member States" and "outside the member States", and the definitions of "relevant country" and "relevant NI transport" inserted, by the Value Added Tax (Miscellaneous Amendments, Northern Ireland Protocol and Savings and Transitional Provisions) (EU Exit) Regulations, SI 2020/1545 regs 95, 96 with effect from IP completion day (11pm UK time on 31 December 2020) by virtue of SI 2020/1641 reg 2, Schedule para 11. The definition of "Community transport" previously read as follows—

  ""Community transport" means the transportation of passengers between the point of departure and the point of arrival in the course of which—

   (*a*)   there is a stop in a Member State other than that in which lies the point of departure and

   (*b*)   there is no stop in a country which is not a Member State".

5 Subject to articles 6 to 8, where goods are supplied on board a ship, aircraft or train in the course of a [relevant NI transport]¹, those goods shall be treated as supplied at the point of departure.

Transitional provisions—Where the Community transport mentioned in SI 2004/3148, Pt 2 (as it had effect immediately before IP completion day) begins before IP completion day; and the goods to which SI 2004/3148 applies are supplied on or after IP completion day, the provisions in SI 2004/3148 concerning the place where the supply of goods is treated as taking place, continue to apply as if that Part had not been amended by SI 2020/1545 (see SI 2020/1545 reg 129).

Amendments—¹ Words substituted for words "Community transport" by the Value Added Tax (Miscellaneous Amendments, Northern Ireland Protocol and Savings and Transitional Provisions) (EU Exit) Regulations, SI 2020/1545 regs 95, 97 with effect from IP completion day (11pm UK time on 31 December 2020) by virtue of SI 2020/1641 reg 2, Schedule para 11.

6 Subject to articles 7 and 8, any goods supplied on board a [ship, aircraft or train]¹ in the course of a [relevant NI transport]² for consumption on board shall be treated as supplied outside the [United Kingdom]².

Transitional provisions—Where the Community transport mentioned in SI 2004/3148, Pt 2 (as it had effect immediately before IP completion day) begins before IP completion day; and the goods to which SI 2004/3148 applies are supplied on or after IP completion day, the provisions in SI 2004/3148 concerning the place where the supply of goods is treated as taking place, continue to apply as if that Part had not been amended by SI 2020/1545 (see SI 2020/1545 reg 129).

Amendments—¹ Words substituted for words "ship or aircraft" by the VAT (Place of Supply of Goods) Order, SI 2009/215 arts 2, 3 with effect from 6 April 2009.
² Words substituted for words "Community transport" and "member States" by the Value Added Tax (Miscellaneous Amendments, Northern Ireland Protocol and Savings and Transitional Provisions) (EU Exit) Regulations, SI 2020/1545 regs 95, 98 with effect from IP completion day (11pm UK time on 31 December 2020) by virtue of SI 2020/1641 reg 2, Schedule para 11.

7 For the purposes of this Part—
(*a*) part of transportation where it is expected that a different means of transport will be used shall be treated as separate transportation and
(*b*) the homeward stage of a return trip shall be treated as separate transportation.

8 This Part shall not apply to any goods supplied as part of a pleasure cruise.

PART 3

SUPPLIES OF GAS[,, ELECTRICITY, HEAT OR COOLING]

Amendments—Words in heading substituted for words "and Electricity" by the VAT (Place of Supply of Goods) (Amendment) Order, SI 2010/2923 art 2(1), (2) with effect in relation to supplies made on or after 1 January 2011.

9 Interpretation of Part 3
In this Part—
(*a*) "the Act" means the Value Added Tax Act 1994
(*b*) "dealer" means a person whose principal activity in respect of receiving supplies of relevant goods is the re-selling of those goods and whose own consumption of those goods is negligible
[(*c*) "relevant goods" means—
 (i) gas supplied through a natural gas system situated within [Northern Ireland or]² the territory of a member State or any network connected to such a system,
 [(ia) gas supplied through a natural gas system situated within Great Britain or any network connected to such a system,]²
 (ii) electricity, and
 (iii) heat or cooling supplied through a network;]¹
(*d*) "re-selling" for the purposes of article 9(*b*) does not include—
 (i) re-sale as part of a single composite supply of other goods or services or
 (ii) re-sale as a supply that falls to be disregarded under section 43(1)(*a*) of the Act where relevant goods are to be effectively used and consumed by a member of a VAT group
(*e*) "VAT group" means any bodies corporate treated under sections 43A to 43C of the Act as members of a group.

Amendments—¹ Para (*c*) substituted by the VAT (Place of Supply of Goods) (Amendment) Order, SI 2010/2923 art 2(1), (3) with effect in relation to supplies made on or after 1 January 2011.
² In para (*c*), in definition of "relevant goods", in sub-para (i) words inserted, and sub-para (ia) inserted, by the Taxation (Post-transition Period) Act 2020 s 3, Sch 2 para 11(1), (2) with effect from IP completion day (11pm on 31 December 2020), by virtue of SI 2020/1642 reg 9. Note that these amendments revise and replace previous amendments that were to have been made by SI 2019/59 reg 83(2) before being withdrawn by SI 2020/1545 reg 104(3)).

10 Relevant goods supplied to a dealer shall be treated as supplied at the place where that dealer has established his business or has a fixed establishment to which the relevant goods are supplied or, in the absence of such a place of business or fixed establishment, the place where he has his permanent address or usually resides.

11 Subject to articles 12 and 13, supplies of relevant goods not falling within article 10 above shall be treated as supplied at-
   (a) the place where the recipient of the supply has effective use and consumption of the goods or
   (b) in relation to any part of the goods not consumed, the place where the recipient of the supply has established his business or has a fixed establishment to which the goods are supplied, or in the absence of such place of business or fixed establishment, the place where he has his permanent address or usually resides.

12 Where the recipient of supplies of relevant goods supplies those goods as part of a single composite supply of other goods or services, that constitutes effective use and consumption by him of the goods for the purposes of article 11(a).

13 The supply of relevant goods to a member of a VAT group, where the goods are effectively used and consumed by a member of that group, shall constitute effective use and consumption of the goods for the purposes of article 11(a).

14 [(1)] For the purposes of section 9A of the Act (reverse charge on [certain goods][1] supplied by persons outside the United Kingdom) a person is outside the United Kingdom if he has established his business or has a fixed establishment outside the United Kingdom or, in the absence of such a place of business or fixed establishment, the place where he has his permanent address or usually resides is outside the United Kingdom.
[(2) For the purposes of that section a person is in Great Britain if—
   (a) the person has established their business or has a fixed establishment in Great Britain, or
   (b) in the absence of such a place of business or fixed establishment, the place where the person has their permanent address, or the place where they usually reside, is in Great Britain.
(3) For the purposes of that section a person is in Northern Ireland if—
   (a) the person has established their business or has a fixed establishment in Northern Ireland, or
   (b) in the absence of such a place of business or fixed establishment, the place where the person has their permanent address, or the place where they usually reside, is in Northern Ireland.][2]

Amendments—[1] Words substituted for words "gas and electricity" by the VAT (Place of Supply of Goods) (Amendment) Order, SI 2010/2923 art 2(1), (4) with effect in relation to supplies made on or after 1 January 2011.
[2] Para (1) numbered as such, and paras (2), (3) inserted, by the Taxation (Post-transition Period) Act 2020 s 3, Sch 2 para 11(1), (3) with effect from IP completion day (11pm on 31 December 2020), by virtue of SI 2020/1642 reg 9.

[PART 4
CHAIN TRANSACTIONS

Amendments—Part 4 (regs 15–18) revoked by the Value Added Tax (Miscellaneous Amendments and Revocations) (EU Exit) Regulations, SI 2019/59 reg 83(1), (3) (as amended by SI 2020/1495 reg 19) with effect from IP completion day (11pm UK time on 31 December 2020).

15 Article 16 applies where the same goods are—
   (a) *supplied successively thorough a chain,* and
   (b) *dispatched or transported from one member State to another member State directly from the first supplier in the chain to the last customer in the chain.*[2]][1]

Amendments—[1] Regs 15–18 inserted by the Value Added Tax (Place of Supply of Goods) (Amendment) Order, SI 2019/1507 with effect from 1 January 2020.
[2] Part 4 (regs 15–18) revoked by the Value Added Tax (Miscellaneous Amendments and Revocations) (EU Exit) Regulations, SI 2019/59 reg 83(1), (3) (as amended by SI 2020/1495 reg 19) with effect from IP completion day (11pm UK time on 31 December 2020).

16 Where this article applies—
   (a) *the intra-Community supply is to be treated as the supply that involves the removal of the goods from or to the United Kingdom;* and
   (b) *all supplies made after the intra-Community supply are to be treated as supplied—*
      (i) *outside the United Kingdom in the case of goods removed or to be removed from the United Kingdom to a customer in another member State;* or
      (ii) *within the United Kingdom in the case of goods removed or to be removed from another member State to a customer in the United Kingdom.*[2]][1]

Amendments—[1] Regs 15–18 inserted by the Value Added Tax (Place of Supply of Goods) (Amendment) Order, SI 2019/1507 with effect from 1 January 2020.
[2] Part 4 (regs 15–18) revoked by the Value Added Tax (Miscellaneous Amendments and Revocations) (EU Exit) Regulations, SI 2019/59 reg 83(1), (3) (as amended by SI 2020/1495 reg 19) with effect from IP completion day (11pm UK time on 31 December 2020).

[**17** The "intra-Community supply" is—
   (a) *the supply in the chain that is made to the intermediary operator ("I"),* or

(b) *where I has provided its supplier with the VAT identification number issued to I by the member State from which the goods are dispatched or transported, the supply in the chain that is made by I.²]¹*

Amendments—¹ Regs 15–18 inserted by the Value Added Tax (Place of Supply of Goods) (Amendment) Order, SI 2019/1507 with effect from 1 January 2020.
² Part 4 (regs 15–18) revoked by the Value Added Tax (Miscellaneous Amendments and Revocations) (EU Exit) Regulations, SI 2019/59 reg 83(1), (3) (as amended by SI 2020/1495 reg 19) with effect from IP completion day (11pm UK time on 31 December 2020).

[18 "Intermediary operator" means a supplier within the chain other than the first supplier in the chain who dispatches or transports the goods either itself or through a third party acting on its behalf.²]¹

Amendments—¹ Regs 15–18 inserted by the Value Added Tax (Place of Supply of Goods) (Amendment) Order, SI 2019/1507 with effect from 1 January 2020.
² Part 4 (regs 15–18) revoked by the Value Added Tax (Miscellaneous Amendments and Revocations) (EU Exit) Regulations, SI 2019/59 reg 83(1), (3) (as amended by SI 2020/1495 reg 19) with effect from IP completion day (11pm UK time on 31 December 2020).

[PART 4A
NORTHERN IRELAND CHAIN TRANSACTIONS]

Part 4A (arts 19–23) inserted by the Value Added Tax (Miscellaneous Amendments, Northern Ireland Protocol and Savings and Transitional Provisions) (EU Exit) Regulations, SI 2020/1545 regs 95, 99 with effect from IP completion day (11pm UK time on 31 December 2020) by virtue of SI 2020/1641 reg 2, Schedule para 11.

[19 Article 20 applies where the same goods—
 (a) are supplied successively through a chain, and
 (b) are dispatched or transported either—
  (i) from a member State to Northern Ireland directly from the first supplier in the chain to the last customer in the chain, or
  (ii) from Northern Ireland to a member State directly from the first supplier in the chain to the last customer in the chain.]¹

Amendments—¹ Part 4A (arts 19–23) inserted by the Value Added Tax (Miscellaneous Amendments, Northern Ireland Protocol and Savings and Transitional Provisions) (EU Exit) Regulations, SI 2020/1545 regs 95, 99 with effect from IP completion day (11pm UK time on 31 December 2020) by virtue of SI 2020/1641 reg 2, Schedule para 11.

[20 Where this article applies—
 (a) the NI-EU supply is to be treated as the supply that involves the removal of the goods from or to Northern Ireland; and
 (b) all supplies made after the NI-EU supply are to be treated as supplied—
  (i) outside the United Kingdom in the case of goods removed or to be removed from Northern Ireland to a customer in a member State;
  (ii) within the United Kingdom in the case of goods removed or to be removed from a member State to a customer in Northern Ireland.]¹

Amendments—¹ Part 4A (arts 19–23) inserted by the Value Added Tax (Miscellaneous Amendments, Northern Ireland Protocol and Savings and Transitional Provisions) (EU Exit) Regulations, SI 2020/1545 regs 95, 99 with effect from IP completion day (11pm UK time on 31 December 2020) by virtue of SI 2020/1641 reg 2, Schedule para 11.

[21 The "NI-EU supply" is—
 (a) the supply in the chain that is made to the intermediary operator ("I"), or
 (b) where I has provided its supplier with the relevant VAT identification number issued to I, the supply in the chain that is made by I.]¹

Amendments—¹ Part 4A (arts 19–23) inserted by the Value Added Tax (Miscellaneous Amendments, Northern Ireland Protocol and Savings and Transitional Provisions) (EU Exit) Regulations, SI 2020/1545 regs 95, 99 with effect from IP completion day (11pm UK time on 31 December 2020) by virtue of SI 2020/1641 reg 2, Schedule para 11.

[22 The "relevant VAT identification number" means—
 (a) where the goods are dispatched or transported from a member State, the VAT identification number issued to I by that member State;
 (b) where the goods are dispatched or transported from Northern Ireland, the VAT identification number issued to I by the United Kingdom along with an NI VAT identifier.]¹

Amendments—¹ Part 4A (arts 19–23) inserted by the Value Added Tax (Miscellaneous Amendments, Northern Ireland Protocol and Savings and Transitional Provisions) (EU Exit) Regulations, SI 2020/1545 regs 95, 99 with effect from IP completion day (11pm UK time on 31 December 2020) by virtue of SI 2020/1641 reg 2, Schedule para 11.

[23 "Intermediary operator" means a supplier within the chain other than the first supplier in the chain who dispatches or transports the goods either itself or through a third party acting on its behalf.]¹

Amendments—[1] Part 4A (arts 19–23) inserted by the Value Added Tax (Miscellaneous Amendments, Northern Ireland Protocol and Savings and Transitional Provisions) (EU Exit) Regulations, SI 2020/1545 regs 95, 99 with effect from IP completion day (11pm UK time on 31 December 2020) by virtue of SI 2020/1641 reg 2, Schedule para 11.

2010/2239

VALUE ADDED TAX (SECTION 55A) (SPECIFIED GOODS AND SERVICES AND EXCEPTED SUPPLIES) ORDER 2010

Made . . . .*13 September 2010*
Laid before the House of Commons . . . .*14 September 2010*
Coming into force . . . .*1 November 2010*

1 Citation, commencement and effect
(1) This Order may be cited as the Value Added Tax (Section 55A) (Specified Goods and Services and Excepted Supplies) Order 2010.
(2) This Order shall come into force on 1st November 2010 and has effect in relation to supplies made on or after that date.

2 Revocation
The Value Added Tax (Section 55A) (Specified Goods and Excepted Supplies) Order 2007 is revoked.

3 Interpretation
In this Order—
"the Act" means the Value Added Tax Act 1994;
"allowance" has the meaning given in Article 3 of the Directive;
"certified emission reduction" has the meaning given in Article 3 of the Directive;
["the Directive" means Directive 2003/87/EC of the European Parliament and of the Council establishing a scheme for greenhouse gas emission allowance trading within the Community, as it has effect in EU law as amended from time to time, before and after exit day;][1]
"emission reduction unit" has the meaning given in Article 3 of the Directive;
"operator" has the meaning given in Article 3 of the Directive;
"public electronic communications service" has the meaning given in section 151 of the Communications Act 2003.

Amendments—[1] Definition of "the Directive" substituted by the Value Added Tax (Miscellaneous Amendments and Revocations) (EU Exit) Regulations, SI 2019/59 reg 84(1), (2) with effect from IP completion day (11pm UK time on 31 December 2020). Definition of "the Directive" previously read as follows—
'"the Directive" means Directive 2003/87/EC of the European Parliament and of the Council establishing a scheme for greenhouse gas emission allowance trading within the Community and amending Council Directive 96/61/EC;"

4 The application of section 55A of the Act to specified goods and services
The goods and services specified in articles 5 and 6 are goods and services to which section 55A of the Act (customers to account for tax on supplies of goods or services of a kind used in missing trader . . . [1] fraud) applies.

Amendments—[1] Words "intra-community" revoked by the Value Added Tax (Miscellaneous Amendments and Revocations) (EU Exit) Regulations, SI 2019/59 reg 84(1), (3) with effect from IP completion day (11pm UK time on 31 December 2020).

5 Specified goods
The goods referred to in article 4 are—
　(*a*) a mobile telephone, whether or not it has any function in addition to the transmitting and receiving of spoken messages;
　(*b*) an integrated circuit device, such as a central processing unit and microprocessor unit, in a state prior to integration into an end user product.

6 Specified services
The services referred to in article 4 are—
　(*a*) a transfer of an allowance;
　(*b*) a transfer of an emission reduction unit which can be used by an operator for compliance with the scheme established by the Directive;
　(*c*) a transfer of a certified emission reduction which can be used by an operator for compliance with the scheme established by the Directive.

7 Excepted supplies
For the purposes of section 55A of the Act a supply of a description specified below is an excepted supply—
　(*a*) a supply of specified goods where the value of the supply is less than £5000;

(b) a supply of specified goods where the supply is of a description specified in an order made under section 50A of the Act (margin schemes) and, in accordance with such an order, the supplier opts to account for the VAT chargeable on the supply on the profit margin on the supply instead of by reference to its value;
(c) a supply of a mobile telephone where, at the time a person enters into the agreement to purchase the telephone—
  (i) he enters into an agreement (including the renewal or extension of an existing agreement) with a provider of a public electronic communications service for the supply, in relation to that telephone, of such a service, and
  (ii) that agreement is not one that requires periodical pre-payments in order to use the service ("Pay as You Go");
(d) a transfer or disposal of specified goods for no consideration that is treated as a supply of goods by virtue of paragraph 5(1) of Schedule 4 to the Act.

8 Article 7(a) does not apply to a supply of specified goods where—
(a) the supply is particularised on the same VAT invoice as a supply, or supplies, of other specified goods, and
(b) the total value of the supplies equals or exceeds £5000.

2010/2924

VALUE ADDED TAX (IMPORTED GAS, ELECTRICITY, HEAT AND COOLING) RELIEF ORDER 2010

Made . . . . *8 December 2010*
Laid before the House of Commons . . . . *9 December 2010*
Coming into force . . . . *1 January 2011*

1 Citation, commencement and effect
(1) This Order may be cited as the Value Added Tax (Imported Gas, Electricity, Heat and Cooling) Relief Order 2010.
(2) This Order comes into force on 1st January 2011 and has effect in relation to goods imported on or after that date.

2 Revocation of the Value Added Tax (Imported Gas and Electricity) Relief Order 2004
(revokes the VAT (Imported Gas and Electricity) Relief Order, SI 2004/3147).

3 Relief from value added tax
The VAT chargeable on the importation . . . [1] of—
(a) gas—
  (i) through a natural gas system or any network connected to such a system, or
  (ii) fed in from a vessel transporting gas into a natural gas system or any upstream pipeline network,
(b) electricity, or
(c) heat or cooling supplied through a network,
shall not be payable.

Amendments—[1] Words "from a place outside the member States" revoked by the Value Added Tax (Miscellaneous Amendments and Revocations) (EU Exit) Regulations, SI 2019/59 reg 85 with effect from IP completion day (11pm UK time on 31 December 2020).

2010/2925

VALUE ADDED TAX (REMOVAL OF GAS, ELECTRICITY, HEAT AND COOLING) ORDER 2010

Made . . . . *8 December 2010*
Laid before the House of Commons . . . . *9 December 2010*
Coming into force . . . . *1 January 2011*

1 Citation, commencement and effect
(1) This Order may be cited as the Value Added Tax (Removal of Gas, Electricity, Heat and Cooling) Order 2010.
(2) This Order comes into force on 1st January 2011 and has effect in relation to supplies made on or after that date.

2 Revocation of the Value Added Tax (Removal of Gas and Electricity) Order 2004
(revokes the VAT (Removal of Gas and Electricity) Order, SI 2004/3150)

3 The application of paragraph 6(1) of Schedule 4 to the Value Added Tax Act 1994
Paragraph 6(1) of Schedule 4 (matters to be treated as supply of goods or services) to the Value Added Tax Act 1994 shall not apply to the removal of—
    (*a*) gas through a natural gas system situated within [Northern Ireland or][1] the territory of a member State or any network connected to such a system,
    (*b*) electricity, or
    (*c*) heat or cooling supplied through a network.

Amendments—[1] In para (*a*) words inserted by the Value Added Tax (Miscellaneous Amendments, Northern Ireland Protocol and Savings and Transitional Provisions) (EU Exit) Regulations, SI 2020/1545 regs 100, 101 with effect from IP completion day (11pm UK time on 31 December 2020) by virtue of SI 2020/1641 reg 2, Schedule para 11.

2011/2931

MARD REGULATIONS 2011

Made . . . .*8th December 2011*
Laid before the House of Commons . . . .*9th December 2011*
Coming into force . . . .*1st January 2012*

1 Citation, commencement and interpretation
(1) These Regulations may be cited as the MARD Regulations 2011 and come into force on 1 January 2012.
(2) The Articles mentioned in these Regulations are those of MARD[, except where otherwise indicated][1].
(3) Regulations 2(1), 4(1), 5(1), 6, 7(2), 7(4) and 13(2) each applies to any Article it mentions only where the relevant UK authority is the requested authority in that Article.
(4) Regulations 9, 10(1), 11, 12 and 13(3) each applies to any Article it mentions only where an applicant authority of the United Kingdom is the applicant authority in that Article.
[(5) Obligations imposed by these Regulations on a relevant UK authority by virtue of a request for assistance relating to a claim in respect of which MARD is made applicable between member States and the United Kingdom by virtue of Article 100 of the withdrawal agreement expire at the end of the period for which MARD is made so applicable by Article 100 of the withdrawal agreement.
(6) In these Regulations—
    "Member State" has the same meaning as it has in MARD, as modified by Article 7(1) of the withdrawal agreement;
    "withdrawal agreement" has the meaning given to it by section 39(1) of the European Union (Withdrawal Agreement) Act 2020.][1]

Amendments—[1] In para (2) words inserted, and paras (5), (6) inserted, by the MARD (Amendment) (EU Exit) Regulations, SI 2020/996 reg 3 with effect from IP completion day (11pm on 31 December 2020).

Claims, etc to the United Kingdom (ie relevant UK authority is the requested authority in MARD)

2 Exchange of information
(1) The relevant UK authority must comply with the provision made by Article 5 in relation to the requested authority.
(2) This is subject to Articles 5(2) and 5(3).

3 A United Kingdom public authority that is to make a refund in Article 6 may follow that Article.

4 (1) The relevant UK authority must make and carry out the agreement and arrangements for which Article 7(1) makes provision in relation to the requested authority, to the extent that this will promote the mutual assistance provided for in MARD.
(2) This is subject to Articles 7(3) and 21(2).

5 Enforcement of foreign claims in the UK
(1) The relevant UK authority must comply with the provision made by Articles 8, 9(1), 13(2), 13(3), 13(5), 14(1), 16, 18(4) and 19(3) in relation to the requested authority.
(2) For Article 8: this is subject to Article 8(2).
(3) For Article 16: paragraph (1) and regulation 7 apply in a way that gives effect to Article 17.

6 (1) The relevant UK authority may follow Article 13(4), first sentence.
(2) Where it does so, that authority must follow Article 13(4), second sentence.

7 (1) Articles 12, 14(1), 14(2), 15(2) second and third sub-paragraphs, and 18 apply to a foreign claim.
(2) The relevant UK authority must follow Article 15(2), first sub-paragraph, second sentence.
(3) The provision in paragraph (1) for Articles 12 and 14 also apply where the foreign claim is based on a revised instrument in Article 15(2), third sub-paragraph.

(4) The relevant UK authority may follow Articles 18(1) and 18(2).
(5) The relevant UK authority may follow Article 18(3) where the United Kingdom is the Member State in that Article.

8 In the application of the Finance Act 2009, Schedule 49 to any kind of foreign claim for which the relevant UK authority is the Commissioners, the sum payable in paragraph 1(1) of that Schedule includes a foreign claim.

Claims, etc from the United Kingdom (ie a UK authority is the applicant authority in MARD)

9 Request for notification of certain documents relating to claims
Any applicant authority of the United Kingdom must ensure compliance or comply with the provision made by Articles 8(1) and 8(2) in relation to the applicant authority.

10 Requests for recovery, and conditions governing them
(1) Any applicant authority of the United Kingdom must comply with the provision made by Articles 10(2) and 11 in relation to the applicant authority.
(2) A request in either Article by an applicant authority of the United Kingdom must comply with Article 12(1) (except for the obligations that Article places on the requested Member State). The request may be accompanied by the other documents as mentioned in Article 12(2).

11 Disputes
Any applicant authority of the United Kingdom must comply with the provision made by Articles 14(3) and 14(4), third sub-paragraph, third sentence in relation to the applicant authority.

12 Amendment or withdrawal of UK request for recovery assistance
Any applicant authority of the United Kingdom must comply with the provision made by Article 15 in relation to the applicant authority.

Claims within MARD: general

13 Questions on limitation
(1) Article 19 applies to a foreign claim and to a claim for which the applicant Member State is the United Kingdom, as appropriate.
(2) The relevant UK authority must comply with the provision made by Article 19(3) in relation to the requested authority.
(3) Any applicant authority of the United Kingdom must comply with the provision made by Article 19(3) in relation to the applicant authority.

14 Costs
(1) The relevant UK authority and an applicant authority of the United Kingdom may follow respectively Article 20(2), second sub-paragraph in relation to the requested and applicant authorities, as appropriate to the circumstances.
(2) United Kingdom public authorities must seek to ensure compliance with Article 20(2), first sub-paragraph and with Article 20(3).

15 Standard forms and means of communication
(1) Article 21(1) applies where the United Kingdom is the requested Member State or the applicant Member State in that Article, as appropriate.
(2) This is subject to Article 21(3).

16 Use of languages
(1) The documents mentioned in Article 22(1) sent from the United Kingdom must comply with that Article.
(2) Where those documents are sent to the United Kingdom, the second sentence of that Article applies provided that the United Kingdom public authority concerned has agreed with the sending Member State as mentioned in that sentence.
(3) This paragraph applies in relation to documents covered by Article 22(3) where the relevant UK authority is the requested authority or an applicant authority of the United Kingdom is the applicant authority in that Article.
The former authority may impose, and the latter authority must obey, the requirement in that Article. Either authority may enter the bilateral agreement in that Article.
(4) English is the only official language in cases where the United Kingdom is the requested Member State in Articles 22(1) and 22(3), or is the applicant Member State in Article 22(2).

17 Disclosure of information and documents
(1) Articles 23(1) and 23(6) apply where the United Kingdom is the Member State receiving the information within those Articles.
(2) Any United Kingdom public authority in question must seek to ensure that the United Kingdom complies with Articles 23(3) and 23(5) where the United Kingdom is the Member State providing the information, or is the Member State from which it originates, within those Articles.
(3) The relevant UK authority may follow Article 23(4), first sentence where it is the requested authority in that Article.

(4) An applicant authority of the United Kingdom may follow Article 23(4), first sentence where it is the applicant authority in that Article.
(5) Paragraphs (3) and (4) are subject to the second and third sentences of Article 23(4), and to Article 23(5), being satisfied.

Statutory instruments revoked

18 Statutory instruments revoked

The Regulations in the table in the Schedule are revoked.

SCHEDULE
TABLE OF STATUTORY INSTRUMENTS REVOKED
Regulation 18

(1) Regulations revoked	(2) References
The Recovery of Duties and Taxes Etc Due in Other Member States (Corresponding UK Claims, Procedure and Supplementary) Regulations 2004	SI 2004/674
The Recovery of Agricultural Levies Due in Other Member States Regulations 2004	SI 2004/800
The Recovery of Duties and Taxes Etc Due in Other Member States (Corresponding UK Claims, Procedure and Supplementary) (Amendment) Regulations 2005	SI 2005/1709
The Recovery of Duties and Taxes Etc Due in Other Member States (Corresponding UK Claims, Procedure and Supplementary) (Amendment) Regulations 2007	SI 2007/3508
The Schedule 39 to the Finance Act 2002 and Recovery of Taxes etc Due in Other Member States (Amendment) Regulations 2010	SI 2010/792

2011/3036

POSTAL PACKETS (REVENUE AND CUSTOMS) REGULATIONS 2011

Made . . . . .19th December 2011
Laid before the House of Commons . . . . .20th December 2011
Coming into force . . . . .10th January 2012

1 Citation and commencement

These Regulations may be cited as the Postal Packets (Revenue and Customs) Regulations 2011 and come into force on 10th January 2012.

2 Definitions

In these Regulations—
"the Act of 1979" means the Customs and Excise Management Act 1979;
"CN22" and "CN23" mean the customs declaration forms for postal items described under those names in the provisions of the Universal Postal Convention and detailed regulations made thereunder which are for the time being in force;
"the Commissioners" means the Commissioners for Her Majesty's Revenue and Customs;
"the customs and excise Acts" has the meaning given by section 1(1) of the Act of 1979;
"the Customs and Excise Acts 1979" has the meaning given by section 1(1) of the Act of 1979;
"customs officer" means an officer of Revenue and Customs;
. . .[1]
"duty" includes value added tax and any other charge on imported goods; and
"exporter" and "importer" have the meanings given by section 1(1) of the Act of 1979.

Amendments—[1] Definition of "the customs territory" revoked by the Customs (Consequential Amendments) (EU Exit) Regulations, SI 2019/140 reg 5(1), (2) with effect from IP completion day (11pm on 31 December 2020) (see EU(WA)A 2020 Sch 5 para 1(1)).
Definition previously read as follows—
" "the customs territory" means the territories which, in accordance with Article 3 of Council Regulation 2913/92/EEC (as amended from time to time), comprise the customs territory of the Community;".

3 Revocations

The Postal Packets (Customs and Excise) Regulations 1986 are revoked.

4 The Postal Packets (Revenue and Customs) Regulations 2007 are revoked.

5 Application of Section 105 of the Postal Services Act 2000

Section 105 of the Postal Services Act 2000 applies to all foreign postal packets.

6 Modifications and Exceptions

In its application to foreign postal packets, the Act of 1979 is subject to the modifications and exceptions made by regulations 7 and 8.

7   Section 159 (power to examine and take account of goods) has effect as if—
   (a) in subsection (2), for "at such place as the Commissioners appoint for the purpose" there were substituted "at the place of importation, the place of exportation or any premises where loading, unloading, sorting, distribution, handling or storage of foreign postal packets (within the meaning of section 105 of the Postal Services Act 2000) takes place", and
   (b) in subsection (8), for the words after "the Commissioners may" there were substituted "accept as the account of those goods for that purpose an account taken by the postal operator concerned or by a person authorised for that purpose by that postal operator.".

8   Paragraph 1(1) of Schedule 3 (notice of seizure) does not apply where the seizure was made in the presence of an officer of the postal operator concerned, authorised for the purpose by that postal operator.

9   In its application to foreign postal packets carried by a universal service provider acting in that capacity, the Act of 1979 is subject to the modifications and exceptions made by regulations 10 to 16.

10 Section 5 (time of importation, exportation, etc) has effect as if—
   (a) subsections (3) and (5) were omitted, and
   (b) for subsection (4) there were substituted—
   "(4) The time of exportation of goods is the time when they are posted (or redirected) in the United Kingdom for transmission to a place outside the [United Kingdom][1].".

Amendments—[1] In reg (10)(b), in the substituted text, words substituted for words "customs territory" by the Customs (Consequential Amendments) (EU Exit) Regulations, SI 2019/140 reg 5(1), (3) with effect from IP completion day (11pm on 31 December 2020) (see EU(WA)A 2020 Sch 5 para 1(1)).

11 Subsection (3) of section 40 (sale of uncleared goods deposited in Queen's warehouse) applies to goods deposited under regulation 22(4) as it applies to goods deposited by a proper officer under that section.

12 Section 43 (duty on imported goods) has effect as if—
   (a) subsection (1) were omitted, and
   (b) in subsection (2)(c), for sub-paragraphs (i) and (ii) there were substituted "those in force at the time when the officer assesses the amount of duty".

13 Section 49 (forfeiture of goods improperly imported) has effect as if subsection (1)(a) were omitted.

14 Section 53 (entry outwards of goods) has effect as if in subsection (8)—
   (a) for "shipped for exportation or as stores or are waterborne for such shipment" there were substituted "exported"; and
   (b) for "shipping or making waterborne" there were substituted "exportation".

15 Section 77 (information in relation to goods imported or exported) applies in relation to any foreign postal packet and its contents as it applies in relation to goods.

16 Section 99 (provisions as to deposit in Queen's warehouse) applies to any goods deposited in a Queen's Warehouse under regulation 22(4) as it applies to goods so deposited under or by virtue of the Customs and Excise Acts 1979.

17 Customs declarations for foreign postal packets carried by a universal service provider
All foreign postal packets carried by a universal service provider—
   (a) posted to the United Kingdom from a place outside the [United Kingdom][1], or
   (b) posted in the United Kingdom to a place outside the [United Kingdom][1],
must be accompanied by a customs declaration in form CN22 or CN23 as appropriate, completed accurately and in full.

Amendments—[1] Words substituted for words "customs territory" in both places by the Customs (Consequential Amendments) (EU Exit) Regulations, SI 2019/140 reg 5(1), (4) with effect from IP completion day (11pm on 31 December 2020) (see EU(WA)A 2020 Sch 5 para 1(1)).

18 Declarations and labelling of packets for exportation
(1) Except where regulation 17 applies, every postal packet containing goods to be exported by post without payment of any duty to which they are subject, or on drawback or repayment of such duty, must—
   (a) be accompanied by a customs declaration fully stating the nature, quantity and value of the goods which it contains or of which it consists and such other particulars as the Commissioners or the postal operator concerned may require,

(b) have affixed to its outer cover in the form and manner required by the Commissioners a label printed with the words "Exported by Post under Revenue and Customs control" or be distinguished in such other manner as the Commissioners may require.

(2) Where the requirements of paragraph (b) have been fulfilled, the postal operator concerned must endorse a certificate of posting on the appropriate document and give it to the sender.

19 Language of declarations

The declarations referred to in regulations 17 and 18 shall be completed legibly in English, French or the language of the destination country.

20 Liability to forfeiture of non-compliant foreign postal packets

(1) Where—
- (a) the contents of a foreign postal packet are not in accordance with the accompanying customs declaration, or
- (b) a foreign postal packet is not accompanied by the prescribed declaration, completed in accordance with these Regulations, or
- (c) a foreign postal packet is not labelled in accordance with these Regulations,

the packet and all its contents shall be liable to forfeiture.

(2) Subject to regulation 8, section 139 (provisions as to detention, seizure and condemnation of goods, etc) of and Schedule 3 to the Act of 1979 shall apply to anything liable to forfeiture under paragraph (1) above as they apply to goods liable to forfeiture under that Act.

21 Production and examination of postal packets

Where a customs officer so requires, in relation to any foreign postal packet, the proper officer of the postal operator concerned must—
- (a) produce the packet to that customs officer; or
- (b) open the packet for examination by that customs officer.

22 Power to require an entry or account and disposal of goods for which no entry or no proper account is given

(1) This regulation applies to goods contained in postal packets which are brought into the United Kingdom . . . [1].

(2) A customs officer may send to the addressee of the postal packet in which the goods are contained, or to any other person who is for the time being the importer of the goods, a notice requiring entry to be made of them or requiring a full and accurate account of them to be delivered to the officer.

(3) Where such entry is not made or such account is not delivered within 28 days of the date of the notice or within such longer period as the Commissioners may allow, then the postal operator concerned shall either—
- (a) return the goods to the sender of the packet in which they were contained or otherwise export them from the customs territory in accordance with any request or indication appearing on the packet, or
- (b) in accordance with arrangements agreed with the Commissioners, destroy the goods, or
- (c) if required by the Commissioners, deliver them to any customs officer.

(4) Where the goods have been delivered to a customs officer under paragraph (3)(c) of this regulation, that officer may deposit the goods in a Queen's warehouse.

(5) This regulation is without prejudice to the Commissioners' powers of seizure if the goods are liable to forfeiture under these Regulations or any other provisions of the customs and excise Acts.

(6) This regulation is without prejudice to the Commissioners' power to refuse customs clearance for the goods.

Amendments—[1] In para (1) words "from outside the customs territory" revoked by the Customs (Consequential Amendments) (EU Exit) Regulations, SI 2019/140 reg 5(1), (5) with effect from IP completion day (11pm on 31 December 2020) (see EU(WA)A 2020 Sch 5 para 1(1)).

23 Payment of duty and other sums

(1) A postal operator must pay over to the Commissioners any sums due to them which are recovered by that postal operator pursuant to section 105(3) of the Postal Services Act 2000.

(2) Where any sums due to the Commissioners and demanded by a postal operator pursuant to section 105(3) of the Postal Services Act 2000 are not paid to that postal operator, that postal operator may, with the agreement of the Commissioners, dispose of the goods contained in the postal packet concerned as that postal operator sees fit.

24 Authorisation of postal operator to perform duties of importer or exporter

The postal operator concerned is authorised to perform, in relation to any postal packet or its contents, such of the duties which the customs and excise Acts require the importer or exporter to perform as the Commissioners may require.

25 The Postal Services Act 2000

Nothing in these Regulations authorises any article to be brought into or sent out of the United Kingdom by post contrary to any provision of the Postal Services Act 2000.

26 UK Border Agency

References in these Regulations to the Commissioners shall include a reference to the Secretary of State by whom general customs functions are exercisable and the Director of Border Revenue.

2012/2907

VALUE ADDED TAX (RELIEF FOR EUROPEAN RESEARCH INFRASTRUCTURE CONSORTIA) ORDER 2012

Made . . . . .20th November 2012
Laid before the House of Commons . . . . .21st November 2012
Coming into force . . . . .1st January 2013

1 Citation, commencement and effect

(1) This Order may be cited as the Value Added Tax (Relief for European Research Infrastructure Consortia) Order 2012 and comes into force on 1st January 2013.
(2) This Order has effect in relation to importations, acquisitions or supplies made on or after 1st January 2013.

2 Relief from value added tax on importation or acquisition of goods

(1) No VAT shall be chargeable on the importation of goods . . . [1], or on the acquisition of goods from [a][1] member State, by an ERIC.
(2) Paragraph (1) applies only where the following requirements are met—
  (a) the statutory seat of the ERIC referred to in Article 8(1) of Council Regulation (EC) No 723/2009 on the Community legal framework for a European Research Infrastructure Consortium is located in [the United Kingdom, a member State or an associated country (within the meaning given by Article 2(c) of that Regulation)][1],
  (b) the goods are for the official use of the ERIC,
  (c) relief is not precluded by the limitations and conditions laid down in the agreement between the members of the ERIC referred to in Article 5(1)(d) of Council Regulation (EC) No 723/2009, and
  (d) a certificate in writing has been given to the Commissioners on behalf of the ERIC that the requirements in paragraphs (a), (b) and (c) are met in relation to the importation or acquisition.
(3) In this article "ERIC" means a body set up as a European Research Infrastructure Consortium by a decision under Article 6(1)(a) of Council Regulation (EC) No 723/2009.

Amendments—[1] In para (1) words "from a place outside the member States" revoked and word substituted for word "another", and in para (2)(a) words substituted for words "a member State", by the Taxation (Post-transition Period) Act 2020 s 3, Sch 2 para 12 with effect from IP completion day (11pm on 31 December 2020), by virtue of SI 2020/1642 reg 9. These amendments supersede amendments that were to have been made by SI 2019/513 reg 7 (which itself is revoked by TPTPA 2020 Sch 2 para 13).

3 Amendment of Schedule 8 to the Value Added Tax Act 1994

(inserts Group 18 (European Research Infrastructure Consortia) into VATA 1994 Sch 8)

2014/1458

VALUE ADDED TAX (SECTION 55A) (SPECIFIED GOODS AND EXCEPTED SUPPLIES) ORDER 2014

Made . . . . .9 June 2014
Laid before the House of Commons . . . . .9 June 2014
Coming into force . . . . .1 July 2014

1 Citation and commencement

(1) This Order may be cited as the Value Added Tax (Section 55A) (Specified Goods and Excepted Supplies) Order 2014.
(2) This Order comes into force on 1st July 2014 and has effect in relation to supplies made on or after that date.

2 Interpretation

In this Order—
  "accredited FIT installation" has the meaning specified in article 2(1) of the Feed-in Tariffs Order 2012;

"the Act" means the Value Added Tax Act 1994;
"directed utility" means a person who is treated as a gas or electricity utility pursuant to a direction made under sub-paragraph 1, or regulations made under sub-paragraph 2, of paragraph 151 of Part 14 of Schedule 6 to the Finance Act 2000;
"specified goods" means the goods specified in article 4;
"supply licence" means —
- (a) a licence granted under section 7A(1) of the Gas Act 1986 (licensing of gas suppliers and gas shippers);
- (b) a licence granted under section 6(1)(d) of the Electricity Act 1989 (licences authorising supply, etc.);
- (c) a licence granted under article 8(1)(c) of the Gas (Northern Ireland) Order 1996 (licences authorising supply, etc.); or
- (d) a licence granted under article 10(1)(c) of the Electricity (Northern Ireland) Order 1992 (licences authorising supply, etc.);

"third party intermediary" means a person who purchases specified goods from a utility in order to make an onward supply of those goods to an end user for consumption, in circumstances where the goods are delivered directly to the end user by the utility;
"utility" has the meaning given by paragraph 150(1) of Part 14 of Schedule 6 to the Finance Act 2000.

3 Application of section 55A of the Act

(1) Section 55A of the Act (customers to account for tax on supplies of goods or services of a kind used in missing trader intra-Community fraud) applies to goods of a description specified in article 4.
(2) The supplies specified in article 5 are excepted supplies for the purposes of section 55A of the Act.

Amendments—[1] In para (1), words "intra-Community" revoked by the Value Added Tax (Miscellaneous Amendments and Revocations) (EU Exit) Regulations, SI 2019/59 reg 86(1), (2) with effect from IP completion day (11pm UK time on 31 December 2020).

4 Specified goods

The goods referred to in article 3(1) are—
- [(a) gas supplied through a natural gas system situated in Great Britain or any network connected to a natural gas system in Great Britain;
- (aa) gas supplied through a natural gas system situated within Northern Ireland or the territory of a member State or any network connected to such a system; and][1]
- (b) electricity.

Amendments—[1] Paras (a), (aa) substituted for previous para (a) by the Value Added Tax (Miscellaneous Amendments, Northern Ireland Protocol and Savings and Transitional Provisions) (EU Exit) Regulations, SI 2020/1545 regs 102, 103 with effect from IP completion day (11pm UK time on 31 December 2020) by virtue of SI 2020/1641 reg 2, Schedule para 11. Para (a) previously read as follows—

> "(a) gas supplied through a natural gas system situated within the territory of a member State or any network connected to such a system; and"

5 Excepted supplies

The supplies referred to in article 3(2) are—
- (a) a supply of specified goods made by a person who holds a supply licence in relation to that supply;
- (b) a supply of specified goods by a directed utility to an end user for consumption;
- (c) a supply of specified goods deemed to have been made pursuant to a contract under—
   - (i) paragraph 3(1) or (2) of Schedule 6 to the Electricity Act 1989 (the electricity code: deemed contracts in certain cases);
   - (ii) paragraph 8(1) or (2) of Schedule 2B to the Gas Act 1986 (the gas code: deemed contracts in certain cases);
   - (iii) paragraph 3(1) or (2) of Schedule 6 to the Electricity (Northern Ireland) Order 1992 (the electricity supply code: deemed contracts); or
   - (iv) section 12(1) or (2) of the Energy Act (Northern Ireland) 2011 (gas: deemed contracts for supply in certain cases);
- (d) a supply of specified goods made to a directed utility for the purpose of —
   - (i) consumption by the directed utility, or
   - (ii) onward supply by the directed utility to an end user for consumption;
- (e) a supply of specified goods made by a person who, in relation to that supply, is exempted from the requirement to hold a supply licence under —
   - (i) article 5 of the Gas Exemptions Order 2011 (supplier exemptions);
   - (ii) paragraph 1, 2, 4 or 5 of Schedule 2A to the Gas Act 1986 (exceptions to prohibition on unlicensed activities);
   - (iii) article 7(1) of the Gas (Northern Ireland) Order 1996 (exemptions);

(iv) article 3(1)(c) of, and Schedule 4 to, the Electricity (Class Exemptions from the Requirements for a Licence) Order 2001;
(v) article 9(1) of the Electricity (Northern Ireland) Order 1992 (exemptions); or
(vi) article 3(1)(c) of, and Schedule 3 to, the Electricity (Class Exemptions from the Requirement for a Licence) Order (Northern Ireland) 2013;

(f) a supply to which section 9A of the Act (reverse charge on gas, electricity, heat or cooling supplied by persons outside the United Kingdom) applies;
(g) a supply of electricity made by an accredited FIT installation;
(h) a supply of specified goods—
   (i) to a third party intermediary; or
   (ii) by a third party intermediary;
(i) any other supply of specified goods which is not a wholesale supply.

2016/12

VALUE ADDED TAX (SECTION 55A) (SPECIFIED SERVICES AND EXCEPTED SUPPLIES) ORDER 2016

Made . . . . .7 January 2016
Laid before the House of Commons . . . . .11 January 2016
Coming into force . . . . .1 February 2016

1 Citation, commencement and effect
(1) This Order may be cited as the Value Added Tax (Section 55A) (Specified Services and Excepted Supplies) Order 2016.
(2) This Order comes into force on 1st February 2016 and has effect in relation to supplies made on or after that date.

2 Interpretation
In this Order—
   "the Act" means the Value Added Tax Act 1994;
   "specified services" means the services specified in article 4.

3 Application of section 55A of the Act
(1) Section 55A of the Act (customers to account for tax on supplies of goods or services of a kind used in missing trader . . . [1] fraud) applies to services of a description specified in article 4.
(2) The supplies specified in article 5 are excepted supplies for the purposes of section 55A of the Act.

Amendments—[1]   In para (1), words "intra-community" revoked by the Value Added Tax (Miscellaneous Amendments and Revocations) (EU Exit) Regulations, SI 2019/59 reg 87 with effect from IP completion day (11pm UK time on 31 December 2020).

4 Specified services
(1) The services referred to in article 3(1) are telecommunication services which enable—
   (a) speech communication instantly or with only a negligible delay between the transmission and the receipt of signals; or
   (b) the transmission of writing, images and sounds or information of any nature when provided in connection with services described in sub-paragraph (a).
(2) In this article "telecommunication services" has the meaning given by paragraph [9E(2)][1] of Schedule 4A to the Act.

Amendments—[1]   Reference in para (2) substituted for reference "9(2)" by the Value Added Tax (Place of Supply of Services) (Telecommunication Services) Order, SI 2017/778 art 8 with effect in relation to supplies of services made on or after 1 November 2017.

5 Excepted Supplies
The supplies referred to in article 3(2) are—
   (a) a supply of specified services which is not a wholesale supply;
   (b) a supply of specified services to which section 8 of the Act (reverse charge on supplies received from abroad) applies.

2017/1216

INDIRECT TAXES (NOTIFIABLE ARRANGEMENTS) REGULATIONS 2017

Made . . . . .7 December 2017

Laid before the House of Commons . . . . *8 December 2017*
Coming into force . . . . *1 January 2018*

PART 1
INTRODUCTION

1 Citation and coming into force

These Regulations may be cited as the Indirect Taxes (Notifiable Arrangements) Regulations 2017 and come into force on 1st January 2018.

2 Interpretation

(1) In these Regulations—

"element", in relation to a notifiable arrangement, includes the way in which the arrangement is structured;

"material date" means the following dates, as applicable—

(*a*) where paragraph 11(1) of the Schedule applies to a promoter, the relevant date as defined by paragraph 11(3) of the Schedule;

(*b*) where paragraph 12(1) of the Schedule applies to a promoter, the date on which the promoter first becomes aware of any transaction forming part of the arrangements;

(*c*) where paragraph 17(1) or 18(1) of the Schedule applies to a person, the date on which the person enters into any transaction forming part of any notifiable arrangements;

"the Schedule" means Schedule 17 to the Finance (No 2) Act 2017;

"VAT advantage" means a tax advantage in relation to VAT.

(2) The following have the same meaning in these Regulations as they do in the stated provisions of the Value Added Tax Act 1994—

"belongs", section 9;
"exempt supply", section 31 and Schedule 9;
"reduced rate of VAT", section 29A;
"standard rate of VAT", the rate in force under section 2(1).

PART 2
NOTIFIABLE ARRANGEMENTS – VAT

3 Notifiable arrangements in relation to VAT

The arrangements described in this Part are prescribed as notifiable arrangements in relation to VAT.

4 Retail supplies—splitting and value shifting

(1) An arrangement which meets the following description is a notifiable arrangement.

(2) A person ("A") makes a supply ("supply 1") of goods or services to a retail customer ("C").

(3) A, or another person ("B"), makes a supply ("supply 2") of other goods or services to C.

(4) In relation to supply 1 and supply 2—
  (*a*) condition 1 or 2 is met; and
  (*b*) condition 3 is met.

(5) Condition 1 is met if—
  (*a*) were supply 1 and supply 2 made as a single supply or part of a single supply to C, that single supply would be taxable at the standard or reduced rate of VAT; and
  (*b*) supply 1 or supply 2 is, or both are,—
    (i) taxable at the reduced rate of VAT;
    (ii) a zero-rated supply; or
    (iii) an exempt supply, except a supply which is subject to insurance premium tax at the higher rate.

(6) Condition 2 is met if—
  (*a*) were supply 1 and supply 2 made as a single supply or part of a single supply to C, that single supply would be an exempt supply; and
  (*b*) supply 1 or supply 2 is, or both are,—
    (i) taxable at the standard or reduced rate of VAT; or
    (ii) a zero-rated supply.

(7) Condition 3 is met if it would be reasonable to conclude that two or more of the following apply—
  (*a*) C would not agree to receive supply 1 without also agreeing to receive supply 2;
  (*b*) where supply 2 is made to C by B, B makes the supply with the agreement of A;
  (*c*) supply 1 and supply 2 would be made as a single supply or part of a single supply to C were it not for a VAT advantage which is obtained, or which may be obtained, by making those supplies separately to C;
  (*d*) the business model of A or B (or both) assumes that—
    (i) only A will make supply 1 to C;

(ii) only A or B (as the case may be) will make supply 2 to C; and
(iii) the agreements to make supply 1 and supply 2 will be entered into with C at or about the same time;
(e) of supply 1 and supply 2, at least one is dependent on the other;
(f) were supply 1 and supply 2 made as a single supply or part of a single supply to C, that supply would be made at or about the same price as the price of both supply 1 and supply 2 are made to C;
(g) a higher profit is generated from whichever of supply 1 or supply 2 is the supply which obtains the greater VAT advantage.
(8) In this regulation, "zero-rated supply" has the meaning given by section 30 of the Value Added Tax Act 1994, excluding a supply of goods or services within items 2(d) and (g) and 8 to 13 of Group 12 in Part 2 of Schedule 8 to that Act.

5 Offshore supplies—insurance and finance

(1) An arrangement which meets the following description is a notifiable arrangement.
(2) A person ("D") who carries on business in the United Kingdom makes a supply of services to a person ("E") who belongs outside the [United Kingdom][1] and the supply is an exempt supply, or would be an exempt supply if made in the United Kingdom, by virtue of any item of Group 2 or any of items 1 to 6 and 8 of Group 5.
[(3) E makes a supply of services to a person ("F") who belongs in the United Kingdom and—
   (a) where the place of supply of the services is the United Kingdom, it is an exempt supply; or
   (b) in any other case, it would be an exempt supply if it were made in the United Kingdom.][1]
(4) The supply which D makes to E is used to make the supply by E to F.
(5) For the purposes of determining whether or not an arrangement meets the description in the preceding paragraphs, a supply of services is made by D to E or E to F notwithstanding that the supply—
   (a) is incorporated within a supply made by another person;
   (b) is split into separate supplies; or
   (c) is effected by means of a chain of supplies involving one or more intermediate suppliers.
(6) In this regulation, "Group 2" and "Group 5" have the meanings given by Schedule 9 to the Value Added Tax Act 1994.

Amendments—[1] In para (2), words "EU" substituted, and para (3) substituted, by the Value Added Tax (Miscellaneous Amendments and Revocations) (EU Exit) Regulations, SI 2019/59 reg 88(1), (2) with effect from IP completion day (11pm UK time on 31 December 2020). Para (3) previously read as follows—
   "(3) E makes a supply of services to a person ("F") who belongs in the EU, where the supply would be an exempt supply if made in the United Kingdom."

6 Offshore supplies—relevant business persons

(1) An arrangement which meets the following description is a notifiable arrangement.
(2) A person ("G") who carries on business in the United Kingdom makes a supply of services to a relevant business person ("H") who belongs outside the [United Kingdom][1].
(3) The supply by G to H would be taxable at the standard or reduced rate of VAT were H a relevant business person who belongs in the United Kingdom.
(4) H makes a supply of services to a person ("I") who belongs in the [United Kingdom][1] and the supply—
   [(a) is an exempt supply made in the United Kingdom; or][1]
   (b) is made in the place where H belongs.
(5) The supply which G makes to H is used to make the supply by H to I.
(6) For the purposes of determining whether or not an arrangement meets the description in the preceding paragraphs, a supply of services is made by G to H or H to I notwithstanding that the supply—
   (a) is incorporated within a supply made by another person;
   (b) is split into separate supplies; or
   (c) is effected by means of a chain of supplies involving one or more intermediate suppliers.
(7) In this regulation, "relevant business person" has the meaning given by section 7A(4) of the Value Added Tax Act 1994;

Amendments—[1] In paras (2), (4), word "EU" substituted, and para (4)(a) substituted, by the Value Added Tax (Miscellaneous Amendments and Revocations) (EU Exit) Regulations, SI 2019/59 reg 88(1), (3) with effect from IP completion day (11pm UK time on 31 December 2020). Para (4)(a) previously read as follows—
   "(a) would be an exempt supply if made in the United Kingdom; or"

7 Options to tax—land

(1) An arrangement which meets the following description is a notifiable arrangement.
(2) A person ("J") has exercised the option to tax in respect of land, as provided by paragraph 2 of Part 1 of Schedule 10 to the Value Added Tax Act 1994, and that option has not been revoked as described in paragraph 23 or 24 of that Schedule.
(3) Fewer than 20 years have expired since the date on which the option had effect.

(4) A supply is made in respect of the land by—
   (a) J; or
   (b) a relevant associate of J,
such that the supply is not a taxable supply, by virtue of paragraph 12(1) of Part 1 of Schedule 10 to the Value Added Tax Act 1994.
(5) In this regulation, "relevant associate" has the meaning given by paragraph 3 of Part 1 of Schedule 10 to the Value Added Tax Act 1994.

PART 3
NOTIFIABLE ARRANGEMENTS – GENERAL

8   Notifiable arrangements in relation to any indirect tax
The arrangements described in this Part are prescribed as notifiable arrangements in relation to any indirect tax.

9   Confidentiality—promoters
(1) An arrangement which meets the following description is a notifiable arrangement.
(2) It might reasonably be expected, were it not for this regulation, that a promoter of the arrangement would wish that after the material date—
   (a) the arrangement; or
   (b) any element of the arrangement which obtains, or which may obtain, a tax advantage,
be kept confidential from HMRC or another promoter.
(3) Such a wish may reasonably be expected where—
   (a) it is reasonable to conclude that the promoter intends to continue or to repeat the use after the material date of—
      (i) the arrangement; or
      (ii) any element of the arrangement which obtains, or which may obtain, a tax advantage or substantially the same as such an element; or
   (b) the promoter—
      (i) does not provide supplementary material to a client or to a person who is to be a party to the arrangement; or
      (ii) does provide supplementary material to such a person but discourages the person from retaining it.
(4) For the purposes of paragraph (2), regulation 5 (persons who are not to be treated as promoters by virtue of legal professional privilege) of the Indirect Taxes (Disclosure of Avoidance Schemes) Regulations 2017 is to be ignored.
(5) In paragraph (3)(b), "supplementary material" means any promotional material, data or written professional advice concerning the arrangement.

10   Small and medium–sized enterprises
(1) In regulation 11, "small or medium-sized enterprise" means a small or medium-sized enterprise as defined in this regulation.
(2) A small or medium-sized enterprise means a business carried on by a person where in respect of the relevant period—
   (a) fewer than 250 persons were employed in the business; and
   (b) the turnover of the business was less than £50 million.
(3) Where the relevant period is an accounting period of more or less than 12 months, the amount of the turnover for that period must be increased or decreased proportionately on a time basis, or, if it appears that that method would work unreasonably or unjustly, on a just and reasonable basis.
(4) Where the person who carries on the business—
   (a) is a body corporate and that body and one or more other bodies corporate are eligible to be treated as members of a group; or
   (b) is associated with another person,
in paragraph (2)(a) and (b), "the business" includes the business of each body corporate eligible to be treated as a member of the group or of each associated person, as appropriate.
(5) In this regulation—
   (a) "associated" has the meaning given by paragraph 48 of Schedule 18 to the Finance Act 2016;
   (b) "eligible to be treated as members of a group" has the meaning given by section 43A of the Value Added Tax Act 1994; and
   (c) "relevant period" means—
      (i) the accounting period of the business which applies to the indirect tax in question; or
      (ii) where there is no such accounting period, the period of 12 months,

      which ended immediately before the date on which it is reasonable to conclude that the arrangement to which regulation 11 applies commenced.

11 Confidentiality—other persons
(1) An arrangement which meets the following description is a notifiable arrangement.
(2) In respect of the arrangement there is no promoter but a person ("P")—
   (*a*) is, or is likely to be, a party to the arrangement; or
   (*b*) uses, or is likely to use, the arrangement,
for the purposes of a business carried on by P.
(3) Paragraph (2) does not apply where the business carried on by P is a small or medium-sized enterprise.
(4) It might reasonably be expected, were it not for this regulation, that P would wish that after the material date—
   (*a*) the arrangement; or
   (*b*) any element of the arrangement which obtains, or which may obtain, a tax advantage,
be kept confidential from HMRC.
(5) Such a wish may reasonably be expected where it is reasonable to conclude that P intends—
   (*a*) to continue or to repeat the use after the material date of—
      (i) the arrangement; or
      (ii) any element of the arrangement which obtains, or which may obtain, a tax advantage or substantially the same as such an element; or
   (*b*) to reduce the risk that, were HMRC to have the information which may be required to be provided to it by virtue of the arrangement being a notifiable arrangement, HMRC may—
      (i) investigate or examine any return, claim or declaration made by P or another person to HMRC; or
      (ii) withhold payment of any or all of an amount claimed from HMRC by P or another person.

12 Premium fees
(1) An arrangement which meets the following description is a notifiable arrangement.
(2) It might reasonably be expected, were it not for this regulation, that a promoter ("P") of the arrangement or another person ("Q") would be able to obtain a premium fee in relation to—
   (*a*) the arrangement; or
   (*b*) any element of the arrangement which obtains, or which may obtain, a tax advantage.
(3) In paragraph (2), "premium fee" means a fee which is—
   (*a*) obtained from a person experienced in receiving services of the type provided by P or Q;
   (*b*) to a significant extent attributable to the tax advantage obtained, or which may be obtained, by the arrangement or any element of the arrangement; and
   (*c*) to any extent contingent upon that tax advantage being obtained as a matter of law.

13 Standardised tax products
(1) An arrangement which meets the following description is a notifiable arrangement.
(2) A promoter of the arrangement makes it available for implementation by more than one other person.
(3) It might reasonably be concluded by a person who has studied the arrangement and who has had regard to all relevant circumstances that conditions 1 to 3 are met.
(4) Condition 1 is that the arrangement has standardised or substantially standardised documentation—
   (*a*) the purpose of which is to enable a person other than the promoter to implement the arrangement;
   (*b*) the form of which is determined by the promoter; and
   (*c*) the substance of which does not need to be tailored to any material extent to enable a person to implement the arrangement.
(5) Condition 2 is that—
   (*a*) a person who intends to implement the arrangement must enter into a specific transaction or series of specific transactions; and
   (*b*) the transaction or series of transactions is standardised or substantially standardised in form.
(6) Condition 3 is that—
   (*a*) the main purpose of the arrangement is to enable a person to obtain a tax advantage; or
   (*b*) it is unlikely that a person would enter into the arrangement were it not that the person or another person may obtain a tax advantage.

2018/326

FULFILMENT BUSINESSES REGULATIONS 2018

Made ....7 March 2018
Laid before the House of Commons ....8 March 2018
Coming into force in accordance with regulation 1

PART 1
PRELIMINARY PROVISIONS

1 Citation and commencement
(1) These Regulations may be cited as the Fulfilment Businesses Regulations 2018.
(2) Subject to paragraphs (3) and (4), these Regulations come into force on 1st April 2018.
(3) Parts 3 and 4 come into force on—
    (a) 1st April 2018 in relation to dealing with contraventions mentioned in regulation 14(1)(a), and
    (b) 1st April 2019 for all other purposes.
(4) Part 5 comes into force on 9th March 2018.

2 Interpretation
In these Regulations—
    "application" means an application under regulation 4;
    "customer" means, in relation to [an imported goods][1] fulfilment business, the person referred to in section 48(1)(a) or (b) of the Finance (No 2) Act 2017;
    "notice" means a notice in writing, including writing in electronic form;
    "notice of approval" means, in relation to an application for approval made under regulation 4(1)(a), a notice given by the Commissioners in accordance with regulation 6(1)(a) or (3)(a);
    "specified" means specified in a notice published by the Commissioners for the purposes of these Regulations, and "specify" is construed accordingly.

Amendments—[1] In the definition of "customer" words substituted for words "a third country goods" by the Value Added Tax (Miscellaneous Amendments and Transitional Provisions) (EU Exit) Regulations, SI 2019/1214 reg 7(1), (2) with effect from IP completion day (11pm UK time on 31 December 2020).

3 Applications and other communications with the Commissioners
(1) An application or notification made or given under these Regulations must be made or given—
    (a) in any specified form,
    (b) by any specified method, and
    (c) providing any specified information.
(2) The Commissioners may specify that an application, or other communication with the Commissioners, is to be made electronically.

PART 2
APPROVAL, VARIATION AND REVOCATION PROCEDURE

4 Applications for approval and to vary an approval
(1) An application must be made to the Commissioners—
    (a) for an approval to carry on [an imported goods][1] fulfilment business, or
    (b) to vary any condition or restriction to which an approval is subject.
[(2) An application under paragraph (1)(a) must be made on or before the day on which a person commences carrying on an imported goods fulfilment business.][1]
(3) An application under paragraph (1)(b) cannot be made if the variation is in respect of a decision which—
    (a) is subject to—
        (i) review under section 15C (review by HMRC) or section 15E (review out of time) of the Finance Act 1994, or
        (ii) appeal under section 16 (appeals to a tribunal) of the Finance Act 1994, or
    (b) was confirmed on such review or appeal.

Cross-references—See the Value Added Tax (Miscellaneous Amendments and Transitional Provisions) (EU Exit) Regulations, SI 2019/1214 regs 10–15 for transitional provisions for persons who before IP completion day were not carrying on a "third country goods fulfilment business" but who, as a result of amendments made by the Taxation (Cross-border Trade) Act 2018 Sch 8 para 123 to F(No 2) A 2017 s 48, are carrying on "an imported goods fulfilment business" at IP completion day or commence doing so during the nine-month period following that day.

Amendments—[1] In para (1)(a) words substituted for words "a third country goods", and para (2) substituted, by the Value Added Tax (Miscellaneous Amendments and Transitional Provisions) (EU Exit) Regulations, SI 2019/1214 reg 7(1), (3) with effect from IP completion day (11pm UK time on 31 December 2020). Para (2) previously read as follows—
    "(2) An application under paragraph (1)(a) must be made on or before—

(a) 30th June 2018, in the case of a person carrying on a third country goods fulfilment business as at 31st March 2018,
(b) 30th September 2018, in the case of a person who commences carrying on a third country goods fulfilment business between 1st April 2018 and 30th June 2018, and
(c) the later of 1st October 2018 and the day on which a person commences carrying on a third country goods fulfilment business, in all other cases."

5 Amendment of an application
(1) An application may be amended by notification to the Commissioners at any time before the Commissioners have given notice under regulation 6(1) in relation to that application.
(2) Where such an amendment is notified, the application is treated as made to the Commissioners on the day the notification is received by the Commissioners.

6 Response to an application
(1) The Commissioners must, as soon as reasonably practicable after receiving an application, give notice to the applicant—
   (a) accepting the application,
   (b) rejecting the application, or
   (c) requesting additional information or permission for the Commissioners to inspect any premises from which the applicant will carry on the [imported goods][1] fulfilment business, or both, by or on a specific date.
(2) Where an applicant—
   (a) fails to provide the additional information by the specific date, or
   (b) fails to permit the inspection of premises on the specific date,
the application is treated as withdrawn on that date.
(3) Where the Commissioners have received the additional information requested or inspected the premises, the Commissioners must, as soon as reasonably practicable after the later of the date of receipt or inspection, give notice to the applicant—
   (a) accepting the application, or
   (b) rejecting the application.
(4) Where an application for approval is accepted, the notice under paragraph (1)(a) or (3)(a) must—
   (a) include the unique reference number assigned by the Commissioners to the approved person,
   (b) state the date from which approval has effect,
   (c) contain any condition or restriction imposed by the Commissioners, and
   (d) refer to the obligations set out in Part 3 of these Regulations.
(5) Where an application to vary any condition or restriction is accepted, the notice under paragraph (1)(a) or (3)(a) must—
   (a) state how the approval is varied, and
   (b) state the date on which the variation has effect.
(6) Where an application is rejected, the notice under paragraph (1)(b) or (3)(b) must give the reasons for the rejection.

Amendments—[1] In para (1)(c) words substituted for words "third country goods", and para (2) substituted, by the Value Added Tax (Miscellaneous Amendments and Transitional Provisions) (EU Exit) Regulations, SI 2019/1214 reg 7(1), (4) with effect from IP completion day (11pm UK time on 31 December 2020).

7 Variation or revocation of approval by the Commissioners
Where the Commissioners vary any condition or restriction to which an approval is subject or revoke an approval, the Commissioners must give notice of the variation or revocation to the approved person which—
   (a) states the date on which the variation or revocation has effect, which cannot be earlier than the day after the notice is given,
   (b) in the case of a variation, states how the approval is varied, and
   (c) gives the reasons for the variation or revocation.

PART 3
OBLIGATIONS IMPOSED ON APPROVED PERSONS

8 Customer not meeting UK obligations
(1) An approved person must notify the Commissioners where the approved person knows or has reasonable grounds to suspect that a customer has not met a relevant obligation.
(2) Notification must be given within 30 days beginning with the day on which the approved person first knows or has reasonable grounds to suspect that the customer has not met the relevant obligation.

(3) If after 60 days beginning with the day on which the approved person first knows or has reasonable grounds to suspect that a customer has not met a relevant obligation, the approved person still knows or has reasonable grounds to suspect that the customer is not meeting a relevant obligation, the approved person must cease to carry on [an imported goods][1] fulfilment business with that customer as soon as reasonably practicable.

(4) An approved person must not commence business by way of [an imported goods][1] fulfilment business with a person where the approved person knows or has reasonable grounds to suspect that that person has not met a relevant obligation.

(5) In this regulation and regulation 9, a "relevant obligation" means a VAT or customs duty obligation under legislation in the United Kingdom in relation to [imported goods][1].

Amendments—[1] In paras (3), (4), in each place, words substituted for words "a third country goods", and in para (5), words substituted for words "third country goods", by the Value Added Tax (Miscellaneous Amendments and Transitional Provisions) (EU Exit) Regulations, SI 2019/1214 reg 7(1), (5) with effect from IP completion day (11pm UK time on 31 December 2020).

9 Notice to a customer of UK obligations

(1) An approved person must give a notice to each customer that—
   (*a*) contains specified information relating to relevant obligations,
   (*b*) states that the approved person must notify the Commissioners where the approved person knows or has reasonable grounds to suspect that the customer has not met a relevant obligation,
   (*c*) states that the approved person must as soon as reasonably practicable cease to carry on [an imported goods][1] fulfilment business with that customer if, within 60 days beginning with the day on which the approved person first knows or has reasonable grounds to suspect that the customer has not met a relevant obligation, the approved person knows or has reasonable grounds to suspect that the customer is still not meeting a relevant obligation, and
   (*d*) states that if the approved person fails to comply with the approved person's obligations under regulation 8(1) and (2) (referred to in paragraph (*b*) and (*c*)), the approved person may be liable to a penalty of £3,000 for each failure and may have approval to carry on [an imported goods][1] fulfilment business revoked.

(2) A notice under paragraph (1) must be given to a customer on or before the latest of—
   (*a*) 30th April 2019,
   (*b*) the end of the period of 30 days beginning with the day on which the approved person receives a notice of approval, and
   (*c*) the end of the period of 30 days beginning with the day on which the approved person begins to carry on [an imported goods][1] fulfilment business with that customer.

(3) Where the specified information referred to in paragraph (1)(*a*) is amended by the Commissioners, an approved person must give further notice to all of that person's customers containing the amended specified information within 30 days beginning with the day on which the approved person is notified by the Commissioners of the amendment.

Amendments—[1] In para (1)(*c*), (*d*), in each place, and in para (2)(*c*) words substituted for words "a third country goods", by the Value Added Tax (Miscellaneous Amendments and Transitional Provisions) (EU Exit) Regulations, SI 2019/1214 reg 7(1), (6) with effect from IP completion day (11pm UK time on 31 December 2020).

10 Customer due diligence and record keeping

(1) An approved person must maintain a record of the following information—
   (*a*) the name and contact details of each customer,
   (*b*) the VAT registration number of each customer or, in cases where a customer is exempt from VAT registration, the reference number relating to that customer's exemption from VAT registration issued by the Commissioners,
   (*c*) a description of the type and quantity of the [imported goods][1] stored for each customer,
   (*d*) any import entry number of the [imported goods][1] stored for each customer,
   (*e*) the country to which the [imported goods][1] are delivered from storage,
   (*f*) a copy of the notice required to be given to each customer under regulation 9, and
   (*g*) any specified further information relating to customers and [imported goods][1].

(2) The information in paragraph (1) must be—
   (*a*) preserved for a period of six years beginning on the date the information is first held by the approved person, and
   (*b*) made available for inspection by an officer when required.

(3) In this regulation, "officer" means a person appointed under section 2(1) of the Commissioners for Revenue and Customs Act 2005.

Amendments—[1] In para (1)(*c*), (*d*), (*e*), and (*g*), words substituted for words "third country goods", by the Value Added Tax (Miscellaneous Amendments and Transitional Provisions) (EU Exit) Regulations, SI 2019/1214 reg 7(1), (7) with effect from IP completion day (11pm UK time on 31 December 2020).

11 Verification of a customer's VAT registration number

(1) An approved person must verify the—
   (*a*) VAT registration number, or

(b) reference number relating to a customer's exemption from VAT registration issued by the Commissioners ("VAT exemption reference number")

held in relation to each customer in accordance with any specified verification process.

(2) Verification in relation to each customer, must be—
 (a) carried out for the first time on or before the latest of—
  (i) 30th April 2019,
  (ii) the end of the period of 30 days beginning with the day on which the approved person receives a notice of approval, and
  (iii) the end of the period of 60 days beginning with the day on which the approved person begins to carry on [an imported goods][1] fulfilment business with a customer, and
 (b) repeated in accordance with a specified frequency or, if different, the frequency set out in the notice of approval.

(3) If the verification process does not verify a customer VAT registration number or VAT exemption reference number, an approved person must notify the Commissioners, within 30 days beginning with the day on which the verification is carried out.

Amendments—[1] In para (2)(a)(iii) words substituted for words "a third country goods", by the Value Added Tax (Miscellaneous Amendments and Transitional Provisions) (EU Exit) Regulations, SI 2019/1214 reg 7(1), (8) with effect from IP completion day (11pm UK time on 31 December 2020).

12 Change to registered details

(1) An approved person must notify the Commissioners of any change in the registered details relating to that person.

(2) Notification must be given on or before the later of 30th April 2019 and the end of the period of 30 days beginning with the day on which the change occurred.

(3) In this regulation, "registered details" means such specified information relating to approved persons which is contained in the register of approved persons.

13 Ceasing to carry on [an imported goods][1] fulfilment business

Where an approved person has ceased to carry on [an imported goods][1] fulfilment business, that person must notify the Commissioners within 30 days beginning with the day on which the activity ceased.

Amendments—[1] In the heading, and in the paragraph, words substituted for words "a third country goods", by the Value Added Tax (Miscellaneous Amendments and Transitional Provisions) (EU Exit) Regulations, SI 2019/1214 reg 7(1), (9) with effect from IP completion day (11pm UK time on 31 December 2020).

PART 4
PENALTIES

14 Penalty assessment

(1) The Commissioners may assess a penalty where a person fails to comply with—
 (a) the requirements set out in regulation 4(2),
 (b) any condition or restriction to which an approval is subject, or
 (c) the obligations set out in Part 3.

(2) In this Part references to a "contravention" are to failing to comply with the requirements, conditions, restrictions or obligations mentioned in paragraph (1)(a) to (c).

(3) If the Commissioners assess a penalty they must give notice to the person who is liable for the penalty.

(4) A notice under paragraph (3) must state the contravention in respect of which the penalty is assessed.

(5) An assessment of a penalty under this Part may not be made later than one year after evidence of facts sufficient in the opinion of the Commissioners to indicate the contravention comes to their knowledge.

(6) Two or more contraventions may be treated by the Commissioners as a single contravention for the purposes of assessing a penalty under this Part.

15 Amount of penalty

(1) The amount of the penalty is—
 (a) £500 for a contravention of the requirement imposed under regulation 4(2),
 (b) subject to paragraph (2), £500 for each month that a contravention referred to in sub-paragraph (a) continues,
 (c) £3,000 for each contravention of the obligations imposed under regulation 8, and
 (d) in all other cases, £500 for each contravention.

(2) The total amount of penalties under paragraph (1)(a) and (b) must not exceed £3,000.

16 Special reduction

(1) If the Commissioners think it right because of special circumstances, they may reduce a penalty under this Part.

(2) In paragraph (1), "special circumstances" does not include inability to pay.

17 Reasonable excuse

(1) Liability to a penalty does not arise under this Part if the person who would otherwise be liable for the penalty satisfies the Commissioners or (on an appeal made to the appeal tribunal) the tribunal that there is a reasonable excuse for the contravention.

(2) For the purposes of paragraph (1), reliance on another person to do anything is not a reasonable excuse unless the person otherwise liable for the penalty took reasonable care to avoid the contravention.

(3) In this regulation "appeal tribunal" has the same meaning as in Chapter 2 of Part 1 of the Finance Act 1994.

18 Payment and recovery

(1) A penalty payable under this Part must be paid before the end of the period of 30 days beginning with the day on which notification of the penalty is issued.

(2) A penalty under this Part is recoverable as a debt due to the Crown.

PART 5

19 Revocation

The Fulfilment Businesses (Approval Scheme) Regulations 2018 are revoked.

2018/1228

VALUE ADDED TAX (DISCLOSURE OF INFORMATION RELATING TO VAT REGISTRATION) (EU EXIT) REGULATIONS 2018

Made . . . .*26 November 2018*
Laid before the House of Commons . . . .*27 November 2018*
Coming into force in accordance with regulation 1

1 Citation and commencement

These Regulations may be cited as the Value Added Tax (Disclosure of Information Relating to VAT Registration) (EU Exit) Regulations 2018 and come into force on such day or days as the Treasury may by regulations under section 52 of the Taxation (Cross-border Trade) Act 2018 appoint.

Commencement—1 December 2020 is the day appointed for the coming into force of these Regulations (see SI 2020/1333).

2 Interpretation

In these Regulations—

"HMRC Commissioners" means the Commissioners for Her Majesty's Revenue and Customs; and

"registration number" has the same meaning as in regulation 2(1) (interpretation–general) of the Value Added Tax Regulations 1995.

3 Disclosure of information relating to VAT registration

HMRC Commissioners may disclose the information in regulation 4 to a person in response to an enquiry made to them by that person which specifies a number.

4 The information is—

(a) whether or not the specified number is a registration number which is allocated to a person registered in the register kept by HMRC Commissioners pursuant to section 3(3) of the Value Added Tax Act 1994; and

(b) the name and address of the person to whom the registration number is allocated.

2018/1376

VALUE ADDED TAX (POSTAL PACKETS AND AMENDMENT) (EU EXIT) REGULATIONS 2018

Made . . . .*17th December 2018*
Laid before the House of Commons . . . .*18th December 2018*
Coming into force in accordance with regulation 1(2)

Amendments—These regulations revoked (before coming into force) by the Value Added Tax (Miscellaneous and Transitional Provisions, Amendment and Revocation) (EU Exit) Regulations, SI 2020/1495 reg 26 with effect from IP completion day (11pm UK time on 31 December 2020).

2019/60

VALUE ADDED TAX (ACCOUNTING PROCEDURES FOR IMPORT VAT FOR VAT REGISTERED PERSONS AND AMENDMENT) (EU EXIT) REGULATIONS 2019

Made . . . . 21 January 2019
Laid before the House of Commons . . . . 22 January 2019
Coming into force in accordance with regulation 1.

1 Citation and commencement

These Regulations may be cited as the Value Added Tax (Accounting Procedures for Import VAT for VAT Registered Persons and Amendment) (EU Exit) Regulations 2019 and come into force on such day as the Treasury may by regulations under section 52 of the Taxation (Cross-border) Trade Act 2018 appoint.

Commencement—IP completion day (11pm UK time on 31 December 2020) is the day appointed for the coming into force of these Regulations (see SI 2020/1641 reg 2, Schedule para 2.)

2 Interpretation

In these Regulations—

"the Act" means the Value Added Tax Act 1994;
"the Commissioners" means the Commissioners for Her Majesty's Revenue and Customs;
["import VAT" means value added tax chargeable by virtue of section 1(1)(c) of the Act but not pursuant to any other provision by or under that Act;][2]
"prescribed accounting period" has the meaning given by section 25(1) of the Act (payment by reference to accounting periods and credit for input tax against output tax);
"registered person" means a person registered under Schedule 1, 1A or 3A to the Act;
["relevant goods" means goods imported into the United Kingdom by a registered person which are used or to be used for the purposes of any business carried on by the registered person, but does not include goods which are the subject of a declaration by a qualifying traveller within the meaning of regulation 39B of the Customs (Import Duty) (EU Exit) Regulations 2018;][1]
"return" means a return which is required to be made in accordance with regulation 25 of the VAT Regulations 1995;
"TCTA 2018" means the Taxation (Cross-border Trade) Act 2018;
"tribunal" has the meaning given by section 82 of the Act;
["Union customs legislation" has the meaning given by paragraph 1(8) of Schedule 9ZB to the Act;][2]
"VAT registration number" means the number allocated by the Commissioners to a person for the purposes of registration under Schedule 1, 1A or 3A of the Act.

Commencement—IP completion day (11pm UK time on 31 December 2020) is the day appointed for the coming into force of these Regulations (see SI 2020/1641 reg 2, Schedule para 2.)

Amendments—[1] The definition of "relevant goods" substituted by the Value Added Tax (Miscellaneous and Transitional Provisions, Amendment and Revocation) (EU Exit) Regulations, SI 2020/1495 reg 20(1), (2) with effect from IP completion day (11pm UK time on 31 December 2020). The definition of "relevant goods" previously read as follows—

""relevant goods" means goods imported into the United Kingdom by a registered person used or to be used for the purposes of any business carried on by the registered person but does not include goods which are the subject of a qualifying importation within the meaning of regulation 3 of the Value Added Tax (Postal Packets and Amendment) (EU Exit) Regulations 2018;"

[2] The definition of "import VAT" substituted, and the definition of "Union customs legislation" inserted, by the Value Added Tax (Miscellaneous Amendments, Northern Ireland Protocol and Savings and Transitional Provisions) (EU Exit) Regulations, SI 2020/1545 reg 105(1), (2) with effect from IP completion day (11pm UK time on 31 December 2020) by virtue of SI 2020/1641 reg 2, Schedule para 11. The definition of "import VAT" previously read as follows—

""import VAT" means value added tax chargeable by virtue of section 1(1)(c) of the Act;"

3 Application of these regulations

(1) These Regulations apply to a registered person who is liable for import VAT on relevant goods [(but this is subject to Part 2 of the Value Added Tax (Miscellaneous and Transitional Provisions, Amendment and Revocation) (EU Exit) Regulations 2020)][1].

[(1A) These regulations do not apply to a person who is treated as having imported goods for the purposes of paragraph 4(2) of Schedule 9ZC(b) to the Act.][2]

(2) A person to whom these Regulations apply (P) may have those relevant goods delivered or removed without payment of the VAT chargeable on the importation and may instead account for that VAT in accordance with these Regulations.

(3) The effect of section 16(2) of the Act (application of customs enactments) is modified to the extent that these Regulations make different provision for accounting for import VAT on relevant goods.

Commencement—IP completion day (11pm UK time on 31 December 2020) is the day appointed for the coming into force of these Regulations (see SI 2020/1641 reg 2, Schedule para 2.)

Amendments—[1] Words inserted by the Value Added Tax (Miscellaneous and Transitional Provisions, Amendment and Revocation) (EU Exit) Regulations, SI 2020/1495 reg 20(1), (3) with effect from IP completion day (11pm UK time on 31 December 2020).
[2] Para (1A) inserted by the Value Added Tax (Miscellaneous Amendments, Northern Ireland Protocol and Savings and Transitional Provisions) (EU Exit) Regulations, SI 2020/1545 reg 105(1), (3) with effect from IP completion day (11pm UK time on 31 December 2020) by virtue of SI 2020/1641 reg 2, Schedule para 11.

4 Accounting for import VAT

Subject to regulation 9, P may account for import VAT on relevant goods on the return P is required to make for the prescribed accounting period in which the liability to the import VAT on those goods is incurred if the conditions set out in regulation 5 are met.

Commencement—IP completion day (11pm UK time on 31 December 2020) is the day appointed for the coming into force of these Regulations (see SI 2020/1641 reg 2, Schedule para 2.)

5 (1) Where the relevant goods are declared for the free-circulation procedure for the purposes of Part 1 of TCTA 2018, P's VAT registration number must be shown on that declaration; and
(2) Where the relevant goods are declared for a special customs procedure for the purposes of Part 1 of TCTA 2018, P must in relation to those goods comply with any conditions imposed by or under Part 1 of TCTA 2018 so far as relating to the special customs procedure for which those goods were declared.
[(3) Where the relevant goods are declared for the free circulation procedure for the purposes of Union customs legislation, P's VAT registration number must be shown on that declaration; and
(4) Where the relevant goods are declared for a special procedure for the purposes of Union customs legislation P must in relation to those goods comply with any conditions imposed by or under the Union customs legislation so far as relating to the special procedure for which those goods were declared.][1]

Commencement—IP completion day (11pm UK time on 31 December 2020) is the day appointed for the coming into force of these Regulations (see SI 2020/1641 reg 2, Schedule para 2.)

Amendments—[1] Paras (3) and (4) inserted by the Value Added Tax (Miscellaneous Amendments, Northern Ireland Protocol and Savings and Transitional Provisions) (EU Exit) Regulations, SI 2020/1545 reg 105(1), (4) with effect from IP completion day (11pm UK time on 31 December 2020) by virtue of SI 2020/1641 reg 2, Schedule para 11.

6 P is required, and is presumed to be so required, for the purposes of the Act, to account for import VAT on relevant goods in accordance with these Regulations if, by the last day on which P is required to furnish a return for a prescribed accounting period in which liability to import VAT on those goods is incurred, P has not otherwise accounted for the import VAT.

Commencement—IP completion day (11pm UK time on 31 December 2020) is the day appointed for the coming into force of these Regulations (see SI 2020/1641 reg 2, Schedule para 2.)

7 Estimation of import VAT

Regulation 28 of the Value Added Tax Regulations 1995 (estimation of output tax) applies for the purpose of these Regulations as if the reference to "output tax" in that regulation includes import VAT chargeable on the importation of relevant goods.

Commencement—IP completion day (11pm UK time on 31 December 2020) is the day appointed for the coming into force of these Regulations (see SI 2020/1641 reg 2, Schedule para 2.)

8 Interest in cases of official error

Section 78 of the Act applies for the purposes of these Regulations as if references to "output tax" in both paragraph (1)(a) and paragraph (5)(a) include import VAT chargeable on the importation of relevant goods.

Commencement—IP completion day (11pm UK time on 31 December 2020) is the day appointed for the coming into force of these Regulations (see SI 2020/1641 reg 2, Schedule para 2.)

Modifications—Regulation 8 applies as if the reference to the importation of relevant goods were a reference to a relevant importation.

9 Withdrawal of the option of a registered person to account for and pay import VAT under these Regulations

(1) The Commissioners may direct that a registered person may not account for and pay import VAT as provided for in these Regulations where they consider it necessary to do so for the protection of the revenue.
(2) A direction of the Commissioners under this Regulation must be given by notice in writing to the registered person and takes effect from a date not earlier than the date of the direction.

Commencement—IP completion day (11pm UK time on 31 December 2020) is the day appointed for the coming into force of these Regulations (see SI 2020/1641 reg 2, Schedule para 2.)

10 Appeals

(1) An appeal lies to a tribunal with respect to any of the following—
  (a) a decision as to any liability of the Commissioners to pay interest under regulation 8 or the amount of interest so payable;
  (b) a direction of the Commissioners under regulation 9.

(2) Part 5 of the Act (reviews and appeals), and any order or regulations made under that Part, have effect as if an appeal under this regulation were an appeal which lies to the tribunal under section 83(1) of the Act (but not under any particular paragraph of that subsection).

Commencement—IP completion day (11pm UK time on 31 December 2020) is the day appointed for the coming into force of these Regulations (see SI 2020/1641 reg 2, Schedule para 2.)

11 Where an appeal is against a direction of the Commissioners under regulation 9 the tribunal must not allow the appeal unless it considers that the Commissioners could not reasonably have been satisfied that there were grounds for the direction.

Commencement—IP completion day (11pm UK time on 31 December 2020) is the day appointed for the coming into force of these Regulations (see SI 2020/1641 reg 2, Schedule para 2.)

12 Amendments to the Value Added Tax Regulations 1995
(1) The Value Added Tax Regulations 1995 are amended as follows.
(2) In regulation 2(1) omit the definitions of "datapost packet", "post office", "postal packet" and "universal service provider";
(3) In regulation 32—
  (a) . . . [2]
  (b) insert at the appropriate place in paragraph (3) "(baa) a total of the import VAT which the taxable person is accounting for on his return for that period in accordance with the Value Added Tax (Accounting Procedures for Import VAT for VAT Registered Persons and Amendment) (EU Exit) Regulations 2019,";
(4) In regulation 39—
  [(a) in paragraph (2), omit ", except that the total of the output tax due" to the end except for the final full stop; and][1]
  (b) . . . [2]
(5) In regulation 40(1)—
  (a) at the appropriate place insert "(ba) all import VAT for which he is accounting on that return in accordance with the Value Added Tax (Accounting Procedures for Import VAT for VAT Registered Persons and Amendment) (EU Exit) Regulations 2019"; and
  (b) . . . [2]
(6) Omit regulation 122.

Commencement—IP completion day (11pm UK time on 31 December 2020) is the day appointed for the coming into force of these Regulations (see SI 2020/1641 reg 2, Schedule para 2.)

Amendments—[1] Sub-para (4)(a) substituted by the Value Added Tax (Miscellaneous and Transitional Provisions, Amendment and Revocation) (EU Exit) Regulations, SI 2020/1495 reg 20(1), (4) with effect from IP completion day (11pm UK time on 31 December 2020). Sub-para (4)(a) previously read as follows—

  "(a) in paragraph (2) for "the total of the output tax" to the end substitute "the total of the import VAT to be accounted for on the return for the period shall be entered instead in the box opposite the legend "VAT due in this period on imports accounted for through postponed accounting""; and"

[2] Sub-paras (3)(a), (4)(b) and (5)(b) revoked by the Value Added Tax (Miscellaneous Amendments, Northern Ireland Protocol and Savings and Transitional Provisions) (EU Exit) Regulations, SI 2020/1545 reg 105(1), (5) with effect from IP completion day (11pm UK time on 31 December 2020) by virtue of SI 2020/1641 reg 2, Schedule para 11. Sub-para (3)(a) previously read as follows—

  "(a) omit paragraphs (3)(b) and (4)(b); and"

Sub-para (4)(b) previously read as follows—

  "(b) in paragraph (3) for "(including acquisitions from other member States)" substitute "(including imports)";"

Sub-para (5)(b) previously read as follows—

  "(b) omit paragraph (d)(iii), but not the final "and";"

2019/105

TAXATION (CROSS-BORDER TRADE) ACT 2018 (VALUE ADDED TAX TRANSITIONAL PROVISIONS) (EU EXIT) REGULATIONS 2019

Made . . . . .24 January 2019
Coming into force in accordance with regulation 1(2)

1 Citation and commencement
(1) These Regulations may be cited as the Taxation (Cross-border Trade) Act 2018 (Value Added Tax Transitional Provisions) (EU Exit) Regulations 2019.
(2) These Regulations come into force on such day or days as the Treasury may by regulations under section 52(2) of the Taxation (Cross-border Trade) Act 2018 ("the Act") appoint.

Commencement—IP completion day (11pm UK time on 31 December 2020) is the day appointed for the coming into force of these Regulations (see SI 2020/1641 reg 2, Schedule para 5.)

2 Interpretation
In these Regulations—
  "the Act" has the meaning given by regulation 1(2),

"VATA 1994" means the Value Added Tax Act 1994,
. . .[1]

Commencement—IP completion day (11pm UK time on 31 December 2020) is the day appointed for the coming into force of these Regulations (see SI 2020/1641 reg 2, Schedule para 5.)

Amendments—[1] The definition of "Chapter 7" revoked by the Value Added Tax (Miscellaneous and Transitional Provisions, Amendment and Revocation) (EU Exit) Regulations, SI 2020/1495 reg 21(1), (2) with effect from IP completion day (11pm UK time on 31 December 2020). The definition of "Chapter 7" previously read as follows—

""Chapter 7" means Chapter 7 of Part 15 of the Customs (Import Duty) (EU Exit) Regulations 2018."

3 Transitional provisions etc

(1) The amendments made by Part 3 of the Act (value added tax) do not have effect in relation to supplies made, and acquisitions taking place, before [IP completion day][1].

(2) In determining for the purposes of this regulation the time when a supply or acquisition of goods is made ignore sections 18(4)(a) and 18B(4) of VATA 1994.

(3) In determining for the purposes of this regulation the time when a supply of services is made—
   (a) invoices and other documents provided to any person before [IP completion day][1] are to be disregarded,
   (b) so much (if any) of any payment received by the supplier before [IP completion day][1] as relates to times on or after [IP completion day][1] are to be treated as received on [IP completion day][1], and
   (c) so much (if any) of any payment received by the supplier on or after [IP completion day][1] as relates to times before [IP completion day][1] are to be treated as if they were received before [IP completion day][1].

(4) A payment in respect of any services is to be taken for the purposes of paragraph (3) to relate to the time of the performance of those services.

(5) But where a payment is received in respect of any services the performance of which takes place over a period a part of which falls before [IP completion day][1] and a part of which does not—
   (a) an apportionment is to be made, on a just and reasonable basis, of the extent to which the payment is attributable to so much of the performance of those services as took place before [IP completion day][1];
   (b) the payment is, to that extent to be taken for the purposes of paragraph (3) to relate to a time before [IP completion day][1]; and
   (c) the remainder, if any, of the payment is to be taken for the purposes of paragraph (3) to relate to times on or after [IP completion day][1].

Commencement—IP completion day (11pm UK time on 31 December 2020) is the day appointed for the coming into force of these Regulations (see SI 2020/1641 reg 2, Schedule para 5.)

Amendments—[1] Words "IP completion day" substituted for words "exit day" in each place by the Value Added Tax (Miscellaneous and Transitional Provisions, Amendment and Revocation) (EU Exit) Regulations, SI 2020/1495 reg 21(1), (3) with effect from IP completion day (11pm UK time on 31 December 2020).

[4 The amendments made by Part 3 of the Act do not have effect in relation to a supply of goods dispatched or transported from the territory of the United Kingdom to the territory of a member State of the EU, or vice versa, provided that the dispatch or transport started before IP completion day and ended thereafter.][1]

Commencement—IP completion day (11pm UK time on 31 December 2020) is the day appointed for the coming into force of these Regulations (see SI 2020/1641 reg 2, Schedule para 5.)

Amendments—[1] Reg 4 substituted by the Value Added Tax (Miscellaneous and Transitional Provisions, Amendment and Revocation) (EU Exit) Regulations, SI 2020/1495 reg 21(1), (4) with effect from IP completion day (11pm UK time on 31 December 2020). Reg 4 previously read as follows—

"4

(1) The amendments made by Part 3 of the Act do not have effect in relation to a supply of goods that involves the removal of the goods to the United Kingdom from a member State of the European Union, or an acquisition of goods in pursuance of such a supply, if by reason of Chapter 7 no import duty is chargeable in respect of the goods.

(2) Those amendments do not have effect in relation to a supply of goods that involves the removal of the goods to a member State of the European Union from the United Kingdom if by reason of EU legislation corresponding to Chapter 7 no customs duty is chargeable in respect of the goods."

5 Any reference to a section 55A statement in—
   (a) section 65 of VATA 1994 (inaccuracies in section 55A statement), or
   (b) section 66 of VATA 1994 (failure to submit section 55A statement),
is to be read after [IP completion day][1] as including a reference to a statement which in accordance with regulations under paragraph 2(3) of Schedule 11 to VATA 1994 was required to be submitted before [IP completion day][1].

Commencement—IP completion day (11pm UK time on 31 December 2020) is the day appointed for the coming into force of these Regulations (see SI 2020/1641 reg 2, Schedule para 5.)

Amendments—[1] Words "IP completion day" substituted for words "exit day" in each place by the Value Added Tax (Miscellaneous and Transitional Provisions, Amendment and Revocation) (EU Exit) Regulations, SI 2020/1495 reg 21(1), (5) with effect from IP completion day (11pm UK time on 31 December 2020).

2019/385

CUSTOMS (CROWN DEPENDENCIES CUSTOMS UNION) (EU EXIT) REGULATIONS 2019

Made . . . . *27 February 2019*
Laid before the House of Commons . . . . *28 February 2019*
Coming into force in accordance with regulation 1(2)

1 Citation, commencement and interpretation
(1) These Regulations may be cited as the Customs (Crown Dependencies Customs Union) (EU Exit) Regulations 2019.
(2) These Regulations come into force on such day as the Treasury may appoint.
(3) In these Regulations—
"the Act" means the Taxation (Cross-border Trade) Act 2018;
"established" in a particular place means—
  (a) in the case of an individual, where the individual is resident in that place; or
  (b) in any other case, where the person has—
    (i) a registered office in that place, or
    (ii) a permanent place in that place from which the person carries out activities for which the person is constituted to perform;
"Guernsey" means the Bailiwick of Guernsey;
"Jersey" means the Bailiwick of Jersey.
["the United Kingdom-Crown Dependencies Customs union" means, collectively, the customs union arrangements which were specified in the Exchange of Letters and the Arrangements referred to in the following Orders in Council—
  (a) The Crown Dependencies Customs Union (Isle of Man) (EU Exit) Order 2019
  (b) The Crown Dependencies Customs Union (Guernsey) (EU Exit) Order 2019;
  (c) The Crown Dependencies Customs Union (Jersey) (EU Exit) Order 2019;][1]

Amendments—[1] The entry for "the United Kingdom-Crown Dependencies Customs union" inserted by the Customs (Northern Ireland) (EU Exit) Regulations, SI 2020/1605 reg 40(1), (2) with effect from IP completion day (11pm UK time on 31 December 2020) (see SI 2020/1643).

2 Isle of Man: modifications of UK customs provisions
The Act (as modified by regulation 3) and the provisions referred to in regulations 4 to [6A][1] (as modified by those regulations) shall apply in respect of the following Customs matters—
  (a) the entitlement of persons established in the Isle of Man in relation to Customs procedures,
  (b) the treatment of goods that are imported into the United Kingdom and then moved to the Isle of Man, and
  (c) any other purposes related to customs union arrangements having effect between the United Kingdom and the Isle of Man.

Amendments—[1] Word "6" substituted by the Customs (Reliefs from a Liability to Import Duty and Miscellaneous Amendments) (EU Exit) Regulations, SI 2020/1431 reg 23(1), (2) with effect from IP completion day (11pm UK time on 31 December 2020) (see SI 2020/1643).

3 (1) The Act is modified as follows.
(2) For the purposes of section 33 (meaning of domestic goods), the definition of "domestic goods" shall be read as including goods which are specified as being domestic goods or are regarded as such under equivalent customs legislation in force in the Isle of Man.
(3) For the purposes of paragraph 17(1) of Schedule 1 (customs declarations) where goods under the control of any HMRC officer are located in the Isle of Man—
  (a) the goods shall be treated as remaining subject to the control of an HMRC officer pursuant to that paragraph, and
  (b) any control for the purposes of that paragraph which is exercised by the Isle of Man Treasury on behalf of HMRC shall be treated as if it were exercised by HMRC.
(4) Schedule 2 (special Customs procedures) is modified as follows.
(5) In paragraph 9 (meaning of goods declared for "an inward processing procedure" in the standard form)—
  (a) in sub-paragraph (1)(a), the reference to "[Great Britain]"[1] shall be read as a reference to [Great Britain][1] or the Isle of Man,
  (b) in sub-paragraph (5)—
    (i) the reference to "applicable export provisions" shall be read, where relevant, as a reference to the applicable export provisions in force in the Isle of Man, and
    (ii) the reference to "[Great Britain]"[1] shall be read as a reference to the [Great Britain][1] and the Isle of Man, and
  (c) in sub-paragraph (6)(a), the reference to "[Great Britain]"[1] shall be read as a reference to the [Great Britain][1] and the Isle of Man.

(6) In paragraph 11(a) (meaning of goods declared for "an inward processing procedure" in the supplementary form), the reference to "free circulation in [Great Britain][1]" shall be read as including a reference to any equivalent free circulation procedures in force in the Isle of Man.
(7) In paragraph 15(b) (meaning of goods declared for "a temporary admission procedure")—
  (a) the reference to "the United Kingdom" shall be read as a reference to the United Kingdom or the Isle of Man, and
  (b) the reference to "applicable export provisions" shall be read, where relevant, as a reference to the applicable export provisions in force in the Isle of Man.
(8) In paragraph 18(2) (discharge of special customs procedures: rules applicable to all procedures)—
  (a) in paragraph (a), the reference to "another Customs procedure" shall be read as including, where relevant, a reference to a declaration for an Isle of Man Customs procedure, and
  (b) in paragraph (b), the reference to "HMRC accept the declaration" shall be read as including, where relevant, acceptance of the declaration for an Isle of Man Customs procedure by the Isle of Man Treasury.
(9) In paragraph 19(3) (discharge of special Customs procedures: rules applicable to particular procedures)—
  (a) the reference to "the United Kingdom" shall be read as a reference to the United Kingdom or the Isle of Man, and
  (b) the reference to "applicable export provisions" shall be read, where relevant, as a reference to the applicable export provisions in force in the Isle of Man.

Amendments—[1] In sub-para (5)(a) words substituted for words "processed there" and "processed in the United Kingdom", in sub-paras (5)(b)(ii) and (c), and in para (6), words substituted for words "the United Kingdom", by the Customs (Northern Ireland) (EU Exit) Regulations, SI 2020/1605 reg 40(1), (3) with effect from IP completion day (11pm UK time on 31 December 2020) (see SI 2020/1643).

Note—Omitted regulations are outside the scope of this work.

[6A (1) The Customs (Reliefs from a Liability to Import Duty and Miscellaneous Amendments) (EU Exit) Regulations 2020 are modified as follows.
(2) Subject to paragraph (3), for the purposes of those Regulations, references to the "United Kingdom" or the "UK" in the UK Reliefs document are to be read as including references to the Isle of Man.
(3) Paragraph (2) does not apply to any references to the "United Kingdom" or the "UK" in the UK Reliefs document which are specified in a notice published by HMRC.
(4) HMRC may publish a notice specifying references in the UK Reliefs document for the purposes of paragraph (3).
(5) In this regulation, "UK Reliefs document" has the meaning given by regulation 2 of the Customs (Reliefs from a Liability to Import Duty and Miscellaneous Amendments) (EU Exit) Regulations 2020.][1]

Amendments—[1] Regulation 6A inserted by the Customs (Reliefs from a Liability to Import Duty and Miscellaneous Amendments) (EU Exit) Regulations, SI 2020/1431 reg 23(1), (3) with effect from IP completion day (11pm UK time on 31 December 2020) (see SI 2020/1643).

7 Crown Dependencies: modification of UK customs provisions

(1) Any provisions made under section 24 (rulings as to application of customs tariff or place of origin) of the Act by HMRC Commissioners by public notice shall apply to applications for rulings received from persons intending to import goods from outside any of the territories included in the United Kingdom-Crown Dependencies Customs union into Guernsey, Jersey or the Isle of Man (as the case may be) in the same way as those provisions apply to such applications from persons intending to import goods into the United Kingdom.
(2) . . .[1]
(3) Regulation 97 (single and comprehensive guarantees) of the Customs (Import Duty) (EU Exit) Regulations 2018 shall apply to persons established in any of the territories included in the United Kingdom-Crown Dependencies [Customs union][1] with the following modifications—
  (a) in paragraph (4)(a), the reference to "the United Kingdom" shall be read as a reference to the United Kingdom, the Isle of Man, Guernsey or Jersey, and
  (b) in paragraph (4)(b), the reference to "Customs obligation" shall be read, where relevant, as including a reference to any obligation or requirement imposed by or under equivalent legislation which is in force in the Isle of Man, Guernsey or Jersey.
[(4) In regulation 16E(1)(a)(i) of the Customs (Northern Ireland) (EU Exit) Regulations 2020 (eligibility criteria), the reference to "established in the United Kingdom" shall be read as a reference to established in any of the territories included in the United Kingdom-Crown Dependencies Custom union.][2]

Amendments—[1] Para (2) revoked and in para (3) words substituted for words "Custom union", by the Customs (Northern Ireland) (EU Exit) Regulations, SI 2020/1605 reg 40(1), (5) with effect from IP completion day (11pm UK time on 31 December 2020) (see SI 2020/1643). Para (2) previously read as follows—

"(2) For the purposes of paragraph (1) "the United Kingdom-Crown Dependencies Custom union" means, collectively, the customs union arrangements which were specified in the Exchange of Letters and the Arrangements referred to in the following Orders in Council—
   (a)   The Crown Dependencies Customs Union (Isle of Man) (EU Exit) Order 2019;
   (b)   The Crown Dependencies Customs Union (Guernsey) (EU Exit) Order 2019;
   (c)   The Crown Dependencies Customs Union (Jersey) (EU Exit) Order 2019."

[2] Para (4) inserted by the Customs (Modification and Amendment) (EU Exit) Regulations, SI 2020/1629 reg 8 with effect from IP completion day (11pm on 31 December 2020).

2019/429

TAXATION (CROSS-BORDER TRADE) ACT 2018 (APPOINTED DAYS NO 4 AND TRANSITIONAL PROVISIONS) (MODIFICATION) (EU EXIT) REGULATIONS 2019

Made . . . .*at 11.30 am on 4 March 2019*

1 Citation and Interpretation

(1) These Regulations may be cited as the Taxation (Cross-border Trade) Act 2018 (Appointed Days No 4 and Transitional Provisions) (Modification) (EU Exit) Regulations 2019.

(2) In these Regulations, "the Act" means the Taxation (Cross-border Trade) Act 2018.

2 Appointed Days

The day appointed for the coming into force of section 13 of, and Schedules 4 and 5 to, the Act (excluding paragraphs 22 and 30 in Schedule 4 and paragraphs 22 and 29 in Schedule 5), is at 11.59 am on 4th March 2019.

3 The day appointed for the coming into force of paragraph 1 of Schedule 7 to the Act, so far as it relates to EU trade duties, is immediately after the coming into force of section 3 of the European Union (Withdrawal) Act 2018.

4 Transitional Provisions

The provisions of the Act that are commenced by virtue of regulation 2 have effect subject to the modifications in the Schedule until the Trade Remedies Authority ("the TRA") is established.

5 Following the establishment of the TRA, any provisional decision or determination made by the Secretary of State under Part 3 or 4 of Schedule 4 to the Act or under Part 3 or 4 of Schedule 5 to the Act, as modified by the Schedule to these Regulations, has effect as though it were a recommendation made by the TRA under the corresponding unmodified provision.

6 Following the establishment of the TRA, anything done (or having effect as if done) by the Secretary of State in pursuance of a transitional function has effect as if done by the TRA, so far as that is required for continuing its effect.

7 Following the establishment of the TRA, anything done (or having effect as if done) in relation to the Secretary of State in connection with a transitional function has effect as if done in relation to the TRA, so far as that is required for continuing its effect.

8 If, on the establishment of the TRA, anything is in the process of being done by or in relation to the Secretary of State in connection with a transitional function, it may, following the establishment of the TRA, be continued by or in relation to the TRA.

9 A "transitional function" is a function which—
   (a)   is conferred on the Secretary of State by the Schedule to these Regulations;
   (b)   corresponds to a function that will, following the establishment of the TRA, be exercisable by the TRA under Schedule 4 or 5 to the Act; and
   (c)   following the establishment of the TRA, will not be exercisable by the Secretary of State.

SCHEDULE
TRANSITIONAL PROVISIONS
Regulation 4

PART 1
GENERAL MODIFICATIONS

1 Unless otherwise specified in this Schedule, the provisions coming into force by virtue of regulation 2 have effect as if for "TRA", in each place where this occurs, there were substituted "Secretary of State".

PART 2
MODIFICATIONS TO SECTION 13 OF THE ACT

2   Section 13 of the Act has effect as if—
   (a) in sub-section (1), for "the Trade Remedies Authority ("the TRA")", there were substituted "the Secretary of State"; and
   (b) in sub-sections (2), (3) and (4)—
      (i) for "accepts a recommendation by the TRA", in each place where this occurs, there were substituted "decides to give effect to a preliminary decision"; and
      (ii) for "the recommendation", in each place where it occurs, there were substituted "the preliminary decision".

PART 3
FURTHER MODIFICATIONS TO SCHEDULE 4 TO THE ACT

Modifications to Part 2 (dumping and subsidisation investigations)

3   Paragraph 9 (initiation of a dumping or a subsidisation investigation) of Schedule 4 to the Act has effect as if, for that paragraph, there were substituted—

"9

(1)   The Secretary of State may initiate a dumping or a subsidisation investigation in relation to goods only if—
   (a) the Secretary of State—
      (i) is requested to initiate an investigation in an application made by or on behalf of a UK industry in the goods ("the applicant UK industry"), or
      (ii) in exceptional circumstances, decides that an investigation should be initiated in the absence of such an application,
   (b) the Secretary of State is satisfied that the application contains sufficient evidence (or, if sub-paragraph (1)(a)(i) does not apply, that there is otherwise sufficient evidence), that—
      (i) the goods have been or are being dumped in the United Kingdom and the dumping has caused or is causing injury to a UK industry in those goods, or
      (ii) as the case may be, the goods have been or are being imported into the United Kingdom and are subsidised, and the importation of the subsidised goods has caused or is causing injury to a UK industry in those goods,
   (c) the Secretary of State is satisfied that it appears from that evidence that—
      (i) the volume of dumped goods (whether actual or potential), and the injury, is more than negligible, and the margin of dumping in relation to those goods is more than minimal, or
      (ii) as the case may be, the volume of subsidised goods (whether actual or potential), and the injury, is more than negligible, and the amount of the subsidy in relation to those goods is more than minimal, and
   (d) the market share requirement is met or the Secretary of State waives the requirement.
(2)   The market share requirement is met if—
   (a) in the case of an application under sub-paragraph (1)(a)(i), the Secretary of State is satisfied that the applicant UK industry has a share of the market for like goods for consumption in the United Kingdom (whether produced there or elsewhere) which is sufficient to justify initiating the investigation;
   (b) in the case of a decision under sub-paragraph (1)(a)(ii), the Secretary of State is satisfied that a UK industry in the goods has a share of the market for like goods for consumption in the United Kingdom (whether produced there or elsewhere) which is sufficient to justify initiating the investigation.
(3)   Regulations may make provision about—
   (a) what constitutes or does not constitute an application made by or on behalf of a UK industry for the purposes of sub-paragraph (1)(a)(i);
   (b) when an application is made for the purposes of sub-paragraph (1)(a)(i);
   (c) the information to be contained in such an application;
   (d) the time limit for determining such an application;
   (e) the Secretary of State's assessment of any information obtained or held by the Secretary of State for the purposes of a decision under sub-paragraph (1)(a)(ii);

(f) what constitutes or does not constitute "negligible" and "minimal" for the purposes of sub-paragraph (1)(c)(i) or (ii);
(g) how it is to be determined for those purposes whether those thresholds have been exceeded;
(h) what constitutes or does not constitute "the market for like goods for consumption in the United Kingdom" and a UK industry's "share" of that market for the purposes of sub-paragraphs (1)(d) and (2);
(i) how any of those matters are to be determined for the purposes of sub-paragraphs (1)(d) and (2).

(4) In the case of an application under sub-paragraph (1)(a)(i), if any of the requirements of sub-paragraph (1)(b) to (d) in respect of a dumping or a subsidisation investigation (as the case may be) are not met, the Secretary of State must reject the application and notify the applicant accordingly.

(5) If the requirements of sub-paragraph (1)(a) to (d) in respect of a dumping investigation are met, the Secretary of State must—
(a) in the case of an application under sub-paragraph (1)(a)(i), accept the application,
(b) notify the governments of the relevant foreign countries or territories,
(c) initiate the investigation,
(d) publish notice of the decision to initiate the investigation (including notice of the goods which are the subject of the investigation), and
(e) notify interested parties (see paragraph 32(3)) accordingly.

(6) If the requirements of sub-paragraph (1)(a) to (d) in respect of a subsidisation investigation are met, the Secretary of State must—
(a) in the case of an application under sub-paragraph (1)(a)(i), accept the application,
(b) after the governments of the relevant foreign countries or territories have been invited to participate in consultations, initiate the investigation,
(c) publish notice of the decision to initiate the investigation (including notice of the goods which are the subject of the investigation), and
(d) notify interested parties accordingly.

(7) "Relevant foreign country or territory" means—
(a) in the case of a potential dumping investigation, the exporting foreign country or territory (within the meaning of paragraph 1(2)) of the alleged dumped goods;
(b) in the case of a potential subsidisation investigation, a foreign country or territory within whose territory is located a foreign authority which is alleged to have granted one or more of the subsidies in question.

(8) Notices under sub-paragraphs (5)(d) and (e) and (6)(c) and (d) must specify the date of the initiation of the investigation.

(9) Nothing in this paragraph prevents the Secretary of State initiating both a dumping investigation and a subsidisation investigation in relation to the same goods if the requirements of sub-paragraph (1)(a) to (d) are met in the case of each investigation.".

4 Paragraph 11 (provisional affirmative determinations and final affirmative or negative determinations) of Schedule 4 to the Act has effect as if—
(a) in sub-paragraphs (3), (4) and (6)(b), for "it", in each place where it occurs, there were substituted "the Secretary of State";
(b) in sub-paragraph (8)(a), for "its", there were substituted "the"; and
(c) in sub-paragraph (8)(b), "the Secretary of State and" were omitted.

5 Paragraph 12 (termination of a dumping or a subsidisation investigation) of Schedule 4 to the Act has effect as if, for that paragraph, there were substituted—

"**12**

A dumping or a subsidisation investigation in relation to goods terminates (if it has not already terminated by virtue of provision made under paragraph 10(1))—
(a) in a case where the Secretary of State makes a final negative determination in relation to the goods, when notice of that determination is published under paragraph 11(8)(a),
(b) in a case where the Secretary of State makes a final affirmative determination in relation to the goods and determines that there is no preliminary decision which the Secretary of State could make under paragraph 17(3) or (4) in relation to them, when notice of that determination is published under paragraph 17(10)(b),

(c) in a case where the Secretary of State makes a final affirmative determination in relation to the goods, and makes a preliminary decision under paragraph 17(3) or (4) in relation to them, but decides not to give effect to the preliminary decision, when notice of that decision is published under paragraph 20(3)(a), or

(d) in a case where the Secretary of State makes a final affirmative determination in relation to the goods, and makes a preliminary decision under paragraph 17(3) or (4) in relation to them, which the Secretary of State decides to give effect to, at the end of the day of publication of the public notice under section 13 giving effect to the preliminary decision.".

Modifications to Part 3 (provisional remedy: requiring a guarantee)

6 Part 3 of Schedule 4 (provisional remedy: requiring a guarantee) to the Act has effect as if, for that Part, there were substituted—

"PART 3
PROVISIONAL REMEDY: REQUIRING A GUARANTEE

13 Secretary of State's power to make a preliminary decision to require a guarantee

(1) This paragraph applies where the Secretary of State makes a provisional affirmative determination in relation to goods which are the subject of a dumping or a subsidisation investigation.

(2) Goods in relation to which that determination is made are referred to in this paragraph as relevant goods.

(3) The Secretary of State may make a preliminary decision—

(a) in the case of a dumping investigation that, in respect of all the relevant goods, all importers of those goods should be required to give a guarantee in respect of any additional amount of import duty which would have been applicable, or potentially applicable, to the goods under section 13 if an anti-dumping amount had been applied to the goods based on the provisional affirmative determination ("an estimated anti-dumping amount"), or

(b) in the case of a subsidisation investigation that, in respect of all the relevant goods, all importers of those goods should be required to give a guarantee in respect of any additional amount of import duty which would have been applicable, or potentially applicable, to the goods under section 13 if a countervailing amount had been applied to the goods based on the provisional affirmative determination ("an estimated countervailing amount").

(4) The Secretary of State may make a preliminary decision under sub-paragraph (3) only if the Secretary of State is satisfied that requiring a guarantee in accordance with the preliminary decision—

(a) is necessary to prevent injury being caused during the investigation to a UK industry in the relevant goods, and

(b) meets the economic interest test (see paragraph 25).

(5) The Secretary of State may make different preliminary decisions under sub-paragraph (3) for different relevant goods or descriptions of relevant goods, including by reference to—

(a) specified overseas exporters or descriptions of overseas exporter;

(b) specified foreign countries or territories or descriptions of foreign countries or territories.

(6) But the Secretary of State may only make one preliminary decision under paragraph (a) or, as the case may be, paragraph (b) of sub-paragraph (3) in relation to any particular relevant good.

(7) And the Secretary of State may make different preliminary decisions under paragraph (a) or (b) of sub-paragraph (3) for different relevant goods or descriptions of relevant goods only if the preliminary decisions which the Secretary of State makes under that paragraph when taken together cover all the relevant goods.

(8) If the Secretary of State determines that there are one or more preliminary decisions which the Secretary of State could make under paragraph (a) or, as the case may be paragraph (b), of sub-paragraph (3), the Secretary of State must make that preliminary decision or those preliminary decisions (subject to sub-paragraphs (6) and (7)).

(9) If the Secretary of State determines that there is no preliminary decision which the Secretary of State could make under sub-paragraph (3), the Secretary of State must—

(a) publish notice of the provisional affirmative determination in relation to the goods,

(b) publish notice of the determination that there is no preliminary decision which the Secretary of State could make under sub-paragraph (3), and

(c) notify interested parties (see paragraph 32(3)) accordingly.

14 Preliminary decisions to require a guarantee

(1) A preliminary decision under paragraph 13(3) to require the giving of a guarantee in respect of goods must specify those goods and include—
- (a) the Secretary of State's preliminary decision regarding—
  - (i) the form of the guarantee,
  - (ii) the estimated anti-dumping amount or the estimated countervailing amount for the purpose of calculating the amount of the guarantee,
  - (iii) the amount of the guarantee,
  - (iv) the period during which the requirement to give a guarantee should apply, and
- (b) such other content as regulations may require.

(2) The form of guarantee referred to in sub-paragraph (1)(a)(i) may be cash, a bond or a bank guarantee.

(3) The preliminary decision referred to in sub-paragraph (1)(a)(ii) must be such that the estimated anti-dumping amount or an estimated countervailing does not exceed—
- (a) the margin of dumping or, as the case may be, the amount of the subsidy, in relation to the goods as determined by the Secretary of State as part of the provisional affirmative determination, or
- (b) the amount which the Secretary of State is satisfied would be adequate to remove the injury to a UK industry in the goods if that amount is less than the margin of dumping or, as the case may be, the amount of the subsidy referred to in paragraph (a).

(4) Regulations may make provision for the purposes of sub-paragraph (3)(b) about how the amount which the Secretary of State is satisfied would be adequate to remove the injury described in that provision is to be determined.

(5) The period referred to in sub-paragraph (1)(a)(iv)—
- (a) must not exceed 6 months in the case of a dumping investigation (but see paragraph 16 regarding extensions), or 4 months in the case of a subsidisation investigation, and
- (b) if the Secretary of State decides to give effect to the preliminary decision, must begin—
  - (i) on the day after the date of publication of the notice under paragraph 15(4)(b), or
  - (ii) if later, on the day which is the day after the end of the period of 60 days beginning with the date of the initiation of the investigation.

15 Secretary of State's decision whether to give effect to a preliminary decision to require a guarantee

(1) If the Secretary of State makes a preliminary decision under paragraph 13(3), the Secretary of State must decide whether to give effect to the preliminary decision.

(2) The Secretary of State may decide not to give effect to the preliminary decision only if the Secretary of State is satisfied that it is not in the public interest to give effect to it.

(3) If the Secretary of State decides not to give effect to the preliminary decision, the Secretary of State must—
- (a) publish notice of the provisional affirmative determination in relation to the goods, of the preliminary decision and of the decision not to give effect to it,
- (b) notify interested parties (see paragraph 32(3)) accordingly, and
- (c) lay a statement before the House of Commons setting out the reasons for deciding not to give effect to the preliminary decision.

(4) If the Secretary of State decides to give effect to the preliminary decision, the Secretary of State must—
- (a) publish notice of the provisional affirmative determination in relation to the goods and of the preliminary decision,
- (b) publish a notice that all importers of the goods specified in the preliminary decision are required to give a guarantee in accordance with the preliminary decision and regulations under paragraph 6 of Schedule 6, and
- (c) notify interested parties accordingly.

(5) The notice under sub-paragraph (4)(b) must—

(a) specify, in accordance with the preliminary decision, the matters referred to in paragraph 14(1)(a)(i) to (iv), and
(b) include such other content as regulations may require.

(6) For the purposes of this Schedule, "the period of a provisional remedy" in respect of goods means the period during which the requirement to give a guarantee in respect of the goods applies.

(7) The period of a provisional remedy in respect of goods ceases (if it has not already expired) when the dumping investigation or, as the case may be, the subsidisation investigation in relation to the goods terminates.

16 Extension of the period of a provisional remedy in a dumping investigation

(1) Regulations may make provision for, or in connection with, the extension by the Secretary of State, in accordance with a preliminary decision made by the Secretary of State, of the period of a provisional remedy which has been applied in respect of goods in the case of a dumping investigation.

(2) Any such extension must not result in the period of the provisional remedy being a period of more than 9 months beginning with the date when the requirement to give a guarantee in respect of goods first applied.

(3) The regulations must require that if the period of a provisional remedy is extended, the Secretary of State—
(a) publishes a revised notice under paragraph 15(4)(b) containing the revised period of the provisional remedy, and
(b) notifies interested parties (see paragraph 32(3)) accordingly.".

Modifications to Part 4 (definitive remedies: anti-dumping amount or countervailing amount)

7 Paragraph 17 (TRA's duty to recommend an anti-dumping amount or countervailing amount) of Schedule 4 to the Act has effect as if—

(a) for the heading of that paragraph, there were substituted—
"Secretary of State's power to make a preliminary decision regarding the application of an anti-dumping amount or a countervailing amount"; and

(b) for that paragraph, there were substituted—

"17

(1) This paragraph applies where the Secretary of State makes a final affirmative determination in relation to goods which are the subject of a dumping or a subsidisation investigation.

(2) Goods in relation to which that determination is made are referred to in this paragraph as relevant goods.

(3) In the case of a dumping investigation, the Secretary of State may make a preliminary decision—
(a) that an additional amount of import duty (referred to in this Schedule as an "anti-dumping amount") should be applicable for a specified period to all the relevant goods except, in the case of goods in respect of which an undertaking is accepted under provision made by or under Part 5, during any period when the undertaking applies, and
(b) regarding the anti-dumping amount that should be applicable to the relevant goods.

(4) In the case of a subsidisation investigation, the Secretary of State may make a preliminary decision—
(a) that an additional amount of import duty (referred to in this Schedule as a "countervailing amount") should be applicable for a specified period to all the relevant goods except, in the case of goods in respect of which an undertaking is accepted under provision made by or under Part 5, during any period when the undertaking applies, and
(b) regarding the countervailing amount that should be applicable to the relevant goods.

(5) The Secretary of State may make a preliminary decision under sub-paragraph (3) or (4) only if the Secretary of State is satisfied that the application of an anti-dumping amount or a countervailing amount in accordance with the preliminary decision meets the economic interest test (see paragraph 25).

(6) The Secretary of State may make different preliminary decisions under sub-paragraph (3) or (4) for different relevant goods or descriptions of relevant goods, including by reference to—
(a) specified overseas exporters or descriptions of overseas exporters;
(b) specified foreign countries or territories or descriptions of foreign countries or territories.

(7) But the Secretary of State may only make one preliminary decision under sub-paragraph (3) or, as the case may be, sub-paragraph (4) in relation to any particular relevant good.
(8) And the Secretary of State may make different preliminary decisions under sub-paragraph (3) or (4) for different relevant goods or descriptions of relevant goods only if the preliminary decisions which the Secretary of State makes under that sub-paragraph when taken together cover all the relevant goods.
(9) If the Secretary of State determines that there are one or more preliminary decisions which the Secretary of State could make under sub-paragraph (3) or, as the case may be, sub-paragraph (4), then the Secretary of State must make that preliminary decision or those preliminary decisions (subject to sub-paragraphs (7) and (8)).
(10) If the Secretary of State determines that there is no preliminary decision that the Secretary of State could make under sub-paragraph (3) or (4) (as the case may be), the Secretary of State must—
- (a) publish notice of the final affirmative determination in relation to the goods,
- (b) publish notice of the determination that there is no preliminary decision which the Secretary of State could make under sub-paragraph (3) or (4), and
- (c) notify interested parties (see paragraph 32(3)) accordingly.".

8 Paragraph 18 (TRA's recommendations about an anti-dumping amount or a countervailing amount) of Schedule 4 to the Act has effect as if—
(1) for the heading of that paragraph, there were substituted—
"Secretary of State's preliminary decisions regarding the application of an anti-dumping amount or a countervailing amount"; and
(2) for that paragraph, there were substituted—

"**18**
(1) This paragraph applies to a preliminary decision made by the Secretary of State under paragraph 17(3) or (4) in relation to goods.
(2) The specified period referred to in paragraph 17(3)(a) or (4)(a)—
- (a) must be a period of 5 years unless the Secretary of State considers that a lesser period is sufficient to counteract—
  - (i) the dumping of the goods which has caused or is causing injury to a UK industry in the goods, or
  - (ii) the importation of the subsidised goods which has caused or is causing injury to a UK industry in the goods, and
- (b) if the Secretary of State decides to give effect to the preliminary decision, must begin on the day after the date of publication of the public notice under section 13 giving effect to the preliminary decision (see paragraph 20(4)(c)) unless the Secretary of State is authorised by regulations made under paragraph 19 to determine a date before then.

(3) In the case of a determination of such a prior date made by virtue of paragraph 19, the reference in sub-paragraph (2)(a) to a period of 5 years is to be read as a reference to a period of 5 years plus the relevant period (within the meaning of paragraph 19).
(4) See also paragraph 21 regarding the possibility, following a review, of extensions or variations to the period for which an anti-dumping amount or countervailing amount applies to goods.
(5) The preliminary decision referred to in paragraph 17(3)(b) or (4)(b) regarding the anti-dumping amount or a countervailing amount that should be applicable to goods, may be made by reference to either or both of the following—
- (a) the value of the goods, and
- (b) the weight or volume of the goods or any other measure of their quantity or size.

(6) But that preliminary decision must be such that an anti-dumping amount or a countervailing amount applicable to goods does not exceed—
- (a) the margin of dumping or, as the case may be, the amount of the subsidy, in relation to the goods, or
- (b) the amount which the Secretary of State is satisfied would be adequate to remove the injury to a UK industry in the goods if that amount is less than the margin of dumping or, as the case may be, the amount of the subsidy referred to in paragraph (a).

(7) Regulations may make provision for the purposes of sub-paragraph (6)(b) about how the amount which the Secretary of State is satisfied would be adequate to remove the injury described in that provision is to be determined.

(8) A preliminary decision made under paragraph 17(3) or (4) must include such other content as regulations may require.".

9 Paragraph 19 of Schedule 4 to the Act has effect as if, for that paragraph, there were substituted—

"**19**
(1) Regulations may make provision authorising the Secretary of State, in specified circumstances, to make a determination, as part of a preliminary decision under paragraph 17(3) or (4), that the specified period for which an anti-dumping amount or a countervailing amount should apply to goods begins on a date ("the relevant date") before the day after the date of publication of the public notice under section 13 giving effect to the preliminary decision.
(2) Such a preliminary decision may only be made in relation to goods in respect of which a requirement to give a guarantee under paragraph 15 is applied ("the provisional remedy").
(3) "The relevant date" must be—
  (a) in a case where a notice under paragraph 29(1) (registration) has been published in respect of the goods—
     (i) a date during the period of 90 days before the beginning of the period of the provisional remedy provided it is not a date before the date of publication of that notice, or
     (ii) a date during the period of the provisional remedy, or
  (b) in any other case, a date during the period of the provisional remedy.
(4) Regulations may provide that, in the case of a preliminary decision made by virtue of sub-paragraph (1), the preliminary decision as to the anti-dumping amount or a countervailing amount must be such that an anti-dumping amount or a countervailing amount applicable for all or part of the relevant period must not exceed a particular amount.
(5) "The relevant period" is the period—
  (a) beginning with the relevant date, and
  (b) ending with the date of publication of the public notice under section 13 giving effect to the preliminary decision.".

10 Paragraph 20 (Secretary of State's power to accept or reject a recommendation) of Schedule 4 to the Act has effect as if—
(a) for the heading of that paragraph, there were substituted—
"*Secretary of State's decision whether to give effect to a preliminary decision regarding the application of an anti-dumping amount or a countervailing amount*"; and
(b) for that paragraph, there were substituted—

"**20**
(1) If the Secretary of State makes a preliminary decision under paragraph 17(3) or (4), the Secretary of State must decide whether to give effect to the preliminary decision.
(2) The Secretary of State may decide not to give effect to the preliminary decision only if the Secretary of State is satisfied that it is not in the public interest to give effect to it.
(3) If the Secretary of State decides not to give effect to the preliminary decision, the Secretary of State must—
  (a) publish notice of the final affirmative determination in relation to the goods, of the preliminary decision, and of the decision not to give effect to it,
  (b) notify interested parties (see paragraph 32(3)) accordingly, and
  (c) lay a statement before the House of Commons setting out the reasons for deciding not to give effect to the preliminary decision.
(4) If the Secretary of State decides to give effect to the preliminary decision, the Secretary of State—
  (a) must publish notice of the final affirmative determination in relation to the goods, of the preliminary decision, and of the decision to give effect to it,
  (b) must notify interested parties accordingly, and
  (c) is required under section 13 to make provision by public notice to give effect to the preliminary decision.
(5) See paragraphs 21 and 22 for variation or revocation of the application of an anti-dumping amount or a countervailing amount.".

11 Paragraph 21 (reviews of continuing application of an anti-dumping amount or a countervailing amount) of Schedule 4 to the Act has effect as if, for sub-paragraphs (6) to (10) of that paragraph, there were substituted—

"(6) Regulations may make provision for or in connection with the Secretary of State—
   (a) making a preliminary decision that the application of an anti-dumping amount or a countervailing amount to goods should be varied or revoked, and
   (b) deciding whether to give effect to such a preliminary decision.
(7) Where, by virtue of provision made under sub-paragraph (6), the Secretary of State decides to give effect to a preliminary decision that the application of an anti-dumping amount or a countervailing amount to goods should be varied or revoked, the Secretary of State—
   (a) must publish notice of the preliminary decision and of the decision to give effect to it,
   (b) must notify interested parties (see paragraph 32(3)) accordingly, and
   (c) is required under section 13 to make provision by public notice to give effect to the preliminary decision.
(8) Where the Secretary of State makes a preliminary decision to vary the application of an anti-dumping amount or a countervailing amount to goods, by virtue of regulations under sub-paragraph (6), such a decision may among other things include—
   (a) varying the goods or descriptions of goods to which an anti-dumping amount or a countervailing amount is applicable (including so that it is applicable to goods or descriptions of goods to which it has not previously been applicable);
   (b) varying the period for which an anti-dumping amount or a countervailing amount is applicable (including extending it beyond the period referred to in paragraph 18(2)(a));
   (c) varying an anti-dumping amount or a countervailing amount.
(9) Regulations under sub-paragraph (6) may provide that the Secretary of State may decide that the application of an anti-dumping amount or a countervailing amount as varied should be applicable to goods from a date ("the relevant date") before the date of publication of the public notice under section 13 giving effect to the preliminary decision.
(10) Such a decision may only be made if—
   (a) a notice under paragraph 29(1) (registration) has been published in respect of the goods, and
   (b) the relevant date is not a date before the date of publication of that notice.".

Modifications to Part 5 (undertakings)

12 Paragraph 23 (acceptance of undertakings) of Schedule 4 to the Act has effect as if—
 (a) for sub-paragraph (1), there were substituted—
"(1) Where the Secretary of State makes a preliminary decision under paragraph 17(3) or (4) that an anti-dumping amount or a countervailing amount should be applicable to goods, the Secretary of State may also—
   (a) request an undertaking in respect of the goods, and
   (b) accept an undertaking in respect of the goods (whether as a result of a request made under paragraph (a) or otherwise)."; and
 (b) for sub-paragraphs (4) to (6), there were substituted—
"(4) Regulations may make provision about—
   (a) requests for undertakings under sub-paragraph (1), and
   (b) the acceptance of undertakings (whether as a result of a request made under sub-paragraph (1)(a) or otherwise).
(5) The regulations must secure that the Secretary of State may request an undertaking in respect of goods only—
   (a) at a time after the Secretary of State has made a provisional affirmative determination in relation to the goods, and
   (b) if such other requirements as the regulations may specify are met.
(6) The regulations must secure that the Secretary of State may accept an undertaking in respect of goods only if satisfied that—
   (a) the undertaking is sufficient to eliminate the injurious effect of—
      (i) the dumping of the goods to a UK industry in those goods, or
      (ii) the importation of the subsidised goods to a UK industry in those goods,
   (b) acceptance of the undertaking meets the economic interest test (see paragraph 25), and
   (c) it is appropriate to accept the undertaking.".

13 Paragraph 24 (reviews of undertakings etc) of Schedule 4 to the Act has effect as if sub-paragraph (4) were omitted.

Modifications to Part 6 (supplementary)

14 Paragraph 25 (the economic interest test) of Schedule 4 to the Act has effect as if—
  (a) in sub-paragraphs (1), (3) and (4), "the TRA or", in each place this occurs, were omitted; and
  (b) in sub-paragraphs (3) and (4)(b), ", as the case may be," were omitted.

15 Paragraph 26 (suspension of anti-dumping or anti-subsidy remedies) of Schedule 4 to the Act has effect as if—
  (a) in sub-paragraph (1)—
    (i) for "recommending to the Secretary of State", there were substituted "making a preliminary decision";
    (ii) for "accepting or rejecting such a recommendation", there were substituted "deciding whether to give effect to such a preliminary decision";
  (b) in sub-paragraph (2), for "recommendation to the Secretary of State", there were substituted "preliminary decision"; and
  (c) in sub-paragraph (6)—
    (i) for "accepts a recommendation", there were substituted "decides to give effect to a preliminary decision";
    (ii) in paragraph (a), for "recommendation and of the acceptance of it", there were substituted "preliminary decision and of the decision to give effect to it"; and
    (iii) in paragraph (c), for "recommendation", at the end, there were substituted "preliminary decision".

16 Paragraph 32 (interpretation) of Schedule 4 to the Act has effect as if, in sub-paragraph (1), in the definition of "the period of a provisional remedy", for "paragraph 15(7)", there were substituted "paragraph 15(6)".

PART 4
FURTHER MODIFICATIONS TO SCHEDULE 5 TO THE ACT

Modifications to Part 2 (safeguarding investigations)

17 Paragraph 7 (initiation of a safeguarding investigation) of Schedule 5 to the Act has effect as if, for that paragraph, there were substituted—

"7
(1) The Secretary of State may initiate a safeguarding investigation in relation to goods only if—
  (a) the Secretary of State—
    (i) is requested to initiate an investigation in an application made by or on behalf UK producers of the goods ("the applicant UK producers"), or
    (ii) decides that an investigation should be initiated in the absence of such an application,
  (b) the Secretary of State is satisfied that the application contains sufficient evidence (or, if sub-paragraph (1)(a)(i) does not apply, that there is otherwise sufficient evidence), that—
    (i) the goods have been or are being imported into the United Kingdom in increased quantities, and
    (ii) the importation of the goods in increased quantities has caused or is causing serious injury to UK producers of those goods,
  (c) the market share requirement is met or the Secretary of State waives the requirement, and
  (d)
    (i) in the case of an application under sub-paragraph (1)(a)(i), the application is accompanied by a preliminary adjustment plan or the Secretary of State waives the requirement for the application to be accompanied by such a plan, or
    (ii) in the case of a decision under sub-paragraph (1)(a)(ii), a preliminary adjustment plan has been prepared by, or on behalf of, the Secretary of State or the Secretary of State waives the requirement for such a plan to be prepared.

(2) The market share requirement is met if—
   (a) in the case of an application under sub-paragraph (1)(a)(i), the Secretary of State is satisfied that the applicant UK producers have a share of the market for like goods and directly competitive goods for consumption in the United Kingdom (whether produced there or elsewhere) which is sufficient to justify initiating the investigation;
   (b) in the case of a decision under sub-paragraph (1)(a)(ii), the Secretary of State is satisfied that UK producers of the goods have a share of the market for like goods and directly competitive goods for consumption in the United Kingdom (whether produced there or elsewhere) which is sufficient to justify initiating the investigation.
(3) A preliminary adjustment plan is—
   (a) in the case of an application under sub-paragraph (1)(a)(i), a plan setting out how the applicant UK producers think they might be able to adjust to the importation of the goods in increased quantities;
   (b) in the case of a decision under sub-paragraph (1)(a)(ii), a plan setting out how UK producers of the goods might be able to adjust to the importation of the goods in increased quantities.
(4) Regulations may make provision about—
   (a) what constitutes or does not constitute an application made by or on behalf of UK producers for the purposes of sub-paragraph (1)(a)(i);
   (b) when an application is made for the purposes of sub-paragraph (1)(a)(i);
   (c) the information to be contained in such an application;
   (d) the time limit for determining such an application;
   (e) the Secretary of State's assessment of any information obtained or held by the Secretary of State for the purposes of a decision under sub-paragraph (1)(a)(ii);
   (f) the form and content of a preliminary adjustment plan;
   (g) what constitutes or does not constitute "the market for like goods and directly competitive goods for consumption in the United Kingdom" and UK producers' "share" of that market for the purposes of sub-paragraphs (1)(c) and (2);
   (h) how any of those matters are to be determined for the purposes of sub-paragraphs (1)(c) and (2).
(5) In the case of an application under sub-paragraph (1)(a)(i), if any of the requirements of sub-paragraph (1)(b) to (d) in respect of a safeguarding investigation are not met, the Secretary of State must reject the application and notify the applicant accordingly.
(6) If the requirements of sub-paragraph (1)(a) to (d) in respect of a safeguarding investigation are met, the Secretary of State must—
   (a) in the case of an application under sub-paragraph (1)(a)(i), accept the application,
   (b) initiate the investigation,
   (c) publish notice of the decision to initiate the investigation (including notice of the goods which are the subject of the investigation), and
   (d) notify interested parties (see paragraph 31(3)) accordingly.
(7) Notices under sub-paragraph (6)(c) and (d) must specify the date of the initiation of the investigation.".

18 Paragraph 9 (provisional affirmative determinations and final affirmative or negative determinations) of Schedule 5 to the Act has effect as if—
(a) in sub-paragraphs (2), (3) and (5)(b), for "it", in each place where it occurs, there were substituted "the Secretary of State";
(b) in sub-paragraph (7)(a), for "its" there were substituted "the"; and
(c) in sub-paragraph (7)(b), "the Secretary of State and" were omitted.

19 Paragraph 10 (termination of a safeguarding investigation) of Schedule 5 to the Act has effect as if, for that paragraph, there were substituted—

"**10**
A safeguarding investigation in relation to goods terminates (if it has not already terminated by virtue of provision made under paragraph 8(1))—
   (a) in a case where the Secretary of State makes a final negative determination in relation to the goods, when notice of that determination is published under paragraph 9(7)(a),

(b) in a case where the Secretary of State makes a final affirmative determination in relation to the goods and determines that there is no preliminary decision which the Secretary of State could make under paragraph 16(3) in relation to them, when notice of that determination is published under paragraph 16(11)(b),

(c) in a case where the Secretary of State makes a final affirmative determination in relation to the goods, and makes a preliminary decision under paragraph 16(3) in relation to them, but decides not to give effect to that preliminary decision, when notice of that decision is published under paragraph 19(3)(a) or 20(3)(a), or

(d) in a case where the Secretary of State makes a final affirmative determination in relation to the goods, and makes a preliminary decision under paragraph 16(3) in relation to them, which the Secretary of State decides to give effect to, at the end of the day of publication of the public notice under section 13 giving effect to the preliminary decision.".

Modifications to Part 3 (provisional remedies: provisional safeguarding amount & provisional tariff rate quotas)

20 Part 3 of Schedule 5 (provisional remedies: provisional safeguarding amount & provisional tariff rate quotas) to the Act has effect as if, for that Part, there were substituted—

"PART 3
PROVISIONAL REMEDIES: PROVISIONAL SAFEGUARDING AMOUNT & PROVISIONAL TARIFF RATE QUOTAS

11 Secretary of State's power to make a preliminary decision regarding the application of a provisional safeguarding amount or a provisional tariff rate quota

(1) This paragraph applies where the Secretary of State makes a provisional affirmative determination in relation to goods which are the subject of a safeguarding investigation.

(2) Goods in relation to which that determination is made are referred to in this paragraph as relevant goods.

(3) The Secretary of State may make a preliminary decision—

(a) that an additional amount of import duty (referred to in this Schedule as a "provisional safeguarding amount") should be applicable for a specified period to all the relevant goods or to specified relevant goods;

(b) that all the relevant goods, or specified relevant goods, should be subject to a quota for a specified period during which a lower rate of import duty should be applicable to imports of goods within the amount of the quota than is applicable to imports of goods outside the amount of the quota (referred to in this Schedule as a "provisional tariff quota").

(4) Where the Secretary of State makes a preliminary decision under sub-paragraph (3)(a) in relation to relevant goods the Secretary of State must, as part of that decision, make a preliminary decision regarding the provisional safeguarding amount that should be applicable to those goods.

(5) The Secretary of State may make a preliminary decision under sub-paragraph (3) only if the Secretary of State is satisfied that applying a provisional safeguarding amount to relevant goods, or making relevant goods subject to a provisional tariff rate quota, in accordance with the preliminary decision—

(a) is necessary to prevent serious injury which it would be difficult to repair from being caused during the investigation to UK producers of the goods, and

(b) meets the economic interest test (see paragraph 23).

(6) The Secretary of State may only make a preliminary decision under one or other of paragraphs (a) and (b) of sub-paragraph (3) in relation to any particular relevant good.

(7) The Secretary of State may make a preliminary decision under paragraph (a) or (b) of sub-paragraph (3) in relation to specified relevant goods (rather than all the relevant goods) only if the preliminary decisions the Secretary of State makes under that sub-paragraph, when taken together, cover all the relevant goods.

(8) If the Secretary of State determines that there are one or more preliminary decisions which the Secretary of State could make under sub-paragraph (3) in relation to all the relevant goods, or that there are one or more preliminary decisions which the Secretary of State could make under sub-paragraph (3) in relation to specified relevant goods, the Secretary of State must make that preliminary decision or one of those preliminary decisions (subject to sub-paragraphs (6) and (7)).

(9) If the Secretary of State determines that there is no preliminary decision which the Secretary of State could make under sub-paragraph (3), the Secretary of State must—

(a) publish notice of the provisional affirmative determination in relation to the goods,

(b) publish notice of the determination that there is no preliminary decision which the Secretary of State could make under sub-paragraph (3), and
(c) notify interested parties (see paragraph 31(3)) accordingly.

12 Secretary of State's preliminary decisions about a provisional safeguarding amount
(1) This paragraph applies to a preliminary decision made by the Secretary of State under paragraph 11(3)(a) in relation to goods.
(2) The specified period referred to in paragraph 11(3)(a)—
　　(a) must not exceed 200 days, and
　　(b) if the Secretary of State decides to give effect to the preliminary decision, must begin on the day after the date of publication of the public notice under section 13 giving effect to the preliminary decision.
(3) A preliminary decision under paragraph 11(3)(a) regarding a provisional safeguarding amount that should be applicable to goods (see paragraph 11(4)) may be made by reference to either or both of the following—
　　(a) the value of the goods, and
　　(b) the weight or volume of the goods or any other measure of their quantity or size.
(4) But that preliminary decision must be such that a provisional safeguarding amount applicable to goods does not exceed the amount which the Secretary of State is satisfied is necessary to prevent serious injury which it would be difficult to repair from being caused during the investigation to UK producers of the goods.
(5) Regulations may make provision for the purposes of sub-paragraph (4) about how the amount which the Secretary of State is satisfied is necessary to prevent the serious injury described in that provision is to be determined.
(6) A preliminary decision under paragraph 11(3)(a), must include such other content as regulations may require.

13 Secretary of State's preliminary decisions regarding provisional tariff rate quotas
(1) This paragraph applies to a preliminary decision made by the Secretary of State under paragraph 11(3)(b) in relation to goods.
(2) The specified period referred to in paragraph 11(3)(b)—
　　(a) must not exceed 200 days, and
　　(b) if the Secretary of State decides to give effect to the preliminary decision, must begin on the day after the date of publication of the public notice under section 13 giving effect to the preliminary decision.
(3) The preliminary decision must (in addition to the specified period) include—
　　(a) the amount of the quota,
　　(b) how the quota should be allocated,
　　(c) the rates of import duty that should be applied to goods subject to the quota, and
　　(d) such other content as regulations may require.
(4) The things decided by the Secretary of State by virtue of sub-paragraph (3)(a) to (c) must be such as the Secretary of State is satisfied are necessary to prevent serious injury which it would be difficult to repair from being caused during the investigation to UK producers of the goods.
(5) Regulations may make provision for the purposes of sub-paragraph (4) about how the things which the Secretary of State is satisfied are necessary to prevent the serious injury described in that provision are to be determined.

14 Secretary of State's power to apply a provisional safeguarding amount
(1) If the Secretary of State makes a preliminary decision under paragraph 11(3)(a), the Secretary of State must decide whether to give effect to the preliminary decision.
(2) The Secretary of State may decide not to give effect to the preliminary decision only if the Secretary of State is satisfied that it is not in the public interest to give effect to it.
(3) If the Secretary of State decides not to give effect to the preliminary decision, the Secretary of State must—
　　(a) publish notice of the provisional affirmative determination in relation to the goods, of the preliminary decision and of the decision not to give effect to it,
　　(b) notify interested parties (see paragraph 31(3)) accordingly, and
　　(c) lay a statement before the House of Commons setting out the reasons for deciding not to give effect to the preliminary decision.
(4) If the Secretary of State decides to give effect to the preliminary decision, the Secretary of State—

(a) must publish notice of the Secretary of State's provisional affirmative determination in relation to the goods, of the preliminary decision and of the decision to give effect to it,
(b) must notify interested parties accordingly, and
(c) is required under section 13 to make provision by public notice to give effect to the preliminary decision.

(5) The period for which a provisional safeguarding amount applies to goods ceases (if it has not already expired) when the safeguarding investigation in relation to the goods terminates.

15 Secretary of State's power to subject goods to a provisional tariff rate quota
(1) If the Secretary of State makes a preliminary decision under paragraph 11(3)(b), the Secretary of State must decide whether to give effect to the preliminary decision.
(2) The Secretary of State may decide not to give effect to the preliminary decision only if the Secretary of State is satisfied that it is not in the public interest to give effect to it.
(3) If the Secretary of State decides not to give effect to the preliminary decision, the Secretary of State must—
(a) publish notice of the provisional affirmative determination in relation to the goods, of the preliminary decision and of the decision not to give effect to it,
(b) notify interested parties (see paragraph 31(3)) accordingly, and
(c) lay a statement before the House of Commons setting out the reasons for deciding not give effect to the preliminary decision.
(4) If the Secretary of State decides to give effect to the preliminary decision, the Secretary of State—
(a) must publish notice of the provisional affirmative determination in relation to the goods, of the preliminary decision and of the decision to give effect to it,
(b) must notify interested parties accordingly, and
(c) is required under section 13 to make provision by public notice to give effect to the preliminary decision.
(5) The period for which goods are subject to a provisional tariff rate quota ceases (if it has not already expired) when the safeguarding investigation in relation to the goods terminates.".

Modifications to Part 4 (definitive remedies: definitive safeguarding amount & tariff rate quotas)

21 Paragraph 16 (TRA's duty to recommend a definitive safeguarding amount or tariff rate quota) of Schedule 5 to the Act has effect as if—
(a) for the heading of that paragraph, there were substituted—
"*Secretary of State's power to make a preliminary decision regarding the application of a definitive safeguarding amount or tariff rate quota*"; and
(b) for that paragraph, there were substituted—

"**16**
(1) This paragraph applies where the Secretary of State makes a final affirmative determination in relation to goods which are the subject of a safeguarding investigation.
(2) Goods in relation to which that determination is made are referred to in this paragraph as relevant goods.
(3) The Secretary of State may make a preliminary decision—
(a) that an additional amount of import duty (referred to in this Schedule as a "definitive safeguarding amount") should be applicable for a specified period to all the relevant goods or to specified relevant goods;
(b) that all the relevant goods, or specified relevant goods, should be subject to a quota for a specified period during which a lower rate of import duty should be applicable to imports of goods within the amount of the quota than is applicable to imports of goods outside the amount of the quota (referred to in this Schedule as a "tariff rate quota").
(4) Where the Secretary of State makes a preliminary decision under sub-paragraph (3)(a) in relation to relevant goods the Secretary of State must, as part of the decision, make a preliminary decision regarding the definitive safeguarding amount that should be applicable to those goods.
(5) The Secretary of State may make a preliminary decision under sub-paragraph (3) only if the Secretary of State is satisfied that—
(a) applying a definitive safeguarding amount to relevant goods, or making relevant goods subject to a tariff rate quota, in accordance with the preliminary decision meets the economic interest test (see paragraph 23), and

(b) there is in place an adjustment plan setting out how UK producers of the relevant goods intend to adjust to the importation of the goods in increased quantities.

(6) But sub-paragraph (5) is to be read as if paragraph (b) were omitted if—

(a) in the case of an application under paragraph 7(1)(a)(i), the Secretary of State waived the requirement for the application to initiate a safeguarding investigation in relation to the relevant goods to be accompanied by a preliminary adjustment plan, or

(b) in the case of a decision under paragraph 7(1)(a)(ii), the Secretary of State has waived the requirement for a preliminary adjustment plan to be prepared.

(7) Regulations may make provision about the form and content of an adjustment plan.

(8) The Secretary of State may only make a preliminary decision under one or other of paragraphs (a) and (b) of sub-paragraph (3) in relation to any particular relevant good.

(9) The Secretary of State may make a preliminary decision under paragraph (a) or (b) of sub-paragraph (3) in relation to specified relevant goods (rather than all the relevant goods) only if the preliminary decisions which the Secretary of State makes under that sub-paragraph, when taken together, cover all the relevant goods.

(10) If the Secretary of State determines that there are one or more preliminary decisions which the Secretary of State could make under sub-paragraph (3) in relation to all the relevant goods, or that there are one or more preliminary decisions which the Secretary of State could make in relation to specified relevant goods, the Secretary of State must make that preliminary decision or one of those preliminary decisions (subject to sub-paragraphs (8) and (9)).

(11) If the Secretary of State determines that there is no preliminary decision which the Secretary of State could make under sub-paragraph (3) the Secretary of State must—

(a) publish notice of the final affirmative determination in relation to the goods,

(b) publish notice of the determination that there is no preliminary decision which the Secretary of State could make under sub-paragraph (3), and

(c) notify interested parties (see paragraph 31(3)) accordingly.".

22 Paragraph 17 (TRA's recommendations about a definitive safeguarding amount) of Schedule 5 to the Act has effect as if—

(a) for the heading of that paragraph, there were substituted—

"Secretary of State's preliminary decisions regarding the application of a definitive safeguarding amount"; and

(b) for that paragraph, there were substituted—

"17

(1) This paragraph applies to a preliminary decision made by the Secretary of State under paragraph 16(3)(a) in relation to goods.

(2) The specified period referred to in paragraph 16(3)(a)—

(a) must be such period as the Secretary of State is satisfied is necessary—

(i) to remove the serious injury, or to prevent further serious injury, caused by the importation of the goods in increased quantities to UK producers of the goods, and

(ii) to facilitate the adjustment of those UK producers to the importation of the goods in increased quantities,

(b) must not exceed 4 years (but see paragraph 21 regarding the possibility of extensions or variations to that period following a review), and

(c) if the Secretary of State decides to give effect to the preliminary decision, must begin on the day after the date of publication of the public notice under section 13 giving effect to the preliminary decision.

(3) A preliminary decision under paragraph 16(3)(a) regarding the definitive safeguarding amount that should be applicable to goods (see paragraph 16(4)) may be made by reference to either or both of the following—

(a) the value of the goods, and

(b) the weight or volume of the goods or any other measure of their quantity or size.

(4) But that preliminary decision must be such that—

(a) a definitive safeguarding amount applicable to goods does not exceed the amount which the Secretary of State is satisfied is necessary—

(i) to remove serious injury to UK producers of the goods, and

(ii) to facilitate the adjustment of those UK producers to the importation of the goods in increased quantities, and

(b) where the specified period referred to in paragraph 16(3)(a) exceeds 1 year, a definitive safeguarding amount applicable to goods becomes progressively smaller as the period progresses.

(5) Regulations may make provision for the purposes of sub-paragraph (4)(a) about how the amount which the Secretary of State is satisfied is necessary for the purposes mentioned is to be determined.

(6) A preliminary decision made under paragraph 16(3)(a) must include such other content as regulations may require.

(7) If a provisional safeguarding remedy has been applied to some or all of the goods as part of the same safeguarding investigation, sub-paragraph (8) applies for the purposes of sub-paragraphs (2)(b) and (4)(b).

(8) The length of the specified period referred to in paragraph 16(3)(a), so far as relating to goods to which a provisional safeguarding remedy has been applied, is to be treated as extended by the length of the specified period for which the Secretary of State decides that a provisional safeguarding remedy should be applied to them.

(9) Where the application of sub-paragraph (8) results in the length of the specified period referred to in paragraph 16(3)(a), so far as relating to goods to which a provisional safeguarding remedy has been applied, exceeding 1 year, sub-paragraph (4)(b) is to be read as if references to goods were references to the goods to which the provisional safeguarding remedy has been applied.

(10) In this paragraph, references to the application of a provisional safeguarding remedy are to—

 (a) applying a provisional safeguarding amount to goods, or

 (b) making goods subject to a provisional tariff rate quota.".

23 Paragraph 18 (TRA's recommendations regarding tariff rate quotas) of Schedule 5 to the Act has effect as if—

 (a) for the heading of that paragraph, there were substituted—

"Secretary of State's preliminary decisions regarding tariff rate quotas"; and

 (b) for that paragraph, there were substituted—

"**18**

(1) This paragraph applies to a preliminary decision made by the Secretary of State under paragraph 16(3)(b) in relation to goods.

(2) The specified period referred to in paragraph 16(3)(b)—

 (a) must be such period as the Secretary of State is satisfied is necessary—

  (i) to remove the serious injury, or to prevent further serious injury, caused by the importation of the goods in increased quantities to UK producers of the goods, and

  (ii) to facilitate the adjustment of those UK producers to the importation of the goods in increased quantities,

 (b) must not exceed 4 years (but see paragraph 21 regarding the possibility of extensions or variations to that period following a review), and

 (c) if the Secretary of State decides to give effect to the preliminary decision, must begin on the day after the date of publication of the public notice under section 13 giving effect to the preliminary decision.

(3) The preliminary decision must (in addition to the specified period) include—

 (a) the amount of the quota,

 (b) how the quota should be allocated,

 (c) the rates of import duty that should be applied to goods subject to the quota, and

 (d) such other content as regulations may require.

(4) The things decided by the Secretary of State by virtue of sub-paragraph (3)(a) to (c)—

 (a) must be such as the Secretary of State is satisfied are necessary—

  (i) to remove serious injury to UK producers of the goods, and

  (ii) to facilitate the adjustment of those UK producers to the importation of the goods in increased quantities, and

 (b) where the specified period referred to in paragraph 16(3)(b) exceeds 1 year, must be such that the amount of import duty applicable to goods subject to the quota becomes progressively smaller as the period progresses (whether by increases in the amount of the quota, decreases in the rates of import duty, or both).

(5) Regulations may make provision for the purposes of sub-paragraph (4)(a) about how the things which the Secretary of State is satisfied are necessary for the purposes mentioned are to be determined.

(6) If a provisional safeguarding remedy has been applied to some or all of the goods as part of the same safeguarding investigation, sub-paragraph (7) applies for the purposes of sub-paragraphs (2)(b) and (4)(b).

(7) The length of the specified period referred to in paragraph 16(3)(b), so far as relating to goods to which a provisional safeguarding remedy has been applied, is to be treated as extended by the length of the specified period for which the Secretary of State decides that a provisional safeguarding remedy should be applied to them.

(8) Where the application of sub-paragraph (7) results in the length of the specified period referred to in paragraph 16(3)(b), so far as relating to goods to which a provisional safeguarding remedy has been applied, exceeding 1 year, sub-paragraph (4)(b) is to be read as if references to goods were references to the goods to which the provisional safeguarding remedy has been applied.

(9) In this paragraph, references to the application of a provisional safeguarding remedy are to—
- (a) applying a provisional safeguarding amount to goods, or
- (b) making goods subject to a provisional tariff rate quota.".

24 Paragraph 19 (Secretary of State's power to apply a definitive safeguarding amount) of Schedule 5 to the Act has effect as if, for that paragraph, there were substituted—

"**19**

(1) If the Secretary of State makes a preliminary decision under paragraph 16(3)(a) that a definitive safeguarding amount should be applicable to goods, the Secretary of State must decide whether to give effect to the preliminary decision.

(2) The Secretary of State may decide not to give effect to the preliminary decision only if the Secretary of State is satisfied that it is not in the public interest to give effect to it.

(3) If the Secretary of State decides not to give effect to the preliminary decision, the Secretary of State must—
- (a) publish notice of the final affirmative determination in relation to the goods, of the preliminary decision and of the decision not to give effect to it,
- (b) notify interested parties (see paragraph 31(3)) accordingly, and
- (c) lay a statement before the House of Commons setting out the reasons for deciding not give effect to the preliminary decision.

(4) If the Secretary of State decides to give effect to the preliminary decision, the Secretary of State—
- (a) must publish notice of the final affirmative determination in relation to the goods, of the preliminary decision and of the decision to give effect to it,
- (b) must notify interested parties accordingly, and
- (c) is required under section 13 to make provision by public notice to give effect to the preliminary decision.

(5) See paragraphs 21 and 22 for variation or revocation of the application of a definitive safeguarding amount.".

25 Paragraph 20 (Secretary of State's power to subject goods to a tariff rate quota) of Schedule 5 to the Act has effect as if, for that paragraph, there were substituted—

"**20**

(1) If the Secretary of State makes a preliminary decision under paragraph 16(3)(b) that goods should be subject to a tariff rate quota, the Secretary of State must decide whether to give effect to the preliminary decision.

(2) The Secretary of State may decide not to give effect to the preliminary decision only if the Secretary of State is satisfied that it is not in the public interest to give effect to it.

(3) If the Secretary of State decides not to give effect to the preliminary decision, the Secretary of State must—
- (a) publish notice of the final affirmative determination in relation to the goods, of the preliminary decision and of the decision not to give effect to it,
- (b) notify interested parties (see paragraph 31(3)) accordingly, and
- (c) lay a statement before the House of Commons setting out the reasons for deciding not give effect to the preliminary decision.

(4) If the Secretary of State decides to give effect to the preliminary decision, the Secretary of State—

(a) must publish notice of the final affirmative determination in relation to the goods, of the preliminary decision and of the decision to give effect to it,
(b) must notify interested parties accordingly, and
(c) is required under section 13 to make provision by public notice to give effect to the preliminary decision.

(5) See paragraphs 21 and 22 for variation or revocation of a tariff rate quota.".

26 Paragraph 21 (reviews) of Schedule 5 to the Act has effect as if, for sub-paragraphs (6) to (10) of that paragraph, there were substituted—

"(6) Regulations may make provision for or in connection with the Secretary of State—
 (a) making a preliminary decision that—
  (i) the application of a definitive safeguarding amount to goods should be varied, revoked or replaced with a tariff rate quota, or
  (ii) a tariff rate quota to which goods are subject should be varied, revoked or replaced with the application of a definitive safeguarding amount, and
 (b) deciding whether to give effect to such a preliminary decision.

(7) Where, by virtue of provision made under sub-paragraph (6), the Secretary of State decides to give effect to a preliminary decision that the application of a definitive safeguarding amount to goods, or a tariff rate quota to which goods are subject, should be varied or revoked, the Secretary of State—
 (a) must publish notice of the preliminary decision and of the decision to give effect to it,
 (b) must notify interested parties (see paragraph 31(3)) accordingly, and
 (c) is required under section 13 to make provision by public notice to give effect to the preliminary decision.

(8) Where the Secretary of State makes a preliminary decision to vary the application of a definitive safeguarding amount to goods, by virtue of regulations under sub-paragraph (6), this may take the form of one or both of the following—
 (a) varying the period for which a definitive safeguarding amount is applicable (including extending it beyond the period referred to in paragraph 17(2)(b));
 (b) varying a definitive safeguarding amount such that a lower amount of import duty is applicable.

(9) Where the Secretary of State makes a preliminary decision to vary a tariff rate quota, by virtue of regulations under sub-paragraph (6), this may take the form of one or more of the following—
 (a) increasing the amount of the quota;
 (b) varying the allocation of the quota;
 (c) reducing the rates of import duty that apply to goods subject to the quota;
 (d) reducing the part of the period for which the amount of the quota is lower or for which import duty at a higher rate applies (so that the amount of the quota is increased, or import duty applies at a lower rate, more quickly);
 (e) varying the period for which goods are subject to the quota (including extending it beyond the period referred to in paragraph 18(2)(b)).

(10) Where, by virtue of provision made under sub-paragraph (6), the Secretary of State decides to give effect to a preliminary decision that, for the first time, a definitive safeguarding amount should be applicable to goods or goods should be subject to a tariff rate quota, the Secretary of State—
 (a) must publish notice of the preliminary decision and of the decision to give effect to it,
 (b) must notify interested parties accordingly, and
 (c) is required under section 13 to make provision by public notice to give effect to the preliminary decision.".

Modifications to Part 5 (supplementary)

27 Paragraph 23 (the economic interest test) of Schedule 5 to the Act has effect as if—
(a) in sub-paragraphs (1) and (3), "the TRA or", in each place where this occurs, were omitted; and
(b) in sub-paragraph (3)(b), ", as the case may be," were omitted.

28 Paragraph 24 (suspension of safeguarding remedies) of Schedule 5 to the Act has effect as if—
(a) in sub-paragraph (1)—

(i) for "recommending to the Secretary of State", there were substituted "making a preliminary decision";
(ii) for "accepting or rejecting such a recommendation", there were substituted "deciding whether to give effect to such a preliminary decision";
(b) in sub-paragraph (2), for "recommendation to the Secretary of State", there were substituted "preliminary decision"; and
(c) in sub-paragraph (6)—
(i) for "accepts a recommendation", there were substituted "decides to give effect to a preliminary decision";
(ii) in paragraph (a), for "recommendation and of the acceptance of it", there were substituted "preliminary decision and of the decision to give effect to it";
(iii) in paragraph (c), for "recommendation", at the end, there were substituted "preliminary decision".

29 Paragraph 25 (exceptions) of Schedule 5 to the Act has effect as if, in sub-paragraph (2), for "recommendation", there were substituted "preliminary decision".

30 Paragraph 26 (restrictions on successive safeguarding remedies) of Schedule 5 to the Act has effect as if—
(a) in sub-paragraph (1), for "recommendation", in both places where it occurs, there were substituted "preliminary decision";
(b) in sub-paragraph (3), for "accept the recommendation", there were substituted "decide to give effect to the preliminary decision"; and
(c) in sub-paragraph (5)—
(i) for "accepting the recommendation", there were substituted "deciding to give effect to the preliminary decision"; and
(ii) for "the recommended period", in each place this occurs, there were substituted "the identified period".

2019/1015

VALUE ADDED TAX (SECTION 55A) (SPECIFIED SERVICES) ORDER 2019

Made . . . . .12th June 2019
Laid before the House of Commons . . . . .13th June 2019
Coming into force . . . . .14th June 2019

1 Citation, commencement and effect
(1) This Order may be cited as the Value Added Tax (Section 55A) (Specified Services) Order 2019.
(2) This Order comes into force on 14th June 2019 and has effect in relation to supplies of specified services made on or after that date.

2 Interpretation
In this Order—
"gas" means gas supplied through the natural gas distribution system;
"a gas or an electricity certificate" is an electronic document which contains information on the source of the energy and its method of production;
"specified services" means the services specified in article 4.

3 Application of section 55A of the Act
Section 55A of the Value Added Tax Act 1994 (customers to account for tax on supplies of goods or services of a kind used in missing trader . . . [1] fraud) applies to services of a description specified in article 4.

Amendments—[1] Words "intra-community" revoked by the Taxation (Cross-border Trade) (Miscellaneous Provisions) (EU Exit) (No 2) Regulations, SI 2019/1346 reg 11 with effect from IP completion day (11pm on 31 December 2020).

4 Specified services
The services referred to in article 3 are gas and electricity certificates.

2020/1454

DEFINITION OF QUALIFYING NORTHERN IRELAND GOODS (EU EXIT) REGULATIONS 2020

Made . . . . .4 December 2020
Coming into force . . . . .5 December 2020

1 Citation and commencement
(1) These Regulations may be cited as the Definition of Qualifying Northern Ireland Goods (EU Exit) Regulations 2020.
(2) These Regulations shall come into force on the day after the day they are made.

2 Interpretation
In these Regulations, "Northern Ireland" does not include any part of the territorial waters of the United Kingdom.

3 Definition of qualifying Northern Ireland goods
(1) For the purposes of the European Union (Withdrawal) Act 2018, "qualifying Northern Ireland goods" means goods which—
    (a) meet or have met the condition at paragraph (2), or
    (b) are NI processed products.
(2) The condition is that the goods are present in Northern Ireland and are not subject to any customs supervision, restriction or control which does not arise from the goods being taken out of the territory of Northern Ireland or the European Union.
(3) For the purposes of this regulation—
"NI processed products" are goods which—
    (a) have undergone processing operations carried out in Northern Ireland only, and
    (b) incorporate only goods which—
        (i) were not at the time of processing under any form of customs supervision, restriction or control, or
        (ii) have been domestic goods within the meaning of section 33 of the Taxation (Cross-border Trade) Act 2018;
"processing operations" means any of the following carried out under customs supervision—
    (a) the working of goods, including erecting or assembling them or fitting them to other goods;
    (b) the processing of goods;
    (c) the destruction of goods;
    (d) the repair of goods, including restoring them and putting them in order;
    (e) the use of goods which are not to be found in the processed products, but which allow or facilitate the production of those products, even if they are entirely or partially used up in the process;
    (f) the usual forms of handling intended to preserve the goods, improve their appearance or marketable quality or otherwise prepare them for distribution or resale; and
    (g) any operation on goods intended to ensure their compliance with technical requirements for their release for free circulation in the United Kingdom.

2020/1495

VALUE ADDED TAX (MISCELLANEOUS AND TRANSITIONAL PROVISIONS AMENDMENT AND REVOCATION) (EU EXIT) REGULATIONS 2020

Made . . . . .9 December 2020
Laid before the House of Commons . . . . .10 December 2020
Coming into force in accordance with regulations 1(2)

PART 1
PRELIMINARY

1 Citation and commencement
(1) These Regulations may be cited as the Value Added Tax (Miscellaneous and Transitional Provisions, Amendment and Revocation) (EU Exit) Regulations 2020.
(2) These Regulations come into force on such day or days as the Treasury may by regulations under section 52 of the Taxation (Cross-border Trade) Act 2018 appoint.

Commencement—IP completion day (11pm UK time on 31 December 2020) is the day appointed for the coming into force of these Regulations (see SI 2020/1641 reg 2, Schedule para 10.)

2 Interpretation—general
In these Regulations—
"Commissioners" means HMRC Commissioners;
"TCTA 2018" means the Taxation (Cross-border Trade) Act 2018;
"the VAT Regulations" means the Value Added Tax Regulations 1995;
"VATA 1994" means the Value Added Tax Act 1994.

Commencement—IP completion day (11pm UK time on 31 December 2020) is the day appointed for the coming into force of these Regulations (see SI 2020/1641 reg 2, Schedule para 10.)

PART 2
PHASING IN OF BORDER CONTROLS: ACCOUNTING FOR IMPORT VAT

CHAPTER 1
PRELIMINARY

3 Interpretation of Part 2

In Part 2—

"import VAT" means value added tax chargeable by virtue of section 1(1)(c) of VATA 1994;
"prescribed accounting period" has the meaning given by section 25(1) of VATA 1994;
"registered for VAT" refers to registration under Schedule 1 or 3A to VATA 1994;
"relevant importation" has the meaning given by regulation 6;
"transitional EIDR procedure" has the meaning given by regulation 29D(1) of the Customs (Import Duty) (EU Exit) Regulations 2018 and "transitional simplified Customs declaration" has the meaning given by regulation 14 of those Regulations.

Commencement—IP completion day (11pm UK time on 31 December 2020) is the day appointed for the coming into force of these Regulations (see SI 2020/1641 reg 2, Schedule para 10.)

CHAPTER 2

ACCOUNTING FOR IMPORT VAT BY VAT REGISTERED PERSONS MAKING TRANSITIONAL SIMPLIFIED CUSTOMS DECLARATIONS USING THE EIDR PROCEDURE

4 Application of this Chapter

This Chapter applies to a person who—
  (a) makes a transitional simplified Customs declaration in accordance with regulation 29C(1)(a) of the Customs (Import Duty) (EU Exit) Regulations 2018, or makes a declaration that is treated as being made for the purposes of that regulation by regulation 37(1A) of those Regulations, in respect of an importation of goods into Great Britain from the EU, and
  (b) is registered, or required to be registered, for VAT at the time the person makes that declaration.

Commencement—IP completion day (11pm UK time on 31 December 2020) is the day appointed for the coming into force of these Regulations (see SI 2020/1641 reg 2, Schedule para 10.)

5 Obligation to account for and pay import VAT in accordance with this Chapter

(1) A person to whom this Chapter applies (P) must account for and pay import VAT on goods which comprise a relevant importation in accordance with the provision made by this Chapter.

(2) The effect of section 16(2) of VATA 1994 (application of customs enactments) is modified to the extent that this Chapter makes different provision for accounting for import VAT, including the timing of such accounting, on a relevant importation.

Commencement—IP completion day (11pm UK time on 31 December 2020) is the day appointed for the coming into force of these Regulations (see SI 2020/1641 reg 2, Schedule para 10.)

6 Relevant importation

In this Chapter a "relevant importation" is an importation of goods into Great Britain from the EU where the goods are—
  (a) chargeable with import VAT for which P is liable,
  (b) used or to be used by P for the purposes of a business P carries on,
  (c) required to be declared for the free circulation procedure under Part 1 of TCTA 2018 during the period beginning at IP completion day and ending on 30th June 2021, and
  (d) not of a description excluded from the transitional EIDR procedure by virtue of regulation 29C(4) of the Customs (Import Duty) (EU Exit) Regulations 2018.

Commencement—IP completion day (11pm UK time on 31 December 2020) is the day appointed for the coming into force of these Regulations (see SI 2020/1641 reg 2, Schedule para 10.)

7 Obligation to account for import VAT on VAT return

P must account for and pay the import VAT on goods which comprise a relevant importation on the return that P is required to make for the prescribed accounting period in which the liability for the import VAT is incurred.

Commencement—IP completion day (11pm UK time on 31 December 2020) is the day appointed for the coming into force of these Regulations (see SI 2020/1641 reg 2, Schedule para 10.)

8 Application with modifications of the Value Added Tax (Accounting Procedures for Import VAT for VAT Registered Persons and Amendment) (EU Exit) Regulations 2019

The following provisions of the Value Added Tax (Accounting Procedures for Import VAT for VAT Registered Persons and Amendment) (EU Exit) Regulations 2019 apply for the purposes of this Chapter with, where applicable, the stated modification—
  (a) regulation 8 (interest in cases of official error) applies as if the reference to the importation of relevant goods were a reference to a relevant importation;

(b) regulation 10(1)(a) and (2) (appeals).

Commencement—IP completion day (11pm UK time on 31 December 2020) is the day appointed for the coming into force of these Regulations (see SI 2020/1641 reg 2, Schedule para 10.)

9 Modification of the VAT Regulations where this Chapter applies

Where this Chapter applies the following provisions of the VAT Regulations are to be applied with the stated modifications—
- (a) regulation 28 (estimation of output tax) is to be read as if—
    - (i) the reference to "output tax" includes import VAT chargeable on goods comprising a relevant importation; and
    - (ii) the words from "in the next prescribed accounting period" to the end were "in the prescribed accounting period in which the Commissioners make available to the person details of the amount of import duty due from the person on goods comprising a relevant importation (and in this regulation "import duty" means import duty charged under section 1 of the Taxation (Cross-border Trade) Act 2018).";
- (b) regulation 29(3) (claims for input tax) is to be read as if the words from "in the next prescribed accounting period" to the end read "in the prescribed accounting period in which the Commissioners make available to the person details of the amount of import duty due from the person in that prescribed accounting period on goods comprising a relevant importation (and "import duty" in this regulation means import duty charged under section 1 of the Taxation (Cross-border Trade) Act 2018).";
- (c) regulation 32(3)(baa) (the VAT account) and regulation 40(1)(ba) (VAT to be accounted for on returns and payment of VAT) are to be read as if after "2019" were added "or Chapter 2 of Part 2 of the Value Added Tax (Miscellaneous and Transitional Provisions, Amendment and Revocation) (EU Exit) Regulations 2020,".

Commencement—IP completion day (11pm UK time on 31 December 2020) is the day appointed for the coming into force of these Regulations (see SI 2020/1641 reg 2, Schedule para 10.)

CHAPTER 3

ACCOUNTING FOR IMPORT VAT: OTHER CIRCUMSTANCES

10 Power to make provision by public notice for bringing into account import VAT

(1) The Commissioners may by public notice make such provision for, or in connection with, the bringing into account of import VAT as they consider appropriate in the circumstances specified in paragraph (2).

(2) The circumstances referred to in paragraph (1) are that a person purports to make a transitional simplified Customs declaration in accordance with regulation 29C(1)(a) of the Customs (Import Duty) (EU Exit) Regulations 2018 in respect of an importation of goods into Great Britain from the EU but—
- (a) the person is ineligible to do so;
- (b) the person purports to do so in respect of goods which are of a description not eligible for the transitional EIDR procedure; or
- (c) the declaration is incomplete.

Commencement—IP completion day (11pm UK time on 31 December 2020) is the day appointed for the coming into force of these Regulations (see SI 2020/1641 reg 2, Schedule para 10.)

PART 3
SAVING AND TRANSITIONAL PROVISION FOR REPAYMENTS TO COMMUNITY TRADERS

11 Saving and transitional provision for repayments to Community traders

(1) The omission of Part 20 (repayments to Community traders) (regulations 173 to 184) of the VAT Regulations by regulation 71 of the Value Added Tax (Miscellaneous Amendments and Revocations) (EU Exit) Regulations 2019 does not have effect where—
- (a) a relevant claim is made on or after IP completion day; or
- (b) a relevant claim is made before IP completion day but is still being processed by the Commissioners at IP completion day; or
- (c) a claimant who has made a relevant claim is required to repay an amount to the Commissioners under regulation 173D(3) on or after IP completion day.

(2) In this regulation a relevant claim is a claim—
- (a) for a repayment of VAT under regulation 173B, or
- (b) for an additional repayment of VAT under regulation 173D(2),

that, in either case, as at IP completion day the claimant was entitled to make under Part 20 as it had effect immediately before IP completion day.

(3) A person may make a relevant claim in accordance with this regulation provided that the person does so on or before 31st March 2021.

(4) Where paragraph (1)(a) applies, a relevant claim must relate to either of the following periods, which are "repayment periods" for the purpose of regulation 173G—
    (a) the period from 1st January to 31st December 2019, or
    (b) the period from 1st January 2020 to IP completion day.
(5) Where the Commissioners receive a relevant claim they must forward it on or before 30th April 2021 to the tax authorities of the member State from which the repayment or additional repayment is claimed, and to this extent the omission of section 39A (applications for forwarding of VAT repayment claims to other member States) of the Value Added Tax Act 1994 by paragraph 42 of Schedule 8 to the Taxation (Cross-border Trade) Act 2018 does not have effect.
(6) Where, in relation to a relevant claim that falls within paragraph (1)(a) or (b), the Commissioners make a request under regulation 173R (requests for further information or a document), for paragraph (1)(b) of that regulation read "a request made to the competent authority of a member State of the EU".
(7) Where paragraph (1)(c) applies, the amount must be repaid to the Commissioners in such form or manner and at such time as the Commissioners may prescribe in a public notice.
(8) Where a person has made a relevant claim in relation to the period in paragraph (4)(a) and that claim was based on a provisional attribution of input tax under Article 175(2) of Directive 2006/112/EC as applied in the claimant's member State, the subsequent adjustment to the attribution of input tax under Article 175(3) of that Directive must be made on or before 31st March 2021.
(9) Where a person has made a relevant claim in relation to the period in paragraph (4)(b) and the claim is based on a provisional attribution of input tax under Article 175(2) of Directive 2006/112/EC as applied in the claimant's member State, any subsequent adjustment to the attribution of input tax must be made under regulation 12 of these Regulations.

Commencement—IP completion day (11pm UK time on 31 December 2020) is the day appointed for the coming into force of these Regulations (see SI 2020/1641 reg 2, Schedule para 10.)

12 Transitional provision for partial exemption adjustments relating to the period from 1st January 2020 to IP completion day

(1) Subject to paragraph (2), where regulation 11(9) applies and a person is required or wishes to make an adjustment to a provisional attribution of input tax for the period from 1st January 2020 to IP completion day, the person must do so by making a claim using the procedure in Part 21 (regulations 185 to 197) of the VAT Regulations as it has effect on and after IP completion day.
(2) Any claim relating to the period from 1st January 2020 to IP completion day must be made on or before 31st December 2021.

Commencement—IP completion day (11pm UK time on 31 December 2020) is the day appointed for the coming into force of these Regulations (see SI 2020/1641 reg 2, Schedule para 10.)

PART 4
SAVING PROVISION FOR ELECTRONIC, TELECOMMUNICATION AND BROADCASTING SERVICES: NON-UNION AND UNION SCHEMES

13 Interpretation of Part 4
In Part 4—
  "Part 26" means Part 26 (UK Union and non-Union special accounting schemes: registration, notification of changes, and returns) (regulations 214 to 218) of the VAT Regulations;
  "Part 27" means Part 27 (non-UK Union and non-Union special accounting schemes: adjustments, claims and error correction) (regulations 219 to 223) of the VAT Regulations;
  "Schedule 3B" means Schedule 3B (electronic, telecommunication and broadcasting services: non-Union scheme) to VATA 1994;
  "Schedule 3BA" means Schedule 3BA (electronic, telecommunication and broadcasting services: Union scheme) to the VATA 1994.

Commencement—IP completion day (11pm UK time on 31 December 2020) is the day appointed for the coming into force of these Regulations (see SI 2020/1641 reg 2, Schedule para 10.)

14 Saving provision for electronic, telecommunication and broadcasting services: non-Union scheme

(1) Schedule 3B continues to apply in relation to supplies made before IP completion day despite its omission by paragraph 86 of Schedule 8 to TCTA 2018.
(2) To the extent that it continues to apply, Schedule 3B has effect subject to such modifications as may be specified in a notice published by the Commissioners.

Commencement—IP completion day (11pm UK time on 31 December 2020) is the day appointed for the coming into force of these Regulations (see SI 2020/1641 reg 2, Schedule para 10.)

15 Saving provision for electronic, telecommunication and broadcasting services: Union scheme

(1) Schedule 3BA continues to apply in relation to supplies made before IP completion day despite its omission by paragraph 87 of Schedule 8 to TCTA 2018.

(2) To the extent that it continues to apply, Schedule 3BA has effect subject to such modifications as may be specified in a notice published by the Commissioners.

Commencement—IP completion day (11pm UK time on 31 December 2020) is the day appointed for the coming into force of these Regulations (see SI 2020/1641 reg 2, Schedule para 10.)

16 Saving provision for references to Schedules 3B and 3BA in VATA 1994

(1) Any references to Schedule 3B or to Schedule 3BA in VATA 1994 (other than those mentioned in regulations 14 and 15) that have been omitted by Schedule 8 to TCTA 2018 continue to apply in relation to supplies made before IP completion day as if they had not been so omitted, but only to the extent that Schedules 3B and 3BA continue to have effect in accordance with these Regulations.

(2) To the extent that they continue to apply, references to Schedule 3B or to Schedule 3BA in VATA 1994 have effect subject to such modifications as may be specified in a notice published by the Commissioners.

Commencement—IP completion day (11pm UK time on 31 December 2020) is the day appointed for the coming into force of these Regulations (see SI 2020/1641 reg 2, Schedule para 10.)

17 Saving Provision for Part 26 of the Value Added Tax Regulations 1995 (UK Union and Non-Union Special Accounting Schemes: Registration, Notification of Changes, and Returns)

(1) Part 26 continues to apply in relation to supplies made before IP completion day despite its omission by regulation 79 of the Value Added Tax (Miscellaneous Amendments and Revocations) (EU Exit) Regulations 2019.

(2) To the extent that it continues to apply, Part 26 has effect subject to such modifications as may be specified in a notice published by the Commissioners.

Commencement—IP completion day (11pm UK time on 31 December 2020) is the day appointed for the coming into force of these Regulations (see SI 2020/1641 reg 2, Schedule para 10.)

18 Saving provision for part 27 of the Value Added Tax Regulations 1995 (Non-UK Union and Non-Union special accounting schemes: adjustments, claims and error correction)

(1) Part 27 continues to apply in relation to supplies made before IP completion day despite its omission by regulation 80 of the Value Added Tax (Miscellaneous Amendments and Revocations) (EU Exit) Regulations 2019.

(2) To the extent that it continues to apply, Part 27 has effect subject to such modifications as may be specified in a notice published by the Commissioners.

Commencement—IP completion day (11pm UK time on 31 December 2020) is the day appointed for the coming into force of these Regulations (see SI 2020/1641 reg 2, Schedule para 10.)

PART 5
AMENDMENTS TO EU EXIT REGULATIONS

19 Amendment of the Value Added Tax (Miscellaneous Amendments and Revocations) (EU Exit) Regulations 2019

(1) The Value Added Tax (Miscellaneous Amendments and Revocations) (EU Exit) Regulations 2019 are amended as follows.

(2) In regulation 83 (amendment of the Value Added Tax (Place of Supply of Goods) Order 2004), after paragraph (2) insert—

"(3) Omit Part 4 (chain transactions) (regulations 15 to 18)."

Commencement—IP completion day (11pm UK time on 31 December 2020) is the day appointed for the coming into force of these Regulations (see SI 2020/1641 reg 2, Schedule para 10.)

20 Amendment of the Value Added Tax (Accounting Procedures for Import VAT for VAT Registered Persons and Amendment) (EU Exit) Regulations 2019

(1) The Value Added Tax (Accounting Procedures for Import VAT for VAT Registered Persons and Amendment) (EU Exit) Regulations 2019 are amended as follows.

(2) In regulation 2 (interpretation), for the definition of "relevant goods" substitute—

""relevant goods" means goods imported into the United Kingdom by a registered person which are used or to be used for the purposes of any business carried on by the registered person, but does not include goods which are the subject of a declaration by a qualifying traveller within the meaning of regulation 39B of the Customs (Import Duty) (EU Exit) Regulations 2018;".

(3) In regulation 3(1), after "relevant goods" insert " (but this is subject to Part 2 of the Value Added Tax (Miscellaneous and Transitional Provisions, Amendment and Revocation) (EU Exit) Regulations 2020)".

(4) In regulation 12—
  (a) in paragraph (3)(b), for the full stop after "2019" substitute a comma;
  (b) for sub-paragraph (a) of paragraph (4) substitute—
    "(a) in paragraph (2), omit ", except that the total of the output tax due" to the end except for the final full stop; and".

Commencement—IP completion day (11pm UK time on 31 December 2020) is the day appointed for the coming into force of these Regulations (see SI 2020/1641 reg 2, Schedule para 10.)

21 Amendment of the Taxation (Cross-Border Trade) Act 2018 (Value Added Tax Transitional Provisions) (EU Exit) Regulations 2019
(1) The Taxation (Cross-border Trade) Act 2018 (Value Added Tax Transitional Provisions) (EU Exit) Regulations 2019 are amended as follows.
(2) In regulation 2, omit the definition for "Chapter 7".
(3) In regulation 3, in each place it occurs, for "exit day" substitute "IP completion day".
(4) For regulation 4, substitute—

"**4** The amendments made by Part 3 of the Act do not have effect in relation to a supply of goods dispatched or transported from the territory of the United Kingdom to the territory of a member State of the EU, or vice versa, provided that the dispatch or transport started before IP completion day and ended thereafter.".
(5) In regulation 5, in each place it occurs, for "exit day" substitute "IP completion day".

Commencement—IP completion day (11pm UK time on 31 December 2020) is the day appointed for the coming into force of these Regulations (see SI 2020/1641 reg 2, Schedule para 10.)

22 Amendment of the Value Added Tax (Miscellaneous Amendments, Revocation and Transitional Provisions) (EU Exit) Regulations 2019
(1) The Value Added Tax (Miscellaneous Amendments, Revocation and Transitional Provisions) (EU Exit) Regulations 2019 are amended as follows.
(2) Omit regulation 8.
(3) In regulation 9, in each place it occurs, for "exit day" substitute "IP completion day".
(4) For regulation 10, substitute—

"**10** The amendments made in relation to value added tax by any regulations made by the appropriate Minister under the Taxation (Cross-border Trade) Act 2018, or by statutory instrument under any other enactment in consequence of, or otherwise in connection with, the United Kingdom's withdrawal from the EU, do not have effect in relation to a supply of goods dispatched or transported from the territory of the United Kingdom to the territory of a member State of the EU, or vice versa, provided that the dispatch or transport started before IP completion day and ended thereafter.".
(5) Omit Part 4 (regulation 15).

Commencement—IP completion day (11pm UK time on 31 December 2020) is the day appointed for the coming into force of these Regulations (see SI 2020/1641 reg 2, Schedule para 10.)

23 Amendment of the Value Added Tax (Miscellaneous Amendments and Transitional Provisions) (EU Exit) Regulations 2019
(1) The Value Added Tax (Miscellaneous Amendments and Transitional Provisions) (EU Exit) Regulations 2019 are amended as follows.
(2) Omit Part 4 (transitional provisions in relation to value added tax) (regulations 4 and 5).
(3) In Part 5 (fulfilment businesses) (regulations 6 to 15), in each place it occurs (including the headings), for "exit day" substitute "IP completion day".

Commencement—IP completion day (11pm UK time on 31 December 2020) is the day appointed for the coming into force of these Regulations (see SI 2020/1641 reg 2, Schedule para 10.)

PART 6
REVOCATION OF RETAINED DIRECT EU LEGISLATION CONCERNING SIMPLIFICATION MEASURES FOR VAT ON FUEL AND HIRING OR LEASING A CAR WHERE CAR IS NOT USED ENTIRELY FOR BUSINESS PURPOSES

24 Interpretation
In Part 6 "the EU legislation" means—
  (a) Council Implementing Decision (EU) 2018/1918 authorising the United Kingdom to apply a special measure derogating from Articles 16 and 168 of Directive 2006/112/EC on the common system of value added tax; and
  (b) Council Implementing Decision (EU) 2019/2230 of 19 December 2019 amending Decision 2007/884/EC authorising the United Kingdom to continue to apply a measure derogating from Articles 26(1)(a), 168 and 169 of Directive 2006/112/EC on the common system of value added tax.

Commencement—IP completion day (11pm UK time on 31 December 2020) is the day appointed for the coming into force of these Regulations (see SI 2020/1641 reg 2, Schedule para 10.)

25 The EU legislation ceases to have effect.

Commencement—IP completion day (11pm UK time on 31 December 2020) is the day appointed for the coming into force of these Regulations (see SI 2020/1641 reg 2, Schedule para 10.)

PART 7
OTHER REVOCATIONS

26 The following Regulations are revoked, so far as not already revoked—
  (a) The Value Added Tax (Postal Packets and Amendment) (EU Exit) Regulations 2018;
  (b) The Data-gathering Powers (Relevant Data) (Amendment) (EU Exit) Regulations 2019.

Commencement—IP completion day (11pm UK time on 31 December 2020) is the day appointed for the coming into force of these Regulations (see SI 2020/1641 reg 2, Schedule para 10.)

2020/1525

EUROPEAN UNION (WITHDRAWAL) ACT 2018 (RELEVANT COURT) (RETAINED EU CASE LAW) REGULATIONS 2020

Made . . . . .9 December 2020
Coming into force in accordance with regulation 1

The Secretary of State makes these Regulations in exercise of the powers conferred by section 6(5A)(a), (b) and (c) and (5B)(a) of the European Union (Withdrawal) Act 2018.

In accordance with section 6(5C) of that Act, the Secretary of State has carried out the necessary consultations.

In accordance with paragraph 9A of Schedule 7 to that Act, a draft of this instrument has been laid before, and approved by a resolution of, each House of Parliament.

1 Citation and commencement
These Regulations may be cited as the European Union (Withdrawal) Act 2018 (Relevant Court) (Retained EU Case Law) Regulations 2020 and come into force on IP completion day.

2 Interpretation
In these Regulations—
  "the 2018 Act" means the European Union (Withdrawal) Act 2018;
  "post-transition case law" means any principles laid down by, and any decisions of, a court or tribunal in the United Kingdom, as they have effect on or after IP completion day.

3 Relevant courts
For the purposes of section 6 of the 2018 Act, each of the following is a relevant court—
  (a) the Court Martial Appeal Court,
  (b) the Court of Appeal in England and Wales,
  (c) the Inner House of the Court of Session,
  (d) the High Court of Justiciary when sitting as a court of appeal in relation to a compatibility issue (within the meaning given by section 288ZA(2) of the Criminal Procedure (Scotland) Act 1995) or a devolution issue (within the meaning given by paragraph 1 of Schedule 6 to the Scotland Act 1998),
  (e) the court for hearing appeals under section 57(1)(b) of the Representation of the People Act 1983,
  (f) the Lands Valuation Appeal Court, and
  (g) the Court of Appeal in Northern Ireland.

4 Extent to which a relevant court is not bound by retained EU case law
(1) A relevant court is not bound by any retained EU case law except as provided in paragraph (2).
(2) A relevant court is bound by retained EU case law so far as there is post-transition case law which modifies or applies that retained EU case law and which is binding on the relevant court.

5 Test to be applied
In deciding whether to depart from any retained EU case law by virtue of section 6(4)(ba) of the 2018 Act and these Regulations, a relevant court must apply the same test as the Supreme Court would apply in deciding whether to depart from the case law of the Supreme Court.

2020/1545

VALUE ADDED TAX (MISCELLANEOUS AMENDMENTS, NORTHERN IRELAND PROTOCOL AND SAVINGS AND TRANSITIONAL PROVISIONS) (EU EXIT) REGULATIONS 2020

Made . . . . .18 December 2020
Laid before the House of Commons . . . . .21 December 2020

Coming into force in accordance with regulation 1

The Treasury make these Regulations in exercise of the powers conferred by sections 51(1)(a) and (3) and 52(2) of the Taxation (Cross-border Trade) Act 2018.

In accordance with section 51(1) of that Act, the Treasury consider it appropriate in consequence of, or otherwise in connection with, the withdrawal of the United Kingdom from the EU to make the following provision in relation to value added tax, including to make such provision as might be made by Act of Parliament. In accordance with section 52(2) of that Act, the Treasury consider it appropriate in consequence of, or otherwise in connection with, the withdrawal of the United Kingdom from the EU for these Regulations to come into force on such day or days as the Treasury may by regulations under section 52 of that Act appoint.

Commencement—IP completion day (11pm UK time on 31 December 2020) is the day appointed for the coming into force of these Regulations (see SI 2020/1641 reg 2, Schedule para 11.)

PART 4
SAVINGS AND TRANSITIONAL PROVISIONS

109 Interpretation of this Part

(1) In this Part—

"the accounting procedures Regulations" means the Value Added Tax (Accounting Procedures for Import VAT for VAT Registered Persons and Amendment) (EU Exit) Regulations 2019;

"acquisition VAT" means VAT charged in accordance with VATA 1994 (as it had effect immediately before IP completion day) on the acquisition in the United Kingdom of goods from a member State;

"Commissioners" means the Commissioners for Her Majesty's Revenue and Customs;

"import VAT" means VAT charged in accordance with section 1(1)(c) of VATA 1994;

"the Part 3 amendments" means the amendments made by Part 3 of TCTA 2018;

"the secondary legislation amendments" means the amendments made in relation to value added tax by any regulations made by the appropriate Minister under TCTA 2018, or by statutory instrument under any other enactment in consequence of, or otherwise in connection with, the United Kingdom's withdrawal from the EU;

"TCTA 2018" means the Taxation (Cross-border Trade) Act 2018;

"VATA 1994" means the Value Added Tax Act 1994.

(2) For the purposes of this Part, any reference in the provisions of VATA 1994 and in subordinate legislation made under that Act (as they had effect immediately before IP completion day) to "another member State" is treated as if it were a reference to "a member State".

Commencement—IP completion day (11pm UK time on 31 December 2020) is the day appointed for the coming into force of these Regulations (see SI 2020/1641 reg 2, Schedule para 11.)

110 Transitional provision in relation to acquisition VAT

(1) Paragraph (2) applies where—
  (a) the time that an acquisition in the United Kingdom of goods from a member State is treated as taking place, as determined by section 12 of VATA 1994 (as it had effect immediately before IP completion day), falls on or after IP completion day; and
  (b) the goods enter the territory of the United Kingdom before IP completion day.

(2) Where this paragraph applies, acquisition VAT is charged, and the person who is liable for the acquisition VAT must account for it, as if the Part 3 amendments and the secondary legislation amendments, insofar as they relate to acquisition VAT, had no effect.

Commencement—IP completion day (11pm UK time on 31 December 2020) is the day appointed for the coming into force of these Regulations (see SI 2020/1641 reg 2, Schedule para 11.)

111 (1) Paragraph (2) applies where—
  (a) the time that an acquisition in the United Kingdom of goods from a member State is treated as taking place, as determined by section 12 of VATA 1994 (as it had effect immediately before IP completion day), falls before IP completion day; and
  (b) the goods so acquired enter the territory of the United Kingdom on or after IP completion day.

(2) Where this paragraph applies—
  (a) the person who is liable for the acquisition VAT must account for it as if the Part 3 amendments and the secondary legislation amendments, insofar as they relate to acquisition VAT, had no effect;
  (b) in cases where the person mentioned in sub-paragraph (a) is also liable for import VAT on the importation of the same goods, that person must—
    (i) account for the import VAT in the manner prescribed by regulation 4 of the accounting procedures Regulations, as if that provision required (rather than permitted) the person to account for import VAT in that manner, provided that the conditions in regulation 5 of those Regulations are met, and

(ii) when accounting for the import VAT—
- (aa) reduce its amount by the amount of the acquisition VAT for which that person is also liable in relation to the same goods, or
- (bb) if the liability for acquisition VAT is greater than the corresponding liability for import VAT, reduce the amount accounted for in respect of import VAT to nil; and

(c) the person liable for the import VAT, if otherwise entitled to credit for input tax in respect of that charge under section 25 of VATA 1994, is not entitled to such credit for any sum greater than the net amount of import VAT accounted for under sub-paragraph (b).

Commencement—IP completion day (11pm UK time on 31 December 2020) is the day appointed for the coming into force of these Regulations (see SI 2020/1641 reg 2, Schedule para 11.)

112 (1) Paragraph (2) applies where—
- (a) a supply of goods as is mentioned in section 14(2) of VATA 1994 (as it had effect immediately before IP completion day) is treated as an acquisition of goods from a member State;
- (b) the time that such acquisition is treated as taking place, as determined by section 12 of VATA 1994 (as it had effect immediately before IP completion day), falls on or after IP completion day; and
- (c) the goods so supplied enter the territory of the United Kingdom before IP completion day.

(2) Where this paragraph applies, acquisition VAT is charged, and the person who is liable for the acquisition VAT must account for it, as if the Part 3 amendments and the secondary legislation amendments, insofar as they relate to acquisition VAT, had no effect.

Commencement—IP completion day (11pm UK time on 31 December 2020) is the day appointed for the coming into force of these Regulations (see SI 2020/1641 reg 2, Schedule para 11.)

113 (1) Paragraph (2) applies where—
- (a) a supply of goods as is mentioned in section 14(2) of VATA 1994 (as it had effect immediately before IP completion day) is treated as an acquisition of goods from a member State;
- (b) the time that such acquisition is treated as taking place, as determined by section 12 of VATA 1994 (as it had effect immediately before IP completion day), falls before IP completion day; and
- (c) the goods so supplied (or any part of them) enter the territory of the United Kingdom on or after IP completion day.

(2) Where this paragraph applies—
- (a) the person who is liable for the acquisition VAT charged in relation to the transaction described in paragraph (1) must account for the full value of the supply, including that which relates to the installation or assembly (as the case may be) of the goods, as if the Part 3 amendments and the secondary legislation amendments, insofar as they relate to acquisition VAT, had no effect;
- (b) in cases where the person mentioned in sub-paragraph (a) is also liable for import VAT on the importation of the same goods, that person must—
    - (i) account for the import VAT in the manner prescribed by regulation 4 of the accounting procedures Regulations, as if that provision required (rather than permitted) the person to account for import VAT in that manner, provided that the conditions in regulation 5 of those Regulations are met, and
    - (ii) when accounting for the import VAT—
        - (aa) reduce its amount by the amount of the acquisition VAT for which that person is also liable in relation to the same goods, or
        - (bb) if the liability for acquisition VAT is greater than the corresponding liability for import VAT, reduce the amount accounted for in respect of import VAT to nil; and
- (c) the person liable for the import VAT, if otherwise entitled to credit for input tax in respect of that charge under section 25 of VATA 1994, is not entitled to such credit for any sum greater than the net amount of import VAT accounted for under sub-paragraph (b).

Commencement—IP completion day (11pm UK time on 31 December 2020) is the day appointed for the coming into force of these Regulations (see SI 2020/1641 reg 2, Schedule para 11.)

114 (1) Regulations 110 to 113 do not apply in relation to transactions involving the removal of goods from a member State to the United Kingdom as a result of their entry into Northern Ireland (as to which see provision relating to VAT on acquisitions in Northern Ireland from member States in Schedule 9ZA to VATA 1994).

(2) Regulations 115 to 118 apply in relation to the transactions referred to in paragraph (1).

Commencement—IP completion day (11pm UK time on 31 December 2020) is the day appointed for the coming into force of these Regulations (see SI 2020/1641 reg 2, Schedule para 11.)

115 Where an acquisition in Northern Ireland of goods from a member State is treated as taking place on or after IP completion day in accordance with paragraph 4(1) of Schedule 9ZA to VATA 1994 and the time of acquisition is determined by reference to a first removal of the goods occurring before IP completion day, the fact that the first removal occurs at that time does not affect the charge to VAT that is imposed under paragraph 1 of that Schedule.

Commencement—IP completion day (11pm UK time on 31 December 2020) is the day appointed for the coming into force of these Regulations (see SI 2020/1641 reg 2, Schedule para 11.)

116 Where an acquisition in Northern Ireland of goods from a member State is treated as taking place before IP completion day in accordance with section 12 of VATA 1994 (as it had effect immediately before IP completion day), the charge to VAT is to be treated as NI acquisition VAT under Schedule 9ZA to VATA 1994 for all purposes relating to things that arise, occur or are done in consequence of or in relation to that charge on or after IP completion day.

Commencement—IP completion day (11pm UK time on 31 December 2020) is the day appointed for the coming into force of these Regulations (see SI 2020/1641 reg 2, Schedule para 11.)

117 Where—
(a) goods are supplied in the circumstances described in paragraph 6(3) of Schedule 9ZA to VATA 1994,
(b) the supply is treated as an acquisition of goods taking place on or after IP completion day in accordance with paragraph 4(1) of that Schedule,
(c) and the goods are removed from a member State to Northern Ireland before IP completion day,

the fact that the removal occurs at that time does not affect the application of the provision in paragraph 6(3) of Schedule 9ZA and does not affect the charge to VAT that is imposed under paragraph 1 of that Schedule.

Commencement—IP completion day (11pm UK time on 31 December 2020) is the day appointed for the coming into force of these Regulations (see SI 2020/1641 reg 2, Schedule para 11.)

118 (1) Paragraph (2) applies where—
(a) goods are supplied in the circumstances described in paragraph 6(3) of Schedule 9ZA to VATA 1994;
(b) the supply is treated as an acquisition of goods taking place before IP completion day in accordance with section 12 and section 14(2) of VATA 1994 (as those sections had effect immediately before IP completion day); and
(c) the goods (or any part of them) are removed from a member State to Northern Ireland on or after IP completion day.

(2) Where this paragraph applies—
(a) the supply of goods is to be treated as involving their removal from a member State to Northern Ireland in accordance with paragraph 6(3) of Schedule 9ZA to VATA 1994;
(b) the fact that the removal of the goods (or part of them) takes place on or after IP completion day does not affect the application of that paragraph; and
(c) the charge to VAT is to be treated as NI acquisition VAT under Schedule 9ZA to VATA 1994 for all purposes relating to things that arise, occur or are done in consequence of or in relation to that charge on or after IP completion day

Commencement—IP completion day (11pm UK time on 31 December 2020) is the day appointed for the coming into force of these Regulations (see SI 2020/1641 reg 2, Schedule para 11.)

119 Transitional provision in relation to the movement of goods between Great Britain and Northern Ireland

(1) Paragraph (2) applies where—
(a) there is a removal of goods from Great Britain to Northern Ireland in the course of a taxable supply made by a taxable person;
(b) the time that a supply in relation to the goods is treated as taking place, as determined by section 6 of VATA 1994, falls before IP completion day;
(c) the goods enter the territory of Northern Ireland on or after IP completion day;
(d) a person is liable for VAT on the supply; and
(e) the person who is liable for VAT on the supply is also liable for VAT charged on the entry of the goods into Northern Ireland by para 3(4) of Schedule 9ZB to VATA 1994.

(2) Where this paragraph applies—
(a) the person liable for the VAT charged on the entry of the goods into Northern Ireland must, when accounting for that VAT—
(i) reduce its amount by the amount of the VAT for which that person is also liable in relation to the supply of the same goods by virtue of the supply (or some part of its amount) being treated as taking place before IP completion day, or

(ii) if the liability for the VAT on the supply is greater than the corresponding liability for VAT on the entry of the goods into Northern Ireland, reduce the amount accounted for in respect of the VAT charged on the entry of the goods into Northern Ireland to nil; and
 (b) any person who would otherwise be entitled to credit under section 25 of VATA 1994 for input tax in respect of the VAT charged on the entry of the goods into Northern Ireland, is not entitled to such credit for any sum greater than the net amount of that VAT accounted for under sub-paragraph (a).

Commencement—IP completion day (11pm UK time on 31 December 2020) is the day appointed for the coming into force of these Regulations (see SI 2020/1641 reg 2, Schedule para 11.)

120 (1) Paragraph (2) applies where—
 (a) there is a removal of goods from Northern Ireland to Great Britain in the course of a taxable supply made by a taxable person;
 (b) the time that a supply in relation to the goods is treated as taking place, as determined by section 6 of VATA 1994, falls before IP completion day;
 (c) the goods enter the territory of Great Britain on or after IP completion day;
 (d) a person is liable for VAT on the supply; and
 (e) the person who is liable for VAT on the supply is also liable for VAT charged on the entry of the goods into Great Britain by para 3(2) of Schedule 9ZB to VATA 1994.
(2) Where this paragraph applies—
 (a) the person liable for the VAT charged on the entry of the goods into Great Britain must, when accounting for that VAT—
  (i) reduce its amount by the amount of the VAT for which that person is also liable in relation to the supply of the same goods by virtue of the supply (or some part of its amount) being treated as taking place before IP completion day, or
  (ii) if the liability for the VAT on the supply is greater than the corresponding liability for VAT on the entry of the goods into Great Britain, reduce the amount accounted for in respect of the VAT charged on the entry of the goods into Great Britain to nil; and
 (b) any person who would otherwise be entitled to credit under section 25 of VATA 1994 for input tax in respect of the VAT charged on the entry of the goods into Great Britain, is not entitled to such credit for any sum greater than the net amount of that VAT accounted for under sub-paragraph (a).

Commencement—IP completion day (11pm UK time on 31 December 2020) is the day appointed for the coming into force of these Regulations (see SI 2020/1641 reg 2, Schedule para 11.)

121 Transitional provision in relation to secondary legislation amended by these Regulations
The amendments made by regulation 11(2) to the Value Added Tax (Cars) Order 1992 do not apply where—
 (a) a person ("P") took possession of the used motor car in Great Britain or the Isle of Man before IP completion day and P would have been eligible to opt to account for the VAT chargeable on a supply of the motor car on the profit margin in accordance with article 8 had it been so supplied before IP completion day; and
 (b) the ownership of the used motor car remained with P from the time P took possession of it under paragraph (a) to the time of the supply of the motor car on which P elects to account for the VAT chargeable on that supply on the profit margin in accordance with article 8.

Commencement—IP completion day (11pm UK time on 31 December 2020) is the day appointed for the coming into force of these Regulations (see SI 2020/1641 reg 2, Schedule para 11.)

122 (1) Paragraph (2) applies where—
 (a) there is a removal of gold as described in the Value Added Tax (Treatment of Transactions) (No 2) Order 1992; and
 (b) acquisition VAT would (but for the provisions made in that Order) be charged on or after IP completion day in accordance with transitional provision made in these Regulations or other regulations made under TCTA 2018.
(2) Where this paragraph applies, the treatment of the acquisition of gold specified in that Order continues to apply as if the Order had not been amended by these Regulations.

Commencement—IP completion day (11pm UK time on 31 December 2020) is the day appointed for the coming into force of these Regulations (see SI 2020/1641 reg 2, Schedule para 11.)

123 (1) Paragraph (2) applies where acquisition VAT is charged on or after IP completion day in accordance with transitional provision made in these Regulations or other regulations made under TCTA 2018.
(2) Where this paragraph applies, the provisions of the Value Added Tax (Input Tax) Order 1992 concerning the disallowance of input tax in relation to goods acquired in the United Kingdom from a member State in accordance with provisions of VATA 1994 (as it had effect immediately before IP completion day), continue to apply as if the Order had not been amended by these Regulations.

124 The amendment made by regulation 30(5)(c) to the Value Added Tax (Special Provisions) Order 1995 does not apply where—
- (a) a person ("P") took possession of the goods in Great Britain or the Isle of Man before IP completion day and P would have been eligible to opt to account for the VAT chargeable on a supply of the goods on the profit margin in accordance with article 12 of the Order had they been so supplied before IP completion day; and
- (b) the ownership of the goods remained with P from the time P took possession of the goods under paragraph (a) to the time of the supply of the goods on which P elects to account for the VAT chargeable on that supply on the profit margin in accordance with article 12 of the Order.

Commencement—IP completion day (11pm UK time on 31 December 2020) is the day appointed for the coming into force of these Regulations (see SI 2020/1641 reg 2, Schedule para 11.)

125 (1) Subject to paragraph (2), regulation 121D of the Value Added Tax Regulations 1995 additionally applies to goods that are—
- (a) transported from the United Kingdom to a member State prior to IP completion day, and remain located in a member State as at IP completion day; or
- (b) exported from a member State prior to IP completion day and remain located outside the member States as at IP completion day.

(2) For the purposes of paragraph (1), the terms "unpaid" and "paid" in regulation 121D(5) of those Regulations also refer to—
- (a) an acquisition of goods in the United Kingdom before the re-importation;
- (b) an importation of the goods from outside the member States before the re-importation;
- (c) a supply or acquisition of the goods in a member State before the re-importation.

Commencement—IP completion day (11pm UK time on 31 December 2020) is the day appointed for the coming into force of these Regulations (see SI 2020/1641 reg 2, Schedule para 11.)

126 In the application of regulation 121D of the Value Added Tax Regulations 1995 to goods which are in the United Kingdom as at IP completion day, the terms "unpaid" and "paid" in paragraph (5) are to have the additional meanings given in regulation 125(2).

Commencement—IP completion day (11pm UK time on 31 December 2020) is the day appointed for the coming into force of these Regulations (see SI 2020/1641 reg 2, Schedule para 11.)

127 Regulation 121D of the Value Added Tax Regulations 1995 does not apply to goods supplied at any time to any person pursuant to regulation 131 of those Regulations.

Commencement—IP completion day (11pm UK time on 31 December 2020) is the day appointed for the coming into force of these Regulations (see SI 2020/1641 reg 2, Schedule para 11.)

128 (1) Paragraph (2) applies where acquisition VAT would, but for the provisions made in the Value Added Tax (Acquisitions) Relief Order 2002, be charged on or after IP completion day in accordance with transitional provision made in these Regulations or other regulations made under TCTA 2018.
(2) Where this paragraph applies, the relief from acquisition VAT provided for in that Order continues to apply as if the Order had not been amended by these Regulations.

Commencement—IP completion day (11pm UK time on 31 December 2020) is the day appointed for the coming into force of these Regulations (see SI 2020/1641 reg 2, Schedule para 11.)

129 (1) Paragraph (2) applies where—
- (a) the Community transport mentioned in Part 2 (goods supplied on board ships, aircraft and trains) of the Value Added Tax (Place of Supply of Goods) Order 2004 (as it had effect immediately before IP completion day) begins before IP completion day; and
- (b) the goods to which that Order applies are supplied on or after IP completion day.

(2) Where this paragraph applies, the provisions in that Order concerning the place where the supply of goods is treated as taking place, continue to apply as if that Part had not been amended by these Regulations.

Commencement—IP completion day (11pm UK time on 31 December 2020) is the day appointed for the coming into force of these Regulations (see SI 2020/1641 reg 2, Schedule para 11.)

130 Supplementary provision to be made by the Commissioners

Where, in this Part, a person is required to account for acquisition VAT, import VAT or VAT for which that person is liable by virtue of paragraph 4(3) of Schedule 9ZB to VATA 1994—
- (a) the Commissioners may make such supplementary provision in a notice published by them as they consider necessary for the accounting for that VAT (including specifying the box in a person's VAT return in which entries are to be made); and
- (b) in relation to cases where VAT is required to be accounted for in the manner prescribed by regulation 4 of the accounting procedures Regulations subject to the conditions in

regulation 5 of those Regulations being met, and those conditions are not met, the VAT for which that person is liable on the importation of the goods must be accounted for in accordance with provision set out in a notice published by the Commissioners.

Commencement—IP completion day (11pm UK time on 31 December 2020) is the day appointed for the coming into force of these Regulations (see SI 2020/1641 reg 2, Schedule para 11.)

131 The Commissioners may make such further supplementary provision in a notice published by them as they consider necessary in connection with the transitional provision made in this Part.

Commencement—IP completion day (11pm UK time on 31 December 2020) is the day appointed for the coming into force of these Regulations (see SI 2020/1641 reg 2, Schedule para 11.)

2020/1546

VALUE ADDED TAX (NORTHERN IRELAND) (EU EXIT) REGULATIONS 2020

Made . . . . .18 December 2020
Laid before the House of Commons . . . . .21 December 2020
Coming into force in accordance with regulation 1

The Treasury make these Regulations in exercise of the powers conferred by sections 51(1)(a) and (3) and 52(2) of the Taxation (Cross-border Trade) Act 2018.
In accordance with section 51(1) of that Act, the Treasury consider it appropriate in consequence of, or otherwise in connection with, the withdrawal of the United Kingdom from the EU to make the following provision in relation to value added tax, including to make such provision as might be made by Act of Parliament. In accordance with section 52(2) of that Act, the Treasury consider it appropriate in consequence of, or otherwise in connection with, the withdrawal of the United Kingdom from the EU for these Regulations to come into force on such day or days as the Treasury may by regulations under section 52 of that Act appoint.

Commencement—IP completion day (11pm UK time on 31 December 2020) is the day appointed for the coming into force of these Regulations (see SI 2020/1641 reg 2, Schedule para 12.)

PART 1
PRELIMINARY

1 Citation and commencement

These Regulations may be cited as the Value Added Tax (Northern Ireland) (EU Exit) Regulations 2020 and come into force on such day or days as the Treasury may by regulations made under section 52 of the Taxation (Cross-border Trade) Act 2018 appoint.

Commencement—IP completion day (11pm UK time on 31 December 2020) is the day appointed for the coming into force of these Regulations (see SI 2020/1641 reg 2, Schedule para 12.)

2 Interpretation

(1) Terms used in both these Regulations and the Value Added Tax Act 1994 have the same meaning in these Regulations as they have in that Act.
(2) That Act is referred to in these Regulations as "VATA".

Commencement—IP completion day (11pm UK time on 31 December 2020) is the day appointed for the coming into force of these Regulations (see SI 2020/1641 reg 2, Schedule para 12.)

PART 2
LIABILITY FOR VAT ON REMOVALS: EXCEPTIONS

3 Removals of gold: customer to account

(1) Paragraph (2) applies where—
  (a) a taxable person makes a taxable supply of gold within the meaning of section 55(5) of VATA (customers to account for tax on supplies of gold etc) to a person (P) who—
    (i) is a taxable person at the time the supply is made; and
    (ii) is supplied in connection with the carrying on by P of a business; and
  (b) the supply involves the removal of the gold from Great Britain to Northern Ireland; or vice versa.
(2) Where this paragraph applies, P (and only P) is treated as having imported the gold for the purpose of paragraph 4 of Schedule 9ZB to VATA (liability for VAT on movements between Great Britain and Northern Ireland) instead of the supplier.
(3) This regulation is subject to regulation 6 (special customs procedures).

Commencement—IP completion day (11pm UK time on 31 December 2020) is the day appointed for the coming into force of these Regulations (see SI 2020/1641 reg 2, Schedule para 12.)

4 Removals of investment gold: person to account is the person who would have accounted for VAT on the supply

(1) Paragraph (2) applies where—

(a) a taxable person makes a supply of gold of a description which but for Note 4(b) to Group 15 of Schedule 9 to VATA (investment gold) would have fallen within that Group; and
(b) the supply involves the removal of the gold from Great Britain to Northern Ireland, or vice versa.

(2) Where this paragraph applies, the person who is treated as having imported the gold for the purpose of paragraph 4 of Schedule 9ZB to VATA is the person (and only that person) who would be required to account for VAT on the supply of the gold if the supply were a taxable but not a zero-rated supply.

(3) This regulation is subject to regulation 6 (special customs procedures).

Commencement—IP completion day (11pm UK time on 31 December 2020) is the day appointed for the coming into force of these Regulations (see SI 2020/1641 reg 2, Schedule para 12.)

5 Section 55A supplies: customer to account

(1) Paragraph (2) applies where—
(a) a taxable person receives a taxable supply of goods which are of a description specified in an order made under section 55A(9) of VATA (customers to account for tax on supplies of goods or services of a kind used in missing trader fraud) and which are not excepted supplies for the purposes of that section; and
(b) the supply involves the removal of the goods from Great Britain to Northern Ireland, or vice versa.

(2) Where this paragraph applies, the taxable person who receives the supply (and only that person) is treated as having imported the goods for the purpose of paragraph 4 of Schedule 9ZB to VATA instead of the supplier.

(3) This regulation is subject to regulation 6 (special customs procedures).

Commencement—IP completion day (11pm UK time on 31 December 2020) is the day appointed for the coming into force of these Regulations (see SI 2020/1641 reg 2, Schedule para 12.)

6 Removals where goods declared to special customs procedure

(1) Paragraph (2) applies where goods are—
(a) removed from Great Britain to Northern Ireland or vice versa; and
(b) declared to a special customs procedure on their entry into that other territory.

(2) Where this paragraph applies, the person who is treated as having imported the goods for the purpose of paragraph 4 of Schedule 9ZB to VATA is the person who causes the goods to be placed into free circulation, and not the person described in paragraph 4(3) or (4) of that Schedule, or any person described in this Part.

(3) A person (P) who (but for this regulation) would be treated as having imported the goods for the purpose of paragraph 4 of Schedule 9ZB to VATA is so treated if, on or before the date on which P would have to pay the VAT charged on the removal of those goods, P does not hold evidence of a description specified in a public notice made by the Commissioners of the goods having been placed into a special customs procedure.

(4) In this regulation—
(a) "special customs procedure" means—
(i) a procedure listed in Article 210 of Regulation (EU) No 952/2013 of the European Parliament and of the Council of 9 October 2013 laying down the Union Customs Code, as it has effect in Northern Ireland as a result of section 7A of the European Union (Withdrawal) Act 2018; or
(ii) a procedure listed in section 3(4) of the Taxation (Cross-border Trade) Act 2018;
(b) the reference to causing goods to be placed into free circulation is a reference to placing goods on the market, or putting them to private use or consumption, in Northern Ireland or Great Britain, as the case may be.

Commencement—IP completion day (11pm UK time on 31 December 2020) is the day appointed for the coming into force of these Regulations (see SI 2020/1641 reg 2, Schedule para 12.)

7 Movement of own goods and on behalf of third party: remover to account

(1) Paragraph (2) applies where a taxable person (T) makes a relevant removal of goods from Great Britain to Northern Ireland in the course of T's business but otherwise than in the course of a taxable supply and as a result of which ownership in the goods does not pass.

(2) Where this paragraph applies, T (and only T) is treated as having imported the goods for the purpose of paragraph 4 of Schedule 9ZB to VATA.

(3) In this regulation a "relevant removal of goods" is a removal by T or under T's direction of goods of which T has possession and in relation to which T exercises control, whether or not T is the owner of the goods, but does not include a removal which consists only of the physical delivery of the goods by a person to whom the goods are consigned for that purpose.

(4) This regulation is subject to regulation 6 (special customs procedures).

Commencement—IP completion day (11pm UK time on 31 December 2020) is the day appointed for the coming into force of these Regulations (see SI 2020/1641 reg 2, Schedule para 12.)

8 Removals from Northern Ireland to Great Britain—zero-rating of supplies for export

(1) Paragraph (2) applies where—
  (a) a taxable person (P) treats a supply of goods as zero-rated as a result of the Commissioners being satisfied that the conditions in regulation 133B of the Value Added Tax Regulations 1995 (supplies to persons outside the relevant states) are met; and
  (b) paragraph (2) of that regulation is satisfied by the goods being removed from Northern Ireland to Great Britain.

(2) Where this paragraph applies, P (and only P) is treated as having imported the goods for the purpose of paragraph 4 of Schedule 9ZB to VATA.

9

(1) Paragraph (2) applies where—
  (a) a taxable person (P) treats a supply of goods as zero-rated as a result of the Commissioners being satisfied that the conditions in regulation 133C of the Value Added Tax Regulations 1995 (VAT retail export scheme) are met; and
  (b) sub-paragraph (1)(c) of that regulation is satisfied by the goods being removed from Northern Ireland to Great Britain.

(2) Where this paragraph applies, P (and only P) is treated as having imported the goods for the purpose of paragraph 4 of Schedule 9ZB to VATA.

Commencement—IP completion day (11pm UK time on 31 December 2020) is the day appointed for the coming into force of these Regulations (see SI 2020/1641 reg 2, Schedule para 12.)

10

(1) Paragraph (2) applies where—
  (a) a taxable person (P) treats a supply of goods as zero-rated as a result of the Commissioners being satisfied that the conditions in regulation 133D of the Value Added Tax Regulations 1995 (supplies to persons departing the relevant states) are met; and
  (b) the requirement in paragraph (1) of that regulation that the goods be for export is satisfied by the goods being removed from Northern Ireland to Great Britain.

(2) Where this paragraph applies, P (and only P) is treated as having imported the goods for the purpose of paragraph 4 of Schedule 9ZB to VATA.

Commencement—IP completion day (11pm UK time on 31 December 2020) is the day appointed for the coming into force of these Regulations (see SI 2020/1641 reg 2, Schedule para 12.)

11

(1) Paragraph (2) applies where—
  (a) a taxable person (P) treats a supply of goods as zero-rated as a result of the Commissioners being satisfied that the conditions in regulation 133E of the Value Added Tax Regulations 1995 (supplies to persons departing the relevant states), are met; and
  (b) the requirement in paragraph (1) of that regulation that the goods be for export was satisfied by the goods being removed from Northern Ireland to Great Britain.

(2) Where this regulation applies, P (and only P) is treated as having imported the goods for the purpose of paragraph 4 of Schedule 9ZB to VATA.

Commencement—IP completion day (11pm UK time on 31 December 2020) is the day appointed for the coming into force of these Regulations (see SI 2020/1641 reg 2, Schedule para 12.)

12 Gifts from Great Britain to Northern Ireland: sender to account

(1) Paragraph (3) applies where goods are removed from Great Britain to Northern Ireland in a consignment of a non-commercial character.

(2) In this regulation, a consignment is of a non-commercial character only if the following requirements are met—
  (a) it is sent by one private individual to another;
  (b) it is not sent in return for any consideration in money or money's worth; and
  (c) it is intended solely for the personal use of the consignee or that of the consignee's family and not for any commercial purpose.

(3) Where this paragraph applies, the sender of the goods (and only the sender) is treated as having imported the goods for the purpose of paragraph 4 of Schedule 9ZB to VATA.

Commencement—IP completion day (11pm UK time on 31 December 2020) is the day appointed for the coming into force of these Regulations (see SI 2020/1641 reg 2, Schedule para 12.)

13 Other removals by non-taxable persons

(1) Paragraph (2) applies where goods are removed from Great Britain to Northern Ireland, otherwise than for the purposes of, or in the course or furtherance of, any business carried on by a registered person (but otherwise than as described in regulation 12 (gifts)).

(2) Where this paragraph applies, the person removing the goods (and only that person) is treated as having imported the goods for the purposes of paragraph 4 of Schedule 9ZB to VATA.

Commencement—IP completion day (11pm UK time on 31 December 2020) is the day appointed for the coming into force of these Regulations (see SI 2020/1641 reg 2, Schedule para 12.)

14 Removals from the Isle of Man to Northern Ireland

This Part applies to goods removed to Northern Ireland from the Isle of Man as it applies to goods removed from Great Britain to Northern Ireland and, in applying this Part for that purpose, references to provisions in VATA, other than references to Schedule 9ZB, are to be read as the corresponding provisions of an Act of Tynwald.

Commencement—IP completion day (11pm UK time on 31 December 2020) is the day appointed for the coming into force of these Regulations (see SI 2020/1641 reg 2, Schedule para 12.)

PART 3

ACCOUNTING FOR VAT ON REMOVALS: TAXABLE PERSONS

15 VAT on removals to be payable by a taxable person as if it were VAT on a supply

This Part applies to a taxable person who is treated as having imported goods for the purpose of paragraph 4 of Schedule 9ZB, or paragraph 4A(2) of Schedule 9ZC, to VATA.

Commencement—IP completion day (11pm UK time on 31 December 2020) is the day appointed for the coming into force of these Regulations (see SI 2020/1641 reg 2, Schedule para 12.)

16 (1) A person to whom this Part applies (P) must account for and pay the VAT charged under paragraph 3(2) or, as the case may be, paragraph 3(4) of Schedule 9ZB to VATA as if that VAT were VAT on a supply made by P.

(2) Accordingly—
  (a) P must in the prescribed accounting period in which the goods are treated as imported account for and pay that VAT together with the VAT chargeable on the supply of goods or services due from P in that period;
  (b) the relevant enforcement provisions apply for the purposes of this regulation, in relation to P's obligation under paragraph (1) to account for and pay any VAT, as if that VAT were VAT on a supply made by P; and
  (c) the effect of section 16 of VATA (application of customs enactments) as applied by paragraph 3(3) or 3(5), as the case may be, of Schedule 9ZB to VATA is disapplied to the extent that it would make alternative provision for the accounting and payment of that VAT.

(3) In this regulation "the relevant enforcement provisions" means so much of—
  (a) VATA and any other enactment, and
  (b) any subordinate legislation,

as has effect for the purposes of, or in connection with, the enforcement of any obligation to account for and pay VAT, and includes, without prejudice to the generality of the foregoing, Part 5 of the Value Added Tax Regulations 1995.

Commencement—IP completion day (11pm UK time on 31 December 2020) is the day appointed for the coming into force of these Regulations (see SI 2020/1641 reg 2, Schedule para 12.)

17 Requirement to produce import document

(1) A taxable person who—
  (a) makes a supply of goods which is zero-rated by virtue of paragraph 3(1) of Schedule 9ZB to VATA or a corresponding provision of an Act of Tynwald; and
  (b) is treated as having imported the goods for the purposes of paragraph 4 of Schedule 9ZB to VATA,

must provide the person to whom the goods are supplied with an invoice, to be known as an import document, containing the information specified in paragraph (4).

(2) A taxable person (T) who is treated by virtue of regulation 7 (movement of own goods and on behalf of third party) as having imported goods for the purposes of paragraph 4 of Schedule 9ZB to VATA must provide the owner of the goods (where that is not T) with an invoice, to be known as an import document, containing the information specified in paragraph (4).

(3) The import document must be provided—
  (a) within a period of 30 days beginning with the day on which the supply is treated as taking place for the purposes of VATA, in the case of the circumstance described in paragraph (1);
  (b) within a period of 30 days beginning with the day on which the goods are treated as having been imported for the purposes of VATA, in the case of the circumstance described in paragraph (2); or
  (c) within such longer period as the Commissioners may allow either generally or in a particular case.

(4) The information required to be included is—
  (a) a sequential number based on one or more series which uniquely identifies the document;
  (b) the time of the supply (where relevant), and removal;
  (c) the date of the issue of the document;
  (d) the name and address of the person to whom the goods are consigned;
  (e) a description sufficient to identify the goods supplied or removed;
  (f) for each description, the quantity of the goods and the amount payable excluding VAT;
  (g) the total amount of VAT chargeable on the removal.

(5) The following provisions of the VAT Regulations 1995 apply in relation to the import document required to be provided under paragraph (1) and (2) as they apply to a VAT invoice required to be provided under regulation 13(1) of those Regulations—
  (a) paragraphs (7) and (8) of regulation 13 (preservation of invoices);
  (b) regulation 13A (electronic invoicing);
  (c) regulation 13B (language).

Commencement—IP completion day (11pm UK time on 31 December 2020) is the day appointed for the coming into force of these Regulations (see SI 2020/1641 reg 2, Schedule para 12.)

18 Penalties

The obligation imposed by regulation 17 is to be treated for the purposes of section 69(1) of VATA (breaches of regulatory provisions) as if it was imposed pursuant to regulations made under VATA, and section 76 of VATA (assessment of amounts due by way of penalty, interest or surcharge) and section 83(1) (appeals) are to be interpreted accordingly.

Commencement—IP completion day (11pm UK time on 31 December 2020) is the day appointed for the coming into force of these Regulations (see SI 2020/1641 reg 2, Schedule para 12.)

PART 4
ACCOUNTING FOR VAT ON REMOVALS: NON-TAXABLE PERSONS

19 Credit for VAT on goods removed from Great Britain to Northern Ireland

(1) Paragraph (2) applies where—
  (a) goods are removed from Great Britain or the Isle of Man to Northern Ireland and a person ("P") is liable for the VAT payable as a result of their entry into Northern Ireland, and
  (b) the goods are not removed for the purposes of, or in the course or furtherance of, any business carried on by a registered person.

(2) Where this paragraph applies and subject to paragraph (5)—
  (a) P is granted a credit in accordance with paragraph (3), and
  (b) P is deemed to have made a payment equal to that credit in respect of the VAT payable as a result of the entry.

(3) The credit referred to in sub-paragraph (2)(a) is—
  (a) the total of the VAT incurred on the purchase or importation of the goods in Great Britain by P or, where the goods were given to P, the VAT which was incurred in Great Britain on those goods by the person who gave the goods to P; or
  (b) if the goods have been manufactured by P, the total of the VAT incurred on the purchase or importation of the materials used in the manufacture of the goods,

but in either case the credit may not be greater than the VAT payable as a result of the entry.

(4) The total of the VAT referred to in sub-paragraphs (3)(a) and (b) is to be calculated in accordance with the directions of the Commissioners specified in a public notice.

(5) If the amount of the VAT due on the entry of the goods exceeds the amount of the credit allowed under sub-paragraph (2)(a) P must account for and pay the balance in such form and manner, and at such time, as may be specified by the Commissioners in a public notice, or as they may direct in a particular case.

(6) This regulation is to be treated, for the purposes of VATA, as if it had been made under that Act.

Commencement—IP completion day (11pm UK time on 31 December 2020) is the day appointed for the coming into force of these Regulations (see SI 2020/1641 reg 2, Schedule para 12.)

PART 5
ENTITLEMENT OF TAXABLE PERSONS TO DEDUCT INPUT TAX

20 (1) This regulation applies where a taxable person (T)—
  (a) receives a supply of goods which is zero-rated pursuant to paragraph 3(1) of Schedule 9ZB to VATA, or a corresponding provision of an Act of Tynwald;
  (b) is not treated as having imported the goods for the purposes of paragraph 4 of Schedule 9ZB; and
  (c) has been provided with an import document in accordance with regulation 17.

(2) This regulation also applies where a taxable person (T)—
  (a) is the owner of goods removed in the circumstances described in regulation 7 (movement of own goods and on behalf of third party);
  (b) is not treated as having imported the goods for the purposes of paragraph 4 of Schedule 9ZB to VATA; and
  (c) has been provided with an import document in accordance with regulation 17.

(3) Where this regulation applies, T may claim deduction of the total amount of the VAT ("the chargeable VAT") shown on the import document as being chargeable on the entry of the goods as if it were input tax as defined in section 24(1) VATA but only if and to the extent that T would have been entitled to deduct it if it had been VAT chargeable on a supply of those goods.

(4) Accordingly, any provision made by or under any enactment that is relevant to the accounting for, or deduction of input VAT, applies in relation to the chargeable VAT that is deductible under paragraph (3) as it does to input VAT as if it were input tax except that references to the date on which input tax becomes chargeable are to be read as referring to the date of the import document provided in accordance with regulation 17.

Commencement—IP completion day (11pm UK time on 31 December 2020) is the day appointed for the coming into force of these Regulations (see SI 2020/1641 reg 2, Schedule para 12.)

21 Where regulation 20 applies, a taxable person (P) who is treated as having imported goods pursuant to paragraph 4 of Schedule 9ZB to VATA may not treat the VAT payable as a result of that importation as P's input VAT allowable under section 25 VATA (where P would otherwise, apart from this regulation, be permitted to do so).

Commencement—IP completion day (11pm UK time on 31 December 2020) is the day appointed for the coming into force of these Regulations (see SI 2020/1641 reg 2, Schedule para 12.)

PART 6

IDENTIFICATION FOR THE PURPOSES OF VAT IN NORTHERN IRELAND

22 Interpretation

(1) In this Part "relevant Northern Ireland trader" means a person of the description referred to in paragraph 7(3) of Schedule 9ZA to VATA who on any day has in the period of 180 days ending on that day undertaken a relevant transaction.
(2) A person undertakes a relevant transaction if the person—
 (a) makes any supply of goods which are in Northern Ireland at the time of the supply and the supply does not involve the removal of the goods from or to Northern Ireland;
 (b) makes any taxable acquisition of goods in Northern Ireland that falls within paragraph 2(3) of Schedule 9ZA to VATA;
 (c) makes a supply of goods which involves their removal from Northern Ireland to a member State, where the supply is to a person who is identified for the purposes of VAT in a member State;
 (d) makes a supply of goods which are treated as supplied in the United Kingdom by virtue of paragraph 29 of Schedule 9ZB to VATA; or
 (e) makes a supply of goods within paragraph 30 of Schedule 9ZB to VATA.

Commencement—IP completion day (11pm UK time on 31 December 2020) is the day appointed for the coming into force of these Regulations (see SI 2020/1641 reg 2, Schedule para 12.)

23 The Commissioners to make arrangements for identification

(1) The Commissioners must make arrangements to ensure that—
 (a) a person who they are satisfied is a relevant Northern Ireland trader is identified for the purposes of VAT in Northern Ireland, and
 (b) a person who may be, or may become, a relevant Northern Ireland trader is identified for the purposes of VAT in Northern Ireland where the Commissioners consider that such identification is appropriate.
(2) The arrangements referred to in paragraph (1) must include—
 (a) identifying such a person on the electronic system required to be maintained by the United Kingdom pursuant to Article 17 of Council Regulation (EU) No 904/2010 on administrative co-operation and combatting fraud in the field of value added tax as it has effect in Northern Ireland as a result of section 7A of the European Union (Withdrawal) Act 2018; and
 (b) notifying that person that such identification has been made.
(3) The Commissioners may identify a person with effect from a past date and in respect of a period of time during which the Commissioners are satisfied that the person may have been a relevant Northern Ireland trader, whether or not the person remains a relevant Northern Ireland trader at the time when the Commissioners identify the person.

Commencement—IP completion day (11pm UK time on 31 December 2020) is the day appointed for the coming into force of these Regulations (see SI 2020/1641 reg 2, Schedule para 12.)

24 Request to be identified and obligation to request to be identified

(1) A person who has not been notified in accordance with regulation 23 (T) must within 30 days of undertaking a relevant transaction—
 (a) request the Commissioners to identify T for the purposes of VAT in Northern Ireland; and
 (b) notify the Commissioners of such details of the relevant transactions T has undertaken as the Commissioners may specify in a notice.
(2) The Commissioners must specify in a notice the form and manner in which the request referred to in paragraph (1)(a) and the notification referred to in paragraph (1)(b) must be given.
(3) In such a case the Commissioners must where they are satisfied that T is a relevant Northern Ireland trader identify T for the purposes of VAT in Northern Ireland with effect from the date on which T first undertook a relevant transaction.

Commencement—IP completion day (11pm UK time on 31 December 2020) is the day appointed for the coming into force of these Regulations (see SI 2020/1641 reg 2, Schedule para 12.)

25 Where T—
(a) is not a relevant Northern Ireland trader;
(b) requests that the Commissioners identify T for the purposes of VAT in Northern Ireland; and
(c) satisfies the Commissioners that T intends to undertake a relevant transaction in the period of 30 days beginning on the date of the request,

the Commissioners must identify T for the purposes of VAT in Northern Ireland with effect from the date of T's request.

Commencement—IP completion day (11pm UK time on 31 December 2020) is the day appointed for the coming into force of these Regulations (see SI 2020/1641 reg 2, Schedule para 12.)

26 Communication of the fact of a person's identification for the purposes of VAT in Northern Ireland

The use of the prefix "XI" to the number assigned to a person for the purposes of VAT in the United Kingdom is the means by which that person communicates that the person is identified for the purpose of VAT in Northern Ireland.

Commencement—IP completion day (11pm UK time on 31 December 2020) is the day appointed for the coming into force of these Regulations (see SI 2020/1641 reg 2, Schedule para 12.)

27 Ceasing to be identified

Where the Commissioners are satisfied that a person has ceased to be a relevant Northern Ireland trader they may cancel that person's identification for the purposes of VAT in Northern Ireland with effect from the day on which the person so ceased or from such later date as may be agreed between them and the person.

Commencement—IP completion day (11pm UK time on 31 December 2020) is the day appointed for the coming into force of these Regulations (see SI 2020/1641 reg 2, Schedule para 12.)

28 Where the Commissioners are satisfied that on the date on which a person was identified for the purposes of VAT in Northern Ireland the person was not a relevant Northern Ireland trader, they may cancel the person's identification with effect from that date.

Commencement—IP completion day (11pm UK time on 31 December 2020) is the day appointed for the coming into force of these Regulations (see SI 2020/1641 reg 2, Schedule para 12.)

29 Where a person satisfies the Commissioners that the person has ceased to be a relevant Northern Ireland trader and the person requests that the person's identification be cancelled, the Commissioners must cancel the person's identification with effect from the day on which the person so ceased or from such later date as may be agreed between them and the person.

Commencement—IP completion day (11pm UK time on 31 December 2020) is the day appointed for the coming into force of these Regulations (see SI 2020/1641 reg 2, Schedule para 12.)

30 Where a person satisfies the Commissioners that the person was not a relevant Northern Ireland trader on the date on which the person was identified for the purposes of VAT in Northern Ireland and the person requests that the person's identification be cancelled, the Commissioners must cancel the person's identification with effect from the date on which the person was identified for the purposes of VAT in Northern Ireland.

Commencement—IP completion day (11pm UK time on 31 December 2020) is the day appointed for the coming into force of these Regulations (see SI 2020/1641 reg 2, Schedule para 12.)

31 Application of section 9A VATA: treating a person as if identified

The reference in subsection (1A) of section 9A of VATA to a person identified for the purposes of VAT in Northern Ireland includes a registered person who is not so identified but who undertakes a business activity from a place in Northern Ireland.

Commencement—IP completion day (11pm UK time on 31 December 2020) is the day appointed for the coming into force of these Regulations (see SI 2020/1641 reg 2, Schedule para 12.)

32 This Part to be treated as made under VATA

The provisions contained in this Part are to be treated for the purposes of VATA as if they had been made under paragraph 7 of Schedule 9ZA to VATA.

Commencement—IP completion day (11pm UK time on 31 December 2020) is the day appointed for the coming into force of these Regulations (see SI 2020/1641 reg 2, Schedule para 12.)

PART 7
ACCOUNTING FOR IMPORT VAT ON LOW VALUE IMPORTATIONS

33 VAT return accounting for low value importations

This Part applies to a person who is treated as having imported goods for the purposes of paragraph 4(2) of Schedule 9ZC to VATA.

Commencement—IP completion day (11pm UK time on 31 December 2020) is the day appointed for the coming into force of these Regulations (see SI 2020/1641 reg 2, Schedule para 12.)

34 (1) A person to whom this Part applies (P) must account for and pay the VAT charged under section 1(1)(c) of VATA, as applied by paragraph 1(3) of Schedule 9ZB to VATA, on the importation of those goods into the United Kingdom by reason of their entry into Northern Ireland, as if that VAT were VAT on a supply made by P.
(2) Accordingly—
   (a) P must in the prescribed accounting period in which the goods are treated as imported account for and pay that VAT together with the VAT chargeable on the supply of goods or services due from P in that period;
   (b) the relevant enforcement provisions apply for the purposes of this regulation, in relation to P's obligation under paragraph (1) to account for and pay any VAT, as if that VAT were VAT on a supply made by P; and
   (c) the effect of section 16 of VATA (application of customs enactments), as modified by paragraph 1(6) of Schedule 9ZB to VATA, is disapplied to the extent that it would make alternative provision for the accounting and payment of that VAT.
(3) In this regulation "the relevant enforcement provisions" means so much of—
   (a) VATA and any other enactment, and
   (b) any subordinate legislation,
as has effect for the purposes of, or in connection with, the enforcement of any obligation to account for and pay VAT, and includes, without prejudice to the generality of the foregoing, Part 5 of the Value Added Tax Regulations 1995.

Commencement—IP completion day (11pm UK time on 31 December 2020) is the day appointed for the coming into force of these Regulations (see SI 2020/1641 reg 2, Schedule para 12.)

2020/1622

EUROPEAN UNION (WITHDRAWAL) ACT 2018 AND EUROPEAN UNION (WITHDRAWAL AGREEMENT) ACT 2020 (COMMENCEMENT, TRANSITIONAL AND SAVINGS PROVISIONS) REGULATIONS 2020

Made . . . .*21st December 2020*

The Secretary of State, in exercise of the powers conferred by sections 23(6) and 25(4) of, and paragraphs 23(3) and 26 of Schedule 7 to, the European Union (Withdrawal) Act 2018 and by sections 41(5) and 42(7) of, and paragraph 68(1) of Schedule 5 to, the European Union (Withdrawal Agreement) Act 2020, makes the following Regulations:

PART 1
CITATION, COMMENCEMENT AND INTERPRETATION

1 Citation, commencement and interpretation
(1) These Regulations may be cited as the European Union (Withdrawal) Act 2018 and European Union (Withdrawal Agreement) Act 2020 (Commencement, Transitional and Savings Provisions) Regulations 2020.
(2) Part 3 (transitional and saving provisions) comes into force on IP completion day.
(3) In these Regulations—
   "ECA 1972" means the European Communities Act 1972;
   "EU(A)A 2008" means the European Union (Amendment) Act 2008;
   "EU(W)A 2018" means the European Union (Withdrawal) Act 2018;
   "EU(WA)A 2020" means the European Union (Withdrawal Agreement) Act 2020;
   "GOWA 2006" means the Government of Wales Act 2006;
   "IA 1978" means the Interpretation Act 1978;
   "ILR(S)A 2010" means the Interpretation and Legislative Reform (Scotland) Act 2010;
   "NIA 1998" means the Northern Ireland Act 1998;
   "SA 1998" means the Scotland Act 1998.

PART 2
PROVISIONS COMING INTO FORCE

2 EU(W)A 2018 provisions coming into force on 31st December 2020
The day appointed for the coming into force of the following provisions of EU(W)A 2018 is 31st December 2020—
   (a) section 23(8) (consequential and transitional provision) insofar as it relates to the repeal of—
      (i) the European Parliamentary Elections Act 2002 to the extent that it is not already repealed; and

(ii) the European Parliament (Representation) Act 2003;
(b) Schedule 9 (additional repeals) insofar as it relates to the repeal of those Acts.

3 EU(W)A 2018 provisions coming into force on IP completion day
The following provisions of EU(W)A 2018 come into force on IP completion day—
(a) section 2 (saving for EU-derived domestic legislation);
(b) section 3 (incorporation of direct EU legislation);
(c) section 4 (saving for rights etc under section 2(1) of ECA 1972);
(d) section 5 (exceptions to savings and incorporation) to the extent that it is not already in force;
(e) section 6(1) to (6) (interpretation of retained EU law) to the extent that it is not already in force;
(f) section 7 (status of retained EU law) to the extent that it is not already in force;
(g) section 12 (retaining EU restrictions in devolution legislation etc) to the extent that it is not already in force;
(h) section 15(2) (publication and rules of evidence) to the extent that it is not already in force;
(i) section 23(5) and (7) (consequential and transitional provision) to the extent that it is not already in force;
(j) section 23(8) (consequential and transitional provision) insofar as it relates to the repeal of—
  (i) the EU(A)A 2008 to the extent that it is not already repealed;
  (ii) the European Union (Finance) Act 2015 to the extent it is not already repealed;
(k) Schedule 1 (further provision about exceptions to savings and incorporation) to the extent that it is not already in force;
(l) Schedule 3 (further amendments of devolution legislation and reporting requirement) to the extent that it is not already in force;
(m) paragraph 3 of Schedule 5 (rules of evidence: questions as to meaning of EU law);
(n) Schedule 8 (consequential, transitional, transitory and saving provision) to the extent that it is not already in force;
(o) Schedule 9 (additional repeals) to the extent that it relates to the repeal of—
  (i) the EU(A)A 2008 to the extent that it is not already repealed;
  (ii) the European Union (Finance) Act 2015 to the extent it is not already repealed.

4 EU(WA)A 2020 provisions coming into force on 31st December 2020
The day appointed for the coming into force of the following provisions of EU(WA)A 2020 is 31st December 2020—
(a) section 41(4) so far as relating to paragraph 57 of Schedule 5, and
(b) paragraph 57 of Schedule 5.

5 EU(WA)A 2020 provisions coming into force on IP completion day
The following provisions of EU(WA)A 2020 come into force on IP completion day—
(a) section 15(3) (Independent Monitoring Authority for the Citizens' Rights Agreements) to the extent that it is not already in force;
(b) section 23 (protection for certain rights, safeguards etc in Belfast Agreement) to the extent that it is not already in force;
(c) section 24 (no alteration of North-South co-operation);
(d) section 25 (retention of saved EU law at end of implementation period) to the extent that it is not already in force;
(e) section 26(1) (interpretation of retained EU law and relevant separation agreement law) to the extent that it is not already in force;
(f) section 30 (certain dispute procedures under withdrawal agreement);
(g) subject to regulation 4 above and except insofar as it concerns paragraph 56(7)(b) of Schedule 5 in relation to the making of regulations under Part 1 of Schedule 2 to EU(W)A 2018, section 41(4) and (6) (consequential and transitional provision etc) to the extent that it is not already in force;
(h) Schedule 2 (Independent Monitoring Authority for the Citizens' Rights Agreements) to the extent that it is not already in force;
(i) Schedule 3 (protection for certain rights, safeguards etc in Belfast Agreement) to the extent that it is not already in force;
(j) subject to regulation 4 above and with the exception of paragraph 56(7)(b) insofar as it relates to the making of regulations under Part 1 of Schedule 2 to EU(W)A 2018, Schedule 5 (consequential and transitional provision etc) to the extent that it is not already in force.

PART 3
TRANSITIONAL AND SAVING PROVISIONS

6 European Communities Act 1972

Despite the ECA 1972 ceasing to have effect by virtue of section 1A(5) of EU(W)A 2018, section 11(2) of ECA 1972 continues to have effect on and after IP completion day in relation to the communication, or public disclosure, of any classified information on or after IP completion day by a person who acquired, or obtained cognisance of, the classified information before IP completion day.

7 Interpretation Act 1978

(1) The repeal by paragraph 22(a) of Schedule 8 to EU(W)A 2018 of the definitions of "the Treaties" and "the EU Treaties" (as defined by section 1(2) of ECA 1972) in Schedule 1 to IA 1978, and the insertion by paragraph 22(e) of Schedule 8 to EU(W)A 2018 of definitions of those expressions in Schedule 1 to IA 1978, do not affect the interpretation of those expressions in pre-IPCD legislation on and after IP completion day in relation to a time before IP completion day.
(2) In its application to an Act passed, or subordinate legislation made, before 19th June 2008, the definition of "the Communities" in Schedule 1 to IA 1978, as inserted by paragraph 22(e) of Schedule 8 to EU(W)A 2018, has effect on and after IP completion day, in its application in relation to a time before 19th June 2008, as if the words from "but" to the end were omitted.
(3) In this regulation—
 "pre-IPCD legislation" means an Act passed, or subordinate legislation made, before IP completion day;
 "subordinate legislation" has the same meaning as in IA 1978.

8 European Union (Amendment) Act 2008

(1) Despite the repeal of EU(A)A 2008 by section 23(8) of, and Schedule 9 to, EU(W)A 2018—
 (a) section 3(2) of EU(A)A 2008 continues to have effect on and after IP completion day in relation to any reference to the EU to which it applied immediately before IP completion day, and
 (b) section 3(6) of EU(A)A 2008 continues to have effect on and after IP completion day in relation to any reference to all or any of the Communities to which it applied immediately before IP completion day.
(2) Paragraph (1)(a) does not apply where the reference to the EU is to be construed in accordance with a new definition of "the EU".
(3) Paragraph (1)(b) does not apply where the reference to all or any of the Communities is to be construed in accordance with a new definition of "the Communities".
(4) In this regulation, "new definition" means a definition—
 (a) inserted into Schedule 1 to IA 1978 by paragraph 22(e) of Schedule 8 to EU(W)A 2018,
 (b) inserted into Schedule 1 to ILR(S)A 2010 by paragraph 35(b) of Schedule 8 to EU(W)A 2018, or
 (c) treated as inserted into Schedule 2 to the Scotland Act 1998 (Transitory and Transitional Provisions) (Publication and Interpretation etc of Acts of the Scottish Parliament) Order 1999 by virtue of regulation 4(5) of the European Union (Withdrawal) Act 2018 (Consequential Modifications and Repeals and Revocations) (EU Exit) Regulations 2019.

9 Further savings in relation to the European Union (Amendment) Act 2008

The repeal of section 3(3), (4) and (5) of, and the Schedule to, EU(A)A 2008 by section 23(8) of, and Schedule 9 to, EU(W)A 2018 does not affect an amendment of an enactment made under section 3(3), (4) or (5) of, or the Schedule to, EU(A)A 2008 so far as—
 (a) the enactment as amended otherwise continues to have effect (whether by virtue of transitional or saving provision or otherwise), or
 (b) any other transitional or saving provision relating to the enactment as amended otherwise continues to have effect.

10 Devolution

(1) Paragraphs 41(1) and (2) and 42 of Schedule 8 to EU(W)A 2018 apply on and after IP completion day to the amendments made by—
 (a) Part 3 of Schedule 3 to that Act;
 (b) paragraph 29 of Schedule 8 to that Act; and
 (c) paragraphs 18, 19, 21, 23, 25, 26, 28, 29 and 30 of Schedule 5 to EU(WA)A 2020;
as they apply to the amendments made by Part 1 of Schedule 3 to that Act.
(2) Paragraph 42 of Schedule 8 to EU(W)A 2018 applies on and after IP completion day to acts (other than the making, confirming or approving of subordinate legislation) done before IP completion day by any person.

(3) The amendments made by—
  (a) section 12 of EU(W)A 2018;
  (b) Parts 1 and 3 of Schedule 3 to that Act;
  (c) paragraph 29 of Schedule 8 to that Act; and
  (d) paragraphs 18, 19, 21, 23, 25, 26, 28, 29 and 30 of Schedule 5 to EU(WA)A 2020
do not apply on and after IP completion day in relation to any pre-IPCD failure.
(4) Accordingly—
  (a) for the purposes of determining whether a question relating to pre-IPCD legislation, a pre-IPCD act or a pre-IPCD failure is a devolution issue within the meaning of Schedule 6 to SA 1998, paragraph 1 of that Schedule continues to have effect on and after IP completion day without the amendments made by paragraph 23 of Schedule 3 to EU(W)A 2018,
  (b) for the purposes of determining whether a question relating to pre-IPCD legislation, a pre-IPCD act or a pre-IPCD failure is a compatibility issue within the meaning of section 288ZA of the Criminal Procedure (Scotland) Act 1995, that section continues to have effect on and after IP completion day without the amendments made by paragraph 29 of Schedule 8 to EU(W)A 2018,
  (c) for the purposes of determining whether a question relating to a pre-IPCD act or a pre-IPCD failure is a devolution issue within the meaning of Schedule 10 to NIA 1998, paragraph 1 of that Schedule continues to have effect on and after IP completion day without the amendment made by paragraph 62 of Schedule 3 to EU(W)A 2018, and
  (d) for the purposes of determining whether a question relating to a pre-IPCD act or a pre-IPCD failure is a devolution issue within the meaning of Schedule 9 to GOWA 2006, paragraphs 1(1)(c) and (d) of that Schedule continue to have effect on and after IP completion day as if the references to section 80(1), (7) and (8) of that Act were to those provisions without the amendments made by paragraph 2 or 37 of Schedule 3 to EU(W)A 2018.
(5) It does not matter whether the question referred to in paragraph (4)(a), (b), (c) or (d) arises before or on or after IP completion day or whether it arises in proceedings which begin before or on or after IP completion day.
(6) In this regulation—
  "pre-IPCD legislation" means an Act of the Scottish Parliament, or a provision of such an Act, the Bill for which received Royal Assent before IP completion day;
  "pre-IPCD act" means an act, or a purported or proposed act, before IP completion day;
  "pre-IPCD failure" means a failure to act before IP completion day;
  and references to Part 3 of Schedule 3 to EU(W)A 2018 do not include any provisions of that Part which have come into force before IP completion day.

11 Scotland Act 1998
(1) Despite its repeal by paragraph 11 of Schedule 3 to EU(W)A 2018, section 34 of SA 1998 continues to have effect on and after IP completion day in relation to a Bill where—
  (a) a reference has been made in relation to the Bill under section 33 of SA 1998 before IP completion day,
  (b) a reference for a preliminary ruling (within the meaning of section 34 of that Act) has been made before IP completion day by the Supreme Court in connection with that reference, and
  (c) neither of those references has been decided or otherwise disposed of before IP completion day.
(2) Where section 34 of SA 1998 continues to have effect in relation to a Bill by virtue of paragraph (1), the following do not apply in relation to the Bill—
  (a) the amendments made to section 32 of SA 1998 by paragraph 10 of Schedule 3 to EU(W)A 2018, and
  (b) the amendments made to section 36 of SA 1998 by paragraph 12 of Schedule 3 to EU(W)A 2018.

12 Scottish Taxpayers
(1) The amendments made to sections 80D and 80DA of SA 1998 by paragraphs 14 and 15 of Schedule 3 to EU(W)A 2018 have effect in relation to the tax year 2020–21 and subsequent tax years.
(2) In paragraph (1), "tax year" means a year beginning on 6th April and ending on the following 5th April.

13 Interpretation and Legislative Reform (Scotland) Act 2010
(1) The repeal by paragraph 35(a) of Schedule 8 to EU(W)A 2018 of the definitions of "the Treaties" and "the EU Treaties" (as defined by section 1(2) of ECA 1972) in Schedule 1 to ILR(S)A 2010 and the insertion by paragraph 35(b) of Schedule 8 to EU(W)A 2018 of definitions of those expressions in Schedule 1 to ILR(S)A 2010 and the amendment of those definitions by paragraph 37(f) of Schedule 5 to EU(WA)A 2020 do not affect the interpretation of those expressions in pre-IPCD legislation on and after IP completion day in relation to a time before IP completion day.

(2) In this regulation—
  (a) "pre-IPCD legislation" means an Act of the Scottish Parliament the Bill for which received Royal Assent before IP completion day or a Scottish instrument made before IP completion day;
  (b) "Scottish instrument" has the same meaning as in Part 1 of ILR(S)A 2010.

14 Government of Wales Act 2006
(1) Despite its repeal by paragraph 39 of Schedule 3 to EU(W)A 2018, section 113 of GOWA 2006 continues to have effect on and after IP completion day in relation to a Bill where—
  (a) a reference has been made in relation to the Bill under section 112 of GOWA 2006 before IP completion day,
  (b) a reference for a preliminary European Court ruling (within the meaning of section 113 of that Act) has been made before IP completion day by the Supreme Court in connection with that reference, and
  (c) neither of those references has been decided or otherwise disposed of before IP completion day.
(2) Where section 113 of GOWA 2006 continues to have effect in relation to a Bill by virtue of paragraph (1), the following do not apply in relation to the Bill—
  (a) the amendments made to section 111 of GOWA 2006 by paragraph 38 of Schedule 3 to EU(W)A 2018, and
  (b) the amendments made to section 115 of GOWA 2006 by paragraph 40 of Schedule 3 to EU(W)A 2018.

15 Welsh taxpayers
(1) The amendments made to sections 116E and 116F of GOWA 2006 by paragraphs 41 and 42 of Schedule 3 to EU(W)A 2018 have effect in relation to the tax year 2020–21 and subsequent tax years.
(2) In paragraph (1), "tax year" means a year beginning on 6th April and ending on the following 5th April.

16 Northern Ireland Act 1998
(1) Despite its repeal by paragraph 52 of Schedule 3 to EU(W)A 2018, section 12 of NIA 1998 continues to have effect on and after IP completion day in relation to a Bill where—
  (a) a reference has been made in relation to the Bill under section 11 of NIA 1998 before IP completion day,
  (b) a reference for a preliminary ruling (within the meaning of section 12 of that Act) has been made before IP completion day by the Supreme Court in connection with that reference, and
  (c) neither of those references has been decided or otherwise disposed of before IP completion day.
(2) Where section 12 of NIA 1998 continues to have effect in relation to a Bill by virtue of paragraph (1), the following do not apply in relation to the Bill—
  (a) the amendment made to section 13 of NIA 1998 by paragraph 53 of Schedule 3 to EU(W)A 2018, and
  (b) the amendments made to section 14 of NIA 1998 by paragraph 54 of Schedule 3 to EU(W)A 2018.

17 Transitional provision for section 5A of EU(W)A 2018
Nothing in section 5A of EU(W)A 2018 prevents the modification on or after IP completion day of retained EU law by an enactment passed or made before IP completion day and coming into force or otherwise having effect on or after IP completion day (whether or not that enactment is itself retained EU law).

18 Transitional provision for paragraph 14 of Schedule 8 to EU(W)A 2018
Paragraph 14 of Schedule 8 to EU(W)A 2018 does not apply to a statutory instrument which was made before IP completion day but which would otherwise be subject to that paragraph.

19 Cross-references
(1) Paragraphs 1 and 2A(3) of Schedule 8 to EU(W)A 2018 do not apply to any reading on or after IP completion day of a reference so far as the reference relates to a time before IP completion day (unless a contrary intention appears in relation to the reference concerned).
(2) Paragraph 2 of that Schedule does not apply to any reading on or after IP completion day of a reference so far as the reference relates to a time before IP completion day which is earlier than immediately before IP completion day (unless a contrary intention appears in relation to the reference concerned).

20 Relation to interpretation legislation

(1) Parts 3 and 4 of Schedule 8 to EU(W)A 2018, Part 3 of Schedule 5 to EU(WA)A 2020, these Regulations and other regulations made under section 23(6) of EU(W)A 2018 or section 41(5) of EU(WA)A 2020 are without prejudice (so far as it is required) to section 16 of IA 1978 or any provision of interpretation legislation which corresponds to that section.

(2) In this regulation, "interpretation legislation" means ILR(S)A 2010, the Scotland Act 1998 (Transitory and Transitional Provisions) (Publication and Interpretation etc of Acts of the Scottish Parliament) Order 1999, the Interpretation Act (Northern Ireland) 1954 or the Legislation (Wales) Act 2019.

21 General saving provision

Any saving of a provision by Part 4 of Schedule 8 to EU(W)A 2018, these Regulations or other regulations made under section 23(6) of that Act or section 41(5) of EU(WA)A 2020 includes, so far as is required for the operation of the saved provision, the saving of any other provision relating to that provision.

22 General provision relating to repeals

The repeal of an enactment by EU(W)A 2018 does not affect an amendment of an enactment made by the repealed enactment so far as—

(a) the enactment as amended otherwise continues to have effect (whether by virtue of transitional or saving provision or otherwise), or

(b) any other transitional or saving provision relating to the enactment as amended otherwise continues to have effect.

2020/1642

FINANCE ACT 2016, SECTION 126 (APPOINTED DAY), THE TAXATION (CROSS-BORDER TRADE) ACT 2018 (APPOINTED DAY NO 8, TRANSITION AND SAVING PROVISIONS) AND THE TAXATION (POST-TRANSITION PERIOD) ACT 2020 (APPOINTED DAY NO 1) (EU EXIT) REGULATIONS 2020

Made . . . . 23rd December 2020

The Treasury make these Regulations in exercise of the powers conferred by section 126(5) and (6) of the Finance Act 2016, sections 56 and 57 of the Taxation (Cross-border Trade) Act 2018 and section 11 of the Taxation (Post-transition Period) Act 2020.

The Treasury consider it appropriate to make regulations 5, 6, 7 and 8 in accordance with section 56(4) of the Taxation (Cross-border Trade) Act 2018.

1 Citation

These Regulations may be cited as The Finance Act 2016, Section 126 (Appointed Day), the Taxation (Cross-border Trade) Act 2018 (Appointed Day No 8, Transition and Saving Provisions) and the Taxation (Post-transition Period) Act 2020 (Appointed Day No 1) (EU Exit) Regulations 2020.

2 Interpretation

In these Regulations "EUCL" means the direct EU legislation referred to in paragraph 1(1) of Schedule 7 to the Taxation (Cross-border Trade) Act 2018.

3 Appointed day—Finance Act 2016

The amendments to the Value Added Tax Act 1994 made by section 126 of the Finance Act 2016 (VAT: women's sanitary products) have effect in relation to supplies made, and acquisitions and importations taking place, on or after IP completion day.

4 Appointed day, saving and transitional provisions—Taxation (Cross-Border Trade) Act 2018

The day appointed for the coming into force of the following provisions of the Taxation (Cross-border Trade) Act 2018, so far as not already in force, is IP completion day—

(a) Part 1 (import duty), other than paragraph 90 of Schedule 7;
(b) Part 3 (value added tax);
(c) Part 4 (excise duties).

5

Section 5 of the Customs and Excise Duties (General Reliefs) Act 1979 shall continue to have effect as it had effect immediately before IP completion day in relation to goods removed to Great Britain from the Channel Islands.

6 The amendment made by paragraph 8(1) of Schedule 9 to the Taxation (Cross-border Trade) Act 2018 has no effect in relation to failures, omissions or inaccuracies occurring before IP completion day.

7 Any subordinate legislation that was made under any powers that are amended, modified or repealed by or under any provisions of the Taxation (Cross-border Trade) Act 2018 that come into force on IP completion day by virtue of regulation 4(b) shall continue to have effect as it had effect immediately before IP completion day.

8 Where EUCL (or any part of it) continues to have effect in relation to a release for free circulation in accordance with Title II of Part 3 of the Agreement on the Withdrawal of the United Kingdom of Great Britain and Northern Ireland from the European Union and the European Atomic Energy Community, the amendment made by paragraph 9 of Schedule 9 to the Taxation (Cross-border Trade) Act 2018 is to be read as if for "Part 1 of the Taxation (Cross-border Trade) Act 2018" there were substituted "Article 201 of Regulation (EU) No 952/2013 of the European Parliament and of the Council of 9 October 2013 laying down the Union Customs Code".

9 Appointed day—Taxation (Post-Transition Period) Act 2020
The day appointed for the coming into force of the provisions of the Taxation (Post-transition Period) Act 2020, so far as not already in force, is IP completion day, other than paragraph 7(3) of Schedule 2.

Part 3

VAT EU Directives at 31 December 2020

Contents

Note—The following "Archived" Directives are set out as they had effect on 31 December 2020 (IP completion day).

Archived EU Council Directives (as at 31 December 2020)

86/560: Thirteenth Council Directive of 17 November 1986.
2006/79: Council Directive of 5 October 2006 on the exemption from taxes of imports of small consignments of goods of a non-commercial character from third countries (codified version).
2006/112: Council Directive of 28 November 2006 on the common system of value added tax.
2007/74: Council Directive of 20 December 2007 on the exemption from value added tax and excise duty of goods imported by persons travelling from third countries.
2008/9: Council Directive of 12 February 2008 laying down detailed rules for the refund of value added tax, provided for in Directive 2006/112/EC, to taxable persons not established in the Member State of refund but established in another Member State.
2009/132: Council Directive 2009/132/EC of 19 October 2009 determining the scope of Article 143(b) and (c) of Directive 2006/112/EC as regards exemption from value added tax on the final importation of certain goods.
2010/24: Council Directive of 16 March 2010 concerning mutual assistance for the recovery of claims relating to taxes, duties and other measures.
2011/16: Council Directive of 15 February 2011 on administrative cooperation in the field of taxation and repealing Directive 77/799/EEC.

ARCHIVED THIRTEENTH COUNCIL DIRECTIVE (86/560/EEC) OF 17 NOVEMBER 1986 ON THE HARMONISATION OF THE LAWS OF THE MEMBER STATES RELATING TO TURNOVER TAXES—ARRANGEMENTS FOR THE REFUND OF VALUE ADDED TAX TO TAXABLE PERSONS NOT ESTABLISHED IN COMMUNITY TERRITORY

(86/560/EEC)

Article 1
For the purposes of this Directive—
1. "A taxable person not established in the territory of the Community" shall mean a taxable person as referred to in Article 4(1) of Directive 77/388/EEC who, during the period referred to in Article 3(1) of this Directive, has had in that territory neither his business nor a fixed establishment from which business transactions are effected, nor, if no such business or fixed establishment exists, his permanent address or usual place of residence, and who, during the same period, has supplied no goods or services deemed to have been supplied in the Member State referred to in Article 2, with the exception of—
   (a) transport services and services ancillary thereto, exempted pursuant to Article 14(1)(i), Article 15 or Article 16(1), B, C and D of Directive 77/388/EEC;
   (b) services provided in cases where tax is payable solely by the person to whom they are supplied, pursuant to Article 21(1)(b) of Directive 77/388/EEC;
2. "Territory of the Community" shall mean the territories of the Member States in which Directive 77/388/EEC is applicable.

Article 2
1. Without prejudice to Articles 3 and 4, each Member State shall refund to any taxable person not established in the territory of the Community, subject to the conditions set out below, any value added tax charged in respect of services rendered or moveable property supplied to him in the territory or the country by other taxable persons or charged in respect of the importation of goods into the country, in so far as such goods and services are used for the purposes of the transactions referred to in Article 17(3)(a) and (b) of Directive 77/388/EEC or of the provision of services referred to in point 1(b) of Article 1 of this Directive.
2. Member States may make the refunds referred to in paragraph 1 conditional upon the granting by third States of comparable advantages regarding turnover taxes.
3. Member States may require the appointment of a tax representative.

Article 3
1. The refunds referred to in Article 2(1) shall be granted upon application by the taxable person. Member States shall determine the arrangements for submitting applications, including the time limits for doing so, the period which applications should cover, the authority competent to receive them and the minimum amounts in respect of which applications may be submitted. They shall also determine the arrangements for making refunds, including the time limits for doing so. They shall impose on the applicant such obligations as are necessary to determine whether the application is justified and to prevent fraud, in particular the obligation to provide proof that he is engaged in an economic activity in accordance with Article 4(1) of Directive 77/388/EEC. The applicant must certify, in a written declaration, that, during the period prescribed, he has not carried out any transaction which does not fulfil the conditions laid down in point 1 of Article 1 of this Directive.
2. Refunds may not be granted under conditions more favourable than those applied to Community taxable persons.

Article 4
1. For the purposes of this Directive, eligibility for refunds shall be determined in accordance with Article 17 of Directive 77/388/EEC as applied in the Member State where the refund is paid.
2. Member States may, however, provide for the exclusion of certain expenditure or make refunds subject to additional conditions.
3. This Directive shall not apply to supplies of goods which are or may be exempted under point 2 of Article 15 of Directive 77/388/EEC.

Article 5
1. Member States shall bring into force the laws, regulations and administrative provisions necessary to comply with this Directive by 1 January 1988 at the latest. This Directive shall apply only to applications for refunds concerning value added tax charged on purchases of goods or services invoiced or on imports effected on or after that date.

2. Member States shall communicate to the Commission the main provisions of national law which they adopt in the field covered by this Directive and shall inform the Commission of the use they make of the option afforded by Article 2(2). The Commission shall inform the other Member States thereof.

Article 6
Within three years of the date referred to in Article 5, the Commission shall, after consulting the Member States, submit a report to the Council and to the European Parliament on the application of this Directive, particularly as regards the application of Article 2(2).

Article 7
As from the date on which this Directive is implemented, and at all events by the date mentioned in Article 5, the last sentence of Article 17(4) of Directive 77/388/EEC and Article 8 of Directive 79/1072/EEC shall cease to have effect in each Member State.

Article 8
This Directive is addressed to the Member States.
Done at Brussels, 17 November 1986.

ARCHIVED COUNCIL DIRECTIVE (2006/79/EC)
OF 5 OCTOBER 2006
ON THE EXEMPTION FROM TAXES OF IMPORTS OF SMALL CONSIGNMENTS OF GOODS OF A NON-COMMERCIAL CHARACTER FROM THIRD COUNTRIES (CODIFIED VERSION)

(2006/79/EC)

Article 1
1. Goods in small consignments of a non-commercial character sent from a third country by private persons to other private persons in a Member State shall be exempt on importation from turnover tax and excise duty.
2. For the purposes of paragraph 1, "small consignments of a non-commercial character" shall mean consignments which:
   (*a*) are of an occasional nature;
   (*b*) contain only goods intended for the personal or family use of the consignees, the nature and quantity of which do not indicate that they are being imported for any commercial purpose;
   (*c*) contain goods with a total value not exceeding EUR 45;
   (*d*) are sent by the sender to the consignee without payment of any kind.

Article 2
1. Article I shall apply to the goods listed below subject to the following quantitative limits:
   (*a*) tobacco products
      (i) 50 cigarettes,
         or
      (ii) 25 cigarillos (cigars of a maximum weight of three grams each),
         or
      (iii) 10 cigars,
         or
      (iv) 50 grams of smoking tobacco;
   (*b*) alcohol and alcoholic beverages:
      (i) distilled beverages and spirits of an alcoholic strength exceeding 22% vol.; undenatured ethyl alcohol of 80% vol. and over: one standard bottle (up to 1 litre),
         or
      (ii) distilled beverages and spirits, and aperitifs with a wine or alcohol base, tafia, saké or similar beverages of an alcoholic strength of 22% vol. or less; sparkling wines, fortified wines: one standard bottle (up to 1 litre),
         or
      (iii) still wines: two litres;
   (*c*) perfumes: 50 grams,
      or
         toilet waters: 0,25 litre or eight ounces;
   (*d*) coffee: 500 grams,
      or
         coffee extracts and essences: 200 grams;

(e) tea: 100 grams,
or
tea extracts and essences: 40 grams.

2. Member States shall have the right to reduce the quantities of the products referred to in paragraph 1 eligible for exemption from turnover tax and excise duties, or to abolish exemption for such products altogether.

Article 3
Any goods listed in Article 2 which are contained in a small consignment of a non-commercial character in quantities exceeding those laid down in the said Article shall be excluded in their entirety from exemption.

Article 4
1. The euro equivalent in national currency which shall apply for the implementation of this Directive shall be fixed once a year. The rates applicable shall be those obtaining on the first working day of October with effect from 1 January of the following year.
2. Member States may round off the amounts in national currency resulting from the conversion of the amounts in euros provided for in Article 1(2), provided such rounding-off does not exceed EUR 2.
3. Member States may maintain the amount of the exemption in force at the time of the annual adjustment provided for in paragraph 1 if, prior to the rounding-off provided for in paragraph 2, conversion of the amount of the exemption expressed in euros would result in a change of less than 5% in the exemption expressed in national currency.

Article 5
Member States shall communicate to the Commission the text of the main provisions of national law which they adopt in the field covered by this Directive. The Commission shall inform the other Member States thereof.

Article 6
Directive 78/1035/EEC shall be repealed, without prejudice to the obligations of the Member States relating to the time-limits for transposition into national law of the Directives set out in Annex I, Part B.

References to the repealed Directive shall be construed as references to this Directive and shall be read in accordance with the correlation table in Annex II.

Article 7
This Directive shall enter into force on the 20th day following its publication in the Official Journal of the European Union.

Article 8
This Directive is addressed to the Member States.

Done at Luxembourg, ...5 October 2006.

For the Council
The President
K. Rajamäki

ANNEX I

PART A
REPEALED DIRECTIVE WITH ITS SUCCESSIVE AMENDMENTS

Council Directive 78/1035/EEC[1] (OJ L 366, 28.12.1978, p. 34)
Council Directive 81/933/EEC (OJ L 338, 25.11.1981, p. 24)   only Article 2
Council Directive 85/576/EEC (OJ L 372, 31.12.1985, p. 30)

Notes—[1] Directive 78/1035/EEC was also amended by the 1994 Act of Accession.

PART B
TIME-LIMITS FOR TRANSPOSITION INTO NATIONAL LAW
(referred to in Article 6)

Directive	Time-limit for transposition
78/1035/EEC	1 January 1979
81/933/EEC	31 December 1981
85/576/EEC	30 June 1986

ANNEX II
CORRELATION TABLE

Directive 78/1035/EEC	This Directive
Article 1(1)	Article 1(1)
Article 1(2), first indent	Article 1(2)(*a*)
Article 1(2), second indent	Article 1(2)(*b*)
Article 1(2), third indent	Article 1(2)(*c*)
Article 1(2), fourth indent	Article 1(2)(*d*)
Article 2(1)(*a*), from "50 cigarettes" to "50 grams of smoking tobacco"	Article 2(1)(*a*)(i) to (iv)
Article 2(1)(*b*)	Article 2(1)(*b*)
Article 2(1)(*b*), first indent	Article 2(1)(*b*)(i)
Article 2(1)(*b*), second indent	Article 2(1)(*b*)(ii)
Article 2(1)(*b*), third indent	Article 2(1)(*b*)(iii)
Article 2(1)(*c*), (*d*) and (*e*)	Article 2(1)(*c*), (*d*) and (*e*)
Article 2(2)	Article 2(2)
Article 2(3)	—
Article 3	Article 3
Article 4(1)	—
Article 4(2)	Article 4(1)
Article 4(3)	Article 4(2)
Article 4(4)	Article 4(3)
Article 5(1)	—
Article 5(2)	Article 5
—	Article 6
—	Article 7
Article 6	Article 8
—	Annex I
—	Annex II

ARCHIVED COUNCIL DIRECTIVE 2006/112/EC
OF 28 NOVEMBER 2006
ON THE COMMON SYSTEM OF VALUE ADDED TAX

(2006/112/EC)

Note—This Directive repeals Council Directives 67/227/EEC (First Council Directive of 11 April 1967) and 77/388 (Sixth Council Directive of 17 May 1977). For correlation table, see Annex XII.

ARRANGEMENT OF CONTENTS

TITLE I:
SUBJECT MATTER AND SCOPE

TITLE II:
TERRITORIAL SCOPE

TITLE III:
TAXABLE PERSONS

TITLE IV:
TAXABLE TRANSACTIONS

CHAPTER 1:
SUPPLY OF GOODS

CHAPTER 2:
INTRA-COMMUNITY ACQUISITION OF GOODS

CHAPTER 3:
SUPPLY OF SERVICES

CHAPTER 4:
IMPORTATION OF GOODS

TITLE V:
PLACE OF TAXABLE TRANSACTIONS.

CHAPTER 1:
PLACE OF SUPPLY OF GOODS

SECTION 1:
Supply of goods without transport

SECTION 2:
Supply of goods with transport

SECTION 3:
Supply of goods on board ships, aircraft or trains

SECTION 4:
Supply of goods through distribution systems

CHAPTER 2:
PLACE OF AN INTRA-COMMUNITY ACQUISITION OF GOODS

CHAPTER 3:
PLACE OF SUPPLY OF SERVICES

SECTION 1:
General rule

SECTION 2:
Particular provisions

SUBSECTION 1:
Supply of services by intermediaries

SUBSECTION 2:
Supply of services connected with immovable property.

SUBSECTION 3:
Supply of transport

SUBSECTION 4:
Supply of cultural and similar services, ancillary transport services or services relating to movable tangible property

SUBSECTION 5:
Supply of miscellaneous services

SUBSECTION 6:
Criterion of effective use and enjoyment

CHAPTER 4:
PLACE OF IMPORTATION OF GOODS

TITLE VI:
CHARGEABLE EVENT AND CHARGEABILITY OF VAT

CHAPTER 1:
GENERAL PROVISIONS

CHAPTER 2:
SUPPLY OF GOODS OR SERVICES

CHAPTER 3:
INTRA-COMMUNITY ACQUISITION OF GOODS

CHAPTER 4:
IMPORTATION OF GOODS

TITLE VII:
TAXABLE AMOUNT

CHAPTER 1:
DEFINITION

CHAPTER 2:
SUPPLY OF GOODS OR SERVICES

CHAPTER 3:
INTRA-COMMUNITY ACQUISITION OF GOODS

CHAPTER 4:
IMPORTATION OF GOODS

CHAPTER 5:
MISCELLANEOUS PROVISIONS

TITLE VIII:
RATES

CHAPTER 1:
APPLICATION OF RATES

CHAPTER 2:
STRUCTURE AND LEVEL OF RATES

SECTION 1:
Standard rate

SECTION 2:
Reduced rates

SECTION 3:
Particular provisions

CHAPTER 3:
TEMPORARY PROVISIONS FOR PARTICULAR LABOUR-INTENSIVE SERVICES

CHAPTER 4:
SPECIAL PROVISIONS APPLYING UNTIL THE ADOPTION OF DEFINITIVE ARRANGEMENTS

CHAPTER 5:
TEMPORARY PROVISIONS

TITLE IX:
EXEMPTIONS

CHAPTER 1:
GENERAL PROVISIONS

CHAPTER 2:
EXEMPTIONS FOR CERTAIN ACTIVITIES IN THE PUBLIC INTEREST

CHAPTER 3:
EXEMPTIONS FOR OTHER ACTIVITIES

CHAPTER 4:
EXEMPTIONS FOR INTRA-COMMUNITY TRANSACTIONS

SECTION 1:
Exemptions related to the supply of goods

SECTION 2:
Exemptions for intra-Community acquisitions of goods

SECTION 3:
Exemptions for certain transport services

CHAPTER 5:
EXEMPTIONS ON IMPORTATION

CHAPTER 6:
EXEMPTIONS ON EXPORTATION

CHAPTER 7:
EXEMPTIONS RELATED TO INTERNATIONAL TRANSPORT

CHAPTER 8:
EXEMPTIONS RELATING TO CERTAIN TRANSACTIONS TREATED AS EXPORTS

CHAPTER 9:
EXEMPTIONS FOR THE SUPPLY OF SERVICES BY INTERMEDIARIES

CHAPTER 10:
EXEMPTIONS FOR TRANSACTIONS RELATING TO INTERNATIONAL TRADE

SECTION 1:
Customs warehouses, warehouses other than customs warehouses and similar arrangements

SECTION 2:
Transactions exempted with a view to export and in the framework of trade between the Member States

SECTION 3:
Provisions common to Sections 1 and 2

TITLE X:
DEDUCTIONS

CHAPTER 1:

ORIGIN AND SCOPE OF RIGHT OF DEDUCTION

CHAPTER 2:

PROPORTIONAL DEDUCTION

CHAPTER 3:

RESTRICTIONS ON THE RIGHT OF DEDUCTION

CHAPTER 4:

RULES GOVERNING EXERCISE OF THE RIGHT OF DEDUCTION

CHAPTER 5:

ADJUSTMENT OF DEDUCTIONS

TITLE XI:
OBLIGATIONS OF TAXABLE PERSONS AND CERTAIN NON-TAXABLE PERSONS

CHAPTER 1:

OBLIGATION TO PAY

SECTION 1:

Persons liable for payment of VAT to the tax authorities

SECTION 2:

Payment arrangements

CHAPTER 2:

IDENTIFICATION

CHAPTER 3:

INVOICING

SECTION 1:

Definition

SECTION 2:

Concept of invoice

SECTION 3:

Issue of invoices

SECTION 4:

Content of invoices

SECTION 5:

Sending invoices by electronic means

SECTION 6:

Simplification measures

CHAPTER 4:

ACCOUNTING

SECTION 1:

Definition

SECTION 2:

General obligations

SECTION 3:

Specific obligations relating to the storage of all invoices

SECTION 4:

Right of access to invoices stored by electronic means in another Member State

CHAPTER 5:

RETURNS

CHAPTER 6:
RECAPITULATIVE STATEMENTS

CHAPTER 7:
MISCELLANEOUS PROVISIONS

CHAPTER 8:
OBLIGATIONS RELATING TO CERTAIN IMPORTATIONS AND EXPORTATIONS

SECTION 1:
Importation

SECTION 2:
Exportation

TITLE XII:
SPECIAL SCHEMES

CHAPTER 1:
SPECIAL SCHEME FOR SMALL ENTERPRISES

SECTION 1:
Simplified procedures for charging and collection

SECTION 2:
Exemptions or graduated relief

SECTION 3:
Reporting and review

CHAPTER 2:
COMMON FLAT-RATE SCHEME FOR FARMERS

CHAPTER 3:
SPECIAL SCHEME FOR TRAVEL AGENTS

CHAPTER 4:
SPECIAL ARRANGEMENTS FOR SECOND-HAND GOODS, WORKS OF ART, COLLECTORS' ITEMS AND ANTIQUES

SECTION 1:
Definitions

SECTION 2:
Special arrangements for taxable dealers

SUBSECTION 1:
Margin scheme

SUBSECTION 2:
Transitional arrangements for second-hand means of transport

SECTION 3:
Special arrangements for sales by public auction

SECTION 4:
Measures to prevent distortion of competition and tax evasion

CHAPTER 5:
SPECIAL SCHEME FOR INVESTMENT GOLD

SECTION 1:
General provisions

SECTION 2:

Exemption from VAT

SECTION 3:
Taxation option

SECTION 4:
Transactions on a regulated gold bullion market

SECTION 5:
Special rights and obligations for traders in investment gold

CHAPTER 6:
SPECIAL SCHEME FOR NON-ESTABLISHED TAXABLE PERSONS SUPPLYING ELECTRONIC SERVICES TO NON-TAXABLE PERSONS

SECTION 1:
General provisions

SECTION 2:
Special scheme for electronically supplied services

TITLE XIII:
DEROGATIONS

CHAPTER 1:
DEROGATIONS APPLYING UNTIL THE ADOPTION OF DEFINITIVE ARRANGEMENTS

SECTION 1:
Derogations for States which were members of the Community on 1 January 1978

SECTION 2:
Derogations for States which acceded to the Community after 1 January 1978

SECTION 3:
Provisions common to Sections 1 and 2

CHAPTER 2:
DEROGATIONS SUBJECT TO AUTHORISATION

SECTION 1:
Simplification measures and measures to prevent tax evasion or avoidance

SECTION 2:
International agreements

TITLE XIV:
MISCELLANEOUS

CHAPTER 1:
IMPLEMENTING MEASURES

CHAPTER 2:
VAT COMMITTEE

CHAPTER 3:
CONVERSION RATES

CHAPTER 4:
OTHER TAXES, DUTIES AND CHARGES

TITLE XV:
FINAL PROVISIONS

CHAPTER 1:
TRANSITIONAL ARRANGEMENTS FOR THE TAXATION OF TRADE BETWEEN MEMBER STATES

CHAPTER 2:

TRANSITIONAL MEASURES APPLICABLE IN THE CONTEXT OF ACCESSION TO THE EUROPEAN UNION

CHAPTER 3:

TRANSPOSITION AND ENTRY INTO FORCE

Annex I: List of the activities referred to in the third subparagraph of article 13(1)

Annex II: Indicative list of the electronically supplied services referred to in point (K) of article 56(1)

Annex III: Lists of supplies of goods and services to which the reduced rates referred to in article 98 may be applied

Annex IV: List of the services referred to in article 106

Annex V: Categories of goods covered by warehousing arrangements other than customs warehousing as provided for under article 160(2)

Annex VI: List of supplies of goods and services as referred to in point (D) of article 199 (1)

Annex VII: List of the agricultural production activities referred to in point (4) of article 295(1)

Annex VIII: Indicative list of the agricultural services referred to in point (5) of article 295(1)

Annex IX: Works of art, collectors' items and antiques, as referred to in points (2), (3) and (4) of article 311(1)

Part A—Works of art
Part B—Collectors' items
Part C—Antiques

Annex X: List of transactions covered by the derogations referred to in articles 370 and 371 and articles 380 to 390

Part A—Transactions which Member States may continue to tax
Part B—Transactions which Member States may continue to exempt

Annex XI

Part A—Repealed Directives with their successive amendments
Part B—Time limits for transposition into national law (referred to in Article 411)

Annex XII: Correlation table

TITLE I
SUBJECT MATTER AND SCOPE

Article 1

1. This Directive establishes the common system of value added tax (VAT).

2. The principle of the common system of VAT entails the application to goods and services of a general tax on consumption exactly proportional to the price of the goods and services, however many transactions take place in the production and distribution process before the stage at which the tax is charged.

On each transaction, VAT, calculated on the price of the goods or services at the rate applicable to such goods or services, shall be chargeable after deduction of the amount of VAT borne directly by the various cost components.

The common system of VAT shall be applied up to and including the retail trade stage.

Article 2

1. The following transactions shall be subject to VAT:
   (a) the supply of goods for consideration within the territory of a Member State by a taxable person acting as such;
   (b) the intra-Community acquisition of goods for consideration within the territory of a Member State by:
      [(i) a taxable person acting as such, or a non-taxable legal person, where the vendor is a taxable person acting as such who is not eligible for the exemption for small enterprises provided for in Article 284 and who is not covered by Article 33 or 36;][2]
      (ii) in the case of new means of transport, a taxable person, or a non-taxable legal person, whose other acquisitions are not subject to VAT pursuant to Article 3(1), or any other non-taxable person;
      (iii) in the case of products subject to excise duty, where the excise duty on the intra-Community acquisition is chargeable, pursuant to Directive 92/12/EEC, within the territory of the Member State, a taxable person, or a non-taxable legal person, whose other acquisitions are not subject to VAT pursuant to Article 3(1);
   (c) the supply of services for consideration within the territory of a Member State by a taxable person acting as such;
   (d) the importation of goods.

2. (a) For the purposes of point (ii) of paragraph 1(b), the following shall be regarded as 'means of transport', where they are intended for the transport of persons or goods:

(i) motorised land vehicles the capacity of which exceeds 48 cubic centimetres or the power of which exceeds 7,2 kilowatts;
(ii) vessels exceeding 7,5 metres in length, with the exception of vessels used for navigation on the high seas and carrying passengers for reward, and of vessels used for the purposes of commercial, industrial or fishing activities, or for rescue or assistance at sea, or for inshore fishing;
(iii) aircraft the take-off weight of which exceeds 1 550 kilograms, with the exception of aircraft used by airlines operating for reward chiefly on international routes.
(b) These means of transport shall be regarded as 'new' in the cases:
(i) of motorised land vehicles, where the supply takes place within six months of the date of first entry into service or where the vehicle has travelled for no more than 6 000 kilometres;
(ii) of vessels, where the supply takes place within three months of the date of first entry into service or where the vessel has sailed for no more than 100 hours;
(iii) of aircraft, where the supply takes place within three months of the date of first entry into service or where the aircraft has flown for no more than 40 hours.
(c) Member States shall lay down the conditions under which the facts referred to in point (b) may be regarded as established.
[3. "Products subject to excise duty" shall mean energy products, alcohol and alcoholic beverages and manufactured tobacco, as defined by current Community legislation, but not gas supplied through a natural gas system situated within the territory of the Community or any network connected to such a system.][1]

Amendments—[1] Article 2(3) substituted by Council Directive 2009/162/EU art 1 with effect from 15 January 2010 (OJ L 10, 15.1.2010, p 14).
[2] Point (1)(b)(i) substituted by Council Directive 2020/285/EU art 1(1) with effect from 22 March 2020 (OJ L 62, 2.3.2020, p 13).

Article 3

1. By way of derogation from Article 2(1)(b)(i), the following transactions shall not be subject to VAT:
(a) the intra-Community acquisition of goods by a taxable person or a non-taxable legal person, where the supply of such goods within the territory of the Member State of acquisition would be exempt pursuant to Articles 148 and 151;
(b) the intra-Community acquisition of goods, other than those referred to in point (a) and Article 4, and other than new means of transport or products subject to excise duty, by a taxable person for the purposes of his agricultural, forestry or fisheries business subject to the common flat-rate scheme for farmers, or by a taxable person who carries out only supplies of goods or services in respect of which VAT is not deductible, or by a non-taxable legal person.
2. Point (b) of paragraph 1 shall apply only if the following conditions are met:
(a) during the current calendar year, the total value of intra-Community acquisitions of goods does not exceed a threshold which the Member States shall determine but which may not be less than EUR 10 000 or the equivalent in national currency;
(b) during the previous calendar year, the total value of intra-Community acquisitions of goods did not exceed the threshold provided for in point (a).
The threshold which serves as the reference shall consist of the total value, exclusive of VAT due or paid in the Member State in which dispatch or transport of the goods began, of the intra-Community acquisitions of goods as referred to under point (b) of paragraph 1.
3. Member States shall grant taxable persons and non-taxable legal persons eligible under point (b) of paragraph 1 the right to opt for the general scheme provided for in Article 2(1)(b)(i).
Member States shall lay down the detailed rules for the exercise of the option referred to in the first subparagraph, which shall in any event cover a period of two calendar years.

Article 4

In addition to the transactions referred to in Article 3, the following transactions shall not be subject to VAT:
(a) the intra-Community acquisition of second-hand goods, works of art, collectors' items or antiques, as defined in points (1) to (4) of Article 311(1), where the vendor is a taxable dealer acting as such and VAT has been applied to the goods in the Member State in which their dispatch or transport began, in accordance with the margin scheme provided for in Articles 312 to 325;
(b) the intra-Community acquisition of second-hand means of transport, as defined in Article 327(3), where the vendor is a taxable dealer acting as such and VAT has been applied to the means of transport in the Member State in which their dispatch or transport began, in accordance with the transitional arrangements for second-hand means of transport;
(c) the intra-Community acquisition of second-hand goods, works of art, collectors' items or antiques, as defined in points (1) to (4) of Article 311(1), where the vendor is an organiser of

sales by public auction, acting as such, and VAT has been applied to the goods in the Member State in which their dispatch or transport began, in accordance with the special arrangements for sales by public auction.

TITLE II
TERRITORIAL SCOPE

Article 5
For the purposes of applying this Directive, the following definitions shall apply:
(1) 'Community' and 'territory of the Community' mean the territories of the Member States as defined in point (2);
(2) 'Member State' and 'territory of a Member State' mean the territory of each Member State of the Community to which the Treaty establishing the European Community is applicable, in accordance with Article 299 of that Treaty, with the exception of any territory referred to in Article 6 of this Directive;
(3) 'third territories' means those territories referred to in Article 6;
(4) 'third country' means any State or territory to which the Treaty is not applicable.

Article 6
1. This Directive shall not apply to the following territories forming part of the customs territory of the Community:
   (a) Mount Athos;
   (b) the Canary Islands;
   [(c) the French territories referred to in Article 349 and Article 355(1) of the Treaty on the Functioning of the European Union;][1]
   (d) the Åland Islands;
   (e) the Channel Islands.
   [(f) Campione d'Italia;
   (g) the Italian waters of Lake Lugano.][2]
2. This Directive shall not apply to the following territories not forming part of the customs territory of the Community:
   (a) the Island of Heligoland;
   (b) the territory of Büsingen;
   (c) Ceuta;
   (d) Melilla;
   (e) Livigno;
   (f) *Campione d'Italia;*[2]
   (g) *the Italian waters of Lake Lugano.*[2]

Amendments—[1] Para 1(c) substituted by Council Directive 2013/61/EU art 1 with effect from 1 January 2014 (OJ L 353, 28.12.2013, p 5).
[2] In para 1, points (f), (g) inserted, and in para 2, points (f), (g) repealed, by Council Directive (EU) 2019/475 art 1 with effect from 14 April 2019 (OJ L 83, 25.3.2019, p 42).

Article 7
1. In view of the conventions and treaties concluded with France, the United Kingdom and Cyprus respectively, the Principality of Monaco, the Isle of Man and the United Kingdom Sovereign Base Areas of Akrotiri and Dhekelia shall not be regarded, for the purposes of the application of this Directive, as third countries.
2. Member States shall take the measures necessary to ensure that transactions originating in or intended for the Principality of Monaco are treated as transactions originating in or intended for France, that transactions originating in or intended for the Isle of Man are treated as transactions originating in or intended for the United Kingdom, and that transactions originating in or intended for the United Kingdom Sovereign Base Areas of Akrotiri and Dhekelia are treated as transactions originating in or intended for Cyprus.

Article 8
If the Commission considers that the provisions laid down in Articles 6 and 7 are no longer justified, particularly in terms of fair competition or own resources, it shall present appropriate proposals to the Council.

TITLE III
TAXABLE PERSONS

Article 9
1. 'Taxable person' shall mean any person who, independently, carries out in any place any economic activity, whatever the purpose or results of that activity.

Any activity of producers, traders or persons supplying services, including mining and agricultural activities and activities of the professions, shall be regarded as 'economic activity'. The exploitation of tangible or intangible property for the purposes of obtaining income therefrom on a continuing basis shall in particular be regarded as an economic activity.

2. In addition to the persons referred to in paragraph 1, any person who, on an occasional basis, supplies a new means of transport, which is dispatched or transported to the customer by the vendor or the customer, or on behalf of the vendor or the customer, to a destination outside the territory of a Member State but within the territory of the Community, shall be regarded as a taxable person.

Commentary—*De Voil Indirect Tax Service* **V2.101, V2.108**.

Article 10

The condition in Article 9(1) that the economic activity be conducted 'independently' shall exclude employed and other persons from VAT in so far as they are bound to an employer by a contract of employment or by any other legal ties creating the relationship of employer and employee as regards working conditions, remuneration and the employer's liability.

Article 11

After consulting the advisory committee on value added tax (hereafter, the 'VAT Committee'), each Member State may regard as a single taxable person any persons established in the territory of that Member State who, while legally independent, are closely bound to one another by financial, economic and organisational links.

A Member State exercising the option provided for in the first paragraph, may adopt any measures needed to prevent tax evasion or avoidance through the use of this provision.

Article 12

1. Member States may regard as a taxable person anyone who carries out, on an occasional basis, a transaction relating to the activities referred to in the second subparagraph of Article 9(1) and in particular one of the following transactions:
   (*a*) the supply, before first occupation, of a building or parts of a building and of the land on which the building stands;
   (*b*) the supply of building land.

2. For the purposes of paragraph 1(*a*), 'building' shall mean any structure fixed to or in the ground.

Member States may lay down the detailed rules for applying the criterion referred to in paragraph 1(a) to conversions of buildings and may determine what is meant by 'the land on which a building stands'.

Member States may apply criteria other than that of first occupation, such as the period elapsing between the date of completion of the building and the date of first supply, or the period elapsing between the date of first occupation and the date of subsequent supply, provided that those periods do not exceed five years and two years respectively.

3. For the purposes of paragraph 1(*b*), 'building land' shall mean any unimproved or improved land defined as such by the Member States.

Article 13

1. States, regional and local government authorities and other bodies governed by public law shall not be regarded as taxable persons in respect of the activities or transactions in which they engage as public authorities, even where they collect dues, fees, contributions or payments in connection with those activities or transactions.

However, when they engage in such activities or transactions, they shall be regarded as taxable persons in respect of those activities or transactions where their treatment as non-taxable persons would lead to significant distortions of competition.

In any event, bodies governed by public law shall be regarded as taxable persons in respect of the activities listed in Annex I, provided that those activities are not carried out on such a small scale as to be negligible.

[2. Member States may regard activities, exempt under Articles 132, 135, 136 and 371, Articles 374 to 377, Article 378(2), Article 379(2) or Articles 380 to 390b, engaged in by bodies governed by public law as activities in which those bodies engage as public authorities.]

Commentary—*De Voil Indirect Tax Service* **V2.108**.

Amendments—Article 13(2) substituted by Council Directive 2009/162/EU art 1(2) with effect from 15 January 2010 (OJ L 10, 15.1.2010, p 14).

TITLE IV
TAXABLE TRANSACTIONS

CHAPTER 1
SUPPLY OF GOODS

Article 14

1. 'Supply of goods' shall mean the transfer of the right to dispose of tangible property as owner.
2. In addition to the transaction referred to in paragraph 1, each of the following shall be regarded as a supply of goods:
    (a) the transfer, by order made by or in the name of a public authority or in pursuance of the law, of the ownership of property against payment of compensation;
    (b) the actual handing over of goods pursuant to a contract for the hire of goods for a certain period, or for the sale of goods on deferred terms, which provides that in the normal course of events ownership is to pass at the latest upon payment of the final instalment;
    (c) the transfer of goods pursuant to a contract under which commission is payable on purchase or sale.
3. Member States may regard the handing over of certain works of construction as a supply of goods.

Commentary—*De Voil Indirect Tax Service* **V3.119**.

Article 15

[1. Electricity, gas, heat or cooling energy and the like shall be treated as tangible property.]
2. Member States may regard the following as tangible property:
    (a) certain interests in immovable property;
    (b) rights in rem giving the holder thereof a right of use over immovable property;
    (c) shares or interests equivalent to shares giving the holder thereof de jure or de facto rights of ownership or possession over immovable property or part thereof.

Amendments—Article 15(1) substituted by Council Directive 2009/162/EU art 1(3) with effect from 15 January 2010 (OJ L 10, 15.1.2010, p 14).

Article 16

The application by a taxable person of goods forming part of his business assets for his private use or for that of his staff, or their disposal free of charge or, more generally, their application for purposes other than those of his business, shall be treated as a supply of goods for consideration, where the VAT on those goods or the component parts thereof was wholly or partly deductible.

However, the application of goods for business use as samples or as gifts of small value shall not be treated as a supply of goods for consideration.

Article 17

1. The transfer by a taxable person of goods forming part of his business assets to another Member State shall be treated as a supply of goods for consideration.

'Transfer to another Member State' shall mean the dispatch or transport of movable tangible property by or on behalf of the taxable person, for the purposes of his business, to a destination outside the territory of the Member State in which the property is located, but within the Community.
2. The dispatch or transport of goods for the purposes of any of the following transactions shall not be regarded as a transfer to another Member State:
    (a) the supply of the goods by the taxable person within the territory of the Member State in which the dispatch or transport ends, in accordance with the conditions laid down in Article 33;
    (b) the supply of the goods, for installation or assembly by or on behalf of the supplier, by the taxable person within the territory of the Member State in which dispatch or transport of the goods ends, in accordance with the conditions laid down in Article 36;
    (c) the supply of the goods by the taxable person on board a ship, an aircraft or a train in the course of a passenger transport operation, in accordance with the conditions laid down in Article 37;
    [(d) the supply of gas through a natural gas system situated within the territory of the Community or any network connected to such a system, the supply of electricity or the supply of heat or cooling energy through heating or cooling networks, in accordance with the conditions laid down in Articles 38 and 39;]
    (e) the supply of the goods by the taxable person within the territory of the Member State, in accordance with the conditions laid down in Articles 138, 146, 147, 148, 151 or 152;
    [(f) the supply of a service performed for the taxable person and consisting in valuations of, or work on, the goods in question physically carried out within the territory of the Member State in which dispatch or transport of the goods ends, provided that the goods, after being valued or worked upon, are returned to that taxable person in the Member State from which they were initially dispatched or transported;]

(g) the temporary use of the goods within the territory of the Member State in which dispatch or transport of the goods ends, for the purposes of the supply of services by the taxable person established within the Member State in which dispatch or transport of the goods began;

(h) the temporary use of the goods, for a period not exceeding twenty-four months, within the territory of another Member State, in which the importation of the same goods from a third country with a view to their temporary use would be covered by the arrangements for temporary importation with full exemption from import duties.

3. If one of the conditions governing eligibility under paragraph 2 is no longer met, the goods shall be regarded as having been transferred to another Member State. In such cases, the transfer shall be deemed to take place at the time when that condition ceases to be met.

Amendments—Article 17(2)(d) substituted by Council Directive 2009/162/EU art 1(3) with effect from 15 January 2010 (OJ L 10, 15.1.2010, p 14).

Article 17(2)(f) substituted by Council Directive 2010/45 art 1(1) with effect from 11 August 2010 (OJ L 189, 22.7.2010, p 1). The deadline for implementation of Directive 2010/45/EU is 31 December 2012.

[Article 17a

1. The transfer by a taxable person of goods forming part of his business assets to another Member State under call-off stock arrangements shall not be treated as a supply of goods for consideration.

2. For the purposes of this Article, call-off stock arrangements shall be deemed to exist where the following conditions are met:
   (a) goods are dispatched or transported by a taxable person, or by a third party on his behalf, to another Member State with a view to those goods being supplied there, at a later stage and after arrival, to another taxable person who is entitled to take ownership of those goods in accordance with an existing agreement between both taxable persons;
   (b) the taxable person dispatching or transporting the goods has not established his business nor has a fixed establishment in the Member State to which the goods are dispatched or transported;
   (c) the taxable person to whom the goods are intended to be supplied is identified for VAT purposes in the Member State to which the goods are dispatched or transported and both his identity and the VAT identification number assigned to him by that Member State are known to the taxable person referred to in point (b) at the time when the dispatch or transport begins;
   (d) the taxable person dispatching or transporting the goods records the transfer of the goods in the register provided for in Article 243(3) and includes the identity of the taxable person acquiring the goods and the VAT identification number assigned to him by the Member State to which the goods are dispatched or transported in the recapitulative statement provided for in Article 262(2).

3. Where the conditions laid down in paragraph 2 are met, the following rules shall apply at the time of the transfer of the right to dispose of the goods as owner to the taxable person referred to in point (c) of paragraph 2, provided that the transfer occurs within the deadline referred to in paragraph 4:
   (a) a supply of goods in accordance with Article 138(1) shall be deemed to be made by the taxable person that dispatched or transported the goods either by himself or by a third party on his behalf in the Member State from which the goods were dispatched or transported;
   (b) an intra-Community acquisition of goods shall be deemed to be made by the taxable person to whom those goods are supplied in the Member State to which the goods were dispatched or transported.

4. If, within 12 months after the arrival of the goods in the Member State to which they were dispatched or transported, the goods have not been supplied to the taxable person for whom they were intended, referred to in point (c) of paragraph 2 and paragraph 6, and none of the circumstances laid down in paragraph 7 have occurred, a transfer within the meaning of Article 17 shall be deemed to take place on the day following the expiry of the 12-month period.

5. No transfer within the meaning of Article 17 shall be deemed to take place where the following conditions are met:
   (a) the right to dispose of the goods has not been transferred, and those goods are returned to the Member State from which they were dispatched or transported within the time limit referred to in paragraph 4; and
   (b) the taxable person who dispatched or transported the goods records their return in the register provided for in Article 243(3).

6. Where, within the period referred to in paragraph 4, the taxable person referred to in point (c) of paragraph 2 is substituted by another taxable person, no transfer within the meaning of Article 17 shall be deemed to take place at the time of the substitution, provided that:
   (a) all other applicable conditions in paragraph 2 are met; and
   (b) the substitution is recorded by the taxable person referred to in point (b) of paragraph 2 in the register provided for in Article 243(3).

CHAPTER 4
IMPORTATION OF GOODS

Article 30

'Importation of goods' shall mean the entry into the Community of goods which are not in free circulation within the meaning of Article 24 of the Treaty.

In addition to the transaction referred to in the first paragraph, the entry into the Community of goods which are in free circulation, coming from a third territory forming part of the customs territory of the Community, shall be regarded as importation of goods.

[CHAPTER 5
PROVISIONS COMMON TO CHAPTERS 1 AND 3

Article 30a

For the purposes of this Directive, the following definitions shall apply:
(1) 'voucher' means an instrument where there is an obligation to accept it as consideration or part consideration for a supply of goods or services and where the goods or services to be supplied or the identities of their potential suppliers are either indicated on the instrument itself or in related documentation, including the terms and conditions of use of such instrument;
(2) 'single-purpose voucher' means a voucher where the place of supply of the goods or services to which the voucher relates, and the VAT due on those goods or services, are known at the time of issue of the voucher;
(3) 'multi-purpose voucher' means a voucher, other than a single-purpose voucher.][1]

Amendments—[1] Articles 30a, 30b inserted by Council Directive 2016/1065/EU Article 1(1) with effect from 2 July 2017 (OJ L 177, 1.7.2016, p 9). Note that member states are required to adopt and publish, by 31 December 2018 at the latest, the laws, regulations and administrative provisions necessary to comply with Directive 2016/1065/EU and that those provisions will apply from 1 January 2019.

[Article 30b

1. Each transfer of a single-purpose voucher made by a taxable person acting in his own name shall be regarded as a supply of the goods or services to which the voucher relates. The actual handing over of the goods or the actual provision of the services in return for a single-purpose voucher accepted as consideration or part consideration by the supplier shall not be regarded as an independent transaction.

Where a transfer of a single-purpose voucher is made by a taxable person acting in the name of another taxable person, that transfer shall be regarded as a supply of the goods or services to which the voucher relates made by the other taxable person in whose name the taxable person is acting.

Where the supplier of goods or services is not the taxable person who, acting in his own name, issued the single-purpose voucher, that supplier shall however be deemed to have made the supply of the goods or services related to that voucher to that taxable person.

2. The actual handing over of the goods or the actual provision of the services in return for a multi-purpose voucher accepted as consideration or part consideration by the supplier shall be subject to VAT pursuant to Article 2, whereas each preceding transfer of that multi-purpose voucher shall not be subject to VAT.

Where a transfer of a multi-purpose voucher is made by a taxable person other than the taxable person carrying out the transaction subject to VAT pursuant to the first subparagraph, any supply of services that can be identified, such as distribution or promotion services, shall be subject to VAT.][1]

Amendments—[1] Articles 30a, 30b inserted by Council Directive 2016/1065/EU Article 1(1) with effect from 2 July 2017 (OJ L 177, 1.7.2016, p 9). Note that member states are required to adopt and publish, by 31 December 2018 at the latest, the laws, regulations and administrative provisions necessary to comply with Directive 2016/1065/EU and that those provisions will apply from 1 January 2019.

TITLE V
PLACE OF TAXABLE TRANSACTIONS

CHAPTER 1

PLACE OF SUPPLY OF GOODS

SECTION 1

Supply of goods without transport

Article 31

Where goods are not dispatched or transported, the place of supply shall be deemed to be the place where the goods are located at the time when the supply takes place.

Commentary—*De Voil Indirect Tax Service* **V3.171–178**.

SECTION 2
Supply of goods with transport

Article 32
Where goods are dispatched or transported by the supplier, or by the customer, or by a third person, the place of supply shall be deemed to be the place where the goods are located at the time when dispatch or transport of the goods to the customer begins.

However, if dispatch or transport of the goods begins in a third territory or third country, both the place of supply by the importer designated or recognised under Article 201 as liable for payment of VAT and the place of any subsequent supply shall be deemed to be within the Member State of importation of the goods.

Commentary—*De Voil Indirect Tax Service* **V3.112**.

Article 33
1. By way of derogation from Article 32, the place of supply of goods dispatched or transported by or on behalf of the supplier from a Member State other than that in which dispatch or transport of the goods ends shall be deemed to be the place where the goods are located at the time when dispatch or transport of the goods to the customer ends, where the following conditions are met:
   (a) the supply of goods is carried out for a taxable person, or a non-taxable legal person, whose intra-Community acquisitions of goods are not subject to VAT pursuant to Article 3 (1) or for any other non-taxable person;
   (b) the goods supplied are neither new means of transport nor goods supplied after assembly or installation, with or without a trial run, by or on behalf of the supplier.
2. Where the goods supplied are dispatched or transported from a third territory or a third country and imported by the supplier into a Member State other than that in which dispatch or transport of the goods to the customer ends, they shall be regarded as having been dispatched or transported from the Member State of importation.

Article 34
1. Provided the following conditions are met, Article 33 shall not apply to supplies of goods all of which are dispatched or transported to the same Member State, where that Member State is the Member State in which dispatch or transport of the goods ends:
   (a) the goods supplied are not products subject to excise duty;
   (b) the total value, exclusive of VAT, of such supplies effected under the conditions laid down in Article 33 within that Member State does not in any one calendar year exceed EUR 100 000 or the equivalent in national currency;
   (c) the total value, exclusive of VAT, of the supplies of goods, other than products subject to excise duty, effected under the conditions laid down in Article 33 within that Member State did not in the previous calendar year exceed EUR 100 000 or the equivalent in national currency.
2. The Member State within the territory of which the goods are located at the time when their dispatch or transport to the customer ends may limit the threshold referred to in paragraph 1 to EUR 35 000 or the equivalent in national currency, where that Member State fears that the threshold of EUR 100 000 might cause serious distortion of competition.

Member States which exercise the option under the first subparagraph shall take the measures necessary to inform accordingly the competent public authorities in the Member State in which dispatch or transport of the goods begins.
3. The Commission shall present to the Council at the earliest opportunity a report on the operation of the special EUR 35 000 threshold referred to in paragraph 2, accompanied, if necessary, by appropriate proposals.
4. The Member State within the territory of which the goods are located at the time when their dispatch or transport begins shall grant those taxable persons who carry out supplies of goods eligible under paragraph 1 the right to opt for the place of supply to be determined in accordance with Article 33.

The Member States concerned shall lay down the detailed rules governing the exercise of the option referred to in the first subparagraph, which shall in any event cover two calendar years.

Article 35
Articles 33 and 34 shall not apply to supplies of second-hand goods, works of art, collectors' items or antiques, as defined in points (1) to (4) of Article 311(1), nor to supplies of second-hand means of transport, as defined in Article 327(3), subject to VAT in accordance with the relevant special arrangements.

Article 36
Where goods dispatched or transported by the supplier, by the customer or by a third person are installed or assembled, with or without a trial run, by or on behalf of the supplier, the place of supply shall be deemed to be the place where the goods are installed or assembled.

Where the installation or assembly is carried out in a Member State other than that of the supplier, the Member State within the territory of which the installation or assembly is carried out shall take the measures necessary to ensure that there is no double taxation in that Member State.

Commentary—*De Voil Indirect Tax Service* **V3.171–178**.

[**Article 36a**

1. Where the same goods are supplied successively and those goods are dispatched or transported from one Member State to another Member State directly from the first supplier to the last customer in the chain, the dispatch or transport shall be ascribed only to the supply made to the intermediary operator.
2. By way of derogation from paragraph 1, the dispatch or transport shall be ascribed only to the supply of goods by the intermediary operator where the intermediary operator has communicated to his supplier the VAT identification number issued to him by the Member State from which the goods are dispatched or transported.
3. For the purposes of this Article, 'intermediary operator' means a supplier within the chain other than the first supplier in the chain who dispatches or transports the goods either himself or through a third party acting on his behalf.
4. This Article shall not apply to the situations covered by Article 14a.][1]

Amendments—[1] Article 36a inserted by Council Directive (EU) 2018/1910 Article 1(2) with effect from 27 December 2018 (OJ L 311, 7.12.2018, p 3).

[**Article 36b**

Where a taxable person is deemed to have received and supplied goods in accordance with Article 14a, the dispatch or transport of the goods shall be ascribed to the supply made by that taxable person.][1]

Amendments—[1] Article 36b inserted by Council Directive 2019/1995/EU art 1(1) with effect from 22 December 2019 (OJ L 310, 2.12.2019, p 1).

SECTION 3
Supply of goods on board ships, aircraft or trains

Article 37

1. Where goods are supplied on board ships, aircraft or trains during the section of a passenger transport operation effected within the Community, the place of supply shall be deemed to be at the point of departure of the passenger transport operation.
2. For the purposes of paragraph 1, 'section of a passenger transport operation effected within the Community' shall mean the section of the operation effected, without a stopover outside the Community, between the point of departure and the point of arrival of the passenger transport operation. 'Point of departure of a passenger transport operation' shall mean the first scheduled point of passenger embarkation within the Community, where applicable after a stopover outside the Community.

'Point of arrival of a passenger transport operation' shall mean the last scheduled point of disembarkation within the Community of passengers who embarked in the Community, where applicable before a stopover outside the Community.

In the case of a return trip, the return leg shall be regarded as a separate transport operation.
3. The Commission shall, at the earliest opportunity, present to the Council a report, accompanied if necessary by appropriate proposals, on the place of taxation of the supply of goods for consumption on board and the supply of services, including restaurant services, for passengers on board ships, aircraft or trains.

Pending adoption of the proposals referred to in the first subparagraph, Member States may exempt or continue to exempt, with deductibility of the VAT paid at the preceding stage, the supply of goods for consumption on board in respect of which the place of taxation is determined in accordance with paragraph 1.

Commentary—*De Voil Indirect Tax Service* **V3.177**.

[SECTION 4
Supplies of gas through a natural gas system, of electricity and of heat or cooling energy through heating and cooling networks

Article 38

1. In the case of the supply of gas through a natural gas system situated within the territory of the Community or any network connected to such a system, the supply of electricity, or the supply of heat or cooling energy through heating or cooling networks to a taxable dealer, the place of supply shall be deemed to be the place where that taxable dealer has established his business or has a fixed establishment for which the goods are supplied or, in the absence of such a place of business or fixed establishment, the place where he has his permanent address or usually resides.

2. For the purposes of paragraph 1, "taxable dealer" shall mean a taxable person whose principal activity in respect of purchases of gas, electricity, heat or cooling energy is reselling those products and whose own consumption of those products is negligible.

Amendments—Section 4 (Arts 38, 39) substituted by Council Directive 2009/162/EU art 1(5) with effect from 15 January 2010 (OJ L 10, 15.1.2010, p 14).

Article 39

In the case of the supply of gas through a natural gas system situated within the territory of the Community or any network connected to such a system, the supply of electricity or the supply of heat or cooling energy through heating or cooling networks, where such a supply is not covered by Article 38, the place of supply shall be deemed to be the place where the customer effectively uses and consumes the goods.

Where all or part of the gas, electricity or heat or cooling energy is not effectively consumed by the customer, those non-consumed goods shall be deemed to have been used and consumed at the place where the customer has established his business or has a fixed establishment for which the goods are supplied. In the absence of such a place of business or fixed establishment, the customer shall be deemed to have used and consumed the goods at the place where he has his permanent address or usually resides.]

Amendments—Section 4 (Arts 38, 39) substituted by Council Directive 2009/162/EU art 1(5) with effect from 15 January 2010 (OJ L 10, 15.1.2010, p 14).

CHAPTER 2

PLACE OF AN INTRA-COMMUNITY ACQUISITION OF GOODS

Article 40

The place of an intra-Community acquisition of goods shall be deemed to be the place where dispatch or transport of the goods to the person acquiring them ends.

Article 41

Without prejudice to Article 40, the place of an intra-Community acquisition of goods as referred to in Article 2(1)(*b*)(i) shall be deemed to be within the territory of the Member State which issued the VAT identification number under which the person acquiring the goods made the acquisition, unless the person acquiring the goods establishes that VAT has been applied to that acquisition in accordance with Article 40.

If VAT is applied to the acquisition in accordance with the first paragraph and subsequently applied, pursuant to Article 40, to the acquisition in the Member State in which dispatch or transport of the goods ends, the taxable amount shall be reduced accordingly in the Member State which issued the VAT identification number under which the person acquiring the goods made the acquisition.

Article 42

The first paragraph of Article 41 shall not apply and VAT shall be deemed to have been applied to the intra-Community acquisition of goods in accordance with Article 40 where the following conditions are met:
   (*a*) the person acquiring the goods establishes that he has made the intra-Community acquisition for the purposes of a subsequent supply, within the territory of the Member State identified in accordance with Article 40, for which the person to whom the supply is made has been designated in accordance with Article 197 as liable for payment of VAT;
   (*b*) the person acquiring the goods has satisfied the obligations laid down in Article 265 relating to submission of the recapitulative statement.

[CHAPTER 3
PLACE OF SUPPLY OF SERVICES

SECTION 1
Definitions

Article 43

For the purpose of applying the rules concerning the place of supply of services:
1. a taxable person who also carries out activities or transactions that are not considered to be taxable supplies of goods or services in accordance with Article 2(1) shall be regarded as a taxable person in respect of all services rendered to him;
2. a non-taxable legal person who is identified for VAT purposes shall be regarded as a taxable person.]

Commentary—*De Voil Indirect Tax Service* **V2.101**, **V3.166, V3.192**.
Amendments—Chapter 3 substituted by Council Directive 2008/8/EC art 2 with effect from 1 January 2010 (OJ L 44, 20.2.2008 p 11).

[SECTION 2
General rules

Article 44

The place of supply of services to a taxable person acting as such shall be the place where that person has established his business. However, if those services are provided to a fixed establishment of the taxable person located in a place other than the place where he has established his business, the place of supply of those services shall be the place where that fixed establishment is located. In the absence of such place of establishment or fixed establishment, the place of supply of services shall be the place where the taxable person who receives such services has his permanent address or usually resides.]

Amendments—Chapter 3 substituted by Council Directive 2008/8/EC art 2 with effect from 1 January 2010 (OJ L 44, 20.2.2008 p 11).

[Article 45

The place of supply of services to a non-taxable person shall be the place where the supplier has established his business. However, if those services are provided from a fixed establishment of the supplier located in a place other than the place where he has established his business, the place of supply of those services shall be the place where that fixed establishment is located. In the absence of such place of establishment or fixed establishment, the place of supply of services shall be the place where the supplier has his permanent address or usually resides.]

Commentary—*De Voil Indirect Tax Service* **V3.188**.

Amendments—Chapter 3 substituted by Council Directive 2008/8/EC art 2 with effect from 1 January 2010 (OJ L 44, 20.2.2008 p 11).

[SECTION 3
Particular provisions
SUBSECTION 1
Supply of services by intermediaries

Article 46

The place of supply of services rendered to a non-taxable person by an intermediary acting in the name and on behalf of another person shall be the place where the underlying transaction is supplied in accordance with this Directive.]

Commentary—*De Voil Indirect Tax Service* **V2.101**, **V3.166**, **V3.192**.

Amendments—Chapter 3 substituted by Council Directive 2008/8/EC art 2 with effect from 1 January 2010 (OJ L 44, 20.2.2008 p 11).

[SUBSECTION 2
Supply of services connected with immovable property

Article 47

The place of supply of services connected with immovable property, including the services of experts and estate agents, the provision of accommodation in the hotel sector or in sectors with a similar function, such as holiday camps or sites developed for use as camping sites, the granting of rights to use immovable property and services for the preparation and coordination of construction work, such as the services of architects and of firms providing on-site supervision, shall be the place where the immovable property is located.]

Amendments—Chapter 3 substituted by Council Directive 2008/8/EC art 2 with effect from 1 January 2010 (OJ L 44, 20.2.2008 p 11).

[SUBSECTION 3
Supply of transport

Article 48

The place of supply of passenger transport shall be the place where the transport takes place, proportionate to the distances covered.]

Amendments—Chapter 3 substituted by Council Directive 2008/8/EC art 2 with effect from 1 January 2010 (OJ L 44, 20.2.2008 p 11).

[Article 49

The place of supply of the transport of goods, other than the intra-Community transport of goods, to non-taxable persons shall be the place where the transport takes place, proportionate to the distances covered.]

Amendments—Chapter 3 substituted by Council Directive 2008/8/EC art 2 with effect from 1 January 2010 (OJ L 44, 20.2.2008 p 11).

[Article 50

The place of supply of the intra-Community transport of goods to non-taxable persons shall be the place of departure.]

Amendments—Chapter 3 substituted by Council Directive 2008/8/EC art 2 with effect from 1 January 2010 (OJ L 44, 20.2.2008 p 11).

[Article 51
"Intra-Community transport of goods" shall mean any transport of goods in respect of which the place of departure and the place of arrival are situated within the territories of two different Member States.
"Place of departure" shall mean the place where transport of the goods actually begins, irrespective of distances covered in order to reach the place where the goods are located and "place of arrival" shall mean the place where transport of the goods actually ends.]
Amendments—Chapter 3 substituted by Council Directive 2008/8/EC art 2 with effect from 1 January 2010 (OJ L 44, 20.2.2008 p 11).

[Article 52
Member States need not apply VAT to that part of the intra-Community transport of goods to non-taxable persons taking place over waters which do not form part of the territory of the Community.]
Amendments—Chapter 3 substituted by Council Directive 2008/8/EC art 2 with effect from 1 January 2010 (OJ L 44, 20.2.2008 p 11).

[SUBSECTION 4
Supply of cultural, artistic, sporting, scientific, educational, entertainment and similar services, ancillary transport services and valuations of and work on movable property.]
Amendments—Chapter 3 substituted by Council Directive 2008/8/EC art 2 with effect from 1 January 2010 (OJ L 44, 20.2.2008 p 11).

[Article 53
The place of supply of services in respect of admission to cultural, artistic, sporting, scientific, educational, entertainment or similar events, such as fairs and exhibitions, and of ancillary services related to the admission, supplied to a taxable person, shall be the place where those events actually take place.]
Amendments—Chapter 3 substituted by Council Directive 2008/8/EC art 2 with effect from 1 January 2010 (OJ L 44, 20.2.2008 p 11).
Articles 53, 54 substituted, by Council Directive 2008/8/EC art 3 with effect from 1 January 2011 (OJ L 44, 20.2.2008 p 11).
Simon's Tax Cases—*R&C Comrs v Finmeccanica Group Services SpA* [2015] UKUT 378 (TCC), [2016] STC 916.

[Article 54
(1) The place of supply of services and ancillary services, relating to cultural, artistic, sporting, scientific, educational, entertainment or similar activities, such as fairs and exhibitions, including the supply of services of the organisers of such activities, supplied to a non-taxable person shall be the place where those activities actually take place.
(2) The place of supply of the following services to a nontaxable person shall be the place where the services are physically carried out:
   (*a*) ancillary transport activities such as loading, unloading, handling and similar activities;
   (*b*) valuations of and work on movable tangible property.]
Amendments—Chapter 3 substituted by Council Directive 2008/8/EC art 2 with effect from 1 January 2010 (OJ L 44, 20.2.2008 p 11).
Articles 53, 54 substituted by Council Directive 2008/8/EC art 3 with effect from 1 January 2011 (OJ L 44, 20.2.2008 p 11).

[SUBSECTION 5
Supply of restaurant and catering services

Article 55
The place of supply of restaurant and catering services other than those physically carried out on board ships, aircraft or trains during the section of a passenger transport operation effected within the Community, shall be the place where the services are physically carried out.]
Amendments—Chapter 3 substituted by Council Directive 2008/8/EC art 2 with effect from 1 January 2010 (OJ L 44, 20.2.2008 p 11).

[SUBSECTION 6
Hiring of means of transport

Article 56
1. The place of short-term hiring of a means of transport shall be the place where the means of transport is actually put at the disposal of the customer.
[2. The place of hiring, other than short-term hiring, of a means of transport to a non-taxable person shall be the place where the customer is established, has his permanent address or usually resides.
However, the place of hiring a pleasure boat to a non-taxable person, other than short-term hiring, shall be the place where the pleasure boat is actually put at the disposal of the customer, where this service is actually provided by the supplier from his place of business or a fixed establishment situated in that place.

3. For the purposes of paragraphs 1 and 2, "short-term" shall mean the continuous possession or use of the means of transport throughout a period of not more than thirty days and, in the case of vessels, not more than 90 days.]]

Amendments—Chapter 3 substituted by Council Directive 2008/8/EC art 2 with effect from 1 January 2010 (OJ L 44, 20.2.2008 p 11).

New paras 2, 3 substituted for previous para 2, by Council Directive 2008/8/EC art 4 with effect from 1 January 2013 (OJ L 44, 20.2.2008 p 11).

[SUBSECTION 7

Supply of restaurant and catering services for consumption on board ships, aircraft or trains

Article 57

1. The place of supply of restaurant and catering services which are physically carried out on board ships, aircraft or trains during the section of a passenger transport operation effected within the Community, shall be at the point of departure of the passenger transport operation.

2. For the purposes of paragraph 1, "section of a passenger transport operation effected within the Community" shall mean the section of the operation effected, without a stopover outside the Community, between the point of departure and the point of arrival of the passenger transport operation.

"Point of departure of a passenger transport operation" shall mean the first scheduled point of passenger embarkation within the Community, where applicable after a stopover outside the Community.

"Point of arrival of a passenger transport operation" shall mean the last scheduled point of disembarkation within the Community of passengers who embarked in the Community, where applicable before a stop-over outside the Community.

In the case of a return trip, the return leg shall be regarded as a separate transport operation.]

Amendments—Chapter 3 substituted by Council Directive 2008/8/EC art 2 with effect from 1 January 2010 (OJ L 44, 20.2.2008 p 11).

[SUBSECTION 8

Supply of telecommunications, broadcasting and electronic services to non-taxable persons

[Article 58

1. The place of supply of the following services to a non-taxable person shall be the place where that person is established, has his permanent address or usually resides:
   (a) telecommunications services;
   (b) radio and television broadcasting services;
   (c) electronically supplied services, in particular those referred to in Annex II.

Where the supplier of a service and the customer communicate via electronic mail, that shall not of itself mean that the service supplied is an electronically supplied service.

2. Paragraph 1 shall not apply where the following conditions are met:
   (a) the supplier is established or, in the absence of an establishment, has his permanent address or usually resides in only one Member State; and
   (b) services are supplied to non-taxable persons who are established, have their permanent address or usually reside in any Member State other than the Member State referred to in point (a); and
   (c) the total value, exclusive of VAT, of the supplies referred to in point (b) does not in the current calendar year exceed EUR 10 000, or the equivalent in national currency, and did not do so in the course of the preceding calendar year.

3. Where, during a calendar year, the threshold referred to in point (c) of paragraph 2 is exceeded, paragraph 1 shall apply as of that time.

4. The Member State within the territory of which the suppliers referred to in paragraph 2 are established or, in the absence of an establishment, have their permanent address or usually reside, shall grant those suppliers the right to opt for the place of supply to be determined in accordance with paragraph 1, which shall in any event cover two calendar years.

5. Member States shall take appropriate measures to monitor the fulfilment by the taxable person of the conditions referred to in paragraphs 2, 3 and 4.

6. The corresponding value in national currency of the amount referred to in point (c) of paragraph 2 shall be calculated by applying the exchange rate published by the European Central Bank on the date of adoption of Council Directive (EU) 2017/2455.(*1)

(*1) Council Directive (EU) 2017/2455 of 5 December 2017 amending Directive 2006/112/EC and Directive 2009/132/EC as regards certain value added tax obligations for supplies of services and distance sales of goods (OJ L 348, 29.12.2017, p. 7).]

AMENDMENTS—

Article 58 substituted by Council Directive 2017/2455/EU art 1(1) with effect from 1 January 2019 (OJ L 348, 29.12.2017 p 7).

[SUBSECTION 9]

Supply of services to non-taxable persons outside the Community

Article 59

The place of supply of the following services to a non-taxable person who is established or has his permanent address or usually resides outside the Community, shall be the place where that person is established, has his permanent address or usually resides:
  (a) transfers and assignments of copyrights, patents, licences, trade marks and similar rights;
  (b) advertising services;
  (c) the services of consultants, engineers, consultancy firms, lawyers, accountants and other similar services, as well as data processing and the provision of information;
  (d) obligations to refrain from pursuing or exercising, in whole or in part, a business activity or a right referred to in this Article;
  (e) banking, financial and insurance transactions including reinsurance, with the exception of the hire of safes;
  (f) the supply of staff;
  (g) the hiring out of movable tangible property, with the exception of all means of transport;
  [(h) the provision of access to a natural gas system situated within the territory of the Community or to any network connected to such a system, to the electricity system or to heating or cooling networks, or the transmission or distribution through these systems or networks, and the provision of other services directly linked thereto;][2]
  (i) telecommunications services;[3]
  (j) radio and television broadcasting services;[3]
  (k) electronically supplied services, in particular those referred to in Annex II.[3]
Where the supplier of a service and the customer communicate via electronic mail, that shall not of itself mean that the service supplied is an electronically supplied service.]][1]

Commentary—*De Voil Indirect Tax Service* **V2.101, V3.166, V3.192**.
Amendments—[1]   Chapter 3 substituted by Council Directive 2008/8/EC art 2 with effect from 1 January 2010 (OJ L 44, 20.2.2008 p 11).
[2]   Point (h) substituted by Council Directive 2009/162/EU art 1(6) with effect from 15 January 2010 (OJ L 10, 15.1.2010, p 14).
[3]   Points (i), (j), (k) repealed by Council Directive 2008/8/EC art 5(2) with effect from 1 January 2015 (OJ L 44, 20.2.2008 p 11).

[SUBSECTION 10]

Prevention of double taxation or non-taxation

[Article 59a

In order to prevent double taxation, non-taxation or distortion of competition, Member States may, with regard to services the place of supply of which is governed by Articles 44, 45, 56, 58 and 59:
  (a) consider the place of supply of any or all of those services, if situated within their territory, as being situated outside the Community if the effective use and enjoyment of the services takes place outside the Community;
  (b) consider the place of supply of any or all of those services, if situated outside the Community, as being situated within their territory if the effective use and enjoyment of the services takes place within their territory.][1]

Amendments—[1]   Article 59a substituted by Council Directive 2008/8/EC art 5(3) with effect from 1 January 2015 (OJ L 44, 20.2.2008 p 11).

Article 59b

Member States shall apply Article 59a(b) to telecommunications services and radio and television broadcasting services, as referred to in point (j) of the first paragraph of Article 59, supplied to non-taxable persons who are established in a Member State, or who have their permanent address or usually reside in a Member State, by a taxable person who has established his business outside the Community or has a fixed establishment there from which the services are supplied, or who, in the absence of such a place of business or fixed establishment, has his permanent address or usually resides outside the Community.[1]

Amendments—[1]   Article 59b repealed by Council Directive 2008/8/EC art 5(3) with effect from 1 January 2015 (OJ L 44, 20.2.2008 p 11).

CHAPTER 4

PLACE OF IMPORTATION OF GOODS

Article 60

The place of importation of goods shall be the Member State within whose territory the goods are located when they enter the Community.

Article 61

By way of derogation from Article 60, where, on entry into the Community, goods which are not in free circulation are placed under one of the arrangements or situations referred to in Article 156, or under temporary importation arrangements with total exemption from import duty, or under external transit arrangements, the place of importation of such goods shall be the Member State within whose territory the goods cease to be covered by those arrangements or situations.

Similarly, where, on entry into the Community, goods which are in free circulation are placed under one of the arrangements or situations referred to in Articles 276 and 277, the place of importation shall be the Member State within whose territory the goods cease to be covered by those arrangements or situations.

TITLE VI
CHARGEABLE EVENT AND CHARGEABILITY OF VAT

CHAPTER 1
GENERAL PROVISIONS

Article 62

For the purposes of this Directive:
(1) 'chargeable event' shall mean the occurrence by virtue of which the legal conditions necessary for VAT to become chargeable are fulfilled;
(2) VAT shall become 'chargeable' when the tax authority becomes entitled under the law, at a given moment, to claim the tax from the person liable to pay, even though the time of payment may be deferred.

CHAPTER 2
SUPPLY OF GOODS OR SERVICES

Article 63

The chargeable event shall occur and VAT shall become chargeable when the goods or the services are supplied.

Article 64

1. Where it gives rise to successive statements of account or successive payments, the supply of goods, other than that consisting in the hire of goods for a certain period or the sale of goods on deferred terms, as referred to in point (b) of Article 14 (2), or the supply of services shall be regarded as being completed on expiry of the periods to which such statements of account or payments relate.
[2. Continuous supplies of goods over a period of more than one calendar month which are dispatched or transported to a Member State other than that in which the dispatch or transport of those goods begins and which are supplied VAT-exempt or which are transferred VAT-exempt to another Member State by a taxable person for the purposes of his business, in accordance with the conditions laid down in Article 138, shall be regarded as being completed on expiry of each calendar month until such time as the supply comes to an end.
Supplies of services for which VAT is payable by the customer pursuant to Article 196, which are supplied continuously over a period of more than one year and which do not give rise to statements of account or payments during that period, shall be regarded as being completed on expiry of each calendar year until such time as the supply of services comes to an end.
Member States may provide that, in certain cases other than those referred to in the first and second subparagraphs, the continuous supply of goods or services over a period of time is to be regarded as being completed at least at intervals of one year.][1]

Amendments—[1] Para 2 substituted by Council Directive 2010/45 art 1(2) with effect from 11 August 2010 (OJ L 189, 22.7.2010, p 1).

Article 65

Where a payment is to be made on account before the goods or services are supplied, VAT shall become chargeable on receipt of the payment and on the amount received.

Article 66

By way of derogation from Articles 63, 64 and 65, Member States may provide that VAT is to become chargeable, in respect of certain transactions or certain categories of taxable person at one of the following times:
(a) no later than the time the invoice is issued;
(b) no later than the time the payment is received;
[(c) where an invoice is not issued, or is issued late, within a specified time no later than on expiry of the time- limit for issue of invoices imposed by Member States pursuant to the second paragraph of Article 222 or where no such time-limit has been imposed by the Member State, within a specified period from the date of the chargeable event.

The derogation provided for in the first paragraph shall not, however, apply to supplies of services in respect of which VAT is payable by the customer pursuant to Article 196 and to supplies or transfers of goods referred to in Article 67.][1]

Amendments—[1] Words substituted by Council Directive 2010/45 art 1(3) with effect from 11 August 2010 (OJ L 189, 22.7.2010, p 1). The deadline for implementation of Directive 2010/45/EU is 31 December 2012.

[Article 66a

By way of derogation from Articles 63, 64 and 65, the chargeable event of the supply of goods by a taxable person who is deemed to have received and supplied the goods in accordance with Article 14a and of the supply of goods to that taxable person shall occur and VAT shall become chargeable at the time when the payment has been accepted.][1]

Amendments—[1] Article 66a substituted by Council Directive 2019/1995/EU art 1(2) with effect from 22 December 2019 (OJ L 310, 2.12.2019, p 1).

[Article 67

Where, in accordance with the conditions laid down in Article 138, goods dispatched or transported to a Member State other than that in which dispatch or transport of the goods begins are supplied VAT-exempt or where goods are transferred VAT-exempt to another Member State by a taxable person for the purposes of his business, VAT shall become chargeable on issue of the invoice, or on expiry of the time limit referred to in the first paragraph of Article 222 if no invoice has been issued by that time.

Article 64(1), the third subparagraph of Article 64(2) and Article 65 shall not apply with respect to the supplies and transfers of goods referred to in the first paragraph.][1]

Amendments—[1] Article substituted by Council Directive 2010/45 art 1(4) with effect from 11 August 2010 (OJ L 189, 22.7.2010, p 1).

CHAPTER 3

INTRA-COMMUNITY ACQUISITION OF GOODS

Article 68

The chargeable event shall occur when the intra-Community acquisition of goods is made.

The intra-Community acquisition of goods shall be regarded as being made when the supply of similar goods is regarded as being effected within the territory of the relevant Member State.

[Article 69

In the case of the intra-Community acquisition of goods, VAT shall become chargeable on issue of the invoice, or on expiry of the time limit referred to in the first paragraph of Article 222 if no invoice has been issued by that time.][1]

Amendments—[1] Article substituted by Council Directive 2010/45 art 1(5) with effect from 11 August 2010 (OJ L 189, 22.7.2010, p 1).

CHAPTER 4

IMPORTATION OF GOODS

Article 70

The chargeable event shall occur and VAT shall become chargeable when the goods are imported.

Article 71

1. Where, on entry into the Community, goods are placed under one of the arrangements or situations referred to in Articles 156, 276 and 277, or under temporary importation arrangements with total exemption from import duty, or under external transit arrangements, the chargeable event shall occur and VAT shall become chargeable only when the goods cease to be covered by those arrangements or situations.

However, where imported goods are subject to customs duties, to agricultural levies or to charges having equivalent effect established under a common policy, the chargeable event shall occur and VAT shall become chargeable when the chargeable event in respect of those duties occurs and those duties become chargeable.

2. Where imported goods are not subject to any of the duties referred to in the second subparagraph of paragraph 1, Member States shall, as regards the chargeable event and the moment when VAT becomes chargeable, apply the provisions in force governing customs duties.

TITLE VII
TAXABLE AMOUNT

CHAPTER 4
IMPORTATION OF GOODS

Article 72
For the purposes of this Directive, 'open market value' shall mean the full amount that, in order to obtain the goods or services in question at that time, a customer at the same marketing stage at which the supply of goods or services takes place, would have to pay, under conditions of fair competition, to a supplier at arm's length within the territory of the Member State in which the supply is subject to tax.

Where no comparable supply of goods or services can be ascertained, 'open market value' shall mean the following:
  (1) in respect of goods, an amount that is not less than the purchase price of the goods or of similar goods or, in the absence of a purchase price, the cost price, determined at the time of supply;
  (2) in respect of services, an amount that is not less than the full cost to the taxable person of providing the service.

CHAPTER 2
SUPPLY OF GOODS OR SERVICES

Article 73
In respect of the supply of goods or services, other than as referred to in Articles 74 to 77, the taxable amount shall include everything which constitutes consideration obtained or to be obtained by the supplier, in return for the supply, from the customer or a third party, including subsidies directly linked to the price of the supply.

[Article 73a
Without prejudice to Article 73, the taxable amount of the supply of goods or services provided in respect of a multi-purpose voucher shall be equal to the consideration paid for the voucher or, in the absence of information on that consideration, the monetary value indicated on the multi-purpose voucher itself or in the related documentation, less the amount of VAT relating to the goods or services supplied.][1]

Amendments—[1] Article 73a inserted by Council Directive 2016/1065/EU Article 1(2) with effect from 2 July 2016 (OJ L 177, 1.7.2016, p 9). Note that member states are required to adopt and publish, by 31 December 2018 at the latest, the laws, regulations and administrative provisions necessary to comply with Directive 2016/1065/EU and that those provisions will apply from 1 January 2019.

Article 74
Where a taxable person applies or disposes of goods forming part of his business assets, or where goods are retained by a taxable person, or by his successors, when his taxable economic activity ceases, as referred to in Articles 16 and 18, the taxable amount shall be the purchase price of the goods or of similar goods or, in the absence of a purchase price, the cost price, determined at the time when the application, disposal or retention takes place.

Article 75
In respect of the supply of services, as referred to in Article 26, where goods forming part of the assets of a business are used for private purposes or services are carried out free of charge, the taxable amount shall be the full cost to the taxable person of providing the services.

Article 76
In respect of the supply of goods consisting in transfer to another Member State, the taxable amount shall be the purchase price of the goods or of similar goods or, in the absence of a purchase price, the cost price, determined at the time the transfer takes place.

Article 77
In respect of the supply by a taxable person of a service for the purposes of his business, as referred to in Article 27, the taxable amount shall be the open market value of the service supplied.

Article 78
The taxable amount shall include the following factors:
  (a) taxes, duties, levies and charges, excluding the VAT itself;
  (b) incidental expenses, such as commission, packing, transport and insurance costs, charged by the supplier to the customer.

For the purposes of point (b) of the first paragraph, Member States may regard expenses covered by a separate agreement as incidental expenses.

Article 79

The taxable amount shall not include the following factors:
   (a) price reductions by way of discount for early payment;
   (b) price discounts and rebates granted to the customer and obtained by him at the time of the supply;
   (c) amounts received by a taxable person from the customer, as repayment of expenditure incurred in the name and on behalf of the customer, and entered in his books in a suspense account.

The taxable person must furnish proof of the actual amount of the expenditure referred to in point (c) of the first paragraph and may not deduct any VAT which may have been charged.

Article 80

1. In order to prevent tax evasion or avoidance, Member States may in any of the following cases take measures to ensure that, in respect of the supply of goods or services involving family or other close personal ties, management, ownership, membership, financial or legal ties as defined by the Member State, the taxable amount is to be the open market value:
   (a) where the consideration is lower than the open market value and the recipient of the supply does not have a full right of deduction under Articles 167 to 171 and Articles 173 to 177;
   (b) where the consideration is lower than the open market value and the supplier does not have a full right of deduction under Articles 167 to 171 and Articles 173 to 177 and the supply is subject to an exemption under Articles 132, 135, 136, 371, 375, 376, 377, 378(2), 379(2) or [Articles 380 to 390b];
   (c) where the consideration is higher than the open market value and the supplier does not have a full right of deduction under Articles 167 to 171 and Articles 173 to 177.

For the purposes of the first subparagraph, legal ties may include the relationship between an employer and employee or the employee's family, or any other closely connected persons.

2. Where Member States exercise the option provided for in paragraph 1, they may restrict the categories of suppliers or recipients to whom the measures shall apply.

3. Member States shall inform the VAT Committee of national legislative measures adopted pursuant to paragraph 1 in so far as these are not measures authorised by the Council prior to 13 August 2006 in accordance with Article 27 (1) to (4) of Directive 77/388/EEC, and which are continued under paragraph 1 of this Article.

Amendments—In para (1)(b), the words substituted for "Articles 380 to 390" by Council Directive 2009/162/EU art 1(7) with effect from 15 January 2010 (OJ L 10, 15.1.2010, p 14).

Article 81

Member States which, at 1 January 1993, were not availing themselves of the option under Article 98 of applying a reduced rate may, if they avail themselves of the option under Article 89, provide that in respect of the supply of works of art, as referred to in Article 103(2), the taxable amount is to be equal to a fraction of the amount determined in accordance with Articles 73, 74, 76, 78 and 79.

The fraction referred to in the first paragraph shall be determined in such a way that the VAT thus due is equal to at least 5% of the amount determined in accordance with Articles 73, 74, 76, 78 and 79.

Article 82

Member States may provide that, in respect of the supply of goods and services, the taxable amount is to include the value of exempt investment gold within the meaning of Article 346, which has been provided by the customer to be used as basis for working and which as a result, loses its VAT exempt investment gold status when such goods and services are supplied. The value to be used is the open market value of the investment gold at the time that those goods and services are supplied.

CHAPTER 3

INTRA-COMMUNITY ACQUISITION OF GOODS

Article 83

In respect of the intra-Community acquisition of goods, the taxable amount shall be established on the basis of the same factors as are used in accordance with Chapter 1 to determine the taxable amount for the supply of the same goods within the territory of the Member State concerned. In the case of the transactions, to be treated as intra-Community acquisitions of goods, referred to in Articles 21 and 22, the taxable amount shall be the purchase price of the goods or of similar goods or, in the absence of a purchase price, the cost price, determined at the time of the supply.

Article 84

1. Member States shall take the measures necessary to ensure that the excise duty due from or paid by the person making the intra-Community acquisition of a product subject to excise duty is included in the taxable amount in accordance with point (a) of the first paragraph of Article 78.

2. Where, after the intra-Community acquisition of goods has been made, the person acquiring the goods obtains a refund of the excise duty paid in the Member State in which dispatch or transport of the goods began, the taxable amount shall be reduced accordingly in the Member State in the territory of which the acquisition was made.

CHAPTER 4
IMPORTATION OF GOODS

Article 85
In respect of the importation of goods, the taxable amount shall be the value for customs purposes, determined in accordance with the Community provisions in force.

Article 86
1. The taxable amount shall include the following factors, in so far as they are not already included:
   (a) taxes, duties, levies and other charges due outside the Member State of importation, and those due by reason of importation, excluding the VAT to be levied;
   (b) incidental expenses, such as commission, packing, transport and insurance costs, incurred up to the first place of destination within the territory of the Member State of importation as well as those resulting from transport to another place of destination within the Community, if that other place is known when the chargeable event occurs.
2. For the purposes of point (b) of paragraph 1, 'first place of destination' shall mean the place mentioned on the consignment note or on any other document under which the goods are imported into the Member State of importation. If no such mention is made, the first place of destination shall be deemed to be the place of the first transfer of cargo in the Member State of importation.

Article 87
The taxable amount shall not include the following factors:
   (a) price reductions by way of discount for early payment;
   (b) price discounts and rebates granted to the customer and obtained by him at the time of importation.

Article 88
Where goods temporarily exported from the Community are reimported after having undergone, outside the Community, repair, processing, adaptation, making up or re-working, Member States shall take steps to ensure that the tax treatment of the goods for VAT purposes is the same as that which would have been applied had the repair, processing, adaptation, making up or re-working been carried out within their territory.

Article 89
Member States which, at 1 January 1993, were not availing themselves of the option under Article 98 of applying a reduced rate may provide that in respect of the importation of works of art, collectors' items and antiques, as defined in points (2), (3) and (4) of Article 311(1), the taxable amount is to be equal to a fraction of the amount determined in accordance with Articles 85, 86 and 87.

The fraction referred to in the first paragraph shall be determined in such a way that the VAT thus due on the importation is equal to at least 5% of the amount determined in accordance with Articles 85, 86 and 87.

CHAPTER 5
MISCELLANEOUS PROVISIONS

Article 90
1. In the case of cancellation, refusal or total or partial nonpayment, or where the price is reduced after the supply takes place, the taxable amount shall be reduced accordingly under conditions which shall be determined by the Member States.
2. In the case of total or partial non-payment, Member States may derogate from paragraph 1.

Article 91
1. Where the factors used to determine the taxable amount on importation are expressed in a currency other than that of the Member State in which assessment takes place, the exchange rate shall be determined in accordance with the Community provisions governing the calculation of the value for customs purposes.
2. Where the factors used to determine the taxable amount of a transaction other than the importation of goods are expressed in a currency other than that of the Member State in which assessment takes place, the exchange rate applicable shall be the latest selling rate recorded, at the time VAT becomes chargeable, on the most representative exchange market or markets of the Member State concerned, or a rate determined by reference to that or those markets, in accordance with the rules laid down by that Member State.

[Member States shall accept instead the use of the latest exchange rate published by the European Central Bank at the time the tax becomes chargeable. Conversion between currencies other than the euro shall be made by using the euro exchange rate of each currency. Member States may require that they be notified of the exercise of this option by the taxable person.

However, for some of the transactions referred to in the first subparagraph or for certain categories of taxable persons, Member States may use the exchange rate determined in accordance with the Community provisions in force governing the calculation of the value for customs purposes.][1]

Amendments—[1]   In para 2, second and third sub-paras substituted by Council Directive 2010/45 art 1(6) with effect from 11 August 2010 (OJ L 189, 22.7.2010, p 1).

Article 92

As regards the costs of returnable packing material, Member States may take one of the following measures:
  (a) exclude them from the taxable amount and take the measures necessary to ensure that this amount is adjusted if the packing material is not returned;
  (b) include them in the taxable amount and take the measures necessary to ensure that this amount is adjusted if the packing material is in fact returned.

TITLE VIII
RATES

CHAPTER 1
APPLICATION OF RATES

Article 93

The rate applicable to taxable transactions shall be that in force at the time of the chargeable event.

However, in the following situations, the rate applicable shall be that in force when VAT becomes chargeable:
  (a) in the cases referred to in Articles 65 and 66;
  (b) in the case of an intra-Community acquisition of goods;
  (c) in the cases, concerning the importation of goods, referred to in the second subparagraph of Article 71(1) and in Article 71(2).

Article 94

1. The rate applicable to the intra-Community acquisition of goods shall be that applied to the supply of like goods within the territory of the Member State.
2. Subject to the option under Article 103(1) of applying a reduced rate to the importation of works of art, collectors' items or antiques, the rate applicable to the importation of goods shall be that applied to the supply of like goods within the territory of the Member State.

Article 95

Where rates are changed, Member States may, in the cases referred to in Articles 65 and 66, effect adjustments in order to take account of the rate applying at the time when the goods or services were supplied.

Member States may also adopt all appropriate transitional measures.

CHAPTER 2
STRUCTURE AND LEVEL OF RATES

SECTION 1
Standard rate

Article 96

Member States shall apply a standard rate of VAT, which shall be fixed by each Member State as a percentage of the taxable amount and which shall be the same for the supply of goods and for the supply of services.

[Article 97

The standard rate shall not be lower than 15%.][1]

Commentary—*De Voil Indirect Tax Service* **V4.401.**
Amendments—[1]   Article 97 substituted by Council Directive 2018/912 Article 1 with effect from 17 July 2018 (OJ L 162, 27.6.2018, p 1).

SECTION 2
Reduced rates
Article 98
1. Member States may apply either one or two reduced rates.
2. The reduced rates shall apply only to supplies of goods or services in the categories set out in Annex III.

[The reduced rates shall not apply to electronically supplied services with the exception of those falling under point (6) of Annex III.][1]

3. When applying the reduced rates provided for in paragraph 1 to categories of goods, Member States may use the Combined Nomenclature to establish the precise coverage of the category concerned.

Commentary—*De Voil Indirect Tax Service* **V4.401**.
Amendments—[1] Second sub-para substituted by Council Directive (EU) 2018/1713 Article 1(1) with effect from 4 December 2018 (OJ L 286, 14.11.2018, p 20).

Article 99
1. The reduced rates shall be fixed as a percentage of the taxable amount, which may not be less than 5%.
2. Each reduced rate shall be so fixed that the amount of VAT resulting from its application is such that the VAT deductible under Articles 167 to 171 and Articles 173 to 177 can normally be deducted in full.

[3. By way of derogation from paragraphs 1 and 2 of this Article, and in addition to the rates referred to in paragraph 1 of Article 98, Member States which, on 1 January 2017, applied, in accordance with Union law, reduced rates lower than the minimum laid down in this Article or granted exemptions with deductibility of the VAT paid at the preceding stage to the supply of certain goods referred to in point (6) of Annex III, may also apply the same VAT treatment where that supply is supplied electronically, as referred to in point (6) of Annex III.][1]

Amendments—[1] Para 3 inserted by Council Directive (EU) 2018/1713 Article (2) with effect from 4 December 2018 (OJ L 286, 14.11.2018, p 20).

Article 100
On the basis of a report from the Commission, the Council shall, starting in 1994, review the scope of the reduced rates every two years.

The Council may, in accordance with Article 93 of the Treaty, decide to alter the list of goods and services set out in Annex III.

Article 101
By 30 June 2007 at the latest the Commission shall present to the European Parliament and the Council an overall assessment report on the impact of reduced rates applying to locally supplied services, including restaurant services, notably in terms of job creation, economic growth and the proper functioning of the internal market, based on a study carried out by an independent economic think-tank.

SECTION 3
Particular provisions
[Article 102
After consultation of the VAT Committee, each Member State may apply a reduced rate to the supply of natural gas, electricity or district heating.]

Amendments—Article 102 substituted by Council Directive 2009/162/EU art 1(8) with effect from 15 January 2010 (OJ L 10, 15.1.2010, p 14).

Article 103
1. Member States may provide that the reduced rate, or one of the reduced rates, which they apply in accordance with Articles 98 and 99 is also to apply to the importation of works of art, collectors' items and antiques, as defined in points (2), (3) and (4) of Article 311(1).
2. If Member States avail themselves of the option under paragraph 1, they may also apply the reduced rate to the following transactions:
   (*a*) the supply of works of art, by their creator or his successors in title;
   (*b*) the supply of works of art, on an occasional basis, by a taxable person other than a taxable dealer, where the works of art have been imported by the taxable person himself, or where they have been supplied to him by their creator or his successors in title, or where they have entitled him to full deduction of VAT.

Article 104
Austria may, in the communes of Jungholz and Mittelberg (Kleines Walsertal), apply a second standard rate which is lower than the corresponding rate applied in the rest of Austria but not less than 15%.

[Article 104a
Cyprus may apply one of the two reduced rates provided for in Article 98 to the supply of liquid petroleum gas (LPG) in cylinders.][1]

Amendments—[1] Article 104a inserted by Council Directive 2009/47/EC art 1 with effect from 1 June 2009 (OJ L 116, 9.5.2009 p 18).

[Article 105
1. Portugal may apply one of the two reduced rates provided for in Article 98 to the tolls on bridges in the Lisbon area.

2. Portugal may, in the case of transactions carried out in the autonomous regions of the Azores and Madeira and of direct importation into those regions, apply rates lower than those applying on the mainland.][1]

Amendments—[1] Article 105 substituted by Council Directive 2009/47/EC art 1 with effect from 1 June 2009 (OJ L 116, 9.5.2009 p 18).

CHAPTER 3
TEMPORARY PROVISIONS FOR PARTICULAR LABOUR-INTENSIVE SERVICES[1]

Amendments—[1] Chapter 3 repealed by Council Directive 2009/47/EC art 1 with effect from 1 June 2009 (OJ L 116, 9.5.2009 p 18).

CHAPTER 4
SPECIAL PROVISIONS APPLYING UNTIL THE ADOPTION OF DEFINITIVE ARRANGEMENTS

Article 109
Pending introduction of the definitive arrangements referred to in Article 402, the provisions laid down in this Chapter shall apply.

Article 110
Member States which, at 1 January 1991, were granting exemptions with deductibility of the VAT paid at the preceding stage or applying reduced rates lower than the minimum laid down in Article 99 may continue to grant those exemptions or apply those reduced rates.

The exemptions and reduced rates referred to in the first paragraph must be in accordance with Community law and must have been adopted for clearly defined social reasons and for the benefit of the final consumer.

Article 111
Subject to the conditions laid down in the second paragraph of Article 110, exemptions with deductibility of the VAT paid at the preceding stage may continue to be granted in the following cases:
   (a) by Finland in respect of the supply of newspapers and periodicals sold by subscription and the printing of publications distributed to the members of corporations for the public good;
   (b) by Sweden in respect of the supply of newspapers, including radio and cassette newspapers for the visually impaired, pharmaceutical products supplied to hospitals or on prescription, and the production of, or other related services concerning, periodicals of non-profit-making organisations;
   [(c) by Malta in respect of the supply of foodstuffs for human consumption and pharmaceuticals.][1]

Amendments—[1] Para (c) inserted by Council Directive 2009/47/EC art 1 with effect from 1 June 2009 (OJ L 116, 9.5.2009 p 18).

Article 112
If the provisions of Article 110 cause for Ireland distortion of competition in the supply of energy products for heating and lighting, Ireland may, on specific request, be authorised by the Commission to apply a reduced rate to such supplies, in accordance with Articles 98 and 99.

In the case referred to in the first paragraph, Ireland shall submit a request to the Commission, together with all necessary information. If the Commission has not taken a decision within three months of receiving the request, Ireland shall be deemed to be authorised to apply the reduced rates proposed.

Article 113
Member States which, at 1 January 1991, in accordance with Community law, were granting exemptions with deductibility of the VAT paid at the preceding stage or applying reduced rates lower than the minimum laid down in Article 99, in respect of goods and services other than those specified in Annex III, may apply the reduced rate, or one of the two reduced rates, provided for in Article 98 to the supply of such goods or services.

Article 114
1. Member States which, on 1 January 1993, were obliged to increase their standard rate in force at 1 January 1991 by more than 2% may apply a reduced rate lower than the minimum laid down in Article 99 to the supply of goods and services in the categories set out in Annex III.

[The Member States referred to in the first subparagraph may also apply such a rate to children's clothing and children's footwear and housing.][1]

2. Member States may not rely on paragraph 1 to introduce exemptions with deductibility of the VAT paid at the preceding stage.

Amendments—[1] In para 1, second sub-para substituted by Council Directive 2009/47/EC art 1 with effect from 1 June 2009 (OJ L 116, 9.5.2009 p 18).

[Article 115
Member States which, at 1 January 1991, were applying a reduced rate to children's clothing, children's footwear or housing may continue to apply such a rate to the supply of those goods or services.][1]

Amendments—[1] Article 115 substituted by Council Directive 2009/47/EC art 1 with effect from 1 June 2009 (OJ L 116, 9.5.2009 p 18).

Article 117
1. *For the purposes of applying Article 115, Austria may continue to apply a reduced rate to restaurant services.*[1]

2. Austria may apply one of the two reduced rates provided for in Article 98 to the letting of immovable property for residential use, provided that the rate is not lower than 10%.

Amendments—[1] Para 1 repealed by Council Directive 2009/47/EC art 1 with effect from 1 June 2009 (OJ L 116, 9.5.2009 p 18).

Article 118
Member States which, at 1 January 1991, were applying a reduced rate to the supply of goods or services other than those specified in Annex III may apply the reduced rate, or one of the two reduced rates, provided for in Article 98 to the supply of those goods or services, provided that the rate is not lower than 12%.

The first paragraph shall not apply to the supply of second-hand goods, works of art, collectors' items or antiques, as defined in points (1) to (4) of Article 311(1), subject to VAT in accordance with the margin scheme provided for in Articles 312 to 325 or the arrangements for sales by public auction.

Article 119
For the purposes of applying Article 118, Austria may apply a reduced rate to wines produced on an agricultural holding by the producer-farmer, provided that the rate is not lower than 12%.

Article 120
Greece may apply rates up to 30% lower than the corresponding rates applied in mainland Greece in the departments of Lesbos, Chios, Samos, the Dodecanese and the Cyclades, and on the islands of Thassos, the Northern Sporades, Samothrace and Skiros.

Article 121
Member States which, at 1 January 1993, regarded work under contract as the supply of goods may apply to the delivery of work under contract the rate applicable to the goods obtained after execution of the work under contract.

For the purposes of applying the first paragraph, 'delivery of work under contract' shall mean the handing over by a contractor to his customer of movable property made or assembled by the contractor from materials or objects entrusted to him by the customer for that purpose, whether or not the contractor has provided any part of the materials used.

Article 122
Member States may apply a reduced rate to the supply of live plants and other floricultural products, including bulbs, roots and the like, cut flowers and ornamental foliage, and of wood for use as firewood.

CHAPTER 5

TEMPORARY PROVISIONS

[Article 123

The Czech Republic may, until 31 December 2010, continue to apply a reduced rate of not less than 5% to the supply of construction work for residential housing not provided as part of a social policy, excluding building materials.][1]

Amendments—[1] Article 123 substituted by Council Directive 2007/75/EC of 20 December 2007, art 1(1) with effect from 1 January 2008.

Article 125

1. Cyprus may, [until 31 December 2010][1], continue to grant an exemption with deductibility of VAT paid at the preceding stage in respect of the supply of pharmaceuticals and foodstuffs for human consumption, with the exception of ice cream, ice lollies, frozen yoghurt, water ice and similar products and savoury food products (potato crisps/sticks, puffs and similar products packaged for human consumption without further preparation).

2. *Cyprus may continue to apply a reduced rate of not less than 5% to the supply of restaurant services, [until 31 December 2010][1] or until the introduction of definitive arrangements, as referred to in Article 402, whichever is the earlier.*[2]

Amendments—[1] Words substituted by Council Directive 2007/75/EC of 20 December 2007, art 1(3) with effect from 1 January 2008.
[2] Para 2 repealed by Council Directive 2009/47/EC art 1 with effect from 1 June 2009 (OJ L 116, 9.5.2009 p 18).

[Article 128

1. Poland may, until 31 December 2010, grant an exemption with deductibility of VAT paid at the preceding stage in respect of the supply of certain books and specialist periodicals.

2. *Poland may, until 31 December 2010 or until the introduction of definitive arrangements, as referred to in Article 402, whichever is the earlier, continue to apply a reduced rate of not less than 7% to the supply of restaurant services.*[2]

3. Poland may, until 31 December 2010, continue to apply a reduced rate of not less than 3% to the supply of foodstuffs as referred to in point (1) of Annex III.

4. Poland may, until 31 December 2010, continue to apply a reduced rate of not less than 7% to the supply of services, not provided as part of a social policy, for construction, renovation and alteration of housing, excluding building materials, and to the supply before first occupation of residential buildings or parts of residential buildings, as referred to in Article 12(1)(a).][1]

Amendments—[1] Article 128 substituted by Council Directive 2007/75/EC of 20 December 2007, art 1(6) with effect from 1 January 2008.
[2] Para 2 repealed by Council Directive 2009/47/EC art 1 with effect from 1 June 2009 (OJ L 116, 9.5.2009 p 18).

Article 129

1. *Slovenia may, [until 31 December 2010][1] or until the introduction of definitive arrangements as referred to in Article 402, whichever is the earlier, continue to apply a reduced rate of not less than 8.5% to the preparation of meals.*[2]

2. Slovenia may, [until 31 December 2010][1], continue to apply a reduced rate of not less than 5% to the supply of construction, renovation and maintenance work for residential housing not provided as part of a social policy, excluding building materials.

Amendments—[1] Words substituted by Council Directive 2007/75/EC of 20 December 2007, art 1(7) with effect from 1 January 2008.
[2] Para 1 repealed by Council Directive 2009/47/EC art 1 with effect from 1 June 2009 (OJ L 116, 9.5.2009 p 18).

[Article 129a

1. Member States may take one of the following measures:
   (a) apply a reduced rate to the supply of COVID-19 in vitro diagnostic medical devices and services closely linked to those devices;
   (b) grant an exemption with deductibility of VAT paid at the preceding stage in respect of the supply of COVID-19 in vitro diagnostic medical devices and services closely linked to those devices.

Only COVID-19 in vitro diagnostic medical devices that are in conformity with the applicable requirements set out in Directive 98/79/EC of the European Parliament and of the Council or Regulation (EU) 2017/746 of the European Parliament and of the Council and other applicable Union legislation shall be eligible for the measures provided for in the first subparagraph.

2. Member States may grant an exemption with deductibility of VAT paid at the preceding stage in respect of the supply of COVID-19 vaccines and services closely linked to those vaccines.

Only COVID-19 vaccines authorised by the Commission or by Member States shall be eligible for the exemption provided for in the first subparagraph.

3. This Article shall apply until 31 December 2022.][1]

Amendments—[1] Article 129a inserted by Council Directive (EU) 2020/2020 art 1 with effect from 12 December 2020 (OJ L 419, 11.12.2020, p 1).

TITLE IX
EXEMPTIONS

CHAPTER 1
GENERAL PROVISIONS

Article 131

The exemptions provided for in Chapters 2 to 9 shall apply without prejudice to other Community provisions and in accordance with conditions which the Member States shall lay down for the purposes of ensuring the correct and straightforward application of those exemptions and of preventing any possible evasion, avoidance or abuse.

CHAPTER 2
EXEMPTIONS FOR CERTAIN ACTIVITIES IN THE PUBLIC INTEREST

Article 132

1. Member States shall exempt the following transactions:
    (a) the supply by the public postal services of services other than passenger transport and telecommunications services, and the supply of goods incidental thereto;
    (b) hospital and medical care and closely related activities undertaken by bodies governed by public law or, under social conditions comparable with those applicable to bodies governed by public law, by hospitals, centres for medical treatment or diagnosis and other duly recognised establishments of a similar nature;
    (c) the provision of medical care in the exercise of the medical and paramedical professions as defined by the Member State concerned;
    (d) the supply of human organs, blood and milk;
    (e) the supply of services by dental technicians in their professional capacity and the supply of dental prostheses by dentists and dental technicians;
    (f) the supply of services by independent groups of persons, who are carrying on an activity which is exempt from VAT or in relation to which they are not taxable persons, for the purpose of rendering their members the services directly necessary for the exercise of that activity, where those groups merely claim from their members exact reimbursement of their share of the joint expenses, provided that such exemption is not likely to cause distortion of competition;
    (g) the supply of services and of goods closely linked to welfare and social security work, including those supplied by old people's homes, by bodies governed by public law or by other bodies recognised by the Member State concerned as being devoted to social wellbeing;
    (h) the supply of services and of goods closely linked to the protection of children and young persons by bodies governed by public law or by other organisations recognised by the Member State concerned as being devoted to social wellbeing;
    (i) the provision of children's or young people's education, school or university education, vocational training or retraining, including the supply of services and of goods closely related thereto, by bodies governed by public law having such as their aim or by other organisations recognised by the Member State concerned as having similar objects;
    (j) tuition given privately by teachers and covering school or university education;
    (k) the supply of staff by religious or philosophical institutions for the purpose of the activities referred to in points (b), (g), (h) and (i) and with a view to spiritual welfare;
    (l) the supply of services, and the supply of goods closely linked thereto, to their members in their common interest in return for a subscription fixed in accordance with their rules by non-profit-making organisations with aims of a political, trade-union, religious, patriotic, philosophical, philanthropic or civic nature, provided that this exemption is not likely to cause distortion of competition;
    (m) the supply of certain services closely linked to sport or physical education by non-profit-making organisations to persons taking part in sport or physical education;
    (n) the supply of certain cultural services, and the supply of goods closely linked thereto, by bodies governed by public law or by other cultural bodies recognised by the Member State concerned;
    (o) the supply of services and goods, by organisations whose activities are exempt pursuant to points (b), (g), (h), (i), (l), (m) and (n), in connection with fund-raising events organised exclusively for their own benefit, provided that exemption is not likely to cause distortion of competition;
    (p) the supply of transport services for sick or injured persons in vehicles specially designed for the purpose, by duly authorised bodies;
    (q) the activities, other than those of a commercial nature, carried out by public radio and television bodies.

2. For the purposes of point (*o*) of paragraph 1, Member States may introduce any restrictions necessary, in particular as regards the number of events or the amount of receipts which give entitlement to exemption.
Commentary—*De Voil Indirect Tax Service* **V4.146**, **V4.161**.

Article 133
Member States may make the granting to bodies other than those governed by public law of each exemption provided for in points (*b*), (*g*), (*h*), (*i*), (*l*), (*m*) and (*n*) of Article 132(1) subject in each individual case to one or more of the following conditions:
- (*a*) the bodies in question must not systematically aim to make a profit, and any surpluses nevertheless arising must not be distributed, but must be assigned to the continuance or improvement of the services supplied;
- (*b*) those bodies must be managed and administered on an essentially voluntary basis by persons who have no direct or indirect interest, either themselves or through intermediaries, in the results of the activities concerned;
- (*c*) those bodies must charge prices which are approved by the public authorities or which do not exceed such approved prices or, in respect of those services not subject to approval, prices lower than those charged for similar services by commercial enterprises subject to VAT;
- (*d*) the exemptions must not be likely to cause distortion of competition to the disadvantage of commercial enterprises subject to VAT.

Member States which, pursuant to Annex E of Directive 77/388/ EEC, on 1 January 1989 applied VAT to the transactions referred to in Article 132(1)(m) and (n) may also apply the conditions provided for in point (d) of the first paragraph when the said supply of goods or services by bodies governed by public law is granted exemption.
Commentary—*De Voil Indirect Tax Service* **V4.146**.

Article 134
The supply of goods or services shall not be granted exemption, as provided for in points (*b*), (*g*), (*h*), (*i*), (*l*), (*m*) and (*n*) of Article 132(1), in the following cases:
- (*a*) where the supply is not essential to the transactions exempted;
- (*b*) where the basic purpose of the supply is to obtain additional income for the body in question through transactions which are in direct competition with those of commercial enterprises subject to VAT.

Commentary—*De Voil Indirect Tax Service* **V4.146**.

CHAPTER 3

EXEMPTIONS FOR OTHER ACTIVITIES

Article 135
1. Member States shall exempt the following transactions:
- (*a*) insurance and reinsurance transactions, including related services performed by insurance brokers and insurance agents;
- (*b*) the granting and the negotiation of credit and the management of credit by the person granting it;
- (*c*) the negotiation of or any dealings in credit guarantees or any other security for money and the management of credit guarantees by the person who is granting the credit;
- (*d*) transactions, including negotiation, concerning deposit and current accounts, payments, transfers, debts, cheques and other negotiable instruments, but excluding debt collection;
- (*e*) transactions, including negotiation, concerning currency, bank notes and coins used as legal tender, with the exception of collectors' items, that is to say, gold, silver or other metal coins or bank notes which are not normally used as legal tender or coins of numismatic interest;
- (*f*) transactions, including negotiation but not management or safekeeping, in shares, interests in companies or associations, debentures and other securities, but excluding documents establishing title to goods, and the rights or securities referred to in Article 15(2);
- (*g*) the management of special investment funds as defined by Member States;
- (*h*) the supply at face value of postage stamps valid for use for postal services within their respective territory, fiscal stamps and other similar stamps;
- (*i*) betting, lotteries and other forms of gambling, subject to the conditions and limitations laid down by each Member State;
- (*j*) the supply of a building or parts thereof, and of the land on which it stands, other than the supply referred to in point (*a*) of Article 12(1);
- (*k*) the supply of land which has not been built on other than the supply of building land as referred to in point (*b*) of Article 12(1);
- (*l*) the leasing or letting of immovable property.

2. The following shall be excluded from the exemption provided for in point (*l*) of paragraph 1:

(a) the provision of accommodation, as defined in the laws of the Member States, in the hotel sector or in sectors with a similar function, including the provision of accommodation in holiday camps or on sites developed for use as camping sites;
(b) the letting of premises and sites for the parking of vehicles;
(c) the letting of permanently installed equipment and machinery;
(d) the hire of safes.

Member States may apply further exclusions to the scope of the exemption referred to in point (l) of paragraph 1.

Commentary—*De Voil Indirect Tax Service* **V4.111, V4.131, V4.136**.

Article 136

Member States shall exempt the following transactions:
(a) the supply of goods used solely for an activity exempted under Articles 132, 135, 371, 375, 376 and 377, Article 378 (2), Article 379(2) and [Articles 380 to 390b], if those goods have not given rise to deductibility;
(b) the supply of goods on the acquisition or application of which VAT was not deductible, pursuant to Article 176.

Amendments—In Article 136(a), the words substituted for "Articles 380 to 390" by Council Directive 2009/162/EU art 1(9) with effect from 15 January 2010 (OJ L 10, 15.1.2010, p 14).

[Article 136a

Where a taxable person is deemed to have received and supplied goods in accordance with Article 14a(2), Member States shall exempt the supply of those goods to that taxable person.][1]

Amendments—[1] Article 136a inserted by Council Directive 2019/1995/EU art 1(3) with effect from 22 December 2019 (OJ L 310, 2.12.2019, p 1).

Article 137

1. Member States may allow taxable persons a right of option for taxation in respect of the following transactions:
    (a) the financial transactions referred to in points (b) to (g) of Article 135(1);
    (b) the supply of a building or of parts thereof, and of the land on which the building stands, other than the supply referred to in point (a) of Article 12(1);
    (c) the supply of land which has not been built on other than the supply of building land referred to in point (b) of Article 12(1);
    (d) the leasing or letting of immovable property.
2. Member States shall lay down the detailed rules governing exercise of the option under paragraph 1.

Member States may restrict the scope of that right of option.

Commentary—*De Voil Indirect Tax Service* **V4.115**.

CHAPTER 4

EXEMPTIONS FOR INTRA-COMMUNITY TRANSACTIONS

SECTION 1

Exemptions related to the supply of goods

Article 138

[1. Member States shall exempt the supply of goods dispatched or transported to a destination outside their respective territory but within the Community, by or on behalf of the vendor or the person acquiring the goods, where the following conditions are met:
    (a) the goods are supplied to another taxable person, or to a non-taxable legal person acting as such in a Member State other than that in which dispatch or transport of the goods begins;
    (b) the taxable person or non-taxable legal person for whom the supply is made is identified for VAT purposes in a Member State other than that in which the dispatch or transport of the goods begins and has indicated this VAT identification number to the supplier.][1]

[1a. The exemption provided for in paragraph 1 shall not apply where the supplier has not complied with the obligation provided for in Articles 262 and 263 to submit a recapitulative statement or the recapitulative statement submitted by him does not set out the correct information concerning this supply as required under Article 264, unless the supplier can duly justify his shortcoming to the satisfaction of the competent authorities.][1]

2. In addition to the supply of goods referred to in paragraph 1, Member States shall exempt the following transactions:
    (a) the supply of new means of transport, dispatched or transported to the customer at a destination outside their respective territory but within the Community, by or on behalf of the vendor or the customer, for taxable persons, or non-taxable legal persons, whose intra-Community acquisitions of goods are not subject to VAT pursuant to Article 3(1), or for any other non-taxable person;

(b) the supply of products subject to excise duty, dispatched or transported to a destination outside their respective territory but within the Community, to the customer, by or on behalf of the vendor or the customer, for taxable persons, or non-taxable legal persons, whose intra-Community acquisitions of goods other than products subject to excise duty are not subject to VAT pursuant to Article 3(1), where those products have been dispatched or transported in accordance with Article 7(4) and (5) or Article 16 of Directive 92/12/EEC;

(c) the supply of goods, consisting in a transfer to another Member State, which would have been entitled to exemption under paragraph 1 and points (a) and (b) if it had been made on behalf of another taxable person.

Amendments—[1] Para 1 substituted and para 1a inserted by Council Directive (EU) 2018/1910 Article 1(3) with effect from 27 December 2018 (OJ L 311, 7.12.2018, p 3).

Article 139

1. [The exemption provided for in Article 138(1) shall not apply to the supply of goods carried out by taxable persons who, within the Member State in which the supply is carried out, are covered by the exemption for small enterprises provided for in Article 284.][1]

Nor shall that exemption apply to the supply of goods to taxable persons, or non-taxable legal persons, whose intra-Community acquisitions of goods are not subject to VAT pursuant to Article 3(1).

[2. The exemption provided for in point (b) of Article 138(2) shall not apply to the supply of products subject to excise duty by taxable persons who, within the Member State in which the supply is carried out, are covered by the exemption for small enterprises provided for in Article 284.][1]

3. The exemption provided for in Article 138(1) and (2)(b) and (c) shall not apply to the supply of goods subject to VAT in accordance with the margin scheme provided for in Articles 312 to 325 or the special arrangements for sales by public auction.

The exemption provided for in Article 138(1) and (2)(c) shall not apply to the supply of second-hand means of transport, as defined in Article 327(3), subject to VAT in accordance with the transitional arrangements for second-hand means of transport.

Amendments—[1] First subparagraph of para 1, and whole of para 2, substituted, by Council Directive 2020/285/EU art 1(2) with effect from 22 March 2020 (OJ L 62, 2.3.2020, p 13).

SECTION 2

Exemptions for intra-community acquisitions of goods

Article 140

Member States shall exempt the following transactions:

(a) the intra-Community acquisition of goods the supply of which by taxable persons would in all circumstances be exempt within their respective territory;

[(b) the intra-Community acquisition of goods the importation of which would in all circumstances be exempt under points (a), (b) and (c) and (e) to (l) of Article 143(1);]

(c) the intra-Community acquisition of goods where, pursuant to Articles 170 and 171, the person acquiring the goods would in all circumstances be entitled to full reimbursement of the VAT due under Article 2(1)(b).

Amendments—Point (b) substituted by Council Directive 2009/69/EC art 1 with effect from 24 July 2009. See OJ L 175, 4.7.2009 p 12).

Article 141

Each Member State shall take specific measures to ensure that VAT is not charged on the intra-Community acquisition of goods within its territory, made in accordance with Article 40, where the following conditions are met:

(a) the acquisition of goods is made by a taxable person who is not established in the Member State concerned but is identified for VAT purposes in another Member State;

(b) the acquisition of goods is made for the purposes of the subsequent supply of those goods, in the Member State concerned, by the taxable person referred to in point (a);

(c) the goods thus acquired by the taxable person referred to in point (a) are directly dispatched or transported, from a Member State other than that in which he is identified for VAT purposes, to the person for whom he is to carry out the subsequent supply;

(d) the person to whom the subsequent supply is to be made is another taxable person, or a non-taxable legal person, who is identified for VAT purposes in the Member State concerned;

(e) the person referred to in point (d) has been designated in accordance with Article 197 as liable for payment of the VAT due on the supply carried out by the taxable person who is not established in the Member State in which the tax is due.

SECTION 3
Exemptions for certain transport services

Article 142

Member States shall exempt the supply of intra-Community transport of goods to and from the islands making up the autonomous regions of the Azores and Madeira, as well as the supply of transport of goods between those islands.

CHAPTER 5
EXEMPTIONS ON IMPORTATION

Article 143

[1.] Member States shall exempt the following transactions:
  (a) the final importation of goods of which the supply by a taxable person would in all circumstances be exempt within their respective territory;
  (b) the final importation of goods governed by Council Directives 69/169/EEC ([1]), 83/181/EEC ([2]) and 2006/79/ EC ([3]);
  (c) the final importation of goods, in free circulation from a third territory forming part of the Community customs territory, which would be entitled to exemption under point (b) if they had been imported within the meaning of the first paragraph of Article 30;
  (d) the importation of goods dispatched or transported from a third territory or a third country into a Member State other than that in which the dispatch or transport of the goods ends, where the supply of such goods by the importer designated or recognised under Article 201 as liable for payment of VAT is exempt under Article 138;
  (e) the reimportation, by the person who exported them, of goods in the state in which they were exported, where those goods are exempt from customs duties;
  (f) the importation, under diplomatic and consular arrangements, of goods which are exempt from customs duties;
  [(fa) the importation of goods by the European Community, the European Atomic Energy Community, the European Central Bank or the European Investment Bank, or by the bodies set up by the Communities to which the Protocol of 8 April 1965 on the privileges and immunities of the European Communities applies, within the limits and under the conditions of that Protocol and the agreements for its implementation or the headquarters agreements, in so far as it does not lead to distortion of competition;][2]
  [(g) the importation of goods by international bodies, other than those referred to in point (fa), recognised as such by the public authorities of the host Member State, or by members of such bodies, within the limits and under the conditions laid down by the international conventions establishing the bodies or by headquarters agreements;][2]
  [(ga) the importation of goods into Member States by the armed forces of other Member States for the use of those forces, or of the civilian staff accompanying them, or for supplying their messes or canteens when such forces take part in a defence effort carried out for the implementation of a Union activity under the common security and defence policy;][3]
  (h) the importation of goods, into Member States party to the North Atlantic Treaty, by the armed forces of other States party to that Treaty for the use of those forces or the civilian staff accompanying them or for supplying their messes or canteens where such forces take part in the common defence effort;
  (i) the importation of goods by the armed forces of the United Kingdom stationed in the island of Cyprus pursuant to the Treaty of Establishment concerning the Republic of Cyprus, dated 16 August 1960, which are for the use of those forces or the civilian staff accompanying them or for supplying their messes or canteens;
  (j) the importation into ports, by sea fishing undertakings, of their catches, unprocessed or after undergoing preservation for marketing but before being supplied;
  (k) the importation of gold by central banks;
  [(l) the importation of gas through a natural gas system or any network connected to such a system or fed in from a vessel transporting gas into a natural gas system or any upstream pipeline network, of electricity or of heat or cooling energy through heating or cooling networks][1].
[2. The exemption provided for in paragraph 1(d) shall apply in cases when the importation of goods is followed by the supply of goods exempted under Article 138(1) and (2)(c) only if at the time of importation the importer has provided to the competent authorities of the Member State of importation at least the following information:
  (a) his VAT identification number issued in the Member State of importation or the VAT identification number of his tax representative, liable for payment of the VAT, issued in the Member State of importation;

(b) the VAT identification number of the customer, to whom the goods are supplied in accordance with Article 138(1), issued in another Member State, or his own VAT identification number issued in the Member State in which the dispatch or transport of the goods ends when the goods are subject to a transfer in accordance with Article 138(2)(c);
  (c) the evidence that the imported goods are intended to be transported or dispatched from the Member State of importation to another Member State.
However, Member States may provide that the evidence referred to in point (c) be indicated to the competent authorities only upon request.][1]

Notes—[(1)] Council Directive 69/169/EEC of 28 May 1969 on the harmonisation of provisions laid down by Law, Regulation or Administrative Action relating to exemption from turnover tax and excise duty on imports in international travel (OJ L 133, 4.6.1969, p. 6). Directive as last amended by Directive 2005/93/EC (OJ L 346, 29.12.2005, p. 16).
[(2)] Council Directive 83/181/EEC of 28 March 1983 determining the scope of Article 14(1)(d) of Directive 77/388/EEC as regards exemption from value added tax on the final importation of certain goods (OJ L 105, 23.4.1983, p. 38). Directive as last amended by the 1994 Act of Accession.
[(3)] Council Directive 2006/79/EC of 5 October 2006 on the exemption from taxes of imports of small consignments of goods of a non-commercial character from third countries (codified version) (OJ L 286, 17.10.2006, p. 15).
Amendments—[1] Introductory words numbered as para 1, and para 2 inserted, by Council Directive 2009/69/EC art 1 with effect from 24 July 2009. See OJ L 175, 4.7.2009 p 12).
[2] In para 1, point (fa) inserted and point (g) substituted by Council Directive 2009/162/EU art 1(10) with effect from 15 January 2010 (OJ L 10, 15.1.2010, p 14).
[3] Point (ga) inserted by Council Directive 2019/2235/EU art 1(2) with effect from 19 January 2020 (OJ L 336, 30.12.2019, p 10).

Article 144
Member States shall exempt the supply of services relating to the importation of goods where the value of such services is included in the taxable amount in accordance with Article 86(1)(b).

Article 145
1. The Commission shall, where appropriate, as soon as possible, present to the Council proposals designed to delimit the scope of the exemptions provided for in Articles 143 and 144 and to lay down the detailed rules for their implementation.
2. Pending the entry into force of the rules referred to in paragraph 1, Member States may maintain their national provisions in force.
  Member States may adapt their national provisions so as to minimise distortion of competition and, in particular, to prevent non-taxation or double taxation within the Community.
  Member States may use whatever administrative procedures they consider most appropriate to achieve exemption.
3. Member States shall notify to the Commission, which shall inform the other Member States accordingly, the provisions of national law which are in force, in so far as these have not already been notified, and those which they adopt pursuant to paragraph 2.

CHAPTER 6

EXEMPTIONS ON EXPORTATION

Article 146
1. Member States shall exempt the following transactions:
  (a) the supply of goods dispatched or transported to a destination outside the Community by or on behalf of the vendor;
  (b) the supply of goods dispatched or transported to a destination outside the Community by or on behalf of a customer not established within their respective territory, with the exception of goods transported by the customer himself for the equipping, fuelling and provisioning of pleasure boats and private aircraft or any other means of transport for private use;
  (c) the supply of goods to approved bodies which export them out of the Community as part of their humanitarian, charitable or teaching activities outside the Community;
  (d) the supply of services consisting in work on movable property acquired or imported for the purpose of undergoing such work within the Community, and dispatched or transported out of the Community by the supplier, by the customer if not established within their respective territory or on behalf of either of them;
  (e) the supply of services, including transport and ancillary transactions, but excluding the supply of services exempted in accordance with Articles 132 and 135, where these are directly connected with the exportation or importation of goods covered by Article 61 and Article 157(1)(a).
2. The exemption provided for in point (c) of paragraph 1 may be granted by means of a refund of the VAT.

Article 147

1. Where the supply of goods referred to in point (*b*) of Article 146(1) relates to goods to be carried in the personal luggage of travellers, the exemption shall apply only if the following conditions are met:
   (*a*) the traveller is not established within the Community;
   (*b*) the goods are transported out of the Community before the end of the third month following that in which the supply takes place;
   (*c*) the total value of the supply, including VAT, is more than EUR 175 or the equivalent in national currency, fixed annually by applying the conversion rate obtaining on the first working day of October with effect from 1 January of the following year.

However, Member States may exempt a supply with a total value of less than the amount specified in point (c) of the first subparagraph.

2. For the purposes of paragraph 1, 'a traveller who is not established within the Community' shall mean a traveller whose permanent address or habitual residence is not located within the Community. In that case 'permanent address or habitual residence' means the place entered as such in a passport, identity card or other document recognised as an identity document by the Member State within whose territory the supply takes place.

Proof of exportation shall be furnished by means of the invoice or other document in lieu thereof, endorsed by the customs office of exit from the Community.

Each Member State shall send to the Commission specimens of the stamps it uses for the endorsement referred to in the second subparagraph. The Commission shall forward that information to the tax authorities of the other Member States.

CHAPTER 7
EXEMPTIONS RELATED TO INTERNATIONAL TRANSPORT

Article 148

Member States shall exempt the following transactions:
   (*a*) the supply of goods for the fuelling and provisioning of vessels used for navigation on the high seas and carrying passengers for reward or used for the purpose of commercial, industrial or fishing activities, or for rescue or assistance at sea, or for inshore fishing, with the exception, in the case of vessels used for inshore fishing, of ships' provisions;
   (*b*) the supply of goods for the fuelling and provisioning of fighting ships, falling within the combined nomenclature (CN) code 8906 10 00, leaving their territory and bound for ports or anchorages outside the Member State concerned;
   (*c*) the supply, modification, repair, maintenance, chartering and hiring of the vessels referred to in point (*a*), and the supply, hiring, repair and maintenance of equipment, including fishing equipment, incorporated or used therein;
   (*d*) the supply of services other than those referred to in point (*c*), to meet the direct needs of the vessels referred to in point (*a*) or of their cargoes;
   (*e*) the supply of goods for the fuelling and provisioning of aircraft used by airlines operating for reward chiefly on international routes;
   (*f*) the supply, modification, repair, maintenance, chartering and hiring of the aircraft referred to in point (*e*), and the supply, hiring, repair and maintenance of equipment incorporated or used therein;
   (*g*) the supply of services, other than those referred to in point (*f*), to meet the direct needs of the aircraft referred to in point (*e*) or of their cargoes.

Article 149

Portugal may treat sea and air transport between the islands making up the autonomous regions of the Azores and Madeira and between those regions and the mainland as international transport.

Article 150

1. The Commission shall, where appropriate, as soon as possible, present to the Council proposals designed to delimit the scope of the exemptions provided for in Article 148 and to lay down the detailed rules for their implementation.

2. Pending the entry into force of the provisions referred to in paragraph 1, Member States may limit the scope of the exemptions provided for in points (*a*) and (*b*) of Article 148.

CHAPTER 8
EXEMPTIONS RELATING TO CERTAIN TRANSACTIONS TREATED AS EXPORTS

Article 151

1. Member States shall exempt the following transactions:
   (*a*) the supply of goods or services under diplomatic and consular arrangements;

[(aa) the supply of goods or services to the European Community, the European Atomic Energy Community, the European Central Bank or the European Investment Bank, or to the bodies set up by the Communities to which the Protocol of 8 April 1965 on the privileges and immunities of the European Communities applies, within the limits and under the conditions of that Protocol and the agreements for its implementation or the headquarters agreements, in so far as it does not lead to distortion of competition;][1]

[(b) the supply of goods or services to international bodies, other than those referred to in point (aa), recognised as such by the public authorities of the host Member States, and to members of such bodies, within the limits and under the conditions laid down by the international conventions establishing the bodies or by headquarters agreements;][1]

[(ba) the supply of goods or services within a Member State, intended either for the armed forces of other Member States for the use of those forces, or of the civilian staff accompanying them, or for supplying their messes or canteens when such forces take part in a defence effort carried out for the implementation of a Union activity under the common security and defence policy;

(bb) the supply of goods or services to another Member State, intended for the armed forces of any Member State other than the Member State of destination itself, for the use of those forces, or of the civilian staff accompanying them, or for supplying their messes or canteens when such forces take part in a defence effort carried out for the implementation of a Union activity under the common security and defence policy;][2]

(c) the supply of goods or services within a Member State which is a party to the North Atlantic Treaty, intended either for the armed forces of other States party to that Treaty for the use of those forces, or of the civilian staff accompanying them, or for supplying their messes or canteens when such forces take part in the common defence effort;

(d) the supply of goods or services to another Member State, intended for the armed forces of any State which is a party to the North Atlantic Treaty, other than the Member State of destination itself, for the use of those forces, or of the civilian staff accompanying them, or for supplying their messes or canteens when such forces take part in the common defence effort;

(e) the supply of goods or services to the armed forces of the United Kingdom stationed in the island of Cyprus pursuant to the Treaty of Establishment concerning the Republic of Cyprus, dated 16 August 1960, which are for the use of those forces, or of the civilian staff accompanying them, or for supplying their messes or canteens.

Pending the adoption of common tax rules, the exemptions provided for in the first subparagraph shall be subject to the limitations laid down by the host Member State.

2. In cases where the goods are not dispatched or transported out of the Member State in which the supply takes place, and in the case of services, the exemption may be granted by means of a refund of the VAT.

Amendments—[1] In para (1), point (aa) inserted and point (b) substituted, by Council Directive 2009/162/EU art 1(11) with effect from 15 January 2010 (OJ L 10, 15.1.2010, p 14).

[2] Points (ba), (bb) inserted by Council Directive 2019/2235/EU art 1(3) with effect from 19 January 2020 (OJ L 336, 30.12.2019, p 10).

Article 152
Member States shall exempt the supply of gold to central banks.

CHAPTER 9
EXEMPTIONS FOR THE SUPPLY OF SERVICES BY INTERMEDIARIES

Article 153
Member States shall exempt the supply of services by intermediaries, acting in the name and on behalf of another person, where they take part in the transactions referred to in Chapters 6, 7 and 8, or of transactions carried out outside the Community.

The exemption referred to in the first paragraph shall not apply to travel agents who, in the name and on behalf of travellers, supply services which are carried out in other Member States.

CHAPTER 10
EXEMPTIONS FOR TRANSACTIONS RELATING TO INTERNATIONAL TRADE
SECTION 1
Customs warehouses, warehouses other than customs warehouses and similar arrangements

Article 154

For the purposes of this Section, 'warehouses other than customs warehouses' shall, in the case of products subject to excise duty, mean the places defined as tax warehouses by Article 4(*b*) of Directive 92/12/EEC and, in the case of products not subject to excise duty, the places defined as such by the Member States.

Article 155

Without prejudice to other Community tax provisions, Member States may, after consulting the VAT Committee, take special measures designed to exempt all or some of the transactions referred to in this Section, provided that those measures are not aimed at final use or consumption and that the amount of VAT due on cessation of the arrangements or situations referred to in this Section corresponds to the amount of tax which would have been due had each of those transactions been taxed within their territory.

Article 156

1. Member States may exempt the following transactions:
    (*a*) the supply of goods which are intended to be presented to customs and, where applicable, placed in temporary storage;
    (*b*) the supply of goods which are intended to be placed in a free zone or in a free warehouse;
    (*c*) the supply of goods which are intended to be placed under customs warehousing arrangements or inward processing arrangements;
    (*d*) the supply of goods which are intended to be admitted into territorial waters in order to be incorporated into drilling or production platforms, for purposes of the construction, repair, maintenance, alteration or fitting-out of such platforms, or to link such drilling or production platforms to the mainland;
    (*e*) the supply of goods which are intended to be admitted into territorial waters for the fuelling and provisioning of drilling or production platforms.
2. The places referred to in paragraph 1 shall be those defined as such by the Community customs provisions in force.

Article 157

1. Member States may exempt the following transactions:
    (*a*) the importation of goods which are intended to be placed under warehousing arrangements other than customs warehousing;
    (*b*) the supply of goods which are intended to be placed, within their territory, under warehousing arrangements other than customs warehousing.
2. Member States may not provide for warehousing arrangements other than customs warehousing for goods which are not subject to excise duty where those goods are intended to be supplied at the retail stage.

Article 158

1. By way of derogation from Article 157(2), Member States may provide for warehousing arrangements other than customs warehousing in the following cases:
    (*a*) where the goods are intended for tax-free shops, for the purposes of the supply of goods to be carried in the personal luggage of travellers taking flights or sea crossings to third territories or third countries, where that supply is exempt pursuant to point (*b*) of Article 146(1);
    (*b*) where the goods are intended for taxable persons, for the purposes of carrying out supplies to travellers on board an aircraft or a ship in the course of a flight or sea crossing where the place of arrival is situated outside the Community;
    (*c*) where the goods are intended for taxable persons, for the purposes of carrying out supplies which are exempt from VAT pursuant to Article 151.
2. Where Member States exercise the option of exemption provided for in point (*a*) of paragraph 1, they shall take the measures necessary to ensure the correct and straightforward application of this exemption and to prevent any evasion, avoidance or abuse.
3. For the purposes of point (*a*) of paragraph 1, 'tax-free shop' shall mean any establishment which is situated within an airport or port and which fulfils the conditions laid down by the competent public authorities.

Article 159

Member States may exempt the supply of services relating to the supply of goods referred to in Article 156, Article 157(1)(*b*) or Article 158.

Article 160
1. Member States may exempt the following transactions:
    (a) the supply of goods or services carried out in the locations referred to in Article 156(1), where one of the situations specified therein still applies within their territory;
    (b) the supply of goods or services carried out in the locations referred to in Article 157(1)(b) or Article 158, where one of the situations specified in Article 157(1)(b) or in Article 158 (1) still applies within their territory.
2. Where Member States exercise the option under point (a) of paragraph 1 in respect of transactions effected in customs warehouses, they shall take the measures necessary to provide for warehousing arrangements other than customs warehousing under which point (b) of paragraph 1 may be applied to the same transactions when they concern goods listed in Annex V and are carried out in warehouses other than customs warehouses.

Article 161
Member States may exempt supply of the following goods and of services relating thereto:
    (a) the supply of goods referred to in the first paragraph of Article 30 while they remain covered by arrangements for temporary importation with total exemption from import duty or by external transit arrangements;
    (b) the supply of goods referred to in the second paragraph of Article 30 while they remain covered by the internal Community transit procedure referred to in Article 276.

Article 162
Where Member States exercise the option provided for in this Section, they shall take the measures necessary to ensure that the intra-Community acquisition of goods intended to be placed under one of the arrangements or in one of the situations referred to in Article 156, Article 157(1)(b) or Article 158 is covered by the same provisions as the supply of goods carried out within their territory under the same conditions.

Article 163
If the goods cease to be covered by the arrangements or situations referred to in this Section, thus giving rise to importation for the purposes of Article 61, the Member State of importation shall take the measures necessary to prevent double taxation.

SECTION 2
Transactions exempted with a view to export and in the framework of trade between the Member States

Article 164
1. Member States may, after consulting the VAT Committee, exempt the following transactions carried out by, or intended for, a taxable person up to an amount equal to the value of the exports carried out by that person during the preceding 12 months:
    (a) intra-Community acquisitions of goods made by the taxable person, and imports for and supplies of goods to the taxable person, with a view to their exportation from the Community as they are or after processing;
    (b) supplies of services linked with the export business of the taxable person.
2. Where Member States exercise the option of exemption under paragraph 1, they shall, after consulting the VAT Committee, apply that exemption also to transactions relating to supplies carried out by the taxable person, in accordance with the conditions specified in Article 138, up to an amount equal to the value of the supplies carried out by that person, in accordance with the same conditions, during the preceding 12 months.

Article 165
Member States may set a common maximum amount for transactions which they exempt pursuant to Article 164.

SECTION 3
Provisions common to Sections 1 and 2

Article 166
The Commission shall, where appropriate, as soon as possible, present to the Council proposals concerning common arrangements for applying VAT to the transactions referred to in Sections 1 and 2.

TITLE X
DEUCTIONS

CHAPTER 1
ORIGIN AND SCOPE OF RIGHT OF DEDUCTION

Article 167
A right of deduction shall arise at the time the deductible tax becomes chargeable.

[Article 167a
Member States may provide within an optional scheme that the right of deduction of a taxable person whose VAT solely becomes chargeable in accordance with Article 66(b) be postponed until the VAT on the goods or services supplied to him has been paid to his supplier.
[Member States which apply the optional scheme referred to in the first paragraph shall set a threshold for taxable persons using that scheme within their territory, based on the annual turnover of the taxable person calculated in accordance with Article 288. That threshold may not be higher than EUR 2 000 000 or the equivalent in national currency.][2]
. . .[2]]1

Amendments—[1] Article inserted by Council Directive 2010/45 art 1(7) with effect from 11 August 2010 (OJ L 189, 22.7.2010, p 1). The deadline for implementation of Directive 2010/45/EU is 31 December 2012.
[2] Second para substituted and third para repealed, by Council Directive 2020/285/EU art 1(3) with effect from 22 March 2020 (OJ L 62, 2.3.2020, p 13).

Article 168
In so far as the goods and services are used for the purposes of the taxed transactions of a taxable person, the taxable person shall be entitled, in the Member State in which he carries out these transactions, to deduct the following from the VAT which he is liable to pay:
   (*a*) the VAT due or paid in that Member State in respect of supplies to him of goods or services, carried out or to be carried out by another taxable person;
   (*b*) the VAT due in respect of transactions treated as supplies of goods or services pursuant to Article 18(*a*) and Article 27;
   (*c*) the VAT due in respect of intra-Community acquisitions of goods pursuant to Article 2(1)(*b*)(i);
   (*d*) the VAT due on transactions treated as intra-Community acquisitions in accordance with Articles 21 and 22;
   (*e*) the VAT due or paid in respect of the importation of goods into that Member State.

[168a
1. In the case of immovable property forming part of the business assets of a taxable person and used both for purposes of the taxable person's business and for his private use or that of his staff, or, more generally, for purposes other than those of his business, VAT on expenditure related to this property shall be deductible in accordance with the principles set out in Articles 167, 168, 169 and 173 only up to the proportion of the property's use for purposes of the taxable person's business.
By way of derogation from Article 26, changes in the proportion of use of immovable property referred to in the first subparagraph shall be taken into account in accordance with the principles provided for in Articles 184 to 192 as applied in the respective Member State.
2. Member States may also apply paragraph 1 in relation to VAT on expenditure related to other goods forming part of the business assets as they specify.]

Amendments—Article 168a inserted by Council Directive 2009/162/EU art 1(12) with effect from 15 January 2010 (OJ L 10, 15.1.2010, p 14).

Article 169
In addition to the deduction referred to in Article 168, the taxable person shall be entitled to deduct the VAT referred to therein in so far as the goods and services are used for the purposes of the following:
   [(*a*) transactions other than those exempt under Article 284 relating to the activities referred to in the second subparagraph of Article 9(1), carried out outside the Member State in which that tax is due or paid, in respect of which VAT would be deductible if they had been carried out within that Member State;][2]
   [(*b*) transactions which are exempt pursuant to Articles 136a, 138, 142 or 144, Articles 146 to 149, Articles 151, 152, 153 or 156, Article 157(1)(b), Articles 158 to 161 or Article 164;][1]
   (*c*) transactions which are exempt pursuant to points (*a*) to (*f*) of Article 135(1), where the customer is established outside the Community or where those transactions relate directly to goods to be exported out of the Community.

Amendments—[1] point (b) substituted by Council Directive 2019/1995/EU art 1(4) with effect from 22 December 2019 (OJ L 310, 2.12.2019, p 1).
[2] Point (a) substituted by Council Directive 2020/285/EU art 1(4) with effect from 22 March 2020 (OJ L 62, 2.3.2020, p 13).

Article 170
[All taxable persons who, within the meaning of Article 1 of Directive 86/560/EEC, Article 2(1) and Article 3 of Directive 2008/9/EC and Article 171 of this Directive, are not established in the Member State in which they purchase goods and services or import goods subject to VAT shall be entitled to obtain a refund of that VAT insofar as the goods and services are used for the purposes of the following:][1]
   (a) transactions referred to in Article 169;
   (b) transactions for which the tax is solely payable by the customer in accordance with Articles 194 to 197 or Article 199.

Amendments—[1] Introductory sentence substituted by Council Directive 2008/8/EC art 2(3) with effect from 1 January 2010 (OJ L 44, 20.2.2008 p 11).

Article 171
[1. VAT shall be refunded to taxable persons who are not established in the Member State in which they purchase goods and services or import goods subject to VAT but who are established in another Member State, in accordance with the detailed rules laid down in Directive 2008/9/EC.[1]

The taxable persons referred to in Article 1 of Directive 79/1072/ EEC shall also, for the purposes of applying that Directive, be regarded as taxable persons who are not established in the Member State concerned where, in the Member State in which they purchase goods and services or import goods subject to VAT, they have only carried out the supply of goods or services to a person designated in accordance with Articles 194 to 197 or Article 199 as liable for payment of VAT.
2. VAT shall be refunded to taxable persons who are not established within the territory of the Community in accordance with the detailed implementing rules laid down in Directive 86/560/EEC.

The taxable persons referred to in Article 1 of Directive 86/560/ EEC shall also, for the purposes of applying that Directive, be regarded as taxable persons who are not established in the Community where, in the Member State in which they purchase goods and services or import goods subject to VAT, they have only carried out the supply of goods or services to a person designated in accordance with Articles 194 to 197 or Article 199 as liable for payment of VAT.
[3. Directive 86/560/EEC shall not apply to:
   (a) amounts of VAT which according to the legislation of the Member State of refund have been incorrectly invoiced;
   (b) invoiced amounts of VAT in respect of supplies of goods the supply of which is, or may be, exempt pursuant to Article 138 or Article 146(1)(b).][1]

Amendments—[1] Paras 1, 3 substituted by Council Directive 2008/8/EC art 2(4) with effect from 1 January 2010 (OJ L 44, 20.2.2008 p 11).

[Article 171a
Member States may, instead of granting a refund of VAT pursuant to Directives 86/560/EEC or 2008/9/EC on those supplies of goods or services to a taxable person in respect of which the taxable person is liable to pay the tax in accordance with Articles 194 to 197 or Article 199, allow deduction of this tax pursuant to the procedure laid down in Article 168. The existing restrictions pursuant to Article 2(2) and Article 4(2) of Directive 86/560/EEC may be retained.

To that end, Member States may exclude the taxable person who is liable to pay the tax from the refund procedure pursuant to Directives 86/560/EEC or 2008/9/EC.][1]

Amendments—[1] Article 171A inserted by Council Directive 2008/8/EC art 2(4) with effect from 1 January 2010 (OJ L 44, 20.2.2008 p 11).

Article 172
1. Any person who is regarded as a taxable person by reason of the fact that he supplies, on an occasional basis, a new means of transport in accordance with the conditions specified in Article 138(1) and (2)(a) shall, in the Member State in which the supply takes place, be entitled to deduct the VAT included in the purchase price or paid in respect of the importation or the intra-Community acquisition of this means of transport, up to an amount not exceeding the amount of VAT for which he would be liable if the supply were not exempt.

A right of deduction shall arise and may be exercised only at the time of supply of the new means of transport.
2. Member States shall lay down detailed rules for the implementation of paragraph 1.

CHAPTER 2

PROPORTIONAL DEDUCTION

Article 173

1. In the case of goods or services used by a taxable person both for transactions in respect of which VAT is deductible pursuant to Articles 168, 169 and 170, and for transactions in respect of which VAT is not deductible, only such proportion of the VAT as is attributable to the former transactions shall be deductible.

The deductible proportion shall be determined, in accordance with Articles 174 and 175, for all the transactions carried out by the taxable person.

2. Member States may take the following measures:
   (a) authorise the taxable person to determine a proportion for each sector of his business, provided that separate accounts are kept for each sector;
   (b) require the taxable person to determine a proportion for each sector of his business and to keep separate accounts for each sector;
   (c) authorise or require the taxable person to make the deduction on the basis of the use made of all or part of the goods and services;
   (d) authorise or require the taxable person to make the deduction in accordance with the rule laid down in the first subparagraph of paragraph 1, in respect of all goods and services used for all transactions referred to therein;
   (e) provide that, where the VAT which is not deductible by the taxable person is insignificant, it is to be treated as nil.

Commentary—*De Voil Indirect Tax Service* **V2.101, V.3.401, V3.460.**

Article 174

1. The deductible proportion shall be made up of a fraction comprising the following amounts:
   (a) as numerator, the total amount, exclusive of VAT, of turnover per year attributable to transactions in respect of which VAT is deductible pursuant to Articles 168 and 169;
   (b) as denominator, the total amount, exclusive of VAT, of turnover per year attributable to transactions included in the numerator and to transactions in respect of which VAT is not deductible.

Member States may include in the denominator the amount of subsidies, other than those directly linked to the price of supplies of goods or services referred to in Article 73.

2. By way of derogation from paragraph 1, the following amounts shall be excluded from the calculation of the deductible proportion:
   (a) the amount of turnover attributable to supplies of capital goods used by the taxable person for the purposes of his business;
   (b) the amount of turnover attributable to incidental real estate and financial transactions;
   (c) the amount of turnover attributable to the transactions specified in points (b) to (g) of Article 135(1) in so far as those transactions are incidental.

3. Where Member States exercise the option under Article 191 not to require adjustment in respect of capital goods, they may include disposals of capital goods in the calculation of the deductible proportion.

Commentary—*De Voil Indirect Tax Service* **V3.460.**

Article 175

1. The deductible proportion shall be determined on an annual basis, fixed as a percentage and rounded up to a figure not exceeding the next whole number.

2. The provisional proportion for a year shall be that calculated on the basis of the preceding year's transactions. In the absence of any such transactions to refer to, or where they were insignificant in amount, the deductible proportion shall be estimated provisionally, under the supervision of the tax authorities, by the taxable person on the basis of his own forecasts.

However, Member States may retain the rules in force at 1 January 1979 or, in the case of the Member States which acceded to the Community after that date, on the date of their accession.

3. Deductions made on the basis of such provisional proportions shall be adjusted when the final proportion is fixed during the following year.

Commentary—*De Voil Indirect Tax Service* **V3.460.**

CHAPTER 3
RESTRICTIONS ON THE RIGHT OF DEDUCTION

Article 176
The Council, acting unanimously on a proposal from the Commission, shall determine the expenditure in respect of which VAT shall not be deductible. VAT shall in no circumstances be deductible in respect of expenditure which is not strictly business expenditure, such as that on luxuries, amusements or entertainment.

Pending the entry into force of the provisions referred to in the first paragraph, Member States may retain all the exclusions provided for under their national laws at 1 January 1979 or, in the case of the Member States which acceded to the Community after that date, on the date of their accession.

Commentary—*De Voil Indirect Tax Service* **V2.101**, **V.3.401**, **V3.460**.

Article 177
After consulting the VAT Committee, each Member State may, for cyclical economic reasons, totally or partly exclude all or some capital goods or other goods from the system of deductions.

In order to maintain identical conditions of competition, Member States may, instead of refusing deduction, tax goods manufactured by the taxable person himself or goods which he has purchased within the Community, or imported, in such a way that the tax does not exceed the amount of VAT which would be charged on the acquisition of similar goods.

CHAPTER 4
RULES GOVERNING EXERCISE OF THE RIGHT OF DEDUCTION

Article 178
In order to exercise the right of deduction, a taxable person must meet the following conditions:
- [(*a*) for the purposes of deductions pursuant to Article 168(*a*), in respect of the supply of goods or services, he must hold an invoice drawn up in accordance with Sections 3 to 6 of Chapter 3 of Title XI;][1]
- (*b*) for the purposes of deductions pursuant to Article 168(*b*), in respect of transactions treated as the supply of goods or services, he must comply with the formalities as laid down by each Member State;
- [(*c*) for the purposes of deductions pursuant to Article 168(*c*), in respect of the intra-Community acquisition of goods, he must set out in the VAT return provided for in Article 250 all the information needed for the amount of VAT due on his intra-Community acquisitions of goods to be calculated and he must hold an invoice drawn up in accordance with Sections 3 to 5 of Chapter 3 of Title XI;][1]
- (*d*) for the purposes of deductions pursuant to Article 168(*d*), in respect of transactions treated as intra-Community acquisitions of goods, he must complete the formalities as laid down by each Member State;
- (*e*) for the purposes of deductions pursuant to Article 168(*e*), in respect of the importation of goods, he must hold an import document specifying him as consignee or importer, and stating the amount of VAT due or enabling that amount to be calculated;
- (*f*) when required to pay VAT as a customer where Articles 194 to 197 or Article 199 apply, he must comply with the formalities as laid down by each Member State.

Amendments—[1] Paras (*a*), (*c*) substituted by Council Directive 2010/45 art 1(8) with effect from 11 August 2010 (OJ L 189, 22.7.2010, p 1).

Article 179
The taxable person shall make the deduction by subtracting from the total amount of VAT due for a given tax period the total amount of VAT in respect of which, during the same period, the right of deduction has arisen and is exercised in accordance with Article 178.

However, Member States may require that taxable persons who carry out occasional transactions, as defined in Article 12, exercise their right of deduction only at the time of supply.

Article 180
Member States may authorise a taxable person to make a deduction which he has not made in accordance with Articles 178 and 179.

[Article 181
Member States may authorise a taxable person who does not hold an invoice drawn up in accordance with Sections 3 to 5 of Chapter 3 of Title XI to make the deduction referred to in Article 168(c) in respect of his intra- Community acquisitions of goods.][1]

Amendments—[1] Article substituted by Council Directive 2010/45 art 1(9) with effect from 11 August 2010 (OJ L 189, 22.7.2010, p 1).

Article 182
Member States shall determine the conditions and detailed rules for applying Articles 180 and 181.

Article 183
Where, for a given tax period, the amount of deductions exceeds the amount of VAT due, the Member States may, in accordance with conditions which they shall determine, either make a refund or carry the excess forward to the following period.

However, Member States may refuse to refund or carry forward if the amount of the excess is insignificant.

Commentary—*De Voil Indirect Tax Service* **V3.401**.

CHAPTER 5
ADJUSTMENT OF DEDUCTIONS

Article 184
The initial deduction shall be adjusted where it is higher or lower than that to which the taxable person was entitled.

Article 185
1. Adjustment shall, in particular, be made where, after the VAT return is made, some change occurs in the factors used to determine the amount to be deducted, for example where purchases are cancelled or price reductions are obtained.
2. By way of derogation from paragraph 1, no adjustment shall be made in the case of transactions remaining totally or partially unpaid or in the case of destruction, loss or theft of property duly proved or confirmed, or in the case of goods reserved for the purpose of making gifts of small value or of giving samples, as referred to in Article 16.

However, in the case of transactions remaining totally or partially unpaid or in the case of theft, Member States may require adjustment to be made.

Commentary—*De Voil Indirect Tax Service* **V3.470**.

Article 186
Member States shall lay down the detailed rules for applying Articles 184 and 185.

Article 187
1. In the case of capital goods, adjustment shall be spread over five years including that in which the goods were acquired or manufactured.

Member States may, however, base the adjustment on a period of five full years starting from the time at which the goods are first used.

In the case of immovable property acquired as capital goods, the adjustment period may be extended up to 20 years.
2. The annual adjustment shall be made only in respect of one-fifth of the VAT charged on the capital goods, or, if the adjustment period has been extended, in respect of the corresponding fraction thereof.

The adjustment referred to in the first subparagraph shall be made on the basis of the variations in the deduction entitlement in subsequent years in relation to that for the year in which the goods were acquired, manufactured or, where applicable, used for the first time.

Commentary—*De Voil Indirect Tax Service* **V3.470**.

Article 188
1. If supplied during the adjustment period, capital goods shall be treated as if they had been applied to an economic activity of the taxable person up until expiry of the adjustment period.

The economic activity shall be presumed to be fully taxed in cases where the supply of the capital goods is taxed.

The economic activity shall be presumed to be fully exempt in cases where the supply of the capital goods is exempt.
2. The adjustment provided for in paragraph 1 shall be made only once in respect of all the time covered by the adjustment period that remains to run. However, where the supply of capital goods is exempt, Member States may waive the requirement for adjustment in so far as the purchaser is a taxable person using the capital goods in question solely for transactions in respect of which VAT is deductible.

Commentary—*De Voil Indirect Tax Service* **V3.470**.

Article 189
For the purposes of applying Articles 187 and 188, Member States may take the following measures:
   (*a*) define the concept of capital goods;
   (*b*) specify the amount of the VAT which is to be taken into consideration for adjustment;
   (*c*) adopt any measures needed to ensure that adjustment does not give rise to any unjustified advantage;

(*d*) permit administrative simplifications.

Article 190
For the purposes of Articles 187, 188, 189 and 191, Member States may regard as capital goods those services which have characteristics similar to those normally attributed to capital goods.

Article 191
If, in any Member State, the practical effect of applying Articles 187 and 188 is negligible, that Member State may, after consulting the VAT Committee, refrain from applying those provisions, having regard to the overall impact of VAT in the Member State concerned and the need for administrative simplification, and provided that no distortion of competition thereby arises.

Article 192
Where a taxable person transfers from being taxed in the normal way to a special scheme or vice versa, Member States may take all measures necessary to ensure that the taxable person does not enjoy unjustified advantage or sustain unjustified harm.

TITLE XI
OBLIGATIONS OF TAXABLE PERSONS AND CERTAIN NON-TAXABLE PERSONS

CHAPTER 1
OBLIGATION TO PAY

SECTION 1
Persons liable for payment of VAT to the tax authorities

[Article 192a
For the purposes of this Section, a taxable person who has a fixed establishment within the territory of the Member State where the tax is due shall be regarded as a taxable person who is not established within that Member State when the following conditions are met:
   (*a*) he makes a taxable supply of goods or of services within the territory of that Member State;
   (*b*) an establishment which the supplier has within the territory of that Member State does not intervene in that supply.][1]

Amendments—[1]   Article 192a inserted by Council Directive 2008/8/EC art 2(5) with effect from 1 January 2010 (OJ L 44, 20.2.2008 p 11).

Article 193
VAT shall be payable by any taxable person carrying out a taxable supply of goods or services, except where it is payable by another person in the cases referred to in [Articles 194 to 199b][1] and Article 202.

Amendments—[1]   Words substituted for words "Articles 194 to 199" by Council Directive 2013/43/EU art 1(1) with effect from 15 August 2013 until 31 December 2018 (OJ L 201, 26.7.2013, p 4).

Article 194
1. Where the taxable supply of goods or services is carried out by a taxable person who is not established in the Member State in which the VAT is due, Member States may provide that the person liable for payment of VAT is the person to whom the goods or services are supplied.
2. Member States shall lay down the conditions for implementation of paragraph 1.

Amendments—[1]   Words substituted for words "Articles 194 to 199" by Council Directive 2013/43/EU art 1(1) with effect from 15 August 2013 until 31 December 2018 (OJ L 201, 26.7.2013, p 4).

Article 195
VAT shall be payable by any person who is identified for VAT purposes in the Member State in which the tax is due and to whom goods are supplied in the circumstances specified in Articles 38 or 39, if the supplies are carried out by a taxable person not established within that Member State.

[Article 196
VAT shall be payable by any taxable person, or non-taxable legal person identified for VAT purposes, to whom the services referred to in Article 44 are supplied, if the services are supplied by a taxable person not established within the territory of the Member State.][1]

Amendments—[1]   Article 196 substituted, by Council Directive 2008/8/EC art 2(7) with effect from 1 January 2010 (OJ L 44, 20.2.2008 p 11).

Article 197
1. VAT shall be payable by the person to whom the goods are supplied when the following conditions are met:
   (*a*) the taxable transaction is a supply of goods carried out in accordance with the conditions laid down in Article 141;
   (*b*) the person to whom the goods are supplied is another taxable person, or a non-taxable legal person, identified for VAT purposes in the Member State in which the supply is carried out;

[(c) the invoice issued by the taxable person not established in the Member State of the person to whom the goods are supplied is drawn up in accordance with Sections 3 to 5 of Chapter 3.]¹
2. Where a tax representative is appointed as the person liable for payment of VAT pursuant to Article 204, Member States may provide for a derogation from paragraph 1 of this Article.

Amendments—¹ Para 1(c) substituted by Council Directive 2010/45 art 1(10) with effect from 11 August 2010 (OJ L 189, 22.7.2010, p 1).

Article 198

1. Where specific transactions relating to investment gold between a taxable person who is a member of a regulated gold bullion market and another taxable person who is not a member of that market are taxed pursuant to Article 352, Member States shall designate the customer as the person liable for payment of VAT.

If the customer who is not a member of the regulated gold bullion market is a taxable person required to be identified for VAT purposes in the Member State in which the tax is due solely in respect of the transactions referred to in Article 352, the vendor shall fulfil the tax obligations on behalf of the customer, in accordance with the law of that Member State.

2. Where gold material or semi-manufactured products of a purity of 325 thousandths or greater, or investment gold as defined in Article 344(1) is supplied by a taxable person exercising one of the options under Articles 348, 349 and 350, Member States may designate the customer as the person liable for payment of VAT.

3. Member States shall lay down the procedures and conditions for implementation of paragraphs 1 and 2.

Article 199

1. Member States may provide that the person liable for payment of VAT is the taxable person to whom any of the following supplies are made:
    (a) the supply of construction work, including repair, cleaning, maintenance, alteration and demolition services in relation to immovable property, as well as the handing over of construction works regarded as a supply of goods pursuant to Article 14(3);
    (b) the supply of staff engaged in activities covered by point (a);
    (c) the supply of immovable property, as referred to in Article 135(1)(j) and (k), where the supplier has opted for taxation of the supply pursuant to Article 137;
    (d) the supply of used material, used material which cannot be re-used in the same state, scrap, industrial and non industrial waste, recyclable waste, part processed waste and certain goods and services, as listed in Annex VI;
    (e) the supply of goods provided as security by one taxable person to another in execution of that security;
    (f) the supply of goods following the cession of a reservation of ownership to an assignee and the exercising of this right by the assignee;
    (g) the supply of immovable property sold by a judgment debtor in a compulsory sale procedure.
2. When applying the option provided for in paragraph 1, Member States may specify the supplies of goods and services covered, and the categories of suppliers or recipients to whom these measures may apply.
3. For the purposes of paragraph 1, Member States may take the following measures:
    (a) provide that a taxable person who also carries out activities or transactions that are not considered to be taxable supplies of goods or services in accordance with Article 2 shall be regarded as a taxable person in respect of supplies received as referred to in paragraph 1 of this Article;
    (b) provide that a non-taxable body governed by public law, shall be regarded as a taxable person in respect of supplies received as referred to in points (e), (f) and (g) of paragraph 1.
4. Member States shall inform the VAT Committee of national legislative measures adopted pursuant to paragraph 1 in so far as these are not measures authorised by the Council prior to 13 August 2006 in accordance with Article 27(1) to (4) of Directive 77/388/EEC, and which are continued under paragraph 1 of this Article.

[Article 199a

1. [Until 30 June 2022, Member States may provide that the person liable for the payment of VAT is the taxable person to whom any of the following supplies are made:]³
    (a) the transfer of allowances to emit greenhouse gases as defined in Article 3 of Directive 2003/87/EC of the European Parliament and of the Council of 13 October 2003 establishing a scheme for greenhouse gas emission allowance trading within the Community [], transferable in accordance with Article 12 of that Directive;
    (b) the transfer of other units that may be used by operators for compliance with the same Directive.
    (c) supplies of mobile telephones, being devices made or adapted for use in connection with a licensed network and operated on specified frequencies, whether or not they have any other use;

(d) supplies of integrated circuit devices such as microprocessors and central processing units in a state prior to integration into end user products;
(e) supplies of gas and electricity to a taxable dealer as defined in Article 38(2);
(f) supplies of gas and electricity certificates;
(g) supplies of telecommunication services as defined in Article 24(2);
(h) supplies of game consoles, tablet PC's and laptops;
(i) supplies of cereals and industrial crops including oil seeds and sugar beet, that are not normally used in the unaltered state for final consumption;
(j) supplies of raw and semi-finished metals, including precious metals, where they are not otherwise covered by point (d) of Article 199(1), the special arrangements for second-hand goods, works of art, collector's items and antiques pursuant to Articles 311 to 343 or the special scheme for investment gold pursuant to Articles 344 to 356.][2]

1a. Member States may lay down the conditions for the application of the mechanism provided for in paragraph 1.

1b. The application of the mechanism provided for in paragraph 1 to the supply of any of the goods or services listed in points (c) to (j) of that paragraph is subject to the introduction of appropriate and effective reporting obligations on taxable persons who supply the goods or services to which the mechanism provided for in paragraph 1 applies.][2]

[2. Member States shall inform the VAT Committee of the application of the mechanism provided for in paragraph 1 on the introduction of any such mechanism and shall provide the following information to the VAT Committee:
(a) the scope of the measure applying the mechanism together with the type and the features of the fraud, and a detailed description of accompanying measures, including any reporting obligations on taxable persons and any control measures;
(b) actions taken to inform the relevant taxable persons of the introduction of the application of the mechanism;
(c) evaluation criteria to enable comparison between fraudulent activities in relation to the goods and services listed in paragraph 1 before and after the application of the mechanism, fraudulent activities in relation to other goods and services before and after the application of the mechanism, and any increase in other types of fraudulent activities before and after the application of the mechanism;
(d) the date of commencement and the period to be covered by the measure applying the mechanism.][2]

3. [Member States applying the mechanism provided for in paragraph 1 shall, on the basis of the evaluation criteria provided for under point (c) of paragraph 2, submit a report to the Commission no later than 30 June 2017.][2]
[(a) the impact on fraudulent activities in relation to supplies of goods or services covered by the measure;][2]
(b) the possible shift of fraudulent activities to goods or other services;
(c) the compliance costs for taxable persons resulting from the measure.

[4. Each Member State that has detected a shift in trends of fraudulent activities in its territory in relation to the goods or services listed in paragraph 1 from the date of entry into force of this Article with respect to such goods or services, shall submit a report to the Commission in that respect no later than 30 June 2017.

5. Before 1 January 2018, the Commission shall present to the European Parliament and to the Council an overall assessment report on the effects of the mechanism provided for in paragraph 1 on combatting fraud.][2][1]

Amendments—[1] Article 199a inserted by Council Directive 2010/23/EU with effect from 9 April 2010 (OJ L 72, 20.03.2010, p 1).
[2] In para 1, first sentence substituted and sub-paras (c)–(j) inserted, paras 1a, 1b inserted, para 2 substituted, in para 3, first sentence and sub-para (a) substituted, and paras 4, 5 substituted for previous para 4, by Council Directive 2013/43/EU art 1(2) with effect from 15 August 2013 until 31 December 2018 (OJ L 201, 26.7.2013, p 4).
[3] In para 1, opening words substituted by Council Directive (EU) 2018/1695 Art 1(1) with effect from 2 December 2018 (OJ L 282, 12.11.2018, p 5).

[Article 199b
1. A Member State may, in cases of imperative urgency and in accordance with paragraphs 2 and 3, designate the recipient as the person liable to pay VAT on specific supplies of goods and services by derogation from Article 193 as a Quick Reaction Mechanism (QRM) special measure to combat sudden and massive fraud liable to lead to considerable and irreparable financial losses.

The QRM special measure shall be subject to appropriate control measures by the Member State with respect to taxable persons who supply the goods or services to which that measure applies, and shall be for a period not exceeding nine months.

2. A Member State wishing to introduce a QRM special measure as provided for in paragraph 1 shall send a notification to the Commission using the standardised form established in accordance with paragraph 4 and at the same time send it to the other Member States. The Member State shall provide the Commission with the information indicating the sector concerned, the type and the features of the

fraud, the existence of imperative grounds of urgency, the sudden and massive character of the fraud and its consequences in terms of considerable and irreparable financial losses. If the Commission considers that it does not have all the necessary information, it shall contact the Member State concerned within two weeks of receipt of the notification and specify what additional information is required. Any additional information provided by the Member State concerned to the Commission shall at the same time be sent to the other Member States. If the additional information provided is not sufficient, the Commission shall inform the Member State concerned thereof within one week. The Member State wishing to introduce a QRM special measure as provided for in paragraph 1 of this Article shall at the same time also make an application to the Commission in accordance with the procedure laid down in Article 395(2) and (3).

In cases of imperative urgency as set out in paragraph 1 of this Article, the procedure laid down in Article 395(2) and (3) shall be completed within six months of receipt of the application by the Commission.

3. Once the Commission has all the information it considers necessary for appraisal of the notification referred to in the first subparagraph of paragraph 2, it shall notify the Member States thereof. Where it objects to the QRM special measure, it shall produce a negative opinion within one month of that notification, and shall inform the Member State concerned and the VAT Committee thereof. Where the Commission does not object, it shall confirm this in writing to the Member State concerned and to the VAT Committee within the same time period. The Member State may adopt the QRM special measure from the date of receipt of that confirmation. In appraising the notification, the Commission shall take into account the views of any other Member State sent to it in writing.

4. The Commission shall adopt an implementing act establishing a standardised form for the submission of the notification for the QRM special measure referred to in paragraph 2 and of the information referred to in the first subparagraph of paragraph 2. That implementing act shall be adopted in accordance with the examination procedure referred to in paragraph 5.

5. Where reference is made to this paragraph, Article 5 of Regulation (EU) No 182/2011 of the European Parliament and of the Council (*) shall apply and for this purpose the committee shall be the committee established by Article 58 of Council Regulation (EU) No 904/2010 (**).

6. The QRM special measure as provided for in paragraph 1 shall apply until 30 June 2022.][1]

* Regulation (EU) No 182/2011 of the European Parliament and of the Council of 16 February 2011 laying down the rules and general principles concerning mechanisms for control by Member States of the Commission's exercise of implementing powers (OJ L 55, 28.2.2011, p. 13).
** Council Regulation (EU) No 904/2010 of 7 October 2010 on administrative cooperation and combating fraud in the field of value added tax (OJ L 268, 12.10.2010, p. 1).

Amendments—[1] Article 199b substituted by Council Directive (EU) 2018/1695 Art 1(2) with effect from 2 December 2018 (OJ L 282, 12.11.2018, p 5).

[Article 199c

1. By way of derogation from Article 193, a Member State may, until 30 June 2022, introduce a generalised reverse charge mechanism ('GRCM') on non-cross-border supplies, providing that the person liable for payment of VAT is the taxable person to whom all supplies of goods and services are made above a threshold of EUR 17 500 per transaction.

A Member State wishing to introduce the GRCM shall comply with all of the following conditions:
   (a) it had in 2014, in accordance with the method and figures set out in the 2016 final report dated 23 August 2016 on the VAT gap published by the Commission, a VAT gap, expressed as a percentage of the VAT total tax liability, of at least 5 percentage points above the Community median VAT gap;
   (b) it has, based on the impact assessment that accompanied the legislative proposal for this Article, a carousel fraud level within its total VAT gap of more than 25%;
   (c) it establishes that other control measures are not sufficient to combat carousel fraud on its territory, in particular by specifying the control measures applied and the particular reasons for their lack of effectiveness, as well as the reasons why administrative cooperation in the field of VAT has proven insufficient;
   (d) it establishes that the estimated gains in tax compliance and collection expected as a result of the introduction of the GRCM outweigh the expected overall additional burden on businesses and tax authorities by at least 25 %; and
   (e) it establishes that the introduction of the GRCM will not result in businesses and tax authorities incurring costs that are higher than those incurred as a result of the application of other control measures.

The Member State shall attach to the request referred to in paragraph 3 the calculation of the VAT gap according to the method and figures available in the report on the VAT gap published by the Commission, as referred to in point (a) of the second subparagraph of this paragraph.

2. Member States that apply the GRCM shall establish appropriate and effective electronic reporting obligations for all taxable persons and, in particular, for taxable persons who supply or receive goods or services to which the GRCM applies to ensure the effective functioning and monitoring of the application of the GRCM.

3. Member States wishing to apply the GRCM shall submit a request to the Commission and provide the following information:
   (a) a detailed justification of fulfilment of the conditions referred to in paragraph 1;
   (b) the starting date of application of the GRCM and the period to be covered by the GRCM;
   (c) actions to be taken to inform taxable persons of the introduction of the application of the GRCM; and
   (d) a detailed description of the accompanying measures referred to in paragraph 2.

If the Commission considers that it does not have all the necessary information, it shall request additional information, including underlying methods, assumptions, studies and other supporting documents, within one month of receipt of the request. The requesting Member State shall submit the required information within a month of receipt of the notification.

4. Where the Commission considers that a request complies with the requirements set out in paragraph 3, it shall, no later than three months after it has received all the necessary information, submit a proposal to the Council. The Council, acting unanimously on such a proposal from the Commission, may authorise the requesting Member State to apply the GRCM. Where the Commission considers that a request is not compliant with the requirements set out in paragraph 3, it shall, within the same deadline, communicate its reasons to the requesting Member State and to the Council.

5. Where a considerable negative impact on the internal market has been established in accordance with the second subparagraph of this paragraph, the Commission shall, no later than three months after it has received all the necessary information, propose the repeal of all the implementing decisions referred to in paragraph 4, at the earliest six months after the entry into force of the first implementing decision authorising a Member State to apply the GRCM. Such repeal shall be deemed to be adopted by the Council unless the Council decides by unanimity to reject the Commission's proposal within 30 days of the Commission's adoption thereof.

A considerable negative impact shall be considered established where the following conditions are fulfilled:
   (a) at least one Member State that does not apply the GRCM informs the Commission of an increase of VAT fraud on its territory due to the application of the GRCM; and
   (b) the Commission establishes, including on the basis of the information provided by the Member States referred to in point (a) of this subparagraph, that the increase of VAT fraud on their territory is related to the application of the GRCM in one or more Member States.

6. Member States that apply the GRCM shall submit the following information in electronic format to all Member States:
   (a) the names of the persons who, in the 12 months preceding the starting date of application of the GRCM, have been subject to proceedings, whether criminal or administrative, for VAT fraud; and
   (b) the names of the persons, including in the case of legal persons the names of their directors, whose VAT registration in that Member State is terminated after the introduction of the GRCM; and
   (c) the names of the persons, including in the case of legal persons the names of their directors, who have failed to submit a VAT return for two consecutive tax periods after the introduction of the GRCM.

The information referred to in points (a) and (b) of the first subparagraph shall be submitted no later than three months after the introduction of the GRCM and shall be updated every three months thereafter. The information referred to in point (c) of the first subparagraph shall be submitted no later than nine months after the introduction of the GRCM and shall be updated every three months thereafter.

Member States that apply the GRCM shall submit an interim report to the Commission no later than one year after the start of application of the GRCM. That report shall provide a detailed assessment of the effectiveness of the GRCM. Three months after the end of the application of the GRCM, Member States that apply the GRCM shall submit a final report on its overall impact.

7. Member States that do not apply the GRCM shall submit an interim report to the Commission as regards the impact in their territory of the application of GRCM by other Member States. That report shall be submitted to the Commission within three months following the application of the GRCM for at least one year in one Member State.

If at least one Member State applies the GRCM, Member States that do not apply the GRCM shall, by 30 September 2022, submit a final report to the Commission as regards the impact in their territory of the GRCM applied by other Member States.

8. In the reports referred to in paragraph 6, Member States shall assess the impact of the application of the GRCM on the basis of the following evaluation criteria:
   (a) the evolution of the VAT gap;
   (b) the evolution of VAT fraud, in particular carousel fraud and fraud at retail level;
   (c) the evolution of the administrative burden on taxable persons;
   (d) the evolution of administrative costs for the tax authorities.

9. In the reports referred to in paragraph 7, Member States shall assess the impact of the application of the GRCM on the basis of the following evaluation criteria:
   (a) the evolution of VAT fraud, in particular carousel fraud and fraud at retail level;
   (b) a shift in fraud from those Member States that apply or have applied the GRCM.][1]

AMENDMENTS—

[1] Article 199c inserted by Council Directive (EU) 2018/2057 Art 1 with effect from 16 January 2019. Note: this amendment applies until 30 June 2022 (OJ L 329, 27.12.2018, p 3). Article 199c is therefore included in this "frozen" version of the Directive, as it had effect as part of the Directive as at 31 December 2020.

Article 200
VAT shall be payable by any person making a taxable intra-Community acquisition of goods.

Article 201
On importation, VAT shall be payable by any person or persons designated or recognised as liable by the Member State of importation.

Article 202
VAT shall be payable by any person who causes goods to cease to be covered by the arrangements or situations listed in Articles 156, 157, 158, 160 and 161.

Article 203
VAT shall be payable by any person who enters the VAT on an invoice.

Article 204
1. Where, pursuant to Articles 193 to 197 and Articles 199 and 200, the person liable for payment of VAT is a taxable person who is not established in the Member State in which the VAT is due, Member States may allow that person to appoint a tax representative as the person liable for payment of the VAT.

Furthermore, where the taxable transaction is carried out by a taxable person who is not established in the Member State in which the VAT is due and no legal instrument exists, with the country in which that taxable person is established or has his seat, relating to mutual assistance similar in scope to that provided for in Directive 76/308/EEC[1] and Regulation (EC) No 1798/2003 [2], Member States may take measures to provide that the person liable for payment of VAT is to be a tax representative appointed by the non-established taxable person.

[However, Member States may not apply the option referred to in the second subparagraph to a taxable person within the meaning of point (1) of Article 358a who has opted for the special scheme for services supplied by taxable persons not established within the Community.][1]

2. The option under the first subparagraph of paragraph 1 shall be subject to the conditions and procedures laid down by each Member State.

(1) Council Directive 76/308/EEC of 15 March 1976 on mutual assistance for the recovery of claims relating to certain levies, duties, taxes and other measures (OJ L 73, 19.3.1976, p. 18.). Directive as last amended by the Act of Accession of 2003.

Amendments—[1] In para 1, third sub-para substituted by Council Directive 2019/1995/EU art 1(5) with effect from 22 December 2019 (OJ L 310, 2.12.2019, p 1).

Article 205
In the situations referred to in Articles 193 to 200 and Articles 202, 203 and 204, Member States may provide that a person other than the person liable for payment of VAT is to be held jointly and severally liable for payment of VAT.

SECTION 2
Payment arrangements

Article 206
Any taxable person liable for payment of VAT must pay the net amount of the VAT when submitting the VAT return provided for in Article 250. Member States may, however, set a different date for payment of that amount or may require interim payments to be made.

Article 207
Member States shall take the measures necessary to ensure that persons who are regarded as liable for payment of VAT in the stead of a taxable person not established in their respective territory, in accordance with Articles 194 to 197 and Articles 199 and 204, comply with the payment obligations set out in this Section.

Member States shall also take the measures necessary to ensure that those persons who, in accordance with Article 205, are held to be jointly and severally liable for payment of the VAT comply with these payment obligations.

Article 208
Where Member States designate the customer for investment gold as the person liable for payment of VAT pursuant to Article 198(1) or if, in the case of gold material, semi-manufactured products, or investment gold as defined in Article 344(1), they exercise the option provided for in Article 198(2) of designating the customer as the person liable for payment of VAT, they shall take the measures necessary to ensure that he complies with the payment obligations set out in this Section.

Article 209
Member States shall take the measures necessary to ensure that non-taxable legal persons who are liable for payment of VAT due in respect of intra-Community acquisitions of goods, as referred to in Article 2(1)(b)(i), comply with the payment obligations set out in this Section.

Article 210
Member States shall adopt arrangements for payment of VAT on intra-Community acquisitions of new means of transport, as referred to in Article 2(1)(b)(ii), and on intra-Community acquisitions of products subject to excise duty, as referred to in Article 2(1)(b)(iii).

Article 211
Member States shall lay down the detailed rules for payment in respect of the importation of goods.

In particular, Member States may provide that, in the case of the importation of goods by taxable persons or certain categories thereof, or by persons liable for payment of VAT or certain categories thereof, the VAT due by reason of the importation need not be paid at the time of importation, on condition that it is entered as such in the VAT return to be submitted in accordance with Article 250.

Article 212
Member States may release taxable persons from payment of the VAT due where the amount is insignificant.

CHAPTER 2
IDENTIFICATION

Article 213
1. Every taxable person shall state when his activity as a taxable person commences, changes or ceases.

Member States shall allow, and may require, the statement to be made by electronic means, in accordance with conditions which they lay down.

2. Without prejudice to the first subparagraph of paragraph 1, every taxable person or non-taxable legal person who makes intra-Community acquisitions of goods which are not subject to VAT pursuant to Article 3(1) must state that he makes such acquisitions if the conditions, laid down in that provision, for not making such transactions subject to VAT cease to be fulfilled.

Article 214
1. Member States shall take the measures necessary to ensure that the following persons are identified by means of an individual number:
   (a) every taxable person, with the exception of those referred to in Article 9(2), who within their respective territory carries out supplies of goods or services in respect of which VAT is deductible, other than supplies of goods or services in respect of which VAT is payable solely by the customer or the person for whom the goods or services are intended, in accordance with Articles 194 to 197 and Article 199;
   (b) every taxable person, or non-taxable legal person, who makes intra-Community acquisitions of goods subject to VAT pursuant to Article 2(1)(b) and every taxable person, or non-taxable legal person, who exercises the option under Article 3(3) of making their intra-Community acquisitions subject to VAT;
   (c) every taxable person who, within their respective territory, makes intra-Community acquisitions of goods for the purposes of transactions which relate to the activities referred to in the second subparagraph of Article 9(1) and which are carried out outside that territory.
   [(d) every taxable person who within their respective territory receives services for which he is liable to pay VAT pursuant to Article 196;
   (e) every taxable person, established within their respective territory, who supplies services within the territory of another Member State for which VAT is payable solely by the recipient pursuant to Article 196.][1]

2. Member States need not identify certain taxable persons who carry out transactions on an occasional basis, as referred to in Article 12.

Amendments—[1] Para 1(d), (e) inserted, by Council Directive 2008/8/EC art 2(8) with effect from 1 January 2010 (OJ L 44, 20.2.2008 p 11).

Article 215
Each individual VAT identification number shall have a prefix in accordance with ISO code 3166 — alpha 2 — by which the Member State of issue may be identified.

Nevertheless, Greece may use the prefix 'EL'.

[The prefix "XI" shall be used for Northern Ireland.][1]

Amendments—[1] Words inserted by Council Directive (EU) 2020/1756 art 1 with effect from 26 November 2020 (OJ L 396, 25.11.2020, p 1).

Article 216

Member States shall take the measures necessary to ensure that their identification systems enable the taxable persons referred to in Article 214 to be identified and to ensure the correct application of the transitional arrangements for the taxation of intra-Community transactions, as referred to in Article 402.

CHAPTER 3
INVOICING
SECTION 1
Definition

[Article 217

For the purposes of this Directive, "electronic invoice" means an invoice that contains the information required in this Directive, and which has been issued and received in any electronic format.][1]

Amendments—[1] Article substituted by Council Directive 2010/45 art 1(11) with effect from 11 August 2010 (OJ L 189, 22.7.2010, p 1).

SECTION 2
Concept of invoice

Article 218

For the purposes of this Directive, Member States shall accept documents or messages on paper or in electronic form as invoices if they meet the conditions laid down in this Chapter.

Article 219

Any document or message that amends and refers specifically and unambiguously to the initial invoice shall be treated as an invoice.

SECTION 3
Issue of invoices

[Article 219a

1. Invoicing shall be subject to the rules applying in the Member State in which the supply of goods or services is deemed to be made, in accordance with the provisions of Title V.
2. By way of derogation from paragraph 1, invoicing shall be subject to the following rules:
    (a) the rules applying in the Member State in which the supplier has established his business or has a fixed establishment from which the supply is made or, in the absence of such place of establishment or fixed establishment, the Member State where the supplier has his permanent address or usually resides, where:
        (i) the supplier is not established in the Member State in which the supply of goods or services is deemed to be made, in accordance with the provisions of Title V, or his establishment in that Member State does not intervene in the supply within the meaning of point (b) of Article 192a, and the person liable for the payment of the VAT is the person to whom the goods or services are supplied unless the customer issues the invoice (self-billing);
        (ii) the supply of goods or services is deemed not to be made within the Community, in accordance with the provisions of Title V;
    (b) the rules applying in the Member State where the supplier making use of one of the special schemes referred to in Chapter 6 of Title XII is identified.
3. Paragraphs 1 and 2 of this Article shall apply without prejudice to Articles 244 to 248.]

Amendments—Article 219a substituted by Council Directive 2017/2455/EU art 1(2) with effect from 1 July 2019 (OJ L 348, 29.12.2017 p 7).

[Article 220

1 Every taxable person shall ensure that, in respect of the following, an invoice is issued, either by himself or by his customer or, in his name and on his behalf, by a third party:
    (1) supplies of goods or services which he has made to another taxable person or to a non-taxable legal person;
    (2) supplies of goods as referred to in Article 33;
    (3) supplies of goods carried out in accordance with the conditions specified in Article 138;
    (4) any payment on account made to him before one of the supplies of goods referred to in points (1) and (2) was carried out;

(5) any payment on account made to him by another taxable person or non-taxable legal person before the provision of services was completed.

2 By way of derogation from paragraph 1, and without prejudice to Article 221(2), the issue of an invoice shall not be required in respect of supplies of services exempted under points (a) to (g) of Article 135(1).][1]

Amendments—[1] Article substituted by Council Directive 2010/45 art 1(13) with effect from 11 August 2010 (OJ L 189, 22.7.2010, p 1).

[**Article 220a**

1 Member States shall allow taxable persons to issue a simplified invoice in any of the following cases:
   (a) where the amount of the invoice is not higher than EUR 100 or the equivalent in national currency;
   (b) where the invoice issued is a document or message treated as an invoice pursuant to Article 219.
   [(c) where the taxable person is benefitting from the exemption for small enterprises provided for in Article 284.][2]

2 Member States shall not allow taxable persons to issue a simplified invoice where invoices are required to be issued pursuant to points (2) and (3) of Article 220(1) or where the taxable supply of goods or services is carried out by a taxable person who is not established in the Member State in which the VAT is due, or whose establishment in that Member State does not intervene in the supply within the meaning of Article 192a, and the person liable for the payment of VAT is the person to whom the goods or services are supplied.][1]

Amendments—[1] Article inserted by Council Directive 2010/45 art 1(14) with effect from 11 August 2010 (OJ L 189, 22.7.2010, p 1). The deadline for implementation of Directive 2010/45/EU is 31 December 2012.
[2] Para 1(c) inserted by Council Directive 2020/285/EU art 1(5) with effect from 22 March 2020 (OJ L 62, 2.3.2020, p 13).

[**Article 221**

1 Member States may impose on taxable persons an obligation to issue an invoice in accordance with the details required under Article 226 or 226b in respect of supplies of goods or services other than those referred to in Article 220(1).

2 Member States may impose on taxable persons who have established their business in their territory or who have a fixed establishment in their territory from which the supply is made, an obligation to issue an invoice in accordance with the details required in Article 226 or 226b in respect of supplies of services exempted under points (a) to (g) of Article 135(1) which those taxable persons have made in their territory or outside the Community.

3 Member States may release taxable persons from the obligation laid down in Article 220(1) or in Article 220a to issue an invoice in respect of supplies of goods or services which they have made in their territory and which are exempt, with or without deductibility of the VAT paid in the preceding stage, pursuant to Articles 110 and 111, Article 125(1), Article 127, Article 128(1), Article 132, points (h) to (l) of Article 135(1), Articles 136, 371, 375, 376 and 377, Articles 378(2) and 379(2) and Articles 380 to 390b.][1]

Amendments—[1] Articles 221–225 substituted by Council Directive 2010/45 art 1(15) with effect from 11 August 2010 (OJ L 189, 22.7.2010, p 1).

[**Article 222**

For supplies of goods carried out in accordance with the conditions specified in Article 138 or for supplies of services for which VAT is payable by the customer pursuant to Article 196, an invoice shall be issued no later than on the fifteenth day of the month following that in which the chargeable event occurs.

For other supplies of goods or services Member States may impose time limits on taxable persons for the issue of invoices.][1]

Amendments—[1] Articles 221–225 substituted by Council Directive 2010/45 art 1(15) with effect from 11 August 2010 (OJ L 189, 22.7.2010, p 1).

[**Article 223**

Member States shall allow taxable persons to issue summary invoices which detail several separate supplies of goods or services provided that VAT on the supplies mentioned in the summary invoice becomes chargeable during the same calendar month.

Without prejudice to Article 222, Member States may allow summary invoices to include supplies for which VAT has become chargeable during a period of time longer than one calendar month.[1]

Amendments—[1] Articles 221–225 substituted by Council Directive 2010/45 art 1(15) with effect from 11 August 2010 (OJ L 189, 22.7.2010, p 1).

[**Article 224**

Invoices may be drawn up by the customer in respect of the supply to him, by a taxable person, of goods or services, where there is a prior agreement between the two parties and provided that a procedure exists for the acceptance of each invoice by the taxable person supplying the goods or services. Member State may require that such invoices be issued in the name and on behalf of the taxable person.[1]

Amendments—[1] Articles 221–225 substituted by Council Directive 2010/45 art 1(15) with effect from 11 August 2010 (OJ L 189, 22.7.2010, p 1).

[**Article 225**
Member States may impose specific conditions on taxable persons in cases where the third party, or the customer, who issues invoices is established in a country with which no legal instrument exists relating to mutual assistance similar in scope to that provided for in Directive 2010/24/EU (*) and Regulation (EC) No 1798/2003 (**).

Amendments—[1] Articles 221–225 substituted by Council Directive 2010/45 art 1(15) with effect from 11 August 2010 (OJ L 189, 22.7.2010, p 1).

SECTION 4
Content of invoices

Article 226
Without prejudice to the particular provisions laid down in this Directive, only the following details are required for VAT purposes on invoices issued pursuant to Articles 220 and 221:
(1) the date of issue;
(2) a sequential number, based on one or more series, which uniquely identifies the invoice;
(3) the VAT identification number referred to in Article 214 under which the taxable person supplied the goods or services;
(4) the customer's VAT identification number, as referred to in Article 214, under which the customer received a supply of goods or services in respect of which he is liable for payment of VAT, or received a supply of goods as referred to in Article 138;
(5) the full name and address of the taxable person and of the customer;
(6) the quantity and nature of the goods supplied or the extent and nature of the services rendered;
(7) the date on which the supply of goods or services was made or completed or the date on which the payment on account referred to in points (4) and (5) of Article 220 was made, in so far as that date can be determined and differs from the date of issue of the invoice;
[(7a) where the VAT becomes chargeable at the time when the payment is received in accordance with Article 66(b) and the right of deduction arises at the time the deductible tax becomes chargeable, the mention "Cash accounting";][1]
(8) the taxable amount per rate or exemption, the unit price exclusive of VAT and any discounts or rebates if they are not included in the unit price;
(9) the VAT rate applied;
(10) the VAT amount payable, except where a special arrangement is applied under which, in accordance with this Directive, such a detail is excluded;
[(10a) where the customer receiving a supply issues the invoice instead of the supplier, the mention "Self-billing";][1]
[(11) in the case of an exemption, reference to the applicable provision of this Directive, or to the corresponding national provision, or any other reference indicating that the supply of goods or services is exempt;][1]
[(11a) where the customer is liable for the payment of the VAT, the mention "Reverse charge";][1]
(12) in the case of the supply of a new means of transport made in accordance with the conditions specified in Article 138 (1) and (2)(*a*), the characteristics as identified in point (*b*) of Article 2(2);
[(13) where the margin scheme for travel agents is applied, the mention "Margin scheme — Travel agents";][1]
(14) where one of the special arrangements applicable to second-hand goods, works of art, collectors' items and antiques is applied, the mention "Margin scheme — Second-hand goods"; "Margin scheme — Works of art", or "Margin scheme — Collector's items and antiques" respectively;][1]
(15) where the person liable for payment of VAT is a tax representative for the purposes of Article 204, the VAT identification number, referred to in Article 214, of that tax representative, together with his full name and address.

Amendments—[1] Paras (7a), (10a), (11a) inserted, paras (11), (13), (14) substituted, by Council Directive 2010/45 art 1(16) with effect from 11 August 2010 (OJ L 189, 22.7.2010, p 1).

[**226a**
Where the invoice is issued by a taxable person, who is not established in the Member State where the tax is due or whose establishment in that Member State does not intervene in the supply within the meaning of Article 192a, and who is making a supply of goods or services to a customer who is liable for payment of VAT, the taxable person may omit the details referred to in points (8), (9) and (10) of Article 226 and instead indicate, by reference to the quantity or extent of the goods or services supplied and their nature, the taxable amount of those goods or services.][1]

Amendments—[1]   Article nserted by Council Directive 2010/45 art 1(17) with effect from 11 August 2010 (OJ L 189, 22.7.2010, p 1). The deadline for implementation of Directive 2010/45/EU is 31 December 2012.

[226b

As regards simplified invoices issued pursuant to Article 220a and Article 221(1) and (2), Member States shall require at least the following details:
   (*a*) the date of issue;
   (*b*) identification of the taxable person supplying the goods or services;
   (*c*) identification of the type of goods or services supplied;
   (*d*) the VAT amount payable or the information needed to calculate it;
   (*e*) where the invoice issued is a document or message treated as an invoice pursuant to Article 219, specific and unambiguous reference to that initial invoice and the specific details which are being amended.
They may not require details on invoices other than those referred to in Articles 226, 227 and 230.';][1]

Amendments—[1]   Article nserted by Council Directive 2010/45 art 1(17) with effect from 11 August 2010 (OJ L 189, 22.7.2010, p 1). The deadline for implementation of Directive 2010/45/EU is 31 December 2012.

Article 227

Member States may require taxable persons established in their territory and supplying goods or services there to indicate the VAT identification number, referred to in Article 214, of the customer in cases other than those referred to in point (4) of Article 226.

Article 228

Member States in whose territory goods or services are supplied may allow some of the compulsory details to be omitted from documents or messages treated as invoices pursuant to Article 219.[1]

Amendments—[1]   Article repealed by Council Directive 2010/45 art 1(18) with effect from 11 August 2010 (OJ L 189, 22.7.2010, p 1). The deadline for implementation of Directive 2010/45/EU is 31 December 2012.

Article 229

Member States shall not require invoices to be signed.

[Article 230

The amounts which appear on the invoice may be expressed in any currency, provided that the amount of VAT payable or to be adjusted is expressed in the national currency of the Member State, using the conversion rate mechanism provided for in Article 91.][1]

Amendments—[1]   Article substituted by Council Directive 2010/45 art 1(19) with effect from 11 August 2010 (OJ L 189, 22.7.2010, p 1).

Article 231

For control purposes, Member States may require invoices in respect of supplies of goods or services in their territory and invoices received by taxable persons established in their territory to be translated into their national languages.[1]

Amendments—[1]   Article repealed by Council Directive 2010/45 art 1(20) with effect from 11 August 2010 (OJ L 189, 22.7.2010, p 1). The deadline for implementation of Directive 2010/45/EU is 31 December 2012.

SECTION 5
[Paper invoices and electronic invoices]

[Article 232

The use of an electronic invoice shall be subject to acceptance by the recipient.][1]

Amendments—[1]   Section 5 heading, and Article 232 substituted, by Council Directive 2010/45 art 1(21) with effect from 11 August 2010 (OJ L 189, 22.7.2010, p 1).

[Article 233

1. The authenticity of the origin, the integrity of the content and the legibility of an invoice, whether on paper or in electronic form, shall be ensured from the point in time of issue until the end of the period for storage of the invoice.

Each taxable person shall determine the way to ensure the authenticity of the origin, the integrity of the content and the legibility of the invoice. This may be achieved by any business controls which create a reliable audit trail between an invoice and a supply of goods or services.

"Authenticity of the origin" means the assurance of the identity of the supplier or the issuer of the invoice.

"Integrity of the content" means that the content required according to this Directive has not been altered.

2. Other than by way of the type of business controls described in paragraph 1, the following are examples of technologies that ensure the authenticity of the origin and the integrity of the content of an electronic invoice:
   (*a*) an advanced electronic signature within the meaning of point (2) of Article 2 of Directive 1999/93/EC of the European Parliament and of the Council of 13 December 1999 on

a Community framework for electronic signatures (*), based on a qualified certificate and created by a secure signature creation device, within the meaning of points (6) and (10) of Article 2 of Directive 1999/93/EC;

(b) electronic data interchange (EDI), as defined in Article 2 of Annex 1 to Commission Recommendation 1994/820/EC of 19 October 1994 relating to the legal aspects of electronic data interchange (**), where the agreement relating to the exchange provides for the use of procedures guaranteeing the authenticity of the origin and integrity of the data.]¹

Amendments—¹ Article 233 substituted, by Council Directive 2010/45 art 1(23) with effect from 11 August 2010 (OJ L 189, 22.7.2010, p 1).

Article 234

Member States may not impose on taxable persons supplying goods or services in their territory any other obligations or formalities relating to the sending or making available of invoices by electronic means.

[Article 235

Member States may lay down specific conditions for electronic invoices issued in respect of goods or services supplied in their territory from a country with which no legal instrument exists relating to mutual assistance similar in scope to that provided for in Directive 2010/24/EU and Regulation (EC) No 1798/2003.]¹

Amendments—¹ Articles 235–237 substituted by Council Directive 2010/45 art 1(24) with effect from 11 August 2010 (OJ L 189, 22.7.2010, p 1).

[Article 236

Where batches containing several electronic invoices are sent or made available to the same recipient, the details common to the individual invoices may be mentioned only once where, for each invoice, all the information is accessible.]¹

Amendments—¹ Articles 235–237 substituted by Council Directive 2010/45 art 1(24) with effect from 11 August 2010 (OJ L 189, 22.7.2010, p 1).

[Article 237

By 31 December 2016 at the latest, the Commission shall present to the European Parliament and the Council an overall assessment report, based on an independent economic study, on the impact of the invoicing rules applicable from 1 January 2013 and notably on the extent to which they have effectively led to a decrease in administrative burdens for businesses, accompanied where necessary by an appropriate proposal to amend the relevant rules.]¹

Amendments—¹ Articles 235–237 substituted by Council Directive 2010/45 art 1(24) with effect from 11 August 2010 (OJ L 189, 22.7.2010, p 1).

SECTION 6
Simplification measures

Article 238

[1. After consulting the VAT Committee, Member States may, in accordance with conditions which they may lay down, provide that in the following cases only the information required pursuant to Article 226b shall be entered on invoices in respect of supplies of goods or services:

(a) where the amount of the invoice is higher than EUR 100 but not higher than EUR 400, or the equivalent in national currency;

(b) where commercial or administrative practice in the business sector concerned or the technical conditions under which the invoices are issued make it particularly difficult to comply with all the obligations referred to in Article 226 or 230.]¹

2. . . .¹

[3. The simplified arrangements provided for in paragraph 1 shall not be applied where invoices are required to be issued pursuant to points (2) and (3) of Article 220(1) or where the taxable supply of goods or services is carried out by a taxable person who is not established in the Member State in which the VAT is due or whose establishment in that Member State does not intervene in the supply within the meaning of Article 192a and the person liable for the payment of VAT is the person to whom the goods or services are supplied.]¹

Amendments—¹ Paras 1, 3 substituted, and para 2 repealed, by Council Directive 2010/45 art 1(25) with effect from 11 August 2010 (OJ L 189, 22.7.2010, p 1).

Article 239

In cases where Member States make use of the option under point (b) of the first subparagraph of Article 272(1) of not allocating a VAT identification number to taxable persons who do not carry out any of the transactions referred to in Articles 20, 21, 22, 33, 36, 138 and 141, and where the supplier or the customer has not been allocated an identification number of that type, another number called the tax reference number, as defined by the Member States concerned, shall be entered on the invoice instead.

Article 240
Where the taxable person has been allocated a VAT identification number, the Member States exercising the option under point (*b*) of the first subparagraph of Article 272(1) may also require the invoice to show the following:
(1) in respect of the supply of services, as referred to in Articles 44, 47, 50, 53, 54 and 55, and the supply of goods, as referred to in Articles 138 and 141, the VAT identification number and the tax reference number of the supplier;
(2) in respect of other supplies of goods or services, only the tax reference number of the supplier or only the VAT identification number.

CHAPTER 4
ACCOUNTING

SECTION 1
Definition

Article 241
For the purposes of this Chapter, 'storage of an invoice by electronic means' shall mean storage of data using electronic equipment for processing (including digital compression) and storage, and employing wire, radio, optical or other electromagnetic means.

SECTION 2
General obligations

Article 242
Every taxable person shall keep accounts in sufficient detail for VAT to be applied and its application checked by the tax authorities.

[Article 243
1. Every taxable person shall keep a register of the goods dispatched or transported by him, or on his behalf, to a destination outside the territory of the Member State of departure but within the Community for the purposes of transactions consisting in valuations of those goods or work on them or their temporary use as referred to in points (f), (g) and (h) of Article 17(2).
2. Every taxable person shall keep accounts in sufficient detail to enable the identification of goods dispatched to him from another Member State, by or on behalf of a taxable person identified for VAT purposes in that other Member State, and used for services consisting in valuations of those goods or work on those goods.
[3. Every taxable person who transfers goods under the call-off stock arrangements referred to in Article 17a shall keep a register that permits the tax authorities to verify the correct application of that Article.
Every taxable person to whom goods are supplied under the call-off stock arrangements referred to in Article 17a shall keep a register of those goods.][2]][1]

Amendments—[1] Article 243 substituted by Council Directive 2010/45 art 1(26) with effect from 11 August 2010 (OJ L 189, 22.7.2010, p 1).
[2] Para 3 inserted by Council Directive (EU) 2018/1910 Article 1(4) with effect from 27 December 2018 (OJ L 311, 7.12.2018, p 3).

[SECTION 2A
General obligations of payment service providers

Article 243a
For the purposes of this Section, the following definitions apply:
(1) "payment service provider" means any of the categories of payment service providers listed in points (a) to (d) of Article 1(1) of Directive (EU) 2015/2366 of the European Parliament and of the Council ([1]) or a natural or legal person benefiting from an exemption in accordance with Article 32 of that Directive;
(2) "payment service" means any of the business activities set out in points (3) to (6) of Annex I to Directive (EU) 2015/2366;
(3) "payment" means, subject to the exclusions provided for in Article 3 of Directive (EU) 2015/2366, a "payment transaction " as defined in point (5) of Article 4 of that Directive or a "money remittance" as defined in point (22) of Article 4 of that Directive;
(4) "payer" means "payer" as defined in point (8) of Article 4 of Directive (EU) 2015/2366;
(5) "payee" means "payee"as defined in point (9) of Article 4 of Directive (EU) 2015/2366;
(6) "home Member State" means "home Member State " as defined in point (1) of Article 4 of Directive (EU) 2015/2366;
(7) "host Member State" means "host Member State" as defined in point (2) of Article 4 of Directive (EU) 2015/2366;

(8) "payment account" means "payment account" as defined in point (12) of Article 4 of Directive (EU) 2015/2366;
(9) "IBAN" means "IBAN" as defined in point (15) of Article 2 of Regulation (EU) No 260/2012 of the European Parliament and of the Council ([2]);
(10) "BIC" means "BIC" as defined in point (16) of Article 2 of Regulation (EU) No 260/2012.][1]

[1] Opinion of 17 December 2019 (not yet published in the Official Journal).
[2] OJ C 240, 16.7.2019, p. 33.

Amendments—[1] Section 2a (arts 243a–243d) inserted by Council Directive 2020/284/EU art 1 with effect from 22 March 2020 (OJ L 62, 2.3.2020, p 7).

[Article 243b

1. Member States shall require payment service providers to keep sufficiently detailed records of payees and of payments in relation to the payment services they provide for each calendar quarter to enable the competent authorities of the Member States to carry out controls of the supplies of goods and services which, in accordance with the provisions of Title V, are deemed to take place in a Member State, in order to achieve the objective of combating VAT fraud.
The requirement referred to in the first subparagraph shall apply only to payment services provided as regards cross-border payments. A payment shall be considered a cross-border payment when the payer is located in a Member State and the payee is located in another Member State, in a third territory or in a third country.
2. The requirement to which payment service providers are subject under paragraph 1 shall apply where, in the course of a calendar quarter, a payment service provider provides payment services corresponding to more than 25 cross-border payments to the same payee.
The number of cross-border payments referred to in the first subparagraph of this paragraph shall be calculated by reference to the payment services provided by the payment service provider per Member State and per identifier as referred to in Article 243c(2). Where the payment service provider has information that the payee has several identifiers the calculation shall be made per payee.
3. The requirement laid down in paragraph 1 shall not apply to payment services provided by the payment service providers of the payer as regards any payment where at least one of the payment service providers of the payee is located in a Member State, as shown by that payment service provider's BIC or any other business identifier code that unambiguously identifies the payment service provider and its location. The payment service providers of the payer shall nevertheless include those payment services in the calculation referred to in paragraph 2.
4. Where the requirement for payment service providers laid down in paragraph 1 applies, the records shall:
   (a) be kept by the payment service provider in electronic format for a period of three calendar years from the end of the calendar year of the date of the payment;
   (b) be made available in accordance with Article 24b of Regulation (EU) No 904/2010 to the home Member State of the payment service provider, or to the host Member States when the payment service provider provides payment services in Member States other than the home Member State.][1]

Amendments—[1] Section 2a (arts 243a–243d) inserted by Council Directive 2020/284/EU art 1 with effect from 22 March 2020 (OJ L 62, 2.3.2020, p 7).

[Article 243c

1. For the application of the second subparagraph of Article 243b(1) and without prejudice to the provisions of Title V, the location of the payer shall be considered to be in the Member State corresponding to:
   (a) the IBAN of the payer's payment account or any other identifier which unambiguously identifies, and gives the location of, the payer, or in the absence of such identifiers,
   (b) the BIC or any other business identifier code that unambiguously identifies, and gives the location of, the payment service provider acting on behalf of the payer.
2. For the application of the second subparagraph of Article 243b(1), the location of the payee shall be considered to be in the Member State, third territory or third country corresponding to:
   (a) the IBAN of the payee's payment account or any other identifier which unambiguously identifies, and gives the location of, the payee, or in the absence of such identifiers,
   (b) the BIC or any other business identifier code that unambiguously identifies, and gives the location of, the payment service provider acting on behalf of the payee.][1]

Amendments—[1] Section 2a (arts 243a–243d) inserted by Council Directive 2020/284/EU art 1 with effect from 22 March 2020 (OJ L 62, 2.3.2020, p 7).

[Article 243d

1. The records to be kept by the payment service providers, pursuant to Article 243b, shall contain the following information:
   (a) the BIC or any other business identifier code that unambiguously identifies the payment service provider;

(b) the name or business name of the payee, as it appears in the records of the payment services provider;
(c) if available, any VAT identification number or other national tax number of the payee;
(d) the IBAN or, if the IBAN is not available, any other identifier which unambiguously identifies, and gives the location of, the payee;
(e) the BIC or any other business identifier code that unambiguously identifies, and gives the location of, the payment service provider acting on behalf of the payee where the payee receives funds without having any payment account;
(f) if available, the address of the payee as it appears in the records of the payment services provider;
(g) the details of any cross-border payment as referred to in Article 243b(1);
(h) the details of any payment refunds identified as relating to the cross-border payments referred to in point (g).

2. The information referred to in points (g) and (h) of paragraph 1 shall contain the following details:
(a) the date and time of the payment or of the payment refund;
(b) the amount and the currency of the payment or of the payment refund;
(c) the Member State of origin of the payment received by or on behalf of the payee, the Member State of destination of the refund, as appropriate, and the information used to determine the origin or the destination of the payment or of the payment refund in accordance with Article 243c;
(d) any reference which unambiguously identifies the payment;
(e) where applicable, information that the payment is initiated at the physical premises of the merchant.][1]

Amendments—[1] Section 2a (arts 243a–243d) inserted by Council Directive 2020/284/EU art 1 with effect from 22 March 2020 (OJ L 62, 2.3.2020, p 7).

SECTION 3

Specific obligations relating to the storage of all invoices

Article 244

Every taxable person shall ensure that copies of the invoices issued by himself, or by his customer or, in his name and on his behalf, by a third party, and all the invoices which he has received, are stored.

Article 245

1. For the purposes of this Directive, the taxable person may decide the place of storage of all invoices provided that he makes the invoices or information stored in accordance with Article 244 available to the competent authorities without undue delay whenever they so request.
2. Member States may require taxable persons established in their territory to notify them of the place of storage, if it is outside their territory.
Member States may also require taxable persons established in their territory to store within that territory invoices issued by themselves or by their customers or, in their name and on their behalf, by a third party, as well as all the invoices that they have received, when the storage is not by electronic means guaranteeing full on-line access to the data concerned.

Article 246

The authenticity of the origin and the integrity of the content of the invoices stored, as well as their legibility, must be guaranteed throughout the storage period.

In respect of the invoices referred to in the second subparagraph of Article 233(1), the details they contain may not be altered and must remain legible throughout the storage period.[1]

Amendments—[1] Article 246 repealed by Council Directive 2010/45 art 1(27) with effect from 11 August 2010 (OJ L 189, 22.7.2010, p 1). The deadline for implementation of Directive 2010/45/EU is 31 December 2012.

Article 247

1. Each Member State shall determine the period throughout which taxable persons must ensure the storage of invoices relating to the supply of goods or services in its territory and invoices received by taxable persons established in its territory.
[2. In order to ensure that the requirements laid down in Article 233 are met, the Member State referred to in paragraph 1 may require that invoices be stored in the original form in which they were sent or made available, whether paper or electronic. Additionally, in the case of invoices stored by electronic means, the Member State may require that the data guaranteeing the authenticity of the origin of the invoices and the integrity of their content, as provided for in Article 233, also be stored by electronic means.
3. The Member State referred to in paragraph 1 may lay down specific conditions prohibiting or restricting the storage of invoices in a country with which no legal instrument exists relating to mutual assistance similar in scope to that provided for in Directive 2010/24/EU and Regulation (EC) No 1798/2003 or to the right referred to in Article 249 to access by electronic means, to download and to use.][1]

Amendments—[1] Paras 2, 3 substituted by Council Directive 2010/45 art 1(28) with effect from 11 August 2010 (OJ L 189, 22.7.2010, p 1).

Article 248

Member States may, subject to conditions which they lay down, require the storage of invoices received by non-taxable persons.

[Article 248a

For control purposes, and as regards invoices in respect of supplies of goods or services supplied in their territory and invoices received by taxable persons established in their territory, Member States may, for certain taxable persons or certain cases, require translation into their official languages. Member States may, however, not impose a general requirement that invoices be translated.][1]

Amendments—[1] Article 248a inserted by Council Directive 2010/45 art 1(29) with effect from 11 August 2010 (OJ L 189, 22.7.2010, p 1). The deadline for implementation of Directive 2010/45/EU is 31 December 2012.

SECTION 4
Right of access to invoices stored by electronic means in another Member State

[Article 249

For control purposes, where a taxable person stores, by electronic means guaranteeing online access to the data concerned, invoices which he issues or receives, the competent authorities of the Member State in which he is established and, where the VAT is due in another Member State, the competent authorities of that Member State, shall have the right to access, download and use those invoices.][1]

Amendments—[1] Article 249 substituted by Council Directive 2010/45 art 1(30) with effect from 11 August 2010 (OJ L 189, 22.7.2010, p 1).

CHAPTER 5
RETURNS

Article 250

1. Every taxable person shall submit a VAT return setting out all the information needed to calculate the tax that has become chargeable and the deductions to be made including, in so far as is necessary for the establishment of the basis of assessment, the total value of the transactions relating to such tax and deductions and the value of any exempt transactions.
2. Member States shall allow, and may require, the VAT return referred to in paragraph 1 to be submitted by electronic means, in accordance with conditions which they lay down.

Article 251

In addition to the information referred to in Article 250, the VAT return covering a given tax period shall show the following:
  (*a*) the total value, exclusive of VAT, of the supplies of goods referred to in Article 138 in respect of which VAT has become chargeable during this tax period;
  (*b*) the total value, exclusive of VAT, of the supplies of goods referred to in Articles 33 and 36 carried out within the territory of another Member State, in respect of which VAT has become chargeable during this tax period, where the place where dispatch or transport of the goods began is situated in the Member State in which the return must be submitted;
  (*c*) the total value, exclusive of VAT, of the intra-Community acquisitions of goods, or transactions treated as such, pursuant to Articles 21 or 22, made in the Member State in which the return must be submitted and in respect of which VAT has become chargeable during this tax period;
  (*d*) the total value, exclusive of VAT, of the supplies of goods referred to in Articles 33 and 36 carried out in the Member State in which the return must be submitted and in respect of which VAT has become chargeable during this tax period, where the place where dispatch or transport of the goods began is situated within the territory of another Member State;
  (*e*) the total value, exclusive of VAT, of the supplies of goods carried out in the Member State in which the return must be submitted and in respect of which the taxable person has been designated, in accordance with Article 197, as liable for payment of VAT and in respect of which VAT has become chargeable during this tax period.

Article 252

1. The VAT return shall be submitted by a deadline to be determined by Member States. That deadline may not be more than two months after the end of each tax period.
2. The tax period shall be set by each Member State at one month, two months or three months. Member States may, however, set different tax periods provided that those periods do not exceed one year.

Article 253
Sweden may apply a simplified procedure for small and medium-sized enterprises, whereby taxable persons carrying out only transactions taxable at national level may submit VAT returns three months after the end of the annual direct tax period.

Article 254
In the case of supplies of new means of transport carried out in accordance with the conditions specified in Article 138(2)(*a*) by a taxable person identified for VAT purposes for a customer not identified for VAT purposes, or by a taxable person as defined in Article 9(2), Member States shall take the measures necessary to ensure that the vendor communicates all the information needed for VAT to be applied and its application checked by the tax authorities.

Article 255
Where Member States designate the customer of investment gold as the person liable for payment of VAT pursuant to Article 198 (1) or if, in the case of gold material, semi-manufactured products or investment gold as defined in Article 344(1), they exercise the option provided for in Article 198(2) of designating the customer as the person liable for payment of VAT, they shall take the measures necessary to ensure that he complies with the obligations relating to submission of a VAT return set out in this Chapter.

Article 256
Member States shall take the measures necessary to ensure that persons who are regarded as liable for payment of VAT in the stead of a taxable person not established within their territory, in accordance with Articles 194 to 197 and Article 204, comply with the obligations relating to submission of a VAT return, as laid down in this Chapter.

Article 257
Member States shall take the measures necessary to ensure that non-taxable legal persons who are liable for payment of VAT due in respect of intra-Community acquisitions of goods, as referred to in Article 2(1)(*b*)(i), comply with the obligations relating to submission of a VAT return, as laid down in this Chapter.

Article 258
Member States shall lay down detailed rules for the submission of VAT returns in respect of intra-Community acquisitions of new means of transport, as referred to in Article 2(1)(*b*)(ii), and intra-Community acquisitions of products subject to excise duty, as referred to in Article 2(1)(*b*)(iii).

Article 259
Member States may require persons who make intra-Community acquisitions of new means of transport as referred to in Article 2 (1)(*b*)(ii), to provide, when submitting the VAT return, all the information needed for VAT to be applied and its application checked by the tax authorities.

Article 260
Member States shall lay down detailed rules for the submission of VAT returns in respect of the importation of goods.

Article 261
1. Member States may require the taxable person to submit a return showing all the particulars specified in Articles 250 and 251 in respect of all transactions carried out in the preceding year. That return shall provide all the information necessary for any adjustments.
2. Member States shall allow, and may require, the return referred to in paragraph 1 to be submitted by electronic means, in accordance with conditions which they lay down.

CHAPTER 6
RECAPITULATIVE STATEMENTS

[Article 262
1. Every taxable person identified for VAT purposes shall submit a recapitulative statement of the following:
   - (a) the acquirers identified for VAT purposes to whom he has supplied goods in accordance with the conditions specified in Article 138(1) and point (c) of Article 138(2);
   - (b) the persons identified for VAT purposes to whom he has supplied goods which were supplied to him by way of intra-Community acquisition of goods referred to in Article 42;
   - (c) the taxable persons, and the non-taxable legal persons identified for VAT purposes, to whom he has supplied services other than services that are exempted from VAT in the Member State where the transaction is taxable and for which the recipient is liable to pay the tax pursuant to Article 196.

2. In addition to the information referred to in paragraph 1, every taxable person shall submit information about the VAT identification number of the taxable persons for whom goods, dispatched or transported under call-off stock arrangements in accordance with the conditions set out in Article 17a, are intended and about any change in the submitted information.][1]

Amendments—[1] Article 262 substituted by Council Directive (EU) 2018/1910 Article 1(4) with effect from 27 December 2018 (OJ L 311, 7.12.2018, p 3).

[Article 263

1. The recapitulative statement shall be drawn up for each calendar month within a period not exceeding one month and in accordance with procedures to be determined by the Member States.

1a. However, Member States, in accordance with the conditions and limits which they may lay down, may allow taxable persons to submit the recapitulative statement for each calendar quarter within a time limit not exceeding one month from the end of the quarter, where the total quarterly amount, excluding VAT, of the supplies of goods as referred to in Articles 264(1)(d) and 265(1)(c) does not exceed either in respect of the quarter concerned or in respect of any of the previous four quarters the sum of EUR 50000 or its equivalent in national currency.

The option provided for in the first subparagraph shall cease to be applicable after the end of the month during which the total value, excluding VAT, of the supplies of goods as referred to in Article 264(1)(d) and 265(1)(c) exceeds, in respect of the current quarter, the sum of EUR 50000 or its equivalent in national currency. In this case, a recapitulative statement shall be drawn up for the month(s) which has (have) elapsed since the beginning of the quarter, within a time limit not exceeding one month.

1b. Until 31 December 2011, Member States are allowed to set the sum mentioned in paragraph 1a at EUR 100000 or its equivalent in national currency.

1c. In the case of supplies of services as referred to in Article 264(1)(d), Member States, in accordance with the conditions and limits which they may lay down, may allow taxable persons to submit the recapitulative statement for each calendar quarter within a time limit not exceeding one month from the end of the quarter.

Member States may, in particular, require the taxable persons who carry out supplies of both goods and services as referred to in Article 264(1)(d) to submit the recapitulative statement in accordance with the deadline resulting from paragraphs 1 to 1b.

2. Member States shall allow, and may require, the recapitulative statement referred to in paragraph 1 to be submitted by electronic file transfer, in accordance with conditions which they lay down.][1]

Amendments—[1] Article 263 substituted by Council Directive 2008/117/EC art 1 with effect from 21 January 2009. The deadline for implementation of this Directive is 1 January 2010 (OJ L 14, 20.1.2009 p 7).

Article 264

1. The recapitulative statement shall set out the following information:

[(a) the VAT identification number of the taxable person in the Member State in which the recapitulative statement must be submitted and under which he has carried out the supply of goods in accordance with the conditions specified in Article 138(1) and under which he effected taxable supplies of services in accordance with the conditions laid down in Article 44;

(b) the VAT identification number of the person acquiring the goods or receiving the services in a Member State other than that in which the recapitulative statement must be submitted and under which the goods or services were supplied to him;][1]

(c) the VAT identification number of the taxable person in the Member State in which the recapitulative statement must be submitted and under which he has carried out a transfer to another Member State, as referred to in Article 138(2)(c), and the number by means of which he is identified in the Member State in which the dispatch or transport ended;

[(d) for each person who acquired goods or received services, the total value of the supplies of goods and the total value of the supplies of services carried out by the taxable person;][1]

(e) in respect of supplies of goods consisting in transfers to another Member State, as referred to in Article 138(2)(c), the total value of the supplies, determined in accordance with Article 76;

(f) the amounts of adjustments made pursuant to Article 90.

[2. The value referred to in paragraph 1(d) shall be declared for the period of submission established in accordance with Article 263(1) to (1 c) during which VAT became chargeable.

The amounts referred to in paragraph 1(f) shall be declared for the period of submission established in accordance with Article 263(1) to (1 c) during which the person acquiring the goods was notified of the adjustment.][2]

Amendments—[1] Para 1(a), (b), (d) substituted, by Council Directive 2008/8/EC art 2(10) with effect from 1 January 2010 (OJ L 44, 20.2.2008 p 11).

[2] Para 2 substituted by Council Directive 2008/117/EC art 1 with effect from 21 January 2009. The deadline for implementation of this Directive is 1 January 2010 (OJ L 14, 20.1.2009 p 7).

Article 265
1. In the case of intra-Community acquisitions of goods, as referred to in Article 42, the taxable person identified for VAT purposes in the Member State which issued him with the VAT identification number under which he made such acquisitions shall set the following information out clearly on the recapitulative statement:
   (a) his VAT identification number in that Member State and under which he made the acquisition and subsequent supply of goods;
   (b) the VAT identification number, in the Member State in which dispatch or transport of the goods ended, of the person to whom the subsequent supply was made by the taxable person;
   (c) for each person to whom the subsequent supply was made, the total value, exclusive of VAT, of the supplies made by the taxable person in the Member State in which dispatch or transport of the goods ended.
[2. The value referred to in paragraph 1(c) shall be declared for the period of submission established in accordance with Article 263(1) to (1 b) during which VAT became chargeable.][1]

Amendments—[1] Para 2 substituted by Council Directive 2008/117/EC art 1 with effect from 21 January 2009. The deadline for implementation of this Directive is 1 January 2010 (OJ L 14, 20.1.2009 p 7).

Article 266
By way of derogation from Articles 264 and 265, Member States may provide that additional information is to be given in recapitulative statements.

Article 267
Member States shall take the measures necessary to ensure that those persons who, in accordance with Articles 194 and 204, are regarded as liable for payment of VAT, in the stead of a taxable person who is not established in their territory, comply with the obligation to submit a recapitulative statement as provided for in this Chapter.

Article 268
Member States may require that taxable persons who, in their territory, make intra-Community acquisitions of goods, or transactions treated as such, pursuant to Articles 21 or 22, submit statements giving details of such acquisitions, provided, however, that such statements are not required in respect of a period of less than one month.

Article 269
Acting unanimously on a proposal from the Commission, the Council may authorise any Member State to introduce the special measures provided for in Articles 270 and 271 to simplify the obligation, laid down in this Chapter, to submit a recapitulative statement. Such measures may not jeopardise the proper monitoring of intra-Community transactions.

Article 270
By virtue of the authorisation referred to in Article 269, Member States may permit taxable persons to submit annual recapitulative statements indicating the VAT identification numbers, in another Member State, of the persons to whom those taxable persons have supplied goods in accordance with the conditions specified in Article 138(1) and (2)(c), where the taxable persons meet the following three conditions:
   [(a) the total annual value, exclusive of VAT, of their supplies of goods and services does not exceed by more than EUR 35 000, or the equivalent in national currency, the amount of the annual turnover which is used as a reference for taxable persons covered by the exemption for small enterprises provided for in Article 284;][1]
   (b) the total annual value, exclusive of VAT, of supplies of goods carried out by them in accordance with the conditions specified in Article 138 does not exceed EUR 15 000 or the equivalent in national currency;
   (c) none of the supplies of goods carried out by them in accordance with the conditions specified in Article 138 is a supply of new means of transport.

Amendments—[1] Point (a) substituted by Council Directive 2020/285/EU art 1(6) with effect from 22 March 2020 (OJ L 62, 2.3.2020, p 13).

Article 271
By virtue of the authorisation referred to in Article 269, Member States which set at over three months the tax period in respect of which taxable persons must submit the VAT return provided for in Article 250 may permit such persons to submit recapitulative statements in respect of the same period where those taxable persons meet the following three conditions:
   (a) the total annual value, exclusive of VAT, of their supplies of goods and services does not exceed EUR 200 000 or the equivalent in national currency;
   (b) the total annual value, exclusive of VAT, of supplies of goods carried out by them in accordance with the conditions specified in Article 138 does not exceed EUR 15 000 or the equivalent in national currency;

(c) none of the supplies of goods carried out by them in accordance with the conditions specified in Article 138 is a supply of new means of transport.

CHAPTER 7
MISCELLANEOUS PROVISIONS

Article 272

1. Member States may release the following taxable persons from certain or all obligations referred to in Chapters 2 to 6:
   (a) taxable persons whose intra-Community acquisitions of goods are not subject to VAT pursuant to Article 3(1);
   [(b) taxable persons carrying out none of the transactions referred to in Articles 20, 21, 22, 33, 36, 136a, 138 and 141;][2]
   (c) taxable persons carrying out only supplies of goods or of services which are exempt pursuant to Articles 132, 135 and 136, Articles 146 to 149 and Articles 151, 152 or 153;
   (d) . . .[3]
   (e) taxable persons covered by the common flat-rate scheme for farmers.
   [Member States may not release the taxable persons referred to in point (b) of the first subparagraph from the invoicing obligations laid down in Sections 3 to 6 of Chapter 3 and Section 3 of Chapter 4.][1]
2. If Member States exercise the option under point (e) of the first subparagraph of paragraph 1, they shall take the measures necessary to ensure the correct application of the transitional arrangements for the taxation of intra-Community transactions.
3. Member States may release taxable persons other than those referred to in paragraph 1 from certain of the accounting obligations referred to in Article 242.

Amendments—[1] In para 1, second sub-para substituted by Council Directive 2010/45 art 1(31) with effect from 11 August 2010 (OJ L 189, 22.7.2010, p 1).
[2] In para 1, point (b) substituted by Council Directive 2019/1995/EU art 1(6) with effect from 22 December 2019 (OJ L 310, 2.12.2019, p 1).
[3] Point 1(d) repealed by Council Directive 2020/285/EU art 1(7) with effect from 22 March 2020 (OJ L 62, 2.3.2020, p 13).

Article 273

Member States may impose other obligations which they deem necessary to ensure the correct collection of VAT and to prevent evasion, subject to the requirement of equal treatment as between domestic transactions and transactions carried out between Member States by taxable persons and provided that such obligations do not, in trade between Member States, give rise to formalities connected with the crossing of frontiers.

The option under the first paragraph may not be relied upon in order to impose additional invoicing obligations over and above those laid down in Chapter 3.

CHAPTER 8

OBLIGATIONS RELATING TO CERTAIN IMPORTATIONS AND EXPORTATIONS

SECTION 1

Importation

Article 274

Articles 275, 276 and 277 shall apply to the importation of goods in free circulation which enter the Community from a third territory forming part of the customs territory of the Community.

Article 275

The formalities relating to the importation of the goods referred to in Article 274 shall be the same as those laid down by the Community customs provisions in force for the importation of goods into the customs territory of the Community.

Article 276

Where dispatch or transport of the goods referred to in Article 274 ends at a place situated outside the Member State of their entry into the Community, they shall circulate in the Community under the internal Community transit procedure laid down by the Community customs provisions in force, in so far as they have been the subject of a declaration placing them under that procedure on their entry into the Community.

Article 277

Where, on their entry into the Community, the goods referred to in Article 274 are in one of the situations which would entitle them, if they were imported within the meaning of the first paragraph of Article 30, to be covered by one of the arrangements or situations referred to in Article 156, or by a temporary importation arrangement with full exemption from import duties, Member States shall take the measures necessary to ensure that the goods may remain in the Community under the same conditions as those laid down for the application of those arrangements or situations.

SECTION 2
Exportation

Article 278
Articles 279 and 280 shall apply to the exportation of goods in free circulation which are dispatched or transported from a Member State to a third territory forming part of the customs territory of the Community.

Article 279
The formalities relating to the exportation of the goods referred to in Article 278 from the territory of the Community shall be the same as those laid down by the Community customs provisions in force for the exportation of goods from the customs territory of the Community.

Article 280
In the case of goods which are temporarily exported from the Community, in order to be reimported, Member States shall take the measures necessary to ensure that, on reimportation into the Community, such goods may be covered by the same provisions as would have applied if they had been temporarily exported from the customs territory of the Community.

TITLE XII
SPECIAL SCHEMES

CHAPTER 1
SPECIAL SCHEME FOR SMALL ENTERPRISES

[SECTION -1
Definitions

Article 280a
For the purposes of this Chapter, the following definitions apply:
(1) "Member State annual turnover" means the total annual value of supplies of goods and services, exclusive of VAT, made by a taxable person within that Member State during a calendar year;
(2) "Union annual turnover" means the total annual value of supplies of goods and services, exclusive of VAT, made by a taxable person within the territory of the Community during a calendar year.][1]

Amendments—[1] Section -1 inserted by Council Directive 2020/285/EU art 1(8) with effect from 22 March 2020 (OJ L 62, 2.3.2020, p 13).

SECTION 1
Simplified procedures for charging and collection

Article 281
Member States which might encounter difficulties in applying the normal VAT arrangements to small enterprises, by reason of the activities or structure of such enterprises, may, subject to such conditions and limits as they may set, and after consulting the VAT Committee, apply simplified procedures, such as flat-rate schemes, for charging and collecting VAT provided that they do not lead to a reduction thereof.

SECTION 2
[Exemptions]

[Article 282
The exemptions provided for in this Section shall apply to the supply of goods and services by small enterprises.][1]

Amendments—[1] Section heading and art 282 substituted by Council Directive 2020/285/EU art 1(9), (10) with effect from 22 March 2020 (OJ L 62, 2.3.2020, p 13).

Article 283
1. The arrangements provided for in this Section shall not apply to the following transactions:
   (*a*) transactions carried out on an occasional basis, as referred to in Article 12;
   (*b*) supplies of new means of transport carried out in accordance with the conditions specified in Article 138(1) and (2)(*a*);
   (*c*) . . .[1]
2. Member States may exclude transactions other than those referred to in paragraph 1 from the arrangements provided for in this Section.

Amendments—[1] Point 1(c) repealed by Council Directive 2020/285/EU art 1(11) with effect from 22 March 2020 (OJ L 62, 2.3.2020, p 13).

[Article 284

1. Member States may exempt the supply of goods and services made within their territory by taxable persons who are established in that territory and whose Member State annual turnover, attributable to such supplies, does not exceed the threshold fixed by those Member States for the application of this exemption. That threshold shall be no higher than EUR 85 000 or the equivalent in national currency.
Member States may fix varying thresholds for different business sectors based on objective criteria. However, none of those thresholds shall exceed the threshold of EUR 85 000 or the equivalent in national currency.
Member States shall ensure that a taxable person eligible to benefit from more than one sectoral threshold can only use one of those thresholds.
Thresholds set by a Member State shall not differentiate between taxable persons who are established and those who are not established in that Member State.
2. Member States that have put in place the exemption under paragraph 1 shall also grant that exemption to the supplies of goods and services in their own territory made by taxable persons established in another Member State, provided that the following conditions are fulfilled:
    (a) the Union annual turnover of that taxable person does not exceed EUR 100 000; (b) the value of the supplies in the Member State where the taxable person is not established does not exceed the threshold applicable in that Member State for granting the exemption to taxable persons established in that Member State.
3. Notwithstanding Article 292b, in order for a taxable person to avail itself of the exemption in a Member State in which that taxable person is not established, the taxable person shall:
    (a) give prior notification to the Member State of establishment; and
    (b) be identified for the application of the exemption by an individual number in the Member State of establishment only.
Member States may use the individual VAT identification number already allocated to the taxable person in respect of that person's obligations under the internal system or apply the structure of a VAT number or any other number for the purpose of the identification referred to in point (b) of the first subparagraph.
The individual identification number referred to in point (b) of the first subparagraph shall have the suffix "EX", or the suffix "EX" shall be added to that number.
4. The taxable person shall inform the Member State of establishment in advance, by means of an update to a prior notification, of any changes to the information previously provided in accordance with the first subparagraph of paragraph 3, including the intention to avail itself of the exemption in a Member State or Member States other than the ones indicated in the prior notification and the decision to cease applying the exemption scheme in a Member State or Member States in which that taxable person is not established.
The cessation shall be effective as of the first day of the next calendar quarter following the receipt of the information from the taxable person or, where such information is received during the last month of a calendar quarter, as of the first day of the second month of the next calendar quarter.
5. The exemption shall apply as regards the Member State in which the taxable person is not established and where that taxable person intends to avail itself of the exemption according to:
    (a) a prior notification, from the date of informing the taxable person of the individual identification number by the Member State of establishment; or
    (b) an update to a prior notification, from the date of confirming the number to the taxable person in consequence of his update by the Member State of establishment.
The date referred to in the first subparagraph shall be no later than 35 working days following the receipt of the prior notification or the update to the prior notification referred to in the first subparagraph of paragraph 3 and in the first subparagraph of paragraph 4, except in specific cases where in order to prevent tax evasion or avoidance Member States may require additional time to carry out the necessary checks.
6. The corresponding value in national currency of the amount referred to in this Article shall be calculated by applying the exchange rate published by the European Central Bank on 18 January 2018.][1]

Amendments—[1] Art 284 substituted by Council Directive 2020/285/EU art 1(12) with effect from 22 March 2020 (OJ L 62, 2.3.2020, p 13).

[Article 284a

1. The prior notification referred to in point (a) of the first subparagraph of Article 284(3) shall contain at least the following information:
    (a) the name, activity, legal form and address of the taxable person;
    (b) the Member State or Member States in which the taxable person intends to avail itself of the exemption;
    (c) the total value of supplies of goods and/or services carried out in the Member State in which the taxable person is established and in each of the other Member States during the previous calendar year;

(d) the total value of supplies of goods and/or services carried out in the Member State in which the taxable person is established and in each of the other Member States during the current calendar year prior to the notification.

The information referred to in point (c) of the first subparagraph of this paragraph has to be given for each previous calendar year belonging to the period referred to in the first subparagraph of Article 288a(1) as regards any Member State which applies the option stipulated therein.

2. Where the taxable person informs the Member State of establishment in accordance with Article 284(4) that it intends to avail itself of the exemption in a Member State or Member States other than the ones indicated in the prior notification, that person is not obliged to give the information referred to in paragraph 1 of this Article in so far as that information has already been included in reports previously submitted under Article 284b.

The update to a prior notification referred to in the first subparagraph shall include the individual identification number referred to in point (b) of Article 284(3).][1]

Amendments—[1] Arts 284a–284e inserted by Council Directive 2020/285/EU art 1(13) with effect from 22 March 2020 (OJ L 62, 2.3.2020, p 13).

[Article 284b
1. A taxable person availing itself of the exemption provided for in Article 284(1) in a Member State in which that person is not established in accordance with the procedure under Article 284(3) and (4) shall report for each calendar quarter to the Member State of establishment the following information, including the individual identification number referred to in point (b) of Article 284(3):
    (a) the total value of supplies carried out during the calendar quarter in the Member State of establishment or "0" if no supplies have been made;
    (b) the total value of supplies carried out during the calendar quarter in each of the Member States other than the Member State of establishment or "0" if no supplies have been made.
2. The taxable person shall communicate the information set out in paragraph 1 within one month from the end of the calendar quarter.
3. When the Union annual turnover threshold referred to in point (a) of Article 284(2) is exceeded, the taxable person shall inform the Member State of establishment within 15 working days. At the same time, the taxable person shall be required to report the value of the supplies referred to in paragraph 1 that have been made from the beginning of the current calendar quarter up until the date the Union annual turnover threshold was exceeded.][1]

Amendments—[1] Arts 284a–284e inserted by Council Directive 2020/285/EU art 1(13) with effect from 22 March 2020 (OJ L 62, 2.3.2020, p 13).

[Article 284c
1. For the purposes of points (c) and (d) of Article 284a(1) and Article 284b(1) the following shall apply:
    (a) the values shall consist of the amounts listed in Article 288;
    (b) the values shall be denominated in euro;
    (c) where the Member State granting the exemption applies varying thresholds as referred to in the second subparagraph of Article 284(1), the taxable person shall be obliged in respect of that Member State to report separately the total value of supplies of goods and/or services as regards each threshold that may be applicable.

For the purposes of point (b) of the first subparagraph, Member States which have not adopted the euro may require the values to be expressed in their national currencies. If the supplies have been made in other currencies, the taxable person shall use the exchange rate applying on the first day of the calendar year. The conversion shall be made by applying the exchange rate published by the European Central Bank for that day, or, if there is no publication on that day, on the next day of publication.

2. The Member State of establishment may require the information referred to in Article 284(3) and (4) and in Article 284b(1) and (3) to be submitted by electronic means, in accordance with conditions laid down by that Member State.][1]

Amendments—[1] Arts 284a–284e inserted by Council Directive 2020/285/EU art 1(13) with effect from 22 March 2020 (OJ L 62, 2.3.2020, p 13).

[Article 284d
1. A taxable person availing itself of the exemption in a Member State in which that taxable person is not established shall not be required in respect of the supplies covered by the exemption in that Member State:
    (a) to be registered for VAT purposes pursuant to Articles 213 and 214;
    (b) to submit a VAT return pursuant to Article 250.
2. A taxable person availing itself of the exemption in the Member State of establishment and in any Member State in which that taxable person is not established shall not be required, in respect of the supplies covered by the exemption in the Member State of establishment, to submit a VAT return pursuant to Article 250.

3. By derogation from paragraphs 1 and 2 of this Article, where a taxable person fails to comply with the rules provided for in Article 284b, Member States may require such a taxable person to fulfil VAT obligations such as those referred to in paragraph 1 of this Article.][1]

Amendments—[1] Arts 284a–284e inserted by Council Directive 2020/285/EU art 1(13) with effect from 22 March 2020 (OJ L 62, 2.3.2020, p 13).

[Article 284e

The Member State of establishment shall, without delay, either deactivate the identification number referred to in point (b) of Article 284(3) or, if the taxable person continues to avail itself of the exemption in another Member State or other Member States, adapt the information received pursuant to Article 284(3) and (4) as regards the Member State or Member States concerned, in the following cases:
- (a) the total value of supplies reported by the taxable person exceeds the amount referred to in point (a) of Article 284(2);
- (b) the Member State granting the exemption has notified that the taxable person is not eligible for the exemption or the exemption has ceased to apply in that Member State;
- (c) the taxable person has informed of its decision to cease to apply the exemption; or
- (d) the taxable person has informed, or it may otherwise be assumed, that his activities have ceased.][1]

Amendments—[1] Arts 284a–284e inserted by Council Directive 2020/285/EU art 1(13) with effect from 22 March 2020 (OJ L 62, 2.3.2020, p 13).

Articles 285, 286, 287

Amendments—[1] Arts 285–287 repealed by Council Directive 2020/285/EU art 1(14) with effect from 22 March 2020 (OJ L 62, 2.3.2020, p 13).

[Article 288

1. The annual turnover serving as a reference for applying the exemption provided for in Article 284 shall consist of the following amounts, exclusive of VAT:
   - (a) the value of supplies of goods and services, in so far as they would be taxed were they supplied by a non-exempt taxable person;
   - (b) the value of transactions which are exempt, with deductibility of the VAT paid at the preceding stage, pursuant to Article 110 or 111 or Article 125(1);
   - (c) the value of transactions which are exempt pursuant to Articles 146 to 149 and Articles 151, 152 and 153;
   - (d) the value of transactions which are exempt pursuant to Article 138 where the exemption provided for in that Article applies;
   - (e) the value of real estate transactions, financial transactions as referred to in points (b) to (g) of Article 135(1), and insurance and reinsurance services, unless those transactions are ancillary transactions.
2. Disposals of the tangible or intangible capital assets of a taxable person shall not be taken into account for the purposes of calculating the turnover referred to in paragraph 1.][1]

Amendments—[1] Art 288 substituted by Council Directive 2020/285/EU art 1(15) with effect from 22 March 2020 (OJ L 62, 2.3.2020, p 13).

[Article 288a

1. A taxable person, whether or not established in the Member State granting the exemption provided for in Article 284(1), shall not be able to benefit from that exemption during a period of one calendar year where the threshold laid down in accordance with that paragraph was exceeded in the preceding calendar year. The Member State granting the exemption may extend this period to two calendar years.

Where, during a calendar year, the threshold referred to in Article 284(1) is exceeded by:
- (a) not more than 10 %, a taxable person shall be able to continue to benefit from the exemption provided for in Article 284(1) during that calendar year;
- (b) more than 10 %, the exemption provided for in Article 284(1) shall cease to apply as of that time.

Notwithstanding points (a) and (b) of the second subparagraph, Member States may set a ceiling of 25 % or allow the taxable person to continue to benefit from the exemption provided for in Article 284(1) without any ceiling during the calendar year when the threshold is exceeded. However, the application of this ceiling or option may not result in exempting a taxable person whose turnover within the Member State granting the exemption exceeds EUR 100 000.

By derogation from the second and third subparagraphs, Member States may determine that the exemption provided for in Article 284(1) shall cease to apply as of the time when the threshold laid down in accordance with that paragraph is exceeded.

2. A taxable person not established in the Member State granting the exemption provided for in Article 284(1) shall not be able to benefit from that exemption, where the Union annual turnover threshold referred to in point (a) of Article 284(2) was exceeded in the preceding calendar year.

Where, during a calendar year, the Union annual turnover threshold referred to in point (a) of Article 284(2) is exceeded, the exemption provided for in Article 284(1) granted to a taxable person not established in the Member State granting that exemption shall cease to apply as of that time.
3. The corresponding value in national currency of the amount referred to in paragraph 1 shall be calculated by applying the exchange rate published by the European Central Bank on 18 January 2018.]¹

Amendments—¹ Art 288a inserted by Council Directive 2020/285/EU art 1(16) with effect from 22 March 2020 (OJ L 62, 2.3.2020, p 13).

Article 289

Taxable persons exempt from VAT shall not be entitled to deduct VAT in accordance with Articles 167 to 171 and Articles 173 to 177, and may not show the VAT on their invoices.

Article 290

Taxable persons who are entitled to exemption from VAT may opt either for the normal VAT arrangements or for the simplified procedures provided for in Article 281. [Member States may lay down the detailed rules and conditions for applying that option.]¹

Amendments—¹ Words substituted by Council Directive 2020/285/EU art 1(17) with effect from 22 March 2020 (OJ L 62, 2.3.2020, p 13).

Articles 291, 292

Amendments—Arts 291, 292 repealed, by Council Directive 2020/285/EU art 1(18) with effect from 22 March 2020 (OJ L 62, 2.3.2020, p 13).

[SECTION 2A

Simplification of obligations for exempt small enterprises

Article 292a

For the purposes of this Section, "exempt small enterprise" means any taxable person benefitting from the exemption in the Member State in which the VAT is due as provided for in Article 284(1) and (2).]¹

Amendments—¹ Section 2a (arts 292a–292d) inserted by Council Directive 2020/285/EU art 1(19) with effect from 22 March 2020 (OJ L 62, 2.3.2020, p 13).

[Article 292b

Without prejudice to Article 284(3), Member States may release exempt small enterprises established in their territory, that avail themselves of the exemption only within that territory, from the obligation to state the beginning of their activity pursuant to Article 213 and to be identified by means of an individual number pursuant to Article 214, except where those enterprises carry out transactions covered by point (b), (d) or (e) of Article 214.
Where the option referred to in the first paragraph is not exercised, Member States shall put in place a procedure for the identification of such exempt small enterprises by means of an individual number. The identification procedure shall not take longer than 15 working days except in specific cases where in order to prevent tax evasion or avoidance Member States may require additional time to carry out the necessary checks.]¹

Amendments—¹ Section 2a (arts 292a–292d) inserted by Council Directive 2020/285/EU art 1(19) with effect from 22 March 2020 (OJ L 62, 2.3.2020, p 13).

[Article 292c

Member States may release exempt small enterprises established in their territory that avail themselves of the exemption only within that territory from the obligation to submit a VAT return laid down in Article 250.
Where the option referred to in the first paragraph is not exercised, Member States shall allow such exempt small enterprises to submit a simplified VAT return to cover the period of a calendar year. However, exempt small enterprises may opt for the application of the tax period set in accordance with Article 252.]¹

Amendments—¹ Section 2a (arts 292a–292d) inserted by Council Directive 2020/285/EU art 1(19) with effect from 22 March 2020 (OJ L 62, 2.3.2020, p 13).

[Article 292d

Member States may release exempt small enterprises from certain or all obligations referred to in Articles 217 to 271.]¹

Amendments—¹ Section 2a (arts 292a–292d) inserted by Council Directive 2020/285/EU art 1(19) with effect from 22 March 2020 (OJ L 62, 2.3.2020, p 13).

SECTION 3

Reporting and review

Amendments—Section 3 (arts 293, 294) repealed by Council Directive 2020/285/EU art 1(20) with effect from 22 March 2020 (OJ L 62, 2.3.2020, p 13).

CHAPTER 2
COMMON FLAT-RATE SCHEME FOR FARMERS

Article 295
1. For the purposes of this Chapter, the following definitions shall apply:
   (1) 'farmer' means any taxable person whose activity is carried out in an agricultural, forestry or fisheries undertaking;
   (2) 'agricultural, forestry or fisheries undertaking' means an undertaking regarded as such by each Member State within the framework of the production activities listed in Annex VII;
   (3) 'flat-rate farmer' means any farmer covered by the flat-rate scheme provided for in this Chapter;
   (4) 'agricultural products' means goods produced by an agricultural, forestry or fisheries undertaking in each Member State as a result of the activities listed in Annex VII;
   (5) 'agricultural services' means services, and in particular those listed in Annex VIII, supplied by a farmer using his labour force or the equipment normally employed in the agricultural, forestry or fisheries undertaking operated by him and normally playing a part in agricultural production;
   (6) 'input VAT charged' means the amount of the total VAT attaching to the goods and services purchased by all agricultural, forestry and fisheries undertakings of each Member State subject to the flat-rate scheme where such tax would be deductible in accordance with Articles 167, 168 and 169 and Articles 173 to 177 by a farmer subject to the normal VAT arrangements;
   (7) 'flat-rate compensation percentages' means the percentages fixed by Member States in accordance with Articles 297, 298 and 299 and applied by them in the cases specified in Article 300 in order to enable flat-rate farmers to offset at a fixed rate the input VAT charged;
   (8) 'flat-rate compensation' means the amount arrived at by applying the flat-rate compensation percentage to the turnover of the flat-rate farmer in the cases specified in Article 300.
2. Where a farmer processes, using means normally employed in an agricultural, forestry or fisheries undertaking, products deriving essentially from his agricultural production, such processing activities shall be treated as agricultural production activities, as listed in Annex VII.

Article 296
1. Where the application to farmers of the normal VAT arrangements, or the special scheme provided for in Chapter 1, is likely to give rise to difficulties, Member States may apply to farmers, in accordance with this Chapter, a flat-rate scheme designed to offset the VAT charged on purchases of goods and services made by the flat-rate farmers.
2. Each Member State may exclude from the flat-rate scheme certain categories of farmers, as well as farmers for whom application of the normal VAT arrangements, or of the simplified procedures provided for in Article 281, is not likely to give rise to administrative difficulties.
3. Every flat-rate farmer may opt, subject to the rules and conditions to be laid down by each Member State, for application of the normal VAT arrangements or, as the case may be, the simplified procedures provided for in Article 281.

Article 297
Member States shall, where necessary, fix the flat-rate compensation percentages. They may fix varying percentages for forestry, for the different sub-divisions of agriculture and for fisheries.

Member States shall notify the Commission of the flat-rate compensation percentages fixed in accordance with the first paragraph before applying them.

Article 298
The flat-rate compensation percentages shall be calculated on the basis of macro-economic statistics for flat-rate farmers alone for the preceding three years.

The percentages may be rounded up or down to the nearest half-point. Member States may also reduce such percentages to a nil rate.

Article 299
The flat-rate compensation percentages may not have the effect of obtaining for flat-rate farmers refunds greater than the input VAT charged.

Article 300
The flat-rate compensation percentages shall be applied to the prices, exclusive of VAT, of the following goods and services:
   (1) agricultural products supplied by flat-rate farmers to taxable persons other than those covered, in the Member State in which these products were supplied, by this flat-rate scheme;
   (2) agricultural products supplied by flat-rate farmers, in accordance with the conditions specified in Article 138, to non-taxable legal persons whose intra-Community acquisitions of goods are subject to VAT, pursuant to Article 2(1)(b), in the Member State in which dispatch or transport of those agricultural products ends;

(3) agricultural services supplied by flat-rate farmers to taxable persons other than those covered, in the Member State in which these services were supplied, by this flat-rate scheme.

Article 301
1. In the case of the supply of agricultural products or agricultural services specified in Article 300, Member States shall provide that the flat-rate compensation is to be paid either by the customer or by the public authorities.
2. In respect of any supply of agricultural products or agricultural services other than those specified in Article 300, the flat-rate compensation shall be deemed to be paid by the customer.

Article 302
If a flat-rate farmer is entitled to flat-rate compensation, he shall not be entitled to deduction of VAT in respect of activities covered by this flat-rate scheme.

Article 303
1. Where the taxable customer pays flat-rate compensation pursuant to Article 301(1), he shall be entitled, in accordance with the conditions laid down in Articles 167, 168 and 169 and Articles 173 to 177 and the procedures laid down by the Member States, to deduct the compensation amount from the VAT for which he is liable in the Member State in which his taxed transactions are carried out.
2. Member States shall refund to the customer the amount of the flat-rate compensation he has paid in respect of any of the following transactions:
   (a) the supply of agricultural products, carried out in accordance with the conditions specified in Article 138, to taxable persons, or to non-taxable legal persons, acting as such in another Member State within the territory of which their intra-Community acquisitions of goods are subject to VAT pursuant to Article 2(1)(b);
   (b) the supply of agricultural products, carried out in accordance with the conditions specified in Articles 146, 147, 148 and 156, Article 157(1)(b) and Articles 158, 160 and 161, to a taxable customer established outside the Community, in so far as the products are used by that customer for the purposes of the transactions referred to in Article 169(a) and (b) or for the purposes of supplies of services which are deemed to take place within the territory of the Member State in which the customer is established and in respect of which VAT is payable solely by the customer pursuant to Article 196;
   (c) the supply of agricultural services to a taxable customer established within the Community but in another Member State or to a taxable customer established outside the Community, in so far as the services are used by the customer for the purposes of the transactions referred to in Article 169(a) and (b) or for the purposes of supplies of services which are deemed to take place within the territory of the Member State in which the customer is established and in respect of which VAT is payable solely by the customer pursuant to Article 196.
3. Member States shall determine the method by which the refunds provided for in paragraph 2 are to be made. In particular, they may apply the provisions of Directives 79/1072/EEC and 86/560/EEC.

Article 304
Member States shall take all measures necessary to verify payments of flat-rate compensation to flat-rate farmers.

Article 305
Whenever Member States apply this flat-rate scheme, they shall take all measures necessary to ensure that the supply of agricultural products between Member States, carried out in accordance with the conditions specified in Article 33, is always taxed in the same way, whether the supply is effected by a flat-rate farmer or by another taxable person.

CHAPTER 3
SPECIAL SCHEME FOR TRAVEL AGENTS

Article 306
1. Member States shall apply a special VAT scheme, in accordance with this Chapter, to transactions carried out by travel agents who deal with customers in their own name and use supplies of goods or services provided by other taxable persons, in the provision of travel facilities. This special scheme shall not apply to travel agents where they act solely as intermediaries and to whom point (c) of the first paragraph of Article 79 applies for the purposes of calculating the taxable amount.
2. For the purposes of this Chapter, tour operators shall be regarded as travel agents.

Article 307
Transactions made, in accordance with the conditions laid down in Article 306, by the travel agent in respect of a journey shall be regarded as a single service supplied by the travel agent to the traveller.

The single service shall be taxable in the Member State in which the travel agent has established his business or has a fixed establishment from which the travel agent has carried out the supply of services.

Article 308
The taxable amount and the price exclusive of VAT, within the meaning of point (8) of Article 226, in respect of the single service provided by the travel agent shall be the travel agent's margin, that is to say, the difference between the total amount, exclusive of VAT, to be paid by the traveller and the actual cost to the travel agent of supplies of goods or services provided by other taxable persons, where those transactions are for the direct benefit of the traveller.

Article 309
If transactions entrusted by the travel agent to other taxable persons are performed by such persons outside the Community, the supply of services carried out by the travel agent shall be treated as an intermediary activity exempted pursuant to Article 153.

If the transactions are performed both inside and outside the Community, only that part of the travel agent's service relating to transactions outside the Community may be exempted.

Article 310
VAT charged to the travel agent by other taxable persons in respect of transactions which are referred to in Article 307 and which are for the direct benefit of the traveller shall not be deductible or refundable in any Member State.

CHAPTER 4
SPECIAL ARRANGEMENTS FOR SECOND-HAND GOODS, WORKS OF ART, COLLECTORS' ITEMS AND ANTIQUES

SECTION 1
Definitions

Article 311
1. For the purposes of this Chapter, and without prejudice to other Community provisions, the following definitions shall apply:
    (1) 'second-hand goods' means movable tangible property that is suitable for further use as it is or after repair, other than works of art, collectors' items or antiques and other than precious metals or precious stones as defined by the Member States;
    (2) 'works of art' means the objects listed in Annex IX, Part A;
    (3) 'collectors' items' means the objects listed in Annex IX, Part B;
    (4) 'antiques' means the objects listed in Annex IX, Part C;
    (5) 'taxable dealer' means any taxable person who, in the course of his economic activity and with a view to resale, purchases, or applies for the purposes of his business, or imports, second-hand goods, works of art, collectors' items or antiques, whether that taxable person is acting for himself or on behalf of another person pursuant to a contract under which commission is payable on purchase or sale;
    (6) 'organiser of a sale by public auction' means any taxable person who, in the course of his economic activity, offers goods for sale by public auction with a view to handing them over to the highest bidder;
    (7) 'principal of an organiser of a sale by public auction' means any person who transmits goods to an organiser of a sale by public auction pursuant to a contract under which commission is payable on a sale.
2. Member States need not regard as works of art the objects listed in points (5), (6) or (7) of Annex IX, Part A.
3. The contract under which commission is payable on a sale, referred to in point (7) of paragraph 1, must provide that the organiser of the sale is to put up the goods for public auction in his own name but on behalf of his principal and that he is to hand over the goods, in his own name but on behalf of his principal, to the highest bidder at the public auction.

Commentary—*De Voil Indirect Tax Service* V3.532.

SECTION 2
Special arrangements for taxable dealers

SUBSECTION 1
Margin scheme

Article 312
For the purposes of this Subsection, the following definitions shall apply:
    (1) 'selling price' means everything which constitutes the consideration obtained or to be obtained by the taxable dealer from the customer or from a third party, including subsidies directly linked to the transaction, taxes, duties, levies and charges and incidental expenses such as commission, packaging, transport and insurance costs charged by the taxable dealer to the customer, but excluding the amounts referred to in Article 79;

(2) 'purchase price' means everything which constitutes the consideration, for the purposes of point (1), obtained or to be obtained from the taxable dealer by his supplier.

Article 313
1. In respect of the supply of second-hand goods, works of art, collectors' items or antiques carried out by taxable dealers, Member States shall apply a special scheme for taxing the profit margin made by the taxable dealer, in accordance with the provisions of this Subsection.
2. Pending introduction of the definitive arrangements referred to in Article 402, the scheme referred to in paragraph 1 of this Article shall not apply to the supply of new means of transport, carried out in accordance with the conditions specified in Article 138(1) and (2)(*a*).

Article 314
The margin scheme shall apply to the supply by a taxable dealer of second-hand goods, works of art, collectors' items or antiques where those goods have been supplied to him within the Community by one of the following persons:
- (*a*) a non-taxable person;
- (*b*) another taxable person, in so far as the supply of goods by that other taxable person is exempt pursuant to Article 136;
- [(*c*) another taxable person, in so far as the supply of goods by that other taxable person is covered by the exemption for small enterprises provided for in Article 284 and involves capital goods;][1]
- (*d*) another taxable dealer, in so far as VAT has been applied to the supply of goods by that other taxable dealer in accordance with this margin scheme.

Amendments—[1] Point (c) substituted by Council Directive 2020/285/EU art 1(21) with effect from 22 March 2020 (OJ L 62, 2.3.2020, p 13).

Article 315
The taxable amount in respect of the supply of goods as referred to in Article 314 shall be the profit margin made by the taxable dealer, less the amount of VAT relating to the profit margin.

The profit margin of the taxable dealer shall be equal to the difference between the selling price charged by the taxable dealer for the goods and the purchase price.

Article 316
1. Member States shall grant taxable dealers the right to opt for application of the margin scheme to the following transactions:
- (*a*) the supply of works of art, collectors' items or antiques, which the taxable dealer has imported himself;
- (*b*) the supply of works of art supplied to the taxable dealer by their creators or their successors in title;
- (*c*) the supply of works of art supplied to the taxable dealer by a taxable person other than a taxable dealer where the reduced rate has been applied to that supply pursuant to Article 103.

2. Member States shall lay down the detailed rules for exercise of the option provided for in paragraph 1, which shall in any event cover a period of at least two calendar years.

Article 317
If a taxable dealer exercises the option under Article 316, the taxable amount shall be determined in accordance with Article 315.

In respect of the supply of works of art, collectors' items or antiques which the taxable dealer has imported himself, the purchase price to be taken into account in calculating the profit margin shall be equal to the taxable amount on importation, determined in accordance with Articles 85 to 89, plus the VAT due or paid on importation.

Article 318
1. In order to simplify the procedure for collecting the tax and after consulting the VAT Committee, Member States may provide that, for certain transactions or for certain categories of taxable dealers, the taxable amount in respect of supplies of goods subject to the margin scheme is to be determined for each tax period during which the taxable dealer must submit the VAT return referred to in Article 250.

In the event that such provision is made in accordance with the first subparagraph, the taxable amount in respect of supplies of goods to which the same rate of VAT is applied shall be the total profit margin made by the taxable dealer less the amount of VAT relating to that margin.

2. The total profit margin shall be equal to the difference between the following two amounts:
- (*a*) the total value of supplies of goods subject to the margin scheme and carried out by the taxable dealer during the tax period covered by the return, that is to say, the total of the selling prices;

(b) the total value of purchases of goods, as referred to in Article 314, effected by the taxable dealer during the tax period covered by the return, that is to say, the total of the purchase prices.

3. Member States shall take the measures necessary to ensure that the taxable dealers referred to in paragraph 1 do not enjoy unjustified advantage or sustain unjustified harm.

Article 319

The taxable dealer may apply the normal VAT arrangements to any supply covered by the margin scheme.

Article 320

1. Where the taxable dealer applies the normal VAT arrangements to the supply of a work of art, a collectors' item or an antique which he has imported himself, he shall be entitled to deduct from the VAT for which he is liable the VAT due or paid on the import.

Where the taxable dealer applies the normal VAT arrangements to the supply of a work of art supplied to him by its creator, or the creator's successors in title, or by a taxable person other than a taxable dealer, he shall be entitled to deduct from the VAT for which he is liable the VAT due or paid in respect of the work of art supplied to him.

2. A right of deduction shall arise at the time when the VAT due on the supply in respect of which the taxable dealer opts for application of the normal VAT arrangements becomes chargeable.

Article 321

If carried out in accordance with the conditions specified in Articles 146, 147, 148 or 151, the supply of second-hand goods, works of art, collectors' items or antiques subject to the margin scheme shall be exempt.

Article 322

In so far as goods are used for the purpose of supplies carried out by him and subject to the margin scheme, the taxable dealer may not deduct the following from the VAT for which he is liable:
  (a) the VAT due or paid in respect of works of art, collectors' items or antiques which he has imported himself;
  (b) the VAT due or paid in respect of works of art which have been, or are to be, supplied to him by their creator or by the creator's successors in title;
  (c) the VAT due or paid in respect of works of art which have been, or are to be, supplied to him by a taxable person other than a taxable dealer.

Article 323

Taxable persons may not deduct from the VAT for which they are liable the VAT due or paid in respect of goods which have been, or are to be, supplied to them by a taxable dealer, in so far as the supply of those goods by the taxable dealer is subject to the margin scheme.

Article 324

Where the taxable dealer applies both the normal VAT arrangements and the margin scheme, he must show separately in his accounts the transactions falling under each of those arrangements, in accordance with the rules laid down by the Member States.

Article 325

The taxable dealer may not enter separately on the invoices which he issues the VAT relating to supplies of goods to which he applies the margin scheme.

SUBSECTION 2

Transitional arrangements for second-hand means of transport

Article 326

Member States which, at 31 December 1992, were applying special tax arrangements other than the margin scheme to the supply by taxable dealers of second-hand means of transport may, pending introduction of the definitive arrangements referred to in Article 402, continue to apply those arrangements in so far as they comply with, or are adjusted to comply with, the conditions laid down in this Subsection.

Denmark is authorised to introduce tax arrangements as referred to in the first paragraph.

Article 327

1. These transitional arrangements shall apply to supplies of second-hand means of transport carried out by taxable dealers, and subject to the margin scheme.

2. These transitional arrangements shall not apply to the supply of new means of transport carried out in accordance with the conditions specified in Article 138(1) and (2)(a).

3. For the purposes of paragraph 1, the land vehicles, vessels and aircraft referred to in point (a) of Article 2(2) shall be regarded as 'second-hand means of transport' where they are second-hand goods which do not meet the conditions necessary to be regarded as new means of transport.

Article 328

The VAT due in respect of each supply referred to in Article 327 shall be equal to the amount of VAT that would have been due if that supply had been subject to the normal VAT arrangements, less the amount of VAT regarded as being incorporated by the taxable dealer in the purchase price of the means of transport.

Article 329

The VAT regarded as being incorporated by the taxable dealer in the purchase price of the means of transport shall be calculated in accordance with the following method:
   (a) the purchase price to be taken into account shall be the purchase price within the meaning of point (2) of Article 312;
   (b) that purchase price paid by the taxable dealer shall be deemed to include the VAT that would have been due if the taxable dealer's supplier had applied the normal VAT arrangements to the supply;
   (c) the rate to be taken into account shall be the rate applicable, pursuant to Article 93, in the Member State in the territory of which the place of the supply to the taxable dealer, as determined in accordance with Articles 31 and 32, is deemed to be situated.

Article 330

The VAT due in respect of each supply of means of transport as referred to in Article 327(1), determined in accordance with Article 328, may not be less than the amount of VAT that would be due if that supply were subject to the margin scheme.

Member States may provide that, if the supply is subject to the margin scheme, the margin may not be less than 10% of the selling price within the meaning of point (1) of Article 312.

Article 331

Taxable persons may not deduct from the VAT for which they are liable the VAT due or paid in respect of second-hand means of transport supplied to them by a taxable dealer, in so far as the supply of those goods by the taxable dealer is subject to VAT in accordance with these transitional arrangements.

Article 332

The taxable dealer may not enter separately on the invoices he issues the VAT relating to supplies to which he applies these transitional arrangements.

SECTION 3

Special arrangements for sales by public auction

Article 333

1. Member States may, in accordance with the provisions of this Section, apply special arrangements for taxation of the profit margin made by an organiser of a sale by public auction in respect of the supply of second-hand goods, works of art, collectors' items or antiques by that organiser, acting in his own name and on behalf of the persons referred to in Article 334, pursuant to a contract under which commission is payable on the sale of those goods by public auction.
2. The arrangements referred to in paragraph 1 shall not apply to the supply of new means of transport, carried out in accordance with the conditions specified in Article 138(1) and (2)(a).

Article 334

These special arrangements shall apply to supplies carried out by an organiser of a sale by public auction, acting in his own name, on behalf of one of the following persons:
   (a) a non-taxable person;
   (b) another taxable person, in so far as the supply of goods, carried out by that taxable person in accordance with a contract under which commission is payable on a sale, is exempt pursuant to Article 136;
   [(c) another taxable person, in so far as the supply of goods, carried out by that taxable person in accordance with a contract under which commission is payable on a sale, is covered by the exemption for small enterprises provided for in Article 284 and involves capital goods;][1]
   (d) a taxable dealer, in so far as the supply of goods, carried out by that taxable dealer in accordance with a contract under which commission is payable on a sale, is subject to VAT in accordance with the margin scheme.

Amendments—[1]   Point (c) substituted by Council Directive 2020/285/EU art 1(22) with effect from 22 March 2020 (OJ L 62, 2.3.2020, p 13).

Article 335

The supply of goods to a taxable person who is an organiser of sales by public auction shall be regarded as taking place when the sale of those goods by public auction takes place.

Article 336

The taxable amount in respect of each supply of goods referred to in this Section shall be the total amount invoiced in accordance with Article 339 to the purchaser by the organiser of the sale by public auction, less the following:
- (a) the net amount paid or to be paid by the organiser of the sale by public auction to his principal, as determined in accordance with Article 337;
- (b) the amount of the VAT payable by the organiser of the sale by public auction in respect of his supply.

Article 337

The net amount paid or to be paid by the organiser of the sale by public auction to his principal shall be equal to the difference between the auction price of the goods and the amount of the commission obtained or to be obtained by the organiser of the sale by public auction from his principal pursuant to the contract under which commission is payable on the sale.

Article 338

Organisers of sales by public auction who supply goods in accordance with the conditions laid down in Articles 333 and 334 must indicate the following in their accounts, in suspense accounts:
- (a) the amounts obtained or to be obtained from the purchaser of the goods;
- (b) the amounts reimbursed or to be reimbursed to the vendor of the goods.

The amounts referred to in the first paragraph must be duly substantiated.

Article 339

The organiser of the sale by public auction must issue to the purchaser an invoice itemising the following:
- (a) the auction price of the goods;
- (b) taxes, duties, levies and charges;
- (c) incidental expenses, such as commission, packing, transport and insurance costs, charged by the organiser to the purchaser of the goods.

The invoice issued by the organiser of the sale by public auction must not indicate any VAT separately.

Article 340

1. The organiser of the sale by public auction to whom the goods have been transmitted pursuant to a contract under which commission is payable on a public auction sale must issue a statement to his principal. The statement issued by the organiser of the sale by public auction must specify separately the amount of the transaction, that is to say, the auction price of the goods less the amount of the commission obtained or to be obtained from the principal.

2. The statement drawn up in accordance with paragraph 1 shall serve as the invoice which the principal, where he is a taxable person, must issue to the organiser of the sale by public auction in accordance with Article 220.

Article 341

Member States which apply the arrangements provided for in this Section shall also apply these arrangements to supplies of second-hand means of transport, as defined in Article 327(3), carried out by an organiser of sales by public auction, acting in his own name, pursuant to a contract under which commission is payable on the sale of those goods by public auction, on behalf of a taxable dealer, in so far as those supplies by that taxable dealer would be subject to VAT in accordance with the transitional arrangements for second-hand means of transport.

SECTION 4

Measures to prevent distortion of competition and tax evasion

Article 342

Member States may take measures concerning the right of deduction in order to ensure that the taxable dealers covered by special arrangements as provided for in Section 2 do not enjoy unjustified advantage or sustain unjustified harm.

Article 343

Acting unanimously on a proposal from the Commission, the Council may authorise any Member State to introduce special measures to combat tax evasion, pursuant to which the VAT due under the margin scheme may not be less than the amount of VAT which would be due if the profit margin were equal to a certain percentage of the selling price.

The percentage of the selling price shall be fixed in the light of the normal profit margins made by economic operators in the sector concerned.

CHAPTER 5
SPECIAL SCHEME FOR INVESTMENT GOLD
SECTION 1
General provisions

Article 344

1. For the purposes of this Directive, and without prejudice to other Community provisions, 'investment gold' shall mean:
   (1) gold, in the form of a bar or a wafer of weights accepted by the bullion markets, of a purity equal to or greater than 995 thousandths, whether or not represented by securities;
   (2) gold coins of a purity equal to or greater than 900 thousandths and minted after 1800, which are or have been legal tender in the country of origin, and are normally sold at a price which does not exceed the open market value of the gold contained in the coins by more than 80%.
2. Member States may exclude from this special scheme small bars or wafers of a weight of 1 g or less.
3. For the purposes of this Directive, the coins referred to in point (2) of paragraph 1 shall not be regarded as sold for numismatic interest.

Article 345

Starting in 1999, each Member State shall inform the Commission by 1 July each year of the coins meeting the criteria laid down in point (2) of Article 344(1) which are traded in that Member State. The Commission shall, before 1 December each year, publish a comprehensive list of those coins in the 'C' series of the *Official Journal of the European Union*. Coins included in the published list shall be deemed to fulfil those criteria throughout the year for which the list is published.

SECTION 2
Exemption from VAT

Article 346

Member States shall exempt from VAT the supply, the intra-Community acquisition and the importation of investment gold, including investment gold represented by certificates for allocated or unallocated gold or traded on gold accounts and including, in particular, gold loans and swaps, involving a right of ownership or claim in respect of investment gold, as well as transactions concerning investment gold involving futures and forward contracts leading to a transfer of right of ownership or claim in respect of investment gold.

Article 347

Member States shall exempt the services of agents who act in the name and on behalf of another person, when they take part in the supply of investment gold for their principal.

SECTION 3
Taxation option

Article 348

Member States shall allow taxable persons who produce investment gold or transform gold into investment gold the right to opt for the taxation of supplies of investment gold to another taxable person which would otherwise be exempt pursuant to Article 346.

Article 349

1. Member States may allow taxable persons who, in the course of their economic activity, normally supply gold for industrial purposes, the right to opt for the taxation of supplies of gold bars or wafers, as referred to in point (1) of Article 344(1), to another taxable person, which would otherwise be exempt pursuant to Article 346.
2. Member States may restrict the scope of the option provided for in paragraph 1.

Article 350

Where the supplier has exercised the right under Articles 348 and 349 to opt for taxation, Member States shall allow the agent to opt for taxation of the services referred to in Article 347.

Article 351

Member States shall lay down detailed rules for the exercise of the options provided for in this Section, and shall inform the Commission accordingly.

SECTION 4
Transactions on a regulated gold bullion market

Article 352

Each Member State may, after consulting the VAT Committee, apply VAT to specific transactions relating to investment gold which take place in that Member State between taxable persons who are members of a gold bullion market regulated by the Member State concerned or between such a taxable person and another taxable person who is not a member of that market. However, the Member State may not apply VAT to supplies carried out in accordance with the conditions specified in Article 138 or to exports of investment gold.

Article 353

Member States which, pursuant to Article 352, tax transactions between taxable persons who are members of a regulated gold bullion market shall, for the purposes of simplification, authorise suspension of the tax to be collected and relieve taxable persons of the accounting requirements in respect of VAT.

SECTION 5
Special rights and obligations for traders in investment gold

Article 354

Where his subsequent supply of investment gold is exempt pursuant to this Chapter, the taxable person shall be entitled to deduct the following:

(a) the VAT due or paid in respect of investment gold supplied to him by a person who has exercised the right of option under Articles 348 and 349 or supplied to him in accordance with Section 4;

(b) the VAT due or paid in respect of a supply to him, or in respect of an intra-Community acquisition or importation carried out by him, of gold other than investment gold which is subsequently transformed by him or on his behalf into investment gold;

(c) the VAT due or paid in respect of services supplied to him consisting in a change of form, weight or purity of gold including investment gold.

Article 355

Taxable persons who produce investment gold or transform gold into investment gold shall be entitled to deduct the VAT due or paid by them in respect of the supply, intra-Community acquisition or importation of goods or services linked to the production or transformation of that gold, as if the subsequent supply of the gold exempted pursuant to Article 346 were taxed.

Article 356

1. Member States shall ensure that traders in investment gold keep, as a minimum, accounts of all substantial transactions in investment gold and keep the documents which enable the customers in such transactions to be identified.

Traders shall keep the information referred to in the first subparagraph for a period of at least five years.

2. Member States may accept equivalent obligations under measures adopted pursuant to other Community legislation, such as Directive 2005/60/EC of the European Parliament and of the Council of 26 October 2005 on the prevention of the use of the financial system for the purpose of money laundering and terrorist financing [1], to comply with the requirements under paragraph 1.

3. Member States may lay down obligations which are more stringent, in particular as regards the keeping of special records or special accounting requirements.

[1] OJ L 309, 25.11.2005, p. 15.

CHAPTER 6
[SPECIAL SCHEMES FOR TAXABLE PERSONS SUPPLYING SERVICES TO NON-TAXABLE PERSONS OR MAKING DISTANCE SALES OF GOODS OR CERTAIN DOMESTIC SUPPLIES OF GOODS]

Amendments—Heading to Chapter 6 substituted by Council Directive 2019/1995/EU art 1(7) with effect from 22 December 2019 (OJ L 310, 2.12.2019, p 1).

SECTION 1
General provisions

Article 357

This Chapter shall apply until 31 December 2014.[1]

Amendments—[1] Article 357 repealed by Council Directive 2008/8/EC art 5(7) with effect from 1 January 2015 (OJ L 44, 20.2.2008 p 11).

[Article 358

For the purposes of this Chapter, and without prejudice to other Community provisions, the following definitions shall apply:

1. "telecommunications services" and "broadcasting services" mean the services referred to in points (a) and (b) of the first paragraph of Article 58;

2. "electronic services" and "electronically supplied services" mean the services referred to in point (c) of the first paragraph of Article 58;

3. "Member State of consumption" means the Member State in which the supply of the telecommunications, broadcasting or electronic services is deemed to take place according to Article 58;
4. "VAT return" means the statement containing the information necessary to establish the amount of VAT due in each Member State.][1]
Amendments—[1] Article 358 substituted by Council Directive 2008/8/EC art 5(8) with effect from 1 January 2015 (OJ L 44, 20.2.2008 p 11).

SECTION 2
[Special scheme for telecommunications, broadcasting or electronic services supplied by taxable persons not established within the Community]

Amendments—Heading to Section 2 substituted by Council Directive 2008/8/EC art 5(9) with effect from 1 January 2015 (OJ L 44, 20.2.2008 p 11).

[Article 358a
For the purposes of this Section, and without prejudice to other Community provisions, the following definitions shall apply:
[1. 'taxable person not established within the Community' means a taxable person who has not established his business in the territory of the Community and who has no fixed establishment there;][2]
2. "Member State of identification" means the Member State which the taxable person not established within the Community chooses to contact to state when his activity as a taxable person within the territory of the Community commences in accordance with the provisions of this Section.][1]
Amendments—[1] Article 358a inserted by Council Directive 2008/8/EC art 5(10) with effect from 1 January 2015 (OJ L 44, 20.2.2008 p 11).
[2] Para 1 substituted by Council Directive 2017/2455/EU art 1(3) with effect from 1 January 2019 (OJ L 348, 29.12.2017 p 7).

[Article 359
Member States shall permit any taxable person not established within the Community supplying telecommunications, broadcasting or electronic services to a non-taxable person who is established in a Member State or has his permanent address or usually resides in a Member State, to use this special scheme. This scheme applies to all those services supplied within the Community.][1]
Amendments—[1] Articles 359–365 substituted by Council Directive 2008/8/EC art 5(11) with effect from 1 January 2015 (OJ L 44, 20.2.2008 p 11).

[Article 360
The taxable person not established within the Community shall state to the Member State of identification when he commences or ceases his activity as a taxable person, or changes that activity in such a way that he no longer meets the conditions necessary for use of this special scheme. He shall communicate that information electronically.][1]
Amendments—[1] Articles 359–365 substituted by Council Directive 2008/8/EC art 5(11) with effect from 1 January 2015 (OJ L 44, 20.2.2008 p 11).

[Article 361
1. The information which the taxable person not established within the Community must provide to the Member State of identification when he commences a taxable activity shall contain the following details:
    (a) name;
    (b) postal address;
    (c) electronic addresses, including websites;
    (d) national tax number, if any;
    [(e) a statement that the person has not established his business in the territory of the Community and has no fixed establishment there.][2]
2. The taxable person not established within in the Community shall notify the Member State of identification of any changes in the information provided.][1]
Amendments—[1] Articles 359–365 substituted by Council Directive 2008/8/EC art 5(11) with effect from 1 January 2015 (OJ L 44, 20.2.2008 p 11).
[2] Para 1(e) substituted by Council Directive 2017/2455/EU art 1(4) with effect from 1 January 2019 (OJ L 348, 29.12.2017 p 7).

[Article 362
The Member State of identification shall allocate to the taxable person not established within the Community an individual VAT identification number and shall notify him of that number by electronic means. On the basis of the information used for that identification, Member States of consumption may have recourse to their own identification systems.][1]
Amendments—[1] Articles 359–365 substituted by Council Directive 2008/8/EC art 5(11) with effect from 1 January 2015 (OJ L 44, 20.2.2008 p 11).

[Article 363

The Member State of identification shall delete the taxable person not established within the Community from the identification register in the following cases:
  (a) if he notifies that Member State that he no longer supplies telecommunications, broadcasting or electronic services;
  (b) if it may otherwise be assumed that his taxable activities have ceased;
  (c) if he no longer meets the conditions necessary for use of this special scheme;
  (d) if he persistently fails to comply with the rules relating to this special scheme.][1]

Amendments—[1] Articles 359–365 substituted by Council Directive 2008/8/EC art 5(11) with effect from 1 January 2015 (OJ L 44, 20.2.2008 p 11).

[Article 364

The taxable person not established within the Community shall submit by electronic means to the Member State of identification a VAT return for each calendar quarter, whether or not telecommunications, broadcasting or electronic services have been supplied. The VAT return shall be submitted within 20 days following the end of the tax period covered by the return.][1]

Amendments—[1] Articles 359–365 substituted by Council Directive 2008/8/EC art 5(11) with effect from 1 January 2015 (OJ L 44, 20.2.2008 p 11).

[Article 365

The VAT return shall show the identification number and, for each Member State of consumption in which VAT is due, the total value, exclusive of VAT, of supplies of telecommunications, broadcasting and electronic services carried out during the tax period and total amount per rate of the corresponding VAT. The applicable rates of VAT and the total VAT due must also be indicated on the return.][1]

Amendments—[1] Articles 359–365 substituted by Council Directive 2008/8/EC art 5(11) with effect from 1 January 2015 (OJ L 44, 20.2.2008 p 11).

Article 366

[1. The VAT return shall be made out in euro.
Member States which have not adopted the euro may require the VAT return to be made out in their national currency. If the supplies have been made in other currencies, the taxable person not established within the Community shall, for the purposes of completing the VAT return, use the exchange rate applying on the last day of the tax period.][1]
2. The conversion shall be made by applying the exchange rates published by the European Central Bank for that day, or, if there is no publication on that day, on the next day of publication.

Amendments—[1] Para 1 substituted by Council Directive 2008/8/EC art 5(12) with effect from 1 January 2015 (OJ L 44, 20.2.2008 p 11).

[Article 367

The taxable person not established within the Community shall pay the VAT, making reference to the relevant VAT return, when submitting the VAT return, at the latest, however, at the expiry of the deadline by which the return must be submitted.
Payment shall be made to a bank account denominated in euro, designated by the Member State of identification. Member States which have not adopted the euro may require the payment to be made to a bank account denominated in their own currency.][1]

Amendments—[1] Articles 367, 368 substituted by Council Directive 2008/8/EC art 5(13) with effect from 1 January 2015 (OJ L 44, 20.2.2008 p 11).

[Article 368

The taxable person not established within the Community making use of this special scheme may not deduct VAT pursuant to Article 168 of this Directive. Notwithstanding Article 1(1) of Directive 86/560/EEC, the taxable person in question shall be refunded in accordance with the said Directive. Articles 2(2) and (3) and Article 4(2) of Directive 86/560/EEC shall not apply to refunds relating to telecommunications, broadcasting or electronic services covered by this special scheme.][1]

Amendments—[1] Articles 367, 368 substituted by Council Directive 2008/8/EC art 5(13) with effect from 1 January 2015 (OJ L 44, 20.2.2008 p 11).

Article 369

[1. The taxable person not established within the Community shall keep records of the transactions covered by this special scheme. Those records must be sufficiently detailed to enable the tax authorities of the Member State of consumption to verify that the VAT return is correct.][1]
2. The records referred to in paragraph 1 must be made available electronically on request to the Member State of identification and to the Member State of consumption.
Those records must be kept for a period of ten years from the end of the year during which the transaction was carried out.

Amendments—[1] Para 1 substituted by Council Directive 2008/8/EC art 5(14) with effect from 1 January 2015 (OJ L 44, 20.2.2008 p 11).

[SECTION 3]

[Special scheme for intra-Community distance sales of goods, for supplies of goods within a Member State made by electronic interfaces facilitating those supplies and for services supplied by taxable persons established within the Community but not in the Member State of consumption]

Amendments—Heading substituted by Council Directive 2019/1995/EU art 1(7) with effect from 22 December 2019 (OJ L 310, 2.12.2019, p 1).

[Article 369a]

For the purposes of this Section, and without prejudice to other Community provisions, the following definitions shall apply:
(1) taxable person not established in the Member State of consumption" means a taxable person who has established his business in the Community or has a fixed establishment there but who has not established his business and has no fixed establishment within the territory of the Member State of consumption;
(2) "Member State of identification" means the Member State in the territory of which the taxable person has established his business or, if he has not established his business in the Community, where he has a fixed establishment.
Where a taxable person has not established his business in the Community, but has more than one fixed establishment therein, the Member State of identification shall be the Member State with a fixed establishment where that taxable person indicates that he will make use of this special scheme. The taxable person shall be bound by that decision for the calendar year concerned and the two calendar years following.
Where a taxable person has not established his business in the Community and has no fixed establishment therein, the Member State of identification shall be the Member State in which the dispatch or transport of the goods begins. Where there is more than one Member State in which the dispatch or transport of the goods begins, the taxable person shall indicate which of those Member States shall be the Member State of identification. The taxable person shall be bound by that decision for the calendar year concerned and the two calendar years following;
(3) Member State of consumption" means one of the following:
   (a) in the case of the supply of services, the Member State in which the supply is deemed to take place according to Chapter 3 of Title V;
   (b) in the case of intra-Community distance sales of goods, the Member State where the dispatch or transport of the goods to the customer ends;
   (c) in the case of the supply of goods made by a taxable person facilitating those supplies in accordance with Article 14a(2) where the dispatch or transport of the goods supplied begins and ends in the same Member State, that Member State.][1]

Amendments—[1] Article 369a substituted by Council Directive 2019/1995/EU art 1(9) with effect from 22 December 2019 (OJ L 310, 2.12.2019, p 1).

[Article 369b]

Member States shall permit the following taxable persons to use this special scheme:
   (a) a taxable person carrying out intra-Community distance sales of goods;
   (b) a taxable person facilitating the supply of goods in accordance with Article 14a(2) where the dispatch or transport of the goods supplied begins and ends in the same Member State;
   (c) a taxable person not established in the Member State of consumption supplying services to a non-taxable person.
This special scheme applies to all those goods or services supplied in the Community by the taxable person concerned.][1]

Amendments—[1] Article 369b substituted by Council Directive 2019/1995/EU art 1(10) with effect from 22 December 2019 (OJ L 310, 2.12.2019, p 1).

[Article 369c]

The taxable person not established in the Member State of consumption shall state to the Member State of identification when he commences and ceases his taxable activities covered by this special scheme, or changes those activities in such a way that he no longer meets the conditions necessary for use of this special scheme. He shall communicate that information electronically.][1]

Amendments—[1] Section 3 (articles 369a–369k) inserted by Council Directive 2008/8/EC art 5(15) with effect from 1 January 2015 (OJ L 44, 20.2.2008 p 11).

[Article 369d]

A taxable person making use of this special scheme shall, for the taxable transactions carried out under this scheme, be identified for VAT purposes in the Member State of identification only. For that purpose the Member State shall use the individual VAT identification number already allocated to the taxable person in respect of his obligations under the internal system.
On the basis of the information used for that identification, Member States of consumption may have recourse to their own identification systems.][1]

Amendments—[1] Section 3 (articles 369a–369k) inserted by Council Directive 2008/8/EC art 5(15) with effect from 1 January 2015 (OJ L 44, 20.2.2008 p 11).

[**Article 369e**

The Member State of identification shall exclude the taxable person not established in the Member State of consumption from this special scheme in any of the following cases:
   [(a) if he notifies that he no longer carries out supplies of goods and services covered by this special scheme;][2]
   (b) if it may otherwise be assumed that his taxable activities covered by this special scheme have ceased;
   (c) if he no longer meets the conditions necessary for use of this special scheme;
   (d) if he persistently fails to comply with the rules relating to this special scheme.][1]

Amendments—[1]   Section 3 (articles 369a–369k) inserted by Council Directive 2008/8/EC art 5(15) with effect from 1 January 2015 (OJ L 44, 20.2.2008 p 11).
[2]   Point (a) substituted by Council Directive 2019/1995/EU art 1(11) with effect from 22 December 2019 (OJ L 310, 2.12.2019, p 1).

[**Article 369f**

The taxable person making use of this special scheme shall submit by electronic means to the Member State of identification a VAT return for each calendar quarter, whether or not supplies of goods and services covered by this special scheme have been carried out. The VAT return shall be submitted by the end of the month following the end of the tax period covered by the return.][1]

Amendments—[1]   Article 369f substituted by Council Directive 2019/1995/EU art 1(12) with effect from 22 December 2019 (OJ L 310, 2.12.2019, p 1).

[**Article 369g**

[1. The VAT return shall show the VAT identification number referred to in Article 369d and, for each Member State of consumption in which VAT is due, the total value exclusive of VAT, the applicable rates of VAT, the total amount per rate of the corresponding VAT and the total VAT due in respect of the following supplies covered by this special scheme carried out during the tax period:
   (a) intra-Community distance sales of goods;
   (b) supplies of goods in accordance with Article 14a(2) where the dispatch or transport of those goods begins and ends in the same Member State;
   (c) supplies of services.
The VAT return shall also include amendments relating to previous tax periods as provided in paragraph 4 of this Article.
2. Where goods are dispatched or transported from Member States other than the Member State of identification, the VAT return shall also include the total value exclusive of VAT, the applicable rates of VAT, the total amount per rate of the corresponding VAT and the total VAT due in respect of the following supplies covered by this special scheme, for each Member State where such goods are dispatched or transported from:
   (a) intra-Community distance sales of goods other than those made by a taxable person in accordance with Article 14a(2);
   (b) intra-Community distance sales of goods and supplies of goods where the dispatch or transport of those goods begins and ends in the same Member State, made by a taxable person in accordance with Article 14a(2).
In relation to the supplies referred to in point (a), the VAT return shall also include the individual VAT identification number or the tax reference number allocated by each Member State where such goods are dispatched or transported from.
In relation to the supplies referred to in point (b), the VAT return shall also include the individual VAT identification number or the tax reference number allocated by each Member State where such goods are dispatched or transported from, if available.
The VAT return shall include the information referred to in this paragraph broken down by Member State of consumption.
3. Where the taxable person supplying services covered by this special scheme has one or more fixed establishments, other than that in the Member State of identification, from which the services are supplied, the VAT return shall also include the total value exclusive of VAT, the applicable rates of VAT, the total amount per rate of the corresponding VAT and the total VAT due of such supplies, for each Member State in which he has an establishment, together with the individual VAT identification number or the tax reference number of this establishment, broken down by Member State of consumption.][2]][1]

Amendments—[1]   Section 3 (articles 369a–369k) inserted by Council Directive 2008/8/EC art 5(15) with effect from 1 January 2015 (OJ L 44, 20.2.2008 p 11).
[2]   Paras substituted by Council Directive 2019/1995/EU art 1(13) with effect from 22 December 2019 (OJ L 310, 2.12.2019, p 1).

[**Article 369h**

1. The VAT return shall be made out in euro.

Member States which have not adopted the euro may require the VAT return to be made out in their national currency. If the supplies have been made in other currencies, the taxable person not established in the Member State of consumption shall, for the purposes of completing the VAT return, use the exchange rate applying on the last date of the tax period.

2. The conversion shall be made by applying the exchange rates published by the European Central Bank for that day, or, if there is no publication on that day, on the next day of publication.][1]

Amendments—[1] Section 3 (articles 369a–369k) inserted by Council Directive 2008/8/EC art 5(15) with effect from 1 January 2015 (OJ L 44, 20.2.2008 p 11).

[Article 369i

The taxable person not established in the Member State of consumption shall pay the VAT, making reference to the relevant VAT return, when submitting the VAT return, at the latest, however, at the expiry of the deadline by which the return must be submitted.

Payment shall be made to a bank account denominated in euro, designated by the Member State of identification. Member States which have not adopted the euro may require the payment to be made to a bank account denominated in their own currency.][1]

Amendments—[1] Section 3 (articles 369a–369k) inserted by Council Directive 2008/8/EC art 5(15) with effect from 1 January 2015 (OJ L 44, 20.2.2008 p 11).

[Article 369j

The taxable person not established in the Member State of consumption making use of this special scheme may not, in respect of his taxable activities covered by this scheme, deduct VAT pursuant to Article 168 of this Directive. Notwithstanding Article 2(1) and Article 3 of Directive 2008/9/EC, the taxable person in question shall be refunded in accordance with the said Directive.

If the taxable person not established in the Member State of consumption making use of this special scheme also carries out in the Member State of consumption activities not covered by this scheme in respect of which he is obliged to be registered for VAT purposes, he shall deduct VAT in respect of his taxable activities which are covered by this scheme in the VAT return to be submitted pursuant to Article 250.][1]

Amendments—[1] Section 3 (articles 369a–369k) inserted by Council Directive 2008/8/EC art 5(15) with effect from 1 January 2015 (OJ L 44, 20.2.2008 p 11).

[Article 369k

1. The taxable person not established in the Member State of consumption shall keep records of the transactions covered by this special scheme. Those records must be sufficiently detailed to enable the tax authorities of the Member State of consumption to verify that the VAT return is correct.

2. The records referred to in paragraph 1 must be made available electronically on request to the Member State of consumption and to the Member State of identification.

Those records must be kept for a period of 10 years from 31 December of the year during which the transaction was carried out.][1]

Amendments—[1] Section 3 (articles 369a–369k) inserted by Council Directive 2008/8/EC art 5(15) with effect from 1 January 2015 (OJ L 44, 20.2.2008 p 11).

TITLE XIII
DEROGATIONS

CHAPTER 1

DEROGATIONS APPLYING UNTIL THE ADOPTION OF DEFINITIVE ARRANGEMENTS

SECTION 1

Derogations for States which were members of the Community on 1 January 1978

Article 370

Member States which, at 1 January 1978, taxed the transactions listed in Annex X, Part A, may continue to tax those transactions.

Article 371

Member States which, at 1 January 1978, exempted the transactions listed in Annex X, Part B, may continue to exempt those transactions, in accordance with the conditions applying in the Member State concerned on that date.

Commentary—*De Voil Indirect Tax Service* **V4.275**.

Article 372

Member States which, at 1 January 1978, applied provisions derogating from the principle of immediate deduction laid down in the first paragraph of Article 179 may continue to apply those provisions.

Article 373
Member States which, at 1 January 1978, applied provisions derogating from Article 28 or from point (c) of the first paragraph of Article 79 may continue to apply those provisions.

Article 374
By way of derogation from Articles 169 and 309, Member States which, at 1 January 1978, exempted, without deductibility of the VAT paid at the preceding stage, the services of travel agents, as referred to in Article 309, may continue to exempt those services. That derogation shall apply also in respect of travel agents acting in the name and on behalf of the traveller.

SECTION 2
Derogations for States which acceded to the Community after 1 January 1978

Article 375
Greece may continue to exempt the transactions listed in points (2), (8), (9), (11) and (12) of Annex X, Part B, in accordance with the conditions applying in that Member State on 1 January 1987.

Article 376
Spain may continue to exempt the supply of services performed by authors, listed in point (2) of Annex X, Part B, and the transactions listed in points (11) and (12) of Annex X, Part B, in accordance with the conditions applying in that Member State on 1 January 1993.

Article 377
Portugal may continue to exempt the transactions listed in points (2), (4), (7), (9), (10) and (13) of Annex X, Part B, in accordance with the conditions applying in that Member State on 1 January 1989.

Article 378
1. Austria may continue to tax the transactions listed in point (2) of Annex X, Part A.
2. For as long as the same exemptions are applied in any of the Member States which were members of the Community on 31 December 1994, Austria may, in accordance with the conditions applying in that Member State on the date of its accession, continue to exempt the following transactions:
    (a) the transactions listed in points (5) and (9) of Annex X, Part B;
    (b) with deductibility of the VAT paid at the preceding stage, all parts of international passenger transport operations, carried out by air, sea or inland waterway, other than passenger transport operations on Lake Constance.

Article 379
1. Finland may continue to tax the transactions listed in point (2) of Annex X, Part A, for as long as the same transactions are taxed in any of the Member States which were members of the Community on 31 December 1994.
2. Finland may, in accordance with the conditions applying in that Member State on the date of its accession, continue to exempt the supply of services by authors, artists and performers, listed in point (2) of Annex X, Part B, and the transactions listed in points (5), (9) and (10) of Annex X, Part B, for as long as the same exemptions are applied in any of the Member States which were members of the Community on 31 December 1994.

Article 380
Sweden may, in accordance with the conditions applying in that Member State on the date of its accession, continue to exempt the supply of services by authors, artists and performers, listed in point (2) of Annex X, Part B, and the transactions listed in points (1), (9) and (10) of Annex X, Part B, for as long as the same exemptions are applied in any of the Member States which were members of the Community on 31 December 1994.

Article 381
The Czech Republic may, in accordance with the conditions applying in that Member State on the date of its accession, continue to exempt the international transport of passengers, as referred to in point (10) of Annex X, Part B, for as long as the same exemption is applied in any of the Member States which were members of the Community on 30 April 2004.

Article 382
Estonia may, in accordance with the conditions applying in that Member State on the date of its accession, continue to exempt the international transport of passengers, as referred to in point (10) of Annex X, Part B, for as long as the same exemption is applied in any of the Member States which were members of the Community on 30 April 2004.

Article 383
Cyprus may, in accordance with the conditions applying in that Member State on the date of its accession, continue to exempt the following transactions:

(a) the supply of building land referred to in point (9) of Annex X, Part B, until 31 December 2007;
(b) the international transport of passengers, as referred to in point (10) of Annex X, Part B, for as long as the same exemption is applied in any of the Member States which were members of the Community on 30 April 2004.

Article 384
For as long as the same exemptions are applied in any of the Member States which were members of the Community on 30 April 2004, Latvia may, in accordance with the conditions applying in that Member State on the date of its accession, continue to exempt the following transactions:
(a) the supply of services by authors, artists and performers, as referred to in point (2) of Annex X, Part B;
(b) the international transport of passengers, as referred to in point (10) of Annex X, Part B.

Article 385
Lithuania may, in accordance with the conditions applying in that Member State on the date of its accession, continue to exempt the international transport of passengers, as referred to in point (10) of Annex X, Part B, for as long as the same exemption is applied in any of the Member States which were members of the Community on 30 April 2004.

Article 386
Hungary may, in accordance with the conditions applying in that Member State on the date of its accession, continue to exempt the international transport of passengers, as referred to in point (10) of Annex X, Part B, for as long as the same exemption is applied in any of the Member States which were members of the Community on 30 April 2004.

Article 387
For as long as the same exemptions are applied in any of the Member States which were members of the Community on 30 April 2004, Malta may, in accordance with the conditions applying in that Member State on the date of its accession, continue to exempt the following transactions:
(a) without deductibility of the VAT paid at the preceding stage, the supply of water by a body governed by public law, as referred to in point (8) of Annex X, Part B;
(b) without deductibility of the VAT paid at the preceding stage, the supply of buildings and building land, as referred to in point (9) of Annex X, Part B;
(c) with deductibility of the VAT paid at the preceding stage, inland passenger transport, international passenger transport and domestic inter-island sea passenger transport, as referred to in point (10) of Annex X, Part B.

Article 388
Poland may, in accordance with the conditions applying in that Member State on the date of its accession, continue to exempt the international transport of passengers, as referred to in point (10) of Annex X, Part B, for as long as the same exemption is applied in any of the Member States which were members of the Community on 30 April 2004.

Article 389
Slovenia may, in accordance with the conditions applying in that Member State on the date of its accession, continue to exempt the international transport of passengers, as referred to in point (10) of Annex X, Part B, for as long as the same exemption is applied in any of the Member States which were members of the Community on 30 April 2004.

Article 390
Slovakia may, in accordance with the conditions applying in that Member State on the date of its accession, continue to exempt the international transport of passengers, as referred to in point (10) of Annex X, Part B, for as long as the same exemption is applied in any of the Member States which were members of the Community on 30 April 2004.

[Article 390a
Bulgaria may, in accordance with the conditions applying in that Member State on the date of its accession, continue to exempt the international transport of passengers as referred to in point 10 of Annex X, Part B, for as long as the same exemption is applied in any of the Member States which were members of the Community on 31 December 2006.]

Amendments—Articles 390a, 390b inserted by Council Directive 2009/162/EU art 1(15) with effect from 15 January 2010 (OJ L 10, 15.1.2010, p 14).

[**Article 390b**

Romania may, in accordance with the conditions applying in that Member State on the date of its accession, continue to exempt the international transport of passengers, as referred to in point 10 of Annex X, Part B, for as long as the same exemption is applied in any of the Member States which were members of the Community on 31 December 2006.]

Amendments—Articles 390a, 390b inserted by Council Directive 2009/162/EU art 1(15) with effect from 15 January 2010 (OJ L 10, 15.1.2010, p 14).

SECTION 3

Provisions common to Sections 1 and 2

Article 391

Member States which exempt the transactions referred to in Articles 371, 375, 376 or 377, Article 378(2), Article 379(2) or [Articles 380 to 390b] may grant taxable persons the right to opt for taxation of those transactions.

Commentary—*De Voil Indirect Tax Service* **V4.275**.

Amendments—Words substituted for "Articles 380 to 390" by Council Directive 2009/162/EU art 1(16) with effect from 15 January 2010 (OJ L 10, 15.1.2010, p 14).

Article 392

Member States may provide that, in respect of the supply of buildings and building land purchased for the purpose of resale by a taxable person for whom the VAT on the purchase was not deductible, the taxable amount shall be the difference between the selling price and the purchase price.

Article 393

1. With a view to facilitating the transition to the definitive arrangements referred to in Article 402, the Council shall, on the basis of a report from the Commission, review the situation with regard to the derogations provided for in Sections 1 and 2 and shall, acting in accordance with Article 93 of the Treaty decide whether any or all of those derogations is to be abolished.

2. By way of definitive arrangements, passenger transport shall be taxed in the Member State of departure for that part of the journey taking place within the Community, in accordance with the detailed rules to be laid down by the Council, acting in accordance with Article 93 of the Treaty.

CHAPTER 2

DEROGATIONS SUBJECT TO AUTHORISATION

SECTION 1

Simplification measures and measures to prevent tax evasion or avoidance

Article 394

Member States which, at 1 January 1977, applied special measures to simplify the procedure for collecting VAT or to prevent certain forms of tax evasion or avoidance may retain them provided that they have notified the Commission accordingly before 1 January 1978 and that such simplification measures comply with the criterion laid down in the second subparagraph of Article 395(1).

Article 395

1. The Council, acting unanimously on a proposal from the Commission, may authorise any Member State to introduce special measures for derogation from the provisions of this Directive, in order to simplify the procedure for collecting VAT or to prevent certain forms of tax evasion or avoidance.

Measures intended to simplify the procedure for collecting VAT may not, except to a negligible extent, affect the overall amount of the tax revenue of the Member State collected at the stage of final consumption.

2. A Member State wishing to introduce the measure referred to in paragraph 1 shall send an application to the Commission and provide it with all the necessary information. If the Commission considers that it does not have all the necessary information, it shall contact the Member State concerned within two months of receipt of the application and specify what additional information is required.

Once the Commission has all the information it considers necessary for appraisal of the request it shall within one month notify the requesting Member State accordingly and it shall transmit the request, in its original language, to the other Member States.

3. Within three months of giving the notification referred to in the second subparagraph of paragraph 2, the Commission shall present to the Council either an appropriate proposal or, should it object to the derogation requested, a communication setting out its objections.

4. The procedure laid down in paragraphs 2 and 3 shall, in any event, be completed within eight months of receipt of the application by the Commission.

5. In cases of imperative urgency as set out in Article 199b(1), the procedure laid down in paragraphs 2 and 3 shall be completed within six months of receipt of the application by the Commission.[1]

Amendments—[1] Para 5 repealed by Coundcil Directive (EU) 2018/1695 Art 1(3) with effect from 2 December 2018 (OJ L 282, 12.11.2018, p 5).

SECTION 2
International agreements

Article 396

1. The Council, acting unanimously on a proposal from the Commission, may authorise any Member State to conclude with a third country or an international body an agreement which may contain derogations from this Directive.

2. A Member State wishing to conclude an agreement as referred to in paragraph 1 shall send an application to the Commission and provide it with all the necessary information. If the Commission considers that it does not have all the necessary information, it shall contact the Member State concerned within two months of receipt of the application and specify what additional information is required.

Once the Commission has all the information it considers necessary for appraisal of the request it shall within one month notify the requesting Member State accordingly and it shall transmit the request, in its original language, to the other Member States.

3. Within three months of giving the notification referred to in the second subparagraph of paragraph 2, the Commission shall present to the Council either an appropriate proposal or, should it object to the derogation requested, a communication setting out its objections.

4. The procedure laid down in paragraphs 2 and 3 shall, in any event, be completed within eight months of receipt of the application by the Commission.

TITLE XIV
MISCELLANEOUS

CHAPTER 1
IMPLEMENTING MEASURES

Article 397

The Council, acting unanimously on a proposal from the Commission, shall adopt the measures necessary to implement this Directive.

CHAPTER 2
VAT COMMITTEE

Article 398

1. An advisory committee on value added tax, called 'the VAT Committee', is set up.

2. The VAT Committee shall consist of representatives of the Member States and of the Commission.
   The chairman of the Committee shall be a representative of the Commission.
   Secretarial services for the Committee shall be provided by the Commission.

3. The VAT Committee shall adopt its own rules of procedure.

4. In addition to the points forming the subject of consultation pursuant to this Directive, the VAT Committee shall examine questions raised by its chairman, on his own initiative or at the request of the representative of a Member State, which concern the application of Community provisions on VAT.

CHAPTER 3
CONVERSION RATES

Article 399

Without prejudice to any other particular provisions, the equivalents in national currency of the amounts in euro specified in this Directive shall be determined on the basis of the euro conversion rate applicable on 1 January 1999. Member States having acceded to the European Union after that date, which have not adopted the euro as single currency, shall use the euro conversion rate applicable on the date of their accession.

Article 400

When converting the amounts referred to in Article 399 into national currencies, Member States may adjust the amounts resulting from that conversion either upwards or downwards by up to 10%.

CHAPTER 4
OTHER TAXES, DUTIES AND CHARGES

Article 401

Without prejudice to other provisions of Community law, this Directive shall not prevent a Member State from maintaining or introducing taxes on insurance contracts, taxes on betting and gambling, excise duties, stamp duties or, more generally, any taxes, duties or charges which cannot be characterised as turnover taxes, provided that the collecting of those taxes, duties or charges does not give rise, in trade between Member States, to formalities connected with the crossing of frontiers.

TITLE XV
FINAL PROVISIONS

CHAPTER 1
TRANSITIONAL ARRANGEMENTS FOR THE TAXATION OF TRADE BETWEEN MEMBER STATES

Article 402

1. The arrangements provided for in this Directive for the taxation of trade between Member States are transitional and shall be replaced by definitive arrangements based in principle on the taxation in the Member State of origin of the supply of goods or services.
2. Having concluded, upon examination of the report referred to in Article 404, that the conditions for transition to the definitive arrangements are met, the Council shall, acting in accordance with Article 93 of the Treaty, adopt the provisions necessary for the entry into force and for the operation of the definitive arrangements.

Article 403

The Council shall, acting in accordance with Article 93 of the Treaty, adopt Directives appropriate for the purpose of supplementing the common system of VAT and, in particular, for the progressive restriction or the abolition of derogations from that system.

Amendments—Articles 403, 404 repealed by Council Directive (EU) 2018/1910 Article 1(6) with effect from 27 December 2018 (OJ L 311, 7.12.2018, p 3).

Article 404

Every four years starting from the adoption of this Directive, the Commission shall, on the basis of information obtained from the Member States, present a report to the European Parliament and to the Council on the operation of the common system of VAT in the Member States and, in particular, on the operation of the transitional arrangements for taxing trade between Member States. That report shall be accompanied, where appropriate, by proposals concerning the definitive arrangements.

Amendments—Articles 403, 404 repealed by Council Directive (EU) 2018/1910 Article 1(6) with effect from 27 December 2018 (OJ L 311, 7.12.2018, p 3).

CHAPTER 2
TRANSITIONAL MEASURES APPLICABLE IN THE CONTEXT OF ACCESSION TO THE EUROPEAN UNION

Article 405

For the purposes of this Chapter, the following definitions shall apply:
  (1) 'Community' means the territory of the Community as defined in point (1) of Article 5 before the accession of new Member States;
  (2) 'new Member States' means the territory of the Member States which acceded to the European Union after 1 January 1995, as defined for each of those Member States in point (2) of Article 5;
  (3) 'enlarged Community' means the territory of the Community as defined in point (1) of Article 5 after the accession of new Member States.

Article 406

The provisions in force at the time the goods were placed under temporary importation arrangements with total exemption from import duty or under one of the arrangements or situations referred to in Article 156, or under similar arrangements or situations in one of the new Member States, shall continue to apply until the goods cease to be covered by these arrangements or situations after the date of accession, where the following conditions are met:
  (*a*) the goods entered the Community or one of the new Member States before the date of accession;
  (*b*) the goods were placed, on entry into the Community or one of the new Member States, under these arrangements or situations;

(c) the goods have not ceased to be covered by these arrangements or situations before the date of accession.

Article 407
The provisions in force at the time the goods were placed under customs transit arrangements shall continue to apply until the goods cease to be covered by these arrangements after the date of accession, where the following conditions are met:
   (a) the goods were placed, before the date of accession, under customs transit arrangements;
   (b) the goods have not ceased to be covered by these arrangements before the date of accession.

Article 408
1. The following shall be treated as an importation of goods where it is shown that the goods were in free circulation in one of the new Member States or in the Community:
   (a) the removal, including irregular removal, of goods from temporary importation arrangements under which they were placed before the date of accession under the conditions provided for in Article 406;
   (b) the removal, including irregular removal, of goods either from one of the arrangements or situations referred to in Article 156 or from similar arrangements or situations under which they were placed before the date of accession under the conditions provided for in Article 406;
   (c) the cessation of one of the arrangements referred to in Article 407, started before the date of accession in the territory of one of the new Member States, for the purposes of a supply of goods for consideration effected before that date in the territory of that Member State by a taxable person acting as such;
   (d) any irregularity or offence committed during customs transit arrangements started under the conditions referred to in point (c).
2. In addition to the case referred to in paragraph 1, the use after the date of accession within the territory of a Member State, by a taxable or non-taxable person, of goods supplied to him before the date of accession within the territory of the Community or one of the new Member States shall be treated as an importation of goods where the following conditions are met:
   (a) the supply of those goods has been exempted, or was likely to be exempted, either under points (a) and (b) of Article 146(1) or under a similar provision in the new Member States;
   (b) the goods were not imported into one of the new Member States or into the Community before the date of accession.

Article 409
In the cases referred to in Article 408(1), the place of import within the meaning of Article 61 shall be the Member State within whose territory the goods cease to be covered by the arrangements or situations under which they were placed before the date of accession.

Article 410
1. By way of derogation from Article 71, the importation of goods within the meaning of Article 408 shall terminate without the occurrence of a chargeable event if one of the following conditions is met:
   (a) the imported goods are dispatched or transported outside the enlarged Community;
   (b) the imported goods within the meaning of Article 408(1)(a) are other than means of transport and are redispatched or transported to the Member State from which they were exported and to the person who exported them;
   (c) the imported goods within the meaning of Article 408(1)(a) are means of transport which were acquired or imported before the date of accession in accordance with the general conditions of taxation in force on the domestic market of
one of the new Member States or of one of the Member States of the Community or which have not been subject, by reason of their exportation, to any exemption from, or refund of, VAT.
2. The condition referred to in paragraph 1(c) shall be deemed to be fulfilled in the following cases:
   (a) when the date of first entry into service of the means of transport was more than eight years before the accession to the European Union.
   (b) when the amount of tax due by reason of the importation is insignificant.

[CHAPTER 2A
TRANSITIONAL MEASURES FOR THE APPLICATION OF NEW LEGISLATION
Article 410a
Articles 30a, 30b and 73a shall apply only to vouchers issued after 31 December 2018.][1]

Amendments—[1] Articles 410a, 410b inserted by Council Directive 2016/1065/EU Article 1(3) with effect from 2 July 2017 (OJ L 177, 1.7.2016, p 9). Note that member states are required to adopt and publish, by 31 December 2018 at the latest, the laws, regulations and administrative provisions necessary to comply with Directive 2016/1065/EU and that those provisions will apply from 1 January 2019.

[**Article 410b**

By 31 December 2022 at the latest, the Commission shall, on the basis of information obtained from the Member States, present to the European Parliament and to the Council an assessment report on the application of the provisions of this Directive as regards the VAT treatment of vouchers, with particular regard to the definition of vouchers, the VAT rules relating to taxation of vouchers in the distribution chain and to non-redeemed vouchers, accompanied where necessary by an appropriate proposal to amend the relevant rules.][1]

Amendments—[1] Articles 410a, 410b inserted by Council Directive 2016/1065/EU Article 1(3) with effect from 2 July 2017 (OJ L 177, 1.7.2016, p 9). Note that member states are required to adopt and publish, by 31 December 2018 at the latest, the laws, regulations and administrative provisions necessary to comply with Directive 2016/1065/EU and that those provisions will apply from 1 January 2019.

CHAPTER 3

TRANSPOSITION AND ENTRY INTO FORCE

Article 411

1. Directive 67/227/EEC and Directive 77/388/EEC are repealed, without prejudice to the obligations of the Member States concerning the time-limits, listed in Annex XI, Part B, for the transposition into national law and the implementation of those Directives.

2. References to the repealed Directives shall be construed as references to this Directive and shall be read in accordance with the correlation table in Annex XII.

Article 412

1. Member States shall bring into force the laws, regulations and administrative provisions necessary to comply with Article 2 (3), Article 44, Article 59(1), Article 399 and Annex III, point (18) with effect from 1 January 2008. They shall forthwith communicate to the Commission the text of those provisions and a correlation table between those provisions and this Directive.

When Member States adopt those provisions, they shall contain a reference to this Directive or be accompanied by such a reference on the occasion of their official publication. Member States shall determine how such reference is to be made.

2. Member States shall communicate to the Commission the text of the main provisions of national law which they adopt in the field covered by this Directive.

Article 413

This Directive shall enter into force on 1 January 2007.

Article 414

This Directive is addressed to the Member States.

ANNEX I

LIST OF THE ACTIVITIES REFERRED TO IN THE THIRD SUBPARAGRAPH OF ARTICLE 13(1)

(1) Telecommunications services;
(2) supply of water, gas, electricity and thermal energy;
(3) transport of goods;
(4) port and airport services;
(5) passenger transport;
(6) supply of new goods manufactured for sale;
(7) transactions in respect of agricultural products, carried out by agricultural intervention agencies pursuant to Regulations on the common organisation of the market in those products;
(8) organisation of trade fairs and exhibitions;
(9) warehousing;
(10) activities of commercial publicity bodies;
(11) activities of travel agents;
(12) running of staff shops, cooperatives and industrial canteens and similar institutions;
(13) activities carried out by radio and television bodies in so far as these are not exempt pursuant to Article 132(1)(q).

ANNEX II

[INDICATIVE LIST OF THE ELECTRONICALLY SUPPLIED SERVICES REFERRED TO IN POINT (C) OF THE FIRST PARAGRAPH OF ARTICLE 58]

Amendments—Heading to Annex II substituted by Council Directive 2008/8/EC art 5(16) with effect from 1 January 2015 (OJ L 44, 20.2.2008 p 11).

(1) Website supply, web-hosting, distance maintenance of programmes and equipment;
(2) supply of software and updating thereof;
(3) supply of images, text and information and making available of databases;
(4) supply of music, films and games, including games of chance and gambling games, and of political, cultural, artistic, sporting, scientific and entertainment broadcasts and events;
(5) supply of distance teaching.

ANNEX III

LIST OF SUPPLIES OF GOODS AND SERVICES TO WHICH THE REDUCED RATES REFERRED TO IN ARTICLE 98 MAY BE APPLIED

(1) Foodstuffs (including beverages but excluding alcoholic beverages) for human and animal consumption; live animals, seeds, plants and ingredients normally intended for use in the preparation of foodstuffs; products normally used to supplement foodstuffs or as a substitute for foodstuffs;
(2) supply of water;
(3) pharmaceutical products of a kind normally used for health care, prevention of illnesses and as treatment for medical and veterinary purposes, including products used for contraception and sanitary protection;
(4) medical equipment, aids and other appliances normally intended to alleviate or treat disability, for the exclusive personal use of the disabled, including the repair of such goods, and supply of children's car seats;
(5) transport of passengers and their accompanying luggage;
[(6) supply, including on loan by libraries, of books, newspapers and periodicals either on physical means of support or supplied electronically or both (including brochures, leaflets and similar printed matter, children's picture, drawing or colouring books, music printed or in manuscript form, maps and hydrographic or similar charts), other than publications wholly or predominantly devoted to advertising and other than publications wholly or predominantly consisting of video content or audible music;][1]
(7) admission to shows, theatres, circuses, fairs, amusement parks, concerts, museums, zoos, cinemas, exhibitions and similar cultural events and facilities;
(8) reception of radio and television broadcasting services;
(9) supply of services by writers, composers and performing artists, or of the royalties due to them;
(10) provision, construction, renovation and alteration of housing, as part of a social policy;
[(10a) renovation and repairing of private dwellings, excluding materials which account for a significant part of the value of the service supplied;
(10b) window-cleaning and cleaning in private households;][1]
(11) supply of goods and services of a kind normally intended for use in agricultural production but excluding capital goods such as machinery or buildings;
(12) accommodation provided in hotels and similar establishments, including the provision of holiday accommodation and the letting of places on camping or caravan sites;
[(12a) restaurant and catering services, it being possible to exclude the supply of (alcoholic and/or non-alcoholic) beverages;][1]
(13) admission to sporting events;
(14) use of sporting facilities;
(15) supply of goods and services by organisations recognised as being devoted to social wellbeing by Member States and engaged in welfare or social security work, in so far as those transactions are not exempt pursuant to Articles 132, 135 and 136;
(16) supply of services by undertakers and cremation services, and the supply of goods related thereto;
(17) provision of medical and dental care and thermal treatment in so far as those services are not exempt pursuant to points (*b*) to (*e*) of Article 132(1);
(18) supply of services provided in connection with street cleaning, refuse collection and waste treatment, other than the supply of such services by bodies referred to in Article 13.
[(19) minor repairing of bicycles, shoes and leather goods, clothing and household linen (including mending and alteration);
(20) domestic care services such as home help and care of young, elderly, sick or disabled;
(21) hairdressing.][1]

Amendments—[1] Points (10a), (10b), (12a), (19)–(21) inserted by Council Directive 2009/47/EC art 1, Annex, with effect from 1 June 2009 (OJ L 116, 9.5.2009 p 18).
Point 6 substituted by Council Directive (EU) 2018/1713 Article (3) with effect from 4 December 2018 (OJ L 286, 14.11.2018, p 20).

ANNEX IV
LIST OF THE SERVICES REFERRED TO IN ARTICLE 106

(1) Minor repairing of:
  (a) bicycles;
  (b) shoes and leather goods;
  (c) clothing and household linen (including mending and alteration);
(2) renovation and repairing of private dwellings, excluding materials which account for a significant part of the value of the service supplied;
(3) window-cleaning and cleaning in private households;
(4) domestic care services such as home help and care of the young, elderly, sick or disabled;
(5) hairdressing.[1]

Amendments—[1] Annex IV repealed by Council Directive 2009/47/EC art 1, Annex, with effect from 1 June 2009 (OJ L 116, 9.5.2009 p 18).

ANNEX V
CATEGORIES OF GOODS COVERED BY WAREHOUSING ARRANGEMENTS OTHER THAN CUSTOMS WAREHOUSING AS PROVIDED FOR UNDER ARTICLE 160(2)

	CN-code	Description of goods
(1)	0701	Potatoes
(2)	0711 20	Olives
(3)	0801	Coconuts, Brazil nuts and cashew nuts
(4)	0802	Other nuts
(5)	0901 11 00 0901 12 00	Coffee, not roasted
(6)	0902	Tea
(7)	1001 to 1005 1007 to 1008	Cereals
(8)	1006	Husked rice
(9)	1201 to 1207	Grains and oil seeds (including soya beans) and oleaginous fruits
(10)	1507 to 1515	Vegetable oils and fats and their fractions, whether or not refined, but not chemically modified
(11)	1701 11 1701 12	Raw sugar
(12)	1801	Cocoa beans, whole or broken, raw or roasted
(13)	2709 2710 2711 12 2711 13	Mineral oils (including propane and butane; also including crude petroleum oils)
(14)	Chapters 28 and 29	Chemicals in bulk
(15)	4001 4002	Rubber, in primary forms or in plates, sheets or strip
(16)	5101	Wool
(17)	7106	Silver
(18)	7110 11 00 7110 21 00 7110 31 00	Platinum (palladium, rhodium)
(19)	7402 7403 7405 7408	Copper
(20)	7502	Nickel
(21)	7601	Aluminium
(22)	7801	Lead

	CN-code	Description of goods
(23)	7901	Zinc
(24)	8001	Tin
(25)	ex 8112 92 ex 8112 99	Indium

ANNEX VI
LIST OF SUPPLIES OF GOODS AND SERVICES AS REFERRED TO IN POINT (D) OF ARTICLE 199(1)

(1) Supply of ferrous and non ferrous waste, scrap, and used materials including that of semi-finished products resulting from the processing, manufacturing or melting down of ferrous and non-ferrous metals and their alloys;
(2) supply of ferrous and non-ferrous semi-processed products and certain associated processing services;
(3) supply of residues and other recyclable materials consisting of ferrous and non-ferrous metals, their alloys, slag, ash, scale and industrial residues containing metals or their alloys and supply of selection, cutting, fragmenting and pressing services of these products;
(4) supply of, and certain processing services relating to, ferrous and non-ferrous waste as well as parings, scrap, waste and used and recyclable material consisting of cullet, glass, paper, paperboard and board, rags, bone, leather, imitation leather, parchment, raw hides and skins, tendons and sinews, twine, cordage, rope, cables, rubber and plastic;
(5) supply of the materials referred to in this annex after processing in the form of cleaning, polishing, selection, cutting, fragmenting, pressing or casting into ingots;
(6) supply of scrap and waste from the working of base materials.

ANNEX VII
LIST OF THE AGRICULTURAL PRODUCTION ACTIVITIES REFERRED TO IN POINT (4) OF ARTICLE 295(1)

(1) Crop production:
 (a) general agriculture, including viticulture;
 (b) growing of fruit (including olives) and of vegetables, flowers and ornamental plants, both in the open and under glass;
 (c) production of mushrooms, spices, seeds and propagating materials;
 (d) running of nurseries;
(2) stock farming together with cultivation:
 (a) general stock farming;
 (b) poultry farming;
 (c) rabbit farming;
 (d) beekeeping;
 (e) silkworm farming;
 (f) snail farming;
(3) forestry;
(4) fisheries:
 (a) freshwater fishing;
 (b) fish farming;
 (c) breeding of mussels, oysters and other molluscs and crustaceans;
 (d) frog farming.

ANNEX VIII
INDICATIVE LIST OF THE AGRICULTURAL SERVICES REFERRED TO IN POINT (5) OF ARTICLE 295(1)

(1) Field work, reaping and mowing, threshing, baling, collecting, harvesting, sowing and planting;
(2) packing and preparation for market, such as drying, cleaning, grinding, disinfecting and ensilage of agricultural products;
(3) storage of agricultural products;
(4) stock minding, rearing and fattening;
(5) hiring out, for agricultural purposes, of equipment normally used in agricultural, forestry or fisheries undertakings;
(6) technical assistance;
(7) destruction of weeds and pests, dusting and spraying of crops and land;

(8) operation of irrigation and drainage equipment;
(9) lopping, tree felling and other forestry services.

ANNEX IX
WORKS OF ART, COLLECTORS' ITEMS AND ANTIQUES, AS REFERRED TO IN POINTS (2), (3) AND (4) OF ARTICLE 311(1)

PART A
WORKS OF ART

(1) Pictures, collages and similar decorative plaques, paintings and drawings, executed entirely by hand by the artist, other than plans and drawings for architectural, engineering, industrial, commercial, topographical or similar purposes, hand-decorated manufactured articles, theatrical scenery, studio back cloths or the like of painted canvas (CN code 9701);
(2) original engravings, prints and lithographs, being impressions produced in limited numbers directly in black and white or in colour of one or of several plates executed entirely by hand by the artist, irrespective of the process or of the material employed, but not including any mechanical or photomechanical process (CN code 9702 00 00);
(3) original sculptures and statuary, in any material, provided that they are executed entirely by the artist; sculpture casts the production of which is limited to eight copies and supervised by the artist or his successors in title (CN code 9703 00 00); on an exceptional basis, in cases determined by the Member States, the limit of eight copies may be exceeded for statuary casts produced before 1 January 1989;
(4) tapestries (CN code 5805 00 00) and wall textiles (CN code 6304 00 00) made by hand from original designs provided by artists, provided that there are not more than eight copies of each;
(5) individual pieces of ceramics executed entirely by the artist and signed by him;
(6) enamels on copper, executed entirely by hand, limited to eight numbered copies bearing the signature of the artist or the studio, excluding articles of jewellery and goldsmiths' and silversmiths' wares;
(7) photographs taken by the artist, printed by him or under his supervision, signed and numbered and limited to 30 copies, all sizes and mounts included.

PART B
COLLECTORS' ITEMS

(1) Postage or revenue stamps, postmarks, first-day covers, pre-stamped stationery and the like, used, or if unused not current and not intended to be current (CN code 9704 00 00);
(2) collections and collectors' pieces of zoological, botanical, mineralogical, anatomical, historical, archaeological, palaeontological, ethnographic or numismatic interest (CN code 9705 00 00).

PART C
ANTIQUES

Goods, other than works of art or collectors' items, which are more than 100 years old (CN code 9706 00 00).

ANNEX X
LIST OF TRANSACTIONS COVERED BY THE DEROGATIONS REFERRED TO IN ARTICLES 370 AND 371 AND ARTICLES 375 TO 390B

Amendments—Annex X title substituted for "List of Transactions Covered By the Derogations Referred to in Articles 370 and 371 and Articles 375 to 390" by Council Directive 2009/162/EU art 1(17) with effect from 15 January 2010 (OJ L 10, 15.1.2010, p 14).

PART A
TRANSACTIONS WHICH MEMBER STATES MAY CONTINUE TO TAX

(1) The supply of services by dental technicians in their professional capacity and the supply of dental prostheses by dentists and dental technicians;
(2) the activities of public radio and television bodies other than those of a commercial nature;
(3) the supply of a building, or parts thereof, or of the land on which it stands, other than as referred to in point (*a*) of Article 12(1), where carried out by taxable persons who were entitled to deduction of the VAT paid at the preceding stage in respect of the building concerned;
(4) the supply of the services of travel agents, as referred to in Article 306, and those of travel agents acting in the name and on behalf of the traveller, in relation to journeys outside the Community.

PART B
TRANSACTIONS WHICH MEMBER STATES MAY CONTINUE TO EXEMPT

(1) Admission to sporting events;

(2) the supply of services by authors, artists, performers, lawyers and other members of the liberal professions, other than the medical and paramedical professions, with the exception of the following:
- (a) assignments of patents, trade marks and other similar rights, and the granting of licences in respect of such rights;
- (b) work, other than the supply of contract work, on movable tangible property, carried out for a taxable person;
- (c) services to prepare or coordinate the carrying out of construction work, such as services provided by architects and by firms providing on-site supervision of works;
- (d) commercial advertising services;
- (e) transport and storage of goods, and ancillary services;
- (f) hiring out of movable tangible property to a taxable person;
- (g) provision of staff to a taxable person;
- (h) provision of services by consultants, engineers, planning offices and similar services in scientific, economic or technical fields;
- (i) compliance with an obligation to refrain from exercising, in whole or in part, a business activity or a right covered by points (a) to (h) or point (j);
- (j) the services of forwarding agents, brokers, business agents and other independent intermediaries, in so far as they relate to the supply or importation of goods or the supply of services covered by points (a) to (i);

(3) the supply of telecommunications services, and of goods related thereto, by public postal services;

(4) the supply of services by undertakers and cremation services and the supply of goods related thereto;

(5) transactions carried out by blind persons or by workshops for the blind, provided that those exemptions do not cause significant distortion of competition;

(6) the supply of goods and services to official bodies responsible for the construction, setting out and maintenance of cemeteries, graves and monuments commemorating the war dead;

(7) transactions carried out by hospitals not covered by point (b) of Article 132(1);

(8) the supply of water by a body governed by public law;

(9) the supply before first occupation of a building, or parts thereof, or of the land on which it stands and the supply of building land, as referred to in Article 12;

(10) the transport of passengers and, in so far as the transport of the passengers is exempt, the transport of goods accompanying them, such as luggage or motor vehicles, or the supply of services relating to the transport of passengers;

(11) the supply, modification, repair, maintenance, chartering and hiring of aircraft used by State institutions, including equipment incorporated or used in such aircraft;

(12) the supply, modification, repair, maintenance, chartering and hiring of fighting ships;

(13) the supply of the services of travel agents, as referred to in Article 306, and those of travel agents acting in the name and on behalf of the traveller, in relation to journeys within the Community.

ANNEX XI

PART A

REPEALED DIRECTIVES WITH THEIR SUCCESSIVE AMENDMENTS

(1) Directive 67/227/EEC (OJ 71, 14.4.1967, p. 1301)
Directive 77/388/EEC

(2) Directive 77/388/EEC (OJ L 145, 13.6.1977, p. 1)
Directive 78/583/EEC (OJ L 194, 19.7.1978, p. 16)
Directive 80/368/EEC (OJ L 90, 3.4.1980, p. 41)
Directive 84/386/EEC (OJ L 208, 3.8.1984, p. 58)
Directive 89/465/EEC (OJ L 226, 3.8.1989, p. 21)
Directive 91/680/EEC (OJ L 376, 31.12.1991, p. 1) — (except for Article 2)
Directive 92/77/EEC (OJ L 316, 31.10.1992, p. 1)
Directive 92/111/EEC (OJ L 384, 30.12.1992, p. 47)
Directive 94/4/EC (OJ L 60, 3.3.1994, p. 14) — (only Article 2)
Directive 94/5/EC (OJ L 60, 3.3.1994, p. 16)
Directive 94/76/EC (OJ L 365, 31.12.1994, p. 53)
Directive 95/7/EC (OJ L 102, 5.5.1995, p. 18)
Directive 96/42/EC (OJ L 170, 9.7.1996, p. 34)
Directive 96/95/EC (OJ L 338, 28.12.1996, p. 89)

Directive 98/80/EC (OJ L 281, 17.10.1998, p. 31)
Directive 1999/49/EC (OJ L 139, 2.6.1999, p. 27)
Directive 1999/59/EC (OJ L 162, 26.6.1999, p. 63)
Directive 1999/85/EC (OJ L 277, 28.10.1999, p. 34)
Directive 2000/17/EC (OJ L 84, 5.4.2000, p. 24)
Directive 2000/65/EC (OJ L 269, 21.10.2000, p. 44)
Directive 2001/4/EC (OJ L 22, 24.1.2001, p. 17)
Directive 2001/115/EC (OJ L 15, 17.1.2002, p. 24)
Directive 2002/38/EC (OJ L 128, 15.5.2002, p. 41)
Directive 2002/93/EC (OJ L 331, 7.12.2002, p. 27)
Directive 2003/92/EC (OJ L 260, 11.10.2003, p. 8)
Directive 2004/7/EC (OJ L 27, 30.1.2004, p. 44)
Directive 2004/15/EC (OJ L 52, 21.2.2004, p. 61)
Directive 2004/66/EC (OJ L 168, 1.5.2004, p. 35) — (only Point V of the Annex)
Directive 2005/92/EC (OJ L 345, 28.12.2005, p. 19)
Directive 2006/18/EC (OJ L 51, 22.2.2006, p. 12)
Directive 2006/58/EC (OJ L 174, 28.6.2006, p. 5)
Directive 2006/69/EC (OJ L 221, 12.8.2006, p. 9 — (only Article 1)
Directive 2006/98/EC (OJ L . . . , . . . , p. . . . (*) — (only point 2 of the Annex)

PART B
TIME LIMITS FOR TRANSPOSITION INTO NATIONAL LAW (REFERRED TO IN ARTICLE 411)

Directive	Deadline for transposition
Directive 67/227/EEC	1 January 1970
Directive 77/388/EEC	1 January 1978
Directive 78/583/EEC	1 January 1979
Directive 80/368/EEC	1 January 1979
Directive 84/386/EEC	1 July 1985
Directive 89/465/EEC	1 January 1990
	1 January 1991
	1 January 1992
	1 January 1993
	1 January 1994 for Portugal
Directive 91/680/EEC	1 January 1993
Directive 92/77/EEC	31 December 1992
Directive 92/111/EEC	1 January 1993
	1 January 1994
	1 October 1993 for Germany
Directive 94/4/EC	1 April 1994
Directive 94/5/EC	1 January 1995
Directive 94/76/EC	1 January 1995
Directive 95/7/EC	1 January 1996
	1 January 1997 for Germany and Luxembourg
Directive 96/42/EC	1 January 1995
Directive 96/95/EC	1 January 1997
Directive 98/80/EC	1 January 2000
Directive 1999/49/EC	1 January 1999
Directive 1999/59/EC	1 January 2000
Directive 1999/85/CE	—
Directive 2000/17/EC	—
Directive 2000/65/EC	31 December 2001
Directive 2001/4/EC	1 January 2001
Directive 2001/115/EC	1 January 2004
Directive 2002/38/EC	1 July 2003
Directive 2002/93/EC	—

Directive	Deadline for transposition
Directive 2003/92/EC	1 January 2005
Directive 2004/7/EC	30 January 2004
Directive 2004/15/EC	—
Directive 2004/66/EC	1 May 2004
Directive 2005/92/EC	1 January 2006
Directive 2006/18/EC	—
Directive 2006/58/EC	1 July 2006
Directive 2006/69/EC	1 January 2008

ANNEX XII
CORRELATION TABLE

Directive 67/227/EEC	Directive 77/388/EEC	Amending Directives	Other acts	This Directive
Article 1, first paragraph				Article 1(1)
Article 1, second and third paragraphs				—
Article 2, first, second and third paragraphs				Article 1(2), first, second and third subparagraphs
Articles 3, 4 and 6				—
	Article 1			—
	Article 2, point (1)			Article 2(1)(a) and (c)
	Article 2, point (2)			Article 2(1)(d)
	Article 3(1), first indent			Article 5, point (2)
	Article 3(1), second indent			Article 5, point (1)
	Article 3(1), third indent			Article 5, points (3) and (4)
	Article 3(2)			—
	Article 3(3), first subparagraph, first indent			Article 6(2)(a) and (b)
	Article 3(3), first subparagraph, second indent			Article 6(2)(c) and (d)
	Article 3(3), first subparagraph, third indent			Article 6(2)(e), (f) and (g)
	Article 3(3) second subparagraph, first indent			Article 6(1)(b)
	Article 3(3) second subparagraph, second indent			Article 6(1)(c)
	Article 3(3), second subparagraph, third indent			Article 6(1)(a)
	Article 3(4), first subparagraph, first and second indents			Article 7(1)
	Article 3(4), second subparagraph, first second and third indents			Article 7(2)
	Article 3(5)			Article 8
	Article 4(1) and (2)			Article 9(1), first and second subparagraphs
	Article 4(3)(a), first subparagraph, first sentence			Article 12(1)(a)
	Article 4(3)(a), first subparagraph, second sentence			Article 12(2), second subparagraph
	Article 4(3)(a), second subparagraph			Article 12(2), third subparagraph
	Article 4(3)(a), third subparagraph			Article 12(2), first subparagraph
	Article 4(3)(b), first subparagraph			Article 12(1)(b)

Correlation Table

Directive 67/227/EEC	Directive 77/388/EEC	Amending Directives	Other acts	This Directive
	Article 4(3)(b), second subparagraph			Article 12(3)
	Article 4(4), first subparagraph			Article 10
	Article 4(4), second and third subparagraphs			Article 11, first and second paragraphs
	Article 4(5), first, second and third subparagraphs			Article 13(1), first, second and third subparagraphs
	Article 4(5), fourth subparagraph			Article 13(2)
	Article 5(1)			Article 14(1)
	Article 5(2)			Article 15(1)
	Article 5(3)(a), (b) and (c)			Article 15(2)(a), (b) and (c)
	Article 5(4)(a), (b) and (c)			Article 14(2)(a), (b) and (c)
	Article 5(5)			Article 14(3)
	Article 5(6), first and second sentences			Article 16, first and second paragraphs
	Article 5(7)(a), (b) and (c)			Article 18(a), (b) and (c)
	Article 5(8), first sentence			Article 19, first paragraph
	Article 5(8), second and third sentences			Article 19, second paragraph
	Article 6(1), first subparagraph			Article 24(1)
	Article 6(1), second subparagraph, first, second and third indents			Article 25(a), (b) and (c)
	Article 6(2), first subparagraph, points (a) and (b)			Article 26(1)(a) and (b)
	Article 6(2), second subparagraph			Article 26(2)
	Article 6(3)			Article 27
	Article 6(4)			Article 28
	Article 6(5)			Article 29
	Article 7(1)(a) and (b)			Article 30, first and second subparagraphs
	Article 7(2)			Article 60
	Article 7(3), first and second subparagraphs			Article 61, first and second paragraphs
	Article 8(1)(a), first sentence			Article 32, first paragraph
	Article 8(1)(a), second and third sentences			Article 36, first and second paragraphs

Directive 67/227/EEC	Directive 77/388/EEC	Amending Directives	Other acts	This Directive
	Article 8(1)(b)			Article 31
	Article 8(1)(c), first subparagraph			Article 37(1)
	Article 8(1)(c), second subparagraph, first indent			Article 37(2), first subparagraph
	Article 8(1)(c), second subparagraph, second and third indents			Article 37(2), second and third subparagraphs
	Article 8(1)(c), third subparagraph			Article 37(2), fourth subparagraph
	Article 8(1)(c), fourth subparagraph			Article 37(3), first subparagraph
	Article 8(1)(c), fifth subparagraph			—
	Article 8(1)(c), sixth subparagraph			Article 37(3), second subparagraph
	Article 8(1)(d), first and second subparagraphs			Article 38(1) and (2)
	Article 8(1)(e), first sentence			Article 39, first paragraph
	Article 8(1)(e), second and third sentences			Article 39, second paragraph
	Article 8(2)			Article 32, second paragraph
	Article 9(1)			Article 43
	Article 9(2) introductory sentence			—
	Article 9(2)(a)			Article 45
	Article 9(2)(b)			Article 46
	Article 9(2)(c), first and second indents			Article 52(a) and (b)
	Article 9(2)(c), third and fourth indents			Article 52(c)
	Article 9(2)(e), first to sixth indents			Article 56(1)(a) to (f)
	Article 9(2)(e), seventh indent			Article 56(1)(l)
	Article 9(2)(e), eighth indent			Article 56(1)(g)
	Article 9(2)(e), ninth indent			Article 56(1)(h)
	Article 9(2)(e), tenth indent, first sentence			Article 56(1)(i)
	Article 9(2)(e), tenth indent, second sentence			Article 24(2)
	Article 9(2)(e), tenth indent, third sentence			Article 56(1)(i)
	Article 9(2)(e), eleventh and twelfth indents			Article 56(1)(j) and (k)
	Article 9(2)(f)			Article 57(1)
	Article 9(3)			Article 58, first and second paragraphs

Directive 67/227/EEC	Directive 77/388/EEC	Amending Directives	Other acts	This Directive
	Article 9(3)(a) and (b)			Article 58, first paragraph, points (a) and (b)
	Article 9(4)			Article 59(1) and (2)
	Article 10(1)(a) and (b)			Article 62, points (1) and (2)
	Article 10(2), first subparagraph, first sentence			Article 63
	Article 10(2), first subparagraph, second and third sentences			Article 64(1) and (2)
	Article 10(2), second subparagraph			Article 65
	Article 10(2), third subparagraph, first, second and third indents			Article 66(a), (b) and (c)
	Article 10(3), first subparagraph, first sentence			Article 70
	Article 10(3), first subparagraph, second sentence			Article 71(1), first subparagraph
	Article 10(3), second subparagraph			Article 71(1), second subparagraph
	Article 10(3), third subparagraph			Article 71(2)
	Article 11(A)(1)(a)			Article 73
	Article 11(A)(1)(b)			Article 74
	Article 11(A)(1)(c)			Article 75
	Article 11(A)(1)(d)			Article 77
	Article 11(A)(2)(a)			Article 78, first paragraph, point (a)
	Article 11(A)(2)(b), first sentence			Article 78, first paragraph, point (b)
	Article 11(A)(2)(b), second sentence			Article 78, second paragraph
	Article 11(A)(3)(a) and (b)			Article 79, first paragraph, points (a) and (b) Article 87(a) and (b)
	Article 11(A)(3)(c), first sentence			Article 79, first paragraph, point (c)
	Article 11(A)(3)(c), second sentence			Article 79, second paragraph
	Article 11(A)(4), first and second subparagraphs			Article 81, first and second paragraphs
	Article 11(A)(5)			Article 82

Directive 67/227/EEC	Directive 77/388/EEC	Amending Directives	Other acts	This Directive
	Article 11(A)(6), first subparagraph, first and second sentences			Article 80(1), first subparagraph
	Article 11(A)(6), first subparagraph, third sentence			Article 80(1), second subparagraph
	Article 11(A)(6), second subparagraph			Article 80(1), first subparagraph
	Article 11(A)(6), third subparagraph			Article 80(2)
	Article 11(A)(6), fourth subparagraph			Article 80(3)
	Article 11(A)(7), first and second subparagraphs			Article 72, first and second paragraphs
	Article 11(B)(1)			Article 85
	Article 11(B)(3)(a)			Article 86(1)(a)
	Article 11(B)(3)(b), first subparagraph			Article 86(1)(b)
	Article 11(B)(3)(b), second subparagraph			Article 86(2)
	Article 11(B)(3)(b), third subparagraph			Article 86(1)(b)
	Article 11(B)(4)			Article 87
	Article 11(B)(5)			Article 88
	Article 11(B)(6), first and second subparagraphs			Article 89, first and second paragraphs
	Article 11(C)(1), first and second subparagraphs			Article 90(1) and (2)
	Article 11(C)(2), first subparagraph			Article 91(1)
	Article 11(C)(2), second subparagraph, first and second sentences			Article 91(2), first and second subparagraphs
	Article 11(C)(3), first and second indents			Article 92(a) and (b)
	Article 12(1)			Article 93, first paragraph
	Article 12(1)(a)			Article 93, second paragraph, point (a)
	Article 12(1)(b)			Article 93, second paragraph, point (c)
	Article 12(2), first and second indents			Article 95, first and second paragraphs
	Article 12(3)(a), first subparagraph, first sentence			Article 96
	Article 12(3)(a), first subparagraph, second sentence			Article 97(1)
	Article 12(3)(a), second subparagraph			Article 97(2)
	Article 12(3)(a), third subparagraph, first sentence			Article 98(1)

Directive 67/227/EEC	Directive 77/388/EEC	Amending Directives	Other acts	This Directive
	Article 12(3)(a), third subparagraph, second sentence			Article 98(2), first subparagraph Article 99(1)
	Article 12(3)(a), fourth subparagraph			Article 98(2), second subparagraph
	Article 12(3)(b), first sentence			Article 102, first paragraph
	Article 12(3)(b), second, third and fourth sentences			Article 102, second paragraph
	Article 12(3)(c), first subparagraph			Article 103(1)
	Article 12(3)(c), second subparagraph, first and second indents			Article 103(2)(a) and (b)
	Article 12(4), first subparagraph			Article 99(2)
	Article 12(4), second subparagraph, first and second sentences			Article 100, first and second paragraphs
	Article 12(4), third subparagraph			Article 101
	Article 12(5)			Article 94(2)
	Article 12(6)			Article 105
	Article 13(A)(1), introductory sentence			Article 131
	Article 13(A)(1)(a) to (n)			Article 132(1)(a) to (n)
	Article 13(A)(1)(o), first sentence			Article 132(1)(o)
	Article 13(A)(1)(o), second sentence			Article 132(2)
	Article 13(A)(1)(p) and (q)			Article 132(1)(p) and (q)
	Article 13(A)(2)(a), first to fourth indents			Article 133(a) to (d)
	Article 13(A)(2)(b), first and second indents			Article 134(a) and (b)
	Article 13(B), introductory sentence			Article 131
	Article 13(B)(a)			Article 135(1)(a)
	Article 13(B)(b), first subparagraph			Article 135(1)(l)
	Article 13(B)(b), first subparagraph, points (1) to (4)			Article 135(2), first subparagraph, points (a) to (d)
	Article 13(B)(b), second subparagraph			Article 135(2), second subparagraph
	Article 13(B)(c)			Article 136(a) and (b)
	Article 13(B)(d)			—
	Article 13(B)(d), points (1) to (5)			Article 135(1)(b) to (f)
	Article 13(B)(d), point (5), first and second indents			Article 135(1)(f)

Directive 67/227/EEC	Directive 77/388/EEC	Amending Directives	Other acts	This Directive
	Article 13(B)(d), point (6)			Article 135(1)(g)
	Article 13(B)(e) to (h)			Article 135(1)(h) to (k)
	Article 13(C), first subparagraph, point (a)			Article 137(1)(d)
	Article 13(C), first subparagraph, point (b)			Article 137(1)(a), (b) and (c)
	Article 13(C), second subparagraph			Article 137(2), first and second subparagraphs
	Article 14(1), introductory sentence			Article 131
	Article 14(1)(a)			Article 140(a)
	Article 14(1)(d), first and second subparagraphs			Article 143(b) and (c)
	Article 14(1)(e)			Article 143(e)
	Article 14(1)(g), first to fourth indents			Article 143(f) to (i)
	Article 14(1)(h)			Article 143(j)
	Article 14(1)(i)			Article 144
	Article 14(1)(j)			Article 143(k)
	Article 14(1)(k)			Article 143(l)
	Article 14(2), first subparagraph			Article 145(1)
	Article 14(2), second subparagraph, first, second and third indents			Article 145(2), first, second and third subparagraphs
	Article 14(2), third subparagraph			Article 145(3)
	Article 15, introductory sentence			Article 131
	Article 15, point (1)			Article 146(1)(a)
	Article 15, point (2), first subparagraph			Article 146(1)(b)
	Article 15, point (2), second subparagraph, first and second indents			Article 147(1), first subparagraph, points (a) and (b)
	Article 15, point (2), second subparagraph, third indent, first part of the sentence			Article 147(1), first subparagraph, point (c)
	Article 15, point (2), second subparagraph, third indent, second part of the sentence			Article 147(1), second subparagraph
	Article 15, point (2), third subparagraph, first and second indents			Article 147(2), first and second subparagraphs
	Article 15, point (2), fourth subparagraph			Article 147(2), third subparagraph
	Article 15, point (3)			Article 146(1)(d)

Directive 67/227/EEC	Directive 77/388/EEC	Amending Directives	Other acts	This Directive
	Article 15, point (4), first subparagraph, points (a) and (b)			Article 148(a)
	Article 15, point (4), first subparagraph, point (c)			Article 148(b)
	Article 15, point (4), second subparagraph, first and second sentences			Article 150(1) and (2)
	Article 15, point (5)			Article 148(c)
	Article 15, point (6)			Article 148(f)
	Article 15, point (7)			Article 148(e)
	Article 15, point (8)			Article 148(d)
	Article 15, point (9)			Article 148(g)
	Article 15, point (10), first subparagraph, first to fourth indents			Article 151(1), first subparagraph, points (a) to (d)
	Article 15, point (10), second subparagraph			Article 151(1), second subparagraph
	Article 15, point (10), third subparagraph			Article 151(2)
	Article 15, point (11)			Article 152
	Article 15, point (12), first sentence			Article 146(1)(c)
	Article 15, point (12), second sentence			Article 146(2)
	Article 15, point (13)			Article 146(1)(e)
	Article 15, point (14), first and second subparagraphs			Article 153, first and second paragraphs
	Article 15, point (15)			Article 149
	Article 16(1)			—
	Article 16(2)			Article 164(1)
	Article 16(3)			Article 166
	Article 17(1)			Article 167
	Article 17(2), (3) and (4)			—
	Article 17(5), first and second subparagraphs			Article 173(1), first and second subparagraphs
	Article 17(5), third subparagraph, points (a) to (e)			Article 173(2)(a) to (e)
	Article 17(6)			Article 176
	Article 17(7), first and second sentences			Article 177, first and second paragraphs

Directive 67/227/EEC	Directive 77/388/EEC	Amending Directives	Other acts	This Directive
	Article 18(1)			—
	Article 18(2), first and second subparagraphs			Article 179, first and second paragraphs
	Article 18(3)			Article 180
	Article 18(4), first and second subparagraphs			Article 183, first and second paragraphs
	Article 19(1), first subparagraph, first indent			Article 174(1), first subparagraph, point (a)
	Article 19(1), first subparagraph, second indent, first sentence			Article 174(1), first subparagraph, point (b)
	Article 19(1), first subparagraph, second indent, second sentence			Article 174(1), second subparagraph
	Article 19(1), second subparagraph			Article 175(1)
	Article 19(2), first sentence			Article 174(2)(a)
	Article 19(2), second sentence			Article 174(2)(a) and (b)
	Article 19(2), third sentence			Article 174(3)
	Article 19(3), first subparagraph, first and second sentences			Article 175(2), first subparagraph
	Article 19(3), first subparagraph, third sentence			Article 175(2), second subparagraph
	Article 19(3), second subparagraph			Article 175(3)
	Article 20(1), introductory sentence			Article 186
	Article 20(1)(a)			Article 184
	Article 20(1)(b), first part of the first sentence			Article 185(1)
	Article 20(1)(b), second part of the first sentence			Article 185(2), first subparagraph
	Article 20(1)(b), second sentence			Article 185(2), second subparagraph
	Article 20(2), first subparagraph, first sentence			Article 187(1), first subparagraph
	Article 20(2), first subparagraph, second and third sentences			Article 187(2), first and second subparagraphs
	Article 20(2), second and third subparagraphs			Article 187(1), second and third subparagraphs
	Article 20(3), first subparagraph, first sentence			Article 188(1), first subparagraph

Directive 67/227/EEC	Directive 77/388/EEC	Amending Directives	Other acts	This Directive
	Article 20(3), first subparagraph, second sentence			Article 188(1), second and third subparagraphs
	Article 20(3), first subparagraph, third sentence			Article 188(2)
	Article 20(3), second subparagraph			Article 188(2)
	Article 20(4), first subparagraph, first to fourth indents			Article 189(a) to (d)
	Article 20(4), second subparagraph			Article 190
	Article 20(5)			Article 191
	Article 20(6)			Article 192
	Article 21			—
	Article 22			—
	Article 22a			Article 249
	Article 23, first paragraph			Article 211, first paragraph Article 260
	Article 23, second paragraph			Article 211, second paragraph
	Article 24(1)			Article 281
	Article 24(2)			Article 292
	Article 24(2)(a), first subparagraph			Article 284(1)
	Article 24(2)(a), second and third subparagraphs			Article 284(2), first and second subparagraphs
	Article 24(2)(b), first and second sentences			Article 285, first and second paragraphs
	Article 24(2)(c)			Article 286
	Article 24(3), first subparagraph			Article 282
	Article 24(3), second subparagraph, first sentence			Article 283(2)
	Article 24(3), second subparagraph, second sentence			Article 283(1)(a)
	Article 24(4), first subparagraph			Article 288, first paragraph, points (1) to (4)
	Article 24(4), second subparagraph			Article 288, second paragraph
	Article 24(5)			Article 289
	Article 24(6)			Article 290
	Article 24(7)			Article 291
	Article 24(8)(a), (b) and (c)			Article 293, points (1), (2) and (3)
	Article 24(9)			Article 294

Directive 67/227/EEC	Directive 77/388/EEC	Amending Directives	Other acts	This Directive
	Article 24a, first paragraph, first to twelfth indents			Article 287, points (7) to (16)
	Article 25(1)			Article 296(1)
	Article 25(2), first to eighth indents			Article 295(1), points (1) to (8)
	Article 25(3), first subparagraph, first sentence			Article 297, first paragraph, first sentence and second paragraph
	Article 25(3), first subparagraph, second sentence			Article 298, first paragraph
	Article 25(3), first subparagraph, third sentence			Article 299
	Article 25(3), first subparagraph, fourth and fifth sentences			Article 298, second paragraph
	Article 25(3), second subparagraph			Article 297, first paragraph, second sentence
	Article 25(4), first subparagraph			Article 272(1), first subparagraph, point (e)
	Article 25(5) and (6)			—
	Article 25(7)			Article 304
	Article 25(8)			Article 301(2)
	Article 25(9)			Article 296(2)
	Article 25(10)			Article 296(3)
	Article 25(11) and (12)			—
	Article 26(1) first and second sentences			Article 306(1), first and second subparagraphs
	Article 26(1) third sentence			Article 306(2)
	Article 26(2), first and second sentences			Article 307, first and second paragraphs
	Article 26(2), third sentence			Article 308
	Article 26(3), first and second sentences			Article 309, first and second paragraphs
	Article 26(4)			Article 310
	Article 26a(A)(a), first subparagraph			Article 311(1), point (2)
	Article 26a(A)(a), second subparagraph			Article 311(2)
	Article 26a(A)(b) and (c)			Article 311(1), points (3) and (4)
	Article 26a(A)(d)			Article 311(1), point (1)
	Article 26a(A)(e) and (f)			Article 311(1), points (5) and (6)

Directive 67/227/EEC	Directive 77/388/EEC	Amending Directives	Other acts	This Directive
	Article 26a(A)(g), introductory sentence			Article 311(1), point (7)
	Article 26a(A)(g), first and second indents			Article 311(3)
	Article 26a(B)(1)			Article 313(1)
	Article 26a(B)(2)			Article 314
	Article 26a(B)(2), first and second indents			Article 314(a) to (d)
	Article 26a(B)(3), first subparagraph, first and second sentences			Article 315, first and second paragraphs
	Article 26a(B)(3), second subparagraph			Article 312
	Article 26a(B)(3), second subparagraph, first and second indents			Article 312, points (1) and (2)
	Article 26a(B)(4), first subparagraph			Article 316(1)
	Article 26a(B)(4), first subparagraph, points (a), (b) and (c)			Article 316(1)(a), (b) and (c)
	Article 26a(B)(4), second subparagraph			Article 316(2)
	Article 26a(B)(4), third subparagraph, first and second sentences			Article 317, first and second paragraphs
	Article 26a(B)(5)			Article 321
	Article 26a(B)(6)			Article 323
	Article 26a(B)(7)			Article 322
	Article 26a(B)(7)(a), (b) and (c)			Article 322(a), (b) and (c)
	Article 26a(B)(8)			Article 324
	Article 26a(B)(9)			Article 325
	Article 26a(B)(10) first and second subparagraphs			Article 318(1), first and second subparagraphs
	Article 26a(B)(10), third subparagraph, first and second indents			Article 318(2)(a) and (b)
	Article 26a(B)(10), fourth subparagraph			Article 318(3)
	Article 26a(B)(11), first subparagraph			Article 319
	Article 26a(B)(11), second subparagraph, point (a)			Article 320(1), first subparagraph
	Article 26a(B)(11), second subparagraph, points (b) and (c)			Article 320(1), second subparagraph
	Article 26a(B)(11), third subparagraph			Article 320(2)
	Article 26a(C)(1), introductory sentence			Article 333(1) Article 334

Directive 67/227/EEC	Directive 77/388/EEC	Amending Directives	Other acts	This Directive
	Article 26a(C)(1), first to fourth indents			Article 334(a) to (d)
	Article 26a(C)(2), first and second indents			Article 336(a) and (b)
	Article 26a(C)(3)			Article 337
	Article 26a(C)(4), first subparagraph, first, second and third indents			Article 339, first paragraph, points (a), (b) and (c)
	Article 26a(C)(4), second subparagraph			Article 339, second paragraph
	Article 26a(C)(5), first and second subparagraphs			Article 340(1), first and second subparagraphs
	Article 26a(C)(5), third subparagraph			Article 340(2)
	Article 26a(C)(6), first subparagraph, first and second indents			Article 338, first paragraph, points (a) and (b)
	Article 26a(C)(6), second subparagraph			Article 338, second paragraph
	Article 26a(C)(7)			Article 335
	Article 26a(D), introductory sentence			—
	Article 26a(D)(a)			Article 313(2) Article 333(2)
	Article 26a(D)(b)			Article 4(a) and (c)
	Article 26a(D)(c)			Article 35 Article 139(3), first subparagraph
	Article 26b(A), first subparagraph, point (i), first sentence			Article 344(1), point (1)
	Article 26b(A), first subparagraph, point (i), second sentence			Article 344(2)
	Article 26b(A), first subparagraph, point (ii), first to fourth indents			Article 344(1), point (2)
	Article 26b(A), second subparagraph			Article 344(3)
	Article 26b(A), third subparagraph			Article 345
	Article 26b(B), first subparagraph			Article 346
	Article 26b(B), second subparagraph			Article 347
	Article 26b(C), first subparagraph			Article 348
	Article 26b(C), second subparagraph, first and second sentences			Article 349(1) and (2)
	Article 26b(C), third subparagraph			Article 350
	Article 26b(C), fourth subparagraph			Article 351
	Article 26b(D)(1)(a), (b) and (c)			Article 354(a), (b) and (c)

Correlation Table

Directive 67/227/EEC	Directive 77/388/EEC	Amending Directives	Other acts	This Directive
	Article 26b(D)(2)			Article 355
	Article 26b(E), first and second subparagraphs			Article 356(1), first and second subparagraphs
	Article 26b(E), third and fourth subparagraphs			Article 356(2) and (3)
	Article 26b(F), first sentence			Article 198(2) and (3)
	Article 26b(F), second sentence			Articles 208 and 255
	Article 26b(G)(1), first subparagraph			Article 352
	Article 26b(G)(1), second subparagraph			—
	Article 26b(G)(2)(a)			Article 353
	Article 26b(G)(2)(b), first and second sentences			Article 198(1) and (3)
	Article 26c(A)(a) to (e)			Article 358, points (1) to (5)
	Article 26c(B)(1)			Article 359
	Article 26c(B)(2), first subparagraph			Article 360
	Article 26c(B)(2), second subparagraph, first part of the first sentence			Article 361(1)
	Article 26c(B)(2), second subparagraph, second part of the first sentence			Article 361(1)(a) to (e)
	Article 26c(B)(2), second subparagraph, second sentence			Article 361(2)
	Article 26c(B)(3), first and second subparagraphs			Article 362
	Article 26c(B)(4)(a) to (d)			Article 363(a) to (d)
	Article 26c(B)(5), first subparagraph			Article 364
	Article 26c(B)(5), second subparagraph			Article 365
	Article 26c(B)(6), first sentence			Article 366(1), first subparagraph
	Article 26c(B)(6), second and third sentences			Article 366(1), second subparagraph
	Article 26c(B)(6), fourth sentence			Article 366(2)
	Article 26c(B)(7), first sentence			Article 367, first paragraph
	Article 26c(B)(7), second and third sentences			Article 367, second paragraph
	Article 26c(B)(8)			Article 368
	Article 26c(B)(9), first sentence			Article 369(1)
	Article 26c(B)(9), second and third sentences			Article 369(2), first and second subparagraphs
	Article 26c(B)(10)			Article 204(1), third subparagraph

Directive 67/227/EEC	Directive 77/388/EEC	Amending Directives	Other acts	This Directive
	Article 27(1) first and second sentences			Article 395(1) first and second subparagraphs
	Article 27(2), first and second sentences			Article 395(2), first subparagraphs
	Article 27(2), third sentence			Article 395(2), second subparagraph
	Article 27(3) and (4)			Article 395(3) and (4)
	Article 27(5)			Article 394
	Article 28(1) and (1a)			—
	Article 28(2), introductory sentence			Article 109
	Article 28(2)(a), first subparagraph			Article 110, first and second paragraphs
	Article 28(2)(a), second subparagraph			—
	Article 28(2)(a), third subparagraph, first sentence			Article 112, first paragraph
	Article 28(2)(a), third subparagraph, second and third sentences			Article 112, second paragraph
	Article 28(2)(b)			Article 113
	Article 28(2)(c), first and second sentences			Article 114(1), first and second subparagraphs
	Article 28(2)(c), third sentence			Article 114(2)
	Article 28(2)(d)			Article 115
	Article 28(2)(e), first and second subparagraphs			Article 118, first and second paragraphs
	Article 28(2)(f)			Article 120
	Article 28(2)(g)			—
	Article 28(2)(h), first and second subparagraphs			Article 121, first and second paragraphs
	Article 28(2)(i)			Article 122
	Article 28(2)(j)			Article 117(2)
	Article 28(2)(k)			Article 116
	Article 28(3)(a)			Article 370
	Article 28(3)(b)			Article 371
	Article 28(3)(c)			Article 391
	Article 28(3)(d)			Article 372

Directive 67/227/EEC	Directive 77/388/EEC	Amending Directives	Other acts	This Directive
	Article 28(3)(e)			Article 373
	Article 28(3)(f)			Article 392
	Article 28(3)(g)			Article 374
	Article 28(3a)			Article 376
	Article 28(4) and (5)			Article 393(1) and (2)
	Article 28(6), first subparagraph, first sentence			Article 106, first and second paragraphs
	Article 28(6), first subparagraph, second sentence			Article 106, third paragraph
	Article 28(6), second subparagraph, points (a), (b) and (c),			Article 107, first paragraph, points (a), (b) and (c)
	Article 28(6), second subparagraph, point (d)			Article 107, second paragraph
	Article 28(6), third subparagraph			Article 107, second paragraph
	Article 28(6), fourth subparagraph, points (a), (b) and (c)			Article 108(a), (b) and (c)
	Article 28(6), fifth and sixth subparagraphs			—
	Article 28a(1), introductory sentence			Article 2(1)
	Article 28a(1)(a), first subparagraph			Article 2(1)(b)(i)
	Article 28a(1)(a), second subparagraph			Article 3(1)
	Article 28a(1)(a), third subparagraph			Article 3(3)
	Article 28a(1)(b)			Article 2(1)(b)(ii)
	Article 28a(1)(c)			Article 2(1)(b)(iii)
	Article 28a(1a)(a)			Article 3(1)(a)
	Article 28a(1a)(b), first subparagraph, first indent			Article 3(1)(b)
	Article 28a(1a)(b), first subparagraph, second and third indents			Article 3(2), first subparagraph, points (a) and (b)
	Article 28a(1a)(b), second subparagraph			Article 3(2), second subparagraph
	Article 28a(2), introductory sentence			—
	Article 28a(2)(a)			Article 2(2), point (a) (i), (ii), and (iii)
	Article 28a(2)(b), first subparagraph			Article 2(2), point (b)
	Article 28a(2)(b), first subparagraph, first and second indents			Article 2(2), point (b) (i), (ii), and (iii)
	Article 28a(2)(b), second subparagraph			Article 2(2), point (c)

Directive 67/227/EEC	Directive 77/388/EEC	Amending Directives	Other acts	This Directive
	Article 28a(3), first and second subparagraphs			Article 20, first and second paragraphs
	Article 28a(4), first subparagraph			Article 9(2)
	Article 28a(4), second subparagraph, first indent			Article 172(1), second subparagraph
	Article 28a(4), second subparagraph, second indent			Article 172(1), first subparagraph
	Article 28a(4), third subparagraph			Article 172(2)
	Article 28a(5)(b), first subparagraph			Article 17(1), first subparagraph
	Article 28a(5)(b), second subparagraph,			Article 17(1), second subparagraph and (2), introductory sentence
	Article 28a(5)(b), second subparagraph, first indent			Article 17(2)(a) and (b)
	Article 28a(5)(b), second subparagraph, second indent			Article 17(2)(c)
	Article 28a(5)(b), second subparagraph, third indent			Article 17(2)(e)
	Article 28a(5)(b), second subparagraph, fifth, sixth and seventh indents			Article 17(2)(f), (g) and (h)
	Article 28a(5)(b), second subparagraph, eighth indent			Article 17(2)(d)
	Article 28a(5)(b), third subparagraph			Article 17(3)
	Article 28a(6), first subparagraph			Article 21
	Article 28a(6), second subparagraph			Article 22
	Article 28a(7)			Article 23
	Article 28b(A)(1)			Article 40
	Article 28b(A)(2), first and second subparagraphs			Article 41, first and second paragraphs
	Article 28b(A)(2), third subparagraph, first and second indents			Article 42(a) and (b)
	Article 28b(B)(1), first subparagraph, first and second indents			Article 33(1)(a) and (b)
	Article 28b(B)(1), second subparagraph			Article 33(2)
	Article 28b(B)(2), first subparagraph			Article 34(1)(a)
	Article 28b(B)(2), first subparagraph, first and second indents			Article 34(1)(b) and (c)
	Article 28b(B)(2), second subparagraph, first and second sentences			Article 34(2), first and second subparagraphs

Directive 67/227/EEC	Directive 77/388/EEC	Amending Directives	Other acts	This Directive
	Article 28b(B)(2), third subparagraph, first sentence			Article 34(3)
	Article 28b(B)(2), third subparagraph, second and third sentences			—
	Article 28b(B)(3), first and second subparagraphs			Article 34(4), first and second subparagraphs
	Article 28b(C)(1), first indent, first subparagraph			Article 48, first paragraph
	Article 28b(C)(1), first indent, second subparagraph			Article 49
	Article 28b(C)(1), second and third indents			Article 48, second and third paragraphs
	Article 28b(C)(2) and (3)			Article 47, first and second paragraphs
	Article 28b(C)(4)			Article 51
	Article 28b(D)			Article 53
	Article 28b(E)(1), first and second subparagraphs			Article 50, first and second paragraphs
	Article 28b(E)(2), first and second subparagraphs			Article 54, first and second paragraphs
	Article 28b(E)(3), first and second subparagraphs			Article 44, first and second paragraphs
	Article 28b(F), first and second paragraphs			Article 55, first and second paragraphs
	Article 28c(A), introductory sentence			Article 131
	Article 28c(A)(a), first subparagraph			Article 138(1)
	Article 28c(A)(a), second subparagraph			Article 139(1), first and second subparagraphs
	Article 28c(A)(b)			Article 138(2)(a)
	Article 28c(A)(c), first subparagraph			Article 138(2)(b)
	Article 28c(A)(c), second subparagraph			Article 139(2)
	Article 28c(A)(d)			Article 138(2)(c)
	Article 28c(B), introductory sentence			Articles 131
	Article 28c(B)(a), (b) and (c)			Article 140(a), (b) and (c)
	Article 28c(C)			Article 142
	Article 28c(D), first subparagraph			Article 143(d)
	Article 28c(D), second subparagraph			Article 131

Directive 67/227/EEC	Directive 77/388/EEC	Amending Directives	Other acts	This Directive
	Article 28c(E), point (1), first indent, replacing Article 16(1)			
	— paragraph 1, first subparagraph			Article 155
	— paragraph 1, first subparagraph, point (A)			Article 157(1)(a)
	— paragraph 1, first subparagraph, point (B), first subparagraph, points (a), (b) and (c)			Article 156(1)(a), (b) and (c)
	— paragraph 1, first subparagraph, point (B), first subparagraph, point (d), first and second indents			Article 156(1)(d) and (e)
	— paragraph 1, first subparagraph, point (B), first subparagraph, point (e), first subparagraph			Article 157(1)(b)
	— paragraph 1, first subparagraph, point (B), first subparagraph, point (e), second subparagraph, first indent			Article 154
	— paragraph 1, first subparagraph, point (B), first subparagraph, point (e), second subparagraph, second indent, first sentence			Article 154
	— paragraph 1, first subparagraph, point (B), first subparagraph, point (e), second subparagraph, second indent, second sentence			Article 157(2)
	— paragraph 1, first subparagraph, point (B), first subparagraph, point (e), third subparagraph, first indent			—
	— paragraph 1, first subparagraph, point (B), first subparagraph, point (e), third subparagraph, second, third and fourth indents			Article 158(1)(a), (b) and (c)
	— paragraph 1, first subparagraph, point (B), second subparagraph			Article 156(2)
	— paragraph 1, first subparagraph, point (C)			Article 159
	— paragraph 1, first subparagraph, point (D), first subparagraph, points (a) and (b)			Article 160(1)(a) and (b)
	— paragraph 1, first subparagraph, point (D), second subparagraph			Articles 160(2)
	— paragraph 1, first subparagraph, point (E), first and second indents			Article 161(a) and (b)
	— paragraph 1, second subparagraph			Article 202
	— paragraph 1, third subparagraph			Article 163

Directive 67/227/EEC	Directive 77/388/EEC	Amending Directives	Other acts	This Directive
	Article 28c(E), point (1), second indent, inserting paragraph 1a into Article 16			
	— paragraph 1a			Article 162
	Article 28c(E), point (2), first indent, amending Article 16(2)			Article 164(1)
	— paragraph 2, first subparagraph			
	Article 28c(E), point (2), second indent, inserting the second and third subparagraphs into Article 16(2)			
	— paragraph 2, second subparagraph			Article 164(2)
	— paragraph 2, third subparagraph			Article 165
	Article 28c(E), point (3), first to fifth indents			Article 141(a) to (e)
	Article 28d(1), first and second sentences			Article 68, first and second paragraphs
	Article 28d(2) and (3)			Article 69(1) and (2)
	Article 28d(4), first and second subparagraphs			Article 67(1) and (2)
	Article 28e(1), first subparagraph			Article 83
	Article 28e(1), second subparagraph, first and second sentences			Article 84(1) and (2)
	Article 28e(2)			Article 76
	Article 28e(3)			Article 93, second paragraph, point (b)
	Article 28e(4)			
	Article 28f, point (1) replacing Article 17(2), (3) and (4)			Article 94(1)
	— paragraph 2(a)			Article 168(a)
	— paragraph 2(b)			Article 168(e)
	— paragraph 2(c)			Article 168(b) and (d)
	— paragraph 2(d)			Article 168(c)
	— paragraph 3(a), (b) and (c)			Article 169(a), (b) and (c) Article 170(a) and (b)
	— paragraph 4, first subparagraph, first indent			Article 171(1), first subparagraph
	— paragraph 4, first subparagraph, second indent			Article 171(2), first subparagraph
	— paragraph 4, second subparagraph, point (a)			Article 171(1), second subparagraph

Directive 67/227/EEC	Directive 77/388/EEC	Amending Directives	This Directive
	— paragraph 4, second subparagraph, point (b)		Article 171(2), second subparagraph
	— paragraph 4, second subparagraph, point (c)		Article 171(3)
	Article 28f, point (2) replacing Article 18(1)		
	— paragraph 1(a)		Article 178(a)
	— paragraph 1(b)		Article 178(e)
	— paragraph 1(c)		Article 178(b) and (d)
	— paragraph 1(d)		Article 178(f)
	— paragraph 1(e)		Article 178(c)
	Article 28f, point (3) inserting paragraph 3a into Article 18		
	— paragraph 3a, first part of the sentence		Article 181
	— paragraph 3a, second part of the sentence		Article 182
	Article 28g replacing Article 21		
	— paragraph 1(a), first subparagraph		Article 193
	— paragraph 1(a), second subparagraph		Article 194(1) and (2)
	— paragraph 1(b)		Article 196
	— paragraph 1(c), first subparagraph, first, second and third indents		Article 197(1)(a), (b) and (c)
	— paragraph 1(c), second subparagraph		Article 197(2)
	— paragraph 1(d)		Article 203
	— paragraph 1(e)		Article 200
	— paragraph 1(f)		Article 195
	— paragraph 2		—
	— paragraph 2(a), first sentence		Article 204(1), first subparagraph
	— paragraph 2(a), second sentence		Article 204(2)
	— paragraph 2(b)		Article 204(1), second subparagraph
	— paragraph 2(c), first subparagraph		Article 199(1)(a) to (g)
	— paragraph 2(c), second, third and fourth subparagraphs		Article 199(2), (3) and (4)
	— paragraph 3		Article 205
	— paragraph 4		Article 201

Directive 67/227/EEC	Directive 77/388/EEC	Amending Directives	Other acts	This Directive
	Article 28h replacing Article 22			
	— paragraph 1(a), first and second sentences			Article 213(1), first and second subparagraphs
	— paragraph 1(b)			Article 213(2)
	— paragraph 1(c), first indent, first sentence			Article 214(1)(a)
	— paragraph 1(c), first indent, second sentence			Article 214(2)
	— paragraph 1(c), second and third indents			Article 214(1)(b) and (c)
	— paragraph 1(d), first and second sentences			Article 215, first and second paragraphs
	— paragraph 1(e)			Article 216
	— paragraph 2(a)			Article 242
	— paragraph 2(b), first and second indents			Article 243(1) and (2)
	— paragraph 3(a), first subparagraph, first sentence			Article 220, point (1)
	— paragraph 3(a), first subparagraph, second sentence			Article 220, points (2) and (3)
	— paragraph 3(a), second subparagraph			Article 220, points (4) and (5)
	— paragraph 3(a), third subparagraph, first and second sentences			Article 221(1), first and second subparagraphs
	— paragraph 3(a), fourth subparagraph			Article 221(2)
	— paragraph 3(a), fifth subparagraph, first sentence			Article 219
	— paragraph 3(a), fifth subparagraph, second sentence			Article 228
	— paragraph 3(a), sixth subparagraph			Article 222
	— paragraph 3(a), seventh subparagraph			Article 223
	— paragraph 3(a), eighth subparagraph, first and second sentences			Article 224(1) and (2)
	— paragraph 3(a), ninth subparagraph, first and second sentences			Article 224(3), first subparagraph
	— paragraph 3(a), ninth subparagraph, third sentence			Article 224(3), second subparagraph
	— paragraph 3(a), tenth subparagraph			Article 225
	— paragraph 3(b), first subparagraph, first to twelfth indents			Article 226, points (1) to (12)

Directive 67/227/EEC	Directive 77/388/EEC	Amending Directives	Other acts	This Directive
	— paragraph 3(b), first subparagraph, thirteenth indent			Article 226, points (13) and (14)
	— paragraph 3(b), first subparagraph, fourteenth indent			Article 226, point (15)
	— paragraph 3(b), second subparagraph			Article 227
	— paragraph 3(b), third subparagraph			Article 229
	— paragraph 3(b), fourth subparagraph			Article 230
	— paragraph 3(b), fifth subparagraph			Article 231
	— paragraph 3(c), first subparagraph			Article 232
	— paragraph 3(c), second subparagraph, introductory sentence			Article 233(1), first subparagraph
	— paragraph 3(c), second subparagraph, first indent, first sentence			Article 233(1), first subparagraph, point (a)
	— paragraph 3(c), second subparagraph, first indent, second sentence			Article 233(2)
	— paragraph 3(c), second subparagraph, second indent, first sentence			Article 233(1), first subparagraph, point (b)
	— paragraph 3(c), second subparagraph, second indent, second sentence			Article 233(3)
	— paragraph 3(c), third subparagraph, first sentence			Article 233(1), second subparagraph
	— paragraph 3(c), third subparagraph, second sentence			Article 237
	— paragraph 3(c), fourth subparagraph, first and second sentences			Article 234
	— paragraph 3(c), fifth subparagraph			Article 235
	— paragraph 3(c), sixth subparagraph			Article 236
	— paragraph 3(d), first subparagraph			Article 244
	— paragraph 3(d), second subparagraph, first sentence			Article 245(1)
	— paragraph 3(d), second subparagraph, second and third sentences			Article 245(2), first and second subparagraphs
	— paragraph 3(d), third subparagraph, first and second sentences			Article 246, first and second paragraphs

Directive 67/227/EEC	Directive 77/388/EEC	Amending Directives	Other acts	This Directive
—	paragraph 3(d), fourth, fifth and sixth subparagraphs			Article 247(1), (2) and (3)
—	paragraph 3(d), seventh subparagraph			Article 248
—	paragraph 3(e), first subparagraph			Articles 217 and 241
—	paragraph 3(e), second subparagraph			Article 218
—	paragraph 4(a), first and second sentences			Article 252(1)
—	paragraph 4(a), third and fourth sentences			Article 252(2), first and second subparagraphs
—	paragraph 4(a), fifth sentence			Article 250(2)
—	paragraph 4(b)			Article 250(1)
—	paragraph 4(c), first indent, first and second subparagraphs			Article 251(a) and (b)
—	paragraph 4(c), second indent, first subparagraph			Article 251(c)
—	paragraph 4(c), second indent, second subparagraph			Article 251(d) and (e)
—	paragraph 5			Article 206
—	paragraph 6(a), first and second sentences			Article 261(1)
—	paragraph 6(a), third sentence			Article 261(2)
—	paragraph 6(b), first subparagraph			Article 262
—	paragraph 6(b), second subparagraph, first sentence			Article 263(1), first subparagraph
—	paragraph 6(b), second subparagraph, second sentence			Article 263(2)
—	paragraph 6(b), third subparagraph, first and second indents			Article 264(1)(a) and (b)
—	paragraph 6(b), third subparagraph, third indent, first sentence			Article 264(1)(d)
—	paragraph 6(b), third subparagraph, third indent, second sentence			Article 264(2), first subparagraph
—	paragraph 6(b), fourth subparagraph, first indent			Article 264(1)(c) and (e)
—	paragraph 6(b), fourth subparagraph, second indent, first sentence			Article 264(1)(f)
—	paragraph 6(b), fourth subparagraph, second indent, second sentence			Article 264(2), second subparagraph

Directive 67/227/EEC	Directive 77/388/EEC	Amending Directives	Other acts	This Directive
	— paragraph 6(b), fifth subparagraph, first and second indents			Article 265(1)(a) and (b)
	— paragraph 6(b), fifth subparagraph, third indent, first sentence			Article 265(1)(c)
	— paragraph 6(b), fifth subparagraph, third indent, second sentence			Article 265(2)
	— paragraph 6(c), first indent			Article 263(1), second subparagraph
	— paragraph 6(c), second indent			Article 266
	— paragraph 6(d)			Article 254
	— paragraph 6(e), first subparagraph			Article 268
	— paragraph 6(e), second subparagraph			Article 259
	— paragraph 7, first part of the sentence			Article 207, first paragraph Article 256 Article 267
	— paragraph 7, second part of the sentence			Article 207, second paragraph
	— paragraph 8, first and second subparagraphs			Article 273, first and second paragraphs
	— paragraph 9(a), first subparagraph, first indent			Article 272(1), first subparagraph, point (c)
	— paragraph 9(a), first subparagraph, second indent			Article 272(1), first subparagraph, points (a) and (d)
	— paragraph 9(a), first subparagraph, third indent			Article 272(1), first subparagraph, point (b)
	— paragraph 9(a), second subparagraph			Article 272(1), second subparagraph
	— paragraph 9(b)			Article 272(3)
	— paragraph 9(c)			Article 212
	— paragraph 9(d), first subparagraph, first and second indents			Article 238(1)(a) and (b)
	— paragraph 9(d), second subparagraph, first to fourth indents			Article 238(2)(a) to (d)
	— paragraph 9(d), third subparagraph			Article 238(3)
	— paragraph 9(e), first subparagraph			Article 239
	— paragraph 9(e), second subparagraph, first and second indents			Article 240, points (1) and (2)

Directive 67/227/EEC	Directive 77/388/EEC	Amending Directives	Other acts	This Directive
	— paragraph 10			Articles 209 and 257
	— paragraph 11			Articles 210 and 258
	— paragraph 12, introductory sentence			Article 269
	— paragraph 12(a), first, second and third indents			Article 270(a), (b) and (c)
	— paragraph 12(b), first second and third indents			Article 271(a), (b) and (c)
	Article 28i inserting a third subparagraph into Article 24(3)			
	— paragraph 3, third subparagraph			Article 283(1)(b) and (c)
	Article 28j, point (1) inserting a second subparagraph into Article 25(4)			
	— paragraph 4, second subparagraph			Article 272(2)
	Article 28j, point (2) replacing Article 25(5) and (6)			
	— paragraph 5, first subparagraph, points (a), (b) and (c)			Article 300, points (1), (2) and (3)
	— paragraph 5, second subparagraph			Article 302
	— paragraph 6(a), first subparagraph, first sentence			Article 301(1)
	— paragraph 6(a), first subparagraph, second sentence			Article 303(1)
	— paragraph 6(a), second subparagraph, first, second and third indents			Article 303(2)(a), (b) and (c)
	— paragraph 6(a), third subparagraph			Article 303(3)
	— paragraph 6(b)			Article 301(1)
	Article 28j, point (3) inserting a second subparagraph into Article 25(9)			
	— paragraph 9, second subparagraph			Article 305
	Article 28k, point (1), first subparagraph			—
	Article 28k, point (1), second subparagraph, point (a)			Article 158(3)
	Article 28k, point (1), second subparagraph, points (b) and (c)			—
	Article 28k, points (2), (3) and (4)			—
	Article 28k, point (5)			Article 158(2)
	Article 28l, first paragraph			—
	Article 28l, second and third paragraphs			Article 402(1) and (2)

Directive 67/227/EEC	Directive 77/388/EEC	Amending Directives	Other acts	This Directive
	Article 28l, fourth paragraph			—
	Article 28m			Article 399, first paragraph
	Article 28n			—
	Article 28o(1), introductory sentence			Article 326, first paragraph
	Article 28o(1)(a), first sentence			Article 327(1) and (3)
	Article 28o(1)(a), second sentence			Article 327(2)
	Article 28o(1)(b)			Article 328
	Article 28o(1)(c), first second and third indents			Article 329(a), (b) and (c)
	Article 28o(1)(d), first and second subparagraphs			Article 330, first and second paragraphs
	Article 28o(1)(e)			Article 332
	Article 28o(1)(f)			Article 331
	Article 28o(1)(g)			Article 4(b)
	Article 28o(1)(h)			Article 35 Article 139(3), second subparagraph
	Article 28o(2)			Article 326, second paragraph
	Article 28o(3)			Article 341
	Article 28o(4)			—
	Article 28p(1), first, second and third indents			Article 405, points (1), (2) and (3)
	Article 28p(2)			Article 406
	Article 28p(3), first subparagraph, first and second indents			Article 407(a) and (b)
	Article 28p(3), second subparagraph			—
	Article 28p(4)(a) to (d)			Article 408(1)(a) to (d)
	Article 28p(5), first and second indents			Article 408(2)(a) and (b)
	Article 28p(6)			Article 409
	Article 28p(7), first subparagraph, points (a), (b) and (c)			Article 410(1)(a), (b) and (c)
	Article 28p(7), second subparagraph, first indent			—
	Article 28p(7), second subparagraph, second, third and fourth indents			Article 410(2)(a), (b) and (c)
	Article 29(1) to (4)			Article 398(1) to (4)
	Article 29a			Article 397

Directive 67/227/EEC	Directive 77/388/EEC	Amending Directives	Other acts	This Directive
	Article 30(1)			Article 396(1)
	Article 30(2), first and second sentences			Article 396(2), first subparagraph
	Article 30(2), third sentence			Article 396(2), second subparagraph
	Article 30(3) and (4)			Article 396(3) and (4)
	Article 31(1)			—
	Article 31(2)			Article 400
	Article 33(1)			Article 401
	Article 33(2)			Article 2(3)
	Article 33a(1), introductory sentence			Article 274
	Article 33a(1)(a)			Article 275
	Article 33a(1)(b)			Article 276
	Article 33a(1)(c)			Article 277
	Article 33a(2), introductory sentence			Article 278
	Article 33a(2)(a)			Article 279
	Article 33a(2)(b)			Article 280
	Article 34			Article 404
	Article 35			Article 403
	Articles 36 and 37			—
	Article 38			Article 414
	Annex A(I)(1) and (2)			Annex VII, point (1)(a) and (b)
	Annex A(I)(3)			Annex VII, points (1)(c) and (d)
	Annex A(II)(1) to (6)			Annex VII, points (2)(a) to (f)
	Annex A(III) and (IV)			Annex VII, points (3) and (4)
	Annex A(IV)(1) to (4)			Annex VII, points (4)(a) to (d)
	Annex A(V)			Article 295(2)
	Annex B, introductory sentence			Article 295(1), point (5)
	Annex B, first to ninth indents			Annex VIII, points (1) to (9)
	Annex C			—
	Annex D(1) to (13)			Annex I, points (1) to (13)
	Annex E(2)			Annex X, Part A, point (1)

Directive 67/227/EEC	Directive 77/388/EEC	Amending Directives	Other acts	This Directive
	Annex E(7)			Annex X, Part A, point (2)
	Annex E(11)			Annex X, Part A, point (3)
	Annex E(15)			Annex X, Part A, point (4)
	Annex F(1)			Annex X, Part B, point (1)
	Annex F(2)			Annex X, Part B, points (2)(a) to (j)
	Annex F(5) to (8)			Annex X, Part B, points (3) to (6)
	Annex F(10)			Annex X, Part B, point (7)
	Annex F(12)			Annex X, Part B, point (8)
	Annex F(16)			Annex X, Part B, point (9)
	Annex F(17), first and second subparagraphs			Annex X, Part B, point (10)
	Annex F(23)			Annex X, Part B, point (11)
	Annex F(25)			Annex X, Part B, point (12)
	Annex F(27)			Annex X, Part B, point (13)
	Annex G(1) and (2)			Article 391
	Annex H, first paragraph			Article 98(3)
	Annex H, second paragraph, introductory sentence			—
	Annex H, second paragraph, points (1) to (6)			Annex III, points (1) to (6)
	Annex H, second paragraph, point (7), first and second subparagraphs			Annex III, points (7) and (8)
	Annex H, second paragraph, points (8) to (17)			Annex III, points (9) to (18)
	Annex I, introductory sentence			—
	Annex I(a), first to seventh indents			Annex IX, Part A, points (1) to (7)
	Annex I(b), first and second indents			Annex IX, Part B, points (1) and (2)
	Annex I(c)			Annex IX, Part C
	Annex J, introductory sentence			Annex V, introductory sentence
	Annex J			Annex V, points (1) to (25)
	Annex K(1), first, second and third indents			Annex IV, points (1)(a), (b) and (c)
	Annex K(2) to (5)			Annex IV, points (2) to (5)
	Annex L, first paragraph, points (1) to (5)			Annex II, points (1) to (5)

Directive 67/227/EEC	Directive 77/388/EEC	Amending Directives	Other acts	This Directive
	Annex L, second paragraph			Article 56(2)
	Annex M, points (a) to (f)			Annex VI, points (1) to (6)
		Article 1, point (1), second subparagraph, of Directive 89/465/EEC		Article 133, second paragraph
		Article 2 of Directive 94/5/EC		Article 342
		Article 3, first and second sentences, of Directive 94/5/EC		Article 343, first and second paragraphs
		Article 4 of Directive 2002/38/EC		Article 56(3) Article 57(2) Article 357
		Article 5 of Directive 2002/38/EC		—
			Annex VIII(II), point (2)(a) of the Act of Accession of Greece	Article 287, point (1)
			Annex VIII(II), point (2)(b) of the Act of Accession of Greece	Article 375
			Annex XXXII(IV), point (3)(a), first indent and second indent, first sentence, of the Act of Accession of Spain and Portugal	Article 287, points (2) and (3)
			Annex XXXII(IV), point (3)(b), first subparagraph, of the Act of Accession of Spain and Portugal	Article 377
			Annex XV(IX), point (2)(b), first subparagraph, of the Act of Accession of Austria, Finland and Sweden	Article 104
			Annex XV(IX), point (2)(c), first subparagraph, of the Act of Accession of Austria, Finland and Sweden	Article 287, point (4)
			Annex XV(IX), point (2)(f), first subparagraph, of the Act of Accession of Austria, Finland and Sweden	Article 117(1)
			Annex XV(IX), point (2)(g), first subparagraph, of the Act of Accession of Austria, Finland and Sweden	Article 119
			Annex XV(IX), point (2)(h), first subparagraph, first and second indents, of the Act of Accession of Austria, Finland and Sweden	Article 378(1)

Directive 67/227/EEC	Directive 77/388/EEC	Amending Directives	Other acts	This Directive
			Annex XV(IX), point (2)(i), first subparagraph, first indent, of the Act of Accession of Austria, Finland and Sweden	—
			Annex XV(IX), point (2)(i), first subparagraph, second and third indents, of the Act of Accession of Austria, Finland and Sweden	Article 378(2)(a) and (b)
			Annex XV(IX), point (2)(j) of the Act of Accession of Austria, Finland and Sweden	Article 287, point (5)
			Annex XV(IX), point (2)(l), first subparagraph, of the Act of Accession of Austria, Finland and Sweden	Article 111(a)
			Annex XV(IX), point (2)(m), first subparagraph, of the Act of Accession of Austria, Finland and Sweden	Article 379(1)
			Annex XV(IX), point (2)(n), first subparagraph, first and second indents, of the Act of Accession of Austria, Finland and Sweden	Article 379(2)
			Annex XV(IX), point (2)(x), first indent, of the Act of Accession of Austria, Finland and Sweden	Article 253
			Annex XV(IX), point (2)(x), second indent, of the Act of Accession of Austria, Finland and Sweden	Article 287, point (6)
			Annex XV(IX), point (2)(z), first subparagraph, of the Act of Accession of Austria, Finland and Sweden	Article 111(b)
			Annex XV(IX), point (2)(aa), first subparagraph, first and second indents, of the Act of Accession of Austria, Finland and Sweden	Article 380
			Protocol No 2 of the Act of Accession of Austria, Finland and Sweden concerning the Åland Islands	Article 6(1)(d)

Directive 67/227/EEC	Directive 77/388/EEC	Amending Directives	Other acts	This Directive
			Annex V(5), point (1)(a) of the 2003 Act of Accession of the Czech Republic, Estonia, Cyprus, Latvia, Lithuania, Hungary, Malta, Poland Slovenia and Slovakia	Article 123
			Annex V(5), point (1)(b) of the 2003 Act of Accession	Article 381
			Annex VI(7), point (1)(a) of the 2003 Act of Accession	Article 124
			Annex VI(7), point (1)(b) of the 2003 Act of Accession	Article 382
			Annex VII(7), point (1), first and second subparagraphs, of the 2003 Act of Accession	Article 125(1) and (2)
			Annex VII(7), point (1), third subparagraph, of the 2003 Act of Accession	—
			Annex VII(7), point (1), fourth subparagraph, of the 2003 Act of Accession	Article 383(a)
			Annex VII(7), point (1), fifth subparagraph, of the 2003 Act of Accession	—
			Annex VII(7), point (1), sixth subparagraph, of the 2003 Act of Accession	Article 383(b)
			Annex VIII(7), point (1)(a) of the 2003 Act of Accession	—
			Annex VIII(7), point (1)(b), second subparagraph, of the 2003 Act of Accession	Article 384(a)
			Annex VIII(7), point (1), third subparagraph, of the 2003 Act of Accession	Article 384(b)
			Annex IX(8), point (1) of the 2003 Act of Accession	Article 385
			Annex X(7), point (1)(a)(i) and (ii) of the 2003 Act of Accession	Article 126(a) and (b)

Directive 67/227/EEC	Directive 77/388/EEC	Amending Directives	Other acts	This Directive
			Annex X(7), point (1)(c) of the 2003 Act of Accession	Article 386
			Annex XI(7), point (1) of the 2003 Act of Accession	Article 127
			Annex XI(7), point (2)(a) of the 2003 Act of Accession	Article 387(c)
			Annex XI(7), point (2)(b) of the 2003 Act of Accession	Article 387(a)
			Annex XI(7), point (2)(c) of the 2003 Act of Accession	Article 387(b)
			Annex XIII(9), point (1)(a) of the 2003 Act of Accession	Article 128(1) and (2)
			Annex XII(9), point (1)(b) of the 2003 Act of Accession	Article 128(3), (4) and (5)
			Annex XII(9), point (2) of the 2003 Act of Accession	Article 388
			Annex XIII(9), point (1)(a) of the 2003 Act of Accession	Article 129(1) and (2)
			Annex XIII(9), point (1)(b) of the 2003 Act of Accession	Article 389
			Annex XIV(7), first subparagraph, of the 2003 Act of Accession	Article 130(a) and (b)
			Annex XIV(7), second subparagraph, of the 2003 Act of Accession	—
			Annex XIV(7), third subparagraph, of the 2003 Act of Accession	Article 390

ARCHIVED COUNCIL DIRECTIVE 2007/74/EC
OF 20 DECEMBER 2007
ON THE EXEMPTION FROM VALUE ADDED TAX AND EXCISE DUTY OF GOODS IMPORTED BY PERSONS TRAVELLING FROM THIRD COUNTRIES

(2007/74/EC)

CHAPTER 1

SUBJECT-MATTER AND DEFINITIONS

Article 1

This Directive lays down rules relating to the exemption from value added tax (VAT) and excise duty of goods imported in the personal luggage of persons travelling from a third country or from a territory where the Community provisions on VAT or excise duty, or both, as defined in Article 3, do not apply.

Article 2

Where a journey involves transit through the territory of a third country, or begins in a territory as referred to in Article 1, this Directive shall apply if the traveller is unable to establish that the goods transported in his luggage have been acquired subject to the general conditions governing taxation on the domestic market of a Member State and do not qualify for any refunding of VAT or excise duty. Overflying without landing shall not be regarded as transit.

Article 3

For the purposes of this Directive, the following definitions shall apply:
1. "third country" means any country which is not a Member State of the European Union;
In view of the Fiscal Agreement between France and the Principality of Monaco dated 18 May 1963 and the Agreement of friendship and neighbourly relations between Italy and the Republic of San Marino dated 31 March 1939, Monaco shall not be regarded as a third country and San Marino shall not be regarded as a third country in respect of excise duty;
2. "territory where the Community provisions on VAT or excise duty, or both do not apply" means any territory, other than a territory of a third country, where Directives 2006/112/EC[1] or 92/12/EEC, or both do not apply;
In view of the Agreement between the Governments of the United Kingdom and the Isle of Man on Customs and Excise and associated matters dated 15 October 1979, the Isle of Man shall not be regarded as a territory where the Community provisions on VAT or excise duty, or both do not apply;
3. "air travellers" and "sea travellers" means any passengers travelling by air or sea other than private pleasure-flying or private pleasure-sea-navigation;
4. "private pleasure-flying" and "private pleasure-sea-navigation" means the use of an aircraft or a sea-going vessel by its owner or the natural or legal person who enjoys its use either through hire or through any other means, for purposes other than commercial and in particular other than for the carriage of passengers or goods or for the supply of services for consideration or for the purposes of public authorities;
5. "frontier zone" means a zone which, as the crow flies, does not extend more than 15 kilometres from the frontier of a Member State and which includes the local administrative districts part of the territory of which lies within the zone; Member States may grant exemptions therefrom;
6. "frontier-zone worker" means any person whose normal activities require that he should go to the other side of the frontier on his work days.

Note—[1] OJ L 347, 11.12.2006 p 1. Directive as amended by Directive 2006/138/EC (OJ L 384, 29.12. 2006 p 92).

CHAPTER 2

EXEMPTIONS

Section 1
COMMON PROVISIONS

Article 4

Member States shall, on the basis of either monetary thresholds or quantitative limits, exempt from VAT and excise duty goods imported in the personal luggage of travellers, provided that the imports are of a non-commercial character.

Article 5

For the purposes of the application of the exemptions, personal luggage shall be regarded as the whole of the luggage which a traveller is able to present to the customs authorities upon arrival, as well as luggage which he presents later to the same authorities, subject to proof that such luggage was registered as ac-companied luggage, at the time of his departure, with the company which has been responsible for conveying him. Fuel other than that referred to in Article 11 shall not be regarded as personal luggage.

Article 6
For the purposes of the application of the exemptions, imports shall be regarded as being of a non-commercial character if they meet the following conditions:
   (a) they take place occasionally;
   (b) they consist exclusively of goods for the personal or family use of the travellers, or of goods intended as presents.

The nature or quantity of the goods must not be such as to indicate that they are being imported for commercial reasons.

Article 7
1. Member States shall exempt from VAT and excise duty imports of goods, other than those referred to in Section 3, the total value of which does not exceed EUR 300 per person.
In the case of air and sea travellers, the monetary threshold specified in the first subparagraph shall be EUR 430.
2. Member States may lower the monetary threshold for travellers under 15 years old, whatever their means of transport. However, the monetary threshold may not be lower than EUR 150.
3. For the purposes of applying the monetary thresholds, the value of an individual item may not be split up.
4. The value of the personal luggage of a traveller, which is imported temporarily or is re-imported following its temporary export, and the value of medicinal products required to meet the personal needs of a traveller shall not be taken into consideration for the purposes of applying the exemptions referred to in paragraphs 1 and 2.

Section 3
QUANTITATIVE LIMITS

Article 8
1. Member States shall exempt from VAT and excise duty imports of the following types of tobacco product, subject either to the following higher or lower quantitative limits:
   (a) 200 cigarettes or 40 cigarettes;
   (b) 100 cigarillos or 20 cigarillos;
   (c) 50 cigars or 10 cigars;
   (d) 250g smoking tobacco or 50g smoking tobacco.

Each amount specified in points (a) to (d) shall represent, for the purposes of paragraph 4, 100% of the total allowance for tobacco products.
Cigarillos are cigars of a maximum weight of 3 grams each.
2. Member States may choose to distinguish between air travellers and other travellers by applying the lower quantitative limits specified in paragraph 1 only to travellers other than air travellers.
3. By derogation from paragraphs 1 and 2, Austria may, as long as the tax system in the Swiss enclave of Samnauntal differs from that applicable in the rest of the Kanton of Graubünden, limit the application of the lower quantitative limit to tobacco products brought into the territory of that Member State by travellers who enter its territory directly from the Swiss enclave of Samnauntal.
4. In the case of any one traveller, the exemption may be applied to any combination of tobacco products, provided that the aggregate of the percentages used up from the individual allowances does not exceed 100%.

Article 9
1. Member States shall exempt from VAT and excise duty alcohol and alcoholic beverages other than still wine and beer, subject to the following quantitative limits:
   (a) a total of 1 litre of alcohol and alcoholic beverages of an alcoholic strength exceeding 22% vol, or un-denatured ethyl alcohol of 80% vol and over;
   (b) a total of 2 litres of alcohol and alcoholic beverages of an alcoholic strength not exceeding 22% vol.

Each of the amounts specified in points (a) and (b) represent, for the purposes of paragraph 2, 100% of the total allowance for alcohol and alcoholic beverages.
2. In the case of any one traveller, the exemption may be applied to any combination of the types of alcohol and alcoholic beverage referred to in paragraph 1, provided that the aggregate of the percentages used up from the individual allowances does not exceed 100%.
3. Member States shall exempt from VAT and excise duty a total of 4 litres of still wine and 16 litres of beer.

Article 10
Exemptions under Articles 8 or 9 shall not apply in the case of travellers under 17 years of age.

Article 11
Member States shall exempt from VAT and excise duty, in the case of any one means of motor transport, the fuel contained in the standard tank and a quantity of fuel not exceeding 10 litres contained in a port-able container.

Article 12
The value of goods referred to in Articles 8, 9 or 11 shall not be taken into consideration for the purposes of applying the exemption provided for in Article 7(1).

CHAPTER 3
SPECIAL CASES

Article 13
1. Member States may lower the monetary thresholds or the quantitative limits, or both, in the case of travellers in the following categories:
    (*a*) persons resident in a frontier zone;
    (*b*) frontier-zone workers;
    (*c*) the crew of a means of transport used to travel from a third country or from a territory where the Community provisions on VAT or excise duty, or both do not apply.
2. Paragraph 1 shall not apply where a traveller in one of the categories listed therein produces evidence to show that he is going beyond the frontier zone of the Member State or that he is not returning from the frontier zone of the neighbouring third country.
However, it shall apply where frontier-zone workers or the crew of the means of transport used in international travel import goods when travelling in the course of their work.

CHAPTER IV
GENERAL AND FINAL PROVISIONS

Article 14
Member States may choose not to levy VAT or excise duty on the import of goods by a traveller when the amount of the tax which should be levied is equal to, or less than, EUR 10.

Article 15
1. The euro equivalent in national currency which shall apply for the implementation of this Directive shall be fixed once a year. The rates applicable shall be those obtaining on the first working day of October. They shall be published in the Official Journal of the European Union and shall apply from 1 January of the following year.
2. Member States may round off the amounts in national currency resulting from the conversion of the amounts in euro provided for in Article 7, provided such rounding-off does not exceed EUR 5.
3. Member States may maintain the monetary thresholds in force at the time of the annual adjustment provided for in paragraph 1 if, prior to the rounding-off provided for in paragraph 2, conversion of the corresponding amounts expressed in euro would result in a change of less than 5% in the exemption expressed in national currency or in a lowering of this exemption.

Article 16
Every four years and for the first time in 2012 the Commission shall forward a report on the implementation of this Directive to the Council, where appropriate accompanied by a proposal for amendment.

Article 17
In Article 5(9) of Directive 69/169/EEC the date of 31 December 2007 shall be replaced by 30 November 2008.

Article 18
Directive 69/169/EEC shall be repealed and replaced by this Directive with effect from 1 December 2008.
References to the repealed Directive shall be construed as references to this Directive and shall be read in accordance with the correlation table in the Annex.

Article 19
1. Member States shall bring into force the laws, regulations and administrative provisions necessary to comply with Articles 1 to 15 of this Directive with effect from 1 December 2008. They shall forthwith communicate to the Commission the text of those measures.
When Member States adopt those measures, they shall contain a reference to this Directive or be accompanied by such reference on the occasion of their official publication. Member States shall determine how such reference is to be made.
2. Member States shall communicate to the Commission the text of the main provisions of national law which they adopt in the field covered by this Directive.

Article 20
This Directive shall enter into force on the day of its publication in the Official Journal of the European Union.
It shall apply with effect from 1 December 2008.
However, Article 17 shall apply with effect from 1 January 2008.

Article 21
This Directive is addressed to the Member States.

Done at Brussels, ...20 December 2007.

For the Council
The President
F. Nunes Correia

ANNEX
CORRELATION TABLE

Directive 69/169/EEC	This Directive
Article 1(1)	Article 7(1)
Article 1(2)	Article 7(2)
Article 1(3)	Article 7(3)
Article 2	–
Article 3, point one	Article 7(4)
Article 3, point two	Article 6
Article 3, point three, first subparagraph	Article 5
Article 3, point three, second subparagraph	Article 5 and 11
Article 4(1), introductory phrase	Article 8(1) introductory phrase, Article 9(1) introductory phrase
Article 4(1), second column	–
Article 4(1)(*a*), first column	Article 8(1)
Article 4(1)(*b*), first column	Article 9(1)
Article 4(1)(*c*), (*d*) and (*e*), first column	–
Article 4(2) first subparagraph	Article 10
Article 4(2) second subparagraph	–
Article 4(3)	Article 12
Article 4(4)	Article 2
Article 4(5)	–
Article 5(1)	–
Article 5(2)	Article 13(1)
Article 5(3)	–
Article 5(4)	Article 13(2)
Article 5(5)	–
Article 5(6), introductory phrase, first indent	Article 3(5)
Article 5(6), introductory phrase, second indent	Article 3(6)
Article 5(7)	–
Article 5(8)	–
Article 5(9)	–
Article 7(1)	–
Article 7(2)	Article 15(1)
Article 7(3)	Article 15(2)
Article 7(4)	Article 15(3)
Article 7(5)	–
Article 7a(1)	–
Article 7a(2)	Article 14
Article 7b	–
Article 7c	–
Article 7d	–
Article 8(1)	Article 19(1), first subparagraph
Article 8(2), first subparagraph	Article 19(1), first subparagraph

Directive 69/169/EEC	This Directive
Article 8(2), second subparagraph	–
Article 9	Article 21

ARCHIVED COUNCIL DIRECTIVE 2008/9/EC
OF 12 FEBRUARY 2008
LAYING DOWN DETAILED RULES FOR THE REFUND OF VALUE ADDED TAX, PROVIDED FOR IN DIRECTIVE 2006/112/EC, TO TAXABLE PERSONS NOT ESTABLISHED IN THE MEMBER STATE OF REFUND BUT ESTABLISHED IN ANOTHER MEMBER STATE

(2008/9/EC)

Article 1
This Directive lays down the detailed rules for the refund of value added tax (VAT), provided for in Article 170 of Directive 2006/112/EC, to taxable persons not established in the Member State of refund, who meet the conditions laid down in Article 3.

Article 2
For the purposes of this Directive, the following definitions shall apply:
1. "taxable person not established in the Member State of refund" means a taxable person within the meaning of Article 9(1) of Directive 2006/112/EC who is not established in the Member State of refund but established in the territory of another Member State;
2. "Member State of refund" means the Member State in which the VAT was charged to the taxable person not established in the Member State of refund in respect of goods or services supplied to him by other taxable persons in that Member State or in respect of the importation of goods into that Member State;
3. "refund period" means the period mentioned in Article 16 covered by the refund application;
4. "refund application" means the application for refund of VAT charged in the Member State of refund to the taxable person not established in the Member State of refund in respect of goods or services supplied to him by other taxable persons in that Member State or in respect of the importation of goods into that Member State;
5. "applicant" means the taxable person not established in the Member State of refund making the refund application.

Article 3
This Directive shall apply to any taxable person not established in the Member State of refund who meets the following conditions:
   (a) during the refund period, he has not had in the Member State of refund, the seat of his economic activity, or a fixed establishment from which business transactions were effected, or, if no such seat or fixed establishment existed, his domicile or normal place of residence;
   (b) during the refund period, he has not supplied any goods or services deemed to have been supplied in the Member State of refund, with the exception of the following transactions:
      (i) the supply of transport services and services ancillary thereto, exempted pursuant to Articles 144, 146, 148, 149, 151, 153, 159 or 160 of Directive 2006/112/EC;
      (ii) the supply of goods and services to a person who is liable for payment of VAT in accordance with Articles 194 to 197 and Article 199 of Directive 2006/112/EC.

Article 4
This Directive shall not apply to:
   (a) amounts of VAT which, according to the legislation of the Member State of refund, have been incorrectly invoiced;
   (b) amounts of VAT which have been invoiced in respect of supplies of goods the supply of which is, or may be, exempt under Article 138 or Article 146(1)(b) of Directive 2006/112/EC.

Article 5
Each Member State shall refund to any taxable person not established in the Member State of refund any VAT charged in respect of goods or services supplied to him by other taxable persons in that Member State or in respect of the importation of goods into that Member State, insofar as such goods and services are used for the purposes of the following transactions:
   (a) transactions referred to in Article 169(a) and (b) of Directive 2006/112/EC;
   (b) transactions to a person who is liable for payment of VAT in accordance with Articles 194 to 197 and Article 199 of Directive 2006/112/EC as applied in the Member State of refund.

Without prejudice to Article 6, for the purposes of this Directive, entitlement to an input tax refund shall be determined pursuant to Directive 2006/112/EC as applied in the Member State of refund.

Article 6
To be eligible for a refund in the Member State of refund, a taxable person not established in the Member State of refund has to carry out transactions giving rise to a right of deduction in the Member State of establishment.

When a taxable person not established in the Member State of refund carries out in the Member State in which he is established both transactions giving rise to a right of deduction and transactions not giving rise to a right of deduction in that Member State, only such proportion of the VAT which is refundable in accordance with Article 5 may be refunded by the Member State of refund as is attributable to the former trans-actions in accordance with Article 173 of Directive 2006/112/EC as applied by the Member State of establishment.

Article 7
To obtain a refund of VAT in the Member State of refund, the taxable person not established in the Member State of refund shall address an electronic refund application to that Member State and submit it to the Member State in which he is established via the electronic portal set up by that Member State.

Article 8
1. The refund application shall contain the following information:
    (a) the applicant's name and full address;
    (b) an address for contact by electronic means;
    (c) a description of the applicant's business activity for which the goods and services are acquired;
    (d) the refund period covered by the application;
    (e) a declaration by the applicant that he has supplied no goods and services deemed to have been sup-plied in the Member State of refund during the refund period, with the exception of transactions referred to in points (i) and (ii) of Article 3(b);
    (f) the applicant's VAT identification number or tax reference number;
    (g) bank account details including IBAN and BIC codes.
2. In addition to the information specified in paragraph 1, the refund application shall set out, for each Member State of refund and for each invoice or importation document, the following details:
    (a) name and full address of the supplier;
    (b) except in the case of importation, the VAT identification number or tax reference number of the supplier, as allocated by the Member State of refund in accordance with the provisions of Articles 239 and 240 of Directive 2006/112/EC;
    (c) except in the case of importation, the prefix of the Member State of refund in accordance with Article 215 of Directive 2006/112/EC;
    (d) date and number of the invoice or importation document;
    (e) taxable amount and amount of VAT expressed in the currency of the Member State of refund;
    (f) the amount of deductible VAT calculated in accordance with Article 5 and the second paragraph of Article 6 expressed in the currency of the Member State of refund;
    (g) where applicable, the deductible proportion calculated in accordance with Article 6, expressed as a percentage;
    (h) nature of the goods and services acquired, described according to the codes in Article 9.

Article 9
1. In the refund application, the nature of the goods and services acquired shall be described by the following codes:
1 = fuel;
2 = hiring of means of transport;
3 = expenditure relating to means of transport (other than the goods and services referred to under codes 1 and 2);
4 = road tolls and road user charge;
5 = travel expenses, such as taxi fares, public transport fares;
6 = accommodation;
7 = food, drink and restaurant services;
8 = admissions to fairs and exhibitions;
9 = expenditure on luxuries, amusements and entertainment;
10 = other.
If code 10 is used, the nature of the goods and services supplied shall be indicated.

2. The Member State of refund may require the applicant to provide additional electronic coded information as regards each code set out in paragraph 1 to the extent that such information is necessary because of any restrictions on the right of deduction under Directive 2006/112/EC, as applicable in the Member State of refund or for the implementation of a relevant derogation received by the Member State of refund under Articles 395 or 396 of that Directive.

Article 10
Without prejudice to requests for information under Article 20, the Member State of refund may require the applicant to submit by electronic means a copy of the invoice or importation document with the refund application where the taxable amount on an invoice or importation document is EUR 1000 or more or the equivalent in national currency. Where the invoice concerns fuel, the threshold is EUR 250 or the equivalent in national currency.

Article 11
The Member State of refund may require the applicant to provide a description of his business activity by using the harmonised codes determined in accordance with the second subparagraph of Article 34a(3) of Council Regulation (EC) No 1798/2003[1].
Note—[1] OJ L 264, 15.10.2003 p 1.

Article 12
The Member State of refund may specify which language or languages shall be used by the applicant for the provision of information in the refund application or of possible additional information.

Article 13
If subsequent to the submission of the refund application the deductible proportion is adjusted pursuant to Article 175 of Directive 2006/112/EC, the applicant shall make a correction to the amount applied for or already refunded.
The correction shall be made in a refund application during the calendar year following the refund period in question or, if the applicant makes no refund applications during that calendar year, by submitting a separate declaration via the electronic portal established by the Member State of establishment.

Article 14
1. The refund application shall relate to the following:
   (a) the purchase of goods or services which was invoiced during the refund period, provided that the VAT became chargeable before or at the time of the invoicing, or in respect of which the VAT became chargeable during the refund period, provided that the purchase was invoiced before the tax became chargeable;
   (b) the importation of goods during the refund period.
2. In addition to the transactions referred to in paragraph 1, the refund application may relate to invoices or import documents not covered by previous refund applications and concerning transactions completed during the calendar year in question.

Article 15
1. The refund application shall be submitted to the Member State of establishment at the latest on 30 September of the calendar year following the refund period. The application shall be considered submitted only if the applicant has filled in all the information required under Articles 8, 9 and 11. [Refund applications which relate to refund periods in 2009 shall be submitted to the Member State of establishment on 31 March 2011 at the latest.][1]
2. The Member State of establishment shall send the applicant an electronic confirmation of receipt with-out delay.
Amendments—[1]   In para 1, second sub-para inserted by Council Directive 2010/66 Art 1 with effect from 1 October 2010.

Article 16
The refund period shall not be more than one calendar year or less than three calendar months. Refund applications may, however, relate to a period of less than three months where the period represents the remainder of a calendar year.

Article 17
If the refund application relates to a refund period of less than one calendar year but not less than three months, the amount of VAT for which a refund is applied for may not be less than EUR 400 or the equivalent in national currency.
If the refund application relates to a refund period of a calendar year or the remainder of a calendar year, the amount of VAT may not be less than EUR 50 or the equivalent in national currency.

Article 18
1. The Member State of establishment shall not forward the application to the Member State of refund where, during the refund period, any of the following circumstances apply to the applicant in the Member State of establishment:
   (a) he is not a taxable person for VAT purposes;

(b) he carries out only supplies of goods or of services which are exempt without deductibility of the VAT paid at the preceding stage pursuant to Articles 132, 135, 136, 371, Articles 374 to 377, Article 378(2)(a), Article 379(2) or Articles 380 to 390 of Directive 2006/112/EC or provisions providing for identical exemptions contained in the 2005 Act of Accession;
(c) he is covered by the exemption for small enterprises provided for in Articles 284, 285, 286 and 287 of Directive 2006/112/EC;
(d) he is covered by the common flat-rate scheme for farmers provided for in Articles 296 to 305 of Directive 2006/112/EC.

2. The Member State of establishment shall notify the applicant by electronic means of the decision it has taken pursuant to paragraph 1.

Article 19

1. The Member State of refund shall notify the applicant without delay, by electronic means, of the date on which it received the application.
2. The Member State of refund shall notify the applicant of its decision to approve or refuse the refund application within four months of its receipt by that Member State.

Article 20

1. Where the Member State of refund considers that it does not have all the relevant information on which to make a decision in respect of the whole or part of the refund application, it may request, by electronic means, additional information, in particular from the applicant or from the competent authorities of the Member State of establishment, within the four-month period referred to in Article 19(2). Where the additional information is requested from someone other than the applicant or a competent authority of a Member State, the request shall be made by electronic means only if such means are available to the recipient of the request.
If necessary, the Member State of refund may request further additional information.
The information requested in accordance with this paragraph may include the submission of the original or a copy of the relevant invoice or import document where the Member State of refund has reasonable doubts regarding the validity or accuracy of a particular claim. In that case, the thresholds mentioned in Article 10 shall not apply.
2. The Member State of refund shall be provided with the information requested under paragraph 1 within one month of the date on which the request reaches the person to whom it is addressed.

Article 21

Where the Member State of refund requests additional information, it shall notify the applicant of its decision to approve or refuse the refund application within two months of receiving the requested information or, if it has not received a reply to its request, within two months of expiry of the time limit laid down in Article 20(2). However, the period available for the decision in respect of the whole or part of the refund application shall always be at least six months from the date of receipt of the application by the Member State of refund.
Where the Member State of refund requests further additional information, it shall notify the applicant of its decision in respect of the whole or part of the refund application within eight months of receipt of the application by that Member State.

Article 22

1. Where the refund application is approved, refunds of the approved amount shall be paid by the Member State of refund at the latest within 10 working days of the expiry of the deadline referred to in Article 19(2) or, where additional or further additional information has been requested, the deadlines referred to in Article 21.
2. The refund shall be paid in the Member State of refund or, at the applicant's request, in any other Member State. In the latter case, any bank charges for the transfer shall be deducted by the Member State of refund from the amount to be paid to the applicant.

Article 23

1. Where the refund application is refused in whole or in part, the grounds for refusal shall be notified by the Member State of refund to the applicant together with the decision.
2. Appeals against decisions to refuse a refund application may be made by the applicant to the competent authorities of the Member State of refund in the forms and within the time limits laid down for appeals in the case of refund applications from persons who are established in that Member State.
If, under the law of the Member State of refund, failure to take a decision on a refund application within the time limits specified in this Directive is not regarded either as approval or as refusal, any administrative or judicial procedures which are available in that situation to taxable persons established in that Member State shall be equally available to the applicant. If no such procedures are available, failure to take a decision on a refund application within these time limits shall mean that the application is deemed to be rejected.

Article 24

1. Where a refund has been obtained in a fraudulent way or otherwise incorrectly, the competent authority in the Member State of refund shall proceed directly to recover the amounts wrongly paid and any penal-ties and interest imposed in accordance with the procedure applicable in the Member State of refund, without prejudice to the provisions on mutual assistance for the recovery of VAT.
2. Where an administrative penalty or interest has been imposed but has not been paid, the Member State of refund may suspend any further refund to the taxable person concerned up to the unpaid amount.

Article 25

The Member State of refund shall take into account as a decrease or increase of the amount of the refund any correction made concerning a previous refund application in accordance with Article 13 or, where a separate declaration is submitted, in the form of separate payment or recovery.

Article 26

Interest shall be due to the applicant by the Member State of refund on the amount of the refund to be paid if the refund is paid after the last date of payment pursuant to Article 22(1).

If the applicant does not submit the additional or further additional information requested to the Member State of refund within the specified time limit, the first paragraph shall not apply. It shall also not apply until the documents to be submitted electronically pursuant to Article 10 have been received by the Member State of refund.

Article 27

1. Interest shall be calculated from the day following the last day for payment of the refund pursuant to Article 22(1) until the day the refund is actually paid.
2. Interest rates shall be equal to the interest rate applicable with respect to refunds of VAT to taxable persons established in the Member State of refund under the national law of that Member State.

If no interest is payable under national law in respect of refunds to established taxable persons, the interest payable shall be equal to the interest or equivalent charge which is applied by the Member State of refund in respect of late payments of VAT by taxable persons.

Article 28

1. This Directive shall apply to refund applications submitted after 31 December 2009.
2. Directive 79/1072/EEC shall be repealed with effect from 1 January 2010. However, its provisions shall continue to apply to refund applications submitted before 1 January 2010.

References to the repealed Directive shall be construed as references to this Directive except for refund applications submitted before 1 January 2010.

Article 29

1. Member States shall bring into force the laws, regulations and administrative provisions necessary to comply with this Directive with effect from 1 January 2010. They shall forthwith inform the Commission thereof.

When such provisions are adopted by Member States, they shall contain a reference to this Directive or be accompanied by such reference on the occasion of their official publication. The methods of making such reference shall be laid down by Member States.
2. Member States shall communicate to the Commission the text of the main provisions of national law which they adopt in the field covered by this Directive.

Article 30

This Directive shall enter into force on the day of its publication in the Official Journal of the European Union.

Article 31

This Directive is addressed to the Member States.

Done at Brussels, ...12 February 2008.

For the Council
The President
A. Bajuk

ARCHIVED COUNCIL DIRECTIVE 2009/132/EC OF 19 OCTOBER 2009 DETERMINING THE SCOPE OF ARTICLE 143(B) AND (C) OF DIRECTIVE 2006/112/EC AS REGARDS EXEMPTION FROM VALUE ADDED TAX ON THE FINAL IMPORTATION OF CERTAIN GOODS

2009/132/EC

TITLE I
SCOPE AND DEFINITIONS

Article 1

The scope of the exemptions from value added tax (hereinafter VAT) referred to in Article 143(b) and (c) of Directive 2006/112/EC and the rules for their implementation, referred to in Article 145 of that Directive, shall be defined by this Directive.

In accordance with Article 131 and Article 143(b) and (c) of Directive 2006/112/EC, the Member States shall apply the exemptions laid down in this Directive under the conditions fixed by them in order to ensure that such exemptions are correctly and simply applied and to prevent any evasion, avoidance or abuses.

Article 2

1. For the purposes of this Directive:
   (a) 'imports' means imports as defined in Article 30 of Directive 2006/112/EC and the entry for home use after being subject to one of the systems provided for in Article 157(1)(a) of that Directive or a system of temporary admission or transit;
   (b) 'personal property' means any property intended for the personal use of the persons concerned or for meeting their household needs, including household effects, cycles and motor-cycles, private motor vehicles and their trailers, camping caravans, pleasure craft and private aeroplanes, as well as household provisions appropriate to normal family requirements, and household pets and saddle animals;
   (c) 'household effects' means personal effects, household linen and furnishings and items of equipment intended for the personal use of the persons concerned or for meeting their household needs;
   (d) 'alcoholic products' means products (beer, wine, aperitifs with a wine or alcohol base, brandies, liqueurs and spirituous beverages, etc.) falling within CN codes 2203 to 2208;
   (e) 'Community' means the territory of the Member States where Directive 2006/112/EC applies.
2. The nature or quantity of personal property shall not reflect any commercial interest, nor shall they be intended for an economic activity within the meaning of Article 9(1) of Directive 2006/112/EC. However, portable instruments of the applied or liberal arts, required by the person concerned for the pursuit of his trade or profession, shall also constitute personal property.

TITLE II
IMPORTATION OF PERSONAL PROPERTY BELONGING TO INDIVIDUALS COMING FROM THIRD COUNTRIES OR THIRD TERRITORIES

CHAPTER 1

PERSONAL PROPERTY OF NATURAL PERSONS TRANSFERRING THEIR NORMAL PLACE OF RESIDENCE TO THE COMMUNITY

Article 3

Subject to Articles 4 to 11, exemption from VAT on importation shall be granted on personal property imported by natural persons transferring their normal place of residence from outside the Community to a Member State of the Community.

Article 4

Exemption shall be limited to personal property which:
   (a) except in special cases justified by the circumstances, has been in the possession of and, in the case of non-consumable goods, used by the person concerned at his former normal place of residence for a minimum of six months before the date on which he ceases to have his normal place of residence outside the Community;
   (b) is intended to be used for the same purpose at his new normal place of residence.

The Member States may in addition make exemption of personal property conditional upon such property having borne, either in the country of origin or in the country of departure, the customs and/or fiscal charges to which it is normally liable.

Article 5

Exemption may be granted only to persons whose normal place of residence has been outside the Community for a continuous period of at least 12 months.

However, the competent authorities may grant exceptions to this rule provided that the intention of the person concerned was clearly to reside outside the Community for a continuous period of at least 12 months.

Article 6
Exemption shall not be granted in respect of:
(a) alcoholic products;
(b) tobacco or tobacco products;
(c) commercial means of transport;
(d) articles for use in the exercise of a trade or profession, other than portable instruments of the applied or liberal arts.

Vehicles intended for mixed use for commercial or professional purposes may also be excluded from exemption.

Article 7
1. Except in special cases, exemption shall be granted only in respect of personal property entered for permanent importation within 12 months of the date of establishment, by the person concerned, of his normal place of residence in the Community.
2. The personal property may be imported in several separate consignments within the period referred to in paragraph 1.

Article 8
1. Until 12 months have elapsed from the date of the declaration for its final importation, personal property which has been imported exempt from tax may not be lent, given as security, hired out or transferred, whether for a consideration or free of charge, without prior notification to the competent authorities.
2. Any loan, giving as security, hiring out or transfer before the expiry of the period referred to in paragraph 1 shall entail payment of the relevant VAT on the goods concerned, at the rate applying on the date of such loan, giving as security, hiring out or transfer, on the basis of the type of goods and the customs value ascertained or accepted on that date by the competent authorities.

Article 9
1. By way of derogation from Article 7(1), exemption may be granted in respect of personal property permanently imported before the person concerned establishes his normal place of residence in the Community, provided that he undertakes actually to establish his normal place of residence there within a period of six months. Such undertaking shall be accompanied by a security, the form and amount of which shall be determined by the competent authorities.
2. Where use is made of paragraph 1, the period laid down in point (a) of the first paragraph of Article 4 shall be calculated from the date of importation into the Community.

Article 10
1. Where, owing to occupational commitments, the person concerned leaves the third country or third territory where he had his normal place of residence without simultaneously establishing his normal place of residence on the territory of a Member State the Community, although having the intention of ultimately doing so, the competent authorities may authorise exemption in respect of the personal property which he transfers into the said territory for this purpose.
2. Exemption in respect of the personal property referred to in paragraph 1 shall be granted in accordance with the conditions laid down in Articles 3 to 8, on the understanding that:
    (a) the periods laid down in point (a) of the first paragraph of Article 4 and paragraph 1 of Article 7 shall be calculated from the date of importation;
    (b) the period referred to in Article 8(1) shall be calculated from the date when the person concerned actually establishes his normal place of residence on the territory of the Community.
3. Exemption shall also be subject to an undertaking from the person concerned that he will actually establish his normal place of residence on the territory of the Community within a period laid down by the competent authorities in keeping with the circumstances. The latter may require this undertaking to be accompanied by a security, the form and amount of which they shall determine.

Article 11
The competent authorities may derogate from points (a) and (b) of the first paragraph of Article 4, points (c) and (d) of the first paragraph of Article 6 and Article 8 when a person has to transfer his normal place of residence to the territory of a Member State as a result of exceptional political circumstances.

CHAPTER 2
GOODS IMPORTED ON THE OCCASION OF A MARRIAGE

Article 12

1. Subject to Articles 13 to 16, exemption shall be granted in respect of trousseaux and household effects, whether or not new, belonging to a person transferring his or her normal place of residence to the territory of the Community on the occasion of his or her marriage.

Exemption shall also be granted in respect of presents customarily given on the occasion of a marriage which are received by a person fulfilling the conditions laid down in the first subparagraph from persons having their normal place of residence outside the Community. The exemption shall apply to presents of a value of not more than EUR 200. Member States may, however, grant exemption for more than EUR 200 provided that the value of each exempt present does not exceed EUR 1,000.

2. The Member State may make exemption of the goods referred to in the first subparagraph of paragraph 1 conditional on their having borne, either in the country or territory of origin or in the country or territory of departure, the customs and fiscal charges to which they are normally liable.

Article 13

The exemption may be granted only to persons:
   (a) whose normal place of residence has been outside the Community for a continuous period of at least 12 months;
   (b) who produce evidence of their marriage.

However, derogations from the rule referred to in the first subparagraph may be granted provided that the intention of the person concerned was clearly to reside outside the Community for a continuous period of at least 12 months.

Article 14

No exemption shall be granted for alcoholic products, tobacco or tobacco products.

Article 15

1. Save in exceptional circumstances, exemption shall be granted only in respect of goods permanently imported:
   (a) not earlier than two months before the date fixed for the wedding; and
   (b) not later than four months after the date of the wedding.

In the case referred to in point (a), exemption may be made subject to the lodging of appropriate security, the form and amount of which shall be determined by the competent authorities.

2. Goods to which exemption is granted may be imported in several separate consignments, within the period referred to in paragraph 1.

Article 16

1. Until 12 months have elapsed from the date of the declaration for their final importation, personal property which has been imported exempt from tax may not be lent, given as security, hired out or transferred, whether for a consideration or free of charge, without prior notification to the competent authorities.

2. Any loan, giving as security, hiring out or transfer before the expiry of the period referred to in paragraph 1 shall entail payment of the relevant VAT on the goods concerned, at the rate applying on the date of such loan, giving as security, hiring out or transfer, on the basis of the type of goods and the value ascertained or accepted on that date by the competent authorities.

CHAPTER 3
PERSONAL PROPERTY ACQUIRED BY INHERITANCE

Article 17

Subject to Articles 18, 19 and 20, exemption shall be granted in respect of personal property acquired by inheritance by a natural person having his normal place of residence in the Community.

Article 18

Exemption shall not be granted in respect of:
   (a) alcoholic products;
   (b) tobacco or tobacco products;
   (c) commercial means of transport;
   (d) articles for use in the exercise of a trade or profession, other than portable instruments of the applied or liberal arts, which were required for the exercise of the trade or profession of the deceased;
   (e) stocks of raw materials and finished or semi-finished products;
   (f) livestock and stocks of agricultural products exceeding the quantities appropriate to normal family requirements.

Article 19

1. Exemption shall be granted only in respect of personal property permanently imported not later than two years from the date on which the person becomes entitled to the goods (final settlement of the inheritance).
However, this period may be extended by the competent authorities on special grounds.
2. The goods may be imported in several separate consignments within the period referred to in paragraph 1.

Article 20

Articles 17, 18 and 19 shall apply *mutatis mutandis* to personal property acquired by inheritance by legal persons engaged in a non-profit-making activity who are established on the territory of the Community.

TITLE III
IMPORTATION OF SCHOOL OUTFITS, EDUCATIONAL MATERIALS AND RELATED HOUSEHOLD EFFECTS

Article 21

1. Exemption shall be granted in respect of outfits, educational materials and household effects representing the usual furnishings for a student's room and belonging to pupils or students coming to stay in the Community for the purposes of studying there and intended for their personal use during the period of their studies.
2. For the purposes of this Article:
   (a) 'pupil or student' means any person enrolled in an educational establishment in order to attend, full-time, the courses offered therein;
   (b) 'outfit' means underwear and household linen as well as clothing, whether or not new;
   (c) 'educational materials' means articles and instruments (including calculators and typewriters) normally used by pupils or students for the purposes of their studies.

Article 22

Exemption shall be granted at least once per school year.

TITLE IV
IMPORTS OF NEGLIGIBLE VALUE

Article 23

Goods of a total value not exceeding EUR 10 shall be exempt on admission. Member States may grant exemption for imported goods of a total value of more than EUR 10, but not exceeding EUR 22.
However, Member States may exclude goods which have been imported on mail order from the exemption provided for in the first sentence of the first subparagraph.

Article 24

Exemption shall not apply to the following:
   (a) alcoholic products;
   (b) perfumes and toilet waters;
   (c) tobacco or tobacco products.

TITLE V
CAPITAL GOODS AND OTHER EQUIPMENT IMPORTED ON THE TRANSFER OF ACTIVITIES

Article 25

1. Without prejudice to the measures in force in the Member State with regard to industrial and commercial policy, and subject to Articles 26 to 29, Member States may allow exemption, on admission, for imports of capital goods and other equipment belonging to undertakings which definitively cease their activity in the third country or third territory of origin in order to carry on a similar activity in the Community and which, in accordance with Article 213(1) of Directive 2006/112/EC, have given advance notice to the competent authorities of the Member State of importation of the commencement of such activity.
Where the undertaking transferred is an agricultural holding, its livestock shall also be exempt on admission.
2. For the purposes of paragraph 1:
   (a) 'activity' means an economic activity as referred to in Article 9(1) of Directive 2006/112/EC;
   (b) 'undertaking' means an independent economic unit of production or of the service industry.

Article 26

1. The exemption shall be limited to capital goods and equipment which:
    (a) except in special cases justified by the circumstances, have actually been used in the undertaking for a minimum of 12 months prior to the date on which the undertaking ceased to operate in the third country or third territory from which it is transferring its activity;
    (b) are intended to be used for the same purposes after the transfer;
    (c) are to be used for the purposes of an activity not exempted under Articles 132, 133, 135 and 136 of Directive 2006/112/EC;
    (d) are appropriate to the nature and size of the undertaking in question.
2. Pending entry into force of the common rules referred to in the first paragraph of Article 176 of Directive 2006/112/EC, Member States may exclude from the exemption, in whole or in part, capital goods in respect of which they have availed themselves of the second subparagraph of Article 176 of that Directive.

Article 27

No exemption shall be granted to undertakings established outside the Community and the transfer of which to the territory of the Community is consequent upon or is for the purpose of merging with, or being absorbed by, an undertaking established in the Community, without a new activity being set up.

Article 28

No exemption shall be granted for:
(a) means of transport which are not in the nature of instruments of production or of the service industry;
(b) supplies of all kinds intended for human consumption or for animal feed;
(c) fuel and stocks of raw materials or finished or semi-finished products;
(d) livestock in the possession of dealers.

Article 29

Except in special cases justified by the circumstances, the exemption shall be granted only in respect of capital goods and other equipment imported before the expiry of a period of 12 months from the date when the undertaking ceased its activities in the third country or third territory of origin.

TITLE VI
IMPORTATION OF CERTAIN AGRICULTURAL PRODUCTS AND PRODUCTS INTENDED FOR AGRICULTURAL USE

CHAPTER 1
PRODUCTS OBTAINED BY COMMUNITY FARMERS ON PROPERTIES LOCATED IN THIRD COUNTRIES OR THIRD TERRITORIES

Article 30

1. Subject to Articles 31 and 32, agricultural, stock-farming, bee-keeping, horticultural and forestry products from properties located in a third country or third territory adjoining the territory of the Community which are operated by agricultural producers having their principal undertaking in the Community and adjacent to the country or territory concerned shall be exempt on admission. Pure-bred horses, not more than six months old and born in a third country or third territory of an animal covered in the Community and then exported temporarily to give birth, shall also be exempt on admission.
2. To be eligible for the exemption under the first subparagraph of paragraph 1, stock-farming products must be obtained from animals reared, acquired or imported in accordance with the general tax arrangements applicable in the Member State of importation.

Article 31

Exemption shall be limited to products which have not undergone any treatment other than that which normally follows their harvest or production.

Article 32

Exemption shall be granted only in respect of products imported by the agricultural producer or on his behalf.

Article 33

This Chapter shall apply *mutatis mutandis* to the products of fishing or fish-farming activities carried out in the lakes or waterways bordering the territory of the Community by fishermen established in the Community and to the products of hunting activities carried out on such lakes or waterways by sportsmen established in the Community.

CHAPTER 2
SEEDS, FERTILISERS AND PRODUCTS FOR THE TREATMENT OF SOIL AND CROPS

Article 34

Subject to Article 35, seeds, fertilisers and products for the treatment of soil and crops, intended for use on property located in the Community, and adjoining a third country or third territory and operated by agricultural producers having their principal undertaking in the said country or territory adjacent to the territory of the Community shall be exempt on admission.

Article 35

1. Exemption shall be limited to the quantities of seeds, fertilisers or other products required for the purpose of operating the property.
It shall be granted only for seeds, fertilisers or other products introduced directly into the Community by the agricultural producer or on his behalf.
2. Member States may make exemption conditional upon the granting of reciprocal treatment.

TITLE VII
IMPORTATION OF THERAPEUTIC SUBSTANCES, MEDICINES, LABORATORY ANIMALS AND BIOLOGICAL OR CHEMICAL SUBSTANCES

CHAPTER 1
LABORATORY ANIMALS AND BIOLOGICAL OR CHEMICAL SUBSTANCES INTENDED FOR RESEARCH

Article 36

1. The following shall be exempt on admission:
    (a) animals specially prepared and sent free of charge for laboratory use;
    (b) biological or chemical substances which are imported subject to the limits and conditions laid down in Article 60 of Council Regulation (EC) No 918/83 of 28 March 1983 setting up a Community system of reliefs from customs duty.[1]
2. The exemption referred to in paragraph 1 shall be limited to animals and biological or chemical substances which are intended for either of the following:
    (a) public establishments principally engaged in education or scientific research, including those departments of public establishments which are principally engaged in education or scientific research;
    (b) private establishments principally engaged in education or scientific research and authorised by the competent authorities of the Member States to receive such articles exempt from tax.

CHAPTER 2
THERAPEUTIC SUBSTANCES OF HUMAN ORIGIN AND BLOOD-GROUPING AND TISSUE-TYPING REAGENTS

Article 37

1. Without prejudice to the exemption provided for in Article 143(a) of Directive 2006/112/EC and subject to Article 38 of this Directive, the following shall be exempted:
    (a) therapeutic substances of human origin;
    (b) blood-grouping reagents;
    (c) tissue-typing reagents.
2. For the purposes of paragraph 1:
    (a) 'therapeutic substances of human origin' means human blood and its derivatives (whole human blood, dried human plasma, human albumin and fixed solutions of human plasma protein, human immunoglobulin and human fibrinogen);
    (b) 'blood-grouping reagents' means all reagents, whether of human, animal, plant or other origin used for blood-type grouping and for the detection of blood incompatibilities;
    (c) 'tissue-typing reagents' means all reagents whether of human, animal, plant or other origin used for the determination of human tissue-types.

Article 38

Exemption shall be limited to products which:
   (a) are intended for institutions or laboratories approved by the competent authorities, for use exclusively for noncommercial medical or scientific purposes;
   (b) are accompanied by a certificate of conformity issued by a duly authorised body in the country or territory of departure;
   (c) are in containers bearing a special label identifying them.

Article 39
Exemption shall include the special packaging essential for the transport of therapeutic substances of human origin or blood-grouping or tissue-typing reagents and also any solvents and accessories needed for their use which may be included in the consignments.

CHAPTER 3
REFERENCE SUBSTANCES FOR THE QUALITY CONTROL OF MEDICAL PRODUCTS
Article 40
Consignments which contain samples of reference substances approved by the World Health Organisation for the quality control of materials used in the manufacture of medicinal products and which are addressed to consignees authorised by the competent authorities of the Member States to receive such consignments free of tax shall be exempt on admission.

CHAPTER 4
PHARMACEUTICAL PRODUCTS USED AT INTERNATIONAL SPORTS EVENTS
Article 41
Pharmaceutical products for human or veterinary medical use by persons or animals participating in international sports events shall, within the limits necessary to meet their requirements during their stay in the Community, be exempt on admission.

Notes[1]   OJ L105, 23.4.1983, p 1.

TITLE VIII
GOODS FOR CHARITABLE OR PHILANTHROPIC ORGANISATIONS

CHAPTER 1
GENERAL PROVISION
Article 42
Member States may impose a limit on the quantity or value of the goods, exempt under Chapters 2, 3 or 4 in order to remedy any abuse and to combat major distortions of competition.

CHAPTER 2
GOODS IMPORTED FOR GENERAL PURPOSES
Article 43
1. Subject to Articles 44, 45 and 46, the following shall be exempt on admission:
    (a) basic necessities obtained free of charge and imported by State organisations or other charitable or philanthropic organisations approved by the competent authorities for distribution free of charge to needy persons;
    (b) goods of every description sent free of charge, by a person or organisation established outside the Community, and without any commercial intent on the part of the sender, to State organisations or other charitable or philanthropic organisations approved by the competent authorities, to be used for fund-raising at occasional charity events for the benefit of needy persons;
    (c) equipment and office materials sent free of charge, by a person or organisation established outside the Community, and without any commercial intent on the part of the sender, to charitable or philanthropic organisations approved by the competent authorities, to be used solely for the purpose of meeting their operating needs or carrying out their stated charitable or philanthropic aims.
2. For the purposes of paragraph 1(a) 'basic necessities' means those goods required to meet the immediate needs of human beings, such as food, medicine, clothing and bed-clothes.

Article 44
Exemption shall not be granted in respect of:
    (a) alcoholic products;
    (b) tobacco or tobacco products;
    (c) coffee and tea;
    (d) motor vehicles other than ambulances.

Article 45
Exemption shall be granted only to organisations accounting procedures of which enable the competent authorities to supervise their operations and which offer all the guarantees considered necessary.

Article 46
1. The organisation entitled to exemption may not lend, hire out or transfer, whether for a consideration or free of charge, the goods referred to in Article 43 for purposes other than those laid down in Article 43(1)(a) and (b), unless the competent authorities have been informed thereof in advance.
2. Should goods and equipment be lent, hired out or transferred to an organisation entitled to benefit from exemption pursuant to Articles 43 and 45, the exemption shall continue to be granted provided that the latter uses the goods and equipment for purposes which confer the right to such exemption.
In other cases, loan, hiring out or transfer shall be subject to prior payment of VAT at the rate applying on the date of the loan, hiring out or transfer, on the basis of the type of goods and equipment and the value ascertained or accepted on that date by the competent authorities.

Article 47
1. Organisations referred to in Article 43 which cease to fulfil the conditions giving entitlement to exemption, or which are proposing to use goods and equipment exempt on admission for purposes other than those provided for by that Article, shall so inform the competent authorities.
2. Goods remaining in the possession of organisations which cease to fulfil the conditions giving entitlement to exemption shall be liable to the relevant import VAT at the rate applying on the date on which those conditions cease to be fulfilled, on the basis of the type of goods and equipment and the value as ascertained or accepted on that date by the competent authorities.
3. Goods used by the organisation benefiting from the exemption for purposes other than those provided for in Article 43 shall be liable to the relevant import VAT at the rate applying on the date on which they are put to another use on the basis of the type of goods and equipment and the value as ascertained on that date by the competent authorities.

CHAPTER 3
ARTICLES IMPORTED FOR THE BENEFIT OF HANDICAPPED PERSONS

Article 48
1. Articles specially designed for the education, employment or social advancement of blind or other physically or mentally handicapped persons shall be exempt on admission where:
   (a) they are imported by institutions or organisations that are principally engaged in the education of or the provision of assistance to handicapped persons and are authorised by the competent authorities of the Member States to receive such articles exempt from tax; and
   (b) they are donated to such institutions or organisations free of charge and with no commercial intent on the part of the donor.
2. Exemption shall apply to specific spare parts, components or accessories specifically for the articles in question and to the tools to be used for the maintenance, checking, calibration and repair of the said articles, provided that such spare parts, components, accessories or tools are imported at the same time as the said articles or, if imported subsequently, that they can be identified as being intended for articles previously exempt on admission or which would be eligible to be so exempt at the time when such entry is requested for the specific spare parts, components or accessories and tools in question.
3. Articles exempt on admission may not be used for purposes other than the education, employment or social advancement of blind or other handicapped persons.

Article 49
1. Goods exempt on admission may be lent, hired out or transferred, whether for a consideration or free of charge, by the beneficiary institutions or organisations on a non-profit-making basis to the persons referred to in Article 48 with whom they are concerned, without payment of VAT on importation.
2. No loan, hiring out or transfer may be effected under conditions other than those provided for in paragraph 1 unless the competent authorities have first been informed.
Should an article be lent, hired out or transferred to an institution or organisation itself entitled to benefit from this exemption, the exemption shall continue to be granted, provided the latter uses the article for purposes which confer the right to such exemption.
In other cases, loan, hiring out or transfer shall be subject to prior payment of VAT, at the rate applying on the date of the loan, hiring out or transfer, on the basis of the type of goods and the value ascertained or accepted on that date by the competent authorities.

Article 50
1. Institutions or organisations referred to in Article 48 which cease to fulfil the conditions giving entitlement to exemption, or which are proposing to use articles exempt on admission for purposes other than those provided for by that Article shall so inform the competent authorities.

2. Articles remaining in the possession of institutions or organisations which cease to fulfil the conditions giving entitlement to exemption shall be liable to the relevant import VAT at the rate applying on the date on which those conditions cease to be fulfilled, on the basis of the type of goods and the value ascertained or accepted on that date by the competent authorities.

3. Articles used by the institution or organisation benefiting from the exemption for purposes other than those provided for in Article 48 shall be liable to the relevant import VAT at the rate applying on the date on which they are put to another use on the basis of the type of goods and the value ascertained or accepted on that date by the competent authorities.

CHAPTER 4
GOODS IMPORTED FOR THE BENEFIT OF DISASTER VICTIMS

Article 51

Subject to Articles 52 to 57 goods imported by State organisations or other charitable or philanthropic organisations approved by the competent authorities shall be exempt on admission where they are intended:

(a) for distribution free of charge to victims of disasters affecting the territory of one or more Member States; or

(b) to be made available free of charge to the victims of such disasters, while remaining the property of the organisations in question.

Goods imported by disaster-relief agencies in order to meet their needs during the period of their activity shall also benefit upon admission from the exemption under the same conditions.

Article 52

No exemption shall be granted for materials and equipment intended for rebuilding disaster areas.

Article 53

Granting of the exemption shall be subject to a decision by the Commission, acting at the request of the Member State or States concerned in accordance with an emergency procedure entailing the consultation of the other Member States. This decision shall, where necessary, lay down the scope and the conditions of the exemption.

Pending notification of the Commission's decision, Member States affected by a disaster may authorise the suspension of any import VAT chargeable on goods imported for the purposes described in Article 51, subject to an undertaking by the importing organisation to pay such tax if exemption is not granted.

Article 54

Exemption shall be granted only to organisations the accounting procedures of which enable the competent authorities to supervise their operations and which offer all the guarantees considered necessary.

Article 55

1. The organisations benefiting from the exemption may not lend, hire out or transfer, whether for a consideration or free of charge, the goods referred to in the first paragraph of Article 51 under conditions other than those laid down in that Article without prior notification thereof to the competent authorities.

2. Should goods be lent, hired out or transferred to an organisation itself entitled to benefit from exemption pursuant to Article 51, the exemption shall continue to be granted, provided the latter uses the goods for purposes which confer the right to such exemption.

In other cases, loan, hiring out or transfer shall be subject to prior payment of VAT, at the rate applying on the date of the loan, hiring out or transfer, on the basis of the type of goods and the value ascertained or accepted on that date by the competent authorities.

Article 56

1. The goods referred to in point (b) of the first paragraph of Article 51, after they cease to be used by disaster victims, may not be lent, hired out or transferred, whether for a consideration or free of charge, unless the competent authorities are notified in advance.

2. Should goods be lent, hired out or transferred to an organisation itself entitled to benefit from exemption pursuant to Article 51 or, if appropriate, to an organisation entitled to benefit from exemption pursuant to Article 43(1)(a), the exemption shall continue to be granted, provided such organisations use the goods concerned for purposes which confer the right to such exemption.

In other cases, loan, hiring out or transfer shall be subject to prior payment of VAT, at the rate applying on the date of the loan, hiring out or transfer, on the basis of the type of goods and the value ascertained or accepted on that date by the competent authorities.

Article 57

1. Organisations referred to in Article 51 which cease to fulfil the conditions giving entitlement to exemption, or which are proposing to use the goods exempt on admission for purposes other than those provided for by that Article shall so inform the competent authorities.

2. In the case of goods remaining in the possession of organisations which cease to fulfil the conditions giving entitlement to exemption, when these are transferred to an organisation itself entitled to benefit from exemption pursuant to this Chapter or, if appropriate, to an organisation entitled to benefit from exemption pursuant to Article 43, the exemption shall continue to be granted, provided the organisation uses the goods in question for purposes which confer the right to such exemptions. In other cases, the goods shall be liable to the relevant import VAT at the rate applying on the date on which those conditions cease to be fulfilled, on the basis of the type of goods and the value ascertained or accepted on that date by the competent authorities.

3. Goods used by the organisation benefiting from the exemption for purposes other than those provided for in this Chapter shall be liable to the relevant import VAT at the rate applying on the date on which they are put to another use, on the basis of the type of goods and the value ascertained or accepted on that date by the competent authorities.

TITLE IX
IMPORTATION IN THE CONTEXT OF CERTAIN ASPECTS OF INTERNATIONAL RELATIONS

CHAPTER 1
HONORARY DECORATIONS OR AWARDS

Article 58

On production of satisfactory evidence to the competent authorities by the persons concerned, and provided the operations involved are not in any way of a commercial character, exemption shall be granted in respect of:
  (a) decorations conferred by the government of a third country on persons whose normal place of residence is in the Community;
  (b) cups, medals and similar articles of an essentially symbolic nature which, having been awarded in a third country or third territory to persons having their normal place of residence in the Community as a tribute to their activities in fields such as the arts, the sciences, sport or the public service or in recognition of merit at a particular event, are imported by such persons themselves;
  (c) cups, medals and similar articles of an essentially symbolic nature which are given free of charge by authorities or persons established in a third country, to be presented on the territory of the Community for the same purposes as those referred to in point (b);
  (d) awards, trophies and souvenirs of a symbolic nature and of limited value intended for distribution free of charge to persons normally resident in a third country or third territory, at business conferences or similar international events; their nature, unitary value or other features, must not be such as might indicate that they are intended for commercial purposes.

CHAPTER 2
PRESENTS RECEIVED IN THE CONTEXT OF INTERNATIONAL RELATIONS

Article 59

Without prejudice, where relevant, to the provisions applicable to the international movement of travellers, and subject to Articles 60 and 61, exemption shall be granted in respect of goods:
  (a) imported by persons who have paid an official visit in a third country or third territory and who have received such goods on that occasion as gifts from the host authorities;
  (b) imported by persons coming to pay an official visit in the Community and who intend to offer them on that occasion as gifts to the host authorities;
  (c) sent as gifts, in token of friendship or goodwill, by an official body, public authority or group carrying on an activity in the public interest which is located in a third country or third territory, to an official body, public authority or group carrying on an activity in the public interest which is located in the Member State of importation and approved by the competent authorities to receive such goods exempt from tax.

Article 60

No exemption shall be granted for alcoholic products, tobacco or tobacco products.

Article 61

Exemption shall be granted only:
  (a) where the articles intended as gifts are offered on an occasional basis;
  (b) where they do not, by their nature, value or quantity, reflect any commercial interest;
  (c) if they are not used for commercial purposes.

CHAPTER 3
GOODS TO BE USED BY MONARCHS OR HEADS OF STATE

Article 62

1. Exemption from tax, within the limits and under the conditions laid down by the competent authorities, shall be granted in respect of:
    (a) gifts to reigning monarchs and heads of State;
    (b) goods to be used or consumed by reigning monarchs and heads of State of a third country, or by persons officially representing them, during their official stay in the Community.
2. The exemption referred to in paragraph 1(b) may be made subject, by the Member State of importation, to reciprocal treatment.
3. The exemption referred to in paragraph 1 is also applicable to persons enjoying prerogatives at international level analogous to those enjoyed by reigning monarchs or heads of State.

TITLE X
IMPORTATION OF GOODS FOR THE PROMOTION OF TRADE

CHAPTER 1
SAMPLES OF NEGLIGIBLE VALUE

Article 63

1. Without prejudice to Article 67(1)(a), samples of goods which are of negligible value and which can be used only to solicit orders for goods of the type they represent shall be exempt on admission.
2. The competent authorities may require that certain articles, to qualify for exemption on admission, be rendered permanently unusable by being torn, perforated, or clearly and indelibly marked, or by any other process, provided such operation does not destroy their character as samples.
3. For the purposes of paragraph 1, 'samples of goods' means any article representing a type of goods whose manner of presentation and quantity, for goods of the same type or quality, rule out its use for any purpose other than that of seeking orders.

CHAPTER 2
PRINTED MATTER AND ADVERTISING MATERIAL

Article 64

Subject to Article 65, printed advertising matter such as catalogues, price lists, directions for use or brochures shall be exempt on admission provided that they relate to:
   (a) goods for sale or hire by a person established outside the Community; or
   (b) transport, commercial insurance or banking services offered by a person established outside the Community.

Article 65

1. The exemption shall be limited to printed advertisements which fulfil the following conditions:
    (a) printed matter must clearly display the name of the undertaking which produces, sells or hires out the goods, or which offers the services to which it refers;
    (b) each consignment must contain no more than one document or a single copy of each document if it is made up of several documents;
    (c) printed matter must not be the subject of grouped consignments from the same consignor to the same consignee.
2. By way of derogation from paragraph 1(b), consignments comprising several copies of the same document may nevertheless be granted exemption provided their total gross weight does not exceed one kilogram.

Article 66

Articles for advertising purposes, of no intrinsic commercial value, sent free of charge by suppliers to their customers which, apart from their advertising function, are not capable of being used shall be exempt on admission.

CHAPTER 3
GOODS USED OR CONSUMED AT A TRADE FAIR OR SIMILAR EVENT

Article 67

1. Subject to Articles 68, 69, 70 and 71, the following shall be exempt on admission:
    (a) small representative samples of goods intended for a trade fair or similar event;
    (b) goods imported solely in order to be demonstrated or in order to demonstrate machines and apparatus displayed at a trade fair or similar event;
    (c) various materials of little value, such as paints, varnishes and wallpaper, which are to be used in the building, fitting-out and decoration of temporary stands at a trade fair or similar event, which are destroyed by being used;

(d) printed matter, catalogues, prospectuses, price lists, advertising posters, calendars, whether or not illustrated, unframed photographs and other articles supplied free of charge in order to advertise goods displayed at a trade fair or similar event.
2. For the purposes of paragraph 1, 'trade fair or similar event' means:
 (a) exhibitions, fairs, shows and similar events connected with trade, industry, agriculture or handicrafts;
 (b) exhibitions and events held mainly for charitable reasons;
 (c) exhibitions and events held mainly for scientific, technical, handicraft, artistic, educational or cultural or sporting reasons, for religious reasons or for reasons of worship, trade union activity or tourism, or in order to promote international understanding;
 (d) meetings of representatives of international organisations or collective bodies;
 (e) official or commemorative ceremonies and gatherings;
However, that definition shall not cover exhibitions staged for private purposes in commercial stores or premises to sell goods.

Article 68
The exemption referred to in Article 67(1)(a) shall be limited to samples which:
 (a) are imported free of charge as such or are obtained at the exhibition from goods imported in bulk;
 (b) are exclusively distributed free of charge to the public at the exhibition for use or consumption by the persons to whom they have been offered;
 (c) are identifiable as advertising samples of low unitary value;
 (d) are not easily marketable and, where appropriate, are packaged in such a way that the quantity of the item involved is lower than the smallest quantity of the same item actually sold on the market;
 (e) in the case of foodstuffs and beverages not packaged as referred to in point (d), are consumed on the spot at the exhibition;
 (f) in their total value and quantity, are appropriate to the nature of the exhibition, the number of visitors and the extent of the exhibitor's participation.

Article 69
The exemption referred to in Article 67(1)(b) shall be limited to goods which are:
 (a) consumed or destroyed at the exhibition; and
 (b) appropriate, in their total value and quantity, to the nature of the exhibition, the number of visitors and the extent of the exhibitor's participation.

Article 70
The exemption referred to in Article 67(1)(d) shall be limited to printed matter and articles for advertising purposes which:
 (a) are intended exclusively to be distributed free of charge to the public at the place where the exhibition is held; and
 (b) in their total value and quantity, are appropriate to the nature of the exhibition, the number of visitors and the extent of the exhibitor's participation.

Article 71
The exemption referred to in Article 67(1)(a) and (b) shall not be granted for:
 (a) alcoholic products;
 (b) tobacco or tobacco products;
 (c) fuels, whether solid, liquid or gaseous.

TITLE XI
GOODS IMPORTED FOR EXAMINATION, ANALYSIS OR TEST PURPOSES

Article 72
Subject to Articles 73 to 78, goods which are to undergo examination, analysis or tests to determine their composition, quality or other technical characteristics for purposes of information or industrial or commercial research shall be exempt on admission.

Article 73
Without prejudice to Article 76, the exemption shall be granted only on condition that the goods to be examined, analysed or tested are completely used up or destroyed in the course of the examination, analysis or testing.

Article 74
No exemption shall be granted in respect of goods used in examination, analysis or tests which in themselves constitute sales promotion operations.

Article 75
Exemption shall be granted only in respect of the quantities of goods which are strictly necessary for the purpose for which they are imported. These quantities shall in each case be determined by the competent authorities, taking into account the said purpose.

Article 76
1. The exemption shall cover goods which are not completely used up or destroyed during examination, analysis or testing, provided that the products remaining are, with the agreement and under the supervision of the competent authorities:
    (a) completely destroyed or rendered commercially valueless on completion of examination, analysis or testing; or
    (b) surrendered to the State without causing it any expense, where this is possible under national law; or
    (c) in duly justified circumstances, exported outside the Community.
2. For the purposes of paragraph 1, 'products remaining' means products resulting from the examinations, analyses or tests or goods not actually used.

Article 77
Save where Article 76(1) is applied, products remaining at the end of the examinations, analyses or tests referred to in Article 72 shall be subject to the relevant import VAT, at the rate applying on the date of completion of the examinations, analyses or tests, on the basis of the type of goods and the value ascertained or accepted on that date by the competent authorities.

However, the interested party may, with the agreement and under the supervision of the competent authorities, convert products remaining to waste or scrap. In this case, the import duties shall be those applying to such waste or scrap at the time of conversion.

Article 78
The period within which the examinations, analyses or tests must be carried out and the administrative formalities to be completed in order to ensure the use of the goods for the purposes intended shall be determined by the competent authorities.

TITLE XII
MISCELLANEOUS IMPORTS

CHAPTER 1
CONSIGNMENTS SENT TO ORGANISATIONS PROTECTING COPYRIGHTS OR INDUSTRIAL AND COMMERCIAL PATENT RIGHTS

Article 79
Trademarks, patterns or designs and their supporting documents, as well as applications for patents for invention or the like, to be submitted to the bodies competent to deal with the protection of copyrights or the protection of industrial or commercial patent rights shall be exempt on admission.

CHAPTER 2
TOURIST INFORMATION LITERATURE

Article 80
The following shall be exempt on admission:
   (a) documentation (leaflets, brochures, books, magazines, guidebooks, posters, whether or not framed, unframed photographs and photographic enlargements, maps, whether or not illustrated, window transparencies, and illustrated calendars) intended to be distributed free of charge and the principal purpose of which is to encourage the public to visit foreign countries, in particular in order to attend cultural, tourist, sporting, religious or trade or professional meetings or events, provided that such literature contains not more than 25 % of private commercial advertising and that the general nature of its promotional aims is evident;
   (b) foreign hotel lists and yearbooks published by official tourist agencies, or under their auspices, and timetables for foreign transport services, provided that such literature is intended for distribution free of charge and contains not more than 25 % of private commercial advertising;
   (c) reference material supplied to accredited representatives or correspondents appointed by official national tourist agencies and not intended for distribution, that is to say, yearbooks, lists of telephone or telex numbers, hotel lists, fairs catalogues, specimens of craft goods of negligible value, and literature on museums, universities, spas or other similar establishments.

CHAPTER 3
MISCELLANEOUS DOCUMENTS AND ARTICLES

Article 81

1. The following shall be exempt on admission:
   (a) documents sent free of charge to the public services of Member States;
   (b) publications of foreign governments and publications of official international bodies intended for distribution without charge;
   (c) ballot papers for elections organised by bodies set up in countries outside the Community;
   (d) objects to be submitted as evidence or for like purposes to the courts or other official agencies of the Member States;
   (e) specimen signatures and printed circulars concerning signatures sent as part of customary exchanges of information between public services or banking establishments;
   (f) official printed matter sent to the central banks of the Member States;
   (g) reports, statements, notes, prospectuses, application forms and other documents drawn up by companies with headquarters outside the Community and sent to the bearers or subscribers of securities issued by such companies;
   (h) recorded media (punched cards, sound recordings, microfilms, etc.) used for the transmission of information sent free of charge to the addressee, in so far as exemption does not give rise to abuses or to major distortions of competition;
   (i) files, archives, printed forms and other documents to be used in international meetings, conferences or congresses, and reports on such gatherings;
   (j) plans, technical drawings, traced designs, descriptions and other similar documents imported with a view to obtaining or fulfilling orders outside the Community or to participating in a competition held in the Community;
   (k) documents to be used in examinations held in the Community by institutions set up outside the Community;
   (l) printed forms to be used as official documents in the international movement of vehicles or goods, within the framework of international conventions;
   (m) printed forms, labels, tickets and similar documents sent by transport undertakings or by undertakings of the hotel industry located outside the Community to travel agencies set up in the Community;
   (n) printed forms and tickets, bills of lading, way-bills and other commercial or office documents which have been used;
   (o) official printed forms from national or international authorities, and printed matter conforming to international standards sent for distribution by associations established outside the Community to corresponding associations located in the Community;
   (p) photographs, slides and stereotype mats for photographs, whether or not captioned, sent to press agencies or newspaper or magazine publishers;
   (q) articles listed in Annex I which are produced by the United Nations or one of its specialised agencies whatever the use for which they are intended;
   (r) collectors' pieces and works of art of an educational, scientific or cultural character which are not intended for sale and which are imported by museums, galleries and other institutions approved by the competent authorities of the Member States for the purpose of duty-free admission of these goods;
   (s) importations of official publications issued under the authority of the country or territory of export, international institutions, regional or local authorities and bodies under public law established in the country or territory of export, and printed matter distributed on the occasion of elections to the European Parliament or on the occasion of national elections in the country in which the printed matter originates by foreign political organisations officially recognised as such in the Member States, in so far as such publications and printed matter have been subject to tax in the country or territory of export and have not benefited from remission of tax on export.

2. The exemption referred to in paragraph 1(r) is granted only on condition that the articles in question are imported free of charge or, if they are imported against payment, that they are not supplied by a taxable person.

CHAPTER 4
ANCILLARY MATERIALS FOR THE STOWAGE AND PROTECTION OF GOODS DURING THEIR TRANSPORT

Article 82

The various materials such as rope, straw, cloth, paper and cardboard, wood and plastics which are used for the stowage and protection — including heat protection — of goods during their transport on the territory of the Community, shall be exempt on admission, provided that:
   (a) they are not normally reusable; and

(b) the consideration paid for them forms part of the taxable amount on importation as defined in Chapter 4 of Title VII of Directive 2006/112/EC.

CHAPTER 5
LITTER, FODDER AND FEEDINGSTUFFS FOR ANIMALS DURING THEIR TRANSPORT

Article 83
Litter, fodder and feedingstuffs of any description put on board the means of transport used to convey animals on the territory of the Community for the purpose of distribution to the said animals during the journey shall be exempt on admission.

CHAPTER 6
FUELS AND LUBRICANTS PRESENT IN LAND MOTOR VEHICLES AND SPECIAL CONTAINERS

Article 84
1. Subject to Articles 85, 86 and 87, the following shall be exempt on admission:
   (a) fuel contained in the standard tanks of:
       (i) private and commercial motor vehicles and motorcycles;
       (ii) special containers;
   (b) fuel contained in portable tanks carried by private motor vehicles and motorcycles, up to a maximum of 10 litres per vehicle and without prejudice to national provisions on the holding and transport of fuel.
2. For the purpose of paragraph 1:
   (a) 'commercial motor vehicle' means any motorised road vehicle (including tractors with trailers) which, by its type of construction and equipment, is designed for, and capable of, transporting, whether for payment or not, more than nine persons including the driver, or goods, and any road vehicle for a special purpose other than transport as such;
   (b) 'private motor vehicle' means any motor vehicle not covered by the definition set out in point (a);
   (c) 'standard tanks' means:
       (i) the tanks permanently fixed by the manufacturer to all motor vehicles of the same type as the vehicle in question and whose permanent fitting enables fuel to be used directly, both for the purpose of propulsion and, where appropriate, for the operation, during transport, of refrigeration systems and other systems;
       (ii) tanks permanently fixed by the manufacturer to all containers of the same type as the container in question and whose permanent fitting enables fuel to be used directly for the operation, during transport, of refrigeration systems and other systems with which special containers are equipped;
   (d) 'special container' means any container fitted with specially designed apparatus for refrigeration systems, oxygenation systems, thermal insulation systems, or other systems.

In addition to the tanks referred to in point (c)(i) of the first subparagraph, gas tanks fitted to motor vehicles designed for the direct use of gas as a fuel and tanks fitted to ancillary systems with which the vehicle may be equipped shall also be considered to be standard tanks.

Article 85
Member States may limit the application of the exemption for fuel contained in the standard fuel tanks of commercial motor vehicles and special containers:
   (a) when the vehicle comes from a third country or third territory, to 200 litres per vehicle and per journey;
   (b) to 200 litres per special container and per journey.

Article 86
Member States may limit the amount of fuel exempt on admission in the case of:
   (a) commercial motor vehicles engaged in international transport coming from third countries or third territories to their frontier zone, to a maximum depth of 25 kilometres as the crow flies, where such transport consists of journeys made by persons residing in that zone;
   (b) private motor vehicles belonging to persons residing in the frontier zone, to a maximum depth of 15 km as the crow flies, contiguous with a third country or third territory.

Article 87
1. Fuel exempt on admission may not be used in a vehicle other than that in which it was imported nor be removed from that vehicle and stored, except during necessary repairs to that vehicle, or transferred for a consideration or free of charge by the person granted the exemption.

2. Non-compliance with paragraph 1 shall give rise to application of the import VAT relating to the products in question at the rate in force on the date of such non-compliance, on the basis of the type of goods and the value ascertained or accepted on that date by the competent authorities.

Article 88

The exemption shall also apply to lubricants carried in motor vehicles and required for their normal operation during the journey in question.

CHAPTER 7
GOODS FOR THE CONSTRUCTION, UPKEEP OR ORNAMENTATION OF MEMORIALS TO, OR CEMETERIES FOR, WAR VICTIMS

Article 89

Exemption from tax shall be granted in respect of goods imported by organisations authorised for that purpose by the competent authorities, for use in the construction, upkeep or ornamentation of cemeteries and tombs of, and memorials to, war victims of a third country who are buried in the Community.

CHAPTER 8
COFFINS, FUNERARY URNS AND ORNAMENTAL FUNERARY ARTICLES

Article 90

The following shall be exempt on admission:
(a) coffins containing bodies and urns containing the ashes of deceased persons, as well as the flowers, funeral wreaths and other ornamental objects normally accompanying them;
(b) flowers, wreaths and other ornamental objects brought by persons resident outside the Community, attending a funeral or coming to decorate graves on the territory of the Community provided these importations do not reflect, by either their nature or their quantity, any commercial intent.

TITLE XIII
GENERAL AND FINAL PROVISIONS

Article 91

Where this Directive provides that the granting of an exemption shall be subject to the fulfilment of certain conditions, the person concerned shall, to the satisfaction of the competent authorities, furnish proof that those conditions have been met.

Article 92

1. The exchange value in national currency of the euro to be taken into consideration for the purposes of this Directive shall be fixed once a year. The rates to be applied shall be those obtaining on the first working day in October and shall take effect on 1 January the following year.
2. Member States may round off the amounts in national currency arrived at by converting the amounts in euro.
3. Member States may continue to apply the amounts of the exemptions in force at the time of the annual adjustment provided for in paragraph 1, if conversion of the amounts of the exemptions expressed in euro leads, before the rounding-off provided for in paragraph 2, to an alteration of less than 5 % in the exemption expressed in national currency or to a reduction in that exemption.

Article 93

This Directive shall not prevent Member States from continuing to grant:
(a) the privileges and immunities granted by them under cultural, scientific or technical cooperation agreements concluded between Member States and third countries;
(b) the special exemptions justified by the nature of frontier traffic which are granted by them under frontier agreements concluded between Member States and third countries;
(c) exemptions in the context of agreements entered into on the basis of reciprocity with third countries that are Contracting Parties to the Convention on International Civil Aviation, signed at Chicago on 7 December 1944, for the purpose of implementing Recommended Practices 4.42 and 4.44 in Annex 9 to the Convention.

Article 94

Until the establishment of Community exemptions upon importation, Member States may retain the exemptions granted to:
(a) merchant-navy seamen;
(b) workers returning to their country of origin after having resided for at least six months outside the Community on account of their occupation.

Article 95
Member States shall inform the Commission of the measures which they adopt to give effect to this Directive, indicating, where the case arises, those measures which they adopt by simple reference to identical provisions of Regulation (EEC) No 918/83.

Article 96
Directive 83/181/EEC, as amended by the Directives listed in Annex II, Part A, is repealed, without prejudice to the obligations of the Member States relating to the time limits for transposition into national law of the Directives set out in Annex II, Part B.

References to the repealed Directive shall be construed as references to this Directive and shall be read in accordance with the correlation table in Annex III.

Article 97
This Directive shall enter into force on the 20th day following its publication in the *Official Journal of the European Union*.

Article 98
This Directive is addressed to the Member States.

Done at Luxembourg, ...19 October 2009.

For the Council
The President
E. ERLANDSSON

ANNEX I
VISUAL AND AUDITORY MATERIALS OF AN EDUCATIONAL, SCIENTIFIC OR CULTURAL CHARACTER

CN code	Description
3704 00	Photographic plates, film, paper, paperboard and textiles, exposed but not developed:
ex 3704 00 10	– Plates and film:
	— Cinematograph film, positives, of an educational, scientific or cultural character
ex 3705	Photographic plates and film, exposed and developed, other than cinematograph film:
	— Of an educational, scientific or cultural character
3706	Cinematograph film, exposed and developed, whether or not incorporating sound track or consisting only of sound track:
3706 10	– Of a width of 35 mm or more:
	– – Other:
ex 3706 10 99	– – – Other positives:
	— Newsreels (with or without sound track) depicting events of current news value at the time of importation, and imported up to a limit of two copies of each subject for copying purposes
	— Archival film material (with or without sound track) intended for use in connection with newsreel films
	— Recreational films particularly suited for children and young people
	— Other films of educational, scientific or cultural character
3706 90	– Other:
	– – Other:
	– – – Other positives:
ex 3706 90 51	— Newsreels (with or without sound track) depicting events of current news value at the time of importation, and imported up to a limit of two copies of each subject for copying purposes
ex 3706 90 91	— Archival film material (with or without sound track) intended for use in connection with newsreel films
ex 3706 90 99	— Recreational films particularly suited for children and young people
	— Other films of educational, scientific or cultural character
4911	Other printed matter, including printed pictures and photographs:
	– Other:
4911 99	– – Other:
ex 4911 99 00	– – Other:

CN code	Description
	— Microcards or other information storage media required in computerised information and documentation services of an educational, scientific or cultural character
	— Wall charts designed solely for demonstration and education
ex 8523	Records, tapes and other recorded media for sound or other similarly recorded phenomena including matrices and masters for the production of records, but excluding products of Chapter 37:
	— Of an educational, scientific or cultural character
ex 9023 00	Instruments, apparatus and models, designed for demonstrational purposes (for example, in education or exhibitions), unsuitable for others uses:
	— Patterns, models and wall charts of an educational, scientific or cultural character, designed solely for demonstration and education
	— Mock-ups or visualisations of abstract concepts such as molecular structures or mathematical formulae
Various	Holograms for laser projection
	Multimedia kits
	Materials for programmed instructions, including materials in kit form with the corresponding printed materials

ANNEX II

PART A

REPEALED DIRECTIVE WITH THE LIST OF ITS SUCCESSIVE AMENDMENTS

(referred to in Article 96)

Council Directive 83/181/EEC
(OJ) L105, 23.4.1983, p 38)
    Council Directive 85/346/EEC
    (OJ L183, 16.7.1985, p 21)
    Council Directive 88/331/EEC
    (OJ L151, 17.6.1988, p 79)
    Commission Directive 89/219/EEC
    (OJ L92, 5.4.1989, p 13)
    Council Directive 91/680/EEC   only as regards Article 2(1) first indent
    (OJ L376, 31.12.1991, p 1)
    1994 Act of Accession, Annex I, point XIII.B.4
    (OJ C241, 29.8.1994, p 276)

PART B

LIST OF TIME LIMITS FOR TRANSPOSITION INTO NATIONAL LAW

(referred to in Article 96)

Directive	Time limit for transposition
83/181/EEC	30 June 1984
85/346/EEC	1 October 1985
88/331/EEC	1 January 1989
89/219/EEC	1 July 1989
91/680/EEC	31 December 1992

ANNEX III

CORRELATION TABLE

Directive 83/181/EEC	This Directive
—	Title I
Article 1(1)	Article 1(1), first and second subparagraphs
Article 1(2) introductory sentence	Article 2(1) introductory sentence
Article 1(2)(a)	Article 2(1)(a)

Directive 83/181/EEC	This Directive
Article 1(2)(b) first subparagraph	Article 2(1)(b)
Article 1(2)(b) second subparagraph, first and second indents	Article 2(1)(b)
Article 1(2)(b) third subparagraph	Article 2(1)(b)
Article 1(2)(b) fourth subparagraph	Article 2(2)
Article 1(2)(c), (d) and (e)	Article 2(1)(c), (d) and (e)
Title I	Title II
Chapter I	Chapter 1
Articles 2 to 5	Articles 3 to 6
Article 6 first and second paragraphs	Article 7(1) and (2)
Articles 7 to 10	Articles 8 to 11
Chapter II	Chapter 2
Article 11(1) and (2)	Article 12(1), first and second subparagraphs
Article 11(3)	Article 12(2)
Article 12, introductory sentence	Article 13, first subparagraph, introductory sentence
Article 12(a), first sentence	Article 13, first subparagraph, point (a)
Article 12(a), second sentence	Article 13, second subparagraph
Article 12(b)	Article 13, first subparagraph, point (b)
Article 13	Article 14
Article 14(1) introductory sentence	Article 15(1), first subparagraph, introductory sentence
Article 14(1) first indent, opening words	Article 15(1), first subparagraph, point (a)
Article 14(1) first indent, words in parentheses	Article 15(1), second subparagraph
Article 14(1), second indent	Article 15(1), first subparagraph, point (b)
Article 14(2)	Article 15(2)
Article 15	Article 16
Chapter III	Chapter 3
Articles 16 to 19	Articles 17 to 20
Title II	Title III
Articles 20 and 21	Articles 21 and 22
Title III	Title IV
Articles 22 and 23	Articles 23 and 24
Title IV	Title V
Article 24(1)	Article 25(1)
Article 24(2) introductory sentence	Article 25(2) introductory sentence
Article 24(2) first and second indents	Article 25(2)(a) and (b)
Article 25(1)	Article 26(1)
Article 25(2)	—
Article 25(3)	Article 26(2)
Articles 26, 27 and 28	Articles 27, 28 and 29
Title V	Title VI
Chapter I	Chapter 1
Article 29(1)	Article 30(1), first subparagraph
Article 29(2)	Article 30(2)
Article 29(3)	Article 30(1), second subparagraph
Articles 30, 31 and 32	Articles 31, 32 and 33
Chapter II	Chapter 2
Article 33	Article 34
Article 34(1) and (2)	Article 35(1), first and second subparagraphs
Article 34(3)	Article 35(2)
Title VI	Title VII
Chapter I	Chapter 1
Article 35(1) introductory sentence	Article 36(1) introductory sentence
Article 35(1)(a)	Article 36(1)(a)
Article 35(1)(b) introductory sentence	Article 36(1)(b)
Article 35(1)(b) first indent	—

Directive 83/181/EEC	This Directive
Article 35(1)(b) second indent	Article 36(1)(b)
Article 35(2) introductory sentence	Article 36(2), introductory sentence
Article 35(2) first and second indents	Article 36(2)(a) and (b)
Chapter II	Chapter 2
Article 36(1)	Article 37(1)
Article 36(2) introductory sentence	Article 37(2) introductory sentence
Article 36(2) first, second and third indents	Article 37(2)(a), (b) and (c)
Articles 37 and 38	Articles 38 and 39
Chapter IIa	Chapter 3
Article 38a	Article 40
Chapter III	Chapter 4
Article 39	Article 41
Title VII	Title VIII
—	Chapter 1
Article 40	Article 42
Chapter I	Chapter 2
Articles 41 to 45	Articles 43 to 47
Chapter II	Chapter 3
Articles 46, 47 and 48	Articles 48, 49 and 50
Chapter III	Chapter 4
Article 49(1) and (2)	Article 51, first and second paragraphs
Articles 50 to 55	Articles 52 to 57
Title VIII	Title IX
Chapter I	Chapter 1
Article 56	Article 58
Chapter II	Chapter 2
Articles 57 and 58	Articles 59 and 60
Article 59, introductory sentence	Article 61, introductory sentence
Article 59, first, second and third indents	Article 61(a), (b) and (c)
Chapter III	Chapter 3
Article 60 first paragraph, introductory sentence	Article 62(1), introductory sentence
Article 60, first paragraph, point (a)	Article 62(1)(a)
Article 60, first paragraph, point (b), first sentence	Article 62(1)(b)
Article 60, first paragraph, point (b), second sentence	Article 62(2)
Article 60, second paragraph	Article 62(3)
Title IX	Title X
Chapter I	Chapter 1
Article 61	Article 63
Chapter II	Chapter 2
Article 62, introductory sentence	Article 64, introductory sentence
Article 62(a)	Article 64(a)
Article 62(b)	—
Article 62(c)	Article 64(b)
Article 63, first paragraph, introductory sentence	Article 65(1), introductory sentence
Article 63, first paragraph, point (a)	Article 65(1)(a)
Article 63, first paragraph, point (b), first sentence	Article 65(1)(b)
Article 63, first paragraph, point (b), second sentence	Article 65(2)
Article 63, first paragraph, point (c)	Article 65(1)(c)
Article 63, second paragraph	—
Article 64	Article 66
Chapter III	Chapter 3
Article 65(1)	Article 67(1)
Article 65(2), introductory sentence	Article 67(2), first subparagraph, introductory sentence
Article 65(2)(a) to (e)	Article 67(2) first subparagraph, points (a) to (e)
Article 65(2), final sentence	Article 67(2), second subparagraph

Directive 83/181/EEC	This Directive
Articles 66 to 69	Articles 68 to 71
Title X	Title XI
Articles 70 to 73	Articles 72 to 75
Article 74(1) introductory sentence	Article 76(1) introductory sentence
Article 74(1), first, second and third indents	Article 76(1)(a), (b) and (c)
Article 74(2)	Article 76(2)
Articles 75 and 76	Articles 77 and 78
Title XI	Title XII
Chapter I	Chapter 1
Article 77	Article 79
Chapter II	Chapter 2
Article 78	Article 80
Chapter III	Chapter 3
Article 79(a) to (q)	Article 81(1)(a) to (q)
Article 79(r), first sentence	Article 81(1)(r)
Article 79(r), second sentence	Article 81(2)
Article 79(s)	Article 81(1)(s)
Chapter IV	Chapter 4
Article 80	Article 82
Chapter V	Chapter 5
Article 81	Article 83
Chapter VI	Chapter 6
Article 82(1) introductory sentence	Article 84(1) introductory sentence
Article 82(1)(a) first and second indents	Article 84(1)(a)(i) and (ii)
Article 82(1)(b)	Article 84(1)(b)
Article 82(2) introductory sentence	Article 84(2) first subparagraph, introductory sentence
Article 82(2)(a) first subparagraph, first and second indents and second subparagraph	Article 84(2), first subparagraph, point (a)
Article 82(2)(b)	Article 84(2), first subparagraph, point (b)
Article 82(2)(c) introductory sentence	Article 84(2), first subparagraph, point (c) introductory sentence
Article 82(2)(c) first indent, first subparagraph	Article 84(2), first subparagraph, point (c)(i)
Article 82(2)(c) first indent, second subparagraph	Article 84(2), second subparagraph
Article 82(2)(c), second indent	Article 84(2), first subparagraph, point (c)(ii)
Article 82(2)(d)	Article 84(2), first subparagraph, point (d)
Article 83 first paragraph introductory sentence	Article 85 introductory sentence
Article 83(a)	Article 85(a)
Article 83(b)	—
Article 83(c)	Article 85(b)
Article 83 second subparagraph	—
Article 84	Article 86
Article 85 first and second paragraphs	Article 87(1) and (2)
Article 86	Article 88
Chapter VII	Chapter 7
Article 87	Article 89
Chapter VIII	Chapter 8
Article 88	Article 90
Title XII	Title XIII
Articles 89, 90 and 91	Articles 91, 92 and 93
Article 92	Article 94
Article 93(1)	—
Article 93(2)	Article 95
—	Article 96
—	Article 97
Article 94	Article 98

Directive 83/181/EEC	This Directive
Annex	Annex I
—	Annex II
—	Annex III

ARCHIVED COUNCIL DIRECTIVE 2010/24/EU OF 16 MARCH 2010 CONCERNING MUTUAL ASSISTANCE FOR THE RECOVERY OF CLAIMS RELATING TO TAXES, DUTIES AND OTHER MEASURES

2010/24/EU

CHAPTER I
GENERAL PROVISIONS

Article 1 Subject matter

This Directive lays down the rules under which the Member States are to provide assistance for the recovery in a Member State of any claims referred to in Article 2 which arise in another Member State.

Article 2 Scope

1. This Directive shall apply to claims relating to the following:
    (a) all taxes and duties of any kind levied by or on behalf of a Member State or its territorial or administrative subdivisions, including the local authorities, or on behalf of the Union;
    (b) refunds, interventions and other measures forming part of the system of total or partial financing of the European Agricultural Guarantee Fund (EAGF) and the European Agricultural Fund for Rural Development (EAFRD), including sums to be collected in connection with these actions;
    (c) levies and other duties provided for under the common organisation of the market for the sugar sector.
2. The scope of this Directive shall include:
    (a) administrative penalties, fines, fees and surcharges relating to the claims for which mutual assistance may be requested in accordance with paragraph 1, imposed by the administrative authorities that are competent to levy the taxes or duties concerned or carry out administrative enquiries with regard to them, or confirmed by administrative or judicial bodies at the request of those administrative authorities;
    (b) fees for certificates and similar documents issued in connection with administrative procedures related to taxes and duties;
    (c) interest and costs relating to the claims for which mutual assistance may be requested in accordance with paragraph 1 or point (a) or (b) of this paragraph.
3. This Directive shall not apply to:
    (a) compulsory social security contributions payable to the Member State or a subdivision of the Member State, or to social security institutions established under public law;
    (b) fees not referred to in paragraph 2;
    (c) dues of a contractual nature, such as consideration for public utilities;
    (d) criminal penalties imposed on the basis of a public prosecution or other criminal penalties not covered by paragraph 2(a).

Article 3 Definitions

For the purposes of this Directive:
   (a) 'applicant authority' means a central liaison office, a liaison office or a liaison department of a Member State which makes a request for assistance concerning a claim referred to in Article 2;
   (b) 'requested authority' means a central liaison office, a liaison office or a liaison department of a Member State to which a request for assistance is made;
   (c) 'person' means:
      (i) a natural person;
      (ii) a legal person;
      (iii) where the legislation in force so provides, an association of persons recognised as having the capacity to perform legal acts but lacking the legal status of a legal person; or
      (iv) any other legal arrangement of whatever nature and form, which has legal personality or not, owning or managing assets which, including income derived therefrom, are subject to any of the taxes covered by this Directive;

(d) 'by electronic means' means using electronic equipment for the processing, including digital compression, and storage of data, and employing wires, radio transmission, optical technologies or other electromagnetic means;
(e) 'CCN network' means the common platform based on the common communication network (CCN) developed by the Union for all transmissions by electronic means between competent authorities in the area of customs and taxation.

Article 4 Organisation
1. Each Member State shall inform the Commission by 20 May 2010 of its competent authority or authorities (hereinafter respectively referred to as the 'competent authority') for the purpose of this Directive and shall inform the Commission without delay of any changes thereof.
The Commission shall make the information received available to the other Member States and publish a list of the competent authorities of the Member States in the Official Journal of the European Union.
2. The competent authority shall designate a central liaison office which shall have principal responsibility for contacts with other Member States in the field of mutual assistance covered by this Directive.
The central liaison office may also be designated as responsible for contacts with the Commission.
3. The competent authority of each Member State may designate liaison offices which shall be responsible for contacts with other Member States concerning mutual assistance with regard to one or more specific types or categories of taxes and duties referred to in Article 2.
4. The competent authority of each Member State may designate offices, other than the central liaison office or liaison offices, as liaison departments. Liaison departments shall request or grant mutual assistance under this Directive in relation to their specific territorial or operational competences.
5. Where a liaison office or a liaison department receives a request for mutual assistance requiring action outside the competence assigned to it, it shall forward the request without delay to the competent office or department, if known, or to the central liaison office, and inform the applicant authority thereof.
6. The competent authority of each Member State shall inform the Commission of its central liaison office and any liaison offices or liaison departments which it has designated. The Commission shall make the information received available to the Member States.
7. Every communication shall be sent by or on behalf or, on a case by case basis, with the agreement of the central liaison office, which shall ensure effectiveness of communication.

CHAPTER II
EXCHANGE OF INFORMATION

Article 5 Request for information
1. At the request of the applicant authority, the requested authority shall provide any information which is foreseeably relevant to the applicant authority in the recovery of its claims as referred to in Article 2.
For the purpose of providing that information, the requested authority shall arrange for the carrying-out of any administrative enquiries necessary to obtain it.
2. The requested authority shall not be obliged to supply information:
   (a) which it would not be able to obtain for the purpose of recovering similar claims arising in the requested Member State;
   (b) which would disclose any commercial, industrial or professional secrets;
   (c) the disclosure of which would be liable to prejudice the security of or be contrary to the public policy of the requested Member State.
3. Paragraph 2 shall in no case be construed as permitting a requested authority of a Member State to decline to supply information solely because this information is held by a bank, other financial institution, nominee or person acting in an agency or a fiduciary capacity or because it relates to ownership interests in a person.
4. The requested authority shall inform the applicant authority of the grounds for refusing a request for information.

Article 6 Exchange of information without prior request
Where a refund of taxes or duties, other than value-added tax, relates to a person established or resident in another Member State, the Member State from which the refund is to be made may inform the Member State of establishment or residence of the upcoming refund.

Article 7 Presence in administrative offices and participation in administrative enquiries
1. By agreement between the applicant authority and the requested authority and in accordance with the arrangements laid down by the requested authority, officials authorised by the applicant authority may, with a view to promoting mutual assistance provided for in this Directive:
   (a) be present in the offices where the administrative authorities of the requested Member State carry out their duties;

(b) be present during administrative enquiries carried out in the territory of the requested Member State;
(c) assist the competent officials of the requested Member State during court proceedings in that Member State.

2. In so far as it is permitted under the legislation in force in the requested Member State, the agreement referred to in paragraph 1(b) may provide that officials of the applicant Member State may interview individuals and examine records.

3. Officials authorised by the applicant authority who make use of the possibilities offered by paragraphs 1 and 2 shall at all times be able to produce written authority stating their identity and their official capacity.

CHAPTER III
ASSISTANCE FOR THE NOTIFICATION OF DOCUMENTS

Article 8 Request for notification of certain documents relating to claims

1. At the request of the applicant authority, the requested authority shall notify to the addressee all documents, including those of a judicial nature, which emanate from the applicant Member State and which relate to a claim as referred to in Article 2 or to its recovery.

The request for notification shall be accompanied by a standard form containing at least the following information:
  (a) name, address and other data relevant to the identification of the addressee;
  (b) the purpose of the notification and the period within which notification should be effected;
  (c) a description of the attached document and the nature and amount of the claim concerned;
  (d) name, address and other contact details regarding:
     (i) the office responsible with regard to the attached document, and, if different;
     (ii) the office where further information can be obtained concerning the notified document or concerning the possibilities to contest the payment obligation.

2. The applicant authority shall make a request for notification pursuant to this article only when it is unable to notify in accordance with the rules governing the notification of the document concerned in the applicant Member State, or when such notification would give rise to disproportionate difficulties.

3. The requested authority shall forthwith inform the applicant authority of any action taken on its request for notification and, more especially, of the date of notification of the document to the addressee.

Article 9 Means of notification

1. The requested authority shall ensure that notification in the requested Member State is effected in accordance with the national laws, regulations and administrative practices in force in the requested Member State.

2. Paragraph 1 shall be without prejudice to any other form of notification made by a competent authority of the applicant Member State in accordance with the rules in force in that Member State. A competent authority established in the applicant Member State may notify any document directly by registered mail or electronically to a person within the territory of another Member State.

CHAPTER IV
RECOVERY OR PRECAUTIONARY MEASURES

Article 10 Request for recovery

1. At the request of the applicant authority, the requested authority shall recover claims which are the subject of an instrument permitting enforcement in the applicant Member State.

2. As soon as any relevant information relating to the matter which gave rise to the request for recovery comes to the knowledge of the applicant authority, it shall forward it to the requested authority.

Article 11 Conditions governing a request for recovery

1. The applicant authority may not make a request for recovery if and as long as the claim and/or the instrument permitting its enforcement in the applicant Member State are contested in that Member State, except in cases where the third subparagraph of Article 14(4) applies.

2. Before the applicant authority makes a request for recovery, appropriate recovery procedures available in the applicant Member State shall be applied, except in the following situations:
  (a) where it is obvious that there are no assets for recovery in the applicant Member State or that such procedures will not result in the payment in full of the claim, and the applicant authority has specific information indicating that the person concerned has assets in the requested Member State;
  (b) where recourse to such procedures in the applicant Member State would give rise to disproportionate difficulty.

Article 12 Instrument permitting enforcement in the requested Member State and other accompanying documents
1. Any request for recovery shall be accompanied by a uniform instrument permitting enforcement in the requested Member State.
This uniform instrument permitting enforcement in the requested Member State shall reflect the substantial contents of the initial instrument permitting enforcement, and constitute the sole basis for the recovery and precautionary measures taken in the requested Member State. It shall not be subject to any act of recognition, supplementing or replacement in that Member State.
The uniform instrument permitting enforcement shall contain at least the following information:
  (a) information relevant to the identification of the initial instrument permitting enforcement, a description of the claim, including its nature, the period covered by the claim, any dates of relevance to the enforcement process, and the amount of the claim and its different components such as principal, interest accrued, etc.;
  (b) name and other data relevant to the identification of the debtor;
  (c) name, address and other contact details regarding:
    (i) the office responsible for the assessment of the claim, and, if different;
    (ii) the office where further information can be obtained concerning the claim or the possibilities for contesting the payment obligation.
2. The request for recovery of a claim may be accompanied by other documents relating to the claim issued in the applicant Member State.

Article 13 Execution of the request for recovery
1. For the purpose of the recovery in the requested Member State, any claim in respect of which a request for recovery has been made shall be treated as if it was a claim of the requested Member State, except where otherwise provided for in this Directive. The requested authority shall make use of the powers and procedures provided under the laws, regulations or administrative provisions of the requested Member State applying to claims concerning the same or, in the absence of the same, a similar tax or duty, except where otherwise provided for in this Directive.
If the requested authority considers that the same or similar taxes or duties are not levied on its territory, it shall make use of the powers and procedures provided under the laws, regulations or administrative provisions of the requested Member State which apply to claims concerning the tax levied on personal income, except where otherwise provided for in this Directive.
The requested Member State shall not be obliged to grant other Member States' claims preferences accorded to similar claims arising in that Member State, except where otherwise agreed between the Member States concerned or provided in the law of the requested Member State. A Member State which grants preferences to another Member State's claims may not refuse to grant the same preferences to the same or similar claims of other Member States on the same conditions.
The requested Member State shall recover the claim in its own currency.
2. The requested authority shall inform the applicant authority with due diligence of any action it has taken on the request for recovery.
3. From the date on which the recovery request is received, the requested authority shall charge interest for late payment in accordance with the laws, regulations and administrative provisions in force in the requested Member State.
4. The requested authority may, where the laws, regulations or administrative provisions in force in the requested Member State so permit, allow the debtor time to pay or authorise payment by instalment and it may charge interest in that respect. It shall subsequently inform the applicant authority of any such decision.
5. Without prejudice to Article 20(1), the requested authority shall remit to the applicant authority the amounts recovered with respect to the claim and the interest referred to in paragraphs 3 and 4 of this Article.

Article 14 Disputes
1. Disputes concerning the claim, the initial instrument permitting enforcement in the applicant Member State or the uniform instrument permitting enforcement in the requested Member State and disputes concerning the validity of a notification made by a competent authority of the applicant Member State shall fall within the competence of the competent bodies of the applicant Member State. If, in the course of the recovery procedure, the claim, the initial instrument permitting enforcement in the applicant Member State or the uniform instrument permitting enforcement in the requested Member State is contested by an interested party, the requested authority shall inform that party that such an action must be brought by the latter before the competent body of the applicant Member State in accordance with the laws in force there.
2. Disputes concerning the enforcement measures taken in the requested Member State or concerning the validity of a notification made by a competent authority of the requested Member State shall be brought before the competent body of that Member State in accordance with its laws and regulations.

3. Where an action as referred to in paragraph 1 has been brought before the competent body of the applicant Member State, the applicant authority shall inform the requested authority thereof and shall indicate the extent to which the claim is not contested.
4. As soon as the requested authority has received the information referred to in paragraph 3, either from the applicant authority or from the interested party, it shall suspend the enforcement procedure, as far as the contested part of the claim is concerned, pending the decision of the body competent in the matter, unless the applicant authority requests otherwise in accordance with the third subparagraph of this paragraph.
At the request of the applicant authority, or where otherwise deemed to be necessary by the requested authority, and without prejudice to Article 16, the requested authority may take precautionary measures to guarantee recovery in so far as the laws or regulations in force in the requested Member State allow such action.
The applicant authority may, in accordance with the laws, regulations and administrative practices in force in the applicant Member State, ask the requested authority to recover a contested claim or the contested part of a claim, in so far as the relevant laws, regulations and administrative practices in force in the requested Member State allow such action. Any such request shall be reasoned. If the result of contestation is subsequently favourable to the debtor, the applicant authority shall be liable for reimbursing any sums recovered, together with any compensation due, in accordance with the laws in force in the requested Member State.
If a mutual agreement procedure has been initiated by the competent authorities of the applicant Member State or the requested Member State, and the outcome of the procedure may affect the claim in respect of which assistance has been requested, the recovery measures shall be suspended or stopped until that procedure has been terminated, unless it concerns a case of immediate urgency because of fraud or insolvency. If the recovery measures are suspended or stopped, the second subparagraph shall apply.

Article 15 Amendment or withdrawal of the request for recovery assistance

1. The applicant authority shall inform the requested authority immediately of any subsequent amendment to its request for recovery or of the withdrawal of its request, indicating the reasons for amendment or withdrawal.
2. If the amendment of the request is caused by a decision of the competent body referred to in Article 14(1), the applicant authority shall communicate this decision together with a revised uniform instrument permitting enforcement in the requested Member State. The requested authority shall then proceed with further recovery measures on the basis of the revised instrument.
Recovery or precautionary measures already taken on the basis of the original uniform instrument permitting enforcement in the requested Member State may be continued on the basis of the revised instrument, unless the amendment of the request is due to invalidity of the initial instrument permitting enforcement in the applicant Member State or the original uniform instrument permitting enforcement in the requested Member State.
Articles 12 and 14 shall apply in relation to the revised instrument.

Article 16 Request for precautionary measures

1. At the request of the applicant authority, the requested authority shall take precautionary measures, if allowed by its national law and in accordance with its administrative practices, to ensure recovery where a claim or the instrument permitting enforcement in the applicant Member State is contested at the time when the request is made, or where the claim is not yet the subject of an instrument permitting enforcement in the applicant Member State, in so far as precautionary measures are also possible, in a similar situation, under the national law and administrative practices of the applicant Member State.
The document drawn up for permitting precautionary measures in the applicant Member State and relating to the claim for which mutual assistance is requested, if any, shall be attached to the request for precautionary measures in the requested Member State. This document shall not be subject to any act of recognition, supplementing or replacement in the requested Member State.
2. The request for precautionary measures may be accompanied by other documents relating to the claim, issued in the applicant Member State.

Article 17 Rules governing the request for precautionary measures

In order to give effect to Article 16, Articles 10(2), 13(1) and (2), 14, and 15 shall apply *mutatis mutandis*.

Article 18 Limits to the requested authority's obligations

1. The requested authority shall not be obliged to grant the assistance provided for in Articles 10 to 16 if recovery of the claim would, because of the situation of the debtor, create serious economic or social difficulties in the requested Member State, in so far as the laws, regulations and administrative practices in force in that Member State allow such exception for national claims.

2. The requested authority shall not be obliged to grant the assistance provided for in Articles 5 and 7 to 16, if the initial request for assistance pursuant to Article 5, 7, 8, 10 or 16 is made in respect of claims which are more than 5 years old, dating from the due date of the claim in the applicant Member State to the date of the initial request for assistance.
However, in cases where the claim or the initial instrument permitting enforcement in the applicant Member State is contested, the 5-year period shall be deemed to begin from the moment when it is established in the applicant Member State that the claim or the instrument permitting enforcement may no longer be contested.
Moreover, in cases where a postponement of the payment or instalment plan is granted by the competent authorities of the applicant Member State, the 5-year period shall be deemed to begin from the moment when the entire payment period has come to its end.
However, in those cases the requested authority shall not be obliged to grant the assistance in respect of claims which are more than 10 years old, dating from the due date of the claim in the applicant Member State.
3. A Member State shall not be obliged to grant assistance if the total amount of the claims covered by this Directive, for which assistance is requested, is less than EUR 1 500.
4. The requested authority shall inform the applicant authority of the grounds for refusing a request for assistance.

Article 19 Questions on limitation
1. Questions concerning periods of limitation shall be governed solely by the laws in force in the applicant Member State.
2. In relation to the suspension, interruption or prolongation of periods of limitation, any steps taken in the recovery of claims by or on behalf of the requested authority in pursuance of a request for assistance which have the effect of suspending, interrupting or prolonging the period of limitation according to the laws in force in the requested Member State shall be deemed to have the same effect in the applicant Member State, on condition that the corresponding effect is provided for under the laws in force in the applicant Member State.
If suspension, interruption or prolongation of the period of limitation is not possible under the laws in force in the requested Member State, any steps taken in the recovery of claims by or on behalf of the requested authority in pursuance of a request for assistance which, if they had been carried out by or on behalf of the applicant authority in its Member State, would have had the effect of suspending, interrupting or prolonging the period of limitation according to the laws in force in the applicant Member State shall be deemed to have been taken in the latter State, in so far as that effect is concerned.
The first and second subparagraphs shall not affect the right of the competent authorities in the applicant Member State to take measures to suspend, interrupt or prolong the period of limitation in accordance with the laws in force in that Member State.
3. The applicant authority and the requested authority shall inform each other of any action which interrupts, suspends or prolongs the limitation period of the claim for which the recovery or precautionary measures were requested, or which may have this effect.

Article 20 Costs
1. In addition to the amounts referred to in Article 13(5), the requested authority shall seek to recover from the person concerned and retain the costs linked to the recovery that it incurred, in accordance with the laws and regulations of the requested Member State.
2. Member States shall renounce all claims on each other for the reimbursement of costs arising from any mutual assistance they grant each other pursuant to this Directive.
However, where recovery creates a specific problem, concerns a very large amount in costs or relates to organised crime, the applicant and requested authorities may agree reimbursement arrangements specific to the cases in question.
3. Notwithstanding paragraph 2, the applicant Member State shall remain liable to the requested Member State for any costs and any losses incurred as a result of actions held to be unfounded, as far as either the substance of the claim or the validity of the instrument permitting enforcement and/or precautionary measures issued by the applicant authority are concerned.

CHAPTER V
GENERAL RULES GOVERNING ALL TYPES OF ASSISTANCE REQUESTS

Article 21 Standard forms and means of communication
1. Requests pursuant to Article 5(1) for information, requests pursuant to Article 8(1) for notification, requests pursuant to Article 10(1) for recovery or requests pursuant to Article 16(1) for precautionary measures shall be sent by electronic means, using a standard form, unless this is impracticable for technical reasons. As far as possible, these forms shall also be used for any further communication with regard to the request.

The uniform instrument permitting enforcement in the requested Member State, the document permitting precautionary measures in the applicant Member State and the other documents referred to in Articles 12 and 16 shall also be sent by electronic means, unless this is impracticable for technical reasons.

Where appropriate, the standard forms may be accompanied by reports, statements and any other documents, or certified true copies or extracts thereof, which shall also be sent by electronic means, unless this is impracticable for technical reasons.

Standard forms and communication by electronic means may also be used for the exchange of information pursuant to Article 6.

2. Paragraph 1 shall not apply to the information and documentation obtained through the presence in administrative offices in another Member State or through the participation in administrative enquiries in another Member State, in accordance with Article 7.

3. If communication is not made by electronic means or with use of standard forms, this shall not affect the validity of the information obtained or of the measures taken in the execution of a request for assistance.

Article 22 Use of languages

1. All requests for assistance, standard forms for notification and uniform instruments permitting enforcement in the requested Member States shall be sent in, or shall be accompanied by a translation into, the official language, or one of the official languages, of the requested Member State. The fact that certain parts thereof are written in a language other than the official language, or one of the official languages, of the requested Member State, shall not affect their validity or the validity of the procedure, in so far as that other language is one agreed between the Member States concerned.

2. The documents for which notification is requested pursuant to Article 8 may be sent to the requested authority in an official language of the applicant Member State.

3. Where a request is accompanied by documents other than those referred to in paragraphs 1 and 2, the requested authority may, where necessary, require from the applicant authority a translation of such documents into the official language, or one of the official languages of the requested Member State, or into any other language bilaterally agreed between the Member States concerned.

Article 23 Disclosure of information and documents

1. Information communicated in any form pursuant to this Directive shall be covered by the obligation of official secrecy and enjoy the protection extended to similar information under the national law of the Member State which received it.

Such information may be used for the purpose of applying enforcement or precautionary measures with regard to claims covered by this Directive. It may also be used for assessment and enforcement of compulsory social security contributions.

2. Persons duly accredited by the Security Accreditation Authority of the European Commission may have access to this information only in so far as it is necessary for care, maintenance and development of the CCN network.

3. The Member State providing the information shall permit its use for purposes other than those referred to in paragraph 1 in the Member State receiving the information, if, under the legislation of the Member State providing the information, the information may be used for similar purposes.

4. Where the applicant or requested authority considers that information obtained pursuant to this Directive is likely to be useful for the purposes referred to in paragraph 1 to a third Member State, it may transmit that information to that third Member State, provided this transmission is in accordance with the rules and procedures laid down in this Directive. It shall inform the Member State of origin of the information about its intention to share that information with a third Member State. The Member State of origin of the information may oppose such a sharing of information within ten working days of the date at which it received the communication from the Member State wishing to share the information.

5. Permission to use information pursuant to paragraph 3 which has been transmitted pursuant to paragraph 4 may be granted only by the Member State from which the information originates.

6. Information communicated in any form pursuant to this Directive may be invoked or used as evidence by all authorities within the Member State receiving the information on the same basis as similar information obtained within that State.

CHAPTER VI
FINAL PROVISIONS

Article 24 Application of other agreements on assistance

1. This Directive shall be without prejudice to the fulfilment of any obligation to provide wider assistance ensuing from bilateral or multilateral agreements or arrangements, including for the notification of legal or extra-legal acts.

2. Where the Member States conclude such bilateral or multilateral agreements or arrangements on matters covered by this Directive other than to deal with individual cases, they shall inform the Commission thereof without delay. The Commission shall in turn inform the other Member States.

3. When providing such greater measure of mutual assistance under a bilateral or multilateral agreement or arrangement, Member States may make use of the electronic communication network and the standard forms adopted for the implementation of this Directive.

Article 25 Committee
1. The Commission shall be assisted by the Recovery Committee.
2. Where reference is made to this paragraph, Articles 5 and 7 of Decision 1999/468/EC shall apply. The period referred to in Article 5(6) of Decision 1999/468/EC shall be set at 3 months.

Article 26 Implementing provisions
The Commission shall adopt, in accordance with the procedure referred to in Article 25(2), detailed rules for implementing Article 4(2), (3) and (4), Article 5(1), Articles 8, 10, 12(1), Article 13(2), (3), (4) and (5), Articles 15, 16(1) and 21(1).
Those rules shall relate to at least the following:
   (a) the practical arrangements with regard to the organisation of the contacts between the central liaison offices, the other liaison offices and the liaison departments, referred to in Article 4(2), (3) and (4), of different Member States, and the contacts with the Commission;
   (b) the means by which communications between authorities may be transmitted;
   (c) the format and other details of the standard forms to be used for the purposes of Article 5(1), Articles 8, 10(1), Article 12(1) and Article 16(1);
   (d) the conversion of the sums to be recovered and the transfer of sums recovered.

Article 27 Reporting
1. Each Member State shall inform the Commission annually by 31 March of the following:
   (a) the number of requests for information, notification and recovery or for precautionary measures which it sends to each requested Member State and which it receives from each applicant Member State each year;
   (b) the amount of the claims for which recovery assistance is requested and the amounts recovered.
2. Member States may also provide any other information that may be useful for evaluating the provision of mutual assistance under this Directive.
3. The Commission shall report every 5 years to the European Parliament and the Council on the operation of the arrangements established by this Directive.

Article 28 Transposition
1. Member States shall adopt and publish, by 31 December 2011, the laws, regulations and administrative provisions necessary to comply with this Directive. They shall forthwith inform the Commission thereof.
They shall apply these provisions from 1 January 2012.
When these provisions are adopted by Member States, they shall contain a reference to this Directive or shall be accompanied by such a reference on the occasion of their official publication. The methods of making such reference shall be laid down by Member States.
2. Member States shall communicate to the Commission the text of the main provisions of national law which they adopt in the field covered by this Directive.

Article 29 Repeal of Directive 2008/55/EC
Directive 2008/55/EC is repealed with effect from 1 January 2012.
References to the repealed Directive shall be construed as references to this Directive.

Article 30 Entry into force
This Directive shall enter into force on the 20th day following its publication in the Official Journal of the European Union.

Article 31 Addressees
This Directive is addressed to the Member States.
Done at Brussels, 16 March 2010.

ARCHIVED COUNCIL DIRECTIVE 2011/16/EU OF 15 FEBRUARY 2011 ON ADMINISTRATIVE COOPERATION IN THE FIELD OF TAXATION AND REPEALING DIRECTIVE 77/799/EEC

CHAPTER I
GENERAL PROVISIONS

Article 1 **Subject matter**

1. This Directive lays down the rules and procedures under which the Member States shall cooperate with each other with a view to exchanging information that is foreseeably relevant to the administration and enforcement of the domestic laws of the Member States concerning the taxes referred to in Article 2.
2. This Directive also lays down provisions for the exchange of information referred to in paragraph 1 by electronic means, as well as rules and procedures under which the Member States and the Commission are to cooperate on matters concerning coordination and evaluation.
3. This Directive shall not affect the application in the Member States of the rules on mutual assistance in criminal matters. It shall also be without prejudice to the fulfilment of any obligations of the Member States in relation to wider administrative cooperation ensuing from other legal instruments, including bilateral or multilateral agreements.

Article 2 **Scope**

1. This Directive shall apply to all taxes of any kind levied by, or on behalf of, a Member State or the Member State's territorial or administrative subdivisions, including the local authorities.
2. Notwithstanding paragraph 1, this Directive shall not apply to value added tax and customs duties, or to excise duties covered by other Union legislation on administrative cooperation between Member States. This Directive shall also not apply to compulsory social security contributions payable to the Member State or a subdivision of the Member State or to social security institutions established under public law.
3. In no case shall the taxes referred to in paragraph 1 be construed as including:
   (a) fees, such as for certificates and other documents issued by public authorities; or
   (b) dues of a contractual nature, such as consideration for public utilities.
4. This Directive shall apply to the taxes referred to in paragraph 1 levied within the territory to which the Treaties apply by virtue of Article 52 of the Treaty on the European Union.

Article 3 **Definitions**

For the purposes of this Directive the following definitions shall apply:
1. 'competent authority' of a Member State means the authority which has been designated as such by that Member State. When acting pursuant to this Directive, the central liaison office, a liaison department or a competent official shall also be deemed to be competent authorities by delegation according to Article 4;
2. 'central liaison office' means the office which has been designated as such with principal responsibility for contacts with other Member States in the field of administrative cooperation;
3. 'liaison department' means any office other than the central liaison office which has been designated as such to directly exchange information pursuant to this Directive;
4. 'competent official' means any official who is authorised to directly exchange information pursuant to this Directive;
5. 'requesting authority' means the central liaison office, a liaison department or any competent official of a Member State who makes a request for assistance on behalf of the competent authority;
6. 'requested authority' means the central liaison office, a liaison department or any competent official of a Member State who receives a request for assistance on behalf of the competent authority;
7. 'administrative enquiry' means all controls, checks and other action taken by Member States in the performance of their duties with a view to ensuring the proper application of tax legislation;
8. 'exchange of information on request' means the exchange of information based on a request made by the requesting Member State to the requested Member State in a specific case;
[9. "automatic exchange" means,
   [(a) for the purposes of Article 8(1) and Articles 8a, 8aa and 8ab, the systematic communication of predefined information to another Member State, without prior request, at pre-established regular intervals. For the purposes of Article 8(1), reference to available information relates to information in the tax files of the Member State communicating the information, which is retrievable in accordance with the procedures for gathering and processing information in that Member State;][3]

(b) for the purposes of Article 8(3a), the systematic communication of predefined information on residents in other Member States to the relevant Member State of residence, without prior request, at pre-established regular intervals;
(c) for the purposes of provisions of this Directive other than Article 8(1) and (3a) and Articles 8a, 8aa and 8ab, the systematic communication of predefined information provided in points (a) and (b) of this point.][3]

[In the context of Articles 8(3a), 8(7a) and 21(2), Article 25(2) and (3) and Annex IV, any capitalised term shall have the meaning that it has under the corresponding definitions set out in Annex I.][3] In the context of Article 8aa and Annex III, any capitalised term shall have the meaning that it has under the corresponding definitions set out in Annex III.][2]

10. 'spontaneous exchange' means the non-systematic communication, at any moment and without prior request, of information to another Member State;
11. 'person' means:
    (a) a natural person;
    (b) a legal person;
    (c) where the legislation in force so provides, an association of persons recognised as having the capacity to perform legal acts but lacking the status of a legal person; or
    (d) any other legal arrangement of whatever nature and form, regardless of whether it has legal personality, owning or managing assets, which, including income derived therefrom, are subject to any of the taxes covered by this Directive;
12. 'by electronic means' means using electronic equipment for the processing, including digital compression, and storage of data, and employing wires, radio transmission, optical technologies or other electromagnetic means;
13. 'CCN network' means the common platform based on the common communication network (CCN), developed by the Union for all transmissions by electronic means between competent authorities in the area of customs and taxation.
[14. "advance cross-border ruling" means any agreement, communication, or any other instrument or action with similar effects, including one issued, amended or renewed in the context of a tax audit, and which meets the following conditions:
    (a) is issued, amended or renewed by, or on behalf of, the government or the tax authority of a Member State, or the Member State's territorial or administrative subdivisions, including local authorities, irrespective of whether it is effectively used;
    (b) is issued, amended or renewed, to a particular person or a group of persons, and upon which that person or a group of persons is entitled to rely;
    (c) concerns the interpretation or application of a legal or administrative provision concerning the administration or enforcement of national laws relating to taxes of the Member State, or the Member State's territorial or administrative subdivisions, including local authorities;
    (d) relates to a cross-border transaction or to the question of whether or not activities carried on by a person in another jurisdiction create a permanent establishment; and
    (e) is made in advance of the transactions or of the activities in another jurisdiction potentially creating a permanent establishment or in advance of the filing of a tax return covering the period in which the transaction or series of transactions or activities took place.
    The cross-border transaction may involve, but is not restricted to, the making of investments, the provision of goods, services, finance or the use of tangible or intangible assets and does not have to directly involve the person receiving the advance cross-border ruling;
15. "advance pricing arrangement" means any agreement, communication or any other instrument or action with similar effects, including one issued, amended or renewed in the context of a tax audit, and which meets the following conditions:
    (a) is issued, amended or renewed by, or on behalf of, the government or the tax authority of one or more Member States, including any territorial or administrative subdivision thereof, including local authorities, irrespective of whether it is effectively used;
    (b) is issued, amended or renewed, to a particular person or a group of persons and upon which that person or a group of persons is entitled to rely; and
    (c) determines in advance of cross-border transactions between associated enterprises, an appropriate set of criteria for the determination of the transfer pricing for those transactions or determines the attribution of profits to a permanent establishment.
    Enterprises are associated enterprises where one enterprise participates directly or indirectly in the management, control or capital of another enterprise or the same persons participate directly or indirectly in the management, control or capital of the enterprises.

Transfer prices are the prices at which an enterprise transfers physical goods and intangible property or provides services to associated enterprises, and "transfer pricing" is to be construed accordingly.

16. For the purpose of point 14 "cross-border transaction" means a transaction or series of transactions where:
    (a) not all of the parties to the transaction or series of transactions are resident for tax purposes in the Member State issuing, amending or renewing the advance cross-border ruling;
    (b) any of the parties to the transaction or series of transactions is simultaneously resident for tax purposes in more than one jurisdiction;
    (c) one of the parties to the transaction or series of transactions carries on business in another jurisdiction through a permanent establishment and the transaction or series of transactions forms part or the whole of the business of the permanent establishment. A cross-border transaction or series of transactions shall also include arrangements made by a person in respect of business activities in another jurisdiction which that person carries on through a permanent establishment; or
    (d) such transactions or series of transactions have a cross border impact.
    For the purpose of point 15, "cross-border transaction" means a transaction or series of transactions involving associated enterprises which are not all resident for tax purposes in the territory of a single jurisdiction or a transaction or series of transactions which have a cross border impact.
17. For the purpose of point 15 and 16, "enterprise" means any form of conducting business.][1]
[18. "cross-border arrangement" means an arrangement concerning either more than one Member State or a Member State and a third country where at least one of the following conditions is met:
    (a) not all of the participants in the arrangement are resident for tax purposes in the same jurisdiction;
    (b) one or more of the participants in the arrangement is simultaneously resident for tax purposes in more than one jurisdiction;
    (c) one or more of the participants in the arrangement carries on a business in another jurisdiction through a permanent establishment situated in that jurisdiction and the arrangement forms part or the whole of the business of that permanent establishment;
    (d) one or more of the participants in the arrangement carries on an activity in another jurisdiction without being resident for tax purposes or creating a permanent establishment situated in that jurisdiction;
    (e) such arrangement has a possible impact on the automatic exchange of information or the identification of beneficial ownership.
    For the purposes of points 18 to 25 of this Article, Article 8ab and Annex IV, an arrangement shall also include a series of arrangements. An arrangement may comprise more than one step or part.
19. "reportable cross-border arrangement" means any cross-border arrangement that contains at least one of the hallmarks set out in Annex IV.
20. "hallmark" means a characteristic or feature of a cross-border arrangement that presents an indication of a potential risk of tax avoidance, as listed in Annex IV.
21. "intermediary" means any person that designs, markets, organises or makes available for implementation or manages the implementation of a reportable cross-border arrangement.
    It also means any person that, having regard to the relevant facts and circumstances and based on available information and the relevant expertise and understanding required to provide such services, knows or could be reasonably expected to know that they have undertaken to provide, directly or by means of other persons, aid, assistance or advice with respect to designing, marketing, organising, making available for implementation or managing the implementation of a reportable cross-border arrangement. Any person shall have the right to provide evidence that such person did not know and could not reasonably be expected to know that that person was involved in a reportable cross-border arrangement. For this purpose, that person may refer to all relevant facts and circumstances as well as available information and their relevant expertise and understanding.
    In order to be an intermediary, a person shall meet at least one of the following additional conditions:
    (a) be resident for tax purposes in a Member State;
    (b) have a permanent establishment in a Member State through which the services with respect to the arrangement are provided;
    (c) be incorporated in, or governed by the laws of, a Member State;
    (d) be registered with a professional association related to legal, taxation or consultancy services in a Member State.

22. "relevant taxpayer" means any person to whom a reportable cross-border arrangement is made available for implementation, or who is ready to implement a reportable cross-border arrangement or has implemented the first step of such an arrangement.
23. for the purposes of Article 8ab, "associated enterprise" means a person who is related to another person in at least one of the following ways:
    (a) a person participates in the management of another person by being in a position to exercise a significant influence over the other person;
    (b) a person participates in the control of another person through a holding that exceeds 25 % of the voting rights;
    (c) a person participates in the capital of another person through a right of ownership that, directly or indirectly, exceeds 25 % of the capital;
    (d) a person is entitled to 25 % or more of the profits of another person.

If more than one person participates, as referred to in points (a) to (d), in the management, control, capital or profits of the same person, all persons concerned shall be regarded as associated enterprises.

If the same persons participate, as referred to in points (a) to (d), in the management, control, capital or profits of more than one person, all persons concerned shall be regarded as associated enterprises.

For the purposes of this point, a person who acts together with another person in respect of the voting rights or capital ownership of an entity shall be treated as holding a participation in all of the voting rights or capital ownership of that entity that are held by the other person.

In indirect participations, the fulfilment of requirements under point (c) shall be determined by multiplying the rates of holding through the successive tiers. A person holding more than 50 % of the voting rights shall be deemed to hold 100 %.

An individual, his or her spouse and his or her lineal ascendants or descendants shall be treated as a single person.

24. "marketable arrangement" means a cross-border arrangement that is designed, marketed, ready for implementation or made available for implementation without a need to be substantially customised.
25. "bespoke arrangement" means any cross-border arrangement that is not a marketable arrangement.][3]

Amendments—[1] Paras 14–17 inserted, by Council Directive 2015/2376/EU Art 1(1) with effect from 18 December 2015. Note that member states are required to adopt and publish, by 31 December 2016, the laws, regulations and administrative provisions necessary to comply with Directive 2015/2376/EU, and to apply those measures from 1 January 2017 (OJ L 332, 18.12.2015, p 1).

[2] Para 9 substituted by Council Directive 2016/881/EU Article 1(1) with effect from 3 June 2016. Note that member states are required to adopt and publish, by 4 June 2017, the laws, regulations and administrative provisions necessary to comply with Directive 2016/881/EU, and to apply those measures from 5 June 2017 (OJ L 146, 3.6.2016, p 8).

[3] In point 9, words substituted and points 18–25 inserted, by Council Directive (EU) 2018/822 art 1(1) with effect from 25 June 2018 (OJ L 139, 5.6.2018, p 1).

Article 4 Organisation

1. Each Member State shall inform the Commission, within one month from 11 March 2011, of its competent authority for the purposes of this Directive and shall inform the Commission without delay of any change thereto.

The Commission shall make the information available to the other Member States and publish a list of the authorities of the Member States in the *Official Journal of the European Union*.

2. The competent authority shall designate a single central liaison office. The competent authority shall be responsible for informing the Commission and the other Member States thereof.

The central liaison office may also be designated as responsible for contacts with the Commission. The competent authority shall be responsible for informing the Commission thereof.

3. The competent authority of each Member State may designate liaison departments with the competence assigned according to its national legislation or policy. The central liaison office shall be responsible for keeping the list of liaison departments up to date and making it available to the central liaison offices of the other Member States concerned and to the Commission.

4. The competent authority of each Member State may designate competent officials. The central liaison office shall be responsible for keeping the list of competent officials up to date and making it available to the central liaison offices of the other Member States concerned and to the Commission.

5. The officials engaged in administrative cooperation pursuant to this Directive shall in any case be deemed to be competent officials for that purpose, in accordance with arrangements laid down by the competent authorities.

6. Where a liaison department or a competent official sends or receives a request or a reply to a request for cooperation, it shall inform the central liaison office of its Member State under the procedures laid down by that Member State.

7. Where a liaison department or a competent official receives a request for cooperation requiring action which falls outside the competence it is assigned according to the national legislation or policy of its Member State, it shall forward such request without delay to the central liaison office of its Member State and inform the requesting authority thereof. In such a case, the period laid down in Article 7 shall start the day after the request for cooperation is forwarded to the central liaison office.

CHAPTER II
EXCHANGE OF INFORMATION

SECTION I
EXCHANGE OF INFORMATION ON REQUEST

Article 5 Procedure for the exchange of information on request
At the request of the requesting authority, the requested authority shall communicate to the requesting authority any information referred to in Article 1(1) that it has in its possession or that it obtains as a result of administrative enquiries.

Article 6 Administrative enquiries
1. The requested authority shall arrange for the carrying out of any administrative enquiries necessary to obtain the information referred to in Article 5.
2. The request referred to in Article 5 may contain a reasoned request for a specific administrative enquiry. If the requested authority takes the view that no administrative enquiry is necessary, it shall immediately inform the requesting authority of the reasons thereof.
3. In order to obtain the requested information or to conduct the administrative enquiry requested, the requested authority shall follow the same procedures as it would when acting on its own initiative or at the request of another authority in its own Member State.
4. When specifically requested by the requesting authority, the requested authority shall communicate original documents provided that this is not contrary to the provisions in force in the Member State of the requested authority.

Article 7 Time limits
1. The requested authority shall provide the information referred to in Article 5 as quickly as possible, and no later than six months from the date of receipt of the request.
However, where the requested authority is already in possession of that information, the information shall be transmitted within two months of that date.
2. In certain special cases, time limits other than those provided for in paragraph 1 may be agreed upon between the requested and the requesting authorities.
3. The requested authority shall confirm immediately and in any event no later than seven working days from receipt, if possible by electronic means, receipt of a request to the requesting authority.
4. Within one month of receipt of the request, the requested authority shall notify the requesting authority of any deficiencies in the request and of the need for any additional background information. In such a case, the time limits provided for in paragraph 1 shall start the day after the requested authority has received the additional information needed.
5. Where the requested authority is unable to respond to the request by the relevant time limit, it shall inform the requesting authority immediately and in any event within three months of the receipt of the request, of the reasons for its failure to do so, and the date by which it considers it might be able to respond.
6. Where the requested authority is not in possession of the requested information and is unable to respond to the request for information or refuses to do so on the grounds provided for in Article 17, it shall inform the requesting authority of the reasons thereof immediately and in any event within one month of receipt of the request.

SECTION II
MANDATORY AUTOMATIC EXCHANGE OF INFORMATION

Article 8 Scope and conditions of mandatory automatic exchange of information
1. The competent authority of each Member State shall, by automatic exchange, communicate to the competent authority of any other Member State, information regarding taxable periods as from 1 January 2014 that is available concerning residents in that other Member State, on the following specific categories of income and capital as they are to be understood under the national legislation of the Member State which communicates the information:
    (a) income from employment;
    (b) director's fees;
    (c) life insurance products not covered by other Union legal instruments on exchange of information and other similar measures;
    (d) pensions;
    (e) ownership of and income from immovable property.

2. Before 1 January 2014, Member States shall inform the Commission of the categories listed in paragraph 1 in respect of which they have information available. They shall inform the Commission of any subsequent changes thereto.

[3. The competent authority of a Member State may indicate to the competent authority of any other Member State that it does not wish to receive information on one or several of the categories of income and capital referred to in paragraph 1. It shall also inform the Commission thereof.

A Member State may be considered as not wishing to receive information in accordance with paragraph 1, if it does not inform the Commission of any single category in respect of which it has information available.][1]

[3a. Each Member State shall take the necessary measures to require its Reporting Financial Institutions to perform the reporting and due diligence rules included in Annexes I and II and to ensure effective implementation of, and compliance with, such rules in accordance with Section IX of Annex I.

Pursuant to the applicable reporting and due diligence rules contained in Annexes I and II, the competent authority of each Member State shall, by automatic exchange, communicate within the deadline laid down in point (b) of paragraph 6 to the competent authority of any other Member State, the following information regarding taxable periods as from 1 January 2016 concerning a Reportable Account:

(a) the name, address, TIN(s) and date and place of birth (in the case of an individual) of each Reportable Person that is an Account Holder of the account and, in the case of any Entity that is an Account Holder and that, after application of due diligence rules consistent with the Annexes, is identified as having one or more Controlling Persons that is a Reportable Person, the name, address, and TIN(s) of the Entity and the name, address, TIN(s) and date and place of birth of each Reportable Person;

(b) the account number (or functional equivalent in the absence of an account number);

(c) the name and identifying number (if any) of the Reporting Financial Institution;

(d) the account balance or value (including, in the case of a Cash Value Insurance Contract or Annuity Contract, the Cash Value or surrender value) as of the end of the relevant calendar year or other appropriate reporting period or, if the account was closed during such year or period, the closure of the account;

(e) in the case of any Custodial Account:

(i) the total gross amount of interest, the total gross amount of dividends, and the total gross amount of other income generated with respect to the assets held in the account, in each case paid or credited to the account (or with respect to the account) during the calendar year or other appropriate reporting period; and

(ii) the total gross proceeds from the sale or redemption of Financial Assets paid or credited to the account during the calendar year or other appropriate reporting period with respect to which the Reporting Financial Institution acted as a custodian, broker, nominee, or otherwise as an agent for the Account Holder;

(f) in the case of any Depository Account, the total gross amount of interest paid or credited to the account during the calendar year or other appropriate reporting period; and

(g) in the case of any account not described in point (e) or point (f), the total gross amount paid or credited to the Account Holder with respect to the account during the calendar year or other appropriate reporting period with respect to which the Reporting Financial Institution is the obligor or debtor, including the aggregate amount of any redemption payments made to the Account Holder during the calendar year or other appropriate reporting period.

For the purposes of the exchange of information under this paragraph, unless otherwise foreseen in this paragraph or in the Annexes, the amount and characterisation of payments made with respect to a Reportable Account shall be determined in accordance with national legislation of the Member State which communicates the information.

The first and second subparagraphs of this paragraph shall prevail over point (c) of paragraph 1 or any other Union legal instrument, including Council Directive 2003/48/EC*, to the extent that the exchange of information at issue would fall within the scope of point (c) of paragraph 1 or of any other Union legal instrument, including Directive 2003/48/EC.

4, 5 . . .[2]

[6. The communication of information shall take place as follows:

(a) for the categories laid down in paragraph 1: at least once a year, within six months following the end of the tax year of the Member State during which the information became available;

(b) for the information laid down in paragraph 3a: annually, within nine months following the end of the calendar year or other appropriate reporting period to which the information relates.][1]

7. The Commission shall adopt the practical arrangements for the automatic exchange of information, in accordance with the procedure referred to in Article 26(2), before the dates referred to in Article 29(1).

[7a. For the purposes of subparagraphs B.1(c) and C.17(g) of Section VIII of Annex I, each Member State shall, by 31 July 2015, provide to the Commission the list of entities and accounts that are to be treated, respectively, as Non-Reporting Financial Institutions and Excluded Accounts. Each Member State shall also inform the Commission if any changes in this respect occur. The Commission shall publish in the Official Journal of the European Union a compiled list of the information received and shall update the list as necessary.

Member States shall ensure that those types of Non-Reporting Financial Institutions and Excluded Accounts satisfy all the requirements listed in subparagraphs B.1(c) and C.17(g) of Section VIII of Annex I, and in particular that the status of a Financial Institution as a Non-Reporting Financial Institution or the status of an account as an Excluded Account does not frustrate the purposes of this Directive.][1]

8. Where Member States agree on the automatic exchange of information for additional categories of income and capital in bilateral or multilateral agreements which they conclude with other Member States, they shall communicate those agreements to the Commission which shall make those agreements available to all the other Member States

Amendments—[*]   Council Directive 2003/48/EC of 3 June 2003 on taxation of savings income in the form of interest payments (OJ L 157, 26.6.2003, p. 38).

[1]   Paras 3, 6 substituted and paras 3a, 7a inserted, by Council Directive 2014/107/EU Art 1(2) with effect from 5 January 2015. See Art 2 for implementation provisions (deadline for implementation is 31 December 2015, with measures to apply from 1 January 2016) (OJ L 359, 16.12.2014, p 1).

[2]   Paras 4, 5 repealed by Council Directive 2015/2376/EU Art 1(2) with effect from 18 December 2015. Note that member states are required to adopt and publish, by 31 December 2016, the laws, regulations and administrative provisions necessary to comply with Directive 2015/2376/EU, and to apply those measures from 1 January 2017 (OJ L 332, 18.12.2015, p 1).

[**Article 8a Scope and conditions of mandatory automatic exchange of information on advance cross-border rulings and advance pricing arrangements**

1. The competent authority of a Member State, where an advance cross-border ruling or an advance pricing arrangement was issued, amended or renewed after 31 December 2016 shall, by automatic exchange, communicate information thereon to the competent authorities of all other Member States as well as to the European Commission, with the limitation of cases set out in paragraph 8 of this Article, in accordance with applicable practical arrangements adopted pursuant to Article 21.

2. The competent authority of a Member State shall, in accordance with applicable practical arrangements adopted pursuant to Article 21, also communicate information to the competent authorities of all other Member States as well as to the European Commission, with the limitation of cases set out in paragraph 8 of this Article, on advance cross-border rulings and advance pricing arrangements issued, amended or renewed within a period beginning five years before 1 January 2017.

If advance cross-border rulings and advance pricing arrangements are issued, amended or renewed between 1 January 2012 and 31 December 2013, such communication shall take place under the condition that they were still valid on 1 January 2014.

If advance cross-border rulings and advance pricing arrangements are issued, amended or renewed between 1 January 2014 and 31 December 2016, such communication shall take place irrespective of whether they are still valid.

Member States may exclude from the communication referred to in this paragraph, information on advance cross-border rulings and advance pricing arrangements issued, amended or renewed before 1 April 2016 to a particular person or a group of persons, excluding those conducting mainly financial or investment activities, with a group-wide annual net turnover, as defined in point (5) of Article 2 of Directive 2013/34/EU of the European Parliament and of the Council[*], of less than EUR 40 000 000 (or the equivalent amount in any other currency) in the fiscal year preceding the date of issuance, amendment or renewal of those cross-border rulings and advance pricing arrangements.

3. Bilateral or multilateral advance pricing arrangements with third countries shall be excluded from the scope of automatic exchange of information under this Article where the international tax agreement under which the advance pricing arrangement was negotiated does not permit its disclosure to third parties. Such bilateral or multilateral advance pricing arrangements will be exchanged under Article 9, where the international tax agreement under which the advance pricing arrangement was negotiated permits its disclosure, and the competent authority of the third country gives permission for the information to be disclosed.

However, where the bilateral or multilateral advance pricing arrangements would be excluded from the automatic exchange of information under the first sentence of the first subparagraph of this paragraph, the information identified in paragraph 6 of this Article referred to in the request that lead to issuance of such a bilateral or multilateral advance pricing arrangement shall instead be exchanged under paragraphs 1 and 2 of this Article.

4. Paragraphs 1 and 2 shall not apply in a case where an advance cross-border ruling exclusively concerns and involves the tax affairs of one or more natural persons.

5. The exchange of information shall take place as follows:

(a) in respect of the information exchanged pursuant to paragraph 1 — within three months following the end of the half of the calendar year during which the advance cross-border rulings or advance pricing arrangements have been issued, amended or renewed;
(b) in respect of the information exchanged pursuant to paragraph 2 — before 1 January 2018.

6. The information to be communicated by a Member State pursuant to paragraphs 1 and 2 of this Article shall include the following:
   (a) the identification of the person, other than a natural person, and where appropriate the group of persons to which it belongs;
   (b) a summary of the content of the advance cross-border ruling or advance pricing arrangement, including a description of the relevant business activities or transactions or series of transactions provided in abstract terms, without leading to the disclosure of a commercial, industrial or professional secret or of a commercial process, or of information whose disclosure would be contrary to public policy;
   (c) the dates of issuance, amendment or renewal of the advance cross-border ruling or advance pricing arrangement;
   (d) the start date of the period of validity of the advance cross-border ruling or advance pricing arrangement, if specified;
   (e) the end date of the period of validity of the advance cross-border ruling or advance pricing arrangement, if specified;
   (f) the type of the advance cross-border ruling or advance pricing arrangement;
   (g) the amount of the transaction or series of transactions of the advance cross-border ruling or advance pricing arrangement if such amount is referred to in the advance cross-border ruling or advance pricing arrangement;
   (h) the description of the set of criteria used for the determination of the transfer pricing or the transfer price itself in the case of an advance pricing arrangement;
   (i) the identification of the method used for determination of the transfer pricing or the transfer price itself in the case of an advance pricing arrangement;
   (j) the identification of the other Member States, if any, likely to be concerned by the advance cross-border ruling or advance pricing arrangement;
   (k) the identification of any person, other than a natural person, in the other Member States, if any, likely to be affected by the advance cross-border ruling or advance pricing arrangement (indicating to which Member States the affected persons are linked); and
   (l) the indication whether the information communicated is based upon the advance cross-border ruling or advance pricing arrangement itself or upon the request referred to in the second subparagraph of paragraph 3 of this Article.

7. To facilitate the exchange of information referred to in paragraph 6 of this Article, the Commission shall adopt the practical arrangements necessary for the implementation of this Article, including measures to standardise the communication of the information set out in paragraph 6 of this Article, as part of the procedure for establishing the standard form provided for in Article 20(5).

8. Information as defined under points (a), (b), (h) and (k) of paragraph 6 of this Article shall not be communicated to the European Commission.

9. The competent authority of the Member States concerned, identified under paragraph 6(j), shall confirm, if possible by electronic means, the receipt of the information to the competent authority which provided the information without delay and in any event no later than seven working days. This measure shall be applicable until the directory referred to in Article 21(5) becomes operational.

10. Member States may, in accordance with Article 5, and having regard to Article 21(4), request additional information, including the full text of an advance cross-border ruling or an advance pricing arrangement.][1]

Amendments—[*] Directive 2013/34/EU of the European Parliament and of the Council of 26 June 2013 on the annual financial statements, consolidated financial statements and related reports of certain types of undertakings, amending Directive 2006/43/EC of the European Parliament and of the Council and repealing Council Directives 78/660/EEC and 83/349/EEC (OJ L 182, 29.6.2013, p. 19).

[1] Articles 8a, 8b inserted by Council Directive 2015/2376/EU Art 1(3) with effect from 18 December 2015. Note that member states are required to adopt and publish, by 31 December 2016, the laws, regulations and administrative provisions necessary to comply with Directive 2015/2376/EU, and to apply those measures from 1 January 2017 (OJ L 332, 18.12.2015, p 1).

[*Article 8aa* **Scope and conditions of mandatory automatic exchange of information on the country-by-country report**

1. Each Member State shall take the necessary measures to require the Ultimate Parent Entity of an MNE Group that is resident for tax purposes in its territory, or any other Reporting Entity in accordance with Section II of Annex III, to file a country-by-country report with respect to its Reporting Fiscal Year within 12 months of the last day of the Reporting Fiscal Year of the MNE Group in accordance with Section II of Annex III.

2. The competent authority of a Member State where the country-by-country report was received pursuant to paragraph 1 shall, by means of automatic exchange and within the deadline laid down in paragraph 4, communicate the country-by-country report to any other Member State in which, on the basis of the information in the country- by-country report, one or more Constituent Entities of the MNE Group of the Reporting Entity are either resident for tax purposes or subject to tax with respect to the business carried out through a permanent establishment.

3. The country-by-country report shall contain the following information with respect to the MNE Group:
   (a) aggregate information relating to the amount of revenue, profit (loss) before income tax, income tax paid, income tax accrued, stated capital, accumulated earnings, number of employees, and tangible assets other than cash or cash equivalents with regard to each jurisdiction in which the MNE Group operates;
   (b) an identification of each Constituent Entity of the MNE Group setting out the jurisdiction of tax residence of that Constituent Entity and, where different from that jurisdiction of tax residence, the jurisdiction under the laws of which that Constituent Entity is organised, and the nature of the main business activity or activities of that Constituent Entity.

4. The communication shall take place within 15 months of the last day of the Fiscal Year of the MNE Group to which the country-by-country report relates. The first country-by-country report shall be communicated for the Fiscal Year of the MNE Group commencing on or after 1 January 2016, which shall take place within 18 months of the last day of that Fiscal Year.][1]

Amendments—[1] Article 8aa inserted by Council Directive 2016/881/EU Article 1(2) with effect from 3 June 2016. Note that member states are required to adopt and publish, by 4 June 2017, the laws, regulations and administrative provisions necessary to comply with Directive 2016/881/EU, and to apply those measures from 5 June 2017 (OJ L 146, 3.6.2016, p 8).

[Article 8ab Scope and conditions of mandatory automatic exchange of information on reportable cross-border arrangements

1. Each Member State shall take the necessary measures to require intermediaries to file information that is within their knowledge, possession or control on reportable cross-border arrangements with the competent authorities within 30 days beginning:
   (a) on the day after the reportable cross-border arrangement is made available for implementation; or
   (b) on the day after the reportable cross-border arrangement is ready for implementation; or
   (c) when the first step in the implementation of the reportable cross-border arrangement has been made,
whichever occurs first.

Notwithstanding the first subparagraph, intermediaries referred to in the second paragraph of point 21 of Article 3 shall also be required to file information within 30 days beginning on the day after they provided, directly or by means of other persons, aid, assistance or advice.

2. In the case of marketable arrangements, Member States shall take the necessary measures to require that a periodic report be made by the intermediary every 3 months providing an update which contains new reportable information as referred to in points (a), (d), (g) and (h) of paragraph 14 that has become available since the last report was filed.

3. Where the intermediary is liable to file information on reportable cross-border arrangements with the competent authorities of more than one Member State, such information shall be filed only in the Member State that features first in the list below:
   (a) the Member State where the intermediary is resident for tax purposes;
   (b) the Member State where the intermediary has a permanent establishment through which the services with respect to the arrangement are provided;
   (c) the Member State which the intermediary is incorporated in or governed by the laws of;
   (d) the Member State where the intermediary is registered with a professional association related to legal, taxation or consultancy services.

4. Where, pursuant to paragraph 3, there is a multiple reporting obligation, the intermediary shall be exempt from filing the information if it has proof, in accordance with national law, that the same information has been filed in another Member State.

5. Each Member State may take the necessary measures to give intermediaries the right to a waiver from filing information on a reportable cross-border arrangement where the reporting obligation would breach the legal professional privilege under the national law of that Member State. In such circumstances, each Member State shall take the necessary measures to require intermediaries to notify, without delay, any other intermediary or, if there is no such intermediary, the relevant taxpayer of their reporting obligations under paragraph 6.

Intermediaries may only be entitled to a waiver under the first subparagraph to the extent that they operate within the limits of the relevant national laws that define their professions.

6. Each Member State shall take the necessary measures to require that, where there is no intermediary or the intermediary notifies the relevant taxpayer or another intermediary of the application of a waiver under paragraph 5, the obligation to file information on a reportable cross-border arrangement lie with the other notified intermediary, or, if there is no such intermediary, with the relevant taxpayer.

7. The relevant taxpayer with whom the reporting obligation lies shall file the information within 30 days, beginning on the day after the reportable cross-border arrangement is made available for implementation to that relevant taxpayer, or is ready for implementation by the relevant taxpayer, or when the first step in its implementation has been made in relation to the relevant taxpayer, whichever occurs first.

Where the relevant taxpayer has an obligation to file information on the reportable cross-border arrangement with the competent authorities of more than one Member State, such information shall be filed only with the competent authorities of the Member State that features first in the list below:
  (a) the Member State where the relevant taxpayer is resident for tax purposes;
  (b) the Member State where the relevant taxpayer has a permanent establishment benefiting from the arrangement;
  (c) the Member State where the relevant taxpayer receives income or generates profits, although the relevant taxpayer is not resident for tax purposes and has no permanent establishment in any Member State;
  (d) the Member State where the relevant taxpayer carries on an activity, although the relevant taxpayer is not resident for tax purposes and has no permanent establishment in any Member State.

8. Where, pursuant to paragraph 7, there is a multiple reporting obligation, the relevant taxpayer shall be exempt from filing the information if it has proof, in accordance with national law, that the same information has been filed in another Member State.

9. Each Member State shall take the necessary measures to require that, where there is more than one intermediary, the obligation to file information on the reportable cross-border arrangement lie with all intermediaries involved in the same reportable cross-border arrangement.

An intermediary shall be exempt from filing the information only to the extent that it has proof, in accordance with national law, that the same information referred to in paragraph 14 has already been filed by another intermediary.

10. Each Member State shall take the necessary measures to require that, where the reporting obligation lies with the relevant taxpayer and where there is more than one relevant taxpayer, the relevant taxpayer that is to file information in accordance with paragraph 6 be the one that features first in the list below:
  (a) the relevant taxpayer that agreed the reportable cross-border arrangement with the intermediary;
  (b) the relevant taxpayer that manages the implementation of the arrangement.

Any relevant taxpayer shall only be exempt from filing the information to the extent that it has proof, in accordance with national law, that the same information referred to in paragraph 14 has already been filed by another relevant taxpayer.

11. Each Member State may take the necessary measures to require that each relevant taxpayer file information about their use of the arrangement to the tax administration in each of the years for which they use it.

12. Each Member State shall take the necessary measures to require intermediaries and relevant taxpayers to file information on reportable cross-border arrangements the first step of which was implemented between the date of entry into force and the date of application of this Directive. Intermediaries and relevant taxpayers, as appropriate, shall file information on those reportable cross-border arrangements by 31 August 2020.

13. The competent authority of a Member State where the information was filed pursuant to paragraphs 1 to 12 of this Article shall, by means of an automatic exchange, communicate the information specified in paragraph 14 of this Article to the competent authorities of all other Member States, in accordance with the practical arrangements adopted pursuant to Article 21.

14. The information to be communicated by the competent authority of a Member State under paragraph 13 shall contain the following, as applicable:
  (a) the identification of intermediaries and relevant taxpayers, including their name, date and place of birth (in the case of an individual), residence for tax purposes, TIN and, where appropriate, the persons that are associated enterprises to the relevant taxpayer;
  (b) details of the hallmarks set out in Annex IV that make the cross-border arrangement reportable;
  (c) a summary of the content of the reportable cross-border arrangement, including a reference to the name by which it is commonly known, if any, and a description in abstract terms of the relevant business activities or arrangements, without leading to the disclosure of a commercial, industrial or professional secret or of a commercial process, or of information the disclosure of which would be contrary to public policy;

- (d) the date on which the first step in implementing the reportable cross-border arrangement has been made or will be made;
- (e) details of the national provisions that form the basis of the reportable cross-border arrangement;
- (f) the value of the reportable cross-border arrangement;
- (g) the identification of the Member State of the relevant taxpayer(s) and any other Member States which are likely to be concerned by the reportable cross-border arrangement;
- (h) the identification of any other person in a Member State likely to be affected by the reportable cross-border arrangement, indicating to which Member States such person is linked.

15. The fact that a tax administration does not react to a reportable cross-border arrangement shall not imply any acceptance of the validity or tax treatment of that arrangement.

16. To facilitate the exchange of information referred to in paragraph 13 of this Article, the Commission shall adopt the practical arrangements necessary for the implementation of this Article, including measures to standardise the communication of the information set out in paragraph 14 of this Article, as part of the procedure for establishing the standard form provided for in Article 20(5).

17. The Commission shall not have access to information referred to in points (a), (c) and (h) of paragraph 14.

18. The automatic exchange of information shall take place within one month of the end of the quarter in which the information was filed. The first information shall be communicated by 31 October 2020.][1]

Amendments—[1] Article 8ab inserted by Council Directive (EU) 2018/822 art 1(2) with effect from 25 June 2018 (OJ L 139, 5.6.2018, p 1).

[Article 8b

1. Before 1 January 2018, Member States shall provide the Commission on an annual basis with statistics on the volume of automatic exchanges under Articles 8 and 8a and, to the extent possible, with information on the administrative and other relevant costs and benefits relating to exchanges that have taken place and any potential changes, for both tax administrations and third parties.

2. Before 1 January 2019, the Commission shall submit a report that provides an overview and an assessment of the statistics and information received under paragraph 1 of this Article, on issues such as the administrative and other relevant costs and benefits of the automatic exchange of information, as well as practical aspects linked thereto. If appropriate, the Commission shall present a proposal to the Council regarding the categories and the conditions laid down in Article 8(1), including the condition that information concerning residents in other Member States has to be available, or the items referred to in Article 8(3a), or both.

When examining a proposal presented by the Commission, the Council shall assess further strengthening of the efficiency and functioning of the automatic exchange of information and raising the standard thereof, with the aim of providing that:
- (a) the competent authority of each Member State shall, by automatic exchange, communicate to the competent authority of any other Member State, information regarding taxable periods as from 1 January 2019 concerning residents in that other Member State, on all categories of income and capital listed in Article 8(1), as they are to be understood under the national legislation of the Member State communicating the information; and
- (b) the lists of categories and items laid down in Articles 8(1) and 8(3a) be extended to include other categories and items, including royalties.][1]

Amendments—[1] Articles 8a, 8b inserted by Council Directive 2015/2376/EU Art 1(3) with effect from 18 December 2015. Note that member states are required to adopt and publish, by 31 December 2016, the laws, regulations and administrative provisions necessary to comply with Directive 2015/2376/EU, and to apply those measures from 1 January 2017 (OJ L 332, 18.12.2015, p 1).

SECTION III

SPONTANEOUS EXCHANGE OF INFORMATION

Article 9 Scope and conditions of spontaneous exchange of information

1. The competent authority of each Member State shall communicate the information referred to in Article 1(1) to the competent authority of any other Member State concerned, in any of the following circumstances:
- (a) the competent authority of one Member State has grounds for supposing that there may be a loss of tax in the other Member State;
- (b) a person liable to tax obtains a reduction in, or an exemption from, tax in one Member State which would give rise to an increase in tax or to liability to tax in the other Member State;
- (c) business dealings between a person liable to tax in one Member State and a person liable to tax in the other Member State are conducted through one or more countries in such a way that a saving in tax may result in one or the other Member State or in both;

(d) the competent authority of a Member State has grounds for supposing that a saving of tax may result from artificial transfers of profits within groups of enterprises;
(e) information forwarded to one Member State by the competent authority of the other Member State has enabled information to be obtained which may be relevant in assessing liability to tax in the latter Member State.

2. The competent authorities of each Member State may communicate, by spontaneous exchange, to the competent authorities of the other Member States any information of which they are aware and which may be useful to the competent authorities of the other Member States.

Article 10 Time limits

1. The competent authority to which information referred to in Article 9(1) becomes available, shall forward that information to the competent authority of any other Member State concerned as quickly as possible, and no later than one month after it becomes available.

2. The competent authority to which information is communicated pursuant to Article 9 shall confirm, if possible by electronic means, the receipt of the information to the competent authority which provided the information immediately and in any event no later than seven working days.

CHAPTER III
OTHER FORMS OF ADMINISTRATIVE COOPERATION

SECTION I
PRESENCE IN ADMINISTRATIVE OFFICES AND PARTICIPATION IN ADMINISTRATIVE ENQUIRIES

Article 11 Scope and conditions

1. By agreement between the requesting authority and the requested authority and in accordance with the arrangements laid down by the latter, officials authorised by the requesting authority may, with a view to exchanging the information referred to in Article 1(1):
   (a) be present in the offices where the administrative authorities of the requested Member State carry out their duties;
   (b) be present during administrative enquiries carried out in the territory of the requested Member State.

Where the requested information is contained in documentation to which the officials of the requested authority have access, the officials of the requesting authority shall be given copies thereof.

2. In so far as this is permitted under the legislation of the requested Member State, the agreement referred to in paragraph 1 may provide that, where officials of the requesting authority are present during administrative enquiries, they may interview individuals and examine records.

Any refusal by the person under investigation to respect the inspection measures of the officials of the requesting authority shall be treated by the requested authority as if that refusal was committed against officials of the latter authority.

3. Officials authorised by the requesting Member State present in another Member State in accordance with paragraph 1 shall at all times be able to produce written authority stating their identity and their official capacity.

SECTION II
SIMULTANEOUS CONTROLS

Article 12 Simultaneous controls

1. Where two or more Member States agree to conduct simultaneous controls, in their own territory, of one or more persons of common or complementary interest to them, with a view to exchanging the information thus obtained, paragraphs 2, 3 and 4 shall apply.

2. The competent authority in each Member State shall identify independently the persons for whom it intends to propose a simultaneous control. It shall notify the competent authority of the other Member States concerned of any cases for which it proposes a simultaneous control, giving reasons for its choice.

It shall specify the period of time during which those controls are to be conducted.

3. The competent authority of each Member State concerned shall decide whether it wishes to take part in simultaneous controls. It shall confirm its agreement or communicate its reasoned refusal to the authority that proposed a simultaneous control.

4. The competent authority of each Member State concerned shall appoint a representative with responsibility for supervising and coordinating the control operation.

SECTION III
ADMINISTRATIVE NOTIFICATION

Article 13 **Request for notification**

1. At the request of the competent authority of a Member State, the competent authority of another Member State shall, in accordance with the rules governing the notification of similar instruments in the requested Member State, notify the addressee of any instruments and decisions which emanate from the administrative authorities of the requesting Member State and concern the application in its territory of legislation on taxes covered by this Directive.
2. Requests for notification shall indicate the subject of the instrument or decision to be notified and shall specify the name and address of the addressee, together with any other information which may facilitate identification of the addressee.
3. The requested authority shall inform the requesting authority immediately of its response and, in particular, of the date of notification of the instrument or decision to the addressee.
4. The requesting authority shall only make a request for notification pursuant to this Article when it is unable to notify in accordance with the rules governing the notification of the instruments concerned in the requesting Member State, or where such notification would give rise to disproportionate difficulties. The competent authority of a Member State may notify any document by registered mail or electronically directly to a person within the territory of another Member State.

SECTION IV
FEEDBACK

Article 14 **Conditions**

1. Where a competent authority provides information pursuant to Articles 5 or 9, it may request the competent authority which receives the information to send feedback thereon. If feedback is requested, the competent authority which received the information shall, without prejudice to the rules on tax secrecy and data protection applicable in its Member State, send feedback to the competent authority which provided the information as soon as possible and no later than three months after the outcome of the use of the requested information is known. The Commission shall determine the practical arrangements in accordance with the procedure referred to in Article 26(2).
2. Member States' competent authorities shall send feedback on the automatic exchange of information to the other Member States concerned once a year, in accordance with practical arrangements agreed upon bilaterally.

SECTION V
SHARING OF BEST PRACTICES AND EXPERIENCE

Article 15 **Scope and conditions**

1. Member States shall, together with the Commission, examine and evaluate administrative cooperation pursuant to this Directive and shall share their experience, with a view to improving such cooperation and, where appropriate, drawing up rules in the fields concerned.
2. Member States may, together with the Commission, produce guidelines on any aspect deemed necessary for sharing best practices and sharing experience.

CHAPTER IV
CONDITIONS GOVERNING ADMINISTRATIVE COOPERATION

Article 16 **Disclosure of information and documents**

1. Information communicated between Member States in any form pursuant to this Directive shall be covered by the obligation of official secrecy and enjoy the protection extended to similar information under the national law of the Member State which received it. Such information may be used for the administration and enforcement of the domestic laws of the Member States concerning the taxes referred to in Article 2.
Such information may also be used for the assessment and enforcement of other taxes and duties covered by Article 2 of Council Directive 2010/24/EU of 16 March 2010 concerning mutual assistance for the recovery of claims relating to taxes, duties and other measures[1], or for the assessment and enforcement of compulsory social security contributions.
In addition, it may be used in connection with judicial and administrative proceedings that may involve penalties, initiated as a result of infringements of tax law, without prejudice to the general rules and provisions governing the rights of defendants and witnesses in such proceedings.
2. With the permission of the competent authority of the Member State communicating information pursuant to this Directive, and only in so far as this is allowed under the legislation of the Member State of the competent authority receiving the information, information and documents received pursuant to this Directive may be used for other purposes than those referred to in paragraph 1. Such permission shall be granted if the information can be used for similar purposes in the Member State of the competent authority communicating the information.

3. Where a competent authority of a Member State considers that information which it has received from the competent authority of another Member State is likely to be useful for the purposes referred to in paragraph 1 to the competent authority of a third Member State, it may transmit that information to the latter competent authority, provided that transmission is in accordance with the rules and procedures laid down in this Directive. It shall inform the competent authority of the Member State from which the information originates about its intention to share that information with a third Member State. The Member State of origin of the information may oppose such a sharing of information within 10 working days of receipt of the communication from the Member State wishing to share the information.

4. Permission to use information pursuant to paragraph 2, which has been transmitted pursuant to paragraph 3, may be granted only by the competent authority of the Member State from which the information originates.

5. Information, reports, statements and any other documents, or certified true copies or extracts thereof, obtained by the requested authority and communicated to the requesting authority in accordance with this Directive may be invoked as evidence by the competent bodies of the requesting Member State on the same basis as similar information, reports, statements and any other documents provided by an authority of that Member State.

[6. Notwithstanding paragraphs 1 to 4 of this Article, information communicated between Member States pursuant to Article 8aa shall be used for the purposes of assessing high-level transfer-pricing risks and other risks related to base erosion and profit shifting, including assessing the risk of non-compliance by members of the MNE Group with applicable transfer-pricing rules, and where appropriate for economic and statistical analysis. Transfer- pricing adjustments by the tax authorities of the receiving Member State shall not be based on the information exchanged pursuant to Article 8aa. Notwithstanding the above, there is no prohibition on using the information communicated between Member States pursuant to Article 8aa as a basis for making further enquiries into the MNE Group's transfer-pricing arrangements or into other tax matters in the course of a tax audit, and, as a result, appropriate adjustments to the taxable income of a Constituent Entity may be made.][2]

Amendments—[1]   OJ L 84, 31.3.2010, p. 1.
[2] Para 6 inserted by Council Directive 2016/881/EU Article 1(3) with effect from 3 June 2016. Note that member states are required to adopt and publish, by 4 June 2017, the laws, regulations and administrative provisions necessary to comply with Directive 2016/881/EU, and to apply those measures from 5 June 2017 (OJ L 146, 3.6.2016, p 8).

Article 17 Limits

1. A requested authority in one Member State shall provide a requesting authority in another Member State with the information referred to in Article 5 provided that the requesting authority has exhausted the usual sources of information which it could have used in the circumstances for obtaining the information requested, without running the risk of jeopardising the achievement of its objectives.

2. This Directive shall impose no obligation upon a requested Member State to carry out enquiries or to communicate information, if it would be contrary to its legislation to conduct such inquiries or to collect the information requested for its own purposes.

3. The competent authority of a requested Member State may decline to provide information where the requesting Member State is unable, for legal reasons, to provide similar information.

4. The provision of information may be refused where it would lead to the disclosure of a commercial, industrial or professional secret or of a commercial process, or of information whose disclosure would be contrary to public policy.

5. The requested authority shall inform the requesting authority of the grounds for refusing a request for information.

Article 18 Obligations

1. If information is requested by a Member State in accordance with this Directive, the requested Member State shall use its measures aimed at gathering information to obtain the requested information, even though that Member State may not need such information for its own tax purposes. That obligation is without prejudice to paragraphs 2, 3 and 4 of Article 17, the invocation of which shall in no case be construed as permitting a requested Member State to decline to supply information solely because it has no domestic interest in such information.

2. In no case shall Article 17(2) and (4) be construed as permitting a requested authority of a Member State to decline to supply information solely because this information is held by a bank, other financial institution, nominee or person acting in an agency or a fiduciary capacity or because it relates to ownership interests in a person.

3. Notwithstanding paragraph 2, a Member State may refuse the transmission of requested information where such information concerns taxable periods prior to 1 January 2011 and where the transmission of such information could have been refused on the basis of Article 8(1) of Directive 77/799/EEC if it had been requested before 11 March 2011.

Article 19 **Extension of wider cooperation provided to a third country**
Where a Member State provides a wider cooperation to a third country than that provided for under this Directive, that Member State may not refuse to provide such wider cooperation to any other Member State wishing to enter into such mutual wider cooperation with that Member State.

Article 20 **Standard forms and computerised formats**
1. Requests for information and for administrative enquiries pursuant to Article 5 and their replies, acknowledgements, requests for additional background information, inability or refusal pursuant to Article 7 shall, as far as possible, be sent using a standard form adopted by the Commission in accordance with the procedure referred to in Article 26(2).
The standard forms may be accompanied by reports, statements and any other documents, or certified true copies or extracts thereof.
2. The standard form referred to in paragraph 1 shall include at least the following information to be provided by the requesting authority:
   (a) the identity of the person under examination or investigation;
   (b) the tax purpose for which the information is sought.
The requesting authority may, to the extent known and in line with international developments, provide the name and address of any person believed to be in possession of the requested information as well as any element that may facilitate the collection of information by the requested authority.
3. Spontaneous information and its acknowledgement pursuant to Articles 9 and 10 respectively, requests for administrative notifications pursuant to Article 13 and feedback information pursuant to Article 14 shall be sent using the standard form adopted by the Commission in accordance with the procedure referred to in Article 26(2).
[4. The automatic exchange of information pursuant to Article 8 shall be sent using a standard computerised format aimed at facilitating such automatic exchange and based on the existing computerised format pursuant to Article 9 of Directive 2003/48/EC, to be used for all types of automatic exchange of information, adopted by the Commission in accordance with the procedure referred to in Article 26(2).
[5. The Commission shall adopt standard forms, including the linguistic arrangements, in accordance with the procedure referred to in Article 26(2), in the following cases:
   (a) for the automatic exchange of information on advance cross-border rulings and advance pricing arrangements pursuant to Article 8a before 1 January 2017;
   (b) for the automatic exchange of information on reportable cross-border arrangements pursuant to Article 8ab before 30 June 2019.
Those standard forms shall not exceed the components for the exchange of information listed in Articles 8a(6) and 8ab(14), and such other related fields which are linked to these components which are necessary to achieve the objectives of Articles 8a and 8ab, respectively.
The linguistic arrangements referred to in the first subparagraph shall not preclude Member States from communicating the information referred to in Articles 8a and 8ab in any of the official languages of the Union. However, those linguistic arrangements may provide that the key elements of such information shall also be sent in another official language of the Union.][4]
[(6) The automatic exchange of information on the country-by-country report pursuant to Article 8aa shall be carried out using the standard form provided in Tables 1, 2 and 3 of Section III of Annex III. The Commission shall, by means of implementing acts, adopt the linguistic arrangements for that exchange by 31 December 2016. They shall not preclude Member States from communicating information referred to in Article 8aa in any of the official and working languages of the Union. However, those linguistic arrangements may provide that the key elements of such information also be sent in another official language of the Union. Those implementing acts shall be adopted in accordance with the procedure referred to in Article 26(2).][3][1]

Amendments—[1] Para 4 substituted by Council Directive 2014/107/EU Art 1(3) with effect from 5 January 2015. See Art 2 for implementation provisions (deadline for implementation is 31 December 2015, with measures to apply from 1 January 2016) (OJ L 359, 16.12.2014, p 1).
[3] Para 6 inserted by Council Directive 2016/881/EU Article 1(4) with effect from 3 June 2016. Note that member states are required to adopt and publish, by 4 June 2017, the laws, regulations and administrative provisions necessary to comply with Directive 2016/881/EU, and to apply those measures from 5 June 2017 (OJ L 146, 3.6.2016, p 8).
[4] Para 5 substituted by Council Directive (EU) 2018/822 art 1(3) with effect from 25 June 2018 (OJ L 139, 5.6.2018, p 1).

Article 21 **Practical arrangements**
1. Information communicated pursuant to this Directive shall, as far as possible, be provided by electronic means using the CCN network.
Where necessary, the Commission shall adopt practical arrangements necessary for the implementation of the first subparagraph in accordance with the procedure referred to in Article 26(2).
[2. The Commission shall be responsible for whatever development of the CCN network is necessary to permit the exchange of that information between Member States and for ensuring the security of the CCN network.

Member States shall be responsible for whatever development of their systems is necessary to enable that information to be exchanged using the CCN network and for ensuring the security of their systems.
Member States shall ensure that each individual Reportable Person is notified of a breach of security with regard to his data when that breach is likely to adversely affect the protection of his personal data or privacy.
Member States shall waive all claims for the reimbursement of expenses incurred in applying this Directive except, where appropriate, in respect of fees paid to experts.][1]
[3. Persons duly accredited by the Security Accreditation Authority of the Commission may have access to that information only in so far as it is necessary for the care, maintenance and development of the directory referred to in paragraph 5 and of the CCN network.][2]
4. Requests for cooperation, including requests for notification, and attached documents may be made in any language agreed between the requested and requesting authority.
Those requests shall be accompanied by a translation into the official language or one of the official languages of the Member State of the requested authority only in special cases when the requested authority states its reason for requesting a translation.
[5. The Commission shall by 31 December 2017 develop and provide with technical and logistical support a secure Member State central directory on administrative cooperation in the field of taxation where information to be communicated in the framework of Article 8a(1) and (2) shall be recorded in order to satisfy the automatic exchange provided for in those paragraphs.
The Commission shall by 31 December 2019 develop and provide with technical and logistical support a secure Member State central directory on administrative cooperation in the field of taxation where information to be communicated in the framework of Article 8ab(13), (14) and (16) shall be recorded in order to satisfy the automatic exchange provided for in those paragraphs.
The competent authorities of all Member States shall have access to the information recorded in that directory. The Commission shall also have access to the information recorded in that directory, however within the limitations set out in Articles 8a(8) and 8ab(17). The necessary practical arrangements shall be adopted by the Commission in accordance with the procedure referred to in Article 26(2).
Until that secure central directory is operational, the automatic exchange provided for in Article 8a(1) and (2) and Article 8ab(13), (14) and (16) shall be carried out in accordance with paragraph 1 of this Article and the applicable practical arrangements.][4]
[6. Information communicated pursuant to Article 8aa(2) shall be provided by electronic means using the CCN network. The Commission shall, by means of implementing acts, adopt the necessary practical arrangements for the upgrading of the CCN network. Those implementing acts shall be adopted in accordance with the procedure referred to in Article 26(2).][3]

Amendments—[1]   Para 2 substituted by Council Directive 2014/107/EU Art 1(4) with effect from 5 January 2015. See Art 2 for implementation provisions (deadline for implementation is 31 December 2015, with measures to apply from 1 January 2016) (OJ L 359, 16.12.2014, p 1).
[2]   Para 3 substituted by Council Directive 2015/2376/EU Art 1(5) with effect from 18 December 2015. Note that member states are required to adopt and publish, by 31 December 2016, the laws, regulations and administrative provisions necessary to comply with Directive 2015/2376/EU, and to apply those measures from 1 January 2017 (OJ L 332, 18.12.2015, p 1).
[3]   Para 6 inserted by Council Directive 2016/881/EU Article 1(5) with effect from 3 June 2016. Note that member states are required to adopt and publish, by 4 June 2017, the laws, regulations and administrative provisions necessary to comply with Directive 2016/881/EU, and to apply those measures from 5 June 2017 (OJ L 146, 3.6.2016, p 8).
[4]   Para 5 substituted by Council Directive (EU) 2018/822 art 1(4) with effect from 25 June 2018 (OJ L 139, 5.6.2018, p 1).

Article 22 Specific obligations

1. Member States shall take all necessary measures to:
    (a) ensure effective internal coordination within the organisation referred to in Article 4;
    (b) establish direct cooperation with the authorities of the other Member States referred to in Article 4;
    (c) ensure the smooth operation of the administrative cooperation arrangements provided for in this Directive.
[(1a) For the purpose of the implementation and enforcement of the laws of the Member States giving effect to this Directive and to ensure the functioning of the administrative cooperation it establishes, Member States shall provide by law for access by tax authorities to the mechanisms, procedures, documents and information referred to in Articles 13, 30, 31 and 40 of Directive (EU) 2015/849 of the European Parliament and of the Council.(*)][1]
2. The Commission shall communicate to each Member State any general information concerning the implementation and application of this Directive which it receives and which it is able to provide.

Amendments—[*]   Opinion of 22 November 2016 (not yet published in the Official Journal).
[1]   Para (1a) inserted by Council Directive 2016/2258/EU Article 1 with effect from 6 December 2016. Member states are required to adopt and publish, by 31 December 2017, the laws, regulations and administrative provisions necessary to comply with Council Directive 2016/2258/EU and to apply those measures from 1 January 2018.

CHAPTER V
RELATIONS WITH THE COMMISSION

Article 23 Evaluation
1. Member States and the Commission shall examine and evaluate the functioning of the administrative cooperation provided for in this Directive.
2. Member States shall communicate to the Commission any relevant information necessary for the evaluation of the effectiveness of administrative cooperation in accordance with this Directive in combating tax evasion and tax avoidance.
[3. Member States shall communicate to the Commission a yearly assessment of the effectiveness of the automatic exchange of information referred to in Articles 8, 8a, 8aa and 8ab as well as the practical results achieved. The Commission shall, by means of implementing acts, adopt the form and the conditions of communication for that yearly assessment. Those implementing acts shall be adopted in accordance with the procedure referred to in Article 26(2).][2]
4. The Commission shall, in accordance with the procedure referred to in Article 26(2), determine a list of statistical data which shall be provided by the Member States for the purposes of evaluation of this Directive.
5, 6 . . . [1]

Amendments—[1] Paras 5, 6 repealed by Council Directive 2015/2376/EU Art 1(6) with effect from 18 December 2015. Note that member states are required to adopt and publish, by 31 December 2016, the laws, regulations and administrative provisions necessary to comply with Directive 2015/2376/EU, and to apply those measures from 1 January 2017 (OJ L 332, 18.12.2015, p 1).
[2] Para 3 substituted by Council Directive (EU) 2018/822 art 1(5) with effect from 25 June 2018 (OJ L 139, 5.6.2018, p 1).

[Article 23a Confidentiality of information
1. Information communicated to the Commission pursuant to this Directive shall be kept confidential by the Commission in accordance with the provisions applicable to Union authorities and may not be used for any purposes other than those required to determine whether and to what extent Member States comply with this Directive.
2. Information communicated to the Commission by a Member State under Article 23, as well as any report or document produced by the Commission using such information, may be transmitted to other Member States. Such transmitted information shall be covered by the obligation of official secrecy and enjoy the protection extended to similar information under the national law of the Member State which received it.
Reports and documents produced by the Commission, referred to in the first subparagraph, may be used by the Member States only for analytical purposes, and shall not be published or made available to any other person or body without the express agreement of the Commission.][1]

Amendments—[1] Article 23a inserted by Council Directive 2015/2376/EU Art 1(7) with effect from 18 December 2015. Note that member states are required to adopt and publish, by 31 December 2016, the laws, regulations and administrative provisions necessary to comply with Directive 2015/2376/EU, and to apply those measures from 1 January 2017 (OJ L 332, 18.12.2015, p 1).

CHAPTER VI
RELATIONS WITH THIRD COUNTRIES

Article 24 Exchange of information with third countries
1. Where the competent authority of a Member State receives from a third country information that is foreseeably relevant to the administration and enforcement of the domestic laws of that Member State concerning the taxes referred to in Article 2, that authority may, in so far as this is allowed pursuant to an agreement with that third country, provide that information to the competent authorities of Member States for which that information might be useful and to any requesting authorities.
2. Competent authorities may communicate, in accordance with their domestic provisions on the communication of personal data to third countries, information obtained in accordance with this Directive to a third country, provided that all of the following conditions are met:
   (a) the competent authority of the Member State from which the information originates have consented to that communication;
   (b) the third country concerned has given an undertaking to provide the cooperation required to gather evidence of the irregular or illegal nature of transactions which appear to contravene or constitute an abuse of tax legislation.

CHAPTER VII
GENERAL AND FINAL PROVISIONS

Article 25 Data protection

[1.] [1] All exchange of information pursuant to this Directive shall be subject to the provisions implementing Directive 95/46/EC. However, Member States shall, for the purpose of the correct application of this Directive, restrict the scope of the obligations and rights provided for in Article 10, Article 11(1), Articles 12 and 21 of Directive 95/46/EC to the extent required in order to safeguard the interests referred to in Article 13(1)(e) of that Directive.

[1a. Regulation (EC) No 45/2001 applies to any processing of personal data under this Directive by the Union institutions and bodies. However, for the purpose of the correct application of this Directive, the scope of the obligations and rights provided for in Article 11, Article 12(1), Articles 13 to 17 of Regulation (EC) No 45/2001 is restricted to the extent required in order to safeguard the interests referred to in point (b) of Article 20(1) of that Regulation.][2]

[2. Reporting Financial Institutions and the competent authorities of each Member State shall be considered to be data controllers for the purposes of Directive 95/46/EC.

3. Notwithstanding paragraph 1, each Member State shall ensure that each Reporting Financial Institution under its jurisdiction informs each individual Reportable Person concerned that the information relating to him referred to in Article 8(3a) will be collected and transferred in accordance with this Directive and shall ensure that the Reporting Financial Institution provides to that individual all information that he is entitled to under its domestic legislation implementing Directive 95/46/EC in sufficient time for the individual to exercise his data protection rights and, in any case, before the Reporting Financial Institution concerned reports the information referred to in Article 8(3a) to the competent authority of its Member State of residence.

4. Information processed in accordance with this Directive shall be retained for no longer than necessary to achieve the purposes of this Directive, and in any case in accordance with each data controller's domestic rules on statute of limitations.][1]

Amendments—[1] Paras 2–4 inserted by Council Directive 2014/107/EU Art 1(5) with effect from 5 January 2015. See Art 2 for implementation provisions (deadline for implementation is 31 December 2015, with measures to apply from 1 January 2016) (OJ L 359, 16.12.2014, p 1).

[2] Para 1a inserted by Council Directive 2015/2376/EU Art 1(8) with effect from 18 December 2015. Note that member states are required to adopt and publish, by 31 December 2016, the laws, regulations and administrative provisions necessary to comply with Directive 2015/2376/EU, and to apply those measures from 1 January 2017 (OJ L 332, 18.12.2015, p 1).

[Article 25a Penalties

Member States shall lay down the rules on penalties applicable to infringements of national provisions adopted pursuant to this Directive and concerning Articles 8aa and 8ab, and shall take all measures necessary to ensure that they are implemented. The penalties provided for shall be effective, proportionate and dissuasive.][1]

Amendments—[1] Article 25a substituted by Council Directive (EU) 2018/822 art 1(6) with effect from 25 June 2018 (OJ L 139, 5.6.2018, p 1).

Article 26 Committee procedure

1. The Commission shall be assisted by the Committee on administrative cooperation for taxation. That committee shall be a committee within the meaning of Regulation (EU) No 182/2011 of the European Parliament and of the Council[*].

2. Where reference is made to this paragraph, Article 5 of Regulation (EU) No 182/2011 shall apply.][1]

Amendments—[*] Regulation (EU) No 182/2011 of the European Parliament and of the Council of 16 February 2011 laying down the rules and general principles concerning mechanisms for control by the Member States of the Commission's exercise of implementing powers (OJ L 55, 28.2.2011, p. 13).

[1] Article 25 substituted by Council Directive 2016/881/EU Article 1(7) with effect from 3 June 2016. Note that member states are required to adopt and publish, by 4 June 2017, the laws, regulations and administrative provisions necessary to comply with Directive 2016/881/EU, and to apply those measures from 5 June 2017 (OJ L 146, 3.6.2016, p 8).

[Article 27 Reporting

1. Every five years after 1 January 2013, the Commission shall submit a report on the application of this Directive to the European Parliament and to the Council.

2. Every two years after 1 July 2020, the Member States and the Commission shall evaluate the relevance of Annex IV and the Commission shall present a report to the Council. That report shall, where appropriate, be accompanied by a legislative proposal.][1]

Amendments—[1] Article 27 substituted by Council Directive (EU) 2018/822 art 1(7) with effect from 25 June 2018 (OJ L 139, 5.6.2018, p 1).

[Article 27a Optional deferral of time limits because of the COVID-19 pandemic

1. Notwithstanding the time limits for filing information on reportable cross-border arrangements as specified in Article 8ab(12), Member States may take the measures necessary to allow intermediaries and relevant taxpayers to file, by 28 February 2021, information on reportable cross-border arrangements the first step of which was implemented between 25 June 2018 and 30 June 2020.

2. Where Member States take measures as referred to in paragraph 1, they shall also take the measures necessary to allow:
  (a) notwithstanding Article 8ab(18), the first information to be communicated by 30 April 2021;
  (b) the period of 30 days for filing information referred to in Article 8ab(1) and (7) to begin by 1 January 2021 where:
    (i) a reportable cross-border arrangement is made available for implementation or is ready for implementation, or where the first step in its implementation has been made between 1 July 2020 and 31 December 2020; or
    (ii) intermediaries within the meaning of the second paragraph of point 21 of Article 3 provide, directly or by means of other persons, aid, assistance or advice between 1 July 2020 and 31 December 2020;
  (c) in the case of marketable arrangements, the first periodic report in accordance with Article 8ab(2) to be made by the intermediary by 30 April 2021.
3. Notwithstanding the time limit laid down in point (b) of Article 8(6), Member States may take the measures necessary to allow the communication of information referred to in Article 8(3a) that relates to the calendar year 2019 or another appropriate reporting period to take place within 12 months following the end of the calendar year 2019 or the other appropriate reporting period.][1]

Amendments—[1] Articles 27a, 27b inserted by Council Directive 2020/876/EU art 1 with effect from 27 June 2020 (OJ L 204, 26.6.2020, p 46).

[Article 27b Extension of the period of deferral
1. The Council, acting unanimously on a proposal from the Commission, may take an implementing decision to extend the period of deferral of the time limits set out in Article 27a by three months, provided that severe risks to public health, hindrances and economic disturbance caused by the COVID-19 pandemic continue to exist and Member States apply lockdown measures.
2. The proposal for a Council implementing decision shall be submitted to the Council at least one month before the expiry of the relevant deadline.][1]

Amendments—[1] Articles 27a, 27b inserted by Council Directive 2020/876/EU art 1 with effect from 27 June 2020 (OJ L 204, 26.6.2020, p 46).

Article 28 Repeal of Directive 77/799/EEC
Directive 77/799/EEC is repealed with effect from 1 January 2013.
References made to the repealed Directive shall be construed as references to this Directive.

Article 29 Transposition
1. Member States shall bring into force the laws, regulations and administrative provisions necessary to comply with this Directive with effect from 1 January 2013.
However, they shall bring into force the laws, regulations and administrative provisions necessary to comply with Article 8 of this Directive with effect from 1 January 2015.
They shall forthwith inform the Commission thereof.
When Member States adopt those measures, they shall contain a reference to this Directive or shall be accompanied by such a reference on the occasion of their official publication. The methods of making such reference shall be laid down by the Member States.
2. Member States shall communicate to the Commission the text of the main provisions of national law which they adopt in the field covered by this Directive.

Article 30 Entry into force
This Directive shall enter into force on the day of its publication in the *Official Journal of the European Union*.

Article 31 Addressees
This Directive is addressed to the Member States.

Done at Brussels, ...15 February 2011.
For the Council
The President
MATOLCSY Gy.

[ANNEX I

REPORTING AND DUE DILIGENCE RULES FOR FINANCIAL ACCOUNT INFORMATION
This Annex lays down the reporting and due diligence rules that have to be applied by Reporting Financial Institutions in order to enable the Member States to communicate, by automatic exchange, the information referred to in Article 8(3a) of this Directive. This Annex also describes the rules and administrative procedures that Member States shall have in place to ensure effective implementation of, and compliance with, the reporting and due diligence procedures set out below.

SECTION I
GENERAL REPORTING REQUIREMENTS

A Subject to paragraphs C through E, each Reporting Financial Institution must report to the competent authority of its Member State the following information with respect to each Reportable Account of such Reporting Financial Institution:

1. the name, address, Member State(s) of residence, TIN(s) and date and place of birth (in the case of an individual) of each Reportable Person that is an Account Holder of the account and, in the case of any Entity that is an Account Holder and that, after application of the due diligence procedures consistent with Sections V, VI and VII, is identified as having one or more Controlling Persons that is a Reportable Person, the name, address, Member State(s) and (if any) other jurisdiction(s) of residence and TIN(s) of the Entity and the name, address, Member State(s) of residence, TIN(s) and date and place of birth of each Reportable Person;
2. the account number (or functional equivalent in the absence of an account number);
3. the name and identifying number (if any) of the Reporting Financial Institution;
4. the account balance or value (including, in the case of a Cash Value Insurance Contract or Annuity Contract, the Cash Value or surrender value) as of the end of the relevant calendar year or other appropriate reporting period or, if the account was closed during such year or period, the closure of the account;
5. in the case of any Custodial Account:
   (a) the total gross amount of interest, the total gross amount of dividends, and the total gross amount of other income generated with respect to the assets held in the account, in each case paid or credited to the account (or with respect to the account) during the calendar year or other appropriate reporting period; and
   (b) the total gross proceeds from the sale or redemption of Financial Assets paid or credited to the account during the calendar year or other appropriate reporting period with respect to which the Reporting Financial Institution acted as a custodian, broker, nominee, or otherwise as an agent for the Account Holder;
6. in the case of any Depository Account, the total gross amount of interest paid or credited to the account during the calendar year or other appropriate reporting period; and
7. in the case of any account not described in subparagraph A(5) or (6), the total gross amount paid or credited to the Account Holder with respect to the account during the calendar year or other appropriate reporting period with respect to which the Reporting Financial Institution is the obligor or debtor, including the aggregate amount of any redemption payments made to the Account Holder during the calendar year or other appropriate reporting period.

B The information reported must identify the currency in which each amount is denominated.

C Notwithstanding subparagraph A(1), with respect to each Reportable Account that is a Pre-existing Account, the TIN(s) or date of birth is not required to be reported if such TIN(s) or date of birth is not in the records of the Reporting Financial Institution and is not otherwise required to be collected by such Reporting Financial Institution under domestic law or any Union legal instrument. However, a Reporting Financial Institution is required to use reasonable efforts to obtain the TIN(s) and date of birth with respect to Pre-existing Accounts by the end of the second calendar year following the year in which Pre-existing Accounts were identified as Reportable Accounts.

D Notwithstanding subparagraph A(1), the TIN is not required to be reported if a TIN is not issued by the relevant Member State or other jurisdiction of residence.

E Notwithstanding subparagraph A(1), the place of birth is not required to be reported unless:
(1) the Reporting Financial Institution is otherwise required to obtain and report it under domestic law or the Reporting Financial Institution is or has been otherwise required to obtain and report it under any Union legal instrument in effect or that was in effect on 5 January 2015; and
(2) it is available in the electronically searchable data maintained by the Reporting Financial Institution.

SECTION II
GENERAL DUE DILIGENCE REQUIREMENTS

A An account is treated as a Reportable Account beginning as of the date it is identified as such pursuant to the due diligence procedures in Sections II through VII and, unless otherwise provided, information with respect to a Repor

B The balance or value of an account is determined as of the last day of the calendar year or other appropriate reporting period.

C   Where a balance or value threshold is to be determined as of the last day of a calendar year, the relevant balance or value must be determined as of the last day of the reporting period that ends with or within that calendar year.

D   Each Member State may allow Reporting Financial Institutions to use service providers to fulfil the reporting and due diligence obligations imposed on such Reporting Financial Institutions, as contemplated in domestic law, but these obligations shall remain the responsibility of the Reporting Financial Institutions.

E   Each Member State may allow Reporting Financial Institutions to apply the due diligence procedures for New Accounts to Pre-existing Accounts, and the due diligence procedures for High Value Accounts to Lower Value Accounts. Where a Member State allows New Account due diligence procedures to be used for Pre-existing Accounts, the rules otherwise applicable to Pre-existing Accounts continue to apply.

SECTION III
DUE DILIGENCE FOR PRE-EXISTING INDIVIDUAL ACCOUNTS

A   Introduction. The following procedures apply for purposes of identifying Reportable Accounts among Pre-existing Individual Accounts.

B   Lower Value Accounts. The following procedures apply with respect to Lower Value Accounts.
1. Residence Address. If the Reporting Financial Institution has in its records a current residence address for the individual Account Holder based on Documentary Evidence, the Reporting Financial Institution may treat the individual Account Holder as being a resident for tax purposes of the Member State or other jurisdiction in which the address is located for purposes of determining whether such individual Account Holder is a Reportable Person.
2. Electronic Record Search. If the Reporting Financial Institution does not rely on a current residence address for the individual Account Holder based on Documentary Evidence as set forth in subparagraph B(1), the Reporting Financial Institution must review electronically searchable data maintained by the Reporting Financial Institution for any of the following indicia and apply subparagraphs B(3) to (6):

   (a) identification of the Account Holder as a resident of a Member State;

   (b) current mailing or residence address (including a post office box) in a Member State;

   (c) one or more telephone numbers in a Member State and no telephone number in the Member State of the Reporting Financial Institution;

   (d) standing instructions (other than with respect to a Depository Account) to transfer funds to an account maintained in a Member State;

   (e) currently effective power of attorney or signatory authority granted to a person with an address in a Member State; or

   (f) a "hold mail" instruction or "in-care-of" address in a Member State if the Reporting Financial Institution does not have any other address on file for the Account Holder.
3. If none of the indicia listed in subparagraph B(2) are discovered in the electronic search, then no further action is required until there is a change in circumstances that results in one or more indicia being associated with the account, or the account becomes a High Value Account.
4. If any of the indicia listed in subparagraph B(2)(a) through (e) are discovered in the electronic search, or if there is a change in circumstances that results in one or more indicia being associated with the account, then the Reporting Financial Institution must treat the Account Holder as a resident for tax purposes of each Member State for which an indicium is identified, unless it elects to apply subparagraph B(6) and one of the exceptions in that subparagraph applies with respect to that account.
5. If a "hold mail" instruction or "in-care-of" address is discovered in the electronic search and no other address and none of the other indicia listed in subparagraph B(2)(a) through (e) are identified for the Account Holder, the Reporting Financial Institution must, in the order most appropriate to the circumstances, apply the paper record search described in subparagraph C(2), or seek to obtain from the Account Holder a self-certification or Documentary Evidence to establish the residence(s) for tax purposes of such Account Holder. If the paper search fails to establish an indicium and the attempt to obtain the self-certification or Documentary Evidence is not successful, the Reporting Financial Institution must report the account to the competent authority of its Member State as an undocumented account.
6. Notwithstanding a finding of indicia under subparagraph B(2), a Reporting Financial Institution is not required to treat an Account Holder as a resident of a Member State if:

(a) the Account Holder information contains a current mailing or residence address in that Member State, one or more telephone numbers in that Member State (and no telephone number in the Member State of the Reporting Financial Institution) or standing instructions (with respect to Financial Accounts other than Depository Accounts) to transfer funds to an account maintained in a Member State, and the Reporting Financial Institution obtains, or has previously reviewed and maintains, a record of:

    (i) a self-certification from the Account Holder of the Member State(s) or other jurisdiction(s) of residence of such Account Holder that does not include that Member State; and

    (ii) Documentary Evidence establishing the Account Holder's non-reportable status;

(b) the Account Holder information contains a currently effective power of attorney or signatory authority granted to a person with an address in that Member State, and the Reporting Financial Institution obtains, or has previously reviewed and maintains, a record of:

    (i) a self-certification from the Account Holder of the Member State(s) or other jurisdiction(s) of residence of such Account Holder that does not include that Member State; or

    (ii) Documentary Evidence establishing the Account Holder's non-reportable status.

C Enhanced Review Procedures for High Value Accounts. The following enhanced review procedures apply with respect to High Value Accounts.

1. Electronic Record search. With respect to High Value Accounts, the Reporting Financial Institution must review electronically searchable data maintained by the Reporting Financial Institution for any of the indicia described in subparagraph B(2).

2. Paper Record Search. If the Reporting Financial Institution's electronically searchable databases include fields for, and capture all of the information described in, subparagraph C(3), then a further paper record search is not required. If the electronic databases do not capture all of this information, then with respect to a High Value Account, the Reporting Financial Institution must also review the current customer master file and, to the extent not contained in the current customer master file, the following documents associated with the account and obtained by the Reporting Financial Institution within the last five years for any of the indicia described in subparagraph B(2):

(a) the most recent Documentary Evidence collected with respect to the account;

(b) the most recent account opening contract or documentation;

(c) the most recent documentation obtained by the Reporting Financial Institution pursuant to AML/KYC Procedures or for other regulatory purposes;

(d) any power of attorney or signature authority forms currently in effect; and

(e) any standing instructions (other than with respect to a Depository Account) to transfer funds currently in effect.

3. Exception To The Extent Databases Contain Sufficient Information. A Reporting Financial Institution is not required to perform the paper record search described in subparagraph C(2) to the extent the Reporting Financial Institution's electronically searchable information includes the following:

(a) the Account Holder's residence status;

(b) the Account Holder's residence address and mailing address currently on file with the Reporting Financial Institution;

(c) the Account Holder's telephone number(s) currently on file, if any, with the Reporting Financial Institution;

(d) in the case of Financial Accounts other than Depository Accounts, whether there are standing instructions to transfer funds in the account to another account (including an account at another branch of the Reporting Financial Institution or another Financial Institution);

(e) whether there is a current "in-care-of" address or "hold mail" instruction for the Account Holder; and

(f) whether there is any power of attorney or signatory authority for the account.

4. Relationship Manager Inquiry for Actual Knowledge. In addition to the electronic and paper record searches described in subparagraphs C(1) and (2), the Reporting Financial Institution must treat as a Reportable Account any High Value Account assigned to a relationship manager (including any Financial Accounts aggregated with that High Value Account) if the relationship manager has actual knowledge that the Account Holder is a Reportable Person.

5. Effect of Finding Indicia.

(a) If none of the indicia listed in subparagraph B(2) are discovered in the enhanced review of High Value Accounts described in paragraph C, and the account is not identified as held by a Reportable Person in subparagraph C(4), then further action is not required until there is a change in circumstances that results in one or more indicia being associated with the account.
(b) If any of the indicia listed in subparagraphs B(2)(a) through (e) are discovered in the enhanced review of High Value Accounts described in paragraph C, or if there is a subsequent change in circumstances that results in one or more indicia being associated with the account, then the Reporting Financial Institution must treat the account as a Reportable Account with respect to each Member State for which an indicium is identified unless it elects to apply subparagraph B(6) and one of the exceptions in that subparagraph applies with respect to that account.
(c) If a "hold mail" instruction or "in-care-of" address is discovered in the enhanced review of High Value Accounts described in paragraph C, and no other address and none of the other indicia listed in subparagraphs B(2)(a) through (e) are identified for the Account Holder, the Reporting Financial Institution must obtain from such Account Holder a self-certification or Documentary Evidence to establish the residence(s) for tax purposes of the Account Holder. If the Reporting Financial Institution cannot obtain such self-certification or Documentary Evidence, it must report the account to the competent authority of its Member State as an undocumented account.
6. If a Pre-existing Individual Account is not a High Value Account as of 31 December 2015, but becomes a High Value Account as of the last day of a subsequent calendar year, the Reporting Financial Institution must complete the enhanced review procedures described in paragraph C with respect to such account within the calendar year following the year in which the account becomes a High Value Account. If based on this review such account is identified as a Reportable Account, the Reporting Financial Institution must report the required information about such account with respect to the year in which it is identified as a Reportable Account and subsequent years on an annual basis, unless the Account Holder ceases to be a Reportable Person.
7. Once a Reporting Financial Institution applies the enhanced review procedures described in paragraph C to a High Value Account, the Reporting Financial Institution is not required to reapply such procedures, other than the relationship manager inquiry described in subparagraph C(4), to the same High Value Account in any subsequent year unless the account is undocumented where the Reporting Financial Institution should reapply them annually until such account ceases to be undocumented.
8. If there is a change of circumstances with respect to a High Value Account that results in one or more indicia described in subparagraph B(2) being associated with the account, then the Reporting Financial Institution must treat the account as a Reportable Account with respect to each Member State for which an indicium is identified unless it elects to apply subparagraph B(6) and one of the exceptions in that subparagraph applies with respect to that account.
9. A Reporting Financial Institution must implement procedures to ensure that a relationship manager identifies any change in circumstances of an account. For example, if a relationship manager is notified that the Account Holder has a new mailing address in a Member State, the Reporting Financial Institution is required to treat the new address as a change in circumstances and, if it elects to apply subparagraph B(6), is required to obtain the appropriate documentation from the Account Holder.

D   Review of Pre-existing High Value Individual Accounts must be completed by 31 December 2016. Review of Preexisting Lower Value Individual Accounts must be completed by 31 December 2017.

E   Any Pre-existing Individual Account that has been identified as a Reportable Account under this Section must be treated as a Reportable Account in all subsequent years, unless the Account Holder ceases to be a Reportable Person.

SECTION IV
DUE DILIGENCE FOR NEW INDIVIDUAL ACCOUNTS

The following procedures apply for purposes of identifying Reportable Accounts among New Individual Accounts.

A   With respect to New Individual Accounts, upon account opening, the Reporting Financial Institution must obtain a self-certification, which may be part of the account opening documentation, that allows the Reporting Financial Institution to determine the Account Holder's residence(s) for tax purposes and confirm the reasonableness of such selfcertification based on the information obtained by the Reporting Financial Institution in connection with the opening of the account, including any documentation collected pursuant to AML/KYC Procedures.

B   If the self-certification establishes that the Account Holder is resident for tax purposes in a Member State, the Reporting Financial Institution must treat the account as a Reportable Account and the self-certification must also include the Account Holder's TIN with respect to such Member State (subject to paragraph D of Section I) and date of birth.

C   If there is a change of circumstances with respect to a New Individual Account that causes the Reporting Financial Institution to know, or have reason to know, that the original self-certification is incorrect or unreliable, the Reporting Financial Institution cannot rely on the original self-certification and must obtain a valid self-certification that establishes the residence(s) for tax purposes of the Account Holder.

SECTION V
DUE DILIGENCE FOR PRE-EXISTING ENTITY ACCOUNTS

The following procedures apply for purposes of identifying Reportable Accounts among Pre-existing Entity Accounts.

A   Entity Accounts Not Required to Be Reviewed, Identified or Reported. Unless the Reporting Financial Institution elects otherwise, either with respect to all Pre-existing Entity Accounts or, separately, with respect to any clearly identified group of such accounts, a Pre-existing Entity Account with an aggregate account balance or value that does not exceed, as of 31 December 2015, an amount denominated in the domestic currency of each Member State that corresponds to USD 250 000, is not required to be reviewed, identified, or reported as a Reportable Account until the aggregate account balance or value exceeds that amount as of the last day of any subsequent calendar year.

B   Entity Accounts Subject to Review. A Pre-existing Entity Account that has an aggregate account balance or value that exceeds, as of 31 December 2015, an amount denominated in the domestic currency of each Member State that corresponds to USD 250 000, and a Pre-existing Entity Account that does not exceed, as of 31 December 2015, that amount but the aggregate account balance or value of which exceeds such amount as of the last day of any subsequent calendar year, must be reviewed in accordance with the procedures set forth in paragraph D.

C   Entity Accounts With Respect to Which Reporting Is Required. With respect to Pre-existing Entity Accounts described in paragraph B, only accounts that are held by one or more Entities that are Reportable Persons, or by Passive NFEs with one or more Controlling Persons who are Reportable Persons, shall be treated as Reportable Accounts.

D   Review Procedures for Identifying Entity Accounts With Respect to Which Reporting Is Required. For Pre-existing Entity Accounts described in paragraph B, a Reporting Financial Institution must apply the following review procedures to determine whether the account is held by one or more Reportable Persons, or by Passive NFEs with one or more Controlling Persons who are Reportable Persons:

1. Determine Whether the Entity Is a Reportable Person.

   (a) Review information maintained for regulatory or customer relationship purposes (including information collected pursuant to AML/KYC Procedures) to determine whether the information indicates that the Account Holder is resident in a Member State. For this purpose, information indicating that the Account Holder is resident in a Member State includes a place of incorporation or organisation, or an address in a Member State.

   (b) If the information indicates that the Account Holder is resident in a Member State, the Reporting Financial Institution must treat the account as a Reportable Account unless it obtains a self-certification from the Account Holder, or reasonably determines based on information in its possession or that is publicly available, that the Account Holder is not a Reportable Person.

2. Determine Whether the Entity is a Passive NFE with One or More Controlling Persons who are Reportable Persons. With respect to an Account Holder of a Pre-existing Entity Account (including an Entity that is a Reportable Person), the Reporting Financial Institution must determine whether the Account Holder is a Passive NFE with one or more Controlling Persons who are Reportable Persons. If any of the Controlling Persons of a Passive NFE is a Reportable Person, then the account must be treated as a Reportable Account. In making these determinations the Reporting Financial Institution must follow the guidance in subparagraphs D(2)(a) through (c) in the order most appropriate under the circumstances.

   (a) Determining whether the Account Holder is a Passive NFE. For purposes of determining whether the Account Holder is a Passive NFE, the Reporting Financial Institution must obtain a self-certification from the Account Holder to establish its status, unless it has information in its possession or that is publicly available, based on which it can reasonably determine that the Account Holder is an Active NFE or a Financial Institution other than an Investment Entity described in subparagraph A(6)(b) of Section VIII that is not a Participating Jurisdiction Financial Institution.

(b) Determining the Controlling Persons of an Account Holder. For the purposes of determining the Controlling Persons of an Account Holder, a Reporting Financial Institution may rely on information collected and maintained pursuant to AML/KYC Procedures.

(c) Determining whether a Controlling Person of a Passive NFE is a Reportable Person. For the purposes of determining whether a Controlling Person of a Passive NFE is a Reportable Person, a Reporting Financial Institution may rely on:

(i) information collected and maintained pursuant to AML/KYC Procedures in the case of a Pre-existing Entity Account held by one or more NFEs with an aggregate account balance or value that does not exceed an amount denominated in the domestic currency of each Member State that corresponds to USD 1 000 000; or

(ii) a self-certification from the Account Holder or such Controlling Person of the Member State(s) or other jurisdiction(s) in which the controlling person is resident for tax purposes.

E Timing of Review and Additional Procedures Applicable to Pre-existing Entity Accounts 1. Review of Pre-existing Entity Accounts with an aggregate account balance or value that exceeds, as of 31 December 2015, an amount denominated in the domestic currency of each Member State that corresponds to USD 250 000, must be completed by 31 December 2017.

2. Review of Pre-existing Entity Accounts with an aggregate account balance or value that does not exceed, as of 31 December 2015, an amount denominated in the domestic currency of each Member State that corresponds to USD 250 000 but exceeds that amount as of 31 December of a subsequent year, must be completed within the calendar year following the year in which the aggregate account balance or value exceeds such amount.

3. If there is a change of circumstances with respect to a Pre-existing Entity Account that causes the Reporting Financial Institution to know, or have reason to know, that the self-certification or other documentation associated with an account is incorrect or unreliable, the Reporting Financial Institution must re-determine the status of the account in accordance with the procedures set forth in paragraph D.

SECTION VI
DUE DILIGENCE FOR NEW ENTITY ACCOUNTS

The following procedures apply for purposes of identifying Reportable Accounts among New Entity Accounts.

Review Procedures for Identifying Entity Accounts With Respect to Which Reporting Is Required. For New Entity Accounts, a Reporting Financial Institution must apply the following review procedures to determine whether the account is held by one or more Reportable Persons, or by Passive NFEs with one or more Controlling Persons who are Reportable Persons:

1. Determine Whether the Entity Is a Reportable Person.

(a) Obtain a self-certification, which may be part of the account opening documentation, that allows the Reporting Financial Institution to determine the Account Holder's residence(s) for tax purposes and confirm the reasonableness of such self-certification based on the information obtained by the Reporting Financial Institution in connection with the opening of the account, including any documentation collected pursuant to AML/KYC Procedures. If the Entity certifies that it has no residence for tax purposes, the Reporting Financial Institution may rely on the address of the principal office of the Entity to determine the residence of the Account Holder.

(b) If the self-certification indicates that the Account Holder is resident in a Member State, the Reporting Financial Institution must treat the account as a Reportable Account, unless it reasonably determines based on information in its possession or that is publicly available that the Account Holder is not a Reportable Person with respect to such Member State.

2. Determine Whether the Entity is a Passive NFE with One or More Controlling Persons Who Are Reportable Persons. With respect to an Account Holder of a New Entity Account (including an Entity that is a Reportable Person), the Reporting Financial Institution must determine whether the Account Holder is a Passive NFE with one or more Controlling Persons who are Reportable Persons. If any of the Controlling Persons of a Passive NFE is a Reportable Person, then the account must be treated as a Reportable Account. In making these determinations the Reporting Financial Institution must follow the guidance in subparagraphs A(2)(a) through (c) in the order most appropriate under the circumstances.

a) Determining whether the Account Holder is a Passive NFE. For purposes of determining whether the Account Holder is a Passive NFE, the Reporting Financial Institution must rely on a self-certification from the Account Holder to establish its status, unless it has information in its possession or that is publicly available, based on which it can reasonably determine that the Account Holder is an Active NFE or a Financial Institution other than an Investment Entity described in subparagraph A(6)(b) of Section VIII that is not a Participating Jurisdiction Financial Institution.

(b) Determining the Controlling Persons of an Account Holder. For purposes of determining the Controlling Persons of an Account Holder, a Reporting Financial Institution may rely on information collected and maintained pursuant to AML/KYC Procedures.

(c) Determining whether a Controlling Person of a Passive NFE is a Reportable Person. For purposes of determining whether a controlling person of a Passive NFE is a Reportable Person, a Reporting Financial Institution may rely on a self-certification from the Account Holder or such Controlling Person.

SECTION VII
SPECIAL DUE DILIGENCE RULES

The following additional rules apply in implementing the due diligence procedures described above:

A Reliance on Self-Certifications and Documentary Evidence. A Reporting Financial Institution may not rely on a selfcertification or Documentary Evidence if the Reporting Financial Institution knows or has reason to know that the self-certification or Documentary Evidence is incorrect or unreliable.

B Alternative Procedures for Financial Accounts held by Individual Beneficiaries of a Cash Value Insurance Contract or an Annuity Contract and for a Group Cash Value Insurance Contract or Group Annuity Contract. A Reporting Financial Institution may presume that an individual beneficiary (other than the owner) of a Cash Value Insurance Contract or an Annuity Contract receiving a death benefit is not a Reportable Person and may treat such Financial Account as other than a Reportable Account unless the Reporting Financial Institution has actual knowledge, or reason to know, that the beneficiary is a Reportable Person. A Reporting Financial Institution has reason to know that a beneficiary of a Cash Value Insurance Contract or an Annuity Contract is a Reportable Person if the information collected by the Reporting Financial Institution and associated with the beneficiary contains indicia as described in paragraph B of Section III. If a Reporting Financial Institution has actual knowledge, or reason to know, that the beneficiary is a Reportable Person, the Reporting Financial Institution must follow the procedures in paragraph B of Section III.

A Reporting Financial Institution may treat a Financial Account that is a member's interest in a Group Cash Value Insurance Contract or Group Annuity Contract as a Financial Account that is not a Reportable Account until the date on which an amount is payable to the employee/certificate holder or beneficiary, if the Financial Account that is a member's interest in a Group Cash Value Insurance Contract or Group Annuity Contract meets the following requirements:

(i) the Group Cash Value Insurance Contract or Group Annuity Contract is issued to an employer and covers 25 or more employees/certificate holders;

(ii) the employee/certificate holders are entitled to receive any contract value related to their interests and to name beneficiaries for the benefit payable upon the employee's death; and

(iii) the aggregate amount payable to any employee/certificate holder or beneficiary does not exceed an amount denominated in the domestic currency of each Member State that corresponds to USD 1 000 000.

The term "Group Cash Value Insurance Contract" means a Cash Value Insurance Contract that (i) provides coverage on individuals who are affiliated through an employer, trade association, labour union, or other association or group; and (ii) charges a premium for each member of the group (or member of a class within the group) that is determined without regard to the individual health characteristics other than age, gender, and smoking habits of the member (or class of members) of the group.

The term "Group Annuity Contract" means an Annuity Contract under which the obligees are individuals who are affiliated through an employer, trade association, labour union, or other association or group.

C Account Balance Aggregation and Currency Rules

1. Aggregation of Individual Accounts. For purposes of determining the aggregate balance or value of Financial Accounts held by an individual, a Reporting Financial Institution is required to aggregate all Financial Accounts maintained by the Reporting Financial Institution, or by a Related Entity, but only to the extent that the Reporting Financial Institution's computerised systems link the Financial

Accounts by reference to a data element such as client number or TIN, and allow account balances or values to be aggregated. Each holder of a jointly held Financial Account shall be attributed the entire balance or value of the jointly held Financial Account for purposes of applying the aggregation requirements described in this subparagraph.

2. Aggregation of Entity Accounts. For purposes of determining the aggregate balance or value of Financial Accounts held by an Entity, a Reporting Financial Institution is required to take into account all Financial Accounts that are maintained by the Reporting Financial Institution, or by a Related Entity, but only to the extent that the Reporting Financial Institution's computerised systems link the Financial Accounts by reference to a data element such as client number or TIN, and allow account balances or values to be aggregated. Each holder of a jointly held Financial Account shall be attributed the entire balance or value of the jointly held Financial Account for purposes of applying the aggregation requirements described in this subparagraph.

3. Special Aggregation Rule Applicable to Relationship Managers. For purposes of determining the aggregate balance or value of Financial Accounts held by a person to determine whether a financial account is a High Value Account, a Reporting Financial Institution is also required, in the case of any Financial Accounts that a relationship manager knows, or has reason to know, are directly or indirectly owned, controlled, or established (other than in a fiduciary capacity) by the same person, to aggregate all such accounts.

4. Amounts Read to Include Equivalent in Other Currencies. All amounts denominated in the domestic currency of each Member State shall be read to include equivalent amounts in other currencies, as determined by domestic law.

SECTION VIII
DEFINED TERMS

The following terms have the meanings set forth below:

A Reporting Financial Institution

1. The term "Reporting Financial Institution" means any Member State Financial Institution that is not a NonReporting Financial Institution. The term "Member State Financial Institution" means: (i) any Financial Institution that is resident in a Member State, but excludes any branch of that Financial Institution that is located outside that Member State; and (ii) any branch of a Financial Institution that is not resident in a Member State, if that branch is located in that Member State.

2. The term "Participating Jurisdiction Financial Institution" means (i) any Financial Institution that is resident in a Participating Jurisdiction, but excludes any branch of that Financial Institution that is located outside such Participating Jurisdiction; and (ii) any branch of a Financial Institution that is not resident in a Participating Jurisdiction, if that branch is located in such Participating Jurisdiction.

3. The term "Financial Institution" means a Custodial Institution, a Depository Institution, an Investment Entity, or a Specified Insurance Company.

4. The term "Custodial Institution" means any Entity that holds, as a substantial portion of its business, Financial Assets for the account of others. An Entity holds Financial Assets for the account of others as a substantial portion of its business if the Entity's gross income attributable to the holding of Financial Assets and related financial services equals or exceeds 20 % of the Entity's gross income during the shorter of: (i) the three-year period that ends on 31 December (or the final day of a non-calendar year accounting period) prior to the year in which the determination is being made; or (ii) the period during which the Entity has been in existence.

5. The term "Depository Institution" means any Entity that accepts deposits in the ordinary course of a banking or similar business.

6. The term "Investment Entity" means any Entity:

   (a) which primarily conducts as a business one or more of the following activities or operations for or on behalf of a customer:

       (i) trading in money market instruments (cheques, bills, certificates of deposit, derivatives, etc.); foreign exchange; exchange, interest rate and index instruments; transferable securities; or commodity futures trading;

       (ii) individual and collective portfolio management; or

       (iii) otherwise investing, administering, or managing Financial Assets or money on behalf of other persons;

   or

   (b) the gross income of which is primarily attributable to investing, reinvesting, or trading in Financial Assets, if the Entity is managed by another Entity that is a Depository Institution, a Custodial Institution, a Specified Insurance Company, or an Investment Entity described in subparagraph A(6)(a).

An Entity is treated as primarily conducting as a business one or more of the activities described in subparagraph A(6)(a), or an Entity's gross income is primarily attributable to investing, reinvesting, or trading in Financial Assets for the purposes of subparagraph A(6)(b), if the Entity's gross income attributable to the relevant activities equals or exceeds 50 % of the Entity's gross income during the shorter of: (i) the three-year period ending on 31 December of the year preceding the year in which the determination is made; or (ii) the period during which the Entity has been in existence. The term "Investment Entity" does not include an Entity that is an Active NFE because that Entity meets any of the criteria in subparagraphs D(8)(d) through (g).

This paragraph shall be interpreted in a manner consistent with similar language set forth in the definition of "financial institution" in the Financial Action Task Force Recommendations.

7. The term "Financial Asset" includes a security (for example, a share of stock in a corporation; partnership or beneficial ownership interest in a widely held or publicly traded partnership or trust; note, bond, debenture, or other evidence of indebtedness), partnership interest, commodity, swap (for example, interest rate swaps, currency swaps, basis swaps, interest rate caps, interest rate floors, commodity swaps, equity swaps, equity index swaps, and similar agreements), Insurance Contract or Annuity Contract, or any interest (including a futures or forward contract or option) in a security, partnership interest, commodity, swap, Insurance Contract, or Annuity Contract. The term "Financial Asset" does not include a non-debt, direct interest in real property.

8. The term "Specified Insurance Company" means any Entity that is an insurance company (or the holding company of an insurance company) which issues, or is obligated to make payments with respect to, a Cash Value Insurance Contract or an Annuity Contract.

B Non-Reporting Financial Institution

1. The term "Non-Reporting Financial Institution" means any Financial Institution which is:

(a) a Governmental Entity, International Organisation or Central Bank, other than with respect to a payment that is derived from an obligation held in connection with a commercial financial activity of a type engaged in by a Specified Insurance Company, Custodial Institution, or Depository Institution;

(b) a Broad Participation Retirement Fund; a Narrow Participation Retirement Fund; a Pension Fund of a Governmental Entity, International Organisation or Central Bank; or a Qualified Credit Card Issuer;

(c) any other Entity that presents a low risk of being used to evade tax, has substantially similar characteristics to any of the Entities described in subparagraphs B(1)(a) and (b), and is included in the list of Non-Reporting Financial Institutions referred to in Article 8(7a) of this Directive, provided that the status of such Entity as a Non-Reporting Financial Institution does not frustrate the purposes of this Directive;

(d) an Exempt Collective Investment Vehicle; or

(e) a trust to the extent that the trustee of the trust is a Reporting Financial Institution and reports all information required to be reported pursuant to Section I with respect to all Reportable Accounts of the trust.

2. The term "Governmental Entity" means the government of a Member State or other jurisdiction, any political subdivision of a Member State or other jurisdiction (which, for the avoidance of doubt, includes a state, province, county, or municipality), or any wholly owned agency or instrumentality of a Member State or other jurisdiction or of any one or more of the foregoing (each, a "Governmental Entity"). This category is comprised of the integral parts, controlled entities, and political subdivisions of a Member State or other jurisdiction.

(a) An "integral part" of a Member State or other jurisdiction means any person, organisation, agency, bureau, fund, instrumentality, or other body, however designated, that constitutes a governing authority of a Member State or other jurisdiction. The net earnings of the governing authority must be credited to its own account or to other accounts of the Member State or other jurisdiction, with no portion inuring to the benefit of any private person. An integral part does not include any individual who is a sovereign, official, or administrator acting in a private or personal capacity.

(b) A "controlled entity" means an Entity which is separate in form from the Member State or other jurisdiction or which otherwise constitutes a separate juridical entity, provided that:

(i) the Entity is wholly owned and controlled by one or more Governmental Entities directly or through one or more controlled entities;

(ii) the Entity's net earnings are credited to its own account or to the accounts of one or more Governmental Entities, with no portion of its income inuring to the benefit of any private person; and

(iii) the Entity's assets vest in one or more Governmental Entities upon dissolution.

(c) Income does not inure to the benefit of private persons if such persons are the intended beneficiaries of a governmental programme, and the programme activities are performed for the general public with respect to the common welfare or relate to the administration of some phase of government. Notwithstanding the foregoing, however, income is considered to inure to the benefit of private persons if the income is derived from the use of a Governmental Entity to conduct a commercial business, such as a commercial banking business, that provides financial services to private persons.

3. The term "International Organisation" means any international organisation or wholly owned agency or instrumentality thereof. This category includes any intergovernmental organisation (including a supranational organisation) (i) that is comprised primarily of governments; (ii) that has in effect a headquarters or substantially similar agreement with the Member State; and (iii) the income of which does not inure to the benefit of private persons.

4. The term "Central Bank" means an institution that is by law or government sanction the principal authority, other than the government of the Member State itself, issuing instruments intended to circulate as currency. Such an institution may include an instrumentality that is separate from the government of the Member State, whether or not owned in whole or in part by the Member State.

5. The term "Broad Participation Retirement Fund" means a fund established to provide retirement, disability, or death benefits, or any combination thereof, to beneficiaries who are current or former employees (or persons designated by such employees) of one or more employers in consideration for services rendered, provided that the fund:

(a) does not have a single beneficiary with a right to more than 5 % of the fund's assets;

(b) is subject to government regulation and provides information reporting to the tax authorities; and

(c) satisfies at least one of the following requirements:

(i) the fund is generally exempt from tax on investment income, or taxation of such income is deferred or taxed at a reduced rate, due to its status as a retirement or pension plan;

(ii) the fund receives at least 50 % of its total contributions (other than transfers of assets from other plans described in subparagraphs B(5) through (7) or from retirement and pension accounts described in subparagraph C(17)(a)) from the sponsoring employers;

(iii) distributions or withdrawals from the fund are allowed only upon the occurrence of specified events related to retirement, disability, or death (except rollover distributions to other retirement funds described in subparagraphs B(5) through (7) or retirement and pension accounts described in subparagraph C(17)(a)), or penalties apply to distributions or withdrawals made before such specified events; or

(iv) contributions (other than certain permitted make-up contributions) by employees to the fund are limited by reference to earned income of the employee or may not exceed, annually, an amount denominated in the domestic currency of each Member State that corresponds to USD 50 000, applying the rules set forth in paragraph C of Section VII for account aggregation and currency translation.

6. The term "Narrow Participation Retirement Fund" means a fund established to provide retirement, disability, or death benefits to beneficiaries who are current or former employees (or persons designated by such employees) of one or more employers in consideration for services rendered, provided that:

(a) the fund has fewer than 50 participants;

(b) the fund is sponsored by one or more employers that are not Investment Entities or Passive NFEs;

(c) the employee and employer contributions to the fund (other than transfers of assets from retirement and pension accounts described in subparagraph C(17)(a)) are limited by reference to earned income and compensation of the employee, respectively;

(d) participants that are not residents of the Member State in which the fund is established are not entitled to more than 20 % of the fund's assets; and

(e) the fund is subject to government regulation and provides information reporting to the tax authorities.

7. The term "Pension Fund of a Governmental Entity, International Organisation or Central Bank" means a fund established by a Governmental Entity, International Organisation or Central Bank to provide retirement, disability, or death benefits to beneficiaries or participants who are current or former employees (or persons designated by such employees), or who are not current or former employees, if the benefits provided to such beneficiaries or participants are in consideration of personal services performed for the Governmental Entity, International Organisation or Central Bank.

8. The term "Qualified Credit Card Issuer" means a Financial Institution satisfying the following requirements:

(a) the Financial Institution is a Financial Institution solely because it is an issuer of credit cards that accepts deposits only when a customer makes a payment in excess of a balance due with respect to the card and the overpayment is not immediately returned to the customer; and

(b) beginning on or before 1 January 2016, the Financial Institution implements policies and procedures either to prevent a customer from making an overpayment in excess of an amount denominated in the domestic currency of each Member State that corresponds to USD 50 000, or to ensure that any customer overpayment in excess of that amount is refunded to the customer within 60 days, in each case applying the rules set forth in paragraph C of Section VII for account aggregation and currency translation. For this purpose, a customer overpayment does not refer to credit balances to the extent of disputed charges but does include credit balances resulting from merchandise returns.

9. The term "Exempt Collective Investment Vehicle" means an Investment Entity that is regulated as a collective investment vehicle, provided that all of the interests in the collective investment vehicle are held by or through individuals or Entities that are not Reportable Persons, except a Passive NFE with Controlling Persons who are Reportable Persons.

An Investment Entity that is regulated as a collective investment vehicle does not fail to qualify under subparagraph B(9) as an Exempt Collective Investment Vehicle, solely because the collective investment vehicle has issued physical shares in bearer form, provided that:

(a) the collective investment vehicle has not issued, and does not issue, any physical shares in bearer form after 31 December 2015;

(b) the collective investment vehicle retires all such shares upon surrender;

(c) the collective investment vehicle performs the due diligence procedures set forth in Sections II through VII and reports any information required to be reported with respect to any such shares when such shares are presented for redemption or other payment; and

(d) the collective investment vehicle has in place policies and procedures to ensure that such shares are redeemed or immobilised as soon as possible, and in any event prior to 1 January 2018.

C Financial Account

1. The term "Financial Account" means an account maintained by a Financial Institution, and includes a Depository Account, a Custodial Account and:

(a) in the case of an Investment Entity, any equity or debt interest in the Financial Institution. Notwithstanding the foregoing, the term "Financial Account" does not include any equity or debt interest in an Entity that is an Investment Entity solely because it (i) renders investment advice to, and acts on behalf of; or (ii) manages portfolios for, and acts on behalf of, a customer for the purpose of investing, managing, or administering Financial Assets deposited in the name of the customer with a Financial Institution other than such Entity;

(b) in the case of a Financial Institution not described in subparagraph C(1)(a), any equity or debt interest in the Financial Institution, if the class of interests was established with the purpose of avoiding reporting in accordance with Section I; and

(c) any Cash Value Insurance Contract and any Annuity Contract issued or maintained by a Financial Institution, other than a non-investment-linked, non-transferable immediate life annuity that is issued to an individual and monetises a pension or disability benefit provided under an account that is an Excluded Account.

The term "Financial Account" does not include any account that is an Excluded Account.

2. The term "Depository Account" includes any commercial, checking, savings, time, or thrift account, or an account that is evidenced by a certificate of deposit, thrift certificate, investment certificate, certificate of indebtedness, or other similar instrument maintained by a Financial Institution in the ordinary course of a banking or similar business. A Depository Account also includes an amount held by an insurance company pursuant to a guaranteed investment contract or similar agreement to pay or credit interest thereon.

3. The term "Custodial Account" means an account (other than an Insurance Contract or Annuity Contract) which holds one or more Financial Assets for the benefit of another person.

4. The term "Equity Interest" means, in the case of a partnership that is a Financial Institution, either a capital or profits interest in the partnership. In the case of a trust that is a Financial Institution, an Equity Interest is considered to be held by any person treated as a settlor or beneficiary of all or a portion of the trust, or any other natural person exercising ultimate effective control over the trust. A Reportable Person will be treated as being a beneficiary of a trust if such Reportable Person has the right to receive directly or indirectly (for example, through a nominee) a mandatory distribution or may receive, directly or indirectly, a discretionary distribution from the trust.

5. The term "Insurance Contract" means a contract (other than an Annuity Contract) under which the issuer agrees to pay an amount upon the occurrence of a specified contingency involving mortality, morbidity, accident, liability, or property risk.

6. The term "Annuity Contract" means a contract under which the issuer agrees to make payments for a period of time determined in whole or in part by reference to the life expectancy of one or more individuals. The term also includes a contract that is considered to be an Annuity Contract in accordance with the law, regulation, or practice of the Member State or other jurisdiction in which the contract was issued, and under which the issuer agrees to make payments for a term of years.

7. The term "Cash Value Insurance Contract" means an Insurance Contract (other than an indemnity reinsurance contract between two insurance companies) that has a Cash Value.

8. The term "Cash Value" means the greater of (i) the amount that the policyholder is entitled to receive upon surrender or termination of the contract (determined without reduction for any surrender charge or policy loan); and (ii) the amount the policyholder can borrow under or with regard to the contract. Notwithstanding the foregoing, the term "Cash Value" does not include an amount payable under an Insurance Contract:

 (a) solely by reason of the death of an individual insured under a life insurance contract;

 (b) as a personal injury or sickness benefit or other benefit providing indemnification of an economic loss incurred upon the occurrence of the event insured against;

 (c) as a refund of a previously paid premium (less cost of insurance charges whether or not actually imposed) under an Insurance Contract (other than an investment-linked life insurance or annuity contract) due to cancellation or termination of the contract, decrease in risk exposure during the effective period of the contract, or arising from the correction of a posting or similar error with regard to the premium for the contract;

 (d) as a policyholder dividend (other than a termination dividend) provided that the dividend relates to an Insurance Contract under which the only benefits payable are described in subparagraph C(8)(b); or

 (e) as a return of an advance premium or premium deposit for an Insurance Contract for which the premium is payable at least annually if the amount of the advance premium or premium deposit does not exceed the next annual premium that will be payable under the contract.

9. The term "Pre-existing Account" means:

 (a) a Financial Account maintained by a Reporting Financial Institution as of 31 December 2015;

 (b) any Financial Account of an Account Holder, regardless of the date such Financial Account was opened, if:

  (i) the Account Holder also holds with the Reporting Financial Institution (or with a Related Entity within the same Member State as the Reporting Financial Institution) a Financial Account that is a Pre-existing Account under subparagraph C(9)(a);

  (ii) the Reporting Financial Institution (and, as applicable, the Related Entity within the same Member State as the Reporting Financial Institution) treats both of the aforementioned Financial Accounts, and any other Financial Accounts of the Account Holder that are treated as Pre-existing Accounts under point (b), as a single Financial Account for purposes of satisfying the standards of knowledge requirements set forth in paragraph A of Section VII, and for purposes of determining the balance or value of any of the Financial Accounts when applying any of the account thresholds;

  (iii) with respect to a Financial Account that is subject to AML/KYC Procedures, the Reporting Financial Institution is permitted to satisfy such AML/KYC Procedures for the Financial Account by relying upon the AML/KYC Procedures performed for the Pre-existing Account described in subparagraph C(9)(a); and

  (iv) the opening of the Financial Account does not require the provision of new, additional or amended customer information by the Account Holder other than for the purposes of this Directive.

10. The term "New Account" means a Financial Account maintained by a Reporting Financial Institution opened on or after 1 January 2016 unless it is treated as a Pre-existing Account under subparagraph C(9)(b).

11. The term "Pre-existing Individual Account" means a Pre-existing Account held by one or more individuals.

12. The term "New Individual Account" means a New Account held by one or more individuals.

13. The term "Pre-existing Entity Account" means a Pre-existing Account held by one or more Entities.

14. The term "Lower Value Account" means a Pre-existing Individual Account with an aggregate balance or value as of 31 December 2015 that does not exceed an amount denominated in the domestic currency of each Member State that corresponds to USD 1 000 000.

15. The term "High Value Account" means a Pre-existing Individual Account with an aggregate balance or value that exceeds, as of 31 December 2015, or 31 December of any subsequent year, an amount denominated in the domestic currency of each Member State that corresponds to USD 1 000 000.

16. The term "New Entity Account" means a New Account held by one or more Entities.

17. The term "Excluded Account" means any of the following accounts:

   (a) a retirement or pension account that satisfies the following requirements:

      (i) the account is subject to regulation as a personal retirement account or is part of a registered or regulated retirement or pension plan for the provision of retirement or pension benefits (including disability or death benefits);

      (ii) the account is tax-favoured (i.e., contributions to the account that would otherwise be subject to tax are deductible or excluded from the gross income of the Account Holder or taxed at a reduced rate, or taxation of investment income from the account is deferred or taxed at a reduced rate);

      (iii) information reporting is required to the tax authorities with respect to the account;

      (iv) withdrawals are conditioned on reaching a specified retirement age, disability, or death, or penalties apply to withdrawals made before such specified events; and

      (v) either (i) annual contributions are limited to an amount denominated in the domestic currency of each Member State that corresponds to USD 50 000 or less; or (ii) there is a maximum lifetime contribution limit to the account of an amount denominated in the domestic currency of each Member State that corresponds to USD 1 000 000 or less, in each case applying the rules set forth in paragraph C of Section VII for account aggregation and currency translation.

      A Financial Account that otherwise satisfies the requirement of subparagraph C(17)(a)(v) will not fail to satisfy such requirement solely because such Financial Account may receive assets or funds transferred from one or more Financial Accounts that meet the requirements of subparagraph C(17)(a) or (b) or from one or more retirement or pension funds that meet the requirements of any of subparagraphs B(5) through (7);

   (b) an account that satisfies the following requirements:

      (i) the account is subject to regulation as an investment vehicle for purposes other than for retirement and is regularly traded on an established securities market, or the account is subject to regulation as a savings vehicle for purposes other than for retirement;

      (ii) the account is tax-favoured (i.e., contributions to the account that would otherwise be subject to tax are deductible or excluded from the gross income of the Account Holder or taxed at a reduced rate, or taxation of investment income from the account is deferred or taxed at a reduced rate);

      (iii) withdrawals are conditioned on meeting specific criteria related to the purpose of the investment or savings account (for example, the provision of educational or medical benefits), or penalties apply to withdrawals made before such criteria are met; and

      (iv) annual contributions are limited to an amount denominated in the domestic currency of each Member State that corresponds to USD 50 000 or less, applying the rules set forth in paragraph C of Section VII for account aggregation and currency translation.

      A Financial Account that otherwise satisfies the requirement of subparagraph C(17)(b)(iv) will not fail to satisfy such requirement solely because such Financial Account may receive assets or funds transferred from one or more Financial Accounts that meet the requirements of subparagraph C(17)(a) or (b) or from one or more retirement or pension funds that meet the requirements of any of subparagraphs B(5) through (7);

   (c) a life insurance contract with a coverage period that will end before the insured individual attains age 90, provided that the contract satisfies the following requirements:

      (i) periodic premiums, which do not decrease over time, are payable at least annually during the period the contract is in existence or until the insured attains age 90, whichever is shorter;

(ii) the contract has no contract value that any person can access (by withdrawal, loan, or otherwise) without terminating the contract;

(iii) the amount (other than a death benefit) payable upon cancellation or termination of the contract cannot exceed the aggregate premiums paid for the contract, less the sum of mortality, morbidity, and expense charges (whether or not actually imposed) for the period or periods of the contract's existence and any amounts paid prior to the cancellation or termination of the contract; and

(iv) the contract is not held by a transferee for value;

(d) an account that is held solely by an estate if the documentation for such account includes a copy of the deceased's will or death certificate;

(e) an account established in connection with any of the following:

(i) a court order or judgment.

(ii) a sale, exchange, or lease of real or personal property, provided that the account satisfies the following requirements:

— the account is funded solely with a down payment, earnest money, deposit in an amount appropriate to secure an obligation directly related to the transaction, or a similar payment, or is funded with a Financial Asset that is deposited in the account in connection with the sale, exchange, or lease of the property,

— the account is established and used solely to secure the obligation of the purchaser to pay the purchase price for the property, the seller to pay any contingent liability, or the lessor or lessee to pay for any damages relating to the leased property as agreed under the lease,

— the assets of the account, including the income earned thereon, will be paid or otherwise distributed for the benefit of the purchaser, seller, lessor, or lessee (including to satisfy such person's obligation) when the property is sold, exchanged, or surrendered, or the lease terminates,

— the account is not a margin or similar account established in connection with a sale or exchange of a Financial Asset, and

— the account is not associated with an account described in subparagraph C(17)(f);

(iii) an obligation of a Financial Institution servicing a loan secured by real property to set aside a portion of a payment solely to facilitate the payment of taxes or insurance related to the real property at a later time;

(iv) an obligation of a Financial Institution solely to facilitate the payment of taxes at a later time;

(f) a Depository Account that satisfies the following requirements:

(i) the account exists solely because a customer makes a payment in excess of a balance due with respect to a credit card or other revolving credit facility and the overpayment is not immediately returned to the customer; and

(ii) beginning on or before 1 January 2016, the Financial Institution implements policies and procedures either to prevent a customer from making an overpayment in excess of an amount denominated in the domestic currency of each Member State that corresponds to USD 50 000, or to ensure that any customer overpayment in excess of that amount is refunded to the customer within 60 days, in each case applying the rules set forth in paragraph C of Section VII for currency translation. For this purpose, a customer overpayment does not refer to credit balances to the extent of disputed charges but does include credit balances resulting from merchandise returns;

(g) any other account that presents a low risk of being used to evade tax, has substantially similar characteristics to any of the accounts described in subparagraphs C(17)(a) through (f), and is included in the list of Excluded Accounts referred to in Article 8(7a) of this Directive, provided that the status of such account as an Excluded Account does not frustrate the purposes of this Directive.

D Reportable Account

1. The term "Reportable Account" means a Financial Account that is maintained by a Member State Reporting Financial Institution and is held by one or more Reportable Persons or by a Passive NFE with one or more Controlling Persons that is a Reportable Person, provided it has been identified as such pursuant to the due diligence procedures described in Sections II through VII.

2. The term "Reportable Person" means a Member State Person other than: (i) a corporation the stock of which is regularly traded on one or more established securities markets; (ii) any corporation that is a Related Entity of a corporation described in clause (i); (iii) a Governmental Entity; (iv) an International Organisation; (v) a Central Bank; or (vi) a Financial Institution.

3. The term "Member State Person" with regard to each Member State means an individual or Entity that is resident in any other Member State under the tax laws of that other Member State, or an estate of a decedent that was a resident of any other Member State. For this purpose, an Entity such as a partnership, limited liability partnership or similar legal arrangement, which has no residence for tax purposes shall be treated as resident in the jurisdiction in which its place of effective management is situated.

4. The term "Participating Jurisdiction" with regard to each Member State means:

    (a) any other Member State;

    (b) any other jurisdiction (i) with which the Member State concerned has an agreement in place pursuant to which that jurisdiction will provide the information specified in Section I; and (ii) which is identified in a list published by that Member State and notified to the European Commission;

    (c) any other jurisdiction (i) with which the Union has an agreement in place pursuant to which that jurisdiction will provide the information specified in Section I; and (ii) which is identified in a list published by the European Commission.

5. The term "Controlling Persons" means the natural persons who exercise control over an Entity. In the case of a trust, that term means the settlor(s), the trustee(s), the protector(s) (if any), the beneficiary(ies) or class(es) of beneficiaries, and any other natural person(s) exercising ultimate effective control over the trust, and in the case of a legal arrangement other than a trust, such term means persons in equivalent or similar positions. The term "Controlling Persons" must be interpreted in a manner consistent with the Financial Action Task Force Recommendations.

6. The term "NFE" means any Entity that is not a Financial Institution.

7. The term "Passive NFE" means any: (i) NFE that is not an Active NFE; or (ii) an Investment Entity described in subparagraph A(6)(b) that is not a Participating Jurisdiction Financial Institution.

8. The term "Active NFE" means any NFE that meets any of the following criteria:

    (a) less than 50 % of the NFE's gross income for the preceding calendar year or other appropriate reporting period is passive income and less than 50 % of the assets held by the NFE during the preceding calendar year or other appropriate reporting period are assets that produce or are held for the production of passive income;

    (b) the stock of the NFE is regularly traded on an established securities market or the NFE is a Related Entity of an Entity the stock of which is regularly traded on an established securities market;

    (c) the NFE is a Governmental Entity, an International Organisation, a Central Bank, or an Entity wholly owned by one or more of the foregoing;

    (d) substantially all of the activities of the NFE consist of holding (in whole or in part) the outstanding stock of, or providing financing and services to, one or more subsidiaries that engage in trades or businesses other than the business of a Financial Institution, except that an Entity does not qualify for this status if the Entity functions (or holds itself out) as an investment fund, such as a private equity fund, venture capital fund, leveraged buyout fund, or any investment vehicle whose purpose is to acquire or fund companies and then hold interests in those companies as capital assets for investment purposes;

    (e) the NFE is not yet operating a business and has no prior operating history, but is investing capital into assets with the intent to operate a business other than that of a Financial Institution, provided that the NFE does not qualify for this exception after the date that is 24 months after the date of the initial organisation of the NFE;

    (f) the NFE was not a Financial Institution in the past five years, and is in the process of liquidating its assets or is reorganising with the intent to continue or recommence operations in a business other than that of a Financial Institution;

    (g) the NFE primarily engages in financing and hedging transactions with, or for, Related Entities that are not Financial Institutions, and does not provide financing or hedging services to any Entity that is not a Related Entity, provided that the group of any such Related Entities is primarily engaged in a business other than that of a Financial Institution; or

    (h) the NFE meets all of the following requirements:

        (i) it is established and operated in its Member State or other jurisdiction of residence exclusively for religious, charitable, scientific, artistic, cultural, athletic, or educational purposes; or it is established and operated in its Member State or other jurisdiction of residence and it is a professional organisation, business league, chamber of commerce, labour organisation, agricultural or horticultural organisation, civic league or an organisation operated exclusively for the promotion of social welfare;

(ii) it is exempt from income tax in its Member State or other jurisdiction of residence;

(iii) it has no shareholders or members who have a proprietary or beneficial interest in its income or assets;

(iv) the applicable laws of the NFE's Member State or other jurisdiction of residence or the NFE's formation documents do not permit any income or assets of the NFE to be distributed to, or applied for the benefit of, a private person or non-charitable Entity other than pursuant to the conduct of the NFE's charitable activities, or as payment of reasonable compensation for services rendered, or as payment representing the fair market value of property which the NFE has purchased; and

(v) the applicable laws of the NFE's Member State or other jurisdiction of residence or the NFE's formation documents require that, upon the NFE's liquidation or dissolution, all of its assets be distributed to a Governmental Entity or other non-profit organisation, or escheat to the government of the NFE's Member State or other jurisdiction of residence or any political subdivision thereof.

E Miscellaneous

1. The term "Account Holder" means the person listed or identified as the holder of a Financial Account by the Financial Institution that maintains the account. A person, other than a Financial Institution, holding a Financial Account for the benefit or account of another person as agent, custodian, nominee, signatory, investment advisor, or intermediary, is not treated as holding the account for purposes of this Directive, and such other person is treated as holding the account. In the case of a Cash Value Insurance Contract or an Annuity Contract, the Account Holder is any person entitled to access the Cash Value or change the beneficiary of the contract. If no person can access the Cash Value or change the beneficiary, the Account Holder is any person named as the owner in the contract and any person with a vested entitlement to payment under the terms of the contract. Upon the maturity of a Cash Value Insurance Contract or an Annuity Contract, each person entitled to receive a payment under the contract is treated as an Account Holder.

2. The term "AML/KYC Procedures" means the customer due diligence procedures of a Reporting Financial Institution pursuant to the anti-money laundering or similar requirements to which such Reporting Financial Institution is subject.

3. The term "Entity" means a legal person or a legal arrangement, such as a corporation, partnership, trust, or foundation.

4. An Entity is a "Related Entity" of another Entity if (i) either Entity controls the other Entity; (ii) the two Entities are under common control; or (iii) the two Entities are Investment Entities described in subparagraph A(6)(b), are under common management, and such management fulfils the due diligence obligations of such Investment Entities. For this purpose control includes direct or indirect ownership of more than 50 % of the vote and value in an Entity.

5. The term "TIN" means Taxpayer Identification Number (or functional equivalent in the absence of a Taxpayer Identification Number).

6. The term "Documentary Evidence" includes any of the following:

(a) a certificate of residence issued by an authorised government body (for example, a government or agency thereof, or a municipality) of the Member State or other jurisdiction in which the payee claims to be a resident;

(b) with respect to an individual, any valid identification issued by an authorised government body (for example, a government or agency thereof, or a municipality), that includes the individual's name and is typically used for identification purposes;

(c) with respect to an Entity, any official documentation issued by an authorised government body (for example, a government or agency thereof, or a municipality) that includes the name of the Entity and either the address of its principal office in the Member State or other jurisdiction in which it claims to be a resident or the Member State or other jurisdiction in which the Entity was incorporated or organised;

(d) any audited financial statement, third-party credit report, bankruptcy filing, or securities regulator's report.

With respect to a Pre-existing Entity Account, Reporting Financial Institutions may use as Documentary Evidence any classification in the Reporting Financial Institution's records with respect to the Account Holder that was determined based on a standardised industry coding system, that was recorded by the Reporting Financial Institution consistent with its normal business practices for purposes of AML/KYC Procedures or another regulatory purposes (other than for tax purposes) and that was implemented by the Reporting Financial Institution prior to the date used to classify the Financial Account as a Pre-existing Account, provided that the Reporting Financial Institution does not know or does not have reason to know that such classification is incorrect or unreliable. The term "standardised industry coding system" means a coding system used to classify establishments by business type for purposes other than tax purposes.

SECTION IX
EFFECTIVE IMPLEMENTATION

Pursuant to Article 8(3a) of this Directive, Member States must have rules and administrative procedures in place to ensure effective implementation of, and compliance with, the reporting and due diligence procedures set out above including:
(1) rules to prevent any Financial Institutions, persons or intermediaries from adopting practices intended to circumvent the reporting and due diligence procedures;
(2) rules requiring Reporting Financial Institutions to keep records of the steps undertaken and any evidence relied upon for the performance of the above procedures and adequate measures to obtain those records;
(3) administrative procedures to verify Reporting Financial Institutions' compliance with the reporting and due diligence procedures; administrative procedures to follow up with a Reporting Financial Institution when undocumented accounts are reported;
(4) administrative procedures to ensure that the Entities and accounts defined in domestic law as Non-Reporting Financial Institutions and Excluded Accounts continue to have a low risk of being used to evade tax; and
(5) effective enforcement provisions to address non-compliance.

SECTION X
IMPLEMENTATION DATES AS REGARDS REPORTING FINANCIAL INSTITUTIONS LOCATED IN AUSTRIA

In the case of Reporting Financial Institutions located in Austria, all references to "2016" and "2017" in this Annex should be read as references to "2017" and "2018" respectively.

In the case of Pre-existing Accounts held by Reporting Financial Institutions located in Austria, all references to "31 December 2015" in this Annex should be read as references to "31 December 2016".][1]

Amendments—[1] Annex I inserted by Council Directive 2014/107/EU Art 1(6), Annex, with effect from 5 January 2015. See Art 2 for implementation provisions (deadline for implementation is 31 December 2015, with measures to apply from 1 January 2016) (OJ L 359, 16.12.2014, p 1).

[ANNEX II
COMPLEMENTARY REPORTING AND DUE DILIGENCE RULES FOR FINANCIAL ACCOUNT INFORMATION

1 Change in circumstances

A "change in circumstances" includes any change that results in the addition of information relevant to a person's status or otherwise conflicts with such person's status. In addition, a change in circumstances includes any change or addition of information to the Account Holder's account (including the addition, substitution, or other change of an Account Holder) or any change or addition of information to any account associated with such account (applying the account aggregation rules described in subparagraphs C(1) through (3) of Section VII of Annex I) if such change or addition of information affects the status of the Account Holder.

If a Reporting Financial Institution has relied on the residence address test described in subparagraph B(1) of Section III of Annex I and there is a change in circumstances that causes the Reporting Financial Institution to know or have reason to know that the original Documentary Evidence (or other equivalent documentation) is incorrect or unreliable, the Reporting Financial Institution must, by the later of the last day of the relevant calendar year or other appropriate reporting period, or 90 calendar days following the notice or discovery of such change in circumstances, obtain a self-certification and new Documentary Evidence to establish the residence(s) for tax purposes of the Account Holder. If the Reporting Financial Institution cannot obtain the self-certification and new Documentary Evidence by such date, the Reporting Financial Institution must apply the electronic record search procedure described in subparagraphs B(2) through (6) of Section III of Annex I.

2 Self-certification for New Entity Accounts

With respect to New Entity Accounts, for the purposes of determining whether a Controlling Person of a Passive NFE is a Reportable Person, a Reporting Financial Institution may only rely on a self-certification from either the Account Holder or the Controlling Person.

3 Residence of a Financial Institution

A Financial Institution is "resident" in a Member State if it is subject to the jurisdiction of such Member State (i.e., the Member State is able to enforce reporting by the Financial Institution). In general, where a Financial Institution is resident for tax purposes in a Member State, it is subject to the jurisdiction of such Member State and it is, thus, a Member State Financial Institution. In the case of a trust that is a Financial Institution (irrespective of whether it is resident for tax purposes in a Member State), the trust is considered to be subject to the jurisdiction of a Member State if one or more of its trustees are resident in such Member State except if the trust reports all the information required to be reported pursuant to this Directive with respect to Reportable Accounts maintained by the trust to another Member State because it is resident for tax purposes in such other Member State. However, where a Financial Institution (other than a trust) does not have a residence for tax purposes (e.g., because it is treated as fiscally transparent, or it is located in a jurisdiction that does not have an income tax), it is considered to be subject to the jurisdiction of a Member State and it is, thus, a Member State Financial Institution if:

    (a) it is incorporated under the laws of the Member State;
    (b) it has its place of management (including effective management) in the Member State; or
    (c) it is subject to financial supervision in the Member State.

Where a Financial Institution (other than a trust) is resident in two or more Member States, such Financial Institution will be subject to the reporting and due diligence obligations of the Member State in which it maintains the Financial Account(s).

4 Account maintained

In general, an account would be considered to be maintained by a Financial Institution as follows:

    (a) in the case of a Custodial Account, by the Financial Institution that holds custody over the assets in the account (including a Financial Institution that holds assets in street name for an Account Holder in such institution);

    (b) in the case of a Depository Account, by the Financial Institution that is obligated to make payments with respect to the account (excluding an agent of a Financial Institution regardless of whether such agent is a Financial Institution);

    (c) in the case of any equity or debt interest in a Financial Institution that constitutes a Financial Account, by such Financial Institution;

    (d) in the case of a Cash Value Insurance Contract or an Annuity Contract, by the Financial Institution that is obligated to make payments with respect to the contract.

5 Trusts that are Passive NFEs

An Entity such as a partnership, limited liability partnership or similar legal arrangement that has no residence for tax purposes, according to subparagraph D(3) of Section VIII of Annex I, shall be treated as resident in the jurisdiction in which its place of effective management is situated. For these purposes, a legal person or a legal arrangement is considered "similar" to a partnership and a limited liability partnership where it is not treated as a taxable unit in a Member State under the tax laws of such Member State. However, in order to avoid duplicate reporting (given the wide scope of the term "Controlling Persons" in the case of trusts), a trust that is a Passive NFE may not be considered a similar legal arrangement.

6 Address of Entity's principal office

One of the requirements described in subparagraph E(6)(c) of Section VIII of Annex I is that, with respect to an Entity, the official documentation includes either the address of the Entity's principal office in the Member State or other jurisdiction in which it claims to be a resident or the Member State or other jurisdiction in which the Entity was incorporated or organised. The address of the Entity's principal office is generally the place in which its place of effective management is situated. The address of a Financial Institution with which the Entity maintains an account, a post office box, or an address used solely for mailing purposes is not the address of the Entity's principal office unless such address is the only address used by the Entity and appears as the Entity's registered address in the Entity's organisational documents. Further, an address that is provided subject to instructions to hold all mail to that address is not the address of the Entity's principal office.][1]

Amendments—[1]   Annex II I inserted by Council Directive 2014/107/EU Art 1(6), Annex, with effect from 5 January 2015. See Art 2 for implementation provisions (deadline for implementation is 31 December 2015, with measures to apply from 1 January 2016) (OJ L 359, 16.12.2014, p 1).

[ANNEX III

FILING RULES FOR GROUPS OF MULTINATIONAL ENTERPRISES

SECTION I
DEFINED TERMS

1. The term "Group" means a collection of enterprises related through ownership or control such that it is either required to prepare Consolidated Financial Statements for financial reporting purposes under applicable accounting principles or would be so required if equity interests in any of the enterprises were traded on a public securities exchange.

2. The term "Enterprise" means any form of conducting business by any person referred to in points (b), (c) and (d) of Article 3, point 11.

3. The term "MNE Group" means any Group that includes two or more enterprises the tax residence for which is in different jurisdictions, or includes an enterprise that is resident for tax purposes in one jurisdiction and is subject to tax with respect to the business carried out through a permanent establishment in another jurisdiction, and is not an Excluded MNE Group.

4. The term "Excluded MNE Group" means, with respect to any Fiscal Year of the Group, a Group having total consolidated group revenue of less than EUR 750 000 000 or an amount in local currency approximately equivalent to EUR 750 000 000 as of January 2015 during the Fiscal Year immediately preceding the Reporting Fiscal Year as reflected in its Consolidated Financial Statements for such preceding Fiscal Year.

5. The term "Constituent Entity" means any of the following:
   (a) any separate business unit of an MNE Group that is included in the Consolidated Financial Statements of the MNE Group for financial reporting purposes, or would be so included if equity interests in such business unit of an MNE Group were traded on a public securities exchange;
   (b) any such business unit that is excluded from the MNE Group's Consolidated Financial Statements solely on size or materiality grounds;
   (c) any permanent establishment of any separate business unit of the MNE Group included in (a) or (b) provided the business unit prepares a separate financial statement for such permanent establishment for financial reporting, regulatory, tax reporting, or internal management control purposes.

6. The term "Reporting Entity" means the Constituent Entity that is required to file a country-by-country report conforming to the requirements in Article 8aa(3) in its jurisdiction of tax residence on behalf of the MNE Group. The Reporting Entity may be the Ultimate Parent Entity, the Surrogate Parent Entity, or any entity described in point 1 of Section II.

7. The term "Ultimate Parent Entity" means a Constituent Entity of an MNE Group that meets the following criteria:
   (a) it owns directly or indirectly a sufficient interest in one or more other Constituent Entities of such MNE Group such that it is required to prepare Consolidated Financial Statements under accounting principles generally applied in its jurisdiction of tax residence, or would be so required if its equity interests were traded on a public securities exchange in its jurisdiction of tax residence;
   (b) there is no other Constituent Entity of such MNE Group that owns directly or indirectly an interest described in point (a) in the first mentioned Constituent Entity.

8. The term "Surrogate Parent Entity" means one Constituent Entity of the MNE Group that has been appointed by such MNE Group, as a sole substitute for the Ultimate Parent Entity, to file the country-by-country report in that Constituent Entity's jurisdiction of tax residence, on behalf of such MNE Group, when one or more of the conditions set out in point (b) of the first paragraph of point 1 of Section II apply.

9. The term "Fiscal Year" means an annual accounting period with respect to which the Ultimate Parent Entity of the MNE Group prepares its financial statements.

10. The term "Reporting Fiscal Year" means that Fiscal Year the financial and operational results of which are reflected in the country-by-country report referred to in Article 8aa(3).

11. The term "Qualifying Competent Authority Agreement" means an agreement that is between authorised representatives of an EU Member State and a non-Union jurisdiction that are parties to an International Agreement and that requires the automatic exchange of country-by-country reports between the party jurisdictions.

12. The term "International Agreement" means the Multilateral Convention on Mutual Administrative Assistance in Tax Matters, any bilateral or multilateral tax convention, or any tax information exchange agreement to which the Member State is a party, and that by its terms provides legal authority for the exchange of tax information between jurisdictions, including automatic exchange of such information.

13. The term "Consolidated Financial Statements" means the financial statements of an MNE Group in which the assets, liabilities, income, expenses and cash flows of the Ultimate Parent Entity and the Constituent Entities are presented as those of a single economic entity.

14. The term "Systemic Failure" with respect to a jurisdiction means either that a jurisdiction has a Qualifying Competent Authority Agreement in effect with a Member State but has suspended automatic exchange (for reasons other than those that are in accordance with the terms of that Agreement), or that a jurisdiction otherwise persistently failed to automatically provide to a Member State country-by-country reports in its possession of MNE Groups that have Constituent Entities in that Member State.

SECTION II
GENERAL REPORTING REQUIREMENTS

1. A Constituent Entity resident in a Member State which is not the Ultimate Parent Entity of an MNE Group shall file a country-by-country report with respect to the Reporting Fiscal Year of an MNE Group of which it is a Constituent Entity, if the following criteria are satisfied:
   (a) the entity is resident for tax purposes in a Member State;
   (b) one of the following conditions applies:
      (i) the Ultimate Parent Entity of the MNE Group is not obligated to file a country-by-country report in its jurisdiction of tax residence;
      (ii) the jurisdiction in which the Ultimate Parent Entity is resident for tax purposes has a current International Agreement to which the Member State is a party but does not have a Qualifying Competent Authority Agreement in effect to which the Member State is a party by the time specified in Article 8aa(1) for filing the country-by-country report for the Reporting Fiscal Year;
      (iii) there has been a Systemic Failure of the jurisdiction of tax residence of the Ultimate Parent Entity that has been notified by the Member State to the Constituent Entity resident for tax purposes in the Member State.

      Without prejudice to the obligation of the Ultimate Parent Entity referred to in Article 8aa(1) or its Surrogate Parent Entity to file the first country-by-country report for the Fiscal Year of the MNE Group commencing on or after 1 January 2016, Member States may decide that the obligation for Constituent Entities set out in point 1 of this Section shall apply for country-by-country reports with respect to the Reporting Fiscal Years commencing on or after 1 January 2017 onwards.

      A Constituent Entity resident in a Member State as defined in the first paragraph of this point shall request its Ultimate Parent Entity to provide it with all information required to enable it to meet its obligations to file a country-by-country report, in accordance with Article 8aa(3). If despite that, that Constituent Entity has not obtained or acquired all the required information to report for the MNE Group, this Constituent Entity shall file a country-by-country report containing all information in its possession, obtained or acquired, and notify the Member State of its residence that the Ultimate Parent Entity has refused to make the necessary information available. This shall be without prejudice to the right of the Member State concerned to apply penalties provided for in its national legislation and this Member State shall inform all Member States of this refusal.

      Where there are more than one Constituent Entities of the same MNE Group that are resident for tax purposes in the Union and one or more of the conditions set out in point (b) of the first paragraph apply, the MNE Group may designate one of such Constituent Entities to file the country-by-country report conforming to the requirements of Article 8aa(3) with respect to any Reporting Fiscal Year within the deadline specified in Article 8aa(1) and to notify the Member State that the filing is intended to satisfy the filing requirement of all the Constituent Entities of such MNE Group that are resident for tax purposes in the Union. That Member State shall, pursuant to Article 8aa(2), communicate the country-by-country report received to any other Member State in which, on the basis of the information in the country-by-country report, one or more Constituent Entities of the MNE Group of the Reporting Entity are either resident for tax purposes or are subject to tax with respect to the business carried out through a permanent establishment.

      Where a Constituent Entity cannot obtain or acquire all the information required to file a country-by-country report, in line with Article 8aa(3), then such Constituent Entity shall not be eligible to be designated to be the Reporting Entity for the MNE Group in accordance with the fourth paragraph of this point. This rule shall be without prejudice to the obligation of the Constituent Entity to notify the Member State of its residence that the Ultimate Parent Entity has refused to make the necessary information available.

2. By derogation from point 1, when one or more of the conditions set out in point (b) of the first paragraph of point 1 apply, an entity described in point 1 shall not be required to file a country-by-country report with respect to any Reporting Fiscal Year if the MNE Group of which it is a Constituent Entity has made available a country-by- country report in accordance with Article 8aa(3) with respect to such Fiscal Year through a Surrogate Parent Entity that files that country-by-country report with the tax authority of its jurisdiction of tax residence on or before the date specified in Article 8aa(1) and that, in case the Surrogate Parent Entity is tax resident in a jurisdiction outside the Union, satisfies the following conditions:

(a) the jurisdiction of tax residence of the Surrogate Parent Entity requires filing of country-by-country reports conforming to the requirements of Article 8aa(3);

(b) the jurisdiction of tax residence of the Surrogate Parent Entity has a Qualifying Competent Authority Agreement in effect to which the Member State is a party by the time specified in Article 8aa(1) for filing the country-by- country report for the Reporting Fiscal Year;

(c) the jurisdiction of tax residence of the Surrogate Parent Entity has not notified the Member State of a Systemic Failure;

(d) the jurisdiction of tax residence of the Surrogate Parent Entity has been notified no later than the last day of the Reporting Fiscal Year of such MNE Group by the Constituent Entity resident for tax purposes in its jurisdiction that it is the Surrogate Parent Entity;

(e) a notification has been provided to the Member State in accordance with point 4.

3. Member States shall request that any Constituent Entity of an MNE Group that is resident for tax purposes in that Member State notifies the Member State whether it is the Ultimate Parent Entity or the Surrogate Parent Entity or the Constituent Entity designated under point 1, no later than the last day of the Reporting Fiscal Year of such MNE Group. Member States may extend that deadline to the last day for filing of a tax return of that Constituent Entity for the preceding fiscal year.

4. Member States shall request that where a Constituent Entity of an MNE Group, that is resident for tax purposes in that Member State, is not the Ultimate Parent Entity nor the Surrogate Parent Entity nor the Constituent Entity designated under point 1, it shall notify the Member State of the identity and tax residence of the Reporting Entity, no later than the last day of the Reporting Fiscal Year of such MNE Group. Member States may extend that deadline to the last day for filing of a tax return of that Constituent Entity for the preceding fiscal year.

5. The country-by-country report shall specify the currency of the amounts referred to in that report.

SECTION III
COUNTRY-BY-COUNTRY REPORT

A. Template for the country-by-country report

Note—Please specify the nature of the activity of the Constituent Entity in the "Additional information"

B. General instructions for filling in the country-by-country report

1. Purpose

The template shall be used for reporting a multinational enterprise's (MNE) Group allocation of income, taxes and business activities on a tax jurisdiction-by-tax jurisdiction basis.

2. Treatment of branches and permanent establishments

The permanent establishment data shall be reported by reference to the tax jurisdiction in which it is situated and not by reference to the tax jurisdiction of residence of the business unit of which the permanent establishment is a part. Residence tax jurisdiction reporting for the business unit of which the permanent establishment is a part shall exclude financial data related to the permanent establishment.

3. Period covered by the annual template

The template shall cover the Fiscal Year of the reporting MNE. For Constituent Entities, at the discretion of the reporting MNE, the template shall reflect on a consistent basis either of the following information:

(a) information for the Fiscal Year of the relevant Constituent Entities ending on the same date as the Fiscal Year of the reporting MNE, or ending within the 12 month period preceding such date;

(b) information for all the relevant Constituent Entities reported for the Fiscal Year of the reporting MNE.

4. Source of data

The reporting MNE shall consistently use the same sources of data from year to year in completing the template. The reporting MNE may choose to use data from its consolidation reporting packages, from separate entity statutory financial statements, regulatory financial statements, or internal management accounts. It is not necessary to reconcile the revenue, profit and tax reporting in the template to the Consolidated Financial Statements. If statutory financial statements are used as the basis for reporting, all amounts shall be translated to the stated functional currency of the reporting MNE at the average exchange rate for the year stated in the "Additional information" section of the template. Adjustments need not be made, however, for differences in accounting principles applied from tax jurisdiction to tax jurisdiction.

The reporting MNE shall provide a brief description of the sources of data used in preparing the template in the "Additional information" section of the template. If a change is made in the source of data used from year to year, the reporting MNE shall explain the reasons for the change and its consequences in the "Additional information" section of the template.

C. Specific instructions for filling in the country-by-country report

1. Overview of allocation of income, taxes and business activities by tax jurisdiction (Table 1)

1.1. Tax jurisdiction

In the first column of the template, the reporting MNE shall list all of the tax jurisdictions in which Constituent Entities of the MNE Group are resident for tax purposes. A tax jurisdiction is defined as a State as well as a non-State jurisdiction which has fiscal autonomy. A separate line shall be included for all Constituent Entities in the MNE Group deemed by the reporting MNE not to be resident in any tax jurisdiction for tax purposes. Where a Constituent Entity is resident in more than one tax jurisdiction, the applicable tax treaty tie breaker shall be applied to determine the tax jurisdiction of residence. Where no applicable tax treaty exists, the Constituent Entity shall be reported in the tax jurisdiction of the Constituent Entity's place of effective management. The place of effective management shall be determined with internationally agreed standards.

1.2. Revenues

In the three columns of the template under the heading "Revenues", the reporting MNE shall report the following information:

(a) the sum of revenues of all the Constituent Entities of the MNE Group in the relevant tax jurisdiction generated from transactions with associated enterprises;

(b) the sum of revenues of all the Constituent Entities of the MNE Group in the relevant tax jurisdiction generated from transactions with independent parties;

(c) the total of the sums referred to in points (a) and (b). Revenues shall include revenues from sales of inventory and properties, services, royalties, interest, premiums and any other amounts.

Revenues shall exclude payments received from other Constituent Entities that are treated as dividends in the payer's tax jurisdiction.

1.3. Profit (loss) before income tax

In the fifth column of the template, the reporting MNE shall report the sum of the profit (loss) before income tax for all the Constituent Entities resident for tax purposes in the relevant tax jurisdiction. The profit (loss) before income tax shall include all extraordinary income and expense items.

1.4. Income tax paid (on cash basis) In the sixth column of the template, the reporting MNE shall report the total amount of income tax actually paid during the relevant Fiscal Year by all the Constituent Entities resident for tax purposes in the relevant tax jurisdiction. Taxes paid shall include cash taxes paid by the Constituent Entity to the residence tax jurisdiction and to all other tax jurisdictions. Taxes paid shall include withholding taxes paid by other entities (associated enterprises and independent enterprises) with respect to payments to the Constituent Entity. Thus, if company A resident in tax jurisdiction A earns interest in tax jurisdiction B, the tax withheld in tax jurisdiction B shall be reported by company A.

1.5. Income tax accrued (current year)

In the seventh column of the template, the reporting MNE shall report the sum of the accrued current tax expense recorded on taxable profits or losses of the year of reporting of all the Constituent Entities resident for tax purposes in the relevant tax jurisdiction. The current tax expense shall reflect only operations in the current year and shall not include deferred taxes or provisions for uncertain tax liabilities.

1.6. Stated capital

In the eighth column of the template, the reporting MNE shall report the sum of the stated capital of all the Constituent Entities resident for tax purposes in the relevant tax jurisdiction. With regard to permanent establishments, the stated capital shall be reported by the legal entity of which it is a permanent establishment unless there is a defined capital requirement in the permanent establishment tax jurisdiction for regulatory purposes.

1.7. Accumulated earnings

In the ninth column of the template, the reporting MNE shall report the sum of the total accumulated earnings of all the Constituent Entities resident for tax purposes in the relevant tax jurisdiction as of the end of the year. With regard to permanent establishments, accumulated earnings shall be reported by the legal entity of which it is a permanent establishment.

1.8. Number of employees

In the tenth column of the template, the reporting MNE shall report the total number of employees on a full-time equivalent (FTE) basis of all the Constituent Entities resident for tax purposes in the relevant tax jurisdiction. The number of employees may be reported as of the year-end, on the basis of average employment levels for the year, or on any other basis consistently applied across tax jurisdictions and from year to year. For this purpose, independent contractors participating in the ordinary operating activities of the Constituent Entity may be reported as employees. Reasonable rounding or approximation of the number of employees is permissible, providing that such rounding or approximation does not materially distort the relative distribution of employees across the various tax jurisdictions. Consistent approaches shall be applied from year to year and across entities.

1.9. Tangible assets other than cash and cash equivalents

In the eleventh column of the template, the reporting MNE shall report the sum of the net book values of tangible assets of all the Constituent Entities resident for tax purposes in the relevant tax jurisdiction. With regard to permanent establishments, assets shall be reported by reference to the tax jurisdiction in which the permanent establishment is situated. Tangible assets for this purpose do not include cash or cash equivalents, intangibles, or financial assets.

2. List of all the Constituent Entities of the MNE Group included in each aggregation per tax jurisdiction (Table 2)

2.1. Constituent Entities resident in the tax jurisdiction The reporting MNE shall list, on a tax jurisdiction-by-tax jurisdiction basis and by legal entity name, all the Constituent Entities of the MNE Group which are resident for tax purposes in the relevant tax jurisdiction. As stated in point 2 of the general instructions with regard to permanent establishments, however, the permanent establishment shall be listed by reference to the tax jurisdiction in which it is situated. The legal entity of which it is a permanent establishment shall be noted.

2.2. Tax jurisdiction of organisation or incorporation if different from tax jurisdiction of residence The reporting MNE shall report the name of the tax jurisdiction under whose laws the Constituent Entity of the MNE Group is organised or incorporated if it is different from the tax jurisdiction of residence.

2.3. Main business activity(ies)

The reporting MNE shall determine the nature of the main business activity(ies) carried out by the Constituent Entity in the relevant tax jurisdiction, by ticking one or more of the appropriate boxes.'

[ANNEX IV

HALLMARKS

PART I

MAIN BENEFIT TEST

Generic hallmarks under category A and specific hallmarks under category B and under points (b)(i), (c) and (d) of paragraph 1 of category C may only be taken into account where they fulfil the "main benefit test".

That test will be satisfied if it can be established that the main benefit or one of the main benefits which, having regard to all relevant facts and circumstances, a person may reasonably expect to derive from an arrangement is the obtaining of a tax advantage.

In the context of hallmark under paragraph 1 of category C, the presence of conditions set out in points (b)(i), (c) or (d) of paragraph 1 of category C can not alone be a reason for concluding that an arrangement satisfies the main benefit test.

PART II

CATEGORIES OF HALLMARKS

A

GENERIC HALLMARKS LINKED TO THE MAIN BENEFIT TEST

1. An arrangement where the relevant taxpayer or a participant in the arrangement undertakes to comply with a condition of confidentiality which may require them not to disclose how the arrangement could secure a tax advantage vis-à-vis other intermediaries or the tax authorities.

2. An arrangement where the intermediary is entitled to receive a fee (or interest, remuneration for finance costs and other charges) for the arrangement and that fee is fixed by reference to:

   (a) the amount of the tax advantage derived from the arrangement; or
   (b) whether or not a tax advantage is actually derived from the arrangement. This would include an obligation on the intermediary to partially or fully refund the fees where the intended tax advantage derived from the arrangement was not partially or fully achieved.

3. An arrangement that has substantially standardised documentation and/or structure and is available to more than one relevant taxpayer without a need to be substantially customised for implementation.

B

SPECIFIC HALLMARKS LINKED TO THE MAIN BENEFIT TEST

1. An arrangement whereby a participant in the arrangement takes contrived steps which consist in acquiring a loss-making company, discontinuing the main activity of such company and using its losses in order to reduce its tax liability, including through a transfer of those losses to another jurisdiction or by the acceleration of the use of those losses.

2. An arrangement that has the effect of converting income into capital, gifts or other categories of revenue which are taxed at a lower level or exempt from tax.

3. An arrangement which includes circular transactions resulting in the round-tripping of funds, namely through involving interposed entities without other primary commercial function or transactions that offset or cancel each other or that have other similar features.

C

SPECIFIC HALLMARKS RELATED TO CROSS-BORDER TRANSACTIONS

1. An arrangement that involves deductible cross-border payments made between two or more associated enterprises where at least one of the following conditions occurs:
   (a) he recipient is not resident for tax purposes in any tax jurisdiction;
   (b) although the recipient is resident for tax purposes in a jurisdiction, that jurisdiction either:
       (i) does not impose any corporate tax or imposes corporate tax at the rate of zero or almost zero; or
       (ii) is included in a list of third-country jurisdictions which have been assessed by Member States collectively or within the framework of the OECD as being non-cooperative;
   (c) the payment benefits from a full exemption from tax in the jurisdiction where the recipient is resident for tax purposes;
   (d) the payment benefits from a preferential tax regime in the jurisdiction where the recipient is resident for tax purposes;

2. Deductions for the same depreciation on the asset are claimed in more than one jurisdiction.

3. Relief from double taxation in respect of the same item of income or capital is claimed in more than one jurisdiction.

4. There is an arrangement that includes transfers of assets and where there is a material difference in the amount being treated as payable in consideration for the assets in those jurisdictions involved.

D

SPECIFIC HALLMARKS CONCERNING AUTOMATIC EXCHANGE OF INFORMATION AND BENEFICIAL OWNERSHIP

1. An arrangement which may have the effect of undermining the reporting obligation under the laws implementing Union legislation or any equivalent agreements on the automatic exchange of Financial Account information, including agreements with third countries, or which takes advantage of the absence of such legislation or agreements. Such arrangements include at least the following:
   (a) the use of an account, product or investment that is not, or purports not to be, a Financial Account, but has features that are substantially similar to those of a Financial Account;
   (b) the transfer of Financial Accounts or assets to, or the use of jurisdictions that are not bound by the automatic exchange of Financial Account information with the State of residence of the relevant taxpayer;
   (c) the reclassification of income and capital into products or payments that are not subject to the automatic exchange of Financial Account information;
   (d) the transfer or conversion of a Financial Institution or a Financial Account or the assets therein into a Financial Institution or a Financial Account or assets not subject to reporting under the automatic exchange of Financial Account information;
   (e) the use of legal entities, arrangements or structures that eliminate or purport to eliminate reporting of one or more Account Holders or Controlling Persons under the automatic exchange of Financial Account information;
   (f) arrangements that undermine, or exploit weaknesses in, the due diligence procedures used by Financial Institutions to comply with their obligations to report Financial Account information, including the use of jurisdictions with inadequate or weak regimes of enforcement of anti-money-laundering legislation or with weak transparency requirements for legal persons or legal arrangements.

2. An arrangement involving a non-transparent legal or beneficial ownership chain with the use of persons, legal arrangements or structures:
   (a) that do not carry on a substantive economic activity supported by adequate staff, equipment, assets and premises; and
   (b) that are incorporated, managed, resident, controlled or established in any jurisdiction other than the jurisdiction of residence of one or more of the beneficial owners of the assets held by such persons, legal arrangements or structures; and
   (c) where the beneficial owners of such persons, legal arrangements or structures, as defined in Directive (EU) 2015/849, are made unidentifiable.

E

SPECIFIC HALLMARKS CONCERNING TRANSFER PRICING

1. An arrangement which involves the use of unilateral safe harbour rules.

2. An arrangement involving the transfer of hard-to-value intangibles. The term "hard-to-value intangibles" covers intangibles or rights in intangibles for which, at the time of their transfer between associated enterprises:
   (a) no reliable comparables exist; and
   (b) at the time the transaction was entered into, the projections of future cash flows or income expected to be derived from the transferred intangible, or the assumptions used in valuing the intangible are highly uncertain, making it difficult to predict the level of ultimate success of the intangible at the time of the transfer.

3. An arrangement involving an intragroup cross-border transfer of functions and/or risks and/or assets, if the projected annual earnings before interest and taxes (EBIT), during the three-year period after the transfer, of the transferor or transferors, are less than 50 % of the projected annual EBIT of such transferor or transferors if the transfer had not been made.][1]

Amendments—[1] Annex IV inserted by Council Directive (EU) 2018/822 art 1(8) with effect from 25 June 2018 (OJ L 139, 5.6.2018, p 1).

VAT Retained EU Regulations

Brexit Notes—See the European Union (Withdrawal) Act 2018 s 3 for general provision on the incorporation of "direct EU legislation" (including EU regulations) into domestic law.
Under the Taxation (Cross-border Trade) Act 2018 s 42(1), any EU regulation so far as applying in relation to VAT, and any "direct EU legislation" so far as relevant to any such regulation, that form part of the law of the UK as a result of EUWA 2018 s 3, cease to have effect.
Note, however, that where the principal VAT Directive (2006/112/EC) remains relevant for determining the meaning and effect of the law relating to VAT, that Directive is to be read for that purpose in the light of the provision made by the Implementing VAT Regulation (282/2011/EU) but ignoring such of its provisions as are excluded by regulations made by the Treasury by statutory instrument.

RETAINED COUNCIL IMPLEMENTING REGULATION 282/2011/EU
OF 15 MARCH 2011
LAYING DOWN IMPLEMENTING MEASURES FOR DIRECTIVE 2006/112/EC ON THE COMMON SYSTEM OF VALUE ADDED TAX

THE COUNCIL OF THE EUROPEAN UNION,

Having regard to the Treaty on the Functioning of the European Union,

Having regard to Council Directive 2006/112/EC of 28 November 2006 on the common system of value added tax , and in particular Article 397 thereof,

Having regard to the proposal from the European Commission,

Whereas:

(1) A number of substantial changes are to be made to Council Regulation (EC) No 1777/2005 of 17 October 2005 laying down implementing measures for Directive 77/388/EEC on the common system of value added tax . It is desirable, for reasons of clarity and rationalisation, that the provisions in question should be recast.

(2) Directive 2006/112/EC contains rules on value added tax (VAT) which, in some cases, are subject to interpretation by the Member States. The adoption of common provisions implementing Directive 2006/112/EC should ensure that application of the VAT system complies more fully with the objective of the internal market, in cases where divergences in application have arisen or may arise which are incompatible with the proper functioning of such internal market. These implementing measures are legally binding only from the date of the entry into force of this Regulation and are without prejudice to the validity of the legislation and interpretation previously adopted by the Member States.

(3) Changes resulting from the adoption of Council Directive 2008/8/EC of 12 February 2008 amending Directive 2006/112/EC as regards the place of supply of services should be reflected in this Regulation.

(4) The objective of this Regulation is to ensure uniform application of the current VAT system by laying down rules implementing Directive 2006/112/EC, in particular in respect of taxable persons, the supply of goods and services, and the place of taxable transactions. In accordance with the principle of proportionality as set out in Article 5(4) of the Treaty on European Union, this Regulation does not go beyond what is necessary in order to achieve this objective. Since it is binding and directly applicable in all Member States, uniformity of application will be best ensured by a Regulation.

(5) These implementing provisions contain specific rules in response to selective questions of application and are designed to bring uniform treatment throughout the Union to those specific circumstances only. They are therefore not conclusive for other cases and, in view of their formulation, are to be applied restrictively.

(6) If a non-taxable person changes residence and transfers a new means of transport, or a new means of transport returns to the Member State from which it was originally supplied exempt of VAT to the non-taxable person returning it, it should be clarified that such a transfer does not constitute the intra-Community acquisition of a new means of transport.

(7) For certain services, it is sufficient for the supplier to demonstrate that the customer for these services, whether or not a taxable person, is located outside the Community for the supply of those services to fall outside the scope of VAT.

(8) It should be specified that the allocation of a VAT identification number to a taxable person who makes or receives a supply of services to or from another Member State, and for which the VAT is payable solely by the customer, does not affect the right of that taxable person

to benefit from non-taxation of his intra- Community acquisitions of goods. However, if the taxable person communicates his VAT identification number to the supplier in respect of an intra- Community acquisition of goods, he is in any event deemed to have opted to make those transactions subject to VAT.

(9) The further integration of the internal market has led to an increased need for cooperation by economic operators established in different Member States across internal borders and the development of European economic interest groupings (EEIGs), constituted in accordance with Council Regulation (EEC) No 2137/85 of 25 July 1985 on the European Economic Interest Grouping (EEIG) . It should therefore be clarified that EEIGs are taxable persons where they supply goods or services for consideration.

(10) It is necessary to clearly define restaurant and catering services, the distinction between the two, and the appropriate treatment of these services.

(11) In order to enhance clarity, the transactions identified as electronically supplied services should be listed without the lists being definitive or exhaustive.

(12) It is necessary, on the one hand, to establish that a transaction which consists solely of assembling the various parts of a machine provided by a customer must be considered as a supply of services, and, on the other hand, to establish the place of such supply when the service is supplied to a non-taxable person.

(13) The sale of an option as a financial instrument should be treated as a supply of services separate from the underlying transactions to which the option relates.

(14) To ensure the uniform application of rules relating to the place of taxable transactions, concepts such as the place where a taxable person has established his business, fixed establishment, permanent address and the place where a person usually resides should be clarified. While taking into account the case law of the Court of Justice, the use of criteria which are as clear and objective as possible should facilitate the practical application of these concepts.

(15) Rules should be established to ensure the uniform treatment of supplies of goods once a supplier has exceeded the distance selling threshold for supplies to another Member State.

(16) It should be clarified that the journey of the means of transport determines the section of a passenger transport operation effected within the Community, and not the journey of the passengers within it.

(17) In the case of intra-Community acquisition of goods, the right of the Member State of acquisition to tax the acquisition should remain unaffected by the VAT treatment of the transaction in the Member States of departure.

(18) The correct application of the rules governing the place of supply of services relies mainly on the status of the customer as a taxable or non-taxable person, and on the capacity in which he is acting. In order to determine the customer's status as a taxable person, it is necessary to establish what the supplier should be required to obtain as evidence from his customer.

(19) It should be clarified that when services supplied to a taxable person are intended for private use, including use by the customer's staff, that taxable person cannot be deemed to be acting in his capacity as a taxable person. Communication by the customer of his VAT identification number to the supplier is sufficient to establish that the customer is acting in his capacity as a taxable person, unless the supplier has information to the contrary. It should also be ensured that a single service acquired for the business but also used for private purposes is only taxed in one place.

(20) In order to determine the customer's place of establishment precisely, the supplier of the service is required to verify the information provided by the customer.

(21) Without prejudice to the general rule on the place of supply of services to a taxable person, where services are supplied to a customer established in more than one place, there should be rules to help the supplier determine the customer's fixed establishment to which the service is provided, taking account of the circumstances. If the supplier of the services is not able to determine that place, there should be rules to clarify the supplier's obligations. Those rules should not interfere with or change the customer's obligations.

(22) The time at which the supplier of the service must determine the status, the capacity and the location of the customer, whether a taxable person or not, should also be specified.

(23) Without prejudice to the general application of the principle with respect to abusive practices to the provisions of this Regulation, it is appropriate to draw specific attention to its application to certain provisions of this Regulation.

(24) Certain specific services such as the assignment of television broadcasting rights in respect of football matches, the translation of texts, services for claiming VAT refunds, and services as an intermediary to a non- taxable person involve cross-border scenarios or even the participation of economic operators established outside the Community. The place of supply of these services needs to be clearly determined in order to create greater legal certainty.

(25) It should be specified that services supplied by an intermediary acting in the name and on behalf of another person who takes part in the provision of accommodation in the hotel sector are not governed by the specific rule for the supply of services connected with immovable property.

(26) Where various services supplied in the framework of organising a funeral form part of a single service, the rule on the place of supply should also be determined.

(27) In order to ensure uniform treatment of supplies of cultural, artistic, sporting, scientific, educational, entertainment and similar services, admission to such events and ancillary services which are related to admission need to be defined.

(28) It is necessary to clarify the treatment of restaurant services and catering services supplied on board a means of transport when passenger transport is being carried out on the territory of several countries.

(29) Given that particular rules for the hiring of a means of transport depend on the duration of its possession or use, it is necessary not only to establish which vehicles should be considered means of transport, but also to clarify the treatment of such a supply where one successive contract follows another. It is also necessary to determine the place where a means of transport is actually put at the disposal of the customer.

(30) In certain specific circumstances a credit or debit card handling fee which is paid in connection with a transaction should not reduce the taxable amount for that transaction.

(31) It is necessary to clarify that the reduced rate may be applied to the hiring out of tents, caravans and mobile homes installed on camping sites and used as accommodation.

(32) Vocational training or retraining should include instruction relating directly to a trade or profession as well as any instruction aimed at acquiring or updating knowledge for vocational purposes, regardless of the duration of a course.

(33) Platinum nobles should be treated as being excluded from the exemptions for currency, bank notes and coins.

(34) It should be specified that the exemption of the supply of services relating to the importation of goods the value of which is included in the taxable amount of those goods should cover transport services carried out during a change of residence.

(35) Goods transported outside the Community by the purchaser thereof and used for the equipping, fuelling or provisioning of means of transport used for non- business purposes by persons other than natural persons, such as bodies governed by public law and associations, should be excluded from the exemption for export transactions.

(36) To guarantee uniform administrative practices for the calculation of the minimum value for exemption on exportation of goods carried in the personal luggage of travellers, the provisions on such calculations should be harmonised.

(37) It should be specified that the exemption for certain transactions treated as exports should also apply to services covered by the special scheme for electronically supplied services.

(38) A body to be set up under the legal framework for a European Research Infrastructure Consortium (ERIC) should only qualify as an international body for the purposes of exemption from VAT where it fulfils certain conditions. The features necessary for it to benefit from exemption should therefore be identified.

(39) Supplies of goods and services under diplomatic and consular arrangements, or to recognised international bodies, or to certain armed forces are exempt from VAT subject to certain limits and conditions. In order that a taxable person making such a supply from another Member State can establish that the conditions and limits for this exemption are met, an exemption certificate should be established.

(40) Electronic import documents should also be admitted to exercise the right to deduct, where they fulfil the same requirements as paper-based documents.

(41) Where a supplier of goods or services has a fixed establishment within the territory of the Member State where the tax is due, the circumstances under which that establishment should be liable for payment of VAT should be specified.

(42) It should be clarified that a taxable person who has established his business within the territory of the Member State where the tax is due must be deemed to be a taxable person established in that Member State for the purposes of liability for the tax, even when that place of business is not involved in the supply of goods or services.

(43) It should be clarified that every taxable person is required to communicate his VAT identification number, as soon as he has one, for certain taxable transactions in order to ensure fairer collection of the tax.

(44) Weights for investment gold which are definitely accepted by the bullion market should be named and a common date for establishing the value of gold coins be determined to ensure equal treatment of economic operators.

(45) The special scheme for taxable persons not established in the Community, supplying

services electronically to non-taxable persons established or resident within the Community, is subject to certain conditions. Where those conditions are no longer fulfilled, the consequences thereof should, in particular, be made clear.

(46) Certain changes result from Directive 2008/8/EC. Since those changes concern, on the one hand, the taxation of the long-term hiring of means of transport as from 1 January 2013 and, on the other, the taxation of electronically supplied services as from 1 January 2015, it should be specified that the corresponding Articles of this Regulation apply only as from those dates,

HAS ADOPTED THIS REGULATION:

CHAPTER I
SUBJECT MATTER

Article 1

This Regulation lays down measures for the implementation of certain provisions of Titles I to V, and VII to XII of Directive 2006/112/EC.

CHAPTER II
SCOPE
(TITLE I OF DIRECTIVE 2006/112/EC)

Article 2

The following shall not result in intra-Community acquisitions within the meaning of point (b) of Article 2(1) of Directive 2006/112/EC:
   (a) the transfer of a new means of transport by a non-taxable person upon change of residence provided that the exemption provided for in point (a) of Article 138(2) of Directive 2006/112/EC could not apply at the time of supply;
   (b) the return of a new means of transport by a non-taxable person to the Member State from which it was initially supplied to him under the exemption provided for in point (a) of Article 138(2) of Directive 2006/112/EC.

Article 3

Without prejudice to point (b) of the first paragraph of Article 59a of Directive 2006/112/EC, the supply of the following services is not subject to VAT if the supplier demonstrates that the place of supply determined in accordance with Subsections 3 and 4 of Section 4 of Chapter V of this Regulation is outside the Community:
   (a) from 1 January 2013, the service referred to in the first subparagraph of Article 56(2) of Directive 2006/112/EC;
   (b) from 1 January 2015, the services listed in Article 58 of Directive 2006/112/EC;
   (c) the services listed in Article 59 of Directive 2006/112/EC.

Article 4

A taxable person who is entitled to non-taxation of his intra-Community acquisitions of goods, in accordance with Article 3 of Directive 2006/112/EC, shall remain so where, pursuant to Article 214(1)(d) or (e) of that Directive, a VAT identification number has been attributed to that taxable person for the services received for which he is liable to pay VAT or for the services supplied by him within the territory of another Member State for which VAT is payable solely by the recipient. However, if that taxable person communicates this VAT identification number to a supplier in respect of an intra-Community acquisition of goods, he shall be deemed to have exercised the option provided for in Article 3(3) of that Directive.

CHAPTER III
TAXABLE PERSONS
(TITLE III OF DIRECTIVE 2006/112/EC)

Article 5

A European Economic Interest Grouping (EEIG) constituted in accordance with Regulation (EEC) No 2137/85 which supplies goods or services for consideration to its members or to third parties shall be a taxable person within the meaning of Article 9(1) of Directive 2006/112/EC.

CHAPTER IV
TAXABLE TRANSACTIONS
(ARTICLES 24 TO 29 OF DIRECTIVE 2006/112/EC)

Article 6

1. Restaurant and catering services mean services consisting of the supply of prepared or unprepared food or beverages or both, for human consumption, accompanied by sufficient support services allowing for the immediate consumption thereof. The provision of food or beverages or both is only

one component of the whole in which services shall predominate. Restaurant services are the supply of such services on the premises of the supplier, and catering services are the supply of such services off the premises of the supplier.

2. The supply of prepared or unprepared food or beverages or both, whether or not including transport but without any other support services, shall not be considered restaurant or catering services within the meaning of paragraph 1.

[Article 6a
1. Telecommunications services within the meaning of Article 24(2) of Directive 2006/112/EC shall cover, in particular, the following:
    (a) fixed and mobile telephone services for the transmission and switching of voice, data and video, including telephone services with an imaging component (videophone services);
    (b) telephone services provided through the internet, including voice over internet Protocol (VoIP);
    (c) voice mail, call waiting, call forwarding, caller identification, three-way calling and other call management services;
    (d) paging services;
    (e) audiotext services;
    (f) facsimile, telegraph and telex;
    (g) access to the internet, including the World Wide Web;
    (h) private network connections providing telecommunications links for the exclusive use of the client.
2. Telecommunications services within the meaning of Article 24(2) of Directive 2006/112/EC shall not cover the following:
    (a) electronically supplied services;
    (b) radio and television broadcasting (hereinafter "broadcasting") services.][1]

Amendments—[1]   Articles 6a, 6b inserted by Council Implementing Regulation (EU) No 1042/2013 art 1(1)(a) with effect from 1 January 2015 (OJ L 284, 26.10.2013, p 1).

[Article 6b
1. Broadcasting services shall include services consisting of audio and audiovisual content, such as radio or television programmes which are provided to the general public via communications networks by and under the editorial responsibility of a media service provider, for simultaneous listening or viewing, on the basis of a programme schedule.
2. Paragraph 1 shall cover, in particular, the following:
    (a) radio or television programmes transmitted or retransmitted over a radio or television network;
    (b) radio or television programmes distributed via the internet or similar electronic network (IP streaming), if they are broadcast simultaneous to their being transmitted or retransmitted over a radio or television network.
3. Paragraph 1 shall not cover the following:
    (a) telecommunications services;
    (b) electronically supplied services;
    (c) the provision of information about particular programmes on demand;
    (d) the transfer of broadcasting or transmission rights;
    (e) the leasing of technical equipment or facilities for use to receive a broadcast;
    (f) radio or television programmes distributed via the internet or similar electronic network (IP streaming), unless they are broadcast simultaneous to their being transmitted or retransmitted over a radio or television network.][1]

Amendments—[1]   Articles 6a, 6b inserted by Council Implementing Regulation (EU) No 1042/2013 art 1(1)(a) with effect from 1 January 2015 (OJ L 284, 26.10.2013, p 1).

Article 7

1. 'Electronically supplied services' as referred to in Directive 2006/112/EC shall include services which are delivered over the Internet or an electronic network and the nature of which renders their supply essentially automated and involving minimal human intervention, and impossible to ensure in the absence of information technology.
2. Paragraph 1 shall cover, in particular, the following:
    (a) the supply of digitised products generally, including software and changes to or upgrades of software;
    (b) services providing or supporting a business or personal presence on an electronic network such as a website or a webpage;
    (c) services automatically generated from a computer via the Internet or an electronic network, in response to specific data input by the recipient;

(d) the transfer for consideration of the right to put goods or services up for sale on an Internet site operating as an online market on which potential buyers make their bids by an automated procedure and on which the parties are notified of a sale by electronic mail automatically generated from a computer;
  (e) Internet Service Packages (ISP) of information in which the telecommunications component forms an ancillary and subordinate part (i.e. packages going beyond mere Internet access and including other elements such as content pages giving access to news, weather or travel reports; playgrounds; website hosting; access to online debates etc.);
  (f) the services listed in Annex I.
3. [Paragraph 1 shall not cover the following:][1]
  [(a) broadcasting services;][1]
  (b) telecommunications services;
  (c) goods, where the order and processing is done electronically;
  (d) CD-ROMs, floppy disks and similar tangible media;
  (e) printed matter, such as books, newsletters, newspapers or journals;
  (f) CDs and audio cassettes;
  (g) video cassettes and DVDs;
  (h) games on a CD-ROM;
  (i) services of professionals such as lawyers and financial consultants, who advise clients by e-mail;
  (j) teaching services, where the course content is delivered by a teacher over the Internet or an electronic network (namely via a remote link);
  (k) offline physical repair services of computer equipment;
  (l) offline data warehousing services;
  (m) advertising services, in particular as in newspapers, on posters and on television;
  (n) telephone helpdesk services;
  (o) teaching services purely involving correspondence courses, such as postal courses;
  (p) conventional auctioneers' services reliant on direct human intervention, irrespective of how bids are made;
  (q) . . .[1]
  (r) . . .[1]
  (s) . . .[1]
  [(t) tickets to cultural, artistic, sporting, scientific, educational, entertainment or similar events booked online;
  (u) accommodation, car-hire, restaurant services, passenger transport or similar services booked online.][1]

Amendments—[1] Words substituted by Council Implementing Regulation (EU) No 1042/2013 art 1(1)(b) with effect from 1 January 2015 (OJ L 284, 26.10.2013, p 1).

Article 8
If a taxable person only assembles the various parts of a machine all of which were provided to him by his customer, that transaction shall be a supply of services within the meaning of Article 24(1) of Directive 2006/112/EC.

Article 9
The sale of an option, where such a sale is a transaction falling within the scope of point (f) of Article 135(1) of Directive 2006/112/EC, shall be a supply of services within the meaning of Article 24(1) of that Directive. That supply of services shall be distinct from the underlying transactions to which the services relate.

[Article 9a
1. For the application of Article 28 of Directive 2006/112/EC, where electronically supplied services are supplied through a telecommunications network, an interface or a portal such as a marketplace for applications, a taxable person taking part in that supply shall be presumed to be acting in his own name but on behalf of the provider of those services unless that provider is explicitly indicated as the supplier by that taxable person and that is reflected in the contractual arrangements between the parties.
In order to regard the provider of electronically supplied services as being explicitly indicated as the supplier of those services by the taxable person, the following conditions shall be met:
  (a) the invoice issued or made available by each taxable person taking part in the supply of the electronically supplied services must identify such services and the supplier thereof;
  (b) the bill or receipt issued or made available to the customer must identify the electronically supplied services and the supplier thereof.
For the purposes of this paragraph, a taxable person who, with regard to a supply of electronically supplied services, authorises the charge to the customer or the delivery of the services, or sets the general terms and conditions of the supply, shall not be permitted to explicitly indicate another person as the supplier of those services.

2. Paragraph 1 shall also apply where telephone services provided through the internet, including voice over internet Protocol (VoIP), are supplied through a telecommunications network, an interface or a portal such as a marketplace for applications and are supplied under the same conditions as set out in that paragraph.

3. This Article shall not apply to a taxable person who only provides for processing of payments in respect of electronically supplied services or of telephone services provided through the internet, including voice over internet Protocol (VoIP), and who does not take part in the supply of those electronically supplied services or telephone services.][1]

Amendments—[1] Article 9a inserted by Council Implementing Regulation (EU) No 1042/2013 art 1(1)(c) with effect from 1 January 2015 (OJ L 284, 26.10.2013, p 1).

CHAPTER V
PLACE OF TAXABLE TRANSACTIONS

SECTION 1
CONCEPTS

Article 10

1. For the application of Articles 44 and 45 of Directive 2006/112/EC, the place where the business of a taxable person is established shall be the place where the functions of the business's central administration are carried out.

2. In order to determine the place referred to in paragraph 1, account shall be taken of the place where essential decisions concerning the general management of the business are taken, the place where the registered office of the business is located and the place where management meets.

Where these criteria do not allow the place of establishment of a business to be determined with certainty, the place where essential decisions concerning the general management of the business are taken shall take precedence.

3. The mere presence of a postal address may not be taken to be the place of establishment of a business of a taxable person.

Article 11

1. For the application of Article 44 of Directive 2006/112/EC, a 'fixed establishment' shall be any establishment, other than the place of establishment of a business referred to in Article 10 of this Regulation, characterised by a sufficient degree of permanence and a suitable structure in terms of human and technical resources to enable it to receive and use the services supplied to it for its own needs.

2. For the application of the following Articles, a 'fixed establishment' shall be any establishment, other than the place of establishment of a business referred to in Article 10 of this Regulation, characterised by a sufficient degree of permanence and a suitable structure in terms of human and technical resources to enable it to provide the services which it supplies:
    (a) Article 45 of Directive 2006/112/EC;
    (b) from 1 January 2013, the second subparagraph of Article 56(2) of Directive 2006/112/EC;
    (c) until 31 December 2014, Article 58 of Directive 2006/112/EC;
    (d) Article 192a of Directive 2006/112/EC.

3. The fact of having a VAT identification number shall not in itself be sufficient to consider that a taxable person has a fixed establishment.

Article 12

For the application of Directive 2006/112/EC, the 'permanent address' of a natural person, whether or not a taxable person, shall be the address entered in the population or similar register, or the address indicated by that person to the relevant tax authorities, unless there is evidence that this address does not reflect reality.

Article 13

The place where a natural person 'usually resides', whether or not a taxable person, as referred to in Directive 2006/112/EC shall be the place where that natural person usually lives as a result of personal and occupational ties.

Where the occupational ties are in a country different from that of the personal ties, or where no occupational ties exist, the place of usual residence shall be determined by personal ties which show close links between the natural person and a place where he is living.

[*Article 13a*

The place where a non-taxable legal person is established, as referred to in the first subparagraph of Article 56(2) and Articles 58 and 59 of Directive 2006/112/EC, shall be:
    (a) the place where the functions of its central administration are carried out; or
    (b) the place of any other establishment characterised by a sufficient degree of permanence and a suitable structure in terms of human and technical resources to enable it to receive and use the services supplied to it for its own needs.][1]

Amendments—[1]   Articles 13a, 13b inserted by Council Implementing Regulation (EU) No 1042/2013 art 1(2)(a) with effect from 1 January 2015 (OJ L 284, 26.10.2013, p 1). Article 13b applies from 1 January 2017.

[Article 13b
For the application of Directive 2006/112/EC, the following shall be regarded as "immovable property":
- (a) any specific part of the earth, on or below its surface, over which title and possession can be created;
- (b) any building or construction fixed to or in the ground above or below sea level which cannot be easily dismantled or moved;
- (c) any item that has been installed and makes up an integral part of a building or construction without which the building or construction is incomplete, such as doors, windows, roofs, staircases and lifts;
- (d) any item, equipment or machine permanently installed in a building or construction which cannot be moved without destroying or altering the building or construction.][1]

Amendments—[1]   Articles 13a, 13b inserted by Council Implementing Regulation (EU) No 1042/2013 art 1(2)(a) with effect from 1 January 2015 (OJ L 284, 26.10.2013, p 1).

SECTION 2

PLACE OF SUPPLY OF GOODS
(ARTICLES 31 TO 39 OF DIRECTIVE 2006/112/EC)

Article 14
Where in the course of a calendar year the threshold applied by a Member State in accordance with Article 34 of Directive 2006/112/EC is exceeded, Article 33 of that Directive shall not modify the place of supplies of goods other than products subject to excise duty carried out in the course of the same calendar year which are made before the threshold applied by the Member State for the calendar year then current is exceeded provided that all of the following conditions are met:
- (a) the supplier has not exercised the option provided for under Article 34(4) of that Directive;
- (b) the value of his supplies of goods did not exceed the threshold in the course of the preceding calendar year.

However, Article 33 of Directive 2006/112/EC shall modify the place of the following supplies to the Member State in which the dispatch or transport ends:
- (a) the supply of goods by which the threshold applied by the Member State for the calendar year then current was exceeded in the course of the same calendar year;
- (b) any subsequent supplies of goods within that Member State in that calendar year;
- (c) supplies of goods within that Member State in the calendar year following the calendar year in which the event referred to in point (a) occurred.

Article 15
The section of a passenger transport operation effected within the Community referred to in Article 37 of Directive 2006/112/EC, shall be determined by the journey of the means of transport and not by the journey completed by each of the passengers.

SECTION 3

PLACE OF INTRA-COMMUNITY ACQUISITIONS OF GOODS
(ARTICLES 40, 41 AND 42 OF DIRECTIVE 2006/112/EC)

Article 16
Where an intra-Community acquisition of goods within the meaning of Article 20 of Directive 2006/112/EC has taken place, the Member State in which the dispatch or transport ends shall exercise its power of taxation irrespective of the VAT treatment applied to the transaction in the Member State in which the dispatch or transport began.

Any request by a supplier of goods for a correction in the VAT invoiced by him and reported by him to the Member State where the dispatch or transport of the goods began shall be treated by that Member State in accordance with its own domestic rules.

SECTION 4
PLACE OF SUPPLY OF SERVICES
(ARTICLES 43 TO 59 OF DIRECTIVE 2006/112/EC)

SUBSECTION 1
STATUS OF THE CUSTOMER

Article 17

1. If the place of supply of services depends on whether the customer is a taxable or non-taxable person, the status of the customer shall be determined on the basis of Articles 9 to 13 and Article 43 of Directive 2006/112/EC.

2. A non-taxable legal person who is identified or required to be identified for VAT purposes under point (b) of Article 214(1) of Directive 2006/112/EC because his intra-Community acquisitions of goods are subject to VAT or because he has exercised the option of making those operations subject to VAT shall be a taxable person within the meaning of Article 43 of that Directive.

Article 18

1. Unless he has information to the contrary, the supplier may regard a customer established within the Community as a taxable person:
    (a) where the customer has communicated his individual VAT identification number to him, and the supplier obtains confirmation of the validity of that identification number and of the associated name and address in accordance with Article 31 of Council Regulation (EC) No 904/2010 of 7 October 2010 on administrative cooperation and combating fraud in the field of value added tax;
    (b) where the customer has not yet received an individual VAT identification number, but informs the supplier that he has applied for it and the supplier obtains any other proof which demonstrates that the customer is a taxable person or a non-taxable legal person required to be identified for VAT purposes and carries out a reasonable level of verification of the accuracy of the information provided by the customer, by normal commercial security measures such as those relating to identity or payment checks.

2. Unless he has information to the contrary, the supplier may regard a customer established within the Community as a non-taxable person when he can demonstrate that the customer has not communicated his individual VAT identification number to him.
[However, irrespective of information to the contrary, the supplier of telecommunications, broadcasting or electronically supplied services may regard a customer established within the Community as a non-taxable person as long as that customer has not communicated his individual VAT identification number to him.][1]

3. Unless he has information to the contrary, the supplier may regard a customer established outside the Community as a taxable person:
    (a) if he obtains from the customer a certificate issued by the customer's competent tax authorities as confirmation that the customer is engaged in economic activities in order to enable him to obtain a refund of VAT under Council Directive 86/560/EEC of 17 November 1986 on the harmonization of the laws of the Member States relating to turnover taxes – Arrangements for the refund of value added tax to taxable persons not established in Community territory
    (b) where the customer does not possess that certificate, if the supplier has the VAT number, or a similar number attributed to the customer by the country of establishment and used to identify businesses or any other proof which demonstrates that the customer is a taxable person and if the supplier carries out a reasonable level of verification of the accuracy of the information provided by the customer, by normal commercial security measures such as those relating to identity or payment checks.

Amendments—[1] Words inserted by Council Implementing Regulation (EU) No 1042/2013 art 1(2)(b) with effect from 1 January 2015 (OJ L 284, 26.10.2013, p 1).

SUBSECTION 2
CAPACITY OF THE CUSTOMER

Article 19

For the purpose of applying the rules concerning the place of supply of services laid down in Articles 44 and 45 of Directive 2006/112/EC, a taxable person, or a non-taxable legal person deemed to be a taxable person, who receives services exclusively for private use, including use by his staff, shall be regarded as a non-taxable person.

Unless he has information to the contrary, such as information on the nature of the services provided, the supplier may consider that the services are for the customer's business use if, for that transaction, the customer has communicated his individual VAT identification number.

Where one and the same service is intended for both private use, including use by the customer's staff, and business use, the supply of that service shall be covered exclusively by Article 44 of Directive 2006/112/EC, provided there is no abusive practice.

SUBSECTION 3
LOCATION OF THE CUSTOMER

Article 20

Where a supply of services carried out for a taxable person, or a non-taxable legal person deemed to be a taxable person, falls within the scope of Article 44 of Directive 2006/112/EC, and where that taxable person is established in a single country, or, in the absence of a place of establishment of a business or a fixed establishment, has his permanent address and usually resides in a single country, that supply of services shall be taxable in that country.

The supplier shall establish that place based on information from the customer, and verify that information by normal commercial security measures such as those relating to identity or payment checks.

The information may include the VAT identification number attributed by the Member State where the customer is established.

Article 21

Where a supply of services to a taxable person, or a non-taxable legal person deemed to be a taxable person, falls within the scope of Article 44 of Directive 2006/112/EC, and the taxable person is established in more than one country, that supply shall be taxable in the country where that taxable person has established his business.

However, where the service is provided to a fixed establishment of the taxable person located in a place other than that where the customer has established his business, that supply shall be taxable at the place of the fixed establishment receiving that service and using it for its own needs.

Where the taxable person does not have a place of establishment of a business or a fixed establishment, the supply shall be taxable at his permanent address or usual residence.

Article 22

1. In order to identify the customer's fixed establishment to which the service is provided, the supplier shall examine the nature and use of the service provided.

Where the nature and use of the service provided do not enable him to identify the fixed establishment to which the service is provided, the supplier, in identifying that fixed establishment, shall pay particular attention to whether the contract, the order form and the VAT identification number attributed by the Member State of the customer and communicated to him by the customer identify the fixed establishment as the customer of the service and whether the fixed establishment is the entity paying for the service.

Where the customer's fixed establishment to which the service is provided cannot be determined in accordance with the first and second subparagraphs of this paragraph or where services covered by Article 44 of Directive 2006/112/EC are supplied to a taxable person under a contract covering one or more services used in an unidentifiable and non-quantifiable manner, the supplier may legitimately consider that the services have been supplied at the place where the customer has established his business.

2. The application of this Article shall be without prejudice to the customer's obligations.

Article 23

1. From 1 January 2013, where, in accordance with the first subparagraph of Article 56(2) of Directive 2006/112/EC, a supply of services is taxable at the place where the customer is established, or, in the absence of an establishment, where he has his permanent address or usually resides, the supplier shall establish that place based on factual information provided by the customer, and verify that information by normal commercial security measures such as those relating to identity or payment checks.

2. Where, in accordance with Articles 58 and 59 of Directive 2006/112/EC, a supply of services is taxable at the place where the customer is established, or, in the absence of an establishment, where he has his permanent address or usually resides, the supplier shall establish that place based on factual information provided by the customer, and verify that information by normal commercial security measures such as those relating to identity or payment checks.

[*Article 24*

Where services covered by the first subparagraph of Article 56(2) or Articles 58 and 59 of Directive 2006/112/EC are supplied to a non-taxable person who is established in more than one country or who has his permanent address in one country and his usual residence in another, priority shall be given:

    (a) in the case of a non-taxable legal person, to the place referred to in point (a) of Article 13a of this Regulation, unless there is evidence that the service is used at the establishment referred to in point (b) of that article;

(b) in the case of a natural person, to the place where he usually resides, unless there is evidence that the service is used at his permanent address.][1]

Amendments—[1] Article 24 substituted by Council Implementing Regulation (EU) No 1042/2013 art 1(2)(c) with effect from 1 January 2015 (OJ L 284, 26.10.2013, p 1).

[SUBSECTION 3A

PRESUMPTIONS FOR THE LOCATION OF THE CUSTOMER

Article 24a

1. For the application of Articles 44, 58 and 59a of Directive 2006/112/EC, where a supplier of telecommunications, broadcasting or electronically supplied services provides those services at a location such as a telephone box, a telephone kiosk, a wi-fi hot spot, an internet café, a restaurant or a hotel lobby where the physical presence of the recipient of the service at that location is needed for the service to be provided to him by that supplier, it shall be presumed that the customer is established, has his permanent address or usually resides at the place of that location and that the service is effectively used and enjoyed there.

2. If the location referred to in paragraph 1 of this Article is on board a ship, aircraft or train carrying out a passenger transport operation effected within the Community pursuant to Articles 37 and 57 of Directive 2006/112/EC, the country of the location shall be the country of departure of the passenger transport operation.

[Article 24b

For the application of Article 58 of Directive 2006/112/EC, where telecommunications, broadcasting or electronically supplied services are supplied to a non-taxable person:
   (a) through his fixed land line, it shall be presumed that the customer is established, has his permanent address or usually resides at the place of installation of the fixed land line;
   (b) through mobile networks, it shall be presumed that the place where the customer is established, has his permanent address or usually resides is the country identified by the mobile country code of the SIM card used when receiving those services;
   (c) for which the use of a decoder or similar device or a viewing card is needed and a fixed land line is not used, it shall be presumed that the customer is established, has his permanent address or usually resides at the place where that decoder or similar device is located, or if that place is not known, at the place to which the viewing card is sent with a view to being used there;
   (d) under circumstances other than those referred to in Article 24a and in points (a), (b) and (c) of this Article, it shall be presumed that the customer is established, has his permanent address or usually resides at the place identified as such by the supplier on the basis of two items of non-contradictory evidence as listed in Article 24f of this Regulation.

Without prejudice to point (d) of the first paragraph, for supplies of services falling under that point, where the total value of such supplies, exclusive of VAT, provided by a taxable person from his business establishment or a fixed establishment located in a Member State, does not exceed EUR 100 000, or the equivalent in national currency, in the current and the preceding calendar year, the presumption shall be that the customer is established, has his permanent address or usually resides at the place identified as such by the supplier on the basis of one item of evidence provided by a person involved in the supply of the services other than the supplier or the customer, as listed in points (a) to (e) of Article 24f.

Where, during a calendar year, the threshold provided in the second paragraph has been exceeded, that paragraph shall not apply as of that time and until such time as the conditions provided in that paragraph are fulfilled again.

The corresponding value in national currency of the amount shall be calculated by applying the exchange rate published by the European Central Bank on the date of adoption of Council Implementing Regulation (EU) 2017/2459.][1]

Amendments—[1] Article 24b substituted by Council Implementing Regulation (EU) 2017/2459 art 1 with effect from 1 January 2019 (OJ L 348, 29.12.2017, p 32).

Article 24c

For the application of Article 56(2) of Directive 2006/112/EC, where the hiring, other than short-term hiring, of means of transport is supplied to a non-taxable person, it shall be presumed that the customer is established, has his permanent address or usually resides at the place identified as such by the supplier on the basis of two items of non- contradictory evidence as listed in Article 24e of this Regulation.][1]

Amendments—[1] Subsections 3a–3c inserted by Council Implementing Regulation (EU) No 1042/2013 art 1(2)(d)(i) with effect from 1 January 2015 (OJ L 284, 26.10.2013, p 1).

[SUBSECTION 3B]
REBUTTAL OF PRESUMPTIONS

Article 24d

1. Where a supplier supplies a service listed in Article 58 of Directive 2006/112/EC, he may rebut a presumption referred to in Article 24a or in point (a), (b) or (c) of Article 24b of this Regulation on the basis of three items of non-contradictory evidence indicating that the customer is established, has his permanent address or usually resides elsewhere.

2. A tax authority may rebut presumptions that have been made under Article 24a, 24b or 24c where there are indications of misuse or abuse by the supplier.][1]

Amendments—[1] Subsections 3a–3c inserted by Council Implementing Regulation (EU) No 1042/2013 art 1(2)(d)(i) with effect from 1 January 2015 (OJ L 284, 26.10.2013, p 1).

[SUBSECTION 3C

EVIDENCE FOR THE IDENTIFICATION OF THE LOCATION OF THE CUSTOMER AND REBUTTAL OF PRESUMPTIONS

Article 24e

For the purposes of applying the rules in Article 56(2) of Directive 2006/112/EC and fulfilling the requirements of Article 24c of this Regulation, the following shall, in particular, serve as evidence:
  (a) the billing address of the customer;
  (b) bank details such as the location of the bank account used for payment or the billing address of the customer held by that bank;
  (c) registration details of the means of transport hired by the customer, if registration of that means of transport is required at the place where it is used, or other similar information;
  (d) other commercially relevant information.

Article 24f

For the purpose of applying the rules in Article 58 of Directive 2006/112/EC and fulfilling the requirements of point (d) of Article 24b or Article 24d(1) of this Regulation, the following shall, in particular, serve as evidence:
  (a) the billing address of the customer;
  (b) the internet Protocol (IP) address of the device used by the customer or any method of geolocation;
  (c) bank details such as the location of the bank account used for payment or the billing address of the customer held by that bank;
  (d) the Mobile Country Code (MCC) of the International Mobile Subscriber Identity (IMSI) stored on the Subscriber Identity Module (SIM) card used by the customer;
  (e) the location of the customer's fixed land line through which the service is supplied to him;
  (f) other commercially relevant information.][1]

Amendments—[1] Subsections 3a–3c inserted by Council Implementing Regulation (EU) No 1042/2013 art 1(2)(d)(i) with effect from 1 January 2015 (OJ L 284, 26.10.2013, p 1).

SUBSECTION 4

COMMON PROVISION REGARDING DETERMINATION OF THE STATUS, THE CAPACITY AND THE LOCATION OF THE CUSTOMER

Article 25

For the application of the rules governing the place of supply of services, only the circumstances existing at the time of the chargeable event shall be taken into account. Any subsequent changes to the use of the service received shall not affect the determination of the place of supply, provided there is no abusive practice.

SUBSECTION 5

SUPPLY OF SERVICES GOVERNED BY THE GENERAL RULES

Article 26

A transaction whereby a body assigns television broadcasting rights in respect of football matches to taxable persons, shall be covered by Article 44 of Directive 2006/112/EC.

Article 27

The supply of services which consist in applying for or receiving refunds of VAT under Council Directive 2008/9/EC of 12 February 2008 laying down detailed rules for the refund of value added tax, provided for in Directive 2006/112/EC, to taxable persons not established in the Member State of refund but established in another Member State shall be covered by Article 44 of Directive 2006/112/EC.

Article 28

In so far as they constitute a single service, the supply of services made in the framework of organising a funeral shall fall within the scope of Articles 44 and 45 of Directive 2006/112/EC.

Article 29

Without prejudice to Article 41 of this Regulation, the supply of services of translation of texts shall fall within the scope of Articles 44 and 45 of Directive 2006/112/EC.

SUBSECTION 6
SUPPLY OF SERVICES BY INTERMEDIARIES

Article 30

The supply of services of intermediaries as referred to in Article 46 of Directive 2006/112/EC shall cover the services of intermediaries acting in the name and on behalf of the recipient of the service procured and the services performed by intermediaries acting in the name and on behalf of the provider of the services procured.

Article 31

Services supplied by intermediaries acting in the name and on behalf of another person consisting of the intermediation in the provision of accommodation in the hotel sector or in sectors having a similar function shall fall within the scope of:
   (a) Article 44 of Directive 2006/112/EC if supplied to a taxable person acting as such, or a non-taxable legal person deemed to be a taxable person;
   (b) Article 46 of that Directive, if supplied to a non-taxable person.

[SUBSECTION 6A
SUPPLY OF SERVICES CONNECTED WITH IMMOVABLE PROPERTY

Article 31a

1. Services connected with immovable property, as referred to in Article 47 of Directive 2006/112/EC, shall include only those services that have a sufficiently direct connection with that property. Services shall be regarded as having a sufficiently direct connection with immovable property in the following cases:
   (a) where they are derived from an immovable property and that property makes up a constituent element of the service and is central to, and essential for, the services supplied;
   (b) where they are provided to, or directed towards, an immovable property, having as their object the legal or physical alteration of that property.
2. Paragraph 1 shall cover, in particular, the following:
   (a) the drawing up of plans for a building or parts of a building designated for a particular plot of land regardless of whether or not the building is erected;
   (b) the provision of on site supervision or security services;
   (c) the construction of a building on land, as well as construction and demolition work performed on a building or parts of a building;
   (d) the construction of permanent structures on land, as well as construction and demolition work performed on permanent structures such as pipeline systems for gas, water, sewerage and the like;
   (e) work on land, including agricultural services such as tillage, sowing, watering and fertilisation;
   (f) surveying and assessment of the risk and integrity of immovable property;
   (g) the valuation of immovable property, including where such service is needed for insurance purposes, to determine the value of a property as collateral for a loan or to assess risk and damages in disputes;
   (h) the leasing or letting of immovable property other than that covered by point (c) of paragraph 3, including the storage of goods for which a specific part of the property is assigned for the exclusive use of the customer;
   (i) the provision of accommodation in the hotel sector or in sectors with a similar function, such as holiday camps or sites developed for use as camping sites, including the right to stay in a specific place resulting from the conversion of timeshare usage rights and the like;
   (j) the assignment or transfer of rights other than those covered by points (h) and (i) to use the whole or parts of an immovable property, including the licence to use part of a property, such as the granting of fishing and hunting rights or access to lounges in airports, or the use of an infrastructure for which tolls are charged, such as a bridge or tunnel;
   (k) the maintenance, renovation and repair of a building or parts of a building, including work such as cleaning, tiling, papering and parqueting;
   (l) the maintenance, renovation and repair of permanent structures such as pipeline systems for gas, water, sewerage and the like;

(m) the installation or assembly of machines or equipment which, upon installation or assembly, qualify as immovable property;
(n) the maintenance and repair, inspection and supervision of machines or equipment if those machines or equipment qualify as immovable property;
(o) property management other than portfolio management of investments in real estate covered by point (g) of paragraph 3, consisting of the operation of commercial, industrial or residential real estate by or on behalf of the owner of the property;
(p) intermediation in the sale, leasing or letting of immovable property and in the establishment or transfer of certain interests in immovable property or rights in rem over immovable property (whether or not treated as tangible property), other than intermediation covered by point (d) of paragraph 3;
(q) legal services relating to the transfer of a title to immovable property, to the establishment or transfer of certain interests in immovable property or rights in rem over immovable property (whether or not treated as tangible property), such as notary work, or to the drawing up of a contract to sell or acquire immovable property, even if the underlying transaction resulting in the legal alteration of the property is not carried through.

3. Paragraph 1 shall not cover the following:
   (a) the drawing up of plans for a building or parts of a building if not designated for a particular plot of land;
   (b) the storage of goods in an immovable property if no specific part of the immovable property is assigned for the exclusive use of the customer;
   (c) the provision of advertising, even if it involves the use of immovable property;
   (d) intermediation in the provision of hotel accommodation or accommodation in sectors with a similar function, such as holiday camps or sites developed for use as camping sites, if the intermediary is acting in the name and on behalf of another person;
   (e) the provision of a stand location at a fair or exhibition site together with other related services to enable the exhibitor to display items, such as the design of the stand, transport and storage of the items, the provision of machines, cable laying, insurance and advertising;
   (f) the installation or assembly, the maintenance and repair, the inspection or the supervision of machines or equipment which is not, or does not become, part of the immovable property;
   (g) portfolio management of investments in real estate;
   (h) legal services other than those covered by point (q) of paragraph 2, connected to contracts, including advice given on the terms of a contract to transfer immovable property, or to enforce such a contract, or to prove the existence of such a contract, where such services are not specific to a transfer of a title on an immovable property.

Article 31b

Where equipment is put at the disposal of a customer with a view to carrying out work on immovable property, that transaction shall only be a supply of services connected with immovable property if the supplier assumes responsibility for the execution of the work.

A supplier who provides the customer with equipment together with sufficient staff for its operation with a view to carrying out work shall be presumed to have assumed responsibility for the execution of that work. The presumption that the supplier has the responsibility for the execution of the work may be rebutted by any relevant means in fact or law.

Article 31c

For the purpose of determining the place of supply of telecommunications, broadcasting or electronically supplied services provided by a taxable person acting in his own name together with accommodation in the hotel sector or in sectors with a similar function, such as holiday camps or sites developed for use as camping sites, those services shall be regarded as being supplied at those locations.][1]

Amendments—[1] Subsection 6a inserted by Council Implementing Regulation (EU) No 1042/2013 art 1(2)(d)(ii) with effect from 1 January 2015 (OJ L 284, 26.10.2013, p 1). Articles 31a, 31b apply from 1 January 2017.

SUBSECTION 7

SUPPLY OF CULTURAL, ARTISTIC, SPORTING, SCIENTIFIC, EDUCATIONAL, ENTERTAINMENT, AND SIMILAR SERVICES

Article 32

1. Services in respect of admission to cultural, artistic, sporting, scientific, educational, entertainment or similar events as referred to in Article 53 of Directive 2006/112/EC shall include the supply of services of which the essential characteristics are the granting of the right of admission to an event in exchange for a ticket or payment, including payment in the form of a subscription, a season ticket or a periodic fee.
2. Paragraph 1 shall apply in particular to:

(a) the right of admission to shows, theatrical performances, circus performances, fairs, amusement parks, concerts, exhibitions, and other similar cultural events;
(b) the right of admission to sporting events such as matches or competitions;
(c) the right of admission to educational and scientific events such as conferences and seminars.
3. Paragraph 1 shall not cover the use of facilities such as gymnastics halls and suchlike, in exchange for the payment of a fee.

Article 33

The ancillary services referred to in Article 53 of Directive 2006/112/EC shall include services which are directly related to admission to cultural, artistic, sporting, scientific, educational, entertainment or similar events and which are supplied separately for a consideration to a person attending an event. Such ancillary services shall include in particular the use of cloakrooms or sanitary facilities but shall not include mere intermediary services relating to the sale of tickets.

[Article 33a

The supply of tickets granting access to a cultural, artistic, sporting, scientific, educational, entertainment or similar event by an intermediary acting in his own name but on behalf of the organiser or by a taxable person, other than the organiser, acting on his own behalf, shall be covered by Article 53 and Article 54(1) of Directive 2006/112/EC.][1]

Amendments—[1] Article 33a inserted by Council Implementing Regulation (EU) No 1042/2013 art 1(2)(d)(iii) with effect from 1 January 2015 (OJ L 284, 26.10.2013, p 1).

SUBSECTION 8
SUPPLY OF ANCILLARY TRANSPORT SERVICES AND VALUATIONS OF AND WORK ON MOVABLE PROPERTY

Article 34

Except where the goods being assembled become part of immovable property, the place of the supply of services to a non-taxable person consisting only of the assembly by a taxable person of the various parts of a machine, all of which were provided to him by his customer, shall be established in accordance with Article 54 of Directive 2006/112/EC.

SUBSECTION 9
SUPPLY OF RESTAURANT AND CATERING SERVICES ON BOARD MEANS OF TRANSPORT

Article 35

The section of a passenger transport operation effected within the Community as referred to in Article 57 of Directive 2006/112/EC shall be determined by the journey of the means of transport and not by the journey completed by each of the passengers.

Article 36

Where restaurant services and catering services are supplied during the section of a passenger transport operation effected within the Community, that supply shall be covered by Article 57 of Directive 2006/112/EC.

Where restaurant services and catering services are supplied outside such a section but on the territory of a Member State or a third country or third territory, that supply shall be covered by Article 55 of that Directive.

Article 37

The place of supply of a restaurant service or catering service carried out within the Community partly during a section of a passenger transport operation effected within the Community, and partly outside such a section but on the territory of a Member State, shall be determined in its entirety according to the rules for determining the place of supply applicable at the beginning of the supply of the restaurant or catering service.

SUBSECTION 10
HIRING OF MEANS OF TRANSPORT

Article 38

1. 'Means of transport' as referred to in Article 56 and point (g) of the first paragraph of Article 59 of Directive 2006/112/EC shall include vehicles, whether motorised or not, and other equipment and devices designed to transport persons or objects from one place to another, which might be pulled, drawn or pushed by vehicles and which are normally designed to be used and actually capable of being used for transport.
2. The means of transport referred to in paragraph 1 shall include, in particular, the following vehicles:
    (a) land vehicles, such as cars, motor cycles, bicycles, tricycles and caravans;

(b) trailers and semi-trailers;
(c) railway wagons;
(d) vessels;
(e) aircraft;
(f) vehicles specifically designed for the transport of sick or injured persons;
(g) agricultural tractors and other agricultural vehicles;
(h) mechanically or electronically propelled invalid carriages.

3. Vehicles which are permanently immobilised and containers shall not be considered to be means of transport as referred to in paragraph 1.

Article 39

1. For the application of Article 56 of Directive 2006/112/EC, the duration of the continuous possession or use of a means of transport which is the subject of hiring shall be determined on the basis of the contract between the parties involved.

The contract shall serve as a presumption which may be rebutted by any means in fact or law in order to establish the actual duration of the continuous possession or use.

The fact that the contractual period of short-term hiring within the meaning of Article 56 of Directive 2006/112/EC is exceeded on grounds of force majeure shall have no bearing on the determination of the duration of the continuous possession or use of the means of transport.

2. Where hiring of one and the same means of transport is covered by consecutive contracts between the same parties, the duration shall be that of the continuous possession or use of the means of transport provided for under the contracts as a whole.

For the purposes of the first subparagraph a contract and its extensions shall be consecutive contracts. However, the duration of the short-term hire contract or contracts preceding a contract which is regarded as long-term shall not be called into question provided there is no abusive practice.

3. Unless there is abusive practice, consecutive contracts between the same parties for different means of transport shall not be considered to be consecutive contracts for the purposes of paragraph 2.

Article 40

The place where the means of transport is actually put at the disposal of the customer as referred to in Article 56(1) of Directive 2006/112/EC, shall be the place where the customer or a third party acting on his behalf takes physical possession of it.

SUBSECTION 11
SUPPLY OF SERVICES TO NON-TAXABLE PERSONS OUT SIDE THE COMMUNITY

Article 41

The supply of services of translation of texts to a non-taxable person established outside the Community shall be covered by point (c) of the first paragraph of Article 59 of Directive 2006/112/EC.

CHAPTER VI
TAXABLE AMOUNT
(TITLE VII OF DIRECTIVE 2006/112/EC)

Article 42

Where a supplier of goods or services, as a condition of accepting payment by credit or debit card, requires the customer to pay an amount to himself or another undertaking, and where the total price payable by that customer is unaffected irrespective of how payment is accepted, that amount shall constitute an integral part of the taxable amount for the supply of the goods or services, under Articles 73 to 80 of Directive 2006/112/EC.

CHAPTER VII
RATES

Article 43

'Provision of holiday accommodation' as referred to in point (12) of Annex III to Directive 2006/112/EC shall include the hiring out of tents, caravans or mobile homes installed on camping sites and used as accommodation.

CHAPTER VIII
EXEMPTIONS

SECTION 1
EXEMPTIONS FOR CERTAIN ACTIVITIES IN THE PUBLIC INTEREST
(ARTICLES 132, 133 AND 134 OF DIRECTIVE 2006/112/EC)

Article 44

Vocational training or retraining services provided under the conditions set out in point (i) of Article 132(1) of Directive 2006/112/EC shall include instruction relating directly to a trade or profession as well as any instruction aimed at acquiring or updating knowledge for vocational purposes. The duration of a vocational training or retraining course shall be irrelevant for this purpose.

SECTION 2
EXEMPTIONS FOR OTHER ACTIVITIES
(ARTICLES 135, 136 AND 137 OF DIRECTIVE 2006/112/EC)

Article 45

The exemption provided for in point (e) of Article 135(1) of Directive 2006/112/EC shall not apply to platinum nobles.

[SECTION 2A
EXEMPTIONS FOR INTRA-COMMUNITY TRANSACTIONS
(ARTICLES 138 TO 142 OF DIRECTIVE 2006/112/EC)

Article 45a

1. For the purpose of applying the exemptions laid down in Article 138 of Directive 2006/112/EC, it shall be presumed that goods have been dispatched or transported from a Member State to a destination outside its territory but within the Community in either of the following cases:
    (a) the vendor indicates that the goods have been dispatched or transported by him or by a third party on his behalf, and either the vendor is in possession of at least two items of non-contradictory evidence referred to in point (a) of paragraph 3 which were issued by two different parties that are independent of each other, of the vendor and of the acquirer, or the vendor is in possession of any single item referred to in point (a) of paragraph 3 together with any single item of non-contradictory evidence referred to in point (b) of paragraph 3 confirming the dispatch or transport which were issued by two different parties that are independent of each other, of the vendor and of the acquirer;
    (b) the vendor is in possession of the following:
        (i) a written statement from the acquirer, stating that the goods have been dispatched or transported by the acquirer, or by a third party on behalf of the acquirer, and identifying the Member State of destination of the goods; that written statement shall state: the date of issue; the name and address of the acquirer; the quantity and nature of the goods; the date and place of the arrival of the goods; in the case of the supply of means of transport, the identification number of the means of transport; and the identification of the individual accepting the goods on behalf of the acquirer; and
        (ii) at least two items of non-contradictory evidence referred to in point (a) of paragraph 3 that were issued by two different parties that are independent of each other, of the vendor and of the acquirer, or any single item referred to in point (a) of paragraph 3 together with any single item of non-contradictory evidence referred to in point (b) of paragraph 3 confirming the dispatch or transport which were issued by two different parties that are independent of each other, of the vendor and of the acquirer.
The acquirer shall furnish the vendor with the written statement referred to in point (b)(i) by the tenth day of the month following the supply.
2. A tax authority may rebut a presumption that has been made under paragraph 1.
3. For the purposes of paragraph 1, the following shall be accepted as evidence of dispatch or transport:
    (a) documents relating to the dispatch or transport of the goods, such as a signed CMR document or note, a bill of lading, an airfreight invoice or an invoice from the carrier of the goods;
    (b) the following documents:
        (i) an insurance policy with regard to the dispatch or transport of the goods, or bank documents proving payment for the dispatch or transport of the goods;
        (ii) official documents issued by a public authority, such as a notary, confirming the arrival of the goods in the Member State of destination;
        (iii) a receipt issued by a warehouse keeper in the Member State of destination, confirming the storage of the goods in that Member State.][1]

Amendments—[1] Section 2A inserted by Council Implementing Regulation (EU) 2018/1912 art 1(1) with effect from 1 January 2020 (OJ L 311, 7.12.2018, p 10).

SECTION 3
EXEMPTIONS ON IMPORTATION
(ARTICLES 143, 144 AND 145 OF DIRECTIVE 2006/112/EC)

Article 46
The exemption provided for in Article 144 of Directive 2006/112/EC shall apply to transport services connected with the importation of movable property carried out as part of a change of residence.

SECTION 4
EXEMPTIONS ON EXPORTATION
(ARTICLES 146 AND 147 OF DIRECTIVE 2006/112/EC)

Article 47
'Means of transport for private use' as referred to in point (b) of Article 146(1) of Directive 2006/112/EC shall include means of transport used for non-business purposes by persons other than natural persons, such as bodies governed by public law within the meaning of Article 13 of that Directive and associations.

Article 48
In order to determine whether, as a condition for the exemption of the supply of goods carried in the personal luggage of travellers, the threshold set by a Member State in accordance with point (c) of the first subparagraph of Article 147(1) of Directive 2006/112/EC has been exceeded, the calculation shall be based on the invoice value. The aggregate value of several goods may be used only if all those goods are included on the same invoice issued by the same taxable person supplying goods to the same customer.

SECTION 5
EXEMPTIONS RELATING TO CERTAIN TRANSACTIONS TREATED AS EXPORTS
(ARTICLES 151 AND 152 OF DIRECTIVE 2006/112/EC)

Article 49
The exemption provided for in Article 151 of Directive 2006/112/EC shall also apply to electronic services where these are provided by a taxable person to whom the special scheme for electronically supplied services provided for in Articles 357 to 369 of that Directive applies.

Article 50
1. In order to qualify for recognition as an international body for the application of point (g) of Article 143(1) and point (b) of the first subparagraph of Article 151(1) of Directive 2006/112/EC a body which is to be set up as a European Research Infrastructure Consortium (ERIC), as referred to in Council Regulation (EC) No 723/2009 of 25 June 2009 on the Community legal framework for a European Research Infrastructure Consortium (ERIC) shall fulfil all of the following conditions:
    (a) it shall have a distinct legal personality and full legal capacity;
    (b) it shall be set up under and shall be subject to European Union law;
    (c) its membership shall include Member States and, where appropriate, third countries and inter-governmental organisations, but exclude private bodies;
    (d) it shall have specific and legitimate objectives that are jointly pursued and essentially non-economic in nature.
2. The exemption provided for in point (g) of Article 143(1) and point (b) of the first subparagraph of Article 151(1) of Directive 2006/112/EC shall apply to an ERIC referred to in paragraph 1 where it is recognised as an international body by the host Member State.
The limits and conditions of such an exemption shall be laid down by agreement between the members of the ERIC in accordance with point (d) of Article 5(1) of Regulation (EC) No 723/2009. Where the goods are not dispatched or transported out of the Member State in which the supply takes place, and in the case of services, the exemption may be granted by means of a refund of the VAT in accordance with Article 151(2) of Directive 2006/112/EC.

Article 51
1. Where the recipient of a supply of goods or services is established within the Community but not in the Member State in which the supply takes place, the VAT and/or excise duty exemption certificate set out in Annex II to this Regulation shall, subject to the explanatory notes set out in the Annex to that certificate, serve to confirm that the transaction qualifies for the exemption under Article 151 of Directive 2006/112/EC.
When making use of that certificate, the Member State in which the recipient of the supply of goods or services is established may decide to use either a common VAT and excise duty exemption certificate or two separate certificates.

2. The certificate referred to in paragraph 1 shall be stamped by the competent authorities of the host Member State. However, if the goods or services are intended for official use, Member States may dispense the recipient from the requirement to have the certificate stamped under such conditions as they may lay down. This dispensation may be withdrawn in the case of abuse.
Member States shall inform the Commission of the contact point designated to identify the services responsible for stamping the certificate and the extent to which they dispense with the requirement to have the certificate stamped. The Commission shall inform the other Member States of the information received from Member States.
3. Where direct exemption is applied in the Member State in which the supply takes place, the supplier shall obtain the certificate referred to in paragraph 1 of this Article from the recipient of the goods or services and retain it as part of his records. If the exemption is granted by means of a refund of the VAT, pursuant to Article 151(2) of Directive 2006/112/EC, the certificate shall be attached to the request for refund submitted to the Member State concerned.

CHAPTER IX
DEDUCTIONS
(TITLE X OF DIRECTIVE 2006/112/EC)

Article 52
Where the Member State of importation has introduced an electronic system for completing customs formalities, the term 'import document' in point (e) of Article 178 of Directive 2006/112/EC shall cover electronic versions of such documents, provided that they allow for the exercise of the right of deduction to be checked.

CHAPTER X
OBLIGATIONS OF TAXABLE PERSONS AND CERTAIN NON-TAXABLE PERSONS
(TITLE XI OF DIRECTIVE 2006/112/EC)

SECTION 1
PERSONS LIABLE TO PAY THE VAT
(ARTICLES 192A TO 205 OF DIRECTIVE 2006/112/EC)

Article 53
1. For the application of Article 192a of Directive 2006/112/EC, a fixed establishment of the taxable person shall be taken into consideration only when it is characterised by a sufficient degree of permanence and a suitable structure in terms of human and technical resources to enable it to make the supply of goods or services in which it intervenes.
2. Where a taxable person has a fixed establishment within the territory of the Member State where the VAT is due, that establishment shall be considered as not intervening in the supply of goods or services within the meaning of point (b) of Article 192a of Directive 2006/112/EC, unless the technical and human resources of that fixed establishment are used by him for transactions inherent in the fulfilment of the taxable supply of those goods or services made within that Member State, before or during this fulfilment.
Where the resources of the fixed establishment are only used for administrative support tasks such as accounting, invoicing and collection of debt-claims, they shall not be regarded as being used for the fulfilment of the supply of goods or services.
However, if an invoice is issued under the VAT identification number attributed by the Member State of the fixed establishment, that fixed establishment shall be regarded as having intervened in the supply of goods or services made in that Member State unless there is proof to the contrary.

Article 54
Where a taxable person has established his place of business within the territory of the Member State where the VAT is due, Article 192a of Directive 2006/112/EC shall not apply whether or not that place of business intervenes in the supply of goods or services he makes within that Member State.

[SECTION 1A
GENERAL OBLIGATIONS
(ARTICLES 242 TO 243 OF DIRECTIVE 2006/112/EC)

Article 54a
1. The register referred to in Article 243(3) of Directive 2006/112/EC that is to be kept by every taxable person who transfers goods under call-off stock arrangements shall contain the following information:
   (a) the Member State from which the goods were dispatched or transported, and the date of dispatch or transport of the goods;
   (b) the VAT identification number of the taxable person for whom the goods are intended, issued by the Member State to which the goods are dispatched or transported;

(c) the Member State to which the goods are dispatched or transported, the VAT identification number of the warehouse keeper, the address of the warehouse at which the goods are stored upon arrival, and the date of arrival of the goods in the warehouse;
(d) the value, description and quantity of the goods that arrived in the warehouse;
(e) the VAT identification number of the taxable person substituting for the person referred to in point (b) of this paragraph under the conditions referred to in Article 17a(6) of Directive 2006/112/EC;
(f) the taxable amount, description and quantity of the goods supplied and the date on which the supply of the goods referred to in point (a) of Article 17a(3) of Directive 2006/112/EC is made and the VAT identification number of the buyer;
(g) the taxable amount, description and quantity of the goods, and the date of occurrence of any of the conditions and the respective ground in accordance with Article 17a(7) of Directive 2006/112/EC;
(h) the value, description and quantity of the returned goods and the date of the return of the goods referred to in Article 17a(5) of Directive 2006/112/EC.

2. The register referred to in Article 243(3) of Directive 2006/112/EC that is to be kept by every taxable person to whom goods are supplied under call-off stock arrangements shall contain the following information:
(a) the VAT identification number of the taxable person who transfers goods under call-off stock arrangements;
(b) the description and quantity of the goods intended for him;
(c) the date on which the goods intended for him arrive in the warehouse;
(d) the taxable amount, description and quantity of the goods supplied to him and the date on which the intra-Community acquisition of the goods referred to in point (b) of Article 17a(3) of Directive 2006/112/EC is made;
(e) the description and quantity of the goods, and the date on which the goods are removed from the warehouse by order of the taxable person referred to in point (a);
(f) the description and quantity of the goods destroyed or missing and the date of destruction, loss or theft of the goods that previously arrived in the warehouse or the date on which the goods were found to be destroyed or missing.

Where the goods are dispatched or transported under call-off stock arrangements to a warehouse keeper different from the taxable person for whom the goods are intended to be supplied, the register of that taxable person does not need to contain the information referred to in points (c), (e) and (f) of the first subparagraph.][1]

Amendments—[1] Section 1A inserted by Council Implementing Regulation (EU) 2018/1912 art 1(12) with effect from 1 January 2020 (OJ L 311, 7.12.2018, p 10).

SECTION 1B

ACCOUNTING (ARTICLES 241 TO 249 OF DIRECTIVE 2006/112/EC)

Article 54b

1. For the application of Article 242a of Directive 2006/112/EC, the term "facilitates" means the use of an electronic interface to allow a customer and a supplier offering services or goods for sale through the electronic interface to enter into contact which results in a supply of goods or services through that electronic interface. However, the term "facilitates" shall not cover a supply of goods or services where all of the following conditions are met:
(a) the taxable person does not set, either directly or indirectly, any of the terms and conditions under which the supply is made;
(b) the taxable person is not, either directly or indirectly, involved in authorising the charge to the customer in respect of the payment made;
(c) the taxable person is not, either directly or indirectly, involved in the ordering or delivery of the goods or in the supply of the services.

2. For the application of Article 242a of Directive 2006/112/EC, the term "facilitates" shall not cover instances where a taxable person only provides any of the following:
(a) the processing of payments in relation to the supply of goods or services;
(b) the listing or advertising of the goods or services;
(c) the redirecting or transferring of customers to other electronic interfaces where goods or services are offered, without any further intervention in the supply.

Article 54c

1. The taxable person referred to in Article 242a of Directive 2006/112/EC shall keep the following records in respect of supplies where he is deemed to have received and supplied goods himself in accordance with Article 14a of Directive 2006/112/EC or where he takes part in a supply of electronically-supplied services for which he is presumed to be acting in his own name in accordance with Article 9a of this Regulation:

(a) the records as set out in Article 63c of this Regulation, where the taxable person has opted to apply one of the special schemes provided for Chapter 6 of Title XII of Directive 2006/112/EC;
(b) the records as set out in Article 242 of Directive 2006/112/EC, where the taxable person has not opted to apply any of the special schemes provided for in Chapter 6 of Title XII of Directive 2006/112/EC.

2. The taxable person referred to in Article 242a of Directive 2006/112/EC shall keep the following information in respect of supplies other than those referred to in paragraph 1:
   (a) the name, postal address and electronic address or website of the supplier whose supplies are facilitated through the use of the electronic interface and, if available:
      (i) the VAT identification number or national tax number of the supplier;
      (ii) the bank account number or number of virtual account of the supplier;
   (b) a description of the goods, their value, the place where the dispatch or transport of the goods ends, together with the time of supply and, if available, the order number or unique transaction number;
   (c) a description of the services, their value, information in order to establish the place of supply and time of supply and, if available, the order number or unique transaction number.

SECTION 2
MISCELLANEOUS PROVISIONS
(ARTICLES 272 AND 273 OF DIRECTIVE 2006/112/EC)

Article 55

For the transactions referred to in Article 262 of Directive 2006/112/EC, taxable persons to whom a VAT identification number has been attributed in accordance with Article 214 of that Directive and non-taxable legal persons identified for VAT purposes shall be required, when acting as such, to communicate their VAT identification number forthwith to those supplying goods and services to them.

The taxable persons referred to in point (b) of Article 3(1) of Directive 2006/112/EC, who are entitled to non-taxation of their intra-Community acquisitions of goods in accordance with the first paragraph of Article 4 of this Regulation, shall not be required to communicate their VAT identification number to those supplying goods to them when a VAT identification number has been attributed to them in accordance with Article 214(1)(d) or (e) of that Directive.

CHAPTER XI
SPECIAL SCHEMES

SECTION 1
SPECIAL SCHEME FOR INVESTMENT GOLD
(ARTICLES 344 TO 356 OF DIRECTIVE 2006/112/EC)

Article 56

'Weights accepted by the bullion markets' as referred to in point (l) of Article 344(1) of Directive 2006/112/EC shall at least cover the units and the weights traded as set out in Annex III to this Regulation.

Article 57

For the purposes of establishing the list of gold coins referred to in Article 345 of Directive 2006/112/EC, 'price' and 'open market value' as referred to in point (2) of Article 344(1) of that Directive shall be the price and open market value on 1 April of each year. If 1 April does not fall on a day on which those values are fixed, the values of the next day on which they are fixed shall be used.

[SECTION 2
SPECIAL SCHEMES FOR NON-ESTABLISHED TAXABLE PERSONS SUPPLYING TELECOMMUNICATIONS SERVICES, BROADCASTING SERVICES OR ELECTRONIC SERVICES TO NON-TAXABLE PERSONS (ARTICLES 358 TO 369K OF DIRECTIVE 2006/112/EC)

SUBSECTION 1
Definitions

Article 57a

For the purposes of this Section, the following definitions shall apply:

(1) "non-Union scheme" means the special scheme for telecommunications services, broadcasting services or electronic services supplied by taxable persons not established within the Community provided for in Section 2 of Chapter 6 of Title XII of Directive 2006/112/EC;
(2) "Union scheme" means the special scheme for telecommunications services, broadcasting services or electronic services supplied by taxable persons established within the Community but not established in the Member State of consumption provided for in Section 3 of Chapter 6 of Title XII of Directive 2006/112/EC;
(3) "special scheme" means the "non-Union scheme" and/or the "Union scheme" as the context requires;
(4) "taxable person" means a taxable person not established within the Community as defined in point (1) of Article 358a of Directive 2006/112/EC, or a taxable person not established in the Member State of consumption, as defined in point (1) of the first paragraph of Article 369a of that Directive.

SUBSECTION 2
Application of the Union scheme

Article 57b

Where a taxable person using the Union scheme has established his business within the Community, the Member State in which his place of business is established shall be the Member State of identification.

Where a taxable person using the Union scheme has established his business outside the Community, but has more than one fixed establishment in the Community, he may choose any Member State in which he has a fixed establishment as the Member State of identification, in accordance with the second paragraph of Article 369a of Directive 2006/112/EC.

SUBSECTION 3
Scope of the Union scheme

Article 57c

The Union scheme shall not apply to telecommunications, broadcasting or electronic services supplied in a Member State where the taxable person has established his business or has a fixed establishment. The supplies of those services shall be declared to the competent tax authorities of that Member State in the VAT return as provided for under Article 250 of Directive 2006/112/EC.

SUBSECTION 4
Identification

Article 57d

When a taxable person informs the Member State of identification that he intends to make use of one of the special schemes, that special scheme shall apply as from the first day of the following calendar quarter.

However, where the first supply of services to be covered by that special scheme takes place before the date referred to in the first paragraph, the special scheme shall apply as from the date of that first supply, provided the taxable person informs the Member State of identification of the commencement of his activities to be covered by the scheme no later than the tenth day of the month following that first supply.

Article 57e

The Member State of identification shall identify the taxable person using the Union scheme by means of his VAT identification number as referred to in Articles 214 and 215 of Directive 2006/112/EC.

Article 57f

1. Where a taxable person using the Union scheme ceases to meet the conditions of the definition laid down in point (2) of the first paragraph of Article 369a of Directive 2006/112/EC, the Member State in which he has been identified shall cease to be the Member State of identification. Where that taxable person still fulfils the conditions for using that special scheme, he shall, to continue using that scheme, indicate as the new Member State of identification the Member State in which he has established his business or, if he has not established his business in the Community, a Member State where he has a fixed establishment.

2. Where the Member State of identification changes in accordance with paragraph 1, that change shall apply as from the date on which the taxable person ceases to have a business establishment or a fixed establishment in the Member State previously indicated as the Member State of identification.

Article 57g

A taxable person using a special scheme may cease using that special scheme regardless of whether he continues to supply services which can be eligible for that special scheme. The taxable person shall inform the Member State of identification at least 15 days before the end of the calendar quarter prior to that in which he intends to cease using the scheme. Cessation shall be effective as of the first day of the next calendar quarter.

VAT obligations relating to supplies of telecommunications, broadcasting or electronic services arising after the date on which the cessation became effective shall be discharged directly with the tax authorities of the Member State of consumption concerned.

Where a taxable person ceases using a special scheme in accordance with the first paragraph, he shall be excluded from using that scheme in any Member State for two calendar quarters from the date of cessation.

SUBSECTION 5
Reporting obligations

Article 57h

1. A taxable person shall, no later than the tenth day of the next month, inform the Member State of identification by electronic means of:
   — the cessation of his activities covered by a special scheme,
   — any changes to his activities covered by a special scheme whereby he no longer meets the conditions necessary for using that special scheme, and
   — any changes to the information previously provided to the Member State of identification.
2. Where the Member State of identification changes in accordance with Article 57f, the taxable person shall inform both relevant Member States of the change no later than the tenth day of the month following the change of establishment. He shall communicate to the new Member State of identification the registration details required when a taxable person makes use of a special scheme for the first time.

SUBSECTION 6
Exclusion

Article 58

Where at least one of the criteria for exclusion laid down in Article 363 or Article 369e of Directive 2006/112/EC applies to a taxable person using one of the special schemes, the Member State of identification shall exclude that taxable person from that scheme.

Only the Member State of identification can exclude a taxable person from using one of the special schemes.

The Member State of identification shall base its decision on exclusion on any information available, including information provided by any other Member State.

The exclusion shall be effective as from the first day of the calendar quarter following the day on which the decision on exclusion is sent by electronic means to the taxable person.

However where the exclusion is due to a change of place of business or fixed establishment, the exclusion shall be effective as from the date of that change.

Article 58a

A taxable person using a special scheme who has, for a period of eight consecutive calendar quarters, made no supplies of services covered by that scheme in any Member State of consumption, shall be assumed to have ceased his taxable activities within the meaning of point (b) of Article 363 or point (b) of Article 369e of Directive 2006/112/EC respectively. This cessation shall not preclude him from using a special scheme if he recommences his activities covered by either scheme.

Article 58b

1. Where a taxable person is excluded from one of the special schemes for persistent failure to comply with the rules relating to that scheme, that taxable person shall remain excluded from using either scheme in any Member State for eight calendar quarters following the calendar quarter during which the taxable person was excluded.

2. A taxable person shall be regarded as having persistently failed to comply with the rules relating to one of the special schemes, within the meaning of point (d) of Article 363 or point (d) of Article 369e of Directive 2006/112/EC, in at least the following cases:
   (a) where reminders pursuant to Article 60a have been issued to him by the Member State of identification, for three immediately preceding calendar quarters and the VAT return has not been submitted for each and every one of these calendar quarters within 10 days after the reminder has been sent;
   (b) where reminders pursuant to Article 63a have been issued to him by the Member State of identification, for three immediately preceding calendar quarters and the full amount of VAT

declared has not been paid by him for each and every one of these calendar quarters within 10 days after the reminder has been sent, except where the remaining unpaid amount is less than EUR 100 for each calendar quarter;
　(c) where following a request from the Member State of identification or the Member State of consumption and one month after a subsequent reminder by the Member State of identification, he has failed to make electronically available the records referred to in Articles 369 and 369k of Directive 2006/112/EC.

Article 58c
A taxable person who has been excluded from one of the special schemes shall discharge all VAT obligations relating to supplies of telecommunications, broadcasting or electronic services arising after the date on which the exclusion became effective directly with the tax authorities of the Member State of consumption concerned.

SUBSECTION 7
VAT return

Article 59
1. Any return period within the meaning of Article 364 or Article 369f of Directive 2006/112/EC shall be a separate return period.
2. Where, in accordance with the second paragraph of Article 57d, a special scheme applies from the date of the first supply, the taxable person shall submit a separate VAT return for the calendar quarter during which the first supply took place.
3. Where a taxable person has been registered under each of the special schemes during a return period, he shall submit VAT returns and make the corresponding payments to the Member State of identification for each scheme in respect of the supplies made and the periods covered by that scheme.
4. Where the Member State of identification changes in accordance with Article 57f after the first day of the calendar quarter in question, the taxable person shall submit VAT returns and make corresponding payments to both the former and the new Member State of identification covering the supplies made during the respective periods in which the Member States have been Member State of identification.

Article 59a
Where a taxable person using a special scheme has supplied no services in any Member State of consumption under that special scheme during a return period, he shall submit a VAT return indicating that no supplies have been made during that period (a nil-VAT return).

Article 60
Amounts on VAT returns made under the special schemes shall not be rounded up or down to the nearest whole monetary unit. The exact amount of VAT shall be reported and remitted.

Article 60a
The Member State of identification shall remind, by electronic means, taxable persons who have failed to submit a VAT return under Article 364 or Article 369f of Directive 2006/112/EC, of their obligation to submit such a return. The Member State of identification shall issue the reminder on the tenth day following that on which the return should have been submitted, and shall inform the other Member States by electronic means that a reminder has been issued.
Any subsequent reminders and steps taken to assess and collect the VAT shall be the responsibility of the Member State of consumption concerned.
Notwithstanding any reminders issued, and any steps taken, by a Member State of consumption, the taxable person shall submit the VAT return to the Member State of identification.

Article 61
1. Changes to the figures contained in a VAT return shall, after its submission, be made only by means of amendments to that return and not by adjustments to a subsequent return.
2. The amendments referred to in paragraph 1 shall be submitted electronically to the Member State of identification within three years of the date on which the initial return was required to be submitted.
However, the rules of the Member State of consumption on assessments and amendments shall remain unaffected.

Article 61a
If a taxable person:
　(a) ceases to use one of the special schemes;
　(b) is excluded from one of the special schemes; or
　(c) changes the Member State of identification in accordance with Article 57f;
he shall submit his final VAT return and the corresponding payment, and any corrections to or late submissions of previous returns, and the corresponding payments, to the Member State which was

the Member State of identification at the time of the cessation, exclusion or change.

SUBSECTION 8
Currency

Article 61b

Where a Member State of identification whose currency is not the euro determines that VAT returns are to be made out in its national currency, that determination shall apply to the VAT returns of all taxable persons using the special schemes.

SUBSECTION 9
Payments

Article 62

Without prejudice to the third paragraph of Article 63a, and to Article 63b, a taxable person shall make any payment to the Member State of identification.

Payments of VAT made by the taxable person under Article 367 or Article 369i of Directive 2006/112/EC shall be specific to the VAT return submitted pursuant to Article 364 or Article 369f of that Directive. Any subsequent adjustment to the amounts paid shall be effected by the taxable person only by reference to that return and may neither be allocated to another return, nor adjusted on a subsequent return. Each payment shall refer to the reference number of that specific return.

Article 63

A Member State of identification which receives a payment in excess of that resulting from the VAT return submitted under Article 364 or Article 369f of Directive 2006/112/EC shall reimburse the overpaid amount directly to the taxable person concerned.

Where a Member State of identification has received an amount in respect of a VAT return subsequently found to be incorrect, and that Member State has already distributed that amount to the Member States of consumption, those Member States of consumption shall each reimburse their respective part of any overpaid amount directly to the taxable person.

However, where overpayments relate to periods up to and including the last return period in 2018, the Member State of identification shall reimburse the relevant portion of the corresponding part of the amount retained in accordance with Article 46(3) of Regulation (EU) No 904/2010 and the Member State of consumption shall reimburse the overpayment less the amount that shall be reimbursed by the Member State of identification.

The Member States of consumption shall, by electronic means, inform the Member State of identification of the amount of those reimbursements.

Article 63a

Where a taxable person has submitted a VAT return under Article 364 or Article 369f of Directive 2006/112/EC, but no payment has been made or the payment is less than that resulting from the return, the Member State of identification shall, by electronic means on the tenth day following the latest day on which the payment should have been made in accordance with Article 367 or Article 369i of Directive 2006/112/EC, remind the taxable person of any VAT payment outstanding. The Member State of identification shall by electronic means inform the Member States of consumption that the reminder has been sent.

Any subsequent reminders and steps taken to collect the VAT shall be the responsibility of the Member State of consumption concerned. When such subsequent reminders have been issued by a Member State of consumption, the corresponding VAT shall be paid to that Member State.

The Member State of consumption shall, by electronic means, inform the Member State of identification that a reminder has been issued.

Article 63b

Where no VAT return has been submitted, or where the VAT return has been submitted late or is incomplete or incorrect, or where the payment of VAT is late, any interest, penalties or any other charges shall be calculated and assessed by the Member State of consumption. The taxable person shall pay such interests, penalties or any other charges directly to the Member State of consumption.

SUBSECTION 10
Records

Article 63c

1. In order to be regarded as sufficiently detailed within the meaning of Articles 369 and 369k of Directive 2006/112/EC, the records kept by the taxable person shall contain the following information:
    (a) the Member State of consumption to which the service is supplied;
    (b) the type of service supplied;
    (c) the date of the supply of service;
    (d) the taxable amount indicating the currency used;
    (e) any subsequent increase or reduction of the taxable amount;

(f) the VAT rate applied;
(g) the amount of VAT payable indicating the currency used;
(h) the date and amount of payments received;
(i) any payments on account received before the supply of service;
(j) where an invoice is issued, the information contained on the invoice;
(k) the name of the customer, where known to the taxable person;
(l) the information used to determine the place where the customer is established or has his permanent address or usually resides.

2. The information referred to in paragraph 1 shall be recorded by the taxable person in such a way that it can be made available by electronic means without delay and for each single service supplied.][1]

Amendments—[1] Section 2 substituted by Council Regulation (EU) No 967/2012 art 2 with effect from 1 January 2015 (OJ L 290, 20.10.2012, p 1).

CHAPTER XII
FINAL PROVISIONS

Article 64

Regulation (EC) No 1777/2005 is hereby repealed.
References made to the repealed Regulation shall be construed as references to this Regulation and shall be read in accordance with the correlation table set out in Annex IV.

Article 65

This Regulation shall enter into force on the 20th day following its publication in the *Official Journal of the European Union*.
It shall apply from 1 July 2011.
However:
— point (a) of Article 3, point (b) of Article 11(2), Article 23(1) and Article 24(1) shall apply from 1 January 2013,
— point (b) of Article 3 shall apply from 1 January 2015,
— point (c) of Article 11(2) shall apply until 31 December 2014.

This Regulation shall be binding in its entirety and directly applicable in all Member States.

Done at Brussels, ... *15 March 2011.*
For the Council
The President
MATOLCSY Gy.

ANNEX I
ARTICLE 7 OF THIS REGULATION

(1) Point (1) of Annex II to Directive 2006/112/EC:
  (a) Website hosting and webpage hosting;
  (b) automated, online and distance maintenance of programmes;
  (c) remote systems administration;
  (d) online data warehousing where specific data is stored and retrieved electronically;
  (e) online supply of on-demand disc space.
(2) Point (2) of Annex II to Directive 2006/112/EC:
  (a) Accessing or downloading software (including procurement/accountancy programmes and anti-virus software) plus updates;
  (b) software to block banner adverts showing, otherwise known as Bannerblockers;
  (c) download drivers, such as software that interfaces computers with peripheral equipment (such as printers);
  (d) online automated installation of filters on websites;
  (e) online automated installation of firewalls.
(3) Point (3) of Annex II to Directive 2006/112/EC:
  (a) Accessing or downloading desktop themes;
  (b) accessing or downloading photographic or pictorial images or screensavers;
  (c) the digitised content of books and other electronic publications;
  (d) subscription to online newspapers and journals;
  (e) weblogs and website statistics;
  (f) online news, traffic information and weather reports;
  (g) online information generated automatically by software from specific data input by the customer, such as legal and financial data, (in particular such data as continually updated stock market data, in real time);
  (h) the provision of advertising space including banner ads on a website/web page;

(i) use of search engines and Internet directories.
(4) Point (4) of Annex II to Directive 2006/112/EC:
   (a) Accessing or downloading of music on to computers and mobile phones;
   (b) accessing or downloading of jingles, excerpts, ringtones, or other sounds;
   (c) accessing or downloading of films;
   (d) downloading of games on to computers and mobile phones;
   (e) accessing automated online games which are dependent on the Internet, or other similar electronic networks, where players are geographically remote from one another.
   [(f) receiving radio or television programmes distributed via a radio or television network, the internet or similar electronic network for listening to or viewing programmes at the moment chosen by the user and at the user's individual request on the basis of a catalogue of programmes selected by the media service provider such as TV or video on demand;
   (g) receiving radio or television programmes distributed via the internet or similar electronic network (IP streaming) unless they are broadcast simultaneously to their being transmitted or retransmitted over a radio and television network;
   (h) the supply of audio and audiovisual content via communications networks which is not provided by and under the editorial responsibility of a media service provider;
   (i) the onward supply of the audio and audiovisual output of a media service provider via communications networks by someone other than the media service provider.][1]
(5) Point (5) of Annex II to Directive 2006/112/EC:
   (a) Automated distance teaching dependent on the Internet or similar electronic network to function and the supply of which requires limited or no human intervention, including virtual classrooms, except where the Internet or similar electronic network is used as a tool simply for communication between the teacher and student;
   (b) workbooks completed by pupils online and marked automatically, without human intervention.

Amendments—[1] Point (4)(f)–(i) inserted by Council Implementing Regulation (EU) No 1042/2013 art 1(3) with effect from 1 January 2015 (OJ L 284, 26.10.2013, p 1).

ANNEX II
ARTICLE 51 OF THIS REGULATION

The form from Annex II can be found at www.eur-lex.europa.eu/LexUriServ/LexUriServ.do?uri=OJ:L:2011:077:0001:0022:EN:PDF.

EXPLANATORY NOTES

1. For the supplier and/or the authorised warehousekeeper, this certificate serves as a supporting document for the tax exemption of the supplies of goods and services or the consignments of goods to the eligible bodies/individuals referred to in Article 151 of Directive 2006/112/EC and Article 13 of Directive 2008/118/EC. Accordingly, one certificate shall be drawn up for each supplier/warehousekeeper. Moreover, the supplier/warehousekeeper is required to keep this certificate as part of his records in accordance with the legal provisions applicable in his Member State.

2.
   (a) The general specification of the paper to be used is as laid down in the *Official Journal of the European Communities* C 164 of 1.7.1989, p. 3.

   The paper is to be white for all copies and should be 210 millimetres by 297 millimetres with a maximum tolerance of 5 millimetres less or 8 millimetres more with regard to their length.

   For an exemption from excise duty the exemption certificate shall be drawn up in duplicate:
   — one copy to be kept by the consignor,
   — one copy to accompany the movement of the products subject to excise duty.
   (b) Any unused space in box 5.B. is to be crossed out so that nothing can be added.
   (c) The document must be completed legibly and in a manner that makes entries indelible. No erasures or overwriting are permitted. It shall be completed in a language recognised by the host Member State.
   (d) If the description of the goods and/or services (box 5.B of the certificate) refers to a purchase order form drawn up in a language other than a language recognised by the host Member Stale, a translation must be attached by the eligible body/individual.
   (e) On the other hand, if the certificate is drawn up in a language other than a language recognised by the Member State of the supplier/warehousekeeper, a translation of the information concerning the goods and services in box 5.B must be attached by the eligible body/individual.

(f) A recognised language means one of the languages officially in use in the Member State or any other official language of the Union which the Member State declares can be used for this purpose.

3. By its declaration in box 3 of the certificate, the eligible body/individual provides the information necessary for the evaluation of the request for exemption in the host Member State.

4. By its declaration in box 4 of the certificate, the body confirms the details in boxes 1 and 3(a) of the document and certifies that the eligible individual is a staff member of the body.

5.
   (a) The reference to the purchase order form (box 5.B of the certificate) must contain at least the date and order number. The order form should contain all the elements that figure at box 5 of the certificate. If the certificate has to be stamped by the competent authority of the host Member State, the order form shall also be stamped.
   (b) The indication of the excise identification number as defined in Article 22(2)(a) of Council Regulation (EC) No 2073/2004 of 16 November 2004 on administrative cooperation in the field of excise duties is optional; the VAT identification number or tax reference number must be indicated.
   (c) The currencies should be indicated by means of a three-letter code in conformity with the ISO code 4217 standard established by the International Standards Organisation .

6. The abovementioned declaration by the eligible body/individual; shall be authenticated at box 6 by the stamp of the competent authority of the host Member State. That authority can make its approval dependent on the agreement of another authority in its Member State. It is up to the competent tax authority to obtain such an agreement.

7. To simplify the procedure, the competent authority can dispense with the obligation on the eligible body to ask for the stamp in the case of exemption for official use. The eligible body should mention this dispensation at box 7 of the certificate.

ANNEX III
ARTICLE 56 OF THIS REGULATION

Unit	Weights traded
Kg	12,5/1
Gram	500/250/100/50/20/10/5/2,5/2
Ounce (1 oz = 31,1035 g)	100/10/5/1/^{1}/$_2$/^{1}/$_4$
Tael (1 tael = 1,193 oz) 10	10/5/1
Tola (10 tolas = 3,75 oz)	10

ANNEX IV
CORRELATION TABLE

Regulation (EC) No 1777/2005	This Regulation
Chapter I	Chapter I
Article 1	Article 1
Chapter II	Chapters III and IV
Section 1 of Chapter II	Chapter III
Article 2	Article 5
Section 2 of Chapter II	Chapter IV
Article 3(1)	Article 9
Article 3(2)	Article 8
Chapter II	Chapter V
Section 1 of Chapter III	Section 4 of Chapter V
Article 4	Article 28
Section 2 of Chapter III	Section 4 of Chapter V
Article 5	Article 34
Article 6	Articles 29 and 41
Article 7	Article 26
Article 8	Article 27
Article 9	Article 30
Article 10	Article 38(2)(b) and (c)
Article 11(1) and (2)	Article 7(1) and (2)

Regulation (EC) No 1777/2005	This Regulation
Article 12	Article 7(3)
Chapter IV	Chapter VI
Article 13	Article 42
Chapter V	Chapter VIII
Section 1 of Chapter V	Section 1 of Chapter VIII
Article 14	Article 44
Article 15	Article 45
Section 2 of Chapter V	Section 4 of Chapter VIII
Article 16	Article 47
Article 17	Article 48
Chapter VI	Chapter IX
Article 18	Article 52
Chapter VII	Chapter XI
Article 19(1)	Article 56
Article 19(2)	Article 57
Article 20(1)	Article 58
Article 20(2)	Article 62
Article 20(3), first subparagraph	Article 59
Article 20(3), second subparagraph	Article 60
Article 20(3), third subparagraph	Article 63
Article 20(4)	Article 61
Chapter VIII	Section 3 of Chapter V
Article 21	Article 16
Article 22	Article 14
Chapter IX	Chapter XII
Article 23	Article 65
Annex I	Annex I
Annex II	Annex III

EU-UK Trade and Cooperation Agreement (protocol: combating VAT fraud etc)

TRADE AND COOPERATION AGREEMENT BETWEEN THE EUROPEAN UNION AND THE EUROPEAN ATOMIC ENERGY COMMUNITY, OF THE ONE PART, AND THE UNITED KINGDOM OF GREAT BRITAIN AND NORTHERN IRELAND, OF THE OTHER PART

Notes—The following text is as agreed between the EU and UK on 24 December 2020. At the time of going to print, the Agreement had not been formally ratified by the EU.

PROTOCOL ON ADMINISTRATIVE COOPERATION AND COMBATING FRAUD IN THE FIELD OF VALUE ADDED TAX AND ON MUTUAL ASSISTANCE FOR THE RECOVERY OF CLAIMS RELATING TO TAXES AND DUTIES

Title I:

GENERAL PROVISIONS

Article 1 Objective

The objective of this Protocol is to establish the framework for administrative cooperation between the Member States and the United Kingdom, in order to enable their authorities to assist each other in ensuring compliance with VAT legislation and in protecting VAT revenue and in recovering claims relating to taxes and duties.

Article 2 Scope

1. This Protocol lays down rules and procedures for cooperation:
   (a) to exchange any information that may help to effect a correct assessment of VAT, monitor the correct application of VAT, and combat VAT fraud; and
   (b) for the recovery of:
      (i) claims relating to VAT, customs duties and excise duties, levied by or on behalf of a State or its territorial or administrative subdivisions, excluding the local authorities, or on behalf of the Union;
      (ii) administrative penalties, fines, fees and surcharges relating to the claims referred to in point (i) imposed by the administrative authorities that are competent to levy the taxes or duties concerned or carry out administrative enquiries with regard to them, or confirmed by administrative or judicial bodies at the request of those administrative authorities; and
      (iii) interest and costs relating to the claims referred to in points (i) and (ii).

2. This Protocol does not affect the application of the rules on administrative cooperation and combating fraud in the field of VAT and assistance for the recovery of claims between Member States.

3. This Protocol does not affect the application of the rules on mutual assistance in criminal matters

Article 3 Definitions

For the purpose of this Protocol, the following definitions shall apply:
   (a) "administrative enquiry" means all the controls, checks and other action taken by the States in the performance of their duties with a view to ensuring the proper application of the VAT legislation;
   (b) "applicant authority" means a central liaison office or a liaison department of a State which makes a request under Title III [Recovery assistance];
   (c) "automatic exchange" means the systematic communication of predefined information to another State, without prior request;
   (d) "by electronic means" means using electronic equipment for the processing (including digital compression) and storage of data, and employing wires, radio transmission, optical technologies or other electromagnetic means;
   (e) "CCN/CSI network" means the common platform based on the common communication network ('CCN') and common system interface ('CSI'), developed by the Union to ensure all transmissions by electronic means between competent authorities in the area of taxation.
   (f) "central liaison office" means the office designated pursuant to paragraph 2 of Article 4 [Organisation] with the principal responsibility for contacts for the application of Title II [Administrative Cooperation and Combating VAT Fraud] or Title III [Recovery assistance];

(g) "competent authority" means the authority designated pursuant to paragraph 1 of Article 4 [Organisation];
(h) "competent official" means any official designated pursuant to paragraph 4 of Article 4 [Organisation] who can directly exchange information under Title II [Administrative Cooperation and Combating VAT Fraud];
(i) "customs duties" means the duty payable on goods entering or leaving the customs territory of each Party in accordance with the rules set out in the customs legislation of the respective Parties;
(j) "excise duties" means those duties and charges defined as such under the domestic legislation of the State in which the applicant authority is located;
(k) "liaison department" means any office other than the central liaison office designated as such pursuant to paragraph 3 of Article 4) [Organisation] to request or grant mutual assistance under Title II [Administrative Cooperation and Combating VAT Fraud] or Title III [Recovery assistance];
(l) "person" means any person as defined in point (m) of Article OTH.1(l), of Title XVII [OTHER PROVISIONS] of Part Two of this Agreement. (m) "requested authority" means the central liaison office, the liaison department or – as far as cooperation under Title II [Administrative Cooperation and Combating VAT Fraud] is concerned – the competent official who receives a request from a requesting or an applicant authority;
(n) "requesting authority" means a central liaison office, a liaison department or a competent official who makes a request for assistance under Title II [Administrative Cooperation and Combating VAT Fraud], on behalf of a competent authority;
(o) "simultaneous control" means the coordinated checking of the tax situation of a taxable person or of two or more related taxable persons organised by two or more States with common or complementary interests;
(p) "Specialised Committee" means the Trade Specialised Committee on Administrative cooperation in VAT and Recovery of Taxes and Duties;
(q) "spontaneous exchange" means the non-systematic communication, at any moment and without prior request, of information to another State;
(r) "State" means a Member State, or the United Kingdom, as the context requires;
(s) "third country" means a country that is neither a Member State nor the United Kingdom;
(t) "VAT" means value added tax pursuant to Council Directive 2006/112/EC on the common system of value added tax for the Union and means value added tax pursuant to the Value Added Tax Act 1994 for the United Kingdom.

Article 4 Organisation
1. Each State shall designate a competent authority responsible for the application of this Protocol.
2. Each State shall designate:
   (a) one central liaison office with the principal responsibility for the application of Title II [Administrative Cooperation and Combating VAT Fraud] of this Protocol; and
   (b) one central liaison office with the principal responsibility for the application of Title III [Recovery assistance] of this Protocol.
3. Each competent authority may designate, directly or by delegation:
   (a) liaison departments to exchange directly information under Title II [Administrative Cooperation and Combating VAT Fraud] of this Protocol;
   (b) liaison departments to request or grant mutual assistance under Title III [Recovery assistance] of this Protocol, in relation to their specific territorial or operational competences.
4. Each competent authority may designate, directly or by delegation, competent officials who can directly exchange information on the basis of Title II [Administrative Cooperation and Combating VAT Fraud] of this Protocol.
5. Each central liaison office shall keep the list of liaison departments and competent officials up-to-date and make it available to the other central liaison offices.
6. Where a liaison department or a competent official sends or receives a request for assistance under this Protocol, it shall inform its central liaison office thereof.
7. Where a central liaison office, a liaison department or a competent official receives a request for mutual assistance requiring action outside its competence, it shall forward the request without delay to the competent central liaison office or liaison department, and shall inform the requesting or applicant authority thereof. In such a case, the period laid down in Article 8 [Time limit for providing information] shall start the day after the request for assistance has been forwarded to the competent central liaison office or the competent liaison department.
8. Each Party shall inform the Specialised Committee of its competent authorities for the purposes of this Protocol within one month of the signature of this Agreement and of any changes regarding those competent authorities without delay. The Specialised Committee shall keep the list of competent authorities updated.

Article 5 Service level agreement
A service level agreement ensuring the technical quality and quantity of the services for the functioning of the communication and information exchange systems shall be concluded according to a procedure established by the Specialised Committee.

Article 6 Confidentiality
1. Any information obtained by a State under this Protocol shall be treated as confidential and shall be protected in the same manner as information obtained under its domestic law.
2. Such information may be disclosed to persons or authorities (including courts and administrative or supervisory bodies) concerned with the application of VAT laws and for the purpose of a correct assessment of VAT as well as for the purpose of applying enforcement measures including recovery or precautionary measures with regard to claims referred to in point (b) of paragraph 1 of Article 2 [Scope].
3. The information referred to in paragraph 1 may also be used for assessment of other taxes and for assessment and enforcement, including recovery or precautionary measures, with regard to claims relating to compulsory social security contributions. If the information exchanged reveals or helps to prove the existence of breaches of the tax law, it may also be used for imposing administrative or criminal sanctions. Only the persons or authorities mentioned in paragraph 2 may use the information and then only for purposes set out in the preceding sentences of this paragraph. They may disclose it in public court proceedings or in judicial decisions.
4. Notwithstanding paragraphs 1 and 2, the State providing the information shall, on the basis of a reasoned request, permit its use for purposes other than those referred to in paragraph 1 of Article 2 [Scope] by the State which receives the information if, under the legislation of the State providing the information, the information may be used for similar purposes. The requested authority shall accept or refuse any such request within one month.
5. Reports, statements and any other documents, or certified true copies or extracts thereof, obtained by a State under the assistance provided by this Protocol may be invoked as evidence in that State on the same basis as similar documents provided by another authority of that State.
6. Information provided by a State to another State may be transmitted by the latter to another State, subject to prior authorisation by the competent authority from which the information originated. The State of origin of the information may oppose such a sharing of information within ten working days of the date on which it received the communication from the State wishing to share the information.
7. The States may transmit information obtained in accordance with this Protocol to third countries subject to the following conditions:
   (a) the competent authority from which the information originates has consented to that transmission; and
   (b) the transmission is permitted by assistance arrangements between the State transmitting the information and that particular third country.
8. When a State receives information from a third country, the States may exchange that information, in so far as permitted by the assistance arrangements with that particular third country.
9. Each State shall immediately notify the other States concerned regarding any breach of confidentiality, and any sanctions and remedial actions consequently imposed.
10. Persons duly accredited by the Security Accreditation Authority of the European Commission may have access to this information only in so far as it is necessary for care, maintenance and development of the electronic systems hosted by the European Commission and used by the States to implement this Protocol.

Title II:

ADMINISTRATIVE COOPERATION AND COMBATING VAT FRAUD

CHAPTER ONE

Exchange of information on request

Article 7 Exchange of information and administrative enquiries
1. At the request of the requesting authority, the requested authority shall communicate the information referred to point (a) of paragraph 1 of Article 2 [Scope], including any information relating to a specific case or cases.
2. For the purpose of forwarding the information referred to in paragraph 1, the requested authority shall arrange for the conduct of any administrative enquiries necessary to obtain such information.
3. The request referred to in paragraph 1 may contain a reasoned request for a specific administrative enquiry. The requested authority shall undertake the administrative enquiry in consultation with the requesting authority where necessary. If the requested authority takes the view that no administrative enquiry is necessary, it shall immediately inform the requesting authority of the reasons thereof.
4. Where the requested authority refuses to undertake an administrative enquiry into amounts that were declared or amounts that should have been declared by a taxable person established in the State of the requested authority in connection with supplies of goods or services and imports of goods

which are made by that taxable person and which are taxable in the State of the requesting authority, the requested authority shall at least provide to the requesting authority the dates and values of any relevant supplies and imports made by the taxable person in the State of the requesting authority over the previous two years, unless the requested authority does not hold and is not required to hold this information under domestic legislation.

5. In order to obtain the information sought or to conduct the administrative enquiry requested, the requested authority or the administrative authority to which it has recourse shall proceed as though acting on its own account or at the request of another authority in its own State.

6. At the request of the requesting authority, the requested authority shall communicate to it any pertinent information it obtains or has in its possession as well as the results of administrative enquiries, in the form of reports, statements and any other documents, or certified true copies or extracts thereof.

7. Original documents shall be provided only where this is not contrary to the provisions in force in the State of the requested authority.

Article 8 Time limit for providing information

1. The requested authority shall provide the information referred to in Article 7 as quickly as possible and no later than 90 days following the date of receipt of the request. However, where the requested authority is already in possession of that information, the time limit shall be reduced to a maximum period of 30 days.

2. In certain special categories of cases, time limits which are different from those provided for in paragraph 1 may be agreed between the requested and the requesting authorities.

3. Where the requested authority is unable to respond to the request within the time limits referred to in paragraphs 1 and 2, it shall forthwith inform the requesting authority in writing of the reasons for its failure to do so, and when it considers it would be likely to be able to respond.

CHAPTER 2

Exchange of information without prior request

Article 9 Types of exchange of information

The exchange of information without prior request shall either be spontaneous exchanges, as provided for in Article 10, or automatic exchanges, as provided for in Article 11.

Article 10 Spontaneous exchange of information

The competent authority of a State shall, without prior request, forward to the competent authority of another State the information referred to in point (a) of paragraph 1 of Article 2 [Scope] which has not been forwarded under the automatic exchange referred to in Article 11 [Automatic exchange of information] and of which it is aware of in the following cases:

(a) where taxation is deemed to take place in another State and information is necessary for the effectiveness of the control system of that State;

(b) where a State has grounds to believe that a breach of VAT legislation has been committed or is likely to have been committed in the other State;

(c) where there is a risk of tax loss in the other State.

Article 11 Automatic exchange of information

1. The categories of information subject to automatic exchange shall be determined by the Specialised Committee in accordance with Article 39 [Trade Specialised Committee on Administrative Cooperation in VAT and Recovery of Taxes and Duties].

2. A State may abstain from taking part in the automatic exchange of one or more categories of information referred to in paragraph 1 where the collection of information for such exchange would require the imposition of new obligations on persons liable for VAT or would impose a disproportionate administrative burden on that State.

3. Each State shall notify the Specialised Committee in writing of its decision taken in accordance with the previous paragraph.

CHAPTER 3

Other forms of cooperation

Article 12 Administrative notification

1. The requested authority shall, at the request of the requesting authority and in accordance with the rules governing the notification of similar instruments and decisions in the State of the requested authority, notify the addressee of all instruments and decisions which have been sent from the requesting authorities and concern the application of VAT legislation in the State of the requesting authority.

2. Requests for notification, mentioning the subject of the instrument or decision to be notified, shall indicate the name, address and any other relevant information for identifying the addressee.

3. The requested authority shall inform the requesting authority immediately of its response to the request for notification and notify it, in particular, of the date of notification of the decision or instrument to the addressee.

Article 13 Presence in administrative offices and participation in administrative enquiries

1. By agreement between the requesting authority and the requested authority, and in accordance with the arrangements laid down by the latter, the requested authority may allow officials authorised by the requesting authority to be present in the offices of the requested authority, or any other place where those authorities carry out their duties, with a view to exchanging the information referred to in point (a) of paragraph 1 of Article 2 [Scope]. Where the requested information is contained in documentation to which the officials of the requested authority have access, the officials of the requesting authority shall be given copies thereof on request.

2. By agreement between the requesting authority and the requested authority, and in accordance with the arrangements laid down by the latter, the requested authority may allow officials authorised by the requesting authority to be present during the administrative enquiries carried out in the territory of the State of the requested authority, with a view to exchanging the information referred to in point (a) of paragraph 1 of Article 2 [Scope]. Such administrative enquiries shall be carried out exclusively by the officials of the requested authority. The officials of the requesting authority shall not exercise the powers of inspection conferred on officials of the requested authority. They may, however, have access to the same premises and documents as the latter, through the intermediation of the officials of the requested authority and for the sole purpose of carrying out the administrative enquiry.

3. By agreement between the requesting authorities and the requested authority, and in accordance with the arrangements laid down by the latter, officials authorised by the requesting authorities may take part in the administrative enquiries carried out in the territory of the requested State with a view to collecting and exchanging the information referred to in point (a) of paragraph 1 of Article 2 [Scope]. Such administrative enquiries shall be carried out jointly by the officials of the requesting and requested authorities and shall be conducted under the direction and according to the legislation of the requested State. The officials of the requesting authorities shall have access to the same premises and documents as the officials of the requested authority and, in so far as it is permitted under the legislation of the requested State for its officials, shall be able to interview taxable persons. Where it is permitted under the legislation of the requested State, the officials of the requesting States shall exercise the same inspection powers as those conferred on officials of the requested State.

The inspection powers of the officials of the requesting authorities shall be exercised for the sole purpose of carrying out the administrative enquiry.

By agreement between the requesting authorities and the requested authority and in accordance with the arrangements laid down by the requested authority, the participating authorities may draft a common enquiry report.

4. The officials of the requesting authority present in another State in accordance with paragraphs 1, 2 and 3 must at all times be able to produce written authority stating their identity and their official capacity.

Article 14 Simultaneous controls

1. The States may agree to conduct simultaneous controls whenever they consider such controls to be more effective than controls carried out by only one State.

2. A State shall identify independently the taxable persons which it intends to propose for a simultaneous control. The competent authority of that State shall notify the competent authority of the other State concerned of the cases proposed for a simultaneous control. It shall give reasons for its choice, as far as possible, by providing the information which led to its decision. It shall specify the period of time during which such controls should be conducted.

3. A competent authority that receives the proposal for a simultaneous control shall confirm its agreement or communicate its reasoned refusal to the counterpart authority, in principle within two weeks of receipt of the proposal, but within a month of receipt of the proposal at the latest.

4. Each competent authority concerned shall appoint a representative to be responsible for supervising and coordinating the control operation.

CHAPTER 4

General provisions

Article 15 Conditions governing the exchange of information

1. The requested authority shall provide a requesting authority with the information referred to in point (a) of paragraph 1 of Article 2 [Scope] or carry out an administrative notification referred to in Article 12 [Administrative notification] provided that:
   (a) the number and nature of the requests for information or administrative notification made by the requesting authority do not impose a disproportionate administrative burden on that requested authority; and

(b) the requesting authority has exhausted the usual sources of information which it could have used in the circumstances to obtain the information requested or measures which it could reasonably have taken to carry out the administrative notification requested, without running the risk of jeopardising the achievement of the desired end.

2. This Protocol shall impose no obligation to have enquiries carried out or to provide information on a particular case if the laws or administrative practices of the State which would have to supply the information do not authorise that State to carry out those enquiries or collect or use that information for its own purposes.

3. A requested authority may refuse to provide information where the requesting authority is unable, for legal reasons, to provide similar information. The requested authority shall inform the Specialised Committee of the grounds for the refusal.

4. The provision of information may be refused where it would lead to the disclosure of a commercial, industrial or professional secret or of a commercial process, or of information whose disclosure would be contrary to public policy.

5. Paragraphs 2, 3 and 4 should in no case be interpreted as authorising the requested authority to refuse to supply information on the sole grounds that this information is held by a bank, other financial institution, nominee or person acting in an agency or fiduciary capacity or because it relates to ownership interests in a legal person.

6. The requested authority shall inform the requesting authority of the grounds for refusing a request for assistance.

Article 16 Feedback

Where a competent authority provides information pursuant to Article 7 [Exchange of information and administrative enquiries] or 10 [Spontaneous exchange of information], it may request the competent authority which receives the information to give feedback thereon. If such request is made, the competent authority which receives the information shall, without prejudice to the rules on tax secrecy and data protection applicable in its State, send feedback as soon as possible, provided that this does not impose a disproportionate administrative burden on it.

Article 17 Language

Requests for assistance, including requests for notification and attached documents, shall be made in a language agreed between the requested and requesting authority.

Article 18 Statistical data

1. By 30 June each year, the Parties shall communicate by electronic means to the Specialised Committee statistical data on the application of this Title.

2. The content and format of the statistical data to be communicated under paragraph 1 shall be determined by the Specialised Committee.

Article 19 Standard forms and means of communication

1. Any information communicated pursuant to Articles 7 [Exchange of information and administrative enquiries], 10 [Spontaneous exchange of information], 11 [Automatic exchange of information], 12 [Administrative notification] and 16 [Feedback] and the statistics pursuant to Article 18 [Statistical data] shall be provided using a standard form referred to in point (d) of paragraph 2 of Article 39 [Trade Specialised Committee on Administrative Cooperation in VAT and Recovery of Taxes and Duties], except in the cases referred to in paragraphs 7 and 8 of Article 6 [Confidentiality]or in specific cases where the respective competent authorities deem other secure means more appropriate and agree to use those means.

2. The standard forms shall be transmitted, in so far as possible, by electronic means.

3. Where the request has not been lodged completely through the electronic systems, the requested authority shall confirm receipt of the request by electronic means without delay and, in any event, no later than five working days after receipt.

4. Where an authority has received a request or information of which it is not the intended recipient, it shall send a message by electronic means to the sender without delay and, in any event, no later than five working days after receipt.

5. Pending the adoption by the Specialised Committee of the decisions referred to in paragraph 2 of Article 39 [Trade Specialised Committee on Administrative Cooperation in VAT and Recovery of Taxes and Duties], the competent authorities shall make use of the rules set out in the Annex to this Protocol, including the standard forms.

Title III:
RECOVERY ASSISTANCE
CHAPTER ONE
Exchange of information

Article 20 Request for information

1. At the request of the applicant authority, the requested authority shall provide any information which is foreseeably relevant to the applicant authority in the recovery of its claims as referred to in point (b) of paragraph 1 of Article 2 [Scope]. The request for information shall include, where available, the name and any other data relevant to the identification of the persons concerned. For the purpose of providing that information, the requested authority shall arrange for the carryingout of any administrative enquiries necessary to obtain it.

2. The requested authority shall not be obliged to supply information:
    (a) which it would not be able to obtain for the purpose of recovering similar claims on its own behalf;
    (b) which would disclose any commercial, industrial or professional secrets; or
    (c) the disclosure of which would be liable to prejudice the security of or be contrary to the public policy of the State of the requested authority.

3. Paragraph 2 shall in no case be construed as permitting a requested authority to decline to supply information solely because this information is held by a bank, other financial institution, nominee or person acting in an agency or a fiduciary capacity or because it relates to ownership interests in a legal person.

4. The requested authority shall inform the applicant authority of the grounds for refusing a request for information.

Article 21 Exchange of information without prior request

Where a refund of taxes or duties relates to a person established or resident in another State, the State from which the refund is to be made may inform the State of establishment or residence of the pending refund.

Article 22 Presence in administrative offices and participation in administrative enquiries

1. By agreement between the applicant authority and the requested authority, and in accordance with the arrangements laid down by the latter, officials authorised by the applicant authority may, with a view to promoting mutual assistance provided for in this Title:
    (a) be present in the offices where officials of the requested State carry out their duties;
    (b) be present during administrative enquiries carried out in the territory of the requested State; and
    (c) assist the competent officials of the requested State during court proceedings in that State.

2. In so far as it is permitted under applicable legislation in the requested State, the agreement referred to in point (b) of paragraph 1 may provide that officials of the applicant authority may interview individuals and examine records.

3. Officials authorised by the applicant authority who make use of the possibility offered by paragraphs 1 and 2 must at all times be able to produce written authority stating their identity and their official capacity.

CHAPTER TWO
Assistance for the notification of documents

Article 23 Request for notification of certain documents relating to claims

1. At the request of the applicant authority, the requested authority shall notify to the addressee all documents, including those of a judicial nature, which have been sent from the State of the applicant authority and which relate to a claim as referred to in point (b) of paragraph 1 of Article 2 [Scope] or to its recovery.

The request for notification shall be accompanied by a standard form containing at least the following information:
    (a) name, address and other data relevant to the identification of the addressee;
    (b) the purpose of the notification and the period within which notification should be effected;
    (c) a description of the attached document and the nature and amount of the claim concerned; and
    (d) name, address and other contact details regarding:
        (i) the office responsible with regard to the attached document; and
        (ii) if different, the office where further information can be obtained concerning the notified document or concerning the possibilities for contesting the payment obligation.

2. The applicant authority shall make a request for notification pursuant to this Article only when it is unable to notify in accordance with the rules governing the notification of the document concerned in its own State or when such notification would give rise to disproportionate difficulties.

3. The requested authority shall forthwith inform the applicant authority of any action taken on its request for notification and in particular of the date of notification of the document to the addressee.

Article 24 Means of notification

1. The requested authority shall ensure that notification in the requested State is effected in accordance with the applicable national laws, regulations and administrative practices.
2. Paragraph 1 shall be without prejudice to any other form of notification made by a competent authority of the applicant State in accordance with the rules in force in that State.
A competent authority established in the applicant State may notify any document directly by registered mail or electronically to a person within the territory of another State.

CHAPTER THREE

Recovery or precautionary measures

Article 25 Request for recovery

1. At the request of the applicant authority, the requested authority shall recover claims which are the subject of an instrument permitting enforcement in the State of the applicant authority.
2. As soon as any relevant information relating to the matter which gave rise to the request for recovery comes to the knowledge of the applicant authority, it shall forward it to the requested authority.

Article 26 Conditions governing a request for recovery

1. The applicant authority may not make a request for recovery if and as long as the claim or the instrument permitting its enforcement are contested in the State of the applicant authority, except in cases where the third subparagraph of paragraph 4 of Article 29 [Disputed claims and enforcement measures] applies.
2. Before the applicant authority makes a request for recovery, appropriate recovery procedures available in the State of the applicant authority shall be applied, except in the following situations:
   (a) where it is obvious that there are no assets for recovery in that State or that such procedures will not result in the payment of a substantial amount, and the applicant authority has specific information indicating that the person concerned has assets in the State of the requested authority;
   (b) where recourse to such procedures in the State of the applicant authority would give rise to disproportionate difficulty.

Article 27 Instrument permitting enforcement in the State of the requested authority and other accompanying documents

1. Any request for recovery shall be accompanied by a uniform instrument permitting enforcement in the State of the requested authority.
This uniform instrument permitting enforcement shall reflect the substantial contents of the initial instrument permitting enforcement in the State of the applicant authority, and constitute the sole basis for recovery and precautionary measures in the State of the requested authority. No act of recognition, supplementing or replacement shall be required in that State.
The uniform instrument permitting enforcement shall contain at least the following information:
   (a) information relevant to the identification of the initial instrument permitting enforcement, a description of the claim, including its nature, the period covered by the claim, any dates of relevance to the enforcement process, and the amount of the claim and its different components such as principal, interest accrued, etc.;
   (b) name and other data relevant to the identification of the debtor; and
   (c) name, address and other contact details regarding:
      (i) the office responsible for the assessment of the claim; and
      (ii) if different, the office where further information can be obtained concerning the claim or the possibilities for contesting the payment obligation.
2. The request for recovery of a claim may be accompanied by other documents relating to the claim issued by the State of the applicant authority.

Article 28 Execution of the request for recovery

1. For the purpose of the recovery in the State of the requested authority, any claim in respect of which a request for recovery has been made shall be treated as if it was a claim of that State, except where otherwise provided for in this Protocol. The requested authority shall make use of the powers and procedures provided under the laws, regulations or administrative provisions of that State applying to its claims except where otherwise provided for in this Protocol.
The State of the requested authority shall not be obliged to grant to claims whose recovery is requested preferences accorded to similar claims arising in the State of the requested authority, except where otherwise agreed or provided under the law of that State.
The State of the requested authority shall recover the claim in its own currency.
2. The requested authority shall inform the applicant authority with due diligence of any action it has taken on the request for recovery.

3. From the date on which the recovery request is received, the requested authority shall charge interest for late payment in accordance with the laws, regulations and administrative provisions applicable to its own claims.

4. The requested authority may, where the applicable laws, regulations or administrative provisions so permit, allow the debtor time to pay or authorise payment by instalment and it may charge interest in that respect. It shall inform the applicant authority of any such decision.

5. Without prejudice to paragraph 1 of Article 35 [Costs], the requested authority shall remit to the applicant authority the amounts recovered with respect to the claim and the interest referred to in paragraphs 3 and 4 of this Article.

Article 29 Disputed claims and enforcement measures

1. Disputes concerning the claim, the initial instrument permitting enforcement in the State of the applicant authority or the uniform instrument permitting enforcement in the State of the requested authority and disputes concerning the validity of a notification made by an applicant authority shall fall within the competence of the competent bodies of the State of the applicant authority. If, in the course of the recovery procedure, the claim, the initial instrument permitting enforcement in the State of the applicant authority or the uniform instrument permitting enforcement in the State of the requested authority is contested by an interested party, the requested authority shall inform that party that such an action must be brought by the latter before the competent body of the State of the applicant authority in accordance with the laws in force there.

2. Disputes concerning enforcement measures taken in the State of the requested authority or concerning the validity of a notification made by an authority of the requested State shall be brought before the competent body of that State in accordance with its laws and regulations.

3. Where an action as referred to in paragraph 1 has been brought, the applicant authority shall inform the requested authority thereof and shall indicate the extent to which the claim is not contested.

4. As soon as the requested authority has received the information referred to in paragraph 3, either from the applicant authority or from the interested party, it shall suspend the enforcement procedure, as far as the contested part of the claim is concerned, pending the decision of the body competent in the matter, unless the applicant authority requests otherwise in accordance with the third subparagraph of this paragraph.

At the request of the applicant authority, or where otherwise deemed to be necessary by the requested authority, and without prejudice to Article 31 [Request for precautionary measures], the requested authority may take precautionary measures to guarantee recovery in so far as the applicable laws or regulations allow.

The applicant authority may, in accordance with the laws, regulations and administrative practices in force in its State, ask the requested authority to recover a contested claim or the contested part of a claim, in so far as the laws, regulations and administrative practices in force in the State of the requested authority allow. Any such request shall be reasoned. If the result of contestation is subsequently favourable to the debtor, the applicant authority shall be liable for reimbursing any sums recovered, together with any compensation due, in accordance with the laws in force in the State of the requested authority.

If a mutual agreement procedure has been initiated between the State of the applicant authority and the State of requested authority, and the outcome of the procedure may affect the claim in respect of which assistance has been requested, the recovery measures shall be suspended or stopped until that procedure has been terminated, unless it concerns a case of immediate urgency because of fraud or insolvency. If the recovery measures are suspended or stopped, the second subparagraph shall apply.

Article 30 Amendment or withdrawal of the request for recovery assistance

1. The applicant authority shall inform the requested authority immediately of any subsequent amendment to its request for recovery or of the withdrawal of its request, indicating the reasons for amendment or withdrawal.

2. If the amendment of the request is caused by a decision of the competent body referred to in paragraph 1 of Article 29 [Disputed claims and enforcement measures], the applicant authority shall communicate this decision together with a revised uniform instrument permitting enforcement in the State of the requested authority. The requested authority shall then proceed with further recovery measures on the basis of the revised instrument.

Recovery or precautionary measures already taken on the basis of the original uniform instrument permitting enforcement in the State of the requested authority may be continued on the basis of the revised instrument, unless the amendment of the request is due to invalidity of the initial instrument permitting enforcement in the State of the applicant authority or the original uniform instrument permitting enforcement in the State of the requested authority.

Articles 27 [Instruments permitting enforcement in the State of the requested authority and other accompanying documents] and 29 [Disputed claims and enforcement measures] shall apply in relation to the revised instrument.

Article 31 Request for precautionary measures

1. At the request of the applicant authority, the requested authority shall take precautionary measures, if allowed by its national law and in accordance with its administrative practices, to ensure recovery where a claim or the instrument permitting enforcement in the State of the applicant authority is contested at the time when the request is made, or where the claim is not yet the subject of an instrument permitting enforcement in the State of the applicant authority, in so far as precautionary measures are possible in a similar situation under the law and administrative practices of the State of the applicant authority.

The document drawn up for permitting precautionary measures in the State of the applicant authority and relating to the claim for which mutual assistance is requested, if any, shall be attached to the request for precautionary measures in the State of the requested authority. This document shall not be subject to any act of recognition, supplementing or replacement in the State of the requested authority.

2. The request for precautionary measures may be accompanied by other documents relating to the claim.

Article 32 Rules governing the request for precautionary measures

In order to give effect to Article 31 [Request for precautionary measures], paragraph 2 of Article 25 [Request for recovery], paragraphs 1 and 2 of Article 28 [Execution of the request for recovery], Articles 29 [Disputed claims and enforcement measures] and 30 [Amendment or withdrawal of the request for recovery assistance] shall apply mutatis mutandis.

Article 33 Limits to the requested authority's obligation

1. The requested authority shall not be obliged to grant the assistance provided for in Articles 25 [Request for recovery] to 31 [Request for precautionary measures] if recovery of the claim would, because of the situation of the debtor, create serious economic or social difficulties in the State of the requested authority, in so far as the laws, regulations and administrative practices in force in that State allow such exception for national claims.

2. The requested authority shall not be obliged to grant the assistance provided for in Articles 25 [Request for recovery] to 31 [Request for precautionary measures] where the costs or administrative burdens for the requested State would be clearly disproportionate to the monetary benefit to be derived by the applicant State.

3. The requested authority shall not be obliged to grant the assistance provided for in Article 20 [Request for information] and Articles 22 [Presence in administrative offices and participation in administrative enquiries] to 31 [Request for precautionary measures] if the initial request for assistance pursuant to Article 20 [Request for information], 22 [Presence in administrative offices and participation in administrative enquiries], 23 [Request for notification of certain documents relating to claims], 25 [Request for recovery] or 31 [Request for precautionary measures] is made in respect of claims which are more than 5 years old, dating from the due date of the claim in the State of the applicant authority to the date of the initial request for assistance.

However, in cases where the claim or the initial instrument permitting enforcement in the State of the applicant authority is contested, the 5-year period shall be deemed to begin from the moment when it is established in the State of the applicant authority that the claim or the instrument permitting enforcement may no longer be contested.

Moreover, in cases where a postponement of the payment or payment by instalments arrangement has been granted by the State of the applicant authority, the 5-year period shall be deemed to begin from the moment when the entire extended payment period has come to its end.

However, in those cases the requested authority shall not be obliged to grant assistance in respect of claims which are more than 10 years old, dating from the due date of the claim in the State of the applicant authority.

4. A State shall not be obliged to grant assistance if the total amount for which assistance is requested is less than GBP 5000.

5. The requested authority shall inform the applicant authority of the grounds for refusing a request for assistance.

Article 34 Questions on limitation

1. Questions concerning periods of limitation shall be governed solely by the laws in force in the State of the applicant authority.

2. In relation to the suspension, interruption or prolongation of periods of limitation, any steps taken in the recovery of claims by or on behalf of the requested authority in pursuance of a request for assistance which have the effect of suspending, interrupting or prolonging the period of limitation according to the laws in force in the State of the requested authority shall have the same effect in the State of the applicant authority, on condition that the corresponding effect is provided for under the law of the latter State.

If suspension, interruption or prolongation of the period of limitation is not possible under the laws in force in the State of the requested authority, any steps taken in the recovery of claims by or on behalf of the requested authority in pursuance of a request for assistance which, if they had been carried out by or on behalf of the applicant authority in its own State, would have had the effect of

suspending, interrupting or prolonging the period of limitation according to the laws of that State shall be deemed to have been taken in the latter State, in so far as that effect is concerned.
The first and second subparagraphs shall not affect the right of the State of the applicant authority to take measures which have the effect of suspending, interrupting or prolonging the period of limitation in accordance with the laws in force in that State.
3. The applicant authority and the requested authority shall inform each other of any action which interrupts, suspends or prolongs the limitation period of the claim for which the recovery or precautionary measures were requested, or which may have this effect.

Article 35 Costs
1. In addition to the amounts referred to in paragraph 5 of Article 28 [Execution of the request for recovery], the requested authority shall seek to recover from the person concerned and retain the costs linked to the recovery that it incurred, in accordance with the laws and regulations of its State.2. The States shall renounce all claims on each other for the reimbursement of costs arising from any mutual assistance they grant each other pursuant to this Protocol.
2. However, where recovery creates a specific problem, concerns a very large amount in costs or relates to organised crime, the applicant and requested authorities may agree reimbursement arrangements specific to the cases in question.
3. Notwithstanding paragraph 2, the State of the applicant authority shall be liable to the State of the requested authority for any costs and any losses incurred as a result of actions held to be unfounded, as far as either the substance of the claim or the validity of the instrument permitting enforcement and/or precautionary measures issued by the applicant authority are concerned.

CHAPTER FOUR

General rules governing all types of recovery assistance requests

Article 36 Use of languages
1. All requests for assistance, standard forms for notification and uniform instruments permitting enforcement in the State of the requested authority shall be sent in, or shall be accompanied by a translation into, the official language, or one of the official languages, of the State of the requested authority. The fact that certain parts thereof are written in a language other than the official language, or one of the official languages, of that State, shall not affect their validity or the validity of the procedure, in so far as that other language is one agreed between the States concerned.
2. The documents for which notification is requested pursuant to Article 23 [Request for notification of certain documents relating to claims] may be sent to the requested authority in an official language of the State of the applicant authority.
3. Where a request is accompanied by documents other than those referred to in paragraphs 1 and 2, the requested authority may, where necessary, require from the applicant authority a translation of such documents into the official language, or one of the official languages of the State of the requested authority, or into any other language agreed between the States concerned.

Article 37 Statistical data
1. By 30 June each year, the Parties shall communicate by electronic means to the Specialised Committee the statistical data on the application of this Title.
2. The content and format of the statistical data to be communicated under paragraph 1 shall be determined by the Specialised Committee.

Article 38 Standard forms and means of communication
1. Requests pursuant to paragraph 1 of Article 20 [Request for information] for information, requests pursuant to paragraph 1 of Article 23 [Request for notification of certain documents relating to claims] for notification, requests pursuant to paragraph 1 of Article 25 [Request for recovery] for recovery or requests pursuant to paragraph 1 of Article 31 [Request for precautionary measures] for precautionary measures, and communication of statistical data pursuant to Article 37 [Statistical data] shall be sent by electronic means, using a standard form, unless this is impracticable for technical reasons. As far as possible, these forms shall also be used for any further communication with regard to the request.
The uniform instrument permitting enforcement in the State of the requested authority, the document permitting precautionary measures in the State of the applicant authority and the other documents referred to in Articles 27 [Instrument permitting enforcement in the State of the requested authority and other accompanying documents] and 31 [Request for precautionary measures] shall also be sent by electronic means, unless this is impracticable for technical reasons.
Where appropriate, the standard forms may be accompanied by reports, statements and any other documents, or certified true copies or extracts thereof, which shall also be sent by electronic means, unless this is impracticable for technical reasons.
Standard forms and communication by electronic means may also be used for the exchange of information pursuant to Article 21 [Exchange of information without prior request].

2. Paragraph 1 shall not apply to the information and documentation obtained through the presence of officials in administrative offices in another State or through participation in administrative enquiries in another State, in accordance with Article 22 [Presence in administrative offices and participation in administrative enquiries].
3. If communication is not made by electronic means or with use of standard forms, this shall not affect the validity of the information obtained or of the measures taken in the execution of a request for assistance.
4. The electronic communication network and the standard forms adopted for the implementation of this Protocol may also be used for recovery assistance regarding other claims than the claims referred to in point (b) of paragraph 1 of Article 2 [Scope], if such recovery assistance is possible under other bilateral or multilateral legally binding instruments on administrative cooperation between the States.
5. Pending the adoption by the Specialised Committee of the decisions referred to in paragraph 2 of Article 39 [Trade Specialised Committee on Administrative Cooperation in VAT and Recovery of Taxes and Duties], the competent authorities shall make use of the rules set out in the Annex to this Protocol, including the standard forms.
6. The State of the requested authority shall use its official currency for the transfer of the recovered amounts to the State of the applicant authority, unless otherwise agreed between the States concerned.

Title IV:
IMPLEMENTATION AND APPLICATION

Article 39 Trade Specialised Committee on Administrative cooperation in VAT and Recovery of Taxes and Duties
1. The Specialised Committee shall:
   (a) hold regular consultations; and
   (b) review the operation and effectiveness of this Protocol at least every 5 years.
2. The Specialised Committee shall adopt decisions or recommendations to:
   (a) determine the frequency of, the practical arrangements for and the exact categories of information subject to automatic exchange referred to in Article 11 [Automatic exchange of information];
   (b) review the result of the automatic exchange of information for each category established pursuant to point (a) of paragraph 2 so as to ensure that this type of exchange takes place only where it is the most efficient means for the exchange of information;
   (c) establish new categories of information to be exchanged pursuant to Article 11 [Automatic exchange of information], should the automatic exchange be the most efficient means of cooperation;
   (d) define the standard forms for the communications pursuant to paragraph 1 of Article 19 [Standard forms and means of communication] and paragraph 1 of Article 38 [Standard forms and means of communication];
   (e) review the availability, collection, and processing of statistical data referred to in Articles 18 [Statistical data] and 37 [Statistical data], so as to ensure that the obligations set out in those Articles do not impose a disproportionate administrative burden on the Parties;
   (f) establish what shall be transmitted via the CCN/CSI network or other means;
   (g) determine the amount and the modalities of the financial contribution to be made by the United Kingdom to the general budget of the Union in respect of the cost generated by its participation in the European information systems, taking into account the decisions referred to in points (d) and (f);
   (h) establish implementing rules on the practical arrangements with regard to the organisation of the contacts between the central liaison offices and liaison departments referred to in paragraphs 2 and 3 of Article 4 [Organisation];
   (i) establish the practical arrangements between the central liaison offices for the implementation of paragraph 5 of Article 4 [Organisation];
   (j) establish implementing rules for Title III [Recovery assistance], including rules on the conversion of the sums to be recovered and the transfer of sums recovered; and
   (k) establish the procedure for concluding the service level agreement referred to in Article 5 [Service level agreement] and also conclude that service level agreement.

Title V
FINAL PROVISIONS

Article 40 Execution of on-going requests

1. Where requests for information and for administrative enquiries sent in accordance with Regulation (EU) No 904/2010 in relation to the transactions covered by Article 99(1) of the Withdrawal Agreement are not yet closed within four years after the end of the transition period, the requested State shall ensure that those requests are executed in accordance with the rules of this Protocol.

2. Where assistance requests relating to taxes and duties within the scope of Article 2 [Scope] of this Protocol sent in accordance with Directive 2010/24/EU in relation to the claims referred to in Article 100(1) of the Withdrawal Agreement are not closed within five years after the end of the transition period, the requested State shall ensure that those assistance requests are executed in accordance with the rules of this Protocol. The standard uniform form for notification or the instrument permitting enforcement in the requested State established in accordance with the legislation referred to in this paragraph shall retain its validity for the purposes of such execution. A revised uniform instrument permitting enforcement in the requested State may be established after the end of that five year period in relation to claims for which assistance was requested before that time. Such revised uniform instruments shall refer to the legal basis used for the initial assistance request.

Article 41 Relation to other agreements or arrangements

This Protocol shall take precedence over the provisions of any bilateral or multilateral agreements or arrangements on administrative cooperation in the field of VAT, or on recovery assistance relating to the claims covered by this Protocol, which have been concluded between Member States and the United Kingdom, insofar as their provisions are incompatible with those of this Protocol.

ANNEX TO THE PROTOCOL ON ADMINISTRATIVE COOPERATION AND COMBATING FRAUD IN THE FIELD OF VALUE ADDED TAX AND ON MUTUAL ASSISTANCE FOR THE RECOVERY OF CLAIMS RELATING TO TAXES AND DUTIES

Pending the adoption by the Specialised Committee of the decisions referred to in paragraph 2 of Article 39 [Trade Specialised Committee on Administrative Cooperation in VAT and Recovery of Taxes and Duties] of the Protocol on administrative cooperation and combating fraud in the field of Value Added Tax and on mutual assistance for the recovery of claims relating to taxes and duties (the "Protocol"), the following rules and standard forms apply.

SECTION 1
Organisation of contacts

1.1

Until further notice, the central liaison offices having the principal responsibility for the application of Title II [Administrative Cooperation and Combating VAT Fraud] of the Protocol are:
   (a) for the United Kingdom: Her Majesty's Revenue and Customs, UK VAT Central Liaison Office;
   (b) for the Member States: the central liaison offices designated for administrative cooperation between the Member States in the area of VAT.

1.2

Until further notice, the central liaison offices having the principal responsibility for the application of Title III [Recovery assistance] of this Protocol are:
   (a) for the United Kingdom: Her Majesty's Revenue and Customs, Debt Management;
   (b) for the Member States: the central liaison offices designated for recovery assistance between the Member States.

SECTION 2
Administrative cooperation and combating fraud in the field of Value Added Tax

2.1

Communication The communication of information under Title II [Administrative Cooperation and Combating VAT Fraud] of this Protocol shall be done, as far as possible, by electronic means and via the Common Communication Network (CCN), between the respective mailboxes of the States for the exchange of information on administrative cooperation or the mailboxes for combating fraud in the field of VAT.

2.2

Standard form For the exchange of information under Title II [Administrative Cooperation and Combating VAT Fraud] of this Protocol, the States shall use the following model:
[See Forms in the UK Government version of the TCA]

SECTION 3
Recovery assistance

Article 3.1 Communication

A request sent by electronic means for the application of Title III of the Protocol shall be sent between the CCN mailboxes that are set up for the type of tax or duty to which the request relates, unless the central liaison offices of the applicant and requested States agree that one of the mailboxes can be used for requests concerning different types of taxes or duties.

However, if a request for notification of documents relates to more than one type of tax or duty, the applicant authority shall send that request to a mailbox set up for at least one of the types of claims mentioned in the documents to be notified.

Article 3.2 Implementing rules relating to the uniform instrument permitting enforcement in the requested State

1. The administrative penalties, fines, fees and surcharges and the interest and costs referred to in point (b) of paragraph 1 of Article 2 of the Protocol which, in accordance with the rules in force in the applicant State, may be due from the date of the initial instrument permitting enforcement until the day before the date on which the recovery request is sent, may be added in the uniform instrument permitting enforcement in the requested State.
2. A single uniform instrument permitting enforcement in the requested State may be issued in respect of several claims and several persons, corresponding to the initial instrument or instruments permitting enforcement in the applicant State.
3. In so far as initial instruments permitting enforcement for several claims in the applicant State have already been replaced by a global instrument permitting enforcement for all those claims in that State, the uniform instrument permitting enforcement in the requested State may be based on the initial instruments permitting enforcement in the applicant State or on that global instrument regrouping those initial instruments in the applicant State.
4. Where the initial instrument referred to in paragraph 2 or the global instrument referred to in paragraph 3 contains several claims, one or more of which have already been collected or recovered, the uniform instrument permitting enforcement in the requested State shall only refer to those claims for which recovery assistance is requested.
5. Where the initial instrument referred to in paragraph 2 or the global instrument referred to in paragraph 3 contains several claims, the applicant authority may list those claims in different uniform instruments permitting enforcement in the requested State, in line with the tax type related division of competences of the respective recovery offices in the requested State.
6. If a request cannot be transmitted by CCN network and is transmitted by post, the uniform instrument permitting enforcement in the requested State shall be signed by a duly authorised official of the applicant authority.

Article 3.3 Conversion of the sums to be recovered

1. The applicant authority shall express the amount of the claim to be recovered in the currency of the applicant State and in the currency of the requested State.
2. For requests sent to the United Kingdom, the exchange rate to be used for the purposes of the recovery assistance shall be the exchange rate published by the European Central Bank on the day before the date on which the request is sent. Where there is no such rate available on that date, the exchange rate used shall be the latest exchange rate published by the European Central Bank before the date the request is sent.
For requests sent to a Member State, the exchange rate to be used for the purposes of the recovery assistance shall be the exchange rate published by the Bank of England on the day before the date on which the request is sent. Where there is no such rate available on that date, the exchange rate used shall be the latest exchange rate published by the Bank of England before the date the request is sent.
3. In order to convert the amount of the claim resulting from the adjustment, referred to in paragraph 2 of Article 30 of the Protocol, into the currency of the State of the requested authority, the applicant authority shall use the exchange rate used in its initial request.

Article 3.4 Transfer of recovered amounts

1. The transfer of the recovered amounts shall take place within two months of the date on which recovery was effected, unless otherwise agreed between the States.
2. However, if recovery measures applied by the requested authority are contested for a reason not falling within the responsibility of the applicant State, the requested authority may wait to transfer any sums recovered in relation to the applicant State's claim, until the dispute is settled, if the following conditions are simultaneously fulfilled:
    (a) the requested authority finds it likely that the outcome of this contestation will be favourable to the party concerned; and
    (b) the applicant authority has not declared that it will reimburse the sums already transferred if the outcome of that contestation is favourable to the party concerned.

3. If the applicant authority has made a declaration to reimburse in accordance with point (b) of the second paragraph, it shall return the recovered amounts already transferred by the requested authority within one month of the receipt of the request for reimbursement. Any other compensation due shall, in that case, be borne solely by the requested authority.

Article 3.5 Reimbursement of recovered amounts

The requested authority shall notify any action taken in the requested State for reimbursement of sums recovered or for compensation in relation to recovery of contested claims to the applicant authority immediately after the requested authority has been informed of such action.

The requested authority shall as far as possible involve the applicant authority in the procedures for settling the amount to be reimbursed and the compensation due. Upon receipt of a reasoned request from the requested authority, the applicant authority shall transfer the sums reimbursed and the compensation paid within two months of the receipt of that request.

Article 3.6 Standard forms

1. For the uniform notification form accompanying the request for notification, referred to in Article 23 of the Protocol, the States shall use the form established in accordance with model A.

2. For the uniform instrument permitting enforcement in the requested State, referred to in Article 27 of the Protocol, accompanying the request for recovery or the request for precautionary measures, or the revised uniform instrument permitting enforcement in the requested State, referred to in paragraph 2 of Article 30 of the Protocol, the States shall use the form established in accordance with model B.

3. For the request for information referred to in Article 20 of the Protocol, the States shall use the form established in accordance with model C.

4. For the request for notification referred to in Article 23 of the Protocol, the States shall use the form established in accordance with model D.

5. For the request for recovery or for precautionary measures referred to in Articles 25 and 31 of the Protocol, the States shall use the form established in accordance with model E.

6. Where forms are transmitted by electronic means, their structure and lay-out may be adapted to the requirements and possibilities of the electronic communication system, provided that the set of data and information contained therein is not substantially altered when compared to the models set out below.

[See the UK Government version of the TCA for the following—
- Model A Uniform notification form providing information about notified document(s)
- Model B Uniform instrument permitting enforcement of claims covered by Article 27 of the Protocol between the European Union and the United Kingdom on administrative cooperation and combating fraud in the field of Value Added Tax and on mutual assistance for the recovery of claims relating to taxes and duties
- Model form C – request for information
- Model form D – request for notification
- Model form E – request for recovery or precautionary measures]

VAT Index

A

ACADEMIES
refund of tax, VATA 1994 s 33B

ACCOMMODATION
boarding houses–
  exemption, VATA 1994 Sch 9 Group 1 item 1(d)
  stays of over four weeks, VATA 1994 Sch 6 para 9
caravans–
  generally, VATA 1994 Sch 8, Group 9, note (b)
  provision of facilities at caravan parks, VATA 1994 Sch 9 Group 1
directors, VATA 1994 s 24(3)
employees, for, VATA 1994 Sch 6 para 10
holiday accommodation, VATA 1994 Sch 9 Group 1
hotels–
  exemption, VATA 1994 Sch 9 Group 1 item 1(d)
  stays of over four weeks, VATA 1994 Sch 6 para 9
houseboat, VATA 1994 Sch 8, Group 9, note (b)
inns–
  exemption, VATA 1994 Sch 9 Group 1 item 1(d)
  stays of over four weeks, VATA 1994 Sch 6 para 9
stays of over four weeks, VATA 1994 Sch 6 para 9
supplied to employees, VATA 1994 Sch 6 para 10

ACCOUNTANTS
services–
  reverse charge, VATA 1994 s 8
  services supplied where received, VATA 1994 Sch 5 para 3
  supply to overseas person, VATA 1994 Sch 8 Group 1

ACCOUNTING PERIODS
See PRESCRIBED ACCOUNTING PERIOD

ACCOUNTS
See also RECORDS
adjustments, SI 1995/2518 reg 38
form, SI 1995/2518 reg 32
generally, 2006/112/EC arts 241–249

ADMINISTRATION AND COLLECTION
assessments–
  acquisition by non-taxable persons, VATA 1994 s 75
  amounts due by way of penalty, interest or surcharge, VATA 1994 s 76
  appeals, VATA 1994 s 83(p)–(r)
  best of judgment, VATA 1994 s 73(1), (7)
  combined assessments, VATA 1994 s 73(4)

ADMINISTRATION AND COLLECTION – cont.
assessments– – cont.
  Commissioners power to make a judgement, VATA 1994 s 73(1), (7)
  de-registration, VATA 1994 s 73(3)
  failure to make return, VATA 1994 s 73
  further assessment for greater amount, VATA 1994 s 73(8)
  grounds for making, VATA 1994 ss 73(1), 76(1)
  incorrect refund/payment, VATA 1994 s 73(2)
  information to be furnished, VATA 1994 ss 73, 74, 76
  interest overpayment, VATA 1994 s 78A
  manner of notification, VATA 1994 s 73, 76(1)
  penalty for failure to notify of understatement, VATA 1994 s 76
  person acting in representative capacity, VATA 1994 s 73(5)
  recovery of tax, VATA 1994 s 73
  supplementary assessments, VATA 1994 s 77
  time limits, VATA 1994 s 73(6)
bad debt relief–
  administration procedure, SI 1995/2518
  appeal, VATA 1994 s 83(h)
  claim, SI 1995/2518 regs 167–169
  flat rate scheme for small businesses, SI 1995/2518 reg 55V
  generally, VATA 1994 s 36
  margin schemes, SI 1995/2518 reg 172A
  notice to purchaser, SI 1995/2518 reg 166A
  refund, repayment of, SI 1995/2518 reg 171
  repayment of input tax, SI 1995/2518 regs 172C–172E
  time limits for claims, SI 1995/2518 reg 165A
  tour operators' margin scheme, SI 1995/2518 reg 172B
  transfer of going concern, SI 1995/2158 reg 6(3)(d)
  transitional provisions, VATA 1994 Sch 13 para 9
  writing off debts, SI 1995/2518 reg 172
cash accounting, VATA 1994 Sch 11 para 2(7)
co-operation, 1798/2003/EC, 1925/2004/EC
documents–
  production, VATA 1994 Sch 11 para 4(1), (7)
  removal, VATA 1994 Sch 11 para 12B
duty to keep records, VATA 1994 Sch 11 para 6
enforcement–
  diligence, levy of, SI 1995/2518 reg 213
  distress, levy of, SI 1995/2518 reg 212
  poinding of goods, SI 1995/2518 reg 213
entry and search. See ENTRY AND SEARCH

ADMINISTRATION AND COLLECTION – cont.

evidence by certificate, VATA 1994 Sch 11 para 14
exchange of information, 1798/2003/EC
furnishing of information and production of documents, VATA 1994 Sch 11 para 7
generally, VATA 1994 s 58
international VAT arrangements, VATA 1994 s 58ZA
invoices–
   generally, VATA 1994 Sch 11 para 2
   produced by computer, VATA 1994 Sch 11 para 3
   time limits, VATA 1994 Sch 11 para 2(2)
money collected, security, VATA 1994 Sch 11 para 1(2)
order for access to recorded information, VATA 1994 Sch 11 para 11
payment of tax. *See* PAYMENT OF TAX
power of entry and search, VATA 1994 Sch 11 para 10
power to require security and production of evidence, VATA 1994 Sch 11 para 4
power to take samples, VATA 1994 Sch 11 para 8
powers to require the opening of gaming machines, VATA 1994 Sch 11 para 9
procedure where documents are removed, VATA 1994 Sch 11 paras 12, 13
recovery of tax–
   generally, VATA 1994 Sch 11 para 5
   retailers, VATA 1994 Sch 11 para 2(6)
security for tax, VATA 1994 Sch 11 para 4
VAT arrangements internationally, VATA 1994 s 58ZA

ADMISSION CHARGES

deemed to be carrying on a business, VATA 1994 s 94
gaming club, VATA 1994 Sch 9, Group 4 note 1

ADVERTISING

reverse charge, VATA 1994 s 8
supplied where received, VATA 1994 Sch 5 para 2
supply to overseas person, VATA 1994 Sch 8 Group 7

ADVOCATES

time of supply, SI 1995/2518 reg 92

AEROPLANES

See AIRCRAFT

AGENTS

margin scheme, VATA 1994 s 50A
refund of VAT to overseas trader through, VATA 1994 s 39(3)
services–
   margin scheme, VATA 1994 s 50A(6)
   reverse charge, VATA 1994 s 8
   supplied where received, VATA 1994 Sch 5 para 8
supply of services through–
   generally, VATA 1994 s 47(3)
zero rating, VATA 1994 Sch 8 Group 7

AGRICULTURE

production activities, 2006/112/EC Annex VII
products–
   import, 83/81/EEC arts 29–34

AIR AMBULANCE CHARITIES

refund of tax–
   generally, VATA 1994 s 33C
   meaning, VATA 1994 s 33D

AIR FREIGHT

zero rating, VATA 1994 Sch 8 Group 8 item 5

AIR NAVIGATION

zero rating, VATA 1994 Sch 8 Group 8 item 6A

AIRCRAFT

adapted value, VATA 1994 s 22(3), (4)
charters–
   supplies of services, VATA 1994 Sch 8 Group 8 note (1)
classification, VATA 1994 Sch 8 Group 9 item 9
freight transportation, VATA 1994 Sch 8 Group 8
handling services, VATA 1994 Sch 8 Group 8 item 6
housing or storage, VATA 1994 Sch 9 Group 1
repair and maintenance, VATA 1994 Sch 8 Group 8
supply etc, VATA 1994 Sch 8 Group 8 item 2
surveys, VATA 1994 Sch 8 Group 8 item 9
transport of passengers, VATA 1994 Sch 8 Group 8 item 4
value adapted, VATA 1994 s 22(3), (4)
zero-rating, VATA 1994 Sch 8 Group 8

AIRPORTS

Customs and Excise–
   handling services, VATA 1994 Sch 8 Group 8 item 6
   meaning, CEMA 1979 s 21
free zone designations. *See* FREE ZONES

ALCOHOLIC BEVERAGES

zero-rating–
   generally, VATA 1994 Sch 8 Group 1
   tax free shops, VATA 1994 Sch 8 Group 14

ALTERATIONS

construction services, VATA 1994 Sch 8 Group 5 note (9)
meaning, VATA 1994 Sch 8 Group 6 note (4)
protected building, VATA 1994 Sch 8, Group 6

AMBULANCES

charities, VATA 1994 Sch 8 Group 15 note (3)(b)
services exemption, VATA 1994 Sch 9 Group 11 item 11

ANIMAL FEEDING STUFFS

pet food, VATA 1994 Sch 8 Group 1 excepted item 6
zero-rating, VATA 1994 Sch 8 Group 1 general item 4

ANIMALS

charities–
   research of medicinal products, VATA 1994 Sch 8 Group 15 item 9
   substances used directly for synthesis or testing, VATA 1994 Sch 8 Group 15 item 10
human consumption, VATA 1994 Sch 8 Group item 4
meaning, VATA 1994 Sch 8 Group 1 note 2, Group 15 note (2), Group 16 note (3)

ANNUAL ACCOUNTING SCHEME

application to use, SI 1995/2518 reg 51
authorisation, SI 1995/2518 reg 50

ANNUAL ACCOUNTING SCHEME – *cont.*
cancellation of registration, SI 1995/2518 reg 53
eligibility, SI 1995/2518 reg 51
enforced withdrawal, SI 1995/2518 regs 53–55
insolvency, SI 1995/2518 reg 54
leaving–
  cancellation of registration, SI 1995/2518 reg 53
  minimum participation period, SI 1995/2518 reg 52
  turnover limit, SI 1995/2518 reg 51
withdrawal–
  enforced, SI 1995/2518 regs 53–55
  voluntary, SI 1995/2518 reg 53

ANTI-AVOIDANCE PROVISIONS
designation of provisions in schemes, VATA Sch 11A para 4
designation of schemes, VATA Sch 11A para 3
disclosure of schemes–
  generally, VATA 1994 Sch 11A
  duty to notify Commissioners–
    exemption, VATA Sch 11A paras 7–8
    generally, VATA Sch 11A para 6
    penalty for failure to notify, VATA Sch 11A paras 10–12
group directions–
  assessment in consequence, VATA 1994 ss 83(*wa*), 84(7A), Sch 9A para 5
  form, VATA 1994 Sch 9A para 2
  manner of giving directions, VATA 1994 Sch 9A para 4
  power to give, VATA 1994 Sch 9A para 1
  time limits, VATA 1994 Sch 9A para 3
groups, and–
  application of VATA 1994 Sch 9A provisions directions, VATA 1994 Sch 9A
  generally, VATA 1994 Sch 9A para 6
'notifiable scheme', VATA Sch 11A para 5
obtaining tax advantage, VATA Sch 11A para 2
voluntary notification of scheme, VATA Sch 11A para 9

ANTIQUES
exemption for certain sales, VATA 1994 Sch 9, Group 11
margin scheme, VATA 1994 s 50A
special scheme, 2006/112/EC arts 311–343, Annex IX

APPEALS
See also VAT AND DUTIES TRIBUNALS
bringing, VATA 1994 s 83G
burden of proof–
  direction to register, VATA 1994 s 84(7)
  dishonest conduct, VATA 1994 s 60
conditions–
  furnishing of returns, VATA 1994 s 84(2)
  payment of tax, VATA 1994 s 84(3), (2), (8)
Court of Appeal, VATA 1994 s 86
default surcharge, VATA 1994 s 84(6)
HMRC review–
  extensions of time, VATA 1994 s 83D
  nature, VATA 1994 s 83F
  offer, VATA 1994 s 83A
  out of time, VATA 1994 s 83E

APPEALS – *cont.*
HMRC review– – *cont.*
  requirement, VATA 1994 s 83C
  right to require, VATA 1994 s 83B
  time limits, VATA 1994 s 83D
interest on tax, VATA 1994 s 84(8)
payment of outstanding tax–
  extension, VATA 1994 Sch 12 para 9
  further appeal, where, VATA 1994 s 85B
  generally, VATA 1994 ss 84(2), (3), 85A
permissible grounds, VATA 1994 s 83
procedural rules, VATA 1994 s 97, Sch 12 paras 9, 10
requirement to furnish return, VATA 1994 s 84(2)
settlement by agreement, VATA 1994 s 85
time limits, VATA 1994 s 83G
'tribunal', FA 1994 s 7, VATA 1994 s 82

APPROVED ALTERATIONS
construction services, VATA 1994 Sch 8 Group 5 note (9)
meaning, VATA 1994 Sch 8 Group 6 note (4)
protected building, VATA 1994 Sch 8, Group 6

ARBITRATION
procedures to be used before appeal, VATA 1994 s 84(9)

ARREST
See also ENTRY AND SEARCH
customs officers, by, VATA 1994 s 72(9), CEMA 1979 ss 15(3), 16(3), 167(1), 168(1)

ART WORKS
meaning, VATA 1994 s 21(6)
sales from stately homes, VATA 1994 Sch 9 Group 11
special scheme, 2006/112/EC arts 311–343, Annex IX

ASSESSMENTS
acquisition by non-taxable persons, VATA 1994 s 75
amounts due by way of penalty, interest or surcharge, VATA 1994 s 76
appeal, VATA 1994 s 83(p), (q), (r)
best of judgment, VATA 1994 s 73(1), (7)
combined, VATA 1994 s 73(4)
Commissioners power to make a judgement, VATA 1994 s 73(1), (7)
de-registration, VATA 1994 s 73(3)
failure to make return, VATA 1994 s 73
further assessment for greater amount, VATA 1994 s 73(8)
grounds for making, VATA 1994 ss 73(1), 76(1)
incorrect refund/payment, VATA 1994 s 73(2)
information to be furnished, VATA 1994 ss 73, 74, 76
interest overpayment, VATA 1994 s 78A
manner of notification, VATA 1994 s 73, 76(1)
person acting in representative capacity, VATA 1994 s 73(5)
supplementary, VATA 1994 s 77
tax assessed–
  penalty for failure to notify of understatement, VATA 1994 s 76
  recovery, VATA 1994 s 73

VAT Index

ASSESSMENTS – *cont.*
  time limits–
    generally, VATA 1994 s 73(6)
    supplementary assessment, VATA 1994 s 77
ASSIGNMENT OF INTEREST IN LAND
  exemption, VATA 1994 Sch 9 Group 1 item 1 note (1)
AVOIDANCE OF TAX
  anti-avoidance provisions–
    See ANTI-AVOIDANCE PROVISIONS
  conduct involving dishonesty, VATA 1994 s 60
  directors liability, VATA 1994 s 61

B

BAD DEBT RELIEF
  administration procedure, SI 1995/2518
  appeals, VATA 1994 s 83(h)
  claims–
    evidence supporting, SI 1995/2518 reg 167
    making, SI 1995/2518 reg 167
    preservation of documents, SI 1995/2518 reg 169
    records to be kept, SI 1995/2518 reg 168
    time limit, SI 1995/2518 reg 165A
  flat rate scheme for small businesses–
    amount, SI 1995/2518 reg 55V
  generally, VATA 1994 s 36
  margin schemes, SI 1995/2518 reg 172A
  notice to purchaser, SI 1995/2518 reg 166A
  repayments–
    input tax, SI 1995/2518 regs 172C–172E
    refund, SI 1995/2518 reg 171
    tour operators' margin scheme, SI 1995/2518 reg 172B
    transfer of going concern, SI 1995/2158 reg 6(3)(d)
  transitional provisions, VATA 1994 Sch 13 para 9
  writing off debts, SI 1995/2518 reg 172
BANKING SERVICES
  exemption, VATA 1994 Sch 9 Group 5
  received from abroad, VATA 1994 s 8
  supplied where received, VATA 1994 Sch 5 para 5
BANK NOTES
  zero-rating, VATA 1994 Sch 8, Group 11
BANKRUPTCY
  See INSOLVENCY
BARRISTERS
  time of supply, SI 1995/2518 reg 92
BATHROOM
  supply to handicapped person, VATA 1994 Sch 8 Group 12 items 10–12
BELONGING
  place of–
    recipient of services, VATA 1994 s 9
    supplier, VATA 1994 s 9
BEST OF JUDGEMENT ASSESSMENTS
  See ASSESSMENTS
BETTING, GAMING AND LOTTERIES
  See also GAMING MACHINES

BETTING, GAMING AND LOTTERIES – *cont.*
  admission charge to gambling club, VATA 1994 Sch 9 Group 4 note (1)
  exemption, VATA 1994 Sch 9 Group 4
  gaming machines–
    'game of chance', VATA 1994 s 23(7)
    generally, VATA 1994 s 23, Sch 9 Group 4
    meaning, VATA 1994 s 23(4)
    power to open and check contents, VATA 1994 Sch 11 para 9
    token, VATA 1994 s 23(3)
    valuation, VATA 1994 s 23(2)
BEVERAGES
  zero-rating, VATA 1994 Sch 8 Group 1
BISCUITS
  zero-rating, VATA 1994 Sch 8 Group 1
BLIND PERSONS
  zero-rating–
    cassette players, VATA 1994 Sch 8 Group 4 item 2(*a*)
    talking books, VATA 1994 Sch 8 Group 4 item 1
    wireless sets, VATA 1994 Sch 8 Group 4 item 2
BLOOD AND BLOOD PRODUCTS
  exemption, VATA 1994 Sch 9 Group 7 items 6, 7
BOARDING HOUSE
  stays of over four weeks, VATA 1994 Sch 6 para 9
BOATS
  anchoring facilities, VATA 1994 Sch 9 Group 1 item 1(*k*)
  berthing facilities, VATA 1994 Sch 9 Group 1 item 1(*k*)
  designed or adapted for handicapped person, VATA 1994 Sch 8 Group 12 item 2(i)
  facilities, VATA 1994 Sch 9 Group 1 item 1(*k*)
  lifeboat, VATA 1994 Sch 8 Group 8 item 3
  mooring facilities, VATA 1994 Sch 9 Group 1 item 1(*k*)
  storing facilities, VATA 1994 Sch 9 Group 1 item 1(*k*)
BODY CORPORATE
  See also GROUP OF COMPANIES
  business carried on in divisions, VATA 1994 s 46(1)
  domestic accommodation for directors, VATA 1994 s 24(3)
  incorporation–
    pre-acquired goods and services, SI 1995/2518 reg 111
  liability of directors, VATA 1994 s 61
  liquidators, SI 1995/2518 reg 9(1), (3)
  officers–
    liability to criminal penalties, CEMA 1979 s 171(4)
  persons exercising control, VATA 1994 s 43
  receivers, SI 1995/2518 reg 9(1), (3)
  registration–
    pre-acquired goods and services, SI 1995/2518 reg 111, VATA 1994
BONDS
  exemption, VATA 1994 Sch 9 Group 5 item 6, 7 note (5)

BOOKLETS
  zero-rating, VATA 1994 Sch 8 Group 3 item 1
BOOKS
  zero-rating–
    children's picture and painting, VATA 1994 Sch 8 Group 3 item 3
    generally, VATA 1994 Sch 8 Group 3
    minor accessories supplied with, VATA 1994 Sch 8 Group 3 item 6
    talking books for handicapped and blind, VATA 1994 Sch 8 Group 4
BOOTS
  See CLOTHING AND FOOTWEAR
'BREXIT'
  abolition of acquisition VAT, T(CBT)A 2018 s 41
  amendments to VAT, T(CBT)A 2018 s 43, Sch 8
  commencement of provisions, T(CBT)A 2018 s 57
  consequential amendments, T(CBT)A 2018 Sch 7
  consequential provision, T(CBT)A 2018 s 56
  EU law relating to VAT, T(CBT)A 2018 s 42
  extension of import VAT, T(CBT)A 2018 s 41
  Northern Ireland Protocol–
    commencement of provisions, T(PTP)A 2020 s 11
    duty on goods imported into or removed from NI, T(PTP)A 2020 s 2, Sch 1
    duty on goods removed to NI, T(PTP)A 2020 s 1
    excise duty on removal of goods to NI, T(PTP)A 2020 ss 4–5
    low value importations, T(PTP)A 2020 s 7, Sch 3
    online sale by overseas persons, T(PTP)A 2020 s 7, Sch 3
    rate of fuel duty on aviation gasoline, T(PTP)A 2020 s 6
    recovery of unlawful state aid, T(PTP)A 2020 Sch 4
    VAT in NI, T(PTP)A 2020 s 3, Sch 2
  other amendments connected with withdrawal from EU, T(CBT)A 2018 s 43, Sch 8
  other provisions connected with withdrawal from EU, T(CBT)A 2018 s 51
  postal packets sent from overseas–
    withdrawal from EU, SI 2018/1376
  post-transition period–
    Northern Ireland Protocol, T(PTP)A 2020 ss 1–7, Schs 1–4
  power to make provision as VAT or customs or excise duty–
    general provision, T(CBT)A 2018 s 51
    Regulations, SI 2019/60
  prohibition on collection of taxies and duties without reciprocity, T(CBT)A 2018 s 54
  single UK customs territory, T(CBT)A 2018 s 55
  subordinate legislation as VAT or customs or excise duty, T(CBT)A 2018 s 52
  transitional provision, T(CBT)A 2018 s 56
BRITISH BROADCASTING CORPORATION (BBC)
  refund of tax, VATA 1994 s 33
BUILDINGS
  adjustment to deduction of input tax, SI 1995/2518 reg 112

BUILDINGS – *cont.*
  alterations, VATA 1994 Sch 8 note 9
  building materials, VATA 1994 Sch 8 Group 5 item 4, Sch 8 Group 6 item 3
  change of use, VATA 1994 Sch 10
  commercial buildings–
    exempt use or supply, VATA 1994 Sch 10 para 5
    refurbished, VATA 1994 Sch 10 para 5
  consideration accruing to other than to grantor, VATA 1994 Sch 10 para 8
  construction–
    generally, VATA 1994 Sch 8 Group 5
  conversion–
    building control approval, obtaining, VATA 1994 Sch A1 para 15
    'changed numbers of dwellings', VATA 1994 Sch A1 para 10
    generally, VATA 1994 Sch 8 Group 5
    'house in multiple occupation', VATA 1994 Sch A1 para 11
    planning consent, VATA 1994 Sch A1 para 15
    qualifying conversions, VATA 1994 Sch A1 para 9
    qualifying residential purpose, VATA 1994 Sch A1 paras 17-21
    qualifying services, VATA 1994 Sch A1 paras 16, 21
    reduced rate of VAT, VATA 1994 Sch A1 paras 6-8, Sch 7A para 4A
    related garage works, VATA 1994 Sch A1 para 14
    services qualifying, VATA 1994 Sch A1 paras 16, 21
    'special residential conversion', VATA 1994 Sch A1 para 12
    supplies to intended user, VATA 1994 Sch A1 para 13
  co-owners–
    registration, VATA 1994 s 51A
  developers of non-residential buildings, VATA 1994 Sch 10 paras 5–7
  do-it-yourself builders–
    refund of tax, VATA 1994 s 35
  election to waive exemption, VATA 1994 Sch 10 paras 2–4
  exempt use or supply–
    commercial buildings, VATA 1994 Sch 10 para 5
    refurbished, VATA 1994 Sch 10 para 5
  grant of major interest, VATA 1994 Sch 8 Group 5 item 1
  leases–
    building used for charitable purpose, VATA 1994 Sch 8 Group 5 item note 4, Group 6
    building used for residential purpose, VATA 1994 Sch 8 Groups 2, 6
    dwelling, VATA 1994 Sch 8 Groups 5, 6
    grant, VATA 1994 Sch 9 Group 1
    holiday accommodation, VATA 1994 Sch 9 Group 1
    listed building, VATA 1994 Sch 9 Group 6
    monument, VATA 1994 Sch 8 Group 6
    protected building, VATA 1994 Sch 8 Group 6

BUILDINGS – *cont.*
  leases– – *cont.*
    reverse surrender, VATA 1994 Sch 9 Group 1 item 1 notes (1), (1A)
    supply of goods as, SI 1995/2518 reg 85
    treatment as supply of goods, VATA 1994 Sch 4 para 4
  listed buildings–
    approved alterations, VATA 1994 Sch 8 Group 6 note (6)
    meaning, VATA 1994 Sch 8 Group 6 note (1)
    zero-rating, VATA 1994 Sch 8 Group 6
  meaning, SI 1995/2518 reg 2
  protected buildings–
    approved alterations, VATA 1994 Sch 8 Group 6 note (6)
    meaning, VATA 1994 Sch 8 Group 6 note (1)
    zero-rating, VATA 1994 Sch 8 Group 6
  residential and charitable, VATA 1994 Sch 10 para 1
  services related to overseas building, VATA 1994 Sch 8 Group 7
  stage payments, time of supply, SI 1995/2518 reg 93
  transitional provisions, VATA 1994 Sch 13 para 10

BURIAL AND CREMATION
  exemption, VATA 1994 Sch 9 Group 8

BUSINESS
  See also BUSINESS ASSETS
  admission charges, VATA 1994 s 94(2)(*b*)
  artificial separation of business activities, counteracting, VATA 1994 Sch 1 paras 1A, 2
  associations deemed to be carrying on, VATA 1994 s 94(2)
  certificate of status of person, SI 1995/2518 Sch 1 Form 10
  change of name, constitution or ownership–
    notification, SI 1995/2518 reg 5 (2)
  meaning, VATA 1994 s 94
  office not treated, VATA 1994 s 94(4)
  transfer to member of group, VATA 1994 s 44

BUSINESS ASSETS
  deemed supply–
    deregistration, at, VATA 1994 Sch 4 para 7
  disposal, VATA 1994 s 94(6), Sch 4
  held at cessation of business, VATA 1994 Sch 4 para 8
  private or non-business use–
    imported goods, VATA 1994 s 27
  removal from member states, VATA 1994 Sch 4 para 6
  sale by third party, VATA 1994 Sch 4 para 6
  time of supply, VATA 1994 s 6(12)
  transfer as going concern–
    generally, VATA 1994 s 49
    group of companies, VATA 1994 s 44

BUSINESS GIFTS
  cost to donor no more than £10.00, VATA 1994 Sch 4 para 5(2)(*a*)
  valuation, VATA 1994 Sch 6 para 6(1)(*a*)

BUSINESS PROMOTION SCHEMES
  value of goods exchanged for trading stamps, VATA 1994 s 19

C

CAMPING
  grant of facilities, VATA 1994 Sch 9 Group 1 item 1(*g*)

CAPITAL GAINS TAX
  disposals of heritage objects–
    exemption, VATA 1994 Sch 9 Group 11 item 4

CAPITAL GOODS
  credit for input tax, SI 1995/2518 regs 112–116
  tax relief, VATA 1994 s 34

CAPITAL TRANSFER TAX
  disposals of heritage objects–
    exemption, VATA 1994 Sch 9 Group 11 item 1

CARAVANS
  holiday accommodation, VATA 1994 Sch 9 Group 1 item 1
  option to tax, VATA 1994 Sch 10 para 2(2)
  pitches and facilities, VATA 1994 Sch 9 Group 1 item 1(*f*)
  zero-rating, VATA 1994 Sch 8 Group 9 item 1

CARS
  See COMPANY CARS; MOTOR CARS

CASH ACCOUNTING SCHEME
  accounting for VAT, SI 1995/2518 reg 65
  admission to scheme, SI 1995/2518 reg 58
  cancellation of registration, SI 1995/2518 reg 61
  eligibility for scheme, SI 1995/2518 reg 58
  insolvency, SI 1995/2518 reg 62
  leaving–
    cancellation of registration, SI 1995/2518 reg 61
    sale of business, SI 1995/2518 reg 63
  regulations, VATA 1994 Sch 11 para 2(7)
  selling business, SI 1995/2518 reg 63
  turnover limit, SI 1995/2518 reg 58
  variation, SI 1995/2518 reg 59
  withdrawal–
    enforced, SI 1995/2518 regs 60–64
    voluntary, SI 1995/2518 regs 60–61

CASSETTE PLAYERS
  blind persons–
    zero-rating, VATA 1994 Sch 8 Group 4 item 2(*a*)

CATERING
  employer provided–
    value of supply, VATA 1994 Sch 6 para 10(1)(*a*)
  food supplied in the course, VATA 1994 Sch 8 Group 1
  supplies by groups, VATA 1994 s 44(4)
  take-away food, VATA 1994 Sch 8 Group 1 note (3)

CEMETERIES
See BURIAL AND CREMATION
CENTRAL BANKS
gold supplied to and by, VATA 1994 Sch 8 Group 10
CERTIFICATES OF DEPOSIT
exemption, VATA 1994 Sch 9 Group 5 items 6, 7, note (5)
CESSATION OF BUSINESS
deemed supply of stock held, VATA 1994 Sch 4 para 8
CHANGE OF USE
relevant charitable or residential building, VATA 1994 Sch 10 para 1
CHANNEL TUNNEL
tax free shops, VATA 1994 Sch 8 Group 14
'terminal', VATA 1994 Sch 8 Group 14 note (2)
CHARGECARDS
exemption, VATA 1994 Sch 9 Group 5 note (4)
CHARGEABLE EVENTS
meaning, 2006/112/EC art 62
CHARTER OF HMRC
publication of details, FA 2009 s 92
CHARITABLE PURPOSES
change of use, VATA 1994 Sch 10 para 1
option to tax excluded, VATA 1994 Sch 10 para 2(2)
relevant charitable purpose, meaning, VATA 1994 Sch 8 Group 5 note (6)
CHARITIES
buildings–
alteration, VATA 1994 Sch 8 Group 12 items 4, 7, 9, 11, 12
change of use, VATA 1994 Sch 10 para 1
construction, VATA 1994 Sch 8 Group 5
handicapped persons, VATA 1994 Sch 8 Group 12 items 4, 7, 9, 11, 12
cassette players for the blind, VATA 1994 Sch 8 Group 4 item 2(*a*)
donations, VATA 1994 Sch 8 Group 15 items 1–2
exports, VATA 1994 Sch 8 Group 12 items 2, 3
fuel and power, VATA 1994 Sch 13 para 7
fund-raising events, VATA 1994 Sch 9 Group 12 item 1
handicapped persons–
care etc for, VATA 1994 s 2(1A)–(1C), Sch A1, Sch 8 Group 15 notes (4A)–(5B)
medical care and products, VATA 1994 Sch 8 Group 15
refund of tax–
generally, VATA 1994 s 33C
relevant charities, VATA 1994 s 33D
rents charged, VATA 1994 Sch 10 para 4(5)
repair and maintenance of goods, VATA 1994 Sch 8 Group 15 items 6, 7
talking books for the blind, VATA 1994 Sch 8 Group 4
wireless sets for the blind, VATA 1994 Sch 8 Group 4 item 1
CHART
zero-rating, VATA 1994 Sch 8 Group 3 item 5
CHEMIST
exemption, VATA 1994 Sch 9 Group 7 item 3

CHEMIST – *cont.*
retail scheme, use of, Notice 727 para 9
zero-rating, VATA 1994 Sch 8 Group 12 item 1
CHILDREN
car seats, VATA 1994 Sch A1 paras 1(5), 7
clothing and footwear, VATA 1994 Sch 8 Group 16 item 1
picture and painting books VATA 1994 Sch 8 Group 3 item 3
CHIROPODISTS
exemption, VATA 1994 Sch 9 Group 7 item 1(*c*)
CIGARS AND CIGARETTES
See TOBACCO
CIVIL ENGINEERING WORKS
capital goods scheme SI 1995/2518 regs 112–116
construction, VATA 1994 Sch 8 Group 5 item 2,
exempt use or supply, VATA 1994 Sch 10
self-supply, VATA 1994 Sch 10 paras 5, 6
services situated abroad, VATA 1994 Sch 8 Group 7
standard rating, VATA 1994 Sch 9 Group 1 items 1(*a*)–(*k*)
zero-rating, VATA 1994 Sch 8 Group 5, 7
CLOTHING AND FOOTWEAR
zero-rating–
handicapped persons, VATA 1994 Sch 8 Group 12 note (4)(*a*)
protective boots and helmets, VATA 1994 Sch 8 Group 16 items 2, 3
young children, VATA 1994 Sch 8 Group 16 item 1
CLUBS AND ASSOCIATIONS
business deemed to be carried on, VATA 1994 s 94(2)
change of members, VATA 1994 s 46(3)
generally, VATA 1994 s 46(2)
non-business activities, VATA 1994 s 10(2), (3)
registration, VATA 1994 s 46(3)
representation, SI 1995/2518 reg 8
responsibility, SI 1995/2518 reg 8
youth clubs, VATA 1994 Sch 9 Group 6 item 6
COASTING SHIP
definition, CEMA 1979 s 1(1)
COFFEE
zero-rating, VATA 1994 Sch 8 Group 1
COINS
See GOLD; MONEY
COLLECTION OF TAX
See ADMINISTRATION AND COLLECTION
COLLECTORS ITEMS
See ANTIQUES; SCIENTIFIC COLLECTIONS
COMMERCIAL BUILDING
exempt use or supply, VATA 1994 Sch 10 para 5
COMMISSION FOR THE NEW TOWNS
refund of tax, VATA 1994 s 33(3)(*g*)
COMMISSIONERS FOR REVENUE AND CUSTOMS
certificate from, VATA 1994 Sch 11 para 14
contravention of relevant rule–
penalty, SI 2003/3113
disclosure of information–
generally, VATA 1994 s 91(1), (2)
errors made, VATA 1994 s 78

COMMISSIONERS FOR REVENUE AND CUSTOMS – *cont.*
facilities–
  power to require, CEMA 1979 s 158
interest payable–
  given by way of credit, VATA 1994 s 81(1), (2)
  official error, VATA 1994 s 78
meaning, VATA 1994 s 96(1)
power to–
  require production of evidence, VATA 1994 Sch 11 para 4
  require security, VATA 1994 Sch 11 para 4
regulations–
  See REGULATIONS

COMMUNITY CUSTOMS CODE
Committee, 450/2008/EC arts 183–185
currency conversion, 450/2008/EC art 31
customs procedure, placing goods under, 450/2008/EC arts 104–107
customs status of goods, 450/2008/EC art 102
customs territory, 450/2008/EC art 3
definitions in Code establishing, 450/2008/EC art 4
disposal of goods, 450/2008/EC art 125, 126
duties based on, 450/2008/EC art 33
end-use procedure, 450/2008/EC art 166
formalities and controls, simplification, 450/2008/EC art 116
free circulation, release of goods for, 450/2008/EC art 129
goods brought into customs territory –
  arrival of goods, 450/2008/EC arts 91–94
  customs territory, 450/2008/EC art 3
  entry summary declaration, 450/2008/EC arts 87–90
  entry of goods, 450/2008/EC arts 87–90
  presentation, unloading and examination, 450/2008/EC arts 95–97
mission of customs authorities, 450/2008/EC art 2
modernised, 450/2008/EC
origin of goods, 450/2008/EC arts 35–39
provisions for the implementation of, 2454/93/EEC
recovery and payment of duty, 450/2008/EC arts 66, 78
release of goods, 450/2008/EC art s123, 24
rights and duties of persons–
  appeals, 450/2008/EC arts 22–24
  application of customs legislation, 450/2008/EC arts 16–20
  authorised economic operator, 450/2008/EC arts 13–15
  control of goods, 450/2008/EC arts 25–28
  customs representation, 450/2008/EC arts 11, 12
  data protection, 450/2008/EC art 6
  documents and other information, keeping, 450/2008/EC arts 29, 30
  information, 450/2008/EC arts 5–10
  penalties, 450/2008/EC art 21
  provision of information, 450/2008/EC arts 5–10
special procedures, 450/2008/EC arts 135–139
tariff classification of goods, 450/2008/EC art 34
time limits, 450/2008/EC art 32

COMMUNITY TRADER
repayment of tax to, SI 1995/2518

COMMUNITY TRANSIT GOODS
definition, CEMA 1979 s 1(1)

COMPANY
See BODY CORPORATE; GROUP OF COMPANIES

COMPLIANCE
powers to enforce, VATA 1994 s 73

COMPUTER
admissibility of computer produced documents, VATA 1994 Sch 11 para 6(6)
data processing. *See* DATA PROCESSING
input tax, adjustment of, SI 1995/2518 regs 112–116
meaning, VATA 1994 s 96(6)
preparation of tax invoice, VATA 1994 Sch 11 para 3
preservation of information, VATA 1994 Sch 11 para 6
self-supply, VATA 1994 s 44(4)
zero-rating, VATA 1994 Sch 8 Group 15 note (3a)

CONFECTIONERY
See FOOD

CONFIRMING HOUSE
exemption, VATA 1994 Sch 9 Group 5

CONNECTED PERSON
acquisition from other member states, VATA 1994 Sch 7 para 1(5)
value of supply, VATA 1994 Sch 6 para 1(4)

CONSIDERATION
acquisition from other member states, VATA 1994 s 20
apportionment, VATA 1994 s 33(4)
discounts for prompt payment, VATA 1994 Sch 6 para 4
gaming machines–
  generally, VATA 1994 s 23(1)
  tokens, VATA 1994 s 23(2)
  value of supply, VATA 1994 s 23(3)
paid by third party, VATA 1994 Sch 6 para 12
received by person other than grantor, VATA 1994 Sch 10 para 8
value–
  provision for employees, VATA 1994 Sch 6 para 10(1)
  supply of goods and services, VATA 1994 s 19
  tokens, stamps and vouchers, VATA 1994 Sch 6 para 5

CONSTRUCTION INDUSTRY
authenticated receipt treated as tax invoice, SI 1995/2518 reg 13(4)
exemption, VATA 1994 Sch 9 Group 1
self-supply of materials, SI 1989/472
time of supply, SI 1995/2518 reg 93
zero-rating, VATA 1994 Sch 8 Groups 5 and 6

CONSTRUCTION SERVICES
See BUILDING; CIVIL ENGINEERING WORK; CONSTRUCTION INDUSTRY; LAND

CONSULTANCY SERVICES
reverse charge, VATA 1994 s 8
supplied where received, VATA 1994 Sch 5 para 3

CONTRACT
  effect of change of rate of tax, VATA 1994 s 89
CONTRAVENTION OF RELEVANT RULE
  penalties–
    appeals, FA 2003 s 33F
    exceptions, FA 2003 s 27
    generally, FA 2003 s 26
    no prosecution after demand notice, FA 2003 s 32
    reasonable excuse, FA 2003 s 27
    review of decisions, FA 2003 ss 33–37
    right to appeal, FA 2003 s 33
    time limit for demands, FA 2003 s 31
CONTROL POWERS
  arrest of persons, CEMA 1979 ss 167, 168
CO-OWNERS
  registration, VATA 1994 s 51A
COPYRIGHT
  services supplied where received, VATA 1994 Sch 5 para 1
  transfer or assignment–
    reverse charge, VATA 1994 s 8
    zero-rating to overseas, VATA 1994 Sch 8 Group 7
COURT OF APPEAL
  appeal from VAT tribunal, VATA 1994 s 86
CRASH HELMETS
  See MOTORCYCLE
CREDIT CARD
  exemption, Sch 9 Group 5 note (4)
CREDIT NOTES
  change in rate of tax on, SI 1995/2518 reg 15
CRIMINAL INVESTIGATIONS
  Northern Ireland, in, FA 2007 s 83
  powers of Revenue and Customs, FA 2007 s 82
  Scotland, in, FA 2007 s 85
  supplementary provisions, FA 2007 s 84
CROSS-BORDER TRADE
  abolition of acquisition VAT, T(CBT)A 2018 s 41
  commencement of provisions, T(CBT)A 2018 s 57
  consequential amendments, T(CBT)A 2018 Sch 7
  consequential provision, T(CBT)A 2018 s 56
  EU law relating to VAT, T(CBT)A 2018 s 42
  extension of import VAT, T(CBT)A 2018 s 41
  other amendments connected with withdrawal from EU, T(CBT)A 2018 s 43, Sch 8
  other provisions connected with withdrawal from EU, T(CBT)A 2018 s 51
  prohibition on collection of taxies and duties without reciprocity, T(CBT)A 2018 s 54
  single UK customs territory, T(CBT)A 2018 s 55
  subordinate legislation, T(CBT)A 2018 s 52
  transitional provision, T(CBT)A 2018 s 56
CROWN
  liability to VAT, VATA 1994 s 41
CROWN ESTATE COMMISSIONERS
  supplies to and by, VATA 1994 s 41
CULTURAL SERVICES
  eligible body supplies, VATA 1994 Sch 9 Group 13 item 2
  generally, VATA 1994 Sch 9 Group 13
  performed outside UK, VATA 1994 Sch 8 Group 7

CULTURAL SERVICES – *cont.*
  public body supplies, VATA 1994 Sch 9 Group 13 item 1
  supply of services by public body, VATA 1994 Sch 9 Group 13 item 1
  supply of services by eligible body, VATA 1994 Sch 9 Group 13 item 2
CURRENCY
  treated as money, VATA 1994 s 96(1)
CURRENT ACCOUNT
  exemption, VATA 1994 Sch 9 Group 5
CUSTOMS AND EXCISE ACT 1979
  application, VATA 1994 s 16
CUSTOMS AND EXCISE AIRPORT
  meaning, CEMA 1979 s 21
CUSTOMS AND EXCISE COMMISSIONERS
  See COMMISSIONERS FOR REVENUE AND CUSTOMS
CUSTOMS DEBT
  extinguishment, 450/2008/EC art 86
  incurrence, 450/2008/EC arts 44–55
CUSTOMS DECLARATIONS
  acceptance, 450/2008/EC art 112
  amendment, 450/2008/EC art 113
  examination and sampling of goods, 450/2008/EC arts 118, 119
  goods under different tariff subheadings, 450/2008/EC art 115
  identification procedures, 450/2008/EC art 121
  invalidation, 450/2008/EC art 114
  person lodging, 450/2008/EC art 111
  simplified, 450/2008/EC art 109
  standard, 450/2008/EC art 108
  supplementation, 450/2008/EC art 110
  verification, 450/2008/EC arts 117–120
CUSTOMS DUTY
  Community Customs Code, 2454/93/EEC
CUSTOMS ENTRY
  zero-rating, VATA 1994 Sch 8 Group 13 item 1
CUSTOMS FORMALITIES
  definition, CEMA 1979 s 1(1)
CUSTOMS VALUE
  air transport costs, including, 2454/93/EEC art 166, annex 25
  carrier media, 2454/93/EEC art 167
  declaration of particulars, 2454/93/EEC arts 178–181a
  documents to be furnished, 2454/93/EEC arts 178–181a
  generally, 450/2008/EC arts 40–43
  generally accepted accounting principles, 2454/93/EEC annex 24
  goods sent by post, 2454/93/EEC art 165
  interpretative notes on, 2454/93/EEC annex 23
  perishable goods, simplified procedures for, 2454/93/EEC arts 173–177
  place of introduction of goods, 2454/93/EEC art 163
  rates of exchange, 2454/93/EEC arts 168–172
  royalties and licence fees, incidence of, 2454/93/EEC arts 157–162
  transport costs, 2454/93/EEC arts 164–166

CUSTOMS WAREHOUSE
  meaning, CEMA 1979 s 1(1)

D

DATA GATHERING
  generally, F(No 2)A 2017 s 69
DATA PROCESSING
  zero-rating, VATA 1994 Sch 8 Group 7
DEATH
  continuation of registration on, SI 1995/2518 reg 9
  notification of, to Commissioners, SI 1995/2518 reg 9
  payment of tax, SI 1995/2518 regs 25(1), 54, 63
  returns, furnishing, SI 1995/2518 regs 25(1), 54, 63
  taxable person, of, SI 1995/2518 reg 9
  termination of prescribed accounting period on, SI 1995/2518 reg 25(3)
DEBENTURES
  exemption, VATA 1994 Sch 9 Group 5 items 6, 7 note (5)
DEBT
  bad. *See* BAD DEBT RELIEF
  goods sold in satisfaction of, VATA 1994 Sch 4 para 7, Sch 11 para 2(1), (2)
DEBTORS
  obtaining contact details, FA 2009 s 97, Sch 49
DEDUCTIONS
  adjustments, 2006/112/EC arts 184–192
  origin and scope of right to deduct, 2006/112/EC arts 167–172
  proportional, 2006/112/EC arts 173–175
  restrictions on right of, 2006/112/EC arts 176, 177
  rules governing exercise of right to deduct, 2006/112/EC arts 178–183
DEEMED SUPPLY
  agent, VATA 1994 s 16
  assets held at deregistration, VATA 1994 Sch 4 para 8(1), (2)
  charge to tax, VATA 1994 s 1(1)
  facilitated by online marketplaces
    exception from liability, VATA 1994 s 77F
    generally, VATA 1994 s 5A
  gaming machine, VATA 1994 s 23
  online marketplaces
    exception from liability, VATA 1994 s 77F
    generally, VATA 1994 s 5A
  removal of goods to another member state, VATA 1994 Sch 4 para 6
  services of office holder, VATA 1994 s 95(7)
  services received from abroad, VATA 1994 s 8
  zero-rated transactions, VATA 1994 s 30(5)
DEFAULT INTEREST
  appeal against assessment, VATA 1994 s 82, 83(*q*)
  assessment, VATA 1994 s 76, 77
  period of, VATA 1994 s 74
  prescribed rate, VATA 1994 s 59
DEFAULT SURCHARGE
  amount, VATA 1994 s 59(4), (5)
  appeal, VATA 1994 s 83(n)

DEFAULT SURCHARGE – *cont.*
  assessment, VATA 1994 s 76, 77
  default, meaning, VATA 1994 s 59(1), (1A)
  exempted defaults, VATA 1994 s 59(7), (9)
  generally, VATA 1994 s 59
  payments on account–
    aggregate value of defaults, calculating, VATA 1994 s 59A(6), (7)
    amount, VATA 1994 s 59A(4), (5)
    continuation of surcharge period, VATA 1994 s 59A(3)
    default left out of account, VATA 1994 s 59A(10), (11)
    exempted defaults, VATA 1994 s 59A(8), (9)
    generally, VATA 1994 s 59A
    method of payment, VATA 1994 s 59A(12), (13)
    person in default, VATA 1994 s 59A(1)
    surcharge liability notice, service of, VATA 1994 s 59A(2)
    surcharge period, VATA 1994 s 59A(2)
  rate, VATA 1994 s 59(1)
  surcharge period generally, VATA 1994 s 59(2)
  customs duties, of, SI 1976/1223
  suspension of penalties during currency of agreement, FA 2009 s 108
DELIBERATE TAX DEFAULTERS
  publication of details, FA 2009 s 97
DELIVERY OF TAX INFORMATION
  software, through–
    ancillary metadata, SI 2019/360
DEMOLITION
  property situated abroad, VATA 1994 Sch 8 Group 7
DENTAL TECHNICIANS
  exemption, VATA 1994 Sch 9 Group 7 item 2
DENTISTS
  exemption, VATA 1994 Sch 9 Group 7 item 2
DEPOSIT ACCOUNTS
  exemption, VATA 1994 Sch 9 Group 5 item 8
DEPOSITS
  time of supply, VATA 1994 s 6(4)
DEREGISTRATION
  acquisitions from other member states, VATA 1994 Sch 3 para 2(1)
  appeal against decision, VATA 1994 s 83(*a*)
  assessment, VATA 1994 s 73(3)
  circumstances–
    ceasing to be liable to registration, VATA 1994 Sch 1 para 13
    ceasing to make taxable supplies, VATA 1994 Sch 1 paras 3–4 11
    void registration, VATA 1994 Sch 1 para 18
  refund of tax, VATA 1994 s 24(6)
  supplies from other member states, VATA 1994 Sch 2 para 2
DEVELOPMENT CORPORATIONS
  refund of tax to, VATA 1994 s 33(3)
DIETICIANS
  exemption, VATA 1994 Sch 9 Group 7
DIGITAL REPORTING AND RECORD-KEEPING
  See also MAKING TAX DIGITAL

DIGITAL REPORTING AND RECORD-KEEPING – *cont.*
  generally, F(No 2)A 2017 s 62
DILIGENCE
  recovery of tax by, SI 1995/2518 reg 213
DIPLOMATS
  importation of goods, reliefs for
    conditions attaching to, SI 1992/3156 arts 3–4
    entitled persons, SI 1992/3156 art 14
    motor vehicles, SI 1992/3156 art 16
    remission or refund, duty or tax subject to, SI 1992/3156 art 17
    tobacco or alcohol products, SI 1992/3156 art 15
DIRECT SELLERS
  direction as to value of supply, VATA 1994 Sch 6 para 2
DIRECTIONS
  anti-avoidance provisions–
    See ANTI-AVOIDANCE PROVISIONS
  registration, VATA 1994 Sch 1 para 2
  value of supplies–
    acquisitions, VATA 1994 Sch 7,
    open market value, VATA 1994 Sch 6 para 1(1)–(3)
DIRECTORS
  holder of office, VATA 1994 s 25(7)
  liability for evasion of tax–
    appeal, VATA 1994 s 83(*n*), (*o*)
    assessment, VATA 1994 s 76, 77
    generally, VATA 1994 s 61
  meaning, VATA 1994 s 24(7)
  provision of domestic accommodation, VATA 1994 s 24(3)
DISABILITY LIVING ALLOWANCE
  meaning, VATA 1994 Sch 8 Group 12 note (7)
  person in receipt, VATA 1994 Sch 8 Group 12 item 14
DISCLOSURE OF INFORMATION
  See also INFORMATION
  EEC member states, between, 77/799/EEC, 79/1070
  penalties, VATA 1994 s 91(3)
  statistical purposes, VATA 1994 s 91
DISCLOSURE OF TAX AVOIDANCE SCHEMES
  Regulations–
    generally, SI 2017/1215
    notifiable arrangements, SI 2017/1216
  VAT and other indirect taxes, F(No 2)A 2017 s 66, Sch 17
DISCOUNT
  imported goods, VATA 1994 s 20(3)
  prompt payment, VATA 1994 Sch 6 para 4(1)
DISPOSAL OF ASSETS
  generally, VATA 1994 s 94(6)
DISTANCE SALES
  option, exercise of, SI 1995/2518 reg 98
DISTRESS
  enforcement, FA 1997 s 51
  recovery of tax, VATA 1994 Sch 11 para 5(4), SI 1995/2518 reg 212
DOCTOR
  exemption, VATA 1994 Sch 9 Group 7 item 1(*a*)

DOCTORS DEPUTISING SERVICE
  exemption, VATA 1994 Sch 9 Group 7 item 5
DOCUMENTS
  admissibility, VATA 1994 Sch 11 para 6(6)
  bad debt relief, SI 1995/2518 reg 169
  compensation for loss or damage, VATA 1994 Sch 11 para 7(1)
  computer produced, VATA 1994 Sch 11 para 6(4)
  failure to keep, VATA 1994 s 73(1)
  false, VATA 1994 s 72
  meaning, VATA 1994 s 96(1), (6)
  power to inspect, copy and remove, VATA 1994 Sch 11 para 7
  production, VATA 1994 Sch 11 para 7
  removal under search warrant, VATA 1994 Sch 11 paras 11–13
DO-IT-YOURSELF BUILDER
  appeal to tribunal, VATA 1994 s 83(*g*)
  claims by, SI 1995/2518 regs 200, 201 Sch 1
  refund of tax, VATA 1994 s 35, SI 1995/2518 Sch 1 Form 11
DOMESTIC ACCOMMODATION
  See ACCOMMODATION
DOMESTIC APPLIANCES
  supply with new buildings, VATA 1994 Sch 8 Group 5 note (12)
DONATIONS
  charities, VATA 1994 Sch 8 Group 5 items 1, 2
DRAINAGE BOARDS
  refund of tax, VATA 1994 s 33(3)
DRUGS
  zero-rating–
    generally, SI 1995/2518 reg 74
    goods on prescription, VATA 1994 Sch 8 Group 12
    supplied to charities, VATA 1994 Sch 8 Group 15
DUTIABLE GOODS
  regulations, VATA 1994 Sch 11 para 2(8)
  removal to UK, VATA 1994 Sch 9 para 3
  warehoused goods. *See* WAREHOUSE
DWELLING
  See BUILDING

E

ECCLESIASTICAL BUILDING
  alteration, VATA 1994 Sch 8 Group 6 item 2
EC SALES STATEMENTS
  See also SECTION 55 STATEMENTS
  EC sales list (VAT 101), SI 1995/2518 regs 21–23, Sch 1 Form 12
EDUCATION
  eligible body, meaning, VATA 1994 Sch 9 Group 6 note (1)
  exemption, VATA 1994 Sch 9 Group 6 items 1–6
  vocational training, VATA 1994 Sch 9 Group 6 note (3)
  youth club, VATA 1994 Sch 9 Group 6 note (6)
E-FILING
  mandatory use, FA 2003 s 204

E-FILING – *cont.*
  returns, SI 1995/2518 reg 25A
  use under other provisions, FA 2003 s 205
ELECTION TO WAIVE EXEMPTION
  See OPTION TO TAX
ELECTRICAL APPLIANCES
  supply to new building, VATA 1994 Sch 8 Group 5 note (12)
ELECTRICITY
  supplied by persons outside UK, reverse charge, VATA 1994 s 9A
ELECTRONIC COMMUNICATIONS
  returns, SI 1995/2518 reg 25A
  use under other provisions, FA 2003 s 205
ELECTRONICALLY SUPPLIED SERVICES
  amendments to VATA 1994, FA 2014 s 103, Sch 22, Sch 3BA, Sch 3B
  appeals, VATA 1994 Sch 3B para 20
  definitions, VATA 1994 Sch 3B para 23
  Directive, 2006/112/EC arts 357–369
  establishment of, VATA 1994 s 3A
  liability for VAT, VATA 1994 Sch 3B para 10
  payment of VAT, VATA 1994 Sch 3B para 13
  payment on account, VATA 1994 Sch 3B para 21
  place of supply, 2006/112/EC Annex II
  qualifying supplies, VATA 1994 Sch 3B para 3
  records, VATA 1994 Sch 3B paras 14, 15
  refund of UK tax, VATA 1994 Sch 3B para 22
  register, VATA 1994 Sch 3B para 1
  registered persons, conditions, VATA 1994 Sch 3B para 2
  registration–
    cancellation, VATA 1994 Sch 3B para 8
    changes, obligation to notify, VATA 1994 Sch 3B para 7
    conditions, VATA 1994 Sch 3B para 2
    date of, VATA 1994 Sch 3B para 5
    number, VATA 1994 Sch 3B para 6
    obligations following, VATA 1994 Sch 3B paras 10–15
    persistent defaulter, of, VATA 1994 Sch 3B para 9
    request, VATA 1994 Sch 3B para 4
  returns, VATA 1994 Sch 3B paras 11, 12, 18(6)
  understatement or overstatement of VAT, VATA 1994 Sch 3B para 16
  VAT provisions, application of, VATA 1994 Sch 3B paras 17–22
  VAT registration, VATA 1994 Sch 3B paras 17, 18
  VAT representatives, VATA 1994 Sch 3B para 19
ELIGIBLE INSTITUTIONS
  See also EDUCATION
  for educated, meaning, VATA 1994 Sch 9 Group 6 note (1)
EMISSIONS TRADING
  charges for allocations, FA 2007 s 16
EMPLOYEES
  domestic accommodation supplied–
    generally, VATA 1994 Sch 6 para 10(1)
    value, VATA 1994 Sch 6 para 10(2)
  services–
    reverse charge, VATA 1994 s 8

EMPLOYEES – *cont.*
  services– – *cont.*
    supplied to overseas person, VATA 1994 Sch 8 Group 7
ENFORCEMENT
  See ADMINISTRATION AND COLLECTION
ENGINEERS
  services–
    reverse charge, VATA 1994 s 8
    supplied where received, VATA 1994 Sch 5 para 3
    zero-rating, VATA 1994 Sch 8 Group 7
ENTERTAINMENT
  services performed abroad, VATA 1994 Sch 8 para 7
ENTRY AND SEARCH
  fraud, VATA 1994 s 72, Sch 11 para 10(3), (4)
  power to search–
    authorised person, VATA 1994 Sch 11 para 10(1), CEMA 1979 s 100F
    entry and inspection, VATA 1994 Sch 11 para 10(2)
  powers conferred by warrant, VATA 1994 Sch 11 para 10(5)
ERRORS IN RETURN
  correction, SI 1995/2518 reg 34
  penalties, FA 2007 Sch 24
ESTABLISHMENT
  place of belonging, VATA 1994 s 9
EU
  acquisition of goods from another member state–
    assessment, VATA 1994 s 75
    meaning, VATA 1994 s 11
    place of supply, VATA 1994 s 13
    scope of tax, VATA 1994 s 10
    timing, VATA 1994 s 12
    valuation, VATA 1994 Sch 7
    value, VATA 1994 s 20
  administrative co-operation, 1798/2003/EC, 1925/2004/EC
  alphabetical codes, SI 1995/2518 reg 2(1)
  approximation of laws, EC Treaty arts 100–102
  common system of VAT–
    conversion rates, 2006/112/EC arts 399, 400
    derogations, 2006/112/EC arts 370–396, Annex X
    implementation of Directive, 1777/2005/EC, 2006/112/EC art 397
    subject matter and scope of, 2006/112/EC arts 1–4
    territorial scope, 2006/112/EC arts 5–8
    transitional provisions, 2006/112/EC arts 402–411
    VAT Committee, 2006/112/EC art 398
  Court of Justice, EC Treaty arts 164–188
  Customs Code. *See* COMMUNITY CUSTOMS CODE
  custom controls, VATA 1994 s 16
  Customs territory, 450/2008/EC art 3
  duties and taxes due in other Member States–
    recovery, SI 2011/2931
  excluded territories, SI 1995/2518 regs 136, 137
  included territories, SI 1995/2518 reg 139

EU – *cont.*
　intra-Community acquisitions–
　　accounting for tax by reference to duty point, SI 1995/2518 reg 41(1)
　　accounting for tax by reference to value shown on invoice, SI 1995/2518 reg 26
　　gas, of, SI 1995/2518 reg 87
　　heat, of, SI 1995/2518 reg 87
　　notification and payment of tax by non-taxable persons, SI 1995/2518 reg 36
　　power, of, SI 1995/2518 reg 87
　　refrigeration, of, SI 1995/2518 reg 87
　　taxable amount, 92/546
　　time, SI 1995/2518 reg 83
　　valuation, SI 1992/2099
　　ventilation, SI 1995/2518 reg 87
　　water, of, SI 1995/2518 reg 87
　legislation, EC Treaty art 189
　member states–
　　removal of goods from, SI 1992/3111 arts 2–4, SI 1995/2518
　mutual assistance, FA 2011 Sch 25, 77/799/EEC, 2002/94/EC, 2008/55/EC, 2010/24/EU
　refund of tax, VATA 1994 s 39
　register of temporary movement of goods, SI 1995/2518 reg 33
　removal of goods from member state–
　　accounting for, SI 1995/2518
　　definitions, SI 1992/3111 art 2
　　establishment in member state, SI 1992/3111 art 3
　　place of supply, SI 1992/3111 art 4
　sales list, SI 1995/2518 Sch 1 Form 12
　sales statements–
　　definitions, SI 1995/2518 reg 21
　　final, SI 1995/2518 reg 23
　　submission of, SI 1992/3096 reg 5
　statistics of trade, 638/2004/EC
　tax provisions, EC Treaty, arts 95–99
　taxation under laws of other member states, VATA 1994 s 92
　temporary movement of goods–
　　register, SI 1995/2518 reg 33
　territories included in references to other member states, VATA 1994 s 93
　transitional provisions, 2006/112/EC arts 402–411
　triangular transactions, VATA 1994 s 14
　valuation of acquisitions, VATA 1994 s 20

EUROPEAN COMMUNITIES/UNION
See EC/EU

EVASION OF TAX
　appeal, VATA 1994 s 83(*n*)
　assessment, VATA 1994 s 76, 77
　conduct involving dishonesty, VATA 1994 s 60
　imported goods, VATA 1994 s 72(10)
　liability of directors, VATA 1994 s 61
　mitigation, VATA 1994 s 70
　penalties. *See* PENALTIES

EVIDENCE
　bad debt relief, SI 1995/2518 reg 167
　certificate of Commissioners, VATA 1994 Sch 11 para 14
　computer documents, VATA 1994 Sch 11 para 6(6)

EXAMINATION SERVICES
　exemption, VATA 1994 Sch 9 Group 6 item 3
　meaning, VATA 1994 Sch 9 Group 6 note (4)

EXCISE DUTIES
　definitions, T(CBT)A 2018 s 49
　effect of 'Brexit', T(CBT)A 2018 s 50, Sch 9
　EU law, T(CBT)A 2018 s 47
　exercise of information powers, T(CBT)A 2018 s 46
　postal packets sent from overseas–
　　general provision, T(CBT)A 2018 s 44
　　withdrawal from EU, SI 2018/1376
　regulation-making powers, T(CBT)A 2018 s 45
　regulations, T(CBT)A 2018 s 48
　remote gambling–
　　withdrawal from EU, and, T(CBT)A 2018 s 50, Sch 9

EXCISE WAREHOUSE
　procedures for goods, SI 1988/890 regs 10–19
　returns and records, SI 1988/809 regs 20–25, Schs 2, 3
　s 46 goods, SI 1988/809 reg 10A
　warehoused goods–
　　duty chargeable, SI 1988/809 regs 26–30
　　operations, SI 1988/809 Sch 1

EXEMPTIONS
　ambulance services, VATA 1994 Sch 9 Group 7 item 11
　anti-forestalling charge, FA 2012 Sch 26
　banking, VATA 1994 Sch 9 Group 5
　betting, gaming and lotteries, VATA 1994 Sch 9 Group 4
　burial and cremations, VATA 1994 Sch 9 Group 8
　capital goods, VATA 1994 s 34
　charities fund-raising, VATA 1994 Sch 9 Group 12 item 1
　credit transactions, VATA 1994 Sch 9 Group 5
　cultural services, VATA 1994 Sch 9 Group 13
　education, research or vocational training–
　　eligible body, meaning, VATA 1994 Sch 9 Group 6 note (1)
　　examination services, VATA 1994 Sch 9 Group 6 item 3
　　generally, VATA 1994 Sch 9 Group 6
　　youth clubs, VATA 1994 Sch 9 Group 9 item 6
　election to tax, VATA 1994 Sch 10 paras 2, 4
　exportation, 2006/112/EC arts 146, 147
　exports, transactions treated as, 2006/112/EC arts 151, 152
　fund-raising events by charities, VATA 1994 Sch 9 Group 12
　generally, VATA 1994 s 31, 2006/112/EC art 131
　health and welfare–
　　ambulance services, VATA 1994 Sch 9 Group 7 item 11
　　chemists, VATA 1994 Sch 9 Group 7 item 3
　　dental technician, VATA 1994 Sch 9 Group 7 item 2(*c*)
　　dentists, VATA 1994 Sch 7 Group 7 item 2
　　doctors, VATA 1994 Sch 9 Group 7 item 1(*a*)
　　generally, VATA 1994 Sch 9 Group 7
　　health visitors, VATA 1994 Sch 7 Group 7 item (*d*)

EXEMPTIONS – *cont.*
  health and welfare– – *cont.*
    hearing aid dispensers, VATA 1994 Sch 7 Group 7 item (*e*)
    human blood, VATA 1994 Sch 9 Group 7 item 6
    human organs, VATA 1994 Sch 9 Group 7 item 8
    medical care and surgical treatment, VATA 1994 Sch 9 Group 7 item 4
    midwives, VATA 1994 Sch 7 Group 7 item (*d*)
    nurses, VATA 1994 Sch 7 Group 7 item (*d*)
    opticians, VATA 1994 Sch 9 Group 7 item 1(*b*)
    welfare services, VATA 1994 Sch 9 Group 7 item 9 note (7)
  importation of goods, 2006/112/EC arts 143–145
  intermediaries, supply of services by, 2006/112/EC art 153
  intra-Community transactions, 2006/112/EC arts 138–142
  investment gold, VATA 1994 Sch 9 Group 15
  insurance, VATA 1994 Sch 9 Group 2
  international trade, transactions relating to, 2006/112/EC arts 154–166, Annex V
  international transport, 2006/112/EC arts 148–150
  land–
    election to tax, VATA 1994 Sch 10 paras 2–4
    grant of interest, right over, VATA 1994 Sch 9 Group 1 item 1
  list of, 2006/112/EC arts 135–137
  postal services, VATA 1994 Sch 9 Group 3
  private tuition, VATA 1994 Sch 9 Group 6 item 12
  professional bodies, VATA 1994 Sch 9 Group 9
  public interest activities, 2006/112/EC arts 132–134
  public interest bodies, VATA 1994 Sch 9 Group 9
  reinsurance, VATA 1994 Sch 9 Group 2
  schools, VATA 1994 Sch 9 Group 6
  securities, VATA 1994 Sch 9 Group 5 item 6
  sports, sports competitions and physical education, VATA 1994 Sch 9 Group 10
  supplies of services involving cost-sharing, VATA 1994 Sch 9 Group 16
  supplies where input tax cannot be recovered, VATA 1994 Sch 9 Group 14
  trade unions, VATA 1994 Sch 9 Group 9
  unit trust management, VATA 1994 Sch 9 Group 5 item 9
  universities, VATA 1994 Sch 9 Group 6
  vocational training, VATA 1994 Sch 9 Group 6
  works of art, VATA 1994 Sch 9 Group 11
  youth club, VATA 1994 Sch 9 Group 6 item 6
EXEMPT SUPPLY
  tax invoice, for, SI 1995/2518 reg 14(4)
EXHIBITION, FAIR
  zero-rating, VATA 1994 Sch 8 Group 7
EXPORT OF GOODS
  arrivals and dispatches, provision of information, SI 1995/2518 regs 23E, 23F
  conditions, VATA 1994 s 30(6)
  exemptions, 2006/112/EC arts 151, 152
  forfeiture of goods, VATA 1994 s 30(10)
  retail export scheme, SI 1995/2518 regs 52–54

EXPORT OF GOODS – *cont.*
  time of, CEMA 1979 s 5
  zero-rating–
    charity, VATA 1994 Sch 8 Group 15 items 2, 3
    financial services, VATA 1994 Sch 8
    goods, VATA 1994 s 30(6)
    handling goods, VATA 1994 Sch 8 Group 8
    insurance, VATA 1994 Sch 8 Group 7
    international defence project, VATA 1994 Sch 8 Group 13
    overseas authority, VATA 1994 Sch 8 Group 13
EXPORTATION OF GOODS
  containers, SI 1995/2518 reg 1282518
  exemptions, 2006/112/EC arts 146, 147
  formalities, 2454/93, SI 1995/2518 reg 140
  overseas persons, supplies to, SI 1995/2518 reg 129
  persons departing from the EC, supplies to, SI 1995/2518 regs 130–133
  time of, CEMA 1979 s 5

F

FARMERS
  certification, VATA 1994 s 54
  flat rate scheme. *See* FLAT RATE SCHEME FOR FARMERS
FINANCIAL SERVICES
  exemption, VATA 1994 Sch 9 Group 4
  reverse charge, VATA 1994 ss 8, 9
  zero-rating, VATA 1994 Sch 8 Group 7
FINANCIAL STATEMENTS
  inspection by customs officers, VATA 1994 Sch 11 para 7
FIREARMS
  used–
    appeal, VATA 1994 s 83(*m*)
    qualifying conditions, VATA 1994 s 54
FISCAL WAREHOUSING
  application procedure, VATA 1994 s 18A(7)
  approval, VATA 1994 s 18A(1), (8)
  assessment for failure to pay tax, VATA 1994 s 73(7A)
  certificates–
    general, SI 1995/2518 regs 145B, 145C
    secure relief on purchased or acquired goods, to, SI 1995/2518 Sch 1 Form 17
    services, connected with, SI 1995/2518 reg 145C
  cessation, VATA 1994 s 18A(5)
  charge in nature of goods, VATA 1994 s 18F(4)
  conditions, imposition of, VATA 1994 s 18A(6)
  deficient goods, VATA 1994 s 18E
  eligible goods, VATA 1994 s 18B(6), Sch 5A
  entitlement to keep fiscal warehouse, VATA 1994 s 18A(2)
  'fiscal warehouse', VATA 1994 s 18A(3), SI 1995/2518 reg 145A(1)
  'fiscal warehousekeeper', VATA 1994 ss 18A(1), 18F(1), SI 1995/2518 reg 145A(2)
  generally, VATA 1994 ss 18A, 18F

FISCAL WAREHOUSING – *cont.*
goods ceasing to be eligible, VATA 1994 s 18F(5)
matters for consideration by Commissioners, VATA 1994 s 18A(4)
missing goods, VATA 1994 s 18E
record and stock control, SI 1995/2518 reg 145F, Sch 1A
regime–
  generally, SI 1995/2518 reg 145E
  interpretation, SI 1995/2518 reg 145A(2)
  stock control and record, SI 1995/2518 reg 145F, Sch 1A
regulations–
  power to make, VATA 1994 ss 18D(3), 18F(7), (8)
relief–
  certificate to secure, SI 1995/2518 Sch 1 Form 17
  generally, VATA 1994 s 18B
removal of goods–
  accountability, VATA 1994 s 18D
  circumstances in which allowed, SI 1995/2518 reg 145H(1)
  deemed removal, VATA 1994 s 18F(6)
  failure to pay tax, VATA 1994 s 73(7B)
  payment of VAT, SI 1995/2518 reg 43, SI 1995/2518 reg 145J
  procedure on non-receipt of relevant documents, SI 1995/2518 reg 145H(3), (4)
  prohibition on, SI 1995/2518 reg 145I
  supply of services, VATA 1994 s 18C
  treated as transferred, SI 1995/2518 reg 145H(2)
  withdrawal of approval, VATA 1994 s 18A(6), (8)
  withdrawal of status, VATA 1994 s 18A(6)
  zero-rated supplies, VATA 1994 s 18C
services–
  connected certificate, SI 1995/2518 reg 145C
  generally, VATA 1994 s 18C
stock control and record, SI 1995/2518 reg 145F Sch 1A
transaction treated as supply of goods, SI 1966/1255
transfers in the UK, SI 1995/2518 reg 145G
VAT invoices relating to services performed in, SI 1995/2518 reg 145D
zero-rating of services performed in, certificate to secure, SI 1995/2518 Sch 1 Form 18

FISHING RIGHTS
liability, VATA 1994 Sch 9 Group 1

FLAT RATE SCHEME FOR FARMERS
admission, SI 1995/2518 reg 206
appeal, VATA 1994 s 83(*m*)
certificate–
  cancellation, SI 1995/2518 reg 206
  effective date, SI 1995/2518 reg 205
certification–
  application, SI 1995/2518 Sch 1 Form 14
  Commissioners, by, SI 1995/2518 reg 203
  further, SI 1995/2518 reg 208
certified person–
  bankruptcy, SI 1995/2518 reg 207

FLAT RATE SCHEME FOR FARMERS – *cont.*
certified person– – *cont.*
  death, SI 1995/2518 reg 207
  incapacity, SI 1995/2518 reg 207
  meaning, SI 1995/2518 reg 202
credit for input tax, claims for amounts to be treated as, SI 1995/2518 reg 209
EC provisions, 2006/112/EC arts 295–305, Annexes VII, VIII
percentage addition, SI 1992/3221
qualifying conditions, VATA 1994 s 54
records–
  duty to keep, SI 1995/2518 reg 210
  production of, SI 1995/2518 reg 211

FLAT RATE SCHEME FOR SMALL BUSINESSES
accounting, method of, SI 1995/2518 reg 55D
admission to, SI 1995/2518 reg 55L
amendment by notice, SI 1995/2518 reg 55T
appropriate percentage applied–
  generally, SI 1995/2518 regs 55H, 55J
  limited cost traders, SI 1995/2518 reg 55KA
  notification of differing percentage, SI 1995/2518 reg 55N
associated persons, SI 1995/2518 reg 55A(2)
authorisation–
  generally, SI 1995/2518 reg 55B
  termination, SI 1995/2518 reg 55P
bad debt relief, SI 1995/2518 reg 55V
categories of business, SI 1995/2518 reg 55K
definitions, SI 1995/2518 reg 55A
determination–
  liability, VATA 1994 s 26B
input tax credit, SI 1995/2518 reg 55E
limited cost traders, SI 1995/2518 reg 55KA
newly registered period–
  reduced appropriate percentage, SI 1995/2518 reg 55JB
regulation-making power, VATA 1994 s 26B
relevant supplies and purchases, SI 1995/2518 reg 55C
relevant turnover, SI 1995/2518 reg 55G
relief–
  exceptional claims, SI 1995/2518 reg 55F
reverse charges, SI 1995/2518 reg 55U
withdrawal–
  date, SI 1995/2518 reg 55Q
  generally, SI 1995/2518 reg 55M
  self-supply, SI 1995/2518 reg 55R
  stock on hand adjustments, SI 1995/2518 reg 55S

FOOD
See also CATERING
animal food. *See* ANIMAL FEEDING STUFFS
hot take-away, VATA 1994 Sch 8 Group 1
supplies by retailers, SI 1995/2518 reg 73
supply in the course of catering, VATA 1994 Sch 8 Group 1
value of supply to employee, VATA 1994 Sch 6 para 10(1), (2)
zero-rating, VATA 1994 Sch 8 Group 1

FOOTWEAR
See CLOTHING AND FOOTWEAR

FOREIGN CURRENCY
  acquisition, VATA 1994 Sch 7 para 4
  value, VATA 1994 Sch 6 para 11
FORMS
  application for registration (VAT 1), SI 1995/2518 reg 5(1), Sch 1
    acquisitions in respect of (VAT 1B), SI 1995/2518 reg 5(1), Sch 1
    distance sales in respect of (VAT 1A), SI 1995/2518 reg 5(1), Sch 1
    partnership by (VAT 2), SI 1995/2518 reg 5(1), Sch 1
  appointment of tax representative (Form 8), SI 1995/2518 reg 10, Sch 1
  diplomats, purchase of EC vehicle (C428), SI 1992/3156 Sch 1
  EC sales list (VAT 101), SI 1995/2518 regs 21–23, Sch 1 Form 12
  electronic communications, use of, SI 1995/258 reg 25A
  flat rate scheme for farmers, application for certification (VAT 98), SI 1995/2518 Sch 1
  generally, SI 1995/2518 reg 2 (3)
  refund of tax, third country trader, SI 1995/2518 Sch 1
    DIY builders, SI 1995/2518 Sch 1
  transfer of business as a going concern (form 3), SI 1995/2518 reg 6 (1), Sch 1
  VAT return (VAT 100), SI 1995/2518 reg 25(1), Sch 1
    final (VAT 193), SI 1995/2518 reg 25(4), Sch 1
  visiting forces–
    importation of motor vehicle (C941), SI 1992/3156 Sch
    purchase of motor vehicle (C&E 941A), SI 1992/3156 Sch
FRAUD
  anti-fraud measures–
  Missing Trader Intra Community–
    accounting for tax, adjustments, SI 1995/2518 reg 38A
    output tax adjustment, VATA 1994 s 26AB, SI 1995/2518 regs 172K–172N
    payments on account, SI 1993/2001 art 2A
    specified goods and services and excepted supplies, SI 2010/2239
    supplies of goods, accounting for tax on, VATA 1994 s 55A
  penalties for transactions connected with–
    generally, VATA 1994 s 69C, F(No 2)A 2017 s 69
    officers' liability, VATA 1994 s 69D
    publication of persons liable, VATA 1994 s 69E
FRAUDULENT EVASION OF TAX
  See EVASION OF TAX
FREE ZONES
  Birmingham Airport as. See BIRMINGHAM AIRPORT FREE ZONE
  free zone goods, meaning, VATA 1994 s 17(3)
  goods, CEMA 1979 s 100A
  Humberside, SI 1994/144
  Liverpool as. See LIVERPOOL FREE ZONE
  offences, SI 1991/2727 reg 6

FREE ZONES – *cont.*
  Prestwick Airport as. See PRESTWICK AIRPORT FREE ZONE
  regulations, VATA 1994 s 17
  search, powers of, CEMA 1979 s 100F
  Sheerness, port of, See SHEERNESS (PORT OF) FREE ZONE
  Southampton as. See SOUTHAMPTON FREE ZONE
  Tilbury, port of, See TILBURY (PORT OF) FREE ZONE
FREEHOLDS
  building used for–
    charitable purposes, VATA 1994 Sch 8 Groups 5, 6
    residential purposes, VATA 1994 Sch 8 Groups 5, 6
    holiday accommodation, VATA 1994 Sch 9 Group 1
  listed building, VATA 1994 Sch 8 Group 6
  monument, VATA 1994 Sch 8 Group 6
  protected building, VATA 1994 Sch 8 Group 6
  supply of goods, VATA 1994 Sch 5 para 4(5)
  zero-rating ambulance services, VATA 1994 Sch 9 Group 11 item 11
FREIGHT
  containers, supply of, Notice 703/1
  zero-rating, VATA 1994 Sch 8 Group 8
FUEL
  domestic/charitable use, VATA 1994 s 2(1A)–(1C), Sch A1
  reduced rate of VAT, VATA 1994 s 2(1A), (1B), Sch A1
FULFILMENT BUSINESSES
  approval scheme, SI 2018/299
  appeals, F(No 2)A 2017 s 56
  commencement, F(No 2)A 2017 s 59
  definitions, F(No 2)A 2017 s 58
  disclosure of information by HMRC, F(No 2)A 2017 s 52
  forfeiture, F(No 2)A 2017 s 54
  generally, F(No 2)A 2017 s 48
  offence, F(No 2)A 2017 s 53
  penalties, F(No 2)A 2017 s 55, Sch 13
  register of approved persons, F(No 2)A 2017 s 50
  regulations, F(No 2)A 2017 ss 51, 57, SI 2018/326
  requirements for approval, F(No 2)A 2017 s 49
FUND RAISING EVENTS
  charities–
    advertising, VATA 1994 Sch 9 Group 15 item 8
    exemption, VATA 1994 Sch 9 Group 12
FUNERALS
  See BURIAL AND CREMATION
FUR
  skin, meaning, VATA 1994 Sch 8 Group 16

G

GAMBLING
  reference to, VATA 1994 s 23(B)

GAME
  granting right to take, VATA 1994 Sch 9 Group 1
GAMING
  See BETTING, GAMING AND LOTTERIES
GAMING MACHINES
  game of chance, meaning, VATA 1994 s 23(7)
  generally, VATA 1994 s 23, Sch 9 Group 4
  meaning, VATA 1994 s 23(4)
  power to open and check contents, VATA 1994 Sch 11 para 9
  valuation–
    generally, VATA 1994 s 23(2)
    token, VATA 1994 s 23(3)
GAS
  supplied by persons outside UK, reverse charge, VATA 1994 s 9A
GAS APPLIANCES
  new buildings, VATA 1994 Sch 8 Group 5 note (12)
GENERAL LIGHTHOUSE AUTHORITY
  refund of tax, VATA 1994 s 33(3)
GIFTS
  deemed supply of goods, VATA 1994 Sch 4 para 5(6)
  gifts to charities, VATA 1994 Sch 8 Group 15 item 1
  visiting forces to, relief on import, SI 1992/3156 art 21
GOING CONCERN
  transfer, Notice 700/9
GOLD AND GOLD COINS
  Central Bank–
    another member state, supply to, SI 1992/3132
    importation by, SI 1992/3124
  investment–
    special scheme, VATA 1994 Sch 9 Group 15; SI 1995/2518 regs 31A, 103A, 2006/112/EC arts 344–356
  meaning, VATA 1994 Sch 8 Group 10 note (1)
  record-keeping requirements, VATA 1994 s 69A
  specified transactions, FA 1999 s 13
  supply of, VATA 1994 s 55
  zero-rating, VATA 1994 Sch 8 Group 10
GOODS
  See also EXPORTED GOODS; IMPORTED GOODS; SUPPLY OF GOODS
  capital, SI 1995/2518 regs 112–116
  exportation. *See* EXPORTED GOODS
  failure to account, VATA 1994 s 73
  handling services VATA 1994 Sch 8 Group 8
  importation. *See* IMPORTED GOODS
  input tax relief on capital goods, VATA 1994 s 34
  intra-community acquisition–
    charge to tax, 2006/112/EC arts 68, 69
    meaning, 2006/112/EC art 20
    place of supply, 2006/112/EC arts 40–42
    taxable transactions, 2006/112/EC arts 20–23
  place of supply, VATA 1994 s 7, 2006/112/EC arts 31–39
  requirement to account, VATA 1994 s 73
  sale in satisfaction of debt, VATA 1994 Sch 4 para 7
  second-hand. *See* SECOND HAND GOODS

GOODS – *cont.*
  supply of. *See* SUPPLY OF GOODS
  transfer, VATA 1994 Sch 4 para 4
  use for non-business purpose, VATA 1994 Sch 4 para 5, SI 1995/2518 regs 116A–116N
  valuation. *See* VALUE
GOODS FOR USE IN A SHIP OR AIRCRAFT
  definition, CEMA 1979 s 1(4)
GOVERNMENT DEPARTMENTS
  generally, VATA 1994 s 41
  meaning, VATA 1994 s 41(6)
GOVERNMENT SECURITIES
  exemption, VATA 1994 Sch 9 Group 5 item 6, 7 note (5)
GROUP OF COMPANIES
  activities deemed to be carried on, VATA 1994 s 43(1), (1AA), (1AB), (2A)–(2E)
  anti-avoidance provisions. *See under* ANTI-AVOIDANCE PROVISIONS
  appeal, VATA 1994 s 83(*k*)
  capital goods scheme, SI 1995/2518 reg 114 5(A)–(B)
  generally, VATA 1994 s 43
  members, treatment as–
    appeals, VATA 1994 s 84(4A)
    application, VATA 1994 s 43B
    eligibility, VATA 1994 s 43A
    termination, VATA 1994 s 43C
  overseas member, FA 1997 s 41
  payment on account, SI 1993/2001 art 17
  representative member, VATA 1994 Sch 10 paras 5, 6
  supplies to, VATA 1994 s 44
  supplies using overseas member, FA 1997 s 41
  transfer of business, VATA 1994 s 44

H

HANDICAPPED PERSONS
  aids, VATA 1994 Sch 8 Group 12
  blind persons, provision of cassette players, talking books and wireless sets, VATA 1994 Sch 8 Group 4
  care and treatment, whether charitable institution providing, VATA 1994 Sch 8 Group 15 notes (4A)–(5B)
  meaning, VATA 1994 Sch 8 Group 12 note (3), Group 15 note (5)
  motor car let on hire–
    generally, VATA 1994 Sch 8 Group 12 item 14
    subsequent sale, VATA 1994 Sch 8 Group 12 item 15
  provision of care and treatment by charity, VATA 1994 Sch 8 Group 15 item 5
HANDLING SERVICES
  zero-rating, VATA 1994 Sch 8 Group 8 item 6
HEADQUARTERS
  See VISITING FORCES
HEALTH AND WELFARE
  exemptions–
    ambulance services, VATA 1994 Sch 9 Group 7 item 11

HEALTH AND WELFARE – *cont.*
  exemptions– – *cont.*
    chemists, VATA 1994 Sch 9 Group 7 item 3
    dental technicians, VATA 1994 Sch 9 Group 7 item 2(*c*)
    dentists, VATA 1994 Sch 9 Group 7 item 2
    doctors, VATA 1994 Sch 9 Group 7 item 1(*a*)
    health visitors, VATA 1994 Sch 9 Group 7 item 1(*d*)
    hearing aid dispensers, VATA 1994 Sch 9 Group 7 item 1(*e*)
    human blood, VATA 1994 Sch 9 Group 7 item 6
    human organs, VATA 1994 Sch 9 item 7 item 8
    midwives, VATA 1994 Sch 9 Group 7 item 1(*d*)
    nurses, VATA 1994 Sch 9 Group 7 item 1(*d*)
    opticians, VATA 1994 Sch 9 Group 7 item 1(*b*)
  health visitor. *See* HEALTH VISITORS
  import relief on goods for, SI 1984/746 Sch 2
  welfare services, meaning, VATA 1994 Sch 9 Group 7 note (6)
HEALTH SERVICE BODIES
  refunds–
    generally, VATA 1994 s 41(7)
HEALTH VISITORS
  exemption, VATA 1994 Sch 9 Group 7 item 1(*d*)
HEARING AID DISPENSER
  exemption, VATA 1994 Sch 9 Group 7 item 1(*e*)
HEAT
  supply, VATA 1994 Sch 4 para 3
HEAT AND COOLING
  imported, relief for, SI 2010/2924
  intra-Community acquisitions, of, SI 1995/2518 reg 87
  place of supply, SI 2004/3148 Pt 3
  removal through network, SI 2010/2925
  reverse charge on, VATA 1994 s 9A
  time of supply, SI 1995/2518 reg 86
HELMETS
  See CLOTHING AND FOOTWEAR
HER MAJESTY'S REVENUE AND CUSTOMS
  data-gathering powers–
    consequential provisions, FA 2011 Sch 23 Pt 6
    interpretation, FA 2011 Sch 23 paras 47–49
    notices, appeals against, FA 2011 Sch 23 Pt 3
    obtaining data, FA 2011 Sch 23 Pt 1
    penalties, FA 2011 Sch 23 Pt 4
    regulations, FA 2011 Sch 23 para 44
    relevant data, SI 2012/847
    relevant data-holders, FA 2011 Sch 23 Pt 2
    statutory records, FA 2011 Sch 23 para 46
    tax, meaning, FA 2011 Sch 23 para 45
HERITAGE OBJECTS
  exemption, VATA 1994 Sch 9 Group 11
HIRE
  zero-rating, transport, VATA 1994 Sch 8 Group 8 note (2)
HMRC CHARTER
  publication of details, FA 2009 s 92
HOLIDAY
  accommodation–
    meaning, VATA 1994 Sch 9 Group 1 note (13)
    supply of, VATA 1994 Sch 9 Group 1 item 1(*e*)

HOLIDAY – *cont.*
  accommodation– – *cont.*
    time sharing, VATA 1994 Sch 8 Group 5 note (7)
  tour operators. *See* TOUR OPERATORS
HOSPITALS
  See also HEALTH AND WELFARE
  exemption, VATA 1994 Sch 9 Group 7 item 4
HOT FOOD
  meaning, VATA 1994 Sch 8 Group 1 note (3)(b)
  zero-rating, VATA 1994 Sch 8 Group 1
HOUSE OF COMMONS
  disqualification of members from tribunals, VATA 1994 Sch 12 para 8
HOUSEBOAT
  holiday accommodation, VATA 1994 Sch 9 Group 1
  option to tax excluded, VATA 1994 Sch 10 para 2(2)
  zero-rating, VATA 1994 Sch 8 Group 9
HOVERCRAFT
  adapted, value, VATA 1994 s 22(3), (4)
  defined as a ship, VATA 1994 s 96(1), SI 1995/2518 reg 117(9)
HUMAN BLOOD, ORGANS AND TISSUE
  exemption, VATA 1994 Sch 9 Group 7 items 6–8

I

IMPORT RELIEF
  acquisitions, on, VATA 1994 s 36A
  antiques, VATA 1994 s 21(4)
  capital goods, VATA 1994 s 34, SI 1984/746 Sch 2
  charitable or philanthropic organisations, for, SI 1984/746 Sch 2
  coffins and funerary items, SI 1984/746 Sch 2
  collector's pieces, VATA 1994 s 21(4)
  description of goods in zero-rate schedule, VATA 1994 s 30(10)
  diplomats–
    conditions attaching to, SI 1992/3156 arts 3–4
    entitled persons, SI 1992/3156 art 14
    motor vehicles, SI 1992/3156 art 16, Sch
    remission of refund, duty or tax subject to, SI 1992/3156 art 17
    special visitors, SI 1992/3156
    tobacco or alcohol products, SI 1992/3156 art 15
  examination, analysis or test for, SI 1984/746 Sch 2
  general provisions, VATA 1994 s 37
  goods of private use, VATA 1994 s 27
  honorary decorations and awards, SI 1992/3193 art 17
  human blood, organs, tissue, SI 1994/746 Sch 2
  importation by taxable persons, VATA 1994 s 38
  inheritance, goods acquired by, SI 1995/2518 SI 1992/3193 art 21
  laboratory animals, SI 1984/746 Sch 2, Group 5
  marriage, import on, SI 1992/3193 arts 13–15
  medical products, SI 1984/746 Sch 2

IMPORT RELIEF – *cont.*
  normal residence, transfer of, SI 1992/3193 art 3
  official visitors, gifts to or from, SI 1992/3193 arts 18–19
  personal property–
    declaration for relief, SI 1992/3193 art 8
    disposal, restriction on, SI 1992/3193 art 7
    enforcement, SI 1992/3193 art 10
    fulfilment of intention to become normally resident, SI 1992/3193 art 9
    security, conditions as to, SI 1992/3193 art 6
    separate consignments in, SI 1992/3193 art 5
  place of residence, SI 1992/3193 art 3
  printed matter, SI 1984/746 Sch 2
  promotion of trade, for, SI 1984/746 Sch 2
  research, biological or chemical substances for, SI 1984/746 Sch 2
  scholastic materials, SI 1992/3193 art 16
  sports events, pharmaceutical products used at, SI 1984/746 Sch 2
  United Nations, produced by, SI 1984/746 Sch 1
  visiting forces, SI 1992/3156 arts 5–13, 18–22, Sch
  war victims, memorials or cemeteries for, SI 1984/746 Sch 2

IMPORTATION OF GOODS
  See also IMPORTS
  charge to tax, 2006/112/EC arts 70, 71
  Community transit procedure, use, SI 1995/2518 reg 141
  Customs & Excise legislation applied, SI 1995/2518 regs 142, 143
  excepted provisions–
    Community legislation, SI 1995/2518 reg 120(1)–(3)
    enactments, SI 1995/2518 reg 118
    regulations, SI 1995/2518 reg 118
  exemptions on, 2006/112/EC arts 143–145
  formalities, SI 1995/2518 reg 140, 2454/93
  gold, SI 1992/3124
  legacies, CED(GR)A 1979 s 7, SI 1992/3193 art 21
  meaning, 2006/112/EC art 30
  person travelling from third party, by, 2007/74/EC
  place of, 2006/112/EC arts 60–61
  postal, SI 1995/2518 reg 122, SI 1986/260
  small non-commercial consignment–
    conditions of relief, SI 1986/939 art 4
    quantitative restrictions on relief, SI 1986/939 art 5
    relief, generally, SI 1986/939
    traveller's baggage, relief not applicable to, SI 1986/939 art 6
  taxable amount, 2006/112/EC arts 72, 85–89
  temporary, SI 1995/2518 reg 123
  time of, CEMA 1979 s 5
  travellers' allowances, SI 1994/955

IMPORTED GOODS
  agents, VATA 1994 s 47(2)
  antiques, VATA 1994 s 21(5)
  appeals, VATA 1994 s 83(*b*), (*f*)
  application of customs and excise legislation, VATA 1994 s 16

IMPORTED GOODS – *cont.*
  apportionment of tax, VATA 1994 s 24(5)
  arrivals and dispatches, provision of information, SI 1995/2518 regs 23E, 23F
  capital goods, VATA 1994 s 34
  charge to tax, VATA 1994 s 1(1)
  collector's pieces, VATA 1994 s 21(5)
  evasion of tax, VATA 1994 s 72(10)
  forfeiture where improperly imported, CEMA 1979 s 49
  free zone regulations, VATA 1994 s 17
  generally, VATA 1994 s 15
  improperly imported–
    forfeiture, CEMA 1979 s 49
    penalty, CEMA 1979 s 50
  information, VATA 1994 Sch 11 para 7(2)–(8)
  input tax credit, VATA 1994 s 24(1)
  member states, from outside–
    scope, VATA 1994 s 1(4)
    value, VATA 1994 s 21
    warehousing regime, VATA 1994 s 18
  movement of–
    application relating to, SI 1984/1176 regs 8–9
    Community transit procedures, SI 1984/1176 reg 4 (1)
    definition, SI 1984/1176 reg 3
    international convention, SI 1984/1176 reg 4 (2)
    local export control, SI 1984/1176 reg 9
    removal document–
      meaning of, SI 1984/1176 reg 3
      necessity of, SI 1984/1176 reg 11
    removals, accidents during–
      completion of, SI 1984/1176 reg 16
      fine for, SI 1984/1176 reg 17
      generally, SI 1984/1176 reg 18
    restriction on, SI 1984/1176 regs 5–7
    standing permission for, SI 1984/1176 reg 10
    vehicles and containers, route for–
      generally, SI 1984/1176 reg 13
      security of, SI 1984/1176 reg 14
      specification of, SI 1984/1176 reg 12
      tampering with, SI 1984/1176 reg 15
  overseas authority, VATA 1994 Sch 8 Group 13 items 2, 3
  penalty for improper importation, CEMA 1979 s 50
  place of supply, VATA 1994 s 7(6)
  private purposes, VATA 1994 s 27
  rate of tax, VATA 1994 s 2(1)(*c*)
  refund of tax–
    generally, VATA 1994 s 33
    new means of transport, VATA 1994 s 40
  re-importation–
    goods exported for treatment or process, SI 1995/2518 reg 126
    non-taxable persons, by, SI 1995/2518 reg 124
    taxable persons, by, SI 1995/2518 reg 125
  relief. *See* IMPORT RELIEF
  supply of, VATA 1994 s 18
  taxable person, VATA 1994 s 38
  transitional provisions, VATA 1994 Sch 13 para 19
  value of supply, VATA 1994 s 21
  zero-rating, VATA 1994 s 30

IMPORTED GOODS – *cont.*
  wedding gift, SI 1992/3193 art 14
  work of art, VATA 1994 s 21(4), SI 1995/658
IMPORTED SERVICES
  reverse charge, VATA 1994 s 8
  supplied where received, VATA 1994 Sch 5
IMPORTER
  agent, VATA 1994 s 47(1)
  meaning, CEMA 1979 s 1
IMPORTS
  See also IMPORTATION OF GOODS
  time of, CEMA 1979 s 5
INCAPACITY
  registered person, VATA 1994 s 46(4), 47(2)
  taxable person, of, SI 1995/2518 reg 9
INCOME TAX
  no deduction for default interest, VATA 1994 s 59(8), (9)
INDEPENDENT TELEVISION NEWS LTD
  refund of tax, VATA 1994 s 33
INFORMATION
  Commissioners power to obtain, VATA 1994 Sch 11 para 7
  false use, VATA 1994 s 72
  penalty for making false statement, VATA 1994 s 72(3)
  power of access to recorded information, VATA 1994 Sch 11 para 11
  services–
    reverse charge, VATA 1994 s 8
INFORMATION POWERS
  amendment, FA 2009 s 95, Sch 47
  extension, FA 2009 s 96, Sch 48
  obtaining contact details for debtors, FA 2009 s 97, Sch 49
INHERITANCE TAX
  conditionally exempt supplies, VATA 1994 Sch 9 Group 11 items 2, 3
INPUT TAX
  agency supplies, VATA 1994 s 47
  amount allowable, VATA 1994 s 26
  appeals, VATA 1994 s 83(c), (e)
  apportionment, VATA 1994 s 24(5)
  business entertainment, SI 1992/3222 art 5
  business assets–
    non-business use of, VATA 1994 s 24, F(No 3)A 2010 Sch 8
  capital items–
    application of scheme, SI 1995/2518 reg 113
    method of adjustment, SI 1995/2518 reg 114
    period of adjustment, SI 1995/2518 reg 114
    references to, SI 1995/2518 reg 112
    taxable use, ascertainment of, SI 1995/2518 reg 116
  cash accounting scheme, SI 1995/2518 reg 57
  claims–
    generally, SI 1995/2518 reg 29
  credit, VATA 1994 s 25, SI 1995/2518 reg 25
  designated travel service–
    goods supplied as, SI 1987/1086 art 12
  disallowance–
    antiques, SI 1992/3222 art 4
    capital goods, SI 1995/2518 regs 112–116

INPUT TAX – *cont.*
  disallowance– – *cont.*
    collectors' pieces, SI 1992/3222 art 4
    consideration not paid, where, VATA 1994 ss 26A–26AA
    designated travel services, SI 1987/1806 art 12
    goods incorporated into a building, SI 1992/3222 art 6
    imported goods owned by third party, VATA 1994 s 27
    land acquired with sporting rights, VATA 1994 Sch 9 Group 1 item 1(c) note (8)
    motor cars, SI 1992/3222 art 7
    used aircraft, SI 1992/3222 art 4
    used boats, SI 1992/3222 art 4
    used caravans, SI 1992/3222 art 4
    used electronic organs, SI 1992/3222 art 4
    used firearms, SI 1992/3222 art 4
    used motor cycles, SI 1992/3222 art 4
    works of art, SI 1992/3222 art 4
  documents to support claim, SI 1995/2518 reg 29(2)
  domestic accommodation, VATA 1994 s 24(3)
  dwellings–
    goods incorporated in, SI 1992/3222 art 6
  election, VATA 1994 Sch 10 para 2
  estimation of, SI 1995/2518 reg 29(3)
  fuel for private use, SI 2013/2911
  generally, VATA 1994 s 24
  imported goods, VATA 1994 s 24(1), (2), 37
  meaning, VATA 1994 s 24(1)
  motor cars, SI 1992/3222 art 7
  new dwellings–
    goods incorporated in, SI 1992/3222 art 6
  non-deductible input tax–
    relief for, VATA 1994 Sch 9 Group 14
  partial exemption–
    See PARTIAL EXEMPTION
  period in which credit claimed. SI 1995/2518 reg 29(1)
  pre-incorporation purchases, SI 1995/2518 reg 111
  pre-registration purchases, SI 1995/2518 reg 111
  repayment of tax–
    See REFUND OF TAX
  reverse charge, VATA 1994 s 8
  self-supplies, on, SI 1995/2518 reg 104
  specified supplies, SI 1999/3121
  taxable supplies–
    accounting for difference, SI 1995/2518 regs 107A–107E
    attributable to, SI 1995/2518 regs 106–106A
  three-year time limit, SI 1995/2518 reg 29 (1A)
  travel services, designated, SI 1987/1806 art 12
  warehoused goods, VATA 1994 s 18
INSOLVENCY
  assessment on receiver, VATA 1994 s 73
  bad debt relief–
    administration procedure, SI 1995/2518
    appeal, VATA 1994 s 83(h)
    claim, SI 1995/2518 regs 167–169
    flat rate scheme for small businesses, SI 1995/2518 reg 55V
    generally, VATA 1994 s 36

INSOLVENCY – *cont.*
  bad debt relief– – *cont.*
    margin schemes, SI 1995/2518 reg 172A
    notice to purchaser, SI 1995/2518 reg 166A
    refund, repayment of, SI 1995/2518 reg 171
    repayment of input tax, SI 1995/2518 regs 172C–172E
    time limits for claims, SI 1995/2518 reg 165A
    tour operators' margin scheme, SI 1995/2518 reg 172B
    transfer of going concern, SI 1995/2158 reg 6(3)(d)
    transitional provisions, VATA 1994 Sch 13 para 9
    writing off debts, SI 1995/2518 reg 172
  bankrupts, VATA 1994 s 46(4)
  body corporate, VATA 1994 s 46(5)
  certificates–
    form of, SI 1986/385 reg 4
    issue of, SI 1986/385 reg 3
    notification to creditors, SI 1986/385 reg 5
  fees, SI 1985/1784
  individual, SI 1995/2518 reg 9
  notification of assessment, VATA 1994 s 73(10)(*q*)
  set off credits, VATA 1994 s 81
  transitional provisions, VATA 1994 Sch 13 para 12, FA 1997 s 49
INSPECTION POWERS
  amendment, FA 2009 s 95, Sch 47
  extension, FA 2009 s 96, Sch 48
INSTALMENT CREDIT FINANCE
  exemption, VATA 1994 Sch 9 Group 5
  supply of goods, VATA 1994 Sch 4 para 1
  zero-rating, VATA 1994 Sch 8 Group 8
INSURANCE
  agents, VATA 1994 Sch 9 Group 2 item 4
  brokers, VATA 1994 Sch 9 Group 2 item 4
  claim under policy of, goods acquired in settlement of, SI 1992/3129 art 4
  exemption, VATA 1994 Sch 9 Group 2
  Export Credits Guarantee Department, provision by, VATA 1994 Sch 9 Group 2 item 3
  intermediary, services of, VATA 1994 Sch 9 Group 2 item 4 notes (1)–(10)
  provider–
    generally, VATA 1994 Sch 9 item 1
    resident outside UK, VATA 1994 Sch 9 item 2
  services–
    reverse charge, VATA 1994 s 8
    supplied where received, VATA 1994 Sch 5 para 5
INTELLECTUAL PROPERTY
  See COPYRIGHT; PATENT; TRADEMARK
INTENDING TRADER
  deregistration, VATA 1994 Sch 1 paras 11, 12
  registration, VATA 1994 Sch 1 paras 9, 10
INTEREST
  appeal, VATA 1994 s 83(s)
  applicable rate, SI 1998/1461
  assessment, VATA 1994 s 76, 77
  exemption, VATA 1994 Sch 9 Group 5

INTEREST – *cont.*
  given by way of credits and set off of credits, VATA 1994 s 81 FA 1997 s 49
  late payment, for, FA 2009 s 101, Sch 53
  official error, in case of, VATA 1994 s 78
  overpayment–
    assessment for overpayment of, VATA 1994 s 78A
  period, VATA 1994 s 74
  prescribed rate–
    meaning, VATA 1994 s 74(6)
  recovery of tax, VATA 1994 s 74
  refund. *See under* REFUND OF TAX
  repayment by HMRC, on, FA 2009 s 102, Sch 54
  repayment supplement, VATA 1994 s 79
  zero-rating, VATA 1994 Sch 8 Group 7
INTERNATIONAL COLLABORATION AGREEMENTS,
  zero-rating, VATA 1994 Sch 8 Group 13 items 2, 3
INTERNATIONAL SERVICES
  zero-rating, VATA 1994 Sch 8 Group 7
INTERNATIONAL TRAVEL
  Imports by persons travelling from third countries, 2007/74/EC
INVESTIGATIONS
  Northern Ireland, in, FA 2007 s 83
  powers of Revenue and Customs, FA 2007 s 82
  Scotland, in, FA 2007 s 85
  supplementary provisions, FA 2007 s 84
INVOICE
  meaning, VATA 1994 s 96(1)
  tax. *See* TAX INVOICE
ISSUE OF SECURITIES
  exemption, VATA 1994 Sch 9 Group 5 item 1

J

JOINT AND SEVERAL LIABILITY
  non-UK sellers in breach of Sch 1A registration, VATA 1994 s 77BA
  online marketplaces, VATA 1994 ss 77B–77BA
  ss 77B–77BA assessment, under, VATA 1994 s 77C
  ss 77B–77BA interest, under, VATA 1994 s 77D
  sellers identified as non-compliant by Commissioners, VATA 1994 s 77B
  traders in supply chain, of, VATA 1994 s 77A
  unpaid VAT of another, for, VATA 1994 s 77A
JOINT PORT LOCAL AUTHORITY
  refund of tax, VATA 1994 s 33
JOURNAL
  charity advertisement, VATA 1994 Sch 8 Group 15 item 8
  zero-rating, VATA 1994 Sch 8 Group 3 item 2
JURY SERVICE
  exemption, VATA 1994 Sch 12 para 8
JUSTICE OF THE PEACE
  issue of warrant, VATA 1994 Sch 11 paras 11–13

L

LAND
  assignment or surrender, VATA 1994 Sch 9 Group 1 item 1 note (1)
  compulsory purchase of, SI 1995/2518 reg 84
  co-owners, registration of, VATA 1994 s 51A
  election to tax, VATA 1994 Sch 10 paras 2–4
  freehold, grant of. *See* FREEHOLD
  grant made without consideration, VATA 1994 Sch 4 paras 5, 9
  grant or assignment of fee simple, consideration not determinable for, SI 1995/2518 reg 84
  held at date of deregistration, VATA 1994 Sch 4 paras 8, 9
  interests in, VATA 1994 Sch 9 Group 1 item 1
  lease. *See* LEASE
  major interest, VATA 1994 s 96(1)
  self-supply, VATA 1994 s 44(4)
  services relating to, place of supply, SI 1992/3121 art 5
  situated abroad, VATA 1994 Sch 8 Group 1 item 1
  supply of, VATA 1994 Sch 9 Group 1
  surrender, VATA 1994 Sch 9 Group 1 note (1)

LATE PAYMENT INTEREST
  sums due to HMRC, on, FA 2009 s 101, Sch 53

LAVATORY
  supply to handicapped person, VATA 1994 Sch 8 Group 12 item 10

LEAFLET
  advertising by charities, VATA 1994 Sch 8 Group 15 item 8
  zero-rating, VATA 1994 Sch 8 Group 3 item 1

LEARNED SOCIETY
  exemption, VATA 1994 Sch 9 Group 9

LEASE
  building used for–
    charitable purpose, VATA 1994 Sch 8 Group 5 item note 4, Group 6
    residential purpose, VATA 1994 Sch 8 Groups 2, 6
  changes to accounting standards etc, FA 2019 s 36, Sch 14
  dwelling, VATA 1994 Sch 8 Groups 5, 6
  grant, VATA 1994 Sch 9 Group 1
  holiday accommodation, VATA 1994 Sch 9 Group 1
  listed building, VATA 1994 Sch 9 Group 6
  monument, VATA 1994 Sch 8 Group 6
  protected building, VATA 1994 Sch 8 Group 6
  reverse surrender, VATA 1994 Sch 9 Group 1 item 1 notes (1), (1A)
  supply of goods as, SI 1995/2518 reg 85
  treatment as supply of goods, VATA 1994 Sch 4 para 4

LEGACIES
  imported, relief for, CED(GR)A 1979 s 7, SI 1992/3193 art 21

LEGAL SERVICES
  insurance claims, VATA 1994 Sch 9 Group 2 note (8)
  reverse charge, VATA 1994 s 8
  supplied where received, VATA 1994 Sch 5 para 3

LEGAL SERVICES – *cont.*
  supply to overseas person, VATA 1994 Sch 8 Group 9
  time of supply, SI 1995/2518 reg 92

LIABILITY TO TAX
  generally, VATA 1994 s 1

LICENCE
  services supplied where received, VATA 1994 Sch 5 para 1
  transfer or assignment–
    reverse charge, VATA 1994 s 8
    zero-rating, VATA 1994 Sch 8 Group 9

LIFEBOAT
  meaning, VATA 1994 Sch 8 Group 8 note (3)
  zero-rating, VATA 1994 Sch 8 Group 8 item 3

LIFT
  supply to handicapped person, VATA 1994 Sch 8 Group 12 item 2, 16–18

LIGHTHOUSE AUTHORITY
  refund of tax, VATA 1994 s 33(3)

LIQUIDATION
  See INSOLVENCY

LISTED BUILDINGS
  See PROTECTED BUILDINGS

LOCAL AUTHORITY
  meaning, VATA 1994 s 96(4)
  refund of tax, VATA 1994 s 33
  registration, VATA 1994 s 42

LONG STAY ACCOMMODATION
  See ACCOMMODATION

LOW VALUE GOODS
  Northern Ireland Protocol, VATA 1994 Sch 9ZC

M

MACHINE TOOLS SUPPLIED TO OVERSEAS AUTHORITY
  zero-rating, VATA 1994 Sch 8 Group 13

MACHINERY AND PLANT
  capital goods tax relief, VATA 1994 s 34

MAGAZINE
  advertising by charities, VATA 1994 Sch 8, Group 15 item 8
  zero-rating, VATA 1994 Sch 8 Group 3

MAGISTRATES COURT COMMITTEE
  refund of tax, SI 1986/336

MAP
  zero-rating, VATA 1994 Sch 8 Group 3

MARGIN SCHEMES
  bad debt relief, SI 1995/2518 reg 172A
  calculation of output tax, VATA 1994 s 50A(1)
  eligible supplies, VATA 1994 s 50A(2)
  global accounting, VATA 1994 s 50A(7)

MARKETPLACES
  online, VATA 1994 ss 77B-77C

MEAL
  provided by employer, VATA 1994 Sch 6 para 10(1), (2)

MEDIA
  advertising by charity, VATA 1994 Sch 8 Group 15

MEDICAL CARE
  exemption, VATA 1994 Sch 9 Group 7 item 4
  provided by charities, VATA 1994 Sch 8 Group 15 item 9
MEDICAL COURIER CHARITIES
  refund of tax–
    generally, VATA 1994 s 33C
    meaning, VATA 1994 s 33D
MEDICAL EQUIPMENT
  zero-rating, VATA 1994 Sch 8 Group 12 items 2–7
MEDICAL LABORATORY TECHNICIAN
  exemption, VATA 1994 Sch 9 Group 7
MEDICAL PRACTITIONER
  exemption, VATA 1994 Sch 9 Group 7
  zero-rating, VATA 1994 Sch 8 Group 12 item 1A
MEDICAL RESEARCH
  charities, VATA 1994 Sch 8 Group 15 items 9, 10
MEDICAL SERVICES
  exemption, VATA 1994 Sch 9 Group 7
  import relief. SI 1984/746 Sch 2
MEMBER STATES
  See EC
MIDWIFE
  exemption, VATA 1994 Sch 9 Group 7 item 1(*d*)
MISDECLARATION
  penalty. *See* PENALTIES
  repeated, VATA 1994 s 64
  resulting in loss of tax, VATA 1994 s 63
MONEY
  exemption, VATA 1994 Sch 9 Group 5
MOORING
  facilities, VATA 1994 Sch 9 Group 1 item 1(*k*)
  meaning, VATA 1994 Sch 9 Group 1 note (15)
MORTGAGE
  aircraft, supply of, repossessed under, SI 1992/3129 art 4
  marine, supply of ship, repossessed under, SI 1992/3129 art 4
MOTOR ASSESSOR
  services, VATA 1994 Sch 9 Group 2 note (1)
MOTOR CARS
  diplomat, purchase by, SI 1992/3156 art 16
  exclusion of input tax credit, SI 1992/3222 art 7
  fuel. *See* FUEL
  handicapped person, VATA 1994 Sch 8 Group 12
  meaning, 2518, SI 1992/3122 art 2, SI 1992/3222 art 2
  overseas visitor, supply to, of, SI 1995/2518 reg 132
  parking facilities, VATA 1994 Sch 9 Group 1 item 1(*h*)
  person departing from UK, SI 1995/2518 reg 113
  second-hand, SI 1992/3122 art 8
  self supply of, SI 1992/3122 arts 5–7
  stock in trade, use for consideration less than market value, VATA 1994 Sch 6 para 1A
  treatment of transactions, SI 1992/3122 art 4
  visiting forces, purchase by, SI 1992/3156 reg 19
MOTOR CYCLES
  acquisition in settlement of insurance claim, SI 1992/3129 art 4
  meaning, SI 1992/3129 art 2

MOTOR CYCLES – *cont.*
  protective helmet, VATA 1994 Sch 8 Group 16 item 3
  second hand–
    exclusion of input tax credit, SI 1992/3222 art 4
    relief for certain supplies, SI 1992/3129 art 8
  repossession under finance agreement, SI 1992/3129 art 4
MUSIC
  printed, duplicated or manuscript, VATA 1994 Sch 8 Group 3

N

'NAMING AND SHAMING'
  publication of details of deliberate tax defaulters, FA 2009 s 97
NEGLECT
  penalties. *See* PENALTIES
  resulting understatement, VATA 1994 s 63(1)
NEW MEANS OF TRANSPORT
  See TRANSPORT
NEW TOWN COMMISSION
  refund of tax, VATA 1994 s 33
NEWSPAPERS
  zero-rating, VATA 1994 Sch 8 Group 3–
    advertisement by charity, VATA 1994 Sch 8 Group 15 item 8
NEWS PROVIDERS
  refund of tax, VATA 1994 s 33
NON-PROFIT MAKING ORGANISATION
  exemption–
    competition entry fees, VATA 1994 Sch 9 Group 10
    education, training and research, VATA 1994 Sch 9 Group 6 items 2, 4, 5
    fund raising events for charity, VATA 1994 Sch 9 Group 12 item 2
    health and welfare services, VATA 1994 Sch 9 Group 7 item 9
    subscriptions to defined bodies, VATA 1994 Sch 9 Group 9
  meaning, VATA 1994 Sch 9 Group 10 note (3)
NON-RESIDENTIAL BUILDINGS
  developers, VATA 1994 Sch 10 paras 5–7
  meaning, VATA 1994 Sch 8 Group 5 note (7)
NORTHERN IRELAND
  acquisition of goods in NI from member states, VATA 1994 Sch 9ZA
  application of VAT, VATA 1994 ss 1, 7charge to tax on acquisitions of goods, VATA 1994 Sch 9ZA
  charge to tax on goods imported, VATA 1994 Sch 9ZB
  computer, meaning, VATA 1994 s 96(6)(b)
  copy, meaning, VATA 1994 s 96(6)(b)
  document, meaning, VATA 1994 s 96(6)(b)
  enforcement of tribunal decisions, VATA 1994 s 87(3)
  EU Exit Regulations, SI 2020/1546
  import of goods into UK as result of entry into NI, VATA 1994 Sch 9ZB

NORTHERN IRELAND – *cont.*
  import of low value goods, VATA 1994 Sch 9ZC
  low value goods, VATA 1994 Sch 9ZC
  Northern Ireland Protocol, VATA 1994 s 40A
  online marketplaces, VATA 1994 Sch 9ZC
  post-transition period–
    commencement of provisions, T(PTP)A 2020 s 11
    duty on goods imported into or removed from NI, T(PTP)A 2020 s 2, Sch 1
    duty on goods removed to NI, T(PTP)A 2020 s 1
    excise duty on removal of goods to NI, T(PTP)A 2020 ss 4–5
    low value importations, T(PTP)A 2020 s 7, Sch 3
    online sale by overseas persons, T(PTP)A 2020 s 7, Sch 3
    rate of fuel duty on aviation gasoline, T(PTP)A 2020 s 6
    recovery of unlawful state aid, T(PTP)A 2020 Sch 4
    VAT in NI, T(PTP)A 2020 s 3, Sch 2
  'qualifying Northern Ireland goods', SI 2020/1454
  recovery of tax, VATA 1994 Sch 11 para 5(4)
  refund of tax to Government, VATA 1994 s 99
  savings, SI 2020/1545
  supply of goods by persons established outside UK facilitated by online marketplaces, VATA 1994 Sch 9ZC
  transitional provisions, SI 2020/1545
NOTICES
  partnerships, by–
    generally, SI 1995/2518 reg 7(1)
    Scotland, SI 1995/2518 reg 7(2)
NOTIFICATION
  bankruptcy, death or incapacity of an individual, SI 1995/2518 reg 9
  business establishment opened in Isle of Man, SI 1982/1067 reg 11
  ceasing to make taxable supplies, VATA 1994 Sch 1 paras 11, 12
  change in–
    constitution of partnership, SI 1995/2518 regs 5, 6
    name, constitution or ownership of business, SI 1995/2518 reg 5(2)
    registered particulars, SI 1995/2518 regs 5, 6
  installation or assembly of goods in UK, SI 1995/2518 reg 12
  liability and registration, VATA 1994 Sch 1 paras 5–8
  liquidation or receivership or body corporate, SI 1995/2518 reg 9
  partnership, by, SI 1995/2518 regs 5(1), 7
  penalties for failure to notify, VATA 1994 s 67
  registration–
    liability to, SI 1995/2518, regs 5, 6
    end of liability, SI 1995/2518 reg 5(3)
  service, VATA 1994 s 98
  tax representative, appointment of, SI 1995/2518 reg 10
  triangulation supplies, SI 1995/2518 reg 11

NURSE
  exemption, VATA 1994 Sch 9 Group 7 item 1(*d*)
NURSERIES
  exemption, VATA 1994 Sch 9 Group 7
NURSING HOME
  exemption, VATA 1994 Sch 9 Group 7

O

OCCUPATIONAL THERAPIST
  exemption, VATA 1994 Sch 9 Group 7
OFFENCES
  breach of walking possession agreements, VATA 1994 s 68
  contravention of relevant rule, penalty for, SI 2003/3113
  evasion of tax. *See* EVASION OF TAX
  failure to make return, VATA 1994 s 73
  failure to notify of acquisition, VATA 1994 s 67
  failure to notify of registration, VATA 1994 s 67
  failure to submit section 55 statements, VATA 1994 s 66
  false information, providing, VATA 1994 s 72
  fraudulent evasion of tax, VATA 1994 s 72
  goods used in breach of condition, CED(GR)A 1979 s 13C
  inaccuracies in EC sales statements, VATA 1994 s 65
  incorrect certificates, VATA 1994 s 62
  neglect, VATA 1994 s 63
  outlying enactments, saving for, CEMA 1979 s 156
  power of arrest, VATA 1994 s 72(9)
  proceedings for, CEMA 1979 ss 45–48
  receiving goods knowing tax to be evaded, VATA 1994 s 72(10)
  repeated misdeclarations, VATA 1994 s 63, 64
  statistics of trade, in relation to, SI 1992/2790 reg 6
  unauthorised disclosure of information, VATA 1994 s 91(4)
  unauthorised issue of invoices, VATA 1994 s 67
  untrue declarations, etc, CEMA 1979 s 167
OFFICE
  meaning, VATA 1994 s 94
OFFICE FOR NATIONAL STATISTICS
  disclosure of information to, VATA 1994 s 91
OFFICIAL ERROR
  appeal, VATA 1994 s 83(s)
  interest, VATA 1994 s 78
ONLINE MARKETPLACES
  deemed supply–
    exception from liability, VATA 1994 s 77F
    generally, VATA 1994 s 5A
  display of VAT registration numbers, VATA 1994 s 77E
  joint and several liability, VATA 1994 ss 77B–77D
  meaning, VATA 1994 s 95A
  'operator', VATA 1994 s 95A
  supply of goods facilitated by–
    deemed supply, VATA 1994 s 5A

ONLINE MARKETPLACES – *cont.*
Northern Ireland Protocol, and, VATA 1994 Sch 9ZC

OPEN MARKET VALUE
See VALUE

OPERATOR
meaning, VATA 1994 s 95A

OPTICAL APPLIANCE
exemption, VATA 1994 Sch 9 Group 7

OPTICIAN
exemption, VATA 1994 Sch 9 Group 7 item 1(b)
refund of tax to, RI 129

OPTION TO TAX (ELECTION TO WAIVE EXEMPTION)
effect of, VATA 1994 Sch 10 paras 2–4
contracts, VATA 1994 s 89
guide to, Notice 742A
manner of election, VATA 1994 Sch 10 paras 2, 3

OUTPUT TAX
accounting for, SI 1995/2518 regs 2(1), 25, 40(a), 108(2)
bad debt relief–
See BAD DEBT RELIEF
calculation–
generally, VATA 1994 Sch 4 para 7, SI 1995/2518 reg 27–
goods sold under a power, SI 1995/2518 reg 27
motor cars, SI 1992/3122 art 8
second-hand goods, SI 1992/3129 art 8
tour operators' services, SI 1987/1806
estimation, SI 1995/2518 reg 28
general provisions, VATA 1994 s 24
margin scheme, VATA 1994 ss 32, 50A
meaning, VATA 1994 s 24(2)
missing trader inter-community fraud–
adjustment in relation to supplies, VATA 1994 s 26AB
persons liable, VATA 1994 s 1(2)
security, VATA 1994 Sch 11 para 4(2)
tour operators–
See TOUR OPERATORS

OVERPAID TAX
recovery–
generally, SI 1995/2518 reg 37

OVERSEAS PERSON
EC trader, VATA 1994 Sch 9 Group 7
overseas body, VATA 1994 Sch 8 Group 13
overseas branch, VATA 1994 Sch 8 Group 13
overseas trader, VATA 1994 Sch 8 Group 13
registration of agent, VATA 1994 s 47

OVERSEAS RESIDENTS
See OVERSEAS PERSON

OVERSEAS SUPPLIER
customers, accounting through, SI 1995/2518 reg 11

OVERSEAS TRADERS
See OVERSEAS PERSON

OVERSTATEMENT OF TAX
persistent misdeclaration, VATA 1994 s 64
serious misdeclaration, VATA 1994 s 63

P

PALLIATIVE CARE CHARITIES
refund of tax–
generally, VATA 1994 s 33C
meaning, VATA 1994 s 33D

PAMPHLET
advertising by charities, VATA 1994 Sch 8 Group 15 item 8
zero-rating, VATA 1994 Sch 8 Group 3

PARKING FACILITIES
exemption, VATA 1994 Sch 9 Group 1 item 1(*h*)

PARTIAL EXEMPTION
attribution of input tax–
adjustment of, SI 1995/2518 regs 107–110
amount under £625, SI 1995/2518 reg 105A
change in intended use, SI 1995/2518 regs 114–116
exempt supplies, SI 1995/2518 reg 105
immediately preceding longer period, amount incurred in, SI 1995/2518 reg 106ZA
method of–
foreign supplies, SI 1995/2518 reg 103
self-supplies, SI 1995/2518 reg 104
special, SI 1995/2518 regs 102-102C
specified exempt supplies, SI 1995/2518 regs 103–106
standard, SI 1995/2518 reg 101
building, adjustment of input tax, SI 1995/2518 regs 112–116
capital items (capital goods scheme), SI 1995/2518 regs 112–116
computers and computer equipment, SI 1995/2518 regs 112–116
exempt input tax, SI 1995/2518 reg 99(1)
generally, VATA 1994 s 26
tax year, SI 1995/2518 reg 99(1)

PARTNERSHIPS
appeal to VAT tribunal by partners, SI 1986/590 reg 12
business carried on by, VATA 1994 s 46(2)
deemed partnership, VATA 1994 Sch 1 para 2(7)
details, SI 1995/2518 Sch 1 Form 2
generally, VATA 1994 s 45
notices by–
generally, SI 1995/2518 reg 7(1)
Scotland, SI 1995/2518 reg 7(2)
notification of liability to register by, SI 1995/2518 reg 5(1)

PASSAGE
widening for handicapped persons, VATA 1994 Sch 8 Group 12 item 8

PASSENGER
transportation, VATA 1994 Sch 8 Group 8

PASSENGER TRANSPORT AUTHORITY
refund of tax, VATA 1994 s 33

PATENT
transfer or assignment–
reverse charge, VATA 1994 s 8
zero-rating, VATA 1994 Sch 8 Group 7

PAYMENT OF VAT
amounts less than 1.00, VATA 1994 Sch 11 para 2
appeal, VATA 1994 s 83

PAYMENT OF VAT – *cont.*
  breach of provisions–
    assessment, VATA 1994 ss 76, 77
    generally, VATA 1994 s 69
  credit for input tax, VATA 1994 ss 25, 26
  errors–
    correction of, SI 1995/2518 reg 35
    voluntary disclosure, SI 1995/2518 reg 34
  failure to make on time–
    penalty, FA 2009 Sch 56
  goods sold in satisfaction of debt, VATA 1994 Sch 4 para 7, Sch 11 para 2(1)
  imported goods–
    deposit, CEMA 1979 ss 43(1), 44
    postponed accounting scheme, SI 1995/2518 reg 122
    security, CEMA 1979 s 37B
  input tax, VATA 1994 s 24
  output tax, VATA 1994 s 24
  payment by reference to accounting periods, VATA 1994 s 25(1)
  payments on account–
    body corporate, SI 1995/2518 reg 48
    calculation of amounts, SI 1993/2001 arts 11–15
    cessation of duty, SI 1993/2001 art 7
    divisions, business carried on in, SI 1993/2001 art 16
    duty to pay, SI 1993/2001 art 4
    eligible persons, SI 1993/2001 art 5
    excess, repayment of, SI 1995/2518 reg 46
    failure to make, SI 1995/2518 reg 47
    generally, VATA 1994 s 28, SI 1995/2518 regs 40A, 45–48
    groups of companies, SI 1993/2001 art 17
    missing trader intra-community fraud, supplies used in, SI 1993/2001 art 2A
    notification in writing, SI 1992/1844 regs 4, 7, SI 1995/2518 reg 45
    overpayment, SI 1995/2518 reg 46
    time for payments, SI 1993/2001 arts 8–9
  penalties–
    failure to make on time, FA 2009 s 107, Sch 56
    non-payment, VATA 1994 s 66, 76
  procedure–
    goods sold in satisfaction of a debt, SI 1995/2518 reg 27
    Post Office, to, SI 1986/260 reg 15
    postponed accounting system, SI 1995/2518 reg 122
    proper officer, to, CEMA 1979 s 43
    repayment, VATA 1994 s 25(3)
    standing deposit, CEMA 1979 s 44
    tax returns, SI 1995/2518 reg 40(2), (3), SI 1995/2518 regs 40A, 46A
  security, VATA 1994 s 73
  shipping and forwarding agent, by, CEMA 1979 s 43(1)
  time limit, SI 1995/2518 regs 25, 40(2), (3), 50, 54, 62, 63
  unpaid tax–
    distress for, SI 1995/2518 reg 212

PAYMENT OF VAT – *cont.*
  unpaid tax– – *cont.*
    joint and several liability of traders in supply chain, VATA 1994 s 77A
  warehoused goods, time of, VATA 1994 s 18(4)–(5A)

PENALTIES
  breach of regulations, VATA 1994 s 69
  breach of walking possession agreements, VATA 1994 s 68
  contravention of relevant rule, for–
    appeals, FA 2003 s 33F
    exceptions, FA 2003 s 27
    generally, FA 2003 s 26, SI 2003/3113
    no prosecution after demand notice, FA 2003 s 32
    reasonable excuse, FA 2003 s 27
    review of decisions, FA 2003 ss 33–37
    right to appeal, FA 2003 s 33
    time limit for demands, FA 2003 s 31
  demands, FA 2003 s 30
  errors, for, FA 2007 Sch 24
  evasion of tax–
    directors of body corporate, liability of, FA 2003 s 28
    generally, VATA 1994 s 72, FA 2003 s 25
    reduction of penalty, FA 2003 s 29
    time limit for demands, FA 2003 s 31
  failure to make payments on time, FA 2009 s 107, Sch 56
  failure to make returns, VATA 1994 s 73, FA 2009 s 106, Sch 55
  failure to pay tax, FA 2009 s 107, Sch 56
  failure to notify, VATA 1994 s 67
  false information, providing, VATA 1994 s 72
  fraudulent evasion of tax, VATA 1994 s 72
  fraudulent transactions, for–
    generally, VATA 1994 s 69C
    officers' liability, VATA 1994 s 69D
    publication of persons liable, VATA 1994 s 69E
  imposition of liability, FA 2003 s 24
  misdeclaration, for–
    generally, VATA 1994 s 63
    repeated, VATA 1994 s 64
  mitigation, VATA 1994 s 70
  negligence, VATA 1994 ss 70, 76, 77
  offshore income–
    designation of territories, SI 2011/976
    generally, FA 2010 Sch 10
  offshore matters and transfers, FA 2015 s 120, Sch 20
  regulations and orders, FA 2003 s 41
  relevant tax or duty, on, FA 2003 s 24(2)
  review of decisions, and–
    appeals, FA 2003 ss 36–37
    extensions of time, FA 2003 s 33C
    further, FA 2003 s 34
    nature, FA 2003 s 33E
    offer, FA 2003 s 33A
    out of time, FA 2003 s 33D
    power of Commissioners on, FA 2003 s 35
    requirement, FA 2003 s 33B
    right, FA 2003 s 33

PENALTIES – *cont.*
  review of decisions, and– – *cont.*
    time extensions, FA 2003 s 33C
    time limit, FA 2003 s 34
  service of notices, FA 2003 s 39
  statements and documents, admissibility of, FA 2003 s 36
  suspension during currency of agreement for deferred payment, FA 2009 s 108
  transactions connected with fraud, for–
    generally, VATA 1994 s 69C
    officers' liability, VATA 1994 s 69D
    publication of persons liable, VATA 1994 s 69E
  unauthorised disclosure of information, VATA 1994 s 91
  unauthorised issue of invoices, VATA 1994 s 67
PENSIONS
  Pensions Act 2008, tax provision consequential on, FA 2011 s 71
PERIODICALS
  zero-rating, VATA 1994 Sch 8 Group 3
PERSISTENT MISDECLARATION
  penalties, VATA 1994 s 64
PERSON
  belonging, VATA 1994 s 9
  intending to make taxable supplies, VATA 1994 Sch 1 paras 9, 14, 15
  notification, VATA 1994 Sch 11 para 2(4), (5)
PET FOOD
  See ANIMAL FEEDING STUFFS
PETROL
  See FUEL
PHOTOGRAPHS
  admissibility in evidence, VATA 1994 Sch 11 paras 12(4)–(7), 14(2)
PHYSIOTHERAPISTS
  exemption, VATA 1994 Sch 9 Group 7 item 2
PICTURE BOOKS
  zero-rating, VATA 1994 Sch 8 Group 3
PILOTAGE SERVICES
  zero-rating, VATA 1994 Sch 8 Group 8 item 7
PLACE OF BELONGING
  amendments to VATA 1994, FA 2014 s 104
  generally, VATA 1994 s 9
PLACE OF SUPPLY
  acquisition of goods, VATA 1994 ss 13, 18, SI 1992/3283, 2006/112/EC arts 31–39
  generally, SI 1992/3121
  goods, of–
    reverse charge on supply from abroad, VATA 1994 s 7AA
    rules for determining, VATA 1994 s 7
  services, of–
    amendments, FA 2009 Sch 36
    customer's registration number, SI 1992/3121 art 14
    determining country in which supplied, VATA 1994 s 7A
    Directive, 2006/112/EC arts 43–59
    generally, VATA 1994 s 7
    hire of transport, SI 1992/3121 arts 17–18
    intermediaries, of, SI 1992/3121 arts 11–13
    land relating to, SI 1992/3121 art 5

PLACE OF SUPPLY – *cont.*
  services, of– – *cont.*
    performed, where, SI 1992/3121 art 15
    place to which supplier or recipient belongs, VATA 1994 s 9
    received, where, SI 1992/3121 art 16
    rules for determining, SI 1992/3121 arts 4, 18
    special rules, VATA 1994 Sch 4A
    transport, SI 1992/3121 arts 6–10
  services supplied where received, VATA 1994 Sch 5
PLACE OF SUPPLY ORDERS
  disapplication of transitional provisions, FA 2014 s 105
  generally, VATA 1994 s 7A
PLANT AND MACHINERY
  generally, VATA 1994 s 34
PLANTS
  zero-rating, VATA 1994 Sch 8 Group 1
PLAY GROUPS
  exemption, VATA 1994 Sch 9 Group 7
POLICE AUTHORITY
  refund of tax, VATA 1994 s 33, SI 1985/1101
POLITICAL PARTY
  subscription income, VATA 1994 s 94
PORTS
  authorities, refund of tax, VATA 1994 s 33
  zero-rating, VATA 1994 Sch 8 Group 8
POSTAL PACKETS
  conveyance, exemption, VATA 1994 Sch 9 Group 3
  meaning, VATA 1994 Sch 9 Group 3 note(1)
  overseas, from–
    general provision, T(CBT)A 2018 s 44
    withdrawal from EU, SI 2018/1376
  postponed accounting system, SI 1995/2518 reg 122
POSTAL SERVICES
  exemption, VATA 1994 Sch 9 Group 3
POSTPONED ACCOUNTING SYSTEM
  payment of tax, SI 1995/2518 reg 122
POWERS
  access to recorded information, VATA 1994 Sch 11 para 11
  arrest, VATA 1994 s 72(9)
  enforcing compliance, VATA 1994 s 73
  entry, search and inspection of premises, VATA 1994 Sch 11 para 10
  inspect, copy and remove documents, VATA 1994 Sch 11 para 7
  obtain information, VATA 1994 Sch 11 para 7
  take samples, VATA 1994 Sch 11 para 8
  trader required to account for goods, VATA 1994 s 73
  visiting uncooperative traders, VATA 1994 s 73(4), (7)
PRESCRIBED ACCOUNTING PERIOD
  generally, VATA 1994 s 25(1)
  length, SI 1995/2518 reg 25
  tax charged in different period, VATA 1994 Sch 11 para 2(10)(*a*)

PRESCRIPTIONS
  zero-rating–
    general, VATA 1994 Sch 8 Group 12 item 1
PRINTED MATTER
  import relief, SI 1984/746 Sch 2
  zero-rating, VATA 1994 Sch 8, group 3
PRIVATE TUITION
  exemption, VATA 1994 Sch 9 Group 6 item 3
PROBATION COMMITTEE
  refund of tax, SI 1986/336
PROFESSION
  business, VATA 1994 s 94
PROFESSIONAL ASSOCIATION
  exemption, VATA 1994 Sch 6 Groups 9, 12
PROFESSIONAL BODIES
  subscriptions, exemption, VATA 1994 Sch 9 Group 9
PROJECT ORGANISATION FOR SELF BUILD PROJECTS
  refund scheme, VATA 1994 s 35
PROTECTED BUILDINGS
  approved alterations, VATA 1994 Sch 8 Group 6 note (6)
  meaning, VATA 1994 Sch 8 Group 6 note (1)
  zero-rating, VATA 1994 Sch 8 Group 6
PUBLIC BODIES
  See also LOCAL AUTHORITY
  meaning, VATA 1994 Sch 9 Group 7 note (5)
  refund of tax, VATA 1994 s 33
  supply of goods and services by, VATA 1994 s 41A
PUBLIC DOMAIN
  bodies with objects in, VATA 1994 s 94
PUBLIC INTEREST BODIES
  subscriptions, exemption, VATA 1994 Sch 9 Group 9
PUBLICATIONS
  zero-rating, VATA 1994 Sch 8 Group 3
PURCHASE TAX
  vehicle re-imported to UK, VATA 1994 Sch 13 para 3

Q

QUARTER
  meaning, VATA 1994 s 96(1)

R

RADIO
  advertising by charities, VATA 1994 Sch 8 Group 15 item 8
  supplies to the blind, VATA 1994 Sch 8 Group 4 item 2
RADIOGRAPHER
  exemption, VATA 1994 Sch 9 Group 7 item 1(c)
RAILWAY CUSTOMS AREA
  definition, CEMA 1979 s 1(1)

RAMP
  construction for handicapped person, VATA 1994 Sch 8 Group 12 items 8, 9, 11
RATE OF TAX
  application of, 2006/112/EC arts 93–95
  change in–
    adjustments of contracts, VATA 1994 s 89
    effect, SI 1995/2518 reg 15
    flat rate scheme for farmers, percentage addition, SI 1992/3221
    supplementary charge, FA 2009 Sch 3
    supplies spanning, VATA 1994 s 88
  fuel and power, on, VATA 1994 s 2(1A)–(1C), Sch A1
  level, 2006/112/EC arts 96–105
  Provisional Collection of Taxes Act 1968, VATA 1994 s 90
  reduced–
    conversion of buildings, for, VATA 1994 Sch A1 paras 6-8, Sch 7A para 4A
    fuel, for, VATA 1994 s 2(1A), (1B), Sch A1
    generally, VATA 1994 s 29A, 2006/112/EC arts 98–101, Annex III
    labour-intensive services, for, 2006/112/EC arts 106–108, Annex IV, 2006/774
    special provisions applying until adoption of definitive arrangements, 2006/112/EC arts 109–122
    special residential building, VATA 1994 Sch A1 para 13
    temporary provisions, 2006/112/EC arts 123–130
  standard–
    generally, VATA 1994 s 2, 2006/112/EC arts 96, 97
  structure, 2006/112/EC arts 96–105
  supplementary charge–
    administration, FA 2009 Sch 3 Pt 5
    conditions, SI 2009/3127
    exceptions, FA 2009 Sch 3 Pt 2
    generally, FA 2009 Sch 3 Pt 1
    interpretation, FA 2009 Sch 3 Pt 5
    invoices, SI 1995/2518 reg 15A
    liability and amount, FA 2009 Sch 3 Pt 3
    listed supplies, FA 2009 Sch 3 Pt 4
REASONABLE EXCUSE
  failure to notify of acquisitions, VATA 1994 s 67(8)
  failure to submit section 55 statements, VATA 1994 s 66(7)(b)
  insufficient funds, VATA 1994 s 71(1)(a)
  misdeclaration, VATA 1994 s 63(10)(a)
  reliance on another to perform task, VATA 1994 s 71(1)(b)
  unauthorised issue of invoices, VATA 1994 s 67(8)
RECEIVER FOR THE METROPOLITAN POLICE DISTRICT
  refund of tax, VATA 1994 s 33
RECIPIENT OF SERVICES
  invoice provided, VATA 1994 s 29
  place of belonging, VATA 1994 s 9
RECKONABLE DATE
  date from which interest runs, VATA 1994 s 74

RECORDED INFORMATION
   generally, VATA 1994 Sch 11 para 11
RECORDS
   See also DOCUMENTS; TAX RETURN
   breach of requirements, VATA 1994 s 69B
   Commissioners powers, VATA 1994 Sch 11
      para 6(1)
   computer records, VATA 1994 Sch 11 para 6(6)
   duty to keep, VATA 1994 Sch 11 para 6, SI
      1995/2518 reg 31
   failure to keep, VATA 1994 s 69(1)
   farmers flat rate scheme–
      duty to keep records, SI 1995/2518 reg 210
      generally, VATA 1994 s 54
      production, SI 1995/2518 reg 211
   free zone goods, SI 1984/1177 reg 24
   gold transactions, VATA 1994 s 69A
   horses and ponies, SI 1983/1099 art 3(*c*)
   motor cars, SI 1992/3122 art 8(2)(*d*)
   orders for access, VATA 1994 Sch 11 para 11
   preservation–
      discharge of duty, VATA 1994 Sch 11 para 6(4),
         (5)
      generally, VATA 1994 Sch 11 para 6(3)
   second hand goods, SI 1992/3129 art 8(3)(*c*)
   statistics of trade, SI 1992/2790 reg 5,
      638/2004/EC
   VAT account, SI 1995/2518 reg 32
RECOVERY OF TAX
   See ADMINISTRATION AND COLLECTION
REDUCED-RATE OF TAX
   conversion of buildings, for, VATA 1994 Sch A1
      paras 6-8, Sch 7A para 4A
   fuel, for, VATA 1994 s 2(1A), (1B), Sch A1
   generally, VATA 1994 s 29A, 2006/112/EC
      arts 98–101, Annex III
   labour-intensive services, for, 2006/112/EC
      arts 106–108, Annex IV, 2006/774
   special provisions applying until adoption of
      definitive arrangements, 2006/112/EC
      arts 109–122
   special residential buildings–
      supplies to intended user, VATA 1994 Sch A1
         para 13
   temporary provisions, 2006/112/EC arts 123–130
REFRIGERATION
   supply, VATA 1994 Sch 4 para 3
   zero-rating, VATA 1994 Sch 8 Group 15
REFUND OF TAX
   academies, to, VATA 1994 s 33B
   air ambulance charities, VATA 1994 ss 33C–33D
   appeal, VATA 1994 s 83(*d*)
   application contents, SI 1995/2518
      regs 173L–173O
   Bournemouth Charter Trustees, SI/2020/1113
   British Broadcasting Authority, VATA 1994 s 33
   capital goods, VATA 1994 s 34
   change in tax rate, VATA 1994 s 90
   charities–
      generally, VATA 1994 s 33C
      relevant charities, VATA 1994 s 33D

REFUND OF TAX – *cont.*
   claims–
      disposal of assets, registration in respect of,
         VATA 1994 Sch 3A
      imported goods, SI 1995/2518 regs 173A–173X
      minimum total claim, SI 1995/2518 reg 173H
      requirements, SI 1995/2518 regs 173I–173K
      time when VAT incurred, SI 1995/2518
         reg 173F
   construction of certain buildings, VATA 1994 s 35
   contents of application, SI 1995/2518
      regs 173L–173O
   deregistration. *See* DEREGISTRATION
   development corporation, VATA 1994 s 33
   discretion, VATA 1994 s 46(1)
   do-it-yourself builders, VATA 1994 s 35
   drainage boards, VATA 1994 s 33
   EC trader, VATA 1994 s 39
   eligible persons, VATA 1994 s 25
   entitlement, notification of, SI 1995/2518
      reg 173Q
   Essex Police, Fire and Crime Commissioner, SI
      2018/16
   extension of 30 day period, SI 1995/2518
   farmers in business overseas, VATA 1994 s 54(5)
   forwarding of claims to other member States,
      VATA 1994 s 39A
   further information or document, requests for, SI
      1995/2518 reg 173R
   generally, SI 1995/1978, SI 1995/2999
   goods imported for private use, VATA 1994 s 27
   government departments, VATA 1994 s 41
   interest–
      awarded by tribunal, VATA 1994 s 73(2)
      claim in writing, need for, VATA 1994 s 78(10)
      delay caused by claimant's conduct, VATA 1994
         s 78(8A)–(9)
      paid to claimant, VATA 1994 s 78(1)
      time limit for making claim, VATA 1994
         s 78(11)
   late payments, interest on, SI 1995/2518
      regs 173W, 173X
   lighthouse authorities, VATA 1994 s 33
   local authorities, VATA 1994 s 33
   medical courier charities, VATA 1994 ss 33C–33D
   museums and galleries, to, VATA 1994 s 33A
   news provider, nominated, VATA 1994 s 33
   Northern Ireland Government, VATA 1994 s 99
   Northumbria Interim Police Authority, SI
      1985/1101
   offset against amount due from trader, VATA 1994
      s 49
   other persons, VATA 1994 Pt 2 s 33E
   overpaid tax–
      arrangements for reimbursing taxpayer, VATA
         1994 s 80A
      assessments of amounts due, VATA 1994 s 80B
      generally, VATA 1994 s 80
   palliative care charities, VATA 1994 ss 33C–33D
   police authority, VATA 1994 s 33
   port authority, VATA 1994 s 33
   power to withhold, VATA 1994 s 25

REFUND OF TAX – *cont.*
  Provisional Collection of Taxes Act 1968, VATA 1994 s 90(3)
  reimbursement–
    arrangements made before 11 February 1998, SI 1995/2518 reg 43H
    arrangements, meaning, SI 1995/2518 reg 43A
    claim, meaning, SI 1995/2518 reg 43A
    interest, SI 1995/2518 reg 43C
    means of, SI 1995/2518 reg 43C
    records, SI 1995/2518 regs 43E, 43F
    repayments, making, SI 1995/2518 reg 43D
    undertakings, SI 1995/2518 reg 43G
    unjust enrichment, arrangements disregarded as, SI 1995/2518 reg 43B
  relevant period, SI 1995/2518 reg 173S
    extension of SI 1995/2518 regs 173T, 173U
  repayment period, SI 1995/2518 reg 173G
  repayment supplement, VATA 1994 s 79
  search and rescue charities, VATA 1994 ss 33C–33D
  statutory bodies, VATA 1994 s 33
  taxable persons not established in Member State of refund but in another Member State, 2008/9/EC
  taxable person not established in territory of country, to, 86/560
  third country traders to, SI 1995/2518
  time for, SI 1995/2518 reg 173V
  transport authority, VATA 1994 s 33
  water authorities, VATA 1994 s 33, SI 1973/2121

REGISTER OF TAXABLE PERSONS
  change in registered particulars, VATA 1994 Sch 1 paras 11, 13, SI 1995/2518 reg 5(2)
  register kept by Commissioners, VATA 1994 Sch 1 para 19

REGISTRATION
  acquisitions from other member states–
    cancellation, VATA 1994 Sch 3 para 6
    conditions for, VATA 1994 Sch 3 para 7
    entitlement for registration, VATA 1994 Sch 3 para 4
    exemption, VATA 1994 Sch 3 para 8
    generally, VATA 1994 Sch 3
    liability, VATA 1994 Sch 3 paras 1, 2
    matters affecting continuance of registration, VATA 1994 Sch 3 para 5
    notification, VATA 1994 Sch 3 para 3
    relevant acquisition, meaning, VATA 1994 Sch 3 para 11
  appeal, VATA 1994 s 83(*a*)
  application forms, SI 1995/2518 reg 5(1), Sch 1, Forms 1, 6, 7
  artificial separation of business activities, counteracting, VATA 1994 Sch 1 paras 1A, 2
  associations, VATA 1994 s 46(3)
  cancellation, VATA 1994 Sch 1 para 13, SI 1995/2518 reg 5(3)
  change in particulars, VATA 1994 Sch 1 para 13(3)
  co-owners of buildings and land, VATA 1994 s 51A
  deregistration. *See* **DEREGISTRATION**

REGISTRATION – *cont.*
  direction–
    conditions, VATA 1994 Sch 1 para 2(2)
    service, VATA 1994 Sch 1 para 2(3)
    supplementary direction, VATA 1994 Sch 1 para 2(4)
  discretion, VATA 1994 Sch 1 para 1(3)
  disposal of assets for which VAT repayment claimed, in respect of, VATA 1994 Sch 3A
  division of business, VATA 1994 s 46(1)
  entitlement, VATA 1994 Sch 1 para 9, 10
  exemption, VATA 1994 Sch 1 para 14
  failure to notify of liability, VATA 1994 s 67
  group of companies, VATA 1994 s 43
  intending trader, VATA 1994 Sch 1 paras 9, 10
  liability–
    cessation of liability, VATA 1994 Sch 1 para 3
    end of, notification, VATA 1994 Sch 1 para 11
    generally, VATA 1994 Sch 1 paras 1–7
  limits–
    generally, VATA 1994 Sch 1 para 1(2), (3)
    supplies from other member states, VATA 1994 Sch 2 para 1(1), (7)
  local authorities, VATA 1994 s 42
  notification–
    failure to make–
      generally, VATA 1994 s 4, 67(1)
      penalty, VATA 1994 ss 67(1), 72(11)
    form, VATA 1994 Sch 1 para 17, SI 1995/2518 Sch 1
    liability, VATA 1994 Sch 1 para 5(1)
  partnership, VATA 1994 s 45
  persons previously exempt, VATA 1994 Sch 1 para 14
  power to vary specified sums, VATA 1994 Sch 1 para 15
  quarter, meaning, VATA 1994 s 96(1)
  register, VATA 1994 s 3
  registrable, meaning, VATA 1994 Sch 1 para 18
  representative member of Group of companies, VATA 1994 s 43,
  single taxable person, VATA 1994 Sch 1 paras 1A, 2
  supplies from other member states, VATA 1994 Sch 2–
    cancellation, VATA 1994 Sch 2 para 6
    conditions for, VATA 1994 Sch 2 para 7
    liability, VATA 1994 Sch 2 paras 1, 2
    notification, VATA 1994 Sch 2 para 3–
      affecting continuance of registration, VATA 1994 Sch 2 para 5
    relevant supply, meaning, VATA 1994 Sch 2 para 10
    request for registration, VATA 1994 Sch 2 para 4
  taxable person, meaning, VATA 1994 s 3
  transfer of business as a going concern, VATA 1994 s 49, Sch 1 para 1(2)
  VAT groups,
    duplication, VATA 1994 s 43D
    eligibility, power to alter, VATA 1994 s 43AA
  VAT representatives, of, VATA 1994 s 48(4)
  voluntary, VATA 1994 Sch 1 paras 9, 10

REGISTRATION CERTIFICATE
  particulars, VATA 1994 Sch 1 paras 11, 12
REGISTRATION NUMBERS
  display, VATA 1994 s 77E
REGULATIONS
  accounting for tax, VATA 1994 Sch 11 para 2
  breach of, VATA 1994 s 69
  contravention of relevant rule, penalty for, SI 2003/3113
  fiscal warehousing, as to, VATA 1994 ss 18D(3), 18F(7), (8)
  imported goods, VATA 1994 ss 37(2), (3), 38
  meaning, VATA 1994 s 96(1)
  parliamentary procedure, VATA 1994 s 97
  payment of VAT, deferring, VATA 1994 s 18D(3)
  recovery of tax, VATA 1994 Sch 11 para 5(4)
  tax representatives, VATA 1994 s 48(6)
  transfers of going concerns, VATA 1994 s 49(2), (3)
  unincorporated bodies, VATA 1994 s 46
  value of supply, SI 1995/2518
REINSURANCE
  exemption, VATA 1994 Sch 9 Group 2
  services–
    reverse charge, VATA 1994 s 8
    supplied where received, VATA 1994 Sch 5 para 5
RELEVANT PURPOSE
  change of use, VATA 1994 Sch 10 para 1
  charitable, VATA 1994 Sch 8 Group 6
  residential, VATA 1994 Sch 8 Group 6
RELIEFS
  See BAD DEBT RELIEF; EXEMPTIONS; IMPORT RELIEF; INPUT TAX; TEMPORARY IMPORTATION RELIEF; ZERO-RATING
RELIGIOUS COMMUNITY
  business carried on, VATA 1994 s 95(3)
  exemption, VATA 1994 Sch 9 Group 7 item 10
RENT
  See LEASES
REPAIRS AND MAINTENANCE
  handicapped aids, VATA 1994 Sch 8 Group 12 item 5
  protected buildings, VATA 1994 Sch 8 Group 6 note (6)
  talking books, VATA 1994 Sch 8 Group 4 item 1(1)
REPAYMENT INTEREST
  sums to be paid by HMRC, on, FA 2009 s 102, Sch 54
REPAYMENT OF TAX
  See REFUND OF TAX
REPAYMENT SUPPLEMENT
  qualifying refunds, VATA 1994 s 79
REPRESENTATIVE MEMBER
  registration, VATA 1994 s 43
REPRESENTATIVES AND SECURITY
  appointment form, SI 1995/2518 Sch 1 Form 8
  enforcement by diligence, VATA 1994 s 48
  enforcement by distress, VATA 1994 s 48

REPRESENTATIVES AND SECURITY – *cont.*
  obligation, VATA 1994 s 48, SI 1995/2518 regs 10, 30
  return, SI 1995/2518 reg 25(3)
RESEARCH
  exemption, VATA 1994 Sch 9 Group 6 item 1
RESIDENTIAL PURPOSE
  change of use of building, VATA 1994 Sch 10 para 1
  option to tax excluded, VATA 1994 Sch 10 para 2(2)
  relevant residential purpose, meaning, VATA 1994 Sch 8 Group 5 note (3)
RESIDUARY BODY
  refund of tax, SI 1985/1101
RETAIL SCHEME
  appeal, VATA 1994 s 83(*y*)
  regulations, VATA 1994 Sch 11 para 2(6)
RETAILER
  calculation of output tax, VATA 1994 s 30(8)
  invoice, SI 1995/2518 reg 71
  methods for calculating output tax, caterers' scheme, SI 1995/2518 reg 73
  requirement to issue tax invoice, SI 1995/2518 reg 16
  scheme agreed with Commissioners, SI 1995/2518 reg 67
  value of supply by, SI 1995/2518
RETENTION PAYMENT
  item of supply, SI 1995/2518 reg 89
RETURNS
  See VAT RETURNS
REVERSE CHARGES
  cessation and recommencement of relevant supplies, notification of, SI 1995/2518 reg 23D
  first relevant supply, notification of, SI 1995/2518 reg 23B
  gas, electricity, heat and cooling supplied from abroad, on, VATA 1994 s 9A
  goods supplied from abroad, on, VATA 1994 s 7AA
  input tax credit, VATA 1994 ss 8(1), 24(1), (2), SI 1995/2518 reg 29(2)
  interpretation, SI 1995/2518 reg 23A
  services received from abroad, VATA 1994 s 8, SI 1997/1523
  services supplied where received, VATA 1994 Sch 5
  submission of statements, SI 1995/2518 reg 23C
  supplies disregarded for partial exemption, VATA 1994 s 8(3)
REVERSE SURRENDER
  exemption, VATA 1994 Sch 9 Group 1 item 1 notes (1), (1A)
ROAD FUEL
  See FUEL
ROAD VEHICLES
  See COMPANY CARS; MOTOR CARS; VEHICLES
ROYALTIES
  time of supply, SI 1995/2518 reg 91

VAT Index

S

SALE OR RETURN
  time of supply, VATA 1994 s 6
SALES INVOICES
  See TAX INVOICE
SALVAGE
  zero-rating, VATA 1994 Sch 8 Group 8 item 8
SAMPLES
  Commissioners power to take, VATA 1994 Sch 11 para 8(1)
  compensation, VATA 1994 Sch 11 para 8(3)
  gift to actual or potential customers, VATA 1994 Sch 4 para 5(2)(*b*), (3)
SANITARY PRODUCTS
  zero-rating, VATA 1994 Sch 8
SAVINGS ACCOUNT
  exemption, VATA 1994 Sch 9, Group 5 item 8
SCHOOLS
  See EDUCATION
SCIENTIFIC COLLECTION
  exemption, VATA 1994 Sch 9 Group 11
  import relief, SI 1984/746 art 5, Sch 2
  margin scheme, VATA 1994 s 50A
SCIENTIFIC EQUIPMENT
  zero-rating, VATA 1994 Sch 8 Group 15
SCIENTIFIC SERVICES
  zero-rating, VATA 1994 Sch 8 Group 7
SCOTLAND
  assignment, VATA 1994 s 96(1)
  copy, meaning, VATA 1994 s 96(7)
  distress, VATA 1994 Sch 11 para 5
  document, meaning, VATA 1994 s 96(7)
  enforcement of tribunal decisions, VATA 1994 s 87(2)
  entry and search, VATA 1994 Sch 11 para 10
  evidence, VATA 1994 Sch 11 para 6
  insolvency, VATA 1994 Sch 11 para 15
  order for access to recorded information, VATA 1994 Sch 11 para 11
  partnership, notices by, SI 1995/2518 reg 7(2)
  recovery of tax, VATA 1994 Sch 11 para 5(5), (6), (9), SI 1995/2518 reg 213
SEARCH
  See ENTRY AND SEARCH
SEARCH AND RESCUE CHARITIES
  refund of tax–
    generally, VATA 1994 s 33C
    meaning, VATA 1994 s 33D
SECOND HAND GOODS
  margin schemes, VATA 1994 ss 32, 50A, SI 1992/3129 art 8
  special scheme, 2006/112/EC arts 311–343, Annex IX
SECONDARY SECURITIES
  exemption, VATA 1994 Sch 9 Group 5 item 6
SECTION 55 STATEMENTS
  failure to submit, VATA 1994 s 66
  generally, VATA 1994 s 55A
  inaccuracies, VATA 1994 s 65
  meaning, VATA 1994 Sch 11 para 2(3)
SECURITIES
  exemption, VATA 1994 Sch 9 Group 5 item 6

SECURITY FOR TAX
  appeal, VATA 1994 s 83(1)
  failure to provide, VATA 1994 s 72(11)
  provision, VATA 1994 Sch 11 para 4
  recovery of tax, VATA 1994 Sch 11 para 5(10)
  requirement to give, CEMA 1979 s 157
SEEDS
  zero-rating, VATA 1994 Sch 8 Group 1
SELF-BILLING INVOICE
  procedure, VATA 1994 ss 6(9), 29
SELF-BUILD PROJECTS
  refund scheme, VATA 1994 s 35(1)
SELF-SUPPLY
  capital items, VATA 1994 s 44(4)
  developers of non-residential buildings, VATA 1994 Sch 10 para 6
  generally, VATA 1994 s 5
  group of companies, VATA 1994 s 43
  input tax, credit–
    attribution of, SI 1995/2518 reg 104
    generally, VATA 1994 ss 24(1), (2), 80
  motor cars, SI 1992/3122 arts 5–7
  printed matter, treatment of, SI 1995/1268 art 11
  time of supply, VATA 1994 s 6
  Treasury orders, VATA 1994 s 5(5), (6)
SENIOR ACCOUNTING OFFICERS
  duties, FA 2009 s 93, Sch 46
SERVICE OF NOTICES
  generally, VATA 1994 s 98
  partnership's registered name, VATA 1994 s 45(4)
SERIOUS MISDECLARATION
  See also MISDECLARATION
  consequences, VATA 1994 s 63
SERVICES
  See also PLACE OF SUPPLY; SUPPLY OF SERVICES
  change in rate of tax, VATA 1994 s 89
  consideration, supplied without, SI 1995/2518 reg 81
  continuous supply, SI 1995/2518 regs 90, 90A, 90B
  deregistration, received after, SI 1995/2518 reg 111(5)
  incorporation, received before, SI 1995/2518 reg 111
  partly used for business purposes, VATA 1994 s 24(5)
  registration, received before, SI 1995/2518 reg 111
  self-supply, VATA 1994 s 5
SET-OFF CREDITS
  Commissioners' power, VATA 1994 s 81(3)
  transitional provisions, VATA 1994 Sch 13 para 21
SEWAGE SERVICES
  zero-rating, VATA 1994 Sch 8 Group 2
SHARES
  exemption, VATA 1994 Sch 9 Group 5 item 6, 7 note (5)
SHEET MUSIC
  See MUSIC
SHIP
  facilities for–
    mooring or storage, VATA 1994 Sch 9 Group 1

SHIP – *cont.*
  facilities for– – *cont.*
    playing game of chance aboard, VATA 1994 Sch 9 Group 4
    handling services, VATA 1994 Sch 8 Group 8 item 6
  meaning, VATA 1994 s 96(1)
  pilotage services, VATA 1994 Sch 8 Group 8 item 7
  supplies, repair or maintenance, VATA 1994 Sch 8 Group 8 items 1, 2A, 2B
  zero-rating–
    charter or hire, VATA 1994 Sch 8 Group 8
    classification, VATA 1994 Sch 8 Group 8
    handling in port, VATA 1994 Sch 8 Group 8
    repair and maintenance, VATA 1994 Sch 8 Group 8
    survey of, VATA 1994 Sch 8 Group 8
    transport of passengers, VATA 1994 Sch 8 Group 8
SHOES
  See CLOTHING AND FOOTWEAR
SHOOTING RIGHTS
  liability for VAT, VATA 1994 Sch 9 Group 1
SIMPLIFICATION
  procedures, 2006/112/EC arts 238–240
SINGLE TAXABLE PERSON
  generally, VATA 1994 Sch 1 paras 1A, 2, 2006/112/EC art 11
SMALL ENTERPRISES
  Special schemes, 2006/112/EC arts 281–294
SOLICITOR
  insurance claims, VATA 1994 Sch 9 Group 2
  reverse charge, VATA 1994 s 8
  supply to overseas person, VATA 1994 Sch 8, Group 7
SPIRITUAL WELFARE
  exemption, VATA 1994 Sch 9 Group 7 item 10
SPORT
  exemption, VATA 1994 Sch 9 Group 10
  facilities for playing, VATA 1994 Sch 9 Group 1 letting
  fund-raising events, VATA 1994 Sch 9 Group 12 note (3)(*b*)
  services performed abroad, VATA 1994 Sch 8 Group 7
SPORTING RIGHTS
  liability for VAT, VATA 1994 Sch 9 Group 1 item 1(*c*) note (8)
SPORTING SERVICES
  performed abroad, VATA 1994 Sch 8 Group 7
STAMPS, TOKENS AND VOUCHERS
  treatment, VATA 1994 s 23, Sch 6 para 5
STANDARD RATE
  See also RATE OF TAX
  generally, VATA 1994 s 2, 2006/112/EC arts 96, 97
STATEMENTS
  admissibility of computer statements, VATA 1994 Sch 11 para 6(6)
STATISTICS OF TRADE
  ancillary costs sample surveys, SI 1992/2790 reg 4A

STATISTICS OF TRADE – *cont.*
  assimilation threshold, SI 1992/2790 reg 3
  collection system, 91/3330 arts 6–16
  Committee, 91/3330 arts 29–30
  Community, 638/2004/EC
  evidence, SI 1992/2970 regs 7–8
  implementing regulation, 92/3046
  Intrastat System–
    application, SI 1992/2790 reg 2, 91/3330 art 7, 92/2256 art 1, 92/3046
  offences, SI 1992/2790 reg 6
  recorded information, access to, SI 1992/2790 regs 9–11
  records, SI 1992/2790 reg 5
  regulations, 91/3330, 92/2256
  supplementary declarations, SI 1992/2790 regs 3–4, Sch.
  thresholds, 92/2256
STATUTORY INSTRUMENTS
  annulment, VATA 1994 s 97(2), (5)
  change in rate of tax, VATA 1994 s 2(1)
STATUTORY WATER UNDERTAKER
  refund of tax, VATA 1994 s 33(3)
STOCKS
  exemption, VATA 1994 Sch 9 Group 5 items 6, 7
STORAGE
  ships/aircraft, VATA 1994 Sch 9 Group 1 item 1(k)
STORES
  zero-rating of goods supplied, VATA 1994 s 30(6)
STRATEGIC HIGHWAYS COMPANIES
  refund of tax, VATA 1994 s 67
STUDENTS
  importation reliefs, SI 1992/3193 art 16
SUBSCRIPTION
  club, association or organisation, VATA 1994 s 94(2), (3), Sch 6 Group 4
  exemption–
    trade union, professional and public interest bodies, VATA 1994 Sch 9 Group 9
    youth club, VATA 1994 Sch 9 Group 6
  gaming club, VATA 1994 Sch 6 Group 4 note (1)(*a*)
SUMMONS
  non-compliance, VATA 1994 Sch 12 para 10
SUPPLEMENTARY CHARGE
  administration, FA 2009 Sch 3 Pt 5
  conditions, SI 2009/3127
  exceptions, FA 2009 Sch 3 Pt 2
  generally, FA 2009 Sch 3 Pt 1
  interpretation, FA 2009 Sch 3 Pt 5
  invoices, SI 1995/2518 reg 15A
  liability and amount, FA 2009 Sch 3 Pt 3
  listed supplies, FA 2009 Sch 3 Pt 4
SUPPLY
  See also PLACE OF SUPPLY
  exempt, determining whether, after grant of interest etc, VATA 1994 s 96 (10A)
  input tax, SI 1995/2518 reg 29
  place of–
    goods, SI 1992/3283
    services, SI 1992/3121
  zero-rated, determining whether, after grant of interest etc, VATA 1994 s 96 (10A)

SUPPLY OF GOODS
abroad, from, VATA 1994 s 7AA
agent, VATA 1994 s 47(1)–(2A)
appeal, VATA 1994 s 83(*b*)
apportionment of tax, VATA 1994 s 24(5)
approval on, VATA 1994 s 6(2)
business assets–
    ceases to be taxable, VATA 1994 Sch 4 para 8
    disposed of, VATA 1994 Sch 4, para 5
    gift of, VATA 1994 Sch 4 para 5(2)
    removal from member states, VATA 1994 Sch 4 para 6
capital goods, VATA 1994 s 34
change in rate of tax–
    adjustment of contract, VATA 1994 s 89
    generally, VATA 1994 s 88
charge to tax, VATA 1994 s 1–3, 2006/112/EC arts 63–67
classification, VATA 1994 s 5, Sch 4
deemed. *See* DEEMED SUPPLY
discounts for prompt payment, VATA 1994 Sch 6 para 4(1)
distinguished from supply of services, VATA 1994 Sch 4
do-it-yourself builders, VATA 1994 s 35
exemptions. *See* EXEMPTIONS
facilitated by online marketplaces
    exception from liability, VATA 1994 s 77F
    generally, VATA 1994 s 5A
generally, VATA 1994 s 5
gift of business assets, VATA 1994 Sch 4 para 5(2)
government departments, VATA 1994 s 41
group of companies, VATA 1994 s 43
heat, VATA 1994 Sch 4 para 3
input tax, VATA 1994 s 24
intermediate, supplies by, SI 1995/2518 regs 11, 18
intra-community acquisition, 2006/112/EC arts 20–23
lease, as, SI 1995/2518 reg 85
major interest in land, VATA 1994 Sch 4 para 4
meaning, 2006/112/EC art 14
online marketplaces, by
    exception from liability, VATA 1994 s 77F
    generally, VATA 1994 s 5A
output tax, VATA 1994 s 24
partner's liability for tax, VATA 1994 s 45(5)
persons belonging in another member state, to, SI 1995/2518 regs 11, 18
persons belonging in other member states, SI 1995/2518 regs 12, 19
place of supply., VATA 1994 s 7, 2006/112/EC arts 31–39. *See also* PLACE OF SUPPLY
power, VATA 1994 Sch 4 para 3
refrigeration, VATA 1994 Sch 4 para 3
refund of tax. *See* REFUND OF TAX
reverse charge on supply from abroad, VATA 1994 s 7AA
self supply. *See* SELF SUPPLY
taxable amount, 2006/112/EC arts 73–82
taxable supply, meaning, VATA 1994 s 4
taxable transactions, 2006/112/EC arts 14–19
timing. *See* TIME OF SUPPLY

SUPPLY OF GOODS – *cont.*
tour operators, VATA 1994 s 53
transfer of possession of goods, VATA 1994 Sch 4 para 1(2)
treasury orders, VATA 1994 s 5
unincorporated bodies, VATA 1994 s 46(3)
value. *See* VALUE
ventilation, VATA 1994 Sch 4 para 3
zero-rating, VATA 1994 s 30

SUPPLY OF NEITHER GOODS NOR SERVICES
generally, VATA 1994 ss 18, 43(1)

SUPPLY OF SERVICES
abroad, from, VATA 1994 s 8
acts or omission, VATA 1994 Sch 5 para 4
agents, through–
    generally, VATA 1994 s 47(3)
appeal, VATA 1994 s 83(*b*)
apportionment of tax, VATA 1994 s 24(5)
change in rate of tax, VATA 1994 s 88, 89
charge to tax, VATA 1994 s 1–3, 2006/112/EC arts 63–67
continuous, SI 1995/2518 regs 90, 90A, 90B
deemed supply–
    services received from abroad, VATA 1994 s 8
exemption. *See* EXEMPTIONS
gaming machines. *See* GAMING MACHINES
generally, VATA 1994 s 5
group of companies, VATA 1994 s 43
input tax, VATA 1994 s 24
meaning, 2006/112/EC art 24
output tax, VATA 1994 s 24
place of supply. *See* PLACE OF SUPPLY
place where recipient belongs, VATA 1994 s 9
private use of assets, VATA 1994 Sch 4 para 5(4), (5)
rate of tax, VATA 1994 s 2(1)(*a*)
recipient. *See* RECIPIENT OF SERVICES
refund of tax, VATA 1994 s 33
reverse charge on supply from abroad, VATA 1994 s 8
self supply. *See* SELF SUPPLY
taxable amount, 2006/112/EC arts 73–82
taxable supply, meaning, VATA 1994 s 4
taxable transactions, 2006/112/EC art 24–29
timing. *See* TIME OF SUPPLY
tour operators, VATA 1994 s 53
transfer of property in goods, VATA 1994 Sch 4 para 1(1)
treasury orders, VATA 1994 s 5
treatment or process to goods, application of, VATA 1994 s 30(2A)
value, *See* VALUE
zero-rating, VATA 1994 s 30, SI 1995/2518 Sch 1 Form 18

SURCHARGE
See DEFAULT SURCHARGE

SURCHARGE LIABILITY NOTICE
See also DEFAULT SURCHARGE
generally, VATA 1994 s 59

SURRENDER OF INTEREST IN LAND
exemption, VATA 1994 Sch 8 Group 1 item 1 note (1)

SURVEYORS
services, VATA 1994 Sch 9 Group 9

T

TAKE-AWAY FOOD
See FOOD
TALKING BOOKS
zero-rating, VATA 1994 Sch 8 Group 4
TAPE RECORDERS
zero-rating of supplies for the blind, VATA 1994 Sch 8 Group 4
TAX AVOIDANCE
disclosure of tax avoidance schemes–
Regulations, SI 2017/1216
VAT and other indirect taxes, F(No 2)A 2017 s 66, Sch 17
penalties for enablers of defeated tax avoidance–
abusive tax arrangements, F(No 2)A 2017 Sch 16, Pt 2
amount of penalty, F(No 2)A 2017 Sch 16, Pt 5
appeals F(No 2)A 2017 Sch 16, Pt 8
assessment of penalty F(No 2)A 2017 Sch 16, Pt 6
TAX EVASION
See EVASION OF TAX
TAX–FREE SHOPS
meaning, VATA 1994 Sch 8 Group 14 note (2)
relevant journey, meaning, VATA 1994 Sch 8 Group 14 note (3)
traveller, meaning, VATA 1994 Sch 8 Group 14 note (4)
zero-rating of goods, VATA 1994 Sch 8 Group 14
TAX INVOICES
alphabetical codes, SI 1995/2518 reg 2(1)
assessment, VATA 1994 ss 76, 77
auctioneer, SI 1995/2518 reg 13(2)
authenticated receipt, construction industry, SI 1995/2518 reg 13(4)
concept of, 2006/112/EC arts 218, 219
contents, VATA 1994 Sch 11 para 2A, SI 1995/2518 reg 14(1), (2). 2006/112/EC arts 226–231
correction, VATA 1994 s 88(5)
credit note, information to be shown in, SI 1995/2518 reg 15
electronic means, sending by, 2006/112/EC arts 232–237
electronic signatures, SI 1995/2518 regs A13-13B
exceptions, SI 1995/2518 reg 20
generally, SI 1995/2518 reg 13(1)–(5)
goods sold under power, VATA 1994 Sch 4 para 7, SI 1995/2518 regs 13(2), 27
issue o, 2006/112/EC arts 220–225
meaning, VATA 1994 s 3(1), 2006/112/EC art 217
persons required to provide, SI 1995/2518 reg 13(1)
prepared by computer, VATA 1994 Sch 11 para 3(1), (3)
provision, VATA 1994 Sch 11 para 2
registration. See REGISTRATION
requirement of, VATA 1994 Sch 11 para 2A

TAX INVOICES – *cont.*
retailers, SI 1995/2518. reg 16
self-billing, VATA 1994 Sch 11 para 2B, SI 1995/2518 reg 13(3)
self-provided, VATA 1994 s 6(9)–
recipients of goods and services, VATA 1994 s 29
services relating to, SI 1995/2518 reg 145D
simplification measures, 2006/112/EC arts 238–240
supplies for which must be provided, SI 1995/2518 regs 13, 20
tax point, VATA 1994 s 6–
acquisition, VATA 1994 s 12
time, SI 1995/2518 reg 13(5)
unauthorised issue–
effect on input tax credit, SI 1995/2518 reg 29
mitigation, VATA 1994 s 70
penalty, VATA 1994 s 67
VAT invoice, meaning, VATA 1994 s 6(15)
zero-rated supplies–
distinguished, SI 1995/2518 reg 14(4)
excepted, SI 1995/2518 reg 20
TAX POINT
See TIME OF SUPPLY
TAX REPRESENTATIVES
appointment , VATA 1994 s 48
notification of appointment, SI 1995/2518 reg 10
service of notices, VATA 1994 s 98
TAXABLE AMOUNTS
foreign currency, in, 2006/112/EC art 91
importation of goods, 2006/112/EC arts 72, 85–89
intra-Community acquisitions, 92/546, 2006/112/EC arts 83, 84
packing materials, 2006/112/EC art 92
reduction, 2006/112/EC art 90
supply of goods and services, 2006/112/EC arts 73–82
TAXABLE PERSON
activities of, 2006/112/EC Annex I
agent acting, VATA 1994 s 47
bankrupt. See INSOLVENCY
certificate of status, SI 1995/2518 Sch 1 Form 16
cancellation of registration. See DEREGISTRATION
death, SI 1995/2518 reg 9
economic activity, 2006/112/EC art 10
exemption from registration, VATA 1994 Sch 1 para 14
identification, 2006/112/EC arts 213–216
importations and exportations, obligations relating to, 2006/112/EC arts 274–280
imported goods–
general, VATA 1994 s 38
private purposes, VATA 1994 s 27
incapacity. See INCAPACITY
invoicing, 2006/112/EC arts 217–240. See also TAX INVOICE
meaning, VATA 1994 s 96(1), 2006/112/EC art 9
non-established taxable person supplying electronic services to, 2006/112/EC arts 357–369

TAXABLE PERSON – *cont.*
  non-established, registration–
    cancellation, VATA 1994 Sch 1A paras 8–12
    exemption, VATA 1994 Sch 1A para 13
    liability to be registered, VATA 1994 Sch 1A paras 1–6
    making notifications, VATA 1994 Sch 1A para 14
    notification of end, VATA 1994 Sch 1A para 7
  not established in territory of country, refund to, 86/560
  obligation to pay, 2006/112/EC arts 193–212, Annex VI
  obligations imposed on, 2006/112/EC art 273
  occasional transactions, 2006/112/EC art 12
  payment on account of tax, VATA 1994 s 28, SI 1995/2518 art 40A
  private purposes, VATA 1994 s 27
  recapitulative statements, 2006/112/EC arts 262–271
  register, VATA 1994 Sch 1 para 19
  registration. *See* REGISTRATION
  release from obligations, 2006/112/EC art 272
  single. *See* SINGLE TAXABLE PERSONS
  states and government authorities, exclusion of, 2006/112/EC art 13
  taxation under laws of other member states, VATA 1994 s 92

TAXABLE SUPPLIES
  See also SUPPLY OF GOODS; SUPPLY OF SERVICES
  charge to tax. *See* OUTPUT TAX
  deemed. *See* DEEMED SUPPLY
  meaning, VATA 1994 s 4

TELECOMMUNICATIONS
  continuous supplies of services, SI 1995/2518 regs 90 90A, 90B
  services supplied where received, VATA 1994 Sch 5 para 7A

TELEVISIONS
  advertising by charities, VATA 1994 Sch 8 Group 15 item 8

TEMPLATES
  zero-rating, VATA 1994 Sch 8 Group 13 item 3

TEMPORARY IMPORTATION EXEMPTION
  Community legislation relating to, SI 1992/3111 Sch
  meaning, SI 1992/3111 art 4
  treatment of supply, SI 1992/3130

TEMPORARY STORAGE FACILITY
  definition, CEMA 1979 s 1(1)

TENANCY
  See LEASE

TENTS
  camping facilities, VATA 1994 Sch 9 Group 1 item 1(*g*)

TERMINAL MARKETS
  Treasury orders, VATA 1994 s 50

TERRITORIAL SEA
  extension of tax, VATA 1994 s 96(1)

THEATRES
  accommodation, VATA 1994 Sch 9 Group 1 item 1(1)

THEATRES – *cont.*
  admission, VATA 1994 s 94

THIRD COUNTRY GOODS FULFILMENT BUSINESSES
  appeals, F(No 2)A 2017 s 56
  commencement, F(No 2)A 2017 s 59
  definitions, F(No 2)A 2017 s 58
  disclosure of information by HMRC, F(No 2)A 2017 s 52
  forfeiture, F(No 2)A 2017 s 54
  generally, F(No 2)A 2017 s 48
  offence, F(No 2)A 2017 s 53
  penalties, F(No 2)A 2017 s 55, Sch 13
  register of approved persons, F(No 2)A 2017 s 50
  regulations, F(No 2)A 2017 ss 51, 57, SI 2018/326
  requirements for approval, F(No 2)A 2017 s 49

THIRD COUNTRY TRADERS
  repayment of tax, SI 1995/2518

TIMBER
  granting right to fell and remove, VATA 1994 Sch 9 Group 1 item 1(1)

TIME LIMITS
  assessment, VATA 1994 s 73(6), 77
  correction of errors, SI 1995/2518 reg 34(1A) VATA 1994
  documents, VATA 1994 Sch 11 para 12
  election to tax, VATA 1994 Sch 10 para 3(6)
  error correction, SI 1995/2518 reg 34(1A) VATA 1994
  input tax limit, SI 1995/2518 reg 29(1A)
  invoices, VATA 1994 Sch 11 para 2(2)
  notification–
    ceasing to make taxable supplies, VATA 1994 Sch 1 para 11
    change in registered particulars, VATA 1994 Sch 1 paras 11–13(3)
    liability to register, VATA 1994 Sch 1 paras 5, 6
  payment of interest in case of official error, VATA 1994 s 78 (11)
  recovery of tax, VATA 1994 s 80(4), (5)
  retention of records, VATA 1994 Sch 11 para 6(3)

TIME OF IMPORT/EXPORT OF GOODS
  general, CEMA 1979 s 5

TIME OF SUPPLY
  acquisition of goods–
    generally, VATA 1994 s 12
    triangular transactions, VATA 1994 s 14(4)
    warehousing, VATA 1994 s 18
  alteration by Commissioners, VATA 1994 s 6(10)
  basic tax point, VATA 1994 s 6(1)–(3)
  change of rate of tax, SI 1995/2518 reg 95
  election for basic tax point to apply, VATA 1994 s 88(2)
  free zone goods, VATA 1994 s 17(5)(*b*)
  fuel for private use, SI 2013/2911
  gas, SI 1995/2518 reg 86
  generally, VATA 1994 s 6, SI 1995/2518 reg 94
  gift of goods, VATA 1994 s 6(12)
  goods–
    approval, sale or return, VATA 1994 s 6(2), (4)
    buyer's possession, SI 1995/2518 reg 88
    private use, for, SI 1995/2518 reg 81(1)
    retention payments, SI 1995/2518 reg 89

TIME OF SUPPLY – *cont.*
  invoice issued–
    after basic tax point, VATA 1994 s 6(5), (6)
    before basic tax point, VATA 1994 s 6(4)
  land–
    compulsory purchase, SI 1995/2518 reg 82(1)
    consideration not determinable, SI 1995/2518 reg 82(2)
    leases, SI 1995/2518 reg 85
    meaning, VATA 1994 s 6(15)
    payment received before basic tax point, VATA 1994 s 6(4)
    power, heat, refrigeration, cooling or ventilation, SI 1995/2518 reg 86
    receipt of payment, reference to, SI 1995/2518 reg 94A
  regulations, VATA 1994 s 88(3), Sch 11 para 2(9)
  removal of goods, VATA 1994 s 6
  royalties, SI 1995/2518 reg 91
  self-supplied, VATA 1994 s 6(11)
  services–
    barristers and advocates, SI 1995/2518 reg 92
    construction industry, SI 1995/2518 reg 93
    continuous supplies of, SI 1995/2518 reg 90
    free supplies of, SI 1995/2518 reg 81(2)
    outside the UK, from, SI 1995/2518 reg 82
    private use of goods, SI 1995/2518 reg 81(1)
    retention payments, SI 1995/2518 reg 89
    together with goods in construction industry, SI 1995/2518 reg 93
  transaction treated as a supply, VATA 1994 ss 6, 56
  water, SI 1995/2518 reg 86

TIME SHARING
  holiday accommodation, VATA 1994 Sch 8 Group 7 item 7

TOBACCO
  products–
    diplomats, import by, SI 1992/3156 art 15
    small non-commercial consignment, SI 1986/939
    travellers' allowance, SI 1994/955
    tax-free shops, zero-rating, VATA 1994 Sch 8 Group 14

TOILET WATER
  travellers' allowance, SI 1994/955

TOKENS
  gaming machines, VATA 1994 s 23(3)
  valuation, VATA 1994 Sch 6 para 5

TOPOGRAPHICAL PLANS
  zero-rating, VATA 1994 Sch 8 Group 3

TOUR OPERATORS
  bad debt relief, SI 1995/2518 reg 172B
  margin scheme,
    designated travel services, incidental supplies, SI 1987/1806 art 14
    meaning, SI 1987/1806 art 3
    place of supply, SI 1987/1806 art 5
    tax chargeable on, SI 1987/1806 art 10
    time of supply, SI 1987/1806 art 4
    value, SI 1987/1806 arts 7–9
  meaning, VATA 1994 s 53(3)

TOUR OPERATORS – *cont.*
  special schemes for, SI 1987/1806, 2006/112/EC arts 306–310
  supplies of goods and services, VATA 1994 s 53

TOWAGE
  zero-rating, VATA 1994 Sch 8 Group 8 item 8

TRADE ASSOCIATIONS
  exemption, VATA 1994 Sch 9 Group 9

TRADE UNIONS
  exemption, VATA 1994 Sch 9 Group 9

TRADEMARKS
  transfer or assignment–
    reverse charge, VATA 1994 s 8
    services supplied where received, VATA 1994 Sch 5 para 1
    zero-rating to overseas, VATA 1994 Sch 8 Group 7

TRADING STAMPS
  schemes, VATA 1994 s 52
  value of goods exchanged for, VATA 1994 Sch 6 para 5

TRAINING
  exemption, VATA 1994 Sch 9 Group 6
  zero-rating, VATA 1994 Sch 8 Group 7

TRANSFER OF BUSINESS AS GOING CONCERN (TOGCs)
  capital goods scheme, SI 1995/2518 reg 114,
  generally, VATA 1994 s 49, SI 1995/1268 reg 5
  second-hand cars, SI 1992/3122 reg 8(c)(d)
  supply made in course of furtherance of business, VATA 1994 s 94(6)
  transfer to members of Group, VATA 1994 s 44

TRANSHIPMENT
  definition, CEMA 1979 s 1(1)

TRANSIT GOODS
  definition, CEMA 1979 s 1(1)

TRANSIT SHED
  definition, CEMA 1979 s 1(1)

TRANSITIONAL PROVISIONS
  assessments, VATA 1994 Sch 13 para 20
  bad debt relief, VATA 1994 Sch 13 para 9
  generally, VATA 1994 Sch 13 para 1
  importation of goods, VATA 1994 Sch 13 para 19
  introduction of VATA, VATA 1994 Sch 13 para 3
  Isle of Man, VATA 1994 Sch 13 para 23
  offences and penalties, VATA 1994 Sch 13 paras 11–18
  overseas suppliers account through their customers, VATA 1994 Sch 13 para 6
  president, chairman of tribunals, VATA 1994 Sch 13 para 5
  set-off of credits, VATA 1994 Sch 13 para 21, FA 1997 s 49
  supplies during construction of buildings and works, VATA 1994 Sch 13 para 10
  supply in accordance with pre 1975 arrangements, VATA 1994 Sch 13 para 4
  validity of subordinate legislation, VATA 1994 Sch 13 para 2
  VAT tribunals, VATA 1994 Sch 13 para 22
  zero rated supplies of goods and services, VATA 1994 Sch 13 para 8

TRANSPORT
See also AIRCRAFT; SHIP
international, exemptions, 2006/112/EC arts 148–150
new means of–
  first entry into service, SI 1995/2518 regs 146, 147
  form, SI 1995/2518 Sch 1 Form 13
  meaning, VATA 1994 s 95
  non-taxable persons, notification and payment of tax, SI 1995/2518 reg 148
  persons departing to another member state, supply to, SI 1995/2518 reg 155
  refund to tax, claim for, SI 1995/2518
  place of supply, SI 1992/3121 arts 6–10

TRANSPORT AUTHORITIES
refund of tax, VATA 1994 s 33

TRAVEL AGENTS
See TOUR OPERATORS

TREASURY ORDERS
acquisition from other members states, VATA 1994 s 11(4)
credit for input tax, VATA 1994 s 25(7)
default interest, VATA 1994 s 74(6)
exemption, VATA 1994 s 30
generally, VATA 1994 s 97
import relief, VATA 1994 s 37(1)
payments on account of tax, VATA 1994 s 28, SI 1995/2518 art 40A
place of supply, VATA 1994 s 7(11)
rate of tax, VATA 1994 s 2(2), (3)
repayment supplement, VATA 1994 s 79(7)
tax as common duty of UK and Isle of Man, IMA 1979 s 1(2), (3)
terminal markets, VATA 1994 s 50
tour operators, VATA 1994 s 53
value of certain goods, VATA 1994 s 22(4), (5)

TREATMENT OR PROCESS
goods reimported after, SI 1995/2518 reg 126
tax treatment, VATA 1994 s 22

TRIANGULATION
place of supply, SI 1995/2518 regs 17, 18, VATA 1994 s 14

TRIBUNALS
See also FIRST-TIER TRIBUNAL, TAX AND CHANCERY CHAMBER, UPPER TRIBUNAL, VAT AND DUTIES TRIBUNAL
Administrative Council–
  See ADMINISTRATIVE JUSTICE AND TRIBUNALS COUNCIL
definition, VATA 1994 s 96(1)
meaning, VATA 1994 s 96(1)
transfer of functions–
  consequential amendments, SI 2009/56 Sch s 1, 2
  existing tribunals, meaning, SI 2009/56 reg 2
  transitional and saving provisions, SI 2009/56 Sch 3
transfer of members, SI 2009/56 reg 5

TURNOVER TAXES
harmonisation, 93/609/EEC

TURNOVER TAXES – *cont.*
international travel, exemption from in, 2007/74/EC

U

UNDERWRITERS
issue of securities and secondary securities, VATA 1994 Sch 9 Group 5

UNINCORPORATED BODIES
See CLUBS AND ASSOCIATIONS

UNITED KINGDOM
registration of person making supply outside, VATA 1994 Sch 1 para 14
supplies made, VATA 1994 s 4
territorial extent, VATA 1994 s 96(11)

UNIT TRUST SCHEMES
exemption, VATA 1994 Sch 9 Group 5 item 6 note (5)
management, VATA 1994 Sch 9 Group 5 item 9 note (6)

UNIVERSITIES
See EDUCATION

V

VALUE
accommodation, provision of–
  employees, VATA 1994 Sch 6 para 10
  period over 4 weeks, VATA 1994 Sch 6 para 9
acquisitions from member states, VATA 1994 s 20, Sch 7
aircraft, adapted, VATA 1994 s 22(3), (4)
antique, imported, VATA 1994 s 21(4)
appeal, VATA 1994 s 83(*v*), (*w*), (*x*)
assets supplied at deregistration, VATA 1994 Sch 6 para 6
cash discount, VATA 1994 Sch 6 para 4
catering supplied to employees, VATA 1994 Sch 6 para 10
collector's pieces, imported, VATA 1994 s 21(4)
connected person–
  importation from, VATA 1994 Sch 6 para 12
  supply to, VATA 1994 Sch 6 para 1(4)
consideration, VATA 1994 s 9, Sch 4 para 1
conversion of foreign currency, VATA 1994 Sch 6 para 11
deregistration. See DEREGISTRATION
designated travel services, SI 1987/1806 reg 7
direction, VATA 1994 Sch 6 para 1–
  to direct seller, VATA 1994 Sch 6 para 2
discount for prompt payment, VATA 1994 Sch 6 para 4
duty of customers to account for tax on supplies, FA 2019 s 51
gaming machines, VATA 1994 s 23(2)–
  tokens, VATA 1994 s 23(2), (3)
generally, VATA 1994 s 19

VALUE – *cont.*
goods–
adapted for recreation of pleasure, VATA 1994 s 22
generally, 2454/93/EEC arts 141–181, Annex 23
eligibility hovercraft, adapted, VATA 1994 s 22(3), (4)
imported goods, VATA 1994 s 21
incidental expenses, VATA 1994 s 19
monetary consideration, VATA 1994 s 19(2)
motor car, self-supplied, VATA 1994 Sch 6 para 6
non-monetary consideration, VATA 1994 s 19(3)
open market value, VATA 1994 s 19(5), Sch 6 para 1(1)
part-money consideration, VATA 1994 s 19(3)
price in money, VATA 1994 s 21(2)
removal of goods to UK, VATA 1994 Sch 9 para 3
residential/charitable buildings, VATA 1994 Sch 10 para 1(6)
retailers, SI 1995/2518
services–
generally, VATA 1994 s 19
received from abroad, VATA 1994 s 8(4)
stamps, VATA 1994 Sch 6 para 5
supply of goods–
by employer, VATA 1994 Sch 6 para 10
expressed in foreign currency, VATA 1994 Sch 6 para 11
Treasury order, VATA 1994 Sch 6 para 6
supply of services–
by employer, VATA 1994 Sch 6 para 10
expressed in foreign currency, VATA 1994 Sch 6 para 11
Treasury order, VATA 1994 Sch 6 para 6
tokens, VATA 1994 Sch 6 para 5
trading stamps, VATA 1994 Sch 6 para 5
treatment of vouchers, FA 2019 s 52, Sch 17
voucher, VATA 1994 Sch 6 para 5, SI 1973/293
work of art, VATA 1994 s 21(4)

VAT INVOICES
See TAX INVOICE

VAT AND DUTIES TRIBUNALS
See VAT APPEALS
composition, VATA 1994 Sch 12 para 5
Court of Appeal, to, VATA 1994 s 86
establishment, VATA 1994 Sch 12 para 1
jurisdiction, VATA 1994 s 82(2)
jury service exemption, VATA 1994 Sch 12 para 8
membership, VATA 1994 Sch 12 paras 6, 7
president, of, VATA 1994 Sch 12 paras 2, 3
procedural rules, VATA 1994 Sch 12 paras 9, 10
sittings, VATA 1994 Sch 12 para 4
transfer of functions, SI 2009/56

VAT APPEALS
assessment, VATA 1994 s 83(*p*), (*q*), (*r*)
bad debt relief, VATA 1994 s 83(*h*)
computer produced invoices, VATA 1994 s 83(*z*)
correction for under-assessment, VATA 1994 s 84(5)
credit for income tax, VATA 1994 s 83(4), (11)
directors liability for evasion of tax, VATA 1994 s 83(*n*), (*o*)

VAT APPEALS – *cont.*
enforcement of registered or recorded decisions, VATA 1994 s 87
evasion of tax involving dishonesty, VATA 1994 s 83(*n*)
evasion penalty appeal. *See under* APPEALS
generally, VATA 1994 s 83
group of companies, VATA 1994 s 83(*k*)
imported goods, VATA 1994 s 83(*b*), (*f*)
interest awarded by tribunal, VATA 1994 s 84(8)
interest in cases of official error, VATA 1994 s 83(*s*)
payment made, VATA 1994 s 83(4)
prior decision, dependent on, VATA 1994 s 84(10)
recovery assessment, against, restrictions on, VATA 1994 s 84(3A)
recovery of overpaid tax, VATA 1994 s 83(*t*)
refund of tax, do it yourself builders, VATA 1994 s 83(*g*)
refund of tax, place of acquisition, VATA 1994 s 83(*d*)
registration, VATA 1994 s 83(*u*), 84(7)
retail schemes, VATA 1994 s 83(*y*)
returns, VATA 1994 s 84(2)
security for tax, VATA 1994 s 83(*l*)
settlement by agreement, VATA 1994 s 85
value of acquisition, VATA 1994 s 83(*w*)
value of supply, VATA 1994 s 83(*v*), (*x*)

VAT REGISTRATION NUMBERS
display, VATA 1994 s 77E

VAT RETURNS
accounting for tax, SI 1995/2518 reg 40(1), (3)
assessment, VATA 1994 s 73(1)
calculation, SI 1995/2518 reg 39
correction, SI 1995/2518 reg 34
electronic, SI 1995/2518, reg 25 (4A)–(4K)
errors, SI 1995/2518 reg 35
failure to make–
generally, VATA 1994 s 73, 84(2)
penalty, FA 2009 s 106, Sch 55
forms, SI 1995/2518 reg 25(1), Sch 1 Forms 4, 5
generally, 2006/112/EC arts 250–261
goods sold in satisfaction of debt, VATA 1994 Sch 4 para 7
incomplete or incorrect assessment, VATA 1994 Sch 11 para 2(10)(*b*), (*c*)
making, VATA 1994 Sch 11 para 2(1)
obligation–
to furnish bankruptcy, insolvency, death or incapacity of registered person, SI 1995/2518 reg 25(3)
ceasing to be registered or a taxable person, SI 1995/2518 reg 25(4)
direction of Commissioners, SI 1995/2518 reg 25(2)
generally, SI 1995/2518 reg 25
penalty for failure to make, VATA 1994 s 73, FA 2009 s 106, Sch 55

VEHICLE OPERATOR
definition, CEMA 1979 s 1(1)

VEHICLES
See also MOTOR CAR
definition, CEMA 1979 s 1(1)

VAT Index

VEHICLES – *cont.*
    diplomats, SI 1992/3156 art 16
    fuel. *See* FUEL
    parking facilities, VATA 1994 Sch 9 Group 1
    rates for light passenger vehicles etc, FA 2019 s 58
    taxis capable of zero emissions, FA 2019 s 59
    temporary importation, SI 1961/1523
    visiting forces, SI 1992/3156 art 19
    zero-rating–
        supply to person leaving UK, SI 1995/2518 regs 132, 133

VENTILATION
    supply, VATA 1994 Sch 4 para 3

VICTUALLING WAREHOUSE
    definition, CEMA 1979 s 1(1)

VIDEO EQUIPMENT
    zero-rating, VATA 1994 Sch 8 Group 16

VILLAGE HALLS
    construction, VATA 1994 Sch 8 Group 5

VISITING FORCES
    conditions attaching to, SI 1992/3156 arts 5–13
    entitled persons, SI 1992/3156 art 18
    gift of goods, SI 1992/3156 art 21
    motor vehicles, SI 1992/3156 arts 19, 22, Sch
    warehouse, removal of goods from, SI 1992/3156 art 20

VOLUNTARY BODIES
    See also CHARITIES
    self build projects, VATA 1994 s 35

VOCATIONAL TRAINING
    exemption, VATA 1994 Sch 9 Group 6
    meaning, VATA 1994 Sch 9 Group 6 note (3)

VOLUNTARY DISCLOSURE
    misdeclarations, VATA 1994 s 63(10)(*b*)

VOUCHERS
    face-value,
        credit, treatment of, VATA 1994 Sch 10A para 3
        issue as supply of services, VATA 1994 Sch 10A para 2
        meaning, VATA 1994 Sch 10A para 1
        other goods and services, supplied with, VATA 1994 Sch 10A para 7
        postage stamp as consideration for, VATA 1994 Sch 10A para 5
        rate categories of supplies, VATA 1994 Sch 10A para 8(2)
        retailer, treatment of, VATA 1994 Sch 10A para 4
        supply, charge on, VATA 1994 Sch 10A para 6
    valuation, VATA 1994 Sch 6 para 5

W

WALKING POSSESSION AGREEMENTS
    assessment, VATA 1994 ss 76, 77
    meaning, VATA 1994 s 68(2)
    penalty for breach, VATA 1994 s 68

WAREHOUSING REGIME
    See also CUSTOMS WAREHOUSE; EXCISE WAREHOUSE; FREE WAREHOUS

WAREHOUSING REGIME – *cont.*
    certificate connected with services, SI 1995/2518 reg 145C
    fiscal warehousing–
        application procedure, VATA 1994 s 18A(7)
        approval, VATA 1994 s 18A(1), (8)
        assessment for failure to pay tax, VATA 1994 s 73(7A)
        certificates, SI 1995/2518 regs 145B, 145C
        cessation, VATA 1994 s 18A(5)
        charge in nature of goods, VATA 1994 s 18F(4)
        conditions, imposition of, VATA 1994 s 18A(6)
        deficient goods, VATA 1994 s 18E
        eligible goods, VATA 1994 s 18B(6), Sch 5A
        entitlement to keep fiscal warehouse, VATA 1994 s 18A(2)
        'fiscal warehouse', VATA 1994 s 18A(3), SI 1995/2518 reg 145A(1)
        'fiscal warehousekeeper', VATA 1994 ss 18A(1), 18F(1), SI 1995/2518 reg 145A(2)
        generally, VATA 1994 ss 18A, 18F
        goods ceasing to be eligible, VATA 1994 s 18F(5)
        matters for consideration by Commissioners, VATA 1994 s 18A(4)
        missing goods, VATA 1994 s 18E
        record and stock control, SI 1995/2518 reg 145F, Sch 1A
        regime, SI 1995/2518 reg 145A(2)
        regulations, power to make, VATA 1994 ss 18D(3), 18F(7), (8)
        relief, VATA 1994 s 18B
        removal of goods, VATA 1994 ss 18A–18C, SI 1995/2518
        services, certificate connected with, SI 1995/2518 reg 145C
        stock control and record, SI 1995/2518 reg 145F Sch 1A
        supply of goods, transaction treated as, SI 1966/1255
        transfers in the UK, SI 1995/2518 reg 145G
        VAT invoices relating to services performed in, SI 1995/2518 reg 145D
        zero-rating of services performed, SI 1995/2518 Sch 1 Form 18
    place and time of supply–
        'dutiable goods', VATA 1994 s 18(6)
        'duty point', VATA 1994 s 18(6)
        'material time', VATA 1994 s 18(6)
        regulations, VATA 1994 s 18(5), (5A)
        'warehouse' VATA 1994 s 18(6)
    removal of goods from fiscal warehouses–
        accountability, VATA 1994 s 18D
        circumstances in which allowed, SI 1995/2518 reg 145H(1)
        deemed removal, VATA 1994 s 18F(6)
        failure to pay tax, VATA 1994 s 73(7B)
        payment of VAT, SI 1995/2518 reg 43, SI 1995/2518 reg 145J
        procedure on non-receipt of relevant documents, SI 1995/2518 reg 145H(3), (4)
        prohibition on, SI 1995/2518 reg 145I
        supply of services, VATA 1994 s 18C

WAREHOUSING REGIME – *cont.*
  removal of goods from fiscal warehouses– – *cont.*
    transferred, treated as, SI 1995/2518 reg 145H(2)
    withdrawal of approval, VATA 1994 s 18A(6), (8)
    withdrawal of status, VATA 1994 s 18A(6)
    zero-rated supplies, VATA 1994 s 18C
  services, VATA 1994 s 18C
  supply of goods subject to–
    'dutiable goods', VATA 1994 s 18(6)
    'duty point', VATA 1994 s 18(6)
    'material time', VATA 1994 s 18(6)
    regulations, VATA 1994 s 18(5), (5A)
    'warehouse' VATA 1994 s 18(6)
  VAT invoices relating to services performed in, SI 1995/2518 reg 145D
WASHROOMS
  supply to handicapped person, VATA 1994 Sch 8 Group 12
WATER
  refund of tax to authority, VATA 1994 s 33(3), SI 1973/2121
  supply of goods, as, SI 1989/1114
  time of supply, SI 1995/2518 reg 86
  zero-rating, VATA 1994 Sch 8 Group 2
WELFARE SERVICES
  See also HEALTH AND WELFARE
  exemption, VATA 1994 Sch 9 Group 7 item 10
WELFARE SPIRITUAL
  exemption, VATA 1994 Sch 9 Group 7 item 10
WINDING UP
  See INSOLVENCY
WINE
  tax free shops, VATA 1994 Sch 8 Group 14
  zero-rating, VATA 1994 Sch 8 Group 1
WIRELESS SET
  zero-rating of supplies to blind, VATA 1994 Sch 8 Group 4
WITHDRAWAL FROM EU
  amendments to export duty, T(CBT)A 2018 s 50, Sch 9
  amendments to VAT, T(CBT)A 2018 s 43, Sch 8
  'excise duty', T(CBT)A 2018 s 53
  postal packets sent from overseas–
    general provision, T(CBT)A 2018 s 44
    withdrawal from EU, SI 2018/1376
  power to make provision as VAT or customs or excise duty–
    general provision, T(CBT)A 2018 s 51
    Regulations, SI 2019/60
  subordinate legislation as VAT or customs or excise duty, T(CBT)A 2018 s 52
WOMEN'S
  sanitary products, VATA 1994 Sch 8
WOODLANDS
  See LAND; TIMBER
WORKS OF ART
  acquisition in settlement of insurance claims, SI 1992/3129 art 4
  exclusion of input tax credit, SI 1992/3222 art 4
  import relief, SI 1984/746 Sch 2

WORKS OF ART – *cont.*
  meaning, VATA 1994 s 21(6), SI 1992/3129 art 2, SI 1992/3222 art 2
  relief for certain supplies, SI 1992/3129 art 4
  repossession under finance agreement, SI 1992/3129 art 4
  sales from stately homes, VATA 1994 Sch 9 Group 11
  special scheme, 2006/112/EC arts 311–343, Annex IX

Y

YOUTH CLUBS
  exemption, VATA 1994 Sch 9 Group 6 item 6
  meaning, VATA 1994 Sch 9 Group 6 note (6)

Z

ZERO-RATING
  aircraft, VATA 1994 Sch 8, Group 8 item 2
  air navigation services, VATA 1994 Sch 8 Group 8 item 6A
  alcoholic beverages, VATA 1994 Sch 8 Group 1
  animal feeding stuffs, VATA 1994 Sch 8 Group 1 general item 2
  animals for human consumption, VATA 1994 Sch 8 Group 1 general item 4
  anti-forestalling charge, FA 2012 Sch 26
  bank notes, VATA 1994 Sch 8 Group 11
  biscuits, VATA 1994 Sch 8 Group 1
  books, VATA 1994 Sch 8 Group 3 item 1
  boots, protective, VATA 1994 Sch 8 Group 16
  building materials, VATA 1994 Sch 8 Group 5 item 4, Sch 8 Group 6 item 3
  caravans, VATA 1994 Sch 8 Group 9 item 1
  charities–
    advertising, VATA 1994 Sch 8 Group 15 item 8
    aids for handicapped persons, VATA 1994 Sch 8 Group 12
    building, VATA 1994 Sch 10 Group 1
    construction of buildings, VATA 1994 Sch 8 Group 5
    donations, VATA 1994 Sch 8 Group 15 items 1, 2
    eligible body, meaning, VATA 1994 Sch 8 Group 15 note 4
    medical or surgical treatment, VATA 1994 Sch 8 Group 15 item 9
    medical or veterinary research, VATA 1994 Sch 8 Group 15 item 10
    talking books, VATA 1994 Sch 8 Group 4
    wireless sets for the blind, VATA 1994 Sch 8 Group 4
  children's picture and painting books, VATA 1994 Sch 8 Group 3 item 3
  clothing and footwear, VATA 1994 Sch 8 Group 16
  confectionery, VATA 1994 Sch 8 Group 1 excepted item 2

VAT Index

ZERO-RATING – *cont.*
   construction of dwellings, VATA 1994 Sch 8 Group 5
   conversion of buildings, VATA 1994 Sch 8 Group 5
   dairy products, VATA 1994 Sch 8 Group 1
   dental supplies, VATA 1994 Sch 8 Group 12
   drugs and medicines–
      general, VATA 1994 Sch 8 Group 12
   exports–
      See EXPORT
   food, VATA 1994 Sch 8 Group 1 general item 1
   generally, VATA 1994 s 30
   gold, VATA 1994 Sch 8 Group 10
   handicapped person–
      aids, VATA 1994 Sch 8 Group 12
      supply of services for adapting aids, VATA 1994 Sch 8 Group 12
   hot food, VATA 1994 Sch 8 Group 1 general item 1
   houseboats, VATA 1994 Sch 8 Group 9 item 2
   imports, VATA 1994 Sch 8 Group 13
   international services, VATA 1994 Sch 8 Group 7
   invalid carriages, VATA 1994 Sch 8 Group 12
   letting on hire, VATA 1994 s 30
   lifeboats, VATA 1994 Sch 8 Group 8 item 3
   magazines, VATA 1994 Sch 8 Group 3 item 2
   maps, charts and topographical plans, VATA 1994 Sch 8 Group 3 item 5
   medical supplies and services, VATA 1994 Sch 8 Group 12
   newspapers and journals, VATA 1994 Sch 8 Group 3 item 2
   pet foods, VATA 1994 Sch 8 Group 1 excepted item 6
   pilotage services, VATA 1994 Sch 8 Group 8 item 7
   potato products, VATA 1994 Sch 8 Group 1 excepted item 5
   protected buildings, VATA 1994 Sch 8 Group 6
   protective helmet, VATA 1994 Sch 8 Group 16
   relevant goods, meaning, VATA 1994 Sch 8 Group 15 note (3)

ZERO-RATING – *cont.*
   repair and maintenance, VATA 1994 Sch 8 Group 15 items 6, 7
   residential and charitable buildings construction, VATA 1994 Sch 8 Group 5
   salvage services, VATA 1994 Sch 8 Group 8 item 8
   sanitary products, VATA 1994 Sch 8
   savoury snacks, VATA 1994 Sch 8 Group 1 excepted item 5
   seeds, VATA 1994 Sch 8 Group 1 general item 3
   services performed in warehouse, certificate to secure, SI 1995/2518 Sch 1 Form 18
   sewerage services, VATA 1994 Sch 8 Group 2
   sheet music, VATA 1994 Sch 8 Group 3
   ships, VATA 1994 Sch 8 Group 8 item 1
   surgical appliances, VATA 1994 Sch 8 Group 12
   talking books, VATA 1994 Sch 8 Group 4
   tax free shops, VATA 1994 Sch 8 Group 14
   tax invoices, SI 1995/2518 regs 13(4), 16
   towage services, VATA 1994 Sch 8, Group 8 item 8
   transport–
      designated travel services outside EC, VATA 1994 Sch 8 Group 8 item 12
      salvage or towage services, VATA 1994 Sch 8 Group 8 item 8
      supply, repair or maintenance of aircraft, VATA 1994 Sch 8 Group 8 item 2
      supply, repair or maintenance of lifeboats, VATA 1994 Sch 8 Group 8 item 3
      supply, repair or maintenance of ships, VATA 1994 Sch 8 Group 8 item 1
      survey of ships and aircraft, VATA 1994 Sch 8 Group 8 item 9
      transport of passengers, VATA 1994 Sch 8 Group 8 item 4
      transport of goods outside member states, VATA 1994 Sch 8 Group 8 item 5
      transport to and from Azores or Madeira, VATA 1994 Sch 8 Group 8 item 13
   water, VATA 1994 Sch 8 Group 2
   wireless sets for the blind, VATA 1994 Sch 8 Group 4